PROJECTS

Note: The ● icon indicates projects that are supported [by] graphing-calculator resources on the CD-ROM that accompanies t[he text].

CHAPTER

1
- 1.1 Project: A Square Wading Pool (p. 11) ●
- 1.2 Project: A Broken Tree (p. 23) ●
- 1.3 Project: A Leaning Ladder (p. 33) ●
- 1.4 Project: A Spherical Asteroid (p. 45) ●

2
- 2.1 Project: Numerical Slope Investigations (p. 63) ●
- 2.2 Project: Limits, Slopes, and Logarithms (p. 74) ●
- 2.3 Project: Numerical Epsilon-Delta Limit Investigations (p. 87) ●

3
- 3.5 Project: When Is Your Coffee Cup Stablest? (p. 150) ●
- 3.8 Project: How Deep Does a Floating Ball Sink? (p. 188) ●

4
- 4.1 Project: Investigating the Folium of Descartes (p. 203) ●
- 4.4 Project: Making a Candy Box With Lid (p. 232) ●
- 4.7 Project: Locating Special Points on Exotic Graphs (p. 267) ●

5
- 5.4 Project: Calculator/Computer Riemann Sums (p. 307) ●
- 5.9 Project: Trapezoidal and Simpson Approximations (p. 359) ●

6
- 6.3 Project: Design Your *Own* Ring! (p. 395)

7
- 7.1 Project: Discovering the Number *e* for Yourself (p. 441) ●
- 7.4 Project: Natural Functional Equations (p. 466)

9
- 9.2 Project: Computer-Assisted Slope Fields and Euler's Method (p. 567) ●
- 9.5 Project: Predator-Prey Equations and Your Own Game Preserve (p. 597) ●

10
- 10.4 Project: Trochoid Investigations (p. 652)
- 10.5 Project: Moon Orbits and Race Tracks (p. 660)

11
- 11.2 Project: Nested Radicals and Continued Fractions (p. 691)
- 11.3 Project: Numerical Summation and Geometric Series (p. 701)
- 11.4 Project: Calculating Logarithms on a Deserted Island (p. 715) ●
- 11.5 Project: **The Number π, Once and for All** (p. 722)
- 11.9 Project: Calculating Trigonometric Functions on a Deserted Island (p. 758) ●

12
- 12.5 Project: Does a Pitched Baseball Really Curve? (p. 816)

13
- 13.9 Project: Numerical Solution of Lagrange Multiplier Systems (p. 927) ●
- 13.10 Project: Critical Point Investigations (p. 935) ●

14
- 14.1 Project: Midpoint Sums Approximating Double Integrals (p. 947) ●
- 14.5 Project: Optimal Design of Race-Car Wheels (p. 978)
- 14.6 Project: Archimedes' Floating Paraboloid (p. 987) ●

15
- 15.5 Project: Surface Integrals and Rocket Nose Cones (p. 1057) ●

CALCULUS
Instructor's Edition

CALCULUS
Instructor's Edition

Sixth Edition

C. HENRY EDWARDS
The University of Georgia, Athens

DAVID E. PENNEY
The University of Georgia, Athens

Prentice Hall, Upper Saddle River, New Jersey 07458

Editor in Chief: Sally Yagan
Acquisition Editor: George Lobell
Vice President/Director of Production and Manufacturing: David W. Riccardi
Executive Managing Editor: Kathleen Schiaparelli
Senior Managing Editor: Linda Mihatov Behrens
Assistant Managing Editor: Bayani Mendoza de Leon
Production Editor: Jeanne Audino
Assistant Managing Editor, Math Media Production: John Matthews
Media Production Editors: Donna Crilly, Wendy Perez
Manufacturing Buyer: Alan Fischer
Manufacturing Manager: Trudy Pisciotti
Marketing Manager: Angela Battle
Marketing Assistant: Rachel Beckman
Development Editor: Ed Millman
Editor in Chief, Development: Carol Trueheart
Assistant Editor of Media: Vince Jansen
Editorial Assistant/Supplements Editor: Melanie Van Benthuysen
Art Director: Jonathan Boylan
Assistant to the Art Director: John Christiana
Interior Designer: Donna Young
Cover Designer: Bruce Kenselaar
Art Editor: Thomas Benfatti
Creative Director: Carole Anson
Director of Creative Services: Paul Belfanti
Photo Researcher: Karen Pugliano
Photo Editor: Beth Boyd Brenzel
Cover Photo: Antonio Martinelli/Arche De La Defense, Sunset View–Paris, Arch. J. O. Spreckelsen-P. Andreu.
   David Cardelus/Esto. All rights reserved.
Back Cover Photo: City of Art and Sciences, Valencia, España. Barbara Burg/Oliver Schuh/Palladium Photodesign, Co, Germany.
Art Studio: Network Graphics

Prentice Hall   © 2002, 1998, 1994, 1990, 1986, 1982 by Prentice-Hall, Inc.
Upper Saddle River, New Jersey 07458

All rights reserved. No part of this book may
be reproduced, in any form or by any means,
without written permission from the publisher.

Printed in the United States of America
10 9 8 7 6 5 4 3 2 1

ISBN 0-13-092072-X

Pearson Education LTD.
Pearson Education Australia PTY, Limited
Pearson Education Singapore, Pte. Ltd.
Pearson Education North Asia Ltd.
Pearson Education Canada, Ltd.
Pearson Educacion de Mexico, S.A. de C.V.
Pearson Education–Japan
Pearson Education Malaysia, Pte. Ltd.

CONTENTS

ABOUT THE AUTHORS — xi
PREFACE — xiii
TEXT WALKTHROUGH — xxi

CHAPTER 1 FUNCTIONS, GRAPHS, AND MODELS — 1

1.1 Functions and Mathematical Modeling   2
  PROJECT: A Square Wading Pool   11
1.2 Graphs of Equations and Functions   12
  PROJECT: A Broken Tree   23
1.3 Polynomials and Algebraic Functions   24
  PROJECT: A Leaning Ladder   33
1.4 Transcendental Functions   33
  PROJECT: A Spherical Asteroid   45
1.5 Preview: What *Is* Calculus?   45
REVIEW: Definitions and Concepts   48

CHAPTER 2 PRELUDE TO CALCULUS — 53

2.1 Tangent Lines and Slope Predictors   54
  PROJECT: Numerical Slope Investigations   63
2.2 The Limit Concept   63
  PROJECT: Limits, Slopes, and Logarithms   74
2.3 More About Limits   75
  PROJECT: Numerical Epsilon-Delta Limit Investigations   87
2.4 The Concept of Continuity   88
REVIEW: Definitions, Concepts, Results   99

CHAPTER 3 THE DERIVATIVE — 101

3.1 The Derivative and Rates of Change   102
3.2 Basic Differentiation Rules   115
3.3 The Chain Rule   126
3.4 Derivatives of Algebraic Functions   133

CONTENTS

- 3.5 Maxima and Minima of Functions on Closed Intervals 142
  - **PROJECT:** When Is Your Coffee Cup Stablest? 150
- 3.6 Applied Optimization Problems 152
- 3.7 Derivatives of Trigonometric Functions 165
- 3.8 Successive Approximations and Newton's Method 176
  - **PROJECT:** How Deep Does a Floating Ball Sink? 188
  - **REVIEW: Formulas, Concepts, Definitions** 189

CHAPTER 4 ADDITIONAL APPLICATIONS OF THE DERIVATIVE 193

- 4.1 Implicit Functions and Related Rates 194
  - **PROJECT:** Investigating the Folium of Descartes 203
- 4.2 Increments, Differentials, and Linear Approximation 204
- 4.3 Increasing and Decreasing Functions and the Mean Value Theorem 212
- 4.4 The First Derivative Test and Applications 222
  - **PROJECT:** Making a Candy Box With Lid 232
- 4.5 Simple Curve Sketching 232
- 4.6 Higher Derivatives and Concavity 242
- 4.7 Curve Sketching and Asymptotes 256
  - **PROJECT:** Locating Special Points on Exotic Graphs 267
  - **REVIEW: Definitions, Concepts, Results** 267

CHAPTER 5 THE INTEGRAL 271

- 5.1 Introduction 272
- 5.2 Antiderivatives and Initial Value Problems 272
- 5.3 Elementary Area Computations 286
- 5.4 Riemann Sums and the Integral 298
  - **PROJECT:** Calculator/Computer Riemann Sums 307
- 5.5 Evaluation of Integrals 308
- 5.6 The Fundamental Theorem of Calculus 318
- 5.7 Integration by Substitution 328
- 5.8 Areas of Plane Regions 336
- 5.9 Numerical Integration 346
  - **PROJECT:** Trapezoidal and Simpson Approximations 359
  - **REVIEW: Definitions, Concepts, Results** 361

CHAPTER 6 APPLICATIONS OF THE INTEGRAL 365

- 6.1 Riemann Sum Approximations 366
- 6.2 Volumes by the Method of Cross Sections 376

Please turn to page xxi to see other text versions.

CONTENTS vii

6.3 Volumes by the Method of Cylindrical Shells 387
PROJECT: Design Your Own Ring! 395
6.4 Arc Length and Surface Area of Revolution 396
6.5 Force and Work 405
6.6 Centroids of Plane Regions and Curves 416
REVIEW: Definitions, Concepts, Results 423

CHAPTER 7 CALCULUS OF TRANSCENDENTAL FUNCTIONS 427

7.1 Exponential and Logarithmic Functions 428
PROJECT: Discovering the Number e for Yourself 441
7.2 Indeterminate Forms and L'Hôpital's Rule 441
7.3 More Indeterminate Forms 449
7.4 The Natural Logarithm as an Integral 455
PROJECT: Natural Functional Equations 466
7.5 Inverse Trigonometric Functions 467
7.6 Hyperbolic Functions 477
REVIEW: Formulas, Concepts, Definitions 485

CHAPTER 8 TECHNIQUES OF INTEGRATION 489

8.1 Introduction 490
8.2 Integral Tables and Simple Substitutions 490
8.3 Integration by Parts 494
8.4 Trigonometric Integrals 501
8.5 Rational Functions and Partial Fractions 508
8.6 Trigonometric Substitution 515
8.7 Integrals Involving Quadratic Polynomials 521
8.8 Improper Integrals 526
Summary 539

CHAPTER 9 DIFFERENTIAL EQUATIONS 545

9.1 Simple Equations and Models 546
9.2 Slope Fields and Euler's Method 558
PROJECT: Computer-Assisted Slope Fields and Euler's Method 567
9.3 Separable Equations and Applications 568
9.4 Linear Equations and Applications 575
9.5 Population Models 587
PROJECT: Predator-Prey Equations and Your Own Game Preserve 597
9.6 Linear Second-Order Equations 598
9.7 Mechanical Vibrations 607
REVIEW: Definitions, Concepts, Results 618

Please turn to page xxi to see other text versions.

viii CONTENTS

CHAPTER 10   POLAR COORDINATES AND PARAMETRIC CURVES   623

10.1 Analytic Geometry and the Conic Sections   624
10.2 Polar Coordinates   629
10.3 Area Computations in Polar Coordinates   638
10.4 Parametric Curves   643
  PROJECT: Trochoid Investigations   652
10.5 Integral Computations with Parametric Curves   653
  PROJECT: Moon Orbits and Race Tracks   660
10.6 Conic Sections and Applications   661
  REVIEW: Concepts and Definitions   679

CHAPTER 11   INFINITE SERIES   681

11.1 Introduction   682
11.2 Infinite Sequences   682
  PROJECT: Nested Radicals and Continued Fractions   691
11.3 Infinite Series and Convergence   691
  PROJECT: Numerical Summation and Geometric Series   701
11.4 Taylor Series and Taylor Polynomials   702
  PROJECT: Calculating Logarithms on a Deserted Island   715
11.5 The Integral Test   715
  PROJECT: The Number π, Once and for All   722
11.6 Comparison Tests for Positive-Term Series   722
11.7 Alternating Series and Absolute Convergence   728
11.8 Power Series   737
11.9 Power Series Computations   750
  PROJECT: Calculating Trigonometric Functions on a Deserted Island   758
11.10 Series Solutions of Differential Equations   758
  REVIEW: Definitions, Concepts, Results   767

CHAPTER 12   VECTORS, CURVES, AND SURFACES IN SPACE   771

12.1 Vectors in the Plane   772
12.2 Three-Dimensional Vectors   778
12.3 The Cross Product of Vectors   788
12.4 Lines and Planes in Space   796
12.5 Curves and Motion in Space   803
  PROJECT: Does a Pitched Baseball Really Curve?   816
12.6 Curvature and Acceleration   817
12.7 Cylinders and Quadric Surfaces   830
12.8 Cylindrical and Spherical Coordinates   838
  REVIEW: Definitions, Concepts, Results   845

Please turn to page xxi to see other text versions.

CONTENTS ix

CHAPTER 13   PARTIAL DIFFERENTIATION   849

13.1 Introduction   850
13.2 Functions of Several Variables   850
13.3 Limits and Continuity   860
13.4 Partial Derivatives   868
13.5 Multivariable Optimization Problems   878
13.6 Increments and Linear Approximation   889
13.7 The Multivariable Chain Rule   896
13.8 Directional Derivatives and the Gradient Vector   907
13.9 Lagrange Multipliers and Constrained Optimization   918
   PROJECT: Numerical Solution of Lagrange Multiplier Systems   927
13.10 Critical Points of Functions of Two Variables   927
   PROJECT: Critical Point Investigations   935
   REVIEW: Definitions, Concepts, Results   936

CHAPTER 14   MULTIPLE INTEGRALS   939

14.1 Double Integrals   940
   PROJECT: Midpoint Sums Approximating Double Integrals   947
14.2 Double Integrals over More General Regions   947
14.3 Area and Volume by Double Integration   954
14.4 Double Integrals in Polar Coordinates   961
14.5 Applications of Double Integrals   968
   PROJECT: Optimal Design of Downhill Race-Car Wheels   978
14.6 Triple Integrals   979
   PROJECT: Archimedes' Floating Paraboloid   987
14.7 Integration in Cylindrical and Spherical Coordinates   988
14.8 Surface Area   996
14.9 Change of Variables in Multiple Integrals   1001
   REVIEW: Definitions, Concepts, Results   1009

CHAPTER 15   VECTOR CALCULUS   1013

15.1 Vector Fields   1014
15.2 Line Integrals   1019
15.3 The Fundamental Theorem and Independence of Path   1030
15.4 Green's Theorem   1037
15.5 Surface Integrals   1047
   PROJECT: Surface Integrals and Rocket Nose Cones   1057
15.6 The Divergence Theorem   1057
15.7 Stokes' Theorem   1065
   REVIEW: Definitions, Concepts, Results   1072

Please turn to page xxi to see other text versions.

APPENDICES — A-1

- A: Real Numbers and Inequalities A-1
- B: The Coordinate Plane and Straight Lines A-6
- C: Review of Trigonometry A-13
- D: Proofs of the Limit Laws A-19
- E: The Completeness of the Real Number System A-23
- F: Existence of the Integral A-28
- G: Approximations and Riemann Sums A-33
- H: L'Hôpital's Rule and Cauchy's Mean Value Theorem A-36
- I: Proof of Taylor's Formula A-38
- J: Conic Sections as Sections of a Cone A-39
- K: Proof of the Linear Approximation Theorem A-40
- L: Units of Measurement and Conversion Factors A-41
- M: Formulas from Algebra, Geometry, and Trigonometry A-42
- N: The Greek Alphabet A-44

REFERENCES FOR FURTHER STUDY — A-45

TEACHING OUTLINES — T-1

INDEX — I-1

TABLE OF INTEGRALS — TA-1

PHOTO CREDITS p. 1. CORBIS p. 53 (top left) Getty Images, Inc.; (bottom left) Courtesy of International Business Machines Corporation. Unauthorized use not permitted. (right) Navy Visual News Service p. 101 Wards Science/Science Source; (bottom right) C. H. Edwards p. 163 Richard Megna/Fundamental Photographs p. 193 (top left) The Royal Society of London; (bottom right) David E. Penney p. 271 Art Resource, N.Y. p. 282 Richard Megna/Fundamental Photographs p. 365 The Granger Collection, New York p. 407 Lucas Bruno/AP/World Wide Photos p. 410 Omnia/Getty Images, Inc. p. 427 (top left) from *Portraits of Eminent Mathematicians* by David Eugene Smith published by Pictorial Mathematics, New York, 1936; (bottom right) Getty Images, Inc./PhotoDisc, Inc. p. 489 (top left) Library of Congress; (bottom right) David E. Penney p. 545 CORBIS p. 623 (top left) Stock Montage, Inc./Historical Pictures Collection; (bottom right) Stephen Gerard/Science Service/Photo Researchers, Inc. p. 681 (top left) University of Cambridge; (bottom right) Image by David E. Penney p. 771 (top left) Library of Congress p. 804 Robert Garvey/Black Star p. 849 Courtesy of the Library of Congress p. 939 (top left) The Granger Collection, New York; (bottom right) Jeff Greenberg/PhotoEdit p. 1013 (top left) CORBIS; (bottom right) Chandra X-Ray Center/A. Hobart

Maple is a registered trademark of Waterloo Maple Inc.
Mathematica is a registered trademark of Wolfram Research, Inc.
MATLAB is a registered trademark of The MathWorks, Inc.

Please turn to page xxi to see other text versions.

ABOUT THE AUTHORS

C. Henry Edwards is emeritus professor of mathematics at the University of Georgia. He earned his Ph.D. at the University of Tennessee in 1960, and recently retired after 40 years of classroom teaching (including calculus or differential equations almost every term) at the universities of Tennessee, Wisconsin, and Georgia, with a brief interlude at the Institute for Advanced Study (Princeton) as an Alfred P. Sloan Research Fellow. He has received numerous teaching awards, including the University of Georgia's *honoratus* medal in 1983 (for sustained excellence in honors teaching), its Josiah Meigs award in 1991 (the institution's highest award for teaching), and the 1997 state-wide Georgia Regents award for research university faculty teaching excellence. His scholarly career has ranged from research and dissertation direction in topology to the history of mathematics to computing and technology in the teaching and applications of mathematics. In addition to being author or co-author of calculus, advanced calculus, linear algebra, and differential equations textbooks, he is well-known to calculus instructors as author of *The Historical Development of the Calculus* (Springer-Verlag, 1979). During the 1990s he served as a principal investigator on three NSF-supported projects: (1) A school mathematics project including Maple for beginning algebra students, (2) A Calculus-with-*Mathematica* program, and (3) A MATLAB-based computer lab project for numerical analysis and differential equations students.

David E. Penney, University of Georgia, completed his Ph.D. at Tulane University in 1965 (under the direction of Prof. L. Bruce Treybig) while teaching at the University of New Orleans. Earlier he had worked in experimental biophysics at Tulane University and the Veteran's Administration Hospital in New Orleans under the direction of Robert Dixon McAfee, where Dr. McAfee's research team's primary focus was on the active transport of sodium ions by biological membranes. Penney's primary contribution here was the development of a mathematical model (using simultaneous ordinary differential equations) for the metabolic phenomena regulating such transport, with potential future applications in kidney physiology, management of hypertension, and treatment of congestive heart failure. He also designed and constructed servomechanisms for the accurate monitoring of ion transport, a phenomenon involving the measurement of potentials in microvolts at impedances of millions of megohms. Penney began teaching calculus at Tulane in 1957 and taught that course almost every term with enthusiasm and distinction until his retirement at the end of the last millennium. During his tenure at the University of Georgia he received numerous University-wide teaching awards as well as directing several doctoral dissertations and seven undergraduate research projects. He is the author of research papers in number theory and topology and is the author or co-author of textbooks on calculus, computer programming, differential equations, linear algebra, and liberal arts mathematics.

PREFACE

Contemporary calculus instructors and students face traditional challenges as well as new ones that result from changes in the role and practice of mathematics by scientists and engineers in the world at large. As a consequence, this sixth edition of our calculus textbook is its most extensive revision since the first edition appeared in 1982.

Two chapters of the fifth edition have been combined in a single more tightly organized one. An entirely new chapter now appears in the table of contents, and most of the remaining chapters have been extensively rewritten. About 125 of the book's over 750 worked examples are new for this edition and the 1825 figures in the text include 225 new computer-generated graphics. About 600 of its over 7000 problems are new, and these are augmented by 320 new conceptual discussion questions that now precede the problem sets. Moreover, 1050 new true/false questions are included in the Study Guides on the new CD-ROM that accompanies this edition. In summary, almost 2000 of these 8400-plus problems and questions are new, and the text discussion and explanations have undergone corresponding alteration and improvement.

PRINCIPAL NEW FEATURES

The current revision of the text features

- More unified treatment of **transcendental functions** in Chapter 7, and
- A new Chapter 9 on **differential equations** and applications.

The new chapter on differential equations now appears immediately after Chapter 8 on techniques of integration. It includes both direction fields and Euler's method together with the more elementary symbolic methods (which exploit techniques from Chapter 8) and interesting applications of both first- and second-order equations. Chapter 11 (Infinite Series) now ends with a new section on power series solutions of differential equations, thus bringing full circle a unifying focus of second-semester calculus on elementary differential equations.

NEW LEARNING RESOURCES

Conceptual Discussion Questions The set of problems that concludes each section is now preceded by a brief **Concepts: Questions and Discussion** set consisting of several open-ended conceptual questions that can be used for either individual study or classroom discussion.

The Text CD-ROM The content of the new CD-ROM that accompanies this text is fully integrated with the textbook material, and is designed specifically for

Please turn to page xxi to see other text versions.

use hand-in-hand with study of the book itself. This CD-ROM features the following resources to support learning and teaching:

- **Interactive True/False Study Guides** that reinforce and encourage student reading of the text. Ten author-written questions for each section carefully guide students through the section, and students can request individual hints suggesting where in the section to look for needed information.
- **Live Examples** feature dynamic multimedia and computer algebra presentations—many accompanied by audio explanations—which enhance student intuition and understanding. These interactive examples expand upon many of the textbook's principal examples; students can change input data and conditions and then observe the resulting changes in step-by-step solutions and accompanying graphs and figures. **Walkthrough videos** demonstrate how students can interact with these live examples.
- **Homework Starters** for the principal types of computational problems in each textbook section, featuring both interactive presentations similar to the live examples and (Web-linked) voice-narrated videos of pencil-and-paper investigations illustrating typical initial steps in the solution of selected textbook problems.
- **Computing Project Resources** support most of the almost three dozen projects that follow key sections in the text. For each such project marked in the text by a CD-ROM icon, more extended discussions illustrating Maple, *Mathematica,* MATLAB, and graphing calculator investigations are provided. Computer algebra system commands can be copied and pasted for interactive execution.
- **Hyperlinked Maple Worksheets** contributed by Harald Pleym of Telemark University College (Norway) constitute an interactive version of essentially the whole textbook. Students and faculty using Maple can change input data and conditions in most of the text examples to investigate the resulting changes in step-by-step solutions and accompanying graphs and figures.
- **PowerPoint Presentations** provide classroom projection versions of about 350 of the figures in the text that would be least convenient to reproduce on a blackboard.
- **Web Site** The contents of the CD-ROM together with additional learning and teaching resources are maintained and updated at the textbook Web site **www.prenhall.com/edwards,** which includes a Comments and Suggestions center where we invite response from both students and instructors.

PH Grade Assist (Computerized Homework Grading System)

About 2000 of the textbook problems are incorporated in an automated grading system that is now available. Each problem solution in the system is structured algorithmically so that students can work in a computer lab setting to submit homework assignments for automatic grading. (There is a small annual fee per participating student.)

New Solutions Manuals
The entirely new 1810-page **Instructor's Solutions Manual** (available in two volumes) includes a detailed solution for every problem in the book. These solutions were written exclusively by the authors and have been checked independently by others.

The entirely new 930-page **Student Solutions Manual** (available in two volumes) includes a detailed solution for every odd-numbered problem in the text. The answers (alone) to most of these odd-numbered problems are included in the answers section at the back of this book.

New Technology manuals
Each of the following manuals is available shrink-wrapped with any version of the text for half the normal price of the manual (all of which are inexpensive):

Please turn to page xxi to see other text versions.

- Jensen, *Using MATLAB in Calculus* (0-13-027268-X)
- Freese/Stegenga, *Calculus Concepts Using Derive* (0-13-085152-3)
- Gresser, *TI Graphing Calculator Approach, 2e* (0-13-092017-7)
- Gresser, *A Mathematica Approach, 2e* (0-13-092015-0)
- Gresser, *A Maple Approach, 2e* (0-13-092014-2)

THE TEXT IN MORE DETAIL . . .

In preparing this edition, we have taken advantage of many valuable comments and suggestions from users of the first five editions. This revision was so pervasive that the individual changes are too numerous to be detailed in a preface, but the following paragraphs summarize those that may be of widest interest.

- ▼ **New Problems**   Most of the 600 new problems lie in the intermediate range of difficulty, neither highly theoretical nor computationally routine. Many of them have a new technology flavor, suggesting (if not requiring) the use of technology ranging from a graphing calculator to a computer algebra system.

- ▼ **Discussion Questions and Study Guides**   We hope the 320 conceptual discussion questions and 1050 true/false study-guide questions constitute a useful addition to the traditional fare of student exercises and problems. The True/False Study Guide for each section provides a focus on the key ideas of the section, with the single goal of motivating guided student reading of the section.

- ▼ **Examples and Explanations**   About one-sixth of the book's worked examples are either new or significantly revised, together with a similar percentage of the text discussion and explanations. Additional computational detail has been inserted in worked examples where students have experienced difficulty, together with additional sentences and paragraphs in similar spots in text discussions.

- ▼ **Project Material**   Many of the text's 33 projects are new for this edition. These appear following the problem sets at the ends of key sections throughout the text. Most (but not all) of these projects employ some aspect of modern computational technology to illustrate the principal ideas of the preceding section, and many contain additional problems intended for solution with the use of a graphing calculator or computer algebra system. Where appropriate, project discussions are significantly expanded in the CD-ROM versions of the projects.

- ▼ **Historical Material**   Historical and biographical chapter openings offer students a sense of the development of our subject by real human beings. Indeed, our exposition of calculus frequently reflects the historical development of the subject—from ancient times to the ages of Newton and Leibniz and Euler to our own era of new computational power and technology.

TEXT ORGANIZATION

- ▼ **Introductory Chapters**   Instead of a routine review of precalculus topics, Chapter 1 concentrates specifically on functions and graphs for use in mathematical modeling. It includes a section cataloging informally the elementary transcendental functions of calculus, as background to their more formal treatment using calculus itself. Chapter 1 concludes with a section addressing the question "What *is* calculus?" Chapter 2 on limits begins with a section on tangent lines to motivate the official introduction of limits in Section 2.2. Trigonometric limits are treated throughout Chapter 2 in order to encourage a richer and more visual introduction to the limit concept.

Please turn to page xxi to see other text versions.

▼ **Differentiation Chapters** The sequence of topics in Chapters 3 and 4 differs a bit from the most traditional order. We attempt to build student confidence by introducing topics more nearly in order of increasing difficulty. The chain rule appears quite early (in Section 3.3) and we cover the basic techniques for differentiating algebraic functions before discussing maxima and minima in Sections 3.5 and 3.6 (in order to illustrate early some significant applications of the derivative). Section 3.7 treats the derivatives of all six trigonometric functions. The authors' fondness for Newton's method (Section 3.8) will be apparent.

The mean value theorem and its applications are deferred to Chapter 4 (following implicit differentiation and related rates in Section 4.1, and differentials and linear approximation in Section 4.2). In addition, a dominant theme of Chapter 4 is the use of calculus both to construct graphs of functions and to explain and interpret graphs that have been constructed by a calculator or computer. This theme is developed in Sections 4.4 on the first derivative test and 4.6 on higher derivatives and concavity.

▼ **Integration Chapters** Chapter 5 begins with a section on antiderivatives—which could logically be included in the preceding chapter, but benefits from the use of integral notation. When the definite integral is introduced in Sections 5.3 and 5.4, we emphasize endpoint and midpoint sums rather than upper and lower and more general Riemann sums. This concrete emphasis carries through the chapter to its final section on numerical integration. Chapter 6 begins with a largely new section on Riemann sum approximations, with new examples centering on fluid flow and medical applications. Section 6.6 is a new treatment of centroids of plane regions and curves.

Chapter 8 (Techniques of Integration) is organized to accommodate those instructors who feel that methods of formal integration now require less emphasis, in view of modern techniques for both numerical and symbolic integration. Integration by parts (Section 8.3) precedes trigonometric integrals (Section 8.4). The method of partial fractions appears in Section 8.5, and trigonometric substitutions and integrals involving quadratic polynomials follow in Sections 8.6 and 8.7. Improper integrals appear in Section 8.8, with new and substantial subsections on special functions and probability and random sampling. This rearrangement of Chapter 8 makes it more convenient to stop wherever the instructor desires.

▼ **Calculus of Transcendental Functions** Section 7.1 (much strengthened for this edition) introduces the exponential and logarithmic functions from a fairly intuitive viewpoint; the approach based on the natural logarithm as an integral appears in Section 7.4. Sections 7.2 and 7.3 introduce l'Hôpital's rule and apply it to round out the calculus of exponential and logarithmic functions. Sections 7.5 and 7.6 cover both derivatives of and integrals involving inverse trigonometric functions and hyperbolic functions.

▼ **Differential Equations** This entirely new chapter begins with the most elementary differential equations and applications (Section 9.1) and then proceeds to introduce both graphical (slope field) and numerical (Euler) methods in Section 9.2. Subsequent sections of the chapter treat separable and linear first-order differential equations and (in more depth than usual in a calculus course) applications such as population growth (including logistic and predator-prey populations) and motion with resistance. The final two sections of Chapter 9 treat second-order linear equations and applications to mechanical vibrations. Instructors desiring still more coverage of differential equations can arrange with the publisher to bundle and use appropriate sections of Edwards and Penney, **Differential Equations: Computing and Modeling 2/e** (Prentice-Hall, 2000).

▼ **Parametric Curves and Polar Coordinates** The principal change in Chapter 10 is the replacement of three separate sections in the 5th edition on parabolas, ellipses, and hyperbolas with a single Section 10.6 that provides a unified treatment of all the conic sections.

▼ **Infinite Series** After the usual introduction to convergence of infinite sequences and series in Sections 11.2 and 11.3, a combined treatment of Taylor polynomials and Taylor series appears in Section 11.4. This makes it possible for the instructor to experiment with a briefer treatment of infinite series, but still offer exposure to the Taylor series that are so important for applications. The principal change in Chapter 11 is the addition of a new final section on power series methods and their use to introduce new transcendental functions, thereby concluding the middle third of the book with a return to differential equations.

▼ **Multivariable Calculus** The treatment of calculus of more than a single variable is rather traditional, beginning with vectors, curves, and surfaces in Chapter 12. Chapter 13 features a strong treatment of multivariable maximum-minimum problems in Sections 13.5 (initial approach to these problems), 13.9 (Lagrange multipliers), and 13.10 (critical points of functions of two variables). Chapters 13 (Partial Differentiation), 14 (Multiple Integrals), and 15 (Vector Calculus) have been significantly rewritten for this edition.

OPTIONS IN TEACHING CALCULUS

The Calculus Sequence The present version of the text is accompanied by a less traditional version that treats transcendental functions earlier in single-variable calculus and includes matrices for use in multivariable calculus. Both versions of the complete text are also available in two-volume split editions. By appropriate selection of first and second volumes, the instructor can therefore construct a complete text for a calculus sequence with

- Early transcendentals in single-variable calculus and matrices in multivariable calculus;
- Early transcendentals in single-variable calculus but traditional coverage of multivariable calculus;
- Transcendental functions delayed until after the integral in single-variable calculus, but matrices used in multivariable calculus;
- Neither early transcendentals in single-variable calculus nor matrices in multivariable calculus.

Maximum-Minimum Problems The text includes first coverage of maximum-minimum problems in Chapter 3 (Sections 3.5 and 3.6) to provide early motivation in the form of concrete applications of the derivative, and then returns with the first- and second-derivative tests of Sections 4.4 and 4.6. However, some instructors may prefer to treat these applications later—following trigonometric derivatives and related rates, and along with the bulk of the associated material in Chapter 4. The modular character of the pertinent sections in these two differential calculus chapters permits such desired rearrangements of the material within the typical pair of instructional units (each likely followed by its own hour test). For instance, Sections 3.5 and 3.6 on max-min problems can be deferred and used to begin the second unit on differential calculus, after appending Sections 4.1 (Implicit Differentiation and Related Rates) and 4.2 (Increments, Differentials, and Linear Approximation) to the first unit. Thus the material in Chapters 3 and 4 would be covered in the following order.

Unit I: Differentiation

3.1 The Derivative and Rates of Change
3.2 Basic Differentiation Rules

- **3.3** The Chain Rule
- **3.4** Derivatives of Algebraic Functions
- **3.7** Derivatives of Trigonometric Functions (skipping Example 13 and Problems 78–86)
- **3.8** Successive Approximations and Newton's Method
- **4.1** Implicit Functions and Related Rates
- **4.2** Increments, Differentials, and Linear Approximation

Unit II: Applications of the Derivative

- **3.5** Maxima and Minima of Functions on Closed Intervals
- **3.6** Applied Optimization Problems
- **4.3** Increasing and Decreasing Functions and the Mean Value Theorem
- **4.4** The First Derivative Test and Applications
- **4.5** Simple Curve Sketching
- **4.6** Higher Derivatives and Concavity
- **4.7** Curve Sketching and Asymptotes

ACKNOWLEDGMENTS

All experienced textbook authors know the value of critical reviewing during the preparation and revision of a manuscript. In our work on this edition we have profited greatly from the unusually detailed and constructive advice of the following very able reviewers:

- Kenzu Abdella—Trent University
- Martina Bode—Northwestern University
- David Caraballo—Georgetown University
- Tom Cassidy—Bucknell University
- Lucille Croom—Hunter College
- Yuanan Diao—University of North Carolina at Charlotte
- Victor Elias—University of Western Ontario
- Haitao Fan—Georgetown University
- James J. Faran, V—The State University of New York at Buffalo
- K. N. Gowrisankaran—McGill University
- Qing Han—University of Notre Dame
- Melvin D. Lax—California State University, Long Beach
- Robert H. Lewis—Fordham University
- Allan B. MacIssac—University of Western Ontario
- Rudolph M. Najar—California State University, Fresno
- George Pletsch—Albuquerque Technical and Vocational Institute
- Nancy Rallis—Boston College
- Robert C. Reilly—University of California, Irvine
- James A. Reneke—Clemson University
- Alexander Retakh—Yale University
- Carl Riehm—McMaster University
- Ira Sharenow—University of Wisconsin, Madison
- Kay Strangman—University of Wisconsin, Madison
- Sophie Tryphonas—University of Toronto at Scarborough
- Clifford E. Weil—Michigan State University
- Kamran Vakili—Princeton University
- Cathleen M. Zucco-Teveloff—Trinity College

Many of the best improvements that have been made must be credited to colleagues and users of the previous five editions throughout the United States, Canada, and abroad. We are grateful to all those, especially students, who have written to us, and hope they will continue to do so. We thank the accuracy checkers of M. and N. Toscano, who verified the solution of every worked-out example and odd-numbered answer, as well as all of the solutions in the Instructor's and Student Solutions Manuals. We believe that the appearance and quality of the finished book is clear testimony to the skill, diligence, and talent of an exceptional staff at Prentice-Hall. We owe special thanks to George Lobell, our mathematics editor, whose advice and criticism guided and shaped this revision in many significant and tangible ways, as did the constructive comments and suggestions of Ed Millman, our developmental editor. We also thank Gale Epps and Melanie Van Benthuysen for their highly varied and detailed services in aid of editors and authors throughout the work of revision. The visual graphics of this text have been widely praised in previous editions, and it is time for us to thank Ron Weichart of Network Graphics, who has worked with us through the past three editions. Jeanne Audino, our production editor, expertly and smoothly managed the whole process of book production. Our art director, Jonathan Boylan, supervised and coordinated the attractive design and layout of the text and the cover for this edition. Vince Jansen coordinated the production of the CD-ROM, for which we thank especially Robert Curtis and Lee Wayand for their interactive examples and Harald Pleym for his Maple worksheets. Finally, we again are unable to thank Alice Fitzgerald Edwards and Carol Wilson Penney adequately for their unrelenting assistance, encouragement, support, and patience extending through six editions and over two decades of work on this textbook.

C. Henry Edwards
hedwards@math.uga.edu

David E. Penney
dpenney@math.uga.edu

Please turn to page xxi to see other text versions.

WALK-THROUGH CONTENTS

FEATURES WALK-THROUGH

New Features of the Sixth Edition	xxii
Pedagogy Changes	xxvi
Hallmark Features	xxx

ADDITIONAL TEXTBOOK OPTIONS

Hardcovers:

Calculus, Early Transcendentals, Matrix Version 6e	xxxiv
Calculus, Matrix Version 6e	xxxvi
Calculus, Early Transcendentals 6e	xxxviii

Paperbacks:

Single Variable Calculus 6e	xl
Multivariable Calculus 6e	xlii
Single Variable Calculus, Early Transcendentals 6e	xliv
Multivariable Calculus with Matrices 6e	xlvi

MEDIA RESOURCES FOR INSTRUCTORS

PH Grade Assist	xlviii
Instructor's Resource CD-ROM	xlix

MEDIA RESOURCES FOR STUDENTS

Student CD-ROM	l
Companion Website	li

PRINT SUPPLEMENTS

For Instructors	lii
For Students	liii

Not for resale: Answers missing from the back. Please contact your Prentice Hall rep for full Solutions Manual.

NEW FEATURES OF THE SIXTH EDITION

The new sixth edition is the most extensive revision since the authors crafted the first edition many years ago. The following pages will highlight overall changes to Calculus 6e.

CONTENT CHANGES

Over 120 new worked examples

Now carefully integrated throughout the text. These examples illustrate modern applications to a variety of disciplines, including engineering, physics, environmental science, and medicine.

Flow Rates and Cardiac Output

The determination of flow rates in pipes or streams has important applications ranging from engineering and environmental studies to medical procedures. A common technique involves the injection of a known amount A of a dye or other marker into the flow at time $t = 0$, followed by measurement at periodic intervals of the concentration of the dye by a probe at a fixed point downstream.

Suppose that all the dye has passed the measurement probe by time $t = T$. Subdivide the interval $[0, T]$ into n time intervals all of the same duration $\Delta t = T/n$. If the concentration $c(t)$ of the dye in the stream is measured at times $t_1, t_2, \ldots, t_n$, then we can estimate the amount of dye that passes the probe during the subinterval of time $[t_{i-1}, t_i]$. If the (unknown) constant flow rate is F, then the volume ΔV_i of fluid that passes the probe during the subinterval of time is $\Delta V_i = F \Delta t$. It may help to think of typical units:

$$\left(F \frac{\text{cm}^3}{\text{second}}\right) \times (\Delta t \text{ seconds}) = \Delta V_i \text{ cm}^3.$$

The amount ΔA_i (in mg, for instance) of dye in this volume of fluid is given by

$$\text{amount (mg)} = \text{concentration}\left(\frac{\text{mg}}{\text{cm}^3}\right) \times \text{volume (cm}^3\text{)}.$$

If we use the measured concentration $c(t_i)$ as the approximate concentration throughout the time interval $[t_{i-1}, t_i]$, this gives

$$\Delta A_i \approx c(t_i) \Delta V_i = c(t_i) \cdot F \Delta t = F \cdot c(t_i) \Delta t.$$

Because the total amount A of injected dye passes the probe by time $t = T$, we add the individual amounts ΔA_i for $i = 1, 2, \ldots, n$ and get

$$A = \sum_{i=1}^{n} \Delta A_i \approx F \cdot \sum_{i=1}^{n} c(t_i) \Delta t$$

(using the fact that the flow rate F is constant). Finally, we recognize the Riemann sum on the right and conclude that

$$A = F \int_0^T c(t)\, dt.$$

Thus the previously unknown flow rate is given by

$$F = \frac{A}{\int_0^T c(t)\, dt}, \qquad (18)$$

in terms of the known amount A of dye injected and the downstream concentration $c(t)$ that has been measured at times $t = t_1, t_2, \ldots, t_n$. We can therefore estimate F by substituting in Eq. (18) the Riemann sum approximation

$$\int_0^T c(t)\, dt \approx \sum_{i=1}^{n} c(t_i) \Delta t$$

—or, alternatively, a Simpson approximation to the integral.

In medicine the term *cardiac output* is used for the flow rate of blood pumped through the aorta by the heart. A typical cardiac output for a 70-kg man would be in the range of 5 to 7 liters per minute (L/min). The dye marker is injected into the heart (or into a vein entering the heart), and then concentration readings are taken by a probe inserted into the aorta leaving the heart.

pages 372-373

in (1) yields the differential equation

$$\frac{dP}{dt} = kP^2 - \delta P = kP(P - M) \qquad (13)$$

(where $M = \delta/k > 0$) as a mathematical model of the population.

Note that the right-hand side in Eq. (13) is the *negative* of the right-hand side in the logistic equation in (7). We will see that the constant M is now a **threshold population,** with the way the population behaves in the future depending critically on whether the initial population P_0 is less than or greater than M.

EXAMPLE 7 Consider an animal population $P(t)$ that is modeled by the equation

$$\frac{dP}{dt} = (0.0004)P \cdot (P - 150) = (0.0004)P^2 - (0.06)P. \qquad (14)$$

We want to find $P(t)$ in the following two cases: (a) $P(0) = 200$; (b) $P(0) = 100$.

Solution To solve the equation in (14), we separate the variables and integrate. We get

$$\int \frac{1}{P(P-150)} \, dP = \int (0.0004) \, dt;$$

$$-\frac{1}{150} \int \left(\frac{1}{P} - \frac{1}{P-150} \right) dP = \int (0.0004) \, dt \qquad \text{[partial fractions]};$$

$$\ln|P| - \ln|P - 150| = -(0.06)t + C;$$

$$\frac{P}{P-150} = \pm e^C e^{-(0.06)t} = B e^{-(0.06)t} \qquad \text{[where } B = \pm e^C\text{]}. \qquad (15)$$

(a) Substituting $t = 0$ and $P = 200$ in (15) gives $B = 4$. With this value of B we solve Eq. (15) for

$$P(t) = \frac{600 e^{-(0.06)t}}{4 e^{-(0.06)t} - 1}. \qquad (16)$$

Note that as t increases and approaches $T = (\ln 4)/0.06 \approx 23.105$, the positive denominator on the right in (16) decreases and approaches zero. Consequently $P(t) \to +\infty$ as $t \to T^-$. This is a *doomsday* situation—a real population *explosion*.

(b) Substituting $t = 0$ and $P = 100$ in (15) gives $B = -2$. With this value of B we solve Eq. (15) for

$$P(t) = \frac{300 e^{-(0.06)t}}{2 e^{-(0.06)t} + 1} = \frac{300}{2 + e^{(0.06)t}}. \qquad (17)$$

Note that as t increases without bound, the positive denominator in the right in Eq. (17) approaches $+\infty$. Consequently $P(t) \to 0$ as $t \to +\infty$. This is an (eventual) *extinction* situation. ◆

Thus the population in Example 7 either explodes or is an endangered species threatened with extinction, depending on whether or not its initial size exceeds the threshold population $M = 150$. An approximation to this phenomenon is sometimes observed with animal populations, such as the alligator population in certain areas of the southern United States.

Figure 9.5.4 shows typical solution curves that illustrate the two possibilities for a population $P(t)$ satisfying Eq. (13). If $P_0 = M$ (exactly!), then the population remains constant. But this equilibrium situation is highly unstable. If P_0 exceeds M, no matter how slightly, then $P(t)$ increases rapidly without bound, whereas if the initial (positive) population is less than M (however slightly), then it decreases—more gradually—toward zero as $t \to +\infty$.

FIGURE 9.5.4 Typical solution curves for the explosion-extinction equation $P' = kP(P - M)$.

xxiv FEATURES WALK-THROUGH

Completely New Chapter 9 on Differential Equations and Their Applications ▼

Found in Calculus II. This new chapter appears immediately after the chapter on techniques of integration. It includes both direction fields and Euler's method, together with the more symbolic elementary methods and applications for both first- and second-order equations. Written specifically to show the applications of Calculus to DEs, this early coverage allows professors to introduce more applications in later chapters. A very modern approach (i.e., each equation is solved graphically, numerically, and symbolically) to solving DEs is employed.

9.2 | SLOPE FIELDS AND EULER'S METHOD

Consider a differential equation of the form $dy/dx = F(x, y)$, where $F(x, y)$ contains both the variables x and y. To solve it, we might think of integrating both sides with respect to x, and hence write $y(x) = \int F(x, y(x))\,dx + C$. Unfortunately, this does not provide a solution of the differential equation because the integral involves the unknown function $y(x)$ itself. In fact, there exists *no* straightforward procedure by which a general differential equation can be solved explicitly. Indeed, the solutions of such a simple-looking differential equation as $dy/dx = x^2 + y^2$ cannot be expressed in terms of the ordinary elementary functions studied in calculus. Nevertheless, the graphical and numerical methods of this section can be used to construct *approximate* solutions of differential equations that suffice for many practical purposes.

Slope Fields and Graphical Solutions

There is a simple geometric way to think about solutions of a given differential equation $dy/dx = F(x, y)$. At each point (x, y) of the xy-plane at which F is defined, the value of $F(x, y)$ determines a slope $m = y'(x) = F(x, y)$. A solution of the differential equation is simply a function whose graph has this "correct slope" at each point through which it passes. Thus a **solution curve** of the differential equation $dy/dx = F(x, y)$—the graph of a solution of this equation—is simply a curve in the xy-plane whose tangent line at each point (x, y) has slope $m = F(x, y)$. For instance, Fig. 9.2.1 shows a solution curve of the differential equation $dy/dx = x - y$ together with lines tangent at thre...

FIGURE 9.2.1 A solution curve for the differential equation $y' = x - y$ together with tangent lines having
- slope $m_1 = x_1 - y_1$ at the point (x_1, y_1);
- slope $m_2 = x_2 - y_2$ at the point (x_2, y_2); and
- slope $m_3 = x_3 - y_3$ at the point (x_3, y_3).

page 558

9.6 | LINEAR SECOND-ORDER EQUATIONS

A **second-order** differential equation is one that involves the second derivative y'' (and perhaps also the first derivative y') of the dependent variable y. It is called **linear** provided that it is linear in the unknown function $y(x)$ and its derivatives. Thus a **linear second-order** differential equation is one of the form

$$A(x)\frac{d^2y}{dx^2} + B(x)\frac{dy}{dx} + C(x)y = F(x), \quad (1)$$

where the *coefficients* $A(x)$, $B(x)$, $C(x)$, and $F(x)$ are given continuous functions of the independent variable on an appropriate open interval I where we may hope to determine a solution. A **solution** of (1) is simply a function $y = y(x)$ that satisfies the differential equation at every point of the interval I.

The coefficient functions in (1) need *not* be linear in x. Thus the second-order equation

$$e^x y'' + (\cos x)y' + (1 + \sqrt{x})y = \tan^{-1} x$$

is linear even though the coefficients are quite nonlinear functions of x. By contrast, the equations

$$y'' = yy' \quad \text{and} \quad y'' + 3(y')^2 + 4y^3 = 0$$

are not linear, because products or powers of y or its derivatives appear in each.

In this section we restrict our attention to the case in which $F(x) \equiv 0$ in Eq. (1). Such a linear equation is said to be **homogeneous**. Thus a homogeneous linear second-order differential equation is one of the form

$$A(x)\frac{d^2y}{dx^2} + B(x)\frac{dy}{dx} + C(x)y = 0. \quad (2)$$

Homogeneous linear equations have the useful feature that we can construct new solutions by forming *linear combinations* of known solutions. In particular, any **linear combination** $y = c_1y_1 + c_2y_2$ of two known solutions y_1 and y_2 of Eq. (2) is another solution of the differential equation.

THEOREM 1   Linear Combinations of Solutions

Suppose that the two functions y_1 and y_2 are both solutions of the homogeneous linear equation in (2) and that c_1 and c_2 are constants. Then the new function y defined by

$$y(x) = c_1 y_1(x) + c_2 y_2(x)$$

also satisfies Eq. (2).

PROOF   The fact that y_1 and y_2 are both solutions of Eq. (2) means that

$$Ay_1'' + By_1' + Cy_1 = 0 \quad \text{and} \quad Ay_2'' + By_2' + Cy_2 = 0.$$

It follows (using linearity of differentiation) that

$$Ay'' + By' + Cy = A(c_1y_1 + c_2y_2)'' + B(c_1y_1 + c_2y_2)' + C(c_1y_1 + c_2y_2)$$
$$= A(c_1y_1'' + c_2y_2'') + B(c_1y_1' + c_2y_2') + C(c_1y_1 + c_2y_2)$$
$$= c_1(Ay_1'' + By_1' + Cy_1) + c_2(Ay_2'' + By_2' + Cy_2)$$
$$= c_1 \cdot 0 + c_2 \cdot 0 = 0.$$

Thus we have verified that the linear combination $y = c_1y_1 + c_2y_2$ is also a solution of Eq. (2).   ◂

page 598

Power Series are Used to Solve Differential Equations ▼

For the first time, the Infinite Series chapter is truly integrated into Calculus II by tying power series back to previous chapter on DEs. Unique sections 11.8–11.10 show this connection.

11.10 SERIES SOLUTIONS OF DIFFERENTIAL EQUATIONS

In Section 9.6 we saw that solving a homogeneous linear differential equation with constant coefficients can be reduced to the algebraic problem of finding the roots of its characteristic equation. There is no simple or similarly routine procedure for solving linear differential equations with *variable* coefficients. Even such a simple-looking equation as $y'' - xy = 0$ has no solution that can be expressed in terms of the standard elementary functions of calculus. One of the most important applications of power series is their use to solve such differential equations.

The Power Series Method

The *power series method* for solving a differential equation consists of substituting the power series

$$y = \sum_{n=0}^{\infty} c_n x^n = c_0 + c_1 x + c_2 x^2 + c_3 x^3 + \cdots \qquad (1)$$

in the differential equation, and then attempting to determine what the values of the coefficients $c_0, c_1, c_2, c_3, \ldots$ must be in order that the series in (1) will actually satisfy the given differential equation. At first glance this might seem to be a formidable problem, because we have infinitely many unknowns $c_0, c_1, c_2, c_3, \ldots$ to find. Nevertheless, we will see that the method frequently succeeds. When it does, we obtain a power series representation of a solution, in contrast to the closed form solutions that result from the solution techniques we saw in Chapter 9.

Before we can substitute the series in (1) in a differential equation, we must first know what to substitute for the derivatives $y', y'', \ldots$ of the unknown function $y(x)$. But recall from Theorem 3 in Section 11.8 that the derivative of a power series can be calculated by termwise differentiation. Hence the first and second derivatives of the series in (1) are given by

$$y' = \sum_{n=1}^{\infty} n c_n x^{n-1} = c_1 + 2c_2 x + 3c_3 x^2 + \cdots \qquad (2)$$

and

$$y'' = \sum_{n=2}^{\infty} n(n-1) c_n x^{n-2} = 2c_2 + 6c_3 x + 12c_4 x^2 + \cdots. \qquad (3)$$

Also, these two series have the same radius of convergence as the original series in (1).

The process of determining the coefficients $c_0, c_1, c_2, c_3, \ldots$ in the series so that it will satisfy a given differential equation depends also on the following consequence of termwise differentiation: If two power series represent the same function on an open interval, then they are identical series. That is, they are one and the same power series. (See Problem 66 in Section 11.8.) In particular, if $\sum a_n x^n \equiv 0$ *on an open interval, then it follows that* $a_n = 0$ *for all n*. This fact is sometimes called the **identity principle** for power series.

EXAMPLE 1 Solve the equation $y' + 2y = 0$.

Solution We substitute the series

$$y = \sum_{n=0}^{\infty} c_n x^n \quad \text{and} \quad y' = \sum_{n=1}^{\infty} n c_n x^{n-1},$$

and obtain

$$\sum_{n=1}^{\infty} n c_n x^{n-1} + 2 \sum_{n=0}^{\infty} c_n x^n = 0. \qquad (4)$$

pages 758-759

Not for resale: Answers missing from the back. Please contact your Prentice Hall rep for full Solutions Manual.

PEDAGOGY CHANGES

New True/False Study Guides ▼

New True/False Study Guides
Author-written True/False questions that focus on conceptual understanding are provided to help students review each section. These 1,080 new questions are located on the new free student CD-ROM. In-text icons direct students to these questions.

3.1 TRUE/FALSE STUDY GUIDE

3.1 CONCEPTS: QUESTIONS AND DISCUSSION

1. The slope line in Fig. 3.1.5 looks as if it might be tangent to the parabola. Is it? If not, what's a simple way you could alter the equation of the parabola—without changing its slope line—in order to ensure that the line will be tangent to the altered parabola?

2. When a ball is tossed straight upward, it may appear to hover at the apex of its trajectory for a brief period of time. Does it?

3. You are pulled over by a policeman who claims that you did not stop properly at a stop sign. You argue that as you braked your car, its velocity was zero at a certain instant before you removed your foot from the brake pedal and proceeded through the intersection. The policeman replies that you nevertheless did not come to a full stop—that he is certain your velocity did not remain zero for even a hundredth of a second. What's the cause of this disagreement? Explain it with such convincing clarity that the judge will let you off without you paying a fine.

4. The ball of Example 6 took the same amount of time to rise from the ground to its highest point as to fall back to the ground. Is this always the case for a ball governed by Eqs. (17) and (18) of this section? *Suggestion:* In lieu of a blizzard of algebra, think about the symmetry of the parabola in Fig. 3.1.19.

page 112

New End-of-Section Concept Questions and Discussions

330 New Questions
These questions can serve as the basis for either writing assignments or for individual and group discussion. Also added are more challenging problems at the end of many problem sets.

5.9 TRUE/FALSE STUDY GUIDE

5.9 CONCEPTS: QUESTIONS AND DISCUSSION

1. Suppose that f is an increasing function on $[a, b]$. Which is larger—the left-hand sum or the right-hand sum, each with n subintervals? What if f is a decreasing function? Draw sketches illustrating both cases.
2. Suppose that the graph of $y = f(x)$ is concave upward on $[a, b]$. Which is larger—the midpoint sum or the trapezoidal sum, each with n subintervals? What if the graph is concave downward? Draw sketches illustrating both cases.
3. Explain why you cannot set up a Simpson's sum beginning with a partition of $[a, b]$ into an odd number of subintervals. If you try to do so, what goes wrong?

page 357

Not for resale: Answers missing from the back. Please contact your Prentice Hall rep for full Solutions Manual.

Updated Examples, Exercises, and Projects

EXAMPLE 3 According to data posted at www.census.gov, the world's total population reached 6 billion persons in mid-1999, and was then increasing at the rate of about 212 thousand persons each day. Assuming that natural population growth at this rate continues, we want to answer these questions:

(a) What is the annual growth rate k?
(b) What will the world population be at the middle of the 21st century?
(c) How long will it take for the world population to increase tenfold—thereby reaching the 60 billion that some demographers believe to be the maximum for which the planet can provide adequate food supplies?

page 549

Examples
Approximately twenty percent of the worked examples are new or significantly revised. Many text discussions and explanations are also new. Additional computational detail has been inserted in worked examples where students have experienced difficulty.

Exercises
More than 2000 new exercises and questions Some exercises encourage the use of technology (graphing calculators or computer algebra systems). All exercise sets have been updated, with the addition of more challenging questions.

13. $x = \sin t - \cos t,\ y = \sin t + \cos t;\ \frac{1}{4}\pi \leq t \leq \frac{1}{2}\pi$
14. $x = e^t \sin t,\ y = e^t \cos t;\ 0 \leq t \leq \pi$
15. $r = e^{\theta/2};\ 0 \leq \theta \leq 4\pi$
16. $r = \theta;\ 2\pi \leq \theta \leq 4\pi$

In Problems 17 through 22, find the area of the surface of revolution generated by revolving the given curve around the indicated axis.

17. $x = 1 - t,\ y = 2\sqrt{t},\ 1 \leq t \leq 4$; the x-axis
18. $x = 2t^2 + t^{-1},\ y = 8\sqrt{t},\ 1 \leq t \leq 2$; the x-axis
19. $x = t^3,\ y = 2t + 3,\ -1 \leq t \leq 1$; the y-axis
20. $x = 2t + 1,\ y = t^2 + t,\ 0 \leq t \leq 3$; the y-axis
21. $r = 4\sin\theta,\ 0 \leq \theta \leq \pi$; the x-axis
22. $r = e^\theta,\ 0 \leq \theta \leq \frac{1}{2}\pi$; the y-axis
23. Find the volume generated by revolving around the x-axis the region under the cycloidal arch of Example 2.
24. Find the area of the surface generated by revolving around the x-axis the cycloidal arch of Example 2.
25. Use the parametrization $x = a\cos t,\ y = b\sin t$ to find: (a) the area bounded by the ellipse $x^2/a^2 + y^2/b^2 = 1$; (b) the volume of the ellipsoid generated by revolving this ellipse around the x-axis.
26. Find the area bounded by the loop of the parametric curve $x = t^2,\ y = t^3 - 3t$ of Problem 25 in Section 10.4.
27. Use the parametrization $x = t\cos t,\ y = t\sin t$ of the Archimedean spiral to find the arc length of the first full turn of this spiral (corresponding to $0 \leq t \leq 2\pi$).
28. The circle $(x - b)^2 + y^2 = a^2$ with radius $a < b$ and center $(b, 0)$ can be parametrized by
$$x = b + a\cos t,\quad y = a\sin t,\quad 0 \leq t \leq 2\pi.$$
Find the surface area of the torus obtained by revolving this circle around the y-axis (Fig. 10.5.8).

FIGURE 10.5.8 The torus of Problem 28.

29. The *astroid* (four-cusped hypocycloid) has equation $x^{2/3} + y^{2/3} = a^{2/3}$ (Fig. 10.4.15) and the parametrization
$$x = a\cos^3 t,\quad y = a\sin^3 t,\quad 0 \leq t \leq 2\pi.$$
Find the area of the region bounded by the astroid.
30. Find the total length of the astroid of Problem 29.

31. Find the area of the surface obtained by revolving the astroid of Problem 29 around the x-axis.
32. Find the area of the surface generated by revolving the lemniscate $r^2 = 2a^2 \cos 2\theta$ around the y-axis (Fig. 10.5.9). [Suggestion: Use Eq. (10); note that $r\,dr = -2a^2 \sin 2\theta\,d\theta$.]

FIGURE 10.5.9 The surface generated by rotating the lemniscate of Problem 32 around the y-axis.

33. Figure 10.5.10 shows the graph of the parametric curve
$$x = t^2\sqrt{3},\quad y = 3t - \tfrac{1}{3}t^3.$$
The shaded region is bounded by the part of the curve for which $-3 \leq t \leq 3$. Find its area.

FIGURE 10.5.10 The parametric curve of Problems 33 through 36.

34. Find the arc length of the loop of the curve of Problem 33.
35. Find the volume of the solid obtained by revolving around the x-axis the shaded region in Fig. 10.5.10.
36. Find the surface area of revolution generated by revolving around the x-axis the loop of Fig. 10.5.10.
37. (a) With reference to Problem 30 and Fig. 10.4.14 in Section 10.4, show that the arc length of the first-quadrant loop of the folium of Descartes is
$$s = 6\int_0^1 \frac{\sqrt{1 + 4t^2 - 4t^3 - 4t^5 + 4t^6 + t^8}}{(1 + t^3)^2}\,dt.$$
(b) Use a programmable calculator or a computer to approximate this length.
38. Find the surface area generated by rotating around the y-axis the cycloidal arch of Example 2. [Suggestion: $\sqrt{x^2} = x$ only if $x \geq 0$.]

page 658

Revised Optional Technology Projects ▼

About three dozen projects are included after key sections. Projects are designed to illustrate the principal ideas of their preceding sections and contain additional problems intended for solution with the use of a calculator or computer. Now briefer, with the deletion of in-text technology details. Maple/*Mathematica*/MATLAB/Calculator resources for each Project are included on the free student CD-ROM. Optional technology manuals are available at half price when packaged with the text.

3.5 Project: When Is Your Coffee Cup Stablest?

Your car has no cupholder, so you must place your filled coffee cup on the passenger seat beside you when you start out in the morning. Bitter experience has taught you that the cup is least stable—and most prone to spill—when it's completely full, but becomes more stable as you drink the coffee and thereby lower its level in the cup. Now you're ready to apply calculus to analyze this phenomenon.

Figure 3.5.22 shows a coffee cup partially filled with coffee. We will assume that it is stablest when the *centroid* of the cup-plus-coffee is lowest. The **centroid** of a solid cylinder or cylindrical shell is its geometric central point, and the y-coordinate $\overline{y}$ of the centroid of a composite body consisting of several pieces with masses $m_1, m_2,$ and m_3 having centroids with respective y-coordinates $y_1, y_2,$ and y_3 is given by

$$\overline{y} = \frac{m_1 y_1 + m_2 y_2 + m_3 y_3}{m_1 + m_2 + m_3}. \tag{1}$$

This formula means that $\overline{y}$ is an average of the y-coordinates $y_1, y_2,$ and y_3 of the individual centroids, each weighted by the corresponding mass.

The simplified model of the coffee cup shown in Fig. 3.5.22 consists of the following:

- A side surface that is a cylindrical shell with height H, inner radius R, and thickness T, and
- A bottom that is a solid cylinder with radius $R + T$ and height B.

FIGURE 3.5.22 Coffee cup partially filled with coffee to depth y.

FIGURE 3.5.23 Centroid height $f(y)$ as a function of coffee depth y.

pages 150-151

Not for resale: Answers missing from the back. Please contact your Prentice Hall rep for full Solutions Manual.

HALLMARK FEATURES

The following pages detail hallmark features that have always characterized the essence of the Edwards/Penney Calculus series.

Accuracy ▶

Even more than its predecessors, this edition was subjected to a comprehensive reviewing process to ensure accuracy. For example, every answer appearing in the Answers section at the back of the book in this edition has been verified using *Mathematica*.

The Fundamental Theorem

We state the fundamental theorem of calculus in two parts. The first part is the fact that every function f that is continuous on an interval I has an antiderivative on I. In particular, an antiderivative of f can be obtained by integrating f in a certain way. Intuitively, in the case $f(x) > 0$, we let $F(x)$ denote the area under the graph of f from a fixed point a of I to x, a point of I with $x > a$. We shall prove that $F'(x) = f(x)$. We show the construction of the function F in Fig. 5.6.3. More precisely, we define the function F as follows:

$$F(x) = \int_a^x f(t)\,dt,$$

where we use the dummy variable t in the integrand to avoid confusion with the upper limit x. The proof that $F'(x) = f(x)$ will be independent of the supposition that $x > a$.

FIGURE 5.6.3 The area function F is an antiderivative of f.

THE FUNDAMENTAL THEOREM OF CALCULUS
Suppose that f is continuous on the closed interval $[a, b]$.

Part 1: If the function F is defined on $[a, b]$ by

$$F(x) = \int_a^x f(t)\,dt, \qquad (7)$$

then F is an antiderivative of f. That is, $F'(x) = f(x)$ for x in $[a, b]$.

Part 2: If G is any antiderivative of f on $[a, b]$, then

$$\int_a^b f(x)\,dx = \Big[G(x)\Big]_a^b = G(b) - G(a). \qquad (8)$$

PROOF OF PART 1 By the definition of the derivative,

$$F'(x) = \lim_{h\to 0} \frac{F(x+h) - F(x)}{h} = \lim_{h\to 0} \frac{1}{h}\left(\int_a^{x+h} f(t)\,dt - \int_a^x f(t)\,dt\right).$$

But

$$\int_a^{x+h} f(t)\,dt = \int_a^x f(t)\,dt + \int_x^{x+h} f(t)\,dt$$

page 321

---

makes it clear that the equation

$$1 - x = 3\cos x$$

has one negative solution and two positive solutions. They could be approximated by (separately) zooming in on the three intersection points. ◆

Can You Believe What You See on Your Calculator/Computer Screen?

The examples we give next show that the short answer to this question is "not always." One reason is that a typical graphing calculator or simple computer program plots only a finite number of equally spaced points on the curve $y = f(x)$, $a \leq x \leq b$, joining the selected points with straight line segments. If the plotted points are sufficiently close, then the resulting graph may look to the unaided eye like a smooth curve, but it may miss some essential features that would be revealed if more points were plotted.

FIGURE 1.4.20 Solving the equation $1 - x = 3\cos x$ of Example 12.

EXAMPLE 13 A 1-ampere alternating current with frequency 60 Hz (Hertz; cycles per second) is described by the function

$$I(t) = \sin 120\pi t. \qquad (15)$$

The absolute value $|I(t)|$ gives the magnitude (in amperes) of the current at time t, which flows in one direction when $I > 0$ the opposite direction when $I < 0$. A simple computer program was used to plot the alleged graphs of $I(t)$ shown in Figs. 1.4.21 through 1.4.23. The graph in Fig. 1.4.21 is plotted on the interval $-1 \leq t \leq 1$, where we should see 120 complete oscillations because the period of $I(t)$ in Eq. (15) is 1/60 s. But instead the figure shows exactly one oscillation, so something has gone badly wrong. The graph in Fig. 1.4.22 is plotted on the interval $-\frac{1}{2} \leq t \leq \frac{1}{2}$, and whatever it is has gone from merely wrong to outright bizarre. Finally, in Fig. 1.4.23 the graph is plotted on the interval $-\frac{1}{30} \leq t \leq \frac{1}{30}$ of length $\frac{4}{60}$, so we should see exactly 4 complete oscillations. And indeed we do, so we've finally got a correct graph of the current function in Eq. (15). ◆

Here's an explanation of what went wrong at first in Example 13. The computer was programmed to plot values at exactly 120 equally spaced points of the interval desired. So in Fig. 1.4.21 we're plotting only 1 point per cycle—not nearly enough to capture the actual shape of the curve—and only 2 points per cycle in Fig. 1.4.22. But in Fig. 1.4.23 we're plotting 30 points per cycle, and this gives an accurate representation of the actual graph.

The incorrect graph in Fig. 1.4.21—which seems to portray an oscillation with the incorrect period of 2 s, instead of the correct $\frac{1}{60}$ s—is an example of the phenomenon of *aliasing*. Another example of aliasing, occasionally seen in old Western movies, is the wagon wheel that appears to rotate slowly in the wrong direction.

FIGURE 1.4.21 On the interval $[-1, 1]$ it's wrong.

FIGURE 1.4.22 On the interval $[-1/2, 1/2]$ it's bizarre.

FIGURE 1.4.23 On the interval $[-1/30, 1/30]$ it's correct!

page 41

◀ Exposition

A lively and accessible writing style
From an author team renowned for its clarity and expert presentation of topics. Their crisp exposition, both intuitive and precise, makes calculus more accessible. An intuitive approach emphasizes both conceptual understanding and care in the formulation of definitions and key concepts of calculus. Some proofs that may be omitted at the discretion of the instructor are placed at the ends of sections and others are deferred to the book's appendices.

Not for resale: Answers missing from the back. Please contact your Prentice Hall rep for full Solutions Manual.

Applications

From a Wide Variety of Disciplines
Its diverse applications are what attract many students to calculus, and realistic applications provide valuable motivation and reinforcement for all students. This book is well-known for its broad range of applications, but it is neither necessary nor desirable that the course cover all of the applications in the book. This provides flexibility for each instructor to determine his or her own flavor and emphasis.

Elastic Springs

Consider a spring whose left end is held fixed and whose right end is free to move along the x-axis. We assume that the right end is at the origin $x = 0$ when the spring has its **natural length**—that is, when the spring is in its rest position, neither compressed nor stretched by outside forces.

According to **Hooke's law** for elastic springs, the force $F(x)$ that must be exerted on the spring to hold its right end at the point x is proportional to the displacement x of the right end from its rest position. That is,

$$F(x) = kx, \qquad (5)$$

where k is a positive constant. The constant k, called the **spring constant**, is a characteristic of the particular spring under study.

Figure 6.5.4 shows the arrangement of such a spring along the x-axis. The right end of the spring is held at position x on the x-axis by a force $F(x)$. The figure shows the situation for $x > 0$, so the spring is stretched. The force that the spring exerts on its right-hand end is directed to the left, so—as the figure indicates—the external force $F(x)$ must act to the right. The right is the positive direction here, so $F(x)$ must be a positive number. Because x and $F(x)$ have the same sign, k must also be positive. You can check that k is positive as well in the case $x < 0$.

FIGURE 6.5.4 The stretch x is proportional to the impressed force F.

Work in the sense of physics is different from work in the sense of physiology. At this moment the weightlifter is doing no work in the physics sense because he is holding the weight still.

pages 406–407

Real-life Examples

The exposition is centered around examples of the use of calculus to solve real problems of interest to real people. In selecting such problems for examples and exercises, the authors took the view that stimulating interest and motivating effective study go hand in hand. Students are shown that the knowledge gained with each new concept or technique will be worth the effort expended. In theoretical discussions, especially, the authors try to provide an intuitive picture of the goal before we set off in

FIGURE 6.5.5 A satellite in orbit 1000 mi above the surface of the earth (Example 3).

If distance is measured in miles and force in pounds, then this integral gives the work in mile-pounds. This is a very unconventional unit of work. We shall multiply by 5280 (ft/mi) to convert any such result into foot-pounds.

EXAMPLE 3 (Satellite Launch) How much work must be done to lift a 1000-lb satellite vertically from the earth's surface to an orbit 1000 mi above the surface? See Fig. 6.5.5, and take $R = 4000$ (mi) to be the radius of the earth.

Solution Because $F = 1000$ (lb) when $r = R = 4000$ (mi), we find from Eq. (6) that

$$k = 4000^2 \cdot 1000 = 16 \times 10^9 \quad (\text{mi}^2\cdot\text{lb}).$$

Then by Eq. (7), the work done is

$$W = \int_{4000}^{5000} \frac{k}{r^2}\, dr = \left[-\frac{k}{r}\right]_{4000}^{5000}$$

$$= (16 \times 10^9) \cdot \left(\tfrac{1}{4000} - \tfrac{1}{5000}\right) = 8 \times 10^5 \quad (\text{mi}\cdot\text{lb}).$$

We multiply by 5280 (ft/mi) and write the answer as

$$4.224 \times 10^9 = 4{,}224{,}000{,}000 \quad (\text{ft}\cdot\text{lb}). \qquad \blacklozenge$$

We can instead express the answer to Example 3 in terms of the power that the launch rocket must provide. **Power** is the rate at which work is done. For instance, 1 **horsepower** (hp) is defined to be 33,000 ft·lb/min. If the ascent to orbit takes 15 min and if only 2% of the power generated by the rocket is effective in lifting the satellite (the rest is used to lift the rocket and its fuel), we can convert the answer in Example 3 to horsepower. The *average* power that the rocket engine must produce during the 15-min ascent is

$$P = \frac{50 \cdot (4.224 \times 10^9)}{15 \cdot 33{,}000} \approx 427{,}000 \quad (\text{hp}).$$

The factor of 50 in the numerator comes from the 2% "efficiency" of the rocket: The total power must be multiplied by $1/(0.02) = 50$.

page 408

Not for resale: Answers missing from the back. Please contact your Prentice Hall rep for full Solutions Manual.

xxxii FEATURES WALK-THROUGH

4.7 Project: Locating Special Points on Exotic Graphs

The investigations described here deal with fairly exotic curves having critical and inflection points that are not clearly visible on their graphs if plotted on a "natural" scale. The reason is that different scales on the x- and y-axes are required to see the unusual behavior in question. In both investigations you are to begin with a graph that you generate with calculator or computer, and then analyze the curve—locating accurately all critical and inflection points—in order to plot additional graphs that demonstrate clearly all of the major features of the curve.

Investigation A Choose in advance a single-digit integer n (perhaps the final nonzero digit of your student I.D. number). Then your task is to analyze the structure of the curve

$$y = x^7 + 5x^6 - 11x^5 - 21x^4 + 31x^3 - 57x^2 - (101 + 2n)x + (89 - 3n).$$

Find the local maximum and minimum points and the inflection point (or points) on this curve, giving their coordinates accurate to four decimal places. To display all these points, you probably will need to produce separate plots with different scales, showing different parts of this curve. In the end, use all the information accumulated to produce a careful hand sketch (*not* to scale) displaying all the maxima, minima, and inflection points with their (approximate) coordinates labeled.

Investigation B Explore in the detail the structure of the graph of the function

$$f(x) = -1,234,567,890 + 2,695,140,459x^2 + 605,435,400x^3$$
$$- 411,401,250x^4 - 60,600,000x^5 + 25,000,000x^6.$$

The graph $y = f(x)$ is shown in Fig. 4.7.19. At a glance, it might appear that we have only three critical points—a local minimum near the origin and two critical points that are also inflection points, as well as two more inflection points that are not critical points. Settle the matter. How many of each, in fact, are there? Find and exhibit all of them in a graph; your graph may be a neat hand sketch and need not be to scale.

FIGURE 4.7.19 The "big picture" in Investigation B.

CHAPTER 4 REVIEW: DEFINITIONS, CONCEPTS, RESULTS

Use the following list as a guide to concepts that you may need to review.

1. Implicitly defined functions
2. Implicit differentiation
3. Solving related-rates problems
4. Increment Δy
5. Increasing functions and decreasing functions
6. Significance of the sign of the first derivative
7. Rolle's theorem
8. The mean value theorem
9. Consequences of the mean value theorem
10. First derivative test

page 267

◀ Integrated Technology

A new free CD-ROM accompanies the book and contains text examples animated with "What-If" scenarios. There are 550 text examples animated and accompanied by 2–3 questions each. In addition, 235 text problems are animated with hints and have related movies (running 3–5 minutes) that teach students how to get started in solving that problem. The whole text is now available in interactive Maple worksheets. The instructor version of the CD also contains 300 PowerPoint slides of the text art for use in lecture.

Visualization ▶

An increased emphasis on graphical visualization is provided by the computer-generated artwork. Over 800 MATLAB- or *Mathematica*-generated figures illustrate the kinds of figures that students using graphing calculators can produce for themselves. Many of these are included with new graphical problem material. *Mathematica*-generated color graphics are included to highlight all sections involving three-dimensional material. The goal is to develop students' intuition of three-dimensional geometry.

FIGURE 12.7.12 The ellipsoid of Example 8.

FIGURE 12.7.13 The traces of the ellipsoid $\frac{x^2}{a^2} + \frac{y^2}{b^2} + \frac{z^2}{c^2}$ (Example 8).

which is the equation of an ellipse with semiaxes $(a/c)\sqrt{c^2 - z_0^2}$ and $(b/c)\sqrt{c^2 - z_0^2}$. Figure 12.7.12 shows this ellipsoid with semiaxes a, b, and c labeled. Figure 12.7.13 shows its trace ellipses in planes parallel to the three coordinate planes.

EXAMPLE 9 The **elliptic paraboloid**

$$\frac{x^2}{a^2} + \frac{y^2}{b^2} = \frac{z}{c} \quad (6)$$

is shown in Fig. 12.7.14. Its trace in the horizontal plane $z = z_0 > 0$ is the ellipse $x^2/a^2 + y^2/b^2 = z_0/c$ with semiaxes $a\sqrt{z_0/c}$ and $b\sqrt{z_0/c}$. Its trace in any vertical plane is a parabola. For instance, its trace in the plane $y = y_0$ has equation $x^2/a^2 + y_0^2/b^2 = z/c$, which can be written in the form $z - z_1 = k(x - x_1)^2$ by taking $z_1 = cy_0^2/b^2$ and $x_1 = 0$. The paraboloid opens upward if $c > 0$ and downward if $c < 0$. If $a = b$, then the paraboloid is said to be **circular**. Figure 12.7.15 shows the traces of a circular paraboloid in planes parallel to the xz- and yz-planes.

FIGURE 12.7.14 An elliptic paraboloid (Example 9).

EXAMPLE 10 The **elliptical cone**

$$\frac{x^2}{a^2} + \frac{y^2}{b^2} = \frac{z^2}{c^2} \quad (7)$$

is shown in Fig. 12.7.16. Its trace in the horizontal plane $z = z_0 \neq 0$ is an ellipse with semiaxes $a|z_0|/c$ and $b|z_0|/c$.

FIGURE 12.7.15 Trace parabolas of a circular paraboloid (Example 9).

FIGURE 12.7.16 An elliptic cone (Example 10).

page 834

Not for resale: Answers missing from the back. Please contact your Prentice Hall rep for full Solutions Manual.

◀ Comprehensive Exercise Sets

Comprised of varying levels of difficulty, these exercises test both computational and conceptual understanding of topics. The exercises in the book, the exercises on the student CD, and the exercises on the website combine to provide more problems than in any other calculus text on the market.

2.4 PROBLEMS

In Problems 1 through 8, apply the limit laws and the theorems of this section to show that the given function is continuous for all x.

1. $f(x) = 2x^5 - 7x^2 + 13$
2. $f(x) = 7x^3 - (2x+1)^5$
3. $g(x) = \dfrac{2x-1}{4x^2+1}$
4. $g(x) = \dfrac{x^3}{x^2+2x+5}$
5. $h(x) = \sqrt{x^2+4x+5}$
6. $h(x) = \sqrt[3]{1-5x}$
7. $f(x) = \dfrac{1-\sin x}{1+\cos^2 x}$
8. $g(x) = \sqrt[4]{1-\sin^2 x}$

In Problems 9 through 14, apply the limit laws and the theorems of this section to show that the given function is continuous on the indicated interval.

9. $f(x) = \dfrac{1}{x+1}, \quad x > -1$
10. $f(x) = \dfrac{x-1}{x^2-4}, \quad -2 < x < 2$
11. $g(t) = \sqrt{9-4t^2}, \quad -\tfrac{3}{2} \le t \le \tfrac{3}{2}$
12. $h(z) = \sqrt{(z-1)(3-z)}, \quad 1 \le z \le 3$
13. $f(x) = \dfrac{x}{\cos x}, \quad -\tfrac{1}{2}\pi < x < \tfrac{1}{2}\pi$
14. $g(t) = \sqrt{1-2\sin t}, \quad -\tfrac{1}{6}\pi < t < \tfrac{1}{6}\pi$

In Problems 15 through 36, tell where the given function is continuous. Recall that when the domain of a function is not specified, it is the set of all real numbers for which the formula of the function is meaningful.

15. $f(x) = 2x + \sqrt[3]{x}$
16. $g(x) = x^2 + \dfrac{1}{x}$
17. $f(x) = \dfrac{1}{x+3}$
18. $f(t) = \dfrac{5}{5-t}$
29. $f(x) = \dfrac{x}{\sqrt{4-x^2}}$
30. $f(x) = \sqrt{\dfrac{1-x^2}{4-x^2}}$
31. $f(x) = \dfrac{\sin x}{x^2}$
32. $g(\theta) = \dfrac{\theta}{\cos \theta}$
33. $f(x) = \dfrac{1}{\sin 2x}$
34. $f(x) = \sqrt{\sin x}$
35. $f(x) = \sin|x|$
36. $G(u) = \dfrac{1}{\sqrt{1+\cos u}}$

In Problems 37 through 48, find the points where the given function is not defined and is therefore not continuous. For each such point a, tell whether or not this discontinuity is removable.

37. $f(x) = \dfrac{x}{(x+3)^3}$
38. $f(t) = \dfrac{t}{t^2-1}$
39. $f(x) = \dfrac{x-2}{x^2-4}$
40. $G(u) = \dfrac{u+1}{u^2-u-6}$
41. $f(x) = \dfrac{1}{1-|x|}$
42. $h(x) = \dfrac{|x-1|}{(x-1)^3}$
43. $f(x) = \dfrac{x-17}{|x-17|}$
44. $g(x) = \dfrac{x^2+5x+6}{x+2}$
45. $f(x) = \begin{cases} -x & \text{if } x < 0; \\ x^2 & \text{if } x > 0 \end{cases}$
46. $f(x) = \begin{cases} x+1 & \text{if } x < 1; \\ 3-x & \text{if } x > 1 \end{cases}$

page 97

---

11 INFINITE SERIES

Srinivasa Ramanujan (1887–1920)

On a cold January day in 1913, the eminent Cambridge mathematics professor G. H. Hardy received a letter from an unknown 25-year-old clerk in the accounting department of a government office in Madras, India. Its author, Srinivasa Ramanujan, had no university education, he admitted—he had flunked out—but "after leaving school I have employed the spare time at my disposal to work at Mathematics ... I have not trodden through the conventional regular course ... but am striking out a new path for myself." The ten pages that followed listed in neat handwritten script approximately 50 formulas, most dealing with integrals and infinite series that Ramanujan had discovered, and asked Hardy's advice whether they contained anything of value. The formulas were of such exotic and unlikely appearance that Hardy at first suspected a hoax, but he and his colleague J. E. Littlewood soon realized that they were looking at the work of an extraordinary mathematical genius.

Thus began one of the most romantic episodes in the history of mathematics. In April 1914 Ramanujan arrived in England a poor, self-taught Indian mathematical amateur called to collaborate as an equal with the most sophisticated professional mathematicians of the day. For the next three years a steady stream of remarkable discoveries poured forth from his pen. But in 1917 he fell seriously ill, apparently with tuberculosis. The following year he returned to India to attempt to regain his health but never recovered, and he died in 1920 at the age of 32. Up to the very end he worked feverishly to record his final discoveries. He left behind notebooks outlining work whose completion occupied prominent mathematicians throughout the twentieth century.

With the possible exception of Euler, no one before or since has exhibited Ramanujan's virtuosity with infinite series. An example of his discoveries is the infinite series

$$\dfrac{1}{\pi} = \dfrac{\sqrt{8}}{9801} \sum_{n=0}^{\infty} \dfrac{(4n)!}{(n!)^4} \cdot \dfrac{(1103 + 26390n)}{396^{4n}},$$

whose first term yields the familiar approximation $\pi \approx 3.14159$, and with each additional term giving π to roughly eight more decimal places of accuracy. For instance, just four terms of Ramanujan's series are needed to calculate the 30-place approximation

$$\pi \approx 3.14159\,26535\,89793\,23846\,26433\,83279$$

that suffices for virtually any imaginable "practical" application—if the universe were a sphere with a radius of 10 billion light years, then this value of π would give its circumference accurate to the nearest hundredth of an inch. But in recent years Ramanujan's ideas have been used to calculate the value of π accurate to a *billion* decimal places. Indeed, such gargantuan computations of π are commonly used to check the accuracy of new supercomputers.

A typical page of Ramanujan's letter to Hardy, listing formulas Ramanujan had discovered, but with no hint of proof or derivation.

681

page 681

◀ Historical Material

Historical and biographical chapter openings offer students a sense of the development of our subject by real mathematicians. Both authors are fond of the history of mathematics and believe that it can favorably influence both our teaching and students' learning of mathematics. For this reason, numerous historical comments appear in the text

---

Not for resale: Answers missing from the back. Please contact your Prentice Hall rep for full Solutions Manual.

TEXTBOOK OPTIONS

This edition of Edwards/Penney Calculus is one of four hardcover versions. The other three are outlined here. There are also two different Single Variable Calculus paperbacks (early and late transcendental functions) and two different Multivariable Calculus paperbacks (with and without Matrices), also outlined here.

CALCULUS, EARLY TRANSCENDENTALS, MATRIX VERSION
0-13-093700-2

INSTRUCTOR'S EDITION
0-13-093711-8

INSTRUCTOR'S SOLUTIONS MANUAL TO ACCOMPANY *SINGLE VARIABLE CALCULUS, EARLY TRANSCENDENTALS*
0-13-066154-6

INSTRUCTOR'S SOLUTIONS MANUAL TO ACCOMPANY *MULTIVARIABLE CALCULUS WITH MATRICES*
0-13-066159-7

STUDENT SOLUTIONS MANUAL TO ACCOMPANY *SINGLE VARIABLE CALCULUS, EARLY TRANSCENDENTALS*
0-13-066155-4

STUDENT SOLUTIONS MANUAL TO ACCOMPANY *MULTIVARIABLE CALCULUS WITH MATRICES*
0-13-066150-3

TEST ITEM FILE
0-13-008845-5

TESTGEN-EQ
0-13-092075-4

THIS TEXT COVERS TRANSCENDENTAL FUNCTIONS IN CALC I AND INCLUDES MATRICES IN CALC III

Contents

1. **Functions, Graphs, and Models**
   - 1.1 Functions and Mathematical Modeling
   - 1.2 Graphs of Equations and Functions
   - 1.3 Polynomials and Algebraic Functions
   - 1.4 Transcendental Functions
   - 1.5 Preview: What *Is* Calculus?

2. **Prelude to Calculus**
   - 2.1 Tangent Lines and Slope Predictors
   - 2.2 The Limit Concept
   - 2.3 More About Limits
   - 2.4 The Concept of Continuity

3. **The Derivative**
   - 3.1 The Derivative and Rates of Change
   - 3.2 Basic Differentiation Rules
   - 3.3 The Chain Rule
   - 3.4 Derivatives of Algebraic Functions
   - 3.5 Maxima and Minima of Functions on Closed Intervals
   - 3.6 Applied Optimization Problems
   - 3.7 Derivatives of Trigonometric Functions
   - 3.8 Exponential and Logarithmic Functions
   - 3.9 Implicit Differentiation and Related Rates
   - 3.10 Successive Approximations and Newton's Method

4. **Additional Applications of the Derivative**
   - 4.1 Introduction
   - 4.2 Increments, Differentials, and Linear Approximation
   - 4.3 Increasing and Decreasing Functions and the Mean Value Theorem
   - 4.4 The First Derivative Test and Applications
   - 4.5 Simple Curve Sketching
   - 4.6 Higher Derivatives and Concavity
   - 4.7 Curve Sketching and Asymptotes
   - 4.8 Intermediate Forms and L'Hôpital's Rule
   - 4.9 More Intermediate Forms

5. **The Integral**
   - 5.1 Introduction
   - 5.2 Antiderivatives and Initial Value Problems
   - 5.3 Elementary Area Computations
   - 5.4 Riemann Sums and the Integral
   - 5.5 Evaluation of Integrals

Not for resale: Answers missing from the back. Please contact your Prentice Hall rep for full Solutions Manual.

- 5.6 The Fundamental Theorem of Calculus
- 5.7 Integration by Substitution
- 5.8 Areas of Plane Regions
- 5.9 Numerical Integration

6. Applications of the Integral
- 6.1 Riemann Sum Approximations
- 6.2 Volumes by the Method of Cross Sections
- 6.3 Volumes by the Method of Cylindrical Shells
- 6.4 Arc Length and Surface Area of Revolution
- 6.5 Force and Work
- 6.6 Centroids of Plane Regions and Curves
- 6.7 The Natural Logarithm as an Integral
- 6.8 Inverse Trigonometric Functions
- 6.9 Hyperbolic Functions

7. Techniques of Integration
- 7.1 Introduction
- 7.2 Integral Tables and Simple Substitutions
- 7.3 Integration by Parts
- 7.4 Trigonometric Integrals
- 7.5 Rational Functions and Partial Fractions
- 7.6 Trigonometric Substitutions
- 7.7 Integrals Involving Quadratic Polynomials
- 7.8 Improper Integrals

8. Differential Equations
- 8.1 Simple Equations and Models
- 8.2 Slope Fields and Euler's Method
- 8.3 Separable Equations and Applications
- 8.4 Linear Equations and Applications
- 8.5 Population Models
- 8.6 Linear Second-Order Equations
- 8.7 Mechanical Vibrations

9. Polar Coordinates and Parametric Curves
- 9.1 Analytic Geometry and the Conic Sections
- 9.2 Polar Coordinates
- 9.3 Area Computations in Polar Coordinates
- 9.4 Parametric Curves
- 9.5 Integral Computations with Parametric Curves
- 9.6 Conic Sections and Applications
- 9.7 Mechanical Vibrations

10. Infinite Series
- 10.1 Introduction
- 10.2 Infinite Sequences
- 10.3 Infinite Series and Convergence
- 10.4 Taylor Series and Taylor Polynomials
- 10.5 The Integral Test
- 10.6 Comparison Tests for Positive-Term Series
- 10.7 Alternating Series and Absolute Convergence
- 10.8 Power Series
- 10.9 Power Series Computations
- 10.10 Series Solutions of Differential Equations

11. Vectors and Matrices
- 11.1 Vectors in the Plane
- 11.2 Three-Dimensional Vectors
- 11.3 The Cross Product of Vectors
- 11.4 Lines and Planes in Space
- 11.5 Linear Systems and Matrices
- 11.6 Matrix Operations
- 11.7 Eigenvalues and Rotated Conics

12. Curves and Surfaces in Space
- 12.1 Curves and Motion in Space
- 12.2 Curvature and Acceleration
- 12.3 Cylinders and Quadratic Surfaces
- 12.4 Cylindrical and Spherical Coordinates

13. Partial Differentiation
- 13.1 Introduction
- 13.2 Functions of Several Variables
- 13.3 Limits and Continuity
- 13.4 Partial Derivatives
- 13.5 Multivariable Optimization Problems
- 13.6 Linear Approximation and Matrix Derivatives
- 13.7 The Multivariable Chain Rule
- 13.8 Directional Derivatives and the Gradient Vector
- 13.9 Lagrange Multipliers and Constrained Optimization
- 13.10 Critical Points of Multivariable Functions

14. Multiple Integrals
- 14.1 Double Integrals
- 14.2 Double Integrals over More General Regions
- 14.3 Area and Volume by Double Integration
- 14.4 Double Integrals in Polar Coordinates
- 14.5 Applications of Double Integrals
- 14.6 Triple Integrals
- 14.7 Integration in Cylindrical and Spherical Coordinates
- 14.8 Surface Area
- 14.9 Change of Variables in Multiple Integrals

15. Vector Calculus
- 15.1 Vector Fields
- 15.2 Line Integrals
- 15.3 The Fundamental Theorem and Independence of Path
- 15.4 Green's Theorem
- 15.5 Surface Integrals
- 15.6 The Divergence Theorem
- 15.7 Stokes' Theorem

Not for resale: Answers missing from the back. Please contact your Prentice Hall rep for full Solutions Manual.

CALCULUS, MATRIX VERSION
0-13-008406-9

INSTRUCTOR'S SOLUTIONS MANUAL TO ACCOMPANY
SINGLE VARIABLE CALCULUS
0-13-066158-9

INSTRUCTOR'S SOLUTIONS MANUAL TO ACCOMPANY
MULTIVARIABLE CALCULUS WITH MATRICES
0-13-066159-7

STUDENT SOLUTIONS MANUAL TO ACCOMPANY
SINGLE VARIABLE CALCULUS
0-13-092077-0

STUDENT SOLUTIONS MANUAL TO ACCOMPANY
MULTIVARIABLE CALCULUS WITH MATRICES
0-13-066150-3

TEST ITEM FILE
0-13-066162-7
0-13-008845-5
(PLEASE ORDER BOTH)

TESTGEN-EQ
0-13-066161-9
0-13-092075-4
(PLEASE ORDER BOTH)

THIS TEXT COVERS TRANSCENDENTAL FUNCTIONS IN CALC II AND MATRICES IN CALC III

Contents

1. **Functions, Graphs, and Models**
   1.1 Functions and Mathematical Modeling
   1.2 Graphs of Equations and Functions
   1.3 Polynomials and Algebraic Functions
   1.4 Transcendental Functions
   1.5 Preview: What *Is* Calculus?

2. **Prelude to Calculus**
   2.1 Tangent Lines and Slope Predictors
   2.2 The Limit Concept
   2.3 More About Limits
   2.4 The Concept of Continuity

3. **The Derivative**
   3.1 The Derivative and Rates of Change
   3.2 Basic Differentiation Rules
   3.3 The Chain Rule
   3.4 Derivatives of Algebraic Functions
   3.5 Maxima and Minima of Functions on Closed Intervals
   3.6 Applied Optimization Problems
   3.7 Derivatives of Trigonometric Functions
   3.8 Successive Approximations and Newton's Method

4. **Additional Applications of the Derivative**
   4.1 Introduction
   4.2 Increments, Differentials, and Linear Approximation
   4.3 Increasing and Decreasing Functions and the Mean Value Theorem
   4.4 The First Derivative Test and Applications
   4.5 Simple Curve Sketching
   4.6 Higher Derivatives and Concavity
   4.7 Curve Sketching and Asymptotes
   4.8 Implicit Differentiation and Related Rates

5. **The Integral**
   5.1 Introduction
   5.2 Antiderivatives and Initial Value Problems
   5.3 Elementary Area Computations
   5.4 Riemann Sums and the Integral
   5.5 Evaluation of Integrals
   5.6 The Fundamental Theorem of Calculus
   5.7 Integration by Substitution
   5.8 Areas of Plane Regions
   5.9 Numerical Integration

6. **Applications of the Integral**
   6.1 Riemann Sum Approximations
   6.2 Volumes by the Method of Cross Sections
   6.3 Volumes by the Method of Cylindrical Shells
   6.4 Arc Length and Surface Area of Revolution
   6.5 Force and Work

Not for resale: Answers missing from the back. Please contact your Prentice Hall rep for full Solutions Manual.

- 6.6 Centroids of Plane Regions and Curves

7. Calculus of Transcendental Functions
- 7.1 Exponential and Logarithmic Functions
- 7.2 Indeterminate Forms and L'Hôpital's Rule
- 7.3 More Indeterminate Forms
- 7.4 The Logarithm as an Integral
- 7.5 Inverse Trigonometric Functions
- 7.6 Hyperbolic Functions

8. Techniques of Integration
- 8.1 Introduction
- 8.2 Integral Tables and Simple Substitutions
- 8.3 Integration by Parts
- 8.4 Trigonometric Integrals
- 8.5 Rational Functions and Partial Fractions
- 8.6 Trigonometric Substitutions
- 8.7 Integrals Involving Quadratic Polynomials
- 8.8 Improper Integrals

9. Differential Equations
- 9.1 Simple Equations and Models
- 9.2 Slope Fields and Euler's Method
- 9.3 Separable Equations and Applications
- 9.4 Linear Equations and Applications
- 9.5 Population Models
- 9.6 Linear Second-Order Equations
- 9.7 Mechanical Vibrations

10. Polar Coordinates and Parametric Curves
- 10.1 Analytic Geometry and the Conic Sections
- 10.2 Polar Coordinates
- 10.3 Area Computations in Polar Coordinates
- 10.4 Parametric Curves
- 10.5 Integral Computations with Parametric Curves
- 10.6 Conic Sections and Applications

11. Infinite Series
- 11.1 Introduction
- 11.2 Infinite Sequences
- 11.3 Infinite Series and Convergence
- 11.4 Taylor Series and Taylor Polynomials
- 11.5 The Integral Test
- 11.6 Comparison Tests for Positive-Term Series
- 11.7 Alternating Series and Absolute Convergence
- 11.8 Power Series
- 11.9 Power Series Computations
- 11.10 Series Solutions of Differential Equations

12. Vectors and Matrices
- 12.1 Vectors in the Plane
- 12.2 Three-Dimensional Vectors
- 12.3 The Cross Product of Two Vectors
- 12.4 Lines and Planes in Space
- 12.5 Linear Systems and Matrices
- 12.6 Matrix Operations
- 12.7 Eigenvalues and Rotated Conics

13. Curves and Surfaces in Space
- 13.1 Curves and Motion in Space
- 13.2 Curvature and Acceleration
- 13.3 Cylinders and Quadric Surfaces
- 13.4 Cylindrical and Spherical Coordinates

14. Partial Differentiation
- 14.1 Introduction
- 14.2 Functions of Several Variables
- 14.3 Limits and Continuity
- 14.4 Partial Derivatives
- 14.5 Multivariable Optimizations Problems
- 14.6 Linear Approximation and Matrix Derivatives
- 14.7 The Multivariable Chain Rule
- 14.8 Directional Derivatives and Gradient Vectors
- 14.9 Lagrange Multipliers and Constrained Optimization
- 14.10 Critical Points of Multivariable Functions

15. Multiple Integrals
- 15.1 Double Integrals
- 15.2 Double Integrals over More General Regions
- 15.3 Area and Volume by Double Integration
- 15.4 Double Integrals in Polar Coordinates
- 15.5 Applications of Double Integrals
- 15.6 Triple Integrals
- 15.7 Integration in Cylindrical and Spherical Coordinates
- 15.8 Surface Area
- 15.9 Change of Variables in Multiple Integrals

16. Vector Calculus
- 16.1 Vector Fields
- 16.2 Line Integrals
- 16.3 The Fundamental Theorem and Independence of Path
- 16.4 Green's Theorem
- 16.5 Surface Integrals
- 16.6 The Divergence Theorem
- 16.7 Stokes' Theorem

Not for resale: Answers missing from the back. Please contact your Prentice Hall rep for full Solutions Manual.

TEXTBOOK OPTIONS

CALCULUS, EARLY TRANSCENDENTALS
0-13-008407-7

INSTRUCTOR'S SOLUTIONS MANUAL TO ACCOMPANY
SINGLE VARIABLE CALCULUS, EARLY TRANSCENDENTALS
0-13-066154-6

INSTRUCTOR'S SOLUTIONS MANUAL TO ACCOMPANY
MULTIVARIABLE CALCULUS
0-13-066145-7

STUDENT SOLUTIONS MANUAL TO ACCOMPANY
SINGLE VARIABLE CALCULUS, EARLY TRANSCENDENTALS
0-13-066155-4

STUDENT SOLUTIONS MANUAL TO ACCOMPANY
MULTIVARIABLE CALCULUS
0-13-062023-8

TEST ITEM FILE
0-13-066162-7
0-13-008845-5
(PLEASE ORDER BOTH)

TESTGEN-EQ
0-13-092075-4
0-13-066161-9
(PLEASE ORDER BOTH)

THIS TEXT COVERS TRANSCENDENTAL FUNCTIONS IN CALC I AND DOES NOT COVER MATRICES

Contents

1. **Functions, Graphs, and Models**
   - 1.1 Functions and Mathematical Modeling
   - 1.2 Graphs of Equations and Functions
   - 1.3 Polynomials and Algebraic Functions
   - 1.4 Transcendental Functions
   - 1.5 Preview: What *Is* Calculus?

2. **Prelude to Calculus**
   - 2.1 Tangent Lines and Slope Predictors
   - 2.2 The Limit Concept
   - 2.3 More About Limits
   - 2.4 The Concept of Continuity

3. **The Derivative**
   - 3.1 The Derivative and Rates of Change
   - 3.2 Basic Differentiation Rules
   - 3.3 The Chain Rule
   - 3.4 Derivatives of Algebraic Functions
   - 3.5 Maxima and Minima of Functions on Closed Intervals
   - 3.6 Applied Optimization Problems
   - 3.7 Derivatives of Trigonometric Functions
   - 3.8 Exponential and Logarithmic Functions
   - 3.9 Implicit Differentiation and Related Rates
   - 3.10 Successive Approximations and Newton's Method

4. **Additional Applications of the Derivative**
   - 4.1 Introduction
   - 4.2 Increments, Differentials, and Linear Approximation
   - 4.3 Increasing and Decreasing Functions and the Mean Value Theorem
   - 4.4 The First Derivative Test and Applications
   - 4.5 Simple Curve Sketching
   - 4.6 Higher Derivatives and Concavity
   - 4.7 Curve Sketching and Asymptotes
   - 4.8 Indeterminate Forms and L'Hôpital's Rule
   - 4.9 More Indeterminate Forms

5. **The Integral**
   - 5.1 Introduction
   - 5.2 Antiderivatives and Initial Value Problems
   - 5.3 Elementary Area Computations
   - 5.4 Riemann Sums and the Integral
   - 5.5 Evaluation of Integrals
   - 5.6 The Fundamental Theorem of Calculus
   - 5.7 Integration by Substitution
   - 5.8 Areas of Plane Regions
   - 5.9 Numerical Integration

Not for resale: Answers missing from the back. Please contact your Prentice Hall rep for full Solutions Manual.

6. Applications of the Integral
- 6.1 Riemann Sum Approximations
- 6.2 Volumes by the Method of Cross Sections
- 6.3 Volumes by the Method of Cylindrical Shells
- 6.4 Arc Length and Surface Area of Revolution
- 6.5 Force and Work
- 6.6 Centroids of Plane Regions and Curves
- 6.7 The Logarithm as an Integral
- 6.8 Inverse Trigonometric Functions
- 6.9 Hyperbolic Functions

7. Techniques of Integration
- 7.1 Introduction
- 7.2 Integral Tables and Simple Substitutions
- 7.3 Integration by Parts
- 7.4 Trigonometric Integrals
- 7.5 Rational Functions and Partial Fractions
- 7.6 Trigonometric Substitutions
- 7.7 Integrals Involving Quadratic Polynomials
- 7.8 Improper Integrals

8. Differential Equations
- 8.1 Simple Equations and Models
- 8.2 Slope Fields and Euler's Method
- 8.3 Separable Equations and Applications
- 8.4 Linear Equations and Applications
- 8.5 Population Models
- 8.6 Linear Second-Order Equations
- 8.7 Mechanical Vibrations

9. Polar Coordinates and Parametric Curves
- 9.1 Analytic Geometry and the Conic Sections
- 9.2 Polar Coordinates
- 9.3 Area Computations in Polar Coordinates
- 9.4 Parametric Curves
- 9.5 Integral Computations with Parametric Curves
- 9.6 Conic Sections and Applications

10. Infinite Series
- 10.1 Introduction
- 10.2 Infinite Sequences
- 10.3 Infinite Series and Convergence
- 10.4 Taylor Series and Taylor Polynomials
- 10.5 The Integral Test
- 10.6 Comparison Tests for Positive-Term Series
- 10.7 Alternating Series and Absolute Convergence
- 10.8 Power Series
- 10.9 Power Series Computations
- 10.10 Series Solutions of Differential Equations

11. Vectors, Curves, and Surfaces in Space
- 11.1 Vectors in the Plane
- 11.2 Three-Dimensional Vectors
- 11.3 The Cross Product of Two Vectors
- 11.4 Lines and Planes in Space
- 11.5 Curves and Motion in Space
- 11.6 Curvature and Acceleration
- 11.7 Cylinders and Quadric Surfaces
- 11.8 Cylindrical and Spherical Coordinates

12. Partial Differentiation
- 12.1 Introduction
- 12.2 Functions of Several Variables
- 12.3 Limits and Continuity
- 12.4 Partial Derivatives
- 12.5 Multivariable Optimization Problems
- 12.6 Increments and Linear Approximation
- 12.7 The Multivariable Chain Rule
- 12.8 Directional Derivatives and Gradient Vectors
- 12.9 Lagrange Multipliers and Constrained Optimization
- 12.10 Critical Points of Functions of Two Variables

13. Multiple Integrals
- 13.1 Double Integrals
- 13.2 Double Integrals over More General Regions
- 13.3 Area and Volume by Double Integration
- 13.4 Double Integrals in Polar Coordinates
- 13.5 Applications of Double Integrals
- 13.6 Triple Integrals
- 13.7 Integration in Cylindrical and Spherical Coordinates
- 13.8 Surface Area
- 13.9 Change of Variables in Multiple Integrals

14. Vector Calculus
- 14.1 Vector Fields
- 14.2 Line Integrals
- 14.3 The Fundamental Theorem and Independence of Path
- 14.4 Green's Theorem
- 14.5 Surface Integrals
- 14.6 The Divergence Theorem
- 14.7 Stokes' Theorem

Not for resale: Answers missing from the back. Please contact your Prentice Hall rep for full Solutions Manual.

xl TEXTBOOK OPTIONS

SINGLE VARIABLE CALCULUS
0-13-062041-6

INSTRUCTOR'S SOLUTIONS MANUAL TO ACCOMPANY
SINGLE VARIABLE CALCULUS
0-13-066158-9

STUDENT SOLUTIONS MANUAL TO ACCOMPANY
SINGLE VARIABLE CALCULUS
0-13-092077-0

TEST ITEM FILE
0-13-066162-7

TESTGEN-EQ
0-13-066161-9

Contents

1. **Functions, Graphs, and Models**
   1.1 Functions and Mathematical Modeling
   1.2 Graphs of Equations and Functions
   1.3 Polynomials and Algebraic Functions
   1.4 Transcendental Functions
   1.5 Preview: What *Is* Calculus?

2. **Prelude to Calculus**
   2.1 Tangent Lines and Slope Predictors
   2.2 The Limit Concept
   2.3 More About Limits
   2.4 The Concept of Continuity

3. **The Derivative**
   3.1 The Derivative and Rates of Change
   3.2 Basic Differentiation Rules
   3.3 The Chain Rule
   3.4 Derivatives of Algebraic Functions
   3.5 Maxima and Minima of Functions on Closed Intervals
   3.6 Applied Optimization Problems
   3.7 Derivatives of Trigonometric Functions
   3.8 Successive Approximations and Newton's Method

4. **Additional Applications of the Derivative**
   4.1 Implicit Functions and Related Rates
   4.2 Increments, Differentials, and Linear Approximation
   4.3 Increasing and Decreasing Functions and the Mean Value Theorem
   4.4 The First Derivative Test and Applications
   4.5 Simple Curve Sketching
   4.6 Higher Derivatives and Concavity
   4.7 Curve Sketching and Asymptotes

Edwards & Penney

Not for resale: Answers missing from the back. Please contact your Prentice Hall rep for full Solutions Manual.

5. The Integral

- 5.1 Introduction
- 5.2 Antiderivatives and Initial Value Problems
- 5.3 Elementary Area Computations
- 5.4 Riemann Sums and the Integral
- 5.5 Evaluation of Integrals
- 5.6 The Fundamental Theorem of Calculus
- 5.7 Integration by Substitution
- 5.8 Areas of Plane Regions
- 5.9 Numerical Integration

6. Applications of the Integral

- 6.1 Riemann Sum Approximations
- 6.2 Volumes by the Method of Cross Sections
- 6.3 Volumes by the Method of Cylindrical Shells
- 6.4 Arc Length and Surface Area of Revolution
- 6.5 Force and Work
- 6.6 Centroids of Plane Regions and Curves

7. Calculus of Transcendental Functions

- 7.1 Exponential and Logarithmic Functions
- 7.2 Indeterminate Forms and L'Hôpital's Rule
- 7.3 More Indeterminate Forms
- 7.4 The Natural Logarithm as an Integral
- 7.5 Inverse Trigonometric Functions
- 7.6 Hyperbolic Functions

8. Techniques of Integration

- 8.1 Introduction
- 8.2 Integral Tables and Simple Substitutions
- 8.3 Integration by Parts
- 8.4 Trigonometric Integrals
- 8.5 Rational Functions and Partial Fractions
- 8.6 Trigonometric Substitutions
- 8.7 Integrals Involving Quadratic Polynomials
- 8.8 Improper Integrals

9. Differential Equations

- 9.1 Simple Equations and Models
- 9.2 Slope Fields and Euler's Method
- 9.3 Separable Equations and Applications
- 9.4 Linear Equations and Applications
- 9.5 Population Models
- 9.6 Linear Second-Order Equations
- 9.7 Mechanical Vibrations

10. Polar Coordinates and Parametric Curves

- 10.1 Analytic Geometry and the Conic Sections
- 10.2 Polar Coordinates
- 10.3 Area Computations in Polar Coordinates
- 10.4 Parametric Curves
- 10.5 Integral Computations with Parametric Curves
- 10.6 Conic Sections and Applications

11. Infinite Series

- 11.1 Introduction
- 11.2 Infinite Sequences
- 11.3 Infinite Series and Convergence
- 11.4 Taylor Series and Taylor Polynomials
- 11.5 The Integral Test
- 11.6 Comparison Tests for Positive-Term Series
- 11.7 Alternating Series and Absolute Convergence
- 11.8 Power Series
- 11.9 Power Series Computations
- 11.10 Series Solutions of Differential Equations

Not for resale: Answers missing from the back. Please contact your Prentice Hall rep for full Solutions Manual.

MULTIVARIABLE CALCULUS
0-13-033967-9

INSTRUCTOR'S SOLUTIONS MANUAL TO ACCOMPANY
MULTIVARIABLE CALCULUS
0-13-066145-7

STUDENT SOLUTIONS MANUAL TO ACCOMPANY
MULTIVARIABLE CALCULUS
0-13-062023-8

TEST ITEM FILE
0-13-066162-7

TESTGEN-EQ
0-13-066161-9

Contents

10. Polar Coordinates and Parametric Curves
- 10.1 Analytic Geometry and the Conic Sections
- 10.2 Polar Coordinates
- 10.3 Area Computations in Polar Coordinates
- 10.4 Parametric Curves
- 10.5 Integral Computations with Parametric Curves
- 10.6 Conic Sections and Applications

11. Infinite Series
- 11.1 Introduction
- 11.2 Infinite Sequences
- 11.3 Infinite Series and Convergence
- 11.4 Taylor Series and Taylor Polynomials
- 11.5 The Integral Test
- 11.6 Comparison Tests for Positive-Term Series
- 11.7 Alternating Series and Absolute Convergence
- 11.8 Power Series
- 11.9 Power Series Computations
- 11.10 Series Solutions of Differential Equations

12. Vectors, Curves, and Surfaces in Space
- 12.1 Vectors in the Plane

Not for resale: Answers missing from the back. Please contact your Prentice Hall rep for full Solutions Manual.

- 12.2 Three-Dimensional Vectors
- 12.3 The Cross Product of Two Vectors
- 12.4 Lines and Planes in Space
- 12.5 Curves and Motion in Space
- 12.6 Curvature and Acceleration
- 12.7 Cylinders and Quadric Surfaces
- 12.8 Cylindrical and Spherical Coordinates

13. Partial Differentiation
- 13.1 Introduction
- 13.2 Functions of Several Variables
- 13.3 Limits and Continuity
- 13.4 Partial Derivatives
- 13.5 Multivariable Optimization Problems
- 13.6 Increments and Linear Approximation
- 13.7 The Multivariable Chain Rule
- 13.8 Directional Derivatives and the Gradient Vector
- 13.9 Lagrange Multipliers and Constrained Optimization
- 13.10 Critical Points of Functions of Two Variables

14. Multiple Integrals
- 14.1 Double Integrals
- 14.2 Double Integrals over More General Regions
- 14.3 Area and Volume by Double Integration
- 14.4 Double Integrals in Polar Coordinates
- 14.5 Applications of Double Integrals
- 14.6 Triple Integrals
- 14.7 Integration in Cylindrical and Spherical Coordinates
- 14.8 Surface Area
- 14.9 Change of Variables in Multiple Integrals

15. Vector Calculus
- 15.1 Vector Fields
- 15.2 Line Integrals
- 15.3 The Fundamental Theorem and Independence of Path
- 15.4 Green's Theorem
- 15.5 Surface Integrals
- 15.6 The Divergence Theorem

Not for resale: Answers missing from the back. Please contact your Prentice Hall rep for full Solutions Manual.

Single Variable Calculus, Early Transcendentals
0-13-041407-7

Instructor's Solutions Manual to Accompany
Single Variable Calculus, Early Transcendentals
0-13-066154-6

Student Solutions Manual to Accompany
Single Variable Calculus, Early Transcendentals
0-13-066155-4

Test Item File
0-13-008845-5

TestGen-EQ
0-13-092075-4

Contents

1. **Functions, Graphs, and Models**
   - 1.1 Functions and Mathematical Modeling
   - 1.2 Graphs of Equations and Functions
   - 1.3 Polynomials and Algebraic Functions
   - 1.4 Transcendental Functions
   - 1.5 Preview: What *Is* Calculus?

2. **Prelude to Calculus**
   - 2.1 Tangent Lines and Slope Predictors
   - 2.2 The Limit Concept
   - 2.3 More About Limits
   - 2.4 The Concept of Continuity

3. **The Derivative**
   - 3.1 The Derivative and Rates of Change
   - 3.2 Basic Differentiation Rules
   - 3.3 The Chain Rule
   - 3.4 Derivatives of Algebraic Functions
   - 3.5 Maxima and Minima of Functions on Closed Intervals
   - 3.6 Applied Optimization Problems
   - 3.7 Derivatives of Trigonometric Functions
   - 3.8 Exponential and Logarithmic Functions
   - 3.9 Implicit Differentiation and Related Rates
   - 3.10 Successive Approximations and Newton's Method

4. **Additional Applications of the Derivative**
   - 4.1 Introduction
   - 4.2 Increments, Differentials, and Linear Approximation
   - 4.3 Increasing and Decreasing Functions and the Mean Value Theorem
   - 4.4 The First Derivative Test and Applications
   - 4.5 Simple Curve Sketching
   - 4.6 Higher Derivatives and Concavity
   - 4.7 Curve Sketching and Asymptotes

Not for resale: Answers missing from the back. Please contact your Prentice Hall rep for full Solutions Manual.

- 4.8 Indeterminate Forms and L'Hôpital's Rule
- 4.9 More Indeterminate Forms

5. The Integral
- 5.1 Introduction
- 5.2 Antiderivatives and Initial Value Problems
- 5.3 Elementary Area Computations
- 5.4 Riemann Sums and the Integral
- 5.5 Evaluation of Integrals
- 5.6 The Fundamental Theorem of Calculus
- 5.7 Integration by Substitution
- 5.8 Areas of Plane Regions
- 5.9 Numerical Integration

6. Applications of the Integral
- 6.1 Riemann Sum Approximations
- 6.2 Volumes by the Method of Cross Sections
- 6.3 Volumes by the Method of Cylindrical Shells
- 6.4 Arc Length and Surface Area of Revolution
- 6.5 Force and Work
- 6.6 Centroids of Plane Regions and Curves
- 6.7 The Natural Logarithm as an Integral
- 6.8 Inverse Trigonometric Functions
- 6.9 Hyperbolic Functions

7. Techniques of Integration
- 7.1 Introduction
- 7.2 Integral Tables and Simple Substitutions
- 7.3 Integration by Parts
- 7.4 Trigonometric Integrals
- 7.5 Rational Functions and Partial Fractions
- 7.6 Trigonometric Substitution
- 7.7 Integrals Involving Quadratic Polynomials
- 7.8 Improper Integrals

8. Differential Equations
- 8.1 Simple Equations and Models
- 8.2 Slope Fields and Euler's Method
- 8.3 Separable Equations and Applications
- 8.4 Linear Equations and Applications
- 8.5 Population Models
- 8.6 Linear Second-Order Equations
- 8.7 Mechanical Vibrations

9. Polar Coordinates and Parametric Curves
- 9.1 Analytic Geometry and the Conic Sections
- 9.2 Polar Coordinates
- 9.3 Area Computations in Polar Coordinates
- 9.4 Parametric Curves
- 9.5 Integral Computations with Parametric Curves
- 9.6 Conic Sections and Applications

10. Infinite Series
- 10.1 Introduction
- 10.2 Infinite Sequences
- 10.3 Infinite Series and Convergence
- 10.4 Taylor Series and Taylor Polynomials
- 10.5 The Integral Test
- 10.6 Comparison Tests for Positive-Term Series
- 10.7 Alternating Series and Absolute Convergence
- 10.8 Power Series
- 10.9 Power Series Computations
- 10.10 Series Solutions of Differential Equations

Not for resale: Answers missing from the back. Please contact your Prentice Hall rep for full Solutions Manual.

MULTIVARIABLE CALCULUS WITH MATRICES
0-13-064818-3

INSTRUCTOR'S SOLUTIONS MANUAL TO ACCOMPANY
MULTIVARIABLE CALCULUS WITH MATRICES
0-13-066159-7

STUDENT SOLUTIONS MANUAL TO ACCOMPANY
MULTIVARIABLE CALCULUS WITH MATRICES
0-13-066150-3

TEST ITEM FILE
0-13-008845-5

TESTGEN-EQ
0-13-092075-4

Contents

10. Infinite Series
- 10.1 Introduction
- 10.2 Infinite Sequences
- 10.3 Infinite Series and Convergence
- 10.4 Taylor Series and Taylor Polynomials
- 10.5 The Integral Test
- 10.6 Comparison Tests for Positive-Term Series
- 10.7 Alternating Series and Absolute Convergence
- 10.8 Power Series
- 10.9 Power Series Computations
- 10.10 Series Solutions of Differential Equations

11. Vectors and Matrices
- 11.1 Vectors in the Plane
- 11.2 Three-Dimensional Vectors
- 11.3 The Cross Product of Vectors
- 11.4 Lines and Planes in Space
- 11.5 Linear Systems and Matrices
- 11.6 Matrix Operations
- 11.7 Eigenvalues and Rotated Conics

12. Curves and Surfaces in Space
- 12.1 Curves and Motion in Space
- 12.2 Curvature and Acceleration
- 12.3 Cylinders and Quadric Surfaces

12.4 Cylindrical and Spherical Coordinates

13. Partial Differentiation
13.1 Introduction
13.2 Functions of Several Variables
13.3 Limits and Continuity
13.4 Partial Derivatives
13.5 Multivariable Optimization Problems
13.6 Linear Approximation and Matrix Derivatives
13.7 The Multivariable Chain Rule
13.8 Directional Derivatives and the Gradient Vector
13.9 Lagrange Multipliers and Constrained Optimization
13.10 Critical Points of Multivariable Functions

14. Multiple Integrals
14.1 Double Integrals
14.2 Double Integrals over More General Regions
14.3 Area and Volume by Double Integration
14.4 Double Integrals in Polar Coordinates
14.5 Applications of Double Integrals
14.6 Triple Integrals
14.7 Integration in Cylindrical and Spherical Coordinates
14.8 Surface Area
14.9 Change of Variables in Multiple Integrals

15. Vector Calculus
15.1 Vector Fields
15.2 Line Integrals
15.3 The Fundamental Theorem and Independence of Path
15.4 Green's Theorem
15.5 Surface Integrals
15.6 The Divergence Theorem
15.7 Stokes' Theorem

Not for resale: Answers missing from the back. Please contact your Prentice Hall rep for full Solutions Manual.

MEDIA RESOURCES

FOR INSTRUCTORS

Prentice Hall Grade Assist

Assessment and Homework Management

This web-based system is deigned to help you teach and help your students learn. This system was developed to automate the production and delivery of web-based assignments ranging from both homework and self-paced practice to secure, proctored testing. For instructors, the system provides a more natural transition from traditional paper-based assignments to timesaving, automatically graded online homework, improving on the limitations of current course management systems. Students prefer this system because it provides immediate, individualized performance feedback and the opportunity to generate unlimited practice through algorithm-driven study sessions. During assignment creation, instructors determine rules and policies for assignments, and then publish them for use by students, at which time the system controls assignment access, grading, and recording of grades in the grade book.

What can you do with the PH Grade Assist?

You can . . .
- Easily create self-scoring, web-delivered tests and homework assignments from your own time-tested problem files.
- Use the 2000 even-numbered textbook problems already loaded for use.
- Edit, modify, or expand existing question banks (whether publisher-provided or homegrown).
- Control the rules and policies surrounding your assignments, including time limitations, ability to retake assignments, feedback content, results reporting, low-stakes or high-stakes forms, and formats.
- Publish your assignments to your own class-specific website, where your students will log in to complete the work.

Scientific, Mathematical, and Technical Question Content

To support the unique requirements of mathematics, the PH Grade Assist provides the following capabilities and question types:

- **Dynamic Editing and Display of Math Expressions** Questions and user responses can include symbolic mathematics input/editing and dynamic display of math expressions and equations. We support **WYSIWYG** editing and display of math formulas as well as text-style editing and display of math using "graphing-calculator-style" syntax that is almost identical to the syntax used by the TI-85 calculator.
- **Integrated Math Parser** Unlike standard quiz engines, PH Grade Assist contains a powerful math parser designed to provide intelligent evaluation of algebraically equivalent equations and expressions, numerically equivalent responses, and mathematically equivalent physical units within student responses. The system uses rules for the order of precedence of operators to determine which parts of expressions should be evaluated first.
- **Math ML** is employed to preserve both style and content in math expressions within question banks.
- **LaTeX Macros** are provided to streamline authoring conversion of scientific and technical content in PH Grade Assist compatible format.
- **Graphing Components** can be integrated into problems to require students to perform curve sketching and other graphical problem-solving techniques.
- **Reference Objects** Questions with static reference figures, graphics, or other reference objects can be incorporated into any question using HTML syntax.
- **Applets and other interactive objects** can be integrated into questions to create student response objects (SROs). PH Grade Assist uses SROs to interactive simulations in which the system records and interprets student responses, automatically scoring them against pre-programmed correct answers. Support is provided for Java applets but can be extended to include other interactive formats (e.g. Shockwave, Flash) using the API.
- **Randomly generated data** Randomly generated formulas and data can be included in problem statements and their corresponding answers to produce limitless surface variations of problems from a single deep question structure. In the case of mathematics questions, expressions with randomly generated data can be generated from MathML and rendered dynamically each time the question is served.

Not for resale: Answers missing from the back. Please contact your Prentice Hall rep for full Solutions Manual.

MEDIA RESOURCES xlix

Instructor's Resource CD-ROM

This CD-ROM contains all the content of the student CD-ROM, plus links to electronic instructor's solutions and PowerPoint slides of text art (described below). The student CD-ROM is designed to enhance students' computational and conceptual understanding of calculus. This CD is not an add-on supplement to the textbook, but rather an extraordinarily useful extension of the text, to be used hand in hand with study of the book itself.

Live Examples
The heart of this CD is in the Live Examples. Nearly every geometric text example is animated. The traditional text environment is now enhanced and brought to life with animations and questions exploring what-if scenarios. Algebraic solutions are paired with geometric solutions. There are more than 500 live examples.

Homework Starters
Each text section includes teaching hints for 3-5 homework problems. These hints often include geometric animations. There are more than 200 Homework Starters included, 2/3 of which also have short 3-5 minute movies supplying instruction at a blackboard detailing how to think about getting started.

True/False Study Guides
There are 10 T/F questions per text section: more than 1000 in total. These questions focus on the core ideas of calculus. These questions are specifically designed to encourage students to read (not just thumb through the text to find examples matching the questions).

Computing Projects
Three dozen projects are scattered throughout both the text and CD. Each project is like an extended homework problem that typically requires some use of technology to help solve the problem. Projects included on the CD greatly expand the text detail and teach students how to use a given technology whether it be Maple or *Mathematica*, MATLAB or a TI Calculator.

Maple Worksheets
The whole text has been translated into Maple worksheets. (Users must have Maple software to use this part of the CD.) The full computing power and graphics package of Maple is now at your fingertips. Students can manipulate each text example with different parameters and graphics. These worksheets stress calculus, not the learning of Maple code.

PowerPoint Slides
Included for instructors' classroom use are 300 PowerPoint slides of text art that you would find difficult to draw freehand.

Full Solutions Available Electronically
Over 1800 text pages that contain all the solutions (step-by-step) to all text problems are available on a secure website (password protected), with a link on this CD to the website. You must contact your local Prentice Hall (or Pearson) sales representative for the password.

Not for resale: Answers missing from the back. Please contact your Prentice Hall rep for full Solutions Manual.

MEDIA RESOURCES

For Students

Student CD-ROM

The new student CD-ROM is designed to enhance students' computational and conceptual understanding of calculus. This CD is not an add-on supplement to the textbook, but rather an extraordinarily useful extension of the text, to be used hand in hand with study of the book itself.

Live Examples
The heart of this CD is in the Live Examples. Nearly every geometric text example is animated. The traditional text environment is now enhanced and brought to life with animations and questions exploring what-if scenarios. Algebraic solutions are paired with geometric solutions. There are more than 500 live examples.

Homework Starters
Each text section includes teaching hints for 3-5 homework problems. These hints often include geometric animations. There are more than 200 Homework Starters included, 2/3 of which also have short 3-5 minute movies supplying instruction at a blackboard detailing how to think about getting started.

True/False Study Guides
There are 10 T/F questions per text section: more than 1000 in total. These questions focus on the core ideas of calculus. These questions are specifically designed to encourage students to read (not just thumb through the text to find examples matching the questions).

Computing Projects
Three dozen projects are scattered throughout both the text and CD. Each project is like an extended homework problem that typically requires some use of technology to help solve the problem. Projects included on the CD greatly expand the text detail and teach students how to use a given technology whether it be Maple or *Mathematica*, MATLAB or a TI Calculator.

Maple Worksheets
The whole text has been translated into Maple worksheets. (Users must have Maple software to use this part of the CD.) The full computing power and graphics package of Maple is now at your fingertips. Students can manipulate each text example with different parameters and graphics. These worksheets stress calculus, not the learning of Maple code.

Not for resale: Answers missing from the back. Please contact your Prentice Hall rep for full Solutions Manual.

Companion Website: www.prenhall.com/edwards

This companion website contains much of what is on the CD-ROM with other activities better suited to the Internet.

Links and Destinations
There are roughly five to ten links per text section to other Internet based sites with calculus oriented or related material. For example, one fascinating link is the enormous History Archive Site in St. Andrews, Scotland, which is loaded with hundreds, if not thousands, of biographies and other fascinating historical material.

Live Examples
The heart of this website is in the Live Examples. Nearly every geometric text example is animated. The traditional text environment is now enhanced and brought to life with animations and questions exploring what-if scenarios. Algebraic solutions are paired with geometric solutions. There are more than 500 live examples.

Homework Starters
Each text section includes teaching hints for 3-5 homework problems. These hints often include geometric animations. There are more than 200 Homework Starters included, 2/3 of which also have short 3-5 minute movies supplying instruction at a blackboard detailing how to think about getting started.

True/False Study Guides
There are 10 T/F questions per text section: more than 1000 in total. These questions focus on the core ideas of calculus. These questions are specifically designed to encourage students to read (not just thumb through the text to find examples matching the questions).

Computing Projects
Three dozen projects are scattered throughout both the text and this website. Each project is like an extended homework problem that typically requires some use of technology to help solve the problem. Projects included here greatly expand the text detail and teach students how to use a given technology whether it be Maple or *Mathematica*, MATLAB or a TI Calculator.

Not for resale: Answers missing from the back. Please contact your Prentice Hall rep for full Solutions Manual.

PRINT SUPPLEMENTS

FOR INSTRUCTORS

Instructor's Solutions Manual Pack

This solutions manual has been tripled in size as the authors provide nearly every step to every text problem solution. 1800+ pages are now also available electronically on a secure website, where you can download or post pdf files section by section. Please contact your local Prentice Hall (or Pearson) sales representative for the password. Please see the textbook options section of this walk-through (pages xxxiv-xlvii) for specific ISBN numbers.

Test Item File

This print resource provides a full complement of additional problems that correlate specifically to the text. A cross-platform computerized version of this test bank is also available. Please see the textbook options section of this walk-through (pages xxxiv-xlvii) for specific ISBN numbers.

Not for resale: Answers missing from the back. Please contact your Prentice Hall rep for full Solutions Manual.

FOR STUDENTS

Student Solutions Manual

Each of the Student Solutions Manuals has been greatly expanded. The full manual is now 900+ pages. Nearly every solution to odd-numbered problems is provided in step-by-step detail. Please see the textbook options section of this walk-through (pages xxxiv-xlvii) for specific ISBN numbers.

Technology Manuals

The following inexpensive manuals can be shrink-wrapped with any text version for half the manual price:

Gresser, *TI Graphing Calculator Approach to Calculus, 2e* (0-13-092017-7)
Gresser, *A Mathematica Approach to Calculus, 2e* (0-13-092015-0)
Gresser, *A Maple Approach to Calculus, 2e* (0-13-092014-2)
Jensen, *Using MATLAB in Calculus* (0-13-027268-X)
Freese/Stegenga, *Calculus Concepts Using Derive* (0-13-085152-3)

History Supplement

Lewinter & Widulski's *The Saga of Mathematics, A Brief History* (0-13-034079-0) is an inexpensive 300-page paperback putting math in a historical context and illustrating its relation to art, music, science, and technology. Available shrink-wrapped to any version of the text for half price.

Student Edition (0-13-092071-1)

Not for resale: Answers missing from the back. Please contact your Prentice Hall rep for full Solutions Manual.

FUNCTIONS, GRAPHS, AND MODELS

The seventeenth-century French scholar René Descartes is perhaps better remembered today as a philosopher than as a mathematician. But most of us are familiar with the "Cartesian plane" in which the location of a point P is specified by its coordinates (x, y).

As a schoolboy Descartes was often permitted to sleep late because of allegedly poor health. He claimed that he always thought most clearly about philosophy, science, and mathematics while he was lying comfortably in bed on cold mornings. After graduating from college, where he studied law (apparently with little enthusiasm), Descartes traveled with various armies for a number of years, but more as a gentleman soldier than as a professional military man.

In 1637, after finally settling down (in Holland), Descartes published his famous philosophical treatise *Discourse on the Method* (of Reasoning Well and Seeking Truth in the Sciences). One of three appendices to this work sets forth his new "analytic" approach to geometry. His principal idea (published almost simultaneously by his countryman Pierre de Fermat) was the correspondence between an *equation* and its *graph*, generally a curve in the plane. The equation could be used to study the curve and vice versa.

René Descartes (1596–1650)

Suppose that we want to solve the equation $f(x) = 0$. Its solutions are the intersection points of the graph of $y = f(x)$ with the x-axis, so an accurate picture of the curve shows the number and approximate locations of the solutions of the equation. For instance, the graph

$$y = x^3 - 3x^2 + 1$$

has three x-intercepts, showing that the equation

$$x^3 - 3x^2 + 1 = 0$$

has three real solutions—one between -1 and 0, one between 0 and 1, and one between 2 and 3. A modern graphing calculator or computer program can approximate these solutions more accurately by magnifying the regions in which they are located. For instance, the magnified center region shows that the corresponding solution is $x \approx 0.65$.

The graph $y = x^3 - 3x^2 + 1$

1.1 FUNCTIONS AND MATHEMATICAL MODELING

Calculus is one of the supreme accomplishments of the human intellect. This mathematical discipline stems largely from the seventeenth-century investigations of Isaac Newton (1642–1727) and Gottfried Wilhelm Leibniz (1646–1716). Yet some of its ideas date back to the time of Archimedes (287–212 B.C.) and originated in cultures as diverse as those of Greece, Egypt, Babylonia, India, China, and Japan. Many of the scientific discoveries that have shaped our civilization during the past three centuries would have been impossible without the use of calculus.

The principal objective of calculus is the analysis of problems of change (of motion, for example) and of content (the computation of area and volume, for instance). These problems are fundamental because we live in a world of ceaseless change, filled with bodies in motion and phenomena of ebb and flow. Consequently, calculus remains a vibrant subject, and today this body of conceptual understanding and computational technique continues to serve as the principal quantitative language of science and technology.

Functions

Most applications of calculus involve the use of real numbers or *variables* to describe changing quantities. The key to the mathematical analysis of a geometric or scientific situation is typically the recognition of relationships among the variables that describe the situation. Such a relationship may be a formula that expresses one variable as a *function* of another. For example:

- The area A of a circle of radius r is given by $A = \pi r^2$ (Fig. 1.1.1). The volume V and surface area S of a sphere of radius r are given by

$$V = \tfrac{4}{3}\pi r^3 \quad \text{and} \quad S = 4\pi r^2,$$

respectively (Fig. 1.1.2).

- After t seconds (s) a body that has been dropped from rest has fallen a distance

$$s = \tfrac{1}{2}gt^2$$

feet (ft) and has speed $v = gt$ feet per second (ft/s), where $g \approx 32$ ft/s² is gravitational acceleration.

- The volume V (in liters, L) of 3 grams (g) of carbon dioxide at 27°C is given in terms of its pressure p in atmospheres (atm) by $V = 1.68/p$.

FIGURE 1.1.1 Circle: area $A = \pi r^2$, circumference $C = 2\pi r$.

FIGURE 1.1.2 Sphere: volume $V = \tfrac{4}{3}\pi r^3$, surface area $S = 4\pi r^2$.

DEFINITION **Function**
A real-valued **function** f defined on a set D of real numbers is a rule that assigns to each number x in D exactly one real number, denoted by $f(x)$.

The set D of all numbers for which $f(x)$ is defined is called the **domain** (or **domain of definition**) of the function f. The number $f(x)$, read "f of x," is called the **value** of the function f at the number (or point) x. The set of all values $y = f(x)$ is called the **range** of f. That is, the range of f is the set

$$\{y : y = f(x) \quad \text{for some } x \text{ in } D\}.$$

In this section we will be concerned more with the domain of a function than with its range.

EXAMPLE 1 The squaring function defined by

$$f(x) = x^2$$

assigns to each real number x its square x^2. Because every real number *can* be squared, the domain of f is the set $\mathbf{R}$ of all real numbers. But only nonnegative numbers are squares. Moreover, if $a \geq 0$, then $a = (\sqrt{a})^2 = f(\sqrt{a})$, so a is a square. Hence the range of the squaring function f is the set $\{y : y \geq 0\}$ of all nonnegative real numbers. ◆

Functions can be described in various ways. A *symbolic* description of the function f is provided by a formula that specifies how to compute the number $f(x)$ in terms of the number x. Thus the symbol $f(\ )$ may be regarded as an operation that is to be performed whenever a number or expression is inserted between the parentheses.

EXAMPLE 2 The formula

$$f(x) = x^2 + x - 3 \tag{1}$$

defines a function f whose domain is the entire real line $\mathbf{R}$. Some typical values of f are $f(-2) = -1$, $f(0) = -3$, and $f(3) = 9$. Some other values of the function f are

$$f(4) = 4^2 + 4 - 3 = 17,$$
$$f(c) = c^2 + c - 3,$$
$$f(2+h) = (2+h)^2 + (2+h) - 3$$
$$= (4 + 4h + h^2) + (2+h) - 3 = h^2 + 5h + 3, \quad \text{and}$$
$$f(-t^2) = (-t^2)^2 + (-t^2) - 3 = t^4 - t^2 - 3.$$
◆

When we describe the function f by writing a formula $y = f(x)$, we call x the **independent variable** and y the **dependent variable** because the value of y depends—through f—upon the choice of x. As the independent variable x changes, or varies, then so does the dependent variable y. The way that y varies is determined by the rule of the function f. For example, if f is the function of Eq. (1), then $y = -1$ when $x = -2$, $y = -3$ when $x = 0$, and $y = 9$ when $x = 3$.

You may find it useful to visualize the dependence of the value $y = f(x)$ on x by thinking of the function f as a kind of machine that accepts as input a number x and then produces as output the number $f(x)$, perhaps displayed or printed (Fig. 1.1.3).

One such machine is the square root key of a simple pocket calculator. When a nonnegative number x is entered and this key is pressed, the calculator displays (an approximation to) the number $\sqrt{x}$. Note that the domain of this *square root function* $f(x) = \sqrt{x}$ is the set $[0, +\infty)$ of all nonnegative real numbers, because no negative number has a real square root. The range of f is also the set of all nonnegative real numbers, because the symbol $\sqrt{x}$ always denotes the *nonnegative* square root of x. The calculator illustrates its "knowledge" of the domain by displaying an error message if we ask it to calculate the square root of a negative number (or perhaps a complex number, if it's a more sophisticated calculator).

FIGURE 1.1.3 A "function machine."

EXAMPLE 3 Not every function has a rule expressible as a simple one-part formula such as $f(x) = \sqrt{x}$. For instance, if we write

$$h(x) = \begin{cases} x^2 & \text{if } x \geq 0, \\ \sqrt{-x} & \text{if } x < 0, \end{cases}$$

then we have defined a perfectly good function with domain $\mathbf{R}$. Some of its values are $h(-4) = 2$, $h(0) = 0$, and $h(2) = 4$. By contrast, the function g in Example 4 is defined initially by means of a verbal description rather than by means of formulas. ◆

EXAMPLE 4 For each real number x, let $g(x)$ denote the greatest integer that is less than or equal to x. For instance, $g(2.5) = 2$, $g(0) = 0$, $g(-3.5) = -4$, and $g(\pi) = 3$. If n is an integer, then $g(x) = n$ for every number x such that $n \leq x < n + 1$. This function g is called the **greatest integer function** and is often denoted by

$$g(x) = [\![x]\!].$$

Thus $[\![2.5]\!] = 2$, $[\![-3.5]\!] = -4$, and $[\![\pi]\!] = 3$. Note that although $[\![x]\!]$ is defined for all x, the range of the greatest integer function is not all of $\mathbf{R}$, but the set $\mathbf{Z}$ of all integers. ◆

The name of a function need not be a single letter such as f or g. For instance, think of the trigonometric functions $\sin(x)$ and $\cos(x)$ with the names sin and cos.

EXAMPLE 5 Another descriptive name for the greatest integer function of Example 4 is

$$\text{Floor}(x) = [\![x]\!]. \tag{2}$$

(We think of the integer n as the "floor" beneath the real numbers lying between n and $n + 1$.) Similarly, we may use $\text{Round}(x)$ to name the familiar function that "rounds off" the real number x to the nearest integer n, except that $\text{Round}(x) = n + 1$ if $x = n + \frac{1}{2}$ (so we "round upward" in case of ambiguity). Round off enough different numbers to convince yourself that

$$\text{Round}(x) = \text{Floor}\left(x + \tfrac{1}{2}\right) \tag{3}$$

for all x.

Closely related to the Floor and Round functions is the "ceiling function" used by the U.S. Postal Service; $\text{Ceiling}(x)$ denotes the least integer that is not less than the number x. In 2001 the postage rate for a first-class letter was 34¢ for the first ounce and 21¢ for each additional ounce or fraction thereof. For a letter weighing $w > 0$ ounces, the number of "additional ounces" involved is $\text{Ceiling}(w) - 1$. Therefore the postage $s(w)$ due on this letter is given by

$$s(w) = 34 + 21 \cdot [\text{Ceiling}(w) - 1] = 13 + 21 \cdot \text{Ceiling}(w). \qquad ◆$$

Domains and Intervals

The function f and the value or expression $f(x)$ are different in the same sense that a machine and its output are different. Nevertheless, it is common to use an expression like "the function $f(x) = x^2$" to define a function merely by writing its formula. In this situation the domain of the function is not specified. Then, by convention, the **domain of the function** f is the set of all real numbers x for which the expression $f(x)$ makes sense and produces a real number y. For instance, the domain of the function $h(x) = 1/x$ is the set of all nonzero real numbers (because $1/x$ is defined precisely when $x \neq 0$).

FIGURE 1.1.4 Some examples of intervals of real numbers.

Domains of functions frequently are described in terms of *intervals* of real numbers (Fig. 1.1.4). (Interval notation is reviewed in Appendix A.) Recall that a **closed interval** $[a, b]$ contains both its endpoints $x = a$ and $x = b$, whereas the **open interval** (a, b) contains neither endpoint. Each of the **half-open intervals** $[a, b)$ and $(a, b]$ contains exactly one of its two endpoints. The **unbounded interval** $[a, \infty)$

contains its endpoint $x = a$, whereas $(-\infty, a)$ does not. The previously mentioned domain of $h(x) = 1/x$ is the *union* of the unbounded intervals $(-\infty, 0)$ and $(0, \infty)$.

EXAMPLE 6 Find the domain of the function $g(x) = \dfrac{1}{2x + 4}$.

Solution Division by zero is not allowed, so the value $g(x)$ is defined precisely when $2x + 4 \neq 0$. This is true when $2x \neq -4$, and thus when $x \neq -2$. Hence the domain of g is the set $\{x : x \neq 2\}$, which is the union of the two unbounded open intervals $(-\infty, -2)$ and $(-2, \infty)$, shown in Fig. 1.1.5. ◆

FIGURE 1.1.5 The domain of $g(x) = 1/(2x + 4)$ is the union of two unbounded open intervals.

EXAMPLE 7 Find the domain of $h(x) = \dfrac{1}{\sqrt{2x + 4}}$.

Solution Now it is necessary not only that the quantity $2x + 4$ be nonzero, but also that it be positive, in order that the square root $\sqrt{2x + 4}$ is defined. But $2x + 4 > 0$ when $2x > -4$, and thus when $x > -2$. Hence the domain of h is the single unbounded open interval $(-2, \infty)$. ◆

Mathematical Modeling

The investigation of an applied problem often hinges on defining a function that captures the essence of a geometrical or physical situation. Examples 8 and 9 illustrate this process.

EXAMPLE 8 A rectangular box with a square base has volume 125. Express its total surface area A as a function of the edge length x of its base.

Solution The first step is to draw a sketch and to label the relevant dimensions. Figure 1.1.6 shows a rectangular box with square base of edge length x and with height y. We are given that the volume of the box is

$$V = x^2 y = 125. \tag{4}$$

Both the top and the bottom of the box have area x^2 and each of its four vertical sides has area xy, so its total surface area is

$$A = 2x^2 + 4xy. \tag{5}$$

FIGURE 1.1.6 The box of Example 8.

But this is a formula for A in terms of the *two* variables x and y rather than a function of the *single* variable x. To eliminate y and thereby obtain A in terms of x alone, we solve Eq. (4) for $y = 125/x^2$ and then substitute this result in Eq. (5) to obtain

$$A = 2x^2 + 4x \cdot \frac{125}{x^2} = 2x^2 + \frac{500}{x}.$$

Thus the surface area is given as a function of the edge length x by

$$A(x) = 2x^2 + \frac{500}{x}, \quad 0 < x < +\infty. \tag{6}$$

It is necessary to specify the domain because negative values of x make sense in the *formula* in (5) but do not belong in the domain of the *function* A. Because every $x > 0$ determines such a box, the domain does, in fact, include all positive real numbers. ◆

COMMENT In Example 8 our goal was to express the dependent variable A as a *function* of the independent variable x. Initially, the geometric situation provided us instead with

1. The *formula* in Eq. (5) expressing A in terms of both x and the additional variable y, and
2. The *relation* in Eq. (4) between x and y, which we used to eliminate y and thereby express A as a function of x alone.

6 CHAPTER 1 Functions, Graphs, and Models

We will see that this is a common pattern in many different applied problems, such as the one that follows.

The Animal Pen Problem You must build a rectangular holding pen for animals. To save material, you will use an existing wall as one of its four sides. The fence for the other three sides costs $5/ft, and you must spend $1/ft to paint the portion of the wall that forms the fourth side of the pen. If you have a total of $180 to spend, what dimensions will maximize the area of the pen you can build?

Figure 1.1.7 shows the animal pen and its dimensions x and y, along with the cost per foot of each of its four sides. When we are confronted with a verbally stated applied problem such as this, our first question is, How on earth do we get started on it? The function concept is the key to getting a handle on such a situation. If we can express the quantity to be maximized—the dependent variable—as a function of some independent variable, then we have something tangible to do: Find the maximum value attained by the function. Geometrically, what is the highest point on that function's graph?

FIGURE 1.1.7 The animal pen.

EXAMPLE 9 In connection with the animal pen problem, express the area A of the pen as a function of the length x of its wall side.

Solution The area A of the rectangular pen of length x and width y is

$$A = xy. \tag{7}$$

When we multiply the length of each side in Fig. 1.1.7 by its cost per foot and then add the results, we find that the total cost C of the pen is

$$C = x + 5y + 5x + 5y = 6x + 10y.$$

So

$$6x + 10y = 180, \tag{8}$$

because we are given $C = 180$. Choosing x to be the independent variable, we use the relation in Eq. (8) to eliminate the additional variable y from the area formula in Eq. (7). We solve Eq. (8) for y and substitute the result

$$y = \tfrac{1}{10}(180 - 6x) = \tfrac{3}{5}(30 - x) \tag{9}$$

in Eq. (7). Thus we obtain the desired function

$$A(x) = \tfrac{3}{5}(30x - x^2)$$

that expresses the area A as a function of the length x.

In addition to this formula for the function A, we must also specify its domain. Only if $x > 0$ will actual rectangles be produced, but we find it convenient to include the value $x = 0$ as well. This value of x corresponds to a "degenerate rectangle" of base length zero and height

$$y = \tfrac{3}{5} \cdot 30 = 18,$$

a consequence of Eq. (9). For similar reasons, we have the restriction $y \geq 0$. Because

$$y = \tfrac{3}{5}(30 - x),$$

it follows that $x \leq 30$. Thus the complete definition of the area function is

$$A(x) = \tfrac{3}{5}(30x - x^2), \quad 0 \leq x \leq 30. \tag{10}$$

◆

COMMENT The domain of a function is a necessary part of its definition, and for each function we must specify the domain of values of the independent variable. In applications, we use the values of the independent variable that are relevant to the problem at hand.

Functions and Mathematical Modeling   SECTION 1.1   7

Example 9 illustrates an important part of the solution of a typical applied problem—the formulation of a **mathematical model** of the physical situation under study. The area function $A(x)$ defined in (10) provides a mathematical model of the animal pen problem. The shape of the optimal animal pen can be determined by finding the maximum value attained by the function A on its domain of definition.

x	$A(x)$
0	0
5	75
10	120
15	135 ←
20	120
25	75
30	0

FIGURE 1.1.8 Area $A(x)$ of a pen with side of length x.

Numerical Investigation

Armed with the result of Example 9, we might attack the animal pen problem by calculating a table of values of the area function $A(x)$ in Eq. (10). Such a table is shown in Fig. 1.1.8. The data in this table suggest strongly that the maximum area is $A = 135 \text{ ft}^2$, attained with side length $x = 15$ ft, in which case Eq. (9) yields $y = 9$ ft. This conjecture appears to be corroborated by the more refined data shown in Fig. 1.1.9.

Thus it seems that the animal pen with maximal area (costing $180) is $x = 15$ ft long and $y = 9$ ft wide. The tables in Figs. 1.1.8 and 1.1.9 show only *integral* values of x, however, and it is quite possible that the length x of the pen of maximal area is *not* an integer. Consequently, numerical tables alone do not settle the matter. A new mathematical idea is needed in order to *prove* that $A(15) = 135$ is the maximum value of

$$A(x) = \tfrac{3}{5}(30x - x^2), \quad 0 \leq x \leq 30$$

for *all* x in its domain. We attack this problem again in Section 1.2.

x	$A(x)$
10	120
11	125.4
12	129.6
13	132.6
14	134.4
15	135 ←
16	134.4
17	132.6
18	129.6
19	125.4
20	120

FIGURE 1.1.9 Further indication that $x = 15$ yields maximal area $A = 135$.

Tabulation of Functions

Many scientific and graphing calculators allow the user to program a given function for repeated evaluation, and thereby to painlessly compute tables like those in Figs. 1.1.8 and 1.1.9. For instance, Figs. 1.1.10 and 1.1.11 show displays of a calculator prepared to calculate values of the dependent variable

$$y_1 = A(x) = (3/5)(30x - x^2),$$

and Fig. 1.1.12 shows the calculator's resulting version of the table in Fig. 1.1.9.

The use of a calculator or computer to tabulate values of a function is a simple technique with surprisingly many applications. Here we illustrate a method of solving approximately an equation of the form $f(x) = 0$ by *repeated tabulation* of values $f(x)$ of the function f.

As a specific example, suppose that we ask what value of x in Eq. (10) yields an animal pen of area $A = 100$. Then we need to solve the equation

$$A(x) = \tfrac{3}{5}(30x - x^2) = 100,$$

which is equivalent to the equation

$$f(x) = \tfrac{3}{5}(30x - x^2) - 100 = 0. \tag{11}$$

FIGURE 1.1.10 A calculator programmed to evaluate $A(x) = (3/5)(30x - x^2)$.

FIGURE 1.1.11 The table setup.

FIGURE 1.1.12 The resulting table.

This is a quadratic equation that could be solved using the quadratic formula of basic algebra, but we want to take a more direct, numerical approach. The reason is that the numerical approach is applicable even when no simple formula (such as the quadratic formula) is available.

The data in Fig. 1.1.8 suggest that one value of x for which $A(x) = 100$ lies somewhere between $x = 5$ and $x = 10$ and that a second such value lies between $x = 20$ and $x = 25$. Indeed, substitution in Eq. (11) yields

$$f(5) = -25 < 0 \quad \text{and} \quad f(10) = 20 > 0.$$

The fact that $f(x)$ is *negative* at one endpoint of the interval [5, 10] but *positive* at the other endpoint suggests that $f(x)$ is *zero* somewhere between $x = 5$ and $x = 10$.

To see *where*, we tabulate values of $f(x)$ on [5, 10]. In the table of Fig. 1.1.13 we see that $f(7) < 0$ and $f(8) > 0$, so we focus next on the interval [7, 8]. Tabulating $f(x)$ on [7, 8] gives the table of Fig. 1.1.14, where we see that $f(7.3) < 0$ and $f(7.4) > 0$.

We therefore tabulate $f(x)$ once more, this time on the interval [7.3, 7.4]. In Fig. 1.1.15 we see that

$$f(7.36) \approx -0.02 \quad \text{and} \quad f(7.37) \approx 0.07.$$

Because $f(7.36)$ is considerably closer to zero than is $f(7.37)$, we conclude that the desired solution of Eq. (11) is given approximately by $x \approx 7.36$, accurate to two decimal places. If greater accuracy were needed, we could continue to tabulate $f(x)$ on smaller and smaller intervals.

If we were to begin with the interval [20, 25] and proceed similarly, we would find the second value $x \approx 22.64$ such that $f(x) = 0$. (You should do this for practice.)

Finally, let's calculate the corresponding values of the width y of the animal pen such that $A = xy = 100$:

- If $x \approx 7.36$, then $y \approx 13.59$.
- If $x \approx 22.64$, then $y \approx 4.42$.

Thus, under the cost constraint of the animal pen problem, we can construct either a 7.36-ft by 13.59-ft or a 22.64-ft by 4.42-ft rectangle, both of area 100 ft^2.

The layout of Figs. 1.1.13 through 1.1.15 suggests the idea of repeated tabulation as a process of successive numerical magnification. This method of repeated tabulation can be applied to a wide range of equations of the form $f(x) = 0$. If the interval [a, b] contains a solution and the endpoint values $f(a)$ and $f(b)$ differ in sign, then we can approximate this solution by tabulating values on successively

x	$f(x)$
5	−25.0
6	−13.6
7	−3.4
8	5.6
9	13.4
10	20.0

FIGURE 1.1.13 Values of $f(x)$ on [5, 10].

x	$f(x)$
7.0	−3.400
7.1	−2.446
7.2	−1.504
7.3	−0.574
7.4	0.344
7.5	1.250
7.6	2.144
7.7	3.026
7.8	3.896
7.9	4.754
8.0	5.600

FIGURE 1.1.14 Values of $f(x)$ on [7, 8].

x	$f(x)$
7.30	−0.5740
7.31	−0.4817
7.32	−0.3894
7.33	−0.2973
7.34	−0.2054
7.35	−0.1135
7.36	−0.0218
7.37	0.0699
7.38	0.1614
7.39	0.2527
7.40	0.3440

FIGURE 1.1.15 Values of $f(x)$ on [7.3, 7.4].

smaller subintervals. Problems 57 through 66 and the project at the end of this section are applications of this concrete numerical method for the approximate solution of equations.

1.1 TRUE/FALSE STUDY GUIDE

1.1 CONCEPTS: QUESTIONS AND DISCUSSION

1. Can a function have the same value at two different points? Can it have two different values at the same point x?
2. Explain the difference between a dependent variable and an independent variable. A change in one both causes and determines a change in the other. Which one is the "controlling variable"?
3. What is the difference between an open interval and a closed interval? Is every interval on the real line either open or closed? Justify your answer.
4. Suppose that S is a set of real numbers. Is there a function whose domain of definition is precisely the set S? Is there a function defined on the whole real line whose range is precisely the set S? Is there a function that has the value 1 at each point of S and the value 0 at each point of the real line R not in S?
5. Figure 1.1.6 shows a box with square base and height y. Which of the following two formulas would suffice to define the volume V of this box as a function of y?

    (a) $V = x^2 y$; (b) $V = y(10 - 2y)^2$.

    Discuss the difference between a formula and a function.
6. In the following table, y is a function of x. Determine whether or not x is a function of y.

x	0	2	4	6	8	10
y	−1	3	8	7	3	−2

1.1 PROBLEMS

In Problems 1 through 4, find and simplify each of the following values: (a) $f(-a)$; (b) $f(a^{-1})$; (c) $f(\sqrt{a})$; (d) $f(a^2)$.

1. $f(x) = \dfrac{1}{x}$
2. $f(x) = x^2 + 5$
3. $f(x) = \dfrac{1}{x^2 + 5}$
4. $f(x) = \sqrt{1 + x^2 + x^4}$

In Problems 5 through 10, find all values of a such that $g(a) = 5$.

5. $g(x) = 3x + 4$
6. $g(x) = \dfrac{1}{2x - 1}$
7. $g(x) = \sqrt{x^2 + 16}$
8. $g(x) = x^3 - 3$
9. $g(x) = \sqrt[3]{x + 25}$
10. $g(x) = 2x^2 - x + 4$

In Problems 11 through 16, compute and then simplify the quantity $f(a + h) - f(a)$.

11. $f(x) = 3x - 2$
12. $f(x) = 1 - 2x$
13. $f(x) = x^2$
14. $f(x) = x^2 + 2x$
15. $f(x) = \dfrac{1}{x}$
16. $f(x) = \dfrac{2}{x + 1}$

In Problems 17 through 20, find the range of values of the given function.

17. $f(x) = \begin{cases} \dfrac{x}{|x|} & \text{if } x \neq 0; \\ 0 & \text{if } x = 0 \end{cases}$
18. $f(x) = [\![3x]\!]$ (Recall that $[\![x]\!]$ is the largest integer not exceeding x.)
19. $f(x) = (-1)^{[\![x]\!]}$
20. $f(x)$ is the first-class postage (in cents) for a letter mailed in the United States and weighing x ounces, $0 < x < 12$. As of January 7, 2001 the postage rate for such a letter was 34¢ for the first ounce plus 21¢ for each additional ounce or fraction thereof.

In Problems 21 through 35, find the largest domain (of real numbers) on which the given formula determines a (real-valued) function.

21. $f(x) = 10 - x^2$
22. $f(x) = x^3 + 5$
23. $f(t) = \sqrt{t^2}$
24. $g(t) = \left(\sqrt{t}\right)^2$

25. $f(x) = \sqrt{3x-5}$ **26.** $g(t) = \sqrt[3]{t+4}$

27. $f(t) = \sqrt{1-2t}$ **28.** $g(x) = \dfrac{1}{(x+2)^2}$

29. $f(x) = \dfrac{2}{3-x}$ **30.** $g(t) = \sqrt{\dfrac{2}{3-t}}$

31. $f(x) = \sqrt{x^2+9}$ **32.** $h(z) = \dfrac{1}{\sqrt{4-z^2}}$

33. $f(x) = \sqrt{4-\sqrt{x}}$ **34.** $f(x) = \sqrt{\dfrac{x+1}{x-1}}$

35. $g(t) = \dfrac{t}{|t|}$

36. Express the area A of a square as a function of its perimeter P.

37. Express the circumference C of a circle as a function of its area A.

38. Express the volume V of a sphere as a function of its surface area S.

39. Given: $0°$C is the same as $32°$F, and a temperature change of $1°$C is the same as a change of $1.8°$F. Express the Celsius temperature C as a function of the Fahrenheit temperature F.

40. Show that if a rectangle has base x and perimeter 100 (Fig. 1.1.16), then its area A is given by the function

$$A(x) = x(50-x), \quad 0 \leq x \leq 50.$$

FIGURE 1.1.16 $A = xy$ (Problem 40).

41. A rectangle with base of length x is inscribed in a circle of radius 2 (Fig 1.1.17). Express the area A of the rectangle as a function of x.

FIGURE 1.1.17 $A = xy$ (Problem 41).

42. An oil field containing 20 wells has been producing 4000 barrels of oil daily. For each new well that is drilled, the daily production of each well decreases by 5 barrels per day. Write the total daily production of the oil field as a function of the number x of new wells drilled.

43. Suppose that a rectangular box has volume 324 cm³ and a square base of edge length x centimeters. The material for the base of the box costs 2¢/cm², and the material for its top and four sides costs 1¢/cm². Express the total cost of the box as a function of x. See Fig. 1.1.18.

FIGURE 1.1.18 $V = x^2 y$ (Problem 43).

44. A rectangle of fixed perimeter 36 is rotated around one of its sides S to generate a right circular cylinder. Express the volume V of this cylinder as a function of the length x of the side S. See Fig. 1.1.19.

FIGURE 1.1.19 $V = \pi x y^2$ (Problem 44).

45. A right circular cylinder has volume 1000 in.³ and the radius of its base is r inches. Express the total surface area A of the cylinder as a function of r. See Fig. 1.1.20.

FIGURE 1.1.20 $V = \pi r^2 h$ (Problem 45).

46. A rectangular box has total surface area 600 cm² and a square base with edge length x centimeters. Express the volume V of the box as a function of x.

47. An open-topped box is to be made from a square piece of cardboard of edge length 50 in. First, four small squares, each of edge length x inches, are cut from the corners of the cardboard (Fig. 1.1.21). Then the four resulting flaps are turned up—folded along the dotted lines—to form the four sides of the box, which will thus have a square base and a depth of x inches (Fig. 1.1.22). Express its volume V as a function of x.

FIGURE 1.1.21 Fold the edges up to make a box (Problem 47).

FIGURE 1.1.22 The box of Problem 47.

48. Continue Problem 40 by numerically investigating the area of a rectangle of perimeter 100. What dimensions (length and width) would appear to maximize the area of such a rectangle?

49. Determine numerically the number of new oil wells that should be drilled to maximize the total daily production of the oil field of Problem 42.

50. Investigate numerically the total surface area A of the rectangular box of Example 8. Assuming that both $x \geq 1$ and $y \geq 1$, what dimensions x and y would appear to minimize A?

Problems 51 through 56 deal with the functions CEILING, FLOOR, *and* ROUND *of Example 5.*

51. Show that $\text{CEILING}(x) = -\text{FLOOR}(-x)$ for all x.

52. Suppose that k is a constant. What is the range of the function $g(x) = \text{ROUND}(kx)$?

53. What is the range of the function $g(x) = \frac{1}{10}\text{ROUND}(10x)$?

54. Recalling that $\pi \approx 3.14159$, note that $\frac{1}{100}\text{ROUND}(100\pi) = 3.14$. Hence define (in terms of ROUND) a function $\text{ROUND2}(x)$ that gives the value of x rounded accurate to two decimal places.

55. Define a function $\text{ROUND4}(x)$ that gives the value of x rounded accurate to four decimal places, so that $\text{ROUND4}(\pi) = 3.1416$.

56. Define a function $\text{CHOP4}(x)$ that "chops off" (or discards) all decimal places of x beyond the fourth one, so that $\text{CHOP4}(\pi) = 3.1415$.

In Problems 57 through 66, a quadratic equation $ax^2+bx+c = 0$ and an interval $[p, q]$ containing one of its solutions are given. Use the method of repeated tabulation to approximate this solution with two digits correct or correctly rounded to the right of the decimal. Check that your result agrees with one of the two solutions given by the quadratic formula,

$$x = \frac{-b \pm \sqrt{b^2 - 4ac}}{2a}.$$

57. $x^2 - 3x + 1 = 0$, $[0, 1]$
58. $x^2 - 3x + 1 = 0$, $[2, 3]$
59. $x^2 + 2x - 4 = 0$, $[1, 2]$
60. $x^2 + 2x - 4 = 0$, $[-4, -3]$
61. $2x^2 - 7x + 4 = 0$, $[0, 1]$
62. $2x^2 - 7x + 4 = 0$, $[2, 3]$
63. $x^2 - 11x + 25 = 0$, $[3, 4]$
64. $x^2 - 11x + 25 = 0$, $[7, 8]$
65. $3x^2 + 23x - 45 = 0$, $[1, 2]$
66. $3x^2 + 23x - 45 = 0$, $[-10, -9]$

1.1 Project: A Square Wading Pool

Beginning with a given square piece of tin, you want to design a wading pool in the manner indicated in Figs. 1.1.21 and 1.1.22. Your task is to investigate the maximum volume of the pool that can be constructed and how to design a wading pool of specified volume. The key is to express the volume of the wading pool as a function $V(x)$ of the edge length x of each corner square (as in Problem 47). You can then use a calculator or computer for appropriate repeated tabulation of this function.

12 CHAPTER 1 Functions, Graphs, and Models

1.2 GRAPHS OF EQUATIONS AND FUNCTIONS

Graphs and equations of *straight lines* in the xy-coordinate plane are reviewed in Appendix B. Recall the **slope-intercept equation**

$$y = mx + b \tag{1}$$

of the straight line with **slope** $m = \tan\phi$, **angle of inclination** ϕ, and **y-intercept** b (Fig. 1.2.1). The "rise over run" definition

$$m = \frac{\text{rise}}{\text{run}} = \frac{\Delta y}{\Delta x} = \frac{y_2 - y_1}{x_2 - x_1} \tag{2}$$

of the slope (Fig. 1.2.2) leads to the **point-slope equation**

$$y - y_0 = m(x - x_0) \tag{3}$$

of the straight line with slope m that passes through the point (x_0, y_0)—see Fig. 1.2.3. In either case a point (x, y) in the xy-plane lies on the line if and only if its coordinates x and y satisfy the indicated equation.

If $\Delta y = 0$ in Eq. (2), then $m = 0$ and the line is *horizontal*. If $\Delta x = 0$, then the line is *vertical* and (because we cannot divide by zero) the slope of the line is not defined. Thus:

- Horizontal lines have slope zero.
- Vertical lines have no defined slope at all.

FIGURE 1.2.1 A line with y-intercept b and inclination angle ϕ.

FIGURE 1.2.2 Slope $m = \tan\phi = \dfrac{\Delta y}{\Delta x}$.

EXAMPLE 1 Write an equation of the line L that passes through the point $P(3, 5)$ and is parallel to the line having equation $y = 2x - 4$.

Solution The two parallel lines have the same angle of inclination ϕ (Fig. 1.2.4) and therefore have the same slope m. Comparing the given equation $y = 2x - 4$ with the slope-intercept equation in (1), we see that $m = 2$. The point-slope equation therefore gives

$$y - 5 = 2(x - 3)$$

—alternatively, $y = 2x - 1$, for an equation of the line L. ◆

FIGURE 1.2.3 The line through (x_0, y_0) with slope m.

FIGURE 1.2.4 Parallel lines have the same slope $m = \tan\phi$.

Equations (1) and (3) can both be put into the form of the general linear equation

$$Ax + By = C. \tag{4}$$

Conversely, if $B \neq 0$, then we can divide the terms in Eq. (4) by B and solve for y, thereby obtaining the point-slope equation of a straight line. If $A = 0$, then the resulting equation has the form $y = H$, the equation of a *horizontal line* with slope zero. If $B = 0$ but $A \neq 0$, then Eq. (4) can be solved for $x = K$, the equation of a *vertical line* (having no slope at all). In summary, we see that if the coefficients A and B are not both zero, then Eq. (4) is the equation of some straight line in the plane.

Graphs of More General Equations

A straight line is a simple example of the graph of an equation. By contrast, a computer-graphing program produced the exotic curve shown in Fig. 1.2.5 when asked to picture the set of all points (x, y) satisfying the equation

$$x^2 + y^2 = (x^2 + y^2 - 2x)^2.$$

FIGURE 1.2.5 The graph of the equation $x^2 + y^2 = (x^2 + y^2 - 2x)^2$.

Both a straight line and this complicated curve are examples of *graphs* of equations.

DEFINITION Graph of an Equation
The **graph** of an equation in two variables x and y is the set of all points (x, y) in the plane that satisfy the equation.

For example, the distance formula of Fig. 1.2.6 tells us that the graph of the equation

$$x^2 + y^2 = r^2 \tag{5}$$

is the circle of radius r centered at the origin $(0, 0)$. More generally, the graph of the equation

$$(x - h)^2 + (y - k)^2 = r^2 \tag{6}$$

FIGURE 1.2.6 The Pythagorean theorem implies the **distance formula** $d = \sqrt{(x_2 - x_1)^2 + (y_2 - y_1)^2}$.

is the circle of radius r with center (h, k). This also follows from the distance formula, because the distance between the points (x, y) and (h, k) in Fig. 1.2.7 is r.

EXAMPLE 2 The equation of the circle with center $(3, 4)$ and radius 10 is

$$(x - 3)^2 + (y - 4)^2 = 100,$$

which may also be written in the form

$$x^2 + y^2 - 6x - 8y - 75 = 0. \qquad \blacklozenge$$

Translates of Graphs

Suppose that the xy-plane is shifted rigidly (or *translated*) by moving each point h units to the right and k units upward. (A negative value of h or k corresponds to a leftward or downward movement.) That is, each point (x, y) of the plane is moved to the point $(x + h, y + k)$; see Fig. 1.2.8. Then the circle with radius r and center $(0, 0)$

FIGURE 1.2.7 A translated circle.

FIGURE 1.2.8 Translating a point.

is translated to the circle with radius r and center (h, k). Thus the general circle described by Eq. (6) is a *translate* of the origin-centered circle. Note that the equation of the translated circle is obtained from the original equation by replacing x with $x - h$ and y with $y - k$. This observation illustrates a general principle that describes equations of translated (or "shifted") graphs.

Translation Principle
When the graph of an equation is translated h units to the right and k units upward, the equation of the translated curve is obtained from the original equation by replacing x with $x - h$ and y with $y - k$.

Observe that we can write the equation of a translated circle in Eq. (6) in the general form

$$x^2 + y^2 + ax + by = c. \tag{7}$$

What, then, can we do when we encounter an equation already of the form in Eq. (7)? We first recognize that the graph is likely to be a circle. If so, we can discover its center and radius by the technique of *completing the square*. To do so, we note that

$$x^2 + ax = \left(x + \frac{a}{2}\right)^2 - \frac{a^2}{4},$$

which shows that $x^2 + ax$ can be made into the perfect square $(x + \frac{1}{2}a)^2$ by adding to it the square of *half* the coefficient of x.

EXAMPLE 3 Find the center and radius of the circle that has the equation

$$x^2 + y^2 - 4x + 6y = 12.$$

Solution We complete the square separately for each of the variables x and y. This gives

$$(x^2 - 4x + 4) + (y^2 + 6y + 9) = 12 + 4 + 9;$$
$$(x - 2)^2 + (y + 3)^2 = 25.$$

Hence the circle—shown in Fig. 1.2.9—has center $(2, -3)$ and radius 5. Solving the last equation for y gives

$$y = -3 \pm \sqrt{25 - (x - 2)^2}.$$

Thus the whole circle consists of the graphs of the *two* equations

$$y = -3 + \sqrt{25 - (x - 2)^2}$$

and

$$y = -3 - \sqrt{25 - (x - 2)^2}$$

that describe its upper and lower semicircles. ◆

FIGURE 1.2.9 The circle of Example 3.

Graphs of Functions
The graph of a function is a special case of the graph of an equation.

DEFINITION Graph of a Function
The **graph** of the function f is the graph of the equation $y = f(x)$.

Thus the graph of the function f is the set of all points in the plane that have the form $(x, f(x))$, where x is in the domain of f. (See Fig. 1.2.10.) Because the second

FIGURE 1.2.10 The graph of the function f.

coordinate of such a point is uniquely determined by its first coordinate, we obtain the following useful principle:

The Vertical Line Test
Each vertical line through a point in the domain of a function meets its graph in exactly one point.

Thus no vertical line can intersect the graph of a function in more than one point. For instance, it follows that the curve in Fig. 1.2.5 cannot be the graph of a *function*, although it *is* the graph of an equation. Similarly, a circle cannot be the graph of a function.

EXAMPLE 4 Construct the graph of the absolute value function $f(x) = |x|$.

Solution Recall that

$$|x| = \begin{cases} x & \text{if } x \geq 0, \\ -x & \text{if } x < 0. \end{cases}$$

So the graph of $y = |x|$ consists of the right half of the line $y = x$ together with the left half of the line $y = -x$, as shown in Fig. 1.2.11. ◆

FIGURE 1.2.11 The graph of the absolute value function $y = |x|$ of Example 4.

EXAMPLE 5 Sketch the graph of the reciprocal function

$$f(x) = \frac{1}{x}.$$

Solution Let's examine four natural cases.

1. When x is positive and numerically large, $f(x)$ is small and positive.
2. When x is positive and near zero, $f(x)$ is large and positive.
3. When x is negative and numerically small (negative and close to zero), $f(x)$ is large and negative.
4. When x is large and negative (x is negative but $|x|$ is large), $f(x)$ is small and negative (negative and close to zero).

To get started with the graph, we can plot a few points, such as

$$(1, 1), (-1, -1), \left(5, \tfrac{1}{5}\right), \left(\tfrac{1}{5}, 5\right), \left(-5, -\tfrac{1}{5}\right), \text{ and } \left(-\tfrac{1}{5}, -5\right).$$

The locations of these points, together with the four cases just discussed, suggest that the actual graph resembles the one shown in Fig. 1.2.12. ◆

FIGURE 1.2.12 The graph of the reciprocal function $y = 1/x$ of Example 5.

Figure 1.2.12 exhibits a "gap," or "discontinuity," in the graph of $y = 1/x$ at $x = 0$. Indeed, the gap is called an *infinite discontinuity* because y increases without

FIGURE 1.2.13 The graph of the greatest integer function $f(x) = [\![x]\!]$ of Example 6.

bound as x approaches zero from the right, whereas y decreases without bound as x approaches zero from the left. This phenomenon generally is signaled by the presence of denominators that are zero at certain values of x, as in the case of the functions

$$f(x) = \frac{1}{1-x} \quad \text{and} \quad f(x) = \frac{1}{x^2},$$

which we ask you to graph in the problems.

EXAMPLE 6 Figure 1.2.13 shows the graph of the greatest integer function $f(x) = [\![x]\!]$ in Example 4 in Section 1.1. Note the "jumps" that occur at integral values of x. On calculators, the greatest integer function is sometimes denoted by $\boxed{\text{INT}}$; in some programming languages, it is called FLOOR. ◆

EXAMPLE 7 Graph the function with the formula

$$f(x) = x - [\![x]\!] - \tfrac{1}{2}.$$

Solution Recall that $[\![x]\!] = n$, where n is the greatest integer not exceeding x—thus $n \leq x < n+1$. Hence if n is an integer, then

$$f(n) = n - n - \tfrac{1}{2} = -\tfrac{1}{2}.$$

This implies that the point $(n, -\tfrac{1}{2})$ lies on the graph of f for each integer n. Next, if $n \leq x < n+1$ (where, again, n is an integer), then

$$f(x) = x - n - \tfrac{1}{2}.$$

Because $y = x - n - \tfrac{1}{2}$ has as its graph a straight line of slope 1, it follows that the graph of f takes the form shown in Fig. 1.2.14. This *sawtooth function* is another example of a discontinuous function. The values of x where the value of $f(x)$ makes a jump are called **points of discontinuity** of the function f. Thus the points of discontinuity of the sawtooth function are the integers. As x approaches the integer n from the left, the value of $f(x)$ approaches $+\tfrac{1}{2}$, but $f(x)$ abruptly jumps to the value $-\tfrac{1}{2}$ when $x = n$. A precise definition of continuity and discontinuity for functions appears in Section 2.4. Figure 1.2.15 shows a graphing calculator prepared to graph the sawtooth function. ◆

FIGURE 1.2.14 The graph of the sawtooth function $f(x) = x - [\![x]\!] - \tfrac{1}{2}$ of Example 7.

FIGURE 1.2.15 A graphing calculator prepared to graph the sawtooth function of Example 7.

Parabolas

The graph of a *quadratic* function of the form

$$f(x) = ax^2 + bx + c \quad (a \neq 0) \tag{8}$$

is a *parabola* whose shape resembles that of the particular parabola in Example 8.

EXAMPLE 8 Construct the graph of the parabola $y = x^2$.

Graphs of Equations and Functions SECTION 1.2   17

Solution We plot some points in a short table of values.

x	-3	-2	-1	0	1	2	3
$y = x^2$	9	4	1	0	1	4	9

When we draw a smooth curve through these points, we obtain the curve shown in Fig. 1.2.16. ◆

The parabola $y = -x^2$ would look similar to the one in Fig. 1.2.16 but would open downward instead of upward. More generally, the graph of the equation

$$y = ax^2 \tag{9}$$

is a parabola with its *vertex* at the origin, provided that $a \neq 0$. This parabola opens upward if $a > 0$ and downward if $a < 0$. [For the time being, we may regard the vertex of a parabola as the point at which it "changes direction." The vertex of a parabola of the form $y = ax^2$ ($a \neq 0$) is always at the origin. A precise definition of the *vertex* of a parabola appears in Chapter 10.]

FIGURE 1.2.16 The graph of the parabola $y = x^2$ of Example 8.

EXAMPLE 9 Construct the graphs of the functions $f(x) = \sqrt{x}$ and $g(x) = -\sqrt{x}$.

Solution After plotting and connecting points satisfying $y = \pm\sqrt{x}$, we obtain the parabola $y^2 = x$ shown in Fig. 1.2.17. This parabola opens to the right. The upper half is the graph of $f(x) = \sqrt{x}$, the lower half is the graph of $g(x) = -\sqrt{x}$. Thus the union of the graphs of these two functions is the graph of the *single* equation $y^2 = x$. (Compare this with the circle of Example 3.) More generally, the graph of the equation

$$x = by^2 \tag{10}$$

is a parabola with its vertex at the origin, provided that $b \neq 0$. This parabola opens to the right if $b > 0$ (as in Fig. 1.2.17), but to the left if $b < 0$. ◆

FIGURE 1.2.17 The graph of the parabola $x = y^2$ of Example 9.

The *size* of the coefficient a in Eq. (9) [or of b in Eq. (10)] determines the "width" of the parabola; its *sign* determines the direction in which the parabola opens. Specifically, the larger $a > 0$ is, the steeper the curve rises and hence the narrower the parabola is. (See Fig. 1.2.18.)

The parabola in Fig. 1.2.19 has the shape of the "standard parabola" in Example 8, but its vertex is located at the point (h, k). In the indicated uv-coordinate

FIGURE 1.2.18 Parabolas with different widths.

FIGURE 1.2.19 A translated parabola.

system, the equation of this parabola is $v = u^2$, in analogy with Eq. (9) with $a = 1$. But the uv-coordinates and xy-coordinates are related as follows:

$$u = x - h, \quad v = y - k.$$

Hence the xy-coordinate equation of this parabola is

$$y - k = (x - h)^2. \tag{11}$$

Thus when the parabola $y = x^2$ is translated h units to the right and k units upward, the equation in (11) of the translated parabola is obtained by replacing x with $x - h$ and y with $y - k$. This is another instance of the *translation principle* that we observed in connection with circles.

More generally, the graph of any equation of the form

$$y = ax^2 + bx + c \quad (a \neq 0) \tag{12}$$

can be recognized as a translated parabola by first completing the square in x to obtain an equation of the form

$$y - k = a(x - h)^2. \tag{13}$$

The graph of this equation is a parabola with its vertex at (h, k).

EXAMPLE 10 Determine the shape of the graph of the equation

$$y = 2x^2 - 4x - 1. \tag{14}$$

Solution If we complete the square in x, Eq. (14) takes the form

$$y = 2(x^2 - 2x + 1) - 3;$$
$$y + 3 = 2(x - 1)^2.$$

Hence the graph of Eq. (14) is the parabola shown in Fig. 1.2.20. It opens upward and its vertex is at $(1, -3)$. ◆

FIGURE 1.2.20 The parabola $y = 2x^2 - 4x - 1$ of Example 10.

Applications of Quadratic Functions

In Section 1.1 we saw that a certain type of applied problem may call for us to find the maximum or minimum attained by a certain function f. If the function f is a quadratic function as in Eq. (8), then the graph of $y = f(x)$ is a parabola. In this case the maximum (or minimum) value of $f(x)$ corresponds to the highest (or lowest) point of the parabola. We can therefore find this maximum (or minimum) value graphically—at least approximately—by zooming in on the vertex of the parabola.

For instance, recall the animal pen problem of Section 1.1. In Example 9 there we saw that the area A of the pen (see Fig. 1.2.21) is given as a function of its base length x by

$$A(x) = \tfrac{3}{5}(30x - x^2), \quad 0 \leq x \leq 30. \tag{15}$$

FIGURE 1.2.21 The animal pen.

Figure 1.2.22 shows the graph $y = A(x)$, and Figs. 1.2.23, 1.2.24, and 1.2.25 show successive magnifications of the region near the high point (vertex) of the parabola. The dashed rectangle in each figure is the viewing window for the next. Figure 1.2.25 makes it *seem* that the maximum area of the pen is $A(15) = 135$. It is clear from the figure that the maximum value of $A(x)$ is within 0.001 of $A = 135$.

FIGURE 1.2.22 The graph $y = A(x)$.

FIGURE 1.2.23 The first zoom.

FIGURE 1.2.24 The second zoom.

FIGURE 1.2.25 The third zoom.

We can verify by completing the square as in Example 10 that the maximum value is *precisely* $A(15) = 135$:

$$A = -\tfrac{3}{5}(x^2 - 30x) = -\tfrac{3}{5}(x^2 - 30x + 225 - 225)$$
$$= -\tfrac{3}{5}(x^2 - 30x + 225) + 135;$$

that is,

$$A - 135 = -\tfrac{3}{5}(x - 15)^2. \quad (16)$$

It follows from Eq. (16) that the graph of Eq. (15) is the parabola shown in Fig. 1.2.26, which opens downward from its vertex (15, 135). This *proves* that the maximum value of $A(x)$ on the interval $[0, 30]$ is the value $A(15) = 135$, as both our numerical investigations in Section 1.1 and our graphical investigations here suggest. And when we glance at Eq. (16) in the form

$$A(x) = 135 - \tfrac{3}{5}(x - 15)^2,$$

it's clear and unarguable that the maximum possible value of $135 - \tfrac{3}{5}u^2$ is 135 when $u = x - 15 = 0$—that is, when $x = 15$.

The technique of completing the square is quite limited: It can be used to find maximum or minimum values only of *quadratic* functions. One of the goals in calculus is to develop a more general technique that can be applied to a far wider variety of functions.

The basis of this more general technique lies in the following observation. Visual inspection of the graph of

$$A(x) = \tfrac{3}{5}(30x - x^2)$$

in Fig. 1.2.26 suggests that the line tangent to the curve at its highest point is horizontal. If we *knew* that the tangent line to a graph at its highest point must be horizontal,

FIGURE 1.2.26 The graph of $A(x) = \tfrac{3}{5}(30x - x^2)$ for $0 \leq x \leq 30$.

20 CHAPTER 1 Functions, Graphs, and Models

then our problem would reduce to showing that (15, 135) is the only point of the graph of $y = A(x)$ at which the tangent line is horizontal.

But what do we mean by the *tangent line* to an arbitrary curve? We pursue this question in Section 2.1. The answer will open the door to the possibility of finding the maximum and minimum values of a wide variety of functions.

Graphic, Numeric, and Symbolic Viewpoints

An equation $y = f(x)$ provides a *symbolic* description of the function f. A table of values of f (like those in Section 1.1) is a *numeric* representation of the function, whereas this section deals largely with *graphic* representations of functions. Interesting applications often involve looking at the same function from at least two of these three viewpoints.

EXAMPLE 11 Suppose that a car begins (at time $t = 0$ hours) in Athens, Georgia (position $x = 0$ miles) and travels to Atlanta (position $x = 60$) with a constant speed of 60 mi/h. The car stays in Atlanta for exactly one hour, then returns to Athens, again with a constant speed of 60 mi/h. Describe the car's "position function" both graphically and symbolically.

Solution It's fairly clear that $x = 60t$ during the 1-hour trip from Athens to Atlanta; for instance, after $t = \frac{1}{2}$ hour the car has traveled halfway, so $x = 30 = \frac{1}{2} \cdot 60$. During the next hour, $1 \leq t \leq 2$, the car's position is constant, $x \equiv 60$. And perhaps you can see that during the return trip of the third hour, $2 \leq t \leq 3$, the car's position is given by

$$x = 60 - 60(t - 2) = 180 - 60t$$

(so that $x(2) = 60$ and $x(3) = 0$). Thus the position function $x(t)$ is defined symbolically by

$$x(t) = \begin{cases} 60t & \text{if } 0 \leq t \leq 1, \\ 60 & \text{if } 1 < t \leq 2, \\ 180 - 60t & \text{if } 2 < t \leq 3. \end{cases}$$

The domain of this function is the t-interval $[0, 3]$ and its graph is shown in Fig. 1.2.27, where we denote both the function and the dependent variable by the same symbol x (an abuse of notation that's not uncommon in applications). ◆

FIGURE 1.2.27 The graph of the position function $x(t)$ in Example 11.

EXAMPLE 12 During the decade of the 1980s the population P (in thousands) of a small but rapidly growing city was recorded in the following table.

Year	1980	1982	1984	1986	1988	1990
t	0	2	4	6	8	10
P	27.00	29.61	32.48	35.62	39.07	42.85

Estimate the population of this city in the year 1987.

Solution Figure 1.2.28 shows a graph of the population function $P(t)$ obtained by connecting the six given data points $(t, P(t))$ with a smooth curve. A careful measurement of the height of the point on this curve at which $t = 7$ yields the approximate population $P(7) \approx 37.4$ (thousand) of the city in 1987. ◆

FIGURE 1.2.28 The population function of Example 12.

1.2 TRUE/FALSE STUDY GUIDE

1.2 CONCEPTS: QUESTIONS AND DISCUSSION

1. Two general forms of equations of straight lines are reviewed at the beginning of this section. Describe a straight line for which the *slope-intercept equation* would be the one more convenient to use in writing an equation of the line. Then describe a line for which the *point-slope equation* would be more convenient.

2. (a) What is the difference between a line that has slope zero and a line that has no slope? If two lines are perpendicular and one of them has slope zero, what is the slope of the other line? (b) Let L_1 and L_2 be two perpendicular lines having slopes m_1 and m_2, respectively. Theorem 2 in Appendix B asserts that L_1 and L_2 are perpendicular if and only if $m_1 m_2 = -1$. Is this assertion true in case L_1 is the x-axis and L_2 is the y-axis? Or is there an oversight in the statement of Theorem 2 in Appendix B?

3. (a) Sketch the graph of the equation $|x| + |y| = 1$. Is this graph the graph of some function? Justify your answer. (b) Repeat part (a), but with the equation $|x + y| = 1$.

4. (a) Suppose that f is a function such that $f(x) > 0$ for all real x. Discuss the question of whether the graph of the given equation is the graph of *some* function.

   (i) $y^2 = f(x)$;   (ii) $|y| = f(x)$;   (iii) $y = |f(x)|$.

   (b) Repeat part (a), but assume that $f(x) < 0$ for all x. (c) Repeat part (a), but assume that f has both positive and negative values. For instance, sketch the graphs of the equations in (i), (ii), and (iii) if $f(x) = x^2 - 1$.

5. Newspaper articles often describe or refer to functions (either explicitly or implicitly) but rarely contain equations. Find and discuss examples of numeric and graphic representations of functions in a typical issue of your local newspaper. Also see if you can find a reference to a function that is described verbally but without either a graphic or a numeric representation.

1.2 PROBLEMS

In Problems 1 through 10, write an equation of the line L described and sketch its graph.

1. L passes through the origin and the point $(2, 3)$.
2. L is vertical and has x-intercept 7.
3. L is horizontal and passes through $(3, -5)$.
4. L has x-intercept 2 and y-intercept -3.
5. L passes through $(2, -3)$ and $(5, 3)$.
6. L passes through $(-1, -4)$ and has slope $\frac{1}{2}$.
7. L passes through $(4, 2)$ and has angle of inclination $135°$.
8. L has slope 6 and y-intercept 7.
9. L passes through $(1, 5)$ and is parallel to the line with equation $2x + y = 10$.
10. L passes through $(-2, 4)$ and is perpendicular to the line with equation $x + 2y = 17$.

Sketch the translated circles in Problems 11 through 16. Indicate the center and radius of each.

11. $x^2 + y^2 = 4x$
12. $x^2 + y^2 + 6y = 0$
13. $x^2 + y^2 + 2x + 2y = 2$
14. $x^2 + y^2 + 10x - 20y + 100 = 0$
15. $2x^2 + 2y^2 + 2x - 2y = 1$
16. $9x^2 + 9y^2 - 6x - 12y = 11$

Sketch the translated parabolas in Problems 17 through 22. Indicate the vertex of each.

17. $y = x^2 - 6x + 9$
18. $y = 16 - x^2$
19. $y = x^2 + 2x + 4$
20. $2y = x^2 - 4x + 8$
21. $y = 5x^2 + 20x + 23$
22. $y = x - x^2$

The graph of the equation $(x - h)^2 + (y - k)^2 = C$ is a circle if $C > 0$, is the single point (h, k) if $C = 0$, and contains no points if $C < 0$. (Why?) Identify the graphs of the equations in Problems 23 through 26. If the graph is a circle, give its center and radius.

23. $x^2 + y^2 - 6x + 8y = 0$
24. $x^2 + y^2 - 2x + 2y + 2 = 0$
25. $x^2 + y^2 + 2x + 6y + 20 = 0$
26. $2x^2 + 2y^2 - 2x + 6y + 5 = 0$

Sketch the graphs of the functions in Problems 27 through 50. Take into account the domain of definition of each function, and plot points as necessary.

27. $f(x) = 2 - 5x, \quad -1 \leq x \leq 1$
28. $f(x) = 2 - 5x, \quad 0 \leq x < 2$
29. $f(x) = 10 - x^2$
30. $f(x) = 1 + 2x^2$
31. $f(x) = x^3$
32. $f(x) = x^4$
33. $f(x) = \sqrt{4 - x^2}$
34. $f(x) = -\sqrt{9 - x^2}$
35. $f(x) = \sqrt{x^2 - 9}$
36. $f(x) = \dfrac{1}{1-x}$
37. $f(x) = \dfrac{1}{x+2}$
38. $f(x) = \dfrac{1}{x^2}$
39. $f(x) = \dfrac{1}{(x-1)^2}$
40. $f(x) = \dfrac{|x|}{x}$
41. $f(x) = \dfrac{1}{2x+3}$
42. $f(x) = \dfrac{1}{(2x+3)^2}$
43. $f(x) = \sqrt{1-x}$
44. $f(x) = \dfrac{1}{\sqrt{1-x}}$
45. $f(x) = \dfrac{1}{\sqrt{2x+3}}$
46. $f(x) = |2x - 2|$
47. $f(x) = |x| + x$
48. $f(x) = |x - 3|$
49. $f(x) = |2x + 5|$
50. $f(x) = \begin{cases} |x| & \text{if } x < 0, \\ x^2 & \text{if } x \geq 0 \end{cases}$

Sketch graphs of the functions given in Problems 51 through 56. Indicate any points of discontinuity.

51. $f(x) = \begin{cases} 0 & \text{if } x < 0, \\ 1 & \text{if } x \geq 0 \end{cases}$
52. $f(x) = \begin{cases} 1 & \text{if } x \text{ is an integer}, \\ 0 & \text{otherwise} \end{cases}$
53. $f(x) = [\![2x]\!]$
54. $f(x) = \dfrac{x-1}{|x-1|}$
55. $f(x) = [\![x]\!] - x$
56. $f(x) = [\![x]\!] + [\![-x]\!] + 1$

In Problems 57 through 64, use a graphing calculator or computer to find (by zooming) the highest or lowest (as appropriate) point P on the given parabola. Determine the coordinates of P with two digits to the right of the decimal correct or correctly rounded. Then verify your result by completing the square to find the actual vertex of the parabola.

57. $y = 2x^2 - 6x + 7$
58. $y = 2x^2 - 10x + 11$
59. $y = 4x^2 - 18x + 22$
60. $y = 5x^2 - 32x + 49$
61. $y = -32 + 36x - 8x^2$
62. $y = -53 - 34x - 5x^2$
63. $y = 3 - 8x - 3x^2$
64. $y = -28 + 34x - 9x^2$

In Problems 65 through 68, use the method of completing the square to graph the appropriate function and thereby determine the maximum or minimum value requested.

65. If a ball is thrown straight upward with initial velocity 96 ft/s, then its height t seconds later is $y = 96t - 16t^2$ (ft). Determine the maximum height that the ball attains.
66. Find the maximum possible area of the rectangle described in Problem 40 of Section 1.1.
67. Find the maximum possible value of the product of two positive numbers whose sum is 50.
68. In Problem 42 of Section 1.1, you were asked to express the daily production of a specific oil field as a function $P = f(x)$ of the number x of new oil wells drilled. Construct the graph of f and use it to find the value of x that maximizes P.

In Problems 69 through 72 write a symbolic description of the function whose graph is pictured. You may use the greatest integer function of Examples 6 and 7.

69. Figure 1.2.29

FIGURE 1.2.29 Problem 69.

70. Figure 1.2.30

FIGURE 1.2.30 Problem 70.

71. Figure 1.2.31

FIGURE 1.2.31 Problem 71.

72. Figure 1.2.32

FIGURE 1.2.32 Problem 72.

Each of Problems 73 through 76 describes a trip you made along a straight road connecting two cities 120 miles apart. Sketch the graph of the distance x from your starting point (in miles) as a function of the time t elapsed (in hours). Also describe the function x(t) symbolically.

73. You traveled for one hour at 45 mi/h, then realized you were going to be late, and therefore traveled at 75 mi/h for the next hour.

74. You traveled for one hour at 60 mi/h, stopped for a half hour while a herd of caribou crossed the road, then drove on toward your destination for the next hour at 60 mi/h.

75. You traveled for one hour at 60 mi/h, were suddenly engulfed in a dense fog, and drove back home at 30 mi/h.

76. You traveled for a half hour at 60 mi/h, suddenly remembered you had left your wallet at home, drove back at 60 mi/h to get it, and finally drove for two hours at 60 mi/h toward your original destination.

77. Suppose that the cost C of printing a pamphlet of at most 100 pages is a linear function of the number p of pages it contains. It costs $1.70 to print a pamphlet with 34 pages, whereas a pamphlet with 79 pages costs $3.05. (a) Express C as a function of p. Use this function to find the cost of printing a pamphlet with 50 pages. (b) Sketch the straight line graph of the function $C(p)$. Tell what the slope and the C-intercept of this line mean—perhaps in terms of the "fixed cost" to set up the press for printing and the "marginal cost" of each additional page printed.

78. Suppose that the cost C of renting a car for a day is a linear function of the number x of miles you drive that day. On day 1 you drove 207 miles and the cost was $99.45. On day 2 you drove 149 miles and the cost was $79.15. (a) Express C as a function of x. Use this function to find the cost for day 3 if you drove 175 miles. (b) Sketch the straight line graph of the function $C(x)$. Tell what the slope and the C-intercept of this line mean—perhaps in terms of fixed and marginal costs as in Problem 77.

79. For a Federal Express letter weighing at most one pound sent to a certain destination, the charge C is $8.00 for the first 8 ounces plus 80¢ for each additional ounce or fraction thereof. Sketch the graph of this function C of the total number x of ounces, and describe it symbolically in terms of the greatest integer function of Examples 6 and 7.

80. In a certain city, the charge C for a taxi trip of at most 20 miles is $3.00 for the first 2 miles (or fraction thereof), plus 50¢ for each half-mile (or part thereof) up to a total of 10 miles, plus 50¢ for each mile (or part thereof) over 10 miles. Sketch the graph of this function C of the number x of miles and describe it symbolically in terms of the greatest integer function of Examples 6 and 7.

81. The volume V (in liters) of a sample of 3 g of carbon dioxide at 27°C was measured as a function of its pressure p (in atmospheres) with the results shown in the following table:

p	0.25	1.00	2.50	4.00	6.00
V	6.72	1.68	0.67	0.42	0.27

Sketch the graph of the function $V(p)$ and use the graph to estimate the volumes of the gas sample at pressures of 0.5 and 5 atmospheres.

82. The average temperature T (in °F) in Athens, Georgia was measured at two-month intervals, with the results shown in the following table:

Date	Jul 15	Sep 15	Nov 15	Jan 15	Mar 15	May 15
T	79.1	70.2	52.3	43.4	52.2	70.1

Sketch the graph of T as a function of the number of days after July 15. Then use your graph to estimate the average temperature on October 15 and on April 15.

1.2 Project: A Broken Tree

A 50-ft tree stands 10 ft from a fence 10 feet high. The tree is suddenly "broken" part of the way up. You are to determine the height of the break so that the tree falls with its trunk barely touching the top of the fence when the tip of the tree strikes the ground on the other side of the fence. The key is the use of simple geometry to derive the equations

$$y = \frac{100}{x - 10}, \qquad (1)$$

$$(y + 10)^2 = 2500 - 100x \qquad (2)$$

24 CHAPTER 1 Functions, Graphs, and Models

FIGURE 1.2.33 The broken tree.

FIGURE 1.2.34 The hyperbola and parabola in the broken tree investigation.

relating the lengths x and y indicated in Fig. 1.2.33. The graph of Eq. (1) is a translated *rectangular hyperbola*, while the graph of Eq. (2) is a translated parabola (Fig. 1.2.34). You can use a graphing calculator or computer to locate the pertinent point(s) of intersection of these two graphs.

1.3 | POLYNOMIALS AND ALGEBRAIC FUNCTIONS

In this section and the next we briefly survey a variety of functions that are used in applications of calculus to describe and model changing phenomena in the world around us. Our viewpoint here is largely graphical. The objective is for you to attain a general understanding of major differences between different types of functions. In later chapters we use calculus to investigate further the graphs presented here.

Power Functions

A function of the form $f(x) = x^k$ (where k is a constant) is called a **power function**. If $k = 0$ then we have the constant function $f(x) \equiv 1$. The shape of the graph of a power function with exponent $k = n$, a positive integer, depends on whether n is even or odd.

EXAMPLE 1 The graphs of the *even*-degree power functions $x^2, x^4, x^6, \ldots$ all "cup upward," as indicated in Fig. 1.3.1. If $n > 2$ is an *even* integer then the graph $y = x^n$ resembles the parabola $y = x^2$, but is flatter near the origin and steeper when $|x| > 1$.

The graphs of the *odd*-degree power functions $x^1, x^3, x^5, \ldots$ all go "from southwest to northeast," as indicated in Fig. 1.3.2. If $n > 1$ is an *odd* integer then the graph $y = x^n$ resembles that of $y = x^3$, but again is flatter near the origin and steeper when $|x| > 1$. ◆

FIGURE 1.3.1 Graphs of power functions of even degree (Example 1).

Note that all the power function graphs in Figs. 1.3.1 and 1.3.2 pass through the origin, through the point $(1, 1)$, and either through $(-1, 1)$ or $(-1, -1)$, depending on whether n is even or odd. In either case, x^n increases numerically (either positively or negatively) as x does. Would you agree that the notation

$$x^n \to +\infty \text{ as } x \to +\infty, \quad x^n \to \begin{cases} +\infty & \text{as } x \to -\infty \text{ if } n \text{ is even,} \\ -\infty & \text{as } x \to -\infty \text{ if } n \text{ is odd} \end{cases}$$

(with the arrow signifying "goes to") provides a convenient and suggestive description of the general features, when $|x|$ becomes large, of the graphs in Figs. 1.3.1 and 1.3.2?

The graph $y = x^k$ may have a quite different appearance if the exponent k is not a positive integer. If k is a negative integer—say, $k = -m$ where m is a positive integer—then

$$f(x) = x^k = x^{-m} = \frac{1}{x^m},$$

FIGURE 1.3.2 Graphs of power functions of odd degree (Example 1).

FIGURE 1.3.3 $y = \dfrac{1}{x}$.

FIGURE 1.3.4 $y = \dfrac{1}{x^2}$.

so in this case the power function is the reciprocal of a function like those in Example 1. Figures 1.3.3 and 1.3.4 show the graphs of

$$y = x^{-1} = \frac{1}{x} \quad \text{and} \quad y = x^{-2} = \frac{1}{x^2},$$

respectively. Observe that 0 is not in the domain of such a function. Moreover, the reciprocal of a number close to zero is very large in magnitude, which explains the behavior of these graphs near zero: In both graphs, $|y|$ is very large—so the point (x, y) is either very high or very low—when x is close to zero.

The graph $y = x^k$ may be undefined if $x \leq 0$ and k is not an integer. In the simplest such case, when k is *irrational*, we do not attempt to define x^k if $x < 0$, so the graph of x^k exists only for $x \geq 0$.

The situation is still more complicated if the exponent k is not an integer. We do not (at present) attempt to define the expression x^k if k is irrational—that is, not a quotient of integers. But if $k = m/n$ is rational, with the integers m and n having no common integral factor larger than 1, then we can write

$$x^k = x^{m/n} = \sqrt[n]{x^m},$$

FIGURE 1.3.5 $y = x^{1/2}$.

and thereby interpret $f(x) = x^k$ as a "root function." If n is odd then $\sqrt[n]{x^m}$ is defined for all real x if m is positive and for all nonzero values of x if m is negative. But if n is even and m is odd, then the root $\sqrt[n]{x^m}$ is not defined for negative x values.

The typical behavior of such root functions is illustrated by the graphs of $y = x^{1/2} = \sqrt{x}$ and $y = x^{1/3} = \sqrt[3]{x}$ shown in Figs. 1.3.5 and 1.3.6. The square root $\sqrt{x}$ is defined only for $x \geq 0$. The cube root $\sqrt[3]{x}$ is defined for all x, but observe that its graph appears to be tangent to the y-axis at the origin.

Combinations of Functions

Many varied and complicated functions can be assembled out of simple "building-block functions." Here we discuss some of the ways of combining functions to obtain new ones.

FIGURE 1.3.6 $y = x^{1/3}$.

Suppose that f and g are functions and that c is a fixed real number. The **(scalar) multiple** cf, the **sum** $f + g$, the **difference** $f - g$, the **product** $f \cdot g$, and the **quotient** f/g are the new functions with the following formulas:

$$(cf)(x) = c \cdot f(x), \tag{1}$$

$$(f + g)(x) = f(x) + g(x), \tag{2}$$

$$(f - g)(x) = f(x) - g(x), \tag{3}$$

$$(f \cdot g)(x) = f(x) \cdot g(x), \quad \text{and} \tag{4}$$

$$\left(\frac{f}{g}\right)(x) = \frac{f(x)}{g(x)}. \tag{5}$$

26 CHAPTER 1 Functions, Graphs, and Models

The combinations in Eqs. (2) through (4) are defined for every number x that lies both in the domain of f *and* in the domain of g. In Eq. (5) we must also require that $g(x) \neq 0$.

EXAMPLE 2 Let $f(x) = x^2 + 1$ and $g(x) = x - 1$. Then:

$$(3f)(x) = 3(x^2 + 1),$$
$$(f + g)(x) = (x^2 + 1) + (x - 1) = x^2 + x,$$
$$(f - g)(x) = (x^2 + 1) - (x - 1) = x^2 - x + 2,$$
$$(f \cdot g)(x) = (x^2 + 1)(x - 1) = x^3 - x^2 + x - 1, \quad \text{and}$$
$$\left(\frac{f}{g}\right)(x) = \frac{x^2 + 1}{x - 1} \quad (x \neq 1).$$

EXAMPLE 3 If $f(x) = \sqrt{1-x}$ for $x \leq 1$ and $g(x) = \sqrt{1+x}$ for $x \geq -1$, then the sum and product of f and g are defined where *both* f and g are defined. Thus the domain of both

$$f(x) + g(x) = \sqrt{1-x} + \sqrt{1+x}$$

and

$$f(x) \cdot g(x) = \sqrt{1-x}\,\sqrt{1+x} = \sqrt{1-x^2}$$

is the closed interval $[-1, 1]$. But the domain of the quotient

$$\frac{f(x)}{g(x)} = \frac{\sqrt{1-x}}{\sqrt{1+x}} = \sqrt{\frac{1-x}{1+x}}$$

is the half-open interval $(-1, 1]$, because $g(-1) = 0$.

The results of algebraic operations can sometimes be visualized with the aid of geometric interpretations of the operations. Figures 1.3.7 through 1.3.10 show the results of various operations involving the function $f(x) = 20x^2(x^2 - 1)^2$. Adding a constant simply shifts the graph vertically, as in Fig. 1.3.7, which shows $y = f(x) + c$ for $c = -2, 0, 2,$ and 4. Multiplication by a positive constant c expands (if $c > 1$) or contracts (if $0 < c < 1$) the graph in the vertical direction, as in Fig. 1.3.8, which shows $y = cf(x)$ for $c = 1, 2,$ and 3. Figure 1.3.9 shows $y = f(x)$ and the parabola $y = 2x^2$, whereas Fig. 1.3.10 shows the graph $y = 2x^2 + f(x)$, obtained by adding the ordinates of the two curves.

FIGURE 1.3.7 $y = 20x^2(x^2 - 1)^2 + c$ for $c = -2, 0, 2, 4$.

FIGURE 1.3.8 $y = c \cdot 20x^2(x^2 - 1)^2$ for $c = 1, 2, 3$.

FIGURE 1.3.9 $y = 2x^2$ and $y = 20x^2(x^2 - 1)^2$.

FIGURE 1.3.10 $y = 2x^2$ and $y = 2x^2 + 20x^2(x^2 - 1)^2$.

Polynomials

A **polynomial** of **degree** n is a function of the form

$$p(x) = a_n x^n + a_{n-1} x^{n-1} + \cdots + a_2 x^2 + a_1 x + a_0 \qquad (6)$$

where the coefficients $a_0, a_1, \ldots, a_n$ are fixed real numbers and $a_n \neq 0$. Thus an nth-degree polynomial is a sum of constant multiples of the **power functions**

$$1, \quad x, \quad x^2, \quad \ldots, \quad x^{n-1}, \quad x^n.$$

A first-degree polynomial is simply a *linear function* $a_1 x + a_0$ whose graph is a straight line. A second-degree polynomial is a *quadratic function* whose graph $y = a_2 x^2 + a_1 x + a_0$ is a parabola (see Section 1.2).

Recall that a **zero** of the function f is a solution of the equation

$$f(x) = 0.$$

Is it obvious to you that *the zeros of $f(x)$ are precisely the x-intercepts of the graph*

$$y = f(x)?$$

Indeed, a major reason for being interested in the graph of a function is to see the number and approximate locations of its zeros.

A key to understanding graphs of higher-degree polynomials is the *fundamental theorem of algebra*. It states that every nth-degree polynomial has n zeros (possibly complex, possibly repeated). It follows that an nth-degree polynomial has *no more than n distinct real zeros*.

FIGURE 1.3.11 $f(x) = x^3 - 3x^2 + 1$ has three real zeros (Example 4).

EXAMPLE 4 Figures 1.3.11 and 1.3.12 exhibit polynomials that both have the maximum number of real zeros allowed by the fundamental theorem of algebra. But the graphs of power functions in Figs. 1.3.1 and 1.3.2 show that a high-degree polynomial may have only a single real zero. And the quadratic function

$$f(x) = x^2 + 4x + 13 = (x+2)^2 + 9$$

has no real zeros at all. (Why not?) Figure 1.3.7 includes graphs of sixth-degree polynomials having six, three, or no zeros. Indeed, an nth-degree polynomial can have any number of zeros from 0 to n if n is even (from 1 to n if n is odd).   ◆

A polynomial behaves "near infinity"—that is, outside an interval on the x-axis containing its real zeros—in much the same way as a power function of the same degree. If $p(x)$ is a polynomial of *odd* degree, then $y = p(x)$ goes in opposite (vertical) directions as x goes to $-\infty$ and to $+\infty$ (like the cubic polynomial graph in Fig. 1.3.11). But if $p(x)$ is a polynomial of *even* degree, then $y = p(x)$ goes in the same (vertical) direction as x goes to $-\infty$ and to $+\infty$ (like the 4th-degree polynomial graph in Fig. 1.3.12).

FIGURE 1.3.12 $f(x) = x^4 - 4x^2 + x + 1$ has four real zeros (Example 4).

Between the extremes to the left and right, where $|x|$ is large, an nth-degree polynomial has at most $n-1$ "bends"—like the 2 bends of the 3rd-degree polynomial graph in Fig. 1.3.11 and the 3 bends of the 4th-degree polynomial graph in Fig. 1.3.12. In Chapter 4 we will use calculus to see why this is so (and to make precise the notion of a "bend" in a curve).

Calculator/Computer Graphing

A typical calculator or computer graphing utility shows (on its graphics screen or monitor) only that portion of a graph $y = f(x)$ that lies within a selected rectangular **viewing window** of the form

$$\{(x, y) : a \leqq x \leqq b \quad \text{and} \quad c \leqq y \leqq d\}.$$

28 CHAPTER 1 Functions, Graphs, and Models

FIGURE 1.3.13 The viewing window $a \leq x \leq b$, $c \leq y \leq d$.

The parts of the graph that lie outside this viewing window remain unseen (Fig. 1.3.13). With a calculator the maximum and minimum x- and y-values may be entered explicitly in a form such as

$$\text{Xmin} = a \qquad \text{Ymin} = c$$
$$\text{Xmax} = b \qquad \text{Ymax} = d$$

Frequently the user must specify the x-**range** $[a, b]$ and the y-**range** $[c, d]$ carefully so that the viewing window will show the desired portion of the graph. The calculator or computer's "default window" may provide only a starting point.

EXAMPLE 5 Construct a graph that exhibits the principal features of the cubic polynomial

$$y = x^3 + 12x^2 + 5x - 66. \tag{7}$$

Solution We anticipate a graph that looks somewhat like the cubic graph in Fig. 1.3.11, one that goes "from southwest to northeast," perhaps with a couple of bends in between. But when we enter Eq. (7) in a typical graphing calculator with default viewing window $-10 \leq x \leq 10$, $-10 \leq y \leq 10$, we get the result shown in Fig. 1.3.14. Evidently our viewing window is not large enough to show the expected behavior.

Doubling each dimension of the viewing window, we get the result in Fig. 1.3.15. Now we see the three zeros that a cubic polynomial can have, as well as some possibility of two bends, but it appears that magnification in the y-direction is indicated. Perhaps we need a y-range measuring in the hundreds rather than the tens. With the viewing window $-20 \leq x \leq 20$, $-200 \leq y \leq 200$ we finally get the satisfying graph shown in Fig. 1.3.16.

FIGURE 1.3.14 $y = x^3 + 12x^2 + 5x - 66$ with viewing window $-10 \leq x \leq 10$, $-10 \leq y \leq 10$.

FIGURE 1.3.15 $y = x^3 + 12x^2 + 5x - 66$ with viewing window $-20 \leq x \leq 20$, $-20 \leq y \leq 20$.

FIGURE 1.3.16 $y = x^3 + 12x^2 + 5x - 66$ with viewing window $-20 \leq x \leq 20$, $-200 \leq y \leq 200$.

Once we have zoomed out to see the "big picture," we can zoom in on points of interest. For instance, Fig. 1.3.16 indicates "zoom boxes" locating the three zeros of the polynomial in (7). Apparently these zeros are located at or near the points $x = -11$, $x = -3$, and $x = 2$. Each can be approximated graphically as closely as you please (subject to the limitations of your computer) by the method of successive magnifications. (See if you can convince yourself that these three zeros are *exactly* the indicated integers. How could you verify that this actually is true?) ◆

EXAMPLE 6 Investigate the graph of the quartic (fourth-degree) polynomial

$$f(x) = (x^2 - 1)(x - 10)(x - 10.1) = x^4 - (20.1)x^3 + 100x^2 + (20.1)x - 101. \quad (8)$$

FIGURE 1.3.17 $y = (x^2 - 1)(x - 10)(x - 10.1)$ with viewing window $-5 \leq x \leq 15$, $-1000 \leq y \leq 1000$.

Solution Here we know the zeros $x = -1, 1, 10,$ and 10.1 in advance, so it makes sense to choose an x-range that includes all four. Noting that $f(0) = -101$, we suspect that a y-range measuring in the hundreds is indicated. Thus with the viewing window $-5 \leq x \leq 15, -1000 \leq y \leq 1000$, we get the attractive graph in Fig. 1.3.17. Observe that with its three bends it resembles the quartic graph in Fig. 1.3.12.

But now the behavior of the graph near the point $x = 10$ is unclear. Does it dip beneath the x-axis or not? We select the viewing window $9.5 \leq x \leq 10.5, -1 \leq y \leq 1$ to magnify this area and get the result in Fig. 1.3.18. This is a case where it appears that different plots on different scales are required to show all the behavior of the graph. ◆

Our graphs in Examples 5 and 6 exhibit the maximum possible number of zeros and bends for the polynomials in Eqs. (7) and (8), so we are fairly confident that our investigations reveal the main qualitative features of the graphs of these polynomials. But only with the calculus techniques of Chapter 4 can we be certain of the structure of a graph. For instance, a polynomial graph can exhibit fewer than the maximum possible number of bends, but at this stage we cannot be certain that more bends are not hidden somewhere, perhaps visible only on a scale different from that of the viewing window we have selected.

FIGURE 1.3.18 $y = (x^2 - 1)(x - 10)(x - 10.1)$ with viewing window $9.5 \leq x \leq 10.5$, $-1 \leq y \leq 1$.

Rational Functions

Just as a rational number is a quotient of two integers, a **rational function** is a quotient

$$f(x) = \frac{p(x)}{q(x)} \quad (9)$$

of two polynomials $p(x)$ and $q(x)$. Graphs of rational functions and polynomials have several features in common. For instance, a rational function has only a finite number of zeros, because $f(x)$ in Eq. (9) can be zero only when the numerator polynomial $p(x)$ is zero. Similarly, the graph of a rational function has only a finite number of bends.

But the denominator polynomial $q(x)$ in Eq. (9) may have a zero at a point $x = a$ where the numerator is nonzero. In this case the value of $f(x)$ will be very large in magnitude when x is close to a. This observation implies that the graph of a rational function may have a feature that no polynomial graph can have—an *asymptote*.

FIGURE 1.3.19 The graph of the rational function in Eq. (10) (Example 7).

EXAMPLE 7 Figure 1.3.19 shows the graph of the rational function

$$f(x) = \frac{(x+2)(x-1)}{x(x+1)(x-2)}. \quad (10)$$

Note the x-intercepts $x = -2$ and $x = 1$, corresponding to the zeros of the numerator $(x + 2)(x - 1)$. The vertical lines $x = -1$, $x = 0$, and $x = 2$ shown in the graph correspond to the zeros of the denominator $x(x + 1)(x - 2)$. These vertical lines are *asymptotes* of the graph of f. ◆

EXAMPLE 8 Figure 1.3.20 shows the graph of the rational function

$$f(x) = \frac{x(x+2)(x-1)}{(x+1)(x-2)}.\qquad(11)$$

The x-intercepts $x = -2$, $x = 0$, and $x = 1$ correspond to the zeros of the numerator, whereas the asymptotes $x = -1$ and $x = 2$ correspond to the zeros of the denominator. ◆

It should be clear that—by counting x-intercepts and asymptotes—you could match the rational functions in Eqs. (10) and (11) with their graphs in Figs. 1.3.19 and 1.3.20 without knowing in advance which was which.

FIGURE 1.3.20 The graph of the rational function in Eq. (11) (Example 8).

Algebraic Functions

An **algebraic function** is one whose formula can be constructed beginning with power functions and applying the algebraic operations of addition, subtraction, multiplication by a real number, multiplication, division, and/or root-taking. Thus polynomials and rational functions are algebraic functions. But whereas every polynomial is defined everywhere on the real line, and every rational function is defined everywhere except at the (finitely many) real zeros of its denominator (which correspond to vertical asymptotes), the domain of definition of an algebraic function may be quite limited. For instance, Figs. 1.3.21 and 1.3.22 show the graphs of the algebraic functions

$$f(x) = \sqrt[4]{16 - x^4} \quad \text{and} \quad g(x) = \sqrt{x^2 - 16}$$

on the bounded and unbounded intervals (respectively) where they are defined.

The graph of every polynomial or rational function looks "smooth" at every point where it is defined, but the graph of an algebraic function may exhibit "corners" or sharp "cusps" where it does not look smooth. For instance, look at the graphs in Figs. 1.3.23 and 1.3.24 of the algebraic functions

$$f(x) = \sqrt{x^2} = |x| \quad \text{and} \quad g(x) = \sqrt[3]{x^2(x-2)^2}.$$

In Chapter 3 we will use concepts of calculus to say precisely what is meant by a smooth graph.

FIGURE 1.3.21 $y = \sqrt[4]{16 - x^4}$ on $[-2, 2]$.

FIGURE 1.3.22 $y = \sqrt{x^2 - 16}$ on $(-\infty, -4) \cup (4, \infty)$.

FIGURE 1.3.23 $y = |x|$ with a "corner" at the origin.

FIGURE 1.3.24 $y = \sqrt[3]{x^2(x-2)^2}$ with "cusps" at (0, 0) and (2, 0).

FIGURE 1.3.25 $y = \pm(0.2969\sqrt{x} - 0.126x - 0.3516x^2 + 0.2843x^3 - 0.10151x^4)$.

Figure 1.3.25 shows the graphs of the two algebraic functions defined by

$$y = \pm(0.2969\sqrt{x} - 0.126x - 0.3516x^2 + 0.2843x^3 - 0.10151x^4). \quad \textbf{(12)}$$

The loop describes the cross-sectional profile of the NASA 0012 airfoil as designed by aeronautical engineers.

1.3 TRUE/FALSE STUDY GUIDE

1.3 CONCEPTS: QUESTIONS AND DISCUSSION

1. In each of the following eight cases, give an example of a function as described or explain why no such function exists.
   (a) A polynomial function of degree less than 2 whose graph lies entirely above the x-axis.
   (b) A polynomial of positive degree whose graph lies entirely beneath the x-axis.
   (c) A polynomial of positive degree and with positive leading coefficient whose graph lies entirely below the x-axis (the *leading coefficient* of a polynomial is the coefficient of its term of highest degree).
   (d) A polynomial of odd degree with negative leading coefficient whose graph does not intersect the x-axis.
   (e) A polynomial whose graph lies entirely between the lines $y = -1$ and $y = 1$.
   (f) A polynomial whose graph contains points above the line $y = 1$ and below the line $y = -1$, but contains no points between those two lines.
   (g) A rational function that has both positive and negative values but is never zero.
   (h) A nonconstant rational function that is never zero and has no vertical asymptote.

2. In each of the following five cases write the formula of a specific function as described. Also sketch a typical graph of such a function (not necessarily the same one you defined symbolically).
   (a) A quadratic polynomial with no real zeros.
   (b) A cubic polynomial with exactly one real zero $x \neq 0$.
   (c) A cubic polynomial with exactly two distinct real zeros.
   (d) A quartic polynomial with exactly two distinct real zeros.
   (e) A quartic polynomial with exactly three distinct real zeros.

3. Which of the following algebraic functions agrees with some polynomial function?
   (a) $f(x) = \sqrt{x^2 + 2x + 1}$
   (b) $f(x) = \sqrt{x^4 + 4x + 4}$
   (c) $f(x) = \sqrt[3]{(x-1)^3}$
   (d) $f(x) = \sqrt[3]{(x-2)^2}$

1.3 PROBLEMS

In Problems 1 through 6, find $f + g$, $f \cdot g$, and f/g, and give the domain of definition of each of these new functions.

1. $f(x) = x + 1$, $g(x) = x^2 + 2x - 3$
2. $f(x) = \dfrac{1}{x-1}$, $g(x) = \dfrac{1}{2x+1}$
3. $f(x) = \sqrt{x}$, $g(x) = \sqrt{x-2}$
4. $f(x) = \sqrt{x+1}$, $g(x) = \sqrt{5-x}$
5. $f(x) = \sqrt{x^2+1}$, $g(x) = \dfrac{1}{\sqrt{4-x^2}}$
6. $f(x) = \dfrac{x-1}{x-2}$, $g(x) = \dfrac{x+1}{x+2}$

In Problems 7 through 12, match the given polynomial with its graph among those shown in Figs. 1.3.26 through 1.3.31. Do not use a graphing calculator or a computer. Instead, consider the degree of the polynomial, its indicated number of zeros, and its behavior for |x| large.

7. $f(x) = x^3 - 3x + 1$
8. $f(x) = 1 + 4x - x^3$
9. $f(x) = x^4 - 5x^3 + 13x + 1$
10. $f(x) = 2x^5 - 10x^3 + 6x - 1$
11. $f(x) = 16 + 2x^2 - x^4$
12. $f(x) = x^5 + x$

FIGURE 1.3.26

FIGURE 1.3.27

FIGURE 1.3.28

FIGURE 1.3.29

FIGURE 1.3.30

FIGURE 1.3.31

In Problems 13 through 16, use the vertical asymptotes of the given rational function (rather than a graphing calculator or computer) to match it with its graph among those shown in Figs. 1.3.32 through 1.3.35.

13. $f(x) = \dfrac{1}{(x+1)(x-2)}$
14. $f(x) = \dfrac{x}{x^2 - 9}$
15. $f(x) = \dfrac{3}{x^2 + 1}$
16. $f(x) = \dfrac{x^2 + 1}{x^3 - 1}$

FIGURE 1.3.32

FIGURE 1.3.33

FIGURE 1.3.34

FIGURE 1.3.35

In Problems 17 through 20, use primarily the domain of definition of the given algebraic function (rather than a graphing calculator or computer) to match it with its graph among those in Figs. 1.3.36 through 1.3.39.

17. $f(x) = x\sqrt{x+2}$
18. $f(x) = \sqrt{2x - x^2}$
19. $f(x) = \sqrt{x^2 - 2x}$
20. $f(x) = 2\sqrt[3]{x^2 - 2x}$

FIGURE 1.3.36

FIGURE 1.3.37

FIGURE 1.3.38

FIGURE 1.3.39

In Problems 21 through 30 use a graphing calculator or computer to determine one or more appropriate viewing windows to exhibit the principal features of the graph $y = f(x)$. In particular, determine thereby the number of real solutions of the equation $f(x) = 0$ and the approximate location (to the nearest integer) of each of these solutions.

21. $f(x) = x^3 - 3x + 1$
22. $f(x) = x^3 - 3x + 2$
23. $f(x) = x^3 - 3x + 3$
24. $f(x) = 2x^4 - 6x^3 + 10x - 5$
25. $f(x) = 2x^4 - 6x^3 + 10x - 6$
26. $f(x) = 2x^4 - 6x^3 + 10x - 7$
27. $f(x) = x^3 - 50x - 100$
28. $f(x) = x^4 + 20x^3 - 50x - 30$
29. $f(x) = x^5 + 5x^4 - 100x^3 - 200x^2 + 2500x - 3500$
30. $f(x) = x^6 - 250x^4 + 2500x^2 - 2500$

In Problems 31 through 37, determine how the graph $y = f(x)$ changes when the value of c is changed within the given interval. With a graphing calculator or computer you should be able to plot graphs with different values of c on the same screen.

31. $f(x) = x^3 - 3x + c$, $-5 \leq c \leq 5$
32. $f(x) = x^3 + cx$, $-5 \leq c \leq 5$
33. $f(x) = x^3 + cx^2$, $-5 \leq c \leq 5$
34. $f(x) = x^4 + cx^2$, $-5 \leq c \leq 5$
35. $f(x) = x^5 + cx^3 + x$, $-5 \leq c \leq 5$
36. $f(x) = \dfrac{1}{1 + cx^2}$, $1 \leq c \leq 10$
37. $f(x) = \sqrt{\dfrac{x^2}{c^2 - x^2}}$, $1 \leq c \leq 10$, x in $(-c, c)$
38. Use the graphical method of repeated magnifications to find both the length and the maximum width of the airfoil shown in Fig. 1.3.25. Determine each accurate to three decimal places.

1.3 Project: A Leaning Ladder

A 12-ft ladder leans across a 5-ft fence and touches a high wall located 3 ft behind the fence. You are to find the distance from the foot of the ladder to the bottom of the fence. The key is the use of simple geometry to derive the equations

$$xy = 15 \quad \text{and} \quad (x + 3)^2 + (y + 5)^2 = 144$$

relating the lengths x and y indicated in Fig. 1.3.40. Can you eliminate y to find a quartic polynomial equation that x must satisfy? If so, then you can use a graphing calculator or computer to approximate the possible values of x by the method of repeated magnification.

FIGURE 1.3.40 The leaning ladder.

1.4 TRANSCENDENTAL FUNCTIONS

Continuing the survey of elementary functions begun in Section 1.3, we now review briefly the most familiar nonalgebraic functions that are studied in calculus. These include the *trigonometric functions* that are used to model periodic phenomena—phenomena of ebb and flow, involving quantities that oscillate with the passage of time—and the *exponential* and *logarithmic functions* that are used to model phenomena of growth and decay—involving quantities that either increase steadily or decrease steadily as time passes. We also introduce *composition* of functions, a new

Trigonometric Functions

A review of trigonometry is included in Appendix C. In elementary trigonometry a trigonometric function such as sin A, cos A, or tan A ordinarily is first defined as a function of an *angle* A in a right triangle. But here a trigonometric function of a *real number* x corresponds to that function of an angle measuring x radians. Thus

$$\sin\frac{\pi}{6} = \frac{1}{2}, \quad \cos\frac{\pi}{6} = \frac{\sqrt{3}}{2}, \quad \text{and} \quad \tan\frac{\pi}{6} = \frac{\sin\frac{\pi}{6}}{\cos\frac{\pi}{6}} = \frac{1}{\sqrt{3}}$$

because $\pi/6$ is the radian measure of an angle of 30°. Recall that

$$\pi \text{ radians} = 180 \text{ degrees,} \tag{1}$$

so

$$1 \text{ rad} = \frac{180}{\pi} \text{ deg} \quad \text{and} \quad 1 \text{ deg} = \frac{\pi}{180} \text{ rad.}$$

FIGURE 1.4.1 $y = \sin x$.

FIGURE 1.4.2 $y = \cos x$.

Figures 1.4.1 and 1.4.2 show the graphs $y = \sin x$ and $y = \cos x$ of the sine and cosine functions, respectively. The value of each oscillates between $+1$ and -1, exhibiting the characteristic *periodicity* of the trigonometric functions:

$$\sin(x + 2\pi) = \sin x \quad \text{and} \quad \cos(x + 2\pi) = \cos x \tag{2}$$

for all x.

If we translate the graph $y = \cos x$ by $\pi/2$ units to the right, we get the graph $y = \sin x$. This observation corresponds to the familiar relation

$$\cos\left(x - \frac{\pi}{2}\right) = \cos\left(\frac{\pi}{2} - x\right) = \sin x. \tag{3}$$

EXAMPLE 1 Figure 1.4.3 shows the translated sine curve obtained by translating the origin to the point $(1, 2)$. Its equation is obtained upon replacing x and y in $y = \sin x$ with $x - 1$ and $y - 2$, respectively:

$$y - 2 = \sin(x - 1); \quad \text{that is,}$$

$$y = 2 + \sin(x - 1). \quad ◆$$

The world around us is full of quantities that oscillate like the trigonometric functions. Think of the alternation of day and night, the endless repetition of the

FIGURE 1.4.3 The translated sine curve $y - 2 = \sin(x - 1)$.

seasons, the monthly cycle of the moon, the rise and fall of the tides, the beat of your heart.

EXAMPLE 2 Figure 1.4.4 shows the cosine-like behavior of temperatures in Athens, Georgia. The average temperature T (in °F) during a 24-hr day t months after July 15 is given approximately by

$$T = T(t) = 61.3 + 17.9 \cos \frac{\pi t}{6}. \tag{4}$$

For instance, on a typical October 15 (three months after July 15) the average temperature is

$$T(3) = 61.3 + 17.9 \cos \frac{3\pi}{6} = 61.3 \quad (°F)$$

because $\cos(3\pi/6) = \cos(\pi/2) = 0$. Thus the "midpoint" of fall weather in Athens—when the average daily temperature is midway between summer's high and winter's low—occurs about three weeks after the official beginning of fall (on or about September 22). Note also that

$$T(t+12) = 61.3 + 17.9 \cos\left(\frac{\pi t}{6} + 2\pi\right) = 61.3 + 17.9 \cos\left(\frac{\pi t}{6}\right) = T(t)$$

(why?), in agreement with the yearly 12-month cycle of average weather. ◆

FIGURE 1.4.4 Average daily temperature in Athens, Georgia, t months after July 15 (Example 2).

The periodicity and oscillatory behavior of the trigonometric functions make them quite unlike polynomial functions. Because

$$\sin n\pi = 0 \quad \text{and} \quad \cos\left(\frac{2n+1}{2}\pi\right) = 0 \tag{5}$$

for $n = 0, 1, 2, 3, \ldots$, we see that the simple trigonometric equations

$$\sin x = 0 \quad \text{and} \quad \cos x = 0 \tag{6}$$

have *infinitely many solutions*. In contrast, a polynomial equation can have only a finite number of solutions.

Figure 1.4.5 shows the graph of $y = \tan x$. The x-intercepts correspond to the zeros of the numerator $\sin x$ in the relation

$$\tan x = \frac{\sin x}{\cos x}, \tag{7}$$

whereas the vertical asymptotes correspond to the zeros of the denominator $\cos x$. Observe the "infinite gaps" in the graph $y = \tan x$ at these odd-integral multiples of $\pi/2$. We call these gaps *discontinuities*, phenomena we discuss further in Chapter 2.

FIGURE 1.4.5 $y = \tan x$.

Composition of Functions

Many varied and complex functions can be "put together" by using quite simple "building-block" functions. In addition to adding, subtracting, multiplying, or dividing two given functions, we can also combine functions by letting one function act on the output of the other.

> **DEFINITION** Composition of Functions
> The **composition** of the two functions f and g is the function $h = f \circ g$ defined by
> $$h(x) = f(g(x)) \qquad (8)$$
> for all x in the domain of g such that $u = g(x)$ is in the domain of f. (The right-hand side in Eq. (8) is read "f of g of x.")

Thus the output $u = g(x)$ of the function g is used as the input to the function f (Fig. 1.4.6). We sometimes refer to g as the *inner function* and to f as the *outer function* in Eq. (8).

FIGURE 1.4.6 The composition of f and g.

EXAMPLE 3 If $f(x) = \sqrt{x}$ and $g(x) = 1 - x^2$, then
$$f(g(x)) = \sqrt{1 - x^2} \quad \text{for } |x| \leq 1,$$
whereas
$$g(f(x)) = 1 - \left(\sqrt{x}\right)^2 = 1 - x \quad \text{for } x \geq 0. \qquad \blacklozenge$$

The $f(g(x))$ notation for compositions is most commonly used in ordinary computations, whereas the $f \circ g$ notation emphasizes that the composition may be regarded as a new kind of combination of the functions f and g. But Example 3 shows that $f \circ g$ is quite unlike the product fg of the two functions f and g, for
$$f \circ g \neq g \circ f,$$
whereas $fg = gf$ (because $f(x) \cdot g(x) = g(x) \cdot f(x)$ whenever $f(x)$ and $g(x)$ are defined). So remember that composition is quite different in character from ordinary multiplication of functions.

EXAMPLE 4 If
$$f(x) = x^2 \quad \text{and} \quad g(x) = \cos x,$$
then the functions
$$f(x)g(x) = x^2 \cos x,$$
$$f(g(x)) = \cos^2 x = (\cos x)^2, \quad \text{and}$$
$$g(f(x)) = \cos x^2 = \cos(x^2)$$
are defined for all x. Figures 1.4.7 through 1.4.9 illustrate vividly how different these three functions are. $\blacklozenge$

FIGURE 1.4.7 $y = x^2 \cos x$ (Example 4).

FIGURE 1.4.8 $y = \cos^2 x$ (Example 4).

FIGURE 1.4.9 $y = \cos x^2$ (Example 4).

EXAMPLE 5 Given the function $h(x) = (x^2 + 4)^{3/2}$, find two functions f and g such that $h(x) = f(g(x))$.

Solution It is technically correct—but useless—simply to let $g(x) = x$ and $f(u) = (u^2 + 4)^{3/2}$. We seek a nontrivial answer here. To calculate $(x^2 + 4)^{3/2}$, we must first calculate $x^2 + 4$. So we choose $g(x) = x^2 + 4$ as the inner function. The last step is to raise $u = g(x)$ to the power $\frac{3}{2}$, so we take $f(u) = u^{3/2}$ as the outer function. Thus if

$$f(x) = x^{3/2} \quad \text{and} \quad g(x) = x^2 + 4,$$

then $f(g(x)) = f(x^2 + 4) = (x^2 + 4)^{3/2} = h(x)$. ◆

Exponential Functions

An **exponential function** is a function of the form

$$f(x) = a^x, \tag{9}$$

where the **base** a is a fixed positive real number—a constant. Note the difference between an exponential function and a power function. In the power function x^n, the *variable* x is raised to a *constant* power; in the exponential function a^x, a *constant* is raised to a *variable* power.

Many computers and programmable calculators use the notation a ∧ x to denote the exponential a^x (a few use a ↑ x). If $a > 1$, then the graph $y = a^x$ looks much like those in Fig. 1.4.10, which shows $y = 2^x$ and $y = 10^x$. The graph of an exponential function with base a, $a > 1$, lies entirely above the x-axis and rises steadily from left to right. Therefore, such a graph is nothing like the graph of a polynomial or trigonometric function. The larger the base a, the more rapid the rate at which the curve $y = a^x$ rises (for $x > 0$). Thus $y = 10^x$ climbs more steeply than $y = 2^x$.

FIGURE 1.4.10 Increasing exponential functions $y = 2^x$ and $y = 10^x$.

EXAMPLE 6 Every exponential function (with base $a > 1$) increases *very rapidly* when x is large. The following table comparing values of x^2 with 2^x exhibits vividly the rapid rate of increase of the exponential function 2^x, even compared with the power function x^2, which increases at a more restrained rate as x increases.

x	x^2	2^x
10	100	1024
20	400	1048576
30	900	1073741824
40	1600	1099511627776
50	2500	1125899906842624
60	3600	1152921504606846976
70	4900	1180591620717411303424
80	6400	1208925819614629174706176
90	8100	1237940039285380274899124224
100	10000	1267650600228229401496703205376

38 CHAPTER 1 Functions, Graphs, and Models

FIGURE 1.4.11 $y = x^2$ and $y = 2^x$.

FIGURE 1.4.12 A magnification of 1.4.11 showing the negative solution.

FIGURE 1.4.13 Decreasing exponential functions $y = 3^{-x}$ and $y = 7^{-x}$.

The comparison between x^2 and 2^x for smaller values of x is interesting in a different way. The graphs of $y = x^2$ and $y = 2^x$ in Fig. 1.4.11 indicate that the equation $x^2 = 2^x$ has three solutions between $x = -2$ and $x = 5$. Is it clear to you that $x = 2$ and $x = 4$ are *exact* solutions? The "zoom" shown in Fig. 1.4.12 indicates that the negative solution is a bit less than -0.75. Perhaps you can zoom once more and find the value of this negative solution accurate to at least two decimal places. ◆

If we replace x in Eq. (9) with $-x$, we get the function a^{-x}. Its graph $y = a^{-x}$ *falls* from left to right if $a > 1$. Figure 1.4.13 shows the graphs $y = 3^{-x}$ and $y = 7^{-x}$.

Whereas trigonometric functions are used to describe periodic phenomena of ebb and flow, exponential functions are used to describe natural processes of steady growth or steady decline.

EXAMPLE 7 Let $P(t)$ denote the number of rodents after t months in a certain prolific population that doubles every month. If there are $P(0) = 10$ rodents initially, then there are

- $P(1) = 10 \cdot 2^1 = 20$ rodents after 1 month,
- $P(2) = 10 \cdot 2^2 = 40$ rodents after 2 months,
- $P(3) = 10 \cdot 2^3 = 80$ rodents after 3 months,

and so forth. Thus the rodent population after t months is given by the exponential function

$$P(t) = 10 \cdot 2^t \tag{10}$$

if t is a nonnegative integer. Under appropriate conditions, Eq. (10) gives an accurate approximation to the rodent population even when t is not an integer. For instance, this formula predicts that after $t = 4\frac{1}{2}$ months, there will be

$$P(4.5) = 10 \cdot 2^{4.5} \approx 226.27 \approx 226 \quad \text{rodents.} \quad ◆$$

EXAMPLE 8 Suppose that you invest $5000 in a money-market account that pays 8% interest compounded annually. This means that the amount in the account is multiplied by 1.08 at the end of each year. Let $A(t)$ denote the amount in your account at the end of t years. Then,

- $A(1) = 5000 \cdot 1.08^1$ ($5400.00) after 1 yr,
- $A(2) = 5000 \cdot 1.08^2$ ($5832.00) after 2 yr,
- $A(3) = 5000 \cdot 1.08^3$ ($6298.56) after 3 yr,

and so on. Thus after t years (t a nonnegative integer), the amount in your account is given by the exponential function

$$A(t) = 5000 \cdot 1.08^t. \tag{11}$$

Figure 1.4.14 shows the graph $A(t) = 5000 \cdot 1.08^t$ as well as the horizontal line $A = 10{,}000$. From this graph we see, for instance, that the amount in the account has doubled (to $10,000) after approximately $t = 9$ yr. We could approximate the "doubling time" more accurately by magnifying the graph near the intersection of the horizontal line and the rising curve. ◆

FIGURE 1.4.14 The graph for Example 8.

Example 9 exhibits a function that combines the steady decrease of an exponential function with negative exponent with the oscillation of a trigonometric function.

EXAMPLE 9 The function

$$y(t) = 3 \cdot 2^{-t} \cos 4\pi t \tag{12}$$

might describe the amplitude y, in inches, of the up-and-down vibrations of a car with very poor shock absorbers t seconds after it hits a deep pothole. Can you see that Eq. (12) describes an initial ($t = 0$) amplitude of 3 inches that halves every second, while two complete up-and-down oscillations occur every second? (The factor $3 \cdot 2^{-t}$ is the decreasing amplitude of the vibrations, while the function $\cos 4\pi t$ has period $\frac{1}{2}$ s.) Figure 1.4.15 shows the graph of $y(t)$. The curve described in Eq. (12) oscillates between the two curves $y(t) = \pm 3 \cdot 2^{-t}$. It appears that the car's vibrations subside and are negligible after 7 or 8 seconds. ◆

FIGURE 1.4.15 $y(t) = 3 \cdot 2^{-t} \cos 4\pi t$ (Example 9).

Logarithmic Functions

In analogy with the inverse trigonometric functions that you may have seen in trigonometry, logarithms are "inverse" to exponential functions. The **base a logarithm** of the positive number x is the power to which a must be raised to get x. That is,

$$y = \log_a x \quad \text{if} \quad a^y = x. \tag{13}$$

The LOG key on most calculators gives the base 10 (*common*) *logarithm* $\log_{10} x$. The LN key gives the *natural logarithm*

$$\ln x = \log_e x,$$

where e is a special irrational number:

$$e = 2.71828182845904523536\ldots.$$

You'll see the significance of this strange-looking base in Chapter 7.

Figure 1.4.16 shows the graphs $y = \ln x$ and $y = \log_{10} x$. Both graphs pass through the point $(1, 0)$ and rise steadily (though slowly) from left to right. Because exponential functions never take on zero or negative values, neither zero nor any negative number is in the domain of any logarithmic function.

The facts that $\log_{10} 100{,}000 = 5$ and $\log_{10} 1{,}000{,}000 = 6$ indicate that the function $\log x = \log_{10} x$ increases quite slowly as x increases. Whereas Example 6 above illustrates the fact that an exponential function a^x (with $a > 1$) increases more rapidly than any power function as $x \to \infty$, Example 10 illustrates the fact that a logarithmic function increases *more slowly* than any power function.

FIGURE 1.4.16 The common and natural logarithm functions.

EXAMPLE 10 In the following table we compare the rate of growth of the power function $f(x) = \frac{1}{2}x^{1/5}$ with that of the logarithm function $g(x) = \log x$.

x	$f(x) = \frac{1}{2}x^{1/5}$	$g(x) = \log x$
20000	3.62390	4.30103
40000	4.16277	4.60206
60000	4.51440	4.77815
80000	4.78176	4.90309
100000	5	5
120000	5.18569	5.07918
140000	5.34805	5.14613
160000	5.49279	5.20412
180000	5.62373	5.25527
200000	5.74349	5.30103

It appears here and in Fig. 1.4.17 that $\log x$ is smaller than $\frac{1}{2}x^{1/5}$ when $x > 100{,}000$. Figure 1.4.18 shows that $\log x$ initially is smaller than $\frac{1}{2}x^{1/5}$, but "catches up and passes" $\frac{1}{2}x^{1/5}$ somewhere around (although a bit less than) $x = 5$. Then $\frac{1}{2}x^{1/5}$ in turn catches up and passes $\log x$ at $x = 100{,}000$. When $x = 10^{50}$, $\frac{1}{2}x^{1/5} = 5{,}000{,}000{,}000$, but the value of $\log x$ is only 50. ◆

FIGURE 1.4.17 $\frac{1}{2}x^{1/5}$ passes $\log x$.

FIGURE 1.4.18 $\log x$ passes $\frac{1}{2}x^{1/5}$.

Transcendental Equations

The trigonometric, exponential, and logarithmic functions are called *transcendental* functions. As we saw in Eqs. (5) and (6), an equation that includes transcendental functions can have infinitely many solutions. But it also may have only a finite number of solutions. Determining whether the number of solutions is finite or infinite can be difficult. One approach is to write the given equation in the form

$$f(x) = g(x), \tag{14}$$

where both the functions f and g are readily graphed. Then the real solutions of Eq. (14) correspond to the intersections of the two graphs $y = f(x)$ and $y = g(x)$.

EXAMPLE 11 The single point of intersection of the graphs $y = x$ and $y = \cos x$, shown in Fig. 1.4.19, indicates that the equation

$$x = \cos x$$

has only a single solution. Moreover, from the graph you can glean the additional information that the solution lies in the interval $(0, 1)$. ◆

FIGURE 1.4.19 Solving the equation $x = \cos x$ of Example 11.

EXAMPLE 12 The graphs of $y = 1 - x$ and $y = 3\cos x$ are shown in Fig. 1.4.20. In contrast with Example 11, there are three points of intersection of the graphs. This

FIGURE 1.4.20 Solving the equation $1 - x = 3\cos x$ of Example 12.

makes it clear that the equation

$$1 - x = 3\cos x$$

has one negative solution and two positive solutions. They could be approximated by (separately) zooming in on the three intersection points. ◆

Can You Believe What You See on Your Calculator/Computer Screen?

The examples we give next show that the short answer to this question is "not always." One reason is that a typical graphing calculator or simple computer program plots only a finite number of equally spaced points on the curve $y = f(x), a \leq x \leq b$, joining the selected points with straight line segments. If the plotted points are sufficiently close, then the resulting graph may look to the unaided eye like a smooth curve, but it may miss some essential features that would be revealed if more points were plotted.

EXAMPLE 13 A 1-ampere alternating current with frequency 60 Hz (Hertz; cycles per second) is described by the function

$$I(t) = \sin 120\pi t. \tag{15}$$

The absolute value $|I(t)|$ gives the magnitude (in amperes) of the current at time t, which flows in one direction when $I > 0$ the opposite direction when $I < 0$. A simple computer program was used to plot the alleged graphs of $I(t)$ shown in Figs. 1.4.21 through 1.4.23. The graph in Fig. 1.4.21 is plotted on the interval $-1 \leq t \leq 1$, where we should see 120 complete oscillations because the period of $I(t)$ in Eq. (15) is 1/60 s. But instead the figure shows exactly one oscillation, so something has gone badly wrong. The graph in Fig. 1.4.22 is plotted on the interval $-\frac{1}{2} \leq t \leq \frac{1}{2}$, and whatever it is has gone from merely wrong to outright bizarre. Finally, in Fig. 1.4.23 the graph is plotted on the interval $-\frac{1}{30} \leq t \leq \frac{1}{30}$ of length $\frac{4}{60}$, so we should see exactly 4 complete oscillations. And indeed we do, so we've finally got a correct graph of the current function in Eq. (15). ◆

Here's an explanation of what went wrong at first in Example 13. The computer was programmed to plot values at exactly 120 equally spaced points of the interval desired. So in Fig. 1.4.21 we're plotting only 1 point per cycle—not nearly enough to capture the actual shape of the curve—and only 2 points per cycle in Fig. 1.4.22. But in Fig. 1.4.23 we're plotting 30 points per cycle, and this gives an accurate representation of the actual graph.

The incorrect graph in Fig. 1.4.21—which seems to portray an oscillation with the incorrect period of 2 s, instead of the correct $\frac{1}{60}$ s—is an example of the phenomenon of *aliasing*. Another example of aliasing, occasionally seen in old Western movies, is the wagon wheel that appears to rotate slowly in the wrong direction.

FIGURE 1.4.21 On the interval $[-1, 1]$ it's wrong.

FIGURE 1.4.22 On the interval $[-1/2, 1/2]$ it's bizarre.

FIGURE 1.4.23 On the interval $[-1/30, 1/30]$ it's correct!

FIGURE 1.4.24 Individual plotted points that are joined by line segments in Fig. 1.4.22.

FIGURE 1.4.25 $I(t) = \sin 120\pi t + 0.01 \sin 12000\pi t$ on the interval $-1/60 \leq t \leq 1/60$.

FIGURE 1.4.26 $I(t) = \sin 120\pi t + 0.01 \sin 12000\pi t$ on the interval $-1/2400 \leq t \leq 1/2400$.

REMARK The aliasing phenomenon exhibited in Figs. 1.4.21 and 1.4.22 is heavily dependent on the precise number of points being plotted. A plotting device (such as graphing calculator) that uses a fixed number of plotting points is susceptible to aliasing. More sophisticated graphing utilities may avoid aliasing by using a variable number of nonuniformly spaced plotting points.

Figure 1.4.22 consists largely of line segments joining consecutive points that are far apart. Figure 1.4.24 shows how that incorrect graph came about; points 1, 3, 5, 7, ..., 117, 119 in the interval $[-0.5, 0.5]$ are plotted in red, whereas points 2, 4, 6, ..., 118, 120 are plotted in blue. Now you can see what happened when the computer plotted line segments joining point 1 to point 2, point 2 to point 3, and so forth.

One moral of Example 13 is that it pays to know what you're looking for in a graph. If the graph looks markedly different in windows of different sizes, this is a clue that something's wrong.

Whereas in Example 13 we got anomalous results by plotting the graph in windows of different sizes, the next example illustrates a situation where we *must* plot graphs on different scales in order to see the whole picture.

EXAMPLE 14 Now suppose that a high-frequency (6000 Hz) current of 0.01 ampere is added to the current in Eq. (15), so the resulting current is described by

$$I(t) = \sin 120\pi t + (0.01) \sin 12000\pi t. \tag{16}$$

When we plot Eq. (16) on the interval $-\frac{1}{60} \leq t \leq \frac{1}{60}$, we get the graph shown in Fig. 1.4.25. It looks like two cycles of the original current in (15), although the plot is perhaps a bit "fuzzy." To see the effect of the added second term in Eq. (16) we must plot the graph on a much magnified scale, as in Fig. 1.4.26. The "fuzz" in Fig. 1.4.25 has now been magnified to show clearly the high-frequency oscillations with period $\frac{1}{6000}$ s. ◆

1.4 TRUE/FALSE STUDY GUIDE

1.4 CONCEPTS: QUESTIONS AND DISCUSSION

Each of the following items describes a particular population numbering $P(t)$ at time t. Tell whether you think the function $P(t)$ seems more likely to be a linear, quadratic, polynomial, root, rational, trigonometric, exponential, or logarithmic function of t. In each case write a specific function satisfying the given description.

1. The population triples every five years.
2. The population increases by the same amount each year.
3. The population oscillates every five years between a maximum of 120 and a minimum of 80.

4. The population decreases for a time, reaches a minimum value, then increases thereafter (getting larger and larger as time goes on).
5. The population increases for a time and reaches a maximum value, then decreases for a time and reaches a minimum value, and thereafter increases (becoming larger and larger).
6. The population increases each year, but by a smaller percentage than it increased in the preceding year.
7. The population decreases by the same percentage each year.
8. The population increases for a time, reaches a maximum value, and decreases thereafter (apparently dying out) with $P(t)$ approaching zero as t increases.

1.4 PROBLEMS

In Problems 1 through 10, match the given function with its graph among those shown in Figs. 1.4.27 through 1.4.36. Try to do this without using your graphing calculator or computer.

1. $f(x) = 2^x - 1$
2. $f(x) = 2 - 3^{-x}$
3. $f(x) = 1 + \cos x$
4. $f(x) = 2 - 2\sin x$
5. $f(x) = 1 + 2\cos x$
6. $f(x) = 2 - \sin x$

FIGURE 1.4.27

FIGURE 1.4.28

FIGURE 1.4.29

FIGURE 1.4.30

FIGURE 1.4.31

FIGURE 1.4.32

FIGURE 1.4.33

FIGURE 1.4.34

FIGURE 1.4.35

FIGURE 1.4.36

7. $f(x) = \dfrac{x}{2^x}$
8. $f(x) = \dfrac{\log x}{x}$
9. $f(x) = \dfrac{1 + \cos 6x}{1 + x^2}$
10. $f(x) = 2^{-x} \sin 10x$

In Problems 11 through 20, find $f(g(x))$ and $g(f(x))$.

11. $f(x) = 1 - x^2,\ g(x) = 2x + 3$
12. $f(x) = -17,\ g(x) = |x|$
13. $f(x) = \sqrt{x^2 - 3},\ g(x) = x^2 + 3$
14. $f(x) = x^2 + 1,\ g(x) = \dfrac{1}{x^2 + 1}$
15. $f(x) = x^3 - 4,\ g(x) = \sqrt[3]{x + 4}$
16. $f(x) = \sqrt{x},\ g(x) = \cos x$
17. $f(x) = \sin x,\ g(x) = x^3$
18. $f(x) = \sin x,\ g(x) = \cos x$
19. $f(x) = 1 + x^2,\ g(x) = \tan x$
20. $f(x) = 1 - x^2,\ g(x) = \sin x$

In Problems 21 through 30, find a function of the form $f(x) = x^k$ (you must specify k) and a function g such that $f(g(x)) = h(x)$.

21. $h(x) = (2 + 3x)^2$
22. $h(x) = (4 - x)^3$
23. $h(x) = \sqrt{2x - x^2}$
24. $h(x) = (1 + x^4)^{17}$
25. $h(x) = (5 - x^2)^{3/2}$
26. $h(x) = \sqrt[3]{(4x - 6)^4}$
27. $h(x) = \dfrac{1}{x + 1}$
28. $h(x) = \dfrac{1}{1 + x^2}$
29. $h(x) = \dfrac{1}{\sqrt{x + 10}}$
30. $h(x) = \dfrac{1}{(1 + x + x^2)^3}$

In Problems 31–40, use a graphing calculator or computer to determine the number of real solutions by inspecting the graph of the given equation.

31. $x = 2^{-x}$
32. $x + 1 = 3 \cos x$
33. $x - 1 = 3 \cos x$
34. $x = 5 \cos x$
35. $x = 7 \cos x$
36. $2 \log_{10} x = \cos x \quad (x > 0)$
37. $\log_{10} x = \cos x \quad (x > 0)$
38. $x^2 = 10 \cos x$
39. $x^2 = 100 \sin x$
40. $x = 5 \cos x + 10 \log_{10} x \quad (x > 0)$

41. Consider the population of Example 7 in this section, which starts with 10 rodents and doubles every month. Determine graphically (that is, by zooming) how long it will take this population to grow to 100 rodents. (Assume that each month is 30 days long and obtain an answer correct to the nearest day.)

42. Consider the money-market account of Example 8, which pays 8% annually. Determine graphically how long it will take the initial investment of $5000 to triple.

43. In 1980 the population P of Mexico was 67.4 million and was growing at the rate of 2.6% per year. If the population continues to grow at this rate, then t years after 1980 it will be $P(t) = 67.4 \cdot (1.026)^t$ (millions). Determine graphically how long it will take the population of Mexico to double.

44. Suppose that the amount A of ozone in the atmosphere decreases at the rate of 0.25% per year, so that after t years the amount remaining is $A(t) = A_0(0.9975)^t$, where A_0 denotes the initial amount. Determine graphically how long it will take for only half the original amount of ozone to be left. Does the numerical value of A_0 affect this answer?

45. The nuclear accident at Chernobyl left the surrounding region contaminated with strontium-90, which initially was emitting radiation at approximately 12 times the level safe for human habitation. When an atom of strontium-90 emits radiation, it decays to a nonradioactive isotope. In this way, about 2.5% of the strontium-90 disappears each year. Then the amount of radiation left after t years will be $A(t) = 12 \cdot (0.975)^t$ (measured in "safe units" of radiation). Determine graphically how long (after the original accident) it will be until the region measures only 1 safe unit, and it is therefore safe for humans to return.

46. Refer to Example 6 of this section; determine graphically the value (accurate to three decimal places) of the negative solution of the equation $x^2 = 2^x$.

47. Refer to Example 10 of this section; determine graphically the value (accurate to three decimal places) of the solution near $x = 5$ of the equation $\log_{10} x = \frac{1}{2} x^{1/5}$.

48. The equation $x^{10} = 3^x$ has three real solutions. Graphically approximate each of them accurate to two decimal places.

1.4 Project: A Spherical Asteroid

You land your spaceship on a spherical asteroid between Earth and Mars. Your copilot walks 1000 feet away along the asteroid's smooth surface carrying a 10-ft rod and thereby vanishes over the horizon. When she places one end of the rod on the ground and holds it straight up and down, you—lying flat on the ground—can just barely see the tip of the rod. Use this information to find the radius R of this asteroid (in miles). The key will be to derive a pair of equations relating R and the angle θ indicated in Fig. 1.4.37. (Think of the right triangle shown there and of the relationship between circular arc length and subtended central angle.) You can then attempt to solve these equations graphically. You should find plenty of solutions. But which of them gives the radius of the asteroid?

FIGURE 1.4.37 The asteroid problem.

1.5 PREVIEW: WHAT *IS* CALCULUS?

Surely this question is on your mind as you begin a study of calculus that may extend over two or three terms. Following our review of functions and graphs in Sections 1.1 through 1.4, we can preview here at least the next several chapters, where the central concepts of calculus are developed.

The Two Fundamental Problems

The body of computational technique that constitutes "the calculus" revolves around two fundamental geometric problems that people have been investigating for more than 2000 years. Each problem involves the graph $y = f(x)$ of a given function.

The first fundamental problem is this: What do we mean by the *line tangent* to the curve $y = f(x)$ at a given point? The word *tangent* stems from the Latin word *tangens,* for "touching." Thus a line tangent to a curve is one that "just touches" the curve. Lines tangent to circles (Fig. 1.5.1) are well known from elementary geometry. Figure 1.5.2 shows the line tangent to the parabola $y = x^2$ at the point $(1, 1)$. We will see in Section 2.1 that this particular tangent line has slope 2, so its point-slope equation is

$$y - 1 = 2 \cdot (x - 1); \quad \text{that is,} \quad y = 2x - 1.$$

Our first problem is how to find tangent lines in more general cases.

FIGURE 1.5.1 The tangent line L touches the circle at the point P.

FIGURE 1.5.2 The line tangent to the parabola $y = x^2$ at the point $(1, 1)$.

The Tangent Problem

Given a point $P(x, f(x))$ on the curve $y = f(x)$, how do we calculate the slope of the tangent line at P (Fig. 1.5.3)?

We begin to explore the answer to this question in Chapter 2. If we denote by $m(x)$ the slope of the tangent line at $P(x, f(x))$, then m is a *new function*. It might informally be called a *slope-predictor* for the curve $y = f(x)$. In calculus this slope-predictor function is called the **derivative** of the function f. In Chapter 3 we learn to calculate derivatives of a variety of functions, and in both Chapter 3 and Chapter 4 we see numerous applications of derivatives in solving real-world problems. These three chapters introduce part of calculus called *differential calculus*.

The tangent problem is a geometric problem—a purely mathematical question. But its answer (in the form of derivatives) is the key to the solution of diverse applied problems in many scientific and technical areas. Examples 1 and 2 may suggest to you the *connections* that are the key to the pivotal role of calculus in science and technology.

FIGURE 1.5.3 What is the slope of the line L tangent to the graph $y = f(x)$ at the point $P(x, f(x))$?

FIGURE 1.5.4 A car on a straight road (Example 1).

FIGURE 1.5.5 The slope of the tangent line at the point $(t, f(t))$ is the velocity at the time t (Example 1).

EXAMPLE 1 Suppose that you're driving a car along a long, straight road (Fig. 1.5.4). If $f(t)$ denotes the *distance* (in miles) the car has traveled at time t (in hours), then the slope of the line tangent to the curve $y = f(t)$ at the point $(t, f(t))$ (Fig. 1.5.5) is the *velocity* (in miles per hour) of the car at time t. ◆

EXAMPLE 2 Suppose that $f(t)$ denotes the number of people in the United States who have a certain serious disease at time t (measured in days from the beginning of the year). Then the slope of the line tangent to the curve $y = f(t)$ at the point $(t, f(t))$ (Fig. 1.5.6) is the *rate of growth* (the number of persons newly affected per day) of the diseased population at time t. ◆

Note The truth of the statements made in these two examples is *not* obvious. To understand such things is one reason you study calculus! We return to the concepts of velocity and rate of change at the beginning of Chapter 3.

Here we will be content with the observation that the slopes of the tangent lines in Examples 1 and 2 at least have the correct *units*. If in the time-distance plane of Example 1 we measure time t (on the horizontal axis) in seconds and distance y (on the vertical axis) in feet (or meters), then the slope (ratio of rise to run) of a straight line has the dimensions of feet (or meters) per second—the proper units for velocity (Fig. 1.5.7). Similarly, if in the ty-plane of Example 2 time t is measured in months and y is measured in persons, then the slope of a straight line has the proper units of persons per month for measuring the rate of growth of the afflicted population (Fig. 1.5.8).

The second fundamental problem of calculus is the problem of *area*. Given the graph $y = f(x)$, what is the area between this graph and the x-axis over the interval $[a, b]$?

FIGURE 1.5.6 The rate of growth of $f(t)$ at the time t is the slope of the tangent line at the point $(t, f(t))$ (Example 2).

FIGURE 1.5.7 Here slope has the dimensions of velocity (ft/s).

FIGURE 1.5.8 Here slope has the dimensions of rate of change of population.

FIGURE 1.5.9 The area problem.

FIGURE 1.5.10 The area A under the velocity curve is equal to the distance traveled during the time interval $a \leqq t \leqq b$ (Example 3).

FIGURE 1.5.11 The area A under the rate-of-change curve is equal to the net change in the population from time $t = a$ to $t = b$ (Example 4).

The Area Problem

If $f(x) \geq 0$ for x in the interval $[a, b]$, how do we calculate the area A of the plane region that lies between the curve $y = f(x)$ and the x-axis over the interval $[a, b]$ (Fig. 1.5.9)?

We begin to explore the answer to this second question in Chapter 5. In calculus the area A is called an *integral* of the function f. Chapters 5 and 6 are devoted to the calculation and application of integrals. These two chapters introduce the other part of calculus, which is called *integral calculus*.

Like the tangent problem, the area problem is a purely mathematical question, but its answer (in the form of integrals) has extensive ramifications of practical importance. Examples 3 and 4 have an obvious kinship with Examples 1 and 2.

EXAMPLE 3 If $f(t)$ denotes the *velocity* of a car at time t, then the area under the curve $y = f(t)$ over the time interval $[a, b]$ is equal to the *distance* traveled by the car between time $t = a$ and time $t = b$ (Fig. 1.5.10). ◆

EXAMPLE 4 If $f(t)$ denotes the *rate of growth* of a diseased population at time t, then the area under the curve $y = f(t)$ over the time interval $[a, b]$ is equal to the net change in the *size* of this population between time $t = a$ and time $t = b$ (Fig. 1.5.11). ◆

When we discuss integrals in Chapter 5, you will learn why the statements in Examples 3 and 4 are true.

The Fundamental Relationship

Examples 1 and 3 are two sides of a certain coin: There is an "inverse relationship" between the *distance* traveled and the *velocity* of a moving car. Examples 2 and 4 exhibit a similar relationship between the *size* of a population and its *rate of change*.

Both the distance/velocity relationship and the size/rate-of-change relationship illustrated by Examples 1 through 4 are consequences of a deep and fundamental relationship between the tangent problem and the area problem. This more general relationship is described by the *fundamental theorem of calculus*, which we discuss in Chapter 5. It was discovered in 1666 by Isaac Newton at the age of 23 while he was still a student at Cambridge University. A few years later it was discovered independently by Gottfried Wilhelm Leibniz, who was then a German diplomat in Paris who studied mathematics privately. Although the tangent problem and the area problem had, even then, been around for almost 2000 years, and much progress on separate solutions had been made by predecessors of Newton and Leibniz, their joint discovery of the fundamental relationship between the area and tangent problems made them famous as "the inventors of the calculus."

Applications of Calculus

So calculus centers around the computation *and application* of derivatives and integrals—that is, of tangent line slopes and areas under graphs. Throughout this textbook, you will see concrete applications of calculus to different areas of science and technology. The following list of a dozen such applications gives just a brief indication of the extraordinary range and real-world power of calculus.

- Suppose that you make and sell tents. How can you make the biggest tent from a given amount of cloth and thereby maximize your profit? (Section 3.6)
- You throw into a lake a cork ball that has one-fourth the density of water. How deep will it sink in the water? (Section 3.8)

- A driver involved in an accident claims he was going only 25 mi/h. Can you determine from his skid marks the actual speed of his car at the time of the accident? (Section 5.2)
- The great pyramid of Khufu at Gizeh, Egypt, was built well over 4000 years ago. No personnel records from the construction remain, but nevertheless we can calculate the approximate number of laborers involved. (Section 6.5)
- Suppose that you win the Florida lottery and decide to use part of your winning to purchase a "perpetual annuity" that will pay you and your heirs (and theirs, *ad infinitum*) $10,000 per year. What is a fair price for an insurance company to charge you for such an annuity? (Section 8.8)
- If the earth's population continues to grow at its present rate, when will there be "standing room only"? (Section 9.1)
- The factories polluting Lake Erie are forced to cease dumping wastes into the lake immediately. How long will it take for natural processes to restore the lake to an acceptable level of purity? (Section 9.4)
- In 1845 the Belgian demographer Verhulst used calculus to predict accurately the course of U.S. population growth (to within 1%) well into the twentieth century, long after his death. How? (Section 9.5)
- What explains the fact that a well-positioned reporter can eavesdrop on a quiet conversation between two diplomats 50 feet away in the Whispering Gallery of the U.S. Senate, even if this conversation is inaudible to others in the same room? (Section 10.6)
- Suppose that Paul and Mary alternately toss a fair six-sided die in turn until one wins the pot by getting the first "six." How advantageous is it to be the one who tosses first? (Section 11.3)
- How can a submarine traveling in darkness beneath the polar icecap keep accurate track of its position without being in radio contact with the rest of the world? (Section 12.5)
- Suppose that your club is designing an unpowered race car for the annual downhill derby. You have a choice of solid wheels, bicycle wheels with thin spokes, or even solid spherical wheels (like giant ball bearings). Can you determine (without time-consuming experimentation) which will make the race car go the fastest? (Section 14.5)
- Some bullets have flattened tips. Is it possible that an artillery shell with a flat-tipped "nose cone" may experience less air resistance—and therefore travel farther—than a shell with a smoothly rounded tip? (Section 15.5)

1.5 TRUE/FALSE STUDY GUIDE

CHAPTER 1 REVIEW: DEFINITIONS AND CONCEPTS

Use this list as a guide to key topics that you may need to review or discuss.

1. The definition of a function
2. The domain and range of a function
3. Dependent and independent variables
4. Open and closed interval notation
5. The idea of a mathematical model
6. Numerical investigation of values of functions by repeated tabulation
7. Slope-intercept and point-slope equations of straight lines
8. The graph of an equation
9. The graph of a function
10. The translation principle for graphs of equations
11. The vertical line test for graphs of functions
12. Equations and translates of circles
13. Parabolas and graphs of quadratic functions
14. Contrasting graphic, numeric, and symbolic views of functions
15. Graphical solution of equations by the method of repeated magnification
16. Algebraic combinations of functions

17. The maximum possible number of zeros of a polynomial
18. The behavior of the polynomial $p(x)$ for $|x|$ large
19. Location of the vertical asymptotes of a rational function
20. Qualitative comparison of graphs of power functions, polynomials, rational functions, and algebraic functions
21. Periods of trigonometric functions
22. Rates of growth of exponential and logarithmic functions
23. Qualitative comparison of the graphs of trigonometric, exponential, and logarithmic functions
24. Composition of functions
25. Determining a viewing window that exhibits the principal features of the graph of a function
26. Possible pitfalls of calculator and computer graphing

CHAPTER 1 MISCELLANEOUS PROBLEMS

In Problems 1 through 10, find the domain of definition of the function with the given formula.

1. $f(x) = \sqrt{x-4}$
2. $f(x) = \dfrac{1}{2-x}$
3. $f(x) = \dfrac{1}{x^2-9}$
4. $f(x) = \dfrac{x}{x^2+1}$
5. $f(x) = \left(1+\sqrt{x}\right)^3$
6. $f(x) = \dfrac{x+1}{x^2-2x}$
7. $f(x) = \sqrt{2-3x}$
8. $f(x) = \dfrac{1}{\sqrt{9-x^2}}$
9. $f(x) = (x-2)(4-x)$
10. $f(x) = \sqrt{(x-2)(4-x)}$

11. In accord with Boyle's law, the pressure p (lb/in.^{2}) and volume V (in.^{3}) of a certain gas satisfy the condition $pV = 800$. What is the range of possible values of p, given $100 \leq V \leq 200$?

12. The relationship between the Fahrenheit temperature F and the Celsius temperature C is given by
$$F = 32 + \tfrac{9}{5}C.$$
If the temperature on a given day ranges from a low of $70°$F to a high of $90°$F, what is the range of temperature in degrees Celsius?

13. An electric circuit contains a battery that supplies E volts in series with a resistance of R ohms (Fig. 1.MP.1). Then the current of I amperes that flows in the circuit satisfies Ohm's law, $E = IR$. If $E = 100$ and $25 < R < 50$, what is the range of possible values of I?

FIGURE 1.MP.1 The simple electric circuit of Problem 13.

14. The period T (in seconds) of a simple pendulum of length L (in feet) is given by $T = 2\pi\sqrt{L/32}$. If $3 < L < 4$, what is the range of possible values of T?

15. Express the volume V of a cube as a function of its total surface area S.

16. The height of a certain right circular cylinder is equal to its radius. Express its total surface area A (including both ends) as a function of its volume V.

17. Express the area A of an equilateral triangle as a function of its perimeter P.

18. A piece of wire 100 in. long is cut into two pieces of lengths x and $100 - x$. The first piece is bent into the shape of a square, the second into the shape of a circle. Express as a function of x the sum A of the areas of the square and circle.

In Problems 19 through 24, write an equation of the straight line L described.

19. L passes through $(-3, 5)$ and $(1, 13)$.
20. L passes through $(4, -1)$ and has slope -3.
21. L has slope $\tfrac{1}{2}$ and y-intercept -5.
22. L passes through $(2, -3)$ and is parallel to the line with equation $3x - 2y = 4$.
23. L passes through $(-3, 7)$ and is perpendicular to the line with equation $y - 2x = 10$. (Appendix B reviews slopes of perpendicular lines.)
24. L is the perpendicular bisector of the segment joining $(1, -5)$ and $(3, -1)$.

In Problems 25 through 34, match the given function with its graph among those shown in Figs. 1.MP.2 through 1.MP.11. Do this without using your graphing calculator or computer. Instead, rely on your knowledge of the general characteristics of polynomial, rational, algebraic, trigonometric, exponential, and logarithmic functions.

FIGURE 1.MP.2

FIGURE 1.MP.3

FIGURE 1.MP.4

FIGURE 1.MP.5

FIGURE 1.MP.6

FIGURE 1.MP.7

FIGURE 1.MP.8

FIGURE 1.MP.9

FIGURE 1.MP.10

FIGURE 1.MP.11

25. $f(x) = 2 - 2x - x^2$

26. $f(x) = x^3 - 4x^2 + 5$

27. $f(x) = x^4 - 4x^3 + 5$

28. $f(x) = \dfrac{5}{x^2 - x - 6}$

29. $f(x) = \dfrac{5}{x^2 - x + 6}$

30. $f(x) = \sqrt{8 + 2x - x^2}$

31. $f(x) = 2^{-x} - 1$

32. $f(x) = \log_{10}(x + 1)$

33. $f(x) = 1 + 3\sin x$

34. $f(x) = x + 3\sin x$

Sketch the graphs of the equations and functions given in Problems 35 through 44.

35. $2x - 5y = 7$

36. $|x - y| = 1$

37. $x^2 + y^2 = 2x$

38. $x^2 + y^2 = 4y - 6x + 3$

39. $y = 2x^2 - 4x - 1$

40. $y = 4x - x^2$

41. $f(x) = \dfrac{1}{x + 5}$

42. $f(x) = \dfrac{1}{4 - x^2}$

43. $f(x) = |x - 3|$

44. $f(x) = |x - 3| + |x + 2|$

45. Apply the triangle inequality (of Appendix A) twice to show that
$$|a + b + c| \leq |a| + |b| + |c|$$
for arbitrary real numbers a, b, and c.

46. Write $a = (a - b) + b$ to deduce from the triangle inequality (of Appendix A) that
$$|a| - |b| \leq |a - b|$$
for arbitrary real numbers a and b.

47. Solve the inequality $x^2 - x - 6 > 0$. [*Suggestion:* Conclude from the factorization
$$x^2 - x - 6 = (x - 3)(x + 2)$$
that the quantities $x - 3$ and $x + 2$ must be either both positive or both negative for the inequality to hold. Consider the two cases separately to conclude that the solution set is $(-\infty, -2) \cup (3, +\infty)$.]

Use the method of Problem 47 to solve the inequalities in Problems 48 through 50.

48. $x^2 - 3x + 2 < 0$
49. $x^2 - 2x - 8 > 0$
50. $2x \geq 15 - x^2$

The remaining problems require the use of an appropriate calculator or computer. In Problems 51 through 56, use either the method of repeated tabulation or the method of successive zooms (or both) to find the two roots (with three digits to the right of the decimal point correct or correctly rounded) of the given quadratic equation. You may check your work with the aid of the quadratic formula and an ordinary calculator.

51. $x^2 - 5x - 7 = 0$
52. $3x^2 - 10x - 11 = 0$
53. $4x^2 - 14x + 11 = 0$
54. $5x^2 + 24x - 35 = 0$
55. $8x^2 + 33x - 36 = 0$
56. $9x^2 + 74x - 156 = 0$

In Problems 57 through 62, apply either the method of repeated tabulation or the method of successive zooms (or both) to find the lowest point on the given parabola. You may check your work by completing the square.

57. $y = x^2 - 5x + 7$
58. $y = 3x^2 - 10x + 11$
59. $y = 4x^2 - 14x + 11$
60. $y = 5x^2 + 24x + 35$
61. $y = 8x^2 + 33x + 35$
62. $y = 9x^2 + 74x + 156$

63. Figure 1.MP.12 shows a 10-cm by 7-cm portrait that includes a border of width x on the top and bottom and of width $2x$ on either side. The area of the border is itself 20 cm^2. Use either repeated tabulation or successive zooms to find x.

FIGURE 1.MP.12 The bordered portrait of Problem 63.

64. A mail-order catalog lists a 60-in. by 35-in. tablecloth that shrinks 7% in area when first washed. The catalog description also implies that the length and width will *both* decrease by the same amount x. Use numerical (tabulation) or graphical (zoom) methods to find x.

Determine graphically the number of real solutions of each equation in Problems 65 through 70.

65. $x^3 - 7x + 3 = 0$
66. $x^4 - 3x^2 + 4x - 5 = 0$
67. $\sin x = x^3 - 3x + 1$
68. $\cos x = x^4 - x$
69. $\cos x = \log_{10} x$
70. $10^{-x} = \log_{10} x$

PRELUDE TO CALCULUS

2

Ada Byron (1815–1852)

The modern computer programming language Ada is named in honor of Ada Byron, daughter of the English poet Lord Byron. Her interest in science and mathematics led her around 1840 to study the Difference Engine, a gear-based mechanical calculator that the mathematician Charles Babbage had built to compute tables of values of functions. By then he was designing his much more advanced Analytic Engine, an elaborate computing machine that would have been far ahead of its time if it had been completed. In 1843 Ada Byron wrote a series of brief essays explaining the planned operation of the Analytical Engine and its underlying mathematical principles. She included a prototype "computer program" to illustrate how its calculations were to be "programmed" in advance, using a deck of punched cards to specify its instructions.

Calculus has been called "the calculating engine par excellence." But in our own time the study and applications of calculus have been reshaped by electronic computers. Throughout this book we illustrate concepts of calculus by means of graphic, numeric, and symbolic results generated by computers. In Chapter 2 we exploit computational technology systematically in the investigation of limits.

Grace Murray Hopper (1906–1992)

Almost exactly a century after the death of Ada Byron, the first modern computer compiler (for translation of human-language programs into machine-language instructions) was developed by Grace Murray Hopper. As a mathematician and U.S. Navy officer, Hopper had worked with the very first modern electronic computers developed during and immediately after World War II. In 1967 she was recalled to active duty to lead efforts to standardize the computer language COBOL for the Navy. In 1985 at the age of 79, she became Rear Admiral Grace Hopper. In 1986 she was retired—as the Navy's oldest commissioned officer on active duty—in a ceremony held aboard the U.S.S. Constitution, the Navy's oldest commissioned warship.

The Difference Engine

2.1 TANGENT LINES AND SLOPE PREDICTORS

In Sections 1.2 and 1.5 we saw that certain applied problems raise the question of what is meant by the *tangent line* at a specified point of a general curve $y = f(x)$. In this section we see that this "tangent-line problem" leads to the limit concept, which we pursue further in Section 2.2.

In elementary geometry the line tangent to a circle at a point P is defined as the straight line through P that is perpendicular to the radius (OP) to that point (Fig. 2.1.1). A general graph $y = f(x)$ has no radius for us to use, but the line tangent to the graph at the point P should be the straight line through P that has—in some sense—the same direction at P as the curve itself. Because a line's "direction" is determined by its slope, our plan for defining a line tangent to a curve amounts to finding an appropriate "slope-prediction formula" that will give the proper slope of the tangent line. Example 1 illustrates this approach in the case of one of the simplest of all nonstraight curves, the parabola with equation $y = x^2$.

FIGURE 2.1.1 The line tangent to the circle at the point P is perpendicular to the radius OP.

EXAMPLE 1 Determine the slope of the line L tangent to the parabola $y = x^2$ at the point $P(a, a^2)$.

Solution Figure 2.1.2 shows the parabola $y = x^2$ and a typical point $P(a, a^2)$ on it. The figure also shows a visual guess of the direction of the desired tangent line L at P. We must find the slope of L.

FIGURE 2.1.2 The tangent line at P should have the same direction as the curve does at P (Example 1).

We cannot immediately calculate the slope of L, because we know the coordinates of only *one* point $P(a, a^2)$ of L. Hence we begin with another line whose slope we *can* compute. Figure 2.1.3 shows the **secant line** K that passes through the point P and the nearby point $Q(b, b^2)$ of the parabola $y = x^2$. Let us write

$$h = \Delta x = b - a$$

for the difference of the x-coordinates of P and Q. (The notation Δx is as old as calculus itself, and it means now what it did 300 years ago: an **increment,** or *change*, in the value of x.) Then the coordinates of Q are given by the formulas

$$b = a + h \quad \text{and} \quad b^2 = (a + h)^2.$$

Hence the difference in the y-coordinates of P and Q is

$$\Delta y = b^2 - a^2 = (a + h)^2 - a^2.$$

FIGURE 2.1.3 The secant line K passes through the two points P and Q, which we can use to determine its slope (Example 1).

Because P and Q are two different points, we can use the definition of slope to calculate the slope m_{PQ} of the secant line K through P and Q. If you change the value of $h = \Delta x$, you change the line K and thereby change its slope. Therefore, m_{PQ} depends on h:

$$m_{PQ} = \frac{\Delta y}{\Delta x} = \frac{(a+h)^2 - a^2}{(a+h) - a}$$
$$= \frac{(a^2 + 2ah + h^2) - a^2}{h} = \frac{2ah + h^2}{h} = \frac{h(2a+h)}{h}. \quad (1)$$

Because h is nonzero, we may cancel it in the final fraction. Thus we find that the slope of the secant line K is given by

$$m_{PQ} = 2a + h. \quad (2)$$

Now imagine what happens as you move the point Q along the curve closer and closer to the point P. (This situation corresponds to h approaching zero.) The line K still passes through P and Q, but it pivots around the fixed point P. As h approaches zero, the secant line K comes closer to coinciding with the tangent line L. This phenomenon is suggested in Fig. 2.1.4, which shows the secant line K approaching the tangent line L.

FIGURE 2.1.4 As $h \to 0$, Q approaches P, and K moves into coincidence with the tangent line L (Example 1).

Our idea is to *define* the tangent line L as the limiting position of the secant line K. To see precisely what this means, examine what happens to the slope of K as

K pivots into coincidence with *L*:

As *h* approaches zero,

Q approaches *P*, and so

K approaches *L*; meanwhile,

the slope of K approaches the slope of L.

Hence our question is this: As the number *h* approaches zero, what value does the slope $m_{PQ} = 2a + h$ approach? We can state this question of the "limiting value" of $2a + h$ by writing

$$\lim_{h \to 0}(2a + h) = ? \tag{3}$$

Here, "lim" is an abbreviation for the word "limit," and "$h \to 0$" is an abbreviation for the phrase "*h* approaches zero." Thus Eq. (3) asks, "What is the limit of $2a + h$ as *h* approaches zero?"

For any specific value of *a* we can investigate this question numerically by calculating values of $2a + h$ with values of *h* that become closer and closer to zero—such as the values $h = 0.1, h = -0.01, h = 0.001, h = -0.0001, \ldots$, or the values $h = 0.5, h = 0.1, h = 0.05, h = 0.01, \ldots$. For instance, the tables of values in Figs. 2.1.5 and 2.1.6 indicate that with $a = 1$ and $a = -2$ we should conclude that

$$\lim_{h \to 0}(2 + h) = 2 \quad \text{and} \quad \lim_{h \to 0}(-4 + h) = -4.$$

More generally, it seems clear from the table in Fig. 2.1.7 that

$$\lim_{h \to 0} m_{PQ} = \lim_{h \to 0}(2a + h) = 2a. \tag{4}$$

h	$2+h$
0.1	2.1
0.01	2.01
0.001	2.001
0.0001	2.0002
↓	↓
0	2

FIGURE 2.1.5 As $h \to 0$ (first column), $2 + h$ approaches 2 (second column).

h	$-4+h$
0.5	−3.5
0.1	−3.9
0.05	−3.95
0.01	−3.99
0.005	−3.995
0.001	−3.999
↓	↓
0	−4

FIGURE 2.1.6 As $h \to 0$ (first column), $-4 + h$ approaches -4 (second column).

h	$2a+h$
0.01	$2a + 0.01$
0.001	$2a + 0.001$
⋮	⋮
↓	↓
0	$2a$

FIGURE 2.1.7 As $h \to 0$ (first column), $2a + h$ approaches $2a$ (second column) (Example 1).

This, finally, answers our original question: The slope $m = m(a)$ of the line tangent to the parabola $y = x^2$ at the point (a, a^2) is given by

$$m = 2a. \tag{5}$$

◆

The formula in Eq. (5) is a "slope predictor" for (lines tangent to) the parabola $y = x^2$. Once we know the slope of the line tangent to the curve at a given point of the curve, we can then use the point-slope formula to write an equation of this tangent line.

EXAMPLE 2 With $a = 1$, the slope predictor in Eq. (5) gives $m = 2$ for the slope of the line tangent to $y = x^2$ at the point $(1, 1)$. Hence an equation of this line is

$$y - 1 = 2(x - 1); \quad \text{that is,} \quad y = 2x - 1.$$

With $a = -3$, Eq. (5) gives $m = -6$ as the slope of the line tangent at $(-3, 9)$, so an equation of the line tangent to the curve at this point is

$$y - 9 = -6(x + 3); \quad \text{that is,} \quad y = -6x - 9.$$ ◆

In Fig. 2.1.8 the parabola $y = x^2$ and its tangent line $y = 2x - 1$ passing through $(1, 1)$ are both graphed. The relationship between the curve and its tangent line is such that as we "zoom in" on the point of tangency, successive magnifications show less and less of a difference between the curve and the tangent line. This phenomenon is illustrated in Figs. 2.1.9 through 2.1.11.

FIGURE 2.1.8 The parabola $y = x^2$ and its tangent line at $P(1, 1)$.

FIGURE 2.1.9 First magnification.

FIGURE 2.1.10 Second magnification.

FIGURE 2.1.11 Can you see the difference?

REMARK In Example 1 we proceeded as though the concept of a tangent line to a curve were self-evident. The actual meaning of the slope-predictor result $m = 2a$ in Eq. (5) is this: Whatever is meant by the line tangent to the parabola $y = x^2$ at the point $P(a, a^2)$, it can only be the unique straight line through P with slope $m = 2a$. Thus we must *define* the line tangent to $y = x^2$ at P to be the line whose point-slope equation is $y - a^2 = 2a(x - a)$. Pictures like those in Figs. 2.1.8 through 2.1.11 certainly support our conviction that this definition is the correct one.

More General Slope Predictors

The general case of the line tangent to a curve $y = f(x)$ is scarcely more complicated than the special case $y = x^2$ of Example 1. Given the function f, suppose that we want to find the slope of the line L tangent to $y = f(x)$ at the point $P(a, f(a))$. As indicated in Fig. 2.1.12, let K be the secant line passing through the point P and the nearby point $Q(a + h, f(a + h))$ on the graph. The slope of this secant line is the **difference quotient**

$$m_{PQ} = \frac{\Delta y}{\Delta x} = \frac{f(a + h) - f(a)}{h} \quad \text{(with } h \neq 0\text{)}. \tag{6}$$

FIGURE 2.1.12 As $h \to 0$, $Q \to P$, and the slope of K approaches the slope of the tangent line L.

FIGURE 2.1.13 The slope of the tangent line at $(a, f(a))$ is
$$m(a) = \lim_{h \to 0} \frac{f(a+h) - f(a)}{h}.$$

We now force Q to approach the fixed point P along the curve $y = f(x)$ by making h approach zero. We ask whether m_{PQ} approaches some limiting value m as $h \to 0$. If so, we write

$$m = \lim_{h \to 0} \frac{f(a+h) - f(a)}{h}$$

and conclude that this number m is the slope of the line tangent to the graph $y = f(x)$ at the point $(a, f(a))$. Actually, this slope depends on a and we can indicate this by writing

$$m_a = \lim_{h \to 0} \frac{f(a+h) - f(a)}{h}. \tag{7}$$

If we can express the limiting value on the right explicitly in terms of a, then Eq. (7) yields a *slope predictor* for lines tangent to the curve $y = f(x)$. In this case the line tangent to the curve at the point $P(a, f(a))$ is *defined* to be the straight line through P that has slope m_a. This tangent line is indicated in Fig. 2.1.13.

In Chapter 3 we will acknowledge the fact that the slope m_a is somehow "derived" from the function f by calling this number the **derivative** of the function f at the point a. Indeed, much of Chapter 3 will be devoted to methods of calculating derivatives of various familiar functions. Most of these methods are based on the limit techniques of Sections 2.2 and 2.3, but the case of quadratic functions is sufficiently simple for inclusion here. Recall from Section 1.2 that the graph of any quadratic function is a parabola that opens either upward or downward.

THEOREM Parabolas and Tangent Lines
Consider the parabola $y = f(x)$ where

$$f(x) = px^2 + qx + r \tag{8}$$

(with $p \neq 0$). Then the line tangent to this parabola at the point $P(a, f(a))$ has slope

$$m_a = 2pa + q. \tag{9}$$

PROOF The slope of the secant line given in (6) may be simplified as follows:

$$m_{PQ} = \frac{f(a+h) - f(a)}{h} = \frac{[p(a+h)^2 + q(a+h) + r] - [pa^2 + qa + r]}{h}$$

$$= \frac{[p(a^2 + 2ah + h^2) + q(a+h) + r] - [pa^2 + qa + r]}{h} = \frac{2pah + ph^2 + qh}{h},$$

and therefore
$$m_{PQ} = 2pa + q + ph.$$

The numbers p, q, and a are fixed, so as $h \to 0$ the product ph approaches zero, much as in our computations in Example 1. Thus
$$m_a = \lim_{h \to 0} m_{PQ} = \lim_{h \to 0}(2pa + q + ph) = 2pa + q,$$

as claimed in Eq. (9). ◀

REMARK 1 Thus the formula $m_a = 2pa + q$ provides a ready slope predictor for lines tangent to the parabola with equation
$$y = px^2 + qx + r.$$

Given the coefficients p, q, r, and the number a, we need only substitute in this slope-predictor formula to obtain the slope m_a of the line tangent to the parabola at the point where $x = a$. We need *not* repeat the computational steps that were carried out in the derivation of the slope-predictor formula.

REMARK 2 If we replace a with x we get the **slope-predictor function**
$$m(x) = 2px + q. \qquad (10)$$

Here m is a *function* whose value $m(x)$ at x is the slope of the line tangent to the parabola $y = f(x)$ at the point $P(x, f(x))$. Perhaps the visual scheme
$$f(x) = px^2 + qx + r$$
$$\downarrow \quad \downarrow \quad \downarrow \quad \downarrow$$
$$m(x) = 2px + q + 0$$

makes this slope predictor easy for you to remember.

EXAMPLE 3 Find an equation of the line tangent to the parabola $y = 2x^2 - 3x + 5$ at the point where $x = -1$.

Solution Here we have $p = 2, q = -3, r = 5$, and the y-coordinate of our point is $2 \cdot (-1)^2 - 3 \cdot (-1) + 5 = 10$. Then Eq. (10) gives the slope predictor
$$m(x) = 2 \cdot 2x + (-3) = 4x - 3,$$
so the slope of the line tangent to the parabola at the point $(-1, 10)$ is $m(-1) = 4 \cdot (-1) - 3 = -7$. The point-slope equation of this tangent line is therefore
$$y - 10 = (-7)(x + 1); \quad \text{that is,} \quad y = -7x + 3. \qquad \blacklozenge$$

FIGURE 2.1.14 The normal line N from the point $(3, 0)$ to the point (c, c^2) on the parabola $y = x^2$.

Normal Lines

How would you find the point $P(c, c^2)$ that lies on the parabola $y = x^2$ and is closest to the point $(3, 0)$? Intuitively, the line segment N with endpoints $(3, 0)$ and P should be perpendicular, or *normal*, to the parabola's tangent line at P (Fig. 2.1.14). But if the slope of the tangent line is m, then—by Theorem 2 in Appendix B—the slope of the normal line is
$$m_N = -\frac{1}{m}. \qquad (11)$$

(Theorem 2 tells us that if two perpendicular lines have nonzero slopes m_1 and m_2, then $m_1 m_2 = -1$.) More precisely, the **normal line** at a point P of a curve where the tangent line has slope m is *defined* to be the line through P with slope $m_N = -1/m$ (Fig. 2.1.15). Consequently, the parabolic slope predictor in (9) enables us to write equations of lines normal to parabolas as easily as equations of tangent lines.

FIGURE 2.1.15 The tangent line and normal line through the point P on a curve.

EXAMPLE 4 In Example 3 we found that the line tangent to the parabola $y = 2x^2 - 3x + 5$ at the point $P(-1, 10)$ has slope -7. Therefore the slope of the line normal to that parabola at P is $m_N = -1/(-7) = \frac{1}{7}$. So the point-slope equation of the normal line is

$$y - 10 = \tfrac{1}{7}(x + 1); \quad \text{that is,} \quad y = \tfrac{1}{7}x + \tfrac{71}{7}. \qquad \blacklozenge$$

The Animal Pen Problem Completed

Now we can apply our newfound knowledge of slope-predictor formulas to wrap up our continuing discussion of the animal pen problem of Section 1.1. In Example 9 there we found that the area A of the pen (see Fig. 2.1.16) is given as a function of its base length x by

$$A(x) = \tfrac{3}{5}(30x - x^2) = -\tfrac{3}{5}x^2 + 18x \tag{12}$$

for $0 \leq x \leq 30$. Therefore our problem is to find the maximum value of $A(x)$ for x in the closed interval $[0, 30]$.

FIGURE 2.1.16 The animal pen.

Let us accept as intuitively obvious—we will see a proof in Chapter 3—the fact that the maximum value of $A(x)$ occurs at the high point where the line tangent to the parabola $y = A(x)$ is *horizontal*, as indicated in Fig. 2.1.17. But the function $A(x)$ in Eq. (12) is quadratic with $p = -\tfrac{3}{5}$ and $q = 18$ (compare (12) with (8)). Therefore the slope predictor in (10) implies that the slope of the tangent line at an arbitrary point $(x, A(x))$ of the parabola is given by

$$m = m(x) = 2px + q = -\tfrac{6}{5}x + 18.$$

We ask when $m = 0$ and find that this happens when

$$-\tfrac{6}{5}x + 18 = 0,$$

and thus when $x = 15$. In agreement with the result found by algebraic methods in Section 1.2, we find that the maximum possible area of the pen is

$$A(15) = \tfrac{3}{5}(30 \cdot 15 - 15^2) = 135 \quad (\text{ft}^2).$$

FIGURE 2.1.17 The graph of $y = A(x)$, $0 \leq x \leq 30$.

Numerical Investigation of Slopes

Suppose that you are given the function f and a specific numerical value of a. You can then use a calculator to investigate the value

$$m = \lim_{h \to 0} \frac{f(a+h) - f(a)}{h} \tag{13}$$

of the slope of the line tangent to the curve $y = f(x)$ at the point $(a, f(a))$. Simply calculate the values of the difference quotient

$$\frac{f(a+h) - f(a)}{h} \tag{14}$$

with successively smaller nonzero values of h to see whether a limiting numerical value is apparent.

EXAMPLE 5 Find by numerical investigation (an approximation to) the line tangent to the graph of

$$f(x) = x + \frac{1}{x} \tag{15}$$

at the point $(2, \tfrac{5}{2})$.

Solution Figure 2.1.18 shows a TI calculator prepared to calculate the difference quotient in Eq. (14) with the function f in Eq. (15). As indicated in Fig. 2.1.19, successive values of this quotient can then be calculated by brief "one-liners." Figure 2.1.20 shows an HP calculator prepared to define the same quotient; then evaluation of the expression 'M(2,0.0001)' yields the approximate value $m \approx 0.75001$. In

FIGURE 2.1.18 A calculator prepared to calculate $\dfrac{f(a+h) - f(a)}{h}$ with $f(x) = x + \dfrac{1}{x}$.

FIGURE 2.1.19 Approximating $\lim\limits_{h \to 0} \dfrac{f(a+h) - f(a)}{h}$.

FIGURE 2.1.20 A calculator prepared to compute $\dfrac{f(x+h) - f(x)}{h}$.

h	$\dfrac{f(2+h) - f(2)}{h}$
0.1	0.76190
0.01	0.75124
0.001	0.75012
0.0001	0.75001
0.00001	0.75000
↓	↓
0	$\dfrac{3}{4}$

FIGURE 2.1.21 Numerical investigation of the limit in (13) with $f(x) = x + \dfrac{1}{x}$, $a = 2$.

this way we get the table shown in Fig. 2.1.21, which suggests that the slope of the line tangent to the graph of $f(x)$ at the point $(2, \frac{5}{2})$ is $m = \frac{3}{4}$. If so, then the tangent line at this point has the point-slope equation

$$y - \tfrac{5}{2} = \tfrac{3}{4}(x - 2); \quad \text{that is,} \quad y = \tfrac{3}{4}x + 1.$$

Our numerical investigation does not constitute a rigorous proof that this actually is the desired tangent line, but Figs. 2.1.22 and 2.1.23 showing the computer-generated graphs

$$y = x + \frac{1}{x} \quad \text{and} \quad y = \frac{3}{4}x + 1$$

are strong evidence that we've got it right. (Do you agree?) ◆

FIGURE 2.1.22 The curve and its tangent line (Example 5).

FIGURE 2.1.23 The curve and its tangent line magnified near $(2, \frac{5}{2})$.

2.1 TRUE/FALSE STUDY GUIDE

2.1 CONCEPTS: QUESTIONS AND DISCUSSION

1. What is the slope-predictor function for the straight line with equation $y = 17x - 21$?

2. Can two different parabolas with equations of the form $y = px^2 + qx + r$ have the same slope-predictor function?

3. The vertex of the parabola with equation $y = px^2 + qx + r$ is its highest point (if $p < 0$) or its lowest point (if $p > 0$). As indicated in Fig. 2.1.17, it is apparent that this vertex is the single point of the parabola at which the tangent line is horizontal. Is it true—for *any* given curve $y = f(x)$—that a point on the graph at which the tangent line is horizontal is either the highest or the lowest point on the graph?

2.1 PROBLEMS

In Problems 1 through 14, first apply the slope-predictor formula in (10) for quadratic functions to write the slope $m(a)$ of the line tangent to $y = f(x)$ at the point where $x = a$. Then write an equation of the line tangent to the graph of f at the point $(2, f(2))$.

1. $f(x) \equiv 5$
2. $f(x) = x$
3. $f(x) = x^2$
4. $f(x) = 1 - 2x^2$
5. $f(x) = 4x - 5$
6. $f(x) = 7 - 3x$
7. $f(x) = 2x^2 - 3x + 4$
8. $f(x) = 5 - 3x - x^2$
9. $f(x) = 2x(x + 3)$
10. $f(x) = 3x(5 - x)$
11. $f(x) = 2x - \left(\dfrac{x}{10}\right)^2$
12. $f(x) = 4 - (3x + 2)^2$
13. $f(x) = (2x + 1)^2 - 4x$
14. $f(x) = (2x+3)^2 - (2x-3)^2$

In Problems 15 through 24, find all points of the curve $y = f(x)$ at which the tangent line is horizontal.

15. $y = 10 - x^2$
16. $y = 10x - x^2$
17. $y = x^2 - 2x + 1$
18. $y = x^2 + x - 2$
19. $y = x - \left(\dfrac{x}{10}\right)^2$
20. $y = x(100 - x)$
21. $y = (x + 3)(x - 5)$
22. $y = (x - 5)^2$
23. $y = 70x - x^2$
24. $y = 100\left(1 - \dfrac{x}{10}\right)^2$

In Problems 25 through 35, use the slope-predictor formula for quadratic functions as necessary. In Problems 25 through 27, write equations for both the line tangent to, and the line normal to, the curve $y = f(x)$ at the given point P.

25. $y = x^2$; $P(-2, 4)$
26. $y = 5 - x - 2x^2$; $P(-1, 4)$
27. $y = 2x^2 + 3x - 5$; $P(2, 9)$
28. Prove that the line tangent to the parabola $y = x^2$ at the point (x_0, y_0) intersects the x-axis at the point $(x_0/2, 0)$. See Fig. 2.1.24.

FIGURE 2.1.24 The parabola and tangent line of Problem 28.

29. If a ball is thrown straight upward with initial velocity 96 ft/s, then its height t seconds later is $y(t) = 96t - 16t^2$ feet. Determine the maximum height the ball attains by finding the point in the parabola $y(t) = 96t - 16t^2$ where the tangent line is horizontal.

30. According to Problem 40 of Section 1.1, the area of a rectangle with base of length x and perimeter 100 is $A(x) = x(50 - x)$. Find the maximum possible area of this rectangle by finding the point on the parabola $A = x(50-x)$ at which the tangent line is horizontal.

31. Find the maximum possible value of the product of two positive numbers whose sum is 50.

32. Suppose that a projectile is fired at an angle of 45° from the horizontal. Its initial position is the origin in the xy-plane, and its initial velocity is $100\sqrt{2}$ ft/s (Fig. 2.1.25). Then its trajectory will be the part of the parabola $y = x - (x/25)^2$ for which $y \geq 0$. (a) How far does the projectile travel (horizontally) before it hits the ground? (b) What is the maximum height above the ground that the projectile attains?

FIGURE 2.1.25 The trajectory of the projectile of Problem 32.

33. One of the two lines that pass through the point $(3, 0)$ and are tangent to the parabola $y = x^2$ is the x-axis. Find an equation for the *other* line. (*Suggestion:* First find the value of the number a shown in Fig. 2.1.26.)

FIGURE 2.1.26 Two lines tangent to the parabola of Problem 33.

34. Write equations for the two straight lines that pass through the point $(2, 5)$ and are tangent to the parabola $y = 4x - x^2$. (*Suggestion:* Draw a figure like Fig. 2.1.26.)

35. Between Examples 3 and 4 we raised—but did not answer—the question of how to locate the point on the graph of $y = x^2$ closest to the point $(3, 0)$. It's now time for you to find that point. (*Suggestion:* Draw a figure like Fig. 2.1.26. The cubic equation you should obtain has one solution that is apparent by inspection.)

Let $P(a, f(a))$ be a fixed point on the graph of $y = f(x)$. If $h > 0$, then $Q(a + h, f(a + h))$ lies to the right, and $R(a - h, f(a - h))$ lies to the left, of P. Does Fig. 2.1.27 make it appear plausible—for $h > 0$ and h very small—that the slope

$$m_{RQ} = \dfrac{f(a+h) - f(a-h)}{2h} = \dfrac{1}{2}(m_{PQ} + m_{RP})$$

The Limit Concept SECTION 2.2 63

FIGURE 2.1.27 Three different approximations to the slope of a tangent line.

is generally an especially good approximation to the slope m of the line tangent to the graph at P? In particular, the "symmetric difference quotient" m_{RQ} is generally a better approximation to m than either the standard right-hand difference quotient

$$m_{PQ} = \frac{f(a+h) - f(a)}{h}$$

or the left-hand difference quotient

$$m_{RP} = \frac{f(a) - f(a-h)}{h}.$$

In Problems 36 through 48, use a calculator or computer to investigate numerically the slope m of the line tangent to the given graph at $P(a, f(a))$ by calculating both m_{PQ} and m_{RQ} for $h = 0.1, 0.01, 0.001, \ldots$. Check the resulting value of m by plotting both the graph of $y = f(x)$ and the alleged tangent line.

36. $f(x) = x^2; a = -1$
37. $f(x) = x^3; a = 2$
38. $f(x) = x^3; a = -1$
39. $f(x) = \sqrt{x}; a = 1$
40. $f(x) = \sqrt{x}; a = 4$
41. $f(x) = \frac{1}{x}; a = 1$
42. $f(x) = \frac{1}{x}; a = -\frac{1}{2}$
43. $f(x) = \cos x; a = 0$
44. $f(x) = \sin 10\pi x; a = 0$
45. $f(x) = \cos x; a = \frac{1}{4}\pi$
46. $f(x) = \sin 10\pi x; a = \frac{1}{20}$
47. $f(x) = \sqrt{25 - x^2}; a = 0$
48. $f(x) = \sqrt{25 - x^2}; a = 3$

2.1 Project: Numerical Slope Investigations

This project consists of numerical investigations of slopes based on the fact that a curve $y = f(x)$ and its tangent line at a fixed point $P(a, f(a))$ are virtually indistinguishable at a sufficiently high level of magnification (as illustrated in Figs. 2.1.8 through 2.1.11). Suppose that we plot the graph on a calculator or computer having a facility that lets us "grab" the xy-coordinates of selected points on the graph. For example, with some graphing calculators, you can simply press the TRACE key and then move the cursor along the graph, pausing to read the coordinates of any desired point. Suppose that you "zoom in" on the point P, and at the kth zoom record the coordinates (x_1, y_1) and (x_2, y_2) of two points located on opposite sides of P (as indicated in Fig. 2.1.28). Then you can approximate the slope m of the line tangent to the graph at P by calculating the value of the difference quotient

$$m_k = \frac{\Delta y}{\Delta x} = \frac{y_2 - y_1}{x_2 - x_1}.$$

After several successive zooms you may have a very accurate approximation to m. The CD-ROM material for this project lists several tangent line problems for you to investigate in this manner.

FIGURE 2.1.28 Points on either side of P.

2.2 THE LIMIT CONCEPT

In Section 2.1 we defined the slope m of the line tangent to the graph $y = f(x)$ at the point $P(a, f(a))$ to be

$$m = \lim_{h \to 0} \frac{f(a+h) - f(a)}{h}. \tag{1}$$

The graph that motivated this definition is repeated in Fig. 2.2.1, with $a + h$ relabeled as x (so that $h = x - a$). We see that x approaches a as h approaches zero, so Eq. (1) can be written in the form

$$m = \lim_{x \to a} \frac{f(x) - f(a)}{x - a}. \tag{2}$$

FIGURE 2.2.1 The slope m at $P(a, f(a))$ can be defined in this way: $m = \lim\limits_{x \to a} \dfrac{f(x) - f(a)}{x - a}$.

Thus the computation of m amounts to the determination of the limit, as x approaches a, of the function

$$g(x) = \frac{f(x) - f(a)}{x - a}. \tag{3}$$

In order to develop general methods for calculating such limits, we need to investigate more fully the meaning of the statement

$$\lim_{x \to a} f(x) = L. \tag{4}$$

This is read "the limit of $f(x)$ as x approaches a is L." We sometimes write Eq. (4) in the concise form

$$f(x) \to L \quad \text{as} \quad x \to a.$$

The function f need not be defined at the point $x = a$ in order for us to discuss the limit of f at a. The actual value of $f(a)$—if any—actually is immaterial. It suffices for $f(x)$ to be defined for all points *other than* a in some **neighborhood** of a—that is, for all $x \neq a$ is some open interval containing a. This is exactly the situation for the function in Eq. (3), which is defined *except* at a (where the denominator is zero). The following statement presents the meaning of Eq. (4) in intuitive language.

Idea of the Limit

We say that the number L is the *limit* of $f(x)$ as x approaches a provided that we can make the number $f(x)$ as close to L as we please merely by choosing x sufficiently near, though not equal to, the number a.

What this means, roughly, is that $f(x)$ tends to get closer and closer to L as x gets closer and closer to a. Once we decide how close to L we want $f(x)$ to be, it is necessary that $f(x)$ be that close to L for *all* x sufficiently close to (but not equal to) a.

Figure 2.2.2 shows a graphical interpretation of the limit concept. As x approaches a (from either side), the point $(x, f(x))$ on the graph $y = f(x)$ must approach the point (a, L).

In this section we explore the idea of the limit, mainly through the investigation of specific examples. A precise statement of the definition of the limit appears in Section 2.3.

FIGURE 2.2.2 Graphical interpretation of the limit concept.

EXAMPLE 1 Investigate the value of $\lim\limits_{x \to 3} \dfrac{x - 1}{x + 2}$.

Investigation This is an investigation (rather than a solution) because numerical calculations may strongly suggest the value of a limit but cannot establish its value with certainty. The table in Fig. 2.2.3 gives values of

$$f(x) = \frac{x - 1}{x + 2},$$

correct to six rounded decimal places, for values of x that approach 3 (but are not equal to 3). The first and third columns of the table show values of x that approach 3 both from the left and from the right.

x	$\dfrac{x-1}{x+2}$	x	$\dfrac{x-1}{x+2}$
2	0.250000	4	0.500000
2.9	0.387755	3.1	0.411765
2.99	0.398798	3.01	0.401198
2.999	0.399880	3.001	0.400120
2.9999	0.399988	3.0001	0.400012
↓	↓	↓	↓
3	0.4	3	0.4

FIGURE 2.2.3 Investigating the limit in Example 1.

Now examine the table—read down the columns for x, because *down* is the table's direction for "approaches"—to see what happens to the corresponding values of $f(x)$. The data clearly suggest that

$$\lim_{x \to 3} \frac{x-1}{x+2} = \frac{2}{5}.$$

◆

REMARK 1 The graph of $f(x) = (x-1)/(x+2)$ in Fig. 2.2.4 reinforces our guess that $f(x)$ is near $\frac{2}{5}$ when x is near 3. For still more reinforcement you can use a graphing calculator or computer to zoom in on the point on the graph where $x = 3$.

REMARK 2 Note that we did not simply substitute the value $x = 3$ into the function $f(x) = (x-1)/(x+2)$ to obtain the apparent value $\frac{2}{5} = 0.4$ of the limit. Although such substitution would produce the correct answer in this particular case, in many limits it produces either an incorrect answer or no answer at all. (See Examples 2 and 3 and Problems 19 through 36 and 47 through 56.)

EXAMPLE 2 Investigate the value of $\displaystyle\lim_{x \to 2} \frac{x^2-4}{x^2+x-6}$.

Investigation The numerical data shown in Fig. 2.2.5 certainly suggest that

$$\lim_{x \to 2} \frac{x^2-4}{x^2+x-6} = \frac{4}{5}.$$

◆

x	$\dfrac{x^2-4}{x^2+x-6}$	x	$\dfrac{x^2-4}{x^2+x-6}$
1	0.750000	3	0.833333
1.5	0.777778	2.5	0.818182
1.9	0.795918	2.1	0.803922
1.99	0.799599	2.01	0.800399
1.999	0.799960	2.001	0.800040
1.9999	0.799996	2.0001	0.800004
↓	↓	↓	↓
2	0.8	2	0.8

FIGURE 2.2.5 Investigating the limit in Example 2.

FIGURE 2.2.4 The limit in Example 1.

REMARK The function

$$f(x) = \frac{x^2-4}{x^2+x-6}$$

66 CHAPTER 2 Prelude to Calculus

FIGURE 2.2.6 The limit in Example 2.

t	$\dfrac{\sqrt{t+25}-5}{t}$
1.0	0.099020
0.5	0.099505
0.1	0.099900
0.05	0.099950
0.01	0.099990
0.005	0.099995
↓	↓
0	0.1

FIGURE 2.2.7 Investigating the limit in Example 3.

is not defined at $x = 2$, so we cannot merely substitute 2 for x. But if we let

$$g(x) = \begin{cases} \dfrac{x^2 - 4}{x^2 + x - 6} & \text{if } x \neq 2, \\ \dfrac{6}{5} & \text{if } x = 2, \end{cases}$$

then $g(x)$ *is* defined at $x = 2$ (and agrees with $f(x)$ elsewhere). Is it clear to you that f and g must have the same limit at $x = 2$? Figure 2.2.6 shows the graph $y = g(x)$, including the isolated point $(2, 1.2)$ on its graph.

EXAMPLE 3 Investigate the value of $\lim\limits_{t \to 0} \dfrac{\sqrt{t+25}-5}{t}$.

Investigation Here we cannot make a guess by substituting $t = 0$ because the fraction

$$g(t) = \dfrac{\sqrt{t+25}-5}{t}$$

is not defined when $t = 0$. But the numerical data shown in Fig. 2.2.7 indicate that

$$\lim_{t \to 0} \dfrac{\sqrt{t+25}-5}{t} = \dfrac{1}{10}.$$

We can attempt to corroborate this result graphically by zooming in on the point $(1, \frac{1}{10})$. The plot shown in Fig. 2.2.8 does not contradict the indicated limit, but somehow is unconvincing because it "goes too far" and suggests (incorrectly!) that $g(t) = \frac{1}{10}$ for $t \neq 0$. The problem is that the scale on the y-axis is too coarse. The magnification shown in Fig. 2.2.9 *does* appear to substantiate the limiting value of $\frac{1}{10}$. ◆

FIGURE 2.2.8 Graph of $g(t) = \dfrac{\sqrt{t+25}-5}{t}$ for $-1 \leq t \leq +1$, $-1 \leq y \leq +1$.

FIGURE 2.2.9 Graph of $g(t) = \dfrac{\sqrt{t+25}-5}{t}$ for $-1 \leq t \leq +1$, $0.099 \leq y \leq 0.101$.

REMARK Can you see that, upon dividing each number in the second column of Fig. 2.2.7 by 10000, one might well suspect that

$$\lim_{t \to 0} \dfrac{\sqrt{t+25}-5}{10000\,t} = 0? \qquad \text{(Wrong!)}$$

In fact, the value of this limit (as we will see in Example 13) is exactly $10^{-5} = 0.00001$, not zero. This fact constitutes a warning that numerical investigations of limits are not conclusive.

The numerical investigation in Example 3 is incomplete because the table in Fig. 2.2.7 shows values of the function $g(t)$ on only one side of the point $t = 0$. But in order that $\lim_{x \to a} f(x) = L$, it is necessary for $f(x)$ to approach L *both* as x approaches a from the left *and* as x approaches a from the right. If $f(x)$ approaches different values as x approaches a from different sides, then $\lim_{x \to a} f(x)$ does not exist. In Section 2.3 we discuss such *one-sided* limits in more detail.

EXAMPLE 4 Investigate $\lim_{x \to 0} f(x)$, given

$$f(x) = \frac{x}{|x|} = \begin{cases} 1 & \text{if } x > 0, \\ -1 & \text{if } x < 0. \end{cases}$$

Solution From the graph of f shown in Fig. 2.2.10, it is apparent that $f(x) \to 1$ as $x \to 0$ from the right and that $f(x) \to -1$ as $x \to 0$ from the left. In particular, there are positive values of x as close to zero as we please such that $f(x) = 1$ and negative values of x equally close to zero such that $f(x) = -1$. Hence we cannot make $f(x)$ as close as we please to any *single* value of L merely by choosing x sufficiently close to zero. Therefore,

$$\lim_{x \to 0} \frac{x}{|x|} \quad \text{does not exist.} \qquad \blacklozenge$$

FIGURE 2.2.10 The graph of $f(x) = \dfrac{x}{|x|}$ (Example 4).

In Example 5 the value obtained by substituting $x = a$ in $F(x)$ to find $\lim_{x \to a} F(x)$ is incorrect.

EXAMPLE 5 Evaluate $\lim_{x \to 0} F(x)$ where

$$F(x) = \begin{cases} 1 & \text{if } x \neq 0, \\ 0 & \text{if } x = 0. \end{cases}$$

The graph of F is shown in Fig. 2.2.11.

Solution The fact that $F(x) = 1$ for *every* value of $x \neq 0$ in any neighborhood of zero implies that

$$\lim_{x \to 0} F(x) = 1.$$

But note that the value of the limit at $x = 0$ is *not* equal to the functional value $F(0) = 0$ there. $\qquad \blacklozenge$

FIGURE 2.2.11 The graph of the function F of Example 5.

The Limit Laws

Numerical investigations such as those in Examples 1 through 3 provide us with an intuitive feeling for limits and typically suggest the correct value of a limit. But most limit computations are based neither on merely suggestive (and imprecise) numerical estimates nor on direct (but difficult) applications of the definition of limit. Instead, such computations are performed most easily and naturally with the aid of the *limit laws* that we give next. These "laws" actually are *theorems*, whose proofs (based on the precise definition of the limit) are included in Appendix D.

Constant Law
If $f(x) \equiv C$, where C is a constant [so $f(x)$ is a **constant function**], then

$$\lim_{x \to a} f(x) = \lim_{x \to a} C = C. \tag{5}$$

Sum Law
If both of the limits

$$\lim_{x \to a} f(x) = L \quad \text{and} \quad \lim_{x \to a} g(x) = M$$

exist, then

$$\lim_{x \to a} [f(x) \pm g(x)] = \left[\lim_{x \to a} f(x)\right] \pm \left[\lim_{x \to a} g(x)\right] = L \pm M. \tag{6}$$

(The limit of a sum is the sum of the limits; the limit of a difference is the difference of the limits.)

Product Law

If both of the limits

$$\lim_{x \to a} f(x) = L \quad \text{and} \quad \lim_{x \to a} g(x) = M$$

exist, then

$$\lim_{x \to a}[f(x)g(x)] = \left[\lim_{x \to a} f(x)\right]\left[\lim_{x \to a} g(x)\right] = LM. \qquad (7)$$

(The limit of a product is the product of the limits.)

Quotient Law

If both of the limits

$$\lim_{x \to a} f(x) = L \quad \text{and} \quad \lim_{x \to a} g(x) = M$$

exist *and* if $M \neq 0$, then

$$\lim_{x \to a} \frac{f(x)}{g(x)} = \frac{\lim_{x \to a} f(x)}{\lim_{x \to a} g(x)} = \frac{L}{M}. \qquad (8)$$

(The limit of a quotient is the quotient of the limits, provided that the limit of the denominator is not zero.)

Root Law

If n is a positive integer and if $a > 0$ for even values of n, then

$$\lim_{x \to a} \sqrt[n]{x} = \sqrt[n]{a}. \qquad (9)$$

The case $n = 1$ of the root law is obvious:

$$\lim_{x \to a} x = a. \qquad (10)$$

Examples 6 and 7 show how the limit laws can be used to evaluate limits of polynomials and rational functions.

EXAMPLE 6

$$\lim_{x \to 3}(x^2 + 2x + 4) = \left(\lim_{x \to 3} x^2\right) + \left(\lim_{x \to 3} 2x\right) + \left(\lim_{x \to 3} 4\right)$$

$$= \left(\lim_{x \to 3} x\right)^2 + 2\left(\lim_{x \to 3} x\right) + \left(\lim_{x \to 3} 4\right) = 3^2 + 2 \cdot 3 + 4 = 19. \quad \blacklozenge$$

EXAMPLE 7

$$\lim_{x \to 3} \frac{2x + 5}{x^2 + 2x + 4} = \frac{\lim_{x \to 3}(2x + 5)}{\lim_{x \to 3}(x^2 + 2x + 4)}$$

$$= \frac{2 \cdot 3 + 5}{3^2 + 2 \cdot 3 + 4} = \frac{11}{19}. \quad \blacklozenge$$

Note In Examples 6 and 7, we systematically applied the limit laws until we could simply substitute 3 for $\lim_{x \to 3} x$ at the final step. To determine the limit of a quotient of polynomials, we must verify before this final step that the limit of the denominator is not zero. If the denominator limit is zero, then the limit *may* fail to exist.

EXAMPLE 8 Investigate $\lim_{x \to 1} \dfrac{1}{(x-1)^2}$.

Solution Because $\lim_{x \to 1}(x-1)^2 = 0$, we cannot apply the quotient law. Moreover, we can make $1/(x-1)^2$ arbitrarily large by choosing x sufficiently close to 1. Hence $1/(x-1)^2$ cannot approach any (finite) number L as x approaches 1. Therefore, the limit in this example does not exist. You can see the geometric reason if you examine the graph of $y = 1/(x-1)^2$ in Fig. 2.2.12. As $x \to 1$, the corresponding point (x, y) ascends the curve near the vertical line $x = 1$. It must therefore leave the indicated strip between the two horizontal lines $x = L-\epsilon$ and $x = L+\epsilon$ that bracket the proposed limit L. Thus, the point (x, y) cannot approach the point $(1, L)$ as $x \to 1$. ◆

FIGURE 2.2.12 The graph of $y = \dfrac{1}{(x-1)^2}$ (Example 8).

EXAMPLE 9 Investigate $\lim\limits_{x \to 2} \dfrac{x^2 - 4}{x^2 + x - 6}$.

Solution We cannot immediately apply the quotient law (as we did in Example 7) because the denominator approaches zero as x approaches 2. If the numerator were approaching some number *other* than zero as $x \to 2$, then the limit would fail to exist (as in Example 8). But here the numerator *does* approach zero, so there is a possibility that a factor of the numerator can be canceled with the same factor of the denominator, thus removing the zero-denominator problem. Indeed,

$$\lim_{x \to 2} \frac{x^2 - 4}{x^2 + x - 6} = \lim_{x \to 2} \frac{(x-2)(x+2)}{(x-2)(x+3)}$$

$$= \lim_{x \to 2} \frac{x+2}{x+3} = \frac{4}{5}.$$

We can cancel the factor $x - 2$ because it is nonzero: $x \neq 2$ when we evaluate the limit as x approaches 2. Moreover, this verifies the numerical limit of 0.8 that we found in Example 2. ◆

Substitution of Limits

It is tempting to write

$$\lim_{x \to -4} \sqrt{x^2 + 9} = \sqrt{\lim_{x \to -4}(x^2 + 9)}$$

$$= \sqrt{(-4)^2 + 9} = \sqrt{25} = 5. \tag{11}$$

But can we simply "move the limit inside the radical" in Eq. (11)? To analyze this question, let us write

$$f(x) = \sqrt{x} \quad \text{and} \quad g(x) = x^2 + 9.$$

Then the function that appears in Eq. (11) is the composite function

$$f(g(x)) = \sqrt{g(x)} = \sqrt{x^2 + 9}.$$

(Recall that the left-hand expression in this equation is read "f of g of x.") Hence our question is whether or not

$$\lim_{x \to a} f(g(x)) = f\left(\lim_{x \to a} g(x)\right).$$

The next limit law answers this question in the affirmative, provided that the "outside function" f meets a certain condition; if so, then the limit of the composite function $f(g(x))$ as $x \to a$ may be found by substituting into the function f the limit of $g(x)$ as $x \to a$.

Substitution Law Limits of Compositions

Suppose that

$$\lim_{x \to a} g(x) = L \quad \text{and that} \quad \lim_{x \to L} f(x) = f(L).$$

Then

$$\lim_{x \to a} f(g(x)) = f\left(\lim_{x \to a} g(x)\right) = f(L). \tag{12}$$

Thus the condition under which Eq. (12) holds is that the limit of the *outer* function f not only exists at $x = L$, but also is equal to the "expected" value of f—namely, $f(L)$. In particular, because

$$\lim_{x \to -4} (x^2 + 9) = 25 \quad \text{and} \quad \lim_{x \to 25} \sqrt{x} = \sqrt{25} = 5,$$

this condition is satisfied in Eq. (11). Hence the computations shown there are valid.

In this section we use only the following special case of the substitution law. With $f(x) = x^{1/n}$, where n is a positive integer, Eq. (12) takes the form

$$\lim_{x \to a} \sqrt[n]{g(x)} = \sqrt[n]{\lim_{x \to a} g(x)}, \tag{13}$$

under the assumption that the limit of $g(x)$ exists as $x \to a$ (and is positive if n is even). With $g(x) = x^m$, where m is a positive integer, Eq. (13) in turn yields

$$\lim_{x \to a} x^{m/n} = a^{m/n}, \tag{14}$$

with the condition that $a > 0$ if n is even. Equations (13) and (14) may be regarded as generalized root laws. Example 10 illustrates the use of these special cases of the substitution law.

EXAMPLE 10

$$\lim_{x \to 4} \sqrt[3]{3\sqrt{x^3} + 20\sqrt{x}} = \sqrt[3]{\lim_{x \to 4}(3x^{3/2} + 20\sqrt{x})} \quad \text{[using Eq. (13)]}$$

$$= \left(\lim_{x \to 4} 3x^{3/2} + \lim_{x \to 4} 20\sqrt{x}\right)^{1/3} \quad \text{[using the sum law]}$$

$$= \left(3 \cdot 4^{3/2} + 20\sqrt{4}\right)^{1/3} \quad \text{[using Eq. (14)]}$$

$$= (24 + 40)^{1/3} = \sqrt[3]{64} = 4. \quad \blacklozenge$$

Slope-Predictor Functions

Our discussion of limits began with the slope

$$m_a = \lim_{h \to 0} \frac{f(a+h) - f(a)}{h} \tag{15}$$

of the line tangent to the graph $y = f(x)$ at the point $(a, f(a))$. The lines tangent to $y = f(x)$ at different points have different slopes. Thus if we replace a with x in Eq. (15), we get a *new function* defined by

$$m(x) = \lim_{h \to 0} \frac{f(x+h) - f(x)}{h}. \tag{16}$$

This function m may be regarded as a "slope predictor" for lines tangent to the graph $y = f(x)$. It is a new function *derived* from the original function $f(x)$, and in Chapter 3 we will call it the *derivative* of f.

EXAMPLE 11 In Section 2.1 we saw that the line tangent to the graph $y = px^2 + qx + r$ at the point where $x = a$ has slope $m_a = 2pa + q$. Hence the slope-predictor function for the quadratic function

$$f(x) = px^2 + qx + r \tag{17}$$

is the linear function

$$m(x) = 2px + q. \tag{18}$$

Figure 2.2.13 illustrates the case $p = 1, q = 4, r = -12$. It is worth noting that the x-intercept where $m(x) = 0$ corresponds to the point of the parabola $y = f(x)$ where the tangent line is horizontal. ◆

The slope-predictor definition in Eq. (16) calls for us to carry out the following four steps.

1. Write the definition of $m(x)$.
2. Substitute into this definition the formula of the given function f.
3. Make algebraic simplifications until Step 4 can be carried out.
4. Determine the value of the limit as $h \to 0$.

Note that x may be thought of as a *constant* throughout this computation—it is h that is the variable in this four-step process.

EXAMPLE 12 Find the slope-predictor function for the function

$$f(x) = x + \frac{1}{x}$$

that was investigated numerically in Example 5 of Section 2.1.

Solution The first two steps in the preceding list yield

$$m(x) = \lim_{h \to 0} \frac{f(x+h) - f(x)}{h} = \lim_{h \to 0} \frac{\left(x + h + \frac{1}{x+h}\right) - \left(x + \frac{1}{x}\right)}{h}.$$

We cancel the two copies of x in the numerator and proceed to simplify algebraically, first finding a common denominator in the numerator:

$$m(x) = \lim_{h \to 0} \frac{h + \frac{1}{x+h} - \frac{1}{x}}{h}$$

$$= \lim_{h \to 0} \frac{h(x+h)x + x - (x+h)}{h(x+h)x}$$

$$= \lim_{h \to 0} \frac{h(x+h)x - h}{h(x+h)x}.$$

Now we can divide numerator and denominator by h (because $h \neq 0$) and finally apply the sum, product, and quotient laws to evaluate the limit as $h \to 0$:

$$m(x) = \lim_{h \to 0} \frac{h(x+h)x - h}{h(x+h)x}$$

$$= \lim_{h \to 0} \frac{(x+h)x - 1}{(x+h)x} = \frac{x^2 - 1}{x^2} = 1 - \frac{1}{x^2}.$$

For instance, the slope of the line tangent to

$$y = x + \frac{1}{x}$$

at the point $(2, \frac{5}{2})$ is $m(2) = \frac{3}{4}$ (thus verifying the result in Example 5 of Section 2.1). ◆

FIGURE 2.2.13 The parabola $y = x^2 + 4x - 12$ and its slope predictor $m(x) = 2x + 4$.

Example 13 illustrates an algebraic procedure often used in "preparing" functions before taking limits. This procedure can be applied when roots are present and resembles the simple computation

$$\frac{1}{\sqrt{5}-\sqrt{2}} = \frac{1}{\sqrt{5}-\sqrt{2}} \cdot \frac{\sqrt{5}+\sqrt{2}}{\sqrt{5}+\sqrt{2}}$$
$$= \frac{\sqrt{5}+\sqrt{2}}{5-2} = \frac{\sqrt{5}+\sqrt{2}}{3}.$$

EXAMPLE 13 Find the slope-predictor function for the function $f(x) = \sqrt{x}$.

Solution

$$m(x) = \lim_{h \to 0} \frac{\sqrt{x+h} - \sqrt{x}}{h}. \quad (19)$$

To prepare the fraction for evaluation of the limit, we first multiply the numerator and denominator by the *conjugate* $\sqrt{x+h} + \sqrt{x}$ of the numerator:

$$m(x) = \lim_{h \to 0} \frac{\sqrt{x+h} - \sqrt{x}}{h} \cdot \frac{\sqrt{x+h} + \sqrt{x}}{\sqrt{x+h} + \sqrt{x}}$$

$$= \lim_{h \to 0} \frac{(x+h) - x}{h(\sqrt{x+h} + \sqrt{x})}$$

$$= \lim_{h \to 0} \frac{1}{\sqrt{x+h} + \sqrt{x}}.$$

Thus

$$m(x) = \frac{1}{2\sqrt{x}}. \quad (20)$$

(In the final step we used the sum, quotient, and root laws—we did not simply substitute 0 for h.) ◆

Note that if we equate the right-hand sides of Eqs. (19) and (20) and take $x = 25$, then we get the limit in Example 3:

$$\lim_{h \to 0} \frac{\sqrt{25+h} - 5}{h} = \frac{1}{10}.$$

(The t in Example 3 has been replaced here with h.) And if we divide both sides by 10000 we find that

$$\lim_{h \to 0} \frac{\sqrt{25+h} - 5}{10000h} = \frac{1}{100000} = 0.00001,$$

as claimed in the remark following Example 3.

2.2 TRUE/FALSE STUDY GUIDE

2.2 CONCEPTS: QUESTIONS AND DISCUSSION

1. The sum, product, and quotient laws imply that *if* the limits

$$\lim_{x \to a} f(x) \quad \text{and} \quad \lim_{x \to a} g(x) \quad (21)$$

both exist, *then* the limit

$$\lim_{x \to a} [f(x) \odot g(x)] \quad (22)$$

also exists—with the symbol $\odot$ denoting either $+$, $-$, $\times$, or $\div$ (and assuming in the case of division that $\lim_{x \to a} g(x) \neq 0$). Can you produce examples—in all four cases—of functions such that *neither* of the limits in (21) exists, but nevertheless the limit in (22) does exist? It may help to review the examples of nonexisting limits in this section.

2. Can you produce examples of functions f and g such that both
$$\lim_{x \to a} g(x) = b \quad \text{and} \quad \lim_{x \to b} f(x) = c$$
exist, but
$$\lim_{x \to a} f(g(x)) \neq f\left(\lim_{x \to a} g(x)\right)?$$
If so, why does this not contradict the substitution law of limits?

2.2 PROBLEMS

Apply the limit laws of this section to evaluate the limits in Problems 1 through 18. Justify each step by citing the appropriate limit law.

1. $\lim_{x \to 3} (3x^2 + 7x - 12)$

2. $\lim_{x \to -2} (x^3 - 3x^2 + 5)$

3. $\lim_{x \to 1} (x^2 - 1)(x^7 + 7x - 4)$

4. $\lim_{x \to -2} (x^3 - 3x + 3)(x^2 + 2x + 5)$

5. $\lim_{x \to 1} \dfrac{x+1}{x^2 + x + 1}$

6. $\lim_{t \to -2} \dfrac{t+2}{t^2 + 4}$

7. $\lim_{x \to 3} \dfrac{(x^2 + 1)^3}{(x^3 - 25)^3}$

8. $\lim_{z \to -1} \dfrac{(3z^2 + 2z + 1)^{10}}{(z^3 + 5)^5}$

9. $\lim_{x \to 1} \sqrt{4x + 5}$

10. $\lim_{y \to 4} \sqrt{27 - \sqrt{y}}$

11. $\lim_{x \to 3} (x^2 - 1)^{3/2}$

12. $\lim_{t \to -4} \sqrt{\dfrac{t+8}{25 - t^2}}$

13. $\lim_{z \to 8} \dfrac{z^{2/3}}{z - \sqrt{2z}}$

14. $\lim_{t \to 2} \sqrt[3]{3t^3 + 4t - 5}$

15. $\lim_{w \to 0} \sqrt{(w-2)^4}$

16. $\lim_{t \to -4} \sqrt[3]{(t+1)^6}$

17. $\lim_{x \to -2} \sqrt[3]{\dfrac{x+2}{(x-2)^2}}$

18. $\lim_{y \to 5} \left(\dfrac{2y^2 + 2y + 4}{6y - 3}\right)^{1/3}$

In Problems 19 through 28, note first that the numerator and denominator have a common algebraic factor (as in Example 9). Use this fact to help evaluate the given limit.

19. $\lim_{x \to -1} \dfrac{x+1}{x^2 - x - 2}$

20. $\lim_{t \to 3} \dfrac{t^2 - 9}{t - 3}$

21. $\lim_{x \to 1} \dfrac{x^2 + x - 2}{x^2 - 4x + 3}$

22. $\lim_{y \to -1/2} \dfrac{4y^2 - 1}{4y^2 + 8y + 3}$

23. $\lim_{t \to -3} \dfrac{t^2 + 6t + 9}{t^2 - 9}$

24. $\lim_{x \to 2} \dfrac{x^2 - 4}{3x^2 - 2x - 8}$

25. $\lim_{z \to -2} \dfrac{(z+2)^2}{z^4 - 16}$

26. $\lim_{t \to 3} \dfrac{t^3 - 9t}{t^2 - 9}$

27. $\lim_{x \to 1} \dfrac{x^3 - 1}{x^4 - 1}$

28. $\lim_{y \to -3} \dfrac{y^3 + 27}{y^2 - 9}$

In Problems 29 through 36, evaluate those limits that exist.

29. $\lim_{x \to 3} \dfrac{\frac{1}{x} - \frac{1}{3}}{x - 3}$

30. $\lim_{t \to 0} \dfrac{\frac{1}{2+t} - \frac{1}{2}}{t}$

31. $\lim_{x \to 4} \dfrac{x - 4}{\sqrt{x} - 2}$

32. $\lim_{x \to 9} \dfrac{3 - \sqrt{x}}{9 - x}$

33. $\lim_{t \to 0} \dfrac{\sqrt{t+4} - 2}{t}$

34. $\lim_{h \to 0} \dfrac{1}{h}\left(\dfrac{1}{\sqrt{9+h}} - \dfrac{1}{3}\right)$

35. $\lim_{x \to 4} \dfrac{x^2 - 16}{2 - \sqrt{x}}$

36. $\lim_{x \to 0} \dfrac{\sqrt{1+x} - \sqrt{1-x}}{x}$

In Problems 37 through 46, use the four-step process illustrated in Examples 12 and 13 to find a slope-predictor function for the given function $f(x)$. Then write an equation for the line tangent to the curve $y = f(x)$ at the point where $x = 2$.

37. $f(x) = x^3$

38. $f(x) = \dfrac{1}{x}$

39. $f(x) = \dfrac{1}{x^2}$

40. $f(x) = \dfrac{1}{x+1}$

41. $f(x) = \dfrac{2}{x - 1}$

42. $f(x) = \dfrac{x}{x - 1}$

43. $f(x) = \dfrac{1}{\sqrt{x+2}}$

44. $f(x) = x^2 + \dfrac{3}{x}$

45. $f(x) = \sqrt{2x + 5}$

46. $f(x) = \dfrac{x^2}{x + 1}$

In Problems 47 through 56, the actual value of the given limit $\lim_{x \to a} f(x)$ is a rational number that is a ratio of two single-digit integers. Guess this limit on the basis of a numerical investigation in which you calculate $f(x)$ for $x = a \pm 0.1$, $x = a \pm 0.05$, $x = a \pm 0.01$, $x = a \pm 0.005$, and so on. Use other similar values of x near a as you wish.

47. $\lim_{x \to 0} \dfrac{(1+x)^2 - 1}{x}$

48. $\lim_{x \to 1} \dfrac{x^4 - 1}{x - 1}$

49. $\lim_{x \to 0} \dfrac{\sqrt{x+9} - 3}{x}$

50. $\lim_{x \to 4} \dfrac{x^{3/2} - 8}{x - 4}$

51. $\lim_{x \to 0} \dfrac{1}{x}\left[\dfrac{2}{(2+x)^3} - \dfrac{1}{4}\right]$

52. $\lim_{x \to 0} \dfrac{(3+x)^{-1} - (3-x)^{-1}}{x}$

53. $\lim_{x \to 0} \dfrac{\sin x}{x}$

54. $\lim_{x \to 0} \dfrac{1 - \cos x}{x^2}$

55. $\lim_{x \to 0} \dfrac{x - \sin x}{x^3}$

56. $\lim_{x \to 0} \left(1 + \dfrac{1}{|x|}\right)^x$

57. In contrast with the rational-valued limits in Problems 47 through 56, the value of the limit
$$\lim_{x \to 0}(1+x)^{1/x}$$
is the famous irrational number e (of Chapter 7), whose three-place decimal approximation is $e \approx 2.718$. Numerically investigate this limit to approximate e accurate to five decimal places. Corroborate this value graphically by zooming in on the y-intercept of the curve $y = (1+x)^{1/x}$.

58. Verify graphically the limit
$$\lim_{x \to 0} \frac{\sin x}{x}$$
of Problem 53 by zooming in on the y-intercept of the curve $y = (\sin x)/x$.

59. Investigate the limit
$$\lim_{x \to 0} \frac{x - \tan x}{x^3}$$
both numerically and graphically. Determine its value accurate to four decimal places.

60. The value of
$$\lim_{x \to 0} \frac{\sin 2x}{\tan 5x}$$
is the ratio of two single-digit integers. Determine this value both numerically and graphically.

61. Calculate the value of
$$f(x) = \sin \frac{\pi}{x}$$
for $x = \frac{1}{2}, \frac{1}{4}, \frac{1}{8}, \frac{1}{16}, \ldots$. What do you now conjecture to be the value of
$$\lim_{x \to 0} \sin \frac{\pi}{x}?$$
Next calculate $f(x)$ for $x = \frac{2}{3}, \frac{2}{9}, \frac{2}{27}, \frac{2}{81}, \ldots$. Now what do you conclude?

62. To investigate the limit of $f(x) = \sin x + 10^{-5} \cos x$ as $x \to 0$, set your graphing calculator or computer to display exactly four digits to the right of the decimal point. After calculating $f(x)$ with $x = 0.1, 0.001, 0.00001, 0.0000001, \ldots$, what do you conclude? (Your answer may depend on how your particular calculator works.) Now zoom in on the y-intercept of the curve $y = f(x)$ sufficiently to show that the value of the limit is nonzero. What is it?

63. Investigate numerically or graphically (or both) the value of the limit
$$\lim_{x \to 0} \left(\log_{10} \frac{1}{|x|} \right)^{-1/32}.$$
The actual value of this limit is zero, so you'll see that your calculator or computer cannot always be believed.

64. (a) Show that the slope of the line tangent to the graph of $y = 10^x$ at the point $(0, 1)$ is the number
$$L = \lim_{h \to 0} \frac{10^h - 1}{h}.$$
Investigate this limit numerically and graphically. Do your results substantiate the fact that $L = \ln 10$, the value produced by the **LN** key on your calculator? (b) Show that the slope-predictor function for lines tangent to the graph $y = 10^x$ is $m(x) = L \cdot 10^x$. Corroborate this fact by using a calculator or computer to plot the graph of $y = 10^x$ and its predicted tangent lines at several different points.

2.2 Project: Limits, Slopes, and Logarithms

Generalize the result in Problem 64 of this section. First refer to Fig. 2.2.14. Then suppose that a is a positive constant. Show that the slope of the line tangent to the graph of $y = a^x$ at the point $(0, 1)$ is the number

$$L(a) = \lim_{h \to 0} \frac{a^h - 1}{h}. \tag{1}$$

(Note how the notation of functions is used in Eq. (1) to emphasize the dependence of the slope on the base constant a.) Next choose at random a pair of positive integers a and b and investigate the numerical values of $L(a)$, $L(b)$, and $L(ab)$. Are your results consistent with the fact that

$$L(ab) = L(a) + L(b), \tag{2}$$

in analogy with the law of logarithms

$$\log ab = \log a + \log b? \tag{3}$$

At this point the connection between Eqs. (2) and (3) is surely an enigma rather than an explanation. The mystery will be explained in Section 7.1, in which we study *natural logarithms*. For now, use the **LN** key on your calculator to find $\ln a$, $\ln b$, and $\ln ab$; compare these with your earlier values of $L(a)$, $L(b)$, and $L(ab)$. You can also follow up these investigations with a computer algebra system: Use it to attempt to evaluate the limit in Eq. (1) symbolically, and then compare the symbolic result with your numerical results.

FIGURE 2.2.14 The graph of $y = a^x$ and its tangent line at the point $(0,1)$.

2.3 MORE ABOUT LIMITS

To investigate limits of trigonometric functions, we begin with Fig. 2.3.1, which shows an angle θ with its vertex at the origin, its initial side along the positive x-axis, and its terminal side intersecting the unit circle at the point P. By the definition of the sine and cosine functions, the coordinates of P are $P(\cos\theta, \sin\theta)$. From geometry we see that, as $\theta \to 0$, the point $P(\cos\theta, \sin\theta)$ approaches the point $R(1, 0)$. Hence $\cos\theta \to 1$ and $\sin\theta \to 0$ as $\theta \to 0$ through positive values. A similar picture gives the same result for negative values of θ, so we see that

$$\lim_{\theta\to 0}\cos\theta = 1 \quad \text{and} \quad \lim_{\theta\to 0}\sin\theta = 0. \tag{1}$$

FIGURE 2.3.1 An angle θ.

Equation (1) says simply that the *limits* of the functions $\cos\theta$ and $\sin\theta$ as $\theta \to 0$ are equal to their respective *values* at $\theta = 0$: $\cos 0 = 1$ and $\sin 0 = 0$.

The limit of the quotient $(\sin\theta)/\theta$ as $\theta \to 0$ plays a special role in the calculus of trigonometric functions. For instance, it is needed to find slopes of lines tangent to trigonometric graphs such as $y = \cos x$ and $y = \sin x$.

Note that the value of the quotient $(\sin\theta)/\theta$ is not defined when $\theta = 0$. (Why not?) But a calculator set in *radian mode* provides us with the numerical evidence shown in Fig. 2.3.2. This table strongly suggests that the limit of $(\sin\theta)/\theta$ is 1 as $\theta \to 0$. This conclusion is supported by the graph of $y = (\sin x)/x$ shown in Fig. 2.3.3, where it appears that the point (x, y) on the curve is near $(0, 1)$ when x is near zero. Later in this section we provide a proof of the following result.

θ	$\dfrac{\sin\theta}{\theta}$
± 1.0	0.84147
± 0.5	0.95885
± 0.1	0.99833
± 0.05	0.99958
± 0.01	0.99998
± 0.005	1.00000
± 0.001	1.00000
$\vdots$	$\vdots$
$\downarrow$	$\downarrow$
0	1

FIGURE 2.3.2 The numerical data suggest that $\lim_{\theta\to 0}\dfrac{\sin\theta}{\theta} = 1$.

THEOREM 1 The Basic Trigonometric Limit

$$\lim_{x\to 0}\frac{\sin x}{x} = 1. \tag{2}$$

As in Examples 1 and 2, many other trigonometric limits can be reduced to the one in Theorem 1.

EXAMPLE 1 Show that

$$\lim_{x\to 0}\frac{1 - \cos x}{x} = 0. \tag{3}$$

Solution We multiply the numerator and denominator in Eq. (3) by the "conjugate" $1 + \cos x$ of the numerator $1 - \cos x$. Then we apply the identity $1 - \cos^2 x = \sin^2 x$. This gives

$$\lim_{x\to 0}\frac{1-\cos x}{x} = \lim_{x\to 0}\frac{1-\cos x}{x}\cdot\frac{1+\cos x}{1+\cos x} = \lim_{x\to 0}\frac{\sin^2 x}{x(1+\cos x)}$$

$$= \left(\lim_{x\to 0}\frac{\sin x}{x}\right)\left(\lim_{x\to 0}\frac{\sin x}{1+\cos x}\right) = 1\cdot\frac{0}{1+1} = 0.$$

In the last step we used *all* the limits in Eqs. (1) and (2). ◆

FIGURE 2.3.3 $y = \dfrac{\sin x}{x}$ for $x \neq 0$.

EXAMPLE 2 Evaluate $\lim_{x\to 0}\dfrac{\tan 3x}{x}$.

Solution

$$\lim_{x\to 0}\frac{\tan 3x}{x} = 3\left(\lim_{x\to 0}\frac{\tan 3x}{3x}\right) = 3\left(\lim_{\theta\to 0}\frac{\tan\theta}{\theta}\right) \quad (\theta = 3x)$$

$$= 3\left(\lim_{\theta\to 0}\frac{\sin\theta}{\theta\cos\theta}\right) \quad \left(\text{because } \tan\theta = \frac{\sin\theta}{\cos\theta}\right)$$

$$= 3\left(\lim_{\theta\to 0}\frac{\sin\theta}{\theta}\right)\left(\lim_{\theta\to 0}\frac{1}{\cos\theta}\right) \quad \text{(by the product law of limits)}$$

$$= 3\cdot 1\cdot\frac{1}{1} = 3.$$

76 CHAPTER 2 Prelude to Calculus

x	$\sin \dfrac{\pi}{x}$
1	0
0.5	0
0.1	0
0.05	0
0.01	0
0.005	0
0.001	0

FIGURE 2.3.4 Do you think that $\lim\limits_{x \to 0} \sin \dfrac{\pi}{x} = 0$ (Example 3)?

FIGURE 2.3.5 The graph of $y = \sin \dfrac{\pi}{x}$ shows infinite oscillation as $x \to 0$ (Example 3).

x	$\sin \dfrac{\pi}{x}$
$\dfrac{2}{9}$	$+1$
$\dfrac{2}{11}$	-1
$\dfrac{2}{101}$	$+1$
$\dfrac{2}{103}$	-1
$\dfrac{2}{1001}$	$+1$
$\dfrac{2}{1003}$	-1

FIGURE 2.3.6 Verify the entries in the second column (Example 3).

FIGURE 2.3.7 How the squeeze law works.

We used the fact that $\tan \theta = (\sin \theta)/(\cos \theta)$ as well as some of the limits in Eqs. (1) and (2). ◆

Example 3 constitutes a *warning:* The results of a numerical investigation can be misleading unless they are interpreted with care.

EXAMPLE 3 The numerical data shown in the table of Fig. 2.3.4 suggest that the limit

$$\lim_{x \to 0} \sin \frac{\pi}{x} \quad (4)$$

has the value zero. But it appears in the graph of $y = \sin(\pi/x)$ (for $x \neq 0$), shown in Fig. 2.3.5, that the value of $\sin(\pi/x)$ oscillates infinitely often between $+1$ and -1 as $x \to 0$. Indeed, this fact follows from the periodicity of the sine function, because π/x increases without bound as $x \to 0$. Hence $\sin(\pi/x)$ cannot approach zero (or any other number) as $x \to 0$. Therefore the limit in (4) *does not exist.*

We can explain the potentially misleading results tabulated in Fig. 2.3.4 as follows: Each value of x shown there just happens to be of the form $1/n$, the reciprocal of an integer. Therefore,

$$\sin \frac{\pi}{x} = \sin \frac{\pi}{1/n} = \sin n\pi = 0$$

for every nonzero integer n. But with a different selection of "trial values" of x, we might have obtained the results shown in Fig. 2.3.6, which immediately suggest the nonexistence of the limit in (4). ◆

The Squeeze Law of Limits

A final property of limits that we will need is the *squeeze law* (also known as the "sandwich theorem"). It is related to the fact that taking limits preserves inequalities among functions.

Figure 2.3.7 illustrates how and why the squeeze law works and how it got its name. The idea is that $g(x)$ is trapped between $f(x)$ and $h(x)$ near a; both $f(x)$ and $h(x)$ approach the same limit L, so $g(x)$ must approach L as well. A formal proof of the squeeze law can be found in Appendix D.

> **Squeeze Law**
>
> Suppose that $f(x) \leq g(x) \leq h(x)$ for all $x \neq a$ in some neighborhood of a and also that
>
> $$\lim_{x \to a} f(x) = L = \lim_{x \to a} h(x).$$
>
> Then
>
> $$\lim_{x \to a} g(x) = L$$
>
> as well.

EXAMPLE 4 Figures 2.3.8 and 2.3.9 show two views of the graph of the function g defined for $x \neq 0$ by

$$g(x) = x \sin \frac{1}{x}.$$

As in Example 3, $\sin(1/x)$ oscillates infinitely often between $+1$ and -1 as $x \to 0$. Therefore the graph $y = g(x)$ bounces back and forth between the lines $y = +x$

FIGURE 2.3.8 The graph of $g(x) = x \sin \dfrac{1}{x}$ for $x \neq 0$ (Example 4).

FIGURE 2.3.9 The graph magnified near the origin (Example 4).

and $y = -x$. Because $|\sin(1/x)| \leq 1$ for all $x \neq 0$,

$$-|x| \leq x \sin \frac{1}{x} \leq +|x|$$

for all $x \neq 0$. Moreover, $\pm|x| \to 0$ as $x \to 0$, so with $f(x) = -|x|$ and $h(x) = +|x|$, it follows from the squeeze law of limits that

$$\lim_{x \to 0} x \sin \frac{1}{x} = 0. \tag{5}$$

◆

QUESTION Why *doesn't* the limit in Eq. (5) follow from the product law of limits with $f(x) = x$ and $g(x) = \sin(1/x)$?

One-Sided Limits

In Example 4 of Section 2.2 we examined the function

$$f(x) = \frac{x}{|x|} = \begin{cases} 1 & \text{if } x > 0; \\ -1 & \text{if } x < 0. \end{cases}$$

FIGURE 2.3.10 The graph of $f(x) = \dfrac{x}{|x|}$ again.

The graph of $y = f(x)$ is shown in Fig. 2.3.10. We argued that the limit of $f(x)$ as $x \to 0$ does not exist because $f(x)$ approaches $+1$ as x approaches zero from the right, whereas $f(x) \to -1$ as x approaches zero from the left. A natural way of describing this situation is to say that at $x = 0$ the *right-hand limit* of $f(x)$ is $+1$ and the *left-hand limit* of $f(x)$ is -1.

Here we define and investigate such one-sided limits. Their definitions will be stated initially in the informal language we used in Section 2.2 to describe the "idea of the limit." To define the right-hand limit of $f(x)$ at $x = a$, we must assume that f is defined on an open interval immediately to the right of a. To define the left-hand limit, we must assume that f is defined on an open interval immediately to the left of a.

The Right-Hand Limit of a Function

Suppose that f is defined on the interval (a, c) immediately to the right of a. Then we say that the number L is the **right-hand limit** of $f(x)$ as x approaches a (from the right), and we write

$$\lim_{x \to a^+} f(x) = L, \tag{6}$$

provided that we can make the number $f(x)$ as close to L as we please merely by choosing the point x in (a, c) sufficiently close to a.

We may describe the right-hand limit in Eq. (6) by saying that $f(x) \to L$ as $x \to a^+$; that is, as x approaches a from the right. The symbol a^+ denotes the right-hand, or "positive," side of the number a (which may be positive, negative, or zero).

For instance, we see in Fig. 2.3.10 that

$$\lim_{x \to 0^+} \frac{|x|}{x} = +1 \qquad (7)$$

because $|x|/x$ is equal to $+1$ for all x to the right of zero. See Fig. 2.3.11(a) for a more general geometric interpretation of right-hand limits.

The Left-Hand Limit of a Function

Suppose that f is defined on the interval (c, a) immediately to the left of a. Then we say that the number L is the **left-hand limit** of $f(x)$ as x approaches a (from the left), and we write

$$\lim_{x \to a^-} f(x) = L, \qquad (8)$$

provided that we can make the number $f(x)$ as close to L as we please merely by choosing the point x in (c, a) sufficiently close to a.

FIGURE 2.3.11 (a) The right-hand limit of $f(x)$ is L. (b) The left-hand limit of $f(x)$ is L.

We may describe the left-hand limit in Eq. (8) by saying that $f(x) \to L$ as $x \to a^-$; that is, as x approaches a from the left. The symbol a^- denotes the left-hand or "negative" side of a.

For instance, we see in Fig. 2.3.10 that

$$\lim_{x \to 0^-} \frac{|x|}{x} = -1 \qquad (9)$$

because $|x|/x$ is equal to -1 for all x to the left of zero. See Fig. 2.3.11(b) for a more general geometric interpretation of left-hand limits.

In Example 4 of Section 2.2 we argued (in essence) that, because the limits in Eqs. (7) and (9) are not equal, the corresponding two-sided limit

$$\lim_{x \to 0} \frac{|x|}{x}$$

does not exist. More generally, Theorem 2 (next) follows from careful consideration of the definitions of all the limits involved.

THEOREM 2 One-Sided Limits and Two-Sided Limits

Suppose that the function f is defined for $x \neq a$ in a neighborhood of the point a. Then the two-sided limit

$$\lim_{x \to a} f(x)$$

exists and is equal to the number L if and only if the one-sided limits

$$\lim_{x \to a^+} f(x) \quad \text{and} \quad \lim_{x \to a^-} f(x)$$

both exist and are equal to L.

Theorem 2 is particularly useful in showing that certain (two-sided) limits do *not* exist, frequently by showing that the left-hand and right-hand limits are not equal to each other.

EXAMPLE 5 The graph of the greatest integer function $f(x) = [\![x]\!]$ is shown in Fig. 2.3.12. It should be apparent that if a is not an integer, then

$$\lim_{x \to a^+} [\![x]\!] = \lim_{x \to a^-} [\![x]\!] = \lim_{x \to a} [\![x]\!] = [\![a]\!].$$

But if $a = n$, an integer, then

$$\lim_{x \to n^-} [\![x]\!] = n - 1 \quad \text{and} \quad \lim_{x \to n^+} [\![x]\!] = n.$$

FIGURE 2.3.12 The graph of the greatest integer function $f(x) = [\![x]\!]$ (Example 5).

Because these left-hand and right-hand limits are not equal, it follows from Theorem 2 that the limit of $f(x) = [\![x]\!]$ does not exist as x approaches an integer n. ◆

EXAMPLE 6 According to the root law in Section 2.2,
$$\lim_{x \to a} \sqrt{x} = \sqrt{a} \quad \text{if } a > 0.$$
But the limit of $f(x) = \sqrt{x}$ as $x \to 0^-$ is not defined because the square root of a negative number is undefined. Hence f is undefined on every open interval containing zero. What we can say in the case $a = 0$ is that
$$\lim_{x \to 0^+} \sqrt{x} = 0,$$
and that the left-hand limit
$$\lim_{x \to 0^-} \sqrt{x}$$
does not exist. ◆

To each of the limit laws in Section 2.2 there correspond two *one-sided limit laws*—a right-hand version and a left-hand version. You may apply these one-sided limit laws in the same way you apply the two-sided limit laws in the evaluation of limits.

EXAMPLE 7 Figure 2.3.13 shows the graph of the function f defined by
$$f(x) = \begin{cases} x^2 & \text{if } x \leq 0; \\ x \sin \dfrac{1}{x} & \text{if } x > 0. \end{cases}$$
Clearly
$$\lim_{x \to 0^-} f(x) = 0 \quad \text{and} \quad \lim_{x \to 0^+} f(x) = 0$$
by a one-sided version of the squeeze law (as in Example 4). It therefore follows from Theorem 2 that
$$\lim_{x \to 0} f(x) = 0.$$
◆

FIGURE 2.3.13 $y = f(x)$ (Example 7).

EXAMPLE 8 Upon applying the appropriate one-sided limit laws, we find that
$$\lim_{x \to 3^-} \left(\frac{x^2}{x^2 + 1} + \sqrt{9 - x^2} \right) = \frac{\lim_{x \to 3^-} x^2}{\lim_{x \to 3^-} (x^2 + 1)} + \sqrt{\lim_{x \to 3^-} (9 - x^2)}$$
$$= \frac{9}{9 + 1} + \sqrt{0} = \frac{9}{10}.$$
Note that the two-sided limit at 3 is not defined because $\sqrt{9 - x^2}$ is not defined when $x > 3$. ◆

Existence of Tangent Lines

Recall that the slope of the line tangent to the graph $y = f(x)$ at the point $P(a, f(a))$ is defined to be
$$m = \lim_{x \to a} \frac{f(x) - f(a)}{x - a} \tag{10}$$
provided that this (two-sided) limit exists. In this case an equation of the line tangent to the graph $y = f(x)$ at $P(a, f(a))$ is
$$y - f(a) = m(x - a).$$
If the limit in (10) does not exist, then we say that the curve $y = f(x)$ does not have a tangent line at the point P. The following example gives perhaps the simplest example of a function whose graph has a tangent line everywhere except at a single isolated point.

FIGURE 2.3.14 The graph of $f(x) = |x|$ has a corner point at $(0, 0)$.

EXAMPLE 9 Show that the graph $y = |x|$ has no tangent line at the origin.

Solution Figure 2.3.14 shows the graph of the function $f(x) = |x|$. The sharp corner at the point $(0, 0)$ makes it intuitively clear that there can be no tangent line there—surely no single straight line can be a good approximation to the shape of the graph at the origin. To verify this intuitive observation, note that when $a = 0$ we have

$$\frac{f(a+h) - f(a)}{h} = \frac{|h|}{h} = \begin{cases} -1 & \text{if } h < 0, \\ +1 & \text{if } h > 0. \end{cases}$$

Hence the left-hand limit of the quotient is -1, whereas the right-hand limit is $+1$. Therefore the two-sided limit in (10) does not exist, so the graph $y = |x|$ has no tangent line at the origin, where $a = 0$. ◆

QUESTION Does Fig. 2.3.14 make it clear to you that for $f(x) = |x|$ and $a \neq 0$, the value of the "slope limit" in (10) is given by

$$m = \begin{cases} -1 & \text{if } a < 0; \\ +1 & \text{if } a > 0? \end{cases}$$

It follows (as is apparent from Fig. 2.3.14) that the line $y = x$ is tangent to the graph $y = |x|$ at any point of the graph to the right of the origin, and that the line $y = -x$ is the tangent line at any point of the graph to the left of the origin.

Infinite Limits

In Example 8 of Section 2.2, we investigated the function $f(x) = 1/(x-1)^2$; the graph of f is shown in Fig. 2.3.15. The value of $f(x)$ increases without bound (that is, eventually exceeds any preassigned number) as x approaches 1 either from the right or from the left. This situation can be described by writing

$$\lim_{x \to 1^-} \frac{1}{(x-1)^2} = +\infty = \lim_{x \to 1^+} \frac{1}{(x-1)^2}, \tag{11}$$

and we say that each of these one-sided limits is equal to "plus infinity."

CAUTION The expression

$$\lim_{x \to 1^+} \frac{1}{(x-1)^2} = +\infty \tag{12}$$

does not mean that there exists an "infinite real number" denoted by $+\infty$—there does not! Neither does it mean that the limit on the left-hand side in Eq. (12) exists—it does not! Instead, Eq. (12) is just a convenient way of saying *why* the right-hand limit in Eq. (12) does not exist: because the quantity $1/(x-2)^2$ increases without bound as $x \to 1^+$.

With similar provisos we may write

$$\lim_{x \to 1} \frac{1}{(x-1)^2} = +\infty \tag{13}$$

despite the fact that the (two-sided) limit in Eq. (13) does not exist. The expression in Eq. (13) is merely a convenient way of saying that the limit in Eq. (13) does not exist because $1/(x-1)^2$ increases without bound as $x \to 1$ from either side.

Now consider the function $f(x) = 1/x$; its graph is shown in Fig. 2.3.16. This function increases without bound as x approaches zero from the right but decreases without bound—it becomes less than any preassigned negative number—as x approaches zero from the left. We therefore write

$$\lim_{x \to 0^-} \frac{1}{x} = -\infty \quad \text{and} \quad \lim_{x \to 0^+} \frac{1}{x} = +\infty. \tag{14}$$

FIGURE 2.3.15 The graph of the function $f(x) = \dfrac{1}{(x-1)^2}$.

FIGURE 2.3.16 The graph of the function $f(x) = \dfrac{1}{x}$.

There is no shorthand for the two-sided limit in this case. We may say only that

$$\lim_{x \to 0} \frac{1}{x} \text{ does not exist.}$$

EXAMPLE 10 Investigate the behavior of the function

$$f(x) = \frac{2x+1}{x-1}$$

near the point $x = 1$, where the limit of $f(x)$ does not exist.

Solution First we look at the behavior of $f(x)$ just to the right of the number 1. If x is greater than 1 but close to 1, then $2x + 1$ is close to 3 and $x - 1$ is a small *positive* number. In this case the quotient $(2x+1)/(x-1)$ is a large positive number, and the closer x is to 1, the larger this positive quotient will be. For such x, $f(x)$ increases without bound as x approaches 1 from the right. That is,

$$\lim_{x \to 1^+} \frac{2x+1}{x-1} = +\infty, \qquad (15)$$

as the data in Fig. 2.3.17 suggest.

x	$\dfrac{2x+1}{x-1}$	x	$\dfrac{2x+1}{x-1}$
1.1	32	0.9	−28
1.01	302	0.99	−298
1.001	3002	0.999	−2998
1.0001	30002	0.9999	−29998
⋮	⋮	⋮	⋮
↓	↓	↓	↓
1	$+\infty$	1	$-\infty$

FIGURE 2.3.17 The behavior of $f(x) = \dfrac{2x+1}{x-1}$ for x near 1 (Example 10).

If instead x is less than 1 but still close to 1, then $2x + 1$ is still close to 3, but now $x - 1$ is a *negative* number close to zero. In this case the quotient $(2x+1)/(x-1)$ is a (numerically) large negative number and decreases without bound as $x \to 1^-$. Hence we conclude that

$$\lim_{x \to 1^-} \frac{2x+1}{x-1} = -\infty. \qquad (16)$$

The results in Eqs. (15) and (16) provide a concise description of the behavior of $f(x) = (2x+1)/(x-1)$ near the point $x = 1$. (See Fig. 2.3.18.) Finally, to remain consistent with Theorem 2 on one-sided and two-sided limits, we do *not* write

$$\lim_{x \to 1} \frac{2x+1}{x-1} = \infty. \qquad \textbf{(Wrong!)}$$

Do you see, however, that it would be correct to write

$$\lim_{x \to 1} \left| \frac{2x+1}{x-1} \right| = +\infty?$$

◆

EXAMPLE 11 The graph of $f(x) = \log_{10} x$ is shown in Fig. 2.3.19. The graph makes it clear that

$$\lim_{x \to 0^+} \log_{10} x = -\infty.$$

But the left-hand limit of $f(x)$ at $x = 0$ does not exist because $\log_{10} x$ is not defined if $x \leq 0$.

◆

FIGURE 2.3.18 Graph of $f(x) = \dfrac{2x+1}{x-1}$.

FIGURE 2.3.19 Graph of $f(x) = \log_{10} x$.

EXAMPLE 12 Look at the graph of $y = 2^x$ in Fig. 1.4.10 to see that

$$\lim_{x \to 0^-} \frac{1}{x} = -\infty \quad \text{implies that} \quad \lim_{x \to 0^-} 2^{1/x} = 0$$

(because $2^t \to 0$ as $t \to -\infty$), whereas

$$\lim_{x \to 0^+} \frac{1}{x} = \infty \quad \text{implies that} \quad \lim_{x \to 0^+} 2^{1/x} = \infty$$

(because $2^t \to +\infty$ as $t \to +\infty$). These one-sided limits of $2^{1/x}$ at $x = 0$ are illustrated in Fig. 2.3.20. ◆

FIGURE 2.3.20 Graph of $f(x) = 2^{1/x}$.

The Basic Trigonometric Limit

We now provide a geometric proof that

$$\lim_{\theta \to 0} \frac{\sin \theta}{\theta} = 1. \tag{17}$$

PROOF Figure 2.3.21 shows the angle θ, the triangles OPQ and ORS, and the circular sector OPR that contains the triangle OPQ and is contained in the triangle ORS. Hence

$$\text{area}(\triangle OPQ) < \text{area}(\text{sector } OPR) < \text{area}(\triangle ORS).$$

In terms of θ, this means that

$$\frac{1}{2} \sin \theta \cos \theta < \frac{1}{2} \theta < \frac{1}{2} \tan \theta = \frac{\sin \theta}{2 \cos \theta}.$$

Here we use the standard formula for the area of a triangle to obtain the area of $\triangle OPQ$ and $\triangle ORS$. We also use the fact that the area of a circular sector in a circle of radius r is $A = \frac{1}{2}r^2\theta$ if the sector is subtended by a central angle of θ radians; here, $r = 1$. If $0 < \theta < \pi/2$, then we can divide each member of the last inequality by $\frac{1}{2} \sin \theta$ to obtain

FIGURE 2.3.21 Aid to the proof of the basic trigonometric limit.

$$\cos \theta < \frac{\theta}{\sin \theta} < \frac{1}{\cos \theta}.$$

We take reciprocals, which reverses the inequalities:

$$\cos \theta < \frac{\sin \theta}{\theta} < \frac{1}{\cos \theta}.$$

Now we apply the squeeze law of limits with

$$f(\theta) = \cos \theta, \quad g(\theta) = \frac{\sin \theta}{\theta}, \quad \text{and} \quad h(\theta) = \frac{1}{\cos \theta}.$$

Because it is clear from Eq. (1) (at the beginning of this section) that $f(\theta)$ and $h(\theta)$ both approach 1 as $\theta \to 0^+$, so does $g(\theta) = (\sin \theta)/\theta$. This geometric argument shows that $(\sin \theta)/\theta \to 1$ for *positive* values of θ that approach zero. But the same result follows for negative values of θ, because $\sin(-\theta) = -\sin \theta$. So we have proved Eq. (17). ◄

The Precise Definition of the Limit

When we say that $f(x)$ approaches the limiting value L as x approaches a, we imply that the behavior of the variable x *controls* the behavior of the value $f(x)$. As x approaches a, this *forces* the value of $f(x)$ to approach L. In Section 2.2 we said that $\lim_{x \to a} f(x) = L$ provided that we can make $f(x)$ as close to L as we please merely by choosing x sufficiently close to a (though not equal to a).

But how close is "sufficiently close"? We can say how close to L we want $f(x)$ to be by prescribing an *error tolerance*. Then the question is this: How close to a must x be in order to force the numerical difference $|f(x) - L|$—the "discrepancy" between $f(x)$ and L—to be less than the prescribed error tolerance. For instance:

- How close to a must x be to guarantee that $|f(x) - L| < 0.1$?
- How close to a must x be to guarantee that $|f(x) - L| < 0.01$?
- How close to a must x be to guarantee that $|f(x) - L| < 0.001$?

For any given error tolerance—however small it may be—we need to determine how close to a (but not equal to a) the variable x must be in order to satisfy that error tolerance.

EXAMPLE 13 Suppose that $a = 2$ and $f(x) = 5x - 3$. We could easily use the limit laws to show that $\lim_{x \to 2} (5x - 3) = 7$, so that $L = 7$. But let's instead begin afresh. We note first that

$$|f(x) - L| = |(5x - 3) - 7| = |5x - 10| = 5 \cdot |x - 2|.$$

Thus $|(5x - 3) - 7|$ is always 5 times $|x - 2|$. It follows that

- If $|x - 2| < 0.02$ then $|5x - 10| = 5 \cdot |x - 2| < 5 \cdot (0.02) = 0.1$.
- If $|x - 2| < 0.002$ then $|5x - 10| = 5 \cdot |x - 2| < 5 \cdot (0.002) = 0.01$.
- If $|x - 2| < 0.0002$ then $|5x - 10| = 5 \cdot |x - 2| < 5 \cdot (0.0002) = 0.001$.

More generally, we need only divide any given error tolerance $\epsilon > 0$ by 5 to get the "variance" in x that works:

$$\text{If} \quad |x - 2| < \frac{\epsilon}{5} \quad \text{then} \quad |(5x - 3) - 7| = 5 \cdot |x - 2| < 5 \cdot \frac{\epsilon}{5} = \epsilon. \tag{18}$$

Thus we can force $f(x) = 5x - 3$ to be within ϵ of $L = 7$ merely by requiring that x be within $\epsilon/5$ of $a = 2$. In this example it is also harmless if $x = 2$ as well—in which case $|(5x - 3) - 7| = 0$—but we include the requirement that $x \neq 2$ by writing $0 < |x - 2| < \epsilon/5$. Finally, if we write $\delta = \epsilon/5$ for this variance in x that forces an acceptable discrepancy in $f(x) = 5x - 3$, we conclude from (18) that

$$|(5x - 3) - 7| < \epsilon \quad \text{for all } x \text{ such that} \quad 0 < |x - 2| < \delta. \tag{19}$$

◆

The exact meaning of limits was debated vigorously—sometimes acrimoniously—during the 17th and 18th centuries. The condition in (19) illustrates the precise definition of the limit that was finally formulated by the German mathematician Karl Weierstrass (1815–1897) and is the definition accepted to this day.

DEFINITION The Limit
Suppose that $f(x)$ is defined in an open interval containing the point a (except possibly not at a itself). Then we say that the number L is the **limit of** $f(x)$ **as** x **approaches** a—and we write

$$\lim_{x \to a} f(x) = L$$

—provided that the following criterion is satisfied: Given any number $\epsilon > 0$, there exists a corresponding number $\delta > 0$ such that

$$|f(x) - L| < \epsilon \quad \text{for all } x \text{ such that} \quad 0 < |x - a| < \delta. \tag{20}$$

The condition in (20) can be rewritten in the form

$$\text{If} \quad 0 < |x - a| < \delta \quad \text{then} \quad |f(x) - L| < \epsilon,$$

or even more simply in the form

$$0 < |x - a| < \delta \quad \text{implies that} \quad |f(x) - L| < \epsilon. \tag{21}$$

FIGURE 2.3.22 Geometric illustration of the limit definition.

Figure 2.3.22 illustrates this definition, which for obvious reasons is often called the "epsilon-delta" definition of limits. The points on the graph of $y = f(x)$ that satisfy the inequality $|f(x) - L| < \epsilon$ are those that lie between the horizontal lines $y = L - \epsilon$ and $y = L + \epsilon$. The points on this graph that satisfy the inequality $|x - a| < \delta$ are those that lie between the vertical lines $x = a - \delta$ and $x = a + \delta$. Consequently, the definition of the limit implies that $\lim_{x \to a} f(x) = L$ if and only if the following statement is true:

> Suppose that the two horizontal lines $y = L - \epsilon$ and $y = L + \epsilon$ (with $\epsilon > 0$) are given. Then it is possible to choose two vertical lines $x = a - \delta$ and $x = a + \delta$ (with $\delta > 0$) so that every point (with $x \neq a$) on the graph of $y = f(x)$ that lies between the two vertical lines must also lie between the two horizontal lines.

Figure 2.3.22 suggests that the closer together are the two horizontal lines, the closer together the two vertical lines will need to be. This is precisely what we mean by "making $f(x)$ closer to L by making x closer to a."

Application of the epsilon-delta definition of limits to establish a limit is usually a two-step process:

- Given $\epsilon > 0$, we first analyze the first inequality $|f(x) - L| < \epsilon$ in (20) to *estimate* or *deduce* a value of $\delta > 0$ that works.
- Then we attempt to *prove* that this value of δ works—that is, prove that $0 < |x - a| < \delta$ implies that $|f(x) - L| < \epsilon$.

EXAMPLE 14 Use the epsilon-delta definition of limits to prove that

$$\lim_{x \to 3} (13x - 29) = 10.$$

Solution Our analysis of the first inequality in (20) consists of noting that it takes the form

$$|(13x - 29) - 10| = |13x - 39| = 13 \cdot |x - 3| < \epsilon,$$

which boils down to $|x - 3| < \epsilon/13$. This leads us to *guess*—on the basis of rather strong circumstantial evidence—that the value $\delta = \epsilon/13$ will work. To *prove* this, we need only note that if $\delta = \epsilon/13$, then

$$0 < |x - 3| < \delta \quad \text{implies that} \quad |(13x - 29) - 10| = 13 \cdot |x - 3| < 13 \cdot \frac{\epsilon}{13} = \epsilon.$$

Thus $0 < |x - 3| < \delta$ implies that $|(13x - 29) - 10| < \epsilon$, as desired. ◆

EXAMPLE 15 Use the epsilon-delta definition of limits to prove that $\lim_{x \to 0} \sqrt[3]{x} = 0$.

Solution Our analysis of the first inequality in (20) consists of noting that it takes the form

$$\left|\sqrt[3]{x} - 0\right| = \left|\sqrt[3]{x}\right| = \sqrt[3]{|x|} < \epsilon,$$

which can be simplified to $|x| < \epsilon^3$. This leads us to *guess* that the value $\delta = \epsilon^3$ will work. To *prove* this, we need only note that if $\delta = \epsilon^3$, then

$$0 < |x - 0| < \delta \quad \text{implies that} \quad \left|\sqrt[3]{x} - 0\right| = \sqrt[3]{|x|} < \sqrt[3]{\epsilon^3} = \epsilon.$$

Thus $0 < |x - 0| < \delta$ implies that $|\sqrt[3]{x} - 0| < \epsilon$, as desired. ◆

Given a value of $\epsilon > 0$, it is frequently more difficult to *guess* a value of δ that works than to *prove* that it does; see Problems 75–84 and this section's project for additional practice. In Appendix D we use the epsilon-delta definition of limits to establish rigorously the laws of limits.

2.3 TRUE/FALSE STUDY GUIDE

2.3 CONCEPTS: QUESTIONS AND DISCUSSION

1. We have interpreted the statement $\lim_{x \to a} f(x) = L$ to mean (roughly) that "$f(x)$ tends to get closer and closer to L as x gets closer and closer to a." What would be meant by the statement that "$f(x)$ gets *steadily* closer to L as x gets steadily closer to a"? State it precisely, something along the lines that "$f(x)$ is still closer to L whenever x is still closer to a" (which is still not sufficiently precise). Does this follow from the statement that $\lim_{x \to a} f(x) = L$? It may help to think about the oscillatory function of Example 4.

2. Formulate precise epsilon-delta definitions of one-sided limits, as well as an M-delta definition of the infinite limit $\lim_{x \to a} f(x) = +\infty$. The latter definition should involve the inequality $f(x) > M$; illustrate it with a figure that is similar to Fig. 2.3.22, but involves only a single horizontal line.

2.3 PROBLEMS

Find the trigonometric limits in Problems 1 through 24. If you have a graphing calculator or a computer with graphing facility, verify that graphical evidence supports your answer.

1. $\lim\limits_{\theta \to 0} \dfrac{\theta^2}{\sin \theta}$

2. $\lim\limits_{\theta \to 0} \dfrac{\sin^2 \theta}{\theta^2}$

3. $\lim\limits_{\theta \to 0} \dfrac{1 - \cos \theta}{\theta^2}$

4. $\lim\limits_{\theta \to 0} \dfrac{\tan \theta}{\theta}$

5. $\lim\limits_{t \to 0} \dfrac{2t}{(\sin t) - t}$

6. $\lim\limits_{\theta \to 0} \dfrac{\sin(2\theta^2)}{\theta^2}$

7. $\lim\limits_{x \to 0} \dfrac{\sin 5x}{x}$

8. $\lim\limits_{z \to 0} \dfrac{\sin 2z}{z \cos 3z}$

9. $\lim\limits_{x \to 0} \dfrac{\sin x}{\sqrt{x}}$

10. $\lim\limits_{x \to 0} \dfrac{1 - \cos 2x}{x}$

11. $\lim\limits_{x \to 0} \dfrac{1}{x} \sin \dfrac{x}{3}$

12. $\lim\limits_{\theta \to 0} \dfrac{(\sin 3\theta)^2}{\theta^2 \cos \theta}$

13. $\lim\limits_{x \to 0} \dfrac{1 - \cos x}{\sin x}$

14. $\lim\limits_{x \to 0} \dfrac{\tan 3x}{\tan 5x}$

15. $\lim\limits_{x \to 0} x \sec x \csc x$

16. $\lim\limits_{\theta \to 0} \dfrac{\sin 2\theta}{\theta}$

17. $\lim\limits_{\theta \to 0} \dfrac{1 - \cos \theta}{\theta \sin \theta}$

18. $\lim\limits_{\theta \to 0} \dfrac{\sin^2 \theta}{\theta}$

19. $\lim\limits_{z \to 0} \dfrac{\tan z}{\sin 2z}$

20. $\lim\limits_{x \to 0} \dfrac{\tan 2x}{3x}$

21. $\lim\limits_{x \to 0} x \cot 3x$

22. $\lim\limits_{x \to 0} \dfrac{x - \tan x}{\sin x}$

23. $\lim\limits_{t \to 0} \dfrac{1}{t^2} \sin^2 \left(\dfrac{t}{2}\right)$

24. $\lim\limits_{x \to 0} \dfrac{\sin 2x}{\sin 5x}$

Use the squeeze law of limits to find the limits in Problems 25 through 28. Also illustrate each of these limits by graphing the functions f, g, and h (in the notation of the squeeze law) on the same screen.

25. $\lim\limits_{x \to 0} x^2 \cos 10x$

26. $\lim\limits_{x \to 0} x^2 \sin \dfrac{1}{x^2}$

27. $\lim\limits_{x \to 0} x^2 \cos \dfrac{1}{\sqrt[3]{x}}$

28. $\lim\limits_{x \to 0} \sqrt[3]{x} \sin \dfrac{1}{x}$

Use one-sided limit laws to find the limits in Problems 29 through 48 or to determine that they do not exist.

29. $\lim_{x \to 0^+} (3 - \sqrt{x})$

30. $\lim_{x \to 0^+} (4 + 3x^{3/2})$

31. $\lim_{x \to 1^-} \sqrt{x - 1}$

32. $\lim_{x \to 4^-} \sqrt{4 - x}$

33. $\lim_{x \to 2^+} \sqrt{x^2 - 4}$

34. $\lim_{x \to 3^+} \sqrt{9 - x^2}$

35. $\lim_{x \to 5^-} \sqrt{x(5 - x)}$

36. $\lim_{x \to 2^-} x\sqrt{4 - x^2}$

37. $\lim_{x \to 4^+} \sqrt{\dfrac{4x}{x - 4}}$

38. $\lim_{x \to -3^+} \sqrt{6 - x - x^2}$

39. $\lim_{x \to 5^-} \dfrac{x - 5}{|x - 5|}$

40. $\lim_{x \to -4^+} \dfrac{16 - x^2}{\sqrt{16 - x^2}}$

41. $\lim_{x \to 3^+} \dfrac{\sqrt{x^2 - 6x + 9}}{x - 3}$

42. $\lim_{x \to 2^+} \dfrac{x - 2}{x^2 - 5x + 6}$

43. $\lim_{x \to 2^+} \dfrac{2 - x}{|x - 2|}$

44. $\lim_{x \to 7^-} \dfrac{7 - x}{|x - 7|}$

45. $\lim_{x \to 1^+} \dfrac{1 - x^2}{1 - x}$

46. $\lim_{x \to 0^-} \dfrac{x}{x - |x|}$

47. $\lim_{x \to 5^+} \dfrac{\sqrt{(5 - x)^2}}{5 - x}$

48. $\lim_{x \to -4^-} \dfrac{4 + x}{\sqrt{(4 + x)^2}}$

For each of the functions in Problems 49 through 58, there is exactly one point a where both the right-hand and left-hand limits of $f(x)$ fail to exist. Describe (as in Example 10) the behavior of $f(x)$ for x near a.

49. $f(x) = \dfrac{1}{x - 1}$

50. $f(x) = \dfrac{2}{3 - x}$

51. $f(x) = \dfrac{x - 1}{x + 1}$

52. $f(x) = \dfrac{2x - 5}{5 - x}$

53. $f(x) = \dfrac{1 - x^2}{x + 2}$

54. $f(x) = \dfrac{1}{(x - 5)^2}$

55. $f(x) = \dfrac{|1 - x|}{(1 - x)^2}$

56. $f(x) = \dfrac{x + 1}{x^2 + 6x + 9}$

57. $f(x) = \dfrac{x - 2}{4 - x^2}$

58. $f(x) = \dfrac{x - 1}{x^2 - 3x + 2}$

In Problems 59 and 60, find the left-hand and right-hand limits of $f(x)$ at $a = 2$. Does the two-sided limit of f exist there? Sketch the graph of $y = f(x)$.

59. $f(x) = \dfrac{x^2 - 4}{|x - 2|}$

60. $f(x) = \dfrac{x^4 - 8x + 16}{|x - 2|}$

In Problems 61 through 68, do the following:

(a) Sketch the graph of the given function f.
(b) For each integer n, evaluate the one-sided limits

$$\lim_{x \to n^-} f(x) \quad \text{and} \quad \lim_{x \to n^+} f(x)$$

in terms of n.
(c) Determine those values of a for which $\lim_{x \to a} f(x)$ exists.

Recall that $[\![x]\!]$ denote the greatest integer that does not exceed x.

61. $f(x) = \begin{cases} 2 & \text{if } x \text{ is not an integer;} \\ 2 + (-1)^x & \text{if } x \text{ is an integer.} \end{cases}$

62. $f(x) = \begin{cases} x & \text{if } x \text{ is not an integer;} \\ 0 & \text{if } x \text{ is an integer.} \end{cases}$

63. $f(x) = [\![10x]\!]$

64. $f(x) = (-1)^{[\![x]\!]}$

65. $f(x) = x - [\![x]\!] - \tfrac{1}{2}$

66. $f(x) = \left[\!\!\left[\dfrac{x}{2} \right]\!\!\right]$

67. $f(x) = [\![x]\!] + [\![-x]\!]$

68. $f(x) = \begin{cases} \dfrac{[\![x]\!]}{x} & \text{if } x \neq 0; \\ 0 & \text{if } x = 0. \end{cases}$

69. If $g(x) = \tfrac{1}{10}[\![10x]\!]$, the value of x to one decimal place rounded down, sketch the graph of g and determine the values of a such that $\lim_{x \to a} g(x)$ exists.

70. The **sign function** $\text{sgn}(x)$ is defined as follows:

$$\text{sgn}(x) = \begin{cases} \dfrac{x}{|x|} & \text{if } x \neq 0; \\ 0 & \text{if } x = 0. \end{cases}$$

Use the sign function to define two functions f and g whose limits as $x \to 0$ do not exist, but such that

(a) $\lim_{x \to 0} [f(x) + g(x)]$ does exist;
(b) $\lim_{x \to 0} f(x) \cdot g(x)$ does exist.

71. Let

$$f(x) = \begin{cases} x^2 & \text{if } x \text{ is rational;} \\ 0 & \text{if } x \text{ is irrational.} \end{cases}$$

Use the squeeze law of limits to show that $\lim_{x \to 0} f(x) = f(0) = 0$.

72. Sketch the graph of the function

$$f(x) = \dfrac{1}{1 + 2^{1/x}}$$

for $x \neq 0$. Then determine whether or not $\lim_{x \to 0} f(x)$ exists.

In Problems 73 and 74, first examine the value of $f(x)$ on intervals of the form

$$\dfrac{1}{n + 1} < x < \dfrac{1}{n}$$

where n is an integer. Then determine whether or not $\lim_{x \to 0} f(x)$ exists. If your graphing calculator or computer has a greatest integer (or "floor") function, graph f to corroborate your answer.

73. $f(x) = x \cdot \left[\!\!\left[\dfrac{1}{x} \right]\!\!\right]$

74. $f(x) = x^2 \cdot \left[\!\!\left[\dfrac{1}{x} \right]\!\!\right]$

In Problems 75 through 84, use the epsilon-delta definition of limits to prove the given equation.

75. $\lim_{x \to -3} (7x - 9) = -30$

76. $\lim_{x \to 5} (17x - 35) = 50$

77. $\lim_{x \to 0^+} \sqrt{x} = 0$ *Suggestion:* First formulate a precise epsilon-delta definition of right-hand limits.

78. $\lim_{x \to 0} x^2 = 0$

79. $\lim_{x \to 2} x^2 = 4$ *Suggestion:* Note that

$$|x^2 - 4| = |x + 2| \cdot |x - 2|.$$

Then argue that if we agree to choose $\delta < 1$, then $|x-2| < \delta$ will imply that $|x + 2| < 3$. (Why?) Then show that it works to choose δ to be the smaller of the two numbers 1 and $\epsilon/3$.

80. $\lim_{x \to 7} (x^2 - 5x - 4) = 10$ *Suggestion:* Note that

$$|(x^2 - 5x - 4) - 10| = |x + 2| \cdot |x - 7|.$$

Then argue that if we agree to choose $\delta < 1$, then $|x-7| < \delta$ will imply that $|x + 2| < 9$. (Why?)

81. $\lim_{x \to 10} (2x^2 - 13x - 25) = 45$ *Suggestion:* Write

$$|(2x^2 - 13x - 25) - 45| = |2x + 7| \cdot |x - 10|.$$

Then argue that if we agree to choose $\delta < 1$, then $|x-10| < \delta$ will imply that $|2x + 7| < 29$. (Why?)

82. $\lim_{x \to 2} x^3 = 8$ *Suggestion:* First verify that

$$|x^3 - 8| = |x^2 + 2x + 4| \cdot |x - 2|.$$

Then argue that if we agree to choose $\delta < 1$, then $|x-2| < \delta$ will imply that $|x^2 + 2x + 4| < 19$. (Why?)

83. Generalize the approach of Problem 79 to prove that $\lim_{x \to a} x^2 = a^2$.

84. Generalize the approach of Problem 82 to prove that $\lim_{x \to a} x^3 = a^3$.

2.3 Project: Numerical Epsilon-Delta Limit Investigations

Figure 2.3.23 shows a steadily rising graph $y = f(x)$ that passes through the point (a, L). Given a single numerical value of $\epsilon > 0$, we can illustrate the limit $\lim_{x \to a} f(x) = L$ by solving the equations $f(x) = L \pm \epsilon$ graphically or numerically for the indicated values x_1 to the left of a such that $f(x_1) = L - \epsilon$ and x_2 to the right of a such that $f(x_2) = L + \epsilon$. If $\delta > 0$ is chosen smaller than either of the two indicated distances $\delta_1 = a - x_1$ and $\delta_2 = x_2 - a$, then the figure suggests that

$$0 < |x - a| < \delta \quad \text{implies that} \quad |f(x) - L| < \epsilon. \tag{21}$$

FIGURE 2.3.23 Finding $\delta = \min(\delta_1, \delta_2)$ graphically.

You should understand that an actual *proof* that $\lim_{x \to a} f(x) = L$ must show that, given *any* $\epsilon > 0$ whatsoever, there exists a $\delta > 0$ that works for *this* ϵ—meaning that the implication in (21) holds.

Doing it for a single value of ϵ does not constitute a proof, but doing it for several successively smaller values of ϵ can be instructive and perhaps convincing. Suppose, for example, that

$$f(x) = x^3 + 5x^2 + 10x + 98, \quad a = 3, \quad \text{and} \quad L = 200.$$

Then, for a particular fixed value of $\epsilon > 0$, you can use a calculator or computer algebra system to solve the equations

$$x^3 + 5x^2 + 10x + 98 = 200 - \epsilon \quad \text{and} \quad x^3 + 5x^2 + 10x + 98 = 200 + \epsilon$$

numerically for the solutions x_1 and x_2 near 3. With $\epsilon = 1$, $\epsilon = 0.2$, and $\epsilon = 0.04$ you should obtain the following results.

ϵ	x_1	x_2	δ_1	δ_2	δ
1	2.98503	3.01488	0.01497	0.01488	0.01
0.2	2.99701	3.00298	0.00299	0.00298	0.002
0.04	2.99940	3.00060	0.00060	0.00060	0.0005

In the final column, each value of δ is (for safety) chosen a bit smaller than either δ_1 or δ_2, to be sure that it works with the corresponding value of ϵ. You might try a still smaller value such as $\epsilon = 0.001$ to find a corresponding value of δ that works. Then carry out a similar investigation to "verify" numerically a polynomial limit of your own selection.

2.4 THE CONCEPT OF CONTINUITY

Anyone can see a drastic difference between the graphs in Figs. 2.4.1 and 2.4.2. Figure 2.4.1 is intended to suggest that the graph $y = f(x)$ can be traced with a continuous motion—without any jumps—of the pen from left to right. But in Fig. 2.4.2 the pen must make a sudden jump at $x = a$.

The concept of continuity isolates the property that the function f of Fig. 2.4.1 possesses but that the function g of Fig. 2.4.2 lacks. We first define *continuity* of a function at a single point.

FIGURE 2.4.1 A continuous graph.

DEFINITION Continuity at a Point
Suppose that the function f is defined in a neighborhood of a. We say that f is **continuous at** a provided that $\lim_{x \to a} f(x)$ exists and, moreover, that the value of this limit is $f(a)$. In other words, f is continuous at a provided that

$$\lim_{x \to a} f(x) = f(a). \tag{1}$$

Briefly, continuity of f at a means this:

The limit of f at a is equal to the value of f there.

FIGURE 2.4.2 A graph that is not continuous.

Another way to put it is this: The limit of f at a is the "expected" value—the value that you would assign if you knew the values of f for $x \neq a$ in a neighborhood of a and you knew f to be "predictable." Alternatively, continuity of f at a means this: When x is close to a, $f(x)$ is close to $f(a)$.

Analysis of the definition of continuity shows us that to be continuous at the point a, the function f must satisfy the following three conditions:

1. The function f must be defined at a [so that $f(a)$ exists].
2. The limit of $f(x)$ as x approaches a must exist.
3. The numbers in conditions 1 and 2 must be equal:

$$\lim_{x \to a} f(x) = f(a).$$

If any one of these conditions is not satisfied, then f is not continuous at a. Examples 1 through 3 illustrate these three possibilities for *discontinuity* at a point. If the function f is *not* continuous at a, then we say that it is **discontinuous** there,

The Concept of Continuity SECTION 2.4   89

or that a is a **discontinuity** of f. Intuitively, a discontinuity of f is a point where the graph of f has a "gap," or "jump," of some sort.

EXAMPLE 1 Figure 2.4.3 shows the graph of the function f defined by

$$f(x) = \frac{1}{x-2} \quad \text{for } x \neq 2.$$

Because f is not defined at the point $x = 2$, it is not continuous there. Moreover, f has what might be called an *infinite discontinuity* at $x = 2$. ◆

FIGURE 2.4.3 The function $f(x) = 1/(x-2)$ has an infinite discontinuity at $x = 2$ (Example 1).

EXAMPLE 2 Figure 2.4.4 shows the graph of the function g defined by

$$g(x) = \text{sgn}(x) = \begin{cases} +1 & \text{if } x \geq 0; \\ -1 & \text{if } x < 0. \end{cases}$$

Its left-hand and right-hand limits at $x = 0$ are unequal, so $g(x)$ has no limit as $x \to 0$. Consequently, the function g is not continuous at $x = 0$; it has what might be called a *finite jump discontinuity* there. ◆

EXAMPLE 3 Figure 2.4.5 shows the graph of the function h defined by

$$h(x) = \begin{cases} \dfrac{\sin x}{x} & \text{if } x \neq 0; \\ 0 & \text{if } x = 0. \end{cases}$$

Because we saw in Section 2.3 that

$$\lim_{x \to 0} h(x) = \lim_{x \to 0} \frac{\sin x}{x} = 1,$$

whereas $h(0) = 0$, we see that the limit and the value of h at $x = 0$ are not equal. Thus the function h is not continuous there. As x moves from negative values through $x = 0$ to positive values, the value of $h(x)$ jumps from "near 1" to zero and back again. ◆

FIGURE 2.4.4 The function g has a finite jump discontinuity at $x = 0$ (Example 2).

The discontinuity at the origin in Example 3 is an example of a *removable* discontinuity. The point a where the function f is discontinuous is called a **removable discontinuity** provided that there exists a function F such that

- $F(x) = f(x)$ for all $x \neq a$ in the domain of definition of f, and
- This new function F is continuous at a.

The original function f may or may not be defined at a, but in any event the graphs of f and F differ only at $x = a$. Sometimes it is simpler to speak of "old" and "new" versions of the same function f. Thus we might say that a removable discontinuity of a function is one that can be removed by suitable definition—or, if necessary, redefinition—of the function at that single point.

FIGURE 2.4.5 The point $(0, 0)$ is on the graph; the point $(0, 1)$ is not (Example 3).

REMARK The discontinuity at the origin of the function h in Example 3 is removable. The reason is that if we change the original value $h(0) = 0$ to $h(0) = 1$, then

$$\lim_{x \to 0} h(x) = \lim_{h \to 0} \frac{\sin x}{x} = 1 = h(0),$$

so h is now continuous at $x = 0$. By contrast, the discontinuities in the sawtooth function f of the next example are not removable, because we see genuine jumps or gaps in the graph that obviously cannot be removed simply by changing the values of f at these discontinuities.

EXAMPLE 4 Figure 2.4.6 shows the graph of the function f defined by

$$f(x) = x - [\![x]\!].$$

FIGURE 2.4.6 The "sawtooth function" of Example 4.

As before, $[\![x]\!]$ denotes the largest integer no greater than x. If $x = n$, an integer, then $[\![n]\!] = n$, so $f(n) = 0$. On the open interval $(n, n+1)$, the graph of f is linear and has slope 1. It should be clear that f is

- Continuous at x if x is *not* an integer;
- Discontinuous at each integer point on the x-axis.

Combinations of Continuous Functions

Frequently we are most interested in functions that *are* continuous. Suppose that the function f is defined on an open interval or a union of open intervals. Then we say simply that f is **continuous** if it is continuous at each point of its domain of definition.

It follows readily from the limit laws in Section 2.2 that *any constant multiple, sum, difference, or product of continuous functions is continuous.* That is, if c is a constant and the functions f and g are continuous at a, then so are the functions

$$cf, \quad f+g, \quad f-g, \quad \text{and} \quad f \cdot g.$$

For instance, if f and g are continuous at a, then

$$\lim_{x \to a}[f(x) + g(x)] = \left(\lim_{x \to a} f(x)\right) + \left(\lim_{x \to a} g(x)\right) = f(a) + g(a),$$

so it follows that the sum $f+g$ is also continuous at a.

EXAMPLE 5 Because $f(x) = x$ and constant-valued functions are clearly continuous everywhere, it follows that the cubic polynomial function

$$f(x) = x^3 - 3x^2 + 1 = x \cdot x \cdot x + (-3) \cdot x \cdot x + 1$$

is continuous everywhere. ◆

More generally, it follows in a similar way that *every* **polynomial function**

$$p(x) = b_n x^n + b_{n-1} x^{n-1} + \cdots + b_1 x + b_0$$

is continuous at each point of the real line. In short, every polynomial is continuous everywhere.

If $p(x)$ and $q(x)$ are polynomials, then the quotient law for limits and the continuity of polynomials imply that

$$\lim_{x \to a} \frac{p(x)}{q(x)} = \frac{\lim_{x \to a} p(x)}{\lim_{x \to a} q(x)} = \frac{p(a)}{q(a)}$$

provided that $q(a) \neq 0$. Thus every **rational function**

$$f(x) = \frac{p(x)}{q(x)} \tag{2}$$

is continuous wherever it is defined—that is, wherever the denominator polynomial is nonzero. More generally, *the quotient of any two continuous functions is continuous at every point where the denominator is nonzero.*

At a point $x = a$ where the denominator in Eq. (2) is zero, $q(a) = 0$, there are two possibilities:

- If $p(a) \neq 0$, then f has an infinite discontinuity (as in Figs. 2.4.3 and 2.4.7) at $x = a$.
- Otherwise, f may have a removable discontinuity at $x = a$.

FIGURE 2.4.7 The function $f(x) = 1/(x-2)^2$ has an infinite discontinuity at $x = 2$.

EXAMPLE 6 Suppose that

$$f(x) = \frac{x-2}{x^2 - 3x + 2}. \tag{3}$$

We factor the denominator: $x^2 - 3x + 2 = (x-1)(x-2)$. This shows that f is not defined at $x = 1$ and at $x = 2$. Thus the rational function defined in Eq. (3) is continuous except at these two points. Because cancellation gives

$$f(x) = \frac{x-2}{x^2 - 3x + 2} = \frac{1}{x-1}$$

except at the single point $x = 2$, the new function

$$F(x) = \frac{1}{x-1} \qquad (4)$$

agrees with $f(x)$ if $x \neq 2$ but is continuous at $x = 2$ also, where $F(2) = 1$. Thus f has a removable discontinuity at $x = 2$; the discontinuity at $x = 1$ is not removable. (See Fig. 2.4.8.) ◆

FIGURE 2.4.8 In Example 6, the graph $y = F(x)$ consists of the graph $y = f(x)$ with the single point (2,1) adjoined.

Continuity of Trigonometric Functions

At the beginning of Section 2.3 we noted that

$$\lim_{x \to 0} \cos x = 1 \quad \text{and} \quad \lim_{x \to 0} \sin x = 0. \qquad (5)$$

Because $\cos 0 = 1$ and $\sin 0 = 0$, the sine and cosine functions are continuous at $x = 0$ by definition. But this fact implies that they are continuous everywhere.

THEOREM 1 Continuity of Sine and Cosine

The functions $f(x) = \sin x$ and $g(x) = \cos x$ are continuous functions of x on the whole real line.

PROOF We give the proof only for $\sin x$; the proof for $\cos x$ is similar. (See Problem 67.) We want to show that $\lim_{x \to a} \sin x = \sin a$ for every real number a. If we write $x = a + h$, so that $h = x - a$, then $h \to 0$ as $x \to a$. Thus we need only show that

$$\lim_{h \to 0} \sin(a + h) = \sin a.$$

But the addition formula for the sine function yields

$$\lim_{h \to 0} \sin(a + h) = \lim_{h \to 0} (\sin a \cos h + \cos a \sin h)$$

$$= (\sin a) \left(\lim_{h \to 0} \cos h \right) + (\cos a) \left(\lim_{h \to 0} \sin h \right) = \sin a$$

as desired; we used the limits in Eq. (5) in the last step. ◀

REMARK It now follows that the function

$$\tan x = \frac{\sin x}{\cos x} \qquad (6)$$

is continuous except where $\cos x = 0$—that is, except when x is an *odd* integral multiple of $\pi/2$. As illustrated in Fig. 2.4.9, $\tan x$ has an infinite discontinuity at each such point.

Composition of Continuous Functions

Recall from Section 1.4 that the **composition** of the two functions f and g is the function $h = f \circ g$ defined by

$$h(x) = f(g(x))$$

for all x in the domain of g such that $u = g(x)$ is in the domain of f. Theorem 2 implies that functions built by forming compositions of *continuous* functions are themselves continuous.

FIGURE 2.4.9 The function tan x has infinite discontinuities at $x = \pm\pi/2$, $\pm 3\pi/2$, ...

THEOREM 2 Continuity of Compositions
The composition of two continuous functions is continuous. More precisely, if g is continuous at a and f is continuous at $g(a)$, then $f \circ g$ is continuous at a.

PROOF The continuity of g at a means that $g(x) \to g(a)$ as $x \to a$, and the continuity of f at $g(a)$ implies that $f(x) \to f(g(a))$ as $x \to g(a)$. Hence the substitution law for limits (Section 2.2) yields

$$\lim_{x \to a} f(g(x)) = f\left(\lim_{x \to a} g(x)\right) = f(g(a)),$$

as desired. ◄

Recall from the root law in Section 2.2 that

$$\lim_{x \to a} \sqrt[n]{x} = \sqrt[n]{a}$$

under the conditions that n is an integer and that $a > 0$ if n is even. Thus the nth-root function $f(x) = \sqrt[n]{x}$ is continuous everywhere if n is odd; f is continuous for $x > 0$ if n is even.

We may combine this result with Theorem 2. Then we see that *a root of a continuous function is continuous wherever it is defined.* That is, the composition

$$h(x) = \sqrt[n]{g(x)} = [g(x)]^{1/n}$$

of $f(x) = \sqrt[n]{x}$ and the function $g(x)$ is continuous at a if g is, assuming that $g(a) > 0$ if n is even (so that $\sqrt[n]{g(a)}$ is defined).

EXAMPLE 7 Show that the function

$$f(x) = \left(\frac{x - 7}{x^2 + 2x + 2}\right)^{2/3}$$

is continuous on the whole real line.

Solution Note first that the denominator

$$x^2 + 2x + 2 = (x + 1)^2 + 1$$

is never zero, because its smallest value (when $x = -1$) is $0^2 + 1 = 1$. Hence the rational function

$$r(x) = \frac{x - 7}{x^2 + 2x + 2}$$

is defined and continuous everywhere. It then follows from Theorem 2 and the continuity of the cube root function that

$$f(x) = [r(x)]^{2/3} = \sqrt[3]{[r(x)]^2}$$

is continuous everywhere—as suggested by its graph in Fig. 2.4.10, where we see the high point $(-1, 4)$ corresponding to the minimum value (at $x = -1$) of the denominator of $r(x)$. ◆

FIGURE 2.4.10 The graph $y = \left(\dfrac{x-7}{x^2+2x+2}\right)^{2/3}$.

EXAMPLE 8 (a) The exponential function $f(x) = 2^x$ is continuous everywhere, and therefore so is the composition $h(x) = 2^{\sin x}$ of f and the sine function. Refer to Fig. 2.4.11, where we see high and low points on the graph of $y = 2^{\sin x}$ corresponding to the high and low points on the graph of $y = \sin x$. (b) By contrast, the tangent function $\tan x$ has infinite discontinuities at odd integral multiples of $\pi/2$ (as shown in Fig. 2.4.9), and we see corresponding discontinuities in the composition $h(x) = 2^{\tan x}$ when we look at the graph in Fig. 2.4.12. These discontinuities are interesting in that, if a is an odd integral multiple of $\pi/2$, then

$$\lim_{x \to a^-} h(x) = \lim_{x \to a^-} 2^{\tan x} = +\infty,$$

whereas

$$\lim_{x \to a^+} h(x) = \lim_{x \to a^+} 2^{\tan x} = 0 = h(a).$$

◆

FIGURE 2.4.11 The function $h(x) = 2^{\sin x}$ is continuous everywhere.

FIGURE 2.4.12 The function $h(x) = 2^{\tan x}$ has infinite discontinuities.

The function $h(x) = 2^{\tan x}$ of Example 8(b) illustrates the concept of *one-sided continuity*. It is convenient to say that the function f is

- **continuous from the left at** a if $\lim\limits_{x \to a^-} = f(a)$, and is
- **continuous from the right at** a if $\lim\limits_{x \to a^+} = f(a)$.

Thus $h(x) = 2^{\tan x}$ is continuous from the right at a if a is an odd integral multiple of $\pi/2$, but is *not* continuous from the left at a. Of course, a function that is continuous at a is automatically continuous at a both from the left and from the right.

Continuous Functions on Closed Intervals

An applied problem typically involves a function whose domain is a *closed interval*. For example, in the animal pen problem of Section 1.1, we found that the area A of the rectangular pen in Fig. 2.4.13 was expressed as a function of its base length x by

$$A = f(x) = \frac{3}{5}x(30 - x).$$

Although this formula for f is meaningful for all x, only values in the closed interval $[0, 30]$ correspond to actual rectangles, so only such values are pertinent to the animal pen problem.

FIGURE 2.4.13 The animal pen.

The function f defined on the closed interval $[a, b]$ is said to be **continuous on** $[a, b]$ provided that

- f is continuous at each point of the open integral (a, b),
- f is continuous from the right at the left-hand endpoint a, and
- f is continuous from the left at the right-hand endpoint b.

The last two conditions imply that, at each endpoint, the value of the function is equal to its limit from *within* the interval. For instance, every polynomial is continuous on every closed interval. The square root function $f(x) = \sqrt{x}$ is continuous from the right at 0 because $\lim_{x \to 0^+} \sqrt{x} = 0 = \sqrt{0}$. Therefore f is continuous on the closed interval $[0, 1]$ even though f is not defined for $x < 0$.

Continuous functions defined on closed intervals have very special properties. For example, every such function has the *intermediate value property* of Theorem 3. (A proof of this theorem is given in Appendix E.) We suggested earlier that continuity of a function is related to the possibility of tracing its graph without lifting the pen from the paper. Theorem 3, the *intermediate value theorem*, expresses this fact with precision.

THEOREM 3 Intermediate Value Property
Suppose that the function f is continuous on the closed interval $[a, b]$. Then $f(x)$ assumes every intermediate value between $f(a)$ and $f(b)$. That is, if K is any number between $f(a)$ and $f(b)$, then there exists at least one number c in (a, b) such that $f(c) = K$.

Figure 2.4.14 shows the graph of a typical continuous function f whose domain is the closed interval $[a, b]$. The number K is located on the y-axis, somewhere between $f(a)$ and $f(b)$. In the figure $f(a) < f(b)$, but this is not important. The horizontal line through K must cross the graph of f somewhere, and the x-coordinate of the point where graph and line meet yields the value of c. The number c is the one whose existence is guaranteed by the intermediate value property of the continuous function f.

FIGURE 2.4.14 The continuous function f attains the intermediate value K at $x = c$.

Thus the intermediate value theorem implies that each horizontal line meeting the y-axis between $f(a)$ and $f(b)$ must cross the graph of the continuous function f somewhere. This is a way of saying that the graph has no gaps or jumps, suggesting that the idea of being able to trace such a graph without lifting the pen from the paper is accurate.

EXAMPLE 9 The discontinuous function defined on $[-1, 1]$ as

$$f(x) = \begin{cases} 0 & \text{if } x < 0, \\ 1 & \text{if } x \geq 0 \end{cases}$$

does *not* attain the intermediate value $\frac{1}{2}$. See Fig. 2.4.15.

FIGURE 2.4.15 This discontinuous function does not have the intermediate value property (Example 9).

Existence of Solutions of Equations

An important application of the intermediate value theorem is the verification of the existence of solutions of equations written in the form

$$f(x) = 0. \tag{7}$$

EXAMPLE 10 You could attempt to approximate the number $\sqrt{2}$ graphically by zooming in on the intersection of the parabola $y = x^2 - 2$ with the positive x-axis (Fig. 2.4.16). The x-coordinate of the intersection yields the positive solution of the equation

$$f(x) = x^2 - 2 = 0. \tag{8}$$

Perhaps it makes no sense to zoom in on this point unless we know that it's "really there." But we can see from Eq. (8) that

$$f(1) = -1 < 0, \quad \text{whereas} \quad f(2) = 2 > 0.$$

We note that the function f is continuous on $[1, 2]$ (it is continuous everywhere) and that $K = 0$ is an intermediate value of f on the interval $[1, 2]$. Therefore, it follows from Theorem 3 that $f(c) = c^2 - 2 = 0$ for some number c in $(1, 2)$—that is, that

$$c^2 = 2.$$

This number c is the desired square root of 2. Thus it is the intermediate value property of continuous functions that guarantees the existence of the number $\sqrt{2}$: There *is* a real number whose square is 2. ◆

FIGURE 2.4.16 The graph of $f(x) = x^2 - 2$ (Example 10).

As indicated in Fig. 2.4.17, the solutions of Eq. (7) are simply the points where the graph $y = f(x)$ crosses the x-axis. Suppose that f is continuous and that we can find a closed interval $[a, b]$ (such as the interval $[1, 2]$ of Example 10) such that the value of f is positive at one endpoint of $[a, b]$ and negative at the other. That is, suppose that $f(x)$ *changes sign* on the closed interval $[a, b]$. Then the intermediate value property ensures that $f(x) = 0$ at some point of $[a, b]$.

FIGURE 2.4.17 The solution of the equation $f(x) = 0$.

FIGURE 2.4.18 The equation $x^3 - x - 2 = 0$ of Example 11 appears to have a solution somewhere between $x = 1$ and $x = 2$.

EXAMPLE 11 The graph $y = x^3 - x - 2$ shown in Fig. 2.4.18 indicates that the equation

$$f(x) = x^3 - x - 2 = 0$$

has a solution somewhere between $x = 1$ and $x = 2$. Apply the intermediate value theorem to show that this actually is so.

Solution The function $f(x)$ is continuous on $[1, 2]$ because it is a polynomial and, therefore, is continuous everywhere. Because $f(1) = -2$ and $f(2) = +4$, the intermediate value theorem implies that every number between -2 and $+4$ is a value of $f(x)$ on $[1, 2]$. In particular,

$$-2 = f(1) < 0 < f(2) = +4,$$

so the intermediate value property of f implies that f attains the value 0 at some number c between $x = 1$ and $x = 2$. That is,

$$f(c) = c^3 - c - 2 = 0,$$

so $x = c$ is a solution in $(1, 2)$ of the equation $x^3 - x - 2 = 0$. ◆

The following example shows that not every suspected root of an equation $f(x) = 0$ that seems to be visible on a computer-plotted figure is actually there. Indeed, a graphing calculator or computer ordinarily is programmed to plot close but isolated points on the desired graph $y = f(x)$ and then join these points with line segments so short that the result looks like a smooth curve. In effect, the computer is *assuming* that the function f is continuous, whether or not it actually is continuous.

EXAMPLE 12 Figure 2.4.19 shows a computer plot of the graph of the function

$$f(x) = \frac{10 \cdot [\![1000x]\!] - 4995}{10000}.$$

The graph $y = f(x)$ appears indistinguishable from the line $y = x - \frac{1}{2}$, and in particular it appears that the equation $f(x) = 0$ has the solution $x = \frac{1}{2}$. But when we zoom in near this alleged solution we see the graph shown in Fig. 2.4.20. Now we see that the function f is discontinuous, and actually "jumps" across the x-axis without intersecting it. Thus the equation $f(x) = 0$ has no solution at all. ◆

FIGURE 2.4.19 The graph $y = f(x)$ of Example 12 appears to have x-intercept $x = 0.5$.

FIGURE 2.4.20 The graph in Example 12 jumps across the x-axis—there is no x-intercept.

2.4 TRUE/FALSE STUDY GUIDE

2.4 CONCEPTS: QUESTIONS AND DISCUSSION

1. Suppose that $a < b < c$. If the function f is continuous both on the closed interval $[a, b]$ and on the closed interval $[b, c]$, does it follow that f is continuous on $[a, c]$? If f is continuous on the closed interval $[n, n + 1]$ for every integer n, does it follow that f is continuous on the entire real line?

2. Suppose that the function f is continuous everywhere and that the composition $f(g(x))$ is continuous at $x = a$. Does it follow that $g(x)$ is continuous at a? *Suggestion:* Consider the possibility that $f(x) = |x|$.

3. Suppose that $p(x)$ is a polynomial of odd degree with positive leading coefficient. Then its graph $y = p(x)$ "heads southwest in the third quadrant" and "northeast in the first quadrant." Can you state more precisely what these

intuitive statements mean? Why does it follow that the equation $p(x) = 0$ always has at least one solution?

4. If $10^L = y$, then we call the number L the *base* 10 *logarithm* of y and write $L = \log y$. Assume that the exponential function $f(x) = 10^x$ is continuous everywhere (it is!) and—as suggested by its graph in Fig. 1.4.10—it has both arbitrarily large positive values and values arbitrarily close to zero. Then explain why the intermediate value theorem implies that every positive number has a base 10 logarithm.

2.4 PROBLEMS

In Problems 1 through 8, apply the limit laws and the theorems of this section to show that the given function is continuous for all x.

1. $f(x) = 2x^5 - 7x^2 + 13$
2. $f(x) = 7x^3 - (2x+1)^5$
3. $g(x) = \dfrac{2x-1}{4x^2+1}$
4. $g(x) = \dfrac{x^3}{x^2+2x+5}$
5. $h(x) = \sqrt{x^2 + 4x + 5}$
6. $h(x) = \sqrt[3]{1 - 5x}$
7. $f(x) = \dfrac{1 - \sin x}{1 + \cos^2 x}$
8. $g(x) = \sqrt[4]{1 - \sin^2 x}$

In Problems 9 through 14, apply the limit laws and the theorems of this section to show that the given function is continuous on the indicated interval.

9. $f(x) = \dfrac{1}{x+1}$, $x > -1$
10. $f(x) = \dfrac{x-1}{x^2-4}$, $-2 < x < 2$
11. $g(t) = \sqrt{9 - 4t^2}$, $-\tfrac{3}{2} \leq t \leq \tfrac{3}{2}$
12. $h(z) = \sqrt{(z-1)(3-z)}$, $1 \leq z \leq 3$
13. $f(x) = \dfrac{x}{\cos x}$, $-\tfrac{1}{2}\pi < x < \tfrac{1}{2}\pi$
14. $g(t) = \sqrt{1 - 2\sin t}$, $-\tfrac{1}{6}\pi < t < \tfrac{1}{6}\pi$

In Problems 15 through 36, tell where the given function is continuous. Recall that when the domain of a function is not specified, it is the set of all real numbers for which the formula of the function is meaningful.

15. $f(x) = 2x + \sqrt[3]{x}$
16. $g(x) = x^2 + \dfrac{1}{x}$
17. $f(x) = \dfrac{1}{x+3}$
18. $f(t) = \dfrac{5}{5-t}$
19. $f(x) = \dfrac{1}{x^2+1}$
20. $g(z) = \dfrac{1}{z^2-1}$
21. $f(x) = \dfrac{x-5}{|x-5|}$
22. $h(x) = \dfrac{x^2+x+1}{x^2+1}$
23. $f(x) = \dfrac{x^2+4}{x-2}$
24. $f(t) = \sqrt[4]{4+t^4}$
25. $f(x) = \sqrt[3]{\dfrac{x+1}{x-1}}$
26. $F(u) = \sqrt[3]{3-u^3}$
27. $f(x) = \dfrac{3}{x^2-x}$
28. $f(z) = \sqrt{9-z^2}$
29. $f(x) = \dfrac{x}{\sqrt{4-x^2}}$
30. $f(x) = \sqrt{\dfrac{1-x^2}{4-x^2}}$
31. $f(x) = \dfrac{\sin x}{x^2}$
32. $g(\theta) = \dfrac{\theta}{\cos \theta}$
33. $f(x) = \dfrac{1}{\sin 2x}$
34. $f(x) = \sqrt{\sin x}$
35. $f(x) = \sin|x|$
36. $G(u) = \dfrac{1}{\sqrt{1+\cos u}}$

In Problems 37 through 48, find the points where the given function is not defined and is therefore not continuous. For each such point a, tell whether or not this discontinuity is removable.

37. $f(x) = \dfrac{x}{(x+3)^3}$
38. $f(t) = \dfrac{t}{t^2-1}$
39. $f(x) = \dfrac{x-2}{x^2-4}$
40. $G(u) = \dfrac{u+1}{u^2-u-6}$
41. $f(x) = \dfrac{1}{1-|x|}$
42. $h(x) = \dfrac{|x-1|}{(x-1)^3}$
43. $f(x) = \dfrac{x-17}{|x-17|}$
44. $g(x) = \dfrac{x^2+5x+6}{x+2}$
45. $f(x) = \begin{cases} -x & \text{if } x < 0; \\ x^2 & \text{if } x > 0 \end{cases}$
46. $f(x) = \begin{cases} x+1 & \text{if } x < 1; \\ 3-x & \text{if } x > 1 \end{cases}$
47. $f(x) = \begin{cases} 1+x^2 & \text{if } x < 0; \\ \dfrac{\sin x}{x} & \text{if } x > 0 \end{cases}$
48. $f(x) = \begin{cases} \dfrac{1-\cos x}{x} & \text{if } x < 0; \\ x^2 & \text{if } x > 0 \end{cases}$

In Problems 49 through 52, find a value of the constant c so that the function $f(x)$ is continuous for all x.

49. $f(x) = \begin{cases} x+c & \text{if } x < 0, \\ 4-x^2 & \text{if } x \geq 0 \end{cases}$
50. $f(x) = \begin{cases} 2x+c & \text{if } x \leq 3, \\ 2c-x & \text{if } x > 3 \end{cases}$

51. $f(x) = \begin{cases} c^2 - x^2 & \text{if } x < 0, \\ 2(x-c)^2 & \text{if } x \geq 0 \end{cases}$

52. $f(x) = \begin{cases} c^3 - x^3 & \text{if } x \leq \pi, \\ c \sin x & \text{if } x > \pi \end{cases}$

In Problems 53 through 58, apply the intermediate value property of continuous functions to show that the given equation has a solution in the given interval.

53. $x^2 - 5 = 0$ on $[2, 3]$
54. $x^3 + x + 1 = 0$ on $[-1, 0]$
55. $x^3 - 3x^2 + 1 = 0$ on $[0, 1]$
56. $x^3 = 5$ on $[1, 2]$
57. $x^4 + 2x - 1 = 0$ on $[0, 1]$
58. $x^5 - 5x^3 + 3 = 0$ on $[-3, -2]$

In Problems 59 and 60, show that the given equation has three distinct roots by calculating the values of the left-hand side at $x = -3, -3, -1, 0, 1, 2,$ and 3 and then applying the intermediate value property of continuous functions on appropriate closed intervals.

59. $x^3 - 4x + 1 = 0$
60. $x^3 - 3x^2 + 1 = 0$

61. Suppose that you accept a job now (time $t = 0$) at an annual salary of $25,000 and are promised a 6% raise at the end of each year of employment. Explain why your salary in thousands of dollars after t years is given by the formula

$$S(t) = 25 \cdot (1.06)^{[\![t]\!]}.$$

Graph this function for the first 5 years and comment on its continuity.

62. Suppose that you accept the same job as in Problem 61, but now are promised a 1.5% raise at the end of each quarter (three months). (a) Write a formula for your salary (in thousands of dollars) after t years. (b) Graph this new salary function and comment on its continuity. (c) Which is the better deal, the promised salary of Problem 61 or the one of this problem?

63. Suppose that f and g are two functions both continuous on the interval $[a, b]$, and such that $f(a) = g(b) = p$ and $f(b) = g(a) = q$ where $p \neq q$. Sketch typical graphs of two such functions. Then apply the intermediate value theorem to the function $h(x) = f(x) - g(x)$ to show that $f(c) = g(c)$ at some point c of (a, b).

64. Suppose that today you leave your home in Estes Park, CO at 1 P.M. and drive to Grand Lake, arriving at 2 P.M. Tomorrow you leave your destination in Grand Lake at 1 P.M. and retrace the same route, arriving home at 2 P.M. Use Problem 63 as a suggestion to show that at some instant between 1 and 2 P.M. you are at precisely the same point on the road both days. What must you assume about the functions describing your location as a function of time each day?

65. Apply the intermediate value property of continuous functions to show that every positive number a has a square root. That is, given $a > 0$, prove that there exists a number r such that $r^2 = a$.

66. Apply the intermediate value property to prove that every real number has a cube root.

67. Show that the cosine function is continuous on the set of all real numbers. (*Suggestion:* Alter the proof of Theorem 1 of the continuity of the sine function.)

68. Determine where the function $f(x) = x + [\![x]\!]$ is continuous.

69. Suppose that $f(x) = 0$ if x is a rational number, whereas $f(x) = 1$ if x is irrational. Prove that f is discontinuous at every real number.

70. Suppose that $f(x) = 0$ if x is a rational number, whereas $f(x) = x^2$ if x is irrational. Prove that f is continuous only at the single point $x = 0$.

71. Figure 2.4.21 suggests that the equation $x = \cos x$ has a solution in the interval $(0, \pi/2)$. Use the intermediate value theorem to show that this is true. Then use your calculator to approximate this solution accurate to two decimal places.

FIGURE 2.4.21 The graphs $y = x$ and $y = \cos x$ (Problem 71).

72. Figure 2.4.22 suggests that the equation $x = -5\cos x$ has at least three distinct solutions. Use the intermediate value theorem to show that this is true. Then use your calculator to approximate each of these solutions accurate to two decimal places.

FIGURE 2.4.22 The graphs $y = x$ and $y = -5\cos x$ (Problem 72).

Investigate the continuity of each of the functions defined in Problems 73 through 78. For each discontinuity, determine whether the given function is continuous from the right and whether it is continuous from the left. Use a graphing calculator or computer if you find it helpful.

73. $f(x) = 2^{1/x}$ if $x \neq 0$; $f(0) = 0$

74. $f(x) = 2^{-1/x^2}$ if $x \neq 0$; $f(0) = 0$

75. $f(x) = \dfrac{1}{1 + 2^{1/x}}$ if $x \neq 0$; $f(0) = 1$

76. $f(x) = \dfrac{1}{1 + 2^{-1/x^2}}$ if $x \neq 0$; $f(0) = 1$

77. $f(x) = \dfrac{1}{1 + 2^{\tan x}}$ where meaningful; $f(x) = 1$ otherwise

78. $f(x) = \dfrac{1}{1 + 2^{1/\sin x}}$ where meaningful; $f(x) = 0$ otherwise

CHAPTER 2 REVIEW: DEFINITIONS, CONCEPTS, RESULTS

Use the following list as a guide to topics that you may need to review.

1. Slope predictors for tangent lines
2. Lines tangent to parabolas
3. Numerical investigation of slopes of lines tangent to more general curves
4. The idea of the limit of $f(x)$ as x approaches a
5. Numerical and graphical investigations of limits
6. The limit laws: constant, addition, product, quotient, root, substitution, and squeeze
7. Slope-predictor functions
8. The four-step process for finding slope-predictor functions
9. The basic trigonometric limit
10. Evaluation of limits of trigonometric functions
11. Right-hand and left-hand limits
12. The relation between one-sided and two-sided limits
13. The precise definition of the limit
14. Existence of tangent lines
15. Infinite limits
16. Continuity of a function at a point
17. Combinations of continuous functions
18. Continuity of polynomials and rational functions
19. Removable discontinuities
20. Continuity of trigonometric functions
21. Compositions of continuous functions
22. The intermediate value property of continuous functions
23. Existence of solutions of equations

CHAPTER 2 MISCELLANEOUS PROBLEMS

Apply the limit laws to evaluate the limits in Problems 1 through 40 or to show that the indicated limit does not exist, as appropriate.

1. $\lim\limits_{x \to 0} (x^2 - 3x + 4)$

2. $\lim\limits_{x \to -1} (3 - x + x^3)$

3. $\lim\limits_{x \to 2} (4 - x^2)^{10}$

4. $\lim\limits_{x \to 1} (x^2 + x - 1)^{17}$

5. $\lim\limits_{x \to 2} \dfrac{1 + x^2}{1 - x^2}$

6. $\lim\limits_{x \to 3} \dfrac{2x}{x^2 - x - 3}$

7. $\lim\limits_{x \to 1} \dfrac{x^2 - 1}{1 - x}$

8. $\lim\limits_{x \to -2} \dfrac{x + 2}{x^2 + x - 2}$

9. $\lim\limits_{t \to -3} \dfrac{t^2 + 6t + 9}{9 - t^2}$

10. $\lim\limits_{x \to 0} \dfrac{4x - x^3}{3x + x^2}$

11. $\lim\limits_{x \to 3} (x^2 - 1)^{2/3}$

12. $\lim\limits_{x \to 2} \sqrt{\dfrac{2x^2 + 1}{2x}}$

13. $\lim\limits_{x \to 3} \left(\dfrac{5x + 1}{x^2 - 8}\right)^{3/4}$

14. $\lim\limits_{x \to 1} \dfrac{x^4 - 1}{x^2 + 2x - 3}$

15. $\lim\limits_{x \to 7} \dfrac{\sqrt{x + 2} - 3}{x - 7}$

16. $\lim\limits_{x \to 1^+} \left(x - \sqrt{x^2 - 1}\right)$

17. $\lim\limits_{x \to -4} \dfrac{\dfrac{1}{\sqrt{13 + x}} - \dfrac{1}{3}}{x + 4}$

18. $\lim\limits_{x \to 1^+} \dfrac{1 - x}{|1 - x|}$

19. $\lim\limits_{x \to 2^+} \dfrac{2 - x}{\sqrt{4 - 4x + x^2}}$

20. $\lim\limits_{x \to -2^-} \dfrac{x + 2}{|x + 2|}$

21. $\lim\limits_{x \to 4^+} \dfrac{x - 4}{|x - 4|}$

22. $\lim\limits_{x \to 3^-} \sqrt{x^2 - 9}$

23. $\lim\limits_{x \to 2^+} \sqrt{4 - x^2}$

24. $\lim\limits_{x \to -3} \dfrac{x}{(x + 3)^2}$

25. $\lim\limits_{x \to 2} \dfrac{x + 2}{(x - 2)^2}$

26. $\lim\limits_{x \to 1^-} \dfrac{x}{x - 1}$

27. $\lim\limits_{x \to 3^+} \dfrac{x}{x - 3}$

28. $\lim\limits_{x \to 1^-} \dfrac{x - 2}{x^2 - 3x + 2}$

29. $\lim\limits_{x \to 1^-} \dfrac{x + 1}{(x - 1)^3}$

30. $\lim\limits_{x \to 5^+} \dfrac{25 - x^2}{x^2 - 10x + 25}$

31. $\lim\limits_{x \to 0} \dfrac{\sin 3x}{x}$

32. $\lim\limits_{x \to 0} \dfrac{\tan 5x}{x}$

33. $\lim\limits_{x \to 0} \dfrac{\sin 3x}{\sin 2x}$

34. $\lim\limits_{x \to 0} \dfrac{\tan 2x}{\tan 3x}$

35. $\lim\limits_{x \to 0^+} \dfrac{x}{\sin \sqrt{x}}$

36. $\lim\limits_{x \to 0} \dfrac{1 - \cos 3x}{2x}$

37. $\lim\limits_{x \to 0} \dfrac{1 - \cos 3x}{2x^2}$

38. $\lim\limits_{x \to 0} x^3 \cot x \csc x$

39. $\lim\limits_{x \to 0} \dfrac{\sec 2x \tan 2x}{x}$

40. $\lim\limits_{x \to 0} x^2 \cot^2 3x$

In Problems 41 through 46, apply your knowledge of lines tangent to parabolas (Section 2.1) to write a slope-predictor formula for the given curve $y = f(x)$. Then write an equation for the line tangent to $y = f(x)$ at the point $(1, f(1))$.

41. $f(x) = 3 + 2x^2$

42. $f(x) = x - 5x^2$

43. $f(x) = 3x^2 + 4x - 5$

44. $f(x) = 1 - 2x - 3x^2$

45. $f(x) = (x-1)(2x-1)$

46. $f(x) = \dfrac{x}{3} - \left(\dfrac{x}{4}\right)^2$

In Problems 47 through 53, use the "four-step process" of Section 2.3 to find a slope-predictor formula for the graph $y = f(x)$.

47. $f(x) = 2x^2 + 3x$

48. $f(x) = x - x^3$

49. $f(x) = \dfrac{1}{3-x}$

50. $f(x) = \dfrac{1}{2x+1}$

51. $f(x) = x - \dfrac{1}{x}$

52. $f(x) = \dfrac{x}{x+1}$

53. $f(x) = \dfrac{x+1}{x-1}$

54. Find a slope-predictor formula for the graph
$$f(x) = 3x - x^2 + |2x + 3|$$
at the points where a tangent line exists. Find the point (or points) where no tangent line exists. Sketch the graph of f.

55. Write equations of the two lines through $(3, 4)$ that are tangent to the parabola $y = x^2$. (*Suggestion:* Let (a, a^2) denote either point of tangency; first solve for a.)

56. Write an equation for the circle with center $(2, 3)$ that is tangent to the line with equation $x + y + 3 = 0$.

In Problems 57 through 60, explain why each function is continuous wherever it is defined by the given formula. For each point a where f is not defined by the formula, tell whether a value can be assigned to $f(a)$ in such a way as to make f continuous at a.

57. $f(x) = \dfrac{1-x}{1-x^2}$

58. $f(x) = \dfrac{1-x}{(2-x)^2}$

59. $f(x) = \dfrac{x^2 + x - 2}{x^2 + 2x - 3}$

60. $f(x) = \dfrac{|x^2 - 1|}{x^2 - 1}$

61. Apply the intermediate value property of continuous functions to prove that the equation $x^5 + x = 1$ has a solution.

62. Apply the intermediate value property of continuous functions to prove that the equation $x^3 - 4x^2 + 1 = 0$ has three different solutions.

63. Show that there is a number x between 0 and $\pi/2$ such that $x = \cos x$.

64. Show that there is a number x between $\pi/2$ and π such that $\tan x = -x$. (*Suggestion:* First sketch the graphs of $y = \tan x$ and $y = -x$.)

65. Find how many straight lines through the point $(12, \frac{15}{2})$ are normal to the graph of $y = x^2$ and find the slope of each. (*Suggestion:* The cubic equation you should obtain has one root evident by inspection.)

66. A circle of radius r is dropped into the parabola $y = x^2$. If r is too large, the circle will not fall all the way to the bottom; if r is sufficiently small, the circle will touch the parabola at its vertex $(0, 0)$. (See Fig. 2.MP.1.) Find the largest value of r so that the circle will touch the vertex of the parabola.

FIGURE 2.MP.1 If the circle is too large, it cannot touch the bottom of the parabola (Problem 66).

THE DERIVATIVE

3

Isaac Newton was born in a rural English farming village on Christmas Day in 1642, three months after his father's death. When the boy was three, his mother remarried and left him with his grandmother. Nothing known about his childhood and early schooling hinted that his life and work would constitute a turning point in the history of humanity.

Isaac Newton (1642–1727)

But due to the influence of an uncle who suspected hidden potential in young Isaac, Newton was able to enter Cambridge University in 1661. During the years 1665 and 1666, when Cambridge closed because of the bubonic plague then sweeping Europe, he returned to his country home and there laid the foundations for the three towering achievements of his scientific career—the invention of the calculus, the discovery of the spectrum of colors in light, and the theory of gravitation. Of these two years he later wrote that "in those days I was in the prime of my age of invention and minded mathematics and philosophy more than at any time since." Indeed, his thirties were devoted more to smoky chemical (and even alchemical) experiments than to serious mathematical investigations.

In his forties, while a mathematics professor at Cambridge, Newton wrote the *Principia Mathematica* (1687), perhaps the single most influential scientific treatise ever published. In it he applied the concepts of the calculus to explore the workings of the universe, including the motions of the earth, moon, and planets about the sun. A student is said to have remarked, "There goes the man that wrote a book that neither he nor anyone else understands." But it established for Newton such fame that upon his death in 1727 he was buried alongside his country's greats in Westminster Abbey with such pomp that the French philosopher Voltaire remarked, "I have seen a professor of mathematics ... buried like a king who had done good to his subjects."

Shortly after his Cambridge graduation in 1665, Newton discovered a new method for solving an equation of the form $f(x) = 0$. Unlike special methods such as the quadratic formula that apply only to equations of special form, *Newton's method* can be used to approximate numerical solutions of virtually any equation. In Section 3.8 we present an iterative formulation of Newton's method that is especially adaptable to calculators and computers. There we describe how the combination of Newton's method with modern computer graphics has led to the generation of striking fractal images associated with the science of *chaos*. The pictures here result from the application of a complex-number version of Newton's method to the simple equation $x^3 + 1 = 0$.

3.1 THE DERIVATIVE AND RATES OF CHANGE

In Section 2.1 we saw that the line tangent to the curve $y = f(x)$ (Fig. 3.1.1) at the point $P(a, f(a))$ has slope

$$m = m(a) = \lim_{h \to 0} \frac{f(a+h) - f(a)}{h} \tag{1}$$

provided that this limit exists. As in the slope-prediction formulas of Section 2.2, we get a new function f'—the *derivative* of the original function f—when we replace the constant a in (1) with the independent variable x.

DEFINITION The Derivative
The **derivative** of the function f is the function f' defined by

$$f'(x) = \lim_{h \to 0} \frac{f(x+h) - f(x)}{h} \tag{2}$$

for all x for which this limit exists.

FIGURE 3.1.1 The geometric motivation for the definition of the derivative.

It is important to understand that when the limit in (2) is evaluated, we hold x fixed while h approaches zero. When we are specifically interested in the value $f'(a)$ of the derivative f' at the number $x = a$, we sometimes rewrite Eq. (2) in the form

$$f'(a) = \lim_{h \to 0} \frac{f(a+h) - f(a)}{h} = \lim_{x \to a} \frac{f(x) - f(a)}{x - a}. \tag{3}$$

The second limit in Eq. (3) is obtained from the first by writing $x = a+h$, $h = x-a$, and by noting that $x \to a$ as $h \to 0$ (Fig. 3.1.2). The statement that these equivalent limits exist can be abbreviated as "$f'(a)$ exists." In this case we say that the function f is **differentiable** at $x = a$. The process of finding the derivative f' is called **differentiation** of f.

However it is found, the derivative f' is a slope predictor for lines tangent to the graph $y = f(x)$ of the original function f (Fig. 3.1.1).

FIGURE 3.1.2 The notation in Eq. (3).

The Derivative as Slope Predictor
The slope m of the line tangent to the graph $y = f(x)$ at the point $(a, f(a))$ where $x = a$ is

$$m = f'(a). \tag{4}$$

Application of the point-slope formula gives

$$y - f(a) = f'(a) \cdot (x - a) \tag{5}$$

as an equation of this tangent line.

Differentiating a given function f by direct evaluation of the limit in Eq. (3) involves carrying out four steps:

1. Write the definition in Eq. (2) of the derivative.
2. Substitute the expressions $f(x+h)$ and $f(x)$ as determined by the particular function f.
3. Simplify the result by algebraic methods until it is possible to . . .
4. Apply appropriate limit laws to finally evaluate the limit.

In Section 2.2 we used this same "four-step process" to calculate several slope-predictor functions—that is, derivatives. The limit calculations of Examples 12 and 13 in Section 2.2—where we found the derivatives of the functions

$$f(x) = x + \frac{1}{x} \quad \text{and} \quad f(x) = \sqrt{x}$$

—illustrate algebraic simplification techniques that frequently are useful in the evaluation of derivatives directly from the definition in Eq. (2).

EXAMPLE 1 First apply the definition of the derivative directly to differentiate the function

$$f(x) = \frac{x}{x+3}.$$

Then find the line tangent to the graph of f at the origin, where $f(0) = 0$.

Solution Steps 1 and 2 above give

$$f'(x) = \lim_{h \to 0} \frac{f(x+h) - f(x)}{h} = \lim_{h \to 0} \frac{\dfrac{x+h}{(x+h)+3} - \dfrac{x}{x+3}}{h}.$$

Then an algebraic simplification suggested by the common-denominator calculation

$$\frac{\dfrac{a}{b} - \dfrac{c}{d}}{h} = \frac{\dfrac{ad - bc}{bd}}{h} = \frac{ad - bc}{hbd}$$

yields

$$f'(x) = \lim_{h \to 0} \frac{(x+h)(x+3) - x(x+h+3)}{h(x+h+3)(x+3)}$$

$$= \lim_{h \to 0} \frac{3h}{h(x+h+3)(x+3)} = \lim_{h \to 0} \frac{3}{(x+h+3)(x+3)}$$

$$= \frac{3}{\left(\lim\limits_{h \to 0}(x+h+3)\right)\left(\lim\limits_{h \to 0}(x+3)\right)}.$$

We therefore find finally that

$$f'(x) = \frac{3}{(x+3)(x+3)} = \frac{3}{(x+3)^2}.$$

Substituting $a = 0$, $f(0) = 0$, and $f'(0) = \frac{1}{3}$ in Eq. (5) gives the equation $y = \frac{1}{3}x$ of the line tangent to the graph $y = x/(x+3)$ at the origin $(0, 0)$ (Fig. 3.1.3). ◆

FIGURE 3.1.3 The tangent line $y = \frac{1}{3}x$ to the curve $y = x/(x+3)$ at the origin.

$$y = (px^2) + (qx) + r$$
$$\downarrow \quad \downarrow \quad \downarrow$$
$$m(x) = 2(px) + q + 0$$

FIGURE 3.1.4 Termwise construction of the slope-predictor function $m(x) = 2px + q$ for a parabola $y = px^2 + qx + r$. Note that the exponent 2 in the quadratic term px^2 comes "down out front"—yielding the linear term $2px$—while the linear term qx simply yields the constant q, and the constant term r just "disappears."

Even when the function f is rather simple, this four-step process for computing f' directly from the definition of the derivative can be time consuming. Also, Step 3 may require considerable ingenuity. Moreover, it would be very repetitious to continue to rely on this process. To avoid tedium, we want a fast, easy, short method for computing $f'(x)$.

That new method is one focus of this chapter: the development of systematic methods ("rules") for differentiating those functions that occur most frequently. Such functions include polynomials, rational functions, the trigonometric functions $\sin x$ and $\cos x$, and combinations of such functions. Once we establish these general differentiation rules, we can apply them formally, almost mechanically, to compute derivatives. Only rarely should we need to return to the definition of the derivative.

Figure 3.1.4 illustrates the slope-predictor function for a parabola that we exhibited in Eq. (10) of Section 2.1. Restated in the language of derivatives, this is an example of a "differentiation rule."

RULE Differentiation of Quadratic Functions

The derivative of the quadratic function

$$f(x) = ax^2 + bx + c \tag{6}$$

is the linear function

$$f'(x) = 2ax + b. \tag{7}$$

Note that this rule works in the same way no matter whether we denote the coefficients by a, b, and c as in Eqs. (6) and (7), or by p, q, and r as in Fig. 3.1.4.

It may be instructive to derive the differentiation formula in (7) directly from the definition of the derivative:

$$f'(x) = \lim_{h \to 0} \frac{f(x+h) - f(x)}{h}$$

$$= \lim_{h \to 0} \frac{[a(x+h)^2 + b(x+h) + c] - [ax^2 + bx + c]}{h}$$

$$= \lim_{h \to 0} \frac{(ax^2 + 2ahx + ah^2 + bx + bh + c) - (ax^2 + bx + c)}{h}$$

$$= \lim_{h \to 0} \frac{2ahx + ah^2 + bh}{h}$$

$$= \lim_{h \to 0} (2ax + ah + b).$$

Therefore

$$f'(x) = 2ax + b.$$

Once we know this rule, we need never again apply the definition of the derivative to differentiate a quadratic function.

EXAMPLE 2 (a) If $f(x) = 3x^2 - 4x + 5$, we can apply Eq. (7) to write the derivative immediately, without going through the four-step process:

$$f'(x) = 2 \cdot (3x) + (-4) = 6x - 4.$$

Figure 3.1.5 compares the graph of f with that of its derivative f'.

(b) Similarly, if $g(t) = 2t - 5t^2$, then

$$g'(t) = (2) + 2 \cdot (-5t) = 2 - 10t. \qquad \blacklozenge$$

It makes no difference what the name for the function is or whether we write x or t for the independent variable. This flexibility is valuable—in general, it is such adaptability that makes mathematics applicable to virtually every other branch of human knowledge. In any case, you should learn every differentiation rule in a form independent of the notation used to state it.

We develop additional differentiation rules in Sections 3.2 through 3.4. First, however, we must introduce new notation and a new interpretation of the derivative.

FIGURE 3.1.5 Note that the curve $y = f(x)$ is falling (from left to right) where the derivative $f'(x)$ is negative, and is rising where the derivative is positive.

Differential Notation

An important alternative notation for the derivative originates from the early custom of writing Δx in place of h (because $h = \Delta x$ is an increment in x) and

$$\Delta y = f(x + \Delta x) - f(x)$$

for the resulting change (or increment) in y. The slope of the secant line K of Fig. 3.1.6

FIGURE 3.1.6 Origin of the dy/dx notation.

is then
$$m_{\text{sec}} = \frac{\Delta y}{\Delta x} = \frac{f(x+h) - f(x)}{h},$$
and the slope of the tangent line is
$$m = \frac{dy}{dx} = \lim_{\Delta x \to 0} \frac{\Delta y}{\Delta x}. \tag{8}$$
Hence, if $y = f(x)$, we often write
$$\frac{dy}{dx} = f'(x). \tag{9}$$

(The so-called *differentials* dy and dx are discussed carefully in Chapter 4.) The symbols $f'(x)$ and dy/dx for the derivative of the function $y = f(x)$ are used almost interchangeably in mathematics and its applications, so you need to be familiar with both versions of the notation. You also need to know that dy/dx is a single symbol representing the derivative; it is *not* the quotient of two separate quantities dy and dx.

EXAMPLE 2 (Continued) If $y = ax^2 + bx + c$, then the derivative in Eq. (7) in differential notation takes the form
$$\frac{dy}{dx} = 2ax + b.$$
Consequently,

$$\text{if} \quad y = 3x^2 - 4x + 5, \quad \text{then} \quad \frac{dy}{dx} = 6x - 4;$$

$$\text{if} \quad z = 2t - 5t^2, \quad \text{then} \quad \frac{dz}{dt} = 2 - 10t. \quad \blacklozenge$$

The letter d in the notation dy/dx stands for the word "differential." Whether we write dy/dx or dz/dt, the dependent variable appears "upstairs" and the independent variable "downstairs."

Rates of Change

The derivative of a function serves as a slope predictor for straight lines tangent to the graph of that function. Now we introduce the equally important interpretation of the derivative of a function as the rate of change of that function with respect to the independent variable.

We begin with the *instantaneous rate of change* of a function whose independent variable is time t. Suppose that Q is a quantity that varies with time t, and write $Q = f(t)$ for the value of Q at time t. For example, Q might be

- The size of a population (such as kangaroos, people, or bacteria);
- The number of dollars in a bank account;

- The volume of a balloon being inflated;
- The amount of water in a reservoir with variable inflow and outflow;
- The amount of a chemical product produced in a reaction; or
- The distance traveled t hours after the beginning of a journey.

The change in Q from time t to time $t + \Delta t$ is the **increment**

$$\Delta Q = f(t + \Delta t) - f(t).$$

The **average rate of change** of Q (per unit of time) is, by definition, the ratio of the change ΔQ in Q to the change Δt in t. Thus it is the quotient

$$\frac{\Delta Q}{\Delta t} = \frac{f(t + \Delta t) - f(t)}{\Delta t} \tag{10}$$

illustrated in Fig. 3.1.7.

FIGURE 3.1.7 Average rate of change as a slope.

We define the **instantaneous rate of change** of Q (per unit of time) to be the limit of this average rate as $\Delta t \to 0$. That is, the instantaneous rate of change of Q is

$$\lim_{\Delta t \to 0} \frac{\Delta Q}{\Delta t} = \lim_{\Delta t \to 0} \frac{f(t + \Delta t) - f(t)}{\Delta t}. \tag{11}$$

But the right-hand limit in Eq. (11) is simply the derivative $f'(t)$. So we see that the instantaneous rate of change of $Q = f(t)$ is the derivative

$$\frac{dQ}{dt} = f'(t). \tag{12}$$

To interpret intuitively the concept of instantaneous rate of change, think of the point $P(t, f(t))$ moving along the graph of the function $Q = f(t)$. As Q changes with time t, the point P moves along the curve. But suppose that suddenly, at the instant t, the point P begins to follow a straight-line path—like a whirling particle suddenly cut loose from its string. Then the new path of P would appear as in Fig. 3.1.8. The dashed curve in the figure corresponds to the "originally planned" behavior of Q (before P decided to fly off along the straight-line path). But the straight-line path of P (of constant slope) corresponds to the quantity Q "changing at a constant rate." Because the straight line is tangent to the graph $Q = f(t)$, we can interpret dQ/dt as the instantaneous rate of change of the quantity Q at the instant t:

FIGURE 3.1.8 The relation between the tangent line at $(t, f(t))$ and the instantaneous rate of change of f at t.

The instantaneous rate of change of $Q = f(t)$ at time t is equal to the slope of the line tangent to the curve $Q = f(t)$ at the point $(t, f(t))$.

We can draw additional important conclusions. Because a positive slope corresponds to a rising tangent line and a negative slope corresponds to a falling tangent line (as in Figs. 3.1.9 and 3.1.10), we say that

$$Q \text{ is } \textit{increasing} \text{ at time } t \text{ if } \frac{dQ}{dt} > 0;$$

$$Q \text{ is } \textit{decreasing} \text{ at time } t \text{ if } \frac{dQ}{dt} < 0.$$

(13)

FIGURE 3.1.9 Quantity increasing—derivative positive.

Note The meaning of the phrase "$Q = f(t)$ is increasing *over* (or *during*) the time interval from $t = a$ to $t = b$" should be intuitively clear. The expressions in (13) give us a way to make precise what we mean by "$Q = f(t)$ is increasing *at time t*"—that is, at the instant t. Note also that the fact that a function is increasing at some instant does not necessarily imply that it continues to increase throughout some interval of time; this question is discussed in Section 4.3.

EXAMPLE 3 The cylindrical tank in Fig. 3.1.11 has a vertical axis and is initially filled with 600 gal of water. This tank takes 60 min to empty after a drain in its bottom is opened. Suppose that the drain is opened at time $t = 0$. Suppose also that the volume V of water remaining in the tank after t minutes is

$$V(t) = \tfrac{1}{6}(60 - t)^2 = 600 - 20t + \tfrac{1}{6}t^2$$

gallons. Find the instantaneous rate at which water is flowing out of the tank at time $t = 15$ (min) *and* at time $t = 45$ (min). Also find the average rate at which water flows out of the tank during the half hour from $t = 15$ to $t = 45$.

FIGURE 3.1.10 Quantity decreasing—derivative negative.

Solution The instantaneous rate of change of the volume $V(t)$ of water in the tank is given by the derivative

$$\frac{dV}{dt} = -20 + \tfrac{1}{3}t.$$

At the instants $t = 15$ and $t = 45$ we obtain

$$V'(15) = -20 + \tfrac{1}{3} \cdot 15 = -15$$

and

$$V'(45) = -20 + \tfrac{1}{3} \cdot 45 = -5.$$

The units here are gallons per minute (gal/min). The fact that $V'(15)$ and $V'(45)$ are negative is consistent with the observation that V is a decreasing function of t (as t increases, V decreases). One way to indicate this is to say that after 15 min, the water is flowing *out* of the tank at 15 gal/min; after 45 min, the water is flowing *out* at 5 gal/min. The instantaneous rate of change of V at $t = 15$ is -15 gal/min, and the instantaneous rate of change of V at $t = 45$ is -5 gal/min. We could have predicted the units, because $\Delta V / \Delta t$ is a ratio of gallons to minutes, and therefore its limit $V'(t) = dV/dt$ must be expressed in the same units.

FIGURE 3.1.11 The draining tank of Example 3.

During the time interval of length $\Delta t = 30$ min from time $t = 15$ to time $t = 45$, the *average* rate of change of the volume $V(t)$ is

$$\frac{\Delta V}{\Delta t} = \frac{V(45) - V(15)}{45 - 15}$$

$$= \frac{\tfrac{1}{6}(60 - 45)^2 - \tfrac{1}{6}(60 - 15)^2}{45 - 15} = \frac{-300}{30}.$$

Each numerator in the last equation is measured in gallons—this is especially apparent when you examine the second numerator—and each denominator is measured in minutes. Hence the ratio in the last fraction is a ratio of gallons to minutes, so the average rate of change of the volume V of water *in* the tank is -10 gal/min. Thus the average rate of flow of water *out* of the tank during this half-hour interval is 10 gal/min. ◆

108   CHAPTER 3   The Derivative

Our examples of functions up to this point have been restricted to those with formulas or verbal descriptions. Scientists and engineers often work with tables of values obtained from observations or experiments. Example 4 shows how the instantaneous rate of change of such a tabulated function can be estimated.

EXAMPLE 4 The table in Fig. 3.1.12 gives the U.S. population P (in millions) in the nineteenth century at 10-year intervals. Estimate the instantaneous rate of population growth in 1850.

Solution We take $t = 0$ (yr) in 1800, so $t = 50$ corresponds to the year 1850. In Fig. 3.1.13 we have plotted the given data and then added a freehand sketch of a smooth curve that fits these data.

t	Year	U.S. Population (Millions)
0	1800	5.3
10	1810	7.2
20	1820	9.6
30	1830	12.9
40	1840	17.1
50	1850	23.2
60	1860	31.4
70	1870	38.6
80	1880	50.2
90	1890	62.9
100	1900	76.0

FIGURE 3.1.12 Data for Example 4.

FIGURE 3.1.13 A smooth curve that fits the data of Fig. 3.1.12 well (Example 4).

We hope that this curve fitting the data is a good approximation to the true graph of the unknown function $P = f(t)$. The instantaneous rate of change dP/dt in 1850 is then the slope of the tangent line at the point $(50, 23.2)$. We draw the tangent line as accurately as we can by visual inspection and then measure the base and height of the triangle in Fig. 3.1.13. In this way we approximate the slope of the tangent at $t = 50$ as

$$\frac{dP}{dt} \approx \frac{36}{51} \approx 0.71$$

millions of people per year (in 1850). Although there was no national census in 1851, we would expect the U.S. population then to have been approximately $23.2 + 0.7 = 23.9$ million. ◆

Velocity and Acceleration

Suppose that a particle moves along a horizontal straight line, with its location x at time t given by its **position function** $x = f(t)$. Thus we make the line of motion a coordinate axis with an origin and a positive direction; $f(t)$ is merely the x-coordinate of the moving particle at time t (Fig. 3.1.14).

FIGURE 3.1.14 The particle in motion is at the point $x = f(t)$ at time t.

Think of the time interval from t to $t + \Delta t$. The particle moves from position $f(t)$ to position $f(t + \Delta t)$ during this interval. Its displacement is then the increment

$$\Delta x = f(t + \Delta t) - f(t).$$

We calculate the *average velocity* of the particle during this time interval exactly as we would calculate average speed on a long motor trip: We divide the distance by the time to obtain an average speed in miles per hour. In this case we divide the displacement of the particle by the elapsed time to obtain the **average velocity**

$$\bar{v} = \frac{\Delta x}{\Delta t} = \frac{f(t + \Delta t) - f(t)}{\Delta t}. \tag{14}$$

(The overbar is a standard symbol that usually connotes an average of some sort.) We define the **instantaneous velocity** v of the particle at the time t to be the limit of the average velocity $\bar{v}$ as $\Delta t \to 0$. That is,

$$v = \lim_{\Delta t \to 0} \frac{\Delta x}{\Delta t} = \lim_{\Delta t \to 0} \frac{f(t + \Delta t) - f(t)}{\Delta t}. \tag{15}$$

We recognize the limit on the right in Eq. (15)—it is the definition of the derivative of f at time t. Therefore, the velocity of the moving particle at time t is simply

$$v = \frac{dx}{dt} = f'(t). \tag{16}$$

Thus *velocity is instantaneous rate of change of position*. The velocity of a moving particle may be positive or negative, depending on whether the particle is moving in the positive or negative direction along the line of motion. We define the **speed** of the particle to be the *absolute value* $|v|$ of the velocity.

EXAMPLE 5 Figure 3.1.15 shows a car moving along the (horizontal) x-axis. Suppose that its position (in feet) at time t (in seconds) is given by

$$x(t) = 5t^2 + 100.$$

FIGURE 3.1.15 The car of Example 5.

Then its velocity at time t is

$$v(t) = x'(t) = 10t.$$

Because $x(0) = 100$ and $v(0) = 0$, the car starts at time $t = 0$ from rest—$v(0) = 0$—at the point $x = 100$. Substituting $t = 10$, we see that $x(10) = 600$ and $v(10) = 100$, so after 10 s the car has traveled 500 ft (from its starting point $x = 100$), and its speed then is 100 ft/s. ◆

Vertical Motion

In the case of vertical motion—such as that of a ball thrown straight upward—it is common to denote the position function by $y(t)$ rather than by $x(t)$. Typically, $y(t)$ denotes the height above the ground at time t, as in Fig. 3.1.16. But velocity is still the derivative of position:

$$v(t) = \frac{dy}{dt}.$$

Upward motion with y increasing corresponds to *positive velocity*, $v > 0$ (Fig. 3.1.17). *Downward motion* with y decreasing corresponds to *negative velocity*, $v < 0$.

The case of vertical motion under the influence of constant gravity is of special interest. If a particle is projected straight upward from an initial height y_0 (ft) above the ground at time $t = 0$ (s) and with initial velocity v_0 (ft/s) *and* if air resistance is negligible, then its height y (in feet above the ground) at time t is given by a formula known from physics,

$$y(t) = -\tfrac{1}{2}gt^2 + v_0 t + y_0. \tag{17}$$

FIGURE 3.1.16 Vertical motion with position function $y(t)$.

FIGURE 3.1.17 Upward motion and downward motion.

Here g denotes the *acceleration* due to the force of gravity. Near the surface of the earth, g is nearly constant, so we assume that it is exactly constant, and at the surface of the earth, $g \approx 32$ ft/s^2, or $g \approx 9.8$ m/s^2.

If we differentiate y with respect to time t, we obtain the velocity of the particle at time t:

$$v(t) = \frac{dy}{dt} = -gt + v_0. \tag{18}$$

The **acceleration** of the particle is defined to be the instantaneous time rate of change (derivative) of its velocity:

$$a = \frac{dv}{dt} = -g. \tag{19}$$

Your intuition should tell you that a body projected upward in this way will reach its maximum height at the instant that its velocity becomes zero—when $v(t) = 0$. (We shall see in Section 3.5 why this is true.)

EXAMPLE 6 Find the maximum height attained by a ball thrown straight upward from the ground with initial velocity $v_0 = +96$ ft/s. Also find the velocity with which it hits the ground upon its return.

Solution To begin the solution of a motion problem such as this, we sketch a diagram like Fig. 3.1.18, indicating both the given data and the data that are unknown at the time instants in question. Here we focus on the time $t = 0$ when the ball leaves the ground ($y = 0$), the unknown time when it reaches its maximum height with velocity $v = 0$, and the unknown time when it returns to the ground.

We begin by substituting $y_0 = 0$, $v_0 = 96$, and $g = 32$ in Eq. (17). Then the height of the ball at time t (so long as it remains aloft) is given by

$$y(t) = -16t^2 + 96t.$$

Then differentiation gives its velocity at time t,

$$v(t) = y'(t) = -32t + 96$$

(see Fig. 3.1.19). The ball attains its maximum height when $v = 0$; that is, when

$$v(t) = -32t + 96 = 0.$$

This occurs when $t = 3$ (s). Substituting $t = 3$ in the height function $y(t)$ gives the maximum height of the ball,

$$y_{max} = y(3) = -16 \cdot (3)^2 + 96 \cdot (3) = 144 \quad \text{(ft)}.$$

The ball returns to the ground when $y(t) = 0$. The equation

$$y(t) = -16t^2 + 96t = -16t(t - 6) = 0$$

has the two solutions $t = 0$ and $t = 6$. Thus the ball returns to the ground at time $t = 6$. The velocity with which it strikes the ground is

$$v(t) = (-32)(6) + 96 = -96 \quad \text{(ft/s)}. \quad \blacklozenge$$

FIGURE 3.1.18 Data for the ball of Example 6.

FIGURE 3.1.19 Note that the ball is rising when its velocity $v > 0$, falling when $v < 0$, and is at its apex when $v = 0$.

Other Rates of Change

The derivative of any function—not merely a function of time—may be interpreted as its instantaneous rate of change with respect to the independent variable. If $y = f(x)$, then the **average rate of change** of y (per unit change in x) on the interval $[x, x + \Delta x]$ is the quotient

$$\frac{\Delta y}{\Delta x} = \frac{f(x + \Delta x) - f(x)}{\Delta x}.$$

The **instantaneous rate of change** of y **with respect to** x is the limit, as $\Delta x \to 0$, of the average rate of change. Thus the instantaneous rate of change of y with respect to x is

$$\lim_{\Delta x \to 0} \frac{\Delta y}{\Delta x} = \frac{dy}{dx} = f'(x). \tag{20}$$

Example 7 illustrates the fact that a dependent variable may sometimes be expressed as two different functions of two different independent variables. The derivatives of these functions are then rates of change of the dependent variable with respect to the two different independent variables.

EXAMPLE 7 The area of a square with edge length x centimeters is $A = x^2$, so the derivative of A with respect to x,

$$\frac{dA}{dx} = 2x, \tag{21}$$

is the rate of change of its area A with respect to x. (See the computations in Fig. 3.1.20.) The units of dA/dx are square centimeters *per centimeter*. Now suppose that the edge length of the square is increasing with time: $x = 5t$, with time t in seconds. Then the area of the square at time t is

$$A = (5t)^2 = 25t^2.$$

The derivative of A with respect to t is

$$\frac{dA}{dt} = 2 \cdot 25t = 50t; \tag{22}$$

this is the rate of change of A with respect to time t, with units of square centimeters *per second*. For instance, when $t = 10$ (so $x = 50$), the values of the two derivatives of A in Eqs. (21) and (22) are

$$\left.\frac{dA}{dx}\right|_{x=50} = 2 \cdot 50 = 100 \quad (\text{cm}^2/\text{cm})$$

and

$$\left.\frac{dA}{dt}\right|_{t=10} = 50 \cdot 10 = 500 \quad (\text{cm}^2/\text{s}).$$

Thus A is increasing at the rate of 100 cm² per cm increase in x, and at the rate of 500 cm² per second increase in t. ◆

FIGURE 3.1.20 The square of Example 7:
$A + \Delta A = (x + \Delta x)^2$;
$\Delta A = 2x\Delta x + (\Delta x)^2$;
$\frac{\Delta A}{\Delta x} = 2x + \Delta x$;
$\frac{dA}{dx} = 2x$.

The notation dA/dt for the derivative suffers from the minor inconvenience of not providing a "place" to substitute a particular value of t, such as $t = 10$. The last lines of Example 7 illustrate one way around this difficulty.

Just as we can speak of whether the quantity $Q(t)$ is increasing or decreasing at time $t = a$—according as $Q'(a) > 0$ or $Q'(a) < 0$—we can ask whether the function $y = f(x)$ is an increasing or decreasing function of x. Thinking of rising tangent lines with positive slopes, and falling tangent lines with negative slopes, we say in analogy with (13) that

y is *increasing* at the point $x = a$ if $f'(a) > 0$;

y is *decreasing* at the point $x = a$ if $f'(a) < 0$.

EXAMPLE 8 Figure 3.1.21 shows the graphs $y = f(x)$ of a function and $y = f'(x)$ of its derivative. Observe that

- $y = f(x)$ has a horizontal tangent line at points where $f'(x) = 0$;
- $f(x)$ is increasing on open intervals where $f'(x) > 0$; and
- $f(x)$ is decreasing on open intervals where $f'(x) < 0$. ◆

FIGURE 3.1.21 Correspondence between the function graph $y = f(x)$ and the derivative graph $y = f'(x)$.

3.1 TRUE/FALSE STUDY GUIDE
3.1 CONCEPTS: QUESTIONS AND DISCUSSION

1. The slope line in Fig. 3.1.5 looks as if it might be tangent to the parabola. Is it? If not, what's a simple way you could alter the equation of the parabola—without changing its slope line—in order to ensure that the line will be tangent to the altered parabola?
2. When a ball is tossed straight upward, it may appear to hover at the apex of its trajectory for a brief period of time. Does it?
3. You are pulled over by a policeman who claims that you did not stop properly at a stop sign. You argue that as you braked your car, its velocity was zero at a certain instant before you removed your foot from the brake pedal and proceeded through the intersection. The policeman replies that you nevertheless did not come to a full stop—that he is certain your velocity did not remain zero for even a hundredth of a second. What's the cause of this disagreement? Explain it with such convincing clarity that the judge will let you off without you paying a fine.
4. The ball of Example 6 took the same amount of time to rise from the ground to its highest point as to fall back to the ground. Is this always the case for a ball governed by Eqs. (17) and (18) of this section? *Suggestion:* In lieu of a blizzard of algebra, think about the symmetry of the parabola in Fig. 3.1.19.

3.1 PROBLEMS

In Problems 1 through 10, find the indicated derivative by using the differentiation rule in Eqs. (6) and (7):

If $f(x) = ax^2 + bx + c$, then $f'(x) = 2ax + b$.

1. $f(x) = 4x - 5$; find $f'(x)$.
2. $g(t) = 100 - 16t^2$; find $g'(t)$.
3. $h(z) = z(25 - z)$; find $h'(z)$.
4. $f(x) = 16 - 49x$; find $f'(x)$.
5. $y = 2x^2 + 3x - 17$; find dy/dx.
6. $x = 16t - 100t^2$; find dx/dt.
7. $z = 5u^2 - 3u$; find dz/du.
8. $v = 5y(100 - y)$; find dv/dy.
9. $x = -5y^2 + 17y + 300$; find dx/dy.
10. $u = 7t^2 + 13t$; find du/dt.

In Problems 11 through 20, apply the definition of the derivative (as in Example 1) to find $f'(x)$.

11. $f(x) = 2x - 1$
12. $f(x) = 2 - 3x$
13. $f(x) = x^2 + 5$
14. $f(x) = 3 - 2x^2$
15. $f(x) = \dfrac{1}{2x+1}$
16. $f(x) = \dfrac{1}{3-x}$
17. $f(x) = \sqrt{2x+1}$
18. $f(x) = \dfrac{1}{\sqrt{x+1}}$
19. $f(x) = \dfrac{x}{1-2x}$
20. $f(x) = \dfrac{x+1}{x-1}$

In Problems 21 through 25, the position function $x = f(t)$ of a particle moving in a horizontal straight line is given. Find its location x when its velocity v is zero.

21. $x = 100 - 16t^2$
22. $x = -16t^2 + 160t + 25$
23. $x = -16t^2 + 80t - 1$
24. $x = 100t^2 + 50$
25. $x = 100 - 20t - 5t^2$

In Problems 26 through 29, the height $y(t)$ (in feet at time t seconds) of a ball thrown vertically upward is given. Find the maximum height that the ball attains.

26. $y = -16t^2 + 160t$
27. $y = -16t^2 + 64t$
28. $y = -16t^2 + 128t + 25$
29. $y = -16t^2 + 96t + 50$

In Problems 30 through 35 (Figs. 3.1.22 through 3.1.27), match the given graph of the function f with that of its derivative, which appears among those in Fig. 3.1.28, parts (a) through (f).

30. Figure 3.1.22
31. Figure 3.1.23

FIGURE 3.1.22

FIGURE 3.1.23

32. Figure 3.1.24   **33.** Figure 3.1.25   **34.** Figure 3.1.26   **35.** Figure 3.1.27

FIGURE 3.1.24

FIGURE 3.1.25

FIGURE 3.1.26

FIGURE 3.1.27

FIGURE 3.1.28(a)

FIGURE 3.1.28(b)

FIGURE 3.1.28(c)

FIGURE 3.1.28(d)

FIGURE 3.1.28(e)

FIGURE 3.1.28(f)

36. The Celsius temperature C is given in terms of the Fahrenheit temperature F by $C = \frac{5}{9}(F - 32)$. Find the rate of change of C with respect to F and the rate of change of F with respect to C.

37. Find the rate of change of the area A of a circle with respect to its circumference C.

38. A stone dropped into a pond at time $t = 0$ s causes a circular ripple that travels out from the point of impact at 5 m/s. At what rate (in square meters per second) is the area within the circle increasing when $t = 10$?

39. A car is traveling at 100 ft/s when the driver suddenly applies the brakes ($x = 0, t = 0$). The position function of the skidding car is $x(t) = 100t - 5t^2$. How far and for how long does the car skid before it comes to a stop?

40. A water bucket containing 10 gal of water develops a leak at time $t = 0$, and the volume V of water in the bucket t seconds later is given by

$$V(t) = 10\left(1 - \frac{t}{100}\right)^2$$

until the bucket is empty at time $t = 100$. (a) At what rate is water leaking from the bucket after exactly 1 min has passed? (b) When is the instantaneous rate of change of V equal to the average rate of change of V from $t = 0$ to $t = 100$?

41. A population of chipmunks moves into a new region at time $t = 0$. At time t (in months), the population numbers

$$P(t) = 100[1 + (0.3)t + (0.04)t^2].$$

(a) How long does it take for this population to double its initial size $P(0)$? (b) What is the rate of growth of the population when $P = 200$?

42. The following data describe the growth of the population P (in thousands) of Gotham City during a 10-year period. Use the graphical method of Example 4 to estimate its rate of growth in 1989.

Year	1984	1986	1988	1990	1992	1994
P	265	293	324	358	395	427

43. The following data give the distance x in feet traveled by an accelerating car (that starts from rest at time $t = 0$) in the first t seconds. Use the graphical method of Example 4 to estimate its speed (in miles per hour) when $t = 20$ and again when $t = 40$.

t	0	10	20	30	40	50	60
x	0	224	810	1655	2686	3850	5109

In Problems 44 through 49, use the fact (proved in Section 3.2) that the derivative of $y = ax^3 + bx^2 + cx + d$ is $dy/dx = 3ax^2 + 2bx + c$.

44. Prove that the rate of change of the volume V of a cube with respect to its edge length x is equal to half the surface area A of the cube (Fig. 3.1.29).

FIGURE 3.1.29 The cube of Problem 44—volume $V = x^3$, surface area $S = 6x^2$.

45. Show that the rate of change of the volume V of a sphere with respect to its radius R is equal to its surface area S (Fig. 3.1.30).

FIGURE 3.1.30 The sphere of Problem 45—volume $V = \frac{4}{3}\pi r^3$ surface area $S = 4\pi r^2$.

46. The height h of a certain cylinder whose height changes is always twice its radius r. Show that the rate of change of its volume V with respect to r is equal to its total surface area S (Fig. 3.1.31).

FIGURE 3.1.31 The cylinder of Problem 46—volume $V = \pi r^2 h$, surface area $S = 2\pi r^2 + 2\pi rh$.

47. A spherical balloon with an initial radius r of 5 in. begins to leak at time $t = 0$, and its radius t seconds later is $r = (60 - t)/12$ in. At what rate (in cubic inches per second) is air leaking from the balloon when $t = 30$?

48. The volume V (in liters) of 3 g of CO_2 at $27°C$ is given in terms of its pressure p (in atmospheres) by the formula $V = 1.68/p$. What is the rate of change of V with respect to p when $p = 2$ (atm)? (*Suggestion:* Use the fact that the derivative of $f(x) = c/x$ is $f'(x) = -c/x^2$ if c is a constant; you can establish this by using the definition of the derivative.)

49. As a snowball with an initial radius of 12 cm melts, its radius decreases at a constant rate. It begins to melt when $t = 0$ (h) and takes 12 h to disappear. (a) What is its rate of change of volume when $t = 6$? (b) What is its average rate of change of volume from $t = 3$ to $t = 9$?

50. A ball thrown vertically upward at time $t = 0$ (s) with initial velocity 96 ft/s and with initial height 112 ft has height function $y(t) = -16t^2 + 96t + 112$. (a) What is the maximum height attained by the ball? (b) When and with what impact speed does the ball hit the ground?

51. A spaceship approaching touchdown on the planet Gzyx has height y (meters) at time t (seconds) given by $y = 100 - 100t + 25t^2$. When and with what speed does it hit the ground?

52. The population (in thousands) of the city Metropolis is given by

$$P(t) = 100[1 + (0.04)t + (0.003)t^2],$$

with t in years and with $t = 0$ corresponding to 1980. (a) What was the rate of change of P in 1986? (b) What was the average rate of change of P from 1983 to 1988?

53. Suppose that during the 1990s the population P of a small city was given by

$$P(t) = 10 + t - 0.1t^2 + 0.006t^3$$

(with t in years and P is thousands). Taking $t=0$ on January 1, 1990, find the time(s) during the 1990s at which the instantaneous rate of change of this population was equal to its average rate of change during the whole decade. (Use the differentiation formulas given in the instructions for Problem 44–49.)

*Problems 54 through 60 involve the **left-hand** and **right-hand** derivatives of f at a that are defined by*

$$f'_-(a) = \lim_{h \to 0^-} \frac{f(a+h) - f(a)}{h}$$

and

$$f'_+(a) = \lim_{h \to 0^+} \frac{f(a+h) - f(a)}{h},$$

(assuming these limits exist). Then $f'(a)$ exists if and only both the left-hand and right-hand derivatives exist and $f'_-(a) = f'_+(a)$.

54. (a) Find $f'_-(0)$ and $f'_+(0)$ given $f(x) = |x|$. (b) The function $f(x) = |2x - 10|$ is differentiable except at a single point. What is this point, and what are the values of its left-hand and right-hand derivatives of f there?

55. Sketch the graph of the given function f and determine if it is differentiable at $x = 0$:

   (a) $f(x) = \begin{cases} x & \text{if } x < 0, \\ 2x & \text{if } x \geq 0; \end{cases}$

   (b) $f(x) = \begin{cases} x^2 & \text{if } x < 0, \\ 2x^2 & \text{if } x \geq 0. \end{cases}$

56. Investigate the differentiability of the function f defined by
$$f(x) = \begin{cases} 2x + 1 & \text{if } x < 1, \\ 4x - x^2 & \text{if } x \geq 1. \end{cases}$$

57. Investigate the differentiability of the function f defined by
$$f(x) = \begin{cases} 11 + 6x - x^2 & \text{if } x < 3, \\ x^2 - 6x + 29 & \text{if } x \geq 3. \end{cases}$$

58. Sketch the graph of the function $f(x) = x \cdot |x|$ and show that it is differentiable everywhere. Can you write a single (one-part) formula that gives the value of $f'(x)$ both for $x > 0$ and for $x < 0$?

59. Sketch the graph of the function $f(x) = x + |x|$. Then investigate its differentiability. Find the derivative $f'(x)$ where it exists; find the one-sided derivatives at the points where $f'(x)$ does not exist.

60. Repeat Problem 59, except with the function $f(x) = x \cdot (x + |x|)$.

3.2 | BASIC DIFFERENTIATION RULES

Here we begin our systematic development of formal rules for finding the derivative f' of the function f:

$$f'(x) = \lim_{h \to 0} \frac{f(x+h) - f(x)}{h}. \quad (1)$$

Some alternative notation for derivatives will be helpful.

When we interpreted the derivative in Section 3.1 as a rate of change, we found it useful to employ the dependent-independent variable notation

$$y = f(x), \quad \Delta x = h, \quad \Delta y = f(x + \Delta x) - f(x). \quad (2)$$

This led to the "differential notation"

$$\frac{dy}{dx} = \lim_{\Delta x \to 0} \frac{\Delta y}{\Delta x} = \lim_{\Delta x \to 0} \frac{f(x + \Delta x) - f(x)}{\Delta x} \quad (3)$$

for the derivative. When you use this notation, remember that the symbol dy/dx is simply another notation for the derivative $f'(x)$; it is *not* the quotient of two separate entities dy and dx.

A third notation is sometimes used for the derivative $f'(x)$; it is $D_x f(x)$. Here, think of D_x as a "machine" that operates on the function f to produce its derivative $D_x f$ with respect to x (Fig. 3.2.1). Thus we can write the derivative of $y = f(x) = x^3$ in any of three ways:

$$f'(x) = \frac{dy}{dx} = D_x x^3 = 3x^2.$$

These three notations for the derivative—the function notation $f'(x)$, the differential notation dy/dx, and the operator notation $D_x f(x)$—are used almost interchangeably in mathematical and scientific writing, so you need to be familiar with each.

The Derivative of a Constant

Our first differentiation rule says that *the derivative of a constant function is identically zero*. Geometry makes this obvious, because the graph of a constant function is a horizontal straight line that is its own tangent line, with slope zero at every point (Fig. 3.2.2).

FIGURE 3.2.1 The "differentiation machine" D_x.

FIGURE 3.2.2 The derivative of a constant-valued function is zero (Theorem 1).

THEOREM 1 Derivative of a Constant
If $f(x) = c$ (a constant) for all x, then $f'(x) = 0$ for all x. That is,

$$\frac{dc}{dx} = D_x c = 0. \tag{4}$$

PROOF Because $f(x+h) = f(x) = c$, we see that

$$f'(x) = \lim_{h \to 0} \frac{f(x+h) - f(x)}{h} = \lim_{h \to 0} \frac{c - c}{h} = \lim_{h \to 0} \frac{0}{h} = 0. \qquad \blacktriangleleft$$

The Power Rule

As motivation for the next rule, consider the following list of derivatives, all of which have already appeared in the text (or as problems). The first two are special cases of the formula $D_x(ax^2 + bx + c) = 2ax + b$.

$D_x x = 1$

$D_x x^2 = 2x = 2 \cdot x^1$

$D_x x^3 = 3 \cdot x^2$ (Problem 37, Section 2.2)

$D_x \dfrac{1}{x} = D_x x^{-1} = -\dfrac{1}{x^2} = -1 \cdot x^{-2}$ (Problem 38, Section 2.2)

$D_x \dfrac{1}{x^2} = D_x x^{-2} = -\dfrac{2}{x^3} = -2 \cdot x^{-3}$ (Problem 39, Section 2.2)

$D_x \sqrt{x} = D_x x^{1/2} = \dfrac{1}{2\sqrt{x}} = \dfrac{1}{2} \cdot x^{-1/2}$ (Example 13, Section 2.2)

Each of these formulas fits the simple pattern

$$D_x x^n = n x^{n-1}, \tag{5}$$

in which the exponent n is simultaneously placed before the variable and, in the exponent, is decreased by 1. Thus it appears that the blanks in the pattern

$$D_x x^{\square} = \square x^{\square - 1}$$

can be filled with any (single) integer you please, or even the fraction $\frac{1}{2}$. But Eq. (5)—inferred from the preceding list of derivatives—is as yet only a conjecture. Nevertheless, many discoveries in mathematics are made by detecting such patterns, then proving that they hold universally.

Eventually we shall see that the formula in Eq. (5), called the **power rule,** is valid for all real numbers n. At this time we give a proof only for the case in which the exponent n is a *positive integer.*

THEOREM 2 Power Rule for a Positive Integer n
If n is a positive integer and $f(x) = x^n$, then

$$f'(x) = n x^{n-1}. \tag{6}$$

PROOF For a positive integer n, the identity

$$b^n - a^n = (b - a)(b^{n-1} + b^{n-2} a + b^{n-3} a^2 + \cdots + b a^{n-2} + a^{n-1})$$

is easy to verify by multiplication. Thus, if $b \neq a$, then

$$\frac{b^n - a^n}{b - a} = b^{n-1} + b^{n-2} a + b^{n-3} a^2 + \cdots + b a^{n-2} + a^{n-1}.$$

Because each of the n terms on the right-hand side approaches a^{n-1} as $b \to a$, this tells us that

$$\lim_{b \to a} \frac{b^n - a^n}{b - a} = na^{n-1}$$

by various limit laws. Now let $b = x + h$ and $a = x$, so that $h = b - a$. Then $h \to 0$ as $b \to a$, and hence

$$f'(x) = \lim_{h \to 0} \frac{(x+h)^n - x^n}{h} = nx^{n-1}. \tag{7}$$

This establishes Theorem 2. ◄

We need not always use the same symbols x and n for the independent variable and the constant exponent in the power rule. For instance,

$$D_t t^m = mt^{m-1} \quad \text{and} \quad D_z z^k = kz^{k-1}.$$

If it is perfectly clear what the independent variable is, the subscript may be dropped from D_x (or D_t, or D_z), as in Example 1.

EXAMPLE 1 $Dx^7 = 7x^6, \qquad Dt^{17} = 17t^{16}, \qquad Dz^{100} = 100z^{99}.$ ◆

The Derivative of a Linear Combination

To use the power rule to differentiate polynomials, we need to know how to differentiate *linear combinations*. A **linear combination** of the functions f and g is a function of the form $af + bg$ where a and b are constants. It follows from the sum and product laws for limits that

$$\lim_{x \to c} [af(x) + bg(x)] = a \left(\lim_{x \to c} f(x) \right) + b \left(\lim_{x \to c} g(x) \right) \tag{8}$$

provided that the two limits on the right in Eq. (8) both exist. The formula in Eq. (8) is called the **linearity property** of the limit operation. It implies an analogous linearity property of differentiation.

THEOREM 3 Derivative of a Linear Combination

If f and g are differentiable functions and a and b are fixed real numbers, then

$$D_x[af(x) + bg(x)] = a[D_x f(x)] + b[D_x g(x)]. \tag{9}$$

With $u = f(x)$ and $v = g(x)$, this takes the form

$$\frac{d(au + bv)}{dx} = a\frac{du}{dx} + b\frac{dv}{dx}. \tag{9'}$$

PROOF The linearity property of limits immediately gives

$$D_x[af(x) + bg(x)] = \lim_{h \to 0} \frac{[af(x+h) + bg(x+h)] - [af(x) + bg(x)]}{h}$$

$$= a \left(\lim_{h \to 0} \frac{f(x+h) - f(x)}{h} \right) + b \left(\lim_{h \to 0} \frac{g(x+h) - g(x)}{h} \right)$$

$$= a[D_x f(x)] + b[D_x g(x)],$$

as desired. ◄

Now take $a = c$ and $b = 0$ in Eq. (9). The result is

$$D_x[cf(x)] = cD_x f(x); \tag{10}$$

alternatively,

$$\frac{d(cu)}{dx} = c\frac{du}{dx}, \tag{10'}$$

Thus *the derivative of a constant multiple of a function is the same constant multiple of its derivative.*

EXAMPLE 2

(a) $D_x(16x^6) = 16 \cdot 6x^5 = 96x^5$.
(b) If $f(z) = 7z^3$, then $f'(z) = 21z^2$.
(c) $\dfrac{d}{du}(99u^{100}) = 9900u^{99}$.

◆

Next, take $a = b = 1$ in Eq. (9). We find that

$$D_x[f(x) + g(x)] = [D_x f(x)] + [D_x g(x)]. \tag{11}$$

In differential notation,

$$\frac{d(u+v)}{dx} = \frac{du}{dx} + \frac{dv}{dx}. \tag{11'}$$

Thus *the derivative of the sum of two functions is the sum of their derivatives.* Similarly, for differences we have

$$\frac{d(u-v)}{dx} = \frac{du}{dx} - \frac{dv}{dx}. \tag{12}$$

It's easy to see that these rules generalize to sums and differences of more than two functions. For example, repeated application of Eq. (11) to the sum of a finite number of differentiable functions gives

$$\frac{d(u_1 + u_2 + \cdots + u_n)}{dx} = \frac{du_1}{dx} + \frac{du_2}{dx} + \cdots + \frac{du_n}{dx}. \tag{13}$$

REMARK Equation (13) tells us that, when differentiating a sum of terms, we simply differentiate each term and then add the results.

EXAMPLE 3

$$D_x(36 + 26x + 7x^5 - 5x^9) = 0 + 26 \cdot 1 + 7 \cdot 5x^4 - 5 \cdot 9x^8$$
$$= 26 + 35x^4 - 45x^8.$$

◆

The Derivative of a Polynomial

When we apply Eqs. (10) and (13) and the power rule to the polynomial

$$p(x) = a_n x^n + a_{n-1} x^{n-1} + \cdots + a_2 x^2 + a_1 x + a_0$$

(and thus differentiate termwise), we find the derivative *as fast as we can write it:*

$$p'(x) = na_n x^{n-1} + (n-1)a_{n-1} x^{n-2} + \cdots + 3a_3 x^2 + 2a_2 x + a_1. \tag{14}$$

With this result, it becomes a routine matter to write an equation for a line tangent to the graph of a polynomial.

EXAMPLE 4 Write an equation for the straight line that is tangent to the graph of $y = 2x^3 - 7x^2 + 3x + 4$ at the point $(1, 2)$.

Solution We compute the derivative as in Eq. (14):

$$\frac{dy}{dx} = 2 \cdot 3x^2 - 7 \cdot 2x + 3 + 0 = 6x^2 - 14x + 3.$$

We substitute $x = 1$ in dy/dx and find that the slope of the tangent line at $(1, 2)$ is $m = -5$. So the point-slope equation of the tangent line is

$$y - 2 = -5(x - 1);$$

that is,

$$y = -5x + 7.$$

A calculator- or computer-generated picture like Fig. 3.2.3 provides suggestive visual evidence of the validity of this tangent line computation. ◆

FIGURE 3.2.3 The graph $y = 2x^3 - 7x^2 + 3x + 4$ and its tangent line $y = -5x + 7$ at the point $(1, 2)$.

EXAMPLE 5 The volume V (in cubic centimeters) of a given sample of water varies with changing temperature T. For T between $0°C$ and $30°C$, the relation is given almost exactly by the formula

$$V = V_0[1 - (6.427 \times 10^{-5})T + (8.505 \times 10^{-6})T^2 - (6.790 \times 10^{-8})T^3],$$

where V_0 is the volume of the water (*not* ice) sample at $0°C$. Suppose that $V_0 = 10^5$ cm^3. Find both the volume and the rate of change of volume with respect to temperature when $T = 20°C$.

Solution Substituting $V_0 = 10^5 = 100{,}000$ in the given volume formula yields

$$V(T) = 100{,}000 - (6.427)T + (0.8505)T^2 - (0.00679)T^3.$$

Then substituting $T = 20$ yields $V(20) \approx 100{,}157.34$, so the sample would expand by about 157 cm^3 if heated from $0°C$ to $20°C$. The rate of change of volume V with respect to temperature T is given by

$$\frac{dV}{dT} = -6.427 + (1.7010)T - (0.02037)T^2,$$

and substituting $T = 20$ here yields

$$\left.\frac{dV}{dT}\right|_{T=20} \approx 19.45 \quad (\text{cm}^3/°C).$$

Thus we should expect the volume of the water sample to increase by slightly more than 19 cm^3 if it is heated by $1°C$ from $20°C$ to $21°C$. In fact, direct substitution into the original volume formula gives

$$V(21) - V(20) \approx 19.88.$$

Finally, we note that the average rate of change of V with respect to T on the interval $19.5 \leq T \leq 20.5$ centered at $T = 20$ is

$$\frac{\Delta V}{\Delta T} = \frac{V(20.5) - V(19.5)}{20.5 - 19.5} \approx 19.44 \quad (\text{cm}^3/°C),$$

which is very close to the derivative dV/dT at $T = 20$. ◆

The Product Rule and the Quotient Rule

It might be natural to conjecture that the derivative of a product $f(x)g(x)$ is the product of the derivatives. This is *false!* For example, if $f(x) = g(x) = x$, then

$$D_x[f(x)g(x)] = D_x x^2 = 2x.$$

But
$$[D_x f(x)] \cdot [D_x g(x)] = (D_x x) \cdot (D_x x) = 1 \cdot 1 = 1.$$

In general, the derivative of a product is *not* merely the product of the derivatives. Theorem 4 tells us what it *is*.

THEOREM 4 The Product Rule
If f and g are differentiable at x, then fg is differentiable at x, and
$$D_x[f(x)g(x)] = f'(x)g(x) + f(x)g'(x). \tag{15}$$
With $u = f(x)$ and $v = g(x)$, this **product rule** takes the form
$$\frac{d(uv)}{dx} = u\frac{dv}{dx} + v\frac{du}{dx}. \tag{15'}$$
When it is clear what the independent variable is, we can write the product rule even more briefly:
$$(uv)' = u'v + uv'. \tag{15''}$$

PROOF We use an "add and subtract" device.
$$D_x[f(x)g(x)] = \lim_{h \to 0} \frac{f(x+h)g(x+h) - f(x)g(x)}{h}$$
$$= \lim_{h \to 0} \frac{f(x+h)g(x+h) - f(x)g(x+h) + f(x)g(x+h) - f(x)g(x)}{h}$$
$$= \lim_{h \to 0} \frac{f(x+h)g(x+h) - f(x)g(x+h)}{h} + \lim_{h \to 0} \frac{f(x)g(x+h) - f(x)g(x)}{h}$$
$$= \left(\lim_{h \to 0} \frac{f(x+h) - f(x)}{h} \right) \left(\lim_{h \to 0} g(x+h) \right) + f(x) \left(\lim_{h \to 0} \frac{g(x+h) - g(x)}{h} \right)$$
$$= f'(x)g(x) + f(x)g'(x). \quad \blacktriangleleft$$

In this proof we used the sum law and product law for limits, the definitions of $f'(x)$ and $g'(x)$, and the fact that
$$\lim_{h \to 0} g(x+h) = g(x).$$

This last equation holds because g is differentiable and therefore continuous at x (as we will see in Theorem 2 in Section 3.4).

In words, the product rule says that *the derivative of the product of two functions is formed by multiplying the derivative of each by the other and then adding the results.*

EXAMPLE 6 Find the derivative of
$$f(x) = (1 - 4x^3)(3x^2 - 5x + 2)$$
without first multiplying out the two factors.

Solution
$$D_x[(1 - 4x^3)(3x^2 - 5x + 2)]$$
$$= [D_x(1 - 4x^3)](3x^2 - 5x + 2) + (1 - 4x^3)[D_x(3x^2 - 5x + 2)]$$
$$= (-12x^2)(3x^2 - 5x + 2) + (1 - 4x^3)(6x - 5)$$
$$= -60x^4 + 80x^3 - 24x^2 + 6x - 5. \quad \blacklozenge$$

We can apply the product rule repeatedly to find the derivative of a product of three or more differentiable functions $u_1, u_2, \ldots, u_n$ of x. For example,

$$\begin{aligned} D[u_1 u_2 u_3] &= (u_1 u_2)' u_3 + (u_1 u_2) u_3' \\ &= (u_1' u_2 + u_1 u_2') u_3 + u_1 u_2 u_3' \\ &= u_1' u_2 u_3 + u_1 u_2' u_3 + u_1 u_2 u_3'. \end{aligned}$$

Note that the derivative of each factor in the original product is multiplied by the other two factors and then the three resulting products are added. This is, indeed, the general result:

$$D(u_1 u_2 \cdots u_n) = u_1' u_2 u_3 \cdots u_{n-1} u_n + u_1 u_2' u_3 \cdots u_{n-1} u_n + \cdots + u_1 u_2 u_3 \cdots u_{n-1} u_n', \tag{16}$$

where the sum in Eq. (16) has one term corresponding to each of the n factors in the product $u_1 u_2 \cdots u_n$. It is easy to establish this **extended product rule** (see Problem 62) one step at a time—next with $n = 4$, then with $n = 5$, and so forth.

Our next result tells us how to find the derivative of the reciprocal of a function if we know the derivative of the function itself.

THEOREM The Reciprocal Rule
If f is differentiable at x and $f(x) \neq 0$, then

$$D_x \left[\frac{1}{f(x)} \right] = -\frac{f'(x)}{[f(x)]^2}. \tag{17}$$

With $u = f(x)$, the reciprocal rule takes the form

$$\frac{d}{dx} \left(\frac{1}{u} \right) = -\frac{1}{u^2} \cdot \frac{du}{dx}. \tag{17'}$$

If there can be no doubt what the independent variable is, we can write

$$\left(\frac{1}{u} \right)' = -\frac{u'}{u^2}. \tag{17''}$$

PROOF As in the proof of Theorem 4, we use the limit laws, the definition of the derivative, and the fact that a function is continuous wherever it is differentiable (by Theorem 2 of Section 3.4). Moreover, note that $f(x+h) \neq 0$ for h near zero because $f(x) \neq 0$ and f is continuous at x. (See Problem 16 in Appendix D.) Therefore

$$D_x \left[\frac{1}{f(x)} \right] = \lim_{h \to 0} \frac{1}{h} \left(\frac{1}{f(x+h)} - \frac{1}{f(x)} \right) = \lim_{h \to 0} \frac{f(x) - f(x+h)}{h f(x+h) f(x)}$$

$$= -\left(\lim_{h \to 0} \frac{1}{f(x+h) f(x)} \right) \left(\lim_{h \to 0} \frac{f(x+h) - f(x)}{h} \right) = -\frac{f'(x)}{[f(x)]^2}. \triangleleft$$

EXAMPLE 7 With $f(x) = x^2 + 1$ in Eq. (17), we get

$$D_x \left(\frac{1}{x^2+1} \right) = -\frac{D_x(x^2+1)}{(x^2+1)^2} = -\frac{2x}{(x^2+1)^2}. \blacklozenge$$

We now combine the reciprocal rule with the power rule for positive integral exponents to establish the power rule for negative integral exponents.

THEOREM 5 Power Rule for a Negative Integer n
If n is a negative integer, then $D_x x^n = n x^{n-1}$.

PROOF Let $m = -n$, so that m is a *positive* integer. If $x \neq 0$ then we can apply the reciprocal rule with $f(x) = x^m \neq 0$ and $f'(x) = mx^{m-1}$ (the latter by the power rule with positive integer exponent). This gives

$$D_x x^n = D_x \left(\frac{1}{x^m}\right) = -\frac{D_x(x^m)}{(x^m)^2} = -\frac{mx^{m-1}}{x^{2m}} = (-m)x^{-m-1} = nx^{n-1}.$$

Thus we have established that the rule in Theorem 5 holds precisely where the function being differentiated is defined—that is, where $x \neq 0$. ◂

EXAMPLE 8

$$D_x \left(\frac{5x^4 - 6x + 7}{2x^2}\right) = D_x \left(\tfrac{5}{2}x^2 - 3x^{-1} + \tfrac{7}{2}x^{-2}\right)$$

$$= \tfrac{5}{2}(2x) - 3(-x^{-2}) + \tfrac{7}{2}(-2x^{-3}) = 5x + \frac{3}{x^2} - \frac{7}{x^3}.$$

The key here was to "divide out" before differentiating. ◆

Now we apply the product rule and reciprocal rule to get a rule for differentiation of the quotient of two functions.

THEOREM 6 The Quotient Rule
If f and g are differentiable at x and $g(x) \neq 0$, then f/g is differentiable at x and

$$D_x \left[\frac{f(x)}{g(x)}\right] = \frac{f'(x)g(x) - f(x)g'(x)}{[g(x)]^2}. \tag{18}$$

With $u = f(x)$ and $v = g(x)$, this rule takes the form

$$\frac{d}{dx}\left(\frac{u}{v}\right) = \frac{v\dfrac{du}{dx} - u\dfrac{dv}{dx}}{v^2} \tag{18'}$$

If it is clear what the independent variable is, we can write the quotient rule in the form

$$\left(\frac{u}{v}\right)' = \frac{u'v - uv'}{v^2}. \tag{18''}$$

PROOF We apply the product rule to the factorization

$$\frac{f(x)}{g(x)} = f(x) \cdot \frac{1}{g(x)}.$$

This gives

$$D_x \left[\frac{f(x)}{g(x)}\right] = [D_x f(x)] \cdot \frac{1}{g(x)} + f(x) \cdot D_x \left[\frac{1}{g(x)}\right]$$

$$= \frac{f'(x)}{g(x)} + f(x) \cdot \left(-\frac{g'(x)}{[g(x)]^2}\right) = \frac{f'(x)g(x) - f(x)g'(x)}{[g(x)]^2}. \quad ◂$$

Note that the numerator in Eq. (18) is *not* the derivative of the product of f and g. And the minus sign means that the *order* of terms in the numerator is important.

EXAMPLE 9 Find $z'(t) = dz/dt$ if z is given by

$$z = \frac{1 - t^3}{1 + t^4}.$$

FIGURE 3.2.4 Graphs of the function $z(t)$ of Example 9 and its derivative $z'(t)$.

Solution Here, primes denote derivatives with respect to t. With t (rather than x) as the independent variable, the quotient rule gives

$$\frac{dz}{dt} = \frac{(1-t^3)'(1+t^4) - (1-t^3)(1+t^4)'}{(1+t^4)^2}$$

$$= \frac{(-3t^2)(1+t^4) - (1-t^3)(4t^3)}{(1+t^4)^2} = \frac{t^6 - 4t^3 - 3t^2}{(1+t^4)^2}.$$

Figure 3.2.4 shows computer-generated graphs of the function $z(t)$ and its derivative $z'(t)$. Observe that $z(t)$ is increasing on intervals where $z'(t)$ is positive and is decreasing on intervals where $z'(t)$ is negative (thus corroborating our computation of the derivative). A quick computer or calculator graph of a function and its alleged derivative will often reveal an error if one has been made. ◆

3.2 TRUE/FALSE STUDY GUIDE

3.2 CONCEPTS: QUESTIONS AND DISCUSSION

1. Theorems 2 and 5 in this section imply that the power rule $D_x x^n = nx^{n-1}$ holds provided that the integer n is nonzero. Does it also hold if $n = 0$? Can you think of a simple algebraic function whose derivative is a nonzero constant multiple of $1/x$?

2. Example 1 and the discussion preceding it may seem to imply that the power rule holds in the very general form $D[\text{whatever}]^n = n[\text{whatever}]^{n-1}$—more precisely, $D_x[f(x)]^n = n[f(x)]^{n-1}$. Is this true or false? When you're confronted with a question like this, don't just sit there. *Check it out!* Test the conjecture with specific choices for n and $f(x)$—perhaps $n = 7$ and $f(x) = x^{11}$. What are the simplest choices you can use to resolve the matter?

3.2 PROBLEMS

Apply the differentiation rules of this section to find the derivatives of the functions in Problems 1 through 40.

1. $f(x) = 3x^2 - x + 5$
2. $g(t) = 1 - 3t^2 - 2t^4$
3. $f(x) = (2x+3)(3x-2)$
4. $g(x) = (2x^2 - 1)(x^3 + 2)$
5. $h(x) = (x+1)^3$
6. $g(t) = (4t-7)^2$
7. $f(y) = y(2y-1)(2y+1)$
8. $f(x) = 4x^4 - \frac{1}{x^2}$
9. $g(x) = \frac{1}{x+1} - \frac{1}{x-1}$
10. $f(t) = \frac{1}{4-t^2}$
11. $h(x) = \frac{3}{x^2 + x + 1}$
12. $f(x) = \frac{1}{1 - \frac{2}{x}}$
13. $g(t) = (t^2 + 1)(t^3 + t^2 + 1)$
14. $f(x) = (2x^3 - 3)(17x^4 - 6x + 2)$
15. $g(z) = \frac{1}{2z} - \frac{1}{3z^2}$
16. $f(x) = \frac{2x^3 - 3x^2 + 4x - 5}{x^2}$
17. $g(y) = 2y(3y^2 - 1)(y^2 + 2y + 3)$
18. $f(x) = \frac{x^2 - 4}{x^2 + 4}$
19. $g(t) = \frac{t-1}{t^2 + 2t + 1}$
20. $u(x) = \frac{1}{(x+2)^2}$
21. $v(t) = \frac{1}{(t-1)^3}$
22. $h(x) = \frac{2x^3 + x^2 - 3x + 17}{2x - 5}$
23. $g(x) = \frac{3x}{x^3 + 7x - 5}$
24. $f(t) = \frac{1}{\left(t + \frac{1}{t}\right)^2}$
25. $g(x) = \frac{\frac{1}{x} - \frac{2}{x^2}}{\frac{2}{x^3} - \frac{3}{x^4}}$
26. $f(x) = \frac{x^3 - \frac{1}{x^2 + 1}}{x^4 + \frac{1}{x^2 + 1}}$
27. $y(x) = x^3 - 6x^5 + \frac{3}{2}x^{-4} + 12$
28. $x(t) = \frac{3}{t} - \frac{4}{t^2} - 5$
29. $y(x) = \frac{5 - 4x^2 + x^5}{x^3}$
30. $u(x) = \frac{2x - 3x^2 + 2x^4}{5x^2}$
31. $y(x) = 3x - \frac{1}{4x^2}$
32. $f(z) = \frac{1}{z(z^2 + 2z + 2)}$
33. $y(x) = \frac{x}{x-1} + \frac{x+1}{3x}$
34. $u(t) = \frac{1}{1 - 4t^{-2}}$
35. $y(x) = \frac{x^3 - 4x + 5}{x^2 + 9}$
36. $w(z) = z^2 \left(2z^3 - \frac{3}{4z^4}\right)$

37. $y(x) = \dfrac{2x^2}{3x - \dfrac{4}{5x^4}}$

38. $z(t) = \dfrac{4}{(t^2 - 3)^2}$

39. $y(x) = \dfrac{x^2}{x+1}$

40. $h(w) = \dfrac{w+10}{w^2}$

In Problems 41 through 50, write an equation of the line tangent to the curve $y = f(x)$ at the given point P on the curve. Express the answer in the form $ax + by = c$.

41. $y = x^3$; $P(2, 8)$

42. $y = 3x^2 - 4$; $P(1, -1)$

43. $y = \dfrac{1}{x-1}$; $P(2, 1)$

44. $y = 2x - \dfrac{1}{x}$; $P(0.5, -1)$

45. $y = x^3 + 3x^2 - 4x - 5$; $P(1, -5)$

46. $y = \left(\dfrac{1}{x} - \dfrac{1}{x^2}\right)^{-1}$; $P(2, 4)$

47. $y = \dfrac{3}{x^2} - \dfrac{4}{x^3}$; $P(-1, 7)$

48. $y = \dfrac{3x - 2}{3x + 2}$; $P(2, 0.5)$

49. $y = \dfrac{3x^2}{x^2 + x + 1}$; $P(-1, 3)$

50. $y = \dfrac{6}{1 - x^2}$; $P(2, -2)$

51. Apply the formula in Example 5 to answer the following two questions. (a) If 1000 cm^3 of water at 0°C is heated, does it initially expand or contract? (b) What is the rate (in cm^3/°C) at which it initially contracts or expands?

52. Susan's weight in pounds is given by the formula $W = (2 \times 10^9)/R^2$, where R is her distance in miles from the center of the earth. What is the rate of change of W with respect to R when $R = 3960$ mi? If Susan climbs a mountain, beginning at sea level, at what rate in ounces per (vertical) mile does her weight initially decrease?

53. The conical tank shown in Fig. 3.2.5 has radius 160 cm and height 800 cm. Water is running out of a small hole in the bottom of the tank. When the height h of water in the tank is 600 cm, what is the rate of change of its volume V with respect to h?

FIGURE 3.2.5 The leaky tank of Problem 53.

54. Find the x- and y-intercepts of the straight line that is tangent to the curve $y = x^3 + x^2 + x$ at the point $(1, 3)$ (Fig. 3.2.6).

FIGURE 3.2.6 The tangent line of Problem 54.

55. Find an equation for the straight line that passes through the point $(1, 5)$ and is tangent to the curve $y = x^3$. [*Suggestion:* Denote by (a, a^3) the point of tangency, as indicated in Fig 3.2.7. Find by inspection small integral solutions of the resulting cubic equation in a.]

FIGURE 3.2.7 The tangent line of Problem 55.

56. Find *two* lines through the point $(2, 8)$ that are tangent to the curve $y = x^3$. [See the suggestion for Problem 55.]

57. Prove that no straight line can be tangent to the curve $y = x^2$ at two different points.

58. Find the two straight lines of slope -2 that are tangent to the curve $y = 1/x$.

59. Let $n \geq 2$ be a fixed but unspecified integer. Find the x-intercept of the line that is tangent to the curve $y = x^n$ at the point $P(x_0, y_0)$.

60. Prove that the curve $y = x^5 + 2x$ has no horizontal tangents. What is the smallest slope that a line tangent to this curve can have?

61. Apply Eq. (16) with $n = 3$ and $u_1 = u_2 = u_3 = f(x)$ to show that

$$D_x([f(x)]^3) = 3[f(x)]^2 \cdot f'(x).$$

62. (a) First write $u_1 u_2 u_3 u_4 = (u_1 u_2 u_3) u_4$ to verify Eq. (16) for $n = 4$. (b) Then write $u_1 u_2 u_3 u_4 u_5 = (u_1 u_2 u_3 u_4) u_5$ and apply the result in part (a) to verify Eq. (16) for $n = 5$.

63. Apply Eq. (16) to show that

$$D_x([f(x)]^n) = n[f(x)]^{n-1} \cdot f'(x)$$

if n is a positive integer and $f'(x)$ exists.

64. Use the result of Problem 63 to compute $D_x[(x^2+x+1)^{100}]$.

65. Use the result of Problem 63 to find $g'(x)$ given $g(x) = (x^3 - 17x + 35)^{17}$.

66. Find constants a, b, c, and d such that the graph of

$$f(x) = ax^3 + bx^2 + cx + d$$

has horizontal tangent lines at the points $(0, 1)$ and $(1, 0)$.

In connection with Problems 67 through 71, Figs. 3.2.8 through 3.2.11 show the curves

$$y = \frac{x^n}{1+x^2}$$

for $n = 0$, 1, 2, and 3.

FIGURE 3.2.8 The graph of $y = \dfrac{1}{1+x^2}$.

FIGURE 3.2.9 The graph of $y = \dfrac{x}{1+x^2}$.

FIGURE 3.2.10 The graph of $y = \dfrac{x^2}{1+x^2}$.

FIGURE 3.2.11 The graph of $y = \dfrac{x^3}{1+x^2}$.

67. Show that for $n = 0$ and $n = 2$, the curve has only a single point where the tangent line is horizontal (Figs. 3.2.8 and 3.2.10).

68. When $n = 1$, there are two points on the curve where the tangent line is horizontal (Fig. 3.2.9). Find them.

69. Show that for $n \geq 3$, $(0, 0)$ is the only point on the graph of

$$y = \frac{x^n}{1+x^2}$$

at which the tangent line is horizontal (Fig. 3.2.11).

70. Figure 3.2.12 shows the graph of the derivative $f'(x)$ of the function

$$f(x) = \frac{x^3}{1+x^2}.$$

There appear to be two points on the graph of $y = f'(x)$ at which the tangent line has slope 1. Find them.

FIGURE 3.2.12 The graph of
$$y = D_x\left(\frac{x^3}{1+x^2}\right)$$
of Problems 70 and 71.

71. It appears in Fig. 3.2.12 that there are three points on the curve $y = f'(x)$ at which the tangent line is horizontal. Find them.

72. Much of life on earth (as we know it) depends critically on the variation of water density with temperature. Consider a sample of water than has a volume of exactly $1000\,\text{cm}^3$ when measured at precisely $0°\text{C}$. Figure 3.2.13 shows a graph of its volume function $V(T)$ as given by the formula in Example 5. The surprise is that, as the temperature is increased, the sample initially contracts rather than expands in volume. Evidently a minimal volume $V_m = V(T_m)$ occurs at a critical temperature $T_m \approx 4$ (°C). Given that the tangent line to the graph of V is horizontal at the point (T_m, V_m), find: (a) the numerical values of T_m and V_m, and (b) the temperature $T_1 \approx 8$ (°C) at which the volume of the sample is again exactly $1000\,\text{cm}^3$. *Comment:* Because water that's slightly warmer than the freezing point of $0°\text{C}$ is slightly denser than water at $0°\text{C}$, the warmer water sinks to the bottom as a cooling lake freezes. But ice is less dense, so it floats on the surface. Consequently, ice at the surface traps somewhat warmer water at the bottom of the lake—which otherwise might freeze solid. This phenomenon is responsible for the survival and evolution of life forms that can withstand cold water but not freezing.

FIGURE 3.2.13 The temperature-volume graph of Problem 72.

In Problems 73 through 78, sketch the graph of the given function f and determine where it is differentiable. Recall the definition *of one-sided derivatives in Problem 54 of Section 3.1, as well as the fact that $f'(a)$ exists if and only if $f'_-(a) = f'_+(a)$.*

73. $f(x) = |x^3|$

74. $f(x) = x^3 + |x^3|$

75. $f(x) = \begin{cases} 2 + 3x^2 & \text{if } x < 1, \\ 3 + 2x^3 & \text{if } x \geq 1 \end{cases}$

76. $f(x) = \begin{cases} x^4 & \text{if } x < 1, \\ 2 - \dfrac{1}{x^4} & \text{if } x \geq 1 \end{cases}$

77. $f(x) = \begin{cases} \dfrac{1}{2-x} & \text{if } x < 1, \\ x & \text{if } x \geq 1 \end{cases}$

78. $f(x) = \begin{cases} \dfrac{12}{(5-x)^2} & \text{if } x < 3, \\ x^2 - 3x + 3 & \text{if } x \geq 3 \end{cases}$

3.3 THE CHAIN RULE

We saw in Section 3.2 how to differentiate powers of the independent variable, but we often need to differentiate powers of rather general (or even unknown) functions. For instance, suppose that

$$y = u^3 \tag{1}$$

where u is in turn a function of x. Then the extended product rule [Eq. (16) in Section 3.2] yields

$$\frac{dy}{dx} = D_x u^3 = D_x(u \cdot u \cdot u) = u' \cdot u \cdot u + u \cdot u' \cdot u + u \cdot u \cdot u'$$

where $u' = du/dx$. After we collect terms, we find that

$$\frac{dy}{dx} = 3u^2 u' = 3u^2 \frac{du}{dx}. \tag{2}$$

Is it a surprise that the derivative of u^3 is *not* simply $3u^2$, which you might expect in analogy with the correct formula $D_x x^3 = 3x^2$? There is an additional factor du/dx, whose presence may seem more natural if we differentiate y in Eq. (1) with respect to u, and write

$$\frac{dy}{du} = 3u^2.$$

Then the derivative formula in (2) takes the form

$$\frac{dy}{dx} = \frac{dy}{du} \cdot \frac{du}{dx}. \tag{3}$$

Equation (3), the **chain rule**, holds for *any* two differentiable functions $y = f(u)$ and $u = g(x)$. The formula in Eq. (2) is simply the special case of (3) with $f(u) = u^3$.

EXAMPLE 1 If

$$y = (3x^2 + 5)^{17},$$

it would be impractical to write the binomial expansion of the seventeenth power of $3x^2 + 5$ before differentiating. The Expand command in a typical computer algebra system yields a polynomial in x having 18 terms, some of which have 15-digit coefficients:

$$(3x^2 + 5)^{17} = 762939453125 + 7781982421857x^2 + \cdots$$
$$+ 186911613281250x^{18} + \cdots + 129140163x^{34}.$$

(Each ellipsis replaces seven omitted terms.) But if we simply write

$$y = u^{17} \quad \text{with} \quad u = 3x^2 + 5,$$

then
$$\frac{dy}{du} = 17u^{16} \quad \text{and} \quad \frac{du}{dx} = 6x.$$

Hence the chain rule yields
$$\frac{dy}{dx} = \frac{dy}{du} \cdot \frac{du}{dx} = 17u^{16} \cdot 6x$$
$$= 17(3x^2 + 5)^{16} \cdot 6x = 102x(3x^2 + 5)^{16}. \quad \blacklozenge$$

The formula in (3) is one that, once learned, is unlikely to be forgotten. Although dy/du and du/dx are *not* fractions—they are merely symbols representing the derivatives $f'(u)$ and $g'(x)$—it is much as though they *were* fractions, with the du in the first factor canceling the du in the second factor:

$$\frac{dy}{du} \cdot \frac{du}{dx} = \frac{dy}{d\!\!\!/u} \cdot \frac{d\!\!\!/u}{dx} = \frac{dy}{dx}. \qquad \text{[Invalid cancellation!]}$$

But you should realize that such "cancellation" no more proves the chain rule than canceling two copies of the symbol d proves that

$$\frac{dy}{dx} = \frac{d\!\!\!/y}{d\!\!\!/x} = \frac{y}{x} \qquad \text{[An absurdity!]}.$$

It is nevertheless an excellent way to *remember* the chain rule. Such manipulations with differentials are so suggestive (even when invalid) that they played a substantial role in the early development of calculus in the seventeenth and eighteenth centuries. Many formulas were thereby produced (and later proved valid), as were some formulas that were incorrect.

EXAMPLE 2 For a physical interpretation of the chain rule, imagine an oil refinery that first makes u liters of gasoline from x barrels of crude oil. Then, in a second process, the refinery makes y grams of a marketable petrochemical from the u liters of gasoline. (The two processes are illustrated in Fig. 3.3.1.) Then y is a function of u and u is a function of x, so the final output y is a function also of the input x. Consider the *units* in which the *derivatives* of these functions are measured.

$$\frac{dy}{du} : \frac{\text{g}}{\text{L}} \qquad \text{(grams of petrochemical per liter of gasoline)}$$

$$\frac{du}{dx} : \frac{\text{L}}{\text{barrel}} \qquad \text{(liters of gasoline per barrel of oil)}$$

$$\frac{dy}{dx} : \frac{\text{g}}{\text{barrel}} \qquad \text{(grams of petrochemical per barrel of oil)}$$

When we include the units in the chain rule equation
$$\frac{dy}{dx} = \frac{dy}{du}\frac{du}{dx},$$

we get

$$\frac{dy}{dx}\frac{\text{g}}{\text{barrel}} = \left(\frac{dy}{du}\frac{\text{g}}{\cancel{\text{L}}}\right) \cdot \left(\frac{du}{dx}\frac{\cancel{\text{L}}}{\text{barrel}}\right) = \left(\frac{dy}{du} \cdot \frac{du}{dx}\right)\frac{\text{g}}{\text{barrel}}.$$

The handy cancellation of units seems to confirm the validity of the chain rule (at least in this application). For example, if we get 3 g of petrochemical per liter of gasoline and 75 L of gasoline per barrel of oil, how could we fail to get $225 = 3 \cdot 75$ g of petrochemical per barrel of oil? $\quad \blacklozenge$

x barrels crude oil

Process 1

u liters gasoline

Process 2

y grams petrochemical

FIGURE 3.3.1 The two-process oil refinery (Example 2).

The Chain Rule in Function Notation

Although Eq. (3) is a memorable statement of the chain rule in differential notation, it has the disadvantage of not specifying the values of the variables at which the derivatives are evaluated. This problem can be solved by the use of function notation for the derivatives. Let us write

$$y = f(u), \quad u = g(x) \quad y = h(x) = f(g(x)).$$

Then

$$\frac{du}{dx} = g'(x), \quad \frac{dy}{dx} = h'(x),$$

and

$$\frac{dy}{du} = f'(u) = f'(g(x)).$$

Substituting these derivatives into the chain rule formula

$$\frac{dy}{dx} = \frac{dy}{du} \cdot \frac{du}{dx} \tag{3}$$

recasts it in the form

$$h'(x) = f'(g(x)) \cdot g'(x). \tag{4}$$

This version of the chain rule gives the derivative of the *composition* $h = f \circ g$ of two functions f and g in terms of *their* derivatives.

THEOREM 1 The Chain Rule

Suppose that g is differentiable at x and that f is differentiable at $g(x)$. Then the composition $h = f \circ g$ defined by $h(x) = f(g(x))$ is differentiable at x, and its derivative is

$$h'(x) = f'(g(x)) \cdot g'(x). \tag{4}$$

REMARK The chain rule in (4) shows that the derivative of the composition $h = f \circ g$ is a *product* of the derivatives of f and g. Note, however, that these two derivatives are evaluated at *different* points. The derivative g' of the *inner function* is evaluated at x, whereas the derivative f' of the *outer function* is evaluated at $g(x)$ (rather than at the same point x).

EXAMPLE 3 In Example 1 we applied the differential form of the chain rule in (3) to differentiate the function

$$h(x) = (3x^2 + 5)^{17}.$$

To apply the functional form of the chain rule in (4), we must first identify the outer function

$$f(x) = x^{17}, \quad \text{for which} \quad f'(x) = 17x^{16},$$

and the inner function

$$g(x) = 3x^2 + 5, \quad \text{for which} \quad g'(x) = 6x.$$

Then

$$h'(x) = f'(g(x)) \cdot g'(x)$$
$$= f'(3x^2 + 5) \cdot (3x^2 + 5)'$$
$$= 17(3x^2 + 5)^{16} \cdot 6x = 102x(3x^2 + 5)^{16}. \quad \blacklozenge$$

The Proof of the Chain Rule

To *outline* a proof of the chain rule, suppose that we are given differentiable functions $y = f(u)$ and $u = g(x)$ and want to compute the derivative

$$\frac{dy}{dx} = \lim_{\Delta x \to 0} \frac{\Delta y}{\Delta x} = \lim_{\Delta x \to 0} \frac{f(g(x + \Delta x)) - f(g(x))}{\Delta x}. \tag{5}$$

The differential form of the chain rule suggests the factorization

$$\frac{\Delta y}{\Delta x} = \frac{\Delta y}{\Delta u} \frac{\Delta u}{\Delta x} \tag{6}$$

where

$$\Delta u = g(x + \Delta x) - g(x) \quad \text{and} \quad \Delta y = f(u + \Delta u) - f(u).$$

For x fixed, the factorization in Eq. (6) is valid if $g'(x) \neq 0$, because

$$g'(x) = \frac{du}{dx} = \lim_{\Delta x \to 0} \frac{\Delta u}{\Delta x} \neq 0$$

implies that $\Delta u \neq 0$ if $\Delta x \neq 0$ is sufficiently small—for if so, then $\Delta u = (\Delta u / \Delta x) \cdot \Delta x$ is the product of nonzero numbers. But the fact that g is differentiable, and therefore continuous, at the point x (see Theorem 2 in Section 3.4) implies that

$$\Delta u = g(x + \Delta x) - g(x) \to 0 \quad \text{as} \quad \Delta x \to 0.$$

The product law of limits therefore gives

$$\frac{dy}{dx} = \lim_{\Delta x \to 0} \frac{\Delta y}{\Delta u} \cdot \frac{\Delta u}{\Delta x} = \left(\lim_{\Delta u \to 0} \frac{\Delta y}{\Delta u} \right) \cdot \left(\lim_{\Delta x \to 0} \frac{\Delta u}{\Delta x} \right) = \frac{dy}{du} \cdot \frac{du}{dx}.$$

Thus we have shown that $D_x[f(g(x))] = f'(g(x)) \cdot g'(x)$ at any point x at which $g'(x) \neq 0$. But if $g'(x) = 0$, then it is entirely possible that Δu is zero for some or all nonzero values of Δx approaching zero—in which case the factorization in (6) is invalid. Our proof of the chain rule is therefore incomplete. In Section 4.2 we give a proof that does not require the assumption that $g'(x) \neq 0$.

The Generalized Power Rule

If we substitute $g(x) = u$ and $g'(x) = du/dx$ into Eq. (4) with $h'(x) = D_x f(g(x)) = D_x f(u)$, we get the hybrid form

$$D_x[f(u)] = f'(u) \cdot \frac{du}{dx} \tag{7}$$

of the chain rule that frequently is the most useful form for purely computational purposes. Recall that the subscript x in D_x specifies that $f(u)$ is being differentiated with respect to x, *not* with respect to u.

Let us set $f(u) = u^n$ in Eq. (7), where n is an integer. Because $f'(u) = nu^{n-1}$, we thereby obtain

$$D_x u^n = nu^{n-1} \frac{du}{dx}, \tag{8}$$

the *chain rule version* of the power rule. If $u = g(x)$ is a differentiable function, then Eq. (8) implies that

$$D_x [g(x)]^n = n[g(x)]^{n-1} \cdot D_x[g(x)]. \tag{9}$$

[If $n - 1 < 0$, we must add the proviso that $g(x) \neq 0$ in order for the right-hand side in Eq. (9) to be meaningful.] We refer to this chain rule version of the power rule as the **generalized power rule.**

REMARK We may interpret the operator form in (9) as describing a chain rule procedure in which we work *from the outside to the inside*—differentiating first the outer function and then the inner function. This outside-inside procedure is illustrated in the next example.

EXAMPLE 4 To differentiate
$$y = \frac{1}{(2x^3 - x + 7)^2},$$
we first write
$$y = (2x^3 - x + 7)^{-2}$$
in order to apply the generalized power rule, Eq. (9), with $n = -2$. This gives
$$\frac{dy}{dx} = \underbrace{(-2)(2x^3 - x + 7)^{-3}}_{\text{derivative of outer function}} \cdot D_x(2x^3 - x + 7)$$

$$= (-2)(2x^3 - x + 7)^{-3} \cdot \underbrace{(6x^2 - 1)}_{\text{derivative of inner function}} = \frac{2(1 - 6x^2)}{(2x^3 - x + 7)^3}.$$ ◆

EXAMPLE 5 Find the derivative of the function
$$h(z) = \left(\frac{z-1}{z+1}\right)^5.$$

Solution The key to applying the generalized power rule is observing *what* the given function is a power *of*. Here,
$$h(z) = u^5, \quad \text{where} \quad u = \frac{z-1}{z+1},$$
and z, not x, is the independent variable. Hence we apply first Eq. (8) and then the quotient rule to get
$$h'(z) = 5u^4 \frac{du}{dz} = 5\left(\frac{z-1}{z+1}\right)^4 D_z\left(\frac{z-1}{z+1}\right)$$

$$= 5\left(\frac{z-1}{z+1}\right)^4 \cdot \frac{(1)(z+1) - (z-1)(1)}{(z+1)^2}$$

$$= 5\left(\frac{z-1}{z+1}\right)^4 \cdot \frac{2}{(z+1)^2} = \frac{10(z-1)^4}{(z+1)^6}.$$ ◆

The importance of the chain rule goes far beyond the power function differentiations illustrated in Examples 1, 4, and 5. We shall learn in later sections how to differentiate exponential, logarithmic, and trigonometric functions. Each time we learn a new differentiation formula—for the derivative $f'(x)$ of a new function $f(x)$—the formula in Eq. (7) immediately provides us with the chain rule version of that formula,
$$D_x f(u) = f'(u) D_x u.$$

The step from the power rule $D_x x^n = nx^{n-1}$ to the generalized power rule $D_x u^n = nu^{n-1} D_x u$ is our first instance of this general phenomenon.

Rate-Of-Change Applications

Suppose that the physical or geometric quantity p depends on the quantity q, which in turn depends on time t. Then the *dependent* variable p is a function both of the *intermediate* variable q and of the *independent* variable t. Hence the derivatives that appear in the chain rule formula
$$\frac{dp}{dt} = \frac{dp}{dq}\frac{dq}{dt}$$

are rates of change (as in Section 3.1) of these variables with respect to one another. For instance, suppose that a spherical balloon is being inflated or deflated. Then its volume V and its radius r are changing with time t, and

$$\frac{dV}{dt} = \frac{dV}{dr}\frac{dr}{dt}.$$

Remember that a positive derivative signals an increasing quantity and that a negative derivative signals a decreasing quantity.

EXAMPLE 6 A spherical balloon is being inflated (Fig. 3.3.2). The radius r of the balloon is increasing at the rate of 0.2 cm/s when $r = 5$ cm. At what rate is the volume V of the balloon increasing at that instant?

FIGURE 3.3.2 The spherical balloon with volume $V = \frac{4}{3}\pi r^3$.

Solution Given $dr/dt = 0.2$ cm/s when $r = 5$ cm, we want to find dV/dt at that instant. Because the volume of the balloon is

$$V = \tfrac{4}{3}\pi r^3,$$

we see that $dV/dr = 4\pi r^2$. So the chain rule gives

$$\frac{dV}{dt} = \frac{dV}{dr} \cdot \frac{dr}{dt} = 4\pi r^2 \frac{dr}{dt} = 4\pi(5)^2(0.2) \approx 62.83 \quad (\text{cm}^3/\text{s})$$

at the instant when $r = 5$ cm. ◆

In Example 6 we did not need to know r explicitly as a function of t. But suppose we are told that after t seconds the radius (in centimeters) of an inflating balloon is $r = 3 + (0.2)t$ (until the balloon bursts). Then the volume of this balloon is

$$V = \frac{4}{3}\pi r^3 = \frac{4}{3}\pi \left(3 + \frac{t}{5}\right)^3,$$

so dV/dt is given explicitly as a function of t by

$$\frac{dV}{dt} = \frac{4}{3}\pi(3)\left(3 + \frac{t}{5}\right)^2 \left(\frac{1}{5}\right) = \frac{4}{5}\pi \left(3 + \frac{t}{5}\right)^2.$$

EXAMPLE 7 Imagine a spherical raindrop that is falling through water vapor in the air. Suppose that the vapor adheres to the surface of the raindrop in such a way that the time rate of increase of the mass M of the droplet is proportional to the surface area S of the droplet. If the initial radius of the droplet is, in effect, zero and the radius is $r = 1$ mm after 20 s, when is the radius 3 mm?

Solution We are given

$$\frac{dM}{dt} = kS,$$

where k is some constant that depends upon atmospheric conditions. Now

$$M = \tfrac{4}{3}\pi\rho r^3 \quad \text{and} \quad S = 4\pi r^2,$$

where ρ is the density of water. Hence the chain rule gives

$$4\pi kr^2 = kS = \frac{dM}{dt} = \frac{dM}{dr} \cdot \frac{dr}{dt};$$

that is,

$$4\pi kr^2 = 4\pi\rho r^2 \frac{dr}{dt}.$$

This implies that

$$\frac{dr}{dt} = \frac{k}{\rho},$$

a constant. So the radius of the droplet grows at a *constant* rate. Thus if it takes 20 s for r to grow to 1 mm, it will take 1 min for r to grow to 3 mm. ◆

3.3 TRUE/FALSE STUDY GUIDE

3.3 CONCEPTS: QUESTIONS AND DISCUSSION

1. As a mathematical quiz show contestant, you are asked to calculate the value $F'(7)$ for the composition $F = f \circ g$. The functions f and g are unknown, but you are permitted to ask exactly three questions regarding numerical values of these functions and/or their derivatives at specified points. What three questions should you ask?

2. Write the function-notation form of the chain rule formula in Problem 63 for a composition $F = f \circ g \circ h$ of three functions. What numerical data are now needed to calculate the numerical value $F'(7)$?

3.3 PROBLEMS

Find dy/dx in Problems 1 through 12.

1. $y = (3x + 4)^5$
2. $y = (2 - 5x)^3$
3. $y = \dfrac{1}{3x - 2}$
4. $y = \dfrac{1}{(2x + 1)^3}$
5. $y = (x^2 + 3x + 4)^3$
6. $y = (7 - 2x^3)^{-4}$
7. $y = (2 - x)^4 (3 + x)^7$
8. $y = (x + x^2)^5 (1 + x^3)^2$
9. $y = \dfrac{x + 2}{(3x - 4)^3}$
10. $y = \dfrac{(1 - x^2)^3}{(4 + 5x + 6x^2)^2}$
11. $y = [1 + (1 + x)^3]^4$
12. $y = [x + (x + x^2)^{-3}]^{-5}$

In Problems 13 through 20, express the derivative dy/dx in terms of x.

13. $y = (u + 1)^3$ and $u = \dfrac{1}{x^2}$
14. $y = \dfrac{1}{2u} - \dfrac{1}{3u^2}$ and $u = 2x + 1$
15. $y = (1 + u^2)^3$ and $u = (4x - 1)^2$
16. $y = u^5$ and $u = \dfrac{1}{3x - 2}$
17. $y = u(1 - u)^3$ and $u = \dfrac{1}{x^4}$
18. $y = \dfrac{u}{u + 1}$ and $u = \dfrac{x}{x + 1}$
19. $y = u^2(u - u^4)^3$ and $u = \dfrac{1}{x^2}$
20. $y = \dfrac{u}{(2u + 1)^4}$ and $u = x - \dfrac{2}{x}$

In Problems 21 through 26, identify a function u of x and an integer $n \neq 1$ such that $f(x) = u^n$. Then compute $f'(x)$.

21. $f(x) = (2x - x^2)^3$
22. $f(x) = \dfrac{1}{2 + 5x^3}$
23. $f(x) = \dfrac{1}{(1 - x^2)^4}$
24. $f(x) = (x^2 - 4x + 1)^3$
25. $f(x) = \left(\dfrac{x + 1}{x - 1}\right)^7$
26. $f(x) = \dfrac{(x^2 + x + 1)^4}{(x + 1)^4}$

Differentiate the functions given in Problems 27 through 36.

27. $g(y) = y + (2y - 3)^5$
28. $h(z) = z^2(z^2 + 4)^3$
29. $F(s) = \left(s - \dfrac{1}{s^2}\right)^3$
30. $G(t) = \left(t^2 + 1 + \dfrac{1}{t}\right)^2$
31. $f(u) = (1 + u)^3 (1 + u^2)^4$
32. $g(w) = (w^2 - 3w + 4)(w + 4)^5$
33. $h(v) = \left[v - \left(1 - \dfrac{1}{v}\right)^{-1}\right]^{-2}$
34. $p(t) = \left(\dfrac{1}{t} + \dfrac{1}{t^2} + \dfrac{1}{t^3}\right)^{-4}$
35. $F(z) = \dfrac{1}{(3 - 4z + 5z^5)^{10}}$
36. $G(x) = \{1 + [x + (x^2 + x^3)^4]^5\}^6$

In Problems 37 through 44, dy/dx can be found in two ways— one way using the chain rule, the other way without using it. Use both techniques to find dy/dx and then compare the answers. (They should agree!)

37. $y = (x^3)^4 = x^{12}$
38. $y = x = \left(\dfrac{1}{x}\right)^{-1}$
39. $y = (x^2 - 1)^2 = x^4 - 2x^2 + 1$
40. $y = (1 - x)^3 = 1 - 3x + 3x^2 - x^3$
41. $y = (x + 1)^4 = x^4 + 4x^3 + 6x^2 + 4x + 1$
42. $y = (x + 1)^{-2} = \dfrac{1}{x^2 + 2x + 1}$
43. $y = (x^2 + 1)^{-1} = \dfrac{1}{x^2 + 1}$
44. $y = (x^2 + 1)^2 = (x^2 + 1)(x^2 + 1)$

We shall see in Section 3.7 that $D_x[\sin x] = \cos x$ (provided that x is in radian measure). Use this fact and the chain rule to find the derivatives of the functions in Problems 45 through 48.

45. $f(x) = \sin(x^3)$
46. $g(t) = (\sin t)^3$
47. $g(z) = (\sin 2z)^3$
48. $k(u) = \sin(1 + \sin u)$

49. A pebble dropped into a lake creates an expanding circular ripple (Fig. 3.3.3). Suppose that the radius of the circle is increasing at the rate of 2 in./s. At what rate is its area increasing when its radius is 10 in.?

FIGURE 3.3.3 Expanding circular ripple in a lake (Problem 49).

50. The area of a circle is decreasing at the rate of 2π cm²/s. At what rate is the radius of the circle decreasing when its area is 75π cm²?

51. Each edge x of a square is increasing at the rate of 2 in./s. At what rate is the area A of the square increasing when each edge is 10 in.?

52. Each edge of an equilateral triangle is increasing at 2 cm/s (Fig. 3.3.4). At what rate is the area of the triangle increasing when each edge is 10 cm?

FIGURE 3.3.4 The triangle of Problem 52 with area $A = \frac{1}{2}xh$.

53. A cubical block of ice is melting in such a way that each edge decreases steadily by 2 in. every hour. At what rate is its volume decreasing when each edge is 10 in. long?

54. Find $f'(-1)$, given $f(y) = h(g(y))$, $h(2) = 55$, $g(-1) = 2$, $h'(2) = -1$, and $g'(-1) = 7$.

55. Given: $G(t) = f(h(t))$, $h(1) = 4$, $f'(4) = 3$, and $h'(1) = -6$. Find $G'(1)$.

56. Suppose that $f(0) = 0$ and that $f'(0) = 1$. Calculate the derivative of $f(f(f(x)))$ at $x = 0$.

57. Air is being pumped into a spherical balloon in such a way that its radius r is increasing at the rate of $dr/dt = 1$ cm/s. What is the time rate of increase, in cubic centimeters per second, of the balloon's volume when $r = 10$ cm?

58. Suppose that the air is being pumped into the balloon of Problem 57 at the constant rate of 200π cm³/s. What is the time rate of increase of the radius r when $r = 5$ cm?

59. Air is escaping from a spherical balloon at the constant rate of 300π cm³/s. What is the radius of the balloon when its radius is decreasing at the rate of 3 cm/s?

60. A spherical hailstone is losing mass by melting uniformly over its surface as it falls. At a certain time, its radius is 2 cm and its volume is decreasing at the rate of 0.1 cm³/s. How fast is its radius decreasing at that time?

61. A spherical snowball is melting in such a way that the rate of decrease of its volume is proportional to its surface area. At 10 A.M. its volume is 500 in.³ and at 11 A.M. its volume is 250 in.³. When does the snowball finish melting? (See Example 7.)

62. A cubical block of ice with edges 20 in. long begins to melt at 8 A.M. Each edge decreases at a constant rate thereafter and each is 8 in. long at 4 P.M. What was the rate of change of the block's volume at noon?

63. Suppose that u is a function of v, that v is a function of w, that w is a function of x, and that all these functions are differentiable. Explain why it follows from the chain rule that

$$\frac{du}{dx} = \frac{du}{dv} \cdot \frac{dv}{dw} \cdot \frac{dw}{dx}.$$

64. Let f be a differentiable function such that $f(1) = 1$. If $F(x) = f(x^n)$ and $G(x) = [f(x)]^n$ (where n is a fixed integer), show that $F(1) = G(1)$ and that $F'(1) = G'(1)$.

Recall from Example 13 in Section 2.2 that

$$D_x\left(\sqrt{x}\right) = \frac{1}{2\sqrt{x}}.$$

Use (only) this fact and the chain rule to calculate the derivative of each function given in Problems 65 through 68.

65. $h(x) = \sqrt{x+4}$

66. $h(x) = x^{3/2}$

67. $h(x) = (x^2+4)^{3/2}$

68. $h(x) = |x| = \sqrt{x^2}$

3.4 DERIVATIVES OF ALGEBRAIC FUNCTIONS

We saw in Section 3.3 that the chain rule yields the differentiation formula

$$D_x u^n = n u^{n-1} \frac{du}{dx} \qquad (1)$$

if $u = f(x)$ is a differentiable function and the exponent n is an integer. We shall see in Theorem 1 of this section that this **generalized power rule** holds not only when the exponent is an integer, but also when it is a rational number $r = p/q$ (where p and q

are integers and $q \neq 0$). Recall that rational powers are defined in terms of integral roots and powers as follows:

$$u^{p/q} = \sqrt[q]{u^p} = \left(\sqrt[q]{u}\right)^p.$$

We consider first the special case of the *root function*

$$f(x) = x^{1/q} = \sqrt[q]{x}$$

where q is a positive integer. If $x > 0$, then $y = x^{1/q}$ if and only if $x = y^q$. It follows that the point (x, y) lies on the graph of $y = f(x)$ if and only if its reflection (y, x) in the line $y = x$ lies on the graph of the *power function*

$$g(x) = x^q.$$

See Fig. 3.4.0, in which we show the fixed points $P(a, b)$ and $R(b, a)$ on the two graphs, as well as the variable points $Q(x, y)$ and $S(y, x)$ with $y = x^{1/q}$. Thinking of the limit of the slope of the line PQ as $x \to a$, we see that the derivative of the root function f at a is given by

$$f'(a) = \lim_{x \to a} \frac{y-b}{x-a} = \frac{1}{\lim_{x \to a} \dfrac{x-a}{y-b}} = \frac{1}{\lim_{y \to b} \dfrac{x-a}{y-b}}$$

(because continuity of f implies that $y \to b$ as $x \to a$). But the limit in the last denominator is the limit $g'(b)$ of the slope of the line RS as $y \to b$, so it follows that

$$f'(a) = \frac{1}{g'(b)} = \frac{1}{qb^{q-1}} = \frac{1}{q(a^{1/q})^{q-1}} = \frac{1}{q}a^{(1/q)-1}$$

(using the known derivative of the power function g). Finally, when we replace a with x and y with b, we see that the root function $f(x) = x^{1/q}$ is differentiable with derivative

$$f'(x) = D_x\left[x^{1/q}\right] = \frac{1}{q}x^{(1/q)-1} \tag{2}$$

if $x > 0$. The same argument shows that Eq. (2) also holds for $x < 0$ if q is an odd integer (so that no even root of a negative number is involved). Thus the power rule—which we established in Section 3.2 only for integral exponents—also holds if the exponent of x is the reciprocal $1/q$ of a positive integer q. (See Problems 72 through 75 for a different derivation of Eq. (2).)

Now we consider the case of a general rational power of the independent variable x:

$$y = x^{p/q}, \tag{3}$$

where p and q are integers with q positive. To calculate its derivative dy/dx, we can apply Eq. (1) with $n = p$ and $u = x^{1/q}$. Using Eq. (2) to calculate du/dx, we get

$$D_x\left[x^{p/q}\right] = D_x\left[(x^{1/q})^p\right]$$
$$= p(x^{1/q})^{p-1} \cdot D_x(x^{1/q})$$
$$= p(x^{1/q})^{p-1} \cdot \frac{1}{q}x^{(1/q)-1}$$
$$= \frac{p}{q}x^{(p/q)-(1/q)+(1/q)-1};$$

therefore

$$D_x\left[x^{p/q}\right] = \frac{p}{q}x^{(p/q)-1}.$$

Thus we have shown that the **power rule**

$$D_x x^r = rx^{r-1} \tag{4}$$

FIGURE 3.4.0 The graphs $y = x^{1/q}$ and $y = x^q$ are reflections of each other in the line $y = x$. The points R and S on $y = x^q$ are reflections of the points P and Q on $y = x^{1/q}$, and the tangent lines to the two curves at P and R are reflections of each other.

holds if the exponent $r = p/q$ is a rational number (subject to the conditions previously mentioned).

Using Eq. (4) we can differentiate a simple "radical" (or "root") function by first rewriting it as a power with a fractional exponent.

EXAMPLE 1

(a) $D_x\left[\sqrt{x}\right] = D_x\left[x^{1/2}\right] = \frac{1}{2}x^{-1/2} = \frac{1}{2\sqrt{x}}.$

(b) If $y = \sqrt{x^3}$, then $\frac{dy}{dx} = \frac{3}{2}x^{1/2} = \frac{3}{2}\sqrt{x}.$

(c) If $g(t) = \frac{1}{\sqrt[3]{t^2}} = t^{-2/3}$, then $g'(t) = -\frac{2}{3}t^{-5/3} = -\frac{2}{3\sqrt[3]{t^5}}.$ ◆

REMARK In parts (a) and (b) of Example 1 it is necessary that $x \geq 0$ in order that $\sqrt{x}$ be defined. In part (a) it is, moreover, necessary that $x \neq 0$; if $x = 0$ then the formula

$$D_x\left[\sqrt{x}\right] = \frac{1}{2\sqrt{x}}$$

would involve division by zero. Figure 3.4.1 shows the graphs of the function $f(x) = \sqrt{x}$ and its derivative $f'(x) = 1/(2\sqrt{x})$ for $x > 0$. Note that $f'(x) \to \infty$ as $x \to 0^+$, further emphasizing the fact that $f(x) = \sqrt{x}$ is not differentiable at $x = 0$.

FIGURE 3.4.1 The graphs of $f(x) = \sqrt{x}$ and $f'(x) = \frac{1}{2\sqrt{x}}$.

The Generalized Power Rule

For the more general form of the power rule, let

$$y = u^r$$

where u is a differentiable function of x and $r = p/q$ is rational. Then

$$\frac{dy}{du} = ru^{r-1}$$

by Eq. (4), so the chain rule gives

$$\frac{dy}{dx} = \frac{dy}{du} \cdot \frac{du}{dx} = ru^{r-1}\frac{du}{dx}.$$

Thus

$$D_x u^r = ru^{r-1}\frac{du}{dx}, \tag{5}$$

which is the generalized power rule for rational exponents.

THEOREM 1 Generalized Power Rule

If r is a rational number, then

$$D_x[f(x)]^r = r[f(x)]^{r-1} \cdot f'(x) \tag{6}$$

wherever the function f is differentiable and the right-hand side is defined.

For the right-hand side in Eq. (6) to be "defined" means that $f'(x)$ exists, there is no division by zero, and no even root of a negative number appears.

EXAMPLE 2

$$D_x\left[\sqrt{4-x^2}\right] = D_x\left[(4-x^2)^{1/2}\right] = \tfrac{1}{2}(4-x^2)^{-1/2} \cdot D_x(4-x^2)$$
$$= \tfrac{1}{2}(4-x^2)^{-1/2} \cdot (-2x);$$

$$D_x\left[\sqrt{4-x^2}\right] = -\frac{x}{\sqrt{4-x^2}} \tag{7}$$

except where $x = \pm 2$ (division by zero) or where $|x| > 2$ (square root of a negative number). Thus Eq. (7) holds if $-2 < x < 2$. In writing derivatives of algebraic functions, we ordinarily omit such disclaimers unless they are pertinent to some specific purpose at hand. But note in Fig. 3.4.2 that if $f(x) = \sqrt{4-x^2}$ then $f'(x) \to +\infty$ as $x \to -2^+$ and $f'(x) \to -\infty$ as $x \to +2^-$. ◆

A template for the application of the generalized power rule is

$$D_x([***]^n) = n[***]^{n-1} D_x[***],$$

where $***$ represents a function of x and (as we now know) n can be either an integer or a fraction (a quotient of integers).

But to differentiate a *power of a function*, we must first recognize *what function* it is a power *of*. So to differentiate a function involving roots (or radicals), we first "prepare" it for an application of the generalized power rule by rewriting it as a power function with fractional exponent. Examples 3 through 6 illustrate this technique.

FIGURE 3.4.2 The graphs of $f(x) = \sqrt{4-x^2}$ and $f'(x) = \dfrac{-x}{\sqrt{4-x^2}}$.

EXAMPLE 3 If $y = 5\sqrt{x^3} - \dfrac{2}{\sqrt[3]{x}}$, then

$$y = 5x^{3/2} - 2x^{-1/3},$$

so

$$\frac{dy}{dx} = 5 \cdot \left(\frac{3}{2}x^{1/2}\right) - 2 \cdot \left(-\frac{1}{3}x^{-4/3}\right) = \frac{15}{2}x^{1/2} + \frac{2}{3}x^{-4/3} = \frac{15}{2}\sqrt{x} + \frac{2}{3\sqrt[3]{x^4}}.$$ ◆

EXAMPLE 4 With $f(x) = 3 - 5x$ and $r = 7$, the generalized power rule yields

$$D_x[(3-5x)^7] = 7(3-5x)^6 D_x(3-5x)$$
$$= 7(3-5x)^6(-5) = -35(3-5x)^6.$$ ◆

EXAMPLE 5 With $f(x) = 2x^2 - 3x + 5$ and $r = \frac{1}{2}$, the generalized power rule yields

$$D_x\sqrt{2x^2 - 3x + 5} = D_x(2x^2 - 3x + 5)^{1/2}$$
$$= \frac{1}{2}(2x^2 - 3x + 5)^{-1/2} D_x(2x^2 - 3x + 5)$$
$$= \frac{4x - 3}{2\sqrt{2x^2 - 3x + 5}}.$$ ◆

EXAMPLE 6 If

$$x = \left[5t + \sqrt[3]{(3t-1)^4}\right]^{10}$$

then Eq. (5) with $u = 5t + (3t-1)^{4/3}$ and with independent variable t gives

$$\frac{dx}{dt} = 10u^9 \cdot \frac{du}{dt}$$
$$= 10\left[5t + (3t-1)^{4/3}\right]^9 \cdot D_t\left[5t + (3t-1)^{4/3}\right]$$
$$= 10\left[5t + (3t-1)^{4/3}\right]^9 \cdot \left[D_t(5t) + D_t(3t-1)^{4/3}\right]$$
$$= 10\left[5t + (3t-1)^{4/3}\right]^9 \cdot \left[5 + \tfrac{4}{3}(3t-1)^{1/3} \cdot 3\right];$$
$$\frac{dx}{dt} = 10\left[5t + (3t-1)^{4/3}\right]^9 \cdot \left[5 + 4(3t-1)^{1/3}\right].$$ ◆

Example 6 illustrates the fact that we apply the chain rule (or generalized power rule) by working from the *outside* to the *inside*. At each step the derivative of the outside function is multiplied by the derivative of the inside function. We continue until no "inside function" remains undifferentiated. Does the process remind you of peeling an onion, one layer at a time, until its core is reached?

Differentiability and Vertical Tangent Lines

Whereas polynomials and rational functions are both continuous and differentiable wherever they are defined, simple algebraic functions can be continuous at points where their derivatives do not exist.

EXAMPLE 7 If

$$f(x) = |x| = \sqrt{x^2}$$

denotes the absolute value function, then for $x \neq 0$ we find that

$$f'(x) = D_x\left[(x^2)^{1/2}\right] = \tfrac{1}{2}(x^2)^{-1/2}(2x) = \frac{x}{\sqrt{x^2}} = \frac{x}{|x|} = \begin{cases} -1 & \text{if } x < 0, \\ +1 & \text{if } x > 0. \end{cases}$$

Thus f is differentiable at every point except possibly for the origin $x = 0$. In fact, the graph of $f(x) = |x|$ in Fig. 3.4.3 makes it clear that the difference quotient

$$\frac{f(x) - f(0)}{x - 0} = \frac{|x|}{x}$$

has left-hand limit -1 and right-hand limit $+1$ at $x = 0$. Thus the absolute value function is not differentiable at the isolated point $x = 0$, where the graph $y = |x|$ has a "corner point" rather than a tangent line. (Can you think of a continuous function whose graph has *infinitely many* such corner points?) ◆

FIGURE 3.4.3 The graph of $f(x) = |x|$.

EXAMPLE 8 Figure 3.4.4 shows the graph of the cube-root function

$$y = \sqrt[3]{x} = x^{1/3},$$

and illustrates another way in which a function can fail to be differentiable at an isolated point. Its derivative,

$$\frac{dy}{dx} = \frac{1}{3}x^{-2/3} = \frac{1}{3\sqrt[3]{x^2}},$$

increases without bound as $x \to 0$ but does not exist at $x = 0$. Therefore, the definition of tangent line does not apply to this graph at $(0, 0)$. Nevertheless, from the figure it seems appropriate to regard the vertical line $x = 0$ as the line tangent to the curve $y = x^{1/3}$ at the point $(0, 0)$. ◆

FIGURE 3.4.4 The graph of the cube root function.

DEFINITION Vertical Tangent Line

The curve $y = f(x)$ has a **vertical tangent line** at the point $(a, f(a))$ provided that f is continuous at a and

$$|f'(x)| \to +\infty \quad \text{as} \quad x \to a. \tag{8}$$

Thus the graph of the continuous function $f(x) = x^{1/3}$ of Example 8 has a vertical tangent line at the origin, even though f is not differentiable at $x = 0$. Note that the requirement that f be continuous at $x = a$ implies that $f(a)$ must be defined. Thus it would be pointless to ask about a line (vertical or not) tangent to the curve $y = 1/x$ where $x = 0$.

If f is defined (and differentiable) on only one side of $x = a$, we mean in Eq. (8) that $|f'(x)| \to +\infty$ as x approaches a from that side.

EXAMPLE 9 Find the points on the curve

$$y = f(x) = x\sqrt{1-x^2}, \quad -1 \leq x \leq 1,$$

at which the tangent line is either horizontal or vertical.

Solution We differentiate using first the product rule and then the chain rule:

$$f'(x) = (1-x^2)^{1/2} + \frac{x}{2}(1-x^2)^{-1/2}(-2x)$$

$$= (1-x^2)^{-1/2}[(1-x^2) - x^2] = \frac{1-2x^2}{\sqrt{1-x^2}}.$$

Now $f'(x) = 0$ only when the numerator $1 - 2x^2$ is zero—that is, when $x = \pm 1/\sqrt{2}$. Because $f(\pm 1/\sqrt{2}) = \pm 1/2$, the curve has a horizontal tangent line at each of the two points $(1/\sqrt{2}, 1/2)$ and $(-1/\sqrt{2}, -1/2)$.

We also observe that the denominator $\sqrt{1-x^2}$ approaches zero as $x \to -1^+$ and as $x \to +1^-$. Because $f(\pm 1) = 0$, we see that the curve has a vertical tangent line at each of the two points $(1, 0)$ and $(-1, 0)$. The graph of f is shown in Fig. 3.4.5. ◆

FIGURE 3.4.5 The graph of $f(x) = x\sqrt{1-x^2}$, $-1 \leq x \leq 1$ (Example 9).

FIGURE 3.4.6 The graph of $y = 1 - \sqrt[5]{x^2}$ with a cusp at $(0, 1)$.

EXAMPLE 10 Figure 3.4.6 shows the graph of the function $f(x) = 1 - \sqrt[5]{x^2}$, which appears to have a sharp "cusp" (rather than a corner) at the point $(0, 1)$. Because the absolute value of the derivative $f'(x) = -\frac{2}{5}x^{-3/5}$ approaches $+\infty$ as $x \to 0$, the curve $y = f(x)$ has a vertical tangent at that point. ◆

Whereas the preceding examples show that a function can be continuous without being differentiable, the following theorem says that a function *is* continuous wherever it is differentiable. Thus differentiability of a function is a stronger condition than continuity alone.

THEOREM 2 Differentiability Implies Continuity
Suppose that the function f is defined in a neighborhood of a. If f is differentiable at a, then f is continuous at a.

PROOF Because $f'(a)$ exists, the product law for limits yields

$$\lim_{x \to a}[f(x) - f(a)] = \lim_{x \to a}(x-a) \cdot \frac{f(x) - f(a)}{x - a}$$

$$= \left(\lim_{x \to a}(x-a)\right)\left(\lim_{x \to a}\frac{f(x) - f(a)}{x - a}\right)$$

$$= 0 \cdot f'(a) = 0.$$

Thus $\lim_{x \to a} f(x) = f(a)$, so f is continuous at a. ◂

3.4 TRUE/FALSE STUDY GUIDE

3.4 CONCEPTS: QUESTIONS AND DISCUSSION

1. (a) Can you define a function that is continuous everywhere and has a "corner point" at each integer point $x = n$, but is differentiable at every other point of the real line? (b) Can you define a function that is continuous everywhere and has a vertical tangent line at each integer point $x = n$, but is differentiable at every other point of the real line?

2. Suppose that the function f has the following property: Every point x of the real line lies in a closed interval $[a, b]$ on which the graph of f is a semicircle having this interval as a diameter. Sketch a typical graph of such a function. Discuss the continuity and differentiability of f. *Remark:* The set of all endpoints of the closed intervals mentioned might (or might not) be the set of all integer points on the real line.

3. In Question 2, you may have assumed that each endpoint of the interval $[a, b]$ lies on exactly two such semicircles, one to the right and one to the left. Can you think of a function g whose graph consists entirely of semicircles, but does not satisfy this "two semicircles" condition? If so, discuss the differentiability of g. *Suggestion:* The construction of g might (or might not) involve the set $\{1, \frac{1}{2}, \frac{1}{3}, \frac{1}{4}, \frac{1}{5}, \ldots\}$ of all reciprocals of positive integers.

4. Suppose that the function f is continuous everywhere. At how many points do you suspect that f can fail to be differentiable? What's the worst such function you can think of?

3.4 PROBLEMS

Differentiate the functions given in Problems 1 through 44.

1. $f(x) = 4\sqrt{x^5} + \dfrac{2}{\sqrt{x}}$
2. $g(t) = 9\sqrt[3]{t^4} - \dfrac{3}{\sqrt[3]{t}}$
3. $f(x) = \sqrt{2x + 1}$
4. $h(z) = \dfrac{1}{\sqrt[3]{7 - 6z}}$
5. $f(x) = \dfrac{6 - x^2}{\sqrt{x}}$
6. $\phi(u) = \dfrac{7 + 2u - 3u^4}{\sqrt[3]{u^2}}$
7. $f(x) = (2x + 3)^{3/2}$
8. $g(x) = (3x + 4)^{4/3}$
9. $f(x) = (3 - 2x^2)^{-3/2}$
10. $f(y) = (4 - 3y^3)^{-2/3}$
11. $f(x) = \sqrt{x^3 + 1}$
12. $g(z) = \dfrac{1}{(z^4 + 3)^2}$
13. $f(x) = \sqrt{2x^2 + 1}$
14. $f(t) = \dfrac{t}{\sqrt{1 + t^4}}$
15. $f(t) = \sqrt{2t^3}$
16. $g(t) = \sqrt{\dfrac{1}{3t^5}}$
17. $f(x) = (2x^2 - x + 7)^{3/2}$
18. $g(z) = (3z^2 - 4)^{97}$
19. $g(x) = \dfrac{1}{(x - 2x^3)^{4/3}}$
20. $f(t) = [t^2 + (1 + t)^4]^5$
21. $f(x) = x\sqrt{1 - x^2}$
22. $g(x) = \sqrt{\dfrac{2x + 1}{x - 1}}$
23. $f(t) = \sqrt{\dfrac{t^2 + 1}{t^2 - 1}}$
24. $h(y) = \left(\dfrac{y + 1}{y - 1}\right)^{17}$
25. $f(x) = \left(x - \dfrac{1}{x}\right)^3$
26. $g(z) = \dfrac{z^2}{\sqrt{1 + z^2}}$
27. $f(v) = \dfrac{\sqrt{v + 1}}{v}$
28. $h(x) = \left(\dfrac{x}{1 + x^2}\right)^{5/3}$
29. $f(x) = \sqrt[3]{1 - x^2}$
30. $g(x) = \sqrt{x + \sqrt{x}}$
31. $f(x) = x(3 - 4x)^{1/2}$
32. $g(t) = \dfrac{t - (1 + t^2)^{1/2}}{t^2}$
33. $f(x) = (1 - x^2)(2x + 4)^{1/3}$
34. $f(x) = (1 - x)^{1/2}(2 - x)^{1/3}$
35. $g(t) = \left(1 + \dfrac{1}{t}\right)^2 (3t^2 + 1)^{1/2}$
36. $f(x) = x(1 + 2x + 3x^2)^{10}$
37. $f(x) = \dfrac{2x - 1}{(3x + 4)^5}$
38. $h(z) = (z - 1)^4 (z + 1)^6$

39. $f(x) = \dfrac{(2x+1)^{1/2}}{(3x+4)^{1/3}}$

40. $f(x) = (1-3x^4)^5(4-x)^{1/3}$

41. $h(y) = \dfrac{\sqrt{1+y}+\sqrt{1-y}}{\sqrt[3]{y^5}}$

42. $f(x) = \sqrt{1-\sqrt[3]{x}}$

43. $g(t) = \sqrt{t+\sqrt{t+\sqrt{t}}}$

44. $f(x) = x^3\sqrt{1-\dfrac{1}{x^2+1}}$

For each curve given in Problems 45 through 50, find all points on the graph where the tangent line is either horizontal or vertical.

45. $y = x^{2/3}$

46. $y = x\sqrt{4-x^2}$

47. $y = x^{1/2} - x^{3/2}$

48. $y = \dfrac{1}{\sqrt{9-x^2}}$

49. $y = \dfrac{x}{\sqrt{1-x^2}}$

50. $y = \sqrt{(1-x^2)(4-x^2)}$

In Problems 51 through 56, first write an equation of the line tangent to the given curve $y = f(x)$ at the indicated point P. Then illustrate your result with a graphing calculator or computer by graphing both the curve and the tangent line on the same screen.

51. $y = 2\sqrt{x}$, at the point P where $x = 4$

52. $y = 3\sqrt[3]{x}$, at the point P where $x = 8$

53. $y = 3\sqrt[3]{x^2}$, at the point P where $x = -1$

54. $y = 2\sqrt{1-x}$, at the point P where $x = \frac{3}{4}$

55. $y = x\sqrt{4-x}$, at the point P where $x = 0$

56. $y = (1-x)\sqrt{x}$, at the point P where $x = 4$

In Problems 57 through 62, match the given graph $y = f(x)$ of a function with the graph $y = f'(x)$ of its derivative among those shown in Figs. 3.4.13(a) through 3.4.13(f).

57. Figure 3.4.7

58. Figure 3.4.8

FIGURE 3.4.7 $y = x^{2/3}$ (Problem 57).

FIGURE 3.4.8 $y = x^{1/3}$ (Problem 58).

59. Figure 3.4.9

60. Figure 3.4.10

FIGURE 3.4.9 $y = 1 - x^{2/3}$ (Problem 59).

FIGURE 3.4.10 $y = x\sqrt{2-x}$ (Problem 60).

61. Figure 3.4.11

62. Figure 3.4.12

FIGURE 3.4.11 $y = x\sqrt{4-x^2}$ (Problem 61).

FIGURE 3.4.12 $y = (1-x^2)^2\sqrt{x^{2/3}}$ (Problem 62).

FIGURE 3.4.13(a)

FIGURE 3.4.13(b)

FIGURE 3.4.13(c)

FIGURE 3.4.13(d)

FIGURE 3.4.13(e)

FIGURE 3.4.13(f)

63. The period of oscillation P (in seconds) of a simple pendulum of length L (in feet) is given by $P = 2\pi\sqrt{L/g}$, where $g = 32$ ft/s². Find the rate of change of P with respect to L when $P = 2$.

64. Find the rate of change of the volume $V = \frac{4}{3}\pi r^3$ of a sphere of radius r with respect to its surface area $A = 4\pi r^2$ when $r = 10$.

65. Find the two points on the circle $x^2 + y^2 = 1$ at which the slope of the tangent line is -2 (Fig. 3.4.14).

FIGURE 3.4.14 The two tangent lines of Problem 65.

66. Find the two points on the circle $x^2 + y^2 = 1$ at which the slope of the tangent line is 3.

67. Find a line through the point $P(18, 0)$ that is normal to the tangent line to the parabola $y = x^2$ at some point $Q(a, a^2)$ (see Fig. 3.4.15). (*Suggestion:* You will obtain a cubic equation in the unknown a. Find by inspection a small integral root r. The cubic polynomial is then the product of $a - r$ and a quadratic polynomial; you can find the latter by division of $a - r$ into the cubic.)

FIGURE 3.4.15 The tangent and normal of Problem 67.

68. Find three distinct lines through the point $P(3, 10)$ that are normal to the parabola $y = x^2$ (Fig. 3.4.16). (See the suggestion for Problem 67. This problem will require a certain amount of calculator-aided computation.)

FIGURE 3.4.16 The three normal lines of Problem 68.

69. Find two distinct lines through the point $P(0, \frac{5}{2})$ that are normal to the curve $y = x^{2/3}$ (Fig. 3.4.17).

FIGURE 3.4.17 The two normal lines of Problem 69.

70. Verify that the line tangent to the circle $x^2 + y^2 = a^2$ at the point P is perpendicular to the radius OP (Fig. 3.4.18).

FIGURE 3.4.18 The circle, radius, and tangent line of Problem 70.

71. Consider the cubic equation $x^3 = 3x + 8$. If we differentiate each side with respect to x, we obtain $3x^2 = 3$, which has the two solutions $x = 1$ and $x = -1$. But neither of these is a solution of the original cubic equation. What went wrong? Why does differentiation of both sides of the cubic equation give an invalid result?

142 CHAPTER 3 The Derivative

The derivation of the generalized power rule $D_x u^r = r u^{r-1} \cdot D_x u$ (for $r = p/q$, a rational number) provided in this section depends on the assumed differentiability of the qth root function $f(x) = x^{1/q}$. If $a > 0$ and q is a positive integer, then the derivative of f is given by

$$f'(a) = \lim_{x \to a} \frac{x^{1/q} - a^{1/q}}{x - a} \quad (9)$$

provided that this limit exists. Problems 72 through 75 illustrate the evaluation of this limit using the algebraic identity

$$s^q - t^q = (s - t)\underbrace{(s^{q-1} + s^{q-2}t + \cdots + st^{q-2} + t^{q-1})}_{q \text{ terms}}. \quad (10)$$

For instance, with $s = x^{1/q}$ and $t = a^{1/q}$ this identity yields (with $q = 2, 3,$ and 5) the formulas

$$x - a = \left(x^{1/2} - a^{1/2}\right)\left(x^{1/2} + a^{1/2}\right), \quad (11)$$

$$x - a = \left(x^{1/3} - a^{1/3}\right)\left(x^{2/3} + x^{1/3}a^{1/3} + a^{2/3}\right), \quad (12)$$

and

$$x - a = \left(x^{1/5} - a^{1/5}\right)\left(x^{4/5} + x^{3/5}a^{1/5} \right.$$
$$\left. + x^{2/5}a^{2/5} + x^{1/5}a^{3/5} + a^{4/5}\right). \quad (13)$$

72. Substitute (11) in the denominator in (9) to show that $D_x x^{1/2} = \frac{1}{2} x^{-1/2}$ for $x > 0$.

73. Substitute (12) in the denominator in (9) to show that $D_x x^{1/3} = \frac{1}{3} x^{-2/3}$ for $x > 0$.

74. Substitute (13) in the denominator in (9) to show that $D_x x^{1/5} = \frac{1}{5} x^{-4/5}$ for $x > 0$.

75. Finally, explain how Eq. (10) can be applied in the general case to prove that

$$D_x x^{1/q} = \frac{1}{q} x^{-(q-1)/q}$$

if $x > 0$ and q is a positive integer.

3.5 | MAXIMA AND MINIMA OF FUNCTIONS ON CLOSED INTERVALS

FIGURE 3.5.1 The animal pen.

In applications we often need to find the maximum (largest) or minimum (smallest) value that a specified quantity can attain. The animal pen problem posed in Section 1.1 is a simple yet typical example of an applied maximum-minimum problem. There we investigated the animal pen shown in Fig. 3.5.1, with the indicated dollar-per-foot cost figures for its four sides. We showed that if $180 is allocated for material to construct this pen, then its area $A = f(x)$ is given as a function of its base length x by

$$f(x) = \tfrac{3}{5}x(30 - x), \quad 0 \leq x \leq 30. \quad (1)$$

Hence the question of the largest possible area of the animal pen is equivalent to the purely mathematical problem of finding the maximum value attained by the function $f(x) = \tfrac{3}{5}x(30 - x)$ on the closed interval $[0, 30]$.

DEFINITION Maximum and Minimum Values
If c is in the closed interval $[a, b]$, then $f(c)$ is called the **minimum value** of $f(x)$ on $[a, b]$ if $f(c) \leq f(x)$ for all x in $[a, b]$. Similarly, if d is in $[a, b]$, then $f(d)$ is called the **maximum value** of $f(x)$ on $[a, b]$ if $f(d) \geq f(x)$ for all x in $[a, b]$.

Thus if $f(c)$ is the minimum value and $f(d)$ the maximum value of $f(x)$ on $[a, b]$, then

$$f(c) \leq f(x) \leq f(d) \quad (2)$$

for all x in $[a, b]$, and hence $f(x)$ attains no value smaller than $f(c)$ or larger than $f(d)$. In geometric terms, $(c, f(c))$ is a *low point* and $(d, f(d))$ is a *high point* on the curve $y = f(x), a \leq x \leq b$, as illustrated in Figs. 3.5.2 and 3.5.3.

Theorem 1 (proved in Appendix E) says that a continuous function f on a closed interval $[a, b]$ attains a minimum value $f(c)$ and a maximum value $f(d)$, so the inequalities in (2) hold: The curve $y = f(x)$ over $[a, b]$ has both a lowest point and a highest point.

Maxima and Minima of Functions on Closed Intervals SECTION 3.5   143

FIGURE 3.5.2 $f(c)$ is the minimum value and $f(d)$ is the maximum value of $f(x)$ on $[a, b]$.

FIGURE 3.5.3 Maximum and minimum values can occur at the endpoints of an interval. Here $f(a)$ is the minimum value and $f(b)$ is the maximum value of $f(x)$ on $[a, b]$.

THEOREM 1 Maximum and Minimum Value Property
If the function f is continuous on the closed interval $[a, b]$, then there exist numbers c and d in $[a, b]$ such that $f(c)$ is the minimum value, and $f(d)$ the maximum value, of f on $[a, b]$.

In short, a continuous function defined on a closed and bounded interval attains both a minimum value and a maximum value at points of the interval. Hence we see it is the *continuity* of the function

$$f(x) = \frac{3}{5}x(30 - x)$$

on the *closed* interval $[0, 30]$ that guarantees that the maximum value of f exists and is attained at some point of the interval $[0, 30]$.

Suppose that the function f is defined on the interval I. Examples 1 and 2 show that if *either f is not continuous or I is not closed*, then f may fail to attain maximum and minimum values at points of I. Thus both hypotheses in Theorem 1 are necessary.

FIGURE 3.5.4 The graph of the function of Example 1.

EXAMPLE 1 Let the continuous function $f(x) = 2x$ be defined only for $0 \leq x < 1$, so that its domain of definition is not a closed interval. From the graph shown in Fig. 3.5.4, it is clear that f attains its minimum value 0 at $x = 0$. But $f(x) = 2x$ attains *no* maximum value at any point of $[0, 1)$. The only possible candidate for a maximum value would be the value 2 at $x = 1$, but $f(1)$ is not defined. ◆

EXAMPLE 2 The function f defined on the closed interval $[0, 1]$ with the formula

$$f(x) = \begin{cases} \dfrac{1}{x} & \text{if } 0 < x \leq 1, \\ 1 & \text{if } x = 0 \end{cases}$$

is not continuous on $[0, 1]$ because $\lim_{x \to 0^+}(1/x)$ does not exist (Fig. 3.5.5). This function does attain its minimum value of 1 at $x = 0$ and also at $x = 1$. But it attains no maximum value on $[0, 1]$ because $1/x$ can be made arbitrarily large by choosing x positive and very close to zero. ◆

FIGURE 3.5.5 The graph of the function of Example 2.

For a variation on Example 2, the function $g(x) = 1/x$ with domain the *open* interval $(0, 1)$ attains neither a maximum nor a minimum there.

Local Maxima and Minima

Once we know that the continuous function f *does* attain minimum and maximum values on the closed interval $[a, b]$, the remaining question is this: Exactly *where* are these values located? We solved the animal pen problem in Section 2.1 on the basis of the following assumption, motivated by geometry: The function $f(x) = \frac{3}{5}x(30-x)$ attains its maximum value on $[0, 30]$ at an interior point of that interval, a point at which the tangent line is horizontal. Theorems 2 and 3 of this section provide a rigorous basis for the method we used there.

We say that the value $f(c)$ is a **local maximum value** of the function f if $f(x) \leq f(c)$ for all x sufficiently near c. More precisely, if this inequality holds for all x that are simultaneously in the domain of f and in some open interval containing c, then $f(c)$ is a local maximum of f. Similarly, we say that the value $f(c)$ is a **local minimum value** of f if $f(x) \geq f(c)$ for all x sufficiently near c.

As Fig. 3.5.6 shows, a local maximum is a point such that no nearby points on the graph are higher, and a local minimum is one such that no nearby points on the graph are lower. A **local extremum** of f is a value of f that is either a local maximum or a local minimum.

FIGURE 3.5.6 Local extrema.

THEOREM 2 Local Maxima and Minima
Suppose that f is differentiable at c and is defined on a open interval containing c. If $f(c)$ is either a local maximum value or a local minimum value of f, then $f'(c) = 0$.

Thus a local extremum of a *differentiable* function on an *open* interval can occur only at a point where the derivative is zero and, therefore, where the line tangent to the graph is horizontal.

PROOF OF THEOREM 2 Suppose, for instance, that $f(c)$ is a local maximum value of f. The assumption that $f'(c)$ exists means that the right-hand and left-hand limits

$$\lim_{h \to 0^+} \frac{f(c+h) - f(c)}{h} \quad \text{and} \quad \lim_{h \to 0^-} \frac{f(c+h) - f(c)}{h}$$

both exist and are equal to $f'(c)$.

If $h > 0$, then

$$\frac{f(c+h) - f(c)}{h} \leq 0,$$

because $f(c) \geq f(c+h)$ for all small positive values of h. Hence, by a one-sided version of the squeeze law for limits (in Section 2.2), this inequality is preserved when we take the limit as $h \to 0$. We thus find that

$$f'(c) = \lim_{h \to 0^+} \frac{f(c+h) - f(c)}{h} \leq \lim_{h \to 0^+} 0 = 0.$$

Similarly, in the case $h < 0$, we find that

$$\frac{f(c+h) - f(c)}{h} \geq 0.$$

Therefore,

$$f'(c) = \lim_{h \to 0^-} \frac{f(c+h) - f(c)}{h} \geq \lim_{h \to 0^-} 0 = 0.$$

Because both $f'(c) \leq 0$ and $f'(c) \geq 0$, we conclude that $f'(c) = 0$. This establishes Theorem 2. ◄

FIGURE 3.5.7 There is no extremum at $x = 0$ even though the derivative is zero there.

BEWARE The converse of Theorem 2 is false. That is, the fact that $f'(c) = 0$ is *not enough* to imply that $f(c)$ is a local extremum. For example, consider the function $f(x) = x^3$. Its derivative $f'(x) = 3x^2$ is zero at $x = 0$. But a glance at its graph (Fig. 3.5.7) shows us that $f(0)$ is *not* a local extremum of f.

Thus the equation $f'(c) = 0$ is a *necessary* condition for $f(c)$ to be a local maximum or minimum value for a function f that is differentiable on an open interval containing c. It is not a *sufficient* condition. The reason: $f'(x)$ may well be zero at points other than local maxima and minima. We give sufficient conditions for local maxima and minima in Chapter 4.

The Closed Interval Maximum-Minimum Method

In most types of optimization problems, we are less interested in the local extrema (as such) than in the *absolute*, or *global*, maximum and minimum values attained by a given continuous function. If f is a function with domain D, we call $f(c)$ the **absolute maximum value**, or **global maximum value**, of f on D provided that $f(c) \geqq f(x)$ for all x in D. Briefly, $f(c)$ is the largest value of f on D. It should be clear how the global minimum of f is to be defined. Figure 3.5.8 illustrates some local and global extrema. On the one hand, every global extremum is, of course, local as well. On the other hand, the graph shows local extrema that are not global.

Theorem 3 tells us that the absolute maximum and absolute minimum values of the continuous function f on the closed interval $[a, b]$ occur either at one of the endpoints a or b or at a *critical point* of f. The number c in the domain of f is called a **critical point** of f if either

- $f'(c) = 0$, or
- $f'(c)$ does not exist.

FIGURE 3.5.8 Some extrema are global; others are merely local.

THEOREM 3 Absolute Maxima and Minima

Suppose that $f(c)$ is the absolute maximum (or absolute minimum) value of the continuous function f on the closed interval $[a, b]$. Then c is either a critical point of f or one of the endpoints a and b.

PROOF This result follows almost immediately from Theorem 2. If c is not an endpoint of $[a, b]$, then $f(c)$ is a local extremum of f on the open interval (a, b). In this case Theorem 2 implies that $f'(c) = 0$, provided that f is differentiable at c. ◂

As a consequence of Theorem 3, we can find the (absolute) maximum and minimum values of the function f on the closed interval $[a, b]$ as follows:

1. *Locate* the critical points of f: those points where $f'(x) = 0$ and those points where $f'(x)$ does not exist.
2. *List* the values of x that yield *possible* extrema of f: the two endpoints a and b and those critical points that lie in $[a, b]$.
3. *Evaluate* $f(x)$ at each point in this list of possible extrema.
4. *Inspect* these values of $f(x)$ to see which is the smallest and which is the largest.

The largest of the values in Step 4 is the absolute maximum value of f; the smallest, the absolute minimum. We call this procedure the **closed-interval maximum-minimum method**.

EXAMPLE 3 For our final discussion of the animal pen problem, let us apply the closed-interval maximum-minimum method to find the maximum and minimum values of the differentiable function

$$f(x) = \tfrac{3}{5}x(30 - x) = \tfrac{3}{5}(30x - x^2)$$

on the closed interval [0, 30].

Solution The derivative of f is

$$f'(x) = \tfrac{3}{5}(30 - 2x),$$

which is zero only at the point $x = 15$ in [0, 30]. Including the two endpoints, our list of the only values of x that can yield extrema of f consists of 0, 15, and 30. We evaluate f at each:

$f(0) = 0,$ ← absolute minimum

$f(15) = 135,$ ← absolute maximum

$f(30) = 0.$ ← absolute minimum

Thus the maximum value of $f(x)$ on [0, 30] is 135 (attained at $x = 15$), and the minimum value is 0 (attained both at $x = 0$ and at $x = 30$). ◆

EXAMPLE 4 Find the maximum and minimum values of

$$f(x) = 2x^3 - 3x^2 - 12x + 15$$

on the closed interval [0, 3].

Solution The derivative of f is

$$f'(x) = 6x^2 - 6x - 12 = 6(x - 2)(x + 1).$$

So the critical points of f are the solutions of the equation

$$6(x - 2)(x + 1) = 0$$

and the numbers c for which $f'(c)$ does not exist. There are none of the latter, so the critical points of f occur at $x = -1$ and $x = 2$. The first of these is not in the domain of f; we discard it, and thus the only critical point of f in [0, 3] is $x = 2$. Including the two endpoints, our list of all values of x that yield a possible maximum or minimum value of f consists of 0, 2, and 3. We evaluate the function f at each:

$f(0) = 15,$ ← absolute maximum

$f(2) = -5,$ ← absolute minimum

$f(3) = 6.$

Therefore the maximum value of f on [0, 3] is $f(0) = 15$ and its minimum value is $f(2) = -5$. ◆

If in Example 4 we had asked for the maximum and minimum values of $f(x)$ on the interval [−2, 3] (instead of the interval [0, 3]), then we would have included *both* critical points $x = -1$ and $x = 2$ in our list of possibilities. The resulting values of f would have been

$f(-2) = 11,$

$f(-1) = 22,$ ← absolute maximum

$f(2) = -5,$ ← absolute minimum

$f(3) = 6.$

Maxima and Minima of Functions on Closed Intervals SECTION 3.5   147

Figure 3.5.9 shows both the curve $y = f(x)$ and the graph of its derivative. Note the vertical line segments joining high and low points on $y = f(x)$ with x-intercepts of $dy/dx = f'(x)$. Thus the figure illustrates the following fact:

> The critical points of a differentiable function $f(x)$ are the zeros of its derivative $f'(x)$.

On the basis of this principle, we can approximate a critical point of f graphically by "zooming in" on a zero of f'.

In Example 4 the function f was differentiable everywhere. Examples 5 and 6 illustrate the case of an extremum at a critical point where the function is not differentiable.

FIGURE 3.5.9 The critical points of the differentiable function $f(x)$ are the zeros of $f'(x)$.

EXAMPLE 5 Find the maximum and minimum values of the function $f(x) = 3 - |x - 2|$ on the interval $[1, 4]$.

Solution If $x \leq 2$, then $x - 2 \leq 0$, so

$$f(x) = 3 - (2 - x) = x + 1.$$

If $x \geq 2$, then $x - 2 \geq 0$, so

$$f(x) = 3 - (x - 2) = 5 - x.$$

Consequently, the graph of f looks like the one shown in Fig. 3.5.10. The only critical point of f in $[1, 4]$ is the point $x = 2$, because $f'(x)$ takes on only the two values $+1$ and -1 (and so is never zero), and $f'(2)$ does not exist. (Why not?) Evaluation of f at this critical point and at the two endpoints yields

$$f(1) = 2,$$
$$f(2) = 3, \quad \longleftarrow \text{absolute maximum}$$
$$f(4) = 1. \quad \longleftarrow \text{absolute minimum}$$

FIGURE 3.5.10 Graph of the function of Example 5.

EXAMPLE 6 Find the maximum and minimum values of

$$f(x) = 5x^{2/3} - x^{5/3}$$

on the closed interval $[-1, 4]$.

Solution Differentiating f yields

$$f'(x) = \frac{10}{3}x^{-1/3} - \frac{5}{3}x^{2/3} = \frac{5}{3}x^{-1/3}(2 - x) = \frac{5(2 - x)}{3x^{1/3}}.$$

Hence f has two critical points in the interval: $x = 2$, where $f'(x) = 0$, and $x = 0$, where $f'(x)$ does not exist (the graph of f has a vertical tangent at $(0, 0)$). When we evaluate f at these two critical points and at the two endpoints, we get

$$f(-1) = 6, \quad \longleftarrow \text{absolute maximum}$$
$$f(0) = 0 \quad \longleftarrow \text{absolute minimum}$$
$$f(2) = 5 \cdot 2^{2/3} - 2^{5/3} \approx 4.76,$$
$$f(4) = 5 \cdot 4^{2/3} - 4^{5/3} \approx 2.52.$$

Thus the maximum value $f(-1) = 6$ occurs at an endpoint. The minimum value $f(0) = 0$ occurs at a point where f is not differentiable. ◆

By using a graphics calculator or computer with graphics capabilities, you can verify that the graph of the function f of Example 6 is that shown in Fig. 3.5.11. But in the usual case of a continuous function that has only finitely many critical points in a given closed interval, the closed-interval maximum-minimum method suffices to

148 CHAPTER 3 The Derivative

FIGURE 3.5.11 Graph of the function of Example 6.

FIGURE 3.5.12 The graphs $y = f(x)$ and $y = f'(x)$.

FIGURE 3.5.13 Zooming in on the minimum shown in Fig. 3.5.12.

FIGURE 3.5.14 Zooming in instead on the zero of $f'(x)$ shown in Fig. 3.5.12.

determine its maximum and minimum values without requiring any detailed knowledge of the graph of the function.

EXAMPLE 7 Figure 3.5.12 shows the graphs of the function

$$f(x) = 4x^4 - 11x^2 - 5x - 3$$

and its derivative

$$f'(x) = 16x^3 - 22x - 5$$

in the viewing window $-3 \leq x \leq 3$, $-30 \leq y \leq 30$. Evidently the maximum value of $f(x)$ on the closed interval $[-2, 2]$ is the left-endpoint value $f(-2) = 27$.

The lowest point on the graph of $y = f(x)$ and the corresponding zero of its derivative $dy/dx = f'(x)$ lie within the small boxes in the figure. To find this lowest point exactly we would need to solve the cubic equation $16x^3 - 22x - 5 = 0$. But the lowest point also can be located approximately by using a graphing calculator or computer to zoom in more closely.

If we attempt to zoom in on the lowest point without changing the "range factors" or "aspect ratios" of the viewing window, we get a picture like the one in Fig. 3.5.13. Here the magnified graph is indistinguishable from its horizontal tangent line at the low point, so it's impossible to gauge accurately the x-coordinate of the critical point.

Consequently, it is much more effective to zoom in on the corresponding zero of the derivative $f'(x)$. We can then locate the indicated critical point with much greater precision. Thus it is clear in Fig. 3.5.14 that the minimum value attained by $f(x)$ on $[-2, 2]$ is approximately $f(1.273) \approx -16.686$. ◆

3.5 TRUE/FALSE STUDY GUIDE

3.5 CONCEPTS: QUESTIONS AND DISCUSSION

1. Suppose that the function f is continuous on the closed interval $[a, b]$. In each of the five following cases, sketch a possible graph (if any) of f.
   (a) f has a single critical point c but neither a local minimum nor a local maximum in the open interval (a, b). Discuss the possibility that f is not differentiable at c and the possibility that f is differentiable there.
   (b) f has two critical points but only a single local extremum in (a, b).
   (c) f has both a local maximum and a local minimum, but only one critical point in (a, b).
   (d) f has exactly one local maximum, exactly one local minimum, and exactly three critical points in (a, b).
   (e) f has three local maxima but only a single local minimum in (a, b).

2. Can you give an example of a polynomial of odd degree that has neither a local minimum value nor a local maximum value? Can you give an example of a polynomial of even degree that has neither an absolute minimum value nor an absolute maximum value?

3. Assume that you have located a point on the graph of a differentiable function where a local extremum occurs. Suppose that you zoom in on this point with a graphing calculator or computer, magnifying at each step by the same factor in the x-direction and the y-direction. Should the graph always look like a horizontal line (as in Fig. 3.5.13) after zooming in sufficiently closely in this manner?

3.5 PROBLEMS

In Problems 1 through 10, state whether the given function attains a maximum value or a minimum value (or both) on the given interval. [Suggestion: Begin by sketching a graph of the function.]

1. $f(x) = 1 - x$; $[-1, 1)$
2. $f(x) = 2x + 1$; $[-1, 1)$
3. $f(x) = |x|$; $(-1, 1)$
4. $f(x) = \dfrac{1}{\sqrt{x}}$; $(0, 1]$
5. $f(x) = |x - 2|$; $(1, 4]$
6. $f(x) = 5 - x^2$; $[-1, 2)$
7. $f(x) = x^3 + 1$; $[-1, 1]$
8. $f(x) = \dfrac{1}{x^2 + 1}$; $(-\infty, \infty)$
9. $f(x) = \dfrac{1}{x(1-x)}$; $[2, 3]$
10. $f(x) = \dfrac{1}{x(1-x)}$; $(0, 1)$

In Problems 11 through 40, find the maximum and minimum values attained by the given function on the indicated closed interval.

11. $f(x) = 3x - 2$; $[-2, 3]$
12. $f(x) = 4 - 3x$; $[-1, 5]$
13. $h(x) = 4 - x^2$; $[1, 3]$
14. $f(x) = x^2 + 3$; $[0, 5]$
15. $g(x) = (x - 1)^2$; $[-1, 4]$
16. $h(x) = x^2 + 4x + 7$; $[-3, 0]$
17. $f(x) = x^3 - 3x$; $[-2, 4]$
18. $g(x) = 2x^3 - 9x^2 + 12x$; $[0, 4]$
19. $h(x) = x + \dfrac{4}{x}$; $[1, 4]$
20. $f(x) = x^2 + \dfrac{16}{x}$; $[1, 3]$
21. $f(x) = 3 - 2x$; $[-1, 1]$
22. $f(x) = x^2 - 4x + 3$; $[0, 2]$
23. $f(x) = 5 - 12x - 9x^2$; $[-1, 1]$
24. $f(x) = 2x^2 - 4x + 7$; $[0, 2]$
25. $f(x) = x^3 - 3x^2 - 9x + 5$; $[-2, 4]$
26. $f(x) = x^3 + x$; $[-1, 2]$
27. $f(x) = 3x^5 - 5x^3$; $[-2, 2]$
28. $f(x) = |2x - 3|$; $[1, 2]$
29. $f(x) = 5 + |7 - 3x|$; $[1, 5]$
30. $f(x) = |x + 1| + |x - 1|$; $[-2, 2]$
31. $f(x) = 50x^3 - 105x^2 + 72x$; $[0, 1]$
32. $f(x) = 2x + \dfrac{1}{2x}$; $[1, 4]$
33. $f(x) = \dfrac{x}{x + 1}$; $[0, 3]$
34. $f(x) = \dfrac{x}{x^2 + 1}$; $[0, 3]$
35. $f(x) = \dfrac{1 - x}{x^2 + 3}$; $[-2, 5]$
36. $f(x) = 2 - \sqrt[3]{x}$; $[-1, 8]$
37. $f(x) = x\sqrt{1 - x^2}$; $[-1, 1]$
38. $f(x) = x\sqrt{4 - x^2}$; $[0, 2]$
39. $f(x) = x(2 - x)^{1/3}$; $[1, 3]$
40. $f(x) = x^{1/2} - x^{3/2}$; $[0, 4]$

41. Suppose that $f(x) = Ax + B$ is a linear function and that $A \neq 0$. Explain why the maximum and minimum values of f on a closed interval $[a, b]$ must occur at the endpoints of the interval.

42. Suppose that f is continuous on $[a, b]$ and differentiable on (a, b) and that $f'(x)$ is never zero at any point of (a, b). Explain why the maximum and minimum values of f must occur at the endpoints of the interval $[a, b]$.

43. Explain why every real number is a critical point of the greatest integer function $f(x) = [\![x]\!]$.

44. Prove that every quadratic function

$$f(x) = ax^2 + bx + c \quad (a \neq 0)$$

has exactly one critical point on the real line.

45. Explain why the cubic polynomial function

$$f(x) = ax^3 + bx^2 + cx + d \quad (a \neq 0)$$

can have either two, one, or no critical points on the real line. Produce examples that illustrate each of the three cases.

46. Define $f(x)$ to be the distance from x to the nearest integer. What are the critical points of f?

In Problems 47 through 52, match the given graph of the function with the graph of its derivative f' from those in Fig. 3.5.15, parts (a) through (f).

(a)

(b)

(c)

(d)

(e)

(f)

FIGURE 3.5.15

47. Figure 3.5.16

48. Figure 3.5.17

FIGURE 3.5.16

FIGURE 3.5.17

49. Fig. 3.5.18

FIGURE 3.5.18

50. Fig. 3.5.19

FIGURE 3.5.19

51. Fig. 3.5.20

FIGURE 3.5.20

52. Fig. 3.5.21

FIGURE 3.5.21

In Problems 53 through 60, find good approximations to the maximum and minimum values of the given function on the indicated closed interval by zooming in on the zeros of the derivative.

53. $f(x) = x^3 + 3x^2 - 7x + 10$; $[-2, 2]$

54. $f(x) = x^3 + 3x^2 - 7x + 10$; $[-4, 2]$

55. $f(x) = x^4 - 3x^3 + 7x - 5$; $[-3, 3]$

56. $f(x) = x^4 - 5x^3 + 17x - 5$; $[-3, 3]$

57. $f(x) = x^4 - 5x^3 + 17x - 5$; $[0, 2]$

58. $f(x) = x^5 - 5x^4 - 15x^3 + 17x^2 + 23x$; $[-1, 1]$

59. $f(x) = x^5 - 5x^4 - 15x^3 + 17x^2 + 23x$; $[-3, 3]$

60. $f(x) = x^5 - 5x^4 - 15x^3 + 17x^2 + 23x$; $[0, 10]$

3.5 Project: When Is Your Coffee Cup Stablest?

Your car has no cupholder, so you must place your filled coffee cup on the passenger seat beside you when you start out in the morning. Bitter experience has taught you that the cup is least stable—and most prone to spill—when it's completely full, but becomes more stable as you drink the coffee and thereby lower its level in the cup. Now you're ready to apply calculus to analyze this phenomenon.

Figure 3.5.22 shows a coffee cup partially filled with coffee. We will assume that it is stablest when the *centroid* of the cup-plus-coffee is lowest. The **centroid** of a solid cylinder or cylindrical shell is its geometric central point, and the y-coordinate $\bar{y}$ of the centroid of a composite body consisting of several pieces with masses m_1, m_2, and m_3 having centroids with respective y-coordinates y_1, y_2, and y_3 is given by

$$\bar{y} = \frac{m_1 y_1 + m_2 y_2 + m_3 y_3}{m_1 + m_2 + m_3}. \tag{1}$$

This formula means that $\bar{y}$ is an average of the y-coordinates y_1, y_2, and y_3 of the individual centroids, each weighted by the corresponding mass.

The simplified model of the coffee cup shown in Fig. 3.5.22 consists of the following:

- A side surface that is a cylindrical shell with height H, inner radius R, and thickness T, and
- A bottom that is a solid cylinder with radius $R + T$ and height B.

FIGURE 3.5.22 Coffee cup partially filled with coffee to depth y.

FIGURE 3.5.23 Centroid height $f(y)$ as a function of coffee depth y.

The cup is partially filled with coffee with depth y and density 1 g/cm³. In the CD-ROM discussion of this project, we take $H = 8$, $R = 3$, $T = 0.5$, and $B = 1$ (all units are centimeters). Assuming also that the density of the material of the cup itself is $\delta = 1$ g/cm³, we apply Eq. (1) to derive the function

$$f(y) = \frac{87 + 4y^2}{34 + 8y}, \quad 0 \leq y \leq 8 \tag{2}$$

giving the y-coordinate $\bar{y} = f(y)$ of the centroid of the cup-plus-coffee as a function of the depth y of the coffee in the cup.

Figure 3.5.23 shows the graph of the function f. It appears that the centroid is lowest when $y = 2$, and thus when the cup is about one-quarter filled with coffee. To find when $f'(y) = 0$, you can differentiate the function in (2) and simplify to obtain

$$f'(y) = \frac{2(4y^2 + 34y - 87)}{(4y + 17)^2}. \tag{3}$$

Thus you need only solve a quadratic equation to see where the numerator is zero: when $y = \frac{1}{4}(-17 \pm 7\sqrt{13})$. The positive solution gives the optimal depth $y \approx 2.0597$ cm of the coffee in your cup—just a bit more than a quarter of the height $H = 8$ cm of the cup.

Carry out this analysis with your own favorite coffee cup. Measure its physical dimensions H, R, T, and B. How can you determine the approximate density δ of its material?

3.6 APPLIED OPTIMIZATION PROBLEMS

This section is devoted to applied maximum-minimum problems (like the animal pen problem of Section 1.1) for which the closed-interval maximum-minimum method of Section 3.5 can be used. When we confront such a problem, there is an important first step: We must determine the quantity to be maximized or minimized. This quantity will be the dependent variable in our analysis of the problem.

This dependent variable must then be expressed as a function of an independent variable, one that "controls" the values of the dependent variable. If the domain of values of the independent variable—those that are pertinent to the applied problem—is a closed interval, then we may proceed with the closed-interval maximum-minimum method. This plan of attack can be summarized in the following steps:

1. *Find the quantity to be maximized or minimized.* This quantity, which you should describe with a word or short phrase and label with a descriptive letter, will be the dependent variable. Because it is a *dependent* variable, it depends on something else; that quantity will be the independent variable. Here we call the independent variable x.

2. *Express the dependent variable as a function of the independent variable.* Use the information in the problem to write the dependent variable as a function of x. Always draw a figure and *label the variables;* this is generally the best way to find the relationship between the dependent and independent variables. Use auxiliary variables if they help, but not too many, for you must eventually eliminate them. You *must* express the dependent variable as a function of the *single* independent variable x and various constants before you can compute any derivatives. Find the domain of this function as well as its formula. Force the domain to be a closed and bounded interval if possible—if the natural domain is an open interval, adjoin the endpoints if you can.

3. *Apply calculus to find the critical points.* Compute the derivative f' of the function f that you found in Step 2. Use the derivative to find the critical points—where $f'(x) = 0$ and where $f'(x)$ does not exist. If f is differentiable everywhere, then its only critical points occur where $f'(x) = 0$.

4. *Identify the extrema.* Evaluate f at each critical point in its domain *and* at the two endpoints. The values you obtain will tell you which is the absolute maximum and which is the absolute minimum. Of course, either or both of these may occur at more than one point.

5. *Answer the question posed in the original problem.* In other words, interpret your results. The answer to the original problem may be something other than merely the largest (or smallest) value of f. Give a precise answer to the specific question originally asked.

Observe how we follow this five-step process in Example 1.

EXAMPLE 1 A farmer has 200 yd of fence with which to construct three sides of a rectangular pen; an existing long, straight wall will form the fourth side. What dimensions will maximize the area of the pen?

Solution We want to maximize the area A of the pen shown in Fig. 3.6.1. To get a formula for the *dependent* variable A, we observe that the area of a rectangle is the product of its base and its height. So we let x denote the length of each of the two sides of the pen perpendicular to the wall. We also let y denote the length of the side parallel to the wall. Then the area of the rectangle is given by the *formula*

$$A = xy.$$

FIGURE 3.6.1 The rectangular pen of Example 1.

FIGURE 3.6.2 The relation in Eq. (1) between x and y (Example 1).

FIGURE 3.6.3 The pen with maximal area of Example 1.

FIGURE 3.6.4 Making the box of Example 2.

FIGURE 3.6.5 The 5-ft width of the metal sheet (Example 2).

Now we need to write A as a *function* of either x or y. Because all 200 yd of fence are to be used,

$$2x + y = 200, \quad \text{so} \quad y = 200 - 2x \quad (1)$$

(We chose to express y in terms of x merely because the algebra is slightly simpler.) Next, we substitute this value of y into the formula $A = xy$ to obtain

$$A(x) = x(200 - 2x) = 200x - 2x^2. \quad (2)$$

This equation expresses the dependent variable A as a function of the independent variable x.

Before proceeding, we must find the domain of the function A. It is clear from Fig. 3.6.2 that $0 < x < 100$. But to apply the closed-interval maximum-minimum method, we need a closed interval. In this example, we may adjoin the endpoints to $(0, 100)$ to get the *closed* interval $[0, 100]$. The values $x = 0$ and $x = 100$ correspond to "degenerate" pens of area zero. Because zero cannot be the maximum value of A, there is no harm in thus enlarging the domain of the function A.

Now we compute the derivative of the function A in Eq. (2):

$$\frac{dA}{dx} = 200 - 4x.$$

Because A is differentiable, its only critical points occur when

$$\frac{dA}{dx} = 0;$$

that is, when

$$200 - 4x = 0.$$

So $x = 50$ is the only interior critical point. Including the endpoints, the extrema of A can occur only at $x = 0, 50$, and 100. We evaluate A at each:

$$A(0) = 0,$$
$$A(50) = 5000, \quad \longleftarrow \text{absolute maximum}$$
$$A(100) = 0.$$

Thus the maximal area is $A(50) = 5000$ (yd^2). From Eq. (1) we find that $y = 100$ when $x = 50$. Therefore, for the pen to have maximal area, each of the two sides perpendicular to the wall should be 50 yd long and the side parallel to the wall should be 100 yd long (Fig. 3.6.3). ◆

EXAMPLE 2 A piece of sheet metal is rectangular, 5 ft wide and 8 ft long. Congruent squares are to be cut from its four corners. The resulting piece of metal is to be folded and welded to form an open-topped box (Fig. 3.6.4). How should this be done to get a box of largest possible volume?

Solution The quantity to be maximized—the dependent variable—is the volume V of the box to be constructed. The shape and thus the volume of the box are determined by the length x of the edge of each corner square removed. Hence x is a natural choice for the independent variable.

To write the volume V as a function of x, note that the finished box will have height x and its base will measure $8 - 2x$ ft by $5 - 2x$ ft. Hence its volume is given by

$$V(x) = x(5 - 2x)(8 - 2x) = 4x^3 - 26x^2 + 40x.$$

The procedure described in this example will produce an actual box only if $0 < x < 2.5$ (Fig. 3.6.5). But we make the domain the *closed* interval $[0, 2.5]$ to ensure that a maximum of $V(x)$ exists and to use the closed-interval maximum-minimum method. The values $x = 0$ and $x = 2.5$ correspond to "degenerate" boxes of zero volume, so adjoining these points to $(0, 2.5)$ will affect neither the location of the absolute maximum nor its value.

154 CHAPTER 3 The Derivative

Now we compute the derivative of V:

$$V'(x) = 12x^2 - 52x + 40 = 4(3x - 10)(x - 1).$$

The only critical points of the differentiable function V occur where

$$V'(x) = 0;$$

that is, where

$$4(3x - 10)(x - 1) = 0.$$

The solutions of this equation are $x = 1$ and $x = \frac{10}{3}$. We discard the latter because it does not lie in the domain $[0, 2.5]$ of V. So we examine these values of V:

$$V(0) = 0,$$
$$V(1) = 18, \quad \longleftarrow \text{ absolute maximum}$$
$$V(2.5) = 0.$$

Thus the maximum value of $V(x)$ on $[0, 2.5]$ is $V(1) = 18$. The answer to the question posed is this: The squares cut from the corners should be of edge length 1 ft each. The resulting box will measure 6 ft by 3 ft by 1 ft, and its volume will be 18 ft^3 (Fig. 3.6.6). ◆

FIGURE 3.6.6 The box with maximal volume of Example 2.

For our next application of the closed-interval maximum-minimum method, let us consider a typical problem in business management. Suppose that x units of computer diskettes are to be manufactured at a *total cost* of $C(x)$ dollars. We make the simple (but not always valid) assumption that the cost function $C(x)$ is the sum of two terms:

- A constant term a representing the *fixed cost* of acquiring and maintaining production facilities (overhead), and
- A variable term representing the *additional cost* of making x units at, for example, b dollars each.

Then

   the **total cost** is the **sum** of the **fixed cost** and the **additional cost,**

so the *cost function* $C(x)$ is given by

$$C(x) = a + bx. \tag{3}$$

We also assume that the number of units that can be sold (and hence will be manufactured) is a linear function of the selling price p, so that $x = m - np$ where m and n are positive constants. The minus sign indicates that an increase in selling price will result in a decrease in sales. If we solve this last equation for p, we get the *price function*

$$p(x) = A - Bx \tag{4}$$

(A and B are also constants).

The quantity to be maximized is profit, given here by the *profit function* $P(x)$, which is equal to the sales revenue minus the production costs. Thus

$$P(x) = xp(x) - C(x). \tag{5}$$

EXAMPLE 3 Suppose that the cost of publishing a small book is $10,000 to set up the (annual) press run plus $8 for each book printed. The publisher sold 7000 copies last year at $13 each, but sales dropped to 5000 copies this year when the price was raised to $15 per copy. Assume that up to 10,000 copies can be printed in a single press run. How many copies should be printed, and what should be the selling price of each copy, to maximize the year's profit on this book?

Solution The dependent variable to be maximized is the profit P. As independent variable we choose the number x of copies to be printed; also, $0 \leq x \leq 10{,}000$. The given cost information then implies that

$$C(x) = 10{,}000 + 8x.$$

Now we substitute into Eq. (4) the data $x = 7000$ when $p = 13$ as well as the data $x = 5000$ when $p = 15$. We obtain the equations

$$A - 7000B = 13, \quad A - 5000B = 15.$$

When we solve these equations simultaneously, we find that $A = 20$ and $B = 0.001$. Hence the price function is

$$p(x) = 20 - \frac{x}{1000},$$

and thus the profit function is

$$P(x) = x\left(20 - \frac{x}{1000}\right) - (10{,}000 + 8x).$$

We expand and collect terms to obtain

$$P(x) = 12x - \frac{x^2}{1000} - 10{,}000, \quad 0 \leq x \leq 10{,}000.$$

Now

$$\frac{dP}{dx} = 12 - \frac{x}{500},$$

and the only critical points of the differentiable function P occur when

$$\frac{dP}{dx} = 0;$$

that is, when

$$12 - \frac{x}{500} = 0; \quad x = 12 \cdot 500 = 6000.$$

We check P at this value of x as well as the values of $P(x)$ at the endpoints to find the maximum profit:

$$P(0) = -10{,}000,$$
$$P(6000) = 26{,}000, \quad \longleftarrow \text{absolute maximum}$$
$$P(10{,}000) = 10{,}000.$$

Therefore, the maximum possible annual profit of \$26,000 results from printing 6000 copies of the book. Each copy should be sold for \$14, because

$$p(6000) = 20 - \frac{6000}{1000} = 14.$$
◆

EXAMPLE 4 We need to design a cylindrical can with radius r and height h. The top and bottom must be made of copper, which will cost 2¢/in.² The curved side is to be made of aluminum, which will cost 1¢/in.² We seek the dimensions that will maximize the volume of the can. The only constraint is that the total cost of the can is to be 300π ¢.

Solution We need to maximize the volume V of the can, which we can compute if we know its radius r and its height h (Fig. 3.6.7). With these dimensions, we find that

$$V = \pi r^2 h, \tag{6}$$

FIGURE 3.6.7 The cylindrical can of Example 4.

but we need to express V as a function of r alone (or as a function of h alone).

Both the circular top and bottom of the can have area πr^2 in.², so the area of copper to be used is $2\pi r^2$ and its cost is $4\pi r^2$ cents. The area of the curved side of the can is $2\pi rh$ in.², so the area of aluminum used is the same, and the aluminum costs $2\pi rh$ cents.

We obtain the total cost of the can by adding the cost of the copper to the cost of the aluminum. This sum must be 300π ¢, and therefore

$$4\pi r^2 + 2\pi rh = 300\pi. \tag{7}$$

We eliminate h in Eq. (6) by solving Eq. (7) for h:

$$h = \frac{300\pi - 4\pi r^2}{2\pi r} = \frac{1}{r}(150 - 2r^2). \tag{8}$$

Hence

$$V = V(r) = (\pi r^2)\frac{1}{r}(150 - 2r^2) = 2\pi(75r - r^3). \tag{9}$$

To determine the domain of definition of V, we note from Eq. (7) that $4\pi r^2 < 300\pi$, so $r < \sqrt{75}$ for the desired can; with $r = \sqrt{75} = 5\sqrt{3}$, we get a degenerate can with height $h = 0$. With $r = 0$, we obtain *no* value of h in Eq. (8) and therefore no can, but $V(r)$ is nevertheless continuous at $r = 0$. Consequently, we can take the closed interval $[0, 5\sqrt{3}]$ to be the domain of V.

Calculating the derivative yields

$$V'(r) = 2\pi(75 - 3r^2) = 6\pi(25 - r^2).$$

Because $V(r)$ is a polynomial, $V'(r)$ exists for all values of r, so we obtain all critical points by solving the equation

$$V'(r) = 0;$$

that is,

$$6\pi(25 - r^2) = 0.$$

We discard the solution -5, as it does not lie in the domain of V. Thus we obtain only the single critical point $r = 5$ in $[0, 5\sqrt{3}]$. Now

$$V(0) = 0,$$
$$V(5) = 500\pi, \quad \leftarrow \text{ absolute maximum}$$
$$V(5\sqrt{3}) = 0.$$

FIGURE 3.6.8 The can of maximal volume in Example 4.

Thus the can of maximum volume has radius $r = 5$ in., and Eq. (8) yields its height to be $h = 20$ in. Figure 3.6.8 shows such a can. ◆

EXAMPLE 5 (A Sawmill Problem) Suppose that you need to cut a beam with maximal rectangular cross section from a circular log of radius 1 ft. (This is the geometric problem of finding the rectangle of greatest area that can be inscribed in a circle of radius 1.) What are the shape and cross-sectional area of such a beam?

Solution Let x and y denote half the base and half the height, respectively, of the inscribed rectangle (Fig. 3.6.9). Apply the Pythagorean theorem to the small right triangle in the figure. This yields the equation

$$x^2 + y^2 = 1, \quad \text{so} \quad y = \sqrt{1 - x^2}.$$

The area of the inscribed rectangle is $A = (2x)(2y) = 4xy$. You may now express A as a function of x alone:

$$A(x) = 4x\sqrt{1 - x^2}.$$

The practical domain of definition of A is $(0, 1)$, and there is no harm (and much advantage) in adjoining the endpoints, so you take $[0, 1]$ to be the domain. Next,

FIGURE 3.6.9 A sawmill problem—Example 5.

$$\frac{dA}{dx} = 4 \cdot (1 - x^2)^{1/2} + 2x(1 - x^2)^{-1/2}(-2x) = \frac{4 - 8x^2}{(1 - x^2)^{1/2}}.$$

You observe that $A'(1)$ does not exist, but this causes no trouble, because differentiability at the endpoints is not assumed in Theorem 3 of Section 3.5. Hence you need only solve the equation

$$A'(x) = 0;$$

that is,

$$\frac{4 - 8x^2}{\sqrt{1-x^2}} = 0.$$

A fraction can be zero only when its numerator is zero and its denominator is *not*, so $A'(x) = 0$ when $4 - 8x^2 = 0$. Thus you find the only critical point of A in the open interval $(0, 1)$ to be $x = \sqrt{1/2} = \frac{1}{2}\sqrt{2}$ (and $2x = 2y = \sqrt{2}$). You evaluate A here and at the two endpoints to find that

$$A(0) = 0,$$
$$A(\tfrac{1}{2}\sqrt{2}) = 2, \quad \leftarrow \text{absolute maximum}$$
$$A(1) = 0.$$

Therefore, the beam with rectangular cross section of maximal area is square, with edges $\sqrt{2}$ ft long and with cross-sectional area 2 ft². ◆

In Problem 43 we ask you to maximize the total cross-sectional area of the four planks that can be cut from the four pieces of log that remain after cutting the square beam (Fig. 3.6.10).

FIGURE 3.6.10 Cut four more beams after cutting one large beam.

Plausibility You should always check your answers for *plausibility*. In Example 5, the cross-sectional area of the log from which the beam is to be cut is $\pi \approx 3.14$ ft². The beam of maximal cross-section area 2 ft² thus uses a little less than 64% of the log. This *is* plausible. Had the fraction been an extremely inefficient 3% or a wildly optimistic 98%, you should have searched for an error in arithmetic, algebra, calculus, or logic (as you would had the fraction been −14% or 150%). Check the results of Examples 1 through 4 for plausibility.

Dimensions Another way to check answers is to use *dimensional analysis*. Work the problem with unspecified constants in place of the actual numbers. In Example 5, it would be good practice to find the beam of maximal rectangular cross section that can be cut from a circular log of radius R rather than radius 1 ft. You can always substitute the given value $R = 1$ at the conclusion of the solution. A brief solution to this problem might go as follows:

Dimensions of beam: base $2x$, height $2y$.

Area of beam: $A = 4xy$.

Draw a radius of the log from its center to one corner of the rectangular beam, as in Fig. 3.6.11. This radius has length R, so the Pythagorean theorem gives

$$x^2 + y^2 = R^2; \qquad y = \sqrt{R^2 - x^2}.$$

FIGURE 3.6.11 The log with radius R.

Area of beam:
$$A(x) = 4x\sqrt{R^2 - x^2}, \quad 0 \le x \le R.$$

$$A'(x) = 4(R^2 - x^2)^{1/2} + 2x(R^2 - x^2)^{-1/2}(-2x) = \frac{4R^2 - 8x^2}{\sqrt{R^2 - x^2}}.$$

$A'(x)$ does not exist when $x = R$, but that's an endpoint; we'll check it separately. $A'(x) = 0$ when $x = \frac{1}{2}R\sqrt{2}$ (ignore the negative root; it's not in the domain of A).

$$A(0) = 0,$$
$$A(\tfrac{1}{2}R\sqrt{2}) = 2R^2, \quad \leftarrow \text{absolute maximum}$$
$$A(R) = 0.$$

Figure 3.6.12 shows the dimensions of the inscribed rectangle of maximal area.

Now you can check the results for dimensional accuracy. The value of x that maximizes A is a length (R) multiplied by a pure (dimensionless) numerical constant ($\frac{1}{2}\sqrt{2}$), so x has the dimensions of length—that's correct; had it been anything else, you would need to search for the error. Moreover, the maximum cross-sectional area of the beam is $2R^2$, the product of a pure number and the square of a length, thus having the dimensions of area. This, too, is correct.

FIGURE 3.6.12 The inscribed square beam with maximal cross-sectional area.

EXAMPLE 6 We consider the reflection of a ray of light by a mirror M as in Fig. 3.6.13, which shows a ray traveling from point A to point B via reflection off M at the point P. We assume that the location of the point of reflection is such that the total distance $d_1 + d_2$ traveled by the light ray will be minimized. This is an application of *Fermat's principle of least time* for the propagation of light. The problem is to find P.

Solution Drop perpendiculars from A and B to the plane of the mirror M. Denote the feet of these perpendiculars by A' and B' (Fig. 3.6.13). Let $a, b, c,$ and x denote the lengths of the segments AA', BB', $A'B'$, and $A'P$, respectively. Then $c - x$ is the length of the segment PB'. By the Pythagorean theorem, the distance to be minimized is then

$$d_1 + d_2 = f(x) = \sqrt{a^2 + x^2} + \sqrt{b^2 + (c-x)^2}. \tag{10}$$

FIGURE 3.6.13 Reflection at P of a light ray by a mirror M (Example 6).

We may choose as the domain of f the interval $[0, c]$, because the minimum of f must occur somewhere within that interval. (To see why, examine the picture you get if x is *not* in that interval.)

Then

$$f'(x) = \frac{x}{\sqrt{a^2 + x^2}} + \frac{(c-x)(-1)}{\sqrt{b^2 + (c-x)^2}}. \tag{11}$$

Recognizing the distances d_1 and d_2 in the denominators here, we see that

$$f'(x) = \frac{x}{d_1} - \frac{c-x}{d_2}. \tag{12}$$

Consequently, any horizontal tangent to the graph of f must occur over the point x determined by the equation

$$\frac{x}{d_1} = \frac{c-x}{d_2}. \tag{13}$$

At such a point, $\cos\alpha = \cos\beta$, where α is the angle of the incident light ray and β is the angle of the reflected ray (Fig. 3.6.13). Both α and β lie between 0 and $\pi/2$, and thus we find that $\alpha = \beta$. In short, the point P must be located so that the angle of incidence is equal to the angle of reflection, a familiar principle from physics. ◆

The computation in Example 6 has an alternative interpretation that is interesting, if somewhat whimsical. Figure 3.6.14 shows a feedlot 200 ft long with a water

FIGURE 3.6.14 The feedlot.

trough along one edge and a feed bin located on an adjacent edge. A cow enters the gate at the point A, 90 ft from the water trough. She walks straight to point P, gets a drink from the trough, and then walks straight to the feed bin at point B, 60 ft from the trough. If the cow knew calculus, what point P along the water trough would she select to minimize the total distance she walks?

In comparing Figs. 3.6.13 and 3.6.14, we see that the cow's problem is to minimize the distance function f in Eq. (10) with the numerical values $a = 90$, $b = 60$, and $c = 200$. When we substitute these values and

$$d_1 = \sqrt{a^2 + x^2} \quad \text{and} \quad d_2 = \sqrt{b^2 + (c - x)^2}$$

in Eq. (13), we get

$$\frac{x}{\sqrt{8100 + x^2}} = \frac{200 - x}{\sqrt{3600 + (200 - x)^2}}.$$

We square both sides, clear the equation of fractions, and simplify. The result is

$$x^2[3600 + (200 - x)^2] = (200 - x)^2(8100 + x^2);$$
$$3600x^2 = 8100(200 - x)^2; \quad \text{(Why?)}$$
$$60x = 90(200 - x);$$
$$150x = 18{,}000;$$
$$x = 120.$$

Thus the cow should proceed directly to the point P located 120 ft along the water trough.

These examples indicate that the closed-interval maximum-minimum method is applicable to a wide range of problems. Indeed, applied optimization problems that seem as different as light rays and cows may have essentially identical mathematical models. This is only one illustration of the power of generality that calculus exploits so effectively.

3.6 TRUE/FALSE STUDY GUIDE

3.6 CONCEPTS: QUESTIONS AND DISCUSSION

1. How do you decide what is the dependent variable in an optimization problem? The independent variable? Discuss the differences in the roles played by dependent and independent variables in an optimization problem.
2. Discuss the differences among the following three items:
   - A *relation* among two or more variables describing an applied problem.
   - A *formula* giving the dependent variable in terms of other variables.
   - A *function* expressing the dependent variable in terms of an independent variable.

   Outline and contrast the roles played by relations, formulas, and functions in typical optimization problems.

3.6 PROBLEMS

1. Find two positive real numbers x and y such that their sum is 50 and their product is as large as possible.

2. Find the maximum possible area of a rectangle of perimeter 200 m.

3. A rectangle with sides parallel to the coordinate axes has one vertex at the origin, one on the positive x-axis, one on the positive y-axis, and its fourth vertex in the first quadrant on the line with equation $2x + y = 100$ (Fig. 3.6.15). What is the maximum possible area of such a rectangle?

FIGURE 3.6.15 The rectangle of Problem 3.

4. A farmer has 600 m of fencing with which to enclose a rectangular pen adjacent to a long existing wall. He will use the wall for one side of the pen and the available fencing for the remaining three sides. What is the maximum area that can be enclosed in this way?

5. A rectangular box has a square base with edges at least 1 in. long. It has no top, and the total area of its five sides is 300 in.² (Fig. 3.6.16). What is the maximum possible volume of such a box?

FIGURE 3.6.16 A box with square base and volume $V = x^2 y$ (Problems 5, 17, and 20).

6. If x is in the interval $[0, 1]$, then $x - x^2$ is not negative. What is the maximum value that $x - x^2$ can have on that interval? In other words, what is the greatest amount by which a real number can exceed its square?

7. The sum of two positive numbers is 48. What is the smallest possible value of the sum of their squares?

8. A rectangle of fixed perimeter 36 is rotated around one of its sides, thus sweeping out a figure in the shape of a right circular cylinder (Fig. 3.6.17). What is the maximum possible volume of that cylinder?

FIGURE 3.6.17 The rectangle and cylinder of Problem 8.

9. The sum of two nonnegative real numbers is 10. Find the minimum possible value of the sum of their cubes.

10. Suppose that the strength of a rectangular beam is proportional to the product of the width and the *square* of the height of its cross section. What shape beam should be cut from a cylindrical log of radius r to achieve the greatest possible strength?

11. A farmer has 600 yd of fencing with which to build a rectangular corral. Some of the fencing will be used to construct two interval divider fences, both parallel to the same two sides of the corral (Fig. 3.6.18). What is the maximum possible total area of such a corral?

FIGURE 3.6.18 The divided corral of Problem 11.

12. Find the maximum possible volume of a right circular cylinder if its total surface area—including both circular ends—is 150π.

13. Find the maximum possible area of a rectangle with diagonals of length 16.

14. A rectangle has a line of fixed length L reaching from one vertex to the midpoint of one of the far sides (Fig. 3.6.19). What is the maximum possible area of such a rectangle?

FIGURE 3.6.19 The rectangle of Problem 14.

15. The volume V (in cubic centimeters) of 1 kg of water at temperature T between $0°C$ and $30°C$ is very closely approximated by

$$V = 999.87 - (0.06426)T + (0.0085043)T^2 - (0.0000679)T^3.$$

At what temperature does water have its maximum density?

16. What is the maximum possible area of a rectangle with a base that lies on the x-axis and with two upper vertices that lie on the graph of the equation $y = 4 - x^2$ (Fig. 3.6.20)?

FIGURE 3.6.20 The rectangle of Problem 16.

17. A rectangular box has a square base with edges at least 1 cm long. Its total surface area is 600 cm^2. What is the largest possible volume that such a box can have?

18. You must make a cylindrical can with a bottom but no top from 300π in.^{2} of sheet metal. No sheet metal will be wasted; you are allowed to order a circular piece of any size for its base and any appropriate rectangular piece to make into its curved side so long as the given conditions are met. What is the greatest possible volume of such a can?

19. Three large squares of tin, each with edges 1 m long, have four small, equal squares cut from their corners. All twelve resulting small squares are to be the same size (Fig. 3.6.21). The three large cross-shaped pieces are then folded and welded to make boxes with no tops, and the twelve small squares are used to make two small cubes. How should this be done to maximize the total volume of all five boxes?

FIGURE 3.6.21 One of the three 1-m squares of Problem 19.

20. Suppose that you are to make a rectangular box with a square base from two different materials. The material for the top and four sides of the box costs $1/ft^2; the material for the base costs $2/ft^2. Find the dimensions of the box of greatest possible volume if you are allowed to spend $144 for the material to make it.

21. A piece of wire 80 in. long is cut into at most two pieces. Each piece is bent into the shape of a square. How should this be done to minimize the sum of the area(s) of the square(s)? To maximize it?

22. A wire of length 100 cm is cut into two pieces. One piece is bent into a circle, the other into a square. Where should the cut be made to maximize the sum of the areas of the square and the circle? To minimize that sum?

23. A farmer has 600 m of fencing with which she plans to enclose a rectangular pasture adjacent to a long existing wall. She plans to build one fence parallel to the wall, two to form the ends of the enclosure, and a fourth (parallel to the ends of the enclosure) to divide it equally. What is the maximum area that can be enclosed?

24. A zookeeper needs to add a rectangular outdoor pen to an animal house with a corner notch, as shown in Fig. 3.6.22. If 85 m of new fence is available, what dimensions of the pen will maximize its area? No fence will be used along the walls of the animal house.

FIGURE 3.6.22 The rectangular pen of Problem 24.

25. Suppose that a post office can accept a package for mailing only if the sum of its length and its girth (the circumference of its cross section) is at most 100 in. What is the maximum volume of a rectangular box with square cross section that can be mailed?

26. Repeat Problem 25, but use a cylindrical package; its cross section is circular.

27. A printing company has eight presses, each of which can print 3600 copies per hour. It costs $5.00 to set up each press for a run and $10 + 6n$ dollars to run n presses for 1 h. How many presses should be used to print 50,000 copies of a poster most profitably?

28. A farmer wants to hire workers to pick 900 bushels of beans. Each worker can pick 5 bushels per hour and is paid $1.00 per bushel. The farmer must also pay a supervisor $10 per hour while the picking is in progress, and he has additional miscellaneous expenses of $8 per worker. How many workers should he hire to minimize the total cost? What will then be the cost per bushel picked?

162   CHAPTER 3 The Derivative

29. The heating and cooling costs for a certain uninsulated house are $500/yr, but with $x \leq 10$ in. of insulation, the costs are $1000/(2+x)$ dollars/yr. It costs $150 for each inch (thickness) of insulation installed. How many inches of insulation should be installed to minimize the *total* (initial plus annual) costs over a 10-yr period? What will then be the annual savings resulting from this optimal insulation?

30. A concessionaire had been selling 5000 burritos each game night at 50¢ each. When she raised the price to 70¢ each, sales dropped to 4000 per night. Assume a linear relationship between price and sales. If she has fixed costs of $1000 per night and each burrito costs her 25¢, what price will maximize her nightly profit?

31. A commuter train carries 600 passengers each day from a suburb to a city. It costs $1.50 per person to ride the train. Market research reveals that 40 fewer people would ride the train for each 5¢ increase in the fare, 40 more for each 5¢ decrease. What fare should be charged to get the largest possible revenue?

32. Find the shape of the cylinder of maximal volume that can be inscribed in a sphere of radius R (Fig. 3.6.23). Show that the ratio of the height of the cylinder to its radius is $\sqrt{2}$ and that the ratio of the volume of the sphere to that of the maximal cylinder is $\sqrt{3}$.

FIGURE 3.6.23 The sphere and cylinder of Problem 32.

33. Find the dimensions of the right circular cylinder of greatest volume that can be inscribed in a right circular cone of radius R and height H (Fig. 3.6.24).

FIGURE 3.6.24 The cone and cylinder of Problem 33.

34. Figure 3.6.25 shows a circle of radius 1 in which a trapezoid is inscribed. The longer of the two parallel sides of the trapezoid coincides with a diameter of the circle. What is the maximum possible area of such a trapezoid. (*Suggestion:* A positive quantity is maximized when its square is maximized.)

FIGURE 3.6.25 The circle and trapezoid of Problem 34.

35. Show that the rectangle of maximal perimeter that can be inscribed in a circle is a square.

36. Find the dimensions of the rectangle (with sides parallel to the coordinate axes) of maximal area that can be inscribed in the ellipse with equation

$$\frac{x^2}{25} + \frac{y^2}{9} = 1$$

(Fig. 3.6.26).

FIGURE 3.6.26 The ellipse and rectangle of Problem 36.

37. A right circular cone of radius r and height h has slant height $L = \sqrt{r^2 + h^2}$. What is the maximum possible volume of a cone with slant height 10?

38. Two vertical poles 10 ft apart are both 10 ft tall. Find the length of the shortest rope that can reach from the top of one pole to a point on the ground between them and then to the top of the other pole.

39. The sum of two nonnegative real numbers is 16. Find the maximum possible value and the minimum possible value of the sum of their cube roots.

40. A straight wire 60 cm long is bent into the shape of an L. What is the shortest possible distance between the two ends of the bent wire?

41. What is the shortest possible distance from a point on the parabola $y = x^2$ to the point $(0, 1)$?

42. Given: There is exactly one point on the graph of $y = \sqrt[3]{3x-4}$ that is closest to the origin. Find it. (*Suggestion:* See Fig. 3.6.27, and solve the equation you obtain by inspection.)

FIGURE 3.6.27 The curve of Problem 42.

43. Find the dimensions that maximize the cross-sectional area of the four planks that can be cut from the four pieces of the circular log of Example 5—the pieces that remain after a square beam has been cut from the log (Fig. 3.6.10).

44. Find the maximal area of a rectangle inscribed in an equilateral triangle with edges of length 1, as in Fig. 3.6.28.

FIGURE 3.6.28 The rectangle and equilateral triangle of Problem 44.

45. A small island is 2 km off shore in a large lake. A woman on the island can row her boat 10 km/h and can run at a speed of 20 km/h. If she rows to the closest point of the straight shore, she will land 6 km from a village on the shore. Where should she land to reach the village most quickly by a combination of rowing and running?

46. A factory is located on one bank of a straight river that is 2000 m wide. On the opposite bank but 4500 m downstream is a power station from which the factory draws its electricity. Assume that it costs three times as much per meter to lay an underwater cable as to lay an aboveground cable. What path should a cable connecting the power station to the factory take to minimize the cost of laying the cable?

47. A company has plants that are located (in an appropriate coordinate system) at the points $A(0, 1)$, $B(0, -1)$, and $C(3, 0)$ (Fig. 3.6.29). The company plans to construct a distribution center at the point $P(x, 0)$. What value of x would minimize the sum of the distances from P to A, B, and C?

FIGURE 3.6.29 The locations in Problem 47.

48. Light travels at speed c in air and at a slower speed v in water. (The constant c is approximately 3×10^{10} cm/s; the ratio $n = c/v$, known as the **index of refraction**, depends on the color of the light but is approximate 1.33 for water.) Figure 3.6.30 shows the path of a light ray traveling from point A in air to point B in water, with what appears to be a sudden change in direction as the ray moves through the air-water interface. (a) Write the time T required for the ray to travel from A to B in terms of the variable x and the constants a, b, c, s, and v, all of which have been defined or are shown in the figure. (b) Show that the equation $T'(x) = 0$ for minimizing T is equivalent to the condition

$$\frac{\sin \alpha}{\sin \beta} = \frac{c}{v} = n.$$

This is **Snell's law:** The ratio of the sines of the angles of incidence and refraction is equal to the index of refraction.

FIGURE 3.6.30 Snell's law gives the path of refracted light (Problem 48).

Refraction of light at an air-water interface

49. The mathematics of Snell's law (Problem 48) is applicable to situations other than the refraction of light. Figure 3.6.31 shows an east-west geologic fault that separates two towns at points A and B. Assume that A is a miles north of the fault, that B is b miles south of the fault, and that B is L miles east of A. We want to build a road from A to B. Because of differences in terrain, the cost of construction is C_1 (in millions of dollars per mile) north of the fault and C_2 south of it. Where should the point P be placed to minimize the total cost of road construction? (a) Using the notation in the figure, show that the cost is minimized when $C_1 \sin\theta_1 = C_2 \sin\theta_2$. (b) Take $a = b = C_1 = 1$, $C_2 = 2$, and $L = 4$. Show that the equation in part (a) is equivalent to

$$f(x) = 3x^4 - 24x^3 + 51x^2 - 32x + 64 = 0.$$

To approximate the desired solution of this equation, calculate $f(0)$, $f(1)$, $f(2)$, $f(3)$, and $f(4)$. You should find that $f(3) > 0 > f(4)$. Interpolate between $f(3)$ and $f(4)$ to approximate the desired root of this equation.

FIGURE 3.6.31 Building a road from A to B (Problem 49).

50. The sum of the volumes of two cubes is 2000 in.³ What should their edges x and y be to maximize the sum of their surface areas? To minimize it?

51. The sum of the surface areas of a cube and a sphere is 1000 in.² What should their dimensions be to minimize the sum of their volumes? To maximize it?

52. Your brother has six pieces of wood with which to make the kite frame shown in Fig. 3.6.32. The four outer pieces with the indicated lengths have already been cut. How long should the lengths of the inner struts be to maximize the area of the kite?

FIGURE 3.6.32 The kite frame (Problem 52).

Problems 53 through 55 deal with alternative methods of constructing a tent.

53. Figure 3.6.33 shows a 20-by-20-ft square of canvas tent material. Girl Scout Troop A must cut pieces from its four corners as indicated, so that the four remaining triangular flaps can be turned up to form a tent in the shape of a pyramid with a square base. How should this be done to maximize the volume of the tent?

Let A denote the area of the base of the tent and h its height. With x as indicated in the figure, show that the volume $V = \frac{1}{3}Ah$ of the tent is given by

$$V(x) = \tfrac{4}{3}x^2\sqrt{100 - 20x}, \quad 0 \leq x \leq 5.$$

Maximize V by graphing $V(x)$ and $V'(x)$ and zooming in on the zero of $V'(x)$.

FIGURE 3.6.33 The canvas square—first attempt.

54. Girl Scout Troop B must make a tent in the shape of a pyramid with a square base from a similar 20-by-20-ft square of canvas but in the manner indicated in Fig. 3.6.34. With x as indicated in the figure, show that the volume of the tent is given by

$$V(x) = \tfrac{2}{3}x^2\sqrt{200 - 20x}, \quad 0 \leq x \leq 10.$$

Maximize V graphically as in Problem 53.

FIGURE 3.6.34 The canvas square—second attempt.

55. Solve Problems 53 and 54 analytically to verify that the maximal volume in Problem 54 is exactly $2\sqrt{2}$ times the maximal volume in Problem 53. It pays to think before making a tent!

Problems 56 and 57 deal with rectangular boxes with square base. Such a box is said to be closed if it has both a (square) bottom and a top (as well as four vertical sides), open *if it has a bottom but no top.*

56. Show that, among all closed square-based rectangular boxes with a given fixed total surface area, the one with maximal volume is a cube.

57. Show that, among all open square-based rectangular boxes with a given fixed total surface area, the one with maximal volume has height equal to half the length of the edge of its base.

Problems 58 through 60 deal with right circular cylinders. Such a "can" is said to be closed *if it has both a (circular) bottom and a top (as well as a curved side),* open *if it has a bottom but no top.*

58. Show that, among all closed cylindrical cans with a given fixed total surface area, the one with maximal volume has height equal to the diameter of its base.

59. Show that, among all open cylindrical cans with a given fixed total surface area, the one with maximal volume has height equal to the radius of its base.

60. Suppose that the bottom and curved side surface of a pop-top soft drink can have the same thickness. But, in order that the top not be ripped upon opening, it is three times as thick as the bottom. Show that, among all such soft drink cans made from a fixed total amount of material (including the triple-thick top), the one with maximal volume has height approximately twice its diameter. (Perhaps this is why soft drink cans look somewhat taller than soup or vegetable cans.) *Suggestion:* To simplify the computations, you may assume that the amount of material used to make a can of inner radius r, inner height h, and thickness t (except for the top, of thickness $3t$), is $\pi r^2 t + 2\pi r h t + 3\pi r^2 t$. This will be quite accurate if t is very small in comparison with r and h.

61. Figure 3.6.35 shows a triangle bounded by the nonnegative coordinate axes and the line tangent to the curve $y = 1/(1 + x^2)$ at the first-quadrant point (x, y). Is it apparent that the area $A(x)$ of this triangle is very large when $x > 0$ is very close to zero? But your task is to find the maximum and minimum values of A for $\frac{1}{2} \leq x \leq 2$. It will be convenient to use a computer algebra system, both to find $A(x)$ and to solve the sixth-degree equation you should encounter.

FIGURE 3.6.35 Triangle bounded by coordinate axes and a tangent line to the curve $y = \dfrac{1}{1 + x^2}$.

62. Figure 3.6.36 shows a one-mile-square city park. A local power company needs to run a power line from the northwest corner A of the park to the southeast corner B. To preserve the beauty of the park, only underground lines may be run through the park itself, but overhead lines are permissible along the boundary of the park. The power company plans to construct an overhead line a distance x along the west edge of the park, then from the southern end of this line continue with a straight power line to point B. If overhead lines cost $40 thousand per mile and underground lines cost $100 thousand per mile, how should the power company construct the line to minimize its total cost?

FIGURE 3.6.36 The one-mile-square park in central Villabuena.

3.7 DERIVATIVES OF TRIGONOMETRIC FUNCTIONS

In this section we begin our study of the calculus of trigonometric functions, focusing first on the sine and cosine functions. The definitions and the elementary properties of trigonometric functions are reviewed in Appendix C.

When we write $\sin \theta$ (or $\cos \theta$), we mean the sine (or cosine) of an angle of θ radians (rad). Recall the fundamental relation between radian measure and degree measure of angles:

$$\pi \text{ radians} = 180 \text{ degrees.} \tag{1}$$

Radians	Degrees
0	0
$\pi/6$	30
$\pi/4$	45
$\pi/3$	60
$\pi/2$	90
$2\pi/3$	120
$3\pi/4$	135
$5\pi/6$	150
π	180
$3\pi/2$	270
2π	360
4π	720

FIGURE 3.7.1 Some radian-degree conversions.

Upon division of both sides of this equation by π and 180, respectively, and abbreviating the units, we get the conversion relations

$$1 \text{ rad} = \frac{180}{\pi} \text{ deg} \quad \text{and} \quad 1 \text{ deg} = \frac{\pi}{180} \text{ rad}.$$

Figure 3.7.1 shows radian-degree conversions for some frequently occurring angles. The derivatives of the sine and cosine functions depend on the limits

$$\lim_{\theta \to 0} \frac{\sin \theta}{\theta} = 1, \quad \lim_{\theta \to 0} \frac{1 - \cos \theta}{\theta} = 0 \qquad (2)$$

that we established in Section 2.3. The addition formulas

$$\cos(x + y) = \cos x \cos y - \sin x \sin y,$$
$$\sin(x + y) = \sin x \cos y + \cos x \sin y \qquad (3)$$

are needed as well.

THEOREM 1 Derivatives of Sines and Cosines

The functions $f(x) = \sin x$ and $g(x) = \cos x$ are differentiable for all x, and

$$D_x \sin x = \cos x, \qquad (4)$$

$$D_x \cos x = -\sin x. \qquad (5)$$

PROOF To differentiate $f(x) = \sin x$, we begin with the definition of the derivative,

$$f'(x) = \lim_{h \to 0} \frac{f(x + h) - f(x)}{h} = \lim_{h \to 0} \frac{\sin(x + h) - \sin x}{h}.$$

Next we apply the addition formula for the sine and the limit laws to get

$$f'(x) = \lim_{h \to 0} \frac{(\sin x \cos h + \sin h \cos x) - \sin x}{h}$$

$$= \lim_{h \to 0} \left[(\cos x) \frac{\sin h}{h} - (\sin x) \frac{1 - \cos h}{h} \right]$$

$$= (\cos x) \left(\lim_{h \to 0} \frac{\sin h}{h} \right) - (\sin x) \left(\lim_{h \to 0} \frac{1 - \cos h}{h} \right).$$

The limits in Eq. (2) now yield

$$f'(x) = (\cos x)(1) - (\sin x)(0) = \cos x,$$

which proves Eq. (4). The proof of Eq. (5) is quite similar. (See Problem 72.) ◂

Examples 1 through 4 illustrate the application of Eqs. (4) and (5) in conjunction with the general differentiation formulas of Sections 3.2, 3.3, and 3.4 to differentiate various combinations of trigonometric and other functions.

EXAMPLE 1 The product rule yields

$$D_x(x^2 \sin x) = (D_x x^2)(\sin x) + (x^2)(D_x \sin x)$$
$$= 2x \sin x + x^2 \cos x.$$

◆

Derivatives of Trigonometric Functions SECTION 3.7   167

EXAMPLE 2 If $y = \dfrac{\cos x}{1 - \sin x}$, then the quotient rule yields

$$\frac{dy}{dx} = \frac{(D_x \cos x)(1 - \sin x) - (\cos x)[D_x(1 - \sin x)]}{(1 - \sin x)^2}$$

$$= \frac{(-\sin x)(1 - \sin x) - (\cos x)(-\cos x)}{(1 - \sin x)^2}$$

$$= \frac{-\sin x + \sin^2 x + \cos^2 x}{(1 - \sin x)^2} = \frac{-\sin x + 1}{(1 - \sin x)^2};$$

$$\frac{dy}{dx} = \frac{1}{1 - \sin x}.$$

◆

FIGURE 3.7.2 The curve $y = \cos^2 x$ and its tangent line at the point P where $x = 0.5$.

EXAMPLE 3 If $x = \cos^3 t$ and $u = \cos t$—so that $x = u^3$—then the chain rule yields

$$\frac{dx}{dt} = \frac{dx}{du}\frac{du}{dt} = (3u^2)(-\sin t) = (3\cos^2 t)(-\sin t) = -3\cos^2 t \sin t.$$

◆

EXAMPLE 4 If $g(t) = (2 - 3\cos t)^{3/2}$, then the chain rule yields

$$g'(t) = \tfrac{3}{2}(2 - 3\cos t)^{1/2} D_t(2 - 3\cos t)$$

$$= \tfrac{3}{2}(2 - 3\cos t)^{1/2}(3\sin t) = \tfrac{9}{2}(2 - 3\cos t)^{1/2}\sin t.$$

◆

EXAMPLE 5 Write an equation of the line tangent to the curve $y = \cos^2 x$ at the point P on the graph where $x = 0.5$. Approximations are allowed.

Solution The y-coordinate of P is $y(0.5) = (\cos 0.5)^2 \approx (0.8776)^2 \approx 0.7702$. Because

$$\frac{dy}{dx} = -2\cos x \sin x,$$

the slope of the tangent line at P is

$$m = \left.\frac{dy}{dx}\right|_{x=0.5} = -2(\cos 0.5)(\sin 0.5) \approx -0.8415.$$

Then the point-slope formula gives the (approximate) equation

$$y - 0.7702 = -(0.8415)(x - 0.5);$$

that is, $y = -(0.8415)x + 1.1909$, as the desired equation of the tangent line at P. Figure 3.7.2 shows the result of checking this computation by graphing both the curve $y = \cos^2 x$ and the line with this equation.

◆

The Remaining Trigonometric Functions

It is easy to differentiate the other four trigonometric functions, because they can be expressed in terms of the sine and cosine functions:

$$\tan x = \frac{\sin x}{\cos x}, \qquad \cot x = \frac{\cos x}{\sin x},$$

$$\sec x = \frac{1}{\cos x}, \qquad \csc x = \frac{1}{\sin x}. \tag{6}$$

Each of these formulas is valid except where a zero denominator is encountered. Thus $\tan x$ and $\sec x$ are undefined when x is an odd integral multiple of $\pi/2$, and $\cot x$ and $\csc x$ are undefined when x is an integral multiple of π. The graphs of the six trigonometric functions appear in Fig. 3.7.3. There we show the sine and its reciprocal, the cosecant, in the same coordinate plane; we also pair the cosine with the secant but show the tangent and cotangent functions separately.

FIGURE 3.7.3 Graphs of the six trigonometric functions.

The functions in Eq. (6) can be differentiated by using the quotient rule and the derivatives of the sine and cosine functions. For example,

$$\tan x = \frac{\sin x}{\cos x},$$

so

$$D_x \tan x = \frac{(D_x \sin x)(\cos x) - (\sin x)(D_x \cos x)}{(\cos x)^2}$$

$$= \frac{(\cos x)(\cos x) - (\sin x)(-\sin x)}{\cos^2 x} = \frac{\cos^2 x + \sin^2 x}{\cos^2 x} = \frac{1}{\cos^2 x};$$

$$D_x \tan x = \sec^2 x.$$

As an exercise, you should derive in similar fashion the differentiation formulas in Eqs. (8) through (10) of Theorem 2.

THEOREM 2   Derivatives of Trigonometric Functions

The functions $f(x) = \tan x$, $g(x) = \cot x$, $p(x) = \sec x$, and $q(x) = \csc x$ are differentiable wherever they are defined, and

$$D_x \tan x = \sec^2 x, \tag{7}$$

$$D_x \cot x = -\csc^2 x, \tag{8}$$

$$D_x \sec x = \sec x \tan x, \tag{9}$$

$$D_x \csc x = -\csc x \cot x. \tag{10}$$

The patterns in the formulas of Theorem 2 and in Eqs. (4) and (5) make them easy to remember. The formulas in Eqs. (5), (8), and (10) are the "cofunction analogues" of those in Eqs. (4), (7), and (9), respectively. Note that the derivative formulas for the three cofunctions are those involving minus signs.

EXAMPLE 6

$$D_x(x \tan x) = (D_x x)(\tan x) + (x)(D_x \tan x)$$

$$= (1)(\tan x) + (x)(\sec^2 x) = \tan x + x \sec^2 x.$$

$$D_t(\cot^3 t) = D_t(\cot t)^3 = 3(\cot t)^2 D_t \cot t$$

$$= 3(\cot t)^2(-\csc^2 t) = -3 \csc^2 t \cot^2 t.$$

$$D_z\left(\frac{\sec z}{\sqrt{z}}\right) = \frac{(D_z \sec z)(\sqrt{z}) - (\sec z)(D_z \sqrt{z})}{(\sqrt{z})^2}$$

$$= \frac{(\sec z)(\tan z)(\sqrt{z}) - (\sec z)(\frac{1}{2} z^{-1/2})}{z}$$

$$= \tfrac{1}{2} z^{-3/2}(2z \tan z - 1) \sec z. \quad \blacklozenge$$

Chain Rule Formulas

Recall from Eq. (7) in Section 3.3 that the chain rule gives

$$D_x[g(u)] = g'(u) \frac{du}{dx} \tag{11}$$

for the derivative of the composition $g(u(x))$ of two differentiable functions g and u. This formula yields a *chain rule version* of each new differentiation formula that we learn.

If we apply Eq. (11) first with $g(u) = \sin u$, then with $g(u) = \cos u$, and so on, we get the chain rule versions of the trigonometric differentiation formulas:

$$D_x \sin u = (\cos u) \frac{du}{dx}, \tag{12}$$

$$D_x \cos u = (-\sin u) \frac{du}{dx}, \tag{13}$$

$$D_x \tan u = (\sec^2 u) \frac{du}{dx}, \tag{14}$$

$$D_x \cot u = (-\csc^2 u) \frac{du}{dx}, \tag{15}$$

$$D_x \sec u = (\sec u \tan u) \frac{du}{dx}, \tag{16}$$

$$D_x \csc u = (-\csc u \cot u) \frac{du}{dx}. \tag{17}$$

The cases in which $u = kx$ (where k is a constant) are worth mentioning. For example,

$$D_x \sin kx = k \cos kx \quad \text{and} \quad D_x \cos kx = -k \sin kx. \tag{18}$$

The formulas in (18) provide an explanation of why radian measure is more appropriate than degree measure. Because it follows from Eq. (1) that an angle of degree measure x has radian measure $\pi x/180$, the "sine of an angle of x degrees" is a *new* and *different* function with the formula

$$\sin x° = \sin \frac{\pi x}{180},$$

expressed on the right-hand side in terms of the standard (radian-measure) sine function. Hence the first formula in (18) yields

$$D_x \sin x° = \frac{\pi}{180} \cos \frac{\pi x}{180},$$

so

$$D_x \sin x° \approx (0.01745) \cos x°.$$

The necessity of using the approximate value 0.01745 here—and indeed its very presence—is one reason why radians instead of degrees are used in the calculus of trigonometric functions: When we work with radians, we don't need such approximations.

EXAMPLE 7 If $y = 2 \sin 10t + 3 \cos \pi t$, then

$$\frac{dy}{dt} = 20 \cos 10t - 3\pi \sin \pi t. \qquad \blacklozenge$$

EXAMPLE 8

$$D_x(\sin^2 3x \cos^4 5x)$$
$$= [D_x(\sin 3x)^2](\cos^4 5x) + (\sin^2 3x)[D_x(\cos 5x)^4]$$
$$= 2(\sin 3x)(D_x \sin 3x) \cdot (\cos^4 5x) + (\sin^2 3x) \cdot 4(\cos 5x)^3 \cdot (D_x \cos 5x)$$
$$= 2(\sin 3x)(3 \cos 3x)(\cos^4 5x) + (\sin^2 3x)(4 \cos^3 5x)(-5 \sin 5x)$$
$$= 6 \sin 3x \cos 3x \cos^4 5x - 20 \sin^2 3x \sin 5x \cos^3 5x. \qquad \blacklozenge$$

EXAMPLE 9 Differentiate $f(x) = \cos \sqrt{x}$.

Solution If $u = \sqrt{x}$, then $du/dx = 1/(2\sqrt{x})$, so Eq. (13) yields

$$D_x \cos \sqrt{x} = D_x \cos u = (-\sin u) \frac{du}{dx} = -(\sin \sqrt{x}) \frac{1}{2\sqrt{x}} = -\frac{\sin \sqrt{x}}{2\sqrt{x}}.$$

Alternatively, we can carry out this computation without introducing the auxiliary variable u:

$$D_x \cos \sqrt{x} = (-\sin \sqrt{x}) \cdot D_x(\sqrt{x}) = -\frac{\sin \sqrt{x}}{2\sqrt{x}}.$$

In Fig. 3.7.4 we have plotted both the curve $y = y(x) = \cos \sqrt{x}$ and (to show the vertical scale more clearly) the constant multiple

$$y = 4y'(x) = -\frac{2 \sin \sqrt{x}}{\sqrt{x}}$$

of its derivative. Note the correspondence in this figure between the local maxima and minima of the function $y(x) = \cos \sqrt{x}$ and the zeros of its derivative $y'(x)$ (which are the same as the zeros of $4y'(x)$). ◆

FIGURE 3.7.4 The curve $y = \cos \sqrt{x}$ and the constant multiple $y = -(2 \sin \sqrt{x})/\sqrt{x}$ of its derivative.

EXAMPLE 10 Differentiate

$$y = \sin^2(2x - 1)^{3/2} = \left[\sin(2x - 1)^{3/2}\right]^2.$$

Solution Here, $y = u^2$, where $u = \sin(2x - 1)^{3/2}$, so

$$\frac{dy}{dx} = 2u \frac{du}{dx} = 2\left[\sin(2x - 1)^{3/2}\right] \cdot D_x\left[\sin(2x - 1)^{3/2}\right]$$

$$= 2\left[\sin(2x - 1)^{3/2}\right]\left[\cos(2x - 1)^{3/2}\right] \cdot D_x(2x - 1)^{3/2}$$

$$= 2\left[\sin(2x - 1)^{3/2}\right]\left[\cos(2x - 1)^{3/2}\right]\tfrac{3}{2}(2x - 1)^{1/2} \cdot 2$$

$$= 6(2x - 1)^{1/2}\left[\sin(2x - 1)^{3/2}\right]\left[\cos(2x - 1)^{3/2}\right]. \quad ◆$$

EXAMPLE 11

$$D_x \tan 2x^3 = (\sec^2 2x^3) \cdot D_x(2x^3) = 6x^2 \sec^2 2x^3.$$

$$D_t \cot^3 2t = D_t(\cot 2t)^3 = 3(\cot 2t)^2 \cdot D_t(\cot 2t)$$

$$= (3 \cot^2 2t)(-\csc^2 2t) \cdot D_t(2t)$$

$$= -6 \csc^2 2t \cot^2 2t.$$

$$D_y \sec \sqrt{y} = \left(\sec \sqrt{y} \tan \sqrt{y}\right) \cdot D_y \sqrt{y} = \frac{\sec \sqrt{y} \tan \sqrt{y}}{2\sqrt{y}}.$$

$$D_z \sqrt{\csc z} = D_z(\csc z)^{1/2} = \tfrac{1}{2}(\csc z)^{-1/2} \cdot D_z(\csc z)$$

$$= \tfrac{1}{2}(\csc z)^{-1/2}(-\csc z \cot z) = -\tfrac{1}{2}(\cot z)\sqrt{\csc z}. \quad ◆$$

Examples 12 and 13 illustrate the applications of trigonometric functions to rate-of-change and maximum-minimum problems.

EXAMPLE 12 A rocket is launched vertically and is tracked by a radar station located on the ground 5 mi from the launch pad. Suppose that the elevation angle θ of the line of sight to the rocket is increasing at 3° per second when $\theta = 60°$. What is the velocity of the rocket at this instant?

Solution First we convert the given data from degrees into radians. Because there are $\pi/180$ rad in 1°, the rate of increase of θ becomes

$$\frac{3\pi}{180} = \frac{\pi}{60} \quad \text{(rad/s)}$$

at the instant when

$$\theta = \frac{60\pi}{180} = \frac{\pi}{3} \quad \text{(rad)}.$$

FIGURE 3.7.5 Tracking an ascending rocket (Example 12).

FIGURE 3.7.6 $\sec\frac{\pi}{3} = 2$ (Example 12).

From Fig. 3.7.5 we see that the height y (in miles) of the rocket is

$$y = 5\tan\theta.$$

Hence its velocity is

$$\frac{dy}{dt} = \frac{dy}{d\theta} \cdot \frac{d\theta}{dt} = 5(\sec^2\theta)\frac{d\theta}{dt}.$$

Because $\sec(\pi/3) = 2$ (Fig. 3.7.6), the velocity of the rocket is

$$\frac{dy}{dt} = 5 \cdot 2^2 \cdot \frac{\pi}{60} = \frac{\pi}{3} \quad \text{(mi/s)},$$

about 3770 mi/h, at the instant when $\theta = 60°$. ◆

EXAMPLE 13 A rectangle is inscribed in a semicircle of radius R (Fig. 3.7.7). What is the maximum possible area of such a rectangle?

Solution If we denote the length of *half* the base of the rectangle by x and its height by y, then its area is $A = 2xy$. We see in Fig. 3.7.7 that the right triangle has hypotenuse R, the radius of the circle. So

$$x = R\cos\theta \quad \text{and} \quad y = R\sin\theta. \tag{19}$$

Each value of θ between 0 and $\pi/2$ corresponds to a possible inscribed rectangle. The values $\theta = 0$ and $\theta = \pi/2$ will yield degenerate rectangles.

We substitute the data in Eq. (19) into the formula $A = 2xy$ to obtain the area

$$A = A(\theta) = 2(R\cos\theta)(R\sin\theta)$$
$$= 2R^2\cos\theta\sin\theta \tag{20}$$

FIGURE 3.7.7 The rectangle of Example 13.

as a function of θ on the closed interval $[0, \pi/2]$. To find the critical points, we differentiate:

$$\frac{dA}{d\theta} = 2R^2(-\sin\theta\sin\theta + \cos\theta\cos\theta) = 2R^2(\cos^2\theta - \sin^2\theta).$$

Because $dA/d\theta$ always exists, we have critical points only if

$$\cos^2\theta - \sin^2\theta = 0;$$
$$\sin^2\theta = \cos^2\theta;$$
$$\tan^2\theta = 1;$$
$$\tan\theta = \pm 1.$$

The only value of θ in $[0, \pi/2]$ such that $\tan\theta = \pm 1$ is $\theta = \pi/4$.

Upon evaluation of $A(\theta)$ at each of the possible values $\theta = 0$, $\theta = \pi/4$, and $\theta = \pi/2$ (the endpoints and the critical point), we find that

$$A(0) = 0,$$

$$A\left(\frac{\pi}{4}\right) = 2R^2\left(\frac{1}{\sqrt{2}}\right)\left(\frac{1}{\sqrt{2}}\right) = R^2, \quad \leftarrow \text{absolute maximum}$$

$$A\left(\frac{\pi}{2}\right) = 0.$$

Thus the largest inscribed rectangle has area R^2, and its dimensions are $2x = R\sqrt{2}$ and $y = R/\sqrt{2}$. ◆

3.7 TRUE/FALSE STUDY GUIDE

3.7 CONCEPTS: QUESTIONS AND DISCUSSION

1. The function f is said to be **even** if $f(-x) = f(x)$ for all x, **odd** if $f(-x) = -f(x)$ for all x. For instance, the power function $f(x) = x^n$ is even if n is an even integer, but is odd if n is an odd integer. How can you determine if a function is even or odd by looking at its graph? Which of the six trigonometric functions are even and which are odd?

2. Give an example of a function (with domain the set of all real numbers) that is neither even nor odd. Find every function that is both even and odd.

3. The six trigonometric functions all have period 2π, meaning that $f(x + 2\pi) = f(x)$ for all x. Which of the trigonometric functions have period π? Determine the value of the constant k if the function $f(t) = A\cos kt + B\sin kt$ models:
   - The height of the tide at a certain beachfront location; with t in hours, the values of $f(t)$ repeat periodically every 12 h 25 min.
   - The average monthly rainfall in a certain locale; with t in months, the values of $f(t)$ repeat periodically every 12 months.
   - The average daily temperature in a certain locale; with t in days, the values of $f(t)$ repeat periodically every 365 days.

4. Considering the trigonometric functions $\sin x$, $\tan x$, $\sec x$, and their cofunctions, what is the pattern of *signs* of their derivatives? State a single short sentence telling which of the six derivative formulas include minus signs and which do not.

3.7 PROBLEMS

Differentiate the functions given in Problems 1 through 20.

1. $f(x) = 3\sin^2 x$
2. $f(x) = 2\cos^4 x$
3. $f(x) = x\cos x$
4. $f(x) = \sqrt{x}\sin x$
5. $f(x) = \dfrac{\sin x}{x}$
6. $f(x) = \dfrac{\cos x}{\sqrt{x}}$
7. $f(x) = \sin x \cos^2 x$
8. $f(x) = \cos^3 x \sin^2 x$
9. $g(t) = (1 + \sin t)^4$
10. $g(t) = (2 - \cos^2 t)^3$
11. $g(t) = \dfrac{1}{\sin t + \cos t}$
12. $g(t) = \dfrac{\sin t}{1 + \cos t}$
13. $f(x) = 2x\sin x - 3x^2\cos x$
14. $f(x) = x^{1/2}\cos x - x^{-1/2}\sin x$
15. $f(x) = \cos 2x \sin 3x$
16. $f(x) = \cos 5x \sin 7x$
17. $g(t) = t^3 \sin^2 2t$
18. $g(t) = \sqrt{t}\cos^3 3t$
19. $g(t) = (\cos 3t + \cos 5t)^{5/2}$
20. $g(t) = \dfrac{1}{\sqrt{\sin^2 t + \sin^2 3t}}$

Find dy/dx in Problems 21 through 40.

21. $y = \sin^2\sqrt{x}$
22. $y = \dfrac{\cos 2x}{x}$
23. $y = x^2\cos(3x^2 - 1)$
24. $y = \sin^3 x^4$
25. $y = \sin 2x \cos 3x$
26. $y = \dfrac{x}{\sin 3x}$
27. $y = \dfrac{\cos 3x}{\sin 5x}$
28. $y = \sqrt{\cos\sqrt{x}}$

29. $y = \sin^2 x^2$
30. $y = \cos^3 x^3$
31. $y = \sin 2\sqrt{x}$
32. $y = \cos 3\sqrt[3]{x}$
33. $y = x \sin x^2$
34. $y = x^2 \cos\left(\dfrac{1}{x}\right)$
35. $y = \sqrt{x} \sin \sqrt{x}$
36. $y = (\sin x - \cos x)^2$
37. $y = \sqrt{x}(x - \cos x)^3$
38. $y = \sqrt{x} \sin \sqrt{x + \sqrt{x}}$
39. $y = \cos(\sin x^2)$
40. $y = \sin(1 + \sqrt{\sin x})$

Find dx/dt in Problems 41 through 60.

41. $x = \tan t^7$
42. $x = \sec t^7$
43. $x = (\tan t)^7$
44. $x = (\sec 2t)^7$
45. $x = t^7 \tan 5t$
46. $x = \dfrac{\sec t^5}{t}$
47. $x = \sqrt{t} \sec \sqrt{t}$
48. $x = \sec \sqrt{t} \tan \sqrt{t}$
49. $x = \csc\left(\dfrac{1}{t^2}\right)$
50. $x = \cot\left(\dfrac{1}{\sqrt{t}}\right)$
51. $x = \dfrac{\sec 5t}{\tan 3t}$
52. $x = \sec^2 t - \tan^2 t$
53. $x = t \sec t \csc t$
54. $x = t^3 \tan^3 t^3$
55. $x = \sec(\sin t)$
56. $x = \cot(\sec 7t)$
57. $x = \dfrac{\sin t}{\sec t}$
58. $x = \dfrac{\sec t}{1 + \tan t}$
59. $x = \sqrt{1 + \cot 5t}$
60. $x = \sqrt{\csc \sqrt{t}}$

In Problems 60 through 64, write an equation of the line that is tangent to the given curve $y = f(x)$ at the point P with the given x-coordinate. Then check the plausibility of your result by plotting both the curve and the line you found on the same screen.

61. $y = x \cos x; \quad x = \pi$
62. $y = \cos^2 x; \quad x = \pi/4$
63. $y = \dfrac{4}{\pi} \tan \dfrac{\pi x}{4}; \quad x = 1$
64. $y = \dfrac{3}{\pi} \sin^2 \dfrac{\pi x}{3}; \quad x = 5$

In Problems 65 through 68, find all points on the given curve $y = f(x)$ where the tangent line is horizontal.

65. $y = \cos 2x$
66. $y = x - 2 \sin x$
67. $y = \sin x \cos x$
68. $y = \dfrac{1}{3 \sin^2 x + 2 \cos^2 x}$

69. Figure 3.7.8 shows the graph $y = x - 2 \cos x$ and two lines of slope 1 both tangent to this graph. Write equations of these two lines.

FIGURE 3.7.8 The curve $y = x - 2 \cos x$ and two tangent lines each having slope 1.

70. Figure 3.7.9 shows the graph
$$y = \dfrac{16 + \sin x}{3 + \sin x}$$
and its two horizontal tangent lines. Write equations of these two lines.

FIGURE 3.7.9 The curve $y = \dfrac{16 + \sin x}{3 + \sin x}$ and its two horizontal tangent lines.

71. Derive the differentiation formulas in Eqs. (8) through (10).

72. Use the definition of the derivative to show directly that $g'(x) = -\sin x$ if $g(x) = \cos x$.

73. If a projectile is fired from ground level with initial velocity v_0 and inclination angle α and if air resistance can be ignored, then its range—the horizontal distance it travels—is
$$R = \dfrac{1}{16} v_0^2 \sin \alpha \cos \alpha$$
(Fig. 3.7.10). What value of α maximizes R?

FIGURE 3.7.10 The projectile of Problem 73.

74. A weather balloon that is rising vertically is observed from a point on the ground 300 ft from the spot directly beneath the balloon (Fig. 3.7.11). At what rate is the balloon rising when the angle between the ground and the observer's line of sight is 45° and is increasing at 1° per second?

FIGURE 3.7.11 The weather balloon of Problem 74.

174 CHAPTER 3 The Derivative

75. A rocket is launched vertically upward from a point 2 mi west of an observer on the ground. What is the speed of the rocket when the angle of elevation (from the horizontal) of the observer's line of sight to the rocket is 50° and is increasing at 5° per second?

76. A plane flying at an altitude of 25,000 ft has a defective airspeed indicator. To determine her speed, the pilot sights a fixed point on the ground. At the moment when the angle of depression (from the horizontal) of her line of sight is 65°, she notes that this angle is increasing at 1.5° per second (Fig. 3.7.12). What is the speed of the plane?

FIGURE 3.7.12 The airplane of Problem 76.

77. An observer on the ground sights an approaching plane flying at constant speed and at an altitude of 20,000 ft. From his point of view, the plane's angle of elevation is increasing at 0.5° per second when the angle is 60°. What is the speed of the plane?

78. Find the largest possible area A of a rectangle inscribed in the unit circle $x^2 + y^2 = 1$ by maximizing A as a function of the angle θ indicated in Fig. 3.7.13.

FIGURE 3.7.13 A rectangle inscribed in the unit circle (Problem 78).

79. A water trough is to be made from a long strip of tin 6 ft wide by bending up at an angle θ a 2-ft strip on each side (Fig. 3.7.14). What angle θ would maximize the cross-sectional area, and thus the volume, of the trough?

FIGURE 3.7.14 The water trough of Problem 79.

80. A circular patch of grass of radius 20 m is surrounded by a walkway, and a light is placed atop a lamppost at the circle's center. At what height should the light be placed to illuminate the walkway most strongly? The intensity of illumination I of a surface is given by $I = (k \sin \theta)/D^2$, where D is the distance from the light source to the surface, θ is the angle at which light strikes the surface, and k is a positive constant.

81. Find the minimum possible volume V of a cone in which a sphere of given radius R is inscribed. Minimize V as a function of the angle θ indicated in Fig. 3.7.15.

FIGURE 3.7.15 Finding the smallest cone containing a fixed sphere (Problem 81).

82. A very long rectangular piece of paper is 20 cm wide. The bottom right-hand corner is folded along the crease shown in Fig. 3.7.16, so that the corner just touches the left-hand side of the page. How should this be done so that the crease is as short as possible?

FIGURE 3.7.16 Fold a piece of paper; make the crease of minimal length (Problem 82).

83. Find the maximum possible area A of a trapezoid inscribed in a semicircle of radius 1, as shown in Fig. 3.7.17. Begin by expressing A as a function of the angle θ shown there.

FIGURE 3.7.17 A trapezoid inscribed in a semicircle (Problem 83).

84. A logger must cut a six-sided beam from a circular log of diameter 30 cm so that its cross section is as shown in Fig. 3.7.18. The beam is symmetrical, with only two different internal angles α and β. Show that the cross section is maximal when the cross section is a regular hexagon, with equal sides and angles (corresponding to $\alpha = \beta = 2\pi/3$). Note that $\alpha + 2\beta = 2\pi$. (Why?)

FIGURE 3.7.18 A hexagonal beam cut from a circular log (Problem 84).

85. Consider a circular arc of length s with its endpoints on the x-axis (Fig. 3.7.19). Show that the area A bounded by this arc and the x-axis is maximal when the circular arc is in the shape of a semicircle. [*Suggestion:* Express A in terms of the angle θ subtended by the arc at the center of the circle, as shown in Fig. 3.7.19. Show that A is maximal when $\theta = \pi$.]

FIGURE 3.7.19 Finding the maximum area bounded by a circular arc and its chord (Problem 85).

86. A hiker starting at a point P on a straight road wants to reach a forest cabin that is 2 km from a point Q 3 km down the road from P (Fig. 3.7.20). She can walk 8 km/h along the road but only 3 km/h through the forest. She wants to minimize the time required to reach the cabin. How far down the road should she walk before setting off through the forest straight for the cabin? [*Suggestion:* Use the angle θ between the road and the path she takes through the forest as the independent variable.]

FIGURE 3.7.20 Finding the quickest path to the cabin in the forest (Problem 86).

87. Show that the function (graphed in Fig. 3.7.21)

$$f(x) = \begin{cases} x \sin \dfrac{1}{x} & \text{if } x \neq 0 \\ 0 & \text{if } x = 0 \end{cases}$$

(see Example 4 in Section 2.3) is *not* differentiable at $x = 0$. [*Suggestion:* Show that whether $z = 1$ or $z = -1$, there are arbitrarily small values of h such that $[f(h) - f(0)]/h = z$. Then use the *definition* of the derivative.]

FIGURE 3.7.21 The graph of $y = x \sin \dfrac{1}{x}$ near $x = 0$.

88. Let

$$f(x) = \begin{cases} x^2 \sin \dfrac{1}{x} & \text{if } x \neq 0 \\ 0 & \text{if } x = 0 \end{cases}$$

(the graph of f appears in Figs. 3.7.22 and 3.7.23). Apply the definition of the derivative to show that f is differentiable at $x = 0$ and that $f'(0) = 0$.

176 CHAPTER 3 The Derivative

FIGURE 3.7.22 The graph of $y = x^2 \sin \dfrac{1}{x}$ (Problem 88).

FIGURE 3.7.23 The graph in Fig. 3.7.22 magnified (Problem 88).

3.8 SUCCESSIVE APPROXIMATIONS AND NEWTON'S METHOD

The solution of equations has always been a central task of mathematics. More than two millennia ago, mathematicians of ancient Babylon discovered the method of "completing the square," which leads to the *quadratic formula* for an exact solution of any second-degree equation $ax^2 + bx + c = 0$. Early in the sixteenth century, several Italian mathematicians (Cardan, del Ferro, Ferrari, and Tartaglia) discovered formulas for the exact solutions of third- and fourth-degree equations. (Because they are quite complicated, these formulas are seldom used today except in computer algebra systems.) And in 1824 a brilliant young Norwegian mathematician, Niels Henrik Abel[*] (1802–1829), published a proof that there is *no* general formula giving the solution of an arbitrary polynomial equation of degree 5 (or higher) in terms of algebraic combinations of its coefficients. Thus the exact solution (for all its roots) of an equation such as

$$f(x) = x^5 - 3x^3 + x^2 - 23x + 19 = 0 \tag{1}$$

may be quite difficult or even—as a practical matter—impossible to find. In such a case it may be necessary to resort to *approximate methods*.

For example, the graph of $y = f(x)$ in Fig. 3.8.1 indicates that Eq. (1) has three real solutions (and hence two complex ones as well). The indicated small rectangle $0.5 \leq x \leq 1$, $-5 \leq y \leq 5$ encloses one of these solutions. If we use this small rectangle as a new "viewing window" with a computer or graphics calculator, then we see that this solution is near 0.8 (Fig. 3.8.2). A few additional magnifications might yield greater accuracy, showing that the solution is approximately 0.801.

Graphical methods are good for three- or four-place approximations. Here we shall discuss an analytical method developed by Isaac Newton that can rapidly provide much more accurate approximations.

Iteration and the Babylonian Square Root Method

What it means to solve even so simple an equation as

$$x^2 - 2 = 0 \tag{2}$$

is open to question. The positive exact solution is $x = \sqrt{2}$. But the number $\sqrt{2}$ is irrational and hence cannot be expressed as a terminating or repeating decimal. Thus

---

[*]For the complete story of Abel's remarkable achievements in his brief lifetime, see Oystein Ore's very readable biography *Niels Henrik Abel* (The University of Minnesota and Chelsea Publishing Company, 1974).

FIGURE 3.8.1 The graph $y = f(x)$ in Eq. (1).

FIGURE 3.8.2 Magnification of Fig. 3.8.1 near a solution.

if we mean by a *solution* an exact decimal value for x, then even Eq. (2) can be solved only approximately.

The ancient Babylonians devised an effective way to generate a sequence of better and better approximations to $\sqrt{A}$, the square root of a given positive number A. Here is the *Babylonian square root method:* We begin with a first guess x_0 for the value of $\sqrt{A}$. For $\sqrt{2}$, we might guess $x_0 = 1.5$. If x_0 is too large—that is, if $x_0 > \sqrt{A}$—then

$$\frac{A}{x_0} < \frac{A}{\sqrt{A}} = \sqrt{A},$$

so A/x_0 is too small an estimate of $\sqrt{A}$. Similarly, if x_0 is too small (if $x_0 < \sqrt{A}$), then A/x_0 is too large an estimate of $\sqrt{A}$; that is, $A/x_0 > \sqrt{A}$.

Thus in each case one of the two numbers x_0 and A/x_0 is an underestimate of $\sqrt{A}$ and the other is an overestimate. The Babylonian idea was that we should get a better estimate of $\sqrt{A}$ by *averaging* x_0 and A/x_0. This yields a better approximation

$$x_1 = \frac{1}{2}\left(x_0 + \frac{A}{x_0}\right) \tag{3}$$

to $\sqrt{A}$. But why not repeat this process? We can average x_1 and A/x_1 to get a second approximation x_2, average x_2 and A/x_2 to get x_3, and so on. By repeating this process, we generate a sequence of numbers

$$x_1, \quad x_2, \quad x_3, \quad x_4, \quad \ldots$$

that we have every right to expect will consist of better and better approximations to $\sqrt{A}$.

Specifically, having calculated the nth approximation x_n, we calculate the next one by means of the *iterative formula*

$$x_{n+1} = \frac{1}{2}\left(x_n + \frac{A}{x_n}\right). \tag{4}$$

In other words, we plow each approximation to $\sqrt{A}$ back into the right-hand side in Eq. (4) to calculate the next approximation. This is an *iterative* process—the words *iteration* and *iterative* are derived from the Latin *iterare*, "to plow again."

Suppose we find that after sufficiently many steps in this iteration, $x_{n+1} \approx x_n$ accurate to the number of decimal places we are retaining in our computations. Then Eq. (4) yields

$$x_n \approx x_{n+1} = \frac{1}{2}\left(x_n + \frac{A}{x_n}\right) = \frac{1}{2x_n}(x_n^2 + A),$$

so $2x_n^2 \approx x_n^2 + A$, and hence $x_n^2 \approx A$ to some degree of accuracy.

EXAMPLE 1 With $A = 2$ we begin with the crude first guess $x_0 = 1$ to the value of $\sqrt{A}$. Then successive applications of the formula in Eq. (4) yield

$$x_1 = \frac{1}{2}\left(1 + \frac{2}{1}\right) = \frac{3}{2} = 1.5,$$

$$x_2 = \frac{1}{2}\left(\frac{3}{2} + \frac{2}{3/2}\right) = \frac{17}{12} \approx 1.416666667,$$

$$x_3 = \frac{1}{2}\left(\frac{17}{12} + \frac{2}{17/12}\right) = \frac{577}{408} \approx 1.414215686,$$

$$x_4 = \frac{1}{2}\left(\frac{577}{408} + \frac{2}{577/408}\right) = \frac{665857}{470832} \approx 1.414213562,$$

rounding results to nine decimal places. It happens that x_4 gives $\sqrt{2}$ accurate to all nine places! ◆

The Babylonian iteration defined in Eq. (4) is a method for generating a sequence of approximations to the positive root $r = \sqrt{A}$ of the particular equation $x^2 - A = 0$. We turn next to a method that gives such a sequence of approximations for more general equations.

Newton's Method

Newton's method is an iterative method for generating a sequence $x_1, x_2, x_3, \ldots$ of approximations to a solution r of a given equation written in the general form

$$f(x) = 0. \tag{5}$$

We hope that this sequence of approximations will "converge" to the root r in the sense of the following definition.

DEFINITION Convergence of Approximations
We say that the sequence of approximations $x_1, x_2, x_3, \ldots$ **converges** to the number r provided that we can make x_n as close to r as we please merely by choosing n sufficiently large. More precisely, for any given $\epsilon > 0$, there exists a positive integer N such that $|x_n - r| < \epsilon$ for all $n \geq N$.

As a practical matter such convergence means, as illustrated in Example 1, that for any positive integer k, x_n and r will agree to k or more decimal places once n becomes sufficiently large.

The idea is that we begin with an *initial guess* x_0 that roughly approximates a solution r of the equation $f(x) = 0$. This initial guess may, for example, be obtained by inspection of the graph of $y = f(x)$, perhaps obtained from a computer or graphics calculator. We use x_0 to calculate an approximation x_1, use x_1 to calculate a better approximation x_2, use x_2 to calculate a still better approximation x_3, and so on.

Here is the general step in the process. Having reached the nth approximation x_n, we use the tangent line at $(x_n, f(x_n))$ to construct the next approximation x_{n+1} to the solution r as follows: Begin at the point x_n on the x-axis. Go vertically up (or down) to the point $(x_n, f(x_n))$ on the curve $y = f(x)$. Then follow the tangent line L there to the point where L meets the x-axis (Fig. 3.8.3). That point will be x_{n+1}.

Here is a formula for x_{n+1}. We obtain it by computing the slope of the line L in two ways: from the derivative and from the two-point definition of slope. Thus

$$f'(x_n) = \frac{f(x_n) - 0}{x_n - x_{n+1}},$$

FIGURE 3.8.3 Geometry of the formula of Newton's method.

and we easily solve for

$$x_{n+1} = x_n - \frac{f(x_n)}{f'(x_n)}. \tag{6}$$

This equation is the **iterative formula** of Newton's method, so called because in about 1669, Newton introduced an algebraic procedure (rather than the geometric construction illustrated in Fig. 3.8.3) that is equivalent to the iterative use of Eq. (6). Newton's first example was the cubic equation $x^3 - 2x - 5 = 0$, for which he found the root $r \approx 2.0946$ (as we ask you to do in Problem 18).

Suppose now that we want to apply Newton's method to solve the equation

$$f(x) = 0 \tag{7}$$

to an accuracy of k decimal places (k digits to the right of the decimal correct or correctly rounded). Remember that an equation must be written precisely in the form of Eq. (7) in order to use the formula in Eq. (6). If we reach the point in our iteration at which x_n and x_{n+1} agree to k decimal places, it then follows that

$$x_n \approx x_{n+1} = x_n - \frac{f(x_n)}{f'(x_n)}; \qquad 0 \approx -\frac{f(x_n)}{f'(x_n)}; \qquad f(x_n) \approx 0.$$

Thus we have found an approximate root $x_n \approx x_{n+1}$ of Eq. (7). In practice, then, we retain k decimal places in our computations and persist until $x_n \approx x_{n+1}$ to this degree of accuracy. (We do not consider here the possibility of round-off error, an important topic in numerical analysis.)

EXAMPLE 2 Use Newton's method to find $\sqrt{2}$ accurate to nine decimal places.

Solution More generally, consider the square root of the positive number A as the positive root of the equation

$$f(x) = x^2 - A = 0.$$

Because $f'(x) = 2x$, Eq. (6) gives the iterative formula

$$x_{n+1} = x_n - \frac{x_n^2 - A}{2x_n} = \frac{1}{2}\left(x_n + \frac{A}{x_n}\right). \tag{8}$$

Thus we have derived the Babylonian iterative formula as a special case of Newton's method. The use of Eq. (8) with $A = 2$ therefore yields exactly the values of $x_1, x_2, x_3,$ and x_4 that we computed in Example 1, and after performing another iteration we find that

$$x_5 = \frac{1}{2}\left(x_4 + \frac{2}{x_4}\right) \approx 1.414213562,$$

which agrees with x_4 to nine decimal places. The very rapid convergence here is an important characteristic of Newton's method. As a general rule (with some exceptions), each iteration doubles the number of decimal places of accuracy. ◆

EXAMPLE 3 Figure 3.8.4 shows an open-topped tray constructed by the method of Example 2 in Section 3.6. We begin with a 7-by-11-in. rectangle of sheet metal. We cut a square with edge length x from each of its four corners and then fold up the resulting flaps to obtain a rectangular tray with volume

$$V(x) = x(7-2x)(11-2x)$$
$$= 4x^3 - 36x^2 + 77x, \quad 0 \leq x \leq 3.5. \quad (9)$$

In Section 3.6 we inquired about the maximum possible volume of such a tray. Here we want to find instead the value(s) of x that will yield a tray with volume 40 in.^{3}; we will find x by solving the equation

$$V(x) = 4x^3 - 36x^2 + 77x = 40.$$

FIGURE 3.8.4 The tray of Example 3.

To solve this equation for x, first we write an equation of the form in Eq. (7):

$$f(x) = 4x^3 - 36x^2 + 77x - 40 = 0. \quad (10)$$

Figure 3.8.5 shows the graph of f. We see three solutions: a root r_1 between 0 and 1, a root r_2 slightly greater than 2, and a root r_3 slightly larger than 6. Because

$$f'(x) = 12x^2 - 72x + 77,$$

Newton's iterative formula in Eq. (6) takes the form

$$x_{n+1} = x_n - \frac{f(x_n)}{f'(x_n)}$$
$$= x_n - \frac{4x_n^3 - 36x_n^2 + 77x_n - 40}{12x_n^2 - 72x_n + 77}. \quad (11)$$

Beginning with the initial guess $x_0 = 1$ (because it's reasonably close to r_1), Eq. (11) gives

$$x_1 = 1 - \frac{4 \cdot 1^3 - 36 \cdot 1^2 + 77 \cdot 1 - 40}{12 \cdot 1^2 - 72 \cdot 1 + 77} \approx 0.7059,$$

$$x_2 \approx 0.7736,$$

$$x_3 \approx 0.7780,$$

$$x_4 \approx 0.7780.$$

FIGURE 3.8.5 The graph of $f(x)$ in Eq. 10 of Example 3.

Thus we obtain the root $r_1 \approx 0.7780$, retaining only four decimal places.

If we had begun with a different initial guess, the sequence of Newton iterates might well have converged to a different root of the equation $f(x) = 0$. The approximate solution obtained therefore depends on the initial guess. For example, with $x_0 = 2$ and, later, with $x_0 = 6$, the iteration in Eq. (11) produces the two sequences

$x_0 = 2$	$x_0 = 6$
$x_1 \approx 2.1053$	$x_1 \approx 6.1299$
$x_2 \approx 2.0993$	$x_2 \approx 6.1228$
$x_3 \approx 2.0992$	$x_3 \approx 6.1227$
$x_4 \approx 2.0992$	$x_4 \approx 6.1227$

Thus the other two roots of Eq. (10) are $r_2 \approx 2.0992$ and $r_3 \approx 6.1277$.

With $x = r_1 \approx 0.7780$, the tray in Fig. 3.8.4 has the approximate dimensions 9.4440 in. by 5.4440 in. by 0.7780 in. With $x = r_2 \approx 2.0992$, its approximate dimensions are 6.8015 in. by 2.8015 in. by 2.0992 in. But the third root $r_3 \approx 6.1227$ would *not* lead to a tray that is physically possible. (Why not?) Thus the *two* values of x that yield trays with volume 40 in. are $x \approx 0.7780$ and $x \approx 2.0992$. ◆

FIGURE 3.8.6 Solving the equation $x = \frac{1}{2}\cos x$ (Example 4).

EXAMPLE 4 Figure 3.8.6 indicates that the equation

$$x = \tfrac{1}{2}\cos x \tag{12}$$

has a solution r near 0.5. To apply Newton's method to approximate r, we rewrite Eq. (12) in the form

$$f(x) = 2x - \cos x = 0.$$

Because $f'(x) = 2 + \sin x$, the iterative formula of Newton's method is

$$x_{n+1} = x_n - \frac{2x_n - \cos x_n}{2 + \sin x_n}.$$

Beginning with $x_0 = 0.5$ and retaining five decimal places, this formula yields

$$x_1 \approx 0.45063, \qquad x_2 \approx 0.45018, \qquad x_3 \approx 0.45018.$$

Thus the root is 0.45018 to five decimal places. ◆

EXAMPLE 5 Newton's method is one for which "the proof is in the pudding." If it works, it's obvious that it does, and everything's fine. When Newton's method fails, it may do so spectacularly. For example, suppose that we want to solve the equation

$$x^{1/3} = 0.$$

Here $r = 0$ is the only solution. The iterative formula in Eq. (6) becomes

$$x_{n+1} = x_n - \frac{(x_n)^{1/3}}{\frac{1}{3}(x_n)^{-2/3}} = x_n - 3x_n = -2x_n.$$

If we begin with $x_0 = 1$, Newton's method yields $x_1 = -2$, $x_2 = +4$, $x_3 = -8$, and so on. Figure 3.8.7 indicates why our "approximations" are not converging. ◆

FIGURE 3.8.7 A failure of Newton's method.

When Newton's method fails, a graph will typically indicate the reason why. Then the use of an alternative method such as repeated tabulation or successive magnification is appropriate.

Newton's Method with Calculators and Computers

With calculators and computers that permit user-defined functions, Newton's method is very easy to set up and apply repeatedly. It is helpful to interpret Newton's iteration

$$x_{n+1} = x_n - \frac{f(x_n)}{f'(x_n)}$$

as follows. Having first defined the functions f and f', we then define the "iteration function"

$$g(x) = x - \frac{f(x)}{f'(x)}.$$

FIGURE 3.8.8 Preparing to solve the equation $x^3 - 3x^2 + 1 = 0$.

FIGURE 3.8.9 Solving the equation $x^3 - 3x^2 + 1 = 0$.

FIGURE 3.8.10 Preparing to solve the equation $x^3 - 3x^2 + 1 = 0$.

Newton's method is then equivalent to the following procedure. Begin with an initial estimate x_0 of the solution of the equation

$$f(x) = 0.$$

Calculate successive approximations $x_1, x_2, x_3, \ldots$ to the exact solution by means of the iteration

$$x_{n+1} = g(x_n).$$

That is, apply the function g to each approximation to get the next.

Figure 3.8.8 shows a TI graphics calculator prepared to solve the equation

$$f(x) = x^3 - 3x^2 + 1 = 0.$$

Then we need only store the initial guess, `0.5 → x`, and next enter repeatedly the command `y3 → x`, as indicated in Fig. 3.8.9.

Figure 3.8.10 shows an HP calculator prepared to carry out the same iteration. The functions `F(X)`, `D(X)` (for $f'(x)$), and `G(X)` are each defined by pressing the DEFINE key. Then it is necessary only to ENTER the initial guess x_0 and press the G key repeatedly to generate the desired successive appropriations.

With *Maple* or *Mathematica* you can define the functions f and g and then repeatedly enter the command $x = g(x)$, as shown in Fig. 3.8.11.

Mathematica Command	*Maple* Command	Result

f[x_] := x^3 − 3x^2 + 1
g[x_] := x − f[x]/f'[x]
x = 0.5
x = g[x]
x = g[x]
x = g[x]
x = g[x]
	f := x −> x^3 − 3 ∗ x^2 + 1;
	g := x −> x − f(x)/D(f)(x);
	x := 0.5;
	x := g(x);
	x := g(x);
	x := g(x);
	x := g(x);
		0.500000
		0.666667
		0.652778
		0.652704
		0.652704

FIGURE 3.8.11 *Mathematica* and *Maple* implementations of Newton's method.

Newton's Method and Computer Graphics

Newton's method and similar iterative techniques are often used to generate vividly colored "fractal patterns," in which the same or similar structures are replicated on smaller and smaller scales at successively higher levels of magnification. To describe one way this can be done, we replace the real numbers in our Newton's method computations with *complex* numbers. We illustrate this idea with the cubic equation

$$f(x) = x^3 - 3x^2 + 1 = 0. \tag{13}$$

In the Project we ask you to approximate the three solutions
$$r_1 \approx -0.53, \qquad r_2 \approx 0.65, \qquad r_3 \approx 2.88$$
of this equation.

First, recall that a *complex number* is a number of the form $a + bi$, where $i = \sqrt{-1}$, so $i^2 = -1$. The real numbers a and b are called the *real part* and the *imaginary part*, respectively, of $a + bi$. You add, multiply, and divide complex numbers as if they were binomials, with real and imaginary parts "collected" as in the computations

$$(3 + 4i) + (5 - 7i) = (3 + 5) + (4 - 7)i = 8 - 3i,$$

$$(2 + 5i)(3 - 4i) = 2(3 - 4i) + 5i(3 - 4i)$$
$$= 6 - 8i + 15i - 20i^2 = 26 + 7i,$$

and

$$\frac{2 + 5i}{3 + 4i} = \frac{2 + 5i}{3 + 4i} \cdot \frac{3 - 4i}{3 - 4i} = \frac{26 + 7i}{9 - 16i^2} = \frac{26 + 7i}{25} = 1.04 + (0.28)i.$$

The use of the *conjugate* $3 - 4i$ of the denominator $3 + 4i$ in the last computation is a very common technique for writing a complex fraction in the standard form $a + bi$. (The **conjugate** of $x + yi$ is $x - yi$; it follows that the conjugate of $x - yi$ is $x + yi$.)

Now let us substitute the complex number $z = x + iy$ into the cubic polynomial

$$f(z) = z^3 - 3z^2 + 1$$

of Eq. (13) and into its derivative $f'(z) = 3z^2 - 6z$. We find that

$$f(z) = (x + iy)^3 - 3(x + iy)^2 + 1$$
$$= (x^3 - 3xy^2 - 3x^2 + 3y^2 + 1) + (3x^2y - y^3 - 6xy)i \tag{14}$$

and

$$f'(z) = 3(x + iy)^2 - 6(x + iy)$$
$$= (3x^2 - 3y^2 - 6x) + (6xy - 6y)i. \tag{15}$$

Consequently, there is nothing to prevent us from applying Newton's method to Eq. (13) with complex numbers. Beginning with a *complex* initial guess $z_0 = x_0 + iy_0$, we can substitute Eqs. (14) and (15) into Newton's iterative formula

$$z_{n+1} = z_n - \frac{f(z_n)}{f'(z_n)} \tag{16}$$

to generate the complex sequence $\{z_n\}$, which may yet converge to a (real) solution of Eq. (13).

With this preparation, we can now explain how Fig. 3.8.12 was generated. A computer was programmed to carry out Newton's iteration repeatedly, beginning with many thousands of initial guesses $z_0 = x_0 + iy_0$ that "fill" the rectangle $-2 \leq x \leq 4$, $-2.25 \leq y \leq 2.25$ in the complex plane. The initial point $z_0 = x_0 + iy_0$ was then

FIGURE 3.8.12 $-2 \leq x \leq 4$, $-2.25 \leq y \leq 2.25$.

FIGURE 3.8.13 $1.6 \leq x \leq 2.4$, $-0.3 \leq y \leq 0.3$.

FIGURE 3.8.14 $1.64 \leq x \leq 1.68$, $-0.015 \leq y \leq 0.015$.

FIGURE 3.8.15 $1.648 \leq x \leq 1.650$, $-0.00075 \leq y \leq 0.00075$.

color-coded according to the root (if any) to which the corresponding sequence $\{z_n\}$ converged:

Color z_0 green if $\{z_n\}$ converges to the root $r_1 \approx -0.53$;

Color z_0 red if $\{z_n\}$ converges to the root $r_2 \approx 0.65$;

Color z_0 yellow if $\{z_n\}$ converges to the root $r_3 \approx 2.88$.

Thus we use different colors to distinguish different "*Newton basins* of attraction" for the equation we are investigating. It is not surprising that a red region containing the root r_2 appears in the middle of Fig. 3.8.12, separating a green region to the left that contains r_1 and a yellow region to the right that contains r_3. But why would yellow lobes protrude from the green region into the red region and green lobes protrude from the yellow region into the red one? To see what's happening near these lobes, we generated some blowups.

Figure 3.8.13 shows a blowup of the rectangle $1.6 \leq x \leq 2.4$, $-0.3 \leq y \leq 0.3$ containing the green lobe that's visible in Fig. 3.8.12. Figure 3.8.14 ($1.64 \leq x \leq 1.68$, $-0.015 \leq y \leq 0.015$) and Fig. 3.8.15 ($1.648 \leq x \leq 1.650$, $-0.00075 \leq y \leq 0.00075$) are further magnifications. The rectangle shown in Fig. 3.8.15 corresponds to less than one millionth of a square inch of Fig. 3.8.12.

At every level of magnification, each green lobe has smaller yellow lobes protruding into the surrounding red region, and each of these yellow lobes has still smaller green lobes protruding from it, and so on ad infinitum (just like the proverbial little fleas that are bitten by still smaller fleas, and so on ad infinitum).

Figure 3.8.16 shows the Newton basins picture for the twelfth-degree polynomial equation

$$f(x) = x^{12} - 14x^{10} + 183x^8 - 612x^6 - 2209x^4 - 35374x^2 + 38025 = 0, \quad \textbf{(17)}$$

which has as its solution the twelve complex numbers

$$1, \quad 1 \pm 2i, \quad -1, \quad -1 \pm 2i,$$
$$3, \quad 3 \pm 2i, \quad -3, \quad -3 \pm 2i.$$

Twelve different colors are used to distinguish the Newton basins of these twelve solutions of Eq. (17).

Where the fractal common boundary appears to separate basins of different colors, it is studded with "flowers" like the one at the center of Fig. 3.8.16, which is magnified in Fig. 3.8.17. Each of these flowers has ten "leaves" (in the remaining ten colors). Each of these leaves has "buds" like the one shown in Fig. 3.8.18. Each of these buds is encircled with flowers that have leaves that have buds that are encircled with flowers—and so on ad infinitum.

FIGURE 3.8.16 Newton basis for the twelfth-degree polynomial.

FIGURE 3.8.17 The flower at the center of Fig. 3.8.16.

FIGURE 3.8.18 A bud on a petal of the flower in Fig. 3.8.17.

3.8 TRUE/FALSE STUDY GUIDE

3.8 CONCEPTS: QUESTIONS AND DISCUSSION

1. Example 1 in this section illustrates the use of Babylonian iteration to approximate the square root of a positive number A, beginning with a positive initial guess x_0. How is the number of iterations required for six-place accuracy affected by choosing x_0 very close to zero, or very large? Does it appear that the number of decimal places of accuracy is roughly doubled with each iteration? What happens if a negative initial guess is used? What happens if A itself is negative?

2. The general rule—that each iteration of Newton's method typically doubles the number of decimal places of accuracy—does not hold when the method is used to approximate a solution r of $f(x) = 0$ if r is also a critical point of f. Investigate the "rate of convergence" to the root r if: (a) $f(x) = (x-2)^2$, so that $r = 2$ is a double root; (b) $f(x) = (x-1)^{2/3}$, so that the graph has a cusp and a vertical tangent at $r = 1$.

3. Consider the exotic function $f(x) = x^2 \sin(1/x)$ [with $f(0) = 0$] of Problem 88 in Section 3.7. Investigate what happens when you use a computer algebra system to attempt to approximate the root $r = 0$ by iterating $g(x) = x - f(x)/f'(x)$. Try a variety of different nonzero initial guesses and explain the results.

3.8 PROBLEMS

In Problems 1 through 20, use Newton's method to find the solution of the given equation $f(x) = 0$ in the indicated interval $[a, b]$ accurate to four decimal places. You may choose the initial guess either on the basis of a calculator graph or by interpolation between the values $f(a)$ and $f(b)$.

1. $x^2 - 5 = 0$; $[2, 3]$ (to find the positive square root of 5)
2. $x^3 - 2 = 0$; $[1, 2]$ (to find the cube root of 2)
3. $x^5 - 100 = 0$; $[2, 3]$ (to find the fifth root of 100)
4. $x^{3/2} - 10 = 0$; $[4, 5]$ (to find $10^{2/3}$)
5. $x^2 + 3x - 1 = 0$; $[0, 1]$
6. $x^3 + 4x - 1 = 0$; $[0, 1]$
7. $x^6 + 7x^2 - 4 = 0$; $[-1, 0]$
8. $x^3 + 3x^2 + 2x = 10$; $[1, 2]$
9. $x - \cos x = 0$; $[0, 2]$
10. $x^2 - \sin x = 0$; $[0.5, 1.0]$
11. $4x - \sin x = 4$; $[1, 2]$
12. $5x + \cos x = 5$; $[0, 1]$
13. $x^5 + x^4 = 100$; $[2, 3]$
14. $x^5 + 2x^4 + 4x = 5$; $[0, 1]$
15. $x + \tan x = 0$; $[2, 3]$
16. $x + \tan x = 0$; $[11, 12]$
17. $x^3 - 10 = 0$; $[2, 3]$
18. $x^3 - 2x - 5 = 0$; $[2, 3]$ (Newton's own example)
19. $x^5 - 5x - 10 = 0$; $[1, 2]$
20. $x^5 = 32$; $[0, 5]$

21. (a) Show that Newton's method applied to the equation $x^3 - a = 0$ yields the formula

$$x_{n+1} = \frac{1}{3}\left(2x_n + \frac{a}{x_n^2}\right)$$

for approximating the cube root of a. (b) Use this formula to find $\sqrt[3]{2}$ accurate to five decimal places.

22. (a) Show that Newton's method yields the formula

$$x_{n+1} = \frac{1}{k}\left[(k-1)x_n + \frac{a}{(x_n)^{k-1}}\right]$$

for approximating the kth root of the positive number a.
(b) Use this formula to find $\sqrt[10]{100}$ accurate to five decimal places.

23. Equation (12) has the special form $x = G(x)$, where $G(x) = \frac{1}{2}\cos x$. For an equation of this form, the iterative formula $x_{n+1} = G(x_n)$ produces a sequence of approximations that *sometimes* converges to a root. In the case of Eq. (12), this *repeated substitution* formula is simply $x_{n+1} = \frac{1}{2}\cos x_n$. Begin with $x_0 = 0.5$ as in Example 4 and retain five decimal places in your computation of the solution of Eq. (12). [*Check:* You should find that $x_8 \approx 0.45018$.]

24. The equation $x^4 = x + 1$ has a solution between $x = 1$ and $x = 2$. Use the initial guess $x_0 = 1.5$ and the method of repeated substitution (see Problem 23) to discover that one of the solutions of this equation is approximately 1.220744. Iterate using the formula

$$x_{n+1} = (x_n + 1)^{1/4}.$$

Then compare the result with what happens when you iterate using the formula

$$x_{n+1} = (x_n)^4 - 1.$$

25. The equation $x^3 - 3x^2 + 1 = 0$ has a solution between $x = 0$ and $x = 1$. To apply the method of repeated substitution (see Problem 23) to this equation, you may write it either in the form

$$x = 3 - \frac{1}{x^2}$$

or in the form

$$x = (3x^2 - 1)^{1/3}.$$

If you begin with $x_0 = 0.5$ in the hope of finding the nearby solution (approximately 0.6527) of the original equation by using each of the preceding iterative formulas, you will observe some of the drawbacks of the method. Describe what goes wrong.

26. Show that Newton's method applied to the equation

$$\frac{1}{x} - a = 0$$

yields the iterative formula

$$x_{n+1} = 2x_n - a(x_n)^2$$

and thus provides a method for approximating the reciprocal $1/a$ without performing any divisions. Such a method is useful because, in most high-speed computers, the operation of division is more time consuming than even several additions and multiplications.

27. Prove that the equation $x^5 + x = 1$ has exactly one real solution. Then use Newton's method to find it with four places correct to the right of the decimal point.

In Problems 28 through 30, use Newton's method to find all real roots of the given equation with four digits correct to the right of the decimal point. [Suggestion: In order to determine the number of roots and their approximate locations, graph the left- and right-hand sides of each equation and observe where the graphs cross.]

28. $x^2 = \cos x$ **29.** $x = 2\sin x$

30. $\cos x = -\frac{1}{5}x$ (There are exactly three solutions, as indicated in Fig. 3.8.19.)

FIGURE 3.8.19 Solving the equation in Problem 30.

31. Prove that the equation $x^7 - 3x^3 + 1 = 0$ has at least one solution. Then use Newton's method to find one solution to three-place accuracy.

32. Use Newton's method to approximate $\sqrt[3]{5}$ to four-place accuracy.

33. Use Newton's method to find the value of x for which $x^3 = \cos x$.

34. Use Newton's method to find the smallest positive value of x for which $x = \tan x$.

35. In Problem 49 of Section 3.6, we dealt with the problem of minimizing the cost of building a road to two points on opposite sides of a geologic fault. This problem led to the equation

$$f(x) = 3x^4 - 24x^3 + 51x^2 - 32x + 64 = 0.$$

Use Newton's method to find, to four-place accuracy, the root of this equation that lies in the interval [3, 4].

36. The moon of Planet Gzyx has an elliptical orbit with eccentricity 0.5, and its period of revolution around the planet is 10 days. If the moon is at the position $(a, 0)$ when $t = 0$, then (Fig. 3.8.20) the central angle after t days is given

FIGURE 3.8.20 The elliptical orbit of Problem 36.

by *Kepler's equation*
$$\frac{2\pi t}{100} = \theta - \frac{1}{2}\sin\theta.$$
Use Newton's method to solve for θ when $t = 17$ (days). Take $\theta_0 = 1.5$ (rad) and calculate the first two approximations θ_1 and θ_2. Express θ_2 in degrees as well.

37. A great problem of Archimedes was that of using a plane to cut a sphere into two segments with volumes in a given (preassigned) ratio. Archimedes showed that the volume of a segment of height h of a sphere of radius a is $V = \frac{1}{3}\pi h^2(3a - h)$. If a plane at distance x from the center of a sphere of radius 1 cuts the sphere into two segments, one with twice the volume of the other, show that $3x^3 - 9x + 2 = 0$. Then use Newton's method to find x accurate to four decimal places.

38. The equation $f(x) = x^3 - 4x + 1 = 0$ has three distinct real roots. Approximate their locations by evaluating f at $x = -3, -2, -1, 0, 1, 2,$ and 3. Then use Newton's method to approximate each of the three roots to four-place accuracy.

39. The equation $x + \tan x = 0$ is important in a variety of applications—for example, in the study of the diffusion of heat. It has a sequence $\alpha_1, \alpha_2, \alpha_3, \ldots$ of positive roots, with the nth root slightly larger than $(n - 0.5)\pi$. Use Newton's method to compute α_1 and α_2 to three-place accuracy.

40. Investigate the cubic equation
$$4x^3 - 42x^2 - 19x - 28 = 0.$$
Perhaps you can see graphically that it has only a single real solution. Find it (accurate to four decimal places). First try the initial guess $x_0 = 0$; be prepared for at least 25 iterations. Then try initial guesses $x_0 = 10$ and $x_0 = 100$.

41. A 15-ft ladder and a 20-ft ladder lean in opposite directions against the vertical walls of a hall (Fig. 3.8.21). The ladders cross at a height of 5 ft. You must find the width w of the hall. First, let x and y denote the heights of the tops of the ladders on the walls and u and v the lengths shown in the figure, so that $w = u + v$. Use similar triangles to show that
$$x = 5\left(1 + \frac{u}{v}\right), \quad y = 5\left(1 + \frac{v}{u}\right).$$
Then apply the Pythagorean theorem to show that $t = u/v$ satisfies the equation
$$t^4 + 2t^3 - 7t^2 - 2t - 1 = 0.$$

FIGURE 3.8.21 The crossing ladders of Problem 41.

Finally, use Newton's method to find first the possible values of t, and then those of w, accurate to four decimal places.

42. Figure 3.8.22 suggests that the equation $15 \sin x = 4\sqrt{x}$ has either three or four positive solutions. Use Newton's method to find each of them accurate to three decimal places. Take whatever steps you find necessary to determine whether there is or is not a solution near $x = 14$.

FIGURE 3.8.22 Three positive solutions or four?

43. The spherical asteroid problem in the Section 1.4 Project leads to the equation $(100 + \theta)\cos\theta = 100$, where $R = 1000/\theta$ is the radius of the asteroid, and it is clear from the context that $0 < \theta < \pi/2$. Use Newton's method to solve this problem.

44. This is a famous "railroad track problem." Consider a 1-mile railroad track that was constructed without leaving the usual expansion spaces between consecutive rails. Thus each rail of the track is, in effect, a single steel rail one mile long. Suppose that an increase in the temperature by 20°C increases—by thermal expansion of the steel—the length of this rail by one foot. Also assume that the ends of the track are fixed, so the rail "bows up" in the shape of a circular arc with central angle 2θ and radius R (Fig. 3.8.23). Find the resulting height x (at its midpoint) of the bowed rail above the ground.

FIGURE 3.8.23 The bowed railroad track of Problem 44.

3.8 Project: How Deep Does a Floating Ball Sink?

Figure 3.8.24 shows a large cork ball of radius $a = 1$ floating in water of density 1. If the ball's density ρ is one-fourth that of water, $\rho = \frac{1}{4}$, then Archimedes' law of buoyancy implies that the ball floats in such a way that one-fourth of its total volume is submerged. Because the volume of the ball is $4\pi/3$, it follows that the volume of the part of the ball beneath the waterline is given by

$$V = \rho \cdot \frac{4\pi}{3} = \frac{1}{4} \cdot \frac{4\pi}{3} = \frac{\pi}{3}. \tag{1}$$

FIGURE 3.8.24 The floating cork ball.

The shape of the submerged part of the ball is that of a **spherical segment** with a circular flat top. The volume of a spherical segment of *top radius r* and *depth h = x* (as in Fig. 3.8.24) is given by the formula

$$V = \frac{\pi x}{6}(3r^2 + x^2). \tag{2}$$

This formula is also due to Archimedes and holds for any depth x, whether the spherical segment is smaller or larger than a hemisphere. For instance, note that with $r = 0$ and $x = 2a$ it gives $V = \frac{4}{3}\pi a^3$, the volume of an entire sphere of radius a.

For a preliminary investigation, proceed as follows to find the depth x to which the ball sinks in the water. Equate the two expressions for V in Eqs. (1) and (2), then use the right triangle in Fig. 3.8.24 to eliminate r. You should find that x must be a solution of the cubic equation

$$f(x) = x^3 - 3x^2 + 1 = 0. \tag{3}$$

As the graph $y = f(x)$ in Fig. 3.8.25 indicates, this equation has three real solutions—one in $(-1, 0)$, one in $(0, 1)$, and one in $(2, 3)$. The solution between 0 and 1 gives the actual depth x to which the ball sinks (why?). You can find x using Newton's method.

FIGURE 3.8.25 Graph for the cork-ball equation.

Your Investigation For your very own floating ball to investigate, let its density ρ in Eq. (1) be given by

$$\rho = \frac{10 + k}{20}$$

where k denotes the last nonzero digit in the sum of the final four digits of your student I.D. number. Your objective is to find the depth to which this ball sinks in the water. Begin by deriving the cubic equation that you need to solve, explaining each step carefully. Then find all of its solutions accurate to at least four decimal places. Include in your report a sketch of a spherical ball with the waterline located accurately (to scale) in the position corresponding to your result for the desired depth.

CHAPTER 3 REVIEW: FORMULAS, CONCEPTS, DEFINITIONS

Differentiation Formulas

$$D_x(cu) = c\frac{du}{dx}$$

$$D_x(u+v) = \frac{du}{dx} + \frac{dv}{dx}$$

$$D_x(uv) = u\frac{dv}{dx} + v\frac{du}{dx}$$

$$D_x\frac{u}{v} = \frac{v\frac{du}{dx} - u\frac{dv}{dx}}{v^2}$$

$$D_x g(u) = g'(u)\frac{du}{dx}$$

$$D_x(u^r) = ru^{r-1}\frac{du}{dx}$$

$$D_x \sin u = (\cos u)\frac{du}{dx}$$

$$D_x \cos u = (-\sin u)\frac{du}{dx}$$

$$D_x \tan u = (\sec^2 u)\frac{du}{dx}$$

$$D_x \cot u = (-\csc^2 u)\frac{du}{dx}$$

$$D_x \sec u = (\sec u \tan u)\frac{du}{dx}$$

$$D_x \csc u = (-\csc u \cot u)\frac{du}{dx}$$

Use the following list as a guide to concepts for review.
1. Definition of the derivative
2. Average rate of change of a function
3. Instantaneous rate of change of a function
4. Position function; velocity and acceleration
5. Differential, function, and operator notation for derivatives
6. The power rule
7. The binomial formula
8. Linearity of differentiation
9. The product rule
10. The reciprocal rule
11. The quotient rule
12. The chain rule
13. The generalized power rule
14. Vertical tangent lines
15. Local maxima and minima
16. $f'(c) = 0$ as a necessary condition for local extrema
17. Absolute (or global) extrema
18. Critical points
19. The closed-interval maximum-minimum method
20. Steps in the solution of applied maximum-minimum problems
21. Derivatives of the sine and cosine functions
22. Derivatives of the other four trigonometric functions
23. Newton's method

CHAPTER 3 MISCELLANEOUS PROBLEMS

Find dy/dx in Problems 1 through 35.

1. $y = x^2 + \dfrac{3}{x^2}$
2. $y = \sqrt{x^3}$
3. $y = \sqrt{x} + \dfrac{1}{\sqrt[3]{x}}$
4. $y = (x^2 + 4x)^{5/2}$
5. $y = (x-1)^7(3x+2)^9$
6. $y = \dfrac{x^4 + x^2}{x^2 + x + 1}$
7. $y = \left(3x - \dfrac{1}{2x^2}\right)^4$
8. $y = x^{10}\sin 10x$
9. $y = 9x^{-1}$
10. $y = \sqrt{\dfrac{1}{5x^6}}$
11. $y = \dfrac{1}{\sqrt{(x^3 - x)^3}}$
12. $y = \sqrt[3]{2x+1}\sqrt[5]{3x-2}$
13. $y = \dfrac{1}{1+u^2}$ where $u = \dfrac{1}{1+x^2}$
14. $y = (\sin x)^{2/3}$
15. $y = \left(\sqrt{x} + \sqrt[3]{2x}\right)^{7/3}$
16. $y = \sqrt{3x^5 - 4x^2}$
17. $y = \dfrac{u+1}{u-1}$ where $u = \sqrt{x+1}$
18. $y = \sin(2\cos 3x)$
19. $y = \sqrt{x^6 + x^4}$
20. $y = \sqrt{1 + \sin\sqrt{x}}$
21. $y = \sqrt{x + \sqrt{2x + \sqrt{3x}}}$
22. $y = \dfrac{x + \sin x}{x^2 + \cos x}$
23. $y = \left(4 - \sqrt[3]{x}\right)^3$
24. $y = \sqrt[3]{x^4 + x^3}$
25. $y = (1 + 2u)^3$ where $u = \dfrac{1}{(1+x)^3}$
26. $y = \cos^2(\sin^2 x)$

27. $y = \sqrt{\dfrac{\sin^2 x}{1 + \cos x}}$

28. $y = \left(1 + \sqrt{x}\right)^3 \left(1 - 2\sqrt[3]{x}\right)^4$

29. $y = \dfrac{\cos 2x}{\sqrt{\sin 3x}}$

30. $y = \sqrt{4 + x^2} - \sqrt{4 - x^2}$

31. $y = \sin^3 2x \cos^2 2x$

32. $y = \left[1 + (2 + 3x)^{-3/2}\right]^{2/3}$

33. $y = \sin^5\left(x + \dfrac{1}{x}\right)$

34. $y = \left(\dfrac{1 + x}{1 - x}\right)^{3/2}$

35. $y = \cos^3\left(\sqrt[3]{x^4 + 1}\right)$

Find the derivatives of the functions given in Problems 36 through 57.

36. $f(x) = \sec(x^4 + x^3)$
37. $f(x) = \tan^2(x^4 + x^3)$
38. $f(x) = \sec^3 2x \tan 2x$
39. $f(x) = \sec \sqrt{x} \tan \sqrt{x}$
40. $f(x) = x^3 \sec 2x$
41. $g(t) = \dfrac{\sec 2t}{t}$
42. $g(t) = 3 \sec(t^2 - 1)$
43. $g(t) = \left(\tan \sqrt{t}\right)^3$
44. $f(x) = \dfrac{1 + \tan x}{\sec x}$
45. $g(t) = \dfrac{1 - \sec t}{1 + \sec t}$
46. $f(x) = \sin(\sec x)$
47. $f(x) = \sin x \sec x$
48. $g(t) = \tan(\sin t)$
49. $g(t) = \tan t \sin t$
50. $h(x) = \dfrac{1}{\cos(\tan x)}$
51. $h(x) = \dfrac{1}{\cos x \tan x}$
52. $\phi(t) = \cot(\csc t)$
53. $\phi(t) = \csc t \cot t$
54. $f(x) = (1 + \sin^2 3x)^{1/2}$
55. $g(x) = \sqrt{\sin(1 + x^3)}$
56. $h(t) = \sqrt[3]{1 + \sec^2 6t}$
57. $\phi(t) = \sqrt[5]{(t - \tan t)^3}$

In Problems 58 through 63, write an equation of the line tangent to the given curve at the indicated point.

58. $y = \dfrac{x + 1}{x - 1}$; $(0, -1)$
59. $y = \sin 3x$; $(\pi/6, 1)$
60. $y = \dfrac{1}{1 + \sqrt{x}}$; $(4, \tfrac{1}{3})$
61. $y = \dfrac{2x}{\sqrt[3]{x + 1}}$; $(7, 7)$
62. $y = \sec x - \tan x$; $(0, 1)$
63. $y = (x^2 + 2x)^{1/3}$; $(2, 2)$

Find the limits in Problems 64 through 69.

64. $\lim\limits_{x \to 0} \dfrac{x - \tan x}{\sin x}$
65. $\lim\limits_{x \to 0} x \cot 3x$
66. $\lim\limits_{x \to 0} \dfrac{\sin 2x}{\sin 5x}$
67. $\lim\limits_{x \to 0} x^2 \csc 2x \cot 2x$
68. $\lim\limits_{x \to 0} x^2 \sin \dfrac{1}{x^2}$
69. $\lim\limits_{x \to 0^+} \sqrt{x} \sin \dfrac{1}{x}$

In Problems 70 through 77, identify two functions f and g such that $h(x) = f(g(x))$. Then apply the chain rule to find $h'(x)$.

70. $h(x) = \sqrt[3]{x + x^4}$
71. $h(x) = \dfrac{1}{\sqrt{x^2 + 25}}$
72. $h(x) = \sqrt{\dfrac{x}{x^2 + 1}}$
73. $h(x) = \sqrt[3]{(x - 1)^5}$
74. $h(x) = \dfrac{(x + 1)^{10}}{(x - 1)^{10}}$
75. $h(x) = \cos(x^2 + 1)$
76. $h(x) = (1 + \sin x)^3$
77. $h(x) = \sec 6x$

78. What is an equation for the straight line through $(1, 0)$ that is tangent to the graph of
$$h(x) = x + \dfrac{1}{x}$$
at a point in the first quadrant?

79. A rectangle has its base on the x-axis and its upper two vertices on the graph of $y = \cos x$, $-\pi/2 \leqq x \leqq \pi/2$. Find the maximum possible area of such a rectangle with four places to the right of the decimal point correct or correctly rounded. You may, and should, use Newton's method to help you solve this problem.

80. An oil field containing 20 wells has been producing 4000 barrels of oil daily. For each new well drilled, the daily production of each well decreases by 5 barrels. How many new wells should be drilled to maximize the total daily production of the oil field?

81. A triangle is inscribed in a circle of radius R. One side of the triangle coincides with a diameter of the circle. In terms of R, what is the maximum possible area of such a triangle?

82. Five rectangular pieces of sheet metal measure 210 cm by 336 cm each. Equal squares are to be cut from all their corners, and the resulting five cross-shaped pieces of metal are to be folded and welded to form five boxes without tops. The 20 little squares that remain are to be assembled in groups of four into five larger squares, and these five larger squares are to be assembled into a cubical box with no top. What is the maximum possible total volume of the six boxes that are constructed in this way?

83. A mass of clay of volume V is formed into two spheres. For what distribution of clay is the total surface area of the two spheres a maximum? A minimum?

84. A right triangle has legs of lengths 3 m and 4 m. What is the maximum possible area of a rectangle inscribed in the triangle in the "obvious" way—with one corner at the triangle's right angle, two adjacent sides of the rectangle lying on the triangle's legs, and the opposite corner on the hypotenuse?

85. What is the maximum possible volume of a right circular cone inscribed in a sphere of radius R?

86. A farmer has 400 ft of fencing with which to build a rectangular corral. He will use some or even all of an existing straight wall 100 ft long as part of the perimeter of the corral. What is the maximum area that can be enclosed?

87. In one simple model of the spread of a contagious disease among members of a population of M people, the incidence of the disease, measured as the number of new cases per day, is given in terms of the number x of individuals already infected by
$$R(x) = kx(M - x) = kMx - kx^2,$$
where k is a positive constant. How many individuals in the population are infected when the incidence R is the greatest?

88. Three sides of a trapezoid have length L, a constant. What should be the length of the fourth side if the trapezoid is to have maximal area?

89. A box with no top must have a base twice as long as it is wide, and the total surface area of the box is to be 54 ft². What is the maximum possible volume of such a box?

90. A small right circular cone is inscribed in a larger one (Fig. 3.MP.1). The larger cone has fixed radius R and fixed altitude H. What is the largest fraction of the volume of the larger cone that the smaller one can occupy?

FIGURE 3.MP.1 A small cone inscribed in a larger one (Problem 90).

91. Two vertices of a trapezoid are at $(-2, 0)$ and $(2, 0)$, and the other two lie on the semicircle $x^2 + y^2 = 4$, $y \geq 0$. What is the maximum possible area of the trapezoid? [*Note:* The area of a trapezoid with bases b_1 and b_2 and height h is $A = h(b_1 + b_2)/2$.]

92. Suppose that f is a differentiable function defined on the whole real number line $\boldsymbol{R}$ and that the graph of f contains a point $Q(x, y)$ closest to the point $P(x_0, y_0)$ not on the graph. Show that
$$f'(x) = -\frac{x - x_0}{y - y_0}$$
at Q. Conclude that the segment PQ is perpendicular to the line tangent to the curve at Q. [*Suggestion:* Minimize the square of the distance PQ.]

93. Use the result of Problem 92 to show that the minimum distance from the point (x_0, y_0) to a point of the straight line $Ax + By + C = 0$ is
$$\frac{|Ax_0 + By_0 + C|}{\sqrt{A^2 + B^2}}.$$

94. A race track is to be built in the shape of two parallel and equal straightaways connected by semicircles on each end (Fig. 3.MP.2). The length of the track, one lap, is to be exactly 4 km. What should its design be to maximize the rectangular area within it?

FIGURE 3.MP.2 Design the race track to maximize the rectangular area (Problem 94).

95. Two towns are located near the straight shore of a lake. Their nearest distances to points on the shore are 1 mi and 2 mi, respectively, and these points on the shore are 6 mi apart. Where should a fishing pier be located to minimize the total amount of paving necessary to build a straight road from each town to the pier?

96. A hiker finds herself in a forest 2 km from a long straight road. She wants to walk to her cabin, which is 10 km away in the forest and also 2 km from the road (Fig. 3.MP.3). She can walk at a rate of 8 km/h along the road but only 3 km/h through the forest. So she decides to walk first to the road, then along the road, and finally through the forest to the cabin. What angle θ (shown in the figure) would minimize the total time required for the hiker to reach her cabin? How much time is saved in comparison with the straight route through the forest?

FIGURE 3.MP.3 The hiker's quickest path to the cabin (Problem 96).

97. When an arrow is shot from the origin with initial velocity v and initial angle of inclination α (from the horizontal x-axis, which represents the ground), then its trajectory is the curve
$$y = mx - \frac{16}{v^2}(1 + m^2)x^2,$$
where $m = \tan \alpha$. (a) Find the maximum height reached by the arrow in terms of m and v. (b) For what value of m (and hence, for what α) does the arrow travel the greatest horizontal distance?

98. A projectile is fired with initial velocity v and angle of elevation θ from the base of a plane inclined at 45° from the horizontal (Fig. 3.MP.4). The range of the projectile, as measured up this slope, is given by
$$R = \frac{v^2\sqrt{2}}{16}(\cos\theta \sin\theta - \cos^2\theta).$$
What value of θ maximizes R?

FIGURE 3.MP.4 A projectile fired uphill (Problem 98).

In Problems 99 through 110, use Newton's method to find the solution of the given equation $f(x) = 0$ in the indicated interval $[a, b]$ accurate to four decimal places.

99. $x^2 - 7 = 0$; $[2, 3]$ (to find the positive square root of 7)
100. $x^3 - 3 = 0$; $[1, 2]$ (to find the cube root of 3)

101. $x^5 - 75 = 0$; $[2, 3]$ (to find the fifth root of 75)
102. $x^{4/3} - 10 = 0$; $[5, 6]$ (to approximate $10^{3/4}$)
103. $x^3 - 3x - 1 = 0$; $[-1, 0]$
104. $x^3 - 4x - 1 = 0$; $[-1, 0]$
105. $x^6 + 7x^2 - 4 = 0$; $[0, 1]$
106. $x^3 - 3x^2 + 2x + 10 = 0$; $[-2, -1]$
107. $x + \cos x = 0$; $[-2, 0]$
108. $x^2 + \sin x = 0$; $[-1.0, -0.5]$
109. $4x - \sin x + 4 = 0$; $[-2, -1]$
110. $5x - \cos x + 5 = 0$; $[-1, 0]$

111. Find the depth to which a wooden ball with radius 2 ft sinks in water if its density is one-third that of water. A useful formula appears in Problem 37 of Section 3.8.

112. The equation $x^2 + 1 = 0$ has no real solutions. Try finding a solution by using Newton's method and report what happens. Use the initial estimate $x_0 = 2$.

113. At the beginning of Section 3.8 we mentioned the fifth-degree equation
$$x^5 - 3x^3 + x^2 - 23x + 19 = 0;$$
its graph appears in Fig. 3.8.1. The graph makes it clear that this equation has exactly three real solutions. Find all of them, to four-place accuracy, using Newton's method.

114. The equation
$$\tan x = \frac{1}{x}$$
has a sequence $\alpha_1, \alpha_2, \alpha_3, \ldots$ of positive roots, with α_n slightly larger than $(n-1)\pi$. Use Newton's method to approximate α_1 and α_2 to three-place accuracy.

115. Criticize the following "proof" that $3 = 2$. Begin by writing
$$x^3 = x \cdot x^2 = x^2 + x^2 + \cdots + x^2 \quad (x \text{ summands}).$$
Differentiate to obtain
$$3x^2 = 2x + 2x + \cdots + 2x \quad (\text{still } x \text{ summands}).$$
Thus $3x^2 = 2x^2$, and "therefore" $3 = 2$.

If we substitute $z = x + h$ into the definition of the derivative, the result is
$$f'(x) = \lim_{z \to x} \frac{f(z) - f(x)}{z - x}.$$
Use this formula in Problems 116 and 117, together with the formula
$$a^3 - b^3 = (a - b)(a^2 + ab + b^2)$$
for factoring the difference of two cubes.

116. Show that
$$D_x x^{3/2} = \lim_{z \to x} \frac{z^{3/2} - x^{3/2}}{z - x} = \frac{3}{2} x^{1/2}.$$
[*Suggestion:* Factor the numerator as a difference of cubes and the denominator as a difference of squares.]

117. Prove that
$$D_x x^{2/3} = \lim_{z \to x} \frac{z^{2/3} - x^{2/3}}{z - x} = \frac{2}{3} x^{-1/3}.$$
[*Suggestion:* Factor the numerator as a difference of squares and the denominator as a difference of cubes.]

118. If you sketch the graph of $f(x) = x^4 - 2x^3 - 3x^2 + 6x + 7$, you will see that there appears to be a single straight line that is tangent to the graph of f at two *different* points. Use a computer algebra system to find those two points, or show by your work that there are no such points.

119. Let L be a straight line passing through the fixed point $P(x_0, y_0)$ and tangent to the parabola $y = x^2$ at the point $Q(a, a^2)$. (a) Show that $a^2 - 2ax_0 + y_0 = 0$. (b) Apply the quadratic formula to show that if $y_0 < (x_0)^2$ (that is, if P lies below the parabola), then there are two possible values for a and thus two lines through P that are tangent to the parabola. (c) Similarly, show that if $y_0 > (x_0)^2$ (P lies above the parabola), then no line through P can be tangent to the parabola.

120. Use a computer algebra system to show that no straight line can be tangent to the graph of a general cubic polynomial function,
$$p(x) = ax^2 + bx^2 + cx + d \quad (a \neq 0),$$
at two different points. (Or find a counterexample to this assertion by finding a specific cubic polynomial and a specific straight line tangent to its graph at two different points.)

ADDITIONAL APPLICATIONS OF THE DERIVATIVE

4

G. W. Leibniz (1646–1716)

Gottfried Wilhelm Leibniz entered the University of Leipzig when he was 15, studied philosophy and law, graduated at 17, and received his doctorate in philosophy at 21. Upon completion of his academic work, Leibniz entered the political and governmental service of the Elector of Mainz (Germany). His serious study of mathematics did not begin until 1672 (when he was 26) when he was sent to Paris on a diplomatic mission. During the next four years there he conceived the principal features of calculus. For this work he is remembered (with Newton) as a codiscoverer of the subject. Newton's discoveries had come slightly earlier (in the late 1660s), but Leibniz's were the first to be published, beginning in 1684. Despite an unfortunate priority dispute between supporters of Newton and supporters of Leibniz that raged for more than a century, it is clear now that the discoveries were made independently.

Throughout his life, Leibniz sought a universal language incorporating notation and terminology that would provide *all* educated people with the powers of clear and correct reasoning in all subjects. But only in mathematics did he largely accomplish this goal. His differential notation for calculus is arguably the best example of a system of notation chosen so as to mirror perfectly the basic operations and processes of the subject. Indeed, it can be said that Leibniz's notation for calculus brings within the range of ordinary students problems that once required the ingenuity of an Archimedes or a Newton. For this reason, Leibniz's approach to calculus was dominant during the eighteenth century, even though Newton's somewhat different approach may have been closer to our modern understanding of the subject.

The origin of differential notation was an infinitesimal right triangle with legs dx and dy and with hypotenuse a tiny segment of the curve $y = f(x)$. Leibniz later described the moment he first visualized this "characteristic triangle" as a burst of light that was the inception of his calculus. Indeed, he sometimes referred to his calculus as "my method of the Characteristic Triangle."

Leibniz's characteristic triangle

The following excerpt shows the opening paragraphs of Leibniz's first published article (in the 1684 *Acta Eruditorum*) in which the differential notation initially appeared. In the fifth line of the second paragraph, the product rule for differentiation is expressed as

$$d(xv) = x\,dv + v\,dx.$$

4.1 IMPLICIT DIFFERENTIATION AND RELATED RATES

A formula such as $y = x^3 \sin x$ defines y "explicitly" as a function of x. Most of the functions we have seen so far have been defined explicitly in this way. Nevertheless, a function can also be defined "implicitly" by an equation that can be solved for y in terms of x. Indeed, we will see that a single equation relating the two variables x and y can implicitly define two or more different functions of x.

EXAMPLE 1

(a) When we solve the equation

$$x - y^2 = 0$$

for $y = \pm\sqrt{x}$, we get the two *explicit* functions

$$f(x) = \sqrt{x} \quad \text{and} \quad g(x) = -\sqrt{x}$$

that we say are implicitly defined by the original equation. The graphs of these two functions—both defined for $x \geq 0$—are the upper and lower branches of the parabola shown (in different colors) in Fig. 4.1.1. The whole parabola is the graph of the equation $x - y^2 = 0$ (or $x = y^2$) but is not the graph of any single function. (Why?)

(b) Similarly, the equation

$$x^2 + y^2 = 100$$

implicitly defines the two continuous functions

$$f(x) = \sqrt{100 - x^2} \quad \text{and} \quad g(x) = -\sqrt{100 - x^2}$$

—both defined for $-10 \leq x \leq 10$—that correspond to the solutions $y = \pm\sqrt{100 - x^2}$ for y in terms of x. The graphs of f and g are the upper and lower semicircles of the whole circle $x^2 + y^2 = 100$ (shown in different colors in Fig. 4.1.2). ◆

FIGURE 4.1.1 The equation $x - y^2 = 0$ implicitly defines the two functions $f(x) = \sqrt{x}$ and $g(x) = -\sqrt{x}$.

FIGURE 4.1.2 The equation $x^2 + y^2 = 100$ implicitly defines the two functions $f(x) = \sqrt{100 - x^2}$ and $g(x) = -\sqrt{100 - x^2}$.

Whereas the equations $x - y^2 = 0$ and $x^2 + y^2 = 100$ are readily solved for y in terms of x, an equation such as $x^3 + y^3 = 3xy$ or $\sin(x + 2y) = 2x \cos y$ may be difficult or impossible to solve for an implicitly defined function $y(x)$. And yet the derivative dy/dx can be calculated without first expressing y in terms of x. Here's how: We can use the chain rule and other basic differentiation rules to differentiate both sides of the given equation with respect to x (we think of x as the independent variable, although it is permissible to reverse the roles of x and y). We then solve the resulting equation for the derivative $y'(x) = dy/dx$ of the implicitly defined function $y(x)$. This process is called **implicit differentiation**. In the examples and problems of this section, we proceed on the assumption that our implicitly defined functions actually exist and are differentiable at almost all points in their domains. (The functions with the graphs shown in Fig. 4.1.2 are *not* differentiable at the endpoints of their domains.)

EXAMPLE 2 Use implicit differentiation to find the derivative of a differentiable function $y = f(x)$ implicitly defined by the equation

$$x^2 + y^2 = 100.$$

Solution The equation $x^2 + y^2 = 100$ is to be regarded as an *identity* that implicitly defines $y = y(x)$ as a function of x. Because $x^2 + [y(x)]^2$ is then a function of x, it has the same derivative as the constant function 100 on the right-hand side of the identity. Thus we may differentiate both sides of the *identity* $x^2 + y^2 = 100$ with respect to x and equate the results. We obtain

$$2x + 2y\frac{dy}{dx} = 0.$$

Implicit Differentiation and Related Rates **SECTION 4.1** 195

In this step, it is essential to remember that y is a function of x, so the chain rule yields $D_x(y^2) = 2y D_x y$.

Then we solve for

$$\frac{dy}{dx} = -\frac{x}{y}. \qquad (1)$$

It may be surprising to see a formula for dy/dx containing both x and y, but such a formula can be just as useful as one containing only x. For example, the formula in Eq. (1) tells us that the slope of the line tangent to the circle $x^2 + y^2 = 100$ at the point $(6, 8)$ is

$$\left.\frac{dy}{dx}\right|_{(6,8)} = -\frac{6}{8} = -\frac{3}{4}.$$

The circle and this line are shown in Fig. 4.1.3. ◆

FIGURE 4.1.3 The circle $x^2 + y^2 = 100$ and the tangent line at the point $(6, 8)$.

Note If we solve for $y = \pm\sqrt{100 - x^2}$ in Example 1, then

$$\frac{dy}{dx} = \frac{-x}{\pm\sqrt{100 - x^2}} = -\frac{x}{y},$$

in agreement with Eq. (1). Thus Eq. (1) simultaneously gives us the derivatives of both the functions $y = +\sqrt{100 - x^2}$ and $y = -\sqrt{100 - x^2}$ implicitly defined by the equation $x^2 + y^2 = 100$.

EXAMPLE 3 The *folium of Descartes* is the graph of the equation

$$x^3 + y^3 = 3xy. \qquad (2)$$

This curve was first proposed by René Descartes as a challenge to Pierre de Fermat (1601–1665) to find its tangent line at an arbitrary point. The project for this section tells how we constructed Fig. 4.1.4. It indicates that the second- and fourth-quadrant points on the graph for which $|x|$ and $|y|$ are both large lie very close to the straight line $x + y + 1 = 0$. In the first quadrant we see a loop shaped like a laurel leaf—hence the name *folium*. (Can you see directly from Eq. (2) that the third quadrant contains *no* points of the folium?) Here we want to find Fermat's answer as to the slope of a typical line tangent to the folium of Descartes.

FIGURE 4.1.4 A tangent line and an apparent asymptote to the curve $x^3 + y^3 = 3xy$.

Solution Equation (2) is a cubic equation in x, and we see in Fig. 4.1.4 three different branches of the graph over an interval to the right of the origin. When we ask a computer algebra system to solve the equation for these implicitly defined functions of x, it produces three different expressions, the simplest of which is

$$y = \frac{1}{2}\sqrt[3]{-4x^3 + 4\sqrt{x^6 - 4x^3}} + \frac{2x}{\sqrt[3]{-4x^3 + 4\sqrt{x^6 - 4x^3}}}.$$

(It turns out that this formula describes the upper part of the loop in Fig. 4.1.4.) Surely you would not relish explicit differentiation of this expression to find the slope of a line tangent to the folium. Fortunately, the alternative of implicit differentiation is available. We need only differentiate each side of Eq. (2) with respect to x, remembering that y is a function of x. Hence we use the chain rule to differentiate y^3 and the product rule to differentiate $3xy$. This yields

$$3x^2 + 3y^2 \frac{dy}{dx} = 3y + 3x \frac{dy}{dx}.$$

We can now collect coefficients (those involving dy/dx and those not) and solve for the derivative:

$$(3y^2 - 3x)\frac{dy}{dx} = 3y - 3x^2;$$

$$\frac{dy}{dx} = \frac{y - x^2}{y^2 - x}. \qquad (3)$$

For instance, at the point $P\left(\frac{3}{2}, \frac{3}{2}\right)$ of the folium, the slope of the tangent line is

$$\left.\frac{dy}{dx}\right|_{\left(\frac{3}{2}, \frac{3}{2}\right)} = \frac{\frac{3}{2} - \left(\frac{3}{2}\right)^2}{\left(\frac{3}{2}\right)^2 - \frac{3}{2}} = -1.$$

This result agrees with our intuition about the figure, because the evident symmetry of the folium around the line $y = x$ suggests that the tangent line at P should, indeed, have slope -1. The equation of this tangent line is

$$y - \tfrac{3}{2} = -\left(x - \tfrac{3}{2}\right);$$

that is, $x + y = 3$. ◆

EXAMPLE 4 Figure 4.1.5 shows a computer plot of the graph of the equation

$$\sin(x + 2y) = 2x \cos y. \qquad (4)$$

Write the equation of the line tangent to this curve at the origin $(0, 0)$.

Solution When we differentiate each side in (4) with respect to the independent variable x, regarding y as a function of x, we get

$$[\cos(x + 2y)] \cdot \left(1 + 2\frac{dy}{dx}\right) = 2\cos y - (2x \sin y)\frac{dy}{dx}. \qquad (5)$$

We could collect coefficients and solve for the derivative dy/dx. But because we need only the slope $y'(0)$ at the origin, let us instead substitute $x = y = 0$ in Eq. (5). Noting that $\cos(0) = 1$ and $\sin(0) = 0$, we get the equation

$$1 + 2y'(0) = 2,$$

from which we see that $y'(0) = \frac{1}{2}$. The resulting tangent line $y = \frac{1}{2}x$ plotted in Fig. 4.1.5 "looks right," and thus corroborates the results of our calculations. ◆

FIGURE 4.1.5 The curve $\sin(x + 2y) = 2x \cos y$ and its tangent at the origin.

Related Rates

A **related-rates** problem involves two or more quantities that vary with time and an equation that expresses some relationship between these quantities. Typically, the values of these quantities at some instant are given, together with all their time rates of change but one. The problem is usually to find the time rate of change that is *not* given, at some instant specified in the problem. Implicit differentiation, with respect to time t, of the equation that relates the given quantities will produce an equation that relates the *rates of change* of the given quantities. This is the key to solving a related-rates problem.

EXAMPLE 5 Suppose that $x(t)$ and $y(t)$ are the x- and y-coordinates at time t of a point moving around the circle with equation

$$x^2 + y^2 = 25. \qquad (6)$$

Let us use the chain rule to differentiate both sides of this equation *with respect to time t*. This produces the equation

$$2x\frac{dx}{dt} + 2y\frac{dy}{dt} = 0. \qquad (7)$$

If the values of x, y, and dx/dt are known at a certain instant t, then Eq. (7) can be solved for the value of dy/dt. It is *not* necessary to know x and y as functions of t. Indeed, it is common for a related-rates problem to contain insufficient information to express x and y as functions of t.

For instance, suppose that we are given $x = 3$, $y = 4$, and $dx/dt = 12$ at a certain instant. Substituting these values into Eq. (7) yields

$$2 \cdot 3 \cdot 12 + 2 \cdot 4 \cdot \frac{dy}{dt} = 0,$$

so we find that $dy/dt = -9$ at the same instant. ◆

EXAMPLE 6 A rocket that is launched vertically is tracked by a radar station located on the ground 3 mi from the launch site. What is the vertical speed of the rocket at the instant that its distance from the radar station is 5 mi and this distance is increasing at the rate of 5000 mi/h?

Solution Figure 4.1.6 illustrates this situation. We denote the altitude of the rocket (in miles) by y and its distance from the radar station by z. We are given

$$\frac{dz}{dt} = 5000 \quad \text{when} \quad z = 5.$$

We want to find dy/dt (in miles per hour) at this instant.

FIGURE 4.1.6 The rocket of Example 6.

We apply the Pythagorean theorem to the right triangle in the figure and obtain

$$y^2 + 9 = z^2$$

as a relation between y and z. From this we see that $y = 4$ when $z = 5$. Implicit differentiation then gives

$$2y\frac{dy}{dt} = 2z\frac{dz}{dt}.$$

We substitute the data $y = 4$, $z = 5$, and $dz/dt = 5000$. Thus we find that

$$\frac{dy}{dt} = 6250 \quad \text{(mi/h)}$$

at the instant in question. ◆

Example 6 illustrates the following steps in the solution of a typical related-rates problem of the sort that involves a geometric situation:

1. Draw a diagram and label as variables the various changing quantities involved in the problem.
2. Record the values of the variables and their rates of change, as given in the problem.
3. Use the diagram to determine an equation that relates the important variables in the problem.
4. Differentiate this equation implicitly with respect to time t.
5. Substitute the given numerical data in the resulting equation, and then solve for the unknown.

WARNING The most common error to be avoided is the premature substitution of the given data before differentiating implicitly. If we had substituted $z = 5$ to begin with in Example 5, our equation would have been $y^2 + 9 = 25$, and implicit differentiation would have given the absurd result $dy/dt = 0$.

We use similar triangles (rather than the Pythagorean theorem) in Example 7 to discover the needed relation between the variables.

EXAMPLE 7 A man 6 ft tall walks with a speed of 8 ft/s away from a street light that is atop an 18-ft pole. How fast is the tip of his shadow moving along the ground when he is 100 ft from the light pole?

Solution Let x be the man's distance from the pole and z the distance from the tip of his shadow to the base of the pole (Fig. 4.1.7). Although x and z are functions of time t, we do *not* attempt to find explicit formulas for either.

FIGURE 4.1.7 The moving shadow of Example 7.

We are given $dx/dt = 8$ (in feet per second); we want to find dz/dt when $x = 100$ (ft). We equate ratios of corresponding sides of the two similar triangles of Fig. 4.1.7 and find that

$$\frac{z}{18} = \frac{z-x}{6}.$$

It follows that

$$2z = 3x,$$

and implicit differentiation gives

$$2\frac{dz}{dt} = 3\frac{dx}{dt}.$$

We substitute $dx/dt = 8$ and find that

$$\frac{dz}{dt} = \frac{3}{2} \cdot \frac{dx}{dt} = \frac{3}{2} \cdot 8 = 12.$$

So the tip of the man's shadow is moving at 12 ft/s. ◆

Example 7 is somewhat unusual in that the answer is independent of the man's distance from the light pole—the given value $x = 100$ is superfluous because the tip of the man's shadow is moving at constant speed. Example 8 is a related-rates problem with two relationships between the variables, which is not quite so unusual.

EXAMPLE 8 Two radar stations at A and B, with B 6 km east of A, are tracking a ship. At a certain instant, the ship is 5 km from A, and this distance is increasing at the rate of 28 km/h. At the same instant, the ship is also 5 km from B, but this distance is increasing at only 4 km/h. Where is the ship, how fast is it moving, and in what direction is it moving?

FIGURE 4.1.8 Radar stations tracking a ship (Example 8).

Solution With the distances indicated in Fig. 4.1.8, we find—again with the aid of the Pythagorean theorem—that

$$x^2 + y^2 = u^2 \quad \text{and} \quad (6-x)^2 + y^2 = v^2. \tag{8}$$

We are given the following data: $u = v = 5$, $du/dt = 28$, and $dv/dt = 4$ at the instant in question. Because the ship is equally distant from A and B, it is clear that $x = 3$. Thus $y = 4$. Hence the ship is 3 km east and 4 km north of A.

We differentiate implicitly the two equations in (8), and we obtain

$$2x\frac{dx}{dt} + 2y\frac{dy}{dt} = 2u\frac{du}{dt}$$

and

$$-2(6-x)\frac{dx}{dt} + 2y\frac{dy}{dt} = 2v\frac{dv}{dt}.$$

When we substitute the numerical data given and data deduced, we find that

$$3\frac{dx}{dt} + 4\frac{dy}{dt} = 140 \quad \text{and} \quad -3\frac{dx}{dt} + 4\frac{dy}{dt} = 20.$$

These equations are easy to solve: $dx/dt = dy/dt = 20$. Therefore, the ship is sailing northeast at a speed of

$$\sqrt{20^2 + 20^2} = 20\sqrt{2} \quad \text{(km/h)}$$

—*if* the figure is correct! A mirror along the line AB will reflect *another* ship, 3 km east and 4 km *south* of A, sailing *southeast* at a speed of $20\sqrt{2}$ km/h.

The lesson? Figures are important, helpful, often essential—but potentially misleading. Avoid taking anything for granted when you draw a figure. In this example there would be no real problem, for each radar station could determine whether the ship was generally to the north or to the south. ◆

4.1 TRUE/FALSE STUDY GUIDE

4.1 CONCEPTS: QUESTIONS AND DISCUSSION

1. Figure 4.1.1 shows the graphs of the two functions $f(x) = \sqrt{x}$ and $g(x) = -\sqrt{x}$ that are defined implicitly by the equation $x - y^2 = 0$. Both f and g are continuous for $x \geq 0$. Can you think of a discontinuous function $y = h(x)$ that satisfies the same equation?

2. How many different continuous functions of x (with the same domain of definition) are implicitly defined by a given quadratic equation in x and y? A given cubic equation? A given quartic (fourth-degree) equation? How many different discontinuous functions?

3. How many different continuous functions of x are defined by the following equations?

    (a) $x^2 + y^2 + 1 = 0$ (b) $x^3 + y^3 = 1$ (c) $x^4 + y^4 = 1$

4. How many different continuous functions of x are defined by the transcendental equation $\sin y = x$?

4.1 PROBLEMS

In Problems 1 through 4, first find the derivative dy/dx by implicit differentiation. Then solve the original equation for y explicitly in terms of x and differentiate to find dy/dx. Finally verify that your two results are the same by substituting the explicit expression for $y(x)$ in the implicit form of the derivative.

1. $x^2 - y^2 = 1$
2. $xy = 1$
3. $16x^2 + 25y^2 = 400$
4. $x^3 + y^3 = 1$

In Problems 5 through 14, find dy/dx by implicit differentiation.

5. $\sqrt{x} + \sqrt{y} = 1$
6. $x^4 + x^2y^2 + y^4 = 48$
7. $x^{2/3} + y^{2/3} = 1$
8. $(x-1)y^2 = x+1$
9. $x^2(x-y) = y^2(x+y)$
10. $x^5 + y^5 = 5x^2y^2$
11. $x \sin y + y \sin x = 1$
12. $\cos(x+y) = \sin x \sin y$

200 CHAPTER 4 Additional Applications of the Derivative

13. $\cos^2 x + \cos^2 y = \sin(x+y)$

14. $xy = \tan xy$

In Problems 15 through 28, use implicit differentiation to find an equation of the line tangent to the given curve at the given point.

15. $x^2 + y^2 = 25$; $(3, -4)$

16. $xy = -8$; $(4, -2)$

17. $x^2 y = x + 2$; $(2, 1)$

18. $x^{1/4} + y^{1/4} = 4$; $(16, 16)$

19. $xy^2 + x^2 y = 2$; $(1, -2)$

20. $\dfrac{1}{x+1} + \dfrac{1}{y+1} = 1$; $(1, 1)$

21. $12(x^2 + y^2) = 25xy$; $(3, 4)$

22. $x^2 + xy + y^2 = 7$; $(3, -2)$

23. $\dfrac{1}{x^3} + \dfrac{1}{y^3} = 2$; $(1, 1)$

24. $(x^2 + y^2)^3 = 8x^2 y^2$; $(1, -1)$

25. $x^{2/3} + y^{2/3} = 5$; $(8, 1)$ (Fig. 4.1.9)

FIGURE 4.1.9 Problem 25.

26. $x^2 - xy + y^2 = 19$; $(3, -2)$ (Fig. 4.1.10)

FIGURE 4.1.10 Problem 26.

27. $(x^2 + y^2)^2 = 50xy$; $(2, 4)$ (Fig. 4.1.11)

FIGURE 4.1.11 Problem 27.

28. $y^2 = x^2(x+7)$; $(-3, 6)$ (Fig. 4.1.12)

FIGURE 4.1.12 Problem 28.

29. The curve $x^3 + y^3 = 9xy$ is similar in shape and appearance to the folium of Descartes in Fig. 4.1.4. Find (a) the equation of its tangent line at the point $(2, 4)$ and (b) the equation of its tangent line with slope -1.

30. (a) Factor the left-hand side of the equation
$$2x^2 - 5xy + 2y^2 = 0$$
to show that its graph consists of two straight lines through the origin. Hence the derivative $y'(x)$ has only two possible numerical values (the slopes of these two lines). (b) Calculate dy/dx by implicit differentiation of the equation in part (a). Verify that the expression you obtain yields the proper slope for each of the straight lines of part (a).

31. Find all points on the graph of $x^2 + y^2 = 4x + 4y$ at which the tangent line is horizontal.

32. Find the first-quadrant points of the folium of Example 3 at which the tangent line is either horizontal ($dy/dx = 0$) or vertical (where $dx/dy = 1/(dy/dx) = 0$).

33. The graph of the equation $x^2 - xy + y^2 = 9$ is the rotated ellipse shown in Fig. 4.1.13. Find the lines tangent to this curve at the two points where it intersects the x-axis; then show that these lines are parallel.

FIGURE 4.1.13 The rotated ellipse of Problem 33.

34. Find the points on the curve of Problem 33 where the tangent line is horizontal ($dy/dx = 0$) and those where it is vertical ($dx/dy = 0$).

35. The graph in Fig. 4.1.14 is a *lemniscate* with equation $(x^2 + y^2)^2 = x^2 - y^2$. Find by implicit differentiation the four points on the lemniscate where the tangent line is horizontal. Then find the two points where the tangent line is vertical—that is, where $dx/dy = 1/(dy/dx) = 0$.

FIGURE 4.1.14 The lemniscate of Problem 35.

36. Water is being collected from a block of ice with a square base (Fig. 4.1.15). The water is produced because the ice is melting in such a way that each edge of the base of the block is decreasing at 2 in./h while the height of the block is decreasing at 3 in./h. What is the rate of flow of water into the collecting pan when the base has edge length 20 in. and the height of the block is 15 in.? Make the simplifying assumption that water and ice have the same density.

FIGURE 4.1.15 The ice block of Problem 36.

37. Sand is being emptied from a hopper at the rate of 10 ft³/s. The sand forms a conical pile whose height is always twice its radius (Fig. 4.1.16). At what rate is the radius of the pile increasing when its height is 5 ft?

FIGURE 4.1.16 The conical sand pile of Problem 37 with volume $V = \frac{1}{3}\pi r^2 h$.

38. Suppose that water is being emptied from a spherical tank of radius 10 ft (Fig. 4.1.17). If the depth of the water in the tank is 5 ft and is decreasing at the rate of 3 ft/s, at what rate is the radius r of the top surface of the water decreasing?

FIGURE 4.1.17 The spherical tank of Problem 38.

39. A circular oil slick of uniform thickness is caused by a spill of 1 m³ of oil. The thickness of the oil slick is decreasing at the rate of 0.1 cm/h. At what rate is the radius of the slick increasing when the radius is 8 m?

40. Suppose that an ostrich 5 ft tall is walking at a speed of 4 ft/s directly toward a street light 10 ft high. How fast is the tip of the ostrich's shadow moving along the ground? At what rate is the ostrich's shadow decreasing in length?

41. The width of a rectangle is half its length. At what rate is its area increasing if its width is 10 cm and is increasing at 0.5 cm/s?

42. At what rate is the area of an equilateral triangle increasing if its base is 10 cm long and is increasing at 0.5 cm/s?

43. A gas balloon is being filled at the rate of 100π cm³ of gas per second. At what rate is the radius of the balloon increasing when its radius is 10 cm?

44. The volume V (in cubic inches) and pressure p (in pounds per square inch) of a certain gas satisfy the equation $pV = 1000$. At what rate is the volume of the sample changing if the pressure is 100 lb/in.² and is increasing at the rate of 2 lb/in.² per second?

45. Figure 4.1.18 shows a kite in the air at an altitude of 400 ft. The kite is being blown horizontally at the rate of 10 ft/s away from the person holding the kite string at ground level. At what rate is the string being payed out when 500 ft of string is already out? (Assume that the string forms a straight line.)

FIGURE 4.1.18 The kite of Problem 45.

46. A weather balloon that is rising vertically is being observed from a point on the ground 300 ft from the spot directly beneath the balloon. At what rate is the balloon rising when the angle between the ground and the observer's line of sight is 45° and is increasing at 1° per second?

47. An airplane flying horizontally at an altitude of 3 mi and at a speed of 480 mi/h passes directly above an observer on the ground. How fast is the distance from the observer to the airplane increasing 30 s later?

48. Figure 4.1.19 shows a spherical tank of radius a partly filled with water. The maximum depth of water in the tank is y. A formula for the volume V of water in the tank—a formula you can derive after you study Chapter 6—is $V = \frac{1}{3}\pi y^2(3a-y)$. Suppose that water is being drained from a spherical tank of radius 5 ft at the rate of 100 gal/min. Find the rate at which the depth y of water is decreasing when (a) $y = 7$ (ft); (b) $y = 3$ (ft). [*Note:* One gallon of water occupies a volume of approximately 0.1337 ft^3.]

FIGURE 4.1.19 The spherical water tank of Problem 48.

49. Repeat Problem 48, but use a tank that is hemispherical, flat side on top, with radius 10 ft.

50. A swimming pool is 50 ft long and 20 ft wide. Its depth varies uniformly from 2 ft at the shallow end to 12 ft at the deep end (Fig. 4.1.20). Suppose that the pool is being filled at the rate of 1000 gal/min. At what rate is the depth of water at the deep end increasing when the depth there is 6 ft? [*Note:* One gallon of water occupies a volume of approximately 0.1337 ft^3.]

FIGURE 4.1.20 Cross section of the swimming pool of Problem 50.

51. A ladder 41 ft long that was leaning against a vertical wall begins to slip. Its top slides down the wall while its bottom moves along the level ground at a constant speed of 4 ft/s. How fast is the top of the ladder moving when it is 9 ft above the ground?

52. The base of a rectangle is increasing at 4 cm/s while its height is decreasing at 3 cm/s. At what rate is its area changing when its base is 20 cm and its height is 12 cm?

53. The height of a cone is decreasing at 3 cm/s while its radius is increasing at 2 cm/s. When the radius is 4 cm and the height is 6 cm, is the volume of the cone increasing or decreasing? At what rate is the volume changing then?

54. A square is expanding. When each edge is 10 in., its area is increasing at 120 in.^{2}/s. At what rate is the length of each edge changing then?

55. A rocket that is launched vertically is tracked by a radar station located on the ground 4 mi from the launch site. What is the vertical speed of the rocket at the instant its distance from the radar station is 5 mi and this distance is increasing at the rate of 3600 mi/h?

56. Two straight roads intersect at right angles. At 10 A.M. a car passes through the intersection headed due east at 30 mi/h. At 11 A.M. a truck heading due north at 40 mi/h passes through the intersection. Assume that the two vehicles maintain the given speeds and directions. At what rate are they separating at 1 P.M.?

57. A 10-ft ladder is leaning against a wall. The bottom of the ladder begins to slide away from the wall at a speed of 1 mi/h. (a) Find the rate at which the top of the latter is moving when it is 4 ft from the ground. If the top of the ladder maintained contact with the wall, find the speed with which it would be moving when it is (b) 1 in. above the ground; (c) 1 mm above the ground. Do you believe your answers? The key to the apparent paradox is that when the top of the ladder is about 1.65 ft high, it disengages altogether from the wall and thereafter slides away from it.

58. Two ships are sailing toward a very small island. One ship, the Pinta, is east of the island and is sailing due west at 15 mi/h. The other ship, the Niña, is north of the island and is sailing due south at 20 mi/h. At a certain time the Pinta is 30 mi from the island and the Niña is 40 mi from the island. At what rate are the two ships drawing closer together at that time?

59. At time $t = 0$, a single-engine military jet is flying due east at 12 mi/min. At the same altitude and 208 mi directly ahead of the military jet, still at time $t = 0$, a commercial jet is flying due north at 8 mi/min. When are the two planes closest to each other? What is the minimum distance between them?

60. A ship with a long anchor chain is anchored in 11 fathoms of water. The anchor chain is being wound in at the rate of 10 fathoms/min, causing the ship to move toward the spot directly above the anchor resting on the seabed. The hawsehole—the point of contact between ship and chain—is located 1 fathom above the water line. At what speed is the ship moving when there are exactly 13 fathoms of chain still out?

61. A water tank is in the shape of a cone with vertical axis and vertex downward. The tank has radius 3 ft and is 5 ft high. At first the tank is full of water, but at time $t = 0$ (in seconds), a small hole at the vertex is opened and the water begins to drain. When the height of the water in the tank has dropped to 3 ft, the water is flowing out at 2 ft^3/s. At what rate, in feet per second, is the water level dropping then?

62. A spherical tank of radius 10 ft is being filled with water at the rate of 200 gal/min. How fast is the water level rising when the maximum depth of water in the tank is 5 ft? See Problem 48 for a useful formula and a helpful note.

63. A water bucket is shaped like the frustum of a cone with height 2 ft, base radius 6 in., and top radius 12 in. Water is leaking from the bucket at 10 in.^{3}/min. At what rate is the water level falling when the depth of water in the bucket is 1 ft? [*Note:* The volume V of a conical frustum with height h and base radii a and b is

$$V = \frac{\pi h}{3}(a^2 + ab + b^2).$$

Such a frustum is shown in Fig. 4.1.21.]

FIGURE 4.1.21 The volume of this conical frustum is given in Problem 63.

64. Suppose that the radar stations A and B of Example 8 are now 12.6 km apart. At a certain instant, a ship is 10.4 km from A and its distance from A is increasing at 19.2 km/h. At the same instant, its distance from B is 5 km and is decreasing at 0.6 km/h. Find the location, speed, and direction of motion of the ship.

65. An airplane climbing at an angle of 45° passes directly over a ground radar station at an altitude of 1 mi. A later reading shows that the distance from the radar station to the plane is 5 mi and is increasing at 7 mi/min. What is the speed of the plane then (in miles per hour)? [*Suggestion:* You may find the law of cosines useful—see Appendix C.]

66. The water tank of Problem 62 is completely full when a plug at its bottom is removed. According to *Torricelli's law*, the water drains in such a way that $dV/dt = -k\sqrt{y}$, where V is the volume of water in the tank and k is a positive empirical constant. (a) Find dy/dt as a function of the depth y. (b) Find the depth of water when the water level is falling the *least* rapidly. (You will need to compute the derivative of dy/dt with respect to y.)

67. A person 6 ft tall walks at 5 ft/s along one edge of a road 30 ft wide. On the other edge of the road is a light atop a pole 18 ft high. How fast is the length of the person's shadow (on the horizontal ground) increasing when the person is 40 ft from the point directly across the road from the pole?

68. A highway patrol officer's radar unit is parked behind a billboard 200 ft from a long straight stretch of U.S. 17. Down the highway, 200 ft from the point on the highway closest to the officer, is an emergency call box. The officer points the radar gun at the call box. A minivan passes the call box and, at that moment, the radar unit indicates that the *distance between the officer and the minivan* is increasing at 45 mi/h—that is, 66 ft/s. The posted speed limit is 55 mi/h. Does the officer have any reason to apprehend the driver of the minivan?

4.1 Project: Investigating the Folium of Descartes

Computer graphics often requires lots of mathematics, and much mathematics was used in constructing many of the figures in this book. To see one way to construct Fig. 4.1.4, use a computer algebra system to solve the equation $x^3 + y^3 = 3xy$ for y in terms of x. Verify that the three expressions you get define three different functions f, g, and h whose graphs are the three branches of the curve that are colored differently in Fig. 4.1.22. Investigate the domains of definition and the graphs of these functions to verify that they fit together precisely as shown in the figure.

FIGURE 4.1.22 The equation $x^3 + y^3 = 3xy$ implicitly defines three functions f, g, and h.

4.2 INCREMENTS, DIFFERENTIALS, AND LINEAR APPROXIMATION

Sometimes we need a quick and simple estimate of the change in $f(x)$ that results from a given change in x. We write y for $f(x)$ and suppose first that the change in the independent variable is the *increment* Δx, so that x changes from its original value to the new value $x + \Delta x$. The change in the value of y is the **increment** Δy, computed by subtracting the old value of y from its new value:

$$\Delta y = f(x + \Delta x) - f(x). \tag{1}$$

The increments Δx and Δy are represented geometrically in Fig. 4.2.1.

Now we compare the actual increment Δy with the change that *would* occur in the value of y *if* it continued to change at the *fixed* rate $f'(x)$ while the value of the independent variable changes from x to $x + \Delta x$. This hypothetical change in y is the **differential**

$$dy = f'(x)\,\Delta x. \tag{2}$$

FIGURE 4.2.1 The increments Δx and Δy.

As Fig. 4.2.2 shows, dy is the change in height of a point that moves along the tangent line at the point $(x, f(x))$ rather than along the curve $y = f(x)$.

FIGURE 4.2.2 The estimate dy of the actual increment Δy.

Think of x as fixed. Then Eq. (2) shows that the differential dy is a *linear* function of the increment Δx. For this reason, dy is called the **linear approximation** to the increment Δy. We can approximate $f(x + \Delta x)$ by substituting dy for Δy:

$$f(x + \Delta x) = y + \Delta y \approx y + dy.$$

Because $y = f(x)$ and $dy = f'(x)\Delta x$, this gives the **linear approximation formula**

$$f(x + \Delta x) \approx f(x) + f'(x)\,\Delta x. \tag{3}$$

The point is that this approximation is a "good" one, at least when Δx is relatively small. If we combine Eqs. (1), (2), and (3), we see that

$$\Delta y \approx f'(x)\,\Delta x = dy. \tag{4}$$

Thus the differential $dy = f'(x)\,\Delta x$ is a good approximation to the increment $\Delta y = f(x + \Delta x) - f(x)$.

If we replace x with a in Eq. (3), we get the approximation

$$f(a + \Delta x) \approx f(a) + f'(a)\,\Delta x. \tag{5}$$

If we now write $\Delta x = x - a$, so that $x = a + \Delta x$, the result is

$$f(x) \approx f(a) + f'(a) \cdot (x - a). \tag{6}$$

Because the right-hand side

$$L(x) = f(a) + f'(a) \cdot (x - a) \tag{7}$$

in Eq. (6) is a linear function of x, we call it the **linear approximation** $L(x)$ **to the function** $f(x)$ **near the point** $x = a$. As illustrated in Fig. 4.2.3, the graph $y = L(x)$ is the straight line tangent to the graph $y = f(x)$ at the point $(a, f(a))$.

EXAMPLE 1 Find the linear approximation to the function $f(x) = \sqrt{1 + x}$ near the point $a = 0$.

Solution Note that $f(0) = 1$ and that

$$f'(x) = \frac{1}{2}(1 + x)^{-1/2} = \frac{1}{2\sqrt{1 + x}},$$

so $f'(0) = \frac{1}{2}$. Hence Eq. (6) with $a = 0$ yields

$$f(x) \approx f(0) + f'(0) \cdot (x - 0) = 1 + \tfrac{1}{2}x = L(x).$$

Thus the desired linear approximation is

$$\sqrt{1 + x} \approx 1 + \tfrac{1}{2}x. \tag{8}$$

Figure 4.2.4 illustrates the close approximation near $x = 0$ of the nonlinear function $f(x) = \sqrt{1 + x}$ by its linear approximation $L(x) = 1 + \tfrac{1}{2}x$. ◆

IMPORTANT It is evident in Fig. 4.2.4 that the value of the linear approximation $L(x) = 1 + \tfrac{1}{2}x$ is closer to the actual value of the function $f(x) = \sqrt{1 + x}$ when x is closer to $a = 0$. For instance, the approximate values

$$\sqrt{1.1} \approx 1 + \tfrac{1}{2}(0.1) = 1.05 \qquad \text{(using } x = 0.1 \text{ in (8))}$$

and

$$\sqrt{1.03} \approx 1 + \tfrac{1}{2}(0.03) = 1.015 \qquad \text{(using } x = 0.03 \text{ in (8))}$$

are accurate to two and three decimal places (rounded), respectively. But

$$\sqrt{3} \approx 1 + \tfrac{1}{2} \cdot 2 = 2,$$

using $x = 2$, is a very poor approximation to $\sqrt{3} \approx 1.732$.

The approximation $\sqrt{1 + x} \approx 1 + \tfrac{1}{2}x$ is a special case of the approximation

$$(1 + x)^k \approx 1 + kx \tag{9}$$

(k is a constant, x is near zero), an approximation with numerous applications. The derivation of (9) is similar to that in Example 1. (See Problem 39.)

EXAMPLE 2 Use the linear approximation formula to approximate $(122)^{2/3}$. Note that

$$(125)^{2/3} = \left[(125)^{1/3}\right]^2 = 5^2 = 25.$$

Solution We need to approximate a particular value of $x^{2/3}$, so our strategy is to apply Eq. (6) with $f(x) = x^{2/3}$. We first note that $f'(x) = \tfrac{2}{3}x^{-1/3}$. We choose $a = 125$, because we know the *exact* values

$$f(125) = (125)^{2/3} = 25 \quad \text{and} \quad f'(125) = \tfrac{2}{3}(125)^{-1/3} = \tfrac{2}{15}$$

and because 125 is relatively close to 122. Then the linear approximation in (6) to $f(x) = x^{2/3}$ near $a = 125$ takes the form

$$f(x) \approx f(125) + f'(125) \cdot (x - 125);$$

FIGURE 4.2.3 The graph of the linear approximation $L(x) = f(a) + f'(a) \cdot (x - a)$ is the line tangent to $y = f(x)$ at the point $(a, f(a))$.

FIGURE 4.2.4 The function $f(x) = \sqrt{1 + x}$ and its linear approximation $L(x) = 1 + \tfrac{1}{2}x$ near $a = 0$.

that is,
$$x^{2/3} \approx 25 + \tfrac{2}{15}(x - 125).$$

With $x = 122$ we get
$$(122)^{2/3} \approx 25 + \tfrac{2}{15}(-3) = 24.6.$$

Thus $(122)^{2/3}$ is approximately 24.6. The actual value of $(122)^{2/3}$ is about 24.5984, so the formula in (6) gives a relatively good approximation in this case. ◆

EXAMPLE 3 A hemispherical bowl of radius 10 in. is filled with water to a depth of x inches. The volume V of water in the bowl (in cubic inches) is given by the formula

$$V = \frac{\pi}{3}(30x^2 - x^3) \qquad (10)$$

FIGURE 4.2.5 The bowl of Example 3.

(Fig. 4.2.5). (You will be able to derive this formula after you study Chapter 6.) Suppose that you *measure* the depth of water in the bowl to be 5 in. with a maximum possible measured error of $\tfrac{1}{16}$ in. Estimate the maximum error in the calculated volume of water in the bowl.

Solution The error in the calculated volume $V(5)$ is the difference
$$\Delta V = V(x) - V(5)$$

between the actual volume $V(x)$ and the calculated volume. We do not know the depth x of water in the bowl. We are given only that the difference
$$\Delta x = x - 5$$

between the actual and the measured depths is numerically at most $\tfrac{1}{16}$ in.: $|\Delta x| \leq \tfrac{1}{16}$. Because Eq. (10) yields

$$V'(x) = \frac{\pi}{3}(60x - 3x^2) = \pi(20x - x^2),$$

the linear approximation
$$\Delta V \approx dV = V'(5)\,\Delta x$$

at $x = 5$ gives
$$\Delta V \approx \pi(20 \cdot 5 - 5^2)\,\Delta x = 75\pi\,\Delta x.$$

With the common practice in science of writing $\Delta x = \pm\tfrac{1}{16}$ to signify that $-\tfrac{1}{16} \leq \Delta x \leq \tfrac{1}{16}$, this gives

$$\Delta V \approx (75\pi)\left(\pm\tfrac{1}{16}\right) \approx \pm 14.73 \quad (\text{in.}^3).$$

The formula in Eq. (10) gives the calculated volume $V(5) \approx 654.50$ in.^{3}, but we now see that this may be in error by almost 15 in.^{3} in either direction. ◆

Absolute and Relative Errors

The **(absolute) error** in a measured or approximated value is defined to be the remainder when the approximate value is subtracted from the true value. Hence

"actual value = approximate value + error."

The **relative error** is the ratio of the (absolute) error to the true value,

$$\text{"relative error} = \frac{\text{error}}{\text{value}}\text{,"}$$

and may be given as either a numerical fraction or as a percentage of the value.

EXAMPLE 4 In Example 3, a relative error in the measured depth x of

$$\frac{\Delta x}{x} = \frac{\frac{1}{16}}{5} = 0.0125 = 1.25\%$$

leads to a relative error in the estimated volume of

$$\frac{dV}{V} \approx \frac{14.73}{654.50} \approx 0.0225 = 2.25\%.$$

The relationship between these two relative errors is of some interest. The formulas for dV and V in Example 3 give

$$\frac{dV}{V} = \frac{\pi(20x - x^2)\,\Delta x}{\frac{1}{3}\pi(30x^2 - x^3)} = \frac{3(20-x)}{30-x} \cdot \frac{\Delta x}{x}.$$

When $x = 5$, this gives

$$\frac{dV}{V} = (1.80)\frac{\Delta x}{x}.$$

Hence, to approximate the volume of water in the bowl with a relative error of at most 0.5%, for instance, we would need to measure the depth with a relative error of at most $(0.5\%)/1.8$, thus with a relative error of less than 0.3%. ◆

The Error in Linear Approximation

Now we consider briefly the question of the difference between the values of a function $f(x)$ and its linear approximation $L(x)$ near the point $x = a$. If we let $\Delta x = x - a$ and write

$$y = f(x), \qquad f(a + \Delta x) = f(a) + \Delta y,$$

and

$$L(x) = f(a) + f'(a) \cdot \Delta x = f(a) + dy,$$

it then follows that the error in the linear approximation is given by

$$f(x) - L(x) = \Delta y - dy, \tag{11}$$

as illustrated in Fig. 4.2.6. It appears in the figure that, the smaller Δx is, the closer are the corresponding points on the curve $y = f(x)$ and its tangent line $y = L(x)$. Because Eq. (11) implies that the difference in the heights of two such points is equal to $\Delta y - dy$, the figure suggests that $\Delta y - dy$ approaches zero as $\Delta x \to 0$.

But even more is true: The difference

$$\Delta y - dy = f(a + \Delta x) - f(a) - f'(a)\,\Delta x \tag{12}$$

is a function of Δx that is small *even in comparison with* Δx. To see why, let's write

$$\epsilon(\Delta x) = \frac{\Delta y - dy}{\Delta x} = \frac{f(a + \Delta x) - f(a)}{\Delta x} - f'(a)$$

and note that

$$\lim_{\Delta x \to 0} \epsilon(\Delta x) = f'(a) - f'(a) = 0.$$

Consequently, the **error**

$$\Delta y - dy = \epsilon(\Delta x) \cdot \Delta x \tag{13}$$

FIGURE 4.2.6 The error $\Delta y - dy$ in the linear approximation $\Delta y \approx f'(a)\,\Delta x = dy$.

in the linear approximation $dy = f'(a)\,\Delta x$ to the actual increment Δy is the product of two quantities, *both* of which approach zero as $\Delta x \to 0$. If Δx is "very small"—so that $\epsilon(\Delta x)$ is also "very small"—then we might well describe their product in (13) as "*very* very small." In this case we may finally rewrite Eq. (13) in the form

$$f(a + \Delta x) - f(a) = f'(a)\,\Delta x + \epsilon(\Delta x) \cdot \Delta x, \tag{14}$$

expressing the actual increment $\Delta y = f(a + \Delta x) - f(a)$ as the sum of the very small differential $dy = f'(a)\,\Delta x$ and the very very small error $\epsilon(\Delta x) \cdot \Delta x$ in this differential.

EXAMPLE 5 If $y = f(x) = x^3$, then simple computations (with $\Delta x = x - a$) give

$$\Delta y = f(a + \Delta x) - f(a)$$
$$= (a + \Delta x)^3 - a^3 = 3a^2 \Delta x + 3a(\Delta x)^2 + (\Delta x)^3$$

and

$$dy = f'(a) \Delta x = 3a^2 \Delta x.$$

Hence

$$\Delta y - dy = 3a(\Delta x)^2 + (\Delta x)^3.$$

If $a = 1$ and $\Delta x = 0.1$, for instance, then these formulas yield

$$\Delta y = 0.331, \quad dy = 0.3, \quad \text{and} \quad \Delta y - dy = 0.031,$$

thereby illustrating the smallness in the error $\Delta y - dy$ in the linear approximation in comparison with the values of Δy and dy. ◆

Example 6 indicates how we sometimes can use a graphing calculator or computer to specify *how accurate* a linear approximation is—in terms of its accuracy throughout an entire interval containing the point $x = a$. In concrete situations we often want to determine an interval throughout which the linear approximation provides a specified accuracy.

EXAMPLE 6 Find an interval on which the approximation

$$\sqrt{1+x} \approx 1 + \tfrac{1}{2}x \tag{15}$$

of Example 1 is accurate to within 0.1.

Solution Accuracy to within 0.1 means that the two functions in (15) differ by less than 0.1:

$$\left|\sqrt{1+x} - \left(1 + \tfrac{1}{2}x\right)\right| < 0.1,$$

which is equivalent to

$$\sqrt{1+x} - 0.1 < 1 + \tfrac{1}{2}x < \sqrt{1+x} + 0.1.$$

Thus we want the graph of the linear approximation $y = 1 + \tfrac{1}{2}x$ to lie between the two curves obtained by shifting the graph $y = \sqrt{1+x}$ vertically up and down by the amount 0.1. Figure 4.2.7 shows the graphs of all these curves on the interval $-1 < x < 1.5$. The points at which the linear approximation $y = 1 + \tfrac{1}{2}x$ emerges from the band of width 0.2 around the graph $y = \sqrt{1+x}$ are marked, and we see that a smaller interval around $x = 0$ is needed to confine the linear approximation within the desired range. Indeed, the zoom shown in Fig. 4.2.8 indicates that the approximation in (15) is accurate to within 0.1 for every x in the interval $-0.6 < x < 0.9$. ◆

FIGURE 4.2.7 The function $f(x) = \sqrt{1+x}$ on the interval $-1 < x < 1.5$.

FIGURE 4.2.8 The function $f(x) = \sqrt{1+x}$ on the smaller interval $-0.6 < x < 0.9$.

Differentials

The linear approximation formula in (3) is often written with dx in place of Δx:

$$f(x + dx) \approx f(x) + f'(x)\, dx. \tag{16}$$

In this case dx is an independent variable, called the **differential** of x, and x is fixed. Thus the differentials of x and y are defined to be

$$dx = \Delta x \quad \text{and} \quad dy = f'(x)\, \Delta x = f'(x)\, dx. \tag{17}$$

From this definition it follows immediately that

$$\frac{dy}{dx} = \frac{f'(x)\, dx}{dx} = f'(x),$$

in perfect accord with the notation we have been using. Indeed, Leibniz originated differential notation by visualizing "infinitesimal" increments dx and dy (Fig. 4.2.9), with their ratio dy/dx being the slope of the tangent line. The key to Leibniz's independent discovery of differential calculus in the 1670s was his insight that if dx and dy are sufficiently small, then the segment of the curve $y = f(x)$ and the straight line segment joining (x, y) and $(x + dx, y + dy)$ are virtually indistinguishable. This insight is illustrated by the successive magnifications in Figs. 4.2.10 through 4.2.12 of the curve $y = x^2$ near the point $(1, 1)$.

Differential notation provides us with a convenient way to write derivative formulas. Suppose that $z = f(u)$, so that $dz = f'(u)\, du$. For particular choices of the function f, we get the formulas

$$d(u^n) = nu^{n-1}\, du,$$

$$d(\sin u) = (\cos u)\, du,$$

$$d(\tan u) = (\sec^2 u)\, du,$$

and so on. Thus we can write differentiation rules in differential form without having to identify the independent variable. The sum, product, and quotient rules take the respective forms

$$d(u + v) = du + dv,$$

$$d(uv) = u\, dv + v\, du,$$

and

$$d\left(\frac{u}{v}\right) = \frac{v\, du - u\, dv}{v^2}.$$

If $z = f(u)$ and $u = g(x)$, we may substitute $du = g'(x)\, dx$ into the formula $dz = f'(u)\, du$. This gives

$$dz = f'(g(x)) \cdot g'(x)\, dx.$$

FIGURE 4.2.9 The slope of the tangent line as the ratio of the infinitesimals dy and dx.

FIGURE 4.2.10 $dx = 1$.

FIGURE 4.2.11 $dx = \frac{1}{3}$.

FIGURE 4.2.12 $dx = \frac{1}{10}$.

This is the differential form of the chain rule

$$D_x f(g(x)) = f'(g(x)) \cdot g'(x).$$

Thus the chain rule appears here as though it were the result of mechanical manipulations of the differential notation. This compatibility with the chain rule is one reason for the extraordinary usefulness of differential notation in calculus.

EXAMPLE 7

(a) If $y = 3x^2 - 2x^{3/2}$, then $dy = (6x - 3\sqrt{x}) \, dx$.

(b) If $u = \sin^2 t - \cos 2t$, then

$$du = (2 \sin t \cos t + 2 \sin 2t) \, dt = 3 \sin 2t \, dt$$

(using the trigonometric identity $\sin 2t = 2 \sin t \cos t$).

(c) If $w = z \sec z$, then

$$dw = (1 \cdot \sec z + z \cdot \sec z \tan z) \, dz = (1 + z \tan z) \sec z \, dz. \quad \blacklozenge$$

Proof of the Chain Rule

We can now use our knowledge of the error in linear approximations to give a proof of the chain rule for the composition $f \circ g$ that does not require the assumption $g'(x) \neq 0$ that we needed in Section 3.3. Here we suppose only the existence of the derivatives $g'(a)$ and $f'(b)$ (where $b = g(a)$) of the functions $u = g(x)$ and $y = f(g(x)) = f(u)$. If we write

$$\Delta u = g(a + \Delta x) - g(a) \quad \text{and} \quad \Delta y = f(b + \Delta u) - f(b),$$

then Eq. (14) in this section—with g in place of f—gives

$$\Delta u = g'(a) \, \Delta x + \epsilon_1 \cdot \Delta x = [g'(a) + \epsilon_1] \, \Delta x \qquad (18)$$

where $\epsilon_1 \to 0$ as $\Delta x \to 0$. A second application of Eq. (14)—this time with u in place of x—gives

$$\Delta y = f'(b) \, \Delta u + \epsilon_2 \cdot \Delta u = [f'(b) + \epsilon_2] \, \Delta u$$
$$= [f'(g(a)) + \epsilon_2] \cdot [g'(a) + \epsilon_1] \, \Delta x \qquad (19)$$

where $\epsilon_2 \to 0$ as $\Delta u \to 0$, and hence as $\Delta x \to 0$ (because Eq. (18) shows that $\Delta u \to 0$ as $\Delta x \to 0$). Finally, when we divide by Δx in Eq. (19) and then take the limit as $\Delta x \to 0$, we get

$$\frac{dy}{dx} = \lim_{\Delta x \to 0} \frac{\Delta y}{\Delta x} = \lim_{\Delta x \to 0} [f'(g(a)) + \epsilon_2] \cdot [g'(a) + \epsilon_1] = f'(g(a)) \cdot g'(a).$$

Thus we have shown that the chain rule formula $D_x [f(g(x))] = f'(g(x)) \cdot g'(x)$ holds at $x = a$.

4.2 TRUE/FALSE STUDY GUIDE

4.2 CONCEPTS: QUESTIONS AND DISCUSSION

1. Use Eqs. (11)–(13) of this section to show that the linear function $L(x) = f(a) + f'(a) \cdot (x - a)$ of x satisfies the condition

$$\lim_{x \to a} \frac{f(x) - L(x)}{x - a} = 0. \qquad (20)$$

2. Any linear function $L(x) = mx + b$ satisfying Eq. (20) is called a **linearization** of the function $f(x)$ at the point $x = a$. Can a function have two different linearizations at the same point?

3. Can a function have a linearization (as in Question 2) at a point where it is not differentiable?

4.2 PROBLEMS

In Problems 1 through 16, write dy in terms of x and dx.

1. $y = 3x^2 - \dfrac{4}{x^2}$
2. $y = 2\sqrt{x} - \dfrac{3}{\sqrt[3]{x}}$
3. $y = x - \sqrt{4 - x^3}$
4. $y = \dfrac{1}{x - \sqrt{x}}$
5. $y = 3x^2(x - 3)^{3/2}$
6. $y = \dfrac{x}{x^2 - 4}$
7. $y = x(x^2 + 25)^{1/4}$
8. $y = \dfrac{1}{(x^2 - 1)^{4/3}}$
9. $y = \cos\sqrt{x}$
10. $y = x^2 \sin x$
11. $y = \sin 2x \cos 2x$
12. $y = \cos^3 3x$
13. $y = \dfrac{\sin 2x}{3x}$
14. $y = \dfrac{\cos x}{\sqrt{x}}$
15. $y = \dfrac{1}{1 - x \sin x}$
16. $y = (1 + \cos 2x)^{3/2}$

In Problems 17 through 24, find—as in Example 1—the linear approximation $L(x)$ to the given function $f(x)$ near the point $a = 0$.

17. $f(x) = \dfrac{1}{1 - x}$
18. $f(x) = \dfrac{1}{\sqrt{1 + x}}$
19. $f(x) = (1 + x)^2$
20. $f(x) = (1 - x)^3$
21. $f(x) = (1 - 2x)^{3/2}$
22. $f(x) = \dfrac{1}{(1 + 3x)^{2/3}}$
23. $f(x) = \sin x$
24. $f(x) = \cos x$

In Problems 25 through 34, use—as in Example 2—a linear approximation $L(x)$ to an appropriate function $f(x)$, with an appropriate value of a, to estimate the given number.

25. $\sqrt[3]{25}$
26. $\sqrt{102}$
27. $\sqrt[4]{15}$
28. $\sqrt{80}$
29. $65^{-2/3}$
30. $80^{3/4}$
31. $\cos 43°$
32. $\sin 32°$
33. $\sin 88°$
34. $\cos 62°$

In Problems 35 through 38, compute the differential of each side of the given equation, regarding x and y as dependent variables (as if both were functions of some third, unspecified, variable). Then solve for dy/dx.

35. $x^2 + y^2 = 1$
36. $x \sin y = 1$
37. $x^3 + y^3 = 3xy$
38. $x \sec y = y$

39. Assuming that $D_x x^k = kx^{k-1}$ for any real constant k (which we shall establish in Chapter 7), derive the linear approximation formula $(1 + x)^k \approx 1 + kx$ for x near zero.

In Problems 40 through 47, use linear approximations to estimate the change in the given quantity.

40. The circumference of a circle, if its radius is increased from 10 in. to 10.5 in.
41. The area of a square, if its edge length is decreased from 10 in. to 9.8 in.
42. The surface area of a sphere, if its radius is increased from 5 in. to 5.2 in. (Fig. 4.2.13).

FIGURE 4.2.13 The sphere of Problem 42—area $A = 4\pi r^2$, volume $V = \frac{4}{3}\pi r^3$.

43. The volume of a cylinder, if both its height and its radius are decreased from 15 cm to 14.7 cm (Fig. 4.2.14).

FIGURE 4.2.14 The cylinder of Problem 43—volume $V = \pi r^2 h$.

44. The volume of the conical sandpile of Fig. 4.2.15, if its radius is 14 in. and its height is increased from 7 in. to 7.1 in.

FIGURE 4.2.15 The conical sandpile of Problem 44—volume $V = \frac{1}{3}\pi r^2 h$.

45. The range $R = \frac{1}{16}v^2 \sin 2\theta$ of a shell fired at inclination angle $\theta = 45°$, if its initial velocity v is increased from 80 ft/s to 81 ft/s.
46. The range $R = \frac{1}{16}v^2 \sin 2\theta$ of a projectile fired with initial velocity $v = 80$ ft/s, if its initial inclination angle θ is increased from 45° to 46°.
47. The wattage $W = RI^2$ of a floodlight with resistance $R = 10$ ohms, if the current I is increased from 3 amperes to 3.1 amperes.
48. The equatorial radius of the earth is approximately 3960 mi. Suppose that a wire is wrapped tightly around the earth at the equator. Approximately how much must this wire be lengthened if it is to be strung all the way around the earth on poles 10 ft above the ground? Use the linear approximation formula!
49. The radius of a spherical ball is measured as 10 in., with a maximum error of $\frac{1}{16}$ in. What is the maximum resulting error in its calculated volume?
50. With what accuracy must the radius of the ball of Problem 49 be measured to ensure an error of at most 1 in.³ in its calculated volume?

51. The radius of a hemispherical dome is measured as 100 m with a maximum error of 1 cm (Fig. 4.2.16). What is the maximum resulting error in its calculated surface area?

FIGURE 4.2.16 The hemisphere of Problem 51—curved surface area $A = 2\pi r^2$.

52. With what accuracy must the radius of a hemispherical dome be measured to ensure an error of at most 0.01% in its calculated surface area?

In Problems 53 through 60, a function $f(x)$ and a point $x = a$ are given. Determine graphically an open interval I centered at a so that the function $f(x)$ and its linear approximation $L(x)$ differ by less than the given value ϵ at each point of I.

53. $f(x) = x^2$, $a = 1$, $\epsilon = 0.2$
54. $f(x) = \sqrt{x}$, $a = 1$, $\epsilon = 0.1$
55. $f(x) = \tan x$, $a = 0$, $\epsilon = 0.01$
56. $f(x) = \sqrt[3]{x}$, $a = 8$, $\epsilon = 0.01$
57. $f(x) = \sin x$, $a = 0$, $\epsilon = 0.05$
58. $f(x) = \tan x$, $a = 0$, $\epsilon = 0.01$
59. $f(x) = \sin x$, $a = \pi/4$, $\epsilon = 0.02$
60. $f(x) = \tan x$, $a = \pi/4$, $\epsilon = 0.02$

4.3 INCREASING AND DECREASING FUNCTIONS AND THE MEAN VALUE THEOREM

The significance of the *sign* of the first derivative of a function is simple but crucial:

$f(x)$ is increasing on an interval where $f'(x) > 0$;
$f(x)$ is decreasing on an interval where $f'(x) < 0$.

Geometrically, this means that where $f'(x) > 0$, the graph of $y = f(x)$ is rising as you scan it from left to right. Where $f'(x) < 0$, the graph is falling. We can clarify the terms *increasing* and *decreasing* as follows.

DEFINITION Increasing and Decreasing Functions
The function f is **increasing** on the interval $I = (a, b)$ provided that

$$f(x_1) < f(x_2)$$

for all pairs of numbers x_1 and x_2 in I for which $x_1 < x_2$. The function f is **decreasing** on I provided that

$$f(x_1) > f(x_2)$$

for all pairs of numbers x_1 and x_2 for which $x_1 < x_2$.

FIGURE 4.3.1 (a) An increasing function and (b) a decreasing function.

Figure 4.3.1 illustrates this definition. In short, the function f is increasing on $I = (a, b)$ if the values of $f(x)$ increase as x increases [Fig. 4.3.1(a)]; f is decreasing on I if the values of $f(x)$ decrease as x increases [Fig. 4.3.1(b)].

EXAMPLE 1 As illustrated in Fig. 4.3.2, the simple function $f(x) = x^2$ is decreasing on the interval $(-\infty, 0)$ and increasing on the interval $(0, +\infty)$. This follows immediately from the elementary fact that $u^2 < v^2$ if $0 < u < v$. Because $f'(x) = 2x$, we also see immediately that $f'(x) < 0$ on the interval $(-\infty, 0)$ and that $f'(x) > 0$ on the interval $(0, +\infty)$. But for more general functions, the mean value theorem of this section is needed to establish the precise relationship between the sign of the derivative of a function and its increasing-decreasing behavior. ◆

FIGURE 4.3.2 $f(x) = x^2$ is decreasing for $x < 0$, increasing for $x > 0$.

REMARK We speak of a function as increasing or decreasing *on an interval*, not at a single point. Nevertheless, if we consider the sign of f', the derivative of f, at a single point, we get a useful intuitive picture of the significance of the sign of the derivative. This is because the derivative $f'(x)$ is the slope of the tangent line at the point $(x, f(x))$ on the graph of f. If $f'(x) > 0$, then the tangent line has positive slope.

Therefore, it rises as you scan from left to right. Intuitively, a rising tangent would seem to correspond to a rising graph and thus to an increasing function. Similarly, we expect to see a falling graph where $f'(x)$ is negative (Fig. 4.3.3). One caution: In order to determine whether a function f is increasing or decreasing, we must examine the sign of f' on a whole interval, not merely at a single point. (See Problem 59.)

The Mean Value Theorem

Although pictures of rising and falling graphs are suggestive, they provide no actual *proof* of the significance of the sign of the derivative. To establish rigorously the connection between a graph's rising and falling and the sign of the derivative of the graphed function, we need the *mean value theorem,* stated later in this section. This theorem is the principal theoretical tool of differential calculus, and we shall see that it has many important applications.

A Question As an introduction to the mean value theorem, we pose the following question. Suppose that P and Q are two points on the surface of the sea, with Q lying generally to the east of P (Fig. 4.3.4). Is it possible to sail a boat from P to Q, always sailing roughly east, without *ever* (even for an instant) sailing in the exact direction from P to Q? That is, can we sail from P to Q without our instantaneous line of motion ever being parallel to the line PQ?

The mean value theorem answers this question: No. There will always be at least one instant when we are sailing parallel to the line PQ, no matter which path we choose.

To paraphrase: Let the path of the sailboat be the graph of a differentiable function $y = f(x)$ with endpoints $P(a, f(a))$ and $Q(b, f(b))$. Then we say that there must be some point on this graph where the tangent line (corresponding to the instantaneous line of motion of the boat) to the curve is parallel to the line PQ that joins the curve's endpoints. This is a *geometric interpretation* of the mean value theorem.

The Geometric Formulation The slope of the line tangent at the point $(c, f(c))$ (Fig. 4.3.5) is $f'(c)$, whereas the slope of the line PQ is

$$\frac{f(b) - f(a)}{b - a}.$$

We may think of this last quotient as the average (or *mean*) value of the slope of the curve $y = f(x)$ over the interval $[a, b]$. The mean value theorem guarantees that there is a point c in (a, b) for which the line tangent to $y = f(x)$ at $(c, f(c))$ is indeed parallel to the line PQ. In the language of algebra, there's a number c in (a, b) such that

$$f'(c) = \frac{f(b) - f(a)}{b - a}. \tag{1}$$

A Preliminary Result We first state a "lemma" to expedite the proof of the mean value theorem. This theorem is called *Rolle's theorem,* after Michel Rolle (1652–1719), who discovered it in 1690. In his youth Rolle studied the emerging subject of calculus but later renounced it. He argued that the subject was based on logical fallacies, and he is remembered today only for the single theorem that bears his name. It is ironic that his theorem plays an important role in the rigorous proofs of several calculus theorems.

ROLLE'S THEOREM
Suppose that the function f is continuous on the closed interval $[a, b]$ and is differentiable in its interior (a, b). If $f(a) = 0 = f(b)$, then there exists some number c in (a, b) such that $f'(c) = 0$.

FIGURE 4.3.6 The idea of the proof of Rolle's theorem.

Figure 4.3.6 illustrates the first case in the following proof of Rolle's theorem. The idea of the proof is this: Suppose that the smooth graph $y = f(x)$ starts ($x = a$) at height zero and ends ($x = b$) at height zero. Then if it goes up, it must come back down. But where it stops going up and starts coming back down, its tangent line must be horizontal. Therefore the derivative is zero at that point.

PROOF OF ROLLE'S THEOREM Because f is continuous on $[a, b]$, it must attain both a maximum and a minimum value on $[a, b]$ (by the maximum value property of Section 3.5). If f has any positive values, consider its maximum value $f(c)$. Now c is not an endpoint of $[a, b]$ because $f(a) = 0$ and $f(b) = 0$. Therefore c is a point of (a, b). But we know that f is differentiable at c. So it follows from Theorem 2 of Section 3.5 that $f'(c) = 0$.

Similarly, if f has any negative values, we can consider its minimum value $f(c)$ and conclude much as before that $f'(c) = 0$.

If f has neither positive nor negative values, then f is identically zero on $[a, b]$, and it follows that $f'(c) = 0$ for *every* c in (a, b).

Thus we see that the conclusion of Rolle's theorem is justified in every case. ◀

An important consequence of Rolle's theorem is that between each pair of zeros of a differentiable function, there is *at least one* point at which the tangent line is horizontal. Some possible pictures of the situation are indicated in Fig. 4.3.7.

EXAMPLE 2 Suppose that $f(x) = x^{1/2} - x^{3/2}$ on $[0, 1]$. Find a number c that satisfies the conclusion of Rolle's theorem.

Solution Note that f is continuous on $[0, 1]$ and differentiable on $(0, 1)$. Because the term $x^{1/2}$ is present, f is *not* differentiable at $x = 0$, but this is irrelevant. Also, $f(0) = 0 = f(1)$, so all of the hypotheses of Rolle's theorem are satisfied. Finally,

$$f'(x) = \tfrac{1}{2}x^{-1/2} - \tfrac{3}{2}x^{1/2} = \tfrac{1}{2}x^{-1/2}(1 - 3x),$$

so we see that $f'(c) = 0$ for $c = \tfrac{1}{3}$. An accurate graph of f on $[0, 1]$, including c and the horizontal tangent line, is shown in Fig. 4.3.8. ◆

FIGURE 4.3.7 The existence of the horizontal tangent is a consequence of Rolle's theorem.

EXAMPLE 3 Suppose that $f(x) = 1 - x^{2/3}$ on $[-1, 1]$. Then f satisfies the hypotheses of Rolle's theorem *except* for the fact that $f'(0)$ does not exist. It is clear from the graph of f that there is *no* point where the tangent line is horizontal (Fig. 4.3.9). Indeed,

$$f'(x) = -\frac{2}{3}x^{-1/3} = -\frac{2}{3\sqrt[3]{x}},$$

so $f'(x) \neq 0$ for $x \neq 0$, and we see that $|f'(x)| \to \infty$ as $x \to 0$. Hence the graph of f has a vertical tangent line—rather than a horizontal one—at the point $(0, 1)$. Thus the conclusion of Rolle's theorem—like that of any theorem—may fail to hold if any of its hypotheses are not satisfied. ◆

FIGURE 4.3.8 The number c of Example 2.

FIGURE 4.3.9 The function $f(x) = 1 - x^{2/3}$ of Example 3.

Increasing and Decreasing Functions and the Mean Value Theorem SECTION 4.3

Now we are ready to state formally and prove the mean value theorem.

THE MEAN VALUE THEOREM
Suppose that the function f is continuous on the closed interval $[a, b]$ and differentiable on the open interval (a, b). Then

$$f(b) - f(a) = f'(c) \cdot (b - a) \tag{2}$$

for some number c in (a, b).

COMMENT Because Eq. (2) is equivalent to Eq. (1), the conclusion of the mean value theorem is that there must be at least one point on the curve $y = f(x)$ at which the tangent line is parallel to the line joining its endpoints $P(a, f(a))$ and $Q(b, f(b))$.

MOTIVATION FOR THE PROOF OF THE MEAN VALUE THEOREM   We consider the auxiliary function ϕ suggested by Fig. 4.3.10. The value of $\phi(x)$ is, by definition, the vertical height difference over x between the point $(x, f(x))$ on the curve and the corresponding point on the line PQ. It appears that a point on the curve $y = f(x)$ where the tangent line is parallel to PQ corresponds to a maximum or minimum of ϕ. It's also clear that $\phi(a) = 0 = \phi(b)$, so Rolle's theorem can be applied to the function ϕ on $[a, b]$. So our plan for proving the mean value theorem is this: First, we obtain a formula for the function ϕ. Second, we locate the point c such that $\phi'(c) = 0$. Finally, we show that this number c is exactly the number needed to satisfy the conclusion of the mean value theorem in Eq. (2).

FIGURE 4.3.10 The construction of the auxiliary function ϕ.

PROOF OF THE MEAN VALUE THEOREM   Because the line PQ passes through $P(a, f(a))$ and has slope

$$m = \frac{f(b) - f(a)}{b - a},$$

the point-slope formula for the equation of a straight line gives us the following equation for PQ:

$$y = y_{\text{line}} = f(a) + m(x - a).$$

Thus

$$\phi(x) = y_{\text{curve}} - y_{\text{line}} = f(x) - f(a) - m(x - a).$$

You may verify by direct substitution that $\phi(a) = 0 = \phi(b)$. And, because ϕ is continuous on $[a, b]$ and differentiable on (a, b), we may apply Rolle's theorem to it. Thus there is a point c somewhere in the open interval (a, b) at which $\phi'(c) = 0$. But

$$\phi'(x) = f'(x) - m = f'(x) - \frac{f(b) - f(a)}{b - a}.$$

Because $\phi'(c) = 0$, we conclude that

$$0 = f'(c) - \frac{f(b) - f(a)}{b - a}.$$

That is,

$$f(b) - f(a) = f'(c) \cdot (b - a).$$

◄

The proof of the mean value theorem is an application of Rolle's theorem, whereas Rolle's theorem is the special case of the mean value theorem in which $f(a) = 0 = f(b)$.

EXAMPLE 4 Suppose that we drive from Kristiansand, Norway to Oslo—a road distance of almost exactly 350 km—in exactly 4 h, from time $t = 0$ to time $t = 4$. Let $f(t)$ denote the distance we have traveled at time t, and assume that f is a differentiable function. Then the mean value theorem implies that

$$350 = f(4) - f(0) = f'(c) \cdot (4 - 0) = 4 f'(c)$$

and thus that

$$f'(c) = \tfrac{350}{4} = 87.5$$

at some instant c in $(0, 4)$. But $f'(c)$ is our *instantaneous* velocity at time $t = c$, and 87.5 km/h is our *average* velocity for the trip. Thus the mean value theorem implies that we must have an instantaneous velocity of exactly 87.5 km/h at least once during the trip. ◆

The argument in Example 4 is quite general—during any trip, the instantaneous velocity must at *some* instant equal the average velocity for the whole trip. For instance, it follows that if two toll stations are 70 mi apart and you drive between the two in exactly 1 h, then at some instant you must have been speeding in excess of the posted limit of 65 mi/h. Speeding tickets have been issued by the Pennsylvania State Police to speeders on the Pennsylvania Turnpike on exactly such evidence!

Consequences of the Mean Value Theorem

The first of three important consequences of the mean value theorem is the *non*trivial converse of the trivial fact that the derivative of a constant function is identically zero. That is, we prove that there can be *no* exotic function that is nonconstant but has a derivative that is identically zero. In Corollaries 1 through 3 we assume, as in Rolle's theorem and the mean value theorem, that f and g are continuous on the closed interval $[a, b]$ and differentiable on (a, b).

COROLLARY 1 Functions with Zero Derivative

If $f'(x) \equiv 0$ on (a, b) (that is, $f'(x) = 0$ for all x in (a, b)), then f is a constant function on $[a, b]$. In other words, there exists a constant C such that $f(x) \equiv C$.

PROOF Apply the mean value theorem to the function f on the interval $[a, x]$, where x is a fixed but arbitrary point of the interval $(a, b]$. We find that

$$f(x) - f(a) = f'(c) \cdot (x - a)$$

for some number c between a and x. But $f'(x)$ is always zero on the interval (a, b), so $f'(c) = 0$. Thus $f(x) - f(a) = 0$, and therefore $f(x) = f(a)$.

But this last equation holds for *all* x in $(a, b]$. Therefore, $f(x) = f(a)$ for all x in $(a, b]$ and, indeed, for all x in $[a, b]$. That is, $f(x)$ has the constant value $C = f(a)$. This establishes Corollary 1. ◄

Corollary 1 is usually applied in a different but equivalent form, which we state and prove next.

COROLLARY 2 Functions with Equal Derivatives

Suppose that $f'(x) = g'(x)$ for all x in the open interval (a, b). Then f and g differ by a constant on $[a, b]$. That is, there exists a constant K such that

$$f(x) = g(x) + K$$

for all x in $[a, b]$.

PROOF Given the hypotheses, let $h(x) = f(x) - g(x)$. Then

$$h'(x) = f'(x) - g'(x) = 0$$

for all x in (a, b). So, by Corollary 1, $h(x)$ is a constant K on $[a, b]$. That is, $f(x) - g(x) = K$ for all x in $[a, b]$; therefore,

$$f(x) = g(x) + K$$

for all x in $[a, b]$. This establishes Corollary 2. ◀

EXAMPLE 5 If $f'(x) = 2\cos x$ and $f(0) = 5$, what is the function $f(x)$?

Solution From our knowledge of the derivatives of trigonometric functions, we know that one function with derivative $g'(x) = 2\cos x$ is

$$g(x) = 2\sin x.$$

Hence Corollary 2 implies that there exists a constant K such that

$$f(x) = g(x) + K = 2\sin x + K$$

on any given interval $[a, b]$ containing zero. But we can find the value of K by substituting $x = 0$:

$$f(0) = 2\sin 0 + K;$$

$$5 = 2 \cdot 0 + K;$$

so $K = 5$. Thus the function f is

$$f(x) = 2\sin x + 5.$$ ◆

The following consequence of the mean value theorem verifies the remarks about increasing and decreasing functions with which we opened this section.

COROLLARY 3 Increasing and Decreasing Functions

If $f'(x) > 0$ for all x in (a, b), then f is an increasing function on $[a, b]$. If $f'(x) < 0$ for all x in (a, b), then f is a decreasing function on $[a, b]$.

PROOF Suppose, for example, that $f'(x) > 0$ for all x in (a, b). We need to show the following: If u and v are points of $[a, b]$ with $u < v$, then $f(u) < f(v)$. We apply the mean value theorem to f, but on the closed interval $[u, v]$. This is legitimate because $[u, v]$ is contained in $[a, b]$, so f satisfies the hypotheses of the mean value theorem on $[u, v]$ as well as on $[a, b]$. The result is that

$$f(v) - f(u) = f'(c) \cdot (v - u)$$

for some number c in (u, v). Because $v > u$ and because, by hypothesis, $f'(c) > 0$, it follows that

$$f(v) - f(u) > 0; \quad \text{that is,} \quad f(u) < f(v),$$

as we wanted to show. The proof is similar in the case that $f'(x)$ is negative on (a, b). ◀

218 CHAPTER 4 Additional Applications of the Derivative

$f'(x)$	$f(x)$
Negative	Decreasing
Positive	Increasing

FIGURE 4.3.11 Corollary 3.

FIGURE 4.3.12 The significance of the sign of $f'(x)$.

The meaning of Corollary 3 is summarized in Fig. 4.3.11. Figure 4.3.12 shows a graph $y = f(x)$ labeled in accord with this correspondence between the sign of the derivative $f'(x)$ and the increasing or decreasing behavior of the function $f(x)$.

EXAMPLE 6 Where is the function $f(x) = x^2 - 4x + 5$ increasing, and where is it decreasing?

Solution The derivative of f is $f'(x) = 2x - 4$. Clearly $f'(x) > 0$ if $x > 2$, whereas $f'(x) < 0$ if $x < 2$. Hence f is decreasing on $(-\infty, 2)$ and increasing on $(2, +\infty)$, as we see in Fig. 4.3.13. ◆

EXAMPLE 7 Show that the equation $x^3 + x - 1 = 0$ has exactly one [real] solution.

Solution We need a *function* so that we may apply the tools of this section, so we let $f(x) = x^3 + x - 1$. Because $f(0) = -1 < 0$, $f(1) = 1 > 0$, and f is continuous (everywhere), the intermediate value property guarantees that $f(x)$ has *at least* one real zero in $[0, 1]$. We see this zero in Fig. 4.3.14, but cannot conclude from graphical evidence alone that there is no zero somewhere else (perhaps outside the viewing window of the figure).

But

$$f'(x) = 3x^2 + 1,$$

and it is evident that $f'(x) > 0$ for all x. So Corollary 3 implies that the graph of $y = f(x)$ is increasing on the whole real number line. Therefore the equation $f(x) = 0$ can have *at most* one solution. (Why?)

In summary, the equation $f(x) = 0$ has both at *least* one solution and at *most* one solution. Therefore it has exactly one [real] solution. ◆

FIGURE 4.3.13 The parabola of Example 6.

FIGURE 4.3.14 The increasing function of Example 7.

EXAMPLE 8 Determine the open intervals on the x-axis on which the function

$$f(x) = 3x^4 - 4x^3 - 12x^2 + 5$$

is increasing and those on which it is decreasing.

Solution The derivative of f is

$$f'(x) = 12x^3 - 12x^2 - 24x$$
$$= 12x(x^2 - x - 2) = 12x(x+1)(x-2). \quad (3)$$

The critical points $x = -1, 0$, and 2 separate the x-axis into the four open intervals $(-\infty, -1)$, $(-1, 0)$, $(0, 2)$, and $(2, +\infty)$ (Fig. 4.3.15). The derivative $f'(x)$ does not change sign within any of these intervals, because

- The factor $x + 1$ in Eq. (3) changes sign only at $x = -1$,
- The factor $12x$ changes sign only at $x = 0$, and
- The factor $x - 2$ changes sign only at $x = 2$.

Increasing and Decreasing Functions and the Mean Value Theorem SECTION 4.3 219

FIGURE 4.3.15 The signs of $x + 1$ and $x - 2$ (Example 8).

Figure 4.3.15 indicates the signs of $x + 1$ and $x - 2$ on each of the four intervals. We illustrate two different methods of determining the sign of $f'(x)$ on each interval.

Method 1 The second, third, and fourth columns of the next table record the signs of the factors in Eq. (3) on each of the four intervals listed in the first column. The signs of $f'(x)$ shown in the fifth column are then obtained by multiplication. The sixth column lists the resulting increasing or decreasing behavior of f on the four intervals.

Interval	$x + 1$	$12x$	$x - 2$	$f'(x)$	f
$(-\infty, -1)$	−	−	−	−	Decreasing
$(-1, 0)$	+	−	−	+	Increasing
$(0, 2)$	+	+	−	−	Decreasing
$(2, +\infty)$	+	+	+	+	Increasing

Method 2 Because the derivative $f'(x)$ does not change sign within any of the four intervals, we need only calculate its value at a single point in each interval. Whatever the sign at that point may be, it is the sign of $f'(x)$ throughout that interval.

In $(-\infty, -1)$: $\quad f'(-2) = -96 < 0; \quad f$ is decreasing.
In $(-1, 0)$: $\quad f'(-0.5) = 7.5 > 0; \quad f$ is increasing.
In $(0, 2)$: $\quad f'(1) = -24 < 0; \quad f$ is decreasing.
In $(2, +\infty)$: $\quad f'(3) = 144 > 0; \quad f$ is increasing.

The second method is especially convenient if the derivative is complicated but an appropriate calculator for computation of its values is available.

Finally, note that the results we have obtained in each method are consistent with the graph of $y = f(x)$ shown in Fig. 4.3.16. ◆

FIGURE 4.3.16 The critical points of the polynomial of Example 8.

EXAMPLE 9 The graph in Fig. 4.3.17 suggests that $\sin x < x$ for all $x > 0$. To show that this is indeed so, it suffices to show that the *difference*

$$h(x) = f(x) - g(x) = x - \sin x$$

of the functions $f(x) = x$ and $g(x) = \sin x$ is positive-valued for $x > 0$. But

$$h'(x) = 1 - \cos x > 0$$

for all x in the interval $(0, 2\pi)$, where $\cos x < 1$. Hence Corollary 3 implies that h is an increasing function on the closed interval $[0, 2\pi]$. Because $h(0) = 0$, it therefore follows that $h(x) > 0$ if $0 < x \leq 2\pi$. But if $x > 2\pi$ then certainly

$$h(x) = x - \sin x > 2\pi - \sin x > 0$$

because $|\sin x| \leq 1$ for all x. Thus we have proved that

$$x - \sin x = h(x) > 0,$$

FIGURE 4.3.17 x and $\sin x$ (Example 9).

and hence that $x > \sin x$ for all $x > 0$. (Can you tell why it follows from this that $x < \sin x$ for all $x < 0$?) ◆

4.3 TRUE/FALSE STUDY GUIDE

4.3 CONCEPTS: QUESTIONS AND DISCUSSION

1. It's often said that "what goes up must come down." Can you translate this common saying into a mathematical statement? Does it follow from results in this section?

2. Two toll stations are located 60 miles apart. Half of the highway between them has a posted speed limit of 50 mi/h (miles per hour) and the other 30 miles has a posted speed limit of 70 mi/h. When you arrive at the second station, your toll pass shows that you traveled the total distance of 60 miles in exactly one hour. On this basis you are cited for speeding somewhere along the way. Is this fair? What's the proof of your guilt?

3. Let $f(x) = x^2$. Which result in this section implies that there is exactly one function $g(x)$ defined for all $x > 0$ such that $g(y) = x$ if $f(x) = y$? Explain why it follows that $g(f(x)) = x$ for all $x > 0$. What's the common name for this function g?

4. Let $f(x) = x^2$. Is there a function $g(x)$ defined for all x (negative as well as nonnegative) such that $g(y) = x$ if $f(x) = y$? Why or why not?

5. Repeat Question 4, except with $f(x) = x^3$.

4.3 PROBLEMS

For the functions in Problems 1 through 6, first determine (as in Example 8) the open intervals on the x-axis on which each function is increasing and those where it is decreasing. Then use this information to match the function to its graph, one of the six shown in Fig. 4.3.18.

1. $f(x) = 4 - x^2$
2. $f(x) = x^2 - 2x - 1$
3. $f(x) = x^2 + 4x + 1$
4. $f(x) = \frac{1}{4}x^3 - 3x$
5. $f(x) = \frac{1}{3}x^3 - \frac{1}{2}x^2 - 2x + 1$
6. $f(x) = 2x - \frac{1}{6}x^2 - \frac{1}{9}x^3$

In Problems 7 through 10, the derivative $f'(x)$ and the value $f(0)$ are given. Use the method of Example 5 to find the function $f(x)$.

7. $f'(x) = 4x;\quad f(0) = 5$
8. $f'(x) = 3\sqrt{x};\quad f(0) = 4$
9. $f'(x) = \dfrac{1}{x^2};\quad f(1) = 1$
10. $f'(x) = \dfrac{2}{\sqrt{x}};\quad f(0) = 3$

In Problems 11 through 24, determine (as in Example 8) the open intervals on the x-axis on which the function is increasing as well as those on which it is decreasing. If you have a graphics calculator or computer, plot the graph $y = f(x)$ to see whether it agrees with your results.

11. $f(x) = 3x + 2$
12. $f(x) = 4 - 5x$
13. $f(x) = 8 - 2x^2$
14. $f(x) = 4x^2 + 8x + 13$
15. $f(x) = 6x - 2x^2$
16. $f(x) = x^3 - 12x + 17$
17. $f(x) = x^4 - 2x^2 + 1$
18. $f(x) = \dfrac{x}{x+1}$ [Note: $f'(x)$ doesn't change sign at $x = -1$. Why?]
19. $f(x) = 3x^4 + 4x^3 - 12x^2$
20. $f(x) = x\sqrt{x^2 + 1}$
21. $f(x) = 8x^{1/3} - x^{4/3}$
22. $f(x) = 2x^3 + 3x^2 - 12x + 5$
23. $f(x) = \dfrac{(x-1)^2}{x^2 - 3}$ (See the note for Problem 18.)
24. $f(x) = x^2 + \dfrac{16}{x^2}$ (See the note for Problem 18.)

FIGURE 4.3.18 Problems 1 through 6.

In Problems 25 through 28, show that the given function satisfies the hypotheses of Rolle's theorem on the indicated interval $[a, b]$, and find all numbers x in (a, b) that satisfy the conclusion of that theorem.

25. $f(x) = x^2 - 2x$; $[0, 2]$
26. $f(x) = 9x^2 - x^4$; $[-3, 3]$
27. $f(x) = 2 \sin x \cos x$; $[0, \pi]$
28. $f(x) = 5x^{2/3} - x^{5/3}$; $[0, 5]$

In Problems 29 through 31, show that the given function f does not satisfy the conclusion of Rolle's theorem on the indicated interval. Which of the hypotheses does it fail to satisfy?

29. $f(x) = 1 - |x|$; $[-1, 1]$
30. $f(x) = 1 - (2-x)^{2/3}$; $[1, 3]$
31. $f(x) = x^4 + x^2$; $[0, 1]$

In Problems 32 through 36, show that the given function f satisfies the hypotheses of the mean value theorem on the indicated interval, and find all numbers c in that interval that satisfy the conclusion of that theorem.

32. $f(x) = x^3$; $[-1, 1]$
33. $f(x) = 3x^2 + 6x - 5$; $[-2, 1]$
34. $f(x) = \sqrt{x-1}$; $[2, 5]$
35. $f(x) = (x-1)^{2/3}$; $[1, 2]$
36. $f(x) = x + \dfrac{1}{x}$; $[2, 3]$

In Problems 37 through 40, show that the given function f satisfies neither the hypotheses nor the conclusion of the mean value theorem on the indicated interval.

37. $f(x) = |x - 2|$; $[1, 4]$
38. $f(x) = 1 + |x - 1|$; $[0, 3]$
39. $f(x) = [\![x]\!]$ (the greatest integer function); $[-1, 1]$
40. $f(x) = 3x^{2/3}$; $[-1, 1]$

In Problems 41 through 44, show that the given equation has exactly one solution in the indicated interval.

41. $x^5 + 2x - 3 = 0$; $[0, 1]$
42. $x^{10} = 1000$; $[1, 2]$
43. $x^4 - 3x = 20$; $[2, 3]$
44. $\sin x = 3x - 1$; $[-1, 1]$

45. A car is driving along a rural road where the speed limit is 70 mi/h. At 3:00 P.M. its odometer (measuring distance traveled) reads 8075 mi. At 3:18 P.M. it reads 8100 mi. Prove that the driver violated the speed limit at some instant between 3:00 and 3:18 P.M.

46. Suppose that a car's speedometer reads 50 mi/h at 3:25 P.M. and 65 mi/h at 3:35 P.M. Prove that at some instant in this 10-minute time interval the car's acceleration was exactly 90 mi/h^2.

47. Points A and B along Interstate Highway 80 in Nebraska are 60 miles apart. Two cars both pass point A at 9:00 A.M. and both pass point B at 10:00 A.M. Show that at some instant between 9:00 and 10:00 A.M. the two cars have the same velocity. (*Suggestion:* Consider the difference $h(t) = f(t) - g(t)$ between the position functions of the two cars.)

48. Show that the function $f(x) = x^{2/3}$ does not satisfy the hypotheses of the mean value theorem on $[-1, 27]$ but that nevertheless there is a number c in $(-1, 27)$ such that
$$f'(c) = \frac{f(27) - f(-1)}{27 - (-1)}.$$

49. Prove that the function
$$f(x) = (1+x)^{3/2} - \tfrac{3}{2}x - 1$$
is increasing on $(0, +\infty)$. Explain carefully how you could conclude that
$$(1+x)^{3/2} > 1 + \tfrac{3}{2}x$$
for all $x > 0$.

50. Suppose that f' is a constant function on the interval $[a, b]$. Prove that f must be a linear function (a function whose graph is a straight line).

51. Suppose that $f'(x)$ is a polynomial of degree $n - 1$ on the interval $[a, b]$. Prove that $f(x)$ must be a polynomial of degree n on $[a, b]$.

52. Suppose that there are k different points of $[a, b]$ at which the differentiable function f vanishes (is zero). Prove that f' must vanish on at least $k - 1$ points of $[a, b]$.

53. (a) Apply the mean value theorem to $f(x) = \sqrt{x}$ on $[100, 101]$ to show that
$$\sqrt{101} = 10 + \frac{1}{2\sqrt{c}}$$
for some number c in $(100, 101)$. (b) Show that if $100 < c < 101$, then $10 < \sqrt{c} < 10.5$, and use this fact to conclude from part (a) that $10.0475 < \sqrt{101} < 10.0500$.

54. Prove that the equation $x^7 + x^5 + x^3 + 1 = 0$ has exactly one real solution.

55. (a) Show that $D_x \tan^2 x = D_x \sec^2 x$ on the open interval $(-\pi/2, \pi/2)$. (b) Conclude that there exists a constant C such that $\tan^2 x = \sec^2 x + C$ for all x in $(-\pi/2, \pi/2)$. Then evaluate C.

56. Explain why the mean value theorem does not apply to the function $f(x) = |x|$ on the interval $[-1, 2]$.

57. Suppose that the function f is differentiable on the interval $[-1, 2]$ and that $f(-1) = -1$ and $f(2) = 5$. Prove that there is a point on the graph of f at which the tangent line is parallel to the line with the equation $y = 2x$.

58. Let $f(x) = x^4 - x^3 + 7x^2 + 3x - 11$. Prove that the graph of f has at least one horizontal tangent line.

59. Let the function g be defined as follows:
$$g(x) = \begin{cases} \dfrac{x}{2} + x^2 \sin \dfrac{1}{x} & \text{if } x \neq 0, \\ 0 & \text{if } x = 0. \end{cases}$$

(a) Show that $g'(0) = \frac{1}{2} > 0$. (b) Sketch the graph of g near $x = 0$. Is g increasing on any open interval containing $x = 0$? [*Answer:* No.]

60. Suppose that f is increasing on every closed interval $[a, b]$ provided that $2 \leq a < b$. Prove that f is increasing on the unbounded open interval $(2, +\infty)$. Note that the principle you discover was used implicitly in Example 6 of this section.

Approximations *Problems 61 through 63 illustrate the use of the mean value theorem to approximate numerical values of functions.*

61. Use the method of Example 9 with $f(x) = \cos x$ and $g(x) = 1 - \frac{1}{2}x^2$ to show that

$$\cos x > 1 - \frac{1}{2}x^2$$

for all $x > 0$ (Fig. 4.3.19).

FIGURE 4.3.19 $\cos x$ and $g(x) = 1 - \frac{1}{2}x^2$ (Problem 61).

62. (a) Use the method of Example 9 and the result of Problem 61 to show that

$$\sin x > x - \frac{1}{6}x^3$$

for all $x > 0$ (Fig. 4.3.20). (b) Use the results of Example 9 and part (a) to calculate the sine of a 5° angle accurate to three decimal places.

FIGURE 4.3.20 x, $\sin x$, and $g(x) = x - \frac{1}{6}x^3$ (Problem 62).

63. (a) Use the results of Problem 62(a) to show that

$$\cos x < 1 - \frac{1}{2}x^2 + \frac{1}{24}x^4$$

for all $x > 0$. (b) Use the results of Problem 61 and part (a) to calculate the cosine of a 10° angle accurate to three decimal places.

4.4 THE FIRST DERIVATIVE TEST AND APPLICATIONS

In Section 3.5 we discussed maximum and minimum values of a function defined on a closed and bounded interval $[a, b]$. Now we consider extreme values of functions defined on more general domains, including open or unbounded intervals as well as closed and bounded intervals.

The distinction between *absolute* and *local* extrema is important here. Let c be a point of the domain D of the function f. Then recall from Section 3.5 that $f(c)$ is the **(absolute) maximum value** of $f(x)$ on D provided that $f(c) \geq f(x)$ for all x in D, whereas the value $f(c)$ is a **local maximum value** of $f(x)$ if it is the maximum value of $f(x)$ on some open interval containing c. Similarly, $f(c)$ is the **(absolute) minimum value** of $f(x)$ on D provided that $f(c) \leq f(x)$ for all x in D; $f(c)$ is a **local minimum value** of $f(x)$ if it is the minimum value of $f(x)$ on some open interval containing c. Thus a local maximum value is one that is as large as or greater than any nearby value of $f(x)$, and a local minimum value is one that is as small as or less than any nearby value. Figure 4.4.1 shows a typical example of a function that has neither an absolute maximum nor an absolute minimum value. But each of the two local extrema pictured there is an (absolute) extreme value on a sufficiently small open interval.

FIGURE 4.4.1 Local extrema are absolute extrema on sufficiently small intervals.

REMARK Absolute extreme values are sometimes called **global** extreme values, and local extreme values are sometimes called **relative** extreme values.

FIGURE 4.4.2 The graph of $f(x) = x^2 + 3$. The local minimum value $f(0) = 3$ is also the global minimum value of $f(x)$.

FIGURE 4.4.3 The graph of $f(x) = 4 - (x-1)^2$. The local maximum value $f(1) = 4$ is also the global maximum value of $f(x)$.

FIGURE 4.4.4 The graph of $f(x) = x^3 - 3x^2 - 9x$. The local minimum value $f(3) = -27$ clearly is not the global minimum value. Similarly, the local maximum value $f(-1) = 5$ is not the global maximum value.

FIGURE 4.4.5 The graph of $f(x) = x^3 + 2$. The critical value $f(0) = 2$ is neither a global nor a local extreme value of $f(x)$.

Theorem 2 of Section 3.5 tells us that any extremum of the differentiable function f on an open interval I must occur at a *critical point* where the derivative vanishes:

$$f'(x) = 0.$$

But the mere fact that $f'(c) = 0$ does *not*, by itself, imply that the critical value $f(c)$ is an extreme value of f. Figures 4.4.2 through 4.4.5 illustrate different possibilities for the nature of $f(c)$: whether it is a local or global maximum or minimum value, or neither.

A Test for Local Extrema

What we need is a way to test whether, at the critical point $x = c$, the value $f(c)$ is actually a maximum or a minimum value of $f(x)$, either local or global. Figure 4.4.6 shows how such a test might be developed. Suppose that the function f is continuous at c and that c is an **interior point** of the domain of f—that is, f is defined on some open interval that contains c. If f is decreasing immediately to the left of c and increasing immediately to the right, then $f(c)$ should be a local minimum value of $f(x)$. But if f is increasing immediately to the left of c and decreasing immediately to its right, then $f(c)$ should be a local maximum. If f is increasing on both sides or decreasing on both sides, then $f(c)$ should be neither a maximum value nor a minimum value of $f(x)$.

Moreover, we know from Corollary 3 in Section 4.3 that the *sign* of the derivative $f'(x)$ determines where $f(x)$ is decreasing and where it is increasing:

- $f(x)$ is decreasing where $f'(x) < 0$;
- $f(x)$ is increasing where $f'(x) > 0$.

FIGURE 4.4.6 The first derivative test.

In the following test for local extrema, we say that

- $f'(x) < 0$ *to the left of* c if $f'(x) < 0$ on some interval (a, c) of numbers immediately to the left of c, and that
- $f'(x) > 0$ *to the right of* c if $f'(x) > 0$ on some interval (c, b) of numbers immediately to the right of c,

and so forth. (See Fig. 4.4.7.) Theorem 1 tells us how to use the *signs* of $f'(x)$ to the left and right of the point c to determine whether $f(x)$ has a local maximum or local minimum value at $x = c$.

FIGURE 4.4.7 Open intervals to the left and right of the point c.

THEOREM 1 The First Derivative Test for Local Extrema

Suppose that the function f is continuous on the interval I and also is differentiable there except possibly at the interior point c of I.

1. If $f'(x) < 0$ to the left of c and $f'(x) > 0$ to the right of c, then $f(c)$ is a *local minimum value* of $f(x)$ on I.
2. If $f'(x) > 0$ to the left of c and $f'(x) < 0$ to the right of c, then $f(c)$ is a *local maximum value* of $f(x)$ on I.
3. If $f'(x) > 0$ both to the left of c and to the right of c, *or* if $f'(x) < 0$ both to the left of c and to the right of c, then $f(c)$ is *neither* a maximum nor a minimum value of $f(x)$.

COMMENT Thus $f(c)$ is a local extremum if the first derivative $f'(x)$ *changes sign* as x increases through c, and the direction of this sign change determines whether $f(c)$ is a local maximum or a local minimum. A good way to remember the first derivative test for local extrema is simply to visualize Fig. 4.4.6.

PROOF We will prove only part 1; the other two parts have similar proofs. Suppose that the hypotheses of Theorem 1 hold: that f is continuous on the interval I, that c is an interior point of I, and that f is differentiable on I except possibly at $x = c$. Then there exist two intervals (a, c) and (c, b), each wholly contained in I, such that $f'(x) < 0$ on (a, c) and $f'(x) > 0$ on (c, b).

Suppose that x is in (a, b). Then there are three cases to consider. First, if $x < c$, then x is in (a, c) and f is decreasing on $(a, c]$, so $f(x) > f(c)$. Second, if $x > c$, then x is in (c, b) and f is increasing on $[c, b)$, so again $f(x) > f(c)$. Finally, if $x = c$, then $f(x) = f(c)$. Thus, for each x in (a, b), $f(x) \geqq f(c)$. Therefore, by definition, $f(c)$ is a local minimum value of $f(x)$. ◀

The idea of this proof is illustrated in Fig. 4.4.8. Part (a) shows f decreasing to the left of c and increasing to the right, so there must be a local minimum at $x = c$. Part (b) shows f increasing to the left of c and decreasing to the right, so $f(c)$ is a local maximum value of $f(x)$. In part (c), the derivative has the same sign on each side of c, and so there can be no extremum of any sort at $x = c$.

FIGURE 4.4.8 The three cases in the first derivative test.

REMARK Figures 4.4.9 through 4.4.13 illustrate cases in which Theorem 1 applies, where the interval I is the entire real number line $\mathbf{R}$. In Fig. 4.4.9 through 4.4.11, the origin $c = 0$ is a critical point because $f'(0) = 0$. In Figs. 4.4.12 and 4.4.13, $c = 0$ is a critical point because $f'(0)$ does not exist.

Classification of Critical Points

Suppose that we have found the critical points of a function. Then we can attempt to classify them—as local maxima, local minima, or neither—by applying the first derivative test at each point in turn. Example 1 illustrates a procedure that can be used.

The First Derivative Test and Applications SECTION 4.4   225

FIGURE 4.4.9 $f(x) = x^2$, $f'(x) = 2x$, a local minimum at $x = 0$.

FIGURE 4.4.10 $f(x) = -x^2$, $f'(x) = -2x$, a local maximum at $x = 0$.

FIGURE 4.4.11 $f(x) = -x^3$, $f'(x) = -3x^2$, no extremum at $x = 0$.

FIGURE 4.4.12 $f(x) = x^{2/3}$, $f'(x) = \frac{2}{3}x^{-1/3}$, a local minimum at $x = 0$.

FIGURE 4.4.13 $f(x) = x^{1/3}$, $f'(x) = \frac{1}{3}x^{-2/3}$, no extremum at $x = 0$.

EXAMPLE 1 Find and classify the critical points of the function

$$f(x) = 2x^3 - 3x^2 - 36x + 7.$$

Solution The derivative is

$$f'(x) = 6x^2 - 6x - 36 = 6(x+2)(x-3), \tag{1}$$

so the critical points [where $f'(x) = 0$] are $x = -2$ and $x = 3$. These two points separate the x-axis into the three open intervals $(-\infty, -2)$, $(-2, 3)$, and $(3, +\infty)$. The derivative $f'(x)$ cannot change sign within any of these intervals. One reason is that the factor $x + 2$ in Eq. (1) changes sign only at -2, whereas the factor $x - 3$ changes sign only at 3 (Fig. 4.4.14). As in Example 7 of Section 4.3, we illustrate here two methods of determining the signs of $f'(x)$ on the intervals $(-\infty, -2)$, $(-2, 3)$, and $(3, +\infty)$.

FIGURE 4.4.14 The signs of $x + 2$ and $x - 3$ (Example 1).

Method 1 The second and third columns of the following table record (from Fig. 4.4.14) the signs of the factors $x + 2$ and $x - 3$ in Eq. (1) on the three intervals listed in the first column. The signs of $f'(x)$ in the fourth column are then obtained by multiplication.

226 CHAPTER 4 Additional Applications of the Derivative

Interval	$x+2$	$x-3$	$f'(x)$
$(-\infty, -2)$	−	−	+
$(-2, 3)$	+	−	−
$(3, +\infty)$	+	+	+

Method 2 Because the derivative $f'(x)$ does not change sign within any of the three intervals, we need to calculate its value only at a single point in each interval:

In $(-\infty, -2)$: $f'(-3) = 36 > 0$; f' is positive;
In $(-2, 3)$: $f'(0) = -36 < 0$; f' is negative;
In $(3, +\infty)$: $f'(4) = 36 > 0$; f' is positive.

$f'(x) > 0$ $f'(x) < 0$ $f'(x) > 0$
f increasing f decreasing f increasing
$x = -2$ $x = 3$

FIGURE 4.4.15 The three intervals of Example 1.

Figure 4.4.15 summarizes our information about the signs of $f'(x)$. Because $f'(x)$ is positive to the left and negative to the right of the critical point $x = -2$, the first derivative test implies that $f(-2) = 51$ is a local maximum value. Because $f'(x)$ is negative to the left and positive to the right of $x = 3$, it follows that $f(3) = -74$ is a local minimum value. The graph of $y = f(x)$ in Fig. 4.4.16 confirms this classification of the critical points $x = -2$ and $x = 3$. ◆

FIGURE 4.4.16 $y = f(x)$ (Example 1).

Open-Interval Maximum-Minimum Problems

In Section 3.6 we discussed applied maximum-minimum problems in which the values of the dependent variable are given by a function defined on a closed and bounded interval. Sometimes, though, the function f describing the variable to be maximized (or minimized) is defined on an *open* interval (a, b), possibly an *unbounded* open interval such as $(1, +\infty)$ or $(-\infty, +\infty)$, and we cannot "close" the interval by adjoining endpoints. Typically, the reason is that $|f(x)| \to +\infty$ as x approaches a or b. But if f has only a single critical point in (a, b), then the first derivative test can tell us that $f(c)$ is the desired extreme value and can even determine whether it is a maximum or a minimum value of $f(x)$.

EXAMPLE 2 Find the (absolute) minimum value of

$$f(x) = x + \frac{4}{x} \quad \text{for} \quad 0 < x < +\infty.$$

Solution The derivative is

$$f'(x) = 1 - \frac{4}{x^2} = \frac{x^2 - 4}{x^2}. \tag{2}$$

The roots of the equation

$$f'(x) = \frac{x^2 - 4}{x^2} = 0$$

are $x = -2$ and $x = 2$. But $x = -2$ is not in the open interval $(0, +\infty)$, so we have only the critical point $x = 2$ to consider.

We see immediately from Eq. (2) that

- $f'(x) < 0$ to the left of $x = 2$ (because $x^2 < 4$ there), and
- $f'(x) > 0$ to the right of $x = 2$ (because $x^2 > 4$ there).

The First Derivative Test and Applications SECTION 4.4 227

Therefore, the first derivative test implies that $f(2) = 4$ is a local minimum value. We note also that $f(x) \to +\infty$ as either $x \to 0^+$ or as $x \to +\infty$. Hence the graph of f must resemble Fig. 4.4.17, and we see that $f(2) = 4$ is in fact the absolute minimum value of $f(x)$ on the entire interval $(0, +\infty)$. ◆

EXAMPLE 3 We must make a cylindrical can with volume 125 in.³ (about 2 L) by cutting its top and bottom from squares of metal and forming its curved side by bending a rectangular sheet of metal to match its ends. What radius r and height h of the can will minimize the total amount of material required for the rectangle and the two squares?

Solution We assume that the corners cut from the two squares, shown in Fig. 4.4.18, are wasted but that there is no other waste. As the figure shows, the area of the total amount of sheet metal required is

$$A = 8r^2 + 2\pi rh.$$

FIGURE 4.4.17 The graph of the function of Example 2.

The volume of the resulting can is then

$$V = \pi r^2 h = 125,$$

so $h = 125/(\pi r^2)$. Hence A is given as a function of r by

$$A(r) = 8r^2 + 2\pi r \cdot \frac{125}{\pi r^2} = 8r^2 + \frac{250}{r}, \quad 0 < r < +\infty.$$

The domain of A is the unbounded open interval $(0, +\infty)$ because r can have any positive value, so $A(r)$ is defined for every number r in $(0, +\infty)$. But $A(r) \to +\infty$ as $r \to 0^+$ and as $r \to +\infty$. So we cannot use the closed-interval maximum-minimum method. But we *can* use the first derivative test.

The derivative of $A(r)$ is

$$\frac{dA}{dr} = 16r - \frac{250}{r^2} = \frac{16}{r^2}\left(r^3 - \frac{125}{8}\right). \tag{3}$$

Thus the only critical point in $(0, +\infty)$ is where $r^3 = \frac{125}{8}$; that is,

$$r = \sqrt[3]{\frac{125}{8}} = \frac{5}{2} = 2.5.$$

FIGURE 4.4.18 The parts to make the cylindrical can of Example 3.

We see immediately from Eq. (3) that

- $dA/dr < 0$ to the left of $r = \frac{5}{2}$, because $r^3 < \frac{125}{8}$ there, and
- $dA/dr > 0$ to the right, where $r^3 > \frac{125}{8}$.

Therefore, the first derivative test implies that a local minimum value of $A(r)$ on $(0, +\infty)$ is

$$A\left(\frac{5}{2}\right) = 8 \cdot \left(\frac{5}{2}\right)^2 + \frac{250}{\frac{5}{2}} = 150.$$

Considering that $A(r) \to +\infty$ as $r \to 0^+$ and as $r \to +\infty$, we see that the graph of $A(r)$ on $(0, +\infty)$ looks like Fig. 4.4.19. This clinches the fact that $A(\frac{5}{2}) = 150$ is the *absolute* minimum value of $A(r)$. Therefore, we minimize the amount of material required by making a can with radius $r = 2.5$ in. and height

$$h = \frac{125}{\pi(2.5)^2} = \frac{20}{\pi} \approx 6.37 \quad \text{(in.)}.$$

FIGURE 4.4.19 Graph of the function of Example 3.

The total amount of material used is 150 in.² ◆

FIGURE 4.4.20 Carrying a rod around a corner (Example 4).

FIGURE 4.4.21 $y = \tan x$ (Example 4).

FIGURE 4.4.22 The graph of $L(\theta)$ (Example 4).

EXAMPLE 4 Find the length of the longest rod that can be carried horizontally around the corner from a hall 2 m wide into one that is 4 m wide.

Solution The desired length is the *minimum* length $L = L_1 + L_2$ of the rod being carried around the corner in Fig. 4.4.20. We see from the two similar triangles in the figure that

$$\frac{4}{L_1} = \sin\theta \quad \text{and} \quad \frac{2}{L_2} = \cos\theta,$$

so

$$L_1 = 4\csc\theta \quad \text{and} \quad L_2 = 2\sec\theta.$$

Therefore, the length $L = L_1 + L_2$ of the rod is given as a function of θ by

$$L(\theta) = 4\csc\theta + 2\sec\theta$$

on the open interval $(0, \pi/2)$. Note that $L(\theta) \to +\infty$ as either $\theta \to 0^+$ or as $\theta \to (\pi/2)^-$. (Why?)

The derivative of $L(\theta)$ is

$$\begin{aligned}\frac{dL}{d\theta} &= -4\csc\theta\cot\theta + 2\sec\theta\tan\theta \\ &= -\frac{4\cos\theta}{\sin^2\theta} + \frac{2\sin\theta}{\cos^2\theta} = \frac{2\sin^3\theta - 4\cos^3\theta}{\sin^2\theta\cos^2\theta} \\ &= \frac{(2\cos\theta)(\tan^3\theta - 2)}{\sin^2\theta}.\end{aligned} \quad (4)$$

Hence $dL/d\theta = 0$ exactly when

$$\tan\theta = \sqrt[3]{2}, \quad \text{so} \quad \theta \approx 0.90 \quad (\text{rad}).$$

We now see from Eq. (4) and from the graph of the tangent function (Fig. 4.4.21) that

- $dL/d\theta < 0$ to the left of $\theta \approx 0.90$, where $\tan\theta < \sqrt[3]{2}$, so $\tan^3\theta < 2$, and
- $dL/d\theta > 0$ to the right, where $\tan^3\theta > 2$.

Hence the graph of L resembles Fig. 4.4.22. This means that the absolute minimum value of L—and therefore the maximum length of the rod in question—is about

$$L(0.90) = 4\csc(0.90) + 2\sec(0.90),$$

approximately 8.32 m. ◆

The method we used in Examples 2 through 4 to establish absolute extrema illustrates the following global version of the first derivative test.

THEOREM 2 The First Derivative Test for Global Extrema

Suppose that f is defined on an open interval I, either bounded or unbounded, and that f is differentiable at each point of I except possibly at the critical point c where f is continuous.

1. If $f'(x) < 0$ for all x in I with $x < c$ and $f'(x) > 0$ for all x in I with $x > c$, then $f(c)$ is the absolute minimum value of $f(x)$ on I.
2. If $f'(x) > 0$ for all x in I with $x < c$ and $f'(x) < 0$ for all x in I with $x > c$, then $f(c)$ is the absolute maximum value of $f(x)$ on I.

The proof of this theorem is essentially the same as that of Theorem 1.

REMARK When the function $f(x)$ has only one critical point c in an open interval I, Theorem 2 may apply to tell us either that $f(c)$ is the absolute minimum or that it is the absolute maximum of $f(x)$ on I. But it is good practice to verify your conclusion by sketching the graph as we did in Examples 2 through 4.

4.4 TRUE/FALSE STUDY GUIDE

4.4 CONCEPTS: QUESTIONS AND DISCUSSION

1. Suppose that the function f is continuous on the whole real line R. Sketch a possible graph—if any—of f in each of the following three cases.
   (a) f has two critical points a and b but neither a local minimum nor a local maximum anywhere. Discuss separately the various possibilities: as to whether f is, or is not, differentiable at a and/or b.
   (b) f has three critical points but only a single local extremum.
   (c) f has three local minima but only a single local maximum.
2. Suppose that f is a cubic polynomial with positive leading coefficient. List the possibilities—with a typical graph of each—for the number and types of critical points of f.
3. Repeat Question 2 for a quartic (fourth-degree) polynomial.
4. Repeat Question 2 for a quintic (fifth-degree) polynomial.
5. Can you show that the function f must have an absolute minimum value if f is a polynomial of even degree with positive leading coefficient?
6. Can you show that the function f must have an absolute minimum value if

$$\lim_{x \to a^+} f(x) = \lim_{x \to b^-} f(x) = +\infty$$

and f is continuous on the open interval (a, b)?

4.4 PROBLEMS

Apply the first derivative test to classify each of the critical points of the functions in Problems 1 through 16 (local or global, maximum or minimum, or not an extremum). If you have a graphics calculator or computer, plot $y = f(x)$ to see whether the appearance of the graph corresponds to your classification of the critical points.

1. $f(x) = x^2 - 4x + 5$
2. $f(x) = 6x - x^2$
3. $f(x) = x^3 - 3x^2 + 5$
4. $f(x) = x^3 - 3x + 5$
5. $f(x) = x^3 - 3x^2 + 3x + 5$
6. $f(x) = 2x^3 + 3x^2 - 36x + 17$
7. $f(x) = 10 + 60x + 9x^2 - 2x^3$
8. $f(x) = 27 - x^3$
9. $f(x) = x^4 - 2x^2$
10. $f(x) = 3x^5 - 5x^3$
11. $f(x) = x + \dfrac{9}{x}$
12. $f(x) = x^2 + \dfrac{2}{x}$
13. $f(x) = 2x - \dfrac{1}{x^2}$
14. $f(x) = x^2 - \dfrac{16}{x}$
15. $f(x) = 3 - x^{2/3}$
16. $f(x) = 4 + x^{1/3}$

In Problems 17 through 26, find and classify the critical points of the given function in the indicated open interval. You may find it useful to construct a table of signs as in Example 1.

17. $f(x) = \sin^2 x;\quad (0, 3)$
18. $f(x) = \cos^2 x;\quad (-1, 3)$
19. $f(x) = \sin^3 x;\quad (-3, 3)$
20. $f(x) = \cos^4 x;\quad (0, 4)$
21. $f(x) = \sin x - x \cos x;\quad (-5, 5)$
22. $f(x) = \cos x + x \sin x;\quad (-5, 5)$
23. $f(x) = \tan^2 x;\quad (-1, 1)$
24. $f(x) = \tan^3 x;\quad (-1, 1)$
25. $f(x) = 2 \tan x - \tan^2 x;\quad (0, 1)$
26. $f(x) = (1 - 2 \sin x)^2;\quad (0, 2)$

In Problems 27 through 50, which are applied maximum-minimum problems, use the first derivative test to verify your answer.

27. Determine two real numbers with difference 20 and minimum possible product.
28. A long rectangular sheet of metal is to be made into a rain gutter by turning up two sides at right angles to the remaining center strip (Fig. 4.4.23). The rectangular cross section of the gutter is to have area 18 in.² Find the minimum possible width of the sheet.

FIGURE 4.4.23 The rectangular cross section of the gutter of Problem 28.

29. Find the point (x, y) on the line $2x + y = 3$ that is closest to the point $(3, 2)$.

30. You must construct a closed rectangular box with volume 576 in.^{3} and with its bottom twice as long as it is wide (Fig. 4.4.24). Find the dimensions of the box that will minimize its total surface area.

FIGURE 4.4.24 The box of Problem 30.

31. Repeat Problem 30, but use an open-topped rectangular box with volume 972 in.^{3}

32. An open-topped cylindrical pot is to have volume 125 in.^{3} What dimensions will minimize the total amount of material used in making this pot (Fig. 4.4.25)? Neglect the thickness of the material and possible wastage.

FIGURE 4.4.25 The cylinder of Problems 32, 33, 38, and 39.

33. An open-topped cylindrical pot is to have volume 250 cm^3 (Fig. 4.4.25). The material for the bottom of the pot costs 4¢/cm^2; that for its curved side costs 2¢/cm^2. What dimensions will minimize the total cost of this pot?

34. Find the point (x, y) on the parabola $y = 4 - x^2$ that is closest to the point $(3, 4)$. [*Suggestion:* The cubic equation that you should obtain has a small integer as one of its roots. *Suggestion:* Minimize the *square* of the distance.]

35. Show that the rectangle with area 100 and minimum perimeter is a square.

36. Show that the rectangular solid with a square base, volume 1000, and minimum total surface area is a cube.

37. A box with a square base and an open top is to have volume 62.5 in.^{3} Neglect the thickness of the material used to make the box, and find the dimensions that will minimize the amount of material used.

38. You need a tin can in the shape of a right circular cylinder of volume 16π cm^3 (Fig. 4.4.25). What radius r and height h would minimize its total surface area (including top and bottom)?

39. The metal used to make the top and bottom of a cylindrical can (Fig. 4.4.25) costs 4¢/in.^{2}; the metal used for the sides costs 2¢/in.^{2} The volume of the can must be exactly 100 in.^{3}. What dimensions of the can would minimize its total cost?

40. Each page of a book will contain 30 in.^{2} of print, and each page must have 2-in. margins at top and bottom and a 1-in. margin at each side. What is the minimum possible area of such a page?

41. What point or points on the curve $y = x^2$ are nearest the point $(0, 2)$? [*Suggestion:* The square of a distance is minimized exactly when the distance itself is minimized.]

42. What is the length of the shortest line segment lying wholly in the first quadrant tangent to the graph of $y = 1/x$ and with its endpoints on the coordinate axes?

43. A rectangle has area 64 cm^2. A straight line is to be drawn from one corner of the rectangle to the midpoint of one of the two more distant sides. What is the minimum possible length of such a line?

44. An oil can is to have volume 1000 in.^{3} and is to be shaped like a cylinder with a flat bottom but capped by a hemisphere (Fig. 4.4.26). Neglect the thickness of the material of the can, and find the dimensions that will minimize the total amount of material needed to construct it.

FIGURE 4.4.26 The oil can of Problem 44.

45. Find the exact length L of the longest rod that can be carried horizontally around a corner from a corridor 2 m wide into one 4 m wide. Do this by *minimizing* the length of the rod in Fig. 4.4.27 by minimizing the square of that length as a function of x.

FIGURE 4.4.27 Carrying a rod around a corner (Problem 45).

46. Find the length of the shortest ladder that will reach from the ground, over a wall 8 ft high, to the side of a building 1 ft behind the wall. That is, minimize the length $L = L_1 + L_2$ shown in Fig. 4.4.28.

47. A sphere with fixed radius a is inscribed in a pyramid with a square base so that the sphere touches the base of the pyramid and also each of its four sides. Show that the minimum possible volume of the pyramid is $8/\pi$ times the volume of the sphere. [*Suggestion:* Use the two right triangles

FIGURE 4.4.28 The ladder of Problem 46.

in Fig. 4.4.29 to show that the volume of the pyramid is

$$V = V(y) = \frac{4a^2 y^2}{3(y - 2a)}.$$

This can be done easily with the aid of the angle θ and *without* the formula for $\tan(\theta/2)$.] Don't forget the domain of $V(y)$.

FIGURE 4.4.29 Cross section through the centers of the sphere and pyramid of Problem 47.

48. Two noisy discothèques, one four times as noisy as the other, are located on opposite ends of a block 1000 ft long. What is the quietest point on the block between the two discos? The intensity of noise at a point away from its source is proportional to the noisiness and inversely proportional to the square of the distance from the source.

49. A floored tent with fixed volume V is to be shaped like a pyramid with a square base and congruent sides (Fig. 4.4.30). What height y and base edge $2x$ would minimize its total surface area (including its floor)?

50. Suppose that the distance from the building to the wall in Problem 46 is a and that the height of the wall is b. Show that the minimal length of the ladder is

$$L_{\min} = \left(a^{2/3} + b^{2/3}\right)^{3/2}.$$

FIGURE 4.4.30 The tent of Problem 49.

Problems 51 and 52 deal with square-based rectangular boxes. Such a box is said to be closed *if it has both a square base and a top (as well as four vertical sides),* open *if it has a base but no top. (Problems 51 through 55 here are in a certain sense "dual" to Problems 56 through 60 in Section 3.6. Compare corresponding problems to make sure you see the difference; one will be a closed-interval maximum-minimum problem and the other an open-interval maximum-minimum problem.)*

51. Show that, among all closed rectangular boxes with square bases and a given fixed volume, the one with minimal total surface area is a cube.

52. Show that, among all open rectangular boxes with square bases and a given fixed volume, the one with minimal total surface area has height equal to half the length of the edge of its base.

Problems 53 through 55 deal with cans in the shape of right circular cylinders. Such a can is said to be closed *if it has both a circular base and a top (as well as a curved side),* open *if it has a base but no top.*

53. Show that, among all closed cylindrical cans with a given fixed volume, the one with minimal total surface area has height equal to the diameter of its base.

54. Show that, among all open cylindrical cans with a given fixed volume, the one with minimal total surface area has height equal to the radius of its base.

55. Suppose that the base and curved side of a pop-top soft drink can have the same thickness. But the top is three times as thick as the base to prevent ripping when the can is opened. Show that, among all such cans with a given fixed volume, the one requiring the least amount (volume) of material to make—including the triply thick top—has height twice the diameter of its base. Perhaps this is why soft drink cans look somewhat taller than vegetable or soup cans.

56. Suppose that you want to construct a closed rectangular box with a square base and fixed volume V. Each of the six faces of the box—the base, top, and four vertical sides—costs a cents per square inch, and gluing each of the 12 edges costs b cents per inch of edge length. What shape should this box be in order to minimize its total cost? [*Suggestion:* Show that the critical points of the cost function are roots of a certain quartic equation that you can solve using a computer algebra system. You may even be able to solve it with pencil and paper alone; begin by grouping the two terms of highest degree.]

4.4 Project: Constructing a Candy Box with Lid

A candy maker wants to package jelly beans in boxes each having a fixed volume V. Each box is to be an open rectangular box with square base of edge length x. (See Fig. 4.4.31.) In addition, the box is to have a square lid with a two-inch rim. Thus the box-with-lid actually consists of two open rectangular boxes—the x-by-x-by-y box itself with height $y \geq 2$ (in.) and the x-by-x-by-2 lid (which fits the box very snugly). Your job as the firm's design engineer is to determine the dimensions x and y that will minimize the total cost of the two open boxes that comprise a single candy box with lid. Assume that the box-with-lid is to be made using an attractive foil-covered cardboard that costs $1 per square foot and that its volume is to be $V = 400 + 50n$ cubic inches. (For your personal design problem, choose an integer n between 1 and 10.)

FIGURE 4.4.31 The square-based candy box with lid.

FIGURE 4.4.32 The cylindrical candy box with lid.

Your next task is to design a cylindrical box-with-lid as indicated in Fig. 4.4.32. Now the box proper and its lid are both open circular cylinders, but everything else is the same as in the previous problem—two-inch rim, $1 per square foot foil-covered cardboard, and volume $V = 400 + 50n$. What are the dimensions of the box of minimal cost? Which is less expensive to manufacture—the optimal rectangular box-with-lid or the optimal box-with-lid in the shape of a cylinder?

4.5 SIMPLE CURVE SKETCHING

We can construct a reasonably accurate graph of the polynomial function

$$f(x) = a_n x^n + a_{n-1} x^{n-1} + \cdots + a_2 x^2 + a_1 x + a_0 \qquad (1)$$

by assembling the following information.

1. **The critical points of f**—that is, the points on the graph where the tangent line is horizontal, so that $f'(x) = 0$.
2. **The increasing/decreasing behavior of f**—that is, the intervals on which f is increasing and those on which it is decreasing.
3. **The behavior of f "at" infinity**—that is, the behavior of f as $x \to +\infty$ and as $x \to -\infty$.

The same information often is the key to understanding the structure of a graph that has been plotted with a calculator or computer.

Behavior at Infinity

To carry out the task in item 3, we write $f(x)$ in the form

$$f(x) = x^n \left(a_n + \frac{a_{n-1}}{x} + \cdots + \frac{a_1}{x^{n-1}} + \frac{a_0}{x^n} \right).$$

Thus we conclude that the behavior of $f(x)$ as $x \to \pm\infty$ is much the same as that of its *leading term* $a_n x^n$, because all the terms that have powers of x in the denominator approach zero as $x \to \pm\infty$. In particular, if $a_n > 0$, then

$$\lim_{x \to \infty} f(x) = +\infty, \tag{2}$$

meaning that $f(x)$ increases without bound as $x \to +\infty$. Also

$$\lim_{x \to -\infty} f(x) = \begin{cases} +\infty & \text{if } n \text{ is even;} \\ -\infty & \text{if } n \text{ is odd.} \end{cases} \tag{3}$$

If $a_n < 0$, simply reverse the signs on the right-hand sides in Eqs. (2) and (3). It follows that the graph of any (nonconstant) *polynomial* function exhibits one of the four "behaviors as $x \to \pm\infty$" that are illustrated in Fig. 4.5.1.

(a) Northwest-northeast if n is even and $a_n > 0$

(b) Southwest-southeast if n is even and $a_n < 0$

(c) Southwest-northeast if n is odd and $a_n > 0$

(d) Northwest-southeast if n is odd and $a_n < 0$

FIGURE 4.5.1 The behavior of polynomial graphs as $x \to \pm\infty$.

Critical Points

Every polynomial, such as $f(x)$ in Eq. (1), is differentiable everywhere. So the critical points of $f(x)$ are the roots of the polynomial equation $f'(x) = 0$—that is, solutions of

$$n a_n x^{n-1} + (n-1) a_{n-1} x^{n-2} + \cdots + 2 a_2 x + a_1 = 0. \tag{4}$$

Sometimes we can find all (real) solutions of such an equation by factoring, but most often in practice we must resort to numerical methods aided by calculator or computer.

Increasing/Decreasing Behavior

Suppose that we have somehow found *all* the (real) solutions $c_1, c_2, \ldots, c_k$ of Eq. (4). Then these solutions are the critical points of f. If they are arranged in increasing order, as in Fig. 4.5.2, then they separate the x-axis into the finite number of open intervals

$$(-\infty, c_1), \quad (c_1, c_2), \quad (c_2, c_3), \quad \ldots, \quad (c_{k-1}, c_k), \quad (c_k, +\infty)$$

FIGURE 4.5.2 The zeros of $f'(x)$ divide the x-axis into intervals on which $f'(x)$ does not change sign.

that also appear in the figure. The intermediate value property applied to $f'(x)$ tells us that $f'(x)$ can change sign only at the critical points of f, so $f'(x)$ has only one sign on each of these open intervals. It is typical for $f'(x)$ to be negative on some intervals and positive on others. Moreover, it's easy to find the sign of $f'(x)$ on any one such interval I: We need only substitute *any* convenient number in I into $f'(x)$.

Once we know the sign of $f'(x)$ on each of these intervals, we know where f is increasing and where it is decreasing. We then apply the first derivative test to find which of the critical values are local maxima, which are local minima, and which are neither—merely places where the tangent line is horizontal. With this information, the knowledge of the behavior of f as $x \to \pm\infty$, and the fact that f is continuous, we can sketch its graph. We plot the critical points $(c_i, f(c_i))$ and connect them with a smooth curve that is consistent with our other data.

It may also be helpful to plot the y-intercept $(0, f(0))$ and also any x-intercepts that are easy to find. But we recommend (until inflection points are introduced in Section 4.6) that you plot *only* these points—critical points and intercepts—and rely otherwise on the increasing and decreasing behavior of f.

EXAMPLE 1 Sketch the graph of $f(x) = x^3 - 27x$.

Solution Because the leading term is x^3, we see that

$$\lim_{x \to +\infty} f(x) = +\infty \quad \text{and} \quad \lim_{x \to -\infty} f(x) = -\infty.$$

Moreover, because

$$f'(x) = 3x^2 - 27 = 3(x+3)(x-3), \tag{5}$$

we see that the critical points where $f'(x) = 0$ are $x = -3$ and $x = 3$. The corresponding points on the graph of f are $(-3, 54)$ and $(3, -54)$. The critical points separate the x-axis into the three open intervals $(-\infty, -3)$, $(-3, 3)$, and $(3, +\infty)$ (Fig. 4.5.3). To determine the increasing or decreasing behavior of f on these intervals, let's substitute a number in each interval into the derivative in Eq. (5):

On $(-\infty, -3)$: $f'(-4) = (3)(-1)(-7) = 21 > 0$; f is increasing;

On $(-3, 3)$: $f'(0) = (3)(3)(-3) = -27 < 0$; f is decreasing;

On $(3, +\infty)$: $f'(4) = (3)(7)(1) = 21 > 0$; f is increasing.

FIGURE 4.5.3 The three open intervals of Example 1.

We plot the critical points and the intercepts $(0, 0)$, $(3\sqrt{3}, 0)$, and $(-3\sqrt{3}, 0)$. Then we use the information about where f is increasing or decreasing to connect these points with a smooth curve. Remembering that there are horizontal tangents at the two critical points, we obtain the graph shown in Fig. 4.5.4.

In the figure we use plus and minus signs to mark the sign of $f'(x)$ in each interval. This makes it clear that $(-3, 54)$ is a local maximum and that $(3, -54)$ is a local minimum. The limits we found at the outset show that neither is global. ◆

FIGURE 4.5.4 Graph of the function of Example 1.

EXAMPLE 2 Sketch the graph of $f(x) = 8x^5 - 5x^4 - 20x^3$.

Solution Because

$$f'(x) = 40x^4 - 20x^3 - 60x^2 = 20x^2(x+1)(2x-3), \qquad (6)$$

the critical points where $f'(x) = 0$ are $x = -1$, $x = 0$, and $x = \frac{3}{2}$. These three critical points separate the x-axis into the four open intervals shown in Fig. 4.5.5. This time, let's determine the increasing or decreasing behavior of f by recording the signs of the factors in Eq. (6) on each of the subintervals shown in Fig. 4.5.5. In this way we get the following table:

Interval	$x+1$	$20x^2$	$2x-3$	$f'(x)$	f
$(-\infty, -1)$	−	+	−	+	Increasing
$(-1, 0)$	+	+	−	−	Decreasing
$\left(0, \frac{3}{2}\right)$	+	+	−	−	Decreasing
$\left(\frac{3}{2}, +\infty\right)$	+	+	+	+	Increasing

FIGURE 4.5.5 The four open intervals of Example 2.

The points on the graph that correspond to the critical points are $(-1, 7)$, $(0, 0)$, and $(1.5, -32.0625)$.

We write $f(x)$ in the form

$$f(x) = x^3(8x^2 - 5x - 20)$$

in order to use the quadratic formula to find the x-intercepts. They turn out to be $(-1.30, 0)$, $(1.92, 0)$ (the abscissas are given only approximately), and the origin $(0, 0)$. The latter is also the y-intercept. We apply the first derivative test to the increasing or decreasing behavior shown in the table. It follows that $(-1, 7)$ is a local maximum, $(1.5, -32.0625)$ is a local minimum, and $(0, 0)$ is neither. The graph resembles the one shown in Fig. 4.5.6. ◆

FIGURE 4.5.6 Graph of the function of Example 2.

In Example 3, the function is not a polynomial. Nevertheless, the methods of this section suffice for sketching its graph.

EXAMPLE 3 Sketch the graph of

$$f(x) = x^{2/3}(x^2 - 2x - 6) = x^{8/3} - 2x^{5/3} - 6x^{2/3}.$$

Solution The derivative of f is

$$f'(x) = \tfrac{8}{3}x^{5/3} - \tfrac{10}{3}x^{2/3} - \tfrac{12}{3}x^{-1/3}$$

$$= \tfrac{2}{3}x^{-1/3}(4x^2 - 5x - 6) = \frac{2(4x + 3)(x - 2)}{3x^{1/3}}. \qquad (7)$$

The tangent line is horizontal at the two critical points $x = -\tfrac{3}{4}$ and $x = 2$, where the numerator in the last fraction of Eq. (7) is zero (and the denominator is not). Moreover, because of the presence of the factor $x^{1/3}$ in the denominator, $|f'(x)| \to +\infty$ as $x \to 0$. Thus $x = 0$ (a critical point because f is not differentiable there) is a point where the tangent line is vertical. These three critical points separate the x-axis into the four open intervals shown in Fig. 4.5.7. We determine the increasing or decreasing behavior of f by substituting a number from each interval in $f'(x)$ (Eq. (7)).

FIGURE 4.5.7 The four open intervals of Example 3.

On $\left(-\infty, -\frac{3}{4}\right)$: $\quad f'(-1) = \dfrac{2 \cdot (-1)(-3)}{3 \cdot (-1)} < 0; \quad f$ is decreasing;

On $\left(-\frac{3}{4}, 0\right)$: $\quad f'\left(-\frac{1}{2}\right) = \dfrac{2 \cdot (+1)\left(-\frac{5}{2}\right)}{3 \cdot \left(-\frac{1}{2}\right)^{1/3}} > 0; \quad f$ is increasing;

On $(0, 2)$: $\quad f'(1) = \dfrac{2 \cdot (+7)(-1)}{3 \cdot (+1)} < 0; \quad f$ is decreasing;

On $(2, +\infty)$: $\quad f'(3) = \dfrac{2 \cdot (+15)(+1)}{3 \cdot (+3)^{1/3}} > 0; \quad f$ is increasing.

The three critical points $x = -\frac{3}{4}$, $x = 0$, and $x = 2$ give the points $(-0.75, -3.25)$, $(0, 0)$, and $(2, -9.52)$ on the graph (using approximations where appropriate).

The first derivative test now shows local minima at $(-0.75, -3.25)$ and at $(2, -9.52)$; there is a local maximum at $(0, 0)$. Although $f'(0)$ does not exist, the function f is continuous everywhere (because it involves only positive powers of x).

We use the quadratic formula to find the x-intercepts. In addition to the origin, they occur where $x^2 - 2x - 6 = 0$, and thus they are located at $(1 - \sqrt{7}, 0)$ and at $(1 + \sqrt{7}, 0)$. We then plot the approximations $(-1.65, 0)$ and $(3.65, 0)$. Finally, we note that $f(x) \to +\infty$ as $x \to \pm\infty$. So the graph has the shape shown in Fig. 4.5.8. ◆

FIGURE 4.5.8 The technique is effective for nonpolynomial functions, as in Example 3.

Curve Sketching and Solution of Equations

An important application of curve-sketching techniques is the solution of an equation of the form

$$f(x) = 0. \tag{8}$$

The real (as opposed to complex) solutions of this equation are simply the x-intercepts of the graph of $y = f(x)$. Hence by sketching this graph with reasonable accuracy—either "by hand" or with a calculator or computer—we can glean information about the number of real solutions of Eq. (8) as well as their approximate locations.

For example, Figs. 4.5.9 through 4.5.11 show the graphs of the cubic polynomials on the left-hand sides of the equations

$$x^3 - 3x + 1 = 0, \tag{9}$$

$$x^3 - 3x + 2 = 0, \tag{10}$$

$$x^3 - 3x + 3 = 0. \tag{11}$$

Note that the polynomials differ only in their constant terms.

238 CHAPTER 4 Additional Applications of the Derivative

FIGURE 4.5.9 $y = x^3 - 3x + 1$.

FIGURE 4.5.10 $y = x^3 - 3x + 2$.

FIGURE 4.5.11 $y = x^3 - 3x + 3$.

It is clear from Fig. 4.5.9 that Eq. (9) has three real solutions, one in each of the intervals $[-2, -1]$, $[0, 1]$, and $[1, 2]$. These solutions could be approximated graphically by successive magnification or analytically by Newton's method. (As we have previously mentioned, there are even formulas—*Cardan's formulas*—for the exact solution of an arbitrary cubic equation, but they are unwieldy and are seldom used except in computer algebra programs. For example, these formulas yield (via a computer algebra system) the expressions

$$x_1 = \left(\frac{-1 + i\sqrt{3}}{2}\right)^{-1/3} + \left(\frac{-1 + i\sqrt{3}}{2}\right)^{1/3},$$

$$x_2 = \left(\frac{-1 + i\sqrt{3}}{2}\right)^{4/3} + \left(\frac{-1 + i\sqrt{3}}{2}\right)^{5/3}, \quad (12)$$

and

$$x_3 = \left(\frac{-1 + i\sqrt{3}}{2}\right)^{2/3} + \left(\frac{-1 + i\sqrt{3}}{2}\right)^{7/3}$$

for the three solutions of Eq. (9). Despite the appearance of the imaginary number $i = \sqrt{-1}$ in these three expressions, Fig. 4.5.9—with its three x-intercepts—indicates that all three solutions simplify to ordinary real numbers.)

It appears in Fig. 4.5.10 that Eq. (10) has the two real solutions $x = 1$ and $x = -2$. Once we verify that $x = 1$ is a solution, then it follows from the *factor theorem* of algebra that $x - 1$ is a factor of $x^3 - 3x + 2$. The other factor can be found by division (long or synthetic) of $x - 1$ into $x^3 - 3x + 2$; the quotient is $x^2 + x - 2$. Thus we see that

$$x^3 - 3x + 2 = (x - 1)(x^2 + x - 2) = (x - 1)^2(x + 2).$$

Hence $x = 1$ is a "double root" and $x = -2$ is a "single root" of Eq. (10), thereby accounting for the three solutions that a cubic equation "ought to have."

We see in Fig. 4.5.11 that Eq. (11) has only one real solution. It is given approximately by $x \approx -2.1038$. Problem 55 asks you to divide $x + 2.0138$ into $x^3 - 3x + 3$ to obtain a factorization of the form

$$x^3 - 3x + 3 \approx (x + 2.1038)(x^2 + bx + c). \quad (13)$$

The quadratic equation $x^2 + bx + c = 0$ has two complex conjugate solutions, which are the other two solutions of Eq. (12).

Calculator and Computer Graphing

With a graphing calculator or computer we may construct the graph of a given function with a few keystrokes. Nevertheless, the viewpoint of this section may be useful in analyzing and understanding what we see on the screen.

EXAMPLE 4 Figure 4.5.12 shows a computer-generated graph of the function

$$f(x) = x^4 - 5x^2 + x + 2. \tag{14}$$

Three critical points are visible, separating the x-axis into two intervals on which the function f increases and two on which it decreases. In order to find these critical points, we need to solve the cubic equation

$$f'(x) = 4x^3 - 10x + 1 = 0. \tag{15}$$

For this purpose we could graph the derivative $f'(x)$ and zoom in on its solutions, or use Newton's method to approximate these solutions accurately, or simply use the "solve" command on our calculator or computer. The approximate solutions of Eq. (15) thus found are -1.6289, 0.1004, and 1.5285. The corresponding numerical values of y obtained by substitution in Eq. (14) are -5.8554, 2.0501, and -2.6947. Thus the three critical points that we see on the graph in Fig. 4.5.12 are $(-1.6289, -5.8554)$, $(0.1004, 2.0501)$, and $(1.5285, -2.6947)$. The function f is decreasing on the intervals $-\infty < x < -1.6289$ and $0.1004 < x < 1.5285$ and increasing on the intervals $-1.6289 < x < 0.1004$ and $1.55285 < x < \infty$. ◆

FIGURE 4.5.12 $y = x^4 - 5x^2 + x + 2$.

4.5 TRUE/FALSE STUDY GUIDE

4.5 CONCEPTS: QUESTIONS AND DISCUSSION

1. Suppose that n is a positive integer and that k is an integer such that $0 \leq k \leq n$. Does there always exist a polynomial of degree n having exactly k real zeros? If not, what are the exceptions?

2. Suppose that $f(x)$ is a polynomial of degree n whose graph has p local minima and q local maxima. Explain why $p + q < n$. Discuss any other necessary restrictions on p and q. For instance, if $n = 4$ is it possible that $p = 3$ and $q = 0$? If $n = 5$ is it possible that $p = 3$ and $q = 1$? Justify your answers.

3. Someone asserts that "the graphs of any two nth-degree polynomials with the same term of highest degree look essentially the same when plotted in a sufficiently large viewing window." To what extent is this a reasonable claim? Begin by testing it with two quartic polynomials both having leading term x^4. Do you need to adjust the x-scale, the y-scale, or both, to make the graphs nearly coincide?

4.5 PROBLEMS

In Problems 1 through 4, use behavior "at infinity" to match the given function with its graph in Fig. 4.5.13.

FIGURE 4.5.13 Problems 1 through 4.

240 CHAPTER 4 Additional Applications of the Derivative

1. $f(x) = x^3 - 5x + 2$
2. $f(x) = x^4 - 3x^2 + x - 2$
3. $f(x) = -\frac{1}{3}x^5 - 3x^2 + 3x + 2$
4. $f(x) = -\frac{1}{3}x^6 + 2x^5 - 3x^4 + \frac{1}{2}x + 5$

In Problems 5 through 14 a function $y = f(x)$ and its computer-generated graph are given. Find both the critical points and the increasing/decreasing intervals for $f(x)$.

5. $y = 2x^2 - 10x - 7$ (Fig. 4.5.14)
6. $y = 27 + 12x - 4x^2$ (Fig. 4.5.15)

FIGURE 4.5.14 Problem 5.

FIGURE 4.5.15 Problem 6.

7. $y = 4x^3 - 3x^2 - 90x + 23$ (Fig. 4.5.16)
8. $y = 85 + 70x - 11x^2 - 4x^3$ (Fig. 4.5.17)

FIGURE 4.5.16 Problem 7.

FIGURE 4.5.17 Problem 8.

9. $y = 3x^4 + 4x^3 - 36x^2 + 40$ (Fig. 4.5.18)
10. $y = 125 + 120x^2 - 2x^3 - 9x^4$ (Fig. 4.5.19)

FIGURE 4.5.18 Problem 9.

FIGURE 4.5.19 Problem 10.

11. $y = 3x^5 - 100x^3 + 960x$ (Fig. 4.5.20)
12. $y = 2x^6 - 87x^4 + 600x^2 + 3000$ (Fig. 4.5.21)

FIGURE 4.5.20 Problem 11.

FIGURE 4.5.21 Problem 12.

13. $y = 3x^7 - 84x^5 + 448x^3$ (Fig. 4.5.22)
14. $y = 3x^8 - 52x^6 + 216x^4 - 500$ (Fig. 4.5.23)

FIGURE 4.5.22 Problem 13.

FIGURE 4.5.23 Problem 14.

In Problems 15 through 48, find the intervals on which the function f is increasing and those on which it is decreasing. Sketch the graph of $y = f(x)$ and label the local maxima and minima. Global extrema should be so identified.

15. $f(x) = 3x^2 - 6x + 5$
16. $f(x) = 5 - 8x - 2x^2$
17. $f(x) = x^3 - 12x$
18. $f(x) = x^3 + 3x$
19. $f(x) = x^3 - 6x^2 + 9x$
20. $f(x) = x^3 + 6x^2 + 9x$
21. $f(x) = x^3 + 3x^2 + 9x$
22. $f(x) = x^3 - 27x$
23. $f(x) = (x-1)^2(x+2)^2$
24. $f(x) = (x-2)^2(2x+3)^2$
25. $f(x) = 3\sqrt{x} - x\sqrt{x}$
26. $f(x) = x^{2/3}(5-x)$
27. $f(x) = 3x^5 - 5x^3$
28. $f(x) = x^4 + 4x^3$
29. $f(x) = x^4 - 8x^2 + 7$
30. $f(x) = \dfrac{1}{x}$
31. $f(x) = 2x^2 - 3x - 9$
32. $f(x) = 6 - 5x - 6x^2$
33. $f(x) = 2x^3 + 3x^2 - 12x$
34. $f(x) = x^3 + 4x$
35. $f(x) = 50x^3 - 105x^2 + 72x$
36. $f(x) = x^3 - 3x^2 + 3x - 1$
37. $f(x) = 3x^4 - 4x^3 - 12x^2 + 8$
38. $f(x) = x^4 - 2x^2 + 1$
39. $f(x) = 3x^5 - 20x^3$
40. $f(x) = 3x^5 - 25x^3 + 60x$
41. $f(x) = 2x^3 + 3x^2 + 6x$
42. $f(x) = x^4 - 4x^3$
43. $f(x) = 8x^4 - x^8$
44. $f(x) = 1 - x^{1/3}$
45. $f(x) = x^{1/3}(4-x)$
46. $f(x) = x^{2/3}(x^2 - 16)$
47. $f(x) = x(x-1)^{2/3}$
48. $f(x) = x^{1/3}(2-x)^{2/3}$

In Problems 49 through 54, the values of the function $f(x)$ at its critical points are given, together with the graph $y = f'(x)$ of its derivative. Use this information to construct a sketch of the graph $y = f(x)$ of the function.

49. $f(-3) = 78$, $f(2) = -47$; Fig. 4.5.24

50. $f(-2) = 106$, $f(4) = -110$; Fig. 4.5.25

FIGURE 4.5.24 $y = f'(x)$ of Problem 49.

FIGURE 4.5.25 $y = f'(x)$ of Problem 50.

51. $f(-3) = -66$, $f(2) = 59$; Fig. 4.5.26

52. $f(-3) = -130$, $f(0) = 5$, $f(1) = -2$; Fig. 4.5.27

FIGURE 4.5.26 $y = f'(x)$ of Problem 51.

FIGURE 4.5.27 $y = f'(x)$ of Problem 52.

53. $f(-2) = -107$, $f(1) = 82$, $f(3) = 18$; Fig. 4.5.28

54. $f(-3) = 5336$, $f(0) = 17$, $f(2) = 961$, $f(4) = -495$; Fig. 4.5.29

FIGURE 4.5.28 $y = f'(x)$ of Problem 53.

FIGURE 4.5.29 $y = f'(x)$ of Problem 54.

55. (a) Verify the approximate solution $x \approx -2.0138$ of Eq. (11). (b) Divide $x^3 - 3x + 3$ by $x + 2.1038$ to obtain the factorization in Eq. (13). (c) Use the quotient in part (b) to find (approximately) the complex conjugate pair of solutions of Eq. (11).

56. Explain why Figs. 4.5.9 and 4.5.10 imply that the cubic equation $x^3 - 3x + q = 0$ has exactly one real solution if $|q| > 2$ but has three distinct real solutions if $|q| < 2$. What is the situation if $q = -2$?

57. The computer-generated graph in Fig. 4.5.30 shows how the curve
$$y = [x(x-1)(2x-1)]^2$$
looks on any "reasonable" scale with integral units of measurement on the y-axis. Use the methods of this section to show that the graph really has the appearance shown in Fig. 4.5.31 (the values on the y-axis are in thousandths), with critical points at 0, $\frac{1}{2}$, $\frac{1}{6}(3 \pm \sqrt{3})$, and 1.

FIGURE 4.5.30 The graph $y = [x(x-1)(2x-1)]^2$ on a "reasonable scale" (Problem 57).

FIGURE 4.5.31 The graph $y = [x(x-1)(2x-1)]^2$ on a finer scale: $-0.005 \leq y \leq 0.005$ (Problem 57).

58. Use a computer algebra system to verify that the three expressions x_1, x_2, and x_3 in Eq. (12) are, indeed, distinct real solutions of Eq. (9).

Problems 59 and 60 require the use of a graphing calculator or computer algebra system. If you find it necessary to solve various equations, you may use either a graphing calculator or a "solve" command in a computer algebra system.

59. Show first that, on a "reasonable" scale with integral units of measurement on the y-axis, the graph of the polynomial
$$f(x) = \left[\tfrac{1}{6}x(9x-5)(x-1)\right]^4$$
strongly resembles the graph shown in Fig. 4.5.30, with a seemingly flat section. Then produce a plot that reveals the true structure of the graph, as in Fig. 4.5.31. Finally, find the approximate coordinates of the local maximum and minimum points on the graph.

60. This problem pertains to the plausible suggestion that two polynomials with essentially the same coefficients ought to have essentially the same roots. (a) Show, nevertheless, that the quartic equation
$$f(x) = x^4 - 55x^3 + 505x^2 + 11000x - 110000 = 0$$
has four distinct real solutions, whereas the "similar" equation
$$g(x) = x^4 - 55x^3 + 506x^2 + 11000x - 110000 = 0$$
has only two distinct real solutions (and two complex conjugate solutions). (b) Let $h(x) = f(x) + \epsilon x^2$. Note that if $\epsilon = 0$ then $h(x) = f(x)$, and if $\epsilon = 1$ then $h(x) = g(x)$. Investigate the question of *where*—between $\epsilon = 0$ and $\epsilon = 1$—the transition from four real solutions of $h(x) = 0$ to only two real solutions takes place.

4.6 HIGHER DERIVATIVES AND CONCAVITY

We saw in Section 4.3 that the sign of the first derivative f' of a differentiable function f indicates whether the graph of f is rising or falling. Here we shall see that the sign of the *second* derivative of f, the derivative of f', indicates which way the curve $y = f(x)$ is *bending*, upward or downward.

Higher Derivatives

The **second derivative** of f is the derivative of f'; it is denoted by f'', and its value at x is

$$f''(x) = D_x(f'(x)) = D_x(D_x f(x)) = D_x^2 f(x).$$

(The superscript 2 is not an exponent but only an indication that the operator D_x is to be applied twice.) The derivative of f'' is the **third derivative** f''' of f, and

$$f'''(x) = D_x(f''(x)) = D_x\left(D_x^2 f(x)\right) = D_x^3 f(x).$$

The third derivative is also denoted by $f^{(3)}$. More generally, the result of beginning with the function f and differentiating n times is succession is the **nth derivative** $f^{(n)}$ of f, with $f^{(n)}(x) = D_x^n f(x)$.

If $y = f(x)$, then the first n derivatives are written in operator notation as

$$D_x y, \quad D_x^2 y, \quad D_x^3 y, \quad \ldots, \quad D_x^n y,$$

in function notation as

$$y'(x), \quad y''(x), \quad y'''(x), \quad \ldots, \quad y^{(n)}(x),$$

and in differential notation as

$$\frac{dy}{dx}, \quad \frac{d^2 y}{dx^2}, \quad \frac{d^3 y}{dx^3}, \quad \ldots, \quad \frac{d^n y}{dx^n}.$$

The history of the curious use of superscripts in differential notation for higher derivatives involves the metamorphosis

$$\frac{d}{dx}\left(\frac{dy}{dx}\right) \to \frac{d}{dx}\frac{dy}{dx} \to \frac{(d)^2 y}{(dx)^2} \to \frac{d^2 y}{dx^2}.$$

EXAMPLE 1 Find the first four derivatives of

$$f(x) = 2x^3 + \frac{1}{x^2} + 16x^{7/2}.$$

Solution Write

$$f(x) = 2x^3 + x^{-2} + 16x^{7/2}.$$

Then

$$f'(x) = 6x^2 - 2x^{-3} + 56x^{5/2} = 6x^2 - \frac{2}{x^3} + 56x^{5/2},$$

$$f''(x) = 12x + 6x^{-4} + 140x^{3/2} = 12x + \frac{6}{x^4} + 140x^{3/2},$$

$$f'''(x) = 12 - 24x^{-5} + 210x^{1/2} = 12 - \frac{24}{x^5} + 210\sqrt{x},$$

and

$$f^{(4)}(x) = 120x^{-6} + 105x^{-1/2} = \frac{120}{x^6} + \frac{105}{\sqrt{x}}.$$
◆

Example 2 shows how to find higher derivatives of implicitly defined functions.

EXAMPLE 2 Find the second derivative $y''(x)$ of a function $y(x)$ that is defined implicitly by the equation

$$x^2 - xy + y^2 = 9.$$

Solution A first implicit differentiation of the given equation *with respect to x* gives

$$2x - y - x\frac{dy}{dx} + 2y\frac{dy}{dx} = 0,$$

so

$$\frac{dy}{dx} = \frac{y - 2x}{2y - x}.$$

We obtain d^2y/dx^2 by differentiating implicitly, again with respect to x, using the quotient rule. After that, we substitute the expression we just found for dy/dx:

$$\frac{d^2y}{dx^2} = D_x\left(\frac{y-2x}{2y-x}\right) = \frac{\left(\frac{dy}{dx} - 2\right)(2y-x) - (y-2x)\left(2\frac{dy}{dx} - 1\right)}{(2y-x)^2}$$

$$= \frac{3x\frac{dy}{dx} - 3y}{(2y-x)^2} = \frac{3x\frac{y-2x}{2y-x} - 3y}{(2y-x)^2}.$$

Thus

$$\frac{d^2y}{dx^2} = -\frac{6(x^2 - xy + y^2)}{(2y-x)^3}.$$

We now substitute the original equation, $x^2 - xy + y^2 = 9$, for one final simplification:

$$\frac{d^2y}{dx^2} = -\frac{54}{(2y-x)^3}.$$

The somewhat unexpected final simplification is always available when the original equation is symmetric in x and y. ◆

The Sign of the Second Derivative

Now we shall investigate the significance of the *sign* of the second derivative. If $f''(x) > 0$ on the interval I, then the first derivative f' is an increasing function on I, because *its* derivative $f''(x)$ is positive. Thus, as we scan the graph $y = f(x)$ from left to right, we see the tangent line turning counterclockwise (Fig. 4.6.1). We describe this situation by saying that the curve $y = f(x)$ is **bending upward.** Note that a curve can bend upward without rising, as in Fig. 4.6.2.

FIGURE 4.6.1 The graph is bending upward.

FIGURE 4.6.2 Another graph bending upward.

FIGURE 4.6.3 A graph bending downward.

FIGURE 4.6.4 Another graph bending downward.

$f''(x)$	$y = f(x)$
Negative	Bending downward
Positive	Bending upward

FIGURE 4.6.5 Significance of the sign of $f''(x)$ on an interval.

If $f''(x) < 0$ on the interval I, then the first derivative f' is decreasing on I, so the tangent line turns clockwise as x increases. We say in this case that the curve $y = f(x)$ is **bending downward.** Figures 4.6.3 and 4.6.4 show two ways this can happen.

The two cases are summarized in the brief table in Fig. 4.6.5.

EXAMPLE 3 Figure 4.6.6 shows the graph of the function

$$f(x) = x^3 - 3x^2 + 3.$$

Because

$$f'(x) = 3x^2 - 6x \quad \text{and} \quad f''(x) = 6x - 6 = 6(x - 1),$$

we see that

$$\begin{aligned} f''(x) &< 0 \quad \text{for} \quad x < 1, \\ f''(x) &> 0 \quad \text{for} \quad x > 1. \end{aligned}$$

Observe in the figure that the curve bends downward on $(-\infty, 1)$ but bends upward on $(1, +\infty)$, consistent with the correspondences in Fig. 4.6.5. ◆

FIGURE 4.6.6 The graph of $y = x^3 - 3x^2 + 3$ (Example 3).

The Second Derivative Test

We know from Section 3.5 that a local extremum of a differentiable function f can occur only at a critical point where $f'(c) = 0$, so the tangent line at the point $(c, f(c))$ on the curve $y = f(x)$ is horizontal. But the example $f(x) = x^3$, for which $x = 0$ is a critical point but not an extremum (Fig. 4.6.7), shows that the *necessary condition* $f'(c) = 0$ is *not* a sufficient condition from which to conclude that $f(c)$ is an extreme value of the function f.

Now suppose not only that $f'(c) = 0$, but also that the curve $y = f(x)$ is bending upward on some open interval that contains the critical point $x = c$. It is apparent from Fig. 4.6.8(a) that $f(c)$ is a local minimum value. Similarly, $f(c)$ is a local maximum value if $f'(c) = 0$ while $y = f(x)$ is bending downward on some open interval containing c [Fig. 4.6.8(b)]. But the *sign* of the second derivative $f''(x)$ tells us whether $y = f(x)$ is bending upward or downward and therefore provides us with a *sufficient* condition for a local extremum.

FIGURE 4.6.7 Although $f'(0) = 0$, $f(0)$ is not an extremum.

THEOREM 1 Second Derivative Test

Suppose that the function f is twice differentiable on the open interval I containing the critical point c at which $f'(c) = 0$. Then

1. If $f''(x) > 0$ on I, then $f(c)$ is the minimum value of $f(x)$ on I.
2. If $f''(x) < 0$ on I, then $f(c)$ is the maximum value of $f(x)$ on I.

PROOF We will prove only part 1. If $f''(x) > 0$ on I, then it follows that the first derivative f' is an increasing function on I. Because $f'(c) = 0$, we may conclude

FIGURE 4.6.8 The second derivative test (Theorem 1). (a) $f''(x) > 0$: tangent turning counterclockwise; graph bending upward; local minimum at $x = c$.
(b) $f''(x) < 0$: tangent turning clockwise; graph bending downward; local maximum at $x = c$.

that $f'(x) < 0$ for $x < c$ in I and that $f'(x) > 0$ for $x > c$ in I. Consequently, the first derivative test of Section 4.4 implies that $f(c)$ is the minimum value of $f(x)$ on I. ◂

$f''(x)$	$f(c)$
Positive	Minimum
Negative	Maximum

FIGURE 4.6.9 Significance of the sign of $f''(x)$ on an interval containing the critical point c.

REMARK 1 Rather than memorizing verbatim the conditions in parts 1 and 2 of Theorem 1 (summarized in Fig. 4.6.9), it is easier and more reliable to remember the second derivative test by visualizing continuously turning tangent lines (Fig. 4.6.8).

REMARK 2 Theorem 1 implies that the function f has a local minimum at the critical point c if $f''(x) > 0$ on some open interval about c but a local maximum if $f''(x) < 0$ near c. But the hypothesis on $f''(x)$ in Theorem 1 is *global* in that $f''(x)$ is assumed to have the same sign at *every* point of the open interval I that contains the critical point c. There is a strictly *local* version of the second derivative test that involves only the sign of $f''(c)$ at the critical point c (rather than on a whole open interval). According to Problem 90, if $f'(c) = 0$, then $f(c)$ is a local minimum value of f if $f''(c) > 0$ but a local maximum if $f''(c) < 0$.

REMARK 3 The second derivative test says *nothing* about what happens if $f''(c) = 0$ at the critical point c. Consider the three functions $f(x) = x^4$, $f(x) = -x^4$, and $f(x) = x^3$. For each, $f'(0) = 0$ and $f''(0) = 0$. But their graphs, shown in Fig. 4.6.10, demonstrate that *anything* can happen at such a point—maximum, minimum, or neither.

REMARK 4 Suppose that we want to maximize or minimize the function f on the open interval I, and we find that f has only one critical point in I, a number c at which $f'(c) = 0$. If $f''(x)$ has the same sign at all points of I, then Theorem 1 implies that $f(c)$ is an absolute extremum of f on I—a minimum if $f''(x) > 0$ and a maximum if $f''(x) < 0$. This absolute interpretation of the second derivative test can be useful in applied open-interval maximum-minimum problems.

EXAMPLE 3 (continued) Consider again the function $f(x) = x^3 - 3x^2 + 3$, for which

$$f'(x) = 3x(x-2) \quad \text{and} \quad f''(x) = 6(x-1).$$

FIGURE 4.6.10 No conclusion is possible if $f'(c) = 0 = f''(c)$.

Then f has the two critical points $x = 0$ and $x = 2$, as marked in Fig. 4.6.6. Because $f''(x) < 0$ for x near zero, the second derivative test implies that $f(0) = 3$ is a local maximum value of f. And because $f''(x) > 0$ for x near 2, it follows that $f(2) = -1$ is a local minimum value. ◆

FIGURE 4.6.11 The open-topped box of Example 4.

EXAMPLE 4 An open-topped rectangular box with square base has volume 500 cm^3. Find the dimensions that minimize the total area A of its base and four sides.

Solution We denote by x the edge length of the square base and by y the height of the box (Fig. 4.6.11). The volume of the box is

$$V = x^2 y = 500, \tag{1}$$

and the total area of its base and four sides is

$$A = x^2 + 4xy. \tag{2}$$

When we solve Eq. (1) for $y = 500/x^2$ and substitute this into Eq. (2), we get the area function

$$A(x) = x^2 + \frac{2000}{x}, \quad 0 < x < +\infty.$$

The domain of A is the open and unbounded interval $(0, +\infty)$ because x can take on any positive value; to make the box volume 500, simply choose $y = 500/x^2$. But x cannot be zero or negative.

The first derivative of $A(x)$ is

$$A'(x) = 2x - \frac{2000}{x^2} = \frac{2(x^3 - 1000)}{x^2}. \tag{3}$$

The equation $A'(x) = 0$ yields $x^3 = 1000$, so the only critical point of A in $(0, +\infty)$ is $x = 10$. To investigate this critical point, we calculate the second derivative,

$$A''(x) = 2 + \frac{4000}{x^3}. \tag{4}$$

Because it is clear that $A''(x) > 0$ on $(0, +\infty)$, it follows from the second derivative test and Remark 4 that $A(10) = 300$ is the absolute minimum value of $A(x)$ on $(0, +\infty)$. Finally, because $y = 500/x^2$, $y = 5$ when $x = 10$. Therefore, this absolute minimum corresponds to a box with base 10 cm by 10 cm and height 5 cm. ◆

Concavity and Inflection Points

A comparison of Fig. 4.6.1 with Fig. 4.6.3 suggests that the question of whether the curve $y = f(x)$ is bending upward or downward is closely related to the question of whether it lies above or below its tangent lines. The latter question refers to the important property of *concavity*.

DEFINITION Concavity

Suppose that the function f is differentiable at the point a and that L is the line tangent to the graph $y = f(x)$ at the point $(a, f(a))$. Then the function f (or its graph) is said to be

1. **Concave upward** at a if, on some open interval containing a, the graph of f lies *above* L.
2. **Concave downward** at a if, on some open interval containing a, the graph of f lies *below* L.

Figure 4.6.12(a) shows a graph that is concave upward at $(a, f(a))$. Figure 4.6.12(b) shows a graph that is concave downward at $(a, f(a))$.

Theorem 2 establishes the connection between concavity and the sign of the second derivative. That connection is the one suggested by our discussion of bending.

FIGURE 4.6.12 (a) At $x = a$, f is a concave upward. (b) At $x = a$, f is concave downward.

THEOREM 2   Test for Concavity
Suppose that the function f is twice differentiable on the open interval I.

1. If $f''(x) > 0$ on I, then f is concave upward at each point of I.
2. If $f''(x) < 0$ on I, then f is concave downward at each point of I.

A proof of Theorem 2 based on the second derivative test is given at the end of this section.

Note   The significance of the sign of the *first* derivative must not be confused with the significance of the sign of the *second* derivative. The possibilities illustrated in Figs. 4.6.13 through 4.6.16 show that the signs of f' and f'' are independent of each other.

FIGURE 4.6.13 $f'(x) > 0$, f increasing; $f''(x) > 0$, f concave upward.

FIGURE 4.6.14 $f'(x) > 0$, f increasing; $f''(x) < 0$; f concave downward.

FIGURE 4.6.15 $f'(x) < 0$, f decreasing; $f''(x) > 0$, f concave upward.

FIGURE 4.6.16 $f'(x) < 0$, f decreasing; $f''(x) < 0$, f concave downward.

248 CHAPTER 4 Additional Applications of the Derivative

EXAMPLE 3 (continued again) For the function $f(x) = x^3 - 3x + 3$, the second derivative changes sign from positive to negative at the point $x = 1$. Observe in Fig. 4.6.6 that the corresponding point $(1, 1)$ on the graph of f is where the curve changes from bending downward to bending upward. ◆

Observe that the test for concavity in Theorem 2 says nothing about the case in which $f''(x) = 0$. A point where the second derivative is zero *may or may not* be a point where the function changes from concave upward on one side to concave downward on the other. But a point like $(1, 1)$ in Fig. 4.6.6, where the concavity *does* change in this manner, is called an *inflection point* of the graph of f. More precisely, the point $x = a$ where f is continuous is an **inflection point** of the function f provided that f is concave upward on one side of $x = a$ and concave downward on the other side. We also refer to $(a, f(a))$ as an inflection point on the graph of f.

THEOREM 3 Inflection Point Test
Suppose that the function f is continuous and f'' exists on an open interval containing the point a. Then a is an inflection point of f provided that $f''(x) < 0$ on one side of a and $f''(x) > 0$ on the other side.

The fact that a point where the second derivative changes sign is an inflection point follows from Theorem 2 and the definition of an inflection point.

REMARK At the inflection point itself, either

- $f''(a) = 0$, or
- $f''(a)$ does not exist.

Thus we find *inflection points* of f by examining the *critical points* of f'. Some of the possibilities are indicated in Fig. 4.6.17. We mark the intervals of upward concavity and downward concavity by small cups opening upward and downward, respectively.

FIGURE 4.6.17 Some inflection points.

EXAMPLE 5 Figure 4.6.18 shows the graph of $f(x) = \sin^2 x$ on $[0, \pi]$. Two evident inflection points are marked. Find their coordinates.

Solution We calculate

$$f'(x) = 2 \sin x \cos x$$

and

$$f''(x) = 2\cos^2 x - 2\sin^2 x = 2\cos 2x.$$

Then

$$f''(x) = 2\cos 2x = 0$$

FIGURE 4.6.18 $y = \sin^2 x$ (Example 5).

at $x = \pi/4$ and at $x = 3\pi/4$ in the interval $[0, \pi]$. Now

$$f''(x) = 2\cos 2x > 0 \quad \text{if} \quad 0 < x < \frac{\pi}{4}, \quad \text{so} \quad 0 < 2x < \frac{\pi}{2};$$

$$f''(x) = 2\cos 2x < 0 \quad \text{if} \quad \frac{\pi}{4} < x < \frac{3\pi}{4}, \quad \text{so} \quad \frac{\pi}{2} < 2x < \frac{3\pi}{2};$$

$$f''(x) = 2\cos 2x > 0 \quad \text{if} \quad \frac{3\pi}{4} < x < \pi, \quad \text{so} \quad \frac{3\pi}{2} < 2x < \pi.$$

It follows that $f(x) = \sin^2 x$ has inflection points at $x = \pi/4$ and $x = 3\pi 4$. The corresponding points marked on the graph in Fig. 4.6.18 are $(\pi/4, 1/2)$ and $(3\pi 4, 1/2)$. ◆

Inflection Points and Curve Sketching

Let the function f be twice differentiable for all x. Just as the critical points where $f'(x) = 0$ separate the x-axis into open intervals on which $f'(x)$ does not change sign, the *possible* inflection points where $f''(x) = 0$ separate the x-axis into open intervals on which $f''(x)$ does not change sign. On each of these intervals, the curve $y = f(x)$ either is bending downward $[f''(x) < 0]$ or is bending upward $[f''(x) > 0]$. We can determine the sign of $f''(x)$ in each of these intervals in either of two ways:

1. Evaluation of $f''(x)$ at a typical point of each interval. The sign of $f''(x)$ at that particular point is the sign of $f''(x)$ throughout the interval.
2. Construction of a table of signs of the factors of $f''(x)$. Then the sign of $f''(x)$ on each interval can be deduced from the table.

These are the same two methods we used in Sections 4.4 and 4.5 to determine the sign of $f'(x)$. We use the first method in Example 6 and the second in Example 7.

EXAMPLE 6 Sketch the graph of $f(x) = 8x^5 - 5x^4 - 20x^3$, indicating local extrema, inflection points, and concave structure.

Solution We sketched this curve in Example 2 of Section 4.5; see Fig. 4.5.6 for the graph. In that example we found the first derivative to be

$$f'(x) = 40x^4 - 20x^3 - 60x^2 = 20x^2(x+1)(2x-3),$$

so the critical points are $x = -1$, $x = 0$, and $x = \frac{3}{2}$. The second derivative is

$$f''(x) = 160x^3 - 60x^2 - 120x = 20x(8x^2 - 3x - 6).$$

When we compute $f''(x)$ at each critical point, we find that

$$f''(-1) = -100 < 0, \quad f''(0) = 0, \quad \text{and} \quad f''\left(\tfrac{3}{2}\right) = 225 > 0.$$

Continuity of f'' ensures that $f''(x) < 0$ near the critical point $x = -1$ and that $f''(x) > 0$ near the critical point $x = \frac{3}{2}$. The second derivative test therefore tells us that f has a local maximum at $x = -1$ and a local minimum at $x = \frac{3}{2}$. We cannot determine from the second derivative test the behavior of f at $x = 0$.

Because $f''(x)$ exists everywhere, the possible inflection points are the solutions of the equation

$$f''(x) = 0; \quad \text{that is,} \quad 20x(8x^2 - 3x - 6) = 0.$$

Clearly, one solution is $x = 0$. To find the other two, we use the quadratic formula to solve the equation

$$8x^2 - 3x - 6 = 0.$$

This gives

$$x = \tfrac{1}{16}\left(3 \pm \sqrt{201}\right),$$

so $x \approx 1.07$ and $x \approx -0.70$ are possible inflection points along with $x = 0$.

250 CHAPTER 4 Additional Applications of the Derivative

$x = -0.70$	$x = 0$	$x = 1.07$
$f''(x) < 0$	$f''(x) > 0$	$f''(x) < 0$	$f''(x) > 0$
Bending down	Bending up	Bending down	Bending up

FIGURE 4.6.19 Intervals of concavity of Example 6.

These three possible inflection points separate the x-axis into the intervals indicated in Fig. 4.6.19. We check the sign of $f''(x)$ on each.

On $(-\infty, -0.70)$: $f''(-1) = -100 < 0$; f is concave downward;
On $(-0.70, 0)$: $f''\left(-\frac{1}{2}\right) = 25 > 0$; f is concave upward;
On $(0, 1.07)$: $f''(1) = -20 < 0$; f is concave downward;
On $(1.07, +\infty)$: $f''(2) = 800 > 0$; f is concave upward.

Thus we see that the direction of concavity of f changes at each of the three points $x \approx -0.70$, $x = 0$, and $x \approx 1.07$. These three points are indeed inflection points. This information is shown in the graph of f sketched in Fig 4.6.20. ◆

FIGURE 4.6.20 The graph of the function of Example 6.

Graph of $y = 8x^5 - 5x^4 - 20x^3$ showing:
- Local maximum $(-1, 7)$
- Horizontal tangent, inflection point $(0, 0)$
- $(1.92, 0)$
- $(-1.3, 0)$
- Inflection point $(-0.70, 4.30)$
- Inflection point $(1.07, -19.98)$
- Local minimum $(1.5, -32.06)$

EXAMPLE 7 Sketch the graph of $f(x) = 4x^{1/3} + x^{4/3}$. Indicate local extrema, inflection points, and concave structure.

Solution First,

$$f'(x) = \frac{4}{3}x^{-2/3} + \frac{4}{3}x^{1/3} = \frac{4(x+1)}{3x^{2/3}},$$

so the critical points are $x = -1$ (where the tangent line is horizontal) and $x = 0$ (where it is vertical). Next,

$$f''(x) = -\frac{8}{9}x^{-5/3} + \frac{4}{9}x^{-2/3} = \frac{4(x-2)}{9x^{5/3}},$$

so the possible inflection points are $x = 2$ (where $f''(x) = 0$) and $x = 0$ (where $f''(x)$ does not exist).

Higher Derivatives and Concavity SECTION 4.6   251

To determine where f is increasing and where it is decreasing, we construct the following table.

Interval	$x+1$	$x^{2/3}$	$f'(x)$	f
$(-\infty, -1)$	−	+	−	Decreasing
$(-1, 0)$	+	+	+	Increasing
$(0, +\infty)$	+	+	+	Increasing

Thus f is decreasing when $x = -1$ and increasing when $x > -1$ (Fig. 4.6.21(a)).

FIGURE 4.6.21 (a) Increasing and decreasing intervals of Example 7. (b) Intervals of concavity of Example 7.

To determine the concavity of f, we construct a table to find the sign of $f''(x)$ on each of the intervals separated by its zeros.

Interval	$x^{5/3}$	$x-2$	$f''(x)$	f
$(-\infty, 0)$	−	−	+	Concave upward
$(0, 2)$	+	−	−	Concave downward
$(2, +\infty)$	+	+	+	Concave upward

The table shows that f is concave downward on $(0, 2)$ and concave upward for $x < 0$ and for $x > 2$ (Fig. 4.6.21(b)).

We note that $f(x) \to +\infty$ as $x \to \pm\infty$, and we mark with plus signs the intervals on the x-axis where f is increasing, minus signs where it is decreasing, cups opening upward where f is concave upward, and cups opening downward where f is concave downward. We plot (at least approximately) the points on the graph of f that correspond to the zeros and discontinuities of f' and f''; these are $(-1, -3)$, $(0, 0)$, and $(2, 6\sqrt[3]{2})$. Finally, we use all this information to draw the smooth curve shown in Fig. 4.6.22. ◆

FIGURE 4.6.22 The graph of the function of Example 7.

FIGURE 4.6.23 The ellipse $x^2 - xy + y^2 = 9$ is concave downward at points above the line $y = \frac{1}{2}x$, concave upward at points beneath it.

EXAMPLE 8 The graph of the equation $x^2 - xy + y^2 = 9$ is the rotated ellipse shown in Fig. 4.6.23. In Example 2 we saw that if the function $y(x)$ is implicitly defined by this equation, then

$$\frac{dy}{dx} = \frac{y - 2x}{2y - x}.$$

Hence $y = 2x$ at any critical point (x, y) at which $y'(x) = 0$. Substituting $y = 2x$ into the equation $x^2 - xy + y^2 = 9$ readily gives the two points $(\sqrt{3}, 2\sqrt{3})$ and $(-\sqrt{3}, -2\sqrt{3})$ that are marked in Fig. 4.6.23. We also saw that

$$\frac{d^2y}{dx^2} = -\frac{54}{(2y - x)^3}.$$

It follows that $y''(x) < 0$ when $2y - x > 0$, so the graph is concave downward at any point (x, y) at which $2y > x$; that is, at points above the line $y = \frac{1}{2}x$. Similarly, $y''(x) > 0$ when $2y - x < 0$, so the graph is concave upward at any point (x, y) at which $2y < x$; that is, at points below the line $y = \frac{1}{2}x$. (See Fig. 4.6.23.) ◆

PROOF OF THEOREM 2 We will prove only part 1—the proof of part 2 is similar. Given a fixed point a of the open interval I where $f''(x) > 0$, we want to show that the graph $y = f(x)$ lies above the tangent line at $(a, f(a))$. The tangent line in question has the equation

$$y = T(x) = f(a) + f'(a) \cdot (x - a). \tag{5}$$

Consider the auxiliary function

$$g(x) = f(x) - T(x) \tag{6}$$

illustrated in Fig. 4.6.24. Note first that $g(a) = g'(a) = 0$, so $x = a$ is a critical point of g. Moreover, Eq. (5) implies that $T'(x) \equiv f'(a)$ and that $T''(x) \equiv 0$, so

$$g''(x) = f''(x) - T''(x) = f''(x) > 0$$

at each point of I. Therefore, the second derivative test implies that $g(a) = 0$ is the minimum value of $g(x) = f(x) - T(x)$ on I. It follows that the curve $y = f(x)$ lies above the tangent line $y = T(x)$. ◂

FIGURE 4.6.24 Illustrating the proof of Theorem 2.

4.6 TRUE/FALSE STUDY GUIDE

4.6 CONCEPTS: QUESTIONS AND DISCUSSION

1. Suppose that the function f is differentiable at the point $x = c$ where $f''(c) = 0$. Does it necessarily follow that the point $(c, f(c))$ is an inflection point of the graph of $y = f(x)$?
2. Suppose that the function f is differentiable except at the point $x = c$ where the graph of $y = f(x)$ has a vertical tangent line. Does it necessarily follow that the point $(c, f(c))$ is an inflection point of the graph of $y = f(x)$?
3. Suppose that n is a positive integer and that k is an integer such that $0 \leq k \leq n - 2$. Does there always exist a polynomial of degree n having exactly k inflection points? Justify your answer.
4. Can the graph of a function have more inflection points than critical points? Justify your answer.

4.6 PROBLEMS

Calculate the first three derivatives of the functions given in Problems 1 through 15.

1. $f(x) = 2x^4 - 3x^3 + 6x - 17$
2. $f(x) = 2x^5 + x^{3/2} - \dfrac{1}{2x}$
3. $f(x) = \dfrac{2}{(2x-1)^2}$
4. $g(t) = t^2 + \sqrt{t+1}$
5. $g(t) = (3t-2)^{4/3}$
6. $f(x) = x\sqrt{x+1}$
7. $h(y) = \dfrac{y}{y+1}$
8. $f(x) = \left(1 + \sqrt{x}\right)^3$
9. $g(t) = \dfrac{1}{2\sqrt{t}}$
10. $h(z) = \dfrac{z^2}{z^2 + 4}$
11. $f(x) = \sin 3x$
12. $f(x) = \cos^2 2x$
13. $f(x) = \sin x \cos x$
14. $f(x) = x^2 \cos x$
15. $f(x) = \dfrac{\sin x}{x}$

In Problems 16 through 22, calculate dy/dx and d^2y/dx^2, assuming that y is defined implicitly as a function of x by the given equation.

16. $x^2 + y^2 = 4$
17. $x^2 + xy + y^2 = 3$
18. $x^{1/3} + y^{1/3} = 1$
19. $y^3 + x^2 + x = 5$
20. $\dfrac{1}{x} + \dfrac{1}{y} = 1$
21. $\sin y = xy$
22. $\sin^2 x + \cos^2 y = 1$

In Problems 23 through 30, find the exact coordinates of the inflection points and critical points marked on the given graph.

23. The graph of $f(x) = x^3 - 3x^2 - 45x$ (Fig. 4.6.25)
24. The graph of $f(x) = 2x^3 - 9x^2 - 108x + 200$ (Fig. 4.6.26)

FIGURE 4.6.25 The graph of $f(x) = x^3 - 3x^2 - 45x$ (Problem 23).

FIGURE 4.6.26 The graph of $f(x) = 2x^3 - 9x^2 - 108x + 200$ (Problem 24).

25. The graph of $f(x) = 4x^3 - 6x^2 - 189x + 137$ (Fig. 4.6.27)
26. The graph of $f(x) = -40x^3 - 171x^2 + 2550x + 4150$ (Fig. 4.6.28)

FIGURE 4.6.27 The graph of $f(x) = 4x^3 - 6x^2 - 189x + 137$ (Problem 25).

FIGURE 4.6.28 The graph of $f(x) = -40x^3 - 171x^2 + 2550x + 4150$ (Problem 26).

27. The graph of $f(x) = x^4 - 54x^2 + 237$ (Fig. 4.6.29)
28. The graph of $f(x) = x^4 - 10x^3 - 250$ (Fig. 4.6.30)

FIGURE 4.6.29 The graph of $f(x) = x^4 - 54x^2 - 237$ (Problem 27).

FIGURE 4.6.30 The graph of $f(x) = x^4 - 10x^3 - 250$ (Problem 28).

29. The graph of $f(x) = 3x^5 - 20x^4 + 1000$ (Fig. 4.6.31)
30. The graph of $f(x) = 3x^5 - 160x^3$ (Fig. 4.6.32)

FIGURE 4.6.31 The graph of $f(x) = 3x^5 - 20x^4 + 1000$ (Problem 29).

FIGURE 4.6.32 The graph of $f(x) = 3x^5 - 160x^3$ (Problem 30).

Apply the second derivative test to find the local maxima and local minima of the functions given in Problems 31 through 50, and apply the inflection point test to find all inflection points.

31. $f(x) = x^2 - 4x + 3$
32. $f(x) = 5 - 6x - x^2$
33. $f(x) = x^3 - 3x + 1$

34. $f(x) = x^3 - 3x^2$
35. $f(x) = x^3$
36. $f(x) = x^4$
37. $f(x) = x^5 + 2x$
38. $f(x) = x^4 - 8x^2$
39. $f(x) = x^2(x-1)^2$
40. $f(x) = x^3(x+2)^2$
41. $f(x) = \sin x$ on $(0, 2\pi)$
42. $f(x) = \cos x$ on $(-\pi/2, \pi/2)$
43. $f(x) = \tan x$ on $(-\pi/2, \pi/2)$
44. $f(x) = \sec x$ on $(-\pi/2, \pi/2)$
45. $f(x) = \cos^2 x$ on $(-\pi/2, 3\pi/2)$
46. $f(x) = \sin^3 x$ on $(-\pi, \pi)$
47. $f(x) = \sin x + \cos x$ on $(0, 2\pi)$
48. $f(x) = \cos x - \sin x$ on $(0, 2\pi)$
49. $f(x) = \sin x + 2\cos x$ on $(0, 2\pi)$
50. $f(x) = 3\sin x - 4\cos x$ on $(0, 2\pi)$

In Problems 51 through 62, rework the indicated problem from Section 4.4, now using the second derivative test to verify that you have found the desired absolute maximum or minimum value.

51. Problem 27
52. Problem 28
53. Problem 29
54. Problem 30
55. Problem 31
56. Problem 32
57. Problem 33
58. Problem 36
59. Problem 37
60. Problem 38
61. Problem 39
62. Problem 40

Sketch the graphs of the functions in Problems 63 through 76, indicating all critical points and inflection points. Apply the second derivative test at each critical point. Show the correct concave structure and indicate the behavior of $f(x)$ as $x \to \pm\infty$.

63. $f(x) = 2x^3 - 3x^2 - 12x + 3$
64. $f(x) = 3x^4 - 4x^3 - 5$
65. $f(x) = 6 + 8x^2 - x^4$
66. $f(x) = 3x^5 - 5x^3$
67. $f(x) = 3x^4 - 4x^3 - 12x^2 - 1$
68. $f(x) = 3x^5 - 25x^3 + 60x$
69. $f(x) = x^3(x-1)^4$
70. $f(x) = (x-1)^2(x+2)^3$
71. $f(x) = 1 + x^{1/3}$
72. $f(x) = 2 - (x-3)^{1/3}$
73. $f(x) = (x+3)\sqrt{x}$
74. $f(x) = x^{2/3}(5 - 2x)$
75. $f(x) = (4-x)\sqrt[3]{x}$
76. $f(x) = x^{1/3}(6-x)^{2/3}$

In Problems 77 through 82, the graph of a function $f(x)$ is shown. Match it with the graph of its second derivative $f''(x)$ in Fig. 4.6.33.

FIGURE 4.6.33

77. See Fig. 4.6.34.
78. See Fig. 4.6.35.

FIGURE 4.6.34

FIGURE 4.6.35

79. See Fig. 4.6.36.
80. See Fig. 4.6.37.

FIGURE 4.6.36

FIGURE 4.6.37

81. See Fig. 4.6.38.

82. See Fig. 4.6.39.

FIGURE 4.6.38

FIGURE 4.6.39

83. (a) Show first that the nth derivative of $f(x) = x^n$ is
$$f^{(n)}(x) \equiv n! = n \cdot (n-1) \cdot (n-2) \cdots 3 \cdot 2 \cdot 1.$$
(b) Conclude that if $f(x)$ is a polynomial of degree n, then $f^{(k)}(x) \equiv 0$ if $k > n$.

84. (a) Calculate the first four derivatives of $f(x) = \sin x$. (b) Explain why it follows that $D_x^{n+4} \sin x = D_x^n \sin x$ if n is a positive integer.

85. Suppose that $z = g(y)$ and that $y = f(x)$. Show that
$$\frac{d^2z}{dx^2} = \frac{d^2z}{dy^2}\left(\frac{dy}{dx}\right)^2 + \frac{dz}{dy} \cdot \frac{d^2y}{dx^2}.$$

86. Prove that the graph of a quadratic polynomial has no inflection points.

87. Prove that the graph of a cubic polynomial has exactly one inflection point.

88. Prove that the graph of a polynomial function of degree 4 has either no inflection point or exactly two inflection points.

89. Suppose that the pressure p (in atmospheres), volume V (in cubic centimeters), and temperature T (in kelvins) of n moles of carbon dioxide (CO_2) satisfy van der Waals' equation
$$\left(p + \frac{n^2 a}{V^2}\right)(V - nb) = nRT,$$
where a, b, and R are empirical constants. The following experiment was carried out to find the values of these constants.

One mole of CO_2 was compressed at the constant temperature $T = 304$ K. The measured pressure-volume (pV) data were then plotted as in Fig. 4.6.40, with the pV curve showing an inflection point coinciding with a horizontal tangent at $V = 128.1$, $p = 72.8$. Use this information to calculate a, b, and R. [*Suggestion:* Solve van der Waals' equation for p and then calculate dp/dV and d^2p/dV^2.]

90. Suppose that the function f is differentiable on an open interval containing the point c at which $f'(c) = 0$ and that the second derivative
$$f''(c) = \lim_{h \to 0} \frac{f'(c+h) - f'(c)}{h} = \lim_{h \to 0} \frac{f'(c+h)}{h}$$
exists. (a) First assume that $f''(c) > 0$. Reason that $f'(c+h)$ and h have the same sign if $h \neq 0$ is sufficiently small. Hence apply the first derivative test to show in this case that $f(c)$ is a local minimum value of f. (b) Show similarly that $f(c)$ is a local maximum value of f if $f''(c) < 0$.

Problems 91 and 92 require the use of a graphing calculator or computer algebra system. Any equations you need to solve may be solved graphically or by using a "solve" key or command; you may find it useful to look ahead to the CD-ROM discussion for the Section 4.7 project.

91. Figure 4.6.41 shows the graph of the cubic equation
$$y = 1000x^3 - 3051x^2 + 3102x + 1050$$
on a scale with x measured in units and y in tens of thousands. The graph appears to exhibit a single point near $(1, 2000)$ that is both a critical point and an inflection point. Nevertheless, this curve "has two real wiggles like a *good* cubic should." Find them! In particular, find the local extrema and inflection point (or points) on this curve. Then sketch a graph that plainly exhibits all these points—mark and label each of them.

FIGURE 4.6.40 A problem involving van der Waals' equation.

FIGURE 4.6.41 The cubic graph of Problem 91.

FIGURE 4.6.42 The graph of Problem 92.

92. Figure 4.6.42 shows the graph of
$$y = [x(1-x)(9x-7)(4x-1)]^4$$
on a scale with x and y both measured in units. At first glance it appears that there is a local maximum near $x = \frac{1}{2}$, with "flat spots" along the x-axis to the left and to the right. But no nonconstant polynomial can have a "flat spot" where $y = 0$ on an open interval of the x-axis. (Why not?) Indeed, this graph actually has seven local extrema and six inflection points in the interval $0 \leq x \leq 1$. Find approximate coordinates of all thirteen of these points, then sketch a graph on a scale that makes all these points evident.

4.7 CURVE SKETCHING AND ASYMPTOTES

We now extend the limit concept to include infinite limits and limits at infinity. This extension will add a powerful weapon to our arsenal of curve-sketching techniques, the notion of an *asymptote* to a curve—a straight line that the curve approaches arbitrarily closely in a sense we soon make precise.

Recall from Section 2.3 that $f(x)$ is said to **increase without bound**, or **become infinite**, as x approaches a, and we write

$$\lim_{x \to a} f(x) = +\infty, \tag{1}$$

provided that $f(x)$ can be made arbitrarily large by choosing x sufficiently close (but not equal) to a. The statement that $f(x)$ **decreases without bound**, or **becomes negatively infinite**, as $x \to a$, written

$$\lim_{x \to a} f(x) = -\infty, \tag{2}$$

has an analogous definition.

EXAMPLE 1 It is apparent that

$$\lim_{x \to -2} \frac{1}{(x+2)^2} = +\infty$$

because, as $x \to -2$, $(x+2)^2$ is positive and approaches zero. (See Fig. 4.7.1.) By contrast,

$$\lim_{x \to -2} \frac{x}{(x+2)^2} = -\infty$$

because, as $x \to -2$, the denominator $(x+2)^2$ is still positive and approaches zero, but the numerator x is negative. (See Fig. 4.7.2.) Thus when x is very close to -2, we have in $x/(x+2)^2$ a negative number close to -2 divided by a very small positive number. Hence the quotient becomes a negative number of large magnitude. ◆

One-sided versions of Eqs. (1) and (2) are valid also. For instance, if n is an *odd* positive integer, then it is apparent that

$$\lim_{x \to 2^-} \frac{1}{(x-2)^n} = -\infty \quad \text{and} \quad \lim_{x \to 2^+} \frac{1}{(x-2)^n} = +\infty,$$

because $(x-2)^n$ is negative when x is to the left of 2 and positive when x is to the right of 2. The case $n = 3$ is illustrated in Fig. 4.7.3.

FIGURE 4.7.1 $\dfrac{1}{(x+2)^2} \to \infty$ as $x \to -2$, and the line $x = -2$ is a vertical asymptote.

FIGURE 4.7.2 $\dfrac{x}{(x+2)^2} \to -\infty$ as $x \to -2$, and the line $x = -2$ is a vertical asymptote.

FIGURE 4.7.3 $\dfrac{1}{(x+2)^3}$ has infinite one-sided limits as $x \to -2$, and the line $x = -2$ is a vertical asymptote.

Vertical Asymptotes

The vertical lines at $x = -2$ in Figs. 4.7.1 through 4.7.3 are examples of *vertical asymptotes* associated with infinite limits. The line $x = a$ is a **vertical asymptote** of the curve $y = f(x)$ provided that either

$$\lim_{x \to a^-} f(x) = \pm \infty \tag{3a}$$

or

$$\lim_{x \to a^+} f(x) = \pm \infty \tag{3b}$$

or both. It is usually the case that both one-sided limits, rather than only one, are infinite. If so, we write

$$\lim_{x \to a} f(x) = \pm \infty. \tag{3c}$$

The geometry of a vertical asymptote is illustrated by the graphs in Figs. 4.7.1 through 4.7.3. In each case, as $x \to -2$ and $f(x) \to \pm\infty$, the point $(x, f(x))$ on the curve approaches the vertical asymptote $x = -2$ and the shape and direction of the curve are better and better approximated by the asymptote.

Figure 4.7.4 shows the graph of a function whose left-hand limit is zero at $x = 1$. But the right-hand limit there is $+\infty$, which explains why the line $x = 1$ is a vertical asymptote for this graph. The right-hand limit in Fig. 4.7.5 does not even exist, but because the left-hand limit at $x = 1$ is $-\infty$, the vertical line at $x = 1$ is again a vertical asymptote.

A vertical asymptote typically appears in the case of a rational function $f(x) = p(x)/q(x)$ at a point $x = a$ where $q(a) = 0$ but $p(a) \neq 0$. (See Examples 4 through 8 later in this section.)

FIGURE 4.7.4 A "right-hand only" vertical asymptote.

Limits at Infinity

In Section 4.5 we discussed infinite limits at infinity in connection with the behavior of a polynomial as $x \to \pm\infty$. There is also such a thing as a *finite* limit at infinity. We say that $f(x)$ **approaches the number L as x increases without bound** and write

$$\lim_{x \to +\infty} f(x) = L \tag{4}$$

provided that $|f(x) - L|$ can be made arbitrarily small (close to zero) merely by choosing x sufficiently large. That is, given $\epsilon > 0$, there exists $M > 0$ such that

$$x > M \quad \text{implies} \quad |f(x) - L| < \epsilon. \tag{5}$$

FIGURE 4.7.5 The behavior of the graph to its *left* produces the vertical asymptote.

The statement that

$$\lim_{x \to -\infty} f(x) = L$$

has a definition of similar form—merely replace the condition $x > M$ with the condition $x < -M$.

The analogues for limits at infinity of the limit laws of Section 2.2 all hold, including, in particular, the sum, product, and quotient laws. In addition, it is not difficult to show that if

$$\lim_{x \to +\infty} f(x) = L \quad \text{and} \quad \lim_{x \to +\infty} g(x) = \pm \infty,$$

then

$$\lim_{x \to +\infty} \frac{f(x)}{g(x)} = 0.$$

CHAPTER 4 Additional Applications of the Derivative

It follows from this result that

$$\lim_{x \to +\infty} \frac{1}{x^k} = 0 \qquad (6)$$

for any choice of the positive rational number k.

Using Eq. (6) and the limit laws, we can easily evaluate limits at infinity of rational functions. The general method is this: First divide each term in both the numerator and the denominator by the highest power of x that appears in any of the terms. Then apply the limit laws.

EXAMPLE 2 Find

$$\lim_{x \to +\infty} f(x) \quad \text{if} \quad f(x) = \frac{3x^3 - x}{2x^3 + 7x^2 - 4}.$$

Solution We begin by dividing each term in the numerator and denominator by x^3:

$$\lim_{x \to +\infty} \frac{3x^3 - x}{2x^3 + 7x^2 - 4} = \lim_{x \to +\infty} \frac{3 - \dfrac{1}{x^2}}{2 + \dfrac{7}{x} - \dfrac{4}{x^3}}$$

$$= \frac{\lim_{x \to +\infty} \left(3 - \dfrac{1}{x^2}\right)}{\lim_{x \to +\infty} \left(2 + \dfrac{7}{x} - \dfrac{4}{x^3}\right)} = \frac{3 - 0}{2 + 0 - 0} = \frac{3}{2}.$$

The same computation, but with $x \to -\infty$, also gives the result

$$\lim_{x \to -\infty} f(x) = \frac{3}{2}. \qquad \blacklozenge$$

EXAMPLE 3 Find $\lim_{x \to +\infty} \left(\sqrt{x+a} - \sqrt{x}\right)$.

Solution We use the familiar "divide-and-multiply" technique with the conjugate of $\sqrt{x+a} - \sqrt{x}$:

$$\lim_{x \to +\infty} \left(\sqrt{x+a} - \sqrt{x}\right) = \lim_{x \to +\infty} \left(\sqrt{x+a} - \sqrt{x}\right) \cdot \frac{\sqrt{x+a} + \sqrt{x}}{\sqrt{x+a} + \sqrt{x}}$$

$$= \lim_{x \to +\infty} \frac{a}{\sqrt{x+a} + \sqrt{x}} = 0. \qquad \blacklozenge$$

Horizontal Asymptotes

In geometric terms, the statement

$$\lim_{x \to +\infty} f(x) = L$$

means that the point $(x, f(x))$ on the curve $y = f(x)$ approaches the horizontal line $y = L$ as $x \to +\infty$. In particular, with the numbers M and ϵ of the condition in Eq. (5), the part of the curve for which $x > M$ lies between the horizontal lines $y = L - \epsilon$ and $y = L + \epsilon$ (Fig. 4.7.6). Therefore, we say that the line $y = L$ is a **horizontal asymptote** of the curve $y = f(x)$ if either

$$\lim_{x \to +\infty} f(x) = L \quad \text{or} \quad \lim_{x \to -\infty} f(x) = L.$$

FIGURE 4.7.6 Geometry of the definition of horizontal asymptote.

EXAMPLE 4 Sketch the graph of $f(x) = x/(x-2)$. Indicate any horizontal or vertical asymptotes.

Solution First we note that $x = 2$ is a vertical asymptote because $|f(x)| \to +\infty$ as $x \to 2$. Also,

$$\lim_{x \to \pm\infty} \frac{x}{x-2} = \lim_{x \to \pm\infty} \frac{1}{1 - \frac{2}{x}} = \frac{1}{1-0} = 1.$$

So the line $y = 1$ is a horizontal asymptote. The first two derivatives of f are

$$f'(x) = -\frac{2}{(x-2)^2} \quad \text{and} \quad f''(x) = \frac{4}{(x-2)^3}.$$

Neither $f'(x)$ nor $f''(x)$ is zero anywhere, so the function f has no critical points and no inflection points. Because $f'(x) < 0$ for $x \neq 2$, we see that $f(x)$ is decreasing on the open intervals $(-\infty, 2)$ and $(2, +\infty)$. And because $f''(x) < 0$ for $x < 2$ and $f''(x) > 0$ for $x > 2$, the graph of f is concave downward on $(-\infty, 2)$ and concave upward on $(2, +\infty)$. The graph of f appears in Fig. 4.7.7. ◆

FIGURE 4.7.7 The graph for Example 4.

FIGURE 4.7.8 $\dfrac{x}{(x+2)^2} \to 0$ as $x \to \infty$, so the x-axis $y = 0$ is a horizontal asymptote.

EXAMPLE 5 Let's reexamine the function

$$f(x) = \frac{x}{(x+2)^2}$$

whose graph was shown in Fig. 4.7.2. We note that

$$\lim_{x \to \infty} \frac{x}{(x+2)^2} = \lim_{x \to \infty} \frac{\dfrac{1}{x}}{\left(1 + \dfrac{2}{x}\right)^2} = 0,$$

so the x-axis $y = 0$ is a horizontal asymptote of the graph $y = f(x)$. We must change the viewing window to see clearly the behavior of this curve for $x > 0$. With the window $-10 < x < 40$, $-0.25 < y < 0.25$ of Fig. 4.7.8 we see that $f(x)$ appears to attain a local maximum value near the point where $x = 2$ before approaching zero as $x \to \infty$. Indeed, upon differentiating f and simplifying the result, we see that

$$f'(x) = \frac{2-x}{(x+2)^3},$$

so the indicated maximum point on the curve is $(2, \frac{1}{8})$. The second derivative of f is

$$f''(x) = \frac{2(x-4)}{(x+2)^4},$$

and it follows that the inflection point apparent in Fig. 4.7.8 is at $(4, \frac{1}{9})$. ◆

Curve-Sketching Strategy

The curve-sketching techniques of Sections 4.5 and 4.6, together with those of this section, can be summarized as a list of steps. If you follow these steps, loosely rather than rigidly, you will obtain a qualitatively accurate sketch of the graph of a given function f:

1. Solve the equation $f'(x) = 0$ and also find where $f'(x)$ does not exist. This gives the critical points of f. Note whether the tangent line is horizontal, vertical, or nonexistent at each critical point.
2. Determine the intervals on which f is increasing and those on which it is decreasing.
3. Solve the equation $f''(x) = 0$ and also find where $f''(x)$ does not exist. These points are the *possible* inflection points of the graph.
4. Determine the intervals on which the graph of f is concave upward and those on which it is concave downward.
5. Find the y-intercept and the x-intercepts (if any) of the graph.
6. Plot and label the critical points, possible inflection points, and intercepts.
7. Determine the asymptotes (if any), discontinuities (if any), and *especially* the behavior of $f(x)$ and $f'(x)$ near discontinuities of f. Also determine the behavior of $f(x)$ as $x \to +\infty$ and as $x \to -\infty$.
8. Finally, join the plotted points with a curve that is consistent with the information you have gathered. Remember that corner points are rare and that straight sections of graph are even rarer.

You may follow these steps in any convenient order and omit any that present major computational difficulties. Many problems require fewer than all eight steps; see Example 4. But Example 6 requires them all.

EXAMPLE 6 Sketch the graph of

$$f(x) = \frac{2 + x - x^2}{(x-1)^2}.$$

Solution We notice immediately that

$$\lim_{x \to 1} f(x) = +\infty,$$

because the numerator approaches 2 as $x \to 1$ and the denominator approaches zero through *positive* values. So the line $x = 1$ is a vertical asymptote. Also,

$$\lim_{x \to \pm\infty} \frac{2 + x - x^2}{(x-1)^2} = \lim_{x \to \pm\infty} \frac{\frac{2}{x^2} + \frac{1}{x} - 1}{\left(1 - \frac{1}{x}\right)^2} = -1,$$

so the line $x = -1$ is a horizontal asymptote (in both the positive and the negative directions).

Next we apply the quotient rule and simplify to find that

$$f'(x) = \frac{x - 5}{(x - 1)^3}.$$

Thus the only critical point in the domain of f is $x = 5$, and we plot the point $(5, f(5)) = (5, -\frac{9}{8})$ on a convenient coordinate plane and mark the horizontal tangent there. To determine the increasing or decreasing behavior of f, we use both the critical point $x = 5$ and the point $x = 1$ (where f' is not defined) to separate the x-axis into open intervals. The following table shows the results:

Interval	$(x-1)^3$	$x-5$	$f'(x)$	f
$(-\infty, 1)$	−	−	+	Increasing
$(1, 5)$	+	−	−	Decreasing
$(5, +\infty)$	+	+	+	Increasing

After some simplifications, we find the second derivative to be

$$f''(x) = \frac{2(7 - x)}{(x - 1)^4}.$$

The only possible inflection point is at $x = 7$, corresponding to the point $(7, -\frac{10}{9})$ on the graph. We use both $x = 7$ and $x = 1$ (where f'' is undefined) to separate the x-axis into open intervals. The concave structure of the graph can be deduced with the aid of the next table.

Interval	$(x-1)^4$	$7-x$	$f''(x)$	f
$(-\infty, 1)$	+	+	+	Concave upward
$(1, 7)$	+	+	+	Concave upward
$(7, +\infty)$	+	−	−	Concave downward

The y-intercept of f is $(0, 2)$, and the equation $2 + x - x^2 = 0$ readily yields the x-intercepts $(-1, 0)$ and $(2, 0)$. We plot these intercepts, sketch the asymptotes, and finally sketch the graph with the aid of the two tables; their information now is symbolized along the x-axis in Fig. 4.7.9. ◆

Slant Asymptotes

Not all asymptotes are horizontal or vertical—some are inclined. The nonvertical line $y = mx + b$ is an **asymptote** for the curve $y = f(x)$ provided that either

$$\lim_{x \to +\infty} [f(x) - (mx + b)] = 0 \tag{7a}$$

or

$$\lim_{x \to -\infty} [f(x) - (mx + b)] = 0 \tag{7b}$$

262 CHAPTER 4 Additional Applications of the Derivative

FIGURE 4.7.9 Graphing the function of Example 6.

(or both). These conditions mean that as $x \to +\infty$ or as $x \to -\infty$ (or both), the vertical distance between the point $(x, f(x))$ on the curve and the point $(x, mx + b)$ on the line approaches zero.

Suppose that $f(x) = p(x)/q(x)$ is a rational function for which the degree of $p(x)$ is greater by 1 than the degree of $q(x)$. Then, by long division of $q(x)$ into $p(x)$, we find that $f(x)$ has the form

$$f(x) = mx + b + g(x)$$

where $m \neq 0$ and

$$\lim_{x \to \pm\infty} g(x) = 0.$$

Thus the nonvertical line $y = mx + b$ is an asymptote of the graph of $y = f(x)$. Such an asymptote is called a **slant** asymptote.

EXAMPLE 7 Sketch the graph of

$$f(x) = \frac{x^2 + x - 1}{x - 1}.$$

Solution The long division suggested previously takes the form shown next.

$$\begin{array}{r} x + 2 \\ x - 1 \overline{\smash{)}\, x^2 + x - 1} \\ \underline{x^2 - x} \\ 2x - 1 \\ \underline{2x - 2} \\ 1 \end{array}$$

Thus

$$f(x) = x + 2 + \frac{1}{x - 1}.$$

So $y = x + 2$ is a slant asymptote of the curve. Also,

$$\lim_{x \to 1} |f(x)| = +\infty,$$

so $x = 1$ is a vertical asymptote. The first two derivatives of f are

$$f'(x) = 1 - \frac{1}{(x - 1)^2} = \frac{x(x - 2)}{(x - 1)^2}.$$

and
$$f''(x) = \frac{2}{(x-1)^3}.$$

It follows that f has critical points at $x = 0$ and at $x = 2$ but no inflection points. The sign of f' tells us that f is increasing on $(-\infty, 0)$ and on $(2, +\infty)$, decreasing on $(0, 1)$ and on $(1, 2)$. Examination of $f''(x)$ reveals that f is concave downward on $(-\infty, 1)$ and concave upward on $(1, +\infty)$. In particular, $f(0) = 1$ is a local maximum value and $f(2) = 5$ is a local minimum value. The graph of f looks much like the one in Fig. 4.7.10. ◆

FIGURE 4.7.10 A function with slant asymptote $y = x + 2$ (Example 7).

FIGURE 4.7.11 $y = \dfrac{x^4 - 5x^2 - 5x + 7}{2x^3 - 2x + 1}$.

Calculator/Computer Graphing

Instead of using concepts of calculus to construct a graph from scratch, we can go the other way. That is, we can *begin* with a graph plotted by a calculator or computer, and then use a calculator to analyze the graph and refine our understanding of it. In Sections 1.3 and 1.4 we discussed the fact that a calculator or computer graph can sometimes be misleading or incomplete. But now we can use calculus—and in particular the computation of critical points and inflection points—to make sure that the machine-generated graph exhibits all of its important features. Moreover, with graphing and automatic solution techniques we can investigate graphs of functions that would be too complicated to study without a calculator or computer.

EXAMPLE 8 Figure 4.7.11 shows a computer-generated graph of the function

$$f(x) = \frac{x^4 - 5x^2 - 5x + 7}{2x^3 - 2x + 1}. \tag{8}$$

It appears likely to have a vertical asymptote somewhere near $x = -1$. To test this hypothesis, we need to know where the denominator in (8) is zero. The graph of this denominator, shown in Fig. 4.7.12, indicates that the equation $2x^3 - 2x + 1 = 0$ has a single real solution near $x = -1.2$. We could zoom in graphically to show that the corresponding vertical asymptote is still closer to $x = -1.19$, and a calculator or computer **Solve** command yields the solution $x \approx -1.1915$ accurate to four decimal places.

Noting that the degree of the numerator in (8) exceeds that of the denominator, we find by long division that

$$f(x) = \frac{1}{2}x + \frac{-4x^2 - \frac{11}{2}x + 7}{2x^3 - 2x + 1}.$$

FIGURE 4.7.12 Graph of the denominator in (8).

264 CHAPTER 4 Additional Applications of the Derivative

FIGURE 4.7.13 Now we see both the vertical asymptote and the slant asymptote $y = \frac{1}{2}x$.

FIGURE 4.7.14 Graph of the numerator in (9).

Thus the graph $y = f(x)$ has the slant asymptote $y = \frac{1}{2}x$ (Fig. 4.7.13).

To investigate the critical points of $f(x)$, we calculate the derivative

$$f'(x) = \frac{2x^6 + 4x^4 + 24x^3 - 32x^2 - 10x + 9}{(2x^3 - 2x + 1)^2}. \tag{9}$$

The critical points of $f(x)$ are the zeros of the numerator of $f'(x)$, together with the zero of the denominator that yields the vertical asymptote. The graph of the numerator, shown in Fig. 4.7.14, indicates that the equation

$$2x^6 + 4x^4 + 24x^3 - 32x^2 - 10x + 9 = 0$$

has four real solutions, near the points $x = -2.3, -0.6, 0.5,$ and 1.1. We could zoom in closer to each of these solutions, or use a calculator or computer $\boxed{\text{Solve}}$ command to get the approximations $x \approx -2.3440, -0.5775, 0.4673,$ and 1.0864 that agree with the overall structure of the graph shown in Fig. 4.7.11, where four critical points with horizontal tangent lines are apparent.

The leftmost critical point $x \approx -2.3440$ deserves closer examination. In Fig. 4.7.13 it appears to be just to the left of the point where the left branch of the graph $y = f(x)$ crosses the slant asymptote $y = \frac{1}{2}x$. The zoom shown in Fig. 4.7.15 bears out this observation.

Finally, an examination of the original graph $y = f(x)$ in Fig. 4.7.11 suggests the approximate locations of three inflection points in the first quadrant. But if the graph is to approach the slant asymptote as $x \to -\infty$, then Fig. 4.7.15 suggests the presence of a fourth inflection point somewhere to the left of the leftmost critical point. (Why?) To investigate this possibility, we calculate the second derivative

$$f''(x) = \frac{2(-16x^6 - 66x^5 + 120x^4 + 34x^3 - 18x^2 - 42x + 13)}{(2x^3 - 2x + 1)^3}. \tag{10}$$

The inflection points of $y = f(x)$ have x-coordinates given by the zeros of the numerator in (10). The graph of this numerator, shown in Fig. 4.7.16, indicates that the equation

$$2(-16x^6 - 66x^5 + 120x^4 + 34x^3 - 18x^2 - 42x + 13) = 0$$

has four real solutions—a negative one near -5.5 as well as three positive solutions between 0 and 2 that correspond to the visually apparent first-quadrant inflection points in Fig. 4.7.11. We could zoom in closer to each of these solutions, or use a calculator or computer $\boxed{\text{Solve}}$ command to get the approximations $-5.4303, 0.3152, 0.6503,$ and 1.3937. The larger view shown in Fig. 4.7.17 convinces us that we've found *all* the inflection points of $y = f(x)$. In particular, we see that $y = f(x)$ is concave upward to the right of the inflection point $x \approx -5.4303$, where the denominator in (10) is negative (why?), and is concave downward just to its right (consistent with what we see in Fig. 4.7.15).

FIGURE 4.7.15 Near the leftmost critical point.

FIGURE 4.7.16 Graph of the numerator in (10).

FIGURE 4.7.17 Larger view of the graph of the numerator in (10).

4.7 TRUE/FALSE STUDY GUIDE

4.7 CONCEPTS: QUESTIONS AND DISCUSSION

1. Can you sketch the graph of a function that has two distinct critical points that are not separated by an inflection point? Does such a function exist?
2. Does the graph of a polynomial always have an inflection point? Or does it depend upon whether the degree n of the polynomial is even or odd? Begin by discussing separately the cases $n = 2, 3, 4$, and 5.
3. Can the graph of a polynomial have an asymptote? Does the graph of a rational function always have an asymptote? Justify your answers.
4. What can you say about the degrees of the numerator and denominator of a rational function that has a horizontal asymptote? What can you say about the degrees of the numerator and denominator of a rational function that has a slant asymptote?

4.7 PROBLEMS

Investigate the limits in Problems 1 through 16.

1. $\lim\limits_{x \to +\infty} \dfrac{x}{x+1}$
2. $\lim\limits_{x \to -\infty} \dfrac{x^2+1}{x^2-1}$
3. $\lim\limits_{x \to 1} \dfrac{x^2+x-2}{x-1}$
4. $\lim\limits_{x \to 1} \dfrac{x^2-x-2}{x-1}$
5. $\lim\limits_{x \to +\infty} \dfrac{2x^2-1}{x^2-3x}$
6. $\lim\limits_{x \to +\infty} \dfrac{x^2+3x}{x^3-5}$
7. $\lim\limits_{x \to -1} \dfrac{x^2+2x+1}{(x+1)^2}$
8. $\lim\limits_{x \to +\infty} \dfrac{5x^3-2x+1}{7x^3+4x^2-2}$
9. $\lim\limits_{x \to 4} \dfrac{x-4}{\sqrt{x}-2}$
10. $\lim\limits_{x \to +\infty} \dfrac{2x+1}{x-x\sqrt{x}}$
11. $\lim\limits_{x \to -\infty} \dfrac{8-\sqrt[3]{x}}{2+x}$
12. $\lim\limits_{x \to +\infty} \dfrac{2x^2-17}{x^3-2x+27}$
13. $\lim\limits_{x \to +\infty} \sqrt{\dfrac{4x^2-x}{x^2+9}}$
14. $\lim\limits_{x \to -\infty} \dfrac{\sqrt[3]{x^3-8x+1}}{3x-4}$
15. $\lim\limits_{x \to -\infty} \left(\sqrt{x^2+2x}-x\right)$
16. $\lim\limits_{x \to -\infty} \left(2x-\sqrt{4x^2-5x}\right)$

Apply your knowledge of limits and asymptotes to match each function in Problems 17 through 28 with its graph-with-asymptotes in one of the twelve parts of Fig. 4.7.18.

17. $f(x) = \dfrac{1}{x-1}$
18. $f(x) = \dfrac{1}{1-x}$
19. $f(x) = \dfrac{1}{(x-1)^2}$
20. $f(x) = -\dfrac{1}{(1-x)^2}$
21. $f(x) = \dfrac{1}{x^2-1}$
22. $f(x) = \dfrac{1}{1-x^2}$
23. $f(x) = \dfrac{x}{x^2-1}$
24. $f(x) = \dfrac{x}{1-x^2}$
25. $f(x) = \dfrac{x}{x-1}$
26. $f(x) = \dfrac{x^2}{x^2-1}$
27. $f(x) = \dfrac{x^2}{x-1}$
28. $f(x) = \dfrac{x^3}{x^2-1}$

Sketch by hand the graph of each function in Problems 29 through 54. Identify and label all extrema, inflection points, intercepts, and asymptotes. Show the concave structure clearly as well as the behavior of the graph for $|x|$ large and for x near any discontinuities of the function.

29. $f(x) = \dfrac{2}{x-3}$
30. $f(x) = \dfrac{4}{5-x}$
31. $f(x) = \dfrac{3}{(x+2)^2}$
32. $f(x) = -\dfrac{4}{(3-x)^2}$
33. $f(x) = \dfrac{1}{(2x-3)^3}$
34. $f(x) = \dfrac{x+1}{x-1}$
35. $f(x) = \dfrac{x^2}{x^2+1}$
36. $f(x) = \dfrac{2x}{x^2+1}$
37. $f(x) = \dfrac{1}{x^2-9}$
38. $f(x) = \dfrac{x}{4-x^2}$
39. $f(x) = \dfrac{1}{x^2+x-6}$
40. $f(x) = \dfrac{2x^2+1}{x^2-2x}$
41. $f(x) = x + \dfrac{1}{x}$
42. $f(x) = 2x + \dfrac{1}{x^2}$
43. $f(x) = \dfrac{x^2}{x-1}$
44. $f(x) = \dfrac{2x^3-5x^2+4x}{x^2-2x+1}$
45. $f(x) = \dfrac{1}{(x-1)^2}$
46. $f(x) = \dfrac{1}{x^2-4}$
47. $f(x) = \dfrac{x}{x+1}$
48. $f(x) = \dfrac{1}{(x+1)^3}$
49. $f(x) = \dfrac{1}{x^2-x-2}$
50. $f(x) = \dfrac{1}{(x-1)(x+1)^2}$

266 CHAPTER 4 Additional Applications of the Derivative

FIGURE 4.7.18 Problems 17 through 28.

51. $f(x) = \dfrac{x^2 - 4}{x}$

52. $f(x) = \dfrac{x}{x^2 - 1}$

53. $f(x) = \dfrac{x^3 - 4}{x^2}$

54. $f(x) = \dfrac{x^2 + 1}{x - 2}$

57. $f(x) = \dfrac{(x+1)^2(x-3)}{x^3(x-2)}$

58. $f(x) = \dfrac{(x+1)^2(x-3)^2}{x^3(x-2)}$

59. $f(x) = \dfrac{(x+1)^2(x-3)^2}{x^3(x-2)^2}$

60. $f(x) = \dfrac{(x+1)(x-3)^4}{x^3(x-2)^3}$

In Problems 55 through 60, you can determine by inspection the x-intercepts as well as the vertical and horizontal asymptotes of the curve $y = f(x)$. First sketch the graph by hand, using this information, and without calculating any derivatives. Then use a calculator or computer to locate accurately the critical and inflection points of $f(x)$. Finally, use a calculator or computer to produce graphs that display the major features of the curve.

55. $f(x) = \dfrac{(x+1)(x-3)}{x^2(x-2)}$

56. $f(x) = \dfrac{(x+1)^2(x-3)}{x^2(x-4)}$

In Problems 61 through 68, begin with a calculator- or computer-generated graph of the curve $y = f(x)$. Then use a calculator or computer to locate accurately the vertical asymptotes and the critical and inflection points of $f(x)$. Finally, use a calculator or computer to produce graphs that display the major features of the curve, including any vertical, horizontal, and slant asymptotes.

61. $f(x) = \dfrac{x^2}{x^3 - 3x^2 + 1}$

62. $f(x) = \dfrac{x^2}{x^3 - 3x^2 + 5}$

63. $f(x) = \dfrac{x^4 - 4x + 5}{x^3 - 3x^2 + 5}$

64. $f(x) = \dfrac{x^4 - 4x + 1}{2x^3 - 3x + 2}$

65. $f(x) = \dfrac{x^5 - 4x^2 + 1}{2x^4 - 3x + 2}$

66. $f(x) = \dfrac{x^5 - 4x^3 + 2}{2x^4 - 5x + 5}$

67. $f(x) = \dfrac{x^6 - 4x^3 + 5x}{2x^5 - 5x^3 + 5}$

68. $f(x) = \dfrac{2x^6 - 5x^4 + 6}{3x^5 - 5x^4 + 4}$

69. Suppose that
$$f(x) = x^2 + \dfrac{2}{x}.$$

Note that
$$\lim_{x \to \pm\infty} [f(x) - x^2] = 0,$$

so the curve $y = f(x)$ approaches the parabola $y = x^2$ as $x \to \pm\infty$. Use this observation to make an accurate sketch of the graph of f.

70. Use the method of Problem 69 to make an accurate sketch of the graph of
$$f(x) = x^3 - \dfrac{12}{x-1}.$$

4.7 Project: Locating Special Points on Exotic Graphs

The investigations described here deal with fairly exotic curves having critical and inflection points that are not clearly visible on their graphs if plotted on a "natural" scale. The reason is that different scales on the x- and y-axes are required to see the unusual behavior in question. In both investigations you are to begin with a graph that you generate with calculator or computer, and then analyze the curve—locating accurately all critical and inflection points—in order to plot additional graphs that demonstrate clearly all of the major features of the curve.

Investigation A Choose in advance a single-digit integer n (perhaps the final nonzero digit of your student I.D. number). Then your task is to analyze the structure of the curve
$$y = x^7 + 5x^6 - 11x^5 - 21x^4 + 31x^3 - 57x^2 - (101 + 2n)x + (89 - 3n).$$

Find the local maximum and minimum points and the inflection point (or points) on this curve, giving their coordinates accurate to four decimal places. To display all these points, you probably will need to produce separate plots with different scales, showing different parts of this curve. In the end, use all the information accumulated to produce a careful hand sketch (*not* to scale) displaying all the maxima, minima, and inflection points with their (approximate) coordinates labeled.

Investigation B Explore in the detail the structure of the graph of the function
$$f(x) = -1{,}234{,}567{,}890 + 2{,}695{,}140{,}459x^2 + 605{,}435{,}400x^3$$
$$- 411{,}401{,}250x^4 - 60{,}600{,}000x^5 + 25{,}000{,}000x^6.$$

The graph $y = f(x)$ is shown in Fig. 4.7.19. At a glance, it might appear that we have only three critical points—a local minimum near the origin and two critical points that are also inflection points, as well as two more inflection points that are not critical points. Settle the matter. How many of each, in fact, are there? Find and exhibit all of them in a graph; your graph may be a neat hand sketch and need not be to scale.

FIGURE 4.7.19 The "big picture" in Investigation B.

CHAPTER 4 REVIEW: DEFINITIONS, CONCEPTS, RESULTS

Use the following list as a guide to concepts that you may need to review.

1. Implicitly defined functions
2. Implicit differentiation
3. Solving related-rates problems
4. Increment Δy
5. Differential dy
6. Linear approximation formula
7. Differentiation rules in differential form
8. Increasing functions and decreasing functions
9. Significance of the sign of the first derivative
10. Rolle's theorem
11. The mean value theorem
12. Consequences of the mean value theorem
13. First derivative test
14. Open-interval maximum-minimum problems
15. Graphs of polynomials
16. Calculation of higher derivatives

268   CHAPTER 4   Additional Applications of the Derivative

17. Concave-upward functions and concave-downward functions
18. Test for concavity
19. Second derivative test
20. Inflection points
21. Inflection point test
22. Infinite limits
23. Vertical asymptotes
24. Limits as $x \to \pm\infty$
25. Horizontal asymptotes
26. Slant asymptotes
27. Curve-sketching techniques

CHAPTER 4 MISCELLANEOUS PROBLEMS

Find dy/dx in Problems 1 through 6.

1. $x^3 = \sin^2 y$
2. $x^2 y^2 = x + y$
3. $\sqrt[3]{x} + \sqrt[3]{y} = 4$
4. $x^3 + y^3 = xy$
5. $x^3 - x^2 y + xy^2 - y^3 = 4$
6. $\sqrt{xy} = \sqrt[3]{x+y}$

In Problems 2 through 10, write an equation of the line tangent to the given curve at the indicated point.

7. $xy - x - y = 1$; $(0, -1)$
8. $x = \sin 2y$; $(1, \pi/4)$
9. $x^2 - 3xy + 2y^2 = 0$; $(2, 1)$
10. $y^3 = x^2 + x$; $(0, 0)$

In Problems 11 through 16, write dy in terms of x and dx.

11. $y = (4x - x^2)^{3/2}$
12. $y = 8x^3 \sqrt{x^2 + 9}$
13. $y = \dfrac{x+1}{x-1}$
14. $y = \sin x^2$
15. $y = x^2 \cos \sqrt{x}$
16. $y = \dfrac{x}{\sin 2x}$

In Problems 17 through 26, estimate the indicated number by linear approximation.

17. $\sqrt{6401}$ (Note that $80^2 = 6400$.)
18. $\dfrac{1}{1.000007}$
19. $(2.0003)^{10}$ (Note that $2^{10} = 1024$.)
20. $\sqrt[3]{999}$ (Note that $10^3 = 1000$.)
21. $\sqrt[3]{1005}$
22. $\sqrt[3]{62}$
23. $26^{3/2}$
24. $\sqrt[5]{30}$
25. $\sqrt[4]{17}$
26. $\sqrt[10]{1000}$

In Problems 27 through 32, estimate by linear approximation the change in the indicated quantity.

27. The volume $V = s^3$ of a cube, if its side length s is increased from 5 in. to 5.1 in.
28. The area $A = \pi r^2$ of a circle, if its radius r is decreased from 10 cm to 9.8 cm.
29. The volume $V = \frac{4}{3}\pi r^3$ of a sphere, if its radius r is increased from 5 cm to 5.1 cm.
30. The volume $V = 1000/p$ in.^{3} of a gas, if the pressure p is decreased from 100 lb/in.^{2} to 99 lb/in.^{2}
31. The period of oscillation $T = 2\pi \sqrt{L/32}$ of a pendulum, if its length L is increased from 2 ft to 2 ft 1 in. (Time T is in seconds and L is in feet.)
32. The lifetime $L = 10^{30}/E^{13}$ of a light bulb with applied voltage E volts (V), if the voltage is increased from 110 V to 111 V. Compare your result with the exact change in the function L.

If the mean value theorem applies to the function f on the interval $[a, b]$, it ensures the existence of a solution c in the interval (a, b) of the equation

$$f'(c) = \dfrac{f(b) - f(a)}{b - a}.$$

In Problems 33 through 38, a function f and an interval $[a, b]$ are given. Verify that the hypotheses of the mean value theorem are satisfied for f on $[a, b]$. Then use the given equation to find the value of the number c.

33. $f(x) = x - \dfrac{1}{x}$; $[1, 3]$
34. $f(x) = x^3 + x - 4$; $[-2, 3]$
35. $f(x) = x^3$; $[-1, 2]$
36. $f(x) = x^3$; $[-2, 1]$
37. $f(x) = \frac{11}{5}x^5$; $[-1, 2]$
38. $f(x) = \sqrt{x}$; $[0, 4]$

Sketch the graphs of the functions in Problems 39 through 43. Indicate the local maxima and minima of each function and the intervals on which the function is increasing or decreasing. Show the concave structure of the graph and identify all inflection points.

39. $f(x) = x^2 - 6x + 4$
40. $f(x) = 2x^3 - 3x^2 - 36x$
41. $f(x) = 3x^5 - 5x^3 + 60x$
42. $f(x) = (3 - x)\sqrt{x}$
43. $f(x) = (1 - x)\sqrt[3]{x}$
44. Show that the equation $x^5 + x = 5$ has exactly one real solution.

Calculate the first three derivatives of the functions in Problems 45 through 54.

45. $f(x) = x^3 - 2x$
46. $f(x) = (x + 1)^{100}$
47. $g(t) = \dfrac{1}{t} - \dfrac{1}{2t + 1}$
48. $h(y) = \sqrt{3y - 1}$
49. $f(t) = 2t^{3/2} - 3t^{4/3}$
50. $g(x) = \dfrac{1}{x^2 + 9}$
51. $h(t) = \dfrac{t + 2}{t - 2}$
52. $f(z) = \sqrt[3]{z} + \dfrac{3}{\sqrt[5]{z}}$
53. $g(x) = \sqrt[3]{5 - 4x}$
54. $g(t) = \dfrac{8}{(3 - t)^{3/2}}$

In Problems 55 through 62, calculate dy/dx and $d^2 y/dx^2$ under the assumption that y is defined implicitly as a function of x by the given equation.

55. $x^{1/3} + y^{1/3} = 1$
56. $2x^2 - 3xy + 5y^2 = 25$
57. $y^5 - 4y + 1 = \sqrt{x}$
58. $\sin xy = xy$
59. $x^2 + y^2 = 5xy + 5$
60. $x^5 + xy^4 = 1$
61. $y^3 - y = x^2 y$
62. $(x^2 - y^2)^2 = 4xy$

Sketch the graphs of the functions in Problems 63 through 82, indicating all critical points, inflection points, and asymptotes. Show the concave structure clearly.

63. $f(x) = x^4 - 32x$
64. $f(x) = 18x^2 - x^4$
65. $f(x) = x^6 - 2x^4$
66. $f(x) = x\sqrt{x-3}$
67. $f(x) = x\sqrt[3]{4-x}$
68. $f(x) = \dfrac{x-1}{x+2}$
69. $f(x) = \dfrac{x^2+1}{x^2-4}$
70. $f(x) = \dfrac{x}{x^2-x-2}$
71. $f(x) = \dfrac{2x^2}{x^2-x-2}$
72. $f(x) = \dfrac{x^3}{x^2-1}$
73. $f(x) = 3x^4 - 4x^3$
74. $f(x) = x^4 - 2x^2$
75. $f(x) = \dfrac{x^2}{x^2-1}$
76. $f(x) = x^3 - 12x$
77. $f(x) = -10 + 6x^2 - x^3$
78. $f(x) = \dfrac{x}{1+x^2}$; note that

$$f'(x) = -\dfrac{(x-1)(x+1)}{(x^2+1)^2}$$

and that

$$f''(x) = \dfrac{2x(x^2-3)}{(x^2+1)^3}.$$

79. $f(x) = x^3 - 3x$
80. $f(x) = x^4 - 12x^2$
81. $f(x) = x^3 + x^2 - 5x + 3$
82. $f(x) = \dfrac{1}{x} + \dfrac{1}{x^2}$
83. The function

$$f(x) = \dfrac{1}{x^2 + 2x + 2}$$

has a maximum value, and only one. Find it.

84. You need to manufacture a cylindrical pot, without a top, with a volume of 1 ft³. The cylindrical part of the pot is to be made of aluminum, the bottom of copper. Copper is five times as expensive as aluminum. What dimensions would minimize the total cost of the pot?

85. An open-topped rectangular box is to have a volume of 4500 cm³. If its bottom is a rectangle whose length is twice its width, what dimensions would minimize the total area of the bottom and four sides of the box?

86. A small rectangular box must be made with a volume of 324 in.³ Its bottom is square and costs twice as much (per square inch) as its top and four sides. What dimensions would minimize the total cost of the material needed to make this box?

87. You must make a small rectangular box with a volume of 400 in.³ Its bottom is a rectangle whose length is twice its width. The bottom costs 7¢/in.²; the top and four sides of the box cost 5¢/in.² What dimensions would minimize the cost of the box?

88. Suppose that $f(x)$ is a cubic polynomial with exactly three distinct real zeros. Prove that the two zeros of $f'(x)$ are real and distinct.

89. Suppose that it costs $1 + (0.0003)v^{3/2}$ dollars per mile to operate a truck at v miles per hour. If there are additional costs (such as the driver's pay) of $10/hr, what speed would minimize the total cost of a 1000-mi trip?

90. The numbers $a_1, a_2, \ldots, a_n$ are fixed. Find a simple formula for the number x such that the sum of the squares of the distances of x from the n fixed numbers is as small as possible.

91. Sketch the curve $y^2 = x(x-1)(x-2)$, showing that it consists of two pieces—one bounded and the other unbounded—and has two horizontal tangent lines, three vertical tangent lines, and two inflection points. [*Suggestion:* Note that the curve is symmetric around the x-axis. Begin by determining the intervals on which the product $x(x-1)(x-2)$ is positive. Compute dy/dx and d^2y/dx^2 by implicit differentiation.]

92. Farmer Rogers wants to fence in a rectangular plot of area 2400 ft². She wants also to use additional fencing to build an internal divider fence parallel to two of the boundary sections (Fig. 4.MP.1). What is the minimum total length of fencing that this project will require? Verify that your answer yields the global minimum.

FIGURE 4.MP.1 The fencing of Problem 92.

93. Farmer Simmons wants to fence in a rectangular plot of area 1800 ft². He wants also to use additional fencing to build two internal divider fences, both parallel to the same two outer boundary sections (Fig. 4.MP.2). What is the minimum total length of fencing that this project will require? Verify that your answer yields the global minimum.

FIGURE 4.MP.2 The fencing of Problem 93.

94. Farmer Taylor wants to fence in a rectangular plot of area 2250 m². She wants also to use additional fencing to build three internal divider fences, all parallel to the same two outer boundary sections. What is the minimum total length of fencing that this project will require? Verify that your answer yields the global minimum.

95. Farmer Upshaw wants to fence in a rectangular plot of area A ft². He wants also to use additional fencing to build n (a fixed but unspecified positive integer) internal divider fences, all parallel to the same two outer boundary sections. What is the minimum total length of fencing that this project will require? Verify that your answer yields the global minimum.

96. What is the length of the shortest line segment that lies in the first quadrant with its endpoints on the coordinate axes and is also tangent to the graph of $y = 1/x^2$? Verify that your answer yields the global minimum.

97. A right triangle is formed in the first quadrant by a line segment that is tangent to the graph of $y = 1/x^2$ and whose endpoints lie on the coordinate axes. Is there a maximum possible area of such a triangle? Is there a minimum? Justify your answers.

98. A right triangle is formed in the first quadrant by a line segment that is tangent to the graph of $y = 1/x$ and whose endpoints lie on the coordinate axes. Is there a maximum possible area of such a triangle? Is there a minimum? Justify your answers.

99. A rectangular box (with a top) is to have volume 288 in.^{3}, and its base is to be exactly three times as long as it is wide. What is the minimum possible surface area of such a box? Verify that your answer yields the global minimum.

100. A rectangular box (with a top) is to have volume 800 in.^{3}, and its base is to be exactly four times as long as it is wide. What is the minimum possible surface area of such a box? Verify that your answer yields the global minimum.

101. A rectangular box (with a top) is to have volume 225 cm^3, and its base is to be exactly five times as long as it is wide. What is the minimum possible surface area of such a box? Verify that your answer yields the global minimum.

102. A rectangular box (with a top) is to have volume V, and its base is to be exactly n times as long as it is wide (n is a fixed but unspecified positive integer). What is the minimum possible surface area of such a box? Verify that your answer yields the global minimum.

103. The graph of $f(x) = x^{1/3}(1 - x)^{2/3}$ is shown in Fig. 4.MP.3. Recall from Section 4.7 that this graph has a slant asymptote with equation $y = mx + b$ provided that
$$\lim_{x \to +\infty} [f(x) - (mx + b)] = 0$$
or that
$$\lim_{x \to -\infty} [f(x) - (mx + b)] = 0.$$
(The values of m and b may be different in the two cases $x \to +\infty$ and $x \to -\infty$.) The graph here appears to have such an asymptote as $x \to +\infty$. Find m by evaluating
$$\lim_{x \to +\infty} \frac{f(x)}{x}.$$
Then find b by evaluating
$$\lim_{x \to +\infty} [f(x) - mx].$$
Finally, find m and b for the case $x \to -\infty$.

FIGURE 4.MP.3 The graph of $y = f(x)$ of Problem 103.

104. You are at the southernmost point of a circular lake of radius 1 mi. Your plan is to swim a straight course to another point on the shore of the lake, then jog to the northernmost point. You can jog twice as fast as you can swim. What route gives the minimum time required for your journey?

105. A rectangular block with square base is being squeezed in such a way that its height is decreasing at the rate of 2 cm/min while its volume remains constant. At what rate is the edge x of its base increasing when $x = 30$ cm and $y = 20$ cm?

106. A ladder 10 ft long is leaning against a wall. If the bottom of the ladder slides away from the wall at the constant rate of 1 mi/h, how fast (in miles per hour) is the top of the ladder moving when it is 0.01 ft above the ground? (Assume that the top of the ladder maintains contact with the wall.)

107. Plane A is flying west toward an airport at an altitude of 2 mi. Plane B is flying south toward the same airport at an altitude of 3 mi. When both planes are 2 mi (ground distance) from the airport, the speed of plane A is 500 mi/h and the distance between the two plane is decreasing at 600 mi/h. What is the speed of plane B then?

THE INTEGRAL

5

Archimedes (287–212 B.C.)

Archimedes of Syracuse was the greatest mathematician of the ancient era from the fifth century B.C. to the second century A.D., when the seeds of modern mathematics sprouted in Greek communities located mainly on the shores of the Mediterranean Sea. He was famous in his own time for mechanical inventions—the so-called Archimedean screw for pumping water, lever-and-pulley devices ("give me a place to stand and I can move the earth"), a planetarium that duplicated the motions of heavenly bodies so accurately as to show eclipses of the sun and moon, and machines of war that terrified Roman soldiers in the siege of Syracuse, during which Archimedes was killed. But it is said that for Archimedes himself these inventions were merely the "diversions of geometry at play," and his writings are devoted to mathematical investigations.

Archimedes carried out many area and volume computations that now use integral calculus—ranging from areas of circles, spheres, and segments of conic sections to volumes of cones, spheres, ellipsoids, and paraboloids. It had been proved earlier in Euclid's *Elements* that the area A of a circle is proportional to the square of its radius r, so $A = \pi r^2$ for some proportionality constant π. But it was Archimedes who accurately approximated the numerical value of π, showing that it lies between the value $3\frac{1}{7}$ memorized by elementary school children and the lower bound $3\frac{10}{71}$. Euclid had also proved that the volume V of a sphere of radius r is given by $V = \mu r^3$ (μ constant), but it was Archimedes who discovered (and proved) that $\mu = 4\pi/3$. He also discovered the now-familiar volume formulas $V = \pi r^2 h$ and $V = \frac{1}{3}\pi r^2 h$ for the cylinder and the cone, respectively, of base radius r and height h.

It was long suspected that Archimedes had not originally discovered his area and volume formulas by means of the limit-based arguments he used to establish them rigorously. In 1906 an Archimedean treatise entitled *The Method* was rediscovered virtually by accident after having been lost since ancient times. In it he described a "method of discovery" based on using infinitesimals much as they were employed during the invention and exploration of calculus in the seventeenth and eighteenth centuries.

To commemorate his sphere and cylinder formulas, Archimedes requested that on his tombstone be carved a sphere inscribed in a circular cylinder. If the height of the cylinder is $h = 2r$, can you verify that the total surface areas A_C and A_S of the cylinder and sphere, and their volumes V_C and V_S, are related by Archimedes' formulas

$$A_S = \tfrac{2}{3} A_C \quad \text{and} \quad V_S = \tfrac{2}{3} V_C ?$$

Thus the volumes and surface areas of the sphere and cylinder have the same 2 : 3 ratio.

5.1 INTRODUCTION

Chapters 1 through 4 dealt with **differential calculus,** which is one of two closely related parts of *the* calculus. Differential calculus is centered on the concept of the *derivative.* Recall that the original motivation for the derivative was the problem of defining what it means for a straight line to be tangent to the graph of a function and calculating the slopes of such lines (Fig. 5.1.1). By contrast, the importance of the derivative stems from its applications to diverse problems that may, upon initial inspection, seem to have little connection with tangent lines.

Integral calculus is based on the concept of the *integral.* The definition of the integral is motivated by the problem of defining and calculating the area of the region that lies between the graph of a positive-valued function f and the x-axis over a given closed interval $[a, b]$. The area of the region R of Fig. 5.1.2 is given by the *integral* of f from a to b, denoted by the symbol

$$\int_a^b f(x)\,dx. \tag{1}$$

FIGURE 5.1.1 The tangent-line problem motivates differential calculus.

But the integral, like the derivative, is important due to its applications in many problems that may appear unrelated to its original motivation—problems involving motion and velocity, population growth, volume, arc length, surface area, and center of gravity, among others.

The principal theorem of this chapter is the *fundamental theorem of calculus* in Section 5.6. It provides a vital connection between the operations of differentiation and integration, one that provides an effective method for computing values of integrals. It turns out that, in order to apply this theorem to evaluate the integral in (1), we need to find not the derivative of the function $f(x)$ but rather a new function $F(x)$ whose derivative is $f(x)$:

$$F'(x) = f(x). \tag{2}$$

FIGURE 5.1.2 The area problem motivates integral calculus.

Thus we need to do "differentiation in reverse." We therefore begin in Section 5.2 with an investigation of *antidifferentiation.*

5.2 ANTIDERIVATIVES AND INITIAL VALUE PROBLEMS

The language of change is the natural language for the statement of most scientific laws and principles. For example, Newton's law of cooling says that the *rate of change* of the temperature T of a body is proportional to the difference between T and the temperature of the surrounding medium (Fig. 5.2.1). That is,

$$\frac{dT}{dt} = -k(T - A), \tag{1}$$

where k is a positive constant and A, normally assumed to be constant, is the surrounding temperature. Similarly, the *rate of change* of a population P with constant birth and death rates is proportional to the size of the population:

$$\frac{dP}{dt} = kP \qquad (k \text{ constant}). \tag{2}$$

Torricelli's law of draining (Fig. 5.2.2) implies that the *rate of change* of the depth y of water in a draining tank is proportional to the *square root* of y; that is,

$$\frac{dy}{dt} = -k\sqrt{y} \qquad (k \text{ constant}). \tag{3}$$

Mathematical models of real-world situations frequently involve equations that contain *derivatives* of unknown functions. Such equations, including Eqs. (1) through (3), are called **differential equations.**

FIGURE 5.2.1 Newton's law of cooling (Eq. (1)) describes the cooling of a hot rock in cold water.

FIGURE 5.2.2 Torricelli's law of draining (Eq. (3)) describes the draining of a cylindrical water tank.

Antiderivatives

The simplest kind of differential equation has the form

$$\frac{dy}{dx} = f(x), \tag{4}$$

where f is a given (known) function and the function $y(x)$ is unknown. The process of finding a function from its derivative is the opposite of differentiation and is therefore called **antidifferentiation**. If we can find a function $y(x)$ whose derivative is $f(x)$,

$$y'(x) = f(x),$$

then we call $y(x)$ an *antiderivative* of $f(x)$.

DEFINITION   Antiderivative
An **antiderivative** of the function f is a function F such that

$$F'(x) = f(x)$$

wherever $f(x)$ is defined.

The table in Fig. 5.2.3 shows some examples of functions, each paired with one of its antiderivatives. Figure 5.2.4 illustrates the operations of differentiation and antidifferentiation, beginning with the same function f and going in opposite directions. Figure 5.2.5 illustrates differentiation "undoing" the result of antidifferentiation—the derivative of the antiderivative of $f(x)$ is the original function $f(x)$.

Function $f(x)$	Antiderivative $F(x)$
1	x
$2x$	x^2
x^3	$\frac{1}{4}x^4$
$\cos x$	$\sin x$
$\sin 2x$	$-\frac{1}{2}\cos 2x$

FIGURE 5.2.3 Some antiderivatives.

FIGURE 5.2.4 Differentiation and antidifferentiation are opposites.

FIGURE 5.2.5 Differentiation undoes the result of antidifferentiation.

EXAMPLE 1 Given the function $f(x) = 3x^2$, $F(x) = x^3$ is an antiderivative of $f(x)$, as are the functions

$$G(x) = x^3 + 17, \quad H(x) = x^3 + \pi, \quad \text{and} \quad K(x) = x^3 - \sqrt{2}.$$

Indeed, $J(x) = x^3 + C$ is an antiderivative of $f(x) = 3x^2$ for *any* choice of the constant C. ◆

Thus a single function has *many* antiderivatives, whereas a function can have *only one* derivative. If $F(x)$ is an antiderivative of $f(x)$, then so is $F(x) + C$ for any choice of the constant C. The converse of this statement is more subtle: If $F(x)$ is one antiderivative of $f(x)$ *on the interval I*, then *every* antiderivative of $f(x)$ on I is of the form $F(x) + C$. This follows directly from Corollary 2 of the mean value theorem in Section 4.3, according to which two functions with the same derivative on an interval differ only by a constant on that interval.

Thus the graphs of any two antiderivatives $F(x) + C_1$ and $F(x) + C_2$ of the same function $f(x)$ on the same interval I are "parallel" in the sense illustrated in Figs. 5.2.6 through 5.2.8. There we see that the constant C is the vertical distance between the curves $y = F(x)$ and $y = F(x) + C$ for each x in I. This is the geometric interpretation of Theorem 1.

FIGURE 5.2.6 Graph of $y = x^2 + C$ for various values of C.

FIGURE 5.2.7 Graph of $y = x^3 + C$ for various values of C.

FIGURE 5.2.8 Graph of $y = \sin x + C$ for various values of C.

THEOREM 1 The Most General Antiderivative
If $F'(x) = f(x)$ at each point of the open interval I, then every antiderivative G of f on I has the form

$$G(x) = F(x) + C, \tag{5}$$

where C is a constant.

Thus if F is any single antiderivative of f on the interval I, then the *most general* antiderivative of f on I has the form $F(x) + C$, as given in Eq. (5). The collection of *all* antiderivatives of the function $f(x)$ is called the **indefinite integral** of f with respect to x and is denoted by

$$\int f(x)\, dx.$$

On the basis of Theorem 1, we write

$$\int f(x)\, dx = F(x) + C, \tag{6}$$

where $F(x)$ is any particular antiderivative of $f(x)$. Therefore,

$$\int f(x)\, dx = F(x) + C \quad \text{if and only if} \quad F'(x) = f(x).$$

The integral symbol $\int$ is made like an elongated capital S. It is, in fact, a medieval S, used by Leibniz as an abbreviation for the Latin word *summa* ("sum"). We think of the combination $\int \ldots dx$ as a single symbol; we fill in the "blank" with the formula of the function whose antiderivative we seek. We may regard the differential dx as specifying the independent variable x both in the function $f(x)$ and in its antiderivatives.

EXAMPLE 2 The entries in Fig. 5.2.3 yield the indefinite integrals

$$\int 1\, dx = x + C,$$

$$\int 2x\, dx = x^2 + C,$$

$$\int x^3\, dx = \tfrac{1}{4}x^4 + C,$$

$$\int \cos x\, dx = \sin x + C,$$

and

$$\int \sin 2x\, dx = -\tfrac{1}{2}\cos 2x + C.$$

You can verify each such formula by differentiating the right-hand side. Indeed, this is the *surefire* way to check any antidifferentiation: To verify that $F(x)$ is an antiderivative of $f(x)$, compute $F'(x)$ to see whether or not you obtain $f(x)$. For instance, the differentiation

$$D_x\left(-\tfrac{1}{2}\cos 2x + C\right) = -\tfrac{1}{2}(-2\sin 2x) + 0 = \sin 2x$$

is sufficient to verify the fifth formula of this example. ◆

The differential dx in Eq. (6) specifies that the independent variable is x. But we can describe a specific antidifferentiation in terms of *any* independent variable that is convenient. For example, the indefinite integrals

$$\int 3t^2\, dt = t^3 + C, \quad \int 3y^2\, dy = y^3 + C, \quad \text{and} \quad \int 3u^2\, du = u^3 + C$$

mean exactly the same thing as

$$\int 3x^2\, dx = x^3 + C.$$

Using Integral Formulas

Every differentiation formula yields immediately—by "reversal" of the differentiation—a corresponding indefinite integral formula. The now-familiar derivatives of power functions and trigonometric and exponential functions yield the integral formulas stated in Theorem 2.

THEOREM 2   Some Integral Formulas

$$\int x^k\, dx = \frac{x^{k+1}}{k+1} + C \quad (\text{if } k \neq -1), \tag{7}$$

$$\int \cos kx\, dx = \frac{1}{k}\sin kx + C, \tag{8}$$

$$\int \sin kx\, dx = -\frac{1}{k}\cos kx + C, \tag{9}$$

$$\int \sec^2 kx \, dx = \frac{1}{k} \tan kx + C, \qquad (10)$$

$$\int \csc^2 kx \, dx = -\frac{1}{k} \cot kx + C, \qquad (11)$$

$$\int \sec kx \tan kx \, dx = \frac{1}{k} \sec kx + C, \quad \text{and} \qquad (12)$$

$$\int \csc kx \cot kx \, dx = -\frac{1}{k} \csc kx + C. \qquad (13)$$

REMARK Be sure you see why there is a minus sign in Eq. (9) but none in Eq. (8)!

Recall that the operation of differentiation is *linear*, meaning that

$$D_x[cF(x)] = cF'(x) \qquad \text{(where } c \text{ is a constant)} \qquad (14a)$$

and

$$D_x[F(x) \pm G(x)] = F'(x) \pm G'(x). \qquad (14b)$$

It follows in the notation of antidifferentiation that

$$\int cf(x) \, dx = c \int f(x) \, dx \quad (c \text{ is a constant}) \qquad (15)$$

and

$$\int [f(x) \pm g(x)] \, dx = \int f(x) \, dx \pm \int g(x) \, dx. \qquad (16)$$

We can summarize these two equations by saying that antidifferentiation is **linear.** In essence, then, we antidifferentiate a sum of functions by antidifferentiating each function individually. This is *termwise* (or *term-by-term*) antidifferentiation. Moreover, a constant coefficient in any such term is merely "carried through" the antidifferentiation.

EXAMPLE 3 Find

$$\int \left(x^3 + 3\sqrt{x} - \frac{4}{x^2} \right) dx.$$

Solution Just as in differentiation, we prepare for antidifferentiation by writing roots and reciprocals as powers with fractional or negative exponents. Thus

$$\int \left(x^3 + 3\sqrt{x} - \frac{4}{x^2} \right) dx = \int \left(x^3 + 3x^{1/2} - 4x^{-2} \right) dx$$

$$= \int x^3 \, dx + 3 \int x^{1/2} \, dx - 4 \int x^{-2} \, dx \qquad \text{[using Eqs. (15) and (16)]}$$

$$= \frac{x^4}{4} + 3 \cdot \frac{x^{3/2}}{\frac{3}{2}} - 4 \cdot \frac{x^{-1}}{-1} + C \qquad \text{[using Eq. (7)]}$$

$$= \frac{1}{4}x^4 + 2x\sqrt{x} + \frac{4}{x} + C.$$

There's only one "$+C$" because the surefire check verifies that $\frac{1}{4}x^4 + 2x^{3/2} + 4x^{-1}$ is a particular antiderivative. Hence any other antiderivative differs from this one by only a (single) constant C. ◆

EXAMPLE 4

$$\int (2\cos 3t + 5\sin 4t)\, dt$$

$$= 2\int \cos 3t\, dt + 5\int \sin 4t\, dt \qquad \text{[using Eqs. (15) and (16)]}$$

$$= 2\left(\tfrac{1}{3}\sin 3t\right) + 5\left(-\tfrac{1}{4}\cos 4t\right) + C \qquad \text{[using Eqs. (8) and (9)]}$$

$$= \tfrac{2}{3}\sin 3t - \tfrac{5}{4}\cos 4t + C.$$

◆

Equation (7) is the power rule "in reverse." The generalized power rule in reverse is

$$\int u^k\, du = \frac{u^{k+1}}{k+1} + C \qquad (\text{if } k \neq -1), \tag{17}$$

where

$$u = g(x) \quad \text{and} \quad du = g'(x)\, dx.$$

EXAMPLE 5 With $u = x + 5$ (so that $du = dx$), Eq. (17) yields

$$\int (x+5)^{10}\, dx = \int u^{10}\, du$$

$$= \tfrac{1}{11}u^{11} + C = \tfrac{1}{11}(x+5)^{11} + C.$$

Note that, after substituting $u = x + 5$ and integrating with respect to u, our final step is to express the resulting antiderivative in terms of the original variable x. ◆

EXAMPLE 6 We want to find

$$\int \frac{20}{(4-5x)^3}\, dx.$$

We plan to use Eq. (17) with $u = 4 - 5x$. But we must get the differential $du = -5\, dx$ into the act. The "constant-multiplier rule" of Eq. (15) permits us to do this:

$$\int \frac{20}{(4-5x)^3}\, dx = 20 \int (4-5x)^{-3}\, dx$$

$$= \frac{20}{-5} \int (4-5x)^{-3}(-5\, dx) \tag{18}$$

$$= -4 \int u^{-3}\, du \qquad (u = 4-5x,\ du = -5\, dx)$$

$$= -4 \cdot \frac{u^{-2}}{-2} + C \qquad \text{[Eq. (7) with } k = -3\text{]}.$$

Thus

$$\int \frac{20}{(4-5x)^3}\, dx = \frac{2}{(4-5x)^2} + C.$$

The key step occurs in (18). There we, in effect, multiplied by the *constant* -5 inside the integral and compensated for that by dividing by -5 outside the integral. At the end it was necessary to replace u with $4 - 5x$ to express the antiderivative in terms of the original independent variable x. ◆

Very Simple Differential Equations

The technique of antidifferentiation can often be used to solve a differential equation of the special form

$$\frac{dy}{dx} = f(x) \qquad (19)$$

in which the dependent variable y does not appear on the right-hand side. To *solve* the differential equation in (19) is simply to find a function $y(x)$ that satisfies Eq. (19)—a function whose derivative is the given function $f(x)$. Hence the **general solution** of Eq. (19) is the indefinite integral

$$y(x) = \int f(x)\, dx + C \qquad (20)$$

of the function $f(x)$.

EXAMPLE 7 The general solution of the differential equation

$$\frac{dy}{dx} = 3x^2$$

is given by

$$y(x) = \int 3x^2\, dx = x^3 + C. \qquad \blacklozenge$$

A differential equation of the form in Eq. (19) may appear in conjunction with an **initial condition,** a condition of the form

$$y(x_0) = y_0. \qquad (21)$$

This condition specifies the value $y = y_0$ that the solution function $y(x)$ must have at $x = x_0$. Once we have found the general solution in Eq. (20), we can determine the value of the constant C by substituting the information that $y = y_0$ when $x = x_0$. With this specific value of C, Eq. (20) then gives the **particular solution** of the differential equation in (19) that satisfies the initial condition in Eq. (21). The combination

$$\frac{dy}{dx} = f(x), \quad y(x_0) = y_0 \qquad (22)$$

of a differential equation with an initial condition is called an **initial value problem.**

EXAMPLE 8 Solve the initial value problem

$$\frac{dy}{dx} = 2x + 3, \quad y(1) = 2. \qquad (23)$$

Solution By Eq. (20) the *general solution* of the differential equation $dy/dx = 2x + 3$ is given by

$$y(x) = \int (2x + 3)\, dx = x^2 + 3x + C.$$

Figure 5.2.9 shows the graph $y = x^2 + 3x + C$ for various value of C. The particular solution we seek corresponds to the curve in Fig. 5.2.9 that passes through the point $(1, 2)$, thereby satisfying the initial condition

$$y(1) = (1)^2 + 3 \cdot (1) + C = 2.$$

FIGURE 5.2.9 General solutions $y = x^2 + 3x + C$ of the differential equation in (22) (Example 8).

It follows that $4 + C = 2$, and hence that $C = -2$. So the desired *particular solution* is given by

$$y(x) = x^2 + 3x - 2.$$ ◆

REMARK The method used in Example 8 may be described as "integrating both sides of a differential equation" with respect to x:

$$\int \left(\frac{dy}{dx}\right) dx = \int (2x + 3) \, dx;$$

$$y(x) = x^2 + 3x + C.$$

Rectilinear Motion

Antidifferentiation enables us, in many important cases, to analyze the motion of a particle (or "mass point") in terms of the forces acting on it. If the particle moves in *rectilinear motion* along a straight line—the x-axis, for instance—under the influence of a given (possibly variable) force, then (as in Section 3.1) the motion of the particle is described by its **position function**

$$x = x(t), \tag{24}$$

which gives its x-coordinate at time t (Fig. 5.2.10). The particle's **velocity** $v(t)$ is the time derivative of its position function,

$$v(t) = \frac{dx}{dt}, \tag{25}$$

FIGURE 5.2.10 The position function $x(t)$ of a particle moving along the x-axis.

and its **acceleration** $a(t)$ is the time derivative of its velocity:

$$a(t) = \frac{dv}{dt} = \frac{d^2x}{dt^2}. \tag{26}$$

In a typical situation, the following information is given (Fig. 5.2.11):

$$\begin{aligned} a(t) &\quad \text{the particle's acceleration;} \\ x(0) = x_0 &\quad \text{its } \textit{initial position;} \\ v(0) = v_0 &\quad \text{its } \textit{initial velocity.} \end{aligned} \tag{27}$$

FIGURE 5.2.11 Initial data for linear motion.

In principle, we can then proceed as follows to find the particle's position function $x(t)$. First we solve the initial value problem

$$\frac{dv}{dt} = a(t), \quad v(0) = v_0 \tag{28}$$

for the velocity function $v(t)$. Knowing $v(t)$, we then solve the initial value problem

$$\frac{dx}{dt} = v(t), \quad x(0) = x_0 \tag{29}$$

for the particle's position function $x(t)$. Thus we determine $x(t)$ from the acceleration and initial data given in Eq. (28) by solving two successive initial value problems. For this purpose we can use the integral versions

$$v(t) = \int a(t) \, dt \tag{30}$$

and

$$x(t) = \int v(t) \, dt \tag{31}$$

of the derivative formulas in (25) and (26), remembering that each antidifferentiation involves an arbitrary constant.

EXAMPLE 9 A particle starts from rest (that is, with initial velocity zero) at the point $x = 10$ and moves along the x-axis with acceleration function $a(t) = 12t$. Find its resulting position function $x(t)$.

Solution First we must solve the initial value problem

$$\frac{dv}{dt} = a(t) = 12t, \quad v(0) = 0$$

to find the velocity function $v(t)$. Using Eq. (30) we get

$$v(t) = \int a(t) \, dt = \int 12t \, dt = 6t^2 + C_1.$$

(We write C_1 because we anticipate the appearance of a second constant when we integrate again to find $x(t)$.) Then substituting the initial data $t = 0$, $v = 0$ yields

$$0 = 6 \cdot 0^2 + C_1 = C_1,$$

so it follows that $v(t) = 6t^2$. Next we must solve the initial value problem

$$\frac{dx}{dt} = v(t) = 6t^2, \quad x(0) = 10$$

for $x(t)$. Using Eq. (31) we get

$$x(t) = \int v(t) \, dt = \int 6t^2 \, dt = 2t^3 + C_2.$$

Then substituting the initial data $t = 0$, $x = 10$ yields

$$10 = 2 \cdot 0^3 + C_2 = C_2,$$

so it follows finally that the particle's position function is

$$x(t) = 2t^3 + 10. \quad \blacklozenge$$

Constant Acceleration

The solution of the initial value problems in Eqs. (28) and (29) is simplest when the given acceleration a is *constant*. We begin with

$$\frac{dv}{dt} = a \quad (a \text{ is a constant})$$

and antidifferentiate:

$$v(t) = \int a \, dt.$$

So

$$v(t) = at + C_1. \tag{32}$$

To evaluate the constant C_1, we substitute the initial datum $v(0) = v_0$; this gives

$$v_0 = a \cdot 0 + C_1 = C_1.$$

Therefore, Eq. (32) becomes

$$v(t) = at + v_0. \tag{33}$$

Because $x'(t) = v(t)$, a second antidifferentiation yields

$$x(t) = \int v(t)\, dt$$

$$= \int (at + v_0)\, dt;$$

$$x(t) = \tfrac{1}{2}at^2 + v_0 t + C_2. \tag{34}$$

Now substituting the initial datum $x(0) = x_0$ gives

$$x_0 = \tfrac{1}{2}a \cdot (0)^2 + v_0 \cdot (0) + C_2 = C_2$$

in Eq. (34). Thus the position function of the particle is

$$x(t) = \tfrac{1}{2}at^2 + v_0 t + x_0. \tag{35}$$

WARNING Equations (33) and (35) are valid only in the case of *constant* acceleration a. They do *not* apply to problems in which the acceleration varies.

EXAMPLE 10 The skid marks made by an automobile indicate that its brakes were fully applied for a distance of 160 ft before it came to a stop. Suppose that the car in question has a constant deceleration of 20 ft/s^2 under the conditions of the skid. How fast was the car traveling when its brakes were first applied?

Solution The introduction of a convenient coordinate system is often crucial to the successful solution of a physical problem. Here we take the x-axis to be positively oriented in the direction of motion of the car. We choose the origin so that $x_0 = 0$ when $t = 0$, the time when the brakes were first applied (Fig. 5.2.12). In this coordinate system, the car's velocity $v(t)$ is a decreasing function of time t (in seconds), so its acceleration is $a = -20$ (ft/s^2) rather than $a = +20$. Hence we begin with the constant acceleration equation

$$\frac{dv}{dt} = -20.$$

FIGURE 5.2.12 Skid marks 160 ft long (Example 10).

Antidifferentiation as in Eq. (30) gives

$$v(t) = \int (-20)\, dt = -20t + C_1.$$

Even though the initial velocity is unknown and not given, the initial data $t = 0$, $v = v_0$ still yield $C_1 = v_0$. So the car's velocity function is

$$v(t) = -20t + v_0. \tag{36}$$

A second antidifferentiation as in Eq. (31) gives

$$x(t) = \int (-20t + v_0)\, dt = -10t^2 + v_0 t + C_2.$$

Substituting the initial data $t = 0$, $x_0 = 0$ yields $C_2 = 0$, so the position function of the car is

$$x(t) = -10t^2 + v_0 t. \tag{37}$$

The fact that the skid marks are 160 ft long tells us that $x = 160$ when the car comes to a stop; that is,

$$x = 160 \quad \text{when} \quad v = 0.$$

Substituting these values into the velocity and position equations [Eqs. (36) and (37)] then yields the two simultaneous equations

$$-20t + v_0 = 0, \quad -10t^2 + v_0 t = 160.$$

We now solve these for v_0 and t to find the initial velocity v_0 and the duration t of the car's skid. If we multiply the first equation by $-t$ and add the result to the second equation, we find that $10t^2 = 160$, so $t = 4$ when the car first comes to a stop. It follows that the velocity of the car was

$$v_0 = 20 \cdot 4 = 80 \quad \text{(ft/s)},$$

or about 55 mi/h, when the brakes were first applied. ◆

Vertical Motion with Constant Gravitational Acceleration

One common application of Eqs. (33) and (35) involves vertical motion near the surface of the earth. A particle in such motion is subject to a *downward* acceleration a, which is almost exactly constant if only small vertical distances are involved. The magnitude of this constant is denoted by g, approximately 32 ft/s² or 9.8 m/s². (If you need more accurate values for g, use 32.17 ft/s² in the fps system or 9.807 m/s² in the mks system.)

If we neglect air resistance, we may assume that this acceleration due to gravity is the only outside influence on the moving particle. Because we deal with vertical motion here, it is natural to choose the y-axis as the coordinate system for the position of the particle and to place "ground level" where $y = 0$ (Fig. 5.2.13). If we choose the upward direction to be the positive direction, then the effect of gravity on the particle is to *decrease* its height and also to *decrease* its velocity $v = dy/dt$. Then the acceleration of the particle is

$$a = \frac{dv}{dt} = -g = -32 \quad (\text{ft/s}^2).$$

Equations (33) and (35) then become

$$v(t) = -32t + v_0 \tag{38}$$

and

$$y(t) = -16t^2 + v_0 t + y_0 \tag{39}$$

Here y_0 is the initial height of the particle in feet, v_0 is its initial velocity in feet per second, and time t is measured in seconds.

EXAMPLE 11 Suppose that a bolt was fired vertically upward from a crossbow at ground level and that it struck the ground 20 s later. If air resistance may be neglected, find the initial velocity of the bolt and the maximum altitude that it reached.

Solution We set up the coordinate system illustrated in Fig. 5.2.14, with ground level corresponding to $y = 0$, with the bolt fired at time $t = 0$ (in seconds), and with the positive direction being the upward direction. Units on the y-axis are in feet.

We are given that $y = 0$ when $t = 20$. We lack any information about the initial velocity v_0. But we may use Eqs. (38) and (39) because we have set up a coordinate system in which the acceleration due to gravity acts in the negative direction. Thus

$$y(t) = -16t^2 + v_0 t + y_0 = -16t^2 + v_0 t$$

and

$$v(t) = -32t + v_0.$$

We use the information that $y = 0$ when $t = 20$ in the first equation:

$$0 = -16 \cdot 20^2 + 20 v_0, \quad \text{and thus} \quad v_0 = 16 \cdot 20 = 320 \quad \text{(ft/s)}.$$

To find the maximum altitude of the bolt, we maximize $y(t)$ by finding the value of t for which its derivative is zero. In other words, the bolt reaches its maximum altitude when its velocity is zero:

$$\frac{dy}{dt} = -32t + v_0 = 0,$$

so at maximum altitude, $t = v_0/32 = 10$. At that time, the bolt has reached its maximum altitude of

$$y_{\max} = y(10) = -16 \cdot 10^2 + 320 \cdot 10 = 1600 \quad \text{(ft)}.$$

The result seems contrary to experience. It may well suggest that air resistance cannot always be neglected, particularly not in problems involving long journeys at high velocity. ◆

5.2 TRUE/FALSE STUDY GUIDE

5.2 CONCEPTS: QUESTIONS AND DISCUSSION

List corresponding features of the graphs of a function f and its antiderivative F. Hence describe a strategy whereby—given a plot showing the graphs of f and F—you can determine which is which. Apply your strategy to the following graphs, in which h is either the derivative or the antiderivative of g.

1. Figure 5.2.15

FIGURE 5.2.15

2. Figure 5.2.16

FIGURE 5.2.16

3. Figure 5.2.17

FIGURE 5.2.17

4. Figure 5.2.18

FIGURE 5.2.18

5.2 PROBLEMS

Evaluate the indefinite integrals in Problems 1 through 30.

1. $\int (3x^2 + 2x + 1)\, dx$
2. $\int (3t^4 + 5t - 6)\, dt$
3. $\int (1 - 2x^2 + 3x^3)\, dx$
4. $\int \left(-\dfrac{1}{t^2}\right) dt$
5. $\int \left(\dfrac{3}{x^3} + 2x^{3/2} - 1\right) dx$
6. $\int \left(x^{5/2} - \dfrac{5}{x^4} - \sqrt{x}\right) dx$
7. $\int \left(\tfrac{3}{2}t^{1/2} + 7\right) dt$
8. $\int \left(\dfrac{2}{x^{3/4}} - \dfrac{3}{x^{2/3}}\right) dx$
9. $\int \left(\sqrt[3]{x^2} + \dfrac{4}{\sqrt[4]{x^5}}\right) dx$
10. $\int \left(2x\sqrt{x} - \dfrac{1}{\sqrt{x}}\right) dx$
11. $\int (4x^3 - 4x + 6)\, dx$
12. $\int \left(\tfrac{1}{4}t^5 - \dfrac{5}{t^2}\right) dt$
13. $\int 7\, dx$
14. $\int \left(\sqrt[3]{x^2} - \dfrac{6}{\sqrt[3]{x}}\right) dx$
15. $\int (x+1)^4\, dx$
16. $\int (t+1)^{10}\, dt$
17. $\int \dfrac{1}{(x-10)^7}\, dx$
18. $\int \sqrt{z+1}\, dz$
19. $\int \sqrt{x}\,(1-x)^2\, dx$
20. $\int \sqrt[3]{x}\,(x+1)^3\, dx$
21. $\int \dfrac{2x^4 - 3x^3 + 5}{7x^2}\, dx$
22. $\int \dfrac{(3x+4)^2}{\sqrt{x}}\, dx$
23. $\int (9t+11)^5\, dt$
24. $\int \dfrac{1}{(3z+10)^7}\, dz$
25. $\int \dfrac{7}{(x+77)^2}\, dx$
26. $\int \dfrac{3}{\sqrt{(x-1)^3}}\, dx$
27. $\int (5\cos 10x - 10\sin 5x)\, dx$
28. $\int (2\cos \pi x + 3\sin \pi x)\, dx$
29. $\int (3\cos \pi t + \cos 3\pi t)\, dt$
30. $\int (4\sin 2\pi t - 2\sin 4\pi t)\, dt$

31. Verify by differentiation that the integral formulas
$$\int \sin x \cos x\, dx = \tfrac{1}{2}\sin^2 x + C_1$$
and
$$\int \sin x \cos x\, dx = -\tfrac{1}{2}\cos^2 x + C_2$$
are both valid. Reconcile these seemingly different results. What is the relation between the constants C_1 and C_2?

32. Show that the obviously different functions
$$F_1(x) = \dfrac{1}{1-x} \quad \text{and} \quad F_2(x) = \dfrac{x}{1-x}$$
are both antiderivatives of $f(x) = 1/(1-x)^2$. What is the relation between $F_1(x)$ and $F_2(x)$?

33. Use the identities
$$\sin^2 x = \dfrac{1 - \cos 2x}{2} \quad \text{and} \quad \cos^2 x = \dfrac{1 + \cos 2x}{2}$$
to find the antiderivatives
$$\int \sin^2 x\, dx \quad \text{and} \quad \int \cos^2 x\, dx.$$

34. (a) First explain why $\int \sec^2 x\, dx = \tan x + C$. (b) Then use the identity $1 + \tan^2 x = \sec^2 x$ to find the antiderivative
$$\int \tan^2 x\, dx.$$

Solve the initial value problems in Problems 35 through 46.

35. $\dfrac{dy}{dx} = 2x + 1;\ y(0) = 3$
36. $\dfrac{dy}{dx} = (x-2)^3;\ y(2) = 1$
37. $\dfrac{dy}{dx} = \sqrt{x};\ y(4) = 0$
38. $\dfrac{dy}{dx} = \dfrac{1}{x^2};\ y(1) = 5$
39. $\dfrac{dy}{dx} = \dfrac{1}{\sqrt{x+2}};\ y(2) = -1$
40. $\dfrac{dy}{dx} = \sqrt{x+9};\ y(-4) = 0$
41. $\dfrac{dy}{dx} = 3x^3 + \dfrac{2}{x^2};\ y(1) = 1$
42. $\dfrac{dy}{dx} = x^4 - 3x + \dfrac{3}{x^3};\ y(1) = -1$
43. $\dfrac{dy}{dx} = (x-1)^3;\ y(0) = 2$
44. $\dfrac{dy}{dx} = \sqrt{x+5};\ y(4) = -3$
45. $\dfrac{dy}{dx} = \dfrac{1}{\sqrt{x-13}};\ y(17) = 2$
46. $\dfrac{dy}{dx} = (2x+3)^{3/2};\ y(3) = 100$

In Problems 47 through 52, a particle moves along the x-axis with the given acceleration function $a(t)$, initial position $x(0)$, and initial velocity $v(0)$. Find the particle's position function $x(t)$.

47. $a(t) = 12t - 4;\ x(0) = 0,\ v(0) = -10$
48. $a(t) = 10 - 30t;\ x(0) = 5,\ v(0) = -5$
49. $a(t) = 2t^2;\ x(0) = -7,\ v(0) = 3$
50. $a(t) = 15\sqrt{t};\ x(0) = 5,\ v(0) = 7$
51. $a(t) = \sin t;\ x(0) = 0,\ v(0) = 0$
52. $a(t) = 8\cos 2t;\ x(0) = -2,\ v(0) = 4$

In Problems 53 through 56, a particle starts at the origin and travels along the x-axis with the velocity function $v(t)$ whose graph is shown in Figs. 5.2.19 through 5.2.22. Sketch the graph of the resulting position function x(t) for $0 \leq t \leq 10$.

53. Figure 5.2.19   **54.** Figure 5.2.20   **55.** Figure 5.2.21   **56.** Figure 5.2.22

FIGURE 5.2.19 Graph of the velocity function $v(t)$ of Problem 53.

FIGURE 5.2.20 Graph of the velocity function $v(t)$ of Problem 54.

FIGURE 5.2.21 Graph of the velocity function $v(t)$ of Problem 55.

FIGURE 5.2.22 Graph of the velocity function $v(t)$ of Problem 56.

Problems 57 through 73 deal with vertical motion near the surface of the earth (with air resistance considered negligible). Use $g = 32$ ft/s² for the magnitude of the gravitational acceleration.

57. You throw a ball straight upward from the ground with initial velocity 96 ft/s. How high does the ball rise, and how long does it remain aloft?

58. When Alex shot a marble straight upward from ground level with his slingshot, it reached a maximum height of 400 ft. What was the marble's initial velocity?

59. Laura drops a stone into a well; it hits bottom 3 s later. How deep is the well?

60. Fran throws a rock straight upward alongside a tree (Fig. 5.2.23). The rock rises until it is even with the top of the tree and then falls back to the ground; it remains aloft for 4 s. How tall is the tree?

FIGURE 5.2.23 The tree of Problem 60.

FIGURE 5.2.24 The building of Problem 61.

61. Mickey throws a ball upward with an initial velocity of 48 ft/s from the top of a building 160 ft high. The ball soon falls to the ground at the base of the building (Fig. 5.2.24). How long does the ball remain aloft, and with what speed does it strike the ground?

62. A ball is dropped from the top of a building 576 ft high. With what velocity should a second ball be thrown straight downward 3 s later so that the two balls hit the ground simultaneously?

63. A ball is dropped from the top of the Empire State Building, 960 ft above 34th Street. How long does it take for the ball to reach the street, and with what velocity does it strike the street?

64. Lynda shoots an arrow straight upward from the ground with initial velocity 320 ft/s. (a) How high is the arrow after exactly 3 s have elapsed? (b) At what time is the arrow exactly 1200 ft above the ground? (c) How many seconds after its release does the arrow strike the ground?

65. Bill throws a stone upward from the ground. The stone reaches a maximum height of 225 ft. What was its initial velocity?

66. Sydney drops a rock into a well in which the water surface is 98 m below the ground. How long does it take the rock to reach the water surface? How fast is the rock moving as it penetrates the water surface?

67. Gloria drops a tennis ball from the top of a building 400 ft high. How long does it take the ball to reach the ground? With what velocity does it strike the ground?

68. Kosmo throws a baseball straight downward from the top of a tall building. The initial speed of the ball is 25 ft/s. It hits the ground with a speed of 153 ft/s. How tall is the building?

69. A ball is thrown straight upward from ground level with an initial speed of 160 ft/s. What is the maximum height that the ball attains?

70. Carolyn drops a sandbag from the top of a tall building h feet high. At the same time Jon throws a ball upward from ground level from a point directly below the sandbag. With what (initial) velocity should the ball be thrown so that it meets the sandbag at the halfway point, where both have altitude $h/2$?

71. Kelly throws a baseball straight downward with an initial speed of 40 ft/s from the top of the Washington Monument, 555 ft high. How long does it take the baseball to reach the ground, and with what speed does it strike the ground?

72. A rock is dropped from an initial height of h feet above the surface of the earth. Show that the speed with which the rock strikes the surface is $\sqrt{2gh}$.

73. A bomb is dropped from a balloon hovering at an altitude of 800 ft. From directly below the balloon, a projectile is fired straight upward toward the bomb exactly 2 s after the bomb is released. With what initial speed should the projectile be fired in order to hit the bomb at an altitude of exactly 400 ft?

74. A car's brakes are applied when the car is moving at 60 mi/h (exactly 88 ft/s). The brakes provide a constant deceleration of 40 ft/s^2. How far does the car travel before coming to a stop?

75. A car traveling at 60 mi/h (exactly 88 ft/s) skids 176 ft after its brakes are applied. The deceleration provided by the braking system is constant. What is its value?

76. A spacecraft is in free fall toward the surface of the moon at a speed of 1000 mi/h. Its retrorockets, when fired, provide a deceleration of 20000 mi/h^2. At what height above the surface should the astronauts activate the retrorockets to ensure a "soft touchdown" ($v = 0$ at impact)? (See Fig. 5.2.25.) Ignore the effect of the moon's gravitational field.

77. (a) What initial velocity v_0 must you use to throw a ball to a maximum height of 144 ft? (b) Now suppose that you throw a ball upward with the same initial velocity v_0 on the moon, where the surface gravitational acceleration is only 5.2 ft/s^2. How high will it go, and how long will it remain aloft?

FIGURE 5.2.25 The spacecraft of Problem 76.

78. Arthur C. Clarke's *The Wind from the Sun* (1963) describes *Diana*, a spacecraft propelled by the solar wind. Its 2-mi^2 aluminized sail provides it with an acceleration of $(0.001)g = 0.032$ ft/s^2. If the *Diana* starts from rest and travels in a straight line, calculate its distance x traveled (in miles) and its velocity v (in mi/h) after 1 min, 1 h, and 1 day.

79. A driver involved in an accident claims he was going only 25 mi/h. When police tested his car, they found that when the brakes were applied at 25 mi/h, the car skidded only 45 ft before coming to a stop. The driver's skid marks at the accident scene measured 210 ft. Assuming the same (constant) deceleration, calculate the speed at which he was traveling prior to the accident.

5.3 ELEMENTARY AREA COMPUTATIONS

The indefinite integrals of Section 5.2 stem from the concept of antidifferentiation. The most fundamental type of integral is the one mentioned in Section 5.1, associated with the concept of area. It is called the *definite integral*, or simply *the* integral. Surprisingly, the quite different concepts of area and antidifferentiation have a close and deep relationship. This fact, discovered and exploited by Newton and Leibniz late in the seventeenth century, is the reason the same word, *integral*, is used in both contexts.

FIGURE 5.3.1 The formula for the area of a triangle, $A = \frac{1}{2}bh$, follows with the aid of this figure.

The Concept of Area

Perhaps everyone's first contact with the concept of area is the formula $A = bh$, which gives the area A of a rectangle as the product of its base length b and its height h. We next learn that the area of a triangle is half the product of its base and height. This follows because any triangle can be split into two right triangles, and every right triangle is exactly half a rectangle (Fig. 5.3.1).

Given the formula $A = \frac{1}{2}bh$ for the area of a triangle, we can—in principle—find the area of any polygonal figure (a plane region bounded by a closed "curve" consisting of a finite number of straight line segments). The reason is that any polygonal figure can be divided into nonoverlapping triangles (Fig. 5.3.2), and the area of the polygonal figure is then the sum of the areas of these triangles. This approach to area dates back several thousand years to the ancient civilizations of Egypt and Babylonia.

The ancient Greeks began the investigation of areas of *curvilinear* figures in the fourth and fifth centuries B.C. Given a plane region R whose area they sought, they worked both with a polygonal P inscribed in R (Fig. 5.3.3) and with a polygonal Q circumscribed about R (Fig. 5.3.4). If the polygons P and Q have sufficiently many sides, all short, then it would appear that their areas $a(P)$ and $a(Q)$ closely approximate the area of the region R. Moreover, error control is possible: We see

FIGURE 5.3.2 Every polygon can be represented as a union of nonoverlapping triangles.

FIGURE 5.3.3 (a) A six-sided polygon P inscribed in R; (b) a many-sided inscribed polygon P more closely approximating the area of R.

FIGURE 5.3.4 (a) A six-sided polygon Q circumscribed around R; (b) a many-sided circumscribed polygon Q more closely approximating the area of R.

that
$$a(P) < a(R) < a(Q) \tag{1}$$

because R contains the polygon P but is contained in the polygon Q.

The inequalities in (1) bracket the desired area $a(R)$. Suppose, for instance, that calculations based on triangular dissections (as in Fig. 5.3.2) yield $a(P) = 7.341$ and $a(Q) = 7.343$. Then the resulting inequality,
$$7.341 < a(R) < 7.343,$$
implies that $a(R) \approx 7.34$, accurate to two decimal places.

Our primary objective here is to describe a systematic technique by which to approximate the area of an appropriate curvilinear region using easily calculated polygonal areas.

Areas Under Graphs

We consider the type of region that is determined by a continuous positive-valued function f defined on a closed interval $[a, b]$. Suppose that we want to calculate the area A of the region R that lies *below* the curve $y = f(x)$ and *above* the interval $[a, b]$ on the x-axis (Fig. 5.3.5). The region R is bounded on the left by the vertical line $x = a$ and on the right by the vertical line $x = b$.

We divide the base interval $[a, b]$ into subintervals, all with the same length. Above each subinterval lies a vertical strip (Fig. 5.3.6), and the area of A is the sum of the areas of these strips.

FIGURE 5.3.5 The area under the graph of $y = f(x)$ from $x = a$ to $x = b$.

FIGURE 5.3.6 Vertical strips determined by a division of $[a, b]$ into equal-length subintervals.

On each of these base subintervals, we erect a rectangle that approximates the corresponding vertical strip. We may choose either an "inscribed" or a "circumscribed" rectangle (both possibilities are illustrated in Fig. 5.3.6), or even a rectangle that is intermediate between the two. These rectangles then make up a polygon that approximates the region R, and therefore the sum of the areas of these rectangles *approximates* the desired area A.

For example, suppose that we want to approximate the area A of the region R that lies below the parabola $y = x^2$ above the interval $[0, 3]$ on the x-axis. The computer plots in Fig. 5.3.7 show successively

- 5 inscribed and 5 circumscribed rectangles;
- 10 inscribed and 10 circumscribed rectangles;
- 20 inscribed and 20 circumscribed rectangles;
- 40 inscribed and 40 circumscribed rectangles.

288 CHAPTER 5 The Integral

Inscribed | Circumscribed

(a) (b) (c) (d)

FIGURE 5.3.7 (a) Five inscribed and circumscribed polygons; (b) ten inscribed and circumscribed polygons; (c) twenty inscribed and circumscribed polygons; (d) forty inscribed and circumscribed polygons.

Each collection of inscribed rectangles gives an *underestimate* of A, whereas each collection of circumscribed rectangles gives an *overestimate* of A. The "curvilinear triangles" (by which the rectangular polygons in Fig. 5.3.7 undershoot or overshoot the region R) constitute the *errors* in these estimates. The more rectangles we use, the more accurate the approximation. Thus, to approximate accurately the area of such a region R, we need an effective way to calculate and sum the areas of collections of rectangles like those in Fig. 5.3.7.

EXAMPLE 1 As in Fig. 5.3.7, let R denote the region that lies below the graph of $f(x) = x^2$ and above the interval $[0, 3]$. Calculate the underestimate and the overestimate of the area A of R by using 5 rectangles each of width $\frac{3}{5}$. Then repeat the computations using 10 rectangles each of width $\frac{3}{10}$.

Elementary Area Computations SECTION 5.3 289

Solution First suppose that $n = 5$ rectangles are used. Let $\underline{A}_5$ denote the underestimate and $\overline{A}_5$ the overestimate obtained by using 5 rectangles based on the 5 subintervals of length $\frac{3}{5}$ (Fig. 5.3.8). From Fig. 5.3.7(a) we see that the heights of the 5 inscribed rectangles (the first of which is degenerate—its height is zero) are the values of the function $f(x) = x^2$ at the 5 *left-hand* endpoints $0, \frac{3}{5}, \frac{6}{5}, \frac{9}{5}$, and $\frac{12}{5}$. Because the base of each rectangle has length $\frac{3}{5}$, we see also that

FIGURE 5.3.8 Five subintervals, each of length $\frac{3}{5}$ (Example 1).

$$\underline{A}_5 = \frac{3}{5} \cdot \left[(0)^2 + \left(\frac{3}{5}\right)^2 + \left(\frac{6}{5}\right)^2 + \left(\frac{9}{5}\right)^2 + \left(\frac{12}{5}\right)^2 \right]$$

$$= \frac{3}{5} \cdot \left(0 + \frac{9}{25} + \frac{36}{25} + \frac{81}{25} + \frac{144}{25} \right) = 6.48.$$

The heights of the 5 circumscribed rectangles are the values of $f(x) = x^2$ at the 5 *right-hand* endpoints $\frac{3}{5}, \frac{6}{5}, \frac{9}{5}, \frac{12}{5}$, and 3, so the corresponding overestimate is

$$\overline{A}_5 = \frac{3}{5} \cdot \left[\left(\frac{3}{5}\right)^2 + \left(\frac{6}{5}\right)^2 + \left(\frac{9}{5}\right)^2 + \left(\frac{12}{5}\right)^2 + \left(\frac{15}{5}\right)^2 \right]$$

$$= \frac{3}{5} \cdot \left(\frac{9}{25} + \frac{36}{25} + \frac{81}{25} + \frac{144}{25} + \frac{225}{25} \right) = 11.88.$$

These are crude approximations to the actual area A. On the basis of this information alone, our best estimate of A might well be the average of the under- and overestimates:

$$\frac{\underline{A}_5 + \overline{A}_5}{2} = \frac{6.48 + 11.88}{2} = 9.18.$$

Let us see if doubling the number of subintervals to $n = 10$ increases the accuracy significantly. Looking at Fig. 5.3.7(b), we see that the heights of the 10 inscribed rectangles are the values of $f(x) = x^2$ at the 10 *left-hand* endpoints $0, \frac{3}{10}, \frac{6}{10}, \frac{9}{10}, \frac{12}{10}, \frac{15}{10}, \frac{18}{10}, \frac{21}{10}, \frac{24}{10}$, and $\frac{27}{10}$ of the subintervals in Fig. 5.3.9. The base of each rectangle has length $\frac{3}{10}$, so the resulting underestimate is

FIGURE 5.3.9 Ten subintervals, each of length $\frac{3}{10}$ (Example 1).

$$\underline{A}_{10} = \frac{3}{10} \cdot \left[(0)^2 + \left(\frac{3}{10}\right)^2 + \left(\frac{6}{10}\right)^2 + \left(\frac{9}{10}\right)^2 + \left(\frac{12}{10}\right)^2 \right.$$

$$\left. + \left(\frac{15}{10}\right)^2 + \left(\frac{18}{10}\right)^2 + \left(\frac{21}{10}\right)^2 + \left(\frac{24}{10}\right)^2 + \left(\frac{27}{10}\right)^2 \right]$$

$$= \frac{3}{10} \cdot \left(0 + \frac{9}{100} + \frac{36}{100} + \frac{81}{100} + \frac{144}{100} + \frac{225}{100} + \frac{324}{100} + \frac{441}{100} + \frac{576}{100} + \frac{729}{100} \right)$$

$$= \frac{7695}{1000} = 7.695.$$

Similarly, the sum of the areas of the 10 circumscribed rectangles in Fig. 5.3.7(b) is the overestimate

$$\overline{A}_{10} = \frac{3}{10} \cdot \left[\left(\frac{3}{10}\right)^2 + \left(\frac{6}{10}\right)^2 + \left(\frac{9}{10}\right)^2 + \left(\frac{12}{10}\right)^2 + \left(\frac{15}{10}\right)^2 \right.$$

$$\left. + \left(\frac{18}{10}\right)^2 + \left(\frac{21}{10}\right)^2 + \left(\frac{24}{10}\right)^2 + \left(\frac{27}{10}\right)^2 + \left(\frac{30}{10}\right)^2 \right]$$

$$= \frac{10395}{1000} = 10.395.$$

At this point, our best estimate of the actual area A might be the average

$$\frac{\underline{A}_{10} + \overline{A}_{10}}{2} = \frac{7.695 + 10.395}{2} = 9.045. \qquad \blacklozenge$$

We used a computer to calculate more refined underestimates and overestimates of the area A under the graph $y = x^2$ over $[0, 3]$, with 20, 40, 80, 160, and, finally, 320 rectangles. The results (rounded to four decimal places) are shown in Fig. 5.3.10. The average values in the final column of the table suggest that $A \approx 9$.

Number of rectangles	Underestimate	Overestimate	Average
5	6.4800	11.8800	9.1800
10	7.6950	10.3950	9.0450
20	8.3363	9.6863	9.0113
40	8.6653	9.3403	9.0028
80	8.8320	9.1695	9.0007
160	8.9158	9.0846	9.0002
320	8.9579	9.0422	9.0000

FIGURE 5.3.10 Estimate of the area under $y = x^2$ over $[0,3]$.

Summation Notation

For more convenient computation of area estimates, as in Example 1, we need a concise notation for sums of many numbers. The symbol $\sum_{i=1}^{n} a_i$ is used to abbreviate the sum of the n numbers $a_1, a_2, a_3, \ldots, a_n$:

$$\sum_{i=1}^{n} a_i = a_1 + a_2 + a_3 + \cdots + a_n. \tag{2}$$

The symbol on the left here—$\sum$ is the capital Greek letter sigma (for S, for "sum")—specifies the sum of the **terms** a_i as the **summation index** i takes on the successive integer values from 1 to n. For instance, the sum of the squares of the first 10 positive integers is

$$\sum_{i=1}^{10} i^2 = 1^2 + 2^2 + 3^2 + 4^2 + 5^2 + 6^2 + 7^2 + 8^2 + 9^2 + 10^2$$

$$= 1 + 4 + 9 + 16 + 25 + 36 + 49 + 64 + 81 + 100 = 385.$$

The particular symbol used for the summation index is immaterial:

$$\sum_{i=1}^{10} i^2 = \sum_{k=1}^{10} k^2 = \sum_{r=1}^{10} r^2 = 385.$$

EXAMPLE 2

$$\sum_{k=1}^{7} (k+1) = 2 + 3 + 4 + 5 + 6 + 7 + 8 = 35,$$

$$\sum_{n=1}^{6} 2^n = 2 + 4 + 8 + 16 + 32 + 64 = 126,$$

and

$$\sum_{j=1}^{5} \frac{(-1)^{j+1}}{j^2} = 1 - \tfrac{1}{4} + \tfrac{1}{9} - \tfrac{1}{16} + \tfrac{1}{25} = \tfrac{3019}{3600} \approx 0.8386. \quad \blacklozenge$$

The simple rules of summation

$$\sum_{i=1}^{n} c a_i = c \sum_{i=1}^{n} a_i \tag{3}$$

and

$$\sum_{i=1}^{n} (a_i + b_i) = \left(\sum_{i=1}^{n} a_i \right) + \left(\sum_{i=1}^{n} b_i \right) \tag{4}$$

are easy to verify by writing out each sum in full.

Note that if $a_i = a$ (a constant) for $i = 1, 2, \ldots, n$, then Eq. (4) yields

$$\sum_{i=1}^{n}(a + b_i) = \sum_{i=1}^{n} a + \sum_{i=1}^{n} b_i = \underbrace{\left(a + a + \cdots + a\right)}_{n \text{ terms}} + \sum_{i=1}^{n} b_i,$$

and hence

$$\sum_{i=1}^{n}(a + b_i) = na + \sum_{i=1}^{n} b_i. \tag{5}$$

In particular,

$$\sum_{i=1}^{n} 1 = n. \tag{6}$$

The sum of the kth powers of the first n positive integers,

$$\sum_{i=1}^{n} i^k = 1^k + 2^k + 3^k + \cdots + n^k,$$

commonly occurs in area computations. The values of this sum for $k = 1, 2,$ and 3 are given by the following formulas (see Problems 43 and 44):

$$\sum_{i=1}^{n} i = \frac{n(n+1)}{2} = \tfrac{1}{2}n^2 + \tfrac{1}{2}n, \tag{7}$$

$$\sum_{i=1}^{n} i^2 = \frac{n(n+1)(2n+1)}{6} = \tfrac{1}{3}n^3 + \tfrac{1}{2}n^2 + \tfrac{1}{6}n, \tag{8}$$

$$\sum_{i=1}^{n} i^3 = \frac{n^2(n+1)^2}{4} = \tfrac{1}{4}n^4 + \tfrac{1}{2}n^3 + \tfrac{1}{4}n^2. \tag{9}$$

EXAMPLE 3 The sum of the first 10 positive integers is given by Eq. (7) with $n = 10$:

$$1 + 2 + 3 + \cdots + 10 = \sum_{i=1}^{10} i = \frac{10 \cdot 11}{2} = 55.$$

The sum of their squares and cubes are given by Eqs. (8) and (9):

$$1^2 + 2^2 + 3^2 + \cdots + 10^2 = \sum_{i=1}^{10} i^2 = \frac{10 \cdot 11 \cdot 21}{6} = 385$$

and

$$1^3 + 2^3 + 3^3 + \cdots + 10^3 = \sum_{i=1}^{10} i^3 = \frac{10^2 \cdot 11^2}{4} = 3025. \qquad \blacklozenge$$

EXAMPLE 4 Consider the sum

$$\sum_{i=1}^{10}(7i^2 - 5i) = 2 + 18 + 48 + \cdots + 522 + 650.$$

Using the rules in Eqs. (3) and (4) as well as Eqs. (7) and (8), we find that

$$\sum_{i=1}^{10}(7i^2 - 5i) = 7\sum_{i=1}^{10} i^2 - 5\sum_{i=1}^{10} i$$

$$= 7 \cdot \frac{10 \cdot 11 \cdot 21}{6} - 5 \cdot \frac{10 \cdot 11}{2} = 2420.$$

◆

EXAMPLE 5 We can use Eq. (8) to simplify the evaluation of the sum for $\underline{A}_{10}$ in Example 1, as follows:

$$\underline{A}_{10} = \tfrac{3}{10} \cdot \left[\left(\tfrac{0}{10}\right)^2 + \left(\tfrac{3}{10}\right)^2 + \left(\tfrac{6}{10}\right)^2 + \cdots + \left(\tfrac{27}{10}\right)^2\right] = \tfrac{3}{10}\sum_{i=0}^{9}\left(\tfrac{3}{10}\right)^2 i^2$$

$$= \tfrac{3}{10} \cdot \left(\tfrac{3}{10}\right)^2 \cdot [1^2 + 2^2 + 3^2 + \cdots + 9^2] = \left(\tfrac{3}{10}\right)^3 \sum_{i=1}^{9} i^2$$

$$= \frac{27}{1000} \cdot \frac{9 \cdot 10 \cdot 19}{6} = \frac{7695}{1000} = 7.695.$$

◆

EXAMPLE 6 Evaluate the limit

$$\lim_{n \to +\infty} \frac{1 + 2 + 3 + \cdots + n}{n^2}.$$

Solution Using Eq. (7), we obtain

$$\lim_{n \to +\infty} \frac{1 + 2 + 3 + \cdots + n}{n^2} = \lim_{n \to +\infty} \frac{\tfrac{1}{2}n(n+1)}{n^2}$$

$$= \lim_{n \to +\infty} \frac{n+1}{2n} = \lim_{n \to +\infty}\left(\frac{1}{2} + \frac{1}{2n}\right) = \frac{1}{2},$$

because the term $1/(2n)$ has limit zero as $n \to +\infty$.

◆

Area Sums

Figure 5.3.11 shows the region R that lies below the graph of the positive-valued *increasing* function f and above the interval $[a, b]$. To approximate the area A of R, we have chosen a fixed integer n and divided the interval $[a, b]$ into n subintervals

$$[x_0, x_1], \quad [x_1, x_2], \quad [x_2, x_3], \quad \ldots, \quad [x_{n-1}, x_n],$$

all with the same length

$$\Delta x = \frac{b - a}{n}. \tag{10}$$

On each of the subintervals we have erected one inscribed rectangle and one circumscribed rectangle.

FIGURE 5.3.11 The area under $y = f(x)$ over the interval $[a, b]$.

FIGURE 5.3.12 Inscribed and circumscribed rectangles on the ith subinterval $[x_{i-1}, x_i]$.

As indicated in Fig. 5.3.12, the inscribed rectangle over the ith subinterval $[x_{i-1}, x_i]$ has height $f(x_{i-1})$, whereas the ith circumscribed rectangle has height $f(x_i)$. Because the base of each rectangle has length Δx, the areas of the rectangles are

$$f(x_{i-1})\,\Delta x \quad \text{and} \quad f(x_i)\,\Delta x, \tag{11}$$

respectively. Adding the areas of the inscribed rectangles for $i = 1, 2, 3, \ldots, n$, we get the underestimate

$$\underline{A}_n = \sum_{i=1}^{n} f(x_{i-1})\,\Delta x \tag{12}$$

of the actual area A. Similarly, the sum of the areas of the circumscribed rectangles is the overestimate

$$\overline{A}_n = \sum_{i=1}^{n} f(x_i)\,\Delta x. \tag{13}$$

The inequality $\underline{A}_n \leqq A \leqq \overline{A}_n$ then yields

$$\sum_{i=1}^{n} f(x_{i-1})\,\Delta x \leqq A \leqq \sum_{i=1}^{n} f(x_i)\,\Delta x. \tag{14}$$

The inequalities in (14) would be reversed if $f(x)$ were decreasing (rather than increasing) on $[a, b]$. (Why?)

Areas as Limits

An illustration such as Fig. 5.3.7 suggests that if the number n of subintervals is very large, so that Δx is small, then the areas $\underline{A}_n$ and $\overline{A}_n$ of the inscribed and circumscribed polygons will differ by very little. Hence both will be very close to the actual area A of the region R. We can also see this because, if f either is increasing or is decreasing on the whole interval $[a, b]$, then the small rectangles in Fig. 5.3.11 (representing the difference between $\overline{A}_n$ and $\underline{A}_n$) can be reassembled in a "stack," as indicated on the right in the figure. It follows that

$$|\overline{A}_n - \underline{A}_n| = |f(b) - f(a)|\,\Delta x. \tag{15}$$

But $\Delta x = (b - a)/n \to 0$ as $n \to \infty$. Thus the difference between the left-hand and right-hand sums in (14) is approaching zero as $n \to \infty$, whereas A does not change as $n \to \infty$. It follows that the area of the region R is given by

$$A = \lim_{n \to \infty} \sum_{i=1}^{n} f(x_{i-1})\,\Delta x = \lim_{n \to \infty} \sum_{i=1}^{n} f(x_i)\,\Delta x. \tag{16}$$

The meaning of these limits is simply that A can be found with any desired accuracy by calculating either sum in Eq. (16) with a sufficiently large number n of subintervals.

In applying Eq. (16), recall that

$$\Delta x = \frac{b-a}{n}. \tag{17}$$

Also note that

$$x_i = a + i\,\Delta x \tag{18}$$

for $i = 0, 1, 2, \ldots, n$, because x_i is i "steps" of length Δx to the right of $x_0 = a$.

EXAMPLE 7 We can now compute exactly the area we approximated in Example 1—the area of the region under the graph of $f(x) = x^2$ over the interval $[0, 3]$. If we divide $[0, 3]$ into n subintervals all of the same length, then Eqs. (17) and (18) give

$$\Delta x = \frac{3}{n} \quad \text{and} \quad x_i = 0 + i \cdot \frac{3}{n} = \frac{3i}{n}$$

for $i = 0, 1, 2, \ldots, n$. Therefore,

$$\sum_{i=1}^{n} f(x_i)\,\Delta x = \sum_{i=1}^{n} (x_i)^2\,\Delta x = \sum_{i=1}^{n} \left(\frac{3i}{n}\right)^2 \left(\frac{3}{n}\right) = \frac{27}{n^3} \sum_{i=1}^{n} i^2.$$

Then Eq. (8) for $\sum i^2$ yields

$$\sum_{i=1}^{n} f(x_i)\,\Delta x = \frac{27}{n^3}\left(\frac{1}{3}n^3 + \frac{1}{2}n^2 + \frac{1}{6}n\right) = 27\left(\frac{1}{3} + \frac{1}{2n} + \frac{1}{6n^2}\right).$$

When we take the limit as $n \to \infty$, Eq. (16) gives

$$A = \lim_{n \to \infty} 27\left(\frac{1}{3} + \frac{1}{2n} + \frac{1}{6n^2}\right) = 9,$$

because the terms $1/(2n)$ and $1/(6n^2)$ approach zero as $n \to \infty$. Thus our earlier inference from the data in Fig. 5.3.10 was correct: $A = 9$ *exactly*. ◆

EXAMPLE 8 Find the area under the graph of $f(x) = 100 - 3x^2$ from $x = 1$ to $x = 5$.

Solution As shown in Fig. 5.3.13, the sum $\sum f(x_i)\,\Delta x$ gives the area of the inscribed rectangular polygon. With $a = 1$ and $b = 5$, Eqs. (17) and (18) give

$$\Delta x = \frac{4}{n} \quad \text{and} \quad x_i = 1 + i \cdot \frac{4}{n} = 1 + \frac{4i}{n}.$$

Therefore

$$\sum_{i=1}^{n} f(x_i)\,\Delta x = \sum_{i=1}^{n}\left[100 - 3 \cdot \left(1 + \frac{4i}{n}\right)^2\right]\left(\frac{4}{n}\right)$$

$$= \sum_{i=1}^{n}\left[97 - \frac{24i}{n} - \frac{48i^2}{n^2}\right]\left(\frac{4}{n}\right)$$

$$= \frac{388}{n}\sum_{i=1}^{n} 1 - \frac{96}{n^2}\sum_{i=1}^{n} i - \frac{192}{n^3}\sum_{i=1}^{n} i^2$$

$$= \frac{388}{n} \cdot n - \frac{96}{n^2}\left(\frac{1}{2}n^2 + \frac{1}{2}n\right) - \frac{192}{n^3}\left(\frac{1}{3}n^3 + \frac{1}{2}n^2 + \frac{1}{6}n\right)$$

$$= 276 - \frac{144}{n} - \frac{32}{n^2}.$$

FIGURE 5.3.13 The region of Example 8.

[We have applied Eqs. (6) through (8).] Consequently, the second limit in Eq. (16) yields

$$A = \lim_{n \to \infty} \left(276 - \frac{144}{n} - \frac{32}{n} \right) = 276$$

for the desired area. ◆

Historical Note—The Number π

Mathematicians of ancient times tended to employ inscribed and circumscribed triangles rather than rectangles for area approximations. In the third century B.C., Archimedes, the greatest mathematician of antiquity, used such an approach to derive the famous estimate

$$\tfrac{223}{71} = 3\tfrac{10}{71} < \pi < 3\tfrac{1}{7} = \tfrac{22}{7}.$$

Because the area of a circle of radius r is πr^2, the number π may be *defined* to be the area of the unit circle of radius $r = 1$. We will approximate π, then, by approximating the area of the unit circle.

Let P_n and Q_n be n-sided regular polygons, with P_n inscribed in the unit circle and Q_n circumscribed around it (Fig. 5.3.14). Because both polygons are regular, all their sides and angles are equal, so we need to find the area of only *one* of the triangles that we've shown making up P_n and *one* of those making up Q_n.

Let α_n be the central angle subtended by *half* of one of the polygon's sides. The angle α_n is the same whether we work with P_n or with Q_n. In degrees,

$$\alpha_n = \frac{360°}{2n} = \frac{180°}{n}.$$

We can read various dimensions and proportions from Fig. 5.3.14. For example, we see that the area $a(P_n) = \underline{A}_n$ of P_n is given by

$$\underline{A}_n = a(P_n) = n \cdot 2 \cdot \frac{1}{2} \sin\alpha_n \cos\alpha_n = \frac{n}{2}\sin 2\alpha_n = \frac{n}{2}\sin\left(\frac{360°}{n}\right) \quad (19)$$

and that the area of Q_n is

$$\overline{A}_n = a(Q_n) = n \cdot 2 \cdot \frac{1}{2}\tan\alpha_n = n\tan\left(\frac{180°}{n}\right). \quad (20)$$

We substituted selected values of n into Eqs. (19) and (20) to obtain the entries of the table in Fig. 5.3.15. Because $\underline{A}_n \leq \pi \leq \overline{A}_n$ for all n, we see that $\pi \approx 3.14159$ to five decimal places. Archimedes' reasoning was *not* circular—he used a direct method for computing the sines and cosines in Eqs. (19) and (20) that does not depend upon *a priori* knowledge of the value of π.*

FIGURE 5.3.14 Estimating π by using inscribed and circumscribed regular polygons and the unit circle.

n	$a(P_n)$	$a(Q_n)$
6	2.598076	3.464102
12	3.000000	3.215390
24	3.105829	3.159660
48	3.132629	3.146086
96	3.139350	3.142715
180	3.140955	3.141912
360	3.141433	3.141672
720	3.141553	3.141613
1440	3.141583	3.141598
2880	3.141590	3.141594
5760	3.141592	3.141593

FIGURE 5.3.15 Data for estimating π (rounded to six-place accuracy).

5.3 TRUE/FALSE STUDY GUIDE

5.3 CONCEPTS: QUESTIONS AND DISCUSSION

1. When the German mathematician Carl Friedrich Gauss (1777–1855) was ten years old, his teacher asked the class to find the sum of the integers 1 through 100. Young Gauss almost immediately wrote the answer (and nothing else) on his slate. Apparently he had simply noted that the sum of the first and last of these integers is 101, as is the sum of the second and next-to-last, as is the sum of the third and second-from-last, and so forth. So he simply multiplied

---

*See Chapter 2 of C. H. Edwards, Jr., *The Historical Development of the Calculus* (New York: Springer-Verlag, 1979).

101 by 50—the number of such pairs—to get the sum 5050. Explain carefully how this approach can be used to show that

$$\sum_{i=1}^{n} i = \frac{n(n+1)}{2}.$$

In what way does the argument depend on whether n is even or odd?

2. The area A of the region under the curve $y = f(x)$ in Fig. 5.3.11 satisfies (for every positive integer n) the inequality $\underline{A}_n < A < \overline{A}_n$, where $\underline{A}_n$ and $\overline{A}_n$ are the sums defined in Eqs. (12) and (13). Moreover,

$$|\overline{A}_n - \underline{A}_n| = |f(b) - f(a)| \cdot \frac{b-a}{n}$$

by Eq. (15). Explain carefully why it follows—as asserted in Eq. (16)—that

$$\lim_{n \to \infty} \underline{A}_n = \lim_{n \to \infty} \overline{A}_n = A.$$

That is, explain why it follows that, given $\epsilon > 0$, there exists an integer N such that both $\underline{A}_n$ and $\overline{A}_n$ differ from A by less than ϵ if $n > N$.

5.3 PROBLEMS

Write each of the sums in Problems 1 through 8 in expanded notation.

1. $\sum_{i=1}^{5} 3^i$

2. $\sum_{i=1}^{6} \sqrt{2i}$

3. $\sum_{j=1}^{5} \frac{1}{j+1}$

4. $\sum_{j=1}^{6} (2j - 1)$

5. $\sum_{k=1}^{6} \frac{1}{k^2}$

6. $\sum_{k=1}^{6} \frac{(-1)^{k+1}}{k^2}$

7. $\sum_{n=1}^{5} x^n$

8. $\sum_{n=1}^{5} (-1)^{n+1} x^{2n-1}$

Write the sums in Problems 9 through 18 in summation notation.

9. $1 + 4 + 9 + 16 + 25$

10. $1 - 2 + 3 - 4 + 5 - 6$

11. $1 + \frac{1}{2} + \frac{1}{3} + \frac{1}{4} + \frac{1}{5}$

12. $1 + \frac{1}{4} + \frac{1}{9} + \frac{1}{16} + \frac{1}{25}$

13. $\frac{1}{2} + \frac{1}{4} + \frac{1}{8} + \frac{1}{16} + \frac{1}{32} + \frac{1}{64}$

14. $\frac{1}{3} - \frac{1}{9} + \frac{1}{27} - \frac{1}{81} + \frac{1}{243}$

15. $\frac{2}{3} + \frac{4}{9} + \frac{8}{27} + \frac{16}{81} + \frac{32}{243}$

16. $1 + \sqrt{2} + \sqrt{3} + 2 + \sqrt{5} + \sqrt{6} + \sqrt{7} + 2\sqrt{2} + 3$

17. $x + \frac{x^2}{2} + \frac{x^3}{3} + \cdots + \frac{x^{10}}{10}$

18. $x - \frac{x^3}{3} + \frac{x^5}{5} - \frac{x^7}{7} + \cdots - \frac{x^{19}}{19}$

Use Eqs. (6) through (9) to find the sums in Problems 19 through 28.

19. $\sum_{i=1}^{10} (4i - 3)$

20. $\sum_{j=1}^{8} (5 - 2j)$

21. $\sum_{i=1}^{10} (3i^2 + 1)$

22. $\sum_{k=1}^{6} (2k - 3k^2)$

23. $\sum_{r=1}^{8} (r - 1)(r + 2)$

24. $\sum_{i=1}^{5} (i^3 - 3i + 2)$

25. $\sum_{i=1}^{6} (i^3 - i^2)$

26. $\sum_{k=1}^{10} (2k - 1)^2$

27. $\sum_{i=1}^{100} i^2$

28. $\sum_{i=1}^{100} i^3$

Use the method of Example 6 to evaluate the limits in Problems 29 and 30.

29. $\lim_{n \to \infty} \frac{1^2 + 2^2 + 3^2 + \cdots + n^2}{n^3}$

30. $\lim_{n \to \infty} \frac{1^3 + 2^3 + 3^3 + \cdots + n^3}{n^4}$

Use Eqs. (6) through (9) to derive concise formulas in terms of n for the sums in Problems 31 and 32.

31. $\sum_{i=1}^{n} (2i - 1)$

32. $\sum_{i=1}^{n} (2i - 1)^2$

In Problems 33 through 42, let R denote the region that lies below the graph of $y = f(x)$ over the interval $[a, b]$ on the x-axis. Use the method of Example 1 to calculate both an underestimate $\underline{A}_n$ and an overestimate $\overline{A}_n$ for the area A of R, based on a division of $[a, b]$ into n subintervals all with the same length $\Delta x = (b-a)/n$.

33. $f(x) = x$ on $[0, 1]$; $n = 5$

34. $f(x) = x$ on $[1, 3]$; $n = 5$

35. $f(x) = 2x + 3$ on $[0, 3]$; $n = 6$

36. $f(x) = 13 - 3x$ on $[0, 3]$; $n = 6$ (Fig. 5.3.16)

FIGURE 5.3.16 Problem 36.

37. $f(x) = x^2$ on $[0, 1]$; $n = 5$
38. $f(x) = x^2$ on $[1, 3]$; $n = 5$
39. $f(x) = 9 - x^2$ on $[0, 3]$; $n = 5$ (Fig. 5.3.17)

FIGURE 5.3.17 Problem 39.

40. $f(x) = 9 - x^2$ on $[1, 3]$; $n = 8$
41. $f(x) = x^3$ on $[0, 1]$; $n = 10$
42. $f(x) = \sqrt{x}$ on $[0, 1]$; $n = 10$ (Fig. 5.3.18)

FIGURE 5.3.18 Problem 42.

43. Derive Eq. (7) by adding the equations

$$\sum_{i=1}^{n} i = 1 + 2 + 3 + \cdots + n$$

and

$$\sum_{i=1}^{n} i = n + (n-1) + (n-2) \cdots + 2 + 1.$$

44. Write the n equations obtained by substituting the values $k = 1, 2, 3, \ldots, n$ into the identity

$$(k+1)^3 - k^3 = 3k^2 + 3k + 1.$$

Add these n equations and use their sum to deduce Eq. (8) from Eq. (7).

In Problems 45 through 50, first calculate (in terms of n) the sum

$$\sum_{i=1}^{n} f(x_i) \, \Delta x$$

to approximate the area A of the region under $y = f(x)$ above the interval $[a, b]$. Then find A exactly (as in Examples 7 and 8) by taking the limit as $n \to \infty$.

45. $f(x) = x$ on $[0, 1]$
46. $f(x) = x^2$ on $[0, 2]$
47. $f(x) = x^3$ on $[0, 3]$
48. $f(x) = x + 2$ on $[0, 2]$
49. $f(x) = 5 - 3x$ on $[0, 1]$
50. $f(x) = 9 - x^2$ on $[0, 3]$

51. As in Fig. 5.3.19, the region under the graph of $f(x) = hx/b$ for $0 \leq x \leq b$ is a triangle with base b and height h. Use Eq. (7) to verify—with the notation of Eq. (16)—that

$$\lim_{n \to \infty} \sum_{i=1}^{n} f(x_i) \, \Delta x = \tfrac{1}{2} bh,$$

in agreement with the familiar formula for the area of a triangle.

FIGURE 5.3.19 Problem 51.

In Problems 52 and 53, let A denote the area and C the circumference of a circle of radius r and let A_n and C_n denote the area and perimeter, respectively, of a regular n-sided polygon inscribed in this circle.

52. Figure 5.3.20 shows one side of the n-sided polygon subtending an angle $2\pi/n$ at the center O of the circle. Show that

$$A_n = nr^2 \sin\left(\frac{\pi}{n}\right) \cos\left(\frac{\pi}{n}\right) \quad \text{and that} \quad C_n = 2nr \sin\left(\frac{\pi}{n}\right).$$

FIGURE 5.3.20 Problem 52.

53. Deduce that $A = \tfrac{1}{2} rC$ by taking the limit of A_n/C_n as $n \to \infty$. Then, under the assumption that $A = \pi r^2$, deduce that $C = 2\pi r$. Thus the familiar circumference formula for a circle follows from the familiar area formula for a circle.

5.4 RIEMANN SUMS AND THE INTEGRAL

Suppose that f is a positive-valued and increasing function defined on a set of real numbers that includes the interval $[a, b]$. In Section 5.3 we used inscribed and circumscribed rectangles to set up the sums

$$\sum_{i=1}^{n} f(x_{i-1})\, \Delta x \quad \text{and} \quad \sum_{i=1}^{n} f(x_i)\, \Delta x \tag{1}$$

that approximate the area A under the graph of $y = f(x)$ from $x = a$ to $x = b$. Recall that the notation in Eq. (1) is based on a division of the interval $[a, b]$ into n subintervals, all with the same length $\Delta x = (b - a)/n$, and that $[x_{i-1}, x_i]$ denotes the ith subinterval.

The approximating sums in Eq. (1) are both of the form

$$\sum_{i=1}^{n} f(x_i^\star)\, \Delta x, \tag{2}$$

where $x_i^\star$ denotes a selected point of the ith subinterval $[x_{i-1}, x_i]$ (Fig. 5.4.1). Sums of the form in (2) appear as approximations in a wide range of applications and form the basis for the definition of the integral. Motivated by our discussion of area in Section 5.3, we want to define the integral of f from a to b as some sort of limit, as $\Delta x \to 0$, of sums such as the one in (2). Our goal is to begin with a fairly general function f and define a computable real number I (the *integral* of f) that—in the special case when f is continuous and positive-valued on $[a, b]$—will equal the area under the graph of $y = f(x)$.

FIGURE 5.4.1 The Riemann sum in Eq. (2) as a sum of areas of rectangles.

Riemann Sums

We begin with a function f defined on $[a, b]$ that is *not* necessarily either continuous or positive valued. A **partition** P of $[a, b]$ is a collection of subintervals

$$[x_0, x_1],\quad [x_1, x_2],\quad [x_2, x_3],\quad \ldots,\quad [x_{n-1}, x_n]$$

of $[a, b]$ such that

$$a = x_0 < x_1 < x_2 < x_3 < \cdots < x_{n-1} < x_n = b,$$

as in Fig. 5.4.1. We write $\Delta x_i = x_i - x_{i-1}$ for the length of the ith subinterval $[x_{i-1}, x_i]$. To get a sum such as the one in (2), we need a point $x_i^\star$ in the ith subinterval for each i, $1 \leq i \leq n$. A collection of points

$$S = \{x_1^\star, x_2^\star, x_3^\star, \ldots, x_n^\star\}$$

FIGURE 5.4.2 The selected point $x_i^\star$ in the ith subinterval $[x_{i-1}, x_i]$.

with $x_i^\star$ in $[x_{i-1}, x_i]$ for each i (Fig. 5.4.2) is called a **selection** for the partition P.

DEFINITION Riemann Sum
Let f be a function defined on the interval $[a, b]$. If P is a partition of $[a, b]$ and S is a selection for P, then the **Riemann sum** for f determined by P and S is

$$R = \sum_{i=1}^{n} f(x_i^\star) \Delta x_i. \tag{3}$$

We also say that this Riemann sum is **associated with** the partition P.

The German mathematician G. F. B. Riemann (1826–1866) provided a rigorous definition of the integral. Various special types of "Riemann sums" had appeared in area and volume computations since the time of Archimedes, but it was Riemann who framed the preceding definition in its full generality.

The point $x_i^\star$ in Eq. (3) is simply a selected point of the ith subinterval $[x_{i-1}, x_i]$. That is, it can be *any* point of this subinterval. But when we compute Riemann sums, we usually choose the points of the selection S in some systematic manner, as illustrated in Fig. 5.4.3. There we show different Riemann sums for the function $f(x) = 2x^3 - 6x^2 + 5$ on the interval $[0, 3]$. Figure 5.4.3(a) shows rectangles associated with the *left-endpoint sum*

$$R_{\text{left}} = \sum_{i=1}^{n} f(x_{i-1}) \Delta x, \tag{4}$$

in which each $x_i^\star$ is selected to be x_{i-1}, the *left endpoint* of the ith subinterval $[x_{i-1}, x_i]$ of length $\Delta x = (b - a)/n$. Figure 5.4.3(b) shows rectangles associated with the

FIGURE 5.4.3 Riemann sums for $f(x) = 2x^3 - 6x^2 + 5$ on $[0,3]$: (a) Left-endpoint sum; (b) Right-endpoint sum; (c) Midpoint sum.

right-endpoint sum

$$R_{\text{right}} = \sum_{i=1}^{n} f(x_i)\,\Delta x, \tag{5}$$

in which each $x_i^\star$ is selected to be x_i, the *right endpoint* of $[x_{i-1}, x_i]$. In each figure, some of the rectangles are inscribed and others are circumscribed.

Figure 5.4.3(c) shows rectangles associated with the *midpoint sum*

$$R_{\text{mid}} = \sum_{i=1}^{n} f(m_i)\,\Delta x, \tag{6}$$

in which

$$x_i^\star = m_i = \frac{x_{i-1} + x_i}{2},$$

the *midpoint* of the ith subinterval $[x_{i-1}, x_i]$. The dashed lines in Fig. 5.4.3(c) represent the ordinates of f at these midpoints.

EXAMPLE 1 In Example 1 of Section 5.3 we calculated left- and right-endpoint sums for $f(x) = x^2$ on $[0, 3]$ with $n = 10$ subintervals. We now do this more concisely by using summation notation, and we also calculate the analogous midpoint sum. Figure 5.4.4 shows a typical approximating rectangle for each of these sums. With $a = 0$, $b = 3$, and $\Delta x = (b-a)/n = \frac{3}{10}$, we see that the ith subdivision point is

$$x_i = a + i \cdot \Delta x = \tfrac{3}{10} i.$$

FIGURE 5.4.4 Example 1: (a) The case $x_i^\star = x_{i-1}$; (b) The case $x_i^\star = x_i$; (c) The case $x_i^\star = m_i$.

The ith subinterval, as well as its midpoint

$$m_i = \frac{x_{i-1} + x_i}{2} = \frac{1}{2}\left(\frac{3i-3}{10} + \frac{3i}{10}\right) = \frac{3}{20}(2i-1),$$

are shown in Fig. 5.4.5. With $x_i^\star = x_{i-1} = \frac{3}{10}(i-1)$, we obtain the left-endpoint sum in Eq. (4),

$$R_{\text{left}} = \sum_{i=1}^{n} f(x_{i-1})\,\Delta x = \sum_{i=1}^{10} \left[\tfrac{3}{10}(i-1)\right]^2 \left(\tfrac{3}{10}\right)$$

$$= \tfrac{27}{1000} \cdot \left(0^2 + 1^2 + 2^2 + \cdots + 9^2\right)$$

$$= \tfrac{7695}{1000} = 7.695 \qquad \text{[using Eq. (8) of Section 5.3]}.$$

FIGURE 5.4.5 The ith subinterval of Example 1.

$m_i = \tfrac{3}{20}(2i-1)$

$x_{i-1} = \tfrac{3}{10}(i-1)$ $\quad x_i = \tfrac{3}{10}i$

With $x_i^\star = x_i = \frac{3}{10}i$, we get the right-endpoint sum in Eq. (5),

$$R_{\text{right}} = \sum_{i=1}^{n} f(x_i) \Delta x = \sum_{i=1}^{10} \left[\frac{3}{10}i\right]^2 \left(\frac{3}{10}\right)$$

$$= \frac{27}{1000} \cdot (1^2 + 2^2 + 3^2 + \cdots + 10^2)$$

$$= \frac{10395}{1000} = 10.395 \qquad \text{[using Eq. (8) of Section 5.3].}$$

Finally, with $x_i^\star = m_i = \frac{3}{20}(2i-1)$, we get the midpoint sum in Eq. (6),

$$R_{\text{mid}} = \sum_{i=1}^{n} f(m_i) \Delta x = \sum_{i=1}^{10} \left[\frac{3}{20}(2i-1)\right]^2 \left(\frac{3}{10}\right)$$

$$= \frac{27}{4000} \cdot (1^2 + 3^2 + 5^2 + \cdots + 17^2 + 19^2) = \frac{35910}{4000} = 8.9775.$$

The midpoint sum is much closer than either endpoint sum to the actual value 9 (of the area under the graph of $y = x^2$ over $[0, 3]$) that we found in Example 7 of Section 5.3. ◆

EXAMPLE 2 Figure 5.4.6 illustrates Riemann sums for $f(x) = \sin x$ on $[0, \pi]$ based on $n = 3$ subintervals: $[0, \pi/3]$, $[\pi/3, 2\pi/3]$, and $[2\pi/3, \pi]$, of length $\Delta x = \pi/3$, and with midpoints $\pi/6$, $\pi/2$, and $5\pi/6$. The left-endpoint sum is

$$R_{\text{left}} = (\Delta x) \cdot \left(\sum_{i=1}^{n} f(x_{i-1})\right) = \frac{\pi}{3} \cdot \left(\sin 0 + \sin \frac{\pi}{3} + \sin \frac{2\pi}{3}\right)$$

$$= \frac{\pi}{3} \cdot \left(0 + \frac{\sqrt{3}}{2} + \frac{\sqrt{3}}{2}\right) = \frac{\pi\sqrt{3}}{3} \approx 1.81.$$

It is clear from the figure that the right-endpoint sum has the same value. The corresponding midpoint sum is

$$R_{\text{mid}} = \frac{\pi}{3} \cdot \left(\sin \frac{\pi}{6} + \sin \frac{\pi}{2} + \sin \frac{5\pi}{6}\right) = \frac{\pi}{3} \cdot \left(\frac{1}{2} + 1 + \frac{1}{2}\right) = \frac{2\pi}{3} \approx 2.09.$$

(We will soon be able to show that the area under one arch of the sine curve is exactly 2.) ◆

FIGURE 5.4.6 Approximating the area under $y = \sin x$ on $[0, \pi]$ (Example 2): (a) Left-endpoint sum; (b) Right-endpoint sum; (c) Midpoint sum.

The Integral as a Limit

In the case of a function f that has both positive and negative values on $[a, b]$, it is necessary to consider the *signs* indicated in Fig. 5.4.7 when we interpret geometrically the Riemann sum in Eq. (3). On each subinterval $[x_{i-1}, x_i]$, we have a rectangle with width Δx and "height" $f(x_i^\star)$. If $f(x_i^\star) > 0$, then this rectangle stands *above* the x-axis;

FIGURE 5.4.7 A geometric representation of the Riemann sum in Eq. (3).

if $f(x_i^\star) < 0$, it lies *below* the x-axis. The Riemann sum R is then the sum of the **signed** areas of these rectangles—that is, the sum of the areas of those rectangles that lie above the x-axis *minus* the sum of the areas of those that lie below the x-axis.

If the widths Δx_i of these rectangles are all very small, then it appears that the corresponding Riemann sum R will closely approximate the area from $x = a$ to $x = b$ under $y = f(x)$ and above the x-axis, *minus* the area that lies above the graph and below the x-axis. This suggests that the integral of f from a to b should be defined by taking the limit of the Riemann sums as the widths Δx_i all approach zero:

$$I = \lim_{\Delta x_i \to 0} \sum_{i=1}^{n} f(x_i^\star) \Delta x_i. \tag{7}$$

The formal definition of the integral is obtained by saying precisely what it means for this limit to exist. The **norm** of the partition P is the largest of the lengths $\Delta x_i = x_i - x_{i-1}$ of the subintervals in P and is denoted by $|P|$. Briefly, Eq. (7) means that if $|P|$ is sufficiently small, then *all* Riemann sums associated with the partition P are close to the number I.

DEFINITION   The Definite Integral

The **definite integral of the function** f **from** a **to** b is the number

$$I = \lim_{|P| \to 0} \sum_{i=1}^{n} f(x_i^\star) \Delta x_i, \tag{8}$$

provided that this limit exists, in which case we say that f is **integrable** on $[a, b]$. Equation (8) means that, for each number $\epsilon > 0$, there exists a number $\delta > 0$ such that

$$\left| I - \sum_{i=1}^{n} f(x_i^\star) \Delta x_i \right| < \epsilon$$

for every Riemann sum associated with any partition P of $[a, b]$ for which $|P| < \delta$.

The customary notation for the integral of f from a to b, due to the German mathematician and philosopher G. W. Leibniz, is

$$I = \int_a^b f(x)\, dx = \lim_{|P| \to 0} \sum_{i=1}^{n} f(x_i^\star) \Delta x_i. \tag{9}$$

Considering I to be the area under $y = f(x)$ from a to b, Leibniz first thought of a narrow strip with height $f(x)$ and "infinitesimally small" width dx (as in Fig. 5.4.8), so that its area would be the product $f(x)\, dx$. He regarded the integral as a sum of areas of such strips and denoted this sum by the elongated capital S (for *summa*) that appears as the integral sign in Eq. (9).

We shall see that this integral notation is not only highly suggestive, but also is exceedingly useful in manipulations with integrals. The numbers a and b are called the **lower limit** and **upper limit**, respectively, of the integral; they are the endpoints of the interval of integration. The function $f(x)$ that appears between the integral sign and dx is called the **integrand.** The symbol dx that follows the integrand in Eq. (9) should, for the time being, be thought of as simply an indication of what the independent variable is. Like the index of summation, the independent variable x is a "dummy variable"—it may be replaced with any other variable without affecting the meaning of Eq. (9). Thus if f is integrable on $[a, b]$, we can write

$$\int_a^b f(x)\, dx = \int_a^b f(t)\, dt = \int_a^b f(u)\, du.$$

FIGURE 5.4.8 Origin of Leibniz's notation for the integral.

The definition given for the definite integral applies only if $a < b$, but it is convenient to include the cases $a = b$ and $a > b$ as well. The integral is defined in these cases as follows:

$$\int_a^a f(x)\,dx = 0 \tag{10}$$

and

$$\int_a^b f(x)\,dx = -\int_b^a f(x)\,dx, \tag{11}$$

provided that the right-hand integral exists. Thus *interchanging the limits of integration reverses the sign of the integral.*

Just as not all functions are differentiable, not every function is integrable. Suppose that c is a point of $[a, b]$ such that $f(x) \to +\infty$ as $x \to c$. If $[x_{k-1}, x_k]$ is the subinterval of the partition P that contains c, then the Riemann sum in Eq. (3) can be made arbitrarily large by choosing $x_k^\star$ to be sufficiently close to c. For our purposes, however, we need to know only that every continuous function is integrable. The following theorem is proved in Appendix G.

THEOREM 1 Existence of the Integral
If the function f is continuous on $[a, b]$, then f is integrable on $[a, b]$.

Although we omit the details, it is not difficult to show that the definition of the integral can be reformulated in terms of sequences of Riemann sums, as follows.

THEOREM 2 The Integral as a Limit of a Sequence
The function f is integrable on $[a, b]$ with integral I if and only if

$$\lim_{n \to \infty} R_n = I \tag{12}$$

for every sequence $\{R_n\}_1^\infty$ of Riemann sums associated with a sequence of partitions $\{P_n\}_1^\infty$ of $[a, b]$ such that $|P_n| \to 0$ as $n \to +\infty$.

Riemann Sum Computations

The reformulation in Theorem 2 of the definition of the integral is helpful because it is easier to visualize a specific sequence of Riemann sums than to visualize the vast totality of all possible Riemann sums. In the case of a continuous function f (known to be integrable by Theorem 1), the situation can be simplified even more by using only Riemann sums associated with partitions consisting of subintervals all with the same length

$$\Delta x_1 = \Delta x_2 = \cdots = \Delta x_n = \frac{b - a}{n} = \Delta x.$$

Such a partition of $[a, b]$ into equal-length subintervals is called a **regular partition** of $[a, b]$.

Any Riemann sum associated with a regular partition can be written in the form

$$\sum_{i=1}^n f(x_i^\star)\,\Delta x, \tag{13}$$

where the absence of a subscript in Δx signifies that the sum is associated with a regular partition. In such a case the conditions $|P| \to 0$, $\Delta x \to 0$, and $n \to +\infty$ are equivalent, so the integral of a *continuous* function can be defined quite simply:

$$\int_a^b f(x)\,dx = \lim_{n\to\infty} \sum_{i=1}^n f(x_i^\star)\,\Delta x = \lim_{\Delta x\to 0} \sum_{i=1}^n f(x_i^\star)\,\Delta x. \quad (14)$$

Consequently, we henceforth will use only regular partitions; the subintervals will thus have length and endpoints given by

$$\Delta x = \frac{b-a}{n} \quad \text{and} \quad x_i = a + i\cdot\Delta x \quad (15)$$

for $i = 0, 1, 2, 3, \ldots, n$. If we select $x_i^\star = x_i$ then (14) gives

$$\int_a^b f(x)\,dx = \lim_{n\to\infty} \sum_{i=1}^n f(x_i)\,\Delta x. \quad (16)$$

EXAMPLE 3 Use Riemann sums to evaluate $\int_0^4 (x^3 - 2x)\,dx$.

Solution With $a = 0$ and $b = 4$ in (15), we have $\Delta x = 4/n$ and $x_i = 4i/n$. Hence

$$\int_0^4 (x^3 - 2x)\,dx = \lim_{n\to\infty} \sum_{i=1}^n f(x_i)\,\Delta x = \lim_{n\to\infty} \sum_{i=1}^n \left[\left(\frac{4i}{n}\right)^3 - 2\left(\frac{4i}{n}\right)\right]\cdot\frac{4}{n}$$

$$= \lim_{n\to\infty} \frac{4}{n}\sum_{i=1}^n \left[\frac{64i^3}{n^3} - \frac{8i}{n}\right]$$

$$= \lim_{n\to\infty} \left[\frac{256}{n^4}\sum_{i=1}^n i^3 - \frac{32}{n^2}\sum_{i=1}^n i\right].$$

We now use Eqs. (7) and (9) in Section 5.3 to convert each of the last two sums to closed form:

$$\int_0^4 (x^3 - 2x)\,dx = \lim_{n\to\infty} \left[\frac{256}{n^4}\cdot\frac{n^2(n+1)^2}{4} - \frac{32}{n^2}\cdot\frac{n(n+1)}{2}\right]$$

$$= \lim_{n\to\infty} \left[\frac{64}{n^2}(n+1)^2 - \frac{16}{n}(n+1)\right]$$

$$= \lim_{n\to\infty} \left[64\left(1 + \frac{1}{n}\right)^2 - 16\left(1 + \frac{1}{n}\right)\right];$$

$$\int_0^4 (x^3 - 2x)\,dx = 64 - 16 = 48. \quad \blacklozenge$$

EXAMPLE 4 Use Riemann sums to evaluate $\int_a^b x\,dx$ (where $a < b$).

Solution With $f(x) = x$ and $x_i^\star = x_i$ (see Fig. 5.4.9), Eqs. (15) and (16) yield

$$\int_a^b x\,dx = \lim_{n\to\infty} \sum_{i=1}^n f(x_i)\,\Delta x = \lim_{n\to\infty} \sum_{i=1}^n (a + i\cdot\Delta x)\,\Delta x$$

$$= \lim_{n\to\infty} \left[(a\,\Delta x)\sum_{i=1}^n 1 + (\Delta x)^2\sum_{i=1}^n i\right]$$

$$= \lim_{n\to\infty} \left[(a\,\Delta x)\cdot n + (\Delta x)^2\cdot\frac{n(n+1)}{2}\right]$$

FIGURE 5.4.9 Calculating the area under $y = x$ from $x = a$ to $x = b$.

when we use Eqs. (6) and (7) in Section 5.3 to convert the sums to closed form. Then substituting $\Delta x = (b-a)/n$ gives

$$\int_a^b x\,dx = \lim_{n\to\infty}\left[a\cdot\frac{b-a}{n}\cdot n + \left(\frac{b-a}{n}\right)^2\cdot\frac{n(n+1)}{2}\right]$$

$$= \lim_{n\to\infty}\left[a(b-a) + \frac{1}{2}(b-a)^2\left(1+\frac{1}{n}\right)\right]$$

$$= a(b-a) + \frac{1}{2}(b-a)^2 = (b-a)\left(a + \frac{1}{2}b - \frac{1}{2}a\right)$$

$$= (b-a)\cdot\frac{1}{2}(b+a) = \frac{1}{2}(b^2 - a^2).$$

Thus we see finally that

$$\int_a^b x\,dx = \frac{1}{2}b^2 - \frac{1}{2}a^2. \tag{17}$$

◆

REMARK 1 If $0 < a < b$, then $A = \int_a^b x\,dx$ is the area of the trapezoid shown in Fig. 5.4.9. Then Eq. (17) implies that

$$A = (b-a)\cdot\tfrac{1}{2}(a+b) = w\cdot\overline{h},$$

where $w = b - a$ is the width and $\overline{h} = \tfrac{1}{2}(a+b)$ is the average height of the trapezoid.

REMARK 2 Figures 5.4.10 and 5.4.11 illustrate two different cases in Example 4. In each case Eq. (17) agrees with the sum of the indicated *signed* areas. The minus sign in Fig. 5.4.10 represents the fact that area *beneath* the x-axis is measured with a *negative* number. The minus sign in Fig. 5.4.11 signifies that the area of the triangle over $[0, a]$ is subtracted from the area of the triangle over $[0, b]$ to get the area of the trapezoid.

The summation formulas in Eqs. (6) through (9) in Section 5.3 suffice for the integration of polynomials of low degree, but integrals of other functions may require other devices (or a computer algebra system) for the conversion of Riemann sums to closed forms whose limits can be evaluated. (See Problems 56 and 57.)

FIGURE 5.4.10 Example 4 with $a < 0 < b$.

FIGURE 5.4.11 Example 4 with $0 < a < b$.

5.4 TRUE/FALSE STUDY GUIDE

5.4 CONCEPTS: QUESTIONS AND DISCUSSION

1. Explain why you would generally expect the midpoint sum in Eq. (6) to be a more accurate approximation to the actual value $\int_a^b f(x)\,dx$ than either the left-endpoint sum in (4) or the right-endpoint sum in (5).

2. The result in Example 4, with $a = 0$, and Problems 49 and 50 tell us that

$$\int_0^b x\,dx = \frac{1}{2}b^2, \qquad \int_0^b x^2\,dx = \frac{1}{3}b^3, \quad \text{and} \quad \int_0^b x^3\,dx = \frac{1}{4}b^4$$

if $b > 0$. Assuming that the pattern holds (it does), what would you expect to be the value of $\int_a^b x^n\,dx$ with $n > 0$ and $0 < a < b$? Explain how you take into account the nonzero lower limit a.

5.4 PROBLEMS

In Problems 1 through 10, express the given limit as a definite integral over the indicated interval $[a, b]$. Assume that $[x_{i-1}, x_i]$ denotes the ith subinterval of a subdivision of $[a, b]$ into n subintervals, all with the same length $\Delta x = (b - a)/n$, and that $m_i = \frac{1}{2}(x_{i-1} + x_i)$ is the midpoint of the ith subinterval.

1. $\lim\limits_{n \to \infty} \sum\limits_{i=1}^{n} (2x_i - 1)\Delta x$ over $[1, 3]$

2. $\lim\limits_{n \to \infty} \sum\limits_{i=1}^{n} (2 - 3x_{i-1})\Delta x$ over $[-3, 2]$

3. $\lim\limits_{n \to \infty} \sum\limits_{i=1}^{n} (x_i^2 + 4)\Delta x$ over $[0, 10]$

4. $\lim\limits_{n \to \infty} \sum\limits_{i=1}^{n} (x_i^3 - 3x_i^2 + 1)\Delta x$ over $[0, 3]$

5. $\lim\limits_{n \to \infty} \sum\limits_{i=1}^{n} \sqrt{m_i}\,\Delta x$ over $[4, 9]$

6. $\lim\limits_{n \to \infty} \sum\limits_{i=1}^{n} \sqrt{25 - x_i^2}\,\Delta x$ over $[0, 5]$

7. $\lim\limits_{n \to \infty} \sum\limits_{i=1}^{n} \frac{1}{\sqrt{1 + m_i}}\,\Delta x$ over $[3, 8]$

8. $\lim\limits_{n \to \infty} \sum\limits_{i=1}^{n} (\cos 2x_{i-1})\,\Delta x$ over $[0, \pi/2]$

9. $\lim\limits_{n \to \infty} \sum\limits_{i=1}^{n} (\sin 2\pi m_i)\,\Delta x$ over $[0, 1/2]$

10. $\lim\limits_{n \to \infty} \sum\limits_{i=1}^{n} (\tan x_i)\,\Delta x$ over $[0, \pi/4]$

In Problems 11 through 20, compute the Riemann sum

$$\sum_{i=1}^{n} f(x_i^*)\,\Delta x$$

for the indicated function and a regular partition of the given interval into n subintervals. Use $x_i^* = x_i$, the right-hand endpoint of the ith subinterval $[x_{i-1}, x_i]$.

11. $f(x) = x^2$ on $[0, 1]$; $n = 5$
12. $f(x) = x^3$ on $[0, 1]$; $n = 5$
13. $f(x) = \dfrac{1}{x}$ on $[1, 6]$; $n = 5$
14. $f(x) = \sqrt{x}$ on $[0, 5]$; $n = 5$
15. $f(x) = 2x + 1$ on $[1, 4]$; $n = 6$
16. $f(x) = x^2 + 2x$ on $[1, 4]$; $n = 6$
17. $f(x) = x^3 - 3x$ on $[1, 4]$; $n = 5$
18. $f(x) = 1 + 2\sqrt{x}$ on $[2, 3]$; $n = 5$
19. $f(x) = \cos x$ on $[0, \pi]$; $n = 6$
20. $f(x) = \sin \pi x$ on $[0, 1]$; $n = 6$

21. through 30. Repeat Problems 11 through 20, except with $x_i^* = x_{i-1}$, the left-hand endpoint.

31. through 40. Repeat Problems 11 through 20, except with $x_i^* = (x_{i-1} + x_i)/2$, the midpoint of the ith subinterval.

41. Work Problem 13 with $x_i^* = (3x_{i-1} + 2x_i)/5$.

42. Work Problem 14 with $x_i^* = (x_{i-1} + 2x_i)/3$.

In Problems 43 through 48, evaluate the given integral by computing

$$\lim_{n \to \infty} \sum_{i=1}^{n} f(x_i) \, \Delta x$$

for a regular partition of the given interval of integration.

43. $\int_0^2 x^2 \, dx$

44. $\int_0^4 x^3 \, dx$

45. $\int_0^3 (2x + 1) \, dx$

46. $\int_1^5 (4 - 3x) \, dx$

47. $\int_0^3 (3x^2 + 1) \, dx$

48. $\int_0^4 (x^3 - x) \, dx$

49. Show by the method of Example 4 that

$$\int_0^b x^2 \, dx = \frac{1}{3} b^3$$

if $b > 0$.

50. Show by the method of Example 4 that

$$\int_0^b x^3 \, dx = \frac{1}{4} b^4$$

if $b > 0$.

51. Let $f(x) = x$, and let $\{x_0, x_1, x_2, \ldots, x_n\}$ be an arbitrary partition of the closed interval $[a, b]$. For each i $(1 \leq i \leq n)$, let $x_i^* = (x_{i-1} + x_i)/2$. Then show that

$$\sum_{i=1}^{n} x_i^* \, \Delta x_i = \frac{1}{2} b^2 - \frac{1}{2} a^2.$$

Explain why this computation proves that

$$\int_a^b x \, dx = \frac{b^2 - a^2}{2}.$$

52. Suppose that f is a function continuous on $[a, b]$ and that k is a constant. Use Riemann sums to prove that

$$\int_a^b k f(x) \, dx = k \int_a^b f(x) \, dx.$$

53. Suppose that $f(x) \equiv c$, a constant. Use Riemann sums to prove that

$$\int_a^b c \, dx = c(b - a).$$

[Suggestion: First consider the case $a < b$.*]*

54. Suppose that the function f is defined on the interval $[0, 1]$ as follows:

$$f(x) = \begin{cases} \dfrac{1}{x} & \text{if } 0 < x \leq 1, \\ 0 & \text{if } x = 0. \end{cases}$$

Show that the integral $\int_0^1 f(x) \, dx$ does not exist. [*Suggestion:* Show that, whatever n may be, the first term in the Riemann sum $\sum_{i=1}^{n} f(x_i^*) \, \Delta x$ can be made arbitrarily large by the choice of the first selected point x_i^*.] Why does this not contradict Theorem 1?

55. Suppose that the function f is defined as follows:

$$f(x) = \begin{cases} 0 & \text{if } x \text{ is rational}, \\ 1 & \text{if } x \text{ is irrational}. \end{cases}$$

Show that the integral $\int_0^1 f(x) \, dx$ does not exist. [*Suggestion:* Show that, whatever n may be, the Riemann sum $\sum_{i=1}^{n} f(x_i^*) \, \Delta x$ has the value 0 for one possible selection of points $\{x_i^*\}$, but the value 1 for another possible selection.] Why does this not contradict Theorem 1?

In Problems 56 and 57, verify the given result as follows: Use a computer algebra system first to set up the appropriate Riemann sum, then to simplify the sum, and finally to evaluate its limit as $n \to +\infty$.

56. $\int_a^b \sin x \, dx = \cos a - \cos b$

57. $\int_a^b \cos x \, dx = \sin b - \sin a$

5.4 Project: Calculator/Computer Riemann Sums

Suppose that you want to approximate the integral

$$\int_a^b f(x) \, dx$$

numerically using *midpoint sums*. If $\Delta x = (b - a)/n$ and

$$m_i = x_i - \frac{1}{2} \Delta x = (a + i \cdot \Delta x) - \frac{1}{2} \Delta x = a + \left(i - \frac{1}{2}\right) \Delta x$$

is the midpoint of the ith subinterval $[x_{i-1}, x_i]$, then the selection $x_i^* = m_i$ in Eq. (14) gives

$$\int_a^b f(x)\, dx = \lim_{n \to \infty} \sum_{i=1}^n f(m_i)\, \Delta x.$$

Many calculators and computer algebra systems include **Sum** commands that can be used to calculate easily and rapidly the midpoint sum with larger and larger values of n. A common practice is to begin with perhaps $n = 50$ subintervals, then calculate midpoint sums with successively doubled numbers of subintervals; that is, with $n = 50, 100, 200, \ldots$, until successive sums agree to the desired number of decimal places of accuracy. In the CD-ROM resource material for this project we illustrate this procedure using graphing calculators and typical computer algebra systems. You can then carry out the following investigations.

1. Approximate the integral

$$\int_0^\pi \sin x\, dx = 2 = 2.0000$$

of Problem 56 accurate to four decimal places.

2. First explain why Fig. 5.4.12 and the area formula $A = \pi r^2$ for a circle of radius r imply that

$$\int_0^1 4\sqrt{1 - x^2}\, dx = \pi.$$

Then use midpoint sums to approximate this integral and, thereby, the numerical value of π. Begin with $n = 50$ subintervals, then successively double n. How large must n be for you to obtain the familiar four-place approximation $\pi \approx 3.1416$?

FIGURE 5.4.12 Investigation 2.

5.5 EVALUATION OF INTEGRALS

The evaluation of integrals by using Riemann sums, as in Section 5.4, is tedious and time-consuming. Fortunately, we will seldom find it necessary to evaluate an integral in this way. In 1666, Isaac Newton, while still a student at Cambridge University, discovered a much more efficient way to evaluate an integral. A few years later, Gottfried Wilhelm Leibniz, working with a different approach, discovered this method independently.

Newton's key idea was that to evaluate the *number*

$$\int_a^b f(x)\, dx,$$

we should first introduce the *function* $A(x)$ defined as follows:

$$A(x) = \int_a^x f(t)\, dt. \tag{1}$$

FIGURE 5.5.1 The area function $A(x)$.

The independent variable x appears as the *upper limit* of the integral in Eq. (1); the dummy variable t is used in the integrand merely to avoid confusion. If f is positive-valued, continuous, and $x > a$, then $A(x)$ is the area below the curve $y = f(x)$ above the interval $[a, x]$ (Fig. 5.5.1).

It is apparent from Fig. 5.5.1 that $A(x)$ increases as x increases. When x increases by Δx, A increases by the area ΔA of the narrow strip in Fig. 5.5.1 with base $[x, x + \Delta x]$. If Δx is very small, then the area of this strip is very close to the area $f(x)\,\Delta x$ of the rectangle with base $[x, x + \Delta x]$ and height $f(x)$. Thus

$$\Delta A \approx f(x)\,\Delta x; \qquad \frac{\Delta A}{\Delta x} \approx f(x). \tag{2}$$

Moreover, the figure makes it plausible that we get equality in the limit at $\Delta x \to 0$:

$$\frac{dA}{dx} = \lim_{\Delta x \to 0} \frac{\Delta A}{\Delta x} = f(x).$$

That is,

$$A'(x) = f(x), \tag{3}$$

so *the derivative of the area function $A(x)$ is the curve's height function $f(x)$*. In other words, Eq. (3) implies that $A(x)$ is an *antiderivative* of $f(x)$.

Figure 5.5.2 shows a physical interpretation of Eq. (3). A paint roller is laying down a 1-mm-thick coat of paint to cover the region under the curve $y = f(t)$. The paint roller is of adjustable length—as it rolls with a speed of 1 mm/s from left to right, one end traces the x-axis and the other end traces the curve $y = f(t)$. At any time t, the volume V of paint the roller has laid down equals the area of the region already painted:

$$V = A(t) \quad (\text{mm}^3).$$

Then Eq. (3) yields

$$\frac{dV}{dt} = A'(t) = f(t).$$

Thus the instantaneous rate at which the roller is depositing paint is equal to the current length of the roller.

FIGURE 5.5.2 The adjustable-length paint roller.

The Evaluation Theorem

Equation (3) implies that the area function $A(x)$ defined in (1) and illustrated in Fig. 5.5.1 is *one* antiderivative of the given function $f(x)$. Now suppose that $G(x)$ is any other antiderivative of $f(x)$—perhaps one found by the methods of Section 5.2. Then

$$A(x) = G(x) + C, \tag{4}$$

because (by the second corollary to the mean value theorem) two antiderivatives of the same function (on an interval) can differ only by a constant. Also,

$$A(a) = \int_a^a f(t)\,dt = 0 \tag{5}$$

and

$$A(b) = \int_a^b f(t)\, dt = \int_a^b f(x)\, dx \qquad (6)$$

by Eq. (1). So it follows that

$$\int_a^b f(x)\, dx = A(b) - A(a) = [G(b) + C] - [G(a) + C],$$

and thus

$$\int_a^b f(x)\, dx = G(b) - G(a). \qquad (7)$$

Our intuitive discussion has led us to the statement of Theorem 1.

THEOREM 1 Evaluation of Integrals
If G is an antiderivative of the continuous function f on the interval $[a, b]$, then

$$\int_a^b f(x)\, dx = G(b) - G(a). \qquad (7)$$

In Section 5.6 we will fill in the details of the preceding discussion, thus giving a rigorous proof of Theorem 1 (which is part of the fundamental theorem of calculus). Here we concentrate on the computational applications of this theorem. The difference $G(b) - G(a)$ is customarily abbreviated as $[G(x)]_a^b$, so Theorem 1 implies that

$$\int_a^b f(x)\, dx = \left[G(x)\right]_a^b = G(b) - G(a) \qquad (8)$$

if G is any antiderivative of the continuous function f on the interval $[a, b]$. Thus if we can find an antiderivative G of f, we can quickly evaluate the integral *without* having to resort to the paraphernalia of limits of Riemann sums.

If $G'(x) = f(x)$, then (as in Section 5.2) we write

$$\int f(x)\, dx = G(x) + C \qquad (9)$$

for the indefinite integral of f. With the indefinite integral $\int f(x)\, dx$ in place of the antiderivative $G(x)$, Eq. (8) takes the form

$$\int_a^b f(x)\, dx = \left[\int f(x)\, dx\right]_a^b. \qquad (10)$$

This is the connection between the indefinite integral and the definite integral to which we have alluded in the earlier sections of Chapter 5.

EXAMPLE 1 Because

$$\int x^n\, dx = \frac{x^{n+1}}{n+1} + C \quad (\text{if } n \neq -1),$$

it follows that

$$\int_a^b x^n\, dx = \left[\frac{x^{n+1}}{n+1}\right]_a^b = \frac{b^{n+1} - a^{n+1}}{n+1}$$

if $n \neq -1$. For instance,

$$\int_0^3 x^2\, dx = \left[\tfrac{1}{3}x^3\right]_0^3 = \tfrac{1}{3} \cdot 3^3 - \tfrac{1}{3} \cdot 0^3 = 9.$$

Contrast the immediacy of this result with the complexity of the computations of Example 7 in Section 5.3.

EXAMPLE 2 Because
$$\int \cos x \, dx = \sin x + C,$$
it follows that
$$\int_a^b \cos x \, dx = \Big[\sin x\Big]_a^b = \sin b - \sin a.$$
Similarly,
$$\int_a^b \sin x \, dx = \Big[-\cos x\Big]_a^b = \cos a - \cos b.$$
In particular, as we mentioned in Example 2 of Section 5.4,
$$\int_0^\pi \sin x \, dx = \Big[-\cos x\Big]_0^\pi = (-\cos \pi) - (-\cos 0) = (+1) - (-1) = 2.$$

EXAMPLE 3
$$\int_0^2 x^5 \, dx = \Big[\tfrac{1}{6}x^6\Big]_0^2 = \tfrac{64}{6} - 0 = \tfrac{32}{3}.$$
$$\int_1^9 (2x - x^{-1/2} - 3) \, dx = \Big[x^2 - 2x^{1/2} - 3x\Big]_1^9 = 52.$$
$$\int_0^1 (2x+1)^3 \, dx = \Big[\tfrac{1}{8}(2x+1)^4\Big]_0^1 = \tfrac{1}{8} \cdot (81 - 1) = 10.$$
$$\int_0^{\pi/2} \sin 2x \, dx = \Big[-\tfrac{1}{2}\cos 2x\Big]_0^{\pi/2} = -\tfrac{1}{2}(\cos \pi - \cos 0) = 1.$$
$$\int_0^{\pi/4} \sec x \tan x \, dx = \Big[\sec x\Big]_0^{\pi/4} = \sqrt{2} - 1.$$

We have not shown the details of finding the antiderivatives, but you can (and should) check each of these results by showing that the derivative of the function within the evaluation brackets on the right is equal to the integrand on the left. In Example 4 we show the details.

EXAMPLE 4 Evaluate $\int_1^5 \sqrt{3x+1} \, dx$.

Solution We apply the antiderivative form of the generalized power rule,
$$\int u^k \, du = \frac{u^{k+1}}{k+1} + C \quad (k \neq -1),$$
with $k = \tfrac{1}{2}$ and
$$u = 3x+1, \qquad du = 3 \, dx.$$
This gives
$$\int (3x+1)^{1/2} \, dx = \tfrac{1}{3} \int (3x+1)^{1/2} (3 \, dx) = \tfrac{1}{3} \int u^{1/2} \, du$$
$$= \tfrac{1}{3} \cdot \frac{u^{3/2}}{\tfrac{3}{2}} + C = \tfrac{2}{9}(3x+1)^{3/2} + C$$

for the indefinite integral, so it follows from Eq. (10) that

$$\int_1^5 \sqrt{3x+1}\, dx = \left[\tfrac{2}{9}(3x+1)^{3/2}\right]_1^5$$
$$= \tfrac{2}{9}(16^{3/2} - 4^{3/2}) = \tfrac{2}{9}(4^3 - 2^3) = \tfrac{112}{9}.$$

♦

If the derivative $F'(x)$ of the function $F(x)$ is continuous, then the evaluation theorem, with $F'(x)$ in place of $f(x)$ and $F(x)$ in place of $G(x)$, yields

$$\int_a^b F'(x)\, dx = \Big[F(x)\Big]_a^b = F(b) - F(a). \tag{11}$$

The next example provides an immediate application.

EXAMPLE 5 Suppose that an animal population $P(t)$ initially numbers $P(0) = 100$ and that its rate of growth after t months is given by

$$P'(t) = 10 + t + (0.06)t^2.$$

What is the population after 10 months?

Solution By Eq. (11), we know that

$$P(10) - P(0) = \int_0^{10} P'(t)\, dt = \int_0^{10} [10 + t + (0.06)t^2]\, dt$$
$$= \left[10t + \tfrac{1}{2}t^2 + (0.02)t^3\right]_0^{10} = 170.$$

Thus $P(10) = 100 + 170 = 270$ individuals. ♦

EXAMPLE 6 Evaluate

$$\lim_{n\to\infty} \sum_{i=1}^n \frac{2i}{n^2}$$

by recognizing this limit as the value of an integral.

Solution If we write

$$\sum_{i=1}^n \frac{2i}{n^2} = \sum_{i=1}^n \left(\frac{2i}{n}\right)\left(\frac{1}{n}\right),$$

we recognize that we have a Riemann sum for the function $f(x) = 2x$ associated with a partition of the interval $[0, 1]$ into n equal-length subintervals. The ith points of subdivision is $x_i = i/n$, and $\Delta x = 1/n$. Hence it follows from the definition of the integral and from the evaluation theorem that

$$\lim_{n\to\infty} \sum_{i=1}^n \frac{2i}{n^2} = \lim_{n\to\infty} \sum_{i=1}^n 2x_i\, \Delta x = \lim_{n\to\infty} \sum_{i=1}^n f(x_i)\, \Delta x$$
$$= \int_0^1 f(x)\, dx = \int_0^1 2x\, dx.$$

Therefore,

$$\lim_{n\to\infty} \sum_{i=1}^n \frac{2i}{n^2} = \Big[x^2\Big]_0^1 = 1.$$

♦

Basic Properties of Integrals

Problems 59 through 62 outline elementary proofs of the integral properties that are stated next. We assume throughout that each function mentioned is integrable on $[a, b]$.

Integral of a Constant

$$\int_a^b c\, dx = c(b - a).$$

This property is intuitively obvious because the area represented by the integral is simply a rectangle with base $b - a$ and height c (Fig. 5.5.3).

FIGURE 5.5.3 The integral of a constant is the area of a rectangle.

Constant Multiple Property

$$\int_a^b cf(x)\, dx = c\int_a^b f(x)\, dx.$$

Thus a constant can be "moved across" the integral sign. For example,

$$\int_0^{\pi/2} 2\sin x\, dx = 2\int_0^{\pi/2} \sin x\, dx = 2\Big[-\cos x\Big]_0^{\pi/2} = 2.$$

Sum Property

$$\int_a^b [f(x) + g(x)]\, dx = \int_a^b f(x)\, dx + \int_a^b g(x)\, dx.$$

Thus if the functions f and g are both integrable on $[a, b]$, then *the integral of their sum is equal to the sum of their integrals.* This fact sometimes permits a "divide-and-conquer" strategy for the calculation of integrals:

$$\int_0^{\pi} \left(3\sqrt{x} + \cos\frac{x}{2}\right) dx = \int_0^{\pi} 3\sqrt{x}\, dx + \int_0^{\pi} \cos\frac{x}{2}\, dx$$

$$= \Big[2x^{3/2}\Big]_0^{\pi} + \Big[2\sin\frac{x}{2}\Big]_0^{\pi} = 2\pi^{3/2} + 2.$$

Figure 5.5.4 illustrates geometrically the sum property of integrals. The proof of the sum property illustrates a Riemann sums approach that can be adapted to all of

FIGURE 5.5.4 The integral of the sum of two positive-valued functions.

the properties under discussion here. Let us think of partitions of the interval $[a, b]$ into subintervals all having the same length Δx. If the functions f, g, and $f + g$ are all integrable, then Theorem 2 in Section 5.4 gives

$$\int_a^b [f(x) + g(x)]\, dx = \lim_{\Delta x \to 0} \sum_{i=1}^n [f(x_i^\star) + g(x_i^\star)]\, \Delta x$$

$$= \lim_{\Delta x \to 0} \left[\sum_{i=1}^n f(x_i^\star)\, \Delta x + \sum_{i=1}^n g(x_i^\star)\, \Delta x \right]$$

$$= \left[\lim_{\Delta x \to 0} \sum_{i=1}^n f(x_i^\star)\, \Delta x \right] + \left[\lim_{\Delta x \to 0} \sum_{i=1}^n g(x_i^\star)\, \Delta x \right]$$

$$= \int_a^b f(x)\, dx + \int_a^b g(x)\, dx.$$

Interval Union Property

If $a < c < b$, then

$$\int_a^b f(x)\, dx = \int_a^c f(x)\, dx + \int_c^b f(x)\, dx.$$

FIGURE 5.5.5 The way the interval union property works.

Figure 5.5.5 indicates the plausibility of the interval union property.

EXAMPLE 7 If $f(x) = 2|x|$, then

$$f(x) = \begin{cases} -2x & \text{if } x \leq 0, \\ 2x & \text{if } x \geq 0. \end{cases}$$

The graph of f is shown in Fig. 5.5.6. An antiderivative of $f(x)$ is not evident, but the interval union property allows us to split the integral of f on $[-1, 3]$ into two easily calculated integrals:

$$\int_{-1}^3 2|x|\, dx = \int_{-1}^0 (-2x)\, dx + \int_0^3 (2x)\, dx$$

$$= \left[-x^2 \right]_{-1}^0 + \left[x^2 \right]_0^3 = [0 - (-1)] + [9 - 0] = 10.$$

FIGURE 5.5.6 The area under the graph of $y = 2|x|$ over $[-1, 3]$.

Does the result agree with Fig. 5.5.6?

EXAMPLE 8 Evaluate the integral $\int_0^{2\pi} |\cos x - \sin x|\, dx$.

Solution Figure 5.5.7 shows the graph of the function $f(x) = \cos x - \sin x$ and Fig. 5.5.8 shows the graph of its absolute value $|f(x)| = |\cos x - \sin x|$ that we want

FIGURE 5.5.7 $y = \cos x - \sin x$.

FIGURE 5.5.8 $y = |\cos x - \sin x|$.

to integrate. We readily see that $f(x) = 0$ at $x = \pi/4$ and $x = 5\pi/4$, so

$$|f(x)| = \begin{cases} \cos x - \sin x & \text{if } 0 \leq x < \pi/4, \\ \sin x - \cos x & \text{if } \pi/4 \leq x < 5\pi/4, \\ \cos x - \sin x & \text{if } 5\pi/4 \leq x \leq 2\pi. \end{cases}$$

The interval union property therefore gives

$$\int_0^{2\pi} |\cos x - \sin x|\, dx$$

$$= \int_0^{\pi/4} (\cos x - \sin x)\, dx + \int_{\pi/4}^{5\pi/4} (\sin x - \cos x)\, dx + \int_{5\pi/4}^{2\pi} (\cos x - \sin x)\, dx$$

$$= \Big[\sin x + \cos x\Big]_0^{\pi/4} + \Big[-\cos x - \sin x\Big]_{\pi/4}^{5\pi/4} + \Big[\sin x + \cos x\Big]_{5\pi/4}^{2\pi}$$

$$= \left(\tfrac{1}{2}\sqrt{2} + \tfrac{1}{2}\sqrt{2}\right) - (0 + 1) + \left(\tfrac{1}{2}\sqrt{2} + \tfrac{1}{2}\sqrt{2}\right)$$
$$- \left(-\tfrac{1}{2}\sqrt{2} - \tfrac{1}{2}\sqrt{2}\right) + (0 + 1) - \left(-\tfrac{1}{2}\sqrt{2} - \tfrac{1}{2}\sqrt{2}\right)$$

$$= 4\sqrt{2}. \qquad \blacklozenge$$

Comparison Properties

(1) If $f(x) \leq g(x)$ for all x in $[a, b]$, then

$$\int_a^b f(x)\, dx \leq \int_a^b g(x)\, dx.$$

(2) If $m \leq f(x) \leq M$ for all x in $[a, b]$, then

$$m(b - a) \leq \int_a^b f(x)\, dx \leq M(b - a).$$

FIGURE 5.5.9 Plausibility of the comparison property.

The first comparison property says that the larger function has the larger integral. The plausibility of the second comparison property is indicated in Fig. 5.5.9. Note that m and M need not necessarily be the minimum and maximum values of $f(x)$ on $[a, b]$.

EXAMPLE 9 Figure 5.5.10 shows the graphs

$$y = \sqrt{1+x}, \quad y = \sqrt{1+\sqrt{x}}, \quad \text{and} \quad y = 1.2 + (0.3)x,$$

and we see that

$$\sqrt{1+x} \leq \sqrt{1+\sqrt{x}} \leq 1.2 + (0.3)x \qquad (12)$$

for x in $[0, 1]$. Indeed, the fact that $x \leq \sqrt{x}$ for x in $[0, 1]$ implies that $\sqrt{1+x} \leq \sqrt{1+\sqrt{x}}$ there. The graph $y = 1.2 + (0.3)x$ that lies above $y = \sqrt{1+\sqrt{x}}$ was discovered empirically using a graphing calculator. At any rate, the inequalities in (12) and the first comparison property of integrals imply that

$$\int_0^1 \sqrt{1+x}\, dx \leq \int_0^1 \sqrt{1+\sqrt{x}}\, dx \leq \int_0^1 [1.2 + (0.3)x]\, dx;$$

FIGURE 5.5.10 Bounding the graph of $f(x) = \sqrt{1+\sqrt{x}}$.

thus

$$\Big[\tfrac{2}{3}(1+x)^{3/2}\Big]_0^1 \leq \int_0^1 \sqrt{1+\sqrt{x}}\, dx \leq \Big[(1.2)x + (0.15)x^2\Big]_0^1 = 1.35.$$

Now $\frac{2}{3}(2^{3/2} - 1) \approx 1.2190$, so we see finally that

$$1.21 \leq \int_0^1 \sqrt{1 + \sqrt{x}} \, dx \leq 1.35. \tag{13}$$

It turns out (using the methods of Section 5.9) that the actual value of $\int_0^1 \sqrt{1 + \sqrt{x}} \, dx$ is 1.29 rounded to two decimal places—quite close to the average 1.28 of the upper and lower bounds in (13). ◆

The properties of integrals stated here are frequently used in computing and will be applied in the proof of the fundamental theorem of calculus in Section 5.6.

5.5 TRUE/FALSE STUDY GUIDE

5.5 CONCEPTS: QUESTIONS AND DISCUSSION

1. Let f be a continuous function defined on the closed interval $[a, b]$. Explain the difference between the functions g and h defined for t in $[a, b]$ by

$$g(t) = \int_a^b f(x) \, dx \quad \text{and} \quad h(t) = \int_a^t f(x) \, dx.$$

What is the difference between their derivatives $g'(t)$ and $h'(t)$?

2. What is the relation between the integrals

$$\int_a^b f(x) \, dx \quad \text{and} \quad \int_a^b |f(x)| \, dx?$$

What is the difference between their absolute values? Discuss separately the following cases:
   (a) f is positive-valued on the interval $[a, b]$;
   (b) f is negative-valued on the interval $[a, b]$;
   (c) f has both positive and negative values on $[a, b]$.

5.5 PROBLEMS

Apply the evaluation theorem to evaluate the integrals in Problems 1 through 36.

1. $\int_0^1 \left(3x^2 + 2\sqrt{x} + 3\sqrt[3]{x}\right) dx$

2. $\int_1^3 \frac{6}{x^2} \, dx$

3. $\int_0^1 x^3(1 + x)^2 \, dx$

4. $\int_{-2}^{-1} \frac{1}{x^4} \, dx$

5. $\int_0^1 (x^4 - x^3) \, dx$

6. $\int_1^2 (x^4 - x^3) \, dx$

7. $\int_{-1}^0 (x + 1)^3 \, dx$

8. $\int_1^3 \frac{x^4 + 1}{x^2} \, dx$

9. $\int_0^4 \sqrt{x} \, dx$

10. $\int_1^4 \frac{1}{\sqrt{x}} \, dx$

11. $\int_{-1}^2 (3x^2 + 2x + 4) \, dx$

12. $\int_0^1 x^{99} \, dx$

13. $\int_{-1}^1 x^{99} \, dx$

14. $\int_0^4 \left(7x^{5/2} - 5x^{3/2}\right) dx$

15. $\int_1^3 (x - 1)^5 \, dx$

16. $\int_1^2 (x^2 + 1)^3 \, dx$

17. $\int_{-1}^0 (2x + 1)^3 \, dx$

18. $\int_1^3 \frac{10}{(2x + 3)^2} \, dx$

19. $\int_1^8 x^{2/3} \, dx$

20. $\int_1^9 \left(1 + \sqrt{x}\right)^2 dx$

21. $\int_0^1 (x^2 - 3x + 4) \, dx$

22. $\int_0^4 \sqrt{3t} \, dt$

23. $\int_1^9 \left(\sqrt{x} - \frac{2}{\sqrt{x}}\right) dx$

24. $\int_2^3 \frac{du}{u^2}$ (Note the abbreviation for $\frac{1}{u^2} du$.)

25. $\int_1^4 \frac{x^2 - 1}{\sqrt{x}} \, dx$

26. $\int_1^4 (t^2 - 2)\sqrt{t} \, dt$

27. $\int_4^7 \sqrt{3x + 4} \, dx$

28. $\int_0^{\pi/2} \cos 2x \, dx$

29. $\int_0^{\pi/4} \sin x \cos x \, dx$

30. $\int_0^\pi \sin^2 x \cos x \, dx$

31. $\int_0^\pi \sin 5x \, dx$

32. $\int_0^2 \cos \pi t \, dt$

33. $\int_0^{\pi/2} \cos 3x \, dx$

34. $\int_0^5 \sin \frac{\pi x}{10} \, dx$

35. $\int_0^2 \cos \frac{\pi x}{4} \, dx$

36. $\int_0^{\pi/8} \sec^2 2t \, dt$

In Problems 37 through 42, evaluate the given limit by first recognizing the indicated sum as a Riemann sum associated with a regular partition of $[0, 1]$ and then evaluating the corresponding integral.

37. $\lim_{n\to\infty} \sum_{i=1}^n \left(\frac{2i}{n} - 1\right) \frac{1}{n}$

38. $\lim_{n\to\infty} \sum_{i=1}^n \frac{i^2}{n^3}$

39. $\lim_{n\to\infty} \frac{1 + 2 + 3 + \cdots + n}{n^2}$

40. $\lim_{n\to\infty} \frac{1^3 + 2^3 + 3^3 + \cdots + n^3}{n^4}$

41. $\lim_{n\to\infty} \frac{\sqrt{1} + \sqrt{2} + \sqrt{3} + \cdots + \sqrt{n}}{n\sqrt{n}}$

42. $\lim_{n\to\infty} \sum_{i=1}^n \frac{1}{n} \sin \frac{\pi i}{n}$

In Problems 43 through 48, an integral $\int_a^b f(x) \, dx$ is given. First sketch the graph $y = f(x)$ on the interval $[a, b]$. Then, interpreting the integral as the area of a region, evaluate it using known area formulas for rectangles, triangles, and circles.

43. $\int_{-2}^2 |1 - x| \, dx$

44. $\int_{-3}^3 |3x - 2| \, dx$

45. $\int_0^5 (2 - |x|) \, dx$

46. $\int_0^6 |5 - |2x|| \, dx$

47. $\int_0^5 \sqrt{25 - x^2} \, dx$

48. $\int_0^6 \sqrt{6x - x^2} \, dx$ (*Suggestion:* Complete the square.)

In Problems 49 through 54, use properties of integrals to establish each inequality without evaluating the integrals involved.

49. $1 \leq \int_0^1 \sqrt{1 + x^2} \, dx \leq \int_0^1 \sqrt{1 + x} \, dx$

50. $\int_1^2 \sqrt{1 + x} \, dx \leq \int_1^2 \sqrt{1 + x^3} \, dx \leq \sqrt{10}$

51. $\int_0^1 \frac{1}{1 + \sqrt{x}} \, dx \leq \int_0^1 \frac{1}{1 + x^2} \, dx$

52. $\int_2^5 \frac{1}{1 + x^5} \, dx \leq \int_2^5 \frac{1}{1 + x^2} \, dx$

53. $\int_0^2 \sin \sqrt{x} \, dx \leq 2$

54. $\frac{\pi}{8} \leq \int_0^{\pi/4} \frac{1}{1 + \cos^2 x} \, dx \leq \frac{\pi}{6}$

In Problems 55 through 58, use the second comparison property of integrals to estimate—giving both a lower bound and an upper bound as in Problem 54—the value of the given integral.

55. $\int_0^1 \frac{1}{1 + x} \, dx$

56. $\int_4^9 \frac{1}{1 + \sqrt{x}} \, dx$

57. $\int_0^{\pi/6} \cos^2 x \, dx$

58. $\int_0^{\pi/4} \sqrt{16 + 2\sin^2 x} \, dx$

59. Use Riemann sums—as in the proof of the sum property of integrals—to establish the constant multiple property.

60. Use Riemann sums to establish the first comparison property of integrals.

61. Deduce the second comparison property of integrals from the first comparison property.

62. Use sequences of Riemann sums to establish the interval union property of the integral. Note that if R'_n and R''_n are Riemann sums for f on the intervals $[a, c]$ and $[c, b]$, respectively, then $R_n = R'_n + R''_n$ is a Riemann sum for f on $[a, b]$.

63. Suppose that a tank initially contains 1000 gal of water and that the rate of change of its volume after the tank drains for t min is $V'(t) = (0.8)t - 40$ (in gallons per minute). How much water does the tank contain after it has been draining for a half-hour?

64. Suppose that the population of Juneau in 1970 was 125 (in thousands) and that its rate of growth t years later was $P'(t) = 8 + (0.5)t + (0.03)t^2$ (in thousands per year). What was its population in 1990?

65. Figure 5.5.11 shows the graph of $f(x) = 1/x$ on the interval $[1, 2]$, the line joining its endpoints $(1, 1)$ and $(2, \frac{1}{2})$, and its tangent line at the point $(\frac{3}{2}, \frac{2}{3})$. Use this construction to estimate the value of the integral

$$\int_1^2 \frac{1}{x} \, dx$$

(whose exact value is known to be $\ln 2 \approx 0.693$).

FIGURE 5.5.11 Bounding the graph of $f(x) = \dfrac{1}{x}$.

66. Figure 5.5.12 shows the graph of $f(x) = 1/(1+x^2)$ on the interval $[0, 1]$, the line $y = L(x)$ joining its endpoints $(0, 1)$ and $(1, \tfrac{1}{2})$, and the line $y = L(x) + 0.07$. First graph $f(x) - L(x)$ to verify that the latter line lies above $y = f(x)$

on the interval $[0, 1]$. Then use this construction to estimate the value of the integral

$$\int_0^1 \frac{1}{1+x^2}\, dx$$

(whose exact value is known to be $\tfrac{1}{4}\pi \approx 0.785$).

FIGURE 5.5.12 Bounding the graph of $f(x) = \dfrac{1}{1+x^2}$.

5.6 THE FUNDAMENTAL THEOREM OF CALCULUS

Newton and Leibniz are generally credited with the invention of calculus in the latter part of the seventeenth century. Actually, others had earlier calculated areas essentially equivalent to integrals and tangent line slopes essentially equivalent to derivatives. The great accomplishments of Newton and Leibniz were the discovery and computational exploitation of the inverse relationship between differentiation and integration. This relationship is embodied in the *fundamental theorem of calculus*. One part of this theorem is the evaluation theorem of Section 5.5: To evaluate

$$\int_a^b f(x)\, dx,$$

it suffices to find an antiderivative of f on $[a, b]$. The other part of the fundamental theorem tells us that doing so is usually possible, at least in theory: Every continuous function has an antiderivative.

The Average Value of a Function

The concept of the *average value* of a function is useful for the proof of the fundamental theorem and has numerous important applications in its own right. The ordinary (arithmetic) **average** of n given numbers $a_1, a_2, \ldots, a_n$ is defined to be

$$\bar{a} = \frac{a_1 + a_2 + \cdots + a_n}{n} = \frac{1}{n}\sum_{i=1}^n a_i. \tag{1}$$

But a function f defined on an interval generally has infinitely many values $f(x)$, so we cannot simply divide the sum of all these values by their number to find the average value of $f(x)$. We introduce the proper notion with a discussion of average temperature.

EXAMPLE 1 Let the measured temperature T during a particular 24-h day at a certain location be given by the function

$$T = f(t), \quad 0 \leq t \leq 24$$

(with the 24-h clock running from $t = 0$ at one midnight to $t = 24$ at the following midnight). Thus, for example, the temperatures $f(1), f(2), \ldots, f(24)$ are recorded at 1-h intervals during the day. We might define the average temperature $\overline{T}$ for the day as the (ordinary arithmetic) average of the hourly temperatures:

$$\overline{T} = \frac{1}{24} \sum_{i=1}^{24} f(t_i),$$

where $t_i = i$. If we divided the day into n equal subintervals rather than into 24 1-h intervals, we would obtain the more general average

$$\overline{T} = \frac{1}{n} \sum_{i=1}^{n} f(t_i).$$

The larger n is, the closer would we expect $\overline{T}$ to be to the "true" average temperature for the entire day. It is therefore plausible to define the true average temperature by letting n increase without bound. This gives

$$\overline{T} = \lim_{n \to \infty} \frac{1}{n} \sum_{i=1}^{n} f(t_i).$$

The right-hand side resembles a Riemann sum, and we can make it into a Riemann sum by introducing the factor

$$\Delta t = \frac{b-a}{n},$$

where $a = 0$ and $b = 24$. Then

$$\overline{T} = \lim_{n \to \infty} \frac{1}{n} \cdot \frac{n}{b-a} \sum_{i=1}^{n} f(t_i) \cdot \frac{b-a}{n}$$

$$= \lim_{n \to \infty} \frac{1}{b-a} \sum_{i=1}^{n} f(t_i) \cdot \frac{b-a}{n}$$

$$= \frac{1}{b-a} \lim_{n \to \infty} \sum_{i=1}^{n} f(t_i) \, \Delta t = \frac{1}{b-a} \int_{a}^{b} f(t) \, dt.$$

Thus

$$\overline{T} = \frac{1}{24} \int_{0}^{24} f(t) \, dt \tag{2}$$

under the assumption that f is continuous, so the Riemann sums converge to the integral as $n \to \infty$. ◆

The final result in Eq. (2) is the *integral of the function divided by the length of the interval.* Example 1 motivates the following definition:

DEFINITION Average Value of a Function
Suppose that the function f is integrable on $[a, b]$. Then the **average value** $\overline{y}$ of $y = f(x)$ for x in the interval $[a, b]$ is

$$\overline{y} = \frac{1}{b-a} \int_{a}^{b} f(x) \, dx. \tag{3}$$

We can rewrite Eq. (3) in the form

$$\int_{a}^{b} f(x) \, dx = \overline{y} \cdot (b-a). \tag{4}$$

If f is positive-valued on $[a, b]$, then Eq. (4) implies that the area under $y = f(x)$ over $[a, b]$ is equal to the area of a rectangle with base length $b - a$ and height $\overline{y}$ (Fig. 5.6.1).

FIGURE 5.6.1 A rectangle illustrating the average value $\overline{y}$ of a function.

EXAMPLE 2 The average value of $f(x) = x^2$ for x in $[0, 2]$ is

$$\overline{y} = \frac{1}{2} \int_0^2 x^2 \, dx = \frac{1}{2} \left[\frac{1}{3} x^3 \right]_0^2 = \frac{4}{3}.$$

EXAMPLE 3 In Athens, Georgia (USA) the mean daily temperature in degrees Fahrenheit t months after July 15 is closely approximated by

$$T = 61 + 18 \cos \frac{\pi t}{6} = f(t). \tag{5}$$

Find the average temperature between September 15 ($t = 2$) and December 15 ($t = 5$).

Solution Equation (3) gives

$$\overline{T} = \frac{1}{5-2} \int_2^5 \left(61 + 18 \cos \frac{\pi t}{6} \right) dt$$

$$= \frac{1}{3} \left[61t + \frac{6 \cdot 18}{\pi} \sin \frac{\pi t}{6} \right]_2^5 \approx 57°\text{F}.$$

FIGURE 5.6.2 The temperature function $T = f(t)$ of Example 3.

Figure 5.6.2 shows the graphs of $T = f(t)$ and $T \equiv 57$. Can you see that Eq. (4) implies that the two almost-triangular regions in the figure have equal areas? ◆

Theorem 1 tells us that every continuous function on a closed interval *attains* its average value at some point of the interval.

THEOREM 1 Average Value Theorem

If f is continuous on $[a, b]$, then

$$f(\overline{x}) = \frac{1}{b-a} \int_a^b f(x) \, dx \tag{6}$$

for some number $\overline{x}$ in $[a, b]$.

PROOF Let $m = f(c)$ be the minimum value of $f(x)$ on $[a, b]$ and let $M = f(d)$ be its maximum value there. Then, by the comparison property of Section 5.5,

$$m = f(c) \leqq \overline{y} = \frac{1}{b-a} \int_a^b f(x) \, dx \leqq f(d) = M.$$

Because f is continuous, we can now apply the intermediate value property. The number $\bar{y}$ is between the two values m and M of f, and consequently, $\bar{y}$ itself must be a value of f. Specifically, $\bar{y} = f(\bar{x})$ for some number $\bar{x}$ between a and b. This yields Eq. (6). ◄

REMARK Whereas $\bar{y}$ denotes the average value of the function $y = f(x)$, the point $\bar{x}$ where this average value is attained is not itself an average value of x.

EXAMPLE 4 If $v(t)$ denotes the velocity function of a sports car accelerating during the time interval $a \leq t \leq b$, then the car's average velocity is given by

$$\bar{v} = \frac{1}{b-a} \int_a^b v(t)\, dt.$$

The average value theorem implies that $\bar{v} = v(\bar{t})$ for some number $\bar{t}$ in $[a, b]$. Thus $\bar{t}$ is an instant at which the car's instantaneous velocity is equal to its average velocity over the entire time interval. ◆

The Fundamental Theorem

We state the fundamental theorem of calculus in two parts. The first part is the fact that every function f that is continuous on an interval I has an antiderivative on I. In particular, an antiderivative of f can be obtained by integrating f in a certain way. Intuitively, in the case $f(x) > 0$, we let $F(x)$ denote the area under the graph of f from a fixed point a of I to x, a point of I with $x > a$. We shall prove that $F'(x) = f(x)$. We show the construction of the function F in Fig. 5.6.3. More precisely, we define the function F as follows:

$$F(x) = \int_a^x f(t)\, dt,$$

FIGURE 5.6.3 The area function F is an antiderivative of f.

where we use the dummy variable t in the integrand to avoid confusion with the upper limit x. The proof that $F'(x) = f(x)$ will be independent of the supposition that $x > a$.

THE FUNDAMENTAL THEOREM OF CALCULUS
Suppose that f is continuous on the closed interval $[a, b]$.

Part 1: If the function F is defined on $[a, b]$ by

$$F(x) = \int_a^x f(t)\, dt, \tag{7}$$

then F is an antiderivative of f. That is, $F'(x) = f(x)$ for x in $[a, b]$.

Part 2: If G is any antiderivative of f on $[a, b]$, then

$$\int_a^b f(x)\, dx = \Big[G(x)\Big]_a^b = G(b) - G(a). \tag{8}$$

PROOF OF PART 1 By the definition of the derivative,

$$F'(x) = \lim_{h \to 0} \frac{F(x+h) - F(x)}{h} = \lim_{h \to 0} \frac{1}{h}\left(\int_a^{x+h} f(t)\, dt - \int_a^x f(t)\, dt\right).$$

But

$$\int_a^{x+h} f(t)\, dt = \int_a^x f(t)\, dt + \int_x^{x+h} f(t)\, dt$$

by the interval union property of Section 5.5. Thus

$$F'(x) = \lim_{h \to 0} \frac{1}{h} \int_x^{x+h} f(t)\, dt.$$

The average value theorem tells us that

$$\frac{1}{h} \int_x^{x+h} f(t)\, dt = f(\bar{t})$$

for some number $\bar{t}$ in $[x, x+h]$. Finally, we note that $\bar{t} \to x$ as $h \to 0$. Thus, because f is continuous, we see that

$$F'(x) = \lim_{h \to 0} \frac{1}{h} \int_x^{x+h} f(t)\, dt = \lim_{h \to 0} f(\bar{t}) = \lim_{\bar{t} \to x} f(\bar{t}) = f(x).$$

Hence the function F in Eq. (7) is, indeed, an antiderivative of f. ◂

FIGURE 5.6.4 The bead at $\bar{t}$ trapped between the washer at $x + h$ and the flange at x.

REMARK Figure 5.6.4 indicates why $\bar{t}$ must approach x as $h \to 0$. As the moving washer at $x + h$ approaches the fixed flange at x, the bead $\bar{t}$ between them has nowhere else to go.

PROOF OF PART 2 Here we apply Part 1 to give a proof of the evaluation theorem in Section 5.5. If G is *any* antiderivative of f, then—because it and the function F of Part 1 are both antiderivatives of f on the interval $[a, b]$—we know that

$$G(x) = F(x) + C$$

on $[a, b]$ for some constant C. To evaluate C, we substitute $x = a$ and obtain

$$C = G(a) - F(a) = G(a),$$

because

$$F(a) = \int_a^a f(t)\, dt = 0.$$

Hence $G(x) = F(x) + G(a)$. In other words,

$$F(x) = G(x) - G(a)$$

for all x in $[a, b]$. With $x = b$ this gives

$$G(b) - G(a) = F(b) = \int_a^b f(x)\, dx,$$

which establishes Eq. (8) ◂

Sometimes the fundamental theorem of calculus is interpreted to mean that differentiation and integration are *inverse processes*. Part 1 can be written in the form

$$\frac{d}{dx}\left(\int_a^x f(t)\, dt \right) = f(x) \qquad (9)$$

if f is continuous on an open interval containing a and x. That is, if we first integrate the function f (with *variable* upper limit of integration x) and then differentiate with respect to x, the result is the function f again. So differentiation "cancels" the effect of integration of continuous functions.

Moreover, Part 2 of the fundamental theorem can be written in the form

$$\int_a^x G'(t)\, dt = G(x) - G(a) \qquad (10)$$

The Fundamental Theorem of Calculus **SECTION 5.6** 323

if we assume that G' is continuous. If so, this equation means that if we first differentiate the function G and then integrate the result from a to x, the result can differ from the original function G by, at worst, the *constant* $G(a)$. This means that integration "cancels" the effect of differentiation when a is chosen so that $G(a) = 0$.

Computational Applications

Examples 1 through 4 of Section 5.5 illustrate the use of Part 2 of the fundamental theorem in the evaluation of integrals. Additional examples appear in the end-of-section problems, in this section, and in Section 5.7. Example 5 illustrates the necessity of splitting an integral into a sum of integrals when its integrand has different antiderivative formulas on different intervals.

FIGURE 5.6.5 The region of Example 5.

EXAMPLE 5 Figure 5.6.5 shows the graph of the function f defined by

$$f(x) = \begin{cases} \cos x & \text{if } x \geq 0, \\ 1 - x^2 & \text{if } x \leq 0. \end{cases}$$

Find the area A of the region R bounded above by the graph of $y = f(x)$ and below by the x-axis.

Solution The x-intercepts shown in the figure are $x = -1$ (where $1 - x^2 = 0$ and $x < 0$) and $x = \pi/2$ (where $\cos x = 0$ and $x > 0$). Hence

$$A = \int_{-1}^{\pi/2} f(x)\,dx = \int_{-1}^{0} (1 - x^2)\,dx + \int_{0}^{\pi/2} \cos x\,dx$$

$$= \left[x - \frac{1}{3}x^3\right]_{-1}^{0} + \left[\sin x\right]_{0}^{\pi/2} = \frac{2}{3} + 1 = \frac{5}{3}. \quad \blacklozenge$$

EXAMPLE 6 Figure 5.6.6 shows the graph of

$$f(x) = x^3 - x^2 - 6x.$$

Find the area A of the entire region R bounded by the graph of f and the x-axis.

FIGURE 5.6.6 The graph $y = x^3 - x^2 - 6x$ of Example 6.

Solution The region R consists of the two regions R_1 and R_2 and extends from $x = -2$ to $x = 3$. The area of R_1 is

$$A_1 = \int_{-2}^{0} (x^3 - x^2 - 6x)\,dx = \left[\tfrac{1}{4}x^4 - \tfrac{1}{3}x^3 - 3x^2\right]_{-2}^{0} = \tfrac{16}{3}.$$

But on the interval $(0, 3)$, the function $f(x)$ is negative-valued, so to get the (positive) area A_2 of R_2, we must integrate the *negative* of f:

$$A_2 = \int_{0}^{3} (-x^3 + x^2 + 6x)\,dx = \left[-\tfrac{1}{4}x^4 + \tfrac{1}{3}x^3 + 3x^2\right]_{0}^{3} = \tfrac{63}{4}.$$

Consequently the area of the entire region R is

$$A = A_1 + A_2 = \tfrac{16}{3} + \tfrac{63}{4} = \tfrac{253}{12} \approx 21.08.$$

In effect, we have integrated the *absolute value* of $f(x)$:

$$A = \int_{-2}^{3} |f(x)|\,dx$$

$$= \int_{-2}^{0} (x^3 - x^2 - 6x)\,dx + \int_{0}^{3} (-x^3 + x^2 + 6x)\,dx = \tfrac{253}{12}.$$

FIGURE 5.6.7 The graph $y = |x^3 - x^2 - 6x|$ of Example 6.

Compare the graph of $y = |f(x)|$ in Fig. 5.6.7 with that of $y = f(x)$ in Fig. 5.6.6. $\blacklozenge$

EXAMPLE 7 Evaluate

$$\int_{-1}^{2} |x^3 - x|\,dx.$$

Solution We note that $x^3 - x \geq 0$ on $[-1, 0]$, that $x^3 - x \leq 0$ on $[0, 1]$, and that $x^3 - x \geq 0$ on $[1, 2]$. So we write

$$\int_{-1}^{2} |x^3 - x| \, dx = \int_{-1}^{0} (x^3 - x) \, dx + \int_{0}^{1} (x - x^3) \, dx + \int_{1}^{2} (x^3 - x) \, dx$$

$$= \left[\tfrac{1}{4}x^4 - \tfrac{1}{2}x^2\right]_{-1}^{0} + \left[\tfrac{1}{2}x^2 - \tfrac{1}{4}x^4\right]_{0}^{1} + \left[\tfrac{1}{4}x^4 - \tfrac{1}{2}x^2\right]_{1}^{2}$$

$$= \tfrac{1}{4} + \tfrac{1}{4} + \left[2 - \left(-\tfrac{1}{4}\right)\right] = \tfrac{11}{4} = 2.75. \qquad \blacklozenge$$

Part 1 of the fundamental theorem of calculus says that the derivative of an integral with respect to its upper limit is equal to the value of the integrand at the upper limit. For example, if

$$y(x) = \int_{0}^{x} t^3 \sin t \, dt,$$

then

$$\frac{dy}{dx} = x^3 \sin x.$$

Example 8 is a bit more complicated in that the upper limit of the integral is a nontrivial function of the independent variable.

EXAMPLE 8 Find $h'(x)$ given

$$h(x) = \int_{0}^{x^2} t^3 \sin t \, dt.$$

Solution Let $y = h(x)$ and $u = x^2$. Then

$$y = \int_{0}^{u} t^3 \sin t \, dt,$$

so

$$\frac{dy}{du} = u^3 \sin u$$

by the fundamental theorem of calculus. Then the chain rule yields

$$h'(x) = \frac{dy}{dx} = \frac{dy}{du} \cdot \frac{du}{dx} = (u^3 \sin u)(2x) = 2x^7 \sin x^2.$$

Initial Value Problems

Note that if

$$y(x) = \int_{a}^{x} f(t) \, dt, \qquad \qquad (11)$$

then $y(a) = 0$. Hence $y(x)$ is a solution of the initial value problem

$$\frac{dy}{dx} = f(x), \quad y(a) = 0. \qquad \qquad (12)$$

To get a solution of the initial value problem

$$\frac{dy}{dx} = f(x) \quad y(a) = b, \qquad \qquad (13)$$

we need only add the desired initial value:

$$y(x) = b + \int_{a}^{x} f(t) \, dt. \qquad \qquad (14)$$

$\blacklozenge$

EXAMPLE 9 Express as an integral the solution of the initial value problem

$$\frac{dy}{dx} = \sec x, \qquad y(2) = 3. \tag{15}$$

Solution With $a = 2$ and $b = 3$, Eq. (14) gives

$$y(x) = 3 + \int_2^x \sec t \, dt. \tag{16}$$

With our present knowledge, we cannot antidifferentiate $\sec t$, but for a particular value of x the integral in Eq. (16) can be approximated using Riemann sums. For instance, with $x = 4$ a calculator with an **INTEGRATE** key gives

$$\int_2^4 \sec t \, dt \approx -2.5121.$$

Hence the value of the solution in Eq. (16) at $x = 4$ is

$$y(4) \approx 3 - 2.5121 = 0.4879. \qquad \blacklozenge$$

5.6 TRUE/FALSE STUDY GUIDE

5.6 CONCEPTS: QUESTIONS AND DISCUSSION

1. Does every function defined on a closed interval have an average value there?
2. Suppose that the function f defined on the closed interval $[a, b]$ has an average value there. Does f necessarily attain this average value there? Either show that it does or give an example showing it need not.
3. Discuss the validity of the assertion that the fundamental theorem of calculus simply says that "every function is the derivative of its integral and the integral of its derivative." Does the fundamental theorem of calculus say this? Does it say more than this?
4. Suppose that a particle moving along the x-axis has position $x = f(t)$ and velocity $v = f'(t)$ at time t. Interpret the values of the integrals

$$\int_a^b f'(t) \, dt \quad \text{and} \quad \int_a^b |f'(t)| \, dt$$

in terms of the change in position of the particle and the distance it travels. What's the difference?

5.6 PROBLEMS

In Problems 1 through 12, find the average value of the given function on the specified interval.

1. $f(x) = x^4;\quad [0, 2]$
2. $g(x) = \sqrt{x};\quad [1, 4]$
3. $h(x) = 3x^2\sqrt{x^3+1};\quad [0, 2]$
4. $f(x) = 8x;\quad [0, 4]$
5. $g(x) = 8x;\quad [-4, 4]$
6. $h(x) = x^2;\quad [-4, 4]$
7. $f(x) = x^3;\quad [0, 5]$
8. $g(x) = x^{-1/2};\quad [1, 4]$
9. $f(x) = \sqrt{x+1};\quad [0, 3]$
10. $g(x) = \sin 2x;\quad [0, \pi/2]$
11. $f(x) = \sin 2x;\quad [0, \pi]$
12. $g(t) = \cos 2\pi t;\quad \left[-\frac{1}{2}, \frac{1}{2}\right]$

Evaluate the integrals in Problems 13 through 28.

13. $\int_{-1}^{3} dx$ (Here dx stands for $1\, dx$.)
14. $\int_{1}^{2} (y^5 - 1)\, dy$
15. $\int_{1}^{4} \frac{dx}{\sqrt{9x^3}}$
16. $\int_{-1}^{1} (x^3 + 2)^2\, dx$
17. $\int_{1}^{3} \frac{3t - 5}{t^4}\, dt$
18. $\int_{-2}^{-1} \frac{x^2 - x + 3}{\sqrt[3]{x}}\, dx$
19. $\int_{0}^{\pi} \sin x \cos x\, dx$

20. $\int_{-1}^{2} |x|\, dx$

21. $\int_{1}^{2} \left(t - \dfrac{1}{2t}\right)^2 dt$

22. $\int_{-1}^{1} \dfrac{x^2 - 4}{x + 2}\, dx$

23. $\int_{0}^{\sqrt{\pi}} x \cos x^2\, dx$

24. $\int_{0}^{2} |x - \sqrt{x}|\, dx$

25. $\int_{-2}^{2} |x^2 - 1|\, dx$

26. $\int_{0}^{\pi/3} \sin 3x\, dx$

27. $\int_{2}^{7} \sqrt{x + 2}\, dx$

28. $\int_{5}^{10} \dfrac{1}{\sqrt{x - 1}}\, dx$

In Problems 29 through 32, the graph of f and the x-axis divide the xy-plane into several regions, some of which are bounded. Find the total area of the bounded regions in each problem.

29. $f(x) = 1 - x^4$ if $x \leq 0$; $f(x) = 1 - x^3$ if $x \geq 0$ (Fig. 5.6.8)

30. $f(x) = (\pi/2)^2 \sin x$ on $[0, \pi/2]$; $f(x) = x(\pi - x)$ on $[\pi/2, \pi]$ (Fig. 5.6.9)

FIGURE 5.6.8 Problem 29.

FIGURE 5.6.9 Problem 30.

31. $f(x) = x^3 - 9x$ (Fig. 5.6.10)

32. $f(x) = x^3 - 2x^2 - 15x$ (Fig. 5.6.11)

FIGURE 5.6.10 Problem 31.

FIGURE 5.6.11 Problem 32.

33. Rosanne drops a ball from a height of 400 ft. Find the ball's average height and its average velocity between the time it is dropped and the time it strikes the ground.

34. Find the average value of the animal population $P(t) = 100 + 10t + (0.02)t^2$ over the time interval $[0, 10]$.

35. Suppose that a 5000-L water tank takes 10 min to drain and that after t minutes, the amount of water remaining in the tank is $V(t) = 50(10 - t)^2$ liters. What is the average amount of water in the tank during the time it drains?

36. On a certain day the temperature t hours past midnight was
$$T(t) = 80 + 10 \sin\left(\dfrac{\pi}{12}(t - 10)\right).$$
What was the average temperature between noon and 6 P.M.?

37. Suppose that a heated rod lies along the interval $0 \leq x \leq 10$. If the temperature at points of the rod is given by $T(x) = 4x(10 - x)$, what is the rod's average temperature?

38. Figure 5.6.12 shows a cross section at distance x from the center of a sphere of radius 1. Find the average area of the cross section for $0 \leq x \leq 1$.

FIGURE 5.6.12 The sphere of Problem 38.

39. Figure 5.6.13 shows a cross section at distance y from the vertex of a cone with base radius 1 and height 2. Find the average area of this cross section for $0 \leq y \leq 2$.

FIGURE 5.6.13 The cone of Problem 39.

40. A sports car starts from rest ($x = 0$, $t = 0$) and experiences constant acceleration $x''(t) = a$ for T seconds. Find, in terms of a and T, (a) its final and average velocities and (b) its final and average positions.

41. (a) Figure 5.6.14 shows a triangle inscribed in the region that lies between the x-axis and the curve $y = 9 - x^2$. Express the area of this triangle as a function $A(x)$ of the x-coordinate of its upper vertex P. (b) Find the average area $\bar{A}$ of $A(x)$ for x in the interval $[-3, 3]$. (c) Sketch a triangle as in Fig. 5.6.14 that has the area $\bar{A}$ found in part (b). How many different such triangles are there?

FIGURE 5.6.14 The typical triangle of Problem 41.

42. (a) Figure 5.6.15 shows a rectangle inscribed in the first-quadrant region that lies between the x-axis and the line $y = 10 - x$. Express the area of this rectangle as a function $A(x)$ of the x-coordinate of its vertex P on the line. (b) Find the average area $\bar{A}$ of $A(x)$ for x in the interval $[0, 10]$. (c) Sketch a rectangle as in Fig. 5.6.15 that has the area $\bar{A}$ found in part (b). How many different such rectangles are there?

FIGURE 5.6.15 The typical rectangle of Problem 42.

43. (a) Figure 5.6.16 shows a rectangle inscribed in the semicircular region that lies between the x-axis and the graph $y = \sqrt{16 - x^2}$. Express the area of the rectangle as a function $A(x)$ of the x-coordinate of its vertex P on the line. (b) Find the average area $\bar{A}$ of $A(x)$ for x in the interval $[0, 4]$. (c) Sketch a rectangle as in Fig. 5.6.16 that has the area $\bar{A}$ found in part (b). How many different such rectangles are there?

FIGURE 5.6.16 The typical rectangle of Problem 43.

44. Repeat Problem 43 in the case that the rectangle has two vertices on the x-axis and two on the parabola $y = 16 - x^2$

(rather than on the semicircle $y = \sqrt{16 - x^2}$). You may need to use a calculator or computer to find the base of a rectangle whose area is the average $\bar{A}$ of $A(x)$ for x in $[0, 4]$.

In Problems 45 through 49, apply the fundamental theorem of calculus to find the derivative of the given function.

45. $f(x) = \int_{-1}^{x} (t^2 + 1)^{17} \, dt$

46. $g(t) = \int_{0}^{t} \sqrt{x^2 + 25} \, dx$

47. $h(z) = \int_{2}^{z} \sqrt[3]{u - 1} \, du$

48. $A(x) = \int_{1}^{x} \frac{1}{t} \, dt$

49. $f(x) = \int_{x}^{10} \left(t + \frac{1}{t} \right) dt$

In Problems 50 through 53, $G(x)$ is the integral of the given function $f(t)$ over the specified interval of the form $[a, x]$, $x > a$. Apply Part 1 of the fundamental theorem of calculus to find $G'(x)$.

50. $f(t) = \dfrac{t}{t^2 + 1}$; $[2, x]$

51. $f(t) = \sqrt{t + 4}$; $[0, x]$

52. $f(t) = \sin^3 t$; $[0, x]$

53. $f(t) = \sqrt{t^3 + 1}$; $[1, x]$

In Problems 54 through 60, differentiate the function by first writing $f(x)$ in the form $g(u)$, where u denotes the upper limit of integration.

54. $f(x) = \int_{0}^{x^2} \sqrt{1 + t^3} \, dt$

55. $f(x) = \int_{2}^{3x} \sin t^2 \, dt$

56. $f(x) = \int_{0}^{\sin x} \sqrt{1 - t^2} \, dt$

57. $f(x) = \int_{0}^{x^2} \sin t \, dt$

58. $f(x) = \int_{1}^{\sin x} (t^2 + 1)^3 \, dt$

59. $f(x) = \int_{1}^{x^2 + 1} \frac{dt}{t}$

60. $f(x) = \int_{1}^{x^5} \sqrt{1 + t^2} \, dt$

Use integrals (as in Example 9) to solve the initial value problems in Problems 61 through 64.

61. $\dfrac{dy}{dx} = \dfrac{1}{x}$, $y(1) = 0$

62. $\dfrac{dy}{dx} = \dfrac{1}{1 + x^2}$, $y(1) = \dfrac{\pi}{4}$

63. $\dfrac{dy}{dx} = \sqrt{1 + x^2}$, $y(5) = 10$

64. $\dfrac{dy}{dx} = \tan x$, $y(1) = 2$

65. The fundamental theorem of calculus *seems* to say that

$$\int_{-1}^{1} \frac{dx}{x^2} = \left[-\frac{1}{x} \right]_{-1}^{1} = -2,$$

in apparent contradiction to the fact that $1/x^2$ is always positive. What's wrong here?

66. Prove that the average rate of change

$$\frac{f(b) - f(a)}{b - a}$$

of the differentiable function f on $[a, b]$ is equal to the average value of its derivative on $[a, b]$.

67. The graph $y = f(x), 0 \leqq x \leqq 10$ is shown in Fig. 5.6.17. Let

$$g(x) = \int_0^x f(t)\, dt.$$

(a) Find the values $g(0)$, $g(2)$, $g(4)$, $g(6)$, $g(8)$, and $g(10)$. (b) Find the intervals on which $g(x)$ is increasing and those on which it is decreasing. (c) Find the global maximum and minimum values of $g(x)$ for $0 \leqq x \leqq 10$. (d) Sketch a rough graph of $y = g(x)$.

FIGURE 5.6.17 Problem 67.

68. Repeat Problem 67, except use the graph of the function f shown in Fig. 5.6.18.

FIGURE 5.6.18 Problem 68.

69. Figure 5.6.19 shows the graph of the function $f(x) = x \sin x$ on the interval $[0, 4\pi]$. Let

$$g(x) = \int_0^x f(t)\, dt.$$

(a) Find the values of x at which $g(x)$ has local maximum and minimum values on the interval $[0, 4\pi]$. (b) Where does $g(x)$ attain its global maximum and minimum values on $[0, 4\pi]$. (c) Which points on the graph $y = f(x)$ correspond to inflection points on the graph $y = g(x)$? (d) Sketch a rough graph of $y = g(x)$.

FIGURE 5.6.19 Problem 69.

70. Repeat Problem 69, except use the function

$$f(x) = \frac{\sin x}{x}$$

on the interval $[0, 4\pi]$ (as shown in Fig. 5.6.20). Take $f(0) = 1$ because $(\sin x)/x \to 1$ as $x \to 0$.

FIGURE 5.6.20 Problem 70.

5.7 INTEGRATION BY SUBSTITUTION

The fundamental theorem of calculus in the form

$$\int_a^b f(x)\, dx = \left[\int f(x)\, dx\right]_a^b \tag{1}$$

implies that we can readily evaluate the definite integral on the left if we can find the indefinite integral (that is, antiderivative) on the right. We now discuss a powerful method of antidifferentiation that amounts to "the chain rule in reverse." This method is a generalization of the "generalized power rule in reverse,"

$$\int u^n\, du = \frac{u^{n+1}}{n+1} + C \quad (n \neq -1), \tag{2}$$

which we introduced in Section 5.2.

Equation (2) is an abbreviation for the formula

$$\int [g(x)]^n g'(x)\,dx = \frac{[g(x)]^{n+1}}{n+1} + C \quad (n \neq -1) \tag{3}$$

that results when we write

$$u = g(x), \quad du = g'(x)\,dx.$$

So to apply Eq. (2) to a given integral, we must be able to visualize the integrand as a *product* of a power of a differentiable function $g(x)$ and its derivative $g'(x)$.

EXAMPLE 1 With

$$u = 2x + 1, \quad du = 2\,dx,$$

we see that

$$\int (2x+1)^5 \cdot 2\,dx = \int u^5\,du = \frac{u^6}{6} + C = \frac{1}{6}(2x+1)^6 + C. \quad \blacklozenge$$

EXAMPLE 2

$$\int 2x\sqrt{1+x^2}\,dx = \int (1+x^2)^{1/2} \cdot 2x\,dx$$

$$= \int u^{1/2}\,du \quad [u = 1 + x^2, \quad du = 2x\,dx]$$

$$= \frac{u^{3/2}}{\frac{3}{2}} + C = \tfrac{2}{3}(1+x^2)^{3/2} + C. \quad \blacklozenge$$

Equation (3) is the special case $f(u) = u^n$ of the general integral formula

$$\int f(g(x)) \cdot g'(x)\,dx = \int f(u)\,du. \tag{4}$$

The right-hand side of Eq. (4) results when we make the formal substitutions

$$u = g(x), \quad du = g'(x)\,dx$$

on the left-hand side.

One of the beauties of differential notation is that Eq. (4) is not only plausible but is, in fact, true—with the understanding that u is to be replaced with $g(x)$ after the indefinite integration on the right-hand side of Eq. (4) has been carried out. Indeed, Eq. (4) is merely an indefinite integral version of the chain rule. For if $F'(x) = f(x)$, then

$$D_x F(g(x)) = F'(g(x)) \cdot g'(x) = f(g(x)) \cdot g'(x)$$

by the chain rule, so

$$\int f(g(x)) \cdot g'(x)\,dx = \int F'(g(x)) \cdot g'(x)\,dx = F(g(x)) + C$$

$$= F(u) + C \quad [u = g(x)]$$

$$= \int f(u)\,du.$$

Equation (4) is the basis for the powerful technique of indefinite **integration by substitution**. It may be used whenever the integrand function is recognized to be of the form $f(g(x)) \cdot g'(x)$.

EXAMPLE 3 Find

$$\int x^2 \sqrt{x^3 + 9}\,dx.$$

Solution Note that x^2 is, to within a ***constant*** factor, the derivative of $x^3 + 9$. We can, therefore, substitute

$$u = x^3 + 9, \quad du = 3x^2 \, dx. \tag{5}$$

The constant factor 3 can be supplied if we compensate by multiplying the integral by $\frac{1}{3}$. This gives

$$\int x^2 \sqrt{x^3 + 9} \, dx = \frac{1}{3} \int (x^3 + 9)^{1/2} \cdot 3x^2 \, dx = \frac{1}{3} \int u^{1/2} \, du$$

$$= \frac{1}{3} \cdot \frac{u^{3/2}}{\frac{3}{2}} + C = \frac{2}{9} u^{3/2} + C = \frac{2}{9}(x^3 + 9)^{3/2} + C.$$

An alternative way to carry out the substitution in (5) is to solve

$$du = 3x^2 \, dx \quad \text{for} \quad x^2 \, dx = \tfrac{1}{3} \, du,$$

and then write

$$\int (x^3 + 9)^{1/2} \, dx = \int u^{1/2} \cdot \tfrac{1}{3} \, du = \tfrac{1}{3} \int u^{1/2} \, du,$$

concluding the computation as before. ◆

The following three steps in the solution of Example 3 are worth special mention:

- The differential dx along with the rest of the integrand is "transformed," or replaced, in terms of u and du.
- Once the integration has been performed, the constant C of integration is added.
- A final resubstitution is necessary to write the answer in terms of the original variable x.

Substitution in Trigonometric Integrals

By now we know that every differentiation formula yields—upon "reversal"—a corresponding antidifferentiation formula. The familiar formulas for the derivatives of the six trigonometric functions thereby yield the following indefinite-integral formulas:

$$\int \cos u \, du = \sin u + C, \tag{6}$$

$$\int \sin u \, du = -\cos u + C, \tag{7}$$

$$\int \sec^2 u \, du = \tan u + C, \tag{8}$$

$$\int \csc^2 u \, du = -\cot u + C, \tag{9}$$

$$\int \sec u \, \tan u \, du = \sec u + C, \tag{10}$$

$$\int \csc u \, \cot u \, du = -\csc u + C. \tag{11}$$

EXAMPLE 4

$$\int \sin(3x+4)\,dx = \int (\sin u) \cdot \tfrac{1}{3}\,du \qquad (u = 3x+4, \quad du = 3\,dx)$$

$$= \tfrac{1}{3} \int \sin u\,du = -\tfrac{1}{3}\cos u + C$$

$$= -\tfrac{1}{3}\cos(3x+4) + C.$$

EXAMPLE 5

$$\int 3x \cos(x^2)\,dx = 3 \int (\cos x^2) \cdot x\,dx$$

$$= 3 \int (\cos u) \cdot \tfrac{1}{2}\,du \qquad (u = x^2, \quad du = 2x\,dx)$$

$$= \tfrac{3}{2} \int \cos u\,du = \tfrac{3}{2}\sin u + C = \tfrac{3}{2}\sin(x^2) + C.$$

EXAMPLE 6

$$\int \sec^2 3x\,dx = \int (\sec^2 u) \cdot \tfrac{1}{3}\,du \qquad (u = 3x, \quad du = 3\,dx)$$

$$= \tfrac{1}{3} \tan u + C = \tfrac{1}{3}\tan 3x + C.$$

EXAMPLE 7 Evaluate

$$\int 2\sin^3 x \cos x\,dx.$$

Solution None of the integrals in Eqs. (6) through (11) appears to "fit," but the substitution

$$u = \sin x, \qquad du = \cos x\,dx$$

yields

$$\int 2\sin^3 x \cos x\,dx = 2 \int u^3\,du = 2 \cdot \frac{u^4}{4} + C = \frac{1}{2}\sin^4 x + C.$$

Substitution in Definite Integrals

The method of integration by substitution can be used with definite integrals as well as with indefinite integrals. Only one additional step is required—evaluation of the final antiderivative at the original limits of integration.

EXAMPLE 8 The substitution used in Example 3 gives

$$\int_0^3 x^2 \sqrt{x^3+9}\,dx = \int_{-}^{-} u^{1/2} \cdot \tfrac{1}{3}\,du \qquad (u = x^3+9, \quad du = 3x^2\,dx)$$

$$= \tfrac{1}{3}\left[\tfrac{2}{3}u^{3/2}\right]_{-}^{-} = \tfrac{2}{9}\left[(x^3+9)^{3/2}\right]_0^3 \qquad \text{(resubstitute)}$$

$$= \tfrac{2}{9}(216 - 27) = 42.$$

The limits on u were left "blank" above because they weren't calculated—there was no need to know them, because we planned to resubstitute for u in terms of the original variable x before using the original limits of integration.

But sometimes it is more convenient to determine the limits of integration with respect to the new variable u. With the substitution $u = x^3 + 9$, $du = 3x^2\,dx$, we see that

- $u = 9$ when $x = 0$ (lower limit);
- $u = 36$ when $x = 3$ (upper limit).

Use of these limits on u (rather than resubstitution in terms of x) gives

$$\int_0^3 x^2\sqrt{x^3+9}\,dx = \tfrac{1}{3}\int_9^{36} u^{1/2}\,du = \tfrac{1}{3}\left[\tfrac{2}{3}u^{3/2}\right]_9^{36} = 42. \qquad \blacklozenge$$

Theorem 1 says that the "natural" way of transforming an integral's limits under a u-substitution, like the work just done, is in fact correct.

THEOREM 1 Definite Integration by Substitution
Suppose that the function g has a continuous derivative on $[a, b]$ and that f is continuous on the interval $g([a, b])$. Let $u = g(x)$. Then

$$\int_a^b f(g(x)) \cdot g'(x)\,dx = \int_{g(a)}^{g(b)} f(u)\,du. \qquad (12)$$

REMARK Thus we get the new limits on u by applying the substitution function $u = g(x)$ to the old limits on x. Then:

- The new lower limit is $g(a)$, and
- The new upper limit is $g(b)$,

whether or not $g(b)$ is greater than $g(a)$.

PROOF OF THEOREM 1 Choose an antiderivative F of f, so $F' = f$. Then, by the chain rule,

$$D_x[F(g(x))] = F'(g(x)) \cdot g'(x) = f(g(x)) \cdot g'(x).$$

Therefore,

$$\int_a^b f(g(x)) \cdot g'(x)\,dx = \Big[F(g(x))\Big]_a^b = F(g(b)) - F(g(a))$$

$$= \Big[F(u)\Big]_{u=g(a)}^{g(b)} = \int_{g(a)}^{g(b)} f(u)\,du.$$

Note how we used the fundamental theorem to obtain the first and last equalities in this argument. ◂

Whether it is simpler to apply Theorem 1 and transform to new u-limits or to resubstitute $u = g(x)$ and use the old x-limits depends on the specific problem at hand. Examples 9 and 10 illustrate the technique of transforming to new limits.

EXAMPLE 9 Evaluate

$$\int_3^5 \frac{x\,dx}{(30-x^2)^2}.$$

Solution Note that $30 - x^2$ is nonzero on $[3, 5]$, so the integrand is continuous there. We substitute

$$u = 30 - x^2, \qquad du = -2x\,dx,$$

and observe that

If $x = 3$, then $u = 21$ (lower limit);
If $x = 5$, then $u = 5$ (upper limit).

Hence our substitution gives

$$\int_3^5 \frac{x\,dx}{(30-x^2)^2} = \int_{21}^5 \frac{-\frac{1}{2}\,du}{u^2} = -\frac{1}{2}\left[-\frac{1}{u}\right]_{21}^5 = -\frac{1}{2}\left(-\frac{1}{5}+\frac{1}{21}\right) = \frac{8}{105}.\ \blacklozenge$$

EXAMPLE 10 Evaluate

$$\int_0^{\pi/4} \sin^3 2t \cos 2t\,dt.$$

Solution We substitute

$$u = \sin 2t, \quad \text{so that} \quad du = 2\cos 2t\,dt.$$

Then $u = 0$ when $t = 0$; $u = 1$ when $t = \pi/4$. Hence

$$\int_0^{\pi/4} \sin^3 2t \cos 2t\,dt = \frac{1}{2}\int_0^1 u^3\,du = \frac{1}{2}\left[\frac{1}{4}u^4\right]_0^1 = \frac{1}{8}.\ \blacklozenge$$

5.7 TRUE/FALSE STUDY GUIDE

5.7 CONCEPTS: QUESTIONS AND DISCUSSION

1. In Theorem 1, the function g is continuous on the interval $[a, b]$. Give an example in which the range set $g([a, b])$ is *not* simply the closed interval with endpoints $g(a)$ and $g(b)$. Then select a nontrivial function f that is continuous on $g([a, b])$ and verify that Eq. (14) holds.
2. Suppose that the function g is continuous on the interval $[a, b]$. Use properties of continuous functions stated in Sections 2.4 and 3.5 to prove that the range set $g([a, b])$ *is* a closed interval.
3. Discuss the possible advantages and disadvantages of transforming to new u-limits when evaluating a definite integral by substitution. Perhaps you can give one example in which this makes the calculation simpler, another example in which it does not.

5.7 PROBLEMS

In Problems 1 through 10, use the indicated substitution to evaluate the given integral.

1. $\int (3x-5)^{17}\,dx;\quad u = 3x-5$

2. $\int \frac{1}{(4x+7)^6}\,dx;\quad u = 4x+7$

3. $\int x\sqrt{x^2+9}\,dx;\quad u = x^2+9$

4. $\int \frac{x^2}{\sqrt[3]{2x^3-1}}\,dx;\quad u = 2x^3-1$

5. $\int \sin 5x\,dx;\quad u = 5x$

6. $\int \cos kx\,dx;\quad u = kx$

7. $\int x\sin(2x^2)\,dx;\quad u = 2x^2$

8. $\int \sqrt{x}\cos(x^{3/2})\,dx;\quad u = x^{3/2}$

9. $\int (1-\cos x)^5 \sin x\,dx;\quad u = 1-\cos x$

10. $\int \frac{\cos 3x}{\sqrt{5+2\sin 3x}}\,dx;\quad u = 5+2\sin 3x$

Evaluate the indefinite integrals in Problems 11 through 40.

11. $\int (x+1)^6\,dx$

12. $\int (2-x)^5\,dx$

13. $\int (4-3x)^7\,dx$

14. $\int \sqrt{2x+1}\,dx$

15. $\displaystyle\int \frac{dx}{\sqrt{7x+5}}$

16. $\displaystyle\int \frac{1}{(3-5x)^2}\,dx$

17. $\displaystyle\int \sin(\pi x+1)\,dx$

18. $\displaystyle\int \cos\frac{\pi t}{3}\,dt$

19. $\displaystyle\int \sec 2\theta\,\tan 2\theta\,d\theta$

20. $\displaystyle\int \csc^2 5x\,dx$

21. $\displaystyle\int x\sqrt{x^2-1}\,dx$

22. $\displaystyle\int 3t(1-2t^2)^{10}\,dt$

23. $\displaystyle\int x\sqrt{2-3x^2}\,dx$

24. $\displaystyle\int \frac{t\,dt}{\sqrt{2t^2+1}}$

25. $\displaystyle\int x^3\sqrt{x^4+1}\,dx$

26. $\displaystyle\int \frac{x^2}{\sqrt[3]{x^3+1}}\,dx$

27. $\displaystyle\int x^2\cos(2x^3)\,dx$

28. $\displaystyle\int t\sec^2(t^2)\,dt$

29. $\displaystyle\int \frac{x^2}{(x^3+5)^4}\,dx$

30. $\displaystyle\int y^2\sqrt[3]{2-4y^3}\,dy$

31. $\displaystyle\int \cos^3 x\,\sin x\,dx$

32. $\displaystyle\int \sin^5 3z\,\cos 3z\,dz$

33. $\displaystyle\int \tan^3\theta\,\sec^2\theta\,d\theta$

34. $\displaystyle\int \sec^3\theta\,\tan\theta\,d\theta$

35. $\displaystyle\int \frac{\cos\sqrt{x}}{\sqrt{x}}\,dx$ [Suggestion: Try $u=\sqrt{x}$.]

36. $\displaystyle\int \frac{dx}{\sqrt{x}\,(1+\sqrt{x})^2}$

37. $\displaystyle\int (x^2+2x+1)^4(x+1)\,dx$

38. $\displaystyle\int \frac{x+2}{(x^2+4x+3)^3}\,dx$

39. $\displaystyle\int (2+t^2)\sqrt[3]{6t+t^3}\,dt$

40. $\displaystyle\int \frac{2-x^2}{(x^3-6x+1)^5}\,dx$

Evaluate the definite integrals in Problems 41 through 54.

41. $\displaystyle\int_1^2 \frac{dt}{(t+1)^3}$

42. $\displaystyle\int_0^4 \frac{dx}{\sqrt{2x+1}}$

43. $\displaystyle\int_0^4 x\sqrt{x^2+9}\,dx$

44. $\displaystyle\int_1^4 \frac{(1+\sqrt{x})^4}{\sqrt{x}}\,dx$ [Suggestion: Try $u=1+\sqrt{x}$.]

45. $\displaystyle\int_0^8 t\sqrt{t+1}\,dt$ [Suggestion: Try $u=t+1$.]

46. $\displaystyle\int_0^{\pi/2} \sin x\,\cos x\,dx$

47. $\displaystyle\int_0^{\pi/6} \sin 2x\,\cos^3 2x\,dx$

48. $\displaystyle\int_0^{\sqrt{\pi}} t\sin\frac{t^2}{2}\,dt$

49. $\displaystyle\int_0^{\pi/2} (1+3\sin\theta)^{3/2}\cos\theta\,d\theta$ [Suggestion: Try $u=1+3\sin\theta$.]

50. $\displaystyle\int_0^{\pi/2} \sec^2\frac{x}{2}\,dx$

51. $\displaystyle\int_0^4 x\sqrt{4-x}\,dx$ [Suggestion: Try $u=4-x$.]

52. $\displaystyle\int_0^{\pi/2} (\cos x)\sqrt{\sin x}\,dx$ [Suggestion: Try $u=\sin x$.]

53. $\displaystyle\int_0^1 t^3\sin\pi t^4\,dt$

54. $\displaystyle\int_{\pi^2/4}^{\pi^2} \frac{\sin\sqrt{x}\,\cos\sqrt{x}}{\sqrt{x}}\,dx$

Use the half-angle identities

$$\cos^2\theta = \frac{1+\cos 2\theta}{2} \quad\text{and}\quad \sin^2\theta = \frac{1-\cos 2\theta}{2}$$

to evaluate the integrals in Problems 55 through 58.

55. $\displaystyle\int \sin^2 x\,dx$

56. $\displaystyle\int \cos^2 x\,dx$

57. $\displaystyle\int_0^\pi \sin^2 3t\,dt$

58. $\displaystyle\int_0^1 \cos^2 \pi t\,dt$

Use the identity $1+\tan^2\theta = \sec^2\theta$ to evaluate the integrals in Problems 59 and 60.

59. $\displaystyle\int \tan^2 x\,dx$

60. $\displaystyle\int_0^{\pi/12} \tan^2 3t\,dt$

61. Substitute $\sin^3 x = (\sin x)(1-\cos^2 x)$ to show that

$$\int \sin^3 x\,dx = \tfrac{1}{3}\cos^3 x - \cos x + C.$$

62. Evaluate

$$\int_0^{\pi/2} \cos^3 x\,dx$$

by the method of Problem 61.

63. Substitute first $u=\sin\theta$ and then $u=\cos\theta$ to obtain

$$\int \sin\theta\,\cos\theta\,d\theta = \tfrac{1}{2}\sin^2\theta + C_1 = -\tfrac{1}{2}\cos^2\theta + C_2.$$

Reconcile these results. What is the relation between the constants C_1 and C_2? *Suggestion:* Compare the graphs (on the same screen) of

$$f(x) = \tfrac{1}{2}\sin^2\theta \quad\text{and}\quad g(x) = -\tfrac{1}{2}\cos^2\theta.$$

64. Substitute first $u=\tan\theta$ and then $u=\sec\theta$ to obtain

$$\int \sec^2\theta\,\tan\theta\,d\theta = \tfrac{1}{2}\tan^2\theta + C_1 = \tfrac{1}{2}\sec^2\theta + C_2.$$

Reconcile these results. What is the relation between the constants C_1 and C_2? *Suggestion:* Compare the graphs (on the same screen) of

$$f(x) = \tfrac{1}{2}\tan^2\theta \quad\text{and}\quad g(x) = \tfrac{1}{2}\sec^2\theta.$$

65. (a) Verify by differentiation that

$$\int \frac{dx}{(1-x)^2} = \frac{x}{1-x} + C_1.$$

(b) Substitute $u=1-x$ to show that

$$\int \frac{dx}{(1-x)^2} = \frac{1}{1-x} + C_2.$$

(c) Reconcile the results of parts (a) and (b). *Suggestion:* Compare the graphs (on the same screen) of

$$f(x) = \frac{x}{1-x} \quad \text{and} \quad g(x) = \frac{1}{1-x}.$$

66. (a) Substitute $u = x^2$ and apply part (a) of Problem 65 to show that

$$\int \frac{x\,dx}{(1-x^2)^2} = \frac{x^2}{2(1-x^2)} + C_1.$$

(b) Substitute $u = 1 - x^2$ to show that

$$\int \frac{x\,dx}{(1-x^2)^2} = \frac{1}{2(1-x^2)} + C_2.$$

(c) Reconcile the results of parts (a) and (b). *Suggestion:* Compare the graphs (on the same screen) of

$$f(x) = \frac{x^2}{2(1-x^2)} \quad \text{and} \quad g(x) = \frac{1}{2(1-x^2)}.$$

*Problems 67 and 68 deal with even and odd functions. An **even** function f is a function such that*

$$f(-x) = f(x)$$

*for all x. This means that the graph of $y = f(x)$ is symmetric under reflection across the y-axis (Fig. 5.7.1). Examples of even functions include $f(x) = \cos x, 1, x^2, x^4,$ and x^6. An **odd** function f is a function such that*

$$f(-x) = -f(x)$$

for all x. This means that the graph of $y = f(x)$ is symmetric under reflections first across the y-axis, then across the x-axis (Fig. 5.7.2). Examples of odd functions are $f(x) = \sin x, x, x^3,$ and x^5. Think about these reflections with the (even) cosine function (in Fig. 5.7.3) and the (odd) sine function (in Fig. 5.7.4).

FIGURE 5.7.1 The graph of the even function $y = f(x)$ is invariant under reflection through the y-axis.

FIGURE 5.7.2 The graph of the odd function $y = f(x)$ is invariant under successive reflections through both axes.

FIGURE 5.7.3 The cosine function is even.

FIGURE 5.7.4 The sine function is odd.

67. See Fig. 5.7.5. If the continuous function f is odd, substitute $u = -x$ into the integral

$$\int_{-a}^{0} f(x)\,dx \quad \text{to show that} \quad \int_{-a}^{a} f(x)\,dx = 0.$$

FIGURE 5.7.5 Areas cancel when f is odd (Problem 67).

68. See Fig. 5.7.6. If the continuous function f is even, use the method of Problem 67 to show that

$$\int_{-a}^{a} f(x)\,dx = 2\int_{0}^{a} f(x)\,dx.$$

FIGURE 5.7.6 Areas add when f is even (Problem 68).

In Problems 69 and 70, use the results of Problems 67 and 68 to justify the values of the given integrals without extensive computation.

69. $\displaystyle\int_{-1}^{1} \left[\tan x + \frac{\sqrt[3]{x}}{(1+x^2)^7} - x^{17}\cos x\right] dx = 0.$

70. $\displaystyle\int_{-5}^{5} \left(3x^2 - x^{10}\sin x + x^5\sqrt{1+x^4}\right) dx = 2\left[x^3\right]_0^5 = 250.$

71. Suppose that f is continuous everywhere and that k is a constant. Show that

$$\int_a^b f(x+k)\,dx = \int_{a+k}^{b+k} f(x)\,dx.$$

In the case in which $k > 0$ and $f(x) > 0$, illustrate this formula with a sketch showing two regions with bases $[a, b]$

and $[a+k, b+k]$. Why is it plausible that these two regions have equal areas?

72. Suppose that f is continuous everywhere and that k is a constant. Show that

$$\int_{ka}^{kb} f(x)\,dx = k \int_a^b f(kx)\,dx.$$

In the case in which $k > 1$ and $f(x) > 0$, illustrate this formula with a sketch showing two regions with bases $[a, b]$

and $[ka, kb]$. Why is it plausible that the area of one of these regions is k times the area of the other?

73. (a) Verify by differentiation that

$$\int u \sin u\, du = \sin u - u \cos u + C.$$

(b) Use part (a) to show that

$$\int_0^{\pi^2} \sin \sqrt{x}\, dx = 2\pi.$$

5.8 AREAS OF PLANE REGIONS

In Section 5.3 we discussed the area A under the graph of a positive-valued continuous function f on the interval $[a, b]$. This discussion motivated our definition in Section 5.4 of the integral of f from a to b as the limit of Riemann sums. An important result was that

$$A = \int_a^b f(x)\,dx, \tag{1}$$

by definition.

Here we consider the problem of finding the areas of more general regions in the coordinate plane. Regions such as the ones illustrated in Fig. 5.8.1 may be bounded by the graphs of *two* (or more) different functions.

FIGURE 5.8.1 Plane regions bounded by pairs of curves.

Let f and g be continuous functions such that $f(x) \geqq g(x)$ for all x in the interval $[a, b]$. We are interested in the area A of the region R in Fig. 5.8.2, which lies *between* the graphs of $y = f(x)$ and $y = g(x)$ for x in $[a, b]$. Thus R is bounded by

- The curve $y = f(x)$, the upper boundary of R, by
- The curve $y = g(x)$, the lower boundary of R, *and* by
- The vertical lines $x = a$ and $x = b$ (if needed).

To approximate A, we consider a partition of $[a, b]$ into n subintervals, all with the same length $\Delta x = (b - a)/n$. If ΔA_i denotes the area of the region between the graphs of f and g over the ith subinterval $[x_{i-1}, x_i]$, and $x_i^\star$ is a selected number chosen in that subinterval (all this for $i = 1, 2, 3, \ldots, n$), then ΔA_i is approximately equal to the area of a rectangle with height $f(x_i^\star) - g(x_i^\star)$ and width Δx (Fig. 5.8.3). Hence

$$\Delta A_i \approx [f(x_i^\star) - g(x_i^\star)]\, \Delta x;$$

Areas of Plane Regions SECTION 5.8   337

FIGURE 5.8.2 A region between two graphs.

FIGURE 5.8.3 A partition of $[a, b]$ divides R into vertical strips that we approximate with rectangular strips.

so

$$A = \sum_{i=1}^{n} \Delta A_i \approx \sum_{i=1}^{n} [f(x_i^\star) - g(x_i^\star)] \Delta x.$$

We introduce the *height* function $h(x) = f(x) - g(x)$ and observe that A is approximated by a Riemann sum for $h(x)$ associated with our partition of $[a, b]$:

$$A \approx \sum_{i=1}^{n} h(x_i^\star) \Delta x.$$

Both intuition and reason suggest that this approximation can be made arbitrarily accurate by choosing n to be sufficiently large (and hence $\Delta x = (b - a)/n$ to be sufficiently small). We therefore conclude that

$$A = \lim_{\Delta x \to 0} \sum_{i=1}^{n} h(x_i^\star) \Delta x = \int_a^b h(x)\, dx = \int_a^b [f(x) - g(x)]\, dx.$$

Because our discussion is based on an intuitive concept rather than on a precise logical definition of area, it does *not* constitute a proof of this area formula. It does, however, provide justification for the following *definition* of the area in question.

DEFINITION The Area Between Two Curves
Let f and g be continuous with $f(x) \geq g(x)$ for x in $[a, b]$. Then the **area** A of the region bounded by the curves $y = f(x)$ and $y = g(x)$ and by the vertical lines $x = a$ and $x = b$ is

$$A = \int_a^b [f(x) - g(x)]\, dx. \tag{2}$$

EXAMPLE 1 Find the area of the region bounded by the lines $y = x$ and $x = 2$ and by the curve $y = 1/x^2$ (Fig. 5.8.4).

Solution Here the top curve is $y = f(x) = x$, the bottom curve is $y = g(x) = 1/x^2$, $a = 1$, and $b = 2$. The vertical line $x = 2$ is "needed" (to form the right-hand boundary of the region), whereas $x = 1$ is not. Equation (2) yields

$$A = \int_1^2 \left(x - \frac{1}{x^2}\right) dx = \left[\frac{1}{2}x^2 + \frac{1}{x}\right]_1^2 = \left(2 + \frac{1}{2}\right) - \left(\frac{1}{2} + 1\right) = 1. \quad \blacklozenge$$

FIGURE 5.8.4 The region of Example 1.

338 CHAPTER 5 The Integral

FIGURE 5.8.5 The integral $\int_a^b g(x)\,dx$ gives the negative of the geometric area for a region that lies below the x-axis.

Equation (1) is the special case of Eq. (2) in which $g(x)$ is identically zero on $[a, b]$. But if $f(x) \equiv 0$ and $g(x) \leq 0$ on $[a, b]$, then Eq. (2) reduces to

$$A = -\int_a^b g(x)\,dx; \quad \text{that is,} \quad \int_a^b g(x)\,dx = -A.$$

In this case the region R lies beneath the x-axis (Fig. 5.8.5). Thus the integral from a to b of a negative-valued function is the *negative* of the area of the region bounded by its graph, the x-axis, and the vertical lines $x = a$ and $x = b$.

More generally, consider a continuous function f with a graph that crosses the x-axis at finitely many points $c_1, c_2, c_3, \ldots, c_k$ between a and b (Fig. 5.8.6). We write

$$\int_a^b f(x)\,dx = \int_a^{c_1} f(x)\,dx + \int_{c_1}^{c_2} f(x)\,dx + \cdots + \int_{c_k}^b f(x)\,dx.$$

Thus we see that

$$\int_a^b f(x)\,dx$$

is equal to the area below $y = f(x)$ and *above* the x-axis *minus* the area above $y = f(x)$ and *below* the x-axis.

FIGURE 5.8.6 The integral $\int_a^b f(x)\,dx$ computes the area above the x-axis *minus* the area below the x-axis.

The following *heuristic* (suggestive, though nonrigorous) way of setting up integral formulas such as Eq. (2) can be useful. Consider the vertical strip of area that lies above the interval $[x, x + dx]$, shown shaded in Fig. 5.8.7, where we have written

$$y_{\text{top}} = f(x) \quad \text{and} \quad y_{\text{bot}} = g(x)$$

for the top and bottom boundary curves. We think of the length dx of the interval $[x, x + dx]$ as being so small that we can regard this strip as a rectangle with width dx and height $y_{\text{top}} - y_{\text{bot}}$. Its area is then

$$dA = (y_{\text{top}} - y_{\text{bot}})\,dx.$$

Think now of the region over $[a, b]$ that lies between $y_{\text{top}} = f(x)$ and $y_{\text{bot}} = g(x)$ as being made up of many such vertical strips. We can regard its area as a sum of areas of such rectangular strips. If we write $\int$ for *sum*, we get the formula

$$A = \int dA = \int_a^b (y_{\text{top}} - y_{\text{bot}})\,dx.$$

FIGURE 5.8.7 Heuristic (suggestive but nonrigorous) approach to setting up area integrals.

This heuristic approach bypasses the subscript notation associated with Riemann sums. Nevertheless, it *is not* and *should not* be regarded as a *complete* derivation of the last formula. It is best used only as a convenient memory device. For instance, in the figures that accompany many examples, we shall often show a strip of width dx as a visual aid in properly setting up the correct integral.

Areas of Plane Regions SECTION 5.8 339

EXAMPLE 2 Find the area A of the region R bounded by the line $y = x$ and the parabola $y = 6 - x^2$.

Solution The region R is shown in Fig. 5.8.8. We can use Eq. (2) and take $f(x) = 6 - x^2$ and $g(x) = x$. The limits a and b will be the x-coordinates of the two points of intersection of the line and the parabola; our first order of business is to find a and b. To do so, we equate $f(x)$ and $g(x)$ and solve the resulting equation for x:

$$x = 6 - x^2; \quad x^2 + x - 6 = 0;$$
$$(x - 2)(x + 3) = 0; \quad x = -3, 2.$$

Thus $a = -3$ and $b = 2$, so Eq. (2) gives

$$A = \int_{-3}^{2} (6 - x^2 - x)\, dx = \left[6x - \tfrac{1}{3}x^3 - \tfrac{1}{2}x^2\right]_{-3}^{2}$$
$$= \left[6 \cdot 2 - \tfrac{1}{3} \cdot 2^3 - \tfrac{1}{2} \cdot 2^2\right] - \left[6 \cdot (-3) - \tfrac{1}{3} \cdot (-3)^3 - \tfrac{1}{2} \cdot (-3)^2\right] = \tfrac{125}{6}. \quad \blacklozenge$$

FIGURE 5.8.8 The region R of Example 2.

Subdividing Regions Before Integrating

Example 3 shows that it is sometimes necessary to subdivide a region before applying Eq. (2), typically because the formula for either the top or the bottom boundary curve (or both) changes somewhere between $x = a$ and $x = b$.

EXAMPLE 3 Find the area of the region R bounded by the line $y = \tfrac{1}{2}x$ and the parabola $y^2 = 8 - x$.

Solution The region R is shaded in Fig. 5.8.9. The points of intersection $(-8, -4)$ and $(4, 2)$ are found by equating $y = \tfrac{1}{2}x$ and $y = \pm\sqrt{8 - x}$ and then solving for x. The lower boundary of R is given by $y_{\text{bot}} = -\sqrt{8 - x}$ on $[-8, 8]$. But the upper boundary of R is given by

$$y_{\text{top}} = \tfrac{1}{2}x \quad \text{on } [-8, 4], \qquad y_{\text{top}} = +\sqrt{8 - x} \quad \text{on } [4, 8].$$

We must therefore divide R into the two regions R_1 and R_2, as indicated in Fig. 5.8.9. Then Eq. (2) gives

$$A = \int_{-8}^{4} \left(\tfrac{1}{2}x + \sqrt{8 - x}\right) dx + \int_{4}^{8} 2\sqrt{8 - x}\, dx$$
$$= \left[\tfrac{1}{4}x^2 - \tfrac{2}{3}(8 - x)^{3/2}\right]_{-8}^{4} + \left[-\tfrac{4}{3}(8 - x)^{3/2}\right]_{4}^{8}$$
$$= \left[\left(\tfrac{16}{4} - \tfrac{16}{3}\right) - \left(\tfrac{64}{4} - \tfrac{128}{3}\right)\right] + \left[0 + \tfrac{32}{3}\right] = 36. \quad \blacklozenge$$

FIGURE 5.8.9 In Example 3, we split region R into two regions R_1 and R_2.

Determining Area by Integrating with Respect to y

The region in Example 3 appears to be simpler if we consider it to be bounded by graphs of functions of y rather than by graphs of functions of x. Figure 5.8.10 shows a region R bounded by the curves $x = f(y)$ and $x = g(y)$, with $f(y) \geqq g(y)$ for y in $[c, d]$, and by the horizontal lines $y = c$ and $y = d$. To approximate the area A of R, we begin with a partition of $[c, d]$ into n subintervals all with the same length $\Delta y = (d - c)/n$. We choose a point $y_i^\star$ in the ith subinterval $[y_{i-1}, y_i]$ for each i $(1 \leq i \leq n)$. The horizontal strip of R lying opposite $[y_{i-1}, y_i]$ is approximated by a rectangle with width Δy (measured vertically) and height $f(y_i^\star) - g(y_i^\star)$ (measured horizontally). Hence

$$A \approx \sum_{i=1}^{n} [f(y_i^\star) - g(y_i^\star)] \, \Delta y.$$

Recognizing the sum as a Riemann sum for the integral

$$\int_c^d [f(y) - g(y)] \, dy$$

motivates the following definition.

FIGURE 5.8.10 Find area by using an integral with respect to y.

DEFINITION   The Area Between Two Curves

Let f and g be continuous functions of y with $f(y) \geqq g(y)$ for y in $[c, d]$. Then the **area** A of the region bounded by the curves $x = f(y)$ and $x = g(y)$ and by the horizontal lines $y = c$ and $y = d$ is

$$A = \int_c^d [f(y) - g(y)] \, dy. \tag{3}$$

In a more advanced course, we would now prove that Eqs. (2) and (3) yield the same area A for a region that can be described both in the manner shown in Fig. 5.8.2 and in the manner shown in Fig. 5.8.10.

Let us write

$$x_{\text{right}} = f(y) \quad \text{and} \quad x_{\text{left}} = g(y)$$

for the right and left boundary curves, respectively, of the region in Fig. 5.8.10. Then

Eq. (3) takes the form

$$A = \int_c^d [x_{\text{right}} - x_{\text{left}}]\, dy.$$

Comparing Example 3 with Example 4 illustrates the advantage of choosing the "right" variable of integration—the one that makes the resulting computations simpler.

EXAMPLE 4 Integrate with respect to y to find the area of the region R of Example 3.

Solution We see from Fig. 5.8.11 that Eq. (3) applies with $x_{\text{right}} = f(y) = 8 - y^2$ and $x_{\text{left}} = g(y) = 2y$ for y in $[-4, 2]$. This gives

$$A = \int_{-4}^{2} [(8 - y^2) - 2y]\, dy = \left[8y - \tfrac{1}{3}y^3 - y^2 \right]_{-4}^{2} = 36. \qquad \blacklozenge$$

FIGURE 5.8.11 Recomputation of the area of Example 3 (Example 4).

EXAMPLE 5 Use calculus to derive the formula $A = \pi r^2$ for the area of a circle of radius r.

Solution The point is that the formula $A = \pi r^2$, however familiar it seems, requires *proof*—it certainly is not self-evident. We begin with the *definition* (as suggested in Section 5.3) of the famous number π as the area of the unit circle $x^2 + y^2 = 1$. This implies that

$$\int_0^1 \sqrt{1 - x^2}\, dx = \frac{\pi}{4}, \qquad (4)$$

(see Fig. 5.8.12) despite the fact that there is no immediate or obvious way of antidifferentiating $\sqrt{1 - x^2}$ in order to explicitly evaluate the integral in (4).

Now we turn our attention to the general circle of radius r shown in Fig. 5.8.13. We apply Eq. (1) to the first quadrant and then multiply by 4. Thus we find that the

FIGURE 5.8.12 The number π is four times the shaded area.

FIGURE 5.8.13 The shaded area can be expressed as an integral.

total area A of the circle is given by

$$A = 4\int_0^r \sqrt{r^2 - x^2}\, dx = 4r\int_0^r \sqrt{1 - \frac{x^2}{r^2}}\, dx$$

$$= 4r\int_0^1 r\sqrt{1 - u^2}\, du \quad \left(\text{Substitution: } u = \frac{x}{r},\ x = ru,\ dx = r\, du\right)$$

$$= 4r^2 \cdot \frac{\pi}{4}.$$

Here we have applied Eq. (4)—with u in place of x—to get $A = \pi r^2$, as desired. ◆

EXAMPLE 6 Approximate the area A of the first-quadrant region shown in Fig. 5.8.14. This is the region bounded by the curves

$$y = \frac{7x}{(x^2 + 1)^{3/2}} \quad \text{and} \quad y = \frac{x^2}{3}.$$

Solution In order to find the exact coordinates of the first-quadrant intersection point in Fig. 5.8.14, we would need to solve the equation

$$\frac{7x}{(x^2 + 1)^{3/2}} = \frac{x^2}{3}.$$

We might begin by first canceling x, then cross-multiplying and squaring both sides. The result, as you can verify, simplifies to the equation

$$x^8 + 3x^6 + 3x^4 + x^2 - 441 = 0.$$

Now you see why we asked for the *approximate* area. Although it is impractical to solve this eighth-degree equation exactly, we can use a graphing calculator or computer to zoom in on the desired intersection point shown in Fig. 5.8.14. In this way we find that $x \approx 1.963$ is its approximate x-coordinate. (We could also use Newton's method or a calculator root-finder.) We can now proceed to approximate the desired area.

$$A \approx \int_0^{1.963} \left(\frac{7x}{(x^2 + 1)^{3/2}} - \frac{x^2}{3}\right) dx$$

$$= \int_0^{1.963} \frac{7x}{(x^2 + 1)^{3/2}}\, dx - \int_0^{1.963} \frac{x^2}{3}\, dx.$$

We substitute $u = x^2 + 1$, $du = 2x\, dx$ to evaluate the first integral and get

$$A \approx \left[\frac{-7x}{\sqrt{x^2 + 1}} - \frac{x^3}{9}\right]_0^{1.963} \approx -4.018 - (-7) = 2.982. \quad \blacklozenge$$

FIGURE 5.8.14 The region of Example 6.

5.8 TRUE/FALSE STUDY GUIDE

5.8 CONCEPTS: QUESTIONS AND DISCUSSION

*The concept of area is not self-evident, and the area of a plane set must be defined before it can be calculated. The area of a region bounded by curves can be defined in terms of areas of inscribed and circumscribed polygons. We say that the region R has **area** A—and write $a(R) = A$—provided that, given any number $\epsilon > 0$ (however small), there exist a polygon P contained in R and a polygon Q containing R such that*

$$A - \epsilon < a(P) \leq a(Q) < A + \epsilon.$$

The polygonal areas $a(P)$ and $a(Q)$ are defined as sums of areas of nonoverlapping triangles and/or rectangles. If for some $\epsilon > 0$ there do not exist such polygons P and Q, then R does not have area. (There do exist plane sets whose area is not defined!)

1. Suppose that the function f is continuous and positive-valued on the interval $[a, b]$. Let R be the plane region bounded above by the graph of $y = f(x)$,

below by the x-axis, and on the sides by the vertical lines $x = a$ and $x = b$. Then use the fact that f is integrable and the observation that any Riemann sum is the area of a polygon to prove that the area A of R exists and is given by

$$A = \int_a^b f(x)\,dx.$$

Suggestion: Think about the maximum and minimum values of $f(x)$ on a typical subinterval of a partition of $[a, b]$.

2. Suppose that the function f is defined on the interval $[0, 1]$ as follows:

$$f(x) = \begin{cases} 0 & \text{if } x \text{ is rational,} \\ 1 & \text{if } x \text{ is irrational.} \end{cases}$$

Let R be the plane region consisting of all those points (x, y) such that $0 \leq x \leq 1$ and $0 \leq y \leq f(x)$. Show that R does not have area. Note that if the polygon P is contained in R then P is "degenerate," so that it has area $a(P) = 0$. Note also that $a(Q) \geq 1$ if the polygon Q contains R.

5.8 PROBLEMS

Find the areas of the regions shown in Problems 1 through 10.

1. (See Fig. 5.8.15.)

FIGURE 5.8.15 Problem 1.

2. (See Fig. 5.8.16.)

FIGURE 5.8.16 Problem 2.

3. (See Fig. 5.8.17.)

FIGURE 5.8.17 Problem 3.

4. (See Fig. 5.8.18.)

FIGURE 5.8.18 Problem 4.

5. (See Fig. 5.8.19.)

FIGURE 5.8.19 Problem 5.

6. (See Fig. 5.8.20.)

FIGURE 5.8.20 Problem 6.

7. (See Fig. 5.8.21.)

FIGURE 5.8.21 Problem 7.

8. (See Fig. 5.8.22.)

FIGURE 5.8.22 Problem 8.

9. (See Fig. 5.8.23.)

FIGURE 5.8.23 Problem 9.

10. (See Fig. 5.8.24.)

FIGURE 5.8.24 Problem 10.

Find the areas of the regions described in Problems 11 through 20.

11. The region R bounded below by the graph of $y = x^3$ and above by the graph of $y = x$ over the interval $[0, 1]$

12. The region R between the graph of $y = 1/(x+1)^2$ and the x-axis over the interval $[1, 3]$

13. The region R bounded above by the graph of $y = x^3$ and below by the graph of $y = x^4$ over the interval $[0, 1]$

14. The region R bounded above by the graph of $y = x^2$ and below by the horizontal line $y = -1$ over the interval $[-1, 2]$

15. The region R bounded above by the graph of $y = 1/(x+1)^3$ and below by the x-axis over the interval $[0, 2]$

16. The region R bounded above by the graph of $y = 4x - x^2$ and below by the x-axis

17. The region R bounded on the left by the graph of $x = y^2$ and on the right by the vertical line $x = 4$

18. The region R between the graphs of $y = x^4 - 4$ and $y = 3x^2$

19. The region R between the graphs of $x = 8 - y^2$ and $x = y^2 - 8$

20. The region R between the graphs of $y = x^{1/3}$ and $y = x^3$

In Problems 21 through 40, sketch the region bounded by the given curves, then find its area.

21. $y = x^2$, $y = 2x$

22. $y = x^2$, $y = 8 - x^2$

23. $x = y^2$, $x = 25$

24. $x = y^2$, $x = 32 - y^2$

25. $y = x^2$, $y = 2x + 3$

26. $y = x^2$, $y = 2x + 8$

27. $x = y^2$, $x = y + 6$

28. $x = y^2$, $x = 8 - 2y$

29. $y = \cos x$, $y = \sin x$, $0 \leq x \leq \pi/4$

30. $y = \cos x$, $y = \sin x$, $-3\pi/4 \leq x \leq 0$

31. $x = 4y^2$, $x + 12y + 5 = 0$

32. $y = x^2$, $y = 3 + 5x - x^2$

33. $x = 3y^2$, $x = 12y - y^2 - 5$

34. $y = x^2$, $y = 4(x - 1)^2$

35. $x = y^2 - 2y - 2$, $x = 4 + y - 2y^2$

36. $y = x^3$, $y = 32 - x^4$

37. $y = x^3$, $y = 32\sqrt{x}$

38. $y = x^3$, $y = 2x - x^2$

39. $y = x^2$, $y = \sqrt[3]{x^2}$

40. $y^2 = x$, $y^2 = 2(x - 3)$

In Problems 41 and 42, first use a calculator or computer to graph the given curves $y = f(x)$ and $y = g(x)$. You should then be able to find the coordinates of the points of intersection that will be evident in your figure. Finally, find the area of the region bounded by the two curves. Problems 43 and 44 are similar, except that the two curves bound two regions; find the sum of the areas of these two regions.

41. $y = x^2 - x$, $y = 1 - x^3$

42. $y = x^3 - x$, $y = 1 - x^4$

43. $y = x^2$, $y = x^3 - 2x$

44. $y = x^3$, $y = 2x^3 + x^2 - 2x$

45. Evaluate
$$\int_{-3}^{3} (4x + 5)\sqrt{9 - x^2}\, dx$$
by writing this integral as a sum of two integrals and interpreting one of them in terms of a known (circular) area.

46. Evaluate
$$\int_{0}^{3} x\sqrt{81 - x^4}\, dx$$
by making a substitution of the form $u = x^p$ (you choose p) and then interpreting the result in terms of a known area.

47. The *ellipse* $x^2/a^2 + y^2/b^2 = 1$ is shown in Fig. 5.8.25. Use the method of Example 4 to show that the area of the region it bounds is $A = \pi ab$, a pleasing generalization of the area formula for the circle.

FIGURE 5.8.25 The ellipse of Problem 47.

48. Figure 5.8.26 shows a *parabolic segment* bounded by the parabola $y = x^2$ and the line $y = 1$. In the third century B.C., Archimedes showed that the area of a parabolic segment is four-thirds the area of the triangle ABC, where AB is the "base" of the parabolic segment and C is its vertex (as in Fig. 5.8.26). Verify this for the indicated parabolic segment.

FIGURE 5.8.26 The parabolic segment of Problem 48.

49. Let A and B be the points of intersection of the parabola $y = x^2$ and the line $y = x + 2$, and let C be the point on the parabola where the tangent line is parallel to the graph of $y = x + 2$. Show that the area of the parabolic segment cut from the parabola by the line (Fig. 5.8.27) is four-thirds the area of the triangle ABC.

FIGURE 5.8.27 The parabolic segment of Problem 49.

50. Find the area of the unbounded region R shaded in Fig. 5.8.28—regard it as the limit as $b \to \infty$ of the region bounded by $y = 1/x^2$, $y = 0$, $x = 1$, and $x = b > 1$.

FIGURE 5.8.28 The unbounded region of Problem 50.

51. Find the total area of the bounded regions that are bounded by the x-axis and the curve $y = 2x^3 - 2x^2 - 12x$.

52. Suppose that the quadratic function
$$f(x) = px^2 + qx + r$$
is never negative on $[a, b]$. Show that the area under the graph of f from a to b is $A = \frac{1}{3}h[f(a) + 4f(m) + f(b)]$, where $h = (b - a)/2$ and $m = (a + b)/2$. [*Suggestion:* By a horizontal translation of this region, you may assume that $a = -h$, $m = 0$, and $b = h$.]

The curves defined in Problems 53 and 54 include the loops shown in Figs. 5.8.29 and 5.8.30. Find the area of the region bounded by each loop.

53. $y^2 = x(5 - x)^2$ **54.** $y^2 = x^2(x + 3)$

FIGURE 5.8.29 The region of Problem 53.

FIGURE 5.8.30 The region of Problem 54.

In Problems 55 through 58, use a calculator to approximate (graphically or otherwise) the points of intersection of the two given curves. Then integrate to find (approximately) the area of the region bounded by these curves.

55. $y = x^2$, $y = \cos x$

56. $y = x^2 - 2x$, $y = \sin x$

57. $y = x^2 - 1$, $y = \dfrac{1}{1+x^2}$

58. $y = x^4 - 16$, $y = 2x - x^2$

59. Find a number $k > 0$ such that the area bounded by the curves $y = x^2$ and $y = k - x^2$ is 72.

60. Find a number $k > 0$ such that the line $y = k$ divides the region between the parabola $y = 100 - x^2$ and the x-axis into two regions having equal areas.

In Problems 61 through 63 the graphs $y = f(x)$ and $y = g(x)$ of the given functions f and g bound two regions R_1 and R_2 as indicated in Figs. 5.8.31 through 5.8.33. You are to find the sum A of the areas $A_1 = a(R_1)$ and $A_2 = a(R_2)$ of these two regions. If possible, obtain the exact value of A; otherwise, approximate it very accurately. You may use a calculator or a computer algebra system, both to find the points of intersection of the two graphs and to carry out the integrations required to calculate A.

FIGURE 5.8.33 The regions of Problem 63.

61. $f(x) = x$ and $g(x) = x(x-4)^2$. Here you should be able to find A without a calculator or a computer.

62. $f(x) = x^2$ and $g(x) = x(x-4)^2$. Here you can solve manually for the points of intersection, but probably will want to use a calculator or computer for the integrations.

63. $f(x) = (x-2)^2$ and $g(x) = x(x-4)^2$. Here you will need to approximate numerically the coordinates of the points of intersection as well as the value of A.

FIGURE 5.8.31 The regions of Problem 61.

FIGURE 5.8.32 The regions of Problem 62.

5.9 NUMERICAL INTEGRATION

The fundamental theorem of calculus,

$$\int_a^b f(x)\,dx = \Big[G(x)\Big]_a^b,$$

can be used to evaluate an integral only if a convenient formula for the antiderivative G of f can be found. But there are simple functions with antiderivatives that are not elementary functions. An **elementary function** is one that can be expressed in terms of polynomial, trigonometric, exponential, or logarithmic functions by means of finite combinations of sums, differences, products, quotients, roots, and function composition.

The problem is that elementary functions can have nonelementary antiderivatives. For example, it is known that the elementary function $f(x) = \sqrt[3]{1+x^2}$ has no elementary antiderivative. Consequently, we cannot use the fundamental theorem of calculus to evaluate an integral such as

$$\int_0^1 \sqrt[3]{1+x^2}\, dx.$$

Here we discuss the use of Riemann sums to approximate numerically integrals that cannot conveniently be evaluated exactly, whether or not nonelementary functions are involved. Given a continuous function f on $[a, b]$ with an integral to be approximated, consider a partition of $[a, b]$ into n subintervals, each with the same length $\Delta x = (b-a)/n$. Then the value of any Riemann sum of the form

$$S = \sum_{i=1}^{n} f(x_i^{\star})\, \Delta x \tag{1}$$

may be taken to be an approximation to the value of the integral $\int_a^b f(x)\, dx$.

With $x_i^{\star} = x_{i-1}$ and with $x_i^{\star} = x_i$ in Eq. (1), we get the *left-endpoint approximation* L_n and the *right-endpoint approximation* R_n to the definite integral $\int_a^b f(x)\, dx$ associated with the partition of $[a, b]$ into n equal-length subintervals. Thus

$$L_n = \sum_{i=1}^{n} f(x_{i-1})\, \Delta x \tag{2}$$

and

$$R_n = \sum_{i=1}^{n} f(x_i)\, \Delta x. \tag{3}$$

We can simplify the notation for L_n and R_n by writing y_i for $f(x_i)$ (Fig. 5.9.1).

FIGURE 5.9.1 $y_i = f(x_i)$.

DEFINITION Endpoint Approximations
The **left-endpoint approximation** L_n and the **right-endpoint approximation** R_n to $\int_a^b f(x)\, dx$ with $\Delta x = (b-a)/n$ are

$$L_n = (\Delta x)(y_0 + y_1 + y_2 + \cdots + y_{n-1}) \tag{2'}$$

and

$$R_n = (\Delta x)(y_1 + y_2 + y_3 + \cdots + y_n). \tag{3'}$$

In Example 1 of Section 5.3 we calculated the left- and right-endpoint approximations to the integral

$$\int_0^3 x^2\, dx = 9 \tag{4}$$

with $n = 5$ and $n = 10$. The table in Fig. 5.9.2 shows values of L_n and R_n with larger values of n.

n	L_n	R_n	$\frac{1}{2}(L_n + R_n)$
5	6.4800	11.8800	9.1800
10	7.6950	10.3950	9.0450
20	8.3363	9.6863	9.0113
40	8.6653	9.3403	9.0028
80	8.8320	9.1695	9.0007
160	8.9158	9.0846	9.0002
320	8.9579	9.0422	9.0000

FIGURE 5.9.2 Left- and right-endpoint approximations to the integral in Eq. (4).

The final column of this table gives the *average* of the endpoint sums L_n and R_n. It is apparent that (for a given value of n) this average is a considerably more accurate approximation to the integral than is either one-sided approximation by itself.

The Trapezoidal and Midpoint Approximations

The average $T_n = (L_n + R_n)/2$ of the left-endpoint and right-endpoint approximations is called the *trapezoidal approximation* to $\int_a^b f(x)\,dx$ associated with the partition of $[a, b]$ into n equal-length subintervals. Written in full,

$$T_n = \frac{1}{2}(L_n + R_n)$$

$$= \frac{\Delta x}{2} \sum_{i=1}^{n} [f(x_{i-1}) + f(x_i)]$$

$$= \frac{\Delta x}{2} \{[f(x_0) + f(x_1)] + [f(x_1) + f(x_2)] + [f(x_2) + f(x_3)] + \cdots$$
$$+ [f(x_{n-2}) + f(x_{n-1})] + [f(x_{n-1}) + f(x_n)]\};$$

that is,

$$T_n = \frac{\Delta x}{2}[f(x_0) + 2f(x_1) + 2f(x_2) + \cdots + 2f(x_{n-2}) + 2f(x_{n-1}) + f(x_n)]. \quad (5)$$

Note the 1-2-2-·····-2-2-1 pattern of the coefficients.

DEFINITION The Trapezoidal Approximation
The **trapezoidal approximation** to

$$\int_a^b f(x)\,dx \quad \text{with} \quad \Delta x = \frac{b-a}{n}$$

is

$$T_n = \frac{\Delta x}{2}(y_0 + 2y_1 + 2y_2 + \cdots + 2y_{n-2} + 2y_{n-1} + y_n). \quad (6)$$

FIGURE 5.9.3 The area of the trapezoid is $\frac{1}{2}[f(x_{i-1}) + f(x_i)]\Delta x$.

Figure 5.9.3 shows where the trapezoidal approximation gets its name. The partition points $x_0, x_1, x_2, \ldots, x_n$ are used to build trapezoids from the x-axis to the graph of the function f. The trapezoid over the ith subinterval $[x_{i-1}, x_i]$ has height Δx, and its parallel bases have widths $f(x_{i-1})$ and $f(x_i)$. So its area is

$$\frac{\Delta x}{2}[f(x_{i-1}) + f(x_i)] = \frac{\Delta x}{2}(y_{i-1} + y_i).$$

FIGURE 5.9.4 Geometry of the trapezoidal approximation.

Comparing this with Eq. (6) shows that T_n is merely the sum of the areas of the n trapezoids shown in Fig. 5.9.4.

EXAMPLE 1 Calculate the trapezoidal approximation to the integral in Eq. (4) with $n = 6$ and $\Delta x = 0.5$.

Solution The trapezoids in Fig. 5.9.5 indicate why T_6 should be a much better approximation than either of the endpoint approximations L_6 or R_6. The table in Fig. 5.9.6 shows the values of $f(x) = x^2$ that are needed to compute L_6 and R_6. The 1-2-2-$\cdots$-2-2-1 coefficients appear in the final column. Using Eq. (6), we get

$$T_6 = \frac{0.5}{2}[1\cdot(0) + 2\cdot(0.25) + 2\cdot(1)$$
$$+ 2\cdot(2.25) + 2\cdot(4) + 2\cdot(6.25) + 1\cdot(9)]$$
$$= 9.125$$

(as compared with the actual value 9). ◆

n	L_n	$f(x_n) = x_n^2$	Coefficients
0	0	0	1
1	0.5	0.25	2
2	1	1	2
3	1.5	2.25	2
4	2	4	2
5	2.5	6.25	2
6	3	9	1

FIGURE 5.9.5 The area under $y = x^2$ (Example 1).

FIGURE 5.9.6 Data for Example 1.

Another useful approximation to $\int_a^b f(x)\,dx$ is the *midpoint approximation* M_n. It is the Riemann sum obtained by choosing the point x_i^* in $[x_{i-1}, x_i]$ to be its midpoint $m_i = (x_{i-1} + x_i)/2$. Thus

$$M_n = \sum_{i=1}^{n} f(m_i)\,\Delta x = (\Delta x)[f(m_1) + f(m_2) + \cdots + f(m_n)]. \qquad (7)$$

350 CHAPTER 5 The Integral

FIGURE 5.9.7 The ordinates used in the midpoint approximation.

Because m_1 is the midpoint of $[x_0, x_1]$, it is sometimes convenient to write $y_{1/2}$ for $f(m_1)$, $y_{3/2}$ for $f(m_2)$, and so on (Fig. 5.9.7).

DEFINITION The Midpoint Approximation
The **midpoint approximation** to

$$\int_a^b f(x)\,dx \quad \text{with} \quad \Delta x = \frac{b-a}{n}$$

is

$$M_n = (\Delta x)\bigl(y_{1/2} + y_{3/2} + y_{5/2} + \cdots + y_{n-(1/2)}\bigr). \tag{7'}$$

EXAMPLE 2 Figure 5.9.8 illustrates the midpoint approximation to the integral

$$\int_0^3 x^2\,dx = 9$$

of Example 1, with $n = 6$ and $\Delta x = 0.5$, and the table in Fig. 5.9.9 shows the values of $f(x) = x^2$ needed to compute M_6. Using Eq. (7), we obtain

$$\begin{aligned} M_6 &= (0.5)\,[1 \cdot (0.0625) + 1 \cdot (0.5625) + 1 \cdot (1.5625) \\ &\quad + 1 \cdot (3.0625) + 1 \cdot (5.0625) + 1 \cdot (7.5625)] \\ &= 8.9375. \end{aligned}$$

◆

FIGURE 5.9.8 Midpoint rectangles approximating the area under $y = x^2$ (Example 2).

n	m_n	$f(m_i)$	Coefficients
1	0.25	0.0625	1
2	0.75	0.5625	1
3	1.25	1.5625	1
4	1.75	3.0625	1
5	2.25	5.0625	1
6	2.75	7.5625	1

FIGURE 5.9.9 Data for Example 2.

FIGURE 5.9.10 The graph of $f(x) = \dfrac{\sin x}{x}$ (Example 3).

EXAMPLE 3 Figure 5.9.10 shows the graph of the function

$$f(x) = \frac{\sin x}{x}. \tag{8}$$

Recall from Section 2.5 that

$$\lim_{x \to 0} \frac{\sin x}{x} = 1.$$

Hence we *define* $f(0) = 1$; then there will be no difficulty at $x = 0$, even though both the numerator and denominator in Eq. (8) are zero. It happens that the function $f(x)$ has *no* elementary antiderivative, so the fundamental theorem of calculus cannot be used to calculate the value of the integral

$$I = \int_0^1 \frac{\sin x}{x}\, dx. \tag{9}$$

But such integrals are important in the design of precise photographic lenses (among other applications), so we are well motivated to resort to approximating its value numerically.

With $n = 10$ and $\Delta x = 0.1$, the trapezoidal approximation is

$$T_{10} = \frac{0.1}{2}\left[1 \cdot 1 + 2 \cdot \frac{\sin 0.1}{0.1} + 2 \cdot \frac{\sin 0.2}{0.2}\right.$$
$$\left. + 2 \cdot \frac{\sin 0.3}{0.3} + \cdots + 2 \cdot \frac{\sin 0.9}{0.9} + 1 \cdot \frac{\sin 1.0}{1.0}\right];$$

$$T_{10} \approx 0.94583.$$

The corresponding midpoint approximation is

$$M_{10} = (0.1)\left[1 \cdot \frac{\sin 0.05}{0.05} + 1 \cdot \frac{\sin 0.15}{0.15} + 1 \cdot \frac{\sin 0.25}{0.25} + \cdots\right.$$
$$\left. + 1 \cdot \frac{\sin 0.85}{0.85} + 1 \cdot \frac{\sin 0.95}{0.95}\right];$$

$$M_{10} \approx 0.94621.$$

The actual value of the integral in Eq. (9) is $I \approx 0.94608$ (accurate to five decimal places). Thus both T_{10} and M_{10} give the correct value 0.946 when rounded to three places. But

- T_{10} underestimates I by about 0.00025, whereas
- M_{10} overestimates I by about 0.00013.

Thus in this example the midpoint approximation is somewhat more accurate than the trapezoidal approximation. ◆

Simpson's Approximation

The midpoint approximation M_n in Eq. (7) is sometimes called the **tangent-line approximation,** because the area of the rectangle with base $[x_{i-1}, x_i]$ and height $f(m_i)$ is also the area of another approximating figure. As shown in Fig. 5.9.11, we draw a segment tangent to the graph of f at the point $(m_i, f(m_i))$ and use that segment for one side of a trapezoid (somewhat like the method of trapezoidal approximation). The trapezoid and the rectangle mentioned above have the same area, and so the value of M_n is the sum of the areas of trapezoids like the one in Fig. 5.9.11.

The area of the trapezoid associated with the midpoint approximation is generally closer to the true value of

$$\int_{x_{i-1}}^{x_i} f(x)\, dx$$

FIGURE 5.9.11 The midpoint (or tangent) approximation.

FIGURE 5.9.12 Comparison of the midpoint approximation error E_M with the trapezoidal approximation error E_T.

than is the area of the trapezoid associated with the trapezoidal approximation, as was the case in Example 3. Figure 5.9.12 shows this too, in that the midpoint error E_M (above the curve in this figure) is generally smaller than the trapezoidal error E_T (below the curve in this figure). Figure 5.9.12 also indicates that if $y = f(x)$ is concave downward, then M_n will be an overestimate and T_n will be an underestimate of $\int_a^b f(x)\,dx$. If the graph is concave upward, then the situation is reversed.

Such observations motivate the consideration of a *weighted average* of M_n and T_n, with M_n weighted more heavily than T_n, to improve our numerical estimates of the definite integral. The particular weighted average

$$S_{2n} = \tfrac{1}{3}(2M_n + T_n) = \tfrac{2}{3}M_n + \tfrac{1}{3}T_n \tag{10}$$

is called *Simpson's approximation* to $\int_a^b f(x)\,dx$. The reason for the subscript $2n$ is that we associate S_{2n} with a partition of $[a, b]$ into an *even* number, $2n$, of equal-length subintervals with the endpoints

$$a = x_0 < x_1 < x_2 < \cdots < x_{2n-2} < x_{2n-1} < x_{2n} = b.$$

The midpoint and trapezoidal approximations associated with the n subintervals

$$[x_0, x_2],\quad [x_2, x_4],\quad [x_4, x_6],\quad \ldots,\quad [x_{2n-4}, x_{2n-2}],\quad [x_{2n-2}, x_{2n}],$$

all with the same length $2\,\Delta x$, can then be written in the respective forms

$$M_n = (2\,\Delta x)(y_1 + y_3 + y_5 + \cdots + y_{2n-1})$$

and

$$T_n = \frac{2\,\Delta x}{2}(y_0 + 2y_2 + 2y_4 + \cdots + 2y_{2n-2} + y_{2n}).$$

We substitute these formulas for M_n and T_n into Eq. (10) and find—after a bit of algebra—that

$$S_{2n} = \frac{\Delta x}{3}(y_0 + 4y_1 + 2y_2 + 4y_3 + 2y_4 + \cdots + 2y_{2n-2} + 4y_{2n-1} + y_{2n}). \tag{11}$$

To be consistent with our other approximation formulas, we next rewrite Eq. (11) with n (rather than $2n$) to denote the total number of subintervals used.

DEFINITION   Simpson's Approximation
Simpson's approximation to $\int_a^b f(x)\,dx$ with $\Delta x = (b-a)/n$, associated with a partition of $[a, b]$ into an **even** number n of equal-length subintervals, is the sum S_n defined as

$$S_n = \frac{\Delta x}{3}(y_0 + 4y_1 + 2y_2 + 4y_3 + 2y_4 + \cdots + 2y_{n-2} + 4y_{n-1} + y_n). \tag{12}$$

REMARK Note the 1-4-2-4-2- · · · · -2-4-2-4-1 pattern of coefficients in Simpson's approximation. This pattern is symmetric (ending in -2-4-1), as shown, if and only if n is *even*.

EXAMPLE 4 Simpson's approximation (with $n = 6$ and $\Delta x = 0.5$) to the integral

$$\int_0^3 x^2 \, dx = 9$$

of Examples 1 and 2 is

$$S_6 = \frac{0.5}{3}[1 \cdot (0)^2 + 4 \cdot (0.5)^2 + 2 \cdot (1)^2 + 4 \cdot (1.5)^2$$
$$+ 2 \cdot (2)^2 + 4 \cdot (2.5)^2 + 1 \cdot (3)^2];$$
$$S_6 = 9 \quad \text{(exactly)}.$$

Problem 29 explains why Simpson's approximation to this particular integral is *exact* rather than merely a good approximation. ◆

EXAMPLE 5 Simpson's approximation (with $n = 10$ and $\Delta x = 0.1$) to the integral

$$\int_0^1 \frac{\sin x}{x} \, dx$$

of Example 3 is

$$S_{10} = \frac{0.1}{3}\left[1 \cdot 1 + 4 \cdot \frac{\sin 0.1}{0.1} + 2 \cdot \frac{\sin 0.2}{0.2} + 4 \cdot \frac{\sin 0.3}{0.3} + \cdots \right.$$
$$\left. + 2 \cdot \frac{\sin 0.8}{0.8} + 4 \cdot \frac{\sin 0.9}{0.9} + 1 \cdot \frac{\sin 1.0}{1.0}\right];$$
$$S_{10} \approx 0.94608,$$

which is accurate to *all five* decimal places shown. ◆

Examples 4 and 5 illustrate the greater accuracy of Simpson's approximation in comparison with the midpoint and trapezoidal approximations.

The numerical methods of this section are especially useful for approximating integrals of functions that are available only in graphical or in tabular form. This is often the case with functions derived from empirical data or from experimental measurements.

EXAMPLE 6 Suppose that the graph in Fig. 5.9.13 shows the velocity $v(t)$ recorded by instruments on board a submarine traveling under the polar ice cap directly toward the North Pole. Use the trapezoidal approximation and Simpson approximation to

FIGURE 5.9.13 Velocity graph for the submarine of Example 6.

estimate the distance $s = \int_a^b v(t)\,dt$ traveled by the submarine during the 10-h period from $t = 0$ to $t = 10$.

Solution We read the following data from the graph:

t	0	1	2	3	4	5	6	7	8	9	10	h
v	12	14	17	21	22	21	15	11	11	14	17	mi/h

Using the trapezoidal approximation with $n = 10$ and $\Delta x = 1$, we obtain

$$s = \int_0^{10} v(t)\,dt$$
$$\approx \tfrac{1}{2}[12 + 2(14 + 17 + 21 + 22 + 21 + 15 + 11 + 11 + 14) + 17]$$
$$= 160.5 \quad \text{(mi)}.$$

Using Simpson's approximation with $2n = 10$ and $\Delta x = 1$, we obtain

$$s = \int_0^{10} v(t)\,dt$$
$$\approx \tfrac{1}{3}[12 + 4 \cdot 14 + 2 \cdot 17 + 4 \cdot 21 + 2 \cdot 22 + 4 \cdot 21$$
$$+ 2 \cdot 15 + 4 \cdot 11 + 2 \cdot 11 + 4 \cdot 14 + 17]$$
$$= 161 \quad \text{(mi)}$$

as an estimate of the distance traveled by the submarine during this 10-h period. ◆

Parabolic Approximations

Although we have defined Simpson's approximation S_{2n} as a weighted average of the midpoint and trapezoidal approximations, Simpson's approximation has an important interpretation in terms of **parabolic approximations** to the curve $y = f(x)$. Beginning with the partition of $[a, b]$ into $2n$ equal-length subintervals, we define the parabolic function

$$p_i(x) = A_i + B_i x + C_i x^2$$

on $[x_{2i-2}, x_{2i}]$ as follows: We choose the coefficients A_i, B_i, and C_i so that $p_i(x)$ agrees with $f(x)$ at the three points x_{2i-2}, x_{2i-1}, and x_{2i} (Fig. 5.9.14). This can be done by solving the three equations

$$A_i + B_i x_{2i-2} + C_i (x_{2i-2})^2 = f(x_{2i-2}),$$
$$A_i + B_i x_{2i-1} + C_i (x_{2i-1})^2 = f(x_{2i-1}),$$
$$A_i + B_i x_{2i} + C_i (x_{2i})^2 = f(x_{2i})$$

FIGURE 5.9.14 The parabolic approximation $y = p_i(x)$ to $y = f(x)$ on $[x_{2i-2}, x_{2i}]$.

for the three unknowns A_i, B_i, and C_i. A routine (but tedious) algebraic computation—see Problem 52 of Section 5.8—shows that

$$\int_{x_{2i-2}}^{x_{2i}} p_i(x)\,dx = \frac{\Delta x}{3}(y_{2i-2} + 4y_{2i-1} + y_{2i}).$$

We now approximate $\int_a^b f(x)\,dx$ by replacing $f(x)$ with $p_i(x)$ on the interval $[x_{2i-2}, x_{2i}]$ for $i = 1, 2, 3, \ldots, n$. This gives

$$\int_a^b f(x)\,dx = \sum_{i=1}^n \int_{x_{2i-2}}^{x_{2i}} f(x)\,dx \approx \sum_{i=1}^n \int_{x_{2i-2}}^{x_{2i}} p_i(x)\,dx$$

$$= \sum_{i=1}^n \frac{\Delta x}{3}(y_{2i-2} + 4y_{2i-1} + y_{2i})$$

$$= \frac{\Delta x}{3}(y_0 + 4y_1 + 2y_2 + 4y_3 + \cdots + 4y_{2n-3} + 2y_{2n-2} + 4y_{2n-1} + y_{2n}).$$

Thus the parabolic approximation described here results in Simpson's approximation S_{2n} to $\int_a^b f(x)\,dx$.

Error Estimates

The trapezoidal approximation, the midpoint approximation, and Simpson's approximation are widely used for numerical integration, and there are *error estimates* that can be used to predict the maximum possible error in a particular approximation. The trapezoidal error ET_n, the midpoint error EM_n, and Simpson's error ES_n are defined by the equations

$$\int_a^b f(x)\,dx = T_n + ET_n, \tag{13}$$

$$\int_a^b f(x)\,dx = M_n + EM_n, \tag{14}$$

and

$$\int_a^b f(x)\,dx = S_n + ES_n \quad (n \text{ even}). \tag{15}$$

Note that each of these formulas is of the form

$$\int_a^b f(x)\,dx = \{\text{approximation}\} + \{\text{error}\}.$$

The absolute value $|ET_n|$ is the difference between the value of the integral and the trapezoidal approximation with n subintervals (and similarly for $|EM_n|$ and $|ES_n|$). Theorems 1 and 2 are proved in numerical analysis textbooks.

THEOREM 1 Trapezoidal and Midpoint Error Estimates

Suppose that the second derivative f'' is continuous on $[a, b]$ and that $|f''(x)| \leq M_2$ for $a \leq x \leq b$. Then

$$|ET_n| \leq \frac{M_2(b-a)^3}{12n^2} \tag{16}$$

and

$$|EM_n| \leq \frac{M_2(b-a)^3}{24n^2}. \tag{17}$$

REMARK Comparing (16) and (17), we see that the maximal predicted midpoint error is *half* the predicted trapezoidal error. This is the reason for weighting M_n

twice as heavily as T_n when we calculate Simpson's approximation using the formula $S_{2n} = \frac{2}{3}M_n + \frac{1}{3}T_n$ in (10).

THEOREM 2 Simpson's Error Estimate
Suppose that the fourth derivative $f^{(4)}$ is continuous on $[a, b]$ and that $|f^{(4)}(x)| \leq M_4$ for $a \leq x \leq b$. If n is even, then

$$|ES_n| \leq \frac{M_4(b-a)^5}{180n^4}. \tag{18}$$

REMARK The factor n^4 in (18)—compared with the n^2 in (16) and (17)—explains the greater accuracy typical of Simpson's approximation. For instance, if $n = 10$, then $n^2 = 100$ but $n^4 = 10000$, so the denominator in the error formula for Simpson's approximation is much larger.

EXAMPLE 7 In Chapter 7 we will see that the natural logarithm of the number 2 (given approximately by the $\boxed{\text{LN}}$ key on your calculator) is the value of the integral

$$\int_1^2 \frac{1}{x}\,dx = \Big[\ln x\Big]_1^2 = \ln 2 - \ln 1 = \ln 2$$

illustrated in Fig. 5.9.15. Estimate the errors in the trapezoidal, midpoint, and Simpson's approximation to this integral by using $n = 10$ subintervals. (The actual value of $\ln 2$ is approximately 0.693147.)

Solution With $f(x) = 1/x$ we calculate

$$f'(x) = -\frac{1}{x^2}, \qquad f''(x) = \frac{2}{x^3}$$

$$f'''(x) = -\frac{6}{x^4}, \qquad f^{(4)}(x) = \frac{24}{x^5}.$$

The maximum values of all these derivatives for $1 \leq x \leq 2$ occur at $x = 1$, so we may take $M_2 = 2$ and $M_4 = 24$ in Eqs. (16), (17), and (18). From Eqs. (16) and (17) we see that

$$|ET_{10}| \leq \frac{2 \cdot 1^3}{12 \cdot 10^2} \approx 0.0016667 \quad \text{and} \quad |EM_{10}| \leq \frac{2 \cdot 1^3}{24 \cdot 10^2} \approx 0.000833. \tag{19}$$

Hence we would expect both the trapezoidal approximation T_{10} and the midpoint approximation M_{10} to give $\ln 2$ accurate to at least two decimal places. From Eq. (18) we see that

$$|ES_{10}| \leq \frac{24 \cdot 1^5}{180 \cdot 10^4} \approx 0.000013, \tag{20}$$

so we would expect Simpson's approximation S_{10} to be accurate to at least four decimal places. When we calculate these approximations, we find that

$$T_{10} = \frac{0.1}{2}\left(\frac{1}{1} + \frac{2}{1.1} + \frac{2}{1.2} + \frac{2}{1.3} + \cdots + \frac{2}{1.9} + \frac{1}{2}\right) \approx 0.693771,$$

$$M_{10} = (0.1)\left(\frac{1}{1.05} + \frac{1}{1.15} + \frac{1}{1.25} + \cdots + \frac{1}{1.85} + \frac{1}{1.95}\right) \approx 0.692835,$$

and

$$S_{10} = \frac{0.1}{3}\left(\frac{1}{1} + \frac{4}{1.1} + \frac{2}{1.2} + \frac{4}{1.3} + \cdots + \frac{4}{1.9} + \frac{1}{2}\right) \approx 0.693150.$$

FIGURE 5.9.15 The number $\ln 2$ as an area.

It follows that the values of the errors in these approximations (in comparison with the actual value $\ln 2 \approx 0.693147$) are

$$ET_{10} \approx -0.000624, \qquad EM_{10} \approx 0.000312, \quad \text{and} \quad ES_{10} \approx 0.000003.$$

Comparing these actual errors with the maximal predicted errors in (19) and (20), we see that our approximations are somewhat more accurate than predicted—M_{10} actually is accurate to three decimal places and S_{10} is accurate to five. It is fairly typical of numerical integration that the trapezoidal, midpoint, and Simpson approximations are somewhat more accurate than the "worst-case" estimates provided by Theorems 1 and 2. ◆

5.9 TRUE/FALSE STUDY GUIDE

5.9 CONCEPTS: QUESTIONS AND DISCUSSION

1. Suppose that f is an increasing function on $[a, b]$. Which is larger—the left-hand sum or the right-hand sum, each with n subintervals? What if f is a decreasing function? Draw sketches illustrating both cases.
2. Suppose that the graph of $y = f(x)$ is concave upward on $[a, b]$. Which is larger—the midpoint sum or the trapezoidal sum, each with n subintervals? What if the graph is concave downward? Draw sketches illustrating both cases.
3. Explain why you cannot set up a Simpson's sum beginning with a partition of $[a, b]$ into an odd number of subintervals. If you try to do so, what goes wrong?

5.9 PROBLEMS

In Problems 1 through 6, calculate the trapezoidal approximation T_n to the given integral, and compare T_n with the exact value of the integral. Use the indicated number n of subintervals, and round answers to two decimal places.

1. $\int_0^4 x\,dx, \quad n = 4$
2. $\int_1^2 x^2\,dx, \quad n = 5$
3. $\int_0^1 \sqrt{x}\,dx, \quad n = 5$
4. $\int_1^3 \frac{1}{x^2}\,dx, \quad n = 4$
5. $\int_0^{\pi/2} \cos x\,dx, \quad n = 3$
6. $\int_0^{\pi} \sin x\,dx, \quad n = 4$

7. through 12. Calculate the midpoint approximations to the integrals in Problems 1 through 6, using the indicated number of subintervals. In each case compare M_n with the exact value of the integral.

In Problems 13 through 20, calculate both the trapezoidal approximation T_n and Simpson's approximation S_n to the given integral. Use the indicated number of subintervals and round answers to four decimal places. In Problems 13 through 16, also compare these approximations with the exact value of the integral.

13. $\int_1^3 x^2\,dx, \quad n = 4$
14. $\int_1^4 x^3\,dx, \quad n = 4$
15. $\int_2^4 \frac{1}{x^3}\,dx, \quad n = 4$
16. $\int_0^1 \sqrt{1+x}\,dx, \quad n = 4$
17. $\int_0^2 \sqrt{1+x^3}\,dx, \quad n = 6$
18. $\int_0^3 \frac{1}{1+x^4}\,dx, \quad n = 6$
19. $\int_1^5 \sqrt[3]{1+x^2}\,dx, \quad n = 8$
20. $\int_0^1 \frac{\tan x}{x}\,dx, \quad n = 10$

[*Note:* Make the integrand in Problem 20 continuous by assuming that its value at $x = 0$ is its limit there,

$$\lim_{x \to 0} \frac{\tan x}{x} = 1.]$$

In Problems 21 and 22, calculate (a) the trapezoidal approximation and (b) Simpson's approximation to

$$\int_a^b f(x)\,dx,$$

where f is the given tabulated function.

21.

x	$a = 1.00$	1.25	1.50	1.75
$f(x)$	3.43	2.17	0.38	1.87

x	2.00	2.25	$2.50 = b$
$f(x)$	2.65	2.31	1.97

22.

x	$a=0$	1	2	3	4	5	6
$f(x)$	23	8	-4	12	35	47	53

x	7	8	9	$10=b$
$f(x)$	50	39	29	5

23. Figure 5.9.16 shows the measured rate of water flow (in liters per minute) into a tank during a 10-min period. Using 10 subintervals in each case, estimate the total amount of water that flows into the tank during this period by using (a) the trapezoidal approximation and (b) Simpson's approximation.

FIGURE 5.9.16 Water-flow graph for Problem 23.

24. Figure 5.9.17 shows the daily mean temperature recorded during December at Big Frog, California. Using 10 subintervals in each case, estimate the average temperature during that month by using (a) the trapezoidal approximation and (b) Simpson's approximation.

FIGURE 5.9.17 Temperature graph for Problem 24.

25. Figure 5.9.18 shows a tract of land with measurements in feet. A surveyor has measured its width w at 50-ft intervals (the values of x shown in the figure), with the following results.

x	0	50	100	150	200	250	300
w	0	165	192	146	63	42	84

x	350	400	450	500	550	600
w	155	224	270	267	215	0

FIGURE 5.9.18 The tract of land of Problem 25.

Use (a) the trapezoidal approximation and (b) Simpson's approximation to estimate the acreage of this tract. [*Note:* An acre is 4840 yd^2.]

26. The base for natural logarithms is the number $e \approx 2.71828$. In Chapter 7 we will see that

$$\int_1^e \frac{1}{x}\,dx = 1.$$

Approximate the integrals

$$\int_1^{2.7} \frac{1}{x}\,dx \quad \text{and} \quad \int_1^{2.8} \frac{1}{x}\,dx$$

with sufficient accuracy to show that $2.7 < e < 2.8$.

Problems 27 and 28 deal with the integral

$$\ln 2 = \int_1^2 \frac{1}{x}\,dx$$

of Example 7.

27. Use the trapezoidal error estimate to determine how large n must be in order to guarantee that T_n differs from $\ln 2$ by at most 0.0005.

28. Use the Simpson's error estimate to determine how large n must be in order to guarantee that S_n differs from $\ln 2$ by at most 0.000005.

29. Deduce the following from the error estimate for Simpson's approximation: If $p(x)$ is a polynomial of degree at most 3, then Simpson's approximation with $n=2$ subintervals gives the exact value of the integral

$$\int_a^b p(x)\,dx.$$

30. Use the result of Problem 29 to calculate (without explicit integration) the area of the region shown in Fig. 5.9.19. [*Answer:* 1331/216.]

FIGURE 5.9.19 The region of Problem 30.

31. Whereas the carefully weighted average in (10) of the midpoint and trapezoidal approximations M_n and T_n gives Simpson's approximation S_{2n}, show that their equally weighted average gives the trapezoidal approximation with twice as many intervals; that is, $\frac{1}{2}(M_n + T_n) = T_{2n}$.

32. Figure 5.9.20 shows a pendulum of length L. If this pendulum is released from rest at an angle α from the vertical, then it swings back and forth with its period T (for one complete oscillation) given by

$$T = 4\sqrt{\frac{L}{g}} \int_0^{\pi/2} \frac{1}{\sqrt{1 - k^2 \sin^2 x}}\,dx,$$

where $k = \sin(\alpha/2)$. Taking $L = 1$ m and $g = 9.8$ m/s^2, use Simpson's approximation with $n = 10$ subintervals to calculate the pendulum's period of oscillation if its initial angle α is (a) 10°; (b) 50°.

FIGURE 5.9.20 The pendulum of Problem 32.

33. Note in Example 7 that the midpoint and trapezoidal approximations gave under- and over-estimates, respectively, of the value $\int_1^2 (1/x)\,dx = \ln 2$. Show that this is a general phenomenon. That is, if $f(x)$ and $f''(x)$ are both positive for $a \leq x \leq b$, then

$$M_n < \int_a^b f(x)\,dx < T_n,$$

whereas if $f(x)$ is positive but $f''(x)$ is negative for $a \leq x \leq b$ then the inequalities are reversed.

5.9 Project: Trapezoidal and Simpson Approximations

In the CD-ROM resource material for the Section 5.4 project, we illustrated calculator and computer algebra system commands that can be used to calculate the Riemann sums

L_n — the left-endpoint approximation,
R_n — the right-endpoint approximation, and
M_n — the midpoint approximation,

based on a division of $[a, b]$ into n equal-length subintervals, to approximate the integral

$$\int_a^b f(x)\,dx. \tag{1}$$

The Riemann sums L_n, R_n, and M_n suffice, in turn, to calculate the trapezoidal and Simpson sums of this section. In particular, the trapezoidal approximation is given—using Eq. (5) of this section—by

$$T_n = \tfrac{1}{2}(L_n + R_n). \tag{2}$$

Once these sums are known, Simpson's approximation based on a subdivision of $[a, b]$ into $2n$ equal-length subintervals is given—using Eq. (10) of this section—by

$$S_n = \tfrac{1}{3}(2M_{n/2} + T_{n/2}) = \tfrac{1}{6}(L_{n/2} + 4M_{n/2} + R_{n/2}). \tag{3}$$

Here, then, is a practical scheme for approximating accurately the integral in (1). Begin with a selected value of n, such as $n = 5$, and calculate the Riemann sums L_5, R_5, and M_5. Then use Eq. (3) to calculate the Simpson approximation S_{10}. Next, double the value of n and calculate similarly L_{10}, R_{10}, M_{10}, and finally S_{20}. A typical strategy is to continue in this manner, always doubling the current value of n for the next cycle of computations, until two successively calculated Simpson approximations agree to the desired number of decimal places of accuracy.

Investigation A According to Example 7, the natural logarithm (corresponding to the LN or, in some cases, the LOG key on your calculator) of the number 2 is the value of the integral

$$\ln 2 = \int_1^2 \frac{1}{x}\,dx.$$

The value of $\ln 2$ correct to 15 decimal places is

$$\ln 2 \approx 0.69314\,71805\,59945.$$

See how many correct decimal places you can obtain in a reasonable period of time by using a Simpson's approximation procedure.

Investigation B In Section 7.5 we will study the inverse tangent function $y = \arctan x$ (y is the angle between $-\pi/2$ and $\pi/2$ such that $\tan y = x$). There we will discover that the derivative of $y = \arctan x$ is

$$\frac{dy}{dx} = \frac{1}{1 + x^2}.$$

This implies that

$$\int_0^1 \frac{1}{1 + x^2}\,dx = \Big[\arctan x\Big]_0^1 = \arctan 1 - \arctan 0 = \frac{\pi}{4}.$$

It follows that the number π is the value of the integral

$$\pi = \int_0^1 \frac{4}{1 + x^2}\,dx.$$

The value of π to 15 decimal places is

$$\pi \approx 3.14159\,26535\,89793.$$

See how many correct decimal places you can obtain in a reasonable period of time by using a Simpson's approximation procedure.

Investigation C Taking $f(x) = 4/(1 + x^2)$ as the integrand of the integral

$$\int_0^1 \frac{4}{1 + x^2}\,dx = \pi$$

FIGURE 5.9.21 Graph of the second derivative of
$f(x) = \dfrac{4}{1+x^2}$.

FIGURE 5.9.22 Graph of the fourth derivative of
$f(x) = \dfrac{4}{1+x^2}$.

of Investigation B, it would be somewhat lengthy to first calculate and then maximize by hand the derivatives $f''(x)$ and $f^{(4)}(x)$ as needed to apply the error estimates in Theorems 1 and 2 of this section. Instead, a computer algebra system readily yields

$$f''(x) = \frac{8(3x^2 - 1)}{(1+x^2)^3} \quad \text{and} \quad f^{(4)}(x) = \frac{96(5x^4 - 10x^2 + 1)}{(1+x^2)^5}.$$

Figures 5.9.21 and 5.9.22 show the graphs of these two derivatives on the interval [0, 1]. From these graphs it is clear that each of these derivatives attains its maximum absolute value at the left endpoint $x = 0$. Thus you can take

$$M_2 = 8 \quad \text{and} \quad M_4 = 96$$

in Theorems 1 and 2. Use this information to determine how large the integer n must be so that:

1. $|EM_n| < 5 \times 10^{-6}$, so the midpoint approximation M_n will give the number π accurate to five decimal places;
2. $|ES_n| < 5 \times 10^{-11}$, so the Simpson approximation S_n will give the number π accurate to ten decimal places;
3. The Simpson approximation S_n will give the number π accurate to 15 decimal places.

CHAPTER 5 REVIEW: DEFINITIONS, CONCEPTS, RESULTS

Use the following list as a guide to concepts that you may need to review.

1. Antidifferentiation and antiderivatives
2. The most general antiderivative of a function
3. Integral formulas
4. Initial value problems
5. Velocity and acceleration
6. Solution of problems involving constant acceleration
7. Properties of area
8. Summation notation
9. The area under the graph of f from a to b
10. Inscribed and circumscribed rectangular polygons
11. A partition of $[a, b]$
12. The norm of a partition
13. A Riemann sum associated with a partition
14. The definite integral of f from a to b
15. Existence of the integral of a continuous function
16. The integral as the limit of a sequence of Riemann sums
17. Regular partitions and

$$\lim_{\Delta x \to 0} \sum_{i=1}^{n} f(x_i^\star)\, \Delta x$$

18. Riemann sums
19. The constant multiple, interval union, and comparison properties of integrals
20. Evaluation of definite integrals by using antiderivatives

21. The average value of $f(x)$ on the interval $[a, b]$
22. The average value theorem
23. The fundamental theorem of calculus
24. Indefinite integrals
25. The method of integration by substitution
26. Transforming the limits in integration by substitution
27. The area between $y = f(x)$ and $y = g(x)$ by integration with respect to x
28. The area between $x = f(y)$ and $x = g(y)$ by integration with respect to y
29. The right-endpoint and left-endpoint approximations
30. The trapezoidal approximation
31. The midpoint approximation
32. Simpson's approximation
33. Error estimates for the trapezoidal approximation and Simpson's approximation

CHAPTER 5 MISCELLANEOUS PROBLEMS

Find the indefinite integrals in Problems 1 through 24. In Problems 13 through 24, use the indicated substitution.

1. $\int \dfrac{x^5 - 2x + 5}{x^3}\, dx$

2. $\int \sqrt{x}\,(1 + \sqrt{x})^3\, dx$

3. $\int (1 - 3x)^9\, dx$

4. $\int \dfrac{7}{(2x + 3)^3}\, dx$

5. $\int \sqrt[3]{9 + 4x}\, dx$

6. $\int \dfrac{24}{\sqrt{6x + 7}}\, dx$

7. $\int x^3(1 + x^4)^5\, dx$

8. $\int 3x^2 \sqrt{4 + x^3}\, dx$

9. $\int x\sqrt[3]{1 - x^2}\, dx$

10. $\int \dfrac{3x}{\sqrt{1 + 3x^2}}\, dx$

11. $\int (7 \cos 5x - 5 \sin 7x)\, dx$

12. $\int 5 \sin^3 4x \cos 4x\, dx$

13. $\int x^3 \sqrt{1 + x^4}\, dx;\quad u = x^4$

14. $\int \sin^2 x \cos x\, dx;\quad u = \sin x$

15. $\int \dfrac{1}{\sqrt{x}\,(1 + \sqrt{x})^2}\, dx;\quad u = 1 + \sqrt{x}$

16. $\int \dfrac{1}{\sqrt{x}\,(1 + \sqrt{x})^2}\, dx;\quad u = \sqrt{x}$

17. $\int x^2 \cos 4x^3\, dx;\quad u = 4x^3$

18. $\int x(x + 1)^{14}\, dx;\quad u = x + 1$

19. $\int x(x^2 + 1)^{14}\, dx;\quad u = x^2 + 1$

20. $\int x^3 \cos x^4\, dx;\quad u = x^4$

21. $\int x\sqrt{4 - x}\, dx;\quad u = 4 - x$

22. $\int \dfrac{x + 2x^3}{(x^4 + x^2)^3}\, dx;\quad u = x^4 + x^2$

23. $\int \dfrac{2x^3}{\sqrt{1 + x^4}}\, dx;\quad u = x^4$

24. $\int \dfrac{2x + 1}{\sqrt{x^2 + x}}\, dx;\quad u = x^2 + x$

Solve the initial value problems in 25 through 30.

25. $\dfrac{dy}{dx} = 3x^2 + 2x;\quad y(0) = 5$

26. $\dfrac{dy}{dx} = 3\sqrt{x};\quad y(4) = 20$

27. $\dfrac{dy}{dx} = (2x + 1)^5;\quad y(0) = 2$

28. $\dfrac{dy}{dx} = \dfrac{2}{\sqrt{x + 5}};\quad y(4) = 3$

29. $\dfrac{dy}{dx} = \dfrac{1}{\sqrt[3]{x}};\quad y(1) = 1$

30. $\dfrac{dy}{dx} = 1 - \cos x;\quad y(0) = 0$

31. When its brakes are fully applied, a certain automobile has a constant deceleration of 22 ft/s². If its initial velocity is 90 mi/h, how long will it take to come to a stop? How many feet will it travel during that time?

32. In Hal Clement's novel *Mission of Gravity,* much of the action take place in the polar regions of the planet Mesklin, where the acceleration of gravity is 22500 ft/s². A stone is dropped near the north pole of Mesklin from a height of 450 ft. How long does it remain aloft? With what speed does it strike the ground?

33. An automobile is traveling along the x-axis in the positive direction. At time $t = 0$ its brakes are fully applied, and the car experiences a constant deceleration of 40 ft/s² while skidding. The car skids 180 ft before coming to a stop. What was its initial velocity?

34. If a car starts from rest with an acceleration of 8 ft/s², how far has it traveled by the time it reaches a speed of 60 mi/h?

35. On the planet Zorg, a ball dropped from a height of 20 ft hits the ground in 2 s. If the ball is dropped from the top of a 200-ft building on Zorg, how long will it take to reach the ground? With what speed will it hit?

36. Suppose that you can throw a ball from the earth's surface straight upward to a maximum height of 144 ft. (a) How high could you throw it on the planet of Problem 35? (b) How high could you throw it in the polar regions of Mesklin? (See Problem 32.)

37. Suppose that a car skids 44 ft if its velocity is 30 mi/h when the brakes are fully applied. Assuming the same constant deceleration, how far will it skid if its velocity is 60 mi/h when the brakes are fully applied?

38. The graph of the velocity of a model rocket fired at time $t = 0$ is shown in Fig. 5.MP.1. (a) At what time was the fuel exhausted? (b) At what time did the parachute open? (c) At what time did the rocket reach its maximum altitude? (d) At what time did the rocket land? (e) How high did the rocket go? (f) How high was the pole on which the rocket landed?

FIGURE 5.MP.1 Rocket velocity graph for Problem 38.

Find the sums in Problems 39 through 42.

39. $\sum_{i=1}^{100} 17$

40. $\sum_{k=1}^{100} \left(\frac{1}{k} - \frac{1}{k+1} \right)$

41. $\sum_{n=1}^{10} (3n-2)^2$

42. $\sum_{n=1}^{16} \sin \frac{n\pi}{2}$

In Problems 43 through 45, find the limit of the given Riemann sum associated with a regular partition of the indicated interval $[a, b]$. First express it as an integral from a to b; then evaluate that integral.

43. $\lim_{n \to \infty} \sum_{i=1}^{n} \frac{\Delta x}{\sqrt{x_i^\star}}$; $[1, 2]$

44. $\lim_{n \to \infty} \sum_{i=1}^{n} [(x_i^\star)^2 - 3x_i^\star] \Delta x$; $[0, 3]$

45. $\lim_{n \to \infty} \sum_{i=1}^{n} 2\pi x_i^\star \sqrt{1 + (x_i^\star)^2} \, \Delta x$; $[0, 1]$

46. Evaluate

$$\lim_{n \to \infty} \frac{1^{10} + 2^{10} + 3^{10} + \cdots + n^{10}}{n^{11}}$$

by expressing this limit as an integral over $[0, 1]$.

47. Use Riemann sums to prove that if $f(x) \equiv c$ (a constant), then

$$\int_a^b f(x) \, dx = c(b-a).$$

48. Use Riemann sums to prove that if f is continuous on $[a, b]$ and $f(x) \geq 0$ for all x in $[a, b]$, then

$$\int_a^b f(x) \, dx \geq 0.$$

49. Use the comparison property of integrals (Section 5.5) to prove that

$$\int_a^b f(x) \, dx > 0$$

if f is a continuous function with $f(x) > 0$ on $[a, b]$.

Evaluate the integrals in Problems 50 through 63.

50. $\int_0^1 (1-x^2)^3 \, dx$

51. $\int \left(\sqrt{2x} - \frac{1}{\sqrt{3x^3}} \right) dx$

52. $\int \frac{\left(1 + \sqrt[3]{x}\right)^2}{\sqrt{x}} \, dx$

53. $\int \frac{4 - x^3}{2x^2} \, dx$

54. $\int_0^1 \frac{dt}{(3 - 2t)^2}$

55. $\int \sqrt{x} \cos x \sqrt{x} \, dx$

56. $\int_0^2 x^2 \sqrt{9 - x^3} \, dx$

57. $\int \frac{1}{t^2} \sin \frac{1}{t} \, dt$

58. $\int_1^2 \frac{2t + 1}{\sqrt{t^2 + t}} \, dt$

59. $\int \frac{\sqrt[3]{u}}{\left(1 + u^{4/3}\right)^3} \, du$

60. $\int_0^{\pi/4} \frac{\sin t}{\sqrt{\cos t}} \, dt$

61. $\int_1^4 \frac{\left(1 + \sqrt{t}\right)^2}{\sqrt{t}} \, dt$

62. $\int \frac{1}{u^2} \sqrt[3]{1 - \frac{1}{u}} \, du$

63. $\int \frac{\sqrt{4x^2 - 1}}{x^4} \, dx$

Find the areas of the plane regions bounded by the curves given in Problems 64 through 70.

64. $y = x^3$, $x = -1$, $y = 1$
65. $y = x^4$, $y = x^5$
66. $y^2 = x$, $3y^2 = x + 6$
67. $y = x^4$, $y = 2 - x^2$
68. $y = x^4$, $y = 2x^2 - 1$
69. $y = (x-2)^2$, $y = 10 - 5x$
70. $y = x^{2/3}$, $y = 2 - x^2$

71. Evaluate the integral

$$\int_0^2 \sqrt{2x - x^2} \, dx$$

by interpreting it as the area of a region.

72. Evaluate the integral

$$\int_1^5 \sqrt{6x - 5 - x^2} \, dx$$

by interpreting it as the area of a region.

73. Find a function f such that

$$x^2 = 1 + \int_1^x \sqrt{1 + [f(t)]^2} \, dt$$

for all $x > 1$. [*Suggestion:* Differentiate both sides of the equation with the aid of the fundamental theorem of calculus.]

74. Show that $G'(x) = \phi(h(x)) \cdot h'(x)$ if
$$G(x) = \int_a^{h(x)} \phi(t)\,dt.$$

75. Use right-endpoint and left-endpoint approximations to estimate
$$\int_0^1 \sqrt{1+x^2}\,dx$$
with error not exceeding 0.05.

76. Calculate the trapezoidal approximation and Simpson's approximation to
$$\int_0^\pi \sqrt{1-\cos x}\,dx$$
with six subintervals. For comparison, use an appropriate half-angle identity to calculate the exact value of this integral.

77. Calculate the midpoint approximation and trapezoidal approximation to
$$\int_1^2 \frac{1}{x+x^2}\,dx$$
with $n=5$ subintervals. Then explain why the exact value of the integral lies between these two approximations.

In Problems 78 through 80, let $\{x_0, x_1, x_2, \ldots, x_n\}$ be a partition of $[a,b]$, where $a<b$.

78. For $i = 1, 2, 3, \ldots, n$, let x_i^* be given by
$$(x_i^*)^2 = \tfrac{1}{3}[(x_{i-1})^2 + x_{i-1}x_i + (x_i)^2].$$
Show first that $x_{i-1} < x_i^* < x_i$. Then use the algebraic identity
$$(c-d)(c^2 + cd + d^2) = c^3 - d^3$$
to show that
$$\sum_{i=1}^n (x_i^*)^2 \,\Delta x_i = \tfrac{1}{3}(b^3 - a^3).$$
Explain why this computation proves that
$$\int_a^b x^2\,dx = \tfrac{1}{3}(b^3 - a^3).$$

79. Let $x_i^* = \sqrt{x_{i-1}x_i}$ for $i = 1, 2, 3, \ldots, n$, and assume that $0 < a < b$. Show that
$$\sum_{i=1}^n \frac{\Delta x_i}{(x_i^*)^2} = \frac{1}{a} - \frac{1}{b}.$$
Then explain why this computation proves that
$$\int_a^b \frac{dx}{x^2} = \frac{1}{a} - \frac{1}{b}.$$

80. Assume that $0 < a < b$. Define
$$x_i^* = \frac{\tfrac{2}{3}\left[(x_i)^{3/2} - (x_{i-1})^{3/2}\right]}{x_i - x_{i-1}}.$$
First show that $x_{i-1} < x_i^* < x_i$. Then use this selection for the given partition to prove that
$$\int_a^b \sqrt{x}\,dx = \tfrac{2}{3}\left(b^{3/2} - a^{3/2}\right).$$

APPLICATIONS OF THE INTEGRAL 6

G.F.B. Riemann (1826–1866)

The general concept of integration traces back to the area and volume computations of ancient times, but the integrals used by Newton and Leibniz were not defined with sufficient precision for full understanding. We owe to the German mathematician G. F. Bernhard Riemann the modern definition that uses "Riemann sums." The son of a Protestant minister, Riemann studied theology and philology at Göttingen University until he finally gained his father's permission to concentrate on mathematics. He transferred to Berlin University, where he received his Ph.D. in 1851. The work he did in the next decade justifies his place on everyone's short list of the most profound and creative mathematicians of all time. But in 1862 he was stricken ill. He never fully recovered and in 1866 died prematurely at the age of 39.

Riemann's mathematical investigations were as varied as they were deep, ranging from the basic concepts of functions and integrals to such areas as non-Euclidean (differential) geometry and the distribution of prime numbers. Recall that the positive integer p is *prime* if it cannot be factored into smaller integers. In a famous paper of 1859, Riemann analyzed the approximation

$$\pi(x) \approx \int_2^x \frac{dt}{\ln t} = \text{li}(x)$$

to the number $\pi(x)$ of those primes $p \leq x$ (with $\ln x$ denoting the natural logarithm of x). There is a remarkable correspondence between the values of $\pi(x)$ and the "logarithmic integral" approximation $\text{li}(x)$:

x	1,000,000	10,000,000	100,000,000	1,000,000,000
$\text{li}(x)$	78,628	664,918	5,762,209	50,849,235
$\pi(x)$	78,498	664,579	5,761,455	50,847,543
error	0.165%	0.051%	0.013%	0.003%

Thirty years after Riemann's death, his ideas led ultimately to a proof that the percentage error in the approximation $\text{li}(x)$ to $\pi(x)$ approaches 0 as $x \to \infty$.

In his 1851 thesis, Riemann introduced a geometric way of visualizing "multi-valued" functions such as the square root function with two values $\pm\sqrt{x}$. The following graph illustrates the *cube root* function. For each complex number $z = x + iy$ in the unit disk $x^2 + y^2 \leq 1$, the three (complex) cube roots of z are plotted directly above z. Each root is plotted at a height equal to its real part, with color determined by its imaginary part. The result is the "Riemann surface" of the cube root function.

365

6.1 RIEMANN SUM APPROXIMATIONS

In Section 5.4 we defined the integral of the function f on the interval $[a, b]$ as a limit of Riemann sums. Specifically, let the interval $[a, b]$ be divided into n subintervals, all with the same length $\Delta x = (b - a)/n$ (Fig. 6.1.1). Then a selection of numbers $x_1^\star, x_2^\star, \ldots, x_n^\star$ in these subintervals ($x_i^\star$ being a point of the ith subinterval $[x_{i-1}, x_i]$) produces a Riemann sum

$$\sum_{i=1}^{n} f(x_i^\star) \Delta x \tag{1}$$

whose value approximates the integral of f on $[a, b]$. The value of the integral is the limiting value (if any) of such sums as the subinterval length Δx approaches zero. That is,

$$\int_a^b f(x)\, dx = \lim_{\Delta x \to 0} \sum_{i=1}^{n} f(x_i^\star) \Delta x. \tag{2}$$

The wide applicability of the definite integral arises from the fact that many geometric and physical quantities can be approximated arbitrarily closely by Riemann sums. Such approximations lead to integral formulas for the computation of such quantities.

FIGURE 6.1.1 A division (or partition) of $[a, b]$ into n equal-length subintervals.

For example, suppose that $f(x)$ is positive-valued on $[a, b]$ and that our goal—as in Section 5.3—is to calculate the area A of the region that lies below the graph of $y = f(x)$ over the interval $[a, b]$. Beginning with the subdivision (or partition) of $[a, b]$ indicated in Fig. 6.1.1, let ΔA_i denote the area of the vertical "strip" that lies under $y = f(x)$ over the ith subinterval $[x_{i-1}, x_i]$. Then, as illustrated in Fig. 6.1.2, the "strip areas"

$$\Delta A_1, \quad \Delta A_2, \quad \ldots, \quad \Delta A_n$$

add up to the total area A:

$$A = \sum_{i=1}^{n} \Delta A_i. \tag{3}$$

FIGURE 6.1.2 Approximating an area by means of a Riemann sum.

But the ith strip is approximated by a rectangle with base $[x_{i-1}, x_i]$ and height $f(x_i^\star)$, so its area is given approximately by

$$\Delta A_i \approx f(x_i^\star)\,\Delta x. \tag{4}$$

After we substitute Eq. (4) into Eq. (3), it becomes apparent that the total area A under the graph of f is given approximately by

$$A \approx \sum_{i=1}^{n} f(x_i^\star)\,\Delta x. \tag{5}$$

Note that the approximating sum on the right is a Riemann sum for f on $[a, b]$. Moreover,

1. It is intuitively evident that the Riemann sum in (5) approaches the actual area A as $n \to +\infty$ (which forces $\Delta x \to 0$);
2. By the definition of the integral, this Riemann sum approaches $\int_a^b f(x)\,dx$ as $n \to +\infty$.

These observations justify the *definition* of the area A by the formula

$$A = \int_a^b f(x)\,dx. \tag{6}$$

Other Quantities as Integrals

Our justification of the area formula in Eq. (6) illustrates an important general method of setting up integral formulas. Suppose that we want to calculate a certain quantity Q that is associated with an interval $[a, b]$ in such a way that subintervals of $[a, b]$ correspond to specific portions of Q (such as the portion of area lying above a particular subinterval). Then a subdivision of $[a, b]$ into n subintervals produces portions

$$\Delta Q_1, \quad \Delta Q_2, \quad \ldots, \quad \Delta Q_n,$$

which add up to the quantity

$$Q = \sum_{i=1}^{n} \Delta Q_i. \tag{7}$$

Now suppose that we can find a function f such that the ith portion ΔQ_i is given approximately by

$$\Delta Q_i \approx f(x_i^\star)\,\Delta x \tag{8}$$

(for each i, $1 \leqq i \leqq n$) for a selected point $x_i^\star$ of the ith subinterval $[x_{i-1}, x_i]$ of $[a, b]$. Then substituting Eq. (8) into Eq. (7) yields the Riemann sum approximation

$$Q \approx \sum_{i=1}^{n} f(x_i^\star)\,\Delta x \tag{9}$$

analogous to the approximation in Eq. (5). The right-hand sum in Eq. (9) is a Riemann sum that approaches the integral

$$\int_a^b f(x)\,dx \quad \text{as} \quad n \to +\infty.$$

If it is also evident—for geometric or physical reasons, for example—that this Riemann sum must approach the quantity Q as $n \to +\infty$, then Eq. (9) justifies our setting up the integral formula

$$Q = \int_a^b f(x)\,dx. \tag{10}$$

Because the right-hand side in Eq. (10) can be easy to calculate (by the fundamental theorem of calculus), this gives us a practical way of finding the exact numerical value of the quantity Q.

In addition to area, the following are some of the quantities that can be calculated by using integral formulas such as Eq. (10). (The variable x is replaced with t where appropriate.)

- The *mass* of a thin rod of variable density lying along the interval $a \leq x \leq b$.
- The *profit* earned by a company between time $t = a$ and time $t = b$.
- The *number* of people in a city who contract a certain disease between time $t = a$ and time $t = b$.
- The *distance* traveled by a moving particle during the time interval $a \leq t \leq b$.
- The *volume* of water flowing into a tank during the time interval $a \leq t \leq b$.
- The *work* done by a variable force in moving a particle from the point $x = a$ to the point $x = b$.

In each case it is evident that a *subinterval* of $[a, b]$ determines a specific *portion* ΔQ of the whole quantity Q that corresponds to the whole interval $[a, b]$. The question is this: What function f should be integrated from a to b? Examples 1 through 3 illustrate the process of finding the needed function f by approximating the portion ΔQ_i of the quantity Q that corresponds to the subinterval $[x_{i-1}, x_i]$. An approximation of the form

$$\Delta Q_i \approx f(x_i^*) \Delta x \tag{8}$$

leads to the desired integral formula

$$Q = \int_a^b f(x)\, dx. \tag{10}$$

The integral in Eq. (10) results from the summation in Eq. (9) when we make the following replacements:

$$\sum_{i=1}^n \text{ becomes } \int_a^b,$$

$$x_i^* \text{ becomes } x, \quad \text{and}$$

$$\Delta x \text{ becomes } dx.$$

FIGURE 6.1.3 The tank of Example 1.

EXAMPLE 1 Suppose that water is pumped into the initially empty tank of Fig. 6.1.3. The rate of water flow into the tank at time t (in seconds) is $50 - t$ liters (L) per second. How much water flows into the tank during the first 30 s?

Solution We want to compute the amount Q of water that flows into the tank during the time interval $[0, 30]$. Think of a subdivision of $[0, 30]$ into n subintervals, all with the same length $\Delta t = 30/n$.

Next choose a point t_i^* in the ith subinterval $[t_{i-1}, t_i]$. If this subinterval is very short, then the rate of water flow between time t_{i-1} and time t_i remains approximately $50 - t_i^*$ liters per second. So the amount ΔQ_i of water *in liters* that flows into the tank during this subinterval of time is obtained approximately by multiplying the *flow rate in liters per second* by the *duration of flow in seconds*:

$$\left[(50 - t_i^*) \, \frac{\text{liters}}{\text{second}} \right] \cdot [\Delta t \text{ seconds}],$$

and hence

$$\Delta Q_i \approx (50 - t_i^*)\, \Delta t \quad \text{(liters)}.$$

Therefore, the total amount Q that we seek is given approximately by

$$Q = \sum_{i=1}^n \Delta Q_i \approx \sum_{i=1}^n (50 - t_i^*)\, \Delta t \quad \text{(liters)}.$$

We recognize that the sum on the right is a Riemann sum, and—most important—we see that it is a Riemann sum for the function $f(t) = 50 - t$. Hence we may conclude that

$$Q = \lim_{n \to \infty} \sum_{i=1}^{n} (50 - t_i^*) \Delta t = \int_0^{30} (50 - t)\, dt$$

$$= \left[50t - \frac{1}{2}t^2 \right]_0^{30} = 1050 \quad \text{(liters)}. \qquad \blacklozenge$$

EXAMPLE 2 Figure 6.1.4 shows a thin rod 20 cm long. Its (linear) *density* at the point x is $15 + 2x$ grams of mass per centimeter of the rod's length (g/cm). The rod's density thus varies from 15 g/cm at the left end $x = 0$ to 55 g/cm at the right end $x = 20$. Find the total mass M of this rod.

FIGURE 6.1.4 The 20-cm rod of Example 2.

Solution Think of a subdivision of $[0, 20]$ into n subintervals of length $\Delta x = 20/n$ each. Figure 6.1.4 shows the short piece of the rod that corresponds to the typical ith subinterval $[x_{i-1}, x_i]$. If x_i^* is, say, the midpoint of $[x_{i-1}, x_i]$, then the mass ΔM_i of this short piece is obtained approximately by multiplying its *density in grams per centimeter* by its *length in centimeters*:

$$\left[(15 + 2x_i^*) \, \frac{\text{grams}}{\text{centimeter}} \right] \cdot [\Delta x \text{ centimeters}].$$

That is,

$$\Delta M_i \approx (15 + 2x_i^*) \Delta x \quad \text{(grams)}.$$

Therefore, the total mass M of the entire rod is given approximately by

$$M = \sum_{i=1}^{n} \Delta M_i \approx \sum_{i=1}^{n} (15 + 2x_i^*) \Delta x.$$

We recognize a Riemann sum on the right, as in Example 1, although this time for the function $f(x) = 15 + 2x$ on the interval $[0, 20]$. Hence we may conclude that

$$M = \lim_{n \to \infty} \sum_{i=1}^{n} (15 + 2x_i^*) \Delta x = \int_0^{20} (15 + 2x)\, dx$$

$$= \left[15x + x^2 \right]_0^{20} = 700 \quad \text{(g)}. \qquad \blacklozenge$$

The key to setting up an integral formula as in Examples 1 and 2 is the recognition of the definite integral that corresponds to a given Riemann sum approximation to the quantity we wish to calculate.

EXAMPLE 3 Calculate Q if

$$Q = \lim_{n \to \infty} \sum_{i=1}^{n} m_i \sqrt{25 - m_i^2} \, \Delta x,$$

where (for each $i = 1, 2, \ldots, n$) m_i denotes the midpoint of the ith subinterval $[x_{i-1}, x_i]$ of a partition of the interval $[3, 4]$ into n subintervals, all with the same length $\Delta x = 1/n$.

Solution We recognize the given sum as a Riemann sum (with $x_i^* = m_i$) for the function $f(x) = x\sqrt{25 - x^2}$. Hence

$$Q = \int_3^4 x\sqrt{25 - x^2}\, dx = \left[-\frac{1}{3}(25 - x^2)^{3/2} \right]_3^4 = \frac{1}{3}(16^{3/2} - 9^{3/2}) = \frac{37}{3}. \qquad \blacklozenge$$

370 CHAPTER 6 Applications of the Integral

Distance and Velocity

Consider a particle that travels along the x-axis with position $x(t)$ and velocity $v = x'(t)$ at time t. Suppose that it begins its motion at time $t = a$ and ends it at time $t = b$. When we integrate the velocity, we get

$$\int_a^b v(t)\, dt = \int_a^b x'(t)\, dt = \Big[x(t)\Big]_a^b = x(b) - x(a)$$

(using the fundamental theorem of calculus). Because the particle has initial position $x(a)$ and final position $x(b)$, we see that the integral

$$s = \int_a^b v(t)\, dt = x(b) - x(a) \qquad (11)$$

FIGURE 6.1.5 Equation (11) means that the (net) distance traveled is equal to the (signed) area under the velocity curve.

of its velocity gives the **displacement** or **net distance** s traveled by the particle. (See Fig. 6.1.5.)

The velocity function $v(t) = x'(t)$ may have both positive and negative values, as illustrated in Fig. 6.1.6. Then forward distances ($v > 0$) and backward distances ($v < 0$) partially or even totally cancel when we compute the net distance in Eq. (11). But suppose that we want to calculate the *total distance* S traveled—irrespective of direction. We can begin with a partition of $[a, b]$ into n subintervals all having the same length $\Delta t = (b-a)/n$ and set up the approximation

$$S \approx \sum_{i=1}^n |v(t_i^\star)|\, \Delta t. \qquad (12)$$

FIGURE 6.1.6 Velocity curve of a particle that first travels forward, then backward, then forward again.

Here $|v(t_i^\star)|$ is the *speed*—irrespective of direction—of the particle at a typical point $t_i^\star$ of the ith subinterval $[t_{i-1}, t_i]$, and thus $|v(t_i^\star)|\, \Delta t$ is the approximate distance traveled during that time interval. The approximation in (12) is a Riemann sum for the integral that gives the **total distance** traveled:

$$S = \int_a^b |v(t)|\, dt. \qquad (13)$$

In summary, we see that:

- The *net distance* s traveled by the particle is the integral of its (signed) *velocity* v, whereas
- The *total distance* S traveled by the particle is the integral of the (unsigned) *speed* $|v|$ of the particle.

The integral in (13) can be calculated by integrating separately over the subintervals where v is positive and those where v is negative, then adding the absolute values of the results. This is exactly the same procedure we use to find the area between the graph of a function and the x-axis when the function has both positive and negative values.

EXAMPLE 4 Suppose that the velocity of a moving particle is $v(t) = t^2 - 11t + 24$ (ft/s). Find both the net distance s and the total distance S it travels between time $t = 0$ and $t = 10$ (s).

Solution For net distance, we use Eq. (11) and find that

$$s = \int_0^{10} (t^2 - 11t + 24)\, dt = \left[\frac{1}{3}t^3 - \frac{11}{2}t^2 + 24t\right]_0^{10}$$

$$= \frac{1000}{3} - \frac{1100}{2} + 240 = \frac{70}{3} \quad \text{(ft)}.$$

FIGURE 6.1.7 Graph of the velocity function of Example 4.

To find the total distance traveled, we note from the graph of $v(t)$ in Fig. 6.1.7—or from the factorization $v(t) = (t-3)(t-8)$—that $v(t) > 0$ if $0 \leq t < 3$, $v(t) < 0$ if

FIGURE 6.1.8 Graph of the absolute value of the velocity function of Example 4.

$3 < t < 8$, and $v(t) > 0$ if $8 < t \leq 10$. By Eq. (13), we need to integrate the absolute value $|v(t)|$ graphed in Fig. 6.1.8. Now

$$\int_0^3 (t^2 - 11t + 24)\, dt = \left[\frac{1}{3}t^3 - \frac{11}{2}t^2 + 24t\right]_0^3 = \frac{63}{2},$$

$$\int_3^8 (-t^2 + 11t - 24)\, dt = \left[-\frac{1}{3}t^3 + \frac{11}{2}t^2 - 24t\right]_3^8 = \frac{125}{6},$$

and

$$\int_8^{10} (t^2 - 11t + 24)\, dt = \left[\frac{1}{3}t^3 - \frac{11}{2}t^2 + 24t\right]_8^{10} = \frac{38}{3}.$$

Thus the particle travels $\frac{63}{2}$ ft forward, then $\frac{125}{6}$ ft backward, and finally $\frac{38}{3}$ ft forward, for a total distance traveled of $S = \frac{63}{2} + \frac{125}{6} + \frac{38}{3} = 65$ ft. ◆

Fluid Flow in Circular Pipes

We consider the flow of fluid in a straight circular pipe of radius r. Because of the friction with the wall of the pipe, the velocity v of the fluid tends to be greatest along the centerline of the pipe, and decreases with the distance x from the center (Fig. 6.1.9). We therefore write $v(x)$ for the velocity (in units such as cm/s) at distance x. We want to calculate the total *flow rate* F (in units such as cm^3/s).

FIGURE 6.1.9 Fluid flow in a pipe of radius r and length L.

Figure 6.1.10 shows the pipe's circular cross section of radius r divided into washer-shaped *annular rings* by concentric circles whose radii are the points $x_0 = 0, x_1, x_2, \ldots, x_n = r$ of a subdivision of the x-interval $[0, r]$ into n subintervals all having the same length $\Delta x = r/n$. The ith annular ring corresponds to the ith subinterval $[x_{i-1}, x_i]$ and is bounded by the circles of radii x_{i-1} and x_i. To approximate its area ΔA_i, we think of cutting this annular ring and straightening it into a long strip of width Δx, as indicated in Fig. 6.1.11. The lengths of the top and bottom edges of this strip are simply the circumferences $2\pi x_{i-1}$ and $2\pi x_i$ of the two circles bounded the original annular ring. If $\overline{x}_i = \frac{1}{2}(x_{i-1} + x_i)$ denotes the "average radius" of this annular ring—so that $2\pi \overline{x}_i$ is the average length of the straightened strip—it follows that

$$\Delta A_i \approx 2\pi \overline{x}_i\, \Delta x. \tag{14}$$

If we reason that the average velocity of the fluid flowing across this ith annular ring is accurately approximated by $v(\overline{x}_i)$, then the volume that flows across it in one unit of time is approximately a cylindrical shell with base area ΔA_i and height $v(\overline{x}_i)$. It follows that the rate of flow ΔF_i of fluid across this annular ring is given approximately by

$$\Delta F_i \approx v(\overline{x}_i)\, \Delta A_i \approx 2\pi \overline{x}_i v(\overline{x}_i)\, \Delta x.$$

FIGURE 6.1.10 The circular cross section divided into annular rings.

FIGURE 6.1.11 An annular ring "straightened out."

Adding the flow rates across all n annular rings that make up the entire circular cross section of the pipe, we get the approximation

$$F = \sum_{i=1}^{n} \Delta F_i \approx \sum_{i=1}^{n} 2\pi \bar{x}_i v(\bar{x}_i) \, \Delta x.$$

Finally, we see that this approximation is a Riemann sum (with $x_i^* = \bar{x}_i$) for the integral

$$F = \int_0^r 2\pi x v(x) \, dx, \tag{15}$$

which thus gives the total flow rate F of fluid along the pipe.

EXAMPLE 5 If the velocity of the flowing fluid is exactly 1 at each point of the pipe, then the volume of fluid that flows across a circular cross section of radius r and area A in 1 second is a cylinder of volume $A \cdot 1 = A$. Thus $F = A$ in this case. Substituting $v(x) \equiv 1$ in Eq. (15) then yields

$$A = \int_0^r 2\pi x \, dx = \left[\pi x^2\right]_0^r = \pi r^2.$$

Because our derivation of Eq. (15) used only the formula $C = 2\pi r$ for the circumference of a circle—and not its area formula—this is a new and independent derivation of the formula $A = \pi r^2$ for the area of a circle of radius r. ◆

EXAMPLE 6 According to the law of laminar flow—discovered by the French physician Jean-Louis-Marie Poiseuille in 1840—the velocity function for fluid flow in a pipe of length L and radius r is

$$v(x) = \frac{P}{4vL}(r^2 - x^2), \tag{16}$$

where v is the viscosity of the fluid and P is the difference in pressure at the two ends of the pipe. Note that this formula gives $v = 0$ at the wall of the pipe, where $x = r$. Substituting this velocity function in Eq. (15) gives

$$F = \int_0^r 2\pi x \cdot \frac{P}{4vL}(r^2 - x^2) \, dx$$

$$= \frac{\pi P}{2vL} \int_0^r (r^2 x - x^3) \, dx = \frac{\pi P}{2vL} \left[\frac{r^2 x^2}{2} - \frac{x^4}{4}\right]_{x=0}^r;$$

$$F = \frac{\pi P}{2vL} \cdot \frac{r^4}{4} = \frac{\pi P r^4}{8vL}. \tag{17}$$

The formula in (17) is called *Poiseuille's law* for laminar fluid flow in a circular pipe. With a given ratio P/L of pressure difference per length, the flow rate F is proportional to the fourth power of the radius r of the pipe. For instance, because $\sqrt[4]{2} \approx 1.19$, a 20% increase in r more than doubles the flow rate F. ◆

Flow Rates and Cardiac Output

The determination of flow rates in pipes or streams has important applications ranging from engineering and environmental studies to medical procedures. A common technique involves the injection of a known amount A of a dye or other marker into the flow at time $t = 0$, followed by measurement at periodic intervals of the concentration of the dye by a probe at a fixed point downstream.

Suppose that all the dye has passed the measurement probe by time $t = T$. Subdivide the interval $[0, T]$ into n time intervals all of the same duration $\Delta t = T/n$. If the concentration $c(t)$ of the dye in the stream is measured at times $t_1, t_2, \ldots, t_n$, then we can estimate the amount of dye that passes the probe during the subinterval of time $[t_{i-1}, t_i]$. If the (unknown) constant flow rate is F, then the volume ΔV_i of fluid that passes the probe during the subinterval of time is $\Delta V_i = F \, \Delta t$. It may help to think of typical units:

$$\left(F \frac{\text{cm}^3}{\text{second}}\right) \times (\Delta t \text{ seconds}) = \Delta V_i \text{ cm}^3.$$

The amount ΔA_i (in mg, for instance) of dye in this volume of fluid is given by

$$\text{amount (mg)} = \text{concentration}\left(\frac{\text{mg}}{\text{cm}^3}\right) \times \text{volume (cm}^3).$$

If we use the measured concentration $c(t_i)$ as the approximate concentration throughout the time interval $[t_{i-1}, t_i]$, this gives

$$\Delta A_i \approx c(t_i)\,\Delta V_i = c(t_i) \cdot F\,\Delta t = F \cdot c(t_i)\,\Delta t.$$

Because the total amount A of injected dye passes the probe by time $t = T$, we add the individual amounts ΔA_i for $i = 1, 2, \ldots, n$ and get

$$A = \sum_{i=1}^{n} \Delta A_i \approx F \cdot \sum_{i=1}^{n} c(t_i)\,\Delta t$$

(using the fact that the flow rate F is constant). Finally, we recognize the Riemann sum on the right and conclude that

$$A = F \int_0^T c(t)\,dt.$$

Thus the previously unknown flow rate is given by

$$F = \frac{A}{\displaystyle\int_0^T c(t)\,dt}, \tag{18}$$

in terms of the known amount A of dye injected and the downstream concentration $c(t)$ that has been measured at times $t = t_1, t_2, \ldots, t_n$. We can therefore estimate F by substituting in Eq. (18) the Riemann sum approximation

$$\int_0^T c(t)\,dt \approx \sum_{i=1}^{n} c(t_i)\,\Delta t$$

—or, alternatively, a Simpson approximation to the integral.

In medicine the term *cardiac output* is used for the flow rate of blood pumped through the aorta by the heart. A typical cardiac output for a 70-kg man would be in the range of 5 to 7 liters per minute (L/min). The dye marker is injected into the heart (or into a vein entering the heart), and then concentration readings are taken by a probe inserted into the aorta leaving the heart.

EXAMPLE 7 The table in Fig. 6.1.12 lists concentration readings (in mg/L) taken with an aortic probe at 2-second intervals after 6 mg of dye was injected into the heart of a patient undergoing surgery. Approximate the cardiac output of the patient.

Solution Here we have $A = 6$, $T = 20$, and $\Delta t = 2$ with t in seconds. Simpson's approximation gives

$$\int_0^{20} c(t)\,dt \approx \frac{2}{3}[0 + 4 \cdot (1.93) + 2 \cdot (8.17) + 4 \cdot (9.00) + 2 \cdot (6.34) + 4 \cdot (3.65)$$
$$+ 2 \cdot (1.84) + 4 \cdot (0.88) + 2 \cdot (0.39) + 4 \cdot (0.15) + 0]$$
$$\approx 63.95.$$

The formula in (18) therefore gives

$$F = \frac{A}{\displaystyle\int_0^{20} c(t)\,dt} \approx \frac{6}{63.95} \approx 0.0938 \quad (\text{L/s}),$$

approximately 5.63 L/min, for the patient's cardiac output. ◆

t	$c(t)$	t	$c(t)$
0	0	12	1.84
2	1.93	14	0.88
4	8.17	16	0.39
6	9.00	18	0.15
8	6.34	20	0
10	3.65		

FIGURE 6.1.12 Dye concentration data in Example 7.

6.1 TRUE/FALSE STUDY GUIDE

6.1 CONCEPTS: QUESTIONS AND DISCUSSION

1. Describe in your own words—with a minimum of calculus textbook jargon and a maximum of personal understanding—the process of using approximating sums to set up an integral formula for use in calculating a specified quantity.
2. Carry out the process described in Question 1 to derive an integral formula corresponding to an application found in a science, engineering, economics, or medical textbook. (The derivation you see there may be somewhat cursory; do it carefully, as in this section.)

6.1 PROBLEMS

In Problems 1 through 10, x_i^* denotes a selected point, and m_i the midpoint, of the ith subinterval $[x_{i-1}, x_i]$ of a partition of the indicated interval $[a, b]$ into n subintervals each of length Δx. Evaluate the given limit by computing the value of the appropriate related integral.

1. $\lim\limits_{n \to \infty} \sum\limits_{i=1}^{n} 2x_i^* \, \Delta x; \quad a = 0, b = 1$

2. $\lim\limits_{n \to \infty} \sum\limits_{i=1}^{n} \dfrac{\Delta x}{(x_i^*)^2}; \quad a = 1, b = 2$

3. $\lim\limits_{n \to \infty} \sum\limits_{i=1}^{n} (\sin \pi x_i^*) \, \Delta x; \quad a = 0, b = 1$

4. $\lim\limits_{n \to \infty} \sum\limits_{i=1}^{n} \left[3(x_i^*)^2 - 1\right] \Delta x; \quad a = -1, b = 3$

5. $\lim\limits_{n \to \infty} \sum\limits_{i=1}^{n} x_i^* \sqrt{(x_i^*)^2 + 9} \, \Delta x; \quad a = 0, b = 4$

6. $\lim\limits_{n \to \infty} \sum\limits_{i=1}^{n} (x_i)^2 \, \Delta x; \quad a = 2, b = 4$

7. $\lim\limits_{n \to \infty} \sum\limits_{i=1}^{n} (2m_i - 1) \, \Delta x; \quad a = -1, b = 3$

8. $\lim\limits_{n \to \infty} \sum\limits_{i=1}^{n} \sqrt{2m_i + 1} \, \Delta x; \quad a = 0, b = 4$

9. $\lim\limits_{n \to \infty} \sum\limits_{i=1}^{n} \dfrac{m_i}{\sqrt{m_i^2 + 16}} \, \Delta x; \quad a = -3, b = 0$

10. $\lim\limits_{n \to \infty} \sum\limits_{i=1}^{n} m_i \cos(m_i^2) \, \Delta x; \quad a = 0, b = \sqrt{\pi}$

The notation in Problems 11 through 14 is the same as in Problems 1 through 10. Express the given limit as an integral involving the function f.

11. $\lim\limits_{n \to \infty} \sum\limits_{i=1}^{n} 2\pi x_i^* f(x_i^*) \, \Delta x; \quad a = 1, b = 4$

12. $\lim\limits_{n \to \infty} \sum\limits_{i=1}^{n} [f(x_i^*)]^2 \, \Delta x; \quad a = -1, b = 1$

13. $\lim\limits_{n \to \infty} \sum\limits_{i=1}^{n} \sqrt{1 + [f(x_i^*)]^2} \, \Delta x; \quad a = 0, b = 10$

14. $\lim\limits_{n \to \infty} \sum\limits_{i=1}^{n} 2\pi m_i \sqrt{1 + [f(m_i)]^2} \, \Delta x; \quad a = -2, b = 3$

In Problems 15 through 18, a rod coinciding with the interval $[a, b]$ on the x-axis (units in centimeters) has the specified density function $\rho(x)$ that gives its density (in grams per centimeter) at the point x. Find the mass M of the rod.

15. $a = 0, b = 100; \quad \rho(x) = \frac{1}{5}x$
16. $a = 0, b = 25; \quad \rho(x) = 60 - 2x$
17. $a = 0, b = 10; \quad \rho(x) = x(10 - x)$
18. $a = 0, b = 10; \quad \rho(x) = 10 \sin \dfrac{\pi x}{10}$

In Problems 19 through 30, compute both the net distance and the total distance traveled between time $t = a$ and time $t = b$ by a particle moving with the given velocity function $v = f(t)$ along a line.

19. $v = -32; \quad a = 0, b = 10$
20. $v = 2t + 10; \quad a = 1, b = 5$
21. $v = 4t - 25; \quad a = 0, b = 10$
22. $v = |2t - 5|; \quad a = 0, b = 5$
23. $v = 4t^3; \quad a = -2, b = 3$
24. $v = t - \dfrac{1}{t^2}; \quad a = 0.1, b = 1$
25. $v = \sin 2t; \quad a = 0, b = \dfrac{\pi}{2}$
26. $v = \cos 2t; \quad a = 0, b = \dfrac{\pi}{2}$
27. $v = \cos \pi t; \quad a = -1, b = 1$
28. $v = \sin t + \cos t; \quad a = 0, b = \pi$
29. $v = t^2 - 9t + 14; \quad a = 0, b = 10$
30. $v = t^3 - 8t^2 + 15t; \quad a = 0, b = 6$

In Problems 31 through 34, use a calculator or computer to approximate both the net distance and the total distance traveled by a particle with the given velocity function $v(t)$ during the indicated time interval $[a, b]$. Begin by graphing $v = v(t)$ to estimate the intervals where $v(t) > 0$ and where $v(t) < 0$. You may then integrate numerically if your calculator or computer has this facility.

31. $v(t) = t^3 - 7t + 4;\quad a = 0, b = 3$
32. $v(t) = t^3 - 5t^2 + 10;\quad a = 0, b = 5$
33. $v(t) = t\sin t - \cos t;\quad a = 0, b = \pi$
34. $v(t) = \sin t + \sqrt{t}\cos t;\quad a = 0, b = 2\pi$

35. Suppose that the circular disk of Fig. 6.1.10 has mass density $\rho(x)$ (in grams per square centimeter) at distance x from the origin. Then the annular ring of Figs. 6.1.10 and 6.1.11 has density approximately $\rho(x_i^\star)$ at each point. Conclude that the mass M of this disk of radius r is given by

$$M = \int_0^r 2\pi x \rho(x)\, dx.$$

In Problems 36 and 37, use the result of Problem 35 to find the mass of a circular disk with the given radius r and density function ρ.

36. $r = 10,\quad \rho(x) = x$
37. $r = 4,\quad \rho(x) = 25 - x^2$

38. If a particle is thrown straight upward from the ground with an initial velocity of 160 ft/s, then its velocity after t seconds is $v = -32t + 160$ feet per second, and it attains its maximum height when $t = 5$ s (and $v = 0$). Use Eq. (11) to compute this maximum height. Check your answer by the methods of Section 5.2.

39. Suppose that the rate of water flow into an initially empty tank is $100 - 3t$ gallons per minute at time t (in minutes). How much water flows into the tank during the interval from $t = 10$ to $t = 20$ min?

40. Suppose that the birth rate in Calgary t years after 1970 was $13 + t$ thousands of births per year. Set up and evaluate an appropriate integral to compute the total number of births that occurred between 1970 and 1990.

41. Assume that the city of Problem 40 had a death rate of $5 + \frac{1}{2}t$ thousands per year t years after 1970. If the population of the city was 125,000 in 1970, what was its population in 1990? Consider both births and deaths.

42. The average daily rainfall in Sioux City is $r(t)$ inches per day at time t (in days), $0 \leq t \leq 365$. Begin with a partition of the interval $[0, 365]$ and derive the formula

$$R = \int_0^{365} r(t)\, dt$$

for the average total annual rainfall R.

43. Take the average daily rainfall of Problem 42 to be

$$r(t) = a - b\cos\frac{2\pi t}{365},$$

where a and b are constants to be determined. If the value of $r(t)$ on January 1 ($t = 0$) is 0.1 in. and the value of $r(t)$ on July 1 ($t = 182.5$) is 0.5 in., what is the average total annual rainfall in this locale?

44. Suppose that the rate of water flow into a tank is $r(t)$ liters per minute at time t (in minutes). Use the method of Example 1 to derive the formula

$$Q = \int_a^b r(t)\, dt$$

for the amount of water that flows into the tank between times $t = a$ and $t = b$.

45. Evaluate

$$\lim_{n\to\infty} \frac{\sqrt[3]{1} + \sqrt[3]{2} + \sqrt[3]{3} + \cdots + \sqrt[3]{n}}{n^{4/3}}$$

by first finding a function f such that the limit is equal to

$$\int_0^1 f(x)\, dx.$$

46. In this problem you are to derive the volume formula $V = \frac{4}{3}\pi r^3$ for a spherical ball of radius r, assuming as *known* the formula $S = 4\pi r^2$ for the surface area of a sphere of radius r. Assume it follows that the volume of a thin spherical shell of radius r and thickness t (Fig. 6.1.13) is given approximately by $\Delta V \approx S \cdot t = 4\pi r^2 t$. Then divide the spherical ball into concentric spherical shells, analogous to the concentric annular rings of Fig. 6.1.10. Finally, interpret the sum of the volumes of these spherical shells as a Riemann sum.

FIGURE 6.1.13 A thin spherical shell of thickness t and inner radius r (Problem 46).

47. A spherical ball has radius 1 ft and, at distance x from its center, its density is $100(1 + x)$ lb/ft^3. Use Riemann sums to find a function $f(x)$ such that the weight of the ball is

$$W = \int_0^1 f(x)\, dx$$

(in pounds). Then compute W by evaluating this integral. [*Suggestion:* Given a partition $0 = x_0 < x_1 < x_2 < \cdots < x_n = 1$ of $[0, 1]$, estimate the weight ΔW_i of the spherical shell $x_{i-1} \leq x \leq x_i$ of the ball.]

48. Find the flow rate F in a circular pipe of radius r if the velocity of the fluid at distance x from the center of the pipe

is given by

$$v(x) = k \cos \frac{\pi x}{2r}.$$

You may use the formula $\int u \cos u \, du = u \sin u + \cos u + C.$

49. Poiseuille discovered his law of fluid flow in the course of investigating the flow of blood in veins and arteries in the human body. With a given fixed flow rate F through a blood vessel of specified length L, Poiseuille's law in Eq. (17) shows that a decrease in the radius r requires an increase in the blood pressure P. This is why hypertension—high blood pressure—frequently results from constriction of arteries. Construct a table in which the first column shows the percentage decrease in the radius of an artery (in increments of 5% from 0% to 25%) and the second column shows the resulting percentage increase in blood pressure.

50. Find the cardiac output (in L/min) if an injection of 4 mg of dye into a patient's heart results in the aortic concentration function

$$c(t) = \frac{250t}{(3+t^2)^2}$$

for $0 \leq t \leq 10$ (seconds).

51. The table in Fig. 6.1.14 lists concentration readings (in mg/L) taken with an aortic probe at 1-second intervals after 4.5 mg of dye was injected into the heart of a patient undergoing surgery. Approximate the patient's cardiac output.

t	$c(t)$	t	$c(t)$
0	0	6	2.21
1	2.32	7	1.06
2	9.80	8	0.47
3	10.80	9	0.18
4	7.61	10	0
5	4.38		

FIGURE 6.1.14 Dye concentration data for Problem 51.

52. Figure 6.1.15 shows the graph of the concentration function $c(t)$ recorded by an aortic probe connected to a plotter after 5.5 mg of dye was injected into the heart of a patient undergoing surgery. Approximate the cardiac output of the patient.

FIGURE 6.1.15 Graph of concentration $c(t)$ in Problem 52.

6.2 VOLUMES BY THE METHOD OF CROSS SECTIONS

Here we use integrals to calculate the volumes of certain solids or regions in space. We begin with an intuitive idea of volume as a measure of solids, analogous to area as a measure of plane regions. In particular, we assume that every simply expressible bounded solid region R has a volume measured by a nonnegative number $v(R)$ such that

- If R consists of two nonoverlapping pieces, then $v(R)$ is the sum of *their* volumes;
- Two different solids have the same volume if they have the same size and shape.

The **method of cross sections** is a way of computing the volume of a solid that is described in terms of its cross sections (or "slices") in planes perpendicular to a fixed *reference line* (such as the x-axis or y-axis). For instance, Fig. 6.2.1 shows a solid R with volume $V = v(R)$ lying alongside the interval $[a, b]$ on the x-axis. That is, a plane perpendicular to the x-axis intersects the solid if and only if this plane meets the x-axis in a point of $[a, b]$. Let R_x denote the intersection of R with the perpendicular plane that meets the x-axis at the point x of $[a, b]$. We call R_x the (plane) **cross section** of the solid at x.

FIGURE 6.2.1 R_x is the cross section of R in the plane perpendicular to the x-axis at x.

Volumes of Cylinders

This situation is especially simple if all the cross sections of R are congruent to one another and are parallel translations of each other. In this case the solid R is called a **cylinder** with **bases** R_a and R_b and **height** $h = b - a$. If R_a and R_b are circular disks, then R is the familiar **circular cylinder**. Recall that the volume formula for a circular

FIGURE 6.2.2 Every cylinder of height h and base area A has volume $V = Ah$.

cylinder of height h and circular base of radius r and area $A = \pi r^2$ is

$$V = \pi r^2 h = Ah.$$

Figure 6.2.2 shows several (general) cylinders with bases of various shapes. The method of cross sections is based on the fact that the volume V of any cylinder—circular or not—is equal to the product of the cylinder's height h and the area A of its base:

$$V = Ah \quad \text{(volume of a cylinder)}. \tag{1}$$

More General Volumes

The volume of a more general solid, as in Fig. 6.2.1, can be approximated by using cylinders. For each x in $[a, b]$, let $A(x)$ denote the area of the cross section R_x of the solid R:

$$A(x) = \text{area}(R_x). \tag{2}$$

We shall assume that the shape of R is sufficiently simple that this **cross-sectional area function** A is continuous (and therefore integrable).

To set up an integral formula for $V = v(R)$, we begin with a partition of $[a, b]$ into n subintervals, all with the same length $\Delta x = (b - a)/n$. Let R_i denote the slab or slice of the solid R positioned alongside the ith subinterval $[x_{i-1}, x_i]$ (Fig. 6.2.3). We denote the volume of this ith slice of R by $\Delta V_i = v(R_i)$, so

$$V = \sum_{i=1}^{n} \Delta V_i.$$

To approximate ΔV_i, we select a typical point $x_i^\star$ in $[x_{i-1}, x_i]$ and consider the *cylinder* C_i whose height is Δx and whose base is the cross section $R_{x_i^\star}$ of R at $x_i^\star$. Figure 6.2.4 suggests that if Δx is small, then $v(C_i)$ is a good approximation to $\Delta V_i = v(R_i)$:

$$\Delta V_i \approx v(C_i) = \text{area}(R_{x_i^\star}) \cdot \Delta x = A(x_i^\star) \, \Delta x,$$

a consequence of Eq. (1) with $A = A(x_i^\star)$ and $h = \Delta x$.

FIGURE 6.2.3 Planes through the partition points x_0, x_1, x_2, ..., x_n partition the solid R into slabs R_1, R_2, ..., R_n.

FIGURE 6.2.4 The slab R_i is approximated by the cylinder C_i of volume $A(x_i^\star) \Delta x$.

Then we add the volumes of these approximating cylinders for $i = 1, 2, 3, \ldots, n$. We find that

$$V = \sum_{i=1}^{n} \Delta V_i \approx \sum_{i=1}^{n} A(x_i^\star) \, \Delta x.$$

We recognize the approximating sum on the right to be a Riemann sum that approaches $\int_a^b A(x) \, dx$ as $n \to +\infty$. This justifies the following definition of the volume of a solid R in terms of its cross-sectional area function $A(x)$.

DEFINITION Volumes by Cross Sections
If the solid R lies alongside the interval $[a, b]$ on the x-axis and has continuous cross-sectional area function $A(x)$, then its volume $V = v(R)$ is

$$V = \int_a^b A(x) \, dx. \tag{3}$$

Equation (3) is known as **Cavalieri's principle,** after the Italian mathematician Bonaventura Cavalieri (1598–1647), who systematically exploited the fact that the volume of a solid is determined by the areas of its cross sections perpendicular to a given reference line.

EXAMPLE 1 Figure 6.2.5(a) shows a square-based pyramid oriented so that its height h corresponds to the interval $[0, h]$ on the x-axis. Its base is a b-by-b square, and each cross section perpendicular to the x-axis is also a square. To find the area $A(x)$ of the s-by-s cross section at x, we equate height-to-length ratios in the similar triangles of Fig. 6.2.5(b):

$$\frac{s}{x} = \frac{b}{h}, \quad \text{so} \quad s = \frac{b}{h} x.$$

Therefore,

$$A(x) = s^2 = \frac{b^2}{h^2} x^2,$$

and Eq. (3)—with $[0, h]$ as the interval of integration—gives

$$V = \int_0^h A(x) \, dx = \int_0^h \frac{b^2}{h^2} x^2 \, dx = \left[\frac{b^2}{h^2} \cdot \frac{x^3}{3} \right]_{x=0}^{x=h} = \frac{1}{3} b^2 h.$$

With $A = b^2$ denoting the area of the base, our result takes the form

$$V = \tfrac{1}{3} A h$$

for the volume of a pyramid. ◆

Cross Sections Perpendicular to the y-Axis

In the case of a solid R lying alongside the interval $[c, d]$ on the y-axis, we denote by $A(y)$ the area of the solid's cross section R_y in the plane perpendicular to the y-axis at the point y of $[c, d]$ (Fig. 6.2.6). A similar discussion, beginning with a partition of $[c, d]$, leads to the volume formula

$$V = \int_c^d A(y) \, dy. \tag{4}$$

FIGURE 6.2.5 The square-based pyramid of Example 1.

FIGURE 6.2.6 $A(y)$ is the area of the cross section R_y in the plane perpendicular to the y-axis at the point y.

Solids of Revolution

An important special case of Eq. (3) gives the volume of a **solid of revolution.** For example, consider the solid R obtained by revolving around the x-axis the region under the graph of $y = f(x)$ over the interval $[a, b]$, where $f(x) \geq 0$. Such a region and the resulting solid of revolution are shown in Fig. 6.2.7.

Volumes by the Method of Cross Sections SECTION 6.2   379

FIGURE 6.2.7 (a) A region from which we can determine the volume of a (b) solid of revolution around the *x*-axis.

Because the solid R is obtained by revolution, each cross section of R at x is a circular *disk* of radius $f(x)$. The cross-sectional area function is then $A(x) = \pi y^2 = \pi [f(x)]^2$, so Eq. (3) yields

$$V = \int_a^b \pi y^2 \, dx = \int_a^b \pi [f(x)]^2 \, dx \tag{5}$$

for the **volume of a solid of revolution around the *x*-axis.**

Note In the expression $\pi y^2 \, dx$, the differential dx tells us that the independent variable is x. We *must* express the dependent variable y in terms of x in order to perform the indicated integration.

EXAMPLE 2 Figure 6.2.8 shows the region that lies below the parabola $y^2 = x$ and above the *x*-axis over the interval $[0, 2]$. Find the volume V of the solid paraboloid (Fig. 6.2.9) obtained by revolving this region around the *x*-axis.

FIGURE 6.2.8 The parabolic region of Example 2.

FIGURE 6.2.9 The solid paraboloid of Example 2.

Solution Because $y^2 = x$ on the parabola, the cross-sectional area function in Eq. (5) is given in terms of x by

$$A(x) = \pi y^2 = \pi x.$$

Hence integration immediately gives

$$V = \int_0^2 \pi x \, dx = \left[\tfrac{1}{2} \pi x^2 \right]_0^2 = 2\pi.$$

◆

EXAMPLE 3 Use the method of cross sections to verify the familiar formula $V = \tfrac{4}{3}\pi R^3$ for the volume of a sphere of radius R.

380 CHAPTER 6 Applications of the Integral

FIGURE 6.2.10 (a) A semicircular region that we rotate (b) to generate a sphere (Example 3).

Solution We think of the sphere as the solid of revolution obtained by revolving the semicircular plane region in Fig. 6.2.10 around the x-axis. This is the region bounded above by the semicircle

$$y = \sqrt{R^2 - x^2}, \quad -R \leq x \leq R$$

and below by the interval $[-R, R]$ on the x-axis. To use Eq. (5), we take

$$f(x) = \sqrt{R^2 - x^2}, \quad a = -R, \quad \text{and} \quad b = R.$$

This gives

$$V = \int_{-R}^{R} \pi \left(\sqrt{R^2 - x^2} \right)^2 dx = \pi \int_{-R}^{R} (R^2 - x^2) \, dx$$

$$= \pi \left[R^2 x - \tfrac{1}{3} x^3 \right]_{-R}^{R} = \tfrac{4}{3} \pi R^3. \qquad \blacklozenge$$

FIGURE 6.2.11 A region lying between the y-axis and the curve $x = g(y)$, $c \leq y \leq d$, is rotated around the y-axis.

Revolution Around the y-Axis

Figure 6.2.11 shows a solid of revolution around the y-axis. The region being revolved is bounded by the y-axis and the curve $x = g(y)$, $c \leq y \leq d$ (as well as the lines $y = c$ and $y = d$). In this case the *horizontal* circular cross section has radius x, and thus the cross-sectional area at y is πx^2, where $x = g(y)$. Hence the cross-sectional area function is $A(y) = \pi [g(y)]^2$. We therefore obtain the formula

$$V = \int_c^d \pi x^2 \, dy = \int_c^d \pi [g(y)]^2 \, dy \qquad (6)$$

FIGURE 6.2.12 Generating a cone by rotation (Example 4).

(contrast it with (5)) for the **volume of a solid of revolution around the y-axis.**

Note In the expression $\pi x^2 \, dy$, the differential dy tells us that the independent variable is y. So here we must express the dependent variable x in terms of y before integrating.

EXAMPLE 4 Use the method of cross sections to verify the familiar formula $V = \tfrac{1}{3} \pi r^2 h$ for the volume of a right circular cone with base radius r and height h.

Solution Figure 6.2.12 depicts the cone as the solid of revolution obtained by revolving around the y-axis the triangle with vertices $(0, 0)$, $(0, h)$, and (r, h). The similar triangles in Fig. 6.2.13 yield the equation $x/y = r/h$, so the radius of the circular cross section perpendicular to the y-axis at the point y is $x = ry/h$. Then Eq. (6),

FIGURE 6.2.13 Finding the radius x of the circular cross section (Example 4).

with $g(y) = ry/h$, gives

$$V = \int_a^b A(y)\,dy = \int_a^b \pi x^2\,dy = \int_0^h \pi \left(\frac{ry}{h}\right)^2 dy$$

$$= \frac{\pi r^2}{h^2} \int_0^h y^2\,dy = \frac{1}{3}\pi r^2 h = \frac{1}{3}Ah,$$

where $A = \pi r^2$ is the area of the base of the cone. ◆

Revolving the Region Between Two Curves

Sometimes we need to calculate the volume of a solid generated by revolving a plane region that lies between two given curves. Suppose that $f(x) \geqq g(x) \geqq 0$ for x in the interval $[a, b]$ and that the solid R is generated by revolving around the x-axis the region between $y = f(x)$ and $y = g(x)$. Then the cross section at x is an **annular ring** (or **washer**) bounded by two circles (Fig. 6.2.14). The ring has inner radius $r_{\text{in}} = g(x)$ and outer radius $r_{\text{out}} = f(x)$, so the formula for the cross-sectional area at x is

$$A(x) = \pi(r_{\text{out}})^2 - \pi(r_{\text{in}})^2 = \pi[(y_{\text{top}})^2 - (y_{\text{bot}})^2] = \pi\{[f(x)]^2 - [g(x)]^2\},$$

FIGURE 6.2.14 (a) The region between two positive graphs (b) is rotated around the x-axis. Cross sections are annular rings.

FIGURE 6.2.15 The plane region of Example 5.

where we write $y_{\text{top}} = f(x)$ and $y_{\text{bot}} = g(x)$ for the top and bottom curves of the plane region. Therefore, Eq. (3) yields

$$V = \int_a^b \pi[(y_{\text{top}})^2 - (y_{\text{bot}})^2]\,dx = \int_a^b \pi\{[f(x)]^2 - [g(x)]^2\}\,dx \qquad (7)$$

for the volume V of the solid.

Similarly, if $f(y) \geqq g(y) \geqq 0$ for $c \leqq y \leqq d$, then the volume of the solid obtained by revolving around the y-axis the region between $x_{\text{right}} = f(y)$ and $x_{\text{left}} = g(y)$ is

$$V = \int_c^d \pi[(x_{\text{right}})^2 - (x_{\text{left}})^2]\,dy = \int_c^d \pi\{[f(y)]^2 - [g(y)]^2\}\,dy. \qquad (8)$$

EXAMPLE 5 Consider the plane region shown in Fig. 6.2.15, bounded by the curves $y^2 = x$ and $y = x^3$, which intersect at the points $(0, 0)$ and $(1, 1)$. If this region is revolved around the x-axis (Fig. 6.2.16), then Eq. (7) with

$$y_{\text{top}} = \sqrt{x}, \qquad y_{\text{bot}} = x^3$$

gives

$$V = \int_0^1 \pi\left[(\sqrt{x})^2 - (x^3)^2\right]dx = \int_0^1 \pi(x - x^6)\,dx$$

$$= \pi\left[\tfrac{1}{2}x^2 - \tfrac{1}{7}x^7\right]_0^1 = \tfrac{5}{14}\pi$$

FIGURE 6.2.16 Revolution around the x-axis (Example 5).

for the volume of revolution.

FIGURE 6.2.17 Revolution around the y-axis (Example 5).

If the same region is revolved around the y-axis (Fig. 6.2.17), then each cross section perpendicular to the y-axis is an annular ring with outer radius $x_{\text{right}} = y^{1/3}$ and inner radius $x_{\text{left}} = y^2$. Hence Eq. (8) gives the volume of revolution generated by this region as

$$V = \int_0^1 \pi \left[(y^{1/3})^2 - (y^2)^2 \right] dy = \int_0^1 \pi \left(y^{2/3} - y^4 \right) dy$$

$$= \pi \left[\tfrac{3}{5} y^{5/3} - \tfrac{1}{5} y^5 \right]_0^1 = \tfrac{2}{5} \pi. \qquad \blacklozenge$$

EXAMPLE 6 Suppose that the plane region of Example 5 (Fig. 6.2.15) is revolved around the vertical line $x = -1$ (Fig. 6.2.18). Then each cross section of the resulting solid is an annular ring with outer radius

$$r_{\text{out}} = 1 + x_{\text{right}} = 1 + y^{1/3}$$

and inner radius

$$r_{\text{in}} = 1 + x_{\text{left}} = 1 + y^2.$$

FIGURE 6.2.18 The annular ring of Example 6.

The area of such a cross section is

$$A(y) = \pi \left(1 + y^{1/3} \right)^2 - \pi (1 + y^2)^2 = \pi \left(2y^{1/3} + y^{2/3} - 2y^2 - y^4 \right),$$

so the volume of the resulting solid of revolution is

$$V = \int_0^1 \pi \left(2y^{1/3} + y^{2/3} - 2y^2 - y^4 \right) dy$$

$$= \pi \left[\tfrac{3}{2} y^{4/3} + \tfrac{3}{5} y^{5/3} - \tfrac{2}{3} y^3 - \tfrac{1}{5} y^5 \right]_0^1 = \tfrac{37}{30} \pi. \qquad \blacklozenge$$

FIGURE 6.2.19 The wedge and cylinder of Example 7.

FIGURE 6.2.20 A cross section of the wedge—an isosceles triangle (Example 7).

FIGURE 6.2.21 The base of the cylinder of Example 7.

EXAMPLE 7 Find the volume of the wedge that is cut from a circular cylinder with unit radius and unit height by a plane that passes through a diameter of the base of the cylinder and through a point on the circumference of its top.

Solution The cylinder and wedge are shown in Fig. 6.2.19. To form such a wedge, fill a cylindrical glass with cider and then drink slowly, tipping the bottom up as you drink, until half the bottom of the glass is exposed; the remaining cider forms the wedge.

We choose as reference line and x-axis the line through the "edge of the wedge"—the original diameter of the base of the cylinder. We can verify with similar triangles that each cross section of the wedge perpendicular to the diameter is an isosceles right triangle. One of these triangles is shown in Fig. 6.2.20. We denote by y the equal base and height of this triangle.

To determine the cross-sectional area function $A(x)$, we must express y in terms of x. Figure 6.2.21 shows the unit circular base of the original cylinder. We apply the Pythagorean theorem to the right triangle in this figure and find that $y = \sqrt{1-x^2}$. Hence

$$A(x) = \tfrac{1}{2}y^2 = \tfrac{1}{2}(1-x^2),$$

so Eq. (3) gives

$$V = \int_{-1}^{1} A(x)\,dx = 2\int_{0}^{1} A(x)\,dx \qquad \text{(by symmetry)}$$

$$= 2\int_{0}^{1} \tfrac{1}{2}(1-x^2)\,dx = \left[x - \tfrac{1}{3}x^3\right]_{0}^{1} = \tfrac{2}{3}$$

for the volume of the wedge. ◆

COMMENT It is a useful habit to check answers for plausibility whenever convenient. For example, we may compare a given solid with one whose volume is known. Because the volume of the original cylinder in Example 7 is π, we have found that the wedge occupies the fraction

$$\frac{V_{\text{wedge}}}{V_{\text{cyl}}} = \frac{\tfrac{2}{3}}{\pi} \approx 21\%$$

of the volume of the cylinder. A glance at Fig. 6.2.19 indicates that this is plausible. An error in our computations could well have given an unbelievable answer.

HISTORICAL NOTE The wedge of Example 7 has an ancient history. Its volume was first calculated in the third century B.C. by Archimedes, who also derived the formula $V = \tfrac{4}{3}\pi r^3$ for the volume of a sphere of radius r. His work on the wedge is found in a manuscript that was discovered in 1906 after having been lost for centuries. Archimedes used a method of exhaustion for volume similar to that discussed for areas in Section 5.3. For more information, see pp. 73–74 of C. H. Edwards, *The Historical Development of the Calculus* (New York: Springer-Verlag, 1979).

6.2 TRUE/FALSE STUDY GUIDE

6.2 CONCEPTS: QUESTIONS AND DISCUSSION

1. Suppose that the cross sections of a solid perpendicular to two nonparallel axes are all circular disks. Is this solid necessarily a solid sphere?
2. Give your own example of a solid whose volume can be calculated by two essentially different integrals—stemming from cross sections perpendicular to nonparallel axes. Show that both integrals give the same volume for this solid.
3. Question 2 points to the need for a definition of volume that is not based on cross sections perpendicular to a particular axis. Formulate a possible definition based on collections of nonoverlapping rectangular blocks containing and contained by a solid. (Consult the definition of area given in the concepts discussion at the end of Section 5.8.)

6.2 PROBLEMS

In Problems 1 through 24, find the volume of the solid that is generated by rotating around the indicated axis the plane region bounded by the given curves.

1. $y = x^2$, $y = 0$, $x = 1$;   the x-axis
2. $y = \sqrt{x}$, $y = 0$, $x = 4$;   the x-axis
3. $y = x^2$, $y = 4$, $x = 0$ (first quadrant only);   the y-axis (Fig. 6.2.22)
4. $y = 1/x$, $y = 0$, $x = 0.1$, $x = 1$;   the x-axis (Fig. 6.2.23)

FIGURE 6.2.22 Problem 3.

FIGURE 6.2.23 Problem 4.

5. $y = \sin x$ on $[0, \pi]$, $y = 0$;   the x-axis
6. $y = 9 - x^2$, $y = 0$;   the x-axis
7. $y = x^2$, $x = y^2$;   the x-axis (Fig. 6.2.24)
8. $y = x^2$, $y = 4x$;   the line $x = 5$ (Fig. 6.2.25)

FIGURE 6.2.24 Problem 7.

FIGURE 6.2.25 Problem 8.

9. $y = x^2$, $y = 8 - x^2$;   the x-axis
10. $x = y^2$, $x = y + 6$;   the y-axis
11. $y = 1 - x^2$, $y = 0$;   the x-axis (Fig. 6.2.26)
12. $y = x - x^3$, $y = 0$ $(0 \leq x \leq 1)$;   the x-axis (Fig. 6.2.27)

FIGURE 6.2.26 Problem 11.

FIGURE 6.2.27 Problem 12.

13. $y = 1 - x^2$, $y = 0$;   the y-axis
14. $y = 6 - x^2$, $y = 2$;   the x-axis (Fig. 6.2.28)
15. $y = 6 - x^2$, $y = 2$;   the y-axis (Fig. 6.2.28)
16. $y = 1 - x^2$, $y = 0$;   the vertical line $x = 2$
17. $y = x - x^3$, $y = 0$ $(0 \leq x \leq 1)$;   the horizontal line $y = -1$
18. $y = 4$, $x = 0$, $y = x^2$;   the x-axis
19. $y = 4$, $x = 0$, $y = x^2$;   the y-axis
20. $x = 16 - y^2$, $x = 0$, $y = 0$ (first quadrant only);   the x-axis (Fig. 6.2.29)

FIGURE 6.2.28 Problems 14 and 15.

FIGURE 6.2.29 Problem 20.

21. $y = x^2$, $x = y^2$;   the line $y = -2$
22. $y = x^2$, $y = 8 - x^2$;   the line $y = -1$
23. $y = x^2$, $x = y^2$;   the line $x = 3$
24. $y = x^2$, $y = 8 - x^2$;   the line $x = 4$

In Problems 25 through 30, find the volume obtained by revolving the region R around the x-axis. You may use the trigonometric identities

$$\cos^2 x = \frac{1 + \cos 2x}{2} \quad \text{and} \quad \sin^2 x = \frac{1 - \cos 2x}{2}$$

to help you evaluate some of the integrals.

25. R is the region between the graph $y = \sin x$ and the x-axis for $0 \leq x \leq \pi$.
26. R is the region between the graph $y = \cos(\frac{1}{2}\pi x)$ and the x-axis for $-1 \leq x \leq 1$.
27. R is the region between the curves $y = \sin x$ and $y = \cos x$ for $0 \leq x \leq \pi/4$.
28. R is the region between $x = -\pi/3$ and $x = \pi/3$ that is bounded by the curves $y = \cos x$ and $y = 1/2$.
29. R is bounded by the curve $y = \tan x$ and the lines $y = 0$ and $x = \pi/4$.
30. R is bounded by the curve $y = \tan x$ and the lines $x = 0$ and $y = 1$.

In Problems 31 through 34, first use a calculator or computer to approximate (graphically or otherwise) the points of intersection of the two given curves. Let R be the region bounded by these curves. Integrate to approximate the volume of the solid obtained by revolving the region R around the x-axis.

31. $y = x^3 + 1$, $y = 3x^2$
32. $y = x^4$, $y = x + 4$

33. $y = x^2$, $y = \cos x$

34. $y = \sin x$, $y = (x-1)^2$

35. The region R shown in Fig. 6.2.30 is bounded by the parabolas $y^2 = 2(x-3)$ and $y^2 = x$. Find the volume of the solid generated by rotating R around the x-axis.

FIGURE 6.2.30 The region of Problem 35.

36. Find the volume of the ellipsoid generated by rotating around the x-axis the region bounded by the ellipse with equation
$$\left(\frac{x}{a}\right)^2 + \left(\frac{y}{b}\right)^2 = 1$$
(Fig. 6.2.31).

FIGURE 6.2.31 The ellipse of Problems 36 and 37.

37. Repeat Problem 36, except rotate the elliptical region around the y-axis.

38. Find the volume of the unbounded solid generated by rotating the unbounded region of Fig. 6.2.32 around the x-axis. This is the region between the graph of $y = 1/x^2$ and the x-axis for $x \geq 1$. [*Method:* Compute the volume from $x = 1$ to $x = b$, where $b > 1$. Then find the limit of this volume as $b \to +\infty$.]

FIGURE 6.2.32 The unbounded plane region of Problem 38.

39. An observatory (Fig. 6.2.33) is shaped like a solid whose base is a circular disk with diameter AB of length $2a$ (Fig. 6.2.34). Find the volume of this solid if each cross section perpendicular to AB is a square.

FIGURE 6.2.33 The observatory of Problem 39.

FIGURE 6.2.34 The circular base of the observatory (Problem 39).

40. The base of a certain solid is a circular disk with diameter AB of length $2a$. Find the volume of the solid if each cross section perpendicular to AB is a semicircle.

41. The base of a certain solid is a circular disk with diameter AB of length $2a$. Find the volume of the solid if each cross section perpendicular to AB is an equilateral triangle.

42. The base of a solid is the region in the xy-plane bounded by the parabolas $y = x^2$ and $x = y^2$. Find the volume of this solid if every cross section perpendicular to the x-axis is a square with *its* base in the xy-plane.

43. The *paraboloid* generated by rotating around the x-axis the region under the parabola $y^2 = 2px$, $0 \leq x \leq h$, is shown in Fig. 6.2.35. Show that the volume of the paraboloid is one-half that of the circumscribed cylinder also shown in the figure.

FIGURE 6.2.35 The paraboloid and cylinder of Problem 43.

44. A pyramid has height h and rectangular base with area A. Show that its volume is $V = \frac{1}{3}Ah$. [*Suggestion:* Note that each cross section parallel to the base is a rectangle.]

45. Repeat Problem 44, except make the base a triangle with area A.

46. Find the volume that remains after a hole of radius 3 is bored through the center of a solid sphere of radius 5 (Fig. 6.2.36).

FIGURE 6.2.36 The sphere-with-hole of Problem 46.

47. Two horizontal circular cylinders both have radius a, and their axes intersect at right angles. Find the volume of their solid of intersection (Figs. 6.2.37 and 6.2.38, where $a = 1$). Is it clear to you that each horizontal cross section of the solid is a square?

FIGURE 6.2.37 The intersecting cylinders of Problem 47.

FIGURE 6.2.38 The solid of intersection (Problem 47).

48. Figure 6.2.39 shows a "spherical segment" of height h that is cut off from a sphere of radius r by a horizontal plane. Show that its volume is
$$V = \tfrac{1}{3}\pi h^2 (3r - h).$$

FIGURE 6.2.39 A spherical segment (Problem 48).

49. A doughnut-shaped solid, called a *torus* (Fig. 6.2.40), is generated by revolving around the y-axis the circular disk $(x - b)^2 + y^2 \leq a^2$ centered at the point $(b, 0)$, where $0 < a < b$. Show that the volume of this torus is $V = 2\pi^2 a^2 b$. [*Suggestion:* Note that each cross section perpendicular to the y-axis is an annular ring, and recall that
$$\int_0^a \sqrt{a^2 - y^2}\, dy = \tfrac{1}{4}\pi a^2$$
because the integral represents the area of a quarter-circle of radius a.]

FIGURE 6.2.40 The torus of Problem 49.

50. The summit of a hill is 100 ft higher than the surrounding level terrain, and each horizontal cross section of the hill is circular. The following table gives the radius r (in feet) for selected values of the height h (in feet) above the surrounding terrain. Use Simpson's approximation to estimate the volume of the hill.

h	0	25	50	75	100
r	60	55	50	35	0

51. *Newton's Wine Barrel* Consider a barrel with the shape of the solid generated by revolving around the x-axis the region under the parabola
$$y = R - kx^2, \qquad -\tfrac{1}{2}h \leq x \leq \tfrac{1}{2}h$$
(Fig. 6.2.41). (a) Show that the radius of each end of the barrel is $r = R - \delta$, where $4\delta = kh^2$. (b) Then show that the volume of the barrel is
$$V = \tfrac{1}{3}\pi h \left(2R^2 + r^2 - \tfrac{2}{5}\delta^2\right).$$

FIGURE 6.2.41 The region of Problem 51.

52. *The Clepsydra, or Water Clock* Consider a water tank whose side surface is generated by rotating the curve $y = kx^4$ around the y-axis (k is a positive constant). (a) Compute $V(y)$, the volume of water in the tank as a function of the depth y. (b) Suppose that water drains from the tank through a small hole at its bottom. Use the chain rule and Torricelli's law of draining [Eq. (3) of Section 5.2] to show that the water level in this tank falls at a *constant* rate. How could such a tank be used as a clock?

53. A contractor wants to bid on the job of leveling a 60-ft hill. It will cost $3.30/yd^3 of material in the hill to be removed. The following table, based on surveying data, shows areas of horizontal cross sections of the hill at 10-ft height intervals. Use (a) the trapezoidal approximation and (b) Simpson's approximation to estimate how much this job should cost. Round each answer to the nearest hundred dollars.

Height x (ft)	0	10	20	30	40	50	60
Area (ft^2)	1513	882	381	265	151	50	0

54. Water evaporates from an open bowl at a rate proportional to the area of the surface of the water. Show that whatever the shape of the bowl, the water level will drop at a constant rate.

55. A frustum of a right circular cone has height h and volume V. Its base is a circular disk with radius R and its top is a circular disk with radius r (Fig. 6.2.42). Apply the method of cross sections to show that

$$V = \tfrac{1}{3}\pi h(r^2 + rR + R^2).$$

FIGURE 6.2.42 A frustum of a cone (Problem 55).

56. Find the volume of the solid of intersection of two spheres of radius a, if the center of each lies on the surface of the other.

57. Find the volume of the solid of intersection of two spheres of radii a and b (with $b < a$) if the center of the smaller sphere lies on the surface of the larger one.

58. In the third century B.C. Archimedes regarded the sphere of radius r as a solid of revolution in deriving his famous volume formula $V = \tfrac{4}{3}\pi r^3$. A major difference between his method and the method of this section is that his derivation used conical frusta rather than circular cylinders (Fig. 6.2.43). Figure 6.2.44 shows the approximating solid obtained by revolving around the x-axis the polygonal arc $P_0 P_1 P_2 \ldots P_n$, where P_i denotes the point $(x_i, f(x_i))$ on the curve $y = f(x)$. The approximating slice that corresponds to the ith subinterval $[x_{i-1}, x_i]$ is the conical frustum highlighted in Fig. 6.2.44. The volume formula of Problem 55 gives the "frustum approximation"

$$V \approx \sum_{i=1}^{n} \frac{\pi}{3}\left\{[f(x_{i-1})]^2 + f(x_{i-1})f(x_i) + [f(x_i)]^2\right\} \Delta x.$$

Use continuity of f to show that this approximation leads (as $n \to +\infty$) to the same volume formula

$$V = \int_a^b \pi [f(x)]^2 \, dx$$

that we derived using the method of cross sections.

FIGURE 6.2.43 Using cylinders to approximate a solid of revolution.

FIGURE 6.2.44 Using conical frusta to approximate a solid of revolution.

6.3 VOLUMES BY THE METHOD OF CYLINDRICAL SHELLS

The method of cross sections of Section 6.2 is a technique of approximating a solid by a stack of thin slabs or slices. In the case of a solid of revolution, these slices are circular disks or annular rings. The **method of cylindrical shells** is a second way of computing volumes of solids of revolution. It is a technique of approximating a solid of revolution by a collection of thin right cylindrical shells, and it frequently leads to simpler computations than does the method of cross sections.

388 CHAPTER 6 Applications of the Integral

FIGURE 6.3.1 A cylindrical shell.

Volume of a Cylindrical Shell

A **cylindrical shell** is a region bounded by two concentric circular cylinders of the same height h. If, as in Fig. 6.3.1, the inner cylinder has radius r_1 and the outer one has radius r_2, then $\bar{r} = (r_1 + r_2)/2$ is the **average radius** of the cylindrical shell and $t = r_2 - r_1$ is its **thickness.** We then get the volume of the cylindrical shell by subtracting the volume of the inner cylinder from that of the outer one:

$$V = \pi r_2^2 h - \pi r_1^2 h = 2\pi \frac{r_1 + r_2}{2}(r_2 - r_1)h = 2\pi \bar{r} t h. \tag{1}$$

In words, the volume of the shell is the product of 2π, its average radius, its thickness, and its height. Thus the volume of a very thin shell is closely approximated by multiplying its curved surface area by its thickness.

More General Volumes

Now suppose that we want to find the volume V of revolution generated by revolving around the y-axis the region under $y = f(x)$ from $x = a$ to $x = b$. We assume, as indicated in Fig. 6.3.2(a), that $0 \leq a < b$ and that $f(x)$ is continuous and nonnegative on $[a, b]$. The solid will then resemble the one shown in Fig. 6.3.2(b).

To find V, we begin with a partition of $[a, b]$ into n subintervals, all with the same length $\Delta x = (b - a)/n$. Let $\bar{x}_i$ denote the midpoint of the ith subinterval $[x_{i-1}, x_i]$. Consider the rectangle in the xy-plane with base $[x_{i-1}, x_i]$ and height $f(\bar{x}_i)$. Figure 6.3.2(c) shows the cylindrical shell that is obtained by revolving this rectangle around the y-axis. This cylindrical shell approximates the solid with volume ΔV_i that is obtained by revolving the region under $y = f(x)$ and over $[x_{i-1}, x_i]$, and thus Eq. (1) gives

$$\Delta V_i \approx 2\pi \bar{x}_i f(\bar{x}_i) \Delta x.$$

We add the volumes of the n cylindrical shells determined by the partition of $[a, b]$. This sum should approximate V because—as Fig. 6.3.2(d) suggests—the union of these shells physically approximates the solid of revolution. Thus we obtain the

FIGURE 6.3.2 A solid of revolution—note the hole through its center—and a way to approximate it with nested cylindrical shells.

approximation

$$V = \sum_{i=1}^{n} \Delta V_i \approx \sum_{i=1}^{n} 2\pi \overline{x}_i f(\overline{x}_i) \Delta x.$$

This approximation to the volume V is a Riemann sum that approaches the integral

$$\int_a^b 2\pi x f(x)\, dx \quad \text{as} \quad \Delta x \to 0,$$

so it appears that the volume of the solid of revolution is given by

$$V = \int_a^b 2\pi x f(x)\, dx. \tag{2}$$

A complete discussion would require a proof that this formula gives the same volume as that *defined* by the method of cross sections in Section 6.2. (See Appendix G.)

It is more reliable to learn how to set up integral formulas than merely to memorize such formulas. A useful heuristic (suggestive but nonrigorous) device for setting up Eq. (2) is to picture the very narrow rectangular strip of area shown in Fig. 6.3.3. When this strip is revolved around the y-axis, it produces a thin cylindrical shell of radius x, height $y = f(x)$, and thickness dx (Fig. 6.3.4). So, if its volume is denoted by dV, we may write

$$dV = 2\pi x \cdot f(x) \cdot dx = 2\pi x f(x)\, dx.$$

This is easy to remember if you visualize Fig. 6.3.5.

FIGURE 6.3.3 Heuristic device for setting up Eq. (2).

FIGURE 6.3.4 Cylindrical shell of infinitesimal thickness.

FIGURE 6.3.5 Infinitesimal cylindrical shell, flattened out.

We think of $V = \int dV$ as a sum of very many such volumes, nested concentrically around the axis of revolution and forming the solid itself. We can then write

$$V = \int_a^b 2\pi x y\, dx = \int_a^b 2\pi x f(x)\, dx.$$

Do not forget to express y (and any other dependent variable) in terms of the independent variable x (identified here by the differential dx) before you integrate.

EXAMPLE 1 Find the volume V of the solid generated by revolving around the y-axis the region under $y = 3x^2 - x^3$ from $x = 0$ to $x = 3$ (Fig. 6.3.6).

Solution Here it would be impractical to use the method of cross sections, because a cross section perpendicular to the y-axis is an annular ring, and finding its inner and outer radii would require us to solve the equation $y = 3x^2 - x^3$ for x in terms of y. We prefer to avoid this troublesome task, and Eq. (2) provides us with an alternative: We take $f(x) = 3x^2 - x^3$, $a = 0$, and $b = 3$. It immediately follows that

$$V = \int_0^3 2\pi x(3x^2 - x^3)\, dx = 2\pi \int_0^3 (3x^3 - x^4)\, dx$$

$$= 2\pi \left[\tfrac{3}{4} x^4 - \tfrac{1}{5} x^5 \right]_0^3 = \tfrac{243}{10}\pi. \quad \blacklozenge$$

FIGURE 6.3.6 The region of Example 1: Rotate it around the y-axis.

FIGURE 6.3.7 The sphere-with-hole of Example 2.

FIGURE 6.3.8 Middle cross section of the sphere-with-hole (Example 2).

EXAMPLE 2 Find the volume V of the solid that remains after you bore a circular hole of radius a through the center of a solid sphere of radius $b > a$ (Fig. 6.3.7).

Solution We think of the sphere of radius b as generated by revolving the right half of the circular disk $x^2 + y^2 = b^2$ around the y-axis, and we think of the hole as vertical and with its centerline lying on the y-axis. Then the upper *half* of the solid in question is generated by revolving around the y-axis the region shaded in Fig. 6.3.8. This is the region below the graph of $y = \sqrt{b^2 - x^2}$ (and above the x-axis) from $x = a$ to $x = b$. The volume of the entire sphere-with-hole is then double that of the upper half, and Eq. (2) gives

$$V = 2\int_a^b 2\pi x(b^2 - x^2)^{1/2}\,dx = 4\pi\left[-\tfrac{1}{3}(b^2 - x^2)^{3/2}\right]_a^b,$$

so

$$V = \tfrac{4}{3}\pi(b^2 - a^2)^{3/2}.\qquad\blacklozenge$$

A way to check an answer such as this is to test it in some extreme cases. If $a = 0$ and $b = r$, which corresponds to drilling no hole at all through a sphere of radius r, then our result reduces to the volume $V = \tfrac{4}{3}\pi r^3$ of the entire sphere. If $a = b$, which corresponds to using a drill bit as large as the sphere, then $V = 0$; this, too, is correct.

Revolving the Region Between Two Curves

Now let A denote the region between the curves $y = f(x)$ and $y = g(x)$ over the interval $[a, b]$, where $0 \leq a < b$ and $g(x) \leq f(x)$ for x in $[a, b]$. Such a region is shown in Fig. 6.3.9. When A is rotated around the y-axis, it generates a solid of revolution. Suppose that we want to find the volume V of this solid. A development similar to that of Eq. (2) leads to the approximation

$$V \approx \sum_{i=1}^{n} 2\pi \overline{x}_i [f(\overline{x}_i) - g(\overline{x}_i)]\,\Delta x,$$

from which we may conclude that

$$V = \int_a^b 2\pi x [f(x) - g(x)]\,dx. \qquad (3)$$

FIGURE 6.3.9 The region A between the graphs of f and g over $[a, b]$ is to be rotated around the y-axis.

FIGURE 6.3.10 The region A is to be rotated around the x-axis.

Thus

$$V = \int_a^b 2\pi x[y_{\text{top}} - y_{\text{bot}}]\, dx, \qquad (3')$$

where $y_{\text{top}} = f(x)$ and $y_{\text{bot}} = g(x)$.

The method of cylindrical shells is also an effective way to compute volumes of solids of revolution around the x-axis. Figure 6.3.10 shows the region A bounded by the curves $x = f(y)$ and $x = g(y)$ for $c \leq y \leq d$ and by the horizontal lines $y = c$ and $y = d$. Let V be the volume obtained by revolving the region A around the x-axis. To compute V, we begin with a partition of $[c, d]$ into n subintervals, all of the same length $\Delta y = (d - c)/n$. Let $\bar{y}_i$ denote the midpoint of the ith subinterval $[y_{i-1}, y_i]$ of the partition. Then the volume of the cylindrical shell with average radius $\bar{y}_i$, height $f(\bar{y}_i) - g(\bar{y}_i)$, and thickness Δy is

$$\Delta V_i = 2\pi \bar{y}_i [f(\bar{y}_i) - g(\bar{y}_i)]\, \Delta y.$$

We add the volumes of these cylindrical shells and thus obtain the approximation

$$V \approx \sum_{i=1}^n 2\pi \bar{y}_i [f(\bar{y}_i) - g(\bar{y}_i)]\, \Delta y.$$

We recognize the right-hand side to be a Riemann sum for an integral with respect to y from c to d and so conclude that the volume of the solid of revolution is given by

$$V = \int_c^d 2\pi y [f(y) - g(y)]\, dy. \qquad (4)$$

Thus

$$V = \int_c^d 2\pi y [x_{\text{right}} - x_{\text{left}}]\, dy, \qquad (4')$$

where $x_{\text{right}} = f(y)$ and $x_{\text{left}} = g(y)$.

Note To use Eqs. (3') and (4'), the integrand must be expressed in terms of the variable of integration specified by the differential.

FIGURE 6.3.11 The region of Example 3.

EXAMPLE 3 Consider the region in the first quadrant bounded by the curves $y^2 = x$ and $y = x^3$ (Fig. 6.3.11). Use the method of cylindrical shells to compute the volume of the solids obtained by revolving this region first around the y-axis and then around the x-axis.

Solution It is best to use cylindrical shells, as in Figs. 6.3.12 and 6.3.13, rather than memorized formulas, to set up the appropriate integrals. Thus the volume of revolution around the y-axis (Fig. 6.3.12) is given by

$$V = \int_0^1 2\pi x (y_{\text{top}} - y_{\text{bot}})\, dx = \int_0^1 2\pi x \left(\sqrt{x} - x^3\right) dx$$

$$= \int_0^1 2\pi \left(x^{3/2} - x^4\right) dx = 2\pi \left[\tfrac{2}{5} x^{5/2} - \tfrac{1}{5} x^5 \right]_0^1 = \tfrac{2}{5}\pi.$$

FIGURE 6.3.12 Revolution around the y-axis (Example 3).

392 CHAPTER 6 Applications of the Integral

The volume of revolution around the x-axis (Fig. 6.3.13) is given by

$$V = \int_0^1 2\pi y(x_{\text{right}} - x_{\text{left}}) \, dy = \int_0^1 2\pi y(y^{1/3} - y^2) \, dy$$

$$= \int_0^1 2\pi (y^{4/3} - y^3) \, dy = 2\pi \left[\tfrac{3}{7} y^{7/3} - \tfrac{1}{4} y^4 \right]_0^1 = \tfrac{5}{14}\pi.$$

The answers are the same, of course, as those we obtained by using the method of cross sections in Example 5 of Section 6.2. ◆

EXAMPLE 4 Suppose that the region of Example 3 is rotated around the vertical line $x = -1$ (Fig. 6.3.14). Then the area element

$$dA = (y_{\text{top}} - y_{\text{bot}}) \, dx = \left(\sqrt{x} - x^3 \right) dx$$

is revolved through a circle of radius $r = 1 + x$. Hence the volume of the resulting cylindrical shell is

$$dV = 2\pi r \, dA = 2\pi (1+x)\left(x^{1/2} - x^3 \right) dx$$
$$= 2\pi \left(x^{1/2} + x^{3/2} - x^3 - x^4 \right) dx.$$

FIGURE 6.3.13 Revolution around the x-axis (Example 3).

FIGURE 6.3.14 Revolution around the vertical line $x = -1$ (Example 4).

The volume of the resulting solid of revolution is then

$$V = \int_0^1 2\pi \left(x^{1/2} + x^{3/2} - x^3 - x^4 \right) dx$$

$$= 2\pi \left[\tfrac{2}{3} x^{3/2} + \tfrac{2}{5} x^{5/2} - \tfrac{1}{4} x^4 - \tfrac{1}{5} x^5 \right]_0^1 = \tfrac{37}{30}\pi,$$

as we found by using the method of cross sections in Example 6 of Section 6.2. ◆

We may observe finally that the method of cylindrical shells is summarized by the heuristic formula

$$V = \int_*^{**} 2\pi r \, dA,$$

where dA denotes the area of an infinitesimal strip that is revolved through a circle of radius r to generate a thin cylindrical shell. The asterisks indicate limits of integration that you need to find.

6.3 TRUE/FALSE STUDY GUIDE

6.3 CONCEPTS: QUESTIONS AND DISCUSSION

In the text's discussion of the solid of revolution illustrated in Fig. 6.3.2, ΔV_i denotes the part of the entire volume V that is obtained by revolving just the strip that lies under the graph of $y = f(x)$ over the ith subinterval $[x_{i-1}, x_i]$. We argued that ΔV_i is approximated by $\Delta V_i \approx 2\pi \overline{x}_i f(\overline{x}_i) \Delta x$.

1. Explain why continuity of the function f implies that $\Delta V_i = 2\pi \bar{x}_i f(x_i^\star) \Delta x$ *exactly* for some point $x_i^\star$ in the ith subinterval.
2. Then the volume V of the entire solid of revolution is given exactly by

$$V = \sum_{i=1}^{n} \Delta V_i = \sum_{i=1}^{n} 2\pi \bar{x}_i f(x_i^\star) \Delta x$$

$$= \sum_{i=1}^{n} 2\pi x_i^\star f(x_i^\star) \Delta x + \sum_{i=1}^{n} 2\pi (\bar{x}_i - x_i^\star) f(x_i^\star) \Delta x. \quad (5)$$

Explain why continuity of f now implies that the last sum in (5) approaches zero as $n \to +\infty$. Explain why this implies that

$$V = \int_a^b 2\pi x f(x)\, dx.$$

6.3 PROBLEMS

In Problems 1 through 28, use the method of cylindrical shells to find the volume of the solid generated by rotating around the indicated axis the region bounded by the given curves.

1. $y = x^2$, $y = 0$, $x = 2$; the y-axis
2. $x = y^2$, $x = 4$; the y-axis
3. $y = 25 - x^2$, $y = 0$; the y-axis (Fig. 6.3.15)
4. $y = 2x^2$, $y = 8$; the y-axis (Fig. 6.3.16)

FIGURE 6.3.15 Problem 3.

FIGURE 6.3.16 Problem 4.

5. $y = x^2$, $y = 8 - x^2$; the y-axis
6. $x = 9 - y^2$, $x = 0$; the x-axis
7. $x = y$, $x + 2y = 3$, $y = 0$; the x-axis (Fig. 6.3.17)
8. $y = x^2$, $y = 2x$; the line $y = 5$
9. $y = 2x^2$, $y^2 = 4x$; the x-axis
10. $y = 3x - x^2$, $y = 0$; the y-axis
11. $y = 4x - x^3$, $y = 0$; the y-axis (Fig. 6.3.18)

FIGURE 6.3.17 Problem 7.

FIGURE 6.3.18 Problem 11.

12. $x = y^3 - y^4$, $x = 0$; the line $y = -2$ (Fig. 6.3.19)
13. $y = x - x^3$, $y = 0$ $(0 \leq x \leq 1)$; the y-axis
14. $x = 16 - y^2$, $x = 0$, $y = 0$ $(0 \leq y \leq 4)$; the x-axis
15. $y = x - x^3$, $y = 0$ $(0 \leq x \leq 1)$; the line $x = 2$ (Fig. 6.3.20)

FIGURE 6.3.19 Problem 12.

FIGURE 6.3.20 Problem 15.

16. $y = x^3$, $y = 0$, $x = 2$; the y-axis (Fig. 6.3.21)

FIGURE 6.3.21 Problem 16.

17. $y = x^3$, $y = 0$, $x = 2$; the line $x = 3$
18. $y = x^3$, $y = 0$, $x = 2$; the x-axis
19. $y = x^2$, $y = 0$, $x = -1$, $x = 1$; the line $x = 2$

20. $y = x^2$, $y = x$ $(0 \leq x \leq 1)$;   the y-axis
21. $y = x^2$, $y = x$ $(0 \leq x \leq 1)$;   the x-axis
22. $y = x^2$, $y = x$ $(0 \leq x \leq 1)$;   the line $y = 2$
23. $y = x^2$, $y = x$ $(0 \leq x \leq 1)$;   the line $x = -1$
24. $x = y^2$, $x = 2 - y^2$;   the x-axis (Fig. 6.3.22)
25. $x = y^2$, $x = 2 - y^2$;   the line $y = 1$
26. $y = 4x - x^2$, $y = 0$;   the y-axis
27. $y = 4x - x^2$, $y = 0$;   the line $x = -1$
28. $y = x^2$, $x = y^2$;   the line $y = -1$

FIGURE 6.3.22 Problem 24.

In Problems 29 through 34, first use a calculator or computer to approximate (graphically or otherwise) the points of intersection of the two given curves. Let R be the region bounded by these curves. Integrate to approximate the volume of the solid obtained by revolving the region R around the y-axis. In Problems 31 through 34 you will find helpful the integral formula

$$\int u \cos u \, du = \cos u + u \sin u + C,$$

which you can verify by differentiation of the right-hand side.

29. $y = x^3 + 1$, $y = 6x - x^2$ (R lies to the right of the y-axis)
30. $y = x^4$, $y = 10x - 5$
31. $y = \cos x$, $y = x^2$
32. $y = \cos x$, $y = (x - 1)^2$
33. $y = \cos x$, $y = 3x^2 - 6x + 2$
34. $y = 3 \cos x$, $y = -\cos 4x$ (R lies between $x = -2$ and $x = 2$)

35. Verify the formula for the volume of a right circular cone by using the method of cylindrical shells. Apply the method to the figure generated by rotating the triangular region with vertices $(0, 0)$, $(r, 0)$, and $(0, h)$ around the y-axis.

36. Use the method of cylindrical shells to compute the volume of the paraboloid of Problem 43 in Section 6.2.

37. Use the method of cylindrical shells to find the volume of the ellipsoid obtained by revolving the elliptical region bounded by the graph of the equation

$$\left(\frac{x}{a}\right)^2 + \left(\frac{y}{b}\right)^2 = 1$$

around the y-axis.

38. Use the method of cylindrical shells to derive the formula given in Problem 48 of Section 6.2 for the volume of a spherical segment.

39. Use the method of cylindrical shells to compute the volume of the torus in Problem 49 in Section 6.2. [*Suggestion:* Substitute u for $x - b$ in the integral given by the formula in Eq. (2).]

40. (a) Find the volume of the solid generated by revolving the region bounded by the curves $y = x^2$ and $y = x + 2$ around the line $x = -2$. (b) Repeat part (a), but revolve the region around the line $x = 3$.

41. Find the volume of the solid generated by revolving the circular disk $x^2 + y^2 \leq a^2$ around the vertical line $x = a$.

42. (a) Verify by differentiation that

$$\int x \sin x \, dx = \sin x - x \cos x + C.$$

(b) Find the volume of the solid obtained by rotating around the y-axis the area under $y = \sin x$ from $x = 0$ to $x = \pi$.

43. We found in Example 2 that the volume remaining after a hole of radius a is bored through the center of a sphere of radius $b > a$ is

$$V = \tfrac{4}{3}\pi(b^2 - a^2)^{3/2}.$$

(a) Express the volume V in this formula *without* use of the hole radius a; use instead the hole height h. [*Suggestion:* Use the right triangle in Fig. 6.3.8.] (b) What is remarkable about the answer to part (a)?

44. The plane region R is bounded above and on the right by the graph of $y = 25 - x^2$, on the left by the y-axis, and below by the x-axis. A paraboloid is generated by revolving R around the y-axis. Then a vertical hole of radius 3 and centered along the y-axis is bored through the paraboloid. Find the volume of the solid that remains by using (a) the method of cross sections and (b) the method of cylindrical shells.

45. The loop of the curve $y^2 = x(5 - x)^2$ bounds the region shown in Fig. 6.3.23. Find the volume of the solid obtained when this region is revolved around (a) the x-axis; (b) the y-axis; (c) the line $x = 5$.

46. The loop of the curve $y^2 = x^2(x + 3)$ bounds the region shown in Fig. 6.3.24. Find the volume of the solid obtained when this region is revolved around (a) the x-axis; (b) the y-axis; (c) the line $x = -3$. *Suggestion:* If useful, substitute $u = x + 3$ before integrating.

FIGURE 6.3.23 The region of Problem 45.

FIGURE 6.3.24 The region of Problem 46.

that lies between the curves

$$y = 1 + \frac{x^2}{5} - \frac{x^4}{500} \quad \text{and} \quad y = \frac{x^4}{10000}.$$

(a) Calculate the volume of concrete used in making this birdbath. (b) Calculate the volume of water it holds when full.

47. Figure 6.3.25 illustrates the solid concrete birdbath whose shape is obtained by revolving around the y-axis the region

FIGURE 6.3.25 The concrete birdbath of Problem 47.

6.3 Project: Design Your Own Ring!

This project deals with the custom-made gold wedding band pictured in Fig. 6.3.26. Its shape is obtained by revolving the region A shown in Fig. 6.3.27 around the vertical axis shown there. The resulting wedding band has

- Inner radius R,
- Minimum thickness T, and
- Width W.

FIGURE 6.3.26 Wedding band.

FIGURE 6.3.27 Cross section of the wedding band.

The curved boundary of the region A is an arc of a circle whose center lies on the axis of revolution. For a typical wedding band, R might be anywhere from 6 to 12 mm, T might be 0.5 to 1.5 mm, and W might be 4 to 10 mm.

If a customer asks the price of a wedding band with given dimensions R, T, and W, the jeweler must first calculate the volume of the desired band to determine how much gold will be required to make it. Use the methods of this section to show that the volume V is given by the formula

$$V = \frac{\pi W}{6}(W^2 + 12RT + 6T^2). \quad (5)$$

If these dimensions are measured in millimeters, then V is given in cubic millimeters. (There are 1000 mm³ in 1 cm³.)

Suppose that the jeweler plans to charge the customer $1000 per *troy ounce* of alloy (90% gold, 10% silver) used to make the ring. (The profit on the sale, covering the jeweler's time and overhead in making the ring, is fairly substantial because the price of gold is generally under $400/oz, and that of silver under $6/oz.) The inner radius R of the wedding band is determined by the measurement of the customer's finger (in millimeters; there are exactly 25.4 mm per inch). Suppose that the jeweler makes all wedding bands with $T = 1$ (mm). Then, for a given acceptable cost C (in dollars), the customer wants to know the maximum width W of the wedding band he or she can afford.

Investigation Measure your own ring finger to determine R (you can measure its circumference C with a piece of string and then divide by 2π). Then choose a cost figure C in the $100 to $500 price range. Use Eq. (5) with $T = 1$ to find the width W of a band that costs C dollars (at $1000/oz). You will need to know that the density of the gold-silver alloy is 18.4 g/cm³ and that 1 lb contains 12 troy ounces and 453.59 g. Use a graphics calculator or a calculator with a $\boxed{\text{SOLVE}}$ key to solve the resulting cubic equation in W.

6.4 ARC LENGTH AND SURFACE AREA OF REVOLUTION

If you plan to hike the Appalachian Trail, you will need to know the length of this curved path so you'll know how much equipment to take. Here we investigate how to find the length of a curved path and the closely related idea of finding the surface area of a curved surface.

A **smooth arc** is the graph of a smooth function defined on a closed interval; a **smooth function** f on $[a, b]$ is a function whose derivative f' is continuous on $[a, b]$. The continuity of f' rules out the possibility of corner points on the graph of f, points where the direction of the tangent line changes abruptly. The graphs of $f(x) = |x|$ and $g(x) = x^{2/3}$ are shown in Fig. 6.4.1; neither is smooth because each has a corner point at the origin.

FIGURE 6.4.1 Graphs that have corner points.

The Length of a Curve

To investigate the length of a smooth arc, we begin with the length of a straight line segment, which is simply the distance between its endpoints. Then, given a smooth arc C, we pose the following question: If C were a thin wire and we straightened it without stretching it, how long would the resulting straight wire be? The answer is what we call the *length* of C.

To approximate the length s of the smooth arc C, we can inscribe in C a polygonal arc—one made up of straight line segments—and then calculate the length of this polygonal arc. We proceed in the following way, under the assumption that C is the graph of a smooth function f defined on the closed interval $[a, b]$. Consider a partition of $[a, b]$ into n subintervals, all with the same length Δx. Let P_i denote the point $(x_i, f(x_i))$ on the arc C corresponding to the ith subdivision point x_i. Our polygonal arc "inscribed in C" is then the union of the line segments $P_0 P_1$, $P_1 P_2$, $P_2 P_3, \ldots, P_{n-1} P_n$. So an approximation to the length s of C is

$$s \approx \sum_{i=1}^{n} |P_{i-1} P_i|, \tag{1}$$

the sum of the lengths of these line segments (Fig. 6.4.2). Our plan is to take the limit of this sum as $n \to \infty$: We want to evaluate

$$s = \lim_{n \to \infty} \sum_{i=1}^{n} |P_{i-1} P_i|.$$

The length of the typical line segment $P_{i-1} P_i$ is

$$|P_{i-1} P_i| = [(x_i - x_{i-1})^2 + (f(x_i) - f(x_{i-1}))^2]^{1/2}.$$

FIGURE 6.4.2 A polygonal arc inscribed in the smooth curve C.

Arc Length and Surface Area of Revolution **SECTION 6.4** 397

We apply the mean value theorem to the function f on the interval $[x_{i-1}, x_i]$ and thereby conclude the existence of a point $x_i^\star$ in this interval such that

$$f(x_i) - f(x_{i-1}) = f'(x_i^\star) \cdot (x_i - x_{i-1}).$$

Hence

$$|P_{i-1}P_i| = \left[1 + \left(\frac{f(x_i) - f(x_{i-1})}{x_i - x_{i-1}}\right)^2\right]^{1/2} \cdot (x_i - x_{i-1})$$

$$= \sqrt{1 + [f'(x_i^\star)]^2}\, \Delta x,$$

where $\Delta x = x_i - x_{i-1}$.

We next substitute this expression for $|P_{i-1}P_i|$ into Eq. (1) and get the approximation

$$s \approx \sum_{i=1}^{n} \sqrt{1 + [f'(x_i^\star)]^2}\, \Delta x.$$

This sum is a Riemann sum for the function $\sqrt{1 + [f'(x)]^2}$ on $[a, b]$, and therefore—because f' is continuous—such sums approach the integral

$$\int_a^b \sqrt{1 + [f'(x)]^2}\, dx$$

as $\Delta x \to 0$. But our approximation ought to approach, as well, the actual length s as $\Delta x \to 0$. On this basis we *define* the **length** s of the smooth arc C to be

$$s = \int_a^b \sqrt{1 + [f'(x)]^2}\, dx = \int_a^b \sqrt{1 + \left(\frac{dy}{dx}\right)^2}\, dx. \tag{2}$$

EXAMPLE 1 Find the length of the so-called semicubical parabola (it's not really a parabola) $y = x^{3/2}$ on $[0, 5]$ (Fig. 6.4.3).

Solution We first compute the integrand in Eq. (2):

$$\sqrt{1 + \left(\frac{dy}{dx}\right)^2} = \sqrt{1 + \left(\tfrac{3}{2}x^{1/2}\right)^2} = \sqrt{1 + \tfrac{9}{4}x} = \tfrac{1}{2}(4 + 9x)^{1/2}.$$

Hence the length of the arc $y = x^{3/2}$ over the interval $[0, 5]$ is

$$s = \int_0^5 \tfrac{1}{2}(4 + 9x)^{1/2}\, dx = \left[\tfrac{1}{27}(4 + 9x)^{3/2}\right]_0^5 = \tfrac{335}{27} \approx 12.41.$$

FIGURE 6.4.3 The semicubical parabola of Example 1.

As a plausibility check, the endpoints of the arc are $(0, 0)$ and $(5, 5\sqrt{5})$, so the straight line segment connecting these points has length $5\sqrt{6} \approx 12.25$. This is, as it should be, somewhat less than the calculated length of the arc. ◆

EXAMPLE 2 A manufacturer needs to make corrugated metal sheets 36 in. wide with cross sections in the shape of the curve

$$y = \tfrac{1}{2}\sin \pi x, \quad 0 \leqq x \leqq 36$$

(Fig. 6.4.4). How wide must the original flat sheets be for the manufacturer to produce these corrugated sheets?

FIGURE 6.4.4 The corrugated metal sheet in the shape of $y = \tfrac{1}{2}\sin \pi x$ (Example 2).

Solution If
$$f(x) = \tfrac{1}{2}\sin \pi x, \quad \text{then} \quad f'(x) = \tfrac{1}{2}\pi \cos \pi x.$$

Hence Eq. (2) yields the arc length of the graph of f over $[0, 36]$:

$$s = \int_0^{36} \sqrt{1 + \left(\tfrac{1}{2}\pi\right)^2 \cos^2 \pi x} \, dx = 36 \int_0^1 \sqrt{1 + \left(\tfrac{1}{2}\pi\right)^2 \cos^2 \pi x} \, dx.$$

These integrals cannot be evaluated in terms of elementary functions. Because of this, we cannot apply the fundamental theorem of calculus. So we estimate their values with the aid of Simpson's approximation (Section 5.9). Both with $n = 6$ and with $n = 12$ subintervals we find that

$$\int_0^1 \sqrt{1 + \left(\tfrac{1}{2}\pi\right)^2 \cos^2 \pi x} \, dx \approx 1.46$$

inches. Therefore the manufacturer should use flat sheets of approximate width $36 \cdot 1.46 \approx 52.6$ in. ◆

Arc Length by Integration with Respect to y

In the case of a smooth arc given as a graph $x = g(y)$ for y in $[c, d]$, a similar discussion beginning with a subdivision of $[c, d]$ leads to the formula

$$s = \int_c^d \sqrt{1 + [g'(y)]^2} \, dy = \int_c^d \sqrt{1 + \left(\frac{dx}{dy}\right)^2} \, dy \quad (3)$$

for its length. We can compute the length of a more general curve, such as a circle, by dividing it into a finite number of smooth arcs and then applying to each of these arcs whichever of Eqs. (2) and (3) is required.

EXAMPLE 3 Find the length s of the curve (Fig. 6.4.5)

$$x = \frac{1}{6}y^3 + \frac{1}{2y}, \quad 1 \leq y \leq 2.$$

Solution Here y is the natural independent variable, so we use the arc-length formula in Eq. (3). First we calculate

$$1 + \left(\frac{dx}{dy}\right)^2 = 1 + \left(\frac{1}{2}y^2 - \frac{1}{2y^2}\right)^2 = 1 + \frac{1}{4}y^4 - \frac{1}{2} + \frac{1}{4y^4}$$

$$= \frac{1}{4}y^4 + \frac{1}{2} + \frac{1}{4y^4} = \left(\frac{1}{2}y^2 + \frac{1}{2y^2}\right)^2.$$

FIGURE 6.4.5 The curve of Example 3 (although we can calculate its arc length without even visualizing it).

Thus we can "get out from under the radical" in Eq. (3):

$$s = \int_c^d \sqrt{1 + \left(\frac{dx}{dy}\right)^2} \, dy = \int_1^2 \left(\frac{1}{2}y^2 + \frac{1}{2y^2}\right) dy$$

$$= \left[\frac{1}{6}y^3 - \frac{1}{2y}\right]_1^2 = \frac{17}{12}. \quad ◆$$

A Symbolic Device

There is a convenient symbolic device that we can employ to remember both Eqs. (2) and (3) simultaneously. We think of two nearby points $P(x, y)$ and $Q(x + dx, y + dy)$ on the smooth arc C and denote by ds the length of the arc that joins P and Q. Imagine that P and Q are so close together that ds is, for all practical purposes, equal to the length of the straight line segment PQ. Then the Pythagorean theorem applied to the small right triangle in Fig. 6.4.6 gives

$$ds = \sqrt{(dx)^2 + (dy)^2} \tag{4}$$

$$= \sqrt{1 + \left(\frac{dy}{dx}\right)^2}\, dx \tag{4'}$$

$$= \sqrt{1 + \left(\frac{dx}{dy}\right)^2}\, dy. \tag{4''}$$

FIGURE 6.4.6 Heuristic development of the arc-length formula.

Thinking of the entire length s of C as the sum of small pieces such as ds, we write

$$s = \int_{\star}^{\star\star} ds. \tag{5}$$

Then formal (symbolic) substitution of the expressions in Eqs. (4') and (4'') for ds in Eq. (5) yields Eqs. (2) and (3); only the limits of integration remain to be determined.

Cones and Conical Frusta

A **surface of revolution** is a surface obtained by revolving an arc or curve around an axis that lies in the same plane as the arc. The surface of a cylinder or of a sphere and the curved surface of a cone are important as examples of surfaces of revolution.

Our basic approach to finding the area of such a surface is this: First we inscribe a polygonal arc in the curve to be revolved. We then regard the area of the surface generated by revolving the polygonal arc to be an approximation to the surface generated by revolving the original curve. Because a surface generated by revolving a polygonal arc around an axis consists of frusta (sections) of cones, we can calculate its area in a reasonably simple way.

This approach to surface area originated with Archimedes. For example, he used this method to establish the formula $A = 4\pi r^2$ for the surface area of a sphere of radius r.

We will need the formula

$$A = 2\pi \bar{r} L \tag{6}$$

for the curved surface area of a conical frustum with average radius $\bar{r} = \frac{1}{2}(r_1 + r_2)$ and *slant height* L (Fig. 6.4.7). Equation (6) follows from the formula

$$A = \pi r L \tag{7}$$

FIGURE 6.4.7 A frustum of a cone; the slant height is L.

for the area of a conical surface with base radius r and slant height L (Fig. 6.4.8). It is easy to derive Eq. (7) by "unrolling" the conical surface onto a sector of a circle

FIGURE 6.4.8 Surface area of a cone: Cut along L, then unroll the cone onto the circular sector.

of radius L, because the area of this sector is

$$A = \frac{2\pi r}{2\pi L} \cdot \pi L^2 = \pi r L.$$

To derive Eq. (6) from Eq. (7), we think of the frustum as the lower section of a cone with slant height $L_2 = L + L_1$ (Fig. 6.4.9). Then subtracting the area of the upper conical section from that of the entire cone gives

$$A = \pi r_2 L_2 - \pi r_1 L_1 = \pi r_2 (L + L_1) - \pi r_1 L_1 = \pi (r_2 - r_1) L_1 + \pi r_2 L$$

for the area of the frustum. But the similar right triangles in Fig. 6.4.9 yield the proportion

$$\frac{r_1}{L_1} = \frac{r_2}{L_2} = \frac{r_2}{L + L_1},$$

from which we find that $(r_2 - r_1) L_1 = r_1 L$. Hence the area of the frustum is

$$A = \pi r_1 L + \pi r_2 L = 2\pi \bar{r} L,$$

where $\bar{r} = \frac{1}{2}(r_1 + r_2)$. So we have verified Eq. (6).

FIGURE 6.4.9 Derivation of Eq. (6).

Surface Area of Revolution

Suppose that the surface S has area A and is generated by revolving around the x-axis the smooth arc $y = f(x)$, $a \leq x \leq b$; suppose also that $f(x)$ is never negative on $[a, b]$. To approximate A we begin with a division of $[a, b]$ into n subintervals, each of length Δx. As in our discussion of arc length leading to Eq. (2), let P_i denote the point $(x_i, f(x_i))$ on the arc. Then, as before, the line segment $P_{i-1} P_i$ has length

$$L_i = |P_{i-1} P_i| = \sqrt{1 + [f'(x_i^\star)]^2} \, \Delta x$$

for some point $x_i^\star$ in the ith subinterval $[x_{i-1}, x_i]$.

The conical frustum obtained by revolving the segment $P_{i-1} P_i$ around the x-axis has slant height L_i and, as shown in Fig. 6.4.10, average radius

$$\bar{r}_i = \tfrac{1}{2}[f(x_{i-1}) + f(x_i)].$$

Because $\bar{r}_i$ lies between the values $f(x_{i-1})$ and $f(x_i)$, the intermediate value property of continuous functions (Section 2.4) yields a point $x_i^{\star\star}$ in $[x_{i-1}, x_i]$ such that $\bar{r}_i = f(x_i^{\star\star})$. By Eq. (6), the area of this conical frustum is, therefore,

$$2\pi \bar{r}_i L_i = 2\pi f(x_i^{\star\star}) \sqrt{1 + [f'(x_i^\star)]^2} \, \Delta x.$$

FIGURE 6.4.10 Approximating a surface area of revolution by the surface of a frustum of a cone.

We add the areas of these conical frusta for $i = 1, 2, 3, \ldots, n$. This gives the approximation

$$A \approx \sum_{i=1}^{n} 2\pi f(x_i^{**})\sqrt{1 + [f'(x_i^*)]^2}\, \Delta x.$$

If x_i^* and x_i^{**} were the *same* point of the ith subinterval $[x_{i-1}, x_i]$, then this approximation would be a Riemann sum for the integral

$$\int_a^b 2\pi f(x)\sqrt{1 + [f'(x)]^2}\, dx.$$

Even though the numbers x_i^* and x_i^{**} are generally not equal, it still follows (from a result in Appendix G) that our approximation approaches the integral above as $\Delta x \to 0$. Intuitively, this is easy to believe; after all, as $\Delta x \to 0$, the difference between x_i^* and x_i^{**} also approaches zero.

We therefore *define* the **area** A of the surface generated by revolving around the x-axis the smooth arc $y = f(x)$, $a \leq x \leq b$, by the formula

$$A = \int_a^b 2\pi f(x)\sqrt{1 + [f'(x)]^2}\, dx. \tag{8}$$

FIGURE 6.4.11 The tiny arc ds generates a ribbon with circumference $2\pi y$ when it is revolved around the x-axis.

If we write y for $f(x)$ and ds for $\sqrt{1 + (dy/dx)^2}\, dx$, as in Eq. (4'), then we can abbreviate Eq. (8) as

$$A = \int_a^b 2\pi y\, ds \quad (x\text{-axis}). \tag{9}$$

This abbreviated formula is conveniently remembered by thinking of $dA = 2\pi y\, ds$ as the area of the narrow frustum obtained by revolving the tiny arc ds around the x-axis in a circle of radius y (Fig. 6.4.11).

EXAMPLE 4 Figure 6.4.12 shows the horn-shaped surface generated by revolving the curve $y = x^3$, $0 \leq x \leq 2$, around the x-axis. Find its surface area of revolution.

Solution Substituting $y = x^3$ and

$$ds = \sqrt{1 + [y'(x)]^2}\, dx = \sqrt{1 + 9x^4}\, dx$$

in Eq. (9), we get

$$A = \int_0^2 2\pi x^3 (1 + 9x^4)^{1/2}\, dx \qquad (\text{let } u = 1 + 9x^4)$$

$$= \left[\frac{\pi}{27}(1 + 9x^4)^{3/2}\right]_0^2 = \frac{\pi}{27}\left(145^{3/2} - 1\right) \approx 203.04. \qquad \blacklozenge$$

FIGURE 6.4.12 The "horn" generated by revolving the curve $y = x^3$, $0 \leq x \leq 2$, around the x-axis.

If the smooth arc being revolved around the x-axis is given instead by $x = g(y)$, $c \leq y \leq d$, then an approximation based on a subdivision of $[c, d]$ leads to the area formula

$$A = \int_c^d 2\pi y\sqrt{1 + [g'(y)]^2}\, dy. \tag{10}$$

We can obtain Eq. (10) by making the formula substitution $ds = \sqrt{1 + (dx/dy)^2}\, dy$ of Eq. (4'') into the abbreviated formula in Eq. (9) for surface area of revolution and then replacing a and b with the correct limits of integration.

Revolution Around the y-Axis

FIGURE 6.4.13 The tiny arc ds generates a ribbon with circumference $2\pi x$ when it is revolved around the y-axis.

Now let us consider the surface generated by revolving a smooth arc around the y-axis rather than around the x-axis In Fig. 6.4.13 we see that the average radius of the narrow frustum obtained by revolving the tiny arc ds is now x instead of y. This suggests the abbreviated formula

$$A = \int_a^b 2\pi x \, ds \quad (y\text{-axis}) \tag{11}$$

for a surface area of revolution around the y-axis. If the smooth arc is given by $y = f(x)$, $a \leq x \leq b$, then the symbolic substitution $ds = \sqrt{1 + (dy/dx)^2} \, dx$ gives

$$A = \int_a^b 2\pi x \sqrt{1 + [f'(x)]^2} \, dx. \tag{12}$$

But if the smooth arc is presented in the form $x = g(y)$, $c \leq y \leq d$, then the symbolic substitution of $ds = \sqrt{1 + (dx/dy)^2} \, dy$ into Eq. (11) gives

$$A = \int_c^d 2\pi g(y) \sqrt{1 + [g'(y)]^2} \, dy. \tag{13}$$

Equations (12) and (13) may be verified by using approximations similar to the one leading to Eq. (8).

EXAMPLE 5 Find the area of the paraboloid shown in Fig. 6.4.14, which is obtained by revolving the parabolic arc $y = x^2$, $0 \leq x \leq \sqrt{2}$, around the y-axis.

Solution Following the suggestion that precedes the example, we get

$$A = \int_*^{**} 2\pi x \, ds = \int_a^b 2\pi x \sqrt{1 + \left(\frac{dy}{dx}\right)^2} \, dx$$

$$= \int_0^{\sqrt{2}} 2\pi x \sqrt{1 + (2x)^2} \, dx$$

$$= \int_0^{\sqrt{2}} \frac{\pi}{4}(1 + 4x^2)^{1/2} \cdot 8x \, dx = \left[\frac{\pi}{6}(1 + 4x^2)^{3/2}\right]_0^{\sqrt{2}} = \frac{13}{3}\pi. \blacklozenge$$

FIGURE 6.4.14 The paraboloid of Example 5.

SURFACE AREA SUMMARY

In conclusion, we have *four* formulas for areas of surfaces of revolution, summarized in the table in Fig. 6.4.15. Which of these formulas is appropriate for computing the area of a given surface depends on two factors:

1. Whether the smooth arc that generates the surface is presented in the form $y = f(x)$ or in the form $x = g(y)$, and
2. Whether this arc is to be revolved around the x-axis or around the y-axis.

	Axis of revolution	
Description of curve C	x-axis	y-axis
$y = f(x)$, $a \leq x \leq b$	$\int_a^b 2\pi f(x)\sqrt{1 + [f'(x)]^2}\, dx$ \quad (8)	$\int_a^b 2\pi x\sqrt{1 + [f'(x)]^2}\, dx$ \quad (12)
$x = g(y)$, $c \leq y \leq d$	$\int_c^d 2\pi y\sqrt{1 + [g'(y)]^2}\, dy$ \quad (10)	$\int_c^d 2\pi g(y)\sqrt{1 + [g'(y)]^2}\, dy$ \quad (13)

FIGURE 6.4.15 Area formulas for surfaces of revolution.

Memorizing the four formulas in the table is unnecessary. We suggest that you instead remember the abbreviated formulas in Eqs. (9) and (11) in conjunction with Figs. 6.4.11 and 6.4.13 and make either the substitution

$$y = f(x), \qquad ds = \sqrt{1 + \left(\frac{dy}{dx}\right)^2}\, dx$$

or the substitution

$$x = g(y), \qquad ds = \sqrt{1 + \left(\frac{dx}{dy}\right)^2}\, dy,$$

depending on whether the smooth arc is presented as a function of x or as a function of y. It may also be helpful to note that all four of these surface-area formulas have the form

$$A = \int_*^{**} 2\pi r\, ds, \qquad (14)$$

where r denotes the radius of the circle around which the arc length element ds is revolved.

As in earlier sections, we again caution you to identify the independent variable by examining the differential and to express every dependent variable in terms of the independent variable before you antidifferentiate. That is, either express everything, including ds, in terms of x (and dx) or everything in terms of y (and dy).

The decision of which abbreviated formula—Eq. (9) or Eq. (11)—to use is determined by the axis of revolution. In contrast, the decision of whether the variable of integration should be x or y is made by the way in which the smooth arc is given: as a function of x or as a function of y. In some problems, either x or y may be used as the variable of integration, but the integral is usually much simpler to evaluate if you make the correct choice. Experience is very helpful here. Right now, try Example 5 with independent variable y.

6.4 TRUE/FALSE STUDY GUIDE

6.4 CONCEPTS: QUESTIONS AND DISCUSSION

Frequently a concept is enriched when it is viewed from different perspectives.

1. Show that the arc length method of this section gives

$$C = 8 \int_0^{1/\sqrt{2}} \frac{1}{\sqrt{1-x^2}}\, dx$$

for the circumference of the unit circle $x^2 + y^2 = 1$. In Section 6.8 we will see that

$$D_x \sin^{-1} x = \frac{1}{\sqrt{1-x^2}},$$

where $y = \sin^{-1} x$ denotes the angle in $[-\pi/2, \pi/2]$ such that $\sin y = x$. Conclude that

$$C = 8\left[\sin^{-1} x\right]_0^{1/\sqrt{2}} = 8\left(\frac{\pi}{4} - 0\right) = 2\pi.$$

2. Suppose that P_n denotes the perimeter of a regular polygon with n sides inscribed in the unit circle. Assume that the limit $P = \lim_{n\to\infty} P_n$ exists (it does). Can you conclude from the definition of the integral as a limit of Riemann sums that $P = C$ (the circumference of the circle of Question 1)?

3. Can you *prove* that the limit $P = \lim_{n\to\infty} P_n$ in Question 2 exists? Can you show that if Q_m is the perimeter of a regular polygon with m sides

6.4 PROBLEMS

In Problems 1 through 10, set up and simplify the integral that gives the length of the given smooth arc. Do not evaluate the integral.

1. $y = x^2$, $0 \le x \le 1$
2. $y = x^{5/2}$, $1 \le x \le 3$
3. $y = 2x^3 - 3x^2$, $0 \le x \le 2$
4. $y = x^{4/3}$, $-1 \le x \le 1$
5. $y = 1 - x^2$, $0 \le x \le 100$
6. $x = 4y - y^2$, $0 \le y \le 1$
7. $x = y^4$, $-1 \le y \le 2$
8. $x^2 = y$, $1 \le y \le 4$
9. $xy = 1$, $1 \le x \le 2$
10. $x^2 + y^2 = 4$, $0 \le x \le 2$

In Problems 11 through 20, set up and simplify the integral that gives the surface area of revolution generated by rotation of the given smooth arc around the given axis. Do not evaluate the integral.

11. $y = x^2$, $0 \le x \le 4$; the x-axis
12. $y = x^2$, $0 \le x \le 4$; the y-axis
13. $y = x - x^2$, $0 \le x \le 1$; the x-axis
14. $y = x^2$, $0 \le x \le 1$; the line $y = 4$
15. $y = x^2$, $0 \le x \le 1$; the line $x = 2$
16. $y = x - x^3$, $0 \le x \le 1$; the x-axis
17. $y = \sqrt{x}$, $1 \le x \le 4$; the x-axis
18. $y = \sqrt{x}$, $1 \le x \le 4$; the y-axis
19. $y = x^{3/2}$, $1 \le x \le 4$; the line $x = -1$
20. $y = x^{5/2}$, $1 \le x \le 4$; the line $y = -2$

Find the lengths of the smooth arcs in Problems 21 through 28.

21. $y = \frac{2}{3}(x^2 + 1)^{3/2}$ from $x = 0$ to $x = 2$
22. $x = \frac{2}{3}(y - 1)^{3/2}$ from $y = 1$ to $y = 5$
23. $y = \frac{1}{6}x^3 + \frac{1}{2x}$ from $x = 1$ to $x = 3$
24. $x = \frac{1}{8}y^4 + \frac{1}{4y^2}$ from $y = 1$ to $y = 2$
25. $8x^2y - 2x^6 = 1$ from $\left(1, \frac{3}{8}\right)$ to $\left(2, \frac{129}{32}\right)$
26. $12xy - 4y^4 = 3$ from $\left(\frac{7}{12}, 1\right)$ to $\left(\frac{67}{24}, 2\right)$
27. $y^3 = 8x^2$ from $(1, 2)$ to $(8, 8)$
28. $(y - 3)^2 = 4(x + 2)^3$ from $(-1, 5)$ to $(2, 19)$

In Problems 29 through 35, find the area of the surface of revolution generated by revolving the given curve around the indicated axis.

29. $y = \sqrt{x}$, $0 \le x \le 1$; the x-axis
30. $y = x^3$, $1 \le x \le 2$; the x-axis
31. $y = \frac{1}{5}x^5 + \frac{1}{12x^3}$, $1 \le x \le 2$; the y-axis
32. $x = \frac{1}{8}y^4 + \frac{1}{4y^2}$, $1 \le y \le 2$; the x-axis
33. $y^3 = 3x$, $0 \le x \le 9$; the y-axis
34. $y = \frac{2}{3}x^{3/2}$, $1 \le x \le 2$; the y-axis (*Suggestion:* Make the substitution $u = 1 + x$.)
35. $y = (2x - x^2)^{1/2}$, $0 \le x \le 2$; the x-axis
36. Prove that the length of one arch of the sine curve $y = \sin x$ is equal to half the circumference of the ellipse $2x^2 + y^2 = 2$. [*Suggestion:* Substitute $x = \cos\theta$ into the arc length integral for the ellipse.]
37. Use Simpson's approximation with $n = 6$ subintervals to estimate the length of the sine arch of Problem 36.
38. Use Simpson's approximation with $n = 10$ subintervals to estimate the length of the parabola $y = x^2$ from $x = 0$ to $x = 1$.
39. Verify Eq. (6) for the curved surface area of a conical frustum. Think of the frustum as being generated by revolving around the y-axis the line segment from $(r_1, 0)$ to (r_2, h).
40. By considering a sphere of radius r to be a surface of revolution, derive the formula $A = 4\pi r^2$ for its surface area.
41. Find the total length of the *astroid* shown in Fig. 6.4.16. The equation of its graph is $x^{2/3} + y^{2/3} = 1$.

FIGURE 6.4.16 The astroid of Problem 41.

42. Find the area of the surface generated by revolving the astroid of Problem 41 around the y-axis (Fig. 6.4.17).

FIGURE 6.4.17 The surface of Problem 42.

FIGURE 6.4.19 The loop of Problem 44.

43. Figure 6.4.18 shows a *spherical zone* of height h—it is cut out of the sphere by two parallel planes that intersect the sphere. Show that the surface area of this zone is $A = 2\pi rh$, where r is the radius of the sphere and h (the *height* of the zone) is the distance between the two planes. Note that A depends only on the height of the zone, and not (otherwise) on the specific location of the two planes relative to the sphere.

45. Figure 6.4.20 shows a cable for a suspension bridge. The cable has the shape of a parabola with equation $y = kx^2$. The suspension bridge has total span $2S$ and the height of the cable (relative to its lowest point) is H at each end. Show that the total length of the cable is given by

$$L = 2\int_0^S \sqrt{1 + \frac{4H^2}{S^4}x^2}\, dx.$$

FIGURE 6.4.20 The parabolic supporting cable of a suspension bridge.

46. Italian engineers have proposed a single-span suspension bridge across the Strait of Messina (8 km wide) between Italy and Sicily. The plans include suspension towers 380 meters high at each end. Use the integral in Problem 45 to approximate the length L of the parabolic suspension cables for this proposed bridge. Assuming that the given dimensions are exact, use Simpson's approximation to estimate the integral with sufficient accuracy to determine L to the nearest meter.

FIGURE 6.4.18 The spherical zone of Problem 43.

44. Figure 6.4.19 shows a loop of the curve $32y^2 = x^2(4-x^2)$. Find the surface area generated by revolving this loop around the x-axis.

6.5 FORCE AND WORK

The concept of *work* is introduced to measure the cumulative effect of a force in moving a body from one position to another. In the simplest case, a particle is moved along a straight line by the action of a *constant* force. The work done by such a force is defined to be the product of the force and the distance through which it acts. Thus if the constant force has magnitude F and the particle is moved through the distance d, then the work done by the force is given by

$$W = F \cdot d. \tag{1}$$

FIGURE 6.5.1 A 50-N force does 500 N·m of work in pushing a box 10 m.

EXAMPLE 1 If a constant horizontal force of 50 newtons (N) is applied to a heavy box to push it a distance of 10 m along a rough floor (Fig. 6.5.1), then the work done by the force is

$$W = 50 \cdot 10 = 500$$

newton-meters (N·m). Note the units; because of the definition of work, units of work are always products of force units and distance units. For another example, to lift a weight of 75 lb a vertical distance of 5 ft, a constant force of 75 lb must be applied. The work done by this force is

$$W = 75 \cdot 5 = 375$$

foot-pounds (ft·lb). ◆

Work Done by a Variable Force

Here we use the integral to generalize the definition of work to the case in which a particle is moved along a straight line by a *variable* force. Given a **force function** $F(x)$ defined at each point x of the straight line segment $[a, b]$, we want to define the work W done by this variable force in pushing the particle from the point $x = a$ to the point $x = b$ (Fig. 6.5.2).

FIGURE 6.5.2 A variable force pushing a particle from a to b.

We begin with the usual partition of the interval $[a, b]$ into n subintervals, all with the same length $\Delta x = (b - a)/n$. For each i ($1 \leq i \leq n$), let $x_i^\star$ be an arbitrary point of the ith subinterval $[x_{i-1}, x_i]$. The key idea is to approximate the actual work ΔW_i done by the *variable* force $F(x)$ in moving the particle from x_{i-1} to x_i by the work $F(x_i^\star) \Delta x$ (force × distance) done in moving a particle the distance Δx from x_{i-1} to x_i (Fig. 6.5.3). Thus

$$\Delta W_i \approx F(x_i^\star) \Delta x. \tag{2}$$

FIGURE 6.5.3 The *constant* force $F(x_i^\star)$ acting through the ith subinterval.

We approximate the total work W by summing from $i = 1$ to $i = n$:

$$W = \sum_{i=1}^{n} \Delta W_i \approx \sum_{i=1}^{n} F(x_i^\star) \Delta x. \tag{3}$$

But the final sum in (3) is a Riemann sum for $F(x)$ on the interval $[a, b]$, and as $n \to +\infty$ (and $\Delta x \to 0$), such sums approach the *integral* of $F(x)$ from $x = a$ to $x = b$. We therefore are motivated to *define* the **work** W done by the force $F(x)$ in moving the particle from $x = a$ to $x = b$ to be

$$W = \int_a^b F(x)\, dx. \tag{4}$$

The following heuristic way of setting up Eq. (4) is useful in obtaining integrals for work problems. Imagine that dx is so small a number that the value of $F(x)$ does not change appreciably on the tiny interval from x to $x + dx$. Then the work done by the force F in moving a particle from x to $x + dx$ should be very close to

$$dW = F(x)\, dx.$$

The natural additive property of work then implies that we could obtain the total work W by adding these tiny elements of work:

$$W = \int_\star^{\star\star} dW = \int_a^b F(x)\, dx.$$

Elastic Springs

Consider a spring whose left end is held fixed and whose right end is free to move along the x-axis. We assume that the right end is at the origin $x = 0$ when the spring has its **natural length**—that is, when the spring is in its rest position, neither compressed nor stretched by outside forces.

According to **Hooke's law** for elastic springs, the force $F(x)$ that must be exerted on the spring to hold its right end at the point x is proportional to the displacement x of the right end from its rest position. That is,

$$F(x) = kx, \tag{5}$$

where k is a positive constant. The constant k, called the **spring constant,** is a characteristic of the particular spring under study.

Figure 6.5.4 shows the arrangement of such a spring along the x-axis. The right end of the spring is held at position x on the x-axis by a force $F(x)$. The figure shows the situation for $x > 0$, so the spring is stretched. The force that the spring exerts on its right-hand end is directed to the left, so—as the figure indicates—the external force $F(x)$ must act to the right. The right is the positive direction here, so $F(x)$ must be a positive number. Because x and $F(x)$ have the same sign, k must also be positive. You can check that k is positive as well in the case $x < 0$.

FIGURE 6.5.4 The stretch x is proportional to the impressed force F.

Work in the sense of physics is different from work in the sense of physiology. At this moment the weightlifter is doing no work in the physics sense because he is holding the weight still.

EXAMPLE 2 Suppose that a spring has a natural length of 1 ft and that a force of 10 lb is required to hold it compressed to a length of 6 in. How much work is done in stretching the spring from its natural length to a total length of 2 ft?

Solution To move the free end from $x = 0$ (the natural-length position) to $x = 1$ (stretched by 1 ft), we must exert a variable force $F(x)$ determined by Hooke's law. We are given that $F = -10$ (lb) when $x = -0.5$ (ft), so Eq. (5), $F = kx$, implies that the spring constant for this spring is $k = 20$ (lb/ft). Thus $F(x) = 20x$, and so—using Eq. (4)—we find that the work done in stretching this spring in the manner given is

$$W = \int_0^1 20x \, dx = \left[10x^2\right]_0^1 = 10 \quad (\text{ft} \cdot \text{lb}).$$

◆

Work Done Against Gravity

According to Newton's law of gravitation, the force that must be exerted on a body to hold it at a distance r from the center of the earth is inversely proportional to r^2 (if $r \geqq R$, the radius of the earth). In other words, if $F(r)$ denotes the holding force, then

$$F(r) = \frac{k}{r^2} \tag{6}$$

for some positive constant k. The value of this force at the surface of the earth, where $r = R \approx 4000$ mi (about 6370 km), is called the **weight** of the body.

Given the weight $F(R)$ of a particular body, we can find the corresponding value of k by using Eq. (6):

$$k = R^2 \cdot F(R).$$

The work that must be done to lift the body vertically from the surface to a distance $R_1 > R$ from the center of the earth is then

$$W = \int_R^{R_1} \frac{k}{r^2}\, dr. \qquad (7)$$

If distance is measured in miles and force in pounds, then this integral gives the work in mile-pounds. This is a very unconventional unit of work. We shall multiply by 5280 (ft/mi) to convert any such result into foot-pounds.

EXAMPLE 3 (Satellite Launch) How much work must be done to lift a 1000-lb satellite vertically from the earth's surface to an orbit 1000 mi above the surface? See Fig. 6.5.5, and take $R = 4000$ (mi) to be the radius of the earth.

Solution Because $F = 1000$ (lb) when $r = R = 4000$ (mi), we find from Eq. (6) that

$$k = 4000^2 \cdot 1000 = 16 \times 10^9 \quad (\text{mi}^2\cdot\text{lb}).$$

Then by Eq. (7), the work done is

$$W = \int_{4000}^{5000} \frac{k}{r^2}\, dr = \left[-\frac{k}{r}\right]_{4000}^{5000}$$

$$= (16 \times 10^9) \cdot \left(\tfrac{1}{4000} - \tfrac{1}{5000}\right) = 8 \times 10^5 \quad (\text{mi}\cdot\text{lb}).$$

We multiply by 5280 (ft/mi) and write the answer as

$$4.224 \times 10^9 = 4{,}224{,}000{,}000 \quad (\text{ft}\cdot\text{lb}).$$

♦

We can instead express the answer to Example 3 in terms of the power that the launch rocket must provide. **Power** is the rate at which work is done. For instance, 1 **horsepower** (hp) is defined to be 33,000 ft·lb/min. If the ascent to orbit takes 15 min and if only 2% of the power generated by the rocket is effective in lifting the satellite (the rest is used to lift the rocket and its fuel), we can convert the answer in Example 3 to horsepower. The *average* power that the rocket engine must produce during the 15-min ascent is

$$P = \frac{50 \cdot (4.224 \times 10^9)}{15 \cdot 33{,}000} \approx 427{,}000 \quad (\text{hp}).$$

The factor of 50 in the numerator comes from the 2% "efficiency" of the rocket: The total power must be multiplied by $1/(0.02) = 50$.

Work Done in Filling a Tank

Examples 2 and 3 are applications of Eq. (4) for calculating the work done by a variable force in moving a particle a certain distance. Another common type of force-work problem involves the summation of work done by constant forces that act through different distances. For example, consider the problem of pumping a fluid from ground level—where we take $y = 0$—up into an aboveground tank (Fig. 6.5.6).

It is convenient to think of the tank as being filled in thin, horizontal layers of fluid, each lifted from its ground to its final position in the tank. No matter how the fluid actually behaves as the tank is filled, this simple way of thinking about the process gives us a way to compute the work done in the filling process. But when we think of filling the tank in this way, we must allow for the fact that different layers of fluid are lifted different distances to reach their final positions in the tank.

Suppose that the bottom of the tank is at height $y = a$ and that its top is at height $y = b > a$. Let $A(y)$ be the cross-sectional area of the tank at height y. Consider a partition of $[a, b]$ into n subintervals, all with the same length Δy. Then the volume of the horizontal slice (Fig. 6.5.7) of the tank that corresponds to the ith subinterval $[y_{i-1}, y_i]$ is

$$\Delta V_i = \int_{y_{i-1}}^{y_i} A(y)\, dy = A(y_i^\star)\, \Delta y$$

for some number $y_i^\star$ in $[y_{i-1}, y_i]$; this is a consequence of the average value theorem for integrals (Section 5.6). If ρ is the density of the fluid (in pounds per cubic foot, for example), then the force required to lift this slice from the ground to its final position in the tank is simply the (constant) weight of the slice:

$$F_i = \rho\, \Delta V_i = \rho A(y_i^\star)\, \Delta y.$$

But what about the distance through which this force must act? The fluid in question is lifted from ground level to the level of the subinterval $[y_{i-1}, y_i]$, so every particle of the fluid is lifted at least the distance y_{i-1} and at most the distance y_i (remember, the fluid begins its journey at ground level, where $y = 0$). Hence the work ΔW_i needed to lift this ith slice of fluid satisfies the inequalities

$$F_i y_{i-1} \leqq \Delta W_i \leqq F_i y_i;$$

that is,

$$\rho y_{i-1} A(y_i^\star)\, \Delta y \leqq \Delta W_i \leqq \rho y_i A(y_i^\star)\, \Delta y.$$

Now we add these inequalities for $i = 1, 2, 3, \ldots, n$ and find thereby that the total work $W = \sum \Delta W_i$ satisfies the inequalities

$$\sum_{i=1}^{n} \rho y_{i-1} A(y_i^\star)\, \Delta y \leqq W \leqq \sum_{i-1}^{n} \rho y_i A(y_i^\star)\, \Delta y.$$

If the three points y_{i-1}, y_i, and $y_i^\star$ of $[y_{i-1}, y_i]$ were the same, then both the last two sums would be Riemann sums for the function $f(y) = \rho y A(y)$ on $[a, b]$. Although the three points are not the same, it still follows—from a result stated in Appendix G—that both sums approach

$$\int_a^b \rho y A(y)\, dy \quad \text{as} \quad \Delta y \to 0.$$

The squeeze law of limits therefore gives the formula

$$W = \int_a^b \rho y A(y)\, dy. \tag{8}$$

This is the work W done in pumping fluid of density ρ from the ground into a tank that has horizontal cross-sectional area $A(y)$ and is located between heights $y = a$ and $y = b$ above the ground.

A quick heuristic way to set up Eq. (8), and many variants of it, is to think of a thin, horizontal slice of fluid with volume $dV = A(y)\, dy$ and weight $\rho\, dV = \rho A(y)\, dy$. The work required to lift this slice a distance y is

$$dW = y \cdot \rho\, dV = \rho y A(y)\, dy,$$

so the total work required to fill the tank is

$$W = \int_\star^{\star\star} dW = \int_a^b \rho y A(y)\, dy,$$

because the horizontal slices lie between $y = a$ and $y = b$.

EXAMPLE 4 Suppose that it took 20 yr to construct the great pyramid of Khufu at Gizeh, Egypt. This pyramid is 500 ft high and has a square base with edge length 750 ft. Suppose also that the pyramid is made of rock with density $\rho = 120$ lb/ft^3. Finally, suppose that each laborer did 160 ft·lb/h of work in lifting rocks from ground level to their final position in the pyramid and worked 12 h daily for 330 days/yr. How many laborers would have been required to construct the pyramid?

The great pyramid of Khufu.

FIGURE 6.5.8 Vertical cross section of Khufu's pyramid.

Solution We assume a constant labor force throughout the 20-yr construction period. We think of the pyramid as being made up of thin, horizontal slabs of rock, each slab lifted (just like a slice of liquid) from ground level to its ultimate height. Hence we can use Eq. (8) to compute the work W required.

Figure 6.5.8 shows a vertical cross section of the pyramid. The horizontal cross section at height y is a square with edge length s. We see from the similar triangles in Fig. 6.5.8 that

$$\frac{s}{750} = \frac{500 - y}{500}, \quad \text{so} \quad s = \frac{3}{2}(500 - y).$$

Hence the cross-sectional area at height y is

$$A(y) = \tfrac{9}{4}(500 - y)^2.$$

Equation (8) therefore gives

$$W = \int_0^{500} 120 \cdot y \cdot \tfrac{9}{4}(500 - y)^2 \, dy$$

$$= 270 \int_0^{500} (250{,}000 y - 1000 y^2 + y^3) \, dy$$

$$= 270 \left[125{,}000 y^2 - \tfrac{1000}{3} y^3 + \tfrac{1}{4} y^4 \right]_0^{500},$$

so $W \approx 1.406 \times 10^{12}$ ft·lb.

Because each laborer does

$$160 \cdot 12 \cdot 330 \cdot 20 \approx 1.267 \times 10^7 \quad \text{ft·lb}$$

of work, the construction of the pyramid would—under our assumptions—have required

$$\frac{1.406 \times 10^{12}}{1.267 \times 10^7} \approx 111{,}000$$

laborers. ◆

Emptying a Tank

Suppose now that the tank shown in Fig. 6.5.9 is already filled with a liquid of density ρ lb/ft^3, and we want to pump all this liquid from the tank up to the level $y = h$ above the top of the tank. We imagine a thin, horizontal slice of liquid at height y. If its

FIGURE 6.5.9 Pumping liquid from a tank to a higher level.

thickness is dy, then its volume is $dV = A(y)\,dy$, so its weight is $\rho\,dV = \rho A(y)\,dy$. This slice must be lifted the distance $h - y$, so the work done to lift the slice is

$$dW = (h - y)\rho\,dV = \rho(h - y)A(y)\,dy.$$

Hence the total amount of work done on all the liquid originally in the tank is

$$W = \int_a^b \rho(h - y)A(y)\,dy. \tag{9}$$

Problem 14 asks you to use Riemann sums to set up this integral.

EXAMPLE 5 A cylindrical tank of radius 3 ft and length 10 ft is lying on its side on horizontal ground. If this tank initially is full of gasoline weighing 40 lb/ft^3, how much work is done in pumping all this gasoline to a point 5 ft above the top of the tank?

Solution Figure 6.5.10 shows an end view of the tank. To exploit its circular symmetry, we choose $y = 0$ at the *center* of the circular vertical section, so the tank lies between $y = -3$ and $y = 3$. A horizontal cross section of the tank that meets the y-axis is a rectangle of length 10 ft and width w. From the right triangle in Fig. 6.5.10, we see that

$$\tfrac{1}{2}w = \sqrt{9 - y^2},$$

FIGURE 6.5.10 End view of the cylindrical tank of Example 5.

so the area of this cross section is

$$A(y) = 10w = 20\sqrt{9 - y^2}.$$

This cross section must be lifted from its initial position y to the final position $5+3 = 8$, so it is to be lifted the distance $8 - y$. Thus Eq. (9) with $\rho = 40$, $a = -3$, and $b = 3$ yields

$$W = \int_{-3}^{3} 40 \cdot (8 - y) \cdot 20\sqrt{9 - y^2}\,dy$$

$$= 6400 \int_{-3}^{3} \sqrt{9 - y^2}\,dy - 800 \int_{-3}^{3} y\sqrt{9 - y^2}\,dy.$$

We attack the two integrals separately. First,

$$\int_{-3}^{3} y\sqrt{9 - y^2}\,dy = \left[-\tfrac{1}{3}(9 - y^2)^{3/2}\right]_{-3}^{3} = 0.$$

Second,

$$\int_{-3}^{3} \sqrt{9 - y^2}\,dy = \tfrac{1}{2}\pi \cdot 3^2 = \tfrac{9}{2}\pi,$$

because the integral is simply the area of a semicircle of radius 3. Hence

$$W = 6400 \cdot \tfrac{9}{2}\pi = 28800\pi,$$

approximately 90,478 ft·lb. ◆

REMARK As in Example 5, you may use as needed in the problems the integral

$$\int_0^a \sqrt{a^2 - x^2}\,dx = \tfrac{1}{4}\pi a^2, \tag{10}$$

which corresponds to the area of a quarter-circle of radius a.

Force Exerted by a Liquid

The **pressure** p at depth h in a liquid is the force per unit area exerted by the liquid at that depth. Pressure is given by

$$p = \rho h, \tag{11}$$

where ρ is the (weight) density of the liquid. For example, at a depth of 10 ft in water, for which $\rho = 62.4$ lb/ft^3, the pressure is $62.4 \cdot 10 = 624$ lb/ft^2. Hence if a thin, flat plate of area 5 ft^2 is suspended in a horizontal position at a depth of 10 ft in water, then the water exerts a downward force of $624 \cdot 5 = 3120$ lb on the top face of the plate and an equal upward force on its bottom face.

It is an important fact that at a given depth in a liquid, the pressure is the same in all directions. But if a flat plate is submerged in a vertical position in the liquid, then the pressure on the face of the plate is *not* constant, because by Eq. (11) the pressure increases with increasing depth. Consequently, the total force exerted on a vertical plate must be computed by integration.

Consider a thin, vertical, flat plate submerged in a liquid of density ρ (Fig. 6.5.11). The surface of the liquid is at the line $y = c$, and the plate lies alongside the interval $a \leq y \leq b$. The width of the plate at depth $c - y$ is some function of y, which we denote by $w(y)$.

FIGURE 6.5.11 A thin plate suspended vertically in a liquid.

To compute the total force F exerted by the liquid on either face of this plate, we begin with a partition of $[a, b]$ into n subintervals, all with the same length Δy, and denote by y_i^* the midpoint of the subinterval $[y_{i-1}, y_i]$. The horizontal strip of the plate opposite this ith subinterval is approximated by a rectangle of width $w(y_i^*)$ and height Δy, and its average depth in the liquid is $c - y_i^*$. Hence the force ΔF_i exerted by the liquid on this horizontal strip is given approximately by

$$\Delta F_i \approx \rho(c - y_i^*)w(y_i^*)\,\Delta y. \tag{12}$$

The total force on the entire plate is given approximately by

$$F = \sum_{i=1}^{n} \Delta F_i \approx \sum_{i=1}^{n} \rho(c - y_i^*)w(y_i^*)\,\Delta y.$$

We obtain the exact value of F by taking the limit of such Riemann sums as $\Delta y \to 0$:

$$F = \int_a^b \rho(c - y)w(y)\,dy. \tag{13}$$

EXAMPLE 6 A cylindrical tank 8 ft in diameter is lying on its side and is half full of oil of density $\rho = 75$ lb/ft^3. Find the total force F exerted by the oil on one end of the tank.

FIGURE 6.5.12 View of one end of the tank of Example 6.

Solution We locate the y-axis as indicated in Fig. 6.5.12, so that the surface of the oil is at the level $y = 0$. The oil lies alongside the interval $-4 \leq y \leq 0$. We see from the right triangle in the figure that the width of the oil at depth $-y$ (and thus at location y) is

$$w(y) = 2\sqrt{16 - y^2}.$$

Hence Eq. (13) gives

$$F = \int_{-4}^{0} 75(-y)\left(2\sqrt{16 - y^2}\right) dy = 75\left[\tfrac{2}{3}(16 - y^2)^{3/2}\right]_{-4}^{0} = 3200 \quad \text{(lb)}. \quad \blacklozenge$$

6.5 TRUE/FALSE STUDY GUIDE

6.5 CONCEPTS: QUESTIONS AND DISCUSSION

1. Suppose that you lift a heavy weight from the floor to high over your head and then let it fall back to the floor. An observer says you did no work because the weight wound up in its initial position. You disagree. Who's right?
2. Consider a water tank in the shape of a solid of revolution around a vertical axis. The work formula in Eq. (8) was derived using horizontal slices. Is it possible to use cylindrical shells to derive an integral formula to use in calculating the work required to fill the tank?

6.5 PROBLEMS

In Problems 1 through 5, find the work done by the given force $F(x)$ in moving a particle along the x-axis from $x = a$ to $x = b$.

1. $F(x) = 10; \quad a = -2, b = 1$
2. $F(x) = 3x - 1; \quad a = 1, b = 5$
3. $F(x) = \dfrac{10}{x^2}; \quad a = 1, b = 10$
4. $F(x) = -3\sqrt{x}; \quad a = 0, b = 4$
5. $F(x) = \sin \pi x; \quad a = -1, b = 1$
6. A spring has a natural length of 1 m, and a force of 10 N is required to hold it stretched to a total length of 2 m. How much work is done in compressing this spring from its natural length to a length of 60 cm?
7. A spring has a natural length of 2 ft, and a force of 15 lb is required to hold it compressed at a length of 18 in. How much work is done in stretching this spring from its natural length to a length of 3 ft?
8. Apply Eq. (4) to compute the amount of work done in lifting a 100-lb weight a height of 10 ft, assuming that this work is done against the constant force of gravity.
9. Compute the amount of work (in foot-pounds) done in lifting a 1000-lb weight from an orbit 1000 mi above the earth's surface to one 2000 mi above the earth's surface. Use the value of k given in Example 3.
10. A cylindrical tank of radius 5 ft and height 10 ft is resting on the ground with its axis vertical. Use Eq. (8) to compute the amount of work done in filling this tank with water pumped in from ground level. (Use $\rho = 62.4$ lb/ft^3 for the weight density of water.)
11. A conical tank is resting on its base, which is at ground level, and its axis is vertical. The tank has radius 5 ft and height

10 ft (Fig. 6.5.13). Compute the work done in filling this tank with water ($\rho = 62.4$ lb/ft^3) pumped in from ground level.

FIGURE 6.5.13 The conical tank of Problem 11.

12. Repeat Problem 11, except that now the tank is upended: Its vertex is at ground level and its base is 10 ft above the ground.

13. A tank whose lowest point is 10 ft above the ground has the shape of a cup obtained by rotating the parabola $x^2 = 5y$, $-5 \leq y \leq 5$, around the y-axis (Fig. 6.5.14). The units on the coordinate axes are in feet. How much work is done in filling this tank with oil of density 50 lb/ft^3 if the oil is pumped in from ground level?

FIGURE 6.5.14 The cup-shaped tank of Problem 13.

14. Suppose that the tank of Fig. 6.5.9 is filled with fluid of density ρ and that all this fluid must be pumped from the tank to the level $y = h$ above the top of the tank. Use Riemann sums, as in the derivation of Eq. (8), to obtain the formula

$$W = \int_a^b \rho(h-y)A(y)\,dy$$

for the work required to do so.

15. Use the formula in Problem 14 to find the amount of work done in pumping the water in the tank of Problem 10 to a height of 5 ft above the top of the tank.

16. Gasoline at a service station is stored in a cylindrical tank buried on its side, with the highest part of the tank 5 ft below the surface. The tank is 6 ft in diameter and 10 ft long. The density of gasoline is 45 lb/ft^3. Assume that the filler cap of each automobile gas tank is 2 ft above the ground (Fig. 6.5.15). (a) How much work is done in emptying all the gasoline from this tank, initially full, into automobiles?

FIGURE 6.5.15 The gasoline tank of Problem 16.

(b) Recall that 1 hp is equivalent to 33,000 ft·lb/min. For electrical conversions, 1 kW (1000 W) is the same as 1.341 hp. The charge for use of electricity generated by a power company is typically about 7.2¢/kWh. Assume that the electrical motor in the gas pump at this station is 30% efficient. How much does it cost to pump all the gasoline from this tank into automobiles?

17. Consider a spherical water tank whose radius is 10 ft and whose center is 50 ft above the ground. How much work is required to fill this tank by pumping water up from ground level? [*Suggestion:* It may simplify your computations to take $y = 0$ at the center of the tank and to think of the distance each horizontal slice of water must be lifted.]

18. A hemispherical tank of radius 10 ft is located with its flat side down atop a tower 60 ft high (Fig. 6.5.16). How much work is required to fill this tank with oil of density 50 lb/ft^3 if the oil is to be pumped into the tank from ground level?

FIGURE 6.5.16 The hemispherical tank of Problem 18.

19. Water is being drawn from a well 100 ft deep, using a bucket that scoops up 100 lb of water. The bucket is pulled up at the rate of 2 ft/s, but it has a hole in the bottom through which water leaks out at the rate of 0.5 lb/s. How much work is done in pulling the bucket to the top of the well? Neglect the weight of the bucket, the weight of the rope, and the work done in overcoming friction. [*Suggestion:* Take $y = 0$ at the level of the water surface in the well, so that $y = 100$ at ground level. Let $\{y_0, y_1, y_2, \ldots, y_n\}$ be a partition of $[0, 100]$ into n equal-length subintervals. Estimate the amount of work ΔW_i required to raise the bucket from y_{i-1} to y_i. Then set up the sum $W = \sum \Delta W_i$ and proceed to the appropriate integral by letting $n \to +\infty$.]

20. A rope that is 100 ft long and weighs 0.25 lb per linear foot hangs from the edge of a very tall building. How much work is required to pull this rope to the top of the building?

21. Suppose that we plug the hole in the leaky bucket of Problem 19. How much work do we do in lifting the mended bucket, full of water, to the surface, using the rope of Problem 20? Ignore friction and the weight of the bucket, but allow for the weight of the rope.

22. Consider a volume V of gas in a cylinder fitted with a piston at one end, where the pressure p of the gas is a function $p(V)$ of its volume (Fig. 6.5.17). Let A be the area of the face of the piston. Then the force exerted on the piston by gas in the cylinder is $F = pA$. Assume that the gas expands from volume V_1 to volume V_2. Show that the work done by the force F is then given by

$$W = \int_{V_1}^{V_2} p(V)\, dV.$$

[*Suggestion:* If x is the length of the cylinder (from its fixed end to the face of the piston), then $F = A \cdot p(Ax)$. Apply Eq. (4) and substitute $V = Ax$ into the resulting integral.]

FIGURE 6.5.17 A cylinder fitted with a piston (Problem 22).

23. The pressure p and volume V of the steam in a small steam engine satisfy the condition $pV^{1.4} = c$ (where c is a constant). In one cycle, the steam expands from a volume $V_1 = 50$ in.^{3} to $V_2 = 500$ in.^{3} with an initial pressure of 200 lb/in.^{2} Use the formula in Problem 22 to compute the work, in foot-pounds, done by this engine in each such cycle.

24. A tank in the shape of a hemisphere of radius 60 is resting on its flat base with the curved surface on top. It is filled with alcohol of density 40 lb/ft^3. How much work is done in pumping all the alcohol to the level of the top of the tank?

25. A tank has the shape of the surface generated by rotating around the y-axis the graph of $y = x^4$, $0 \leq x \leq 1$. The tank is initially full of oil of density 60 lb/ft^3. The units on the coordinate axes are in feet. How much work is done in pumping all the oil to the level of the top of the tank?

26. A cylindrical tank of radius 3 ft and length 20 ft is lying on its side on horizontal ground. Gasoline weighing 40 lb/ft^3 is at ground level and is to be pumped into the tank. Find the work required to fill the tank.

27. The base of a spherical storage tank of radius 12 ft is at ground level. Find the amount of work done in filling the tank with oil of density 50 lb/ft^3 if all the oil is initially at ground level.

28. A 20-lb monkey is attached to a 50-ft chain that weighs 0.5 lb per (linear) foot. The other end of the chain is attached to the 40-ft-high ceiling of the monkey's cage (Fig. 6.5.18). Find the amount of work the monkey does in climbing up her chain to the ceiling.

FIGURE 6.5.18 The monkey of Problem 28.

29. Tom is flying his kite at a height of 500 ft above the ground. Suppose that the kite string weighs $\frac{1}{16}$ oz per (linear) foot and is stretched in a straight line at a 45° angle to the ground. How much work was done by the wind in lifting the string from ground level up to its flying position?

30. The center of a spherical tank of radius R is at a distance $H > R$ above the ground. A liquid of weight density ρ is at ground level. Show that the work required to pump the initially empty tank full of this liquid is the same as that to lift the full tank the distance H (ignoring the weight of the tank itself).

31. A water trough 10 ft long has a square cross section that is 2 ft wide. If the trough is full of water (density $\rho = 62.4$ lb/ft^3), find the force exerted by the water on one end of the trough.

32. Repeat Problem 31 for a trough whose cross section is an equilateral triangle with edges 2 ft long.

33. Repeat Problem 31 for a trough whose cross section is a trapezoid 3 ft high, 2 ft wide at the bottom, and 4 ft wide at the top.

34. Find the force on one end of the cylindrical tank of Example 5 if the tank is filled with oil of density 50 lb/ft^3. Remember that

$$\int_0^a \sqrt{a^2 - y^2}\, dy = \tfrac{1}{4}\pi a^2,$$

because the integral represents the area of a quarter-circle of radius a.

In Problems 35 through 38, a gate in the vertical face of a dam is described. Find the total force of water on this gate if its top is 10 ft beneath the surface of the water.

35. A square of edge length 5 ft whose top is parallel to the water surface.

36. A circle of radius 3 ft.

37. An isosceles triangle 5 ft high and 8 ft wide at the top.

38. A semicircle of radius 4 ft whose top edge is its diameter (also parallel to the water surface).

39. Suppose that the dam of Fig. 6.5.19 is $L = 200$ ft long and $T = 30$ ft thick at its base. Find the force of water on the dam if the water is 100 ft deep and the *slanted* end of the dam faces the water.

416 CHAPTER 6 Applications of the Integral

FIGURE 6.5.19 View of a model of a dam (Problem 39).

40. The concrete birdbath of Problem 47 in Section 6.3 is obtained by revolving around the y-axis the region that lies between the curves

$$y = 1 + \frac{x^2}{5} - \frac{x^4}{500} \quad \text{and} \quad y = \frac{x^4}{10000}$$

(with x and y in inches). When placed on its stand, the bottom of this birdbath is 40 inches above the ground. How much work (in ft·lb) is done in filling this birdbath with water lifted from ground level? If necessary, use a computer algebra system or table of integrals to help solve this problem.

6.6 CENTROIDS OF PLANE REGIONS AND CURVES

According to the **law of the lever**, two masses m_1 and m_2 on opposite sides and at respective distances d_1 and d_2 from the fulcrum of a lever will balance provided that $m_1 d_1 = m_2 d_2$. (See Fig. 6.6.1.) Think of the x-axis as the location of a (weightless) lever arm supporting various point masses and of the origin as a fulcrum. Then a more general form of the law of the lever states that (particle) masses $m_0, m_1, m_2, \ldots, m_n$ with respective coordinates $x_0, x_1, x_2, \ldots, x_n$ will balance provided that

$$\sum_{i=0}^{n} m_i x_i = m_0 x_0 + m_1 x_1 + m_2 x_2 + \cdots + m_n x_n = 0. \quad (1)$$

FIGURE 6.6.1 Law of the lever: The weights balance when $m_1 d_1 = m_2 d_2$.

Now consider arbitrary masses $m_1, m_2, \ldots, m_n$ at the points $x_1, x_2, \ldots, x_n$. Then a single particle with mass

$$m = m_1 + m_2 + \cdots + m_n = \sum_{i=1}^{n} m_i$$

at position $-\overline{x}$ will balance these n masses provided that

$$-m\overline{x} + \sum_{i=1}^{n} m_i x_i = 0;$$

that is, provided that

$$\overline{x} = \frac{1}{m} \sum_{i=1}^{n} m_i x_i. \quad (2)$$

Thus the original n masses act on the lever like a single particle of mass m located at the point $\overline{x}$. The point $\overline{x}$ is called the *center of mass*, and the sum $\sum_{i=1}^{n} m_i x_i$ that appears in Eq. (2) is called the *moment* of the system of masses about the origin.

Now consider a system of n particles with masses $m_1, m_2, \ldots, m_n$ located in the plane (see Fig. 6.6.2) at the points with respective coordinates $(x_1, y_1), (x_2, y_2), \ldots, (x_n, y_n)$. In analogy with the one-dimensional case just discussed, we define the **moment** M_y of this system of masses **about the y-axis** and its **moment** M_x **about the x-axis** by means of the equations

$$M_y = \sum_{i=1}^{n} m_i x_i \quad \text{and} \quad M_x = \sum_{i=1}^{n} m_i y_i. \quad (3)$$

FIGURE 6.6.2 Point masses in the plane and their moment arms about the x-axis.

Centroids of Plane Regions and Curves SECTION 6.6   417

The **center of mass** of this system of n particles is the point $(\overline{x}, \overline{y})$ with coordinates defined to be

$$\overline{x} = \frac{M_y}{m} \quad \text{and} \quad \overline{y} = \frac{M_x}{m} \tag{4}$$

where $m = m_1 + m_2 + \cdots + m_n$ is the sum of the masses. Thus $(\overline{x}, \overline{y})$ is the point where a single particle of mass m would have the same moments as the original whole system about the two coordinate axes. In elementary physics it is shown that, if the xy-plane were a rigid and weightless plastic sheet with our n particles imbedded in it, then it would balance (horizontally) on the point of an icepick at the point $(\overline{x}, \overline{y})$.

Laminas and Thin Plates

As the number of particles we consider increases while their masses decrease in proportion, their aggregate more and more closely resembles a plane region of varying density. Let us first define the center of mass $(\overline{x}, \overline{y})$ and the moments about the coordinate axes of a thin plate, or **lamina,** of constant density ρ, one that occupies a bounded plane region R. Because ρ is constant, the numbers $\overline{x}$ and $\overline{y}$ should be independent of the value of ρ, so we will assume that $\rho = 1$ (for convenience) in our definitions and computations. In this case $(\overline{x}, \overline{y})$ is called the **centroid** of the plane region R. We shall also define $M_y(R)$ and $M_x(R)$, the moments of the plane region R about the coordinate axes, with $\rho = 1$. The corresponding moments of a lamina of constant density $\rho \neq 1$ would then be $\rho M_y(R)$ and $\rho M_x(R)$.

Our definitions will be based on the following two physical principles. The first is quite natural: If a region has a line of symmetry, as in Fig. 6.6.3, then its centroid lies on this line.

FIGURE 6.6.3 A line of symmetry.

Symmetry Principle

If the plane region R is symmetric with respect to the line L—that is, if R is carried onto itself when the plane is rotated through an angle of 180° about the line L—then the centroid of R (considered as a lamina of constant density) lies on L.

We will find the second principle very useful in locating centroids of regions that are unions of simple regions.

Additivity of Moments

If R is the union of the two nonoverlapping regions S and T, then

$$M_y(R) = M_y(S) + M_y(T) \quad \text{and} \quad M_x(R) = M_x(S) + M_x(T). \tag{5}$$

For example, the symmetry principle implies that the centroid of a rectangle is its geometric center: the intersection of the perpendicular bisectors of its sides. We assume also that the moments of a rectangle R with area A and centroid $(\overline{x}, \overline{y})$ are $M_y(R) = A\overline{x}$ and $M_x(R) = A\overline{y}$. Knowing the centroid of a rectangle, our strategy will be to calculate the moments of a more general region by using additivity of moments and the integral, and finally to define the centroid of this more general region by analogy with the equations in (4).

Integral Formulas for Centroids

Suppose that the function f is continuous and nonnegative on $[a, b]$, and suppose also that the region R is the region between the graph of f and the x-axis for $a \leqq x \leqq b$. We begin with a regular partition of $[a, b]$ into n subintervals all having the same length $\Delta x = (b-a)/n$. Denote by $x_i^\star$ the midpoint of the ith subinterval $[x_{i-1}, x_i]$. As shown in Fig. 6.6.4, the rectangle with base $[x_{i-1}, x_i]$ and height $f(x_i^\star)$ has area $f(x_i^\star)\Delta x$ and centroid $(x_i^\star, \tfrac{1}{2} f(x_i^\star))$. If P_n denotes the union of these rectangles for $i = 1, 2, 3, \ldots, n$, then—because moments are additive—the moments of the rectangular polygon P_n

FIGURE 6.6.4 Locating the centroid of R by approximating R with rectangles.

about the y-axis and the x-axis are

$$M_y(P_n) = \sum_{i=1}^{n} x_i^* \cdot f(x_i^*) \, \Delta x$$

and

$$M_x(P_n) = \sum_{i=1}^{n} \frac{1}{2} f(x_i^*) \cdot f(x_i^*) \, \Delta x,$$

respectively.

We define the moments $M_y(R)$ and $M_x(R)$ of the region R itself by taking the limits of $M_y(P_n)$ and $M_x(P_n)$ as $\Delta x \to 0$. Because the preceding sums are Riemann sums, their limits are the definite integrals

$$M_y(R) = \int_a^b x f(x) \, dx \tag{6}$$

and

$$M_x(R) = \int_a^b \frac{1}{2} [f(x)]^2 \, dx. \tag{7}$$

Finally, we define the **centroid** $(\bar{x}, \bar{y})$ of R by

$$\bar{x} = \frac{M_y(R)}{A} \quad \text{and} \quad \bar{y} = \frac{M_x(R)}{A}, \tag{8}$$

where $A = \int_a^b f(x) \, dx$ is the area of R. Thus

$$\bar{x} = \frac{1}{A} \int_a^b x f(x) \, dx \tag{9}$$

and

$$\bar{y} = \frac{1}{A} \int_a^b \frac{1}{2} [f(x)]^2 \, dx \tag{10}$$

are the coordinates of the centroid of the region under $y = f(x)$ from $x = a$ to $x = b$.

By the symmetry principle, the centroid of a circular disk is its center. But the centroid of a semicircle is more interesting.

EXAMPLE 1 Find the centroid of the upper half D of the circular disk with center $(0, 0)$ and radius r.

Solution By symmetry, the centroid of D lies on the y-axis, so $\bar{x} = 0$. The semicircular disk lies under $y = \sqrt{r^2 - x^2}$ from $x = -r$ to $x = r$, as shown in Fig. 6.6.5. Hence Eq. (7) yields

$$M_x(D) = \int_{-r}^{r} \frac{1}{2} \left(\sqrt{r^2 - x^2} \right)^2 dx$$

$$= \frac{1}{2} \int_{-r}^{r} (r^2 - x^2) \, dx = \left[r^2 x - \frac{x^3}{3} \right]_{-r}^{r} = \frac{2}{3} r^3.$$

FIGURE 6.6.5 The half-disk D of Example 1.

Because $A = \frac{1}{2} \pi r^2$, the second formula in (8) gives

$$\bar{y} = \frac{M_x(D)}{A} = \frac{\frac{2}{3} r^3}{\frac{1}{2} \pi r^2} = \frac{4r}{3\pi} \approx (0.4244) r.$$

Thus the centroid of D is the point $(0, 4r/3\pi)$. Note that our computed value for $\bar{y}$ has the dimensions of length (because r is a length), as it should. Any answer having other dimensions would be suspect. Do you feel that these coordinates are plausible as well? ◆

Centroids of Plane Regions and Curves SECTION 6.6 419

EXAMPLE 2 Find the centroid of the triangle T with vertices $(0, 0)$, $(1, 0)$, and $(0, 1)$.

Solution Figure 6.6.6 shows the triangle T. Note first that $\bar{x} = \bar{y}$ by symmetry. Equation (6), with $y = f(x) = 1 - x$, gives

$$M_y(T) = \int_0^1 x(1-x)\,dx = \left[\frac{1}{2}x^2 - \frac{1}{3}x^3\right]_0^1 = \frac{1}{6}.$$

So, by the first equation in (8),

$$\bar{x} = \frac{M_y(T)}{A} = \frac{\frac{1}{6}}{\frac{1}{2}} = \frac{1}{3}.$$

Thus the centroid of T is $(\frac{1}{3}, \frac{1}{3})$.

FIGURE 6.6.6 The triangle T of Example 2.

Additivity of moments can be used to define the moments and centroid of any plane region that is the union of a finite number of nonoverlapping regions shaped like the one in Fig. 6.6.7. For example, suppose that $f(x) \geq g(x) \geq 0$ on $[a, b]$ and that R is the region between the graphs of $y = f(x)$ and $y = g(x)$ for $a \leq x \leq b$. If R_f and R_g denote the regions under the graphs of f and g, respectively, then $M_y(R) + M_y(R_g) = M_y(R_f)$ by additivity of moments. Therefore

$$M_y(R) = M_y(R_f) - M_y(R_g)$$
$$= \int_a^b x f(x)\,dx - \int_a^b x g(x)\,dx$$

by Eq. (6). Thus

$$M_y(R) = \int_a^b x \cdot [f(x) - g(x)]\,dx. \tag{11}$$

FIGURE 6.6.7 The region R between $y = f(x)$ and $y = g(x)$.

Similarly,

$$M_x(R) = M_x(R_f) - M_x(R_g)$$
$$= \int_a^b \frac{1}{2}[f(x)]^2\,dx - \int_a^b \frac{1}{2}[g(x)]^2\,dx$$

by Eq. (7), and therefore

$$M_x(R) = \int_a^b \frac{1}{2}\{[f(x)]^2 - [g(x)]^2\}\,dx. \tag{12}$$

We then define the centroid of R by means of the equations in (8), with

$$A = \int_a^b [f(x) - g(x)]\,dx. \tag{13}$$

EXAMPLE 3 Let R be the rectangle of Fig. 6.6.8. Following two applications of the symmetry principle, we conclude that its centroid is at the point $(4, 2)$. Let us test Eqs. (11) and (12) to see if they yield the same result. With $a = 2$, $b = 6$, $f(x) \equiv 3$, and $g(x) \equiv 1$, we get

$$M_y(R) = \int_2^6 x(3-1)\,dx = \left[x^2\right]_2^6 = 32,$$

$$M_x(R) = \int_2^6 \frac{1}{2}[(3)^2 - (1)^2]\,dx = \left[4x\right]_2^6 = 16.$$

FIGURE 6.6.8 The rectangle of Example 3.

Because the region has area $A = 4 \cdot 2 = 8$, we find using (8) that

$$\bar{x} = \frac{M_y}{A} = \frac{32}{8} = 4 \quad \text{and} \quad \bar{y} = \frac{M_x}{A} = \frac{16}{8} = 2,$$

exactly as expected.

An interesting theorem relating centroids and volumes of revolution is named for the Greek mathematician who stated it during the third century A.D.

FIRST THEOREM OF PAPPUS Volume of Revolution
Suppose that a plane region R is rotated around an axis in its plane, thereby generating a solid of revolution with volume V. Assume that the axis does not intersect the interior of R. Then V is the product of the area A of R and the distance traveled by the centroid of R during one complete rotation.

PROOF (For the special case of a region shaped like the one shown in Fig. 6.6.9.) This is the region between the two graphs $y = f(x)$ and $y = g(x)$ for $a \leq x \leq b$, and we shall take the axis of rotation to be the y-axis. Then, in one complete rotation around the y-axis, the distance traveled by the centroid of R is $d = 2\pi \bar{x}$. By the method of cylindrical shells of Section 6.3, the volume of the solid generated is

$$V = \int_a^b 2\pi x \, [f(x) - g(x)] \, dx$$
$$= 2\pi \, M_y(R) \quad \text{(by Eq. (11))}$$
$$= 2\pi \bar{x} \cdot A \quad \text{(by Eq. (8))},$$

and thus $V = d \cdot A$, as desired.

FIGURE 6.6.9 A region R between the graphs of two functions.

EXAMPLE 4 Find the volume V of the sphere of radius r generated by rotation of the semicircle D of Example 1 around the x-axis.

Solution The area of D is $A = \frac{1}{2}\pi r^2$, and we found in Example 1 that $\bar{y} = 4r/3\pi$. Hence Pappus's theorem gives

$$V = 2\pi \, \bar{y} A = 2\pi \cdot \frac{4r}{3\pi} \cdot \frac{\pi r^2}{2} = \frac{4}{3}\pi r^3.$$

EXAMPLE 5 Consider the circular disk of Fig. 6.6.10, with radius a and center at the point $(0, b)$ where $0 < a < b$. Find the volume V of the solid torus generated by rotating this disk around the y-axis.

Solution The centroid of the circle is its center $(b, 0)$, so $\bar{x} = b$. Hence the centroid of the disk is moved once around a circle of radius b, thus through the distance $d = 2\pi b$. Consequently

$$V = d \cdot A = 2\pi b \cdot \pi a^2 = 2\pi^2 a^2 b.$$

Note that this result is dimensionally correct.

FIGURE 6.6.10 Rotate the circular disk about the y-axis to produce a torus (Example 5).

Moments and Centroids of Curves

Moments and centroids of plane *curves* are defined in a way that is quite analogous to the method for plane regions, so we shall present this topic in less detail. The moments $M_y(C)$ and $M_x(C)$ of the plane curve C about the y- and x-axes, respectively, are defined to be

$$M_y(C) = \int x \, ds \quad \text{and} \quad M_x(C) = \int y \, ds \qquad (14)$$

(with appropriate limits to be inserted when the integrals are evaluated). The **centroid** of C is then defined to be the point with coordinates

$$\bar{x} = \frac{1}{s} M_y(C) = \frac{1}{s} \int_C x \, ds \quad \text{and} \quad \bar{y} = \frac{1}{s} M_x(C) = \frac{1}{s} \int_C y \, ds \qquad (15)$$

where s is the arc length of C.

The meaning of the integrals in (14) and (15) is that of the notation of Section 6.4. That is, ds is a symbol to be replaced (before evaluation of the integral) by either

$$ds = \sqrt{1 + \left(\frac{dy}{dx}\right)^2}\, dx \quad \text{or} \quad ds = \sqrt{1 + \left(\frac{dx}{dy}\right)^2}\, dy,$$

depending on whether C is a smooth arc of the form $y = f(x)$ or one of the form $x = g(y)$. For example, if C is described by $y = f(x), a \leq x \leq b$, then

$$M_y(C) = \int_a^b x\sqrt{1 + [f'(x)]^2}\, dx \tag{16}$$

and

$$M_x(C) = \int_a^b f(x)\sqrt{1 + [f'(x)]^2}\, dx. \tag{17}$$

EXAMPLE 6 Let J denote the upper half of the circle (not the *disk*) of radius r. Thus the arc J is the graph of

$$y = \sqrt{r^2 - x^2}, \quad -r \leq x \leq r.$$

Find the centroid of J.

Solution Note first that $M_y(J) = 0$ by symmetry. Now

$$\frac{dy}{dx} = -\frac{x}{\sqrt{r^2 - x^2}},$$

so

$$ds = \sqrt{1 + \frac{x^2}{r^2 - x^2}}\, dx = \frac{r}{\sqrt{r^2 - x^2}}\, dx.$$

Hence the second formula in (14) yields

$$M_x(J) = \int_{-r}^{r} \sqrt{r^2 - x^2}\, \frac{r}{\sqrt{r^2 - x^2}}\, dx = \int_{-r}^{r} r\, dx = 2r^2.$$

Because $s = \pi r$, the coordinates of the centroid of J are

$$\bar{x} = \frac{M_y(J)}{s} = 0 \quad \text{and} \quad \bar{y} = \frac{M_x(J)}{s} = \frac{2r^2}{\pi r} = \frac{2r}{\pi}.$$

The answer is dimensionally correct. Is it plausible? ◆

The first theorem of Pappus has an analogue for surface area of revolution.

SECOND THEOREM OF PAPPUS Surface Area of Revolution
Suppose that the plane curve C is rotated around an axis in its plane that does not intersect C. Then the area A of the surface of revolution generated is equal to the product of the length of C and the distance traveled by the centroid of C.

PROOF (For the special case in which C is a smooth arc described by $y = f(x)$, $a \leq x \leq b$, and the axis of revolution is the y-axis.) The distance traveled by the centroid of C is $d = 2\pi \bar{x}$. By Eq. (12) in Section 6.4, the area of the surface of revolution is

$$A = \int_a^b 2\pi x \sqrt{1 + [f'(x)]^2}\, dx$$

$$= 2\pi M_y(C) \quad \text{(Eq. (16))}$$

$$= 2\pi \bar{x} s = d \cdot s \quad \text{(Eq. (15))},$$

as desired. ◂

EXAMPLE 7 Find the surface area A of the sphere of radius r generated by revolving around the x-axis the semicircular arc of Example 6.

Solution Because we found that $\bar{y} = 2r/\pi$ and we know that $S = \pi r$, the second theorem of Pappus gives

$$A = 2\pi \bar{y} s = 2\pi \cdot \frac{2r}{\pi} \cdot \pi r = 4\pi r^2.$$

◆

EXAMPLE 8 Find the surface area A of the torus of Example 5.

Solution Now we think of rotating the circle (*not* the disk) of radius a centered at the point $(b, 0)$. Naturally, the centroid of the circle is located at its center $(b, 0)$; this follows from the symmetry principle and can be verified independently by computations like those in Example 6. Hence the distance traveled by the centroid is $d = 2\pi b$. Because the circumference of the circle is $S = 2\pi a$, the second theorem of Pappus gives

$$A = 2\pi b \cdot 2\pi a = 4\pi^2 ab.$$

Again, note that the answer is dimensionally correct.

◆

6.6 TRUE/FALSE STUDY GUIDE

6.6 CONCEPTS: QUESTIONS AND DISCUSSION

1. Example 6 shows that the centroid of a curve need not be a point of the curve. Must the centroid of a plane region be a point of that region?
2. How could you check the results in Examples 4 and 8 for plausibility?

6.6 PROBLEMS

In Problems 1 through 18, find the centroid of the plane region bounded by the given curves.

1. $x = 0, x = 4, y = 0, y = 6$
2. $x = 1, x = 3, y = 2, y = 4$
3. $x = -1, x = 3, y = -2, y = 4$
4. $x = 0, y = 0, x + y = 3$
5. $x = 0, y = 0, x + 2y = 4$
6. $y = 0, y = x, x + y = 2$
7. $y = 0, y = x^2, x = 2$
8. $y = x^2, y = 9$
9. $y = 0, y = x^2 - 4$
10. $x = -2, x = 2, y = 0, y = x^2 + 1$
11. $y = 4 - x^2, y = 0$
12. $y = x^2, y = 18 - x^2$
13. $y = 3x^2, y = 0, x = 1$
14. $x = y^2, y = 0, x = 4$ (*above* the x-axis)
15. $y = x, y = 6 - x^2$
16. $y = x^2, y^2 = x$
17. $y = x^2, y = x^3$
18. $y = \sin x \ (0 \leq x \leq \pi), y = 0$
19. Find the centroid of the first quadrant of the circular disk $x^2 + y^2 \leq r^2$ by direct computation, as in Example 1.
20. Apply the first theorem of Pappus to find the centroid of the first quadrant of the circular disk $x^2 + y^2 \leq r^2$. Use the facts that $\bar{x} = \bar{y}$ by symmetry and that rotation of this quarter disk about either coordinate axis gives a solid hemisphere with volume $V = \frac{2}{3}\pi r^3$.
21. Find the centroid of the arc consisting of the first-quadrant portion of the circle $x^2 + y^2 = r^2$ by direct computation, as in Example 6.
22. Apply the second theorem of Pappus to find the centroid of the quarter-circular arc of Problem 21. Note that $\bar{x} = \bar{y}$ by symmetry, and that rotation of this arc around either coordinate axis gives a hemisphere with surface area $A = 2\pi r^2$.
23. Show by direct computation that the centroid of the triangle with vertices $(0, 0)$, $(r, 0)$, and $(0, h)$ is the point $(r/3, h/3)$. Verify that this point lies on the line from the vertex $(0, 0)$ to the midpoint of the opposite side of the triangle and two-thirds of the way from the vertex to that midpoint.
24. Apply the first theorem of Pappus and the result of Problem 23 to verify the formula $V = \frac{1}{3}\pi r^2 h$ for the volume of the cone generated by rotating the triangle around the y-axis.
25. Apply the second theorem of Pappus to show that the lateral surface area of the cone of Problem 24 is $A = \pi r L$, where $L = \sqrt{r^2 + h^2}$ is the *slant height* of the cone.
26. (a) Use additivity of moments to find the centroid of the trapezoid shown in Fig. 6.6.11. (b) Apply the first theorem of Pappus and the result of part (a) to show that the volume of the conical frustum generated by rotating the trapezoid

around the y-axis is

$$V = \frac{\pi h}{3}\left(r_1^2 + r_1 r_2 + r_2^2\right).$$

FIGURE 6.6.11 The trapezoid of Problem 26.

27. Apply the second theorem of Pappus to show that the lateral surface area of the conical frustum in Problem 26 is $A = \pi(r_1 + r_2)L$, where

$$L = \sqrt{(r_1 - r_2)^2 + h^2}$$

is the slant height of the frustum.

28. (a) Apply the second theorem of Pappus to verify that the curved surface area of a right circular cylinder with height h and base radius r is $A = 2\pi r h$. (b) Explain how this formula also follows from the result of Problem 27.

29. (a) Use additivity of moments to find the centroid of the plane region shown in Fig. 6.6.12, which consists of a semicircular region of radius a resting atop a rectangular region of width $2a$ and height h. (b) Then apply the first theorem of Pappus to find the volume generated by rotating this region around the x-axis.

FIGURE 6.6.12 The plane region of Problem 29.

30. (a) Consider the plane region shown in Fig. 6.6.13, bounded by $x^2 = 2py$, $x = 0$, and $y = h = r^2/2p$ ($p > 0$). Show that its area is $A = 2rh/3$ and that the x-coordinate of its centroid is $\bar{x} = 3r/8$. (b) Use Pappus's theorem and the result of part (a) to show that the volume of a paraboloid of revolution with radius r and height h is $V = \frac{1}{2}\pi r^2 h$.

FIGURE 6.6.13 The region of Problem 30.

31. The region in the first quadrant bounded by the graphs of $y = x$ and $y = x^2$ is rotated around the line $y = x$. Find first the centroid of the region, then find the volume of revolution thereby generated.

32. Let R be the region in the xy-plane that is bounded by the curves $y = x^m$ and $y = x^n$, where m and n are positive integers such that $m < n$. Use a computer algebra system to show that the centroid $(\bar{x}, \bar{y})$ of R has coordinates

$$\bar{x} = \frac{(m+1)(n+1)}{(m+2)(n+2)} \quad \text{and} \quad \bar{y} = \frac{(m+1)(n+1)}{(2m+1)(2n+1)}.$$

Can you see by visualizing (or plotting) the figure why it is natural to conjecture that, if m is sufficiently large and $n = m + 1$, then the centroid $(\bar{x}, \bar{y})$ does *not* lie within R? Find specific values of m and n such that the centroid of R does not lie within R.

CHAPTER 6 REVIEW: DEFINITIONS, CONCEPTS, RESULTS

Use the following list as a guide to concepts that you may need to review.

1. The general method of setting up an integral formula for a quantity by approximating it and then recognizing the approximation to be a Riemann sum that corresponds to the desired integral: If the interval $[a, b]$ is partitioned into n subintervals of equal length $\Delta x = (b-a)/n$ and if $x_i^\star$ denotes a point of the ith subinterval, then

$$\lim_{n \to \infty} \sum_{i=1}^{n} f(x_i^\star)\,\Delta x = \int_a^b f(x)\,dx.$$

2. Net distance traveled as the integral of velocity:

$$s = \int_a^b v(t)\,dt.$$

3. The method of cross sections for computing volumes:

$$V = \int_a^b A(x)\,dx,$$

where $A(x)$ denotes the area of a slice with infinitesimal thickness dx.

4. Determining the volume of a solid of revolution by the method of cross sections, with the cross sections being either disks or annular rings.
5. Determining the volume of a solid of revolution by the method of cylindrical shells:

$$V = \int_{\star}^{\star\star} 2\pi r \, dA,$$

where r denotes the radius of the circle through which the area element dA is revolved.

6. The arc length of a smooth arc described either in the form $y = f(x), a \leq x \leq b$, or in the form $x = g(y), c \leq y \leq d$:

$$s = \int_{\star}^{\star\star} ds \quad \left(ds = \sqrt{(dx)^2 + (dy)^2}\right),$$

where

$$ds = \sqrt{1 + [f'(x)]^2} \, dx \quad \text{for } y = f(x);$$

$$ds = \sqrt{1 + [g'(y)]^2} \, dy \quad \text{for } x = g(y).$$

7. Determining the area of the surface of revolution generated by revolving a smooth arc, given in the form $y = f(x)$ or in the form $x = g(y)$, around either the x-axis or the y-axis:

$$A = \int_{\star}^{\star\star} 2\pi r \, ds,$$

where r denotes the radius of the circle through which the arc length element ds is revolved.

8. The work done by a force function in moving a particle along a straight line segment:

$$W = \int_a^b F(x) \, dx$$

if the force $F(x)$ acts from $x = a$ to $x = b$.

9. Hooke's law and the work done in stretching or compressing an elastic spring.
10. Work done against the varying force of gravity.
11. Work done in filling a tank or in pumping the liquid in a tank to another level:

$$W = \int_a^b \rho h(y) A(y) \, dy,$$

where $h(y)$ denotes the vertical distance that the horizontal fluid slice of volume $dV = A(y) \, dy$, at the height y, must be lifted.

12. The force exerted by a liquid on the face of a submerged vertical plate:

$$F = \int_{\star}^{\star\star} \rho h \, dA,$$

where h denotes the depth of the horizontal area element dA beneath the surface of the fluid of weight density ρ.

13. The formulas for the coordinates of the centroid of a plane region.
14. The formulas for the coordinates of the centroid of a plane curve.
15. The first and second theorems of Pappus.

CHAPTER 6 MISCELLANEOUS PROBLEMS

In Problems 1 through 3, find both the net distance and the total distance traveled between times $t = a$ and $t = b$ by a particle moving along a line with the given velocity function $v = f(t)$.

1. $v = t^2 - t - 2; \quad a = 0, b = 3$
2. $v = |t^2 - 4|; \quad a = 1, b = 4$
3. $v = \pi \sin \frac{1}{2}\pi(2t - 1); \quad a = 0, b = \frac{3}{2}$

In Problems 4 through 8, a solid extends along the x-axis from $x = a$ to $x = b$, and its cross-section area at x is $A(x)$. Find its volume.

4. $A(x) = x^3; \quad a = 0, b = 1$
5. $A(x) = \sqrt{x}; \quad a = 1, b = 4$
6. $A(x) = x^3; \quad a = 1, b = 2$
7. $A(x) = \pi(x^2 - x^4); \quad a = 0, b = 1$
8. $A(x) = x^{100}; \quad a = -1, b = 1$
9. Suppose that rainfall begins at time $t = 0$ and that the rate after t hours is $(t + 6)/12$ inches per hour. How many inches of rain fall during the first 12 h?
10. The base of a certain solid is the region in the first quadrant bounded by the curves $y = x^3$ and $y = 2x - x^2$. Find the solid's volume if each cross section perpendicular to the x-axis is a square with one edge in the base of the solid.
11. Find the volume of the solid generated by revolving around the x-axis the first-quadrant region of Problem 10.
12. Find the volume of the solid generated by revolving the region bounded by $y = 2x^4$ and $y = x^2 + 1$ around (a) the x-axis; (b) the y-axis.
13. A wire made of copper (density 8.5 g/cm³) is shaped like a helix that spirals around the x-axis from $x = 0$ to $x = 20$. Each cross section of this wire perpendicular to the x-axis is a circular disk of radius 0.25 cm. What is the total mass of the wire?
14. Derive the formula $V = \frac{1}{3}\pi h(r_1^2 + r_1 r_2 + r_2^2)$ for the volume of a frustum of a cone with height h and base radii r_1 and r_2.
15. Suppose that the point P lies on a line perpendicular to the xy-plane at the origin O, with $|OP| = h$. Consider the "elliptical cone" that consists of all points on line segments from P to points on and within the ellipse with equation

$$\left(\frac{x}{a}\right)^2 + \left(\frac{y}{b}\right)^2 = 1.$$

Show that the volume of this elliptical cone is $V = \frac{1}{3}\pi a b h$.

16. Figure 6.MP.1 shows the region R bounded by the ellipse $(x/a)^2 + (y/b)^2 = 1$ and by the line $x = a - h$, where $0 < h < a$. Revolution of R around the x-axis generates a "segment of an ellipsoid" of radius r, height h, and

volume V. Show that

$$r^2 = \frac{b^2(2ah - h^2)}{a^2} \quad \text{and that} \quad V = \frac{1}{3}\pi r^2 h \frac{3a - h}{2a - h}.$$

FIGURE 6.MP.1 A segment of an ellipse (Problem 16).

17. Figure 6.MP.2 shows the region R bounded by the hyperbola $(x/a)^2 - (y/b)^2 = 1$ and the line $x = a + h$, where $h > 0$. Revolving R around the x-axis generates a "segment of a hyperboloid" of radius r, height h, and volume V. Show that

$$r^2 = \frac{b^2(2ah + h^2)}{a^2} \quad \text{and that} \quad V = \frac{1}{3}\pi r^2 h \frac{3a + h}{2a + h}.$$

FIGURE 6.MP.2 The region R of Problem 17.

In Problems 18 through 20, the function $f(x)$ is nonnegative and continuous for $x \geq 1$. When the region lying under $y = f(x)$ from $x = 1$ to $x = t$ is revolved around the indicated axis, the volume of the resulting solid is $V(t)$. Find the function $f(x)$.

18. $V(t) = \pi\left(1 - \frac{1}{t}\right);$ the x-axis
19. $V(t) = \frac{1}{6}\pi[(1 + 3t)^2 - 16];$ the x-axis
20. $V(t) = \frac{2}{9}\pi[(1 + 3t^2)^{3/2} - 8];$ the y-axis
21. Use the integral formula

$$\int u \sin u \, du = \sin u - u \cos u + C$$

to find the volume of the solid generated by revolving around the y-axis the first-quadrant region bounded by $y = x$ and $y = \sin(\frac{1}{2}\pi x)$.

22. Use the method of cylindrical shells to find the volume of the solid generated by revolving around the line $x = -2$ the region bounded by $y = x^2$ and $y = x + 2$.

23. Find the length of the curve $y = \frac{1}{3}x^{3/2} - x^{1/2}$ from $x = 1$ to $x = 4$.

24. Find the area of the surface generated by revolving the curve of Problem 23 around (a) the x-axis; (b) the y-axis.
25. Find the length of the curve $x = \frac{3}{8}(y^{4/3} - 2y^{2/3})$ from $y = 1$ to $y = 8$.
26. Find the area of the surface generated by revolving the curve of Problem 25 around (a) the x-axis; (b) the y-axis.
27. Find the area of the surface generated by revolving the curve of Problem 23 around the line $x = 1$.
28. If $-r \leq a < b \leq r$, then a "spherical zone" of "height" $h = b - a$ is generated by revolving around the x-axis the circular arc $y = \sqrt{r^2 - x^2}$, $a \leq x \leq b$. Show that the area of this spherical zone is $A = 2\pi rh$, the same as that of a cylinder of radius r and height h.
29. Apply the result of Problem 28 to show that the surface area of a sphere of radius r is $A = 4\pi r^2$.
30. Let R denote the region bounded by the curves $y = 2x^3$ and $y^2 = 4x$. Find the volumes of the solids obtained by revolving the region R around (a) the x-axis; (b) the y-axis; (c) the line $y = -1$; (d) the line $x = 2$. In each case use both the method of cross sections and the method of cylindrical shells.
31. Find the natural length L of a spring if five times as much work is required to stretch it from a length of 2 ft to a length of 5 ft as is required to stretch it from a length of 2 ft to a length of 3 ft.
32. A steel beam weighing 1000 lb hangs from a 50-ft cable that weighs 5 lb per linear foot. How much work is done in winding in 25 ft of the cable with a windlass?
33. A spherical tank of radius R (in feet) is initially full of oil of density ρ lb/ft^3. Find the total work done in pumping all the oil from the sphere to a height of $2R$ above the top of the tank.
34. How much work is done by a colony of ants in building a conical anthill of height and diameter 1 ft, using sand initially at ground level and with a density of 150 lb/ft^3?
35. The gravitational attraction below the earth's surface is directly proportional to the distance from the center of the earth. Suppose that a straight cylindrical hole of radius 1 ft is dug from the earth's surface to its center. Assume that the earth has radius 3960 mi and uniform density 350 lb/ft^3. How much work, in foot-pounds, is done in lifting a 1-lb weight from the bottom of this hole to its top?
36. How much work is done in digging the hole of Problem 35—that is, in lifting all the material it initially contained to the earth's surface?
37. Suppose that a dam is shaped like a trapezoid of height 100 ft, 300 ft long at the top and 200 ft long at the bottom. When the water level behind the dam is even with its top, what is the total force that the water exerts on the dam?
38. Suppose that a dam has the same top and bottom lengths as the dam of Problem 37 and the same vertical height of 100 ft, but that its face toward the water is slanted at an angle of 30° from the vertical. What is the total force of water pressure on this dam?
39. For $c > 0$, the graphs of $y = c^2x^2$ and $y = c$ bound a plane region. Revolve this region around the horizontal line $y = -1/c$ to form a solid. For what value of c is the volume of this solid maximal? Minimal?

Find the centroids of the curves in Problems 40 through 43.

40. $y = \dfrac{x^5}{5} + \dfrac{1}{12x^3}$, $1 \leq x \leq 2$

41. $x = \dfrac{y^4}{8} + \dfrac{1}{4y^2}$, $1 \leq y \leq 2$

42. $y = \dfrac{x^{3/2}}{3} - x^{1/2}$, $1 \leq x \leq 4$

43. $x = \dfrac{3}{8}(y^{4/3} - 2y^{2/3})$, $1 \leq y \leq 8$

44. Find the centroid of the plane region in the first quadrant that is bounded by the curves $y = x^3$ and $y = 2x - x^2$.

45. Find the centroid of the plane region bounded by the curves $x = 2y^4$ and $x = y^2 + 1$.

46. Let T be the plane triangle with vertices $(0, 0)$, (a, b), and $(c, 0)$. Show that the centroid of T is the point of intersection of its medians.

47. Use the first theorem of Pappus to find the y-coordinate of the centroid of the upper half of the ellipse

$$\dfrac{x^2}{a^2} + \dfrac{y^2}{b^2} = 1.$$

Use the facts that the area of this semiellipse is $A = \tfrac{1}{2}\pi ab$ and the volume of the ellipsoid it generates when rotated around the x-axis is $V = \tfrac{4}{3}\pi ab^2$.

48. (a) Use the first theorem of Pappus to find the centroid of the first-quadrant part of the annular ring with boundary circles $x^2 + y^2 = a^2$ and $x^2 + y^2 = b^2$, with $0 < a < b$. (b) Show that the limiting position of this centroid as $b \to a$ is the centroid of a quarter-circular arc of radius a.

49. Let T be the triangle in the first quadrant with one vertex at $(0, 0)$ and the opposite side L, of length w, joining the other two vertices (a, b) and (c, d), where $a > c > 0$ and $d > b > 0$. Let A denote the area of T, $\bar{y}$ the y-coordinate of the centroid of T, p the perpendicular distance from $(0, 0)$ to L, V the volume generated by revolving T around the x-axis, and S the surface area generated by revolving L around the x-axis. Derive the following formulas in the order listed.

(a) $A = \tfrac{1}{2}(ad - bc)$

(b) $\bar{y} = \tfrac{1}{3}(b + d)$

(c) $V = \tfrac{1}{3}\pi(b + d)(ad - bc)$

(d) $p = \dfrac{ad - bc}{w}$

(e) $S = \pi(b + d)w$

(f) $V = \tfrac{1}{3}pS$

50. Suppose that n is an even positive integer. Let J be an n-sided regular polygon inscribed in the circle of radius r centered at the origin. Let S be the surface area generated by rotating J around a diameter of the circle through two opposite vertices of J; let V be the volume of the solid enclosed by that surface. Conclude from part (f) of Problem 49 that

$$V = \dfrac{1}{3}\left(r \cos \dfrac{\pi}{n}\right) \cdot S.$$

Archimedes deduced from this result that, if the surface area of a sphere of radius r is $4\pi r^2$, then its volume is $\tfrac{4}{3}\pi r^3$. Supply the details of his reasoning.

51. Suppose that n is a positive integer. Let R_n denote the region bounded by the curves $y = x$ and $y = x^n$ for $0 \leq x \leq 1$. Show that the limiting position as $n \to +\infty$ of the centroid of R_n is the centroid of the triangle with vertices $(0, 0)$, $(1, 0)$, and $(1, 1)$. Why does this seem plausible?

52. Let the region R be the union of the semicircular disk $x^2 + y^2 \leq 9$, $x \geq 0$, and the square with vertices $(1, 0)$, $(-1, 0)$, $(1, -2)$, and $(-1, -2)$. (a) Find the centroid of R. (b) Then find the volume of the solid obtained by rotating R around the line $y = -4$.

CALCULUS OF TRANSCENDENTAL FUNCTIONS

7

John Napier (1550–1617)

John Napier was the eighth baron of Merchiston (near Edinburgh), Scotland. As a landowner, he participated vigorously in local affairs and actively managed crops and cattle on his lands around Merchiston Castle. He is said to have regarded as his most important and lasting contribution his book *A Plaine Discovery of the Whole Revelation of Saint John* (1593), in which (among other things) he predicted that the world would come to an end in the year 1786. But the world—still here over two centuries later—remembers Napier as the inventor of logarithms. The late sixteenth century was an age of numerical computation, as developments in astronomy and navigation called for increasingly accurate and lengthy trigonometric computations. With his theological work behind him, Napier began in 1594 the 20-year labor that was to revolutionize the practical art of numerical computation. The result of this monumental project was his 1614 book *Mirifici Logarithmorum Canonis Descriptio* (Description of the Wonderful Canon of Logarithms), which contained his logarithmic tables along with a brief introduction and guide to their use.

Students today first learn of the "common" base-10 logarithm $\log_{10} x$ as the power to which 10 must be raised to get the number x. Because

$$\log_{10} xy = \log_{10} x + \log_{10} y,$$

multiplying the two numbers x and y effectively reduces to the simpler operation of adding their logarithms. The "logarithm" $\mathrm{Nlog}(x)$ that Napier used was somewhat different. Whereas $\log_{10} 1 = 0$, Napier's definition implies that $\mathrm{Nlog}(10^7) = 0$ with the previous equation replaced by a rule of the form $\mathrm{Nlog}(xy) = \mathrm{Nlog}(x) + \mathrm{Nlog}(y) - C$. Hence the use of Napier's original table of logarithms would involve continual addition or subtraction of the particular constant $C = 10^7 \times \ln 10^7$ (where ln denotes the modern "natural" logarithm).

In 1615 the English mathematics professor Henry Briggs visited Napier in Scotland. Their discussions led to Briggs's construction of a table of "improved" logarithms, ones for which the logarithm of 1 is 0 and the logarithm of 10 is 1. Within a decade after Napier's death, 10-place tables of these common logarithms had been completed. These tables played a central role in scientific computation during the next three centuries.

On a slide rule of the type used universally by calculus students prior to the advent of electronic pocket calculators in the 1970s, numbers are inscribed on the scales at distances proportional to their logarithms. Consequently, the logarithms of x on a fixed scale and of y on a sliding scale are readily added to determine the product xy.

427

7.1 EXPONENTIAL AND LOGARITHMIC FUNCTIONS

Until now, we have concentrated on algebraic and trigonometric functions. Exponential and logarithmic functions complete the list of the so-called *elementary functions* that are most important in applications of calculus.

Exponential Functions

An *exponential function* is a function of the form

$$f(x) = a^x \tag{1}$$

where $a > 0$. Note that the exponent x is the variable here; the number a, called the *base*, is a constant. Thus

- An exponential function $f(x) = a^x$ is a constant raised to a variable power, whereas
- The power function $p(x) = x^k$ is a variable raised to a constant power.

In elementary algebra a *rational* power of the positive real number a is defined in terms of integral roots and powers. If n is a positive integer then

$$a^n = a \cdot a \cdot a \cdots a \qquad (n \text{ factors})$$

and

$$a^{-n} = \frac{1}{a^n}.$$

Next we learn that if $r = p/q$ where p and q are integers (with q positive), then the rational power a^r is defined by

$$a^{p/q} = \sqrt[q]{a^p} = \left(\sqrt[q]{a}\right)^p.$$

The following **laws of exponents** are then established for all *rational* exponents r and s:

$$a^{r+s} = a^r \cdot a^s, \qquad (a^r)^s = a^{r \cdot s},$$
$$a^{-r} = \frac{1}{a^r}, \qquad (ab)^r = a^r \cdot b^r. \tag{2}$$

Moreover, recall that

$$a^0 = 1 \tag{3}$$

for every positive real number a.

The following example illustrates the fact that applications often call for irrational exponents as well as rational exponents.

EXAMPLE 1 Consider a bacteria population $P(t)$ that begins (at time $t = 0$) with initial population $P(0) = 1$ (million) and doubles every hour thereafter. The growing population is given at 1-hour intervals as in the following table:

t	1	2	3	4	5	(hours)
P	2	4	8	16	32	(millions)

It is evident that $P(n) = 2^n$ if n is an integer. Now let's make the plausible assumption that the population increases by the same factor in any two time intervals of the same length—for example, if it grows by 10% in any one eight-minute interval, then it grows by 10% in any *other* eight-minute interval. If q is a positive integer and k denotes the factor by which the population increases during a time interval of length $\Delta t = 1/q$,

Exponential and Logarithmic Functions SECTION 7.1   429

then the population is given at successive time intervals of length $1/q$ as in the next table.

t	$\dfrac{1}{q}$	$\dfrac{2}{q}$	$\dfrac{3}{q}$	$\cdots$	$\dfrac{q}{q}=1$
P	k	k^2	k^3	$\cdots$	$k^q = 2$ (Why?)

We therefore see that $k = 2^{1/q}$. If p is another positive integer, then during p/q hours the population P will increase p times by the factor $k = 2^{1/q}$, so it follows that

$$P(p/q) = k^p = \left(2^{1/q}\right)^p = 2^{p/q}.$$

Thus the bacteria population after t hours is given (in millions) by

$$P(t) = 2^t$$

if the exponent t is a rational number. But because time is not restricted to rational values alone, we surely ought to conclude that $P(t) = 2^t$ for *all* $t \geq 0$. ◆

Investigation   But what do we mean by an expression involving an irrational exponent, such as $2^{\sqrt{2}}$ or 2^π? To find the value of 2^π, we might work with (rational) finite decimal approximations to the irrational number $\pi = 3.1415926\cdots$. For example, a calculator gives

$$2^{3.1} = 2^{31/10} = \left(\sqrt[10]{2}\right)^{31} \approx 8.5742.$$

The approximate values shown in the table in Fig. 7.1.1 indicate that the bacteria population in Example 1 after π hours is

$$P(\pi) \approx 8.8250 \quad \text{(million)}.$$

t	2^t
3.1	8.5742
3.14	8.8152
3.141	8.8214
3.1415	8.8244
3.14159	8.8250
3.141592	8.8250
3.1415926	8.8250
↓	↓
π	2^π

FIGURE 7.1.1 Investigating 2^π.

Because any irrational number can be approximated arbitrarily closely by rational numbers, the preceding investigation suggests that the value of a^x—with irrational exponent x and a fixed base $a > 0$—can be regarded as a limit of the form

$$a^x = \lim_{r \to x} a^r \quad (r \text{ rational}). \tag{4}$$

Indeed, when the meaning of the limit in (4) is made precise, it provides one way of defining as well as calculating values of the exponential function $f(x) = a^x$ for all x.

On a calculator, the $\boxed{\wedge}$ key (sometimes the $\boxed{y^x}$ key) is ordinarily used to calculate values of exponential functions. For instance, Fig. 7.1.2 shows the result of graphing the function defined by **y = 2∧x**. We see the steadily rising graph (from left to right) of a function that is positive-valued for all x. Indeed, if r and s are positive rational numbers with $r < s$ and $a > 1$, then we note first that $a^{s-r} > 1$ (Why?) and then that

$$a^r < a^r \cdot a^{s-r} = a^{r+(s-r)} = a^s.$$

FIGURE 7.1.2 The graph $y = 2^x$.

Thus $a^r < a^s$ whenever $0 < r < s$, so the exponential function $f(x) = a^x$ is certainly an increasing function if only positive rational values of the exponent are involved. A graphing calculator or computer actually plots only finitely many points (x, a^x), but the curve plotted in Fig. 7.1.2 looks connected because these points are plotted too close together for the eye to distinguish them.

By contrast, the graph in Fig. 7.1.3 is shown with a dotted curve to suggest that it is densely filled with tiny holes corresponding to the missing points (x, a^x) for which x is irrational. In Section 7.4 we will use calculus to show that these holes can be filled to obtain the graph of a continuous increasing function f with the following properties:

FIGURE 7.1.3 The graph of $y = a^x$ has "holes" if only rational values of x are used.

- $f(x)$ is defined for every real number x;
- $f(r) = a^r$ if r is rational; and
- the laws of exponents in (2) hold for irrational as well as rational exponents.

430 CHAPTER 7 Calculus of Transcendental Functions

FIGURE 7.1.4 $y = a^x$ for $a = 2, 3, 5, 10$.

FIGURE 7.1.5 Here the graphs $y = 2^x$ and $y = x^2$ look similar for $x > 2$.

FIGURE 7.1.6 But here we see 2^x increasing much more rapidly than x^2.

We therefore write $f(x) = a^x$ for all x and call f the **exponential function with base** a.

As illustrated in Fig. 7.1.4, the exponential function $f(x) = a^x$ with $a > 1$ increases rapidly as $x > 0$ increases, and the graphs of $y = a^x$ look qualitatively similar for different values of the base a so long as $a > 1$. The steep rate of increase of a^x for x positive and increasing is a characteristic feature of exponential functions. Figures 7.1.5 and 7.1.6 compare the graphs of the exponential function $y = 2^x$ and the quadratic function $y = x^2$.

Derivatives of Exponential Functions

To compute the derivative of the exponential function $f(x) = a^x$, we begin with the definition of the derivative and then use the first law of exponents in Eq. (2) to simplify. This gives

$$f'(x) = \lim_{h \to 0} \frac{f(x+h) - f(x)}{h} = \lim_{h \to 0} \frac{a^{x+h} - a^x}{h}$$

$$= \lim_{h \to 0} \frac{a^x a^h - a^x}{h} \qquad \text{(by the laws of exponents)}$$

$$= a^x \left(\lim_{h \to 0} \frac{a^h - 1}{h} \right) \qquad \text{(because } a^x \text{ is ``constant'' with respect to } h\text{).}$$

Under the assumption that $f(x) = a^x$ is differentiable, it follows that the limit

$$m(a) = \lim_{h \to 0} \frac{a^h - 1}{h} \tag{5}$$

exists. Although its value $m(a)$ depends on a, the limit is a constant as far as x is concerned. Thus we find that the derivative of a^x is a *constant multiple* of a^x itself:

$$D_x a^x = m(a) \cdot a^x. \tag{6}$$

h	$\dfrac{2^h - 1}{h}$	$\dfrac{3^h - 1}{h}$
0.1	0.718	1.161
0.01	0.696	1.105
0.001	0.693	1.099
0.0001	0.693	1.099

FIGURE 7.1.7 Investigating the values of $m(2)$ and $m(3)$.

Because $a^0 = 1$, we see from Eq. (6) that the constant $m(a)$ is the slope of the line tangent to the curve $y = a^x$ at the point $(0, 1)$, where $x = 0$.

The numerical data shown in Fig. 7.1.7 suggest that $m(2) \approx 0.693$ and that $m(3) \approx 1.099$. The tangent lines with these slopes are shown in Fig. 7.1.8. Thus it appears that

$$D_x 2^x \approx (0.693) \cdot 2^x \quad \text{and} \quad D_x 3^x \approx (1.099) \cdot 3^x. \tag{7}$$

We would like somehow to avoid awkward numerical factors like those in Eq. (7). It seems plausible that the value $m(a)$ defined in Eq. (5) is a continuous function of a. If so, then because $m(2) < 1$ and $m(3) > 1$, the intermediate value theorem implies that $m(e) = 1$ (exactly) for some number e between 2 and 3. If we use this particular number e as the base, then it follows from Eq. (6) that the derivative of

FIGURE 7.1.8 The graphs (a) $y = 2^x$ and (b) $y = 3^x$.

the resulting exponential function $f(x) = e^x$ is

$$D_x e^x = e^x. \tag{8}$$

Thus the function e^x is its own derivative. We call $f(x) = e^x$ the **natural exponential function.** Its graph is shown in Fig. 7.1.9.

n	$\left(1 + \dfrac{1}{n}\right)^n$
10	2.594
100	2.705
1,000	2.717
10,000	2.718
100,000	2.718

FIGURE 7.1.9 The graph $y = e^x$.

FIGURE 7.1.10 Numerical estimate of the number e.

We will see in Section 7.3 that the number e is given by the limit

$$e = \lim_{n \to \infty} \left(1 + \frac{1}{n}\right)^n.$$

Let us investigate this limit numerically. With a calculator we obtain the values in the table of Fig. 7.1.10. The evidence suggests (but does not prove) that $e \approx 2.718$ to three places. This number e is one of the most important special numbers in mathematics. It is known to be irrational; its value accurate to 15 places is

$$e \approx 2.71828\ 1828\ 459045.$$

The chain rule version of Eq. (8) is the differentiation formula

$$D_x e^u = e^u \frac{du}{dx}, \tag{9}$$

432 CHAPTER 7 Calculus of Transcendental Functions

where u denotes a differentiable function of x. In particular,

$$D_x e^{kx} = k e^{kx}$$

if k is a constant. For instance, $D_x e^{-x} = -e^{-x}$ and $D_x e^{2x} = 2e^{2x}$.

EXAMPLE 2

(a) If $f(x) = x^2 e^{-x}$, then the product rule gives

$$\begin{aligned} f'(x) &= (D_x x^2) e^{-x} + x^2 (D_x e^{-x}) \\ &= (2x) e^{-x} + x^2 (-e^{-x}) \\ &= (2x - x^2) e^{-x}. \end{aligned}$$

FIGURE 7.1.11 The graph of Example 2, part (a).

(b) If $y = \dfrac{e^{2x}}{2x+1}$, then the quotient rule gives

$$\begin{aligned} \frac{dy}{dx} &= \frac{(D_x e^{2x})(2x+1) - (e^{2x}) D_x(2x+1)}{(2x+1)^2} \\ &= \frac{(2e^{2x})(2x+1) - (e^{2x})(2)}{(2x+1)^2} = \frac{4x e^{2x}}{(2x+1)^2}. \end{aligned}$$ ◆

EXAMPLE 3 Figure 7.1.11 shows a computer plot of the graph of $f(x) = x^2 e^{-x}$. Find the coordinates of the indicated local maximum point on the curve in the first quadrant.

Solution The calculation in part (a) of Example 2 yields $f'(x) = 0$ when

$$(2x - x^2) e^{-x} = \frac{x(2-x)}{e^x} = 0,$$

so the only critical points of f are at $x = 0$ and $x = 2$. Thus the indicated first-quadrant critical point on the curve is $(2, f(2)) = (2, 4e^{-2}) \approx (2, 0.5413)$. ◆

Logarithms and Inverse Functions

In precalculus courses, the **base a logarithm function** $\log_a x$ is introduced as the "opposite" of the exponential function $f(x) = a^x$ with base $a > 1$. That is, $\log_a x$ is the power to which a must be raised to get x. Thus

$$y = \log_a x \quad \text{if and only if} \quad a^y = x. \tag{10}$$

With $a = 10$, this is the base 10 *common logarithm* $\log_{10} x$.

EXAMPLE 4

$$\begin{aligned} \log_{10} 1000 &= 3 & \text{because} && 1000 &= 10^3; \\ \log_{10}(0.1) &= -1 & \text{because} && 0.1 &= 10^{-1}; \\ \log_2 16 &= 4 & \text{because} && 16 &= 2^4; \\ \log_3 9 &= 2 & \text{because} && 9 &= 3^2. \end{aligned}$$ ◆

If $y = \log_a x$, then $a^y = x > 0$. Hence it follows that

$$a^{\log_a x} = x \tag{11a}$$

and

$$\log_a(a^y) = y. \tag{11b}$$

Thus the base a exponential and logarithmic functions are natural opposites, in the sense that each undoes the result of applying the other. Apply both in succession—in either order—and you're back where you started (Fig. 7.1.12). Example 5 gives other familiar pairs of functions that are *inverses* of each other.

FIGURE 7.1.12 Inverse functions f and g. Each undoes the effect of the other.

EXAMPLE 5 The following are some pairs of *inverse functions:*

(a) $f(x) = x + 1$ and $g(x) = x - 1$.

Adding 1 and subtracting 1 are inverse operations; doing either undoes the other. Next, doubling and halving are inverse operations:

(b) $f(x) = 2x$ and $g(x) = \dfrac{x}{2}$.

A function can be its own inverse:

(c) $f(x) = \dfrac{1}{x}$ and $g(x) = \dfrac{1}{x}$. ◆

Like $f(x) = a^x$ and $g(x) = \log_a x$, each pair f and g of functions given in Example 5 has the property that

$$f(g(x)) = x \quad \text{and} \quad g(f(x)) = x \tag{12}$$

for all values of x in the domains of g and f, respectively. For instance, the functions $f(x) = x + 1$ and $g(x) = x - 1$ in part (a) of the example are defined for all x, and it is easy to check that

$$f(g(x)) = g(x) + 1 = (x - 1) + 1 = x$$

and

$$g(f(x)) = f(x) - 1 = (x + 1) - 1 = x$$

for every real number x.

DEFINITION Inverse Functions
The two functions f and g are **inverse functions,** or are **inverses** of each other, provided that

- The range of values of each function is the domain of definition of the other, and
- The relations in (12) hold for all x in the domains of g and f, respectively.

The following two examples illustrate the fact that care is required when we specify the domains of definition of the functions f and g to ensure that the condition in (12) is satisfied.

EXAMPLE 6 The function $f(x) = x^2$ is defined for all x and its range is the set of all nonnegative real numbers y; thus we write $f : (-\infty, +\infty) \longrightarrow [0, +\infty)$. As indicated in Fig. 7.1.13, it is a familiar fact that each positive number y has two different square roots, $g_+(y) = +\sqrt{y}$ and $g_-(y) = -\sqrt{y}$. (Recall that the symbol $\sqrt{y}$ unadorned with either sign *always* denotes the nonnegative square root of y.) The positive square root function $g_+(y) = +\sqrt{y}$ is defined for all $y \geq 0$, as is $g_-(y)$, and they are the inverses of the two different squaring functions

$$f_+ : [0, +\infty) \longrightarrow [0, +\infty) \quad \text{defined by} \quad f_+(x) = x^2 \text{ for } x \geqq 0$$

and

$$f_- : (-\infty, 0] \longrightarrow [0, +\infty) \quad \text{defined by} \quad f_-(x) = x^2 \text{ for } x \leqq 0.$$

(The functions f_+ and f_- are obtained by "restricting" the function $f(x) = x^2$ to the nonnegative x-axis and the nonpositive x-axis, respectively.) For instance,

$$f_-(g_-(x)) = (-\sqrt{x})^2 = (\sqrt{x})^2 = x \quad \text{for all} \quad x \geq 0$$

and

$$g_-(f_-(x)) = -\sqrt{x^2} = -\sqrt{(-x)^2} = -(-x) = x \quad \text{for all} \quad x \leqq 0.$$

FIGURE 7.1.13 The function $f(x) = x^2$ and its restrictions f_- and f_+.

FIGURE 7.1.14 The function $f(x) = x^2$ has inverse $g(y) = \sqrt[3]{y}$ defined for all y.

Thus the functions f_- and g_- are inverse functions. You should verify similarly that the functions f_+ and g_+ are inverse functions. ◆

EXAMPLE 7 In contrast with Example 6, the functions $f(x) = x^3$ and $g(x) = \sqrt[3]{x}$ are inverse functions defined for all x. The difference is that any real number x—whether positive, negative, or zero—has one and only one cube root (as indicated in Fig. 7.1.14). ◆

Because $a^x > 0$ for all x (as illustrated in Fig. 7.1.15), it follows that $\log_a x$ is defined *only* for $x > 0$. Because interchanging x and y in $a^y = x$ yields $y = a^x$, it follows from Eq. (10) that the graph of $y = \log_a x$ is the reflection in the line $y = x$ of the graph of $y = a^x$ and therefore has the shape shown in Fig. 7.1.15. Because $a^0 = 1$, it also follows that

$$\log_a 1 = 0,$$

so the intercepts in the figure are independent of the choice of a.

FIGURE 7.1.15 The graph of $x = a^y$ is the graph of the inverse function $\log_a x$ of the exponential function a^x. The case $a > 1$ is shown here.

We can use the inverse-function relationship between $\log_a x$ and a^x to deduce, from the laws of exponents in Eq. (2), the following **laws of logarithms:**

$$\log_a xy = \log_a x + \log_a y, \quad \log_a \frac{1}{x} = -\log_a x,$$
$$\log_a \frac{x}{y} = \log_a x - \log_a y, \quad \log_a x^y = y \log_a x. \tag{13}$$

We will verify these laws of logarithms in Section 7.4.

Derivatives of Inverse Functions

Our interest in inverse-function pairs at this point stems from the following general principle: When we know the derivative of either of two inverse functions, then we can use the inverse-function relationship between them to *discover* the derivative of the other of the two functions. Theorem 1 is usually proved in an advanced calculus course.

THEOREM 1 Differentiation of an Inverse Function

Suppose that the differentiable function f is defined on the open interval I and that $f'(x) > 0$ for all x in I. Then f has an inverse function g, the function g is differentiable, and

$$g'(x) = \frac{1}{f'(g(x))} \tag{14}$$

for all x in the domain of g.

COMMENT 1 Theorem 1 is true also when the condition $f'(x) > 0$ is replaced with the condition $f'(x) < 0$. If we assume that g is differentiable, then we can derive the formula in Eq. (14) by differentiating with respect to x each side in the inverse-function relation

$$f(g(x)) = x.$$

When we differentiate each side, using the fact that this relation is actually an identity on some interval and using the chain rule on the left-hand side, the result is

$$f'(g(x)) \cdot g'(x) = 1.$$

When we solve this equation for $g'(x)$, the result is Eq. (14).

COMMENT 2 In order that the function f in Theorem 1 have an inverse function g, it is necessary (and sufficient) that, for each y in the range of f, there exists exactly one x in the domain of f such that $f(x) = y$. (We can then define $g(y) = x$.) Figure 7.1.14 indicates that this is so for the cubing function $f(x) = x^3$ of Example 7. In contrast, we see in Fig. 7.1.13 that each $y > 0$ in the range of the squaring function $f(x) = x^2$ of Example 6 corresponds to two different values of x—the positive and negative square roots of y. This is why the squaring function $f : (-\infty, +\infty) \longrightarrow [0, +\infty)$ has no (single) inverse function. The graph of f is the entire parabola in the figure. The right and left "halves" of the parabola are the graphs of the restrictions f_+ and f_- with inverse functions g_+ and g_-, respectively.

COMMENT 3 Equation (14) is easy to remember in differential notation. Let us write $x = f(y)$ and $y = g(x)$. Then $dy/dx = g'(x)$ and $dx/dy = f'(y)$. So Eq. (14) becomes the seemingly inevitable formula

$$\frac{dy}{dx} = \frac{1}{\frac{dx}{dy}}. \tag{15}$$

In using Eq. (15), it is important to remember that dy/dx is to be evaluated at x, but dx/dy is to be evaluated at the corresponding value of y; namely, $y = g(x)$.

EXAMPLE 8 In Section 3.4 we verified the power rule $D_x x^r = r x^{r-1}$ for rational values of the exponent r. Here we can investigate more efficiently the derivative of the root function $\sqrt[q]{x}$ (with q a positive integer). We need only observe that the power function $f(x) = x^q$, $x > 0$ certainly has a positive derivative: $f'(x) = q x^{q-1}$ for $x > 0$. Therefore Theorem 1 implies that its inverse function $g(x) = x^{1/q} = \sqrt[q]{x}$ exists and has derivative

$$D_x x^{1/q} = g'(x) = \frac{1}{f'(g(x))} = \frac{1}{q(x^{1/q})^{q-1}} = \frac{1}{q x^{1-(1/q)}} = \frac{1}{q} x^{(1/q)-1},$$

as desired. Alternatively, we could use the approach of Comment 1 and simply write the identity $(x^{1/q})^q = x$. Then differentiation, using the chain rule on the left (and $D_x x \equiv 1$ on the right) gives the equation $q(x^{1/q})^{q-1} \cdot D_x x = 1$, so we can solve for $D_x x^{1/q} = (1/q) x^{(1/q)-1}$. ◆

The Natural Logarithm

The natural exponential function $f(x) = e^x$ is defined for all x and $f'(x) = e^x > 0$. If f is the inverse function that consequently is guaranteed by Theorem 1 in this section, then $f(g(x)) = e^{g(x)} = x$. Thus $g(x)$ is "the power to which e must be raised to get x," and therefore is simply the logarithm function with base e: $g(x) = \log_e x$. The function g is therefore called the **natural logarithm** function. It is commonly denoted (on calculator keys, for instance) by the special symbol ln:

$$\ln x = \log_e x \quad (x > 0). \tag{16}$$

Because $e^x > 0$ for all x, it follows that $\ln x$ is defined only for $x > 0$. The graph of $y = \ln x$ is shown in Fig. 7.1.16, and appears to rise quite slowly when x is large. We note that $\ln 1 = 0$, so the graph has x-intercept $x = 1$, and that $\ln e = 1$ (because $\ln e = \log_e e = 1$).

The inverse function relations between $f(x) = e^x$ and $g(x) = \ln x$ are these:

$$e^{\ln x} = x \quad \text{for all } x > 0 \tag{17a}$$

and

$$\ln(e^x) = x \quad \text{for all } x. \tag{17b}$$

FIGURE 7.1.16 The graph of the natural logarithm function.

Derivatives of Logarithmic Functions

To differentiate the natural logarithm function, we can apply Eq. (14) in Theorem 1 (with $f(x) = e^x$ and $g(x) = \ln x$) and thereby write

$$g'(x) = \frac{1}{f'(g(x))} = \frac{1}{f'(\ln x)} = \frac{1}{e^{\ln x}} = \frac{1}{x}.$$

Alternatively, we could begin with Eq. (17a) and differentiate both sides with respect to x, as follows:

$$D_x e^{\ln x} = D_x x;$$

$$e^{\ln x} \cdot D_x \ln x = 1 \quad \text{(by Eq. (9) with } u = \ln x\text{)};$$

$$x \cdot D_x \ln x = 1.$$

Thus we find either way that the derivative $g'(x) = D_x \ln x$ of the natural logarithm function is given by

$$D_x \ln x = \frac{1}{x} \tag{18}$$

for $x > 0$. Thus $\ln x$ is the hitherto missing function whose derivative is $x^{-1} = 1/x$.

Just as with exponentials, the derivative of a logarithm function with base other than e involves an inconvenient numerical factor. For instance, Problem 74 shows that

$$D_x \log_{10} x \approx \frac{0.4343}{x}. \tag{19}$$

The contrast between Eqs. (18) and (19) illustrates one way in which base e logarithms are "natural."

EXAMPLE 9 Figure 7.1.17 shows the graph of the function

$$f(x) = \frac{\ln x}{x}.$$

Find the coordinates of the indicated first-quadrant critical point on this curve.

FIGURE 7.1.17 The graph of Example 9.

Solution Equation (18) and the quotient rule yield

$$f'(x) = \frac{(D_x \ln x)(x) - (\ln x)(D_x x)}{x^2} = \frac{\frac{1}{x} \cdot x - (\ln x) \cdot 1}{x^2} = \frac{1 - \ln x}{x^2}.$$

Hence the only critical point of f occurs when $\ln x = 1$; that is, when $x = e$. Thus the critical point indicated in Fig. 7.1.17 is $(e, 1/e) \approx (2.718, 0.368)$. ◆

The chain-rule version of Eq. (18) is

$$D_x \ln u = \frac{1}{u} \cdot \frac{du}{dx} = \frac{u'}{u}, \tag{20}$$

where u is a positive-valued function of x and u' denotes $u'(x)$. If $u(x)$ has negative values, then the function $\ln |u|$ is defined wherever u is nonzero, so

$$D_x \ln |u| = \frac{1}{|u|} \cdot \frac{d|u|}{du} \cdot \frac{du}{dx}$$

by Eq. (20) with $|u|$ in place of u. But from the familiar graph of the absolute value function we see that

$$\frac{d|u|}{du} = \frac{|u|}{u} = \begin{cases} -1 & \text{if } u < 0, \\ +1 & \text{if } u > 0. \end{cases}$$

It therefore follows that

$$D_x \ln |u| = \frac{1}{u} \cdot \frac{du}{dx} \tag{21}$$

wherever the differentiable function $u(x)$ is nonzero. In particular,

$$D_x \ln |x| = \frac{1}{x} \tag{22}$$

if $x \neq 0$ (see Fig. 7.1.18).

FIGURE 7.1.18 The function $f(x) = \ln |x|$ and its derivative $f'(x) = 1/x$.

EXAMPLE 10 With $u = 1 + x^2$ as the "inner function" in Eq. (20), we get

$$D_x \ln(1 + x^2) = \frac{u'}{u} = \frac{2x}{1 + x^2}.$$
◆

EXAMPLE 11 Find the derivative of $y = \sqrt{1 + \ln x}$.

Solution Now $u = 1 + \ln x$ is the inner function, so

$$\frac{dy}{dx} = \frac{1}{2}(1 + \ln x)^{-1/2} \cdot D_x(1 + \ln x)$$

$$= \frac{1}{2}(1 + \ln x)^{-1/2} \cdot \frac{1}{x} = \frac{1}{2x\sqrt{1 + \ln x}}.$$
◆

EXAMPLE 12 Find the derivative of $y = \ln \sqrt{\dfrac{2x + 3}{4x + 5}}$.

Solution If we differentiated immediately, we'd find ourselves applying the quotient rule to differentiate the fraction within the radical. (Try it yourself!) It's simpler to apply laws of logarithms to simplify the given function *before* differentiating it:

$$y = \ln \left(\frac{2x + 3}{4x + 5}\right)^{1/2} = \frac{1}{2} \ln \frac{2x + 3}{4x + 5} = \frac{1}{2}[\ln(2x + 3) - \ln(4x + 5)].$$

Then

$$\frac{dy}{dx} = \frac{1}{2}\left(\frac{2}{2x+3} - \frac{4}{4x+5}\right) = \frac{1}{2x+3} - \frac{2}{4x+5} = -\frac{1}{8x^2 + 22x + 15}.$$ ◆

Logarithmic Differentiation

The derivatives of certain functions are most conveniently found by first differentiating their logarithms. This process—called **logarithmic differentiation**—involves the following steps for finding $f'(x)$.

1. Given $\qquad\qquad\qquad\qquad\qquad\qquad\qquad\qquad y = f(x).$

2. Take *natural* logarithms; then simplify, $\qquad\quad \ln y = \ln f(x).$
   using laws of logarithms

3. Differentiate with respect to x $\qquad\qquad\qquad \dfrac{1}{y} \cdot \dfrac{dy}{dx} = D_x[\ln f(x)].$

4. Multiply both sides by $y = f(x)$ $\qquad\qquad\quad \dfrac{dy}{dx} = f(x) D_x[\ln f(x)].$

REMARK If $f(x)$ is not positive-valued everywhere, then Steps 1 and 2 should be replaced with $y = |f(x)|$ and $\ln y = \ln|f(x)|$, respectively. The differentiation in Step 3 then leads to the result $dy/dx = f(x) D_x[\ln|f(x)|]$ in Step 4. In practice, we need not be overly concerned in advance with the sign of $f(x)$, because the appearance of what seems to be the logarithm of a negative quantity will signal the fact that absolute values should be used.

EXAMPLE 13 Find dy/dx, given

$$y = \frac{\sqrt{(x^2+1)^3}}{\sqrt[3]{(x^3+1)^4}}.$$

Solution The laws of logarithms give

$$\ln y = \ln \frac{(x^2+1)^{3/2}}{(x^3+1)^{4/3}} = \frac{3}{2}\ln(x^2+1) - \frac{4}{3}\ln(x^3+1).$$

Then differentiation with respect to x gives

$$\frac{1}{y} \cdot \frac{dy}{dx} = \frac{3}{2} \cdot \frac{2x}{x^2+1} - \frac{4}{3} \cdot \frac{3x^2}{x^3+1} = \frac{3x}{x^2+1} - \frac{4x^2}{x^3+1}.$$

Finally, to solve for dy/dx, we multiply both sides by

$$y = \frac{(x^2+1)^{3/2}}{(x^3+1)^{4/3}},$$

and we obtain

$$\frac{dy}{dx} = \left(\frac{3x}{x^2+1} - \frac{4x^2}{x^3+1}\right) \cdot \frac{(x^2+1)^{3/2}}{(x^3+1)^{4/3}}.$$ ◆

EXAMPLE 14 Find dy/dx, given $y = x^{x+1}$ for $x > 0$.

Solution If $y = x^{x+1}$, then

$$\ln y = \ln(x^{x+1}) = (x+1)\ln x;$$

$$\frac{1}{y} \cdot \frac{dy}{dx} = (1)(\ln x) + (x+1)\left(\frac{1}{x}\right) = 1 + \frac{1}{x} + \ln x.$$

Multiplying by $y = x^{x+1}$ gives

$$\frac{dy}{dx} = \left(1 + \frac{1}{x} + \ln x\right) x^{x+1}.$$

7.1 TRUE/FALSE STUDY GUIDE

7.1 CONCEPTS: QUESTIONS AND DISCUSSION

1. Example 5 lists three inverse function pairs. List several more inverse function pairs f and g of your own. In each case specify the domains of f and g and verify that f and g are indeed inverse functions.
2. Suppose that n is a positive integer. Discuss (as in Examples 6 and 7) the question of whether the power function $f(x) = x^n$ and the root function $g(x) = \sqrt[n]{x}$ are inverse functions defined for all x. How does the situation depend on whether n is even or odd? Discuss positive and negative nth roots if necessary. Specify the domain of definition of each function you mention and verify all claims you make.
3. Sketch the bell-shaped graph of the function

$$f(x) = \frac{1}{1+x^2}.$$

Explain why f (which is defined for all x) does not have an inverse function, but its restrictions f_+ and f_- to the positive and negative x-axes do have inverse functions g_+ and g_- (using notation similar to that in Example 6). Find formulas for $g_+(x)$ and $g_-(x)$ and specify the domain of definition of each of these two inverse functions.
4. Restrict the domain of each of the six trigonometric functions $\sin x$, $\cos x$, $\tan x$, $\cot x$, $\sec x$, and $\csc x$ to those points in the interval $0 < x < \pi$ at which they are defined. Consulting the graphs in Fig. 3.7.3 as necessary, determine which of these functions have inverse functions. Answer the same question if instead the domains are restricted to the interval $0 < x < \pi/2$.

7.1 PROBLEMS

Differentiate the functions in Problems 1 through 38.

1. $f(x) = e^{2x}$
2. $f(x) = e^{3x-1}$
3. $f(x) = e^{x^2}$
4. $f(x) = e^{4-x^3}$
5. $f(x) = e^{1/x^2}$
6. $f(x) = x^2 e^{x^3}$
7. $g(t) = t e^{\sqrt{t}}$
8. $g(t) = (e^{2t} + e^{3t})^7$
9. $g(t) = (t^2 - 1)e^{-t}$
10. $g(t) = \sqrt{e^t - e^{-t}}$
11. $g(t) = e^{\cos t}$
12. $f(x) = x e^{\sin x}$
13. $g(t) = \dfrac{1 - e^{-t}}{t}$
14. $f(x) = e^{-1/x}$
15. $f(x) = \dfrac{1-x}{e^x}$
16. $f(x) = e^{\sqrt{x}} + e^{-\sqrt{x}}$
17. $f(x) = e^{e^x}$
18. $f(x) = \sqrt{e^{2x} + e^{-2x}}$
19. $f(x) = \sin(2e^x)$
20. $f(x) = \cos(e^x + e^{-x})$
21. $f(x) = \ln(3x - 1)$
22. $f(x) = \ln(4 - x^2)$
23. $f(x) = \ln\sqrt{1 + 2x}$
24. $f(x) = \ln[(1+x)^2]$
25. $f(x) = \ln\sqrt[3]{x^3 - x}$
26. $f(x) = \ln(\sin^2 x)$
27. $f(x) = \cos(\ln x)$
28. $f(x) = (\ln x)^3$
29. $f(x) = \dfrac{1}{\ln x}$
30. $f(x) = \ln(\ln x)$
31. $f(x) = \ln\left(x\sqrt{x^2 + 1}\right)$
32. $g(t) = t^{3/2} \ln(t+1)$
33. $f(x) = \ln(\cos x)$
34. $f(x) = \ln(2 \sin x)$
35. $f(t) = t^2 \ln(\cos t)$
36. $f(x) = \sin(\ln 2x)$
37. $g(t) = t(\ln t)^2$
38. $g(t) = \sqrt{t}[\cos(\ln t)]^2$

In Problems 39 through 46, apply laws of logarithms to simplify the given function before finding its derivative.

39. $f(x) = \ln[(2x+1)^3(x^2-4)^4]$
40. $f(x) = \ln\sqrt{\dfrac{1-x}{1+x}}$
41. $f(x) = \ln\sqrt{\dfrac{4-x^2}{9+x^2}}$
42. $f(x) = \ln\dfrac{\sqrt{4x-7}}{(3x-2)^3}$
43. $f(x) = \ln\dfrac{x+1}{x-1}$
44. $f(x) = x^2 \ln\dfrac{1}{2x+1}$
45. $g(t) = \ln\dfrac{t^2}{t^2+1}$
46. $f(x) = \ln\dfrac{\sqrt{x+1}}{(x-1)^3}$

In Problems 47 through 58, find dy/dx by logarithmic differentiation.

47. $y = 2^x$
48. $y = x^x$
49. $y = x^{\ln x}$
50. $y = (1+x)^{1/x}$
51. $y = (\ln x)^{\sqrt{x}}$
52. $y = (3 + 2^x)^x$
53. $y = \dfrac{(1+x^2)^{3/2}}{(1+x^3)^{4/3}}$
54. $y = (x+1)^x$
55. $y = (x^2+1)^{x^2}$
56. $y = \left(1 + \dfrac{1}{x}\right)^x$
57. $y = \left(\sqrt{x}\right)^{\sqrt{x}}$
58. $y = x^{\sin x}$

In Problems 59 through 62, write an equation of the line tangent to the graph of the given function at the indicated point.

59. $y = xe^{2x}$ at the point $(1, e^2)$
60. $y = e^{2x} \cos x$ at the point $(0, 1)$
61. $y = x^3 \ln x$ at the point $(1, 0)$
62. $y = \dfrac{\ln x}{x^2}$ at the point (e, e^{-2})

In Problems 63 and 64, differentiate the given function $f(x)$ and its derivative in turn, several times in succession. Then give a likely formula for the result after n successive differentiations in this manner.

63. $f(x) = e^{2x}$
64. $f(x) = xe^x$

65. Figure 7.1.19 shows the graph of the function $f(x) = e^{-x/6} \sin x$, together with the graphs of its "envelope curves" $y = e^{-x/6}$ and $y = -e^{-x/6}$. Find the first local maximum point and the first local minimum point on the graph of f for $x > 0$.

FIGURE 7.1.19 The graph for Problems 65 and 66.

66. Find the first two points of tangency of the curve $y = e^{-x/6} \sin x$ with the two envelope curves shown in Fig. 7.1.19. Are these the same as the two local extreme points found in Problem 65?

67. Find graphically the coordinates (accurate to three decimal places) of the intersection point of the graphs $y = e^x$ and $y = x^{10}$ indicated in Fig. 7.1.20.

FIGURE 7.1.20 Comparing $y = e^x$ and $y = x^{10}$.

68. See Problem 67. Determine a viewing rectangle that reveals a second intersection point (with $x > 10$) of the graphs $y = e^x$ and $y = x^{10}$. Then determine graphically the first three digits of the larger solution x of the equation $e^x = x^{10}$ (thus writing this solution in the form $p.qr \times 10^k$).

69. If we substitute $n = 10^k$ in $e = \lim\limits_{n \to \infty} \left(1 + \dfrac{1}{n}\right)^n$, we get the limit

$$e = \lim_{k \to \infty} \left(1 + \dfrac{1}{10^k}\right)^{10^k}$$

that "converges" much more rapidly. Using a calculator or computer, substitute $k = 1, 2, 3, \ldots, 8$ in turn to discover that $e \approx 2.71828$ accurate to five decimal places.

70. Suppose that u and v are differentiable functions of x. Show by logarithmic differentiation that

$$D_x(u^v) = v(u^{v-1})\dfrac{du}{dx} + (u^v \ln u)\dfrac{dv}{dx}.$$

Interpret the two terms on the right in relation to the special cases in which (a) u is a constant; (b) v is a constant.

71. Suppose that $y = uvw/pqr$, where $u, v, w, p, q,$ and r are nonzero differentiable functions of x. Show by logarithmic differentiation that

$$\dfrac{dy}{dx} = y \cdot \left(\dfrac{1}{u}\dfrac{du}{dx} + \dfrac{1}{v}\dfrac{dv}{dx} + \dfrac{1}{w}\dfrac{dw}{dx} - \dfrac{1}{p}\dfrac{dp}{dx} - \dfrac{1}{q}\dfrac{dq}{dx} - \dfrac{1}{r}\dfrac{dr}{dx}\right).$$

Is the generalization—for an arbitrary finite number of factors in numerator and denominator—obvious?

72. Show that the number $\log_2 3$ is irrational. [*Suggestion:* Assume to the contrary that $\log_2 3 = p/q$ where p and q are positive integers; then express the consequence of this assumption in exponential form. Under what circumstances can an integral power of 2 equal an integral power of 3?]

73. The $\boxed{\texttt{log}}$ key on the typical calculator denotes the base 10 logarithm $f(x) = \log_{10} x$.
(a) Use the definition of the derivative to show that

$$f'(1) = \lim_{h \to 0} \log_{10}(1 + h)^{1/h}.$$

(b) Investigate the limit in (a) numerically to show that $f'(1) \approx 0.4343$.

74. The object of this problem is to differentiate the base 10 logarithm function of Problem 73.
   (a) First use the known formula for $D_x e^u$ to show that $D_x 10^x = 10^x \ln 10$.
   (b) Conclude from the chain rule that
   $$D_x 10^u = 10^u (\ln 10) \frac{du}{dx}.$$
   (c) Substitute $u = \log_{10} x$ in the inverse function identity $10^{\log_{10} x} = x$ and then differentiate using the result of part (b) to conclude that
   $$D_x \log_{10} x = \frac{1}{x \ln 10} \approx \frac{0.4343}{x},$$
   consistent with the result (for $x = 1$) of Problem 73.

7.1 Project: Discovering the Number e for Yourself

You can investigate the value of e by approximating the value of a such that

$$m(a) = \lim_{h \to 0} \frac{a^h - 1}{h} = 1.$$

You need use only available technology to calculate (with appropriate fixed values of a) values of the function $\phi(h) = (a^h - 1)/h$ with h sufficiently small that you can recognize (to appropriate accuracy) the value of the limit.

For instance, if you calculate $\phi(h)$ with $a = 2$ and with $a = 3$ for $h = 0.1, 0.01, 0.001, 0.0001, \ldots$, you should find that

$$m(2) \approx 0.6931 < 1 \quad \text{whereas} \quad m(3) \approx 1.0986 > 1.$$

It follows that the mysterious number e for which $m(e) = 1$ is somewhere between 2 and 3. Linear interpolation between the values of $m(2) \approx 0.6931$ and $m(3) \approx 1.0986$ suggests that $e \approx 2.7$ or $e \approx 2.8$ accurate to one decimal place.

Investigate the values of $m(2.7)$ and $m(2.8)$ to verify the entries shown in Fig. 7.1.21. Continue in this way to close in on the number e. Don't quit until you're convinced that $e \approx 2.718$ accurate to three decimal places.

a	$m(a)$
2	0.6931
2.7	0.9933
↓	↓
e	1.0000
↑	↑
2.8	1.0296
3	1.0986

FIGURE 7.1.21 Closing in on the number e.

7.2 INDETERMINATE FORMS AND L'HÔPITAL'S RULE

An *indeterminate form* is a certain type of expression with a limit that is not evident by inspection. There are several types of indeterminate forms. If

$$\lim_{x \to a} f(x) = 0 = \lim_{x \to a} g(x),$$

then we say that the quotient $f(x)/g(x)$ has the **indeterminate form** $0/0$ at $x = a$ (or as $x \to a$). For example, to differentiate the trigonometric functions (Section 3.7), we needed to know that

$$\lim_{x \to 0} \frac{\sin x}{x} = 1. \tag{1}$$

Figure 7.2.1 corroborates the fact that $(\sin x)/x$ is close to 1 when x is close to zero.

The quotient $(\sin x)/x$ in Eq. (1) has the indeterminate form $0/0$ at $x = 0$ because the functions $f(x) = \sin x$ and $g(x) = x$ both approach zero as $x \to 0$. Hence the quotient law of limits cannot be used to evaluate this limit. We therefore needed a special geometric argument (see Section 2.3) to find the limit in Eq. (1). Something similar happens whenever we compute a derivative, because the quotient

$$\frac{f(x) - f(a)}{x - a},$$

whose limit as $x \to a$ is the derivative $f'(a)$, has the indeterminate form $0/0$ at $x = a$.

We can sometimes find the limit of an indeterminate form by performing a special algebraic manipulation or construction, as in our earlier computation of derivatives. Often, however, it is more convenient to apply a rule that appeared in the first

FIGURE 7.2.1 Visual evidence that the quotient $(\sin x)/x$ is near 1 when x is near zero.

calculus textbook ever published, by the Marquis de l'Hôpital, in 1696. L'Hôpital was a French nobleman who had hired the Swiss mathematician John Bernoulli as his calculus tutor, and "l'Hôpital's rule" is actually the work of Bernoulli.

THEOREM 1 L'Hôpital's Rule
Suppose that the functions f and g are differentiable and that $g'(x)$ is nonzero in some neighborhood of the point a (except possibly at a itself). Suppose also that

$$\lim_{x \to a} f(x) = 0 = \lim_{x \to a} g(x).$$

Then

$$\lim_{x \to a} \frac{f(x)}{g(x)} = \lim_{x \to a} \frac{f'(x)}{g'(x)}, \qquad (2)$$

provided that the limit on the right either exists (as a finite real number) or is $+\infty$ or $-\infty$.

In essence, l'Hôpital's rule says that if $f(x)/g(x)$ has the indeterminate form $0/0$ at $x = a$, then—subject to a few mild restrictions—this quotient has the same limit at $x = a$ as does the quotient $f'(x)/g'(x)$ of *derivatives*. The proof of l'Hôpital's rule is discussed at the end of this section.

EXAMPLE 1 Find $\lim\limits_{x \to 0} \dfrac{e^x - 1}{\sin 2x}$.

Solution The fraction whose limit we seek has the indeterminate form $0/0$ at $x = 0$. The numerator and denominator are clearly differentiable in some neighborhood of $x = 0$, and the derivative of the denominator is certainly nonzero if the neighborhood is small enough (specifically, if $|x| < \pi/4$). So l'Hôpital's rule applies, and

$$\lim_{x \to 0} \frac{e^x - 1}{\sin 2x} = \lim_{x \to 0} \frac{e^x}{2\cos 2x} = \frac{e^0}{2\cos 0} = \frac{1}{2}$$

because (by continuity) both e^x and $\cos 2x$ approach 1 as $x \to 0$. Figure 7.2.2 corroborates this limit. ◆

If the quotient $f'(x)/g'(x)$ is itself indeterminate, then l'Hôpital's rule may be applied a second (or third, ...) time, as in Example 2. When the rule is applied repeatedly, however, the conditions for its applicability must be checked at each stage.

FIGURE 7.2.2 Visual evidence that the quotient $\dfrac{e^x - 1}{\sin 2x}$ is near $\dfrac{1}{2}$ when x is near 0.

EXAMPLE 2 Find $\lim\limits_{x \to 1} \dfrac{1 - x + \ln x}{1 + \cos \pi x}$.

Solution

$$\lim_{x \to 1} \frac{1 - x + \ln x}{1 + \cos \pi x} = \lim_{x \to 1} \frac{-1 + \dfrac{1}{x}}{-\pi \sin \pi x} \qquad \text{(still of the form 0/0)}$$

$$= \lim_{x \to 1} \frac{x - 1}{\pi x \sin \pi x} \qquad \text{(algebraic simplification)}$$

$$= \lim_{x \to 1} \frac{1}{\pi \sin \pi x + \pi^2 x \cos \pi x} \qquad \text{(l'Hôpital's rule again)}$$

$$= -\frac{1}{\pi^2} \qquad \text{(by inspection).}$$

Because the final limit exists, so do the previous ones; the existence of the final limit in Eq. (2) implies the existence of the first. ◆

When you need to apply l'Hôpital's rule repeatedly in this way, you need only keep differentiating the numerator and denominator separately until at least one of them has a nonzero finite limit. At that point you can recognize the limit of the quotient by inspection, as in the final step in Example 2.

EXAMPLE 3 Find $\lim_{x \to 0} \dfrac{\sin x}{x + x^2}$.

Solution If we simply apply l'Hôpital's rule twice in succession, the result is the *incorrect* computation

$$\lim_{x \to 0} \frac{\sin x}{x + x^2} = \lim_{x \to 0} \frac{\cos x}{1 + 2x}$$
$$= \lim_{x \to 0} \frac{-\sin x}{2} = 0. \quad \textbf{(Wrong!)}$$

The answer is wrong because $(\cos x)/(1 + 2x)$ is *not* an indeterminate form. Thus l'Hôpital's rule cannot be applied to it. The *correct* computation is

$$\lim_{x \to 0} \frac{\sin x}{x + x^2} = \lim_{x \to 0} \frac{\cos x}{1 + 2x} = \frac{\lim_{x \to 0} \cos x}{\lim_{x \to 0} (1 + 2x)} = \frac{1}{1} = 1. \quad \blacklozenge$$

The point of Example 3 is to issue a warning: Verify the hypotheses of l'Hôpital's rule *before* you apply it. It is an oversimplification to say that l'Hôpital's rule works when you need it and doesn't work when you don't, but there is still much truth in this statement.

Indeterminate Forms Involving ∞

L'Hôpital's rule has several variations. In addition to the fact that the limit in Eq. (2) is allowed to be infinite, the real number a in l'Hôpital's rule may be replaced with either $+\infty$ or $-\infty$. For example,

$$\lim_{x \to \infty} \frac{f(x)}{g(x)} = \lim_{x \to \infty} \frac{f'(x)}{g'(x)} \quad \textbf{(3)}$$

provided that the other hypotheses are satisfied in some interval of the form $(c, +\infty)$. In particular, to use Eq. (3), we must first verify that

$$\lim_{x \to \infty} f(x) = 0 = \lim_{x \to \infty} g(x)$$

and that the right-hand limit in Eq. (3) exists. The proof of this version of l'Hôpital's rule is outlined in Problem 70.

L'Hôpital's rule may also be used when $f(x)/g(x)$ has the **indeterminate form** ∞/∞. This means that

$$\lim_{x \to a} f(x) \quad \text{is either } +\infty \text{ or } -\infty$$

and

$$\lim_{x \to a} g(x) \quad \text{is either } +\infty \text{ or } -\infty.$$

The proof of this extension of the rule is difficult and is omitted here. [For a proof, see (for example) A. E. Taylor and W. R. Mann, *Advanced Calculus*, 3rd ed. (New York: John Wiley, 1983), p. 107.]

One-sided indeterminate forms occur, and we may speak of a 0/0 form or an ∞/∞ form as either $x \to a^-$ or as $x \to a^+$.

444 CHAPTER 7 Calculus of Transcendental Functions

EXAMPLE 4 Figure 7.2.3 shows a computer-generated graph of the function

$$f(x) = \frac{\ln 2x}{\ln x}. \tag{4}$$

The vertical asymptote $x = 1$ is explained (without using l'Hôpital's rule) by the facts that

- the numerator $\ln 2x$ is positive at $x = 1$, while
- the denominator $\ln x$ approaches zero through negative values as $x \to 1^-$ and approaches zero through positive values as $x \to 1^+$.

The familiar graph of $y = \ln x$ (Fig. 7.2.4) reminds us that $\ln x \to -\infty$ as $x \to 0^+$ and that $\ln x \to +\infty$ as $x \to +\infty$. Consequently, we see that the function f in Eq. (4) has the indeterminate form ∞/∞, both as $x \to 0^+$ and as $x \to +\infty$. Thus l'Hôpital's rule gives

$$\lim_{x \to 0^+} \frac{\ln 2x}{\ln x} = \lim_{x \to 0^+} \frac{\frac{2}{2x}}{\frac{1}{x}} = \lim_{x \to 0^+} 1 = 1$$

FIGURE 7.2.3 The graph $y = \dfrac{\ln 2x}{\ln x}$ has both the vertical asymptote $x = 1$ and the horizontal asymptote $y = 1$.

and

$$\lim_{x \to +\infty} \frac{\ln 2x}{\ln x} = \lim_{x \to +\infty} \frac{\frac{2}{2x}}{\frac{1}{x}} = \lim_{x \to +\infty} 1 = 1.$$

The fact that

$$\lim_{x \to 0^+} \frac{\ln 2x}{\ln x} = 1$$

explains why the graph in Fig. 7.2.3 appears to "start" at the point (0, 1). And the fact that

$$\lim_{x \to \infty} \frac{\ln 2x}{\ln x} = 1$$

explains the horizontal asymptote $y = 1$ that we see in Fig. 7.2.3. ◆

FIGURE 7.2.4 The graphs $y = e^x$ and $y = \ln x$ are reflections of one another in the line $y = x$.

Order of Magnitude of e^x and $\ln x$

Because $D_x e^x = e^x$ (for all x) and $D_x \ln x = 1/x$ (for all $x > 0$), the functions $\ln x$ and e^x are increasing wherever they are defined. If n is an integer and $x > n$, it follows that $e^x > e^n > 2^n$, and hence that

$$\lim_{x \to +\infty} e^x = +\infty. \tag{5}$$

Similarly, if $x > 2^n$, then $\ln x > \ln 2^n = n \ln 2$, and therefore

$$\lim_{x \to +\infty} \ln x = +\infty \tag{6}$$

as well.

But the graphs in Fig. 7.2.4 suggest that as $x \to +\infty$, $e^x \to +\infty$ much more rapidly than $\ln x \to +\infty$. Indeed, l'Hôpital's rule yields

$$\lim_{x \to +\infty} \frac{e^x}{\ln x} = \lim_{x \to +\infty} \frac{e^x}{\frac{1}{x}} = \lim_{x \to +\infty} x e^x = +\infty.$$

Thus, when x is large positive, e^x is so much larger than $\ln x$ that the quotient $e^x/(\ln x)$ is large positive. This observation seems related to the facts that:

- The second derivative $D_x^2 e^x = e^x > 0$ for all x, so the curve $y = e^x$ is concave upward, and becomes steeper and steeper as x increases.

FIGURE 7.2.5 The graph $y = x^2 e^{-x}$ has two local extrema, two inflection points, and the horizontal asymptote $y = 0$.

- In contrast, $D_x^2 \ln x = -1/x^2 < 0$ for all $x > 0$, so the curve $y = \ln x$ is concave downward, and becomes less and less steep as x increases.

EXAMPLE 5 Explain the principal features of the graph of the function $f(x) = x^2 e^{-x}$ shown in Fig. 7.2.5.

Solution The function $f(x) = x^2/e^x$ has the indeterminate form ∞/∞ as $x \to +\infty$. Hence the horizontal asymptote $y = 0$ is explained by two applications of l'Hôpital's rule:

$$\lim_{x \to \infty} \frac{x^2}{e^x} = \lim_{x \to \infty} \frac{2x}{e^x} = \lim_{x \to \infty} \frac{2}{e^x} = 0. \tag{7}$$

The two local extrema that we see in the figure result from the fact that the derivative

$$f'(x) = 2x \cdot e^{-x} - x^2 \cdot e^{-x} = (2x - x^2)e^{-x} = x(2 - x)e^{-x}$$

has the two zeros $x = 0$ and $x = 2$. The second derivative is

$$f''(x) = (2 - 2x) \cdot e^{-x} - (2x - x^2) \cdot e^{-x} = (x^2 - 4x + 2)e^{-x},$$

and the two solutions $x = 2 \pm \sqrt{2}$ of the quadratic equation $x^2 - 4x + 2 = 0$ provide the two inflection points visible in Fig. 7.2.5. ◆

The exponential function is notable for its very rapid rate of increase with increasing x. In fact, e^x increases more rapidly as $x \to +\infty$ than *any* fixed power of x. Thus the limit in (7) is a special case of the fact that

$$\lim_{x \to \infty} \frac{x^k}{e^x} = 0 \tag{8}$$

or, alternatively,

$$\lim_{x \to \infty} \frac{e^x}{x^k} = +\infty \tag{9}$$

for any fixed real number $k > 0$. For instance, if $k = n$, a positive integer, then n successive applications of l'Hôpital's rule give

$$\lim_{x \to \infty} \frac{x^n}{e^x} = \lim_{x \to \infty} \frac{nx^{n-1}}{e^x} = \lim_{x \to \infty} \frac{n(n-1)x^{n-2}}{e^x}$$

$$= \cdots = \lim_{x \to \infty} \frac{n(n-1) \cdots 2x}{e^x} = \lim_{x \to \infty} \frac{n(n-1) \cdots 2 \cdot 1}{e^x} = 0.$$

In Problem 61 we ask you to consider positive nonintegral values of k.

The table in Fig. 7.2.6 illustrates the case $k = 5$ of Eq. (8). Although both $x^5 \to +\infty$ and $e^x \to +\infty$ as $x \to +\infty$, we see that e^x increases so much more rapidly than x^5 that $x^5/e^x \to 0$.

x	x^5	e^x	x^5/e^x
10	1.00×10^5	2.20×10^4	4.54×10^0
20	3.20×10^6	4.85×10^8	6.60×10^{-3}
30	2.43×10^7	1.07×10^{13}	2.27×10^{-6}
40	1.02×10^8	2.35×10^{17}	4.35×10^{-10}
50	3.13×10^8	5.18×10^{21}	6.03×10^{-14}
↓	↓	↓	↓
∞	∞	∞	

FIGURE 7.2.6 Orders of magnitude of x^5 and e^x.

FIGURE 7.2.7 The graph $y = (\ln x)/\sqrt{x}$ has a local maximum, an inflection point, and the horizontal asymptote $y = 0$.

EXAMPLE 6 Explain the principal features of the graph of the function

$$f(x) = \frac{\ln x}{\sqrt{x}}$$

shown in Fig. 7.2.7.

Solution The function $f(x) = (\ln x)/\sqrt{x}$ has the indeterminate form ∞/∞ as $x \to +\infty$. A single application of l'Hôpital's rule yields

$$\lim_{x \to \infty} \frac{\ln x}{\sqrt{x}} = \lim_{x \to \infty} \frac{\frac{1}{x}}{\frac{1}{2\sqrt{x}}} = \lim_{x \to \infty} \frac{2}{\sqrt{x}} = 0, \tag{10}$$

and thus the graph has the horizontal asymptote $y = 0$. The local maximum that we see in the figure results from the fact that the derivative

$$f'(x) = \frac{\frac{1}{x}\sqrt{x} - \frac{\ln x}{2\sqrt{x}}}{x} = \frac{2 - \ln x}{2x^{3/2}}$$

has the zero $x = e^2$. The inflection point that we see corresponds to the zero $x = e^{8/3}$ of the second derivative

$$f''(x) = \frac{-\frac{1}{x} \cdot 2x^{3/2} - (2 - \ln x)(3x^{1/2})}{4x^3} = \frac{-8 + 3\ln x}{4x^{5/2}}. \qquad \blacklozenge$$

In contrast with the exponential function, the natural logarithm function is notable for its very slow rate of increase with increasing x. In Problem 62 we ask you to generalize the result in Eq. (10) by showing that

$$\lim_{x \to +\infty} \frac{\ln x}{x^k} = 0 \tag{11}$$

if $k > 0$. Thus

- $\ln x$ increases slower than any (positive) power of x, whereas
- e^x increases faster than any power of x.

REMARK Figure 7.2.8 might suggest to the unwary that $\ln x$ is greater than (rather than less than) $x^{1/10}$ when x is large positive. But Eq. (11) implies that the graph of $y = x^{1/10}$ must eventually overtake and recross the graph of $y = \ln x$. (See Problem 74.)

FIGURE 7.2.8 Comparing $y = \ln x$ with $y = x^{1/10}$.

Proof of L'Hôpital's Rule

Suppose that the functions f and g of Theorem 1 are not merely differentiable but have continuous derivatives near $x = a$ and that $g'(a) \neq 0$. Then

$$\lim_{x \to a} \frac{f'(x)}{g'(x)} = \frac{\lim_{x \to a} f'(x)}{\lim_{x \to a} g'(x)} = \frac{f'(a)}{g'(a)} \tag{12}$$

by the quotient law for limits. In this case l'Hôpital's rule in Eq. (2) reduces to the limit

$$\lim_{x \to a} \frac{f(x)}{g(x)} = \frac{f'(a)}{g'(a)}, \tag{13}$$

which is a weak form of the rule. It actually is this weak form that is typically applied in single-step applications of l'Hôpital's rule.

EXAMPLE 7 In Example 1 we had
$$f(x) = e^x - 1, \quad g(x) = \sin 2x$$
so
$$f'(x) = e^x, \quad g'(x) = 2\cos 2x,$$
and $g'(0) = 2 \neq 0$. With $a = 0$, Eq. (13) therefore gives
$$\lim_{x \to 0} \frac{e^x - 1}{\sin 2x} = \lim_{x \to 0} \frac{f(x)}{g(x)} = \frac{f'(0)}{g'(0)} = \frac{1}{2}.$$
◆

THEOREM 2 L'Hôpital's Rule (weak form)
Suppose that the functions f and g are differentiable at $x = a$, that
$$f(a) = 0 = g(a),$$
and that $g'(a) \neq 0$. Then
$$\lim_{x \to a} \frac{f(x)}{g(x)} = \frac{f'(a)}{g'(a)}. \tag{13}$$

PROOF We begin with the right-hand side of Eq. (13) and work toward the left-hand side.

$$\frac{f'(a)}{g'(a)} = \frac{\lim_{x \to a} \dfrac{f(x) - f(a)}{x - a}}{\lim_{x \to a} \dfrac{g(x) - g(a)}{x - a}} \quad \text{(the definition of the derivative)}$$

$$= \lim_{x \to a} \frac{\dfrac{f(x) - f(a)}{x - a}}{\dfrac{g(x) - g(a)}{x - a}} \quad \text{(the quotient law of limits)}$$

$$= \lim_{x \to a} \frac{f(x) - f(a)}{g(x) - g(a)} \quad \text{(algebraic simplification)}$$

$$= \lim_{x \to a} \frac{f(x)}{g(x)}$$

[because $f(a) = 0 = g(a)$]. ◀

Figure 7.2.9 illustrates the meaning and proof of Theorem 2. Appendix H includes a proof of the strong form of l'Hôpital's rule, the form stated in Theorem 1.

FIGURE 7.2.9 Suppose that the point $P(g(t), f(t))$ traces a continuous curve that passes through the origin O when $t = a$. Then the secant line OP approaches the tangent line at O as $t \to a$, so its slope $f(t)/g(t)$ approaches the slope $f'(a)/g'(a)$ of the tangent line at O.

7.2 TRUE/FALSE STUDY GUIDE

7.2 CONCEPTS: QUESTIONS AND DISCUSSION

In the following questions, think of the given functions f and g as a tortoise and a hare racing toward infinity as $x \to +\infty$. Which is the tortoise and which is the hare?

1. $f(x) = x^2$ and $g(x) = x^5$
2. $f(x) = x^{1/2}$ and $g(x) = x^{1/5}$
3. $f(x) = x^{10} \ln x$ and $g(x) = \dfrac{e^x}{x^{10}}$
4. $f(x) = e^x$ and $g(x)$ is a polynomial
5. $f(x) = \ln x$ and $g(x)$ is a polynomial

7.2 PROBLEMS

Find the limits in Problems 1 through 48.

1. $\lim_{x \to 1} \dfrac{x-1}{x^2-1}$
2. $\lim_{x \to \infty} \dfrac{3x-4}{2x-5}$
3. $\lim_{x \to \infty} \dfrac{2x^2-1}{5x^2+3x}$
4. $\lim_{x \to 0} \dfrac{e^{3x}-1}{x}$
5. $\lim_{x \to 0} \dfrac{\sin x^2}{x}$
6. $\lim_{x \to 0^+} \dfrac{1-\cos\sqrt{x}}{x}$
7. $\lim_{x \to 1} \dfrac{x-1}{\sin x}$
8. $\lim_{x \to 0} \dfrac{1-\cos x}{x^3}$
9. $\lim_{x \to 0} \dfrac{e^x - x - 1}{x^2}$
10. $\lim_{z \to \pi/2} \dfrac{1+\cos 2z}{1-\sin 2z}$
11. $\lim_{u \to 0} \dfrac{u \tan u}{1-\cos u}$
12. $\lim_{x \to 0} \dfrac{x-\tan x}{x^3}$
13. $\lim_{x \to \infty} \dfrac{\ln x}{\sqrt[10]{x}}$
14. $\lim_{r \to \infty} \dfrac{e^r}{(r+1)^4}$
15. $\lim_{x \to 10} \dfrac{\ln(x-9)}{x-10}$
16. $\lim_{t \to \infty} \dfrac{t^2+1}{t \ln t}$
17. $\lim_{x \to 0} \dfrac{e^x + e^{-x} - 2}{x \sin x}$
18. $\lim_{x \to (\pi/2)^-} \dfrac{\tan x}{\ln(\cos x)}$
19. $\lim_{x \to 0} \dfrac{\sin 3x}{\tan 5x}$
20. $\lim_{x \to 0} \dfrac{e^x - e^{-x}}{x}$
21. $\lim_{x \to 1} \dfrac{x^3-1}{x^2-1}$
22. $\lim_{x \to 2} \dfrac{x^3-8}{x^4-16}$
23. $\lim_{x \to \infty} \dfrac{x+\sin x}{3x+\cos x}$
24. $\lim_{x \to \infty} \dfrac{\sqrt{x^2+4}}{x}$
25. $\lim_{x \to 0} \dfrac{2^x-1}{3^x-1}$
26. $\lim_{x \to \infty} \dfrac{2^x}{3^x}$
27. $\lim_{x \to \infty} \dfrac{\sqrt{x^2-1}}{\sqrt{4x^2-x}}$
28. $\lim_{x \to \infty} \dfrac{\sqrt{x^3+x}}{\sqrt{2x^3-4}}$
29. $\lim_{x \to 0} \dfrac{\ln(1+x)}{x}$
30. $\lim_{x \to \infty} \dfrac{\ln(\ln x)}{x \ln x}$
31. $\lim_{x \to 0} \dfrac{2e^x - x^2 - 2x - 2}{x^3}$
32. $\lim_{x \to 0} \dfrac{\sin x - \tan x}{x^3}$
33. $\lim_{x \to 0} \dfrac{2 - e^x - e^{-x}}{2x^2}$
34. $\lim_{x \to 0} \dfrac{e^{3x} - e^{-3x}}{2x}$
35. $\lim_{x \to \pi/2} \dfrac{2x - \pi}{\tan 2x}$
36. $\lim_{x \to \pi/2} \dfrac{\sec x}{\tan x}$
37. $\lim_{x \to 2} \dfrac{x - 2\cos \pi x}{x^2 - 4}$
38. $\lim_{x \to 1/2} \dfrac{2x - \sin \pi x}{4x^2 - 1}$
39. $\lim_{x \to 0^+} \dfrac{\ln \sqrt{2x}}{\ln \sqrt[3]{3x}}$
40. $\lim_{x \to 0} \dfrac{\ln(1+x)}{\ln(1-x^2)}$
41. $\lim_{x \to 0} \dfrac{\exp(x^3) - 1}{x - \sin x}$
42. $\lim_{x \to 0} \dfrac{\sqrt{1+3x} - 1}{x}$
43. $\lim_{x \to 0} \dfrac{\sqrt[3]{1+4x} - 1}{x}$
44. $\lim_{x \to 0} \dfrac{\sqrt{3+2x} - \sqrt{3+x}}{x}$
45. $\lim_{x \to 0} \dfrac{\sqrt[3]{1+x} - \sqrt[3]{1-x}}{x}$
46. $\lim_{x \to \pi/4} \dfrac{1 - \tan x}{4x - \pi}$
47. $\lim_{x \to 0} \dfrac{\ln(1+x^2)}{e^x - \cos x}$
48. $\lim_{x \to 2} \dfrac{x^5 - 5x^2 - 12}{x^{10} - 500x - 24}$

Sketch the graphs of the curves in Problems 49 through 60. Even if you use a graphing calculator or computer, apply l'Hôpital's rule as necessary to verify the apparent behavior of the curve as x approaches a point where the function has an indeterminate form.

49. $y = \dfrac{\sin^2 x}{x}$
50. $y = \dfrac{\sin^2 x}{x^2}$
51. $y = \dfrac{\sin x}{x - \pi}$
52. $y = \dfrac{\cos x}{2x - \pi}$
53. $y = \dfrac{1 - \cos x}{x^2}$
54. $y = \dfrac{x - \sin x}{x^3}$
55. $y = xe^{-x}$
56. $y = e^{-x}\sqrt{x}$
57. $y = xe^{-\sqrt{x}}$
58. $y = x^2 e^{-2x}$
59. $y = \dfrac{\ln x}{x}$
60. $y = \dfrac{\ln x}{\sqrt{x} + \sqrt[3]{x}}$

61. Show that $\lim_{x \to \infty} \dfrac{x^k}{e^x} = 0$ if k is a positive real number.

62. Show that $\lim_{x \to \infty} \dfrac{\ln x}{x^k} = 0$ if k is a positive real number.

63. Suppose that n is a fixed positive integer larger than 1. Show that the curve $y = x^n e^{-x}$ has a single local maximum and two inflection points for $x > 0$, and also has the x-axis as an asymptote.

64. Suppose that k is an arbitrary positive real number. Show that the curve $y = x^{-k} \ln x$ has a single local maximum and a single inflection point for $x > 0$, and also has the x-axis as an asymptote.

65. Substitute $y = \dfrac{1}{x}$ in Eq. (11) to show that
$$\lim_{x \to 0^+} x^k \ln x = 0$$
if k is a positive real number.

66. Show that if n is any integer, then
$$\lim_{x \to \infty} \dfrac{(\ln x)^n}{x} = 0.$$

67. Suppose that $f'(x)$ is continuous. Show that
$$\lim_{h \to 0} \dfrac{f(x+h) - f(x-h)}{2h} = f'(x).$$
The *symmetric difference quotient* on the left can be used (with h very small) to approximate the derivative numerically, and turns out to be a better approximation than the one-sided difference quotient $[f(x+h) - f(x)]/h$.

68. Suppose that $f''(x)$ is continuous. Show that
$$\lim_{h \to 0} \dfrac{f(x+h) - 2f(x) + f(x-h)}{h^2} = f''(x).$$
The *second difference quotient* on the left can be used (with h very small) to approximate the second derivative numerically.

69. In his calculus textbook of 1696, l'Hôpital used a limit similar to
$$\lim_{x \to 1} \dfrac{\sqrt{2x - x^4} - \sqrt[3]{x}}{1 - x^{4/3}}$$
to illustrate his rule. Evaluate this limit.

70. Establish the 0/0 version of l'Hôpital's rule for the case $a = \infty$. *Suggestion:* Let $F(t) = f(1/t)$ and $G(t) = g(1/t)$. Then show that
$$\lim_{x \to \infty} \frac{f(x)}{g(x)} = \lim_{t \to 0^+} \frac{F(t)}{G(t)} = \lim_{t \to 0^+} \frac{F'(t)}{G'(t)} = \lim_{x \to \infty} \frac{f'(x)}{g'(x)},$$
using l'Hôpital's rule for the case $a = 0$.

71. Show *without* using l'Hôpital's rule that
$$\lim_{x \to \infty} \left(\frac{x}{e}\right)^x = +\infty.$$
Thus the function $f(x) = x^x$ increases even faster than the exponential function e^x as $x \to +\infty$.

72. If a chemical plant releases an amount A of a pollutant into a canal at time $t = 0$, then the resulting concentration of pollutant at time t in the water at a town on the canal a fixed distance x_0 downstream is
$$C(t) = \frac{A}{\sqrt{\pi k t}} \exp\left(-\frac{x_0^2}{4kt}\right)$$
where k is a constant. Sketch a typical graph of $C(t)$ for $t \geq 0$. Then show that the maximum pollutant concentration that occurs at the town is
$$C_{\max} = \frac{A}{x_0}\sqrt{\frac{2}{\pi e}}.$$

73. (a) If $f(x) = x^n e^{-x}$ (where n is a fixed positive integer) is the function of Problem 63, show that the maximum value of $f(x)$ for $x \geq 0$ is $f(n) = n^n e^{-n}$. (b) Conclude from the fact that $f(n-1)$ and $f(n+1)$ are both less than $f(n)$ that
$$\left(1 + \frac{1}{n}\right)^n < e < \left(1 - \frac{1}{n}\right)^{-n}.$$
Substitute $n = 1{,}000{,}000$ to prove that $e \approx 2.71828$ accurate to five decimal places.

74. (a) Approximate numerically the solution x_1 of the equation $\ln x = x^{1/10}$ that is indicated in Fig. 7.2.8. (b) Use a calculator or computer to plot the graphs of $y = \ln x$ and $y = x^{1/10}$ in a viewing window that shows a second solution x_2 of the equation $\ln x = x^{1/10}$. Then approximate x_2 numerically. *Suggestion:* Plot the graphs on successive intervals of the form $[10^n, 10^{n+1}]$ where $n = 1, 2, 3, \ldots$. By the time you locate x_2 you may well have the feeling of "going boldly where no one has gone before!"

75. Figure 7.2.10 shows an arc of the unit circle $x^2 + y^2 = 1$ with central angle 2α and height $h = 1 - \cos\alpha$. Show that the centroid of this arc is the point
$$\left(0, \frac{\sin\alpha}{\alpha}\right).$$

FIGURE 7.2.10 The circular arc of Problem 75.

76. The centroid C shown in Fig. 7.2.10 appears to lie about one-third of the way from the arc to the horizontal chord joining its endpoints. Prove that this is indeed so for small values of α by showing that $\lim_{\alpha \to 0}(d/h) = 1/3$, where d denotes the distance from the centroid C to the highest point $(0, 1)$ of the circular arc.

7.3 MORE INDETERMINATE FORMS

We saw in Section 7.2 that l'Hôpital's rule can be applied to the indeterminate forms $0/0$ and ∞/∞. There are other indeterminate forms; although l'Hôpital's rule cannot be applied directly to these other forms, it may be possible to convert them into the form $0/0$ or into the form ∞/∞. If so, it may be possible to apply l'Hôpital's rule.

Suppose that
$$\lim_{x \to a} f(x) = 0 \quad \text{and} \quad \lim_{x \to a} g(x) = \infty.$$

Then we say that the product $f(x) \cdot g(x)$ has the **indeterminate form** $0 \cdot \infty$ at $x = a$ (or as $x \to a$). To find the limit of $f(x) \cdot g(x)$ at $x = a$, we can change the problem to one of the forms $0/0$ or ∞/∞ in this way:
$$f(x) \cdot g(x) = \frac{f(x)}{1/g(x)} = \frac{g(x)}{1/f(x)}.$$

Now l'Hôpital's rule may be applied if its other hypotheses are satisfied, as illustrated in Example 1.

EXAMPLE 1 Find $\lim_{x \to \infty} x \ln\left(\frac{x-1}{x+1}\right)$.

Solution We are dealing with the indeterminate form $0 \cdot \infty$, so we write

$$\lim_{x \to \infty} x \ln\left(\frac{x-1}{x+1}\right) = \lim_{x \to \infty} \frac{\ln\left(\frac{x-1}{x+1}\right)}{\frac{1}{x}}.$$

The right-hand limit has the form 0/0, so we can apply l'Hôpital's rule. First we note that

$$D_x \ln\left(\frac{x-1}{x+1}\right) = \frac{2}{x^2 - 1}.$$

Thus

$$\lim_{x \to \infty} x \ln\left(\frac{x-1}{x+1}\right) = \lim_{x \to \infty} \frac{\frac{2}{x^2-1}}{-\frac{1}{x^2}}$$

$$= \lim_{x \to \infty} \frac{-2x^2}{x^2-1} = \lim_{x \to \infty} \frac{-2}{1 - \frac{1}{x^2}} = -2.$$

Hence the curve

$$y = x \ln\frac{x-1}{x+1}, \quad x > 1,$$

has the line $y = -2$ as a horizontal asymptote as $x \to +\infty$. (See Fig. 7.3.1.) It also has the line $x = 1$ as a vertical asymptote as $x \to 1^+$. (Why?) ◆

If

$$\lim_{x \to a} f(x) = +\infty = \lim_{x \to a} g(x),$$

then we say that $f(x) - g(x)$ has the **indeterminate form** $\infty - \infty$ as $x \to a$. To evaluate

$$\lim_{x \to a} [f(x) - g(x)],$$

we try by algebraic manipulation to convert $f(x) - g(x)$ into a form of type 0/0 or ∞/∞ so that it may be possible to apply l'Hôpital's rule. If $f(x)$ or $g(x)$ is expressed as a fraction, we can sometimes do this by finding a common denominator. In most cases, however, subtler methods are required. Example 2 illustrates the technique of finding a common denominator. Example 3 demonstrates a factoring technique that can be effective.

FIGURE 7.3.1 Visual corroboration of the limit in Example 1.

EXAMPLE 2

$$\lim_{x \to 0} \left(\frac{1}{x} - \frac{1}{\sin x}\right) = \lim_{x \to 0} \frac{(\sin x) - x}{x \sin x} \qquad \text{(form 0/0)}$$

$$= \lim_{x \to 0} \frac{(\cos x) - 1}{\sin x + x \cos x} \qquad \text{(still 0/0)}$$

$$= \lim_{x \to 0} \frac{-\sin x}{2 \cos x - x \sin x} = 0. \qquad ◆$$

EXAMPLE 3

$$\lim_{x \to +\infty} \left(\sqrt{x^2 + 3x} - x\right) = \lim_{x \to +\infty} x \left(\sqrt{1 + \frac{3}{x}} - 1\right) \quad \text{(form } \infty \cdot 0\text{)}$$

$$= \lim_{x \to +\infty} \frac{\sqrt{1 + \frac{3}{x}} - 1}{\frac{1}{x}} \quad \text{(form 0/0 now)}$$

$$= \lim_{x \to +\infty} \frac{\frac{1}{2}\left(1 + \frac{3}{x}\right)^{-1/2}\left(-\frac{3}{x^2}\right)}{-\frac{1}{x^2}}$$

$$= \lim_{x \to +\infty} \frac{\frac{3}{2}}{\sqrt{1 + \frac{3}{x}}} = \frac{3}{2}.$$

Thus the curve $y = \sqrt{x^2 + 3x} - x$, $x > 0$, has the line $y = \frac{3}{2}$ as a horizontal asymptote as $x \to +\infty$. (See Fig. 7.3.2.) ◆

FIGURE 7.3.2 Visual corroboration of the limit in Example 3.

The Indeterminate Forms 0^0, ∞^0, and 1^∞

Suppose that we need to find the limit of a quantity

$$y = [f(x)]^{g(x)},$$

where the limits of f and g as $x \to a$ are such that one of the **indeterminate forms** 0^0, ∞^0, or 1^∞ is produced. We first compute the natural logarithm

$$\ln y = \ln\left([f(x)]^{g(x)}\right) = g(x) \ln f(x).$$

For each of the three indeterminate forms mentioned here, $g(x) \ln f(x)$ has the form $0 \cdot \infty$, so we can use our earlier methods to find $L = \lim_{x \to a} \ln y$ (assuming that $f(x) > 0$ near $x = a$, so that $y > 0$). Then

$$\lim_{x \to a} [f(x)]^{g(x)} = \lim_{x \to a} y = \lim_{x \to a} \exp(\ln y) = \exp\left(\lim_{x \to a} \ln y\right) = e^L,$$

because the exponential function is continuous. Thus we have the following four steps for finding the limit of $[f(x)]^{g(x)}$ as $x \to a$:

1. Let $y = [f(x)]^{g(x)}$.
2. Simplify $\ln y = g(x) \ln f(x)$.
3. Evaluate $L = \lim_{x \to a} \ln y$.
4. Conclude that $\lim_{x \to a} [f(x)]^{g(x)} = e^L$.

EXAMPLE 4 Find $\lim_{x \to 0} (\cos x)^{1/x^2}$.

Solution Here we have the indeterminate form 1^∞. If we let $y = (\cos x)^{1/x^2}$, then

$$\ln y = \ln\left[(\cos x)^{1/x^2}\right] = \frac{\ln \cos x}{x^2}.$$

As $x \to 0$, $\cos x \to 1$, and so $\ln \cos x \to 0$; we are now dealing with the indeterminate form 0/0. Hence two applications of l'Hôpital's rule yield

$$\lim_{x \to 0} \ln y = \lim_{x \to 0} \frac{\ln \cos x}{x^2} = \lim_{x \to 0} \frac{(-\sin x)/(\cos x)}{2x} = \lim_{x \to 0} \frac{-\tan x}{2x} \quad \text{(0/0 form)}$$

$$= \lim_{x \to 0} \frac{-\sec^2 x}{2} = -\frac{1}{2}.$$

FIGURE 7.3.3 Visual corroboration of the limit in Example 4.

Consequently, as suggested by Fig. 7.3.3,

$$\lim_{x \to 0}(\cos x)^{1/x^2} = e^{-1/2} = \frac{1}{\sqrt{e}}.$$

EXAMPLE 5 Find $\lim_{x \to 0^+} x^{\tan x}$.

Solution This has the indeterminate form 0^0. If $y = x^{\tan x}$, then

$$\ln y = (\tan x)(\ln x) = \frac{\ln x}{\cot x}.$$

Now we have the indeterminate form ∞/∞, and l'Hôpital's rule yields

$$\lim_{x \to 0^+} \ln y = \lim_{x \to 0^+} \frac{\ln x}{\cot x} = \lim_{x \to 0^+} \frac{\frac{1}{x}}{-\csc^2 x} = -\lim_{x \to 0^+} \frac{\sin^2 x}{x}$$

$$= -\lim_{x \to 0^+} \left(\frac{\sin x}{x}\right)(\sin x) = (-1) \cdot 0 = 0.$$

Therefore, $\lim_{x \to 0^+} x^{\tan x} = e^0 = 1$. The graph of the curve $y = x^{\tan x}$, $0 < x < \pi/2$ in Fig. 7.3.4 provides corroboration of this limit. We note also a local minimum on the curve near $x = 0.4$. (See Problem 45.) ◆

FIGURE 7.3.4 Visual corroboration of the limit in Example 5.

Although $a^0 = 1$ for any *nonzero* constant a, the form 0^0 is indeterminate—the limit is not necessarily 1 (see Problem 52). But the form 0^∞ is not indeterminate; its limit is zero. For example,

$$\lim_{x \to 0^+} x^{1/x} = 0.$$

The Number e as a Limit

Figure 7.3.5 shows the graph of the function

$$f(x) = \left(1 + \frac{1}{x}\right)^x \tag{1}$$

for $x > 0$. The graph appears to begin at the point $(0, 1)$ and to approach a horizontal asymptote as $x \to +\infty$. Note that $f(x)$ has the indeterminate form ∞^0 as $x \to 0^+$ and has the indeterminate form 0^∞ as $x \to +\infty$. In each case our strategy is to calculate the limit of $\ln f(x)$:

$$\lim \left[\ln\left(1 + \frac{1}{x}\right)^x\right] = \lim \left[x \cdot \ln\left(1 + \frac{1}{x}\right)\right] = \lim \frac{\ln\left(1 + \frac{1}{x}\right)}{\frac{1}{x}}.$$

FIGURE 7.3.5 The graph $y = \left(1 + \frac{1}{x}\right)^x$ has the horizontal asymptote $y = e$.

The last limit here has the indeterminate form ∞/∞ as $x \to 0^+$ and has the indeterminate form $0/0$ as $x \to +\infty$. In each case we can apply l'Hôpital's rule to obtain

$$\lim \left[\ln\left(1 + \frac{1}{x}\right)^x\right] = \lim \frac{-\frac{1}{x^2} \cdot \frac{1}{1 + (1/x)}}{-\frac{1}{x^2}} = \lim \frac{x}{x + 1} = \begin{cases} 0 & \text{as } x \to 0^+, \\ 1 & \text{as } x \to +\infty. \end{cases}$$

Thus we find that

$$\lim_{x \to 0^+}\left(1 + \frac{1}{x}\right)^x = e^0 = 1$$

and that
$$\lim_{x \to +\infty} \left(1 + \frac{1}{x}\right)^x = e^1 = e. \quad (2)$$

The last limit shows that the horizontal asymptote in Fig. 7.3.5 is the line $y = e$.

If we write $x = n$ (a positive integer) in Eq. (2), we obtain the famous limit
$$e = \lim_{n \to \infty} \left(1 + \frac{1}{n}\right)^n, \quad (3)$$

which can be used to approximate the number e. In Problem 44 we ask you to use l'Hôpital's rule similarly to derive the more general limit expression
$$e^x = \lim_{n \to \infty} \left(1 + \frac{x}{n}\right)^n \quad (4)$$

for the exponential function.

The limit in (3) can be approximated with a very rudimentary calculator by substituting $n = 2^k$ (a power of 2) to get
$$e = \lim_{k \to \infty} \left(1 + \frac{1}{2^k}\right)^{2^k} = \lim_{k \to \infty} v^{2^k} \quad (5)$$

where $v = 1 + (1/2^k)$. Then
$$(v^2)^2 = v^4, \quad (v^4)^2 = v^8, \quad (v^8)^2 = v^{16}, \quad \ldots, \quad \left(v^{2^{k-1}}\right)^2 = v^{2^k}.$$

Therefore we should get the value $[1 + (1/2^k)]^{2^k}$ if we enter $v = 1 + (1/2^k)$ and then press the $\boxed{x^2}$ key k times in succession. (Try this with your own calculator. Can you see how and why the process may fail if k is too large?) The entries in the table in Fig. 7.3.6 were calculated using a high-precision computer (rather than a simple calculator). They indicate that $e = 2.71828\,1828$ accurate to nine decimal places.

k	$\left(1 + \dfrac{1}{2^k}\right)^{2^k}$
10	2.71695 5729
20	2.71828 0532
30	2.71828 1827
40	2.71828 1828
50	2.71828 1828

FIGURE 7.3.6 Approximating the number e.

7.3 TRUE/FALSE STUDY GUIDE

7.3 CONCEPTS: QUESTIONS AND DISCUSSION

1. List the seven indeterminate forms discussed in Sections 7.2 and 7.3. Illustrate each of these forms with your own example.
2. Explain in your own words why 0^∞ and $0^{-\infty}$ are *not* indeterminate forms.
3. Suppose that someone claims that "calculus is merely the study of indeterminate forms." Based on what you've learned so far, how would you argue for (or against) this claim?

7.3 PROBLEMS

Find the limits in Problems 1 through 34.

1. $\lim\limits_{x \to 0} x \cot x$
2. $\lim\limits_{x \to 0} \left(\dfrac{1}{x} - \cot x\right)$
3. $\lim\limits_{x \to 0} \dfrac{1}{x} \ln\left(\dfrac{7x + 8}{4x + 8}\right)$
4. $\lim\limits_{x \to 0^+} (\sin x)(\ln \sin x)$
5. $\lim\limits_{x \to 0} x^2 \csc^2 x$
6. $\lim\limits_{x \to \infty} e^{-x} \ln x$
7. $\lim\limits_{x \to \infty} x(e^{1/x} - 1)$
8. $\lim\limits_{x \to 2} \left(\dfrac{1}{x - 2} - \dfrac{1}{\ln(x - 1)}\right)$
9. $\lim\limits_{x \to 0^+} x \ln x$
10. $\lim\limits_{x \to \pi/2} (\tan x)(\cos 3x)$
11. $\lim\limits_{x \to \pi} (x - \pi) \csc x$
12. $\lim\limits_{x \to \infty} (x - \sin x) \exp(-x^2)$
13. $\lim\limits_{x \to 0^+} \left(\dfrac{1}{\sqrt{x}} - \dfrac{1}{\sin x}\right)$
14. $\lim\limits_{x \to 0} \left(\dfrac{1}{x} - \dfrac{1}{e^x - 1}\right)$
15. $\lim\limits_{x \to 1^+} \left(\dfrac{x}{x^2 + x - 2} - \dfrac{1}{x - 1}\right)$
16. $\lim\limits_{x \to \infty} \left(\sqrt{x + 1} - \sqrt{x}\right)$
17. $\lim\limits_{x \to 0} \left(\dfrac{1}{x} - \dfrac{1}{\ln(1 + x)}\right)$
18. $\lim\limits_{x \to \infty} \left(\sqrt{x^2 + x} - \sqrt{x^2 - x}\right)$

19. $\lim_{x\to\infty} \left(\sqrt[3]{x^3+2x+5} - x\right)$

20. $\lim_{x\to 0^+} x^x$

21. $\lim_{x\to 0^+} x^{\sin x}$

22. $\lim_{x\to\infty} \left(\frac{2x-1}{2x+1}\right)^x$

23. $\lim_{x\to\infty} (\ln x)^{1/x}$

24. $\lim_{x\to\infty} \left(1 - \frac{1}{x^2}\right)^x$

25. $\lim_{x\to 0} \left(\frac{\sin x}{x}\right)^{1/x^2}$

26. $\lim_{x\to 0^+} (1+2x)^{1/(3x)}$

27. $\lim_{x\to\infty} \left(\cos\frac{1}{x^2}\right)^{x^4}$

28. $\lim_{x\to 0^+} (\sin x)^{\sec x}$

29. $\lim_{x\to 0^+} (x + \sin x)^x$

30. $\lim_{x\to\pi/2} (\tan x - \sec x)$

31. $\lim_{x\to 1} x^{1/(1-x)}$

32. $\lim_{x\to 1^+} (x-1)^{\ln x}$

33. $\lim_{x\to 2^+} \left(\frac{1}{\sqrt{x^2-4}} - \frac{1}{x-2}\right)$

34. $\lim_{x\to\infty} \left(\sqrt[5]{x^5 - 3x^4 + 17} - x\right)$

Figures 7.3.7 through 7.3.9 illustrate the graphs of some of the functions defined for $x > 0$ in Problems 35 through 42. In each of these problems:

(a) *First use your own calculator or computer to graph the given function $f(x)$ with an x-range sufficient to suggest its behavior both as $x \to 0^+$ and as $x \to +\infty$.*
(b) *Then apply l'Hôpital's rule as necessary to verify this suspected behavior near zero and $+\infty$.*
(c) *Finally, estimate graphically and/or numerically the maximum value attained by $f(x)$ for $x \geq 0$. If possible, find this maximum value exactly.*

FIGURE 7.3.7

FIGURE 7.3.8

FIGURE 7.3.9

35. $f(x) = x^{1/x}$

36. $f(x) = x^{(1/x^2)}$

37. $f(x) = (x^2)^{1/x}$

38. $f(x) = x^{-x}$

39. $f(x) = (1+x^2)^{1/x}$

40. $f(x) = \left(1 + \frac{1}{x^2}\right)^x$

41. $f(x) = (x + \sin x)^{1/x}$

42. $f(x) = \left(e^{1/x^2}\right)^{(\cos x - 1)}$

Use l'Hôpital's rule to establish the limits in Problems 43 and 44.

43. $\lim_{h\to 0}(1+hx)^{1/h} = e^x$

44. $\lim_{n\to\infty} \left(1 + \frac{x}{n}\right)^n = e^x$

45. Estimate graphically or numerically the location of the local minimum point on the graph $y = x^{\tan x}$ shown in Fig. 7.3.4.

46. Let n be a fixed positive integer and let $p(x)$ be the polynomial
$$p(x) = x^n + a_1 x^{n-1} + a_2 x^{n-2} + \cdots + a_{n-1}x + a_n;$$
the numbers $a_1, a_2, \ldots, a_n$ are fixed real numbers. Prove that
$$\lim_{x\to\infty} \left([p(x)]^{1/n} - x\right) = \frac{a_1}{n}.$$

47. As we shall see in Problem 52 of Section 8.6, the surface area of the ellipsoid obtained by revolving the ellipse
$$\frac{x^2}{a^2} + \frac{y^2}{b^2} = 1 \quad (a > b > 0)$$
around the x-axis is
$$A = 2\pi ab \left[\frac{b}{a} + \frac{a}{c}\sin^{-1}\left(\frac{c}{a}\right)\right],$$
where $c = \sqrt{a^2 - b^2}$. Use l'Hôpital's rule to show that
$$\lim_{b\to a} A = 4\pi a^2,$$
the surface area of a sphere of radius a.

48. If the amount A_0 is invested in an account that earns interest at the annual rate $r \leq 1$ compounded n times annually, then the amount A in the account after t years is given by
$$A = A_0 \left(1 + \frac{r}{n}\right)^{nt}.$$
(a) Show that A is an increasing function of n (with r and t fixed). Thus the bank that compounds more often pays more interest. (b) Use l'Hôpital's rule to show that
$$\lim_{n\to\infty} A(n) = A_0 e^{rt}.$$
This is the amount after t years if the bank compounds interest "continuously." The "annual yield" is the value of this limit in the case $t = 1$. (c) If a bank advertises an annual interest rate of 8% compounded continuously, what is the annual yield?

49. Graph the function $f(x) = |\ln x|^{1/x}$ for $x > 0$ and determine its behavior as $x \to 0^+$ and as $x \to +\infty$. Estimate graphically and/or numerically the locations of any critical points or inflection points on the graph of f.

50. Graph the function $f(x) = |\ln x|^{1/|\ln x|}$ for $x > 0$ and determine its behavior as $x \to 0^+$, as $x \to +\infty$, and as x approaches 1 from either side.

51. Graph the function $f(x) = |\ln x|^{|\ln x|}$ for $x > 0$ and determine its behavior as $x \to 0^+$, as $x \to +\infty$, and as x

approaches 1 from either side. Explore both graphically (by zooming) and symbolically (by differentiating) the question of whether f is differentiable at $x = 1$.

52. Let α be a fixed real number. (a) Evaluate (in terms of α) the 0^0 indeterminate form
$$\lim_{x \to 0} \left[\exp\left(-\frac{1}{x^2}\right) \right]^{\alpha x^2}.$$
(Note that l'Hôpital's rule is not needed.) Thus the indeterminate form 0^0 may have as its limit any positive real number. Explain why. (b) Can the limit of a 0^0 indeterminate form be zero, negative, or infinite? Explain.

53. Sketch the graph of the function $f(x) = (1 + x)^{1/x}$ for $x \geq -1, x \neq 0$. Explain why you can approximate the number e by zooming in on the *apparent* y-intercept of this graph. Do so, accurate to five decimal places.

54. This problem explores the fact that a lead ball hits the ground with greater speed than a feather when both are dropped simultaneously from the top of a tall building. Assuming that air resistance is proportional to downward velocity v, we will show in Chapter 9 that after t seconds the velocity of a dropped body of mass m is given by
$$v(t) = \frac{mg}{k}\left(1 - e^{-kt/m}\right)$$
where g is the familiar acceleration of gravity and k denotes a constant air-resistance coefficient. (a) Note that
$$\lim_{t \to \infty} v(t) = \frac{mg}{k}.$$
Thus a body's velocity tends to a finite limit after it has fallen a sufficiently long time. (b) Note that
$$\lim_{m \to 0} v(t) = 0.$$
Consequently a light "feathery" body falls very slowly through the air. (c) Show that
$$\lim_{m \to \infty} v(t) = gt = \lim_{k \to 0^+} v(t),$$
the velocity of the body after t seconds in the case of *no* air resistance. Thus a very heavy body tends to fall much as it would with no air resistance.

7.4 THE NATURAL LOGARITHM AS AN INTEGRAL

Our introduction of the functions e^x and $\ln x$ in Section 7.1 was informal and based on an intuitive conception rather than a precise definition of exponentials. Here we provide a solid foundation and careful development of the natural exponential and logarithm functions and their properties.

It is simplest to make the definition of the natural logarithm function our starting point. Guided by the properties of logarithms outlined in Section 7.1, we want to define $\ln x$ for $x > 0$ in such a way that

$$\ln 1 = 0 \quad \text{and} \quad D_x \ln x = \frac{1}{x}. \tag{1}$$

To do so, we recall part 1 of the fundamental theorem of calculus (Section 5.6), from which it follows that

$$D_x \left(\int_a^x f(t)\, dt \right) = f(x) \tag{2}$$

if f is continuous on an interval containing a and x. In order that $\ln x$ satisfy the equations in (1), we take $a = 1$ and $f(t) = 1/t$.

DEFINITION The Natural Logarithm
The **natural logarithm** $\ln x$ of the positive number x is defined to be

$$\ln x = \int_1^x \frac{1}{t}\, dt. \tag{3}$$

Note that $\ln x$ is *not* defined for $x \leq 0$. Geometrically the value $\ln x$ of the natural logarithm of x is equal to:

- The area under the graph of $y = 1/t$ from $t = 1$ to $t = x$ if $x > 1$ (Fig. 7.4.1);
- The negative of this area if $0 < x < 1$;
- Zero if $x = 1$.

FIGURE 7.4.1 The natural logarithm function defined by means of an integral.

FIGURE 7.4.2 Using rectangles to estimate ln 2.

EXAMPLE 1 The number

$$\ln 2 = \int_1^2 \frac{1}{t}\,dt = \int_1^2 \frac{1}{x}\,dx$$

is equal to the area under the graph of $y = 1/x$ from $x = 1$ to $x = 2$. Examining the inscribed and circumscribed rectangles in Fig. 7.4.2, we see immediately that

$$\frac{1}{2} < \ln 2 < 1.$$

We can use Simpson's approximation to estimate $\ln 2$ more closely. The regular partition of $[1, 2]$ into $n = 10$ subintervals, each of length $\Delta x = \frac{1}{10}$, and with endpoints $1, \frac{11}{10}, \frac{12}{10}, \ldots, \frac{19}{10}, 2$ yields

$$\ln 2 = \frac{\frac{1}{10}}{3} \cdot \left(1 + 4 \cdot \frac{10}{11} + 2 \cdot \frac{10}{12} + 4 \cdot \frac{10}{13} + 2 \cdot \frac{10}{14} + 4 \cdot \frac{10}{15}\right.$$
$$\left. + 2 \cdot \frac{10}{16} + 4 \cdot \frac{10}{17} + 2 \cdot \frac{10}{18} + 4 \cdot \frac{10}{19} + \frac{1}{2}\right) \approx 0.69315.$$

This approximation is accurate to five decimal places because the actual value of $\ln 2$ to six places is 0.693147. ◆

The Graph of $y = \ln x$

The fact that $D_x \ln x = 1/x$ follows immediately from the fundamental theorem of calculus in (2). And by Theorem 2 in Section 3.4, the fact that the function $\ln x$ is differentiable for $x > 0$ implies that it is continuous for $x > 0$. Because

$$D_x \ln x = \frac{1}{x} > 0 \quad \text{and} \quad D_x^2 \ln x = -\frac{1}{x^2} < 0$$

for $x > 0$, we see that $\ln x$ is an increasing function whose graph is concave downward everywhere (by Theorem 2 in Section 4.6). Using the laws of logarithms (in Theorem 1) we see, from the facts that

$$\ln 2^n = n \ln 2 \to +\infty \quad \text{and} \quad \ln 2^{-n} = -n \ln 2 \to -\infty$$

as $n \to +\infty$, that

$$\lim_{x \to \infty} \ln x = +\infty \quad \text{and} \quad \lim_{x \to 0^+} \ln x = -\infty. \tag{4}$$

When we assemble these facts, we see that the graph of $y = \ln x$ has the familiar shape shown in Fig. 7.4.3.

FIGURE 7.4.3 The graph of the natural logarithm function.

The Number e

Because $\ln x$ is an increasing function, the intermediate value property of continuous functions implies that the curve $y = \ln x$ crosses the horizontal line $y = 1$ precisely once. (See Fig. 7.4.4.) The x-coordinate of the point of intersection is the famous number $e \approx 2.71828$ introduced differently in Section 7.1.

DEFINITION The Number e
The number e is the (unique) real number such that
$$\ln e = 1. \tag{5}$$

FIGURE 7.4.4 The fact that $\ln e = 1$ is expressed graphically here.

The number e has been used to denote the number whose natural logarithm is 1 ever since this number was introduced by the great Swiss mathematician Leonhard Euler (1707–1783), who used e for "exponential." [Euler also popularized the use of π for the area (approximately 3.14159) of the unit circle as well as the symbol i for the imaginary number $\sqrt{-1}$.]

EXAMPLE 2 With a graphing calculator or computer you can zoom in on the intersection of the graphs of $y = \ln x$ and $y = 1$ to verify the first few decimal places of e. For instance, the viewing window $2.71 \leq x \leq 2.72$, $0.99 \leq y \leq 1.01$ of Fig. 7.4.5 suffices to verify that $e \approx 2.718$ to three decimal places. ◆

FIGURE 7.4.5 Zooming in on the number e.

The Laws of Logarithms

We now use our ability to differentiate logarithms to establish rigorously the laws of logarithms.

THEOREM 1 Laws of Logarithms
If x and y are positive numbers and r is a rational number, then

$$\ln xy = \ln x + \ln y; \tag{6}$$

$$\ln\left(\frac{1}{x}\right) = -\ln x; \tag{7}$$

$$\ln\left(\frac{x}{y}\right) = \ln x - \ln y; \tag{8}$$

$$\ln(x^r) = r \ln x. \tag{9}$$

The restriction that r is rational is removed later in this section, when we examine general exponential functions (those with bases other than e).

PROOF OF EQUATION (6) We temporarily fix y, so that we may regard x as the independent variable and y as a constant in what follows. Then

$$D_x \ln xy = \frac{D_x(xy)}{xy} = \frac{y}{xy} = \frac{1}{x} = D_x \ln x.$$

Thus $\ln xy$ and $\ln x$ have the same derivative with respect to x. We antidifferentiate both and conclude that

$$\ln xy = \ln x + C$$

for some constant C. To evaluate C, we substitute $x = 1$ into both sides of the last equation. The fact that $\ln 1 = 0$ then implies that $C = \ln y$, and this is enough to establish Eq. (6). ◂

PROOF OF EQUATION (7) We differentiate $\ln(1/x)$:

$$D_x\left(\ln\frac{1}{x}\right) = \frac{-\frac{1}{x^2}}{\frac{1}{x}} = -\frac{1}{x} = D_x(-\ln x).$$

Thus $\ln(1/x)$ and $-\ln x$ have the same derivative. Hence antidifferentiation gives

$$\ln\left(\frac{1}{x}\right) = -\ln x + C,$$

where C is a constant. We substitute $x = 1$ into this last equation. Because $\ln 1 = 0$, it follows that $C = 0$, and this proves Eq. (7). ◄

PROOF OF EQUATION (8) Because $x/y = x \cdot (1/y)$, Eq. (8) follows immediately from Eqs. (6) and (7). ◄

PROOF OF EQUATION (9) We know that $D_x x^r = r x^{r-1}$ if r is rational. So

$$D_x(\ln x^r) = \frac{r x^{r-1}}{x^r} = \frac{r}{x} = D_x(r \ln x).$$

Antidifferentiation then gives

$$\ln(x^r) = r \ln x + C$$

for some constant C. As before, substituting $x = 1$ then gives $C = 0$, which proves Eq. (9). We show later in this section that Eq. (9) holds whether or not r is rational. ◄

The proofs of Eqs. (6), (7), and (9) are all quite similar—we differentiate the left-hand side, apply the fact that two functions with the same derivative (on an interval) differ by a constant C (on that interval), and evaluate C by using the fact that $\ln 1 = 0$.

Logarithms and Experimental Data

Certain empirical data can be explained by assuming that the observed dependent variable is a **power function** of the independent variable x. In other words, y is described by a mathematical model of the form

$$y = kx^m,$$

where k and m are constants. If so, the laws of logarithms imply that

$$\ln y = \ln k + m \ln x.$$

An experimenter can then plot values of $\ln y$ against values of $\ln x$. If the power-function model is valid, the resulting data points will lie on a straight line of slope m and with y-intercept $\ln k$ (Fig. 7.4.6). This technique makes it easy to see whether or not the data lie on a straight line. And if they do, this technique makes it easy also to measure the slope and y-intercept of the line and thereby find the values of k and m.

FIGURE 7.4.6 Plotting the logarithms of data may reveal a hidden relationship.

EXAMPLE 3 (Planetary Motion) The table in Fig. 7.4.7 gives the period of revolution T and the major semiaxis a of the elliptical orbit of each of the first six planets around the sun, together with the logarithms of these numbers. If we plot $\ln T$ against $\ln a$, it is immediately apparent that the resulting points lie on a straight line of slope $m = \frac{3}{2}$. Hence T and a satisfy an equation of the form $T = ka^{3/2}$, so

$$T^2 = Ca^3.$$

Planet	T (in days)	a (in 10^6 km)	ln T	ln a
Mercury	87.97	58	4.48	4.06
Venus	224.70	108	5.41	4.68
Earth	365.26	149	5.90	5.00
Mars	686.98	228	6.53	5.43
Jupiter	4332.59	778	8.37	6.66
Saturn	10,759.20	1426	9.28	7.26

FIGURE 7.4.7 Data for Example 3.

This means that the square of the period T is proportional to the cube of the major semiaxis a. This is Kepler's third law of planetary motion, which Johannes Kepler (1571–1630) discovered empirically in 1619. ◆

The Natural Exponential Function

We know that the natural logarithm function $\ln x$ is continuous and increasing for $x > 0$ and that it attains arbitrarily large positive and negative values (because of the limits in (4)). It follows that $\ln x$ has an inverse function that is defined for all x. To see this, let y be any (fixed) real number. If a and b are positive numbers such that $\ln a < y < \ln b$, then the intermediate value property gives a number $x > 0$, with x between a and b, such that $\ln x = y$. Because $\ln x$ is an increasing function, there is only *one* such number x such that $\ln x = y$ (Fig. 7.4.8). Because y determines precisely one such value x, we see that x is a *function* of y.

FIGURE 7.4.8 To get $x = \exp y$, move straight over from y to the graph $y = \ln x$, then move straight down (or up) to x.

This function x of y is the inverse function of the natural logarithm function, and it is called the *natural exponential function*. It is commonly denoted by exp (for "exponential"), so

$$x = \exp y \quad \text{provided that} \quad y = \ln x.$$

Interchanging x and y yields the following definition.

DEFINITION The Natural Exponential Function
The **natural exponential function** exp is defined for all x as follows:

$$\exp x = y \quad \text{if and only if} \quad \ln y = x. \tag{10}$$

460 CHAPTER 7 Calculus of Transcendental Functions

Thus $\exp x$ is simply that (positive) number whose natural logarithm is x. It is an immediate consequence of Eq. (10) that

$$\ln(\exp x) = x \quad \text{for all } x \tag{11}$$

and that

$$\exp(\ln y) = y \quad \text{for all } y > 0. \tag{12}$$

As in the case of the graphs of $y = a^x$ and $y = \log_a x$ discussed informally in Section 7.1, the fact that $\exp x$ and $\ln x$ are inverse functions implies that the graphs of $y = \exp x$ and $y = \ln x$ are reflections of each other across the line $y = x$. (See Fig. 7.4.9.) Therefore, the graph of the exponential function looks like the one shown in Fig. 7.4.10. In particular, $\exp x$ is positive-valued for all x, and

$$\exp 0 = 1, \tag{13}$$

$$\lim_{x \to \infty} \exp x = +\infty, \quad \text{and} \tag{14}$$

$$\lim_{x \to -\infty} \exp x = 0. \tag{15}$$

These facts follow from the equation $\ln 1 = 0$ and the limits in (4).

FIGURE 7.4.9 The graphs $y = e^x$ and $y = \ln x$ are reflections of each other across the 45° line $y = x$.

FIGURE 7.4.10 The graph of the natural exponential function, exp.

Exponentials and Powers of e

Recall that we have now defined the number $e \approx 2.71828$ as the number whose natural logarithm is 1. If r is any rational number, it follows that

$$\ln(e^r) = r \ln e = r.$$

But Eq. (10) implies that $\ln(e^r) = r$ if and only if

$$\exp r = e^r.$$

Thus $\exp x$ is equal to e^x (e raised to the power x) if x is a rational number. We therefore *define* e^x for irrational as well as rational values of x by

$$e^x = \exp x. \tag{16}$$

This is our first legitimate instance of powers with irrational exponents.

Equation (16) is the reason for calling exp the natural exponential function. With this notation, Eqs. (10) through (12) become

$$e^x = y \quad \text{if and only if} \quad \ln y = x, \tag{17}$$

$$\ln(e^x) = x \quad \text{for all } x, \tag{18}$$

and

$$e^{\ln x} = x \quad \text{for all } x > 0. \tag{19}$$

To justify Eq. (16), we should show rigorously that powers of e satisfy the laws of exponents. We can do this immediately.

THEOREM 2 Laws of Exponents
If x and y are real numbers and r is rational, then

$$e^x e^y = e^{x+y}, \tag{20}$$

$$e^{-x} = \frac{1}{e^x}, \tag{21}$$

and

$$(e^x)^r = e^{rx}. \tag{22}$$

PROOF The laws of logarithms and Eq. (18) give

$$\ln(e^x e^y) = \ln(e^x) + \ln(e^y) = x + y = \ln(e^{x+y}).$$

Then Eq. (20) follows from the fact that ln is an increasing function and therefore is one-to-one—if $x_1 \ne x_2$, then $\ln x_1 \ne \ln x_2$. Similarly,

$$\ln\bigl([e^x]^r\bigr) = r \ln(e^x) = rx = \ln(e^{rx}).$$

So Eq. (22) follows in the same way. The proof of Eq. (21) is almost identical. We will see presently that the restriction that r is rational in Eq. (22) is unnecessary; that is, the equation $(e^x)^y = e^{xy}$ holds for *all* real numbers x and y. ◂

General Exponential Functions

The natural exponential function e^x and the natural logarithm function $\ln x$ are often called the exponential and logarithm functions with *base e*. We now define general exponential and logarithm functions, with the forms a^x and $\log_a x$, whose base is a positive number $a \ne 1$. But it is convenient here to reverse the order of treatment, so we first consider the general exponential function.

If r is a rational number, then the law of exponents in Eq. (22) gives

$$a^r = (e^{\ln a})^r = e^{r \ln a}.$$

We therefore *define* arbitrary powers (rational *and* irrational) of the positive number a in this way:

$$a^x = e^{x \ln a} \tag{23}$$

for all x. Thus

$$3^{\sqrt{2}} = e^{\sqrt{2} \ln 3} \approx e^{1.5537} \approx 4.7289$$

and

$$(0.5)^{-\pi} = e^{-\pi \ln(0.5)} \approx e^{2.1776} \approx 8.8251.$$

Then $f(x) = a^x$ is called the **exponential function with base** a. Note that $a^x > 0$ for all x and that $a^0 = e^0 = 1$ for all $a > 0$.

The *laws of exponents* for general exponentials follow almost immediately from the definition in Eq. (23) and from the laws of exponents for the natural exponential function:

$$a^x a^y = a^{x+y}, \tag{24}$$

$$a^{-x} = \frac{1}{a^x}, \tag{25}$$

and

$$(a^x)^y = a^{xy} \tag{26}$$

for all x and y. To prove Eq. (24), we write

$$a^x a^y = e^{x \ln a} e^{y \ln a} = e^{(x \ln a)+(y \ln a)} = e^{(x+y) \ln a} = a^{x+y}.$$

To derive Eq. (26), note first from Eq. (23) that $\ln a^x = x \ln a$. Then

$$(a^x)^y = e^{y \ln(a^x)} = e^{xy \ln a} = a^{xy}.$$

This follows for all real numbers x and y, so the restriction that r is rational in the formula $(e^x)^r = e^{rx}$ (Eq. (22)) has now been removed.

If $a > 1$, so that $\ln a > 0$, then Eqs. (14) and (15) immediately give us the results

$$\lim_{x \to \infty} a^x = +\infty \quad \text{and} \quad \lim_{x \to -\infty} a^x = 0. \tag{27}$$

Because

$$D_x a^x = D_x(e^{x \ln a}) = (\ln a) e^{x \ln a} = a^x \ln a \tag{28}$$

is positive for all x if $a > 1$, we see that—in this case—$f(x) = a^x$ is an *increasing* function of x. The graph $y = a^x$ then resembles that of the natural exponential function $y = e^x$, but its relative steepness depends on the magnitude of a (Fig. 7.4.11).

If $0 < a < 1$, then $\ln a < 0$. In this case it therefore follows from (28) that $f(x) = a^x$ is a *decreasing* function, and the values of the two limits in (27) are interchanged (Fig. 7.4.12). Whether $a > 1$ or $0 < a < 1$, it follows from (28) that $f''(x) = a^x (\ln a)^2 > 0$ for all x, so the graphs in both Figs. 7.4.11 and 7.4.12 are concave upward for all x.

FIGURE 7.4.11 If $a > 1$ then $\lim_{x \to -\infty} a^x = 0$, $\lim_{x \to \infty} a^x = +\infty$.

FIGURE 7.4.12 If $0 < a < 1$ then $\lim_{x \to -\infty} a^x = +\infty$, $\lim_{x \to \infty} a^x = 0$.

Derivatives and Integrals

If $u = u(x)$ is a differentiable function of x, then Eq. (28) combined with the chain rule gives

$$D_x a^u = (a^u \ln a) \frac{du}{dx}. \tag{29}$$

The corresponding integral formula is

$$\int a^u \, du = \frac{a^u}{\ln a} + C. \tag{30}$$

But rather than using these general formulas, it usually is simpler to rely solely on the definition in Eq. (23), as in Examples 3, 4, and 5.

EXAMPLE 4 To differentiate $f(x) = 3^{x^2}$, we may first write

$$3^{x^2} = (e^{\ln 3})^{x^2} = e^{x^2 \ln 3}.$$

Then

$$D_x 3^{x^2} = D_x e^{x^2 \ln 3} = e^{x^2 \ln 3} D_x(x^2 \ln 3) = 3^{x^2} (\ln 3)(2x). \quad \blacklozenge$$

EXAMPLE 5 Find $\int \dfrac{10^{\sqrt{x}}}{\sqrt{x}}\,dx$.

Solution We first write $10^{\sqrt{x}} = (e^{\ln 10})^{\sqrt{x}} = e^{\sqrt{x}\ln 10}$. Then

$$\int \dfrac{10^{\sqrt{x}}}{\sqrt{x}}\,dx = \int \dfrac{e^{\sqrt{x}\ln 10}}{\sqrt{x}}\,dx$$

$$= \int \dfrac{2e^{u}}{\ln 10}\,du \qquad \left(u = \sqrt{x}\,\ln 10,\quad du = \dfrac{\ln 10}{2\sqrt{x}}\,dx\right)$$

$$= \dfrac{2e^{u}}{\ln 10} + C = \dfrac{2}{\ln 10}10^{\sqrt{x}} + C. \qquad \blacklozenge$$

EXAMPLE 6 The function

$$P(t) = 3 \cdot (1.07)^{t}$$

describes a population that starts with $P(0) = 3$ (million) bacteria at time $t = 0$ (h) and increases in number by 7% every hour. After 10 hours the population is

$$P(10) = 3 \cdot (1.07)^{10} \approx 5.90 \quad \text{(million)},$$

so the population has almost doubled. The derivative of $P(t)$ is

$$P'(t) = D_t[3 \cdot (1.07)^t] = 3 \cdot D_t\left(e^{t\ln(1.07)}\right)$$
$$= 3 \cdot [\ln(1.07)]e^{t\ln(1.07)} = 3(\ln 1.07)(1.07)^t,$$

so at time $t = 10$ the rate of growth of this bacteria population is

$$P'(10) = 3(\ln 1.07)(1.07)^{10} \approx 0.40 \quad \text{(million per hour)}. \qquad \blacklozenge$$

Whether or not the exponent r is rational, the **general power function** $f(x) = x^r$ is now defined for $x > 0$ by

$$x^r = e^{r\ln x}.$$

We may now prove the power rule of differentiation for an *arbitrary* (constant) exponent as follows:

$$D_x x^r = D_x(e^{r\ln x}) = e^{r\ln x}D_x(r\ln x) = x^r \cdot \dfrac{r}{x} = rx^{r-1}.$$

For example, we now know that

$$D_x x^{\pi} = \pi x^{\pi - 1} \approx (3.14159)x^{2.14159}.$$

General Logarithm Functions

If $a > 1$, then the general exponential function a^x is continuous and increasing for all x and attains all positive values. It therefore has an inverse function that is defined for all $x > 0$. This inverse function of a^x is called the **logarithm function with base** a and is denoted by $\log_a x$. Thus

$$y = \log_a x \quad \text{if and only if} \quad x = a^y. \tag{31}$$

The logarithm function with base e is the natural logarithm function: $\log_e x = \ln x$.

The following *laws of logarithms* are easy to derive from the laws of exponents in Eqs. (24) through (26).

$$\log_a xy = \log_a x + \log_a y, \tag{32}$$

$$\log_a \left(\frac{1}{x}\right) = -\log_a x, \tag{33}$$

$$\log_a x^y = y \log_a x. \tag{34}$$

These formulas hold for any positive base $a \neq 1$ and for all positive values of x and y; in Eq. (34), y may be negative or zero as well.

Logarithms with one base are related to logarithms with another base, and the relationship is most easily expressed by the formula

$$(\log_a b)(\log_b c) = \log_a c. \tag{35}$$

This formula holds for all values of a, b, and c for which it makes sense—the bases a and b are positive numbers other than 1 and c is positive. The proof of this formula is outlined in Problem 39. Equation (35) should be easy to remember—it is as if some arcane cancellation law applies.

If we take $c = a$ in Eq. (35), this gives

$$(\log_a b)(\log_b a) = 1, \tag{36}$$

which in turn, with $b = e$, gives

$$\ln a = \frac{1}{\log_a e}. \tag{37}$$

If we replace a with e, b with a, and c with x in Eq. (35), we obtain

$$(\log_e a)(\log_a x) = \log_e x,$$

so

$$\log_a x = \frac{\log_e x}{\log_e a} = \frac{\ln x}{\ln a}. \tag{38}$$

On most calculators, the $\boxed{\text{LOG}}$ key denotes common (base 10) logarithms: $\log x = \log_{10} x$. In contrast, in many programming languages, such as BASIC, and some symbolic algebra programs, such as *Mathematica*, only the natural logarithm appears explicitly—as `LOG(X)` (in BASIC) and as `Log[x]` (in *Mathematica*). To get $\log_{10} x$ we write `LOG(X)/LOG(10)` and `Log[10,x]`, respectively.

Differentiating both sides of Eq. (38) yields

$$D_x \log_a x = \frac{1}{x \ln a} = \frac{\log_a e}{x}. \tag{39}$$

For example,

$$D_x \log_{10} x = \frac{\log_{10} e}{x} \approx \frac{0.4343}{x}.$$

If we combine the formula $D_x \ln |x| = 1/x$ (see Eq. (22) in Section 7.1) and Eq. (38) with u in place of x, the chain rule gives

$$D_x \log_a |u| = \frac{D_x \ln |u|}{\ln a} = \frac{1}{u \ln a} \cdot \frac{du}{dx} = \frac{\log_a e}{u} \cdot \frac{du}{dx} \tag{40}$$

if u is a differentiable function of x.

EXAMPLE 7

$$D_x \log_2 \sqrt{x^2 + 1} = \frac{1}{2} D_x \log_2(x^2 + 1) = \frac{1}{2} \cdot \frac{\log_2 e}{x^2 + 1} \cdot 2x \approx \frac{(1.4427)x}{x^2 + 1}.$$

In the last step we substituted $\log_2 e = 1/(\ln 2) \approx 1/0.68315 \approx 1.4427$. ◆

7.4 TRUE/FALSE STUDY GUIDE

7.4 CONCEPTS: QUESTIONS AND DISCUSSION

1. Contrast the "e^x first" approach to exponentials and logarithms in Section 7.1 with the "$\ln x$ first" approach in this section. Outline each approach and point out key differences. What, if anything, is not fully defined in each approach? How is the number e introduced in each approach? How do the derivations of the differentiation formulas $D_x e^x = e^x$ and $D_x \ln x = 1/x$ differ in the two approaches?

2. Outline the way in which the precise definitions of the exponential and logarithm functions in this section are used to define and differentiate the power function $f(x) = x^r$ (for both positive and negative values of x and both rational and irrational values of the exponent r).

7.4 PROBLEMS

In Problems 1 through 24, find the derivative of the given function $f(x)$.

1. $f(x) = 10^x$
2. $f(x) = 2^{1/x^2}$
3. $f(x) = \dfrac{3^x}{4^x}$
4. $f(x) = \log_{10} \cos x$
5. $f(x) = 7^{\cos x}$
6. $f(x) = 2^x 3^{x^2}$
7. $f(x) = 2^{x\sqrt{x}}$
8. $f(x) = \log_{100} 10^x$
9. $f(x) = 2^{\ln x}$
10. $f(x) = 7^{8^x}$
11. $f(x) = 17^x$
12. $f(x) = 2^{\sqrt{x}}$
13. $f(x) = 10^{1/x}$
14. $f(x) = 3^{\sqrt{1-x^2}}$
15. $f(x) = 2^{2^x}$
16. $f(x) = \log_2 x$
17. $f(x) = \log_3 \sqrt{x^2+4}$
18. $f(x) = \log_{10}(e^x)$
19. $f(x) = \log_3(2^x)$
20. $f(x) = \log_{10}(\log_{10} x)$
21. $f(x) = \log_2(\log_3 x)$
22. $f(x) = \pi^x + x^\pi + \pi^\pi$
23. $f(x) = \exp(\log_{10} x)$
24. $f(x) = \pi^{x^3}$

Evaluate the integrals given in Problems 25 through 32.

25. $\displaystyle\int 3^{2x}\, dx$
26. $\displaystyle\int x \cdot 10^{-x^2}\, dx$
27. $\displaystyle\int \dfrac{2^{\sqrt{x}}}{\sqrt{x}}\, dx$
28. $\displaystyle\int \dfrac{10^{1/x}}{x^2}\, dx$
29. $\displaystyle\int x^2 7^{x^3+1}\, dx$
30. $\displaystyle\int \dfrac{1}{x \log_{10} x}\, dx$
31. $\displaystyle\int \dfrac{\log_2 x}{x}\, dx$
32. $\displaystyle\int (2^x) 3^{(2^x)}\, dx$

33. The heart rate R (in beats per minute) and weight W (in pounds) of various mammals were measured, with the results shown in Fig. 7.4.13. Use the method of Example 3 to find a relation between the two of the form $R = kW^m$.

W	25	67	127	175	240	975
R	131	103	88	81	75	53

FIGURE 7.4.13 Data for Problem 33.

34. During the adiabatic expansion of a certain diatomic gas, its volume V (in liters) and pressure p (in atmospheres) were measured, with the results shown in Fig. 7.4.14. Use the method of Example 3 to find a relation between V and p of the form $p = kV^m$.

V	1.46	2.50	3.51	5.73	7.26
p	28.3	13.3	8.3	4.2	3.0

FIGURE 7.4.14 Data for Problem 34.

35. Find the highest point on the curve $f(x) = x \cdot 2^{-x}$ for $x > 0$.

36. Approximate the area of the first-quadrant region bounded by the curves $y = 2^{-x}$ and $y = (x-1)^2$. One of the points of intersection of these two curves should be evident, but you will need to approximate the other point.

37. Approximate the volume of the solid generated by rotation of the region of Problem 36 around the x-axis.

38. Approximate the area of the first-quadrant region bounded by the curves $y = 3^{2-x}$ and $y = (3x-4)^2$. You will need to approximate the two points of intersection of these two curves.

39. Prove Eq. (35). [*Suggestion:* Let $x = \log_a b$, $y = \log_b c$, and $z = \log_a c$. Then show that $a^z = a^{xy}$, and conclude that $z = xy$.]

40. Consider the function
$$f(x) = \dfrac{1}{1 + 2^{1/x}} \quad \text{for } x \neq 0.$$
Show that both the left-hand and right-hand limits of $f(x)$ at $x = 0$ exist but are unequal.

41. Find dy/dx if $y = \log_x 2$.

7.4 Project: Natural Functional Equations

Provide complete details in the proofs of Fact 1 and Fact 2 that are outlined here.

Fact 1 If f is a continuous function such that

$$f(x + y) = f(x) + f(y) \tag{1}$$

for all real numbers x and y, then $f(x) = kx$ for some constant k.

OUTLINE OF PROOF Let us substitute t for y in Eq. (1) and then integrate from $t = 0$ to $t = y$ with x held constant:

$$\int_{t=0}^{y} f(x+t)\,dt = \int_{t=0}^{y} f(x)\,dt + \int_{t=0}^{y} f(t)\,dt.$$

Then substituting $u = u(t) = x + t$, $du = dt$ on the left-hand side yields the equation

$$\int_{u=x}^{x+y} f(u)\,du = y \cdot f(x) + \int_{t=0}^{y} f(t)\,dt,$$

from which we find that

$$y \cdot f(x) = \int_{t=0}^{x+y} f(t)\,dt - \int_{t=0}^{x} f(t)\,dt - \int_{t=0}^{y} f(t)\,dt.$$

The right-hand side is symmetric in the variables x and y, so interchanging them gives

$$y \cdot f(x) = x \cdot f(y), \quad \text{so that} \quad \frac{f(x)}{x} = \frac{f(y)}{y}$$

for all x and y. Because x and y are independent, it follows that the function $f(x)/x$ must be constant-valued, and therefore

$$f(x) = kx$$

for some constant k. ◄

This subtle proof is due to H. N. Shapiro, "A micronote on a functional equation," *Amer. Math. Monthly* **80** (1973), p. 1041. There exist discontinuous functions that satisfy Eq. (1). But it is known that any such function must be truly bizarre—its graph must intersect every circular disk in the xy-plane. Can you see that this implies not only that such a function not only is discontinuous at every point, but also is unbounded near every point?

Fact 2 If f is a positive-valued continuous function such that

$$f(x + y) = f(x) \cdot f(y) \tag{2}$$

for all real numbers x and y, then

$$f(x) = e^{kx}$$

for some constant k.

OUTLINE OF PROOF Let $g(x) = \ln(f(x))$. Taking the natural logarithm of both sides in Eq. (2) gives

$$g(x+y) = \ln(f(x+y)) = \ln(f(x) \cdot f(y)) = \ln(f(x)) + \ln(f(y)) = g(x) + g(y).$$

Application of Fact 1 to g now yields

$$\ln(f(x)) = kx, \quad \text{so that} \quad f(x) = e^{kx}. \quad \blacktriangleleft$$

Challenge Use similar methods to establish the following result:

Fact 3 If f is a continuous function such that

$$f(xy) = f(x) \cdot f(y) \tag{3}$$

for all positive real numbers x and y, then

$$f(x) = x^k$$

for some constant k.

7.5 INVERSE TRIGONOMETRIC FUNCTIONS

Recall that the function f is said to be **one-to-one** on its domain of definition D if, given x_1 and x_2 in D, $x_1 \neq x_2$ implies that $f(x_1) \neq f(x_2)$: "Different inputs give different outputs." (To prove that f is one-to-one, it is usually easier to prove the contrapositive—that if $f(x_1) = f(x_2)$, then $x_1 = x_2$.) What is important here is that if f is one-to-one on its domain of definition, then it has an inverse function f^{-1}. This inverse function is *defined* by

$$f^{-1}(x) = y \quad \text{if and only if} \quad f(y) = x. \tag{1}$$

For example, from Section 7.1 we are familiar with the pair of inverse functions

$$f(x) = e^x \quad \text{and} \quad f^{-1}(x) = \ln x.$$

From a geometric viewpoint, Eq. (1) implies that the graphs $y = f(x)$ and $y = f^{-1}(x)$ are reflections across the 45° line $y = x$, like the familiar graphs $y = e^x$ and $y = \ln x$ in Fig. 7.5.1.

FIGURE 7.5.1 The graphs $y = e^x$ and $y = \ln x$ are reflections across the line $y = x$.

The Inverse Tangent Function

Here we want to define the inverses of the trigonometric functions, beginning with the inverse tangent function. We must, however, confront the fact that the trigonometric functions fail to be one-to-one because the period of each of the six is π or 2π. For example, $\tan x = 1$ if x is $\pi/4$ or $\pi/4$ plus any integral multiple of π. These many values of x, all with tangent equal to 1, correspond to the multiple points of intersection of the graph $y = \tan x$ and the horizontal line $y = 1$ in Fig. 7.5.2.

FIGURE 7.5.2 The tangent function takes on every real number value infinitely often.

FIGURE 7.5.3 Simply reflecting the graph of $y = \tan x$ across the 45°-line $y = x$ does not produce the graph of a function.

Figure 7.5.3 is the reflection of Fig. 7.5.2 across the 45° line $y = x$. The multiple intersections of $x = \tan y$ and the vertical line $x = 1$ indicate that we must make a choice in order to define $\tan^{-1} 1$. That is, we *cannot* define $y = \tan^{-1} x$, the inverse of the tangent function, by saying simply that y is the number such that $\tan y = x$. There are *many* such values of y, and we must specify just which particular one of these is to be used. (Note that the symbol -1 in the notation $\tan^{-1} x$ is not an exponent—it does *not* mean $(\tan x)^{-1}$.)

We do this by suitably restricting the domain of the tangent function. Because the function $\tan x$ is increasing on $(-\pi/2, \pi/2)$ and its range of values is $(-\infty, +\infty)$, for each x in $(-\infty, +\infty)$ there is *one* number y in $(-\pi/2, \pi/2)$ such that $\tan y = x$. This observation leads to the following definition of the *inverse tangent* (or *arctangent*) function, denoted by $\tan^{-1} x$ or $\arctan x$.

DEFINITION   The Inverse Tangent Function
The **inverse tangent** (or **arctangent**) **function** is defined as follows:

$$y = \tan^{-1} x \quad \text{if and only if} \quad \tan y = x \quad \text{and} \quad -\pi/2 < y < \pi/2 \tag{2}$$

where x is an arbitrary real number.

Because the tangent function attains all real values, $\tan^{-1} x$ is defined for all real numbers x; $\tan^{-1} x$ is that number y in the interval $(-\pi/2, \pi/2)$ whose tangent is x. The graph of $y = \tan^{-1} x$ is the reflection of the graph of $y = \tan x$, $-\pi/2 < x < \pi/2$, across the line $y = x$ (Fig. 7.5.4).

It follows from Eq. (2) that

$$\tan(\tan^{-1} x) = x \quad \text{for all } x \tag{3a}$$

and

$$\tan^{-1}(\tan x) = x \quad \text{if } -\pi/2 < x < \pi/2. \tag{3b}$$

FIGURE 7.5.4 The inverse tangent function $\tan^{-1} x$ is defined for all x.

Because the derivative of $\tan x$ is positive for all x in the interval $(-\pi/2, \pi/2)$, it follows from Theorem 1 in Section 7.1 that $\tan^{-1} x$ is differentiable for all x. We may, therefore, differentiate both sides of the identity in Eq. (3a). First we write that identity in the form

$$\tan y = x,$$

where $y = \tan^{-1} x$. Then differentiation with respect to x yields

$$(\sec^2 y) \frac{dy}{dx} = 1;$$

$$\frac{dy}{dx} = \frac{1}{\sec^2 y} = \frac{1}{1 + \tan^2 y} = \frac{1}{1 + x^2}.$$

Thus

$$D_x \tan^{-1} x = \frac{1}{1 + x^2}, \tag{4}$$

and if u is any differentiable function of x, then

$$D_x \tan^{-1} u = \frac{1}{1 + u^2} \cdot \frac{du}{dx}. \tag{5}$$

The definition of the inverse cotangent function is similar to that of the inverse tangent function, except that we begin by restricting the cotangent function to the interval $(0, \pi)$, where it is a decreasing function attaining all real values. Thus the **inverse cotangent** (or **arccotangent**) **function** is defined as

$$y = \cot^{-1} x \quad \text{if and only if} \quad \cot y = x \quad \text{and} \quad 0 < y < \pi \tag{6}$$

where x is any real number. Then differentiation of both sides of the identity $\cot(\cot^{-1} x) = x$ leads, as in the derivation of Eq. (4), to

$$D_x \cot^{-1} x = -\frac{1}{1 + x^2}.$$

If u is a differentiable function of x, then the chain rule gives

$$D_x \cot^{-1} u = -\frac{1}{1+u^2} \cdot \frac{du}{dx}. \tag{7}$$

Upon comparing Eqs. (5) and (7) we see that $D_x \cot^{-1} x = -D_x \tan^{-1} x$, so the two inverse functions are closely related. Indeed, perhaps you can show—using either calculus or just the definitions of the two functions—that $\tan^{-1} x + \cot^{-1} x \equiv \pi/2$.

EXAMPLE 1 A mountain climber on one edge of a deep canyon 800 ft wide sees a large rock fall from the opposite edge at time $t = 0$. As he watches the rock plummet downward, his eyes first move slowly, then faster, then more slowly again. Let α be the angle of depression of his line of sight below the horizontal. At what angle α would the rock *seem* to be moving the most rapidly? That is, when would $d\alpha/dt$ be maximal?

FIGURE 7.5.5 The falling rock of Example 1.

Solution From our study of constant acceleration in Section 5.2, we know that the rock will fall $16t^2$ feet in the first t seconds. We refer to Fig. 7.5.5 and see that the value of α at time t will be

$$\alpha = \alpha(t) = \tan^{-1}\left(\frac{16t^2}{800}\right) = \tan^{-1}\left(\frac{t^2}{50}\right).$$

Hence

$$\frac{d\alpha}{dt} = \frac{1}{1+\left(\frac{t^2}{50}\right)^2} \cdot \frac{2t}{50} = \frac{100t}{t^4+2500}.$$

To find when $d\alpha/dt$ is maximal, we find when *its* derivative is zero:

$$\frac{d}{dt}\left(\frac{d\alpha}{dt}\right) = \frac{100(t^4+2500) - (100t)(4t^3)}{(t^4+2500)^2} = \frac{100(2500-3t^4)}{(t^4+2500)^2}.$$

So $d^2\alpha/dt^2$ is zero when $3t^4 = 2500$—that is, when

$$t = \sqrt[4]{\frac{2500}{3}} \approx 5.37 \quad \text{(s)}.$$

This is the value of t when $d\alpha/dt$ is maximal, and at this time we have $t^2 = 50/\sqrt{3}$. So the angle at this time is

$$\alpha = \arctan\left(\frac{1}{50} \cdot \frac{50}{\sqrt{3}}\right) = \arctan\left(\frac{1}{\sqrt{3}}\right) = \frac{\pi}{6}.$$

The *apparent* speed of the falling rock is greatest when the climber's line of sight is 30° below the horizontal. The actual speed of the rock is then $32t$ with $t \approx 5.37$ and thus is about 172 ft/s. ◆

FIGURE 7.5.6 Multiple values of x such that $\sin x = \frac{1}{2}$.

The Inverse Sine Function

Figure 7.5.6 shows the graph of the sine function and the horizontal line $y = \frac{1}{2}$. Because this line meets the graph of the sine function in more than one point (indeed, at infinitely many points), the sine function takes on the value $\frac{1}{2}$ for many different values of x. For example, $\sin x = \frac{1}{2}$ if x is *either* $\pi/6$ plus any integral multiple of 2π or $5\pi/6$ plus any integral multiple of 2π.

Figure 7.5.7 is the reflection of Fig. 6.8.6 across the 45° line $y = x$. The multiple intersections of $x = \sin y$ and the vertical line $x = \frac{1}{2}$ indicate that we must make a choice in order to define $\sin^{-1}(\frac{1}{2})$. That is, we *cannot* define $y = \sin^{-1} x$, the inverse of the sine function, by saying merely that y is the number such that $\sin y = x$. There are *many* such values of y, and we must specify just which particular one of these is to be used.

FIGURE 7.5.7 There are many possible choices for $y = \sin^{-1}\frac{1}{2}$.

We do this by suitably restricting the domain of the sine function. Because the function $\sin x$ is increasing on $[-\pi/2, \pi/2]$ and its range of values is $[-1, 1]$, for each x in $[-1, 1]$ there is *one* number y in $[-\pi/2, \pi/2]$ such that $\sin y = x$. This observation leads to the following definition of the *inverse sine* (or *arcsine*) function, denoted by $\sin^{-1} x$ or by $\arcsin x$.

DEFINITION The Inverse Sine Function
The **inverse sine** (or **arcsine**) **function** is defined as follows:

$$y = \sin^{-1} x \quad \text{if and only if} \quad \sin y = x \quad \text{and} \quad -\pi/2 \leq y \leq \pi/2 \qquad (8)$$

where $-1 \leq x \leq 1$.

Thus, if x is between -1 and $+1$ (inclusive), then $\sin^{-1} x$ is that number y between $-\pi/2$ and $\pi/2$ such that $\sin y = x$. Even more briefly, $\arcsin x$ is the angle (in radians) nearest zero whose sine is x. For instance,

$$\sin^{-1} 1 = \frac{\pi}{2}, \qquad \sin^{-1} 0 = 0, \qquad \sin^{-1}(-1) = -\frac{\pi}{2},$$

and $\sin^{-1} 2$ does not exist.

Because interchanging x and y in the equation $\sin y = x$ yields $y = \sin x$, it follows from Eq. (8) that the graph of $y = \sin^{-1} x$ is the reflection of the graph of $y = \sin x$, $-\pi/2 \leq x \leq \pi/2$, across the line $y = x$ (Fig. 7.5.8).

(a) Graph of the sine function

(b) Graph of the arcsine function

FIGURE 7.5.8 The graphs $y = \sin x$ and $y = \sin^{-1} x$ are reflections of each other across the line $y = x$.

It also follows from Eq. (8) that

$$\sin(\sin^{-1} x) = x \quad \text{if } -1 \leq x \leq 1 \qquad (9a)$$

and

$$\sin^{-1}(\sin x) = x \quad \text{if } -\pi/2 \leq x \leq \pi/2. \qquad (9b)$$

Because the derivative of $\sin x$ is positive for $-\pi/2 < x < \pi/2$, it follows from Theorem 1 of Section 7.1 that $\sin^{-1} x$ is differentiable on $(-1, 1)$. We may, therefore, differentiate both sides of the identity in (9a), but we begin by writing it in the form

$$\sin y = x,$$

where $y = \sin^{-1} x$. Then differentiation with respect to x gives

$$(\cos y)\frac{dy}{dx} = 1,$$

Inverse Trigonometric Functions   SECTION 7.5   471

so
$$\frac{dy}{dx} = \frac{1}{\cos y} = \frac{1}{\sqrt{1 - \sin^2 y}} = \frac{1}{\sqrt{1 - x^2}}.$$

We are correct in taking the positive square root in this computation because $\cos y > 0$ for $-\pi/2 < y < \pi/2$. Thus

$$D_x \sin^{-1} x = \frac{1}{\sqrt{1 - x^2}} \tag{10}$$

provided that $-1 < x < 1$. When we combine this result with the chain rule, we get

$$D_x \sin^{-1} u = \frac{1}{\sqrt{1 - u^2}} \cdot \frac{du}{dx} \tag{11}$$

if u is a differentiable function with values in the interval $(-1, 1)$.

EXAMPLE 2 If $y = \sin^{-1} x^2$, then Eq. (11) with $u = x^2$ yields

$$\frac{dy}{dx} = \frac{1}{\sqrt{1 - (x^2)^2}} \cdot 2x = \frac{2x}{\sqrt{1 - x^4}}.$$ ◆

FIGURE 7.5.9 The cosine function is decreasing on the interval $0 \leq x \leq \pi$.

The definition of the inverse cosine function is similar to that of the inverse sine function, except that we begin by restricting the cosine function to the interval $[0, \pi]$, where it is a decreasing function (Fig. 7.5.9). Thus the **inverse cosine** (or **arccosine**) **function** is defined by means of the rule

$$y = \cos^{-1} x \quad \text{if and only if} \quad \cos y = x \quad \text{and} \quad 0 \leq y \leq \pi \tag{12}$$

where $-1 \leq x \leq 1$. Thus $\cos^{-1} x$ is the angle in $[0, \pi]$ whose cosine is x. For instance,

$$\cos^{-1} 1 = 0, \qquad \cos^{-1} 0 = \frac{\pi}{2}, \qquad \cos^{-1}(-1) = \pi.$$

We may compute the derivative of $\cos^{-1} x$, also written $\arccos x$, by differentiating both sides of the identity

$$\cos(\cos^{-1} x) = x \quad (-1 < x < 1).$$

FIGURE 7.5.10 The graph $y = \cos^{-1} x$ of the arccosine function.

The computations are similar to those for $D_x \sin^{-1} x$ and lead to the result

$$D_x \cos^{-1} x = -\frac{1}{\sqrt{1 - x^2}}.$$

And if u denotes a differentiable function of x, the chain rule then gives

$$D_x \cos^{-1} u = -\frac{1}{\sqrt{1 - u^2}} \cdot \frac{du}{dx}. \tag{13}$$

Figure 7.5.10 shows the graph of $y = \cos^{-1} x$ as the reflection of the graph of $y = \cos x$, $0 \leq x \leq \pi$, across the line $y = x$.

The Inverse Secant Function

Figure 7.5.11 shows that the secant function is increasing on each of the intervals $[0, \pi/2)$ and $(\pi/2, \pi]$. On the union of these two intervals, the secant function attains all real values y such that $|y| \geq 1$. We may, therefore, define the inverse secant function, denoted by $\sec^{-1} x$ or by $\text{arcsec } x$, by restricting the secant function to the union of the two intervals $[0, \pi/2)$ and $(\pi/2, \pi]$.

FIGURE 7.5.11 Restriction of the secant function to the union of the two intervals $[0, \pi/2)$ and $(\pi/2, \pi]$.

DEFINITION The Inverse Secant Function
The **inverse secant** (or **arcsecant**) **function** is defined as follows:

$$y = \sec^{-1} x \quad \text{if and only if} \quad \sec y = x \quad \text{and} \quad 0 \leq y \leq \pi \quad (14)$$

where $|x| \geq 1$.

REMARK 1 Because $\sec(\pi/2)$ is not defined, the restriction $0 \leq y \leq \pi$ in (14) implies that the range of the inverse secant function is the union $[0, \pi/2) \cup (\pi/2, \pi]$.

REMARK 2 Some textbooks offer alternative definitions of the inverse secant based on different intervals of definition of $\sec x$. The definition given here, however, satisfies the condition that

$$\sec^{-1} x = \cos^{-1} \frac{1}{x} \quad (\text{if } |x| > 1),$$

which is convenient for calculator-computer calculations. (See Problem 62.) Moreover, our definition of $\sec^{-1} x$ is the same as that used in computer algebra systems such as *Maple* and *Mathematica*. (See Problem 61.)

The graph of $y = \sec^{-1} x$ is the reflection of the graph of $y = \sec x$, suitably restricted to the intervals $0 \leq x < \pi/2$ and $\pi/2 < x \leq \pi$, across the line $y = x$ (Fig. 7.5.12). It follows from the definition of the inverse secant that

$$\sec(\sec^{-1} x) = x \quad \text{if } |x| \geq 1, \quad (15a)$$

$$\sec^{-1}(\sec x) = x \quad \text{for } x \text{ in } [0, \pi/2) \cup (\pi/2, \pi]. \quad (15b)$$

FIGURE 7.5.12 The graph of $y = \text{arcsec } x = \sec^{-1} x$.

Following the now-familiar pattern, we find $D_x \sec^{-1} x$ by differentiating both sides of Eq. (15a) in the form

$$\sec y = x,$$

where $y = \sec^{-1} x$. This yields

$$(\sec y \tan y) \frac{dy}{dx} = 1,$$

so

$$\frac{dy}{dx} = \frac{1}{\sec y \tan y} = \frac{1}{\pm x \sqrt{x^2 - 1}},$$

because $\tan y = \pm \sqrt{\sec^2 y - 1} = \pm \sqrt{x^2 - 1}$.

To obtain the correct choice of sign here, note what happens in the two cases $x > 1$ and $x < -1$. In the first case, $0 < y < \pi/2$ and $\tan y > 0$, so we choose the plus sign. If $x < -1$, then $\pi/2 < y < \pi$ and $\tan y < 0$, so we take the minus sign. Thus

$$\frac{dy}{dx} = \frac{1}{|x| \sqrt{x^2 - 1}} \quad (|x| > 1). \quad (16)$$

If u is a differentiable function of x with values that exceed 1 in magnitude, then by the chain rule we have

$$D_x \sec^{-1} u = \frac{1}{|u| \sqrt{u^2 - 1}} \cdot \frac{du}{dx}. \quad (17)$$

EXAMPLE 3 The function $f(x) = \sec^{-1} e^x$ is defined if $x > 0$, because then $e^x > 1$. Then by Eq. (17),

$$D_x \sec^{-1} e^x = \frac{e^x}{|e^x|\sqrt{e^{2x}-1}} = \frac{1}{\sqrt{e^{2x}-1}}$$

because $|e^x| = e^x$ for all x. ◆

The **inverse cosecant** (or **arccosecant**) **function** is the inverse of the function $y = \csc x$, where x is restricted to the union of the intervals $[-\pi/2, 0)$ and $(0, \pi/2]$. Thus

$$y = \csc^{-1} x \quad \text{if and only if} \quad \csc y = x \quad \text{and} \quad -\pi/2 < y < \pi/2 \quad (18)$$

where $|x| \geq 1$. Its derivative formula, which has a derivation similar to that of the inverse secant function, is

$$D_x \csc^{-1} u = -\frac{1}{|u|\sqrt{u^2-1}} \cdot \frac{du}{dx}. \quad (19)$$

SUMMARY

The following table summarizes the domains, ranges, and derivatives of the six inverse trigonometric functions.

Function	Domain of Definition	Range of Values	Derivative
$\sin^{-1} x$	$-1 \leq x \leq 1$	$-\pi/2 \leq y \leq \pi/2$	$\dfrac{1}{\sqrt{1-x^2}}$
$\cos^{-1} x$	$-1 \leq x \leq 1$	$0 \leq y \leq \pi$	$-\dfrac{1}{\sqrt{1-x^2}}$
$\tan^{-1} x$	$-\infty < x < +\infty$	$-\pi/2 < y < \pi/2$	$\dfrac{1}{1+x^2}$
$\cot^{-1} x$	$-\infty < x < +\infty$	$0 < y < \pi$	$-\dfrac{1}{1+x^2}$
$\sec^{-1} x$	$|x| \geq 1$	$0 \leq y < \pi/2,\ \pi/2 < y \leq \pi$	$\dfrac{1}{|x|\sqrt{x^2-1}}$
$\csc^{-1} x$	$|x| \geq 1$	$-\pi/2 < y < 0,\ 0 < y < \pi/2$	$-\dfrac{1}{|x|\sqrt{x^2-1}}$

It is worth noting that

- $\sin^{-1} x$ has the range $[-\pi/2, \pi/2]$ and $\tan^{-1} x$ has the range $(-\pi/2, \pi/2)$, whereas
- $\cos^{-1} x$ has the range $[0, \pi]$ and $\sec^{-1} x$ has the range $[0, \frac{1}{2}\pi) \cup (\frac{1}{2}\pi, \pi]$.

Observe also the "difference only in sign" of the derivatives of function/cofunction pairs of inverse functions. ◆

Integrals Involving Inverse Trigonometric Functions

The derivatives of the six inverse trigonometric functions are all simple *algebraic* functions. As a consequence, inverse trigonometric functions typically occur when we integrate algebraic functions. Moreover, as mentioned earlier, the derivatives of $\cos^{-1} x$, $\cot^{-1} x$, and $\csc^{-1} x$ differ only in sign from the derivatives of their respective cofunctions. For this reason only the arcsine, arctangent, and arcsecant functions are necessary for integration, and only these three are in common use. That is, you need commit to memory the integral formulas only for the latter three functions. They follow immediately from Eqs. (5), (11), and (17) and may be written in the forms shown next:

$$\int \frac{du}{\sqrt{1-u^2}} = \sin^{-1} u + C, \tag{20}$$

$$\int \frac{du}{1+u^2} = \tan^{-1} u + C, \tag{21}$$

$$\int \frac{du}{u\sqrt{u^2-1}} = \sec^{-1} |u| + C. \tag{22}$$

It is easy to verify that the absolute value on the right-hand side in Eq. (22) follows from the one in Eq. (17). (See Problem 57.) And remember that because $\sec^{-1} |u|$ is undefined unless $|u| \geq 1$, the definite integral

$$\int_a^b \frac{du}{u\sqrt{u^2-1}}$$

is meaningful only when the limits a and b are both at least 1 or both at most -1.

EXAMPLE 4 It follows immediately from Eq. (21) that

$$\int_0^1 \frac{dx}{1+x^2} = \left[\tan^{-1} x\right]_0^1 = \tan^{-1} 1 - \tan^{-1} 0 = \frac{\pi}{4}. \quad \blacklozenge$$

EXAMPLE 5 The substitution $u = 3x$, $du = 3\,dx$ gives

$$\int \frac{1}{1+9x^2}\,dx = \frac{1}{3}\int \frac{3}{1+(3x)^2}\,dx$$

$$= \frac{1}{3}\int \frac{du}{1+u^2} = \frac{1}{3}\tan^{-1} u + C = \frac{1}{3}\tan^{-1} 3x + C. \quad \blacklozenge$$

EXAMPLE 6 The substitution $u = \frac{1}{2}x$, $du = \frac{1}{2}dx$ gives

$$\int \frac{1}{\sqrt{4-x^2}}\,dx = \int \frac{1}{2\sqrt{1-(x/2)^2}}\,dx$$

$$= \int \frac{1}{\sqrt{1-u^2}}\,du = \arcsin u + C = \arcsin\left(\frac{x}{2}\right) + C. \quad \blacklozenge$$

EXAMPLE 7 The substitution $u = x\sqrt{2}$, $du = \sqrt{2}\,dx$ gives

$$\int_1^{\sqrt{2}} \frac{1}{x\sqrt{2x^2-1}}\,dx = \int_{\sqrt{2}}^2 \frac{1}{u\sqrt{u^2-1}}\,du$$

$$= \left[\sec^{-1} |u|\right]_{\sqrt{2}}^2 = \sec^{-1} 2 - \sec^{-1}\sqrt{2}$$

$$= \frac{\pi}{3} - \frac{\pi}{4} = \frac{\pi}{12}. \quad \blacklozenge$$

7.5 TRUE/FALSE STUDY GUIDE

7.5 CONCEPTS: QUESTIONS AND DISCUSSION

1. Suppose that f and g are inverse functions. Outline the way the derivative of g can be found if the derivative of f is known.
2. Discuss the differences and similarities in the domains and ranges of the six inverse trigonometric functions.

7.5 PROBLEMS

Find the values indicated in Problems 1 through 4.

1. (a) $\sin^{-1}\left(\frac{1}{2}\right)$; (b) $\sin^{-1}\left(-\frac{1}{2}\right)$; (c) $\sin^{-1}\left(\frac{1}{2}\sqrt{2}\right)$;
   (d) $\sin^{-1}\left(-\frac{1}{2}\sqrt{3}\right)$
2. (a) $\cos^{-1}\left(\frac{1}{2}\right)$; (b) $\cos^{-1}\left(-\frac{1}{2}\right)$; (c) $\cos^{-1}\left(\frac{1}{2}\sqrt{2}\right)$;
   (d) $\cos^{-1}\left(-\frac{1}{2}\sqrt{3}\right)$
3. (a) $\tan^{-1} 0$; (b) $\tan^{-1} 1$; (c) $\tan^{-1}(-1)$; (d) $\tan^{-1}\sqrt{3}$
4. (a) $\sec^{-1} 1$; (b) $\sec^{-1}(-1)$; (c) $\sec^{-1} 2$; (d) $\sec^{-1}\left(-\sqrt{2}\right)$

Differentiate the functions in Problems 5 through 26.

5. $f(x) = \sin^{-1}(x^{100})$
6. $f(x) = \arctan(e^x)$
7. $f(x) = \sec^{-1}(\ln x)$
8. $f(x) = \ln(\tan^{-1} x)$
9. $f(x) = \arcsin(\tan x)$
10. $f(x) = x \arctan x$
11. $f(x) = \sin^{-1} e^x$
12. $f(x) = \arctan \sqrt{x}$
13. $f(x) = \cos^{-1} x + \sec^{-1}\left(\frac{1}{x}\right)$
14. $f(x) = \cot^{-1}\left(\frac{1}{x^2}\right)$
15. $f(x) = \csc^{-1} x^2$
16. $f(x) = \arccos\left(\frac{1}{\sqrt{x}}\right)$
17. $f(x) = \frac{1}{\arctan x}$
18. $f(x) = (\arcsin x)^2$
19. $f(x) = \tan^{-1}(\ln x)$
20. $f(x) = \operatorname{arcsec}\sqrt{x^2+1}$
21. $f(x) = \tan^{-1} e^x + \cos^{-1} e^{-x}$
22. $f(x) = \exp(\arcsin x)$
23. $f(x) = \sin(\arctan x)$
24. $f(x) = \sec(\sec^{-1} e^x)$
25. $f(x) = \dfrac{\arctan x}{(1+x^2)^2}$
26. $f(x) = (\sin^{-1} 2x^2)^{-2}$

In Problems 27 through 30, find dy/dx by implicit differentiation. Then find the line tangent to the graph of the equation at the indicated point P.

27. $\tan^{-1} x + \tan^{-1} y = \dfrac{\pi}{2}$; $P(1, 1)$
28. $\sin^{-1} x + \sin^{-1} y = \dfrac{\pi}{2}$; $P\left(\frac{1}{2}, \frac{1}{2}\sqrt{3}\right)$
29. $(\sin^{-1} x)(\sin^{-1} y) = \dfrac{\pi^2}{16}$; $P\left(\frac{1}{2}\sqrt{2}, \frac{1}{2}\sqrt{2}\right)$
30. $(\sin^{-1} x)^2 + (\sin^{-1} y)^2 = \dfrac{5\pi^2}{36}$; $P\left(\frac{1}{2}, \frac{1}{2}\sqrt{3}\right)$

Evaluate or antidifferentiate, as appropriate, in Problems 31 through 55.

31. $\displaystyle\int_0^1 \dfrac{dx}{1+x^2}$
32. $\displaystyle\int_0^{1/2} \dfrac{dx}{\sqrt{1-x^2}}$
33. $\displaystyle\int_{\sqrt{2}}^{2} \dfrac{dx}{x\sqrt{x^2-1}}$
34. $\displaystyle\int_{-2}^{-2/\sqrt{3}} \dfrac{dx}{x\sqrt{x^2-1}}$
35. $\displaystyle\int_0^3 \dfrac{dx}{9+x^2}$
36. $\displaystyle\int_0^{\sqrt{12}} \dfrac{dx}{\sqrt{16-x^2}}$
37. $\displaystyle\int \dfrac{dx}{\sqrt{1-4x^2}}$
38. $\displaystyle\int \dfrac{dx}{9x^2+4}$
39. $\displaystyle\int \dfrac{dx}{x\sqrt{x^2-25}}$
40. $\displaystyle\int \dfrac{dx}{x\sqrt{4x^2-9}}$
41. $\displaystyle\int \dfrac{e^x}{1+e^{2x}}\,dx$
42. $\displaystyle\int \dfrac{x^2}{x^6+25}\,dx$
43. $\displaystyle\int \dfrac{dx}{x\sqrt{x^6-25}}$
44. $\displaystyle\int \dfrac{\sqrt{x}}{1+x^3}\,dx$
45. $\displaystyle\int \dfrac{dx}{\sqrt{x(1-x)}}$
46. $\displaystyle\int \dfrac{\sec x \tan x}{1+\sec^2 x}\,dx$
47. $\displaystyle\int \dfrac{x^{49}}{1+x^{100}}\,dx$
48. $\displaystyle\int \dfrac{x^4}{\sqrt{1-x^{10}}}\,dx$
49. $\displaystyle\int \dfrac{1}{x[1+(\ln x)^2]}\,dx$
50. $\displaystyle\int \dfrac{\arctan x}{1+x^2}\,dx$
51. $\displaystyle\int_0^1 \dfrac{1}{1+(2x-1)^2}\,dx$
52. $\displaystyle\int_0^1 \dfrac{x^3}{1+x^4}\,dx$
53. $\displaystyle\int_1^e \dfrac{dx}{x\sqrt{1-(\ln x)^2}}$
54. $\displaystyle\int_1^2 \dfrac{dx}{x\sqrt{x^2-1}}$
55. $\displaystyle\int_1^3 \dfrac{dx}{2\sqrt{x}\,(1+x)}$ [*Suggestion:* Let $u = x^{1/2}$.]

56. Conclude from the formula $D_x \cos^{-1} x = -D_x \sin^{-1} x$ that $\sin^{-1} x + \cos^{-1} x = \pi/2$ if $0 \le x \le 1$.

57. The integral formula in (22) is equivalent to

$$D_u \sec^{-1}|u| = \dfrac{1}{u\sqrt{u^2-1}} \quad \text{if } |u| > 1. \qquad (22')$$

This is the same as (16) if $u > 1$. Assuming that $u < -1$, substitute $x = -u$ in $y = \sec^{-1}|u|$ and use the chain rule $dy/du = (dy/dx)(dx/du)$ to verify (22').

In Problems 58 through 60, substitute $u = ax$ (assuming that $a > 0$) to derive the given integral formula.

58. $\displaystyle\int \dfrac{1}{\sqrt{a^2-u^2}}\,du = \sin^{-1}\left(\dfrac{u}{a}\right) + C$ $(u < a)$.
59. $\displaystyle\int \dfrac{1}{a^2+u^2}\,du = \dfrac{1}{a}\tan^{-1}\left(\dfrac{u}{a}\right) + C$.
60. $\displaystyle\int \dfrac{1}{u\sqrt{u^2-a^2}}\,du = \dfrac{1}{a}\sec^{-1}\left|\dfrac{u}{a}\right| + C$ $(u > a)$.

61. If $f(x) = \sec^{-1} x$ then the computer algebra systems *Mathematica* and *Maple* both give

$$f'(x) = \dfrac{1}{x^2\sqrt{1-\dfrac{1}{x^2}}}$$

for the derivative of f. Verify carefully that (if either $x < -1$ or $x > 1$) this result is equivalent to the derivative formula for $\sec^{-1} x$ given in this section.

62. Show that

$$D_x \sec^{-1} x = D_x \cos^{-1} \frac{1}{x} \quad \text{if } |x| > 1,$$

and conclude that

$$\sec^{-1} x = \cos^{-1} \frac{1}{x} \quad \text{if } |x| > 1.$$

This fact can be used to find arcsecant values on a calculator that has a key for the arccosine function, usually written $\boxed{\text{INV}}\ \boxed{\text{COS}}$ or $\boxed{\text{COS}^{-1}}$, but no arcsecant key.

63. Some calculus textbooks define the inverse secant function as that function g such that $y = g(x)$ if and only if $\sec y = x$ with y in either $[0, \pi/2)$ or $[\pi, 3\pi/2)$ (the latter instead of the interval $(\pi/2, \pi]$ used in this text). In contrast with Fig. 7.5.12, show that the graph of this "alternative arcsecant function" is as shown in Fig. 7.5.13. Then show that its derivative is given by

$$g'(x) = \frac{1}{x\sqrt{x^2 - 1}}$$

(with no absolute value on the right).

FIGURE 7.5.13 Graph of the alternative inverse secant function of Problem 63.

64. (a) Deduce from the addition formula for tangents (Problem 28 in Appendix C) that

$$\arctan x + \arctan y = \arctan \frac{x+y}{1-xy}$$

provided that $xy < 1$. (b) Apply part (a) to show that each of the following numbers is equal to $\pi/4$: (i) $\arctan(\frac{1}{2}) + \arctan(\frac{1}{3})$; (ii) $2\arctan(\frac{1}{3}) + \arctan(\frac{1}{7})$; (iii) $\arctan(\frac{120}{119}) - \arctan(\frac{1}{239})$; (iv) $4\arctan(\frac{1}{5}) - \arctan(\frac{1}{239})$.

65. A billboard to be built *parallel* to a highway will be 12 m high and its bottom will be 4 m above the eye level of the average passing motorist. How far from the highway should the billboard be placed in order to maximize the vertical angle it subtends at the motorist's eyes?

66. Use inverse trigonometric functions to prove that the vertical angle subtended by a rectangular painting on a wall is greatest when the painting is hung with its center at the level of the observer's eyes.

67. Show that the circumference of a circle of radius a is $2\pi a$ by finding the length of the circular arc

$$y = \sqrt{a^2 - x^2}$$

from $x = 0$ to $x = a/\sqrt{2}$ and then multiplying by 8.

68. Find the volume generated by revolving around the y-axis the area under $y = 1/(1+x^4)$ from $x = 0$ to $x = 1$.

69. The unbounded region R is bounded on the left by the y-axis, below by the x-axis, and above by the graph of $y = 1/(1+x^2)$. Show that the area of R is finite by evaluating

$$\lim_{a \to \infty} \int_0^a \frac{dx}{1+x^2}.$$

70. A building 250 ft high is equipped with an external elevator. The elevator starts at the top at time $t = 0$ and descends at the constant rate of 25 ft/s. You are watching the elevator from a window that is 100 ft above the ground and in a building 50 ft from the elevator. At what height does the elevator appear to you to be moving the fastest?

71. Suppose that the function f is defined for all x such that $|x| > 1$ and has the property that

$$f'(x) = \frac{1}{x\sqrt{x^2-1}}$$

for all such x. (a) Explain why there exist two constants A and B such that

$$f(x) = \operatorname{arcsec} x + A \quad \text{if } x > 1;$$
$$f(x) = -\operatorname{arcsec} x + B \quad \text{if } x < -1.$$

(b) Determine the values of A and B so that $f(2) = 1 = f(-2)$. Then sketch the graph of $y = f(x)$.

In some computing languages the arctangent is the only inverse trigonometric function that is programmed directly, so it is necessary to express $\sin^{-1} x$ and $\sec^{-1} x$ in terms of $\tan^{-1} x$. In Problems 72 and 73 verify each given identity by differentiating both sides. What else must be done?

72. $\sin^{-1} x = \tan^{-1}\left(\dfrac{x}{\sqrt{1-x^2}}\right)$.

73. (a) $\sec^{-1} x = \tan^{-1}\sqrt{x^2-1}$ if $x > 1$;

(b) $\sec^{-1} x = \pi - \tan^{-1}\sqrt{x^2-1}$ if $x < -1$.

In Problems 74 through 76, estimate the absolute maximum value of $f(x)$ for $x > 0$. You may want to begin by locating the pertinent critical point graphically.

74. $f(x) = x^{-1/2} \tan^{-1} x$

75. $f(x) = e^{-x/10} \tan^{-1} x$

76. $f(x) = e^{-x/100} \sec^{-1} x$

7.6 HYPERBOLIC FUNCTIONS

The **hyperbolic cosine** and the **hyperbolic sine** of the real number x are denoted by $\cosh x$ and $\sinh x$ and are defined to be

$$\cosh x = \frac{e^x + e^{-x}}{2} \quad \text{and} \quad \sinh x = \frac{e^x - e^{-x}}{2}. \tag{1}$$

These particular combinations of familiar exponentials are useful in certain applications of calculus and are also helpful in evaluating certain integrals. The other four hyperbolic functions—the hyperbolic tangent, cotangent, secant, and cosecant—are defined in terms of $\cosh x$ and $\sinh x$ by analogy with trigonometry:

$$\tanh x = \frac{\sinh x}{\cosh x} = \frac{e^x - e^{-x}}{e^x + e^{-x}},$$

$$\coth x = \frac{\cosh x}{\sinh x} = \frac{e^x + e^{-x}}{e^x - e^{-x}} \quad (x \neq 0); \tag{2}$$

$$\operatorname{sech} x = \frac{1}{\cosh x} = \frac{2}{e^x + e^{-x}},$$

$$\operatorname{csch} x = \frac{1}{\sinh x} = \frac{2}{e^x - e^{-x}} \quad (x \neq 0). \tag{3}$$

The trigonometric terminology and notation for these hyperbolic functions stems from the fact that these functions satisfy a list of identities that, apart from an occasional difference of sign, much resemble familiar trigonometric identities:

$$\cosh^2 x - \sinh^2 x = 1; \tag{4}$$

$$1 - \tanh^2 x = \operatorname{sech}^2 x; \tag{5}$$

$$\coth^2 x - 1 = \operatorname{csch}^2 x; \tag{6}$$

$$\sinh(x + y) = \sinh x \cosh y + \cosh x \sinh y; \tag{7}$$

$$\cosh(x + y) = \cosh x \cosh y + \sinh x \sinh y; \tag{8}$$

$$\sinh 2x = 2 \sinh x \cosh x; \tag{9}$$

$$\cosh 2x = \cosh^2 x + \sinh^2 x; \tag{10}$$

$$\cosh^2 x = \tfrac{1}{2}(\cosh 2x + 1); \tag{11}$$

$$\sinh^2 x = \tfrac{1}{2}(\cosh 2x - 1). \tag{12}$$

FIGURE 7.6.1 Relation of the ordinary cosine and sine functions to the circle $x^2 + y^2 = 1$.

The identities in Eqs. (4), (7), and (8) follow directly from the definitions of $\cosh x$ and $\sinh x$, as in Example 1.

EXAMPLE 1 To establish the "fundamental identity" in Eq. (4), we simply substitute the definitions of $\cosh x$ and $\sinh x$ on the left-hand side and write

$$\cosh^2 x - \sinh^2 x = \tfrac{1}{4}(e^x + e^{-x})^2 - \tfrac{1}{4}(e^x - e^{-x})^2$$

$$= \tfrac{1}{4}(e^{2x} + 2 + e^{-2x}) - \tfrac{1}{4}(e^{2x} - 2 + e^{-2x}) = 1.$$

The other identities listed previously may be derived from Eqs. (4), (7), and (8) in ways that parallel the derivations of the corresponding trigonometric identities. ◆

FIGURE 7.6.2 Relation of the hyperbolic cosine and hyperbolic sine functions to the hyperbola $x^2 - y^2 = 1$.

The trigonometric functions are sometimes called the *circular* functions because the point $(\cos\theta, \sin\theta)$ lies on the circle $x^2 + y^2 = 1$ for all θ (Fig. 7.6.1). Similarly, the identity in Eq. (4) tells us that the point $(\cosh\theta, \sinh\theta)$ lies on the hyperbola $x^2 - y^2 = 1$, and this is how the name *hyperbolic* function originated (Fig. 7.6.2).

FIGURE 7.6.3 Graphs of the six hyperbolic functions.

The graphs of $y = \cosh x$ and $y = \sinh x$ are easy to construct. Add (for cosh) or subtract (for sinh) the ordinates of the graphs of $y = \frac{1}{2}e^x$ and $y = \frac{1}{2}e^{-x}$. The graphs of the other four hyperbolic functions can then be constructed by dividing ordinates. The graphs of all six are shown in Fig. 7.6.3.

These graphs show a striking difference between the hyperbolic functions and the ordinary trigonometric functions: None of the hyperbolic functions is periodic. They do, however, have even-odd properties, as the circular functions do. Like cosine and secant, the two functions cosh and sech are even, because

$$\cosh(-x) = \cosh x \quad \text{and} \quad \text{sech}(-x) = \text{sech}\, x$$

for all x. The other four hyperbolic functions, like the sine and tangent functions, are odd:

$$\sinh(-x) = -\sinh x, \qquad \tanh(-x) = -\tanh x,$$

and so on.

Derivatives and Integrals of Hyperbolic Functions

The formulas for the derivatives of the hyperbolic functions parallel those for the trigonometric functions, with occasional sign differences. For example,

$$D_x \cosh x = D_x\left(\tfrac{1}{2}e^x + \tfrac{1}{2}e^{-x}\right) = \tfrac{1}{2}e^x - \tfrac{1}{2}e^{-x} = \sinh x.$$

The chain rule then gives

$$D_x \cosh u = (\sinh u) \frac{du}{dx} \tag{13}$$

if u is a differentiable function of x. The other five differentiation formulas are

$$D_x \sinh u = (\cosh u) \frac{du}{dx}, \tag{14}$$

$$D_x \tanh u = (\text{sech}^2 u) \frac{du}{dx}, \tag{15}$$

$$D_x \coth u = (-\text{csch}^2 u) \frac{du}{dx}, \tag{16}$$

$$D_x \text{sech} \, u = (-\text{sech} \, u \tanh u) \frac{du}{dx}, \tag{17}$$

$$D_x \text{csch} \, u = (-\text{csch} \, u \coth u) \frac{du}{dx}. \tag{18}$$

Equation (14) is derived exactly as Eq. (13) is. Then Eqs. (15) through (18) follow from Eqs. (13) and (14) with the aid of the quotient rule and the identities in Eqs. (5) and (6).

As indicated in Example 2, the differentiation of hyperbolic functions using Eqs. (13) through (18) is very similar to the differentiation of trigonometric functions.

EXAMPLE 2

(a) $D_x \cosh 2x = 2 \sinh 2x$.
(b) $D_x \sinh^2 x = 2 \sinh x \cosh x$.
(c) $D_x(x \tanh x) = \tanh x + x \, \text{sech}^2 x$.
(d) $D_x \text{sech}(x^2) = -2x \, \text{sech}(x^2) \tanh(x^2)$. ◆

The antiderivative versions of the differentiation formulas in Eqs. (13) through (18) are the following integral formulas:

$$\int \sinh u \, du = \cosh u + C, \tag{19}$$

$$\int \cosh u \, du = \sinh u + C, \tag{20}$$

$$\int \text{sech}^2 u \, du = \tanh u + C, \tag{21}$$

$$\int \text{csch}^2 u \, du = -\coth u + C, \tag{22}$$

$$\int \text{sech} \, u \tanh u \, du = -\text{sech} \, u + C, \tag{23}$$

$$\int \text{csch} \, u \coth u \, du = -\text{csch} \, u + C. \tag{24}$$

The integrals in Example 3 illustrate the fact that simple hyperbolic integrals may be treated in much the same way as simple trigonometric integrals.

EXAMPLE 3

(a) With $u = 3x$, we have

$$\int \cosh 3x \, dx = \int (\cosh u) \left(\tfrac{1}{3} du\right) = \tfrac{1}{3} \sinh u + C = \tfrac{1}{3} \sinh 3x + C.$$

(b) With $u = \sinh x$, we have

$$\int \sinh x \cosh x \, dx = \int u \, du = \tfrac{1}{2}u^2 + C = \tfrac{1}{2}\sinh^2 x + C.$$

(c) Using Eq. (12), we find that

$$\int \sinh^2 x \, dx = \int \tfrac{1}{2}(\cosh 2x - 1) \, dx = \tfrac{1}{4}\sinh 2x - \tfrac{1}{2}x + C.$$

(d) Finally, using Eq. (5), we see that

$$\int_0^1 \tanh^2 x \, dx = \int_0^1 (1 - \operatorname{sech}^2 x) \, dx = \Big[x - \tanh x\Big]_0^1$$

$$= 1 - \tanh 1 = 1 - \frac{e - e^{-1}}{e + e^{-1}} = \frac{2}{e^2 + 1}$$

$$\approx 0.238406.$$

Inverse Hyperbolic Functions

Figure 7.6.3 shows that

- The functions $\sinh x$ and $\tanh x$ are increasing for all x;
- The functions $\coth x$ and $\operatorname{csch} x$ are decreasing and defined for all $x \neq 0$;
- The function $\cosh x$ is increasing on the half-line $x \geq 0$; and
- The function $\operatorname{sech} x$ is decreasing on the half-line $x \geq 0$.

It follows that each of the six hyperbolic functions can be "inverted" on the indicated domain where it is either increasing or decreasing. The resulting inverse hyperbolic functions and their domains of definition are listed in the following table:

Inverse Hyperbolic Function	Defined for
$\sinh^{-1} x$	All x
$\cosh^{-1} x$	$x \geq 1$
$\tanh^{-1} x$	$|x| < 1$
$\coth^{-1} x$	$|x| > 1$
$\operatorname{sech}^{-1} x$	$0 < x \leq 1$
$\operatorname{csch}^{-1} x$	$x \neq 0$

EXAMPLE 4 Find the numerical value of $\tanh^{-1}\left(\tfrac{1}{2}\right)$.

Solution If $y = \tanh^{-1} x$, then

$$\tanh y = x;$$

$$\frac{e^y - e^{-y}}{e^y + e^{-y}} = x \qquad \text{[by Eq. (2)]};$$

$$e^y - e^{-y} = xe^y + xe^{-y};$$

$$(1-x)e^y = (1+x)e^{-y};$$

$$e^{2y} = \frac{1+x}{1-x};$$

$$y = \tfrac{1}{2}\ln\frac{1+x}{1-x}.$$

Hence, with $x = \tfrac{1}{2}$, we find that

$$\tanh^{-1}\left(\tfrac{1}{2}\right) = \tfrac{1}{2}\ln 3 \approx 0.549306.$$

Scientific calculators ordinarily are used to find values of hyperbolic and inverse hyperbolic functions. Many calculators give values only of $\sinh^{-1}$, $\cosh^{-1}$, and $\tanh^{-1}$. Values of the other three inverse hyperbolic functions can then be found by using the identities

$$\text{sech}^{-1} x = \cosh^{-1}\left(\frac{1}{x}\right), \tag{25}$$

$$\text{csch}^{-1} x = \sinh^{-1}\left(\frac{1}{x}\right), \tag{26}$$

and

$$\coth^{-1} x = \tanh^{-1}\left(\frac{1}{x}\right). \tag{27}$$

For example,

$$\coth^{-1} 2 = \tanh^{-1}\left(\tfrac{1}{2}\right) \approx 0.549306.$$

Derivatives of Inverse Hyperbolic Functions

Here are the derivatives of the six inverse hyperbolic functions:

$$D_x \sinh^{-1} x = \frac{1}{\sqrt{1+x^2}}, \tag{28}$$

$$D_x \cosh^{-1} x = \frac{1}{\sqrt{x^2-1}}, \tag{29}$$

$$D_x \tanh^{-1} x = \frac{1}{1-x^2}, \tag{30}$$

$$D_x \coth^{-1} x = \frac{1}{1-x^2}, \tag{31}$$

$$D_x \text{sech}^{-1} x = -\frac{1}{x\sqrt{1-x^2}}, \tag{32}$$

$$D_x \text{csch}^{-1} x = -\frac{1}{|x|\sqrt{1+x^2}}. \tag{33}$$

We can derive these formulas by the standard method of finding the derivative of the inverse of a function when the derivative of the function itself is known. The only requirement is that the inverse function is known in advance to be differentiable.

EXAMPLE 5 To differentiate $\tanh^{-1} x$, we begin with the inverse function relation

$$\tanh(\tanh^{-1} x) = x$$

and substitute $u = \tanh^{-1} x$. Then, because this equation is actually an identity,

$$D_x \tanh u = D_x x = 1,$$

so

$$(\text{sech}^2 u)\frac{du}{dx} = 1.$$

Thus

$$D_x \tanh^{-1} x = \frac{du}{dx} = \frac{1}{\text{sech}^2 u} = \frac{1}{1-\tanh^2 u}$$

$$= \frac{1}{1-\tanh^2(\tanh^{-1} x)} = \frac{1}{1-x^2}.$$

This establishes Eq. (30). We can use similar methods to verify the formulas for the derivatives of the other five hyperbolic functions. ◆

The hyperbolic functions are defined in terms of the natural exponential e^x, so it's no surprise that their inverses may be expressed in terms of $\ln x$. (See Example 4.) In fact,

$$\sinh^{-1} x = \ln\left(x + \sqrt{x^2+1}\right) \quad \text{for all } x; \tag{34}$$

$$\cosh^{-1} x = \ln\left(x + \sqrt{x^2-1}\right) \quad \text{for all } x \geq 1; \tag{35}$$

$$\tanh^{-1} x = \tfrac{1}{2}\ln\left(\frac{1+x}{1-x}\right) \quad \text{for } |x| < 1; \tag{36}$$

$$\coth^{-1} x = \tfrac{1}{2}\ln\left(\frac{x+1}{x-1}\right) \quad \text{for } |x| > 1; \tag{37}$$

$$\operatorname{sech}^{-1} x = \ln\left(\frac{1+\sqrt{1-x^2}}{x}\right) \quad \text{if } 0 < x \leq 1; \tag{38}$$

$$\operatorname{csch}^{-1} x = \ln\left(\frac{1}{x} + \frac{\sqrt{1+x^2}}{|x|}\right) \quad \text{if } x \neq 0. \tag{39}$$

Each of these identities may be established by showing that each side has the same derivative and also that the two sides agree for at least one value of x in every interval of their respective domains.

EXAMPLE 6 To establish the identity in (34), we begin by differentiating each side:

$$D_x \ln\left(x + \sqrt{x^2+1}\right) = \frac{1 + \dfrac{x}{\sqrt{x^2+1}}}{x + \sqrt{x^2+1}} = \frac{1}{\sqrt{x^2+1}} = D_x \sinh^{-1} x.$$

Thus

$$\sinh^{-1} x = \ln\left(x + \sqrt{x^2+1}\right) + C.$$

But $\sinh^{-1}(0) = 0 = \ln(0 + \sqrt{0+1})$. This implies that $C = 0$ and thus establishes Eq. (34). It is not quite so easy to show that $C = 0$ in the proofs of Eqs. (37) and (39); see Problems 64 and 65. ◆

Equations (34) through (39) may be used to calculate the values of inverse hyperbolic functions. This is convenient if you own a calculator whose repertoire does not include the inverse hyperbolic functions or if you are programming in a language such as BASIC, most forms of which do not include these functions.

Integrals Involving Inverse Hyperbolic Functions

The principal applications of inverse hyperbolic functions are to the evaluation of algebraic integrals. The differentiation formulas in Eqs. (28) through (33) may, in the usual way, be written as the following integral formulas:

$$\int \frac{du}{\sqrt{u^2+1}} = \sinh^{-1} u + C, \tag{40}$$

$$\int \frac{du}{\sqrt{u^2-1}} = \cosh^{-1} u + C, \tag{41}$$

$$\int \frac{du}{1-u^2} = \tanh^{-1} u + C \quad \text{if } |u| < 1, \tag{42a}$$

$$\int \frac{du}{1-u^2} = \coth^{-1} u + C \quad \text{if } |u| > 1, \tag{42b}$$

$$\int \frac{du}{1-u^2} = \tfrac{1}{2}\ln\left|\frac{1+u}{1-u}\right| + C, \tag{42c}$$

$$\int \frac{du}{u\sqrt{1-u^2}} = -\text{sech}^{-1}|u| + C, \qquad (43)$$

$$\int \frac{du}{u\sqrt{1+u^2}} = -\text{csch}^{-1}|u| + C. \qquad (44)$$

The distinction between the two cases $|u| < 1$ and $|u| > 1$ in Eqs. (42a) and (42b) results from the fact that the inverse hyperbolic tangent is defined for $|x| < 1$, whereas the inverse hyperbolic cotangent is defined for $|x| > 1$.

EXAMPLE 7 The substitution $u = 2x$, $dx = \frac{1}{2}du$ yields

$$\int \frac{dx}{\sqrt{4x^2 - 1}} = \frac{1}{2}\int \frac{du}{\sqrt{u^2 + 1}} = \frac{1}{2}\sinh^{-1} 2x + C. \qquad \blacklozenge$$

EXAMPLE 8

$$\int_0^{1/2} \frac{dx}{1-x^2} = \left[\tanh^{-1} x\right]_0^{1/2}$$

$$= \frac{1}{2}\left[\ln\left|\frac{1+x}{1-x}\right|\right]_0^{1/2} = \frac{1}{2}\ln 3 \approx 0.549306. \qquad \blacklozenge$$

EXAMPLE 9

$$\int_2^5 \frac{dx}{1-x^2} = \left[\coth^{-1} x\right]_2^5 = \frac{1}{2}\left[\ln\left|\frac{1+x}{1-x}\right|\right]_2^5$$

$$= \frac{1}{2}\left[\ln\left(\frac{6}{4}\right) - \ln 3\right] = -\frac{1}{2}\ln 2 \approx -0.346574. \qquad \blacklozenge$$

7.6 TRUE/FALSE STUDY GUIDE

7.6 CONCEPTS: QUESTIONS AND DISCUSSION

1. Discuss the differences and similarities in the domains and ranges of the six inverse hyperbolic functions.
2. Beginning with the graphs of the hyperbolic functions in Fig. 7.6.3, sketch the graphs of the six inverse hyperbolic functions. Then identify the domain and range of each.
3. Discuss the analogy between trigonometric identities (such as $\cos^2 x + \sin^2 x = 1$) and hyperbolic identities (such as $\cosh^2 x - \sinh^2 x = 1$).

7.6 PROBLEMS

Find the derivatives of the functions in Problems 1 through 14.

1. $f(x) = \cosh(3x - 2)$
2. $f(x) = \sinh\sqrt{x}$
3. $f(x) = x^2 \tanh\left(\frac{1}{x}\right)$
4. $f(x) = \text{sech } e^{2x}$
5. $f(x) = \coth^3 4x$
6. $f(x) = \ln \sinh 3x$
7. $f(x) = e^{\text{csch} x}$
8. $f(x) = \cosh \ln x$
9. $f(x) = \sin(\sinh x)$
10. $f(x) = \tan^{-1}(\tanh x)$
11. $f(x) = \sinh x^4$
12. $f(x) = \sinh^4 x$
13. $f(x) = \dfrac{1}{x + \tanh x}$
14. $f(x) = \cosh^2 x - \sinh^2 x$

Evaluate the integrals in Problems 15 through 28.

15. $\int x \sinh x^2 \, dx$
16. $\int \cosh^2 3u \, du$
17. $\int \tanh^2 3x \, dx$
18. $\int \dfrac{\text{sech}\sqrt{x} \, \tanh\sqrt{x}}{\sqrt{x}} dx$
19. $\int \sinh^2 2x \cosh 2x \, dx$
20. $\int \tanh 3x \, dx$
21. $\int \dfrac{\sinh x}{\cosh^3 x} dx$
22. $\int \sinh^4 x \, dx$

23. $\displaystyle\int \coth x \operatorname{csch}^2 x\, dx$
24. $\displaystyle\int \operatorname{sech} x\, dx$
25. $\displaystyle\int \frac{\sinh x}{1 + \cosh x}\, dx$
26. $\displaystyle\int \frac{\sinh \ln x}{x}\, dx$
27. $\displaystyle\int \frac{1}{(e^x + e^{-x})^2}\, dx$
28. $\displaystyle\int \frac{e^x + e^{-x}}{e^x - e^{-x}}\, dx$

Find the derivatives of the functions in Problems 29 through 38.

29. $f(x) = \sinh^{-1} 2x$
30. $f(x) = \cosh^{-1}(x^2 + 1)$
31. $f(x) = \tanh^{-1} \sqrt{x}$
32. $f(x) = \coth^{-1} \sqrt{x^2 + 1}$
33. $f(x) = \operatorname{sech}^{-1}\left(\dfrac{1}{x}\right)$
34. $f(x) = \operatorname{csch}^{-1} e^x$
35. $f(x) = (\sinh^{-1} x)^{3/2}$
36. $f(x) = \sinh^{-1}(\ln x)$
37. $f(x) = \ln(\tanh^{-1} x)$
38. $f(x) = \dfrac{1}{\tanh^{-1} 3x}$

Use inverse hyperbolic functions to evaluate the integrals in Problems 39 through 48.

39. $\displaystyle\int \frac{dx}{\sqrt{x^2 + 9}}$
40. $\displaystyle\int \frac{dy}{\sqrt{4y^2 - 9}}$
41. $\displaystyle\int_{1/2}^{1} \frac{dx}{4 - x^2}$
42. $\displaystyle\int_{5}^{10} \frac{dx}{4 - x^2}$
43. $\displaystyle\int \frac{dx}{x\sqrt{4 - 9x^2}}$
44. $\displaystyle\int \frac{dx}{x\sqrt{x^2 + 25}}$
45. $\displaystyle\int \frac{e^x}{\sqrt{e^{2x} + 1}}\, dx$
46. $\displaystyle\int \frac{x}{\sqrt{x^4 - 1}}\, dx$
47. $\displaystyle\int \frac{1}{\sqrt{1 - e^{2x}}}\, dx$
48. $\displaystyle\int \frac{\cos x}{\sqrt{1 + \sin^2 x}}\, dx$

49. Apply the definitions in Eq. (1) to prove the identity in Eq. (7).

50. Derive the identities in Eqs. (5) and (6) from the identity in Eq. (4).

51. Deduce the identities in Eqs. (10) and (11) from the identity in Eq. (8).

52. Suppose that A and B are constants. Show that the function $x(t) = A\cosh kt + B\sinh kt$ is a solution of the differential equation
$$\frac{d^2x}{dt^2} = k^2 x(t).$$

53. Find the length of the curve $y = \cosh x$ over the interval $[0, a]$.

54. Find the volume of the solid obtained by revolving around the x-axis the area under $y = \sinh x$ from $x = 0$ to $x = \pi$.

55. Show that the area $A(\theta)$ of the shaded sector in Fig. 7.6.2 is $\theta/2$. This corresponds to the fact that the area of the sector of the unit circle between the positive x-axis and the radius to the point $(\cos\theta, \sin\theta)$ is $\theta/2$. [*Suggestion:* Note first that
$$A(\theta) = \tfrac{1}{2}\cosh\theta \sinh\theta - \int_1^{\cosh\theta} \sqrt{x^2 - 1}\, dx.$$
Then use the fundamental theorem of calculus to show that $A'(\theta) = \tfrac{1}{2}$ for all θ.]

56. Evaluate the following limits:
    (a) $\displaystyle\lim_{x \to 0} \frac{\sinh x}{x}$; (b) $\displaystyle\lim_{x \to \infty} \tanh x$; (c) $\displaystyle\lim_{x \to \infty} \frac{\cosh x}{e^x}$.

57. Use the method of Example 4 to find the numerical value of $\sinh^{-1} 1$.

58. Apply Eqs. (34) and (39) to verify the identity
$$\operatorname{csch}^{-1} x = \sinh^{-1}\left(\frac{1}{x}\right) \quad \text{if } x \neq 0.$$

59. Establish the formula for $D_x \sinh^{-1} x$ in Eq. (28).

60. Establish the formula for $D_x \operatorname{sech}^{-1} x$ in Eq. (32).

61. Prove Eq. (36) by differentiating both sides.

62. Establish Eq. (34) by solving the equation
$$x = \sinh y = \frac{e^y - e^{-y}}{2}$$
for y in terms of x.

63. Establish Eq. (37) by solving the equation
$$x = \coth y = \frac{e^y + e^{-y}}{e^y - e^{-y}}$$
for y in terms of x.

64. (a) Differentiate both sides of Eq. (37) to show that they differ by a constant C. (b) Then prove that $C = 0$ by using the definition of $\coth x$ to show that $\coth^{-1} 2 = \tfrac{1}{2}\ln 3$.

65. (a) Differentiate both sides of Eq. (39) to show that they differ by a constant C. (b) Then prove that $C = 0$ by using the definition of $\operatorname{csch} x$ to show that $\operatorname{csch}^{-1} 1 = \ln(1 + \sqrt{2})$.

66. Estimate (graphically or numerically) the points of intersection of the curves $y = x + 2$ and $y = \cosh x$. Then approximate the area of the region bounded by these two curves.

In Problems 67 and 68, show first that $f(x) \to 0$ as $x \to +\infty$. Then estimate (graphically or numerically) the absolute maximum value of $f(x)$ for $x > 0$. Differentiate $f(x)$ to verify that you have an approximate critical point.

67. $f(x) = e^{-2x} \tanh x$
68. $f(x) = e^{-x} \sinh^{-1} x$

Problems 69 and 70 deal with the hanging cable illustrated in Fig. 7.6.4. If the cable is flexible and has uniform density, then elementary principles of physics can be used to show that its

FIGURE 7.6.4 A flexible uniform cable suspended between two points at equal heights.

shape function $y = y(x)$ satisfies the differential equation

$$\frac{d^2y}{dx^2} = k\sqrt{1 + \left(\frac{dy}{dx}\right)^2} \quad (45)$$

where k is a constant determined by the density and tension of the cable.

69. Verify that the function

$$y(x) = y_0 + \frac{1}{k}(-1 + \cosh kx) \quad (46)$$

satisfies the differential equation in (45) and also satisfies the initial conditions $y(0) = y_0$, $y'(0) = 0$. A curve with this shape is called a *catenary*, from the Latin word *catena* (chain).

70. A high-voltage line is to be strung between two 50-ft towers 200 ft apart. (a) If the line sags 20 ft at its middle (where $x = 0$)—so $y_0 = 30$ (ft) in Eq. (46)—estimate graphically or numerically the value of the parameter k. (b) Then approximate the total length of the high-voltage line.

CHAPTER 7 REVIEW: FORMULAS, CONCEPTS, DEFINITIONS

Differentiation and Integration Formulas

$D_x(e^u) = e^u \dfrac{du}{dx}$ $\quad\displaystyle\int e^u \, du = e^u + C$

$D_x(\ln u) = \dfrac{1}{u}\dfrac{du}{dx}$ $\quad\displaystyle\int \dfrac{1}{u} \, du = \ln|u| + C$

$D_x(\tan^{-1} u) = \dfrac{1}{1+u^2}\dfrac{du}{du}$ $\quad\displaystyle\int \dfrac{1}{1+u^2} \, du = \tan^{-1} u + C$

$D_x(\sin^{-1} u) = \dfrac{1}{\sqrt{1-u^2}}\dfrac{du}{dx}$ $\quad\displaystyle\int \dfrac{1}{\sqrt{1-u^2}} \, du = \sin^{-1} u + C$

$D_x(\sec^{-1} u) = \dfrac{1}{|u|\sqrt{u^2-1}}\dfrac{du}{dx}$ $\quad\displaystyle\int \dfrac{1}{u\sqrt{u^2-1}} \, du = \sec^{-1}|u| + C$

$D_x(\sinh u) = (\cosh u)\dfrac{du}{dx}$ $\quad D_x(\cosh u) = (\sinh u)\dfrac{du}{dx}$

$D_x(\tanh u) = (\operatorname{sech}^2 u)\dfrac{du}{dx}$ $\quad D_x(\coth u) = (-\operatorname{csch}^2 u)\dfrac{du}{dx}$

$D_x(\operatorname{sech} u) = (-\operatorname{sech} u \tanh u)\dfrac{du}{dx}$ $\quad D_x(\operatorname{csch} u) = (-\operatorname{csch} u \coth u)\dfrac{du}{dx}$

$D_x(\sinh^{-1} u) = \dfrac{1}{\sqrt{1+u^2}}\dfrac{du}{dx}$ $\quad D_x(\cosh^{-1} u) = \dfrac{1}{\sqrt{u^2-1}}\dfrac{du}{dx}$

$D_x(\tanh^{-1} u) = \dfrac{1}{1-u^2}\dfrac{du}{dx}$ $\quad D_x(\coth^{-1} u) = \dfrac{1}{1-u^2}\dfrac{du}{dx}$

$D_x(\operatorname{sech}^{-1} u) = -\dfrac{1}{u\sqrt{1-u^2}}\dfrac{du}{dx}$ $\quad D_x(\operatorname{csch}^{-1} u) = -\dfrac{1}{|u|\sqrt{1+u^2}}\dfrac{du}{dx}$

Use the following list as a guide to concepts for review.

1. Elementary definitions of the natural exponential and natural logarithm functions
2. Derivatives of the natural exponential and natural logarithm functions
3. The definition of the number e
4. Inverse functions and their derivatives
5. Logarithmic differentiation
6. l'Hôpital's rule and the indeterminate forms $0/0$, ∞/∞, $0\cdot\infty$, $\infty - \infty$, 0^0, ∞^0, and 1^∞
7. The orders of magnitude of exponential and logarithmic functions
8. The number e as a limit
9. Laws of exponents and laws of logarithms
10. The definition of the natural logarithm function $\ln x$ as an integral
11. The definition of the natural exponential function $\exp x$
12. The inverse function relationship between $\ln x$ and $\exp x$
13. Differentiation of $\ln u$ and $\exp u$ where u is a differentiable function of x
14. The definition of the general exponential and logarithm functions with base $a > 0$, $a \neq 1$
15. Differentiation of a^u and $\log_a u$
16. The definitions of the six inverse trigonometric functions
17. The derivatives of the inverse trigonometric functions
18. The integrals formulas corresponding to the derivatives of the inverse tangent, inverse sine, and inverse secant functions
19. The definitions and derivatives of the six hyperbolic functions
20. The definitions and derivatives of the six inverse hyperbolic functions

CHAPTER 7 MISCELLANEOUS PROBLEMS

Find the derivatives of the functions defined in Problems 1 through 22.

1. $f(x) = \cos(1 - e^{-x})$
2. $f(x) = \sin^2(e^{-x})$
3. $f(x) = \ln(x + e^{-x})$
4. $f(x) = e^x \cos 2x$
5. $f(x) = e^{-2x} \sin 3x$
6. $g(t) = \ln\left(te^{t^2}\right)$
7. $g(t) = 3(e^t - \ln t)^5$
8. $g(t) = \sin(e^t)\cos(e^{-t})$
9. $f(x) = \dfrac{2 + 3x}{e^{4x}}$
10. $g(t) = \dfrac{1 + e^t}{1 - e^t}$

In Problems 11 through 16, find dy/dx by implicit differentiation.

11. $xe^y = y$
12. $\sin(xy) = x$
13. $e^x + e^y = e^{xy}$
14. $x = ye^y$
15. $e^{x-y} = xy$
16. $x \ln y = x + y$

In Problems 17 through 22, find dy/dx by logarithmic differentiation.

17. $y = \sqrt{(x^2 - 4)\sqrt{2x + 1}}$

18. $y = \dfrac{(3-x^2)^{1/2}}{(x^4+1)^{1/4}}$

19. $y = \left[\dfrac{(x+1)(x+2)}{(x^2+1)(x^2+2)}\right]^{1/3}$

20. $y = \sqrt{x+1}\sqrt[3]{x+2}\sqrt[4]{x+3}$

21. $y = x^{(e^x)}$

22. $y = (\ln x)^{\ln x}, \quad x > 1$

Find the limits in Problems 23 through 38.

23. $\lim\limits_{x \to 2} \dfrac{x-2}{x^2-4}$

24. $\lim\limits_{x \to 0} \dfrac{\sin 2x}{x}$

25. $\lim\limits_{x \to \pi} \dfrac{1+\cos x}{(x-\pi)^2}$

26. $\lim\limits_{x \to 0} \dfrac{x - \sin x}{x^3}$

27. $\lim\limits_{t \to 0} \dfrac{\tan t - \sin t}{t^3}$

28. $\lim\limits_{x \to \infty} \dfrac{\ln(\ln x)}{\ln x}$

29. $\lim\limits_{x \to 0} (\cot x)\ln(1+x)$

30. $\lim\limits_{x \to 0^+} \left(e^{1/x}-1\right)\tan x$

31. $\lim\limits_{x \to 0} \left(\dfrac{1}{x^2} - \dfrac{1}{1-\cos x}\right)$

32. $\lim\limits_{x \to \infty} \left(\dfrac{x^2}{x+2} - \dfrac{x^3}{x^2+3}\right)$

33. $\lim\limits_{x \to \infty} \left(\sqrt{x^2-x-1} - \sqrt{x}\right)$

34. $\lim\limits_{x \to \infty} x^{1/x}$

35. $\lim\limits_{x \to \infty} (e^{2x} - 2x)^{1/x}$

36. $\lim\limits_{x \to \infty} [1 - \exp(-x^2)]^{1/x^2}$

37. $\lim\limits_{x \to \infty} x\left[\left(1+\dfrac{1}{x}\right)^x - e\right]$ [*Suggestion:* Let $u = 1/x$, and take the limit as $u \to 0^+$.]

38. According to Problem 53 of Section 8.6, the surface area of the ellipsoid obtained by revolving around the x-axis the ellipse with equation

$$\left(\dfrac{x}{a}\right)^2 + \left(\dfrac{y}{b}\right)^2 = 1 \quad (0 < a < b)$$

is

$$A = 2\pi ab\left[\dfrac{b}{a} + \dfrac{a}{c}\ln\left(\dfrac{b+c}{a}\right)\right],$$

where $c = \sqrt{b^2 - a^2}$. Use l'Hôpital's rule to show that

$$\lim\limits_{b \to a} A = 4\pi a^2,$$

the surface area of a sphere of radius a.

Evaluate the indefinite integrals in Problems 39 through 50.

39. $\displaystyle\int \dfrac{dx}{1-2x}$

40. $\displaystyle\int \dfrac{\sqrt{x}}{1+x^{3/2}}\,dx$

41. $\displaystyle\int \dfrac{3-x}{1+6x-x^2}\,dx$

42. $\displaystyle\int \dfrac{e^x - e^{-x}}{e^x + e^{-x}}\,dx$

43. $\displaystyle\int \dfrac{\sin x}{2+\cos x}\,dx$

44. $\displaystyle\int \dfrac{e^{-1/x^2}}{x^3}\,dx$

45. $\displaystyle\int \dfrac{10^{\sqrt{x}}}{\sqrt{x}}\,dx$

46. $\displaystyle\int \dfrac{1}{x(\ln x)^2}\,dx$

47. $\displaystyle\int e^x\sqrt{1+e^x}\,dx$

48. $\displaystyle\int \dfrac{1}{x}\sqrt{1+\ln x}\,dx$

49. $\displaystyle\int 2^x 3^x\,dx$

50. $\displaystyle\int \dfrac{dx}{x^{1/3}(1+x^{2/3})}$

51. A grain warehouse holds B bushels of grain, which is deteriorating in such a way that only $B \cdot 2^{-t/12}$ bushels will be salable after t months. Meanwhile, the grain's market price is increasing linearly: After t months it will be $2 + \frac{1}{12}t$ dollars per bushel. After how many months should the grain to sold to maximize the revenue obtained?

52. You have borrowed \$1000 at 10% annual interest, compounded continuously, to plant timber on a tract of land. Your agreement is to repay the loan, plus interest, when the timber is cut and sold. If the cut timber can be sold after t years for $800\exp(\frac{1}{2}\sqrt{t})$ dollars, when should you cut and sell to maximize the profit?

53. Blood samples from 1000 students are to be tested for a certain disease known to occur in 1% of the population. Each test costs \$5, so it would cost \$5000 to test the samples individually. Suppose, however, that "lots" made up of x samples each are formed by pooling halves of individual samples, and that these lots are tested first (for \$5 each). Only in case a lot tests positive—the probability of this is $1 - (0.99)^x$—will the x samples used to make up this lot be tested individually. (a) Show that the total expected number of tests is

$$f(x) = \dfrac{1000}{x}[(1)(0.99)^x + (x+1)(1-(0.99)^x)]$$

$$= 1000 + \dfrac{1000}{x} - 1000 \cdot (0.99)^x$$

if $x \geq 2$. (b) Show that the value of x that minimizes $f(x)$ is a root of the equation

$$x = \dfrac{(0.99)^{-x/2}}{\sqrt{\ln(100/99)}}.$$

Because the denominator is approximately 0.1, it may be convenient to solve instead the simpler equation $x = 10 \cdot (0.99)^{-x/2}$. (c) From the results in parts (a) and (b), compute the minimum (expected) cost of using this batch method to test the original 1000 samples.

54. Find the length of the curve $y = \frac{1}{2}x^2 - \frac{1}{4}\ln x$ from $x = 1$ to $x = e$.

Differentiate the functions in Problems 55 through 74.

55. $f(x) = \sin^{-1} 3x$

56. $f(x) = \tan^{-1} 7x$

57. $g(t) = \sec^{-1} t^2$

58. $g(t) = \tan^{-1} e^t$

59. $f(x) = \sin^{-1}(\cos x)$

60. $f(x) = \sinh^{-1} 2x$

61. $g(t) = \cosh^{-1} 10t$

62. $h(u) = \tanh^{-1}\left(\dfrac{1}{u}\right)$

63. $f(x) = \sin^{-1}\left(\dfrac{1}{x^2}\right)$

64. $f(x) = \tan^{-1}\left(\dfrac{1}{x}\right)$

65. $f(x) = \arcsin \sqrt{x}$

66. $f(x) = x \sec^{-1} x^2$

67. $f(x) = \tan^{-1}(1 + x^2)$

68. $f(x) = \sin^{-1} \sqrt{1 - x^2}$

69. $f(x) = e^x \sinh e^x$

70. $f(x) = \ln \cosh x$

71. $f(x) = \tanh^2 3x + \text{sech}^2 3x$

72. $f(x) = \sinh^{-1} \sqrt{x^2 - 1}$

73. $f(x) = \cosh^{-1} \sqrt{x^2 - 1}$

74. $f(x) = \tanh^{-1}(1 - x^2)$

Evaluate the integrals in Problems 75 through 94.

75. $\displaystyle\int \dfrac{dx}{\sqrt{1 - 4x^2}}$

76. $\displaystyle\int \dfrac{dx}{1 + 4x^2}$

77. $\displaystyle\int \dfrac{dx}{\sqrt{4 - x^2}}$

78. $\displaystyle\int \dfrac{dx}{4 + x^2}$

79. $\displaystyle\int \dfrac{e^x}{\sqrt{1 - e^{2x}}}\, dx$

80. $\displaystyle\int \dfrac{x}{1 + x^4}\, dx$

81. $\displaystyle\int \dfrac{1}{\sqrt{9 - 4x^2}}\, dx$

82. $\displaystyle\int \dfrac{1}{9 + 4x^2}\, dx$

83. $\displaystyle\int \dfrac{x^2}{1 + x^6}\, dx$

84. $\displaystyle\int \dfrac{\cos x}{1 + \sin^2 x}\, dx$

85. $\displaystyle\int \dfrac{1}{x\sqrt{4x^2 - 1}}\, dx$

86. $\displaystyle\int \dfrac{1}{x\sqrt{x^4 - 1}}\, dx$

87. $\displaystyle\int \dfrac{1}{\sqrt{e^{2x} - 1}}\, dx$

88. $\displaystyle\int x^2 \cosh x^3\, dx$

89. $\displaystyle\int \dfrac{\sinh \sqrt{x}}{\sqrt{x}}\, dx$

90. $\displaystyle\int \text{sech}^2(3x - 2)\, dx$

91. $\displaystyle\int \dfrac{\arctan x}{1 + x^2}\, dx$

92. $\displaystyle\int \dfrac{1}{\sqrt{4x^2 - 1}}\, dx$

93. $\displaystyle\int \dfrac{1}{\sqrt{4x^2 + 9}}\, dx$

94. $\displaystyle\int \dfrac{x}{\sqrt{x^4 + 1}}\, dx$

95. Find the volume generated by revolving around the y-axis the region under $y = 1/\sqrt{1 - x^4}$ from $x = 0$ to $x = 1/\sqrt{2}$.

96. Find the volume generated by revolving around the y-axis the region under $y = 1/\sqrt{x^4 + 1}$ from $x = 0$ to $x = 1$.

97. Use Eqs. (35) through (38) of Section 7.6 to show that

(a) $\coth^{-1} x = \tanh^{-1}\left(\dfrac{1}{x}\right)$;

(b) $\text{sech}^{-1} x = \cosh^{-1}\left(\dfrac{1}{x}\right)$.

98. Show that $x''(t) = k^2 x(t)$ if

$$x(t) = A\cosh kt + B\sinh kt,$$

where A and B are constants. Determine A and B if (a) $x(0) = 1$, $x'(0) = 0$; (b) $x(0) = 0$, $x'(0) = 1$.

99. Use Newton's method to find the least positive solution of the equation $\cos x \cosh x = 1$. Begin by sketching the graphs of $y = \cos x$ and $y = \text{sech}\, x$.

100. (a) Verify by differentiation that

$$\int \sec x\, dx = \sinh^{-1}(\tan x) + C.$$

(b) Show similarly that

$$\int \text{sech}\, x\, dx = \tan^{-1}(\sinh x) + C.$$

101. Figure 7.MP.1 shows the graphs of $f(x) = x^{1/2}$, $g(x) = \ln x$, and $h(x) = x^{1/3}$ plotted on the interval $[0.2, 10]$. You can see that the graph of f remains above the graph of $\ln x$, whereas the graph of h dips below the graph of $\ln x$. But because $\ln x$ increases *less* rapidly than any positive power of x, the graph of h must eventually cross the graph of $\ln x$ and rise above it. Finally, it is easy to believe that, for a suitable choice of p between 2 and 3, the graph of $j(x) = x^{1/p}$ never dips below the graph of $\ln x$ but does drop down just far enough to be tangent to the graph of $\ln x$ at a certain point. (a) Show that $f(x) > \ln x$ for all $x > 0$ by finding the global minimum value of $f(x) - \ln x$ on the interval $(0, +\infty)$. (b) Use Newton's method to find the value at which $h(x)$ crosses the graph of $\ln x$ and rises above it—the value of x *not* shown in Fig. 7.MP.1. (c) Find the value of p for which the graph of $j(x)$ is tangent to the graph of $\ln x$ at the point $(q, \ln q)$.

FIGURE 7.MP.1 The three functions of Problem 101.

TECHNIQUES OF INTEGRATION

8

Leonhard Euler (1707–1783)

The most prolific mathematician in all history was Leonhard Euler, who was born in 1707 in Basel, Switzerland, the home of the Bernoulli family of mathematicians. His father preferred a theological career for his son, but young Euler learned mathematics from John Bernoulli and thereby found his true vocation. During his lifetime Euler published more than 500 books and papers. His work continued unabated even after he lost his sight in 1766. Upon his death in 1783, he left behind more than 300 additional manuscripts whose publication continued in a steady flow for another half century. His collected works fill approximately 75 substantial volumes.

No other mathematician of the past more directly affects the modern student of mathematics, because it was largely Euler who shaped the notation and terminology still used today in teaching high school algebra and trigonometry as well as calculus. His *Introductio in Analysin Infinitorium* (Introduction to Infinitesimal Analysis) is the earliest mathematics textbook whose exposition would (in translation from the original Latin) be accessible to a modern student. Here are some now-familiar notations whose use was popularized and standardized by Euler:

e	for the base of natural logarithms;
a, b, c	for the sides of the triangle ABC;
i	for the square root of -1;
$\sum$	for the summation symbol;
$f(x)$	for function notation;
π	for the area of the unit circle;

and the trigonometric abbreviations sin, cos, tang, cot, sec, and cosec, which are close to their current forms. It was Euler's *Introductio* that once and for all based calculus squarely on the function concept. His 1755 and 1768 calculus treatises provide the original source for much of the content and methods of modern calculus courses and texts.

Euler originally discovered so many of the standard formulas and identities of mathematics that it is customary to attribute a formula to the first mathematician *after* Euler to *re*discover it. But the identity $e^{ix} = \cos x + i \sin x$ relating the exponential and trigonometric functions is still known as Euler's formula. Substituting $x = \pi$ yields the relation $e^{i\pi} + 1 = 0$, which links five of the most important constants in mathematics.

The portrait—part of a page from Chapter VII of the *Introductio*—shows the first appearance in public print of the number $e \approx 2.71828$. Immediately following its definition as the sum of the infinite series

$$\sum_{n=0}^{\infty} \frac{1}{n!} = 1 + \frac{1}{1!} + \frac{1}{2!} + \cdots + \frac{1}{n!} + \cdots,$$

Euler gives the numerical value of e accurate to 23 decimal places.

8.1 INTRODUCTION

We saw in Chapter 6 that many geometric and physical quantities can be expressed as definite integrals. The fundamental theorem of calculus reduces the problem of calculating the definite integral

$$\int_a^b f(x)\,dx$$

to that of finding an antiderivative $G(x)$ of $f(x)$. Once this is accomplished, then

$$\int_a^b f(x)\,dx = \Big[G(x)\Big]_a^b = G(b) - G(a).$$

But as yet we have relied largely on trial-and-error methods for finding the required antiderivative $G(x)$. In some cases a knowledge of elementary derivative formulas, perhaps in combination with a simple substitution, allows us to integrate a given function. This approach can, however, be inefficient and time-consuming, especially in view of the following surprising fact: Some simple-looking integrals, such as

$$\int e^{-x^2}\,dx, \quad \int \frac{\sin x}{x}\,dx, \quad \text{and} \quad \int \sqrt{1+x^4}\,dx,$$

cannot be evaluated in terms of finite combinations of the familiar algebraic and elementary transcendental functions. For example, the antiderivative

$$H(x) = \int_0^x e^{-t^2}\,dt$$

of $\exp(-x^2)$ has no finite expression in terms of elementary functions. Any attempt to find such an expression will, therefore, inevitably be unsuccessful.

The presence of such integrals indicates that we cannot hope to reduce integration to a routine process such as differentiation. In fact, finding antiderivatives is an art, the mastery of which depends on experience and practice. Nevertheless, there are a number of techniques whose systematic use can substantially reduce our dependence on chance and intuition alone. This chapter deals with some of these systematic techniques of integration.

8.2 INTEGRAL TABLES AND SIMPLE SUBSTITUTIONS

Integration would be a simple matter if we had a list of integral formulas, an *integral table*, in which we could locate any integral that we needed to evaluate. But the diversity of integrals that we encounter is too great for such an all-inclusive integral table to be practical. It is more sensible to print or memorize a short table of integrals of the sort seen frequently and to learn techniques by which the range of applicability of this short table can be extended. We begin with the list of integrals in Fig. 8.2.1, which are familiar from earlier chapters. Each formula is equivalent to one of the basic derivative formulas.

A table of 113 integral formulas appears on the inside back cover of this book. Even more extensive integral tables are readily available. For example, the volume of *Standard Mathematical Tables and Formulas,* edited by William H. Beyer and published by the CRC Press, Inc. (Boca Raton, Florida), contains over 700 integral formulas. But even such a lengthy table can be expected to include only a small fraction of the integrals we may need to evaluate. Thus it is necessary to learn techniques for deriving new formulas and for transforming a given integral either into one that's already familiar or into one that appears in an accessible table.

The principal such technique is the *method of substitution*, which we first considered in Section 5.7. Recall that if

$$\int f(u)\, du = F(u) + C,$$

then

$$\int f(g(x)) \cdot g'(x)\, dx = F(g(x)) + C.$$

Thus the substitution

$$u = g(x), \qquad du = g'(x)\, dx$$

transforms the integral

$$\int f(g(x)) \cdot g'(x)\, dx \quad \text{into the simpler integral} \quad \int f(u)\, du.$$

The key to making this simplification lies in spotting the composition $f(g(x))$ in the given integrand. For this integrand to be converted into a function of u alone, the remaining factor must be a *constant* multiple of the derivative $g'(x)$ of the "inside function" $g(x)$. In this case we replace $f(g(x))$ with the simpler $f(u)$ and $g'(x)\, dx$ with the simpler du. Chapter 6 contains numerous illustrations of this method of substitution, and the problems at the end of this section provide an opportunity to review it.

EXAMPLE 1 Find $\int \dfrac{1}{x}(1 + \ln x)^5\, dx$.

Solution We need to spot *both* the inner function $g(x)$ and its derivative $g'(x)$. If we choose $g(x) = 1 + \ln x$, then $g'(x) = 1/x$. Hence the given integral is of the form discussed above with $f(u) = u^5$, $u = 1 + \ln x$, and $du = dx/x$. Therefore,

$$\int \frac{1}{x}(1 + \ln x)^5\, dx = \int u^5\, du = \tfrac{1}{6} u^6 + C = \tfrac{1}{6}(1 + \ln x)^6 + C. \qquad \blacklozenge$$

EXAMPLE 2 Find $\int \dfrac{x}{1 + x^4}\, dx$.

Solution Here it is not so clear what the inside function is. But, looking at the integral formula in Eq. (11) (Fig. 8.2.1), we try the substitution $u = x^2$, $du = 2x\, dx$. We take advantage of the factor $x\, dx = \tfrac{1}{2}\, du$ that is available in the integrand and compute as follows:

$$\int \frac{x}{1 + x^4}\, dx = \tfrac{1}{2} \int \frac{du}{1 + u^2} = \tfrac{1}{2} \tan^{-1} u + C = \tfrac{1}{2} \tan^{-1} x^2 + C.$$

Note that the substitution $u = x^2$ would have been of no use had the integrand been either $1/(1 + x^4)$ or $x^2/(1 + x^4)$. $\qquad \blacklozenge$

Example 2 illustrates how to make a substitution that converts a given integral into a familiar one. This is a kind of *pattern-matching*. Often an integral that does not appear in any integral table can be transformed into one that does by using the techniques of this chapter. In Example 3 we employ an appropriate substitution to match the given integral with the standard integral formula

$$\int \frac{u^2}{\sqrt{a^2 - u^2}}\, du = \frac{a^2}{2} \sin^{-1}\left(\frac{u}{a}\right) - \frac{u}{2}\sqrt{a^2 - u^2} + C, \qquad (13)$$

which is Formula (56) (inside the back cover).

$$\int u^n\, du = \frac{u^{n+1}}{n+1} + C \quad [n \neq -1] \qquad (1)$$

$$\int \frac{du}{u} = \ln |u| + C \qquad (2)$$

$$\int e^u\, du = e^u + C \qquad (3)$$

$$\int \cos u\, du = \sin u + C \qquad (4)$$

$$\int \sin u\, du = -\cos u + C \qquad (5)$$

$$\int \sec^2 u\, du = \tan u + C \qquad (6)$$

$$\int \csc^2 u\, du = -\cot u + C \qquad (7)$$

$$\int \sec u \tan u\, du = \sec u + C \qquad (8)$$

$$\int \csc u \cot u\, du = -\csc u + C \qquad (9)$$

$$\int \frac{du}{\sqrt{1 - u^2}} = \sin^{-1} u + C \qquad (10)$$

$$\int \frac{du}{1 + u^2} = \tan^{-1} u + C \qquad (11)$$

$$\int \frac{du}{u\sqrt{u^2 - 1}} = \sec^{-1} |u| + C \qquad (12)$$

FIGURE 8.2.1 A short table of integrals.

EXAMPLE 3 Find $\int \frac{x^2}{\sqrt{25 - 16x^2}} \, dx$.

Solution So that $25 - 16x^2$ will be equal to $a^2 - u^2$ in Eq. (13), we take $a = 5$ and $u = 4x$. Then $du = 4\,dx$, and so $dx = \frac{1}{4}\,du$. This gives

$$\int \frac{x^2}{\sqrt{25 - 16x^2}} \, dx = \int \frac{\left(\frac{1}{4}u\right)^2}{\sqrt{25 - u^2}} \cdot \frac{1}{4} \, du = \frac{1}{64} \int \frac{u^2}{\sqrt{25 - u^2}} \, du$$

$$= \frac{1}{64} \left[\frac{25}{2} \sin^{-1}\left(\frac{u}{5}\right) - \frac{u}{2}\sqrt{25 - u^2} \right] + C$$

$$= \frac{25}{128} \sin^{-1}\left(\frac{4x}{5}\right) - \frac{x}{32}\sqrt{25 - 16x^2} + C. \quad \blacklozenge$$

In Section 8.6 we will see how to derive integral formulas such as that in Eq. (13).

Computer Algebra Systems

Systems such as *Derive*, *Maple*, and *Mathematica* have integral formulas stored internally and can perform pattern matching substitutions like the one used in Example 3. For instance, the *Mathematica* command

```
Integrate[ x^2 / Sqrt[ 25 - 16 x^2 ], x ]
```

and the *Maple* command

```
int( x^2 / sqrt(25 - 16*x^2), x );
```

as well as the corresponding *Derive* command, all produce precisely the same result as that found in Example 3 (except without adding the arbitrary constant of integration, which computer algebra systems generally omit).

Sometimes different methods (whether manual, table, or computer methods) produce integrals that appear to differ. For instance, *Derive* and *Maple* yield the same antiderivative $\frac{1}{2}\tan^{-1} x^2$ of $x/(1 + x^4)$ found in Example 2, whereas *Mathematica* returns the function $-\frac{1}{2}\tan^{-1} x^{-2}$ as the result. Naturally we wonder whether $\frac{1}{2}\tan^{-1} x^2 \equiv -\frac{1}{2}\tan^{-1} x^{-2}$. Figure 8.2.2 shows that the answer is No! In Problem 55 we ask you to reconcile these apparently different antiderivatives of the same function.

If computer algebra systems can match patterns with tables of integrals stored in computer memory, you may wonder why manual integration techniques should still be learned. One answer is that a hand computation may yield an integral in a simpler or more convenient form than a computer result. For instance, a computer algebra system may yield a result of the form

$$\int \frac{1}{x}(1 + \ln x)^5 \, dx = \ln x + \tfrac{5}{2}(\ln x)^2 + \tfrac{10}{3}(\ln x)^3 + \tfrac{5}{2}(\ln x)^4 + (\ln x)^5 + \tfrac{1}{6}(\ln x)^6$$

that looks considerably less appealing than the hand result $\frac{1}{6}(1 + \ln x)^6$ of Example 1. Is the relationship between the two obvious? See Problem 54.

FIGURE 8.2.2 The graphs $y = \frac{1}{2}\tan^{-1} x^2$ and $y = -\frac{1}{2}\tan^{-1} x^{-2}$ do not agree. What *is* the relationship between them?

8.2 TRUE/FALSE STUDY GUIDE

8.2 CONCEPTS: QUESTIONS AND DISCUSSION

As illustrated at the end of this section (and in Problems 54 through 57), two different methods may yield antiderivatives $G(x)$ and $H(x)$ quite different in appearance, even though they are supposed to be antiderivatives of the same function $f(x)$. Discuss different means for reconciling these antiderivatives, such as:

1. Calculating numerical values of $G(x)$ and $H(x)$ for selected values of x. What can you conclude from such results?

2. Using a calculator or computer to graph $G(x)$ and $H(x)$ simultaneously. What would it mean if the two graphs do not coincide, but intersect at one or more isolated points?
3. Graphing the derivatives $G'(x)$ and $H'(x)$ to see if the graphs coincide. If so, does it follow that $G(x)$ and $H(x)$ are both antiderivatives of $f(x)$?
4. Using a calculator or computer to calculate the numerical values of

$$\int_a^b f(x)\,dx, \quad G(b) - G(a), \quad \text{and} \quad H(b) - H(a)$$

for selected values of a and b. What can you conclude from such results?
5. Simply differentiating $G(x)$ and $H(x)$. Will a glance at the results always settle the matter immediately?

8.2 PROBLEMS

Evaluate the integrals in Problems 1 through 30.

1. $\int (2 - 3x)^4\,dx$
2. $\int \dfrac{1}{(1 + 2x)^2}\,dx$
3. $\int x^2 \sqrt{2x^3 - 4}\,dx$
4. $\int \dfrac{5t}{5 + 2t^2}\,dt$
5. $\int \dfrac{2x}{\sqrt[3]{2x^2 + 3}}\,dx$
6. $\int x \sec^2 x^2\,dx$
7. $\int \dfrac{\cot \sqrt{y} \csc \sqrt{y}}{\sqrt{y}}\,dy$
8. $\int \sin \pi(2x + 1)\,dx$
9. $\int (1 + \sin \theta)^5 \cos \theta\,d\theta$
10. $\int \dfrac{\sin 2x}{4 + \cos 2x}\,dx$
11. $\int e^{-\cot x} \csc^2 x\,dx$
12. $\int \dfrac{e^{\sqrt{x+4}}}{\sqrt{x+4}}\,dx$
13. $\int \dfrac{(\ln t)^{10}}{t}\,dt$
14. $\int \dfrac{t}{\sqrt{1 - 9t^2}}\,dt$
15. $\int \dfrac{1}{\sqrt{1 - 9t^2}}\,dt$
16. $\int \dfrac{e^{2x}}{1 + e^{2x}}\,dx$
17. $\int \dfrac{e^{2x}}{1 + e^{4x}}\,dx$
18. $\int \dfrac{e^{\arctan x}}{1 + x^2}\,dx$
19. $\int \dfrac{3x}{\sqrt{1 - x^4}}\,dx$
20. $\int \sin^3 2x \cos 2x\,dx$
21. $\int \tan^4 3x \sec^2 3x\,dx$
22. $\int \dfrac{1}{1 + 4t^2}\,dt$
23. $\int \dfrac{\cos \theta}{1 + \sin^2 \theta}\,d\theta$
24. $\int \dfrac{\sec^2 \theta}{1 + \tan \theta}\,d\theta$
25. $\int \dfrac{(1 + \sqrt{x})^4}{\sqrt{x}}\,dx$
26. $\int t^{-1/3} \sqrt{t^{2/3} - 1}\,dt$
27. $\int \dfrac{1}{(1 + t^2) \arctan t}\,dt$
28. $\int \dfrac{\sec 2x \tan 2x}{(1 + \sec 2x)^{3/2}}\,dx$
29. $\int \dfrac{1}{\sqrt{e^{2x} - 1}}\,dx$
30. $\int \dfrac{x}{\sqrt{\exp(2x^2) - 1}}\,dx$

In Problems 31 through 35, evaluate the given integral by making the indicated substitution.

31. $\int x^2 \sqrt{x - 2}\,dx; \quad u = x - 2$
32. $\int \dfrac{x^2}{\sqrt{x + 3}}\,dx; \quad u = x + 3$
33. $\int \dfrac{x}{\sqrt{2x + 3}}\,dx; \quad u = 2x + 3$
34. $\int x \sqrt[3]{x - 1}\,dx; \quad u = x - 1$
35. $\int \dfrac{x}{\sqrt[3]{x + 1}}\,dx; \quad u = x + 1$

In Problems 36 through 50, evaluate the given integral. First make a substitution that transforms it into a standard form. The standard forms with the given formula numbers are inside the back cover of this book. If a computer algebra system is available, compare and reconcile (if necessary) the result found using the integral table formula with a machine result.

36. $\int \dfrac{1}{100 + 9x^2}\,dx; \quad$ Formula (17)
37. $\int \dfrac{1}{100 - 9x^2}\,dx; \quad$ Formula (18)
38. $\int \sqrt{9 - 4x^2}\,dx; \quad$ Formula (54)
39. $\int \sqrt{4 + 9x^2}\,dx; \quad$ Formula (44)
40. $\int \dfrac{1}{\sqrt{16x^2 + 9}}\,dx; \quad$ Formula (45)
41. $\int \dfrac{x^2}{\sqrt{16x^2 + 9}}\,dx; \quad$ Formula (49)
42. $\int \dfrac{x^2}{\sqrt{25 + 16x^2}}\,dx; \quad$ Formula (49)
43. $\int x^2 \sqrt{25 - 16x^2}\,dx; \quad$ Formula (57)
44. $\int x \sqrt{4 - x^4}\,dx; \quad$ Formula (54)
45. $\int e^x \sqrt{9 + e^{2x}}\,dx; \quad$ Formula (44)
46. $\int \dfrac{\cos x}{(\sin^2 x) \sqrt{1 + \sin^2 x}}\,dx; \quad$ Formula (50)

47. $\displaystyle\int \frac{\sqrt{x^4-1}}{x}\,dx$; Formula (47)

48. $\displaystyle\int \frac{e^{3x}}{\sqrt{25+16e^{2x}}}\,dx$; Formula (49)

49. $\displaystyle\int \frac{(\ln x)^2}{x}\sqrt{1+(\ln x)^2}\,dx$; Formula (48)

50. $\displaystyle\int x^8\sqrt{4x^6-1}\,dx$; Formula (48)

51. The substitution $u = x^2$, $x = \sqrt{u}$, $dx = du/(2\sqrt{u})$ appears to lead to this result:
$$\int_{-1}^{1} x^2\,dx = \tfrac{1}{2}\int_{1}^{1} \sqrt{u}\,du = 0.$$
Do you believe this result? If not, why not?

52. Use the fact that $x^2+4x+5 = (x+2)^2+1$ to evaluate
$$\int \frac{1}{x^2+4x+5}\,dx.$$

53. Use the fact that $1-(x-1)^2 = 2x-x^2$ to evaluate
$$\int \frac{1}{\sqrt{2x-x^2}}\,dx.$$

54. Use the binomial expansion
$$(1+t)^6 = 1+6t+15t^2+20t^3+15t^4+6t^5+t^6$$
to reconcile the result of Example 1 with the machine result listed at the end of this section. Are the two results precisely equal?

55. Establish the precise relationship between the two functions
$$\tfrac{1}{2}\tan^{-1}x^2 \quad \text{and} \quad -\tfrac{1}{2}\tan^{-1}x^{-2}$$
graphed in Fig. 8.2.2. Are both actually antiderivatives of $x/(1+x^4)$?

56. With $u = x$ and $a = 1$, Formula (54) inside the back cover yields
$$\int \sqrt{x^2+1}\,dx = \tfrac{1}{2}x\sqrt{x^2+1}+\tfrac{1}{2}\ln\left|x+\sqrt{x^2+1}\right|,$$
whereas *Maple* and *Mathematica* both give
$$\int \sqrt{x^2+1}\,dx = \tfrac{1}{2}x\sqrt{x^2+1}+\tfrac{1}{2}\sinh^{-1}x.$$
Consult Section 7.6 to reconcile these two results.

57. According to Formula (44) inside the back covers of this book,
$$\int \sqrt{x^2+1}\,dx = G(x)+C$$
where
$$G(x) = \tfrac{1}{2}x\sqrt{x^2+1}+\tfrac{1}{2}\ln\left(x+\sqrt{x^2+1}\right).$$
But another calculus book states that $\int \sqrt{x^2+1}\,dx = H(x)+C$ where
$$H(x) = \tfrac{1}{8}\Big[\left(x+\sqrt{x^2+1}\right)^2$$
$$+4\ln\left(x+\sqrt{x^2+1}\right)-\left(x+\sqrt{x^2+1}\right)^{-2}\Big].$$
Which book is correct? Use a computer algebra system if you wish.

8.3 INTEGRATION BY PARTS

One reason for transforming a given integral into another is to make its evaluation easier. There are two general ways to accomplish this. We have seen the first, integration by substitution. The second is *integration by parts*.

The formula for integration by parts is a simple consequence of the product rule for derivatives,
$$D_x(uv) = v\frac{du}{dx}+u\frac{dv}{dx}.$$

If we write this formula in the form
$$u(x)v'(x) = D_x[u(x)v(x)]-v(x)u'(x), \tag{1}$$

then antidifferentiation gives
$$\int u(x)v'(x)\,dx = u(x)v(x)-\int v(x)u'(x)\,dx. \tag{2}$$

This is the formula for **integration by parts**. With $du = u'(x)\,dx$ and $dv = v'(x)\,dx$, Eq. (2) becomes
$$\int u\,dv = uv-\int v\,du. \tag{3}$$

To apply the integration by parts formula to a given integral, we must first factor its integrand into two "parts," u and dv, the latter including the differential dx. We try to choose the parts in accordance with two principles:

1. The antiderivative $v = \int dv$ is easy to find.
2. The new integral $\int v\,du$ is easier to compute than the original integral $\int u\,dv$.

An effective strategy is to choose for dv the most complicated factor that can readily be integrated. Then we differentiate the other part, u, to find du.

We begin with two examples in which we have little flexibility in choosing the parts u and dv.

EXAMPLE 1 Find $\int \ln x\,dx$. (See Fig. 8.3.1.)

Solution Here there is little alternative to the natural choice $u = \ln x$ and $dv = dx$. It is helpful to systematize the procedure of integration by parts by writing u, dv, du, and v in a rectangular array like this:

$$\text{Let} \quad u = \ln x \quad \text{and} \quad dv = dx.$$
$$\text{Then} \quad du = \frac{1}{x}dx \quad \text{and} \quad v = x.$$

The first line in the array specifies the choice of u and dv; the second line is computed from the first. Then Eq. (3) gives

$$\int \ln x\,dx = x \ln x - \int dx = x \ln x - x + C.$$

FIGURE 8.3.1 Graphs of the functions $\ln x$ and $x \ln x - x$ of Example 1. If you did not recognize either graph, but noted that the zero of one corresponds to a critical point of the other, which would you conclude is the antiderivative?

COMMENT 1 The constant of integration appears only at the last step. We know that once we have found one antiderivative, any other may be obtained by adding a constant C to the one we have found.

COMMENT 2 In computing $v = \int dv$, we ordinarily take the constant of integration to be zero. Had we written $v = x + C_1$ in Example 1, the answer would have been

$$\int \ln x\,dx = (x + C_1)\ln x - \int \left(1 + \frac{C_1}{x}\right)dx$$
$$= x \ln x + C_1 \ln x - (x + C_1 \ln x) + C = x \ln x - x + C$$

as before, so introducing the extra constant C_1 has no effect.

EXAMPLE 2 Find $\int \arcsin x\,dx$.

Solution Again, there is only one plausible choice for u and dv:

$$\text{Let} \quad u = \arcsin x \quad \text{and} \quad dv = dx.$$
$$\text{Then} \quad du = \frac{dx}{\sqrt{1-x^2}} \quad \text{and} \quad v = x.$$

Then Eq. (3) gives

$$\int \arcsin x\,dx = x \arcsin x - \int \frac{x}{\sqrt{1-x^2}}\,dx$$
$$= x \arcsin x + \sqrt{1-x^2} + C.$$

EXAMPLE 3 Find $\int xe^{-x}\,dx$.

Solution Here we appear to have some flexibility. Suppose that we try

$$u = e^{-x}, \quad dv = x\,dx$$

so that

$$du = -e^{-x}\,dx, \quad v = \tfrac{1}{2}x^2.$$

Then integration by parts gives

$$\int xe^{-x}\,dx = \tfrac{1}{2}x^2 e^{-x} + \tfrac{1}{2}\int x^2 e^{-x}\,dx.$$

The new integral on the right looks more troublesome than the original problem on the left! Let us begin anew.

$$\text{Let} \quad u = x \quad \text{and} \quad dv = e^{-x}\,dx.$$
$$\text{Then} \quad du = dx \quad \text{and} \quad v = -e^{-x}.$$

Now integration by parts gives

$$\int xe^{-x}\,dx = -xe^{-x} + \int e^{-x}\,dx = -xe^{-x} - e^{-x} + C. \quad \blacklozenge$$

Integration by parts can be applied to definite integrals as well as to indefinite integrals. We integrate Eq. (1) from $x = a$ to $x = b$ and apply the fundamental theorem of calculus. This gives

$$\int_a^b u(x)v'(x)\,dx = \int_a^b D_x[u(x)v(x)]\,dx - \int_a^b v(x)u'(x)\,dx$$
$$= \Big[u(x)v(x)\Big]_a^b - \int_a^b v(x)u'(x)\,dx.$$

In the notation of Eq. (3), this equation would be written

$$\int_{x=a}^{x=b} u\,dv = \Big[uv\Big]_a^b - \int_{x=a}^{x=b} v\,du, \qquad (4)$$

although we must not forget that u and v are functions of x. For example, with $u = x$ and $dv = e^{-x}\,dx$, as in Example 3, we obtain

$$\int_0^1 xe^{-x}\,dx = \Big[-xe^{-x}\Big]_0^1 + \int_0^1 e^{-x}\,dx = -e^{-1} + \Big[-e^{-x}\Big]_0^1 = 1 - \frac{2}{e}.$$

EXAMPLE 4 Find $\int x^2 e^{-x}\,dx$.

Solution If we choose $u = x^2$, then $du = 2x\,dx$, so we will reduce the exponent of x by this choice.

$$\text{Let} \quad u = x^2 \quad \text{and} \quad dv = e^{-x}\,dx.$$
$$\text{Then} \quad du = 2x\,dx \quad \text{and} \quad v = -e^{-x}.$$

Then integration by parts gives

$$\int x^2 e^{-x}\,dx = -x^2 e^{-x} + 2\int xe^{-x}\,dx.$$

We apply integration by parts a second time to the right-hand integral and obtain the result

$$\int xe^{-x}\,dx = -xe^{-x} - e^{-x}$$

of Example 3. Substitution then yields

$$\int x^2 e^{-x}\,dx = -x^2 e^{-x} - 2xe^{-x} - 2e^{-x} + C$$
$$= -(x^2 + 2x + 2)e^{-x} + C.$$

In effect, we have annihilated the original factor x^2 by integrating by parts twice in succession. See Fig. 8.3.2. $\quad\blacklozenge$

FIGURE 8.3.2 Graphs of the functions $x^2 e^{-x}$ and $-(x^2 + 2x + 2)e^{-x} + 1$. Noting only that the zero of one corresponds to a critical point of the other, which do you conclude is the antiderivative?

EXAMPLE 5 Find $\int e^{2x} \sin 3x \, dx$.

Solution This is another example in which repeated integration by parts succeeds, but with a twist:

$$\text{Let} \quad u = \sin 3x, \quad dv = e^{2x} \, dx.$$
$$\text{Then} \quad du = 3\cos 3x \, dx, \quad v = \tfrac{1}{2} e^{2x}.$$

Therefore,

$$\int e^{2x} \sin 3x \, dx = \tfrac{1}{2} e^{2x} \sin 3x - \tfrac{3}{2} \int e^{2x} \cos 3x \, dx.$$

At first it might appear that little progress has been made, for the integral on the right is as difficult to integrate as the one on the left. We ignore this objection and try again, applying integration by parts to the new integral:

$$\text{Let} \quad u = \cos 3x, \quad dv = e^{2x} \, dx.$$
$$\text{Then} \quad du = -3\sin 3x \, dx, \quad v = \tfrac{1}{2} e^{2x}.$$

Now we find that

$$\int e^{2x} \cos 3x \, dx = \tfrac{1}{2} e^{2x} \cos 3x + \tfrac{3}{2} \int e^{2x} \sin 3x \, dx.$$

When we substitute this result into the previous equation, we discover that

$$\int e^{2x} \sin 3x \, dx = \tfrac{1}{2} e^{2x} \sin 3x - \tfrac{3}{4} e^{2x} \cos 3x - \tfrac{9}{4} \int e^{2x} \sin 3x \, dx.$$

So we are back where we started. Or *are* we? In fact we are *not*, because we can *solve* this last equation for the desired integral. We add the right-hand integral here to both sides of the last equation. This gives

$$\tfrac{13}{4} \int e^{2x} \sin 3x \, dx = \tfrac{1}{4} e^{2x} (2\sin 3x - 3\cos 3x) + C_1,$$

so

$$\int e^{2x} \sin 3x \, dx = \tfrac{1}{13} e^{2x} (2\sin 3x - 3\cos 3x) + C.$$

(See Fig. 8.3.3.) ◆

FIGURE 8.3.3 Graphs of the functions $e^{2x} \sin 3x$ and $\tfrac{1}{13} e^{2x}(2\sin 3x - 3\cos 3x)$. Noting only that the zeros of one correspond to the critical points of the other, which do you conclude is the antiderivative?

EXAMPLE 6 Find a reduction formula for $\int \sec^n x \, dx$.

Solution The idea is that n is a (large) positive integer and that we want to express the given integral in terms of the integral of a lower power of $\sec x$. The easiest power of $\sec x$ to integrate is $\sec^2 x$, so we proceed as follows:

$$\text{Let} \quad u = \sec^{n-2} x, \quad dv = \sec^2 x \, dx.$$
$$\text{Then} \quad du = (n-2)\sec^{n-2} x \tan x \, dx, \quad v = \tan x.$$

This gives

$$\int \sec^n x \, dx = \sec^{n-2} x \tan x - (n-2) \int \sec^{n-2} x \tan^2 x \, dx$$
$$= \sec^{n-2} x \tan x - (n-2) \int (\sec^{n-2} x)(\sec^2 x - 1) \, dx.$$

Hence

$$\int \sec^n x \, dx = \sec^{n-2} x \tan x - (n-2) \int \sec^n x \, dx + (n-2) \int \sec^{n-2} x \, dx.$$

We solve this equation for the original integral and find that

$$\int \sec^n x \, dx = \frac{\sec^{n-2} x \tan x}{n-1} + \frac{n-2}{n-1} \int \sec^{n-2} x \, dx. \quad (5)$$

This is the desired reduction formula. For example, if we take $n = 3$ in this formula, we find that

$$\int \sec^3 x \, dx = \tfrac{1}{2} \sec x \tan x + \tfrac{1}{2} \int \sec x \, dx$$

and thus

$$\int \sec^3 x \, dx = \tfrac{1}{2} \sec x \tan x + \tfrac{1}{2} \ln |\sec x + \tan x| + C. \quad (6)$$

In the last step we used the integral formula

$$\int \sec x \, dx = \ln |\sec x + \tan x| + C, \quad (7)$$

which is tricky to derive systematically (see Section 8.4) but is easy to verify by differentiation:

$$D_x(\ln |\sec x + \tan x|) = \frac{D_x(\sec x + \tan x)}{\sec x + \tan x}$$

$$= \frac{\sec x \tan x + \sec^2 x}{\sec x + \tan x} = \frac{(\sec x)(\tan x + \sec x)}{\sec x + \tan x} = \sec x.$$

The reason for using the reduction formula in Eq. (5) to integrate $\sec^n x$ is that—if n is a positive integer—repeated application of the formula must yield either Eq. (7) or the elementary integral

$$\int \sec^2 x \, dx = \tan x + C. \qquad \blacklozenge$$

EXAMPLE 7 With $n = 4$ in Eq. (5) we get

$$\int \sec^4 x \, dx = \tfrac{1}{3} \sec^2 x \tan x + \tfrac{2}{3} \int \sec^2 x \, dx$$
$$= \tfrac{1}{3} \sec^2 x \tan x + \tfrac{2}{3} \tan x + C, \quad (8)$$

and with $n = 5$ we get

$$\int \sec^5 x \, dx = \tfrac{1}{4} \sec^3 x \tan x + \tfrac{3}{4} \int \sec^3 x \, dx$$
$$= \tfrac{1}{4} \sec^3 x \tan x + \tfrac{3}{8} \sec x \tan x + \tfrac{3}{8} \ln |\sec x + \tan x| + C, \quad (9)$$

using Eq. (6) in the last step. $\qquad \blacklozenge$

8.3 TRUE/FALSE STUDY GUIDE

8.3 CONCEPTS: QUESTIONS AND DISCUSSION

1. Given an integral $\int f(x) \, dx$, state in your own words, with a minimum of jargon, your strategy for factoring the integrand into a product $f(x) = g(x)h(x)$ so that the separation into parts $u = g(x)$, $dv = h(x) \, dx$ is effective in evaluating the integral.

2. Give an example of an integral $\int f(x)\,dx$ for which the integrand can be factored in at least three different ways—some that lead to a successful integration by parts and some that do not.

8.3 PROBLEMS

Use integration by parts to compute the integrals in Problems 1 through 34.

1. $\int xe^{2x}\,dx$
2. $\int x^2 e^{2x}\,dx$
3. $\int t \sin t\,dt$
4. $\int t^2 \sin t\,dt$
5. $\int x \cos 3x\,dx$
6. $\int x \ln x\,dx$
7. $\int x^3 \ln x\,dx$
8. $\int e^{3z} \cos 3z\,dz$
9. $\int \arctan x\,dx$
10. $\int \dfrac{\ln x}{x^2}\,dx$
11. $\int \sqrt{y} \ln y\,dy$
12. $\int x \sec^2 x\,dx$
13. $\int (\ln t)^2\,dt$
14. $\int t(\ln t)^2\,dt$
15. $\int x\sqrt{x+3}\,dx$
16. $\int x^3\sqrt{1-x^2}\,dx$
17. $\int x^5 \sqrt{x^3+1}\,dx$
18. $\int \sin^2 \theta\,d\theta$
19. $\int \csc^3 \theta\,d\theta$
20. $\int \sin(\ln t)\,dt$
21. $\int x^2 \arctan x\,dx$
22. $\int \ln(1+x^2)\,dx$
23. $\int \sec^{-1}\sqrt{x}\,dx$
24. $\int x \tan^{-1}\sqrt{x}\,dx$
25. $\int \tan^{-1}\sqrt{x}\,dx$
26. $\int x^2 \cos 4x\,dx$
27. $\int x \csc^2 x\,dx$
28. $\int x \arctan x\,dx$
29. $\int x^3 \cos x^2\,dx$
30. $\int e^{-3x} \sin 4x\,dx$
31. $\int \dfrac{\ln x}{x\sqrt{x}}\,dx$
32. $\int \dfrac{x^7}{(1+x^4)^{3/2}}\,dx$
33. $\int x \cosh x\,dx$
34. $\int e^x \cosh x\,dx$

In Problems 35 through 38, first make a substitution of the form $t = x^k$ and then integrate by parts.

35. $\int x^3 \sin x^2\,dx$
36. $\int x^7 \cos x^4\,dx$
37. $\int \exp(-\sqrt{x})\,dx$
38. $\int x^2 \sin x^{3/2}\,dx$

In Problems 39 through 42, use the method of cylindrical shells to calculate the volume of the solid obtained by revolving the region R around the y-axis.

39. R is bounded below by the x-axis and above by the curve $y = \cos x$, $-\pi/2 \le x \le \pi/2$.
40. R is bounded below by the x-axis and above by the curve $y = \sin x$, $0 \le x \le \pi$.
41. R is bounded below by the x-axis, on the right by the line $x = e$, and above by the curve $y = \ln x$.
42. R is bounded below by the x-axis, on the left by the y-axis, on the right by the line $x = 1$, and above by the curve $y = e^{-x}$.

In Problems 43 through 45, first estimate graphically or numerically the points of intersection of the two given curves, then approximate the volume of the solid that is generated when the region bounded by these two curves is revolved around the y-axis.

43. $y = x^2$ and $y = \cos x$
44. $y = 10x - x^2$ and $y = e^x - 1$
45. $y = x^2 - 2x$ and $y = \ln(x+1)$
46. Use integration by parts to evaluate

$$\int 2x \arctan x\,dx,$$

with $dv = 2x\,dx$, but let $v = x^2 + 1$ rather than $v = x^2$. Is there a reason why v should not be chosen in this way?

47. Use integration by parts to evaluate $\int xe^x \cos x\,dx$.
48. Use integration by parts to evaluate $\int \sin 3x \cos x\,dx$.

Derive the reduction formulas given in Problems 49 through 54. Throughout, n denotes a positive integer with an appropriate side condition (such as $n \ge 1$ or $n \ge 2$).

49. $\int x^n e^x\,dx = x^n e^x - n \int x^{n-1} e^x\,dx$
50. $\int x^n e^{-x^2}\,dx = -\dfrac{1}{2} x^{n-1} e^{-x^2} + \dfrac{n-1}{2} \int x^{n-2} e^{-x^2}\,dx$
51. $\int (\ln x)^n\,dx = x(\ln x)^n - n \int (\ln x)^{n-1}\,dx$
52. $\int x^n \cos x\,dx = x^n \sin x - n \int x^{n-1} \sin x\,dx$
53. $\int \sin^n x\,dx = -\dfrac{\sin^{n-1} x \cos x}{n} + \dfrac{n-1}{n} \int \sin^{n-2} x\,dx$
54. $\int \cos^n x\,dx = \dfrac{\cos^{n-1} x \sin x}{n} + \dfrac{n-1}{n} \int \cos^{n-2} x\,dx$

Use appropriate reduction formulas from the preceding list to evaluate the integrals in Problems 55 through 57.

55. $\int_0^1 x^3 e^x \, dx$

56. $\int_0^1 x^5 e^{-x^2} \, dx$

57. $\int_1^e (\ln x)^3 \, dx$

58. Apply the reduction formula in Problem 53 to show that for each positive integer n,

$$\int_0^{\pi/2} \sin^{2n} x \, dx = \frac{\pi}{2} \cdot \frac{1}{2} \cdot \frac{3}{4} \cdot \frac{5}{6} \cdots \frac{2n-1}{2n}$$

and

$$\int_0^{\pi/2} \sin^{2n+1} x \, dx = \frac{2}{3} \cdot \frac{4}{5} \cdot \frac{6}{7} \cdot \frac{8}{9} \cdots \frac{2n}{2n+1}.$$

59. Derive the formula

$$\int \ln(x+10) \, dx = (x+10) \ln(x+10) - x + C$$

in three different ways: (a) by substituting $u = x + 10$ and applying the result of Example 1; (b) by integrating by parts with $u = \ln(x+10)$ and $dv = dx$, noting that

$$\frac{x}{x+10} = 1 - \frac{10}{x+10};$$

and (c) by integrating by parts with $u = \ln(x+10)$ and $dv = dx$, but with $v = x + 10$.

60. Derive the formula

$$\int x^3 \tan^{-1} x \, dx = \tfrac{1}{4}(x^4 - 1) \tan^{-1} x - \tfrac{1}{12} x^3 + \tfrac{1}{4} x + C$$

by integrating by parts with $u = \tan^{-1} x$ and $v = \tfrac{1}{4}(x^4 - 1)$.

61. Let $J_n = \int_0^1 x^n e^{-x} \, dx$ for each integer $n \geq 0$. (a) Show that

$$J_0 = 1 - \frac{1}{e} \quad \text{and that} \quad J_n = nJ_{n-1} - \frac{1}{e}$$

for $n \geq 1$. (b) Deduce by mathematical induction that

$$J_n = n! - \frac{n!}{e} \sum_{k=0}^n \frac{1}{k!}$$

for each integer $n \geq 0$. (c) Explain why $J_n \to 0$ as $n \to +\infty$. (d) Conclude that

$$e = \lim_{n \to \infty} \sum_{k=0}^n \frac{1}{k!}.$$

62. Let m and n be positive integers. Derive the reduction formula

$$\int x^m (\ln x)^n \, dx = \frac{x^{m+1}}{m+1} (\ln x)^n - \frac{n}{m+1} \int x^m (\ln x)^{n-1} \, dx.$$

63. An advertisement for a symbolic algebra program claims that an engineer worked for three weeks on the integral

$$\int (k \ln x - 2x^3 + 3x^2 + b)^4 \, dx,$$

which deals with turbulence in an aerospace application. The advertisement said that the engineer never got the same answer twice in the three weeks. Explain how you could use the reduction formula of Problem 62 to find the engineer's integral (but don't actually do it). Can you see any reason why it should have taken three weeks?

64. Figure 8.3.4 shows the region bounded by the x-axis and the graph of $y = \tfrac{1}{2} x^2 \sin x$, $0 \leq x \leq \pi$. Use Formulas (42) and (43) (inside the back cover)—which are derived by integration by parts—to find (a) the area of this region; (b) the volume obtained by revolving this region around the y-axis.

FIGURE 8.3.4 The region of Problem 64.

65. The top shown in Fig. 8.3.5 has the shape of the solid obtained by revolving the region of Problem 64 around the x-axis. Find the volume of this top.

FIGURE 8.3.5 The top of Problem 65.

66. A particle is set in motion at time $t = 0$ and moves to the right along the x-axis. (a) Suppose that its acceleration at time t is $a = 100 e^{-t}$. Show that the particle moves infinitely far to the right along the x-axis. (b) Suppose that its acceleration at time t is $a = 100(1-t) e^{-t}$. Show that the particle never moves beyond a certain point to the right of its initial position and find that point. Explain why the particle "effectively" comes to a stop at that point.

67. Find the area and centroid of the region that is bounded by the curves $y = x^2$ and $y = 2^x$ for $2 \leq x \leq 4$.

68. For each positive integer k, let

$$I_k = \int_0^{\pi/2} \sin^k x \, dx.$$

(a) Show that $I_{2n} \geq I_{2n+1} \geq I_{2n+2}$ for each positive integer n.
(b) Use Problem 58 to show that

$$\lim_{n \to \infty} \frac{I_{2n+2}}{I_{2n}} = 1.$$

(c) Conclude from parts (a) and (b) that

$$\lim_{n \to \infty} \frac{I_{2n+1}}{I_{2n}} = 1.$$

(d) Conclude from part (c) and Problem 58 that

$$\lim_{n \to \infty} \frac{2}{1} \cdot \frac{2}{3} \cdot \frac{4}{3} \cdot \frac{4}{5} \cdot \frac{6}{5} \cdot \frac{6}{7} \cdots \frac{2n}{2n-1} \cdot \frac{2n}{2n+1} = \frac{\pi}{2}.$$

This result is usually written as the *infinite product*

$$\frac{\pi}{2} = \frac{2}{1} \cdot \frac{2}{3} \cdot \frac{4}{3} \cdot \frac{4}{5} \cdot \frac{6}{5} \cdot \frac{6}{7} \cdots,$$

which was discovered by the English mathematician John Wallis in 1655.

8.4 TRIGONOMETRIC INTEGRALS

Here we discuss the evaluation of certain integrals in which the integrand is either a power of a trigonometric function or the product of two such powers. Such integrals are among the most common trigonometric integrals in applications of calculus.

To evaluate the integrals

$$\int \sin^2 u \, du \quad \text{and} \quad \int \cos^2 u \, du$$

that appear in numerous applications, we use the **half-angle identities**

$$\sin^2 \theta = \tfrac{1}{2}(1 - \cos 2\theta), \tag{1}$$

$$\cos^2 \theta = \tfrac{1}{2}(1 + \cos 2\theta) \tag{2}$$

of Eqs. (11) and (10) in Appendix C.

EXAMPLE 1 Find $\int \sin^2 3x \, dx$. (See Fig. 8.4.1.)

Solution The identity in Eq. (1)—with $3x$ in place of θ—yields

$$\int \sin^2 3x \, dx = \int \tfrac{1}{2}(1 - \cos 6x) \, dx$$

$$= \tfrac{1}{2}\left(x - \tfrac{1}{6}\sin 6x\right) + C = \tfrac{1}{12}(6x - \sin 6x) + C. \quad \blacklozenge$$

To integrate $\tan^2 x$ and $\cot^2 x$, we use the identities

$$1 + \tan^2 x = \sec^2 x \quad \text{and} \quad 1 + \cot^2 x = \csc^2 x. \tag{3}$$

FIGURE 8.4.1 Graphs of the functions $\sin^2 3x$ and $\tfrac{1}{12}(6x - \sin 6x)$ of Example 1. The zeros of which correspond to the critical points of the other? So which is the antiderivative?

The first of these follows from the fundamental identity $\sin^2 x + \cos^2 x = 1$ upon division of both sides by $\cos^2 x$. To obtain the second formula in (3), we divide both sides of the fundamental identity by $\sin^2 x$.

EXAMPLE 2 Compute the antiderivative $\int \cot^2 3x \, dx$.

Solution By using the second identity in (3) with $3x$ in place of x, we obtain

$$\int \cot^2 3x \, dx = \int (\csc^2 3x - 1) \, dx$$

$$= \int (\csc^2 u - 1)(\tfrac{1}{3}du) \qquad (u = 3x)$$

$$= \tfrac{1}{3}(-\cot u - u) + C = -\tfrac{1}{3}\cot 3x - x + C. \quad \blacklozenge$$

Integrals of Products of Sines and Cosines

The substitution $u = \sin x$, $du = \cos x \, dx$ gives

$$\int \sin^3 x \cos x \, dx = \int u^3 \, du = \tfrac{1}{4}u^4 + C = \tfrac{1}{4}\sin^4 x + C.$$

This substitution, or the similar substitution $u = \cos x$, $du = -\sin x \, dx$, can be used to evaluate an integral of the form

$$\int \sin^m x \cos^n x \, dx \qquad (4)$$

in the first of the following two cases:

- **Case 1:** At least one of the two numbers m and n is an *odd positive integer*. If so, then the other may be any real number.
- **Case 2:** Both m and n are *nonnegative even integers*.

Suppose, for example, that $m = 2k+1$ is an odd positive integer. Then we isolate one $\sin x$ factor and use the identity $\sin^2 x = 1 - \cos^2 x$ to express the remaining $\sin^{m-1} x$ factor in terms of $\cos x$, as follows:

$$\int \sin^m x \cos^n x \, dx = \int \sin^{m-1} x \cos^n x \sin x \, dx = \int (\sin^2 x)^k \cos^n x \sin x \, dx$$

$$= \int (1 - \cos^2 x)^k \cos^n x \sin x \, dx.$$

Now the substitution $u = \cos x$, $du = -\sin x \, dx$ yields

$$\int \sin^m x \cos^n x \, dx = -\int (1 - u^2)^k u^n \, du.$$

The exponent $k = (m-1)/2$ is a nonnegative integer because m is an odd positive integer. Thus the factor $(1-u^2)^k$ of the integrand is a polynomial in the variable u, and so its product with u^n is easy to integrate.

In essence, this method consists of peeling off one copy of $\sin x$ (if m is odd) and then converting the remaining sines into cosines. If n is odd, then we can split off one copy of $\cos x$ and convert the remaining cosines into sines.

EXAMPLE 3

(a) $\displaystyle\int \sin^3 x \cos^2 x \, dx = \int (1 - \cos^2 x) \cos^2 x \sin x \, dx$

$$= \int (u^4 - u^2) \, du \qquad (u = \cos x)$$

$$= \tfrac{1}{5}u^5 - \tfrac{1}{3}u^3 + C = \tfrac{1}{5}\cos^5 x - \tfrac{1}{3}\cos^3 x + C.$$

(b) $\displaystyle\int \cos^5 x \, dx = \int (1 - \sin^2 x)^2 \cos x \, dx$

$$= \int (1 - u^2)^2 \, du \qquad (u = \sin x)$$

$$= \int (1 - 2u^2 + u^4) \, du = u - \tfrac{2}{3}u^3 + \tfrac{1}{5}u^5 + C$$

$$= \sin x - \tfrac{2}{3}\sin^3 x + \tfrac{1}{5}\sin^5 x + C. \qquad \blacklozenge$$

In case 2 of the sine-cosine integral in Eq. (4), with both m and n nonnegative even integers, we use the half-angle formulas in Eqs. (1) and (2) to halve the even powers of $\sin x$ and $\cos x$. If we repeat this process with the resulting powers of $\cos 2x$ (if necessary), we get integrals involving odd powers, and we have seen how to handle these in Case 1.

EXAMPLE 4 Use of Eqs. (1) and (2) gives

$$\int \sin^2 x \cos^2 x \, dx = \int \tfrac{1}{2}(1 - \cos 2x)\tfrac{1}{2}(1 + \cos 2x) \, dx$$

$$= \tfrac{1}{4} \int (1 - \cos^2 2x) \, dx = \tfrac{1}{4} \int \left[1 - \tfrac{1}{2}(1 + \cos 4x)\right] dx$$

$$= \tfrac{1}{8} \int (1 - \cos 4x) \, dx = \tfrac{1}{8}x - \tfrac{1}{32} \sin 4x + C.$$

In the third step we used Eq. (2) with $\theta = 2x$. ◆

EXAMPLE 5 Here we apply Eq. (2), first with $\theta = 3x$ and then with $\theta = 6x$.

$$\int \cos^4 3x \, dx = \int \left[\tfrac{1}{2}(1 + \cos 6x)\right]^2 dx$$

$$= \tfrac{1}{4} \int (1 + 2\cos 6x + \cos^2 6x) \, dx$$

$$= \tfrac{1}{4} \int \left(\tfrac{3}{2} + 2\cos 6x + \tfrac{1}{2}\cos 12x\right) dx$$

$$= \tfrac{3}{8}x + \tfrac{1}{12} \sin 6x + \tfrac{1}{96} \sin 12x + C.$$ ◆

Integrals of Products of Secants and Tangents

To integrate $\tan x$, we use the substitution

$$u = \cos x, \qquad du = -\sin x \, dx$$

and get

$$\int \tan x \, dx = \int \frac{\sin x}{\cos x} \, dx = -\int \frac{1}{u} \, du = -\ln |u| + C.$$

Thus

$$\int \tan x \, dx = -\ln |\cos x| + C = \ln |\sec x| + C. \tag{5}$$

In Eq. (5) we used the fact that $|\sec x| = 1/|\cos x|$.

Similarly,

$$\int \cot x \, dx = \ln |\sin x| + C = -\ln |\csc x| + C. \tag{6}$$

The first person to integrate $\sec x$ may well have spent much time doing so. Here is one of several methods. First we "prepare" the function for integration:

$$\sec x = \frac{1}{\cos x} = \frac{\cos x}{\cos^2 x} = \frac{\cos x}{1 - \sin^2 x}.$$

Next we use the algebraic identity

$$\frac{1}{1+z} + \frac{1}{1-z} = \frac{2}{1-z^2},$$

which you can verify by finding a common denominator on the right. Similarly, we see that

$$\frac{2\cos x}{1-\sin^2 x} = \frac{\cos x}{1+\sin x} + \frac{\cos x}{1-\sin x}.$$

Therefore,

$$\int \sec x \, dx = \tfrac{1}{2} \int \left(\frac{\cos x}{1+\sin x} + \frac{\cos x}{1-\sin x} \right) dx$$

$$= \tfrac{1}{2}(\ln|1+\sin x| - \ln|1-\sin x|) + C.$$

It's customary to simplify this result:

$$\int \sec x \, dx = \tfrac{1}{2} \ln \left| \frac{1+\sin x}{1-\sin x} \right| + C = \tfrac{1}{2} \ln \left| \frac{(1+\sin x)^2}{1-\sin^2 x} \right| + C$$

$$= \ln \left| \frac{(1+\sin x)^2}{\cos^2 x} \right|^{1/2} + C = \ln \left| \frac{1+\sin x}{\cos x} \right| + C$$

$$= \ln|\sec x + \tan x| + C.$$

After we verify by differentiation that

$$\int \sec x \, dx = \ln|\sec x + \tan x| + C, \tag{7}$$

we could always "derive" this result by using an unmotivated trick:

$$\int \sec x \, dx = \int (\sec x) \frac{\tan x + \sec x}{\sec x + \tan x} \, dx$$

$$= \int \frac{\sec x \tan x + \sec^2 x}{\sec x + \tan x} \, dx = \ln|\sec x + \tan x| + C.$$

A similar technique yields

$$\int \csc x \, dx = -\ln|\csc x + \cot x| + C. \tag{8}$$

EXAMPLE 6 The substitution $u = \tfrac{1}{2}x$, $du = \tfrac{1}{2} dx$ gives

$$\int_0^{\pi/2} \sec \frac{x}{2} \, dx = 2 \int_0^{\pi/4} \sec u \, du$$

$$= 2 \Big[\ln|\sec u + \tan u| \Big]_0^{\pi/4} = 2 \ln(1+\sqrt{2}) \approx 1.76275. \quad \blacklozenge$$

An integral of the form

$$\int \tan^m x \sec^n x \, dx \tag{9}$$

can be routinely evaluated in either of the following two cases:

- *Case 1: m* is an *odd positive integer.*
- *Case 2: n* is an *even positive integer.*

In Case 1, we split off the factor $\sec x \tan x$ to form, along with dx, the differential $\sec x \tan x \, dx$ of $\sec x$. We then use the identity $\tan^2 x = \sec^2 x - 1$ to convert the remaining even power of $\tan x$ into powers of $\sec x$. This prepares the integrand for the substitution $u = \sec x$.

EXAMPLE 7

$$\int \tan^3 x \sec^3 x \, dx = \int (\sec^2 x - 1) \sec^2 x \sec x \tan x \, dx$$

$$= \int (u^4 - u^2) \, du \qquad (u = \sec x)$$

$$= \tfrac{1}{5} u^5 - \tfrac{1}{3} u^3 + C = \tfrac{1}{5} \sec^5 x - \tfrac{1}{3} \sec^3 x + C. \qquad \blacklozenge$$

To evaluate the integral in Eq. (9) in Case 2, we split off $\sec^2 x$ to form, along with dx, the differential of $\tan x$. We then use the identity $\sec^2 x = 1 + \tan^2 x$ to convert the remaining even power of $\sec x$ into powers of $\tan x$. This prepares the integrand for the substitution $u = \tan x$.

EXAMPLE 8 **Method 1.** Use of the secant-tangent form $\sec^2 u = 1 + \tan^2 u$ of the fundamental identity of trigonometry gives

$$\int \sec^6 2x \, dx = \int (1 + \tan^2 2x)^2 \sec^2 2x \, dx$$

$$= \tfrac{1}{2} \int (1 + \tan^2 2x)^2 (2 \sec^2 2x) \, dx$$

$$= \tfrac{1}{2} \int (1 + u^2)^2 \, du \qquad (u = \tan 2x, \quad du = 2\sec^2 2x \, dx)$$

$$= \tfrac{1}{2} \int (1 + 2u^2 + u^4) \, du = \tfrac{1}{2} u + \tfrac{1}{3} u^3 + \tfrac{1}{10} u^5 + C$$

$$= \tfrac{1}{2} \tan 2x + \tfrac{1}{3} \tan^3 2x + \tfrac{1}{10} \tan^5 2x + C. \qquad (10)$$

Method 2. Alternatively, we could apply the reduction formula

$$\int \sec^n x \, dx = \frac{\sec^{n-2} x \tan x}{n - 1} + \frac{n - 2}{n - 1} \int \sec^{n-2} x \, dx$$

of Section 8.3, first with $n = 6$ and then with $n = 4$. This gives

$$\int \sec^6 2x \, dx = \tfrac{1}{2} \int \sec^6 u \, du \qquad (u = 2x)$$

$$= \tfrac{1}{2} \left(\tfrac{1}{5} \sec^4 u \tan u + \tfrac{4}{5} \int \sec^4 u \, du \right)$$

$$= \tfrac{1}{10} \sec^4 u \tan u + \tfrac{2}{5} \left(\tfrac{1}{3} \sec^2 u \tan u + \tfrac{2}{3} \int \sec^2 u \, du \right)$$

$$= \tfrac{1}{10} \sec^4 2x \tan 2x + \tfrac{2}{15} \sec^2 2x \tan 2x + \tfrac{4}{15} \tan 2x + C. \qquad (11)$$

(See Figs. 8.4.2 and 8.4.3.) $\qquad \blacklozenge$

Similar methods are effective with integrals of the form

$$\int \csc^m x \cot^n x \, dx,$$

because the cotangent and cosecant functions satisfy analogous differentiation formulas and trigonometric identities:

$$1 + \tan^2 x = \sec^2 x, \qquad D_x \tan x = \sec^2 x, \qquad D_x \sec x = \sec x \tan x$$

FIGURE 8.4.2 After an initial attempt to evaluate $\int \sec^6 2x \, dx$ using the two methods of Example 8, a computer was used to plot the two alleged antiderivatives. Why does this figure indicate the presence of an error in the calculations? What is the relationship between any two antiderivatives of a given function?

FIGURE 8.4.3 After the error made initially was found and corrected, this figure resulted when the two antiderivatives in (10) and (11) were plotted simultaneously (each with $C = 0$). It indicates that the two antiderivative formulas are, in fact, equivalent.

and

$$1 + \cot^2 x = \csc^2 x, \qquad D_x \cot x = -\csc^2 x, \qquad D_x \csc x = -\csc x \cot x.$$

The method of Case 1 succeeds with the integral

$$\int \tan^n x \, dx$$

only when n is an odd positive integer, but there is another approach that works equally well whether n is even or odd. We split off the factor $\tan^2 x$ and replace it with $\sec^2 x - 1$:

$$\int \tan^n x \, dx = \int (\tan^{n-2} x)(\sec^2 x - 1) \, dx$$
$$= \int \tan^{n-2} x \sec^2 x \, dx - \int \tan^{n-2} x \, dx.$$

We integrate what we can and find that

$$\int \tan^n x \, dx = \frac{\tan^{n-1} x}{n-1} - \int \tan^{n-2} x \, dx. \tag{12}$$

Equation (12) is another example of a reduction formula. Its use effectively reduces the original exponent from n to $n-2$. If we apply Eq. (12) repeatedly, we eventually get either

$$\int \tan^2 x \, dx = \int (\sec^2 x - 1) \, dx = \tan x - x + C$$

or

$$\int \tan x \, dx = \ln|\sec x| + C.$$

EXAMPLE 9 Two applications of Eq. (12) give

$$\int \tan^6 x \, dx = \tfrac{1}{5} \tan^5 x - \int \tan^4 x \, dx$$
$$= \tfrac{1}{5} \tan^5 x - \left(\tfrac{1}{3} \tan^3 x - \int \tan^2 x \, dx \right)$$
$$= \tfrac{1}{5} \tan^5 x - \tfrac{1}{3} \tan^3 x + \tan x - x + C. \qquad \blacklozenge$$

Finally, in the case of an integral involving an unusual mixture of trigonometric functions—tangents and cosecants, for example—expressing the integrand entirely in terms of sines and cosines may yield an expression that's easy to integrate.

8.4 TRUE/FALSE STUDY GUIDE

8.4 CONCEPTS: QUESTIONS AND DISCUSSION

In the following questions, the term "trigonometric integral" means an integral of a positive whole-number power of a trigonometric function or an integral of the product of two such powers.

1. Describe the types of trigonometric integrals that can be evaluated using the methods of this section.
2. Give examples of several trigonometric integrals that cannot be evaluated using the methods of this section.

8.4 PROBLEMS

Evaluate the integrals in Problems 1 through 44.

1. $\int \sin^2 2x \, dx$
2. $\int \cos^2 5x \, dx$
3. $\int \sec^2 \frac{x}{2} \, dx$
4. $\int \tan^2 \frac{x}{2} \, dx$
5. $\int \tan 3x \, dx$
6. $\int \cot 4x \, dx$
7. $\int \sec 3x \, dx$
8. $\int \csc 2x \, dx$
9. $\int \frac{1}{\csc^2 x} \, dx$
10. $\int \sin^2 x \cot^2 x \, dx$
11. $\int \sin^3 x \, dx$
12. $\int \sin^4 x \, dx$
13. $\int \sin^2 \theta \cos^3 \theta \, d\theta$
14. $\int \sin^3 t \cos^3 t \, dt$
15. $\int \cos^5 x \, dx$
16. $\int \frac{\sin t}{\cos^3 t} \, dt$
17. $\int \frac{\sin^3 x}{\sqrt{\cos x}} \, dx$
18. $\int \sin^3 \phi \cos^4 \phi \, d\phi$
19. $\int \sin^5 2z \cos^2 2z \, dz$
20. $\int \sin^{3/2} x \cos^3 x \, dx$
21. $\int \frac{\sin^3 4x}{\cos^2 4x} \, dx$
22. $\int \cos^6 4\theta \, d\theta$
23. $\int \sec^4 t \, dt$
24. $\int \tan^3 x \, dx$
25. $\int \cot^3 2x \, dx$
26. $\int \tan \theta \sec^4 \theta \, d\theta$
27. $\int \tan^5 2x \sec^2 2x \, dx$
28. $\int \cot^3 x \csc^2 x \, dx$
29. $\int \csc^6 2t \, dt$
30. $\int \frac{\sec^4 t}{\tan^2 t} \, dt$
31. $\int \frac{\tan^3 \theta}{\sec^4 \theta} \, d\theta$
32. $\int \frac{\cot^3 x}{\csc^2 x} \, dx$
33. $\int \frac{\tan^3 t}{\sqrt{\sec t}} \, dt$
34. $\int \frac{1}{\cos^4 2x} \, dx$
35. $\int \frac{\cot \theta}{\csc^3 \theta} \, d\theta$
36. $\int \sin^2 3\alpha \cos^2 3\alpha \, d\alpha$
37. $\int \cos^3 5t \, dt$
38. $\int \tan^4 x \, dx$
39. $\int \cot^4 3t \, dt$
40. $\int \tan^2 2t \sec^4 2t \, dt$
41. $\int \sin^5 2t \cos^{3/2} 2t \, dt$
42. $\int \cot^3 \xi \csc^{3/2} \xi \, d\xi$
43. $\int \frac{\tan x + \sin x}{\sec x} \, dx$
44. $\int \frac{\cot x + \csc x}{\sin x} \, dx$

In Problems 45 through 48, find the area of the region bounded by the two given curves.

45. The x-axis and the curve $y = \sin^3 x$, from $x = 0$ to $x = \pi$
46. $y = \cos^2 x$ and $y = \sin^2 x$, from $x = -\pi/4$ to $x = \pi/4$
47. $y = \sin x \cos x$ and $y = \sin^2 x$, from $x = \pi/4$ to $x = \pi$
48. $y = \cos^3 x$ and $y = \sin^3 x$, from $x = \pi/4$ to $x = 5\pi/4$

In Problems 49 and 50, first graph the integrand function and guess the value of the integral. Then verify your guess by actually evaluating the integral.

49. $\int_0^{2\pi} \sin^3 x \cos^2 x \, dx$
50. $\int_0^{\pi} \sin^5 2x \, dx$

In Problems 51 through 54, find the volume of the solid generated by revolving the given region R around the x-axis.

51. R is bounded by the x-axis and the curve $y = \sin^2 x$, $0 \leq x \leq \pi$.
52. R is the region of Problem 46.
53. R is bounded by $y = 2$ and $y = \sec x$ for $-\pi/3 \leq x \leq \pi/3$.
54. R is bounded by $y = 4\cos x$ and $y = \sec x$ for $-\pi/3 \leq x \leq \pi/3$.
55. Let R denote the region that lies between the curves $y = \tan^2 x$ and $y = \sec^2 x$ for $0 \leq x \leq \pi/4$. Find: (a) the area of R; (b) the volume of the solid obtained by revolving R around the x-axis.
56. Find the length of the graph of $y = \ln(\cos x)$ from $x = 0$ to $x = \pi/4$.
57. Find
$$\int \tan x \sec^4 x \, dx$$
in two different ways. Then show that your two results are equivalent.
58. Find
$$\int \cot^3 x \, dx$$
in two different ways. Then show that your two results are equivalent.

Problems 59 through 62 are applications of the trigonometric identities

$$\sin A \sin B = \tfrac{1}{2}[\cos(A-B) - \cos(A+B)],$$
$$\sin A \cos B = \tfrac{1}{2}[\sin(A-B) + \sin(A+B)],$$
$$\cos A \cos B = \tfrac{1}{2}[\cos(A-B) + \cos(A+B)].$$

59. Find $\int \sin 3x \cos 5x \, dx$.
60. Find $\int \sin 2x \sin 4x \, dx$.
61. Find $\int \cos x \cos 4x \, dx$.

62. Suppose that m and n are positive integers with $m \neq n$. Show that

(a) $\displaystyle\int_0^{2\pi} \sin mx \sin nx \, dx = 0;$

(b) $\displaystyle\int_0^{2\pi} \cos mx \sin nx \, dx = 0;$

(c) $\displaystyle\int_0^{2\pi} \cos mx \cos nx \, dx = 0.$

63. Substitute $\sec x \csc x = (\sec^2 x)/(\tan x)$ to derive the formula

$$\int \sec x \csc x \, dx = \ln|\tan x| + C.$$

64. Show that

$$\csc x = \frac{1}{2\sin\left(\frac{1}{2}x\right)\cos\left(\frac{1}{2}x\right)},$$

then apply the result of Problem 63 to derive the formula

$$\int \csc x \, dx = \ln\left|\tan\frac{x}{2}\right| + C.$$

65. Substitute $x = \frac{1}{2}\pi - u$ into the integral formula of Problem 64 to show that

$$\int \sec x \, dx = \ln\left|\cot\left(\frac{\pi}{4} - \frac{x}{2}\right)\right| + C.$$

66. Use appropriate trigonometric identities to deduce from the result of Problem 65 that

$$\int \sec x \, dx = \ln|\sec x + \tan x| + C.$$

67. Show first that the reduction formula in Eq. (12) gives

$$\int \tan^4 x \, dx = \tfrac{1}{3}\tan^3 x - \tan x + x + C.$$

Then compare this result with the alleged antiderivative

$$\int \tan^4 x \, dx = \tfrac{1}{12}(\sec^3 x)(9x\cos x + 3x\cos 3x - 4\sin 3x)$$

given by some versions of *Mathematica*.

68. Compare the result given in Example 9 with the integral

$$\int \tan^6 x \, dx$$

as given by your favorite computer algebra system.

8.5 RATIONAL FUNCTIONS AND PARTIAL FRACTIONS

We now discuss methods with which every rational function can be integrated in terms of elementary functions. Recall that a rational function $R(x)$ is a function that can be expressed as the quotient of two polynomials. That is,

$$R(x) = \frac{P(x)}{Q(x)}, \qquad (1)$$

where $P(x)$ and $Q(x)$ are polynomials. The **method of partial fractions** is an *algebraic* technique that decomposes $R(x)$ into a sum of terms:

$$R(x) = \frac{P(x)}{Q(x)} = p(x) + F_1(x) + F_2(x) + \cdots + F_k(x), \qquad (2)$$

where $p(x)$ is a polynomial and each expression $F_i(x)$ is a fraction that can be integrated with little difficulty.

EXAMPLE 1 We can verify (by finding a common denominator on the right) that

$$\frac{x^3 - 1}{x^3 + x} = 1 - \frac{1}{x} + \frac{x-1}{x^2+1}. \qquad (3)$$

It follows that

$$\int \frac{x^3 - 1}{x^3 + x}\, dx = \int\left(1 - \frac{1}{x} + \frac{x}{x^2+1} - \frac{1}{x^2+1}\right) dx$$

$$= x - \ln|x| + \tfrac{1}{2}\ln(x^2+1) - \tan^{-1} x + C.$$

The key to this simple integration lies in finding the decomposition given in Eq. (3). The existence of such a decomposition and the technique of finding it are what the method of partial fractions is about. (See Fig. 8.5.1.) ◆

FIGURE 8.5.1 Graphs of the function $f(x) = (x^3 - 1)/(x^3 + x)$ of Example 1 and its indefinite integral with $C = 0$. Which is which?

According to a theorem proved in advanced algebra, every rational function can be written in the form in Eq. (2) with each $F_i(x)$ being a fraction either of the form

$$\frac{A}{(ax+b)^n} \tag{4}$$

or of the form

$$\frac{Bx+C}{(ax^2+bx+c)^n} \tag{5}$$

(where A, B, C, a, b, and c are constants). Here the quadratic polynomial $ax^2 + bx + c$ is **irreducible**: It is not a product of linear factors with real coefficients. This is the same as saying that the equation $ax^2 + bx + c = 0$ has no real roots, and the quadratic formula tells us that this is the case exactly when its discriminant is negative: $b^2 - 4ac < 0$.

Fractions of the forms in Eqs. (4) and (5) are called **partial fractions**, and the sum in Eq. (2) is called the **partial-fraction decomposition** of $R(x)$. Thus Eq. (3) gives the partial-fraction decomposition of $(x^3-1)/(x^3+x)$. A partial fraction of the form in Eq. (4) may be integrated immediately, and we will see in Section 7.7 how to integrate one of the form in Eq. (5).

The first step in finding the partial-fraction decomposition of $R(x)$ is to find the polynomial $p(x)$ in Eq. (2). It turns out that $p(x) \equiv 0$ provided that the degree of the numerator $P(x)$ is *less than* that of the denominator $Q(x)$; such a rational function $R(x) = P(x)/Q(x)$ is said to be **proper**. If $R(x)$ is not proper, then $p(x)$ may be found by dividing $Q(x)$ into $P(x)$, as in Example 2.

EXAMPLE 2 Find $\displaystyle\int \frac{x^3 + x^2 + x - 1}{x^2 + 2x + 2}\, dx$. (See Fig. 8.5.2.)

Solution Long division of denominator into numerator may be carried out as follows:

$$\begin{array}{r}
x - 1 \qquad\qquad\qquad\quad p(x) \quad\text{(quotient)}\\
x^2 + 2x + 2 \overline{\smash{\big)}\, x^3 + x^2 + x - 1} \\
\underline{x^3 + 2x^2 + 2x}\qquad\qquad \\
-x^2 - x - 1 \\
\underline{-x^2 - 2x - 2} \\
x + 1 \qquad\quad r(x) \quad\text{(remainder)}
\end{array}$$

FIGURE 8.5.2 Graphs of the function $f(x) = (x^3 + x^2 + x - 1)/(x^2 + 2x + 2)$ of Example 2 and its indefinite integral with $C = 0$. Which is which?

As in simple arithmetic,

$$\text{"fraction} = \text{quotient} + \frac{\text{remainder}}{\text{divisor}}\text{."}$$

Thus

$$\frac{x^3 + x^2 + x - 1}{x^2 + 2x + 2} = (x - 1) + \frac{x + 1}{x^2 + 2x + 2},$$

and hence

$$\int \frac{x^3 + x^2 + x - 1}{x^2 + 2x + 2}\, dx = \int \left(x - 1 + \frac{x + 1}{x^2 + 2x + 2}\right) dx$$
$$= \tfrac{1}{2}x^2 - x + \tfrac{1}{2}\ln(x^2 + 2x + 2) + C. \quad\blacklozenge$$

By using long division as in Example 2, any rational function $R(x)$ can be written as a sum of a polynomial $p(x)$ and a *proper* rational fraction,

$$R(x) = p(x) + \frac{r(x)}{Q(x)}.$$

To see how to integrate an arbitrary rational function, we therefore need only see how to find the partial-fraction decomposition of a proper rational fraction.

To obtain such a decomposition, the first step is to factor the denominator $Q(x)$ into a product of linear factors (those of the form $ax + b$) and irreducible quadratic factors (those of the form $ax^2 + bx + c$ with $b^2 - 4ac < 0$). This is always possible in principle but may be difficult in practice. But once we have found the factorization of $Q(x)$, we can obtain the partial-fraction decomposition by routine algebraic methods (described next). Each linear or irreducible quadratic factor of $Q(x)$ leads to one or more partial fractions of the forms in Eqs. (4) and (5).

Linear Factors

Let $R(x) = P(x)/Q(x)$ be a *proper* rational fraction, and suppose that the linear factor $ax + b$ occurs n times in the complete factorization of $Q(x)$. That is, $(ax+b)^n$ is the highest power of $ax + b$ that divides "evenly" into $Q(x)$. In this case we call n the **multiplicity** of the factor $ax + b$.

RULE 1 Linear Factor Partial Fractions
The part of the partial-fraction decomposition of $R(x)$ that corresponds to the linear factor $ax + b$ of multiplicity n is a sum of n partial fractions, specifically

$$\frac{A_1}{ax+b} + \frac{A_2}{(ax+b)^2} + \cdots + \frac{A_n}{(ax+b)^n}, \tag{6}$$

where $A_1, A_2, \ldots, A_n$ are constants.

If *all* the factors of $Q(x)$ are linear, then the partial-fraction decomposition of $R(x)$ is a sum of expressions like the one in Eq. (6). The situation is especially simple if each of these linear factors is *nonrepeated*—that is, if each has multiplicity $n = 1$. In this case, the expression in (6) reduces to its first term, and the partial-fraction decomposition of $R(x)$ is a sum of such terms. The solutions in Examples 3 and 4 illustrate how the constant numerators can be determined.

EXAMPLE 3 Find $\displaystyle\int \frac{5}{(2x+1)(x-2)}\,dx$. (See Fig. 8.5.3.)

Solution The linear factors in the denominator are distinct, so we seek a partial-fraction decomposition of the form

$$\frac{5}{(2x+1)(x-2)} = \frac{A}{2x+1} + \frac{B}{x-2}.$$

To find the constants A and B, we multiply both sides of this *identity* by the left-hand (common) denominator $(2x+1)(x-2)$. The result is

$$5 = A(x-2) + B(2x+1) = (A+2B)x + (-2A+B).$$

Next we equate coefficients of x and coefficients of 1 on the left-hand and right-hand sides of this equation. This yields the equations

$$A + 2B = 0,$$
$$-2A + B = 5,$$

which we readily solve for $A = -2$, $B = 1$. Hence

$$\frac{5}{(2x+1)(x-2)} = \frac{-2}{2x+1} + \frac{1}{x-2},$$

and therefore

$$\int \frac{5}{(2x+1)(x-2)}\,dx = -\ln|2x+1| + \ln|x-2| + C = \ln\left|\frac{x-2}{2x+1}\right| + C. \quad\blacklozenge$$

FIGURE 8.5.3 Graphs of the function $f(x) = 5/[(2x+1)(x-2)]$ of Example 3 and its indefinite integral with $C = 0$. Which is which?

Rational Functions and Partial Fractions SECTION 8.5 511

EXAMPLE 4 Find $\int \dfrac{4x^2 - 3x - 4}{x^3 + x^2 - 2x}\,dx$. (See Fig. 8.5.4.)

Solution The rational function to be integrated is proper, so we immediately factor its denominator:

$$x^3 + x^2 - 2x = x(x^2 + x - 2) = x(x-1)(x+2).$$

We are dealing with three nonrepeated linear factors, so the partial-fraction decomposition has the form

$$\dfrac{4x^2 - 3x - 4}{x^3 + x^2 - 2x} = \dfrac{A}{x} + \dfrac{B}{x-1} + \dfrac{C}{x+2}.$$

To find the constants A, B, and C, we multiply both sides of this equation by the common denominator $x(x-1)(x+2)$ and find thereby that

$$4x^2 - 3x - 4 = A(x-1)(x+2) + Bx(x+2) + Cx(x-1). \qquad (7)$$

Then we collect coefficients of like powers of x on the right:

$$4x^2 - 3x - 4 = (A+B+C)x^2 + (A+2B-C)x + (-2A).$$

Because two polynomials are (identically) equal only if the coefficients of corresponding powers of x are the same, we conclude that

$$A + B + C = 4,$$
$$A + 2B - C = -3,$$
$$-2A = -4.$$

We solve these simultaneous equations and thus find that $A = 2$, $B = -1$, and $C = 3$.

There is an alternative way to find A, B, and C that is especially effective in the case of nonrepeated linear factors. Substitute the values of $x=0$, $x=1$, and $x=-2$ (the zeros of the linear factors of the denominator) into Eq. (7). Substituting $x=0$ into Eq. (7) immediately gives $-4 = -2A$, so $A = 2$. Substituting $x=1$ into Eq. (7) gives $-3 = 3B$, so $B = -1$. Substituting $x = -2$ gives $18 = 6C$, so $C = 3$.

With these values of $A=2$, $B=-1$, and $C=3$, however obtained, we find that

$$\int \dfrac{4x^2 - 3x - 4}{x^3 + x^2 - 2x}\,dx = \int \left(\dfrac{2}{x} - \dfrac{1}{x-1} + \dfrac{3}{x+2}\right) dx$$

$$= 2\ln|x| - \ln|x-1| + 3\ln|x+2| + C.$$

Laws of logarithms allow us to write this antiderivative in the more compact form

$$\int \dfrac{4x^2 - 3x - 4}{x^3 + x^2 - 2x}\,dx = \ln\left|\dfrac{x^2(x+2)^3}{x-1}\right| + C. \qquad \blacklozenge$$

EXAMPLE 5 Find $\int \dfrac{x^3 - 4x - 1}{x(x-1)^3}\,dx$.

Solution Here we have the linear factor x of multiplicity 1 but also the linear factor $x-1$ of multiplicity 3. According to Rule 1, the partial-fraction decomposition of the integrand has the form

$$\dfrac{x^3 - 4x - 1}{x(x-1)^3} = \dfrac{A}{x} + \dfrac{B}{x-1} + \dfrac{C}{(x-1)^2} + \dfrac{D}{(x-1)^3}.$$

To find the constants A, B, C, and D, we multiply both sides of this equation by the least common denominator $x(x-1)^3$. We find that

$$x^3 - 4x - 1 = A(x-1)^3 + Bx(x-1)^2 + Cx(x-1) + Dx.$$

FIGURE 8.5.4 Graphs of the function $f(x) = (4x^2 - 3x - 4)/(x^3 + x^2 - 2x)$ of Example 4 and its indefinite integral with $C=0$. Which is which?

We expand and then collect coefficients of like powers of x on the right-hand side. This yields

$$x^3 - 4x + 1 = (A+B)x^3 + (-3A - 2B + C)x^2 + (3A + B - C + D)x - A.$$

Then we equate coefficients of like powers of x on each side of this equation. We get the four simultaneous equations

$$A + B = 1,$$
$$-3A - 2B + C = 0,$$
$$3A + B - C + D = -4,$$
$$-A = -1.$$

The last equation gives $A = 1$, and then the first equation gives $B = 0$. Next, the second equation gives $C = 3$. When we substitute these values into the third equation, we finally get $D = -4$. Hence

$$\int \frac{x^3 - 4x - 1}{x(x-1)^3}\, dx = \int \left(\frac{1}{x} + \frac{3}{(x-1)^2} - \frac{4}{(x-1)^3} \right) dx$$

$$= \ln|x| - \frac{3}{x-1} + \frac{2}{(x-1)^2} + C. \quad \blacklozenge$$

Quadratic Factors

Suppose that $R(x) = P(x)/Q(x)$ is a proper rational fraction and that the irreducible quadratic factor $ax^2 + bx + c$ occurs n times in the factorization. That is, $(ax^2 + bx + c)^n$ is the highest power of $ax^2 + bx + c$ that divides evenly into $Q(x)$. As before, we call n the **multiplicity** of the quadratic factor $ax^2 + bx + c$.

RULE 2 Quadratic Factor Partial Fractions

The part of the partial-fraction decomposition of $R(x)$ that corresponds to the irreducible quadratic factor $ax^2 + bx + c$ of multiplicity n is a sum of n partial fractions. It has the form

$$\frac{B_1 x + C_1}{ax^2 + bx + c} + \frac{B_2 x + C_2}{(ax^2 + bx + c)^2} + \cdots + \frac{B_n x + C_n}{(ax^2 + bx + c)^n}, \quad (8)$$

where $B_1, B_2, \ldots, B_n, C_1, C_2, \ldots,$ and C_n are constants.

If $Q(x)$ has both linear and irreducible quadratic factors, then the partial-fraction decomposition of $R(x)$ is simply the sum of the expressions of the form in (6) that correspond to the linear factors plus the sum of the expressions of the form in (8) that correspond to the quadratic factors. In the case of an irreducible quadratic factor of multiplicity $n = 1$, the expression in (8) reduces to its first term alone.

The most important case is that of a nonrepeated quadratic factor of the sum of squares form $x^2 + k^2$ (where k is a positive constant). The corresponding partial fraction $(Bx + C)/(x^2 + k^2)$ is readily integrated by using the familiar integrals

$$\int \frac{x}{x^2 + k^2}\, dx = \frac{1}{2} \ln(x^2 + k^2) + C,$$

$$\int \frac{1}{x^2 + k^2}\, dx = \frac{1}{k} \arctan \frac{x}{k} + C.$$

We will discuss in Section 8.7 the integration of more general partial fractions involving irreducible quadratic factors.

EXAMPLE 6 Find $\int \dfrac{5x^3 - 3x^2 + 2x - 1}{x^4 + x^2}\, dx.$

Solution The denominator $x^4 + x^2 = x^2(x^2 + 1)$ is the product of an irreducible quadratic factor and a repeated linear factor. The partial-fraction decomposition of the integrand takes the form

$$\frac{5x^3 - 3x^2 + 2x - 1}{x^4 + x^2} = \frac{A}{x} + \frac{B}{x^2} + \frac{Cx + D}{x^2 + 1}.$$

We multiply both sides by $x^4 + x^2$ and obtain

$$5x^3 - 3x^2 + 2x - 1 = Ax(x^2 + 1) + B(x^2 + 1) + (Cx + D)x^2$$
$$= (A + C)x^3 + (B + D)x^2 + Ax + B.$$

As before, we equate coefficients of like powers of x. This yields the four simultaneous equations

$$A + C = 5,$$
$$B + D = -3,$$
$$A = 2,$$
$$B = -1.$$

These equations are easily solved for $A = 2$, $B = -1$, $C = 3$, and $D = -2$. Thus

$$\int \frac{5x^3 - 3x^2 + 2x - 1}{x^4 + x^2}\, dx = \int \left(\frac{2}{x} - \frac{1}{x^2} + \frac{3x - 2}{x^2 + 1} \right) dx$$
$$= 2\ln|x| + \frac{1}{x} + \frac{3}{2}\int \frac{2x\, dx}{x^2 + 1} - 2\int \frac{dx}{x^2 + 1}$$
$$= 2\ln|x| + \frac{1}{x} + \frac{3}{2}\ln(x^2 + 1) - 2\tan^{-1} x + C. \quad \blacklozenge$$

REMARK Numerical solution for the coefficients in a partial-fraction decomposition frequently is more tedious than in Examples 3 through 6. But computer algebra systems can do this work automatically. For instance, if we write

```
f := (5*x^3 - 3*x^2 + 2*x -1)/(x^4 + x^2)
```

then either the *Mathematica* command `Apart[ f ]` or the *Maple* command

```
convert( f, parfrac, x )
```

quickly produces the partial-fraction decomposition found in Example 6. Figure 8.5.5 shows this decomposition as generated by a graphing calculator.

FIGURE 8.5.5 Using the TI-92 `expand` command to produce the partial-fraction decomposition in Example 6.

8.5 TRUE/FALSE STUDY GUIDE
8.5 CONCEPTS: QUESTIONS AND DISCUSSION

1. Suppose that a factorization of the polynomial $Q(x)$ into two or more linear factors of the form $x - a$ is known. Explain why the methods of this section suffice to integrate any rational function of the form $f(x) = P(x)/Q(x)$. Will the integral
$$\int f(x)\,dx$$
ever be a rational function? If so, give an example illustrating this possibility.

2. Suppose that a factorization of the polynomial $Q(x)$ into two or more quadratic factors of the form $x^2 + a^2$ is known. Explain why the methods of this section suffice to integrate any rational function of the form $f(x) = P(x)/Q(x)$. Will the integral
$$\int f(x)\,dx$$
ever be a rational function? If so, give an example illustrating this possibility.

8.5 PROBLEMS

Find the integrals in Problems 1 through 36.

1. $\int \dfrac{x^2}{x+1}\,dx$
2. $\int \dfrac{x^3}{2x-1}\,dx$
3. $\int \dfrac{1}{x^2-3x}\,dx$
4. $\int \dfrac{x}{x^2+4x}\,dx$
5. $\int \dfrac{1}{x^2+x-6}\,dx$
6. $\int \dfrac{x^3}{x^2+x-6}\,dx$
7. $\int \dfrac{1}{x^3+4x}\,dx$
8. $\int \dfrac{1}{(x+1)(x^2+1)}\,dx$
9. $\int \dfrac{x^4}{x^2+4}\,dx$
10. $\int \dfrac{1}{(x^2+1)(x^2+4)}\,dx$
11. $\int \dfrac{x-1}{x+1}\,dx$
12. $\int \dfrac{2x^3-1}{x^2+1}\,dx$
13. $\int \dfrac{x^2+2x}{(x+1)^2}\,dx$
14. $\int \dfrac{2x-4}{x^2-x}\,dx$
15. $\int \dfrac{1}{x^2-4}\,dx$
16. $\int \dfrac{x^4}{x^2+4x+4}\,dx$
17. $\int \dfrac{x+10}{2x^2+5x-3}\,dx$
18. $\int \dfrac{x+1}{x^3-x^2}\,dx$
19. $\int \dfrac{x^2+1}{x^3+2x^2+x}\,dx$
20. $\int \dfrac{x^2+x}{x^3-x^2-2x}\,dx$
21. $\int \dfrac{4x^3-7x}{x^4-5x^2+4}\,dx$
22. $\int \dfrac{2x^2+3}{x^4-2x^2+1}\,dx$
23. $\int \dfrac{x^2}{(x+2)^3}\,dx$
24. $\int \dfrac{x^2+x}{(x^2-4)(x+4)}\,dx$
25. $\int \dfrac{1}{x^3+x}\,dx$
26. $\int \dfrac{6x^3-18x}{(x^2-1)(x^2-4)}\,dx$
27. $\int \dfrac{x+4}{x^3+4x}\,dx$
28. $\int \dfrac{4x^4+x+1}{x^5+x^4}\,dx$
29. $\int \dfrac{x}{(x+1)(x^2+1)}\,dx$
30. $\int \left(\dfrac{x+2}{x^2+4}\right)^2 dx$
31. $\int \dfrac{x^2-10}{2x^4+9x^2+4}\,dx$
32. $\int \dfrac{x^2}{x^4-1}\,dx$
33. $\int \dfrac{x^3+x^2+2x+3}{x^4+5x^2+6}\,dx$
34. $\int \dfrac{x^2+4}{(x^2+1)^2(x^2+2)}\,dx$
35. $\int \dfrac{x^4+3x^2-4x+5}{(x-1)^2(x^2+1)}\,dx$
36. $\int \dfrac{2x^3+5x^2-x+3}{(x^2+x-2)^2}\,dx$

In Problems 37 through 40, make a preliminary substitution before using the method of partial fractions to find the integrals.

37. $\int \dfrac{e^{4t}}{(e^{2t}-1)^3}\,dt$
38. $\int \dfrac{\cos\theta}{\sin^2\theta - \sin\theta - 6}\,d\theta$
39. $\int \dfrac{1+\ln t}{t(3+2\ln t)^2}\,dt$
40. $\int \dfrac{\sec^2 t}{\tan^3 t + \tan^2 t}\,dt$

In Problems 41 through 44, find the area of the region R between the curve and the x-axis over the given interval.

41. $y = \dfrac{x-9}{x^2-3x}$, $1 \leq x \leq 2$
42. $y = \dfrac{x+5}{3+2x-x^2}$, $0 \leq x \leq 2$
43. $y = \dfrac{3x-15-2x^2}{x^3-9x}$, $1 \leq x \leq 2$
44. $y = \dfrac{x^2+10x+16}{x^3+8x^2+16x}$, $2 \leq x \leq 5$

In Problems 45 through 48, find the volume of the solid obtained by revolving the region R around the y-axis.

45. The region R of Problem 41
46. The region R of Problem 42
47. The region R of Problem 43
48. The region R of Problem 44

In Problems 49 and 50, find the volume of the solid obtained by revolving the region R around the x-axis.

49. The region R of Problem 41

50. The region R of Problem 42

51. The plane region R shown in Fig. 8.5.6 is bounded by the curve

$$y^2 = \frac{1-x}{1+x}x^2, \quad 0 \leq x \leq 1.$$

Find the volume generated by revolving R around the x-axis.

FIGURE 8.5.6 The region of Problem 51.

52. Figure 8.5.7 shows the region bounded by the curve

$$y^2 = \frac{(1-x)^2}{(1+x)^2}x^4, \quad 0 \leq x \leq 1.$$

Find the volume generated by revolving this region around: (a) the x-axis; (b) the y-axis.

FIGURE 8.5.7 The region of Problem 52.

In Problems 53 through 56, write the general form of a partial-fraction decomposition of the given rational function $f(x)$ (with coefficients A, B, C, . . . remaining to be determined). Then use a computer algebra system (as in the remark following Example 6) to find the numerical values of the coefficients in the decomposition. Finally, find the indefinite integral $\int f(x)\,dx$ both by hand and using the computer algebra system, and resolve any apparent discrepancy between the two results.

53. $f(x) = \dfrac{98(x^3 - 50x + 100)}{x^2(x^2 - 12x + 35)}$

54. $f(x) = \dfrac{16(2x^3 + 77x - 99)}{(x^2 + 10x + 21)^2}$

55. $f(x) = \dfrac{324(x^3 + 8)}{(x^2 - x - 6)(x^2 + x - 20)^2}$

56. $f(x) = \dfrac{500(4x^4 - 23x^2 + 16)}{(x^2 - 4)^2(x - 3)^2}$

In Problems 57 and 58, first use a computer algebra system to find a partial-fraction decomposition of the given integrand. Then proceed as in Problems 53 through 56 to evaluate the given integral, both manually and automatically.

57. $\displaystyle\int \dfrac{2(54x^4 + 859x^2 - 581x + 85)}{18x^5 - 21x^4 + 458x^3 - 526x^2 + 200x - 25}\,dx$

58. $\displaystyle\int \dfrac{3750x^5 + 125x^4 - 9900x^3 - 495x^2 + 2x - 20}{625x^6 - 2450x^4 - 199x^2 - 4}\,dx$

In Problems 59 through 61, find values of the coefficients a, b, and c (not all zero) such that the given indefinite integral involves no logarithms, and is therefore a rational function.

59. $\displaystyle\int \dfrac{ax^2 + bx + c}{x^2(x-1)}\,dx$

60. $\displaystyle\int \dfrac{ax^2 + bx + c}{x^3(x-1)^2}\,dx$

61. $\displaystyle\int \dfrac{ax^2 + bx + c}{x^3(x-4)^4}\,dx$

8.6 TRIGONOMETRIC SUBSTITUTION

The method of *trigonometric substitution* can be very effective in dealing with integrals when the integrands contain algebraic expressions such as $(a^2 - u^2)^{1/2}$, $(u^2 - a^2)^{3/2}$, and $1/(a^2 + u^2)^2$. There are three basic trigonometric substitutions:

If the integral involves	then substitute	and use the identity
$a^2 - u^2$	$u = a\sin\theta$	$1 - \sin^2\theta = \cos^2\theta$
$a^2 + u^2$	$u = a\tan\theta$	$1 + \tan^2\theta = \sec^2\theta$
$u^2 - a^2$	$u = a\sec\theta$	$\sec^2\theta - 1 = \tan^2\theta$

516 CHAPTER 8 Techniques of Integration

What we mean by the substitution $u = a\sin\theta$ is, more precisely, the *inverse* trigonometric substitution

$$\theta = \sin^{-1}\frac{u}{a}, \qquad -\frac{\pi}{2} \leqq \theta \leqq \frac{\pi}{2},$$

where $|u| \leqq a$. Suppose, for example, that an integral contains the expression $(a^2 - u^2)^{1/2}$. Then this substitution yields

$$(a^2 - u^2)^{1/2} = (a^2 - a^2\sin^2\theta)^{1/2} = (a^2\cos^2\theta)^{1/2} = a\cos\theta.$$

We chose the nonnegative square root in the last step because $\cos\theta \geqq 0$ for $-\pi/2 \leqq \theta \leqq \pi/2$. Thus the troublesome factor $(a^2 - u^2)^{1/2}$ becomes $a\cos\theta$ and, meanwhile, $du = a\cos\theta\, d\theta$. If the trigonometric integral that results from the substitution can be evaluated by earlier methods of this chapter, the result will ordinarily involve $\theta = \sin^{-1}(u/a)$ and trigonometric functions of θ. The final step will be to express the answer in terms of the original variable. For this purpose the values of the various trigonometric functions can be read from the right triangle in Fig. 8.6.1, which contains an angle θ such that $\sin\theta = u/a$ (if u is negative, then θ is negative).

FIGURE 8.6.1 The reference triangle for the substitution $u = a\sin\theta$.

EXAMPLE 1 Evaluate $\displaystyle\int \frac{x^3}{\sqrt{1-x^2}}\, dx$, where $|x| < 1$.

Solution Here $a = 1$ and $u = x$, so we substitute

$$x = \sin\theta, \qquad dx = \cos\theta\, d\theta.$$

This gives

$$\int \frac{x^3}{\sqrt{1-x^2}}\, dx = \int \frac{\sin^3\theta \cos\theta}{\sqrt{1-\sin^2\theta}}\, d\theta$$

$$= \int \sin^3\theta\, d\theta = \int (\sin\theta)(1-\cos^2\theta)\, d\theta$$

$$= \tfrac{1}{3}\cos^3\theta - \cos\theta + C.$$

Figure 8.6.2, in which $\sin\theta = x$, reminds us that

$$\cos\theta = (1-\sin^2\theta)^{1/2} = \sqrt{1-x^2},$$

FIGURE 8.6.2 Reference triangle for the substitution $x = \sin\theta$.

so our final result in terms of x is

$$\int \frac{x^3}{\sqrt{1-x^2}}\, dx = \frac{1}{3}(1-x^2)^{3/2} - \sqrt{1-x^2} + C. \qquad \blacklozenge$$

Example 2 illustrates the use of trigonometric substitution to find integrals like those in Formulas (44) through (62) inside the back cover.

EXAMPLE 2 Find $\displaystyle\int \sqrt{a^2 - u^2}\, du$, where $|u| \leqq a$.

Solution The substitution $u = a\sin\theta$, $du = a\cos\theta\, d\theta$ gives

$$\int \sqrt{a^2 - u^2}\, du = \int \sqrt{a^2 - a^2\sin^2\theta}\, (a\cos\theta)\, d\theta$$

$$= \int a^2\cos^2\theta\, d\theta = \tfrac{1}{2}a^2 \int (1 + \cos 2\theta)\, d\theta$$

$$= \tfrac{1}{2}a^2 \left(\theta + \tfrac{1}{2}\sin 2\theta\right) + C = \tfrac{1}{2}a^2(\theta + \sin\theta\cos\theta) + C.$$

(We used the identity $\sin 2\theta = 2\sin\theta\cos\theta$ in the last step.) Now from Fig. 8.6.1 we see that

$$\sin\theta = \frac{u}{a} \quad \text{and} \quad \cos\theta = \frac{\sqrt{a^2-u^2}}{a}.$$

Hence

$$\int \sqrt{a^2-u^2}\, du = \frac{1}{2}a^2\left(\sin^{-1}\frac{u}{a} + \frac{u}{a}\cdot\frac{\sqrt{a^2-u^2}}{a}\right) + C$$

$$= \frac{u}{2}\sqrt{a^2-u^2} + \frac{a^2}{2}\sin^{-1}\frac{u}{a} + C.$$

Thus we have obtained Formula (54) inside the back cover. ◆

What we mean by the substitution $u = a\tan\theta$ in an integral that contains $a^2 + u^2$ is the substitution

$$\theta = \tan^{-1}\frac{u}{a}, \quad -\frac{\pi}{2} < \theta < \frac{\pi}{2}.$$

In this case

$$\sqrt{a^2+u^2} = \sqrt{a^2+a^2\tan^2\theta} = \sqrt{a^2\sec^2\theta} = a\sec\theta,$$

under the assumption that $a > 0$. We take the positive square root in the last step here because $\sec\theta > 0$ for $-\pi/2 < \theta < \pi/2$. The values of the various trigonometric functions of θ under this substitution can be read from the right triangle of Fig. 8.6.3, which shows a [positive or negative] acute angle θ such that $\tan\theta = u/a$.

FIGURE 8.6.3 The reference triangle for the substitution $u = a\tan\theta$.

EXAMPLE 3 Find $\displaystyle\int \frac{1}{(4x^2+9)^2}\, dx$.

Solution The factor $4x^2 + 9$ corresponds to $u^2 + a^2$ with $u = 2x$ and $a = 3$. Hence the substitution $u = a\tan\theta$ amounts to

$$2x = 3\tan\theta, \quad x = \tfrac{3}{2}\tan\theta, \quad dx = \tfrac{3}{2}\sec^2\theta\, d\theta.$$

This gives

$$\int \frac{1}{(4x^2+9)^2}\, dx = \int \frac{\tfrac{3}{2}\sec^2\theta}{(9\tan^2\theta+9)^2}\, d\theta$$

$$= \tfrac{3}{2}\int \frac{\sec^2\theta}{(9\sec^2\theta)^2}\, d\theta = \tfrac{1}{54}\int \frac{1}{\sec^2\theta}\, d\theta$$

$$= \tfrac{1}{54}\int \cos^2\theta\, d\theta = \tfrac{1}{108}(\theta + \sin\theta\cos\theta) + C.$$

(The integration in the last step is the same as in Example 2.) Now $\theta = \tan^{-1}(2x/3)$, and the triangle of Fig. 8.6.4 gives

$$\sin\theta = \frac{2x}{\sqrt{4x^2+9}}, \quad \cos\theta = \frac{3}{\sqrt{4x^2+9}}.$$

FIGURE 8.6.4 The reference triangle for Example 3.

Hence

$$\int \frac{1}{(4x^2+9)^2}\, dx = \frac{1}{108}\left[\tan^{-1}\left(\frac{2x}{3}\right) + \frac{2x}{\sqrt{4x^2+9}}\cdot\frac{3}{\sqrt{4x^2+9}}\right] + C$$

$$= \frac{1}{108}\tan^{-1}\left(\frac{2x}{3}\right) + \frac{x}{18(4x^2+9)} + C.$$ ◆

518   CHAPTER 8 Techniques of Integration

What we mean by the substitution $u = a\sec\theta$ in an integral that contains $u^2 - a^2$ is the substitution

$$\theta = \sec^{-1}\frac{u}{a}, \quad 0 \leq \theta \leq \pi,$$

where $|u| \geq a > 0$ (because of the domain and range of the inverse secant function). Then

$$\sqrt{u^2 - a^2} = \sqrt{a^2\sec^2\theta - a^2} = \sqrt{a^2\tan^2\theta} = \pm a\tan\theta.$$

Here we must take the plus sign if $u > a$, so that $0 < \theta < \pi/2$ and $\tan\theta > 0$. If $u < -a$, so $\pi/2 < \theta < \pi$ and $\tan\theta < 0$, we take the minus sign. In either case the values of the various trigonometric functions of θ can be read from the right triangle in Fig. 8.6.5.

FIGURE 8.6.5 The reference triangle for the substitution $u = a\sec\theta$.

EXAMPLE 4 Find $\displaystyle\int \frac{\sqrt{x^2 - 25}}{x}\,dx$, where $x > 5$.

Solution We substitute $x = 5\sec\theta$, $dx = 5\sec\theta\tan\theta\,d\theta$. Then

$$\sqrt{x^2 - 25} = \sqrt{25(\sec^2\theta - 1)} = 5\tan\theta,$$

because $x > 5$ implies that $0 < \theta < \pi/2$, so $\tan\theta > 0$. Hence this substitution gives

$$\int \frac{\sqrt{x^2 - 25}}{x}\,dx = \int \frac{5\tan\theta}{5\sec\theta}(5\sec\theta\tan\theta)\,d\theta$$

$$= 5\int \tan^2\theta\,d\theta = 5\int(\sec^2\theta - 1)\,d\theta$$

$$= 5\tan\theta - 5\theta + C = \sqrt{x^2 - 25} - 5\sec^{-1}\left(\frac{x}{5}\right) + C.$$

The substitutions in the last step may be read from the reference triangle in Fig. 8.6.6. ◆

FIGURE 8.6.6 The reference triangle for the substitution $x = 5\sec\theta$.

Hyperbolic substitutions may be used in a similar way—and with the same effect—as trigonometric substitutions. The three basic hyperbolic substitutions, which are not ordinarily memorized, are listed in the following table for reference.

If the integral involves	then substitute	and use the identity
$a^2 - u^2$	$u = a\tanh\theta$	$1 - \tanh^2\theta = \text{sech}^2\theta$
$a^2 + u^2$	$u = a\sinh\theta$	$1 + \sinh^2\theta = \cosh^2\theta$
$u^2 - a^2$	$u = a\cosh\theta$	$\cosh^2\theta - 1 = \sinh^2\theta$

EXAMPLE 5 Find $\displaystyle\int \frac{1}{\sqrt{x^2 - 1}}\,dx$, where $x > 1$.

Solution For purposes of comparison, we evaluate this integral both by trigonometric substitution and by hyperbolic substitution. The trigonometric substitution

$$x = \sec\theta, \quad dx = \sec\theta\tan\theta\,d\theta, \quad \tan\theta = \sqrt{x^2 - 1}$$

gives

$$\int \frac{1}{\sqrt{x^2 - 1}}\,dx = \int \frac{\sec\theta\tan\theta}{\tan\theta}\,d\theta = \int \sec\theta\,d\theta$$

$$= \ln|\sec\theta + \tan\theta| + C \quad \text{[Eq. (7), Section 8.4]}$$

$$= \ln\left|x + \sqrt{x^2 - 1}\right| + C.$$

Using instead the hyperbolic substitution $x = \cosh\theta$, $dx = \sinh\theta\,d\theta$, we have

$$\sqrt{x^2 - 1} = \sqrt{\cosh^2\theta - 1} = \sinh\theta.$$

We take the positive square root here, because $x > 1$ implies that $\theta = \cosh^{-1} x > 0$ and thus that $\sinh\theta > 0$. Hence

$$\int \frac{1}{\sqrt{x^2-1}}\,dx = \int \frac{\sinh\theta}{\sinh\theta}\,d\theta = \int 1\,d\theta = \theta + C = \cosh^{-1} x + C.$$

The two results appear to differ, but Eq. (35) in Section 7.6 shows that they are equivalent. ♦

8.6 TRUE/FALSE STUDY GUIDE

8.6 CONCEPTS: QUESTIONS AND DISCUSSION

1. For each of the three trigonometric substitutions discussed in this section, describe—perhaps by means of examples—the types of integrals for which substitution permits evaluation.
2. Explain why these trigonometric substitutions do not appear to suffice for the evaluation of integrals such as

$$\int \sqrt{1+x^3}\,dx \quad \text{and} \quad \int \sqrt{x^4-1}\,dx.$$

8.6 PROBLEMS

Use trigonometric substitutions to evaluate the integrals in Problems 1 through 36.

1. $\int \frac{1}{\sqrt{16-x^2}}\,dx$
2. $\int \frac{1}{\sqrt{4-9x^2}}\,dx$
3. $\int \frac{1}{x^2\sqrt{4-x^2}}\,dx$
4. $\int \frac{1}{x^2\sqrt{x^2-25}}\,dx$
5. $\int \frac{x^2}{\sqrt{16-x^2}}\,dx$
6. $\int \frac{x^2}{\sqrt{9-4x^2}}\,dx$
7. $\int \frac{1}{(9-16x^2)^{3/2}}\,dx$
8. $\int \frac{1}{(25+16x^2)^{3/2}}\,dx$
9. $\int \frac{\sqrt{x^2-1}}{x^2}\,dx$
10. $\int x^3\sqrt{4-x^2}\,dx$
11. $\int x^3\sqrt{9+4x^2}\,dx$
12. $\int \frac{x^3}{\sqrt{x^2+25}}\,dx$
13. $\int \frac{\sqrt{1-4x^2}}{x}\,dx$
14. $\int \frac{1}{\sqrt{1+x^2}}\,dx$
15. $\int \frac{1}{\sqrt{9+4x^2}}\,dx$
16. $\int \sqrt{1+4x^2}\,dx$
17. $\int \frac{x^2}{\sqrt{25-x^2}}\,dx$
18. $\int \frac{x^3}{\sqrt{25-x^2}}\,dx$
19. $\int \frac{x^2}{\sqrt{1+x^2}}\,dx$
20. $\int \frac{x^3}{\sqrt{1+x^2}}\,dx$
21. $\int \frac{x^2}{\sqrt{4+9x^2}}\,dx$
22. $\int (1-x^2)^{3/2}\,dx$
23. $\int \frac{1}{(1+x^2)^{3/2}}\,dx$
24. $\int \frac{1}{(4-x^2)^2}\,dx$
25. $\int \frac{1}{(4-x^2)^3}\,dx$
26. $\int \frac{1}{(4x^2+9)^3}\,dx$
27. $\int \sqrt{9+16x^2}\,dx$
28. $\int (9+16x^2)^{3/2}\,dx$
29. $\int \frac{\sqrt{x^2-25}}{x}\,dx$
30. $\int \frac{\sqrt{9x^2-16}}{x}\,dx$
31. $\int x^2\sqrt{x^2-1}\,dx$
32. $\int \frac{x^2}{\sqrt{4x^2-9}}\,dx$
33. $\int \frac{1}{(4x^2-1)^{3/2}}\,dx$
34. $\int \frac{1}{x^2\sqrt{4x^2-9}}\,dx$
35. $\int \frac{\sqrt{x^2-5}}{x^2}\,dx$
36. $\int (4x^2-5)^{3/2}\,dx$

Use hyperbolic substitutions to evaluate the integrals in Problems 37 through 41.

37. $\int \frac{1}{\sqrt{25+x^2}}\,dx$
38. $\int \sqrt{1+x^2}\,dx$
39. $\int \frac{\sqrt{x^2-4}}{x^2}\,dx$
40. $\int \frac{1}{\sqrt{1+9x^2}}\,dx$
41. $\int x^2\sqrt{1+x^2}\,dx$

42. Use the result of Example 2 to show that the area bounded by the ellipse

$$\frac{x^2}{a^2} + \frac{y^2}{b^2} = 1$$

of Fig. 8.6.7 is given by $A = \pi ab$. (The special case $b = a$ is the familiar circular area formula $A = \pi a^2$.)

FIGURE 8.6.7 The ellipse of Problem 42.

43. Derive the formula $A = \frac{1}{2}a^2\theta$ for the area of a circular sector with radius a and central angle θ by calculating and adding the areas of the right triangle OAC and the region ABC of Fig. 8.6.8.

FIGURE 8.6.8 The circular sector of Problem 43.

44. Compute the arc length of the parabola $y = x^2$ over the interval $[0, 1]$.

45. Compute the area of the surface obtained by revolving around the x-axis the parabolic arc of Problem 44.

46. Show that the length of one arch of the sine curve $y = \sin x$ is equal to half the circumference of the ellipse $x^2 + \frac{1}{2}y^2 = 1$. [*Suggestion:* Substitute $x = \cos\theta$ into the arc-length integral for the ellipse.] (See Fig. 8.6.9.)

FIGURE 8.6.9 Two arcs with the same length (Problem 46).

47. Compute the arc length of the curve $y = \ln x$ over the interval $[1, 2]$.

48. Compute the area of the surface obtained by revolving around the y-axis the curve of Problem 47.

FIGURE 8.6.10 The torus of Problem 49.

49. A torus (see Fig. 8.6.10) is obtained by revolving around the y-axis the circle
$$(x-b)^2 + y^2 = a^2 \quad (0 < a \leq b).$$
Show that the surface area of the torus is $4\pi^2 ab$.

50. Find the area under the curve $y = \sqrt{9 + x^2}$ over the interval $[0, 4]$.

51. Find the area of the surface obtained by revolving around the x-axis the curve $y = \sin x$, $0 \leq x \leq \pi$. (See Fig. 8.6.11.)

FIGURE 8.6.11 The pointed football of Problem 51.

52. An ellipsoid of revolution is obtained by revolving the ellipse $x^2/a^2 + y^2/b^2 = 1$ around the x-axis. Suppose that $a > b$. Show that the ellipsoid has surface area
$$A = 2\pi ab \left[\frac{b}{a} + \frac{a}{c} \sin^{-1}\left(\frac{c}{a}\right) \right],$$
where $c = \sqrt{a^2 - b^2}$. Assume that $a \approx b$, so that $c \approx 0$ and $\sin^{-1}(c/a) \approx c/a$. Conclude that $A \approx 4\pi a^2$.

53. Suppose that $b > a$ for the ellipsoid of revolution of Problem 52. Show that its surface area is then
$$A = 2\pi ab \left[\frac{b}{a} + \frac{a}{c} \ln\left(\frac{b+c}{a}\right) \right],$$
where $c = \sqrt{b^2 - a^2}$. Use the fact that $\ln(1+x) \approx x$ if $x \approx 0$, and thereby conclude that $A \approx 4\pi a^2$ if $a \approx b$.

54. A road is to be built from the point $(2, 1)$ to the point $(5, 3)$, following the path of the parabola
$$y = -1 + 2\sqrt{x-1}.$$
Calculate the length of this road (the units on the coordinate axes are in miles). [*Suggestion:* Substitute $x = \sec^2\theta$ into the arc-length integral.]

55. Suppose that the cost of the road in Problem 54 is $\sqrt{x}$ million dollars per mile. Calculate the total cost of the road.

56. A kite is flying at a height of 500 ft and at a horizontal distance of 100 ft from the stringholder on the ground. The kite string weighs 1/16 oz/ft and is hanging in the shape of the parabola $y = x^2/20$ that joins the stringholder at $(0, 0)$ to the kite at $(100, 500)$ (Fig. 8.6.12). Calculate the work (in foot-pounds) done in lifting the kite string from the ground to its present position.

FIGURE 8.6.12 The kite string of Problem 56.

8.7 INTEGRALS INVOLVING QUADRATIC POLYNOMIALS

Many integrals containing a square root or negative power of a quadratic polynomial $ax^2 + bx + c$ can be simplified by the process of *completing the square*. For example,

$$x^2 + 2x + 2 = (x+1)^2 + 1,$$

and hence the substitution $u = x+1$, $du = dx$ yields

$$\int \frac{1}{x^2 + 2x + 2}\, dx = \int \frac{1}{u^2 + 1}\, du = \tan^{-1} u + C = \tan^{-1}(x+1) + C.$$

In general, the objective is to convert $ax^2 + bx + c$ into either a sum or difference of two squares—either $u^2 \pm a^2$ or $a^2 - u^2$—so that the method of trigonometric substitution can then be used. To see how this works in practice, suppose first that $a = 1$, so that the quadratic in question has the form $x^2 + bx + c$. The sum $x^2 + bx$ of the first two terms can be completed to a perfect square by adding $b^2/4$, the square of half the coefficient of x, and in turn subtracting $b^2/4$ from the constant term c. This gives

$$x^2 + bx + c = \left(x^2 + bx + \frac{b^2}{4}\right) + \left(c - \frac{b^2}{4}\right)$$

$$= \left(x + \frac{b}{2}\right)^2 + \left(c - \frac{b^2}{4}\right).$$

With $u = x + \frac{1}{2}b$, this result is of the form $u^2 + A^2$ or $u^2 - A^2$, depending on the sign of $c - \frac{1}{4}b^2$. If the coefficient a of x^2 is not 1, we first factor it out and proceed as before:

$$ax^2 + bx + c = a\left(x^2 + \frac{b}{a}x + \frac{c}{a}\right).$$

EXAMPLE 1 Find $\int \dfrac{1}{9x^2 + 6x + 5}\, dx$.

Solution The first step is to complete the square:

$$9x^2 + 6x + 5 = 9\left(x^2 + \tfrac{2}{3}x\right) + 5 = 9\left(x^2 + \tfrac{2}{3}x + \tfrac{1}{9}\right) - 1 + 5$$

$$= 9\left(x + \tfrac{1}{3}\right)^2 + 4 = (3x+1)^2 + 2^2.$$

Hence

$$\int \frac{1}{9x^2 + 6x + 5}\, dx = \int \frac{1}{(3x+1)^2 + 4}\, dx$$

$$= \frac{1}{3}\int \frac{1}{u^2 + 4}\, du \qquad (u = 3x+1)$$

$$= \frac{1}{6}\int \frac{\frac{1}{2}}{\left(\frac{1}{2}u\right)^2 + 1}\, du$$

$$= \frac{1}{6}\int \frac{1}{v^2 + 1}\, dv \qquad (v = \tfrac{1}{2}u)$$

$$= \frac{1}{6}\tan^{-1} v + C = \frac{1}{6}\tan^{-1}\left(\frac{u}{2}\right) + C$$

$$= \frac{1}{6}\tan^{-1}\left(\frac{3x+1}{2}\right) + C. \qquad \blacklozenge$$

EXAMPLE 2 Find $\int \frac{1}{\sqrt{9 + 16x - 4x^2}} \, dx$.

Solution First we complete the square:
$$9 + 16x - 4x^2 = 9 - 4(x^2 - 4x)$$
$$= 9 - 4(x^2 - 4x + 4) + 16 = 25 - 4(x - 2)^2.$$

Hence
$$\int \frac{1}{\sqrt{9 + 16x - 4x^2}} \, dx = \int \frac{1}{\sqrt{25 - 4(x - 2)^2}} \, dx$$
$$= \frac{1}{5} \int \frac{1}{\sqrt{1 - \frac{4}{25}(x - 2)^2}} \, dx$$
$$= \frac{1}{2} \int \frac{1}{\sqrt{1 - u^2}} \, du \qquad \left(u = \tfrac{2}{5}(x - 2)\right)$$
$$= \tfrac{1}{2} \sin^{-1} u + C = \tfrac{1}{2} \sin^{-1}\left(\tfrac{2}{5}(x - 2)\right) + C.$$

An alternative approach is to make the trigonometric substitution
$$2(x - 2) = 5 \sin \theta, \qquad 2 \, dx = 5 \cos \theta \, d\theta$$
immediately after completing the square. This yields
$$\int \frac{1}{\sqrt{9 + 16x - 4x^2}} \, dx = \int \frac{1}{\sqrt{25 - 4(x - 2)^2}} \, dx$$
$$= \int \frac{\tfrac{5}{2} \cos \theta}{\sqrt{25 - 25 \sin^2 \theta}} \, d\theta$$
$$= \frac{1}{2} \int 1 \, d\theta = \frac{1}{2} \theta + C$$
$$= \frac{1}{2} \arcsin \frac{2(x - 2)}{5} + C. \qquad \blacklozenge$$

Some integrals that contain a quadratic expression can be split into two simpler integrals. Examples 3 and 4 illustrate this technique.

EXAMPLE 3 Find $\int \frac{2x + 3}{9x^2 + 6x + 5} \, dx$.

Solution Because $D_x(9x^2 + 6x + 5) = 18x + 6$, this would be a simpler integral if the numerator $2x + 3$ were a constant multiple of $18x + 6$. Our strategy is to write
$$2x + 3 = A \cdot (18x + 6) + B$$
so that we can split the given integral into a sum of two integrals, one of which has numerator $18x + 6$ in its integrand. By matching coefficients in
$$2x + 3 = 18Ax + (6A + B),$$
we find that $A = \tfrac{1}{9}$ and $B = \tfrac{7}{3}$. Hence
$$\int \frac{2x + 3}{9x^2 + 6x + 5} \, dx = \frac{1}{9} \int \frac{18x + 6}{9x^2 + 6x + 5} \, dx + \frac{7}{3} \int \frac{1}{9x^2 + 6 + 5} \, dx.$$

The first integral on the right is a logarithm, and the second is given in Example 1. Thus
$$\int \frac{2x + 3}{9x^2 + 6x + 5} \, dx = \frac{1}{9} \ln(9x^2 + 6x + 5) + \frac{7}{18} \tan^{-1}\left(\frac{3x + 1}{2}\right) + C.$$

Alternatively, we could first complete the square in the denominator. The substitution $u = 3x + 1$, $x = \frac{1}{3}(u - 1)$, $dx = \frac{1}{3} du$ then gives

$$\int \frac{2x + 3}{(3x + 1)^2 + 4} dx = \int \frac{\frac{2}{3}(u - 1) + 3}{u^2 + 4} \cdot \frac{1}{3} du$$

$$= \frac{1}{9} \int \frac{2u}{u^2 + 4} du + \frac{7}{9} \int \frac{1}{u^2 + 4} du$$

$$= \frac{1}{9} \ln(u^2 + 4) + \frac{7}{18} \tan^{-1}\left(\frac{u}{2}\right) + C$$

$$= \frac{1}{9} \ln(9x^2 + 6x + 5) + \frac{7}{18} \tan^{-1}\left(\frac{3x + 1}{2}\right) + C. \quad \blacklozenge$$

EXAMPLE 4 Find $\int \frac{2 + 6x}{(3 + 2x - x^2)^2} dx$ given $|x - 1| < 2$.

Solution Because $D_x(3 + 2x - x^2) = 2 - 2x$, we first write

$$\int \frac{2 + 6x}{(3 + 2x - x^2)^2} dx = -3 \int \frac{2 - 2x}{(3 + 2x - x^2)^2} dx + 8 \int \frac{1}{(3 + 2x - x^2)^2} dx.$$

Then let $u = 3 + 2x - x^2$, $du = (2 - 2x) dx$ in the first integral to obtain

$$-3 \int \frac{2 - 2x}{(3 + 2x - x^2)^2} dx = -3 \int \frac{du}{u^2} = \frac{3}{u} + C_1 = \frac{3}{3 + 2x - x^2} + C_1.$$

Therefore,

$$\int \frac{2 + 6x}{(3 + 2x - x^2)^2} dx = \frac{3}{3 + 2x - x^2} + 8 \int \frac{1}{(3 + 2x - x^2)^2} dx. \quad (1)$$

(We can drop the constant C_1 because it can be absorbed by the constant C, which we will obtain when we evaluate the remaining integral.) To evaluate the remaining integral, we complete the square:

$$3 + 2x - x^2 = 4 - (x^2 - 2x + 1) = 4 - (x - 1)^2.$$

Because $|x - 1| < 2$, this suggests the substitution

$$x - 1 = 2 \sin \theta, \qquad dx = 2 \cos \theta \, d\theta,$$

with which

$$3 + 2x - x^2 = 4 - 4 \sin^2 \theta = 4 \cos^2 \theta.$$

This substitution yields

$$8 \int \frac{1}{(3 + 2x - x^2)^2} dx = 8 \int \frac{2 \cos \theta}{(4 \cos^2 \theta)^2} d\theta = \int \sec^3 \theta \, d\theta$$

$$= \tfrac{1}{2} \sec \theta \tan \theta + \tfrac{1}{2} \int \sec \theta \, d\theta \qquad \text{[Section 8.3, Eq. (5)]}$$

$$= \tfrac{1}{2} \sec \theta \tan \theta + \tfrac{1}{2} \ln |\sec \theta + \tan \theta| + C$$

$$= \frac{x - 1}{3 + 2x - x^2} + \tfrac{1}{2} \ln \left| \frac{x + 1}{\sqrt{3 + 2x - x^2}} \right| + C. \quad (2)$$

In the last step we read the values of $\sec \theta$ and $\tan \theta$ from the right triangle in Fig. 8.7.1. When we substitute Eq. (2) into Eq. (1), we finally obtain the result

$$\int \frac{2 + 6x}{(3 + 2x - x^2)^2} dx = \frac{x + 2}{3 + 2x - x^2} + \frac{1}{2} \ln \left| \frac{x + 1}{\sqrt{3 + 2x - x^2}} \right| + C. \quad \blacklozenge$$

FIGURE 8.7.1 The reference triangle for Example 4.

The method of Example 4 can be used to evaluate a general integral of the form

$$\int \frac{Ax + B}{(ax^2 + bx + c)^n}\, dx, \tag{3}$$

where n is a positive integer. By splitting such an integral into two simpler ones and then completing the square in the quadratic expression in the denominator, the problem of evaluating the integral in Eq. (3) can be reduced to that of computing

$$\int \frac{1}{(a^2 \pm u^2)^n}\, du. \tag{4}$$

If the sign in the denominator of Eq. (4) is the plus sign, then the substitution $u = a \tan\theta$ transforms the integral into the form

$$\int \cos^m \theta\, d\theta.$$

(See Problem 35.) This integral can be handled by the methods of Section 8.4 or by using the reduction formula

$$\int \cos^k \theta\, d\theta = \frac{1}{k} \cos^{k-1}\theta \sin\theta + \frac{k-1}{k} \int \cos^{k-2}\theta\, d\theta$$

of Problem 54 in Section 8.3.

If the sign of the denominator in Eq. (4) is the minus sign, then the substitution $u = a \sin\theta$ transforms the integral into the form

$$\int \sec^m \theta\, d\theta.$$

(See Problem 36.) This integral may be evaluated with the aid of the reduction formula

$$\int \sec^k \theta\, d\theta = \frac{1}{k-1} \sec^{k-2}\theta \tan\theta + \frac{k-2}{k-1} \int \sec^{k-2}\theta\, d\theta$$

[Eq. (5) of Section 8.3].

8.7 TRUE/FALSE STUDY GUIDE

8.7 CONCEPTS: QUESTIONS AND DISCUSSION

1. Suppose that the factorization of the polynomial $Q(x)$ yields two or more quadratic factors. Explain why the methods of this section suffice to integrate any rational function of the form $f(x) = P(x)/Q(x)$.
2. Will the integral $\int f(x)\, dx$ in Question 1 ever be a rational function? If so, give an example illustrating this possibility.

8.7 PROBLEMS

Evaluate the antiderivatives in Problems 1 through 34.

1. $\displaystyle \int \frac{1}{x^2 + 4x + 5}\, dx$

2. $\displaystyle \int \frac{2x + 5}{x^2 + 4x + 5}\, dx$

3. $\displaystyle \int \frac{5 - 3x}{x^2 + 4x + 5}\, dx$

4. $\displaystyle \int \frac{x + 1}{(x^2 + 4x + 5)^2}\, dx$

5. $\displaystyle \int \frac{1}{\sqrt{3 - 2x - x^2}}\, dx$

6. $\displaystyle \int \frac{x + 3}{\sqrt{3 - 2x - x^2}}\, dx$

7. $\displaystyle \int x\sqrt{3 - 2x - x^2}\, dx$

8. $\displaystyle \int \frac{1}{4x^2 + 4x - 3}\, dx$

9. $\displaystyle \int \frac{3x + 2}{4x^2 + 4x - 3}\, dx$

10. $\displaystyle \int \sqrt{4x^2 + 4x - 3}\, dx$

11. $\displaystyle \int \frac{1}{x^2 + 4x + 13}\, dx$

12. $\displaystyle \int \frac{1}{\sqrt{2x - x^2}}\, dx$

13. $\displaystyle \int \frac{1}{3 + 2x - x^2}\, dx$

14. $\displaystyle \int x\sqrt{8 + 2x - x^2}\, dx$

15. $\displaystyle\int \frac{2x-5}{x^2+2x+2}\,dx$

16. $\displaystyle\int \frac{2x-1}{4x^2+4x-15}\,dx$

17. $\displaystyle\int \frac{x}{\sqrt{5+12x-9x^2}}\,dx$

18. $\displaystyle\int (3x-2)\sqrt{9x^2+12x+8}\,dx$

19. $\displaystyle\int (7-2x)\sqrt{9+16x-4x^2}\,dx$

20. $\displaystyle\int \frac{2x+3}{\sqrt{x^2+2x+5}}\,dx$

21. $\displaystyle\int \frac{x+4}{(6x-x^2)^{3/2}}\,dx$

22. $\displaystyle\int \frac{x-1}{(x^2+1)^2}\,dx$

23. $\displaystyle\int \frac{2x+3}{(4x^2+12x+13)^2}\,dx$

24. $\displaystyle\int \frac{x^3}{(1-x^2)^4}\,dx$

25. $\displaystyle\int \frac{3x-1}{x^2+x+1}\,dx$

26. $\displaystyle\int \frac{3x-1}{(x^2+x+1)^2}\,dx$

27. $\displaystyle\int \frac{1}{(x^2-4)^2}\,dx$

28. $\displaystyle\int (x-x^2)^{3/2}\,dx$

29. $\displaystyle\int \frac{x^2+1}{x^3+x^2+x}\,dx$

30. $\displaystyle\int \frac{x^2+2}{(x^2+1)^2}\,dx$

31. $\displaystyle\int \frac{2x^2+3}{x^4-2x^2+1}\,dx$

32. $\displaystyle\int \frac{x^2+4}{(x^2+1)^2(x^2+2)}\,dx$

33. $\displaystyle\int \frac{3x+1}{(x^2+2x+5)^2}\,dx$

34. $\displaystyle\int \frac{x^3-2x}{x^2+2x+2}\,dx$

35. Show that the substitution $u = a\tan\theta$ gives
$$\int \frac{1}{(a^2+u^2)^n}\,du = \frac{1}{a^{2n-1}}\int \cos^{2n-2}\theta\,d\theta.$$

36. Show that the substitution $u = a\sin\theta$ gives
$$\int \frac{1}{(a^2-u^2)^n}\,du = \frac{1}{a^{2n-1}}\int \sec^{2n-2}\theta\,d\theta.$$

In Problems 37 through 39 the region R lies between the curve $y = 1/(x^2 - 2x + 5)$ and the x-axis from $x = 0$ to $x = 5$.

37. Find the area of the region R.

38. Find the volume of the solid generated by revolving R around the y-axis.

39. Find the volume of the solid generated by revolving R around the x-axis.

In Problems 40 through 42 the region R lies between the curve $y = 1/(4x^2 - 20x + 29)$ and the x-axis from $x = 1$ to $x = 4$.

40. Find the area of the region R.

41. Find the volume of the solid generated by revolving R around the y-axis.

42. Find the volume of the solid generated by revolving R around the x-axis.

43. Your task is to build a road that joins the points $(0, 0)$ and $(3, 2)$ and follows the path of the circle with equation $(4x + 4)^2 + (4y - 19)^2 = 377$. Find the length of this road. (Units on the coordinate axes are measured in miles.)

44. Suppose that the road of Problem 43 (Fig. 8.7.2) costs $10/(1+x)$ million dollars per mile. (a) Calculate its total cost. (b) With the same cost per mile, calculate the total cost of a straight line road from $(0, 0)$ to $(3, 2)$. You should find that it is *more* expensive than the *longer* circular road!

FIGURE 8.7.2 According to Problem 44, the circular-arc road is less expensive to construct than the shorter straight road!

In Problems 45 through 47, factor the denominator by first noting by inspection a root r of the denominator and then employing long division by $x - r$. Finally, use the method of partial fractions to aid in finding the indicated antiderivative.

45. $\displaystyle\int \frac{3x+2}{x^3+x^2-2}\,dx$

46. $\displaystyle\int \frac{1}{x^3+8}\,dx$

47. $\displaystyle\int \frac{x^4+2x^2}{x^3-1}\,dx$

48. (a) Find constants a and b such that
$$x^4 + 1 = (x^2 + ax + 1)(x^2 + bx + 1).$$
(b) Prove that
$$\int_0^1 \frac{x^2+1}{x^4+1}\,dx = \frac{\pi}{2\sqrt{2}}.$$
[*Suggestion:* If u and v are positive numbers and $uv = 1$, then
$$\arctan u + \arctan v = \frac{1}{2}\pi.]$$

49. Factor $x^4 + x^2 + 1$ with the aid of ideas suggested in Problem 48. Then evaluate
$$\int \frac{2x^3+3x}{x^4+x^2+1}\,dx.$$

50. Evaluate the integral to show that
$$\int_0^1 \frac{16(x-1)}{x^4-2x^3+4x-4}\,dx = \pi.$$
This integral was (in effect) used by D. Bailey, P. Borwein, and S. Plouffe as a starting point in their recent determination of the 5 billionth hexagesimal digit of the number π (it's a 9). [*Suggestion:* Long divide to verify that $x^2 - 2$ is a factor of the denominator and to find the other factor.]

In Problems 51 through 54, write the general form of a partial-fraction decomposition of the given rational function $f(x)$ (with coefficients $A, B, C, \ldots$ remaining to be determined). Then use a computer algebra system (as in the remark following Example 6 in Section 8.5) to find the numerical values of the coefficients in the decomposition. Finally, find the indefinite integral $\int f(x)\,dx$

both by hand and by using the computer algebra system, and resolve any apparent discrepancy between the two results.

51. $\int \dfrac{7x^4 + 28x^3 + 50x^2 + 67x + 23}{(x-1)(x^2 + 2x + 2)^2}\, dx$

52. $\int \dfrac{35 + 84x + 55x^2 - x^3 + 5x^4 - 4x^5}{(x^2 + 1)^2 (x^2 + 6x + 10)}\, dx$

53. $\int \dfrac{32x^5 + 16x^4 + 19x^3 - 98x^2 - 107x - 15}{(x^2 - 2x - 15)(4x^2 + 4x + 5)^2}\, dx$

54. $\int \dfrac{63x^5 + 302x^4 + 480x^3 + 376x^2 - 240x - 300}{(x^2 + 6x + 10)^2 (4x^2 + 4x + 5)^2}\, dx$

In Problems 55 through 58, find values of the coefficients a, b, c, and d (not all zero) such that the given indefinite integral involves no logarithms or inverse tangents, and is therefore a rational function.

55. $\int \dfrac{ax + b}{(x^2 + 4x + 5)^2}\, dx$

56. $\int \dfrac{ax^2 + bx + c}{(x^2 + 4x + 5)^2}\, dx$

57. $\int \dfrac{ax^2 + bx + c}{(x^2 + 2x + 2)(x^2 + 4x + 5)}\, dx$

58. $\int \dfrac{ax^3 + bx^2 + cx + d}{(x^2 + 4x + 5)^3}\, dx$

8.8 IMPROPER INTEGRALS

To show the existence of the definite integral, we have relied until now on the existence theorem stated in Section 5.4. This is the theorem that guarantees the existence of the definite integral

$$\int_a^b f(x)\, dx$$

provided that the function f is *continuous* on the closed and bounded interval $[a, b]$. Certain applications of calculus, however, lead naturally to the formulation of integrals in which either

1. The interval of integration is not bounded; it has one of the forms

$$[a, +\infty), \quad (-\infty, a], \quad \text{or} \quad (-\infty, +\infty); \quad \text{or}$$

2. The integrand has an infinite discontinuity at some point c in the interval $[a, b]$:

$$\lim_{x \to c} f(x) = \pm\infty.$$

An example of Case 1 is the integral

$$\int_1^\infty \dfrac{1}{x^2}\, dx.$$

A geometric interpretation of this integral is the area of the unbounded region (shaded in Fig. 8.8.1) that lies between the curve $y = 1/x^2$ and the x-axis and to the right of the vertical line $x = 1$. An example of Case 2 is the integral

$$\int_0^1 \dfrac{1}{\sqrt{x}}\, dx.$$

This integral may be interpreted as the area of the unbounded region (shaded in Fig. 8.8.2) that lies under the curve $y = 1/\sqrt{x}$ from $x = 0$ to $x = 1$.

Such integrals are called **improper integrals.** The natural interpretation of an improper integral is the area of an unbounded region. It is perhaps surprising that such an area can nevertheless be finite, and here we shall show how to find such areas—that is, how to evaluate improper integrals.

To see why improper integrals require special care, let us consider the integral

$$\int_{-1}^1 \dfrac{1}{x^2}\, dx.$$

FIGURE 8.8.1 The shaded area cannot be measured by using our earlier techniques.

FIGURE 8.8.2 Another area that must be measured with an improper integral.

This integral is improper because its integrand $f(x) = 1/x^2$ is unbounded as $x \to 0$, and thus f is not continuous at $x = 0$. If we thoughtlessly applied the fundamental theorem of calculus, we would obtain

$$\int_{-1}^{1} \frac{1}{x^2}\, dx = \left[-\frac{1}{x}\right]_{-1}^{1} = (-1) - (+1) = -2. \quad \textbf{(Wrong!)}$$

The negative answer is obviously incorrect, because the area shown in Fig. 8.8.3 lies above the x-axis and hence the integral cannot be negative. This simple example emphasizes that we cannot ignore the hypotheses—*continuous* function and *bounded closed* interval—of the fundamental theorem of calculus.

FIGURE 8.8.3 The area under $y = 1/x^2$, $-1 \leq x \leq 1$.

Infinite Limits of Integration

Suppose that the function f is continuous and nonnegative on the unbounded interval $[a, +\infty)$. Then, for any fixed $t > a$, the area $A(t)$ of the region under $y = f(x)$ from $x = a$ to $x = t$ (shaded in Fig. 8.8.4) is given by the (ordinary) definite integral

$$A(t) = \int_a^t f(x)\, dx.$$

Suppose now that we let $t \to +\infty$ and find that the limit of $A(t)$ exists. Then we may regard this limit as the area of the unbounded region that lies under $y = f(x)$ and over $[a, +\infty)$. For f continuous on $[a, +\infty)$, we therefore *define*

$$\int_a^\infty f(x)\, dx = \lim_{t \to \infty} \int_a^t f(x)\, dx \qquad (1)$$

FIGURE 8.8.4 The shaded area $A(t)$ exists provided that f is continuous.

provided that this limit exists (as a finite real number). If this limit exists, we say that the improper integral on the left **converges;** if the limit does not exist, we say that the improper integral **diverges.** If $f(x)$ is nonnegative on $[a, +\infty)$, then the limit in Eq. (1) either exists or is infinite, and in the latter case we write

$$\int_a^\infty f(x)\, dx = +\infty$$

and say that the improper integral **diverges to infinity.**

If the function f has both positive and negative values on $[a, +\infty)$, then the improper integral can diverge *by oscillation*—that is, without diverging to infinity. This occurs with $\int_0^\infty \sin x\, dx$, because it is easy to verify that $\int_0^t \sin x\, dx$ is zero if t is an even integral multiple of π but is 2 if t is an odd integral multiple of π. Thus $\int_0^t \sin x\, dx$ oscillates between 0 and 2 as $t \to +\infty$, and so the limit in Eq. (1) does not exist.

We handle an infinite lower limit of integration similarly: We define

$$\int_{-\infty}^b f(x)\, dx = \lim_{t \to -\infty} \int_t^b f(x)\, dx \qquad (2)$$

provided that the limit exists. If the function f is continuous on the whole real line, we define

$$\int_{-\infty}^\infty f(x)\, dx = \int_{-\infty}^c f(x)\, dx + \int_c^\infty f(x)\, dx \qquad (3)$$

for any convenient choice of c, provided that both improper integrals on the right-hand side converge. Note that the leftmost integral in Eq. (3) is *not* necessarily equal to

$$\lim_{t \to \infty} \int_{-t}^t f(x)\, dx.$$

(See Problem 52.)

It makes no difference what value of c is used in Eq. (3), because if $c < d$, then

$$\int_{-\infty}^{c} f(x)\,dx + \int_{c}^{\infty} f(x)\,dx = \int_{-\infty}^{c} f(x)\,dx + \int_{c}^{d} f(x)\,dx + \int_{d}^{\infty} f(x)\,dx$$

$$= \int_{-\infty}^{d} f(x)\,dx + \int_{d}^{\infty} f(x)\,dx,$$

under the assumption that the limits involved all exist.

EXAMPLE 1 Investigate the improper integrals

(a) $\displaystyle\int_{1}^{\infty} \frac{1}{x^2}\,dx$ and

(b) $\displaystyle\int_{-\infty}^{0} \frac{1}{\sqrt{1-x}}\,dx.$

Solution

(a) $\displaystyle\int_{1}^{\infty} \frac{1}{x^2}\,dx = \lim_{t \to \infty} \int_{1}^{t} \frac{1}{x^2}\,dx = \lim_{t \to \infty} \left[-\frac{1}{x}\right]_{1}^{t} = \lim_{t \to \infty}\left(-\frac{1}{t}+1\right) = 1.$

Thus this improper integral converges, and this is the area of the region shaded in Fig. 8.8.1.

(b) $\displaystyle\int_{-\infty}^{0} \frac{1}{\sqrt{1-x}}\,dx = \lim_{t \to -\infty} \int_{t}^{0} \frac{1}{\sqrt{1-x}}\,dx$

$$= \lim_{t \to -\infty}\left[-2\sqrt{1-x}\right]_{t}^{0} = \lim_{t \to -\infty}(2\sqrt{1-t}-2) = +\infty.$$

FIGURE 8.8.5 The unbounded region represented by the improper integral in Example 1(b).

Thus the second improper integral of this example diverges to $+\infty$ (Fig. 8.8.5).

EXAMPLE 2 Investigate the improper integral $\displaystyle\int_{-\infty}^{\infty} \frac{1}{1+x^2}\,dx.$

Solution The choice $c = 0$ in Eq. (3) gives

$$\int_{-\infty}^{\infty} \frac{1}{1+x^2}\,dx = \int_{-\infty}^{0} \frac{1}{1+x^2}\,dx + \int_{0}^{\infty} \frac{1}{1+x^2}\,dx$$

$$= \lim_{s \to -\infty} \int_{s}^{0} \frac{1}{1+x^2}\,dx + \lim_{t \to \infty} \int_{0}^{t} \frac{1}{1+x^2}\,dx$$

$$= \lim_{s \to -\infty}\left[\tan^{-1}x\right]_{s}^{0} + \lim_{t \to \infty}\left[\tan^{-1}x\right]_{0}^{t}$$

$$= \lim_{s \to -\infty}(-\tan^{-1}s) + \lim_{t \to \infty}(\tan^{-1}t) = \frac{\pi}{2} + \frac{\pi}{2} = \pi.$$

FIGURE 8.8.6 The area measured by the integral in Example 2.

The shaded region in Fig. 8.8.6 is a geometric interpretation of the integral of Example 2.

Infinite Integrands

Suppose that the function f is continuous and nonnegative on $[a, b]$ but that $f(x) \to +\infty$ as $x \to b^-$. The graph of such a function appears in Fig. 8.8.7. The area $A(t)$ of the region lying under $y = f(x)$ from $x = a$ to $x = t < b$ is the value of the (ordinary) definite integral

$$A(t) = \int_{a}^{t} f(x)\,dx.$$

If the limit of $A(t)$ exists as $t \to b^-$, then this limit may be regarded as the area of the (unbounded) region under $y = f(x)$ from $x = a$ to $x = b$. For f continuous on

FIGURE 8.8.7 An improper integral of the second type: $f(x) \to \infty$ as $x \to b^-$.

$[a, b)$, we therefore *define*

$$\int_a^b f(x)\, dx = \lim_{t \to b^-} \int_a^t f(x)\, dx, \tag{4}$$

provided that this limit exists (as a finite number), in which case we say that the improper integral on the left **converges;** if the limit does not exist, we say that the integral **diverges.** If

$$\int_a^b f(x)\, dx = \lim_{t \to b^-} \int_a^t f(x)\, dx = \infty,$$

then we say that the improper integral **diverges to infinity.**

If f is continuous on $(a, b]$ but the limit of $f(x)$ as $x \to a^+$ is infinite, then we *define*

$$\int_a^b f(x)\, dx = \lim_{t \to a^+} \int_t^b f(x)\, dx, \tag{5}$$

provided that the limit exists. If f is continuous at every point of $[a, b]$ except for the point c in (a, b) and one or both one-sided limits of f at c are infinite, then we *define*

$$\int_a^b f(x)\, dx = \int_a^c f(x)\, dx + \int_c^b f(x)\, dx \tag{6}$$

provided that both improper integrals on the right converge.

EXAMPLE 3 Investigate the improper integrals

(a) $\displaystyle\int_0^1 \frac{1}{\sqrt{x}}\, dx$ and

(b) $\displaystyle\int_1^2 \frac{1}{(x-2)^2}\, dx.$

Solution (a) The integrand $1/\sqrt{x}$ becomes infinite as $x \to 0^+$, so

$$\int_0^1 \frac{1}{\sqrt{x}}\, dx = \lim_{t \to 0^+} \int_t^1 \frac{1}{\sqrt{x}}\, dx$$

$$= \lim_{t \to 0^+} \Big[2\sqrt{x}\Big]_t^1 = \lim_{t \to 0^+} 2(1 - \sqrt{t}) = 2.$$

Thus the area of the unbounded region shown in Fig. 8.8.2 is 2.

(b) Here the integrand becomes infinite as x approaches the right-hand endpoint, so

$$\int_1^2 \frac{1}{(x-2)^2}\,dx = \lim_{t\to 2^-}\int_1^t \frac{1}{(x-2)^2}\,dx$$

$$= \lim_{t\to 2^-}\left[-\frac{1}{x-2}\right]_1^t$$

$$= \lim_{t\to 2^-}\left(-1 - \frac{1}{t-2}\right) = +\infty.$$

Hence this improper integral diverges to infinity (Fig. 8.8.8). It follows that the improper integral

$$\int_1^3 \frac{1}{(x-2)^2}\,dx = \int_1^2 \frac{1}{(x-2)^2}\,dx + \int_2^3 \frac{1}{(x-2)^2}\,dx$$

also diverges, because not both of the right-hand improper integrals converge. (You can verify that the second one also diverges to $+\infty$.) ◆

FIGURE 8.8.8 The unbounded region represented by the improper integral in Example 3(b).

FIGURE 8.8.9 The region of Example 4.

EXAMPLE 4 Investigate the improper integral

$$\int_0^2 \frac{1}{(2x-1)^{2/3}}\,dx.$$

Solution This improper integral corresponds to the region shaded in Fig. 8.8.9. The integrand has an infinite discontinuity at the point $c = \frac{1}{2}$ within the interval of integration, so we write

$$\int_0^2 \frac{1}{(2x-1)^{2/3}}\,dx = \int_0^{1/2} \frac{1}{(2x-1)^{2/3}}\,dx + \int_{1/2}^2 \frac{1}{(2x-1)^{2/3}}\,dx$$

and investigate separately the two improper integrals on the right. We find that

$$\int_0^{1/2} \frac{1}{(2x-1)^{2/3}}\,dx = \lim_{t\to (1/2)^-}\int_0^t \frac{1}{(2x-1)^{2/3}}\,dx$$

$$= \lim_{t\to (1/2)^-}\left[\tfrac{3}{2}(2x-1)^{1/3}\right]_0^t$$

$$= \lim_{t\to (1/2)^-}\tfrac{3}{2}\left[(2t-1)^{1/3} - (-1)^{1/3}\right] = \tfrac{3}{2},$$

and

$$\int_{1/2}^{2} \frac{1}{(2x-1)^{2/3}}\,dx = \lim_{t \to (1/2)^+} \int_{t}^{2} \frac{1}{(2x-1)^{2/3}}\,dx$$
$$= \lim_{t \to (1/2)^+} \left[\tfrac{3}{2}(2x-1)^{1/3}\right]_{t}^{2}$$
$$= \lim_{t \to (1/2)^+} \tfrac{3}{2}\left[3^{1/3} - (2t-1)^{1/3}\right] = \tfrac{3}{2}\sqrt[3]{3}.$$

Therefore,

$$\int_{0}^{2} \frac{1}{(2x-1)^{2/3}}\,dx = \tfrac{3}{2}\left(1 + \sqrt[3]{3}\right).$$ ◆

Special Functions and Improper Integrals

Special functions in advanced mathematics frequently are defined by means of improper integrals. An important example is the **gamma function** $\Gamma(t)$ that the prolific Swiss mathematician Leonhard Euler (1707–1783) introduced to "interpolate" values of the factorial function

$$n! = 1 \cdot 2 \cdot 3 \cdots (n-1) \cdot n.$$

The gamma function is defined for all real numbers $t > 0$ by the improper integral

$$\Gamma(t) = \int_{0}^{\infty} x^{t-1} e^{-x}\,dx. \qquad (7)$$

Thus for a fixed positive number t, the value $\Gamma(t)$ is the area under the curve $y = x^{t-1} e^{-x}$ from $x = 0$ to ∞ (Fig. 8.8.10). It turns out that the improper integral in (7) converges for all $t > 0$. The following example treats the illustrative cases $t = 1$ and $t = 2$.

FIGURE 8.8.10 The graphs $y = x^{t-1} e^{-x}$ for $t = 1, 2, 3, 4$.

EXAMPLE 5 If $t = 1$, then

$$\Gamma(1) = \int_{0}^{\infty} e^{-x}\,dx = \lim_{b \to \infty} \int_{0}^{b} e^{-x}\,dx$$
$$= \lim_{b \to \infty} \left[e^{-x}\right]_{0}^{b} = \lim_{b \to \infty}(1 - e^{-b}) = 1.$$

If $t = 2$, then integration by parts with $u = x$, $dv = e^{-x}\,dx$ yields

$$\Gamma(2) = \int_{0}^{\infty} x e^{-x}\,dx = \lim_{b \to \infty} \int_{0}^{b} x e^{-x}\,dx$$
$$= \lim_{b \to \infty} \left(\left[-xe^{-x}\right]_{0}^{b} + \int_{0}^{b} e^{-x}\,dx\right)$$
$$= \lim_{b \to \infty}(0 - be^{-b}) + \int_{0}^{\infty} e^{-x}\,dx = 0 + 1 = 1$$

as well. ◆

Because $0! = 1$ by definition and $1! = 1$, Example 5 can be interpreted to say that $\Gamma(1) = 0!$ and $\Gamma(2) = 1!$. More generally, it turns out—see Problems 47 and 48—that

$$\Gamma(n+1) = n! \qquad (8)$$

for every nonnegative integer n. But remember, the gamma function is defined for all positive *real numbers*. In Problem 57 we ask you to show that

$$\Gamma\left(\tfrac{1}{2}\right) = 2\int_0^\infty e^{-x^2}\,dx. \tag{9}$$

Figure 8.8.11 shows the graph $y = e^{-x^2}$ in comparison with $y = e^{-x}$ for $x \geq 0$. Because $e^{-x^2} < e^{-x}$ for $x > 1$ and the improper integral

$$\int_0^\infty e^{-x}\,dx$$

FIGURE 8.8.11 The graphs $y = e^{-x}$ and $y = e^{-x^2}$.

converges by Example 5, it is plausible that the area under $y = e^{-x^2}$ for $x \geq 0$ is finite, and hence that the improper integral in (9) converges as well. Indeed, we will see in Section 14.4 that $\Gamma(\tfrac{1}{2}) = \sqrt{\pi}$.

Escape Velocity

We saw in Section 6.5 how to compute the work W_r required to lift a body of mass m from the surface of a planet of mass M and radius R to a distance $r > R$ from the center of the planet. According to Eq. (7) there, the answer is

$$W_r = \int_R^r \frac{GMm}{x^2}\,dx.$$

So the work required to move the mass m "infinitely far" from the planet is

$$W = \lim_{r\to\infty} W_r = \int_R^\infty \frac{GMm}{x^2}\,dx = \lim_{r\to\infty}\left[-\frac{GMm}{x}\right]_R^r = \frac{GMm}{R}.$$

EXAMPLE 6 Suppose that the mass is projected with initial velocity v straight upward from the planet's surface, as in Jules Verne's novel *From the Earth to the Moon* (1865), in which a spacecraft was fired from an immense cannon. Then the initial kinetic energy $\tfrac{1}{2}mv^2$ of the mass is available to supply this work—by conversion into potential energy. From the equation

$$\frac{1}{2}mv^2 = \frac{GMm}{R},$$

we find that

$$v = \sqrt{\frac{2GM}{R}}.$$

Substituting appropriate numerical values for the constants G, M, and R yields the value $v \approx 11{,}175$ m/s (about 25,000 mi/h) for the *escape velocity* from the earth. ◆

Present Value of a Perpetuity

Consider a perpetual annuity, under which you and your heirs (and theirs, ad infinitum) will be paid A dollars annually. The question we pose is this: What is the fair market value of such an annuity? What should you pay to purchase it?

EXAMPLE 7 If the interest is compounded continuously at the annual rate r, then a dollar deposited in a savings account would grow to e^{rt} dollars in t years. Hence e^{-rt} dollars deposited now would yield \$1 after t years. Consequently, the **present value** of the amount you (and your heirs) will receive between time $t = 0$ (the present) and time $t = T > 0$ is defined to be

$$P_T = \int_0^T Ae^{-rt}\,dt.$$

Hence the total present value of the perpetual annuity is

$$P = \lim_{T\to\infty} P_T = \int_0^\infty Ae^{-rt}\,dt = \lim_{T\to\infty}\left[-\frac{A}{r}e^{-rt}\right]_0^T = \frac{A}{r}.$$

Thus $A = rP$. For instance, at an annual interest rate of 8% ($r = 0.08$), you should be able to purchase for $P = (\$50000)/(0.08) = \$625{,}000$ a perpetuity that pays you (and your heirs) an annual sum of $50000 forever. ◆

Statistics and Probability Integrals

Figure 8.8.12 shows the famous *bell-shaped curve* with equation

$$y = \frac{1}{\sqrt{2\pi}} \exp\left(-\tfrac{1}{2}x^2\right).$$

Problem 63 gives the value

$$\frac{1}{\sqrt{2\pi}} \int_{-\infty}^{\infty} \exp\left(-\tfrac{1}{2}x^2\right) dx = 1. \tag{10}$$

FIGURE 8.8.12 The bell-shaped curve $y = \frac{1}{\sqrt{2\pi}} e^{-\frac{1}{2}x^2}$.

Thus the area of the region under the bell-shaped curve—with "infinite tails" extending in both directions—is exactly 1. By numerical integration (using Simpson's approximation, for instance) it can be verified that

$$\frac{1}{\sqrt{2\pi}} \int_{-1}^{1} \exp\left(-\tfrac{1}{2}x^2\right) dx \approx 0.6827, \qquad \frac{1}{\sqrt{2\pi}} \int_{-2}^{2} \exp\left(-\tfrac{1}{2}x^2\right) dx \approx 0.9545,$$

$$\text{and} \qquad \frac{1}{\sqrt{2\pi}} \int_{-3}^{3} \exp\left(-\tfrac{1}{2}x^2\right) dx \approx 0.9973. \tag{11}$$

It follows that:

- Just over two-thirds of the area under the bell-shaped curve lies between $x = -1$ and $x = 1$;
- Almost 95.5% of the area lies between $x = -2$ and $x = 2$; and
- Almost 99.75% of the total area lies between $x = -3$ and $x = 3$.

The bell-shaped curve is used in describing the distributions of a wide range of typical attributes of individual members of large populations. Many such attributes—such as the height, weight, IQ, or SAT score of a college student—are distributed among members of the population in a manner that has both random and systematic aspects. For instance, let $X(s)$ denote the height of the college-age male s. Then X is a real-valued function defined on the set S of all college-age males. In statistics, such a real-valued function defined on a population set is called a **random variable** on S. Given a random variable X defined on a set S and two numbers a and b, we may ask what is the fraction or proportion $P\{a \leq X(s) \leq b\}$ of elements s of the set S such that the value $X(s)$ lies between a and b (inclusive). This fraction may be regarded as the **probability** $P\{a \leq X(s) \leq b\}$ that $X(s)$ lies in $[a, b]$.

A **normal** random variable X with **mean value** μ and **standard deviation** σ is one such that

$$P\left\{a \leq \frac{X(s) - \mu}{\sigma} \leq b\right\} = \frac{1}{\sqrt{2\pi}} \int_a^b \exp\left(-\tfrac{1}{2}x^2\right) dx \tag{12}$$

if $a < b$. You can easily verify that

$$a \leq \frac{X(s) - \mu}{\sigma} \leq b \quad \text{if and only if} \quad \mu + a\sigma \leq X(s) \leq \mu + b\sigma, \tag{13}$$

so Eq. (12) is equivalent to

$$P\{\mu + a\sigma \leq X(s) \leq \mu + b\sigma\} = \frac{1}{\sqrt{2\pi}} \int_a^b \exp\left(-\tfrac{1}{2}x^2\right) dx. \tag{14}$$

The next example reveals the meanings of the parameters μ and σ.

EXAMPLE 8 If we take $a = 0$ and $b = +\infty$ in Eqs. (13) and (14), we see that

$$P\{\mu \leq X(s) < +\infty\} = \frac{1}{\sqrt{2\pi}} \int_0^\infty \exp\left(-\tfrac{1}{2}x^2\right) dx = \tfrac{1}{2}$$

(using (10) and the symmetry of the graph in Fig. 8.8.12). Thus the value $X(s)$ is greater than or equal to the mean value μ for *half* the elements of the set S. If we take $a = -1$ and $b = 1$, we see that

$$P\{\mu - \sigma \leq X(s) \leq \mu + \sigma\} = \frac{1}{\sqrt{2\pi}} \int_{-1}^{1} \exp\left(-\tfrac{1}{2}x^2\right) dx \approx 0.6827$$

(using (11)). Thus the value $X(s)$ lies within one standard deviation σ of the mean value μ for a bit over two-thirds of the elements of S. Similarly,

$$P\{\mu - 2\sigma \leq X(s) \leq \mu + 2\sigma\} = \frac{1}{\sqrt{2\pi}} \int_{-2}^{2} \exp\left(-\tfrac{1}{2}x^2\right) dx \approx 0.9545,$$

so the value $X(s)$ lies within two standard deviations of the mean value for over 95% of the elements of S. ◆

Numerical values of the integral in (12) and (14) are frequently calculated using values of the special function

$$\operatorname{erf}(x) = \frac{2}{\sqrt{\pi}} \int_0^x \exp(-t^2)\, dx \qquad (15)$$

(*erf* is for "error function"), which is tabulated in mathematical handbooks and included in most computer algebra systems. In Problem 64 we ask you to show that

$$\frac{1}{\sqrt{2\pi}} \int_0^u \exp\left(-\tfrac{1}{2}x^2\right) dx = \tfrac{1}{2}\operatorname{erf}\left(\frac{u}{\sqrt{2}}\right). \qquad (16)$$

EXAMPLE 9 Scoring for the Scholastic Aptitude Test (SAT) has been changed in recent years, so that the same performance now receives a higher score than before. This test was originally designed so that the SAT score $X(s)$ of a college-bound student s would (theoretically) be a random variable with mean value $\mu = 1000$ and standard deviation $\sigma = 100$. (a) In this case, what percentage of students tested should score at least 1250? (b) What percentage should score no more than 850?

Solution (a) If we write $\mu + a\sigma = 1000 + 100a = 1250$, we find that $a = 2.5$. Then the proportion of students with scores of at least 1250—that is, $1250 \leq X(s) < +\infty$—is given (with $b = +\infty$) by

$$P\{1250 \leq X(s) < +\infty\} = \frac{1}{\sqrt{2\pi}} \int_{2.5}^{\infty} \exp\left(-\tfrac{1}{2}x^2\right) dx \qquad \text{[using (14)]}$$

$$= \frac{1}{\sqrt{2\pi}} \int_0^{\infty} \exp\left(-\tfrac{1}{2}x^2\right) dx - \frac{1}{\sqrt{2\pi}} \int_0^{2.5} \exp\left(-\tfrac{1}{2}x^2\right) dx$$

$$= \frac{1}{2} - \frac{1}{2}\operatorname{erf}\left(\frac{2.5}{\sqrt{2}}\right) \qquad \text{[using (16)]}$$

$$\approx \frac{1}{2}(1 - 0.98758) = 0.00621$$

(using the approximation $\operatorname{erf}(2.5/\sqrt{2}) \approx 0.98758$ given by a computer algebra system). Thus about 0.62% of all students tested—fewer than one in a hundred—should score at least 1250 (under the original grading system).

(b) If we write $\mu + b\sigma = 1000 + 100b = 850$, we find that $b = -1.5$. Then the proportion of students with scores at most 850—that is, $-\infty < X(s) \leq 850$—is given (with $a = -\infty$) by

$$P\{-\infty < X(s) \leq 850\} = \frac{1}{\sqrt{2\pi}} \int_{-\infty}^{-1.5} \exp\left(-\tfrac{1}{2}x^2\right) dx \quad \text{[using (14)]}$$

$$= \frac{1}{\sqrt{2\pi}} \int_{1.5}^{\infty} \exp\left(-\tfrac{1}{2}x^2\right) dx \quad \text{[by symmetry]}$$

$$= \frac{1}{\sqrt{2\pi}} \int_{0}^{\infty} \exp\left(-\tfrac{1}{2}x^2\right) dx - \frac{1}{\sqrt{2\pi}} \int_{0}^{1.5} \exp\left(-\tfrac{1}{2}x^2\right) dx$$

$$= \frac{1}{2} - \frac{1}{2}\mathrm{erf}\left(\frac{1.5}{\sqrt{2}}\right) \quad \text{[using (16)]}$$

$$\approx \frac{1}{2}(1 - 0.86639) \approx 0.06681$$

(using the value $\mathrm{erf}(1.5/\sqrt{2}) \approx 0.86639$ given by a computer algebra system). Thus about 6.68% of all students tested—about one in fifteen—should score 850 or less. ◆

Random Sampling

A **binary event** is one with two possible outcomes that occur with probabilities p and $q = 1 - p$, respectively. Examples include:

- The toss of a coin with possible outcomes "heads" and "tails."
- Polling the preference of a randomly selected voter who may be either a Democrat or a Republican.
- Quality testing an electronic component chosen at random from a shipment; it may be either defective or not.

Given a particular binary event, the result of carrying out the event N times—for instance, tossing a coin N times—is called an N-**event sample** (or a sample of **size** N). Given an N-event sample s, let $X(s)$ denote the number of "successful" outcomes with probability p. For instance, if s consists of N tosses of a coin, then $X(s)$ might denote the number of heads obtained. Then X is a random variable defined on the set S of all N-event samples.

If the sample size N is large, then the *central limit theorem* of advanced probability theory implies that X is closely approximated by a normal random variable whose mean value and standard deviation are given by

$$\mu = Np \quad \text{and} \quad \sigma = \sqrt{Npq}. \tag{17}$$

The probability that the number of successes lies between $\mu + a\sigma$ and $\mu + b\sigma$ is then given approximately by

$$P\{\mu + a\sigma \leq X(s) \leq \mu + b\sigma\} \approx \frac{1}{\sqrt{2\pi}} \int_{a}^{b} \exp\left(-\tfrac{1}{2}x^2\right) dx. \tag{18}$$

It is common statistical practice to assume equality in (18) if $N > 30$.

EXAMPLE 10 Suppose that a fair coin (one with $p = q = \tfrac{1}{2}$) is tossed $N = 400$ times. (a) Calculate the approximate probability that the number of heads obtained is between 185 and 215 inclusive. (b) Calculate the approximate probability that the number is more than 230.

Solution First note that by the equations in (17), the mean and standard deviation of $X(s)$ are

$$\mu = Np = 400 \cdot \tfrac{1}{2} = 200 \quad \text{and} \quad \sigma = \sqrt{Npq} = \sqrt{400 \cdot \tfrac{1}{2} \cdot \tfrac{1}{2}} = 10.$$

(a) If we write $\mu + a\sigma = 200 + 10a = 185$ and $\mu + b\sigma = 200 + 10b = 215$, we find that $a = -1.5$ and $b = 1.5$. Hence the probability that the number of heads lies in the interval $[185, 215]$ is

$$P\{185 \leq X(s) \leq 215\} \approx \frac{1}{\sqrt{2\pi}} \int_{-1.5}^{1.5} \exp\left(-\tfrac{1}{2}x^2\right) dx \qquad \text{[using (18)]}$$

$$= 2 \cdot \frac{1}{\sqrt{2\pi}} \int_{0}^{1.5} \exp\left(-\tfrac{1}{2}x^2\right) dx \qquad \text{[by symmetry]}$$

$$= 2 \cdot \frac{1}{2}\mathrm{erf}\left(\frac{1.5}{\sqrt{2}}\right) \qquad \text{[using (16)]}$$

$$\approx 0.86639 \qquad \text{[computer algebra system]}.$$

In common language, the probability of getting 185 to 215 heads in 400 tosses of a fair coin is thus about 87%, which is about 7 chances out of 8.

(b) If we write $\mu + a\sigma = 200 + 10a = 230$, we get $a = 3$. Then the probability that the number of heads is at least 230—that is, $230 \leq X(s) < +\infty$—is given (with $b = +\infty$) by

$$P\{230 \leq X(s) < +\infty\}$$

$$\approx \frac{1}{\sqrt{2\pi}} \int_{3}^{\infty} \exp\left(-\tfrac{1}{2}x^2\right) dx \qquad \text{[using (18)]}$$

$$= \frac{1}{\sqrt{2\pi}} \int_{0}^{\infty} \exp\left(-\tfrac{1}{2}x^2\right) dx - \frac{1}{\sqrt{2\pi}} \int_{0}^{3} \exp\left(-\tfrac{1}{2}x^2\right) dx$$

$$= \frac{1}{2} - \frac{1}{2}\mathrm{erf}\left(\frac{3}{\sqrt{2}}\right) \qquad \text{[using (16)]}$$

$$\approx \frac{1}{2}(1 - 0.99730) = 0.00135$$

(using the value $\mathrm{erf}(3/\sqrt{2}) \approx 0.99730$ given by a computer algebra system). Thus there is less than two chances in a thousand of obtaining at least 230 heads in 400 tosses of a fair coin. ◆

REMARK The decimal-place answers calculated in Example 10 are only rough approximations, although the final conclusions—"about 7 chances in 8" in part (a) and "less than two chances in a thousand" in part (b)—are correct. One reason is that (18) is, after all, only an approximation whose accuracy we have not discussed. Moreover, because a count of coin tosses is discrete rather than continuous, one might well argue that in part (a) we should calculate $P\{184.5 \leq X(s) \leq 215.5\}$ rather than $P\{185 \leq X(s) \leq 215\}$, and "extend by half integers" similarly in part (b). Such issues as these are discussed in statistics courses.

8.8 TRUE/FALSE STUDY GUIDE

8.8 CONCEPTS: QUESTIONS AND DISCUSSION

1. List the different types of improper integrals that are discussed in this section. For each type, give examples of both convergent and divergent improper integrals of that type.
2. Discuss and illustrate with examples the difference between "divergence to infinity" and "divergence by oscillation."
3. Discuss the relation between improper integrals and areas of unbounded regions in the plane.

8.8 PROBLEMS

Determine whether or not the improper integrals in Problems 1 through 38 converge. Evaluate those that do converge.

1. $\displaystyle\int_2^\infty \frac{1}{x\sqrt{x}}\,dx$

2. $\displaystyle\int_1^\infty \frac{1}{x^{2/3}}\,dx$

3. $\displaystyle\int_0^4 \frac{1}{x\sqrt{x}}\,dx$

4. $\displaystyle\int_0^8 \frac{1}{x^{2/3}}\,dx$

5. $\displaystyle\int_1^\infty \frac{1}{x+1}\,dx$

6. $\displaystyle\int_3^\infty \frac{1}{\sqrt{x+1}}\,dx$

7. $\displaystyle\int_5^\infty \frac{1}{(x-1)^{3/2}}\,dx$

8. $\displaystyle\int_0^4 \frac{1}{\sqrt{4-x}}\,dx$

9. $\displaystyle\int_0^9 \frac{1}{(9-x)^{3/2}}\,dx$

10. $\displaystyle\int_0^3 \frac{1}{(x-3)^2}\,dx$

11. $\displaystyle\int_{-\infty}^{-2} \frac{1}{(x+1)^3}\,dx$

12. $\displaystyle\int_{-\infty}^0 \frac{1}{\sqrt{4-x}}\,dx$

13. $\displaystyle\int_{-1}^8 \frac{1}{\sqrt[3]{x}}\,dx$

14. $\displaystyle\int_{-4}^4 \frac{1}{(x+4)^{2/3}}\,dx$

15. $\displaystyle\int_2^\infty \frac{1}{\sqrt[3]{x-1}}\,dx$

16. $\displaystyle\int_{-\infty}^\infty \frac{x}{(x^2+4)^{3/2}}\,dx$

17. $\displaystyle\int_{-\infty}^\infty \frac{x}{x^2+4}\,dx$

18. $\displaystyle\int_0^\infty e^{-(x+1)}\,dx$

19. $\displaystyle\int_0^1 \frac{e^{\sqrt{x}}}{\sqrt{x}}\,dx$

20. $\displaystyle\int_0^2 \frac{x}{x^2-1}\,dx$

21. $\displaystyle\int_0^\infty xe^{-3x}\,dx$

22. $\displaystyle\int_{-\infty}^2 e^{2x}\,dx$

23. $\displaystyle\int_0^\infty xe^{-x^2}\,dx$

24. $\displaystyle\int_{-\infty}^\infty |x|e^{-x^2}\,dx$

25. $\displaystyle\int_0^\infty \frac{1}{1+x^2}\,dx$

26. $\displaystyle\int_0^\infty \frac{x}{1+x^2}\,dx$

27. $\displaystyle\int_0^\infty \cos x\,dx$

28. $\displaystyle\int_0^\infty \sin^2 x\,dx$

29. $\displaystyle\int_1^\infty \frac{\ln x}{x}\,dx$

30. $\displaystyle\int_2^\infty \frac{1}{x\ln x}\,dx$

31. $\displaystyle\int_2^\infty \frac{1}{x(\ln x)^2}\,dx$

32. $\displaystyle\int_1^\infty \frac{\ln x}{x^2}\,dx$

33. $\displaystyle\int_0^{\pi/2} \frac{\cos x}{\sqrt{\sin x}}\,dx$

34. $\displaystyle\int_0^{\pi/2} \frac{\sin x}{(\cos x)^{4/3}}\,dx$

35. $\displaystyle\int_0^1 \ln x\,dx$

36. $\displaystyle\int_0^1 \frac{\ln x}{x}\,dx$

37. $\displaystyle\int_0^1 \frac{\ln x}{x^2}\,dx$

38. $\displaystyle\int_0^\infty e^{-x}\cos x\,dx$

In Problems 39 through 42, the given integral is improper both because the interval of integration is unbounded and because the integrand is unbounded near zero. Investigate its convergence by expressing it as a sum of two integrals—one from 0 to 1, the other from 1 to ∞. Evaluate those integrals that converge.

39. $\displaystyle\int_0^\infty \frac{1}{x+x^2}\,dx$

40. $\displaystyle\int_0^\infty \frac{1}{x^2+x^4}\,dx$

41. $\displaystyle\int_0^\infty \frac{1}{x^{1/2}+x^{3/2}}\,dx$

42. $\displaystyle\int_0^\infty \frac{1}{x^{2/3}+x^{4/3}}\,dx$

In Problems 43 through 46, find all real number values of k for which the given improper integral converges. Evaluate the integral for those values of k.

43. $\displaystyle\int_0^1 \frac{1}{x^k}\,dx$

44. $\displaystyle\int_1^\infty \frac{1}{x^k}\,dx$

45. $\displaystyle\int_0^1 x^k \ln x\,dx$

46. $\displaystyle\int_1^\infty \frac{1}{x(\ln x)^k}\,dx$

47. Beginning with the definition of the gamma function in Eq. (7), integrate by parts to show that
$$\Gamma(x+1) = x\Gamma(x)$$
for every positive real number x.

48. Explain how to apply the result of Problem 47 n times in succession to show that if n is a positive integer, then $\Gamma(n+1) = n!\Gamma(1) = n!$.

Problems 49 through 51 deal with Gabriel's horn, the surface obtained by revolving the curve $y = 1/x$, $x \geq 1$, around the x-axis (Fig. 8.8.13).

FIGURE 8.8.13 Gabriel's horn (Problems 49 through 51).

49. Show that the area under the curve $y = 1/x$, $x \geq 1$, is infinite.

50. Show that the volume of revolution enclosed by Gabriel's horn is finite, and compute it.

51. Show that the surface area of Gabriel's horn is infinite. [*Suggestion:* Let A_t denote the surface area from $x = 1$ to $x = t > 1$. Prove that $A_t > 2\pi \ln t$.] In any case, the implication is that we could fill Gabriel's horn with a finite amount of paint (Problem 50), but no finite amount suffices to paint its surface.

52. Show that
$$\int_{-\infty}^{\infty} \frac{1+x}{1+x^2}\,dx$$
diverges, but that
$$\lim_{t\to\infty}\int_{-t}^{t}\frac{1+x}{1+x^2}\,dx = \pi.$$

53. Use the substitution $x = e^{-u}$ and the fact that $\Gamma(n+1) = n!$ (Problem 48) to prove that if m and n are fixed but arbitrary positive integers, then
$$\int_0^1 x^m (\ln x)^n\,dx = \frac{n!(-1)^n}{(m+1)^{n+1}}.$$

54. Consider a perpetual annuity under which you and your heirs will be paid at the rate of $10 + t$ thousand dollars per year t years hence. Thus you will receive $20,000 10 years from now, your heir will receive $110,000 100 years from now, and so on. Assuming a constant annual interest rate of 10%, show that the present value of this perpetuity is
$$P = \int_0^\infty (10+t) e^{-t/10}\,dt,$$
and then evaluate this improper integral.

55. A "semi-infinite" uniform rod occupies the nonnegative x-axis ($x \geq 0$) and has linear density δ; that is, a segment of length dx has mass $\delta\,dx$. Show that the force of gravitational attraction that the rod exerts on a point mass m at $(-a, 0)$ is
$$F = \int_0^\infty \frac{Gm\delta}{(a+x)^2}\,dx = \frac{Gm\delta}{a}.$$

56. A rod of linear density δ (see Problem 55) occupies the entire y-axis. A point mass m is located at $(a, 0)$ on the x-axis, as indicated in Fig. 8.8.14. Show that the total (horizontal) gravitational attraction that the rod exerts on m is
$$F = \int_{-\infty}^\infty \frac{Gm\delta\cos\theta}{r^2}\,dy = \frac{2Gm\delta}{a},$$
where $r^2 = a^2 + y^2$ and $\cos\theta = a/r$.

FIGURE 8.8.14 Gravitational attraction exerted on a point mass by an infinite rod (Problem 56).

57. Verify Eq. (9) by substituting $x = u^2$ in the integral that defines the value $\Gamma(\tfrac{1}{2})$.

58. Given the fact that
$$\int_0^\infty e^{-x^2}\,dx = \tfrac{1}{2}\sqrt{\pi},$$
find the volume of the unbounded solid that is obtained by revolving around the x-axis the unbounded region R between the x-axis and the curve $y = e^{-x^2}$ for $x \geq 0$.

59. Find the volume of the unbounded solid that is obtained by revolving around the y-axis the region R of Problem 58.

60. Recall from Problem 47 that $\Gamma(x+1) = x\Gamma(x)$ if $x > 0$. Suppose that n is a positive integer. Use Eq. (9) to establish that
$$\Gamma\left(n + \tfrac{1}{2}\right) = \frac{1\cdot 3\cdot 5 \cdots (2n-1)}{2^n}\sqrt{\pi}.$$

61. (a) Suppose that $k > 1$. Use integration by parts to show that
$$\int_0^\infty x^k \exp(-x^2)\,dx = \frac{k-1}{2}\int_0^\infty x^{k-2}\exp(-x^2)\,dx.$$
(b) Suppose that n is a positive integer. Prove that
$$\int_0^\infty x^{n-1}\exp(-x^2)\,dx = \frac{1}{2}\Gamma\left(\frac{n}{2}\right).$$

62. Suppose that you win the Florida lottery and decide to use part of your winnings to purchase a perpetual annuity that will pay you and your heirs $10,000 per year (forever). Assuming an annual interest rate of 6%, what is a fair price for an insurance company to charge you for such an annuity?

63. Deduce Eq. (10) in this section from the value
$$\int_{-\infty}^\infty \exp(-t^2)\,dt = \sqrt{\pi}$$
established in Section 14.4.

64. Deduce Eq. (16) in this section from Eq. (15).

In Problems 65 through 70, determine the value of k by using a calculator or computer to evaluate
$$\int_0^b f(x)\,dx$$
for successively larger values of b. Continue until it seems certain that the four-place value of k is an integer.

65. $\displaystyle\int_0^\infty x^5 e^{-x}\,dx = 60k$

66. $\displaystyle\int_0^\infty \frac{\sin x}{x}\,dx = \frac{\pi}{k}$

67. $\displaystyle\int_0^\infty \frac{1}{x^2+2}\,dx = \frac{\pi}{k\sqrt{2}}$

68. $\displaystyle\int_0^\infty \frac{1-e^{-3x}}{x}\,dx = \frac{\ln 10}{k}$

69. $\displaystyle\int_0^\infty \exp(-x^2)\cos 2x\,dx = \frac{\pi}{ke}$

70. $\displaystyle\int_0^\infty \sin(x^2)\,dx = \frac{1}{k}\sqrt{\frac{\pi}{2}}$

71. Suppose that the intelligence quotient (IQ) scores of middle-school students constitute a normal random variable with a mean of 100 and a standard deviation of 15. (a) Calculate the percentage of students that have an IQ score between 90 and 110, inclusive. (b) Calculate the percentage that have an IQ score of 125 or higher.

72. Suppose that the heights of adult U.S. males constitute a normal random variable with a mean of 69 inches and a standard deviation of 3 inches. (a) Calculate the percentage of adult U.S. males who have heights between 67 inches and 72 inches, inclusive. (b) Calculate the percentage having height 76 inches or more.

73. Suppose that the fair coin of Example 10 is tossed $N = 1000$ times. (a) Calculate the probability that the number of heads obtained is between 425 and 475, inclusive. (b) Calculate the probability that 500 or more heads are obtained.

74. Suppose that a biased coin has probability $p = 0.6$ of heads and $q = 0.4$ of tails is tossed $N = 600$ times. (a) Calculate the probability that the number of heads obtained is between 345 and 375, inclusive. (b) Calculate the probability that fewer than 350 heads are obtained.

75. A student randomly guesses the answers on a 50-question true-false test. (a) What is the probability that he passes (60% or more correct)? (b) What is the probability that he makes a C or better (70% or more correct)?

76. A machine prints circuit boards of which 1% are defective. What is the probability that 10 or more circuit boards out of 500 tested are defective?

77. Suppose that 55% of registered voters in a metropolitan population actually favor the Democratic candidate for mayor. If 750 registered voters are randomly polled, what is the probability that between 41% and 49% (inclusive) will favor the Republican candidate?

78. Let
$$I_n = \int_1^\infty \frac{(\ln x)^n}{x^2}\, dx.$$
Show that $(n+1)I_n = I_{n+1}$ for each integer $n \geq 0$. Conclude that $I_n = n!$ if n is a positive integer.

CHAPTER 8 SUMMARY

When you confront the problem of evaluating a particular integral, you must first decide which of the several methods of this chapter to try. There are only two *general* methods of integration:

- Integration by substitution (Section 8.2), and
- Integration by parts (Section 8.3).

These are the analogues for integration of the chain rule and product rule, respectively, for differentiation.

Look first at the given integral to see if you can spot a substitution that would transform it into an elementary or familiar integral or one likely to be found in an integral table. In the case of an integral

$$\int f(x)g(x)\, dx,$$

whose integral is an unfamiliar product of two functions, one of which is easily differentiated and the other easily integrated, then an attempt to integrate by parts is indicated.

Beyond these two general methods, the chapter deals with a number of *special* methods. In the case of an integral that is obviously trigonometric, $\int \text{trig}(x)\, dx$, the simple "spin-off" methods of Section 8.4 may succeed. Remember that reduction formulas [such as Eq. (5) and Problems 53 and 54 of Section 8.3] are available for integrating an integral power of a single trigonometric function.

Any integral of a rational function—that is, an integral of the form

$$\int \frac{p(x)}{q(x)}\, dx,$$

where the integrand is a quotient of polynomials—can be evaluated by the method of partial fractions (Section 8.5). If the degree of the numerator is not less than that of the denominator—that is, if the rational function is not proper—first use long division to express it as the sum of a polynomial (easily integrated) and a proper rational fraction. Then decompose the latter into partial fractions. Partial fractions corresponding to linear factors are easily integrated, and those corresponding to irreducible quadratic factors can be integrated by completing the square and making (if necessary) a trigonometric substitution. As we explained in Section 8.7, the trigonometric integrals that result can always be evaluated.

In the case of an integral involving $\sqrt{ax^2 + bx + c}$, first complete the square (Section 8.7) and then rationalize the integral by making an appropriate trigonometric substitution (Section 8.6). This will leave you with a trigonometric integral.

Some additional special substitutions are introduced in the Miscellaneous Problems that follow. Notable among these is the substitution

$$u = \tan\frac{\theta}{2},$$

which transforms any integral $\int R(\sin\theta, \cos\theta)\, d\theta$ of a rational function of $\sin\theta$ and $\cos\theta$ into an integral of a rational function of u. The latter integral can then be evaluated by the method of partial fractions.

A final comment: Computer algebra systems are increasingly used for the evaluation of integrals such as those studied in this chapter. Nevertheless, the availability of these systems is no panacea. For instance, such computer systems are likely to be stumped by the integral

$$\int (1 + \ln x)\sqrt{1 + (x \ln x)^2}\, dx.$$

But you probably notice that the substitution

$$u = x \ln x, \qquad du = (1 + \ln x)\, dx$$

transforms this integral into the integral

$$\int \sqrt{1 + u^2}\, du,$$

which is amenable to trigonometric substitution (and can be found in almost any integral table). Thus the human factor remains—thankfully—essential. ◆

CHAPTER 8 MISCELLANEOUS PROBLEMS

Evaluate the integrals in Problems 1 through 100.

1. $\int \dfrac{1}{(1+x)\sqrt{x}}\, dx$ [*Suggestion:* Let $x = u^2$.]

2. $\int \dfrac{\sec^2 t}{1 + \tan t}\, dt$

3. $\int \sin x \sec x\, dx$

4. $\int \dfrac{\csc x \cot x}{1 + \csc^2 x}\, dx$

5. $\int \dfrac{\tan\theta}{\cos^2\theta}\, d\theta$

6. $\int \csc^4 x\, dx$

7. $\int x \tan^2 x\, dx$

8. $\int x^2 \cos^2 x\, dx$

9. $\int x^5 \sqrt{2 - x^3}\, dx$

10. $\int \dfrac{1}{\sqrt{x^2 + 4}}\, dx$

11. $\int \dfrac{x^2}{\sqrt{25 + x^2}}\, dx$

12. $\int (\cos x)\sqrt{4 - \sin^2 x}\, dx$

13. $\int \dfrac{1}{x^2 - x + 1}\, dx$

14. $\int \sqrt{x^2 + x + 1}\, dx$

15. $\int \dfrac{5x + 31}{3x^2 - 4x + 11}\, dx$

16. $\int \dfrac{x^4 + 1}{x^2 + 1}\, dx$

17. $\int \sqrt{x^4 + x^7}\, dx$

18. $\int \dfrac{\sqrt{x}}{1 + x}\, dx$ [*Suggestion:* Let $x = u^2$.]

19. $\int \dfrac{\cos x}{\sqrt{4 - \sin^2 x}}\, dx$

20. $\int \dfrac{\cos 2x}{\cos x}\, dx$

21. $\int \dfrac{\tan x}{\ln(\cos x)}\, dx$

22. $\int \dfrac{x^7}{\sqrt{1 - x^4}}\, dx$

23. $\int \ln(1 + x)\, dx$

24. $\int x \sec^{-1} x\, dx$

25. $\int \sqrt{x^2 + 9}\, dx$

26. $\int \dfrac{x^2}{\sqrt{4 - x^2}}\, dx$

27. $\int \sqrt{2x - x^2}\, dx$

28. $\int \dfrac{4x - 2}{x^3 - x}\, dx$

29. $\int \dfrac{x^4}{x^2 - 2}\, dx$

30. $\int \dfrac{\sec x \tan x}{\sec x + \sec^2 x}\, dx$

31. $\int \dfrac{x}{(x^2 + 2x + 2)^2}\, dx$

32. $\int \dfrac{x^{1/3}}{x^{1/2} + x^{1/4}}\, dx$ [*Suggestion:* Let $x = u^{12}$.]

33. $\int \dfrac{1}{1 + \cos 2\theta}\, d\theta$

34. $\int \dfrac{\sec x}{\tan x}\, dx$

35. $\int \sec^3 x \tan^3 x\, dx$

36. $\int x^2 \tan^{-1} x\, dx$

37. $\displaystyle\int x(\ln x)^3\, dx$

38. $\displaystyle\int \frac{1}{x\sqrt{1+x^2}}\, dx$

39. $\displaystyle\int e^x\sqrt{1+e^{2x}}\, dx$

40. $\displaystyle\int \frac{x}{\sqrt{4x-x^2}}\, dx$

41. $\displaystyle\int \frac{1}{x^3\sqrt{x^2-9}}\, dx$

42. $\displaystyle\int \frac{x}{(7x+1)^{17}}\, dx$

43. $\displaystyle\int \frac{4x^2+x+1}{4x^3+x}\, dx$

44. $\displaystyle\int \frac{4x^3-x+1}{x^3+1}\, dx$

45. $\displaystyle\int \tan^2 x \sec x\, dx$

46. $\displaystyle\int \frac{x^2+2x+2}{(x+1)^3}\, dx$

47. $\displaystyle\int \frac{x^4+2x+2}{x^5+x^4}\, dx$

48. $\displaystyle\int \frac{8x^2-4x+7}{(x^2+1)(4x+1)}\, dx$

49. $\displaystyle\int \frac{3x^5-x^4+2x^3-12x^2-2x+1}{(x^3-1)^2}\, dx$

50. $\displaystyle\int \frac{x}{x^4+4x^2+8}\, dx$

51. $\displaystyle\int (\ln x)^6\, dx$

52. $\displaystyle\int \frac{(1+x^{2/3})^{3/2}}{x^{1/3}}\, dx$ [Suggestion: Let $x = u^3$.]

53. $\displaystyle\int \frac{(\arcsin x)^2}{\sqrt{1-x^2}}\, dx$

54. $\displaystyle\int \frac{1}{x^{3/2}(1+x^{1/3})}\, dx$ [Suggestion: Let $x = u^6$.]

55. $\displaystyle\int \tan^3 z\, dz$

56. $\displaystyle\int \sin^2\omega \cos^4\omega\, d\omega$

57. $\displaystyle\int \frac{xe^{x^2}}{1+e^{2x^2}}\, dx$

58. $\displaystyle\int \frac{\cos^3 x}{\sqrt{\sin x}}\, dx$

59. $\displaystyle\int x^3 e^{-x^2}\, dx$

60. $\displaystyle\int \sin\sqrt{x}\, dx$

61. $\displaystyle\int \frac{\arcsin x}{x^2}\, dx$

62. $\displaystyle\int \sqrt{x^2-9}\, dx$

63. $\displaystyle\int x^2\sqrt{1-x^2}\, dx$

64. $\displaystyle\int x\sqrt{2x-x^2}\, dx$

65. $\displaystyle\int \frac{x-2}{4x^2+4x+1}\, dx$

66. $\displaystyle\int \frac{2x^2-5x-1}{x^3-2x^2-x+2}\, dx$

67. $\displaystyle\int \frac{e^{2x}}{e^{2x}-1}\, dx$

68. $\displaystyle\int \frac{\cos x}{\sin^2 x-3\sin x+2}\, dx$

69. $\displaystyle\int \frac{2x^3+3x^2+4}{(x+1)^4}\, dx$

70. $\displaystyle\int \frac{\sec^2 x}{\tan^2 x+2\tan x+2}\, dx$

71. $\displaystyle\int \frac{x^3+x^2+2x+1}{x^4+2x^2+1}\, dx$

72. $\displaystyle\int \sin x \cos 3x\, dx$

73. $\displaystyle\int x^5\sqrt{x^3-1}\, dx$

74. $\displaystyle\int \ln(x^2+2x)\, dx$

75. $\displaystyle\int \frac{\sqrt{1+\sin x}}{\sec x}\, dx$

76. $\displaystyle\int \frac{1}{x^{2/3}(1+x^{2/3})}\, dx$

77. $\displaystyle\int \frac{\sin x}{\sin 2x}\, dx$

78. $\displaystyle\int \sqrt{1+\cos t}\, dt$

79. $\displaystyle\int \sqrt{1+\sin t}\, dt$

80. $\displaystyle\int \frac{\sec^2 t}{1-\tan^2 t}\, dt$

81. $\displaystyle\int \ln(x^2+x+1)\, dx$

82. $\displaystyle\int e^x \sin^{-1}(e^x)\, dx$

83. $\displaystyle\int \frac{\arctan x}{x^2}\, dx$

84. $\displaystyle\int \frac{x^2}{\sqrt{x^2-25}}\, dx$

85. $\displaystyle\int \frac{x^3}{(x^2+1)^2}\, dx$

86. $\displaystyle\int \frac{1}{x\sqrt{6x-x^2}}\, dx$

87. $\displaystyle\int \frac{3x+2}{(x^2+4)^{3/2}}\, dx$

88. $\displaystyle\int x^{3/2}\ln x\, dx$

89. $\displaystyle\int \frac{\sqrt{1+\sin^2 x}}{\sec x \csc x}\, dx$

90. $\displaystyle\int \frac{\exp(\sqrt{\sin x})}{(\sec x)\sqrt{\sin x}}\, dx$

91. $\displaystyle\int xe^x \sin x\, dx$

92. $\displaystyle\int x^2 e^{x^{3/2}}\, dx$

93. $\displaystyle\int \frac{\arctan x}{(x-1)^3}\, dx$

94. $\displaystyle\int \ln(1+\sqrt{x})\, dx$

95. $\displaystyle\int \frac{2x+3}{\sqrt{3+6x-9x^2}}\, dx$

96. $\displaystyle\int \frac{1}{\sqrt{e^{2x}-1}}\, dx$

97. $\displaystyle\int \frac{x^4}{(x-1)^2}\, dx$ [Suggestion: Let $u = x-1$.]

98. $\displaystyle\int x^{3/2}\tan^{-1}(\sqrt{x})\, dx$

99. $\displaystyle\int \operatorname{arcsec}(\sqrt{x})\, dx$

100. $\displaystyle\int x\sqrt{\frac{1-x^2}{1+x^2}}\, dx$

101. Find the area of the surface generated by revolving the curve $y = \cosh x$, $0 \le x \le 1$, around the x-axis.

102. Find the length of the curve $y = e^{-x}$, $0 \le x \le 1$.

103. (a) Find the area A_t of the surface generated by revolving the curve $y = e^{-x}$, $0 \le x \le t$, around the x-axis. (b) Find $\lim_{t\to\infty} A_t$.

104. (a) Find the area A_t of the surface generated by revolving the curve $y = 1/x$, $1 \le x \le t$, around the x-axis. (b) Find $\lim_{t\to\infty} A_t$.

105. Find the area of the surface generated by revolving the curve $y = \sqrt{x^2-1}$, $1 \le x \le 2$, around the x-axis.

106. (a) Derive the reduction formula

$$\int x^m (\ln x)^n\, dx = \frac{1}{m+1}x^{m+1}(\ln x)^n - \frac{n}{m+1}\int x^m (\ln x)^{n-1}\, dx.$$

(b) Evaluate $\int_1^e x^3(\ln x)^3\, dx$.

107. Derive the reduction formula

$$\int \sin^m x \cos^n x\, dx = -\frac{1}{m+n}\sin^{m-1} x \cos^{n+1} x + \frac{m-1}{m+n}\int \sin^{m-2} x \cos^n x\, dx.$$

108. Use the reduction formulas of Problem 107 here and Problem 54 of Section 8.3 to evaluate

$$\int_0^{\pi/2} \sin^6 x \cos^5 x\, dx.$$

109. Find the area bounded by the curve $y^2 = x^5(2-x)$, $0 \le x \le 2$. [Suggestion: Substitute $x = 2\sin^2\theta$, then use the result of Problem 58 of Section 8.3.]

110. Show that
$$0 < \int_0^1 \frac{t^4(1-t)^4}{1+t^2}\, dt$$
and that
$$\int_0^1 \frac{t^4(1-t)^4}{1+t^2}\, dt = \frac{22}{7} - \pi.$$

111. Evaluate
$$\int_0^1 t^4(1-t)^4\, dt;$$
then apply the results of Problem 110 to conclude that
$$\frac{22}{7} - \frac{1}{630} < \pi < \frac{22}{7} - \frac{1}{1260}.$$
Thus $3.1412 < \pi < 3.1421$.

112. Find the length of the curve $y = \frac{4}{5}x^{5/4}$, $0 \leq x \leq 1$.

113. Find the length of the curve $y = \frac{4}{3}x^{3/4}$, $1 \leq x \leq 4$.

114. An initially empty water tank is shaped like a cone whose axis is vertical. Its vertex is at the bottom; the cone is 9 ft deep and has a top radius of 4.5 ft. Beginning at time $t = 0$, water is poured into this tank at 50 ft^3/min. Meanwhile, water leaks from a hole at the tank's bottom at the rate of $10\sqrt{y}$ cubic feet per minute, where y is the depth of water in the tank. (This is consistent with Torricelli's law of draining.) How long does it take to fill the tank?

115. (a) Evaluate
$$\int \frac{1}{1 + e^x + e^{-x}}\, dx.$$
(b) Explain why your substitution in part (a) suffices to integrate any rational function of e^x.

116. (a) The equation $x^3 + x + 1 = 0$ has at least one real root r. Use Newton's method to find it, accurate to at least two places. (b) Use long division to find (approximately) the irreducible quadratic factor of $x^3 + x + 1$. (c) Use the factorization obtained in part (b) to evaluate (approximately)
$$\int_0^1 \frac{1}{x^3 + x + 1}\, dx.$$

117. Evaluate $\displaystyle\int \frac{1}{1+e^x}\, dx$.

118. The integral
$$\int \frac{1 + 2x^2}{x^5(1+x^2)^3}\, dx = \int \frac{x + 2x^3}{(x^4 + x^2)^3}\, dx$$
would require you to solve 11 equations in 11 unknowns if you were to use the method of partial fractions to evaluate it. Use the substitution $u = x^4 + x^2$ to evaluate it much more simply.

119. Evaluate
$$\int \sqrt{\tan\theta}\, d\theta.$$
[*Suggestion:* First substitute $u = \tan\theta$. Then substitute $u = x^2$. Finally, use the method of partial fractions; see Problem 48 of Section 8.7.]

120. Prove that if $p(x)$ is a polynomial, then the substitution $u^n = (ax+b)/(cx+d)$ transforms the integral
$$\int p(x)\left(\frac{ax+b}{cx+d}\right)^{1/n} dx$$
into the integral of a rational function of u. (The substitution indicated here is called a *rationalizing substitution*; its name comes from the fact that it converts the integrand into a *rational* function of u.)

In Problems 121 through 129, use the rationalizing substitution indicated in Problem 120 to evaluate the integral.

121. $\displaystyle\int x^3\sqrt{3x-2}\, dx$

122. $\displaystyle\int x^3\sqrt[3]{x^2+1}\, dx$

123. $\displaystyle\int \frac{x^3}{(x^2-1)^{4/3}}\, dx$

124. $\displaystyle\int x^2(x-1)^{3/2}\, dx$

125. $\displaystyle\int \frac{x^5}{\sqrt{x^3+1}}\, dx$

126. $\displaystyle\int x^7\sqrt[3]{x^4+1}\, dx$

127. $\displaystyle\int \sqrt{\frac{1+x}{1-x}}\, dx$

128. $\displaystyle\int \frac{x}{\sqrt{x+1}}\, dx$

129. $\displaystyle\int \frac{\sqrt[3]{x+1}}{x}\, dx$

130. Substitute $x = u^2$ to find
$$\int \sqrt{1 + \sqrt{x}}\, dx.$$

131. Substitute $u^2 = 1 + e^{2x}$ to find
$$\int \sqrt{1+e^{2x}}\, dx.$$

132. Find the area A of the surface obtained by revolving the curve $y = \frac{2}{3}x^{3/2}$, $3 \leq x \leq 8$, around the x-axis. [*Suggestion:* Substitute $x = u^2$ into the surface area integral. *Note:* $A \approx 732.39$.]

133. Find the area bounded by one loop of the curve
$$y^2 = x^2(1-x), \quad 0 \leq x \leq 1.$$

134. Find the area bounded by the loop of the curve
$$y^2 = x^2\left(\frac{1-x}{1+x}\right), \quad 0 \leq x \leq 1.$$

More General Trigonometric Integrals

As a last resort, any trigonometric integral can be transformed into an integral
$$\int R(\sin\theta, \cos\theta)\, d\theta \qquad (1)$$
of sines and cosines. If the integrand in Eq. (1) is a quotient of polynomials in the variables $\sin\theta$ and $\cos\theta$, then the special substitution
$$u = \tan\frac{\theta}{2} \qquad (2)$$
suffices for its evaluation.

To carry out the substitution indicated in Eq. (2), we must express $\sin\theta$, $\cos\theta$, and $d\theta$ in terms of u and du. Note first that
$$\theta = 2\tan^{-1} u, \quad \text{so} \quad d\theta = \frac{2\, du}{1+u^2}. \qquad (3)$$

We see from the triangle in Fig. 8.MP.1 that

$$\sin\frac{\theta}{2} = \frac{u}{\sqrt{1+u^2}}, \qquad \cos\frac{\theta}{2} = \frac{1}{\sqrt{1+u^2}}.$$

FIGURE 8.MP.1 The special rationalizing substitution $u = \tan\frac{\theta}{2}$.

Hence

$$\sin\theta = 2\sin\frac{\theta}{2}\cos\frac{\theta}{2} = \frac{2u}{1+u^2}, \qquad (4)$$

$$\cos\theta = \cos^2\frac{\theta}{2} - \sin^2\frac{\theta}{2} = \frac{1-u^2}{1+u^2}. \qquad (5)$$

These substitutions will convert the integral in Eq. (1) into an integral of a rational function of u. The latter can then be evaluated by the methods of Section 8.5.

EXAMPLE With the substitutions in Eqs. (3) and (5),

$$\int \frac{1}{5+3\cos\theta}\,d\theta = \int \frac{1}{5+3\cdot\frac{1-u^2}{1+u^2}} \cdot \frac{2}{1+u^2}\,du$$

$$= \int \frac{2}{8+2u^2}\,du = \int \frac{1}{4+u^2}\,du$$

$$= \frac{1}{2}\tan^{-1}\frac{u}{2} + C = \frac{1}{2}\tan^{-1}\left(\frac{1}{2}\tan\frac{\theta}{2}\right) + C. \quad \blacklozenge$$

In Problems 135 through 142, use the rationalizing substitution given in Eqs. (2) through (5).

135. $\int \dfrac{1}{1+\cos\theta}\,d\theta$

136. $\int \dfrac{1}{5+4\cos\theta}\,d\theta$

137. $\int \dfrac{1}{1+\sin\theta}\,d\theta$

138. $\int \dfrac{1}{(1-\cos\theta)^2}\,d\theta$

139. $\int \dfrac{1}{\sin\theta+\cos\theta}\,d\theta$

140. $\int \dfrac{1}{2+\sin\phi+\cos\phi}\,d\phi$

141. $\int \dfrac{\sin\theta}{2+\cos\theta}\,d\theta$

142. $\int \dfrac{\sin\theta-\cos\theta}{\sin\theta+\cos\theta}\,d\theta$

143. (a) Substitute $u = \tan(\theta/2)$ to show that

$$\int \sec\theta\,d\theta = \ln\left|\frac{1+\tan\frac{\theta}{2}}{1-\tan\frac{\theta}{2}}\right| + C.$$

(b) Use the trigonometric identity

$$\tan\frac{\theta}{2} = \sqrt{\frac{1-\cos\theta}{1+\cos\theta}}$$

to derive our earlier formula

$$\int \sec\theta\,d\theta = \ln|\sec\theta+\tan\theta| + C$$

from the solution in part (a).

144. (a) Use the method of Problem 143 to show that

$$\int \csc\theta\,d\theta = \ln\left|\tan\frac{\theta}{2}\right| + C.$$

(b) Use trigonometric identities to derive the formula

$$\int \csc\theta\,d\theta = \ln|\csc\theta-\cot\theta| + C$$

from part (a).

DIFFERENTIAL EQUATIONS

John Bernoulli (1667–1748)

In the eighteenth century the remarkable Swiss family Bernoulli was to mathematics what the Bach family was to music. Eight different Bernoullis were sufficiently prominent that more than two centuries later, they rate entries in the *Dictionary of Scientific Biography*. The brothers James (Jakob, 1654–1705) and John (Johann, 1667–1748) Bernoulli played crucial rules in the early development of Leibniz's version of the calculus based on infinitely small differentials, which in continental European science predominated over Newton's version based more explicitly on limits of ratios. It was James Bernoulli who introduced the word "integral" in suggesting the name *calculus integralis* (instead of Leibniz's original *calculus summatorius*) for the subject inverse to the *calculus differentialis*.

John Bernoulli first studied mathematics under his older brother James at the university in Basel, Switzerland, but soon they were on an equal footing in mathematical understanding. In 1691, John Bernoulli visited Paris and there met the young Marquis de l'Hôpital (1661–1704), who was anxious to learn the secrets of the new infinitesimal calculus. In return for a generous monthly stipend, Bernoulli agreed to tutor the wealthy Marquis and continued the lessons (and the financial arrangement) by mail after his return to Basel. The result of this correspondence was the first differential calculus textbook, published by l'Hôpital in 1696. This text is remembered mainly for its inclusion of the theorem concerning indeterminate forms now known as *l'Hôpital's rule* (Section 7.2), although it was actually discovered by John Bernoulli.

The Bernoulli brothers were pioneers in the use of differential equations to model physical phenomena, and they introduced now-familiar techniques such as "separation of variables" to solve these differential equations. For instance, both James and John worked on the *catenary problem*, which asks for the shape of a hanging cable suspended between two fixed points, assuming that it is inelastic (unstretchable) but perfectly flexible. They showed that the shape function $y(x)$ of the cable satisfies the differential equation

$$a\frac{d^2y}{dx^2} = \sqrt{1 + \left(\frac{dy}{dx}\right)^2},$$

(where the constant $a = T/\rho$ is the ratio of the cable's tension at its lowest point and its density [assumed constant]). They succeeded in solving this differential equation to show that the shape of the hanging cable is described by

$$y = a\cosh\left(\frac{x}{a}\right).$$

What is the shape of a hanging cable?

545

9.1 SIMPLE EQUATIONS AND MODELS

Mathematical models of changing real-world phenomena frequently involve differential equations—that is, equations containing *derivatives* of unknown functions. For instance, in Section 5.2 we mentioned the simple differential equations

$$\frac{dP}{dt} = kP \quad \text{(natural population growth)} \tag{1}$$

and

$$\frac{dy}{dt} = -k\sqrt{y} \quad \text{(Torricelli's law)}. \tag{2}$$

Each equation involves the independent variable t, a proportionality constant k, and an unknown function $P(t)$ or $y(t)$ of t. The dependent variable P in Eq. (1) denotes a population for which the time rate of change is proportional to the size of the population. The dependent variable y in Eq. (2) denotes the depth of water in a tank draining slowly through a small hole in its bottom.

A (first-order) **differential equation** is an equation that can be written in the form

$$\frac{dy}{dx} = F(x, y) \tag{3}$$

where $F(x, y)$ is a given expression involving the independent variable x and the dependent variable y, the latter representing an unknown function $y(x)$ of x. A **solution** of Eq. (3) is a specific function $y(x)$ such that $y'(x) = F(x, y(x))$ for all x in some appropriate interval I. That is, Eq. (3) reduces to an identity in x when the dependent variable y is replaced with the solution function $y(x)$.

A differential equation frequently appears together with an **initial condition** $y(a) = b$ that specifies a desired value b of the solution at the point $x = a$. The two together constitute an **initial value problem**

$$\frac{dy}{dx} = F(x, y), \quad y(a) = b, \tag{4}$$

which asks for a particular solution $y(x)$ of the differential equation that also satisfies the given initial condition.

EXAMPLE 1 To verify that a given function $y(x)$ is a solution of Eq. (3), it suffices to calculate the derivative dy/dx and then to verify that it is equal to $F(x, y(x))$. For instance, if $y = x^7$ then

$$\frac{dy}{dx} = 7x^6 = 7 \cdot \frac{x^7}{x} = \frac{7y}{x}$$

if $x > 0$. This calculation verifies that the function $y(x) = x^7$ is a solution (on the interval $x > 0$) of the differential equation

$$\frac{dy}{dx} = \frac{7y}{x}. \tag{5}$$

You can verify similarly that $y(x) = Cx^7$ satisfies Eq. (5) for any value of the constant C. ◆

When a solution of a differential equation contains an arbitrary constant C, we call the solution a **general solution** of the equation. A general solution actually describes an infinite collection of **particular solutions** of the differential equation, because different choices of C yield different solutions of the equation. Thus the choices $C = 11$ and $C = 23$ in Example 1 yield the two particular solutions $y_1(x) = 11x^7$

and $y_2(x) = 23x^7$. The former satisfies the initial value problem

$$\frac{dy}{dx} = \frac{7y}{x}, \qquad y(1) = 11,$$

while $y_2(x)$ satisfies the initial condition $y(1) = 23$.

Equations with One Variable Missing

If the dependent variable y does not appear explicitly on the right-hand side in (3), then the differential equation reduces to the form

$$\frac{dy}{dx} = f(x) \tag{6}$$

where f is a given function of x. As we noted in Section 5.2, the solution of a differential equation of this simple form reduces to integration:

$$y(x) = \int y'(x)\,dx = \int f(x)\,dx + C.$$

If the indefinite integral $F(x) = \int f(x)\,dx$ can be evaluated, then $y(x) = F(x) + C$ is a general solution of Eq. (6). For instance, a general solution of the differential equation $dy/dx = 21x^6$ is given by

$$y(x) = \int 21x^6\,dx = 3x^7 + C.$$

If, on the other hand, the independent variable x does not appear explicitly on the right-hand side in (3), then the differential equation reduces to the form

$$\frac{dy}{dx} = g(y), \tag{7}$$

which implies that $y'(x) = g(y(x))$ if $y(x)$ is a solution. To solve the equation in (7), we can first divide both sides by $g(y(x))$ and then attempt to integrate with respect to x:

$$\int \frac{y'(x)}{g(y(x))}\,dx = \int 1\,dx; \qquad \text{[substitute } y = y(x),\ dy = y'(x)\,dx\text{]}$$

$$\int \frac{1}{g(y)}\,dy = x + C. \tag{8}$$

If the indefinite integral

$$G(y) = \int \frac{1}{g(y)}\,dy$$

in (8) can be evaluated, then we may call the resulting equation

$$G(y) = x + C \tag{9}$$

an **implicit solution** of Eq. (7)—whether or not we can solve explicitly for y as a function of x.

REMARK Note that Eq. (8) results formally from the differential equation in (7) if we first divide both sides by $g(y)$ and multiply by dx to "separate the variables,"

$$\frac{1}{g(y)}\,dy = dx,$$

then integrate each side with respect to its "own" variable—y on the left and x on the right.

EXAMPLE 2 Solve the initial value problem

$$\frac{dy}{dx} = y^2, \qquad y(0) = 2. \tag{10}$$

Solution Separating the variables as in Eqs. (8) and (9), we write

$$\int \frac{1}{y^2} dy = \int dx; \qquad -\frac{1}{y} = x + C.$$

This is an implicit general solution from which we readily obtain the explicit general solution

$$y(x) = -\frac{1}{x+C}. \tag{11}$$

We find C by substituting the initial values $x = 0$, $y = 2$. This gives $C = -\frac{1}{2}$, so the desired particular solution of the initial value problem in (10) is

$$y(x) = -\frac{1}{x - \frac{1}{2}} = \frac{2}{1 - 2x}.$$

FIGURE 9.1.1 Solution curves of the differential equation $y' = y^2$.

The graph of this solution, passing through the point $(0, 2)$, is highlighted in Fig. 9.1.1. ◆

The graph of a solution of a differential equation is called a **solution curve** of the equation. Figure 9.9.1 shows a variety of different solution curves of the differential equation $dy/dx = y^2$ of Example 2. It appears that these solution curves fill the xy-plane. Indeed, given any fixed point (a, b) of the plane with $b \neq 0$, we can substitute $x = a$ and $y = b$ in Eq. (11) and solve for C to obtain the solution curve that passes through this point. The x-axis is also a solution curve of the differential equation. (Why?)

The Natural Growth Equation

With $x(t)$ in place of $P(t)$ in Eq. (1), we have the differential equation

$$\frac{dx}{dt} = kx, \tag{12}$$

which serves as the mathematical model for an extraordinarily wide range of natural phenomena. It is easily solved if we first separate the variables and then integrate:

$$\frac{dx}{x} = k\,dt;$$

$$\int \frac{dx}{x} = \int k\,dt;$$

$$\ln x = kt + C.$$

We apply the exponential function to both sides of the last equation to solve for x:

$$x = e^{\ln x} = e^{kt+C} = e^{kt}e^C = Ae^{kt}.$$

Here, $A = e^C$ is a constant that remains to be determined. But we see that A is simply the value $x_0 = x(0)$ of $x(t)$ when $t = 0$, and thus $A = x_0$.

THEOREM 1 The Natural Growth Equation

The solution of the initial value problem

$$\frac{dx}{dt} = kx, \qquad x(0) = x_0 \tag{13}$$

is

$$x(t) = x_0 e^{kt}. \tag{14}$$

As a consequence, Eq. (12) is often called the **exponential growth equation,** or the **natural growth equation.** We see from Eq. (14) that, with $x_0 > 0$, the solution $x(t)$ is an increasing function if $k > 0$ and a decreasing function if $k < 0$. (The situation $k < 0$ is sometimes called *exponential decay.*) These two cases are illustrated in Figs. 9.1.2 and 9.1.3, respectively. The remainder of this section concerns examples of natural phenomena for which this differential equation serves as a mathematical model.

FIGURE 9.1.2 Solution of the exponential growth equation for $k > 0$.

FIGURE 9.1.3 Solution of the exponential growth equation—now actually a *decay* equation—for the case $k < 0$.

Population Growth

When we compare Eqs. (1), (12), and (14), we see that a population $P(t)$ with growth rate proportional to its size is given by

$$P(t) = P_0 e^{kt}, \tag{15}$$

where $P_0 = P(0)$. If t is measured in years, then the proportionality constant k in (15) is called the **annual growth rate,** which can be positive, negative, or zero. Its value is often given as a percentage (its decimal value multiplied by 100). If k is close to zero, then this value is fairly close to the annual percentage increase (or decrease) of the population each year.

EXAMPLE 3 According to data posted at www.census.gov, the world's total population reached 6 billion persons in mid-1999, and was then increasing at the rate of about 212 thousand persons each day. Assuming that natural population growth at this rate continues, we want to answer these questions:

(a) What is the annual growth rate k?
(b) What will the world population be at the middle of the 21st century?
(c) How long will it take for the world population to increase tenfold—thereby reaching the 60 billion that some demographers believe to be the maximum for which the planet can provide adequate food supplies?

Solution (a) We measure the world population $P(t)$ in billions and measure time in years. We take $t = 0$ to correspond to mid-1999, so that $P_0 = 6$. The fact that $P(t)$ is increasing by 212,000, or 0.000212 billion, persons per day at time $t = 0$ means that

$$P'(0) = (0.000212)(365.25) \approx 0.07743$$

billion per year. From the natural growth equation $dP/dt = kP$ with $t = 0$ we now obtain

$$k = \frac{P'(0)}{P(0)} \approx \frac{0.07743}{6} \approx 0.0129.$$

Thus the world population was growing at the rate of about 1.29% annually in mid-1999. This value of k gives the world population function

$$P(t) = P_0 e^{kt} = 6e^{(0.0129)t}.$$

(b) With $t = 51$ we obtain the prediction

$$P(51) = 6e^{(0.0129)(51)} \approx 11.58$$

(billion) for the world population in mid-2050, so the population will almost double in the 51 years following 1999.

(c) The world population should reach 60 billion when

$$60 = 6e^{(0.0129)t}; \quad \text{that is, when} \quad t = \frac{\ln 10}{0.0129} \approx 178,$$

thus in the year 2177. ◆

Note Actually, the rate of growth of the world population is expected to slow somewhat during the next half-century, and the best current prediction for the population in the year 2050 is "only" 9.1 billion. A simple mathematical model cannot be expected to mirror precisely the complexity of the real world.

Radioactive Decay and Radiocarbon Dating

Consider a sample of material that contains $N(t)$ atoms of a certain radioactive isotope at time t. Many experiments have confirmed that a constant fraction of these radioactive atoms will spontaneously decay (into atoms of another element or another isotope of the same element) during each given unit of time. Consequently, the sample behaves exactly like a population with a constant death rate but with no births occurring. To write a model for $N(t)$, we use Eq. (1) with N in place of P and with $-k$ in place of k (so that $k > 0$ corresponds to a decreasing number of atoms). We thus obtain the differential equation

$$\frac{dN}{dt} = -kN. \tag{16}$$

From the solution (14) of Eq. (12), with k replaced with $-k$, we conclude that

$$N(t) = N_0 e^{-kt}, \tag{17}$$

where $N_0 = N(0)$, the number of radioactive atoms of the original isotope present in the sample at time $t = 0$.

The value of the *decay constant k* depends on the particular isotope with which we are dealing. If k is large, then the isotope decays rapidly. If k is near zero, the isotope decays quite slowly and thus may be a relatively persistent factor in its environment. The decay constant k is often specified in terms of another empirical parameter that is more convenient, the *half-life* of the isotope. The **half-life** τ of a sample of a radioactive isotope is the time required for *half* of that sample to decay. To find the relationship between k and τ, we set

$$t = \tau \quad \text{and} \quad N = \tfrac{1}{2} N_0$$

in Eq. (17), so that

$$\tfrac{1}{2}N_0 = N_0 e^{-k\tau}. \tag{18}$$

When we solve for τ, we find that

$$\tau = \frac{\ln 2}{k}. \tag{19}$$

Note that the concept of half-life is meaningful—the value of τ depends *only* on k and thus depends only on the particular isotope involved. It does *not* depend on the amount of that isotope present.

The method of *radiocarbon dating* is based on the fact that the radioactive carbon isotope ^{14}C has a known half-life of about 5700 yr. Living organic matter maintains a constant level of ^{14}C by "breathing" air (or by consuming organic matter that does so). But air contains ^{14}C along with the much more common, stable isotope ^{12}C of carbon, mostly in the gas CO_2. Thus all living organisms maintain the same percentage of ^{14}C as in air, because organic processes seem to make no distinction between the two isotopes. But when an organism dies, it ceases to metabolize carbon, and the process of radioactive decay begins to deplete its ^{14}C content. The fraction of ^{14}C in the air remains roughly constant because new ^{14}C is continuously generated by the bombardment of nitrogen atoms in the upper atmosphere by cosmic rays, and this generation has long been in steady-state equilibrium with the loss of ^{14}C through radioactive decay.

EXAMPLE 4 A specimen of charcoal found at Stonehenge contains 63% as much ^{14}C as a sample of present-day charcoal. What is the age of the sample?

Solution We take $t = 0$ (in years) as the time of death of the tree from which the Stonehenge charcoal was made. From Eq. (18), we know that

$$\tfrac{1}{2}N_0 = N_0 e^{-5700k},$$

so

$$k = \frac{\ln 2}{\tau} = \frac{\ln 2}{5700} \approx 0.0001216.$$

We are given that $N = (0.63)N_0$ at present, so we solve the equation

$$(0.63)N_0 = N_0 e^{-kt}$$

with this value of k. We thus find that

$$t = -\frac{\ln(0.63)}{0.0001216} \approx 3800 \quad (\text{yr}).$$

Therefore, the sample is about 3800 yr old. If it is connected in any way with the builders of Stonehenge, our computations suggest that this observatory, monument, or temple—whichever it may be—dates from almost 1800 B.C. ◆

EXAMPLE 5 According to one cosmological theory, there were equal amounts of the uranium isotopes ^{235}U and ^{238}U at the creation of the universe in the "big bang." At present there are 137.7 ^{238}U atoms for each ^{235}U atom. Using the known half-lives

$$4.51 \text{ billion yr for } ^{238}U,$$

$$0.71 \text{ billion yr for } ^{235}U,$$

calculate the age of the universe.

Solution Let $N_8(t)$ and $N_5(t)$ be the numbers of ^{238}U and ^{235}U atoms, respectively, at time t, in billions of years after the creation of the universe. Then

$$N_8(t) = N_0 e^{-kt} \quad \text{and} \quad N_5(t) = N_0 e^{-ct},$$

where N_0 is the initial number of atoms of each isotope. Also,

$$k = \frac{\ln 2}{4.51} \quad \text{and} \quad c = \frac{\ln 2}{0.71},$$

a consequence of Eq. (19). We divide the equation for N_8 by the equation for N_5 and find that when t has the value corresponding to "now,"

$$137.7 = \frac{N_8}{N_5} = e^{(c-k)t}.$$

Finally, we solve this equation for t:

$$t = \frac{\ln(137.7)}{\left(\dfrac{1}{0.71} - \dfrac{1}{4.51}\right) \ln 2} \approx 5.99.$$

Thus we estimate the age of the universe to be about 6 billion years, which is roughly on the same order of magnitude as recent estimates of 10 to 15 billion years (based on astronomical observations of the rate of expansion of the universe). ◆

More Natural Growth and Decay Models

Continuously Compounded Interest Consider a savings account that is opened with an initial deposit of A_0 dollars and earns interest at the annual rate r. If there are $A(t)$ dollars in the account at time t and the interest is compounded at time $t + \Delta t$, this means that $rA(t) \Delta t$ dollars in interest are added to the account then. So

$$A(t + \Delta t) = A(t) + rA(t) \Delta t,$$

and thus

$$\frac{\Delta A}{\Delta t} = \frac{A(t + \Delta t) - A(t)}{\Delta t} = rA(t).$$

Continuous compounding of interest results from taking the limit as $\Delta t \to 0$, so

$$\frac{dA}{dt} = rA. \tag{20}$$

This is an exponential growth equation with solution

$$A(t) = A_0 e^{rt}. \tag{21}$$

EXAMPLE 6 If $A_0 = \$1000$ is invested at an annual interest rate of 6% compounded continuously, then $r = 0.06$, and Eq. (21) gives

$$A(1) = 1000 e^{(0.06)(1)} = \$1061.84$$

for the value of the investment after one year. Hence the *effective annual interest rate* is 6.184%. Thus the more often interest is compounded, the more rapidly savings grow, but bank advertisements sometimes overemphasize this advantage. For instance, 6% compounded *monthly* multiplies your investment by

$$1 + \frac{0.06}{12} = 1.005$$

at the end of each month, so an initial investment of $1000 would grow in one year to

$$(1000)(1.005)^{12} = \$1061.68,$$

only 16¢ less than would be yielded by continuous compounding. ◆

Drug Elimination The amount $A(t)$ of a certain drug in the human bloodstream, as measured by the excess above the natural level of the drug in the bloodstream, typically declines at a rate proportional to that excess amount. That is,

$$\frac{dA}{dt} = -\lambda A, \quad \text{so} \quad A(t) = A_0 e^{-\lambda t}. \tag{22}$$

The parameter λ is called the *elimination constant* of the drug, and $T = 1/\lambda$ is called the *elimination time*.

EXAMPLE 7 The elimination time for alcohol varies from one person to another. If a person's "sobering time" $T = 1/\lambda$ is 2.5 h, how long will it take the excess bloodstream alcohol concentration to be reduced from 0.10% to 0.02%?

Solution We assume that the normal concentration of alcohol in the blood is zero, so any amount is an excess amount. In this problem, we have $\lambda = 1/2.5 = 0.4$, so Eq. (22) yields

$$0.02 = (0.10)e^{-(0.4)t}.$$

Thus

$$t = -\frac{\ln(0.2)}{0.4} \approx 4.02 \quad (\text{h}).\qquad\blacklozenge$$

Sales Decline According to marketing studies, if advertising for a particular product is halted and other market conditions—such things as number and promotion of competing products, their prices, and so on—remain unchanged, then the sales of the unadvertised product will decline at a rate that is proportional at any time t to the current sales S. That is,

$$\frac{dS}{dt} = -\lambda S, \quad \text{so} \quad S(t) = S_0 e^{-\lambda t}.$$

Here S_0 denotes the initial value of the sales, which we take to be sales in the final month of advertising. If we take months as the units for time t, then $S(t)$ gives the number of sales t months after advertising is halted, and λ might be called the *sales decay constant*.

Linguistics Consider a basic list of N_0 words in use in a given language at time $t = 0$. Let $N(t)$ denote the number of these words that are still in use at time t—those that have neither disappeared from the language nor been replaced. According to one theory in linguistics, the rate of decrease of N is proportional to N. That is,

$$\frac{dN}{dt} = -\lambda N, \quad \text{so} \quad N(t) = N_0 e^{-\lambda t}.$$

If t is measured in millennia (as is standard in linguistics), then $k = e^{-\lambda}$ is the fraction of the words in the original list that survive for 1000 yr.

Torricelli's Law

Suppose that a water tank has a hole with area a at its bottom and that water is draining from the hole. Denote by $y(t)$ the depth (in feet) of water in the tank at time t (in seconds) and by $V(t)$ the volume of water (in cubic feet) in the tank then. It is plausible—and true under ideal conditions—that the velocity of the stream of water exiting through the hole is

$$v = \sqrt{2gy} \quad (g \approx 32 \text{ ft/s}^2), \tag{23}$$

which is the velocity that a drop of water would acquire in falling freely from the water surface to the hole. This is *Torricelli's law of draining*.

As indicated in Fig. 9.1.4, the amount of water that leaves through the bottom hole during a short time interval dt amounts to a cylinder with base area a and height $v\,dt$. Hence the resulting change dV in the volume of water in the tank is given by

$$dV = -av\,dt = -a\sqrt{2gy}\,dt. \tag{24}$$

FIGURE 9.1.4 Derivation of Torricelli's law.

554 CHAPTER 9 Differential Equations

But if $A(y)$ denotes the horizontal cross-sectional area of the tank at height y above the hole, then
$$dV = A(y)\,dy, \tag{25}$$
as usual. Comparing Eqs. (24) and (25), we see that $y(t)$ satisfies the differential equation
$$A(y)\frac{dy}{dt} = -a\sqrt{2gy}. \tag{26}$$

In some applications this is a very convenient form of Torricelli's law. In other situations you may prefer to work with the differential equation in (24) in the form
$$\frac{dV}{dt} = -a\sqrt{2gy} \tag{27}$$
or, if the area of the bottom hole is unknown, the form
$$\frac{dV}{dt} = -c\sqrt{y}, \tag{28}$$
where $c = a\sqrt{2g}$ is a positive constant.

Cylindrical water tanks are common (Fig. 9.1.5). In this case the cross-sectional area function in Eq. (26) is constant: $A(y) \equiv A$. Consequently Eq. (26) reduces to the simple differential equation
$$\frac{dy}{dt} = -k\sqrt{y} \tag{29}$$

FIGURE 9.1.5 A cylindrical water tank has constant cross-sectional area.

where $k = (a/A)\sqrt{2g}$ is a positive constant that frequently is determined from given tank-draining data (rather than from a knowledge of the areas a and A).

EXAMPLE 8 The water in a draining cylindrical tank is 10 ft deep at noon. At 1:00 P.M. it is 5 ft deep. When will the tank be empty?

Solution If we write Eq. (29) in the form
$$\frac{1}{\sqrt{y}} \cdot \frac{dy}{dt} = -k,$$
then integration yields
$$2\sqrt{y} = -kt + C.$$
Substituting the initial data $y = 10$ when $t = 0$ (noon) gives $C = 2\sqrt{10}$, so
$$2\sqrt{y} = -kt + 2\sqrt{10}. \tag{30}$$
Then substituting the additional data $y = 5$ when $t = 1$ (1:00 P.M.) gives $k = 2\sqrt{10} - 2\sqrt{5}$. Substituting this value in Eq. (30) and dividing by 2 yields
$$\sqrt{y} = (\sqrt{5} - \sqrt{10})t + \sqrt{10}. \tag{31}$$
Finally, the tank is empty when $y = 0$ in Eq. (31), and thus when
$$t = \frac{\sqrt{10}}{\sqrt{10} - \sqrt{5}} \approx 3.414,$$
about 3 h 25 min. So we see that—whereas a natural (but naive and **wrong**) guess might have been 2:00 P.M. (one more hour for the remaining 5 ft of water to drain)—the tank actually is not empty until about 3:25 P.M. You should use Eq. (31) to show that the actual water depth in the tank at 2:00 P.M. is about 1.72 ft, and the depth at 3:00 P.M. is about 2 in., so it takes about 25 min for the last 2 in. of water in the tank to drain! ◆

EXAMPLE 9 A hemispherical tank has top radius 4 ft and, at time $t = 0$, is full of water. At that moment a circular hole of diameter 1 in. is opened in the bottom of the tank. How long will it take for all the water to drain from the tank?

Solution From the right triangle in Fig. 9.1.6, we see that

$$A(y) = \pi r^2 = \pi[16 - (4-y)^2] = \pi(8y - y^2).$$

With $g = 32$ ft/s^2, Eq. (26) takes the form

$$\pi(8y - y^2)\frac{dy}{dt} = -\pi\left(\frac{1}{24}\right)^2\sqrt{64y};$$

$$\int (8y^{1/2} - y^{3/2})\,dy = -\int \frac{1}{72}\,dt + C;$$

$$\frac{16}{3}y^{3/2} - \frac{2}{5}y^{5/2} = -\frac{1}{72}t + C.$$

Now $y(0) = 4$, so

$$C = \tfrac{16}{3}\cdot 4^{3/2} - \tfrac{2}{5}\cdot 4^{5/2} = \tfrac{448}{15}.$$

The tank is empty when $y = 0$—that is, when

$$t = 72\cdot\tfrac{448}{15} \approx 2150 \text{ (s)},$$

about 35 min 50 s. So it takes slightly less than 36 min for the tank to drain. ◆

FIGURE 9.1.6 Draining a hemispherical tank.

9.1 TRUE/FALSE STUDY GUIDE

9.1 CONCEPTS: QUESTIONS AND DISCUSSION

1. Do the solution curves of the natural growth equation $dy/dx = ky$ (with k a constant) fill the entire xy-plane?
2. Do the solution curves of the differential equation $dy/dx = k\sqrt{y}$ (with k a constant) fill the entire xy-plane?
3. Can one solve the differential equation $dy/dx = xy$ simply by integrating both sides with respect to x? Justify your answer.

9.1 PROBLEMS

In each of Problems 1 through 10, first find a general solution of the given differential equation. Then find a particular solution that satisfies the given initial condition.

1. $\dfrac{dy}{dx} = 2y, \quad y(1) = 3$
2. $\dfrac{dy}{dx} = -3y, \quad y(5) = -10$
3. $\dfrac{dy}{dx} = 2y^2, \quad y(7) = 3$
4. $\dfrac{dy}{dx} = \dfrac{7}{y}, \quad y(0) = 6$
5. $\dfrac{dy}{dx} = 2\sqrt{y}, \quad y(0) = 9$
6. $\dfrac{dy}{dx} = 6y^{2/3}, \quad y(1) = 8$
7. $\dfrac{dy}{dx} = 1 + y, \quad y(0) = 5$
8. $\dfrac{dy}{dx} = (2+y)^2, \quad y(5) = 3$
9. $\dfrac{dy}{dx} = e^{-y}, \quad y(0) = 2$
10. $\dfrac{dy}{dx} = 2\sec y, \quad y(0) = 0$

In Problems 11 through 15, a function $y = g(x)$ is described by a geometric property of its graph. Write a differential equation of the form $dy/dx = F(x, y)$ having the function g as a solution.

11. The slope of the graph of g at the point (x, y) is the sum of x and y.
12. The line tangent to the graph of g at the point (x, y) intersects the x-axis at the point $(x/2, 0)$.
13. Every straight line normal to the graph of g passes through the point $(0, 1)$.
14. The graph of g is normal to every curve of the form $y = kx^2$ (k is a constant) where they meet.
15. The line tangent to the graph of g at the point (x, y) passes through the point $(-y, x)$.

In Problems 16 through 20, write—in the manner of Eqs. (1) and (2) of this section—a differential equation that is a mathematical model of the situation described.

16. The time rate of change of a population $P = P(t)$ is proportional to the square root of P.

17. The time rate of change of the velocity $v = v(t)$ of a coasting motorboat is proportional to the square of v.

18. The acceleration dv/dt of a Lamborghini is proportional to the difference between 250 km/h and the velocity of the car.

19. In a city having a fixed population P of persons, the time rate of change of the number N of those persons who have heard a certain rumor is proportional to the number of those who have not yet heard the rumor.

20. In a city with a fixed population P of persons, the time rate of change of the number N of those persons infected with a certain contagious disease is proportional to the product of the number who have the disease and the number who do not.

21. *Continuously Compounded Interest* Suppose that $1000 is deposited in a savings account that pays 8% annual interest compounded continuously. At what rate (in dollars per year) is it earning interest after 5 yr? After 20 yr?

22. *Population Growth* Coopersville had a population of 25,000 in 1970 and a population of 30,000 in 1980. Assume that its population will continue to grow exponentially at a constant rate. What population can the Coopersville city planners expect in the year 2010?

23. *Population Growth* In a certain culture of bacteria, the number of bacteria increased sixfold in 10 h. Assuming natural growth, how long did it take for their number to double?

24. *Radiocarbon Dating* Carbon extracted from an ancient skull recently unearthed contained only one-sixth as much radioactive ^{14}C as carbon extracted from present-day bone. How old is the skull?

25. *Radiocarbon Dating* Carbon taken from a relic purported to date from A.D. 30 contained 4.6×10^{10} atoms of ^{14}C per gram. Carbon extracted from a present-day specimen of the same substance contained 5.0×10^{10} atoms of ^{14}C per gram. Compute the approximate age of the relic. What is your opinion as to its authenticity?

26. *Continuously Compounded Interest* Upon the birth of their first child, a couple deposited $5000 in a savings account that pays 6% annual interest compounded continuously. The interest payments are allowed to accumulate. How much will the account contain when the child is ready to go to college at age 18?

27. *Continuously Compounded Interest* You discover in your attic an overdue library book on which your great-great-great-grandfather owed a fine of 30¢ exactly 100 years ago. If an overdue fine grows exponentially at a 5% annual interest rate compounded continuously, how much would you have to pay if you returned the book today?

28. *Drug Elimination* Suppose that sodium pentobarbital will anesthetize a dog when its bloodstream contains at least 45 mg of sodium pentobarbital per kilogram of body weight of the dog. Suppose also that sodium pentobarbital is eliminated exponentially from a dog's bloodstream, with a half-life of 5 h. What single dose should be administered to anesthetize a 50-kg dog for 1 h?

29. *Sales Decline* Moonbeam Motors has discontinued advertising of their sports-utility vehicle. The company plans to resume advertising when sales have declined to 75% of their initial rate. If after 1 week without advertising, sales have declined to 95% of their initial rate, when should the company expect to resume advertising?

30. *Linguistics* The English language evolves in such a way that 77% of all words disappear (or are replaced) every 1000 yr. Of a basic list of words used by Chaucer in A.D. 1400, what percentage should we expect to find still in use today?

31. *Radioactive Decay* The half-life of radioactive cobalt is 5.27 yr. Suppose that a nuclear accident has left the level of cobalt radiation in a certain region at 100 times the level acceptable for human habitation. How long will it be before the region is again habitable? (Ignore the likely presence of other radioactive substances.)

32. *Radioactive Decay* Suppose that a rare mineral deposit formed in an ancient cataclysm—such as the collision of a meteorite with the earth—originally contained the uranium isotope ^{238}U (which has a half-life of 4.51×10^9 yr) but none of the lead isotope ^{207}Pb, the end product of the radioactive decay of ^{238}U. If the ratio of ^{238}U atoms to ^{207}Pb atoms in the mineral deposit today is 0.9, when did the cataclysm occur?

33. A bacteria population $P(t)$ undergoing natural growth numbers 49 at 12 noon. (a) Suppose that there are 294 bacteria at 1:00 P.M. Write a formula giving $P(t)$ after t hours. (b) How many bacteria are there at 1:40 P.M.? (c) At what time—to the nearest minute—will there be 20 thousand bacteria?

34. The amount $A(t)$ of atmospheric pollutants in a certain mountain valley satisfies the natural growth equation and triples every 7.5 years. (a) If the initial amount is 10 pu ("pollution units"), write a formula for $A(t)$ giving the amount (in pu) present after t years. (b) What will be the amount of pollutants present in the valley atmosphere after 5 years? (c) If it will be dangerous to stay in the valley when the amount of pollutants reaches 100 pu, how long will this take?

35. An accident at a nuclear power plant has left the surrounding area polluted with radioactive material that undergoes natural decay. The initial amount of radioactive material present is 15 su ("safe units") and 5 months later it is 10 su. (a) Write a formula giving the amount $A(t)$ of radioactive material (in su) remaining after t months. (b) What amount of radioactive material will remain after 8 months? (c) How long—total number of months or fraction thereof—will it be until $A(t) = 1$ (su), so it is safe for people to return to the area?

36. There are now about 3300 different human *language families* in the whole world. Assume that all of these are derived from a single original language and that a language family develops into 1.5 language families every 6 thousand years. About how long ago was the single original human language spoken?

37. Thousand of years ago ancestors of the Native Americans crossed the Bering Strait from Asia and entered the western

hemisphere. Since then, they have fanned out across North and South America. The single language that the original Native Americans spoke has since split into many language families. Assume (as in Problem 36) that the number of these language families has been multiplied by 1.5 every 6000 years. There are now 150 Native American language families in the western hemisphere. About when did the ancestors of today's Native Americans arrive?

38. In 1998 there were 40 million Internet users in the world and this number was then doubling every 100 days. Assuming that this rate of growth continued, how long would it be until all the world's 6 billion human beings were using the Internet?

39. A tank shaped like a vertical cylinder initially contains water to a depth of 9 ft (Fig. 9.1.7). A bottom plug is pulled at time $t = 0$ (t in hours). After 1 h the depth has dropped to 4 ft. How long will it take all the water to drain from this tank?

FIGURE 9.1.7 The cylindrical tank of Problem 39.

40. Suppose that the tank of Problem 39 has a radius of 3 ft and that its bottom hole is circular with radius 1 in. How long will it take for the water, initially 9 ft deep, to drain completely?

41. A water tank is in the shape of a right circular cone with its axis vertical and its vertex at the bottom. The tank is 16 ft high and the radius of its top is 5 ft. At time $t = 0$, a plug at its vertex is removed and the tank, initially full of water, begins to drain. After 1 h the water in the tank is 9 ft deep. When will the tank be empty (Fig. 9.1.8)?

FIGURE 9.1.8 The conical tank of Problem 41.

42. Suppose that a cylindrical tank (axis vertical) initially containing V_0 liters of water drains through a bottom hole in T minutes. Use Torricelli's law to show that the volume of water in the tank after $t \leq T$ minutes is $V(t) = V_0[1 - (t/T)]^2$.

43. The shape of a water tank is obtained by revolving the curve $y = x^{4/3}$ around the y-axis (units on the coordinate axes are in feet). A plug at the bottom is removed at 12 noon, when the water depth in the tank is 12 ft. At 1 P.M. the water depth is 6 ft. When will the tank be empty?

44. The shape of a water tank is obtained by revolving the parabola $y = x^2$ around the y-axis (units on the coordinate axes are in feet; see Fig. 9.1.9). The water depth is 4 ft at 12 noon; at that time, a plug in a circular hole at the bottom of the tank is removed. At 1 P.M. the water level is 1 ft. (a) Find the water depth $y(t)$ after t hours. (b) When will the tank be empty? (c) What is the radius of the circular hole at the bottom?

FIGURE 9.1.9 The tank of Problem 44.

45. A cylindrical tank of length 5 ft and radius 3 ft is situated with its axis horizontal. If a circular bottom hole of radius 1 in. is opened and the tank is initially half full of xylene, how long will it take the liquid to drain completely?

46. A spherical tank of radius 25 cm is full of mercury when a circular bottom hole of radius 5 mm is opened. How long will it be before all of the mercury drains from the tank? (Use $g = 9.8$ m/s^2.)

47. *The Clepsydra, or Water Clock* A 12-h water clock is to be designed with the dimensions shown in Fig. 9.1.10, shaped like the surface obtained by revolving the curve $y = f(x)$ around the y-axis. What equation should this curve have, *and* what radius should the bottom hole have, so that the water level will fall at the *constant* rate of 4 in./h?

FIGURE 9.1.10 The clepsydra of Problem 47.

9.2 SLOPE FIELDS AND EULER'S METHOD

Consider a differential equation of the form $dy/dx = F(x, y)$, where $F(x, y)$ contains both the variables x and y. To solve it, we might think of integrating both sides with respect to x, and hence write $y(x) = \int F(x, y(x))\, dx + C$. Unfortunately, this does not provide a solution of the differential equation because the integral involves the unknown function $y(x)$ itself. In fact, there exists *no* straightforward procedure by which a general differential equation can be solved explicitly. Indeed, the solutions of such a simple-looking differential equation as $dy/dx = x^2 + y^2$ cannot be expressed in terms of the ordinary elementary functions studied in calculus. Nevertheless, the graphical and numerical methods of this section can be used to construct *approximate* solutions of differential equations that suffice for many practical purposes.

Slope Fields and Graphical Solutions

There is a simple geometric way to think about solutions of a given differential equation $dy/dx = F(x, y)$. At each point (x, y) of the xy-plane at which F is defined, the value of $F(x, y)$ determines a slope $m = y'(x) = F(x, y)$. A solution of the differential equation is simply a function whose graph has this "correct slope" at each point through which it passes. Thus a **solution curve** of the differential equation $dy/dx = F(x, y)$—the graph of a solution of this equation—is simply a curve in the xy-plane whose tangent line at each point (x, y) has slope $m = F(x, y)$. For instance, Fig. 9.2.1 shows a solution curve of the differential equation $dy/dx = x - y$ together with lines tangent at three typical points.

This geometric viewpoint suggests a *graphical method* for constructing approximate solutions of the differential equation $dy/dx = F(x, y)$. Through each of a representative collection of points (x, y) in the plane we draw a short line segment having the proper slope $m = F(x, y)$. All these line segments constitute a **slope field** (or **direction field**) for the equation $dy/dx = F(x, y)$.

This slope field suggests visually the general shapes of solution curves of the differential equation. Through each point a solution curve should proceed in such a direction that its tangent line is nearly parallel to the nearby line segments of the slope field. Beginning at any initial point (a, b), we can attempt to sketch freehand a solution curve that threads its way through the slope field, following the visible line segments as closely as possible.

FIGURE 9.2.1 A solution curve for the differential equation $y' = x - y$ together with tangent lines having

- slope $m_1 = x_1 - y_1$ at the point (x_1, y_1);
- slope $m_2 = x_2 - y_2$ at the point (x_2, y_2); and
- slope $m_3 = x_3 - y_3$ at the point (x_3, y_3).

EXAMPLE 1 Construct a slope field for the differential equation $dy/dx = x - y$ and use it to sketch a solution curve that passes through the point $(-4, 4)$.

Solution Figure 9.2.2 shows a table of slopes for the given equation. The numerical slope $m = x - y$ appears at the intersection of the horizontal x-row and the vertical y-column of the table. If you inspect the pattern of upper-left to lower-right diagonals in this table, you can see that it was easily and quickly constructed. (Of course, a more complicated function $F(x, y)$ on the right-hand side of the differential equation would

x \ y	−4	−3	−2	−1	0	1	2	3	4
−4	0	−1	−2	−3	−4	−5	−6	−7	−8
−3	1	0	−1	−2	−3	−4	−5	−6	−7
−2	2	1	0	−1	−2	−3	−4	−5	−6
−1	3	2	1	0	−1	−2	−3	−4	−5
0	4	3	2	1	0	−1	−2	−3	−4
1	5	4	3	2	1	0	−1	−2	−3
2	6	5	4	3	2	1	0	−1	−2
3	7	6	5	4	3	2	1	0	−1
4	8	7	6	5	4	3	2	1	0

FIGURE 9.2.2 Values of the slope $y' = x - y$ for $-4 \leq x, y \leq 4$.

FIGURE 9.2.3 Slope field for $y' = x - y$ corresponding to the table of slopes in Fig. 8.2.2.

FIGURE 9.2.4 The solution curve through $(-4, 4)$.

necessitate more complicated calculations.) Figure 9.2.3 shows the corresponding slope field; Fig. 9.2.4 shows a solution curve sketched through the point $(-4, 4)$ in such a way as to follow this slope field as closely as possible. At each point the solution curve appears to proceed in the direction indicated by the nearby line segments of the slope field. ◆

The 81 slope segments in Fig. 9.2.3 are tedious to construct by hand. Fortunately, most computer algebra systems include commands for quick and ready construction of slope fields with as many line segments as desired; such commands are illustrated in the project material for this section. The more line segments are constructed, the more accurately solution curves can be visualized and sketched. Figure 9.2.4 shows a "finer" slope field for the differential equation $dy/dx = x - y$ of Example 1, together with typical solution curves threading through this slope field.

If you look closely at Fig. 9.2.5, you may detect a solution curve that appears to be a straight line! Indeed, you can verify that the linear function $y = x - 1$ is a solution of the equation $dy/dx = x - y$, and it appears likely that the other solution curves approach this straight line as an asymptote as $x \to +\infty$. This inference illustrates the fact that a slope field can suggest tangible information about solutions that is not at all evident from the differential equation itself. Can you, by tracing the appropriate solution curve in this figure, infer that $y(3) \approx 2$ if $y(x)$ is the solution of the initial value problem $dy/dx = x - y$, $y(-4) = 4$?

FIGURE 9.2.5 Slope field and typical solution curves for $y' = x - y$.

The next two examples illustrate the use of slope fields to glean useful information in physical situations that are modeled by differential equations. Example 2 is based on the fact that a baseball moving through the air at moderate velocity v (less than about 300 ft/s) encounters air resistance that is approximately proportional to the magnitude of v. If the baseball is thrown straight downward from the top of a tall building or from a hovering helicopter, then it experiences both the downward acceleration of gravity and an upward acceleration due to air resistance. If the y-axis is directed *downward*, then the ball's velocity $v = dy/dx$ and its gravitational acceleration $g = 32$ ft/s^2 are both positive, whereas its acceleration due to air resistance is negative. Hence its total acceleration has the form

$$\frac{dv}{dt} = g - kv. \tag{1}$$

A typical value of the air resistance proportionality constant might be $k = 0.16$.

EXAMPLE 2 Suppose that you throw a baseball straight downward from a helicopter hovering at an altitude of 3000 ft. You wonder whether someone standing on the ground directly below could conceivably catch the ball. To estimate the speed with which the ball will land, you use your laptop's computer algebra system to construct a slope field for the differential equation

$$\frac{dv}{dt} = 32 - (0.16)v. \tag{2}$$

FIGURE 9.2.6 Slope field and typical solution curves for $v' = 32 - 0.16v$.

The result is shown in Fig. 9.2.6, together with a number of solution curves corresponding to different values of the initial velocity $v(0)$ with which you might throw the baseball downward. Note that all these solution curves appear to approach the horizontal line $v = 200$ as an asymptote. This means that—however you throw it—the baseball should approach the *limiting velocity* $v = 200$ ft/s instead of accelerating indefinitely (as it would in the absence of air resistance). The useful fact that 60 mi/h is the same speed as 88 ft/s yields

$$v = 200 \, \frac{\text{ft}}{\text{s}} \times \frac{60 \text{ mi/h}}{88 \text{ ft/s}} \approx 136.36 \, \frac{\text{mi}}{\text{h}}.$$

Perhaps a catcher accustomed to 100 mi/h fastballs would have some chance of fielding this speeding ball. ◆

COMMENT If the initial velocity of the ball is $v(0) = 200$, then Eq. (2) gives $v'(0) = 32 - (0.16) \cdot (200) = 0$, so the ball experiences *no* initial acceleration. Its velocity therefore remains unchanged, and hence $v(t) \equiv 200$ is a constant "equilibrium solution" of the differential equation. If the initial velocity is greater than 200, then the initial acceleration given in Eq. (2) is negative, so the ball slows as it falls. But if the initial velocity is less than 200, then the initial acceleration given in (2) is positive, so the ball gains speed as it falls. It therefore seems quite reasonable that, because of air resistance, the baseball will approach a limiting velocity of 200 ft/s, whatever its initial velocity might be. You might like to verify that—in the absence of air resistance—this ball would hit the ground at over 300 mi/h.

In Section 9.5 we will discuss in detail the logistic differential equation

$$\frac{dP}{dt} = kP(M - P), \tag{3}$$

which often is used to model a population $P(t)$ that inhabits an environment with *carrying capacity* M. This means that M is the maximum population that this environment can sustain on a long-term basis (in terms of available food and space, for instance).

EXAMPLE 3 If we take $k = 0.0004$ and $M = 150$, then the logistic equation in (3) takes the form

$$\frac{dP}{dt} = (0.0004) P \cdot (150 - P) = (0.06) P - (0.0004) P^2. \tag{4}$$

The positive term $(0.06)P$ on the right in (4) corresponds to natural growth at a 6% annual rate (with time t measured in years). The negative term $-(0.0004)P^2$ represents the inhibition of growth due to limited resources in the environment.

Figure 9.2.7 shows a slope field for Eq. (4) together with a number of solution curves corresponding to possible different values of the initial population $P(0)$. Note that all these solution curves appear to approach the horizontal line $P = 150$ as an asymptote. This means that—whatever the initial population—the population $P(t)$ approaches the *limiting population* $P = 150$ as $t \to +\infty$. ◆

FIGURE 9.2.7 Slope field and typical solution curves for $P' = 0.06P - 0.0004P^2$.

COMMENT If the initial population is $P(0) = 150$, then Eq. (4) gives

$$P'(0) = (0.0004)(150) \cdot (150 - 150) = 0,$$

so the population experiences *no* initial (instantaneous) change. It therefore remains unchanged, and hence $P(t) \equiv 150$ is a constant "equilibrium solution" of the differential equation in (4). If the initial population is greater than 150, then the initial rate of change given by (4) is negative, so the population immediately begins to decrease. But if the initial population is less than 150 (but positive), then the initial rate of change given by (4) is positive, so the population immediately begins to increase. It therefore seems quite reasonable that the population will approach a limiting value of 150, whatever the (positive) initial population.

Euler's Method and Numerical Solutions

A computer plotter can be programmed to draw a solution curve that begins at the point (x_0, y_0) and threads its way through the slope field of a given differential equation $dy/dx = F(x, y)$. The procedure that the plotter carries out can be described as follows.

- The plotter pen begins at the initial point (x_0, y_0) and moves a tiny distance along the slope segment through (x_0, y_0). This takes it to the point (x_1, y_1).
- At (x_1, y_1) the pen changes direction and now moves a tiny distance along the slope segment through this new starting point (x_1, y_1). This takes it to the next starting point (x_2, y_2).
- At (x_2, y_2) the pen direction changes again and now moves a tiny distance along the slope segment through (x_2, y_2). This takes it to the next starting point (x_3, y_3).

Figure 9.2.8 illustrates the result of continuing in this fashion—by a sequence of discrete straight-line steps from one starting point to the next. In this figure we see a polygonal curve consisting of line segments that connect the successive points (x_0, y_0), (x_1, y_1), (x_2, y_2), (x_3, y_3), ... But suppose that each "tiny distance" that the pen travels along a slope segment—before the course correction that sends it along a fresh new slope segment—is so small that the naked eye cannot distinguish the individual line segments constituting the polygonal curve. Then the resulting polygonal curve looks like a smooth, continuously turning solution curve of the differential equation. Indeed, this is (in essence) how the solution curves shown in the figures of this chapter were computer-generated.

Euler did not have a computer plotter (it was the 18th century), and his idea was to do all this numerically rather than graphically. To approximate the solution of the initial value problem

$$\frac{dy}{dx} = F(x, y), \qquad y(x_0) = y_0, \tag{5}$$

FIGURE 9.2.8 The first few steps in approximating a solution curve.

FIGURE 9.2.9 The step from (x_n, y_n) to (x_{n+1}, y_{n+1}).

we first choose a fixed (horizontal) **step size** h to use in making each step from one point to the next. Suppose that we have begun at the initial point (x_0, y_0) and, after n steps, have reached the point (x_n, y_n). Then the step from (x_n, y_n) to the next point (x_{n+1}, y_{n+1}) is illustrated in Fig. 9.2.9. The slope of the direction segment through (x_n, y_n) is $m = F(x_n, y_n)$. Hence a horizontal change of size h from x_n to x_{n+1} corresponds to a vertical change of size $m \cdot h = h \cdot F(x_n, y_n)$ from y_n to y_{n+1}. Therefore the coordinates of the new point (x_{n+1}, y_{n+1}) are given in terms of the old coordinates by

$$x_{n+1} = x_n + h, \qquad y_{n+1} = y_n + h \cdot F(x_n, y_n). \tag{6}$$

Given the initial value problem in (5), **Euler's method** with step size h consists of beginning with the initial point (x_0, y_0) and applying the formulas

$$\begin{aligned} x_1 &= x_0 + h, & y_1 &= y_0 + h \cdot F(x_0, y_0); \\ x_2 &= x_1 + h, & y_2 &= y_1 + h \cdot F(x_1, y_1); \\ x_3 &= x_2 + h, & y_3 &= y_2 + h \cdot F(x_2, y_2); \\ &\vdots & &\vdots \end{aligned} \tag{7}$$

to calculate successive points $(x_1, y_1), (x_2, y_2), (x_3, y_3), \ldots$ on an approximate solution curve.

But we do not ordinarily sketch the corresponding polygonal approximation. Instead, the numerical result of applying Euler's method is the sequence of *approximations*

$$y_1, \quad y_2, \quad y_3, \quad \ldots, \quad y_n, \quad \ldots$$

to the *true values*

$$y(x_1), \quad y(x_2), \quad y(x_3), \quad \ldots, \quad y(x_n), \quad \ldots$$

at the points $x_1, x_2, x_3, \ldots, x_n, \ldots$ of the *exact* (although unknown) solution of the initial value problem. These results typically are presented in the form of a table of approximate values of the desired solution.

EXAMPLE 4 (a) Apply Euler's method to approximate the solution of the initial value problem

$$\frac{dy}{dx} = x + \frac{1}{5}y, \qquad y(0) = -3, \tag{8}$$

with step size $h = 1$ on the interval $[0, 5]$. (b) Repeat part (a), but use step size $h = 0.2$ and the interval $[0, 1]$.

Solution (a) With $x_0 = 0$, $y_0 = -3$, $F(x, y) = x + \frac{1}{5}y$, and $h = 1$, the equations in (7) yield the approximate values

$$y_1 = y_0 + h \cdot \left[x_0 + \tfrac{1}{5}y_0\right] = (-3) + 1 \cdot \left[0 + \tfrac{1}{5}(-3)\right] = -3.6,$$

$$y_2 = y_1 + h \cdot \left[x_1 + \tfrac{1}{5}y_1\right] = (-3.6) + 1 \cdot \left[1 + \tfrac{1}{5}(-3.6)\right] = -3.32,$$

$$y_3 = y_2 + h \cdot \left[x_2 + \tfrac{1}{5}y_2\right] = (-3.32) + 1 \cdot \left[2 + \tfrac{1}{5}(-3.32)\right] = -1.984,$$

$$y_4 = y_3 + h \cdot \left[x_3 + \tfrac{1}{5}y_3\right] = (-1.984) + 1 \cdot \left[3 + \tfrac{1}{5}(-1.984)\right] = 0.6192, \quad \text{and}$$

$$y_5 = y_4 + h \cdot \left[x_4 + \tfrac{1}{5}y_4\right] = (0.6912) + 1 \cdot \left[4 + \tfrac{1}{5}(0.6912)\right] \approx 4.74304$$

at the points $x_1 = 1$, $x_2 = 2$, $x_3 = 3$, $x_4 = 4$, and $x_5 = 5$. Note how the result of each calculation feeds into the next. The resulting table of approximate values is shown next.

x	0	1	2	3	4	5
Approx. y	-3	-3.6	-3.32	-1.984	0.6912	4.74304

FIGURE 9.2.10 Graphs of Euler approximations with step sizes $h = 1$, $h = 0.2$, and $h = 0.05$.

Figure 9.2.10 shows the graph of this approximation, together with the graphs of the Euler approximations obtained with step sizes $h = 0.2$ and $h = 0.05$. The exact solution is the highest curve in the figure. We see that decreasing the step size increases the accuracy, but with any given step size, the accuracy decreases with distance from the initial point.

(b) We begin anew with $x_0 = 0$, $y_0 = 3$, $F(x, y) = x + \frac{1}{5}y$, and $h = 0.2$. The equations in (7) yield the approximate values

$$y_1 = y_0 + h \cdot \left[x_0 + \tfrac{1}{5}y_0\right] = (-3) + (0.2) \cdot \left[0 + \tfrac{1}{5}(-3)\right] = -3.12,$$

$$y_2 = y_1 + h \cdot \left[x_1 + \tfrac{1}{5}y_1\right] = (-3.12) + (0.2) \cdot \left[0.2 + \tfrac{1}{5}(-3.12)\right] = -3.205,$$

$$y_3 = y_2 + h \cdot \left[x_2 + \tfrac{1}{5}y_2\right] = (-3.205) + (0.2) \cdot \left[0.4 + \tfrac{1}{5}(-3.205)\right] = -3.253,$$

$$y_4 = y_3 + h \cdot \left[x_3 + \tfrac{1}{5}y_3\right] = (-3.253) + (0.2) \cdot \left[0.6 + \tfrac{1}{5}(-3.253)\right] = -3.263, \quad \text{and}$$

$$y_5 = y_4 + h \cdot \left[x_4 + \tfrac{1}{5}y_4\right] = (-3.263) + (0.2) \cdot \left[0.8 + \tfrac{1}{5}(-3.263)\right] \approx -3.234$$

at the points $x_1 = 0.2$, $x_2 = 0.4$, $x_3 = 0.6$, $x_4 = 0.8$, and $x_5 = 1$. The resulting table of values is next.

x	0	0.2	0.4	0.6	0.8	1
Approx. y	-3	-3.12	-3.205	-3.253	-3.263	-3.234

High accuracy with Euler's method usually requires a very small step size, and hence a larger number of steps than can reasonably be carried out by hand. The project material for this section contains calculator and computer programs for automating Euler's method. One of these programs was used to calculate the entries in the table in Fig. 9.2.11. We see that 500 Euler steps (with step size $h = 0.002$) from $x = 0$ to $x = 1$ yield values with errors not exceeding 0.001. ◆

x	Approx. y with $h = 0.2$	Approx. y with $h = 0.02$	Approx. y with $h = 0.002$	Actual Value of y
0	-3.000	-3.000	-3.000	-3.000
0.2	-3.120	-3.104	-3.102	-3.102
0.4	-3.205	-3.172	-3.168	-3.168
0.6	-3.253	-3.201	-3.196	-3.195
0.8	-3.263	-3.191	-3.184	-3.183
1	-3.234	-3.140	-3.130	-3.129

FIGURE 9.2.11 Euler approximations with step sizes $h = 0.2$, $h = 0.02$, and $h = 0.002$.

EXAMPLE 5 Suppose that the baseball of Example 2 is simply dropped (instead of being thrown downward) from the helicopter. Then its velocity $v(t)$ after t seconds satisfies the initial value problem

$$\frac{dv}{dt} = 32 - (0.16)v, \qquad v(0) = 0. \tag{9}$$

We use Euler's method with $h = 1$ to track the ball's increasing velocity at 1-second intervals for the first 10 seconds of fall. With $t_0 = 0$, $v_0 = 0$, $F(t, v) = 32 - (0.16)v$, and $h = 1$, the equations in (7) yield the approximate values

$v_1 = v_0 + h \cdot [32 - (0.16)v_0] = (0) + 1 \cdot [32 - (0.16)(0)] = 32,$

$v_2 = v_1 + h \cdot [32 - (0.16)v_1] = (32) + 1 \cdot [32 - (0.16)(32)] = 58.88,$

$v_3 = v_2 + h \cdot [32 - (0.16)v_2] = (58.88) + 1 \cdot [32 - (0.16)(58.88)] \approx 81.46,$

$v_4 = v_3 + h \cdot [32 - (0.16)v_3] = (81.46) + 1 \cdot [32 - (0.16)(81.46)] \approx 100.43,$ and

$v_5 = v_4 + h \cdot [32 - (0.16)v_4] = (100.43) + 1 \cdot [32 - (0.16)(100.43)] \approx 116.36.$

Continuing in this fashion, we complete the column of values of v corresponding to $h = 1$ in the table of Fig. 9.2.12. (We have rounded velocity to the nearest foot per second). The values corresponding to $h = 0.1$ were calculated using a computer, and we see that they are accurate to within about 1 ft/s. Note also that after 10 seconds the falling ball has attained about 80% of its limiting velocity of 200 ft/s. ◆

t	Approx. v with $h = 1$	Approx. v with $h = 0.1$	Actual Value of v
1	32	30	30
2	59	55	55
3	81	77	76
4	100	95	95
5	116	111	110
6	130	124	123
7	141	135	135
8	150	145	144
9	158	153	153
10	165	160	160

FIGURE 9.2.12 Euler approximations in Example 5 with step sizes $h = 1$ and $h = 0.1$.

Existence and Uniqueness

The initial value problem $dy/dx = 1/x$, $y(0) = 0$ has *no* solution, because no solution $y(x) = \ln|x| + C$ of the differential equation is defined at $x = 0$. On the other hand, you can readily verify that the initial value problem $dy/dx = 2\sqrt{y}$, $y(0) = 0$ has the *two* different solutions $y_1(x) = x^2$ and $y_2(x) \equiv 0$. Consequently, before we speak of "the" solution of a given initial value problem, it is necessary to know that it has *one and only one* solution.

A general existence-uniqueness theorem of differential equations implies that the initial value problem $dy/dx = F(x, y)$, $y(a) = b$ has one and only one solution on some open interval containing the point $x = a$ provided that both the function F and its partial derivative $\partial F/\partial y$ are continuous near the point (a, b) in the xy-plane. (Continuity and partial derivatives of functions of two variables are defined in Chapter 13. Briefly, continuity of F means that $F(x, y)$ is close to $F(a, b)$ if (x, y) is close to (a, b). The partial derivative $\partial F/\partial y$ denotes the derivative of F with respect to y, with x regarded as a constant.) For many subsequent applications in this chapter, it will suffice to know that the hypotheses of this general theorem are satisfied if $F(x, y)$ is a polynomial in the two variables x and y. A precise statement and further discussion of the theorem can be found in Section 1.3 of Edwards and Penney, *Differential Equations: Computing and Modeling*, 2nd ed. (Upper Saddle River, N.J.: Prentice Hall, 2000).

9.2 TRUE/FALSE STUDY GUIDE

9.2 CONCEPTS: QUESTIONS AND DISCUSSION

1. Compare the advantages of graphical and numerical approximation of solutions of differential equations.
2. For what purposes does a graph of one or more solutions give more useful information than a table of values, and for what purposes is a table preferable?
3. Simple examples of the failure of existence and uniqueness of solutions of initial value problem are given near the end of this section. Provide two or three similar examples of your own.

9.2 PROBLEMS

In Problems 1 through 10, we have provided the direction field of the indicated differential equation, together with one or more solution curves. Sketch likely solution curves through the additional points marked in each direction field. (One method: Photocopy the direction field and draw your solution curves in a second color. Another method: Use a computer algebra program to construct and print the given direction field.)

1. $\dfrac{dy}{dx} = -y - \sin x$ (Fig. 9.2.13)

2. $\dfrac{dy}{dx} = x + y$ (Fig. 9.2.14)

FIGURE 9.2.13

FIGURE 9.2.14

3. $\dfrac{dy}{dx} = y - \sin x$ (Fig. 9.2.15)

4. $\dfrac{dy}{dx} = x - y$ (Fig. 9.2.16)

FIGURE 9.2.15

FIGURE 9.2.16

5. $\dfrac{dy}{dx} = y - x + 1$ (Fig. 9.2.17)

6. $\dfrac{dy}{dx} = x - y + 1$ (Fig. 9.2.18)

FIGURE 9.2.17

FIGURE 9.2.18

7. $\dfrac{dy}{dx} = \sin x + \sin y$ (Fig. 9.2.19)

8. $\dfrac{dy}{dx} = x^2 - y$ (Fig. 9.2.20)

FIGURE 9.2.19

FIGURE 9.2.20

9. $\dfrac{dy}{dx} = x^2 - y - 2$ (Fig. 9.2.21)

10. $\dfrac{dy}{dx} = -x^2 + \sin y$ (Fig. 9.2.22)

FIGURE 9.2.21

FIGURE 9.2.22

In Problems 11 through 20, an initial value problem and its exact solution $y(x)$ are given. Apply Euler's method twice to approximate this solution on the interval $[0, \frac{1}{2}]$, first with step size $h = 0.25$, then with step size $h = 0.1$. Compare the three-place values of the two approximations at $x = \frac{1}{2}$ with the value $y(\frac{1}{2})$ of the exact solution.

11. $\dfrac{dy}{dx} = -y, \quad y(0) = 2; \quad y(x) = 2e^{-x}$

12. $\dfrac{dy}{dx} = 2y, \quad y(0) = \dfrac{1}{2}; \quad y(x) = \dfrac{1}{2}e^{2x}$

13. $\dfrac{dy}{dx} = y + 1, \quad y(0) = 1; \quad y(x) = 2e^{x} - 1$

14. $\dfrac{dy}{dx} = x - y, \quad y(0) = 1; \quad y(x) = 2e^{-x} + x - 1$

15. $\dfrac{dy}{dx} = y - x - 1, \quad y(0) = 1; \quad y(x) = 2 + x - e^{x}$

16. $\dfrac{dy}{dx} = -2xy, \quad y(0) = 2; \quad y(x) = 2\exp(-x^2)$

17. $\dfrac{dy}{dx} = -3x^2 y, \quad y(0) = 3; \quad y(x) = 3\exp(-x^3)$

18. $\dfrac{dy}{dx} = e^{-y}, \quad y(0) = 0; \quad y(x) = \ln(x+1)$

19. $\dfrac{dy}{dx} = \dfrac{1}{4}(1 + y^2), \quad y(0) = 1; \quad y(x) = \tan\left(\dfrac{x+\pi}{4}\right)$

20. $\dfrac{dy}{dx} = 2xy^2, \quad y(0) = 1; \quad y(x) = \dfrac{1}{1-x^2}$

In Problems 21 and 22, first use the method of Example 1 to construct a slope field for the given differential equation. Then sketch the solution curve corresponding to the given initial condition. Finally, use this solution curve to estimate the desired value of the solution $y(x)$.

21. $\dfrac{dy}{dx} = x + y, \quad y(0) = 0; \quad y(-4) = ?$

22. $\dfrac{dy}{dx} = y - x, \quad y(4) = 0; \quad y(-4) = ?$

Problems 23 and 24 are like Problems 21 and 22, but now use a computer algebra system to plot and print out a slope field for the given differential equation. If you wish (and know how), you can check your manually sketched solution curve by plotting it with the computer.

23. $\dfrac{dy}{dx} = x^2 + y^2 - 1, \quad y(0) = 0; \quad y(2) = ?$

24. $\dfrac{dy}{dx} = x + \dfrac{1}{2}y^2, \quad y(-2) = 0; \quad y(2) = ?$

25. You bail out of the helicopter of Example 2 and your parachute opens immediately. Now $k = 1.6$ in Eq. (1), so your downward velocity satisfies the initial value problem

$$\dfrac{dv}{dt} = 32 - (1.6)v, \qquad v(0) = 0.$$

To investigate your chances of survival, construct a slope field for this differential equation and sketch the appropriate solution curve. What will your limiting velocity be? Will a strategically located haystack do any good? How long will it take you to reach 95% of your limiting velocity?

26. Suppose that the deer population $P(t)$ in a small forest satisfies the logistic equation

$$\dfrac{dP}{dt} = (0.0225)P - (0.0003)P^2.$$

Construct a slope field and appropriate solution curve to answer the following questions: If there are 25 deer at time $t = 0$ and t is measured in months, how long will it take for the number of deer to double? What will be the limiting deer population?

27. Use Euler's method with a programmable calculator or computer system to find the desired solutions in Problem 23. Begin with step size $h = 0.1$, and then use successively smaller step sizes $h = 0.01, h = 0.001, \ldots,$ until successive approximate solutions at $x = 2$ agree to two decimal places.

28. Use Euler's method with a programmable calculator or computer system to find the desired solutions in Problem 24. Begin with step size $h = 0.1$, and then use successively smaller step sizes $h = 0.01, h = 0.001, \ldots,$ until successive approximate solutions at $x = 2$ agree to two decimal places.

Problems 29 through 32 illustrate the fact that, if the hypotheses of the theorem cited near the end of this section are not satisfied, then the initial value problem $dy/dx = F(x, y), y(a) = b$ may have either no solutions, finitely many solutions, or infinitely many solutions.

29. Show that on the interval $[0, \pi]$, the functions $y_1(x) \equiv 1$ and $y_2(x) = \cos x$ both satisfy the initial value problem

$$\dfrac{dy}{dx} + \sqrt{1 - y^2} = 0, \qquad y(0) = 1.$$

Why does this fact not contradict the existence-uniqueness theorem cited in this section? Explain your answer carefully.

30. Find by inspection two different solutions of the initial value problem

$$\dfrac{dy}{dx} = 3y^{2/3}, \qquad y(0) = 0.$$

Why does the existence of different solutions not contradict the existence-uniqueness theorem of this section?

31. Use Fig. 9.2.23 as a suggestion for showing that the initial value problem

$$\frac{dy}{dx} = 3y^{2/3}, \qquad y(-1) = -1$$

has infinitely many solutions. Why does this not contradict the existence-uniqueness theorem of this section?

32. Verify that if k is a constant, then the function $y(x) = kx$ satisfies the differential equation $x(dy/dx) = y$. Hence conclude that the initial value problem

$$x\frac{dy}{dx} = y, \qquad y(0) = 0$$

has infinitely many solutions on any open interval containing $x = 0$.

FIGURE 9.2.23 A suggestion for Problem 31.

9.2 Project: Computer-Assisted Slope Fields and Euler's Method

The CD-ROM project material illustrates the use of *Maple, Mathematica,* and MATLAB to construct slope fields and solution curves for a given differential equation. Use your system to carry out the following investigation.

Investigation Plot a direction field and typical solution curves for the differential equation $dy/dx = \sin(x - y)$, but with a bigger viewing window than that of Fig. 9.2.24. With $-10 \leq x \leq 10$, $-10 \leq y \leq 10$, for instance, a number of apparent straight-line solution curves should be visible. (a) Substitute $y = ax + b$ in the differential equation to determine what the coefficients a and b must be in order to get a solution. (b) Perhaps your computer algebra system will give the general solution

$$y(x) = x - 2\tan^{-1}\left(\frac{x - 2 + C}{x - C}\right).$$

Can you determine a value of the arbitrary constant C that yields the linear solution $y(x) = x - \frac{1}{2}\pi$ determined by the initial condition $y(\frac{1}{2}\pi) = 0$? (Verify this.)

FIGURE 9.2.24 Direction field and solution curves for $y' = \sin(x - y)$ generated by a TI-89/92+ graphing calculator.

Famous Numbers Investigation

The CD-ROM project material illustrates *Maple, Mathematica,* and MATLAB routines for the implementation of Euler's method. The problems below describe the numbers $e \approx 2.71828$, $\ln 2 \approx 0.69315$, and $\pi \approx 3.14159$ as specific values of solutions of certain initial value problems. In each case, apply Euler's method with $n = 50, 100, 200, \ldots$ subintervals (doubling n each time). How many subintervals are needed to obtain—twice in succession—the correct value of the target number rounded to three decimal places?

1. The number $e = y(1)$, where $y(x)$ is the solution of the initial value problem $dy/dx = y$, $y(0) = 1$.
2. The number $\ln 2 = y(2)$, where $y(x)$ is the solution of the initial value problem $dy/dx = 1/x$, $y(1) = 0$.
3. The number $\pi = y(1)$, where $y(x)$ is the solution of the initial value problem

$$\frac{dy}{dx} = \frac{4}{1 + x^2}, \qquad y(0) = 0.$$

Also, explain in each of these problems what the point is—why the indicated famous number is, indeed, the expected result.

9.3 SEPARABLE EQUATIONS AND APPLICATIONS

In Section 9.1 we saw that a general solution of a differential equation $dy/dx = R(x, y)$ can be written in terms of integrals if either the independent variable x or the dependent variable y is missing from the expression $R(x, y)$ on the right-hand side. The method we used there also can be used if $R(x, y)$ can be expressed as the *product* of a function $g(x)$ of x and a function $h(y)$ of y. In this case the differential equation takes the form

$$\frac{dy}{dx} = g(x)h(y). \tag{1}$$

Such a differential equation is said to be **separable** because—upon formal multiplication of both sides by dx and by $f(y) = 1/h(y)$—it takes the symbolic form

$$f(y)\,dy = g(x)\,dx, \tag{2}$$

in which the variables x and y (and their respective differentials dx and dy) are *separated* on opposite sides of the equation. The equation in (2) is literally an equation relating differentials, a "differential equation," but we take Eq. (2) to be concise notation for the more familiar "derivative" equation

$$f(y)\frac{dy}{dx} = g(x), \tag{3}$$

and abuse the terminology slightly by referring to Eq. (3) as a *differential equation* as well.

The process of rewriting Eq. (1) in the form in (2) is called *separating the variables*. It is then tempting to find a solution of (1) simply by integrating each side in (2) with respect to its "own" variable:

$$\int f(y)\,dy = \int g(x)\,dx. \tag{4}$$

Indeed, if the antiderivatives $F(y) = \int f(y)\,dy$ and $G(x) = \int g(x)\,dx$ can be found, then the resulting equation

$$F(y) = G(x) + C \tag{5}$$

provides an *implicit solution* of Eq. (3). That is, any differentiable function $y(x)$ defined implicitly by (5) is an actual (explicit) solution of Eq. (3).

To verify this claim, suppose that $y = y(x)$ satisfies Eq. (5) for some fixed value of the arbitrary constant C. Then differentiating each side yields

$$D_x[F(y(x))] = D_x[G(x) + C];$$
$$F'(y(x)) \cdot y'(x) = G'(x) \quad \text{[using the chain rule]};$$
$$f(y(x))\frac{dy}{dx} = g(x) \quad \text{[because } F' = f \text{ and } G' = g\text{]}.$$

Thus $y(x)$ does, indeed, satisfy the differential equation in (3).

EXAMPLE 1 (a) Solve the differential equation $dy/dx = -6xy$ with the initial condition $y(0) = 7$. (b) Repeat with the initial condition $y(0) = -4$.

Solution (a) Separation of variables gives

$$\frac{1}{y}\,dy = -6x\,dx.$$

Integration then yields

$$\int \frac{1}{y}\,dy = \int (-6x)\,dx;$$

$$\ln|y| = -3x^2 + C. \tag{6}$$

The initial condition $y(0) = 7$ indicates a positive-valued solution, so we replace $|y|$ with y in the implicit solution in (6). This gives

$$\ln y = -3x^2 + C, \quad \text{so that} \quad y(x) = e^{-3x^2+C} = e^C e^{-3x^2}.$$

Then substituting $x = 0$ and $y = 7$ gives $C = \ln 7$, so the desired particular solution is

$$y(x) = e^{\ln 7} e^{-3x^2} = 7e^{-3x^2}.$$

(b) Beginning with Eq. (6), we note that the initial condition $y(0) = -4$ indicates a negative-valued solution, so we replace $|y|$ with $-y$ in the implicit solution there. This gives

$$\ln(-y) = -3x^2 + C, \quad \text{so that} \quad y(x) = -e^{-3x^2+C} = -e^C e^{-3x^2}.$$

Then substituting $x = 0$, $y = -4$ gives $C = \ln 4$, so the desired particular solution is

$$y(x) = -e^{\ln 4} e^{-3x^2} = -4e^{-3x^2}. \quad \blacklozenge$$

REMARK 1 An alternative approach in Example 1 would be to solve Eq. (6) for

$$|y| = e^C e^{-3x^2} = Be^{-3x^2}, \quad \text{so that} \quad y(x) = \pm Be^{-3x^2}.$$

The constant $B = e^C$ is necessarily positive. (Why?) In spite of this, we can accommodate both positive and negative values of y by writing $A = \pm B$ (thereby absorbing the sign in the coefficient A). This gives the general solution

$$y(x) = Ae^{-3x^2} \tag{7}$$

of the differential equation $dy/dx = -6xy$. The values $A = 7$ and $A = -4$ give the two particular solutions found in parts (a) and (b) of Example 1. The graphs of both of these solutions are shown in color in Fig. 9.3.1.

FIGURE 9.3.1 Three different solutions of the differential equation $\dfrac{dy}{dx} = -6xy$.

REMARK 2 The value $A = 0$ in Eq. (7) gives the trivial solution $y(x) \equiv 0$ of the differential equation $dy/dx = -6xy$. Examine the solution

$$\ln|y| = -3x^2 + C \tag{6}$$

obtained by the method of separation of variables. Can you see that *no* value of C in Eq. (6) yields the trivial solution $y(x) \equiv 0$? This observation illustrates the fact that constant-valued solutions of a differential equation can be "lost" when we separate the variables. That is, if $y = y_0$ is a root of the equation $h(y) = 0$, then the constant-valued solution $y(x) \equiv y_0$ of the differential equation $dy/dx = g(x)h(y)$ may not satisfy the new differential equation obtained upon division by $h(y)$. Therefore, it is important to note in advance any such constant-valued solutions of a given separable differential equation.

EXAMPLE 2 Find all solutions of the differential equation $dy/dx = 6x(y-1)^{2/3}$.

Solution Obviously we intend to divide both sides by the factor $(y-1)^{2/3}$ to separate the variables. But first we note that $(y-1)^{2/3} = 0$ when $y(x) \equiv 1$, and that the latter is a solution of the given differential equation. Putting aside this trivial solution for the time being, we proceed to the separation of variables and integration. This leads to

$$\int \frac{1}{3(y-1)^{2/3}}\,dy = \int 2x\,dx;$$

$$(y-1)^{1/3} = x^2 + C.$$

570 CHAPTER 9 Differential Equations

FIGURE 9.3.2 Solution curves of the differential equation $\dfrac{dy}{dx} = 6x(y-1)^{2/3}$ corresponding to different values of C in Eq. (8).

We can solve this implicit solution for the general solution

$$y(x) = 1 + (x^2 + C)^3. \tag{8}$$

Positive values of the arbitrary constant C give the solution curves that lie above the line $y = 1$ (see Fig. 9.3.2) and negative values of C yield those that dip below this line. The value $C = 0$ gives the solution $y(x) = 1 + x^6$, rather than the so-called "singular" solution $y(x) \equiv 1$. Apparently the latter solution was lost when the variables were separated. (See Questions 1 through 3 at the end of this section.) ◆

EXAMPLE 3 Solve the initial value problem

$$\frac{dy}{dx} = \frac{4 - 2x}{3y^2 - 5}, \qquad y(1) = 3. \tag{9}$$

Solution We proceed to separate the variables and integrate. This gives

$$\int (3y^2 - 5)\, dy = \int (4 - 2x)\, dx;$$

$$y^3 - 5y = 4x - x^2 + C. \tag{10}$$

If we substitute $x = 1$ and $y = 3$ in the implicit solution in Eq. (10), we find that $C = 9$. Hence the desired particular solution $y(x)$ is defined implicitly by the equation

$$y^3 - 5y = 4x - x^2 + 9.$$

The graph of this equation—generated by the contour plotting command of a computer algebra system—is the upper solution curve shown in Fig. 9.3.3. (See Question 4 at the end of this section.) ◆

FIGURE 9.3.3 Solution curves of the differential equation $\dfrac{dy}{dx} = \dfrac{4-2x}{3y^2-5}$ corresponding to different values of C in Eq. (10).

Cooling and Heating

According to **Newton's law of cooling** (or heating), the time rate of change of the temperature $u(t)$ of a body immersed in a medium of constant temperature A (Fig. 9.3.4) is proportional to the temperature difference $u - A$. It follows that

$$\frac{du}{dt} = -k(u - A), \tag{11}$$

where the proportionality constant k is positive. Note that if $u > A$ then $du/dt < 0$, so that the body is cooling. But if $u < A$ then $du/dt > 0$, so the temperature u is increasing.

EXAMPLE 4 A 4-lb roast, initially at 50°F, is placed in a 375° oven at 5:00 P.M. At 6:15 P.M. the temperature of the roast is 125°F. When will it be ready to serve medium rare (at 150°F)?

Solution With $A = 375$, Eq. (11) gives

$$\frac{du}{dt} = -k(u - 375) = k(375 - u).$$

FIGURE 9.3.4 Newton's law of cooling, Eq. (11), describes the cooling of a hot rock in water.

While the roast is cooking, its temperature satisfies the inequality $u < 375$. That noted, we separate the variables and integrate:

$$\int \frac{1}{375 - u}\, du = \int k\, dt;$$

$$-\ln(375 - u) = kt + C;$$

$$375 - u = e^{-(kt+C)} = Be^{-kt}$$

where $B = e^{-C}$. Next, $u(0) = 50$ implies that $B = 375 - 50 = 325$, so

$$u(t) = 375 - 325e^{-kt}.$$

We also know that $u = 125$ when $t = 75$. Substituting these values then yields $k = -\frac{1}{75} \ln\left(\frac{250}{325}\right) \approx 0.003498$. We finally solve the equation $150 = 375 - 325e^{-kt}$ for

$$t = -\frac{\ln\left(\frac{225}{325}\right)}{k} \approx -\frac{\ln\left(\frac{225}{325}\right)}{0.003498} \approx 105.12$$

minutes. This is the total cooking time required for the roast. Because it was placed in the oven at 5:00 P.M., it should be removed at about 6:45 P.M. ◆

Linear Differential Equations

The differential equation

$$\frac{dx}{dt} = ax + b \tag{12}$$

is said to be **linear** in the dependent variable x (and its derivative) if the coefficients a and b do not involve x. The general case in which a and b may involve the independent variable t is discussed in Section 9.4.

Equation (12) is separable if a and b are *constants* (with $a \neq 0$). Separating the variables and integrating, we get

$$\int \frac{a}{ax+b} dx = \int a\, dt;$$

$$\ln|ax+b| = at + C.$$

It follows that

$$ax + b = \pm e^C e^{at} = Ke^{at}.$$

If an initial condition $x(0) = x_0$ is given, we see immediately that $K = ax_0 + b$, so

$$ax + b = (ax_0 + b)e^{at}.$$

Finally, we readily solve for the solution

$$x(t) = x_0 e^{at} + \frac{b}{a}(e^{at} - 1) \tag{13}$$

of the initial value problem $dx/dt = ax + b$, $x(0) = x_0$.

The remaining examples of this section illustrate the numerous applications of the solution in (13) of a linear differential equation with constant coefficients.

Population Growth with Immigration Consider a national population $P(t)$ with constant birth and death rates β and δ (in births or deaths per year per unit of population). If also there is a constant net immigration rate of I persons entering the country annually, then P satisfies the linear differential equation

$$\frac{dP}{dt} = kP + I \tag{14}$$

where $k = \beta - \delta$. According to Eq. (13) with P, k, and I in place of x, a, and b, the solution of Eq. (14) for which $P(0) = P_0$ is

$$P(t) = P_0 e^{kt} + \frac{I}{k}(e^{kt} - 1). \tag{15}$$

The first term on the right-hand side is the net effect after t years of natural population growth via births and deaths; the second term represents the effect of immigration.

EXAMPLE 5 In the year 2000 the U.S. population was approximately $P_0 = 280$ million and about 14.6 births and 8.6 deaths per thousand population were occurring annually. In addition, a net immigration into the country at the rate of about 960 thousand people per year was occurring. Let's examine the effects of these birth, death, and immigration rates, assuming that they hold constant for the next 20 years. With

$$\beta = \frac{14.6}{1000} = 0.0146, \qquad \delta = \frac{8.6}{1000} = 0.0086, \quad k = \beta - \delta = 0.006,$$

and $I = 0.96$ (counting people by the million in each case), the differential equation in (14) takes the form

$$\frac{dP}{dt} = (0.006)P + 0.96.$$

Its solution, given by (15) with $P_0 = 280$, is

$$P(t) = 280e^{(0.006)t} + 160\left(e^{(0.006)t} - 1\right).$$

The predicted population for the year 2020 is $P(20) \approx 336.1$ million. Of the 20-year predicted U.S. population increase of $336.1 - 280 = 56.1$ million, the amount due to the 0.6% natural growth rate (as if there were no immigration) is

$$280e^{(0.006)(20)} - 280 \approx 35.7 \quad \text{(million)},$$

and the remaining amount due ultimately to immigration is

$$160\left(e^{(0.006)(20)} - 1\right) \approx 20.4 \quad \text{(million)}. \qquad \blacklozenge$$

Savings Account with Continuous Deposits Consider a savings account that contains A_0 dollars initially and earns interest at the annual rate r compounded continuously (as in Section 9.1). Now suppose that deposits are added to this account at the rate of Q dollars per year. To simplify the mathematical model, we assume that these deposits are made continuously rather than (for instance) monthly. We may then regard the amount $A(t)$ in the account at time t as a "population" of dollars, with a natural (annual) growth rate r and "immigration" (deposits) at the rate of Q dollars annually. Then by merely changing the notation in Eqs. (14) and (15), we get the differential equation

$$\frac{dA}{dt} = rA + Q, \tag{16}$$

which has the solution

$$A(t) = A_0 e^{rt} + \frac{Q}{r}(e^{rt} - 1). \tag{17}$$

EXAMPLE 6 Suppose that you wish to arrange, at the time of her birth, for your daughter to have $100,000 available for her college expenses when she is 18 years old. You plan to do so by making frequent, small—essentially continuous—deposits in a mutual fund at the rate of Q dollars per year. This fund will accumulate 9% annual interest compounded continuously. What should Q be so that you achieve your goal?

Solution With $A_0 = 0$ and $r = 0.09$, we want the value of Q so that Eq. (17) yields the result

$$A(18) = 100000.$$

That is, we must find Q so that

$$100000 = \frac{Q}{0.09}\left(e^{(0.09)(18)} - 1\right).$$

When we solve this equation we find that $Q \approx 2220.53$. Thus you should deposit $2220.53 per year, or about $185.04 per month, in order to have $100,000 in the fund after 18 years. You may wish to verify that your total deposits will be $39,939.50 and that the total interest accumulated will be $60,030.50. (You should also remember that you will have to pay taxes on an interest income averaging about $3335 per year.) ◆

Diffusion of Information and Spread of Disease Let $N(t)$ denote the number of people (in a fixed population P) who by time t have heard a certain news item spread by the mass media. Under certain common conditions, the time rate of increase of N will be proportional to the number of people who have not yet heard the news. Thus

$$\frac{dN}{dt} = k(P - N). \tag{18}$$

If $N(0) = 0$, the solution of Eq. (18) is

$$N(t) = P \cdot (1 - e^{-kt}). \tag{19}$$

If P and some later value $N(t_1)$ are known, we can then solve for k and thereby determine $N(t)$ for all t. Problem 35 illustrates this situation.

Different infectious diseases spread in different ways. A simple model may be built on the assumption that some infectious diseases spread like information—in a fixed population P, the rate of increase of the number $N(t)$ of people infected with the disease is proportional to the number $P - N$ who are not yet infected. Then N satisfies the differential equation in (18). See Problems 39 and 40 for applications.

9.3 TRUE/FALSE STUDY GUIDE

9.3 CONCEPTS: QUESTIONS AND DISCUSSION

Questions 1 through 3 pertain to the general solution $y(x) = 1 + (x^2 + C)^3$ of the differential equation $dy/dx = 6x(y - 1)^{2/3}$ discussed in Example 2.

1. Is there a value of the arbitrary constant C that yields the constant-valued solution $y(x) \equiv 1$?
2. Does every point of the xy-plane lie on precisely one solution curve of the form $y(x) = 1 + (x^2 + C)^3$? (See Fig. 9.3.2.)
3. Find two different solutions of the differential equation, both of which satisfy the initial condition $y(1) = 1$. Can you show that the entire singular solution curve $y \equiv 1$ consists of points where the differential equation has two different solutions? If so, why does this fact not contradict the existence-uniqueness theorem discussed at the end of Section 9.1?
4. Examine the solution curves of the differential equation

$$\frac{dy}{dx} = \frac{4 - 2x}{3y^2 - 5}$$

shown in Fig. 9.3.3. (a) Explain why the solution satisfying the initial condition $y(0) = 0$ is defined on the interval $0 \leq x \leq 4$ but not on the interval $-2 \leq x \leq 6$. (b) Explain why the solution satisfying the initial condition $y(1) = 3$ is defined on the interval $-1 \leq x \leq 5$ but not on the interval $-3 \leq x \leq 7$.

9.3 PROBLEMS

Find general solutions (implicit if necessary, explicit if possible) of the differential equations in Problems 1 through 10.

1. $\dfrac{dy}{dx} = 2x\sqrt{y}$
2. $\dfrac{dy}{dx} = 2xy^2$
3. $\dfrac{dy}{dx} = x^2 y^2$
4. $\dfrac{dy}{dx} = (xy)^{3/2}$
5. $\dfrac{dy}{dx} = 2x\sqrt{y-1}$
6. $\dfrac{dy}{dx} = 4x^3(y-4)^2$
7. $\dfrac{dy}{dx} = \dfrac{1+\sqrt{x}}{1+\sqrt{y}}$
8. $\dfrac{dy}{dx} = \dfrac{x+x^3}{y+y^3}$
9. $\dfrac{dy}{dx} = \dfrac{x^2+1}{x^2(3y^2+1)}$
10. $\dfrac{dy}{dx} = \dfrac{(x^3-1)y^3}{x^2(2y^3-3)}$

Solve the initial value problems in Problems 11 through 20.

11. $\dfrac{dy}{dx} = y^2$, $y(0) = 1$
12. $\dfrac{dy}{dx} = \sqrt{y}$, $y(0) = 4$
13. $\dfrac{dy}{dx} = \dfrac{1}{4y^3}$, $y(0) = 1$
14. $\dfrac{dy}{dx} = \dfrac{1}{x^2 y}$, $y(1) = 2$
15. $\dfrac{dy}{dx} = \sqrt{xy^3}$, $y(0) = 4$
16. $\dfrac{dy}{dx} = \dfrac{x}{y}$, $y(3) = 5$
17. $\dfrac{dy}{dx} = -\dfrac{x}{y}$, $y(12) = -5$
18. $y^2 \dfrac{dy}{dx} = x^2 + 2x + 1$, $y(1) = 2$
19. $\dfrac{dy}{dx} = 3x^2 y^2 - y^2$, $y(0) = 1$
20. $\dfrac{dy}{dx} = 2xy^3(2x^2+1)$, $y(1) = 1$

In Problems 21 through 30, use the method of derivation of Eq. (13), rather than the equation itself, to find the solution of the given initial value problem.

21. $\dfrac{dy}{dx} = y+1$; $y(0) = 1$
22. $\dfrac{dy}{dx} = 2-y$; $y(0) = 3$
23. $\dfrac{dy}{dx} = 2y-3$; $y(0) = 2$
24. $\dfrac{dy}{dx} = \dfrac{1}{4} - \dfrac{y}{16}$; $y(0) = 20$
25. $\dfrac{dx}{dt} = 2(x-1)$; $x(0) = 0$
26. $\dfrac{dx}{dt} = 2 - 3x$; $x(0) = 4$
27. $\dfrac{dx}{dt} = 5(x+2)$; $x(0) = 25$
28. $\dfrac{dx}{dt} = -3 - 4x$; $x(0) = -5$
29. $\dfrac{dv}{dt} = 10(10-v)$; $v(0) = 0$
30. $\dfrac{dv}{dt} = -5(10-v)$; $v(0) = -10$

31. Zembla had a population of 1.5 million in 1990. Assume that this country's population is growing continuously at a 4% annual rate and that Zembla absorbs 50,000 newcomers per year. What will its population be in the year 2010?

32. When a cake is removed from an oven, the temperature of the cake is 210°F. The cake is left to cool at room temperature, which is 70°F. After 30 min the temperature of the cake is 140°F. When will it be 100°F?

33. Payments are made continuously on a mortgage of original amount P_0 dollars at the constant rate of c dollars per month. Let $P(t)$ denote the balance (amount still owed) after t months and let r denote the monthly interest rate paid by the mortgage holder. (For example, $r = 0.06/12 = 0.005$ if the annual interest rate is 6%.) Derive the differential equation

$$\dfrac{dP}{dt} = rP - c, \qquad P(0) = P_0.$$

34. Your cousin must pay off an auto loan of $3600 continuously over a period of 36 months. Apply the result of Problem 33 to determine the monthly payment required if the annual interest rate is (a) 12%; (b) 18%.

35. A rumor about phenylethylamine in the drinking water began to spread one day in a city with a population of 100,000. Within a week, 10,000 people had heard this rumor. Assuming that the rate of increase of the number of people who have heard the rumor is proportional to the number who have not yet heard it, how long will it be until half the population of the city has heard the rumor?

36. Rework Example 5, assuming that new conditions, effective in the year 2000, result in 17 births and 7 deaths annually per thousand population, as well as an immigration rate of 1.5 million persons per year.

37. You would like to be a multimillionaire but cannot rely on winning the lottery. How much would you need to invest per month—in effect, continuously—in an investment account that pays an annual interest rate of 10%, compounded continuously, in order for the account to be worth $5 million after 30 years?

38. Just before midday the body of an apparent homicide victim is found in a room that is kept at a constant temperature of 70°F. At 12 noon the temperature of the body is 80°F and at 1 P.M. it is 75°F. Assume that the temperature of the body at the time of death was 98.6°F and that is has cooled in accord with Newton's law of cooling. What was the time of death?

39. Pottstown has a fixed population of 10,000 people. On January 1, 1000 people have the flu; on April 1, 2000 people have it. Assume that the rate of increase of the number $N(t)$ who have the flu is proportional to the number who don't have it. How many will have the disease on October 1?

40. Let $x(t)$ denote the number of people in Athens, Georgia, of population 100,000, who have the Tokyo flu. The rate of change of $x(t)$ is proportional to the number of those in Athens who do not yet have the disease. Suppose that 20,000 have the flu on March 1 and that 60,000 have it on March 16. (a) Set up and solve a differential equation to find $x(t)$. (b) On what date will the number of people infected with the disease reach 80,000? (c) What happens in the long run?

41. Early one morning it began to snow at a constant rate. At 7 A.M. a snowplow set off to clear a road. By 8 A.M. it had traveled 2 miles, but it took two more hours (until 10 A.M.) for the snowplow to clear an addition 2 miles of road. (a) Let $t = 0$ when it began to snow and let $x(t)$ denote the distance traveled by the snowplow at time t. Assuming that the snowplow clears snow from the road at a constant rate (in cubic feet per hour, say), show that

$$k\frac{dx}{dt} = \frac{1}{t}$$

where k is a constant. (b) What time did it begin to snow? (*Answer:* 6 A.M.)

42. A snowplow sets off at 7 A.M. as in Problem 41. Suppose now that by 8 A.M. it had traveled 4 miles and that by 9 A.M. it had moved an additional 3 miles. What time did it begin to snow? This is a more difficult snowplow problem because now a transcendental equation must be solved numerically to find the value of k. (*Answer:* 4:27 A.M.)

43. (*The catenary*) Suppose that a uniform flexible cable is suspended between two points ($\pm L, H$) at equal height located symmetrically on either side of the y-axis (Fig. 9.3.5). Principles of physics can be used to show that the shape $y = y(x)$ of the hanging cable satisfies the differential equation

$$a\frac{d^2y}{dx^2} = \sqrt{1 + \left(\frac{dy}{dx}\right)^2},$$

where the constant $a = T/\rho$ is the ratio of the tension T of the cable at its lowest point to its linear (constant) density ρ. Note that the lowest point of the cable occurs where $x = 0$ and that $y'(0) = 0$. Substitute $v = dy/dx$ in this second-order differential equation to show that it becomes the first-order equation

$$a\frac{dv}{dt} = \sqrt{1 + v^2}.$$

Solve this differential equation for $y'(x) = v(x) = \sinh(x/a)$. Then integrate to get the shape function

$$y(x) = a\cosh\left(\frac{x}{a}\right) + C$$

of the hanging cable. This curve is called a *catenary*, from the Latin word for *chain*.

FIGURE 9.3.5 A flexible uniform cable suspended between two points at equal heights.

9.4 LINEAR EQUATIONS AND APPLICATIONS

A **linear** first-order differential equation is one that can be written in the form

$$\frac{dy}{dx} + P(x) \cdot y = Q(x) \tag{1}$$

where $P(x)$ and $Q(x)$ are given functions of x. If the "coefficients" P and Q are actually constants, then the differential equation is separable and can be solved as in Section 9.3.

In this section we discuss the general case of variable coefficients. We will show how to multiply each side in (1) by an appropriately selected function $\rho(x)$ so that each side of the resulting equation can be integrated, thereby eliminating the unknown derivative term dy/dx. Such a function $\rho(x)$, multiplication by which makes it possible to integrate the equation, is called an **integrating factor** for the differential equation. The following example indicates how this can happen.

EXAMPLE 1 The differential equation

$$x^3\frac{dy}{dx} + x^2y = 2x^3 + 1$$

is not of the form in (1). But division of both sides by x^3 gives the linear equation

$$\frac{dy}{dx} + \frac{1}{x}y = 2 + \frac{1}{x^3}, \tag{2}$$

which *is* of the form in (1), with $P(x) = 1/x$ and $Q(x) = 2 + (1/x^3)$. For whatever reason, let us multiply both sides in (2) by the factor $\rho(x) = x$. The result is

$$x\frac{dy}{dx} + y = 2x + \frac{1}{x^2}.$$

We now recognize the left-hand side as the derivative $D_x(x \cdot y) = xy' + y$ of the product $x \cdot y$. Thus the last equation can be written as follows:

$$D_x(x \cdot y) = 2x + \frac{1}{x^2}.$$

We can now integrate both sides with respect to x. An indefinite integral of the derivative on the left is simply the product $x \cdot y$. Because the integrals of the two sides differ by a constant, integration yields

$$x \cdot y = \int \left(2x + \frac{1}{x^2}\right) dx = x^2 - \frac{1}{x} + C.$$

Finally, we divide by x to solve for y and thereby obtain the general solution

$$y(x) = x - \frac{1}{x^2} + \frac{C}{x}$$

of the linear differential equation in (2). ◆

The crucial integrating factor $\rho(x) = x$ in Example 1 was simply "pulled out of a hat." Next we will show that the integrating factor given by

$$\rho(x) = \exp\left(\int P(x)\,dx\right) \tag{3}$$

always effects the solution of the linear equation $y' + P(x)y = Q(x)$. Note first that, in Example 1 where $P(x) = 1/x$, Eq. (3) gives

$$\rho(x) = \exp\left(\int \frac{1}{x}\,dx\right) = e^{\ln x} = x,$$

and this is how we actually obtained the integrating factor $\rho(x) = x$ of Example 1—it was not "pulled out of a hat."

In general, we begin with the linear equation $y' + Py = Q$ and multiply both sides by the integrating factor $\rho(x)$ in Eq. (3). The result is

$$e^{\int P(x)\,dx} \frac{dy}{dx} + P(x)e^{\int P(x)\,dx} y = Q(x)e^{\int P(x)\,dx}. \tag{4}$$

Because

$$D_x\left[\int P(x)\,dx\right] = P(x),$$

the left-hand side in Eq. (4) is the derivative of the *product* $y(x) \cdot e^{\int P(x)\,dx}$, so Eq. (4) is equivalent to

$$D_x\left[y(x) \cdot e^{\int P(x)\,dx}\right] = Q(x)e^{\int P(x)\,dx}.$$

Integrating both sides of this equation yields

$$y(x)e^{\int P(x)\,dx} = \int \left(Q(x)e^{\int P(x)\,dx}\right) dx + C.$$

Finally solving for y, we obtain the general solution of the linear first-order differential equation in (1):

$$y(x) = e^{-\int P(x)\,dx}\left[\int \left(Q(x)e^{\int P(x)\,dx}\right) dx + C\right]. \tag{5}$$

There is no need to memorize such a formula. In a specific problem it generally is simpler to use the *method* by which we developed the formula. That is, in order to solve an equation written in the form in (1) with the coefficient functions $P(x)$ and $Q(x)$ displayed explicitly, you should carry out the following steps.

Method: Solution of First-Order Linear Equations

1. Begin by calculating the integrating factor $\rho(x) = e^{\int P(x)\,dx}$.
2. Then multiply both sides of the differential equation by $\rho(x)$.
3. Next, recognize the left-hand side of the resulting equation as the derivative of a product:

$$D_x[\rho(x)y(x)] = \rho(x)Q(x).$$

4. Finally, integrate this equation to obtain

$$\rho(x)y(x) = \int \rho(x)Q(x)\,dx + C,$$

then solve for y to obtain the general solution of the original differential equation.

REMARK 1 Given an initial condition $y(x_0) = y_0$, you can (as usual) substitute $x = x_0$ and $y = y_0$ in the general solution and solve for the value of C that yields the particular solution satisfying this initial condition.

REMARK 2 The integrating factor $\rho(x)$ is determined only to within a multiplicative constant. If we replace

$$\int P(x)\,dx \quad \text{with} \quad \int P(x)\,dx + K$$

in Eq. (3), the result is

$$\rho(x) = e^{K+\int P(x)\,dx} = e^K e^{\int P(x)\,dx}.$$

But the constant factor e^K does not affect the result of multiplying both sides of the differential equation in (1) by $\rho(x)$. Hence we may choose for $\int P(x)\,dx$ any convenient antiderivative of $P(x)$.

EXAMPLE 2 Solve the initial value problem

$$\frac{dy}{dx} - y = \frac{11}{8}e^{-x/3}, \qquad y(0) = 0.$$

Solution Here we have $P(x) \equiv -1$ and $Q(x) = \frac{11}{8}e^{-x/3}$, so the integrating factor is

$$\rho(x) = e^{\int (-1)\,dx} = e^{-x}.$$

Multiplying both sides of the given equation by e^{-x} yields

$$e^{-x}\frac{dy}{dx} - e^{-x}y = \frac{11}{8}e^{-4x/3}, \tag{6}$$

which we recognize as

$$\frac{d}{dx}(e^{-x}y) = \frac{11}{8}e^{-4x/3}.$$

Hence integration with respect to x gives

$$e^{-x}y = \int \frac{11}{8}e^{-4x/3}\,dx = -\frac{33}{32}e^{-4x/3} + C,$$

and then multiplication by e^x gives the general solution

$$y(x) = Ce^x - \frac{33}{32}e^{-x/3}. \tag{7}$$

Substituting $x = y = 0$ now gives $C = \frac{33}{32}$, so the desired particular solution is

$$y(x) = \frac{33}{32}e^x - \frac{33}{32}e^{-x/3} = \frac{33}{32}\left(e^x - e^{-x/3}\right). \qquad \blacklozenge$$

FIGURE 9.4.1 Solution curves of the differential equation $\frac{dy}{dx} - y = \frac{11}{8}e^{-x/3}$ corresponding to different values of C in Eq. (7).

REMARK Figure 9.4.1 shows some typical solution curves for Eq. (6), including the one passing through the origin. Note that some solutions grow rapidly in the positive direction as x increases, while others grow rapidly in the negative direction. Such behavior of a given solution curve is determined by its initial condition $y(0) = y_0$. The two types of behavior in Example 2 are separated by the particular solution

$$y(x) = -\frac{33}{32}e^{-x/3}$$

for which $C=0$ in Eq. (7), so $y_0 = -\frac{33}{32}$. If $y_0 > -\frac{33}{32}$ then $C > 0$ in Eq. (7), so the term e^x eventually dominates the behavior of $y(x)$, and hence $y(x) \to +\infty$ as $x \to +\infty$. But if $y_0 < -\frac{33}{32}$ then $C < 0$, so both terms in $y(x)$ are negative and therefore $y(x) \to -\infty$ as $x \to +\infty$. Thus the initial condition $y_0 = -\frac{33}{32}$ is *critical* in the sense that solutions that start above $-\frac{33}{32}$ on the y-axis grow in the positive direction, whereas solutions that start lower than $-\frac{33}{32}$ grow in the negative direction as $x \to +\infty$. The interpretation of a mathematical model often hinges on finding such a critical condition that separates one kind of behavior of a solution from a different kind of behavior.

EXAMPLE 3 Find a general solution of

$$(x^2 + 1)\frac{dy}{dx} + 3xy = 6x. \tag{8}$$

Solution After dividing both sides of the equation by $x^2 + 1$, we recognize the result

$$\frac{dy}{dx} + \frac{3x}{x^2 + 1}y = \frac{6x}{x^2 + 1}$$

as a first-order linear equation with $P(x) = 3x/(x^2 + 1)$ and $Q(x) = 6x/(x^2 + 1)$. Multiplication by the integrating factor

$$\rho(x) = \exp\left(\int \frac{3x}{x^2 + 1}\,dx\right) = \exp\left(\tfrac{3}{2}\ln(x^2 + 1)\right) = (x^2 + 1)^{3/2}$$

yields

$$(x^2 + 1)^{3/2}\frac{dy}{dx} + 3x(x^2 + 1)^{1/2}y = 6x(x^2 + 1)^{1/2},$$

and thus

$$D_x\left[(x^2 + 1)^{3/2}y\right] = 6x(x^2 + 1)^{1/2}.$$

Integration then yields

$$(x^2 + 1)^{3/2}y = \int 6x(x^2 + 1)^{1/2}\,dx = 2(x^2 + 1)^{3/2} + C.$$

Multiplying both sides by $(x^2+1)^{-3/2}$ then gives the general solution

$$y(x) = 2 + C(x^2+1)^{-3/2}. \tag{9}$$

◆

REMARK Figure 9.4.2 shows some typical solution curves for Eq. (8). Note that as $x \to +\infty$, all other solution curves approach the constant solution curve $y(x) \equiv 2$ that corresponds to $C=0$ in Eq. (9). This constant solution can be described as an *equilibrium solution* of the differential equation, because $y(0) = 2$ implies that $y(x) = 2$ for all x (and thus the value of the solution remains forever where it begins).

FIGURE 9.4.2 Solution curves of the differential equation $(x^2+1)\dfrac{dy}{dx} + 3xy = 6x$ corresponding to different values of C in Eq. (9).

A Closer Look at the Method

The preceding derivation of the solution in Eq. (5) of the linear first-order equation $y' + Py = Q$ bears closer examination. Suppose that the coefficient functions $P(x)$ and $Q(x)$ are continuous on the (possibly unbounded) open interval I. Then the antiderivatives

$$\int P(x)\,dx \quad \text{and} \quad \int \left(Q(x)e^{\int P(x)\,dx}\right) dx$$

exist on I. Our derivation of Eq. (5) shows that *if* $y = y(x)$ is a solution of Eq. (1) on I, *then* $y(x)$ is given by the formula in (5) for some choice of the constant C. Conversely, you may verify by direct substitution that the function $y(x)$ given in Eq. (5) satisfies Eq. (1). Finally, given a point x_0 of I and any number y_0, there is—as previously noted—a unique value of C such that $y(x_0) = y_0$. Consequently, we have proved the following existence-uniqueness theorem.

THEOREM 1 The Linear First-Order Equation

If the functions $P(x)$ and $Q(x)$ are continuous on the open interval I containing the point x_0, then the initial value problem

$$\frac{dy}{dx} + P(x)y = Q(x), \qquad y(x_0) = y_0 \tag{10}$$

has a unique solution $y(x)$ on I, given by the formula in (5) with an appropriate value of C.

REMARK 1 Theorem 1 gives a solution on the *entire* interval I for a *linear* differential equation, in contrast with the existence-uniqueness theorem mentioned in the last paragraphs of Section 9.2. That theorem guarantees only a solution on a possibly smaller interval J.

REMARK 2 Theorem 1 tells us that every solution of Eq. (1) is included in the general solution given in Eq. (5). Thus a linear first-order differential equation has no "singular solution" that is not included in its general solution.

REMARK 3 The appropriate value of the constant C in Eq. (5)—as needed to solve the initial value problem in (10)—can be selected "automatically" by writing

$$\rho(x) = \exp\left(\int_{x_0}^{x} P(t)\,dt\right),$$

$$y(x) = \frac{1}{\rho(x)}\left[y_0 + \int_{x_0}^{x} \rho(t)Q(t)\,dt\right]. \tag{11}$$

The indicated limits x_0 and x effect a choice of indefinite integrals in Eq. (5) that guarantees in advance that $\rho(x_0) = 1$ and that $y(x_0) = y_0$ (as you can verify directly by substituting $x = x_0$ in the equations in (11)).

EXAMPLE 4 Solve the initial value problem

$$x^2 \frac{dy}{dx} + xy = \sin x, \qquad y(1) = y_0. \tag{12}$$

Solution Division by x^2 gives the linear first-order equation

$$\frac{dy}{dx} + \frac{1}{x} y = \frac{\sin x}{x^2}$$

in which $P(x) = 1/x$ and $Q(x) = (\sin x)/x^2$. With $x_0 = 1$ the integrating factor in (11) is

$$\rho(x) = \exp\left(\int_1^x \frac{1}{t} \, dt \right) = \exp(\ln x) = x,$$

so the desired particular solution is given by

$$y(x) = \frac{1}{x} \left[y_0 + \int_1^x \frac{\sin t}{t} \, dt \right]. \tag{13}$$

In accord with Theorem 1, this solution is defined on the whole positive x-axis. ◆

FIGURE 9.4.3 Solution curves of the differential equation $x^2 \frac{dy}{dx} + xy = \sin x$ corresponding to different values of y_0 in Eq. (13).

COMMENT Ordinarily an integral such as the one in Eq. (13) might (for a given value of x) need to be approximated numerically—using Simpson's approximation, for instance—to find the value $y(x)$ of the solution at x. But the integral serves perfectly well to define the function $y(x)$. For instance, using a computer algebra system, one can use the *Maple* command

```
y := (1/x)*(1 + int(sin(t)/t, t=1..x));
```

or the *Mathematica* command

```
y = (1/x)*(1 + Integrate[Sin[t]/t, { t, 1, x } ]);
```

to define the particular solution with $y(1) = 1$, then plot this solution in the usual manner. Figure 9.4.3 shows solution curves plotted in this way with initial values $y(1) = y_0$ ranging from $y_0 = -2$ to $y_0 = 2$. It appears that on each solution curve, $y(x) \to 0$ as $x \to +\infty$.

Mixture Problems

As a first application of linear first-order equations, we consider a tank containing a solution—a mixture of solute and solvent—such as salt dissolved in water. There is both inflow and outflow, and we want to compute the *amount* $x(t)$ of solute in the tank at time t, given the amount $x(0) = x_0$ at time $t = 0$. Suppose that solution with a concentration of c_i grams of solute per liter of solution flows into the tank at the constant rate of r_i liters per second, and that the solution in the tank—kept thoroughly mixed by stirring—flows out at the constant rate of r_o liters per second.

To set up a differential equation for $x(t)$, we estimate the change Δx in x during the brief time interval $[t, t + \Delta t]$. The amount of solute that flows into the tank during Δt seconds is $r_i c_i \, \Delta t$ grams. To check this, observe how the cancellation of units in

$$\left(r_i \; \frac{\text{liters}}{\text{second}} \right) \times \left(c_i \; \frac{\text{grams}}{\text{liter}} \right) \times (\Delta t \; \text{seconds})$$

yields a quantity measured in grams.

The amount of solute that flows out of the tank during the same time interval depends on the concentration $c_o(t)$ of solute in the solution at time t. But as noted

Linear Equations and Applications   SECTION 9.4   581

Input: r_i L/s, c_i gm/L

Amount $x(t)$
Volume $V(t)$
Concentration $c_o(t) = \frac{x}{V}$

Output:
r_o L/s,
c_o gm/L

FIGURE 9.4.4 The single-tank mixture problem.

in Fig. 9.4.4, $c_o(t) = x(t)/V(t)$, where $V(t)$ denotes the volume (not constant unless $r_i = r_o$) of solution in the tank at time t. Then

$$\Delta x = \{\text{grams input}\} - \{\text{grams output}\} \approx r_i c_i \, \Delta t - r_o c_o \, \Delta t. \quad (14)$$

We now divide by Δt:

$$\frac{\Delta x}{\Delta t} \approx r_i c_i - r_o c_o.$$

Finally, we take the limit as $\Delta t \to 0$; if all the functions involved are continuous and $x(t)$ is differentiable, then the error in this approximation also approaches zero, and we obtain the differential equation

$$\frac{dx}{dt} = r_i c_i - r_o c_o, \quad (15)$$

in which r_i, c_i, and r_o are constants, but c_o denotes the variable concentration

$$c_o(t) = \frac{x(t)}{V(t)} \quad (16)$$

of solute in the tank at time t. Thus the amount $x(t)$ of solution in the tank satisfies the differential equation

$$\frac{dx}{dt} = r_i c_i - \frac{r_o}{V} x. \quad (17)$$

If $V_0 = V(0)$, then $V(t) = V_0 + (r_i - r_o)t$, so Eq. (17) is a linear first-order differential equation for the amount $x(t)$ of solute in the tank at time t.

IMPORTANT Equation (17) is *not* one you should commit to memory. It is the process we used to obtain that equation—examination of the behavior of the system over the short time interval $[t, t+\Delta t]$—that you should strive to understand, because it is a very useful tool for obtaining all sorts of differential equations.

REMARK In deriving Eq. (17) we used g/L mass/volume units for convenience. Any other consistent system of units can be used to measure amounts of solute and volumes of solution. In the following example we measure both in cubic kilometers.

EXAMPLE 5 Assume that Lake Erie has a volume of 480 km³ and that its rates of inflow (from Lake Huron) and outflow (to Lake Ontario) are both 350 km³ per year. Suppose that at the time $t = 0$ (in years), the pollutant concentration of Lake Erie—caused by past industrial pollution that has now been ordered to cease—is five times that of Lake Huron. If the outflow from Lake Erie henceforth is perfectly mixed lake water, how long will it take to reduce the pollution concentration in Lake Erie to twice that of Lake Huron?

Solution Here our "mixing tank" is Lake Erie and $x(t)$ denotes the volume of pollutants in the lake after t years. If c denotes the constant (although unknown) pollutant concentration in Lake Huron, then the initial concentration of pollutants in Lake Erie is $5c$. Summarizing the given information, we therefore have

$$V = 480 \quad (\text{km}^3),$$

$$r_i = r_o = r = 350 \quad (\text{km}^3/\text{yr}),$$

$$c_i = c \quad (\text{the pollutant concentration of Lake Huron}), \text{ and}$$

$$x_0 = x(0) = 5cV.$$

The question is this: When is $x(t) = 2cV$? With this notation, Eq. (17) is the separable equation

$$\frac{dx}{dt} = rc - \frac{r}{V}x, \tag{18}$$

which we rewrite in the linear first-order form

$$\frac{dx}{dt} + px = q \tag{19}$$

with constant coefficients $p = r/V$, $q = rc$, and integrating factor $\rho = e^{pt}$. You can either solve this equation directly or apply the formula in (11). The latter gives

$$x(t) = e^{-pt}\left[x_0 + \int_0^t qe^{pt}\, dt\right] = e^{-pt}\left[x_0 + \frac{q}{p}(e^{pt}-1)\right]$$

$$= e^{-rt/V}\left[5cV + \frac{rc}{r/V}\left(e^{rt/V}-1\right)\right];$$

$$x(t) = cV + 4cVe^{-rt/V}. \tag{20}$$

To find when $x(t) = 2cV$, we therefore need only solve the equation

$$2cV = cV + 4cVe^{-rt/V},$$

which simplifies upon cancellation of cV to $4e^{-rt/V} = 1$:

$$t = \frac{V}{r}\ln 4 = \frac{480}{350}\ln 4 \approx 1.091 \quad \text{(years)}. \qquad \blacklozenge$$

EXAMPLE 6 A 120-gal tank initially contains 90 lb of salt dissolved in 90 gal of water. Brine containing 2 lb/gal of salt flows into the tank at the rate of 4 gal/min, and the well-stirred mixture flows out of the tank at the rate of 3 gal/min. How much salt does the tank contain when it is full?

Solution The interesting feature of this example is that, due to the differing rates of inflow and outflow, the volume of brine in the tank increases steadily with $V(t) = 90 + t$ gallons. The change Δx in the amount x of salt in the tank from time t to time $t + \Delta t$ is given by

$$\Delta x \approx 4 \cdot 2 \cdot \Delta t - 3 \cdot \left(\frac{x}{90+t}\right)\Delta t,$$

so the differential equation that models this example is

$$\frac{dx}{dt} + \frac{3}{90+t}x = 8.$$

An integrating factor is

$$\rho(x) = \exp\left(\int \frac{3}{90+t}\, dt\right) = e^{3\ln(90+t)} = (90+t)^3,$$

which gives

$$D_t[(90+t)^3 x] = 8 \cdot (90+t)^3;$$

$$(90+t)^3 x = 2(90+t)^4 + C.$$

Substituting $x(0) = 90$ gives $C = -(90)^4$, so the amount of salt in the tank at time t is

$$x(t) = 2 \cdot (90+t) - \frac{90^4}{(90+t)^3}.$$

The tank is full after 30 min, and when $t = 30$, we have

$$x(30) = 2 \cdot (90+30) - \frac{90^4}{120^3} \approx 202 \quad \text{(lb)}$$

of salt in the tank. $\qquad \blacklozenge$

Motion with Resistance

In Section 9.2 we explored graphical and numerical solutions of the differential equation

$$\frac{dv}{dt} = g - kv \tag{21}$$

satisfied by the *downward* velocity v of a ball that is dropped from a hovering helicopter and is thereafter affected both by gravity and by air resistance proportional to v. Here we explore symbolic solutions of similar problems.

Suppose that a ball is thrown straight up in the air. We set up a coordinate system with the y-axis directed *upward* and with $y = 0$ at ground level. As illustrated in Fig. 9.4.5, the ball of mass m is acted on by the force $F_G = -mg$ of gravity—negative because it is directed downward—and by the force F_R of air resistance. If the air resistance is proportional to the velocity of the ball, then

$$F_R = -Rv \tag{22}$$

where $R > 0$ is a proportionality constant. Observe that the minus sign here correctly indicates that the force acts downward ($F_R < 0$) when the motion is upward ($v > 0$) and that the force acts upward ($F_R > 0$) when the motion is downward ($v < 0$).

By Newton's second law of motion, the total force $F = F_G + F_R$ is equal to the acceleration $ma = m(dv/dt)$ of the ball, and hence

$$m\frac{dv}{dt} = -mg - Rv. \tag{23}$$

Division by the mass m of the ball yields the equation

$$\frac{dv}{dt} = -g - kv \tag{24}$$

where $k = R/m > 0$ and $g \approx 32$ ft/s² (or 9.8 m/s²). (You should verify that if the positive y-axis were directed downward instead of upward, then this derivation would yield Eq. (21) with a single sign changed on the right-hand side.)

EXAMPLE 7 Suppose that the ball of Section 9.2 (with $k = 0.16$ in fps units) is projected straight upward from the ground—perhaps by a pitching machine—with initial velocity 160 ft/s. Find

(a) the maximum height it attains;
(b) its time of ascent to that height and the time of its descent back to the ground;
(c) the velocity with which it strikes the ground.

Before proceeding with the solution, let's first consider (for the purpose of later comparison) the case of *no* air resistance. With $k = 0$ in Eq. (24), we readily calculate

$$\frac{dv}{dt} = -32, \quad v = -32t + 160, \quad \text{and} \quad y = \int v\,dt = -16t^2 + 160t$$

(with $v_0 = 160$ and $y_0 = 0$) as in Section 5.2. The ball reaches its maximum height when $v = -32t + 160 = 0$, thus when $t = 5$ (s). Hence its maximum height is $y(5) = 400$ (ft). It strikes the ground after 10 seconds, with velocity $v(10) = -160$ ft/s (and thus with the same speed as its launch from the ground).

Solution If we rewrite Eq. (24) in the form

$$\frac{dv}{dt} + (0.16)v = -32,$$

we see that we have a linear differential equation with integrating factor

$$\rho(t) = e^{\int (0.16)\, dt} = e^{(0.16)t}.$$

After we multiply both sides of the differential equation by $\rho(t)$ and integrate, we get

$$e^{(0.16)t} \frac{dv}{dt} + (0.16)e^{(0.16)t} v = -32 e^{(0.16)t};$$

$$D_t \left(e^{(0.16)t} v \right) = -32 e^{(0.16)t};$$

$$e^{(0.16)t} v = \int \left[-32 e^{(0.16)t} \right] dt = -200 e^{(0.16)t} + C_1.$$

Substituting $t = 0$, $v = 160$ gives $C_1 = 360$, so after t seconds the velocity of the ball is

$$v(t) = e^{-(0.16)t} \left(-200 e^{(0.16)t} + 360 \right) = -200 + 360 e^{-(0.16)t}. \qquad (25)$$

Now an easy antidifferentiation yields

$$y = \int v\, dt = \int \left(-200 + 360 e^{-(0.16)t} \right) dt = -200 t - 2250 e^{-(0.16)t} + C_2.$$

Finally, substituting $t = 0$, $y = 0$ gives $C_2 = 2250$, so the height of the ball after t seconds in the air is

$$y(t) = -200 t + 2250 \left(1 - e^{-(0.16)t} \right). \qquad (26)$$

FIGURE 9.4.6 Graph of the ball's height function $y(t)$.

Figure 9.4.6 shows the graph of $y(t)$. We see at a glance that air resistance has reduced the maximum height of the ball from 400 ft to under 300 ft, and its total time in the air from 10 s to a bit over 8 s:

(a) The ball reaches its apex when $y'(t) = v(t) = -200 + 360 e^{-(0.16)t} = 0$, so its time of ascent is

$$t = \frac{\ln(360/200)}{0.16} \approx 3.67 \ \ (\text{s}).$$

Thus its maximum height in the air is given by Eq. (26) as $y(3.67) \approx 265.27$ ft.

(b) The ball returns to the ground when

$$y(t) = 0; \quad \text{that is, when} \quad -200 t + 2250 \left(1 - e^{-(0.16)t} \right) = 0.$$

Using Newton's method, or the `Solve` command on a calculator or computer algebra system, we find that $t \approx 8.24$ s. Thus the time of descent of the ball (from its apex back to the ground) is approximately $8.24 - 3.76 = 4.57$ s. Note that this time of descent is somewhat greater than its time of ascent, as every major-league catcher knows.

(c) Finally, the velocity with which the ball strikes the ground is given by Eq. (25) as $v(8.24) \approx -95.44$ ft/s. Note that the ball's impact speed is considerably less than its initial launch speed of 160 ft/s. ◆

REMARK Suppose that instead of striking the ground, the ball of Example 7 falls into a virtually bottomless pit (such as a deep mine shaft). Note that Eq. (25) implies that it does not fall with uniformly increasing speed—as it would in a vacuum—but instead approaches a *limiting speed* of 200 ft/s (as we observed graphically and numerically in Section 9.2). This phenomenon is analyzed more generally in Problem 43. It explains why one occasionally reads of someone whose parachute failed to open completely but nevertheless survived (perhaps with the aid of a conveniently located haystack).

Linear Equations and Applications SECTION 9.4

9.4 TRUE/FALSE STUDY GUIDE

9.4 CONCEPTS: QUESTIONS AND DISCUSSION

1. Write several differential equations that are linear but not separable.
2. Write several differential equations that are both linear and separable. Compare their solutions by separation of variables with their solutions using the method of this section. Are the two general solutions identical in each case? If not, reconcile the two results. Does one method seem generally easier than the other? Does this depend on the particular differential equation?
3. Consider the up-and-down motion of a ball subject both to gravity and to a force $F_R = -Rv^p$ of air resistance that is proportional to some *power* $p \neq 1$ of the velocity. Is the resulting differential equation—analogous to (24)—still linear? If not, can you think of a value of p for which you might still be able to solve for the velocity function $v(t)$?

9.4 PROBLEMS

Find general solutions of the differential equations in Problems 1 through 20. If an initial condition is given, find the corresponding particular solution.

1. $\dfrac{dy}{dx} + y = 2$, $y(0) = 0$
2. $\dfrac{dy}{dx} - 2y = 3e^{2x}$, $y(0) = 0$
3. $\dfrac{dy}{dx} + 3y = 2xe^{-3x}$
4. $\dfrac{dy}{dx} - 2xy = e^{x^2}$
5. $x\dfrac{dy}{dx} + 2y = 3x$, $y(1) = 5$
6. $x\dfrac{dy}{dx} + 5y = 7x^2$, $y(2) = 5$
7. $2x\dfrac{dy}{dx} + y = 10\sqrt{x}$
8. $3x\dfrac{dy}{dx} + y = 12x$
9. $x\dfrac{dy}{dx} - y = x$, $y(1) = 7$
10. $2x\dfrac{dy}{dx} - 3y = 9x^3$
11. $x\dfrac{dy}{dx} + y = 3xy$, $y(1) = 0$
12. $x\dfrac{dy}{dx} + 3y = 2x^5$, $y(2) = 1$
13. $\dfrac{dy}{dx} + y = e^x$, $y(0) = 1$
14. $x\dfrac{dy}{dx} - 3y = x^3$, $y(1) = 10$
15. $\dfrac{dy}{dx} + 2xy = x$, $y(0) = -2$
16. $\dfrac{dy}{dx} = (1-y)\cos x$, $y(\pi) = 2$
17. $(1+x)\dfrac{dy}{dx} + y = \cos x$, $y(0) = 1$
18. $x\dfrac{dy}{dx} = 2y + x^3 \cos x$
19. $\dfrac{dy}{dx} + y \cot x = \cos x$
20. $\dfrac{dy}{dx} = 1 + x + y + xy$, $y(0) = 0$
21. Express the general solution of $dy/dx = 1 + 2xy$ in terms of the **error function**
$$\text{erf}(x) = \dfrac{2}{\sqrt{\pi}} \int_0^x e^{-t^2}\, dt.$$
22. Express the solution of the initial value problem
$$2x\dfrac{dy}{dx} = y + 2x \cos x, \qquad y(1) = 0$$
as an integral as in Example 4.
23. A tank contains 1000 L of a solution consisting of 100 kg of salt dissolved in water. Pure water is pumped into the tank at the rate of 5 L/s, and the mixture—kept uniform by stirring—is pumped out at the same rate. How long will it be until only 10 kg of salt remains in the tank?
24. Consider a reservoir with a volume of 8 billion cubic feet (ft^3) and an initial pollutant concentration of 0.25%. There is a daily inflow of 500 million ft^3 of water with a pollutant concentration of 0.05% and an equal daily outflow of the well-mixed water in the reservoir. How long will it take to reduce the pollutant concentration in the reservoir to 0.10%?
25. Rework Example 5 for the case of Lake Ontario. The only differences are that this lake has a volume of 1640 km^3 and an inflow-outflow rate of 410 km^3/year.
26. A tank initially contains 60 gal of pure water. Brine containing 1 lb of salt per gallon enters the tank at 2 gal/min, and the (perfectly mixed) solution leaves the tank at 3 gal/min; thus the tank is empty after exactly 1 h. (a) Find the amount of salt in the tank after t minutes. (b) What is the maximum amount of salt ever in the tank?
27. A 400-gal tank initially contains 100 gal of brine containing 50 lb of salt. Brine containing 1 lb of salt per gallon enters the tank at the rate of 5 gal/s, and the well-mixed brine in

the tank flows out at the rate of 3 gal/s. How much salt will the tank contain when it is full of brine?

28. Consider the *cascade* of two tanks shown in Fig. 9.4.7, with $V_1 = 100$ (gal) and $V_2 = 200$ (gal) the volumes of brine in the two tanks. Each tank also initially contains 50 lb of salt. The three flow rates indicated in the figure are each 5 gal/min, with pure water flowing into tank 1. (a) Find the amount $x(t)$ of salt in tank 1 at time t. (b) Suppose that $y(t)$ is the amount of salt in tank 2 at time t. Show first that

$$\frac{dy}{dt} = \frac{5x}{100} - \frac{5y}{200},$$

then solve for $y(t)$, using the function $x(t)$ found in part (a). (c) Finally, find the maximum amount of salt ever in tank 2.

FIGURE 9.4.7 A cascade of two tanks.

29. A 30-year-old woman accepts an engineering position with a starting salary of $30,000 per year. Her salary $S(t)$ increases exponentially, with $S(t) = 30e^{t/20}$ thousand dollars after t years. Meanwhile, 12% of her salary is deposited continuously in a retirement account, which accumulates interest at a continuous annual rate of 6%. (a) Estimate ΔA in terms of Δt to derive the differential equation satisfied by the amount $A(t)$ in her retirement account after t years. (b) Compute $A(40)$, the amount available for her retirement at age 70.

30. Suppose that a falling hailstone with density $\delta = 1$ starts from rest with negligible radius $r = 0$. Thereafter its radius is $r = kt$ (k is a constant) as it grows by accretion during its fall. Set up and solve the initial value problem

$$\frac{d}{dt}(mv) = mg, \quad v(0) = 0,$$

where m is the variable mass of the hailstone, $v = dy/dt$ is its velocity, and the positive y-axis points downward. Then show that $dv/dt = g/4$. Thus the hailstone falls as though it were under *one-fourth* the influence of gravity.

31. The acceleration of a Maserati is proportional to the difference between 250 km/h and the velocity of this sports car. If this machine can accelerate from rest to 100 km/h in 10 s, how long will it take for the car to accelerate from rest to 200 km/h?

32. Suppose that a body moves through a resisting medium with resistance proportional to its velocity v, so that $dv/dt = -kv$. (a) Show that its velocity and position at time t are given by

$$v(t) = v_0 e^{-kt}$$

and

$$x(t) = x_0 + \left(\frac{v_0}{k}\right)(1 - e^{-kt}).$$

(b) Conclude that the body travels only a finite distance, and find that distance.

33. Suppose that a motorboat is moving at 40 ft/s when its motor suddenly quits, and that 10 s later the boat has slowed to 20 ft/s. Assume, as in Problem 32, that the resistance it encounters while coasting is proportional to its velocity. How far will the boat coast in all?

34. Consider a body that moves horizontally through a medium whose resistance is proportional to the *square* of the velocity v, so that $dv/dt = -kv^2$. Show that

$$v(t) = \frac{v_0}{1 + v_0 k t}$$

and that

$$x(t) = x_0 + \frac{1}{k} \ln(1 + v_0 k t).$$

Note that, in contrast with the result of Problem 32, $x(t) \to +\infty$ as $t \to +\infty$.

35. Assuming resistance proportional to the square of the velocity (as in Problem 34), how far does the motorboat of Problem 33 coast in the first minute after its motor quits?

36. Assume that a body moving with velocity v encounters resistance of the form $dv/dt = -kv^{3/2}$. Show that

$$v(t) = \frac{4v_0}{\left(kt\sqrt{v_0} + 2\right)^2}$$

and that

$$x(t) = x_0 + \frac{2}{k}\sqrt{v_0}\left(1 - \frac{2}{kt\sqrt{v_0} + 2}\right).$$

Conclude that under a $\frac{3}{2}$-power resistance a body coasts only a finite distance before coming to a stop.

37. Suppose that a car starts from rest, its engine providing an acceleration of 10 ft/s^2, while air resistance provides 0.1 ft/s^2 of deceleration for each foot per second of the car's velocity. (a) Find the car's maximum possible (limiting) velocity. (b) Find how long it takes the car to attain 90% of its limiting velocity, and how far it travels while doing so.

38. Rework both parts of Problem 37, with the sole difference that the deceleration due to air resistance now is $(0.001)v^2$ ft/s^2 when the car's velocity is v feet per second.

39. A motorboat weighs 32,000 lb and its motor provides a thrust of 5000 lb. Assume that the water resistance is

100 pounds for each foot per second of the speed v of the boat. Then

$$1000\frac{dv}{dt} = 5000 - 100v.$$

If the boat starts from rest, what is the maximum velocity that it can attain?

40. It is proposed to dispose of nuclear wastes—in drums with weight $W = 640$ lb and volume $8\,\text{ft}^3$—by dropping them into the ocean ($v_0 = 0$). The force equation for a drum falling through water is

$$m\frac{dv}{dt} = -W + B + F_R,$$

where the buoyant force B is equal to the weight (at 62.5 lb/ft^3) of the volume of water displaced by the drum (Archimedes' principle) and F_R is the force of water resistance, found empirically to be 1 lb for each foot per second of the velocity of a drum. If the drums are likely to burst upon an impact of more than 75 ft/s, what is the maximum depth to which they can be dropped in the ocean without likelihood of bursting?

41. Rework Example 7, but for a crossbow bolt launched straight upward from the ground with an initial velocity of 49 m/s.

42. Consider anew the ball of Examples 2 and 5 in Section 9.2, which is dropped from a helicopter hovering at a height of 3000 ft. (a) Solve the initial value problem

$$\frac{dv}{dt} = 32 - (0.16)v, \qquad v(0) = 0$$

to find its velocity $v(t)$ after t seconds. (b) Show that the limiting velocity of the ball is exactly 200 ft/s. (c) Find the ball's time of descent to the ground.

43. Solve the general initial velocity problem $dv/dt = -g - kv$, $v(0) = v_0$ for a projectile moving in a vertical line subject to gravity and air resistance. Show that

$$v(t) = v_0 e^{-kt} + \frac{g}{k}(e^{-kt} - 1).$$

Conclude that the projectile approaches a limiting *terminal velocity* given by

$$v_\tau = \lim_{t \to \infty} v(t) = -\frac{g}{k}.$$

44. A woman bails out of an airplane at an altitude of 10,000 ft, falls freely for 20 s, then opens her parachute. How long will it take her to reach the ground? Assume linear air resistance of k feet per second per second, taking $k = 0.15$ without the parachute and $k = 1.5$ with the parachute. (*Suggestion:* First determine her height and velocity when the parachute opens.)

9.5 POPULATION MODELS

In Section 9.1 we introduced the exponential differential equation $dP/dt = kP$, with solution $P(t) = P_0 e^{kt}$, as a mathematical model for natural population growth that occurs as a result of constant birth and death rates. Here we present a more general population model that accommodates birth and death rates that are not necessarily constant. As before, however, our population function $P(t)$ will be a *continuous* approximation to the actual population, which of course grows by integral increments.

Suppose that the population changes only by the occurrence of births and deaths—there is no immigration to or emigration from outside the country or environment under consideration. It is customary to track the growth or decline of a population in terms of its *birth rate* and *death rate* functions defined as follows:

- $\beta(t)$ is the number of births per unit of population per unit of time at time t;
- $\delta(t)$ is the number of deaths per unit of population per unit of time at time t.

Then the numbers of births and deaths that occur during the [short] time interval $[t, t + \Delta t]$ are given (approximately) by

$$\text{births:} \quad \beta(t) \cdot P(t) \cdot \Delta t; \qquad \text{deaths:} \quad \delta(t) \cdot P(t) \cdot \Delta t.$$

Hence the change ΔP in the population during the time interval $[t, t + \Delta t]$ of length Δt is

$$\Delta P = \{\text{births}\} - \{\text{deaths}\} \approx \beta(t) \cdot P(t) \cdot \Delta t - \delta(t) \cdot P(t) \cdot \Delta t,$$

so

$$\frac{\Delta P}{\Delta t} \approx [\beta(t) - \delta(t)] \cdot P(t).$$

The error in this approximation should approach zero as $\Delta t \to 0$, so—taking the limit—we get the differential equation

$$\frac{dP}{dt} = (\beta - \delta) \cdot P, \qquad (1)$$

in which we write $\beta = \beta(t)$, $\delta = \delta(t)$, and $P = P(t)$ for brevity. Equation (1) is the **general population equation.** If β and δ are constant, Eq. (1) reduces to the natural growth equation with $k = \beta - \delta$. But it also includes the possibility that β and δ are variable functions of t. The birth and death rates need not be known in advance; they may well depend on the unknown function $P(t)$.

EXAMPLE 1 Suppose that an alligator population numbers 100 initially, and that its death rate is $\delta = 0$ (so none of the alligators is dying). If the birth rate is $\beta = (0.0005)P$—and thus the rate increases as the population does—then Eq. (1) gives the initial value problem

$$\frac{dP}{dt} = (0.0005)P^2, \qquad P(0) = 100$$

(with t in years). Upon separating the variables we get

$$\int \frac{1}{P^2}\, dP = \int (0.0005)\, dt;$$

$$-\frac{1}{P} = (0.0005)t + C.$$

Substituting $t = 0$, $P = 100$ gives $C = -1/100$, and then we readily solve for

$$P(t) = \frac{2000}{20 - t}.$$

For instance, $P(10) = 2000/10 = 200$, so after 10 years the alligator population has doubled. But we see that $P(t) \to +\infty$ as $t \to 20$, so a real "population explosion" occurs in 20 years. Indeed, the direction field and solution curves shown in Fig. 9.5.1 indicate that a population explosion always occurs, whatever the size of the (positive) initial population $P(0) = P_0$. In particular, it appears that the population always becomes unbounded in a *finite* period of time. ◆

FIGURE 9.5.1 Direction field and solution curves for the equation $dP/dt = (0.0005)P^2$ in Example 1.

Bounded Populations and the Logistic Equation

In situations as diverse as the human population of a nation and a fruit fly population in a closed container, it is often observed that the birth rate decreases as the population itself increases. The reasons may range from increased scientific or cultural sophistication to limitations on available food or space. Suppose, for example, that the birth rate β is a *linear* decreasing function of the population size P, so that $\beta = \beta_0 - \beta_1 P$ where β_0 and β_1 are positive constants. If the death rate $\delta = \delta_0$ remains constant, then Eq. (1) takes the form

$$\frac{dP}{dt} = (\beta_0 - \beta_1 P - \delta_0) P;$$

that is,

$$\frac{dP}{dt} = aP - bP^2 \qquad (2)$$

where $a = \beta_0 - \delta_0$ and $b = \beta_1$.

If the coefficients a and b are both positive, then Eq. (2) is called the **logistic equation.** For the purpose of relating the behavior of the population $P(t)$ to the values of the parameters in the equation, it is useful to rewrite the logistic equation in the form

$$\frac{dP}{dt} = kP(M - P) \qquad (3)$$

where $k = b$ and $M = a/b$ are constants.

EXAMPLE 2 In Example 3 of Section 9.2 we explored graphically a population modeled by the logistic equation

$$\frac{dP}{dt} = (0.0004) P \cdot (150 - P) = (0.06) P - (0.0004) P^2. \qquad (4)$$

To solve this differential equation symbolically, we separate the variables and integrate. We get

$$\int \frac{1}{P(150-P)} \, dP = \int (0.0004) \, dt;$$

$$\frac{1}{150} \int \left(\frac{1}{P} + \frac{1}{150-P} \right) dP = \int (0.0004) \, dt \qquad \text{[partial fractions]};$$

$$\ln |P| - \ln |150 - P| = (0.06)t + C;$$

$$\frac{P}{150 - P} = \pm e^C e^{(0.06)t} = B e^{(0.06)t} \qquad [\text{where } B = \pm e^C].$$

If we substitute $t = 0$ and $P = P_0$ into this last equation, we find that $B = P_0/(150-P_0)$. Hence

$$\frac{P}{150 - P} = \frac{P_0 e^{(0.06)t}}{150 - P_0}.$$

Finally, this last equation is easy to solve for the population

$$P(t) = \frac{150 P_0}{P_0 + (150 - P_0) e^{-(0.06)t}} \qquad (5)$$

at time t in terms of the initial population $P_0 = P(0)$. Figure 9.5.2 shows a number of solution curves corresponding to different values of the initial population ranging from $P_0 = 20$ to $P_0 = 300$. Note that all these solution curves appear to approach the horizontal line $P = 150$ as an asymptote. Indeed, you should be able to see directly from Eq. (5) that $P(t) \to 150$ as $t \to +\infty$, whatever the initial value $P_0 > 0$. ◆

FIGURE 9.5.2 Typical solution curves for the logistic equation $P' = 0.06P - 0.0004P^2$.

Limited Populations and Carrying Capacity

The finite limiting population discovered in Example 2 is characteristic of logistic populations. In Problem 31 we ask you to use the method of solution of Example 2 to show that the solution of the logistic initial value problem

$$\frac{dP}{dt} = kP(M - P), \quad P(0) = P_0 \tag{6}$$

is

$$P(t) = \frac{MP_0}{P_0 + (M - P_0)e^{-kMt}}. \tag{7}$$

Actual populations are positive-valued. If $P_0 = M$ then (7) reduces to the unchanging (constant-valued) *equilibrium population* $P(T) \equiv M$. Otherwise, the behavior of a logistic population depends upon whether $0 < P_0 < M$ or $P_0 > M$. If $0 < P_0 < M$ then we see from Eqs. (6) and (7) that $P'(t) > 0$ and

$$P(t) = \frac{MP_0}{P_0 + (M - P_0)e^{-kMt}} = \frac{MP_0}{P_0 + \{\text{positive number}\}} < \frac{MP_0}{P_0} = M.$$

But if $P_0 > M$ then we see from Eqs. (6) and (7) that $P'(t) < 0$ and

$$P(t) = \frac{MP_0}{P_0 + (M - P_0)e^{-kMt}} = \frac{MP_0}{P_0 + \{\text{negative number}\}} > \frac{MP_0}{P_0} = M.$$

In each case, the "positive number" or "negative number" in the denominator has absolute value less than P_0 and—because of the exponential factor—approaches zero as $t \to +\infty$. It follows that

$$\lim_{t \to \infty} P(t) = \frac{MP_0}{P_0 + 0} = M. \tag{8}$$

Thus a population that satisfies the logistic equation does *not* grow without bound like a naturally growing population modeled by the exponential equation $dP/dt = kP$. Instead, it approaches the finite **limiting population** M as $t \to +\infty$. As illustrated by the typical solution curves of the logistic equation shown in Fig. 9.5.3, the population $P(t)$ steadily increases and approaches M from below if $0 < P_0 < M$, but steadily decreases and approaches M from above if $P_0 > M$. Sometimes M is called the **carrying capacity** of the environment, considering it to be the maximum population that the environment can support on a long-term basis.

FIGURE 9.5.3 Typical solution curves for the logistic equation $P' = kP(M - P)$. Each solution curve that starts below the line $P = M/2$ has an inflection point on this line. (See Problem 33.)

EXAMPLE 3 Suppose that in 1885 the population of a certain country was 50 million and was growing at the rate of 750,000 people per year at that time. Suppose also that in 1940 its population was 100 million and was then growing at the rate of 1 million per year. Assume that this population satisfies the logistic equation. Determine both the limiting population M and the predicted population for the year 2000.

Solution We substitute the two given pairs of data in Eq. (6) and find that

$$0.75 = 50k(M - 50) \quad \text{and} \quad 1.00 = 100k(M - 100).$$

We solve simultaneously for $M = 200$ and $k = 0.0001$. Thus the limiting population of the country in question is 200 million. With these values of M and k, and with $t = 0$ corresponding to the year 1940 (in which $P_0 = 100$), we find that—according to Eq. (7)—the population in the year 2000 will be

$$P(60) = \frac{200 \cdot 100}{100 + (200 - 100)e^{-(0.0001)(200)(60)}},$$

about 153.7 million people. ◆

HISTORICAL NOTE The logistic equation was introduced (around 1840) as a possible model for human population growth by the Belgian mathematician and demographer P. F. Verhulst (1804–1849). In Examples 4 and 5 we compare natural growth and logistic model fits to census data for the U.S. population in the 19th century.

EXAMPLE 4 The U.S. population in 1800 was 5.308 million and in 1900 was 76.212 million. If we take $P_0 = 5.308$ (with $t = 0$ in 1800) in the natural growth model $P(t) = P_0 e^{rt}$ and substitute $t = 100$, $P = 76.212$, we find that

$$76.212 = 5.308 e^{100r}, \quad \text{so} \quad r = \frac{1}{100} \ln \frac{76.212}{5.308} \approx 0.026643.$$

Thus our natural growth model for the U.S. population during the 19th century is

$$P(t) = (5.308) e^{(0.026643)t} \tag{9}$$

(with t in years and P in millions). Because $e^{0.026643} \approx 1.02700$, the average population growth between 1800 and 1900 was about 2.7% per year. This rate of growth was not sustained during the 20th century. Whereas Eq. (9) predicts $P(150) = 288.780$ and $P(200) = 1094.240$ (over a billion), the actual population of the United States in the year 2000 was "only" about 280 million. ◆

EXAMPLE 5 The U.S. population in the year 1850 was 23.192 million. If we take $P_0 = 5.308$ and substitute the data pairs $t = 50$, $P = 23.192$ (for 1850) and $t = 100$, $P = 76.212$ (for 1900) in the logistic model formula in Eq. (7), we get the two equations

$$\frac{(5.308)M}{5.308 + (M - 5.308)e^{-50kM}} = 23.192,$$

$$\frac{(5.308)M}{5.308 + (M - 5.308)e^{-100kM}} = 76.212 \tag{10}$$

in the two unknowns k and M. A computer algebra system yields the approximate solution

$$k = 0.000167716, \quad M = 188.121$$

of the simultaneous equations in (10). Substituting these values in Eq. (7) yields the logistic model

$$P(t) = \frac{998.546}{5.308 + (182.813)e^{-(0.031551)t}}, \tag{11}$$

which agrees with the U.S. population data for 1850 and 1900. It predicts $P(150) = 144.354$, a fairly good approximation to the actual 1950 U.S. population of 151.326 million. Nevertheless, by the year 2000, the U.S. population had already greatly exceeded the limiting population of 188.121 million predicted by Eq. (11). ◆

The moral of Examples 4 and 5 is simply that one cannot expect too much of models that are based on severely limited information (such as a mere pair of data points). Much of the science of statistics is devoted to the analysis of large "data sets" to formulate useful (and perhaps reliable) mathematical models.

More Applications of the Logistic Equation

We next describe some situations that illustrate the varied circumstances in which the logistic equation is a satisfactory mathematical model.

1. *Limited environment situation.* A certain environment can support a population of at most M individuals. It is then reasonable to expect the growth rate $\beta - \delta$ (the combined birth and death rates) to be proportional to $M - P$, because we may think of $M - P$ as the potential for further expansion. Then $\beta - \delta = k(M - P)$, so that

$$\frac{dP}{dt} = (\beta - \delta)P = kP(M - P).$$

The classic example of a limited environment situation is a fruit fly population in a closed container.

2. *Competition situation.* If the birth rate β is constant but the death rate δ is proportional to P, so that $\delta = \alpha P$, then

$$\frac{dP}{dt} = (\beta - \alpha P)P = kP(M - P).$$

This might be a reasonable working hypothesis in a study of a cannibalistic population, in which all deaths result from chance encounters between individuals. Of course, competition between individuals is not usually so deadly, nor its effects so immediate and decisive.

3. *Joint proportion situation.* Let $P(t)$ denote the number of individuals in a constant-size susceptible population M who are infected with a certain contagious and incurable disease. The disease is spread by chance encounters. Then $P'(t)$ should be proportional to the product of the number P of individuals having the disease and the number $M - P$ of those not having it, and therefore $dP/dt = kP(M - P)$. Again we discover that the mathematical model is the logistic equation. The mathematical description of the spread of a rumor in a population of M individuals is identical.

EXAMPLE 6 Suppose that at time $t = 0$ (weeks), 10 thousand people in a city with population $M = 100$ thousand have heard a certain rumor. After 1 week the number $P(t)$ of those who have heard it has increased to $P(1) = 20$ thousand. Assuming that $P(t)$ satisfies a logistic equation, when will 80% of the city's population have heard the rumor?

Solution Substituting $P_0 = 10$ and $M = 100$ (thousand) in Eq. (7), we get

$$P(t) = \frac{1000}{10 + 90e^{-100kt}}. \tag{12}$$

Then substituting $t = 1$, $P = 20$ gives the equation

$$20 = \frac{1000}{10 + 90e^{-100k}}$$

that is readily solved for

$$e^{-100k} = \frac{4}{9}, \quad \text{so} \quad k = \frac{1}{100} \ln \frac{9}{4} \approx 0.008109.$$

With $P(t) = 80$, Eq. (12) takes the form

$$80 = \frac{1000}{10 + 90e^{-100kt}},$$

which we solve for $e^{-100kt} = \frac{1}{36}$. It follows that 80% of the population has heard the rumor when

$$t = \frac{\ln 36}{100k} = \frac{\ln 36}{\ln(9/4)} \approx 4.42,$$

thus after about four weeks and three days. ◆

Doomsday versus Extinction

Consider a population $P(t)$ of unsophisticated animals that rely solely on chance encounters between females and males for reproductive purposes. It is reasonable to expect such encounters to occur at a rate that is proportional to the product of the number $P/2$ of males and the number $P/2$ of females, hence at a rate proportional to P^2. We therefore assume that births occur at the rate kP^2 (per unit time, with k constant). The birth rate (in births per unit time per unit of population) is then given by $\beta = kP$. If the death rate δ is constant, then the general population equation in (1) yields the differential equation

$$\frac{dP}{dt} = kP^2 - \delta P = kP(P - M) \tag{13}$$

(where $M = \delta/k > 0$) as a mathematical model of the population.

Note that the right-hand side in Eq. (13) is the *negative* of the right-hand side in the logistic equation in (7). We will see that the constant M is now a **threshold population,** with the way the population behaves in the future depending critically on whether the initial population P_0 is less than or greater than M.

EXAMPLE 7 Consider an animal population $P(t)$ that is modeled by the equation

$$\frac{dP}{dt} = (0.0004)P \cdot (P - 150) = (0.0004)P^2 - (0.06)P. \tag{14}$$

We want to find $P(t)$ in the following two cases: (a) $P(0) = 200$; (b) $P(0) = 100$.

Solution To solve the equation in (14), we separate the variables and integrate. We get

$$\int \frac{1}{P(P - 150)} dP = \int (0.0004) dt;$$

$$-\frac{1}{150} \int \left(\frac{1}{P} - \frac{1}{P - 150} \right) dP = \int (0.0004) dt \qquad \text{[partial fractions]};$$

$$\ln|P| - \ln|P - 150| = -(0.06)t + C;$$

$$\frac{P}{P - 150} = \pm e^C e^{-(0.06)t} = Be^{-(0.06)t} \qquad \text{[where } B = \pm e^C\text{]}. \tag{15}$$

(a) Substituting $t = 0$ and $P = 200$ in (15) gives $B = 4$. With this value of B we solve Eq. (15) for

$$P(t) = \frac{600 e^{-(0.06)t}}{4 e^{-(0.06)t} - 1}. \tag{16}$$

Note that as t increases and approaches $T = (\ln 4)/0.06 \approx 23.105$, the positive denominator on the right in (16) decreases and approaches zero. Consequently $P(t) \to +\infty$ as $t \to T^-$. This is a *doomsday* situation—a real population *explosion*.

(b) Substituting $t = 0$ and $P = 100$ in (15) gives $B = -2$. With this value of B we solve Eq. (15) for

$$P(t) = \frac{300 e^{-(0.06)t}}{2 e^{-(0.06)t} + 1} = \frac{300}{2 + e^{(0.06)t}}. \tag{17}$$

Note that as t increases without bound, the positive denominator in the right in Eq. (17) approaches $+\infty$. Consequently $P(t) \to 0$ as $t \to +\infty$. This is an (eventual) *extinction* situation. ♦

Thus the population in Example 7 either explodes or is an endangered species threatened with extinction, depending on whether or not its initial size exceeds the threshold population $M = 150$. An approximation to this phenomenon is sometimes observed with animal populations, such as the alligator population in certain areas of the southern United States.

Figure 9.5.4 shows typical solution curves that illustrate the two possibilities for a population $P(t)$ satisfying Eq. (13). If $P_0 = M$ (exactly!), then the population remains constant. But this equilibrium situation is highly unstable. If P_0 exceeds M, no matter how slightly, then $P(t)$ increases rapidly without bound, whereas if the initial (positive) population is less than M (however slightly), then it decreases—more gradually—toward zero as $t \to +\infty$.

FIGURE 9.5.4 Typical solution curves for the explosion-extinction equation $P' = kP(P - M)$.

Predator-Prey Populations

Consider the two differential equations

$$\frac{dx}{dt} = px - axy, \tag{18}$$

$$\frac{dy}{dt} = -qy + bxy \tag{19}$$

with positive coefficients a, b, p, and q. In ecology this system of simultaneous equations is often used to model a *prey population* (such as rabbits) and a *predator population* (such as foxes) that occupy the same environment. Typically, there is a food supply ample to feed the prey, whereas the predators feed on the prey—thereby impeding the growth of the prey population and promoting the growth of the predator population.

Note that if a were zero then Eq. (18) would reduce to the natural growth equation $dx/dt = px$, and thereby would imply that the prey population $x(t)$ would increase without bound as $t \to +\infty$. On the other hand, if b were zero, then Eq. (19) would reduce to the natural decay equation $dy/dx = -qy$, and would therefore imply that the predator population $y(t)$ would decline and die out as $t \to +\infty$. If a and b are positive, then the negative term $-axy$ in (18) represents a decrease in the rate of growth of the prey due to life-threatening "interaction" with the predators, while the positive term bxy in (19) represents a concomitant decrease in the rate of decline of the predators (who prosper at the expense of the prey).

If the coefficients in Eqs. (18) and (19) are all positive, then it generally is impossible to solve for x and y explicitly as elementary functions of the time variable t. But if we think of y as a function of x, then the chain rule in the form

$$\frac{dy}{dt} = \frac{dy}{dx}\frac{dx}{dt}$$

yields

$$\frac{dy}{dx} = \frac{dy/dt}{dx/dt} = \frac{-qy + bxy}{px - axy}. \tag{20}$$

In Problem 34 we ask you to separate the variables in Eq. (20) to derive the implicit general solution

$$x^q y^p = Ce^{bx}e^{ay} \tag{21}$$

of Eq. (20). The value of the arbitrary constant C can be determined by substitution of specific numerical values of the coefficients a, b, p, and q together with initial values $x_0 = x(0)$ and $y_0 = y(0)$ of the two populations.

The graph of Eq. (21) is typically a closed curve in the shape of an oval in the first quadrant of the xy-plane. For instance, with the values $a = 0.0003$, $b = 0.0002$, $p = 0.08$, and $q = 0.07$ of the coefficients and with initial populations of $x_0 = 800$ rabbits and $y_0 = 75$ foxes, the implicit plotting command of a computer algebra system generates the solution curve shown in Fig. 9.5.5.

We can "zoom in" on the leftmost and rightmost points P_1 and P_2 on the curve by plotting it in appropriately selected smaller viewing windows. Of course we may also zoom in on the lowest and highest points Q_1 and Q_2. Doing so, we determine the approximate coordinates $P_1(50, 267)$, $P_2(1146, 267)$, $Q_1(350, 45)$, and $Q_2(350, 820)$ of these extreme points on the solution curve.

A more detailed analysis of Eqs. (18) and (19) reveals that the point $(x(t), y(t))$ traverses the solution curve repeatedly in a counterclockwise direction as time t advances. Consequently, if we begin with $x_0 = 800$ rabbits and $y_0 = 75$ foxes, then:

- The numbers of rabbits and foxes both increase initially until there are 1146 rabbits and 267 foxes (at P_2);

FIGURE 9.5.5 A typical prey-predator solution curve.

- Next the number of rabbits decreases and the number of foxes continues to increase until there are 350 rabbits and 820 foxes (at Q_2);
- Next the numbers of rabbits and foxes both decrease until there are 50 rabbits and 267 foxes (at P_1);
- Next the number of rabbits increases and the number of foxes continues to decrease until there are 350 rabbits and 45 foxes (at Q_1);
- Finally the numbers of rabbits and foxes both increase until there are again 800 rabbits and 75 foxes.

This process of cyclical variation of the rabbit and fox populations continues indefinitely. In particular, we see that the number of rabbits oscillates between 50 and 1146, while the number of foxes oscillates between 45 and 820. This classical model of a predator-prey situation was developed in the 1920s by the Italian mathematician Vito Volterra (1860–1940) in order to analyze the cyclic variations observed in the shark and food fish populations in the Adriatic Sea. The *time lag* of the predator population behind that of the prey population is worthy of note. A similar (but more complicated) analysis might help explain—and even predict—the time lag of economic prosperity of a nation subsequent to certain fiscal policies of its government.

9.5 TRUE/FALSE STUDY GUIDE

9.5 CONCEPTS: QUESTIONS AND DISCUSSION

1. Describe the general features of populations that are modeled by the differential equation $dP/dt = kP(M - P)$ with $k > 0$ and $M > 0$. In what way do solutions depend on the value of the initial population $P(0) = P_0$?
2. Describe the general features of populations that are modeled by the differential equation $dP/dt = kP(P - M)$ with $k > 0$ and $M > 0$. In what way do solutions depend on the value of the initial population $P(0) = P_0$?
3. What are the similarities and differences between the two situations in Questions 1 and 2? Distinguish the roles played by the critical population M in the two cases.
4. Explain the behaviors of the rabbit and fox populations starting at the points P_1, P_2, Q_1, and Q_2 in Fig. 9.5.5; do so by calculating the signs of the derivatives dx/dt and dy/dt at these points.

9.5 PROBLEMS

Use partial fractions to solve the initial value problems in Problems 1 through 8.

1. $\dfrac{dx}{dt} = x - x^2$, $x(0) = 2$
2. $\dfrac{dx}{dt} = 10x - x^2$, $x(0) = 1$
3. $\dfrac{dx}{dt} = 1 - x^2$, $x(0) = 3$
4. $\dfrac{dx}{dt} = 9 - 4x^2$, $x(0) = 0$
5. $\dfrac{dx}{dt} = 3x(5 - x)$, $x(0) = 8$
6. $\dfrac{dx}{dt} = 3x(x - 5)$, $x(0) = 2$
7. $\dfrac{dx}{dt} = 4x(7 - x)$, $x(0) = 11$
8. $\dfrac{dx}{dt} = 7x(x - 13)$, $x(0) = 17$

9. The time rate of change of a rabbit population P is proportional to the square root of P. At time $t = 0$ (in months) the population numbers 100 rabbits and is increasing at the rate of 20 rabbits per month. How many rabbits will there be one year later?

10. Suppose that the fish population $P(t)$ in a lake was attacked by a disease at time $t = 0$, with the result that the fish ceased to reproduce (so that the birth rate was $\beta = 0$) and the death rate δ (deaths per week per fish) was thereafter proportional to $1/\sqrt{P}$. If there were initially 900 fish in the lake and 441 were left after 6 weeks, how long did it take all the fish in the lake to die?

11. Suppose that when a certain lake is stocked with fish, the birth and death rates β and δ are both inversely proportional to $\sqrt{P}$. (a) Show that

$$P(t) = \left(\tfrac{1}{2}kt - \sqrt{P_0}\right)^2$$

where k is a constant. (b) If $P_0 = 100$ and after 6 months there are 169 fish in the lake, how many will there be after one year?

12. The time rate of change of an alligator population P in a swamp is proportional to the square of P. The swamp contained a dozen alligators in 1988, two dozen in 1998. When will there be four dozen alligators in the swamp? What happens thereafter?

13. Consider a prolific breed of rabbits whose birth and death rates, β and δ, are each proportional to the rabbit population $P = P(t)$, with $\beta > \delta$. (a) Show that

$$P(t) = \frac{P_0}{1 - kP_0 t}$$

where k is a constant. Note that $P(t) \to +\infty$ as $t \to 1/(kP_0)$. This is doomsday. (b) Suppose that $P_0 = 6$ and that there are nine rabbits after ten months. When does doomsday occur?

14. Repeat part (a) of Problem 13 in the case $\beta < \delta$. What now happens to the rabbit population in the long run?

15. Suppose that the population $P(t)$ (in millions) of Ruritania satisfies the differential equation

$$\frac{dP}{dt} = k \cdot P \cdot (200 - P) \quad (k \text{ constant}).$$

Its population in 1940 was 100 million and was then growing at the rate of 1 million per year. Predict this country's population for the year 2000.

16. Suppose that a community contains 15000 people who are susceptible to Michaud's syndrome, a contagious disease. At time $t = 0$ the number $N(t)$ of people who have developed Michaud's syndrome is 5000 and is increasing at the rate of 500 per day. Assume that $N'(t)$ is proportional to the product of the numbers of those who have caught the disease and those who have not. How long will it take for another 5000 people to develop Michaud's syndrome?

17. As the salt KNO_3 dissolves in methanol, the number $x(t)$ of grams of the salt in solution after t seconds satisfies the differential equation

$$\frac{dx}{dt} = (0.8)x - (0.004)x^2.$$

(a) If $x = 50$ when $t = 0$, how long will it take an additional 50 g of the salt to dissolve? (b) What is the maximum amount of the salt that will ever dissolve in the methanol?

18. A population $P(t)$ (t in months) of squirrels satisfies the differential equation

$$\frac{dP}{dt} = (0.001)P^2 - kP \quad (k \text{ constant}).$$

If $P(0) = 100$ and $P'(0) = 8$, how long will it take for this population to double to 200 squirrels?

19. Consider an animal population $P(t)$ (t in years) that satisfies the differential equation

$$\frac{dP}{dt} = kP^2 - (0.01)P \quad (k \text{ constant}).$$

Suppose also that $P(0) = 200$ and that $P'(0) = 2$. (a) When is $P = 1000$? (b) When will doomsday occur for this population?

20. Suppose that the number $x(t)$ (t in months) of alligators in a swamp satisfies the differential equation

$$\frac{dx}{dt} = (0.0001)x^2 - (0.01)x.$$

(a) If initially there are 25 alligators, solve this equation to determine what happens to this alligator population in the long run. (b) Repeat part (a), but use 150 alligators initially.

21. Consider a population $P(t)$ satisfying the logistic equation $dP/dt = aP - bP^2$, where $B = aP$ is the time rate at which births occur and $D = bP^2$ is the rate at which deaths occur. If the initial population is $P(0) = P_0$ and B_0 births per month and D_0 deaths per month are occurring at time $t = 0$, show that the limiting population is $M = B_0 P_0 / D_0$.

22. Consider a rabbit population $P(t)$ satisfying the logistic equation as in Problem 21. If the initial population is 120 rabbits and there are 8 births per month and 6 deaths per month occurring at time $t = 0$, how many months does it take for $P(t)$ to reach 95% of the limiting population M?

23. Consider a rabbit population $P(t)$ satisfying the logistic equation as in Problem 21. If the initial population is 240 rabbits and there are 9 births per month and 12 deaths per month occurring at time $t = 0$, how many months does it take for $P(t)$ to reach 105% of the limiting population M?

24. Consider a population $P(t)$ satisfying the extinction/explosion equation

$$\frac{dP}{dt} = aP^2 - bP,$$

where $B = aP^2$ is the time rate at which births occur and $D = bP$ is the rate at which deaths occur. If the initial population is $P(0) = P_0$ and B_0 births per month and D_0 deaths per month are occurring at time $t = 0$, show that the threshold population is $M = D_0 P_0 / B_0$.

25. Consider an alligator population $P(t)$ satisfying the extinction/explosion equation as in Problem 24. If the initial population is 100 alligators and there are 10 births per month and 9 deaths per month occurring at time $t = 0$, how many months does it take for $P(t)$ to reach 10 times the threshold population M?

26. Consider an alligator population $P(t)$ satisfying the extinction/explosion equation as in Problem 24. If the initial population is 110 alligators and there are 11 births per month and 12 deaths per month occurring at time $t = 0$, how many months does it take for $P(t)$ to reach 10% of the threshold population M?

27. Suppose that at time $t = 0$, half of a "logistic" population of 100,000 persons has heard a certain rumor, and that the number of those who have heard it is then increasing at the rate of 1000 persons per day. How long will it take for this rumor to spread to 80% of the population? (*Suggestion:* Find the value of k by substituting $P(0)$ and $P'(0)$ in the logistic equation in (3).)

28. The data in the table in Fig. 9.5.6 are given for a certain population $P(t)$ that satisfies the logistic equation in (3). (a) What is the limiting population M? (*Suggestion:* Use the approximation

$$P'(t) \approx \frac{P(t+h) - P(t-h)}{2h}$$

Year	P (millions)
1924	24.63
1925	25.00
1926	25.38
⋮	⋮
1974	47.04
1975	47.54
1976	48.04

FIGURE 9.5.6 Population data for Problem 28.

with $h=1$ to estimate the values of $P'(t)$ when $P=25.00$ and when $P=47.54$. Then substitute these values in the logistic equation and solve for k and M.) (b) Use the values of k and M found in part (a) to determine when $P = 75$. (*Suggestion:* Take $t = 0$ to correspond to the year 1925.)

29. During the period from 1790 to 1930, the U.S. population $P(t)$ (t in years) grew from 3.9 million to 123.2 million. Throughout this period, $P(t)$ remained close to the solution of the initial value problem

$$\frac{dP}{dt} = (0.03135)P - (0.0001489)P^2, \quad P(0) = 3.9.$$

(a) What population does this logistic equation predict for the year 1930? (b) What limiting population does this equation predict? (c) Has this logistic equation continued since 1930 to accurately model the U.S. population? [This problem is based on a computation by Verhulst, who in 1845 used the 1790–1840 U.S. population data to predict accurately the U.S. population through the year 1930 (long after his own death, of course).]

30. Consider two populations $P_1(t)$ and $P_2(t)$, both of which satisfy the logistic equation with the same limiting population M, but with different values k_1 and k_2 of the constant k in Eq. (3). Assume that $k_1 < k_2$. Which population approaches M more rapidly? You can reason *geometrically* by examining slope fields (especially if appropriate software is available), *symbolically* by analyzing the solution given in Eq. (7), or *numerically* by substituting successive values of t.

31. (a) Derive the solution given in Eq. (7) for the logistic initial value problem in (6). (b) How does this solution behavior (as t increases) if the initial value P_0 is negative?

32. (a) Derive the solution

$$P(t) = \frac{MP_0}{P_0 + (M - P_0)e^{kMt}}$$

satisfying the initial condition $P(0) = P_0$ for the explosion/extinction equation in (13). (b) How does this solution behave (as t increases) if the initial value P_0 is negative?

33. If $P(t)$ satisfies the logistic equation in (3), use the chain rule to show that

$$P''(t) = 2k^2 P \cdot \left(P - \tfrac{1}{2}M\right) \cdot (P - M).$$

Conclude that

$P''(t) > 0$ if $0 < P < \tfrac{1}{2}M$; $\quad P''(t) = 0$ if $P = \tfrac{1}{2}M$;

$P''(t) < 0$ if $\tfrac{1}{2}M < P < M$; and $P''(t) > 0$ if $P > M$.

In particular, it follows that any solution curve that crosses the horizontal line $P = \tfrac{1}{2}M$ has an inflection point where it crosses that line, and therefore resembles one of the lower S-shaped curves in Fig. 9.5.3.

34. Derive the solution in Eq. (21) of the separable differential equation in (20).

9.5 Project: Predator-Prey Equations and Your Own Game Preserve

You own a large forested game preserve that you originally stocked with F_0 foxes and R_0 rabbits. The following differential equations model the numbers $R(t)$ of rabbits and $F(t)$ of foxes t months later.

$$\frac{dR}{dt} = (0.01)pR - (0.0001)aRF,$$

$$\frac{dF}{dt} = -(0.01)qF + (0.0001)bRF$$

where p and q are the two largest digits (with $p < q$), and a and b the two smallest nonzero digits (with $a < b$), in your student I.D. number.

The numbers of foxes and rabbits will oscillate periodically, as in the situation illustrated by Fig. 9.5.5. Choose your initial numbers F_0 of foxes and R_0 of rabbits—perhaps several hundred of each—so that the resulting solution curve in the RF-plane is a fairly eccentric closed curve. (The eccentricity may be increased if you begin with a relatively large number of rabbits and a relatively small number of foxes, as any game preserve manager would naturally do.)

Your task is then to determine the maximum and minimum number of rabbits and foxes that will ever be observed in your game preserve. Use the implicit curve-plotting facility of a graphing calculator or computer algebra system to zoom in on the rightmost, leftmost, lowest, and highest points of the solution curve with sufficient precision to determine their coordinates accurate to the nearest integer.

9.6 LINEAR SECOND-ORDER EQUATIONS

A **second-order** differential equation is one that involves the second derivative y'' (and perhaps also the first derivative y') of the dependent variable y. It is called **linear** provided that it is linear in the unknown function $y(x)$ and its derivatives. Thus a **linear second-order** differential equation is one of the form

$$A(x)\frac{d^2y}{dx^2} + B(x)\frac{dy}{dx} + C(x)y = F(x), \tag{1}$$

where the *coefficients* $A(x)$, $B(x)$, $C(x)$, and $F(x)$ are given continuous functions of the independent variable on an appropriate open interval I where we may hope to determine a solution. A **solution** of (1) is simply a function $y = y(x)$ that satisfies the differential equation at every point of the interval I.

The coefficient functions in (1) need *not* be linear in x. Thus the second-order equation

$$e^x y'' + (\cos x)y' + \left(1 + \sqrt{x}\right)y = \tan^{-1} x$$

is linear even though the coefficients are quite nonlinear functions of x. By contrast, the equations

$$y'' = yy' \quad \text{and} \quad y'' + 3(y')^2 + 4y^3 = 0$$

are not linear, because products or powers of y or its derivatives appear in each.

In this section we restrict our attention to the case in which $F(x) \equiv 0$ in Eq. (1). Such a linear equation is said to be **homogeneous**. Thus a homogeneous linear second-order differential equation is one of the form

$$A(x)\frac{d^2y}{dx^2} + B(x)\frac{dy}{dx} + C(x)y = 0. \tag{2}$$

Homogeneous linear equations have the useful feature that we can construct new solutions by forming *linear combinations* of known solutions. In particular, any **linear combination** $y = c_1 y_1 + c_2 y_2$ of two known solutions y_1 and y_2 of Eq. (2) is another solution of the differential equation.

THEOREM 1 Linear Combinations of Solutions

Suppose that the two functions y_1 and y_2 are both solutions of the homogeneous linear equation in (2) and that c_1 and c_2 are constants. Then the new function y defined by

$$y(x) = c_1 y_1(x) + c_2 y_2(x)$$

also satisfies Eq. (2).

PROOF The fact that y_1 and y_2 are both solutions of Eq. (2) means that

$$Ay_1'' + By_1' + Cy_1 = 0 \quad \text{and} \quad Ay_2'' + By_2' + Cy_2 = 0.$$

It follows (using linearity of differentiation) that

$$\begin{aligned} Ay'' + By' + Cy &= A(c_1 y_1 + c_2 y_2)'' + B(c_1 y_1 + c_2 y_2)' + C(c_1 y_1 + c_2 y_2) \\ &= A(c_1 y_1'' + c_2 y_2'') + B(c_1 y_1' + c_2 y_2') + C(c_1 y_1 + c_2 y_2) \\ &= c_1(Ay_1'' + By_1' + Cy_1) + c_2(Ay_2'' + By_2' + Cy_2) \\ &= c_1 \cdot 0 + c_2 \cdot 0 = 0. \end{aligned}$$

Thus we have verified that the linear combination $y = c_1 y_1 + c_2 y_2$ is also a solution of Eq. (2). ◄

Theorem 1 implies that any constant multiple cy of the solution y is also a solution of the differential equation—choose $c_2 = 0$. But we do not regard y and cy as "really different" solutions. The two solutions y_1 and y_2 are called **independent** provided that neither is a constant multiple of the other. We can always determine whether two given solutions y_1 and y_2 are independent by noting whether either of the two quotients y_1/y_2 or y_2/y_1 is a constant. For instance, the following pairs of functions are obviously independent:

$$x \text{ and } x^2; \quad e^x \text{ and } e^{-2x}; \quad \cos x \text{ and } \sin x.$$

Theorem 1 provides us with the means to solve initial value problems by forming linear combinations of independent solutions.

EXAMPLE 1 (a) Verify that $y_1(x) = x^2$ and $y_2(x) = x^{-3}$ are independent solutions (for $x > 0$) of the homogeneous linear equation

$$x^2 y'' + 2xy' - 6y = 0.$$

(b) Find a solution satisfying the two initial conditions $y(1) = 10$ and $y'(1) = 5$.

Solutions For part (a), we readily calculate

$$x^2 y_1'' + 2xy_1' - 6y_1 = x^2 \cdot 2 + 2x \cdot 2x - 6 \cdot x^2 = (2 + 4 - 6)x^2 = 0$$

and

$$x^2 y_2'' + 2xy_2' - 6y_2 = x^2 \cdot 12x^{-5} + 2x \cdot (-3x^{-4}) - 6 \cdot x^{-3} = (12 - 6 - 6)x^{-3} = 0.$$

Thus both y_1 and y_2 are solutions of the given differential equation. Because neither $y_1/y_2 = x^5$ nor $y_2/y_1 = x^{-5}$ is a constant, it follows that these two solutions are independent.

To solve part (b), we see (by Theorem 1) that the linear combination

$$y(x) = c_1 y_1(x) + c_2 y_2(x) = c_1 x^2 + c_2 x^{-3}$$

is also a solution (for any choice of the constants c_1 and c_2). When we impose the given initial conditions on this new solution and its derivative $y'(x) = 2c_1 x - 3c_2 x^{-4}$, we get the equations

$$c_1 + c_2 = 10 \quad \text{and} \quad 2c_1 - 3c_2 = 5.$$

We readily solve these equations—for instance, by substituting $c_1 = 10 - c_2$ from the first equation into the second—for $c_1 = 7$ and $c_2 = 3$. Consequently, a solution of the initial value problem

$$x^2 y'' + 2xy' - 6y = 0, \quad y(1) = 10, \quad y'(1) = 5$$

is $y(x) = 7x^2 + 3x^{-3}$. ◆

The leading coefficient function $A(x) = x^2$ in the differential equation of Example 1 vanishes at $x = 0$. On any interval where the function $A(x)$ is nonzero, we can divide by $A(x)$ to write the homogeneous equation $Ay'' + By' + Cy = 0$ in the form

$$\frac{d^2 y}{dx^2} + P(x)\frac{dy}{dx} + Q(x)y = 0. \tag{3}$$

One key to solving homogeneous second-order equations is the fact that *every* solution of such an equation is a linear combination of any two given independent solutions. Unlike Theorem 1, the theorem that follows is not elementary, and its proof is therefore omitted.

THEOREM 2 General Solutions

Suppose that y_1 and y_2 are independent solutions of the homogeneous linear equation in (3) on an interval I where the coefficient functions $P(x)$ and $Q(x)$ are continuous. If y is any given solution of the equation on this interval, then there exist constants c_1 and c_2 such that

$$y(x) = c_1 y_1(x) + c_2 y_2(x)$$

for all x in I.

As a result of Theorem 2, we know *every* solution of a homogeneous linear second-order differential equation once we know just *two* independent solutions y_1 and y_2. For this reason, we may call $y = c_1 y_1 + c_2 y_2$ the **general solution** of the differential equation—there is no other solution of it. For instance, $y(x) = c_1 x^2 + c_2 x^{-3}$ is the general solution (for $x > 0$) of the differential equation in Example 1, and no function not of this form can satisfy the equation.

Because the general solution of a second-order differential equation involves *two* arbitrary constants, we can hope to satisfy *two* initial conditions by selecting the values of c_1 and c_2 appropriately. This is why a second-order linear initial value problem typically takes the form

$$Ay'' + By' + Cy = F, \quad y(a) = b_0, \quad y'(a) = b_1 \tag{4}$$

with two initial conditions specifying given values of the solution y and its derivative y' at the same point $x = a$.

A general existence-uniqueness theorem asserts that an initial value problem of the form in (4) has exactly one solution on an interval where the coefficient functions are continuous and $A(x)$ is nonzero. For instance, the coefficient functions in the differential equation of Example 1 are all continuous and $A(x) = x^2$ is nonzero for $x > 0$. Therefore the only solution for $x > 0$ of the initial value problem

$$x^2 y'' + 6xy' - 2y = 0, \quad y(1) = 10, \quad y'(1) = 5$$

is the solution $y(x) = 7x^2 + 3x^{-3}$ that we found in part (b) of Example 1.

Constant-Coefficient Equations

We saw in Section 9.4 that the general solution of a linear first-order equation is given by an explicit integral formula involving the coefficients in the equation. In contrast, this is far from true for second-order linear equations. It can be a formidable task to find the two independent solutions that are needed to construct a general solution of a given homogeneous linear second-order equation. For instance, the general solution of the differential equation $6y'' + 2xy' - x^2 y = 0$—which may appear to resemble superficially the equation of Example 1—cannot be expressed simply in terms of familiar elementary functions. This difficulty somehow arises from the variable coefficients in the last equation.

Fortunately, it *is* possible to solve explicitly a homogeneous linear second-order differential equation of the form

$$a \frac{d^2 y}{dx^2} + b \frac{dy}{dx} + cy = 0 \tag{5}$$

with *constant coefficients* a, b, and c. And we will see in Section 9.7 that such differential equations have important physical applications.

To construct the general solution $y = c_1 y_1 + c_2 y_2$ of the differential equation

$$ay'' + by' + cy = 0 \tag{6}$$

with $a \neq 0$, we need to find two independent particular solutions y_1 and y_2. The key idea is to find a plausible *form* of a possible solution of Eq. (6). Because—if r

is a constant—$D_x(e^{rx})$ is a constant multiple of $y(x) = e^{rx}$, it follows that y'' and y' would have that form as well. Indeed, substitution of $y(x) = e^{rx}$, $y'(x) = re^{rx}$, and $y'' = r^2 e^{rx}$ into Eq. (6) yields the equation

$$ar^2 e^{rx} + bre^{rx} + ce^{rx} = (ar^2 + br + c)e^{rx} = 0.$$

Because e^{rx} is never zero, the product $(ar^2 + br + c)e^{rx}$ is zero exactly when

$$ar^2 + br + c = 0. \tag{7}$$

This is a simple quadratic equation that we can solve to find the value (or values) of r such that $y = e^{rx}$ is, indeed, a solution of Eq. (6).

Equation (7) is called the **characteristic equation** (or **auxiliary equation**) of the homogeneous linear second-order differential equation $ay'' + by' + cy = 0$. We can solve it by any of various techniques; the familiar quadratic formula yields the solutions

$$r_1, r_2 = \frac{-b \pm \sqrt{b^2 - 4ac}}{2a},$$

in which the two possible choices of sign yield the two roots r_1 and r_2. If $b^2 - 4ac > 0$ then both are real, and the two distinct possibilities r_1 and r_2 for the value of r yield the two independent solutions $y_1 = e^{r_1 x}$ and $y_2 = e^{r_2 x}$ of the differential equation in (6). (Do you see why neither is a constant multiple of the other?) Remember that once we have found two independent solutions, we have found them all. Examples 2 through 4 illustrate how to proceed if r_1 and r_2 are distinct and real. It remains to be seen how we should proceed should $b^2 - 4ac$ be zero or negative.

CASE 1   Distinct Real Roots

Suppose that the characteristic equation of the linear homogeneous differential equation $ay'' + by' + cy = 0$ has unequal real roots r_1 and r_2. Then a general solution of this differential equation is

$$y(x) = c_1 e^{r_1 x} + c_2 e^{r_2 x}. \tag{8}$$

Thus, in this case, the solution of the differential equation reduces to the simple matter of solving a quadratic equation.

EXAMPLE 2 Solve the differential equation $3y'' + 7y' + 2y = 0$.

Solution We can solve the characteristic equation $3r^2 + 7r + 2 = 0$ by factoring:

$$3r^2 + 7r + 2 = (3r + 1)(r + 2) = 0.$$

The roots $r_1 = -\frac{1}{3}$ and $r_2 = -2$ are real and distinct. Therefore the general solution of the differential equation—given in (8)—is

$$y(x) = c_1 e^{-x/3} + c_2 e^{-2x}. \qquad \blacklozenge$$

REMARK   A first-order differential equation generally has only a single solution curve passing through a given initial point (a, b) and, therefore, only a single tangent line through the initial point is tangent to a solution curve of the equation. By contrast, Fig. 9.6.1 illustrates the fact that a second-order differential equation generally has infinitely many solution curves passing through a given point (a, b_0)—one for each (real) value of the initial slope $y'(a) = b_1$. That is, every nonvertical straight line through (a, b_0) is tangent to some solution curve. Figure 9.6.1 shows several solution curves of the differential equation $3y'' + 7y' + 2y = 0$ all having the same initial value $y(0) = 1$; Fig. 9.6.2 shows several solution curves all having the same initial slope $y'(0) = 1$.

FIGURE 9.6.1 Solutions of $3y'' + 7y' + 2y = 0$ with the same initial value $y(0) = 1$ but with different values of the initial slope ranging from $y'(0) = -9$ to $y'(0) = 9$.

FIGURE 9.6.2 Solutions of $3y'' + 7y' + 2y = 0$ with the same initial slope $y'(0) = 1$ but with different initial values ranging from $y(0) = -9$ to $y(0) = 9$.

EXAMPLE 3 Solve the differential equation $5y'' - 2y' = 0$.

Solution Here the coefficient of y in the differential equation is zero, corresponding to the constant term zero in its characteristic equation: $5r^2 - 2r = 0$. The factorization

$$5r^2 - 2r = r(5r - 2) = 5r\left(r - \tfrac{2}{5}\right) = 0$$

reveals the distinct real roots $r_1 = 0$ and $r_2 = \tfrac{2}{5}$. Because $e^{r_1 x} = e^{0 \cdot x} = e^0 = 1$, the general solution of the given equation is

$$y(x) = c_1 + c_2 e^{2x/5}.$$

As illustrated in Fig. 9.6.3, the solution curves with a given value of c_1 and different values of c_2 all have the line $y = c_1$ as an asymptote as $x \to -\infty$. ◆

FIGURE 9.6.3 Solutions $y(x) = 1 + c_2 e^{2x/5}$ of $5y'' - 2y' = 0$ with different values of c_2 ranging from $c_2 = -3$ to $c_2 = 3$.

EXAMPLE 4 Solve the differential equation $y'' - 4y = 0$.

Solution Now the coefficient of y' in the differential equation is zero, and hence the coefficient of r is zero in its characteristic equation: $r^2 - 4 = 0$. The factorization $r^2 - 4 = (r + 2)(r - 2)$ reveals the roots $r_1 = -2$ and $r_2 = 2$, and thus we obtain the general solution

$$y(x) = c_1 e^{-2x} + c_2 e^{2x}.$$

But you can readily verify (by differentiating y_3 and y_4 twice each) that $y_3(x) = \cosh 2x$ and $y_4(x) = \sinh 2x$ are also independent solutions of the differential equation $y'' - 4y = 0$. Therefore

$$y(x) = c_1 \cosh 2x + c_2 \sinh 2x$$

is another general solution of the same differential equation. Thus there is nothing unique about the *form* of a given general solution—any two different pairs of independent solutions of the same linear homogeneous second-order differential equation will yield two different expressions for the general solution. Moreover, the graphs of the two functions in one such pair can appear quite different from those in the other pair. Figure 9.6.4 shows the graphs of the four solutions e^{-2x}, e^{2x}, $\cosh 2x$, and $\sinh 2x$ of $y'' - 4y = 0$. ◆

FIGURE 9.6.4 Four different solutions of the equation $y'' - 4y = 0$.

REMARK Because $\cosh 2x$ and $\sinh 2x$ are solutions of the linear differential equation $y'' - 4y = 0$ with general solution $y(x) = c_1 e^{-2x} + c_2 e^{2x}$, it follows from Theorem 2 that each of the functions $\cosh 2x$ and $\sinh 2x$ can be expressed as a linear combination of the functions e^{-2x} and e^{2x}. Of course this is no surprise, because

$$\cosh 2x = \tfrac{1}{2} e^{2x} + \tfrac{1}{2} e^{-2x} \quad \text{and} \quad \sinh 2x = \tfrac{1}{2} e^{2x} - \tfrac{1}{2} e^{-2x}$$

by the definitions of the hyperbolic sine and cosine functions (Section 7.6).

If $b^2 - 4ac = 0$, then the characteristic equation $ar^2 + br + c = 0$ has equal (and necessarily real) roots $r_1 = r_2 = -b/(2a)$. Hence, at first, we obtain only the single solution $y_1(x) = e^{r_1 x}$ of the corresponding differential equation. In this case the problem that remains is to produce the "missing" second independent solution of the differential equation.

A double root $r = r_1$ can occur only if the characteristic equation factors as

$$ar^2 + br + c = a(r - r_1)^2 = a(r^2 - 2r_1 r + r_1^2) = 0.$$

The corresponding differential equation is then a constant multiple of the equation

$$y'' - 2r_1 y' + r_1^2 y = 0.$$

But it is easy to verify (and you should do so) that $y_2 = xe^{r_1 x}$ is a second solution of this differential equation. Obviously the solutions $y_1(x) = e^{r_1 x}$ and $y_2(x) = xe^{r_1 x}$ are independent, and therefore enable us to write a general solution of the given differential equation.

CASE 2 Equal Real Roots
Suppose that the characteristic equation of the linear homogeneous differential equation $ay'' + by' + cy = 0$ has equal real roots $r_1 = r_2$. Then a general solution of this differential equation is

$$y(x) = c_1 e^{r_1 x} + c_2 x e^{r_1 x} = (c_1 + c_2 x) e^{r_1 x}. \qquad (9)$$

EXAMPLE 5 Solve the initial value problem

$$4y'' + 12y' + 9y = 0, \qquad y(0) = 4, \quad y'(0) = -3.$$

Solution The characteristic equation

$$4r^2 + 12r + 9 = (2r + 3)^2 = 0$$

of the given differential equation has equal real roots $r_1 = r_2 = -\frac{3}{2}$. Hence the general solution—as given in Eq. (9)—is

$$y(x) = c_1 e^{-3x/2} + c_2 x e^{-3x/2}.$$

Differentiation gives

$$y'(x) = -\tfrac{3}{2} c_1 e^{-3x/2} + c_2 e^{-3x/2} - \tfrac{3}{2} c_2 x e^{-3x/2}.$$

Therefore the given initial conditions yield the simultaneous equations

$$y(0) = \quad c_1 \quad = 4,$$
$$y'(0) = -\tfrac{3}{2} c_1 + c_2 = -3,$$

which imply that $c_1 = 4$ and $c_2 = 3$. Thus the solution of the given initial value problem is

$$y(x) = 4e^{-3x/2} + 3xe^{-3x/2} = (4 + 3x)e^{-3x/2}.$$

This particular solution of the differential equation is illustrated in Fig. 9.6.5, together with several others of the form $y(x) = c_1 e^{-3x/2} + 3xe^{-3x/2}$. ◆

FIGURE 9.6.5 Solutions $y(x) = (c_1 + 3x)e^{-3x/2}$ of $4y'' + 12y' + 9y = 0$ with different values of c_1 ranging from $c_1 = -4$ to $c_1 = 4$.

Complex Roots

If $b^2 - 4ac < 0$, then solution of the characteristic equation $ar^2 + br + c = 0$ using the quadratic formula gives

$$r = \frac{-b \pm \sqrt{b^2 - 4ac}}{2a} = \frac{-b \pm \sqrt{(-1) \cdot (4ac - b^2)}}{2a} = p \pm iq$$

where

$$p = -\frac{b}{2a}, \quad q = \frac{\sqrt{4ac - b^2}}{2a}, \quad \text{and} \quad i = \sqrt{-1}.$$

Thus we obtain a complex conjugate pair of roots.

But what does $y = e^{rx}$ mean when r is a complex number? The answer stems from **Euler's formula**

$$e^{i\theta} = \cos\theta + i\sin\theta, \tag{10}$$

which we discuss in detail in Section 11.4. If $r = p + iq$, we therefore define the complex exponential e^{rx} (for x real) by writing

$$e^{rx} = e^{(p+iq)x} = e^{px+iqx} = e^{px}e^{iqx},$$

so

$$e^{rx} = e^{px}(\cos qx + i\sin qx), \tag{11}$$

using Euler's formula with $\theta = qx$.

As defined by Eq. (11), the exponential e^{rx} is a complex-valued function of the real variable x. Such a function is differentiated by differentiating separately its real and imaginary parts. That is,

$$D_x(e^{rx}) = D_x(e^{px}\cos qx) + iD_x(e^{px}\sin qx)$$
$$= (pe^{px}\cos qx - qe^{px}\sin qx) + i(pe^{px}\sin qx + qe^{px}\cos qx)$$
$$= (p + iq)(e^{px}\cos qx + ie^{px}\sin qx) = re^{rx}.$$

Thus $D_x e^{rx} = re^{rx}$ when r is complex, exactly as when r is real.

This familiar differentiation formula is the basis for the fact that $y = e^{rx}$ is a solution of the homogeneous linear differential equation $ay'' + by' + cy = 0$ precisely when r is a root of the associated characteristic equation $ar^2 + br + c = 0$. In the case of complex conjugate roots $r_1, r_2 = p \pm qi$, we get the general complex-valued solution

$$y(x) = C_1 e^{r_1 x} + C_2 e^{r_2 x},$$

which we can rewrite as

$$y(x) = C_1 e^{(p+iq)x} + C_2 e^{(p-iq)x}$$
$$= C_1 e^{px}(\cos qx + i\sin qx) + C_2 e^{px}(\cos qx - i\sin qx)$$
$$= (C_1 + C_2)e^{px}\cos qx + i(C_1 - C_2)e^{px}\sin qx;$$

thus

$$y(x) = c_1 e^{px}\cos qx + c_2 e^{px}\sin qx$$

where $c_1 = C_1 + C_2$ and $c_2 = i(C_1 - C_2)$. In the last line here, we have expressed the solution $y(x)$ as a linear combination of the real-valued functions $e^{px}\cos qx$ and $e^{px}\sin qx$. Thus the complex conjugate roots $p \pm iq$ of the characteristic equation lead to the independent *real-valued* solutions $y_1 = e^{px}\cos qx$ and $y_2 = e^{px}\sin qx$ of the differential equation.

CASE 3   Complex Conjugate Roots

Suppose that the characteristic equation of the linear homogeneous differential equation $ay'' + by' + cy = 0$ has complex conjugate roots $p \pm iq$ (with $q \neq 0$). Then a general solution of the differential equation is

$$y(x) = e^{px}(c_1 \cos qx + c_2 \sin qx). \tag{12}$$

EXAMPLE 6 The characteristic equation $r^2 + 4 = 0$ of the differential equation
$$y'' + 4y = 0$$
has complex conjugate roots $\pm 2i$. With $p = 0$ and $q = 2$ in Eq. (12) we get the general solution
$$y(x) = c_1 \cos 2x + c_2 \sin 2x.$$

Figures 9.6.6 and 9.6.7 show some typical solution curves. Each is shaped like the graph of a constant multiple of the sine or cosine of $2x$. Figure 9.6.6 illustrates the effect of varying the *joint amplitude* $c = \sqrt{c_1^2 + c_2^2}$ of the constants c_1 and c_2. Figure 9.6.7 illustrates the effect of varying their ratio. ◆

FIGURE 9.6.6 Solutions $y(x) = c(3 \cos 2x + 4 \sin 2x)$ of $y'' + 4y = 0$ with different values of c ranging from $c = -3$ to $c = 3$.

FIGURE 9.6.7 Solutions $y_1 = 5 \cos 2x$, $y_2 = 5 \sin 2x$, $y_3 = 3 \cos 2x + 4 \sin 2x$, and $y_4 = -4 \cos 2x + 3 \sin 2x$ of $y'' + 4y = 0$. Can you determine which is which?

EXAMPLE 7 Solve the initial value problem
$$9y'' + 6y' + 325y = 0, \quad y(0) = 12, \quad y'(0) = 50.$$

Solution The roots of the characteristic equation $9r^2 + 6r + 325 = 0$ are given by
$$r = \frac{-6 \pm \sqrt{(-6)^2 - 4 \cdot 9 \cdot 325}}{2 \cdot 9} = \frac{-6 \pm 6\sqrt{-324}}{18} = -\frac{1}{3} \pm 6i.$$

Therefore the general solution is
$$y(x) = e^{-x/3}(c_1 \cos 6x + c_2 \sin 6x).$$

Its derivative is
$$y'(x) = -\tfrac{1}{3}e^{-x/3}(c_1 \cos 6x + c_2 \sin 6x) + 6e^{-x/3}(c_2 \cos 6x - c_1 \sin 6x).$$

When we impose the given initial conditions we obtain the simultaneous equations
$$y(0) = \quad c_1 \quad = 12,$$
$$y'(0) = -\tfrac{1}{3}c_1 + 6c_2 = 50$$

with solution $c_1 = 12$, $c_2 = 9$. Thus the solution of the given initial value problem is
$$y(x) = e^{-x/3}(12 \cos 6x + 9 \sin 6x).$$

The graph of this solution is shown in Fig. 9.6.8. It is worth nothing that $y(x) \to 0$ as $x \to +\infty$. ◆

FIGURE 9.6.8 The solution $y(x) = e^{-x/3}(12 \cos 6x + 9 \sin 6x)$ of the initial value problem in Example 7 oscillates between the dashed "envelope curves" $y = +15e^{-x/3}$ and $y = -15e^{-x/3}$.

9.6 TRUE/FALSE STUDY GUIDE

9.6 CONCEPTS: QUESTIONS AND DISCUSSION

1. Complete the entries in the following table summarizing the various cases for the solutions of the constant-coefficient differential equation $ay'' + by' + cy = 0$.

Roots of $ar^2 + br + c = 0$	General Solution

2. For each case in Question 1, give your own example of such a differential equation and its general solution—preferably one with rather large and interesting integer coefficients. (*Suggestion:* Begin with the numerical roots r_1 and r_2 and work backward to construct the corresponding differential equation.)

3. Show that the function $y(x) = |x^{-3}|$ is a solution for $x \neq 0$ of the differential equation $x^2 y'' + 2xy' - 6y = 0$ of Example 1. Is $y(x)$ a linear combination of the independent solutions $y_1(x) = x^2$ and $y_2(x) = x^{-3}$ of this equation? If not, then why does this fact not contradict Theorem 2?

9.6 PROBLEMS

Find general solutions of the differential equations in Problems 1 through 14.

1. $y'' - 7y' + 10y = 0$
2. $y'' + 2y' - 15y = 0$
3. $4y'' - 4y' - 3y = 0$
4. $12y'' + 13y' + 3y = 0$
5. $y'' + 4y' + y = 0$
6. $4y'' - 4y' - 19y = 0$
7. $4y'' + 12y' + 9y = 0$
8. $9y'' - 30y' + 25y = 0$
9. $25y'' - 20y' + 4y = 0$
10. $49y'' + 126y' + 81y = 0$
11. $y'' + 6y' + 13y = 0$
12. $y'' - 10y' + 74y = 0$
13. $9y'' + 6y' + 226y = 0$
14. $9y'' + 90y' + 226y = 0$

Solve the initial value problems in Problems 15 through 26.

15. $2y'' - 11y' + 12y = 0$; $\quad y(0) = 5, \quad y'(0) = 15$
16. $y'' - 2y' - 35y = 0$; $\quad y(0) = 12, \quad y'(0) = 0$
17. $y'' - 18y' + 77y = 0$; $\quad y(0) = 4, \quad y'(0) = 8$
18. $12y'' - y' - 6y = 0$; $\quad y(0) = 2, \quad y'(0) = 10$
19. $y'' + 22y' + 121y = 0$; $\quad y(0) = 2, \quad y'(0) = -25$
20. $9y'' + 42y' + 49y = 0$; $\quad y(0) = 6, \quad y'(0) = -11$
21. $y'' + 25y = 0$; $\quad y(0) = 7, \quad y'(0) = 10$
22. $9y'' + 100y = 0$; $\quad y(0) = 99, \quad y'(0) = 100$
23. $y'' + 4y' + 20y = 0$; $\quad y(0) = 9, \quad y'(0) = 10$
24. $y'' + 10y' + 106y = 0$; $\quad y(0) = 11, \quad y'(0) = -10$
25. $4y'' + 4y' + 101y = 0$; $\quad y(0) = 10, \quad y'(0) = 25$
26. $100y'' + 20y' + 10001y = 0$; $\quad y(0) = 30, \quad y'(0) = -33$

Each of Problems 27 through 34 gives the general solution of a homogeneous linear second-order differential equation with constant coefficients. Find that equation.

27. $y(x) = c_1 + c_2 e^{-10x}$
28. $y(x) = c_1 e^{10x} + c_2 e^{-10x}$
29. $y(x) = c_1 e^{-10x} + c_2 x e^{-10x}$
30. $y(x) = c_1 e^{10x} + c_2 e^{100x}$
31. $y(x) = c_1 + c_2 x$
32. $y(x) = e^x \left[c_1 \exp(x\sqrt{2}) + c_2 \exp(-x\sqrt{2}) \right]$
33. $y(x) = e^{-5x} \left(c_1 \cos \dfrac{x}{5} + c_2 \sin \dfrac{x}{5} \right)$
34. $y(x) = e^{-x/5} (c_1 \cos 5x + c_2 \sin 5x)$
35. Given: The differential equation $y'' + 25y = 0$. (a) Show that this equation has infinitely many different solutions $y(x)$ such that $y(0) = y(\pi) = 0$. (b) Show that this equation has no nontrivial solution $y(x)$ such that $y(0) = y(3) = 0$.
36. Suppose that $y(x)$ is a solution of the equation $ay'' + by' + cy = 0$ and that a, b, and c are all positive. Show that $y(x) \to 0$ as $x \to \pm\infty$.

9.7 MECHANICAL VIBRATIONS

Many natural phenomena exhibit either steady growth (or decline) or periodic oscillations (ebb and flow). Phenomena of steady growth are typically modeled by first-order differential equations (as in Section 9.5), whereas periodic phenomena and vibrations are typically modeled by second-order differential equations.

The motion of a mass attached to a spring serves as a relatively simple example of the vibrations that occur in more complex mechanical systems. For many such systems, the analysis of these vibrations is a problem in the solution of linear differential equations with constant coefficients (Section 9.6).

We consider a body of mass m attached to one end of an ordinary spring that resists compression as well as stretching; the other end of the spring is attached to a fixed structure, as shown in Fig. 9.7.1. Assume that the body rests on a frictionless horizontal plane so that it can move only back and forth as the spring compresses and stretches. Denote by x the distance of the body from its **equilibrium position**—its position when the spring is unstretched. We take $x > 0$ when the spring is stretched, and thus $x < 0$ when it is compressed.

According to Hooke's law, the restorative force F_S that the spring exerts on the mass is proportional to the distance x that the spring has been stretched or compressed. Because this is the same as the displacement x of the mass m from its equilibrium position, it follows that

$$F_S = -kx. \qquad (1)$$

FIGURE 9.7.1 A mass-spring-dashpot system.

The positive constant of proportionality k is called the **spring constant.** Note that F_S and x have opposite signs: $F_S < 0$ when $x > 0$, $F_S > 0$ when $x < 0$.

Figure 9.7.1 shows the mass attached to a dashpot—a device that, like a shock absorber, provides a force directed opposite to the instantaneous direction of motion of the mass m. We assume that the dashpot is so designed that this force F_R is proportional to the velocity $v = dx/dt$ of the mass; that is, that

$$F_R = -cv = -c\frac{dx}{dt}. \qquad (2)$$

The positive constant c is the **damping constant** of the dashpot. More generally, we may regard Eq. (2) as specifying frictional forces in our system (including air resistance to the motion of the mass).

If, in addition to the forces F_S and F_R, the mass is subjected to a given **external force** $F_E = F(t)$, then the total force acting on the mass is $F_T = F_S + F_R + F_E$. Using Newton's second law in the form

$$F_T = ma = m\frac{d^2x}{dt^2} = mx'',$$

we obtain the linear second-order differential equation

$$mx'' + cx' + kx = F(t) \qquad (3)$$

that governs the motion of the mass.

For an alternative example, we might attach the mass to the lower end of a spring that is suspended vertically from a fixed support, as in Fig. 9.7.2. In this case the weight $W = mg$ of the mass would stretch the spring a distance s_0 determined by Eq. (1) with $F_S = -W$ and $x = s_0$. That is, $mg = ks_0$, so that $s_0 = mg/k$. This gives the **static** equilibrium position of the mass. If y denotes the displacement of the mass in motion, measured downward from its static equilibrium position, then we ask you to show (in Problem 23) that $y = y(t)$ satisfies Eq. (3); specifically, that

$$my'' + cy' + ky = F(t) \qquad (4)$$

FIGURE 9.7.2 A mass suspended vertically from a spring.

if we include damping and external forces.

Free Undamped Motion

If there is no external force acting on the spring, then $F(t) \equiv 0$ in Eq. (3), and we call the resulting motion **free**. Thus the homogeneous equation

$$mx'' + cx' + kx = 0 \tag{5}$$

describes free motion of a mass on a spring with dashpot but with no external force applied.

If we have only a mass on a spring, with neither damping nor external force, then $c = 0$ as well, so Eq. (5) reduces to the equation

$$mx'' + kx = 0 \tag{6}$$

that models **free undamped motion**. It is convenient to rewrite Eq. (6) in the form

$$x'' + \omega_0^2 x = 0 \tag{7}$$

where

$$\omega_0 = \sqrt{\frac{k}{m}} \tag{8}$$

is the **natural frequency** of vibration of the mass on the spring. [The Greek letter ω (omega) is often used to denote frequency.]

EXAMPLE 1 A body with mass $m = \frac{1}{2}$ kilograms (kg) is attached to the end of a spring that is stretched 2 meters (m) by a force of 100 Newtons (N). This body is displaced one-half meter to the right (from its equilibrium position when the spring is unstretched) and then released from rest. Describe the motion that results.

Solution The spring constant is $k = 100/2 = 50$ (N/m), so the position function $x(t)$ of the body satisfies the initial value problem

$$\tfrac{1}{2}x'' + 50x = 0; \quad x(0) = \tfrac{1}{2}, \quad x'(0) = 0. \tag{9}$$

The equivalent different equation $x'' + 100x = 0$ has characteristic equation $r^2 + 100 = 0$ with roots $r = \pm 10i$. Therefore the general solution of the differential equation in (9) and its derivative are

$$x(t) = A\cos 10t + B\sin 10t \quad \text{and} \quad x'(t) = -10A\sin 10t + 10B\cos 10t.$$

(We write A and B for the coefficients merely to avoid subscripts.) The initial conditions immediately give $A = \tfrac{1}{2}$ and $B = 0$. Thus the position function of the body is

$$x(t) = \tfrac{1}{2}\cos 10t.$$

This function describes a back-and-forth oscillation between the rightmost position $x = \tfrac{1}{2}$ (when $t = 0, \pi/5, 2\pi/5, \ldots$) and its leftmost position $x = -\tfrac{1}{2}$ (when $t = \pi/10, 3\pi/10, 5\pi/10, \ldots$). ◆

The general solution of Eq. (7) is

$$x(t) = A\cos\omega_0 t + B\sin\omega_0 t. \tag{10}$$

To analyze the motion described by this solution, we choose constants C and α so that

$$C = \sqrt{A^2 + B^2}, \quad \cos\alpha = \frac{A}{C}, \quad \text{and} \quad \sin\alpha = \frac{B}{C}, \tag{11}$$

as indicated in Fig. 9.7.3. Note that, although $\tan\alpha = B/A$, the angle α is *not* given by the principal branch of the inverse tangent function (which gives values only in the

FIGURE 9.7.3 The angle α.

interval $-\pi/2 < x < \pi/2$). Instead, α is the angle between 0 and 2π whose cosine and sine have the signs given in (11), where either A or B or both may be negative. Thus

$$\alpha = \begin{cases} \tan^{-1}(B/A) & \text{if } A > 0, B > 0 \quad \text{(first quadrant)}, \\ \pi + \tan^{-1}(B/A) & \text{if } A < 0 \quad \text{(second or third quadrant)}, \\ 2\pi + \tan^{-1}(B/A) & \text{if } A > 0, B < 0 \quad \text{(fourth quadrant)}, \end{cases}$$

where $\tan^{-1}(B/A)$ is the angle in $(-\pi/2, \pi/2)$ given by a calculator or computer.

In any event, from (10) and (11) we get

$$x(t) = C\left(\frac{A}{C}\cos\omega_0 t + \frac{B}{C}\sin\omega_0 t\right) = C(\cos\alpha\cos\omega_0 t + \sin\alpha\sin\omega_0 t).$$

With the aid of the cosine addition formula, we find that

$$x(t) = C\cos(\omega_0 t - \alpha). \tag{12}$$

Thus the mass oscillates to and fro about its equilibrium position with

Amplitude	C,
Circular frequency	ω_0, and
Phase angle	α.

Such motion is called **simple harmonic motion**. A typical graph of $x(t)$ is shown in Fig. 9.7.4. If time t is measured in seconds, the circular frequency ω_0 has dimensions of radians per second (rad/s). The **period** of the motion is the time required for the system to complete one full oscillation, so it is given by

$$T = \frac{2\pi}{\omega_0} \tag{13}$$

seconds; its **frequency** is

$$\nu = \frac{1}{T} = \frac{\omega_0}{2\pi} \tag{14}$$

FIGURE 9.7.4 Simple harmonic motion.

in hertz (Hz), which measures the number of complete cycles per second. Note that frequency is measured in cycles per second, whereas circular frequency has the dimensions of radians per second.

If the initial position $x(0) = x_0$ and initial velocity $x'(0) = v_0$ of the mass are given, we first determine the values of the coefficients A and B in Eq. (10), then find the amplitude C and phase angle α by carrying out the transformation of $x(t)$ to the form in Eq. (12), as indicated previously.

EXAMPLE 2 Suppose that the mass $m = \frac{1}{2}$ (kg) of Example 1 is attached to the same spring with Hooke's constant $k = 50$ (N/m). But now it is set in motion with initial position $x(0) = \frac{1}{2}$ (m) and initial velocity $x'(0) = -10$ (m/s). (Thus the mass is displaced to the right and moving to the left at time $t = 0$.) Find the position function of the body as well as the amplitude, frequency, period of oscillation, and phase angle of its motion.

Solution With $m = \frac{1}{2}$ and $k = 50$, Eq. (6) yields $\frac{1}{2}x'' + 50x = 0$; that is,

$$x'' + 100x = 0.$$

Consequently, we see from Eq. (8) that the circular frequency will be $\omega_0 = \sqrt{100} = 10$ (rad/s). Hence the body will oscillate with

frequency: $\quad \dfrac{10}{2\pi} \approx 1.59 \quad \text{Hz}$

and

$$\text{period:} \quad \frac{2\pi}{10} \approx 0.63 \quad \text{s.}$$

We now impose the initial conditions $x(0) = 0.5$ and $x'(0) = -10$ on the general solution $x(t) = A\cos 10t + B\sin 10t$, and it follows that $A = 0.5$ and $B = -1$. So the position function of the body is

$$x(t) = \tfrac{1}{2} \cos 10t - \sin 10t.$$

Hence its amplitude of motion is

$$C = \sqrt{\left(\tfrac{1}{2}\right)^2 + (1)^2} = \tfrac{1}{2}\sqrt{5} \approx 1.12 \quad \text{(m)}.$$

To find the phase angle, we use the cosine addition formula to write

$$x(t) = \frac{\sqrt{5}}{2}\left(\frac{1}{\sqrt{5}}\cos 10t - \frac{2}{\sqrt{5}}\sin 10t\right) = \frac{\sqrt{5}}{2}\cos(10t - \alpha).$$

Thus we require

$$\cos \alpha = \frac{1}{\sqrt{5}} > 0 \quad \text{and} \quad \sin \alpha = -\frac{2}{\sqrt{5}} < 0.$$

Hence α is the fourth-quadrant angle

$$\alpha = 2\pi - \tan^{-1}\left(\frac{\tfrac{2}{5}\sqrt{5}}{\tfrac{1}{5}\sqrt{5}}\right) \approx 5.1760 \quad \text{(rad)}.$$

In the form in which the amplitude and phase angle are made explicit, the position function is

$$x(t) \approx \frac{\sqrt{5}}{2}\cos(10t - 5.1760). \qquad \blacklozenge$$

Free Damped Motion

We assume now that $c > 0$ in Eq. (5) and consider **damped motion** of a mass on a spring (still with no external force). The characteristic equation of the differential equation $mx'' + cx' + kx = 0$ has roots

$$r = \frac{-c \pm \sqrt{c^2 - 4km}}{2m}. \tag{15}$$

Therefore the type of motion that occurs depends on whether $c^2 > 4km$ (distinct real roots), $c^2 = 4km$ (equal real roots), or $c^2 < 4km$ (complex conjugate roots).

Overdamped Case $c^2 > 4km$. Because c is relatively large in this case, we are dealing with a strong resistance in comparison with a relatively weak spring (or a small mass). In this case Eq. (15) gives negative distinct real roots $r_1 = -p_1$ and $r_2 = -p_2$ (where $p_1, p_2 > 0$). Hence the position function has the form

$$x(t) = c_1 e^{-p_1 t} + c_2 e^{-p_2 t}. \tag{16}$$

Obviously $x(t) \to 0$ as $t \to +\infty$, and hence the mass m settles to its equilibrium position without any oscillations. That is, any would-be oscillations are damped out. (See Problem 36.) Figure 9.7.5 shows some typical graphs of the position function in this overdamped case.

FIGURE 9.7.5 Overdamped motion. $x(t) = c_1 e^{r_1 t} + c_2 e^{r_2 t}$ with $r_1 < 0$ and $r_2 < 0$. Solution curves are graphed with the same initial position x_0 and different initial velocities.

Critically Damped Case $c^2 = 4km$. In this case Eq. (15) gives equal real roots $r = -p = -c/(2m) < 0$. The position function therefore has the form

$$x(t) = (c_1 + c_2 t)e^{-pt}. \tag{17}$$

Mechanical Vibrations SECTION 9.7 611

Figure 9.7.6 shows some typical graphs of the position function in this critically damped case. The damping is just large enough to damp out any would-be oscillations, but even a slight decrease in the damping brings us to the remaining case, the one that shows the most dramatic behavior.

Underdamped Case $c^2 < 4km$. Now Eq. (15) gives the complex conjugate roots

$$r = \frac{-c \pm \sqrt{-(4km - c^2)}}{2m} = -\frac{c}{2m} \pm i\sqrt{\frac{k}{m} - \left(\frac{c}{2m}\right)^2}.$$

Let us write

$$p = \frac{c}{2m} \quad \text{and} \quad \omega_1 = \sqrt{\omega_0^2 - p^2} \tag{18}$$

(recalling from (8) the undamped circular frequency $\omega_0 = \sqrt{k/m}$). Then the complex conjugate roots of the characteristic equation are $r = -p \pm i\omega_1$, so the general solution of $mx'' + cx' + kx = 0$ is

$$x(t) = e^{-pt}(A\cos\omega_1 t + B\sin\omega_1 t) = Ce^{-pt}\left(\frac{A}{C}\cos\omega_1 t + \frac{B}{C}\sin\omega_1 t\right)$$

where $C = \sqrt{A^2 + B^2}$. Using the cosine addition formula, it follows that $x(t)$ can be written in the form

$$x(t) = Ce^{-pt}\cos(\omega_1 t - \alpha) \tag{19}$$

similar to Eq. (12), with

$$C = \sqrt{A^2 + B^2}, \quad \cos\alpha = \frac{A}{C}, \quad \text{and} \quad \sin\alpha = \frac{B}{C}.$$

The solution in (19) represents exponentially damped oscillations of the body around its equilibrium position. The graph of $x(t)$ lies between the curves $x = -Ce^{-pt}$ and $x = Ce^{-pt}$ and touches them when $\omega_1 t - \alpha$ is an integral multiple of π. The motion is not actually periodic, but it is nevertheless useful to call ω_1 its **circular frequency**, $T_1 = 2\pi/\omega_1$ its **pseudoperiod** of oscillation, and Ce^{-pt} its **time-varying amplitude**. Most of these quantities are shown in the typical graph of underdamped motion shown in Fig. 9.7.7. Note from Eq. (18) that in this case ω_1 is less than the undamped circular frequency ω_0, so T_1 is larger than the period T of oscillation of the same mass without damping on the same spring. Thus the action of the dashpot has at least three effects:

FIGURE 9.7.6 Critically damped motion. $x(t) = (c_1 + c_2 t)e^{-pt}$ with $p > 0$. Solution curves are graphed with the same initial position x_0 and different initial velocities.

FIGURE 9.7.7 Underdamped oscillations: $x(t) = Ce^{-pt}\cos(\omega_1 t - \alpha)$.

1. It exponentially damps the oscillations, in accord with the time-varying amplitude.
2. It slows the motion; that is, the dashpot decreases the frequency of the motion.
3. It delays the motion—this is the effect of the phase angle in Eq. (19).

EXAMPLE 3 The mass and spring of Example 2 are now attached also to a dashpot that provides 6 N of resistance for each meter per second of velocity. The mass is set in motion with the same initial position $x(0) = \frac{1}{2}$ (m) and the same initial velocity $x'(0) = -10$ (m/s). Find the position function of the mass as well as its new frequency of oscillation, its pseudoperiod, and the phase angle of its motion.

Solution Rather than memorizing the various formulas given in the preceding discussion, it is better practice in a particular case to set up the differential equation and then solve it directly. Recall that $m = \frac{1}{2}$ and $k = 50$; we are now given $c = 6$ in mks units. Hence Eq. (3) is $\frac{1}{2}x'' + 6x' + 50x = 0$; that is,

$$x'' + 12x' + 100x = 0.$$

The roots of the characteristic equation $r^2 + 12r + 100 = 0$ are

$$r_1, r_2 = \frac{-12 \pm \sqrt{144 - 400}}{2} = -6 \pm 8i,$$

so the general solution is

$$x(t) = e^{-6t}(A\cos 8t + B\sin 8t). \tag{20}$$

The new circular frequency is $\omega_1 = 8$ (rad/s), and the pseudoperiod and new frequency are

$$T_1 = \frac{2\pi}{8} \approx 0.79 \text{ (s)}$$

and

$$\frac{1}{T_1} = \frac{8}{2\pi} \approx 1.27 \text{ (Hz)}$$

(in contrast with 0.63 s and 1.59 Hz, respectively, in the undamped case).

From Eq. (20) we compute

$$x'(t) = e^{-6t}(-8A\sin 8t + 8B\cos 8t) - 6e^{-6t}(A\cos 8t + B\sin 8t).$$

The initial conditions therefore produce the equations

$$x(0) = A = \tfrac{1}{2} \quad \text{and} \quad x'(0) = -6A + 8B = -10,$$

so $A = \tfrac{1}{2}$ and $B = -\tfrac{7}{8}$. Thus

$$x(t) = e^{-6t}\left(\tfrac{1}{2}\cos 8t - \tfrac{7}{8}\sin 8t\right),$$

and so with

$$C = \sqrt{\left(\tfrac{1}{2}\right)^2 + \left(\tfrac{7}{8}\right)^2} = \tfrac{1}{8}\sqrt{65}$$

we have

$$x(t) = \frac{\sqrt{65}}{8}e^{-6t}\left(\frac{4}{\sqrt{65}}\cos 8t - \frac{7}{\sqrt{65}}\sin 8t\right).$$

We require

$$\cos\alpha = \frac{4}{\sqrt{65}} > 0 \quad \text{and} \quad \sin\alpha = -\frac{7}{\sqrt{65}} < 0,$$

so α is the fourth-quadrant angle

$$\alpha = 2\pi - \tan^{-1}\left(\tfrac{7}{4}\right) \approx 5.2315 \text{ (rad)}.$$

In summary, the position function of the oscillating mass is given approximately by

$$x(t) = \frac{\sqrt{65}}{8}e^{-6t}\cos(8t - 5.2315). \tag{21}$$

FIGURE 9.7.8 Graph of the position function in Eq. (21).

Figure 9.7.8 shows the graph of this position function. Although the oscillations theoretically occur indefinitely, we see that—from a practical point of view—they are effectively damped out after a second or so. ◆

Forced Oscillations

Masses on springs in mechanical systems often are subject to periodic external forces. A typical example would be a car being driven down a road with periodic pavement oscillations. The mass is the car itself; the dashpot and spring consist of its suspension (shock absorbers and leaf or coil springs). The road provides the external force and the driver feels the periodic motion of the car.

Mechanical Vibrations SECTION 9.7

If we include in Eq. (3) a periodic external force $F(t) = F_0 \cos \omega t$ with amplitude F_0 and circular frequency ω, we get the nonhomogeneous differential equation

$$mx'' + cx' + kx = F_0 \cos \omega t. \tag{22}$$

In Section 9.6 we solved only homogeneous differential equations, but a nonhomogeneous equation of the special form in (22) frequently can be solved by a method of "shrewd guessing." Because derivatives of sines and cosines of ωt are again sines and cosines of ωt, it is reasonable to guess that Eq. (22) might have a *particular solution* of the form

$$x_p(t) = A \cos \omega t + B \sin \omega t. \tag{23}$$

If so, we can hope to discover the values of A and B by substituting (23) for x in Eq. (22) and then collecting coefficients of $\cos \omega t$ and $\sin \omega t$.

Now let $x_c(t)$ denote the *general solution*—involving arbitrary constants c_1 and c_2—of the associated (force-free) equation $mx'' + c'x + kx = 0$. Then the sum

$$x(t) = x_c(t) + x_p(t) \tag{24}$$

will be a general solution of Eq. (22), because we find that

$$mx'' + cx' + kx = m(x_c + x_p)'' + c(x_c + x_p)' + k(x_c + x_p)$$
$$= (mx_c'' + cx_c' + kx_c) + (mx_p'' + cx_p' + kx_p)$$
$$= 0 + F_0 \cos \omega t = F_0 \cos \omega t.$$

In summary, the general solution of the nonhomogeneous equation in (22) is the sum of the particular solution x_p and the general solution x_c of the associated homogeneous equation. Finally, we can impose given initial conditions on $x(t)$ to determine the numerical values of the constants c_1 and c_2 that appear in x_c. Examples 4 and 5 illustrate this procedure.

EXAMPLE 4 Suppose that $m = 1$, $c = 0$, $k = 9$, $F_0 = 80$, and $\omega = 5$, so that the nonhomogeneous differential equation in (22) is

$$x'' + 9x = 80 \cos 5t. \tag{25}$$

Find $x(t)$ if $x(0) = x'(0) = 0$.

Solution The associated homogeneous differential equation $x'' + 9x = 0$ has general solution

$$x_c(t) = c_1 \cos 3t + c_2 \sin 3t.$$

The particular solution given by (23) with $\omega = 5$ takes the form $x_p(t) = A \cos 5t + B \sin 5t$. Substituting x_p for x in the nonhomogeneous equation in (25) yields

$$(-25A \cos 5t - 25B \sin 5t) + 9(A \cos 5t + B \sin 5t) = 80 \cos 5t.$$

When we group and compare coefficients of $\cos 5t$ and $\sin 5t$ on the two sides of this equation, we see that $-16A = 80$ and $-16B = 0$. Consequently $A = -5$ and $B = 0$, so the particular solution is $x_p(t) = -5 \cos 5t$. The general solution $x(t) = x_c(t) + x_p(t)$ in (24) is therefore

$$x(t) = c_1 \cos 3t + c_2 \sin 3t - 5 \cos 5t.$$

Finally, we apply the given initial conditions $x(0) = x'(0) = 0$ to $x(t)$ and its derivative

$$x'(t) = -3c_1 \sin 3t + 3c_2 \cos 3t + 25 \sin 5t.$$

We thereby obtain $x(0) = c_1 - 5 = 0$ and $x'(0) = 3c_2 = 0$, so $c_1 = 5$ and $c_2 = 0$. This gives the desired solution

$$x(t) = 5 \cos 3t - 5 \cos 5t$$

FIGURE 9.7.9 The response function $x(t) = 5\cos 3t - 5\cos 5t$ in Example 4.

of the original initial value problem. As indicated in Fig. 9.7.9, the period of $x(t)$ is the least common integral multiple 2π of the periods $2\pi/3$ and $2\pi/5$ of the two cosine terms. ◆

REMARK Suppose that the frequency ω of the external force $F(t) = 80\cos\omega t$ in Example 4 had been equal to the natural frequency $\omega_0 = 3$ of the mass-and-spring system. Then substituting the "trial solution" $x_p(t) = A\cos 3t + B\sin 3t$ in the nonhomogeneous differential equation would have led to the contradictory equation $0 = 80\cos 3t$. (Verify this for yourself.) Thus we would not have been able to determine A and B in this way. The case in which the external and natural frequencies are equal leads to the phenomenon of **resonance,** with oscillations of larger and larger amplitudes occurring. (See Problem 37.) This phenomenon does not occur when nonzero damping is present, as in Example 5.

EXAMPLE 5 Suppose that $m = 1$, $c = 2$, $k = 26$, $F_0 = 82$, and $\omega = 4$, so the nonhomogeneous differential equation in (22) is

$$x'' + 2x' + 26x = 82\cos 4t. \tag{26}$$

Find $x(t)$ if $x(0) = 6$ and $x'(0) = 0$.

Solution The associated homogeneous differential equation $x'' + 2x' + 26x = 0$ has characteristic equation

$$r^2 + 2r + 26 = (r+1)^2 + 25 = 0$$

with complex conjugate roots $r = -1 \pm 5i$. Hence its general solution is

$$x_c(t) = e^{-t}(c_1 \cos 5t + c_2 \sin 5t).$$

The particular solution given in (23) with $\omega = 4$ is $x_p(t) = A\cos 4t + B\sin 4t$. When we substitute this trial solution in the nonhomogeneous equation in (26), collect like terms, and equate coefficients of $\cos 4t$ and $\sin 4t$, we get the equations

$$10A + 8B = 82,$$
$$-8A + 10B = 0$$

with solution $A = 5$, $B = 4$. This gives the particular solution

$$x_p(t) = 5\cos 4t + 4\sin 4t$$

of Eq. (26). The general solution $x(t) = x_c(t) + x_p(t)$ in (24) is therefore

$$x(t) = e^{-t}(c_1 \cos 5t + c_2 \sin 5t) + 5\cos 4t + 4\sin 4t.$$

Finally, we apply the given initial conditions $x(0) = 6$ and $x'(0) = 0$ to $x(t)$ and its derivative

$$x'(t) = -e^{-t}(c_1 \cos 5t + c_2 \sin 5t) + e^{-t}(-5c_1 \sin 5t + 5c_2 \cos 5t) - 20\sin 4t + 16\cos 4t.$$

Thereby we get the simultaneous equations

$$x(0) = c_1 + 5 = 6,$$
$$x'(0) = -c_1 + 5c_2 + 16 = 0$$

with solution $c_1 = 1$, $c_2 = -3$. These coefficients yield the desired solution

$$x(t) = e^{-t}(\cos 5t - 3\sin 5t) + 5\cos 4t + 4\sin 4t \tag{27}$$

of the original initial value problem. ◆

REMARK The solution in (27) is the sum of a **transient solution**

$$x_{tr}(t) = e^{-t}(\cos 5t - 3\sin 5t)$$

FIGURE 9.7.10 Solutions of the initial value problem in (28) with $x_0 = -20, -10, 0, 10, 20$, and also the steady periodic solution $x_{sp}(t)$.

—thus named because it dies out as $t \to +\infty$—and the **steady periodic solution**

$$x_{sp}(t) = 5\cos 4t + 4\sin 4t$$
$$= \sqrt{41}\left(\frac{5}{\sqrt{41}}\cos 4t + \frac{4}{\sqrt{41}}\sin 4t\right) = \sqrt{41}\cos\left(4t - \tan^{-1}\frac{4}{5}\right)$$

that represents a motion in which the mass perpetually continues to oscillate with constant amplitude $\sqrt{41}$ and circular frequency $\omega = 4$.

Figure 9.7.10 shows graphs of the solution $x(t) = x_{tr}(t) + x_{sp}(t)$ of the initial value problem

$$x'' + 2x' + 26x = 82\cos 4t; \qquad x(0) = x_0, \quad x'(0) = 0 \tag{28}$$

for the different initial positions $x_0 = -20, -10, 0, 10,$ and 20. Here we see clearly what it means for the transient solution $x_{tr}(t)$ to "die out with the passage of time," leaving only the steady periodic solution $x_{sp}(t)$. Indeed, because $x_{tr}(t) \to 0$ exponentially, within a very few cycles the graphs of the full solution $x(t)$ and the steady periodic solution $x_{sp}(t)$ are virtually indistinguishable.

9.7 TRUE/FALSE STUDY GUIDE

9.7 CONCEPTS: QUESTIONS AND DISCUSSION

In each of Questions 1 through 4, describe differences between the indicated varieties of motion of a mass attached to a spring.

1. Damped and undamped free motions
2. Overdamped and underdamped free motions
3. Damped and undamped forced motions
4. Transient and steady periodic forced motions

9.7 PROBLEMS

Problems 1 through 4 concern undamped free motion of a mass m on a spring with Hooke's (spring) constant k. Suppose that the mass is set in motion with initial position $x(0) = x_0$ and initial velocity $x'(0) = v_0$. Write the position function of the mass in the form $x(t) = C\cos(\omega_0 t - \alpha)$.

1. $m = 2, k = 50;$ $x_0 = 4, v_0 = 15$
2. $m = 3, k = 48;$ $x_0 = -6, v_0 = 32$
3. $m = 4, k = 36;$ $x_0 = -5, v_0 = -36$
4. $m = 5, k = 80;$ $x_0 = 15, v_0 = -32$

Problems 5 through 10 deal with damped free motion of a mass m that is attached both to a spring with Hooke's constant k and to a dashpot with damping constant c. Suppose that the mass is set in motion with initial position $x(0) = x_0$ and initial velocity $x'(0) = v_0$. Find the position function $x(t)$ of the mass. Determine whether the resulting motion is overdamped, critically damped, or underdamped; in the latter case, write the position function in the form $x(t) = Ce^{-pt}\cos(\omega_1 t - \alpha)$.

5. $m = \frac{1}{2},\ c = 3,\ k = 4,\ x_0 = 2,\ v_0 = 0$
6. $m = 3,\ c = 30,\ k = 63,\ x_0 = 2,\ v_0 = 2$
7. $m = 1,\ c = 8,\ k = 16,\ x_0 = 5,\ v_0 = -10$
8. $m = 2,\ c = 12,\ k = 50,\ x_0 = 0,\ v_0 = -8$
9. $m = 2,\ c = 16,\ k = 40,\ x_0 = 5,\ v_0 = 4$
10. $m = 1,\ c = 10,\ k = 125,\ x_0 = 6,\ v_0 = 50$

The initial value problems in Problems 11 through 14 describe forced undamped motion of a mass on a spring. Express the position function $x(t)$ as the sum of two oscillations (as in Example 4). Throughout, primes denote derivatives with respect to t.

11. $x'' + 9x = 10\cos 2t;$ $x(0) = x'(0) = 0$
12. $x'' + 4x = 5\sin 3t;$ $x(0) = x'(0) = 0$
13. $x'' + 100x = 300\sin 5t;$ $x(0) = 0, x'(0) = 0$
14. $x'' + 25x = 90\cos 4t;$ $x(0) = 25, x'(0) = 10$

In Problems 15 through 18, find the steady periodic solution of the given differential equation. If initial conditions are given, also find the transient solution.

15. $x'' + 4x' + 4x = 130\cos 3t$
16. $x'' + 3x' + 5x = -500\cos 5t$
17. $x'' + 4x' + 5x = 40\cos 3t;$ $x(0) = x'(0) = 0$
18. $x'' + 8x' + 25x = 200\cos t + 520\sin t;$ $x(0) = 5, x'(0) = 0$

19. Determine the period and frequency of the simple harmonic motion of a 4-kg mass on the end of a spring with spring constant 16 N/m.

20. Determine the period and frequency of the simple harmonic motion of a body of mass 0.75 kg on the end of a spring with spring constant 48 N/m.

21. A mass of 3 kg is attached to the end of a spring that is stretched 20 cm by a force of 15 N. It is set in motion with initial position $x_0 = 0$ and initial velocity $v_0 = -10$ m/s. Find the amplitude, period, and frequency of the resulting motion.

22. A body with mass 250 g is attached to the end of a spring that is stretched 25 cm by a force of 9 N. At time $t = 0$ the body is pulled 1 m to the right, stretching the spring, and set in motion with an initial velocity of 5 m/s to the left. (a) Find $x(t)$ in the form $C\cos(\omega_0 t + \alpha)$. (b) Find the amplitude and period of motion of the body.

23. Derive Eq. (4) describing the motion of a mass attached to the bottom of a vertically suspended spring. (*Suggestion:* First denote by $x(t)$ the displacement of the mass below the unstretched position of the spring; set up the differential equation for x. Then substitute $y = x - x_0$ in this differential equation.)

24. Consider a floating cylindrical buoy with radius r, height h, and uniform density $\rho \leq 0.5$ (recall that the density of water is 1 g/cm³). The buoy is initially suspended at rest with its bottom at the top surface of the water and is released at time $t = 0$. Thereafter it is acted on by two forces: a downward gravitational force equal to its weight $mg = \rho\pi r^2 hg$ and an upward force of buoyancy equal to the weight $\pi r^2 xg$ of water displaced, where $x = x(t)$ is the depth of the bottom of the buoy beneath the surface at time t (Fig. 9.7.11). Conclude that the buoy undergoes simple harmonic motion around its equilibrium position $x_e = \rho h$ with period $p = 2\pi\sqrt{\rho h/g}$. Compute p and the amplitude of the motion if $\rho = 0.5$ g/cm³, $h = 200$ cm, and $g = 980$ cm/s².

FIGURE 9.7.11 The buoy of Problem 24.

25. A cylindrical buoy weighing 100 lb (thus of mass $m = 3.125$ slugs in ft-lb-s (fps) units) floats in water with its axis vertical (as in Problem 24). When depressed slightly and released, it oscillates up and down four times every 10 s. Assume that friction is negligible. Find the radius of the buoy.

26. Assume that the earth is a solid sphere of uniform density, with mass M and radius $R = 3960$ (mi). For a particle of mass m *within* the earth at distance r from the center of the earth, the gravitational force attracting m toward the center is $F_r = -GM_r m/r^2$, where M_r is the mass of the part of the earth within a sphere of radius r. (a) Show that $F_r = -GMmr/R^3$. (b) Now suppose that a small hole is drilled straight through the center of the earth, thus connecting two antipodal points on its surface. Let a particle of mass m be dropped at time $t = 0$ into this hole with initial speed zero, and let $r(t)$ be its distance from the center

of the earth at time t (Fig. 9.7.12). Conclude from Newton's second law and part (a) that $r''(t) = -k^2 r(t)$, where $k^2 = GM/R^3 = g/R$. (c) Take $g = 32.2$ ft/s^2, and conclude from part (b) that the particle undergoes simple harmonic motion back and forth between the ends of the hole, with a period of about 84 min. (d) Look up (or derive) the period of a satellite that just skims the surface of the earth; compare it with the result in part (c). How do you explain the coincidence? Or *is* it a coincidence? (e) With what speed (in miles per hour) does the particle pass through the center of the earth? (f) Look up (or derive) the orbital velocity of a satellite that just skims the surface of the earth; compare it with the result in part (e). How do you explain the coincidence? Or *is* it a coincidence?

FIGURE 9.7.12 A mass m falling down a hole through the center of the earth (Problem 26).

27. Suppose that the mass in a free mass-spring-dashpot system with $m = 10$, $c = 9$, and $k = 2$ is set in motion with $x(0) = 0$ and $x'(0) = 5$. (a) Find the position function $x(t)$ and show that its graph looks as indicated in Fig. 9.7.13. (b) Find how far the mass moves to the right before starting back toward the origin.

FIGURE 9.7.13 The position function $x(t)$ of Problem 27.

28. Suppose that the mass in a free mass-spring-dashpot system with $m = 25$, $c = 10$, and $k = 226$ is set in motion with $x(0) = 20$ and $x'(0) = 41$. (a) Find the position function $x(t)$ and show that its graph looks as indicated in Fig. 9.7.14. (b) Find the pseudoperiod of the oscillations and the equations of the "envelope curves" that are dashed in the figure.

FIGURE 9.7.14 The position function $x(t)$ of Problem 28.

29. A 12-lb weight (mass $m = 0.375$ slugs in fps units) is attached both to a vertically suspended spring that it stretches 6 in. and to a dashpot that provides 3 lb of resistance for every foot per second of velocity. (a) If the weight is pulled down 1 ft below its static equilibrium position and then released from rest at time $t = 0$, find its position function $x(t)$. (b) Find the frequency, time-varying amplitude, and phase angle of the motion.

30. This problem deals with a highly simplified model of a car of weight 3200 lb (mass $m = 100$ slugs in fps units). Assume that the suspension system acts like a single spring and its shock absorbers like a single dashpot, so that its vertical vibrations satisfy Eq. (4) with appropriate values of the coefficients. (a) Find the stiffness coefficient k of the spring if the car undergoes free vibrations at 80 cycles per minute (cycles/min) when its shock absorbers are disconnected. (b) With the shock absorbers connected the car is set into vibration by driving it over a bump, and the resulting damped vibrations have a frequency of 78 cycles/min. After how long will the time-varying amplitude be 1% of its initial value?

Problems 31 through 36 deal with damped free vibrations of a mass-spring-dashpot system whose position function satisfies the equation $mx'' + cx' + kx = 0$. The mass is set in motion with initial position $x(0) = x_0$ and initial velocity $x'(0) = v_0$. Recall the notation $p = c/(2m)$ and $\omega_0 = \sqrt{k/m}$ in Eqs. (18) and (8), respectively. The system is critically damped or overdamped as specified in each problem.

31. (Critically damped) Show in this case that
$$x(t) = (x_0 + v_0 t + p x_0 t) e^{-pt}.$$

32. (Critically damped) Deduce from Problem 31 that the mass passes through $x = 0$ at some instant $t > 0$ if and only if x_0 and $v_0 + px_0$ have opposite signs.

33. (Critically damped) Deduce from Problem 31 that $x(t)$ has a local maximum or minimum at some instant $t > 0$ if and only if v_0 and $v_0 + px_0$ have the same sign.

34. (Overdamped) Show in this case that
$$x(t) = \frac{1}{2\gamma} [(v_0 - r_2 x_0) e^{r_1 t} - (v_0 - r_1 x_0) e^{r_2 t}],$$
where $r_1, r_2 = -p \pm \sqrt{p^2 - \omega_0^2}$ and $\gamma = (r_1 - r_2)/2 > 0$.

35. (Overdamped) If $x_0 = 0$, deduce from Problem 34 that
$$x(t) = \frac{v_0}{\gamma} e^{-pt} \sinh \gamma t.$$

36. (Overdamped) Prove that in this case the mass can pass through its equilibrium position $x = 0$ at most once.

37. Consider the mass-and-spring system of Example 4, except with the external force $F(t) = 60 \cos 3t$ having frequency ω equal to the natural frequency $\omega_0 = 3$ of the system. Then the position function of the mass satisfies the differential equation $x'' + 9x = 60 \cos 3t$. (a) Show that this nonhomogeneous differential equation has *no* solution of the form $x(t) = A \cos 3t + B \sin 3t$. (As suggested in the text, try to find one and observe what happens.) (b) Verify that $x_p(t) = 10t \sin 3t$ is a particular solution of $x'' + 9x = 60 \cos 3t$. The graph of $x_p(t)$, which is shown in Fig. 9.7.15, indicates that any solution

$$x(t) = c_1 \cos 3t + c_2 \sin 3t + 10t \sin 3t$$

of this equation exhibits oscillations of unbounded magnitude as $t \to +\infty$.

FIGURE 9.7.15 The resonance solution $x_p(t) = 10t \sin 3t$ of the differential equation $x'' + 9x = 60 \cos 3t$ oscillates between the lines $x = -10t$ and $x = +10t$.

CHAPTER 9 REVIEW: DEFINITIONS, CONCEPTS, RESULTS

Use the following list as a guide to concepts you may need to review.

1. General and particular solutions of a differential equation
2. Solution curves of a differential equation
3. Solution of the equation $dy/dx = f(x, y)$ if either x or y is missing
4. The exponential equation $dx/dt = kx$ and applications to natural growth and decay
5. Torricelli's law and draining tanks
6. Slope fields and approximate solution curves
7. Euler's method and approximate numerical solutions
8. Separable differential equations
9. Separation of variables
10. Newton's law of cooling
11. The constant-coefficient linear equation $dx/dt = ax + b$ and applications
12. The linear first-order equation $dy/dx + P(x)y = Q(x)$
13. The integrating factor $\rho(x) = \exp\left(\int P(x)\,dx\right)$ for a linear equation
14. Mixture problems
15. Motion with resistance proportional to velocity
16. The general population equation $dP/dt = (\beta - \delta)P$
17. Bounded populations and the logistic equation $dP/dt = kP(M - P)$
18. The explosion-extinction equation $dP/dt = kP(P - M)$
19. The characteristic equation of a homogeneous linear second-order differential equation
20. The general solution of a differential equation of the form $ay'' + by' + cy = 0$
21. Oscillation of a mass-spring-dashpot system—free and forced, damped and undamped

CHAPTER 9 MISCELLANEOUS PROBLEMS

In Problems 1 through 26, find the general solution of the given differential equation. If an initial condition is given, find the corresponding particular solution.

1. $\dfrac{dy}{dx} = 2x + \cos x; \quad y(0) = 0$

2. $\dfrac{dy}{dx} = 3\sqrt{x} + \dfrac{1}{\sqrt{x}}; \quad y(1) = 10$

3. $\dfrac{dy}{dx} = (y + 1)^2$

4. $\dfrac{dy}{dx} = \sqrt{y + 1}$

5. $\dfrac{dy}{dx} = 3x^2 y^2; \quad y(0) = 1$

6. $\dfrac{dy}{dx} = \sqrt[3]{xy}; \quad y(1) = 1$

7. $x^2 y^2 \dfrac{dy}{dx} = 1$

8. $\sqrt{xy}\,\dfrac{dy}{dx} = 1$

9. $\dfrac{dy}{dx} = y^2 \cos x; \quad y(0) = 1$

10. $\dfrac{dy}{dx} = \sqrt{y} \sin x; \quad y(0) = 4$

11. $\dfrac{dy}{dx} = \dfrac{y^2\left(1 - \sqrt{x}\right)}{x^2\left(1 - \sqrt{y}\right)}$

12. $\dfrac{dy}{dx} = \dfrac{\sqrt{y}(x+1)^3}{\sqrt{x}(y+1)^3}$

13. $x^3 + 3y - x\dfrac{dy}{dx} = 0$

14. $xy^2 + 3y^2 - x^2\dfrac{dy}{dx} = 0$

15. $3y + x^4\dfrac{dy}{dx} = 2xy$

16. $2xy^2 + x^2\dfrac{dy}{dx} = y^2$

17. $2x^2y + x^3\dfrac{dy}{dx} = 1$

18. $\dfrac{dy}{dx} = 1 + x^2 + y^2 + x^2y^2$

19. $\dfrac{dy}{dx} + 3y = 3x^2e^{-3x}$

20. $3x^5y^2 + x^3\dfrac{dy}{dx} = 2y^2$

21. $x\dfrac{dy}{dx} + 3y = 3x^{-3/2}$

22. $(x^2 - 1)\dfrac{dy}{dx} + (x - 1)y = 1$

23. $9x^2y^2 + x^{3/2}\dfrac{dy}{dx} = y^2$

24. $2y + (x + 1)\dfrac{dy}{dx} = 3x + 3$

25. $\dfrac{dy}{dx} = e^x + y$

26. $y + x\dfrac{dy}{dx} = 2e^{2x}$

Each of the differential equations in Problems 27 and 28 is both separable and linear. Derive and reconcile the two general solutions you find by the two indicated methods.

27. $\dfrac{dy}{dx} = 3(y + 7)x^2$

28. $\dfrac{dy}{dx} = \dfrac{2xy + 2x}{x^2 + 1}$

Solve the initial value problems in 29 and 30.

29. $\dfrac{dx}{dt} = x^2 + 5x + 6;\quad x(0) = 5$

30. $\dfrac{dx}{dt} = 2x^2 + x - 15;\quad x(0) = 10$

31. **Radioactive Decay** A certain moon rock contains equal numbers of potassium atoms and argon atoms. Assume that all the argon is present because of radioactive decay of potassium (its half-life is about 1.28×10^9 yr) and that 1 out of every 9 potassium atom disintegrations yields an atom of argon. What is the age of the rock, measured from the time it contained only potassium?

32. **Newton's Law of Cooling** If a body is cooling in a medium with constant temperature A, then—according to Newton's law of cooling (Section 9.3)—the rate of change of temperature T of the body is proportional to $T - A$. We plan to cool a pitcher of buttermilk initially at 25°C by setting it on the front porch, where the temperature is 0°C. If the temperature of the buttermilk drops to 15°C after 20 min, when will it be at 5°C?

33. When sugar is dissolved in water, the amount A of sugar that remains undissolved after t minutes satisfies the differential equation $dA/dt = -kA\,(k > 0)$. If 25% of the sugar dissolves in 1 min, how long does it take for half the sugar to dissolve?

34. The intensity I of light at a depth x meters below the surface of a lake satisfies the differential equation $dI/dx = -(1.4)I$. (a) At what depth is the intensity half the intensity I_0 at the surface (where $x = 0$)? (b) What is the intensity at a depth of 10 m (as a fraction of I_0)? (c) At what depth will the intensity be 1% of its value at the surface?

35. The barometric pressure p (in inches of mercury) at an altitude x miles above sea level satisfies the differential equation $dp/dx = -(0.2)p$ with initial condition $p(0) = 29.92$. (a) Calculate the barometric pressure at 10,000 ft and again at 30,000 ft. (b) Without prior conditioning, few people can survive when the pressure drops to less than 15 in. of mercury. How high is that? (c) The highest mountain in North America is Mt. McKinley, in Denali National Park, Alaska, U.S.A. What is the atmospheric pressure at its summit, approximately 20,320 ft above sea level?

36. An accident at a nuclear power plant has left the surrounding area polluted with a radioactive element that decays at a rate proportional to its current amount $A(t)$. The initial level of radiation is 10 times the maximum amount S that is safe, and 100 days later it is still 7 times that amount. (a) Set up and solve a differential equation to find $A(t)$. (b) How long (to the nearest day after the original accident) will it be before it is safe for people to return to the area?

37. Suppose that a nuclear accident was confined to a single room of a nuclear research laboratory but has left that room contaminated with polonium-210, which has a half-life of 140 days. If the initial contamination of the room is five times the amount safe for long-term human exposure, how long should laboratory workers wait before entering the room to decontaminate it?

38. Suppose that the national government's current annual budget is $2 trillion, but only $1.85 trillion in taxes is being collected annually (so the current deficit is $150 billion per year). Suppose also that both the annual budget and the annual tax revenues increase exponentially. If revenues increase at 3% annually, what annual percentage increase in the national budget will yield a balanced budget seven years in the future? You may choose either a symbolic approach or a graphical approach (in which case you need to determine the budget's rate of increase so that the budget and revenue graphs intersect seven years from now).

Solve the initial value problems in 39 through 44. Primes denote derivatives with respect to x.

39. $6y'' - 19y' + 15y = 0;\quad y(0) = 13,\ y'(0) = 21$

40. $50y'' - 5y' - 28y = 0;\quad y(0) = 25,\ y'(0) = -10$

41. $121y'' + 154y' + 49y = 0;\quad y(0) = 11,\ y'(0) = 10$

42. $169y'' - 130y' + 25y = 0;\quad y(0) = 26,\ y'(0) = 39$

43. $100y'' + 20y' + 10001y = 0;\quad y(0) = 10,\ y'(0) = 9$

44. $100y'' + 2000y' + 10001y = 0;\quad y(0) = 1,\ y'(0) = -9$

45. (a) In 1979 the typical microcomputer contained 29 thousand transistors. Assuming natural growth at the annual rate r, write a formula giving the number $N(t)$ of transistors

in a typical microcomputer t years later. (b) In 1993 the typical microcomputer CPU contained 3.1 million transistors. Find the annual growth rate r of part (a), expressed as a percentage. (c) At the rate you found in part (b), how many months are required to double the number of transistors in a typical microcomputer? (d) Assuming the rate of parts (b) and (c) remains constant, how many transistors (rounded to the nearest million) did the typical microcomputer contain in the year 2001?

46. Dinosaurs became extinct late in the Cretaceous Era, about 70 million years ago. Suppose that you find a dinosaur bone containing exactly one atom of ^{14}C. Obtain a sound *underestimate* of the weight of the dinosaur. You will need to look up Avogadro's number and perhaps read about what it tells you.

47. Suppose that the fish population $P(t)$ in a lake is attacked by disease at time $t=0$, with the result that

$$\frac{dP}{dt} = -k\sqrt{P} \quad (k > 0)$$

thereafter. If there were initially 900 fish in the lake and only 441 remained after 6 weeks, how long would it take for all of the fish in the lake to die?

48. Prove that the solution of the initial value problem

$$\frac{dP}{dt} = k\sqrt{P}, \qquad P(0) = P_0 \quad (P_0 > 0)$$

is given by

$$P(t) = \left(\tfrac{1}{2}kt + \sqrt{P_0}\right)^2.$$

49. Suppose that the population of Fremont satisfies the differential equation of Problem 48. (a) If $P = 100{,}000$ in 1970 and $P = 121{,}000$ in 1980, what should the population be in 2000? (b) When will the population reach 200,000?

50. The population $P(t)$ of a certain group of rabbits satisfies the initial value problem

$$\frac{dP}{dt} = kP^2, \qquad P(0) = P_0,$$

where k is a positive constant. Derive the solution

$$P(t) = \frac{P_0}{1 - kP_0 t}.$$

51. In Problem 50, suppose that $P_0 = 2$ and that there are 4 rabbits after 3 months. What happens in the next 3 months?

52. Suppose that a motorboat is traveling at $v_0 = 40$ ft/s when its motor is cut off at time $t = 0$. Thereafter its deceleration (due to water resistance) is given by $dv/dt = -kv^2$, where k is a positive constant. (a) Solve this differential equation to show that the speed of the boat at time $t > 0$ is

$$v(t) = \frac{40}{1 + 40kt}$$

feet per second. (b) If the speed of the boat after 10 s is 20 ft/s, how long does it take (since the motor was cut off) for the boat to slow to 5 ft/s?

53. Suppose that the fish population $P(t)$ in a lake is attacked by disease at time $t=0$, with the result that

$$\frac{dP}{dt} = -3\sqrt{P}$$

thereafter. Time t is measured in weeks. Initially there are $P_0 = 900$ fish in the lake. How long will it take for all of the fish to die?

54. A race car sliding along a level surface is decelerated by frictional forces proportional to its speed. Suppose that it decelerates initially at 2 m/s^2 and travels a total distance of 1800 m. What was its initial velocity? (See Problem 32 of Section 9.4.)

55. A home mortgage of \$120,000 is to be paid off continuously over a period of 25 yr. Apply the result of Problem 33 in Section 9.3 to determine the monthly payment if the annual interest rate, compounded continuously, is (a) 8%; (b) 12%.

56. A powerboat weighs 32000 lb and its motor provides a thrust of 5000 lb. Assume that the water resistance is 100 lb for each foot per second of the boat's speed. Then the velocity $v(t)$ (in ft/s) of the boat at time t (in seconds) satisfies the differential equation

$$1000\frac{dv}{dt} = 5000 - 100v.$$

Find the maximum velocity that the boat can attain if it starts from rest.

57. The temperature in my freezer is $-16°C$ and the room temperature is a constant $20°C$. At 11 P.M. one evening the power goes off because of an ice storm. At 6 A.M. the next morning I see that the temperature in the freezer has risen to $-10°C$. At what time will the temperature in the freezer reach the critical value of $0°C$ if the power is not restored?

58. Suppose that the action of fluorocarbons depletes the ozone in the upper atmosphere by 0.25% annually, so that the amount A of ozone in the upper atmosphere satisfies the differential equation

$$\frac{dA}{dt} = -\frac{1}{400}A \quad (t \text{ in years}).$$

(a) What percentage of the original amount A_0 of upper-atmospheric ozone will remain 25 yr from now? (b) How long will it take for the amount of upper-atmospheric ozone to be reduced to half its initial amount?

59. A car starts from rest and travels along a straight and level road. Its engine provides a constant acceleration of a feet per second per second. Air resistance and road friction cause a deceleration of ρ feet per second per second for every foot per second of the car's velocity v. (a) Show that the velocity of the car after t seconds is

$$v(t) = \frac{a}{\rho}(1 - e^{-\rho t}).$$

(b) If $a = 17.6$ ft/s^2 and $\rho = 0.1$, find v when $t = 10$ s and find the limiting velocity of the car as $t \to +\infty$. (Give each answer in miles per hour as well as in feet per second.)

60. Immediately after an accident in a nuclear power plant, the level of radiation there was 10 times the safe limit. After 6 months it dropped to 9 times the safe limit. Assuming exponential decay, how long (in years) after the accident will the radiation level drop to the safe limit?

61. A 22-yr-old engineer accepts a position with a starting salary of \$30,000/yr. Her annual salary S increases exponentially, with

$$S(t) = 30e^{(0.05)t}$$

thousand dollars after t years. Meanwhile, she deposits 12% of her salary continuously in a retirement account that accumulates interest at an annual rate of 6% compounded continuously. (a) Estimate ΔA in terms of Δt to derive this equation for the amount $A(t)$ in her retirement account at time t:

$$\frac{dA}{dt} - (0.06)A = (3.6)e^{(0.05)t}.$$

(b) Solve this equation with the initial condition $A(0) = 0$ and then compute $A(40)$, the amount available for her retirement at age 62.

62. A tumor may be regarded as a population P of multiplying cells. It is found empirically that the "birth rate" β of the cells in a tumor decreases exponentially with time, so that $\beta(t) = \beta_0 e^{-\alpha t}$ (where α and β_0 are positive constants), and hence

$$\frac{dP}{dt} = \beta_0 e^{-\alpha t} P, \qquad P(0) = P_0.$$

Solve this initial value problem to obtain

$$P(t) = P_0 \exp\left(\frac{\beta_0}{\alpha}(1 - e^{-\alpha t})\right).$$

Observe that $P(t)$ approaches the finite limiting population $P_0 \exp(\beta_0/\alpha)$ as $t \to +\infty$.

63. For the tumor of Problem 62, suppose that at time $t = 0$ there are $P_0 = 10^6$ cells and that $P(t)$ is then increasing at the rate of 3×10^5 cells per month. After 6 months the tumor has doubled (in size and in number of cells). Solve numerically for α, and then find the limiting population of the tumor.

Differential Equations and Determinism Given a mass m, a dashpot constant c, and a spring constant k, the differential equation

$$mx'' + cx' + kx = 0 \qquad (1)$$

has a unique solution for $t \geq 0$ satisfying given initial conditions $x(0) = x_0$, $x'(0) = v_0$. Thus the future motion of an ideal mass-spring-dashpot system is completely determined by the differential equation and the initial conditions. Of course, in a real physical system it is impossible to measure the parameters m, c, and k precisely. Problems 64 through 67 explore the resulting uncertainty in predicting the future behavior of a physical system.

64. Suppose that $m = 1$, $c = 2$, and $k = 1$. Show that the solution of Eq. (1) with $x(0) = 0$ and $x'(0) = 1$ is

$$x_1(t) = te^{-t}.$$

65. Suppose that $m = 1$ and $c = 2$ but $k = 1 - 10^{-2n}$. Show that the solution of Eq. (1) with $x(0) = 0$ and $x'(0) = 1$ is

$$x_2(t) = 10^n e^{-t} \sinh 10^{-n} t.$$

66. Suppose that $m = 1$ and $c = 2$ but that $k = 1 + 10^{-2n}$. Show that the solution of Eq. (1) with $x(0) = 0$ and $x'(0) = 1$ is

$$x_3(t) = 10^n e^{-t} \sin 10^{-n} t.$$

67. Whereas the graphs of $x_1(t)$ and $x_2(t)$ resemble those shown in Figs. 9.7.5 and 9.7.6, the graph of $x_3(t)$ exhibits damped oscillations like those illustrated in Fig. 9.7.7, but with a very long pseudoperiod. Nevertheless, show that for each fixed $t > 0$ it is true that

$$\lim_{n \to \infty} x_2(t) = \lim_{n \to \infty} x_3(t) = x_1(t).$$

Conclude that *on a given finite time interval* the three solutions are in "practical" agreement if n is sufficiently large.

POLAR COORDINATES AND PARAMETRIC CURVES

10

Pierre de Fermat (1601–1665)

Pierre de Fermat exemplifies the distinguished tradition of great amateurs in mathematics. Like his contemporary René Descartes, he was educated as a lawyer. But unlike Descartes, Fermat actually practiced law as his profession and served in the regional parliament. His ample leisure time was, however, devoted to mathematics and to other intellectual pursuits, such as the study of ancient Greek manuscripts.

In a margin of one such manuscript (by the Greek mathematician Diophantus) was found a handwritten note that has remained an enigma ever since. Fermat asserts that for *no* integer $n > 2$ do positive integers x, y, and z exist such that $x^n + y^n = z^n$. For instance, although $15^2 + 8^2 = 17^2$, the sum of two (positive integer) cubes cannot be a cube. "I have found an admirable proof of this," Fermat wrote, "but this margin is too narrow to contain it." Despite the publication of many incorrect proofs, "Fermat's last theorem" remained unproved for three and one-half centuries. But in a June 1993 lecture, the British mathematician Andrew Wiles of Princeton University announced a long and complex proof of Fermat's last theorem. Although the proof as originally proposed contained some gaps, these have been repaired, and experts in the field agree that Fermat's last *conjecture* is, finally, a *theorem*.

Descartes and Fermat shared in the discovery of analytic geometry. But whereas Descartes typically used geometrical methods to solve algebraic equations (see the Chapter 1 opening), Fermat concentrated on the investigation of geometric curves defined by algebraic equations. For instance, he introduced the translation methods of this chapter together with rotation methods to show that the graph of an equation of the form $Ax^2 + Bxy + Cy^2 + Dx + Ey + F = 0$ is generally a conic section. Most of his mathematical work remained unpublished during his lifetime, but it contains numerous tangent line (derivative) and area (integral) computations.

The brilliantly colored left-hand photograph is a twentieth-century example of a geometric object defined by means of algebraic operations. Starting with the point $P(a, b)$ in the xy-plane, we interpret P as the complex number $c = a + bi$ and define the sequence $\{z_n\}$ of points of the complex plane iteratively (as in Section 3.8) by the equations

$$z_0 = c, \qquad z_{n+1} = z_n^2 + c \quad (\text{for } n \geqq 0).$$

If this sequence of points remains inside the circle $x^2 + y^2 = 4$ for all n, then the original point $P(a, b)$ is colored black. Otherwise, the color assigned to P is determined by the speed with which this sequence "escapes" that circular disk. The set of all black points is the famous *Mandelbrot set,* discovered in 1980 by the French mathematician Benoit Mandelbrot.

The object in the right-hand figure is a subset of that in the left-hand figure.

623

10.1 ANALYTIC GEOMETRY AND THE CONIC SECTIONS

Plane analytic geometry, a central topic of this chapter, is the use of algebra and calculus to study the properties of curves in the xy-plane. The ancient Greeks used deductive reasoning and the methods of axiomatic Euclidean geometry to study lines, circles, and the **conic sections** (parabolas, ellipses, and hyperbolas). The properties of conic sections have played an important role in diverse scientific applications since the seventeenth century, when Kepler discovered—and Newton explained—the fact that the orbits of planets and other bodies in the Solar System are conic sections.

The French mathematicians Descartes and Fermat, working almost independently of one another, initiated analytic geometry in 1637. The central idea of analytic geometry is the correspondence between an equation $F(x, y) = 0$ and its **locus** (typically, a curve), the set of all those points (x, y) in the plane with coordinates that satisfy this equation.

A central idea of analytic geometry is this: Given a geometric locus or curve, its properties can be derived algebraically or analytically from its defining equation $F(x, y) = 0$. For example, suppose that the equation of a given curve turns out to be the linear equation

$$Ax + By = C, \tag{1}$$

where A, B, and C are constants with $B \neq 0$. This equation may be written in the form

$$y = mx + b, \tag{2}$$

where $m = -A/B$ and $b = C/B$. But Eq. (2) is the slope-intercept equation of the straight line with slope m and y-intercept b. Hence the given curve is this straight line. We use this approach in Example 1 to show that a specific geometrically described locus is a particular straight line.

EXAMPLE 1 Prove that the set of all points equidistant from the points $(1, 1)$ and $(5, 3)$ is the perpendicular bisector of the line segment that joins these two points.

Solution The typical point $P(x, y)$ in Fig. 10.1.1 is equally distant from $(1, 1)$ and $(5, 3)$ if and only if

$$(x - 1)^2 + (y - 1)^2 = (x - 5)^2 + (y - 3)^2;$$
$$x^2 - 2x + 1 + y^2 - 2y + 1 = x^2 - 10x + 25 + y^2 - 6y + 9;$$
$$2x + y = 8;$$
$$y = -2x + 8. \tag{3}$$

FIGURE 10.1.1 The perpendicular bisector of Example 1.

Thus the given locus is the straight line in Eq. (3) whose slope is -2. The straight line through $(1, 1)$ and $(5, 3)$ has equation

$$y - 1 = \tfrac{1}{2}(x - 1) \tag{4}$$

and thus has slope $\tfrac{1}{2}$. Because the product of the slopes of these two lines is -1, it follows (from Theorem 2 in Appendix B) that these lines are perpendicular. If we solve Eqs. (3) and (4) simultaneously, we find that the intersection of these lines is, indeed, the midpoint $(3, 2)$ of the given line segment. Thus the locus described is the perpendicular bisector of this line segment. ◆

FIGURE 10.1.2 The circle with center (h, k) and radius r.

The circle shown in Fig. 10.1.2 has center (h, k) and radius r. It may be described geometrically as the set or locus of all points $P(x, y)$ whose distance from (h, k) is r.

The distance formula then gives

$$(x - h)^2 + (y - k)^2 = r^2 \tag{5}$$

as the equation of this circle. In particular, if $h = k = 0$, then Eq. (5) takes the simple form

$$x^2 + y^2 = r^2. \tag{6}$$

We can see directly from this equation, without further reference to the definition of *circle,* that a circle centered at the origin has the following symmetry properties:

- *Symmetry around the x-axis:* The equation of the curve is unchanged when y is replaced with $-y$.
- *Symmetry around the y-axis:* The equation of the curve is unchanged when x is replaced with $-x$.
- *Symmetry with respect to the origin:* The equation of the curve is unchanged when x is replaced with $-x$ and y is replaced with $-y$.
- *Symmetry around the $45°$ line $y = x$:* The equation is unchanged when x and y are interchanged.

The relationship between Eqs. (5) and (6) is an illustration of the *translation principle* stated informally in Section 1.2. Imagine a translation (or "slide") of the plane that moves each point (x, y) to the new position $(x + h, y + k)$. Under such a translation, a curve C is moved to a new position. The equation of the new translated curve is easy to obtain from the old equation—we simply replace x with $x - h$ and y with $y - k$. Conversely, we can recognize a translated circle from its equation: Any equation of the form

$$x^2 + y^2 + Ax + By + C = 0 \tag{7}$$

can be rewritten in the form

$$(x - h)^2 + (y - k)^2 = p$$

by completing squares, as in Example 2 of Section 1.2. Thus the graph of Eq. (7) is either a circle (if $p > 0$), a single point (if $p = 0$), or no points at all (if $p < 0$). We use this approach in Example 2 to discover that the locus described is a particular circle.

EXAMPLE 2 Determine the locus of a point $P(x, y)$ if its distance $|AP|$ from $A(7, 1)$ is twice its distance $|BP|$ from $B(1, 4)$.

Solution The points A, B, and P appear in Fig. 10.1.3, along with a curve through P that represents the given locus. From

$$|AP|^2 = 4|BP|^2 \quad (\text{because } |AP| = 2|BP|),$$

we get the equation

$$(x - 7)^2 + (y - 1)^2 = 4[(x - 1)^2 + (y - 4)^2].$$

Hence

$$3x^2 + 3y^2 + 6x - 30y + 18 = 0;$$
$$x^2 + y^2 + 2x - 10y = -6;$$
$$(x + 1)^2 + (y - 5)^2 = 20.$$

Thus the locus is a circle with center $(-1, 5)$ and radius $r = \sqrt{20} = 2\sqrt{5}$. ◆

FIGURE 10.1.3 The locus of Example 2.

Conic Sections

Conic sections are so named because they are the curves formed by a plane intersecting a cone. The cone used is a right circular cone with two *nappes* extending infinitely far in both directions (Fig. 10.1.4). There are three types of conic sections, as illustrated in Fig. 10.1.5. If the cutting plane is parallel to some generator of the cone (a line that, when revolved around an axis, forms the cone), then the curve of intersection is a *parabola*. If the plane is not parallel to a generator, then the curve of intersection is either a single closed curve—an *ellipse*—or a *hyperbola* with two *branches*.

FIGURE 10.1.4 A cone with two nappes.

FIGURE 10.1.5 The conic sections.

In Appendix J we use the methods of three-dimensional analytic geometry to show that if an appropriate xy-coordinate system is set up in the intersecting plane, then the equations of the three conic sections take the following forms:

$$\text{Parabola:} \qquad y^2 = kx; \tag{8}$$

$$\text{Ellipse:} \qquad \frac{x^2}{a^2} + \frac{y^2}{b^2} = 1; \tag{9}$$

$$\text{Hyperbola:} \qquad \frac{x^2}{a^2} - \frac{y^2}{b^2} = 1. \tag{10}$$

In Section 10.6 we discuss these conic sections on the basis of definitions that are two-dimensional—they do not require the three-dimensional setting of a cone and an intersecting plane. Example 3 illustrates one such approach to the conic sections.

EXAMPLE 3 Let e be a given positive number (*not* to be confused with the natural logarithm base; in the context of conic sections, e stands for *eccentricity*). Determine the locus of a point $P(x, y)$ if its distance from the fixed point $F(p, 0)$ is e times its distance from the vertical line L whose equation is $x = -p$ (Fig. 10.1.6).

Solution Let PQ be the perpendicular from P to the line L. Then the condition

$$|PF| = e|PQ|$$

takes the analytic form

$$\sqrt{(x-p)^2 + y^2} = e|x - (-p)|.$$

That is,

$$(x^2 - 2px + p^2) + y^2 = e^2(x^2 + 2px + p^2),$$

so

$$x^2(1-e^2) - 2p(1+e^2)x + y^2 = -p^2(1-e^2). \tag{11}$$

FIGURE 10.1.6 The locus of Example 3.

- *Case 1:* $e = 1$. Then Eq. (11) reduces to

$$y^2 = 4px. \tag{12}$$

We see upon comparison with Eq. (8) that the locus of P is a *parabola* if $e = 1$.

- *Case 2:* $e < 1$. Dividing both sides of Eq. (11) by $1 - e^2$, we get

$$x^2 - 2p \cdot \frac{1+e^2}{1-e^2}x + \frac{y^2}{1-e^2} = -p^2.$$

We now complete the square in x. The result is

$$\left(x - p \cdot \frac{1+e^2}{1-e^2}\right)^2 + \frac{y^2}{1-e^2} = p^2\left[\left(\frac{1+e^2}{1-e^2}\right)^2 - 1\right] = a^2.$$

This equation has the form

$$\frac{(x-h)^2}{a^2} + \frac{y^2}{b^2} = 1, \tag{13}$$

where

$$h = +p \cdot \frac{1+e^2}{1-e^2} \quad \text{and} \quad b^2 = a^2(1-e^2). \tag{14}$$

When we compare Eqs. (9) and (13), we see that if $e < 1$, then the locus of P is an *ellipse* with $(0, 0)$ translated to $(h, 0)$, as illustrated in Fig. 10.1.7.

- *Case 3:* $e > 1$. In this case, Eq. (11) reduces to a translated version of Eq. (10), so the locus of P is a *hyperbola*. The details, which are similar to those in Case 2, are left for Problem 35.

FIGURE 10.1.7 An ellipse: $e < 1$ (Example 3).

Thus the locus in Example 3 is a *parabola* if $e = 1$, an *ellipse* if $e < 1$, and a *hyperbola* if $e > 1$. The number e is called the **eccentricity** of the conic section. The point $F(p, 0)$ is commonly called its **focus** in the parabolic case. Figure 10.1.8 shows the parabola of Case 1; Fig. 10.1.9 illustrates the hyperbola of Case 3. ◆

FIGURE 10.1.8 A parabola: $e = 1$ (Example 3).

FIGURE 10.1.9 A hyperbola: $e > 1$ (Example 3).

If we begin with Eqs. (8) through (10), we can derive the general characteristics of the three conic sections shown in Figs. 10.1.7 through 10.1.9. For example, in the case of the parabola of Eq. (8) with $k < 0$, the curve passes through the origin, $x \geq 0$ at each of the curve's points, $y \to \pm\infty$ as $x \to \infty$, and the graph is symmetric around the x-axis (because the curve is unchanged when y is replaced with $-y$).

In the case of the ellipse of Eq. (9), the graph must be symmetric around both coordinate axes. At each point (x, y) of the graph, we must have $|x| \leq a$ and $|y| \leq b$. The graph intersects the axes at the four points $(\pm a, 0)$ and $(0, \pm b)$.

Finally, the hyperbola of Eq. (10)—or its alternative form

$$y = \pm\frac{b}{a}\sqrt{x^2 - a^2}$$

628 CHAPTER 10 Polar Coordinates and Parametric Curves

—is symmetric around both coordinate axes. Its meets the x-axis at the two points $(\pm a, 0)$ and has one branch consisting of points with $x \geq a$ and has another branch where $x \leq -a$. Also, $|y| \to \infty$ as $|x| \to \infty$.

10.1 TRUE/FALSE STUDY GUIDE

10.1 CONCEPTS: QUESTIONS AND DISCUSSION

You may want to use the implicit plotting facility of a computer algebra system to investigate the following questions.

1. The graph of the equation $x^2 - y^2 = 0$ consists of the two lines $x - y = 0$ and $x + y = 0$ through the origin. What is the graph of the equation $x^n - y^n = 0$? Does it depend on whether the positive integer n is even or odd? Explain your answers.
2. How do the graphs of the equations $x^3 + y^3 = 1$ and $x^4 + y^4 = 1$ differ from the unit circle $x^2 + y^2 = 1$ (and from each other)? How does the graph of the equation $x^n + y^n = 1$ change as the positive integer n gets larger and larger? Discuss the possibility of a "limiting set" as $n \to +\infty$. Do these questions depend on whether n is even or odd?
3. The graph of the equation $x^2 - y^2 = 1$ is a hyperbola. Discuss (as in Question 2) the graph of the equation $x^n - y^n = 1$.

10.1 PROBLEMS

In Problems 1 through 6, write an equation of the specified straight line.

1. The line through the point $(1, -2)$ that is parallel to the line with equation $x + 2y = 5$
2. The line through the point $(-3, 2)$ that is perpendicular to the line with equation $3x - 4y = 7$
3. The line that is tangent to the circle $x^2 + y^2 = 25$ at the point $(3, -4)$
4. The line that is tangent to the curve $y^2 = x + 3$ at the point $(6, -3)$
5. The line that is perpendicular to the curve $x^2 + 2y^2 = 6$ at the point $(2, -1)$
6. The perpendicular bisector of the line segment with endpoints $(-3, 2)$ and $(5, -4)$

In Problems 7 through 16, find the center and radius of the circle described in the given equation.

7. $x^2 + 2x + y^2 = 4$
8. $x^2 + y^2 - 4y = 5$
9. $x^2 + y^2 - 4x + 6y = 3$
10. $x^2 + y^2 + 8x - 6y = 0$
11. $4x^2 + 4y^2 - 4x = 3$
12. $4x^2 + 4y^2 + 12y = 7$
13. $2x^2 + 2y^2 - 2x + 6y = 13$
14. $9x^2 + 9y^2 - 12x = 5$
15. $9x^2 + 9y^2 + 6x - 24y = 19$
16. $36x^2 + 36y^2 - 48x - 108y = 47$

In Problems 17 through 20, show that the graph of the given equation consists either of a single point or of no points.

17. $x^2 + y^2 - 6x - 4y + 13 = 0$
18. $2x^2 + 2y^2 + 6x + 2y + 5 = 0$
19. $x^2 + y^2 - 6x - 10y + 84 = 0$
20. $9x^2 + 9y^2 - 6x - 6y + 11 = 0$

In Problems 21 through 24, write the equation of the specified circle.

21. The circle with center $(-1, -2)$ that passes through the point $(2, 3)$
22. The circle with center $(2, -2)$ that is tangent to the line $y = x + 4$
23. The circle with center $(6, 6)$ that is tangent to the line $y = 2x - 4$
24. The circle that passes through the points $(4, 6)$, $(-2, -2)$, and $(5, -1)$

In Problems 25 through 30, derive the equation of the set of all points $P(x, y)$ that satisfy the given condition. Then sketch the graph of the equation.

25. The point $P(x, y)$ is equally distant from the two points $(3, 2)$ and $(7, 4)$.
26. The distance from P to the point $(-2, 1)$ is half the distance from P to the point $(4, -2)$.
27. The point P is three times as far from the point $(-3, 2)$ as it is from the point $(5, 10)$.
28. The distance from P to the line $x = -3$ is equal to its distance from the point $(3, 0)$.

29. The sum of the distances from P to the points $(4, 0)$ and $(-4, 0)$ is 10.

30. The sum of the distances from P to the points $(0, 3)$ and $(0, -3)$ is 10.

31. Find all the lines through the point $(2, 1)$ that are tangent to the parabola $y = x^2$.

32. Find all lines through the point $(-1, 2)$ that are normal to the parabola $y = x^2$.

33. Find all lines that are normal to the curve $xy = 4$ and simultaneously are parallel to the line $y = 4x$.

34. Find all lines that are tangent to the curve $y = x^3$ and are also parallel to the line $3x - y = 5$.

35. Suppose that $e > 1$. Show that Eq. (11) of this section can be written in the form

$$\frac{(x-h)^2}{a^2} - \frac{y^2}{b^2} = 1,$$

thus showing that its graph is a hyperbola. Find a, b, and h in terms of p and e.

10.2 POLAR COORDINATES

A familiar way to locate a point in the coordinate plane is by specifying its rectangular coordinates (x, y)—that is, by giving its abscissa x and ordinate y relative to given perpendicular axes. In some problems it is more convenient to locate a point by means of its *polar coordinates*. The polar coordinates give its position relative to a fixed reference point O (the **pole**) and to a given ray (the **polar axis**) beginning at O.

For convenience, we begin with a given xy-coordinate system and then take the origin as the pole and the nonnegative x-axis as the polar axis. Given the pole O and the polar axis, the point P with **polar coordinates** r and θ, written as the ordered pair (r, θ), is located as follows. First find the terminal side of the angle θ, given in radians, where θ is measured counterclockwise (if $\theta > 0$) from the x-axis (the polar axis) as its initial side. If $r \geq 0$, then P is on the terminal side of this angle at the distance r from the origin. If $r < 0$, then P lies on the ray opposite the terminal side at the distance $|r| = -r > 0$ from the pole (Fig. 10.2.1). The **radial coordinate** r can be described as the *directed* distance of P from the pole along the terminal side of the angle θ. Thus, if r is positive, the point P lies in the same quadrant as θ, whereas if r is negative, then P lies in the opposite quadrant. If $r = 0$, the angle θ does not matter; the polar coordinates $(0, \theta)$ represent the origin whatever the **angular coordinate** θ might be. The origin, or pole, is the only point for which $r = 0$.

FIGURE 10.2.1 The difference between the two cases $r > 0$ and $r < 0$.

FIGURE 10.2.2 The polar coordinates (r, θ) and $(-r, \theta + \pi)$ represent the same point P (Example 1).

EXAMPLE 1 Polar coordinates differ from rectangular coordinates in that any point has more than one representation in polar coordinates. For example, the polar coordinates (r, θ) and $(-r, \theta + \pi)$ represent the same point P, as shown in Fig. 10.2.2. More generally, this point P has the polar coordinates $(r, \theta + n\pi)$ for any even integer n and the coordinates $(-r, \theta + n\pi)$ for any odd integer n. Thus the polar-coordinate pairs

$$\left(2, \frac{\pi}{3}\right), \quad \left(-2, \frac{4\pi}{3}\right), \quad \left(2, \frac{7\pi}{3}\right), \quad \text{and} \quad \left(-2, -\frac{2\pi}{3}\right)$$

FIGURE 10.2.3 The point P of Example 1 can be described in many different ways using polar coordinates.

FIGURE 10.2.4 Read Eqs. (1) and (2)—conversions between polar and rectangular coordinates—from this figure.

FIGURE 10.2.5 The circle $r = a$ centered at the origin (Example 2).

all represent the same point P in Fig. 10.2.3. (The rectangular coordinates of P are $(1, \sqrt{3})$.) ◆

To convert polar coordinates into rectangular coordinates, we use the basic relations

$$x = r\cos\theta, \quad y = r\sin\theta \quad (1)$$

that we read from the right triangle in Fig. 10.2.4. Converting in the opposite direction, we have

$$r^2 = x^2 + y^2, \quad \tan\theta = \frac{y}{x} \text{ if } x \neq 0. \quad (2)$$

Some care is required in making the correct choice of θ in the formula $\tan\theta = y/x$. If $x > 0$, then (x, y) lies in either the first or fourth quadrant, so $-\pi/2 < \theta < \pi/2$, which is the range of the inverse tangent function. Hence if $x > 0$, then $\theta = \arctan(y/x)$. But if $x < 0$, then (x, y) lies in the second or third quadrant. In this case a proper choice for the angle is $\theta = \pi + \arctan(y/x)$. In any event, the signs of x and y in Eq. (1) with $r > 0$ indicate the quadrant in which θ lies.

Polar Coordinate Equations

Some curves have simpler equations in polar coordinates than in rectangular coordinates; this is an important reason for the usefulness of polar coordinates. The **graph** of an equation in the polar-coordinate variables r and θ is the set of all those points P such that P has some pair of polar coordinates (r, θ) that satisfy the given equation. The graph of a polar equation $r = f(\theta)$ can be constructed by computing a table of values of r against θ and then plotting the corresponding points (r, θ) on polar-coordinate graph paper.

EXAMPLE 2 One reason for the importance of polar coordinates is that many real-world problems involve circles, and the polar-coordinate equation (or *polar equation*) of the circle with center $(0, 0)$ and radius $a > 0$ (Fig. 10.2.5) is very simple:

$$r = a. \quad (3)$$

Note that if we begin with the rectangular-coordinates equation $x^2 + y^2 = a^2$ of this circle and transform it using the first relation in (2), we get the polar-coordinate equation $r^2 = a^2$. Then Eq. (3) results upon taking positive square roots. ◆

EXAMPLE 3 Construct the polar-coordinate graph of the equation $r = 2\sin\theta$.

Solution Figure 10.2.6 shows a table of values of r as a function of θ. The corresponding points (r, θ) are plotted in Fig. 10.2.7, using the rays at multiples of $\pi/6$ and the circles (centered at the pole) of radii 1 and 2 to locate these points. A visual inspection of the smooth curve connecting these points suggests that it is a circle of radius 1. Let us assume for the moment that this is so. Note then that the point $P(r, \theta)$ moves *once around this circle counterclockwise* as θ increases from 0 to π and then moves around this circle a *second time* as θ increases from π to 2π. This is because the negative values of r for θ between π and 2π give—in this example—the same geometric points as do the positive values of r for θ between 0 and π. (Why?) ◆

The verification that the graph of $r = 2\sin\theta$ is the indicated circle illustrates the general procedure for transferring back and forth between polar and rectangular coordinates, using the relations in (1) and (2).

θ	r
0	0.00
$\pi/6$	1.00
$\pi/3$	1.73
$\pi/2$	2.00
$2\pi/3$	1.73
$5\pi/6$	1.00
π	0.00
$7\pi/6$	-1.00
$4\pi/3$	-1.73
$3\pi/2$	-2.00
$5\pi/3$	-1.73
$11\pi/6$	-1.00
2π	0.00
(data rounded)	

FIGURE 10.2.6 Values of $r = 2\sin\theta$ (Example 3).

FIGURE 10.2.7 The graph of the polar equation $r = 2\sin\theta$ (Example 3).

EXAMPLE 4 To transform the equation $r = 2\sin\theta$ of Example 3 into rectangular coordinates, we first multiply both sides by r to get

$$r^2 = 2r\sin\theta.$$

Equations (1) and (2) now give

$$x^2 + y^2 = 2y.$$

Finally, after we complete the square in y, we have

$$x^2 + (y-1)^2 = 1,$$

the rectangular-coordinate equation (or *rectangular equation*) of a circle whose center is $(0, 1)$ and whose radius is 1. ◆

FIGURE 10.2.8 The graphs of the circles whose equations appear in Eq. (4) with $a = 1$.

More generally, the graphs of the equations

$$r = 2a\sin\theta \quad \text{and} \quad r = 2a\cos\theta \tag{4}$$

are circles of radius a centered, respectively, at the points $(0, a)$ and $(a, 0)$. This is illustrated (with $a = 1$) in Fig. 10.2.8.

By substituting the equations given in (1), we can transform the rectangular equation $ax + by = c$ of a straight line into

$$ar\cos\theta + br\sin\theta = c.$$

Let us take $a = 1$ and $b = 0$. Then we see that the polar equation of the vertical line $x = c$ is $r = c\sec\theta$, as we can deduce directly from Fig. 10.2.9.

FIGURE 10.2.9 Finding the polar equation of the vertical line $x = c$.

EXAMPLE 5 Sketch the graph of the polar equation $r = 2 + 2\sin\theta$.

Solution If we scan the second column of the table in Fig. 10.2.6, mentally adding 2 to each entry for r, we see that

- r increases from 2 to 4 as θ increases from 0 to $\pi/2$;
- r decreases from 4 to 2 as θ increases from $\pi/2$ to π;
- r decreases from 2 to 0 as θ increases from π to $3\pi/2$;
- r increases from 0 to 2 as θ increases from $3\pi/2$ to 2π.

FIGURE 10.2.10 A cardioid (Example 5).

FIGURE 10.2.11 The rectangular coordinates graph of $r = 2\cos 2\theta$ as a function of θ. Numbered portions of the graph correspond to numbered portions of the polar-coordinates graph in Fig. 10.2.12.

FIGURE 10.2.12 A four-leaved rose (Example 6).

This information tells us that the graph resembles the curve shown in Fig. 10.2.10. This heart-shaped graph is called a **cardioid**. The graphs of the equations

$$r = a(1 \pm \sin\theta) \quad \text{and} \quad r = a(1 \pm \cos\theta)$$

are all cardioids, differing only in size (determined by a), axis of symmetry (horizontal or vertical), and the direction in which the cusp at the pole points. ◆

EXAMPLE 6 Sketch the graph of the equation $r = 2\cos 2\theta$.

Solution Rather than constructing a table of values of r as a function of θ and then plotting individual points, let us begin with a *rectangular-coordinate graph* of r as a function of θ. In Fig. 10.2.11, we see that $r = 0$ if θ is an odd integral multiple of $\pi/4$, and that r is alternately positive and negative on successive intervals of length $\pi/2$ from one odd integral multiple of $\pi/4$ to the next.

Now let's think about how r changes as θ increases, beginning at $\theta = 0$. As θ increases from 0 to $\pi/4$, r decreases in value from 2 to 0, and so we draw the first portion (labeled "1") of the polar curve in Fig. 10.2.12. As θ increases from $\pi/4$ to $3\pi/4$, r first decreases from 0 to -2 and then increases from -2 to 0. Because r is now negative, we draw the second and third portions (labeled "2" and "3") of the polar curve in the third and fourth quadrants (rather than in the first and second quadrants) in Fig. 10.2.12. Continuing in this fashion, we draw the fourth through eighth portions of the polar curve, with those portions where r is negative in the quadrants opposite those in which θ lies. The arrows on the resulting polar curve in Fig. 10.2.12 indicate the direction of motion of the point $P(r, \theta)$ along the curve as θ increases. The whole graph consists of four loops, each of which begins and ends at the pole. ◆

The curve in Example 6 is called a *four-leaved rose*. The equations $r = a\cos n\theta$ and $r = a\sin n\theta$ represent "roses" with $2n$ "leaves," or loops, if n is even and $n \geq 2$ but with n loops if n is odd and $n \geq 3$.

The four-leaved rose exhibits several types of symmetry. The following are some *sufficient* conditions for symmetry in polar coordinates:

- *For symmetry around the x-axis:* The equation is unchanged when θ is replaced with $-\theta$.
- *For symmetry around the y-axis:* The equation is unchanged when θ is replaced with $\pi - \theta$.
- *For symmetry with respect to the origin:* The equation is unchanged when r is replaced with $-r$.

Because $\cos 2\theta = \cos(-2\theta) = \cos 2(\pi - \theta)$, the equation $r = 2\cos 2\theta$ of the four-leaved rose satisfies the first two symmetry conditions, and therefore its graph is symmetric around both the x-axis and the y-axis. Thus it is also symmetric around the origin. Nevertheless, this equation does *not* satisfy the third condition, the one for symmetry around the origin. This illustrates that although the symmetry conditions given are *sufficient* for the symmetries described, they are not *necessary* conditions.

EXAMPLE 7 Figure 10.2.13 shows the lemniscate with equation

$$r^2 = -4\sin 2\theta.$$

To see why it has loops only in the second and fourth quadrants, we examine a table of signs of values of $-4\sin 2\theta$.

θ	2θ	$-4\sin 2\theta$
$0 < \theta < \frac{1}{2}\pi$	$0 < 2\theta < \pi$	Negative
$\frac{1}{2}\pi < \theta < \pi$	$\pi < 2\theta < 2\pi$	Positive
$\pi < \theta < \frac{3}{2}\pi$	$2\pi < 2\theta < 3\pi$	Negative
$\frac{3}{2}\pi < \theta < 2\pi$	$3\pi < 2\theta < 4\pi$	Positive

When θ lies in the first or the third quadrant, the quantity $-4\sin 2\theta$ is negative, so the equation $r^2 = -4\sin 2\theta$ cannot be satisfied for any real values of r. ◆

FIGURE 10.2.13 The lemniscate $r^2 = -4\sin 2\theta$ (Example 7).

Example 6 illustrates a peculiarity of graphs of polar equations, caused by the fact that a single point has multiple representations in polar coordinates. The point with polar coordinates $(2, \pi/2)$ clearly lies on the four-leaved rose, but these coordinates do *not* satisfy the equation $r = 2\cos 2\theta$. This means that a point may have one pair of polar coordinates that satisfy a given equation and others that do not. Hence we must be careful to understand this: The graph of a polar equation consists of all those points with *at least one* polar-coordinate representation that satisfies the given equation.

Another result of the multiplicity of polar coordinates is that the simultaneous solution of two polar equations does not always give all the points of intersection of their graphs. For instance, consider the circles $r = 2\sin\theta$ and $r = 2\cos\theta$ shown in Fig. 10.2.8. The origin is clearly a point of intersection of these two circles. Its polar representation $(0, \pi)$ satisfies the equation $r = 2\sin\theta$, and its representation $(0, \pi/2)$ satisfies the other equation, $r = 2\cos\theta$. But the origin has no *single* polar representation that satisfies both equations simultaneously! If we think of θ as increasing uniformly with time, then the corresponding moving points on the two circles pass through the origin at different times. Hence the origin cannot be discovered as a point of intersection of the two circles merely by solving their equations $r = 2\sin\theta$ and $r = 2\cos\theta$ simultaneously in a straightforward manner. But one fail-safe way to find *all* points of intersection of two polar-coordinate curves is to graph both curves.

EXAMPLE 8 Find all points of intersection of the graphs of the equations $r = 1 + \sin\theta$ and $r^2 = 4\sin\theta$.

Solution The graph of $r = 1 + \sin\theta$ is a scaled-down version of the cardioid of Example 5. In Problem 52 we ask you to show that the graph of $r^2 = 4\sin\theta$ is the figure-eight curve shown with the cardioid in Fig. 10.2.14. The figure shows four points of intersection: A, B, C, and O. Can we find all four using algebra?

Given the two equations, we begin by eliminating r. Because

$$(1 + \sin\theta)^2 = r^2 = 4\sin\theta,$$

it follows that

$$\sin^2\theta - 2\sin\theta + 1 = 0;$$

$$(\sin\theta - 1)^2 = 0;$$

FIGURE 10.2.14 The cardioid $r = 1 + \sin\theta$ and the figure eight $r^2 = 4\sin\theta$ meet in four points (Example 8).

and thus that $\sin\theta = 1$. So θ must be an angle of the form $\frac{1}{2}\pi + 2n\pi$ where n is an integer. All points on the cardioid and all points on the figure-eight curve are produced by letting θ range from 0 to 2π, so $\theta = \pi/2$ will produce all the solutions that we can obtain by simple algebraic elimination. The only such point is $A(2, \pi/2)$, and the other three points of intersection are detected only when the two equations are graphed. ◆

Calculator/Computer-Generated Polar Curves

It might take you quite a while to construct by hand the "butterfly curve" shown in Fig. 10.2.15. But most graphing calculators and computer algebra systems have facilities for plotting polar curves. For instance, with a TI calculator set in "polar graph mode," one need only enter and graph the equation

```
r = e^(cos(θ)) - 2*cos(4θ) + sin(θ/4)^3
```

on the interval $0 \leq \theta \leq 8\pi$. With *Maple* and *Mathematica* the graphics package commands

```
polarplot(exp(cos(t)) - 2*cos(4*t) + sin(t/4)^3, t=0..8*Pi);
```

and

```
PolarPlot[ Exp[Cos[t]] - 2*Cos[4*t] + Sin[t/4]^3, { t, 0, 8*Pi }];
```

FIGURE 10.2.15 $r = e^{\cos\theta} - 2\cos 4\theta + \sin^3(\theta/4)$.

(respectively) give the same result (with t in place of θ).

Because of the presence of the term $\sin^3(\theta/4)$, the more usual interval $0 \leq \theta \leq 2\pi$ gives only a part of the curve shown in Fig. 10.2.15. (Try it to see for yourself.) But

$$\sin^3\left(\frac{\theta + 8\pi}{4}\right) = \sin^3\left(\frac{\theta}{4} + 2\pi\right) = \sin^3\left(\frac{\theta}{4}\right),$$

so values of $\sin^3(\theta/4)$ repeat themselves when θ exceeds 8π. Therefore the interval $0 \leq \theta \leq 8\pi$ suffices to give the entire butterfly curve. You might try plotting a butterfly curve with the term $\sin^3(\theta/4)$ replaced with $\sin^5(\theta/12)$—as originally recommended by Temple H. Fay in his article "The Butterfly Curve" (*American Mathematical Monthly*, May 1989, p. 442). What range of values of θ will now be required to obtain the whole butterfly?

10.2 TRUE/FALSE STUDY GUIDE

10.2 CONCEPTS: QUESTIONS AND DISCUSSION

1. Figures 10.2.16 through 10.2.18 illustrate the polar curve $r = a + b\cos\theta$ for various values of a and b. What determines whether the curve exhibits a cusp (Fig. 10.2.16), a loop (Fig. 10.2.17), or neither (Fig. 10.2.18)? Does your answer apply also to polar curves of the form $r = a + b\sin\theta$? Given a and b, what is the difference between the curves $r = a + b\cos\theta$ and $r = a + b\sin\theta$?

FIGURE 10.2.16 $r = 4 + 4\cos\theta$.

FIGURE 10.2.17 $r = 4 + 7\cos\theta$.

FIGURE 10.2.18 $r = 4 + 3\cos\theta$.

2. Figures 10.2.19 and 10.2.20 show the graphs of the equations $r = \cos 3\theta$ and $r = \sin 4\theta$. Given a positive integer n, what is the difference between the "rose graphs" $r = \cos n\theta$ and $r = \sin n\theta$? Explain precisely how the number of leaves in the complete graph depends on n. What determines whether $0 \leq \theta \leq \pi$ or $0 \leq \theta \leq 2\pi$ gives all the leaves?

FIGURE 10.2.19 $r = \cos 3\theta$.

FIGURE 10.2.20 $r = \sin 4\theta$.

10.2 PROBLEMS

1. Plot the points with the given polar coordinates, and then find the rectangular coordinates of each.
   (a) $(1, \pi/4)$ (b) $(-2, 2\pi/3)$ (c) $(1, -\pi/3)$
   (d) $(3, 3\pi/2)$ (e) $(2, -\pi/4)$ (f) $(-2, -7\pi/6)$
   (g) $(2, 5\pi/6)$

2. Find two polar-coordinate representations, one with $r > 0$ and the other with $r < 0$, for the points with the given rectangular coordinates.
   (a) $(-1, -1)$ (b) $(\sqrt{3}, -1)$ (c) $(2, 2)$
   (d) $(-1, \sqrt{3})$ (e) $(\sqrt{2}, -\sqrt{2})$ (f) $(-3, \sqrt{3})$

In Problems 3 through 10, express the given rectangular equation in polar form.

3. $x = 4$
4. $y = 6$
5. $x = 3y$
6. $x^2 + y^2 = 25$
7. $xy = 1$
8. $x^2 - y^2 = 1$
9. $y = x^2$
10. $x + y = 4$

In Problems 11 through 18, express the given polar equation in rectangular form.

11. $r = 3$
12. $\theta = 3\pi/4$
13. $r = -5\cos\theta$
14. $r = \sin 2\theta$
15. $r = 1 - \cos 2\theta$
16. $r = 2 + \sin\theta$
17. $r = 3\sec\theta$
18. $r^2 = \cos 2\theta$

For the curves described in Problems 19 through 28, write equations in both rectangular and polar form.

19. The vertical line through $(2, 0)$
20. The horizontal line through $(1, 3)$
21. The line with slope -1 through $(2, -1)$
22. The line with slope 1 through $(4, 2)$
23. The line through the points $(1, 3)$ and $(3, 5)$
24. The circle with center $(3, 0)$ that passes through the origin
25. The circle with center $(0, -4)$ that passes through the origin
26. The circle with center $(3, 4)$ and radius 5
27. The circle with center $(1, 1)$ that passes through the origin
28. The circle with center $(5, -2)$ that passes through the point $(1, 1)$

In Problems 29 through 32, transform the given polar-coordinate equation into a rectangular-coordinate equation, then match the equation with its graph among those in Figs. 10.2.21 through 10.2.24.

29. $r = -4\cos\theta$
30. $r = 5\cos\theta + 5\sin\theta$
31. $r = -4\cos\theta + 3\sin\theta$
32. $r = 8\cos\theta - 15\sin\theta$

FIGURE 10.2.21

FIGURE 10.2.22

FIGURE 10.2.23

FIGURE 10.2.24

The graph of a polar equation of the form $r = a + b\cos\theta$ (or $r = a + b\sin\theta$) is called a limaçon (from the French word for snail). In Problems 33 through 36, match the given polar-coordinate equation with its graph among the limaçons in Figs. 10.2.25 through 10.2.28.

33. $r = 8 + 6\cos\theta$
34. $r = 7 + 7\cos\theta$
35. $r = 5 + 9\cos\theta$
36. $r = 3 + 11\cos\theta$

37. Show that the graph of the polar equation $r = a\cos\theta + b\sin\theta$ is a circle if $a^2 + b^2 \neq 0$. Express the center (h, k) and radius r of this circle in terms of a and b.

38. Show that if $0 < a < b$, then the limaçon with polar equation $r = a + b\cos\theta$ has an inner loop (as in Figs. 10.2.25 and 10.2.27). In this case, find (in terms of a and b) the range of values of θ that correspond to points of the inner loop.

FIGURE 10.2.25

FIGURE 10.2.26

FIGURE 10.2.27

FIGURE 10.2.28

Sketch the graphs of the polar equations in Problems 39 through 52. Indicate any symmetries around either coordinate axis or the origin.

39. $r = 2\cos\theta$ (circle)
40. $r = 2\sin\theta + 2\cos\theta$ (circle)
41. $r = 1 + \cos\theta$ (cardioid)
42. $r = 1 - \sin\theta$ (cardioid)
43. $r = 2 + 4\sin\theta$ (limaçon)
44. $r = 4 + 2\cos\theta$ (limaçon)
45. $r^2 = 4\sin 2\theta$ (lemniscate)

46. $r^2 = 4\cos 2\theta$ (lemniscate)
47. $r = 2\sin 2\theta$ (four-leaved rose)
48. $r = 3\sin 3\theta$ (three-leaved rose)
49. $r = 3\cos 3\theta$ (three-leaved rose)
50. $r = 3\theta$ (spiral of Archimedes)
51. $r = 2\sin 5\theta$ (five-leaved rose)
52. $r^2 = 4\sin\theta$ (figure eight)

In Problems 53 through 58, find all points of intersection of the curves with the given polar equations.

53. $r = 1, \quad r = \cos\theta$
54. $r = \sin\theta, \quad r^2 = 3\cos^2\theta$
55. $r = \sin\theta, \quad r = \cos 2\theta$
56. $r = 1 + \cos\theta, \quad r = 1 - \sin\theta$
57. $r = 1 - \cos\theta, \quad r^2 = 4\cos\theta$
58. $r^2 = 4\sin\theta, \quad r^2 = 4\cos\theta$

59. (a) The straight line L passes through the point with polar coordinates (p, α) and is perpendicular to the line segment joining the pole and the point (p, α). Write the polar-coordinate equation of L. (b) Show that the rectangular-coordinate equation of L is

$$x\cos\alpha + y\sin\alpha = p.$$

60. Find a rectangular-coordinate equation of the cardioid with polar equation $r = 1 - \cos\theta$.

61. Use polar coordinates to identify the graph of the rectangular-coordinate equation $a^2(x^2 + y^2) = (x^2 + y^2 - by)^2$.

62. Plot the polar equations

$$r = 1 + \cos\theta \quad \text{and} \quad r = -1 + \cos\theta$$

on the same coordinate plane. Comment on the results.

63. Figures 10.2.29 and 10.2.30 show the graphs of the equations $r = \cos(5\theta/3)$ and $r = \cos(5\theta/2)$. Why does one have five (overlapping) loops while the other has ten loops? In each case, what range of values of θ is required to obtain all the loops? In the more general case $r = (\cos p\theta/q)$ where p and q are positive integers, is it p or q (or both) that determine the number of loops and the range of values of θ required to show all the loops in the complete graph?

64. Figures 10.2.31 and 10.2.32 show the graphs of the equations $r = 1 + 4\sin 3\theta$ and $r = 1 + 4\cos 4\theta$. What determines whether a polar curve of the form $r = a + b\sin(n\theta)$—with a and b positive constants and n a positive integer—has both larger and smaller loops? What determines whether the smaller loops are within or outside of the larger ones?

FIGURE 10.2.29 $r = \cos\left(\dfrac{5\theta}{3}\right)$.

FIGURE 10.2.30 $r = \cos\left(\dfrac{5\theta}{2}\right)$.

FIGURE 10.2.31 $r = 1 + 4\sin 3\theta$.

FIGURE 10.2.32 $r = 1 + 4\cos 4\theta$.

10.3 AREA COMPUTATIONS IN POLAR COORDINATES

The graph of the polar-coordinate equation $r = f(\theta)$ may bound an area, as does the cardioid $r = 2(1 + \cos\theta)$—see Fig. 10.3.1. To calculate the area of this region, we may find it convenient to work directly with polar coordinates rather than to change to rectangular coordinates.

To see how to set up an area integral using polar coordinates, we consider the region R of Fig. 10.3.2. This region is bounded by the two radial lines $\theta = \alpha$ and $\theta = \beta$ and by the curve $r = f(\theta)$, $\alpha \leq \theta \leq \beta$. To approximate the area A of R, we begin with a partition

$$\alpha = \theta_0 < \theta_1 < \theta_2 < \cdots < \theta_n = \beta$$

of the interval $[\alpha, \beta]$ into n subintervals, all with the same length $\Delta\theta = (\beta - \alpha)/n$. We select a point $\theta_i^\star$ in the ith subinterval $[\theta_{i-1}, \theta_i]$ for $i = 1, 2, \ldots, n$.

Let ΔA_i denote the area of the sector bounded by the lines $\theta = \theta_{i-1}$ and $\theta = \theta_i$ and by the curve $r = f(\theta)$. We see from Fig. 10.3.2 that for small values of $\Delta\theta$, ΔA_i is approximately equal to the area of the *circular* sector that has radius $r_i^\star = f(\theta_i^\star)$ and is bounded by the same lines. That is,

$$\Delta A_i \approx \tfrac{1}{2}(r_i^\star)^2 \Delta\theta = \tfrac{1}{2}[f(\theta_i^\star)]^2 \Delta\theta.$$

We add the areas of these sectors for $i = 1, 2, \ldots, n$ and thereby find that

$$A = \sum_{i=1}^{n} \Delta A_i \approx \sum_{i=1}^{n} \tfrac{1}{2}[f(\theta_i^\star)]^2 \Delta\theta.$$

The right-hand sum is a Riemann sum for the integral

$$\int_\alpha^\beta \tfrac{1}{2}[f(\theta)]^2 \, d\theta.$$

Hence, if f is continuous, the value of this integral is the limit, as $\Delta\theta \to 0$, of the preceding sum. We therefore conclude that the *area A of the region R bounded by the lines $\theta = \alpha$ and $\theta = \beta$ and the curve $r = f(\theta)$* is

$$A = \int_\alpha^\beta \tfrac{1}{2}[f(\theta)]^2 \, d\theta. \tag{1}$$

The infinitesimal sector shown in Fig. 10.3.3, with radius r, central angle $d\theta$, and area $dA = \tfrac{1}{2} r^2 \, d\theta$, serves as a useful device for remembering Eq. (1) in the abbreviated

FIGURE 10.3.1 What is the area of the region R bounded by the cardioid $r = 2(1 + \cos\theta)$?

FIGURE 10.3.2 We obtain the area formula from Riemann sums.

FIGURE 10.3.3 Nonrigorous derivation of the area formula in polar coordinates.

Area Computations in Polar Coordinates SECTION 10.3   639

form

$$A = \int_\alpha^\beta \tfrac{1}{2} r^2 \, d\theta. \quad (2)$$

EXAMPLE 1 Find the area of the region bounded by the limaçon with equation $r = 3 + 2\cos\theta$, $0 \leq \theta \leq 2\pi$ (Fig. 10.3.4).

Solution We could apply Eq. (2) with $\alpha = 0$ and $\beta = 2\pi$. Here, instead, we will make use of symmetry. We will calculate the area of the upper half of the region and then double the result. Note that the infinitesimal sector shown in Fig. 10.3.4 sweeps out the upper half of the limaçon as θ increases from 0 to π (Fig. 10.3.5). Hence

$$A = 2\int_\alpha^\beta \tfrac{1}{2} r^2 \, d\theta = \int_0^\pi (3 + 2\cos\theta)^2 \, d\theta$$

$$= \int_0^\pi (9 + 12\cos\theta + 4\cos^2\theta) \, d\theta.$$

FIGURE 10.3.4 The limaçon of Example 1.

FIGURE 10.3.5 Infinitesimal sectors from $\theta = 0$ to $\theta = \pi$ (Example 1).

Because

$$4\cos^2\theta = 4 \cdot \frac{1 + \cos 2\theta}{2} = 2 + 2\cos 2\theta,$$

we now get

$$A = \int_0^\pi (11 + 12\cos\theta + 2\cos 2\theta) \, d\theta$$

$$= \Big[11\theta + 12\sin\theta + \sin 2\theta\Big]_0^\pi = 11\pi. \quad \blacklozenge$$

EXAMPLE 2 Find the area bounded by each loop of the limaçon with equation $r = 1 + 2\cos\theta$ (Fig. 10.3.6).

Solution The equation $1 + 2\cos\theta = 0$ has two solutions for θ in the interval $[0, 2\pi]$: $\theta = 2\pi/3$ and $\theta = 4\pi/3$. The upper half of the outer loop of the limaçon corresponds to values of θ between 0 and $2\pi/3$, where r is positive. Because the curve is symmetric around the x-axis, we can find the total area A_1 bounded by the outer loop by integrating from 0 to $2\pi/3$ and then doubling. Thus

$$A_1 = 2\int_0^{2\pi/3} \tfrac{1}{2}(1 + 2\cos\theta)^2 \, d\theta = \int_0^{2\pi/3} (1 + 4\cos\theta + 4\cos^2\theta) \, d\theta$$

$$= \int_0^{2\pi/3} (3 + 4\cos\theta + 2\cos 2\theta) \, d\theta$$

$$= \Big[3\theta + 4\sin\theta + \sin 2\theta\Big]_0^{2\pi/3} = 2\pi + \tfrac{3}{2}\sqrt{3}.$$

The inner loop of the limaçon corresponds to values of θ between $2\pi/3$ and $4\pi/3$, where r is negative. Hence the area bounded by the inner loop is

FIGURE 10.3.6 The limaçon of Example 2.

$$A_2 = \int_{2\pi/3}^{4\pi/3} \tfrac{1}{2}(1 + 2\cos\theta)^2 \, d\theta$$

$$= \tfrac{1}{2}\Big[3\theta + 4\sin\theta + \sin 2\theta\Big]_{2\pi/3}^{4\pi/3} = \pi - \tfrac{3}{2}\sqrt{3}.$$

The area of the region lying *between* the two loops of the limaçon is then

$$A = A_1 - A_2 = 2\pi + \tfrac{3}{2}\sqrt{3} - \left(\pi - \tfrac{3}{2}\sqrt{3}\right) = \pi + 3\sqrt{3}. \quad \blacklozenge$$

The Area Between Two Polar Curves

Now consider two curves $r = f(\theta)$ and $r = g(\theta)$, with $f(\theta) \geq g(\theta) \geq 0$ for $\alpha \leq \theta \leq \beta$. Then we can find the area of the region bounded by these curves and the rays (radial lines) $\theta = \alpha$ and $\theta = \beta$ (Fig. 10.3.7) by subtracting the area bounded by the inner curve from that bounded by the outer curve. That is, the area A between the two curves is given by

$$A = \int_\alpha^\beta \tfrac{1}{2}[f(\theta)]^2 \, d\theta - \int_\alpha^\beta \tfrac{1}{2}[g(\theta)]^2 \, d\theta,$$

so that

$$A = \tfrac{1}{2} \int_\alpha^\beta \left\{[f(\theta)]^2 - [g(\theta)]^2\right\} d\theta. \tag{3}$$

FIGURE 10.3.7 The area between the graphs of f and g.

With r_{outer} for the outer curve and r_{inner} for the inner curve, we get the abbreviated formula

$$A = \tfrac{1}{2} \int_\alpha^\beta \left[(r_{\text{outer}})^2 - (r_{\text{inner}})^2\right] d\theta \tag{4}$$

for the area of the region shown in Fig. 10.3.8.

FIGURE 10.3.8 The radial line segment illustrates the radii r_{inner} and r_{outer} of Eq. (4).

FIGURE 10.3.9 The region of Example 3.

EXAMPLE 3 Find the area A of the region that lies within the limaçon $r = 1 + 2\cos\theta$ and outside the circle $r = 2$.

Solution The circle and limaçon are shown in Fig. 10.3.9, with the area A between them shaded. The points of intersection of the circle and limaçon are given by

$$1 + 2\cos\theta = 2, \quad \text{so} \quad \cos\theta = \tfrac{1}{2},$$

and the figure shows that we should choose the solutions $\theta = \pm\pi/3$. These two values of θ are the needed limits of integration. When we use Eq. (3), we find that

$$A = \tfrac{1}{2} \int_{-\pi/3}^{\pi/3} \left[(1 + 2\cos\theta)^2 - 2^2\right] d\theta$$

$$= \int_0^{\pi/3} (4\cos\theta + 4\cos^2\theta - 3) \, d\theta \qquad \text{(by symmetry)}$$

$$= \int_0^{\pi/3} (4\cos\theta + 2\cos 2\theta - 1) \, d\theta$$

$$= \left[4\sin\theta + \sin 2\theta - \theta\right]_0^{\pi/3} = \frac{15\sqrt{3} - 2\pi}{6}.$$

◆

Area Computations in Polar Coordinates SECTION 10.3   641

10.3 TRUE/FALSE STUDY GUIDE
10.3 CONCEPTS: QUESTIONS AND DISCUSSION

1. Give an example of a plane region whose area can be calculated both by a rectangular-coordinate integral and a polar-coordinate integral, but the latter is easier to evaluate.
2. Give an example of a plane region whose area can be calculated both by a rectangular-coordinate integral and a polar-coordinate integral, but the former is easier to evaluate.
3. Give an example of an unbounded plane region such that its polar-coordinate area integral is improper but convergent.

10.3 PROBLEMS

In Problems 1 through 6, sketch the plane region bounded by the given polar curve $r = f(\theta)$, $\alpha \leq \theta \leq \beta$, and the rays $\theta = \alpha$, $\theta = \beta$.

1. $r = \theta$, $0 \leq \theta \leq \pi$
2. $r = \theta$, $0 \leq \theta \leq 2\pi$
3. $r = 1/\theta$, $\pi \leq \theta \leq 3\pi$
4. $r = 1/\theta$, $3\pi \leq \theta \leq 5\pi$
5. $r = e^{-\theta}$, $0 \leq \theta \leq \pi$
6. $r = e^{-\theta}$, $\pi/2 \leq \theta \leq 3\pi/2$

In Problems 7 through 16, find the area bounded by the given curve.

7. $r = 2\cos\theta$
8. $r = 4\sin\theta$
9. $r = 1 + \cos\theta$
10. $r = 2 - 2\sin\theta$ (Fig. 10.3.10)
11. $r = 2 - \cos\theta$
12. $r = 3 + 2\sin\theta$ (Fig. 10.3.11)

FIGURE 10.3.10 The cardioid of Problem 10.

FIGURE 10.3.11 The limaçon of Problem 12.

13. $r = -4\cos\theta$
14. $r = 5(1 + \sin\theta)$
15. $r = 3 - \cos\theta$
16. $r = 2 + \sin\theta + \cos\theta$

In Problems 17 through 24, find the area bounded by one loop of the given curve.

17. $r = 2\cos 2\theta$
18. $r = 3\sin 3\theta$ (Fig. 10.3.12)
19. $r = 2\cos 4\theta$ (Fig. 10.3.13)
20. $r = \sin 5\theta$ (Fig. 10.3.14)
21. $r^2 = 4\sin 2\theta$
22. $r^2 = 4\cos 2\theta$ (Fig. 10.3.15)
23. $r^2 = 4\sin\theta$
24. $r = 6\cos 6\theta$

FIGURE 10.3.14 The five-leaved rose of Problem 20.

FIGURE 10.3.15 The lemniscate of Problem 22.

In Problems 25 through 36, find the area of the region described.

25. Inside $r = 2\sin\theta$ and outside $r = 1$
26. Inside both $r = 4\cos\theta$ and $r = 2$
27. Inside both $r = \cos\theta$ and $r = \sqrt{3}\sin\theta$
28. Inside $r = 2 + \cos\theta$ and outside $r = 2$
29. Inside $r = 3 + 2\cos\theta$ and outside $r = 4$
30. Inside $r^2 = 2\cos 2\theta$ and outside $r = 1$
31. Inside $r^2 = \cos 2\theta$ and $r^2 = \sin 2\theta$ (Fig. 10.3.16)
32. Inside the large loop and outside the small loop of $r = 1 - 2\sin\theta$ (Fig. 10.3.17)

FIGURE 10.3.12 The three-leaved rose of Problem 18.

FIGURE 10.3.13 The eight-leaved rose of Problem 19.

FIGURE 10.3.16 Problem 31.

FIGURE 10.3.17 Problem 32.

33. Inside $r = 2(1 + \cos\theta)$ and outside $r = 1$
34. Inside the figure-eight curve $r^2 = 4\cos\theta$ and outside $r = 1 - \cos\theta$
35. Inside both $r = 2\cos\theta$ and $r = 2\sin\theta$
36. Inside $r = 2 + 2\sin\theta$ and outside $r = 2$
37. Find the area of the circle $r = \sin\theta + \cos\theta$ by integration in polar coordinates (Fig. 10.3.18). Check your answer by writing the equation of the circle in rectangular coordinates, finding its radius, and then using the familiar formula for the area of a circle.

FIGURE 10.3.18 The circle $r = \sin\theta + \cos\theta$ (Problem 37).

38. Find the area of the region that lies interior to all three circles $r = 1$, $r = 2\cos\theta$, and $r = 2\sin\theta$.
39. The *spiral of Archimedes*, shown in Fig. 10.3.19, has the simple equation $r = a\theta$ (a is a constant). Let A_n denote the area bounded by the nth turn of the spiral, where $2(n-1)\pi \leq \theta \leq 2n\pi$, and by the portion of the polar axis joining its endpoints. For each $n \geq 2$, let $R_n = A_n - A_{n-1}$

FIGURE 10.3.19 The spiral of Archimedes (Problem 39).

denote the area between the $(n-1)$th and the nth turns. Then derive the following results of Archimedes:

(a) $A_1 = \frac{1}{3}\pi(2\pi a)^2$; (b) $A_2 = \frac{7}{12}\pi(4\pi a)^2$;
(c) $R_2 = 6A_1$; (d) $R_{n+1} = nR_2$ for $n \geq 2$.

40. Two circles both have radius a, and each circle passes through the center of the other. Find the area of the region that lies within both circles.
41. A polar curve of the form $r = ae^{-k\theta}$ is called a *logarithmic spiral*, and the portion given by $2(n-1)\pi \leq \theta \leq 2n\pi$ is called the nth *turn* of this spiral. Figure 10.3.20 shows the first five turns of the logarithmic spiral $r = e^{-\theta/10}$, and the area of the region lying between the second and third turns is shaded. Find:

(a) The area of the region that lies between the first and second turns.

(b) The area of the region that lies between the $(n-1)$th and nth turns for $n > 1$.

FIGURE 10.3.20 The logarithmic spiral of Problem 41.

42. Figure 10.3.21 shows the first turn of the logarithmic spiral $r = 2e^{-\theta/10}$ together with the two circles, both centered at $(0, 0)$, through the endpoints of the spiral. Find the areas of the two shaded regions and verify that their sum is the area of the annular region between the two circles.

FIGURE 10.3.21 The two regions of Problem 42.

43. The shaded region R in Fig. 10.3.22 is bounded by the cardioid $r = 1 + \cos\theta$, the spiral $r = e^{-\theta/5}$, $0 \leq \theta \leq \pi$, and the spiral $r = e^{\theta/5}$, $-\pi \leq \theta \leq 0$. Graphically estimate the points of intersection of the cardioid and the spirals, then approximate the area of the region R.

FIGURE 10.3.22 The region of Problem 43.

FIGURE 10.3.23 The region of Problem 44.

44. The shaded region R in Fig. 10.3.23 lies inside both the cardioid $r = 3 + 3\sin\theta$ and the polar curve $r = 3 + \cos 4\theta$. Graphically estimate the points of intersection of the two curves; then approximate the area of the region R.

10.4 PARAMETRIC CURVES

Until now we have encountered *curves* mainly as graphs of equations. An equation of the form $y = f(x)$ or of the form $x = g(y)$ determines a curve by giving one of the coordinate variables explicitly as a function of the other. An equation of the form $F(x, y) = 0$ may also determine a curve, but then each variable is given implicitly as a function of the other.

Another important type of curve is the trajectory of a point moving in the coordinate plane. The motion of the point can be described by giving its position $(x(t), y(t))$ at time t. Such a description involves expressing both the rectangular-coordinate variables x and y as functions of a third variable, or *parameter*, t rather than as functions of one another. In this context a **parameter** is an independent variable (not a constant, as is sometimes meant in popular usage). This approach motivates the following definition.

DEFINITION Parametric Curve
A **parametric curve** C in the plane is a pair of functions

$$x = f(t), \quad y = g(t), \tag{1}$$

that give x and y as continuous functions of the real number t (the parameter) in some interval I.

Each value of the parameter t determines a point $(f(t), g(t))$, and the set of all such points is the **graph** of the curve C. Often the distinction between the curve—the pair of **coordinate functions** f and g—and the graph is not made. Therefore, we may refer interchangeably to the curve and to its graph when the context makes clear the intended meaning. The two equations in (1) are called the **parametric equations** of the curve.

The graph of a parametric curve may be sketched by plotting enough points to indicate its likely shape. In some cases we can eliminate the parameter t and thus obtain an equation in x and y. This equation may give us more information about the shape of the curve.

EXAMPLE 1 Determine the graph of the curve

$$x = \cos t, \quad y = \sin t, \quad 0 \leqq t \leqq 2\pi. \tag{2}$$

Solution Figure 10.4.1 shows a table of values of x and y that correspond to multiples of $\pi/4$ for the parameter t. These values give the eight points highlighted in Fig. 10.4.2, all of which lie on the unit circle. This suggests that the graph is, in fact, the unit circle. To verify this, we note that the fundamental identity of trigonometry gives

$$x^2 + y^2 = \cos^2 t + \sin^2 t \equiv 1,$$

so every point of the graph lies on the circle with equation $x^2 + y^2 = 1$. Conversely, the point of the circle with angular (polar) coordinate t is the point $(\cos t, \sin t)$ of the graph. Thus the graph is precisely the unit circle. ◆

t	x	y
0	1	0
$\pi/4$	$1/\sqrt{2}$	$1/\sqrt{2}$
$\pi/2$	0	1
$3\pi/4$	$-1/\sqrt{2}$	$1/\sqrt{2}$
π	-1	0
$5\pi/4$	$-1/\sqrt{2}$	$-1/\sqrt{2}$
$3\pi/2$	0	-1
$7\pi/4$	$1/\sqrt{2}$	$-1/\sqrt{2}$
2π	1	0

FIGURE 10.4.1 A table of values for Example 1.

FIGURE 10.4.2 The graph of the parametric functions of Example 1.

What is lost in the process in Example 1 is the information about how the graph is produced as t goes from 0 to 2π. But this is easy to determine by inspection. As t travels from 0 to 2π, the point $(\cos t, \sin t)$ begins at $(1, 0)$ and travels counterclockwise around the circle, ending at $(1, 0)$ when $t = 2\pi$.

A given figure in the plane may be the graph of different curves. To speak more loosely, a given curve may have different **parametrizations.**

EXAMPLE 2 The graph of the parametric curve

$$x = \frac{1-t^2}{1+t^2}, \quad y = \frac{2t}{1+t^2}, \quad -\infty < t < +\infty$$

also lies on the unit circle, because we find that $x^2 + y^2 = 1$ here as well. If t begins at 0 and increases, then the point $P(x(t), y(t))$ begins at $(1, 0)$ and travels along the upper half of the circle. If t begins at 0 and decreases, then the point $P(x(t), y(t))$ travels along the lower half of the circle. As t approaches either $+\infty$ or $-\infty$, the point P approaches the point $(-1, 0)$. Thus the graph consists of the unit circle with the single point $(-1, 0)$ deleted. A slight modification of the curve of Example 1,

$$x = \cos t, \quad y = \sin t, \quad -\pi < t < \pi,$$

is a different parametrization of this same graph. ◆

EXAMPLE 3 Eliminate the parameter to determine the graph of the parametric curve

$$x = t - 1, \quad y = 2t^2 - 4t + 1, \quad 0 \leq t \leq 2.$$

Solution We substitute $t = x + 1$ (from the equation for x) into the equation for y. This yields

$$y = 2(x+1)^2 - 4(x+1) + 1 = 2x^2 - 1$$

for $-1 \leq x \leq 1$. Thus the graph of the given curve is a portion of the parabola $y = 2x^2 - 1$ (Fig. 10.4.3). As t increases from 0 to 2, the point $(t - 1, 2t^2 - 4t + 1)$ travels along the parabola from $(-1, 1)$ to $(1, 1)$. ◆

FIGURE 10.4.3 The curve of Example 3 is part of a parabola.

REMARK The parabolic arc of Example 3 can be reparametrized with

$$x = \sin t, \quad y = 2\sin^2 t - 1.$$

Now, as t increases, the point $(\sin t, 2\sin^2 t - 1)$ travels back and forth along the parabola between the two points $(-1, 1)$ and $(1, 1)$, rather like the bob of a pendulum.

The parametric curve of Example 3 is one in which we can eliminate the parameter and thus obtain an explicit equation $y = f(x)$. Moreover, any explicitly presented curve $y = f(x)$ can be viewed as a parametric curve by writing

$$x = t, \quad y = f(t),$$

with the parameter t taking on values in the original domain of f. By contrast, the circle of Example 1 illustrates a parametric curve whose graph is not the graph of any single function. (Why not?) Example 4 exhibits another way in which parametric curves can differ from graphs of functions—they can have self-intersections.

EXAMPLE 4 The parametric equations

$$x = \cos at, \quad y = \sin bt$$

(with a and b constant) define the *Lissajous curves* that typically appear on oscilloscopes in physics and electronics laboratories. The Lissajous curve with $a = 3$ and $b = 5$ is shown in Fig. 10.4.4. You probably would not want to calculate and plot by hand enough points to produce a Lissajous curve. Figure 10.4.4 was plotted with a computer program that generated it almost immediately. But it is perhaps more instructive to watch a slower graphing calculator plot a parametric curve like this,

FIGURE 10.4.4 The Lissajous curve with $a = 3$, $b = 5$.

because the curve is traced by a point that moves on the screen as the parameter t increases (from 0 to 2π in this case). For instance, with a TI calculator set in "parametric graph mode," one need only enter and graph the equations

$$X_T = \cos(3T) \quad Y_T = \sin(5T)$$

on the interval $0 \leq t \leq 2\pi$. With *Maple* and *Mathematica* the commands

```
plot([cos(3*t),sin(5*t),t=0..2*pi]);
```

and

```
ParametricPlot[{Cos[3*t],Sin[5*t]},{t,0,2*Pi}];
```

(respectively) give the same figure. ◆

The use of parametric equations $x = x(t)$, $y = y(t)$ is most advantageous when elimination of the parameter is either impossible or would lead to an equation $y = f(x)$ that is considerably more complicated than the original parametric equations. This often happens when the curve is a geometric locus or the path of a point moving under specified conditions.

EXAMPLE 5 The curve traced by a point P on the edge of a rolling circle is called a **cycloid.** The circle rolls along a straight line without slipping or stopping. (You will see a cycloid if you watch a patch of bright paint on the tire of a bicycle that crosses your path.) Find parametric equations for the cycloid if the line along which the circle rolls is the x-axis, the circle is above the x-axis but always tangent to it, and the point P begins at the origin.

Solution Evidently the cycloid consists of a series of arches. We take as parameter t the angle (in radians) through which the circle has turned since it began with P at the origin. This is the angle TCP in Fig. 10.4.5.

FIGURE 10.4.5 The cycloid and the right triangle CPQ (Example 5).

The distance the circle has rolled is $|OT|$, so this is also the length of the circumference subtended by the angle TCP. Thus $|OT| = at$ if a is the radius of the circle, so the center C of the rolling circle has coordinates (at, a) when the angle TCP is t. The right triangle CPQ in Fig. 10.4.5 provides us with the relations

$$at - x = a\sin t \quad \text{and} \quad a - y = a\cos t.$$

Therefore the cycloid—the path of the moving point P—has parametric equations

$$x = a(t - \sin t), \quad y = a(1 - \cos t). \tag{3}$$

◆

FIGURE 10.4.6 A bead sliding down a wire—the brachistochrone problem.

HISTORICAL NOTE Figure 10.4.6 shows a bead sliding down a frictionless wire from point P to point Q. The *brachistochrone problem* asks what shape the wire should be to minimize the bead's time of descent from P to Q. In June of 1696, John Bernoulli proposed the brachistochrone problem as a public challenge, with a 6-month deadline (later extended to Easter 1697 at Leibniz's request). Isaac Newton, then retired from academic life and serving as Warden of the Mint in London, received Bernoulli's challenge on January 29, 1697. The very next day he communicated his own solution—the curve of minimal descent time is an arc of an inverted cycloid—to the Royal Society of London.

Lines Tangent to Parametric Curves

The parametric curve $x = f(t)$, $y = g(t)$ is called **smooth** if the derivatives $f'(t)$ and $g'(t)$ are continuous and never simultaneously zero. In some neighborhood of each point of its graph, a smooth parametric curve can be described in one or possibly both of the forms $y = F(x)$ and $x = G(y)$. To see why this is so, suppose (for example) that $f'(t) > 0$ on the interval I. Then $f(t)$ is an increasing function on I and therefore has an inverse function $t = \phi(x)$ there. If we substitute $t = \phi(x)$ into the equation $y = g(t)$, then we get

$$y = g(\phi(x)) = F(x).$$

We can use the chain rule to compute the slope dy/dx of the line tangent to a smooth parametric curve at a given point. Differentiating $y = F(x)$ with respect to t yields

$$\frac{dy}{dt} = \frac{dy}{dx} \cdot \frac{dx}{dt},$$

so

$$\frac{dy}{dx} = \frac{dy/dt}{dx/dt} = \frac{g'(t)}{f'(t)} \qquad (4)$$

at any point where $f'(t) \neq 0$. The tangent line is vertical at any point where $f'(t) = 0$ but $g'(t) \neq 0$.

Equation (4) gives $y' = dy/dx$ as a function of t. Another differentiation with respect to t, again with the aid of the chain rule, results in the formula

$$\frac{dy'}{dt} = \frac{dy'}{dx} \cdot \frac{dx}{dt},$$

so

$$\frac{d^2y}{dx^2} = \frac{dy'}{dx} = \frac{dy'/dt}{dx/dt}. \qquad (5)$$

EXAMPLE 6 Calculate dy/dx and d^2y/dx^2 for the cycloid with the parametric equations in (3).

Solution We begin with

$$x = a(t - \sin t), \quad y = a(1 - \cos t). \qquad (3)$$

Then Eq. (4) gives

$$\frac{dy}{dx} = \frac{dy/dt}{dx/dt} = \frac{a \sin t}{a(1 - \cos t)} = \frac{\sin t}{1 - \cos t}. \qquad (6)$$

This derivative is zero when y is an odd integral multiple of π, so the tangent line is horizontal at the midpoint of each arch of the cycloid. The endpoints of the arches correspond to even integral multiples of π, where both the numerator and the denominator in Eq. (6) are zero. These are isolated points (called *cusps*) at which the cycloid fails to be a smooth curve. (See Fig. 10.4.7.)

FIGURE 10.4.7 Horizontal tangents and cusps of the cycloid.

Next, Eq. (5) yields

$$\frac{d^2y}{dx^2} = \frac{(\cos t)(1-\cos t) - (\sin t)(\sin t)}{(1-\cos t)^2 \cdot a(1-\cos t)} = -\frac{1}{a(1-\cos t)^2}.$$

Because $d^2y/dx^2 < 0$ for all t (except for the isolated even integral multiples of π), this shows that each arch of the cycloid is concave downward (Fig. 10.4.5). ◆

REMARK In Fig. 10.4.7 it appears that the cycloid has a vertical tangent line at each cusp point $(2n\pi a, 0)$. We can verify this observation by calculating the limit as $t \to 2n\pi$ of the derivative in (6). Using l'Hôpital's rule, we get

$$\lim_{t \to 2n\pi} \frac{dy}{dx} = \lim_{t \to 2n\pi} \frac{\sin t}{1 - \cos t} = \lim_{t \to 2n\pi} \frac{\cos t}{\sin t} = \pm\infty,$$

because $\cos t \to 1$ and $\sin t \to 0$ as $t \to 2n\pi$. The limit is $+\infty$ or $-\infty$ according as t approaches $2n\pi$ from the right or the left. In either event, we conclude that the tangent line is, indeed, vertical at the cusp point.

EXAMPLE 7 It would be impractical to attempt to graph the curve

$$x^3 = 2y^6 - 5y^4 + 9y \tag{7}$$

by solving for y as a function of x. But we can parametrize this curve by defining

$$y = t, \quad x = (2t^6 - 5t^4 + 9t)^{1/3}. \tag{8}$$

FIGURE 10.4.8 The parametric curve of Example 7.

Figure 10.4.8 shows a computer plot of this parametric curve for $-2.5 \leq t \leq 2.5$. We see at least four likely critical and inflection points. It appears that there are horizontal tangent lines at the points P_1 and P_2 on the y-axis, and vertical tangent lines at P_3 and P_4. Let's investigate the character of these points by calculating the pertinent derivatives.

To investigate the possibility of horizontal and vertical tangent lines, we use Eq. (4) to calculate the first derivative

$$\frac{dy}{dx} = \frac{dy/dt}{dx/dt} = \frac{3(2t^6 - 5t^4 + 9t)^{2/3}}{12t^5 - 20t^3 + 9}. \tag{9}$$

Using a computer algebra system, we find that the only real zeros of the polynomial $2t^6 - 5t^4 + 9t$ in the numerator are $t = 0$ and $t \approx -1.8065$. These values of t yield the points $P_1(0, 0)$ and $P_2(-0.00002422, -1.86065)$, respectively, that are shown in the figure. Thus P_2 does not lie precisely on the y-axis, after all.

The denominator polynomial $12t^5 - 20t^3 + 9$ in (9) has only the single real zero $t \approx -2.5587$, which yields the single point $P_3(-2.5587, -1.3941)$ on the curve where the tangent line is vertical. In particular, there is *no* vertical tangent line near the point P_4 indicated in the figure.

To investigate the possibility of possible inflection points, we use Eq. (5) and a computer algebra system to calculate the second derivative

$$\frac{d^2y}{dx^2} = \frac{d}{dt}\left(\frac{dy}{dx}\right) \div \frac{dx}{dt}$$

$$= -\frac{6(2t^6 - 5t^4 + 9t)^{1/3}(36t^{10} - 150t^8 + 50t^6 + 594t^5 - 450t^3 - 81)}{(12t^5 - 20t^3 + 9)^3}. \tag{10}$$

The two trinomials that appear in the numerator and denominator here are the same as those in (9), and correspond to the three critical points already found. Our computer algebra system reports that the tenth-degree numerator polynomial in (10) has only two real zeros: $t \approx 1.0009$ and $t \approx -2.2614$. These two zeros of the second derivative yield the two points $P_4(1.8172, 1.0009)$ and $P_5(4.8820, -2.2614)$ that are shown in the figure. It is visually clear that the concavity of the curve changes at P_4—where $dy/dx \approx 0.9063$ so the tangent line is steep but not vertical—but the character of the remaining point is not so obvious. Nevertheless, you can graph the second derivative in (10) to verify that it is positive to the right and negative to the left of P_5—so this final candidate is, indeed, also an inflection point.

Finally, because our viewing window in Fig. 10.4.8 is large enough to include all the critical points and inflection points on the curve in (7)—and since it is clear from the equations in (8) that $|x|$ and $|y| \to \infty$ as $|t| \to \infty$—we are assured that the figure shows all of the principal features of the curve. ◆

Polar Curves as Parametric Curves

A curve given in polar coordinates by the equation $r = f(\theta)$ can be regarded as a parametric curve with parameter θ. To see this, we recall that the equations $x = r \cos\theta$ and $y = r \sin\theta$ allow us to change from polar to rectangular coordinates. We replace r with $f(\theta)$, and this gives the parametric equations

$$x = f(\theta) \cos\theta, \quad y = f(\theta) \sin\theta, \tag{11}$$

which express x and y in terms of the parameter θ.

EXAMPLE 8 The *spiral of Archimedes* has the polar-coordinate equation $r = a\theta$ (Fig. 10.4.9). The equations in (11) give the spiral the parametrization

$$x = a\theta \cos\theta, \quad y = a\theta \sin\theta.$$

◆

FIGURE 10.4.9 The spiral of Archimedes (Example 8).

The slope dy/dx of a tangent line can be computed in terms of polar coordinates as well as rectangular coordinates. Given a polar-coordinate curve $r = f(\theta)$, we use the parametrization shown in (11). Then Eq. (4), with θ in place of t, gives

$$\frac{dy}{dx} = \frac{dy/d\theta}{dx/d\theta} = \frac{f'(\theta) \sin\theta + f(\theta) \cos\theta}{f'(\theta) \cos\theta - f(\theta) \sin\theta}, \tag{12}$$

or, alternatively, denoting $f'(\theta)$ by r',

$$\frac{dy}{dx} = \frac{r'\sin\theta + r\cos\theta}{r'\cos\theta - r\sin\theta}. \tag{13}$$

Equation (13) has the following useful consequence. Let ψ denote the angle between the tangent line at P and the radius OP (extended) from the origin (Fig. 10.4.10). Then

$$\cot\psi = \frac{1}{r}\cdot\frac{dr}{d\theta} \quad (0 \leq \psi \leq \pi). \tag{14}$$

In Problem 32 we indicate how Eq. (14) can be derived from Eq. (13).

FIGURE 10.4.10 The interpretation of the angle ψ. [See Eq. (14).]

FIGURE 10.4.11 The angle ψ is always 45° for the logarithmic spiral (Example 9).

EXAMPLE 9 Consider the *logarithmic spiral* with polar equation $r = e^\theta$. Show that $\psi = \pi/4$ at every point of the spiral, and write an equation of its tangent line at the point $(e^{\pi/2}, \pi/2)$.

Solution Because $dr/d\theta = e^\theta$, Eq. (14) tells us that $\cot\psi = e^\theta/e^\theta = 1$. Thus $\psi = \pi/4$. When $\theta = \pi/2$, Eq. (13) gives

$$\frac{dy}{dx} = \frac{e^{\pi/2}\sin(\pi/2) + e^{\pi/2}\cos(\pi/2)}{e^{\pi/2}\cos(\pi/2) - e^{\pi/2}\sin(\pi/2)} = -1.$$

But when $\theta = \pi/2$, we have $x = 0$ and $y = e^{\pi/2}$. It follows that an equation of the desired tangent line is

$$y - e^{\pi/2} = -x; \quad \text{that is,} \quad x + y = e^{\pi/2}.$$

The line and the spiral appear in Fig. 10.4.11. ◆

10.4 TRUE/FALSE STUDY GUIDE

10.4 CONCEPTS: QUESTIONS AND DISCUSSION

1. Pick two points A and B in the plane. Then define a parametrization $P(t) = (x(t), y(t))$ of the line segment $\overline{AB}$ such that $P(0) = A$ and $P(1) = B$.
2. Pick two points A and B equidistant from the origin. Then define a parametrization of a circular arc AB such that $P(0) = A$ and $P(1) = B$.
3. Pick two points A and B on the parabola $y = x^2$. Then define a parametrization of the parabola such that $P(0) = A$ and $P(1) = B$.
4. Let A and B be two points on a given parametric curve. Is it always possible to define a parametrization of the curve such that $P(0) = A$ and $P(1) = B$?

10.4 PROBLEMS

In Problems 1 through 12, eliminate the parameter and then sketch the curve.

1. $x = t+1$, $y = 2t-1$
2. $x = t^2+1$, $y = 2t^2-1$
3. $x = t^2$, $y = t^3$
4. $x = \sqrt{t}$, $y = 3t-2$
5. $x = t+1$, $y = 2t^2-t-1$
6. $x = t^2+3t$, $y = t-2$
7. $x = e^t$, $y = 4e^{2t}$
8. $x = 2e^t$, $y = 2e^{-t}$
9. $x = 5\cos t$, $y = 3\sin t$
10. $x = \sinh t$, $y = \cosh t$
11. $x = 2\cosh t$, $y = 3\sinh t$
12. $x = \sec t$, $y = \tan t$

In Problems 13 through 16, first eliminate the parameter and sketch the curve. Then describe the motion of the point $(x(t), y(t))$ as t varies in the given interval.

13. $x = \sin 2\pi t$, $y = \cos 2\pi t$; $0 \leq t \leq 1$
14. $x = 3 + 2\cos t$, $y = 5 - 2\sin t$; $0 \leq t \leq 2\pi$
15. $x = \sin^2 \pi t$, $y = \cos^2 \pi t$; $0 \leq t \leq 2$
16. $x = \cos t$, $y = \sin^2 t$; $-\pi \leq t \leq \pi$

In Problems 17 through 20, (a) first write the equation of the line tangent to the given parametric curve at the point that corresponds to the given value of t, and (b) then calculate d^2y/dx^2 to determine whether the curve is concave upward or concave downward at this point.

17. $x = 2t^2+1$, $y = 3t^3+2$; $t = 1$
18. $x = \cos^3 t$, $y = \sin^3 t$; $t = \pi/4$
19. $x = t\sin t$, $y = t\cos t$; $t = \pi/2$
20. $x = e^t$, $y = e^{-t}$; $t = 0$

In Problems 21 through 24, find the angle ψ between the radius OP and the tangent line at the point P that corresponds to the given value of θ.

21. $r = \exp(\theta\sqrt{3})$, $\theta = \pi/2$
22. $r = 1/\theta$, $\theta = 1$
23. $r = \sin 3\theta$, $\theta = \pi/6$
24. $r = 1 - \cos\theta$, $\theta = \pi/3$

In Problems 25 through 28, find

(a) *The points on the curve where the tangent line is horizontal.*
(b) *The slope of each tangent line at any point where the curve intersects the x-axis.*

25. $x = t^2$, $y = t^3 - 3t$ (Fig. 10.4.12)
26. $x = \sin t$, $y = \sin 2t$ (Fig. 10.4.13)
27. $r = 1 + \cos\theta$
28. $r^2 = 4\cos 2\theta$ (See Fig. 10.3.15.)

FIGURE 10.4.12 The curve of Problem 25.

FIGURE 10.4.13 The curve of Problem 26.

29. The curve C is determined by the parametric equations $x = e^{-t}$, $y = e^{2t}$. Calculate dy/dx and d^2y/dx^2 directly from these parametric equations. Conclude that C is concave upward at every point. Then sketch C.

30. The graph of the folium of Descartes with rectangular equation $x^3 + y^3 = 3xy$ appears in Fig. 10.4.14. Parametrize its loop as follows: Let P be the point of intersection of the line $y = tx$ with the loop; then solve for the coordinates x and y of P in terms of t.

FIGURE 10.4.14 The loop of the folium of Descartes (Problem 30).

31. Parametrize the parabola $y^2 = 4px$ by expressing x and y as functions of the slope m of the tangent line at the point $P(x, y)$ of the parabola.

32. Let P be a point of the curve with polar equation $r = f(\theta)$, and let ψ be the angle between the extended radius OP and the tangent line at P. Let α be the angle of inclination of this tangent line, measured counterclockwise from the horizontal. Then $\psi = \alpha - \theta$. Verify Eq. (14) by substituting $\tan\alpha = dy/dx$ from Eq. (13) and $\tan\theta = y/x = (\sin\theta)/(\cos\theta)$ into the identity

$$\cot\psi = \frac{1}{\tan(\alpha - \theta)} = \frac{1 + \tan\alpha \tan\theta}{\tan\alpha - \tan\theta}.$$

33. Let P_0 be the highest point of the circle of Fig. 10.4.5—the circle that generates the cycloid of Example 5. Show that the line through P_0 and the point P of the cycloid (the point P is shown in Fig. 10.4.5) is tangent to the cycloid at P. This fact gives a geometric construction of the line tangent to the cycloid.

34. A circle of radius b rolls without slipping inside a circle of radius $a > b$. The path of a point fixed on the circumference of the rolling circle is called a *hypocycloid* (Fig. 10.4.15). Let P begin its journey at $A(a, 0)$ and let t be the angle AOC, where O is the center of the large circle and C is the center of the rolling circle. Show that the coordinates of P are given by the parametric equations

$$x = (a - b)\cos t + b\cos\left(\frac{a-b}{b}t\right),$$

$$y = (a - b)\sin t - b\sin\left(\frac{a-b}{b}t\right).$$

FIGURE 10.4.15 The hypocycloid of Problem 34.

35. If $b = a/4$ in Problem 34, show that the parametric equations of the hypocycloid reduce to

$$x = a\cos^3 t, \qquad y = a\sin^3 t.$$

36. (a) Prove that the hypocycloid of Problem 35 is the graph of the equation

$$x^{2/3} + y^{2/3} = a^{2/3}.$$

(b) Find all points of this hypocycloid where its tangent line is either horizontal or vertical, and find the intervals on which it is concave upward and those on which it is concave downward. (c) Sketch this hypocycloid.

37. Consider a point P on the spiral of Archimedes, the curve shown in Fig. 10.4.16 with polar equation $r = a\theta$.

FIGURE 10.4.16 The segment PQ is tangent to the spiral (a result of Archimedes; see Problem 37).

Archimedes viewed the path of P as compounded of two motions, one with speed a directly away from the origin O and another a circular motion with unit angular speed around O. This suggests Archimedes' result that the line PQ in the figure is tangent to the spiral at P. Prove that this is indeed true.

38. (a) Deduce from Eq. (6) that if t is not an integral multiple of 2π, then the slope of the tangent line at the corresponding point of the cycloid is $\cot(t/2)$. (b) Conclude that at the cusp of the cycloid where t is an integral multiple of 2π, the cycloid has a vertical tangent line.

39. A *loxodrome* is a curve $r = f(\theta)$ such that the tangent line at P and the radius OP in Fig. 10.4.10 make a constant angle. Use Eq. (14) to prove that every loxodrome is of the form $r = Ae^{k\theta}$, where A and k are constants. Thus every loxodrome is a logarithmic spiral similar to the one considered in Example 9.

40. Let a curve be described in polar coordinates by $r = f(\theta)$ where f is continuous. If $f(\alpha) = 0$, then the origin is the point of the curve corresponding to $\theta = \alpha$. Deduce from the parametrization $x = f(\theta)\cos\theta$, $y = f(\theta)\sin\theta$ that the line tangent to the curve at this point makes the angle α with the positive x-axis. For example, the cardioid $r = f(\theta) = 1 - \sin\theta$ shown in Fig. 10.4.17 is tangent to the y-axis at the origin. And, indeed, $f(\pi/2) = 0$. The y-axis is the line $\theta = \alpha = \pi/2$.

FIGURE 10.4.17 The cardioid of Problem 40.

41. Use the technique of Problem 30 to parametrize the first-quadrant loop of the folium-like curve $x^5 + y^5 = 5x^2y^2$.

42. A line segment of length $2a$ has one endpoint constrained to lie on the x-axis and the other endpoint constrained to lie on the y-axis, but its endpoints are free to move along those axes. As they do so, its midpoint sweeps out a locus in the xy-plane. Obtain a rectangular-coordinate equation of this locus and thereby identify this curve.

In Problems 43–46, investigate (as in Example 7) the given curve and construct a sketch that shows all the critical points and inflection points on it.

43. $x = y^3 - 3y^2 + 1$

44. $x = y^4 - 3y^3 + 5y$

45. $x^3 = y^5 - 5y^3 + 4$

46. $x^5 = 5y^6 - 17y^3 + 13y$

10.4 Project: Trochoid Investigations

A *trochoid* is traced by a point P on a spoke of a wheel of radius a as it rolls along the x-axis. If the distance of P from the center of the rolling wheel is $b > 0$, show that the trochoid is described by the parametric equations

$$x = at - b\sin t, \qquad y = a - b\cos t.$$

FIGURE 10.4.18 The trochoid with $a = 2$ and $b = 4$.

Note that the trochoid is a familiar cycloid if $b = a$. We allow the possibility that $b > a$. Figure 10.4.18 shows the trochoid with $a = 2$ and $b = 4$. Experiment with different values of a and b. What determines whether the trochoid has loops, cusps, or neither?

Hypotrochoids

A hypotrochoid is to a hypocycloid (Problem 34) as a trochoid is to a cycloid. Thus a hypotrochoid is traced by a point P on a spoke of a wheel of radius b as it rolls around inside a circle of radius a. If the distance of P from the center of the rolling wheel is $c > 0$, show that the hypotrochoid is described by the parametric equations

$$x = (a-b)\cos t + c\cos\left(\frac{a-b}{b}t\right), \qquad y = (a-b)\sin t - c\sin\left(\frac{a-b}{b}t\right).$$

FIGURE 10.4.19 The hypotrochoid with $a = 10$, $b = 2$, $c = 4$.

FIGURE 10.4.20 The hypotrochoid with $a = 10$, $b = 4$, $c = 2$.

Note that the hypotrochoid is a hypocycloid if $c = b$. There are a number of different ways a hypotrochoid can look. Figures 10.4.19 and 10.4.20 illustrate two possibilities. Experiment with different values of a, b, and c. What determines whether the trochoid has loops, cusps, or neither? If there are loops, what determines how many there are? Does a hypotrochoid always repeat itself after a finite number of turns around the origin? What happens if a is an integer but b is an irrational number?

Epitrochoids

An *epitrochoid* is generated in the same way as a hypotrochoid, except now the small circle rolls around on the outside of the large circle. With the same notation otherwise, show that the epitrochoid is described by the parametric equations

$$x = (a+b)\cos t - c\cos\left(\frac{a+b}{b}t\right), \qquad y = (a+b)\sin t - c\sin\left(\frac{a+b}{b}t\right).$$

FIGURE 10.4.21 The epitrochoid with $a = 10$, $b = 2$, $c = 2$.

If $b = c$—so the point P lies on the rim of the rolling circle, then the epitrochoid is an *epicycloid* (illustrated in Fig. 10.4.21). Experiment with different values of a, b, and c, and investigate for epitrochoids the same questions posed previously for hypotrochoids.

10.5 INTEGRAL COMPUTATIONS WITH PARAMETRIC CURVES

In Chapter 6 we discussed the computation of a variety of geometric quantities associated with the graph $y = f(x)$ of a nonnegative function on the interval $[a, b]$. These included the following.

- The area under the curve:

$$A = \int_a^b y\, dx. \tag{1}$$

- The volume of revolution around the x-axis:

$$V_x = \int_a^b \pi y^2\, dx. \tag{2a}$$

- The volume of revolution around the y-axis:

$$V_y = \int_a^b 2\pi xy\, dx. \tag{2b}$$

- The arc length of the curve:

$$s = \int_0^s ds = \int_a^b \sqrt{1 + (dy/dx)^2}\, dx. \tag{3}$$

- The area of the surface of revolution around the x-axis:

$$S_x = \int_{x=a}^b 2\pi y\, ds. \tag{4a}$$

- The area of the surface of revolution around the y-axis:

$$S_y = \int_{x=a}^b 2\pi x\, ds. \tag{4b}$$

We substitute $y = f(x)$ into each of these integrals before we integrate from $x = a$ to $x = b$.

We now want to compute these same quantities for a smooth parametric curve

$$x = f(t), \quad y = g(t), \quad \alpha \leq t \leq \beta. \tag{5}$$

The area, volume, arc length, and surface integrals in Eqs. (1) through (4) can then be evaluated by making the formal substitutions

$$\begin{aligned} x &= f(t), & y &= g(t), \\ dx &= f'(t)\, dt, & dy &= g'(t)\, dt, \quad \text{and} \\ ds &= \sqrt{[f'(t)]^2 + [g'(t)]^2}\, dt. \end{aligned} \tag{6}$$

The infinitesimal "right triangle" in Fig. 10.5.1 serves as a convenient device for remembering the latter substitution for ds. The Pythagorean theorem then leads to the symbolic manipulation

FIGURE 10.5.1 Nearly a right triangle for dx and dy close to zero.

$$ds = \sqrt{dx^2 + dy^2} = \sqrt{\left(\frac{dx}{dt}\right)^2 + \left(\frac{dy}{dt}\right)^2}\, dt = \sqrt{[f'(t)]^2 + [g'(t)]^2}\, dt. \tag{7}$$

It simplifies the discussion to assume that the graph of the parametric curve in (5) resembles Fig. 10.5.2, in which $y = g(t) \geq 0$ and $x = f(t)$ is either increasing on

654 CHAPTER 10 Polar Coordinates and Parametric Curves

the entire interval $\alpha \leq t \leq \beta$ or is decreasing there. The two parts of Fig. 10.5.2 illustrate the two possibilities—whether as t increases the curve is traced in the positive x-direction from left to right, or in the negative x-direction from right to left. How and whether to take this direction of motion into account depends on which integral we are computing.

CASE 1 *Area and Volume of Revolution* To evaluate the integrals in (1) and (2), which involve dx, we integrate *either* from $t = \alpha$ to $t = \beta$ or from $t = \beta$ to $t = \alpha$—the proper choice of limits on t being the one that corresponds to traversing the curve in the positive x-direction *from left to right.* Specifically,

$$A = \int_\alpha^\beta g(t) f'(t)\, dt \quad \text{if } f(\alpha) < f(\beta),$$

whereas

$$A = \int_\beta^\alpha g(t) f'(t)\, dt \quad \text{if } f(\beta) < f(\alpha).$$

The validity of this method of evaluating the integrals in Eqs. (1) and (2) follows from Theorem 1 of Section 5.7, on integration by substitution.

CASE 2 *Arc Length and Surface Area* To evaluate the integrals in (3) and (4), which involve ds rather than dx, we integrate from $t = \alpha$ to $t = \beta$ irrespective of the direction of motion along the curve. To see why this is so, recall from Eq. (4) of Section 10.4 that $dy/dx = g'(t)/f'(t)$ if $f'(t) \neq 0$ on $[\alpha, \beta]$. Hence

$$s = \int_a^b \sqrt{1 + \left(\frac{dy}{dx}\right)^2}\, dx = \int_{f^{-1}(a)}^{f^{-1}(b)} \sqrt{1 + \left[\frac{g'(t)}{f'(t)}\right]^2}\, f'(t)\, dt.$$

Assuming that $f'(t) > 0$ if $f(\alpha) = a$ and $f(\beta) = b$, whereas $f'(t) < 0$ if $f(\alpha) = b$ and $f(\beta) = a$, it follows in either event that

$$s = \int_\alpha^\beta \sqrt{1 + \left[\frac{g'(t)}{f'(t)}\right]^2}\, |f'(t)|\, dt,$$

and so

$$s = \int_\alpha^\beta \sqrt{[f'(t)]^2 + [g'(t)]^2}\, dt = \int_\alpha^\beta \sqrt{\left(\frac{dx}{dt}\right)^2 + \left(\frac{dy}{dt}\right)^2}\, dt. \tag{8}$$

This formula, derived under the assumption that $f'(t) \neq 0$ on $[\alpha, \beta]$, may be taken to be the *definition* of arc length for an arbitrary smooth parametric curve. Similarly, the area of a surface of revolution is defined for smooth parametric curves as the result of first substituting Eq. (6) into Eq. (4a) or (4b) and then integrating from $t = \alpha$ to $t = \beta$.

EXAMPLE 1 Use the parametrization $x = a\cos t$, $y = a\sin t$ ($0 \leq t \leq 2\pi$) of the circle with center $(0, 0)$ and radius a to find (a) the area A of this circle; (b) the volume V of the sphere obtained by revolving the circle around the x-axis; and (c) the surface area S of this sphere.

Solution (a) The left-to-right direction along the quarter circle shown in Fig. 10.5.3 is from $t = \pi/2$ to $t = 0$, and $dx = -a\sin t\, dt$. Therefore Eq. (1) and multiplication

FIGURE 10.5.2 Tracing a parametrized curve: (a) $f(t)$ increasing; (b) $f(t)$ decreasing.

FIGURE 10.5.3 The quarter-circle of Example 1.

by 4 give

$$A = 4\int_{t=\pi/2}^{0} y\,dx = 4\int_{\pi/2}^{0} (a\sin t)(-a\sin t)\,dt$$

$$= 4a^2 \int_0^{\pi/2} \sin^2 t\,dt = 2a^2 \int_0^{\pi/2} (1 - \cos 2t)\,dt$$

$$= 2a^2 \left[t - \frac{1}{2}\sin 2t \right]_0^{\pi/2} = 2a^2 \cdot \frac{\pi}{2} = \pi a^2$$

for yet another derivation of the familiar formula $A = \pi a^2$ for the area of a circle of radius a.

(b) To calculate the volume of the sphere, we apply Eq. (2a) and double to get

$$V = 2\int_{t=\pi/2}^{0} \pi y^2\,dx$$

$$= 2\int_{\pi/2}^{0} \pi(a\sin t)^2(-a\sin t\,dt) = 2\pi a^3 \int_0^{\pi/2} (1 - \cos^2 t)\sin t\,dt$$

$$= 2\pi a^3 \left[-\cos t + \frac{1}{3}\cos^3 t \right]_0^{\pi/2} = \frac{4}{3}\pi a^3.$$

(c) To find the surface area of the sphere, we calculate first the arc-length differential

$$ds = \sqrt{(-a\sin t)^2 + (a\cos t)^2}\,dt = a\,dt$$

of the parametrized curve. Then Eq. (4a) gives

$$S = 2\int_{t=0}^{\pi/2} 2\pi y\,ds = 2\int_0^{\pi/2} 2\pi(a\sin t)\cdot a\,dt$$

$$= 4\pi a^2 \int_0^{\pi/2} \sin t\,dt = 4\pi a^2 \left[-\cos t \right]_0^{\pi/2} = 4\pi a^2. \quad\blacklozenge$$

Of course, the results of Example 1 are familiar. In contrast, Example 2 requires the methods of this section.

EXAMPLE 2 Find the area under, and the arc length of, the cycloidal arch of Fig. 10.5.4. Its parametric equations are

$$x = a(t - \sin t), \quad y = a(1 - \cos t), \quad 0 \leqq t \leqq 2\pi.$$

FIGURE 10.5.4 The cycloidal arch of Example 2.

Solution Because $dx = a(1 - \cos t)\,dt$ and the left-to-right direction along the curve is from $t = 0$ to $t = 2\pi$, Eq. (1) gives

$$A = \int_{t=0}^{2\pi} y\,dx$$

$$= \int_0^{2\pi} a(1 - \cos t) \cdot a(1 - \cos t)\,dt = a^2 \int_0^{2\pi} (1 - \cos t)^2\,dt$$

for the area. Now we use the half-angle identity

$$1 - \cos t = 2\sin^2\left(\frac{t}{2}\right)$$

and a consequence of Problem 58 in Section 8.3:

$$\int_0^{\pi} \sin^{2n} u\,du = \pi \cdot \frac{1}{2} \cdot \frac{3}{4} \cdot \frac{5}{6} \cdots \frac{2n-1}{2n}.$$

We thereby get

$$A = 4a^2 \int_0^{2\pi} \sin^4\left(\frac{t}{2}\right) dt = 8a^2 \int_0^{\pi} \sin^4 u\, du \qquad \left(u = \frac{t}{2}\right)$$

$$= 8a^2 \cdot \pi \cdot \frac{1}{2} \cdot \frac{3}{4} = 3\pi a^2$$

for the area under one arch of the cycloid. The arc-length differential is

$$ds = \sqrt{a^2(1-\cos t)^2 + (a \sin t)^2}\, dt$$

$$= a\sqrt{2(1-\cos t)}\, dt = 2a \sin\left(\frac{t}{2}\right) dt,$$

so Eq. (3) gives

$$s = \int_0^{2\pi} 2a \sin\frac{t}{2}\, dt = \left[-4a \cos\frac{t}{2}\right]_0^{2\pi} = 8a$$

for the length of one arch of the cycloid. ◆

Parametric Polar Coordinates

Suppose that a parametric curve is determined by giving its polar coordinates

$$r = r(t), \qquad \theta = \theta(t), \qquad \alpha \leq t \leq \beta$$

as functions of the parameter t. Then this curve is described in rectangular coordinates by the parametric equations

$$x(t) = r(t) \cos \theta(t), \qquad y(t) = r(t) \sin \theta(t), \qquad \alpha \leq t \leq \beta,$$

giving x and y as functions of t. The latter parametric equations may then be used in the integral formulas in Eqs. (1) through (4).

To compute ds, we first calculate the derivatives

$$\frac{dx}{dt} = (\cos \theta)\frac{dr}{dt} - (r \sin \theta)\frac{d\theta}{dt}, \qquad \frac{dy}{dt} = (\sin \theta)\frac{dr}{dt} + (r \cos \theta)\frac{d\theta}{dt}.$$

Upon substituting these expressions for dx/dt and dy/dt in Eq. (8) and making algebraic simplifications, we find that the arc-length differential in parametric polar coordinates is

$$ds = \sqrt{\left(\frac{dr}{dt}\right)^2 + \left(r\frac{d\theta}{dt}\right)^2}\, dt. \tag{9}$$

In the case of a curve with the explicit polar-coordinate equation $r = f(\theta)$, we may use θ itself as the parameter. Then Eq. (9) takes the simpler form

$$ds = \sqrt{\left(\frac{dr}{d\theta}\right)^2 + r^2}\, d\theta. \tag{10}$$

The formula $ds = \sqrt{(dr)^2 + (r\, d\theta)^2}$, equivalent to Eq. (9), is easy to remember with the aid of the tiny "almost-triangle" shown in Fig. 10.5.5.

EXAMPLE 3 Find the perimeter (arc length) s of the cardioid with polar equation $r = 1 + \cos \theta$ (Fig. 10.5.6.). Find also the surface area S generated by revolving the cardioid around the x-axis.

Solution Because $dr/d\theta = -\sin \theta$, Eq. (10) and the identity

$$1 + \cos \theta = 2 \cos^2\left(\frac{\theta}{2}\right) \tag{11}$$

FIGURE 10.5.5 The differential triangle in polar coordinates.

FIGURE 10.5.6 The cardioid of Example 3.

give

$$ds = \sqrt{(-\sin\theta)^2 + (1+\cos\theta)^2}\,d\theta = \sqrt{2(1+\cos\theta)}\,d\theta$$

$$= \sqrt{4\cos^2\left(\frac{\theta}{2}\right)}\,d\theta = \left|2\cos\left(\frac{\theta}{2}\right)\right|d\theta.$$

Hence $ds = 2\cos(\theta/2)\,d\theta$ on the upper half of the cardioid, where $0 \leq \theta \leq \pi$, and thus $\cos(\theta/2) \geq 0$. Therefore

$$s = 2\int_0^\pi 2\cos\frac{\theta}{2}\,d\theta = 8\left[\sin\frac{\theta}{2}\right]_0^\pi = 8.$$

The surface area of revolution around the x-axis (Fig. 10.5.7) is given by

$$S = \int_{\theta=0}^\pi 2\pi y\,ds$$

$$= \int_{\theta=0}^\pi 2\pi (r\sin\theta)\,ds = \int_0^\pi 2\pi(1+\cos\theta)(\sin\theta)\cdot 2\cos\left(\frac{\theta}{2}\right)d\theta$$

$$= 16\pi \int_0^\pi \cos^4\frac{\theta}{2}\sin\frac{\theta}{2}\,d\theta = 16\pi\left[-\frac{2}{5}\cos^5\frac{\theta}{2}\right]_0^\pi = \frac{32\pi}{5},$$

using the identity

$$\sin\theta = 2\sin\left(\frac{\theta}{2}\right)\cos\left(\frac{\theta}{2}\right)$$

as well as the identity in Eq. (11). ◆

FIGURE 10.5.7 The surface generated by rotating the cardioid around the x-axis.

10.5 TRUE/FALSE STUDY GUIDE

10.5 CONCEPTS: QUESTIONS AND DISCUSSION

1. If the circle of radius a is parametrized by $x = a\cos t$, $y = a\sin t$ as in Example 1, explain carefully why the integral

$$\int_{t=0}^{2\pi} y\,dx = \int_{t=0}^\pi y\,dx + \int_{t=\pi}^{2\pi} y\,dx$$

does *not* give the correct area of the circle. Relate the two integrals on the right to the upper and lower halves of the circle.

2. If the circle of radius a is parametrized by $x = a\sin\pi t$, $y = a\cos\pi t$, explain carefully why the integral

$$\int_{t=0}^2 y\,dx = \int_{t=0}^{1/2} y\,dx + \int_{t=1/2}^{3/2} y\,dx + \int_{t=3/2}^2 y\,dx$$

does give the correct area. Relate the three integrals on the right to appropriate parts of the circular area.

10.5 PROBLEMS

In Problems 1 through 6, find the area of the region that lies between the given parametric curve and the x-axis.

1. $x = t^3$, $y = 2t^2 + 1$; $-1 \leq t \leq 1$
2. $x = e^{3t}$, $y = e^{-t}$; $0 \leq t \leq \ln 2$
3. $x = \cos t$, $y = \sin^2 t$; $0 \leq t \leq \pi$
4. $x = 2 - 3t$, $y = e^{2t}$; $0 \leq t \leq 1$
5. $x = \cos t$, $y = e^t$; $0 \leq t \leq \pi$
6. $x = 1 - e^t$, $y = 2t + 1$; $0 \leq t \leq 1$

In Problems 7 through 10, find the volume obtained by revolving around the x-axis the region described in the given problem.

7. Problem 1
8. Problem 2
9. Problem 3
10. Problem 5

In Problems 11 through 16, find the arc length of the given curve.

11. $x = 2t$, $y = \frac{2}{3}t^{3/2}$; $5 \leq t \leq 12$
12. $x = \frac{1}{2}t^2$, $y = \frac{1}{3}t^3$; $0 \leq t \leq 1$

13. $x = \sin t - \cos t$, $y = \sin t + \cos t$; $\frac{1}{4}\pi \leq t \leq \frac{1}{2}\pi$

14. $x = e^t \sin t$, $y = e^t \cos t$; $0 \leq t \leq \pi$

15. $r = e^{\theta/2}$; $0 \leq \theta \leq 4\pi$

16. $r = \theta$; $2\pi \leq \theta \leq 4\pi$

In Problems 17 through 22, find the area of the surface of revolution generated by revolving the given curve around the indicated axis.

17. $x = 1 - t$, $y = 2\sqrt{t}$, $1 \leq t \leq 4$; the x-axis

18. $x = 2t^2 + t^{-1}$, $y = 8\sqrt{t}$, $1 \leq t \leq 2$; the x-axis

19. $x = t^3$, $y = 2t + 3$, $-1 \leq t \leq 1$; the y-axis

20. $x = 2t + 1$, $y = t^2 + t$, $0 \leq t \leq 3$; the y-axis

21. $r = 4 \sin \theta$, $0 \leq \theta \leq \pi$; the x-axis

22. $r = e^\theta$, $0 \leq \theta \leq \frac{1}{2}\pi$; the y-axis

23. Find the volume generated by revolving around the x-axis the region under the cycloidal arch of Example 2.

24. Find the area of the surface generated by revolving around the x-axis the cycloidal arch of Example 2.

25. Use the parametrization $x = a \cos t$, $y = b \sin t$ to find: (a) the area bounded by the ellipse $x^2/a^2 + y^2/b^2 = 1$; (b) the volume of the ellipsoid generated by revolving this ellipse around the x-axis.

26. Find the area bounded by the loop of the parametric curve $x = t^2$, $y = t^3 - 3t$ of Problem 25 in Section 10.4.

27. Use the parametrization $x = t \cos t$, $y = t \sin t$ of the Archimedean spiral to find the arc length of the first full turn of this spiral (corresponding to $0 \leq t \leq 2\pi$).

28. The circle $(x - b)^2 + y^2 = a^2$ with radius $a < b$ and center $(b, 0)$ can be parametrized by

$$x = b + a \cos t, \quad y = a \sin t, \quad 0 \leq t \leq 2\pi.$$

Find the surface area of the torus obtained by revolving this circle around the y-axis (Fig. 10.5.8).

FIGURE 10.5.8 The torus of Problem 28.

29. The *astroid* (four-cusped hypocycloid) has equation $x^{2/3} + y^{2/3} = a^{2/3}$ (Fig. 10.4.15) and the parametrization

$$x = a \cos^3 t, \quad y = a \sin^3 t, \quad 0 \leq t \leq 2\pi.$$

Find the area of the region bounded by the astroid.

30. Find the total length of the astroid of Problem 29.

31. Find the area of the surface obtained by revolving the astroid of Problem 29 around the x-axis.

32. Find the area of the surface generated by revolving the lemniscate $r^2 = 2a^2 \cos 2\theta$ around the y-axis (Fig. 10.5.9). [*Suggestion:* Use Eq. (10); note that $r \, dr = -2a^2 \sin 2\theta \, d\theta$.]

FIGURE 10.5.9 The surface generated by rotating the lemniscate of Problem 32 around the y-axis.

33. Figure 10.5.10 shows the graph of the parametric curve

$$x = t^2\sqrt{3}, \quad y = 3t - \frac{1}{3}t^3.$$

The shaded region is bounded by the part of the curve for which $-3 \leq t \leq 3$. Find its area.

FIGURE 10.5.10 The parametric curve of Problems 33 through 36.

34. Find the arc length of the loop of the curve of Problem 33.

35. Find the volume of the solid obtained by revolving around the x-axis the shaded region in Fig. 10.5.10.

36. Find the surface area of revolution generated by revolving around the x-axis the loop of Fig. 10.5.10.

37. (a) With reference to Problem 30 and Fig. 10.4.14 in Section 10.4, show that the arc length of the first-quadrant loop of the folium of Descartes is

$$s = 6 \int_0^1 \frac{\sqrt{1 + 4t^2 - 4t^3 - 4t^5 + 4t^6 + t^8}}{(1 + t^3)^2} \, dt.$$

(b) Use a programmable calculator or a computer to approximate this length.

38. Find the surface area generated by rotating around the y-axis the cycloidal arch of Example 2. [*Suggestion:* $\sqrt{x^2} = x$ only if $x \geq 0$.]

39. Find the volume generated by rotating around the y-axis the region under the cycloidal arch of Example 2.

40. Suppose that after a string is wound clockwise around a circle of radius a, its free end is at the point $A(a, 0)$. (See Fig. 10.5.11.) Now the string is unwound, always stretched tight so the unwound portion TP is tangent to the circle at T. The locus of the string's free endpoint P is called the **involute** of the circle.
  (a) Show that the parametric equations of the involute (in terms of the angle t of Fig. 10.5.11) are
  $$x = a(\cos t + t \sin t), \quad y = a(\sin t - t \cos t).$$
  (b) Find the length of the involute from $t = 0$ to $t = \pi$.

FIGURE 10.5.11 The involute of a circle.

41. Suppose that the circle of Problem 40 is a water tank and the "string" is a rope of length πa. It is anchored at the point B opposite A. Figure 10.5.12 depicts the total area that can be grazed by a cow tied to the free end of the rope. Find this total area. (The three labeled arcs of the curve in the figure represent, respectively, an involute APQ generated as the cow unwinds the rope in the counterclockwise direction, a semicircle QR of radius πa centered at B, and an involute RSA generated as the cow winds the rope around the tank proceeding in the counterclockwise direction from B to A. These three arcs form a closed curve that resembles a cardioid, and the cow can reach every point that lies inside this curve and outside the original circle.)

FIGURE 10.5.12 The area that the cow of Problem 41 can graze.

42. Now suppose that the rope of the previous problem has length $2\pi a$ and is anchored at the point A before being wound completely around the tank. Now find the total area that the cow can graze. Figure 10.5.13 shows an involute APQ, a semicircle QR of radius $2\pi a$ centered at A, and an involute RSA. The cow can reach every point that lies inside the outer curve and outside the original circle.

FIGURE 10.5.13 The area that the cow of Problem 42 can graze.

In Problems 43 through 54, use a graphing calculator or computer algebra system as appropriate. Approximate (by integrating numerically) the desired quantity if it cannot be calculated exactly.

43. Find the total arc length of the 3-leaved rose $r = 3 \sin 3\theta$ of Fig. 10.3.12.

44. Find the total surface area generated by rotating around the y-axis the 3-leaved rose of Problem 43.

45. Find the total length of the 4-leaved rose $r = 2 \cos 2\theta$ of Fig. 10.2.12.

46. Find the total surface area generated by revolving around the x-axis the 4-leaved rose of Problem 45.

47. Find the total arc length of the limaçon (both loops) $r = 5 + 9 \cos \theta$ of Fig. 10.2.25.

48. Find the total surface area generated by revolving around the x-axis the limaçon of Problem 47.

49. Find the total arc length (all seven loops) of the polar curve $r = \cos(\frac{7}{3}\theta)$ of Fig. 10.5.14.

FIGURE 10.5.14 The curve $r = \cos(\frac{7}{3}\theta)$ of Problem 49.

50. Find the total arc length of the figure-8 curve $x = \sin t$, $y = \sin 2t$ of Fig. 10.4.13.

51. Find the total surface area and volume generated by revolving around the x-axis the figure-8 curve of Problem 50.

52. Find the total surface area and volume generated by revolving around the y-axis the figure-8 curve of Problem 50.

53. Find the total arc length of the Lissajous curve $x = \cos 3t$, $y = \sin 5t$ of Fig. 10.4.4.

54. Find the total arc length of the epitrochoid $x = 8\cos t - 5\cos 4t$, $y = 8\sin t - 5\sin 4t$ of Fig. 10.5.15.

55. Frank A. Farris of Santa Clara University, while designing a computer laboratory exercise for his calculus students, discovered an extremely lovely curve with the parametrization

$$x(t) = \cos t + \tfrac{1}{2}\cos 7t + \tfrac{1}{3}\sin 17t,$$
$$y(t) = \sin t + \tfrac{1}{2}\sin 7t + \tfrac{1}{3}\cos 17t.$$

For information on what these equations represent, see his article "Wheels on Wheels on Wheels—Surprising Symmetry" in the June 1996 issue of *Mathematics Magazine*. Plot these equations so you can enjoy this extraordinary figure, then numerically integrate to approximate the length of its graph. What kind of symmetry does the graph have? Is this predictable from the coefficients of t in the parametric equations?

FIGURE 10.5.15 The epitrochoid of Problem 54.

10.5 Project: Moon Orbits and Race Tracks

The investigations in this project call for the use of numerical integration techniques (using a calculator or computer) to approximate the parametric arc-length integral

$$s = \int_a^b \sqrt{[x'(t)]^2 + [y'(t)]^2}\, dt. \tag{1}$$

Consider the ellipse with equation

$$\frac{x^2}{a^2} + \frac{y^2}{b^2} = 1 \quad (a > b) \tag{2}$$

and *eccentricity* $\epsilon = \sqrt{1 - (b/a)^2}$. Substitute the parametrization

$$x = a\cos t, \quad y = b\sin t \tag{3}$$

into Eq. (1) to show that the perimeter of the ellipse is given by the *elliptic integral*

$$p = 4a \int_0^{\pi/2} \sqrt{1 - \epsilon^2 \cos^2 t}\, dt. \tag{4}$$

This integral is known to be nonelementary if $0 < \epsilon < 1$. A common simple approximation to it is

$$p \approx \pi(A + R), \tag{5}$$

where

$$A = \frac{1}{2}(a+b) \quad \text{and} \quad R = \sqrt{\frac{a^2 + b^2}{2}}$$

denote the arithmetic mean and root-square mean, respectively, of the semiaxes a and b of the ellipse.

Investigation A As a warm-up, consider the ellipse whose major and minor semi-axes a and b are, respectively, the largest and smallest nonzero digits of your student I.D. number. For this ellipse, compare the arc-length estimate given by (5) and by numerical evaluation of the integral in (4).

Investigation B If we ignore the perturbing effects of the sun and the planets other than the earth, the orbit of the moon is an almost perfect ellipse with the earth at one focus. Assume that this ellipse has major semiaxis $a = 384{,}403$ km (exactly) and eccentricity $\epsilon = 0.0549$ (exactly). Approximate the perimeter p of this ellipse [using Eq. (4)] to the nearest meter.

Investigation C Suppose that you are designing an elliptical auto racetrack. Choose semiaxes for *your* racetrack so that its perimeter will be somewhere between a half mile and two miles. Your task is to construct a table with *time* and *speed* columns that an observer can use to determine the average speed of a particular car as it circles the track. The times listed in the first column should correspond to speeds up to perhaps 150 mi/h. The observer clocks a car's circuit of the track and locates its time for the lap in the first column of the table. The corresponding figure in the second column then gives the car's average speed (in miles per hour) for that circuit of the track. Your report should include a convenient table to use in this way—so you can successfully sell it to racetrack patrons attending the auto races.

10.6 CONIC SECTIONS AND APPLICATIONS

Here we discuss in more detail the three types of conic sections—parabolas, ellipses, and hyperbolas—that were introduced in Section 10.1.

The Parabola

The case $e = 1$ of Example 3 in Section 10.1 is motivation for this formal definition.

DEFINITION The Parabola
A **parabola** is the set of all points P in the plane that are equidistant from a fixed point F (called the **focus** of the parabola) and a fixed line L (called the parabola's **directrix**) not containing F.

If the focus of the parabola is $F(p, 0)$ and its directrix is the vertical line $x = -p$, $p > 0$, then it follows from Eq. (12) of Section 10.1 that the equation of this parabola is

$$y^2 = 4px. \qquad (1)$$

When we replace x with $-x$ both in the equation and in the discussion that precedes it, we get the equation of the parabola whose focus is $(-p, 0)$ and whose directrix is the vertical line $x = p$. The new parabola has equation

$$y^2 = -4px. \qquad (2)$$

The old and new parabolas appear in Fig. 10.6.1.

We could also interchange x and y in Eq. (1). This would give the equation of a parabola whose focus is $(0, p)$ and whose directrix is the horizontal line $y = -p$.

FIGURE 10.6.1 Two parabolas with vertical directrices.

662 CHAPTER 10 Polar Coordinates and Parametric Curves

This parabola opens upward, as in Fig. 10.6.2(a); its equation is

$$x^2 = 4py. \qquad (3)$$

Finally, we replace y with $-y$ in Eq. (3). This gives the equation

$$x^2 = -4py \qquad (4)$$

of a parabola opening downward, with focus $(0, -p)$ and with directrix $y = p$, as in Fig. 10.6.2(b).

Each of the parabolas discussed so far is symmetric around one of the coordinate axes. The line around which a parabola is symmetric is called the **axis** of the parabola. The point of a parabola midway between its focus and its directrix is called the **vertex** of the parabola. The vertex of each parabola that we discussed in connection with Eqs. (1) through (4) is the origin $(0, 0)$.

EXAMPLE 1 Determine the focus, directrix, axis, and vertex of the parabola $x^2 = 12y$.

Solution We write the given equation as $x^2 = 4 \cdot (3y)$. In this form it matches Eq. (3) with $p = 3$. Hence the focus of the given parabola is $(0, 3)$ and its directrix is the horizontal line $y = -3$. The y-axis is its axis of symmetry, and the parabola opens upward from its vertex at the origin. ◆

Suppose that we begin with the parabola of Eq. (1) and translate it in such a way that its vertex moves to the point (h, k). Then the translated parabola has equation

$$(y - k)^2 = 4p(x - h). \qquad (1a)$$

The new parabola has focus $F(p + h, k)$ and its directrix is the vertical line $x = -p + h$ (Fig. 10.6.3). Its axis is the horizontal line $y = k$.

We can obtain the translates of the other three parabolas in Eqs. (2) through (4) in the same way. If the vertex is moved from the origin to the point (h, k), then the three equations take these forms:

$$(y - k)^2 = -4p(x - h), \qquad (2a)$$

$$(x - h)^2 = 4p(y - k), \quad \text{and} \qquad (3a)$$

$$(x - h)^2 = -4p(y - k). \qquad (4a)$$

Equations (1a) and (2a) both take the general form

$$y^2 + Ax + By + C = 0 \quad (A \neq 0), \qquad (5)$$

whereas Eqs. (3a) and (4a) both take the general form

$$x^2 + Ax + By + C = 0 \quad (B \neq 0). \qquad (6)$$

What is significant about Eqs. (5) and (6) is what they have in common: Both are linear in one of the coordinate variables and quadratic in the other. In fact, we can reduce *any* such equation to one of the standard forms in Eqs. (1a) through (4a) by completing the square in the coordinate variable that appears quadratically. This means that the graph of any equation of the form of either Eqs. (5) or (6) is a parabola. The features of the parabola can be read from the standard form of its equation, as in Example 2.

EXAMPLE 2 Determine the graph of the equation

$$4y^2 - 8x - 12y + 1 = 0.$$

FIGURE 10.6.2 Two parabolas with horizontal directrices: (a) opening upward; (b) opening downward.

FIGURE 10.6.3 A translation of the parabola $y^2 = 4px$.

FIGURE 10.6.4 The parabola of Example 2.

Solution This equation is linear in x and quadratic in y. We divide through by the coefficient of y^2 and then collect on one side of the equation all terms that include y:

$$y^2 - 3y = 2x - \tfrac{1}{4}.$$

Then we complete the square in the variable y and thus find that

$$y^2 - 3y + \tfrac{9}{4} = 2x - \tfrac{1}{4} + \tfrac{9}{4} = 2x + 2 = 2(x+1).$$

The final step is to write in the form $4p(x-h)$ the terms on the right-hand side that include x:

$$\left(y - \tfrac{3}{2}\right)^2 = 4 \cdot \tfrac{1}{2} \cdot (x+1).$$

This equation has the form of Eq. (1a) with $p = \tfrac{1}{2}$, $h = -1$, and $k = \tfrac{3}{2}$. Thus the graph is a parabola that opens to the right from its vertex at $(-1, \tfrac{3}{2})$. Its focus is at $(-\tfrac{1}{2}, \tfrac{3}{2})$, its directrix is the vertical line $x = -\tfrac{3}{2}$, and its axis is the horizontal line $y = \tfrac{3}{2}$. It appears in Fig. 10.6.4. ◆

Applications of Parabolas

The parabola $y^2 = 4px$ ($p > 0$) is shown in Fig. 10.6.5 along with an incoming ray of light traveling to the left and parallel to the x-axis. This light ray strikes the parabola at the point $Q(a, b)$ and is reflected toward the x-axis, which it meets at the point $(c, 0)$. The light ray's angle of reflection must equal its angle of incidence, which is why both of these angles—measured with respect to the tangent line L at Q—are labeled α in the figure. The angle vertical to the angle of incidence is also equal to α. Hence, because the incoming ray is parallel to the x-axis, the angle the reflected ray makes with the x-axis at $(c, 0)$ is 2α.

Using the points Q and $(c, 0)$ to compute the slope of the reflected light ray, we find that

$$\frac{b}{a-c} = \tan 2\alpha = \frac{2\tan\alpha}{1 - \tan^2\alpha}.$$

(The second equality follows from a trigonometric identity in Problem 64 of Section 7.5.) But the angle α is related to the slope of the tangent line L at Q. To find that slope, we begin with

$$y = 2\sqrt{px} = 2(px)^{1/2}$$

and compute

$$\frac{dy}{dx} = \left(\frac{p}{x}\right)^{1/2}.$$

Hence the slope of L is both $\tan\alpha$ and dy/dx evaluated at (a, b); that is,

$$\tan\alpha = \left(\frac{p}{a}\right)^{1/2}.$$

Therefore,

$$\frac{b}{a-c} = \frac{2\tan\alpha}{1-\tan^2\alpha} = \frac{2\sqrt{\frac{p}{a}}}{1 - \frac{p}{a}} = \frac{2\sqrt{pa}}{a-p} = \frac{b}{a-p},$$

because $b = 2\sqrt{pa}$. Hence $c = p$. The surprise is that c is independent of a and b and depends only on the equation $y^2 = 4px$ of the parabola. Therefore *all* incoming light rays parallel to the x-axis will be reflected to the single point $F(p, 0)$. This is why F is called the *focus* of the parabola.

This **reflection property** of the parabola is exploited in the design of parabolic mirrors. Such a mirror has the shape of the surface obtained by revolving a parabola around its axis of symmetry. Then a beam of incoming light rays parallel to the axis will be focused at F, as shown in Fig. 10.6.6. The reflection property can also be used

FIGURE 10.6.5 The reflection property of the parabola: $\alpha = \beta$.

FIGURE 10.6.6 Incident rays parallel to the axis reflect through the focus.

664 CHAPTER 10 Polar Coordinates and Parametric Curves

in reverse—rays emitted at the focus are reflected in a beam parallel to the axis, thus keeping the light beam intense. Moreover, applications are not limited to light rays alone; parabolic mirrors are used in visual and radio telescopes, radar antennas, searchlights, automobile headlights, microphone systems, satellite ground stations, and solar heating devices.

Galileo discovered early in the seventeenth century that the trajectory of a projectile fired from a gun is a parabola (under the assumptions that air resistance can be ignored and that the gravitational acceleration remains constant). Suppose that a projectile is fired with initial velocity v_0 at time $t = 0$ from the origin and at an angle α of inclination from the horizontal x-axis. Then the initial velocity of the projectile splits into the components

$$v_{0x} = v_0 \cos\alpha \quad \text{and} \quad v_{0y} = v_0 \sin\alpha,$$

FIGURE 10.6.7 Resolution of the initial velocity v_0 into its horizontal and vertical components.

as indicated in Fig. 10.6.7. The fact that the projectile continues to move horizontally with *constant* speed v_{0x}, together with Eq. (34) of Section 5.2, implies that its x- and y-coordinates after t seconds are

$$x = (v_0 \cos\alpha)t, \tag{7}$$

$$y = -\tfrac{1}{2}gt^2 + (v_0 \sin\alpha)t. \tag{8}$$

By substituting $t = x/(v_0 \cos\alpha)$ from Eq. (7) into Eq. (8) and then completing the square, we can derive (as in Problem 70) an equation of the form

$$y - M = -4p\left(x - \tfrac{1}{2}R\right)^2. \tag{9}$$

Here,

$$M = \frac{v_0^2 \sin^2\alpha}{2g} \tag{10}$$

is the maximum height attained by the projectile, and

$$R = \frac{v_0^2 \sin 2\alpha}{g} \tag{11}$$

FIGURE 10.6.8 The trajectory of the projectile, showing its maximum altitude M and its range R.

is its **range**, the horizontal distance the projectile will travel before it returns to the ground. Thus its trajectory is the parabola shown in Fig. 10.6.8.

The Ellipse

An ellipse is a conic section with eccentricity e less than 1, as in Example 3 of Section 10.1.

> **DEFINITION** The Ellipse
> Suppose that $e < 1$, and let F be a fixed point and L a fixed line not containing F. The **ellipse** with **eccentricity** e, **focus** F, and **directrix** L is the set of all points P such that the distance $|PF|$ is e times the (perpendicular) distance from P to the line L.

The equation of the ellipse is especially simple if F is the point $(c, 0)$ on the x-axis and L is the vertical line $x = c/e^2$. The case $c > 0$ is shown in Fig. 10.6.9. If Q is the point $(c/e^2, y)$, then PQ is the perpendicular from $P(x, y)$ to L. The condition $|PF| = e|PQ|$ then gives

$$(x - c)^2 + y^2 = e^2\left(x - \frac{c}{e^2}\right)^2;$$

$$x^2 - 2cx + c^2 + y^2 = e^2 x^2 - 2cx + \frac{c^2}{e^2};$$

$$x^2(1 - e^2) + y^2 = c^2\left(\frac{1}{e^2} - 1\right) = \frac{c^2}{e^2}(1 - e^2).$$

FIGURE 10.6.9 Ellipse: focus F, directrix L, eccentricity e.

Thus
$$x^2(1-e^2) + y^2 = a^2(1-e^2),$$
where
$$a = \frac{c}{e}. \tag{12}$$

We divide both sides of the next-to-last equation by $a^2(1-e^2)$ and get
$$\frac{x^2}{a^2} + \frac{y^2}{a^2(1-e^2)} = 1.$$

Finally, with the aid of the fact that $e < 1$, we may let
$$b^2 = a^2(1-e^2) = a^2 - c^2. \tag{13}$$

Then the equation of the ellipse with focus $(c, 0)$ and directrix $x = c/e^2 = a/e$ takes the simple form
$$\frac{x^2}{a^2} + \frac{y^2}{b^2} = 1. \tag{14}$$

We see from Eq. (14) that this ellipse is symmetric around both coordinate axes. Its x-intercepts are $(\pm a, 0)$ and its y-intercepts are $(0, \pm b)$. The points $(\pm a, 0)$ are called the **vertices** of the ellipse, and the line segment joining them is called its **major axis**. The line segment joining $(0, b)$ and $(0, -b)$ is called the **minor axis** [note from Eq. (13) that $b < a$]. The alternative form
$$a^2 = b^2 + c^2 \tag{15}$$

of Eq. (13) is the Pythagorean relation for the right triangle of Fig. 10.6.10. Indeed, visualization of this triangle is an excellent way to remember Eq. (15). The numbers a and b are the lengths of the major and minor **semiaxes,** respectively.

FIGURE 10.6.10 The parts of an ellipse.

FIGURE 10.6.11 The ellipse as a conic section: two foci, two directrices.

$e = 0.97$ $e = 0.70$ $e = 0$

FIGURE 10.6.12 The relation between the eccentricity of an ellipse and its shape.

Because $a = c/e$, the directrix of the ellipse in Eq. (14) is $x = a/e$. If we had begun instead with the focus $(-c, 0)$ and directrix $x = -a/e$, we would still have obtained Eq. (14), because only the squares of a and c are involved in its derivation. Thus the ellipse in Eq. (14) has *two* foci, $(c, 0)$ and $(-c, 0)$, and *two* directrices, $x = a/e$ and $x = -a/e$ (Fig. 10.6.11).

The larger the eccentricity $e < 1$, the more elongated the ellipse. (Remember that $e = 1$ is the eccentricity of every parabola). But if $e = 0$, then Eq. (13) gives $b = a$, so Eq. (14) reduces to the equation of a circle of radius a. Thus a circle is an ellipse of eccentricity zero. Compare the three cases shown in Fig. 10.6.12.

FIGURE 10.6.13 The ellipse of Example 3.

FIGURE 10.6.14 An ellipse with vertical major axis.

FIGURE 10.6.15 The ellipse of Example 4.

EXAMPLE 3 Find an equation of the ellipse with foci $(\pm 3, 0)$ and vertices $(\pm 5, 0)$.

Solution We are given $c = 3$ and $a = 5$, so Eq. (13) gives $b = 4$. Thus Eq. (14) gives

$$\frac{x^2}{25} + \frac{y^2}{16} = 1$$

for the desired equation. This ellipse is shown in Fig. 10.6.13. ◆

If the two foci of an ellipse are on the y-axis, such as $F_1(0, c)$ and $F_2(0, -c)$, then the equation of the ellipse is

$$\frac{x^2}{b^2} + \frac{y^2}{a^2} = 1, \qquad (16)$$

and it is still true that $a^2 = b^2 + c^2$, as in Eq. (15). But now the major axis of length $2a$ is vertical and the minor axis of length $2b$ is horizontal. The derivation of Eq. (16) is similar to that of Eq. (14); see Problem 79. Figure 10.6.14 shows the case of an ellipse whose major axis is vertical. The vertices of such an ellipse are at $(0, \pm a)$; they are always the endpoints of the major axis.

In practice there is little chance of confusing Eqs. (14) and (16). The equation or the given data will make it clear whether the major axis of the ellipse is horizontal or vertical. Just use the equation to read the ellipse's intercepts. The two intercepts that are farthest from the origin are the endpoints of the major axis; the other two are the endpoints of the minor axis. The two foci lie on the major axis, each at distance c from the center of the ellipse—which will be the origin if the equation of the ellipse has the form of either Eq. (14) or Eq. (16).

EXAMPLE 4 Sketch the graph of the equation

$$\frac{x^2}{16} + \frac{y^2}{25} = 1.$$

Solution The x-intercepts are $(\pm 4, 0)$; the y-intercepts are $(0, \pm 5)$. So the major axis is vertical. We take $a = 5$ and $b = 4$ in Eq. (15) and find that $c = 3$. The foci are thus at $(0, \pm 3)$. Hence this ellipse has the appearance of the one shown in Fig. 10.6.15. ◆

Any equation of the form

$$Ax^2 + Cy^2 + Dx + Ey + F = 0, \qquad (17)$$

in which the coefficients A and C of the squared variables are *both nonzero* and *have the same sign*, may be reduced to the form

$$A(x - h)^2 + C(y - k)^2 = G$$

by completing the square in x and y. We may assume that A and C are both positive. Then if $G < 0$, there are no points that satisfy Eq. (17), and the graph is the empty set. If $G = 0$, then there is exactly one point on the locus—the single point (h, k). And if $G > 0$, we can divide both sides of the last equation by G and get an equation that resembles one of these two:

$$\frac{(x - h)^2}{a^2} + \frac{(y - k)^2}{b^2} = 1, \qquad (18a)$$

$$\frac{(x - h)^2}{b^2} + \frac{(y - k)^2}{a^2} = 1. \qquad (18b)$$

Which equation should you choose? Select the one that is consistent with the condition $a \geqq b > 0$. Finally, note that either of the equations in (18) is the equation of a translated ellipse. Thus, apart from the exceptional cases already noted, the graph of Eq. (17) is an ellipse if $AC > 0$.

EXAMPLE 5 Determine the graph of the equation

$$3x^2 + 5y^2 - 12x + 30y + 42 = 0.$$

Solution We collect terms containing x, terms containing y, and complete the square in each variable. This gives

$$3(x^2 - 4x) + 5(y^2 + 6y) = -42;$$

$$3(x^2 - 4x + 4) + 5(y^2 + 69 + 9) = 15;$$

$$\frac{(x-2)^2}{5} + \frac{(y+3)^2}{3} = 1.$$

Thus the given equation is that of a translated ellipse with center at $(2, -3)$. Its horizontal major semiaxis has length $a = \sqrt{5}$ and its minor semiaxis has length $b = \sqrt{3}$ (Fig. 10.6.16). The distance from the center to each focus is $c = \sqrt{2}$ and the eccentricity is $e = c/a = \sqrt{2/5}$. ◆

FIGURE 10.6.16 The ellipse of Example 5.

Applications of Ellipses

EXAMPLE 6 The orbit of the earth is an ellipse with the sun at one focus. The planet's maximum distance from the center of the sun is 94.56 million miles and its minimum distance is 91.44 million miles. What are the major and minor semiaxes of the earth's orbit, and what is its eccentricity?

Solution As Fig. 10.6.17 shows, we have

$$a + c = 94.56 \quad \text{and} \quad a - c = 91.44,$$

with units in millions of miles. We conclude from these equations that $a = 93.00$, that $c = 1.56$, and then that

$$b = \sqrt{(93.00)^2 - (1.56)^2} \approx 92.99$$

million miles. Finally,

$$e = \frac{c}{a} = \frac{1.56}{93.00} \approx 0.017,$$

a number relatively close to zero. This means that the earth's orbit is nearly circular. Indeed, the major and minor semiaxes are so nearly equal that, on any usual scale, the earth's orbit would appear to be a perfect circle. But the difference between uniform circular motion and the earth's actual motion has some important aspects, including the facts that the sun is 1.56 million miles off center and that the orbital speed of the earth is not constant. ◆

FIGURE 10.6.17 The orbit of the earth with its eccentricity exaggerated (Example 6).

EXAMPLE 7 One of the most famous comets is Halley's comet, named for Edmund Halley (1656–1742), a disciple of Newton. By studying the records of the paths of earlier comets, Halley deduced that the comet of 1682 was the same one that had been sighted in 1607, in 1531, in 1456, and in 1066 (an omen at the Battle of Hastings). In 1682 Halley predicted that this comet would return in 1759, in 1835, and in 1910; he was correct each time. The period of Halley's comet is about 76 years—it can vary a couple of years in either direction because of perturbations of its orbit by the planet Jupiter. The orbit of Halley's comet is an ellipse with the sun at one focus. In terms of astronomical units (1 AU is the mean distance from the earth to the sun), the major and minor semiaxes of this elliptical orbit are 18.09 AU and 4.56 AU, respectively. What are the maximum and minimum distances from the sun of Halley's comet?

668 CHAPTER 10 Polar Coordinates and Parametric Curves

Solution We are given that $a = 18.09$ (all distance measurements are in astronomical units) and that $b = 4.56$, so

$$c = \sqrt{(18.09)^2 - (4.56)^2} \approx 17.51.$$

Hence the maximum distance of the comet from the sun is $a + c \approx 35.60$ AU, and its minimum distance is $a - c \approx 0.58$ AU. The eccentricity of its orbit is

$$e = \frac{c}{a} = \frac{17.51}{18.09} \approx 0.97,$$

a very eccentric orbit (but see Problem 77). ◆

FIGURE 10.6.18 The reflection property: $\alpha = \beta$.

The *reflection property* of the ellipse states that the tangent line at a point P of an ellipse makes equal angles with the two lines PF_1 and PF_2 from P to the two foci of the ellipse (Fig. 10.6.18). This property is the basis of the "whispering gallery" phenomenon, which has been observed in the so-called whispering gallery of the U.S. Senate. Suppose that the ceiling of a large room is shaped like half an ellipsoid obtained by revolving an ellipse around its major axis. Sound waves, like light waves, are reflected with equal angles of incidence and reflection. Thus if two diplomats are holding a quiet conversation near one focus of the ellipsoidal surface, a reporter standing near the other focus—perhaps 50 feet away—might be able to eavesdrop on their conversation even if the conversation were inaudible to others in the same room.

Some billiard tables are manufactured in the shape of an ellipse. The foci of such tables are plainly marked for the convenience of enthusiasts of this unusual game.

A more serious application of the reflection property of ellipses is the nonsurgical kidney-stone treatment called *shockwave lithotripsy*. An ellipsoidal reflector with a transducer (an energy transmitter) at one focus is positioned outside the patient's body so that the offending kidney stone is located at the other focus. The stone then is pulverized by reflected shockwaves emanating from the transducer. (For further details, see the COMAP *Newsletter* **20**, November, 1986.)

An alternative definition of the ellipse with foci F_1 and F_2 and major axis of length $2a$ is this: It is the locus of a point P such that the sum of the distances $|PF_1|$ and $|PF_2|$ is the constant $2a$. (See Problem 82.) This fact gives us a convenient way to draw the ellipse by using two tacks placed at F_1 and F_2, a string of length $2a$, and a pencil (Fig. 10.6.19).

FIGURE 10.6.19 One way to draw an ellipse.

The Hyperbola

A hyperbola is a conic section defined in the same way as is an ellipse, except that the eccentricity e of a hyperbola is greater than 1.

DEFINITION The Hyperbola
Suppose that $e > 1$, and let F be a fixed point and L a fixed line not containing F. Then the **hyperbola** with **eccentricity** e, **focus** F, and **directrix** L is the set of all points P such that the distance $|PF|$ is e times the (perpendicular) distance from P to the line L.

As with the ellipse, the equation of a hyperbola is simplest if F is the point $(c, 0)$ on the x-axis and L is the vertical line $x = c/e^2$. The case $c > 0$ is shown in Fig. 10.6.20. If Q is the point $(c/e^2, y)$, then PQ is the perpendicular from $P(x, y)$ to L. The condition $|PF| = e|PQ|$ gives

$$(x - c)^2 + y^2 = e^2\left(x - \frac{c}{e^2}\right)^2;$$

$$x^2 - 2cx + c^2 + y^2 = e^2 x^2 - 2cx + \frac{c^2}{e^2};$$

$$(e^2 - 1)x^2 - y^2 = c^2\left(1 - \frac{1}{e^2}\right) = \frac{c^2}{e^2}(e^2 - 1).$$

FIGURE 10.6.20 The definition of the hyperbola.

Thus
$$(e^2 - 1)x^2 - y^2 = a^2(e^2 - 1),$$
where
$$a = \frac{c}{e}. \tag{19}$$

If we divide both sides of the next-to-last equation by $a^2(e^2 - 1)$, we get
$$\frac{x^2}{a^2} - \frac{y^2}{a^2(e^2 - 1)} = 1.$$

To simplify this equation, we let
$$b^2 = a^2(e^2 - 1) = c^2 - a^2. \tag{20}$$

This is permissible because $e > 1$. So the equation of the hyperbola with focus $(c, 0)$ and directrix $x = c/e^2 = a/e$ takes the form
$$\frac{x^2}{a^2} - \frac{y^2}{b^2} = 1. \tag{21}$$

The minus sign on the left-hand side is the only difference between the equation of a hyperbola and that of an ellipse. Of course, Eq. (20) also differs from the relation
$$b^2 = a^2(1 - e^2) = a^2 - c^2$$
for the case of the ellipse.

The hyperbola of Eq. (21) is clearly symmetric around both coordinate axes and has x-intercepts $(\pm a, 0)$. But it has no y-intercept. If we rewrite Eq. (21) in the form
$$y = \pm \frac{b}{a} \sqrt{x^2 - a^2}, \tag{22}$$

then we see that there are points on the graph only if $|x| \geq a$. Hence the hyperbola has two **branches,** as shown in Fig. 10.6.21. We also see from Eq. (22) that $|y| \to \infty$ as $|x| \to \infty$.

The x-intercepts $V_1(-a, 0)$ and $V_2(a, 0)$ are the **vertices** of the hyperbola, and the line segment joining them is its **transverse axis** (Fig. 10.6.22). The line segment

FIGURE 10.6.21 A hyperbola has two branches.

FIGURE 10.6.22 The parts of a hyperbola.

joining $W_1(0, -b)$ and $W_2(0, b)$ is its **conjugate axis.** The alternative form

$$c^2 = a^2 + b^2 \tag{23}$$

of Eq. (20) is the Pythagorean relation for the right triangle shown in Fig. 10.6.22.

The lines $y = \pm bx/a$ that pass through the **center** $(0, 0)$ and the opposite vertices of the rectangle in Fig. 10.6.22 are **asymptotes** of the two branches of the hyperbola in both directions. That is, if

$$y_1 = \frac{bx}{a} \quad \text{and} \quad y_2 = \frac{b}{a}\sqrt{x^2 - a^2},$$

then

$$\lim_{x \to \infty}(y_1 - y_2) = 0 = \lim_{x \to -\infty}(y_1 - (-y_2)). \tag{24}$$

To verify the first limit (for instance), note that

$$\lim_{x \to \infty} \frac{b}{a}\left(x - \sqrt{x^2 - a^2}\right) = \lim_{x \to \infty} \frac{b}{a} \cdot \frac{\left(x - \sqrt{x^2 - a^2}\right)\left(x + \sqrt{x^2 - a^2}\right)}{x + \sqrt{x^2 - a^2}}$$

$$= \lim_{x \to \infty} \frac{b}{a} \cdot \frac{a^2}{x + \sqrt{x^2 - a^2}} = 0.$$

Just as in the case of the ellipse, the hyperbola with focus $(c, 0)$ and directrix $x = a/e$ also has focus $(-c, 0)$ and directrix $x = -a/e$ (Fig. 10.6.23). Because $c = ae$ by Eq. (19), the foci $(\pm ae, 0)$ and the directrices $x = \pm a/e$ take the same forms in terms of a and e for both the hyperbola $(e > 1)$ and the ellipse $(e < 1)$.

If we interchange x and y in Eq. (21), we obtain

$$\frac{y^2}{a^2} - \frac{x^2}{b^2} = 1. \tag{25}$$

This hyperbola has foci at $(0, \pm c)$. The foci as well as this hyperbola's transverse axis lie on the y-axis. Its asymptotes are $y = \pm ax/b$, and its graph generally resembles the one in Fig. 10.6.23.

When we studied the ellipse, we saw that its orientation—whether the major axis is horizontal or vertical—is determined by the relative sizes of a and b. In the

FIGURE 10.6.23 The hyperbola of Eq. (25) has horizontal directrices.

case of the hyperbola, the situation is quite different, because the relative sizes of a and b make no such difference: They affect only the slopes of the asymptotes. The direction in which the hyperbola opens—horizontal as in Fig. 10.6.22 or vertical as in Fig. 10.6.23—is determined by the signs of the terms that contain x^2 and y^2.

EXAMPLE 8 Sketch the graph of the hyperbola with equation

$$\frac{y^2}{9} - \frac{x^2}{16} = 1.$$

Solution This is an equation of the form in Eq. (25), so the hyperbola opens vertically. Because $a = 3$ and $b = 4$, we find that $c = 5$ by using Eq. (23): $c^2 = a^2 + b^2$. Thus the vertices are $(0, \pm 3)$, the foci are the two points $(0, \pm 5)$, and the asymptotes are the two lines $y = \pm 3x/4$. This hyperbola appears in Fig. 10.6.24. ◆

FIGURE 10.6.24 The hyperbola of Example 8.

EXAMPLE 9 Find an equation of the hyperbola with foci $(\pm 10, 0)$ and asymptotes $y = \pm 4x/3$.

Solution Because $c = 10$, we have

$$a^2 + b^2 = 100 \quad \text{and} \quad \frac{b}{a} = \frac{4}{3}.$$

Thus $b = 8$ and $a = 6$, and the standard equation of the hyperbola is

$$\frac{x^2}{36} - \frac{y^2}{64} = 1.$$

◆

As we noted earlier, any equation of the form

$$Ax^2 + Cy^2 + Dx + Ey + F = 0 \tag{26}$$

with both A and C nonzero can be reduced to the form

$$A(x - h)^2 + B(y - k)^2 = G$$

by completing the square in x and y. Now suppose that the coefficients A and C of the quadratic terms have *opposite signs*. For example, suppose that $A = p^2$ and $B = -q^2$. The last equation then becomes

$$p^2(x - h)^2 - q^2(y - k)^2 = G. \tag{27}$$

If $G = 0$, then factorization of the difference of squares on the left-hand side yields the equations

$$p(x - h) + q(y - k) = 0 \quad \text{and} \quad p(x - h) - q(y - k) = 0$$

of two straight lines through (h, k) with slopes $m = \pm p/q$. If $G \neq 0$, then division of Eq. (27) by G gives an equation that looks either like

$$\frac{(x - h)^2}{a^2} - \frac{(y - k)^2}{b^2} = 1 \quad \text{(if } G > 0\text{)}$$

or like

$$\frac{(y - k)^2}{a^2} - \frac{(x - h)^2}{b^2} = 1 \quad \text{(if } G < 0\text{)}.$$

Thus if $AC < 0$ in Eq. (26), the graph is either a pair of intersecting straight lines or a hyperbola.

EXAMPLE 10 Determine the graph of the equation

$$9x^2 - 4y^2 - 36x + 8y = 4.$$

Solution We collect the terms that contain x and those that contain y, and we then complete the square in each variable. We find that

$$9(x - 2)^2 - 4(y - 1)^2 = 36,$$

so

$$\frac{(x - 2)^2}{4} - \frac{(y - 1)^2}{9} = 1.$$

Hence the graph is a hyperbola with a horizontal transverse axis and center $(2, 1)$. Because $a = 2$ and $b = 3$, we find that $c = \sqrt{13}$. The vertices of the hyperbola are $(0, 1)$ and $(4, 1)$, and its foci are the two points $(2 \pm \sqrt{13}, 1)$. Its asymptotes are the two lines

$$y - 1 = \pm \tfrac{3}{2}(x - 2),$$

translates of the asymptotes $y = \pm 3x/2$ of the hyperbola $\tfrac{1}{4}x^2 - \tfrac{1}{9}y^2 = 1$. Figure 10.6.25 shows the graph of the translated hyperbola. ◆

FIGURE 10.6.25 The hyperbola of Example 10, a translate of the hyperbola $x^2/4 - y^2/9 = 1$.

Applications of Hyperbolas

The *reflection property* of the hyperbola takes the same form as that for the ellipse. If P is a point on a hyperbola, then the two lines PF_1 and PF_2 from P to the two foci make equal angles with the tangent line at P. In Fig. 10.6.26 this means that $\alpha = \beta$.

FIGURE 10.6.26 The reflection property of the hyperbola.

FIGURE 10.6.27 How a hyperbolic mirror reflects a ray aimed at one focus: $\alpha = \beta$ again.

For an important application of this reflection property, consider a mirror that is shaped like one branch of a hyperbola and is reflective on its outer (convex) surface. An incoming light ray aimed toward one focus will be reflected toward the other focus (Fig. 10.6.27). Figure 10.6.28 indicates the design of a reflecting telescope that makes use of the reflection properties of the parabola and the hyperbola. The parallel incoming light rays first are reflected by the parabola toward its focus at F. Then they are intercepted by an auxiliary hyperbolic mirror with foci at E and F and reflected into the eyepiece located at E.

FIGURE 10.6.28 One type of reflecting telescope: main mirror parabolic, auxiliary mirror hyperbolic.

Example 11 illustrates how hyperbolas are used to determine the positions of ships at sea.

EXAMPLE 11 A ship lies in the Labrador Sea due east of Wesleyville, point A, on the long north-south coastline of Newfoundland. Simultaneous radio signals are transmitted by radio stations at A and at St. John's, point B, which is on the coast 200 km due south of A. The ship receives the signal from A 500 microseconds (μs) before it receives the signal from B. Assume that the speed of radio signals is 300 m/μs. How far out at sea is the ship?

674 CHAPTER 10 Polar Coordinates and Parametric Curves

FIGURE 10.6.29 A navigation problem (Example 11).

Solution The situation is diagrammed in Fig. 10.6.29. The difference between the distances of the ship at S from A and B is

$$|SB| - |SA| = 500 \cdot 300 = 150{,}000$$

meters; that is, 150 km. Thus (by Problem 88) the ship lies on a hyperbola with foci A and B. From Fig. 10.6.29 we see that $c = 100$, so $a = \frac{1}{2} \cdot 150 = 75$, and thus

$$b = \sqrt{c^2 - a^2} = \sqrt{100^2 - 75^2} = 25\sqrt{7}.$$

In the coordinate system of Fig. 10.6.29, the hyperbola has equation

$$\frac{y^2}{75^2} - \frac{x^2}{7 \cdot 25^2} = 1.$$

We substitute $y = 100$ because the ship is due east of A. Thus we find that the ship's distance from the coastline is $x = \frac{175}{3} \approx 58.3$ km. ◆

Conics in Polar Coordinates

In order to investigate orbits of satellites—such as planets or comets orbiting the sun or natural or artificial moons orbiting a planet—we need equations of the conic sections in polar coordinates. As a bonus, we find that all three conic sections have the same general equation in polar coordinates.

To derive the polar equation of a conic section, suppose its focus is the origin O and that its directrix is the vertical line $x = -p$ (with $p > 0$). In the notation of Fig. 10.6.30, the fact that $|OP| = e|PQ|$ then tells us that $r = e(p + r \cos \theta)$. Solution of this equation for r yields

$$r = \frac{pe}{1 - e \cos \theta}.$$

If the directrix is the vertical line $x = +p > 0$ to the right of the origin, then a similar calculation gives the same result, except with a change of sign in the denominator.

FIGURE 10.6.30 A conic section: $|OP| = e|PQ|$.

Polar Coordinate Equation of a Conic Section

The polar equation of a conic section with eccentricity e, focus O, and directrix $x = \pm p$ is

$$r = \frac{pe}{1 \pm e \cos \theta}. \tag{28}$$

Figure 10.6.31 shows an ellipse with eccentricity $e < 1$ and directrix $x = -p$. Its vertices correspond to $\theta = 0$ and $\theta = \pi$, where maximal and minimal radii r_0 and r_1 occur. It follows that the length $2a$ of its major axis is

$$2a = r_0 + r_1 = \frac{pe}{1-e} + \frac{pe}{1+e} = \frac{2pe}{1-e^2}.$$

FIGURE 10.6.31 The maximal radius $r_0 = \dfrac{pe}{1-e}$ and the minimal radius $r_1 = \dfrac{pe}{1+e}$ of the ellipse.

Cross multiplication gives the relation

$$pe = a(1 - e^2), \tag{29}$$

and substituting in (28) then yields the equation

$$r = \frac{a(1 - e^2)}{1 \pm e \cos \theta} \tag{30}$$

of an ellipse with eccentricity e and major semiaxis a.

EXAMPLE 12 Sketch the graph of the equation

$$r = \frac{16}{5 - 3 \cos \theta}.$$

Conic Sections and Applications   SECTION 10.6   675

Solution First we divide numerator and denominator by 5 and find that

$$r = \frac{\frac{16}{5}}{1 - \frac{3}{5}\cos\theta}.$$

Thus $e = \frac{3}{5}$ and $pe = \frac{16}{5}$. Equation (29) then implies that $a = 5$. Finally, $c = ae = 3$ and

$$b = \sqrt{a^2 - c^2} = 4.$$

So we have here an ellipse with major semiaxis $a = 5$, minor semiaxis $b = 4$, and center at $(3, 0)$ in Cartesian coordinates. The ellipse is shown in Fig. 10.6.32. ◆

FIGURE 10.6.32 The ellipse of Example 12.

REMARK 1 The limiting form of Eq. (30) as $e \to 0$ is the equation $r = a$ of a circle. Because $p \to \infty$ as $e \to 0$ with a fixed in Eq. (29), we may therefore regard any circle as an ellipse with eccentricity zero and with directrix at infinity.

REMARK 2 If we begin with an ellipse with eccentricity $e < 1$ and directrix $x = -p$, then the limiting form of Eq. (30) as $e \to 1^-$ is the equation

$$r = \frac{p}{1 - \cos\theta} \tag{31}$$

of a parabola. For instance, Fig. 10.6.33 shows a parabola and an ellipse of eccentricity $e = 0.99$, both with directrix $p = -1$. Observe that the two curves appear to almost coincide near the origin where $30° < \theta < 330°$. This sort of approximation of an ellipse by a parabola is useful in studying comets with highly eccentric elliptical orbits.

FIGURE 10.6.33 The parabola $r = \dfrac{1}{1 - \cos\theta}$ and the ellipse $r = \dfrac{0.99}{1 - 0.99\cos\theta}$.

EXAMPLE 13 A certain comet is known to have a highly eccentric elliptical orbit with the sun at one focus. Two successive observations as this comet approached the sun gave the measurements $r = 6$ AU when $\theta = 60°$, and $r = 2$ AU when $\theta = 90°$ (relative to a fixed polar-coordinate system). Estimate the position of the comet at its point of closest approach to the sun.

Solution Because the elliptical orbit is highly eccentric, we assume that near the sun it can be approximated closely by a parabola. The angle $\theta = \alpha$ of the axis is unknown, but a preliminary sketch indicates that α will be less than the initial angle of observation; thus $0 < \alpha < \pi/3$. Using the polar coordinate system with this unknown polar axis and counterclockwise angular variable $\phi = \theta - \alpha$ (Fig. 10.6.34), the equation in (31) of the parabola takes the form

$$r = \frac{p}{1 - \cos\phi} = \frac{p}{1 - \cos(\theta - \alpha)}. \tag{32}$$

The vertex of a parabola is its point closest to its focus (Problem 65), so the minimum distance of the comet from the sun will be $r = p/2$ when $\theta = \pi + \alpha$. Our problem, then, is to determine the values of p and α.

FIGURE 10.6.34 The comet of Example 13.

676 CHAPTER 10 Polar Coordinates and Parametric Curves

Substituting the given observational data into Eq. (32) yields the two equations

$$6 = \frac{p}{1 - \cos(\pi/3 - \alpha)} \quad \text{and} \quad 2 = \frac{p}{1 - \cos(\pi/2 - \alpha)}. \tag{33}$$

Elimination of p yields

$$6 - 6\cos\left(\frac{\pi}{3} - \alpha\right) = 2 - 2\cos\left(\frac{\pi}{2} - \alpha\right);$$

$$6 - 6\left(\frac{1}{2}\cos\alpha + \frac{\sqrt{3}}{2}\sin\alpha\right) = 2 - 2\sin\alpha.$$

We therefore need to solve the single equation

$$3\cos\alpha + (3\sqrt{3} - 2)\sin\alpha - 4 = 0.$$

A calculator or computer yields the approximate root $\alpha = 0.3956 \approx 22.67°$. Then the second equation in (33) gives $p = 2(1 - \sin\alpha) \approx 1.2293$ (AU). Because 1 astronomical unit is about 93 million miles, the comet's closest approach to the sun is about $\frac{1}{2}p = (0.5)(1.2293)(93) \approx 57.16$ million miles. ◆

10.6 TRUE/FALSE STUDY GUIDE

10.6 CONCEPTS: QUESTIONS AND DISCUSSION

1. Summarize the definitions and alternative constructions of the parabola, ellipse, and hyperbola.
2. Compare the reflection properties of the three types of conic sections.
3. Summarize the applications of the conic sections. You might like to consult an encyclopedia or do a Web search.

10.6 PROBLEMS

In Problems 1 through 5, find the equation and sketch the graph of the parabola with vertex V and focus F.

1. $V(0, 0)$, $F(3, 0)$
2. $V(0, 0)$, $F(0, -2)$
3. $V(2, 3)$, $F(2, 1)$
4. $V(-1, -1)$, $F(-3, -1)$
5. $V(2, 3)$, $F(0, 3)$

In Problems 6 through 10, find the equation and sketch the graph of the parabola with the given focus and directrix.

6. $F(1, 2)$, $x = -1$
7. $F(0, -3)$, $y = 0$
8. $F(1, -1)$, $x = 3$
9. $F(0, 0)$, $y = -2$
10. $F(-2, 1)$, $x = -4$

In Problems 11 through 18, sketch the parabola with the given equation. Show and label its vertex, focus, axis, and directrix.

11. $y^2 = 12x$
12. $x^2 = -8y$
13. $y^2 = -6x$
14. $x^2 = 7y$
15. $x^2 - 4x - 4y = 0$
16. $y^2 - 2x + 6y + 15 = 0$
17. $4x^2 + 4x + 4y + 13 = 0$
18. $4y^2 - 12y + 9x = 0$

In Problems 19 through 33, find an equation of the ellipse specified.

19. Vertices $(\pm 4, 0)$ and $(0, \pm 5)$
20. Foci $(\pm 5, 0)$, major semiaxis 13
21. Foci $(0, \pm 8)$, major semiaxis 17
22. Center $(0, 0)$, vertical major axis 12, minor axis 8
23. Foci $(\pm 3, 0)$, eccentricity $\frac{3}{4}$
24. Foci $(0, \pm 4)$, eccentricity $\frac{2}{3}$
25. Center $(0, 0)$, horizontal major axis 20, eccentricity $\frac{1}{2}$
26. Center $(0, 0)$, horizontal minor axis 10, eccentricity $\frac{1}{2}$
27. Foci $(\pm 2, 0)$, directrices $x = \pm 8$
28. Foci $(0, \pm 4)$, directrices $y = \pm 9$
29. Center $(2, 3)$, horizontal axis 8, vertical axis 4
30. Center $(1, -2)$, horizontal major axis 8, eccentricity $\frac{3}{4}$
31. Foci $(-2, 1)$ and $(4, 1)$, major axis 10
32. Foci $(-3, 0)$ and $(-3, 4)$, minor axis 6
33. Foci $(-2, 2)$ and $(4, 2)$, eccentricity $\frac{1}{3}$

Sketch the graphs of the equations in Problems 34 through 38. Indicate centers, foci, and lengths of axes.

34. $4x^2 + y^2 = 16$
35. $4x^2 + 9y^2 = 144$
36. $4x^2 + 9x^2 = 24x$
37. $9x^2 + 4y^2 - 32y + 28 = 0$
38. $2x^2 + 3y^2 + 12x - 24y + 60 = 0$

In Problems 39 through 52, find an equation of the hyperbola described.

39. Foci $(\pm 4, 0)$, vertices $(\pm 1, 0)$
40. Foci $(0, \pm 3)$, vertices $(0, \pm 2)$
41. Foci $(\pm 5, 0)$, asymptotes $y = \pm 3x/4$
42. Vertices $(\pm 3, 0)$, asymptotes $y = \pm 3x/4$
43. Vertices $(0, \pm 5)$, asymptotes $y = \pm x$
44. Vertices $(\pm 3, 0)$, eccentricity $e = \frac{5}{3}$
45. Foci $(0, \pm 6)$, eccentricity $e = 2$
46. Vertices $(\pm 4, 0)$ and passing through $(8, 3)$
47. Foci $(\pm 4, 0)$, directrices $x = \pm 1$
48. Foci $(0, \pm 9)$, directrices $y = \pm 4$
49. Center $(2, 2)$, horizontal transverse axis of length 6, eccentricity $e = 2$
50. Center $(-1, 3)$, vertices $(-4, 3)$ and $(2, 3)$, foci $(-6, 3)$ and $(4, 3)$
51. Center $(1, -2)$, vertices $(1, 1)$ and $(1, -5)$, asymptotes $3x - 2y = 7$ and $3x + 2y = -1$
52. Focus $(8, -1)$, asymptotes $3x - 4y = 13$ and $3x + 4y = 5$

Sketch the graphs of the equations given in Problems 53 through 58; indicates centers, foci, and asymptotes.

53. $x^2 - y^2 - 2x + 4y = 4$
54. $x^2 - 2y^2 + 4x = 0$
55. $y^2 - 3x^2 - 6y = 0$
56. $x^2 - y^2 - 2x + 6y = 9$
57. $9x^2 - 4y^2 + 18x + 8y = 31$
58. $4y^2 - 9x^2 - 18x - 8y = 41$

In each of Problems 59 through 64, identify and sketch the conic section with the given polar equation.

59. $r = \dfrac{6}{1 + \cos\theta}$
60. $r = \dfrac{6}{1 + 2\cos\theta}$
61. $r = \dfrac{3}{1 - \cos\theta}$
62. $r = \dfrac{8}{8 - 2\cos\theta}$
63. $r = \dfrac{6}{2 - \sin\theta}$
64. $r = \dfrac{12}{3 + 2\cos\theta}$

65. Prove that the point of the parabola $y^2 = 4px$ closest to its focus is its vertex.

66. Find an equation of the parabola that has a vertical axis and passes through the points $(2, 3)$, $(4, 3)$, and $(6, -5)$.

67. Show that an equation of the line tangent to the parabola $y^2 = 4px$ at the point (x_0, y_0) is
$$2px - y_0 y + 2px_0 = 0.$$
Conclude that the tangent line intersects the x-axis at the point $(-x_0, 0)$. This fact provides a quick method for constructing a line tangent to a parabola at a given point.

68. A comet's orbit is a parabola with the sun at its focus. When the comet is $100\sqrt{2}$ million miles from the sun, the line from the sun to the comet makes an angle of $45°$ with the axis of the parabola (Fig. 10.6.35). What will be the minimum distance between the comet and the sun? [*Suggestion:* Write the equation of the parabola with the origin at the focus, then use the result of Problem 65.]

FIGURE 10.6.35 The comet of Problem 68 in parabolic orbit around the sun.

69. Suppose that the angle of Problem 68 increases from $45°$ to $90°$ in 3 days. How much longer will be required for the comet to reach its point of closest approach to the sun? Assume that the line segment from the sun to the comet sweeps out area at a constant rate (Kepler's second law).

70. Use Eqs. (7) and (8) to derive Eq. (9) with the values of M and R given in Eqs. (10) and (11).

71. Deduce from Eq. (11) that, given a fixed initial velocity v_0, the maximum range of the projectile is $R_{\max} = v_0^2/g$ and is attained when $\alpha = 45°$.

In Problems 72 through 74, assume that a projectile is fired with initial velocity $v_0 = 50$ m/s from the origin and at an angle of inclination α. Use $g = 9.8$ m/s^2.

72. If $\alpha = 45°$, find the range of the projectile and the maximum height it attains.

73. For what value or values of α is the range $R = 125$ m?

74. Find the range of the projectile and the length of time it remains above the ground if (a) $\alpha = 30°$; (b) $\alpha = 60°$.

75. The book *Elements of Differential and Integral Calculus* by William Granville, Percey Smith, and William Longley (Ginn and Company: Boston, 1929) lists a number of "curves for reference"; the curve with equation $\sqrt{x} + \sqrt{y} = \sqrt{a}$ is called a parabola. Verify that the curve in question actually is a parabola, or show that it is not.

76. The 1992 edition of the study guide for the national actuarial examinations has a problem quite similar to this one: Every point on the plane curve K is equally distant from the

point $(-1, -1)$ and the line $x + y = 1$, and K has equation
$$x^2 + Bxy + Cy^2 + Dx + Ey + F = 0.$$
Which is the value of D: $-2, 2, 4, 6,$ or 8?

77. (a) The orbit of the comet Kahoutek is an ellipse of extreme eccentricity $e = 0.999925$; the sun is at one focus of this ellipse. The minimum distance between the sun and Kahoutek is 0.13 AU. What is the maximum distance between Kahoutek and the sun? (b) The orbit of the comet Hyakutake is an ellipse of extreme eccentricity $e = 0.999643856$; the sun is at one focus of this ellipse. The minimum distance between the sun and Hyakutake is 0.2300232 AU. What is the maximum distance between Hyakutake and the sun?

78. The orbit of the planet Mercury is an ellipse of eccentricity $e = 0.206$. Its maximum and minimum distances from the sun are 0.467 and 0.307 AU, respectively. What are the major and minor semiaxes of the orbit of Mercury? Does "nearly circular" accurately describe the orbit of Mercury?

79. Derive Eq. (16) for an ellipse whose foci lie on the y-axis.

80. Show that the line tangent to the ellipse
$$\frac{x^2}{a^2} + \frac{y^2}{b^2} = 1$$
at the point $P(x_0, y_0)$ of that ellipse has equation
$$\frac{x_0 x}{a^2} + \frac{y_0 y}{b^2} = 1.$$

81. Use the result of Problem 80 to establish the reflection property of the ellipse. [*Suggestion:* Let m be the slope of the line normal to the ellipse at $P(x_0, y_0)$ and let m_1 and m_2 be the slopes of the lines PF_1 and PF_2, respectively, from P to the two foci F_1 and F_2 of the ellipse. Show that
$$\frac{m - m_1}{1 + m_1 m} = \frac{m_2 - m}{1 + m_2 m};$$
then use the identity for $\tan(A - B)$.]

82. Given $F_1(-c, 0)$ and $F_2(c, 0)$ with $a > c > 0$, prove that the ellipse
$$\frac{x^2}{a^2} + \frac{y^2}{b^2} = 1$$
(with $b^2 = a^2 - c^2$) is the locus of those points P such that $|PF_1| + |PF_2| = 2a$.

83. Find an equation of the ellipse with horizontal and vertical axes that passes through the points $(-1, 0), (3, 0), (0, 2),$ and $(0, -2)$.

84. Derive an equation for the ellipse with foci $(3, -3)$ and $(-3, 3)$ and major axis of length 10. Note that the foci of this ellipse lie on neither a vertical line nor a horizontal line.

85. Show that the graph of the equation
$$\frac{x^2}{15 - c} - \frac{y^2}{c - 6} = 1$$
is (a) a hyperbola with foci $(\pm 3, 0)$ if $6 < c < 15$ and (b) an ellipse if $c < 6$. (c) Identify the graph in the case $c > 15$.

86. Establish that the line tangent to the hyperbola
$$\frac{x^2}{a^2} - \frac{y^2}{b^2} = 1$$
at the point $P(x_0, y_0)$ has equation
$$\frac{x_0 x}{a^2} - \frac{y_0 y}{b^2} = 1.$$

87. Use the result of Problem 86 to establish the reflection property of the hyperbola. (See the suggestion for Problem 81.)

88. Suppose that $0 < a < c$, and let $b = \sqrt{c^2 - a^2}$. Show that the hyperbola $x^2/a^2 - y^2/b^2 = 1$ is the locus of a point P such that the *difference* between the distances $|PF_1|$ and $|PF_2|$ is equal to $2a$ (F_1 and F_2 are the foci of the hyperbola).

89. Derive an equation for the hyperbola with vertices $(\pm 3/\sqrt{2}, \pm 3/\sqrt{2})$ and foci $(\pm 5, \pm 5)$. Use the difference definition of a hyperbola implied by Problem 88.

90. Two radio signaling stations at A and B lie on an east-west line, with A 100 mi west of B. A plane is flying west on a line 50 mi north of the line AB. Radio signals are sent (traveling at 980 ft/μs) simultaneously from A and B, and the one sent from B arrives at the plane 400 μs before the one sent from A. Where is the plane?

91. Two radio signaling stations are located as in Problem 90 and transmit radio signals that travel at the same speed. But now we know only that the plane is generally somewhere north of the line AB, that the signal from B arrives 400 μs before the one sent from A, and that the signal sent from A and reflected by the plane takes a total of 600 μs to reach B. Where is the plane?

92. A comet has a parabolic orbit with the sun at one focus. When the comet is 150 million miles from the sun, the sun-comet line makes an angle of $45°$ with the axis of the parabola. What will be the minimum distance between the comet and the sun?

93. A satellite has an elliptical orbit with the center of the earth (take its radius to be 4000 mi) at one focus. The lowest point of its orbit is 500 mi above the North Pole and the highest point is 5000 mi above the South Pole. What is the height of the satellite above the surface of the earth when the satellite crosses the equatorial plane?

94. Find the closest approach to the sun of a comet as in Example 13 of this section; assume that $r = 2.5$ AU when $\theta = 45°$ and that $r = 1$ AU when $\theta = 90°$.

95. An ellipse has semimajor axis a and semiminor axis b. Use the polar-coordinate equation of an ellipse to derive the formula $A = \pi ab$ for its area.

96. The orbit of a certain comet approaching the sun is the parabola
$$r = \frac{1}{1 - \cos\theta}.$$
The units for r are in astronomical units. Suppose that it takes 15 days for the comet to travel from the position $\theta = 60°$ to the position $\theta = 90°$. How much longer will it require for the comet to reach its point of closest approach to the sun? Assume that the radius from the sun to the comet sweeps out area at a constant rate as the comet moves (Kepler's second law of planetary motion).

CHAPTER 10 REVIEW: CONCEPTS AND DEFINITIONS

Use the following list as a guide to additional concepts that you may need to review.

1. Conic sections
2. The relationship between rectangular and polar coordinates
3. The graph of an equation in polar coordinates
4. The area formula in polar coordinates
5. Definition of a parametric curve and of a smooth parametric curve
6. The slope of the line tangent to a smooth parametric curve (both in rectangular and in polar coordinates)
7. Integral computations with parametric curves [Eqs. (1) through (4) of Section 10.5]
8. Arc length of a parametric curve

REVIEW OF CONIC SECTIONS

The parabola with focus $(p, 0)$ and directrix $x = -p$ has eccentricity $e = 1$ and equation $y^2 = 4px$. The accompanying table compares the properties of an ellipse and a hyperbola, each with foci $(\pm c, 0)$ and major axis of length $2a$.

	Ellipse	Hyperbola
Eccentricity	$e = \dfrac{c}{a} < 1$	$e = \dfrac{c}{a} > 1$
a, b, c relation	$a^2 = b^2 + c^2$	$c^2 = a^2 + b^2$
Equation	$\dfrac{x^2}{a^2} + \dfrac{y^2}{b^2} = 1$	$\dfrac{x^2}{a^2} - \dfrac{y^2}{b^2} = 1$
Vertices	$(\pm a, 0)$	$(\pm a, 0)$
y-intercepts	$(0, \pm b)$	None
Directrices	$x = \pm \dfrac{a}{e}$	$x = \pm \dfrac{a}{e}$
Asymptotes	None	$y = \pm \dfrac{bx}{a}$

CHAPTER 10 MISCELLANEOUS PROBLEMS

Sketch the graphs of the equations in Problems 1 through 30. In Problems 1 through 18, if the graph is a conic section, label its center, foci, and vertices.

1. $x^2 + y^2 - 2x - 2y = 2$
2. $x^2 + y^2 = x + y$
3. $x^2 + y^2 - 6x + 2y + 9 = 0$
4. $y^2 = 4(x + y)$
5. $x^2 = 8x - 2y - 20$
6. $x^2 + 2y^2 - 2x + 8y + 8 = 0$
7. $9x^2 + 4y^2 = 36x$
8. $x^2 - y^2 = 2x - 2y - 1$
9. $y^2 - 2x^2 = 4x + 2y + 3$
10. $9y^2 - 4x^2 = 8x + 18y + 31$
11. $x^2 + 2y^2 = 4x + 4y - 12$
12. $y^2 - 6y + 4x + 5 = 0$
13. $9(x^2 - 2x + 1) = 4(y^2 + 9)$
14. $(x^2 - 4)(y^2 - 1) = 0$
15. $x^2 - 8x + y^2 - 2y + 16 = 0$
16. $(x - 1)^2 + 4(y - 2)^2 = 1$
17. $(x^2 - 4x + y^2 - 4y + 8)(x + y)^2 = 0$
18. $x = y^2 + 4y + 5$
19. $r = -2\cos\theta$
20. $\cos\theta + \sin\theta = 0$
21. $r = \dfrac{1}{\sin\theta + \cos\theta}$
22. $r\sin^2\theta = \cos\theta$
23. $r = 3\csc\theta$
24. $r = 2(\cos\theta - 1)$
25. $r^2 = 4\cos\theta$
26. $r\theta = 1$
27. $r = 3 - 2\sin\theta$
28. $r = \dfrac{1}{1 + \cos\theta}$
29. $r = \dfrac{4}{2 + \cos\theta}$
30. $r = \dfrac{4}{1 - 2\cos\theta}$

In Problems 31 through 38, find the area of the region described.

31. Inside both $r = 2\sin\theta$ and $r = 2\cos\theta$
32. Inside $r^2 = 4\cos\theta$
33. Inside $r = 3 - 2\sin\theta$ and outside $r = 4$
34. Inside $r^2 = 2\sin 2\theta$ and outside $r = 2\sin\theta$
35. Inside $r = 2\sin 2\theta$ and outside $r = \sqrt{2}$
36. Inside $r = 3\cos\theta$ and outside $r = 1 + \cos\theta$
37. Inside $r = 1 + \cos\theta$ and outside $r = \cos\theta$
38. Between the loops of $r = 1 - 2\sin\theta$

In Problems 39 through 43, eliminate the parameter and sketch the curve.

39. $x = 2t^3 - 1$, $y = 2t^3 + 1$
40. $x = \cosh t$, $y = \sinh t$
41. $x = 2 + \cos t$, $y = 1 - \sin t$
42. $x = \cos^4 t$, $y = \sin^4 t$
43. $x = 1 + t^2$, $y = t^3$

In Problems 44 through 48, write an equation of the line tangent to the given curve at the indicated point.

44. $x = t^2$, $y = t^3$; $t = 1$
45. $x = 3\sin t$, $y = 4\cos t$; $t = \pi/4$
46. $x = e^t$, $y = e^{-t}$; $t = 0$
47. $r = \theta$; $\theta = \pi/2$
48. $r = 1 + \sin\theta$; $\theta = \pi/3$

In Problems 49 through 52, find the area of the region between the given curve and the x-axis.

49. $x = 2t + 1$, $y = t^2 + 3$; $-1 \leq t \leq 2$
50. $x = e^t$, $y = e^{-t}$; $0 \leq t \leq 10$
51. $x = 3\sin t$, $y = 4\cos t$; $0 \leq t \leq \pi/2$
52. $x = \cosh t$, $y = \sinh t$; $0 \leq t \leq 1$

In Problems 53 through 57, find the arc length of the given curve.

53. $x = t^2$, $y = t^3$; $0 \leq t \leq 1$
54. $x = \ln(\cos t)$, $y = t$; $0 \leq t \leq \pi/4$
55. $x = 2t$, $y = t^3 + \dfrac{1}{3t}$; $1 \leq t \leq 2$

56. $r = \sin\theta$; $0 \leq \theta \leq \pi$
57. $r = \sin^2(\theta/3)$; $0 \leq \theta \leq \pi$

In Problems 58 through 62, find the area of the surface generated by revolving the given curve around the x-axis.

58. $x = t^2 + 1$, $y = 3t$; $0 \leq t \leq 2$
59. $x = 4\sqrt{t}$, $y = \dfrac{t^3}{3} + \dfrac{1}{2t^2}$; $1 \leq t \leq 4$
60. $r = \cos\theta$
61. $r = e^{\theta/2}$; $0 \leq \theta \leq \pi$
62. $x = e^t \cos t$, $y = e^t \sin t$; $0 \leq t \leq \pi/2$

63. Consider the rolling circle of radius a that was used to generate the cycloid in Example 5 of Section 10.4. Suppose that this circle is the rim of a disk, and let Q be a point of this disk at distance $b < a$ from its center. Find parametric equations for the curve traced by Q as the circle rolls along the x-axis. Assume that Q begins at the point $(0, a - b)$. Sketch this curve, which is called a **trochoid.**

64. If the smaller circle of Problem 34 in Section 10.4 rolls around the *outside* of the larger circle, the path of the point P is called an **epicycloid.** Show that it has parametric equations

$$x = (a+b)\cos t - b\cos\left(\frac{a+b}{b}t\right),$$
$$y = (a+b)\sin t - b\sin\left(\frac{a+b}{b}t\right).$$

65. Suppose that $b = a$ in Problem 64. Show that the epicycloid is then the cardioid $r = 2a(1 - \cos\theta)$ translated a units to the right.

66. Find the area of the surface generated by revolving the lemniscate $r^2 = 2a^2 \cos 2\theta$ around the x-axis.

67. Find the volume generated by revolving around the y-axis the area under the cycloid

$$x = a(t - \sin t), \quad y = a(1 - \cos t), \quad 0 \leq t \leq 2\pi.$$

68. Show that the length of one arch of the hypocycloid of Problem 34 in Section 10.4 is $s = 8b(a-b)/a$.

69. Find a polar-coordinate equation of the circle that passes through the origin and is centered at the point with polar coordinates (p, α).

70. Find a simple equation of the parabola whose focus is the origin and whose directrix is the line $y = x + 4$. Recall from Miscellaneous Problem 93 of Chapter 3 that the distance from the point (x_0, y_0) to the line with equation $Ax + By + C = 0$ is

$$\frac{|Ax_0 + By_0 + C|}{\sqrt{A^2 + B^2}}.$$

71. A **diameter** of an ellipse is a chord through its center. Find the maximum and minimum lengths of diameters of the ellipse with equation

$$\frac{x^2}{a^2} + \frac{y^2}{b^2} = 1.$$

72. Use calculus to prove that the ellipse of Problem 71 is normal to the coordinate axes at each of its four vertices.

73. The parabolic arch of a bridge has base width b and height h at its center. Write its equation, choosing the origin on the ground at the left end of the arch.

74. Use methods of calculus to find the points of the ellipse

$$\frac{x^2}{a^2} + \frac{y^2}{b^2} = 1$$

that are nearest to and farthest from (a) the center $(0,0)$; (b) the focus $(c, 0)$.

75. Consider a line segment QR that contains a point P such that $|QP| = a$ and $|PR| = b$. Suppose that Q is constrained to move on the y-axis, whereas R must remain on the x-axis. Prove that the locus of P is an ellipse.

76. Suppose that $a > 0$ and that F_1 and F_2 are two fixed points in the plane with $|F_1 F_2| > 2a$. Imagine a point P that moves in such a way that $|PF_2| = 2a + |PF_1|$. Prove that the locus of P is one branch of a hyperbola with foci F_1 and F_2. Then—as a consequence—explain how to construct points on a hyperbola by drawing appropriate circles centered at its foci.

77. Let Q_1 and Q_2 be two points on the parabola $y^2 = 4px$. Let P be the point of the parabola at which the tangent line is parallel to $Q_1 Q_2$. Prove that the horizontal line through P bisects the segment $Q_1 Q_2$.

78. Determine the locus of a point P such that the product of its distances from the two fixed points $F_1(-a, 0)$ and $F_2(a, 0)$ is a^2.

79. Find the eccentricity of the conic section with equation $3x^2 - y^2 + 12x + 9 = 0$.

80. Find the area bounded by the loop of the *strophoid*

$$r = \sec\theta - 2\cos\theta$$

shown in Fig. 10.MP.1.

FIGURE 10.MP.1 The strophoid of Problem 80.

FIGURE 10.MP.2 The folium of Descartes $x^3 + y^3 = 3xy$ (Problem 81).

81. Find the area bounded by the loop of the folium of Descartes with equation $x^3 + y^3 = 3xy$ shown in Fig. 10.MP.2. (*Suggestion:* Change to polar coordinates and then substitute $u = \tan\theta$ to evaluate the area integral.)

82. Use the method of Problem 81 to find the area bounded by the first-quadrant loop of the curve $x^5 + y^5 = 5x^2 y^2$ (similar to the folium of Problem 81).

83. The graph of a conic section in the xy-plane has intercepts at $(5, 0)$, $(-5, 0)$, $(0, 4)$, and $(0, -4)$. Deduce all the information you can about this conic. Can you determine whether it is a parabola, a hyperbola, or an ellipse? What if you also know that the graph of this conic is normal to the y-axis at the point $(0, 4)$?

INFINITE SERIES

11

Srinivasa Ramanujan
(1887–1920)

On a cold January day in 1913, the eminent Cambridge mathematics professor G. H. Hardy received a letter from an unknown 25-year-old clerk in the accounting department of a government office in Madras, India. Its author, Srinivasa Ramanujan, had no university education, he admitted—he had flunked out—but "after leaving school I have employed the spare time at my disposal to work at Mathematics ... I have not trodden through the conventional regular course ... but am striking out a new path for myself." The ten pages that followed listed in neat handwritten script approximately 50 formulas, most dealing with integrals and infinite series that Ramanujan had discovered, and asked Hardy's advice whether they contained anything of value. The formulas were of such exotic and unlikely appearance that Hardy at first suspected a hoax, but he and his colleague J. E. Littlewood soon realized that they were looking at the work of an extraordinary mathematical genius.

Thus began one of the most romantic episodes in the history of mathematics. In April 1914 Ramanujan arrived in England a poor, self-taught Indian mathematical amateur called to collaborate as an equal with the most sophisticated professional mathematicians of the day. For the next three years a steady stream of remarkable discoveries poured forth from his pen. But in 1917 he fell seriously ill, apparently with tuberculosis. The following year he returned to India to attempt to regain his health but never recovered, and he died in 1920 at the age of 32. Up to the very end he worked feverishly to record his final discoveries. He left behind notebooks outlining work whose completion occupied prominent mathematicians throughout the twentieth century.

With the possible exception of Euler, no one before or since has exhibited Ramanujan's virtuosity with infinite series. An example of his discoveries is the infinite series

$$\frac{1}{\pi} = \frac{\sqrt{8}}{9801} \sum_{n=0}^{\infty} \frac{(4n)!}{(n!)^4} \cdot \frac{(1103 + 26390n)}{396^{4n}},$$

whose first term yields the familiar approximation $\pi \approx 3.14159$, and with each additional term giving π to roughly eight more decimal places of accuracy. For instance, just four terms of Ramanujan's series are needed to calculate the 30-place approximation

$$\pi \approx 3.14159\ 26535\ 89793\ 23846\ 26433\ 83279$$

that suffices for virtually any imaginable "practical" application—if the universe were a sphere with a radius of 10 billion light years, then this value of π would give its circumference accurate to the nearest hundredth of an inch. But in recent years Ramanujan's ideas have been used to calculate the value of π accurate to a *billion* decimal places. Indeed, such gargantuan computations of π are commonly used to check the accuracy of new supercomputers.

A typical page of Ramanujan's letter to Hardy, listing formulas Ramanujan had discovered, but with no hint of proof or derivation.

681

11.1 INTRODUCTION

In the fifth century B.C., the Greek philosopher Zeno proposed the following paradox: In order for a runner to travel a given distance, the runner must first travel halfway, then half the remaining distance, then half the distance that yet remains, and so on *ad infinitum*. But, Zeno argued, it is clearly impossible for a runner to accomplish infinitely many such tasks in a finite period of time, so motion from one point to another is impossible.

Zeno's paradox suggests the infinite subdivision of [0, 1] indicated in Fig. 11.1.1. There is one subinterval of length $1/2^n$ for each integer $n = 1, 2, 3, \ldots$. If the length of the interval is the sum of the lengths of the subintervals into which it is divided, then it would appear that

$$1 = \frac{1}{2} + \frac{1}{4} + \frac{1}{8} + \frac{1}{16} + \cdots + \frac{1}{2^n} + \cdots,$$

FIGURE 11.1.1 Subdivision of an interval to illustrate Zeno's paradox.

with infinitely many terms somehow adding up to 1. But the formal infinite sum

$$1 + 2 + 3 + \cdots + n + \cdots$$

of all the positive integers seems meaningless—it does not appear to add up to *any* (finite) value.

The question is this: What, if anything, do we mean by the sum of an *infinite* collection of numbers? This chapter explores conditions under which an *infinite* sum

$$a_1 + a_2 + a_3 + \cdots + a_n + \cdots,$$

known as an *infinite series*, is meaningful. We discuss methods for computing the sum of an infinite series and applications of the algebra and calculus of infinite series. Infinite series are important in science and mathematics because many functions either arise most naturally in the form of infinite series or have infinite series representations (such as the Taylor series of Section 11.4) that are useful for numerical computations.

11.2 INFINITE SEQUENCES

An **infinite sequence** of real numbers is an ordered, unending list

$$a_1, a_2, a_3, a_4, \ldots, a_n, a_{n+1}, \ldots \quad (1)$$

of numbers. That this list is *ordered* implies that it has a first term a_1, a second term a_2, a third term a_3, and so forth. That the sequence is unending, or *infinite*, implies that (for every n) the *n*th term a_n has a successor a_{n+1}. Thus, as indicated by the final ellipsis in (1), an infinite sequence never ends and—despite the fact that we write explicitly only a finite number of terms—it actually has an infinite number of terms. Concise notation for the infinite sequence in (1) is

$$\{a_n\}_{n=1}^{\infty}, \quad \{a_n\}_1^{\infty}, \quad \text{or simply} \quad \{a_n\}. \quad (2)$$

Frequently an infinite sequence $\{a_n\}$ of numbers can be described "all at once" by a single function f that gives the successive terms of the sequence as successive values of the function:

$$a_n = f(n) \quad \text{for} \quad n = 1, 2, 3, \ldots. \quad (3)$$

Here $a_n = f(n)$ is simply a *formula for the nth term* of the sequence. Conversely, if the sequence $\{a_n\}$ is given in advance, we can regard (3) as the definition of the function f having the set of positive integers as its domain of definition. Ordinarily we will use the subscript notation a_n in preference to the function notation $f(n)$.

EXAMPLE 1 The following table exhibits several particular infinite sequences. Each is described in three ways: in the concise sequential notation $\{a_n\}$ of (2), by writing the formula as in (3) for its nth term, and in extended list notation as in (1). Note that n need not begin with the initial value 1.

$\left\{\dfrac{1}{n}\right\}_1^\infty \qquad a_n = \dfrac{1}{n} \qquad 1, \dfrac{1}{2}, \dfrac{1}{3}, \dfrac{1}{4}, \ldots, \dfrac{1}{n}, \ldots$

$\left\{\dfrac{1}{10^n}\right\}_0^\infty \qquad a_n = \dfrac{1}{10^n} \qquad 1, \dfrac{1}{10}, \dfrac{1}{100}, \dfrac{1}{1000}, \ldots, \dfrac{1}{10^n}, \ldots$

$\left\{\sqrt{3n-7}\right\}_3^\infty \qquad a_n = \sqrt{3n-7} \qquad \sqrt{2}, \sqrt{5}, \sqrt{8}, \sqrt{11}, \ldots, \sqrt{3n-7}, \ldots$

$\left\{\sin \dfrac{n\pi}{2}\right\}_1^\infty \qquad a_n = \sin \dfrac{n\pi}{2} \qquad 1, 0, -1, 0, \ldots, \sin \dfrac{n\pi}{2}, \ldots$

$\left\{3 + (-1)^n\right\}_1^\infty \qquad a_n = 3 + (-1)^n \qquad 2, 4, 2, 4, \ldots, 3 + (-1)^n, \ldots$

Sometimes it is inconvenient or impossible to give an explicit formula for the nth term of a particular sequence. The following example illustrates how sequences may be defined in other ways. ◆

EXAMPLE 2 Here we give the first ten terms of each sequence.

(a) The sequence of prime integers (those positive integers n having precisely two divisors, 1 and n with $n > 1$),

$$2, 3, 5, 7, 11, 13, 17, 19, 23, 29, \ldots$$

(b) The sequence whose nth term is the nth decimal digit of the number

$$\pi = 3.14159265358979323846\ldots,$$

$$1, 4, 1, 5, 9, 2, 6, 5, 3, 5, \ldots$$

(c) The **Fibonacci sequence** $\{F_n\}$, which may be defined by

$$F_1 = 1, \quad F_2 = 1, \quad \text{and} \quad F_{n+1} = F_n + F_{n-1} \quad \text{for} \quad n \geq 2.$$

Thus each term after the second is the sum of the preceding two terms:

$$1, 1, 2, 3, 5, 8, 13, 21, 34, 55, \ldots$$

This is an example of a *recursively defined* sequence in which each term (after the first few) is given by a formula involving its predecessors. The 13th-century Italian mathematician Fibonacci asked the following question: If we start with a single pair of rabbits that gives birth to a new pair after two months, and each such new pair does the same, how many pairs of rabbits will we have after n months? See Problems 55 and 56.

(d) If the amount $A_0 = 100$ dollars is invested in a savings account that draws 10% interest compounded annually, then the amount A_n in the account at the end of n years is defined (for $n \geq 1$) by the *iterative formula* $A_n = (1.10) A_{n-1}$ (rounded to the nearest number of cents) in terms of the preceding amount:

$$110.00, 121.00, 133.10, 146.41, 161.05, 177.16,$$
$$194.87, 214.36, 235.79, 259.37, \ldots \quad ◆$$

Limits of Sequences

The limit of a sequence is defined in much the same way as the limit of an ordinary function (Section 2.2).

DEFINITION   Limit of a Sequence
We say that the sequence $\{a_n\}$ **converges** to the real number L, or has the **limit** L, and we write

$$\lim_{n \to \infty} a_n = L, \qquad (4)$$

provided that a_n can be made as close to L as we please merely by choosing n to be sufficiently large. That is, given any number $\epsilon > 0$, there exists an integer N such that

$$|a_n - L| < \epsilon \quad \text{for all } n \geqq N. \qquad (5)$$

If the sequence $\{a_n\}$ does *not* converge, then we say that $\{a_n\}$ **diverges.**

FIGURE 11.2.1 The point (n, a_n) approaches the line $y = L$ as $n \to +\infty$.

FIGURE 11.2.2 The inequality $|a_n - L| < \epsilon$ means that a_n lies somewhere between $L - \epsilon$ and $L + \epsilon$.

Figure 11.2.1 illustrates geometrically the definition of the limit of a sequence. Because

$$|a_n - L| < \epsilon \quad \text{means that} \quad L - \epsilon < a_n < L + \epsilon,$$

the condition in (5) means that if $n \geqq N$, then the point (n, a_n) lies between the horizontal lines $y = L - \epsilon$ and $y = L + \epsilon$. Alternatively, if $n \geqq N$, then the number a_n lies between the points $L - \epsilon$ and $L + \epsilon$ on the real line (Fig. 11.2.2).

EXAMPLE 3 Suppose that we want to establish rigorously the intuitively evident fact that the sequence $\{1/n\}_1^\infty$ converges to zero,

$$\lim_{n \to \infty} \frac{1}{n} = 0. \qquad (6)$$

Because $L = 0$ here, we need only convince ourselves that to each positive number ϵ there corresponds an integer N such that

$$\left| \frac{1}{n} \right| = \frac{1}{n} < \epsilon \quad \text{if} \quad n \geqq N.$$

But evidently it suffices to choose any fixed integer $N > 1/\epsilon$. Then $n \geqq N$ implies immediately that

$$\frac{1}{n} \leqq \frac{1}{N} < \epsilon,$$

as desired (Fig. 11.2.3). ◆

FIGURE 11.2.3 If $N > \dfrac{1}{\epsilon}$ and $n \geqq N$ then $0 < \dfrac{1}{n} \leqq \dfrac{1}{N} < \epsilon$.

EXAMPLE 4 (a) The sequence $\{(-1)^n\}$ diverges because its successive terms "oscillate" between the two values $+1$ and -1. Hence $(-1)^n$ cannot approach any single value as $n \to \infty$. (b) The terms of the sequence $\{n^2\}$ increase without bound as $n \to \infty$. Thus the sequence $\{n^2\}$ diverges. In this case, we might also say that $\{n^2\}$ diverges *to infinity*. ◆

Using Limit Laws

The limit laws in Section 2.2 for limits of functions have natural analogues for limits of sequences. Their proofs are based on techniques similar to those used in Appendix D.

THEOREM 1 Limit Laws for Sequences
If the limits
$$\lim_{n \to \infty} a_n = A \quad \text{and} \quad \lim_{n \to \infty} b_n = B$$
exist (so A and B are real numbers), then

1. $\lim_{n \to \infty} c a_n = cA$ (c any real number);
2. $\lim_{n \to \infty} (a_n + b_n) = A + B$;
3. $\lim_{n \to \infty} a_n b_n = AB$;
4. $\lim_{n \to \infty} \dfrac{a_n}{b_n} = \dfrac{A}{B}$.

In part 4 we must assume that $B \neq 0$ (so that $b_n \neq 0$ for all sufficiently large values of n).

THEOREM 2 Substitution Law for Sequences
If $\lim_{n \to \infty} a_n = A$ and the function f is continuous at $x = A$, then
$$\lim_{n \to \infty} f(a_n) = f(A).$$

THEOREM 3 Squeeze Law for Sequences
If $a_n \leqq b_n \leqq c_n$ for all n and
$$\lim_{n \to \infty} a_n = L = \lim_{n \to \infty} c_n,$$
then $\lim_{n \to \infty} b_n = L$ as well.

These theorems can be used to compute limits of many sequences formally, without recourse to the definition. For example, Eq. (6) and the product law of limits yield
$$\lim_{n \to \infty} \frac{1}{n^k} = 0 \tag{7}$$
for every positive integer k.

EXAMPLE 5 Eq. (7) and the limit laws give (after dividing numerator and denominator by the highest power of n that is present)

$$\lim_{n \to \infty} \frac{7n^2}{5n^2 - 3} = \lim_{n \to \infty} \frac{7}{5 - \dfrac{3}{n^2}}$$

$$= \frac{\lim_{n \to \infty} 7}{\left(\lim_{n \to \infty} 5\right) - 3 \cdot \left(\lim_{n \to \infty} \dfrac{1}{n^2}\right)} = \frac{7}{5 - 3 \cdot 0} = \frac{7}{5}.$$ ◆

FIGURE 11.2.4 The points $(n, (\cos n)/n)$ for $n = 1, 2, \ldots, 30$.

EXAMPLE 6 Show that $\lim_{n \to \infty} \dfrac{\cos n}{n} = 0$.

Solution This follows from the squeeze law and the fact that $1/n \to 0$ as $n \to \infty$, because

$$-\frac{1}{n} \leqq \frac{\cos n}{n} \leqq \frac{1}{n}$$

for every positive integer n. ◆

REMARK With a typical graphing calculator (in "dot plot mode") or computer algebra system (using its "list plot" facility), one can plot the points (n, a_n) in the xy-plane corresponding to a given sequence $\{a_n\}$. Figure 11.2.4 shows such a plot for the sequence of Example 6 and provides visual evidence of its convergence to zero.

EXAMPLE 7 Show that if $a > 0$, then $\lim_{n \to \infty} \sqrt[n]{a} = 1$.

Solution We apply the substitution law with $f(x) = a^x$, $a_n = 1/n$, and $A = 0$. Because $1/n \to 0$ as $n \to \infty$ and f is continuous at $x = 0$, this gives

$$\lim_{n \to \infty} a^{1/n} = \lim_{n \to \infty} f(1/n) = f(0) = a^0 = 1.$$ ◆

EXAMPLE 8 The limit laws and the continuity of $f(x) = \sqrt{x}$ at $x = 4$ yield

$$\lim_{n \to \infty} \sqrt{\frac{4n-1}{n+1}} = \left(\lim_{n \to \infty} \frac{4 - \dfrac{1}{n}}{1 + \dfrac{1}{n}} \right)^{1/2} = \sqrt{4} = 2.$$ ◆

EXAMPLE 9 Show that if $|r| < 1$, then $\lim_{n \to \infty} r^n = 0$.

Solution Because $|r^n| = |(-r)^n|$, we may assume that $0 < r < 1$. Then $1/r = 1 + a$ for some number $a > 0$, so the binomial formula yields

$$\frac{1}{r^n} = (1 + a)^n = 1 + na + \{\text{positive terms}\} > 1 + na;$$

$$0 < r^n < \frac{1}{1 + na}.$$

Now $1/(1 + na) \to 0$ as $n \to \infty$. Therefore, the squeeze law implies that $r^n \to 0$ as $n \to \infty$. ◆

Figure 11.2.5 shows the graph of a function f such that $\lim_{x \to \infty} f(x) = L$. If the sequence $\{a_n\}$ is defined by the formula $a_n = f(n)$ for each positive integer n,

FIGURE 11.2.5 If $\lim_{x \to \infty} f(x) = L$ and $a_n = f(n)$, then $\lim_{n \to \infty} a_n = L$.

then all the points $(n, f(n))$ lie on the graph of $y = f(x)$. It therefore follows from the definition of the limit of a function that $\lim_{n \to \infty} a_n = L$ as well.

THEOREM 4 Limits of Functions and Sequences
If $a_n = f(n)$ for each positive integer n, then

$$\lim_{x \to \infty} f(x) = L \quad \text{implies that} \quad \lim_{n \to \infty} a_n = L. \tag{8}$$

The converse of the statement in (8) is generally false. For example, take $f(x) = \sin \pi x$ and, for each positive integer n, let $a_n = f(n) = \sin n\pi$. Then $\sin n\pi \equiv 0$, but $\sin nx$ oscillates between 1 and -1, so

$$\lim_{n \to \infty} a_n = \lim_{n \to \infty} \sin n\pi = 0, \quad \text{but}$$

$$\lim_{x \to \infty} f(x) = \lim_{x \to \infty} \sin \pi x \quad \text{does not exist.}$$

Because of (8) we can use **l'Hôpital's rule for sequences:** If $a_n = f(n)$, $b_n = g(n)$, and $f(x)/g(x)$ has the indeterminate form ∞/∞ as $x \to \infty$, then

$$\lim_{n \to \infty} \frac{a_n}{b_n} = \lim_{x \to \infty} \frac{f(x)}{g(x)} = \lim_{x \to \infty} \frac{f'(x)}{g'(x)}, \tag{9}$$

provided that f and g satisfy the other hypotheses of l'Hôpital's rule, including the important assumption that the right-hand limit exists.

EXAMPLE 10 Show that $\lim_{n \to \infty} \frac{\ln n}{n} = 0$.

Solution The function $(\ln x)/x$ is defined for all $x \geq 1$ and agrees with the given sequence $\{(\ln n)/n\}$ when $x = n$, a positive integer. Because $(\ln x)/x$ has the indeterminate form ∞/∞ as $x \to \infty$, l'Hôpital's rule gives

$$\lim_{n \to \infty} \frac{\ln n}{n} = \lim_{x \to \infty} \frac{\ln x}{x} = \lim_{x \to \infty} \frac{\frac{1}{x}}{1} = 0. \qquad \blacklozenge$$

EXAMPLE 11 Show that $\lim_{n \to \infty} \sqrt[n]{n} = 1$.

Solution First we note that

$$\ln \sqrt[n]{n} = \ln n^{1/n} = \frac{\ln n}{n} \to 0 \quad \text{as } n \to \infty,$$

by Example 10. By the substitution law with $f(x) = e^x$, this gives

$$\lim_{n \to \infty} n^{1/n} = \lim_{n \to \infty} \exp\left(\ln n^{1/n}\right) = e^0 = 1. \qquad \blacklozenge$$

EXAMPLE 12 Find $\lim_{n \to \infty} \frac{3n^3}{e^{2n}}$.

Solution We apply l'Hôpital's rule repeatedly, although we must be careful at each intermediate step to verify that we still have an indeterminate form. Thus we find that

$$\lim_{n \to \infty} \frac{3n^3}{e^{2n}} = \lim_{x \to \infty} \frac{3x^3}{e^{2x}} = \lim_{x \to \infty} \frac{9x^2}{2e^{2x}} = \lim_{x \to \infty} \frac{18x}{4e^{2x}} = \lim_{x \to \infty} \frac{18}{8e^{2x}} = 0. \qquad \blacklozenge$$

Bounded Monotonic Sequences

The set of all *rational* numbers has by itself all of the most familiar elementary algebraic properties of the entire real number system. To guarantee the existence of irrational numbers, we must assume in addition a "completeness property" of the real numbers. Otherwise, the real line might have "holes" where the irrational numbers ought to be. One way of stating this completeness property is in terms of the convergence of an important type of sequence, a bounded monotonic sequence.

The sequence $\{a_n\}_1^\infty$ is said to be **increasing** if

$$a_1 \leq a_2 \leq a_3 \leq \cdots \leq a_n \leq \cdots$$

and **decreasing** if

$$a_1 \geq a_2 \geq a_3 \geq \cdots \geq a_n \geq \cdots.$$

The sequence $\{a_n\}$ is **monotonic** if it is either increasing or decreasing. The sequence $\{a_n\}$ is **bounded** if there is a number M such that $|a_n| \leq M$ for all n. The following assertion may be taken to be an axiom for the real number system.

Bounded Monotonic Sequence Property
Every bounded monotonic infinite sequence converges—that is, has a finite limit.

Suppose, for example, that the increasing sequence $\{a_n\}_1^\infty$ is bounded above by a number M, meaning that $a_n \leq M$ for all $n \geq 1$. Because the sequence is also bounded below (by a_1, for instance), the bounded monotonic sequence property implies that

$$\lim_{n \to \infty} a_n = A \quad \text{for some real number } A \leq M,$$

as in Fig. 11.2.6(a). If the increasing sequence $\{a_n\}$ is not bounded above, then it follows that

$$\lim_{n \to \infty} a_n = +\infty$$

as in Fig. 11.2.6(b). (See Problem 52.) Figure 11.2.7 illustrates the graph of a typical bounded increasing sequence, with the heights of the points (n, a_n) steadily rising toward A.

FIGURE 11.2.6 (a) If the increasing sequence $\{a_n\}$ is bounded above by M, then its terms "pile up" at some point $A \leq M$. (b) If the sequence is unbounded, then its terms "keep going" and diverge to infinity.

FIGURE 11.2.7 Graph of a bounded increasing sequence with limit A.

EXAMPLE 13 Investigate the sequence $\{a_n\}$ that is defined recursively by

$$a_1 = \sqrt{6}, \qquad a_{n+1} = \sqrt{6 + a_n} \quad \text{for} \quad n \geq 1. \tag{10}$$

Solution The first four terms of this sequence are

$$\sqrt{6}, \quad \sqrt{6+\sqrt{6}}, \quad \sqrt{6+\sqrt{6+\sqrt{6}}}, \quad \sqrt{6+\sqrt{6+\sqrt{6+\sqrt{6}}}}. \tag{11}$$

If the sequence $\{a_n\}$ converges, then its limit A would seem to be the natural interpretation of the infinite expression

$$\sqrt{6+\sqrt{6+\sqrt{6+\sqrt{6+\cdots}}}}.$$

A calculator gives 2.449, 2.907, 2.984, and 2.997 for the approximate values of the terms in (11). This suggests that the sequence may be bounded above by $M = 3$. Indeed, if we assume that a particular term a_n satisfies the inequality $a_n < 3$, then it follows that

$$a_{n+1} = \sqrt{6 + a_n} < \sqrt{6 + 3} = 3;$$

that is, $a_{n+1} < 3$ as well. Can you see that this implies that *all* terms of the sequence are less than 3? (If there were a first term not less than 3, then its predecessor would be less than 3, and we would have a contradiction. This is a "proof by mathematical induction.")

In order to apply the bounded monotonic sequence property to conclude that the sequence $\{a_n\}$ converges, it remains to show that it is an increasing sequence. But

$$(a_{n+1})^2 - (a_n)^2 = (6 + a_n) - (a_n)^2 = (2 + a_n)(3 - a_n) > 0$$

because $a_n < 3$. Because all terms of the sequence are positive (why?), it therefore follows that $a_{n+1} > a_n$ for all $n \geq 1$, as desired.

Now that we know that the limit A of the sequence $\{a_n\}$ exists, we can write

$$A = \lim_{n \to \infty} a_{n+1} = \lim_{n \to \infty} \sqrt{6 + a_n} = \sqrt{6 + A},$$

and thus $A^2 = 6 + A$. The roots of this quadratic equation are -2 and 3. Because $A > 0$ (why?), we conclude that $A = \lim_{n \to \infty} a_n = 3$, and so

$$\sqrt{6 + \sqrt{6 + \sqrt{6 + \sqrt{6 + \cdots}}}} = 3. \tag{12}$$

FIGURE 11.2.8 Graph of the sequence of Example 13.

The graph in Fig. 11.2.8 of the first ten terms of the sequence $\{a_n\}$ shows that the convergence to its limit 3 is quite rapid. ◆

To indicate what the bounded monotonic sequence property has to do with the "completeness property" of the real numbers, in Problem 63 we outline a proof, using this property, of the existence of the number $\sqrt{2}$. In Problems 61 and 62, we outline a proof of the equivalence of the bounded monotonic sequence property and another common statement of the completeness of the real number system—the *least upper bound property*.

11.2 TRUE/FALSE STUDY GUIDE

11.2 CONCEPTS: QUESTIONS AND DISCUSSION

1. Can a sequence $\{a_n\}_1^\infty$ converge to two different numbers?
2. Suppose it is known that every open interval containing the point L contains all but finitely many members of the sequence $\{a_n\}_1^\infty$. Does this imply that $\lim_{n \to \infty} a_n = L$?
3. Suppose that the sequence $\{a_n\}_1^\infty$ is obtained by interspersing the members of the two convergent infinite sequences $\{p_n\}_1^\infty$ and $\{q_n\}_1^\infty$. Does it follow that the sequence $\{a_n\}_1^\infty$ also converges?

11.2 PROBLEMS

In Problems 1 through 8, find a pattern in the sequence with given terms a_1, a_2, a_3, a_4 and (assuming that it continues as indicated) write a formula for the general term a_n of the sequence.

1. $1, 4, 9, 16, \ldots$
2. $2, 7, 12, 17, \ldots$
3. $\frac{1}{3}, \frac{1}{9}, \frac{1}{27}, \frac{1}{81}, \ldots$
4. $1, -\frac{1}{2}, \frac{1}{4}, -\frac{1}{8}, \ldots$
5. $\frac{1}{2}, \frac{1}{5}, \frac{1}{8}, \frac{1}{11}, \ldots$
6. $\frac{1}{2}, \frac{1}{5}, \frac{1}{10}, \frac{1}{17}, \ldots$
7. $0, 2, 0, 2, \ldots$
8. $10, 5, 10, 5, \ldots$

In Problems 9 through 42, determine whether or not the sequence $\{a_n\}$ converges, and find its limit if it does converge.

9. $a_n = \dfrac{2n}{5n - 3}$
10. $a_n = \dfrac{1 - n^2}{2 + 3n^2}$
11. $a_n = \dfrac{n^2 - n + 7}{2n^3 + n^2}$
12. $a_n = \dfrac{n^3}{10n^2 + 1}$
13. $a_n = 1 + \left(\frac{9}{10}\right)^n$
14. $a_n = 2 - \left(-\frac{1}{2}\right)^n$

15. $a_n = 1 + (-1)^n$

16. $a_n = \dfrac{1 + (-1)^n}{\sqrt{n}}$

17. $a_n = \dfrac{1 + (-1)^n \sqrt{n}}{\left(\frac{3}{2}\right)^n}$

18. $a_n = \dfrac{\sin n}{3^n}$

19. $a_n = \dfrac{\sin^2 n}{\sqrt{n}}$

20. $a_n = \sqrt{\dfrac{2 + \cos n}{n}}$

21. $a_n = n \sin \pi n$

22. $a_n = n \cos \pi n$

23. $a_n = \pi^{-(\sin n)/n}$

24. $a_n = 2^{\cos \pi n}$

25. $a_n = \dfrac{\ln n}{\sqrt{n}}$

26. $a_n = \dfrac{\ln 2n}{\ln 3n}$

27. $a_n = \dfrac{(\ln n)^2}{n}$

28. $a_n = n \sin\left(\dfrac{1}{n}\right)$

29. $a_n = \dfrac{\tan^{-1} n}{n}$

30. $a_n = \dfrac{n^3}{e^{n/10}}$

31. $a_n = \dfrac{2^n + 1}{e^n}$

32. $a_n = \dfrac{\sinh n}{\cosh n}$

33. $a_n = \left(1 + \dfrac{1}{n}\right)^n$

34. $a_n = (2n + 5)^{1/n}$

35. $a_n = \left(\dfrac{n-1}{n+1}\right)^n$

36. $a_n = (0.001)^{-1/n}$

37. $a_n = \sqrt[n]{2^{n+1}}$

38. $a_n = \left(1 - \dfrac{2}{n^2}\right)^n$

39. $a_n = \left(\dfrac{2}{n}\right)^{3/n}$

40. $a_n = (-1)^n (n^2 + 1)^{1/n}$

41. $a_n = \left(\dfrac{2 - n^2}{3 + n^2}\right)^n$

42. $a_n = \dfrac{\left(\frac{2}{3}\right)^n}{1 - \sqrt[n]{n}}$

In Problems 43 through 50, investigate the given sequence $\{a_n\}$ numerically or graphically. Formulate a reasonable guess for the value of its limit. Then apply limit laws to verify that your guess is correct.

43. $a_n = \dfrac{n-2}{n+13}$

44. $a_n = \dfrac{2n+3}{5n-17}$

45. $a_n = \sqrt{\dfrac{4n^2 + 7}{n^2 + 3n}}$

46. $a_n = \left(\dfrac{n^3 - 5}{8n^3 + 7n}\right)^{1/3}$

47. $a_n = e^{-1/\sqrt{n}}$

48. $a_n = n \sin \dfrac{2}{n}$

49. $a_n = 4 \tan^{-1} \dfrac{n-1}{n+1}$

50. $a_n = 3 \sin^{-1} \sqrt{\dfrac{3n-1}{4n+1}}$

51. Prove that if $\lim_{n \to \infty} a_n = A \ne 0$, then the sequence $\{(-1)^n a_n\}$ diverges.

52. Prove that if the increasing sequence $\{a_n\}$ is not bounded, then $\lim_{n \to \infty} a_n = +\infty$. (It's largely a matter of saying precisely what this means.)

53. Suppose that $A > 0$. Given $x_1 \ne 0$ but otherwise arbitrary, define the sequence $\{x_n\}$ recursively by
$$x_{n+1} = \dfrac{1}{2} \cdot \left(x_n + \dfrac{A}{x_n}\right) \quad \text{if} \quad n \ge 1.$$
Prove that if $L = \lim_{n \to \infty} x_n$ exists, then $L = \pm\sqrt{A}$.

54. Suppose that A is a fixed real number. Given $x_1 \ne 0$ but otherwise arbitrary, define the sequence $\{x_n\}$ recursively by
$$x_{n+1} = \dfrac{1}{3} \cdot \left(2x_n + \dfrac{A}{(x_n)^2}\right) \quad \text{if} \quad n \ge 1.$$
Prove that if $L = \lim_{n \to \infty} x_n$ exists, then $L = \sqrt[3]{A}$.

55. (a) Suppose that every newborn pair of rabbits becomes productive after two months, and thereafter gives birth to a new pair of rabbits every month. If we begin with a single newborn pair of rabbits, denote by F_n the total number of pairs of rabbits we have after n months. Explain carefully why $\{F_n\}$ is the Fibonacci sequence of Example 2. (b) If, instead, every newborn pair of rabbits becomes productive after three months, denote by $\{G_n\}$ the number of pairs of rabbits we have after n months. Give a recursive definition of the sequence $\{G_n\}$ and calculate its first ten terms.

56. Let $\{F_n\}$ be the Fibonacci sequence of Example 2, and assume that
$$\tau = \lim_{n \to \infty} \dfrac{F_{n+1}}{F_n}$$
exists. (It does.) Show that $\tau = \frac{1}{2}(1+\sqrt{5})$. (Suggestion: Write $a_n = F_n/F_{n-1}$ and show that $a_{n+1} = 1 + (1/a_n)$.)

57. Let the sequence $\{a_n\}$ be defined recursively as follows:
$$a_1 = 2; \qquad a_{n+1} = \tfrac{1}{2}(a_n + 4) \quad \text{for } n \ge 1.$$
(a) Prove by induction on n that $a_n < 4$ for each n and that $\{a_n\}$ is an increasing sequence. (b) Find the limit of this sequence.

58. Investigate as in Example 13 the sequence $\{a_n\}$ that is defined recursively by
$$a_1 = \sqrt{2}, \qquad a_{n+1} = \sqrt{2 + a_n} \quad \text{for } n \ge 1.$$
In particular, show that
$$\sqrt{2 + \sqrt{2 + \sqrt{2 + \sqrt{2 + \cdots}}}} = 2.$$

Verify the results stated in Problems 59 and 60.

59. $\sqrt{20 + \sqrt{20 + \sqrt{20 + \sqrt{20 + \cdots}}}} = 5$.

60. $\sqrt{90 + \sqrt{90 + \sqrt{90 + \sqrt{90 + \cdots}}}} = 10$.

Problems 61 and 62 deal with the least upper bound property of the real numbers: If the nonempty set S of real numbers has an upper bound, then S has a least upper bound. The number M is an **upper bound** for the set S if $x \le M$ for all x in S. The upper bound L of S is a **least upper bound** for S if no number smaller than L is an upper bound for S. You can easily show that if the set S has least upper bounds L_1 and L_2, then $L_1 = L_2$; in other words, if a least upper bound for a set exists, then it is unique.

61. Prove that the least upper bound property implies the bounded monotonic sequence property. (Suggestion: If $\{a_n\}$ is a bounded increasing sequence and A is the least upper bound of the set $\{a_n : n \ge 1\}$ of terms of the sequence, you can prove that $A = \lim_{n \to \infty} a_n$.)

62. Prove that the bounded monotonic sequence property implies the least upper bound property. (Suggestion: For each

positive integer n, let a_n be the least integral multiple of $1/10^n$ that is an upper bound of the set S. Prove that $\{a_n\}$ is a bounded decreasing sequence and then that $A = \lim_{n\to\infty} a_n$ is a least upper bound for S.)

63. For each positive integer n, let a_n be the largest integral multiple of $1/10^n$ such that $a_n^2 \leq 2$. (a) Prove that $\{a_n\}$ is a bounded increasing sequence, so $A = \lim_{n\to\infty} a_n$ exists. (b) Prove that if $A^2 > 2$, then $a_n^2 > 2$ for n sufficiently large.

(c) Prove that if $A^2 < 2$, then $a_n^2 < B$ for some number $B < 2$ and all sufficiently large n. (d) Conclude that $A^2 = 2$.

64. Investigate the sequence $\{a_n\}$, where

$$a_n = [\![n + \tfrac{1}{2} + \sqrt{n}]\!].$$

You may need a computer or programmable calculator to discover what is remarkable about this sequence.

11.2 Project: Nested Radicals and Continued Fractions

This project is an investigation of the relation

$$\sqrt{q + p\sqrt{q + p\sqrt{q + p\sqrt{q + \cdots}}}} = p + \cfrac{q}{p + \cfrac{q}{p + \cfrac{q}{p + \cdots}}} \qquad (1)$$

where p and q are positive. We ask not only whether this equation could possibly be true, but also what it means. In the following two numerical explorations, you can (for instance) take p and q to be the last two nonzero digits in your student I.D. number.

Exploration 1 Define the infinite sequence $\{a_n\}$ recursively by

$$a_1 = \sqrt{q} \quad \text{and} \quad a_{n+1} = \sqrt{q + pa_n} \quad \text{for} \quad n \geq 1. \qquad (2)$$

Use a calculator or computer to approximate enough terms of this sequence numerically to determine whether it appears to converge. Assuming that it does, write the first several terms symbolically and conclude that $A = \lim_{n\to\infty} a_n$ is a natural interpretation of the *nested radical* on the left-hand side in (1). Finally, take the limit in the recursion in (2) to show that A is the positive solution of the quadratic equation $x^2 - px - q = 0$. Does the quadratic formula then yield a result consistent with your numerical evidence?

Exploration 2 Define the infinite sequence $\{b_n\}$ recursively by

$$b_1 = p \quad \text{and} \quad b_{n+1} = p + \frac{q}{b_n} \quad \text{for} \quad n \geq 1. \qquad (3)$$

Use a calculator or computer to approximate enough terms of this sequence numerically to determine whether or not it appears to converge. Assuming that it does, write the first several terms symbolically and conclude that $B = \lim_{n\to\infty} b_n$ is a natural interpretation of the *continued fraction* on the right-hand side in (1). Finally, take the limit in the recursion in (3) to show that B is also the positive solution of the quadratic equation $x^2 - px - q = 0$. Conclude thereby that Eq. (1) is indeed true.

11.3 INFINITE SERIES AND CONVERGENCE

An **infinite series** is an expression of the form

$$\sum_{n=1}^{\infty} a_n = a_1 + a_2 + a_3 + \cdots + a_n + \cdots, \qquad (1)$$

where $\{a_n\}$ is an infinite sequence of real numbers. The number a_n is called the ***n*th term** of the series. The symbol $\sum_{n=1}^{\infty} a_n$ is simply an abbreviation for the right-hand side of Eq. (1). In this section we discover what is meant by the **sum** of an infinite series.

692 CHAPTER 11 Infinite Series

EXAMPLE 1 Consider the infinite series

$$\sum_{n=1}^{\infty} \frac{1}{2^n} = \frac{1}{2} + \frac{1}{4} + \frac{1}{8} + \frac{1}{16} + \cdots + \frac{1}{2^n} + \cdots \quad (2)$$

that was mentioned in Section 11.1; its nth term is $a_n = 1/2^n$. Although we cannot literally add an infinite number of terms, we can add any finite number of the terms in (2). For instance, the sum of the first five terms is

$$\frac{1}{2} + \frac{1}{4} + \frac{1}{8} + \frac{1}{16} + \frac{1}{32} = \frac{31}{32} = 0.96875.$$

n	Sum of First n Terms
5	0.96875000
10	0.99902344
15	0.99996948
20	0.99999905
25	0.99999997

FIGURE 11.3.1 Sums of terms in the infinite series of Example 1.

We could add five more terms, then five more, and so forth. The table in Fig. 11.3.1 shows what happens. It appears that the sums get closer and closer to 1 as we add more and more terms. If indeed this is so, then it is natural to say that the sum of the (whole) infinite series in (2) is 1, and hence to write

$$\sum_{n=1}^{\infty} \frac{1}{2^n} = \frac{1}{2} + \frac{1}{4} + \frac{1}{8} + \frac{1}{16} + \cdots + \frac{1}{2^n} + \cdots = 1. \quad \blacklozenge$$

Motivated by Example 1, we introduce the *partial sums* of the general infinite series in (1). The *n*th **partial sum** S_n of the series is the sum of its first n terms:

$$S_n = a_1 + a_2 + a_3 + \cdots + a_n = \sum_{k=1}^{n} a_k. \quad (3)$$

Thus each infinite series has not only an infinite sequence of terms, but also an **infinite sequence of partial sums** $S_1, S_2, S_3, \ldots, S_n, \ldots$, where

$$S_1 = a_1,$$
$$S_2 = a_1 + a_2,$$
$$S_3 = a_1 + a_2 + a_3,$$
$$\vdots$$
$$S_{10} = a_1 + a_2 + a_3 + a_4 + a_5 + a_6 + a_7 + a_8 + a_9 + a_{10},$$

and so forth. We define the sum of the infinite series to be the limit of its sequence of partial sums, provided that this limit exists.

DEFINITION The Sum of an Infinite Series
We say that the infinite series

$$\sum_{n=1}^{\infty} a_n \quad \textbf{converges} \text{ (or is } \textbf{convergent}\text{)}$$

with **sum** S provided that the limit of its sequence of partial sums,

$$S = \lim_{n \to \infty} S_n, \quad (4)$$

exists (and is finite). Otherwise we say that the series **diverges** (or is **divergent**). If a series diverges, then it has no sum.

Thus the sum of an infinite series is a limit of finite sums,

$$S = \sum_{n=1}^{\infty} a_n = \lim_{N \to \infty} \sum_{n=1}^{N} a_n,$$

provided that this limit exists.

EXAMPLE 1 (continued) Show that the series

$$\sum_{n=1}^{\infty} \left(\frac{1}{2}\right)^n = \frac{1}{2} + \frac{1}{4} + \frac{1}{8} + \frac{1}{16} + \cdots$$

converges. Then find its sum.

Solution The first four partial sums are

$$S_1 = \frac{1}{2}, \quad S_2 = \frac{3}{4}, \quad S_3 = \frac{7}{8}, \quad \text{and} \quad S_4 = \frac{15}{16}.$$

It seems likely that $S_n = (2^n - 1)/2^n$, and indeed this follows easily by induction, because

$$S_{n+1} = S_n + \frac{1}{2^{n+1}} = \frac{2^n - 1}{2^n} + \frac{1}{2^{n+1}} = \frac{2^{n+1} - 2 + 1}{2^{n+1}} = \frac{2^{n+1} - 1}{2^{n+1}}.$$

Hence the sum of the given series is

$$S = \lim_{n \to \infty} S_n = \lim_{n \to \infty} \frac{2^n - 1}{2^n} = \lim_{n \to \infty} \left(1 - \frac{1}{2^n}\right) = 1.$$

FIGURE 11.3.2 Graph of the first 20 partial sums of the infinite series in Example 1.

The graph in Fig. 11.3.2 illustrates the convergence of the partial sums to the number 1. ◆

EXAMPLE 2 Show that the series

$$\sum_{n=1}^{\infty} (-1)^{n+1} = 1 - 1 + 1 - 1 + \cdots$$

diverges.

Solution The sequence of partial sums of this series is

$$1, 0, 1, 0, 1, \ldots,$$

which has no limit. Therefore the series diverges. ◆

EXAMPLE 3 Show that the infinite series

$$\sum_{n=1}^{\infty} \frac{1}{n(n+1)}$$

converges. Then find its sum.

Solution We need a formula for the nth partial sum S_n so that we can evaluate its limit as $n \to \infty$. To find such a formula, we begin with the observation that the nth term of the series is

$$a_n = \frac{1}{n(n+1)} = \frac{1}{n} - \frac{1}{n+1}.$$

(In more complicated cases, such as those in Problems 50 through 55, such a decomposition can be obtained by the method of partial fractions.) It follows that the sum of the first n terms of the given series is

$$S_n = \left(1 - \frac{1}{2}\right) + \left(\frac{1}{2} - \frac{1}{3}\right) + \left(\frac{1}{3} - \frac{1}{4}\right)$$

$$+ \left(\frac{1}{4} - \frac{1}{5}\right) + \cdots + \left(\frac{1}{n} - \frac{1}{n+1}\right)$$

$$= 1 - \frac{1}{n+1} = \frac{n}{n+1}.$$

Hence

$$\sum_{n=1}^{\infty} \frac{1}{n(n+1)} = \lim_{n \to \infty} \frac{n}{n+1} = 1.$$ ◆

The sum for S_n in Example 3, called a *telescoping* sum, provides us with a way to find the sums of certain series. The series in Examples 1 and 2 are examples of a more common and more important type of series, the *geometric series*.

DEFINITION   Geometric Series
The series $\sum_{n=0}^{\infty} a_n$ is said to be a **geometric series** if each term after the first is a fixed multiple of the term immediately before it. That is, there is a number r, called the **ratio** of the series, such that

$$a_{n+1} = ra_n \quad \text{for all } n \geq 0.$$

If we write $a = a_0$ for the initial constant term, then $a_1 = ar, a_2 = ar^2, a_3 = ar^3$, and so forth. Thus every geometric series takes the form

$$a + ar + ar^2 + ar^3 + \cdots = \sum_{n=0}^{\infty} ar^n. \tag{5}$$

Note that the summation begins at $n = 0$ (rather than at $n = 1$). It is therefore convenient to regard the sum

$$S_n = a(1 + r + r^2 + r^3 + \cdots + r^n)$$

of the first $n + 1$ terms as the nth partial sum of the series.

EXAMPLE 4   The infinite series

$$\sum_{n=0}^{\infty} \frac{2}{3^n} = 2 + \frac{2}{3} + \frac{2}{9} + \cdots + \frac{2}{3^n} + \cdots$$

is a geometric series whose first term is $a = 2$ and whose ratio is $r = \frac{1}{3}$. ◆

THEOREM 1   The Sum of a Geometric Series
If $|r| < 1$, then the geometric series in Eq. (5) converges, and its sum is

$$S = \sum_{n=0}^{\infty} ar^n = \frac{a}{1-r}. \tag{6}$$

If $|r| \geq 1$ and $a \neq 0$, then the geometric series diverges.

PROOF   If $r = 1$, then $S_n = (n+1)a$, so the series certainly diverges if $a \neq 0$. If $r = -1$ and $a \neq 0$, then the series diverges by an argument like the one in Example 2. So we may suppose that $|r| \neq 1$. Then the elementary identity

$$1 + r + r^2 + r^3 + \cdots + r^n = \frac{1 - r^{n+1}}{1 - r}$$

follows if we multiply each side by $1 - r$. Hence the nth partial sum of the geometric series is

$$S_n = a(1 + r + r^2 + r^3 + \cdots + r^n) = a \left(\frac{1}{1-r} - \frac{r^{n+1}}{1-r} \right).$$

If $|r| < 1$, then $r^{n+1} \to 0$ as $n \to \infty$, by Example 9 in Section 11.2. So in this case the geometric series converges to

$$S = \lim_{n \to \infty} a \cdot \left(\frac{1}{1-r} - \frac{r^{n+1}}{1-r} \right) = \frac{a}{1-r}.$$

Infinite Series and Convergence SECTION 11.3   695

But if $|r| > 1$, then $\lim_{n \to \infty} r^{n+1}$ does not exist, so $\lim_{n \to \infty} S_n$ does not exist. This establishes the theorem. ◂

EXAMPLE 5 With $a = 1$ and $r = -\frac{2}{3}$, we find that

$$1 - \frac{2}{3} + \frac{4}{9} - \frac{8}{27} + \cdots = \sum_{n=0}^{\infty} \left(-\frac{2}{3}\right)^n = \frac{1}{1-\left(-\frac{2}{3}\right)} = \frac{3}{5}.$$

The graph in Fig. 11.3.3 shows the partial sums of this series approaching its sum $\frac{3}{5}$ alternately from above and below. ◆

FIGURE 11.3.3 Graph of the first dozen partial sums of the infinite series in Example 5.

EXAMPLE 6 Determine whether or not the infinite series $\sum_{n=1}^{\infty} \frac{2^{2n-1}}{3^n}$ converges.

Solution If we write this series in the form

$$\sum_{n=1}^{\infty} \frac{2^{2n-1}}{3^n} = \frac{2}{3} + \frac{8}{9} + \frac{32}{27} + \frac{128}{81} + \cdots = \frac{2}{3}\left(1 + \frac{4}{3} + \frac{16}{9} + \frac{64}{27} + \cdots\right),$$

then we recognize it as a geometric series with first term $a = \frac{2}{3}$ and ratio $r = \frac{4}{3}$. Because $r > 1$, the second part of Theorem 1 implies that this series diverges. ◆

Theorem 2 implies that the operations of addition and of multiplication by a constant can be carried out term by term in the case of *convergent* series. Because the sum of an infinite series is the limit of its sequence of partial sums, this theorem follows immediately from the limit laws for sequences (Theorem 1 of Section 11.2).

THEOREM 2 Termwise Addition and Multiplication
If the series $A = \sum a_n$ and $B = \sum b_n$ converge to the indicated sums and c is a constant, then the series $\sum(a_n + b_n)$ and $\sum c a_n$ also converge, with sums

1. $\sum (a_n + b_n) = A + B;$
2. $\sum c a_n = c A.$

The geometric series in Eq. (6) may be used to find the rational number represented by a given infinite repeating decimal.

EXAMPLE 7

$$0.55555\cdots = \frac{5}{10} + \frac{5}{100} + \frac{5}{1000} + \cdots = \frac{5}{10}\left(1 + \frac{1}{10} + \frac{1}{100} + \cdots\right)$$

$$= \sum_{n=0}^{\infty} \frac{5}{10}\left(\frac{1}{10}\right)^n = \frac{\frac{5}{10}}{1 - \frac{1}{10}} = \frac{5}{10} \cdot \frac{10}{9} = \frac{5}{9}.$$

In a more complicated situation, we may need to use the termwise algebra of Theorem 2:

$$0.7282828\cdots = \frac{7}{10} + \frac{28}{10^3} + \frac{28}{10^5} + \frac{28}{10^7} + \cdots$$

$$= \frac{7}{10} + \frac{28}{10^3}\left(1 + \frac{1}{10^2} + \frac{1}{10^4} + \cdots\right)$$

$$= \frac{7}{10} + \frac{28}{1000}\sum_{n=0}^{\infty}\left(\frac{1}{100}\right)^n = \frac{7}{10} + \frac{28}{1000}\left(\frac{1}{1-\frac{1}{100}}\right)$$

$$= \frac{7}{10} + \frac{28}{1000}\cdot\frac{100}{99} = \frac{7}{10} + \frac{28}{990} = \frac{721}{990}.$$

This technique can be used to show that every repeating infinite decimal represents a rational number. Consequently, the decimal expansions of irrational numbers such as π, e, and $\sqrt{2}$ must be nonrepeating as well as infinite. Conversely, if p and q are integers with $q \neq 0$, then long division of q into p yields a repeating decimal expansion for the rational number p/q, because such a division can yield at each stage only q possible different remainders. ◆

EXAMPLE 8 Suppose that Paul and Mary toss a fair six-sided die in turn until one of them wins by getting the first "six." If Paul tosses first, calculate the probability that he will win the game.

Solution Because the die is fair, the probability that Paul gets a "six" on the first round is $\frac{1}{6}$. The probability that he gets the game's first "six" on the second round is $\left(\frac{5}{6}\right)^2 \left(\frac{1}{6}\right)$—the product of the probability $\left(\frac{5}{6}\right)^2$ that neither Paul nor Mary rolls a "six" in the first round and the probability $\frac{1}{6}$ that Paul rolls a "six" in the second round. Paul's probability p of getting the first "six" in the game is the *sum* of his probabilities of getting it in the first round, in the second round, in the third round, and so on. Hence

$$p = \frac{1}{6} + \left(\frac{5}{6}\right)^2 \left(\frac{1}{6}\right) + \left(\frac{5}{6}\right)^2 \left(\frac{5}{6}\right)^2 \left(\frac{1}{6}\right) + \cdots$$

$$= \frac{1}{6}\left[1 + \left(\frac{5}{6}\right)^2 + \left(\frac{5}{6}\right)^4 + \cdots\right]$$

$$= \frac{1}{6} \cdot \frac{1}{1 - \left(\frac{5}{6}\right)^2} = \frac{1}{6} \cdot \frac{36}{11} = \frac{6}{11}.$$

Because he has the advantage of tossing first, Paul has more than the fair probability $\frac{1}{2}$ of getting the first "six" and thus winning the game. ◆

Theorem 3 is often useful in showing that a given series does *not* converge.

THEOREM 3 The *n*th-Term Test for Divergence
If either

$$\lim_{n \to \infty} a_n \neq 0$$

or this limit does not exist, then the infinite series $\sum a_n$ diverges.

PROOF We want to show under the stated hypothesis that the series $\sum a_n$ diverges. It suffices to show that *if* the series $\sum a_n$ does converge, then $\lim_{n \to \infty} a_n = 0$. So suppose that $\sum a_n$ converges with sum $S = \lim_{n \to \infty} S_n$, where

$$S_n = a_1 + a_2 + a_3 + \cdots + a_n$$

is the nth partial sum of the series. Because $a_n = S_n - S_{n-1}$,

$$\lim_{n \to \infty} a_n = \lim_{n \to \infty} (S_n - S_{n-1}) = \left(\lim_{n \to \infty} S_n\right) - \left(\lim_{n \to \infty} S_{n-1}\right) = S - S = 0.$$

Consequently, if $\lim_{n \to \infty} a_n \neq 0$, then the series $\sum a_n$ diverges. ◂

REMARK It is important to remember also the *contrapositive* of the *n*th-term divergence test: *If the infinite series $\sum a_n$ converges with sum S, then its sequence $\{a_n\}$ of terms converges to 0.* Thus we have *two* sequences associated with the single infinite series $\sum a_n$: its sequence $\{a_n\}$ of *terms* and its sequence $\{S_n\}$ of *partial sums*. And

(assuming that the series converges to S) these two sequences have generally different limits:
$$\lim_{n\to\infty} a_n = 0 \quad \text{and} \quad \lim_{n\to\infty} S_n = S.$$

EXAMPLE 9 The series
$$\sum_{n=1}^{\infty} (-1)^{n-1} n^2 = 1 - 4 + 9 - 16 + 25 - \cdots$$
diverges because $\lim_{n\to\infty} a_n$ does not exist, whereas the series
$$\sum_{n=1}^{\infty} \frac{n}{3n+1} = \frac{1}{4} + \frac{2}{7} + \frac{3}{10} + \frac{4}{13} + \cdots$$
diverges because
$$\lim_{n\to\infty} \frac{n}{3n+1} = \frac{1}{3} \neq 0.$$
◆

WARNING The converse of Theorem 3 is *false*! The condition
$$\lim_{n\to\infty} a_n = 0$$
is necessary *but not sufficient* to guarantee convergence of the series
$$\sum_{n=1}^{\infty} a_n.$$
That is, a series may satisfy the condition $a_n \to 0$ as $n \to \infty$ and yet diverge. An important example of a divergent series with terms that approach zero is the **harmonic series**
$$\sum_{n=1}^{\infty} \frac{1}{n} = 1 + \frac{1}{2} + \frac{1}{3} + \frac{1}{4} + \frac{1}{5} + \cdots. \tag{7}$$

THEOREM 4
The harmonic series diverges.

PROOF The nth term of the harmonic series in (7) is $a_n = 1/n$, and Fig. 11.3.4 shows the graph of the related function $f(x) = 1/x$ on the interval $1 \leq x \leq n+1$. For each integer k, $1 \leq k \leq n$, we have erected on the subinterval $[k, k+1]$ a rectangle with height $f(k) = 1/k$. All of these n rectangles have base length 1, and their respective heights are the successive terms $1, 1/2, 1/3, \ldots, 1/n$ of the harmonic series. Hence the sum of their areas is the nth partial sum
$$S_n = 1 + \frac{1}{2} + \frac{1}{3} + \frac{1}{4} + \cdots + \frac{1}{n}$$

FIGURE 11.3.4 Idea of the proof of Theorem 4.

of the series. Because these rectangles circumscribe the area under the curve $y = 1/x$ from $x = 1$ to $x = n + 1$, we therefore see that S_n must exceed this area. That is,

$$S_n > \int_1^{n+1} \frac{1}{x}\, dx = \Big[\ln x\Big]_1^{n+1} = \ln(n+1).$$

But $\ln(n + 1)$ takes on arbitrarily large positive values with increasing n. Because $S_n > \ln(n + 1)$, it follows that the partial sums of the harmonic series also take on arbitrarily large positive values. Now the terms of the harmonic series are positive, so its sequence of partial sums is increasing. We may therefore conclude that $S_n \to +\infty$ as $n \to +\infty$, and hence that the harmonic series diverges. ◄

If the sequence of partial sums of the series $\sum a_n$ diverges to infinity, then we say that the series **diverges to infinity,** and we write

$$\sum_{n=1}^{\infty} a_n = \infty.$$

The series $\sum (-1)^{n+1}$ of Example 2 is a series that diverges but does not diverge to infinity. In the nineteenth century it was common to say that such a series was divergent by *oscillation;* today we say merely that it diverges.

Our proof of Theorem 4 shows that

$$\sum_{n=1}^{\infty} \frac{1}{n} = \infty.$$

But the partial sums of the harmonic series diverge to infinity very slowly. If N_A denotes the smallest integer such that

$$\sum_{n=1}^{N_A} \frac{1}{n} \geq A,$$

then with the aid of a programmable calculator you can verify that $N_5 = 83$. With the aid of a computer and refinements of estimates like those in the proof of Theorem 4, one can show that

$$N_{10} = 12367,$$

$$N_{20} = 272{,}400{,}600,$$

$$N_{100} \approx 1.5 \times 10^{43}, \quad \text{and}$$

$$N_{1000} \approx 1.1 \times 10^{434}.$$

Thus you would need to add more than a quarter of a billion terms of the harmonic series to get a partial sum that exceeds 20. At this point each of the next few terms would be approximately $0.00000004 = 4 \times 10^{-9}$. The number of terms you'd have to add to reach 1000 is far greater than the estimated number of elementary particles in the entire universe (10^{80}). If you enjoy such large numbers, see the article "Partial sums of infinite series, and how they grow," by R. P. Boas, Jr., in *American Mathematical Monthly* **84** (1977): 237–248.

Theorem 5 says that if two infinite series have the same terms from some point on, then either both series converge or both series diverge. The proof is left for Problem 63.

THEOREM 5 Series that Are Eventually the Same
If there exists a positive integer k such that $a_n = b_n$ for all $n > k$, then the series $\sum a_n$ and $\sum b_n$ either both converge or both diverge.

It follows that a *finite* number of terms can be changed, deleted from, or adjoined to an infinite series without altering its convergence or divergence (although the *sum* of a convergent series will generally be changed by such alterations). In particular, taking $b_n = 0$ for $n \leq k$ and $b_n = a_n$ for $n > k$, we see that the series

$$\sum_{n=1}^{\infty} a_n = a_1 + a_2 + a_3 + \cdots + a_k + a_{k+1} + \cdots$$

and the series

$$\sum_{n=k+1}^{\infty} a_n = a_{k+1} + a_{k+2} + a_{k+3} + a_{k+4} + \cdots$$

that is obtained by deleting its first k terms either both converge or both diverge.

11.3 TRUE/FALSE STUDY GUIDE

11.3 CONCEPTS: QUESTIONS AND DISCUSSION

1. Can one ever obtain a convergent infinite series by interspersing the terms of two divergent series?
2. Suppose that an infinite series has the property that, given any positive number, all but finitely many terms of the series are positive and less than this number. Does it follows that this series converges? What if it's true that, given any positive number, all but finitely many partial sums of the series are greater than this number? Does it then follow that this series diverges?
3. Can one determine whether a given infinite series converges or diverges merely by computing a sufficiently large number of partial sums?
4. Can one determine the sum—accurate to a given fixed number of decimal places—of a convergent geometric series merely by computing a sufficiently large number of partial sums?

11.3 PROBLEMS

In Problems 1 through 37, determine whether the given infinite series converges or diverges. If it converges, find its sum.

1. $1 + \dfrac{1}{3} + \dfrac{1}{9} + \cdots + \dfrac{1}{3^n} + \cdots$
2. $1 + e^{-1} + e^{-2} + e^{-3} + \cdots + e^{-n} + \cdots$
3. $1 + 3 + 5 + 7 + \cdots + (2n-1) + \cdots$
4. $\dfrac{1}{2} + \dfrac{1}{\sqrt{2}} + \dfrac{1}{\sqrt[3]{2}} + \cdots + \dfrac{1}{\sqrt[n]{2}} + \cdots$
5. $1 - 2 + 4 - 8 + 16 - \cdots + (-2)^n + \cdots$
6. $1 - \dfrac{1}{4} + \dfrac{1}{16} - \cdots + \left(-\dfrac{1}{4}\right)^n + \cdots$
7. $4 + \dfrac{4}{3} + \dfrac{4}{9} + \dfrac{4}{27} + \cdots + \dfrac{4}{3^n} + \cdots$
8. $\dfrac{1}{3} + \dfrac{2}{9} + \dfrac{4}{27} + \dfrac{8}{81} + \cdots + \dfrac{2^{n-1}}{3^n} + \cdots$
9. $1 + (1.01) + (1.01)^2 + (1.01)^3 + \cdots + (1.01)^n + \cdots$
10. $1 + \dfrac{1}{\sqrt{2}} + \dfrac{1}{\sqrt[3]{3}} + \cdots + \dfrac{1}{\sqrt[n]{n}} + \cdots$
11. $\displaystyle\sum_{n=0}^{\infty} \dfrac{(-1)^n n}{n+1}$
12. $\displaystyle\sum_{n=1}^{\infty} \left(\dfrac{e}{10}\right)^n$
13. $\displaystyle\sum_{n=0}^{\infty} (-1)^n \left(\dfrac{3}{e}\right)^n$
14. $\displaystyle\sum_{n=0}^{\infty} \dfrac{3^n - 2^n}{4^n}$
15. $\displaystyle\sum_{n=1}^{\infty} (\sqrt{2})^{1-n}$
16. $\displaystyle\sum_{n=1}^{\infty} \left(\dfrac{2}{n} - \dfrac{1}{2^n}\right)$
17. $\displaystyle\sum_{n=1}^{\infty} \dfrac{n}{10n+17}$
18. $\displaystyle\sum_{n=1}^{\infty} \dfrac{\sqrt{n}}{\ln(n+1)}$
19. $\displaystyle\sum_{n=1}^{\infty} (5^{-n} - 7^{-n})$
20. $\displaystyle\sum_{n=0}^{\infty} \dfrac{1}{1 + \left(\frac{9}{10}\right)^n}$
21. $\displaystyle\sum_{n=1}^{\infty} \left(\dfrac{e}{\pi}\right)^n$
22. $\displaystyle\sum_{n=1}^{\infty} \left(\dfrac{\pi}{e}\right)^n$
23. $\displaystyle\sum_{n=0}^{\infty} \left(\dfrac{100}{99}\right)^n$
24. $\displaystyle\sum_{n=0}^{\infty} \left(\dfrac{99}{100}\right)^n$
25. $\displaystyle\sum_{n=0}^{\infty} \dfrac{1 + 2^n + 3^n}{5^n}$
26. $\displaystyle\sum_{n=0}^{\infty} \dfrac{1 + 2^n + 5^n}{3^n}$
27. $\displaystyle\sum_{n=0}^{\infty} \dfrac{7 \cdot 5^n + 3 \cdot 11^n}{13^n}$
28. $\displaystyle\sum_{n=1}^{\infty} \sqrt[n]{2}$
29. $\displaystyle\sum_{n=1}^{\infty} \left[\left(\dfrac{7}{11}\right)^n - \left(\dfrac{3}{5}\right)^n\right]$
30. $\displaystyle\sum_{n=1}^{\infty} \dfrac{2n}{\sqrt{4n^2 + 3}}$
31. $\displaystyle\sum_{n=1}^{\infty} \dfrac{n^2 - 1}{3n^2 + 1}$
32. $\displaystyle\sum_{n=1}^{\infty} \sin^n 1$
33. $\displaystyle\sum_{n=1}^{\infty} \tan^n 1$
34. $\displaystyle\sum_{n=1}^{\infty} (\arcsin 1)^n$
35. $\displaystyle\sum_{n=1}^{\infty} (\arctan 1)^n$
36. $\displaystyle\sum_{n=1}^{\infty} \arctan n$

37. $\sum_{n=2}^{\infty} \dfrac{1}{n \ln n}$ (Suggestion: Mimic the proof of Theorem 4 to show divergence.)

38. Use the method of Example 6 to verify that
   (a) $0.666666666\cdots = \frac{2}{3}$;   (b) $0.111111111\cdots = \frac{1}{9}$;
   (c) $0.249999999\cdots = \frac{1}{4}$;   (d) $0.999999999\cdots = 1$.

In Problems 39 through 43, find the rational number represented by the given repeating decimal.

39. $0.4747\,4747\ldots$
40. $0.2525\,2525\ldots$
41. $0.123\,123\,123\ldots$
42. $0.3377\,3377\,3377\ldots$
43. $3.14159\,14159\,14159\ldots$

In Problems 44 through 49, find the set of all those values of x for which the given series is a convergent geometric series, then express the sum of the series as a function of x.

44. $\sum_{n=1}^{\infty}(2x)^n$
45. $\sum_{n=1}^{\infty}\left(\dfrac{x}{3}\right)^n$
46. $\sum_{n=1}^{\infty}(x-1)^n$
47. $\sum_{n=1}^{\infty}\left(\dfrac{x-2}{3}\right)^n$
48. $\sum_{n=1}^{\infty}\left(\dfrac{x^2}{x^2+1}\right)^n$
49. $\sum_{n=1}^{\infty}\left(\dfrac{5x^2}{x^2+16}\right)^n$

In Problems 50 through 55, express the nth partial sum of the infinite series as a telescoping sum (as in Example 3) and thereby find the sum of the series if it converges.

50. $\sum_{n=1}^{\infty}\dfrac{1}{4n^2-1}$
51. $\sum_{n=1}^{\infty}\dfrac{1}{9n^2+3n-2}$
52. $\sum_{n=1}^{\infty}\ln\dfrac{n+1}{n}$
53. $\sum_{n=1}^{\infty}\dfrac{1}{16n^2-8n-3}$
54. $\sum_{n=1}^{\infty}\dfrac{1}{n(n+2)}$
55. $\sum_{n=2}^{\infty}\dfrac{1}{n^2-1}$

In Problems 56 through 60, use a computer algebra system to find the partial fraction decomposition of the general term, then apply the method of Problems 50 through 55 to sum the series.

56. $\sum_{n=1}^{\infty}\dfrac{2n+1}{n^2(n+1)^2}$
57. $\sum_{n=1}^{\infty}\dfrac{6n^2+2n-1}{n(n+1)(4n^2-1)}$
58. $\sum_{n=1}^{\infty}\dfrac{2}{n(n+1)(n+2)}$
59. $\sum_{n=1}^{\infty}\dfrac{6}{n(n+1)(n+2)(n+3)}$
60. $\sum_{n=3}^{\infty}\dfrac{6n}{n^4-5n^2+4}$

61. Prove: If $\sum a_n$ diverges and c is a nonzero constant, then $\sum c a_n$ diverges.

62. Suppose that $\sum a_n$ converges and that $\sum b_n$ diverges. Prove that $\sum (a_n + b_n)$ diverges.

63. Let S_n and T_n denote the nth partial sums of $\sum a_n$ and $\sum b_n$, respectively. Suppose that k is a fixed positive integer and that $a_n = b_n$ for all $n \geq k$. Show that $S_n - T_n = S_k - T_k$ for all $n > k$. Hence prove Theorem 5.

64. A ball has *bounce coefficient* $r < 1$ if, when it is dropped from a height h, it bounces back to a height of rh (Fig. 11.3.5). Suppose that such a ball is dropped from the initial height a and subsequently bounces infinitely many times. Use a geometric series to show that the total up-and-down distance it travels in all its bouncing is

$$D = a \cdot \dfrac{1+r}{1-r}.$$

Note that D is *finite*.

FIGURE 11.3.5 Successive bounces of the ball of Problems 64 and 65.

65. A ball with bounce coefficient $r = 0.64$ (see Problem 64) is dropped from an initial height of $a = 4$ ft. Use a geometric series to compute the total time required for it to complete its infinitely many bounces. The time required for a ball to drop h feet (from rest) is $\sqrt{2h/g}$ seconds, where $g = 32$ ft/s^2.

66. Suppose that the government spends $1 billion and that each recipient of a fraction of this wealth spends 90% of the dollars that he or she receives. In turn, the secondary recipients spend 90% of the dollars they receive, and so on. How much total spending thereby results from the original injection of $1 billion into the economy?

67. A tank initially contains a mass M_0 of air. Each stroke of a vacuum pump removes 5% of the air in the container. Compute: (a) The mass M_n of air remaining in the tank after n strokes of the pump; (b) $\lim_{n\to\infty} M_n$.

68. Paul and Mary toss a fair coin in turn until one of them wins the game by getting the first "head." Calculate for each the probability that he or she wins the game.

69. Peter, Paul, and Mary toss a fair coin in turn until one of them wins by getting the first "head." Calculate for each the probability that he or she wins the game. Check your answer by verifying that the sum of the three probabilities is 1.

70. Peter, Paul, and Mary roll a fair die in turn until one of them wins by getting the first "six." Calculate for each the probability that he or she wins the game. Check your answer by verifying that the sum of the three probabilities is 1.

71. A pane of a certain type of glass reflects half the incident light, absorbs one-fourth, and transmits one-fourth. A window is made of two panes of this glass separated by a small space (Fig. 11.3.6). What fraction of the incident light I is transmitted by the double window?

72. Criticize the following evaluation of the sum of an infinite series:

Let $x = 1 - 2 + 4 - 8 + 16 - 32 + 64 - \cdots$.

Then $2x = 2 - 4 + 8 - 16 + 32 - 64 + \cdots$.

Add the equations to obtain $3x = 1$. Thus $x = \frac{1}{3}$, and "therefore"

$$1 - 2 + 4 - 8 + 16 - 32 + 64 - \cdots = \frac{1}{3}.$$

FIGURE 11.3.6 The double-pane window of Problem 71.

11.3 Project: Numerical Summation and Geometric Series

With a modern calculator or computer, the computation of partial sums of infinite series—historically a tedious and time-consuming task—is now (ordinarily) a simple matter. Graphing calculators and computer algebra systems typically include one-line command such as

`sum(seq(a,k), k,1,n))`	TI calculator
`sum( a(k), k = 1..n )`	*Maple*
`Sum[ a[k], { k, 1, n } ]`	*Mathematica*

for the calculation of the nth partial sum of the infinite series $\sum_{k=1}^{\infty} a_k$ whose kth term is denoted by $a(k)$. For instance, we can check numerically the fact that

$$\sum_{k=0}^{\infty} \left(\frac{1}{5}\right)^k = \frac{5}{4}$$

by very quickly calculating the first seven partial sums 1.0000, 1.2000, 1.2400, 1.2480, 1.2496, 1.2499, and 1.2500. While not conclusive, this numerical evidence is nevertheless reassuring.

Investigation A Calculate partial sums of the geometric series

$$\sum_{n=0}^{\infty} r^n$$

with $r = 0.2, 0.5, 0.75, 0.9$, and 0.99. For each value of r, calculate the partial sums S_n with $n = 10, 20, 30, \ldots$, continuing until two successive results agree to four or five decimal places. (For $r = 0.9$ and 0.99, you may decide to use $n = 100, 200, 300, \ldots$.) How does the apparent rate of convergence—as measured by the number of terms required for the desired accuracy—depend on the value of r?

Investigation B Archaeological evidence indicates that the ancient (pre-Roman) Etruscans played dice using a dodecahedral die having 12 pentagonal faces numbered 1 through 12 (Fig. 11.3.7). One could simulate such a die by drawing a random card from a deck of 12 cards numbered 1 through 12. Here let's think of a deck having k cards numbered 1 through k. For your own personal value of k, begin with the largest digit in the sum of the digits in your student ID number. This is your value of k unless this digit is less than 5, in which case subtract it from 10 to get your value of k.

FIGURE 11.3.7 The 12-sided dodecahedron.

(a) John and Mary draw alternately from a shuffled deck of k cards. The first one to draw an ace—the card numbered 1—wins. Assume that John draws first. Use the formula for the sum of a geometric series to calculate (both as a rational number and as a four-place decimal) the probability J that John wins, and similarly the probability M that Mary wins. Check that $J + M = 1$.

(b) Now John, Mary, and Paul draw alternately from the deck of k cards. Calculate separately their respective probabilities of winning, given that John draws first and Mary draws second. Check that $J + M + P = 1$.

11.4 TAYLOR SERIES AND TAYLOR POLYNOMIALS

The infinite series we studied in Section 11.3 have *constant* terms, and the sum of such a series (assuming it converges) is a *number*. In contrast, much of the practical importance of infinite series derives from the fact that many functions have useful representations as infinite series with *variable* terms.

EXAMPLE 1 If we write $r = x$ for the ratio in a geometric series, then Theorem 1 in Section 11.3 gives the infinite series representation

$$\frac{1}{1-x} = \sum_{n=0}^{\infty} x^n = 1 + x + x^2 + x^3 + \cdots \quad (1)$$

of the function $f(x) = 1/(1-x)$. That is, for each fixed number x with $|x| < 1$, the infinite series in (1) converges to the number $1/(1-x)$. The nth partial sum

$$S_n(x) = 1 + x + x^2 + x^3 + \cdots + x^n \quad (2)$$

of the geometric series in (1) is now an nth-degree *polynomial* that approximates the function $f(x) = 1/(1-x)$. The convergence of the infinite series for $|x| < 1$ suggests that the approximation

$$\frac{1}{1-x} \approx 1 + x + x^2 + x^3 + \cdots + x^n \quad (3)$$

should then be accurate if n is sufficiently large. Figure 11.4.1 shows the graphs of $1/(1-x)$ and the three approximations $S_1(x)$, $S_2(x)$, and $S_3(x)$. It appears that the approximations are more accurate when n is larger and when x is closer to zero. ◆

FIGURE 11.4.1 Graphs of the partial sums $S_1(x)$, $S_2(x)$, and $S_3(x)$ of the power series $\sum_{n=0}^{\infty} x^n = \frac{1}{1-x}$ of Example 1.

REMARK The approximation in (3) could be used to calculate numerical quotients with a calculator that has only $+$, $-$, $\times$ keys (but no $\div$ key). For instance,

$$\frac{329}{73} = \frac{3.29}{0.73} = 3.29 \times \frac{1}{1 - 0.27}$$
$$\approx (3.29)[1 + (0.27) + (0.27)^2 + \cdots + (0.27)^{10}]$$
$$\approx (3.29)(1.36986); \quad \text{thus}$$
$$\frac{329}{73} \approx 4.5068,$$

accurate to four decimal places. This is a simple illustration of the use of polynomial approximation for numerical computation.

The definitions of the various elementary transcendental functions leave it unclear how to compute their values precisely, except at a few isolated points. For example,

$$\ln x = \int_1^x \frac{1}{t} \, dt \quad (x > 0)$$

by definition, so obviously $\ln 1 = 0$, but no other value of $\ln x$ is obvious. The natural exponential function is the inverse of $\ln x$, so it is clear that $e^0 = 1$, but it is not at all clear how to compute e^x for $x \neq 0$. Indeed, even such an innocent-looking expression as $\sqrt{x}$ is not computable (precisely and in a finite number of steps) unless x happens to be the square of a rational number.

But *any* value of a polynomial

$$P(x) = c_0 + c_1 x + c_2 x^2 + \cdots + c_n x^n$$

with known coefficients $c_0, c_1, c_2, \ldots, c_n$ is easy to calculate—as in the preceding remark, only addition and multiplication are required. One goal of this section is to use the fact that polynomial values are so readily computable to help us calculate approximate values of functions such as $\ln x$ and e^x.

Polynomial Approximations

Suppose that we want to calculate (or, at least, closely approximate) a specific value $f(x_0)$ of a given function f. It would suffice to find a polynomial $P(x)$ with a graph that is very close to that of f on some interval containing x_0. For then we could use the value $P(x_0)$ as an approximation to the actual value of $f(x_0)$. Once we know how to find such an approximating polynomial $P(x)$, the next question would be how accurately $P(x_0)$ approximates the desired value $f(x_0)$.

The simplest example of polynomial approximation is the linear approximation

$$f(x) \approx f(a) + f'(a)(x - a)$$

obtained by writing $\Delta x = x - a$ in the linear approximation formula, Eq. (3) of Section 4.2. The graph of the first-degree polynomial

$$P_1(x) = f(a) + f'(a)(x - a) \qquad (4)$$

FIGURE 11.4.2 The tangent line at $(a, f(a))$ is the best linear approximation to $y = f(x)$ near a.

is the line tangent to the curve $y = f(x)$ at the point $(a, f(a))$; see Fig. 11.4.2. This first-degree polynomial agrees with f and with its first derivative at $x = a$. That is,

$$P_1(a) = f(a) \quad \text{and} \quad P_1'(a) = f'(a).$$

EXAMPLE 2 Suppose that $f(x) = \ln x$ and that $a = 1$. Then $f(1) = 0$ and $f'(1) = 1$, so $P_1(x) = x - 1$. Hence we expect that $\ln x \approx x - 1$ for x near 1. With $x = 1.1$, we find that

$$P_1(1.1) = 0.1000, \quad \text{whereas} \quad \ln(1.1) \approx 0.0953.$$

The error in this approximation is about 5%.

To better approximate $\ln x$ near $x = 1$, let us find a second-degree polynomial

$$P_2(x) = c_0 + c_1 x + c_2 x^2$$

that not only has the same value and the same first derivative as does f at $x = 1$, but also has the same second derivative there: $P_2''(1) = f''(1) = -1$. To satisfy these conditions, we must have

$$P_2(1) = c_2 + c_1 + c_0 = 0,$$
$$P_2'(1) = 2c_2 + c_1 = 1, \quad \text{and}$$
$$P_2''(1) = 2c_2 = -1.$$

When we solve these equations, we find that $c_0 = -\frac{3}{2}$, $c_1 = 2$, and $c_2 = -\frac{1}{2}$, so

$$P_2(x) = -\frac{3}{2} + 2x - \frac{1}{2}x^2.$$

With $x = 1.1$ we find that $P_2(1.1) = 0.0950$, which is accurate to three decimal places because $\ln(1.1) \approx 0.0953$. The graph of $y = P_2(x)$ is a parabola through $(1, 0)$ with the same value, slope, *and curvature* there as $y = \ln x$ (Fig. 11.4.3). ◆

The tangent line and the parabola used in the computations of Example 2 illustrate one general approach to polynomial approximation. To approximate the function $f(x)$ near $x = a$, we look for an nth-degree polynomial

$$P_n(x) = c_0 + c_1 x + c_2 x^2 + \cdots + c_n x^n$$

FIGURE 11.4.3 The linear and parabolic approximations to $y = \ln x$ near the point $(1, 0)$ (Example 2).

such that its value at a and the values of its first n derivatives at a agree with the corresponding values of f. That is, we require that

$$P_n(a) = f(a),$$
$$P_n'(a) = f'(a),$$
$$P_n''(a) = f''(a),$$
$$\vdots$$
$$P_n^{(n)}(a) = f^{(n)}(a).$$
(5)

We can use these $n + 1$ conditions to evaluate the values of the $n + 1$ coefficients $c_0, c_1, c_2, \ldots, c_n$.

The algebra involved is much simpler, however, if we begin with $P_n(x)$ expressed as an nth-degree polynomial in powers of $x - a$ rather than in powers of x:

$$P_n(x) = c_0 + c_1(x - a) + c_2(x - a)^2 + \cdots + c_n(x - a)^n.$$
(6)

Then substituting $x = a$ in Eq. (6) yields

$$c_0 = P_n(a) = f(a)$$

by the first condition in Eq. (5). Substituting $x = a$ into

$$P_n'(x) = c_1 + 2c_2(x - a) + 3c_3(x - a)^2 + \cdots + nc_n(x - a)^{n-1}$$

yields

$$c_1 = P_n'(a) = f'(a)$$

by the second condition in Eq. (5). Next, substituting $x = a$ into

$$P_n''(x) = 2c_2 + 3 \cdot 2c_3(x - a) + \cdots + n(n - 1)c_n(x - a)^{n-2}$$

yields $2c_2 = P_n''(a) = f''(a)$, so

$$c_2 = \tfrac{1}{2} f''(a).$$

We continue this process to find $c_3, c_4, \ldots, c_n$. In general, the constant term in the kth derivative $P_n^{(k)}(x)$ is $k!c_k$, because it is the kth derivative of the kth-degree term $b_k(x - a)^k$ in $P_n(x)$:

$$P_n^{(k)}(x) = k!c_k + \{\text{powers of } x - a\}.$$

(Recall that $k! = 1 \cdot 2 \cdot 3 \cdots (k - 1) \cdot k$ denotes the *factorial* of the positive integer k, read "k factorial.") So when we substitute $x = a$ into $P_n^{(k)}(x)$, we find that

$$k!c_k = P_n^{(k)}(a) = f^{(k)}(a)$$

and thus that

$$c_k = \frac{f^{(k)}(a)}{k!} \qquad (7)$$

for $k = 1, 2, 3, \ldots, n$.

Indeed, Eq. (7) holds also for $k = 0$ if we use the universal convention that $0! = 1$ and agree that the zeroth derivative $g^{(0)}$ of the function g is just g itself. With such conventions, our computations establish the following theorem.

THEOREM 1 The *n*th-Degree Taylor Polynomial
Suppose that the first n derivatives of the function $f(x)$ exist at $x = a$. Let $P_n(x)$ be the *n*th-degree polynomial

$$P_n(x) = \sum_{k=0}^{n} \frac{f^{(k)}(a)}{k!}(x-a)^k \qquad (8)$$

$$= f(a) + f'(a)(x-a) + \frac{f''(a)}{2!}(x-a)^2 + \cdots + \frac{f^{(n)}(a)}{n!}(x-a)^n.$$

Then the values of $P_n(x)$ and its first n derivatives agree, at $x = a$, with the values of f and its first n derivatives there. That is, the equations in (5) all hold.

The polynomial in Eq. (8) is called the ***n*th-degree Taylor polynomial of the function f at the point** $x = a$. Note that $P_n(x)$ is a polynomial in powers of $x - a$ rather than in powers of x. To use $P_n(x)$ effectively for the approximation of $f(x)$ near a, we must be able to compute the value $f(a)$ and the values of its derivatives $f'(a)$, $f''(a)$, and so on, all the way to $f^{(n)}(a)$.

The line $y = P_1(x)$ is simply the line tangent to the curve $y = f(x)$ at the point $(a, f(a))$. Thus $y = f(x)$ and $y = P_1(x)$ have the same slope at this point. Now recall from Section 4.6 that the second derivative measures the way the curve $y = f(x)$ is bending as it passes through $(a, f(a))$. Therefore, let us call $f''(a)$ the "concavity" of $y = f(x)$ at $(a, f(a))$. Then, because $P_2''(a) = f''(a)$, it follows that $y = P_2(x)$ has the same value, the same slope, *and* the same concavity at $(a, f(a))$ as does $y = f(x)$. Moreover, $P_3(x)$ and $f(x)$ will also have the same rate of change of concavity at $(a, f(a))$. Such observations suggest that the larger n is, the more closely the *n*th-degree Taylor polynomial will approximate $f(x)$ for x near a.

EXAMPLE 3 Find the *n*th-degree Taylor polynomial of $f(x) = \ln x$ at $a = 1$.

Solution The first few derivatives of $f(x) = \ln x$ are

$$f'(x) = \frac{1}{x}, \quad f''(x) = -\frac{1}{x^2}, \quad f^{(3)}(x) = \frac{2}{x^3}, \quad f^{(4)}(x) = -\frac{3!}{x^4}, \quad f^{(5)}(x) = \frac{4!}{x^5}.$$

The pattern is clear:

$$f^{(k)}(x) = (-1)^{k-1}\frac{(k-1)!}{x^k} \quad \text{for } k \geq 1.$$

Hence $f^{(k)}(1) = (-1)^{k-1}(k-1)!$, so Eq. (8) gives

$$P_n(x) = (x-1) - \frac{1}{2}(x-1)^2 + \frac{1}{3}(x-1)^3 - \frac{1}{4}(x-1)^4 + \cdots + \frac{(-1)^{n-1}}{n}(x-1)^n.$$

With $n = 2$ we obtain the quadratic polynomial

$$P_2(x) = (x-1) - \tfrac{1}{2}(x-1)^2 = -\tfrac{1}{2}x^2 + 2x - \tfrac{3}{2},$$

the same as in Example 2. With the third-degree Taylor polynomial

$$P_3(x) = (x-1) - \tfrac{1}{2}(x-1)^2 + \tfrac{1}{3}(x-1)^3$$

FIGURE 11.4.4 The first three Taylor polynomials approximating $f(x) = \ln x$ near $x = 1$.

we can go a step further in approximating $\ln(1.1) = 0.095310179\ldots \approx 0.0953$. The value

$$P_3(1.1) = (0.1) - \tfrac{1}{2}(0.1)^2 + \tfrac{1}{3}(0.1)^3 \approx 0.095333 \approx 0.0953$$

is accurate to four decimal places (rounded). In Fig. 11.4.4 we see that, the higher the degree and the closer x is to 1, the more accurate the approximation $\ln x \approx P_n(x)$ appears to be. ◆

In the common case $a = 0$, the nth-degree Taylor polynomial in Eq. (8) reduces to

$$P_n(x) = f(0) + f'(0)x + \frac{f''(0)}{2!}x^2 + \cdots + \frac{f^{(n)}(0)}{n!}x^n. \quad (9)$$

EXAMPLE 4 Find the nth-degree Taylor polynomial for $f(x) = e^x$ at $a = 0$.

Solution This is the easiest of all Taylor polynomials to compute, because $f^{(k)}(x) = e^x$ for all $k \geq 0$. Hence $f^{(k)}(0) = 1$ for all $k \geq 0$, so Eq. (9) yields

$$P_n(x) = 1 + x + \frac{x^2}{2!} + \frac{x^3}{3!} + \cdots + \frac{x^n}{n!}. \quad ◆$$

The first few Taylor polynomials of the natural exponential function at $a = 0$ are, therefore,

$$P_0(x) = 1,$$
$$P_1(x) = 1 + x,$$
$$P_2(x) = 1 + x + \tfrac{1}{2}x^2,$$
$$P_3(x) = 1 + x + \tfrac{1}{2}x^2 + \tfrac{1}{6}x^3,$$
$$P_4(x) = 1 + x + \tfrac{1}{2}x^2 + \tfrac{1}{6}x^3 + \tfrac{1}{24}x^4,$$
$$P_5(x) = 1 + x + \tfrac{1}{2}x^2 + \tfrac{1}{6}x^3 + \tfrac{1}{24}x^4 + \tfrac{1}{120}x^5.$$

Figure 11.4.5 shows the graphs of $P_1(x)$, $P_2(x)$, and $P_3(x)$. The table in Fig. 11.4.6 shows how these polynomials approximate $f(x) = e^x$ for $x = 0.1$ and for $x = 0.5$. At least for these two values of x, the closer x is to $a = 0$, the more rapidly $P_n(x)$ appears to approach $f(x)$ as n increases.

FIGURE 11.4.5 The first three Taylor polynomials approximating $f(x) = e^x$ near $x = 0$.

$x = 0.1$

n	$P_n(x)$	e^x	$e^x - P_n(x)$
0	1.00000	1.10517	0.10517
1	1.10000	1.10517	0.00517
2	1.10500	1.10517	0.00017
3	1.10517	1.10517	0.00000
4	1.10517	1.10517	0.00000

$x = 0.5$

n	$P_n(x)$	e^x	$e^x - P_n(x)$
0	1.00000	1.64872	0.64872
1	1.50000	1.64872	0.14872
2	1.62500	1.64872	0.02372
3	1.64583	1.64872	0.00289
4	1.64844	1.64872	0.00028
5	1.64879	1.64872	0.00002

FIGURE 11.4.6 Approximating $y = e^x$ with Taylor polynomials at $a = 0$.

Taylor's Formula

The closeness with which the polynomial $P_n(x)$ approximates the function $f(x)$ is measured by the difference

$$R_n(x) = f(x) - P_n(x),$$

for which

$$f(x) = P_n(x) + R_n(x). \tag{10}$$

This difference $R_n(x)$ is called the **nth-degree remainder for** $f(x)$ **at** $x = a$. It is the *error* made if the value $f(x)$ is replaced with the approximation $P_n(x)$.

The theorem that lets us estimate the error, or remainder, $R_n(x)$ is called **Taylor's formula**, after Brook Taylor (1685–1731), a follower of Newton who introduced Taylor polynomials in an article published in 1715. The particular expression for $R_n(x)$ that we give next is called the *Lagrange form* for the remainder because it first appeared in 1797 in a book written by the French mathematician Joseph Louis Lagrange (1736–1813).

THEOREM 2 Taylor's Formula

Suppose that the $(n+1)$th derivative of the function f exists on an interval containing the points a and b. Then

$$f(b) = f(a) + f'(a)(b-a) + \frac{f''(a)}{2!}(b-a)^2$$
$$+ \frac{f^{(3)}(a)}{3!}(b-a)^3 + \cdots + \frac{f^{(n)}(a)}{n!}(b-a)^n + \frac{f^{(n+1)}(z)}{(n+1)!}(b-a)^{n+1} \tag{11}$$

for some number z between a and b.

REMARK With $n = 0$, Eq. (11) reduces to the equation

$$f(b) = f(a) + f'(z)(b-a),$$

the conclusion of the mean value theorem (Section 4.3). Thus Taylor's formula is a far-reaching generalization of the mean value theorem of differential calculus.

A proof of Taylor's formula is given in Appendix I. If we replace b with x in Eq. (11), we get the **nth-degree Taylor formula with remainder at** $x = a$,

$$f(x) = f(a) + f'(a)(x-a) + \frac{f''(a)}{2!}(x-a)^2 + \frac{f^{(3)}(a)}{3!}(x-a)^3$$
$$+ \cdots + \frac{f^{(n)}(a)}{n!}(x-a)^n + \frac{f^{(n+1)}(z)}{(n+1)!}(x-a)^{n+1}, \tag{12}$$

where z is some number between a and x. Thus the nth-degree remainder term is

$$R_n(x) = \frac{f^{(n+1)}(z)}{(n+1)!}(x-a)^{n+1}, \tag{13}$$

which is easy to remember—it's the same as the *last* term of $P_{n+1}(x)$, except that $f^{(n+1)}(a)$ is replaced with $f^{(n+1)}(z)$.

EXAMPLE 3 (continued) To estimate the accuracy of the approximation

$$\ln 1.1 \approx 0.095333,$$

we substitute $x = 1$ into the formula
$$f^{(k)}(x) = (-1)^{k-1}\frac{(k-1)!}{x^k}$$
for the kth derivative of $f(x) = \ln x$ and get
$$f^{(k)}(1) = (-1)^{k-1}(k-1)!.$$
Hence the third-degree Taylor formula *with remainder* at $x = 1$ is
$$\ln x = (x-1) - \frac{1}{2}(x-1)^2 + \frac{1}{3}(x-1)^3 - \frac{3!}{4!z^4}(x-1)^4$$
with z between $a = 1$ and x. With $x = 1.1$ this gives
$$\ln(1.1) \approx 0.095333 - \frac{(0.1)^4}{4z^4},$$
where $1 < z < 1.1$. The value $z = 1$ gives the largest possible magnitude $(0.1)^4/4 = 0.000025$ of the remainder term. It follows that
$$0.095308 < \ln(1.1) < 0.095334,$$
so we can conclude that $\ln(1.1) = 0.0953$ to four-place accuracy. ◆

Taylor Series

If the function f has derivatives of all orders, then we can write Taylor's formula (Eq. (11)) with any degree n that we please. Ordinarily, the exact value of z in the Taylor remainder term in Eq. (13) is unknown. Nevertheless, we can sometimes use Eq. (13) to show that the remainder approaches zero as $n \to +\infty$:
$$\lim_{n\to\infty} R_n(x) = 0 \tag{14}$$
for some particular *fixed* value of x. Then Eq. (10) gives
$$f(x) = \lim_{n\to\infty}[P_n(x) + R_n(x)] = \lim_{n\to\infty} P_n(x) = \lim_{n\to\infty} \sum_{k=0}^{n}\frac{f^{(k)}(a)}{k!}(x-a)^k;$$
that is,
$$f(x) = \sum_{k=0}^{\infty}\frac{f^{(k)}(a)}{k!}(x-a)^k. \tag{15}$$
The infinite series
$$\sum_{n=0}^{\infty}\frac{f^{(n)}(a)}{n!}(x-a)^n = f(a) + f'(a)(x-a) + \frac{f''(a)}{2!}(x-a)^2$$
$$+ \cdots + \frac{f^{(n)}(a)}{n!}(x-a)^n + \cdots \tag{16}$$
is called the **Taylor series** of the function f at $x = a$. Its partial sums are the successive Taylor polynomials of f at $x = a$.

We can write the Taylor series of a function f without knowing that it converges. But if the limit in Eq. (14) can be established, then it follows as in Eq. (15) that the Taylor series in Eq. (16) actually converges to $f(x)$. If so, then we can approximate the value of $f(x)$ sufficiently accurately by calculating the value of a Taylor polynomial of f of sufficiently high degree.

EXAMPLE 5 In Example 4 we noted that if $f(x) = e^x$, then $f^{(k)}(x) = e^x$ for all integers $k \geq 0$. Hence the Taylor formula
$$f(x) = f(0) + f'(0)x + \frac{f''(0)}{2!}x^2 + \cdots + \frac{f^{(n)}(0)}{n!}x^n + \frac{f^{(n+1)}(z)}{(n+1)!}x^{n+1}$$

at $a = 0$ gives

$$e^x = 1 + x + \frac{x^2}{2!} + \frac{x^3}{3!} + \cdots + \frac{x^n}{n!} + \frac{e^z x^{n+1}}{(n+1)!} \tag{17}$$

for some z between 0 and x. If x and hence z are negative then $e^z < 1$, whereas $e^z < e^x$ if both are positive. Thus the remainder term $R_n(x)$ satisfies the inequalities

$$0 < |R_n(x)| < \frac{|x|^{n+1}}{(n+1)!} \quad \text{if } x < 0,$$

$$0 < |R_n(x)| < \frac{e^x x^{n+1}}{(n+1)!} \quad \text{if } x > 0.$$

Therefore, the fact that

$$\lim_{n \to \infty} \frac{x^n}{n!} = 0 \tag{18}$$

for all x (see Problem 55) implies that $\lim_{n \to \infty} R_n(x) = 0$ for all x. This means that the Taylor series for e^x converges to e^x for all x, and we may write

$$e^x = \sum_{n=0}^{\infty} \frac{x^n}{n!} = 1 + x + \frac{x^2}{2!} + \frac{x^3}{3!} + \frac{x^4}{4!} + \cdots. \tag{19}$$

The series in Eq. (19) is the most famous and most important of all Taylor series. With $x = 1$, Eq. (19) yields a numerical series

$$e = \sum_{n=0}^{\infty} \frac{1}{n!} = 1 + \frac{1}{1!} + \frac{1}{2!} + \frac{1}{3!} + \frac{1}{4!} + \cdots \tag{20}$$

for the number e itself. The 10th and 20th partial sums of this series give the approximations

$$e \approx 1 + \frac{1}{1!} + \frac{1}{2!} + \cdots + \frac{1}{10!} \approx 2.7182818$$

and

$$e \approx 1 + \frac{1}{1!} + \frac{1}{2!} + \cdots + \frac{1}{20!} \approx 2.71828\,18284\,59045\,235,$$

both of which are accurate to the number of decimal places shown. ◆

EXAMPLE 6 To find the Taylor series at $a = 0$ for $f(x) = \cos x$, we first calculate the derivatives

$$f(x) = \cos x, \qquad f'(x) = -\sin x,$$
$$f''(x) = -\cos x, \qquad f^{(3)}(x) = \sin x,$$
$$f^{(4)}(x) = \cos x, \qquad f^{(5)}(x) = -\sin x,$$
$$\vdots \qquad \qquad \vdots$$
$$f^{(2n)}(x) = (-1)^n \cos x, \qquad f^{(2n+1)}(x) = (-1)^{n+1} \sin x.$$

It follows that

$$f^{(2n)}(0) = (-1)^n \quad \text{but} \quad f^{(2n+1)}(0) = 0,$$

so the Taylor polynomials and Taylor series of $f(x) = \cos x$ include only terms of *even* degree. The Taylor formula of degree $2n$ for $\cos x$ at $a = 0$ is

$$\cos x = 1 - \frac{x^2}{2!} + \frac{x^4}{4!} - \cdots + (-1)^n \frac{x^{2n}}{(2n)!} + (-1)^{n+1} \frac{\cos z}{(2n+2)!} x^{2n+2},$$

where z is between 0 and x. Because $|\cos x| \leq 1$ for all z, it follows from Eq. (18) that the remainder term approaches zero as $n \to \infty$ *for all x*. Hence the desired Taylor series of $f(x) = \cos x$ at $a = 0$ converges to $\cos x$ for all x, so we may write

$$\cos x = \sum_{n=0}^{\infty} \frac{(-1)^n x^{2n}}{(2n)!} = 1 - \frac{x^2}{2!} + \frac{x^4}{4!} - \frac{x^6}{6!} + \cdots. \quad (21)$$

♦

In Problem 41 we ask you to show similarly that the Taylor series at $a = 0$ of $f(x) = \sin x$ is

$$\sin x = \sum_{n=0}^{\infty} \frac{(-1)^n x^{2n+1}}{(2n+1)!} = x - \frac{x^3}{3!} + \frac{x^5}{5!} - \frac{x^7}{7!} + \cdots. \quad (22)$$

Figures 11.4.7 and 11.4.8 illustrate the increasingly better approximations to $\cos x$ and $\sin x$ that we get by using more and more terms of the series in Eqs. (21) and (22).

FIGURE 11.4.7 Approximating $\cos x$ with nth-degree Taylor polynomials.

FIGURE 11.4.8 Approximating $\sin x$ with nth-degree Taylor polynomials.

The case $a = 0$ of Taylor's series in (16) is called the **Maclaurin series** of the function $f(x)$,

$$\sum_{n=0}^{\infty} \frac{f^{(n)}(0)}{n!} x^n = f(0) + f'(0)x + \frac{f''(0)}{2!} x^2 + \frac{f^{(3)}(0)}{3!} x^3 + \cdots. \quad (23)$$

Colin Maclaurin (1698–1746) was a Scottish mathematician who used this series as a basic tool in a calculus book he published in 1742. The three Maclaurin series

$$e^x = \sum_{n=0}^{\infty} \frac{x^n}{n!} = 1 + x + \frac{x^2}{2!} + \frac{x^3}{3!} + \frac{x^4}{4!} + \cdots, \quad (19)$$

$$\cos x = \sum_{n=0}^{\infty} \frac{(-1)^n x^{2n}}{(2n)!} = 1 - \frac{x^2}{2!} + \frac{x^4}{4!} - \frac{x^6}{6!} + \cdots, \quad \text{and} \quad (21)$$

$$\sin x = \sum_{n=0}^{\infty} \frac{(-1)^n x^{2n+1}}{(2n+1)!} = x - \frac{x^3}{3!} + \frac{x^5}{5!} - \frac{x^7}{7!} + \cdots \quad (22)$$

(which actually were discovered by Newton) bear careful examination and comparison. Observe that:

- The terms in the *even* cosine series are the *even*-degree terms in the exponential series but with alternating signs.
- The terms in the *odd* sine series are the *odd*-degree terms in the exponential series but with alternating signs.

Equations (19), (21), and (22) are *identities* that hold for all values of x. Consequently, new series can be derived by substitution, as in Examples 7 and 8.

EXAMPLE 7 Substituting $x = -t^2$ into Eq. (19) yields

$$e^{-t^2} = 1 - t^2 + \frac{t^4}{2!} - \frac{t^6}{3!} + \cdots + (-1)^n \frac{t^{2n}}{n!} + \cdots.$$

◆

EXAMPLE 8 Substituting $x = 2t$ into Eq. (22) gives

$$\sin 2t = 2t - \frac{4}{3}t^3 + \frac{4}{15}t^5 - \frac{8}{315}t^7 + \cdots.$$

◆

Euler's Formula

The sum of an infinite series $\sum c_n$ with complex terms $c_n = a_n + ib_n$ is defined by

$$\sum_{n=1}^{\infty} c_n = \sum_{n=1}^{\infty} a_n + i \sum_{n=1}^{\infty} b_n$$

provided that the two infinite series of real terms on the right-hand side converge, in which case we say that the series of complex terms on the left-hand side converges.

It can be shown that the exponential series in (19) converges whenever the number x is replaced with a complex number $z = x + iy$. Consequently, the exponential function e^z can be *defined* (for complex as well as for real arguments) by means of the series

$$e^z = \sum_{n=0}^{\infty} \frac{z^n}{n!} = 1 + z + \frac{z^2}{2!} + \frac{z^3}{3!} + \frac{z^4}{4!} + \cdots.$$

If we substitute the *pure imaginary* number $z = i\theta$ (with θ real), we get

$$e^{i\theta} = \sum_{n=0}^{\infty} \frac{(i\theta)^n}{n!} = 1 + i\theta + \frac{(i\theta)^2}{2!} + \frac{(i\theta)^3}{3!} + \frac{(i\theta)^4}{4!} + \cdots$$

$$= 1 + i\theta - \frac{\theta^2}{2!} - \frac{i\theta^3}{3!} + \frac{\theta^4}{4!} + \frac{i\theta^5}{5!} - \cdots$$

$$= \left(1 - \frac{\theta^2}{2!} + \frac{\theta^4}{4!} - \cdots\right) + i\left(\theta - \frac{\theta^3}{3!} + \frac{\theta^5}{5!} - \cdots\right),$$

using the facts that $i^2 = -1$, $i^3 = -i$, $i^4 = 1$, and so on. We recognize the Maclaurin series for $\cos\theta$ and $\sin\theta$ on the right-hand side and conclude that

$$e^{i\theta} = \cos\theta + i\sin\theta$$

for every real number θ. This is the famous **Euler's formula.** For instance, with $\theta = \pi$ it gives $e^{i\pi} = \cos\pi + i\sin\pi = -1$, and hence the extraordinary relation

$$e^{i\pi} + 1 = 0$$

relating the five most important special numbers in mathematics: $0, 1, i, \pi$, and e.

The Number π

In Section 5.3 we described how Archimedes used polygons inscribed in and circumscribed about the unit circle to show that $3\frac{10}{71} < \pi < 3\frac{1}{7}$. With the aid of electronic computers, π has been calculated to well over a *billion* decimal places. We describe now some of the methods that have been used for such computations. [For a chronicle of humanity's perennial fascination with the number π, see Peter Beckmann, *A History of π*, New York: St. Martin's Press, 1971.]

We begin with the elementary algebraic identity

$$\frac{1}{1+x} = 1 - x + x^2 - x^3 + \cdots + (-1)^{k-1}x^{k-1} + \frac{(-1)^k x^k}{1+x}, \qquad (24)$$

which can be verified by multiplying both sides by $1 + x$. We substitute t^2 for x and

$n+1$ for k and thus find that

$$\frac{1}{1+t^2} = 1 - t^2 + t^4 - t^6 + \cdots + (-1)^n t^{2n} + \frac{(-1)^{n+1} t^{2n+2}}{1+t^2}.$$

Because $D_t \tan^{-1} t = 1/(1+t^2)$, integrating both sides of this last equation from $t = 0$ to $t = x$ gives

$$\tan^{-1} x = x - \frac{x^3}{3} + \frac{x^5}{5} - \frac{x^7}{7} + \cdots + (-1)^n \frac{x^{2n+1}}{2n+1} + R_{2n+1}, \quad (25)$$

where

$$|R_{2n+1}| = \left| \int_0^x \frac{t^{2n+2}}{1+t^2} \, dx \right| \leq \left| \int_0^x t^{2n+2} \, dx \right| = \frac{|x|^{2n+3}}{2n+3}. \quad (26)$$

This estimate of the error makes it clear that

$$\lim_{n \to \infty} R_n = 0$$

if $|x| \leq 1$. Hence we obtain the Taylor series for the inverse tangent function:

$$\tan^{-1} x = \sum_{n=0}^{\infty} (-1)^n \frac{x^{2n+1}}{2n+1} = x - \frac{x^3}{3} + \frac{x^5}{5} - \frac{x^7}{7} + \cdots, \quad (27)$$

valid for $-1 \leq x \leq 1$.

If we substitute $x = 1$ into Eq. (27), we obtain *Leibniz's series*

$$\frac{\pi}{4} = 1 - \frac{1}{3} + \frac{1}{5} - \frac{1}{7} + \cdots.$$

Although this is a beautiful series, it is not an effective way to compute π. But the error estimate in Eq. (26) shows that we can use Eq. (25) to calculate $\tan^{-1} x$ if $|x|$ is small. For example, if $x = \frac{1}{5}$, then the fact that

$$\frac{1}{9 \cdot 5^9} \approx 0.000000057 < 0.0000001$$

implies that the approximation

$$\tan^{-1}\left(\tfrac{1}{5}\right) \approx \tfrac{1}{5} - \tfrac{1}{3}\left(\tfrac{1}{5}\right)^3 + \tfrac{1}{5}\left(\tfrac{1}{5}\right)^5 - \tfrac{1}{7}\left(\tfrac{1}{5}\right)^7$$

is accurate to six decimal places.

Accurate inverse tangent calculations lead to accurate computations of the number π. For example, we can use the addition formula for the tangent function to show (Problem 52) that

$$\frac{\pi}{4} = 4 \tan^{-1}\left(\frac{1}{5}\right) - \tan^{-1}\left(\frac{1}{239}\right). \quad (28)$$

HISTORICAL NOTE In 1706, John Machin used Eq. (28) to calculate the first 100 decimal places of π. (In Problem 54 we ask you to use it to show that $\pi = 3.14159$ to five decimal places.) In 1844 the lightning-fast mental calculator Zacharias Dase of Germany computed the first 200 decimal places of π, using the related formula

$$\frac{\pi}{4} = \tan^{-1}\left(\frac{1}{2}\right) + \tan^{-1}\left(\frac{1}{5}\right) + \tan^{-1}\left(\frac{1}{8}\right). \quad (29)$$

You might enjoy verifying this formula. (See Problem 53.) A recent computation of 1 million decimal places of π used the formula

$$\frac{\pi}{4} = 12 \tan^{-1}\left(\frac{1}{18}\right) + 8 \tan^{-1}\left(\frac{1}{57}\right) - 5 \tan^{-1}\left(\frac{1}{239}\right).$$

For derivations of this formula and others like it, with further discussion of the computations of the number π, see the article "An algorithm for the calculation of π" by George Miel in the *American Mathematical Monthly* **86** (1979), pp. 694–697. Although few practical applications require more than ten or twelve decimal places of π, these computations provide dramatic evidence of the power of Taylor's formula. Moreover, the number π continues to serve as a challenge both to human ingenuity and to the accuracy and efficiency of modern electronic computers. For an account of how investigations of the Indian mathematical genius Srinivasa Ramanujan (1887–1920) have led recently to the computation of over a billion decimal places of π, see the article "Ramanujan and pi," Jonathan M. Borwein and Peter B. Borwein, *Scientific American* (Feb. 1988), pp. 112–117.

11.4 TRUE/FALSE STUDY GUIDE

11.4 CONCEPTS: QUESTIONS AND DISCUSSION

1. Suppose that we take Euler's formula $e^{i\theta} = \cos\theta + i\sin\theta$ as a starting point and *define* the exponential $e^z = e^{x+iy}$ by writing
$$e^z = e^x e^{iy} = e^x(\cos y + i\sin y).$$
Can you then *prove* on this basis that $e^{z+w} = e^z e^w$ if $z = x+iy$ and $w = u+iv$ are complex numbers?

2. Can you use the definition of e^z in Question 1 to prove that $D_x e^{kx} = ke^{kx}$ if $k = a + bi$ is a complex constant and x is a real variable?

11.4 PROBLEMS

In Problems 1 through 10, find Taylor's formula for the given function f at $a = 0$. Find both the Taylor polynomial $P_n(x)$ of the indicated degree n and the remainder term $R_n(x)$.

1. $f(x) = e^{-x}$, $n = 5$
2. $f(x) = \sin x$, $n = 4$
3. $f(x) = \cos x$, $n = 4$
4. $f(x) = \dfrac{1}{1-x}$, $n = 4$
5. $f(x) = \sqrt{1+x}$, $n = 3$
6. $f(x) = \ln(1+x)$, $n = 4$
7. $f(x) = \tan x$, $n = 3$
8. $f(x) = \arctan x$, $n = 2$
9. $f(x) = \sin^{-1} x$, $n = 2$
10. $f(x) = x^3 - 3x^2 + 5x - 7$, $n = 4$

In Problems 11 through 20, find the Taylor polynomial with remainder by using the given values of a and n.

11. $f(x) = e^x$; $a = 1, n = 4$
12. $f(x) = \cos x$; $a = \pi/4, n = 3$
13. $f(x) = \sin x$; $a = \pi/6, n = 3$
14. $f(x) = \sqrt{x}$; $a = 100, n = 3$
15. $f(x) = \dfrac{1}{(x-4)^2}$; $a = 5, n = 5$
16. $f(x) = \tan x$; $a = \pi/4, n = 4$
17. $f(x) = \cos x$; $a = \pi, n = 4$
18. $f(x) = \sin x$; $a = \pi/2, n = 4$
19. $f(x) = x^{3/2}$; $a = 1, n = 4$
20. $f(x) = \dfrac{1}{\sqrt{1-x}}$; $a = 0, n = 4$

In Problems 21 through 28, find the Maclaurin series of the given function f by substituting in one of the known series in Eqs. (19), (21), and (22).

21. $f(x) = e^{-x}$
22. $f(x) = e^{2x}$
23. $f(x) = e^{-3x}$
24. $f(x) = \exp(x^3)$
25. $f(x) = \sin 2x$
26. $f(x) = \sin\dfrac{x}{2}$
27. $f(x) = \sin x^2$
28. $f(x) = \sin^2 x = \tfrac{1}{2}(1 - \cos 2x)$

In Problems 29 through 40, find the Taylor series [Eq. (16)] of the given function at the indicated point a.

29. $f(x) = \ln(1+x)$, $a = 0$
30. $f(x) = \dfrac{1}{1-x}$, $a = 0$
31. $f(x) = e^{-x}$, $a = 0$
32. $f(x) = \sin x$, $a = \pi/2$
33. $f(x) = \ln x$, $a = 1$
34. $f(x) = e^{2x}$, $a = 0$
35. $f(x) = \cos x$, $a = \pi/4$
36. $f(x) = \dfrac{1}{(1-x)^2}$, $a = 0$
37. $f(x) = \dfrac{1}{x}$, $a = 1$
38. $f(x) = \cos x$, $a = \pi/2$
39. $f(x) = \sin x$, $a = \pi/4$
40. $f(x) = \sqrt{1+x}$, $a = 0$

41. Derive, as in Example 5, the Taylor series in Eq. (22) of $f(x) = \sin x$ at $a = 0$.

42. Granted that it is valid to differentiate the sine and cosine Taylor series in a term-by-term manner, use these series to verify that $D_x \cos x = -\sin x$ and $D_x \sin x = \cos x$.

43. Use the differentiation formulas $D_x \sinh x = \cosh x$ and $D_x \cosh x = \sinh x$ to derive the Maclaurin series

$$\cosh x = \sum_{n=0}^{\infty} \frac{x^{2n}}{(2n)!} \quad \text{and} \quad \sinh x = \sum_{n=0}^{\infty} \frac{x^{2n+1}}{(2n+1)!}$$

for the hyperbolic sine and cosine functions. What is their relationship to the Maclaurin series of the ordinary sine and cosine functions?

44. Derive the Maclaurin series stated in Problem 43 by substituting the known Maclaurin series for the exponential function in the definitions

$$\cosh x = \frac{e^x + e^{-x}}{2} \quad \text{and} \quad \sinh x = \frac{e^x - e^{-x}}{2}$$

of the hyperbolic functions.

The sum commands listed for several computer algebra systems in the Section 11.3 Project can be used to calculate Taylor polynomials efficiently. For instance, when the TI graphing calculator definitions

```
Y1 = sin(x)
Y2 = sum(seq((-1)^(N-1)*X^(2N-1)/
      (2N-1)!,N,1,7))
```

are graphed, the result is Fig. 11.4.9, showing that the 13th-degree Taylor polynomial $P_{13}(x)$ approximates $\sin x$ rather closely if $-3\pi/2 < x < 3\pi/2$ but not outside this range. By plotting several successive Taylor polynomials of a function $f(x)$ simultaneously, we can get a visual sense of the way in which they approximate the function. Do this for each function given in Problems 45 through 50.

FIGURE 11.4.9 Graphs of $y = \sin x$ and its 13th-degree Taylor polynomial $P_{13}(x)$.

45. $f(x) = e^{-x}$
46. $f(x) = \sin x$
47. $f(x) = \cos x$
48. $f(x) = \ln(1+x)$
49. $f(x) = \dfrac{1}{1+x}$
50. $f(x) = \dfrac{1}{1-x^2}$

51. Let the function

$$f(x) = \sum_{n=0}^{\infty} \frac{(-1)^n x^n}{(2n)!} = 1 - \frac{x}{2!} + \frac{x^2}{4!} - \frac{x^3}{6!} + \cdots$$

be defined by replacing x with $\sqrt{x}$ in the Maclaurin series for $\cos x$. Plot partial sums of this series to verify graphically that $f(x)$ agrees with the function $g(x)$ defined by

$$g(x) = \begin{cases} \cos \sqrt{x} & \text{if } x \geq 0, \\ \cosh \sqrt{|x|} & \text{if } x < 0. \end{cases}$$

52. Beginning with $\alpha = \tan^{-1}(\frac{1}{5})$, use the addition formula

$$\tan(A+B) = \frac{\tan A + \tan B}{1 - \tan A \tan B}$$

to show in turn that (a) $\tan 2\alpha = \frac{5}{12}$; (b) $\tan 4\alpha = \frac{120}{119}$; (c) $\tan(\pi/4 - 4\alpha) = -\frac{1}{239}$. Finally, show that part (c) implies Eq. (28).

53. Apply the addition formula for the tangent function to verify Eq. (29).

54. Every young person deserves the thrill, just once, of calculating personally the first several decimal places of the number π. The seemingly random nature of this decimal expansion demands an explanation; how, indeed, are the digits 3.14159 26535 89793... determined? For a partial answer, set your calculator to display nine decimal places. Then add enough terms of the arctangent series in (27) with $x = \frac{1}{5}$ to calculate $\arctan(\frac{1}{5})$ accurate to nine places. Next, calculate the value of $\arctan(\frac{1}{239})$ similarly. Finally, substitute these numerical results in Eq. (28) and solve for π. How many accurate decimal places do you get?

55. Prove that

$$\lim_{n \to \infty} \frac{x^n}{n!} = 0$$

if x is a real number. [*Suggestion:* Choose an integer k such that $k > |2x|$, and let $L = |x|^k/k!$. Then show that

$$\frac{|x|^n}{n!} < \frac{L}{2^{n-k}}$$

if $n > k$.]

56. Suppose that $0 < x \leq 1$. Integrate both sides of the identity

$$\frac{1}{1+t} = 1 - t + t^2 - t^3 + \cdots + (-1)^n t^n + \frac{(-1)^{n+1} t^{n+1}}{1+t}$$

from $t = 0$ to $t = x$ to show that

$$\ln(1+x) = x - \frac{x^2}{2} + \frac{x^3}{3} - \cdots + (-1)^n \frac{x^{n+1}}{n+1} + R_n,$$

where $\lim_{n \to \infty} R_n = 0$. Hence conclude that

$$\ln(1+x) = \sum_{n=1}^{\infty} (-1)^{n+1} \frac{x^n}{n}$$

if $0 < x \leq 1$.

57. Criticize the following "proof" that $2 = 1$. Substituting $x = 1$ into the result in Problem 56 yields the fact that

$$\ln 2 = 1 - \tfrac{1}{2} + \tfrac{1}{3} - \tfrac{1}{4} + \cdots.$$

If
$$S = 1 + \tfrac{1}{2} + \tfrac{1}{3} + \tfrac{1}{4} + \cdots,$$
then
$$\ln 2 = S - 2 \cdot \left(\tfrac{1}{2} + \tfrac{1}{4} + \tfrac{1}{6} + \tfrac{1}{8} + \cdots\right) = S - S = 0.$$
Hence $2 = e^{\ln 2} = e^0 = 1$.

58. Deduce from the result of Problem 56 first that
$$\ln(1-x) = -\sum_{n=1}^{\infty} \frac{x^n}{n} = -x - \frac{x^2}{3} - \frac{x^3}{3} - \cdots$$

and then that
$$\ln \frac{1+x}{1-x} = \sum_{n \text{ odd}} \frac{2x^n}{n} = 2\left(x + \frac{x^3}{3} + \frac{x^5}{5} + \cdots\right)$$
if $0 \leq x \leq 1$.

59. Approximate the number $\ln 2 \approx 0.69315$ first by substituting $x = 1$ in the Maclaurin series of Problem 56, and then by substituting $x = \tfrac{1}{3}$ (why?) in the second series of Problem 58. Which approach appears to require the fewest terms to yield the value of $\ln 2$ accurate to a given number of decimal places?

11.4 Project: Calculating Logarithms on a Deserted Island

The problem is that you're stranded for life on a desert island with only a very basic calculator that does not calculate natural logarithms. So to get modern science going on this miserable island, you need to use the infinite series for $\ln[(1+x)/(1-x)]$ in Problem 58 to produce a simple table of logarithms (with five-place accuracy, say), giving $\ln x$ at least for the integers $x = 1, 2, 3, \ldots, 9$, and 10.

The most direct way might be to use the series for $\ln[(1+x)/(1-x)]$ to calculate first $\ln 2$, $\ln 3$, $\ln 5$, and $\ln 7$. Then use the law of logarithms $\ln xy = \ln x + \ln y$ to fill in the other entries in the table by simple addition of logarithms already computed. Unfortunately, larger values of x result in series that are more slowly convergent. So you could save yourself time and work by exercising some ingenuity: Calculate from scratch some four *other* logarithms from which you can build up the rest. For example, if you know $\ln 2$ and $\ln 1.25$, then $\ln 10 = \ln 1.25 + 3 \ln 2$. (Why?) Be as ingenious as you wish. Can you complete your table of ten logarithms by calculating directly (using the series) *fewer* than four logarithms to begin with?

For a finale, calculate somehow (from scratch, and accurate to five rounded decimal places) the natural logarithm $\ln(pq.rs)$, where p, q, r, and s denote the last four *nonzero* digits in your student I.D. number.

11.5 THE INTEGRAL TEST

A Taylor series (as in Section 11.4) is a special type of infinite series with *variable* terms. We saw that Taylor's formula can sometimes be used—as in the case of the exponential, sine, and cosine series—to establish the convergence of such a series.

But given an infinite series $\sum a_n$ with *constant* terms, it is the exception rather than the rule when a simple formula for the nth partial sum of that series can be found and used directly to determine whether the series converges or diverges. There are, however, several *convergence tests* that use the *terms* of an infinite series rather than its partial sums. Such a test, when successful, will tell us whether or not the series converges. Once we know that the series $\sum a_n$ does converge, it is then a separate matter to find its sum S. It may be necessary to approximate S by adding sufficiently many terms; in this case we shall need to know how many terms are required for the desired accuracy.

Here and in Section 11.6, we concentrate our attention on **positive-term series**—that is, series with terms that are all positive. If $a_n > 0$ for all n, then
$$S_1 < S_2 < S_3 < \cdots < S_n < \cdots,$$
so the sequence $\{S_n\}$ of partial sums of the series is increasing. Hence there are just two possibilities. If the sequence $\{S_n\}$ is *bounded*—there exists a number M such that $S_n < M$ for all n—then the bounded monotonic sequence property (Section 11.2)

implies that $S = \lim_{n \to \infty} S_n$ exists, so the series $\sum a_n$ *converges*. Otherwise, it diverges to infinity (by Problem 52 in Section 11.2).

A similar alternative holds for improper integrals. Suppose that the function f is continuous and positive-valued for $x \geq 1$. Then it follows (from Problem 51) that the improper integral

$$\int_1^\infty f(x)\,dx = \lim_{b \to \infty} \int_1^b f(x)\,dx \tag{1}$$

either converges (the limit is a real number) or diverges to infinity (the limit is $+\infty$). This analogy between positive-term series and improper integrals of positive functions is the key to the **integral test**. We compare the behavior of the series $\sum a_n$ with that of the improper integral in Eq. (1), where f is an appropriately chosen function. [Among other things, we require that $f(n) = a_n$ for all n.]

THEOREM 1 The Integral Test

Suppose that $\sum a_n$ is a positive-term series and that f is a positive-valued, decreasing, continuous function for $x \geq 1$. If $f(n) = a_n$ for all integers $n \geq 1$, then the series and the improper integral

$$\sum_{n=1}^\infty a_n \quad \text{and} \quad \int_1^\infty f(x)\,dx$$

either both converge or both diverge.

PROOF Because f is a decreasing function, the rectangular polygon with area

$$S_n = a_1 + a_2 + a_3 + \cdots + a_n$$

shown in Fig. 11.5.1 contains the region under $y = f(x)$ from $x = 1$ to $x = n+1$. Hence

$$\int_1^{n+1} f(x)\,dx \leq S_n. \tag{2}$$

Similarly, the rectangular polygon with area

$$S_n - a_1 = a_2 + a_3 + a_4 + \cdots + a_n$$

shown in Fig. 11.5.2 is contained in the region under $y = f(x)$ from $x = 1$ to $x = n$. Hence

$$S_n - a_1 \leq \int_1^n f(x)\,dx. \tag{3}$$

FIGURE 11.5.1 Underestimating the partial sums with an integral.

FIGURE 11.5.2 Overestimating the partial sums with an integral.

Suppose first that the improper integral $\int_1^\infty f(x)\,dx$ diverges (necessarily to $+\infty$). Then

$$\lim_{n\to\infty} \int_1^{n+1} f(x)\,dx = +\infty,$$

so it follows from (2) that $\lim_{n\to\infty} S_n = +\infty$ as well, and hence the infinite series $\sum a_n$ likewise diverges.

Now suppose instead that the improper integral $\int_1^\infty f(x)\,dx$ converges and has the (finite) value I. Then (3) implies that

$$S_n \leq a_1 + \int_1^n f(x)\,dx \leq a_1 + I,$$

so the increasing sequence $\{S_n\}$ is bounded. Thus the infinite series

$$\sum_{n=1}^\infty a_n = \lim_{n\to\infty} S_n$$

converges as well. Hence we have shown that the infinite series and the improper integral either both converge or both diverge. ◄

EXAMPLE 1 We used a version of the integral test to prove in Section 11.3 that the harmonic series

$$\sum_{n=1}^\infty \frac{1}{n} = 1 + \frac{1}{2} + \frac{1}{3} + \frac{1}{4} + \cdots$$

diverges. Using the test as stated in Theorem 1 is a little simpler: We note that $f(x) = 1/x$ is positive, continuous, and decreasing for $x \geq 1$ and that $f(n) = 1/n$ for each positive integer n. Now

$$\int_1^\infty \frac{1}{x}\,dx = \lim_{b\to\infty} \int_1^b \frac{1}{x}\,dx = \lim_{b\to\infty} \Big[\ln x\Big]_1^b = \lim_{b\to\infty}(\ln b - \ln 1) = +\infty.$$

Thus the improper integral diverges and, therefore, so does the harmonic series. ◆

The harmonic series is the case $p = 1$ of the *p*-**series**

$$\sum_{n=1}^\infty \frac{1}{n^p} = 1 + \frac{1}{2^p} + \frac{1}{3^p} + \cdots + \frac{1}{n^p} + \cdots. \tag{4}$$

Whether the *p*-series converges or diverges depends on the value of p.

EXAMPLE 2 Show that the *p*-series converges if $p > 1$ but diverges if $0 < p \leq 1$.

Solution The case $p = 1$ has already been settled in Example 1. If $p > 0$ but $p \neq 1$, then the function $f(x) = 1/x^p$ satisfies the conditions of the integral test, and

$$\int_1^\infty \frac{1}{x^p}\,dx = \lim_{b\to\infty} \int_1^b \frac{1}{x^p}\,dx = \lim_{b\to\infty}\left[-\frac{1}{(p-1)x^{p-1}}\right]_1^b$$

$$= \lim_{b\to\infty} \frac{1}{p-1}\left(1 - \frac{1}{b^{p-1}}\right).$$

If $p > 1$, then

$$\int_1^\infty \frac{1}{x^p}\,dx = \frac{1}{p-1} < \infty,$$

so the integral and the series both converge. But if $0 < p < 1$, then

$$\int_1^\infty \frac{1}{x^p}\,dx = \lim_{b\to\infty} \frac{1}{1-p}(b^{1-p} - 1) = \infty,$$

and in this case the integral and the series both diverge. ◆

As specific examples, the series

$$\sum_{n=1}^{\infty} \frac{1}{n^2} = 1 + \frac{1}{2^2} + \frac{1}{3^2} + \cdots + \frac{1}{n^2} + \cdots$$

converges ($p = 2 > 1$), whereas the series

$$\sum_{n=1}^{\infty} \frac{1}{\sqrt{n}} = 1 + \frac{1}{\sqrt{2}} + \frac{1}{\sqrt{3}} + \cdots + \frac{1}{\sqrt{n}} + \cdots$$

diverges ($p = \frac{1}{2} \leq 1$).

Now suppose that the positive-term series $\sum a_n$ converges by the integral test and that we wish to approximate its sum by adding sufficiently many of its initial terms. The difference between the sum S of the series and its nth partial sum S_n is the **remainder**

$$R_n = S - S_n = a_{n+1} + a_{n+2} + a_{n+3} + \cdots . \qquad (5)$$

This remainder is the error made when the sum is estimated by using in its place the partial sum S_n.

THEOREM 2 The Integral Test Remainder Estimate
Suppose that the infinite series and improper integral

$$\sum_{n=1}^{\infty} a_n \quad \text{and} \quad \int_1^{\infty} f(x)\,dx$$

satisfy the hypotheses of the integral test, and suppose in addition that both converge. Then

$$\int_{n+1}^{\infty} f(x)\,dx \leq R_n \leq \int_n^{\infty} f(x)\,dx, \qquad (6)$$

where R_n is the remainder given in Eq. (5).

PROOF We see from Fig. 11.5.3 that

$$\int_k^{k+1} f(x)\,dx \leq a_k \leq \int_{k-1}^{k} f(x)\,dx$$

for $k = n+1, n+2, \ldots$. We add these inequalities for all such values of k, and the result is the inequality in (6), because

$$R_n = \sum_{k=n+1}^{\infty} a_k,$$

$$\sum_{k=n+1}^{\infty} \int_k^{k+1} f(x)\,dx = \int_{n+1}^{\infty} f(x)\,dx,$$

and

$$\sum_{k=n+1}^{\infty} \int_{k-1}^{k} f(x)\,dx = \int_n^{\infty} f(x)\,dx. \qquad \blacktriangleleft$$

FIGURE 11.5.3 Establishing the integral test remainder estimate.

If we substitute $R_n = S - S_n$, then it follows from (6) that the sum S of the series satisfies the inequality

$$S_n + \int_{n+1}^{\infty} f(x)\,dx \leq S \leq S_n + \int_n^{\infty} f(x)\,dx. \qquad (7)$$

If the nth partial sum S_n is known and the difference

$$\int_n^{n+1} f(x)\,dx$$

between the two integrals is small, then (7) provides an accurate estimate of the sum S of the infinite series.

EXAMPLE 3 We will see in Section 11.8 that the exact sum of the p-series with $p=2$ is $\pi^2/6$, thus giving the beautiful formula

$$\frac{\pi^2}{6} = 1 + \frac{1}{2^2} + \frac{1}{3^2} + \frac{1}{4^2} + \cdots. \tag{8}$$

Use this series to approximate the number π by applying the integral test remainder estimate, first with $n=50$, then with $n=200$.

Solution Obviously we take $f(x) = 1/x^2$ in the remainder estimate. Because

$$\int_n^\infty \frac{1}{x^2}\,dx = \lim_{b\to\infty}\left[-\frac{1}{x}\right]_n^b = \lim_{b\to\infty}\left(\frac{1}{n} - \frac{1}{b}\right) = \frac{1}{n},$$

Eq. (7) gives

$$S_n + \frac{1}{n+1} \leq \frac{\pi^2}{6} \leq S_n + \frac{1}{n}, \tag{9}$$

where

$$S_n = 1 + \frac{1}{2^2} + \frac{1}{3^2} + \cdots + \frac{1}{n^2}$$

is the nth partial sum of the series in (8). Upon multiplying by 6 and taking square roots, (9) gives the inequality

$$\sqrt{6\left(S_n + \frac{1}{n+1}\right)} \leq \pi \leq \sqrt{6\left(S_n + \frac{1}{n}\right)}. \tag{10}$$

You could add the first 50 terms in (8) one by one in a few minutes using a simple four-function calculator, but this kind of arithmetic is precisely the task for which a modern calculator or computer algebra system is designed. A one-line instruction such as the calculator command `sum(seq(1/n^2,n,1,50))` yields

$$S_{50} = \sum_{n=1}^{50} \frac{1}{n^2} \approx 1.625132734.$$

Then, using (9) for illustration rather than (10), we calculate

$$1.62513273 + \frac{1}{51} < \frac{\pi^2}{6} < 1.62513274 + \frac{1}{50};$$

$$1.64474057 < \frac{\pi^2}{6} < 1.64513274;$$

$$3.14140787 < \pi < 3.14178237.$$

Finally, rounding down on the left and up on the right (why?), we conclude that $3.1414 < \pi < 3.1418$. The average of these two bounds is the traditional four-place approximation $\pi \approx 3.1416$.

The 200th partial sum of the series in (8) is

$$S_{200} = \sum_{n=1}^{200} \frac{1}{n^2} \approx 1.639946546.$$

Substituting this sum and $n = 200$ in (10), we get

$$3.14158081 < \pi < 3.14160457.$$

This proves that $\pi \approx 3.1416$ rounded accurate to four decimal places. ◆

EXAMPLE 4 Show that the series

$$\sum_{n=2}^{\infty} \frac{1}{n(\ln n)^2} \qquad (11)$$

converges, and determine how many terms you would need to add to find its sum accurate to within 0.01. That is, how large must n be in order that the remainder satisfy the inequality $R_n < 0.01$?

Solution We begin the sum at $n = 2$ because $\ln 1 = 0$. Let $f(x) = 1/[x(\ln x)^2]$. Then

$$\int_n^\infty \frac{1}{x(\ln x)^2}\,dx = \lim_{b\to\infty}\left[-\frac{1}{\ln x}\right]_n^b = \lim_{b\to\infty}\left(\frac{1}{\ln n} - \frac{1}{\ln b}\right) = \frac{1}{\ln n}.$$

Substituting $n = 2$ shows that the series in (11) converges (by the integral test). Our calculations and the right-hand inequality in (6) now give $R_n < 1/(\ln n)$, so we need

$$\frac{1}{\ln n} \leqq 0.01; \quad \ln n \geqq 100; \quad n \geqq e^{100} \approx 2.7 \times 10^{43}.$$

A computer that could calculate a billion (10^9) terms per second would require about 8.5×10^{26} years—far longer than the expected lifetime of the universe—to sum this many terms. But you can check that accuracy to only one decimal place—that is, $R_n < 0.05$—would require only about $n = 4.85 \times 10^8$ (fewer than a half billion) terms, well within the range of a powerful desktop computer. ◆

11.5 TRUE/FALSE STUDY GUIDE

11.5 CONCEPTS: QUESTIONS AND DISCUSSION

1. What might it mean to say that one infinite series converges more slowly than another? Perhaps that more terms of one than the other must be added to make the remainder R_n less than a preassigned error? If so, compare the rates at which the series $\sum n^{-2}, \sum n^{-3/2}, \sum n^{-4/3}, \ldots, \sum n^{-101/100}, \ldots,$ converge.

2. Can you use infinite series such as those listed in Question 1 to illustrate the claim that, however slowly one infinite series converges, there's another one that converges even more slowly?

3. Can you think of a way in which the convergent infinite series in Question 1 seem to resemble more and more closely the divergent harmonic series $\sum n^{-1}$? Discuss the possibility that two infinite series can resemble each other arbitrarily closely, yet one converges and the other diverges.

11.5 PROBLEMS

In Problems 1 through 30, use the integral test to test the given series for convergence.

1. $\sum_{n=1}^{\infty} \dfrac{n}{n^2+1}$

2. $\sum_{n=1}^{\infty} \dfrac{n}{e^{n^2}}$

3. $\sum_{n=1}^{\infty} \dfrac{1}{\sqrt{n+1}}$

4. $\sum_{n=1}^{\infty} \dfrac{1}{(n+1)^{4/3}}$

5. $\sum_{n=1}^{\infty} \dfrac{1}{n^2+1}$

6. $\sum_{n=1}^{\infty} \dfrac{1}{n(n+1)}$

7. $\sum_{n=2}^{\infty} \dfrac{1}{n \ln n}$

8. $\sum_{n=1}^{\infty} \dfrac{\ln n}{n}$

9. $\sum_{n=1}^{\infty} \dfrac{1}{2^n}$

10. $\sum_{n=1}^{\infty} \dfrac{n}{e^n}$

11. $\sum_{n=1}^{\infty} \dfrac{n^2}{e^n}$

12. $\sum_{n=1}^{\infty} \dfrac{1}{17n-13}$

13. $\sum_{n=1}^{\infty} \dfrac{\ln n}{n^2}$

14. $\sum_{n=1}^{\infty} \dfrac{n+1}{n^2}$

15. $\sum_{n=1}^{\infty} \dfrac{n}{n^4+1}$

16. $\sum_{n=1}^{\infty} \dfrac{1}{n^3+n}$

17. $\sum_{n=1}^{\infty} \dfrac{2n+5}{n^2+5n+17}$

18. $\sum_{n=1}^{\infty} \ln\left(\dfrac{n+1}{n}\right)$

19. $\sum_{n=1}^{\infty} \ln\left(1 + \dfrac{1}{n^2}\right)$

20. $\sum_{n=1}^{\infty} \dfrac{2^{1/n}}{n^2}$

21. $\sum_{n=1}^{\infty} \dfrac{n}{4n^2+5}$

22. $\sum_{n=1}^{\infty} \dfrac{n}{(4n^2+5)^{3/2}}$

23. $\sum_{n=2}^{\infty} \dfrac{1}{n\sqrt{\ln n}}$

24. $\sum_{n=2}^{\infty} \dfrac{1}{n(\ln n)^3}$

25. $\sum_{n=1}^{\infty} \dfrac{1}{4n^2+9}$

26. $\sum_{n=1}^{\infty} \dfrac{n+1}{n+100}$

27. $\sum_{n=1}^{\infty} \dfrac{n}{n^4+2n^2+1}$

28. $\sum_{n=1}^{\infty} \dfrac{1}{(n+1)^3}$

29. $\sum_{n=1}^{\infty} \dfrac{\arctan n}{n^2+1}$

30. $\sum_{n=3}^{\infty} \dfrac{1}{n(\ln n)[\ln(\ln n)]}$

In Problems 31 through 34, tell why the integral test does not apply to the given series.

31. $\sum_{n=1}^{\infty} \dfrac{(-1)^n}{n}$

32. $\sum_{n=1}^{\infty} e^{-n} \sin n$

33. $\sum_{n=1}^{\infty} \dfrac{2+\sin n}{n^2}$

34. $\sum_{n=1}^{\infty} \left(\dfrac{\sin n}{n}\right)^4$

In Problems 35 through 38, determine the values of p for which the given series converges.

35. $\sum_{n=1}^{\infty} \dfrac{1}{p^n}$

36. $\sum_{n=1}^{\infty} \dfrac{n}{(n^2+1)^p}$

37. $\sum_{n=2}^{\infty} \dfrac{1}{n(\ln n)^p}$

38. $\sum_{n=3}^{\infty} \dfrac{1}{n(\ln n)[\ln(\ln n)]^p}$

In Problems 39 through 42, find the least positive integer n such that the remainder R_n in Theorem 2 is less than E.

39. $\sum_{n=1}^{\infty} \dfrac{1}{n^2}$; $E = 0.0001$

40. $\sum_{n=1}^{\infty} \dfrac{1}{n^2}$; $E = 0.00005$

41. $\sum_{n=1}^{\infty} \dfrac{1}{n^3}$; $E = 0.00005$

42. $\sum_{n=1}^{\infty} \dfrac{1}{n^6}$; $E = 2 \times 10^{-11}$

In Problems 43 through 46, find the sum of the given series accurate to the indicated number k of decimal places. Begin by finding the smallest value of n such that the remainder satisfies the inequality $R_n < 5 \times 10^{-(k+1)}$. Then use a calculator to compute the partial sum S_n and round off appropriately.

43. $\sum_{n=1}^{\infty} \dfrac{1}{n^{3/2}}$; $k = 2$

44. $\sum_{n=1}^{\infty} \dfrac{1}{n^3}$; $k = 3$

45. $\sum_{n=1}^{\infty} \dfrac{1}{n^5}$; $k = 5$

46. $\sum_{n=1}^{\infty} \dfrac{1}{n^7}$; $k = 7$

In Problems 47 and 48, use a computer algebra system (if necessary) to determine the values of p for which the given infinite series converges.

47. $\sum_{n=1}^{\infty} \dfrac{\ln n}{n^p}$

48. $\sum_{n=1}^{\infty} \dfrac{1}{p^{\ln n}}$

49. Deduce from the inequalities in (2) and (3) with the function $f(x) = 1/x$ that
$$\ln n \leq 1 + \dfrac{1}{2} + \dfrac{1}{3} + \cdots + \dfrac{1}{n} \leq 1 + \ln n$$
for $n = 1, 2, 3, \ldots$. If a computer adds 1 millions terms of the harmonic series per second, how long will it take for the partial sum to reach 50?

50. (a) Let
$$c_n = 1 + \dfrac{1}{2} + \dfrac{1}{3} + \cdots + \dfrac{1}{n} - \ln n$$
for $n = 1, 2, 3, \ldots$. Deduce from Problem 49 that $0 \leq c_n \leq 1$ for all n. (b) Note that
$$\int_n^{n+1} \dfrac{1}{x}\, dx \geq \dfrac{1}{n+1}.$$
Conclude that the sequence $\{c_n\}$ is decreasing. Therefore the sequence $\{c_n\}$ converges. The number
$$\gamma = \lim_{n \to \infty} c_n = \lim_{n \to \infty} \left(1 + \dfrac{1}{2} + \dfrac{1}{3} + \cdots + \dfrac{1}{n} - \ln n\right) \approx 0.57722$$
is known as **Euler's constant.**

51. Suppose that the function f is continuous and positive-valued for $x \geq 1$. Let
$$b_n = \int_1^n f(x)\, dx$$
for $n = 1, 2, 3, \ldots$. (a) Suppose that the increasing sequence $\{b_n\}$ is bounded, so that $B = \lim_{n \to \infty} b_n$ exists. Prove that
$$\int_1^\infty f(x)\, dx = B.$$
(b) Prove that if the sequence $\{b_n\}$ is not bounded, then
$$\int_1^\infty f(x)\, dx = +\infty.$$

11.5 Project: The Number π, Once and for All

When we replace the parameter p in the p-series $\sum 1/n^p$ with the variable x, we get one of the most important transcendental functions in higher mathematics, the **Riemann zeta function**

$$\zeta(x) = \sum_{n=1}^{\infty} \frac{1}{n^x} = 1 + \frac{1}{2^x} + \frac{1}{3^x} + \frac{1}{4^x} + \cdots.$$

REMARK One can substitute a complex number $x = a + bi$ in the zeta function. Now that Fermat's last theorem has been proved, the most famous unsolved conjecture in mathematics is the **Riemann hypothesis**—that $\zeta(a + bi) = 0$ implies that $a = \frac{1}{2}$; that is, that the only complex zeros of the Riemann zeta function have real part $\frac{1}{2}$. (The smallest such example is approximately $\frac{1}{2} + 14.13475i$.) The truth of the Riemann hypothesis would have profound implications in number theory, including information about the distribution of the prime numbers.

In Problems 1 through 4, use the given value of the zeta function and the integral-test remainder estimate (as in Example 3 of this section) with the given value of n to determine how accurately the value of the number π is thereby determined. Knowing that

$$\pi \approx 3.14159\,26535\,89793\,23846,$$

write each final answer in the form $\pi \approx 3.abcde\ldots$, giving precisely those digits that are correct or correctly rounded.

1. $\zeta(2) = \dfrac{\pi^2}{6}$ with $n = 25$.
2. $\zeta(4) = \dfrac{\pi^4}{90}$ with $n = 20$.
3. $\zeta(6) = \dfrac{\pi^6}{945}$ with $n = 15$.
4. $\zeta(8) = \dfrac{\pi^8}{9450}$ with $n = 10$.

5. Finally, use one of the preceding four problems and your own careful choice of n to show that $\pi \approx 3.141592654$ with all digits correct or correctly rounded.

Euler showed that if n is even then $\zeta(n)$ is a rational multiple of π^n (as in the cases $n = 2, 4, 6, 8$ cited above). Because any integral power of π is irrational, it follows that the number $\zeta(n)$ is irrational if n is even. But little was known about $\zeta(n)$ for n odd until 1978, when Roger Apéry proved that $\zeta(3)$ is irrational. In Section 7.7 of Andrews, Askey, and Roy, *Special Functions* (Cambridge Univ. Press: 1999), the authors show that there exist infinite sequences $\{A_n\}$ and $\{B_n\}$ of integers such that

$$0 < |A_n + B_n \zeta(3)| < 3 \cdot \left(\frac{9}{10}\right)^n$$

for each integer $n \geqq 1$. Can you explain why this implies that $\zeta(3)$ is irrational? (Assume, to the contrary, that $\zeta(3) = p/q$ is rational.)

11.6 COMPARISON TESTS FOR POSITIVE-TERM SERIES

With the integral test we attempt to determine whether or not an infinite series converges by comparing it with an improper integral. The methods of this section involves comparing the terms of the *positive-term* series $\sum a_n$ with those of another positive-term series $\sum b_n$ whose convergence or divergence is known. We have already developed two families of *reference series* for the role of the known series $\sum b_n$; these are the geometric series of Section 11.3 and the p-series of Section 11.5. They are well adapted for our new purposes because their convergence or divergence is quite easy to determine. Recall that the geometric series $\sum r^n$ converges if $|r|<1$ and diverges if $|r| \geq 1$, and that the p-series $\sum 1/n^p$ converges if $p>1$ and diverges if $0 < p \leq 1$.

Let $\sum a_n$ and $\sum b_n$ be positive-term series. Then we say that the series $\sum b_n$ **dominates** the series $\sum a_n$ provided that $a_n \leq b_n$ for all n. Theorem 1 says that the positive-term series $\sum a_n$ converges if it is dominated by a convergent series and diverges if it dominates a positive-term divergent series.

THEOREM 1 Comparison Test
Suppose that $\sum a_n$ and $\sum b_n$ are positive-term series. Then

1. $\sum a_n$ converges if $\sum b_n$ converges and $a_n \leq b_n$ for all n;
2. $\sum a_n$ diverges if $\sum b_n$ diverges and $a_n \geq b_n$ for all n.

PROOF Denote the nth partial sums of the series $\sum a_n$ and $\sum b_n$ by S_n and T_n, respectively. Then $\{S_n\}$ and $\{T_n\}$ are increasing sequences. To prove part (1), suppose that $\sum b_n$ converges, so $T = \lim_{n \to \infty} T_n$ exists (so that T is a real number). Then the fact that $a_n \leq b_n$ for all n implies that $S_n \leq T_n \leq T$ for all n. Thus the sequence $\{S_n\}$ of partial sums of $\sum a_n$ is bounded and increasing and therefore converges. Thus $\sum a_n$ converges.

Part (2) is merely a restatement of part (1). If the series $\sum a_n$ converged, then the fact that $\sum a_n$ dominates $\sum b_n$ would imply—by part (1), with a_n and b_n interchanged—that $\sum b_n$ converged. But $\sum b_n$ diverges, so it follows that $\sum a_n$ must also diverge. ◂

We know by Theorem 5 of Section 11.3 that the convergence or divergence of an infinite series is not affected by the insertion or deletion of a finite number of terms. Consequently, the conditions $a_n \leq b_n$ and $a_n \geq b_n$ in the two parts of the comparison test really need to hold only for all $n \geq k$, where k is some fixed positive integer. Thus we can say that the positive-term series $\sum a_n$ converges if it is "eventually dominated" by the convergent positive-term series $\sum b_n$.

EXAMPLE 1 Because

$$\frac{1}{n(n+1)(n+2)} < \frac{1}{n^3}$$

for all $n \geq 1$, the series

$$\sum_{n=1}^{\infty} \frac{1}{n(n+1)(n+2)} = \frac{1}{1 \cdot 2 \cdot 3} + \frac{1}{2 \cdot 3 \cdot 4} + \frac{1}{3 \cdot 4 \cdot 5} + \cdots$$

is dominated by the series $\sum 1/n^3$, which is a convergent p-series with $p = 3$. Both are positive-term series, and hence the series $\sum 1/[n(n+1)(n+2)]$ converges by part (1) of the comparison test. ◆

EXAMPLE 2 Because

$$\frac{1}{\sqrt{2n-1}} > \frac{1}{\sqrt{2n}}$$

for all $n \geq 1$, the positive-term series

$$\sum_{n=1}^{\infty} \frac{1}{\sqrt{2n-1}} = 1 + \frac{1}{\sqrt{3}} + \frac{1}{\sqrt{5}} + \frac{1}{\sqrt{7}} + \cdots$$

dominates the series

$$\sum_{n=1}^{\infty} \frac{1}{\sqrt{2n}} = \frac{1}{\sqrt{2}} \sum_{n=1}^{\infty} \frac{1}{n^{1/2}}.$$

But $\sum 1/n^{1/2}$ is a divergent p-series with $p = \frac{1}{2}$, and a constant nonzero multiple of a divergent series diverges. So part (2) of the comparison test implies that the series $\sum 1/\sqrt{2n-1}$ also diverges. ◆

EXAMPLE 3 Test the series

$$\sum_{n=0}^{\infty} \frac{1}{n!} = 1 + \frac{1}{1!} + \frac{1}{2!} + \frac{1}{3!} + \cdots$$

for convergence.

Solution We note first that if $n \geq 1$, then

$$n! = n(n-1)(n-2) \cdots 3 \cdot 2 \cdot 1$$
$$\geq 2 \cdot 2 \cdot 2 \cdots 2 \cdot 2 \cdot 1 \quad \text{(the same number of factors);}$$

that is, $n! \geq 2^{n-1}$ for $n \geq 1$. Thus

$$\frac{1}{n!} \leq \frac{1}{2^{n-1}} \quad \text{for } n \geq 1,$$

so the series

$$\sum_{n=0}^{\infty} \frac{1}{n!} \quad \text{is dominated by the series} \quad 1 + \sum_{n=1}^{\infty} \frac{1}{2^{n-1}} = 1 + \sum_{n=0}^{\infty} \frac{1}{2^n},$$

which is a convergent geometric series (after the first term). Both are positive-term series, so by the comparison test the given series converges. We saw in Section 11.4 that the sum of the series is the number e, so

$$e = 1 + \frac{1}{1!} + \frac{1}{2!} + \frac{1}{3!} + \cdots + \frac{1}{n!} + \cdots.$$

Indeed, this series provides perhaps the simplest way of showing that

$$e \approx 2.71828\ 1828\ 459045\ 23536.$$

◆

Limit Comparison of Terms

Suppose that $\sum a_n$ is a positive-term series such that $a_n \to 0$ as $n \to +\infty$. Then, in connection with the nth-term divergence test of Section 11.3, the series $\sum a_n$ has at least a *chance* of converging. How do we choose an appropriate positive-term series $\sum b_n$ with which to compare it? A good idea is to express b_n as a *simple* function of n, simpler than a_n but such that a_n and b_n approach zero at the same rate as $n \to +\infty$. If the formula for a_n is a fraction, we can try discarding all but the terms of largest magnitude in its numerator and denominator to form b_n. For example, if

$$a_n = \frac{3n^2 + n}{n^4 + \sqrt{n}},$$

then we reason that n is small in comparison with $3n^2$, and that $\sqrt{n}$ is small in comparison with n^4, when n is quite large. This suggests that we choose $b_n = 3n^2/n^4 = 3/n^2$. The series $\sum 3/n^2$ converges ($p = 2$), but when we attempt to compare $\sum a_n$ and $\sum b_n$, we find that $a_n \geq b_n$ (rather than $a_n \leq b_n$). Consequently, the comparison test does not apply immediately—the fact that $\sum a_n$ dominates a convergent series does *not* imply that $\sum a_n$ itself converges. Theorem 2 provides a convenient way of handling such a situation.

THEOREM 2 Limit Comparison Test
Suppose that $\sum a_n$ and $\sum b_n$ are positive-term series. If the limit

$$L = \lim_{n \to \infty} \frac{a_n}{b_n}$$

exists and $0 < L < +\infty$, then either both series converge or both series diverge.

PROOF Choose two fixed positive numbers P and Q such that $P < L < Q$. Then $P < a_n/b_n < Q$ for n sufficiently large, and so

$$Pb_n < a_n < Qb_n$$

for all sufficiently large values of n. If $\sum b_n$ converges, then $\sum a_n$ is eventually dominated by the convergent series $\sum Qb_n = Q\sum b_n$, so part (1) of the comparison test implies that $\sum a_n$ also converges. If $\sum b_n$ diverges, then $\sum a_n$ eventually dominates the divergent series $\sum Pb_n = P\sum b_n$, so part (2) of the comparison test implies that $\sum a_n$ also diverges. Thus the convergence of either series implies the convergence of the other. ◄

EXAMPLE 4 With

$$a_n = \frac{3n^2 + n}{n^4 + \sqrt{n}} \quad \text{and} \quad b_n = \frac{1}{n^2}$$

(motivated by the discussion preceding Theorem 2), we find that

$$\lim_{n \to \infty} \frac{a_n}{b_n} = \lim_{n \to \infty} \frac{3n^4 + n^3}{n^4 + \sqrt{n}} = \lim_{n \to \infty} \frac{3 + \dfrac{1}{n}}{1 + \dfrac{1}{n^{7/2}}} = 3.$$

Because $\sum 1/n^2$ is a convergent p-series ($p=2$), the limit comparison test tells us that the series

$$\sum_{n=1}^{\infty} \frac{3n^2 + n}{n^4 + \sqrt{n}}$$

also converges. ◆

EXAMPLE 5 Test for convergence: $\displaystyle\sum_{n=1}^{\infty} \frac{1}{2n + \ln n}$.

Solution Because $\lim_{n \to \infty} (\ln n)/n = 0$ (by l'Hôpital's rule), $\ln n$ is very small in comparison with $2n$ when n is large. We therefore take $a_n = 1/(2n + \ln n)$ and, ignoring the constant coefficient 2, we take $b_n = 1/n$. Then we find that

$$\lim_{n \to \infty} \frac{a_n}{b_n} = \lim_{n \to \infty} \frac{n}{2n + \ln n} = \lim_{n \to \infty} \frac{1}{2 + \dfrac{\ln n}{n}} = \frac{1}{2}.$$

Because the harmonic series $\sum 1/n = \sum b_n$ diverges, it follows that the given series $\sum a_n$ also diverges. ◆

It is important to remember that if $L = \lim_{n \to \infty}(a_n/b_n)$ is either zero or infinite, then the limit comparison test does not apply. (See Problem 52 for a discussion of what conclusions may sometimes be drawn in these cases.) Note, for example, that if $a_n = 1/n^2$ and $b_n = 1/n$, then $\lim_{n \to \infty}(a_n/b_n) = 0$. But in this case $\sum a_n$ converges, whereas $\sum b_n$ diverges.

Estimating Remainders

Suppose that $0 \leq a_n \leq b_n$ for all n and we know that $\sum b_n$ converges, so the comparison test implies that $\sum a_n$ converges as well. Let us write $s = \sum a_n$ and $S = \sum b_n$. If a numerical estimate is available for the remainder

$$R_n = S - S_n = b_{n+1} + b_{n+2} + \cdots$$

in the dominating series $\sum b_n$, then we can use it to estimate the remainder

$$r_n = s - s_n = a_{n+1} + a_{n+2} + \cdots$$

in the series $\sum a_n$. The reason is that $0 \leq a_n \leq b_n$ (for all n) implies that $0 \leq r_n \leq R_n$. We can apply this fact if, for instance, we have used the integral test remainder estimate to calculate an upper bound for R_n—which is, then, an upper bound for r_n as well.

EXAMPLE 6 The series

$$\sum_{n=1}^{\infty} a_n = \sum_{n=1}^{\infty} \frac{1}{n^3 + \sqrt{n}}$$

converges because it is dominated by the convergent p-series

$$\sum_{n=1}^{\infty} b_n = \sum_{n=1}^{\infty} \frac{1}{n^3}.$$

It therefore follows by the integral test remainder estimate (Section 11.5) that

$$0 < r_n \leq R_n \leq \int_n^{\infty} \frac{1}{x^3}\,dx = \lim_{b \to \infty}\left[-\frac{1}{2x^2}\right]_n^b = \frac{1}{2n^2}.$$

Now a calculator gives

$$s_{100} = \sum_{n=1}^{100} \frac{1}{n^3 + \sqrt{n}} \approx 0.680284 \quad \text{and} \quad R_{100} \leq \frac{1}{2 \cdot 100^2} = 0.00005.$$

It follows that $0.680284 \leq s \leq 0.680334$. In particular,

$$\sum_{n=1}^{\infty} \frac{1}{n^3 + \sqrt{n}} \approx 0.6803$$

rounded accurate to four decimal places. ◆

Rearrangement and Grouping

We close our discussion of positive-term series with the observation that the sum of a convergent *positive*-term series is not altered by grouping or rearranging its terms. For example, let $\sum a_n$ be a convergent positive-term series and consider

$$\sum_{n=1}^{\infty} b_n = (a_1 + a_2 + a_3) + a_4 + (a_5 + a_6) + \cdots.$$

That is, the new series has terms

$$b_1 = a_1 + a_2 + a_3,$$
$$b_2 = a_4,$$
$$b_3 = a_5 + a_6,$$

and so on. Then every partial sum T_n of $\sum b_n$ is equal to some partial sum $S_{n'}$ of $\sum a_n$. Because $\{S_n\}$ is an increasing sequence with limit $S = \sum a_n$, it follows easily that $\{T_n\}$ is an increasing sequence with the same limit. Thus $\sum b_n = S$ as well. The argument is more subtle if terms of $\sum a_n$ are moved "out of place," as in

$$\sum_{n=1}^{\infty} b_n = a_1 + a_2 + a_4 + a_3 + a_6 + a_8 + a_5 + a_{10} + a_{12} + \cdots,$$

but the same conclusion holds: Any rearrangement of a convergent *positive*-term series also converges, and it converges to the same sum.

Similarly, it is easy to prove that any grouping or rearrangement of a divergent positive-term series also diverges. But these observations all fail in the case of an infinite series with both positive and negative terms. For example, the series $\sum(-1)^n$ diverges, but it has the convergent grouping

$$(-1+1) + (-1+1) + (-1+1) + \cdots = 0 + 0 + 0 + \cdots = 0.$$

It follows from Problem 56 of Section 11.4 that

$$\ln 2 = 1 - \frac{1}{2} + \frac{1}{3} - \frac{1}{4} + \frac{1}{5} - \cdots,$$

but the rearrangement

$$1 + \frac{1}{3} - \frac{1}{2} + \frac{1}{5} + \frac{1}{7} - \frac{1}{4} + \frac{1}{9} + \frac{1}{11} - \frac{1}{6} + \cdots$$

converges instead to $\frac{3}{2} \ln 2$. This series for $\ln 2$ even has rearrangements that converge to zero and others that diverge to $+\infty$. (See Problem 64 of Section 11.7.)

11.6 TRUE/FALSE STUDY GUIDE

11.6 CONCEPTS: QUESTIONS AND DISCUSSION

1. Can you give examples of a pair of positive-term infinite series $\sum a_n$ and $\sum b_n$ such that $\lim_{n \to \infty}(a_n/b_n) = 0$ and (a) both series converge; (b) both diverge; (c) one converges and the other diverges?
2. Can you give an example of two convergent positive-term infinite series $\sum a_n$ and $\sum b_n$ such that $\lim_{n \to \infty}(a_n/b_n) = 1$ but neither series dominates the other?
3. Can you give an example of two positive-term infinite series $\sum a_n$ and $\sum b_n$ that either both converge or both diverge, but the limit $\lim_{n \to \infty}(a_n/b_n)$ does not exist?

11.6 PROBLEMS

Use comparison tests to determine whether the infinite series in Problems 1 through 36 converge or diverge.

1. $\sum_{n=1}^{\infty} \dfrac{1}{n^2 + n + 1}$

2. $\sum_{n=1}^{\infty} \dfrac{n^3 + 1}{n^4 + 2}$

3. $\sum_{n=1}^{\infty} \dfrac{1}{n + \sqrt{n}}$

4. $\sum_{n=1}^{\infty} \dfrac{1}{n + n^{3/2}}$

5. $\sum_{n=1}^{\infty} \dfrac{1}{1 + 3^n}$

6. $\sum_{n=1}^{\infty} \dfrac{10n^2}{n^4 + 1}$

7. $\sum_{n=2}^{\infty} \dfrac{10n^2}{n^3 - 1}$

8. $\sum_{n=1}^{\infty} \dfrac{n^2 - n}{n^4 + 2}$

9. $\sum_{n=1}^{\infty} \dfrac{1}{\sqrt{37n^3 + 3}}$

10. $\sum_{n=1}^{\infty} \dfrac{1}{\sqrt{n^2 + 1}}$

11. $\sum_{n=1}^{\infty} \dfrac{\sqrt{n}}{n^2 + n}$

12. $\sum_{n=1}^{\infty} \dfrac{1}{3 + 5^n}$

13. $\sum_{n=2}^{\infty} \dfrac{1}{\ln n}$

14. $\sum_{n=1}^{\infty} \dfrac{1}{n - \ln n}$

15. $\sum_{n=1}^{\infty} \dfrac{\sin^2 n}{n^2 + 1}$

16. $\sum_{n=1}^{\infty} \dfrac{\cos^2 n}{3^n}$

17. $\sum_{n=1}^{\infty} \dfrac{n + 2^n}{n + 3^n}$

18. $\sum_{n=1}^{\infty} \dfrac{1}{2^n + 3^n}$

19. $\sum_{n=2}^{\infty} \dfrac{1}{n^2 \ln n}$

20. $\sum_{n=1}^{\infty} \dfrac{1}{n^{1+\sqrt{n}}}$

21. $\sum_{n=1}^{\infty} \dfrac{\ln n}{n^2}$

22. $\sum_{n=1}^{\infty} \dfrac{\arctan n}{n}$

23. $\sum_{n=1}^{\infty} \dfrac{\sin^2(1/n)}{n^2}$

24. $\sum_{n=1}^{\infty} \dfrac{e^{1/n}}{n}$

25. $\sum_{n=1}^{\infty} \dfrac{\ln n}{e^n}$

26. $\sum_{n=1}^{\infty} \dfrac{n^2 + 2}{n^3 + 3n}$

27. $\sum_{n=1}^{\infty} \dfrac{n^{3/2}}{n^2 + 4}$

28. $\sum_{n=1}^{\infty} \dfrac{1}{n \cdot 2^n}$

29. $\sum_{n=1}^{\infty} \dfrac{3}{4 + \sqrt{n}}$

30. $\sum_{n=1}^{\infty} \dfrac{n^2 + 1}{e^n(n+1)^2}$

31. $\sum_{n=1}^{\infty} \dfrac{2n^2 - 1}{n^2 \cdot 3^n}$

32. $\sum_{n=1}^{\infty} \dfrac{1}{\sqrt[3]{2n^4 + 1}}$

33. $\sum_{n=1}^{\infty} \dfrac{2 + \sin n}{n^2}$

34. $\sum_{n=1}^{\infty} \dfrac{\ln n}{n^3}$

35. $\sum_{n=1}^{\infty} \dfrac{(n+1)^n}{n^{n+1}}$ $\left[\text{Suggestion: } \lim_{n \to \infty} \left(1 + \dfrac{1}{n}\right)^n = e.\right]$

36. $\sum_{n=1}^{\infty} \left(\dfrac{\sin n}{n}\right)^4$

In Problems 37 through 40, calculate the sum of the first ten terms of the series, then estimate the error made in using this partial sum to approximate the sum of the series.

37. $\sum_{n=1}^{\infty} \dfrac{1}{n^2 + 1}$

38. $\sum_{n=1}^{\infty} \dfrac{1}{3^n + 1}$

39. $\sum_{n=1}^{\infty} \dfrac{\cos^2 n}{n^2}$

40. $\sum_{n=2}^{\infty} \dfrac{1}{(n+1)(\ln n)^2}$

In Problems 41 through 44, first determine the smallest positive integer n such that the remainder satisfies the inequality $R_n < 0.005$. Then use a calculator or computer to approximate the sum of the series accurate to two decimal places.

41. $\sum_{n=1}^{\infty} \dfrac{1}{n^3 + 1}$

42. $\sum_{n=1}^{\infty} \dfrac{n}{(n+1)2^n}$

43. $\sum_{n=1}^{\infty} \dfrac{\cos^4 n}{n^4}$

44. $\sum_{n=1}^{\infty} \dfrac{1}{n^{2+(1/n)}}$

45. Show that if $\sum a_n$ is a convergent positive-term series, then the series $\sum \sin(a_n)$ also converges.

46. (a) Prove that $\ln n < n^{1/8}$ for all sufficiently large values of n. (b) Explain why part (a) shows that the series $\sum 1/(\ln n)^8$ diverges.

47. Prove that if $\sum a_n$ is a convergent positive-term series, then $\sum (a_n/n)$ converges.

48. Suppose that $\sum a_n$ is a convergent positive-term series and that $\{c_n\}$ is a sequence of positive numbers with limit zero. Prove that $\sum a_n c_n$ converges.

49. Use the result of Problem 48 to prove that if $\sum a_n$ and $\sum b_n$ are convergent positive-term series, then $\sum a_n b_n$ converges.

50. Prove that the series

$$\sum_{n=1}^{\infty} \dfrac{1}{1 + 2 + 3 + \cdots + n}$$

converges.

51. Use the result of Problem 50 in Section 11.5 to prove that the series

$$\sum_{n=1}^{\infty} \dfrac{1}{1 + \dfrac{1}{2} + \dfrac{1}{3} + \cdots + \dfrac{1}{n}}$$

diverges.

52. Adapt the proof of the limit-comparison test to prove the following two results. (a) Suppose that $\sum a_n$ and $\sum b_n$ are positive-term series and that $\sum b_n$ converges. If

$$L = \lim_{n \to \infty} \dfrac{a_n}{b_n} = 0,$$

then $\sum a_n$ converges. (b) Suppose that $\sum a_n$ and $\sum b_n$ are positive-term series and that $\sum b_n$ diverges. If

$$L = \lim_{n \to \infty} \dfrac{a_n}{b_n} = +\infty,$$

then $\sum a_n$ diverges.

11.7 ALTERNATING SERIES AND ABSOLUTE CONVERGENCE

In Sections 11.5 and 11.6 we considered only positive-term series. Now we discuss infinite series that have both positive terms and negative terms. An important example is a series with terms that are alternatively positive and negative. An **alternating series** is an infinite series of the form

$$\sum_{n=1}^{\infty} (-1)^{n+1} a_n = a_1 - a_2 + a_3 - a_4 + a_5 - \cdots \qquad (1)$$

or of the form $\sum_{n=1}^{\infty} (-1)^n a_n$, where $a_n > 0$ for all n. For example, the *alternating harmonic series*

$$\sum_{n=1}^{\infty} \dfrac{(-1)^{n+1}}{n} = 1 - \dfrac{1}{2} + \dfrac{1}{3} - \dfrac{1}{4} + \dfrac{1}{5} - \cdots$$

and the geometric series

$$\sum_{n=0}^{\infty} \left(-\frac{1}{2}\right)^n = 1 - \frac{1}{2} + \frac{1}{4} - \frac{1}{8} + \frac{1}{16} - \cdots$$

are both alternating series. Theorem 1 shows that both these series converge because the sequence of absolute values of their terms is decreasing and has limit zero.

THEOREM 1 Alternating Series Test
If the alternating series in Eq. (1) satisfies the two conditions

1. $a_n \geq a_{n+1} > 0$ for all n and
2. $\lim_{n \to \infty} a_n = 0$,

then the infinite series converges.

PROOF We first consider the even-numbered partial sums $S_2, S_4, S_6, \ldots, S_{2n}, \ldots$. We may write

$$S_{2n} = (a_1 - a_2) + (a_3 - a_4) + \cdots + (a_{2n-1} - a_{2n}).$$

Because $a_k - a_{k+1} \geq 0$ for all k, the sequence $\{S_{2n}\}$ is increasing. Also, because

$$S_{2n} = a_1 - (a_2 - a_3) - \cdots - (a_{2n-2} - a_{2n-1}) - a_{2n},$$

$S_{2n} \leq a_1$ for all n. So the increasing sequence $\{S_{2n}\}$ is bounded above. Hence the limit

$$S = \lim_{n \to \infty} S_{2n}$$

exists by the bounded monotonic sequence property of Section 11.2. It remains only for us to verify that the odd-numbered partial sums $S_1, S_3, S_5, \ldots$ also converge to S. But $S_{2n+1} = S_{2n} + a_{2n+1}$ and $\lim_{n \to \infty} a_{2n+1} = 0$, so

$$\lim_{n \to \infty} S_{2n+1} = \left(\lim_{n \to \infty} S_{2n}\right) + \left(\lim_{n \to \infty} a_{2n+1}\right) = S.$$

Thus $\lim_{n \to \infty} S_n = S$, and therefore the series in Eq. (1) converges. ◄

Figure 11.7.1 illustrates the way in which the partial sums of a convergent alternating series (with positive first term) approximate its sum S, with the even partial sums $\{S_{2n}\}$ approaching S from below and the odd partial sums $\{S_{2n+1}\}$ approaching S from above.

FIGURE 11.7.1 The even partial sums $\{S_{2n}\}$ increase and the odd partial sums $\{S_{2n+1}\}$ decrease.

EXAMPLE 1 The series

$$\sum_{n=1}^{\infty} \frac{(-1)^{n+1}}{2n-1} = 1 - \frac{1}{3} + \frac{1}{5} - \frac{1}{7} + \frac{1}{9} - \cdots$$

satisfies the conditions of Theorem 1 and therefore converges. The alternating series test does not tell us the sum of this series, but we saw in Section 11.4 that its sum is $\pi/4$. The graph in Fig. 11.7.2 of the partial sums of this series illustrates the typical convergence of an alternating series, with its partial sums approaching its sum alternately from above and below. ◆

FIGURE 11.7.2 Graph of the first 14 partial sums of the alternating series in Example 1.

EXAMPLE 2 The series

$$\sum_{n=1}^{\infty} \frac{(-1)^{n+1}n}{2n-1} = 1 - \frac{2}{3} + \frac{3}{5} - \frac{4}{7} + \frac{5}{9} - \cdots$$

is an alternating series, and by expanding we verify that $n(2n+1) > (n+1)(2n-1)$, so it follows that

$$a_n = \frac{n}{2n-1} > \frac{n+1}{2n+1} = a_{n+1}$$

for all $n \geq 1$. But

$$\lim_{n \to \infty} a_n = \frac{1}{2} \neq 0,$$

so the alternating series test *does not apply*. (This fact alone does not imply that the series in question diverges—many series in Sections 11.5 and 11.6 converge even though the alternating series test does not apply. But the series of this example diverges by the nth-term divergence test.) ◆

If a series converges by the alternating series test, then Theorem 2 shows how to approximate its sum with any desired degree of accuracy—*if* you have a computer fast enough to add a large number of its terms.

THEOREM 2 Alternating Series Remainder Estimate
Suppose that the series $\sum (-1)^{n+1} a_n$ satisfies the conditions of the alternating series test and therefore converges. Let S denote the sum of the series. Denote by $R_n = S - S_n$ the error made in replacing S with the nth partial sum S_n of the series. Then this **remainder** R_n has the same sign as the next term $(-1)^{n+2} a_{n+1}$ of the series, and

$$0 \leq |R_n| < a_{n+1}. \qquad (2)$$

In particular, the *sum S of a convergent alternating series lies between any two consecutive partial sums*. This follows from the proof of Theorem 1, where we saw that $\{S_{2n}\}$ is an increasing sequence and that $\{S_{2n+1}\}$ is a decreasing sequence, both converging to S. The resulting inequalities

$$S_{2n-1} > S > S_{2n} = S_{2n-1} - a_{2n}$$

and

$$S_{2n} < S < S_{2n+1} = S_{2n} + a_{2n+1}$$

(see Fig. 11.7.3) imply the inequality in (2).

FIGURE 11.7.3 Illustrating the proof of the alternating series remainder estimate.

REMARK The inequality in (2) means the following. Suppose that you are given an *alternating series* that satisfies the conditions of Theorem 2 and has sum S. Then, if S is replaced with a partial sum S_n, the error made is numerically less than the first term a_{n+1} not retained and has the same sign as this first neglected term. **Important:** This error estimate *does not* apply to other types of series.

EXAMPLE 3 We saw in Section 11.4 that

$$e^x = \sum_{n=0}^{\infty} \frac{x^n}{n!}$$

for all x and thus (with $x = -1$) that

$$\frac{1}{e} = e^{-1} = 1 - 1 + \frac{1}{2!} - \frac{1}{3!} + \frac{1}{4!} - \cdots.$$

Use this alternating series to compute e^{-1} accurate to four decimal places.

Solution To attain four-place accuracy, we want the error to be less than a half unit in the fourth place. Thus we want

$$|R_n| < \frac{1}{(n+1)!} \leq 0.00005.$$

If we use a calculator to compute the reciprocals of the factorials of the first several integers, we find that the least value of n for which this inequality holds is $n = 7$. Then

$$e^{-1} = 1 - \frac{1}{1!} + \frac{1}{2!} - \frac{1}{3!} + \frac{1}{4!} - \frac{1}{5!} + \frac{1}{6!} - \frac{1}{7!} + R_7 \approx 0.367857 + R_7.$$

(Relying on a common "+2 rule of thumb," we are carrying six decimal places because we want four-place accuracy in the final answer.) Now the first neglected term $1/8!$ is positive, so the inequality in (2) gives

$$0 < R_7 < \frac{1}{8!} < 0.000025.$$

Therefore

$$S_7 \approx 0.367857 < e^{-1} < S_7 + 0.000025 \approx 0.367882.$$

The two bounds here both round to $e^{-1} \approx 0.3679$. Although this approximation is accurate to four decimal places, its reciprocal

$$e = 1/e^{-1} \approx 1/(0.3679) \approx 2.7181 \approx 2.718$$

gives the number e accurate to only three decimal places. ◆

Absolute Convergence

The series

$$\sum_{n=1}^{\infty} \frac{(-1)^{n+1}}{n} = 1 - \frac{1}{2} + \frac{1}{3} - \frac{1}{4} + \frac{1}{5} - \cdots$$

converges, but if we simply replace each term with its absolute value, we get the *divergent* series

$$1 + \frac{1}{2} + \frac{1}{3} + \frac{1}{4} + \frac{1}{5} + \cdots.$$

In contrast, the *convergent* series

$$\sum_{n=0}^{\infty} \frac{(-1)^n}{2^n} = 1 - \frac{1}{2} + \frac{1}{4} - \frac{1}{8} + \cdots = \frac{2}{3}$$

has the property that the associated positive-term series

$$1 + \frac{1}{2} + \frac{1}{4} + \frac{1}{8} + \cdots = 2$$

also converges. Theorem 3 tells us that if a series of *positive* terms converges, then we may insert minus signs in front of any of the terms—every other one, for instance—and the resulting series will also converge.

THEOREM 3 Absolute Convergence Implies Convergence
If the series $\sum |a_n|$ converges, then so does the series $\sum a_n$.

PROOF Suppose that the series $\sum |a_n|$ converges. Note that

$$0 \leqq a_n + |a_n| \leqq 2|a_n|$$

for all n. Let $b_n = a_n + |a_n|$. It then follows from the comparison test that the positive-term series $\sum b_n$ converges, because it is dominated by the convergent series $\sum 2|a_n|$. It is easy to verify, too, that the termwise difference of two convergent series also converges. Hence we now see that the series

$$\sum a_n = \sum (b_n - |a_n|) = \sum b_n - \sum |a_n|$$

converges. ◂

Thus we have another convergence test, one not limited to positive-term series nor limited to alternating series: Given the series $\sum a_n$, test the series $\sum |a_n|$ for convergence. If the latter converges, then so does the former. (But the converse is *not* true!) This phenomenon motivates us to make the following definition.

DEFINITION Absolute Convergence
The series $\sum a_n$ is said to **converge absolutely** (and is called **absolutely convergent**) provided that the series

$$\sum |a_n| = |a_1| + |a_2| + |a_3| + \cdots + |a_n| + \cdots$$

converges.

Thus we have explained the title of Theorem 3, and we can rephrase the theorem as follows: *If a series converges absolutely, then it converges.* The two examples preceding Theorem 3 show that a convergent series may either converge absolutely or fail to do so:

$$1 - \frac{1}{2} + \frac{1}{4} - \frac{1}{8} + \frac{1}{16} - \cdots$$

is an absolutely convergent series because

$$1 + \frac{1}{2} + \frac{1}{4} + \frac{1}{8} + \frac{1}{16} + \cdots$$

converges, whereas

$$1 - \frac{1}{2} + \frac{1}{3} - \frac{1}{4} + \frac{1}{5} - \cdots$$

is a series that, though convergent, is *not* absolutely convergent. A series that converges but does not converge absolutely is said to be **conditionally convergent.** Consequently, the terms *absolutely convergent, conditionally convergent,* and *divergent* are simultaneously all inclusive and mutually exclusive: Any given numerical series belongs to exactly one of those three classes.

There is some advantage in the application of Theorem 3, because to apply it we test the *positive*-term series $\sum |a_n|$ for convergence—and we have a variety of tests, such as comparison tests or the integral test, designed for use on positive-term series.

Note also that absolute convergence of the series $\sum a_n$ means that a *different* series $\sum |a_n|$ converges, and the two sums will generally differ. For example, with $a_n = \left(-\frac{1}{3}\right)^n$, the formula for the sum of a geometric series gives

$$\sum_{n=0}^{\infty} a_n = \sum_{n=0}^{\infty} \left(-\frac{1}{3}\right)^n = \frac{1}{1 - \left(-\frac{1}{3}\right)} = \frac{3}{4},$$

whereas

$$\sum_{n=0}^{\infty} |a_n| = \sum_{n=0}^{\infty} \left(\frac{1}{3}\right)^n = \frac{1}{1 - \frac{1}{3}} = \frac{3}{2}.$$

EXAMPLE 4 Discuss the convergence of the series

$$\sum_{n=1}^{\infty} \frac{\cos n}{n^2} = \cos 1 + \frac{\cos 2}{4} + \frac{\cos 3}{9} + \cdots.$$

Solution Let $a_n = (\cos n)/n^2$. Then

$$|a_n| = \frac{|\cos n|}{n^2} \leq \frac{1}{n^2}$$

for all $n \geq 1$. Hence the positive-term series $\sum |a_n|$ converges by the comparison test, because it is dominated by the convergent p-series $\sum (1/n^2)$. Thus the given series is absolutely convergent, and it therefore converges by Theorem 3. ◆

One reason for the importance of absolute convergence is the fact (proved in advanced calculus) that the terms of an absolutely convergent series may be regrouped or rearranged without changing the sum of the series. As we suggested at the end of Section 11.6, this is *not* true of conditionally convergent series.

The Ratio Test and the Root Test

Our next two convergence tests involve a way of measuring the rate of growth or decrease of the sequence $\{a_n\}$ of terms of a series to determine whether $\sum a_n$ converges absolutely or diverges.

THEOREM 4 The Ratio Test
Suppose that the limit

$$\rho = \lim_{n \to \infty} \left| \frac{a_{n+1}}{a_n} \right| \qquad (3)$$

either exists or is infinite. Then the infinite series $\sum a_n$ of nonzero terms

1. Converges absolutely if $\rho < 1$;
2. Diverges if $\rho > 1$.

If $\rho = 1$, the ratio test is inconclusive.

PROOF If $\rho < 1$, choose a (fixed) number r with $\rho < r < 1$. Then Eq. (3) implies that there exists an integer N such that $|a_{n+1}| \leq r|a_n|$ for all $n \geq N$. It follows that

$$|a_{N+1}| \leq r|a_N|,$$
$$|a_{N+2}| \leq r|a_{N+1}| \leq r^2|a_N|,$$
$$|a_{N+3}| \leq r|a_{N+2}| \leq r^3|a_N|,$$

and in general that

$$|a_{N+k}| \leq r^k |a_N| \quad \text{for } k \geq 0.$$

Hence the series

$$|a_N| + |a_{N+1}| + |a_{N+2}| + \cdots$$

is dominated by the geometric series

$$|a_N|(1 + r + r^2 + r^3 + \cdots),$$

and the latter converges because $|r| < 1$. Thus the series $\sum |a_n|$ converges, so the series $\sum a_n$ converges absolutely.

If $\rho > 1$, then Eq. (3) implies that there exists a positive integer N such that $|a_{n+1}| > |a_n|$ for all $n \geq N$. It follows that $|a_n| > |a_N| > 0$ for all $n > N$. Thus the sequence $\{a_n\}$ cannot approach zero as $n \to +\infty$, and consequently, by the nth-term divergence test, the series $\sum a_n$ diverges. ◀

To see that $\sum a_n$ may either converge or diverge if $\rho = 1$, consider the divergent series $\sum (1/n)$ and the convergent series $\sum (1/n^2)$. You should verify that, for both series, the value of the ratio ρ is 1.

EXAMPLE 5 Consider the series

$$\sum_{n=1}^{\infty} \frac{(-1)^n 2^n}{n!} = -2 + \frac{4}{2!} - \frac{8}{3!} + \frac{16}{4!} - \cdots.$$

Then

$$\rho = \lim_{n\to\infty} \left|\frac{a_{n+1}}{a_n}\right| = \lim_{n\to\infty} \left|\frac{\frac{(-1)^{n+1}2^{n+1}}{(n+1)!}}{\frac{(-1)^n 2^n}{n!}}\right| = \lim_{n\to\infty} \frac{2}{n+1} = 0.$$

Because $\rho < 1$, the series converges absolutely. ◆

EXAMPLE 6 Test for convergence: $\sum_{n=1}^{\infty} \frac{n}{2^n}$.

Solution We have

$$\rho = \lim_{n\to\infty} \left|\frac{a_{n+1}}{a_n}\right| = \lim_{n\to\infty} \frac{\frac{n+1}{2^{n+1}}}{\frac{n}{2^n}} = \lim_{n\to\infty} \frac{n+1}{2n} = \frac{1}{2}.$$

Because $\rho < 1$, this series converges (absolutely). ◆

EXAMPLE 7 Test for convergence: $\sum_{n=1}^{\infty} \frac{3^n}{n^2}$.

Solution Here we have

$$\rho = \lim_{n\to\infty} \left|\frac{a_{n+1}}{a_n}\right| = \lim_{n\to\infty} \frac{\frac{3^{n+1}}{(n+1)^2}}{\frac{3^n}{n^2}} = \lim_{n\to\infty} \frac{3n^2}{(n+1)^2} = 3.$$

In this case $\rho > 1$, so the given series diverges. ◆

THEOREM 5   The Root Test
Suppose that the limit

$$\rho = \lim_{n\to\infty} \sqrt[n]{|a_n|} \qquad (4)$$

exists or is infinite. Then the infinite series $\sum a_n$

1. Converges absolutely if $\rho < 1$;
2. Diverges if $\rho > 1$.

If $\rho = 1$, the root test is inconclusive.

PROOF   If $\rho < 1$, choose a (fixed) number r such that $\rho < r < 1$. Then $|a_n|^{1/n} < r$, and hence $|a_n| < r^n$, for n sufficiently large. Thus the series $\sum |a_n|$ is eventually dominated by the convergent geometric series $\sum r^n$. Therefore $\sum |a_n|$ converges, and so the series $\sum a_n$ converges absolutely.
If $\rho > 1$, then $|a_n|^{1/n} > 1$, and hence $|a_n| > 1$, for n sufficiently large. Therefore the nth-term test for divergence implies that the series $\sum a_n$ diverges. ◂

The ratio test is generally simpler to apply than the root test, and therefore it is ordinarily the one to try first. But there are certain series for which the root test succeeds and the ratio test fails, as in Example 8.

Alternating Series and Absolute Convergence **SECTION 11.7** 735

EXAMPLE 8 Consider the series

$$\sum_{n=0}^{\infty} \frac{1}{2^{n+(-1)^n}} = \frac{1}{2} + \frac{1}{1} + \frac{1}{8} + \frac{1}{4} + \frac{1}{32} + \frac{1}{16} + \cdots.$$

Then $a_{n+1}/a_n = 2$ if n is even, whereas $a_{n+1}/a_n = \frac{1}{8}$ if n is odd. So the limit required for the ratio test does not exist. But

$$\lim_{n\to\infty} |a_n|^{1/n} = \lim_{n\to\infty} \left|\frac{1}{2^{n+(-1)^n}}\right|^{1/n} = \lim_{n\to\infty} \frac{1}{2} \left|\frac{1}{2^{(-1)^n/n}}\right| = \frac{1}{2},$$

so the given series converges by the root test. (Its convergence also follows from the fact that it is a rearrangement of the positive-term convergent geometric series $\sum 1/2^n$.) ◆

11.7 TRUE/FALSE STUDY GUIDE

11.7 CONCEPTS: QUESTIONS AND DISCUSSION

1. Can you give an example of a divergent alternating series $\sum (-1)^{n+1} a_n$ such that $\lim_{n\to\infty} a_n = 0$? In view of the alternating series test stated in Theorem 1 of this section, how is such an example possible?

2. Give your own example of an infinite series such that both $\sum a_n$ and $\sum |a_n|$ converge but have different sums, both of which you can calculate. What can you conclude about the series if $\sum a_n$ and $\sum |a_n|$ have the same sum?

3. Can you give an example of a conditionally convergent positive-term series? Why or why not?

11.7 PROBLEMS

Determine whether or not the alternating series in Problems 1 through 20 converge or diverge.

1. $\sum_{n=1}^{\infty} \frac{(-1)^{n+1}}{n^2}$

2. $\sum_{n=1}^{\infty} \frac{(-1)^{n+1}}{\sqrt{n^2+1}}$

3. $\sum_{n=1}^{\infty} \frac{(-1)^n n}{3n+2}$

4. $\sum_{n=1}^{\infty} \frac{(-1)^n n}{3n^2+2}$

5. $\sum_{n=1}^{\infty} \frac{(-1)^{n+1} n}{\sqrt{n^2+2}}$

6. $\sum_{n=1}^{\infty} \frac{(-1)^{n+1} n^2}{\sqrt{n^5+5}}$

7. $\sum_{n=2}^{\infty} \frac{(-1)^{n+1} n}{\ln n}$

8. $\sum_{n=1}^{\infty} \frac{(-1)^n \ln n}{\sqrt{n}}$

9. $\sum_{n=1}^{\infty} \frac{(-1)^n n}{2^n}$

10. $\sum_{n=1}^{\infty} n \cdot \left(-\frac{2}{3}\right)^{n+1}$

11. $\sum_{n=1}^{\infty} \frac{(-1)^n n}{\sqrt{2^n+1}}$

12. $\sum_{n=1}^{\infty} \left(-\frac{n\pi}{10}\right)^{n+1}$

13. $\sum_{n=1}^{\infty} \frac{1}{n^{2/3}} \sin\left(\frac{n\pi}{2}\right)$

14. $\sum_{n=1}^{\infty} \frac{\cos n\pi}{n^{3/2}}$

15. $\sum_{n=1}^{\infty} (-1)^n \sin\left(\frac{1}{n}\right)$

16. $\sum_{n=1}^{\infty} (-1)^n n \sin\left(\frac{\pi}{n}\right)$

17. $\sum_{n=1}^{\infty} \frac{(-1)^{n+1}}{\sqrt[n]{2}}$

18. $\sum_{n=1}^{\infty} \frac{(-1.01)^{n+1}}{n^4}$

19. $\sum_{n=1}^{\infty} \frac{(-1)^{n+1}}{\sqrt[n]{n}}$

20. $\sum_{n=1}^{\infty} \frac{(-1)^{n+1} n!}{(2n)!}$

Determine whether the series in Problems 21 through 42 converge absolutely, converge conditionally, or diverge.

21. $\sum_{n=1}^{\infty} \frac{(-1)^{n+1}}{2^n}$

22. $\sum_{n=1}^{\infty} \frac{1}{n^2+1}$

23. $\sum_{n=1}^{\infty} \frac{(-1)^n \ln n}{n}$

24. $\sum_{n=1}^{\infty} \frac{1}{n^n}$

25. $\sum_{n=1}^{\infty} \left(\frac{10}{n}\right)^n$

26. $\sum_{n=1}^{\infty} \frac{3^n}{n!n}$

27. $\sum_{n=0}^{\infty} \frac{(-10)^n}{n!}$

28. $\sum_{n=1}^{\infty} \frac{(-1)^{n+1} n!}{n^n}$

29. $\sum_{n=1}^{\infty} (-1)^{n+1} \left(\frac{n}{n+1}\right)^n$

30. $\sum_{n=1}^{\infty} \frac{n!n^2}{(2n)!}$

31. $\sum_{n=1}^{\infty} \left(\frac{\ln n}{n}\right)^n$

32. $\sum_{n=0}^{\infty} \frac{(-1)^n 2^{3n}}{7^n}$

33. $\sum_{n=0}^{\infty} (-1)^n \left(\sqrt{n+1}-\sqrt{n}\right)$

34. $\sum_{n=1}^{\infty} n \cdot \left(\frac{3}{4}\right)^n$

35. $\sum_{n=1}^{\infty} \left[\ln\left(\frac{1}{n}\right)\right]^n$

36. $\sum_{n=0}^{\infty} \frac{(n!)^2}{(2n)!}$

37. $\sum_{n=1}^{\infty} \frac{(-1)^{n+1} 3^n}{n(2^n + 1)}$

38. $\sum_{n=1}^{\infty} \frac{(-1)^{n+1} \arctan n}{n}$

39. $\sum_{n=1}^{\infty} \frac{(-1)^{n+1} n!}{1 \cdot 3 \cdot 5 \cdots (2n-1)}$

40. $\sum_{n=1}^{\infty} (-1)^{n+1} \frac{1 \cdot 3 \cdot 5 \cdots (2n-1)}{1 \cdot 4 \cdot 7 \cdots (3n-2)}$

41. $\sum_{n=1}^{\infty} \frac{(n+2)!}{3^n (n!)^2}$

42. $\sum_{n=1}^{\infty} \frac{(-1)^{n+1} n^n}{3^{n^2}}$

In Problems 43 through 48, sum the indicated number of initial terms of the given alternating series. Then apply the alternating series remainder estimate to estimate the error in approximating the sum of the series with this partial sum. Finally, approximate the sum of the series, writing precisely the number of decimal places that thereby are guaranteed to be correct (after rounding).

43. $\sum_{n=1}^{\infty} \frac{(-1)^{n+1}}{n^3}$, 5 terms

44. $\sum_{n=1}^{\infty} \frac{(-1)^{n+1}}{3^n}$, 8 terms

45. $\sum_{n=1}^{\infty} \frac{(-1)^{n+1}}{n!}$, 6 terms

46. $\sum_{n=1}^{\infty} \frac{(-1)^{n+1}}{n^n}$, 7 terms

47. $\sum_{n=1}^{\infty} \frac{(-1)^{n+1}}{n}$, 12 terms

48. $\sum_{n=1}^{\infty} \frac{(-1)^{n+1}}{n^2}$, 15 terms

In Problems 49 through 54, sum enough terms (tell how many) to approximate the sum of the series, writing the sum rounded to the indicated number of correct decimal places.

49. $\sum_{n=1}^{\infty} \frac{(-1)^{n+1}}{n^4}$, 3 decimal places

50. $\sum_{n=1}^{\infty} \frac{(-1)^{n+1}}{n^5}$, 4 decimal places

51. $\frac{1}{\sqrt{e}} = \sum_{n=0}^{\infty} \frac{(-1)^n}{n! 2^n}$, 4 decimal places

52. $\cos 1 = \sum_{n=0}^{\infty} \frac{(-1)^n}{(2n)!}$, 5 decimal places

53. $\sin 60° = \sum_{n=0}^{\infty} \frac{(-1)^n}{(2n+1)!} \left(\frac{\pi}{3}\right)^{2n+1}$, 5 decimal places

54. $\ln(1.1) = \sum_{n=1}^{\infty} \frac{(-1)^{n+1}}{n \cdot 10^n}$, 7 decimal places

In Problems 55 and 56, show that the indicated alternating series $\sum (-1)^{n+1} a_n$ satisfies the condition that $a_n \to 0$ as $n \to +\infty$, but nevertheless diverges. Tell why the alternating series test does not apply. It may be informative to graph the first 10 or 20 partial sums.

55. $a_n = \begin{cases} \frac{1}{n} & \text{if } n \text{ is odd,} \\ \frac{1}{n^2} & \text{if } n \text{ is even.} \end{cases}$

56. $a_n = \begin{cases} \frac{1}{\sqrt{n}} & \text{if } n \text{ is odd,} \\ \frac{1}{n^3} & \text{if } n \text{ is even.} \end{cases}$

57. Give an example of a pair of convergent series $\sum a_n$ and $\sum b_n$ such that $\sum a_n b_n$ diverges.

58. Prove that $\sum |a_n|$ diverges if the series $\sum a_n$ diverges.

59. Prove that
$$\lim_{n \to \infty} \frac{a^n}{n!} = 0$$
(for any real number a) by applying the ratio test to show that the infinite series $\sum a^n/n!$ converges.

60. (a) Suppose that r is a (fixed) number such that $|r| < 1$. Use the ratio test to prove that the series $\sum_{n=0}^{\infty} nr^n$ converges. Let S denote its sum. (b) Show that
$$(1-r)S = \sum_{n=1}^{\infty} r^n.$$
Show how to conclude that
$$\sum_{n=0}^{\infty} nr^n = \frac{r}{(1-r)^2}.$$

61. Let
$$H_n = \sum_{k=1}^{n} \frac{1}{k} \quad \text{and} \quad S_n = \sum_{k=1}^{n} \frac{(-1)^{k+1}}{k}$$
denote the nth partial sums of the harmonic and alternating harmonic series, respectively. (a) Show that $S_{2n} = H_{2n} - H_n$ for all $n \geq 1$. (b) Problem 50 in Section 11.5 says that
$$\lim_{n \to \infty} (H_n - \ln n) = \gamma$$
(where $\gamma \approx 0.57722$ denotes Euler's constant). Explain why it follows that
$$\lim_{n \to \infty} (H_{2n} - \ln 2n) = \gamma.$$
(c) Conclude from parts (a) and (b) that $\lim_{n \to \infty} S_{2n} = \ln 2$. Thus
$$\ln 2 = 1 - \frac{1}{2} + \frac{1}{3} - \frac{1}{4} + \frac{1}{5} - \frac{1}{6} + \cdots.$$

62. Suppose that $\sum a_n$ is a conditionally convergent infinite series. For each n, let
$$a_n^+ = \frac{a_n + |a_n|}{2} \quad \text{and} \quad a_n^- = \frac{a_n - |a_n|}{2}.$$
(a) Explain why $\sum a_n^+$ consists of the positive terms of $\sum a_n$ and why $\sum a_n^-$ consists of the negative terms of $\sum a_n$. (b) Given a real number r, show that some rearrangement of the conditionally convergent series $\sum a_n$ converges to r. *Suggestion:* If r is positive, for instance, begin with the first partial sum of the positive series $\sum a_n^+$ that exceeds r.

Then add just enough terms of the negative series $\sum a_n^-$ so that the cumulative sum is less than r. Next add just enough terms of the positive series that the cumulative sum is greater than r, and continue in this way to define the desired rearrangement. Why does it follow that this rearranged infinite series converges to r?

63. Use the method of Problem 62 to write the first dozen terms of a rearrangement of the alternating harmonic series (Problem 61) that converges to 1 rather than to $\ln 2$.

64. Describe a way to rearrange the terms of the alternating harmonic series to obtain (a) A rearranged series that converges to -2; (b) A rearranged series that diverges to $+\infty$.

65. Here is another rearrangement of the alternating harmonic series of Problem 61:

$$1 - \frac{1}{2} - \frac{1}{4} - \frac{1}{6} - \frac{1}{8}$$
$$+ \frac{1}{3} - \frac{1}{10} - \frac{1}{12} - \frac{1}{14} - \frac{1}{16}$$
$$+ \frac{1}{5} - \frac{1}{18} - \frac{1}{20} - \frac{1}{22} - \frac{1}{24}$$
$$+ \frac{1}{7} - \frac{1}{26} - \frac{1}{28} - \frac{1}{30} - \frac{1}{32} + \cdots.$$

Use a computer to collect evidence about the value of its sum.

11.8 POWER SERIES

The most important infinite series representations of functions are those whose terms are constant multiples of (successive) integral powers of the independent variable x—that is, series that resemble "infinite polynomials." For example, we discussed in Section 11.4 the geometric series

$$\frac{1}{1-x} = 1 + x + x^2 + x^3 + \cdots \quad (|x| < 1) \tag{1}$$

and the Taylor series

$$e^x = \sum_{n=0}^{\infty} \frac{x^n}{n!} = 1 + x + \frac{x^2}{2!} + \frac{x^3}{3!} + \frac{x^4}{4!} + \cdots, \tag{2}$$

$$\cos x = \sum_{n=0}^{\infty} \frac{(-1)^n x^{2n}}{(2n)!} = 1 - \frac{x^2}{2!} + \frac{x^4}{4!} - \frac{x^6}{6!} + \cdots, \quad \text{and} \tag{3}$$

$$\sin x = \sum_{n=0}^{\infty} \frac{(-1)^n x^{2n+1}}{(2n+1)!} = x - \frac{x^3}{3!} + \frac{x^5}{5!} - \frac{x^7}{7!} + \cdots. \tag{4}$$

There we used Taylor's formula to show that the series in Eqs. (2) through (4) converge, for all x, to the functions e^x, $\cos x$, and $\sin x$, respectively. Here we investigate the convergence of a "power series" without knowing in advance the function (if any) to which it converges.

All the infinite series in Eqs. (1) through (4) have the form

$$\sum_{n=0}^{\infty} a_n x^n = a_0 + a_1 x + a_2 x^2 + \cdots + a_n x^n + \cdots \tag{5}$$

with the constant *coefficients* $a_0, a_1, a_2, \ldots$. An infinite series of this form is called a **power series** in (powers of) x. In order that the initial terms of the two sides of Eq. (5) agree, we adopt here the convention that $x^0 = 1$ even if $x = 0$.

Convergence of Power Series

The partial sums of the power series in (5) are the *polynomials*

$$s_1(x) = a_0 + a_1 x, \quad s_2(x) = a_0 + a_1 x + a_2 x^2, \quad s_3(x) = a_0 + a_1 x + a_2 x^2 + a_3 x^3,$$

and so forth. The nth partial sum is an nth-degree polynomial. When we ask *where* the power series converges, we seek those values of x for which the limit

$$s(x) = \lim_{n \to \infty} s_n(x)$$

exists. The sum $s(x)$ of a power series is then a function of x that is defined wherever the series converges.

The power series in (5) obviously converges when $x = 0$. In general, it will converge for some nonzero values of x and diverge for others. Because of the way in which powers of x are involved, the ratio test of Section 11.7 is particularly effective in determining the values of x for which a given power series converges.

Assume that the limit

$$\rho = \lim_{n \to \infty} \left| \frac{a_{n+1}}{a_n} \right| \tag{6}$$

exists. This is the limit that we need if we want to apply the ratio test to the series $\sum a_n$ of constants. To apply the ratio test to the power series in Eq. (5), we write $u_n = a_n x^n$ and compute the limit

$$\lim_{n \to \infty} \left| \frac{u_{n+1}}{u_n} \right| = \lim_{n \to \infty} \left| \frac{a_{n+1} x^{n+1}}{a_n x^n} \right| = \rho |x|. \tag{7}$$

If $\rho = 0$, then $\sum a_n x^n$ converges absolutely for all x. If $\rho = +\infty$, then $\sum a_n x^n$ diverges for all $x \neq 0$. If ρ is a positive real number, we see from Eq. (7) that $\sum a_n x^n$ converges absolutely for all x such that $\rho \cdot |x| < 1$—that is, when

$$|x| < R = \frac{1}{\rho} = \lim_{n \to \infty} \left| \frac{a_n}{a_{n+1}} \right|. \tag{8}$$

In this case the ratio test also implies that $\sum a_n x^n$ diverges if $|x| > R$ but is inconclusive when $x = \pm R$. We have therefore proved Theorem 1, under the additional hypothesis that the limit in Eq. (6) exists. In Problems 69 and 70 we outline a proof that does not require this additional hypothesis.

THEOREM 1 Convergence of Power Series

If $\sum a_n x^n$ is a power series, then either

1. The series converges absolutely for all x, or
2. The series converges only when $x = 0$, or
3. There exists a number $R > 0$ such that $\sum a_n x^n$ converges absolutely if $|x| < R$ and diverges if $|x| > R$.

The number R of Case 3 is called the **radius of convergence** of the power series $\sum a_n x^n$. We write $R = \infty$ in Case 1 and $R = 0$ in Case 2. The set of all real numbers x for which the series converges is called its **interval of convergence** (Fig. 11.8.1); note that this set *is* an interval. If $0 < R < \infty$, then the interval of convergence is one of the intervals

$$(-R, R), \quad (-R, R], \quad [-R, R), \quad \text{or} \quad [-R, R].$$

FIGURE 11.8.1 The interval of convergence if $0 < R = \lim_{n \to \infty} \left| \frac{a_n}{a_{n+1}} \right| < \infty$.

When we substitute either of the endpoints $x = \pm R$ into the series $\sum a_n x^n$, we obtain an infinite series with constant terms whose convergence must be determined separately. Because these will be numerical series, the earlier tests of this chapter are appropriate.

EXAMPLE 1 Find the interval of convergence of the series

$$\sum_{n=1}^{\infty} \frac{x^n}{n \cdot 3^n}.$$

Solution With $u_n = x^n/(n \cdot 3^n)$ we find that

$$\lim_{n \to \infty} \left| \frac{u_{n+1}}{u_n} \right| = \lim_{n \to \infty} \left| \frac{\frac{x^{n+1}}{(n+1) \cdot 3^{n+1}}}{\frac{x^n}{n \cdot 3^n}} \right| = \lim_{n \to \infty} \frac{n|x|}{3(n+1)} = \frac{|x|}{3}.$$

Now $|x|/3 < 1$ provided that $|x| < 3$, so the ratio test implies that the given series converges absolutely if $|x| < 3$ and diverges if $|x| > 3$. When $x = 3$, we have the divergent harmonic series $\sum (1/n)$, and when $x = -3$ we have the convergent alternating series $\sum (-1)^n/n$. Thus the interval of convergence of the given power series is $[-3, 3)$. We see dramatically in Fig. 11.8.2 the difference between convergence at $x = -3$ and divergence at $x = +3$. ◆

FIGURE 11.8.2 Graphs of the partial sums $S_4(x)$, $S_6(x)$, and $S_{10}(x)$ of the power series $S(x) = \sum_{n=1}^{\infty} \frac{x^n}{n \cdot 3^n}$ of Example 1. We see convergence at $x = -3$, but apparently $S(x) \to \infty$ as x approaches $+3$, where the series diverges harmonically.

EXAMPLE 2 Find the interval of convergence of the power series

$$\sum_{n=0}^{\infty} \frac{(-2)^n x^n}{(2n)!} = 1 - \frac{2x}{2!} + \frac{4x^2}{4!} - \frac{8x^3}{6!} + \frac{16x^4}{8!} - \cdots.$$

Solution With $u_n = (-2)^n x^n/(2n)!$ we find that

$$\lim_{n \to \infty} \left| \frac{u_{n+1}}{u_n} \right| = \lim_{n \to \infty} \left| \frac{\frac{(-2)^{n+1} x^{n+1}}{(2n+2)!}}{\frac{(-2)^n x^n}{(2n)!}} \right| = \lim_{n \to \infty} \frac{2|x|}{(2n+1)(2n+2)} = 0$$

for all x [using the fact that $(2n+2)! = (2n)!(2n+1)(2n+2)$]. Hence the ratio test implies that the given power series converges for all x, and its interval of convergence is therefore $(-\infty, +\infty)$, the entire real line. ◆

REMARK The power series of Example 2 results upon substituting $\sqrt{2x}$ for x in the Taylor series for $\cos x$ [Eq. (3)]. But only for $x > 0$ does the sum $S(x)$ of the series exhibit the oscillatory character of the function $\cos \sqrt{2x}$ (Fig. 11.8.3). For $x < 0$ the power series converges to the quite different (and nonoscillatory) function $\cosh \sqrt{|2x|}$.

FIGURE 11.8.3 Graphs of the partial sums $S_5(x)$, $S_{10}(x)$, $S_{15}(x)$, and $S_{20}(x)$ of the power series $S(x) = \sum_{n=0}^{\infty} \dfrac{(-2x)^n}{(2n)!}$ of Example 2, which converges to $\cos \sqrt{2x}$ for $x > 0$.

EXAMPLE 3 Find the interval of convergence of the series $\sum_{n=1}^{\infty} n^n x^n$.

Solution With $u_n = n^n x^n$ we find that

$$\lim_{n \to \infty} \left| \frac{u_{n+1}}{u_n} \right| = \lim_{n \to \infty} \left| \frac{(n+1)^{n+1} x^{n+1}}{n^n x^n} \right| = \lim_{n \to \infty} (n+1) \left(1 + \frac{1}{n}\right)^n |x| = +\infty$$

for all $x \neq 0$, because

$$\lim_{n \to \infty} \left(1 + \frac{1}{n}\right)^n = e.$$

Thus the given series diverges for all $x \neq 0$, and its interval of convergence consists of the single point $x = 0$. ◆

EXAMPLE 4 Use the ratio test to verify that the Taylor series for $\cos x$ in Eq. (3) converges for all x.

Solution With $u_n = (-1)^n x^{2n}/(2n)!$ we find that

$$\lim_{n \to \infty} \left| \frac{u_{n+1}}{u_n} \right| = \lim_{n \to \infty} \left| \frac{\frac{(-1)^{n+1} x^{2n+2}}{(2n+2)!}}{\frac{(-1)^n x^{2n}}{(2n)!}} \right| = \lim_{n \to \infty} \frac{x^2}{(2n+1)(2n+2)} = 0$$

for all x, so the series converges for all x. ◆

IMPORTANT In Example 4, the ratio test tells us only that the series for $\cos x$ converges to *some* number, *not* necessarily the particular number $\cos x$. The argument of Section 11.4, using Taylor's formula with remainder, is required to establish that the sum of the series is actually $\cos x$.

Power Series in Powers of $x - c$

An infinite series of the form

$$\sum_{n=0}^{\infty} a_n(x-c)^n = a_0 + a_1(x-c) + a_2(x-c)^2 + \cdots, \qquad (9)$$

where c is a constant, is called a **power series in** (powers of) $x - c$. By the same reasoning that led us to Theorem 1, with x^n replaced with $(x - c)^n$ throughout, we conclude that either

1. The series in Eq. (9) converges absolutely for all x, or
2. The series converges only when $x - c = 0$—that is, when $x = c$—or
3. There exists a number $R > 0$ such that the series in Eq. (9) converges absolutely if $|x - c| < R$ and diverges if $|x - c| > R$.

As in the case of a power series with $c = 0$, the number R is called the **radius of convergence** of the series, and the **interval of convergence** of the series $\sum a_n(x-c)^n$ is the set of all numbers x for which it converges (Fig. 11.8.4). As before, when $0 < R < \infty$, the convergence of the series at the endpoints $x = c - R$ and $x = c + R$ of its interval of convergence must be checked separately.

FIGURE 11.8.4 The interval of convergence of $\sum_{n=0}^{\infty} a_n(x-c)^n$.

EXAMPLE 5 Determine the interval of convergence of the series

$$\sum_{n=1}^{\infty} \frac{(-1)^n(x-2)^n}{n \cdot 4^n}.$$

Solution We let $u_n = (-1)^n(x-2)^n/(n \cdot 4^n)$. Then

$$\lim_{n \to \infty} \left| \frac{u_{n+1}}{u_n} \right| = \lim_{n \to \infty} \left| \frac{\frac{(-1)^{n+1}(x-2)^{n+1}}{(n+1) \cdot 4^{n+1}}}{\frac{(-1)^n(x-2)^n}{n \cdot 4^n}} \right|$$

$$= \lim_{n \to \infty} \frac{|x-2|}{4} \cdot \frac{n}{n+1} = \frac{|x-2|}{4}.$$

Hence the given series converges when $|x - 2| < 4$, so the radius of convergence is $R = 4$. Because $c = 2$, the series converges when $-2 < x < 6$ and diverges if either $x < -2$ or $x > 6$. When $x = -2$, the series reduces to the divergent harmonic series, and when $x = 6$ it reduces to the convergent alternating series $\sum(-1)^n/n$. Thus the interval of convergence of the given power series is $(-2, 6]$. ◆

Power Series Representations of Functions

Power series are important tools for computing (or approximating) values of functions. Suppose that the series $\sum a_n x^n$ converges to the value $f(x)$; that is,

$$f(x) = a_0 + a_1 x + a_2 x^2 + \cdots + a_n x^n + \cdots$$

for each x in the interval of convergence of the power series. Then we call $\sum a_n x^n$ a **power series representation** of $f(x)$. For example, the geometric series $\sum x^n$ in Eq. (1) is a power series representation of the function $f(x) = 1/(1-x)$ on the interval $(-1, 1)$.

We saw in Section 11.4 how Taylor's formula with remainder can often be used to find a power series representation of a given function. Recall that the nth-degree Taylor's formula for $f(x)$ at $x = a$ is

$$f(x) = f(a) + f'(a)(x-a) + \frac{f''(a)}{2!}(x-a)^2 + \frac{f^{(3)}(a)}{3!}(x-a)^3$$
$$+ \cdots + \frac{f^{(n)}(a)}{n!}(x-a)^n + R_n(x). \quad \textbf{(10)}$$

The remainder $R_n(x)$ is given by

$$R_n(x) = \frac{f^{(n+1)}(z)}{(n+1)!}(x-a)^{n+1},$$

where z is some number between a and x. If we let $n \to +\infty$ in Eq. (10), we obtain Theorem 2.

THEOREM 2 Taylor Series Representations
Suppose that the function f has derivatives of all orders on some interval containing a and also that

$$\lim_{n \to \infty} R_n(x) = 0 \quad \textbf{(11)}$$

for each x in that interval. Then

$$f(x) = \sum_{n=0}^{\infty} \frac{f^{(n)}(a)}{n!}(x-a)^n \quad \textbf{(12)}$$

for each x in the interval.

The power series in Eq. (12) is the **Taylor series** of the function f **at** $x = a$ (or *in powers of* $x - a$, or *with center a*). If $a = 0$, we obtain the power series

$$f(x) = \sum_{n=0}^{\infty} \frac{f^{(n)}(0)}{n!} x^n = f(0) + f'(0)x + \frac{f''(0)}{2!}x^2 + \cdots, \quad \textbf{(13)}$$

commonly called the **Maclaurin series** of f. Thus the power series in Eqs. (2) through (4) are the Maclaurin series of the functions e^x, $\cos x$, and $\sin x$, respectively.

EXAMPLE 6 New power series can be constructed from old ones. For instance, upon replacing x with $-x$ in the Maclaurin series for e^x, we obtain

$$e^{-x} = 1 - x + \frac{x^2}{2!} - \frac{x^3}{3!} + \cdots + (-1)^n \frac{x^n}{n!} + \cdots.$$

Let us now add the series for e^x and e^{-x} and divide by 2. This gives

$$\cosh x = \frac{e^x + e^{-x}}{2} = \frac{1}{2}\left(1 + x + \frac{x^2}{2!} + \frac{x^3}{3!} + \frac{x^4}{4!} + \cdots\right)$$
$$+ \frac{1}{2}\left(1 - x + \frac{x^2}{2!} - \frac{x^3}{3!} + \frac{x^4}{4!} - \cdots\right),$$

so

$$\cosh x = 1 + \frac{x^2}{2!} + \frac{x^4}{4!} + \frac{x^6}{6!} + \cdots.$$

Similarly,

$$\sinh x = x + \frac{x^3}{3!} + \frac{x^5}{5!} + \frac{x^7}{7!} + \cdots.$$

Note the strong resemblance to Eqs. (3) and (4), the series for $\cos x$ and $\sin x$, respectively.

Upon replacing x with $-x^2$ in the series for e^x, we obtain

$$e^{-x^2} = \sum_{n=0}^{\infty} (-1)^n \frac{x^{2n}}{n!} = 1 - x^2 + \frac{x^4}{2!} - \frac{x^6}{3!} + \cdots.$$

Because this power series converges to $\exp(-x^2)$ for all x, it must be the Maclaurin series for $\exp(-x^2)$. (See Problem 66.) Think how tedious it would be to compute the derivatives of $\exp(-x^2)$ needed to write its Maclaurin series directly from Eq. (13). ◆

EXAMPLE 7 Sometimes a function is originally defined by means of a power series. One of the most important "higher transcendental functions" of applied mathematics is the Bessel function $J_0(x)$ of order zero defined by

$$J_0(x) = \sum_{n=0}^{\infty} \frac{(-1)^n x^{2n}}{2^{2n}(n!)^2} = 1 - \frac{x^2}{4} + \frac{x^4}{64} - \frac{x^6}{2304} + \cdots.$$

Only terms of even degree appear, so let us write $u_n = (-1)^n x^{2n} / [2^{2n}(n!)^2]$ for the nth term in this series (not counting its constant term). Then

$$\lim_{n \to \infty} \left| \frac{u_{n+1}}{u_n} \right| = \lim_{n \to \infty} \left| \frac{\frac{(-1)^{n+1} x^{2n+2}}{2^{2n+2}[(n+1)!]^2}}{\frac{(-1)^n x^{2n}}{2^{2n}(n!)^2}} \right| = \lim_{n \to \infty} \frac{x^2}{4(n+1)^2} = 0$$

for all x, so the ratio test implies that $J_0(x)$ is defined on the whole real line. The series for $J_0(x)$ resembles somewhat the cosine series, but the graph of $J_0(x)$ exhibits *damped* oscillations (Fig. 11.8.5). Bessel functions are important in such applications as the distribution of temperature in a cylindrical steam pipe and distribution of thermal neutrons in a cylindrical reactor. ◆

FIGURE 11.8.5 Graphs of the Bessel function $J_0(x)$ and its Taylor polynomials $P_8(x)$, $P_{14}(x)$, $P_{24}(x)$, and $P_{30}(x)$.

The Binomial Series

Example 8 gives one of the most famous and useful of all series, the *binomial series*, which was discovered by Newton in the 1660s. It is the infinite series generalization of the (finite) binomial theorem of elementary algebra.

EXAMPLE 8 Suppose that α is a nonzero real number. Show that the Maclaurin series of $f(x) = (1+x)^\alpha$ is

$$(1+x)^\alpha = 1 + \sum_{n=1}^{\infty} \frac{\alpha(\alpha-1)(\alpha-2)\cdots(\alpha-n+1)}{n!} x^n$$

$$= 1 + \alpha x + \frac{\alpha(\alpha-1)}{2!} x^2 + \frac{\alpha(\alpha-1)(\alpha-2)}{3!} x^3 + \cdots. \tag{14}$$

Also determine the interval of convergence of this **binomial series.**

Solution To derive the series itself, we simply list all the derivatives of $f(x) = (1+x)^\alpha$, including its "zeroth" derivative:

$$f(x) = (1+x)^\alpha$$
$$f'(x) = \alpha(1+x)^{\alpha-1}$$
$$f''(x) = \alpha(\alpha-1)(1+x)^{\alpha-2}$$
$$f^{(3)}(x) = \alpha(\alpha-1)(\alpha-2)(1+x)^{\alpha-3},$$
$$\vdots$$
$$f^{(n)}(x) = \alpha(\alpha-1)(\alpha-2)\cdots(\alpha-n+1)(1+x)^{\alpha-n}.$$

Thus

$$f^{(n)}(0) = \alpha(\alpha-1)(\alpha-2)\cdots(\alpha-n+1).$$

If we substitute this value of $f^{(n)}(0)$ into the Maclaurin series formula in Eq. (13), we get the binomial series in Eq. (14).

To determine the interval of convergence of the binomial series, we let

$$u_n = \frac{\alpha(\alpha-1)(\alpha-2)\cdots(\alpha-n+1)}{n!} x^n.$$

We find that

$$\lim_{n\to\infty} \left| \frac{u_{n+1}}{u_n} \right| = \lim_{n\to\infty} \left| \frac{\dfrac{\alpha(\alpha-1)(\alpha-2)\cdots(\alpha-n)x^{n+1}}{(n+1)!}}{\dfrac{\alpha(\alpha-1)(\alpha-2)\cdots(\alpha-n+1)x^n}{n!}} \right|$$

$$= \lim_{n\to\infty} \left| \frac{(\alpha-n)x}{n+1} \right| = |x|.$$

Hence the ratio test shows that the binomial series converges absolutely if $|x| < 1$ and diverges if $|x| > 1$. Its convergence at the endpoints $x = \pm 1$ depends on the value of α; we shall not pursue this problem. Problem 67 outlines a proof that the sum of the binomial series actually is $(1+x)^\alpha$ if $|x| < 1$. ◆

If $\alpha = k$, a positive integer, then the coefficient of x^n is zero for $n > k$, and the binomial series reduces to the binomial formula

$$(1+x)^k = \sum_{n=0}^{k} \frac{k!}{n!(k-n)!} x^n.$$

Otherwise Eq. (14) is an infinite series. For example, with $\alpha = \frac{1}{2}$, we obtain

$$\sqrt{1+x} = 1 + \frac{\frac{1}{2}}{1!}x + \frac{\left(\frac{1}{2}\right)\left(-\frac{1}{2}\right)}{2!}x^2 + \frac{\left(\frac{1}{2}\right)\left(-\frac{1}{2}\right)\left(-\frac{3}{2}\right)}{3!}x^3$$

$$+ \frac{\left(\frac{1}{2}\right)\left(-\frac{1}{2}\right)\left(-\frac{3}{2}\right)\left(-\frac{5}{2}\right)}{4!}x^4 + \cdots$$

$$= 1 + \frac{1}{2}x - \frac{1}{8}x^2 + \frac{1}{16}x^3 - \frac{5}{128}x^4 + \cdots. \tag{15}$$

If we replace x with $-x$ and take $\alpha = -\frac{1}{2}$, we get the series

$$\frac{1}{\sqrt{1-x}} = 1 + \frac{-\frac{1}{2}}{1!}(-x) + \frac{\left(-\frac{1}{2}\right)\left(-\frac{3}{2}\right)}{2!}(-x)^2 + \cdots + \frac{1 \cdot 3 \cdot 5 \cdots (2n-1)}{n! \cdot 2^n}x^n + \cdots,$$

which in summation notation takes the form

$$\frac{1}{\sqrt{1-x}} = 1 + \sum_{n=1}^{\infty} \frac{1 \cdot 3 \cdot 5 \cdots (2n-1)}{2 \cdot 4 \cdot 6 \cdots (2n)} x^n. \tag{16}$$

We will find this series quite useful in Example 12 and in Problem 68.

Differentiation and Integration of Power Series

Sometimes it is inconvenient to compute the repeated derivatives of a function in order to find its Taylor series. An alternative method of finding new power series is by the differentiation and integration of known power series.

Suppose that a power series representation of the function $f(x)$ is known. Then Theorem 3 (we leave its proof to advanced calculus) implies that the function $f(x)$ may be differentiated by separately differentiating the individual terms in its power series. That is, the power series obtained by termwise differentiation converges to the derivative $f'(x)$. Similarly, a function can be integrated by termwise integration of its power series.

THEOREM 3 Termwise Differentiation and Integration
Suppose that the function f has a power series representation

$$f(x) = \sum_{n=0}^{\infty} a_n x^n = a_0 + a_1 x + a_2 x^2 + a_3 x^3 + \cdots$$

with nonzero radius of convergence R. Then f is differentiable on $(-R, R)$ and

$$f'(x) = \sum_{n=1}^{\infty} n a_n x^{n-1} = a_1 + 2a_2 x + 3a_3 x^2 + 4a_4 x^3 + \cdots. \tag{17}$$

Also,

$$\int_0^x f(t)\,dt = \sum_{n=0}^{\infty} \frac{a_n x^{n+1}}{n+1} = a_0 x + \tfrac{1}{2}a_1 x^2 + \tfrac{1}{3}a_2 x^3 + \cdots \tag{18}$$

for each x in $(-R, R)$. Moreover, the power series in Eqs. (17) and (18) have the same radius of convergence R.

REMARK 1 Although we omit the proof of Theorem 3, we observe that the radius of convergence of the series in Eq. (17) is

$$R = \lim_{n \to \infty} \left| \frac{n a_n}{(n+1)a_{n+1}} \right| = \left(\lim_{n \to \infty} \frac{n}{n+1} \right) \cdot \left(\lim_{n \to \infty} \left| \frac{a_n}{a_{n+1}} \right| \right) = \lim_{n \to \infty} \left| \frac{a_n}{a_{n+1}} \right|.$$

Thus, by Eq. (8), the power series for $f(x)$ and the power series for $f'(x)$ have the same radius of convergence (under the assumption that the preceding limit exists).

REMARK 2 Theorem 3 has this important consequence: If both the power series $\sum a_n x^n$ and $\sum b_n x^n$ converge and, for all x with $|x| < R$ $(R > 0)$, $\sum a_n x^n = \sum b_n x^n$, then $a_n = b_n$ for all n. In particular, the Taylor series of a function is its unique power series representation (if any). (See Problem 66.)

EXAMPLE 9 Termwise differentiation of the geometric series for

$$f(x) = \frac{1}{1-x}$$

yields

$$\frac{1}{(1-x)^2} = D_x \left(\frac{1}{1-x} \right) = D_x (1 + x + x^2 + x^3 + \cdots)$$
$$= 1 + 2x + 3x^2 + 4x^3 + \cdots .$$

Thus

$$\frac{1}{(1-x)^2} = \sum_{n=1}^{\infty} nx^{n-1} = \sum_{n=0}^{\infty} (n+1)x^n.$$

The series converges to $1/(1-x)^2$ if $-1 < x < 1$. ◆

EXAMPLE 10 Replacing x with $-t$ in the geometric series of Example 9 gives

$$\frac{1}{1+t} = 1 - t + t^2 - t^3 + \cdots + (-1)^n t^n + \cdots .$$

Because $D_t \ln(1+t) = 1/(1+t)$, termwise integration from $t = 0$ to $t = x$ now gives

$$\ln(1+x) = \int_0^x \frac{1}{1+t} \, dt$$
$$= \int_0^x (1 - t + t^2 - \cdots + (-1)^n t^n + \cdots) \, dt;$$

$$\ln(1+x) = x - \frac{1}{2}x^2 + \frac{1}{3}x^3 - \frac{1}{4}x^4 + \cdots + \frac{(-1)^{n+1}}{n} x^n + \cdots \quad (19)$$

if $|x| < 1$. ◆

EXAMPLE 11 Find a power series representation for the arctangent function.

Solution Because $D_t \tan^{-1} t = 1/(1+t^2)$, termwise integration of the geometric series

$$\frac{1}{1+t^2} = 1 - t^2 + t^4 - t^6 + t^8 - \cdots$$

gives

$$\tan^{-1} x = \int_0^x \frac{1}{1+t^2} \, dt = \int_0^x (1 - t^2 + t^4 - t^6 + t^8 - \cdots) \, dt$$

if x is in the interval $(-1, 1)$ where the geometric series converges. Therefore

$$\tan^{-1} x = \sum_{n=1}^{\infty} \frac{(-1)^{n+1} x^{2n-1}}{2n-1} = x - \frac{1}{3}x^3 + \frac{1}{5}x^5 - \frac{1}{7}x^7 + \frac{1}{9}x^9 - \cdots \quad (20)$$

if $-1 < x < 1$. Figure 11.8.6 illustrates both the convergence of the power series within this interval and the divergence outside it. ◆

FIGURE 11.8.6 The graphs of the Taylor polynomials of degrees $n = 3, 5, 7$, and 9 illustrate the convergence within the interval $-1 < x < 1$ and divergence outside this interval.

EXAMPLE 12 Find a power series representation for the arcsine function.

Solution First we substitute t^2 for x in Eq. (16). This yields

$$\frac{1}{\sqrt{1-t^2}} = 1 + \sum_{n=1}^{\infty} \frac{1 \cdot 3 \cdot 5 \cdots (2n-1)}{2 \cdot 4 \cdot 6 \cdots (2n)} t^{2n}$$

if $|t| < 1$. Because $D_t \sin^{-1} t = 1/\sqrt{1-t^2}$, termwise integration of this series from $t = 0$ to $t = x$ gives

$$\sin^{-1} x = \int_0^x \frac{1}{\sqrt{1-t^2}}\, dt = x + \sum_{n=1}^{\infty} \frac{1 \cdot 3 \cdot 5 \cdots (2n-1)}{2 \cdot 4 \cdot 6 \cdots (2n)} \cdot \frac{x^{2n+1}}{2n+1} \qquad (21)$$

if $|x| < 1$. Problem 68 shows how to use this series to derive the series

$$\frac{\pi^2}{6} = 1 + \frac{1}{2^2} + \frac{1}{3^2} + \frac{1}{4^2} + \cdots + \frac{1}{n^2} + \cdots,$$

which we used in Example 3 of Section 11.5 to approximate the number π. ◆

11.8 TRUE/FALSE STUDY GUIDE

11.8 CONCEPTS: QUESTIONS AND DISCUSSION

1. Suppose that you started with the Maclaurin series of the sine and cosine functions as their definitions. How many of the familiar properties of $\cos x$ and $\sin x$—such as their derivatives and addition formulas—could you establish using only these series?
2. Use the Maclaurin series for the sine and cosine functions and the corresponding hyperbolic series in Example 6 to explore relations between function pairs trig ix and trigh x, where trig denotes one of the cos/sin/tan trigonometric functions, and trigh denotes the corresponding hyperbolic function.

11.8 PROBLEMS

Find the interval of convergence of each power series in Problems 1 through 30.

1. $\sum_{n=1}^{\infty} nx^n$

2. $\sum_{n=1}^{\infty} \frac{x^n}{\sqrt{n}}$

3. $\sum_{n=1}^{\infty} \frac{nx^n}{2^n}$

4. $\sum_{n=1}^{\infty} \frac{(-1)^n x^n}{n^{1/2} 5^n}$

5. $\sum_{n=1}^{\infty} n! x^n$

6. $\sum_{n=1}^{\infty} \frac{(-1)^n x^n}{n^n}$

7. $\sum_{n=1}^{\infty} \frac{3^n x^n}{n^3}$

8. $\sum_{n=1}^{\infty} \frac{(-4)^n x^n}{\sqrt{2n+1}}$

9. $\sum_{n=1}^{\infty} (-1)^n n^{1/2} (2x)^n$

10. $\sum_{n=1}^{\infty} \frac{n^2 x^n}{3n-1}$

11. $\sum_{n=1}^{\infty} \frac{(-1)^n nx^n}{2^n(n+1)^3}$

12. $\sum_{n=1}^{\infty} \frac{n^{10} x^n}{10^n}$

13. $\sum_{n=1}^{\infty} \frac{(\ln n) x^n}{3^n}$

14. $\sum_{n=2}^{\infty} \frac{(-1)^n 4^n x^n}{n \ln n}$

15. $\sum_{n=0}^{\infty} (5x-3)^n$

16. $\sum_{n=1}^{\infty} \frac{(2x-1)^n}{n^4 + 16}$

17. $\sum_{n=1}^{\infty} \frac{2^n (x-3)^n}{n^2}$

18. $\sum_{n=1}^{\infty} \frac{n!}{n^n} x^n$ (Do not test the endpoints; the series diverges at each.)

19. $\sum_{n=1}^{\infty} \frac{(2n)!}{n!} x^n$

20. $\sum_{n=1}^{\infty} \frac{1 \cdot 3 \cdot 5 \cdots (2n+1)}{n!} x^n$ (Do not test the endpoints; the series diverges at each.)

21. $\sum_{n=1}^{\infty} \frac{n^3 (x+1)^n}{3^n}$

22. $\sum_{n=1}^{\infty} \frac{(-1)^{n+1}(x-2)^n}{n^2}$

23. $\sum_{n=1}^{\infty} \frac{(3-x)^n}{n^3}$

24. $\sum_{n=1}^{\infty} \frac{(-1)^{n+1} 10^n}{n!}(x-10)^n$

25. $\sum_{n=1}^{\infty} \frac{n!}{2^n}(x-5)^n$

26. $\sum_{n=1}^{\infty} \frac{(-1)^{n+1}}{n \cdot 10^n}(x-2)^n$

27. $\sum_{n=0}^{\infty} x^{(2^n)}$

28. $\sum_{n=0}^{\infty} \left(\frac{x^2+1}{5}\right)^n$

29. $\sum_{n=1}^{\infty} \frac{(-1)^n x^n}{1 \cdot 3 \cdot 5 \cdots (2n-1)}$

30. $\sum_{n=1}^{\infty} \frac{1 \cdot 3 \cdot 5 \cdots (2n-1)}{2 \cdot 5 \cdot 8 \cdots (3n-1)} x^n$

In Problems 31 through 42, use power series established in this section to find a power series representation of the given function. Then determine the radius of convergence of the resulting series.

31. $f(x) = \frac{x}{1-x}$

32. $f(x) = \frac{1}{10+x}$

33. $f(x) = x^2 e^{-3x}$

34. $f(x) = \frac{x}{9-x^2}$

35. $f(x) = \sin(x^2)$

36. $f(x) = \cos^2 2x = \frac{1}{2}(1 + \cos 4x)$

37. $f(x) = \sqrt[3]{1-x}$

38. $f(x) = (1+x^2)^{3/2}$

39. $f(x) = (1+x)^{-3}$

40. $f(x) = \frac{1}{\sqrt{9+x^3}}$

41. $f(x) = \frac{\ln(1+x)}{x}$

42. $f(x) = \frac{x - \arctan x}{x^3}$

In Problems 43 through 48, find a power series representation for the given function $f(x)$ by using termwise integration.

43. $f(x) = \int_0^x \sin t^3 \, dt$

44. $f(x) = \int_0^x \frac{\sin t}{t} \, dt$

45. $f(x) = \int_0^x \exp(-t^3) \, dt$

46. $f(x) = \int_0^x \frac{\arctan t}{t} \, dt$

47. $f(x) = \int_0^x \frac{1 - \exp(-t^2)}{t^2} \, dt$

48. $\tanh^{-1} x = \int_0^x \frac{1}{1-t^2} \, dt$

Beginning with the geometric series $\sum_{n=0}^{\infty} x^n$ as in Example 9, differentiate termwise to find the sums (for $|x| < 1$) of the power series in Problems 49 through 51.

49. $\sum_{n=1}^{\infty} nx^n$

50. $\sum_{n=1}^{\infty} n(n-1)x^n$

51. $\sum_{n=1}^{\infty} n^2 x^n$

52. Use the power series of the preceding problems to sum the numerical series

$$\sum_{n=1}^{\infty} \frac{n}{2^n} \quad \text{and} \quad \sum_{n=1}^{\infty} \frac{n^2}{3^n}.$$

53. Verify by termwise differentiation of its Maclaurin series that the exponential function $y = e^x$ satisfies the differential equation $dy/dx = y$. (Thus the exponential series arises naturally as a power series that is its own termwise derivative.)

54. Verify by termwise differentiation of their Maclaurin series that the sine function $y = \sin x$ and the cosine function $y = \cos x$ both satisfy the differential equation

$$\frac{d^2 y}{dx^2} + y = 0.$$

55. Verify by termwise differentiation of the hyperbolic sine and cosine series in Example 6 that each of the functions $\cosh x$ and $\sinh x$ is the derivative of the other, and that each satisfies the differential equation $y'' - y = 0$.

56. In elementary mathematics one sees various definitions (some circular!) of the trigonometric functions. One approach to a rigorous foundation for these functions is to begin by defining $\cos x$ and $\sin x$ by means of their Maclaurin series. For instance, never having heard of sine, cosine, or the number π, we might define the function

$$S(x) = \sum_{n=1}^{\infty} \frac{(-1)^{n-1} x^{2n-1}}{(2n-1)!}$$

and verify using the ratio test that this series converges for all x. Use a computer algebra system to plot graphs of high-degree partial sums $s_n(x)$ of this series. Does it appear that the function $S(x)$ appears to have a zero somewhere near the number 3? Solve the equation $s_n(x) = 0$ numerically (for some large values of n) to verify that this least positive zero of the sine function is approximately 3.14159 (and thus the famous number π makes a fresh new appearance).

57. The Bessel function of order 1 is defined by

$$J_1(x) = \sum_{n=0}^{\infty} \frac{(-1)^n x^{2n+1}}{2^{2n+1} n! (n+1)!} = \frac{x}{2} - \frac{x^3}{16} + \frac{x^5}{384} - \cdots.$$

Verify that this series converges for all x and that the derivative of the Bessel function of order zero is given by $J_0'(x) = -J_1(x)$. Are the graphs in Fig. 11.8.7 consistent with this latter fact?

FIGURE 11.8.7 Graphs of the Bessel functions $J_0(x)$ and $J_1(x)$. Note that their zeros are interlaced, like the zeros of the cosine and sine functions.

58. Verify by termwise integration that

$$\int x J_0(x)\, dx = x J_1(x) + C.$$

59. Bessel's equation of order n is the second-order differential equation

$$x^2 y'' + x y' + (x^2 - n^2) y = 0.$$

Verify by termwise differentiation that $y = J_0(x)$ satisfies Bessel's equation of order zero.

60. Verify that $y = J_1(x)$ satisfies Bessel's equation of order 1 (Problem 59).

61. First use the sine series to find the Taylor series of $f(x) = (\sin x)/x$. Then use a graphing calculator or computer to illustrate the approximation of $f(x)$ by its Taylor polynomials with center $a = 0$.

62. First find the Taylor series of the function

$$g(x) = \int_0^x \frac{\sin t}{t}\, dt.$$

Then determine where this power series converges. Finally, use a graphing calculator or computer to illustrate the approximation of $g(x)$ by its Taylor polynomials with center $a = 0$.

63. Deduce from the arctangent series (Example 11) that

$$\pi = \frac{6}{\sqrt{3}} \sum_{n=0}^{\infty} \frac{(-1)^n}{2n+1} \left(\frac{1}{3}\right)^n.$$

Then use this alternating series to show that $\pi = 3.14$ accurate to two decimal places.

64. Substitute the Maclaurin series for $\sin x$, and then assume the validity of termwise integration of the resulting series, to derive the formula

$$\int_0^{\infty} e^{-t} \sin xt\, dt = \frac{x}{1+x^2} \quad (|x| < 1).$$

Use the fact from Section 8.8 that

$$\int_0^{\infty} t^n e^{-t}\, dt = \Gamma(n+1) = n!.$$

65. (a) Deduce from the Maclaurin series for e^t that

$$\frac{1}{x^x} = \sum_{n=0}^{\infty} \frac{(-1)^n}{n!} (x \ln x)^n.$$

(b) Assuming the validity of termwise integration of the series in part (a), use the integral formula of Problem 53 in Section 8.8 to conclude that

$$\int_0^1 \frac{1}{x^x}\, dx = \sum_{n=1}^{\infty} \frac{1}{n^n}.$$

66. Suppose that $f(x)$ is represented by the power series

$$\sum_{n=0}^{\infty} a_n x^n$$

for all x in some open interval centered at $x = 0$. Show by repeated differentiation of the series, substituting $x = 0$ after each differentiation, that $a_n = f^{(n)}(0)/n!$ for all $n \geq 0$. Thus the only power series in x that represents a function at and near $x = 0$ is its Maclaurin series.

67. (a) Consider the binomial series

$$f(x) = \sum_{n=0}^{\infty} \frac{\alpha(\alpha-1)(\alpha-2)\cdots(\alpha-n+1)}{n!} x^n,$$

which converges (to *something*) if $|x| < 1$. Compute the derivative $f'(x)$ by termwise differentiation, and show that it satisfies the differential equation $(1+x) f'(x) = \alpha f(x)$.
(b) Solve the differential equation in part (a) to obtain $f(x) = C(1+x)^{\alpha}$ for some constant C. Finally, show that $C = 1$. Thus the binomial series converges to $(1+x)^{\alpha}$ if $|x| < 1$.

68. (a) Show by direct integration that

$$\int_0^1 \frac{\arcsin x}{\sqrt{1-x^2}}\,dx = \frac{\pi^2}{8}.$$

(b) Use the result of Problem 58 in Section 8.3 to show that

$$\int_0^1 \frac{x^{2n+1}}{\sqrt{1-x^2}}\,dx = \frac{2\cdot 4\cdot 6\cdots(2n)}{1\cdot 3\cdot 5\cdots(2n+1)}.$$

(c) Substitute the series of Example 10 for arcsin x into the integral of part (a); then use the integral of part (b) to integrate termwise. Conclude that

$$\int_0^1 \frac{\arcsin x}{\sqrt{1-x^2}}\,dx = 1 + \frac{1}{3^2} + \frac{1}{5^2} + \frac{1}{7^2} + \cdots.$$

(d) Note that

$$\sum_{n=1}^{\infty} \frac{1}{n^2} = \sum_{n=1}^{\infty} \frac{1}{(2n-1)^2} + \sum_{n=1}^{\infty} \frac{1}{(2n)^2}.$$

Use this information and parts (a) and (c) to show that

$$\sum_{n=1}^{\infty} \frac{1}{n^2} = \frac{\pi^2}{6}.$$

69. Prove that if the power series $\sum a_n x^n$ converges for some $x = x_0 \neq 0$, then it converges absolutely for all x such that $|x| < |x_0|$. [*Suggestion:* Conclude from the fact that $\lim_{n\to\infty} a_n x_0^n = 0$ that $|a_n x^n| \leq |x/x_0|^n$ for all n sufficiently large. Thus the series $\sum |a_n x^n|$ is eventually dominated by the geometric series $\sum |x/x_0|^n$, which converges if $|x| < |x_0|$.]

70. Suppose that the power series $\sum a_n x^n$ converges for some but not all nonzero values of x. Let S be the set of real numbers for which the series converges absolutely. (a) Conclude from Problem 69 that the set S is bounded above. (b) Let λ be the least upper bound of the set S. (See Problem 61 of Section 11.2.) Then show that $\sum a_n x^n$ converges absolutely if $|x| < \lambda$ and diverges if $|x| > \lambda$. Explain why this proves Theorem 1 without the additional hypothesis that $\lim_{n\to\infty} |a_{n+1}/a_n|$ exists.

11.9 POWER SERIES COMPUTATIONS

Power series often are used to approximate numerical values of functions and integrals. *Alternating* power series (such as the sine and cosine series) are especially common and useful. Recall the alternating series remainder (or "error") estimate of Theorem 2 in Section 11.7. It applies to a convergent alternating series $\sum (-1)^{n+1} a_n$ whose terms are decreasing (so $a_n > a_{n+1}$ for every n). If we write

$$\sum_{k=1}^{\infty} (-1)^{k+1} a_k = (a_1 - a_2 + a_3 - \cdots \pm a_n) + E, \qquad (1)$$

then $E = \mp a_{n+1} \pm a_{n+2} \mp a_{n+3} \pm \cdots$ is the error made when the series is *truncated*—the terms following $(-1)^{n+1} a_n$ are simply chopped off and discarded, and the n-term partial sum is used in place of the actual sum of the whole series. The remainder estimate then says that the error E has the same sign as the first term not retained, and is less in magnitude than this first neglected term; that is, $|E| < a_{n+1}$.

EXAMPLE 1 Use the first four terms of the binomial series

$$\sqrt{1+x} = 1 + \tfrac{1}{2}x - \tfrac{1}{8}x^2 + \tfrac{1}{16}x^3 - \tfrac{5}{128}x^4 + \cdots \qquad (2)$$

to estimate the number $\sqrt{105}$ and to estimate the accuracy in the approximation.

Solution If $x > 0$ then the binomial series is, after the first term, an alternating series. In order to match the pattern on the left-hand side in Eq. (2), we first write

$$\sqrt{105} = \sqrt{100 + 5} = 10\sqrt{1 + \tfrac{5}{100}} = 10\sqrt{1 + 0.05}.$$

Then with $x = 0.05$ the series in (2) gives

$$\sqrt{105} = 10\left[1 + \tfrac{1}{2}(0.05) - \tfrac{1}{8}(0.05)^2 + \tfrac{1}{16}(0.05)^3 + E\right]$$
$$= 10[1.02469531 + E] = 10.2469531 + 10E.$$

Note that the error $10E$ in our approximation $\sqrt{105} \approx 10.2469531$ is 10 times the error E in the truncated series itself. It follows from the remainder estimate that E

is negative and that

$$|10E| < 10 \cdot \tfrac{5}{128}(0.05)^4 \approx 0.0000024.$$

Therefore,

$$10.2469531 - 0.0000024 = 10.2469507 < \sqrt{105} < 10.2469531,$$

so it follows that $\sqrt{105} \approx 10.24695$ rounded accurate to five decimal places. ◆

REMARK Suppose that we had been asked in advance to approximate $\sqrt{105}$ accurate to five decimal places. A convenient way to do this is to continue writing terms of the series until it is clear that they have become too small in magnitude to affect the fifth decimal place. A good rule of thumb is to use two more decimal places in the computations than are required in the final answer. Thus we use seven decimal places in this case and get

$$\sqrt{105} = 10 \cdot (1+0.05)^{1/2}$$
$$\approx 10 \cdot (1 + 0.025 - 0.0003125 + 0.0000078 - 0.0000002 + \cdots)$$
$$\approx 10.246951 \approx 10.24695.$$

EXAMPLE 2 Figure 11.9.1 shows the graph of the function $f(x) = (\sin x)/x$. Approximate (accurate to three decimal places) the area

$$A = \int_{-\pi}^{\pi} \frac{\sin x}{x}\, dx = 2\int_{0}^{\pi} \frac{\sin x}{x}\, dx \tag{3}$$

of the shaded region lying under the "principal arch" from $x = -\pi$ to π.

Solution When we substitute the Taylor series for $\sin x$ in Eq. (3) and integrate termwise, we get

$$A = 2\int_{0}^{\pi} \frac{1}{x}\left(x - \frac{x^3}{3!} + \frac{x^5}{5!} - \frac{x^7}{7!} + \cdots\right) dx$$
$$= 2\int_{0}^{\pi} \left(1 - \frac{x^2}{3!} + \frac{x^4}{5!} - \frac{x^6}{7!} + \cdots\right) dx$$
$$= 2\left[x - \frac{x^3}{3!3} + \frac{x^5}{5!5} - \frac{x^7}{7!7} + \cdots\right]_{0}^{\pi},$$

FIGURE 11.9.1 The graph $y = \dfrac{\sin x}{x}$ of Example 2.

and thus

$$A = 2\pi - \frac{2\pi^3}{3!3} + \frac{2\pi^5}{5!5} - \frac{2\pi^7}{7!7} + \frac{2\pi^9}{9!9} - \frac{2\pi^{11}}{11!11} + \cdots.$$

Following the "+2 rule of thumb" and retaining five decimal places, we calculate

$$A = 6.28319 - 3.44514 + 1.02007 - 0.17122 + 0.01825 - 0.00134 + 0.00007 - \cdots.$$

The sum of the first six terms gives $A \approx 3.70381$. Because we are summing an alternating series, the error in this approximation is positive and less than the next term 0.00007. Neglecting possible roundoff in the last place, we would conclude that $3.70381 < A < 3.70388$. Thus $A \approx 3.704$ rounded accurate to three decimal places. ◆

The Algebra of Power Series

Theorem 1, which we state without proof, implies that power series may be added and multiplied much like polynomials. The guiding principle is that of collecting coefficients of like powers of x.

THEOREM 1 Adding and Multiplying Power Series

Let $\sum a_n x^n$ and $\sum b_n x^n$ be power series with nonzero radii of convergence. Then

$$\sum_{n=0}^{\infty} a_n x^n + \sum_{n=0}^{\infty} b_n x^n = \sum_{n=0}^{\infty} (a_n + b_n) x^n \qquad (4)$$

and

$$\left(\sum_{n=0}^{\infty} a_n x^n\right)\left(\sum_{n=0}^{\infty} b_n x^n\right) = \sum_{n=0}^{\infty} c_n x^n$$

$$= a_0 b_0 + (a_0 b_1 + a_1 b_0)x + (a_0 b_2 + a_1 b_1 + a_2 b_0)x^2 + \cdots, \qquad (5)$$

where

$$c_n = a_0 b_n + a_1 b_{n-1} + a_2 b_{n-2} + \cdots + a_{n-1} b_1 + a_n b_0. \qquad (6)$$

The series in Eqs. (4) and (5) converge for any x that lies interior to the intervals of convergence of both $\sum a_n x^n$ and $\sum b_n x^n$.

Thus if $\sum a_n x^n$ and $\sum b_n x^n$ are power series representations of the functions $f(x)$ and $g(x)$, respectively, then the product power series $\sum c_n x^n$ found by "ordinary multiplication" and collection of terms is a power series representation of the product function $f(x)g(x)$. This fact can also be used to divide one power series by another, *provided* that the quotient is known to have a power series representation.

EXAMPLE 3 Assume that the tangent function has a power series representation $\tan x = \sum a_n x^n$ (it does). Use the Maclaurin series for $\sin x$ and $\cos x$ to find a_0, a_1, a_2, and a_3.

Solution We multiply series to obtain

$$\sin x = \tan x \cos x$$
$$= (a_0 + a_1 x + a_2 x^2 + a_3 x^3 + \cdots)\left(1 - \frac{x^2}{2} + \frac{x^4}{24} - \cdots\right).$$

If we multiply each term in the first factor by each term in the second, then collect coefficients of like powers, the result is

$$\sin x = a_0 + a_1 x + \left(a_2 - \tfrac{1}{2} a_0\right) x^2 + \left(a_3 - \tfrac{1}{2} a_1\right) x^3 + \cdots.$$

But because

$$\sin x = x - \tfrac{1}{6} x^3 + \tfrac{1}{120} x^5 - \cdots,$$

comparison of coefficients gives the equations

$$\begin{aligned}
a_0 &= 0, \\
a_1 &= 1, \\
-\tfrac{1}{2} a_0 + a_2 &= 0, \\
-\tfrac{1}{2} a_1 + a_3 &= -\tfrac{1}{6}.
\end{aligned}$$

Thus we find that $a_0 = 0$, $a_1 = 1$, $a_2 = 0$, and $a_3 = \tfrac{1}{3}$. So

$$\tan x = x + \tfrac{1}{3} x^3 + \cdots.$$

Things are not always as they first appear. A computer algebra system gives the continuation

$$\tan x = x + \tfrac{1}{3} x^3 + \tfrac{2}{15} x^5 + \tfrac{17}{315} x^7 + \tfrac{62}{2835} x^9 + \tfrac{1382}{155,925} x^{11} + \cdots \qquad (7)$$

of the tangent series. For the general form of the nth coefficient, see K. Knopp's *Theory and Application of Infinite Series* (New York: Hafner Press, 1971), p. 204.

You may also check that the first few terms agree with the result of ordinary division of the Maclaurin series for $\cos x$ into the Maclaurin series for $\sin x$:

$$\begin{array}{r} x + \frac{1}{3}x^3 + \frac{2}{15}x^5 + \cdots \\ 1 - \frac{1}{2}x^2 + \frac{1}{24}x^4 - \cdots \overline{\smash{\big)}\, x - \frac{1}{6}x^3 + \frac{1}{120}x^5 - \cdots} \end{array}$$

Figure 11.9.2 shows the approximation of the tangent function (on $-\pi/2 < x < \pi/2$) by the first four odd-degree polynomial partial sums corresponding to the terms exhibited in Eq. (7). Evidently these polynomial approximations have difficulty "keeping up" with $\tan x$ as it approaches $\pm\infty$ as $x \to \pm\pi/2$. ◆

FIGURE 11.9.2 The graphs of $y = \tan x$ and the first four partial sums of the power series in (7).

Power Series and Indeterminate Forms

According to Theorem 3 of Section 11.8, a power series is differentiable and therefore continuous within its interval of convergence. It follows that

$$\lim_{x \to c} \sum_{n=0}^{\infty} a_n (x - c)^n = a_0. \tag{8}$$

Examples 4 and 5 illustrate the use of this simple observation to find the limit of the indeterminate form $f(x)/g(x)$. The technique is to first substitute power series representations for $f(x)$ and $g(x)$.

EXAMPLE 4 Find $\displaystyle\lim_{x \to 0} \frac{\sin x - \arctan x}{x^2 \ln(1 + x)}$.

Solution The power series of Eqs. (4), (19), and (20) in Section 11.8 give

$$\sin x - \arctan x = \left(x - \tfrac{1}{6}x^3 + \tfrac{1}{120}x^5 - \cdots\right) - \left(x - \tfrac{1}{3}x^3 + \tfrac{1}{5}x^5 - \cdots\right)$$
$$= \tfrac{1}{6}x^3 - \tfrac{23}{120}x^5 + \cdots$$

and

$$x^2 \ln(1 + x) = x^2 \cdot \left(x - \tfrac{1}{2}x^2 + \tfrac{1}{3}x^3 + \cdots\right) = x^3 - \tfrac{1}{2}x^4 + \tfrac{1}{3}x^5 - \cdots.$$

Hence

$$\lim_{x \to 0} \frac{\sin x - \arctan x}{x^2 \ln(1 + x)} = \lim_{x \to 0} \frac{\tfrac{1}{6}x^3 - \tfrac{23}{120}x^5 + \cdots}{x^3 - \tfrac{1}{2}x^4 + \cdots}$$
$$= \lim_{x \to 0} \frac{\tfrac{1}{6} - \tfrac{23}{120}x^2 + \cdots}{1 - \tfrac{1}{2}x + \cdots} = \frac{1}{6}. \quad ◆$$

EXAMPLE 5 Find $\displaystyle\lim_{x \to 1} \frac{\ln x}{x - 1}$.

Solution We first replace x with $x - 1$ in the power series for $\ln(1 + x)$ used in Example 4. [Equation (8) makes it clear that this method requires all series to have center c if we are taking limits as $x \to c$.] This gives us

$$\ln x = (x - 1) - \tfrac{1}{2}(x - 1)^2 + \tfrac{1}{3}(x - 1)^3 - \cdots.$$

Hence

$$\lim_{x \to 1} \frac{\ln x}{x - 1} = \lim_{x \to 1} \frac{(x - 1) - \tfrac{1}{2}(x - 1)^2 + \tfrac{1}{3}(x - 1)^3 - \cdots}{x - 1}$$
$$= \lim_{x \to 1} \left[1 - \tfrac{1}{2}(x - 1) + \tfrac{1}{3}(x - 1)^2 - \cdots\right] = 1. \quad ◆$$

The method of Examples 4 and 5 provides a useful alternative to l'Hôpital's rule, especially when repeated differentiation of numerator and denominator is inconvenient or too time-consuming. (See Problems 59 and 60.)

Numerical and Graphical Error Estimation

The following examples show how to investigate the accuracy in a power-series partial-sum approximation for a specified interval of values of x. We will take the statement that a given approximation is "accurate to p decimal places" to mean that its error E is numerically less than half a unit in the pth decimal place; that is, that $|E| < 0.5 \times 10^{-p}$. For instance, four-place accuracy means that $|E| < 0.00005$. (Note that $p = 4$ is the number of zeros here.) Nevertheless, we should remember that in some cases a result accurate to within a half unit in the pth place may round "the wrong way," so that the result rounded to p places may still be in error by a unit in the pth decimal place (as in Problem 12).

EXAMPLE 6 Consider the polynomial approximation

$$\sin x \approx x - \frac{x^3}{3!} + \frac{x^5}{5!} - \cdots + (-1)^{n+1} \frac{x^{2n-1}}{(2n-1)!} \quad (9)$$

obtained by truncating the alternating Taylor series of the sine function.

(a) How accurate is the cubic approximation $P_3(x) \approx x - x^3/3!$ for angles from $0°$ to $10°$? Use this approximation to estimate $\sin 10°$.

(b) How many terms in (9) are needed to guarantee six-place accuracy in calculating $\sin x$ for angles from $0°$ to $45°$? Use the corresponding polynomial to approximate $\sin 30°$ and $\sin 40°$.

(c) For what values of x does the fifth-degree approximation yield five-place accuracy?

Solution (a) Of course we must substitute x in radians in (9), so we deal here with values of x in the interval $0 \leq x \leq \pi/18$. For any such x, the error E is positive (Why?) and is bounded by the magnitude of the next term:

$$|E| < \frac{x^5}{5!} \leq \frac{(\pi/18)^5}{5!} \approx 0.00000135 < 0.000005.$$

We count five zeros on the right, and thus we have five-place accuracy. For instance, substituting $x = \pi/18$ in the cubic polynomial $P_3(x)$ gives

$$\sin 10° = \sin\left(\frac{\pi}{18}\right) \approx \frac{\pi}{18} - \frac{1}{3!} \cdot \left(\frac{\pi}{18}\right)^3$$

$$\approx 0.1736468 \approx 0.17365.$$

This five-place approximation $\sin 10° \approx 0.17365$ is correct, because the actual seven-place value of $\sin 10°$ is $0.1736482 \approx 0.17365$.

Solution (b) For any x in the interval $0 \leq x \leq \pi/4$, the error E made if we use the polynomial value in (9) in place of the actual value $\sin x$ is bounded by the first neglected term,

$$|E| < \frac{x^{2n+1}}{(2n+1)!} \leq \frac{(\pi/4)^{2n+1}}{(2n+1)!}.$$

The table in Fig. 11.9.3 shows calculator values for $n = 1, 2, 3, \ldots$ of this maximal error (rounded to eight decimal places). For six-place accuracy we want $|E| < 0.0000005$, so we see that $n = 4$ will suffice. We therefore use the seventh-degree Taylor polynomial

$$P_7(x) = x - \frac{x^3}{3!} + \frac{x^5}{5!} - \frac{x^7}{7!} \quad (10)$$

to approximate $\sin x$ for $0 \leq x \leq \pi/4$. With $x = \pi/6$ we get

$$\sin 30° \approx \frac{\pi}{6} - \frac{(\pi/6)^3}{3!} + \frac{(\pi/6)^5}{5!} - \frac{(\pi/6)^7}{7!} \approx 0.49999999 \approx \frac{1}{2},$$

n	$\dfrac{(\pi/4)^{2n+1}}{(2n+1)!}$
1	0.08074551
2	0.00249039
3	0.00003658
4	0.00000031
5	0.00000000

FIGURE 11.9.3 Estimating the error in Example 6(b).

as expected. Substituting $x = 2\pi/9$ in (10) similarly gives $\sin 40° \approx 0.64278750$, whereas the actual eight-place value of $\sin 40°$ is $0.64278761 \approx 0.642788$.

Solution (c) The fifth-degree approximation

$$\sin x \approx P_5(x) = x - \frac{x^3}{3!} + \frac{x^5}{5!} \tag{11}$$

gives five-place accuracy when x is such that the error E satisfies the inequality

$$|E| < \frac{|x|^7}{7!} = \frac{|x|^7}{5040} \leq 0.000005;$$

that is, when $|x| \leq [(5040) \cdot (0.000005)]^{1/7} \approx 0.5910$ (radians). In degrees, this corresponds to angles between $-33.86°$ and $+33.86°$. In Fig. 11.9.4 the graph of $y = x^7/7!$ in the viewing window $-1 \leq x \leq 1$, $-0.00001 \leq y \leq 0.00001$ provides visual corroboration of this analysis—we see clearly that $x^7/7!$ remains between -0.000005 and 0.000005 when x is between -0.59 and 0.59. ◆

FIGURE 11.9.4 The graph of the maximal error $y = \dfrac{x^7}{7!}$ in Example 6(c).

EXAMPLE 7 Suppose now that we want to approximate $f(x) = \sin x$ with three-place accuracy on the whole interval from $0°$ to $90°$. Now it makes sense to begin with a Taylor series centered at the midpoint $x = \pi/4$ of the interval. Because the function $f(x)$ and its successive derivatives are $\sin x$, $\cos x$, $-\sin x$, $-\cos x$, and so forth, their values at $x = \pi/4$ are $\frac{1}{2}\sqrt{2}$, $\frac{1}{2}\sqrt{2}$, $-\frac{1}{2}\sqrt{2}$, $-\frac{1}{2}\sqrt{2}$, and so forth. Consequently Taylor's formula with remainder (Section 11.4) for $f(x) = \sin x$ centered at $x = \pi/4$ takes the form

$$\sin x = \frac{\sqrt{2}}{2} \cdot \left[1 + \left(x - \frac{\pi}{4}\right) - \frac{1}{2!}\left(x - \frac{\pi}{4}\right)^2 \right.$$
$$\left. - \frac{1}{3!}\left(x - \frac{\pi}{4}\right)^3 + \cdots \pm \frac{1}{n!}\left(x - \frac{\pi}{4}\right)^n \right] + E(x) \tag{12}$$

where

$$|E(x)| = \left| \frac{f^{(n+1)}(z)}{(n+1)!}\left(x - \frac{\pi}{4}\right)^{n+1} \right| \leq \frac{1}{(n+1)!}\left|x - \frac{\pi}{4}\right|^{n+1} \tag{13}$$

for some z in the interval $0 \leq x \leq \pi/2$. Observe that the corresponding Taylor series is not alternating—if $x > \pi/4$ it has instead a "$++--++--$" pattern of signs—but we can still use the remainder estimate in (13). For three-place accuracy we need to choose n so that $y = E(x)$ remains within the viewing window $-0.0005 \leq y \leq 0.0005$ on the whole interval $0 \leq x \leq \pi/2$. Looking at the graphs plotted in Fig. 11.9.5, we see that this is so if $n = 5$ but not if $n = 4$. The desired approximation is therefore

FIGURE 11.9.5 Comparing errors in Example 7.

$$\sin x \approx \frac{\sqrt{2}}{2} \cdot \left[1 + \left(x - \frac{\pi}{4}\right) - \frac{1}{2!}\left(x - \frac{\pi}{4}\right)^2 - \frac{1}{3!}\left(x - \frac{\pi}{4}\right)^3 \right.$$
$$\left. + \frac{1}{4!}\left(x - \frac{\pi}{4}\right)^4 + \frac{1}{5!}\left(x - \frac{\pi}{4}\right)^5 \right].$$

For instance, substituting $x = 0$ we get $\sin 0° \approx 0.00020 \approx 0.000$ as desired, and $x = \pi/2$ gives $\sin 90° \approx 1.00025 \approx 1.000$. ◆

11.9 TRUE/FALSE STUDY GUIDE

11.9 CONCEPTS: QUESTIONS AND DISCUSSION

1. Outline how you might use the binomial series (as in Example 1) to construct a *table of roots*—perhaps the square roots, cube roots, and fourth roots of the first 100 positive integers.

11.9 PROBLEMS

In Problems 1 through 10, use an infinite series to approximate the indicated number accurate to three decimal places.

1. $\sqrt[3]{65}$
2. $\sqrt[4]{630}$
3. $\sin(0.5)$
4. $e^{-0.2}$
5. $\tan^{-1}(0.5)$
6. $\ln(1.1)$
7. $\sin\left(\dfrac{\pi}{10}\right)$
8. $\cos\left(\dfrac{\pi}{20}\right)$
9. $\sin 10°$
10. $\cos 5°$

In Problems 11 through 22, use power series to approximate the value of the given integrals accurate to four decimal places.

11. $\displaystyle\int_0^1 \dfrac{\sin x}{x}\,dx$
12. $\displaystyle\int_0^1 \dfrac{\sin x}{\sqrt{x}}\,dx$
13. $\displaystyle\int_0^{1/2} \dfrac{\arctan x}{x}\,dx$
14. $\displaystyle\int_0^1 \sin x^2\,dx$
15. $\displaystyle\int_0^{1/10} \dfrac{\ln(1+x)}{x}\,dx$
16. $\displaystyle\int_0^{1/2} \dfrac{1}{\sqrt{1+x^4}}\,dx$
17. $\displaystyle\int_0^{1/2} \dfrac{1-e^{-x}}{x}\,dx$
18. $\displaystyle\int_0^{1/2} \sqrt{1+x^3}\,dx$
19. $\displaystyle\int_0^1 e^{-x^2}\,dx$
20. $\displaystyle\int_0^1 \dfrac{1-\cos x}{x^2}\,dx$
21. $\displaystyle\int_0^{1/2} \sqrt[3]{1+x^2}\,dx$
22. $\displaystyle\int_0^{1/2} \dfrac{x}{\sqrt{1+x^3}}\,dx$

In Problems 23 through 28, use power series rather than l'Hôpital's rule to evaluate the given limit.

23. $\displaystyle\lim_{x\to 0} \dfrac{1+x-e^x}{x^2}$
24. $\displaystyle\lim_{x\to 0} \dfrac{x-\sin x}{x^3 \cos x}$
25. $\displaystyle\lim_{x\to 0} \dfrac{1-\cos x}{x(e^x-1)}$
26. $\displaystyle\lim_{x\to 0} \dfrac{e^x - e^{-x} - 2x}{x - \arctan x}$
27. $\displaystyle\lim_{x\to 0} \left(\dfrac{1}{x} - \dfrac{1}{\sin x}\right)$
28. $\displaystyle\lim_{x\to 1} \dfrac{\ln(x^2)}{x-1}$

In Problems 29 through 32, calculate the indicated number with the required accuracy using Taylor's formula for an appropriate function centered at the given point $x=a$.

29. $\sin 80°$; $a = \pi/4$, four decimal places
30. $\cos 35°$; $a = \pi/4$, four decimal places
31. $\cos 47°$; $a = \pi/4$, six decimal places
32. $\sin 58°$; $a = \pi/3$, six decimal places

In Problems 33 through 36, determine the number of decimal places of accuracy the given appropriate formula yields for $|x| \leq 0.1$.

33. $e^x \approx 1 + x + \tfrac{1}{2}x^2 + \tfrac{1}{6}x^3 + \tfrac{1}{24}x^4$
34. $\sin x \approx x - \tfrac{1}{6}x^3 + \tfrac{1}{120}x^5$
35. $\ln(1+x) \approx x - \tfrac{1}{2}x^2 + \tfrac{1}{3}x^3 - \tfrac{1}{4}x^4$
36. $\sqrt{1+x} \approx 1 + \tfrac{1}{2}x - \tfrac{1}{8}x^2$

37. Show that the approximation in Problem 33 gives the value of e^x accurate to within 0.001 if $|x| \leq 0.5$. Then calculate $\sqrt[3]{e}$ accurate to two decimal places.

38. For what values of x is the approximation $\sin x \approx x - \tfrac{1}{6}x^3$ accurate to five decimal places?

39. (a) Show that the values of the cosine function for angles between 40° and 50° can be calculated with five-place accuracy using the approximation
$$\cos x \approx \dfrac{\sqrt{2}}{2}\left[1-\left(x-\dfrac{\pi}{4}\right)-\dfrac{1}{2}\left(x-\dfrac{\pi}{4}\right)^2 + \dfrac{1}{6}\left(x-\dfrac{\pi}{4}\right)^3\right].$$
(b) Show that this approximation yields eight-place accuracy for angles between 44° and 46°.

40. Extend the approximation in Problem 39 to one that yields the values of $\cos x$ accurate to five decimal places for angles between 30° and 60°.

In Problems 41 through 44, use termwise integration of an appropriate power series to approximate the indicated area or volume accurate to two decimal places.

41. Figure 11.9.1 shows the region that lies between the graph of $y = (\sin x)/x$ and the x-axis from $x = -\pi$ to $x = \pi$. Substitute $\sin^2 x = \tfrac{1}{2}(1 - \cos 2x)$ to approximate the volume of the solid that is generated by revolving this region around the x-axis.

42. Approximate the area of the region that lies between the graph of $y = (1 - \cos x)/x^2$ and the x-axis from $x = -2\pi$ to $x = 2\pi$ (Fig. 11.9.6).

FIGURE 11.9.6 The region of Problem 42.

43. Approximate the volume of the solid generated by rotating the region of Problem 42 around the y-axis.

44. Approximate the volume of the solid generated by rotating the region of Problem 42 around the x-axis.

45. Derive the geometric series by long division of $1 - x$ into 1.

46. Derive the series for $\tan x$ listed in Example 3 by long division of the Maclaurin series of $\cos x$ into the Maclaurin series of $\sin x$.

47. Derive the geometric series representation of $1/(1-x)$ by finding $a_0, a_1, a_2, \ldots$ such that
$$(1-x)(a_0 + a_1 x + a_2 x^2 + a_3 x^3 + \cdots) = 1.$$

48. Derive the first five coefficients in the binomial series for $\sqrt{1+x}$ by finding a_0, a_1, a_2, a_3, and a_4 such that
$$(a_0 + a_1 x + a_2 x^2 + a_3 x^3 + a_4 x^4 + \cdots)^2 = 1 + x.$$

49. Use the method of Example 3 to find the coefficients a_0, a_1, a_2, a_3, and a_4 in the series
$$\sec x = \frac{1}{\cos x} = \sum_{n=0}^{\infty} a_n x^n.$$

50. Multiply the geometric series for $1/(1-x)$ and the series for $\ln(1-x)$ to show that if $|x| < 1$, then
$$\frac{\ln(1-x)}{1-x} = -x - \left(1 + \tfrac{1}{2}\right)x^2 - \left(1 + \tfrac{1}{2} + \tfrac{1}{3}\right)x^3$$
$$- \left(1 + \tfrac{1}{2} + \tfrac{1}{3} + \tfrac{1}{4}\right)x^4 - \cdots.$$

51. Take as known the logarithmic series
$$\ln(1+x) = x - \tfrac{1}{2}x^2 + \tfrac{1}{3}x^3 - \tfrac{1}{4}x^4 + \cdots.$$
Find the first four coefficients in the series for e^x by finding a_0, a_1, a_2, and a_3 such that
$$1 + x = e^{\ln(1+x)} = \sum_{n=0}^{\infty} a_n \left(x - \tfrac{1}{2}x^2 + \tfrac{1}{3}x^3 - \tfrac{1}{4}x^4 + \cdots\right)^n.$$
This is exactly how the power series for e^x was first discovered (by Newton)!

52. Use the method of Example 3 to show that
$$\frac{x}{\sin x} = 1 + \frac{1}{6}x^2 + \frac{7}{360}x^4 + \cdots.$$

53. Show that long division of power series gives
$$\frac{2+x}{1+x+x^2} = 2 - x - x^2 + 2x^3 - x^4 - x^5 + 2x^6$$
$$- x^7 - x^8 + 2x^9 - x^{10} - x^{11} + \cdots.$$
Show also that the radius of convergence of this series is $R = 1$.

54. Use the series in Problem 53 to approximate with two-place accuracy the value of the integral
$$\int_0^{1/2} \frac{x+2}{x^2+x+1} dx.$$
Compare your estimate with the exact result given by a computer algebra system.

Use the power series in Problem 53 to approximate with two-place accuracy the rather formidable integrals in Problems 55 and 56. Compare your estimates with the exact values given by a computer algebra system.

55. $\displaystyle\int_0^{1/2} \frac{1}{1+x^2+x^4} dx$

56. $\displaystyle\int_0^{1/2} \frac{1}{1+x^4+x^8} dx$

In Problems 57 and 58, graph the given function and several of its Taylor polynomials of the indicated degrees.

57. $f(x) = \dfrac{\sin x}{x}$; degrees $n = 2, 4, 6, \ldots$.

58. $f(x) = \displaystyle\int_0^x \frac{\sin t}{t} dt$; degrees $n = 3, 5, 7, \ldots$.

59. Use known power series to evaluate $\displaystyle\lim_{x \to 0} \frac{\sin x - \tan x}{\sin^{-1} x - \tan^{-1} x}$.

60. Substitute series such as
$$\sin(\tan x) = x + \frac{x^3}{6} - \frac{x^5}{40} - \frac{55x^7}{1008} + \cdots$$
provided by a computer algebra system to evaluate
$$\lim_{x \to 0} \frac{\sin(\tan x) - \tan(\sin x)}{\sin^{-1}(\tan^{-1} x) - \tan^{-1}(\sin^{-1} x)}.$$

61. (a) First use the parametrization $x(t) = a \cos t$, $y(t) = b \sin t$, $0 \leq t \leq 2\pi$ of the ellipse $(x/a)^2 + (y/b)^2 = 1$ to show that its perimeter (arc length) p is given by
$$p = 4a \int_0^{\pi/2} \sqrt{1 - \epsilon^2 \cos^2 t}\, dt$$
where $\epsilon = \sqrt{1 - (b/a)^2}$ is the *eccentricity* of the ellipse. This so-called *elliptic integral* is nonelementary, and so must be approximated numerically. (b) Use the binomial series to expand the integrand in the perimeter formula in part (a). Then integrate termwise—using Formula 113 from the table of integrals inside the back cover—to show that the perimeter of the ellipse is given in terms of its major semiaxis and eccentricity by the power series
$$p = 2\pi a \left(1 - \frac{1}{4}\epsilon^2 - \frac{3}{64}\epsilon^4 - \frac{5}{256}\epsilon^6 - \frac{175}{16384}\epsilon^8 - \cdots\right).$$

62. The *arithmetic mean* of the major and minor semiaxes of the ellipse of Problem 61 is $A = \tfrac{1}{2}(a+b)$; their *root-square mean* is $R = \sqrt{\tfrac{1}{2}(a^2+b^2)}$. Substitute $b = a\sqrt{1-\epsilon^2}$ and use the binomial series to derive the expansions
$$A = a\left(1 - \frac{1}{4}\epsilon^2 - \frac{1}{16}\epsilon^4 - \frac{1}{32}\epsilon^6 - \frac{5}{256}\epsilon^8 - \cdots\right)$$
and
$$R = a\left(1 - \frac{1}{4}\epsilon^2 - \frac{1}{32}\epsilon^4 - \frac{1}{128}\epsilon^6 - \frac{5}{2048}\epsilon^8 - \cdots\right).$$

Something wonderful happens when you average these two series; show that

$$\frac{1}{2}(A+R) = a\left(1 - \frac{1}{4}\epsilon^2 - \frac{3}{64}\epsilon^6 - 5\frac{5}{256}\epsilon^6 - \frac{180}{16384}\epsilon^8 - \cdots\right),$$

and then note that the first four terms of the series within the parentheses here are the same as in the ellipse perimeter series of Problem 61(b). Conclude that the perimeter p of the ellipse is given by

$$p = \pi(A+R) + \frac{5\pi a}{8192}\epsilon^8 + \cdots. \quad (14)$$

If ϵ is quite small—as in a nearly circular ellipse—then the difference between the exact value of p and the simple approximation

$$p \approx \pi(A+R) = \pi\left(\tfrac{1}{2}(a+b) + \sqrt{\tfrac{1}{2}(a^2+b^2)}\right)$$

is extremely small. For instance, suppose that the orbit of the moon around the earth is an ellipse with major semi-axis a exactly 238,857 miles long and eccentricity ϵ exactly 0.0549. Then use Eq. (14) and a computer algebra system with extended-precision arithmetic to find the perimeter of the moon's orbit accurate *to the nearest inch*; give your answer in miles-feet-inches format.

11.9 Project: Calculating Trigonometric Functions on a Deserted Island

Again (as in the 11.4 Project) you're stranded for life on a desert island with only a very basic calculator that doesn't know about transcendental functions. Now your task is to use the (alternating) sine and cosine series to construct a table presenting (with five-place accuracy) the sines, cosines, and tangents of angles from 0° to 90° in increments of 5°.

To begin with, you can find the sine, cosine, and tangent of an angle of 45° from the familiar 1-1-$\sqrt{2}$ right triangle. Then you can find the values of these functions at an angle of 60° from an equilateral triangle. Once you know all about 45° and 60° angles, you can use the sine and cosine addition formulas

$$\sin(\alpha \pm \beta) = \sin\alpha\cos\beta \pm \cos\alpha\sin\beta$$

and

$$\cos(\alpha \pm \beta) = \cos\alpha\cos\beta \mp \sin\alpha\sin\beta$$

and/or equivalent forms to find the sine, cosine, and tangent of such angles as 15°, 30°, 75°, and 90°.

But algebra and simple trigonometric identities will probably never give you the sine or cosine or an angle of 5°. For this you will need to use the power series for sine and cosine. Sum enough terms (and then some) so you know your result is accurate to nine decimal places. Then fill in all the entries in your table, rounding them to five places. Tell—honestly—whether your entries agree with those your *real* calculator gives.

Finally, explain what strategy you would use to complete a similar table of values of trigonometric functions with angles in increments of 1° rather than 5°.

11.10 SERIES SOLUTIONS OF DIFFERENTIAL EQUATIONS

In Section 9.6 we saw that solving a homogeneous linear differential equation with constant coefficients can be reduced to the algebraic problem of finding the roots of its characteristic equation. There is no simple or similarly routine procedure for solving linear differential equations with *variable* coefficients. Even such a simple-looking equation as $y'' - xy = 0$ has no solution that can be expressed in terms of the standard elementary functions of calculus. One of the most important applications of power series is their use to solve such differential equations.

The Power Series Method

The *power series method* for solving a differential equation consists of substituting the power series

$$y = \sum_{n=0}^{\infty} c_n x^n = c_0 + c_1 x + c_2 x^2 + c_3 x^3 + \cdots \quad (1)$$

in the differential equation, and then attempting to determine what the values of the coefficients $c_0, c_1, c_2, c_3, \ldots$ must be in order that the series in (1) will actually satisfy the given differential equation. At first glance this might seem to be a formidable problem, because we have infinitely many unknowns $c_0, c_1, c_2, c_3, \ldots$ to find. Nevertheless, we will see that the method frequently succeeds. When it does, we obtain a power series representation of a solution, in contrast to the closed form solutions that result from the solution techniques we saw in Chapter 9.

Before we can substitute the series in (1) in a differential equation, we must first know what to substitute for the derivatives $y', y'', \ldots$ of the unknown function $y(x)$. But recall from Theorem 3 in Section 11.8 that the derivative of a power series can be calculated by termwise differentiation. Hence the first and second derivatives of the series in (1) are given by

$$y' = \sum_{n=1}^{\infty} nc_n x^{n-1} = c_1 + 2c_2 x + 3c_3 x^2 + \cdots \tag{2}$$

and

$$y'' = \sum_{n=2}^{\infty} n(n-1)c_n x^{n-2} = 2c_2 + 6c_3 x + 12c_4 x^2 + \cdots . \tag{3}$$

Also, these two series have the same radius of convergence as the original series in (1).

The process of determining the coefficients $c_0, c_1, c_2, c_3, \ldots$ in the series so that it will satisfy a given differential equation depends also on the following consequence of termwise differentiation: If two power series represent the same function on an open interval, then they are identical series. That is, they are one and the same power series. (See Problem 66 in Section 11.8.) In particular, *if $\sum a_n x^n \equiv 0$ on an open interval, then it follows that $a_n = 0$ for all n*. This fact is sometimes called the **identity principle** for power series.

EXAMPLE 1 Solve the equation $y' + 2y = 0$.

Solution We substitute the series

$$y = \sum_{n=0}^{\infty} c_n x^n \quad \text{and} \quad y' = \sum_{n=1}^{\infty} nc_n x^{n-1},$$

and obtain

$$\sum_{n=1}^{\infty} nc_n x^{n-1} + 2 \sum_{n=0}^{\infty} c_n x^n = 0. \tag{4}$$

To compare coefficients here, we need the general term in each sum to be the term containing x^n. To accomplish this, we shift the index of summation in the first sum. To see how to do this, note that

$$\sum_{n=1}^{\infty} nc_n x^{n-1} = c_1 + 2c_2 x + 3c_3 x^2 + \cdots = \sum_{n=0}^{\infty} (n+1)c_{n+1} x^n.$$

Thus we can replace n with $n+1$ if, at the same time, we start counting one step lower; that is, at $n = 0$ rather than at $n = 1$. This is a shift of $+1$ in the index of summation. The result of making this shift in Eq. (4) is the identity

$$\sum_{n=0}^{\infty} (n+1)c_{n+1} x^n + 2 \sum_{n=0}^{\infty} c_n x^n = 0;$$

that is,

$$\sum_{n=0}^{\infty} [(n+1)c_{n+1} + 2c_n] x^n = 0.$$

If this equation holds on some interval, then it follows from the identity principle that $(n+1)c_{n+1} + 2c_n = 0$ for all $n \geq 0$; consequently,

$$c_{n+1} = -\frac{2c_n}{n+1} \tag{5}$$

for all $n \geq 0$. Equation (5) is a **recurrence relation** from which we can successively compute $c_1, c_2, c_3, \ldots$ in terms of c_0; the latter will turn out to be the arbitrary constant that we expect to find in a general solution of a first-order differential equation.

With $n = 0$, Eq. (5) gives

$$c_1 = -\frac{2c_0}{1}.$$

With $n = 1$, Eq. (5) gives

$$c_2 = -\frac{2c_1}{2} = +\frac{2^2 c_0}{1 \cdot 2} = \frac{2^2 c_0}{2!}.$$

With $n = 2$, Eq. (5) gives

$$c_3 = -\frac{2c_2}{3} = -\frac{2^3 c_0}{1 \cdot 2 \cdot 3} = -\frac{2^3 c_0}{3!}.$$

By now it should be clear that after n such steps, we will have

$$c_n = (-1)^n \frac{2^n c_0}{n!}, \quad n \geq 1.$$

(This is easy to prove by induction on n.) Consequently, our solution takes the form

$$y(x) = \sum_{n=0}^{\infty} c_n x^n = \sum_{n=0}^{\infty} (-1)^n \frac{2^n c_0}{n!} x^n = c_0 \sum_{n=0}^{\infty} \frac{(-2x)^n}{n!} = c_0 e^{-2x}.$$

In the final step we have used the familiar exponential series to identify our power series solution as the same solution $y(x) = c_0 e^{-2x}$ we could have obtained by the method of separation of variables. ◆

Shift of Index of Summation

In the solution of Example 1 we wrote

$$\sum_{n=1}^{\infty} n c_n x^{n-1} = \sum_{n=0}^{\infty} (n+1) c_{n+1} x^n \tag{6}$$

by shifting the index of summation by $+1$ in the series on the left. That is, we simultaneously *increased* the index of summation by 1 (replacing n with $n+1$, $n \to n+1$) and *decreased* the starting point by 1, from $n = 1$ to $n = 0$, thereby obtaining the series on the right. This procedure is valid because each infinite series in (6) is simply a compact notation for the single series

$$c_1 + 2c_2 x + 3c_3 x^2 + 4c_4 x^3 + \cdots. \tag{7}$$

More generally, we can shift the index of summation by k in an infinite series by simultaneously *increasing* the summation index by k ($n \to n + k$) and *decreasing* the starting point by k. For instance, a shift by $+2$ ($n \to n+2$) yields

$$\sum_{n=3}^{\infty} a_n x^{n-1} = \sum_{n=1}^{\infty} a_{n+2} x^{n+1}.$$

If k is negative we interpret a "decrease by k" as an increase by $-k = |k|$. Thus a shift by -2 ($n \to n-2$) in the index of summation yields

$$\sum_{n=1}^{\infty} n c_n x^{n-1} = \sum_{n=3}^{\infty} (n-2) c_{n-2} x^{n-3};$$

we have *decreased* the index of summation by 2, but *increased* the starting point by 2, from $n = 1$ to $n = 3$. You should check that the summation on the right is merely another representation of the series in (7).

EXAMPLE 2 Solve the equation $(x-3)y' + 2y = 0$.

Solution As before, we substitute

$$y = \sum_{n=0}^{\infty} c_n x^n \quad \text{and} \quad y' = \sum_{n=1}^{\infty} n c_n x^{n-1}$$

to obtain

$$(x-3) \sum_{n=1}^{\infty} n c_n x^{n-1} + 2 \sum_{n=0}^{\infty} c_n x^n = 0,$$

so that

$$\sum_{n=1}^{\infty} n c_n x^n - 3 \sum_{n=1}^{\infty} n c_n x^{n-1} + 2 \sum_{n=0}^{\infty} c_n x^n = 0.$$

In the first sum we can replace $n = 1$ with $n = 0$ with no effect on the sum. In the second sum we shift the index of summation by $+1$. This yields

$$\sum_{n=0}^{\infty} n c_n x^n - 3 \sum_{n=0}^{\infty} (n+1) c_{n+1} x^n + 2 \sum_{n=0}^{\infty} c_n x^n = 0;$$

that is,

$$\sum_{n=0}^{\infty} [n c_n - 3(n+1) c_{n+1} + 2 c_n] x^n = 0.$$

The identity principle then gives

$$n c_n - 3(n+1) c_{n+1} + 2 c_n = 0,$$

from which we obtain the recurrence relation

$$c_{n+1} = \frac{n+2}{3(n+1)} c_n \quad \text{for} \quad n \geq 0.$$

We apply this formula with $n = 0$, $n = 1$, and $n = 2$ in turn, and find that

$$c_1 = \frac{2}{3} c_0, \quad c_2 = \frac{3}{3 \cdot 2} c_1 = \frac{3}{3^2} c_0, \quad \text{and} \quad c_3 = \frac{4}{3 \cdot 3} c_2 = \frac{4}{3^3} c_0.$$

This is almost enough to make the pattern evident; it is not difficult to show by induction on n that

$$c_n = \frac{n+1}{3^n} c_0 \quad \text{if} \quad n \geq 1.$$

Hence our proposed power series solution is

$$y(x) = c_0 \sum_{n=0}^{\infty} \frac{n+1}{3^n} x^n. \tag{8}$$

Its radius of convergence is

$$\rho = \lim_{n \to \infty} \left| \frac{c_n}{c_{n+1}} \right| = \lim_{n \to \infty} \frac{3n+3}{n+2} = 3.$$

Thus the series in (8) converges if $-3 < x < 3$ and diverges if $|x| > 3$. In this particular example we can explain why. An elementary solution (obtained by separation of variables) of our differential equation is $y = 1/(3-x)^2$. If we differentiate termwise the geometric series

$$\frac{1}{3-x} = \frac{\frac{1}{3}}{1 - \frac{x}{3}} = \frac{1}{3}\sum_{n=0}^{\infty}\frac{x^n}{3^n},$$

we get a constant multiple of the series in (8). Thus this series (with the arbitrary constant c_0 appropriately chosen) represents the solution

$$y(x) = \frac{1}{(3-x)^2}$$

on the interval $-3 < x < 3$, and the singularity at $x = 3$ is the reason why the radius of convergence of the power series solution turned out to be $\rho = 3$. ◆

EXAMPLE 3 Solve the equation $x^2 y' = y - x - 1$.

Solution We make the usual substitutions $y = \sum c_n x^n$ and $y' = \sum n c_n x^{n-1}$, which yield

$$x^2 \sum_{n=1}^{\infty} n c_n x^{n-1} = -1 - x + \sum_{n=0}^{\infty} c_n x^n,$$

so that

$$\sum_{n=1}^{\infty} n c_n x^{n+1} = -1 - x + \sum_{n=0}^{\infty} c_n x^n.$$

Because of the presence of the two terms -1 and $-x$ on the right-hand side, we need to split off the first two terms, $c_0 + c_1 x$, of the series on the right for comparison. If we also shift the index of summation on the left by -1 (replace $n = 1$ with $n = 2$ and n with $n - 1$), we get

$$\sum_{n=2}^{\infty}(n-1)c_{n-1}x^n = -1 - x + c_0 + c_1 x + \sum_{n=2}^{\infty} c_n x^n.$$

Because the left-hand side contains neither a constant term nor a term containing x to the first power, the identity principle now yields $c_0 = 1$, $c_1 = 1$, and $c_n = (n-1)c_{n-1}$ for $n \geq 2$. It follows that

$$c_2 = 1 \cdot c_1 = 1!, \qquad c_3 = 2 \cdot c_2 = 2!, \qquad c_4 = 3 \cdot c_3 = 3!,$$

and, in general, that

$$c_n = (n-1)! \quad \text{for} \quad n \geq 2.$$

Thus we obtain the power series

$$y(x) = 1 + x + \sum_{n=2}^{\infty}(n-1)!x^n.$$

But the radius of convergence of this series is

$$\rho = \lim_{n\to\infty}\frac{(n-1)!}{n!} = \lim_{n\to\infty}\frac{1}{n} = 0,$$

so the series converges only for $x = 0$. What does this mean? Simply that the given differential equation does not have a [convergent] power series solution of the assumed form $y = \sum c_n x^n$. This example serves as a warning that the simple act of writing $y = \sum c_n x^n$ involves an assumption that may be false. ◆

EXAMPLE 4 Solve the equation $y'' + y = 0$.

Solution If we assume a solution of the form

$$y = \sum_{n=0}^{\infty} c_n x^n,$$

we find that

$$y' = \sum_{n=1}^{\infty} n c_n x^{n-1} \quad \text{and} \quad y'' = \sum_{n=2}^{\infty} n(n-1) c_n x^{n-2}.$$

Substituting for y and y'' in the differential equation then yields

$$\sum_{n=2}^{\infty} n(n-1) c_n x^{n-2} + \sum_{n=0}^{\infty} c_n x^n = 0.$$

We shift the index of summation in the first sum by $+2$ (replace $n = 2$ with $n = 0$ and n with $n + 2$). This gives

$$\sum_{n=0}^{\infty} (n+2)(n+1) c_{n+2} x^n + \sum_{n=0}^{\infty} c_n x^n = 0.$$

The identity $(n+2)(n+1)c_{n+2} + c_n = 0$ now follows from the identity principle, and thus we obtain the recurrence relation

$$c_{n+2} = -\frac{c_n}{(n+1)(n+2)} \tag{9}$$

for $n \geq 0$. It is evident that this formula will determine the coefficients c_n with even subscript in terms of c_0 and those of odd subscript in terms of c_1; c_0 and c_1 are not predetermined, and thus will be the two arbitrary constants we expect to find in a general solution of a second-order equation.

When we apply the recurrence relation in (9) with $n = 0, 2,$ and 4 in turn, we get

$$c_2 = -\frac{c_0}{2!}, \quad c_4 = \frac{c_0}{4!}, \quad \text{and} \quad c_6 = -\frac{c_0}{6!}.$$

Taking $n = 1, 3,$ and 5 in turn, we find that

$$c_3 = -\frac{c_1}{3!}, \quad c_5 = \frac{c_1}{5!}, \quad \text{and} \quad c_7 = -\frac{c_1}{7!}.$$

Again, the pattern is clear; we leave it for you to show (by induction) that for $k \geq 1$,

$$c_{2k} = \frac{(-1)^k c_0}{(2k)!} \quad \text{and} \quad c_{2k+1} = \frac{(-1)^k c_1}{(2k+1)!}.$$

Thus we get the power series solution

$$y(x) = c_0 \left(1 - \frac{x^2}{2!} + \frac{x^4}{4!} - \frac{x^6}{6!} + \cdots \right) + c_1 \left(x - \frac{x^3}{3!} + \frac{x^5}{5!} - \frac{x^7}{7!} + \cdots \right);$$

that is, $y(x) = c_0 \cos x + c_1 \sin x$. Note that we have no problem with the radius of convergence here; the Taylor series for the sine and cosine functions converge for all x. ◆

Power Series Definitions of Functions

The solution of Example 4 can bear further comment. Suppose that we had never heard of the sine and cosine functions, let alone their Taylor series. We would then have discovered the two power series solutions

$$C(x) = \sum_{n=0}^{\infty} \frac{(-1)^n x^{2n}}{(2n)!} = 1 - \frac{x^2}{2!} + \frac{x^4}{4!} - \cdots \quad (10)$$

and

$$S(x) = \sum_{n=0}^{\infty} \frac{(-1)^n x^{2n+1}}{(2n+1)!} = x - \frac{x^3}{3!} + \frac{x^5}{5!} - \cdots \quad (11)$$

of the differential equation $y'' + y = 0$. It is clear that $C(0) = 1$ and that $S(0) = 0$. After verifying that the two series in (10) and (11) converge for all x, we can differentiate them term by term to find that

$$C'(x) = -S(x) \quad \text{and} \quad S'(x) = C(x). \quad (12)$$

Consequently $C'(0) = 0$ and $S'(0) = 1$. Thus with the aid of the power series method (all the while knowing nothing about the sine and cosine functions), we have discovered that $y = C(x)$ is the unique solution of

$$y'' + y = 0$$

that satisfies the initial conditions $y(0) = 1$ and $y'(0) = 0$, and that $y = S(x)$ is the unique solution that satisfies the initial conditions $y(0) = 0$ and $y'(0) = 1$. It follows that $C(x)$ and $S(x)$ are linearly independent, and—recognizing the importance of the differential equation $y'' + y = 0$—we can agree to call C the *cosine* function and S the *sine* function. Indeed, all the usual properties of these two functions can be established, using only their initial values (at $x = 0$) and the derivatives in (12); there is no need to refer to triangles or even to angles. (Can you use the series in (10) and (11) to show that $[C(x)]^2 + [S(x)]^2 = 1$ for all x?) This demonstrates that the cosine and sine functions are fully determined by the differential equation $y'' + y = 0$ of which they are the natural linearly independent solutions. Figures 11.10.1 and 11.10.2 show how the geometric character of the graphs of $\cos x$ and $\sin x$ is revealed by the graphs of the Taylor polynomial approximations that we get by truncating the infinite series in (10) and (11).

FIGURE 11.10.1 Graphs of $\cos x$ and its Taylor polynomial approximations $P_6(x)$, $P_8(x)$, $P_{14}(x)$, $P_{16}(x)$, $P_{22}(x)$, and $P_{24}(x)$.

FIGURE 11.10.2 Graphs of $\sin x$ and its Taylor polynomial approximations $P_5(x)$, $P_7(x)$, $P_{13}(x)$, $P_{15}(x)$, $P_{21}(x)$, and $P_{23}(x)$.

This is by no means an uncommon situation. Many important special functions of mathematics occur in the first instance as power series solutions of differential equations, and thus are in practice *defined* by means of these power series. Example 5 introduces in this manner the *Airy functions* that appear in applications ranging from the propagation of radio waves to vibrations in atoms and molecules.

EXAMPLE 5 Solve the Airy equation $y'' - xy = 0$.

Solution Substituting $y = \sum c_n x^n$ and $y'' = \sum n(n-1)c_n x^{n-2}$ as usual yields

$$\sum_{n=2}^{\infty} n(n-1)c_n x^{n-2} - \sum_{n=0}^{\infty} c_n x^{n+1} = 0.$$

A shift of indices—replacing n with $n+2$ in the first sum and with $n-1$ in the second—yields

$$\sum_{n=0}^{\infty}(n+2)(n+1)c_{n+2} x^n - \sum_{n=1}^{\infty} c_{n-1} x^n = 0.$$

Splitting off the term corresponding to $n = 0$ in the first sum and combining the remaining terms, we get

$$2c_2 + \sum_{n=1}^{\infty}[(n+2)(n+1)c_{n+2} - c_{n-1}]x^n = 0.$$

The identity principle now gives $c_2 = 0$—because there is no other constant term on the left-hand side—and the recurrence relation $(n+2)(n+1)c_{n+2} - c_{n-1} = 0$ for $n \geq 1$. Replacement of n with $n+1$ gives the recurrence relation

$$c_{n+3} = \frac{c_n}{(n+2)(n+3)} \tag{13}$$

for $n \geq 0$. Thus each coefficient (after the first three) depends on the third previous one. Hence the fact that $c_2 = 0$ implies that

$$c_2 = c_5 = c_8 = \cdots = 0.$$

Beginning with c_0 as an arbitrary constant, we apply (13) with $n = 0$, $n = 3$, and $n = 6$ in turn and calculate

$$c_3 = \frac{c_0}{2 \cdot 3} = \frac{c_0}{6}, \quad c_6 = \frac{c_3}{5 \cdot 6} = \frac{c_0}{180}, \quad \text{and} \quad c_9 = \frac{c_6}{8 \cdot 9} = \frac{c_0}{12960}.$$

Beginning with c_1 as a second arbitrary constant, we calculate similarly

$$c_4 = \frac{c_1}{3 \cdot 4} = \frac{c_1}{12}, \quad c_7 = \frac{c_4}{6 \cdot 7} = \frac{c_1}{504}, \quad \text{and} \quad c_{10} = \frac{c_7}{9 \cdot 10} = \frac{c_1}{45360}.$$

When we collect the terms that involve c_0 and those that involve c_1, we get the general solution

$$y(x) = c_0 \left(1 + \frac{x^3}{6} + \frac{x^6}{180} + \frac{x^9}{12960} + \cdots\right) + c_1\left(x + \frac{x^4}{12} + \frac{x^7}{504} + \frac{x^{10}}{45360} + \cdots\right)$$

of the Airy equation, with arbitrary constants c_0 and c_1. We see here the independent (why?) particular solutions

$$y_1(x) = 1 + \frac{x^3}{6} + \frac{x^6}{180} + \frac{x^9}{12960} + \cdots \quad \text{and} \quad y_2(x) = x + \frac{x^4}{12} + \frac{x^7}{504} + \frac{x^{10}}{45360} + \cdots.$$

Recognizing the pattern of coefficients is not so easy as in Example 4, but you can verify that the terms shown agree with the formulas

$$y_1(x) = 1 + \sum_{k=1}^{\infty} \frac{1 \cdot 4 \cdots (3k-2)}{(3k)!} x^{3k} \quad \text{and} \quad y_2(x) = x + \sum_{k=1}^{\infty} \frac{2 \cdot 5 \cdots (3k-1)}{(3k+1)!} x^{3k+1}.$$

The special combinations

$$\text{Ai}(x) = \frac{y_1(x)}{3^{2/3}\Gamma\left(\frac{2}{3}\right)} - \frac{y_2(x)}{3^{1/3}\Gamma\left(\frac{1}{3}\right)} \quad \text{and} \quad \text{Bi}(x) = \frac{y_1(x)}{3^{1/6}\Gamma\left(\frac{2}{3}\right)} + \frac{y_2(x)}{3^{-1/6}\Gamma\left(\frac{1}{3}\right)}$$

FIGURE 11.10.3 The graphs $y = \text{Ai}(x)$ and $y = \text{Bi}(x)$ of the Airy functions.

—with $\Gamma(x)$ denoting the gamma function defined in Section 8.8—are the standard *Airy functions*, which appear in mathematical tables and computer algebra systems. Their graphs in Fig. 11.10.3 exhibit oscillatory behavior for $x < 0$, but $\text{Ai}(x)$ decreases exponentially and $\text{Bi}(x)$ increases exponentially as $x \to \infty$. ◆

11.10 TRUE/FALSE STUDY GUIDE

11.10 CONCEPTS: QUESTIONS AND DISCUSSION

1. Suppose that the exponential function $E(x) = e^x$ is *defined* as the solution of the initial value problem $y' = y$, $y(0) = 1$. Beginning with this definition, what properties of the function $E(x)$ can be established?
2. Suppose that the hyperbolic functions $\text{Ch}(x) = \cosh x$ and $\text{Sh}(x) = \sinh x$ are *defined* as the solutions of the differential equation $y'' = y$ that satisfy the initial conditions $y(0) = 1$, $y'(0) = 0$ and $y(0) = 0$, $y'(0) = 1$, respectively. Beginning with these definitions, what properties of the functions $\text{Ch}(x)$ and $\text{Sh}(x)$ can be established? Can you discover a connection between these functions and the function $E(x)$ of Question 1?

11.10 PROBLEMS

In Problems 1 through 10, find a power series solution of the given differential equation. Determine the radius of convergence of the resulting series, and use your knowledge of familiar Maclaurin series and the binomial series to identify the series solution in terms of familiar elementary functions. (Of course, no one can prevent you from checking your work by also solving the equations by the methods of Chapter 9!)

1. $y' = y$
2. $y' = 4y$
3. $2y' + 3y = 0$
4. $y' + 2xy = 0$
5. $y' = x^2 y$
6. $(x - 2)y' + y = 0$
7. $(2x - 1)y' + 2y = 0$
8. $2(x + 1)y' = y$
9. $(x - 1)y' + 2y = 0$
10. $2(x - 1)y' = 3y$

In Problems 11 through 14, use the method of Example 4 to find two linearly independent power series solutions of the given differential equation. Determine the radius of convergence of each series, and identify the general solution in terms of familiar elementary functions.

11. $y'' = y$
12. $y'' = 4y$
13. $y'' + 9y = 0$
14. $y'' + y = x$

Show (as in Example 3) that the power series method fails to yield a power series solution of the form $y = \sum c_n x^n$ for the differential equations in Problems 15 through 18.

15. $xy' + y = 0$
16. $2xy' = y$
17. $x^2 y' + y = 0$
18. $x^3 y' = 2y$

In Problems 19 through 22, first derive a recurrence relation giving c_n for $n \geq 2$ in terms of c_0 or c_1 (or both). Then apply the given initial conditions to find the values of c_0 and c_1. Next determine c_n (in terms of n, as in the text) and, finally, identify the particular solution in terms of familiar elementary functions.

19. $y'' + 4y = 0;$ $\quad y(0) = 0, \quad y'(0) = 3$
20. $y'' - 4y = 0;$ $\quad y(0) = 2, \quad y'(0) = 0$
21. $y'' - 2y' + y = 0;$ $\quad y(0) = 0, \quad y'(0) = 1$
22. $y'' + y' - 2y = 0;$ $\quad y(0) = 1, \quad y'(0) = -2$
23. Show that the equation

$$x^2 y'' + x^2 y' + y = 0$$

has no power series solution of the form $y = \sum c_n x^n$.

24. Use the power series method to discover the solution
$$J_0(x) = \sum_{k=0}^{\infty} \frac{(-1)^k x^{2k}}{2^{2k}(k!)^2} = 1 - \frac{x^2}{4} + \frac{x^4}{64} - \frac{x^6}{2304} + \cdots$$
of the Bessel equation $xy'' + y' + xy = 0$. Explain why the series method does not yield an independent second solution.

25. (a) Show that the solution of the initial value problem
$$y' = 1 + y^2, \quad y(0) = 0$$
is $y(x) = \tan x$. (b) Because $y(x) = \tan x$ is an odd function with $y'(0) = 1$, its Taylor series is of the form
$$y = x + c_3 x^3 + c_5 x^5 + c_7 x^7 + \cdots.$$

Substitute this series in $y' = 1 + y^2$ and equate like powers of x to derive the following relations:
$$3c_3 = 1, \qquad 5c_5 = 2c_3,$$
$$7c_7 = 2c_5 + (c_3)^2, \qquad 9c_9 = 2c_7 + 2c_3c_5,$$
$$11c_{11} = 2c_9 + 2c_3c_7 + (c_5)^2.$$

(c) Conclude that
$$\tan x = x + \frac{1}{3}x^3 + \frac{2}{15}x^5 + \frac{17}{315}x^7 + \frac{62}{2835}x^9 + \frac{1382}{155925}x^{11} + \cdots.$$

CHAPTER 11 REVIEW: DEFINITIONS, CONCEPTS, RESULTS

Use the following list as a guide to concepts that you may need to review.

1. Definition of the limit of a sequence
2. The limit laws for sequences
3. The bounded monotonic sequence property
4. Definition of the sum of an infinite series
5. Formula for the sum of a geometric series
6. The nth-term test for divergence
7. Divergence of the harmonic series
8. The nth-degree Taylor polynomial of the function f at the point $x = a$
9. Taylor's formula with remainder
10. The Taylor series of the elementary transcendental functions
11. The integral test
12. Convergence of p-series
13. The comparison and limit comparison tests
14. The alternating series test
15. Absolute convergence: definition *and* the fact that it implies convergence
16. The ratio test
17. The root test
18. Power series; radius of convergence and interval of convergence
19. The binomial series
20. Termwise differentiation and integration of power series
21. The use of power series to approximate values of functions and integrals
22. The sum and product of two power series
23. The use of power series to evaluate indeterminate forms
24. Power series solution of differential equations

CHAPTER 11 MISCELLANEOUS PROBLEMS

In Problems 1 through 15, determine whether or not the sequence $\{a_n\}$ converges, and find its limit if it does converge.

1. $a_n = \dfrac{n^2 + 1}{n^2 + 4}$
2. $a_n = \dfrac{8n - 7}{7n - 8}$
3. $a_n = 10 - (0.99)^n$
4. $a_n = n \sin \pi n$
5. $a_n = \dfrac{1 + (-1)^n \sqrt{n}}{n + 1}$
6. $a_n = \sqrt{\dfrac{1 + (-0.5)^n}{n + 1}}$
7. $a_n = \dfrac{\sin 2n}{n}$
8. $a_n = 2^{-(\ln n)/n}$
9. $a_n = (-1)^{\sin(n\pi/2)}$
10. $a_n = \dfrac{(\ln n)^3}{n^2}$
11. $a_n = \dfrac{1}{n} \sin \dfrac{1}{n}$
12. $a_n = \dfrac{n - e^n}{n + e^n}$
13. $a_n = \dfrac{\sinh n}{n}$
14. $a_n = \left(1 + \dfrac{2}{n}\right)^{2n}$
15. $a_n = (2n^2 + 1)^{1/n}$

Determine whether each infinite series in Problems 16 through 30 converges or diverges.

16. $\sum_{n=1}^{\infty} \dfrac{(n^2)!}{n^n}$
17. $\sum_{n=1}^{\infty} \dfrac{(-1)^{n+1} \ln n}{n}$
18. $\sum_{n=0}^{\infty} \dfrac{3^n}{2^n + 4^n}$
19. $\sum_{n=0}^{\infty} \dfrac{n!}{e^{n^2}}$
20. $\sum_{n=1}^{\infty} \dfrac{1}{n^{3/2}} \sin \dfrac{1}{n}$
21. $\sum_{n=0}^{\infty} \dfrac{(-2)^n}{3^n + 1}$

22. $\sum_{n=1}^{\infty} 2^{-(2/n^2)}$

23. $\sum_{n=2}^{\infty} \frac{(-1)^n n}{(\ln n)^3}$

24. $\sum_{n=1}^{\infty} \frac{(-1)^n}{10^{1/n}}$

25. $\sum_{n=1}^{\infty} \frac{\sqrt{n} + \sqrt[3]{n}}{n^2 + n^3}$

26. $\sum_{n=1}^{\infty} \frac{(-1)^{n+1}}{n^{[1+(1/n)]}}$

27. $\sum_{n=1}^{\infty} \frac{(-1)^{n+1} \arctan n}{\sqrt{n}}$

28. $\sum_{n=1}^{\infty} n \sin \frac{1}{n}$

29. $\sum_{n=3}^{\infty} \frac{1}{n(\ln n)(\ln \ln n)}$

30. $\sum_{n=3}^{\infty} \frac{1}{n(\ln n)(\ln \ln n)^2}$

Find the interval of convergence of the power series in Problems 31 through 40.

31. $\sum_{n=0}^{\infty} \frac{2^n x^n}{n!}$

32. $\sum_{n=0}^{\infty} \frac{(3x)^n}{2^{n+1}}$

33. $\sum_{n=1}^{\infty} \frac{(x-1)^n}{n \cdot 3^n}$

34. $\sum_{n=0}^{\infty} \frac{(2x-3)^n}{4^n}$

35. $\sum_{n=1}^{\infty} \frac{(-1)^n x^n}{4n^2 - 1}$

36. $\sum_{n=0}^{\infty} \frac{(2x-1)^n}{n^2 + 1}$

37. $\sum_{n=0}^{\infty} \frac{n! x^{2n}}{10^n}$

38. $\sum_{n=2}^{\infty} \frac{x^n}{\ln n}$

39. $\sum_{n=0}^{\infty} \frac{1 + (-1)^n}{2(n!)} x^n$

40. $\sum_{n=1}^{\infty} \left(1 + \frac{1}{n}\right)^n (x-1)^n$

Find the set of all values of x for which the series in Problems 41 through 43 converge.

41. $\sum_{n=1}^{\infty} (x - n)^n$

42. $\sum_{n=1}^{\infty} (\ln x)^n$

43. $\sum_{n=0}^{\infty} \frac{e^{nx}}{n!}$

44. Find the rational number that has repeated decimal expansion $2.7\,1828\,1828\,1828\ldots.$

45. Give an example of two convergent numerical series $\sum a_n$ and $\sum b_n$ such that the series $\sum a_n b_n$ diverges.

46. Prove that if $\sum a_n$ is a convergent positive-term series, then $\sum a_n^2$ converges.

47. Let the sequence $\{a_n\}$ be defined recursively as follows:

$$a_1 = 1; \quad a_{n+1} = 1 + \frac{1}{1 + a_n} \quad \text{if } n \geq 1.$$

The limit of the sequence $\{a_n\}$ is the value of the *continued fraction*

$$1 + \cfrac{1}{2 + \cfrac{1}{2 + \cfrac{1}{2 + \cfrac{1}{2 + \cdots}}}}.$$

Assuming that $A = \lim_{n \to \infty} a_n$ exists, prove that $A = \sqrt{2}$.

48. Let $\{F_n\}_1^{\infty}$ be the Fibonacci sequence of Example 2 in Section 11.2. (a) Prove that $0 < F_n \leq 2^n$ for all $n \geq 1$, and hence conclude that the power series

$$F(x) = \sum_{n=1}^{\infty} F_n x^n$$

converges if $|x| < \frac{1}{2}$. (b) Show that $(1 - x - x^2) F(x) = x$, so

$$F(x) = \frac{x}{1 - x - x^2}.$$

49. We say that the *infinite product* indicated by

$$\prod_{n=1}^{\infty} (1 + a_n) = (1 + a_1)(1 + a_2)(1 + a_3) \cdots$$

converges provided that the infinite series

$$S = \sum_{n=1}^{\infty} \ln(1 + a_n)$$

converges, in which case the value of the infinite product is, by definition, e^S. Use the integral test to prove that

$$\prod_{n=1}^{\infty} \left(1 + \frac{1}{n}\right)$$

diverges.

50. Prove that the infinite product (see Problem 49)

$$\prod_{n=1}^{\infty} \left(1 + \frac{1}{n^2}\right)$$

converges, and use the integral test remainder estimate to approximate its value. The actual value of this infinite product is known to be

$$\frac{\sinh \pi}{\pi} \approx 3.67607\,79103\,74977\,72069\,56975.$$

In Problems 51 through 55, use infinite series to approximate the indicated number accurate to three decimal places.

51. $\sqrt[5]{1.5}$

52. $\ln(1.2)$

53. $\int_0^{0.5} e^{-x^2} \, dx$

54. $\int_0^{0.5} \sqrt[3]{1 + x^4} \, dx$

55. $\int_0^1 \frac{1 - e^{-x}}{x} \, dx$

56. Substitute the Maclaurin series for $\sin x$ into that for e^x to obtain

$$e^{\sin x} = 1 + x + \tfrac{1}{2} x^2 - \tfrac{1}{8} x^4 + \cdots.$$

57. Substitute the Maclaurin series for the cosine and then integrate termwise to derive the formula

$$\int_0^{\infty} e^{-t^2} \cos 2xt \, dt = \frac{\sqrt{\pi}}{2} e^{-x^2}.$$

Use the reduction formula

$$\int_0^{\infty} t^{2n} e^{-t^2} \, dt = \frac{2n - 1}{2} \int_0^{\infty} t^{2n-2} e^{-t^2} \, dt$$

that follows from the one derived in Problem 50 of Section 8.3. The validity of this improper termwise integration is subject to verification.

58. Prove that
$$\tanh^{-1} x = \int_0^x \frac{1}{1-t^2}\, dt = \sum_{n=0}^{\infty} \frac{x^{2n+1}}{2n+1}$$
if $|x| < 1$.

59. Prove that
$$\sinh^{-1} x = \int_0^x \frac{1}{\sqrt{1+t^2}}\, dt$$
$$= \sum_{n=0}^{\infty} (-1)^n \frac{1 \cdot 3 \cdot 5 \cdots (2n-1)}{2 \cdot 4 \cdot 6 \cdots (2n)} \cdot \frac{x^{2n+1}}{2n+1}$$
if $|x| < 1$.

60. Suppose that $\tan y = \sum a_n y^n$. Determine $a_0, a_1, a_2,$ and a_3 by substituting the inverse tangent series [Eq. (27) of Section 11.4] into the equation
$$x = \tan(\tan^{-1} x) = \sum_{n=0}^{\infty} a_n (\tan^{-1} x)^n.$$

61. According to *Stirling's series*, the value of $n!$ for large n is given to a close approximation by
$$n! \approx \sqrt{2\pi n}\left(\frac{n}{e}\right)^n e^{\mu(n)},$$
where
$$\mu(n) = \frac{1}{12n} - \frac{1}{360n^3} + \frac{1}{1260n^5}.$$
Substitute $\mu(n)$ into Maclaurin's series for e^x to show that
$$e^{\mu(n)} = 1 + \frac{1}{12n} + \frac{1}{288n^2} - \frac{139}{51840n^3} + \cdots.$$
Can you show that the next term in the last series is $-571/(2{,}488{,}320 n^4)$?

62. Define
$$T(n) = \int_0^{\pi/4} \tan^n x\, dx$$
for $n \geq 0$. (a) Show by "reduction" of the integral that
$$T(n+2) = \frac{1}{n+1} - T(n)$$
for $n \geq 0$. (b) Conclude that $T(n) \to 0$ as $n \to \infty$. (c) Show that $T(0) = \pi/4$ and that $T(1) = \tfrac{1}{2}\ln 2$. (d) Prove by induction on n that
$$T(2n) = (-1)^{n+1}\left(1 - \frac{1}{3} + \frac{1}{5} - \cdots \pm \frac{1}{2n-1} - \frac{\pi}{4}\right).$$
(e) Conclude from parts (b) and (d) that
$$1 - \frac{1}{3} + \frac{1}{5} - \frac{1}{7} + \cdots = \frac{\pi}{4}.$$
(f) Prove by induction on n that
$$T(2n+1) = \frac{1}{2}(-1)^n\left(1 - \frac{1}{2} + \frac{1}{3} - \cdots \pm \frac{1}{n} - \ln 2\right).$$
(g) Conclude from parts (b) and (f) that
$$1 - \tfrac{1}{2} + \tfrac{1}{3} - \tfrac{1}{4} + \cdots = \ln 2.$$

63. Prove as follows that the number e is irrational. First suppose to the contrary that $e = p/q$, where p and q are positive integers. Note that $q > 1$. Write
$$\frac{p}{q} = e = 1 + \frac{1}{1!} + \frac{1}{2!} + \frac{1}{3!} + \cdots + \frac{1}{q!} + R_q,$$
where $0 < R_q < 3/(q+1)!$. (Why?) Then show that multiplying of both sides of this equation by $q!$ would lead to the contradiction that one side of the result is an integer but the other side is not.

64. Evaluate the infinite product (see Problem 49)
$$\prod_{n=2}^{\infty} \frac{n^2}{n^2 - 1}$$
by finding an explicit formula for
$$\prod_{n=2}^{k} \frac{n^2}{n^2-1} \quad (k \geq 2)$$
and then taking the limit as $k \to \infty$.

65. Find a continued fraction representation (see Problem 47)
$$a_0 + \cfrac{1}{a_1 + \cfrac{1}{a_2 + \cfrac{1}{a_3 + \cfrac{1}{a_4 + \cdots}}}}$$
of $\sqrt{5}$.

66. Evaluate
$$1 + \frac{1}{2} - \frac{2}{3} + \frac{1}{4} + \frac{1}{5} - \frac{2}{6} + \frac{1}{7} + \frac{1}{8} - \frac{2}{9} + \frac{1}{10} + \cdots.$$

VECTORS, CURVES, AND SURFACES IN SPACE

12

Johannes Kepler (1571–1630)

Ancient Greek mathematicians and astronomers developed an elaborate mathematical model to account for the complicated motions of the sun, moon, and six planets then known as viewed from the earth. A combination of uniform circular motions was used to describe the motion of each body around the earth— if the earth is arbitrarily placed at the origin of coordinates, then each body *does* orbit the earth.

In this system, it was typical for a planet P to travel uniformly around a small circle (the *epicycle*) with center C, which in turn traveled uniformly around a circle centered at the earth (labeled E in the figure at the lower left). The radii of the circles and the angular speeds of P and C were chosen to match the observed motion of the planet as closely as possible. For greater accuracy, secondary "circles on circles" could be used. In fact, several circles were required for each body in the Greek theory of epicycles, which reached its definitive form in Ptolemy's *Almagest* of the second century A.D.

In 1543, Copernicus altered Ptolemy's approach by placing the center of each primary circle at the sun rather than at the earth. But this change was of greater philosophical than mathematical significance. His *heliocentric system* was still overly complicated, still requiring many secondary circles, and still beset with inaccuracies in representing the motions of the heavenly bodies.

It was Johannes Kepler who finally got rid of all these circles. On the basis of a detailed analysis of planetary observations accumulated by the Danish astronomer Tycho Brahe, Kepler stated his three famous *laws of planetary motion*, which describe elliptical (rather than circular) orbits of planets around the sun (Section 12.6). Ironically, his original goal had been to prove that the placement of Mercury, Venus, Earth, Mars, and Jupiter is determined by the five regular polyhedra as indicated in the figure at the lower right, which appeared in his *Mysterium Cosmographicum* (1596). This model of the solar system shows a cube inscribed in the sphere containing Saturn's orbit, and the sphere of Jupiter's orbit is inscribed in this cube. A tetrahedron (with four triangular faces) is inscribed in Jupiter's sphere, and in this tetrahedron is inscribed the sphere of the orbit of Mars. Continuing in this way, the spheres of the three remaining planets then known were interspersed with the remaining three regular solids—the octahedron (eight triangular faces), the dodecahedron (12 pentagonal faces), and the icosahedron (20 triangular faces). It is said that Kepler always remained prouder of his five solids than of his three laws.

The small circle is the epicycle.

Kepler's regular polyhedron model of the solar system.

771

In his *Principia Mathematica* (1687), Newton showed that Kepler's laws follow from the basic principles of mechanics ($F = ma$ and so on) and the inverse-square law of gravitational attraction. His success in using mathematics to explain natural phenomena ("I now demonstrate the frame of the System of the World") inspired confidence that the universe could be understood and perhaps even mastered. This new confidence permanently altered humanity's perception of itself and of its place in the scheme of things. Newton employed a powerful but now antiquated form of geometrical calculus in the *Principia*. In Section 12.6 we apply the modern calculus of vector-valued functions to outline the relation between Newton's laws and Kepler's laws.

12.1 VECTORS IN THE PLANE

A physical quantity such as length, temperature, or mass can be specified in terms of a single real number, its *magnitude*. Such a quantity is called a **scalar.** Other physical quantities, such as force and velocity, possess both magnitude and *direction;* these quantities are called **vector quantities,** or simply **vectors.**

For example, to specify the velocity of a moving point in the coordinate plane, we must give both the rate at which it moves (its speed) and the direction of that motion. The *velocity vector* of the moving point incorporates both pieces of information—direction and speed. It is convenient to represent this velocity vector by an arrow, with its initial point located at the current position of the moving point on its trajectory (Fig. 12.1.1).

Although the arrow, a directed line segment, carries the desired information—both magnitude (the segment's length) and direction—it is a pictorial representation rather than a quantitative object. The following formal definition of a vector captures the essence of magnitude in combination with direction.

FIGURE 12.1.1 A velocity vector may be represented by an arrow.

DEFINITION   Vector
A **vector v** in the Cartesian plane is an ordered pair of real numbers that has the form $\langle a, b \rangle$. We write $\mathbf{v} = \langle a, b \rangle$ and call a and b the **components** of the vector **v**.

The directed line segment $\overrightarrow{OP}$ from the origin O to the point $P(a, b)$ is one geometric representation of the vector **v**. (See Fig. 12.1.2.) For this reason, the vector $\mathbf{v} = \langle a, b \rangle$ is called the **position vector** of the point $P(a, b)$. In fact, the relationship between $\mathbf{v} = \langle a, b \rangle$ and $P(a, b)$ is so close that, in certain contexts, it is convenient to confuse the two deliberately—to regard **v** and P as the same mathematical object.

The directed line segment from the point $Q(a_1, b_1)$ to the point $R(a_2, b_2)$ has the same direction and magnitude as the directed line segment from the origin $O(0, 0)$ to the point $P(a, b)$ with $a = a_2 - a_1$ and $b = b_2 - b_1$ (Fig. 12.1.2), and consequently they represent the same vector $\mathbf{v} = \overrightarrow{OP} = \overrightarrow{QR}$. This observation makes it easy to find the components of the vector with arbitrary initial point Q and arbitrary terminal point R.

FIGURE 12.1.2 The position vector **v** of the point P and another representation $\overrightarrow{QR}$ of **v**.

REMARK   When discussing vectors we often use the term *scalar* to refer to an ordinary numerical quantity, one that is *not* a vector. In printed work we use **bold** type to distinguish the names of vectors from those of other mathematical objects, such as the scalars a and b that are the components of the vector $\mathbf{v} = \langle a, b \rangle$. In handwritten work a suitable alternative is to place an arrow—or just a bar—over every symbol that denotes a vector. Thus you may write $\vec{v} = \langle a, b \rangle$ or $\bar{v} = \langle a, b \rangle$. There is no need for an arrow or a bar over a vector $\langle a, b \rangle$ already identified by angle brackets, so none should be used there.

A directed line segment has both length and direction. The **length** of the vector $\mathbf{v} = \langle a, b \rangle$ is denoted by $v = |\mathbf{v}|$ and is defined as follows:

$$v = |\mathbf{v}| = |\langle a, b \rangle| = \sqrt{a^2 + b^2}. \tag{1}$$

Vectors in the Plane **SECTION 12.1** 773

The notation $v = |\mathbf{v}|$ is used because the length of a vector is in many ways analogous to the absolute value of a real number (Fig. 12.1.3).

EXAMPLE 1 The length of the vector $\mathbf{v} = \langle 1, -2 \rangle$ is

$$v = |\langle 1, -2 \rangle| = \sqrt{(1)^2 + (-2)^2} = \sqrt{5}.$$

FIGURE 12.1.3 The length $v = |\mathbf{v}|$ of the vector **v**.

The only vector with length zero is the **zero vector** with both components zero, denoted by $\mathbf{0} = \langle 0, 0 \rangle$. The zero vector is unique in that it has no specific direction. Every nonzero vector has a specified direction; the vector represented by the arrow $\overrightarrow{OP}$ from the origin O to another point P in the plane has direction specified (for instance) by the counterclockwise angle from the positive x-axis to $\overrightarrow{OP}$.

What is important about the vector $\mathbf{v} = \langle a, b \rangle$ represented by $\overrightarrow{OP}$ often is not *where* it is, but how long it is and which way it points. If the directed line segment $\overrightarrow{QR}$ with endpoints $Q(a_1, b_1)$ and $R(a_2, b_2)$ has the same length and direction as $\overrightarrow{OP}$, then we say that $\overrightarrow{QR}$ **represents** (or is a **representation** of) the vector **v** (Fig. 12.1.2). Thus a single vector has many representatives (Fig. 12.1.4).

Algebraic Operations with Vectors

The operations of addition and multiplication of real numbers have analogues for vectors. We shall define each of these operations of *vector algebra* in terms of components of vectors and then give a geometric interpretation in terms of arrows.

FIGURE 12.1.4 All these arrows represent the same vector $\mathbf{v} = \langle a, b \rangle$.

DEFINITION Equality of Vectors
The two vectors $\mathbf{u} = \langle u_1, u_2 \rangle$ and $\mathbf{v} = \langle v_1, v_2 \rangle$ are **equal** provided that $u_1 = v_1$ and $u_2 = v_2$.

In other words, two vectors are equal if and only if *corresponding components* are the same. Moreover, two directed line segments $\overrightarrow{PQ}$ and $\overrightarrow{RS}$ represent the same vector provided that they have the same length and direction. This will be the case provided that the segments $\overrightarrow{PQ}$ and $\overrightarrow{RS}$ are opposite sides of a parallelogram (Fig. 12.1.5).

DEFINITION Addition of Vectors
The **sum** $\mathbf{u} + \mathbf{v}$ of the two vectors $\mathbf{u} = \langle u_1, u_2 \rangle$ and $\mathbf{v} = \langle v_1, v_2 \rangle$ is the vector

$$\mathbf{u} + \mathbf{v} = \langle u_1 + v_1, u_2 + v_2 \rangle. \tag{2}$$

FIGURE 12.1.5 Parallel directed segments representing equal vectors.

Thus we add vectors by adding corresponding components—that is, by *componentwise addition*. The geometric interpretation of vector addition is the **triangle law of addition**, illustrated in Fig. 12.1.6, where the labeled lengths indicate why this interpretation is valid. An equivalent interpretation is the **parallelogram law of addition**, illustrated in Fig. 12.1.7.

FIGURE 12.1.6 The triangle law is a geometric interpretation of vector addition.

FIGURE 12.1.7 The parallelogram law for vector addition.

EXAMPLE 2 The sum of the vectors $\mathbf{u} = \langle 4, 3 \rangle$ and $\mathbf{v} = \langle -5, 2 \rangle$ is the vector

$$\mathbf{u} + \mathbf{v} = \langle 4, 3 \rangle + \langle -5, 2 \rangle = \langle 4 + (-5), 3 + 2 \rangle = \langle -1, 5 \rangle.$$ ◆

It is natural to write $2\mathbf{u} = \mathbf{u} + \mathbf{u}$. But if $\mathbf{u} = \langle u_1, u_2 \rangle$, then

$$2\mathbf{u} = \mathbf{u} + \mathbf{u} = \langle u_1, u_2 \rangle + \langle u_1, u_2 \rangle = \langle 2u_1, 2u_2 \rangle.$$

This suggests that multiplication of a vector by a scalar (real number) also is defined in a componentwise manner.

DEFINITION Multiplication of a Vector by a Scalar
If $\mathbf{u} = \langle u_1, u_2 \rangle$ and c is a real number, then the **scalar multiple** $c\mathbf{u}$ is the vector

$$c\mathbf{u} = \langle cu_1, cu_2 \rangle. \tag{3}$$

Note that

$$|c\mathbf{u}| = \sqrt{(cu_1)^2 + (cu_2)^2} = |c|\sqrt{(u_1)^2 + (u_2)^2} = |c| \cdot |\mathbf{u}|.$$

Thus the length of $|c\mathbf{u}|$ is $|c|$ times the length of $\mathbf{u}$. The **negative** of the vector $\mathbf{u}$ is the vector

$$-\mathbf{u} = (-1)\mathbf{u} = \langle -u_1, -u_2 \rangle,$$

with the same length as $\mathbf{u}$ but the opposite direction. We say that the two nonzero vectors $\mathbf{u}$ and $\mathbf{v}$ have

- The **same direction** if $\mathbf{u} = c\mathbf{v}$ for some $c > 0$;
- **Opposite directions** if $\mathbf{u} = c\mathbf{v}$ for some $c < 0$.

FIGURE 12.1.8 The vector $c\mathbf{u}$ may have the same direction as $\mathbf{u}$ or the opposite direction, depending on the sign of c.

The geometric interpretation of scalar multiplication is that $c\mathbf{u}$ is the vector with length $|c| \cdot |\mathbf{u}|$, with the same direction as $\mathbf{u}$ if $c > 0$ but with the opposite direction if $c < 0$ (Fig. 12.1.8).

The **difference** $\mathbf{u} - \mathbf{v}$ of the vectors $\mathbf{u} = \langle u_1, u_2 \rangle$ and $\mathbf{v} = \langle v_1, v_2 \rangle$ is defined to be

$$\mathbf{u} - \mathbf{v} = \mathbf{u} + (-\mathbf{v}) = \langle u_1 - v_1, u_2 - v_2 \rangle. \tag{4}$$

If we think of $\langle u_1, u_2 \rangle$ and $\langle v_1, v_2 \rangle$ as position vectors of the points P and Q, respectively, then $\mathbf{u} - \mathbf{v}$ may be represented by the arrow $\overrightarrow{QP}$ from Q to P. We may therefore write

$$\mathbf{u} - \mathbf{v} = \overrightarrow{OP} - \overrightarrow{OQ} = \overrightarrow{QP},$$

as illustrated in Fig. 12.1.9.

EXAMPLE 3 Suppose that $\mathbf{u} = \langle 4, -3 \rangle$ and $\mathbf{v} = \langle -2, 3 \rangle$. Find $|\mathbf{u}|$ and the vectors $\mathbf{u} + \mathbf{v}, \mathbf{u} - \mathbf{v}, 3\mathbf{u}, -2\mathbf{v}$, and $2\mathbf{u} + 4\mathbf{v}$.

Solution

$$|\mathbf{u}| = \sqrt{4^2 + (-3)^2} = \sqrt{25} = 5.$$

$$\mathbf{u} + \mathbf{v} = \langle 4 + (-2), -3 + 3 \rangle = \langle 2, 0 \rangle.$$

$$\mathbf{u} - \mathbf{v} = \langle 4 - (-2), -3 - 3 \rangle = \langle 6, -6 \rangle.$$

$$3\mathbf{u} = \langle 3 \cdot 4, 3 \cdot (-3) \rangle = \langle 12, -9 \rangle.$$

$$-2\mathbf{v} = \langle -2 \cdot (-2), -2 \cdot 3 \rangle = \langle 4, -6 \rangle.$$

$$2\mathbf{u} + 4\mathbf{v} = \langle 2 \cdot 4 + 4 \cdot (-2), 2 \cdot (-3) + 4 \cdot 3 \rangle = \langle 0, 6 \rangle.$$ ◆

FIGURE 12.1.9 Geometric interpretation of the difference $\mathbf{u} - \mathbf{v}$.

The familiar algebraic properties of real numbers carry over to the following analogous properties of vector addition and scalar multiplication. Let $\mathbf{a}$, $\mathbf{b}$, and $\mathbf{c}$ be vectors and r and s real numbers. Then

1. $\mathbf{a} + \mathbf{b} = \mathbf{b} + \mathbf{a}$,
2. $\mathbf{a} + (\mathbf{b} + \mathbf{c}) = (\mathbf{a} + \mathbf{b}) + \mathbf{c}$,
3. $r(\mathbf{a} + \mathbf{b}) = r\mathbf{a} + r\mathbf{b}$, (5)
4. $(r + s)\mathbf{a} = r\mathbf{a} + s\mathbf{a}$,
5. $(rs)\mathbf{a} = r(s\mathbf{a}) = s(r\mathbf{a})$.

You can easily verify these identities by working with components. For example, if $\mathbf{a} = \langle a_1, a_2 \rangle$ and $\mathbf{b} = \langle b_1, b_2 \rangle$, then

$$r(\mathbf{a} + \mathbf{b}) = r\langle a_1 + b_1, a_2 + b_2 \rangle = \langle r(a_1 + b_1), r(a_2 + b_2) \rangle$$
$$= \langle ra_1 + rb_1, ra_2 + rb_2 \rangle = \langle ra_1, ra_2 \rangle + \langle rb_1, rb_2 \rangle = r\mathbf{a} + r\mathbf{b}.$$

The proofs of the other four identities in (5) are left as exercises.

The Unit Vectors i and j

A **unit** vector is a vector of length 1. If $\mathbf{a} = \langle a_1, a_2 \rangle \neq \mathbf{0}$, then

$$\mathbf{u} = \frac{\mathbf{a}}{|\mathbf{a}|} \quad (6)$$

is the unit vector with the same direction as $\mathbf{a}$, because

$$|\mathbf{u}| = \sqrt{\left(\frac{a_1}{|\mathbf{a}|}\right)^2 + \left(\frac{a_2}{|\mathbf{a}|}\right)^2} = \frac{1}{|\mathbf{a}|}\sqrt{a_1^2 + a_2^2} = 1.$$

For example, if $\mathbf{a} = \langle 3, -4 \rangle$, then $|\mathbf{a}| = 5$. Thus $\langle \frac{3}{5}, -\frac{4}{5} \rangle$ is a unit vector that has the same direction as $\mathbf{a}$.

Two particular unit vectors play a special role, the vectors

$$\mathbf{i} = \langle 1, 0 \rangle \quad \text{and} \quad \mathbf{j} = \langle 0, 1 \rangle.$$

The first points in the positive x-direction; the second points in the positive y-direction (Fig. 12.1.10). Together they provide a useful alternative notation for vectors. If $\mathbf{a} = \langle a_1, a_2 \rangle$, then

$$\mathbf{a} = \langle a_1, 0 \rangle + \langle 0, a_2 \rangle = a_1 \langle 1, 0 \rangle + a_2 \langle 0, 1 \rangle = a_1\mathbf{i} + a_2\mathbf{j}. \quad (7)$$

FIGURE 12.1.10 The vectors **i** and **j**.

Thus every vector in the plane is a **linear combination** of **i** and **j**. The usefulness of this notation is based on the fact that such linear combinations of **i** and **j** may be manipulated as if they were ordinary sums. For example, if

$$\mathbf{a} = a_1\mathbf{i} + a_2\mathbf{j} \quad \text{and} \quad \mathbf{b} = b_1\mathbf{i} + b_2\mathbf{j},$$

then

$$\mathbf{a} + \mathbf{b} = (a_1\mathbf{i} + a_2\mathbf{j}) + (b_1\mathbf{i} + b_2\mathbf{j}) = (a_1 + b_1)\mathbf{i} + (a_2 + b_2)\mathbf{j}.$$

Also,

$$c\mathbf{a} = c(a_1\mathbf{i} + a_2\mathbf{j}) = (ca_1)\mathbf{i} + (ca_2)\mathbf{j}.$$

EXAMPLE 4 Suppose that $\mathbf{a} = 2\mathbf{i} - 3\mathbf{j}$ and $\mathbf{b} = 3\mathbf{i} + 4\mathbf{j}$. Express $5\mathbf{a} - 3\mathbf{b}$ in terms of **i** and **j**.

Solution

$$5\mathbf{a} - 3\mathbf{b} = 5 \cdot (2\mathbf{i} - 3\mathbf{j}) - 3 \cdot (3\mathbf{i} + 4\mathbf{j})$$
$$= (10 - 9)\mathbf{i} + (-15 - 12)\mathbf{j} = \mathbf{i} - 27\mathbf{j}. \quad \blacklozenge$$

776 CHAPTER 12 Vectors, Curves, and Surfaces in Space

FIGURE 12.1.11 The vectors **a**, **b**, and **b** − **a** of Example 5.

FIGURE 12.1.12 Resolution of $\mathbf{a} = \langle a_1, a_2 \rangle$ into its horizontal and vertical components.

FIGURE 12.1.13 The suspended weight of Example 6.

EXAMPLE 5 When the vectors $\mathbf{a} = 8\mathbf{i} + 5\mathbf{j}$ and $\mathbf{b} = -11\mathbf{i} + 17\mathbf{j}$ are plotted carefully (Fig. 12.1.11), they look as though they might be perpendicular. Determine whether or not this is so.

Solution If the vectors **a** and **b** are regarded as position vectors of the points $P(8, 5)$ and $Q(-11, 17)$, then their difference $\mathbf{c} = \mathbf{b} - \mathbf{a} = -19\mathbf{i} + 12\mathbf{j}$ represents the third side $\overrightarrow{PQ}$ of the triangle OPQ (Fig. 12.1.11). According to the Pythagorean theorem, this triangle is a right triangle with hypotenuse PQ if and only if $|\mathbf{c}|^2 = |\mathbf{a}|^2 + |\mathbf{b}|^2$. But

$$|\mathbf{c}|^2 = (-19)^2 + 12^2 = 505 \quad \text{whereas} \quad |\mathbf{a}|^2 + |\mathbf{b}|^2 = [8^2 + 5^2] + [(-11)^2 + 17^2] = 499.$$

It follows that the vectors **a** and **b** are not perpendicular. ◆

Equation (7) expresses the vector $\mathbf{a} = \langle a_1, a_2 \rangle$ as the sum of a horizontal vector $a_1\mathbf{i}$ and a vertical vector $a_2\mathbf{j}$, as Fig. 12.1.12 shows. The decomposition or *resolution* of a vector into its horizontal and vertical components is an important technique in the study of vector quantities. For example, a force **F** may be decomposed into its horizontal and vertical components $F_1\mathbf{i}$ and $F_2\mathbf{j}$, respectively. The physical effect of the single force **F** is the same as the combined effect of the separate forces $F_1\mathbf{i}$ and $F_2\mathbf{j}$. (This is an instance of the empirically verifiable parallelogram law of addition of forces.) Because of this decomposition, many two-dimensional problems can be reduced to one-dimensional problems, the latter solved, and the two results combined (again by vector methods) to give the solution of the original problem.

EXAMPLE 6 A 100-lb weight is suspended from the ceiling by means of two perpendicular flexible cables of equal length (Fig. 12.1.13). Find the tension (in pounds) in each cable.

Solution Each cable is inclined at an angle of 45° from the horizontal, so it follows readily upon calculating horizontal and vertical components that the indicated tension force vectors $\mathbf{T}_1$ and $\mathbf{T}_2$ are given by

$$\mathbf{T}_1 = (T_1 \cos 45°)\mathbf{i} + (T_1 \sin 45°)\mathbf{j} \quad \text{and} \quad \mathbf{T}_2 = (-T_2 \cos 45°)\mathbf{i} + (T_2 \sin 45°)\mathbf{j},$$

where $T_1 = |\mathbf{T}_1|$ and $T_2 = |\mathbf{T}_2|$ are the tension forces we seek. The downward force of gravity acting on the weight is given by $\mathbf{F} = -100\mathbf{j}$. In order that the weight hangs motionless, the three forces must "balance," so that $\mathbf{T}_1 + \mathbf{T}_2 + \mathbf{F} = \mathbf{0}$; that is,

$$[(T_1 \cos 45°)\mathbf{i} + (T_1 \sin 45°)\mathbf{j}] + [(-T_2 \cos 45°)\mathbf{i} + (T_2 \sin 45°)\mathbf{j}] = 100\mathbf{j}.$$

When we equate the components of **i** in this equation and separately equate the components of **j**, we get the two scalar equations

$$T_1 \cos 45° - T_2 \cos 45° = 0 \quad \text{and} \quad T_1 \sin 45° + T_2 \sin 45° = 100.$$

The first of these scalar equations implies that $T_1 = T_2 = T$, and then the second yields $T = 100/(2 \sin 45°) = 50\sqrt{2} \approx 70.71$ (pounds) for the tension in each cable. ◆

12.1 TRUE/FALSE STUDY GUIDE

12.1 CONCEPTS: QUESTIONS AND DISCUSSION

1. Discuss the relation between a 2-dimensional vector and a point in the plane.
2. Give several examples of quantities that possess both magnitude and direction. For each, discuss whether and how such quantities might be added.
3. If a person owns stock in two companies, how might the worth of his portfolio be described by a 2-dimensional vector? If several people owning stock in these same two companies form a partnership, is the "worth vector" of the partnership equal to the sum of the worth vectors of the partners?

12.1 PROBLEMS

In Problems 1 through 4, find a vector $\mathbf{v} = \langle a, b \rangle$ that is represented by the directed line segment $\overrightarrow{RS}$. Then sketch both $\overrightarrow{RS}$ and the position vector of the point $P(a, b)$.

1. $R(1, 2)$, $S(3, 5)$
2. $R(-2, -3)$, $S(1, 4)$
3. $R(5, 10)$, $S(-5, -10)$
4. $R(-10, 20)$, $S(15, -25)$

In Problems 5 through 8, find the sum $\mathbf{w} = \mathbf{u} + \mathbf{v}$ and illustrate it geometrically.

5. $\mathbf{u} = \langle 1, -2 \rangle$, $\mathbf{v} = \langle 3, 4 \rangle$
6. $\mathbf{u} = \langle 4, 2 \rangle$, $\mathbf{v} = \langle -2, 5 \rangle$
7. $\mathbf{u} = 3\mathbf{i} + 5\mathbf{j}$, $\mathbf{v} = 2\mathbf{i} - 7\mathbf{j}$
8. $\mathbf{u} = 7\mathbf{i} + 5\mathbf{j}$, $\mathbf{v} = -10\mathbf{i}$

In Problems 9 through 16, find $|\mathbf{a}|$, $|-2\mathbf{b}|$, $|\mathbf{a} - \mathbf{b}|$, $\mathbf{a} + \mathbf{b}$, and $3\mathbf{a} - 2\mathbf{b}$.

9. $\mathbf{a} = \langle 1, -2 \rangle$, $\mathbf{b} = \langle -3, 2 \rangle$
10. $\mathbf{a} = \langle 3, 4 \rangle$, $\mathbf{b} = \langle -4, 3 \rangle$
11. $\mathbf{a} = \langle -2, -2 \rangle$, $\mathbf{b} = \langle -3, -4 \rangle$
12. $\mathbf{a} = -2\langle 4, 7 \rangle$, $\mathbf{b} = -3\langle -4, -2 \rangle$
13. $\mathbf{a} = \mathbf{i} + 3\mathbf{j}$, $\mathbf{b} = 2\mathbf{i} - 5\mathbf{j}$
14. $\mathbf{a} = 2\mathbf{i} - 5\mathbf{j}$, $\mathbf{b} = \mathbf{i} - 6\mathbf{j}$
15. $\mathbf{a} = 4\mathbf{i}$, $\mathbf{b} = -7\mathbf{j}$
16. $\mathbf{a} = -\mathbf{i} - \mathbf{j}$, $\mathbf{b} = 2\mathbf{i} + 2\mathbf{j}$

In Problems 17 through 20, find a unit vector $\mathbf{u}$ with the same direction as the given vector $\mathbf{a}$. Express $\mathbf{u}$ in terms of $\mathbf{i}$ and $\mathbf{j}$. Also find a unit vector $\mathbf{v}$ with the direction opposite that of $\mathbf{a}$.

17. $\mathbf{a} = \langle -3, -4 \rangle$
18. $\mathbf{a} = \langle 5, -12 \rangle$
19. $\mathbf{a} = 8\mathbf{i} + 15\mathbf{j}$
20. $\mathbf{a} = 7\mathbf{i} - 24\mathbf{j}$

In Problems 21 through 24, find the vector $\mathbf{a}$, expressed in terms of $\mathbf{i}$ and $\mathbf{j}$, that is represented by the arrow $\overrightarrow{PQ}$ in the plane.

21. $P = (3, 2)$, $Q = (3, -2)$
22. $P = (-3, 5)$, $Q = (-3, 6)$
23. $P = (-4, 7)$, $Q = (4, -7)$
24. $P = (1, -1)$, $Q = (-4, -1)$

In Problems 25 through 28, determine whether or not the given vectors $\mathbf{a}$ and $\mathbf{b}$ are perpendicular.

25. $\mathbf{a} = \langle 6, 0 \rangle$, $\mathbf{b} = \langle 0, -7 \rangle$
26. $\mathbf{a} = 3\mathbf{j}$, $\mathbf{b} = 3\mathbf{i} - \mathbf{j}$
27. $\mathbf{a} = 2\mathbf{i} - \mathbf{j}$, $\mathbf{b} = 4\mathbf{j} + 8\mathbf{i}$
28. $\mathbf{a} = 8\mathbf{i} + 10\mathbf{j}$, $\mathbf{b} = 15\mathbf{i} - 12\mathbf{j}$

In Problems 29 and 30, express $\mathbf{i}$ and $\mathbf{j}$ in terms of $\mathbf{a}$ and $\mathbf{b}$.

29. $\mathbf{a} = 2\mathbf{i} + 3\mathbf{j}$, $\mathbf{b} = 3\mathbf{i} + 4\mathbf{j}$
30. $\mathbf{a} = 5\mathbf{i} - 9\mathbf{j}$, $\mathbf{b} = 4\mathbf{i} - 7\mathbf{j}$

In Problems 31 and 32, write $\mathbf{c}$ in the form $r\mathbf{a} + s\mathbf{b}$ where r and s are scalars.

31. $\mathbf{a} = \mathbf{i} + \mathbf{j}$, $\mathbf{b} = \mathbf{i} - \mathbf{j}$, $\mathbf{c} = 2\mathbf{i} - 3\mathbf{j}$
32. $\mathbf{a} = 3\mathbf{i} + 2\mathbf{j}$, $\mathbf{b} = 8\mathbf{i} + 5\mathbf{j}$, $\mathbf{c} = 7\mathbf{i} + 9\mathbf{j}$

33. Find a vector that has the same direction as $5\mathbf{i} - 7\mathbf{j}$ and is (a) three times its length; (b) one-third its length.

34. Find a vector that has the opposite direction from $-3\mathbf{i} + 5\mathbf{j}$ and is (a) four times its length; (b) one-fourth its length.

35. Find a vector of length 5 with (a) the same direction as $7\mathbf{i} - 3\mathbf{j}$; (b) the direction opposite that of $8\mathbf{i} + 5\mathbf{j}$.

36. For what numbers c are the vectors $\langle c, 2 \rangle$ and $\langle c, -8 \rangle$ perpendicular?

37. For what numbers c are the vectors $2c\mathbf{i} - 4\mathbf{j}$ and $3\mathbf{i} + c\mathbf{j}$ perpendicular?

38. Given the three points $A(2, 3)$, $B(-5, 7)$, and $C(1, -5)$, verify by direct computation of the vectors and their sum that $\overrightarrow{AB} + \overrightarrow{BC} + \overrightarrow{CA} = \mathbf{0}$.

In Problems 39 through 42, give a componentwise proof of the indicated property of vector algebra. Take $\mathbf{a} = \langle a_1, a_2 \rangle$, $\mathbf{b} = \langle b_1, b_2 \rangle$, and $\mathbf{c} = \langle c_1, c_2 \rangle$ throughout.

39. $\mathbf{a} + (\mathbf{b} + \mathbf{c}) = (\mathbf{a} + \mathbf{b}) + \mathbf{c}$
40. $(r + s)\mathbf{a} = r\mathbf{a} + s\mathbf{a}$
41. $(rs)\mathbf{a} = r(s\mathbf{a})$
42. If $\mathbf{a} + \mathbf{b} = \mathbf{a}$, then $\mathbf{b} = \mathbf{0}$.

43. Find the tension in each cable of Example 6 if the angle between them is $120°$.

In Problems 44 through 46, a given weight (in pounds) is suspended by two cables as shown in the figure. Find the tension in each cable.

44.

FIGURE 12.1.14

45.

FIGURE 12.1.15

46.

FIGURE 12.1.16

In Problems 47 through 49, assume the following fact: If an airplane flies with velocity vector $\mathbf{v}_a$ relative to the air and the velocity of the wind is $\mathbf{w}$, then the velocity vector of the plane relative to the ground is $\mathbf{v}_g = \mathbf{v}_a + \mathbf{w}$ (Fig. 12.1.17). The vector $\mathbf{v}_a$ is called the apparent velocity vector *and the vector $\mathbf{v}_g$ is called the* true velocity vector.

FIGURE 12.1.17 The vectors of Problems 47 through 49
- Apparent velocity: $\mathbf{v}_a$
- Wind velocity: $\mathbf{w}$
- True velocity: $\mathbf{v}_g = \mathbf{v}_a + \mathbf{w}$

47. Suppose that the wind is blowing from the northeast at 50 mi/h and that the pilot wishes to fly due east at 500 mi/h. What should the plane's apparent velocity vector be?

48. Repeat Problem 47 with the phrase *due east* replaced with *due west*.

49. Repeat Problem 47 in the case that the pilot wishes to fly northwest at 500 mi/h.

50. Given any three points A, B, and C in the plane, show that $\overrightarrow{AB} + \overrightarrow{BC} + \overrightarrow{CA} = \mathbf{0}$. [*Suggestion:* Picture the triangle ABC.]

51. If $\mathbf{a}$ and $\mathbf{b}$ are the position vectors of the points P and Q in the plane and M is the point with position vector $\mathbf{v} = \frac{1}{2}(\mathbf{a} + \mathbf{b})$, show that M is the midpoint of the line segment PQ. Is it sufficient to show that the vectors $\overrightarrow{PM}$ and $\overrightarrow{QM}$ are equal and opposite?

52. In the triangle ABC, let M and N be the midpoints of AB and AC, respectively. Show that $\overrightarrow{MN} = \frac{1}{2}\overrightarrow{BC}$. Conclude that the line segment joining the midpoints of two sides of a triangle is parallel to the third side. How are their lengths related?

53. Prove that the diagonals of a parallelogram $ABCD$ bisect each other. [*Suggestion:* If M and N are the midpoints of the diagonals AC and BD, respectively, and O is the origin, show that $\overrightarrow{OM} = \overrightarrow{ON}$.]

54. Use vectors to prove that the midpoints of the four sides of an arbitrary quadrilateral are the vertices of a parallelogram.

55. Figure 12.1.18 shows the vector $\mathbf{a}_\perp$ obtained by rotating the vector $\mathbf{a} = a_1\mathbf{i} + a_2\mathbf{j}$ through a counterclockwise angle of $90°$. Show that
$$\mathbf{a}_\perp = -a_2\mathbf{i} + a_1\mathbf{j}.$$
[*Suggestion:* Begin by writing $\mathbf{a} = (r\cos\theta)\mathbf{i} + (r\sin\theta)\mathbf{j}$.]

FIGURE 12.1.18 Rotate $\mathbf{a}$ counterclockwise $90°$ to obtain $\mathbf{a}_\perp$ (Problem 55).

12.2 THREE-DIMENSIONAL VECTORS

In the first eleven chapters we discussed many aspects of the calculus of functions of a *single* variable. The geometry of such functions is two-dimensional, because the graph of a function of a single variable is a curve in the coordinate plane. Most of the remaining chapters deal with the calculus of functions of *several* (two or more) independent variables. The geometry of functions of two variables is three-dimensional because the graphs of such functions are generally surfaces in space.

Rectangular coordinates in the plane may be generalized to rectangular coordinates in space. A point in space is determined by giving its location relative to three mutually perpendicular **coordinate axes** that pass through the origin O. We shall usually draw the x-, y-, and z-axes as shown in Fig. 12.2.1, sometimes with arrows indicating the positive direction along each axis; the positive x-axis will always be labeled x, and similarly for the positive y- and z-axes. With this configuration of axes, our rectangular coordinate system is said to be **right-handed:** If you curl the fingers of your right hand in the direction of a $90°$ rotation from the positive x-axis to the positive y-axis, then your thumb points in the direction of the positive z-axis. If the x- and y-axes were interchanged, then the coordinate system would be left-handed. These two coordinate systems are different in that it is impossible to bring one into coincidence with the other by means of rotations and translations. This is why the L- and D-alanine molecules shown in Fig. 12.2.2 are different; you can metabolize the left-handed ("levo") version but not the right-handed ("dextro") version. In this book we shall discuss right-handed coordinate systems exclusively and always draw the x-, y-, and z-axes with the right-handed orientation shown in Fig. 12.2.1.

FIGURE 12.2.1 The right-handed coordinate system.

Three-Dimensional Vectors SECTION 12.2 779

FIGURE 12.2.2 The stereoisomers of the amino acid alanine are physically and biologically different even through they have the same molecular formula.

The three coordinate axes taken in pairs determine the three **coordinate planes** (Fig. 12.2.3):

- The (horizontal) xy-plane, where $z = 0$;
- The (vertical) yz-plane, where $x = 0$; and
- The (vertical) xz-plane, where $y = 0$.

The point P in space is said to have **rectangular coordinates** (x, y, z) if

- x is its signed distance from the yz-plane,
- y is its signed distance from the xz-plane, and
- z is its signed distance from the xy-plane.

FIGURE 12.2.3 The coordinate planes in space.

(See Fig. 12.2.4.) In this case we may describe the location of P simply by calling it "the point $P(x, y, z)$." There is a natural one-to-one correspondence between ordered triples (x, y, z) of real numbers and points P in space; this correspondence is called a **rectangular coordinate system** in space. In Fig. 12.2.5 the point P is located in the **first octant**—the eighth of space in which all three rectangular coordinates are positive.

If we apply the Pythagorean theorem to the right triangles P_1QR and P_1RP_2 in Fig. 12.2.6, we get

$$|P_1P_2|^2 = |RP_2|^2 + |P_1R|^2 = |RP_2|^2 + |QR|^2 + |P_1Q|^2$$
$$= (x_1 - x_2)^2 + (y_1 - y_2)^2 + (z_1 - z_2)^2.$$

Thus the **distance formula** for the **distance** $|P_1P_2|$ between the points P_1 and P_2 is

$$|P_1P_2| = \sqrt{(x_1 - x_2)^2 + (y_1 - y_2)^2 + (z_1 - z_2)^2}. \tag{1}$$

FIGURE 12.2.4 Locating the point P in rectangular coordinates.

FIGURE 12.2.5 Completing the box to show P with the illusion of the third dimension.

FIGURE 12.2.6 The distance between P_1 and P_2 is the length of the long diagonal of the box.

EXAMPLE 1 The distance between the points $A(1, 3, -2)$ and $B(4, -3, 1)$ is

$$|AB| = \sqrt{(4-1)^2 + (-3-3)^2 + (1+2)^2} = \sqrt{54} \approx 7.348.$$ ◆

You can apply the distance formula in Eq. (1) to show that the **midpoint** M of the line segment joining $P_1(x_1, y_1, z_1)$ and $P_2(x_2, y_2, z_2)$ is

$$M\left(\frac{x_1 + x_2}{2}, \frac{y_1 + y_2}{2}, \frac{z_1 + z_2}{2}\right). \tag{2}$$

(See Problem 63.)

The **graph** of an equation in three variables x, y, and z is the set of all points in space with rectangular coordinates that satisfy that equation. In general, the graph of an equation in three variables is a *two-dimensional surface* in $\mathbf{R}^3$ (three-dimensional space with rectangular coordinates).

EXAMPLE 2 Given a fixed point $C(h, k, l)$ and a number $r > 0$, find an equation of the sphere with radius r and center C.

Solution By definition, the sphere is the set of all points $P(x, y, z)$ such that the distance from P to C is r. That is, $|CP| = r$, and thus $|CP|^2 = r^2$. Therefore

$$(x - h)^2 + (y - k)^2 + (z - l)^2 = r^2. \tag{3}$$ ◆

Equation (3) is worth remembering as the equation of the **sphere with radius** r and **center** $C(h, k, l)$ shown in Fig. 12.2.7. Moreover, given an equation of the form

$$x^2 + y^2 + z^2 + Ax + By + Cz + D = 0,$$

we can attempt—by completing the square in each variable—to write it in the form of Eq. (3) and thereby show that its graph is a sphere.

FIGURE 12.2.7 The sphere with center (h, k, l) and radius r.

EXAMPLE 3 Determine the graph of the equation

$$x^2 + y^2 + z^2 + 4x + 2y - 6z - 2 = 0.$$

Solution We complete the square in each variable. The equation then takes the form

$$(x^2 + 4x + 4) + (y^2 + 2y + 1) + (z^2 - 6z + 9) = 2 + (4 + 1 + 9) = 16;$$

that is,

$$(x + 2)^2 + (y + 1)^2 + (z - 3)^2 = 4^2.$$

Thus the graph of the given equation is the sphere with radius 4 and center $(-2, -1, 3)$. ◆

Vectors in Space

The discussion of vectors in space parallels the discussion in Section 12.1 of vectors in the plane. The difference is that a vector in space has three components rather than two. The point $P(x, y, z)$ has **position vector** $\mathbf{v} = \overrightarrow{OP} = \langle x, y, z \rangle$, which is represented by the directed line segment (or arrow) $\overrightarrow{OP}$ from the origin O to the point P (as well as by any parallel translate of this arrow—see Fig. 12.2.8). The distance formula in Eq. (1) gives

$$|\mathbf{v}| = \sqrt{x^2 + y^2 + z^2} \tag{4}$$

for the **length** (or **magnitude**) of the vector $\mathbf{v} = \langle x, y, z \rangle$.

FIGURE 12.2.8 The arrow $\overrightarrow{OP}$ represents the position vector $\mathbf{v} = \langle x, y, z \rangle$.

Three-Dimensional Vectors SECTION 12.2 781

Given two points $A(a_1, a_2, a_3)$ and $B(b_1, b_2, b_3)$ in space, the directed line segment $\overrightarrow{AB}$ in Fig. 12.2.9 represents the vector

$$\mathbf{v} = \langle b_1 - a_1, b_2 - a_2, b_3 - a_3 \rangle.$$

Its length is the distance between the two points A and B:

$$|\mathbf{v}| = |\overrightarrow{AB}| = \sqrt{(b_1 - a_1)^2 + (b_2 - a_2)^2 + (b_3 - a_3)^2}.$$

What it means for two vectors in space to be equal is essentially the same as in the case of two-dimensional vectors: The vectors $\mathbf{a} = \langle a_1, a_2, a_3 \rangle$ and $\mathbf{b} = \langle b_1, b_2, b_3 \rangle$ are **equal** provided that $a_1 = b_1$, $a_2 = b_2$, and $a_3 = b_3$. That is, two vectors are equal exactly when corresponding components are equal.

We define addition and scalar multiplication of three-dimensional vectors exactly as we did in Section 12.1, taking into account that the vectors now have three components rather than two: The **sum** of the vectors $\mathbf{a} = \langle a_1, a_2, a_3 \rangle$ and $\mathbf{b} = \langle b_1, b_2, b_3 \rangle$ is the vector

$$\mathbf{a} + \mathbf{b} = \langle a_1 + b_1, a_2 + b_2, a_3 + b_3 \rangle. \tag{5}$$

FIGURE 12.2.9 The arrow $\overrightarrow{AB}$ represents the vector $\mathbf{v} = \langle b_1 - a_1, b_2 - a_2, b_3 - a_3 \rangle$.

Because $\mathbf{a}$ and $\mathbf{b}$ lie in a plane (although not necessarily the xy-plane) if their initial points coincide, addition of three-dimensional vectors obeys the same **parallelogram law** as in the two-dimensional case (Fig. 12.2.10).

If c is a real number, then the **scalar multiple** $c\mathbf{a}$ is the vector

$$c\mathbf{a} = \langle ca_1, ca_2, ca_3 \rangle. \tag{6}$$

FIGURE 12.2.10 The parallelogram law for addition of vectors.

The length of $c\mathbf{a}$ is $|c|$ times the length of $\mathbf{a}$, and $c\mathbf{a}$ has the same direction as $\mathbf{a}$ if $c > 0$ but the opposite direction if $c < 0$. The following algebraic properties of vector addition and scalar multiplication for three-dimensional vectors are easy to establish; they follow from computations with components, exactly as in Section 12.1:

$$\begin{aligned} \mathbf{a} + \mathbf{b} &= \mathbf{b} + \mathbf{a}, \\ \mathbf{a} + (\mathbf{b} + \mathbf{c}) &= (\mathbf{a} + \mathbf{b}) + \mathbf{c}, \\ r(\mathbf{a} + \mathbf{b}) &= r\mathbf{a} + r\mathbf{b}, \\ (r + s)\mathbf{a} &= r\mathbf{a} + s\mathbf{a}, \\ (rs)\mathbf{a} &= r(s\mathbf{a}) = s(r\mathbf{a}). \end{aligned} \tag{7}$$

EXAMPLE 4 If $\mathbf{a} = \langle 3, 4, 12 \rangle$ and $\mathbf{b} = \langle -4, 3, 0 \rangle$, then

$$\mathbf{a} + \mathbf{b} = \langle 3 - 4, 4 + 3, 12 + 0 \rangle = \langle -1, 7, 12 \rangle,$$
$$|\mathbf{a}| = \sqrt{3^2 + 4^2 + 12^2} = \sqrt{169} = 13,$$
$$2\mathbf{a} = \langle 2 \cdot 3, 2 \cdot 4, 2 \cdot 12 \rangle = \langle 6, 8, 24 \rangle, \quad \text{and}$$
$$2\mathbf{a} - 3\mathbf{b} = \langle 6 + 12, 8 - 9, 24 - 0 \rangle = \langle 18, -1, 24 \rangle. \quad \blacklozenge$$

A **unit vector** is a vector of length 1. We can express any vector in space (or *space vector*) in terms of the three **basic unit vectors**

$$\mathbf{i} = \langle 1, 0, 0 \rangle, \quad \mathbf{j} = \langle 0, 1, 0 \rangle, \quad \mathbf{k} = \langle 0, 0, 1 \rangle.$$

When located with their initial points at the origin, these basic unit vectors form a right-handed triple of vectors pointing in the positive directions along the three coordinate axes (Fig. 12.2.11).

The space vector $\mathbf{a} = \langle a_1, a_2, a_3 \rangle$ can be written as

$$\mathbf{a} = a_1\mathbf{i} + a_2\mathbf{j} + a_3\mathbf{k},$$

FIGURE 12.2.11 The basic unit vectors $\mathbf{i}$, $\mathbf{j}$, and $\mathbf{k}$.

a linear combination of the basic unit vectors. As in the two-dimensional case, the usefulness of this representation is that algebraic operations involving vectors may be carried out simply by collecting coefficients of **i**, **j**, and **k**.

EXAMPLE 5 Given the vectors $\mathbf{a} = \langle 3, -4, 2 \rangle$ and $\mathbf{b} = \langle 5, 2, -7 \rangle$, we can write

$$\mathbf{a} = 3\mathbf{i} - 4\mathbf{j} + 2\mathbf{k} \quad \text{and} \quad \mathbf{b} = 5\mathbf{i} + 2\mathbf{j} - 7\mathbf{k}$$

in order to calculate

$$7\mathbf{a} + 5\mathbf{b} = 7 \cdot (3\mathbf{i} - 4\mathbf{j} + 2\mathbf{k}) + 5 \cdot (5\mathbf{i} + 2\mathbf{j} - 7\mathbf{k})$$
$$= (21 + 25)\mathbf{i} + (-28 + 10)\mathbf{j} + (14 - 35)\mathbf{k}$$
$$= 46\mathbf{i} - 18\mathbf{j} - 21\mathbf{k} = \langle 46, -18, -21 \rangle. \qquad \blacklozenge$$

The Dot Product of Two Vectors

The **dot product** of the two vectors

$$\mathbf{a} = a_1\mathbf{i} + a_2\mathbf{j} + a_3\mathbf{k} \quad \text{and} \quad \mathbf{b} = b_1\mathbf{i} + b_2\mathbf{j} + b_3\mathbf{k}$$

is the number obtained when we multiply corresponding components of **a** and **b** and add the results. That is,

$$\mathbf{a} \cdot \mathbf{b} = a_1b_1 + a_2b_2 + a_3b_3. \tag{8}$$

Thus the dot product of two vectors is the *sum of the products of their corresponding components*. In the case of plane vectors $\mathbf{a} = \langle a_1, a_2 \rangle$ and $\mathbf{b} = \langle b_1, b_2 \rangle$, we simply dispense with third components and write $\mathbf{a} \cdot \mathbf{b} = a_1b_1 + a_2b_2$.

EXAMPLE 6 To apply the definition to calculate the dot product of the two vectors $\mathbf{a} = \langle 3, 4, 12 \rangle$ and $\mathbf{b} = \langle -4, 3, 0 \rangle$, we simply follow the pattern in Eq. (8):

$$\mathbf{a} \cdot \mathbf{b} = (3)(-4) + (4)(3) + (12)(0) = -12 + 12 + 0 = 0.$$

And if $\mathbf{c} = \langle 4, 5, -3 \rangle$, then

$$\mathbf{a} \cdot \mathbf{c} = (3)(4) + (4)(5) + (12)(-3) = 12 + 20 - 36 = -4. \qquad \blacklozenge$$

IMPORTANT The dot product of two *vectors* is a *scalar*—that is, an ordinary real number. For this reason the dot product is often called the **scalar product.** Example 6 illustrates the fact that the scalar product of two nonzero vectors (with positive lengths) may be zero or even a negative number.

The following **properties of the dot product** show that dot products of vectors behave in many ways in analogy to the ordinary algebra of real numbers.

$$\mathbf{a} \cdot \mathbf{a} = |\mathbf{a}|^2,$$
$$\mathbf{a} \cdot \mathbf{b} = \mathbf{b} \cdot \mathbf{a},$$
$$\mathbf{a} \cdot (\mathbf{b} + \mathbf{c}) = \mathbf{a} \cdot \mathbf{b} + \mathbf{a} \cdot \mathbf{c}, \tag{9}$$
$$(r\mathbf{a}) \cdot \mathbf{b} = r(\mathbf{a} \cdot \mathbf{b}) = \mathbf{a} \cdot (r\mathbf{b}).$$

Each of the properties in (9) can be established by working with components of the vectors involved. For instance, to establish the second equation, suppose that $\mathbf{a} = \langle a_1, a_2, a_3 \rangle$ and $\mathbf{b} = \langle b_1, b_2, b_3 \rangle$. Then

$$\mathbf{a} \cdot \mathbf{b} = a_1b_1 + a_2b_2 + a_3b_3 = b_1a_1 + b_2a_2 + b_3a_3 = \mathbf{b} \cdot \mathbf{a}.$$

This derivation makes it clear that the commutative law for the dot product is a consequence of the commutative law $ab = ba$ for multiplication of ordinary real numbers.

Example 6 shows that the *algebraic definition* of the dot product is easy to apply in routine calculations. But what does it mean? The significance and **meaning of the dot product** lie in its *geometric interpretation*.

Let the vectors **a** and **b** be represented as position vectors by the directed segments $\overrightarrow{OP}$ and $\overrightarrow{OQ}$, respectively. Then the angle θ between **a** and **b** is the angle at O in triangle OPQ of Fig. 12.2.12. We say that **a** and **b** are **parallel** if $\theta = 0$ or if $\theta = \pi$ and that **a** and **b** are **perpendicular** if $\theta = \pi/2$. For convenience, we regard the zero vector $\mathbf{0} = \langle 0, 0, 0 \rangle$ as both parallel to *and* perpendicular to *every* vector.

FIGURE 12.2.12 The angle θ between the vectors **a** and **b**.

THEOREM 1 Interpretation of the Dot Product
If θ is the angle between the vectors **a** and **b**, then

$$\mathbf{a} \cdot \mathbf{b} = |\mathbf{a}|\,|\mathbf{b}| \cos \theta. \tag{10}$$

PROOF If either $\mathbf{a} = \mathbf{0}$ or $\mathbf{b} = \mathbf{0}$, then Eq. (10) follows immediately. If the vectors **a** and **b** are parallel, then $\mathbf{b} = t\mathbf{a}$ with either $t > 0$ and $\theta = 0$ or $t < 0$ and $\theta = \pi$. In either case, both sides in Eq. (10) reduce to $t|\mathbf{a}|^2$, so again the conclusion of Theorem 1 follows.

We turn to the general case in which the vector $\mathbf{a} = \overrightarrow{OP}$ and $\mathbf{b} = \overrightarrow{OQ}$ are nonzero and nonparallel. Then

$$|\overrightarrow{QP}|^2 = |\mathbf{a} - \mathbf{b}|^2 = (\mathbf{a} - \mathbf{b}) \cdot (\mathbf{a} - \mathbf{b})$$
$$= \mathbf{a} \cdot \mathbf{a} - \mathbf{a} \cdot \mathbf{b} - \mathbf{b} \cdot \mathbf{a} + \mathbf{b} \cdot \mathbf{b}$$
$$= |\mathbf{a}|^2 + |\mathbf{b}|^2 - 2\mathbf{a} \cdot \mathbf{b}.$$

But $c = |\overrightarrow{QP}|$ is the side of triangle OPQ (Fig. 12.2.12) that is opposite the angle θ included between the sides $a = |\mathbf{a}|$ and $b = |\mathbf{b}|$. Hence the law of cosines (Appendix M) gives

$$|\overrightarrow{QP}|^2 = c^2 = a^2 + b^2 - 2ab \cos \theta$$
$$= |\mathbf{a}|^2 + |\mathbf{b}|^2 - 2\,|\mathbf{a}|\,|\mathbf{b}| \cos \theta.$$

Finally, comparing these two expressions for $|\overrightarrow{QP}|^2$ yields Eq. (10). ◄

This theorem tells us that the angle θ between the nonzero vectors **a** and **b** can be found by using the equation

$$\cos \theta = \frac{\mathbf{a} \cdot \mathbf{b}}{|\mathbf{a}|\,|\mathbf{b}|}. \tag{11}$$

For instance, given the vectors $\mathbf{a} = \langle 8, 5 \rangle$ and $\mathbf{b} = \langle -11, 17 \rangle$ of Example 5 in Section 12.1, we calculate

$$\cos \theta = \frac{\langle 8, 5 \rangle \cdot \langle -11, 17 \rangle}{|\langle 8, 5 \rangle|\,|\langle -11, 17 \rangle|} = \frac{(8)(-11) + (5)(17)}{\sqrt{8^2 + 5^2}\sqrt{(-11)^2 + 17^2}} = \frac{-3}{\sqrt{89}\sqrt{410}}.$$

It follows that $\theta = \arccos(-3/\sqrt{89}\sqrt{410}) \approx 1.5865$ (*radians*) $\approx 90.90° \neq 90°$, so we see again that the vectors **a** and **b** are not perpendicular.

More generally, the two nonzero vectors **a** and **b** are perpendicular if and only if they make a right angle, so that $\theta = \pi/2$. By (11), this in turn is so if and only if $\mathbf{a} \cdot \mathbf{b} = 0$. Hence we have a quick computational check for perpendicularity of vectors.

COROLLARY Test for Perpendicular Vectors
The two nonzero vectors **a** and **b** are perpendicular if and only if $\mathbf{a} \cdot \mathbf{b} = 0$.

EXAMPLE 7 (a) To show that the plane vectors $\mathbf{a} = \langle 8, 5\rangle$ and $\mathbf{b} = \langle -11, 17\rangle$ of Example 5 in Section 12.1 were not perpendicular, we need only have calculated their dot product $\mathbf{a} \cdot \mathbf{b} = -88 + 85 = -3$ and observed that its value is not zero. (b) Given the space vectors $\mathbf{a} = \langle 8, 5, -1\rangle$ and $\mathbf{b} = \langle -11, 17, -3\rangle$, we find that

$$\mathbf{a} \cdot \mathbf{b} = (8)(-11) + (5)(17) + (-1)(-3) = -88 + 85 + 3 = 0.$$

We may therefore conclude that $\mathbf{a}$ and $\mathbf{b}$ *are* perpendicular. ◆

EXAMPLE 8 Find the angles shown in the triangle of Fig. 12.2.13 with vertices at $A(2, -1, 0)$, $B(5, -4, 3)$, and $C(1, -3, 2)$.

Solution We apply Eq. (10) with $\theta = \angle A$, $\mathbf{a} = \overrightarrow{AB} = \langle 3, -3, 3\rangle$, and $\mathbf{b} = \overrightarrow{AC} = \langle -1, -2, 2\rangle$. This yields

$$\angle A = \cos^{-1}\left(\frac{\overrightarrow{AB} \cdot \overrightarrow{AC}}{|\overrightarrow{AB}||\overrightarrow{AC}|}\right) = \cos^{-1}\left(\frac{\langle 3, -3, 3\rangle \cdot \langle -1, -2, 2\rangle}{\sqrt{27}\sqrt{9}}\right)$$

$$= \cos^{-1}\left(\frac{9}{\sqrt{27}\sqrt{9}}\right) \approx 0.9553 \text{ (rad)} \approx 54.74°.$$

Similarly,

$$\angle B = \cos^{-1}\left(\frac{\overrightarrow{BA} \cdot \overrightarrow{BC}}{|\overrightarrow{BA}||\overrightarrow{BC}|}\right) = \cos^{-1}\left(\frac{\langle -3, 3, -3\rangle \cdot \langle -4, 1, -1\rangle}{\sqrt{27}\sqrt{18}}\right)$$

$$= \cos^{-1}\left(\frac{18}{\sqrt{27}\sqrt{18}}\right) \approx 0.6155 \text{ (rad)} \approx 35.26°.$$

Then $\angle C = 180° - \angle A - \angle B \approx 90°$. As a check, note that

$$\overrightarrow{CA} \cdot \overrightarrow{CB} = \langle 1, 2, -2\rangle \cdot \langle 4, -1, 1\rangle = 0.$$

So the angle at C is, indeed, a right angle. ◆

Direction Angles and Projections

The **direction angles** of the nonzero vector $\mathbf{a} = \langle a_1, a_2, a_3\rangle$ are the angles α, β, and γ that it makes with the vectors $\mathbf{i}$, $\mathbf{j}$, and $\mathbf{k}$, respectively (Fig. 12.2.14). The cosines of these angles, $\cos\alpha$, $\cos\beta$, and $\cos\gamma$, are called the **direction cosines** of the vector $\mathbf{a}$. When we replace $\mathbf{b}$ in Eq. (11) with $\mathbf{i}$, $\mathbf{j}$, and $\mathbf{k}$ in turn, we find that

$$\cos\alpha = \frac{\mathbf{a} \cdot \mathbf{i}}{|\mathbf{a}||\mathbf{i}|} = \frac{a_1}{|\mathbf{a}|},$$

$$\cos\beta = \frac{\mathbf{a} \cdot \mathbf{j}}{|\mathbf{a}||\mathbf{j}|} = \frac{a_2}{|\mathbf{a}|}, \quad \text{and} \qquad (12)$$

$$\cos\gamma = \frac{\mathbf{a} \cdot \mathbf{k}}{|\mathbf{a}||\mathbf{k}|} = \frac{a_3}{|\mathbf{a}|}.$$

That is, the direction cosines of $\mathbf{a}$ are the components of the *unit vector* $\mathbf{a}/|\mathbf{a}|$ with the same direction as $\mathbf{a}$. Consequently

$$\cos^2\alpha + \cos^2\beta + \cos^2\gamma = 1. \qquad (13)$$

EXAMPLE 9 Find the direction angles of the vector $\mathbf{a} = 2\mathbf{i} + 3\mathbf{j} - \mathbf{k}$.

Solution Because $|\mathbf{a}| = \sqrt{14}$, the equations in (12) give

$$\alpha = \cos^{-1}\left(\frac{2}{\sqrt{14}}\right) \approx 57.69°, \qquad \beta = \cos^{-1}\left(\frac{3}{\sqrt{14}}\right) \approx 36.70°,$$

$$\text{and} \qquad \gamma = \cos^{-1}\left(\frac{-1}{\sqrt{14}}\right) \approx 105.50°. \qquad ◆$$

FIGURE 12.2.13 The triangle of Example 8.

FIGURE 12.2.14 The direction angles of the vector $\mathbf{a}$.

Sometimes we need to find the component of one vector **a** in the direction of another *nonzero* vector **b**. Think of the two vectors located with the same initial point (Fig. 12.2.15). Then the (scalar) **component of a along b**, denoted by comp$_b$**a**, is numerically the length of the perpendicular projection of **a** onto the straight line determined by **b**. The number comp$_b$**a** is positive if the angle θ between **a** is acute (so **a** and **b** point in the same general direction) and negative if $\theta > \pi/2$. Thus comp$_b$**a** = $|\mathbf{a}|\cos\theta$ in either case. Equation (10) then gives

$$\text{comp}_b\mathbf{a} = \frac{|\mathbf{a}||\mathbf{b}|\cos\theta}{|\mathbf{b}|} = \frac{\mathbf{a}\cdot\mathbf{b}}{|\mathbf{b}|}. \tag{14}$$

There is no need to memorize this formula, for—in practice—we can always read comp$_b$**a** = $|\mathbf{a}|\cos\theta$ from the figure and then apply Eq. (10) to eliminate $\cos\theta$. Note that comp$_b$**a** is a scalar, not a vector.

FIGURE 12.2.15 The component of **a** along **b**.

EXAMPLE 10 Given $\mathbf{a} = \langle 4, -5, 3\rangle$ and $\mathbf{b} = \langle 2, 1, -2\rangle$, express **a** as the sum of a vector $\mathbf{a}_\parallel$ parallel to **b** and a vector $\mathbf{a}_\perp$ perpendicular to **b**.

Solution Our method of solution is motivated by the diagram in Fig. 12.2.16. We take

$$\mathbf{a}_\parallel = (\text{comp}_b\mathbf{a})\frac{\mathbf{b}}{|\mathbf{b}|} = \frac{\mathbf{a}\cdot\mathbf{b}}{|\mathbf{b}|^2}\mathbf{b} = \frac{8-5-6}{9}\mathbf{b}$$

$$= -\frac{1}{3}\langle 2, 1, -2\rangle = \left\langle -\frac{2}{3}, -\frac{1}{3}, \frac{2}{3}\right\rangle,$$

FIGURE 12.2.16 Construction of $\mathbf{a}_\parallel$ and $\mathbf{a}_\perp$.

and

$$\mathbf{a}_\perp = \mathbf{a} - \mathbf{a}_\parallel = \langle 4, -5, 3\rangle - \left\langle -\frac{2}{3}, -\frac{1}{3}, \frac{2}{3}\right\rangle = \left\langle \frac{14}{3}, -\frac{14}{3}, \frac{7}{3}\right\rangle.$$

The diagram makes our choice of $\mathbf{a}_\parallel$ plausible, and we have deliberately chosen $\mathbf{a}_\perp$ so that $\mathbf{a} = \mathbf{a}_\parallel + \mathbf{a}_\perp$. To verify that the vector $\mathbf{a}_\parallel$ is indeed parallel to **b**, we simply note that it is a scalar multiple of **b**. To verify that $\mathbf{a}_\perp$ is perpendicular to **b**, we compute the dot product

$$\mathbf{a}_\perp \cdot \mathbf{b} = \tfrac{28}{3} - \tfrac{14}{3} - \tfrac{14}{3} = 0.$$

Thus $\mathbf{a}_\parallel$ and $\mathbf{a}_\perp$ have the required properties. ◆

One important application of vector components is to the definition and computation of *work*. Recall that the work W done by a constant force F exerted along the line of motion in moving a particle a distance d is given by $W = Fd$. But what if the force is a constant vector **F** pointing in some direction other than the line of motion, as when a child pulls a sled against the resistance of friction (Fig. 12.2.17)? Suppose that **F** moves a particle along the line segment from P to Q, and let $\mathbf{D} = \overrightarrow{PQ}$ be the resulting *displacement vector* of the object (Fig. 12.2.18). Then the **work** W done by the force **F** in moving the object along the line from P to Q is, by definition, the product of the component of **F** along **D** and the distance moved:

$$W = (\text{comp}_\mathbf{D}\mathbf{F})|\mathbf{D}|. \tag{15}$$

FIGURE 12.2.17 The vector force **F** is constant but acts at an angle to the line of motion (Example 10).

FIGURE 12.2.18 The force vector **F** and displacement vector **D** in Eq. (16).

786 CHAPTER 12 Vectors, Curves, and Surfaces in Space

If we use Eq. (14) and substitute $\text{comp}_\mathbf{D} \mathbf{F} = (\mathbf{F} \cdot \mathbf{D})/|\mathbf{D}|$, we get

$$W = \mathbf{F} \cdot \mathbf{D} \tag{16}$$

for the work done by the constant force $\mathbf{F}$ in moving an object along the displacement vector $\mathbf{D} = \overrightarrow{PQ}$. This formula is the vector generalization of the scalar work formula $W = Fd$. Work is measured in foot-pounds (ft·lb) if distance is measured in feet and force in pounds. If metric units of meters (m) for distance and newtons (N) for force are used, then work is measured in joules (J). (One joule is approximately 0.7376 ft·lb.)

EXAMPLE 11 Suppose that the force vector in Fig. 12.2.17 is inclined at an angle of $30°$ from the ground. If the child exerts a constant force of 20 lb, how much work is done in pulling the sled a distance of one mile?

Solution We are given that $|\mathbf{F}| = 20$ (lb) and $|\mathbf{D}| = 5280$ (ft). Because $\cos 30° = \frac{1}{2}\sqrt{3}$, Eq. (16) yields

$$W = \mathbf{F} \cdot \mathbf{D} = |\mathbf{F}| \, |\mathbf{D}| \cos 30° = (20)(5280)\left(\tfrac{1}{2}\sqrt{3}\right) \approx 91452 \quad (\text{ft·lb}).$$

This may seem like a lot of work for a child to do. If the 1-mile trip takes an hour, then the child is generating *power* (work per unit time) at the rate of (91452 ft·lb)/(3600 s) ≈ 25.4 ft·lb/s. Because 1 horsepower (hp) is defined to be 550 ft·lb/s, the child's "power rating" is $25.4/550 \approx \frac{1}{20}$ hp. By comparison, an adult in excellent physical condition can climb the 2570 steps of the staircase of the CN tower in Toronto in less than 40 minutes. On October 29, 1989, Brendon Keenory of Toronto set the world's record for the fastest stairclimb there with a time of 7 min 52 s. Assuming that he climbed 1672 ft and weighed 160 lb, he generated an average of more than 0.988 hp over this time interval. ◆

12.2 TRUE/FALSE STUDY GUIDE

12.2 CONCEPTS: QUESTIONS AND DISCUSSION

1. Discuss the relation between a 3-dimensional vector and a point in space.
2. How does the dot product of two vectors resemble the ordinary product of two numbers? How do the two products differ?
3. Discuss the analogy between the absolute value of a number and the length of a vector.
4. Give an example of a real-world situation described by a triple of real numbers. In your example, do vector addition and scalar multiplication make any sense?

12.2 PROBLEMS

In Problems 1 through 6, find (a) $2\mathbf{a} + \mathbf{b}$, *(b)* $3\mathbf{a} - 4\mathbf{b}$, *(c)* $\mathbf{a} \cdot \mathbf{b}$, *(d)* $|\mathbf{a} - \mathbf{b}|$, *and (e)* $\mathbf{a}/|\mathbf{a}|$.

1. $\mathbf{a} = \langle 2, 5, -4 \rangle$, $\mathbf{b} = \langle 1, -2, -3 \rangle$
2. $\mathbf{a} = \langle -1, 0, 2 \rangle$, $\mathbf{b} = \langle 3, 4, -5 \rangle$
3. $\mathbf{a} = \mathbf{i} + \mathbf{j} + \mathbf{k}$, $\mathbf{b} = \mathbf{j} - \mathbf{k}$
4. $\mathbf{a} = 2\mathbf{i} - 3\mathbf{j} + 5\mathbf{k}$, $\mathbf{b} = 5\mathbf{i} + 3\mathbf{j} - 7\mathbf{k}$
5. $\mathbf{a} = 2\mathbf{i} - \mathbf{j}$, $\mathbf{b} = \mathbf{j} - 3\mathbf{k}$
6. $\mathbf{a} = \mathbf{i} - 2\mathbf{j} + 3\mathbf{k}$, $\mathbf{b} = \mathbf{i} + 3\mathbf{j} - 2\mathbf{k}$

7 through 12. Find, to the nearest degree, the angle between the vectors $\mathbf{a}$ and $\mathbf{b}$ in Problems 1 through 6.

13 through 18. Find $\text{comp}_\mathbf{a} \mathbf{b}$ and $\text{comp}_\mathbf{b} \mathbf{a}$ for the vectors $\mathbf{a}$ and $\mathbf{b}$ given in Problems 1 through 6.

In Problems 19 through 24, write the equation of the indicated sphere.

19. Center $(3, 1, 2)$, radius 5
20. Center $(-2, 1, -5)$, radius $\sqrt{7}$
21. One diameter: the segment joining $(3, 5, -3)$ and $(7, 3, 1)$
22. Center $(4, 5, -2)$, passing through the point $(1, 0, 0)$
23. Center $(0, 0, 2)$, tangent to the xy-plane
24. Center $(3, -4, 3)$, tangent to the xz-plane

In Problems 25 through 28, find the center and radius of the sphere with the given equation.

25. $x^2 + y^2 + z^2 + 4x - 6y = 0$
26. $x^2 + y^2 + z^2 - 8x - 9y + 10z + 40 = 0$
27. $3x^2 + 3y^2 + 3z^2 - 18z - 48 = 0$
28. $2x^2 + 2y^2 + 2z^2 = 7x + 9y + 11z$

In Problems 29 through 38, describe the graph of the given equation in geometric terms, using plain, clear language.

29. $z = 0$ **30.** $x = 0$
31. $z = 10$ **32.** $xy = 0$
33. $xyz = 0$ **34.** $x^2 + y^2 + z^2 + 7 = 0$
35. $x^2 + y^2 + z^2 = 0$ **36.** $x^2 + y^2 + z^2 - 2x + 1 = 0$
37. $x^2 + y^2 + z^2 - 6x + 8y + 25 = 0$
38. $x^2 + y^2 = 0$

*Two vectors are **parallel** provided that one is a scalar multiple of the other. Determine whether the vectors **a** and **b** in Problems 39 through 42 are parallel or perpendicular or neither.*

39. $\mathbf{a} = \langle 4, -2, 6 \rangle$ and $\mathbf{b} = \langle 6, -3, 9 \rangle$
40. $\mathbf{a} = \langle 4, -2, 6 \rangle$ and $\mathbf{b} = \langle 4, 2, 2 \rangle$
41. $\mathbf{a} = 12\mathbf{i} - 20\mathbf{j} + 16\mathbf{k}$ and $\mathbf{b} = -9\mathbf{i} + 15\mathbf{j} - 12\mathbf{k}$
42. $\mathbf{a} = 12\mathbf{i} - 20\mathbf{j} + 17\mathbf{k}$ and $\mathbf{b} = -9\mathbf{i} + 15\mathbf{j} + 24\mathbf{k}$

In Problems 43 and 44, determine whether or not the three given points lie on a single straight line.

43. $P(0, -2, 4)$, $Q(1, -3, 5)$, $R(4, -6, 8)$
44. $P(6, 7, 8)$, $Q(3, 3, 3)$, $R(12, 15, 18)$

In Problems 45 through 48, find (to the nearest degree) the three angles of the triangle with the given vertices.

45. $A(1, 0, 0)$, $B(0, 1, 0)$, $C(0, 0, 1)$
46. $A(1, 0, 0)$, $B(1, 2, 0)$, $C(1, 2, 3)$
47. $A(1, 1, 1)$, $B(3, -2, 3)$, $C(3, 4, 6)$
48. $A(1, 0, 0)$, $B(0, 1, 0)$, $C(-1, -2, -2)$

In Problems 49 through 52, find the direction angles of the vector represented by $\overrightarrow{PQ}$.

49. $P(1, -1, 0)$, $Q(3, 4, 5)$
50. $P(2, -3, 5)$, $Q(1, 0, -1)$
51. $P(-1, -2, -3)$, $Q(5, 6, 7)$
52. $P(0, 0, 0)$, $Q(5, 12, 13)$

*In Problems 53 and 54, find the work W done by the force **F** in moving a particle in a straight line from P to Q.*

53. $\mathbf{F} = \mathbf{i} - \mathbf{k}$; $P(0, 0, 0)$, $Q(3, 1, 0)$
54. $\mathbf{F} = 2\mathbf{i} - 3\mathbf{j} + 5\mathbf{k}$; $P(5, 3, -4)$, $Q(-1, -2, 5)$

55. Suppose that the force vector in Fig. 12.2.17 is inclined at an angle of 40° from the ground. If the child exerts a constant force of 40 N, how much heat energy (in calories) does the child expend in pulling the sled a distance of 1 km along the ground? [*Note:* 1 J of work requires an expenditure of 0.239 calories of energy.]

56. A 1000-lb dog sled has a coefficient of sliding friction of 0.2, so it requires a force with a horizontal component of 200 lb to keep it moving at a constant speed. Suppose that a dog-team harness is attached so that the team's force vector makes an angle of 5° with the horizontal. If the dog team pulls this sled at a speed of 10 mi/h, how much power (in horsepower) are the dogs generating? [*Note:* 1 hp is 550 ft·lb/s.]

57. Suppose that the horizontal and vertical components of the three vectors shown in Fig. 12.2.19 balance (the algebraic sum of the horizontal components is zero, as is the sum of the vertical components). How much work is done by the constant force **F** (parallel to the inclined plane) in pulling the weight mg up the inclined plane a vertical height h?

FIGURE 12.2.19 The inclined plane of Problem 57.

58. Prove the **Cauchy-Schwarz inequality:**

$$|\mathbf{a} \cdot \mathbf{b}| \leqq |\mathbf{a}| \, |\mathbf{b}|$$

for all pairs of vectors **a** and **b**.

59. Given two arbitrary vectors **a** and **b**, prove that they satisfy the **triangle inequality,**

$$|\mathbf{a} + \mathbf{b}| \leqq |\mathbf{a}| + |\mathbf{b}|.$$

[*Suggestion:* Square both sides.]

60. Prove that if **a** and **b** are arbitrary vectors, then

$$|\mathbf{a} - \mathbf{b}| \geqq |\mathbf{a}| - |\mathbf{b}|.$$

[*Suggestion:* Write $\mathbf{a} = (\mathbf{a} - \mathbf{b}) + \mathbf{b}$; then apply the triangle inequality of Problem 59.]

61. Use the dot product to construct a nonzero vector $\mathbf{w} = \langle w_1, w_2, w_3 \rangle$ perpendicular to both of the vectors $\mathbf{u} = \langle 1, 2, -3 \rangle$ and $\mathbf{v} = \langle 2, 0, 1 \rangle$.

62. The unit cube in the first octant in space has opposite vertices $O(0, 0, 0)$ and $P(1, 1, 1)$. Find the angle between the edge of the cube on the x-axis and the diagonal OP.

63. Prove that the point M given in Eq. (2) is indeed the midpoint of the segment $P_1 P_2$. [*Note:* You must prove *both* that M is equally distant from P_1 and P_2 *and* that M lies on the segment $P_1 P_2$.]

64. Given vectors **a** and **b**, let $a = |\mathbf{a}|$ and $b = |\mathbf{b}|$. Prove that the vector

$$\mathbf{c} = \frac{(b\mathbf{a} + a\mathbf{b})}{(a + b)}$$

bisects the angle between **a** and **b**.

65. Let **a**, **b**, and **c** be three vectors in the xy-plane with **a** and **b** nonzero and nonparallel. Show that there exist scalars α and β such that $\mathbf{c} = \alpha \mathbf{a} + \beta \mathbf{b}$. [*Suggestion:* Begin by expressing **a**, **b**, and **c** in terms of **i**, **j**, and **k**.]

66. Let $ax + by + c = 0$ be the equation of the line L in the xy-plane with normal vector $\mathbf{n}$. Let $P_0(x_0, y_0)$ be a point on this line and $P_1(x_1, y_1)$ be a point not on L. Prove that the perpendicular distance from P_1 to L is
$$d = \frac{|\mathbf{n} \cdot \overrightarrow{P_0 P_1}|}{|\mathbf{n}|} = \frac{|ax_1 + by_1 + c|}{\sqrt{a^2 + b^2}}.$$

67. Given the two points $A(3, -2, 4)$ and $B(5, 7, -1)$, write an equation in x, y, and z that says that the point $P(x, y, z)$ is equally distant from the points A and B. Then simplify this equation and give a geometric description of the set of all such points $P(x, y, z)$.

68. Given the fixed point $A(1, 3, 5)$, the point $P(x, y, z)$, and the vector $\mathbf{n} = \mathbf{i} - \mathbf{j} + 2\mathbf{k}$, use the dot product to help you write an equation in x, y, and z that says this: $\mathbf{n}$ and $\overrightarrow{AP}$ are perpendicular. Then simplify this equation and give a geometric description of all such points $P(x, y, z)$.

69. Prove that the points $(0, 0, 0)$, $(1, 1, 0)$, $(1, 0, 1)$, and $(0, 1, 1)$ are the vertices of a regular tetrahedron by showing that each of the six edges has length $\sqrt{2}$. Then use the dot product to find the angle between any two edges of the tetrahedron.

70. The methane molecule CH_4 is arranged with the four hydrogen atoms at the vertices of a regular tetrahedron and with the carbon atom at its center (Fig. 12.2.20). Suppose that the axes and scale are chosen so that the tetrahedron is that of Problem 69, with its center at $(\frac{1}{2}, \frac{1}{2}, \frac{1}{2})$. Find the bond angle α between the lines from the carbon atom to two of the hydrogen atoms.

FIGURE 12.2.20 The methane bond angle α of Problem 70.

12.3 THE CROSS PRODUCT OF VECTORS

We often need to find a vector that is perpendicular to each of two vectors $\mathbf{a}$ and $\mathbf{b}$ in space. A routine way of doing this is provided by the *cross product* $\mathbf{a} \times \mathbf{b}$ of the vectors $\mathbf{a}$ and $\mathbf{b}$. This vector product is quite unlike the dot product $\mathbf{a} \cdot \mathbf{b}$ in that $\mathbf{a} \cdot \mathbf{b}$ is a *scalar*, whereas $\mathbf{a} \times \mathbf{b}$ is a *vector*. For this reason $\mathbf{a} \times \mathbf{b}$ is sometimes called the *vector product* of the two vectors $\mathbf{a}$ and $\mathbf{b}$.

The **cross product** (or **vector product**) of the vectors $\mathbf{a} = \langle a_1, a_2, a_3 \rangle$ and $\mathbf{b} = \langle b_1, b_2, b_3 \rangle$ is defined algebraically by the formula

$$\mathbf{a} \times \mathbf{b} = \langle a_2 b_3 - a_3 b_2, a_3 b_1 - a_1 b_3, a_1 b_2 - a_2 b_1 \rangle. \tag{1}$$

Although this formula seems unmotivated, it has a redeeming feature: The product $\mathbf{a} \times \mathbf{b}$ is perpendicular both to $\mathbf{a}$ and to $\mathbf{b}$, as suggested in Fig. 12.3.1.

FIGURE 12.3.1 The cross product $\mathbf{a} \times \mathbf{b}$ is perpendicular to both $\mathbf{a}$ and $\mathbf{b}$.

THEOREM 1 Perpendicularity of the Cross Product
The cross product $\mathbf{a} \times \mathbf{b}$ is perpendicular both to $\mathbf{a}$ and to $\mathbf{b}$.

PROOF We show that $\mathbf{a} \times \mathbf{b}$ is perpendicular to $\mathbf{a}$ by showing that the dot product of $\mathbf{a}$ and $\mathbf{a} \times \mathbf{b}$ is zero. With the components as in Eq. (1), we find that

$$\mathbf{a} \cdot (\mathbf{a} \times \mathbf{b}) = a_1(a_2 b_3 - a_3 b_2) + a_2(a_3 b_1 - a_1 b_3) + a_3(a_1 b_2 - a_2 b_1)$$
$$= a_1 a_2 b_3 - a_1 a_3 b_2 + a_2 a_3 b_1 - a_2 a_1 b_3 + a_3 a_1 b_2 - a_3 a_2 b_1$$
$$= 0.$$

A similar computation shows that $\mathbf{b} \cdot (\mathbf{a} \times \mathbf{b}) = 0$ as well, so $\mathbf{a} \times \mathbf{b}$ is also perpendicular to the vector $\mathbf{b}$. ◄

You need not memorize Eq. (1), because there is an alternative version involving determinants that is easy both to remember and to use. Recall that a *determinant* of order 2 is defined as follows:

$$\begin{vmatrix} a_1 & a_2 \\ b_1 & b_2 \end{vmatrix} = a_1 b_2 - a_2 b_1. \tag{2}$$

EXAMPLE 1

$$\begin{vmatrix} 2 & -1 \\ 3 & 4 \end{vmatrix} = 2 \cdot 4 - (-1) \cdot 3 = 11. \qquad \blacklozenge$$

A determinant of order 3 can be defined in terms of determinants of order 2:

$$\begin{vmatrix} a_1 & a_2 & a_3 \\ b_1 & b_2 & b_3 \\ c_1 & c_2 & c_3 \end{vmatrix} = +a_1 \begin{vmatrix} b_2 & b_3 \\ c_2 & c_3 \end{vmatrix} - a_2 \begin{vmatrix} b_1 & b_3 \\ c_1 & c_3 \end{vmatrix} + a_3 \begin{vmatrix} b_1 & b_2 \\ c_1 & c_2 \end{vmatrix}. \tag{3}$$

Each element a_i of the first row is multiplied by the 2-by-2 "subdeterminant" obtained by deleting the row *and* column that contain a_i. Note in Eq. (3) that signs are attached to the a_i in accord with the checkerboard pattern

$$\begin{vmatrix} + & - & + \\ - & + & - \\ + & - & + \end{vmatrix}.$$

Equation (3) is an expansion of the 3-by-3 determinant along its first row. It can be expanded along any other row or column as well. For example, its expansion along its second column is

$$\begin{vmatrix} a_1 & a_2 & a_3 \\ b_1 & b_2 & b_3 \\ c_1 & c_2 & c_3 \end{vmatrix} = -a_2 \begin{vmatrix} b_1 & b_3 \\ c_1 & c_3 \end{vmatrix} + b_2 \begin{vmatrix} a_1 & a_3 \\ c_1 & c_3 \end{vmatrix} - c_2 \begin{vmatrix} a_1 & a_3 \\ b_1 & b_3 \end{vmatrix}.$$

In linear algebra it is shown that all such expansions yield the same value for the determinant.

Although we can expand a determinant of order 3 along any row or column, here we will use only expansions along the first row, as in Eq. (3) and Example 2.

EXAMPLE 2

$$\begin{vmatrix} 1 & 3 & -2 \\ 2 & -1 & 4 \\ -3 & 7 & 5 \end{vmatrix} = 1 \cdot \begin{vmatrix} -1 & 4 \\ 7 & 5 \end{vmatrix} - 3 \cdot \begin{vmatrix} 2 & 4 \\ -3 & 5 \end{vmatrix} + (-2) \cdot \begin{vmatrix} 2 & -1 \\ -3 & 7 \end{vmatrix}$$

$$= 1 \cdot (-5 - 28) + (-3) \cdot (10 + 12) + (-2) \cdot (14 - 3)$$

$$= -33 - 66 - 22 = -121. \qquad \blacklozenge$$

Equation (1) for the cross product of the vectors $\mathbf{a} = a_1 \mathbf{i} + a_2 \mathbf{j} + a_3 \mathbf{k}$ and $\mathbf{b} = b_1 \mathbf{i} + b_2 \mathbf{j} + b_3 \mathbf{k}$ is equivalent to

$$\mathbf{a} \times \mathbf{b} = \begin{vmatrix} a_2 & a_3 \\ b_2 & b_3 \end{vmatrix} \mathbf{i} - \begin{vmatrix} a_1 & a_3 \\ b_1 & b_3 \end{vmatrix} \mathbf{j} + \begin{vmatrix} a_1 & a_2 \\ b_1 & b_2 \end{vmatrix} \mathbf{k}. \tag{4}$$

This is easy to verify by expanding the 2-by-2 determinants on the right-hand side and noting that the three components of the right-hand side of Eq. (1) result. Motivated by Eq. (4), we write

$$\mathbf{a} \times \mathbf{b} = \begin{vmatrix} \mathbf{i} & \mathbf{j} & \mathbf{k} \\ a_1 & a_2 & a_3 \\ b_1 & b_2 & b_3 \end{vmatrix}. \tag{5}$$

The "symbolic determinant" in this equation is to be evaluated by expansion along its first row, just as in Eq. (3) and just as though it were an ordinary determinant with real number entries. The result of this expansion is the right-hand side of Eq. (4). The components of the *first* vector **a** in **a** × **b** form the *second* row of the 3-by-3 determinant, and the components of the *second* vector **b** form the *third* row. The order of the vectors **a** and **b** is important because, as we soon shall see, **a** × **b** is generally *not* equal to **b** × **a**: The cross product is *not commutative*.

Equation (5) for the cross product is the form most convenient for computational purposes.

EXAMPLE 3 If $\mathbf{a} = 3\mathbf{i} - \mathbf{j} + 2\mathbf{k}$ and $\mathbf{b} = 2\mathbf{i} + 2\mathbf{j} - \mathbf{k}$, then

$$\mathbf{a} \times \mathbf{b} = \begin{vmatrix} \mathbf{i} & \mathbf{j} & \mathbf{k} \\ 3 & -1 & 2 \\ 2 & 2 & -1 \end{vmatrix} = \begin{vmatrix} -1 & 2 \\ 2 & -1 \end{vmatrix} \mathbf{i} - \begin{vmatrix} 3 & 2 \\ 2 & -1 \end{vmatrix} \mathbf{j} + \begin{vmatrix} 3 & -1 \\ 2 & 2 \end{vmatrix} \mathbf{k}$$

$$= (1 - 4)\mathbf{i} - (-3 - 4)\mathbf{j} + (6 - (-2))\mathbf{k}.$$

Thus

$$\mathbf{a} \times \mathbf{b} = -3\mathbf{i} + 7\mathbf{j} + 8\mathbf{k}.$$

You might now pause to verify (by using the dot product) that the vector $-3\mathbf{i} + 7\mathbf{j} + 8\mathbf{k}$ is perpendicular both to **a** and to **b**. ◆

If the vectors **a** and **b** share the same initial point, then Theorem 1 implies that **a** × **b** is perpendicular to the plane determined by **a** and **b** (Fig. 12.3.2). There are still two possible directions for **a** × **b**, but if $\mathbf{a} \times \mathbf{b} \neq \mathbf{0}$, then the triple **a**, **b**, **a** × **b** is a *right-handed* triple in exactly the same sense as the triple **i**, **j**, **k**. Thus if the thumb of your right hand points in the direction of **a** × **b**, then your fingers curl in the direction of rotation (less than 180°) from **a** to **b**.

Once we have established the direction of **a** × **b**, we can describe the cross product in completely geometric terms by telling what the length |**a** × **b**| of the vector **a** × **b** is. This is given by the formula

$$|\mathbf{a} \times \mathbf{b}|^2 = |\mathbf{a}|^2|\mathbf{b}|^2 - (\mathbf{a} \cdot \mathbf{b})^2. \tag{6}$$

FIGURE 12.3.2 The vectors **a**, **b**, and **a** × **b**—in that order—form a right-handed triple.

We can verify this vector identity routinely (though tediously) by writing $\mathbf{a} = \langle a_1, a_2, a_3 \rangle$ and $\mathbf{b} = \langle b_1, b_2, b_3 \rangle$, computing both sides of Eq. (6), and then noting that the results are equal (Problem 36).

Geometric Significance of the Cross Product

Equation (6) tells us what |**a** × **b**| is, but Theorem 2 reveals the geometric significance of the cross product.

THEOREM 2 Length of the Cross Product
Let θ be the angle between the nonzero vectors **a** and **b** (measured so that $0 \leqq \theta \leqq \pi$). Then

$$|\mathbf{a} \times \mathbf{b}| = |\mathbf{a}|\,|\mathbf{b}| \sin \theta. \tag{7}$$

PROOF We begin with Eq. (6) and use the fact that $\mathbf{a} \cdot \mathbf{b} = |\mathbf{a}|\,|\mathbf{b}| \cos \theta$. Thus

$$|\mathbf{a} \times \mathbf{b}|^2 = |\mathbf{a}|^2|\mathbf{b}|^2 - (\mathbf{a} \cdot \mathbf{b})^2 = |\mathbf{a}|^2|\mathbf{b}|^2 - (|\mathbf{a}|\,|\mathbf{b}| \cos \theta)^2$$
$$= |\mathbf{a}|^2|\mathbf{b}|^2(1 - \cos^2 \theta) = |\mathbf{a}|^2|\mathbf{b}|^2 \sin^2 \theta.$$

Equation (7) now follows after we take the positive square root of both sides. (This is the correct root on the right-hand side because $\sin \theta \geq 0$ for $0 \leqq \theta \leqq \pi$.) ◂

COROLLARY Parallel Vectors

Two nonzero vectors **a** and **b** are parallel ($\theta = 0$ or $\theta = \pi$) if and only if $\mathbf{a} \times \mathbf{b} = \mathbf{0}$.

In particular, the cross product of any vector with itself is the zero vector. Also, Eq. (1) shows immediately that the cross product of any vector with the zero vector is the zero vector itself. Thus

$$\mathbf{a} \times \mathbf{a} = \mathbf{a} \times \mathbf{0} = \mathbf{0} \times \mathbf{a} = \mathbf{0} \tag{8}$$

for every vector **a**.

Equation (7) has an important geometric interpretation. Suppose that **a** and **b** are represented by adjacent sides of a parallelogram $PQRS$, with $\mathbf{a} = \overrightarrow{PQ}$ and $\mathbf{b} = \overrightarrow{PS}$ (Fig. 12.3.3). The parallelogram then has base of length $|\mathbf{a}|$ and height $|\mathbf{b}| \sin \theta$, so its area is

$$A = |\mathbf{a}|\,|\mathbf{b}| \sin \theta = |\mathbf{a} \times \mathbf{b}|. \tag{9}$$

FIGURE 12.3.3 The area of the parallelogram $PQRS$ is $|\mathbf{a} \times \mathbf{b}|$.

Thus *the length of the cross product* $\mathbf{a} \times \mathbf{b}$ *is numerically the same as the area of the parallelogram determined by* **a** *and* **b**. It follows that the area of the triangle PQS in Fig. 12.3.4, whose area is half that of the parallelogram, is

$$\tfrac{1}{2} A = \tfrac{1}{2} |\mathbf{a} \times \mathbf{b}| = \tfrac{1}{2} |\overrightarrow{PQ} \times \overrightarrow{PS}|. \tag{10}$$

Equation (10) gives a quick way to compute the area of a triangle—even one in space—without the need of finding any of its angles.

EXAMPLE 4 Find the area of the triangle with vertices $A(3, 0, -1)$, $B(4, 2, 5)$, and $C(7, -2, 4)$.

Solution $\overrightarrow{AB} = \langle 1, 2, 6 \rangle$ and $\overrightarrow{AC} = \langle 4, -2, 5 \rangle$, so

$$\overrightarrow{AB} \times \overrightarrow{AC} = \begin{vmatrix} \mathbf{i} & \mathbf{j} & \mathbf{k} \\ 1 & 2 & 6 \\ 4 & -2 & 5 \end{vmatrix} = 22\mathbf{i} + 19\mathbf{j} - 10\mathbf{k}.$$

FIGURE 12.3.4 The area of $\triangle PQS$ is $\tfrac{1}{2}|\mathbf{a} \times \mathbf{b}|$.

Therefore, by Eq. (10), the area of triangle ABC is

$$\tfrac{1}{2}\sqrt{22^2 + 19^2 + (-10)^2} = \tfrac{1}{2}\sqrt{945} \approx 15.37. \quad \blacklozenge$$

Now let **u**, **v**, **w** be a right-handed triple of mutually perpendicular *unit* vectors. The angle between any two of these is $\theta = \pi/2$, and $|\mathbf{u}| = |\mathbf{v}| = |\mathbf{w}| = 1$. Thus it follows from Eq. (7) that $\mathbf{u} \times \mathbf{v} = \mathbf{w}$. When we apply this observation to the basic unit vectors **i**, **j**, and **k** (Fig. 12.3.5), we see that

$$\mathbf{i} \times \mathbf{j} = \mathbf{k}, \quad \mathbf{j} \times \mathbf{k} = \mathbf{i}, \quad \text{and} \quad \mathbf{k} \times \mathbf{i} = \mathbf{j}. \tag{11a}$$

But

$$\mathbf{j} \times \mathbf{i} = -\mathbf{k}, \quad \mathbf{k} \times \mathbf{j} = -\mathbf{i}, \quad \text{and} \quad \mathbf{i} \times \mathbf{k} = -\mathbf{j}. \tag{11b}$$

FIGURE 12.3.5 The basic unit vectors in space.

These observations, together with the fact that

$$\mathbf{i} \times \mathbf{i} = \mathbf{j} \times \mathbf{j} = \mathbf{k} \times \mathbf{k} = \mathbf{0}, \tag{11c}$$

also follow directly from the original definition of the cross product [in the form in Eq. (5)]. The products in Eq. (11a) are easily remembered in terms of the sequence

$$\mathbf{i}, \quad \mathbf{j}, \quad \mathbf{k}, \quad \mathbf{i}, \quad \mathbf{j}, \quad \mathbf{k}, \quad \ldots.$$

The product of any two consecutive unit vectors, in the order in which they appear in this sequence, is the next one in the sequence.

Note *The cross product is not commutative:* $\mathbf{i} \times \mathbf{j} \neq \mathbf{j} \times \mathbf{i}$. Instead, it is **anticommutative:** For any two vectors $\mathbf{a}$ and $\mathbf{b}$, $\mathbf{a} \times \mathbf{b} = -(\mathbf{b} \times \mathbf{a})$. This is the first part of Theorem 3.

THEOREM 3 Algebraic Properties of the Cross Product
If $\mathbf{a}$, $\mathbf{b}$, and $\mathbf{c}$ are vectors and k is a real number, then

1. $\mathbf{a} \times \mathbf{b} = -(\mathbf{b} \times \mathbf{a})$; (12)
2. $(k\mathbf{a}) \times \mathbf{b} = \mathbf{a} \times (k\mathbf{b}) = k(\mathbf{a} \times \mathbf{b})$; (13)
3. $\mathbf{a} \times (\mathbf{b} + \mathbf{c}) = (\mathbf{a} \times \mathbf{b}) + (\mathbf{a} \times \mathbf{c})$; (14)
4. $\mathbf{a} \cdot (\mathbf{b} \times \mathbf{c}) = (\mathbf{a} \times \mathbf{b}) \cdot \mathbf{c}$; (15)
5. $\mathbf{a} \times (\mathbf{b} \times \mathbf{c}) = (\mathbf{a} \cdot \mathbf{c})\mathbf{b} - (\mathbf{a} \cdot \mathbf{b})\mathbf{c}$. (16)

The proofs of Eqs. (12) through (15) are straightforward applications of the definition of the cross product in terms of components. See Problem 33 for an outline of the proof of Eq. (16).

We can find cross products of vectors expressed in terms of the basic unit vectors $\mathbf{i}$, $\mathbf{j}$, and $\mathbf{k}$ by means of computations that closely resemble those of ordinary algebra. We simply apply the algebraic properties summarized in Theorem 3 together with the relations in Eq. (11) giving the various products of the three unit vectors. We must be careful to preserve the order of factors, because vector multiplication is not commutative—although, of course, we should not hesitate to use Eq. (12).

EXAMPLE 5 $(\mathbf{i} - 2\mathbf{j} + 3\mathbf{k}) \times (3\mathbf{i} + 2\mathbf{j} - 4\mathbf{k})$

$= 3(\mathbf{i} \times \mathbf{i}) + 2(\mathbf{i} \times \mathbf{j}) - 4(\mathbf{i} \times \mathbf{k}) - 6(\mathbf{j} \times \mathbf{i}) - 4(\mathbf{j} \times \mathbf{j})$
$\quad + 8(\mathbf{j} \times \mathbf{k}) + 9(\mathbf{k} \times \mathbf{i}) + 6(\mathbf{k} \times \mathbf{j}) - 12(\mathbf{k} \times \mathbf{k})$

$= 3 \cdot \mathbf{0} + 2\mathbf{k} - 4 \cdot (-\mathbf{j}) - 6 \cdot (-\mathbf{k}) - 4 \cdot \mathbf{0} + 8\mathbf{i} + 9\mathbf{j} + 6 \cdot (-\mathbf{i}) - 12 \cdot \mathbf{0}$

$= 2\mathbf{i} + 13\mathbf{j} + 8\mathbf{k}.$ ◆

Scalar Triple Products

Let us examine the product $\mathbf{a} \cdot (\mathbf{b} \times \mathbf{c})$ that appears in Eq. (15). This expression would not make sense were the parentheses instead around $\mathbf{a} \cdot \mathbf{b}$, because $\mathbf{a} \cdot \mathbf{b}$ is a scalar, and thus we could not form the cross product of $\mathbf{a} \cdot \mathbf{b}$ with the vector $\mathbf{c}$. This means that we may omit the parentheses—the expression $\mathbf{a} \cdot \mathbf{b} \times \mathbf{c}$ is not ambiguous—but we keep them for extra clarity. The dot product of the vectors $\mathbf{a}$ and $\mathbf{b} \times \mathbf{c}$ is a real number, called the **scalar triple product** of the vectors $\mathbf{a}$, $\mathbf{b}$, and $\mathbf{c}$. Equation (15) implies the curious fact that we can interchange the operations $\cdot$ (dot) and $\times$ (cross) without affecting the value of the expression:

$$\mathbf{a} \cdot (\mathbf{b} \times \mathbf{c}) = (\mathbf{a} \times \mathbf{b}) \cdot \mathbf{c}$$

for all vectors $\mathbf{a}$, $\mathbf{b}$, and $\mathbf{c}$.

To compute the scalar triple product in terms of components, write $\mathbf{a} = \langle a_1, a_2, a_3 \rangle$, $\mathbf{b} = \langle b_1, b_2, b_3 \rangle$, and $\mathbf{c} = \langle c_1, c_2, c_3 \rangle$. Then

$$\mathbf{b} \times \mathbf{c} = (b_2 c_3 - b_3 c_2)\mathbf{i} - (b_1 c_3 - b_3 c_1)\mathbf{j} + (b_1 c_2 - b_2 c_1)\mathbf{k},$$

so

$$\mathbf{a} \cdot (\mathbf{b} \times \mathbf{c}) = a_1(b_2 c_3 - b_3 c_2) - a_2(b_1 c_3 - b_3 c_1) + a_3(b_1 c_2 - b_2 c_1).$$

But the expression on the right is the value of the 3-by-3 determinant

$$\mathbf{a} \cdot (\mathbf{b} \times \mathbf{c}) = \begin{vmatrix} a_1 & a_2 & a_3 \\ b_1 & b_2 & b_3 \\ c_1 & c_2 & c_3 \end{vmatrix}. \tag{17}$$

This is the quickest way to compute the scalar triple product.

EXAMPLE 6 If $\mathbf{a} = 2\mathbf{i} - 3\mathbf{k}$, $\mathbf{b} = \mathbf{i} + \mathbf{j} + \mathbf{k}$, and $\mathbf{c} = 4\mathbf{j} - \mathbf{k}$, then

$$\mathbf{a} \cdot (\mathbf{b} \times \mathbf{c}) = \begin{vmatrix} 2 & 0 & -3 \\ 1 & 1 & 1 \\ 0 & 4 & -1 \end{vmatrix}$$

$$= +2 \cdot \begin{vmatrix} 1 & 1 \\ 4 & -1 \end{vmatrix} - 0 \cdot \begin{vmatrix} 1 & 1 \\ 0 & -1 \end{vmatrix} + (-3) \cdot \begin{vmatrix} 1 & 1 \\ 0 & 4 \end{vmatrix}$$

$$= 2 \cdot (-5) + (-3) \cdot 4 = -22.$$

FIGURE 12.3.6 The volume of the parallelepiped is $|\mathbf{a} \cdot (\mathbf{b} \times \mathbf{c})|$.

The importance of the scalar triple product for applications depends on the following geometric interpretation. Let $\mathbf{a}$, $\mathbf{b}$, and $\mathbf{c}$ be three vectors with the same initial point. Figure 12.3.6 shows the parallelepiped determined by these vectors—that is, with arrows representing these vectors as adjacent edges. If the vectors $\mathbf{a}$, $\mathbf{b}$, and $\mathbf{c}$ are coplanar (lie in a single plane), then the parallelepiped is *degenerate* and its volume is zero. Theorem 4 holds whether or not the three vectors are coplanar, but it is most useful when they are not.

THEOREM 4 **Scalar Triple Products and Volume**
The volume V of the parallelepiped determined by the vectors $\mathbf{a}$, $\mathbf{b}$, and $\mathbf{c}$ is the absolute value of the scalar triple product $\mathbf{a} \cdot (\mathbf{b} \times \mathbf{c})$; that is,

$$V = |\mathbf{a} \cdot (\mathbf{b} \times \mathbf{c})|. \tag{18}$$

PROOF If the three vectors are coplanar, then $\mathbf{a}$ and $\mathbf{b} \times \mathbf{c}$ are perpendicular, so $V = |\mathbf{a} \cdot (\mathbf{b} \times \mathbf{c})| = 0$. Assume, then, that they are not coplanar. By Eq. (9) the area of the base (determined by $\mathbf{b}$ and $\mathbf{c}$) of the parallelepiped is $A = |\mathbf{b} \times \mathbf{c}|$.

Now let α be the *acute* angle between $\mathbf{a}$ and the vector $\mathbf{b} \times \mathbf{c}$ that is perpendicular to the base. Then the height of the parallelepiped is $h = |\mathbf{a}| \cos \alpha$. If θ is the angle between the vectors $\mathbf{a}$ and $\mathbf{b} \times \mathbf{c}$, then either $\theta = \alpha$ or $\theta = \pi - \alpha$. Hence $\cos \alpha = |\cos \theta|$, so

$$V = Ah = |\mathbf{b} \times \mathbf{c}| \, |\mathbf{a}| \cos \alpha = |\mathbf{a}| \, |\mathbf{b} \times \mathbf{c}| \, |\cos \theta| = |\mathbf{a} \cdot (\mathbf{b} \times \mathbf{c})|.$$

Thus we have verified Eq. (18). ◂

EXAMPLE 7 Figure 12.3.7 shows the pyramid $OPQR$ and the parallelepiped both determined by the vectors

$$\mathbf{a} = \overrightarrow{OP} = \langle 3, 2, -1 \rangle, \quad \mathbf{b} = \overrightarrow{OQ} = \langle -2, 5, 1 \rangle, \quad \text{and} \quad \mathbf{c} = \overrightarrow{OR} = \langle 2, 1, 5 \rangle.$$

The volume of the pyramid is $V = \frac{1}{3} Ah$, where h is its height and the area A of its base OPQ is *half* the area of the corresponding base of the parallelepiped. It therefore follows from Eq. (17) and (18) that V is one-sixth the volume of the parallelepiped:

$$V = \frac{1}{6} |\mathbf{a} \cdot (\mathbf{b} \times \mathbf{c})| = \frac{1}{6} \begin{vmatrix} 3 & 2 & -1 \\ -2 & 5 & 1 \\ 2 & 1 & 5 \end{vmatrix} = \frac{108}{6} = 18.$$

FIGURE 12.3.7 The pyramid (and parallelepiped) of Example 7.

EXAMPLE 8 Use the scalar triple product to show that the points $A(1, -1, 2)$, $B(2, 0, 1)$, $C(3, 2, 0)$, and $D(5, 4, -2)$ are coplanar.

Solution It's enough to show that the vectors $\overrightarrow{AB} = \langle 1, 1, -1 \rangle$, $\overrightarrow{AC} = \langle 2, 3, -2 \rangle$, and $\overrightarrow{AD} = \langle 4, 5, -4 \rangle$ are coplanar. But their scalar triple product is

$$\begin{vmatrix} 1 & 1 & -1 \\ 2 & 3 & -2 \\ 4 & 5 & -4 \end{vmatrix} = 1 \cdot (-2) - 1 \cdot 0 + (-1) \cdot (-2) = 0,$$

so Theorem 4 guarantees that the parallelepiped determined by these three vectors has volume zero. Hence the four given points are coplanar. ◆

The cross product occurs quite often in scientific applications. For example, suppose that a body in space is free to rotate around the fixed point O. If a force $\mathbf{F}$ acts at a point P of the body, that force causes the body to rotate. This effect is measured by the **torque vector** τ defined by the relation

$$\tau = \mathbf{r} \times \mathbf{F},$$

where $\mathbf{r} = \overrightarrow{OP}$, the straight line through O determined by τ is the axis of rotation, and the length

$$|\tau| = |\mathbf{r}|\,|\mathbf{F}| \sin\theta$$

is the **moment** of the force $\mathbf{F}$ around this axis (Fig. 12.3.8).

Another application of the cross product involves the force exerted on a moving charged particle by a magnetic field. This force is important in particle accelerators, mass spectrometers, and television picture tubes; controlling the paths of the ions is accomplished through the interplay of electric and magnetic fields. In such circumstances, the force $\mathbf{F}$ on the particle due to a magnetic field depends on three things: the charge q of the particle, its velocity vector $\mathbf{v}$, and the magnetic field vector $\mathbf{B}$ at the instantaneous location of the particle. And it turns out that

$$\mathbf{F} = (q\mathbf{v}) \times \mathbf{B}.$$

FIGURE 12.3.8 The torque vector τ is normal to both $\mathbf{r}$ and $\mathbf{F}$.

12.3 TRUE/FALSE STUDY GUIDE

12.3 CONCEPTS: QUESTIONS AND DISCUSSION

1. How does the cross product of two vectors resemble the ordinary product of two numbers? How do the two products differ?
2. Discuss the differences and the similarities between the dot product and the cross product of two vectors.
3. A surveyor measures a polygonal plot of land by first finding the coordinates of the vertices of its bounding polygon. Outline how the surveyor might then proceed to use cross products to calculate the area of the plot.

12.3 PROBLEMS

Find $\mathbf{a} \times \mathbf{b}$ *in Problems 1 through 4.*

1. $\mathbf{a} = \langle 5, -1, -2 \rangle$, $\mathbf{b} = \langle -3, 2, 4 \rangle$
2. $\mathbf{a} = \langle 3, -2, 0 \rangle$, $\mathbf{b} = \langle 0, 3, -2 \rangle$
3. $\mathbf{a} = \mathbf{i} - \mathbf{j} + 3\mathbf{k}$, $\mathbf{b} = -2\mathbf{i} + 3\mathbf{j} + \mathbf{k}$
4. $\mathbf{a} = 4\mathbf{i} + 2\mathbf{j} - 2\mathbf{k}$, $\mathbf{b} = 2\mathbf{i} - 5\mathbf{j} + 5\mathbf{k}$

In Problems 5 and 6, find the cross product of the given 2-dimensional vectors $\mathbf{a} = \langle a_1, a_2 \rangle$ *and* $\mathbf{b} = \langle b_1, b_2 \rangle$ *by first "extending" them to 3-dimensional vectors* $\mathbf{a} = \langle a_1, a_2, 0 \rangle$ *and* $\mathbf{b} = \langle b_1, b_2, 0 \rangle$.

5. $\mathbf{a} = \langle 2, -3 \rangle$ and $\mathbf{b} = \langle 4, 5 \rangle$
6. $\mathbf{a} = -5\mathbf{i} + 2\mathbf{j}$ and $\mathbf{b} = 7\mathbf{i} - 11\mathbf{j}$

In Problems 7 and 8, find two different unit vectors $\mathbf{u}$ *and* $\mathbf{v}$ *both of which are perpendicular to both the given vectors* $\mathbf{a}$ *and* $\mathbf{b}$.

7. $\mathbf{a} = \langle 3, 12, 0 \rangle$ and $\mathbf{b} = \langle 0, 4, 3 \rangle$
8. $\mathbf{a} = \mathbf{i} + 2\mathbf{j} + 3\mathbf{k}$ and $\mathbf{b} = 2\mathbf{i} + 3\mathbf{j} + 5\mathbf{k}$

9. Apply Eq. (5) to verify the equations in (11a).
10. Apply Eq. (5) to verify the equations in (11b).
11. Prove that the vector product is not associative by comparing $\mathbf{a} \times (\mathbf{b} \times \mathbf{c})$ with $(\mathbf{a} \times \mathbf{b}) \times \mathbf{c}$ in the case $\mathbf{a} = \mathbf{i}$, $\mathbf{b} = \mathbf{i} + \mathbf{j}$, and $\mathbf{c} = \mathbf{i} + \mathbf{j} + \mathbf{k}$.
12. Find nonzero vectors $\mathbf{a}$, $\mathbf{b}$, and $\mathbf{c}$ such that $\mathbf{a} \times \mathbf{b} = \mathbf{a} \times \mathbf{c}$ but $\mathbf{b} \neq \mathbf{c}$.
13. Suppose that the three vectors $\mathbf{a}$, $\mathbf{b}$, and $\mathbf{c}$ are mutually perpendicular. Prove that $\mathbf{a} \times (\mathbf{b} \times \mathbf{c}) = \mathbf{0}$.
14. Find the area of the triangle with vertices $P(1, 1, 0)$, $Q(1, 0, 1)$, and $R(0, 1, 1)$.
15. Find the area of the triangle with vertices $P(1, 3, -2)$, $Q(2, 4, 5)$, and $R(-3, -2, 2)$.
16. Find the volume of the parallelepiped with adjacent edges $\overrightarrow{OP}$, $\overrightarrow{OQ}$, and $\overrightarrow{OR}$, where P, Q, and R are the points given in Problem 14.

17. (a) Find the volume of the parallelepiped with adjacent edges $\overrightarrow{OP}$, $\overrightarrow{OQ}$, and $\overrightarrow{OR}$, where P, Q, and R are the points given in Problem 15. (b) Find the volume of the pyramid with vertices O, P, Q, and R.

18. Find a unit vector **n** perpendicular to the plane through the points P, Q, and R of Problem 15. Then find the distance from the origin to this plane by computing $\mathbf{n} \cdot \overrightarrow{OP}$.

In Problems 19 through 22, determine whether or not the four given points A, B, C, and D are coplanar. If not, find the volume of the pyramid with these four points as its vertices, given that its volume is one-sixth that of the parallelepiped spanned by $\overrightarrow{AB}$, $\overrightarrow{AC}$, and $\overrightarrow{AD}$.

19. $A(1, 3, -2)$, $B(3, 4, 1)$, $C(2, 0, -2)$, and $D(4, 8, 4)$

20. $A(13, -25, -37)$, $B(25, -14, -22)$, $C(24, -38, -25)$, and $D(26, 10, -19)$

21. $A(5, 2, -3)$, $B(6, 4, 0)$, $C(7, 5, 1)$, and $D(14, 14, 18)$

22. $A(25, 22, -33)$, $B(36, 34, -20)$, $C(27, 25, -29)$, and $D(34, 34, -12)$

23. Figure 12.3.9 shows a polygonal plot of land, with angles and lengths measured by a surveyor. First find the coordinates of each vertex. Then use the vector product [as in Eq. (10)] to calculate the area of the plot.

FIGURE 12.3.9 Problem 23.

24. Repeat Problem 23 with the plot shown in Fig. 12.3.10.

FIGURE 12.3.10 Problem 24.

25. Repeat Problem 23 with the plot shown in Fig. 12.3.11. [*Suggestion:* First divide the plot into two triangles.]

FIGURE 12.3.11 Problem 25.

26. Repeat Problem 23 with the plot shown in Fig. 12.3.12.

FIGURE 12.3.12 Problem 26.

27. Apply Eq. (5) to verify Eq. (12), the anticommutativity of the vector product.

28. Apply Eq. (17) to verify the identity for scalar triple products stated in Eq. (15).

29. Suppose that P and Q are points on a line L in space. Let A be a point not on L (Fig. 12.3.13). (a) Calculate in two ways the area of the triangle APQ to show that the perpendicular distance from A to the line L is

$$d = \frac{|\overrightarrow{AP} \times \overrightarrow{AQ}|}{|\overrightarrow{PQ}|}.$$

(b) Use this formula to compute the distance from the point $(1, 0, 1)$ to the line through the two points $P(2, 3, 1)$ and $Q(-3, 1, 4)$.

FIGURE 12.3.13 Problem 29.

30. Suppose that A is a point not on the plane determined by the three points P, Q, and R. Calculate in two ways the volume of the pyramid $APQR$ to show that the perpendicular distance from A to this plane is

$$d = \frac{|\overrightarrow{AP} \cdot (\overrightarrow{AQ} \times \overrightarrow{AR})|}{|\overrightarrow{PQ} \times \overrightarrow{PR}|}.$$

Use this formula to compute the distance from the point $(1, 0, 1)$ to the plane through the points $P(2, 3, 1)$, $Q(3, -1, 4)$, and $R(0, 0, 2)$.

31. Suppose that P_1 and Q_1 are two points on the line L_1 and that P_2 and Q_2 are two points on the line L_2. If the lines L_1 and L_2 are not parallel, then the perpendicular distance d between them is the projection of $\overrightarrow{P_1 P_2}$ onto a vector **n** that is perpendicular both to $\overrightarrow{P_1 Q_1}$ and $\overrightarrow{P_2 Q_2}$. Prove that

$$d = \frac{|\overrightarrow{P_1 P_2} \cdot (\overrightarrow{P_1 Q_1} \times \overrightarrow{P_2 Q_2})|}{|\overrightarrow{P_1 Q_1} \times \overrightarrow{P_2 Q_2}|}.$$

796 CHAPTER 12 Vectors, Curves, and Surfaces in Space

32. Use the following method to establish that the **vector triple product** $(\mathbf{a} \times \mathbf{b}) \times \mathbf{c}$ is equal to $(\mathbf{a} \cdot \mathbf{c})\mathbf{b} - (\mathbf{b} \cdot \mathbf{c})\mathbf{a}$. (a) Let $\mathbf{I}$ be a unit vector in the direction of $\mathbf{a}$ and let $\mathbf{J}$ be a unit vector perpendicular to $\mathbf{I}$ and parallel to the plane of $\mathbf{a}$ and $\mathbf{b}$. Let $\mathbf{K} = \mathbf{I} \times \mathbf{J}$. Explain why there are scalars $a_1, b_1, b_2, c_1, c_2,$ and c_3 such that

$$\mathbf{a} = a_1 \mathbf{I}, \quad \mathbf{b} = b_1 \mathbf{I} + b_2 \mathbf{J}, \quad \text{and} \quad \mathbf{c} = c_1 \mathbf{I} + c_2 \mathbf{J} + c_3 \mathbf{K}.$$

(b) Now show that

$$(\mathbf{a} \times \mathbf{b}) \times \mathbf{c} = -a_1 b_2 c_2 \mathbf{I} + a_1 b_2 c_1 \mathbf{J}.$$

(c) Finally, substitute for $\mathbf{I}$ and $\mathbf{J}$ in terms of $\mathbf{a}$ and $\mathbf{b}$.

33. By permutation of the vectors $\mathbf{a}$, $\mathbf{b}$, and $\mathbf{c}$, deduce from Problem 32 that

$$\mathbf{a} \times (\mathbf{b} \times \mathbf{c}) = (\mathbf{a} \cdot \mathbf{c})\mathbf{b} - (\mathbf{a} \cdot \mathbf{b})\mathbf{c}$$

[this is Eq. (16)].

34. Deduce from the orthogonality properties of the vector product that the vector $(\mathbf{a} \times \mathbf{b}) \times (\mathbf{c} \times \mathbf{d})$ can be written in the form $r_1 \mathbf{a} + r_2 \mathbf{b}$ and in the form $s_1 \mathbf{c} + s_2 \mathbf{d}$.

35. Consider the triangle in the xy-plane that has vertices $(x_1, y_1, 0)$, $(x_2, y_2, 0)$, and $(x_3, y_3, 0)$. Use the vector product to prove that the area of this triangle is *half* the *absolute value* of the determinant

$$\begin{vmatrix} 1 & x_1 & y_1 \\ 1 & x_2 & y_2 \\ 1 & x_3 & y_3 \end{vmatrix}.$$

36. Given the vectors $\mathbf{a} = \langle a_1, a_2, a_3 \rangle$ and $\mathbf{b} = \langle b_1, b_2, b_3 \rangle$, verify Eq. (6),

$$|\mathbf{a} \times \mathbf{b}|^2 = |\mathbf{a}|^2 |\mathbf{b}|^2 - (\mathbf{a} \cdot \mathbf{b})^2,$$

by computing each side in terms of the components of $\mathbf{a}$ and $\mathbf{b}$.

12.4 LINES AND PLANES IN SPACE

Just as in the plane, a straight line in space is determined by any two points P_0 and P_1 that lie on it. We may write $\mathbf{v} = \overrightarrow{P_0 P_1}$—meaning that the directed line segment $\overrightarrow{P_0 P_1}$ represents the vector $\mathbf{v}$—to describe the "direction of the line." Thus, alternatively, a line in space can be specified by giving a point P_0 on it *and* a [nonzero] vector $\mathbf{v}$ that determines the direction of the line.

To investigate equations that describe lines in space, let us begin with a straight line L that passes through the point $P_0(x_0, y_0, z_0)$ and is parallel to the vector $\mathbf{v} = a\mathbf{i} + b\mathbf{j} + c\mathbf{k}$ (Fig. 12.4.1). Then another point $P(x, y, z)$ lies on the line L if and only if the vectors $\mathbf{v}$ and $\overrightarrow{P_0 P}$ are parallel, in which case

$$\overrightarrow{P_0 P} = t\mathbf{v} \tag{1}$$

for some real number t. If $\mathbf{r}_0 = \overrightarrow{OP_0}$ and $\mathbf{r} = \overrightarrow{OP}$ are the position vectors of the points P_0 and P, respectively, then $\overrightarrow{P_0 P} = \mathbf{r} - \mathbf{r}_0$. Hence Eq. (1) gives the **vector equation**

$$\mathbf{r} = \mathbf{r}_0 + t\mathbf{v} \tag{2}$$

describing the line L. As indicated in Fig. 12.4.1, $\mathbf{r}$ is the position vector of an *arbitrary* point P on the line L, and Eq. (2) gives $\mathbf{r}$ in terms of the parameter t, the position vector $\mathbf{r}_0$ of a *fixed* point P_0 on L, and the fixed vector $\mathbf{v}$ that determines the direction of L.

The left- and right-hand sides of Eq. (2) are equal, and each side is a vector. So corresponding components are also equal. When we write the resulting equations, we get a scalar description of the line L. Because $\mathbf{r}_0 = \langle x_0, y_0, z_0 \rangle$ and $\mathbf{r} = \langle x, y, z \rangle$, Eq. (2) thereby yields the three scalar equations

$$x = x_0 + at, \quad y = y_0 + bt, \quad z = z_0 + ct. \tag{3}$$

FIGURE 12.4.1 Finding the equation of the line L that passes through the point P_0 and is parallel to the vector $\mathbf{v}$.

FIGURE 12.4.2 The line L of Example 1.

These are **parametric equations** of the line L that passes through the point (x_0, y_0, z_0) and is parallel to the vector $\mathbf{v} = \langle a, b, c \rangle$.

EXAMPLE 1 Write parametric equations of the line L that passes through the points $P_1(1, 2, 2)$ and $P_2(3, -1, 3)$ of Fig. 12.4.2.

Solution The line L is parallel to the vector

$$\mathbf{v} = \overrightarrow{P_1 P_2} = (3\mathbf{i} - \mathbf{j} + 3\mathbf{k}) - (\mathbf{i} + 2\mathbf{j} + 2\mathbf{k}) = 2\mathbf{i} - 3\mathbf{j} + \mathbf{k},$$

so we take $a = 2$, $b = -3$, and $c = 1$. With P_1 as the fixed point, the equations in (3) give

$$x = 1 + 2t, \quad y = 2 - 3t, \quad z = 2 + t$$

as parametric equations of L. In contrast, with P_2 as the fixed point and with the vector

$$-2\mathbf{v} = -4\mathbf{i} + 6\mathbf{j} - 2\mathbf{k}$$

(parallel to $\mathbf{v}$) as the direction vector, the equations in (3) yield the parametric equations

$$x = 3 - 4t, \quad y = -1 + 6t, \quad z = 3 - 2t.$$

Thus the parametric equations of a line are not unique. ◆

Given two straight lines L_1 and L_2 with parametric equations

$$x = x_1 + a_1 t, \quad y = y_1 + b_1 t, \quad z = z_1 + c_1 t \quad (4)$$

and

$$x = x_2 + a_2 s, \quad y = y_2 + b_2 s, \quad z = z_2 + c_2 s, \quad (5)$$

respectively, we can see at a glance whether or not L_1 and L_2 are parallel. Because L_1 is parallel to $\mathbf{v}_1 = \langle a_1, b_1, c_1 \rangle$ and L_2 is parallel to $\mathbf{v}_2 = \langle a_2, b_2, c_2 \rangle$, it follows that the lines L_1 and L_2 are parallel if and only if the vectors $\mathbf{v}_1$ and $\mathbf{v}_2$ are scalar multiples of each other (Fig. 12.4.3). If the two lines are not parallel, we can attempt to find a point of intersection by solving the equations

$$x_1 + a_1 t = x_2 + a_2 s \quad \text{and} \quad y_1 + b_1 t = y_2 + b_2 s$$

simultaneously for s and t. If these values of s and t also satisfy the equation $z_1 + c_1 t = z_2 + c_2 s$, then we have found a point of intersection. Its rectangular coordinates can be found by substituting the resulting value of t into Eq. (4) [or the resulting value of s into Eq. (5)]. Otherwise, the lines L_1 and L_2 do not intersect. Two nonparallel and nonintersecting lines in space are called **skew lines** (Fig. 12.4.4).

FIGURE 12.4.3 Parallel lines.

FIGURE 12.4.4 Skew lines.

EXAMPLE 2 The line L_1 with parametric equations

$$x = 1 + 2t, \quad y = 2 - 3t, \quad z = 2 + t$$

passes through the point $P_1(1, 2, 2)$ (discovered by substituting $t = 0$) and is parallel to the vector $\mathbf{v}_1 = \langle 2, -3, 1 \rangle$. The line L_2 with parametric equations

$$x = 3 + 4t, \quad y = 1 - 6t, \quad z = 5 + 2t$$

passes through the point $P_2(3, 1, 5)$ and is parallel to the vector $\mathbf{v}_2 = \langle 4, -6, 2 \rangle$. Because $\mathbf{v}_2 = 2\mathbf{v}_1$, we see that L_1 and L_2 are parallel.

But are L_1 and L_2 actually different lines, or are we perhaps dealing with two different parametrizations of the same line? To answer this question, we note that $\overrightarrow{P_1 P_2} = \langle 2, -1, 3 \rangle$ is not a multiple of, and therefore is not parallel to, $\mathbf{v}_1 = \langle 2, -3, 1 \rangle$. Thus the point P_2 does not lie on the line L_1, and hence the lines L_1 and L_2 are indeed distinct. ◆

If all the coefficients a, b, and c in (3) are nonzero, then we can eliminate the parameter t. Simply solve each equation for t and then set the resulting expressions equal to each other. This gives

$$\frac{x - x_0}{a} = \frac{y - y_0}{b} = \frac{z - z_0}{c}. \quad (6)$$

These are called the **symmetric equations** of the line L. If one or more of a or b or c is zero, this means that L lies in a plane parallel to one of the coordinate planes, and in this case the line does not have symmetric equations. For example, if $c = 0$, then L lies in the horizontal plane $z = z_0$. Of course, it is still possible to write equations for L that don't include the parameter t; if $c = 0$, for instance, but a and b are nonzero, then we could describe the line L as the set of points (x, y, z) satisfying the equations

$$\frac{x - x_0}{a} = \frac{y - y_0}{b}, \qquad z = z_0.$$

EXAMPLE 3 Find both parametric and symmetric equations of the line L through the points $P_0(3, 1, -2)$ and $P_1(4, -1, 1)$. Find also the points at which L intersects the three coordinate planes.

Solution The line L is parallel to the vector $\mathbf{v} = \overrightarrow{P_0 P_1} = \langle 1, -2, 3 \rangle$, so we take $a = 1$, $b = -2$, and $c = 3$. The equations in (3) then give the parametric equations

$$x = 3 + t, \qquad y = 1 - 2t, \qquad z = -2 + 3t$$

of L, and the equations in (6) give the symmetric equations

$$\frac{x - 3}{1} = \frac{y - 1}{-2} = \frac{z + 2}{3}.$$

To find the point at which L intersects the xy-plane, we set $z = 0$ in the symmetric equations. This gives

$$\frac{x - 3}{1} = \frac{y - 1}{-2} = \frac{2}{3},$$

and so $x = \frac{11}{3}$ and $y = -\frac{1}{3}$. Thus L meets the xy-plane at the point $(\frac{11}{3}, -\frac{1}{3}, 0)$. Similarly, $x = 0$ gives $(0, 7, -11)$ for the point where L meets the yz-plane, and $y = 0$ gives $(\frac{7}{2}, 0, -\frac{1}{2})$ for its intersection with the xz-plane. ◆

Planes in Space

A plane $\mathcal{P}$ in space is determined by a point $P_0(x_0, y_0, z_0)$ through which $\mathcal{P}$ passes and a line through P_0 that is normal to $\mathcal{P}$. Alternatively, we may be given P_0 on $\mathcal{P}$ and a vector $\mathbf{n} = \langle a, b, c \rangle$ normal to the plane $\mathcal{P}$. The point $P(x, y, z)$ lies on the plane $\mathcal{P}$ if and only if the vectors $\mathbf{n}$ and $\overrightarrow{P_0 P}$ are perpendicular (Fig. 12.4.5), in which case $\mathbf{n} \cdot \overrightarrow{P_0 P} = 0$. We write $\overrightarrow{P_0 P} = \mathbf{r} - \mathbf{r}_0$, where $\mathbf{r}$ and $\mathbf{r}_0$ are the position vectors $\mathbf{r} = \overrightarrow{OP}$ and $\mathbf{r}_0 = \overrightarrow{OP_0}$ of the points P and P_0, respectively. Thus we obtain a **vector equation**

$$\mathbf{n} \cdot (\mathbf{r} - \mathbf{r}_0) = 0 \tag{7}$$

of the plane $\mathcal{P}$.

If we substitute $\mathbf{n} = \langle a, b, c \rangle$, $\mathbf{r} = \langle x, y, z \rangle$, and $\mathbf{r}_0 = \langle x_0, y_0, z_0 \rangle$ into Eq. (7), we thereby obtain a **scalar equation**

FIGURE 12.4.5 Because $\mathbf{n}$ is normal to $\mathcal{P}$, it follows that $\mathbf{n}$ is normal to $\overrightarrow{P_0 P}$ for all points P in $\mathcal{P}$.

$$a(x - x_0) + b(y - y_0) + c(z - z_0) = 0 \tag{8}$$

of the plane through $P_0(x_0, y_0, z_0)$ with **normal vector** $\mathbf{n} = \langle a, b, c \rangle$.

EXAMPLE 4 An equation of the plane through $P_0(-1, 5, 2)$ with normal vector $\mathbf{n} = \langle 1, -3, 2 \rangle$ is

$$1 \cdot (x + 1) + (-3) \cdot (y - 5) + 2 \cdot (z - 2) = 0;$$

that is, $x - 3y + 2z = -12$. ◆

IMPORTANT The coefficients of x, y, and z in the last equation are the components of the normal vector. This is always the case, because we can write Eq. (8) in the form

$$ax + by + cz = d, \tag{9}$$

where $d = ax_0 + by_0 + cz_0$. Conversely, every *linear equation* in x, y, and z of the form in Eq. (9) represents a plane in space provided that the coefficients a, b, and c are not all zero. The reason is that if $c \neq 0$ (for instance), then we can choose x_0 and y_0 arbitrarily and solve the equation $ax_0 + by_0 + cz_0 = d$ for z_0. With these values, Eq. (9) takes the form

$$ax + by + cz = ax_0 + by_0 + cz_0;$$

that is,

$$a(x - x_0) + b(y - y_0) + c(z - z_0) = 0,$$

so this equation represents the plane through (x_0, y_0, z_0) with normal vector $\langle a, b, c \rangle$.

FIGURE 12.4.6 The normal vector **n** as a cross product (Example 5).

EXAMPLE 5 Find an equation for the plane through the three points $P(2, 4, -3)$, $Q(3, 7, -1)$, and $R(4, 3, 0)$.

Solution We want to use Eq. (8), so we first need a vector **n** that is normal to the plane in question. One easy way to obtain such a normal vector is by using the cross product. Let

$$\mathbf{n} = \overrightarrow{PQ} \times \overrightarrow{PR} = \begin{vmatrix} \mathbf{i} & \mathbf{j} & \mathbf{k} \\ 1 & 3 & 2 \\ 2 & -1 & 3 \end{vmatrix} = 11\mathbf{i} + \mathbf{j} - 7\mathbf{k}.$$

Because $\overrightarrow{PQ}$ and $\overrightarrow{PR}$ are in the plane, their cross product **n** is normal to the plane (Fig. 12.4.6). Hence the plane has equation

$$11(x - 2) + (y - 4) - 7(z + 3) = 0.$$

After simplifying, we write the equation as

$$11x + y - 7z = 47.$$

◆

Two planes with normal vectors **n** and **m** are said to be **parallel** provided that **n** and **m** are parallel. Otherwise, the two planes meet in a straight line (Fig. 12.4.7), and we can find the angle θ between the normal vectors **n** and **m** (Fig. 12.4.8). We then define the **angle** between the two planes to be either θ or $\pi - \theta$, whichever is an acute angle.

FIGURE 12.4.7 The intersection of two nonparallel planes is a straight line.

EXAMPLE 6 Find the angle θ between the planes with equations

$$2x + 3y - z = -3 \quad \text{and} \quad 4x + 5y + z = 1.$$

Then write symmetric equations of their line of intersection L.

Solution The vectors $\mathbf{n} = \langle 2, 3, -1 \rangle$ and $\mathbf{m} = \langle 4, 5, 1 \rangle$ are normal to the two planes, so

$$\cos \theta = \frac{\mathbf{n} \cdot \mathbf{m}}{|\mathbf{n}| |\mathbf{m}|} = \frac{22}{\sqrt{14}\sqrt{42}}.$$

FIGURE 12.4.8 Vectors **m** and **n** normal to the planes $\mathcal{P}$ and $\mathcal{Q}$, respectively.

Hence $\theta = \cos^{-1}(\frac{11}{21}\sqrt{3}) \approx 24.87°$.

To determine the line of intersection L of the two planes, we need first to find a point P_0 that lies on L. We can do this by substituting an arbitrarily chosen value of x into the equations of the given planes and then solving the resulting equations for y and z. With $x = 1$ we get the equations

$$2 + 3y - z = -3,$$
$$4 + 5y + z = 1.$$

The common solution is $y = -1$, $z = 2$. Thus the point $P_0(1, -1, 2)$ lies on the line L.

Next we need a vector **v** parallel to L. The vectors **n** and **m** normal to the two planes are both perpendicular to L, so their cross product is parallel to L. Alternatively, we can find a second point P_1 on L by substituting a second value of x into the equations of the given planes and solving for y and z, as before. With $x = 5$ we obtain the equations

$$10 + 3y - z = -3,$$
$$20 + 5y + z = 1,$$

with common solution $y = -4$, $z = 1$. Thus we obtain a second point $P_1(5, -4, 1)$ on L and thereby the vector

$$\mathbf{v} = \overrightarrow{P_0 P_1} = \langle 4, -3, -1 \rangle$$

parallel to L. From Eq. (6) we now find symmetric equations

$$\frac{x-1}{4} = \frac{y+1}{-3} = \frac{z-2}{-1}$$

of the line of intersection of the two given planes. ◆

Finally, we may note that the symmetric equations of a line L present the line as an intersection of planes: We can rewrite the equations in (6) in the form

$$b(x - x_0) - a(y - y_0) = 0,$$
$$c(x - x_0) - a(z - z_0) = 0, \quad \quad (10)$$
$$c(y - y_0) - b(z - z_0) = 0.$$

These are the equations of three planes that intersect in the line L. The first has normal vector $\langle b, -a, 0 \rangle$, a vector parallel to the xy-plane. So the first plane is perpendicular to the xy-plane. Similarly, the second plane is perpendicular to the xz-plane and the third is perpendicular to the yz-plane.

The equations in (10) are symmetric equations of the line that passes through the point $P_0(x_0, y_0, z_0)$ and is parallel to $\mathbf{v} = \langle a, b, c \rangle$. Unlike the equations in (6), these equations are meaningful whether or not all the components a, b, and c are nonzero. They have a special form, though, if one of the three components is zero. If, say, $a = 0$, then the first two equations in (10) take the form $x = x_0$. The line is then the intersection of the two planes $x = x_0$ and $c(y - y_0) = b(z - z_0)$.

EXAMPLE 7 In Example 3 we saw that the line L through the point $P_0(3, 1, -2)$ and $P_1(4, -1, 1)$ has symmetric equations

$$\frac{x-3}{1} = \frac{y-1}{-2} = \frac{z+2}{3}.$$

Proceeding to rewrite these equations as in (10), we obtain first the equations

$$-2(x - 3) = y - 1,$$
$$3(x - 3) = z + 2,$$
$$3(y - 1) = -2(z + 2)$$

and then (upon simplification) the equations

$$2x + y = 7,$$
$$3x - z = 11,$$
$$3y + 2z = -1$$

that represent L as the intersection of three planes, each of them parallel to one of the three coordinate axes in space. Figure 12.4.9 shows a computer plot of these three planes intersecting in the line L. ◆

FIGURE 12.4.9 The line L of Example 7 is the intersection of the plane $\mathcal{P}_1$ parallel to the z-axis, the plane $\mathcal{P}_2$ parallel to the y-axis, and the plane $\mathcal{P}_3$ parallel to the x-axis.

12.4 TRUE/FALSE STUDY GUIDE

12.4 CONCEPTS: QUESTIONS AND DISCUSSION

1. Figure 12.4.10 shows the possible configuration of two lines L_1 and L_2 in the xy-plane. We see that the intersection of L_1 and L_2 can consists of either one point, no points, or infinitely many points. Explain why this geometric observation implies that two linear equations $a_1 x + b_1 y = c_1$ and $a_2 x + b_2 y = c_2$ in two unknowns x and y can have either a single simultaneous solution (x, y), no solution, or infinitely many different solutions.

(a) Two intersecting lines: a unique solution.

(b) Two parallel lines: no solution.

(c) Two coincident lines: infinitely many solutions.

FIGURE 12.4.10 (a) The nonparallel lines L_1 and L_2 intersect in a single point. (b) The distinct parallel lines L_1 and L_2 have no point of intersection. (c) The coincident lines L_1 and L_2 have infinitely many points in common.

In each of the following cases, describe similarly the possible configurations and hence the possible number of points of intersection of the indicated number of lines or planes. Translate your geometric conclusion into a statement about the possible number of solutions of a system of two or three linear equations in two or three unknowns.

2. Three lines in the plane.
3. Two lines in space.
3. Three planes in space.

12.4 PROBLEMS

In Problems 1 through 4, write parametric equations of the straight line that passes through the point P and is parallel to the vector **v**.

1. $P(0, 0, 0)$, $\mathbf{v} = \mathbf{i} + 2\mathbf{j} + 3\mathbf{k}$
2. $P(3, -4, 5)$, $\mathbf{v} = -2\mathbf{i} + 7\mathbf{j} + 3\mathbf{k}$
3. $P(4, 13, -3)$, $\mathbf{v} = 2\mathbf{i} - 3\mathbf{k}$
4. $P(17, -13, -31)$, $\mathbf{v} = \langle -17, 13, 31 \rangle$

In Problems 5 through 8, write parametric equations of the straight line that passes through the points P_1 and P_2.

5. $P_1(0, 0, 0)$, $P_2(-6, 3, 5)$
6. $P_1(3, 5, 7)$, $P_2(6, -8, 10)$
7. $P_1(3, 5, 7)$, $P_2(6, 5, 4)$
8. $P_1(29, -47, 13)$, $P_2(73, 53, -67)$

In Problems 9 through 14, write both parametric and symmetric equations for the indicated straight line.

9. Through $P(2, 3, -4)$ and parallel to $\mathbf{v} = \langle 1, -1, -2 \rangle$
10. Through $P(2, 5, -7)$ and $Q(4, 3, 8)$
11. Through $P(1, 1, 1)$ and perpendicular to the xy-plane
12. Through the origin and perpendicular to the plane with equation $x + y + z = 1$
13. Through $P(2, -3, 4)$ and perpendicular to the plane with equation $2x - y + 3z = 4$
14. Through $P(2, -1, 5)$ and parallel to the line with parametric equations $x = 3t, y = 2 + t, z = 2 - t$

In Problems 15 through 20, determine whether the two lines L_1 and L_2 are parallel, skew, or intersecting. If they intersect, find the point of intersection.

15. L_1: $x - 2 = \frac{1}{2}(y + 1) = \frac{1}{3}(z - 3)$;
    L_2: $\frac{1}{3}(x - 5) = \frac{1}{2}(y - 1) = z - 4$
16. L_1: $\frac{1}{4}(x - 11) = y - 6 = -\frac{1}{2}(z + 5)$;
    L_2: $\frac{1}{6}(x - 13) = -\frac{1}{3}(y - 2) = \frac{1}{8}(z - 5)$
17. L_1: $x = 6 + 2t$, $y = 5 + 2t$, $z = 7 + 3t$;
    L_2: $x = 7 + 3s$, $y = 5 + 3s$, $z = 10 + 5s$
18. L_1: $x = 14 + 3t$, $y = 7 + 2t$, $z = 21 + 5t$;
    L_2: $x = 5 + 3s$, $y = 15 + 5s$, $z = 10 + 7s$

19. L_1: $\frac{1}{6}(x-7) = \frac{1}{4}(y+5) = -\frac{1}{8}(z-9)$;
    L_2: $-\frac{1}{9}(x-11) = -\frac{1}{6}(y-7) = \frac{1}{12}(z-13)$

20. L_1: $x = 13 + 12t$, $y = -7 + 20t$, $z = 11 - 28t$;
    L_2: $x = 22 + 9s$, $y = 8 + 15s$, $z = -10 - 21s$

*In Problems 21 through 24, write an equation of the plane with normal vector **n** that passes through the point P.*

21. $P(0, 0, 0)$, $\mathbf{n} = \langle 1, 2, 3 \rangle$
22. $P(3, -4, 5)$, $\mathbf{n} = \langle -2, 7, 3 \rangle$
23. $P(5, 12, 13)$, $\mathbf{n} = \mathbf{i} - \mathbf{k}$
24. $P(5, 12, 13)$, $\mathbf{n} = \mathbf{j}$

In Problems 25 through 32, write an equation of the indicated plane.

25. Through $P(5, 7, -6)$ and parallel to the xz-plane.
26. Through $P(1, 0, -1)$ with normal vector $\mathbf{n} = \langle 2, 2, -1 \rangle$.
27. Through $P(10, 4, -3)$ with normal vector $\mathbf{n} = \langle 7, 11, 0 \rangle$.
28. Through $P(1, -3, 2)$ with normal vector $\mathbf{n} = \overrightarrow{OP}$.
29. Through the origin and parallel to the plane with equation $3x + 4y = z + 10$.
30. Through $P(5, 1, 4)$ and parallel to the plane with equation $x + y - 2z = 0$.
31. Through the origin and the points $P(1, 1, 1)$ and $Q(1, -1, 3)$.
32. Through the points $A(1, 0, -1)$, $B(3, 3, 2)$, and $C(4, 5, -1)$.

In Problems 33 and 34, write an equation of the plane that contains both the point P and the line L.

33. $P(2, 4, 6)$; L: $x = 7 - 3t$, $y = 3 + 4t$, $z = 5 + 2t$
34. $P(13, -7, 29)$; L: $x = 17 - 9t$, $y = 23 + 14t$, $z = 35 - 41t$

In Problems 35 through 38, determine whether the line L and the plane $\mathcal{P}$ intersect or are parallel. If they intersect, find the point of intersection.

35. L: $x = 7 - 4t$, $y = 3 + 6t$, $z = 9 + 5t$;
    $\mathcal{P}$: $4x + y + 2z = 17$
36. L: $x = 15 + 7t$, $y = 10 + 12t$, $z = 5 - 4t$;
    $\mathcal{P}$: $12x - 5y + 6z = 50$
37. L: $x = 3 + 2t$, $y = 6 - 5t$, $z = 2 + 3t$;
    $\mathcal{P}$: $3x + 2y - 4z = 1$
38. L: $x = 15 - 3t$, $y = 6 - 5t$, $z = 21 - 14t$;
    $\mathcal{P}$: $23x + 29y - 31z = 99$

In Problems 39 through 42, find the angle between the planes with the given equations.

39. $x = 10$ and $x + y + z = 0$
40. $2x - y + z = 5$ and $x + y - z = 1$
41. $x - y - 2z = 1$ and $x - y - 2z = 5$
42. $2x + y + z = 4$ and $3x - y - z = 3$

In Problems 43 through 46, write both parametric and symmetric equations of the line of intersection of the indicated planes.

43. The planes of Problem 39
44. The planes of Problem 40
45. The planes of Problem 41
46. The planes of Problem 42

47. Write symmetric equations for the line through $P(3, 3, 1)$ that is parallel to the line of Problem 46.
48. Find an equation of the plane through $P(3, 3, 1)$ that is perpendicular to the planes $x + y = 2z$ and $2x + z = 10$.
49. Find an equation of the plane through $(1, 1, 1)$ that intersects the xy-plane in the same line as does the plane $3x + 2y - z = 6$.
50. Find an equation for the plane that passes through the point $P(1, 3, -2)$ and contains the line of intersection of the planes $x - y + z = 1$ and $x + y - z = 1$.
51. Find an equation of the plane that passes through the points $P(1, 0, -1)$ and $Q(2, 1, 0)$ and is parallel to the line of intersection of the planes $x + y + z = 5$ and $3x - y = 4$.
52. Prove that the lines $x - 1 = \frac{1}{2}(y+1) = z - 2$ and $x - 2 = \frac{1}{3}(y-2) = \frac{1}{2}(z-4)$ intersect. Find an equation of the [only] plane that contains them both.
53. Prove that the line of intersection of the planes $x + 2y - z = 2$ and $3x + 2y + 2z = 7$ is parallel to the line $x = 1 + 6t$, $y = 3 - 5t$, $z = 2 - 4t$. Find an equation of the plane determined by these two lines.
54. Show that the perpendicular distance D from the point $P_0(x_0, y_0, z_0)$ to the plane $ax + by + cz = d$ is

$$D = \frac{|ax_0 + by_0 + cz_0 - d|}{\sqrt{a^2 + b^2 + c^2}}.$$

[*Suggestion:* The line that passes through P_0 and is perpendicular to the given plane has parametric equations $x = x_0 + at$, $y = y_0 + bt$, $z = z_0 + ct$. Let $P_1(x_1, y_1, z_1)$ be the point of this line, corresponding to $t = t_1$, at which it intersects the given plane. Solve for t_1, and then compute $D = |\overrightarrow{P_0 P_1}|$.]

In Problems 55 and 56, use the formula of Problem 54 to find the distance between the given point and the given plane.

55. The origin and the plane $x + y + z = 10$
56. The point $P(5, 12, -13)$ and the plane with equation $3x + 4y + 5z = 12$
57. Prove that any two skew lines lie in parallel planes.
58. Use the formula of Problem 54 to show that the perpendicular distance D between the two parallel planes $ax + by + cz + d_1 = 0$ and $ax + by + cz + d_2 = 0$ is

$$D = \frac{|d_1 - d_2|}{\sqrt{a^2 + b^2 + c^2}}.$$

59. The line L_1 is described by the equations

$$x - 1 = 2y + 2, \quad z = 4.$$

The line L_2 passes through the points $P(2, 1, -3)$ and $Q(0, 8, 4)$. (a) Show that L_1 and L_2 are skew lines. (b) Use the results of Problems 57 and 58 to find the perpendicular distance between L_1 and L_2.

60. Find the shortest distance between points of the line L_1 with parametric equations

$$x = 7 + 2t, \quad y = 11 - 5t, \quad z = 13 + 6t$$

and the line L_2 of intersection of the planes $3x - 2y + 4z = 10$ and $5x + 3y - 2z = 15$.

12.5 CURVES AND MOTION IN SPACE

In Section 10.4 we discussed parametric curves in the plane. Now think of a point that moves along a curve in three-dimensional space. We can describe this point's changing position by means of *parametric equations*

$$x = f(t), \qquad y = g(t), \qquad z = h(t) \tag{1}$$

that specify its coordinates as functions of time t. A **parametric curve** C in space is (by definition) simply a triple (f, g, h) of such *coordinate functions*. But often it is useful to refer informally to C as the trajectory in space that is traced out by a moving point with these coordinate functions. Space curves exhibit a number of interesting new phenomena that we did not see with plane curves.

EXAMPLE 1 Figure 12.5.1 shows a common *trefoil knot* in space defined by the parametric equations

$$x(t) = \left(2 + \cos \tfrac{3}{2}t\right) \cos t, \qquad y(t) = \left(2 + \cos \tfrac{3}{2}t\right) \sin t, \qquad z(t) = \sin \tfrac{3}{2}t.$$

Actually, to enhance the three-dimensional appearance of this curve's shape, we have plotted in the figure a thin tubular surface whose centerline is the knot itself. The viewpoint for the computer plot is so chosen that we are looking down on the curve from a point on the positive z-axis. ◆

FIGURE 12.5.1 A tubular knot whose centerline is the parametric curve of Example 1.

EXAMPLE 2 Figure 12.5.2 shows simultaneously the circle

$$x(t) = 4 \cos t, \qquad y(t) = 4 \sin t, \qquad z(t) \equiv 0$$

in the xy-plane, the ellipse

$$x(t) = 5 \cos t, \qquad y(t) \equiv 0, \qquad z(t) = 3 \sin t$$

in the xz-plane, and the ellipse

$$x(t) \equiv 0, \qquad y(t) = 3 \cos t, \qquad z(t) = 5 \sin t$$

in the yz-plane. Here, again, we actually have plotted thin tubular tori having these closed curves as centerlines. Can you see that any two of these curves are unlinked, but that the three together apparently cannot be "pulled apart"? ◆

FIGURE 12.5.2 The Borromean rings of Example 2.

FIGURE 12.5.3 The position vector $\mathbf{r} = \langle x, y, z \rangle$ of a moving particle in space.

FIGURE 12.5.4 The point of Example 3 moves in a helical path.

Vector-Valued Functions

The changing location of a point moving along the parametric curve in (1) can be described by giving its **position vector**

$$\mathbf{r}(t) = x(t)\mathbf{i} + y(t)\mathbf{j} + z(t)\mathbf{k} = \langle x(t), y(t), z(t) \rangle, \tag{2}$$

or simply

$$\mathbf{r} = x\mathbf{i} + y\mathbf{j} + z\mathbf{k} = \langle x, y, z \rangle,$$

whose components are the coordinate functions of the moving point (Fig. 12.5.3). Equation (2) defines a **vector-valued function** that associates with the number t the vector $\mathbf{r}(t)$. In the case of a plane curve described by a two-dimensional position vector, we may suppress the third component in Eq. (2) and write $\mathbf{r}(t) = x(t)\mathbf{i} + y(t)\mathbf{j} = \langle x(t), y(t) \rangle$.

EXAMPLE 3 The position vector

$$\mathbf{r}(t) = \mathbf{i}\cos t + \mathbf{j}\sin t + t\mathbf{k} \tag{3}$$

describes the **helix** of Fig. 12.5.4. Because $x^2 + y^2 = \cos^2 t + \sin^2 t = 1$ for all t, the projection $(x(t), y(t))$ into the xy-plane moves around and around the unit circle. Meanwhile, because $z = t$, the point $(\cos t, \sin t, t)$ steadily moves upward on the vertical cylinder in space that stands above and below the circle $x^2 + y^2 = 1$ in the xy-plane. The familiar corkscrew shape of the helix appears everywhere from the coiled springs of an automobile to the *double helix* model of the DNA molecule that carries the genetic information of living cells (Fig. 12.5.5). ◆

Much of the calculus of (ordinary) real-valued functions applies to vector-valued functions. To begin with, the **limit** of a vector-valued function $\mathbf{r} = \langle f, g, h \rangle$ is *defined* as follows:

FIGURE 12.5.5 The intertwined helices that model the DNA molecule served as a model for the DNA Tower in Kings Park, Perth, Australia. For a fascinating account of the discovery of the role of the helix as the genetic basis for life itself, see James D. Watson, *The Double Helix* (New York: Atheneum, 1968).

$$\lim_{t \to a} \mathbf{r}(t) = \left\langle \lim_{t \to a} f(t), \lim_{t \to a} g(t), \lim_{t \to a} h(t) \right\rangle$$
$$= \mathbf{i}\left(\lim_{t \to a} f(t)\right) + \mathbf{j}\left(\lim_{t \to a} g(t)\right) + \mathbf{k}\left(\lim_{t \to a} h(t)\right), \tag{4}$$

provided that the limits in the last three expressions exist. Thus we take limits of vector-valued functions by taking limits of their component functions.

Curves and Motion in Space **SECTION 12.5** 805

We say that $\mathbf{r} = \mathbf{r}(t)$ is **continuous** at the number a provided that

$$\lim_{t \to a} \mathbf{r}(t) = \mathbf{r}(a).$$

This amounts to saying that $\mathbf{r}$ is continuous at a if and only if its component functions f, g, and h are continuous at a.

The **derivative** $\mathbf{r}'(t)$ of the vector-valued function $\mathbf{r}(t)$ is defined in almost exactly the same way as the derivative of a real-valued function. Specifically,

$$\mathbf{r}'(t) = \lim_{\Delta t \to 0} \frac{\mathbf{r}(t + \Delta t) - \mathbf{r}(t)}{\Delta t}, \tag{5}$$

FIGURE 12.5.6 Geometry of the derivative of a vector-valued function.

provided that this limit exists. Figures 12.5.6 and 12.5.7 correctly suggest that the **derivative vector**

$$\mathbf{r}'(t) = \frac{d\mathbf{r}}{dt} = D_t[\mathbf{r}(t)]$$

will be tangent to the curve C with position vector $\mathbf{r}(t)$. For this reason, we call $\mathbf{r}'(t)$ a **tangent vector** to the curve C at the corresponding point P provided that $\mathbf{r}'(t)$ exists and is nonzero there. The **tangent line** to C at this point P with position vector $\mathbf{r}(t)$ is then the line through P determined by $\mathbf{r}'(t)$.

Our next result implies the simple *but important* fact that the derivative vector $\mathbf{r}'(t)$ can be calculated by **componentwise differentiation** of $\mathbf{r}(t)$—that is, by differentiating separately the component functions of $\mathbf{r}(t)$.

THEOREM 1 Componentwise Differentiation

FIGURE 12.5.7 The derivative vector is tangent to the curve at the point of evaluation.

Suppose that

$$\mathbf{r}(t) = \langle f(t), g(t), h(t) \rangle = f(t)\mathbf{i} + g(t)\mathbf{j} + h(t)\mathbf{k},$$

where f, g, and h are differentiable functions. Then

$$\mathbf{r}'(t) = \langle f'(t), g'(t), h'(t) \rangle = f'(t)\mathbf{i} + g'(t)\mathbf{j} + h'(t)\mathbf{k}. \tag{6}$$

That is, if $\mathbf{r} = x\mathbf{i} + y\mathbf{j} + z\mathbf{k}$, then

$$\frac{d\mathbf{r}}{dt} = \frac{dx}{dt}\mathbf{i} + \frac{dy}{dt}\mathbf{j} + \frac{dz}{dt}\mathbf{k}.$$

PROOF We take the limit in Eq. (5) simply by taking limits of components. We find that

$$\mathbf{r}'(t) = \lim_{\Delta t \to 0} \frac{\Delta \mathbf{r}}{\Delta t} = \lim_{\Delta t \to 0} \frac{\mathbf{r}(t + \Delta t) - \mathbf{r}(t)}{\Delta t}$$

$$= \lim_{\Delta t \to 0} \frac{f(t + \Delta t)\mathbf{i} + g(t + \Delta t)\mathbf{j} + h(t + \Delta t)\mathbf{k} - f(t)\mathbf{i} - g(t)\mathbf{j} - h(t)\mathbf{k}}{\Delta t}$$

$$= \left(\lim_{\Delta t \to 0} \frac{f(t + \Delta t) - f(t)}{\Delta t} \right)\mathbf{i} + \left(\lim_{\Delta t \to 0} \frac{g(t + \Delta t) - g(t)}{\Delta t} \right)\mathbf{j}$$

$$+ \left(\lim_{\Delta t \to 0} \frac{h(t + \Delta t) - h(t)}{\Delta t} \right)\mathbf{k}$$

$$= f'(t)\mathbf{i} + g'(t)\mathbf{j} + h'(t)\mathbf{k}. \qquad ◂$$

EXAMPLE 4 Find parametric equations of the line tangent to the helix C of Example 3 at the point $P(-1, 0, \pi)$ where $t = \pi$.

Solution Componentwise differentiation of $\mathbf{r}(t) = \mathbf{i}\cos t + \mathbf{j}\sin t + t\mathbf{k}$ yields

$$\mathbf{r}'(t) = -\mathbf{i}\sin t + \mathbf{j}\cos t + \mathbf{k},$$

so the vector tangent to C at P is $\mathbf{r}'(\pi) = -\mathbf{j} + \mathbf{k} = \langle 0, -1, 1 \rangle$. It follows that the parametric equations of the line tangent at P—with its own position vector $\mathbf{r}(\pi) + t\mathbf{r}'(\pi)$—are

$$x = -1, \qquad y = -t, \qquad z = \pi + t.$$

In particular, we see that this tangent line lies in the vertical plane $x = -1$. ◆

Theorem 2 tells us that the formulas for computing derivatives of sums and products of vector-valued functions are formally similar to those for real-valued functions.

THEOREM 2 Differentiation Formulas
Let $\mathbf{u}(t)$ and $\mathbf{v}(t)$ be differentiable vector-valued functions. Let $h(t)$ be a differentiable real-valued function and let c be a (constant) scalar. Then

1. $D_t[\mathbf{u}(t) + \mathbf{v}(t)] = \mathbf{u}'(t) + \mathbf{v}'(t)$,
2. $D_t[c\mathbf{u}(t)] = c\mathbf{u}'(t)$,
3. $D_t[h(t)\mathbf{u}(t)] = h'(t)\mathbf{u}(t) + h(t)\mathbf{u}'(t)$,
4. $D_t[\mathbf{u}(t) \cdot \mathbf{v}(t)] = \mathbf{u}'(t) \cdot \mathbf{v}(t) + \mathbf{u}(t) \cdot \mathbf{v}'(t)$, and
5. $D_t[\mathbf{u}(t) \times \mathbf{v}(t)] = \mathbf{u}'(t) \times \mathbf{v}(t) + \mathbf{u}(t) \times \mathbf{v}'(t)$.

PROOF We'll prove part (4), working with two-dimensional vectors for simplicity, and leave the other parts as exercises. If

$$\mathbf{u}(t) = \langle f_1(t), f_2(t) \rangle \quad \text{and} \quad \mathbf{v}(t) = \langle g_1(t), g_2(t) \rangle,$$

then

$$\mathbf{u}(t) \cdot \mathbf{v}(t) = f_1(t)g_1(t) + f_2(t)g_2(t).$$

Hence the product rule for ordinary real-valued functions gives

$$\begin{aligned}
D_t[\mathbf{u}(t) \cdot \mathbf{v}(t)] &= D_t[f_1(t)g_1(t) + f_2(t)g_2(t)] \\
&= [f_1'(t)g_1(t) + f_1(t)g_1'(t)] + [f_2'(t)g_2(t) + f_2(t)g_2'(t)] \\
&= [f_1'(t)g_1(t) + f_2'(t)g_2(t)] + [f_1(t)g_1'(t) + f_2(t)g_2'(t)] \\
&= \mathbf{u}'(t) \cdot \mathbf{v}(t) + \mathbf{u}(t) \cdot \mathbf{v}'(t).
\end{aligned}$$
◄

REMARK The order of the factors in part (5) of Theorem 2 *must* be preserved because the cross product is not commutative.

EXAMPLE 5 The trajectory of the parametric curve $\mathbf{r}(t) = a\mathbf{i}\cos t + a\mathbf{j}\sin t$ is the circle of radius a centered at the origin in the xy-plane. Because $\mathbf{r}(t) \cdot \mathbf{r}(t) = a^2$, a constant, part 4 of Theorem 2 gives

$$0 \equiv \frac{d}{dt}(a^2) = \frac{d}{dt}[\mathbf{r}(t) \cdot \mathbf{r}(t)] = \mathbf{r}'(t) \cdot \mathbf{r}(t) + \mathbf{r}(t) \cdot \mathbf{r}'(t) = 2\mathbf{r}'(t) \cdot \mathbf{r}(t).$$

Because $\mathbf{r}'(t) \cdot \mathbf{r}(t) \equiv 0$, we see that (consistent with elementary geometry) the tangent vector $\mathbf{r}'(t)$ is perpendicular to the position vector $\mathbf{r}(t)$ at every point of the circle (Fig. 12.5.8). ◆

FIGURE 12.5.8 The position and tangent vectors for the circle of Example 5.

Velocity and Acceleration Vectors

Looking at Fig. 12.5.6 and the definition of $\mathbf{r}'(t)$ in Eq. (5), we note that $|\mathbf{r}(t + \Delta t) - \mathbf{r}(t)|$ is the distance from the point with position vector $\mathbf{r}(t)$ to the point with position vector $\mathbf{r}(t + \Delta t)$. It follows that the quotient

$$\frac{|\mathbf{r}(t + \Delta t) - \mathbf{r}(t)|}{\Delta t}$$

is the average speed of a particle that travels from $\mathbf{r}(t)$ to $\mathbf{r}(t + \Delta t)$ in time Δt. Consequently, the limit in Eq. (5) yields both the direction of motion and the instantaneous speed of a particle moving along a curve with position vector $\mathbf{r}(t)$.

We therefore define the **velocity vector** $\mathbf{v}(t)$ at time t of a point moving along a curve with position vector $\mathbf{r}(t)$ as the derivative

$$\mathbf{v}(t) = \mathbf{r}'(t) = f'(t)\mathbf{i} + g'(t)\mathbf{j} + h'(t)\mathbf{k}; \tag{7a}$$

in differential notation,

$$\mathbf{v} = \frac{d\mathbf{r}}{dt} = \frac{dx}{dt}\mathbf{i} + \frac{dy}{dt}\mathbf{j} + \frac{dz}{dt}\mathbf{k}. \tag{7b}$$

Its **acceleration vector** $\mathbf{a}(t)$ is given by

$$\mathbf{a}(t) = \mathbf{v}'(t) = f''(t)\mathbf{i} + g''(t)\mathbf{j} + h''(t)\mathbf{k}; \tag{8a}$$

alternatively,

$$\mathbf{a} = \frac{d\mathbf{v}}{dt} = \frac{d^2x}{dt^2}\mathbf{i} + \frac{d^2y}{dt^2}\mathbf{j} + \frac{d^2z}{dt^2}\mathbf{k}. \tag{8b}$$

Thus, for motion in the plane or in space, just as for motion along a line,

velocity is the **time derivative** of **position;**

acceleration is the **time derivative** of **velocity.**

The **speed** $v(t)$ and **scalar acceleration** $a(t)$ of the moving point are the lengths of its velocity and acceleration vectors, respectively:

$$v(t) = |\mathbf{v}(t)| = \sqrt{\left(\frac{dx}{dt}\right)^2 + \left(\frac{dy}{dt}\right)^2 + \left(\frac{dz}{dt}\right)^2} \tag{9}$$

and

$$a(t) = |\mathbf{a}(t)| = \sqrt{\left(\frac{d^2x}{dt^2}\right)^2 + \left(\frac{d^2y}{dt^2}\right)^2 + \left(\frac{d^2z}{dt^2}\right)^2}. \tag{10}$$

Note The scalar acceleration $a = |d\mathbf{v}/dt|$ is generally *not* equal to the derivative dv/dt of the speed of a moving point. The difference between the two is discussed in Section 12.6.

EXAMPLE 6 A particle moving along the parabola $y = x^2$ in the plane has position vector $\mathbf{r}(t) = t\mathbf{i} + t^2\mathbf{j}$. Find its velocity and acceleration vectors and its speed and scalar acceleration at the instant when $t = 2$.

Solution Because $\mathbf{r}(2) = 2\mathbf{i} + 4\mathbf{j}$, the location of the particle at time $t = 2$ is $(2, 4)$. Its velocity vector and speed are given by

$$\mathbf{v} = \mathbf{i} + 2t\mathbf{j} \quad \text{and} \quad v(t) = |\mathbf{v}(t)| = \sqrt{1 + 4t^2},$$

so $\mathbf{v}(2) = \mathbf{i} + 4\mathbf{j}$ (a vector) and $v(2) = \sqrt{17}$ (a scalar). Its acceleration is $\mathbf{a}(t) = \mathbf{v}'(t) = 2\mathbf{j}$ (a constant vector), so $\mathbf{a} = 2\mathbf{j}$ and $a = |\mathbf{a}| = 2$ (scalar acceleration) for all t, including the instant at which $t = 2$. Figure 12.5.9 shows the trajectory of the particle with its velocity and acceleration vectors $\mathbf{v}(2)$ and $\mathbf{a}(2)$ attached at its location $(2, 4)$ when $t = 2$. ◆

FIGURE 12.5.9 The velocity and acceleration vectors at $t = 2$ (Example 6).

EXAMPLE 7 Find the velocity, acceleration, speed, and scalar acceleration of a moving point P whose trajectory is the helix with position vector

$$\mathbf{r}(t) = (a\cos\omega t)\mathbf{i} + (a\sin\omega t)\mathbf{j} + bt\mathbf{k}. \tag{11}$$

Solution Equation (11) is a generalization of the position vector $\mathbf{r}(t) = \mathbf{i}\cos t + \mathbf{j}\sin t + t\mathbf{k}$ of the helix in Example 3. Here $x^2 + y^2 = a^2$, so the xy-projection $(a\cos\omega t, a\sin\omega t)$ of P lies on the circle of radius a centered at the origin. This projection moves around the circle with angular speed ω (radians per unit time). Meanwhile, the point P itself also is moving upward (if $b > 0$) on the vertical cylinder of radius a; the z-component of its velocity is $dz/dt = b$. Except for the radius of the cylinder, the picture looks the same as Fig. 12.5.4.

The derivative of the position vector in (11) is the velocity vector

$$\mathbf{v}(t) = (-a\omega\sin\omega t)\mathbf{i} + (a\omega\cos\omega t)\mathbf{j} + b\mathbf{k}. \tag{12}$$

Another differentiation gives its acceleration vector

$$\mathbf{a}(t) = (-a\omega^2\cos\omega t)\mathbf{i} + (-a\omega^2\sin\omega t)\mathbf{j}$$
$$= -a\omega^2(\mathbf{i}\cos\omega t + \mathbf{j}\sin\omega t). \tag{13}$$

The speed of the moving point is a constant, because

$$v(t) = |\mathbf{v}(t)| = \sqrt{a^2\omega^2 + b^2}.$$

Note that the acceleration vector is a horizontal vector of length $a\omega^2$. Moreover, if we think of $\mathbf{a}(t)$ as attached to the moving point at the time t of evaluation—so that the initial point of $\mathbf{a}(t)$ is the terminal point of $\mathbf{r}(t)$—then $\mathbf{a}(t)$ points directly toward the point $(0, 0, bt)$ on the z-axis. ◆

REMARK The helix of Example 7 is a typical trajectory of a charged particle in a constant magnetic field. Such a particle must satisfy both Newton's law $\mathbf{F} = m\mathbf{a}$ and the magnetic force law $\mathbf{F} = (q\mathbf{v}) \times \mathbf{B}$ mentioned in Section 12.3. Hence its velocity and acceleration vectors must satisfy the equation

$$(q\mathbf{v}) \times \mathbf{B} = m\mathbf{a}. \tag{14}$$

If the constant magnetic field is vertical, $\mathbf{B} = B\mathbf{k}$, then with the velocity vector of Eq. (12) we find that

$$q\mathbf{v} \times \mathbf{B} = q\begin{vmatrix} \mathbf{i} & \mathbf{j} & \mathbf{k} \\ -a\omega\sin\omega t & a\omega\cos\omega t & b \\ 0 & 0 & B \end{vmatrix} = qa\omega B(\mathbf{i}\cos\omega t + \mathbf{j}\sin\omega t).$$

The acceleration vector in Eq. (13) gives

$$m\mathbf{a} = -ma\omega^2(\mathbf{i}\cos\omega t + \mathbf{j}\sin\omega t).$$

When we compare the last two results, we see that the helix of Example 7 satisfies Eq. (14) provided that

$$qa\omega B = -ma\omega^2; \quad \text{that is,} \quad \omega = -\frac{qB}{m}.$$

For example, this equation would determine the angular speed ω for the helical trajectory of electrons ($q < 0$) in a cathode-ray tube placed in a constant magnetic field parallel to the axis of the tube (Fig. 12.5.10).

FIGURE 12.5.10 A spiraling electron in a cathode-ray tube.

Integration of Vector-Valued Functions

Integrals of vector-valued functions are defined by analogy with the definition of an integral of a real-valued function:

$$\int_a^b \mathbf{r}(t)\,dt = \lim_{\Delta t \to 0} \sum_{i=1}^n \mathbf{r}(t_i^\star)\,\Delta t,$$

where $t_i^\star$ is a point of the ith subinterval of a division of $[a,b]$ into n subintervals, all with the same length $\Delta t = (b-a)/n$.

If $\mathbf{r}(t) = f(t)\mathbf{i} + g(t)\mathbf{j}$ is continuous on $[a,b]$, then—by taking limits componentwise—we get

$$\int_a^b \mathbf{r}(t)\,dt = \lim_{\Delta t \to 0} \sum_{i=1}^n \mathbf{r}(t_i^\star)\,\Delta t$$

$$= \mathbf{i}\left(\lim_{\Delta t \to 0} \sum_{i=1}^n f(t_i^\star)\,\Delta t\right) + \mathbf{j}\left(\lim_{\Delta t \to 0} \sum_{i=1}^n g(t_i^\star)\,\Delta t\right).$$

This gives the result that

$$\int_a^b \mathbf{r}(t)\,dt = \mathbf{i}\left(\int_a^b f(t)\,dt\right) + \mathbf{j}\left(\int_a^b g(t)\,dt\right). \tag{15}$$

Thus *a vector-valued function may be integrated componentwise.* The three-dimensional version of Eq. (15) is derived in the same way, merely including third components.

Now suppose that $\mathbf{R}(t)$ is an *antiderivative* of $\mathbf{r}(t)$, meaning that $\mathbf{R}'(t) = \mathbf{r}(t)$. That is, if $\mathbf{R}(t) = F(t)\mathbf{i} + G(t)\mathbf{j}$, then

$$\mathbf{R}'(t) = F'(t)\mathbf{i} + G'(t)\mathbf{j} = f(t)\mathbf{i} + g(t)\mathbf{j} = \mathbf{r}(t).$$

Then componentwise integration yields

$$\int_a^b \mathbf{r}(t)\,dt = \mathbf{i}\left(\int_a^b f(t)\,dt\right) + \mathbf{j}\left(\int_a^b g(t)\,dt\right) = \mathbf{i}\Big[F(t)\Big]_a^b + \mathbf{j}\Big[G(t)\Big]_a^b$$

$$= [F(b)\mathbf{i} + G(b)\mathbf{j}] - [F(a)\mathbf{i} + G(a)\mathbf{j}].$$

Thus the *fundamental theorem of calculus* for vector-valued functions takes the form

$$\int_a^b \mathbf{r}(t)\,dt = \Big[\mathbf{R}(t)\Big]_a^b = \mathbf{R}(b) - \mathbf{R}(a), \tag{16}$$

where $\mathbf{R}'(t) = \mathbf{r}(t)$ is continuous on $[a,b]$.

Indefinite integrals of vector-valued functions may be computed as well. If $\mathbf{R}'(t) = \mathbf{r}(t)$, then every antiderivative of $\mathbf{r}(t)$ is of the form $\mathbf{R}(t) + \mathbf{C}$ for some constant vector $\mathbf{C}$. We therefore write

$$\int \mathbf{r}(t)\,dt = \mathbf{R}(t) + \mathbf{C} \quad \text{if} \quad \mathbf{R}'(t) = \mathbf{r}(t), \tag{17}$$

on the basis of a componentwise computation similar to the one leading to Eq. (16).

If $\mathbf{r}(t)$, $\mathbf{v}(t)$, and $\mathbf{a}(t)$ are the position, velocity, and acceleration vectors of a point moving in space, then the vector derivatives

$$\frac{d\mathbf{r}}{dt} = \mathbf{v} \quad \text{and} \quad \frac{d\mathbf{v}}{dt} = \mathbf{a}$$

imply the indefinite integrals

$$\mathbf{v}(t) = \int \mathbf{a}(t)\,dt \qquad (18)$$

and

$$\mathbf{r}(t) = \int \mathbf{v}(t)\,dt. \qquad (19)$$

Both of these integrals involve a *vector* constant of integration.

EXAMPLE 8 Suppose that a moving point has given initial position vector $\mathbf{r}(0) = 2\mathbf{i}$, initial velocity vector $\mathbf{v}(0) = \mathbf{i} - \mathbf{j}$, and acceleration vector $\mathbf{a}(t) = 2\mathbf{i} + 6t\mathbf{j}$. Find its position and velocity at time t.

Solution Equation (18) gives

$$\mathbf{v}(t) = \int \mathbf{a}(t)\,dt = \int (2\mathbf{i} + 6t\mathbf{j})\,dt = 2t\mathbf{i} + 3t^2\mathbf{j} + \mathbf{C}_1.$$

To evaluate the constant vector $\mathbf{C}_1$, we substitute $t = 0$ in this equation and find that $\mathbf{v}(0) = (0)\mathbf{i} + (0)\mathbf{j} + \mathbf{C}_1$, so $\mathbf{C}_1 = \mathbf{v}(0) = \mathbf{i} - \mathbf{j}$. Thus the velocity vector of the moving point at time t is

$$\mathbf{v}(t) = (2t\mathbf{i} + 3t^2\mathbf{j}) + (\mathbf{i} - \mathbf{j}) = (2t + 1)\mathbf{i} + (3t^2 - 1)\mathbf{j}.$$

A second integration, using Eq. (19), gives

$$\mathbf{r}(t) = \int \mathbf{v}(t)\,dt$$

$$= \int [(2t+1)\mathbf{i} + (3t^2 - 1)\mathbf{j}]\,dt = (t^2 + t)\mathbf{i} + (t^3 - t)\mathbf{j} + \mathbf{C}_2.$$

Again we substitute $t = 0$ and find that $\mathbf{C}_2 = \mathbf{r}(0) = 2\mathbf{i}$. Hence

$$\mathbf{r}(t) = (t^2 + t)\mathbf{i} + (t^3 - t)\mathbf{j} + 2\mathbf{i} = (t^2 + t + 2)\mathbf{i} + (t^3 - t)\mathbf{j}$$

is the position vector of the point at time t. ◆

Vector integration is the basis for at least one method of navigation. If a submarine is cruising beneath the icecap at the North Pole, as in Fig. 12.5.11, and thus can use neither visual nor radio methods to determine its position, there is an alternative. Build a sensitive gyroscope-accelerometer combination and install it in the submarine. The device continuously measures the sub's acceleration vector, beginning at the time $t = 0$ when its position $\mathbf{r}(0)$ and velocity $\mathbf{v}(0)$ are known. Because $\mathbf{v}'(t) = \mathbf{a}(t)$, Eq. (16) gives

$$\int_0^t \mathbf{a}(t)\,dt = \Big[\mathbf{v}(t)\Big]_0^t = \mathbf{v}(t) - \mathbf{v}(0),$$

FIGURE 12.5.11 A submarine beneath the polar icecap.

so
$$\mathbf{v}(t) = \mathbf{v}(0) + \int_0^t \mathbf{a}(t)\,dt.$$

Thus the velocity at every time $t \geq 0$ is known. Similarly, because $\mathbf{r}'(t) = \mathbf{v}(t)$, a second integration gives
$$\mathbf{r}(t) = \mathbf{r}(0) + \int_0^t \mathbf{v}(t)\,dt$$

for the position of the sub at every time $t \geq 0$. On-board computers can be programmed to carry out these integrations (perhaps by using Simpson's approximation) and continuously provide captain and crew with the submarine's (almost) exact position and velocity.

Motion of Projectiles

Suppose that a projectile is launched from the point (x_0, y_0), with y_0 denoting its initial height above the surface of the earth. Let α be the angle of inclination from the horizontal of its initial velocity vector $\mathbf{v}_0$ (Fig. 12.5.12). Then its initial position vector is

$$\mathbf{r}_0 = x_0\mathbf{i} + y_0\mathbf{j}, \tag{20a}$$

and from Fig. 12.5.12 we see that

$$\mathbf{v}_0 = (v_0 \cos\alpha)\mathbf{i} + (v_0 \sin\alpha)\mathbf{j}, \tag{20b}$$

where $v_0 = |\mathbf{v}_0|$ is the initial speed of the projectile.

We suppose that the motion takes place sufficiently close to the surface that we may assume that the earth is flat and that gravity is perfectly uniform. Then, if we also ignore air resistance, the acceleration of the projectile is

$$\mathbf{a} = \frac{d\mathbf{v}}{dt} = -g\mathbf{j},$$

where $g \approx 32$ ft/s² ≈ 9.8 m/s². Antidifferentiation gives

$$\mathbf{v}(t) = -gt\mathbf{j} + \mathbf{C}_1.$$

Put $t = 0$ in both sides of this last equation. This shows that $\mathbf{C}_1 = \mathbf{v}_0$ (as expected!) and thus that

$$\mathbf{v}(t) = \frac{d\mathbf{r}}{dt} = -gt\mathbf{j} + \mathbf{v}_0.$$

Another antidifferentiation gives

$$\mathbf{r}(t) = -\tfrac{1}{2}gt^2\mathbf{j} + \mathbf{v}_0 t + \mathbf{C}_2.$$

Now substituting $t = 0$ yields $\mathbf{C}_2 = \mathbf{r}_0$, so the position vector of the projectile at time t is

$$\mathbf{r}(t) = -\tfrac{1}{2}gt^2\mathbf{j} + \mathbf{v}_0 t + \mathbf{r}_0. \tag{21}$$

FIGURE 12.5.12 Trajectory of a projectile launched at the angle α.

Equations (20a) and (20b) now give

$$\mathbf{r}(t) = [(v_0\cos\alpha)t + x_0]\mathbf{i} + \left[-\tfrac{1}{2}gt^2 + (v_0\sin\alpha)t + y_0\right]\mathbf{j},$$

so parametric equations of the trajectory of the particle are

$$x(t) = (v_0\cos\alpha)t + x_0, \tag{22}$$

$$y(t) = -\tfrac{1}{2}gt^2 + (v_0\sin\alpha)t + y_0. \tag{23}$$

812 CHAPTER 12 Vectors, Curves, and Surfaces in Space

EXAMPLE 9 An airplane is flying horizontally at an altitude of 1600 ft to pass directly over snowbound cattle on the ground and release hay to land there. The plane's speed is a constant 150 mi/h (220 ft/s). At what angle of sight ϕ (between the horizontal and the direct line to the target) should a bale of hay be released in order to hit the target?

Solution See Fig. 12.5.13. We take $x_0 = 0$ where the bale of hay is released at time $t = 0$. Then $y_0 = 1600$ (ft), $v_0 = 220$ (ft/s), and $\alpha = 0$. Then Eqs. (22) and (23) take the forms
$$x(t) = 220t, \qquad y(t) = -16t^2 + 1600.$$
From the second of these equations we find that $t = 10$ (s) when the bale of hay hits the ground ($y = 0$). It has then traveled a horizontal distance
$$x(10) = 220 \cdot 10 = 2200 \quad \text{(ft)}.$$
Hence the required angle of sight is
$$\phi = \tan^{-1}\left(\frac{1600}{2200}\right) \approx 36°.$$

FIGURE 12.5.13 Trajectory of the hay bale of Example 9.

FIGURE 12.5.14 The trajectory of the ball of Example 10.

EXAMPLE 10 A ball is thrown northward into the air from the origin in xyz-space (the xy-plane represents the ground and the positive y-axis points north). The initial velocity (vector) of the ball is
$$\mathbf{v}_0 = \mathbf{v}(0) = 80\mathbf{j} + 80\mathbf{k}.$$
The spin of the ball causes an eastward acceleration of 2 ft/s² in addition to gravitational acceleration. Thus the acceleration vector produced by the combination of gravity and spin is
$$\mathbf{a}(t) = 2\mathbf{i} - 32\mathbf{k}.$$
First find the velocity vector $\mathbf{v}(t)$ of the ball and its position vector $\mathbf{r}(t)$. Then determine where and with what speed the ball hits the ground (Fig. 12.5.14).

Solution When we antidifferentiate $\mathbf{a}(t)$ we get
$$\mathbf{v}(t) = \int \mathbf{a}(t)\, dt = \int (2\mathbf{i} - 32\mathbf{k})\, dt = 2t\mathbf{i} - 32t\mathbf{k} + \mathbf{C}_1.$$
We substitute $t = 0$ to find that $\mathbf{C}_1 = \mathbf{v}_0 = 80\mathbf{j} + 80\mathbf{k}$, so
$$\mathbf{v}(t) = 2t\mathbf{i} + 80\mathbf{j} + (80 - 32t)\mathbf{k}.$$
Another antidifferentiation yields
$$\mathbf{r}(t) = \int \mathbf{v}(t)\, dt = \int [2t\mathbf{i} + 80\mathbf{j} + (80 - 32t)\mathbf{k}]\, dt$$
$$= t^2\mathbf{i} + 80t\mathbf{j} + (80t - 16t^2)\mathbf{k} + \mathbf{C}_2,$$

and substituting $t = 0$ gives $\mathbf{C}_2 = \mathbf{r}(0) = \mathbf{0}$. Hence the position vector of the ball is

$$\mathbf{r}(t) = t^2\mathbf{i} + 80t\mathbf{j} + (80t - 16t^2)\mathbf{k}.$$

The ball hits the ground when $z = 80t - 16t^2 = 0$; that is, when $t = 5$. Its position vector then is

$$\mathbf{r}(5) = 5^2\mathbf{i} + 80 \cdot 5\mathbf{j} = 25\mathbf{i} + 400\mathbf{j},$$

so the ball has traveled 25 ft eastward and 400 ft northward. Its velocity vector at impact is

$$\mathbf{v}(5) = 2 \cdot 5\mathbf{i} + 80\mathbf{j} + (80 - 32 \cdot 5)\mathbf{k} = 10\mathbf{i} + 80\mathbf{j} - 80\mathbf{k},$$

so its speed when it hits the ground is

$$v(5) = |\mathbf{v}(5)| = \sqrt{10^2 + 80^2 + (-80)^2},$$

approximately 113.58 ft/s. Because the ball started with initial speed $v_0 = \sqrt{80^2 + 80^2} \approx 113.14$ ft/s, its eastward acceleration has slightly increased its terminal speed. ◆

12.5 TRUE/FALSE STUDY GUIDE

12.5 CONCEPTS: QUESTIONS AND DISCUSSION

In Questions 1 through 3, let $\mathbf{f} : \mathbf{R} \to \mathbf{R}^3$ be a vector-valued function of a real variable t. In each question you are asked for a "coordinate-free" definition. Compare your definition with the corresponding componentwise definition or calculation. Do the two agree?

1. Give a definition of $\lim_{t \to a} \mathbf{f}(t)$ that does not involve the component functions of $\mathbf{f}$.
2. Give a definition of $\mathbf{f}'(t)$ that does not involve the component functions of $\mathbf{f}$.
3. Give a definition of
$$\int_a^b \mathbf{f}(t)\, dt$$
that does not involve the component functions of $\mathbf{f}$.

12.5 PROBLEMS

In Problems 1 through 4, also match the curves there defined with their three-dimensional plots in Figs. 12.5.15 through 12.5.18.

FIGURE 12.5.15

FIGURE 12.5.16

FIGURE 12.5.17

FIGURE 12.5.18

1. Show that the graph of the curve with parametric equations $x = t$, $y = \sin 5t$, $z = \cos 5t$ lies on the circular cylinder $y^2 + z^2 = 1$ centered along the x-axis.

2. Show that the graph of the curve with parametric equations $x = \sin t$, $y = \cos t$, $z = \cos 8t$ lies on the vertical circular cylinder $x^2 + y^2 = 1$.

3. Show that the graph of the curve with parametric equations $x = t \sin 6t$, $y = t \cos 6t$, $z = t$ lies on the cone $z = \sqrt{x^2 + y^2}$ with its vertex at the origin and opening upward.

4. Show that the graph of the curve with parametric equations $x = \cos t \sin 4t$, $y = \sin t \sin 4t$, $z = \cos 4t$ lies on the surface of the sphere $x^2 + y^2 + z^2 = 1$.

In Problems 5 through 10, find the values of $\mathbf{r}'(t)$ and $\mathbf{r}''(t)$ for the given values of t.

5. $\mathbf{r}(t) = 3\mathbf{i} - 2\mathbf{j}$; $t = 1$
6. $\mathbf{r}(t) = t^2\mathbf{i} - t^3\mathbf{j}$; $t = 2$
7. $\mathbf{r}(t) = e^{2t}\mathbf{i} + e^{-t}\mathbf{j}$; $t = 0$
8. $\mathbf{r}(t) = \mathbf{i}\cos t + \mathbf{j}\sin t$; $t = \pi/4$
9. $\mathbf{r}(t) = 3\mathbf{i}\cos 2\pi t + 3\mathbf{j}\sin 2\pi t$; $t = 3/4$
10. $\mathbf{r}(t) = 5\mathbf{i}\cos t + 4\mathbf{j}\sin t$; $t = \pi$

In Problems 11 through 16, the position vector $\mathbf{r}(t)$ of a particle moving in space is given. Find its velocity and acceleration vectors and its speed at time t.

11. $\mathbf{r}(t) = t\mathbf{i} + t^2\mathbf{j} + t^3\mathbf{k}$
12. $\mathbf{r}(t) = t^2(3\mathbf{i} + 4\mathbf{j} - 12\mathbf{k})$
13. $\mathbf{r}(t) = t\mathbf{i} + 3e^t\mathbf{j} + 4e^t\mathbf{k}$
14. $\mathbf{r}(t) = e^t\mathbf{i} + e^{2t}\mathbf{j} + e^{3t}\mathbf{k}$
15. $\mathbf{r}(t) = (3\cos t)\mathbf{i} + (3\sin t)\mathbf{j} - 4t\mathbf{k}$
16. $\mathbf{r}(t) = 12t\mathbf{i} + (5\sin 2t)\mathbf{j} - (5\cos 2t)\mathbf{k}$

Calculate the integrals in Problems 17 through 20.

17. $\int_0^{\pi/4} (\mathbf{i}\sin t + 2\mathbf{j}\cos t)\, dt$
18. $\int_1^e \left(\frac{1}{t}\mathbf{i} - \mathbf{j}\right) dt$
19. $\int_0^2 t^2(1+t^3)^{3/2}\mathbf{i}\, dt$
20. $\int_0^1 \left(\mathbf{i}e^t - \mathbf{j}te^{-t^2}\right) dt$

In Problems 21 through 24, apply Theorem 2 to compute the derivative $D_t[\mathbf{u}(t) \cdot \mathbf{v}(t)]$.

21. $\mathbf{u}(t) = 3t\mathbf{i} - \mathbf{j}$, $\mathbf{v}(t) = 2\mathbf{i} - 5t\mathbf{j}$
22. $\mathbf{u}(t) = t\mathbf{i} + t^2\mathbf{j}$, $\mathbf{v}(t) = t^2\mathbf{i} - t\mathbf{j}$
23. $\mathbf{u}(t) = \langle \cos t, \sin t \rangle$, $\mathbf{v}(t) = \langle \sin t, -\cos t \rangle$
24. $\mathbf{u} = \langle t, t^2, t^3 \rangle$, $\mathbf{v} = \langle \cos 2t, \sin 2t, e^{-3t} \rangle$

In Problems 25 through 34, the acceleration vector $\mathbf{a}(t)$, the initial position $\mathbf{r}_0 = \mathbf{r}(0)$, and the initial velocity $\mathbf{v}_0 = \mathbf{v}(0)$ of a particle moving in xyz-space are given. Find its position vector $\mathbf{r}(t)$ at time t.

25. $\mathbf{a} = \mathbf{0}$; $\mathbf{r}_0 = \mathbf{i}$; $\mathbf{v}_0 = \mathbf{k}$
26. $\mathbf{a} = 2\mathbf{i}$; $\mathbf{r}_0 = 3\mathbf{j}$; $\mathbf{v}_0 = 4\mathbf{k}$
27. $\mathbf{a}(t) = 2\mathbf{i} - 4\mathbf{k}$; $\mathbf{r}_0 = \mathbf{0}$; $\mathbf{v}_0 = 10\mathbf{j}$
28. $\mathbf{a}(t) = \mathbf{i} - \mathbf{j} + 3\mathbf{k}$; $\mathbf{r}_0 = 5\mathbf{i}$; $\mathbf{v}_0 = 7\mathbf{j}$
29. $\mathbf{a}(t) = 2\mathbf{j} - 6t\mathbf{k}$; $\mathbf{r}_0 = 2\mathbf{i}$; $\mathbf{v}_0 = 5\mathbf{k}$
30. $\mathbf{a}(t) = 6t\mathbf{i} - 5\mathbf{j} + 12t^2\mathbf{k}$; $\mathbf{r}_0 = 3\mathbf{i} + 4\mathbf{j}$; $\mathbf{v}_0 = 4\mathbf{j} - 5\mathbf{k}$
31. $\mathbf{a}(t) = t\mathbf{i} + t^2\mathbf{j} + t^3\mathbf{k}$; $\mathbf{r}_0 = 10\mathbf{i}$; $\mathbf{v}_0 = 10\mathbf{j}$
32. $\mathbf{a}(t) = t\mathbf{i} + e^{-t}\mathbf{j}$; $\mathbf{r}_0 = 3\mathbf{i} + 4\mathbf{j}$; $\mathbf{v}_0 = 5\mathbf{k}$
33. $\mathbf{a}(t) = \mathbf{i}\cos t + \mathbf{j}\sin t$; $\mathbf{r}_0 = \mathbf{j}$; $\mathbf{v}_0 = -\mathbf{i} + 5\mathbf{k}$
34. $\mathbf{a}(t) = 9(\mathbf{i}\sin 3t + \mathbf{j}\cos 3t) + 4\mathbf{k}$; $\mathbf{r}_0 = 3\mathbf{i} + 4\mathbf{j}$; $\mathbf{v}_0 = 2\mathbf{i} - 7\mathbf{k}$

35. The parametric equations of a moving point are
$$x(t) = 3\cos 2t, \quad y(t) = 3\sin 2t, \quad z(t) = 8t.$$
Find its velocity, speed, and acceleration at time $t = 7\pi/8$.

36. Use the equations in Theorem 2 to calculate
$$D_t[\mathbf{u}(t) \cdot \mathbf{v}(t)] \quad \text{and} \quad D_t[\mathbf{u}(t) \times \mathbf{v}(t)]$$
if $\mathbf{u}(t) = \langle t, t^2, t^3 \rangle$ and $\mathbf{v}(t) = \langle e^t, \cos t, \sin t \rangle$.

37. Verify part 5 of Theorem 2 in the special case $\mathbf{u}(t) = \langle 0, 3, 4t \rangle$ and $\mathbf{v}(t) = \langle 5t, 0, -4 \rangle$.

38. Prove part 5 of Theorem 2.

39. A point moves on a sphere centered at the origin. Show that its velocity vector is always tangent to the sphere.

40. A particle moves with constant speed along a curve in space. Show that its velocity and acceleration vectors are always perpendicular.

41. Find the maximum height reached by the ball in Example 10 and also its speed at that height.

42. The **angular momentum** $\mathbf{L}(t)$ and **torque** $\boldsymbol{\tau}(t)$ of a moving particle of mass m with position vector $\mathbf{r}(t)$ are defined to be
$$\mathbf{L}(t) = m\mathbf{r}(t) \times \mathbf{v}(t), \qquad \boldsymbol{\tau}(t) = m\mathbf{r}(t) \times \mathbf{a}(t).$$
Prove that $\mathbf{L}'(t) = \boldsymbol{\tau}(t)$. It follows that $\mathbf{L}(t)$ must be constant if $\boldsymbol{\tau} \equiv \mathbf{0}$; this is the law of conservation of angular momentum.

Problems 43 through 48 deal with a projectile fired from the origin (so $x_0 = y_0 = 0$) with initial speed v_0 and initial angle of inclination α. The **range** *of the projectile is the horizontal distance it travels before it returns to the ground.*

43. If $\alpha = 45°$, what value of v_0 gives a range of 1 mi?

44. If $\alpha = 60°$ and the range is $R = 1$ mi, what is the maximum height attained by the projectile?

45. Deduce from Eqs. (22) and (23) the fact that the range is
$$R = \tfrac{1}{16}v_0^2 \sin\alpha\cos\alpha.$$

46. Given the initial speed v_0, find the angle α that maximizes the range. [*Suggestion:* Use the result of Problem 45.]

47. Suppose that $v_0 = 160$ (ft/s). Find the maximum height $y_{\max}$ and the range R of the projectile if (a) $\alpha = 30°$; (b) $\alpha = 45°$; (c) $\alpha = 60°$.

48. The projectile of Problem 47 is to be fired at a target 600 ft away, and there is a hill 300 ft high midway between the gun site and this target. At what initial angle of inclination should the projectile be fired?

49. A projectile is to be fired horizontally from the top of a 100-m cliff at a target 1 km from the base of the cliff. What should be the initial velocity of the projectile? (Use $g = 9.8$ m/s^2.)

50. A bomb is dropped (initial speed zero) from a helicopter hovering at a height of 800 m. A projectile is fired from a gun located on the ground 800 m west of the point directly beneath the helicopter. The projectile is supposed to intercept the bomb at a height of exactly 400 m. If the projectile is fired at the same instant that the bomb is dropped, what should be its initial velocity and angle of inclination?

51. Suppose, more realistically, that the projectile of Problem 50 is fired 1 s after the bomb is dropped. What should be its initial velocity and angle of inclination?

52. An artillery gun with a muzzle velocity of 1000 ft/s is located atop a seaside cliff 500 ft high. At what initial inclination angle (or angles) should it fire a projectile in order to hit a ship at sea 20,000 ft from the base of the cliff?

53. Suppose that the vector-valued functions $\mathbf{u}(t)$ and $\mathbf{v}(t)$ both have limits as $t \to a$. Prove:
(a) $\lim_{t \to a}(\mathbf{u}(t) + \mathbf{v}(t)) = \lim_{t \to a}\mathbf{u}(t) + \lim_{t \to a}\mathbf{v}(t)$;
(b) $\lim_{t \to a}(\mathbf{u}(t) \cdot \mathbf{v}(t)) = \left(\lim_{t \to a}\mathbf{u}(t)\right) \cdot \left(\lim_{t \to a}\mathbf{v}(t)\right)$.

54. Suppose that both the vector-valued function $\mathbf{r}(t)$ and the real-valued function $h(t)$ are differentiable. Deduce the chain rule for vector-valued functions,
$$D_t[\mathbf{r}(h(t))] = h'(t)\mathbf{r}'(h(t)),$$
in componentwise fashion from the ordinary chain rule.

55. A point moves with constant speed, so its velocity vector $\mathbf{v}$ satisfies the condition
$$|\mathbf{v}|^2 = \mathbf{v} \cdot \mathbf{v} = C \quad \text{(a constant)}.$$
Prove that the velocity and acceleration vectors of the point are always perpendicular to each other.

56. A point moves on a circle whose center is at the origin. Use the dot product to show that the position and velocity vectors of the moving point are always perpendicular.

57. A point moves on the hyperbola $x^2 - y^2 = 1$ with position vector
$$\mathbf{r}(t) = \mathbf{i}\cosh \omega t + \mathbf{j}\sinh \omega t$$
(the number ω is a constant). Prove that the acceleration vector $\mathbf{a}(t)$ satisfies the equation $\mathbf{a}(t) = c\mathbf{r}(t)$, where c is a positive constant. What sort of external force would produce this kind of motion?

58. Suppose that a point moves on the ellipse
$$\frac{x^2}{a^2} + \frac{y^2}{b^2} = 1$$
with position vector $\mathbf{r}(t) = \mathbf{i}a\cos \omega t + \mathbf{j}b\sin \omega t$ (ω is a constant). Prove that the acceleration vector $\mathbf{a}$ satisfies the equation $\mathbf{a}(t) = c\mathbf{r}(t)$, where c is a negative constant. To what sort of external force $\mathbf{F}(t)$ does this motion correspond?

59. A point moves in the plane with constant acceleration vector $\mathbf{a} = a\mathbf{j}$. Prove that its path is a parabola or a straight line.

60. Suppose that a particle is subject to no force, so its acceleration vector $\mathbf{a}(t)$ is identically zero. Prove that the particle travels along a straight line at constant speed (Newton's first law of motion).

61. *Uniform Circular Motion* Consider a particle that moves counterclockwise around the circle with center $(0, 0)$ and radius r at a constant angular speed of ω radians per second (Fig. 12.5.19). If its initial position is $(r, 0)$, then its position vector is
$$\mathbf{r}(t) = \mathbf{i}r\cos \omega t + \mathbf{j}r\sin \omega t.$$
(a) Show that the velocity vector of the particle is tangent to the circle and that the speed of the particle is
$$v(t) = |\mathbf{v}(t)| = r\omega.$$
(b) Show that the acceleration vector $\mathbf{a}$ of the particle is directed opposite to $\mathbf{r}$ and that
$$a(t) = |\mathbf{a}(t)| = r\omega^2.$$

FIGURE 12.5.19 Uniform circular motion (Problem 61).

62. Suppose that a particle is moving under the influence of a *central* force field $\mathbf{R} = k\mathbf{r}$, where k is a scalar function of x, y, and z. Conclude that the trajectory of the particle lies in a *fixed* plane through the origin.

63. A baseball is thrown with an initial velocity of 160 ft/s straight upward from the ground. It experiences a downward gravitational acceleration of 32 ft/s². Because of spin, it experiences also a (horizontal) northward acceleration of 0.1 ft/s²; otherwise, the air has no effect on its motion. How far north of the throwing point will the ball land?

64. A baseball is hit with an initial velocity of 96 ft/s and an initial inclination angle of 15° from ground level straight down a foul line. Because of spin it experiences a horizontal acceleration of 2 ft/s² perpendicular to the foul line; otherwise, the air has no effect on its motion. When the ball hits the ground, how far is it from the foul line?

65. A projectile is fired northward (in the positive y-direction) out to sea from the top of a seaside cliff 384 ft high. The projectile's initial velocity vector is $\mathbf{v}_0 = 200\mathbf{j} + 160\mathbf{k}$. In addition to a downward (negative z-direction) gravitational acceleration of 32 ft/s², it experiences in flight an eastward (positive x-direction) acceleration of 2 ft/s² due to spin.
(a) Find the projectile's velocity and position vectors t seconds after it is fired.
(b) How long is the projectile in the air?
(c) Where does the projectile hit the water ($z = 0$)? Give the answer by telling how far north out to sea and how far east along the coast is its impact position.
(d) What is the maximum height of the projectile above the water?

66. A gun fires a shell with a muzzle velocity of 150 m/s. While the shell is in the air, it experiences a downward (vertical) gravitational acceleration of 9.8 m/s² and an eastward (horizontal) Coriolis acceleration of 5 cm/s²; air resistance may be ignored. The target is 1500 m due north of the gun, and both the gun and target are on level ground. Halfway between them is a hill 600 m high. Tell precisely how to aim the gun—both compass heading and inclination from the horizontal—so that the shell will clear the hill and hit the target.

12.5 Project: Does a Pitched Baseball Really Curve?

Have you ever wondered whether a baseball pitch really curves or whether it's some sort of optical illusion? In this project you'll use calculus to illuminate the matter.

Suppose that a pitcher throws a ball toward home plate (60 ft away, as in Fig. 12.5.20) and gives it a spin of S revolutions per second counterclockwise (as viewed from above) about a vertical axis through the center of the ball. This spin is described by the *spin vector* $\mathbf{S}$ that points along the axis of revolution in the right-handed direction and has length S (Fig. 12.5.21).

FIGURE 12.5.20 The x-axis points toward home plate.

We know from studies of aerodynamics that this spin causes a difference in air pressure on the sides of the ball toward and away from this spin. Studies also show that this pressure difference results in a *spin acceleration*

$$\mathbf{a}_S = c\mathbf{S} \times \mathbf{v} \tag{1}$$

of the ball (where c is an empirical constant). The total acceleration of the ball is then

$$\mathbf{a} = (c\mathbf{S} \times \mathbf{v}) - g\mathbf{k}, \tag{2}$$

where $g \approx 32$ ft/s² is the gravitational acceleration. Here we will ignore any other effects of air resistance.

With the spin vector $\mathbf{S} = S\mathbf{k}$ pointing upward, as in Fig. 12.5.21, show first that

$$\mathbf{S} \times \mathbf{v} = -Sv_y\mathbf{i} + Sv_x\mathbf{j}, \tag{3}$$

where v_x is the component of $\mathbf{v}$ in the x-direction and v_y is the component of $\mathbf{v}$ in the y-direction.

FIGURE 12.5.21 The spin and velocity vectors.

For a ball pitched along the x-axis, v_x is much larger than v_y, and so the approximation $\mathbf{S} \times \mathbf{v} = Sv_x\mathbf{j}$ is sufficiently accurate for our purposes. We may then take the acceleration vector of the ball to be

$$\mathbf{a} = cSv_x\mathbf{j} - g\mathbf{k}. \tag{4}$$

Now suppose that the pitcher throws the ball from the initial position $x_0 = y_0 = 0$, $z_0 = 5$ (ft), with initial velocity vector

$$\mathbf{v}_0 = 120\mathbf{i} - 2\mathbf{j} + 4\mathbf{k} \tag{5}$$

(with components in feet per second, so $v_0 \approx 120$ ft/s, about 82 mi/h) and with a spin of $S = \frac{80}{3}$ rev/s. A reasonable value of c is

$$c = 0.005 \text{ ft/s}^2 \quad \text{per ft/s of velocity and rev/s of spin,}$$

although the precise value depends on whether the pitcher has (accidentally, of course) scuffed the ball or administered some foreign substance to it.

Show first that these values of the parameters yield

$$\mathbf{a} = 16\mathbf{j} - 32\mathbf{k}$$

for the ball's acceleration vector. Then integrate twice in succession to find the ball's position vector

$$\mathbf{r}(t) = x(t)\mathbf{i} + y(t)\mathbf{j} + z(t)\mathbf{k}.$$

Use your results to fill in the following table, giving the pitched ball's horizontal deflection y and height z (above the ground) at quarter-second intervals.

t (s)	x (ft)	y (ft)	z (ft)
0.0	0	0	5
0.25	30	?	?
0.50	60	?	?

Suppose that the batter gets a "fix" on the pitch by observing the ball during the first quarter-second and prepares to swing. After 0.25 s does the pitch still appear to be straight on target toward home plate at a height of 5 ft?

What happens to the ball during the final quarter-second of its approach to home plate—*after* the batter has begun to swing the bat? What were the ball's horizontal and vertical deflections during this brief period? What is your conclusion? Does the pitched ball really "curve" or not?

12.6 CURVATURE AND ACCELERATION

The speed of a moving point is closely related to the arc length of its trajectory. The arc-length formula for parametric curves in space (or *space curves*) is a natural generalization of the formula for parametric plane curves [Eq. (8) of Section 10.5]. The **arc length** s along the smooth curve with position vector

$$\mathbf{r}(t) = f(t)\mathbf{i} + g(t)\mathbf{j} + h(t)\mathbf{k} = x\mathbf{i} + y\mathbf{j} + z\mathbf{k} \tag{1}$$

from the point $\mathbf{r}(a)$ to the point $\mathbf{r}(b)$ is, by definition,

$$s = \int_a^b \sqrt{[x'(t)]^2 + [y'(t)]^2 + [z'(t)]^2}\, dt$$

$$= \int_a^b \sqrt{\left(\frac{dx}{dt}\right)^2 + \left(\frac{dy}{dt}\right)^2 + \left(\frac{dz}{dt}\right)^2}\, dt. \tag{2}$$

We see from Eq. (9) in Section 12.5 that the integrand is the speed $v(t) = |\mathbf{r}'(t)|$ of the moving point with position vector $\mathbf{r}(t)$, so

$$s = \int_a^b v(t)\, dt. \tag{3}$$

EXAMPLE 1 Find the arc length of one turn (from $t = 0$ to $t = 2\pi/\omega$) of the helix shown in Fig. 12.6.1. This helix has the parametric equations

$$x(t) = a \cos \omega t, \quad y(t) = a \sin \omega t, \quad z(t) = bt.$$

Solution We found in Example 7 of Section 12.5 that

$$v(t) = \sqrt{a^2\omega^2 + b^2}.$$

Hence Eq. (3) gives

$$s = \int_0^{2\pi/\omega} \sqrt{a^2\omega^2 + b^2}\, dt = \frac{2\pi}{\omega}\sqrt{a^2\omega^2 + b^2}.$$

For instance, if $a = b = \omega = 1$, then $s = 2\pi\sqrt{2}$, which is $\sqrt{2}$ times the circumference of the circle in the xy-plane over which the helix lies. ◆

FIGURE 12.6.1 The helix of Example 1.

Let $s(t)$ denote the arc length along a smooth curve from its initial point $\mathbf{r}(a)$ to the variable point $\mathbf{r}(t)$. Then, from Eq. (3), we obtain the **arc-length function** $s(t)$

of the curve:

$$s(t) = \int_a^t v(\tau)\,d\tau. \tag{4}$$

The fundamental theorem of calculus then gives

$$\frac{ds}{dt} = v. \tag{5}$$

Thus *the speed of the moving point is the time rate of change of its arc-length function.* If $v(t) > 0$ for all t, then it follows that $s(t)$ is an increasing function of t and therefore has an inverse function $t(s)$. When we replace t with $t(s)$ in the curve's original parametric equations, we obtain the **arc-length parametrization**

$$x = x(s), \qquad y = y(s), \qquad z = z(s).$$

This gives the position of the moving point as a function of arc length measured along the curve from its initial point. (See Fig. 12.6.2.)

FIGURE 12.6.2 A curve parametrized by arc length s.

EXAMPLE 2 If we take $a = 5$, $b = 12$, and $\omega = 1$ for the helix of Example 1, then the velocity formula $v = (a^2\omega^2 + b^2)^{1/2}$ yields

$$v = \sqrt{5^2 \cdot 1^2 + 12^2} = \sqrt{169} = 13.$$

Hence Eq. (5) gives $ds/dt = 13$, so

$$s = 13t,$$

taking $s = 0$ when $t = 0$ and thereby measuring arc length from the natural starting point $(5, 0, 0)$. When we substitute $t = s/13$ and the numerical values of $a, b,$ and ω into the original parametric equations of the helix, we get the arc-length parametrization

$$x(s) = 5\cos\frac{s}{13}, \qquad y(s) = 5\sin\frac{s}{13}, \qquad z(s) = \frac{12s}{13}$$

of the helix. ◆

Curvature of Plane Curves

FIGURE 12.6.3 The intuitive idea of curvature.

The word *curvature* has an intuitive meaning that we need to make precise. Most people would agree that a straight line does not curve at all, whereas a circle of small radius is more curved than a circle of large radius (Fig. 12.6.3). This judgment may be based on a conception of curvature as "rate of change of direction." The direction of a curve is determined by its velocity vector, so you would expect the idea of curvature to have something to do with the rate at which the velocity vector is turning.

Let

$$\mathbf{r}(t) = x(t)\mathbf{i} + y(t)\mathbf{j}, \qquad a \le t \le b \tag{6}$$

be the position vector of a differentiable plane curve that is *smooth*—meaning that the velocity vector $\mathbf{v}(t) = \mathbf{r}'(t)$ is *nonzero*. Then the curve's **unit tangent vector** at the point $\mathbf{r}(t)$ is the unit vector

$$\mathbf{T}(t) = \frac{\mathbf{v}(t)}{|\mathbf{v}(t)|} = \frac{\mathbf{v}(t)}{v(t)}, \tag{7}$$

where $v(t) = |\mathbf{v}(t)|$ is the speed. Now denote by ϕ the angle of inclination of T, measured counterclockwise from the positive x-axis (Fig. 12.6.4). Then

$$\mathbf{T} = \mathbf{i}\cos\phi + \mathbf{j}\sin\phi. \tag{8}$$

FIGURE 12.6.4 The unit tangent vector $\mathbf{T}$.

We can express the unit tangent vector $\mathbf{T}$ of Eq. (8) as a function of the arc-length parameter s indicated in Fig. 12.6.4. Then the rate at which $\mathbf{T}$ is turning is measured by the derivative

$$\frac{d\mathbf{T}}{ds} = \frac{d\mathbf{T}}{d\phi} \cdot \frac{d\phi}{ds} = (-\mathbf{i}\sin\phi + \mathbf{j}\cos\phi)\frac{d\phi}{ds}. \qquad (9)$$

Note that

$$\left|\frac{d\mathbf{T}}{ds}\right| = \left|\frac{d\phi}{ds}\right| \qquad (10)$$

because the vector on the right-hand side of Eq. (9) is a unit vector.

The **curvature** at a point of a plane curve, denoted by κ (lowercase Greek kappa), is therefore defined to be

$$\kappa = \left|\frac{d\phi}{ds}\right|, \qquad (11)$$

the absolute value of the rate of change of the angle ϕ with respect to arc length s. We define the curvature κ in terms of $d\phi/ds$ rather than $d\phi/dt$ because the latter depends not only on the shape of the curve, but also on the speed of the moving point $\mathbf{r}(t)$. For a straight line the angle ϕ is a constant, so the curvature given by Eq. (11) is zero. If you imagine a point that is moving with constant speed along a curve, the curvature is greatest at points where ϕ changes the most rapidly, such as the points P and R on the curve of Fig. 12.6.5. The curvature is least at points such as Q and S, where ϕ is changing the least rapidly.

We need to derive a formula that is effective in computing the curvature of a smooth parametric plane curve $x = x(t)$, $y = y(t)$. First we note that

$$\phi = \tan^{-1}\left(\frac{dy}{dx}\right) = \tan^{-1}\left(\frac{y'(t)}{x'(t)}\right)$$

provided $x'(t) \neq 0$. Hence

$$\frac{d\phi}{dt} = \frac{y''x' - y'x''}{(x')^2} \div \left(1 + \left(\frac{y'}{x'}\right)^2\right) = \frac{x'y'' - x''y'}{(x')^2 + (y')^2},$$

where primes denote derivatives with respect to t. Because $v = ds/dt > 0$, Eq. (11) gives

$$\kappa = \left|\frac{d\phi}{ds}\right| = \left|\frac{d\phi}{dt} \cdot \frac{dt}{ds}\right| = \frac{1}{v}\left|\frac{d\phi}{dt}\right|;$$

thus

$$\kappa = \frac{|x'y'' - x''y'|}{[(x')^2 + (y')^2]^{3/2}} = \frac{|x'y'' - x''y'|}{v^3}. \qquad (12)$$

At a point where $x'(t) = 0$, we know that $y'(t) \neq 0$, because the curve is smooth. Thus we will obtain the same result if we begin with the equation $\phi = \cot^{-1}(x'/y')$.

An explicitly described curve $y = f(x)$ may be regarded as a parametric curve $x = x$, $y = f(x)$. Then $x' = 1$ and $x'' = 0$, so Eq. (12)—with x in place of t as the parameter—becomes

$$\kappa = \frac{|y''|}{[1 + (y')^2]^{3/2}} = \frac{|d^2y/dx^2|}{[1 + (dy/dx)^2]^{3/2}}. \qquad (13)$$

FIGURE 12.6.5 The curvature is large at P and R, small at Q and S.

EXAMPLE 3 Show that the curvature at each point of a circle of radius a is $\kappa = 1/a$.

Solution With the familiar parametrization $x = a\cos t$, $y = a\sin t$ of such a circle centered at the origin, we let primes denote derivatives with respect to t and obtain

$$x' = -a\sin t, \qquad y' = a\cos t,$$
$$x'' = -a\cos t, \qquad y'' = -a\sin t.$$

Hence Eq. (12) gives

$$\kappa = \frac{|(-a\sin t)(-a\sin t) - (-a\cos t)(a\cos t)|}{[(-a\sin t)^2 + (a\cos t)^2]^{3/2}} = \frac{a^2}{a^3} = \frac{1}{a}.$$

Alternatively, we could have used Eq. (13). Our point of departure would then be the equation $x^2 + y^2 = a^2$ of the same circle, and we would compute y' and y'' by implicit differentiation. (See Problem 27.) ◆

It follows immediately from Eqs. (8) and (9) that

$$\mathbf{T} \cdot \frac{d\mathbf{T}}{ds} = 0,$$

so the unit tangent vector $\mathbf{T}$ and its derivative vector $d\mathbf{T}/ds$ are perpendicular. If $|d\mathbf{T}/ds| \neq 0$, then the *unit* vector $\mathbf{N}$ that points in the direction of $d\mathbf{T}/ds$ is called the **principal unit normal vector** to the curve. Because $\kappa = |d\phi/ds| = |d\mathbf{T}/ds|$ by Eq. (10), it follows that

$$\frac{d\mathbf{T}}{ds} = \kappa\mathbf{N}. \quad (14)$$

Intuitively, $\mathbf{N}$ *is the unit normal vector to the curve that points in the direction in which the curve is bending.*

Suppose that P is a point on a parametrized curve at which $\kappa \neq 0$. Consider the circle that is tangent to the curve at P and has the same curvature there. The center of the circle is to lie on the concave side of the curve—that is, on the side toward which the normal vector $\mathbf{N}$ points. This circle is called the **osculating circle** (or **circle of curvature**) of the curve at the given point because it touches the curve so closely there. (*Osculum* is the Latin word for *kiss*.) Let ρ be the radius of the osculating circle and let $\gamma = \overrightarrow{OC}$ be the position vector of its center C (Fig. 12.6.6). Then ρ is called the **radius of curvature** of the curve at the point P and γ is called the (vector) **center of curvature** of the curve at P.

Example 3 implies that the radius of curvature is

$$\rho = \frac{1}{\kappa}, \quad (15)$$

FIGURE 12.6.6 Osculating circle, radius of curvature, and center of curvature.

and the fact that $|\mathbf{N}| = 1$ implies that the position vector of the center of curvature is

$$\gamma = \mathbf{r} + \rho\mathbf{N} \quad (\mathbf{r} = \overrightarrow{OP}). \quad (16)$$

EXAMPLE 4 Determine the vectors $\mathbf{T}$ and $\mathbf{N}$, the curvature κ, and the center of curvature of the parabola $y = x^2$ at the point $(1, 1)$.

Solution If the parabola is parametrized by $x = t$, $y = t^2$, then its position vector is $\mathbf{r}(t) = t\mathbf{i} + t^2\mathbf{j}$, so $\mathbf{v}(t) = \mathbf{i} + 2t\mathbf{j}$. The speed is $v(t) = \sqrt{1 + 4t^2}$, so Eq. (7) yields

$$\mathbf{T}(t) = \frac{\mathbf{v}(t)}{v(t)} = \frac{\mathbf{i} + 2t\mathbf{j}}{\sqrt{1 + 4t^2}}.$$

By substituting $t = 1$, we find that the unit tangent vector at $(1, 1)$ is

$$\mathbf{T} = \frac{1}{\sqrt{5}}\mathbf{i} + \frac{2}{\sqrt{5}}\mathbf{j}.$$

Because the parabola is concave upward at $(1, 1)$, the principal unit normal vector is the upward-pointing unit vector

$$\mathbf{N} = -\frac{2}{\sqrt{5}}\mathbf{i} + \frac{1}{\sqrt{5}}\mathbf{j}$$

that is perpendicular to **T**. (Note that $\mathbf{T} \cdot \mathbf{N} = 0$.) If $y = x^2$, then $dy/dx = 2x$ and $d^2y/dx^2 = 2$, so Eq. (13) yields

$$\kappa = \frac{|y''|}{[1 + (y')^2]^{3/2}} = \frac{2}{(1 + 4x^2)^{3/2}}.$$

So at the point $(1, 1)$ we find the curvature and radius of curvature to be

$$\kappa = \frac{2}{5\sqrt{5}} \quad \text{and} \quad \rho = \frac{5\sqrt{5}}{2},$$

respectively.

Next, Eq. (16) gives the center of curvature as

$$\gamma = \langle 1, 1 \rangle + \frac{5\sqrt{5}}{2} \left\langle -\frac{2}{\sqrt{5}}, \frac{1}{\sqrt{5}} \right\rangle = \left\langle -4, \frac{7}{2} \right\rangle.$$

The equation of the osculating circle to the parabola at $(1, 1)$ is, therefore,

$$(x + 4)^2 + \left(y - \tfrac{7}{2}\right)^2 = \rho^2 = \tfrac{125}{4}.$$

Figure 12.6.7 shows this large osculating circle at the point $(1, 1)$, as well as the smaller osculating circles that are tangent to the parabola at the points $(0, 0)$, $(\tfrac{1}{3}, \tfrac{1}{9})$, and $(\tfrac{2}{3}, \tfrac{4}{9})$. Is it clear to you which of these osculating circles is which? ◆

FIGURE 12.6.7 Osculating circles for the parabola of Example 4.

Curvature of Space Curves

Consider now a moving particle in space with twice-differentiable position vector $\mathbf{r}(t)$. Suppose also that the velocity vector $\mathbf{v}(t)$ is never zero. The **unit tangent vector** at time t is defined, as before, to be

$$\mathbf{T}(t) = \frac{\mathbf{v}(t)}{|\mathbf{v}(t)|} = \frac{\mathbf{v}(t)}{v(t)}, \tag{17}$$

so

$$\mathbf{v} = v\mathbf{T}. \tag{18}$$

We defined the curvature of a plane curve to be $\kappa = |d\phi/ds|$, where ϕ is the angle of inclination of **T** from the positive x-axis. For a space curve, there is no single angle that determines the direction of **T**, so we adopt the following approach (which leads to the same value for curvature when applied to a space curve that happens to lie in the xy-plane). Differentiating the identity $\mathbf{T} \cdot \mathbf{T} = 1$ with respect to arc length s gives

$$\mathbf{T} \cdot \frac{d\mathbf{T}}{ds} = 0.$$

It follows that the vectors **T** and $d\mathbf{T}/ds$ are always perpendicular.

Then we define the **curvature** κ of the curve at the point $\mathbf{r}(t)$ to be

$$\kappa = \left|\frac{d\mathbf{T}}{ds}\right| = \left|\frac{d\mathbf{T}}{dt}\frac{dt}{ds}\right| = \frac{1}{v}\left|\frac{d\mathbf{T}}{dt}\right|. \tag{19}$$

At a point where $\kappa \neq 0$, we define the **principal unit normal vector N** to be

$$\mathbf{N} = \frac{d\mathbf{T}/ds}{|d\mathbf{T}/ds|} = \frac{1}{\kappa}\frac{d\mathbf{T}}{ds}, \tag{20}$$

so

$$\frac{d\mathbf{T}}{ds} = \kappa \mathbf{N}. \tag{21}$$

FIGURE 12.6.8 The principal unit normal vector **N** points in the direction in which the curve is turning.

Equation (21) shows that **N** has the same direction as $d\mathbf{T}/ds$ (Fig. 12.6.8), and Eq. (20) shows that **N** is a unit vector. Because Eq. (21) is the same as Eq. (14), we see that the present definitions of κ and **N** agree with those given earlier in the two-dimensional case.

EXAMPLE 5 Compute the curvature κ of the helix of Example 1, the helix with parametric equations

$$x(t) = a\cos\omega t, \qquad y(t) = a\sin\omega t, \qquad z(t) = bt.$$

Solution In Example 7 of Section 12.5, we computed the velocity vector

$$\mathbf{v} = \mathbf{i}(-a\omega\sin\omega t) + \mathbf{j}(a\omega\cos\omega t) + b\mathbf{k}$$

and speed

$$v = |\mathbf{v}| = \sqrt{a^2\omega^2 + b^2}.$$

Hence Eq. (17) gives the unit tangent vector

$$\mathbf{T} = \frac{\mathbf{v}}{v} = \frac{\mathbf{i}(-a\omega\sin\omega t) + \mathbf{j}(a\omega\cos\omega t) + b\mathbf{k}}{\sqrt{a^2\omega^2 + b^2}}.$$

Then

$$\frac{d\mathbf{T}}{dt} = \frac{\mathbf{i}(-a\omega^2\cos\omega t) + \mathbf{j}(-a\omega^2\sin\omega t)}{\sqrt{a^2\omega^2 + b^2}},$$

so Eq. (19) gives

$$\kappa = \frac{1}{v}\left|\frac{d\mathbf{T}}{dt}\right| = \frac{a\omega^2}{a^2\omega^2 + b^2}$$

for the curvature of the helix. Note that the helix has constant curvature. Also note that, if $b = 0$ (so that the helix reduces to a circle of radius a in the xy-plane), our result reduces to $\kappa = 1/a$, in agreement with our computation of the curvature of a circle in Example 3. ◆

Normal and Tangential Components of Acceleration

We may apply Eq. (21) to analyze the meaning of the acceleration vector of a moving particle with velocity vector $\mathbf{v}$ and speed v. Then Eq. (17) gives $\mathbf{v} = v\mathbf{T}$, so the acceleration vector of the particle is

$$\mathbf{a} = \frac{d\mathbf{v}}{dt} = \frac{dv}{dt}\mathbf{T} + v\frac{d\mathbf{T}}{dt} = \frac{dv}{dt}\mathbf{T} + v\frac{d\mathbf{T}}{ds}\frac{ds}{dt}.$$

But $ds/dt = v$, so Eq. (21) gives

$$\mathbf{a} = \frac{dv}{dt}\mathbf{T} + \kappa v^2 \mathbf{N}. \tag{22}$$

Because $\mathbf{T}$ and $\mathbf{N}$ are unit vectors tangent and normal to the curve, respectively, Eq. (22) provides a *decomposition of the acceleration vector* into its components tangent to and normal to the trajectory. The **tangential component**

$$a_T = \frac{dv}{dt} \tag{23}$$

is the rate of change of speed of the particle, whereas the **normal component**

$$a_N = \kappa v^2 = \frac{v^2}{\rho} \tag{24}$$

measures the rate of change of its direction of motion. The decomposition

$$\mathbf{a} = a_T\mathbf{T} + a_N\mathbf{N} \tag{25}$$

is illustrated in Fig. 12.6.9.

FIGURE 12.6.9 Resolution of the acceleration vector $\mathbf{a}$ into its tangential and normal components.

As an application of Eq. (22), think of a train moving along a straight track with constant speed v, so that $a_T = 0 = a_N$ (the latter because $\kappa = 0$ for a straight line). Suppose that at time $t = 0$, the train enters a circular curve of radius ρ. At that instant, it will *suddenly* be subjected to a normal acceleration of magnitude v^2/ρ, proportional to the *square* of the speed of the train. A passenger in the train will experience a sudden jerk to the side. If v is large, the stresses may be great enough to damage the track or derail the train. It is for exactly this reason that railroads are built not with curves shaped like arcs of circles but with *approach curves* in which the curvature, and hence the normal acceleration, build up smoothly.

EXAMPLE 6 A particle moves in the xy-plane with parametric equations

$$x(t) = \tfrac{3}{2}t^2, \qquad y(t) = \tfrac{4}{3}t^3.$$

Find the tangential and normal components of its acceleration vector when $t = 1$.

Solution The trajectory and the vectors **N** and **T** appear in Fig. 12.6.10. There **N** and **T** are shown attached at the point of evaluation, at which $t = 1$. The particle has position vector

$$\mathbf{r}(t) = \tfrac{3}{2}t^2\mathbf{i} + \tfrac{4}{3}t^3\mathbf{j}$$

and thus velocity

$$\mathbf{v}(t) = 3t\mathbf{i} + 4t^2\mathbf{j}.$$

Hence its speed is

$$v(t) = \sqrt{9t^2 + 16t^4},$$

from which we calculate

$$a_T = \frac{dv}{dt} = \frac{9t + 32t^3}{\sqrt{9t^2 + 16t^4}}.$$

Thus $v = 5$ and $a_T = \tfrac{41}{5}$ when $t = 1$.

To use Eq. (12) to compute the curvature at $t = 1$, we compute $dx/dt = 3t$, $dy/dt = 4t^2$, $d^2x/dt^2 = 3$, and $d^2y/dt^2 = 8t$. Thus at $t = 1$ we have

$$\kappa = \frac{|x'y'' - x''y'|}{v^3} = \frac{|3 \cdot 8 - 3 \cdot 4|}{5^3} = \frac{12}{125}.$$

Hence

$$a_N = \kappa v^2 = \tfrac{12}{125} \cdot 5^2 = \tfrac{12}{5}$$

when $t = 1$. As a check (Problem 28), you might compute **T** and **N** when $t = 1$ and verify that

$$\tfrac{41}{5}\mathbf{T} + \tfrac{12}{5}\mathbf{N} = \mathbf{a} = 3\mathbf{i} + 8\mathbf{j}. \qquad \blacklozenge$$

It remains for us to see how to compute a_T, a_N, and **N** effectively in the case of a space curve. We would prefer to have formulas that explicitly contain only the vectors **r**, **v**, and **a**.

If we compute the dot product of $\mathbf{v} = v\mathbf{T}$ with the acceleration **a** as given in Eq. (22) and use the facts that $\mathbf{T} \cdot \mathbf{T} = 1$ and $\mathbf{T} \cdot \mathbf{N} = 0$, we get

$$\mathbf{v} \cdot \mathbf{a} = v\mathbf{T} \cdot \left(\frac{dv}{dt}\mathbf{T}\right) + (v\mathbf{T}) \cdot (\kappa v^2 \mathbf{N}) = v\frac{dv}{dt}.$$

It follows that

$$a_T = \frac{dv}{dt} = \frac{\mathbf{v} \cdot \mathbf{a}}{v} = \frac{\mathbf{r}'(t) \cdot \mathbf{r}''(t)}{|\mathbf{r}'(t)|}. \tag{26}$$

FIGURE 12.6.10 The moving particle of Example 6.

Similarly, when we compute the cross product of $\mathbf{v} = v\mathbf{T}$ with each side of Eq. (22), we find that

$$\mathbf{v} \times \mathbf{a} = \left(v\mathbf{T} \times \frac{dv}{dt}\mathbf{T}\right) + (v\mathbf{T} \times \kappa v^2 \mathbf{N}) = \kappa v^3 (\mathbf{T} \times \mathbf{N}).$$

Because κ and v are nonnegative and because $\mathbf{T} \times \mathbf{N}$ is a unit vector, we may conclude that

$$\kappa = \frac{|\mathbf{v} \times \mathbf{a}|}{v^3} = \frac{|\mathbf{r}'(t) \times \mathbf{r}''(t)|}{|\mathbf{r}'(t)|^3}. \tag{27}$$

It now follows from Eq. (24) that

$$a_N = \frac{|\mathbf{r}'(t) \times \mathbf{r}''(t)|}{|\mathbf{r}'(t)|}. \tag{28}$$

The curvature of a space curve often is not as easy to compute directly from the definition as we found in the case of the helix of Example 5. It is generally more convenient to use Eq. (27). Once $\mathbf{a}$, $\mathbf{T}$, a_T, and a_N have been computed, we can rewrite Eq. (25) as

$$\mathbf{N} = \frac{\mathbf{a} - a_T \mathbf{T}}{a_N} \tag{29}$$

to find the principal unit normal vector.

EXAMPLE 7 Compute $\mathbf{T}$, $\mathbf{N}$, κ, a_T, and a_N at the point $(1, \frac{1}{2}, \frac{1}{3})$ of the twisted cubic with parametric equations

$$x(t) = t, \qquad y(t) = \tfrac{1}{2}t^2, \qquad z(t) = \tfrac{1}{3}t^3.$$

Solution Differentiating the position vector

$$\mathbf{r}(t) = \langle t, \tfrac{1}{2}t^2, \tfrac{1}{3}t^3 \rangle$$

gives

$$\mathbf{r}'(t) = \langle 1, t, t^2 \rangle \quad \text{and} \quad \mathbf{r}''(t) = \langle 0, 1, 2t \rangle.$$

When we substitute $t = 1$, we obtain

$$\mathbf{v}(1) = \langle 1, 1, 1 \rangle \qquad \text{(velocity)},$$
$$v(1) = |\mathbf{v}(1)| = \sqrt{3} \qquad \text{(speed), and}$$
$$\mathbf{a}(1) = \langle 0, 1, 2 \rangle \qquad \text{(acceleration)}$$

at the point $(1, \frac{1}{2}, \frac{1}{3})$. Then Eq. (26) gives the tangential component of acceleration:

$$a_T = \frac{\mathbf{v} \cdot \mathbf{a}}{v} = \frac{3}{\sqrt{3}} = \sqrt{3}.$$

Because

$$\mathbf{v} \times \mathbf{a} = \begin{vmatrix} \mathbf{i} & \mathbf{j} & \mathbf{k} \\ 1 & 1 & 1 \\ 0 & 1 & 2 \end{vmatrix} = \langle 1, -2, 1 \rangle,$$

Eq. (27) gives the curvature:

$$\kappa = \frac{|\mathbf{v} \times \mathbf{a}|}{v^3} = \frac{\sqrt{6}}{(\sqrt{3})^3} = \frac{\sqrt{2}}{3}.$$

Curvature and Acceleration SECTION 12.6   825

The normal component of acceleration is $a_N = \kappa v^2 = \sqrt{2}$. The unit tangent vector is

$$\mathbf{T} = \frac{\mathbf{v}}{v} = \frac{1}{\sqrt{3}}\langle 1, 1, 1\rangle = \frac{\mathbf{i} + \mathbf{j} + \mathbf{k}}{\sqrt{3}}.$$

Finally, Eq. (29) gives

$$\mathbf{N} = \frac{\mathbf{a} - a_T\mathbf{T}}{a_N} = \frac{1}{\sqrt{2}}(\langle 0, 1, 2\rangle - \langle 1, 1, 1\rangle) = \frac{1}{\sqrt{2}}\langle -1, 0, 1\rangle = \frac{-\mathbf{i} + \mathbf{k}}{\sqrt{2}}.$$

Figure 12.6.11 shows the twisted cubic and its osculating circle at the point P. This osculating circle has radius $a = 1/\kappa = \frac{3}{2}\sqrt{2}$ and its center C has position vector $\overrightarrow{OC} = \overrightarrow{OP} + a\mathbf{N} = \langle -\frac{1}{2}, \frac{1}{2}, \frac{11}{6}\rangle.$ ◆

FIGURE 12.6.11 Osculating circle for the twisted cubic of Example 7. It is plotted as the parametric curve with position vector $\mathbf{r}(t) = \overrightarrow{OC} - (a\cos t)\mathbf{N} + (a\sin t)\mathbf{T}$.

Newton, Kepler, and the Solar System

As outlined on the opening page of this chapter, the modern view of our solar system dates back to the formulation by Johannes Kepler (1571–1630) of the following three propositions, now known as **Kepler's laws of planetary motion.**

1. The orbit of each planet is an ellipse with the sun at one focus.
2. The radius vector from the sun to a planet sweeps out area at a constant rate.
3. The *square* of the period of revolution of a planet about the sun is proportional to the *cube* of the major semiaxis of its elliptical orbit.

Figure 12.6.12 illustrates Kepler's second law. If the planet traverses the paths P_1P_2 and P_3P_4 along its orbit in equal times, then the areas of the shaded elliptical sectors SP_1P_2 and SP_3P_4 are equal.

In his *Principia Mathematica* (1687), Newton employed a powerful but now antiquated form of geometrical calculus to show that Kepler's laws follow from the basic principles of mechanics ($F = ma$, and so on) and the inverse-square law of gravitational attraction. In the remainder of this section we apply the modern calculus of vector-valued functions to outline the relation between Newton's laws and Kepler's laws.

FIGURE 12.6.12 Kepler's law implies that the shaded areas are equal if the planet's times of traversal of the orbital segments P_1P_2 and P_3P_4 are equal.

Radial and Transverse Components of Acceleration

To begin, we set up a coordinate system in which the sun is located at the origin in the plane of motion of a planet. Let $r = r(t)$ and $\theta = \theta(t)$ be the polar coordinates at time t of the planet as it orbits the sun. We want first to split the planet's position, velocity, and acceleration vectors $\mathbf{r}$, $\mathbf{v}$, and $\mathbf{a}$ into *radial* and *transverse* components. To do so, we introduce at each point (r, θ) of the plane (the origin excepted) the *unit* vectors

$$\mathbf{u}_r = \mathbf{i}\cos\theta + \mathbf{j}\sin\theta, \qquad \mathbf{u}_\theta = -\mathbf{i}\sin\theta + \mathbf{j}\cos\theta. \tag{30}$$

If we substitute $\theta = \theta(t)$, then $\mathbf{u}_r$ and $\mathbf{u}_\theta$ become functions of t. The **radial** unit vector $\mathbf{u}_r$ always points directly away from the origin; the **transverse** unit vector $\mathbf{u}_\theta$ is obtained from $\mathbf{u}_r$ by a 90° counterclockwise rotation (Fig. 12.6.13).

In Problem 66 we ask you to verify, by componentwise differentiation of the equations in (30), that

$$\frac{d\mathbf{u}_r}{dt} = \mathbf{u}_\theta\frac{d\theta}{dt} \quad \text{and} \quad \frac{d\mathbf{u}_\theta}{dt} = -\mathbf{u}_r\frac{d\theta}{dt}. \tag{31}$$

FIGURE 12.6.13 The radial and transverse unit vector $\mathbf{u}_r$ and $\mathbf{u}_\theta$.

The position vector $\mathbf{r}$ points directly away from the origin and has length $|\mathbf{r}| = r$, so

$$\mathbf{r} = r\mathbf{u}_r. \tag{32}$$

Differentiating both sides of Eq. (32) with respect to t gives

$$\mathbf{v} = \frac{d\mathbf{r}}{dt} = \mathbf{u}_r\frac{dr}{dt} + r\frac{d\mathbf{u}_r}{dt}.$$

We use the first equation in (31) and find that the planet's velocity vector is

$$\mathbf{v} = \mathbf{u}_r \frac{dr}{dt} + r \frac{d\theta}{dt} \mathbf{u}_\theta. \tag{33}$$

Thus we have expressed the velocity $\mathbf{v}$ in terms of the radial vector $\mathbf{u}_r$ and the transverse vector $\mathbf{u}_\theta$.

We differentiate both sides of Eq. (33) and thereby find that

$$\mathbf{a} = \frac{d\mathbf{v}}{dt} = \left(\mathbf{u}_r \frac{d^2 r}{dt^2} + \frac{dr}{dt} \frac{d\mathbf{u}_r}{dt} \right) + \left(\frac{dr}{dt} \frac{d\theta}{dt} \mathbf{u}_\theta + r \frac{d^2\theta}{dt^2} \mathbf{u}_\theta + r \frac{d\theta}{dt} \frac{d\mathbf{u}_\theta}{dt} \right).$$

Then, by using the equations in (31) and collecting the coefficients of $\mathbf{u}_r$ and $\mathbf{u}_\theta$ (Problem 67), we obtain the decomposition

$$\mathbf{a} = \left[\frac{d^2 r}{dt^2} - r \left(\frac{d\theta}{dt} \right)^2 \right] \mathbf{u}_r + \left[\frac{1}{r} \frac{d}{dt} \left(r^2 \frac{d\theta}{dt} \right) \right] \mathbf{u}_\theta \tag{34}$$

of the acceleration vector into its radial and transverse components.

Planets and Satellites

The key to Newton's analysis was the connection between his law of gravitational attraction and Kepler's *second* law of planetary motion. Suppose that we begin with the inverse-square law of gravitation in its vector form

$$\mathbf{F} = m\mathbf{a} = -\frac{GMm}{r^2} \mathbf{u}_r, \tag{35}$$

where M denotes the mass of the sun and m the mass of the orbiting planet. But the acceleration of the planet is given *also* by

$$\mathbf{a} = -\frac{\mu}{r^2} \mathbf{u}_r, \tag{36}$$

where $\mu = GM$. We equate the transverse components in Eqs. (34) and (36) and thus obtain

$$\frac{1}{r} \cdot \frac{d}{dt} \left(r^2 \frac{d\theta}{dt} \right) = 0.$$

We drop the factor $1/r$, then antidifferentiate both sides. We find that

$$r^2 \frac{d\theta}{dt} = h \quad (h \text{ a constant}). \tag{37}$$

FIGURE 12.6.14 Area swept out by the radius vector.

We know from Section 10.3 that if $A(t)$ denotes the area swept out by the planet's radius vector from time 0 to time t (Fig. 12.6.14), then

$$A(t) = \int_{\theta(0)}^{\theta(t)} \frac{1}{2} r^2 \, d\theta = \int_0^t \frac{1}{2} r^2 \frac{d\theta}{dt} \, dt.$$

Now we apply the fundamental theorem of calculus, which yields

$$\frac{dA}{dt} = \frac{1}{2} r^2 \frac{d\theta}{dt}. \tag{38}$$

When we compare Eqs. (37) and (38), we see that

$$\frac{dA}{dt} = \frac{h}{2}. \tag{39}$$

FIGURE 12.6.15 A polar coordinate ellipse with eccentricity $e = |OP|/|PQ|$.

Because $h/2$ is a constant, we have derived Kepler's second law: The radius vector from sun to planet sweeps out area at a constant rate.

Next we outline the derivation of Newton's law of gravitation from Kepler's first and second laws of planetary motion. Figure 12.6.15 shows an ellipse with eccentricity e and focus at the origin. The defining relation $|OP| = e|PQ|$ of this ellipse gives $r = e(p - r \cos\theta)$. Solving this equation then yields the polar-coordinate equation

$$r = \frac{pe}{1 + e \cos\theta} \tag{40}$$

of an ellipse with eccentricity $e < 1$ and directrix $x = p$. In Problem 64 we ask you to show by differentiating twice, using the chain rule and Kepler's second law in the form in Eq. (37), that Eq. (40) implies that

$$\frac{d^2 r}{dt^2} = \frac{h^2}{r^2}\left(\frac{1}{r} - \frac{1}{pe}\right). \tag{41}$$

Now if Kepler's second law in the form in Eq. (37) holds, then Eq. (34) gives

$$\mathbf{a} = \left[\frac{d^2 r}{dt^2} - r\left(\frac{d\theta}{dt}\right)^2\right]\mathbf{u}_r \tag{42}$$

for the planet's acceleration vector. Finally, upon substituting $d\theta/dt = h/r^2$ from Eq. (37) and the expression in Eq. (41) for d^2r/dt^2, we find (Problem 65) that Eq. (42) can be simplified to the form

$$\mathbf{a} = -\frac{h^2}{per^2}\mathbf{u}_r. \tag{43}$$

This is the inverse-square law of gravitation in the form of Eq. (36) with $\mu = h^2/pe$.

Now suppose that the elliptical orbit of a planet around the sun has major semiaxis a and minor semiaxis b. Then the constant

$$pe = \frac{h^2}{\mu}$$

that appears in Eq. (42) satisfies the equations

$$pe = a(1 - e^2) = a\left(1 - \frac{a^2 - b^2}{a^2}\right) = \frac{b^2}{a}.$$

[See Eq. (29) in Section 10.6.] We equate these two expressions for pe and find that $h^2 = \mu b^2/a$.

Now let T denote the period of revolution of the planet—the time required for it to complete one full revolution in its elliptical orbit around the sun. Then we see from Eq. (39) that the area of the ellipse bounded by this orbit is $A = \frac{1}{2}hT = \pi ab$ and thus that

$$T^2 = \frac{4\pi^2 a^2 b^2}{h^2} = \frac{4\pi^2 a^2 b^2}{\mu b^2 / a}.$$

Therefore

$$T^2 = \gamma a^3, \tag{44}$$

where the proportionality constant $\gamma = 4\pi^2/\mu = 4\pi^2/GM$ [compare Eqs. (35) and (36)] depends on the gravitational constant G and the sun's mass M. Thus we have derived Kepler's third law of planetary motion from his first two laws and Newton's law of gravitational attraction.

EXAMPLE 8 The period of revolution of Mercury in its elliptical orbit around the sun is $T = 87.97$ days, whereas that of the earth is 365.26 days. Compute the major semiaxis (in astronomical units) of the orbit of Mercury. See Fig. 12.6.16.

FIGURE 12.6.16 The inner planets of the solar system (Example 8).

Solution The major semiaxis of the orbit of the earth is, by definition, 1 AU. So Eq. (44) gives the value of the constant $\gamma = (365.26)^2$ (in day^2/AU^3). Hence the major semiaxis of the orbit of Mercury is

$$a = \left(\frac{T^2}{\gamma}\right)^{1/3} = \left(\frac{(87.97)^2}{(365.26)^2}\right)^{1/3} \approx 0.387 \quad (AU).$$

As yet we have considered only planets in orbits around the sun. But Kepler's laws and the equations of this section apply to bodies in orbit around any common central mass, so long as they move solely under the influence of *its* gravitational attraction. Examples include satellites (artificial or natural) orbiting the earth or the moons of Jupiter.

EXAMPLE 9 A communications relay satellite is to be placed in a circular orbit around the earth and is to have a period of revolution of 24 h. This is a *geosynchronous* orbit in which the satellite appears to be stationary in the sky. Assume that the earth's natural moon has a period of 27.32 days in a circular orbit of radius 238,850 mi. What should be the radius of the satellite's orbit? (See Fig. 12.6.17.)

FIGURE 12.6.17 A communications satellite in orbit around the earth (Example 9).

Solution Equation (44), when applied to the moon, yields

$$(27.32)^2 = \gamma(238,850)^3.$$

For the stationary satellite that has period $T = 1$ (day), it yields $1^2 = \gamma r^3$, where r is the radius of the geosynchronous orbit. To eliminate γ, we divide the second of these equations by the first and find that

$$r^3 = \frac{(238,850)^3}{(27.32)^2}.$$

Thus r is approximately 26,330 mi. The radius of the earth is about 3960 mi, so the satellite will be 22370 mi above the surface.

12.6 TRUE/FALSE STUDY GUIDE

12.6 CONCEPTS: QUESTIONS AND DISCUSSION

1. The curvature of a plane curve is defined in Eq. (11) and the curvature of a space curve is defined in Eq. (21). Do these two definitions agree in the case of a curve that lies in the xy-plane? Explain why.
2. Suppose that two bodies move solely under their mutual gravitational attraction. Then each moves in an elliptical orbit about the other. For instance, in a coordinate system with the earth (rather than the sun) at the origin, the orbit of the sun is an ellipse with the earth at one focus. Which is *really* the center of the solar system? Is this a mathematical or a philosophical question?

12.6 PROBLEMS

Find the arc length of each curve described in Problems 1 through 6.

1. $x = 3\sin 2t$, $y = 3\cos 2t$, $z = 8t$; from $t = 0$ to $t = \pi$
2. $x = t$, $y = t^2/\sqrt{2}$, $z = t^3/3$; from $t = 0$ to $t = 1$
3. $x = 6e^t \cos t$, $y = 6e^t \sin t$, $z = 17e^t$; from $t = 0$ to $t = 1$
4. $x = t^2/2$, $y = \ln t$, $z = t\sqrt{2}$; from $t = 1$ to $t = 2$
5. $x = 3t\sin t$, $y = 3t\cos t$, $z = 2t^2$; from $t = 0$ to $t = 4/5$
6. $x = 2e^t$, $y = e^{-t}$, $z = 2t$; from $t = 0$ to $t = 1$

In Problems 7 through 12, find the curvature of the given plane curve at the indicated point.

7. $y = x^3$ at $(0, 0)$
8. $y = x^3$ at $(-1, -1)$
9. $y = \cos x$ at $(0, 1)$
10. $x = t - 1$, $y = t^2 + 3t + 2$, where $t = 2$
11. $x = 5\cos t$, $y = 4\sin t$, where $t = \pi/4$
12. $x = 5\cosh t$, $y = 3\sinh t$, where $t = 0$

In Problems 13 through 16, find the point or points on the given curve at which the curvature is a maximum.

13. $y = e^x$
14. $y = \ln x$
15. $x = 5\cos t$, $y = 3\sin t$
16. $xy = 1$

For the plane curves in Problems 17 through 21, find the unit tangent and normal vectors at the indicated point.

17. $y = x^3$ at $(-1, -1)$
18. $x = t^3, y = t^2$ at $(-1, 1)$
19. $x = 3\sin 2t, y = 4\cos 2t$, where $t = \pi/6$
20. $x = t - \sin t, y = 1 - \cos t$, where $t = \pi/2$
21. $x = \cos^3 t, y = \sin^3 t$, where $t = 3\pi/4$

The position vector of a particle moving in the plane is given in Problems 22 through 26. Find the tangential and normal components of the acceleration vector.

22. $\mathbf{r}(t) = 3\mathbf{i}\sin\pi t + 3\mathbf{j}\cos\pi t$
23. $\mathbf{r}(t) = (2t+1)\mathbf{i} + (3t^2 - 1)\mathbf{j}$
24. $\mathbf{r}(t) = \mathbf{i}\cosh 3t + \mathbf{j}\sinh 3t$
25. $\mathbf{r}(t) = \mathbf{i}t\cos t + \mathbf{j}t\sin t$
26. $\mathbf{r}(t) = \langle e^t \sin t, e^t \cos t \rangle$

27. Use Eq. (13) to compute the curvature of the circle with equation $x^2 + y^2 = a^2$.
28. Verify the equation $\frac{41}{5}\mathbf{T} + \frac{12}{5}\mathbf{N} = 3\mathbf{i} + 8\mathbf{j}$ given at the end of Example 6.

In Problems 29 through 31, find the equation of the osculating circle for the given plane curve at the indicated point.

29. $y = 1 - x^2$ at $(0, 1)$
30. $y = e^x$ at $(0, 1)$
31. $xy = 1$ at $(1, 1)$

Find the curvature κ of the space curves with position vectors given in Problems 32 through 36.

32. $\mathbf{r}(t) = t\mathbf{i} + (2t-1)\mathbf{j} + (3t+5)\mathbf{k}$
33. $\mathbf{r}(t) = t\mathbf{i} + \mathbf{j}\sin t + \mathbf{k}\cos t$
34. $\mathbf{r}(t) = \langle t, t^2, t^3 \rangle$
35. $\mathbf{r}(t) = \langle e^t \cos t, e^t \sin t, e^t \rangle$
36. $\mathbf{r}(t) = \mathbf{i}t\sin t + \mathbf{j}t\cos t + \mathbf{k}t$

37. through 41. Find the tangential and normal components of acceleration a_T and a_N for the curves of Problems 32 through 36, respectively.

In Problems 42 through 45, find the unit vectors $\mathbf{T}$ and $\mathbf{N}$ for the given curve at the indicated point.

42. The curve of Problem 34 at $(1, 1, 1)$.
43. The curve of Problem 33 at $(0, 0, 1)$.
44. The curve of Problem 3 at $(6, 0, 17)$.
45. The curve of Problem 35 at $(1, 0, 1)$.

46. Find $\mathbf{T}$, $\mathbf{N}$, a_T, and a_N as functions of t for the helix of Example 1.

47. Find the arc-length parametrization of the line

$$x(t) = 2 + 4t, \quad y(t) = 1 - 12t, \quad z(t) = 3 + 3t$$

in terms of the arc length s measured from the initial point $(2, 1, 3)$.

48. Find the arc-length parametrization of the circle

$$x(t) = 2\cos t, \quad y(t) = 2\sin t, \quad z = 0$$

in terms of the arc length s measured counterclockwise from the initial point $(2, 0, 0)$.

49. Find the arc-length parametrization of the helix

$$x(t) = 3\cos t, \quad y(t) = 3\sin t, \quad z(t) = 4t$$

in terms of the arc length s measured from the initial point $(3, 0, 0)$.

50. Substitute $x = t$, $y = f(t)$, and $z = 0$ into Eq. (27) to verify that the curvature of the plane curve $y = f(x)$ is

$$\kappa(x) = \frac{|f''(x)|}{[1 + (f'(x))^2]^{3/2}}.$$

51. A particle moves under the influence of a force that is always perpendicular to its direction of motion. Show that the speed of the particle must be constant.

52. Deduce from Eq. (24) that

$$\kappa = \frac{\sqrt{a^2 - (a_T)^2}}{v^2} = \frac{\sqrt{(x''(t))^2 + (y''(t))^2 - (v'(t))^2}}{(x'(t))^2 + (y'(t))^2}.$$

53. Apply the formula of Problem 52 to calculate the curvature of the curve

$$x(t) = \cos t + t\sin t, \quad y(t) = \sin t - t\cos t.$$

54. The folium of Descartes with equation $x^3 + y^3 = 3xy$ is shown in Fig. 12.6.18. Find the curvature and center of curvature of this folium at the point $(\frac{3}{2}, \frac{3}{2})$. Begin by calculating dy/dx and d^2y/dx^2 by implicit differentiation.

FIGURE 12.6.18 The folium of Descartes (Problem 54).

55. Determine the constants A, B, C, D, E, and F so that the curve

$$y = Ax^5 + Bx^4 + Cx^3 + Dx^2 + Ex + F$$

does, simultaneously, all of the following:
- Joins the two points $(0, 0)$ and $(1, 1)$;
- Has slope 0 at $(0, 0)$ and slope 1 at $(1, 1)$;
- Has curvature 0 at both $(0, 0)$ and $(1, 1)$.

The curve in question is shown in color in Fig. 12.6.19. Why would this be a good curve to join the railroad tracks, shown in black in the figure?

FIGURE 12.6.19 Connecting railroad tracks (Problem 55).

59. The earth's moon: $a = 238{,}900$ mi, $e = 0.055$, $T = 27.32$ days

60. An artificial earth satellite: $a = 10{,}000$ mi, $e = 0.5$

61. Assuming the earth to be a sphere with radius 3960 mi, find the altitude above the earth's surface of a satellite in a circular orbit that has a period of revolution of 1 h.

62. Given the fact that Jupiter's period of (almost) circular revolution around the Sun is 11.86 yr, calculate the distance of Jupiter from the Sun.

63. Suppose that an earth satellite in elliptical orbit varies in altitude from 100 to 1000 mi above the earth's surface (assumed spherical). Find this satellite's period of revolution.

64. (a) Beginning with the polar-coordinates equation of an ellipse in Eq. (40), apply the chain rule and Kepler's second law in the form $d\theta/dt = h/r^2$ to differentiate r with respect to t and thereby show that $dr/dt = (h \sin \theta)/p$. (b) Differentiate again to show that $d^2r/dt^2 = (h^2 \cos \theta)/(pr^2)$. (c) Derive Eq. (41) by solving Eq. (40) for $\cos \theta$ and substituting the result in the formula in part (b).

65. Derive Eq. (43) by substituting the expressions for $d\theta/dt$ and d^2r/dt^2 given by Eqs. (37) and (41), respectively, into Eq. (42).

66. Derive both equations in (31) by differentiating the equations in (30).

67. Derive Eq. (34) by differentiating Eq. (33).

56. Consider a body in an elliptical orbit with major and minor semiaxes a and b and period of revolution T. (a) Deduce from Eq. (33) that $v = r(d\theta/dt)$ when the body is nearest to and farthest from its foci. (b) Then apply Kepler's second law to conclude that $v = 2\pi ab/(rT)$ at the body's nearest and farthest points.

In Problems 57 through 60, apply the equation of part (b) of Problem 56 to compute the speed (in miles per second) of the given body at the nearest and farthest points of its orbit. Convert 1 AU, the major semiaxis of the Earth's orbit, into 92,956,000 mi.

57. Mercury: $a = 0.387$ AU, $e = 0.206$, $T = 87.97$ days

58. The earth: $e = 0.0167$, $T = 365.26$ days

12.7 CYLINDERS AND QUADRIC SURFACES

Just as the graph of an equation $f(x, y) = 0$ is generally a curve in the xy-plane, the graph of an equation in three variables is generally a surface in space. A function F of three variables associates a real number $F(x, y, z)$ with each ordered triple (x, y, z) of real numbers. The **graph** of the equation

$$F(x, y, z) = 0 \tag{1}$$

is the set of all points whose coordinates (x, y, z) satisfy this equation. We refer to the graph of such an equation as a **surface**. For instance, the graph of the equation

$$x^2 + y^2 + z^2 - 1 = 0$$

is a familiar surface, the unit sphere centered at the origin. But note that the graph of Eq. (1) does not always agree with our intuitive notion of a surface. For example, the graph of the equation

$$(x^2 + y^2)(y^2 + z^2)(z^2 + x^2) = 0$$

consists of the points lying on the three coordinate axes in space, because

- $x^2 + y^2 = 0$ implies that $x = y = 0$ (the z-axis);
- $y^2 + z^2 = 0$ implies that $y = z = 0$ (the x-axis);
- $z^2 + x^2 = 0$ implies that $z = x = 0$ (the y-axis).

We leave for advanced calculus the precise definition of *surface* as well as the study of conditions sufficient to imply that the graph of Eq. (1) actually is a surface.

Cylinders and Quadric Surfaces   SECTION 12.7   831

Planes and Traces

The simplest example of a surface is a plane with linear equation $Ax + By + Cz + D = 0$. In this section we discuss examples of other simple surfaces that frequently appear in multivariable calculus.

FIGURE 12.7.1 The intersection of the sphere S and the plane $\mathcal{P}$ is a circle.

FIGURE 12.7.2 A sphere as a union of circles (and two points).

In order to sketch a surface S, it is often helpful to examine its intersections with various planes. The **trace** of the surface S in the plane $\mathcal{P}$ is the intersection of $\mathcal{P}$ and S. For example, if S is a sphere, then we can verify by the methods of elementary geometry that the trace of S in the plane $\mathcal{P}$ is a circle (Fig. 12.7.1), provided that $\mathcal{P}$ intersects the sphere but is not merely tangent to it (Problem 49). Figure 12.7.2 illustrates the horizontal trace circles that (together with two "polar points") make up the sphere $x^2 + y^2 + z^2 = 25$.

When we want to visualize a specific surface in space, it often suffices to examine its traces in the coordinate planes and possibly a few planes parallel to them, as in Example 1.

FIGURE 12.7.3 Traces of the plane $3x + 2y + 2z = 6$ in the coordinate planes (Example 1).

EXAMPLE 1 Consider the plane with equation $3x + 2y + 2z = 6$. We find its trace in the xy-plane by setting $z = 0$. The equation then reduces to the equation $3x + 2y = 6$ of a straight line in the xy-plane. Similarly, when we set $y = 0$ we get the line $3x + 2z = 6$ as the trace of the given plane in the xz-plane. To find its trace in the yz-plane, we set $x = 0$, and this yields the line $y + z = 3$. Figure 12.7.3 shows the portions of these three trace lines that lie in the first octant. Together they give us a good picture of how the plane $3x + 2y + 2z = 6$ is situated in space. ◆

Cylinders and Rulings

Let C be a curve in a plane and let L be a line not parallel to that plane. Then the set of points on lines parallel to L that intersect C is called a **cylinder**. These straight lines that make up the cylinder are called **rulings** of the cylinder.

EXAMPLE 2 Figure 12.7.4 shows a vertical cylinder for which C is the circle $x^2 + y^2 = a^2$ in the xy-plane. The trace of this cylinder in any horizontal plane $z = c$ is a circle with radius a and center $(0, 0, c)$ on the z-axis. Thus the point (x, y, z) lies on this cylinder if and only if $x^2 + y^2 = a^2$. Hence this cylinder is the graph of the equation $x^2 + y^2 = a^2$, an equation in **three** variables—even though the variable z is technically missing.

FIGURE 12.7.4 A right circular cylinder.

832 CHAPTER 12 Vectors, Curves, and Surfaces in Space

The fact that the variable z does not appear explicitly in the equation $x^2 + y^2 = a^2$ means that given any point $(x_0, y_0, 0)$ on the *circle* $x^2 + y^2 = a^2$ in the xy-plane, the point (x_0, y_0, z) lies on the cylinder for any and all values of z. The set of all such points is the vertical line through the point $(x_0, y_0, 0)$. Thus this vertical line is a ruling of the *cylinder* $x^2 + y^2 = a^2$. Figure 12.7.5 exhibits the cylinder as the union of its rulings. ◆

A cylinder need not be circular—that is, the curve C can be an ellipse, a rectangle, or a quite arbitrary curve.

EXAMPLE 3 Figure 12.7.6 shows both horizontal traces and vertical rulings on a vertical cylinder through the figure-eight curve C in the xy-plane (C has the parametric equations $x = \sin t$, $y = \sin 2t$, $0 \leq t \leq 2\pi$). ◆

FIGURE 12.7.5 The cylinder $x^2 + y^2 = a^2$; its rulings are parallel to the z-axis.

If the curve C in the xy-plane has equation

$$f(x, y) = 0, \qquad (2)$$

then the cylinder through C with vertical rulings has the same equation in space. This is so because the point $P(x, y, z)$ lies on the cylinder if and only if the point $(x, y, 0)$ lies on the curve C. Similarly, the graph of an equation $g(x, z) = 0$ is a cylinder with rulings parallel to the y-axis, and the graph of an equation $h(y, z) = 0$ is a cylinder with rulings parallel to the x-axis. Thus the graph in space of an equation that includes only two of the three coordinate variables is always a cylinder; its rulings are parallel to the axis corresponding to the *missing* variable.

EXAMPLE 4 The graph of the equation $4y^2 + 9z^2 = 36$ is the **elliptic cylinder** shown in Fig. 12.7.7. Its rulings are parallel to the x-axis, and its trace in every plane perpendicular to the x-axis is an ellipse with semiaxes of lengths 3 and 2 (just like the pictured ellipse $y^2/9 + z^2/4 = 1$ in the yz-plane). ◆

EXAMPLE 5 The graph of the equation $z = 4 - x^2$ is the **parabolic cylinder** shown in Fig. 12.7.8. Its rulings are parallel to the y-axis, and its trace in every plane perpendicular to the y-axis is a parabola that is a parallel translate of the parabola $z = 4 - x^2$ in the xz-plane. ◆

FIGURE 12.7.6 The vertical cylinder through the figure-eight curve $x = \sin t$, $y = \sin 2t$.

Surfaces of Revolution

Another way to use a plane curve C to generate a surface is to revolve the curve in space around a line L in its plane. This gives a **surface of revolution** with **axis** L. For

FIGURE 12.7.7 An elliptical cylinder (Example 4).

FIGURE 12.7.8 The parabolic cylinder $z = 4 - x^2$ (Example 5).

Cylinders and Quadric Surfaces SECTION 12.7 833

example, Fig. 12.7.9 shows the surface generated by revolving the curve $f(x, y) = 0$ in the first quadrant of the xy-plane around the x-axis. The typical point $P(x, y, z)$ lies on this surface of revolution provided that it lies on the vertical circle (parallel to the yz-plane) with center $R(x, 0, 0)$ and radius r such that the point $Q(x, r, 0)$ lies on the given curve C, in which case $f(x, r) = 0$. Because

$$r = |RQ| = |RP| = \sqrt{y^2 + z^2},$$

it is therefore necessary that
$$f\left(x, \sqrt{y^2 + z^2}\right) = 0. \tag{3}$$

FIGURE 12.7.9 The surface generated by rotating C around the x-axis. (For clarity, only a quarter of the surface is shown.)

This, then, is the equation of a **surface of revolution around the x-axis.**

The equations of surfaces of revolution around other coordinate axes are obtained similarly. If the first-quadrant curve $f(x, y) = 0$ is revolved instead around the y-axis, then we replace x with $\sqrt{x^2 + z^2}$ to get the equation $f(\sqrt{x^2 + z^2}, y) = 0$ of the resulting surface of revolution. If the curve $g(y, z) = 0$ in the first quadrant of the yz-plane is revolved around the z-axis, we replace y with $\sqrt{x^2 + y^2}$. Thus the equation of the resulting surface of revolution around the z-axis is $g(\sqrt{x^2 + y^2}, z) = 0$. These assertions are easily verified with the aid of diagrams similar to Fig 12.7.9.

EXAMPLE 6 Write an equation of the **ellipsoid of revolution** obtained by revolving the ellipse $4y^2 + z^2 = 4$ around the z-axis (Fig. 12.7.10).

Solution We replace y with $\sqrt{x^2 + y^2}$ in the given equation. This yields $4x^2 + 4y^2 + z^2 = 4$ as an equation of the ellipsoid. ◆

EXAMPLE 7 Determine the graph of the equation $z^2 = x^2 + y^2$.

Solution First we rewrite the given equation in the form $z = \pm\sqrt{x^2 + y^2}$. Thus the surface is symmetric around the xy-plane, and the upper half has equation $z = \sqrt{x^2 + y^2}$. We can obtain this last equation from the simple equation $z = y$ by replacing y with $\sqrt{x^2 + y^2}$. Thus we obtain the upper half of the surface by revolving the line $z = y$ (for $y \geq 0$) around the z-axis. The graph is the **cone** shown in Fig. 12.7.11. Its upper half has equation $z = \sqrt{x^2 + y^2}$ and its lower half has equation $z = -\sqrt{x^2 + y^2}$. The entire cone $z^2 = x^2 + y^2$ is obtained by revolving the entire line $z = y$ around the z-axis. ◆

FIGURE 12.7.10 The ellipsoid of revolution of Example 6.

Quadric Surfaces

Cones, spheres, circular and parabolic cylinders, and ellipsoids of revolution are all surfaces that are graphs of second-degree equations in x, y, and z. The graph of a second-degree equation in three variables is called a **quadric surface**. We discuss here some important special cases of the equation

$$Ax^2 + By^2 + Cz^2 + Dx + Ey + Fz + H = 0. \tag{4}$$

This is a special second-degree equation in that it contains no terms involving the products xy, xz, or yz.

EXAMPLE 8 The **ellipsoid**

$$\frac{x^2}{a^2} + \frac{y^2}{b^2} + \frac{z^2}{c^2} = 1 \tag{5}$$

FIGURE 12.7.11 The cone of Example 7.

is symmetric around each of the three coordinate planes and has intercepts $(\pm a, 0, 0)$, $(0, \pm b, 0)$, and $(0, 0, \pm c)$ on the three coordinate axes. (There is no loss of generality in assuming that a, b, and c are positive.) Each trace of this ellipsoid in a plane parallel to one of the coordinate planes is either a single point or an ellipse. For example, if $-c < z_0 < c$, then the trace of the ellipsoid of Eq. (5) in the plane $z = z_0$ has equation

$$\frac{x^2}{a^2} + \frac{y^2}{b^2} = 1 - \frac{z_0^2}{c^2} > 0,$$

FIGURE 12.7.12 The ellipsoid of Example 8.

FIGURE 12.7.13 The traces of the ellipsoid $\dfrac{x^2}{a^2} + \dfrac{y^2}{b^2} + \dfrac{z^2}{c^2}$ (Example 8).

which is the equation of an ellipse with semiaxes $(a/c)\sqrt{c^2 - z_0^2}$ and $(b/c)\sqrt{c^2 - z_0^2}$. Figure 12.7.12 shows this ellipsoid with semiaxes a, b, and c labeled. Figure 12.7.13 shows its trace ellipses in planes parallel to the three coordinate planes. ◆

EXAMPLE 9 The **elliptic paraboloid**

$$\frac{x^2}{a^2} + \frac{y^2}{b^2} = \frac{z}{c} \tag{6}$$

is shown in Fig. 12.7.14. Its trace in the horizontal plane $z = z_0 > 0$ is the ellipse $x^2/a^2 + y^2/b^2 = z_0/c$ with semiaxes $a\sqrt{z_0/c}$ and $b\sqrt{z_0/c}$. Its trace in any vertical plane is a parabola. For instance, its trace in the plane $y = y_0$ has equation $x^2/a^2 + y_0^2/b^2 = z/c$, which can be written in the form $z - z_1 = k(x - x_1)^2$ by taking $z_1 = cy_0^2/b^2$ and $x_1 = 0$. The paraboloid opens upward if $c > 0$ and downward if $c < 0$. If $a = b$, then the paraboloid is said to be **circular**. Figure 12.7.15 shows the traces of a circular paraboloid in planes parallel to the xz- and yz-planes. ◆

FIGURE 12.7.14 An elliptic paraboloid (Example 9).

EXAMPLE 10 The **elliptical cone**

$$\frac{x^2}{a^2} + \frac{y^2}{b^2} = \frac{z^2}{c^2} \tag{7}$$

is shown in Fig. 12.7.16. Its trace in the horizontal plane $z = z_0 \neq 0$ is an ellipse with semiaxes $a|z_0|/c$ and $b|z_0|/c$. ◆

FIGURE 12.7.15 Trace parabolas of a circular paraboloid (Example 9).

FIGURE 12.7.16 An elliptic cone (Example 10).

Cylinders and Quadric Surfaces SECTION 12.7   835

EXAMPLE 11 The **hyperboloid of one sheet** with equation

$$\frac{x^2}{a^2} + \frac{y^2}{b^2} - \frac{z^2}{c^2} = 1 \qquad (8)$$

is shown in Fig. 12.7.17. Its trace in the horizontal plane $z = z_0$ is the ellipse $x^2/a^2 + y^2/b^2 = 1 + z_0^2/c^2 > 0$. Its trace in a vertical plane is a hyperbola except when the vertical plane intersects the xy-plane in a line tangent to the ellipse $x^2/a^2 + y^2/b^2 = 1$. In this special case, the trace is a degenerate hyperbola consisting of two intersecting lines. Figure 12.7.18 shows the traces (in planes parallel to the coordinate planes) of a circular ($a = b$) hyperboloid of one sheet.

The graphs of the equations

$$\frac{y^2}{b^2} + \frac{z^2}{c^2} - \frac{z^2}{a^2} = 1 \quad \text{and} \quad \frac{x^2}{a^2} + \frac{z^2}{c^2} - \frac{y^2}{c^2} = 1$$

are also hyperboloids of one sheet, opening along the x- and y-axes, respectively. ◆

FIGURE 12.7.17 A hyperboloid of one sheet (Example 11).

FIGURE 12.7.18 A circular hyperboloid of one sheet (Example 11). Its traces in horizontal planes are circles; its traces in vertical planes are hyperbolas.

EXAMPLE 12 The **hyperboloid of two sheets** with equation

$$\frac{z^2}{c^2} - \frac{x^2}{a^2} - \frac{y^2}{b^2} = 1 \qquad (9)$$

consists of two separate pieces, or *sheets* (Fig. 12.7.19). The two sheets open along the positive and negative z-axis and intersect it at the points $(0, 0, \pm c)$. The trace of this hyperboloid in a horizontal plane $z = z_0$ with $|z_0| > c$ is the ellipse

$$\frac{x^2}{a^2} + \frac{y^2}{b^2} = \frac{z_0^2}{c^2} - 1 > 0.$$

Its trace in any vertical plane is a nondegenerate hyperbola. Figure 12.7.20 shows traces of a circular hyperboloid of two sheets.

The graphs of the equations

$$\frac{x^2}{a^2} - \frac{y^2}{b^2} - \frac{z^2}{c^2} = 1 \quad \text{and} \quad \frac{y^2}{b^2} - \frac{x^2}{a^2} - \frac{z^2}{c^2} = 1$$

FIGURE 12.7.19 A hyperboloid of two sheets (Example 12).

FIGURE 12.7.20 A circular hyperboloid of two sheets (Example 12). Its (nondegenerate) traces in horizontal planes are circles; its traces in vertical planes are hyperbolas.

are also hyperboloids of two sheets, opening along the x-axis and y-axis, respectively. When the equation of a hyperboloid is written in standard form with $+1$ on the right-hand side [as in Eqs. (8) and (9)], then the number of sheets is equal to the number of negative terms on the left-hand side.

FIGURE 12.7.21 A hyperbolic paraboloid is a saddle-shaped surface (Example 13).

FIGURE 12.7.22 The vertical traces of the hyperbolic paraboloid $z = y^2 - x^2$ (Example 13).

FIGURE 12.7.23 The horizontal traces of the hyperbolic paraboloid $z = y^2 - x^2$ (Example 13).

EXAMPLE 13 The **hyperbolic paraboloid**

$$\frac{y^2}{b^2} - \frac{x^2}{a^2} = \frac{z}{c} \quad (c > 0) \tag{10}$$

is saddle shaped, as indicated in Fig. 12.7.21. Its trace in the horizontal plane $z = z_0$ is a hyperbola (or two intersecting lines if $z_0 = 0$). Its trace in a vertical plane parallel to the xz-plane is a parabola that opens downward, whereas its trace in a vertical plane parallel to the yz-plane is a parabola that opens upward. In particular, the trace of the hyperbolic paraboloid in the xz-plane is a parabola opening downward from the origin, whereas its trace in the yz-plane is a parabola opening upward from the origin. Thus the origin looks like a local maximum from one direction but like a local minimum from another. Such a point on a surface is called a **saddle point.**

Figure 12.7.22 shows the parabolic traces in vertical planes of the hyperbolic paraboloid $z = y^2 - x^2$. Figure 12.7.23 shows its hyperbolic traces in horizontal planes.

12.7 TRUE/FALSE STUDY GUIDE

12.7 CONCEPTS: QUESTIONS AND DISCUSSION

The following questions are concerned with possible graphs of the second-degree equation

$$Ax^2 + By^2 + Cz^2 + Dx + Ey + Fz + H = 0. \tag{11}$$

1. Under what conditions on the coefficients A, B, and C is the graph (a) an ellipsoid; (b) a paraboloid; (c) a hyperboloid?
2. Under what conditions on the coefficients is the graph a cone or cylinder?
3. Besides ellipsoids, paraboloids, hyperboloids, cones, and cylinders, what are the other possibilities for the graph of the equation in (11)? Give an example to illustrate each possibility.

12.7 PROBLEMS

Describe and sketch the graphs of the equations given in Problems 1 through 30.

1. $3x + 2y + 10z = 20$
2. $3x + 2y = 30$
3. $x^2 + y^2 = 9$
4. $y^2 = x^2 - 9$
5. $xy = 4$
6. $z = 4x^2 + 4y^2$
7. $z = 4x^2 + y^2$
8. $4x^2 + 9y^2 = 36$
9. $z = 4 - x^2 - y^2$
10. $y^2 + z^2 = 1$
11. $2z = x^2 + y^2$
12. $x = 1 + y^2 + z^2$
13. $z^2 = 4(x^2 + y^2)$
14. $y^2 = 4x$
15. $x^2 = 4z + 8$
16. $x = 9 - z^2$
17. $4x^2 + y^2 = 4$
18. $x^2 + z^2 = 4$
19. $x^2 = 4y^2 + 9z^2$
20. $x^2 - 4y^2 = z$
21. $x^2 + y^2 + 4z = 0$
22. $x = \sin y$
23. $x = 2y^2 - z^2$
24. $x^2 + 4y^2 + 2z^2 = 4$
25. $x^2 + y^2 - 9z^2 = 9$
26. $x^2 - y^2 - 9z^2 = 9$
27. $y = 4x^2 + 9z^2$
28. $y^2 + 4x^2 - 9z^2 = 36$
29. $y^2 - 9x^2 - 4z^2 = 36$
30. $x^2 + 9y^2 + 4z^2 = 36$

Problems 31 through 40 give the equation of a curve in one of the coordinate planes. Write an equation for the surface generated by revolving this curve around the indicated axis. Then sketch the surface.

31. $x = 2z^2$; the x-axis
32. $4x^2 + 9y^2 = 36$; the y-axis
33. $y^2 - z^2 = 1$; the z-axis
34. $z = 4 - x^2$; the z-axis
35. $y^2 = 4x$; the x-axis
36. $yz = 1$; the z-axis
37. $z = \exp(-x^2)$; the z-axis
38. $(y - z)^2 + z^2 = 1$; the z-axis
39. The line $z = 2x$; the z-axis
40. The line $z = 2x$; the x-axis

In Problems 41 through 48, describe the traces of the given surfaces in planes of the indicated type.

41. $x^2 + 4y^2 = 4$; in horizontal planes (those parallel to the xy-plane)
42. $x^2 + 4y^2 + 4z^2 = 4$; in horizontal planes
43. $x^2 + 4y^2 + 4z^2 = 4$; in planes parallel to the yz-plane
44. $z = 4x^2 + 9y^2$; in horizontal planes
45. $z = 4x^2 + 9y^2$; in planes parallel to the yz-plane
46. $z = xy$; in horizontal planes
47. $z = xy$; in vertical planes through the z-axis
48. $x^2 - y^2 + z^2 = 1$; in both horizontal and vertical planes parallel to the coordinate axes
49. Prove that the triangles OAC and OBC in Fig. 12.7.1 are congruent, and thereby conclude that the trace of a sphere in an intersecting plane is a circle.

50. Prove that the projection into the yz-plane of the curve of intersection of the surfaces $x = 1 - y^2$ and $x = y^2 + z^2$ is an ellipse (Fig. 12.7.24).

FIGURE 12.7.24 The paraboloid and parabolic cylinder of Problem 50.

51. Show that the projection into the xy-plane of the intersection of the plane $z = y$ and the paraboloid $z = x^2 + y^2$ is a circle (Fig. 12.7.25).

FIGURE 12.7.25 The plane and paraboloid of Problem 51.

52. Prove that the projection into the xz-plane of the intersection of the paraboloids $y = 2x^2 + 3z^2$ and $y = 5 - 3x^2 - 2z^2$ is a circle (Fig. 12.7.26).

FIGURE 12.7.26 The two paraboloids of Problem 52.

53. Prove that the projection into the xy-plane of the intersection of the plane $x + y + z = 1$ and the ellipsoid $x^2 + 4y^2 + 4z^2 = 4$ is an ellipse.
54. Show that the curve of intersection of the plane $z = ky$ and the cylinder $x^2 + y^2 = 1$ is an ellipse. [*Suggestion:* Introduce uv-coordinates into the plane $z = ky$ as follows: Let the u-axis be the original x-axis and let the v-axis be the line $z = ky, x = 0$.]

12.8 CYLINDRICAL AND SPHERICAL COORDINATES

Rectangular coordinates provide only one of several useful ways of describing points, curves, and surfaces in space. Here we discuss two additional coordinate systems in three-dimensional space. Each is a generalization of polar coordinates in the coordinate plane.

Recall from Section 10.2 that the relationship between the rectangular coordinates (x, y) and the polar coordinates (r, θ) of a point in space is given by

$$x = r\cos\theta, \qquad y = r\sin\theta \tag{1}$$

and

$$r^2 = x^2 + y^2, \qquad \tan\theta = \frac{y}{x} \quad \text{if } x \neq 0. \tag{2}$$

Read these relationships directly from the right triangle in Fig. 12.8.1.

FIGURE 12.8.1 The relation between rectangular and polar coordinates in the xy-plane.

Cylindrical Coordinates

The **cylindrical coordinates** (r, θ, z) of a point P in space are natural hybrids of its polar and rectangular coordinates. We use the polar coordinates (r, θ) of the point in the plane with rectangular coordinates (x, y) and use the same z-coordinate as in rectangular coordinates. (The cylindrical coordinates of a point P in space are illustrated in Fig. 12.8.2.) This means that we can obtain the relations between the rectangular coordinates (x, y, z) of the point P and its cylindrical coordinates (r, θ, z) by simply adjoining the identity $z = z$ to the equations in (1) and (2):

$$x = r\cos\theta, \qquad y = r\sin\theta, \qquad z = z \tag{3}$$

and

$$r^2 = x^2 + y^2, \qquad \tan\theta = \frac{y}{x}, \qquad z = z. \tag{4}$$

We can use these equations to convert from rectangular to cylindrical coordinates and vice versa.

FIGURE 12.8.2 Finding the cylindrical coordinates of the point P.

EXAMPLE 1 (a) Find the rectangular coordinates of the point P having cylindrical coordinates $(4, \frac{5}{3}\pi, 7)$. (b) Find the cylindrical coordinates of the point Q having rectangular coordinates $(-2, 2, 5)$.

Solution (a) We apply the equations in (3) to write

$$x = 4\cos\left(\tfrac{5}{3}\pi\right) = 4 \cdot \tfrac{1}{2} = 2,$$
$$y = 4\sin\left(\tfrac{5}{3}\pi\right) = 4 \cdot \left(-\tfrac{1}{2}\sqrt{3}\right) = -2\sqrt{3},$$
$$z = 7.$$

Thus the point P has rectangular coordinates $(2, -2\sqrt{3}, 7)$.

(b) Noting first that the point Q is in the second quadrant of the xy-plane, we apply the equations in (4) and write

$$r = \sqrt{(-2)^2 + 2^2} = 2\sqrt{2},$$
$$\tan\theta = \frac{-2}{2} = -1, \quad \text{so} \quad \theta = \frac{3\pi}{4},$$
$$z = 5.$$

Thus the point Q has cylindrical coordinates $(2\sqrt{2}, \frac{3}{4}\pi, 5)$. We can add any even integral multiple of π to θ, so other cylindrical coordinates for Q are $(2\sqrt{2}, \frac{11}{4}\pi, 5)$ and $(2\sqrt{2}, -\frac{5}{4}\pi, 5)$. ◆

The **graph** of an equation involving r, θ, and z is the set of all points in space having cylindrical coordinates that satisfy the equation. The name *cylindrical coordinates* arises from the fact that the graph in space of the equation $r = c$ (a constant) is a cylinder of radius c symmetric around the z-axis (Fig. 12.8.3). Cylindrical coordinates are useful in describing other surfaces that are symmetric around the z-axis. The rectangular-coordinate equation of such a surface typically involves x and y only in the combination $x^2 + y^2$, for which we can then substitute r^2 to get the cylindrical-coordinate equation.

FIGURE 12.8.3 The cylinder $r = c$.

EXAMPLE 2 (a) The sphere $x^2 + y^2 + z^2 = a^2$ has cylindrical-coordinate equation $r^2 + z^2 = a^2$.

(b) The cone $z^2 = x^2 + y^2$ has cylindrical-coordinate equation $z^2 = r^2$. Taking square roots, we get $z = \pm r$, and the two signs give (for $r \geq 0$) the two nappes of the cone (Fig. 12.8.4).

(c) The paraboloid $z = x^2 + y^2$ has cylindrical-coordinate equation $z = r^2$ (Fig. 12.8.5).

(d) The ellipsoid $(x/3)^2 + (y/3)^2 + (z/2)^2 = 1$ has cylindrical-coordinate equation $(r/3)^2 + (z/2)^2 = 1$ (Fig. 12.8.6). ◆

FIGURE 12.8.4 The cone $z^2 = r^2$.

FIGURE 12.8.5 The paraboloid $z = r^2$.

FIGURE 12.8.6 The ellipsoid $\dfrac{r^2}{9} + \dfrac{z^2}{4} = 1$.

EXAMPLE 3 Sketch the region that is bounded by the two surfaces with cylindrical-coordinate equations $z = r^2$ and $z = 8 - r^2$.

Solution If we substitute $r^2 = x^2 + y^2$ in the given equations, we get the familiar rectangular equations
$$z = x^2 + y^2 \quad \text{and} \quad z = 8 - x^2 - y^2$$
that describe paraboloids opening upward from $(0, 0, 0)$ and downward from $(0, 0, 8)$, respectively. Figure 12.8.7 shows a computer plot of the region in space that is bounded below by the paraboloid $z = x^2 + y^2$ and above by the paraboloid $z = 8 - x^2 - y^2$. ◆

REMARK The relations $x = r \cos\theta$ and $y = r \sin\theta$ play an important role in the computer plotting of figures symmetric around the z-axis. For instance, the paraboloid $z = 8 - r^2$ of Example 3 can be plotted using computer algebra system syntax like the *Maple* command

```
plot3d( [r*cos(θ), r*sin(θ), 8 - r^2],
        r=0..2,  θ=0..2*Pi );
```

FIGURE 12.8.7 The solid of Example 3.

or the *Mathematica* command

```
ParametricPlot3D[ {r*Cos[θ], r*Sin[θ], 8 - r^2},
                  {r,0,2}, {θ,0,2*Pi} ];
```

FIGURE 12.8.8 Finding the spherical coordinates of the point P.

Spherical Coordinates

Figure 12.8.8 shows the **spherical coordinates** (ρ, ϕ, θ) of the point P in space. The first spherical coordinate ρ is simply the distance $\rho = |OP|$ from the origin O to P. The second spherical coordinate ϕ is the angle between OP and the positive z-axis. Thus we may always choose ϕ in the interval $[0, \pi]$, although it is not restricted to that domain. Finally, θ is the familiar angle θ of cylindrical coordinates. That is, θ is the angular coordinate of the vertical projection Q of P into the xy-plane. Thus we may always choose θ in the interval $[0, 2\pi]$, although it is not restricted to that domain. Both angles ϕ and θ are always measured in radians.

The name *spherical coordinates* is used because the graph of the equation $\rho = c$ (c is a constant) is a sphere—more precisely, a spherical surface—of radius c centered at the origin. The equation $\phi = c$ (a constant) describes (one nappe of) a cone if $0 < c < \pi/2$ or if $\pi/2 < c < \pi$ (Fig. 12.8.9). The spherical equation of the xy-plane is $\phi = \pi/2$.

From the right triangle OPQ of Fig. 12.8.8, we see that

$$r = \rho \sin \phi \quad \text{and} \quad z = \rho \cos \phi. \tag{5}$$

Indeed, these equations are most easily remembered by visualizing this triangle. Substituting the equations in (5) into those in (3) yields

$$x = \rho \sin \phi \cos \theta, \qquad y = \rho \sin \phi \sin \theta, \qquad z = \rho \cos \phi. \tag{6}$$

These three equations give the relationship between rectangular and spherical coordinates. Also useful is the formula

$$\rho^2 = x^2 + y^2 + z^2, \tag{7}$$

a consequence of the distance formula.

FIGURE 12.8.9 The two nappes of a 45° cone; $\phi = \pi/2$ is the spherical equation of the xy-plane.

It is important to note the order in which the spherical coordinates (ρ, ϕ, θ) of a point P are written—first the distance ρ of P from the origin, then the angle ϕ down from the positive z-axis, and last the counterclockwise angle θ measured from the positive x-axis. You may find this mnemonic device to be helpful: The consonants in the word "raft" remind us, in order, of *r*ho, *f*ee (for phi), and *t*heta. Warning: In some other physics and mathematics books, a different order, or even different symbols, may be used.

Given the rectangular coordinates (x, y, z) of the point P, one systematic method for finding the spherical coordinates (ρ, ϕ, θ) of P is this. First we find the cylindrical coordinates r and θ of P with the aid of the triangle in Fig. 12.8.10(a). Then we find ρ and ϕ from the triangle in Fig. 12.8.10(b).

EXAMPLE 4 (a) Find the rectangular coordinates of the point P having the spherical coordinates $(8, \frac{5}{6}\pi, \frac{1}{3}\pi)$. (b) Approximate the spherical coordinates of the point Q having rectangular coordinates $(-3, -4, -12)$.

Solution (a) We apply the equations in (6) to write

$$x = 8 \sin\left(\tfrac{5}{6}\pi\right) \cos\left(\tfrac{1}{3}\pi\right) = 8 \cdot \tfrac{1}{2} \cdot \tfrac{1}{2} = 2,$$

$$y = 8 \sin\left(\tfrac{5}{6}\pi\right) \sin\left(\tfrac{1}{3}\pi\right) = 8 \cdot \tfrac{1}{2} \cdot \left(\tfrac{1}{2}\sqrt{3}\right) = 2\sqrt{3},$$

$$z = 8 \cos\left(\tfrac{5}{6}\pi\right) = 8 \cdot \left(-\tfrac{1}{2}\sqrt{3}\right) = -4\sqrt{3}.$$

Thus the point P has rectangular coordinates $(2, 2\sqrt{3}, -4\sqrt{3})$.

(b) First we note that $r = \sqrt{(-3)^2 + (-4)^2} = \sqrt{25} = 5$ and that

$$\rho = \sqrt{(-3)^2 + (-4)^2 + (-12)^2} = \sqrt{169} = 13.$$

FIGURE 12.8.10 Triangles used in finding spherical coordinates.

Next,
$$\phi = \cos^{-1}\left(\frac{z}{\rho}\right) = \cos^{-1}\left(-\frac{12}{13}\right) \approx 2.7468 \quad (\text{rad}).$$

Finally, the point $(-3, -4)$ lies in the third quadrant of the xy-plane, so
$$\theta = \pi + \tan^{-1}\left(\frac{3}{4}\right) \approx 3.7851 \quad (\text{rad}).$$

Thus the approximate spherical coordinates of the point Q are $(13, 2.7468, 3.7851)$.

EXAMPLE 5 Find a spherical-coordinate equation of the paraboloid with rectangular-coordinates equation $z = x^2 + y^2$.

Solution We substitute $z = \rho \cos \phi$ from Eq. (5) and $x^2 + y^2 = r^2 = \rho^2 \sin^2 \phi$ from Eq. (6). This gives $\rho \cos \phi = \rho^2 \sin^2 \phi$. Cancelling ρ gives $\cos \phi = \rho \sin^2 \phi$; that is,
$$\rho = \csc \phi \cot \phi$$
is the spherical-coordinate equation of the paraboloid. We get the whole paraboloid by using ϕ in the range $0 < \phi \leq \pi/2$. Note that $\phi = \pi/2$ gives the point $\rho = 0$ that might otherwise have been lost by cancelling ρ.

EXAMPLE 6 Determine the graph of the spherical-coordinate equation $\rho = 2 \cos \phi$.

Solution Multiplying by ρ gives
$$\rho^2 = 2\rho \cos \phi;$$
then substituting $\rho^2 = x^2 + y^2 + z^2$ and $z = \rho \cos \phi$ yields
$$x^2 + y^2 + z^2 = 2z$$
as the rectangular-coordinate equation of the graph. Completing the square in z now gives
$$x^2 + y^2 + (z-1)^2 = 1,$$
so the graph is a sphere with center $(0, 0, 1)$ and radius 1. It is tangent to the xy-plane at the origin (Fig. 12.8.11).

FIGURE 12.8.11 The sphere of Example 6.

EXAMPLE 7 Determine the graph of the spherical-coordinate equation $\rho = \sin \phi \sin \theta$.

Solution We first multiply each side by ρ and get $\rho^2 = \rho \sin \phi \sin \theta$. We then use Eqs. (6) and (7) and find that $x^2 + y^2 + z^2 = y$. This is a rectangular-coordinate equation of a sphere with center $(0, \frac{1}{2}, 0)$ and radius $\frac{1}{2}$.

REMARK The relations in (6) are used in computer plotting of spherical-coordinate surfaces. For instance, the spherical surface $\rho = 2 \cos \phi$ of Example 6 can be plotted using computer algebra system syntax like the *Maple* commands

```
ρ := 2*cos(φ);
plot3d( [ρ*sin(φ)*cos(θ), ρ*sin(φ)*sin(θ), ρ*cos(φ)],
        φ = 0..Pi/2, θ = 0..2*Pi );
```

or the *Mathematica* commands

```
ρ = 2 Cos[φ];
ParametricPlot3D[
    {ρ*Sin[φ]*Cos[θ], ρ*Sin[φ]*Sin[θ], ρ*Cos[φ]},
    {φ, 0, Pi/2}, {θ, 0, 2*Pi} ];
```

FIGURE 12.8.12 The relations among latitude, longitude, and spherical coordinates.

In each case the spherical surface is described parametrically by giving x, y, and z in terms of ρ, ϕ, and θ.

Latitude and Longitude

A **great circle** of a spherical surface is a circle formed by the intersection of the surface with a plane through the center of the sphere. Thus a great circle of a spherical surface is a circle (in the surface) that has the same radius as the sphere. Therefore, a great circle is a circle of maximum possible circumference that lies on the sphere. It's easy to see that any two points on a spherical surface lie on a great circle (uniquely determined unless the two points lie on the ends of a diameter of the sphere). In the calculus of variations, it is shown that the shortest distance between two such points—measured along the curved surface—is the shorter of the two arcs of the great circle that contains them. The surprise may be that the *shortest* distance is found by using the *largest* circle.

The spherical coordinates ϕ and θ are closely related to the latitude and longitude of points on the surface of the earth. Assume that the earth is a sphere with radius $\rho = 3960$ mi. We begin with the **prime meridian** (a **meridian** is a great semicircle connecting the North and South Poles) through Greenwich, England, just outside London. This is the point marked G in Fig. 12.8.12.

We take the z-axis through the North Pole and the x-axis through the point where the prime meridian intersects the equator. The **latitude** α and (west) **longitude** β of a point P in the Northern Hemisphere are given by the equations

$$\alpha = 90° - \phi° \quad \text{and} \quad \beta = 360° - \theta°, \tag{8}$$

where $\phi°$ and $\theta°$ are the angular spherical coordinates, measured in *degrees*, of P. (That is, $\phi°$ and $\theta°$ denote the degree equivalents of the angles ϕ and θ, respectively, which are measured in radians unless otherwise specified.) Thus the latitude α is measured northward from the equator and the longitude β is measured westward from the prime meridian.

EXAMPLE 8 Find the great-circle distance between New York (latitude 40.75° north, longitude 74° west) and London (latitude 51.5° north, longitude 0°). (See Fig. 12.8.13.)

Solution From the equations in (8) we find that $\phi° = 49.25°, \theta° = 286°$ for New York, whereas $\phi° = 38.5°, \theta° = 360°$ (or $0°$) for London. Hence the angular spherical coordinates of New York are $\phi = (49.25/180)\pi, \theta = (286/180)\pi$, and those of London are $\phi = (38.5/180)\pi, \theta = 0$. With these values of ϕ and θ and with $\rho = 3960$ (mi),

FIGURE 12.8.13 Finding the great-circle distance d from New York to London (Example 8).

the equations in (6) give the rectangular coordinates

New York: $P_1(826.90, -2883.74, 2584.93)$

and

London: $P_2(2465.16, 0.0, 3099.13)$.

The angle γ between the radius vectors $\mathbf{u} = \overrightarrow{OP_1}$ and $\mathbf{v} = \overrightarrow{OP_2}$ in Fig. 12.8.14 satisfies the equation

$$\cos\gamma = \frac{\mathbf{u}\cdot\mathbf{v}}{|\mathbf{u}||\mathbf{v}|}$$

$$= \frac{826.90 \cdot 2465.16 - 2883.74 \cdot 0 + 2584.93 \cdot 3099.13}{(3960)^2} \approx 0.641.$$

Thus γ is approximately 0.875 (rad). Hence the great-circle distance between New York and London is close to

$$d = 3960 \cdot 0.875 \approx 3465 \quad (\text{mi}),$$

about 5576 km.

FIGURE 12.8.14 The great-circle arc between New York and London (Example 8).

12.8 TRUE/FALSE STUDY GUIDE

12.8 CONCEPTS: QUESTIONS AND DISCUSSION

1. Give several examples of surfaces that are described more simply in rectangular coordinates than in cylindrical or spherical coordinates.
2. Give several examples of surfaces that are described more simply in cylindrical coordinates than in rectangular or spherical coordinates.
3. Give several examples of surfaces that are described more simply in spherical coordinates than in rectangular or cylindrical coordinates.

12.8 PROBLEMS

In Problems 1 through 6, find the rectangular coordinates of the point with the given cylindrical coordinates.

1. $(1, \frac{1}{2}\pi, 2)$
2. $(3, \frac{3}{2}\pi, -1)$
3. $(2, \frac{3}{4}\pi, 3)$
4. $(3, \frac{7}{6}\pi, -1)$
5. $(2, \frac{1}{3}\pi, -5)$
6. $(4, \frac{5}{3}\pi, 6)$

In Problems 7 through 12, find the rectangular coordinates of the points with the given spherical coordinates (ρ, ϕ, θ).

7. $(2, 0, \pi)$
8. $(3, \pi, 0)$
9. $(3, \frac{1}{2}\pi, \pi)$
10. $(4, \frac{1}{6}\pi, \frac{2}{3}\pi)$
11. $(2, \frac{1}{3}\pi, \frac{3}{2}\pi)$
12. $(6, \frac{3}{4}\pi, \frac{4}{3}\pi)$

In Problems 13 through 22, find both the cylindrical coordinates and the spherical coordinates of the point P with the given rectangular coordinates.

13. $P(0, 0, 5)$
14. $P(0, 0, -3)$
15. $P(1, 1, 0)$
16. $P(2, -2, 0)$
17. $P(1, 1, 1)$
18. $P(-1, 1, -1)$
19. $P(2, 1, -2)$
20. $P(-2, -1, -2)$
21. $P(3, 4, 12)$
22. $P(-2, 4, -12)$

In Problems 23 through 38, describe the graph of the given equation. (It is understood that equations including r are in cylindrical coordinates and those including ρ or ϕ are in spherical coordinates.)

23. $r = 5$
24. $\theta = 3\pi/4$
25. $\theta = \pi/4$
26. $\rho = 5$
27. $\phi = \pi/6$
28. $\phi = 5\pi/6$
29. $\phi = \pi/2$
30. $\phi = \pi$
31. $z^2 + 2r^2 = 4$
32. $z^2 - 2r^2 = 4$
33. $r = 4\cos\theta$
34. $\rho = 4\cos\phi$
35. $r^2 - 4r + 3 = 0$
36. $\rho^2 - 4\rho + 3 = 0$
37. $z^2 = r^4$
38. $\rho^3 + 4\rho = 0$

In Problems 39 through 44, convert the given equation both to cylindrical and to spherical coordinates.

39. $x^2 + y^2 + z^2 = 25$
40. $x^2 + y^2 = 2x$
41. $x + y + z = 1$
42. $x + y = 4$
43. $x^2 + y^2 + z^2 = x + y + z$
44. $z = x^2 - y^2$

In Problems 45 through 52, describe and sketch the surface or solid described by the given equations and/or inequalities.

45. $r = 3$, $-1 \leq z \leq 1$
46. $\rho = 2$, $0 \leq \phi \leq \pi/2$
47. $\rho = 2$, $\pi/3 \leq \phi \leq 2\pi/3$
48. $0 \leq r \leq 3$, $-2 \leq z \leq 2$
49. $1 \leq r \leq 3$, $-2 \leq z \leq 2$
50. $0 \leq \rho \leq 2$, $0 \leq \phi \leq \pi/2$
51. $3 \leq \rho \leq 5$
52. $0 \leq \phi \leq \pi/6$, $0 \leq \rho \leq 10$

53. The parabola $z = x^2$, $y = 0$ is rotated around the z-axis. Write a cylindrical-coordinate equation for the surface thereby generated.

54. The hyperbola $y^2 - z^2 = 1$, $x = 0$ is rotated around the z-axis. Write a cylindrical-coordinate equation for the surface thereby generated.

55. A sphere of radius 2 is centered at the origin. A hole of radius 1 is drilled through the sphere, with the axis of the hole lying on the z-axis. Describe the solid region that remains (Fig. 12.8.15) in (a) cylindrical coordinates; (b) spherical coordinates.

FIGURE 12.8.15 The sphere-with-hole of Problem 55.

56. Find the great-circle distance in miles and in kilometers from Atlanta (latitude 33.75° north, longitude 84.40° west) to San Francisco (latitude 37.78° north, longitude 122.42° west).

57. Find the great-circle distance in miles and in kilometers from Fairbanks (latitude 64.80° north, longitude 147.85° west) to St. Petersburg, Russia (latitude 59.91° north, longitude 30.43° *east* of Greenwich—alternatively, longitude 329.57° west).

58. Because Fairbanks and St. Petersburg, Russia (see Problem 57) are at approximately the same latitude, a plane could fly from one to the other roughly along the 62nd parallel of latitude. Accurately estimate the length of such a trip both in kilometers and in miles.

59. In flying the great-circle route from Fairbanks to St. Petersburg, Russia (see Problem 57), how close in kilometers and in miles to the North Pole would a plane fly?

60. The vertex of a right circular cone of radius R and height H is located at the origin and its axis lies on the nonnegative z-axis. Describe the solid cone in cylindrical coordinates.

61. Describe the cone of Problem 60 in spherical coordinates.

62. In flying the great-circle route from New York to London (Example 8), an airplane initially flies generally east-northeast. Does the plane ever fly at a latitude *higher* than that of London? [*Suggestion:* Express the z-coordinate of the plane's route as a function of x, and then maximize z.]

63. Figure 12.8.16 shows the torus that is obtained by revolving around the z-axis the circle of radius b centered at the point $(a, 0)$ in the yz-plane. Write a radical-free equation describing this torus in (a) rectangular coordinates; (b) cylindrical coordinates; (c) spherical coordinates. (d) Investigate the use of one of these descriptions with a computer algebra system to plot this torus with selected values of a and b.

FIGURE 12.8.16 The torus of Problem 63.

64. The bumpy sphere of Fig. 12.8.17 is an exaggerated representation of waves on the surface of a very small planet that is covered by a very deep ocean. Such bumpy or wrinkled spheres may also, perhaps more realistically, be used to model tumors. Use a computer algebra system to plot the spherical-coordinate surface

$$\rho = a + b \cos m\theta \sin n\phi$$

with selected values of the positive numbers a and b and the positive integers m and n. How does the surface depend on the value of each of these four parameters?

FIGURE 12.8.17 The bumpy sphere of Problem 64.

CHAPTER 12 REVIEW: DEFINITIONS, CONCEPTS, RESULTS

Use the following list as a guide to concepts that you may need to review.

1. Vectors: their definition, length, equality, addition, multiplication by scalars, and dot product.
2. The dot (scalar) product of vectors—definition and geometric interpretation.
3. Use of the dot product to test perpendicularity of vectors and, more generally, to find the angle between two vectors.
4. The cross (vector) product of two vectors—definition and geometric interpretation.
5. The scalar triple product of three vectors—definition and geometric interpretation.
6. The parametric and symmetric equations of the straight line that passes through a given point and is parallel to a given vector.
7. The equation of the plane through a given point normal to a given vector.
8. Vector-valued functions, velocity vectors, and acceleration vectors.
9. Componentwise differentiation and integration of vector-valued functions.
10. The equations of motion of a projectile.
11. The velocity and acceleration vectors of a particle moving along a parametric space curve.
12. Arc length of a parametric space curve.
13. The curvature, unit tangent vector, and principal unit normal vector of a parametric curve in the plane or in space.
14. Tangential and normal components of the acceleration vector of a parametric curve.
15. Kepler's three laws of planetary motion.
16. The radial and transverse unit vectors.
17. Polar decomposition of velocity and acceleration vectors.
18. Outline of the derivation of Kepler's laws from Newton's law of gravitation.
19. Equations of cylinders and surfaces of revolution.
20. The standard types of quadric surfaces.
21. Definitions of the cylindrical-coordinate and spherical-coordinate systems; the equations relating cylindrical and spherical coordinates to rectangular coordinates.

CHAPTER 12 MISCELLANEOUS PROBLEMS

1. Suppose that M is the midpoint of the segment PQ in space and that A is another point. Show that
$$\overrightarrow{AM} = \frac{1}{2}(\overrightarrow{AP} + \overrightarrow{AQ}).$$

2. Let $\mathbf{a}$ and $\mathbf{b}$ be nonzero vectors. Define
$$\mathbf{a}_\parallel = (\text{comp}_\mathbf{b} \mathbf{a}) \frac{\mathbf{b}}{|\mathbf{b}|} \quad \text{and} \quad \mathbf{a}_\perp = \mathbf{a} - \mathbf{a}_\parallel.$$
Prove that $\mathbf{a}_\perp$ is perpendicular to $\mathbf{b}$.

3. Let P and Q be different points in space. Show that the point R lies on the line through P and Q *if and only if* there exist numbers a and b such that $a + b = 1$ and $\overrightarrow{OR} = a\overrightarrow{OP} + b\overrightarrow{OQ}$. Conclude that
$$\mathbf{r}(t) = t\overrightarrow{OP} + (1-t)\overrightarrow{OQ}$$
is a parametric equation of this line.

4. Conclude from the result of Problem 3 that the points P, Q, and R are collinear if and only if there exist numbers a, b, and c, not all zero, such that $a + b + c = 0$ and $a\overrightarrow{OP} + b\overrightarrow{OQ} + c\overrightarrow{OR} = \mathbf{0}$.

5. Let $P(x_0, y_0)$, $Q(x_1, y_1)$, and $R(x_2, y_2)$ be points in the xy-plane. Use the cross product to show that the area of the triangle PQR is
$$A = \tfrac{1}{2}|(x_1 - x_0)(y_2 - y_0) - (x_2 - x_0)(y_1 - y_0)|.$$

6. Write both symmetric and parametric equations of the line that passes through $P_1(1, -1, 0)$ and is parallel to $\mathbf{v} = \langle 2, -1, 3\rangle$.

7. Write both symmetric and parametric equations of the line that passes through $P_1(1, -1, 2)$ and $P_2(3, 2, -1)$.

8. Write an equation of the plane through $P(3, -5, 1)$ with normal vector $\mathbf{n} = \mathbf{i} + \mathbf{j}$.

9. Show that the lines with symmetric equations
$$x - 1 = 2(y+1) = 3(z-2)$$
and
$$x - 3 = 2(y-1) = 3(z+1)$$
are parallel. Then write an equation of the plane containing these two lines.

10. Let the lines L_1 and L_2 have symmetric equations
$$\frac{x - x_i}{a_i} = \frac{y - y_i}{b_i} = \frac{z - z_i}{c_i}$$
for $i = 1, 2$. Show that L_1 and L_2 are skew lines if and only if
$$\begin{vmatrix} x_1 - x_2 & y_1 - y_2 & z_1 - z_2 \\ a_1 & b_1 & c_1 \\ a_2 & b_2 & c_2 \end{vmatrix} \neq 0.$$

11. Given the four points $A(2, 3, 2)$, $B(4, 1, 0)$, $C(-1, 2, 0)$, and $D(5, 4, -2)$, find an equation of the plane that passes through A and B and is parallel to the line through C and D.

12. Given the points A, B, C, and D of Problem 11, find points P on the line AB and Q on the line CD such that the line PQ is perpendicular to both AB and CD. What is the perpendicular distance d between the lines AB and CD?

13. Let $P_0(x_0, y_0, z_0)$ be a point of the plane with equation
$$ax + by + cz + d = 0.$$

By projecting $\overrightarrow{OP_0}$ onto the normal vector $\mathbf{n} = \langle a, b, c \rangle$, show that the distance D from the origin to this plane is

$$D = \frac{|d|}{\sqrt{a^2 + b^2 + c^2}}.$$

14. Show that the distance D from the point $P_1(x_1, y_1, z_1)$ to the plane $ax + by + cz + d = 0$ is equal to the distance from the origin to the plane with equation

$$a(x + x_1) + b(y + y_1) + c(z + z_1) + d = 0.$$

Hence conclude from the result of Problem 13 that

$$D = \frac{|ax_1 + by_1 + cz_1 + d|}{\sqrt{a^2 + b^2 + c^2}}.$$

15. Find the perpendicular distance between the parallel planes $2x - y + 2z = 4$ and $2x - y + 2z = 13$.

16. Write an equation of the plane through the point $(1, 1, 1)$ that is normal to the twisted cubic $x = t$, $y = t^2$, $z = t^3$ at this point.

17. Let ABC be an isosceles triangle with $|AB| = |AC|$. Let M be the midpoint of BC. Use the dot product to show that AM and BC are perpendicular.

18. Use the dot product to show that the diagonals of a rhombus (a parallelogram with all four sides of equal length) are perpendicular to each other.

19. The acceleration of a certain particle is

$$\mathbf{a} = \mathbf{i} \sin t - \mathbf{j} \cos t.$$

Assume that the particle begins at time $t = 0$ at the point $(0, 1)$ and has initial velocity $\mathbf{v}_0 = -\mathbf{i}$. Show that its path is a circle.

20. A particle moves in an attracting central force field with force proportional to the distance from the origin. This implies that the particle's acceleration vector is $\mathbf{a} = -\omega^2 \mathbf{r}$, where $\mathbf{r}$ is the position vector of the particle. Assume that the particle's initial position is $\mathbf{r}_0 = p\mathbf{i}$ and that its initial velocity is $\mathbf{v}_0 = q\omega \mathbf{j}$. Show that the trajectory of the particle is the ellipse with equation $x^2/p^2 + y^2/q^2 = 1$. [*Suggestion:* If $x''(t) = -k^2 x(t)$ (where k is constant), then $x(t) = A \cos kt + B \sin kt$ for some constants A and B.]

21. At time $t = 0$, a ground target is 160 ft from a gun and is moving directly away from it with a constant speed of 80 ft/s. If the muzzle velocity of the gun is 320 ft/s, at what angle of elevation α should it be fired in order to strike the moving target?

22. Suppose that a gun with muzzle velocity v_0 is located at the foot of a hill with a 30° slope. At what angle of elevation (from the horizontal) should the gun be fired in order to maximize its range, as measured up the hill?

23. A particle moves in space with parametric equations $x = t$, $y = t^2$, $z = \frac{4}{3}t^{3/2}$. Find the curvature of its trajectory and the tangential and normal components of its acceleration when $t = 1$.

24. The **osculating plane** to a space curve at a point P of that curve is the plane through P that is parallel to the curve's unit tangent and principal unit normal vectors at P. Write an equation of the osculating plane to the curve of Problem 23 at the point $(1, 1, \frac{4}{3})$.

25. Show that the equation of the plane that passes through the point $P_0(x_0, y_0, z_0)$ and is parallel to the vectors $\mathbf{v}_1 = \langle a_1, b_1, c_1 \rangle$ and $\mathbf{v}_2 = \langle a_2, b_2, c_2 \rangle$ can be written in the form

$$\begin{vmatrix} x - x_0 & y - y_0 & z - z_0 \\ a_1 & b_1 & c_1 \\ a_2 & b_2 & c_2 \end{vmatrix} = 0.$$

26. Deduce from Problem 25 that the equation of the osculating plane (Problem 24) to the parametric curve $\mathbf{r}(t)$ at the point $\mathbf{r}(t_0)$ can be written in the form

$$[\mathbf{R} - \mathbf{r}(t_0)] \cdot [\mathbf{r}'(t_0) \times \mathbf{r}''(t_0)] = 0,$$

where $\mathbf{R} = \langle x, y, z \rangle$. Note first that the vectors $\mathbf{T}$ and $\mathbf{N}$ are coplanar with $\mathbf{r}'(t)$ and $\mathbf{r}''(t)$.

27. Use the result of Problem 26 to write an equation of the osculating plane to the twisted cubic $x = t$, $y = t^2$, $z = t^3$ at the point $(1, 1, 1)$.

28. Let a parametric curve in space be described by equations $r = r(t)$, $\theta = \theta(t)$, $z = z(t)$ that give the cylindrical coordinates of a moving point on the curve for $a \leq t \leq b$. Use the equations relating rectangular and cylindrical coordinates to show that the arc length of the curve is

$$s = \int_a^b \left[\left(\frac{dr}{dt}\right)^2 + \left(r\frac{d\theta}{dt}\right)^2 + \left(\frac{dz}{dt}\right)^2 \right]^{1/2} dt.$$

29. A point moves on the *unit* sphere $\rho = 1$ with its spherical angular coordinates at time t given by $\phi = \phi(t)$, $\theta = \theta(t)$, $a \leq t \leq b$. Use the equations relating rectangular and spherical coordinates to show that the arc length of its path is

$$s = \int_a^b \left[\left(\frac{d\phi}{dt}\right)^2 + (\sin^2 \phi)\left(\frac{d\theta}{dt}\right)^2 \right]^{1/2} dt.$$

30. The vector product $\mathbf{B} = \mathbf{T} \times \mathbf{N}$ of the unit tangent vector and the principal unit normal vector is the **unit binormal vector B** of a curve. (a) Differentiate $\mathbf{B} \cdot \mathbf{T} = 0$ to show that $\mathbf{T}$ is perpendicular to $d\mathbf{B}/ds$. (b) Differentiate $\mathbf{B} \cdot \mathbf{B} = 1$ to show that $\mathbf{B}$ is perpendicular to $d\mathbf{B}/ds$. (c) Conclude from parts (a) and (b) that $d\mathbf{B}/ds = -\tau \mathbf{N}$ for some number τ. Called the **torsion** of the curve, τ measures the amount that the curve twists at each point in space.

31. Show that the torsion of the helix of Example 7 of Section 12.5 is constant by showing that its value is

$$\tau = \frac{b\omega}{a^2 \omega^2 + b^2}.$$

32. Deduce from the definition of torsion (Problem 30) that $\tau \equiv 0$ for any curve such that $\mathbf{r}(t)$ lies in a fixed plane.

33. Write an equation in spherical coordinates for the spherical surface with radius 1 and center $x = 0 = y$, $z = 1$.

34. Let C be the circle in the yz-plane with radius 1 and center $y = 1$, $z = 0$. Write equations in both rectangular and cylindrical coordinates of the surface obtained by revolving C around the z-axis.

35. Let C be the curve in the yz-plane with equation $(y^2 + z^2)^2 = 2(z^2 - y^2)$. Write an equation in spherical coordinates of the surface obtained by revolving this curve around the z-axis. Then sketch this surface. [*Suggestion:* Remember that $r^2 = 2 \cos 2\theta$ is the polar equation of a figure-eight curve.]

36. Let A be the area of the parallelogram $PQRS$ in space determined by the vectors $\mathbf{a} = \overrightarrow{PQ}$ and $\mathbf{b} = \overrightarrow{PS}$. Let A' be the area of the perpendicular projection of $PQRS$ into a plane that makes an acute angle γ with the plane of $PQRS$. Assuming that $A' = A\cos\gamma$ in such a situation (this is true), prove that the areas of the perpendicular projections of the parallelogram $PQRS$ into the three coordinate planes are

$$|\mathbf{i}\cdot(\mathbf{a}\times\mathbf{b})|, \quad |\mathbf{j}\cdot(\mathbf{a}\times\mathbf{b})|, \quad \text{and} \quad |\mathbf{k}\cdot(\mathbf{a}\times\mathbf{b})|.$$

Conclude that the square of the area of a parallelogram in space is equal to the sum of the squares of the areas of its perpendicular projections into the three coordinate planes.

37. Take $\mathbf{a} = \langle a_1, a_2, a_3\rangle$ and $\mathbf{b} = \langle b_1, b_2, b_3\rangle$ in Problem 36. Show that

$$A^2 = \begin{vmatrix} a_2 & a_3 \\ b_2 & b_3 \end{vmatrix}^2 + \begin{vmatrix} a_3 & a_1 \\ b_3 & b_1 \end{vmatrix}^2 + \begin{vmatrix} a_1 & a_2 \\ b_1 & b_2 \end{vmatrix}^2.$$

38. Let C be a curve in a plane $\mathcal{P}$ that is not parallel to the z-axis. Suppose that the projection of C into the xy-plane is an ellipse. Introduce uv-coordinates into the plane $\mathcal{P}$ to prove that the curve C is itself an ellipse.

39. Conclude from Problem 38 that the intersection of a nonvertical plane and an elliptic cylinder with vertical sides is an ellipse.

40. Use the result of Problem 38 to prove that the intersection of the plane $z = Ax + By$ and the paraboloid $z = a^2x^2 + b^2y^2$ is either empty, a single point, or an ellipse.

41. Use the result of Problem 38 to prove that the intersection of the plane $z = Ax + By$ and the ellipsoid $x^2/a^2 + y^2/b^2 + z^2/c^2 = 1$ is either empty, a single point, or an ellipse.

42. Suppose that $y = f(x)$ is the graph of a function for which f'' is continuous, and suppose also that the graph has an inflection point at $(a, f(a))$. Prove that the curvature of the graph at $x = a$ is zero.

43. Find the points on the curve $y = \sin x$ where the curvature is maximal and those where it is minimal.

44. The right branch of the hyperbola $x^2 - y^2 = 1$ may be parametrized by $x(t) = \cosh t$, $y(t) = \sinh t$. Find the point where its curvature is minimal.

45. Find the vectors $\mathbf{N}$ and $\mathbf{T}$ at the point of the curve $x(t) = t\cos t$, $y(t) = t\sin t$ that corresponds to $t = \pi/2$.

46. Find the points on the ellipse $x^2/a^2 + y^2/b^2 = 1$ (with $a > b > 0$) where the curvature is maximal and those where it is minimal.

47. Suppose that the plane curve $r = f(\theta)$ is given in polar coordinates. Write r' for $f'(\theta)$ and r'' for $f''(\theta)$. Show that its curvature is given by

$$\kappa = \frac{|r^2 + 2(r')^2 - rr''|}{[r^2 + (r')^2]^{3/2}}.$$

48. Use the formula in Problem 47 to calculate the curvature $\kappa(\theta)$ at the point (r, θ) of the spiral of Archimedes with equation $r = \theta$. Then show that $\kappa(\theta) \to 0$ as $\theta \to +\infty$.

49. A railway curve must join two straight tracks, one extending due west from $(-1, -1)$ and the other extending due east from $(1, 1)$. Determine A, B, and C so that the curve $y = Ax + Bx^3 + Cx^5$ joins $(-1, -1)$ and $(1, 1)$ and so that the slope and curvature of this connecting curve are zero at both its endpoints.

50. A plane passing through the origin and not parallel to any coordinate plane has an equation of the form $Ax + By + Cz = 0$ and intersects the spherical surface $x^2 + y^2 + z^2 = R^2$ in a great circle. Find the highest point on this great circle; that is, find the coordinates of the point with the largest z-coordinate.

51. Suppose that a tetrahedron in space has a solid right angle at one vertex (like a corner of a cube). Suppose that A is the area of the side opposite the solid right angle and that B, C, and D are the areas of the other three sides. (a) Prove that

$$A^2 = B^2 + C^2 + D^2.$$

(b) Of what famous theorem is this a three-dimensional version?

PARTIAL DIFFERENTIATION 13

Joseph Louis Lagrange (1736–1813)

Joseph Louis Lagrange is remembered for his great treatises on analytical mechanics and on the theory of functions that summarized much of eighteenth-century pure and applied mathematics. These treatises—*Mécanique analytique* (1788), *Théorie des fonctions analytiques* (1797), and *Leçons sur le calcul des fonctions* (1806)—systematically developed and applied widely the differential and integral calculus of multivariable functions expressed in terms of the rectangular coordinates x, y, z in three-dimensional space. They were written and published in Paris during the last quarter-century of Lagrange's career. But he grew up and spent his first 30 years in Turin, Italy. His father pointed Lagrange toward the law, but by age 17 Lagrange had decided on a career in science and mathematics. Based on his early work in celestial mechanics (the mathematical analysis of the motions of the planets and satellites in our solar system), Lagrange in 1766 succeeded Leonhard Euler as director of the Berlin Academy in Germany.

Lagrange regarded his far-reaching work on maximum-minimum problems as his best work in mathematics. This work, which continued throughout his long career, dated back to a letter to Euler that Lagrange wrote from Turin when he was only 19. This letter outlined a new approach to a certain class of optimization problems that comprise the calculus of variations. A typical example is the *isoperimetric problem*, which asks what curve of a given arc length encloses a plane region with the greatest area. (The answer: a circle.) In the *Mécanique analytique*, Lagrange applied his "method of multipliers" to investigate the motion of a particle in space that is constrained to move on a surface defined by an equation of the form $g(x, y, z) = 0$. Section 13.9 applies the Lagrange multiplier method to the problem of maximizing or minimizing a function $f(x, y, z)$ subject to a "constraint" of the form

$$g(x, y, z) = 0.$$

Today this method has applications that range from minimizing the fuel required for a spacecraft to achieve its desired trajectory to maximizing the productivity of a commercial enterprise limited by the availability of financial, natural, and personnel resources.

Modern scientific visualization often employs computer graphic techniques to present different interpretations of the same data simultaneously in a single figure. The following color graphic shows both a graph of a surface $z = f(x, y)$ and a contour map showing *level curves* that appear to encircle points (x, y) corresponding to *pits and peaks* on the surface. In Section 13.5 we learn how to locate multivariable maximum-minimum points like those visible on this surface.

13.1 INTRODUCTION

We turn our attention here and in Chapters 14 and 15 to the calculus of functions of more than one variable. Many real-world functions depend on two or more variables. For example:

- In physical chemistry the ideal gas law $pV = nRT$ (where n and R are constants) is used to express any one of the variables p (pressure), V (volume), and T (temperature) as a function of the other two.
- The altitude above sea level at a particular location on the earth's surface depends on the latitude and longitude of the location.
- A manufacturer's profit depends on sales, overhead costs, the cost of each raw material used, and in many cases, additional variables.
- The amount of usable energy a solar panel can gather depends on its efficiency, its angle of inclination to the sun's rays, the angle of elevation of the sun above the horizon, and other factors.

FIGURE 13.1.1 A box whose total cost we want to minimize.

A typical application may call for us to find an extreme value of a function of several variables. For example, suppose that we want to minimize the cost of making a rectangular box with a volume of 48 ft^3, given that its front and back cost \$1/ft^2, its top and bottom cost \$2/ft^2, and its two ends cost \$3/ft^2. Figure 13.1.1 shows such a box of length x, width y, and height z. Under the conditions given, its total cost will be

$$C = 2xz + 4xy + 6yz \quad \text{(dollars)}.$$

But x, y, and z are not independent variables, because the box has fixed volume

$$V = xyz = 48.$$

We eliminate z, for instance, from the first formula by using the second; because $z = 48/(xy)$, the cost we want to minimize is given by

$$C = 4xy + \frac{288}{x} + \frac{96}{y}.$$

Because neither of the variables x or y can be expressed in terms of the other, the single-variable maximum-minimum techniques of Chapter 3 cannot be applied here. We need new optimization techniques applicable to functions of two or more independent variables. In Section 13.5 we shall return to this problem.

The problem of optimization is merely one example. We shall see in this chapter that many of the main ingredients of single-variable differential calculus—limits, derivatives and rates of change, chain rule computations, and maximum-minimum techniques—can be generalized to functions of two or more variables.

13.2 FUNCTIONS OF SEVERAL VARIABLES

Recall from Section 1.1 that a real-valued *function* is a rule or correspondence f that associates a unique real number with each element of a set D. The domain D has always been a subset of the real line for the functions of a single variable that we have studied up to this point. If D is a subset of the plane, then f is a function of *two* variables—for, given a point P of D, we naturally associate with P its rectangular coordinates (x, y).

DEFINITION   Functions of Two or Three Variables

A **function of two variables,** defined on the **domain** D in the plane, is a rule f that associates with each point (x, y) in D a unique real number, denoted by $f(x, y)$.
A **function of three variables,** defined on the **domain** D in space, is a rule f that associates with each point (x, y, z) in D a unique real number $f(x, y, z)$.

We can typically define a function f of two (or three) variables by giving a formula that specifies $f(x, y)$ in terms of x and y (or $f(x, y, z)$ in terms of x, y, and z). In case the domain D of f is not explicitly specified, we take D to consist of all points for which the given formula is meaningful.

EXAMPLE 1 The domain of the function f with formula

$$f(x, y) = \sqrt{25 - x^2 - y^2}$$

is the set of all (x, y) such that $25 - x^2 - y^2 \geq 0$—that is, the circular disk $x^2 + y^2 \leq 25$ of radius 5 centered at the origin. Similarly, the function g defined as

$$g(x, y, z) = \frac{x + y + z}{\sqrt{x^2 + y^2 + z^2}}$$

is defined at all points in space where $x^2 + y^2 + z^2 > 0$. Thus its domain consists of all points in three-dimensional space $\mathbf{R}^3$ other than the origin $(0, 0, 0)$. ◆

EXAMPLE 2 Find the domain of definition of the function with formula

$$f(x, y) = \frac{y}{\sqrt{x - y^2}}. \tag{1}$$

Find also the points (x, y) at which $f(x, y) = \pm 1$.

Solution For $f(x, y)$ to be defined, the *radicand* $x - y^2$ must be positive—that is, $y^2 < x$. Hence the domain of f is the set of points lying strictly to the right of the parabola $x = y^2$. This domain is shaded in Fig. 13.2.1. The parabola in the figure is dashed to indicate that it is not included in the domain of f; any point for which $x = y^2$ would entail division by zero in Eq. (1).

The function $f(x, y)$ has the value ± 1 whenever

$$\frac{y}{\sqrt{x - y^2}} = \pm 1;$$

that is, when $y^2 = x - y^2$, so $x = 2y^2$. Thus $f(x, y) = \pm 1$ at each point of the parabola $x = 2y^2$ [other than its vertex $(0, 0)$, which is not included in the domain of f]. This parabola is shown as a solid curve in Fig. 13.2.1. ◆

FIGURE 13.2.1 The domain of $f(x, y) = \dfrac{y}{\sqrt{x - y^2}}$ (Example 2).

In a geometric, physical, or economic situation, a function typically results from expressing one descriptive variable in terms of others. As we saw in Section 13.1, the cost C of the box discussed there is given by the formula

$$C = 4xy + \frac{288}{x} + \frac{96}{y}$$

in terms of the length x and width y of the box. The value C of this function is a variable that depends on the values of x and y. Hence we call C a **dependent variable,** whereas x and y are **independent variables.** And if the temperature T at the point (x, y, z) in space is given by some formula $T = h(x, y, z)$, then the dependent variable T is a function of the three independent variables x, y, and z.

We can define a function of four or more variables by giving a formula that includes the appropriate number of independent variables. For example, if an amount A of heat is released at the origin in space at time $t = 0$ in a medium with thermal diffusivity k, then—under appropriate conditions—the temperature T at the point (x, y, z) at time $t > 0$ is given by

$$T(x, y, z, t) = \frac{A}{(4\pi k t)^{3/2}} \exp\left(-\frac{x^2 + y^2 + z^2}{4kt}\right).$$

If A and k are constants, then this formula gives the temperature T as a function of the four independent variables x, y, z, and t.

852 CHAPTER 13 Partial Differentiation

We shall see that the main differences between single-variable and multivariable calculus show up when only two independent variables are involved. Hence many of our results will be stated in terms of functions of two variables. Most of these results readily generalize by analogy to the case of three or more independent variables.

Graphs and Level Curves

We can visualize how a function f of two variables "works" in terms of its graph. The **graph** of f is the graph of the equation $z = f(x, y)$. Thus the graph of f is the set of all points in space with coordinates (x, y, z) that satisfy the equation $z = f(x, y)$. (See Fig. 13.2.2.) The planes and quadric surfaces of Sections 12.4 and 12.7 provide some simple examples of graphs of functions of two variables.

FIGURE 13.2.2 The graph of a function of two variables is typically a surface "over" the domain of the function.

EXAMPLE 3 Sketch the graph of the function $f(x, y) = 2 - \frac{1}{2}x - \frac{1}{3}y$.

Solution We know from Section 12.4 that the graph of the equation $z = 2 - \frac{1}{2}x - \frac{1}{3}y$ is a plane, and we can visualize it by using its intercepts with the coordinate axes to plot the portion in the first octant of space. Clearly $z = 2$ if $x = y = 0$. Also the equation gives $y = 6$ if $x = z = 0$ and $x = 4$ if $y = z = 0$. Hence the graph looks as pictured in Fig. 13.2.3. ◆

EXAMPLE 4 The graph of the function $f(x, y) = x^2 + y^2$ is the familiar circular paraboloid $z = x^2 + y^2$ (Section 12.7) shown in Fig. 13.2.4. ◆

FIGURE 13.2.3 The planar graph of Example 3.

EXAMPLE 5 Find the domain of definition of the function

$$g(x, y) = \frac{1}{2}\sqrt{4 - 4x^2 - y^2} \qquad (2)$$

and sketch its graph.

Solution The function g is defined wherever $4 - 4x^2 - y^2 \geq 0$—that is, $x^2 + \frac{1}{4}y^2 \leq 1$—so that Eq. (2) does not involve the square root of a negative number. Thus the domain of g is the set of points in the xy-plane that lie on and within the ellipse $x^2 + \frac{1}{4}y^2 = 1$ (Fig. 13.2.5). If we square both sides of the equation $z = \frac{1}{2}\sqrt{4 - 4x^2 - y^2}$ and simplify the result, we get the equation

$$x^2 + \frac{1}{4}y^2 + z^2 = 1$$

of an ellipsoid with semiaxes $a = 1$, $b = 2$, and $c = 1$ (Section 12.7). But $g(x, y)$ as defined in Eq. (2) is nonnegative wherever it is defined, so the graph of g is the upper half of the ellipsoid (Fig. 13.2.6). ◆

FIGURE 13.2.4 The paraboloid is the graph of the function $f(x, y) = x^2 + y^2$.

FIGURE 13.2.5 The domain of the function $g(x, y) = \frac{1}{2}\sqrt{4 - 4x^2 - y^2}$.

FIGURE 13.2.6 The graph of the function g is the upper half of the ellipsoid.

Functions of Several Variables SECTION 13.2 853

The intersection of the horizontal plane $z = k$ with the surface $z = f(x, y)$ is called the **contour curve** of **height** k on the surface (Fig. 13.2.7). The vertical projection of this contour curve into the xy-plane is the **level curve** $f(x, y) = k$ of the function f. Thus a level curve of f is simply a set in the xy-plane on which the value $f(x, y)$ is *constant*. On a topographic map, such as the one in Fig. 13.2.8, the level curves are curves of constant height above sea level.

FIGURE 13.2.7 A contour curve and the corresponding level curve.

FIGURE 13.2.8 The region near Longs Peak, Rocky Mountain National Park, Colorado, showing contour lines at intervals of 200 feet.

Level curves give a two-dimensional way of representing a three-dimensional surface $z = f(x, y)$, just as the two-dimensional map in Fig. 13.2.8 represents a three-dimensional mountain range. We do this by drawing typical level curves of $z = f(x, y)$ in the xy-plane, labeling each with the corresponding (constant) value of z. Figure 13.2.9 illustrates this process for a simple hill.

EXAMPLE 6 Figure 13.2.10 shows some typical contour curves on the paraboloid $z = 25 - x^2 - y^2$. Figure 13.2.11 shows the corresponding level curves. ◆

FIGURE 13.2.9 Contour curves and level curves for a hill.

FIGURE 13.2.10 Contour curves on the surface $z = 25 - x^2 - y^2$.

FIGURE 13.2.11 Level curves of the function $f(x, y) = 25 - x^2 - y^2$.

FIGURE 13.2.12 Level curves for the function $f(x, y) = y^2 - x^2$.

FIGURE 13.2.13 Contour curves on $z = y^2 - x^2$ (Example 7).

EXAMPLE 7 Sketch some typical level curves for the function $f(x, y) = y^2 - x^2$.

Solution If $k \neq 0$ then the curve $y^2 - x^2 = k$ is a hyperbola (Section 10.6). It opens along the y-axis if $k > 0$, along the x-axis if $k < 0$. If $k = 0$ then we have the equation $y^2 - x^2 = 0$, whose graph consists of the two straight lines $y = x$ and $y = -x$. Figure 13.2.12 shows some of the level curves, each labeled with the corresponding constant value of z. Figure 13.2.13 shows contour curves on the hyperbolic paraboloid $z = y^2 - x^2$ (Section 12.7). Note that the saddle point at the origin on the paraboloid corresponds to the intersection point of the two level curves $y = x$ and $y = -x$ in Fig. 13.2.12. ◆

The graph of a function $f(x, y, z)$ of three variables cannot be drawn in three dimensions, but we can readily visualize its **level surfaces** of the form $f(x, y, z) = k$. For example, the level surfaces of the function $f(x, y, z) = x^2 + y^2 + z^2$ are spheres (spherical surfaces) centered at the origin. Thus the level surfaces of f are the sets in space on which the value $f(x, y, z)$ is constant.

If the function f gives the temperature at the location (x, y) or (x, y, z), then its level curves or surfaces are called **isotherms**. A weather map typically includes level curves of the ground-level atmospheric pressure; these are called **isobars**. Even though you may be able to construct the graph of a function of two variables, that graph might be so complicated that information about the function (or the situation it describes) is obscure. Frequently the level curves themselves give more information, as in weather maps. For example, Fig. 13.2.14 shows level curves for the annual

FIGURE 13.2.14 Days of high air pollution forecast in the United States (from National Atlas of the United States, U.S. Department of the Interior, 1970).

Functions of Several Variables SECTION 13.2 855

numbers of days of *high* air pollution forecast at different localities in the United States. The scale of this figure does not show local variations caused by individual cities. But a glance indicates that western Colorado, south Georgia, and central Illinois all expect the same number (10, in this case) of high-pollution days each year.

EXAMPLE 8 Figure 13.2.15 shows some level surfaces of the function

$$f(x, y, z) = x^2 + y^2 - z^2.$$

If $k > 0$, then the graph of $x^2 + y^2 - z^2 = k$ is a hyperboloid of one sheet, whereas if $k < 0$ it is a hyperboloid of two sheets. The cone $x^2 + y^2 - z^2 = 0$ lies between these two types of hyperboloids. ◆

FIGURE 13.2.15 Some level surfaces of the function $w = f(x, y, z) = x^2 + y^2 - z^2$ (Example 8).

Computer Plots

Many computer systems have surface and contour plotting routines like the *Maple* commands

```
plot3d(y^2 - x^2, x = -3..3, y = -3..3);

with(plots):  contourplot(y^2 - x^2, x = -3..3, y = -3..3);
```

and the *Mathematica* commands

```
Plot3D[ y^2 - x^2, {x,-3,3}, {y,-3,3} ]

ContourPlot[ y^2 - x^2, {x,-3,3}, {y,-3,3} ]
```

for the function $f(x, y) = y^2 - x^2$ of Example 7.

EXAMPLE 9 Figure 13.2.16 shows both the graph and some projected contour curves of the function

$$f(x, y) = (x^2 - y^2)\exp(-x^2 - y^2).$$

Observe the patterns of nested level curves that indicate "pits" and "peaks" on the surface. In Fig. 13.2.17, the level curves that correspond to surface contours above the xy-plane are shown in red, while those that correspond to contours below the xy-plane are shown in blue. In this way we can distinguish between peaks and pits. It appears likely that the surface has peaks above the points $(\pm 1, 0)$ on the x-axis in the xy-plane, and has pits below the points $(0, \pm 1)$ on the y-axis. Because $f(x, \pm x) \equiv 0$, the two 45° lines $y = \pm x$ in Fig. 13.2.17 are also level curves; they intersect at the point $(0, 0)$ in the plane that corresponds to a saddle point or "pass" (as in *mountain pass*) on the surface. ◆

FIGURE 13.2.16 The graph and projected contour curves of the function $f(x, y) = (x^2 - y^2)e^{-x^2-y^2}$.

FIGURE 13.2.17 Level curves for the function $f(x, y) = (x^2 - y^2)e^{-x^2-y^2}$.

REMARK In Section 13.5 we will study analytic methods for locating maximum and minimum points of functions of two variables *exactly*. But Example 9 indicates that plots of level curves provide a valuable tool for locating them *approximately*.

FIGURE 13.2.18 The curve $z = \sin r$ (Example 10).

EXAMPLE 10 The surface

$$z = \sin \sqrt{x^2 + y^2} \tag{3}$$

is symmetrical with respect to the z-axis, because Eq. (3) reduces to the equation $z = \sin r$ (Fig. 13.2.18) in terms of the radial coordinate $r = \sqrt{x^2 + y^2}$ that measures perpendicular distance from the z-axis. The *surface* $z = \sin r$ is generated by revolving the curve $z = \sin x$ around the z-axis. Hence its level curves are circles centered at the origin in the xy-plane. For instance, $z = 0$ if r is an integral multiple of π, whereas $z = \pm 1$ if r is any odd integral multiple of $\pi/2$. Figure 13.2.19 shows traces of this surface in planes parallel to the yz-plane. The "hat effect" was achieved by plotting (x, y, z) for those points (x, y) that lie within a certain ellipse in the xy-plane. ◆

Given an arbitrary function $f(x, y)$, it can be quite a challenge to construct by hand a picture of the surface $z = f(x, y)$. Example 11 illustrates some special techniques that may be useful. Additional surface-sketching techniques will appear in the remainder of this chapter.

FIGURE 13.2.19 The hat surface $z = \sin \sqrt{x^2 + y^2}$ (Example 10).

EXAMPLE 11 Investigate the graph of the function

$$f(x, y) = \tfrac{3}{4} y^2 + \tfrac{1}{24} y^3 - \tfrac{1}{32} y^4 - x^2. \tag{4}$$

Solution The key feature in Eq. (4) is that the right-hand side is the *sum* of a function of x and a function of y. If we set $x = 0$, we get the curve

$$z = \tfrac{3}{4} y^2 + \tfrac{1}{24} y^3 - \tfrac{1}{32} y^4 \tag{5}$$

in which the surface $z = f(x, y)$ intersects the yz-plane. But if we set $y = y_0$ in Eq. (4), we get

$$z = \left(\tfrac{3}{4} y_0^2 + \tfrac{1}{24} y_0^3 - \tfrac{1}{32} y_0^4 \right) - x^2;$$

that is,

$$z = k - x^2, \tag{6}$$

which is the equation of a parabola in the xz-plane. Hence the trace of $z = f(x, y)$ in each plane $y = y_0$ is a parabola of the form in Eq. (6) (Fig. 13.2.20).

We can use the techniques of Section 4.5 to sketch the curve in Eq. (5). Calculating the derivative of z with respect to y, we get

$$\frac{dz}{dy} = \frac{3}{2} y + \frac{1}{8} y^2 - \frac{1}{8} y^3 = -\frac{1}{8} y(y^2 - y - 12) = -\frac{1}{8} y(y + 3)(y - 4).$$

Hence the critical points are $y = -3$, $y = 0$, and $y = 4$. The corresponding values of z are

$$f(0, -3) = \tfrac{99}{32} \approx 3.09, \quad f(0, 0) = 0, \quad \text{and} \quad f(0, 4) = \tfrac{20}{3} \approx 6.67.$$

Because $z \to -\infty$ as $y \to \pm\infty$, it follows readily that the graph of Eq. (5) looks like that in Fig. 13.2.21.

FIGURE 13.2.20 The intersection of $z = f(x, y)$ and the plane $y = y_0$ (Example 11).

FIGURE 13.2.21 The curve $z = \tfrac{3}{4} y^2 + \tfrac{1}{24} y^3 - \tfrac{1}{32} y^4$ (Example 11).

FIGURE 13.2.22 Trace parabolas of $z = f(x, y)$ (Example 11).

FIGURE 13.2.23 Contour curves on $z = f(x, y)$ (Example 11).

Now we can see what the surface $z = f(x, y)$ looks like. Each vertical plane $y = y_0$ intersects the curve in Eq. (5) at a single point, and this point is the vertex of a parabola that opens downward like that in Eq. (6); this parabola is the intersection of the plane and the surface. Thus the surface $z = f(x, y)$ is generated by translating the vertex of such a parabola along the curve

$$z = \tfrac{3}{4}y^2 + \tfrac{1}{24}y^3 - \tfrac{1}{32}y^4,$$

as indicated in Fig. 13.2.22.

Figure 13.2.23 shows some typical contour curves on this surface. They indicate that the surface resembles two peaks separated by a mountain pass. Figure 13.2.24 shows a computer plot of level curves of the function $f(x, y)$. The nested level curves enclosing the points $(0, -3)$ and $(0, 4)$ correspond to the peaks at the point $(0, -3, \tfrac{99}{32})$ and $(0, 4, \tfrac{20}{3})$ on the surface $z = f(x, y)$. The level figure-eight curve through $(0, 0)$ marks the saddle point (or pass) that we see at the origin on the surface in Figs. 13.2.22 and 13.2.23. Extreme values and saddle points of functions of two variables are discussed in Sections 13.5 and 13.10. ◆

FIGURE 13.2.24 Level curves of the function $f(x, y) = \tfrac{3}{4}y^2 + \tfrac{1}{24}y^3 - \tfrac{1}{32}y^4 - x^2$ (Example 11).

13.2 TRUE/FALSE STUDY GUIDE

13.2 CONCEPTS: QUESTIONS AND DISCUSSION

1. Summarize the relationship between the level curves of a function $f(x, y)$ and the pits, peaks, and passes on the surface $z = f(x, y)$. In short, how can you locate likely pits, peaks, and passes by looking at a plot of level curves?

2. Give examples of other types of data for your country that might be presented in the form of a contour (level curve) map like the one shown in Fig. 13.2.14.

3. The function graphed in Example 11 is of the form $z = f(x) + g(y)$, the sum of single-variable functions of the two independent variables x and y. Describe a way of sketching the graph of any such function.

13.2 PROBLEMS

In Problems 1 through 20, state the largest possible domain of definition of the given function f.

1. $f(x, y) = 4 - 3x - 2y$
2. $f(x, y) = \sqrt{x^2 + 2y^2}$
3. $f(x, y) = \dfrac{1}{x^2 + y^2}$
4. $f(x, y) = \dfrac{1}{x - y}$
5. $f(x, y) = \sqrt[3]{y - x^2}$
6. $f(x, y) = \sqrt{2x} + \sqrt[3]{3y}$
7. $f(x, y) = \sin^{-1}(x^2 + y^2)$

8. $f(x, y) = \tan^{-1}\left(\dfrac{y}{x}\right)$

9. $f(x, y) = \exp(-x^2 - y^2)$ (Fig. 13.2.25)

FIGURE 13.2.25 The graph of the function of Problem 9.

10. $f(x, y) = \ln(x^2 - y^2 - 1)$
11. $f(x, y) = \ln(y - x)$
12. $f(x, y) = \sqrt{4 - x^2 - y^2}$
13. $f(x, y) = \dfrac{1 + \sin xy}{xy}$
14. $f(x, y) = \dfrac{1 + \sin xy}{x^2 + y^2}$ (Fig. 13.2.26)

FIGURE 13.2.26 The graph $z = \dfrac{1 + \sin(xy)}{x^2 + y^2}$ of Problem 14.

15. $f(x, y) = \dfrac{xy}{x^2 - y^2}$
16. $f(x, y, z) = \dfrac{1}{\sqrt{z - x^2 - y^2}}$
17. $f(x, y, z) = \exp\left(\dfrac{1}{x^2 + y^2 + z^2}\right)$
18. $f(x, y, z) = \ln(xyz)$
19. $f(x, y, z) = \ln(z - x^2 - y^2)$
20. $f(x, y, z) = \sin^{-1}(3 - x^2 - y^2 - z^2)$

In Problems 21 through 30, describe the graph of the function f.

21. $f(x, y) = 10$
22. $f(x, y) = x$
23. $f(x, y) = x + y$
24. $f(x, y) = \sqrt{x^2 + y^2}$
25. $f(x, y) = x^2 + y^2$
26. $f(x, y) = 4 - x^2 - y^2$
27. $f(x, y) = \sqrt{4 - x^2 - y^2}$
28. $f(x, y) = 16 - y^2$
29. $f(x, y) = 10 - \sqrt{x^2 + y^2}$
30. $f(x, y) = -\sqrt{36 - 4x^2 - 9y^2}$

In Problems 31 through 40, sketch some typical level curves of the function f.

31. $f(x, y) = x - y$
32. $f(x, y) = x^2 - y^2$
33. $f(x, y) = x^2 + 4y^2$
34. $f(x, y) = y - x^2$
35. $f(x, y) = y - x^3$
36. $f(x, y) = y - \cos x$
37. $f(x, y) = x^2 + y^2 - 4x$
38. $f(x, y) = x^2 + y^2 - 6x + 4y + 7$
39. $f(x, y) = \exp(-x^2 - y^2)$
40. $f(x, y) = \dfrac{1}{1 + x^2 + y^2}$

In Problems 41 through 46, describe the level surfaces of the function f.

41. $f(x, y, z) = x^2 + y^2 - z$
42. $f(x, y, z) = z + \sqrt{x^2 + y^2}$
43. $f(x, y, z) = x^2 + y^2 + z^2 - 4x - 2y - 6z$
44. $f(x, y, z) = z^2 - x^2 - y^2$
45. $f(x, y, z) = x^2 + 4y^2 - 4x - 8y + 17$
46. $f(x, y, z) = x^2 + y^2 + 25$

In Problems 47 through 52, the function $f(x, y)$ is the sum of a function of x and a function of y. Hence you can use the method of Example 11 to construct a sketch of the surface $z = f(x, y)$. Match each function with its graph among Figs. 13.2.27 through 13.2.32.

FIGURE 13.2.27

FIGURE 13.2.28

FIGURE 13.2.29

FIGURE 13.2.30

FIGURE 13.2.31

FIGURE 13.2.32

47. $f(x, y) = x^3 + y^2$
48. $f(x, y) = 2x - y^2$
49. $f(x, y) = x^3 - 3x^2 + \frac{1}{2}y^2$
50. $f(x, y) = x^2 - y^2$
51. $f(x, y) = x^2 + y^4 - 4y^2$
52. $f(x, y) = 2y^3 - 3y^2 - 12y + x^2$

Problems 53 through 58 show the graphs of six functions $z = f(x, y)$. Figures 13.2.39 through 13.2.44 show level curve plots for the same functions but in another order; the level curves in each figure correspond to contours at equally spaced heights on the surface $z = f(x, y)$. Match each surface with its level curves.

53. $z = \dfrac{1}{1 + x^2 + y^2}$, $|x| \leq 2, |y| \leq 2$ (Fig. 13.2.33)

FIGURE 13.2.33 $z = \dfrac{1}{1 + x^2 + y^2}$, $|x| \leq 2, |y| \leq 2$.

54. $z = r^2 \exp(-r^2) \cos^2\left(\frac{3}{2}\theta\right)$, $|x| \leq 3, |y| \leq 3$ (Fig. 13.2.34)

FIGURE 13.2.34 $z = r^2 \exp(-r^2) \cos^2\left(\frac{3}{2}\theta\right)$, $|x| \leq 3, |y| \leq 3, r \geq 0$.

55. $z = \cos\sqrt{x^2 + y^2}$, $|x| \leq 10, |y| \leq 10$ (Fig. 13.2.35)

FIGURE 13.2.35 $z = \cos\sqrt{x^2 + y^2}$, $|x| \leq 10, |y| \leq 10$.

56. $z = x \exp(-x^2 - y^2)$, $|x| \leq 2, |y| \leq 2$ (Fig. 13.2.36)

FIGURE 13.2.36 $z = x \exp(-x^2 - y^2)$, $|x| \leq 2, |y| \leq 2$.

57. $z = 3(x^2 + 3y^2) \exp(-x^2 - y^2)$, $|x| \leq 2.5, |y| \leq 2.5$ (Fig. 13.2.37)

FIGURE 13.2.37 $z = 3(x^2 + 3y^2) \exp(-x^2 - y^2)$, $|x| \leq 2.5, |y| \leq 2.5$.

58. $z = xy \exp\left(-\frac{1}{2}(x^2 + y^2)\right)$, $|x| \leq 3.5, |y| \leq 3.5$ (Fig. 13.2.38)

FIGURE 13.2.38 $z = xy \exp\left(-\frac{1}{2}(x^2 + y^2)\right)$, $|x| \leq 3.5, |y| \leq 3.5$.

FIGURE 13.2.39

FIGURE 13.2.40

FIGURE 13.2.41

FIGURE 13.2.42

FIGURE 13.2.43

FIGURE 13.2.44

860 CHAPTER 13 Partial Differentiation

59. Use a computer to investigate surfaces of the form $z = (ax + by)\exp(-x^2 - y^2)$. How do the number and locations of apparent peaks and pits depend on the values of the constants a and b?

60. Use a computer to graph the surface $z = (ax^2 + 2bxy + cy^2)\exp(-x^2 - y^2)$ with different values of the parameters a, b, and c. Describe the different types of surfaces that are obtained in this way. How do the number and locations of apparent peaks and pits depend on the values of the constants a, b, and c?

61. Use a computer to investigate surfaces of the form $z = r^2 \exp(-r^2) \sin n\theta$. How do the number and locations of apparent peaks and pits depend on the value of the integer n?

62. Repeat Problem 61 with surfaces of the form $z = r^2 \exp(-r^2) \cos^2 n\theta$.

13.3 LIMITS AND CONTINUITY

We need limits of functions of several variables for the same reasons that we needed limits of functions of a single variable—so that we can discuss continuity, slopes, and rates of change. Both the definition and the basic properties of limits of functions of several variables are essentially the same as those that we stated in Section 2.2 for functions of a single variable. For simplicity, we shall state them here only for functions of two variables x and y; for a function of three variables, the pair (x, y) should be replaced with the triple (x, y, z).

For a function f of two variables, we ask what number (if any) the values $f(x, y)$ approach as (x, y) approaches the fixed point (a, b) in the coordinate plane. For a function f of three variables, we ask what number (if any) the values $f(x, y, z)$ approach as (x, y, z) approaches the fixed point (a, b, c) in space.

EXAMPLE 1 The numerical data in the table of Fig. 13.3.1 suggest that the values of the function $f(x, y) = xy$ approach 6 as $x \to 2$ and $y \to 3$ simultaneously—that is, as (x, y) approaches the point $(2, 3)$. It therefore is natural to write

$$\lim_{(x,y)\to(2,3)} xy = 6.$$ ◆

x	y	$f(x,y) = xy$ (rounded)
2.2	2.5	5.50000
1.98	3.05	6.03900
2.002	2.995	5.99599
1.9998	3.0005	6.00040
2.00002	2.99995	5.99996
1.999998	3.000005	6.00000
↓	↓	↓
2	3	6

FIGURE 13.3.1 The numerical data of Example 1.

Our intuitive idea of the limit of a function of two variables is this. We say that the number L is the *limit* of the function $f(x, y)$ as (x, y) approaches the point (a, b), and we write

$$\lim_{(x,y)\to(a,b)} f(x, y) = L, \tag{1}$$

provided that the number $f(x, y)$ can be made as close as we please to L merely by choosing the point (x, y) sufficiently close to—but not equal to—the point (a, b).

To make this intuitive idea precise, we must specify how close to L—within the distance $\epsilon > 0$, say—we want $f(x, y)$ to be, and then how close to (a, b) the point (x, y) must be to accomplish this. We think of the point (x, y) as being close to (a, b) provided that it lies within a small circular disk (Fig. 13.3.2) with center (a, b) and radius δ, where δ is a small positive number. The point (x, y) lies within this disk if and only if

$$\sqrt{(x-a)^2 + (y-b)^2} < \delta. \tag{2}$$

This observation serves as motivation for the formal definition, with two additional conditions. First, we define the limit of $f(x, y)$ as $(x, y) \to (a, b)$ *only* under the condition that the domain of definition of f contains points $(x, y) \neq (a, b)$ that lie arbitrarily close to (a, b)—that is, within *every* disk of the sort shown in Fig. 13.3.2 and thus within any and every preassigned positive distance of (a, b). Hence we do not speak of the limit of f at an isolated point of its domain D. Finally, we do *not* require that f be defined at the point (a, b) itself. Thus we deliberately exclude the possibility that $(x, y) = (a, b)$.

FIGURE 13.3.2 The circular disk with center (a, b) and radius δ.

DEFINITION The Limit of $f(x, y)$

We say that the **limit of** $f(x, y)$ **as** (x, y) **approaches** (a, b) **is** L provided that for every number $\epsilon > 0$, there exists a number $\delta > 0$ with the following property: If (x, y) is a point of the domain of f such that if

$$0 < \sqrt{(x-a)^2 + (y-b)^2} < \delta, \tag{2'}$$

then it follows that

$$|f(x, y) - L| < \epsilon. \tag{3}$$

REMARK The "extra" inequality $0 < \sqrt{(x-a)^2 + (y-b)^2}$ in Eq. (2') serves to ensure that $(x, y) \neq (a, b)$.

EXAMPLE 2 The computer-generated graph in Fig. 13.3.3 suggests that

$$\lim_{(x,y) \to (0,0)} \frac{\sin(x^2 + y^2)}{x^2 + y^2} = 1.$$

Show that this is true.

FIGURE 13.3.3 The graph $z = \dfrac{\sin(x^2+y^2)}{x^2+y^2}$ of Example 2.

Solution Here $a = b = 0$ and $L = 1$ in the definition of the limit. Given $\epsilon > 0$, we must find a value $\delta > 0$ such that

$$0 < \sqrt{x^2 + y^2} < \delta \quad \text{implies that} \quad \left| \frac{\sin(x^2 + y^2)}{x^2 + y^2} - 1 \right| < \epsilon.$$

But the familiar single-variable limit

$$\lim_{t \to 0} \frac{\sin t}{t} = 1$$

implies the existence of a number δ_1 such that

$$0 < |t| < \delta_1 \quad \text{implies that} \quad \left| \frac{\sin t}{t} - 1 \right| < \epsilon.$$

When we substitute $t = x^2 + y^2$, we see that

$$0 < |x^2 + y^2| < \delta_1 \quad \text{implies that} \quad \left| \frac{\sin(x^2 + y^2)}{x^2 + y^2} - 1 \right| < \epsilon.$$

Hence we need only choose $\delta = \sqrt{\delta_1}$. Then

$$0 < \sqrt{x^2 + y^2} < \delta \quad \text{implies that} \quad 0 < |x^2 + y^2| < \delta^2 = \delta_1,$$

which (in turn) implies that $\left| \dfrac{\sin(x^2 + y^2)}{x^2 + y^2} - 1 \right| < \epsilon,$

as desired. ◆

Continuity and the Limit Laws

We frequently rely on continuity rather than the formal definition of the limit to evaluate limits of functions of several variables. We say that f is **continuous at the point** (a, b) provided that $f(a, b)$ exists and $f(x, y)$ approaches $f(a, b)$ as (x, y) approaches (a, b). That is,

$$\lim_{(x,y) \to (a,b)} f(x, y) = f(a, b).$$

Thus f is continuous at (a, b) if it is defined there and its limit there is equal to its value there, precisely as in the case of a function of a single variable. The function f is said to be **continuous on the set** D if it is continuous at each point of D, again exactly as in the single-variable case.

EXAMPLE 3 Let D be the circular disk consisting of the points (x, y) such that $x^2 + y^2 \leq 1$ and let $f(x, y) = 1$ at each point of D (Fig. 13.3.4). Then the limit of $f(x, y)$ at each point of D is 1, so f is continuous on D. But let the new function $g(x, y)$ be defined on the entire plane $\mathbf{R}^2$ as follows:

$$g(x, y) = \begin{cases} f(x, y) & \text{if } (x, y) \text{ is in } D; \\ 0 & \text{otherwise.} \end{cases}$$

Then g is *not* continuous on $\mathbf{R}^2$. For instance, the limit of $g(x, y)$ as $(x, y) \to (1, 0)$ does not exist because there exist both points within D arbitrarily close to $(1, 0)$ at which g has the value 1 and points outside of D arbitrarily close to $(1, 0)$ at which g has the value 0. Thus $g(x, y)$ cannot approach any single value as $(x, y) \to (1, 0)$. Because g has no limit at $(1, 0)$, it cannot be continuous there. ◆

FIGURE 13.3.4 The circular disk of Example 3.

The limit laws of Section 2.2 have natural analogues for functions of several variables. If

$$\lim_{(x,y) \to (a,b)} f(x, y) = L \quad \text{and} \quad \lim_{(x,y) \to (a,b)} g(x, y) = M, \tag{4}$$

then the sum, product, and quotient laws for limits are these:

$$\lim_{(x,y) \to (a,b)} [f(x, y) + g(x, y)] = L + M, \tag{5}$$

$$\lim_{(x,y) \to (a,b)} [f(x, y) \cdot g(x, y)] = L \cdot M, \tag{6}$$

and

$$\lim_{(x,y) \to (a,b)} \frac{f(x, y)}{g(x, y)} = \frac{L}{M} \quad \text{if } M \neq 0. \tag{7}$$

EXAMPLE 4 Show that $\lim_{(x,y) \to (a,b)} xy = ab$.

Solution We take $f(x, y) = x$ and $g(x, y) = y$. Then it follows from the definition of limit that

$$\lim_{(x,y) \to (a,b)} f(x, y) = a \quad \text{and} \quad \lim_{(x,y) \to (a,b)} g(x, y) = b.$$

Hence the product law gives

$$\lim_{(x,y) \to (a,b)} xy = \lim_{(x,y) \to (a,b)} [f(x, y) g(x, y)]$$

$$= \left[\lim_{(x,y) \to (a,b)} f(x, y) \right] \left[\lim_{(x,y) \to (a,b)} g(x, y) \right] = ab. \quad ◆$$

More generally, suppose that $P(x, y)$ is a polynomial in the two variables x and y. That is, $P(x, y)$ is a sum of constant multiples of the form $x^i y^j$ where the exponents i and j are nonnegative integers. Thus $P(x, y)$ can be written in the form

$$P(x, y) = \sum c_{ij} x^i y^j.$$

The sum and product laws for limits then imply that

$$\begin{aligned}
\lim_{(x,y)\to(a,b)} P(x, y) &= \lim_{(x,y)\to(a,b)} \sum c_{ij} x^i y^j \\
&= \sum \left(\lim_{(x,y)\to(a,b)} c_{ij} x^i y^j \right) \\
&= \sum c_{ij} \left(\lim_{x \to a} x^i \right) \left(\lim_{y \to b} y^k \right) \\
&= \sum c_{ij} a^i b^j = P(a, b).
\end{aligned}$$

It follows that *every polynomial in two (or more) variables is an everywhere continuous function.*

EXAMPLE 5 The function $f(x, y) = 2x^4 y^2 - 7xy + 4x^2 y^3 - 5$ is a polynomial, so we can find its limit at any point (a, b) simply by evaluating $f(a, b)$. For instance,

$$\lim_{(x,y)\to(-1,2)} f(x, y) = f(-1, 2) = 2 \cdot (-1)^4 (2)^2 - 7 \cdot (-1)(2) + 4 \cdot (-1)^2 (2)^3 - 5 = 49.$$

◆

Just as in the single-variable case, any composition of continuous multivariable functions is also a continuous function. For example, suppose that the functions f and g are both continuous at (a, b) and that h is continuous at the point $(f(a, b), g(a, b))$. Then the composite function

$$H(x, y) = h(f(x, y), g(x, y))$$

is also continuous at (a, b). As a consequence, any finite combination involving sums, products, quotients, and compositions of the familiar elementary functions is continuous, except possibly at points where a denominator is zero or where the formula for the function is otherwise meaningless. This general rule suffices for the evaluation of most limits that we shall encounter.

EXAMPLE 6 The function $g(x, y) = \sin(x^2 + y^2)$ is the composition of the continuous function $\sin t$ and the polynomial $x^2 + y^2$, and is therefore continuous everywhere. Hence the function f defined by

$$f(x, y) = \begin{cases} \dfrac{\sin(x^2 + y^2)}{x^2 + y^2} & \text{unless } x = y = 0, \\ 1 & \text{if } x = y = 0 \end{cases}$$

is continuous except possibly at the origin $(0, 0)$, where the denominator is zero. But we saw in Example 2 that

$$\lim_{(x,y)\to(0,0)} f(x, y) = 1 = f(0, 0),$$

so f is continuous at the origin as well. Thus the function f is continuous everywhere.

◆

EXAMPLE 7 If

$$f(x, y) = e^{xy} \sin \frac{\pi y}{4} + xy \ln \sqrt{y - x},$$

then e^{xy} is the composition of continuous functions, thus continuous; $\sin \frac{1}{4}\pi y$ is continuous for the same reason; their product is continuous because each is continuous.

Also $y - x$, a polynomial, is continuous everywhere; $\sqrt{y - x}$ is therefore continuous if $y \geq x$; $\ln \sqrt{y - x}$ is continuous provided that $y > x$; $xy \ln \sqrt{y - x}$ is the product of functions continuous if $y > x$. And thus the sum

$$f(x, y) = e^{xy} \sin \frac{\pi y}{4} + xy \ln \sqrt{y - x}$$

of functions continuous if $y > x$ is itself continuous if $y > x$. Because $f(x, y)$ is continuous if $y > x$, it follows that

$$\lim_{(x,y) \to (1,2)} \left[e^{xy} \sin \frac{\pi y}{4} + xy \ln \sqrt{y - x} \right] = f(1, 2) = e^2 \cdot 1 + 2 \ln 1 = e^2. \quad \blacklozenge$$

Examples 8 and 9 illustrate techniques that sometimes are successful in handling cases with denominators that approach zero; in such cases the techniques of Examples 5 through 7 cannot be applied.

EXAMPLE 8 Show that $\displaystyle\lim_{(x,y) \to (0,0)} \frac{xy}{\sqrt{x^2 + y^2}} = 0$.

Solution Let (r, θ) be the polar coordinates of the point (x, y). Then $x = r \cos \theta$ and $y = r \sin \theta$, so

$$\frac{xy}{\sqrt{x^2 + y^2}} = \frac{(r \cos \theta)(r \sin \theta)}{\sqrt{r^2 (\cos^2 \theta + \sin^2 \theta)}} = r \cos \theta \sin \theta \quad \text{for } r > 0.$$

Because $r = \sqrt{x^2 + y^2}$, it is clear that $r \to 0$ as both x and y approach zero. It therefore follows that

$$\lim_{(x,y) \to (0,0)} \frac{xy}{\sqrt{x^2 + y^2}} = \lim_{r \to 0} r \cos \theta \sin \theta = 0,$$

because $|\cos \theta \sin \theta| \leq |\cos \theta| \cdot |\sin \theta| \leq 1$ for all θ. So if the function f is defined as

$$f(x, y) = \begin{cases} \dfrac{xy}{\sqrt{x^2 + y^2}} & \text{if } (x, y) \neq (0, 0), \\ 0 & \text{if } x = y = 0, \end{cases}$$

then it follows that f is continuous at the origin $(0, 0)$. Figure 13.3.5 shows the graph of $z = f(x, y)$. It corroborates the zero limit that we found at $(0, 0)$. Near the origin the graph appears to resemble the saddle point on a hyperbolic paraboloid (Fig. 13.2.13), but this doesn't look like a smooth and comfortable saddle. $\quad \blacklozenge$

FIGURE 13.3.5 The graph $z = \dfrac{xy}{\sqrt{x^2 + y^2}}$ (Example 8).

EXAMPLE 9 Show that

$$\lim_{(x,y) \to (0,0)} \frac{xy}{x^2 + y^2}$$

does not exist.

Solution Our plan is to show that $f(x, y) = xy/(x^2 + y^2)$ approaches different values as (x, y) approaches $(0, 0)$ from different directions. Suppose that (x, y) approaches $(0, 0)$ along the straight line of slope m through the origin. On this line we have $y = mx$. So, on this line,

$$f(x, y) = f(x, mx) = \frac{x \cdot mx}{x^2 + m^2 x^2} = \frac{m}{1 + m^2}$$

if $x \neq 0$. If we take $m = 1$, we see that $f(x, y) = \frac{1}{2}$ at every point of the line $y = x$ other than $(0, 0)$. If we take $m = -1$, then $f(x, y) = -\frac{1}{2}$ at every point of the line $y = -x$ other than $(0, 0)$. Thus $f(x, y)$ approaches two different values as (x, y) approaches $(0, 0)$ along these two lines (Fig. 13.3.6). Hence $f(x, y)$ cannot approach any *single* value as (x, y) approaches $(0, 0)$, and this implies that the limit in question cannot exist.

FIGURE 13.3.6 The function f of Example 9 takes on both values $+\frac{1}{2}$ and $-\frac{1}{2}$ at points arbitrarily close to the origin.

FIGURE 13.3.7 The graph of $f(x, y) = \dfrac{xy}{x^2 + y^2}$ (Example 9).

Figure 13.3.7 shows a computer-generated graph of the function $f(x, y) = xy/(x^2 + y^2)$. It consists of linear rays along each of which the polar angular coordinate θ is constant. For each number z between $-\frac{1}{2}$ and $\frac{1}{2}$ (inclusive), there are rays along which $f(x, y)$ has the constant value z. Hence we can make $f(x, y)$ approach any number we please in $[-\frac{1}{2}, \frac{1}{2}]$ by letting (x, y) approach $(0, 0)$ from the appropriate direction. There are also paths along which (x, y) approaches $(0, 0)$ but the limit of $f(x, y)$ does not exist (Problem 53). ◆

REMARK In order for

$$L = \lim_{(x,y) \to (a,b)} f(x, y)$$

to exist, $f(x, y)$ must approach L for *any and every* mode of approach of (x, y) to (a, b). In Problem 51 we give an example of a function f such that $f(x, y) \to 0$ as $(x, y) \to (0, 0)$ along any straight line through the origin, but $f(x, y) \to 1$ as $(x, y) \to (0, 0)$ along the parabola $y = x^2$. Thus the method of Example 9 cannot be used to show that a limit exists, only that it does not. Fortunately, many important applications, including those we discuss in the remainder of this chapter, involve only functions that exhibit no such exotic behavior as the functions of Problems 51 through 53.

Functions of Three or More Variables

Thus far in this section, we have discussed explicitly only functions of two variables, but the concepts of limits and continuity generalize in a straightforward manner to functions of three or more variables. A **function f of n variables** assigns a single real number $f(x_1, x_2, \ldots, x_n)$ to an n-tuple $(x_1, x_2, \ldots, x_n)$ of real numbers. For instance, the function f might assign to the 4-tuple (x, y, z, t) the temperature $u = f(x, y, z, t)$ at time t at the point (x, y, z) in three-dimensional space.

Just as three-dimensional space $\boldsymbol{R}^3$ is the set of all triples (x_1, x_2, x_3) of real numbers, n-**dimensional space** $\boldsymbol{R}^n$ is the set of all n-tuples of real numbers. Thus the temperature function mentioned earlier is defined on four-dimensional space $\boldsymbol{R}^4$. We may therefore write $f : \boldsymbol{R}^4 \to \boldsymbol{R}$, with time t playing the role of the fourth dimension (but without the fanciful implications sometimes enjoyed in science fiction).

It is common practice to identify the n-tuple $(x_1, x_2, \ldots, x_n)$ with the vector $\mathbf{x} = \langle x_1, x_2, \ldots, x_n \rangle$—regarding each notation as simply a way of specifying the same ordered list $x_1, x_2, \ldots, x_n$ of real numbers. Then we may also regard $\boldsymbol{R}^n$ as the set of all n-vectors. This viewpoint enables us to add points in $\boldsymbol{R}^n$ coordinatewise as n-vectors, and similarly to multiply points by scalars. In analogy with lengths of vectors in $\boldsymbol{R}^2$ and $\boldsymbol{R}^3$, we define the **length** $|\mathbf{x}|$ of the vector $\mathbf{x}$ in $\boldsymbol{R}^n$ to be

$$|\mathbf{x}| = \sqrt{x_1^2 + x_2^2 + \cdots + x_n^2}.$$

For instance, the 4-vector $\langle 5, -2, 4, 2\rangle$ has length $\sqrt{25 + 4 + 16 + 4} = \sqrt{49} = 7$.

The function $f : \boldsymbol{R}^n \to \boldsymbol{R}$ may be regarded either as a function of the n independent real variables $x_1, x_2, \ldots, x_n$ or as a function of the single n-vector $\mathbf{x} = \langle x_1, x_2, \ldots, x_n \rangle$. We may then write either $f(x_1, x_2, \ldots, x_n)$ or $f(\mathbf{x})$, depending on which notation seems most natural in a given situation. For instance, with vector notation the limit concept takes the form of the statement that

$$\lim_{\mathbf{x} \to \mathbf{a}} f(\mathbf{x}) = L \tag{8}$$

provided that, for every number $\epsilon > 0$, there exists a corresponding number $\delta > 0$ such that

$$|f(\mathbf{x}) - L| < \epsilon \quad \text{whenever} \quad 0 < |\mathbf{x} - \mathbf{a}| < \delta. \tag{9}$$

Then the function f is continuous at the point $\mathbf{a} = (a_1, a_2, \ldots, a_n)$ provided that

$$\lim_{\mathbf{x} \to \mathbf{a}} f(\mathbf{x}) = f(\mathbf{a}). \tag{10}$$

An attractive feature of vector notation is that the multidimensional statements in (8), (9), and (10) take precisely the same forms as in the case of functions of a single variable, as do the multidimensional limit laws. (See the discussion questions for this section.)

13.3 TRUE/FALSE STUDY GUIDE

13.3 CONCEPTS: QUESTIONS AND DISCUSSION

1. Give precise statements of the limit laws for real-valued functions of three or more variables. Explain why any polynomial in three or more variables is continuous everywhere.
2. State precisely the general principle of the continuity of compositions of continuous multivariable functions. It should apply, for instance, to a function of four variables each of which is itself a function of three variables.
3. Explain how the reasoning of Examples 2 and 6 applies to the function F defined except at the origin in $\mathbf{R}^3$ by

$$F(x, y, z) = \frac{\sin(x^2 + y^2 + z^2)}{x^2 + y^2 + z^2}.$$

What are your conclusions?
4. Give several concrete examples of real-world functions of four or more variables.

13.3 PROBLEMS

Use the limit laws and consequences of continuity to evaluate the limits in Problems 1 through 16.

1. $\lim\limits_{(x,y) \to (0,0)} (7 - x^2 + 5xy)$

2. $\lim\limits_{(x,y) \to (1,-2)} (3x^2 - 4xy + 5y^2)$

3. $\lim\limits_{(x,y) \to (1,-1)} e^{-xy}$

4. $\lim\limits_{(x,y) \to (0,0)} \dfrac{x+y}{1+xy}$

5. $\lim\limits_{(x,y) \to (0,0)} \dfrac{5-x^2}{3+x+y}$

6. $\lim\limits_{(x,y) \to (2,3)} \dfrac{9-x^2}{1+xy}$

7. $\lim\limits_{(x,y) \to (0,0)} \ln \sqrt{1 - x^2 - y^2}$

8. $\lim\limits_{(x,y) \to (2,-1)} \ln \dfrac{1+x+2y}{3y^2 - x}$

9. $\lim\limits_{(x,y) \to (0,0)} e^{x+2y} \cos(3x + 4y)$

10. $\lim\limits_{(x,y) \to (0,0)} \dfrac{\cos(x^2 + y^2)}{1 - x^2 - y^2}$

11. $\lim\limits_{(x,y,z) \to (1,1,1)} \dfrac{x^2 + y^2 + z^2}{1 - x - y - z}$

12. $\lim\limits_{(x,y,z) \to (1,1,1)} (x + y + z) \ln xyz$

13. $\lim\limits_{(x,y,z) \to (1,1,0)} \dfrac{xy - z}{\cos xyz}$

14. $\lim\limits_{(x,y,z) \to (2,-1,3)} \dfrac{x + y + z}{x^2 + y^2 + z^2}$

15. $\lim\limits_{(x,y,z) \to (2,8,1)} \sqrt{xy} \tan \dfrac{3\pi z}{4}$

16. $\lim\limits_{(x,y) \to (1,-1)} \arcsin \dfrac{xy}{\sqrt{x^2 + y^2}}$

In Problems 17 through 20, evaluate the limits

$$\lim_{h \to 0} \frac{f(x+h, y) - f(x, y)}{h} \text{ and }$$

$$\lim_{k \to 0} \frac{f(x, y+k) - f(x, y)}{k}.$$

17. $f(x, y) = xy$
18. $f(x, y) = x^2 + y^2$
19. $f(x, y) = xy^2 - 2$
20. $f(x, y) = x^2 y^3 - 10$

In Problems 21 through 30, find the limit or show that it does not exist.

21. $\lim\limits_{(x,y) \to (1,1)} \dfrac{1 - xy}{1 + xy}$

22. $\lim\limits_{(x,y) \to (2,-2)} \dfrac{4 - xy}{4 + xy}$

23. $\lim\limits_{(x,y,z) \to (1,1,1)} \dfrac{xyz}{yz + xz + xy}$

24. $\lim\limits_{(x,y,z) \to (1,-1,1)} \dfrac{yz + xz + xy}{1 + xyz}$

25. $\lim\limits_{(x,y) \to (0,0)} \ln(1 + x^2 + y^2)$

26. $\lim\limits_{(x,y) \to (1,1)} \ln(2 - x^2 - y^2)$

27. $\lim_{(x,y)\to(0,0)} \dfrac{\cot(x^2+y^2)}{x^2+y^2}$

28. $\lim_{(x,y)\to(0,0)} \sin(\ln(1+x+y))$

29. $\lim_{(x,y)\to(0,0)} \exp\left(-\dfrac{1}{x^2+y^2}\right)$

30. $\lim_{(x,y)\to(0,0)} \arctan\left(-\dfrac{1}{x^2+y^2}\right)$

In Problems 31 through 36, determine the largest set of points in the xy-plane on which the given formula defines a continuous function.

31. $f(x,y)=\sqrt{x+y}$

32. $f(x,y)=\sin^{-1}(x^2+y^2)$

33. $f(x,y)=\ln(x^2+y^2-1)$

34. $f(x,y)=\ln(2x-y)$

35. $f(x,y)=\tan^{-1}\left(\dfrac{1}{x^2+y^2}\right)$

36. $f(x,y)=\tan^{-1}\left(\dfrac{1}{x+y}\right)$

In Problems 37 through 40, evaluate the limit by making the polar coordinates substitution $(x,y)=(r\cos\theta, r\sin\theta)$ and using the fact that $r \to 0$ as $(x,y)\to(0,0)$.

37. $\lim_{(x,y)\to(0,0)} \dfrac{x^2-y^2}{\sqrt{x^2+y^2}} = 0$

38. $\lim_{(x,y)\to(0,0)} \dfrac{x^3-y^3}{x^2+y^2} = 0$

39. $\lim_{(x,y)\to(0,0)} \dfrac{x^4+y^4}{(x^2+y^2)^{3/2}} = 0$

40. $\lim_{(x,y)\to(0,0)} \dfrac{\sin\sqrt{x^2+y^2}}{\sqrt{x^2+y^2}}$

41. Determine whether or not

$$\lim_{(x,y,z)\to(0,0,0)} \dfrac{xyz}{x^2+y^2+z^2}$$

exists; evaluate it if it does exist. [*Suggestion:* Substitute spherical coordinates $x=\rho\sin\phi\cos\theta$, $y=\rho\sin\phi\sin\theta$, $z=\rho\cos\phi$.]

42. Determine whether or not

$$\lim_{(x,y,z)\to(0,0,0)} \arctan \dfrac{1}{x^2+y^2+z^2}$$

exists; evaluate it if it does exist. [See the *Suggestion* for Problem 41.]

In Problems 43 and 44, investigate the existence of the given limit by making the substitution $y=mx$.

43. $\lim_{(x,y)\to(0,0)} \dfrac{x^2-y^2}{x^2+y^2}$

44. $\lim_{(x,y)\to(0,0)} \dfrac{x^4-y^4}{x^4+x^2y^2+y^4}$

In Problems 45 and 46, show that the given limit does not exist by considering points of the form $(x,0,0)$ or $(0,y,0)$ or $(0,0,z)$ that approach the origin along one of the coordinate axes.

45. $\lim_{(x,y,z)\to(0,0,0)} \dfrac{x+y+z}{x^2+y^2+z^2}$

46. $\lim_{(x,y,z)\to(0,0,0)} \dfrac{x^2+y^2-z^2}{x^2+y^2+z^2}$

In Problems 47 through 50, use a computer-plotted graph to explain why the given limit does not exist.

47. $\lim_{(x,y)\to(0,0)} \dfrac{x^2-2y^2}{x^2+y^2}$

48. $\lim_{(x,y)\to(0,0)} \dfrac{x^2y^2}{x^4+y^4}$

49. $\lim_{(x,y)\to(0,0)} \dfrac{xy}{2x^2+3y^2}$

50. $\lim_{(x,y)\to(0,0)} \dfrac{x^2+4xy+y^2}{x^2+xy+y^2}$

51. Let

$$f(x,y)=\dfrac{2x^2 y}{x^4+y^2}.$$

(a) Show that $f(x,y)\to 0$ as $(x,y)\to(0,0)$ along any and every straight line through the origin. (b) Show that $f(x,y)\to 1$ as $(x,y)\to(0,0)$ along the parabola $y=x^2$. Conclude that the limit of $f(x,y)$ as $(x,y)\to(0,0)$ does not exist. The graph of f is shown in Fig. 13.3.8.

FIGURE 13.3.8 The graph $z=\dfrac{2x^2y}{x^4+y^2}$ of Problem 51; note the curve $y=x^2$, $z=1$.

52. Suppose that $f(x,y)=(x-y)/(x^3-y)$ except at points of the curve $y=x^3$, where we *define* $f(x,y)$ to be 1. Show that f is not continuous at the point $(1,1)$. Evaluate the limits of $f(x,y)$ as $(x,y)\to(1,1)$ along the vertical line $x=1$ and along the horizontal line $y=1$. [*Suggestion:* Recall that $a^3-b^3=(a-b)(a^2+ab+b^2)$.]

53. Let

$$\lim_{(x,y)\to(0,0)} \dfrac{xy}{x^2+y^2}$$

be the limit in Example 9. Show that as $(x,y)\to(0,0)$ along the hyperbolic spiral $r\theta=1$, the limit of $f(x,y)$ does not exist.

Discuss the continuity of the functions defined in Problems 54 through 56.

54. $f(x,y)=\begin{cases}\dfrac{\sin xy}{xy} & \text{unless } xy=0,\\ 1 & \text{if } xy=0.\end{cases}$ (See Fig. 13.3.9.)

FIGURE 13.3.9 The graph $z=\dfrac{\sin xy}{xy}$ of Problem 54.

55. $g(x,y)=\begin{cases}\dfrac{\sin(x^2-y^2)}{x^2-y^2} & \text{unless } x^2=y^2,\\ 1 & \text{if } x^2=y^2.\end{cases}$

56. $h(x,y,z)=\begin{cases}\dfrac{\sin xyz}{xyz} & \text{unless } xyz=0,\\ 1 & \text{if } xyz=0.\end{cases}$

13.4 PARTIAL DERIVATIVES

Recall that the derivative of the single-variable function $u = g(x)$ is defined as

$$\frac{du}{dx} = \lim_{\Delta x \to 0} \frac{\Delta u}{\Delta x},$$

where $\Delta u = g(x+h) - g(x)$ is the change in u resulting from the change $h = \Delta x$ in x. This derivative is interpreted as the instantaneous rate of change of u with respect to x. For a function $z = f(x, y)$ of two variables, we need a similar understanding of the rate at which z changes as x and y vary (either singly or simultaneously).

We take a divide-and-conquer approach to this concept. If x is changed by $h = \Delta x$ but y is not changed, then the resulting change in z is

$$\Delta z = f(x+h, y) - f(x, y),$$

and the corresponding instantaneous rate of change of z is

$$\frac{dz}{dx} = \lim_{\Delta x \to 0} \frac{\Delta z}{\Delta x}. \tag{1}$$

On the other hand, if x is not changed but y is changed by the amount $k = \Delta y$, then the resulting change in z is

$$\Delta z = f(x, y+k) - f(x, y),$$

and the corresponding instantaneous rate of change of z is

$$\frac{dz}{dy} = \lim_{\Delta y \to 0} \frac{\Delta z}{\Delta y}. \tag{2}$$

The limits in Eqs. (1) and (2) are the *two* **partial derivatives** of the function $f(x, y)$ with respect to its two independent variables x and y, respectively.

DEFINITION Partial Derivatives
The **partial derivatives** (**with respect to** x **and with respect to** y) of the function $f(x, y)$ are the two functions defined by

$$f_x(x, y) = \lim_{h \to 0} \frac{f(x+h, y) - f(x, y)}{h}, \tag{3}$$

$$f_y(x, y) = \lim_{k \to 0} \frac{f(x, y+k) - f(x, y)}{k} \tag{4}$$

whenever these limits exist.

Note that Eqs. (3) and (4) are simply restatements of Eqs. (1) and (2). Just as with single-variable derivatives, there are several alternative ways of writing partial derivatives.

Notation for Partial Derivatives
If $z = f(x, y)$, then we may express its partial derivatives with respect to x and y, respectively, in these forms:

$$\frac{\partial z}{\partial x} = \frac{\partial f}{\partial x} = f_x(x, y) = \frac{\partial}{\partial x} f(x, y) = D_x[f(x, y)] = D_1[f(x, y)], \tag{5}$$

$$\frac{\partial z}{\partial y} = \frac{\partial f}{\partial y} = f_y(x, y) = \frac{\partial}{\partial y} f(x, y) = D_y[f(x, y)] = D_2[f(x, y)]. \tag{6}$$

Computer algebra systems generally employ variants of the "operator notation" for partial derivatives, such as `diff(f(x,y), x)` and `D[f[x,y], x]` in *Maple* and *Mathematica*, respectively.

Note that if we delete the symbol y throughout Eq. (3), the result is the limit that defines the single-variable derivative $f'(x)$. This means that we can calculate $\partial z/\partial x$ as an "ordinary" derivative with respect to x simply by regarding y as a constant during the process of differentiation. Similarly, we can compute $\partial z/\partial y$ as an ordinary derivative by thinking of y as the *only* variable and treating x as a constant during the computation.

Consequently, we seldom need to evaluate directly the limits in Eqs. (3) and (4) in order to calculate partial derivatives. Ordinarily we simply apply familiar differentiation results to differentiate $f(x, y)$ with respect to either independent variable (x or y) while holding the other variable constant. In short,

- To calculate $\partial f/\partial x$, regard y as a constant and differentiate with respect to x.
- To calculate $\partial f/\partial y$, regard x as a constant and differentiate with respect to y.

EXAMPLE 1 Compute both the partial derivatives $\partial f/\partial x$ and $\partial f/\partial y$ of the function $f(x, y) = x^2 + 2xy^2 - y^3$.

Solution To compute the partial derivative of f with respect to x, we regard y as a constant. Then we differentiate normally and find that

$$\frac{\partial f}{\partial x} = 2x + 2y^2.$$

When we regard x as a constant and differentiate with respect to y, we find that

$$\frac{\partial f}{\partial y} = 4xy - 3y^2.$$

◆

EXAMPLE 2 Find $\partial z/\partial x$ and $\partial z/\partial y$ if $z = (x^2 + y^2)e^{-xy}$.

Solution Because $\partial z/\partial x$ is calculated as if it were an ordinary derivative with respect to x, with y held constant, we use the product rule. This gives

$$\frac{\partial z}{\partial x} = (2x)(e^{-xy}) + (x^2 + y^2)(-ye^{-xy}) = (2x - x^2y - y^3)e^{-xy}.$$

Because x and y appear symmetrically in the expression for z, we get $\partial z/\partial y$ when we interchange x and y in the expression for $\partial z/\partial x$:

$$\frac{\partial z}{\partial y} = (2y - xy^2 - x^3)e^{-xy}.$$

You should check this result by differentiating with respect to y directly in order to find $\partial z/\partial y$.

◆

Instantaneous Rates of Change

To get an intuitive feel for the meaning of partial derivatives, we can think of $f(x, y)$ as the temperature at the point (x, y) of the plane. Then $f_x(x, y)$ is the instantaneous rate of change of temperature at (x, y) per unit increase in x (with y held constant). Similarly, $f_y(x, y)$ is the instantaneous rate of change of temperature per unit increase in y (with x held constant). For instance, we show in the next example that, with the temperature function $f(x, y) = x^2 + 2xy^2 - y^3$ of Example 1, the rate of change of temperature at the point $(1, -1)$ is $+4°$ per unit distance in the positive x-direction and $-7°$ per unit distance in the positive y-direction.

EXAMPLE 3 Suppose that the xy-plane is somehow heated and that its temperature at the point (x, y) is given by the function $f(x, y) = x^2 + 2xy^2 - y^3$, whose partial derivatives $f_x(x, y) = 2x + 2y^2$ and $f_y(x, y) = 4xy - 3y^2$ were calculated in Example 1. Suppose also that distance is measured in miles and temperature in degrees Celsius (°C). Then at the point $(1, -1)$, one mile east and one mile south of the origin, the rate of change of temperature (in degrees per mile) in the (eastward) positive

x-direction is

$$f_x(1, -1) = 2 \cdot (1) + 2 \cdot (-1)^2 = 4 \quad \text{(deg/mi)},$$

and the rate of change in the (northward) positive y-direction is

$$f_y(1, -1) = 4 \cdot 1 \cdot (-1) - 3 \cdot (-1)^2 = -7 \quad \text{(deg/mi)}.$$

Thus, if we start at the point $(1, -1)$ and walk $\frac{1}{10}$ mi east, we expect to experience a temperature increase of about $4 \cdot (0.1) = 0.4°C$. If instead we started at $(1, -1)$ and walked 0.2 mi north, we would expect to experience a temperature change of about $(-7) \cdot (0.2) = -1.4°C$; that is, a temperature decrease of about $1.4°C$. ◆

EXAMPLE 4 The volume V (in cubic centimeters) of 1 mole (mol) of an ideal gas is given by

$$V = \frac{(82.06)T}{p},$$

where p is the pressure (in atmospheres) and T is the absolute temperature (in kelvins (K), where $K = °C + 273$). Find the rates of change of the volume of 1 mol of an ideal gas with respect to pressure and with respect to temperature when $T = 300$ K and $p = 5$ atm.

Solution The partial derivatives of V with respect to its two variables are

$$\frac{\partial V}{\partial p} = -\frac{(82.06)T}{p^2} \quad \text{and} \quad \frac{\partial V}{\partial T} = \frac{82.06}{p}.$$

With $T = 300$ and $p = 5$, we have the values $\partial V/\partial p = -984.72$ (cm³/atm) and $\partial V/\partial T = 16.41$ (cm³/K). These partial derivatives allow us to estimate the effect of a small change in temperature or in pressure on the volume V of the gas, as follows. We are given $T = 300$ and $p = 5$, so the volume of gas with which we are dealing is

$$V = \frac{(82.06)(300)}{5} = 4923.60 \quad \text{(cm}^3\text{)}.$$

We would expect an increase in pressure of 1 atm (with T held constant) to decrease the volume of gas by appropriately 1 L (1000 cm³), because $-984.72 \approx -1000$. An increase in temperature of 1 K (or 1°C) would, with p held constant, increase the volume by about 16 cm³, because $16.41 \approx 16$. ◆

Geometric Interpretation of Partial Derivatives

The partial derivatives f_x and f_y are the slopes of lines tangent to certain curves on the surface $z = f(x, y)$. Figure 13.4.1 illustrates the intersection of this surface with a vertical plane $y = b$ parallel to the xz-coordinate plane. Along the intersection curve, the x-coordinate varies but the y-coordinate is constant: $y = b$ at each point because the curve lies in the vertical plane $y = b$. A curve of intersection of $z = f(x, y)$ with a vertical plane parallel to the xz-plane is therefore called an x-**curve** on the surface.

Figure 13.4.2 shows a point $P(a, b, c)$ in the surface $z = f(x, y)$, the x-curve through P, and the line tangent to this x-curve at P. Figure 13.4.3 shows the parallel projection of the vertical plane $y = b$ onto the xz-plane itself. We can now "ignore" the presence of $y = b$ and regard $z = f(x, b)$ as a function of the *single* variable x. The slope of the line tangent to the original x-curve through P (see Fig. 13.4.2) is equal to the slope of the tangent line in Fig. 13.4.3. But by familiar single-variable calculus, this latter slope is given by

$$\lim_{h \to 0} \frac{f(a + h, b) - f(a, b)}{h} = f_x(a, b).$$

FIGURE 13.4.1 A vertical plane parallel to the xz-plane intersects the surface $z = f(x, y)$ in an x-curve.

FIGURE 13.4.2 An x-curve and its tangent line at P.

FIGURE 13.4.3 Projection into the xz-plane of the x-curve through $P(a, b, c)$ and its tangent line.

FIGURE 13.4.4 A vertical plane parallel to the yz-plane intersects the surface $z = f(x, y)$ in a y-curve.

FIGURE 13.4.5 A y-curve and its tangent line at P.

FIGURE 13.4.6 Projection into the yz-plane of the y-curve through $P(a, b, c)$ and its tangent line.

Thus we see that the geometric meaning of f_x is as follows:

Geometric Interpretation of $\partial f / \partial x$

The value $f_x(a, b)$ is the slope of the line tangent at $P(a, b, c)$ to the x-curve through P on the surface $z = f(x, y)$.

We proceed in much the same way to investigate the geometric meaning of partial differentiation with respect to y. Figure 13.4.4 illustrates the intersection with the surface $z = f(x, y)$ of a vertical plane $x = a$ parallel to the yz-coordinate plane. Now the curve of intersection is a **y-curve** along which y varies but $x = a$ is constant. Figure 13.4.5 shows this y-curve $z = f(a, y)$ and its tangent line at P. The projection of the tangent line in the yz-plane (in Fig. 13.4.6) has slope $\partial z / \partial y = f_y(a, b)$. Thus we see that the geometric meaning of f_y is as follows:

Geometric Interpretation of $\partial f / \partial y$

The value $f_y(a, b)$ is the slope of the line tangent at $P(a, b, c)$ to the y-curve through P on the surface $z = f(x, y)$.

FIGURE 13.4.7 The graph $z = 5xy \exp(-x^2 - 2y^2)$.

FIGURE 13.4.8 The angle of climb in the x-direction.

EXAMPLE 5 Suppose that the graph $z = 5xy \exp(-x^2 - 2y^2)$ in Fig. 13.4.7 represents a terrain featuring two peaks (hills, actually) and two pits. With all distances measured in miles, z is the altitude above the point (x, y) at sea level in the xy-plane. For instance, the height of the pictured point P is $z(-1, -1) = 5e^{-3} \approx 0.2489$ (mi), about 1314 ft above sea level. We ask at what rate we climb if, starting at the point $P(-1, -1, 0.2489)$, we head either due east (the positive x-direction) or due north (the positive y-direction). If we calculate the two partial derivatives of $z(x, y)$, we get

$$\frac{\partial z}{\partial x} = 5y(1 - 2x^2) \exp(-x^2 - 2y^2) \quad \text{and} \quad \frac{\partial z}{\partial y} = 5x(1 - 4y^2) \exp(-x^2 - 2y^2).$$

(You should check this.) Substituting $x = y = -1$ now gives

$$\left. \frac{\partial z}{\partial x} \right|_{(-1,-1)} = 5e^{-3} \approx 0.2489 \quad \text{and} \quad \left. \frac{\partial z}{\partial y} \right|_{(-1,-1)} = 15e^{-3} \approx 0.7468.$$

The units here are in miles per mile—that is, the ratio of rise to run in vertical miles per horizontal mile. So if we head east, we start climbing at an angle of

$$\alpha = \tan^{-1}(0.2489) \approx 0.2440 \quad \text{(rad)},$$

about 13.98°. (See Fig. 13.4.8.) But if we head north, then we start climbing at an angle of

$$\beta = \tan^{-1}(0.7468) \approx 0.6415 \quad \text{(rad)},$$

FIGURE 13.4.9 The angle of climb in the y-direction.

approximately 36.75°. (See Fig. 13.4.9.) Do these results appear to be consistent with Fig. 13.4.7? ◆

Planes Tangent to Surfaces

The two tangent lines illustrated in Figs. 13.4.2 and 13.4.5 determine a unique plane through the point $P(a, b, f(a, b))$. We will see in Section 13.7 that if the partial derivatives f_x and f_y are continuous functions of x and y, then this plane contains the line tangent at P to *every* smooth curve on the surface $z = f(x, y)$ that passes through P. This motivates the following definition of the plane tangent to the surface at P.

DEFINITION   Plane Tangent to $z = f(x, y)$

Suppose that the function $f(x, y)$ has continuous partial derivatives on a circular disk centered at the point (a, b). Then the **plane tangent** to the surface $z = f(x, y)$ at the point $P(a, b, f(a, b))$ is the plane through P that contains the lines tangent at P to the two curves

$$z = f(x, b), \quad y = b \quad (x\text{-curve}) \tag{7}$$

and

$$z = f(a, y), \quad x = a \quad (y\text{-curve}). \tag{8}$$

To find an equation of this tangent plane at the point $P(a, b, c)$ where $c = f(a, b)$, recall from Section 12.4 that a typical nonvertical plane in space that passes through the point P has an equation of the form

$$A(x - a) + B(y - b) + C(z - c) = 0 \tag{9}$$

where $C \neq 0$. If we solve for $z - c$ we get the equation

$$z - c = p(x - a) + q(y - b) \tag{10}$$

where $p = -A/C$ and $q = -B/C$. This plane will be tangent to the surface $z = f(x, y)$ at the point $P(a, b, c)$ provided that the line defined in Eq. (10) with $y = b$ is tangent to the x-curve in Eq. (7), and the line defined in (10) with $x = a$ is tangent to the y-curve in Eq. (8). But the substitution $y = b$ reduces Eq. (10) to

$$z - c = p(x - a), \quad \text{so} \quad \frac{\partial z}{\partial x} = p,$$

and the substitution $x = a$ reduces Eq. (10) to

$$z - c = q(y - b), \quad \text{so} \quad \frac{\partial z}{\partial y} = q.$$

Moreover, our discussion of the geometric interpretation of partial derivatives gave

$$\left.\frac{\partial z}{\partial x}\right|_{(a,b)} = f_x(a, b) \quad \text{and} \quad \left.\frac{\partial z}{\partial y}\right|_{(a,b)} = f_y(a, b)$$

for the slopes of the lines through P that are tangent there to the x-curve and y-curve, respectively. Hence we must have $p = f_x(a, b)$ and $q = f_y(a, b)$ in order for the plane in Eq. (10) to be tangent to the surface $z = f(x, y)$ at the point P. Substituting these values in Eq. (10) yields the following result (under the assumption that the partial derivatives are continuous, so that the tangent plane is defined).

The Plane Tangent to a Surface

The plane tangent to the surface $z = f(x, y)$ at the point $P(a, b, f(a, b))$ has equation

$$z - f(a, b) = f_x(a, b)(x - a) + f_y(a, b)(y - b). \tag{11}$$

Partial Derivatives SECTION 13.4   873

If for variety we write (x_0, y_0, z_0) for the coordinates of P, we can rewrite Eq. (11) in the form

$$f_x(x_0, y_0)(x - x_0) + f_y(x_0, y_0)(y - y_0) + (-1)(z - z_0) = 0, \quad (12)$$

from which we see (by consulting Eq. (8) in Section 12.4) that the plane tangent to the surface $z = f(x, y)$ at the point $P(x_0, y_0, z_0)$ has **normal vector**

$$\mathbf{n} = f_x(x_0, y_0)\mathbf{i} + f_y(x_0, y_0)\mathbf{j} - \mathbf{k} = \left\langle \frac{\partial z}{\partial x}, \frac{\partial z}{\partial y}, -1 \right\rangle. \quad (13)$$

Note that $\mathbf{n}$ is a downward-pointing vector (Why?); its negative $-\mathbf{n}$ is the upward-pointing vector shown in Fig. 13.4.10.

EXAMPLE 6 Write an equation of the plane tangent to the paraboloid $z = 5 - 2x^2 - y^2$ at the point $P(1, 1, 2)$.

Solution If $f(x, y) = 5 - 2x^2 - y^2$, then

$$f_x(x, y) = -4x, \qquad f_y(x, y) = -2y;$$
$$f_x(1, 1) = -4, \qquad f_y(1, 1) = -2.$$

Hence Eq. (11) gives

$$z - 2 = -4(x - 1) - 2(y - 1)$$

(when simplified, $z = 8 - 4x - 2y$) as an equation of the plane tangent to the paraboloid at P. The computer plot in Fig. 13.4.11 corroborates this result. ◆

FIGURE 13.4.10 The surface $z = f(x, y)$, its tangent plane at $P(x_0, y_0, z_0)$, and the vector $-\mathbf{n}$ normal to both at P.

FIGURE 13.4.11 The paraboloid and tangent plane of Example 6.

Functions of Three or More Variables

Just like functions of two variables, a function of three or more variables has partial derivatives with respect to each of its independent variables. The partial derivative with respect to each variable is defined as a limit of a difference quotient involving increments in the selected variable. For instance, a function $f(x, y, z)$ has three partial derivatives, which are defined to be

$$\frac{\partial f}{\partial x} = \lim_{h \to 0} \frac{f(x + h, y, z) - f(x, y, z)}{h},$$
$$\frac{\partial f}{\partial y} = \lim_{h \to 0} \frac{f(x, y + h, z) - f(x, y, z)}{h}, \quad (14)$$
$$\text{and} \quad \frac{\partial f}{\partial z} = \lim_{h \to 0} \frac{f(x, y, z + h) - f(x, y, z)}{h}.$$

Partial derivatives of functions of still more variables are defined in an analogous way. A function $f(x_1, x_2, \ldots, x_n)$ of n variables has n partial derivatives, one with respect to each of its independent variables. Limit quotients corresponding to those in (14) can be written more concisely using vector notation. Let us write

$$f(\mathbf{x}) = f(x_1, x_2, \ldots, x_n) \quad \text{where} \quad \mathbf{x} = \langle x_1, x_2, \ldots, x_n \rangle.$$

If $\mathbf{e}_i = \langle 0, 0, \ldots, 1, \ldots, 0 \rangle$ is the unit n-vector with ith entry 1, then

$$f(\mathbf{x} + h\mathbf{e}_i) = f(x_1, x_2, \ldots, x_{i-1}, x_i + h, x_{i+1}, \ldots, x_n).$$

The partial derivative $\partial f/\partial x_i = f_{x_i} = D_i f = D_{x_i} f$ of f with respect to the ith variable x_i is then defined to be

$$\frac{\partial f}{\partial x_i} = \lim_{h \to 0} \frac{f(\mathbf{x} + h\mathbf{e}_i) - f(\mathbf{x})}{h}. \quad (15)$$

The value of $\partial f/\partial x_i$ can be interpreted as the instantaneous rate of change of the function value $f(\mathbf{x})$ per unit change in the ith variable x_i. Just as in the case of two independent variables, each of these partial derivatives is calculated by differentiating with respect to the selected variable, regarding the others as constants.

EXAMPLE 7 The four partial derivatives of the function $g(x, y, u, v) = e^{ux} \sin vy$ are

$$g_x = ue^{ux} \sin vy, \quad g_y = ve^{ux} \cos vy, \quad g_u = xe^{ux} \sin vy, \quad \text{and} \quad g_v = ye^{ux} \cos vy.$$

Observe that we get these partial derivatives by differentiating $e^{ux} \sin vy$ with respect to the variables $x, y, u,$ and v in turn, in each case holding the remaining three variables constant. ◆

Higher-Order Partial Derivatives

The first-order partial derivatives f_x and f_y are themselves functions of x and y, so they may be differentiated with respect to x or to y. The partial derivatives of $f_x(x, y)$ and $f_y(x, y)$ are called the **second-order partial derivatives** of f. There are four of them, because there are four possibilities in the order of differentiation:

$$(f_x)_x = f_{xx} = \frac{\partial f_x}{\partial x} = \frac{\partial}{\partial x}\left(\frac{\partial f}{\partial x}\right) = \frac{\partial^2 f}{\partial x^2},$$

$$(f_x)_y = f_{xy} = \frac{\partial f_x}{\partial y} = \frac{\partial}{\partial y}\left(\frac{\partial f}{\partial x}\right) = \frac{\partial^2 f}{\partial y\, \partial x},$$

$$(f_y)_x = f_{yx} = \frac{\partial f_y}{\partial x} = \frac{\partial}{\partial x}\left(\frac{\partial f}{\partial y}\right) = \frac{\partial^2 f}{\partial x\, \partial y},$$

$$(f_y)_y = f_{yy} = \frac{\partial f_y}{\partial y} = \frac{\partial}{\partial y}\left(\frac{\partial f}{\partial y}\right) = \frac{\partial^2 f}{\partial y^2}.$$

If we write $z = f(x, y)$, then we can replace each occurrence of the symbol f here with z.

Note The function f_{xy} is the second-order partial derivative of f with respect to x first and then to y; f_{yx} is the result of differentiating with respect to y first and x second. Although f_{xy} and f_{yx} are not necessarily equal, it is proved in advanced calculus that these two "mixed" second-order partial derivatives are equal if they are both continuous. More precisely, if f_{xy} and f_{yx} are continuous on a circular disk centered at the point (a, b), then

$$f_{xy}(a, b) = f_{yx}(a, b). \tag{16}$$

But if the mixed second-order derivatives f_{xy} and f_{yx} are merely defined at (a, b) but not necessarily continuous at and near this point, then it is entirely possible at $f_{xy} \neq f_{yx}$ at (a, b). (See Problem 74.)

Because most functions of interest to us have second-order partial derivatives that are continuous everywhere they are defined, we will ordinarily need to deal with only three distinct second-order partial derivatives (f_{xx}, f_{yy}, and $f_{xy} = f_{yx}$) rather than with four. Similarly, if $f(x, y, z)$ is a function of three variables with continuous second-order partial derivatives, then

$$\frac{\partial^2 f}{\partial x\, \partial y} = \frac{\partial^2 f}{\partial y\, \partial x}, \quad \frac{\partial^2 f}{\partial x\, \partial z} = \frac{\partial^2 f}{\partial z\, \partial x}, \quad \text{and} \quad \frac{\partial^2 f}{\partial y\, \partial z} = \frac{\partial^2 f}{\partial z\, \partial y}.$$

Third-order and higher-order partial derivatives are defined similarly, and the order in which the differentiations are performed is unimportant as long as all derivatives involved are continuous. In such a case, for example, the distinct third-order partial derivatives of the function $z = f(x, y)$ are

$$f_{xxx} = \frac{\partial}{\partial x}\left(\frac{\partial^2 f}{\partial x^2}\right) = \frac{\partial^3 f}{\partial x^3},$$

$$f_{xxy} = \frac{\partial}{\partial y}\left(\frac{\partial^2 f}{\partial x^2}\right) = \frac{\partial^3 f}{\partial y\, \partial x^2},$$

$$f_{xyy} = \frac{\partial}{\partial y}\left(\frac{\partial^2 f}{\partial y\, \partial x}\right) = \frac{\partial^3 f}{\partial y^2\, \partial x}, \quad \text{and}$$

$$f_{yyy} = \frac{\partial}{\partial y}\left(\frac{\partial^2 f}{\partial y^2}\right) = \frac{\partial^3 f}{\partial y^3}.$$

EXAMPLE 8 Show that the partial derivatives of third and higher orders of the function $f(x, y) = x^2 + 2xy^2 - y^3$ are constant.

Solution We find that
$$f_x(x, y) = 2x + 2y^2 \quad \text{and} \quad f_y(x, y) = 4xy - 3y^2.$$
So
$$f_{xx}(x, y) = 2, \quad f_{xy}(x, y) = 4y, \quad \text{and} \quad f_{yy}(x, y) = 4x - 6y.$$
Finally,
$$f_{xxx}(x, y) = 0, \quad f_{xxy}(x, y) = 0, \quad f_{xyy}(x, y) = 4, \quad \text{and} \quad f_{yyy}(x, y) = -6.$$

The function f is a polynomial, so all its partial derivatives are polynomials and are, therefore, continuous everywhere. Hence we need not compute any other third-order partial derivatives; each is equal to one of these four. Moreover, because the third-order partial derivatives are all constant, all higher-order partial derivatives of f are zero. ◆

13.4 TRUE/FALSE STUDY GUIDE

13.4 CONCEPTS: QUESTIONS AND DISCUSSION

1. Recall that the absolute value function $f(x) = |x|$ is differentiable except at the single point $x = 0$. Can you define an analogous function of two variables—one that has partial derivatives except at a single point?
2. Suppose that the surface $z = f(x, y)$ has a peak or a pit (that is, either a high point or a low point) at a point (a, b, c) where the surface has a tangent plane. What can you say about this tangent plane? What can you say about the values of the partial derivatives $f_x(a, b)$ and $f_y(a, b)$?
3. Can a surface $z = f(x, y)$ have a pit or a peak at a point where the partial derivatives f_x and f_y do not exist? Supply an example illustrating your answer.

13.4 PROBLEMS

In Problems 1 through 20, compute the first-order partial derivatives of each function.

1. $f(x, y) = x^4 - x^3 y + x^2 y^2 - xy^3 + y^4$
2. $f(x, y) = x \sin y$
3. $f(x, y) = e^x(\cos y - \sin y)$
4. $f(x, y) = e^2 e^{xy}$
5. $f(x, y) = \dfrac{x + y}{x - y}$
6. $f(x, y) = \dfrac{xy}{x^2 + y^2}$
7. $f(x, y) = \ln(x^2 + y^2)$
8. $f(x, y) = (x - y)^{14}$
9. $f(x, y) = x^y$
10. $f(x, y) = \tan^{-1} xy$
11. $f(x, y, z) = x^2 y^3 z^4$
12. $f(x, y, z) = x^2 + y^3 + z^4$
13. $f(x, y, z) = e^{xyz}$
14. $f(x, y, z) = x^4 - 16yz$
15. $f(x, y, z) = x^2 e^y \ln z$
16. $f(u, v) = (2u^2 + 3v^2)\exp(-u^2 - v^2)$
17. $f(r, s) = \dfrac{r^2 - s^2}{r^2 + s^2}$

18. $f(u, v) = e^{uv}(\cos uv + \sin uv)$
19. $f(u, v, w) = ue^v + ve^w + we^u$
20. $f(r, s, t) = (1 - r^2 - s^2 - t^2)e^{-rst}$

In Problems 21 through 30, verify that $z_{xy} = z_{yx}$.

21. $z = x^2 - 4xy + 3y^2$
22. $z = 2x^3 + 5x^2y - 6y^2 + xy^4$
23. $z = x^2 \exp(-y^2)$
24. $z = xye^{-xy}$
25. $z = \ln(x + y)$
26. $z = (x^3 + y^3)^{10}$
27. $z = e^{-3x} \cos y$
28. $z = (x + y) \sec xy$
29. $z = x^2 \cosh(1/y^2)$
30. $z = \sin xy + \tan^{-1} xy$

In Problems 31 through 40, find an equation of the plane tangent to the given surface $z = f(x, y)$ at the indicated point P.

31. $z = x^2 + y^2$; $P = (3, 4, 25)$
32. $z = \sqrt{50 - x^2 - y^2}$; $P = (4, -3, 5)$
33. $z = \sin \dfrac{\pi xy}{2}$; $P = (3, 5, -1)$
34. $z = \dfrac{4}{\pi} \tan^{-1} xy$; $P = (1, 1, 1)$
35. $z = x^3 - y^3$; $P = (3, 2, 19)$
36. $z = 3x + 4y$; $P = (1, 1, 7)$
37. $z = xy$; $P = (1, -1, -1)$
38. $z = \exp(-x^2 - y^2)$; $P = (0, 0, 1)$
39. $z = x^2 - 4y^2$; $P = (5, 2, 9)$
40. $z = \sqrt{x^2 + y^2}$; $P = (3, -4, 5)$

Recall that $f_{xy} = f_{yx}$ for a function $f(x, y)$ with continuous second-order partial derivatives. In Problems 41 through 44, apply this criterion to determine whether there exists a function $f(x, y)$ having the given first-order partial derivatives. If so, try to determine a formula for such a function $f(x, y)$.

41. $f_x(x, y) = 2xy^3$, $f_y(x, y) = 3x^2y^2$
42. $f_x(x, y) = 5xy + y^2$, $f_y(x, y) = 3x^2 + 2xy$
43. $f_x(x, y) = \cos^2(xy)$, $f_y(x, y) = \sin^2(xy)$
44. $f_x(x, y) = \cos x \sin y$, $f_y(x, y) = \sin x \cos y$

Figures 13.4.12 through 13.4.17 show the graphs of a certain function $f(x, y)$ and its first- and second-order partial derivatives. In Problems 45 through 50, match that function or partial derivative with its graph.

FIGURE 13.4.12

FIGURE 13.4.13

FIGURE 13.4.14

FIGURE 13.4.15

FIGURE 13.4.16

FIGURE 13.4.17

45. $f(x, y)$
46. $f_x(x, y)$
47. $f_y(x, y)$
48. $f_{xx}(x, y)$
49. $f_{xy}(x, y)$
50. $f_{yy}(x, y)$

51. Verify that the mixed second-order partial derivatives f_{xy} and f_{yx} are equal if $f(x, y) = x^m y^n$, where m and n are positive integers.

52. Suppose that $z = e^{x+y}$. Show that e^{x+y} is the result of differentiating z first m times with respect to x, then n times with respect to y.

53. Let $f(x, y, z) = e^{xyz}$. Calculate the distinct second-order partial derivatives of f and the third-order partial derivative f_{xyz}.

54. Suppose that $g(x, y) = \sin xy$. Verify that $g_{xy} = g_{yx}$ and that $g_{xxy} = g_{xyx} = g_{yxx}$.

55. It is shown in physics that the temperature $u(x, t)$ at time t at the point x of a long, insulated rod that lies along the x-axis satisfies the *one-dimensional heat equation*

$$\frac{\partial u}{\partial t} = k \frac{\partial^2 u}{\partial x^2} \qquad (k \text{ is a constant}).$$

Show that the function

$$u = u(x, t) = \exp(-n^2 kt) \sin nx$$

satisfies the one-dimensional heat equation for any choice of the constant n.

56. The *two-dimensional heat equation* for an insulated thin plate is

$$\frac{\partial u}{\partial t} = k \left(\frac{\partial^2 u}{\partial x^2} + \frac{\partial^2 u}{\partial y^2} \right).$$

Show that the function

$$u = u(x, y, t) = \exp(-[m^2 + n^2]kt) \sin mx \cos ny$$

satisfies this equation for any choice of the constants m and n.

57. A string is stretched along the x-axis, fixed at each end, and then set into vibration. It is shown in physics that the displacement $y = y(x, t)$ of the point of the string at location x at time t satisfies the *one-dimensional wave equation*

$$\frac{\partial^2 y}{\partial t^2} = a^2 \frac{\partial^2 y}{\partial x^2},$$

where the constant a depends on the density and tension of the string. Show that the following functions satisfy the one-dimensional wave equation: (a) $y = \sin(x+at)$; (b) $y = \cosh(3[x - at])$; (c) $y = \sin kx \cos kat$ (k is a constant).

58. A steady-state temperature function $u = u(x, y)$ for a thin flat plate satisfies *Laplace's equation*

$$\frac{\partial^2 u}{\partial x^2} + \frac{\partial^2 u}{\partial y^2} = 0.$$

Determine which of the following functions satisfy Laplace's equation:

(a) $u = \ln\left(\sqrt{x^2 + y^2}\right)$;
(b) $u = \sqrt{x^2 + y^2}$;
(c) $u = \arctan(y/x)$;
(d) $u = e^{-x} \sin y$.

59. Suppose that f and g are twice-differentiable functions of a single variable. Show that $y(x, t) = f(x + at) + g(x - at)$ satisfies the one-dimensional wave equation of Problem 57.

60. The electric potential field of a point charge q is defined (in appropriate units) by $\phi(x, y, z) = q/r$ where $r = \sqrt{x^2 + y^2 + z^2}$. Show that ϕ satisfies the *three-dimensional Laplace equation*

$$\frac{\partial^2 \phi}{\partial x^2} + \frac{\partial^2 \phi}{\partial y^2} + \frac{\partial^2 \phi}{\partial z^2} = 0.$$

61. Let $u(x, t)$ denote the underground temperature at depth x and time t at a location where the seasonal variation of surface ($x = 0$) temperature is described by

$$u(0, t) = T_0 + a_0 \cos \omega t,$$

where T_0 is the annual average surface temperature and the constant ω is so chosen that the period of $u(0, t)$ is one year. Show that the function

$$u(x, t) = T_0 + a_0 \exp\left(-x\sqrt{\omega/2k}\right) \cos\left(\omega t - x\sqrt{\omega/2k}\right)$$

satisfies both the "surface condition" and the one-dimensional heat equation of Problem 55.

62. The aggregate electrical resistance R of three resistances R_1, R_2, and R_3 connected in parallel satisfies the equation

$$\frac{1}{R} = \frac{1}{R_1} + \frac{1}{R_2} + \frac{1}{R_3}.$$

Show that

$$\frac{\partial R}{\partial R_1} + \frac{\partial R}{\partial R_2} + \frac{\partial R}{\partial R_3} = \left(\frac{1}{R_1^2} + \frac{1}{R_2^2} + \frac{1}{R_3^2}\right) \div \left(\frac{1}{R_1} + \frac{1}{R_2} + \frac{1}{R_3}\right)^2.$$

63. The **ideal gas law** $pV = nRT$ (n is the number of moles of the gas, R is a constant) determines each of the three variables p (pressure), V (volume), and T (temperature) as functions of the other two. Show that

$$\frac{\partial p}{\partial V} \cdot \frac{\partial V}{\partial T} \cdot \frac{\partial T}{\partial p} = -1.$$

64. It is geometrically evident that every plane tangent to the cone $z^2 = x^2 + y^2$ passes through the origin. Show this by methods of calculus.

65. There is only one point at which the plane tangent to the surface

$$z = x^2 + 2xy + 2y^2 - 6x + 8y$$

is horizontal. Find it.

66. Show that the plane tangent to the paraboloid with equation $z = x^2 + y^2$ at the point (a, b, c) intersects the xy-plane in the line with equation $2ax + 2by = a^2 + b^2$. Then show that this line is tangent to the circle with equation $4x^2 + 4y^2 = a^2 + b^2$.

67. According to van der Waals' equation, 1 mol of a gas satisfies the equation

$$\left(p + \frac{a}{V^2}\right)(V - b) = (82.06)T$$

where p, V, and T are as in Example 4. For carbon dioxide, $a = 3.59 \times 10^6$ and $b = 42.7$, and V is 25,600 cm^3 when p is 1 atm and $T = 313$ K. (a) Compute $\partial V/\partial p$ by differentiating van der Waals' equation with T held constant. Then estimate the change in volume that would result from an increase of 0.1 atm of pressure with T held at 313 K. (b) Compute $\partial V/\partial T$ by differentiating van der Waals' equation with p held constant. Then estimate the change in volume that would result from an increase of 1 K in temperature with p held at 1 atm.

68. A *minimal surface* has the least surface area of all surfaces with the same boundary. Figure 13.4.18 shows *Scherk's minimal surface*. It has the equation

$$z = \ln(\cos x) - \ln(\cos y).$$

A minimal surface $z = f(x, y)$ is known to satisfy the partial differential equation

$$\left(1 + z_y^2\right)z_{xx} - 2z_x z_y z_{xy} + \left(1 + z_x^2\right)z_{yy} = 0.$$

Verify this in the case of Scherk's minimal surface.

FIGURE 13.4.18 Scherk's minimal surface (Problem 68).

69. We say that the function $z = f(x, y)$ is **harmonic** if it satisfies Laplace's equation $z_{xx} + z_{yy} = 0$. (See Problem 58.) Show that each of these four functions is harmonic:

(a) $f_1(x, y) = \sin x \sinh(\pi - y)$;
(b) $f_2(x, y) = \sinh 2x \sin 2y$;
(c) $f_3(x, y) = \sin 3x \sinh 3y$;
(d) $f_4(x, y) = \sinh 4(\pi - x) \sin 4y$.

70. Figure 13.4.19 shows the graph of the sum

$$z(x, y) = \sum_{i=1}^{4} f_i(x, y)$$

of the four functions defined in Problem 69. Explain why $z(x, y)$ is a harmonic function.

FIGURE 13.4.19 The surface $z = f(x, y)$ of Problem 70.

71. You are standing at the point where $x = y = 100$ (ft) on a hillside whose height (in feet above sea level) is given by

$$z = 100 + \frac{1}{100}(x^2 - 3xy + 2y^2),$$

with the positive x-axis to the east and the positive y-axis to the north. (a) If you head due east, will you initially be ascending or descending? At what angle (in degrees) from the horizontal? (b) If you head due north, will you initially be ascending or descending? At what angle (in degrees) from the horizontal?

72. Answer questions (a) and (b) in Problem 71, except that now you are standing at the point where $x = 150$ and $y = 250$ (ft) on a hillside whose height (in feet above sea level) is given by

$$z = 1000 + \frac{1}{1000}(3x^2 - 5xy + y^2).$$

73. Figure 13.3.7 shows the graph of the function f defined by

$$f(x, y) = \begin{cases} \dfrac{xy}{x^2 + y^2} & \text{unless } x = y = 0, \\ 0 & \text{if } x = y = 0. \end{cases}$$

(a) Show that the first-order partial derivatives f_x and f_y are defined everywhere and are continuous except possibly at the origin. (b) Consider behavior on straight lines to show that neither f_x nor f_y is continuous at the origin. (c) Show that the second-order partial derivatives of f are all defined and continuous except possibly at the origin. (d) Show that the second-order partial derivatives f_{xx} and f_{yy} exist at the origin, but that the mixed partial derivatives f_{xy} and f_{yx} do not.

74. Figure 13.4.20 shows the graph of the function g defined by

$$g(x, y) = \begin{cases} \dfrac{xy(x^2 - y^2)}{x^2 + y^2} & \text{unless } x = y = 0, \\ 0 & \text{if } x = y = 0. \end{cases}$$

(a) Show that the first-order partial derivatives g_x and g_y are defined everywhere and are continuous except possibly at the origin. (b) Use polar coordinates to show that g_x and g_y are continuous at $(0, 0)$ as well. (c) Show that the second-order partial derivatives of g are all defined and continuous except possibly at the origin. (d) Show that all four second-order partial derivatives of g exist at the origin, but that $g_{xy}(0, 0) \neq g_{yx}(0, 0)$. (e) Consider behavior on straight lines to show that none of the four second-order partial derivatives of g is continuous at the origin.

FIGURE 13.4.20 The graph $z = \dfrac{x^3 y - xy^3}{x^2 + y^2}$ of Problem 74.

13.5 MULTIVARIABLE OPTIMIZATION PROBLEMS

The single-variable maximum-minimum techniques of Section 3.5 generalize readily to functions of several variables. We consider first a function f of two variables. Suppose that we are interested in the extreme values attained by $f(x, y)$ on a plane region R that consists of the points on and within a simple (nonintersecting) closed curve C (Fig. 13.5.1). We say that the function f attains its **absolute,** or **global, maximum value** M on R at the point (a, b) of R provided that

$$f(x, y) \leq M = f(a, b)$$

for all points (x, y) of R. Similarly, f attains its **absolute,** or **global, minimum value** m at the point (c, d) of R provided that $f(x, y) \geq m = f(c, d)$ for all points (x, y)

Multivariable Optimization Problems SECTION 13.5   879

of R. In plain words, the absolute maximum M and the absolute minimum m are the largest and smallest values (respectively) attained by $f(x, y)$ at points of the domain R of f.

Theorem 1, proved in advanced calculus courses, guarantees the existence of absolute maximum and minimum values in many situations of practical interest.

THEOREM 1 Existence of Extreme Values

Suppose that the function f is continuous on the region R that consists of the points on and within a simple closed curve C in the plane. Then f attains an absolute maximum value at some point (a, b) of R and attains an absolute minimum value at some point (c, d) of R.

FIGURE 13.5.1 A plane region R bounded by the simple closed curve C and a disk D in R centered at the interior point (a, b) of R.

We are interested mainly in the case in which the function f attains its absolute maximum (or minimum) value at an interior point of R. The point (a, b) of R is called an **interior point** of R provided that some circular disk centered at (a, b) lies wholly within R (Fig. 13.5.1). The interior points of a region R of the sort described in Theorem 1 are precisely those that do *not* lie on the boundary curve C.

An absolute extreme value attained by the function at an *interior* point of R is necessarily a local extreme value. We say that $f(a, b)$ is a **local maximum value** of $f(x, y)$ provided that it is the absolute maximum value of f on some disk D that is centered at (a, b) and lies wholly within the domain R. Similarly, a **local minimum value** is an absolute minimum value on some such disk. Thus a local maximum (or minimum) value $f(a, b)$ is not necessarily an absolute maximum (or minimum) value, but is the largest (or smallest) value attained by $f(x, y)$ at points near (a, b).

EXAMPLE 1 Figure 13.5.2 shows a computer-generated graph of the function

$$f(x, y) = 3(x - 1)^2 e^{-x^2 - (y+1)^2} - 10\left(\tfrac{1}{5}x - x^3 - y^5\right)e^{-x^2 - y^2} - \tfrac{1}{3}e^{-(x+1)^2 - y^2}$$

plotted on the rectangle R for which $-3 \leqq x \leqq 3$ and $-3 \leqq y \leqq 3$. Looking at the labeled extreme values of $f(x, y)$, we see

- A local maximum that is not an absolute maximum,
- A local maximum that is also an absolute maximum,
- A local minimum that is not an absolute minimum, and
- A local minimum that is also an absolute minimum.

We can think of the local maxima on the graph as mountain tops or "peaks" and the local minima as valley bottoms or "pits."   ◆

FIGURE 13.5.2 Local extrema contrasted with global extrema.

Finding Local Extrema

We need a criterion that will provide a practical way to find local extrema of functions of two (or more) variables. The desired result—stated in Theorem 2—is analogous to the single-variable criterion of Section 3.5: If $f(c)$ is a local extreme value of the differentiable single-variable function f, then $x = c$ must be a *critical point* where $f'(c) = 0$.

Suppose, for instance, that $f(a, b)$ is a local maximum value of $f(x, y)$ attained at a point (a, b) where both partial derivatives f_x and f_y exist. We consider vertical plane cross-section curves on the graph $z = f(x, y)$, just as when we explored the geometrical interpretation of partial derivatives in Section 13.4. The cross-section curves parallel to the xz- and yz-planes are the graphs (in these planes) of the single-variable functions

$$G(x) = f(x, b) \quad \text{and} \quad H(y) = f(a, y)$$

whose derivatives are the partial derivatives of f:

$$f_x(a, b) = G'(a) \quad \text{and} \quad f_y(a, b) = H'(b). \tag{1}$$

Because $f(a, b)$ is a local maximum value of $f(x, y)$, it follows readily that $G(a)$ and $H(b)$ are local maximum values of $G(x)$ and $H(y)$, respectively. Therefore the single-variable maximum-minimum criterion of Section 3.5 implies that

$$G'(a) = 0 \quad \text{and} \quad H'(b) = 0. \tag{2}$$

Combining (1) and (2), we conclude that

$$f_x(a, b) = 0 \quad \text{and} \quad f_y(a, b) = 0. \tag{3}$$

Essentially the same argument yields the same conclusion if $f(a, b)$ is a local minimum value of $f(x, y)$. This discussion establishes Theorem 2.

THEOREM 2   Necessary Conditions for Local Extrema
Suppose that $f(x, y)$ attains a local maximum value or a local minimum value at the point (a, b) and that both the partial derivatives $f_x(a, b)$ and $f_y(a, b)$ exist. Then

$$f_x(a, b) = 0 = f_y(a, b). \tag{3}$$

The equations in (3) imply that the plane tangent to the surface $z = f(x, y)$ must be horizontal at any local maximum or local minimum point $(a, b, f(a, b))$, in perfect analogy to the single-variable case (in which the tangent line is horizontal at any local maximum or minimum point on the graph of a differentiable function).

EXAMPLE 2 Consider the three familiar surfaces

$$z = f(x, y) = x^2 + y^2,$$
$$z = g(x, y) = 1 - x^2 - y^2, \quad \text{and}$$
$$z = h(x, y) = y^2 - x^2$$

shown in Fig. 13.5.3. In each case $\partial z / \partial x = \pm 2x$ and $\partial z / \partial y = \pm 2y$. Thus both partial derivatives are zero at the origin $(0, 0)$ (and only there). It is clear from the figure that $f(x, y) = x^2 + y^2$ has a local minimum at $(0, 0)$. In fact, because a square cannot be negative, $z = x^2 + y^2$ has the global minimum value 0 at $(0, 0)$. Similarly, $g(x, y)$ has a local (indeed, global) maximum value at $(0, 0)$, whereas $h(x, y)$ has neither a local minimum nor a local maximum there—the origin is a *saddle point* of h. This example shows that a point (a, b) where

$$\frac{\partial z}{\partial x} = 0 = \frac{\partial z}{\partial y}$$

may correspond to either a local minimum, a local maximum, or neither. Thus the necessary condition in Eq. (3) is *not* a sufficient condition for a local extremum. ◆

(a) $f(x, y) = x^2 + y^2$, local minimum at $(0, 0)$

(b) $g(x, y) = 1 - x^2 - y^2$, local maximum at $(0, 0)$

(c) $h(x, y) = y^2 - x^2$, saddle point at $(0, 0)$

FIGURE 13.5.3 Where both partial derivatives are zero, there may be (a) a minimum, (b) a maximum, or (c) neither.

EXAMPLE 3 Find all points on the surface

$$z = \tfrac{3}{4}y^2 + \tfrac{1}{24}y^3 - \tfrac{1}{32}y^4 - x^2$$

at which the tangent plane is horizontal.

Solution We first calculate the partial derivatives $\partial z/\partial x$ and $\partial z/\partial y$:

$$\frac{\partial z}{\partial x} = -2x,$$

$$\frac{\partial z}{\partial y} = \tfrac{3}{2}y + \tfrac{1}{8}y^2 - \tfrac{1}{8}y^3$$
$$= -\tfrac{1}{8}y(y^2 - y - 12) = -\tfrac{1}{8}y(y+3)(y-4).$$

We next equate both $\partial z/\partial x$ and $\partial z/\partial y$ to zero. This yields

$$-2x = 0 \quad \text{and} \quad -\tfrac{1}{8}y(y+3)(y-4) = 0.$$

Simultaneous solution of these equations yields exactly three points where both partial derivatives are zero: $(0, -3)$, $(0, 0)$, and $(0, 4)$. The three corresponding points on the surface where the tangent plane is horizontal are $(0, -3, \tfrac{99}{32})$, $(0, 0, 0)$, and $(0, 4, \tfrac{20}{3})$. These three points are indicated on the graph in Fig. 13.5.4 of the surface. (Recall that we constructed this surface in Example 11 of Section 13.2.) ◆

FIGURE 13.5.4 The surface of Example 3.

Finding Global Extrema

Theorem 2 is a very useful tool for finding the absolute maximum and absolute minimum values attained by a continuous function f on a region R of the type described in Theorem 1. If $f(a, b)$ is the absolute maximum value, for example, then (a, b) is either an interior point of R or a point of the boundary curve C. If (a, b) is an interior point and both the partial derivatives $f_x(a, b)$ and $f_y(a, b)$ exist, then Theorem 2 implies that both these partial derivatives must be zero. Thus we have the following result.

THEOREM 3 Types of Absolute Extrema
Suppose that f is continuous on the plane region R consisting of the points on and within a simple closed curve C. If $f(a, b)$ is either the absolute maximum or the absolute minimum value of $f(x, y)$ on R, then (a, b) is either

1. An interior point of R at which

$$\frac{\partial f}{\partial x} = \frac{\partial f}{\partial y} = 0,$$

2. An interior point of R where not both partial derivatives exist, or
3. A point of the boundary curve C of R.

A point (a, b) where either condition (1) or condition (2) holds is called a **critical point** of the function f. Thus Theorem 3 says that *any extreme value of the continuous function f on the plane region R must occur at an interior critical point or at a boundary point*. Note the analogy with Theorem 3 of Section 3.5, which implies that an extreme value of a single-variable function $f(x)$ on a closed and bounded interval I must occur either at an interior critical point of I or at an endpoint (boundary point) of I.

As a consequence of Theorem 3, we can find the absolute maximum and minimum values of $f(x, y)$ on R as follows:

1. First locate the interior critical points.
2. Next find the possible extreme values of f on the boundary curve C.
3. Finally compare the values of f at the points found in steps 1 and 2.

The technique to be used in the second step will depend on the nature of the boundary curve C, as illustrated in Examples 4 and 5.

FIGURE 13.5.5 The graph of the function of Example 4.

FIGURE 13.5.6 The triangular region of Example 5.

EXAMPLE 4 Let $f(x, y) = \sqrt{x^2 + y^2}$ on the region R consisting of the points on and within the circle $x^2 + y^2 = 1$ in the xy-plane. The graph of f is shown in Fig. 13.5.5. We see that the minimum value 0 of f occurs at the origin $(0, 0)$, where both the partial derivatives f_x and f_y fail to exist (Why?), whereas the maximum value 1 of f on R occurs at *each and every* point of the boundary circle. ◆

EXAMPLE 5 Find the maximum and minimum values attained by the function

$$f(x, y) = xy - x - y + 3$$

at points of the triangular region R in the xy-plane with vertices at $(0, 0)$, $(2, 0)$, and $(0, 4)$.

Solution The region R is shown in Fig. 13.5.6. Its boundary "curve" C consists of the segment $0 \leq x \leq 2$ on the x-axis, the segment $0 \leq y \leq 4$ on the y-axis, and the part of the line $2x + y = 4$ that lies in the first quadrant. Any interior extremum must occur at a point where both

$$\frac{\partial f}{\partial x} = y - 1 \quad \text{and} \quad \frac{\partial f}{\partial y} = x - 1$$

are zero. Hence the only interior critical point is $(1, 1)$.

Along the edge where $y = 0$: The function $f(x, y)$ takes the form

$$\alpha(x) = f(x, 0) = 3 - x, \qquad 0 \leq x \leq 2.$$

Because $\alpha(x)$ is a decreasing function, its extrema for $0 \leq x \leq 2$ occur at the endpoints $x = 0$ and $x = 2$. This gives the two possibilities $(0, 0)$ and $(2, 0)$ for locations of extrema of $f(x, y)$.

Along the edge where $x = 0$: The function $f(x, y)$ takes the form

$$\beta(y) = f(0, y) = 3 - y, \qquad 0 \leq y \leq 4.$$

The endpoints of this interval yield the points $(0, 0)$ and $(0, 4)$ as possibilities for locations of extrema of $f(x, y)$.

On the edge of R where $y = 4 - 2x$: We may substitute $4 - 2x$ for y in the formula for $f(x, y)$ and thus express f as a function of a single variable:

$$\gamma(x) = x(4 - 2x) - x - (4 - 2x) + 3$$
$$= -2x^2 + 5x - 1, \qquad 0 \leq x \leq 2.$$

To find the extreme values of $\gamma(x)$, we first calculate

$$\gamma'(x) = -4x + 5;$$

$\gamma'(x) = 0$ where $x = \frac{5}{4}$. Thus each extreme value of $\gamma(x)$ on $[0, 2]$ must occur either at the interior point $x = \frac{5}{4}$ of the interval $[0, 2]$ or at one of the endpoints $x = 0$ and $x = 2$. This gives the possibilities $(0, 4)$, $(\frac{5}{4}, \frac{3}{2})$, and $(2, 0)$ for locations of extrema of $f(x, y)$.

We conclude by evaluating f at each of the points we have found:

$$f(0, 0) = 3, \qquad \longleftarrow \text{ maximum}$$
$$f(\tfrac{5}{4}, \tfrac{3}{2}) = 2.125$$
$$f(1, 1) = 2,$$
$$f(2, 0) = 1,$$
$$f(0, 4) = -1. \qquad \longleftarrow \text{ minimum}$$

Thus the maximum value of $f(x, y)$ on the region R is $f(0, 0) = 3$ and the minimum value is $f(0, 4) = -1$. ◆

Note the terminology used in this section. In Example 5, the maximum *value* of f is 3, the maximum *occurs at* the point $(0, 0)$ in the domain of f, and the *highest point* on the graph of f is $(0, 0, 3)$.

Highest and Lowest Points of Surfaces

In applied problems we frequently know in advance that the absolute maximum (or minimum) value of $f(x, y)$ on R occurs at an *interior* point of R where both partial derivatives of f exist. In this important case, Theorem 3 tells us that we can locate every possible point at which the maximum (or minimum) might occur by simultaneously solving the two equations

$$f_x(x, y) = 0 \quad \text{and} \quad f_y(x, y) = 0. \qquad (4)$$

If we are lucky, these equations will have only one simultaneous solution (x, y) interior to R. If so, then *that* solution must be the location of the desired maximum (or minimum). If we find that the equations in (4) have several simultaneous solutions interior to R, then we simply evaluate f at each solution to determine which yields the largest (or smallest) value of $f(x, y)$ and is therefore the desired maximum (or minimum) point.

We can use this method to find the lowest point on a surface $z = f(x, y)$ that opens upward, as in Fig. 13.5.7. If R is a sufficiently large rectangle, then $f(x, y)$ attains large positive values everywhere on the boundary of R but smaller values at interior points. It follows that the minimum value of $f(x, y)$ must be attained at an interior point of R.

The question of a highest or lowest point is not pertinent for a surface that opens both upward and downward, as in Fig. 13.5.8.

FIGURE 13.5.7 The surface $z = x^4 + y^4 - x^2y^2$ opens upward.

FIGURE 13.5.8 The surface $z = x^4 + y^4 - 3x^2y^2$ opens both upward and downward.

EXAMPLE 6 Find the highest point on the surface

$$z = f(x, y) = \tfrac{8}{3}x^3 + 4y^3 - x^4 - y^4. \qquad (5)$$

Solution We observe that the negative fourth-degree terms in $f(x, y)$ clearly predominate when $|x|$ and/or $|y|$ is large, so the surface $z = f(x, y)$ opens downward. (See Fig. 13.5.9.) To verify this observation, we factor out $x^4 + y^4$ and write

$$f(x, y) = (x^4 + y^4)\left[\frac{\tfrac{8}{3}x^3 + 4y^3}{x^4 + y^4} - 1\right]. \qquad (6)$$

Now consider a fixed point (x, y) and let m denote the smaller, and M the larger, of the two numbers $|x|$ and $|y|$. Then

$$\left|\frac{\tfrac{8}{3}x^3 + 4y^3}{x^4 + y^4}\right| \leq \frac{4|x|^3 + 4|y|^3}{x^4 + y^4} = \frac{4m^3 + 4M^3}{m^4 + M^4} \leq \frac{4M^3 + 4M^3}{0^4 + M^4} = \frac{8}{M}.$$

For instance, if either $|x|$ or $|y|$ is greater than $M = 10$, then the fraction within brackets in Eq. (6) has absolute value less than $\tfrac{8}{10}$, so it follows that $f(x, y) < 0$.

Thus $f(x, y)$ is negative outside the large square R with vertices $(\pm 10, \pm 10)$ in the xy-plane. But $z = f(x, y)$ certainly attains positive values within R, such as $f(1, 1) = \tfrac{14}{3}$. Consequently Theorem 1 implies that $f(x, y)$ attains an absolute maximum value at some interior point of R. So let us proceed to find this maximum value.

Because the partial derivatives $\partial z/\partial x$ and $\partial z/\partial y$ exist everywhere, Theorem 3 implies that we need only solve the equations $\partial z/\partial x = 0$ and $\partial z/\partial y = 0$ in Eq. (4)—that is,

$$\frac{\partial z}{\partial x} = 8x^2 - 4x^3 = 4x^2(2 - x) = 0,$$

$$\frac{\partial z}{\partial y} = 12y^2 - 4y^3 = 4y^2(3 - y) = 0.$$

FIGURE 13.5.9 The surface $z = \tfrac{8}{3}x^3 + 4y^3 - x^4 - y^4$ opens downward.

If these two equations are satisfied, then

$$\boxed{\text{Either } x = 0 \text{ or } x = 2} \quad \text{and} \quad \boxed{\text{either } y = 0 \text{ or } y = 3.}$$

FIGURE 13.5.10 The critical points of Example 6.

It follows that either

| $x = 0$ and $y = 0$ | or | $x = 0$ and $y = 3$ | or | $x = 2$ and $y = 0$ | or | $x = 2$ and $y = 3$. |

Consequently, we need only inspect the values

$z(0, 0) = 0,$

$z(2, 0) = \frac{16}{3} = 5.333\,333\,333\ldots,$

$z(0, 3) = 27,$

$z(2, 3) = \frac{97}{3} = 32.333\,333\,333\ldots.$ ← maximum

Thus the highest point on the surface is the point $\left(2, 3, \frac{97}{3}\right)$. The four critical points on the surface are indicated in Fig. 13.5.10. ◆

Applied Maximum-Minimum Problems

The analysis of a multivariable applied maximum-minimum problem involves the same general steps that we listed at the beginning of Section 3.6. Here, however, we will express the dependent variable—the quantity to be maximized or minimized—as a function $f(x, y)$ of *two* independent variables. Once we have identified the appropriate region in the xy-plane as the domain of f, the methods of this section are applicable. We often find that a preliminary step is required: If the meaningful domain of definition of f is an unbounded region, then we first restrict f to a *bounded* plane region R on which we know the desired extreme value occurs. This procedure is similar to the one we used with open-interval maximum-minimum problems in Section 4.4.

EXAMPLE 7 Find the minimum cost of a rectangular box with volume 48 ft³ if the front and back cost \$1/ft², the top and bottom cost \$2/ft², and the two ends cost \$3/ft². (We first discussed such a box in Section 13.1.) This box is shown in Fig. 13.5.11.

Solution We found in Section 13.1 that the cost C (in dollars) of this box is given by

$$C(x, y) = 4xy + \frac{288}{x} + \frac{96}{y}$$

in terms of its length x and width y. Let R be a square such as the one shown in Fig. 13.5.12. Two sides of R are so close to the coordinate axes that $288/x > 1000$ on the side nearest the y-axis and $96/y > 1000$ on the side nearest the x-axis. Also, the square is so large that $4xy > 1000$ on both of the other two sides. This means that $C(x, y) > 1000$ at every point (x, y) of the first quadrant that lies on or outside the boundary of the square R. Because $C(x, y)$ attains reasonably small values within R (for instance, $C(1, 1) = 388$), it is clear that the absolute minimum of C must occur at an interior point of R. Thus, although the natural domain of the cost function $C(x, y)$ is the entire first quadrant, we have succeeded in restricting its domain to a region R of the sort to which Theorem 3 applies.

We therefore solve the simultaneous equations

$$\frac{\partial C}{\partial x} = 4y - \frac{288}{x^2} = 0,$$

$$\frac{\partial C}{\partial y} = 4x - \frac{96}{y^2} = 0.$$

We multiply the first equation by x and the second by y. (*Ad hoc* methods are frequently required in the solution of simultaneous nonlinear equations.) This procedure gives

$$\frac{288}{x} = 4xy = \frac{96}{y},$$

FIGURE 13.5.11 A box whose total cost we want to minimize (Example 7).

FIGURE 13.5.12 The cost function $C(x, y)$ of Example 7 takes on large positive values on the boundary of the square.

so that $x = 288y/96 = 3y$. We substitute $x = 3y$ into the equation $\partial C/\partial y = 0$ and find that

$$12y - \frac{96}{y^2} = 0, \quad \text{so} \quad 12y^3 = 96.$$

Hence $y = \sqrt[3]{8} = 2$, so $x = 6$. Therefore, the minimum cost of this box is $C(6, 2) = 144$ (dollars). Because the volume of the box is $V = xyz = 48$, its height is $z = 48/(6 \cdot 2) = 4$ when $x = 6$ and $y = 2$. Thus the optimal box is 6 ft wide, 2 ft deep, and 4 ft high. ◆

REMARK As a check, note that the cheapest surfaces (front and back) are the largest, whereas the most expensive surfaces (the sides) are the smallest.

We have seen that if $f_x(a, b) = 0 = f_y(a, b)$, then $f(a, b)$ may be either a maximum value, a minimum value, or neither. In Section 13.10 we discuss conditions that suffice to distinguish between a local maximum, a local minimum, and a saddle point on the surface $z = f(x, y)$. These conditions involve the second-order derivatives of f.

Functions of Three or More Variables

The methods of this section generalize readily to functions of three or more variables. For instance, suppose that the function $f(x, y, z)$ is continuous on a bounded region R in space bounded by a closed surface S. Then (in analogy with Theorem 1), the function f attains an absolute maximum value at some point (a, b, c) of R (and likewise an absolute minimum value at some point of R). If (a, b, c) is an interior point of R at which the partial derivatives of f exist, then (in analogy with Theorem 3) it follows that all three vanish there:

$$f_x(a, b, c) = f_y(a, b, c) = f_z(a, b, c) = 0. \tag{7}$$

We may therefore attempt to find this point by solving the three simultaneous equations

$$f_x(x, y, z) = 0, \quad f_y(x, y, z) = 0, \quad \text{and} \quad f_z(x, y, z) = 0 \tag{8}$$

for the three unknown values $x = a$, $y = b$, and $z = c$. Thus a key step in the method of solution of a three-variable extreme value problem is essentially the same as in the method for a two-variable problem—"set the partial derivatives equal to zero and solve the resulting equations." But see Problems 68 through 70.

Example 8 illustrates a "line-through-the-point" method that we can sometimes use to show that a point (a, b, c) where the conditions in (8) hold is neither a local maximum nor a local minimum point. (The method is also applicable to functions of two or of more than three variables.)

EXAMPLE 8 Determine whether the function $f(x, y, z) = xy + yz - xz$ has any local extrema.

Solution The necessary conditions in Eq. (8) give the equations

$$f_x(x, y, z) = y - z = 0,$$
$$f_y(x, y, z) = x + z = 0,$$
$$f_z(x, y, z) = y - x = 0.$$

We easily find that the simultaneous solution of these equations is $x = y = z = 0$. On the line $x = y = z$ through $(0, 0, 0)$, the function $f(x, y, z)$ reduces to x^2, which is minimal at $x = 0$. But on the line $x = -y = z$, it reduces to $-3x^2$, which is maximal when $x = 0$. Hence f can have neither a local maximum nor a local minimum at $(0, 0, 0)$. Therefore it has no extrema, local *or* global. ◆

13.5 TRUE/FALSE STUDY GUIDE

13.5 CONCEPTS: QUESTIONS AND DISCUSSION

1. Suppose that the function f is continuous on the disk D bounded by the unit circle $x^2 + y^2 = 1$. Is it possible that $f(x, y)$ attains both its maximum and minimum values on D at points of the boundary circle? Illustrate your answer with an example.
2. Give an example of a function that is defined at every point of the unit disk D but attains no maximum value at any point of D.
3. Give an example of a function f defined on the unit disk D that attains its maximum value at an interior point at which the partial derivatives of D do not exist.
4. How would you alter the proof of Theorem 2 to show that the partial derivatives of a function of three variables vanish at an interior local maximum or minimum point? (What would you mean by an *interior point* of a space region?) Does your proof apply to the function $w = f(x, y, z) = \sqrt{x^2 + y^2 + z^2}$?

13.5 PROBLEMS

In Problems 1 through 12, find every point on the given surface $z = f(x, y)$ at which the tangent plane is horizontal.

1. $z = x - 3y + 5$
2. $z = 4 - x^2 - y^2$
3. $z = xy + 5$
4. $z = x^2 + y^2 + 2x$
5. $z = x^2 + y^2 - 6x + 2y + 5$
6. $z = 10 + 8x - 6y - x^2 - y^2$
7. $z = x^2 + 4x + y^3$
8. $z = x^4 + y^3 - 3y$
9. $z = 3x^2 + 12x + 4y^3 - 6y^2 + 5$ (Fig. 13.5.13)

FIGURE 13.5.13 The surface of Problem 9.

10. $z = \dfrac{1}{1 - 2x + 2y + x^2 + y^2}$
11. $z = (2x^2 + 3y^2)\exp(-x^2 - y^2)$ (Fig. 13.5.14)

FIGURE 13.5.14 The surface of Problem 11.

12. $z = 2xy\exp\left(-\tfrac{1}{8}(4x^2 + y^2)\right)$ (Fig. 13.5.15)

FIGURE 13.5.15 The surface of Problem 12.

Each of the surfaces defined in Problems 13 through 22 either opens downward and has a highest point, or opens upward and has a lowest point. Find this highest or lowest point on the surface $z = f(x, y)$.

13. $z = x^2 - 2x + y^2 - 2y + 3$
14. $z = 6x - 8y - x^2 - y^2$
15. $z = 2x - x^2 + 2y^2 - y^4$
16. $z = 4xy - x^4 - y^4$
17. $z = 3x^4 - 4x^3 - 12x^2 + 2y^2 - 12y$
18. $z = 3x^4 + 4x^3 + 6y^4 - 16y^3 + 12y^2$
19. $z = 2x^2 + 8xy + y^4$
20. $z = \dfrac{1}{10 - 2x - 4y + x^2 + y^4}$
21. $z = \exp(2x - 4y - x^2 - y^2)$
22. $z = (1 + x^2)\exp(-x^2 - y^2)$

In Problems 23 through 28, find the maximum and minimum values attained by the given function $f(x, y)$ on the given plane region R.

23. $f(x, y) = x + 2y$; R is the square with vertices at $(\pm 1, \pm 1)$.
24. $f(x, y) = x^2 + y^2 - x$; R is the square of Problem 23.

25. $f(x, y) = x^2 + y^2 - 2x$; R is the triangular region with vertices at $(0, 0)$, $(2, 0)$, and $(0, 2)$.

26. $f(x, y) = x^2 + y^2 - x - y$; R is the region of Problem 25.

27. $f(x, y) = 2xy$; R is the circular disk $x^2 + y^2 \leq 1$.

28. $f(x, y) = xy^2$; R is the circular disk $x^2 + y^2 \leq 3$.

In Problems 29 through 34, the equation of a plane or surface is given. Find the first-octant point $P(x, y, z)$ on the surface closest to the given fixed point $Q(x_0, y_0, z_0)$. [Suggestion: Minimize the squared distance $|PQ|^2$ as a function of x and y.]

29. The plane $12x + 4y + 3z = 169$ and the fixed point $Q(0, 0, 0)$

30. The plane $2x + 2y + z = 27$ and the fixed point $Q(9, 9, 9)$

31. The plane $2x + 3y + z = 49$ and the fixed point $Q(7, -7, 0)$

32. The surface $xyz = 8$ and the fixed point $Q(0, 0, 0)$

33. The surface $x^2 y^2 z = 4$ and the fixed point $Q(0, 0, 0)$

34. The surface $x^4 y^8 z^2 = 8$ and the fixed point $Q(0, 0, 0)$

35. Find the maximum possible product of three positive numbers whose sum is 120.

36. Find the maximum possible volume of a rectangular box if the sum of the lengths of its 12 edges is 6 meters.

37. Find the dimensions of the box with volume 1000 in.^{3} that has minimal total surface area.

38. Find the dimensions of the open-topped box with volume 4000 cm^3 whose bottom and four sides have minimal total surface area.

In Problems 39 through 42, you are to find the dimensions that minimize the total cost of the material needed to construct the rectangular box that is described. It is either closed (top, bottom, and four sides) or open-topped (four sides and a bottom).

39. The box is to be open-topped with a volume of 600 in.^{3} The material for its bottom costs 6¢/in.^{2} and the material for its four sides costs 5¢/in.^{2}

40. The box is to be closed with a volume of 48 ft^3. The material for its top and bottom costs \$3/ft^2 and the material for its four sides costs \$4/ft^2.

41. The box is to be closed with a volume of 750 in.^{3} The material for its top and bottom costs 3¢/in.^{2}, the material for its front and back costs 6¢/in.^{2}, and the material for its two ends costs 9¢/in.^{2}

42. The box is to be a closed shipping crate with a volume of 12 m^3. The material for its bottom costs *twice* as much (per square meter) as the material for its top and four sides.

43. A rectangular building is to have a volume of 8000 ft^3. Annual heating and cooling costs will amount to \$2/ft^2 for its top, front, and back, and \$4/ft^2 for the two end walls. What dimensions of the building would minimize these annual costs?

44. You want to build a rectangular aquarium with a bottom made of slate costing 28¢/in.^{2} Its sides will be glass, which costs 5¢/in.^{2}, and its top will be stainless steel, which costs 2¢/in.^{2} The volume of this aquarium is to be 24,000 in.^{3} What are the dimensions of the least expensive such aquarium?

45. A rectangular box is inscribed in the first octant with three of its sides in the coordinate planes, their common vertex at the origin, and the opposite vertex on the plane with equation $x + 3y + 7z = 11$. What is the maximum possible volume of such a box?

46. Three sides of a rectangular box lie in the coordinate planes, their common vertex at the origin; the opposite vertex is on the plane with equation
$$\frac{x}{a} + \frac{y}{b} + \frac{z}{c} = 1$$
(a, b, and c are positive constants). In terms of a, b, and c, what is the maximum possible volume of such a box?

47. Find the maximum volume of a rectangular box that a post office will accept for delivery if the sum of its *length* and *girth* cannot exceed 108 in.

48. Repeat Problem 47 for the case of a cylindrical box—one shaped like a hatbox or a fat mailing tube.

49. A rectangular box with its base in the xy-plane is inscribed under the graph of the paraboloid $z = 1 - x^2 - y^2$, $z \geq 0$. Find the maximum possible volume of the box. [*Suggestion:* You may assume that the sides of the box are parallel to the vertical coordinate planes, and it follows that the box is symmetrically placed around these planes.]

50. What is the maximum possible volume of a rectangular box inscribed in a hemisphere of radius R? Assume that one face of the box lies in the planar base of the hemisphere.

51. A buoy is to have the shape of a right circular cylinder capped at each end by identical right circular cones with the same radius as the cylinder. Find the minimum possible surface area of the buoy, given that it has fixed volume V.

52. A pentagonal window is to have the shape of a rectangle surmounted by an isosceles triangle (with horizontal base, so the window is symmetric around its vertical axis), and the perimeter of the window is to be 24 ft. What are the dimensions of such a window that will admit the most light (because its area is the greatest)?

53. Find the point (x, y) in the plane for which the sum of the squares of its distances from $(0, 1)$, $(0, 0)$, and $(2, 0)$ is a minimum.

54. Find the point (x, y) in the plane for which the sum of the squares of its distances from (a_1, b_1), (a_2, b_2), and (a_3, b_3) is a minimum.

55. An A-frame house is to have fixed volume V. Its front and rear walls are in the shape of equal, parallel isosceles triangles with horizontal bases. The roof consists of two rectangles that connect pairs of upper sides of the triangles. To minimize heating and cooling costs, the total area of the A-frame (excluding the floor) is to be minimized. Describe the shape of the A-frame of minimal area.

56. What is the maximum possible volume of a rectangular box whose longest diagonal has fixed length L?

57. A wire 120 cm long is cut into three *or fewer* pieces, and each piece is bent into the shape of a square. How should this be done to minimize the total area of these squares? To maximize it?

58. You must divide a lump of putty of fixed volume V into three or fewer pieces and form the pieces into cubes. How should you do this to maximize the total surface area of the cubes? To minimize it?

59. A very long rectangle of sheet metal has width L and is to be folded to make a rain gutter (Fig. 13.5.16). Maximize its volume by maximizing the cross-sectional area shown in the figure.

FIGURE 13.5.16 Cross section of the rain gutter of Problem 59.

60. Consider the function $f(x, y) = (y - x^2)(y - 3x^2)$. (a) Show that $f_x(0, 0) = 0 = f_y(0, 0)$. (b) Show that for every straight line $y = mx$ through $(0, 0)$, the function $f(x, mx)$ has a local minimum at $x = 0$. (c) Examine the values of f at points of the parabola $y = 2x^2$ to show that f does *not* have a local minimum at $(0, 0)$. This tells us that we cannot use the line-through-the-point method of Example 8 to show that a point *is* a local extremum.

61. Suppose that Alpha, Inc. and Beta, Ltd. manufacture competitive (but not identical) products, with the weekly sales of each product determined by the selling price of that product *and* the price of its competition. Suppose that Alpha sets a sales price of x dollars per unit for its product, while Beta sets a sales price of y dollars per unit for its product. Market research shows that the weekly profit made by Alpha is then

$$P(x) = -2x^2 + 12x + xy - y - 10$$

and that the weekly profit made by Beta is

$$Q(y) = -3y^2 + 18y + 2xy - 2x - 15$$

(both in thousands of dollars). The peculiar notation arises from the fact that x is the only variable under the control of Alpha and y is the only variable under the control of Beta. (If this disturbs you, feel free to write $P(x, y)$ in place of $P(x)$ and $Q(x, y)$ in place of $Q(y)$.) (a) Assume that both company managers know calculus and that each knows that the *other* knows calculus and has some common sense. What price will each manager set to maximize his company's weekly profit? (b) Now suppose that the two managers enter into an agreement (legal or otherwise) by which they plan to maximize their *total* weekly profit. Now what should be the selling price of each product? (We suppose that they will divide the resulting profit in an equitable way, but the details of this intriguing problem are not the issue.)

62. Three firms—Ajax Products (AP), Behemoth Quicksilver (BQ), and Conglomerate Resources (CR)—produce products in quantities A, B, and C, respectively. The weekly profits that accrue to each, in thousands of dollars, obey the following equations:

AP: $P = 1000A - A^2 - 2AB$,
BQ: $Q = 2000B - 2B^2 - 4BC$,
CR: $R = 1500C - 3C^2 - 6AC$.

(a) If each firm acts independently to maximize its weekly profit, what will those profits be? (b) If firms AP and CR join to maximize their total profit while BQ continues to act alone, what effects will this have? Give a *complete* answer to this problem. Assume that the fact of the merger of AP and CR is known to the management of BQ.

63. A farmer can raise sheep, hogs, and cattle. She has space for 80 sheep or 120 hogs or 60 cattle or any combination using the same amount of space; that is, 8 sheep use as much space as 12 hogs or 6 cattle. The anticipated profits per animal are $10 per sheep, $8 per hog, and $20 for each head of cattle. State law requires that a farmer raise as many hogs as sheep and cattle combined. How does the farmer maximize her profit?

Problems 64 and 65 deal with the quadratic form

$$f(x, y) = ax^2 + 2bxy + cy^2. \tag{9}$$

64. Show that the quadratic form f in (9) has only the single critical point $(0, 0)$ unless $ac - b^2 = 0$, in which case every point on a certain line through the origin is a critical point. Experiment with computer graphs to formulate a conjecture about the shape of the surface $z = f(x, y)$ in the exceptional case $ac - b^2 = 0$. Can you substantiate your conjecture?

65. Use a computer algebra system to graph the quadratic form in (9) for a variety of different values of the coefficients a, b, and c in order to corroborate the following two conclusions. (a) If $ac - b^2 > 0$, then the graph of $z = f(x, y)$ is an elliptic paraboloid and f therefore has either a maximum or a minimum value at $(0, 0)$. (b) If $ac - b^2 < 0$, then the graph of $z = f(x, y)$ is a hyperbolic paraboloid and f therefore has a saddle point at $(0, 0)$.

Figures 13.5.7 and 13.5.8 illustrate (and Problems 66 and 67 deal with) the cases $b = -\frac{1}{2}$ and $b = -\frac{3}{2}$ (respectively) of the special quartic form

$$f(x, y) = x^4 + 2bx^2y^2 + y^4. \tag{10}$$

66. Show that the quartic form f in (10) has only the single critical point $(0, 0)$ unless $b = -1$, in which case every point on a certain pair of lines through the origin is a critical point (Fig. 13.5.17). Experiment with computer graphs to formulate a conjecture about the shape of the graph of f in each of the two cases $b > -1$ and $b < -1$.

FIGURE 13.5.17 The graph of the function $f(x, y) = x^4 - x^2y^2 + y^4$ having critical points on the lines $y = \pm x$.

67. To show that the quartic form in (10) has a local minimum at the origin if $b > -1$ and a saddle point if $b < -1$, substitute $x = r\cos\theta$, $y = r\sin\theta$ and write $x^4 + 2bx^2y^2 + y^4 = r^4 g(\theta)$. Then find the maximum and minimum values of $g(\theta)$ for $0 \leq \theta \leq 2\pi$.

68. Find the global maximum and minimum values of
$$f(x, y, z) = x^2 - 6xy + y^2 + 2yz + z^2 + 12.$$
What happens at the point or points at which all three partial derivatives of f are simultaneously zero?

69. Find the global maximum and minimum values of
$$g(x, y, z) = x^4 - 8x^2 y^2 + y^4 + z^4 + 12.$$
What happens at the point or points at which all three partial derivatives of g are simultaneously zero?

70. The plane $\mathcal{P}$ with equation $x + y + z = 1$ meets the first octant in the triangle T for which x, y, and z are all nonnegative. Find the maximum value of the expression $E = x - y + z$ on T. You will probably proceed by solving the equation of the plane $\mathcal{P}$ for $z = 1 - x - y$ and substituting for z in the expression E to obtain the quantity $h(x, y) = x - y + (1 - x - y)$ to be maximized. What happens at the point or points at which both partial derivatives of h are simultaneously zero?

13.6 INCREMENTS AND LINEAR APPROXIMATION

In Section 4.2 we used the *differential*
$$df = f'(x)\,\Delta x$$
to approximate the *increment*, or actual change,
$$\Delta f = f(x + \Delta x) - f(x)$$
in the value of a single-variable function that results from the change Δx in the independent variable. Thus $\Delta f \approx df$; that is,
$$f(x + \Delta x) - f(x) \approx f'(x)\,\Delta x. \tag{1}$$

We now describe the use of the partial derivatives $\partial f/\partial x$ and $\partial f/\partial y$ to approximate the **increment**
$$\Delta f = f(x + \Delta x, y + \Delta y) - f(x, y) \tag{2}$$
in the value of a function f (of two variables) that results when its two independent variables are changed simultaneously. If only x were changed and y were held constant, we could temporarily regard $f(x, y)$ as a function of x alone. Then, with $f_x(x, y)$ playing the role of $f'(x)$, the linear approximation in Eq. (1) would give
$$f(x + \Delta x, y) - f(x, y) \approx f_x(x, y)\,\Delta x \tag{3}$$
for the change in f corresponding to the change Δx in x. Similarly, if only y were changed and x were held constant, then—temporarily regarding $f(x, y)$ as a function of y alone—we would get
$$f(x, y + \Delta y) - f(x, y) \approx f_y(x, y)\,\Delta y \tag{4}$$
for the change in f corresponding to the change Δy in y.

If both x and y are changed simultaneously, we might expect the *sum* of the approximations in (3) and (4) to be a good estimate of the resulting increment in the value of f. On this basis we define the **differential**
$$df = f_x(x, y)\,\Delta x + f_y(x, y)\,\Delta y \tag{5}$$
of a function of two independent variables. The approximation $\Delta f \approx df$ then yields the approximation
$$f(x + \Delta x, y + \Delta y) \approx f(x, y) + f_x(x, y)\,\Delta x + f_y(x, y)\,\Delta y. \tag{6}$$

EXAMPLE 1 Find the differential df of the function $f(x, y) = x^2 + 3xy - 2y^2$. Then compare df and the actual increment Δf when (x, y) changes from $P(3, 5)$ to $Q(3.2, 4.9)$.

Solution The differential of f, as given in Eq. (5), is

$$df = \frac{\partial f}{\partial x}\Delta x + \frac{\partial f}{\partial y}\Delta y = (2x + 3y)\Delta x + (3x - 4y)\Delta y.$$

At the point $P(3, 5)$ this differential is

$$df = (2 \cdot 3 + 3 \cdot 5)\Delta x + (3 \cdot 3 - 4 \cdot 5)\Delta y = 21\Delta x - 11\Delta y.$$

With $\Delta x = 0.2$ and $\Delta y = -0.1$, corresponding to the change from $P(3, 5)$ to $Q(3.2, 4.9)$, we get

$$df = 21 \cdot (0.2) - 11 \cdot (-0.1) = 5.3.$$

The actual change in the value of f from P to Q is the increment

$$\Delta f = f(3.2, 4.9) - f(3, 5) = 9.26 - 4 = 5.26,$$

so in this example the differential seems to be a good approximation to the increment. ◆

At the fixed point $P(a, b)$, the differential

$$df = f_x(a, b)\Delta x + f_y(a, b)\Delta y \tag{7}$$

is a *linear* function of Δx and Δy; the coefficients $f_x(a, b)$ and $f_y(a, b)$ in this linear function depend on a and b. Thus the differential df is a *linear approximation* to the actual increment Δf. The linear approximation theorem (stated later in this section) implies that if the function f has continuous partial derivatives, then df is a *very good approximation* to Δf when the changes Δx and Δy in x and y are sufficiently small. The **linear approximation**

$$f(a + \Delta x, b + \Delta y) \approx f(a, b) + f_x(a, b)\Delta x + f_y(a, b)\Delta y \tag{8}$$

may then be used to estimate the value of $f(a + \Delta x, b + \Delta y)$ when Δx and Δy are small and the values $f(a, b)$, $f_x(a, b)$, and $f_y(a, b)$ are all known.

EXAMPLE 2 Use linear approximation to estimate $\sqrt{2 \cdot (2.02)^3 + (2.97)^2}$.

Solution We begin by letting $f(x, y) = \sqrt{2x^3 + y^2}$, $a = 2$, and $b = 3$. It is then easy to compute the exact value $f(2, 3) = \sqrt{2 \cdot 8 + 9} = \sqrt{25} = 5$. Next,

$$\frac{\partial f}{\partial x} = \frac{3x^2}{\sqrt{2x^3 + y^2}} \quad \text{and} \quad \frac{\partial f}{\partial y} = \frac{y}{\sqrt{2x^3 + y^2}},$$

so

$$f_x(2, 3) = \tfrac{12}{5} \quad \text{and} \quad f_y(2, 3) = \tfrac{3}{5}.$$

Hence Eq. (8) with $\Delta x = 0.02$ and $\Delta y = -0.03$ gives

$$\sqrt{2 \cdot (2.02)^3 + (2.97)^2} = f(2.02, 2.97)$$

$$\approx f(2, 3) + f_x(2, 3) \cdot (0.02) + f_y(2, 3) \cdot (-0.03)$$

$$= 5 + \tfrac{12}{5} \cdot (0.02) - \tfrac{3}{5} \cdot (0.03) = 5.03.$$

The actual value to four decimal places is 5.0305. ◆

If $z = f(x, y)$, we often write dz in place of df. So the differential of the dependent variable z at the point (a, b) is $dz = f_x(a, b)\Delta x + f_y(a, b)\Delta y$. At the arbitrary point (x, y) the differential of z takes the form

$$dz = f_x(x, y)\Delta x + f_y(x, y)\Delta y.$$

More simply, we can write

$$dz = \frac{\partial z}{\partial x} \Delta x + \frac{\partial z}{\partial y} \Delta y. \tag{9}$$

It is customary to write dx for Δx and dy for Δy in this formula. When this is done, Eq. (9) takes the form

$$dz = \frac{\partial z}{\partial x} dx + \frac{\partial z}{\partial y} dy. \tag{10}$$

When we use this notation, we must realize that dx and dy have *no* connotation of being "infinitesimal" or even small. The differential dz is still simply a linear function of the ordinary real variables dx and dy, a function that gives a linear approximation to the change in z when x and y are changed by the amounts dx and dy, respectively.

EXAMPLE 3 In Example 4 of Section 13.4, we considered 1 mole of an ideal gas—its volume V in cubic centimeters given in terms of its pressure p in atmospheres and temperature T in kelvins by the formula $V = (82.06) T/p$. Approximate the change in V when p is increased from 5 atm to 5.2 atm and T is increased from 300 K to 310 K.

Solution The differential of $V = V(p, T)$ is

$$dV = \frac{\partial V}{\partial p} dp + \frac{\partial V}{\partial T} dT = -\frac{82.06 \cdot T}{p^2} dp + \frac{82.06}{p} dT.$$

With $p = 5$, $T = 300$, $dp = 0.2$, and $dT = 10$, we compute

$$dV = -\frac{82.06 \cdot 300}{5^2} \cdot 0.2 + \frac{82.06}{5} \cdot 10 = -32.8 \quad (\text{cm}^3).$$

This indicates that the gas will decrease in volume by about 33 cm³. The actual change is

$$\Delta V = \frac{82.06 \cdot 310}{5.2} - \frac{82.06 \cdot 300}{5} = 4892.0 - 4923.6 = -31.6 \quad (\text{cm}^3). \blacklozenge$$

EXAMPLE 4 The point $(1, 2)$ lies on the curve with equation

$$f(x, y) = 2x^3 + y^3 - 5xy = 0. \tag{11}$$

(See Fig. 13.6.1.) Approximate the y-coordinate of the nearby point (x, y) on this curve for which $x = 1.2$.

Solution The increment between $f(1, 2) = 0$ and $f(x, y) = 0$ on this curve is $\Delta f = 0 \approx df$, so when we compute the differentials in Eq. (11), we get

$$df = \frac{\partial f}{\partial x} dx + \frac{\partial f}{\partial y} dy = (6x^2 - 5y) dx + (3y^2 - 5x) dy = 0.$$

Now when we substitute $x = 1$, $y = 2$, and $dx = 0.2$, we obtain the equation $(-4)(0.2) + (7) dy = 0$. It then follows that $dy = (0.8)/7 \approx 0.114 \approx 0.1$. This yields $(1.2, 2.1)$ for the approximate coordinates of the nearby point. As a check on the accuracy of this approximation, we can substitute $x = 1.2$ into Eq. (11). This gives the equation

$$2 \cdot (1.2)^3 + y^3 - 5 \cdot (1.2) y = y^3 - 6y + 3.456 = 0.$$

The roots of this equation are the x-intercepts of the curve in Fig. 13.6.2. A calculator or computer with an equation solver (or Newton's method) then yields $y \approx 2.084 \approx 2.1$ for the solution near $y = 2$. $\blacklozenge$

FIGURE 13.6.1 The curve of Example 4.

FIGURE 13.6.2 The graph of $g(y) = y^3 - 6y + 3.456$.

Functions of Three or More Variables

Increments and differentials of functions of more than two variables are defined similarly. A function $w = f(x, y, z)$ has **increment**

$$\Delta w = \Delta f = f(x + \Delta x, y + \Delta y, z + \Delta z) - f(x, y, z)$$

and **differential**

$$dw = df = \frac{\partial f}{\partial x} \Delta x + \frac{\partial f}{\partial y} \Delta y + \frac{\partial f}{\partial z} \Delta z;$$

that is,

$$dw = \frac{\partial w}{\partial x} dx + \frac{\partial w}{\partial y} dy + \frac{\partial w}{\partial z} dz$$

if, as in Eq. (10), we write dx for Δx, dy for Δy, and dz for Δz.

EXAMPLE 5 You have constructed a metal cube that is supposed to have edge length 100 mm, but each of its three measured dimensions x, y, and z may be in error by as much as a millimeter. Use differentials to estimate the maximum resulting error in its calculated volume $V = xyz$.

Solution We need to approximate the increment

$$\Delta V = V(100 + dx, 100 + dy, 100 + dz) - V(100, 100, 100)$$

when the errors dx, dy, and dz in x, y, and z are maximal. The differential of $V = xyz$ is

$$dV = yz\, dx + xz\, dy + xy\, dz.$$

When we substitute $x = y = z = 100$ and $dx = \pm 1$, $dy = \pm 1$, and $dz = \pm 1$, we get

$$dV = 100 \cdot 100 \cdot (\pm 1) + 100 \cdot 100 \cdot (\pm 1) + 100 \cdot 100 \cdot (\pm 1) = \pm 30000.$$

It may surprise you to find that an error of only a millimeter in each dimension of a cube can result in an error of 30,000 mm^3 in its volume. (For a cube made of precious metal, an error of 30 cm^3 in its volume could correspond to a difference of hundreds or thousands of dollars in its cost.) ◆

Linear Approximation and Differentiability

Vector notation simplifies the description of differentials and linear approximation for functions of several variables. Let $f(\mathbf{x}) = f(x_1, x_2, \ldots, x_n)$ be a real-valued function of n variables. If

$$\mathbf{x} = \langle x_1, x_2, \ldots, x_n \rangle \quad \text{and} \quad \mathbf{h} = \langle h_1, h_2, \ldots, h_n \rangle,$$

then the linear approximation formula for f takes the form

$$f(\mathbf{x} + \mathbf{h}) \approx f(\mathbf{x}) + \frac{\partial f}{\partial x_1} h_1 + \frac{\partial f}{\partial x_2} h_2 + \cdots + \frac{\partial f}{\partial x_n} h_n \tag{12}$$

with one term for each independent variable. We introduce the **gradient vector**

$$\nabla f(\mathbf{x}) = \langle D_1 f(\mathbf{x}), D_2 f(\mathbf{x}), \ldots, D_n f(\mathbf{x}) \rangle = \left\langle \frac{\partial f}{\partial x_1}, \frac{\partial f}{\partial x_2}, \ldots, \frac{\partial f}{\partial x_n} \right\rangle \tag{13}$$

of the function $f(x_1, x_2, \ldots, x_n)$ of n variables; its elements are the n first-order partial derivatives of f (assuming that they exist). This new vector-valued function is called the *gradient* of f and is denoted by ∇f (pronounced "del f"). In Section 13.8 we explore the meaning of the gradient vector ∇f; here we use it simply as a notational device to simplify the formula in (12).

The dot (or scalar) product of two n-vectors is, exactly as in dimensions 2 and 3, the sum of the products of corresponding elements of the two vectors. That is, if $\mathbf{a} = \langle a_1, a_2, \ldots, a_n \rangle$ and $\mathbf{b} = \langle b_1, b_2, \ldots, b_n \rangle$, then

$$\mathbf{a} \cdot \mathbf{b} = a_1 b_1 + a_2 b_2 + \cdots + a_n b_n.$$

Consequently, the linear approximation formula in (12) takes the concise form

$$f(\mathbf{x} + \mathbf{h}) \approx f(\mathbf{x}) + \nabla f(\mathbf{x}) \cdot \mathbf{h}, \tag{14}$$

in pleasant analogy with the original single-variable approximation $f(x+h) \approx f(x) + f'(x)h$ (writing h for Δx here). Because $\nabla f(\mathbf{x})$ and $\mathbf{h}$ are both vectors with n components, the dot product on the right-hand side in (14) is defined and gives

$$\nabla f(\mathbf{x}) \cdot \mathbf{h} = D_1 f(\mathbf{x}) h_1 + D_2 f(\mathbf{x}) h_2 + \cdots + D_n f(\mathbf{x}) h_n,$$

thus providing the linear terms on the right-hand side in (12). In analogy with the two-variable case in (5), the sum of these n linear terms is the **differential** $df = \nabla f(\mathbf{x}) \cdot \mathbf{h}$ of the function f of n real variables. With $\mathbf{h} = \mathbf{dx} = \langle dx_1, dx_2, \ldots, dx_n \rangle$, this differential takes the form

$$df = \frac{\partial f}{\partial x_1} dx_1 + \frac{\partial f}{\partial x_2} dx_2 + \cdots + \frac{\partial f}{\partial x_n} dx_n$$

that generalizes the two-dimensional differential in Eq. (10).

The gradient vector $\nabla f(\mathbf{x})$ is defined wherever all of the first-order partial derivatives of f exist. In Appendix K we give a proof of the linear approximation theorem stated next. This theorem assures us (in effect) that if the partial derivatives of f are also *continuous*, then the linear approximation in (14) is a *good* approximation when $|\mathbf{h}| = \sqrt{h_1^2 + h_2^2 + \cdots + h_n^2}$ is small.

THEOREM Linear Approximation

Suppose that the function $f(\mathbf{x})$ of n variables has continuous first-order partial derivatives in a region that contains the neighborhood $|\mathbf{x} - \mathbf{a}| < r$ consisting of all points $\mathbf{x}$ at distance less than r from the fixed point $\mathbf{a}$. If $\mathbf{a} + \mathbf{h}$ lies in this neighborhood, then

$$f(\mathbf{a} + \mathbf{h}) = f(\mathbf{a}) + \nabla f(\mathbf{a}) \cdot \mathbf{h} + \boldsymbol{\epsilon}(\mathbf{h}) \cdot \mathbf{h} \tag{15}$$

where $\boldsymbol{\epsilon}(\mathbf{h}) = \langle \epsilon_1(\mathbf{h}), \epsilon_2(\mathbf{h}), \ldots, \epsilon_n(\mathbf{h}) \rangle$ is a vector such that each element $\epsilon_i(\mathbf{h})$ approaches zero as $\mathbf{h} \to \mathbf{0}$.

REMARK 1 The multivariable function f is said to be **continuously differentiable** at a point provided that its first-order partial derivatives not only exist but are continuous at the point. Thus the hypothesis of the linear approximation theorem is that the function f is continuously differentiable in the specified neighborhood of the point $\mathbf{a}$.

REMARK 2 The dot product

$$\boldsymbol{\epsilon}(\mathbf{h}) \cdot \mathbf{h} = \epsilon_1(\mathbf{h}) h_1 + \epsilon_2(\mathbf{h}) h_2 + \cdots + \epsilon_n(\mathbf{h}) h_n \tag{16}$$

in (15) is the **error** in the linear approximation—it measures the extent to which the *approximation* $f(\mathbf{a} + \mathbf{h}) \approx f(\mathbf{a}) + \nabla f(\mathbf{a}) \cdot \mathbf{h}$ fails to be an *equality*. We may regard the conclusion of the linear approximation theorem as saying that if $\mathbf{h}$ is "very small," then each element $\epsilon_i(\mathbf{h})$ of $\boldsymbol{\epsilon}(\mathbf{h})$ is also "very small." In this event, each summand in (16) is a product of two very small terms, so we might say that the error $\boldsymbol{\epsilon}(\mathbf{h}) \cdot \mathbf{h}$ is "very very small."

Now let us divide by $|\mathbf{h}|$ in Eq. (16). Then we see that

$$\frac{\boldsymbol{\epsilon}(\mathbf{h}) \cdot \mathbf{h}}{|\mathbf{h}|} = \epsilon_1(\mathbf{h}) \frac{h_1}{|\mathbf{h}|} + \epsilon_2(\mathbf{h}) \frac{h_2}{|\mathbf{h}|} + \cdots + \epsilon_n(\mathbf{h}) \frac{h_n}{|\mathbf{h}|} \to 0 \tag{17}$$

as $\mathbf{h} \to \mathbf{0}$. The reason is that, for each i ($1 \leq i \leq n$),

$$\frac{h_i}{|\mathbf{h}|} \leq 1 \quad \text{and} \quad \epsilon_i(\mathbf{h}) \to 0$$

as $\mathbf{h} \to \mathbf{0}$. Dividing both sides by $|\mathbf{h}|$ in Eq. (15) therefore gives the limit

$$\lim_{\mathbf{h} \to \mathbf{0}} \frac{f(\mathbf{a} + \mathbf{h}) - f(\mathbf{a}) - \nabla f(\mathbf{a}) \cdot \mathbf{h}}{|\mathbf{h}|} = 0, \tag{18}$$

under the assumption that the function f is continuously differentiable near $\mathbf{a}$.

The condition in Eq. (18) is central to the study of differentiability of multivariable functions. Indeed, the real-valued function $f(\mathbf{x})$ is said to be **differentiable** at the point $\mathbf{a}$ provided that there exists a constant vector $\mathbf{c} = \langle c_1, c_2, \ldots, c_n \rangle$ such that

$$\lim_{\mathbf{h} \to \mathbf{0}} \frac{f(\mathbf{a} + \mathbf{h}) - f(\mathbf{a}) - \mathbf{c} \cdot \mathbf{h}}{|\mathbf{h}|} = 0. \tag{19}$$

In effect, this definition means that f is differentiable at $\mathbf{a}$ if there exists a linear function $\mathbf{c} \cdot \mathbf{h} = c_1 h_1 + c_2 h_2 + \cdots + c_n h_n$ (of the components of $\mathbf{h}$) that approximates the increment $f(\mathbf{a} + \mathbf{h}) - f(\mathbf{a})$ so closely that the error is small even in comparison with $|\mathbf{h}|$. Equation (18) implies that if f is continuously differentiable near $\mathbf{a}$, then the gradient vector $\nabla f(\mathbf{a})$ is precisely such a vector $\mathbf{c}$ (and moreover, by Problem 48, is the only such vector).

Thus *a function is differentiable if it is continuously differentiable*. This says little in the case of a single-variable function, which is called differentiable if its derivative merely exists. In contrast, we have as yet said nothing about the existence of partial derivatives of a differentiable multivariable function. The following example treats the case of just $n = 2$ variables.

EXAMPLE 6 Suppose that the function $f(x, y)$ is differentiable at the point (a, b). By Eq. (19), this means that there exists a constant vector $\mathbf{c} = \langle c_1, c_2 \rangle$ such that

$$\lim_{(h_1, h_2) \to (0,0)} \frac{f(a + h_1, b + h_2) - f(a, b) - (c_1 h_1 + c_2 h_2)}{\sqrt{h_1^2 + h_2^2}} = 0. \tag{20}$$

If $h_1 = h$ and $h_2 = 0$, then Eq. (20) implies that

$$\lim_{h \to 0} \frac{f(a + h, b) - f(a, b) - c_1 h}{h} = 0,$$

and hence that

$$\lim_{h \to 0} \frac{f(a + h, b) - f(a, b)}{h} = c_1.$$

Thus the partial derivative $f_x(a, b)$ exists and is equal to the first element c_1 of $\mathbf{c}$. Similarly, if we substitute $h_1 = 0$ and $h_2 = h$ in (20)—do this yourself—we find that the partial derivative $f_y(a, b)$ exists and is equal to the second element c_2 of $\mathbf{c}$. ◆

Example 6 is the case $n = 2$ of the general theorem that *differentiability at a point implies existence of all first-order partial derivatives at that point*. It is also true that differentiability implies continuity (Problem 47). In summary, we have the following implications for a function f of several variables:

- If f is continuously differentiable, then f is differentiable.
- If f is differentiable, then all partial derivatives of f exist.
- If f is differentiable, then f is continuous.

Problems 43 through 45 show that none of these implications can be reversed for a function f of two or more variables. That is, f can have partial derivatives without being differentiable, and can be differentiable without being continuously differentiable. Moreover, f can have partial derivatives without being continuous (and vice versa). Thus the mere existence of partial derivatives—even all of them—appears to imply much less for a function of several variables than it does for a single-variable function. But all these distinctions disappear in the case of polynomials and rational functions of several variables—which have continuous partial derivatives wherever they are defined.

13.6 TRUE/FALSE STUDY GUIDE

13.6 CONCEPTS: QUESTIONS AND DISCUSSION

1. Compare the concept of differentiability for single-variable functions with that for multivariable functions.
2. Compare the roles of the derivative of a single-variable function and the gradient vector of a multivariable function. For instance, what is the value of the gradient vector at a local maximum or minimum point?
3. Does a surface $z = f(x, y)$ always have a tangent plane at a point **a** where f is differentiable? Describe the way this tangent plane approximates the graph near the point $(\mathbf{a}, f(\mathbf{a}))$.

13.6 PROBLEMS

Find the differential dw in Problems 1 through 16.

1. $w = 3x^2 + 4xy - 2y^3$
2. $w = \exp(-x^2 - y^2)$
3. $w = \sqrt{1 + x^2 + y^2}$
4. $w = xye^{x+y}$
5. $w = \arctan\left(\dfrac{x}{y}\right)$
6. $w = xz^2 - yx^2 + zy^2$
7. $w = \ln(x^2 + y^2 + z^2)$
8. $w = \sin xyz$
9. $w = x \tan yz$
10. $w = xye^{uv}$
11. $w = e^{-xyz}$
12. $w = \ln(1 + rs)$
13. $w = u^2 \exp(-v^2)$
14. $w = \dfrac{s+t}{s-t}$
15. $w = \sqrt{x^2 + y^2 + z^2}$
16. $w = pqr \exp(-p^2 - q^2 - r^2)$

In Problems 17 through 24, use the exact value $f(P)$ and the differential df to approximate the value $f(Q)$.

17. $f(x, y) = \sqrt{x^2 + y^2}$; $P(3, 4)$, $Q(2.97, 4.04)$
18. $f(x, y) = \sqrt{x^2 - y^2}$; $P(13, 5)$, $Q(13.2, 4.9)$
19. $f(x, y) = \dfrac{1}{1 + x + y}$; $P(3, 6)$, $Q(3.02, 6.05)$
20. $f(x, y, z) = \sqrt{xyz}$; $P(1, 3, 3)$, $Q(0.9, 2.9, 3.1)$
21. $f(x, y, z) = \sqrt{x^2 + y^2 + z^2}$; $P(3, 4, 12)$, $Q(3.03, 3.96, 12.05)$
22. $f(x, y, z) = \dfrac{xyz}{x + y + z}$; $P(2, 3, 5)$, $Q(1.98, 3.03, 4.97)$
23. $f(x, y, z) = e^{-xyz}$; $P(1, 0, -2)$, $Q(1.02, 0.03, -2.02)$
24. $f(x, y) = (x - y) \cos 2\pi xy$; $P\left(1, \tfrac{1}{2}\right)$, $Q(1.1, 0.4)$

In Problems 25 through 32, use differentials to approximate the indicated number.

25. $\left(\sqrt{15} + \sqrt{99}\right)^2$
26. $\left(\sqrt{26}\right)\left(\sqrt[3]{28}\right)\left(\sqrt[4]{17}\right)$
27. $e^{0.4} = \exp(1.1^2 - 0.9^2)$
28. $\dfrac{\sqrt[3]{25}}{\sqrt[5]{30}}$
29. $\sqrt{(3.1)^2 + (4.2)^2 + (11.7)^2}$
30. $\sqrt[3]{(5.1)^2 + 2 \cdot (5.2)^2 + 2 \cdot (5.3)^2}$
31. The y-coordinate of the point P near $(1, 2)$ on the curve $2x^3 + 2y^3 = 9xy$, if the x-coordinate of P is 1.1.
32. The x-coordinate of the point P near $(2, 4)$ on the curve $4x^4 + 4y^4 = 17x^2 y^2$, if the y-coordinate of P is 3.9.
33. The base and height of a rectangle are measured as 10 cm and 15 cm, respectively, with a possible error of as much as 0.1 cm in each measurement. Use differentials to estimate the maximum resulting error in computing the area of the rectangle.
34. The base radius r and the height h of a right circular cylinder are measured as 3 cm and 9 cm, respectively. There is a possible error of 1 mm in each measurement. Use differentials to estimate the maximum possible error in computing: (a) the volume of the cylinder; (b) the total surface area of the cylinder.
35. The base radius r and height h of a right circular cone are measured as 5 in. and 10 in., respectively. There is a

possible error of as much as $\frac{1}{10}$ in. in each measurement. Use differentials to estimate the maximum resulting error that might occur in computing the volume of the cone.

36. The dimensions of a closed rectangular box are found by measurement to be 10 cm by 15 cm by 20 cm, but there is a possible error of 0.1 cm in each. Use differentials to estimate the maximum resulting error in computing the total surface area of the box.

37. A surveyor wants to find the area in acres of a certain field (1 acre is 43,560 ft^2). She measures two different sides, finding them to be $a = 500$ ft and $b = 700$ ft, with a possible error of as much as 1 ft in each measurement. She finds the angle between these two sides to be $\theta = 30°$, with a possible error of as much as 0.25°. The field is triangular, so its area is given by $A = \frac{1}{2}ab\sin\theta$. Use differentials to estimate the maximum resulting error, in acres, in computing the area of the field by this formula.

38. Use differentials to estimate the change in the volume of the gas of Example 3 if its pressure is decreased from 5 atm to 4.9 atm and its temperature is decreased from 300 K to 280 K.

39. The period of oscillation of a simple pendulum of length L is given (approximately) by the formula $T = 2\pi\sqrt{L/g}$. Estimate the change in the period of a pendulum if its length is increased from 2 ft to 2 ft 1 in. and it is simultaneously moved from a location where g is exactly 32 ft/s^2 to one where $g = 32.2$ ft^2.

40. Given the pendulum of Problem 39, show that the relative error in the determination of T is half the difference of the relative errors in measuring L and g—that is, that

$$\frac{dT}{T} = \frac{1}{2}\left(\frac{dL}{L} - \frac{dg}{g}\right).$$

41. The range of a projectile fired (in a vacuum) with initial velocity v_0 and inclination angle α from the horizontal is $R = \frac{1}{32}v_0^2\sin 2\alpha$. Use differentials to approximate the change in range if v_0 is increased from 400 to 410 ft/s and α is increased from 30° to 31°.

42. A horizontal beam is supported at both ends and supports a uniform load. The deflection, or sag, at its midpoint is given by

$$S = \frac{k}{wh^3}, \qquad (21)$$

where w and h are the width and height, respectively, of the beam and k is a constant that depends on the length and composition of the beam and the amount of the load. Show that

$$dS = -S\left(\frac{1}{w}dw + \frac{3}{h}dh\right).$$

If $S = 1$ in. when $w = 2$ in. and $h = 4$ in., approximate the sag when $w = 2.1$ in. and $h = 4.1$ in. Compare your approximation with the actual value you compute from Eq. (21).

43. Let the function f be defined on the whole xy-plane by $f(x, y) = 1$ if $x = y \ne 0$, whereas $f(x, y) = 0$ otherwise. (a) Show that f is not continuous at $(0, 0)$. (b) Show that both partial derivatives f_x and f_y exist at $(0, 0)$.

44. Show that the function $f(x, y) = (\sqrt[3]{x} + \sqrt[3]{y})^3$ is continuous and has partial derivatives at the origin $(0, 0)$, but is not differentiable there.

45. Show that the function f defined by $f(x, y) = y^2 + x^3\sin(1/x)$ for $x \ne 0$, and $f(0, y) = y^2$, is differentiable at $(0, 0)$, but is not continuously differentiable there because $f_x(x, y)$ is not continuous at $(0, 0)$.

46. Let $f(x)$ be a function of the single variable x. Show that the ordinary derivative $f'(a)$ exists if and only if f is differentiable in the sense of Eq. (19), meaning that there exists a constant c such that

$$\lim_{h\to 0}\frac{f(a+h) - f(a) - ch}{|h|} = 0,$$

in which case $f'(a) = c$.

47. Deduce from Eq. (19) that the function f is continuous wherever it is differentiable.

48. Deduce from Eq. (19) that if the multivariable function $f(\mathbf{x})$ is differentiable at $\mathbf{a}$, then its first-order partial derivatives at $\mathbf{a}$ exist and are given by $D_i f(\mathbf{a}) = c_i$ for $i = 1, 2, \ldots, n$. Conclude in turn that the vector $\mathbf{c} = \langle c_1, c_2, \ldots, c_n\rangle$ in (19) is unique.

13.7 THE MULTIVARIABLE CHAIN RULE

The single-variable chain rule expresses the derivative of a composite function $f(g(t))$ in terms of the derivatives of f and g:

$$D_t f(g(t)) = f'(g(t)) \cdot g'(t). \qquad (1)$$

With $w = f(x)$ and $x = g(t)$, the chain rule implies that

$$\frac{dw}{dt} = \frac{dw}{dx}\frac{dx}{dt}. \qquad (2)$$

The simplest multivariable chain rule situation involves a function $w = f(x, y)$ where both x and y are functions of the same single variable t: $x = g(t)$ and $y = h(t)$. The composite function $f(g(t), h(t))$ is then a single-variable function of t, and Theorem 1 expresses its derivative in terms of the partial derivatives of f and the ordinary derivatives of g and h. We assume that the stated hypotheses hold on suitable domains such that the composite function is defined.

THEOREM 1 The Chain Rule
Suppose that $w = f(x, y)$ has continuous first-order partial derivatives and that $x = g(t)$ and $y = h(t)$ are differentiable functions. Then w is a differentiable function of t, and

$$\frac{dw}{dt} = \frac{\partial w}{\partial x} \cdot \frac{dx}{dt} + \frac{\partial w}{\partial y} \cdot \frac{dy}{dt}. \tag{3}$$

The variable notation of Eq. (3) ordinarily will be more useful than function notation. Remember, in any case, that the partial derivatives in Eq. (3) are to be evaluated at the point $(g(t), h(t))$, so in function notation Eq. (3) is

$$D_t[f(g(t), h(t))] = f_x(g(t), h(t)) \cdot g'(t) + f_y(g(t), h(t)) \cdot h'(t). \tag{4}$$

A proof of the chain rule is included at the end of this section. In outline, it consists of beginning with the linear approximation

$$\Delta w \approx \frac{\partial w}{\partial x} \Delta x + \frac{\partial w}{\partial y} \Delta y$$

of Section 13.6 and dividing by Δt:

$$\frac{\Delta w}{\Delta t} \approx \frac{\partial w}{\partial x} \frac{\Delta x}{\Delta t} + \frac{\partial w}{\partial y} \frac{\Delta y}{\Delta t}.$$

Then we take the limit as $\Delta t \to 0$ to obtain

$$\frac{dw}{dt} = \frac{\partial w}{\partial x} \cdot \frac{dx}{dt} + \frac{\partial w}{\partial y} \cdot \frac{dy}{dt}.$$

EXAMPLE 1 Suppose that $w = e^{xy}$, $x = t^2$, and $y = t^3$. Then

$$\frac{\partial w}{\partial x} = ye^{xy}, \quad \frac{\partial w}{\partial y} = xe^{yx}, \quad \frac{dx}{dt} = 2t, \quad \text{and} \quad \frac{dy}{dt} = 3t^2.$$

So Eq. (3) yields

$$\frac{dw}{dt} = \frac{\partial w}{\partial x} \cdot \frac{dx}{dt} + \frac{\partial w}{\partial y} \cdot \frac{dy}{dt} = (ye^{xy})(2t) + (xe^{xy})(3t^2)$$

$$= \left(t^3 e^{t^5}\right)(2t) + \left(t^2 e^{t^5}\right)(3t^2) = 5t^4 e^{t^5}. \blacklozenge$$

REMARK Had our purpose not been to illustrate the multivariable chain rule, we could have obtained the same result $dw/dt = 5t^4 \exp t^5$ more simply by writing

$$w = e^{xy} = e^{(t^2)(t^3)} = e^{t^5}$$

and then differentiating w as a single-variable function of t. But this single-variable approach is available only if the functions $x(t)$ and $y(t)$ are known explicitly. Sometimes, however, we know only the *numerical values* of x and y and/or their rates of change at a given instant. In such cases the multivariable chain rule in (3) can then be used to find the numerical rate of change of w at that instant.

EXAMPLE 2 Figure 13.7.1 shows a melting cylindrical block of ice. Because of the sun's heat beating down from above, its height h is decreasing more rapidly than its radius r. If its height is decreasing at 3 cm/h and its radius is decreasing at 1 cm/h when $r = 15$ cm and $h = 40$ cm, what is the rate of change of the volume V of the block at that instant?

FIGURE 13.7.1 Warm sun melting a cylindrical block of ice (Example 2).

Solution With $V = \pi r^2 h$, the chain rule gives

$$\frac{dV}{dt} = \frac{\partial V}{\partial r}\frac{dr}{dt} + \frac{\partial V}{\partial h}\frac{dh}{dt} = 2\pi r h \frac{dr}{dt} + \pi r^2 \frac{dh}{dt}.$$

Substituting the given numerical values $r = 15, h = 40, dr/dt = -1$, and $dh/dt = -3$, we find that

$$\frac{dV}{dt} = 2\pi(15)(40)(-1) + \pi(15)^2(-3) = -1875\pi \approx -5890.49 \quad (\text{cm}^3/\text{h}).$$

Thus the volume of the cylindrical block is decreasing at slightly less than 6 liters per hour at the given instant. ◆

In the context of Theorem 1, we may refer to w as the **dependent variable,** x and y as **intermediate variables,** and t as the **independent variable.** Then note that the right-hand side of Eq. (3) has two terms, one for each intermediate variable, both terms like the right-hand side of the single-variable chain rule in Eq. (2). If there are more than two intermediate variables, then there is still one term on the right-hand side for each intermediate variable. For example, if $w = f(x, y, z)$ with x, y, and z each a function of t, then the chain rule takes the form

$$\frac{dw}{dt} = \frac{\partial w}{\partial x} \cdot \frac{dx}{dt} + \frac{\partial w}{\partial y} \cdot \frac{dy}{dt} + \frac{\partial w}{\partial z} \cdot \frac{dz}{dt}. \tag{5}$$

The proof of Eq. (5) is essentially the same as the proof of Eq. (3); it requires the linear approximation theorem for three variables rather than for two variables.

You may find it useful to envision the three types of variables—dependent, intermediate, and independent—as though they were lying at three different levels, as in Fig. 13.7.2, with the dependent variable at the top and the independent variable at the bottom. Each variable then depends (either directly or indirectly) on those that lie below it.

FIGURE 13.7.2 Levels of chain rule variables.

EXAMPLE 3 Find dw/dt if $w = x^2 + ze^y + \sin xz$ and $x = t$, $y = y^2$, $z = t^3$.

Solution Equation (5) gives

$$\frac{dw}{dt} = \frac{\partial w}{\partial x} \cdot \frac{dx}{dt} + \frac{\partial w}{\partial y} \cdot \frac{dy}{dt} + \frac{\partial w}{\partial z} \cdot \frac{dz}{dt}$$

$$= (2x + z\cos xz)(1) + (ze^y)(2t) + (e^y + x\cos xz)(3t^2)$$

$$= 2t + (3t^2 + 2t^4)e^{t^2} + 4t^3 \cos t^4. \quad ◆$$

In Example 3 we could check the result given by the chain rule by first writing w as an explicit function of t and then computing the ordinary single-variable derivative of w with respect to t.

Several Independent Variables

There may be several independent variables as well as several intermediate variables. For example, if $w = f(x, y, z)$ where $x = g(u, v)$, $y = h(u, v)$, and $z = k(u, v)$, so that

$$w = f(x, y, z) = f(g(u, v), h(u, v), k(u, v)),$$

then we have the three intermediate variables x, y, and z and the two independent variables u and v. In this case we would need to compute the *partial* derivatives $\partial w/\partial u$ and $\partial w/\partial v$ of the composite function. The general chain rule in Theorem 2 implies that each partial derivative of the dependent variable w is given by a chain rule formula such as Eq. (3) or (5). The only difference is that the derivatives with respect to the independent variables are partial derivatives. For instance,

$$\frac{\partial w}{\partial u} = \frac{\partial w}{\partial x} \cdot \frac{\partial x}{\partial u} + \frac{\partial w}{\partial y} \cdot \frac{\partial y}{\partial u} + \frac{\partial w}{\partial z} \cdot \frac{\partial z}{\partial u}.$$

The "molecular model" in Fig. 13.7.3 illustrates this formula. The "atom" at the top represents the dependent variable w. The atoms at the next level represent the intermediate variables x, y, and z. The atoms at the bottom represent the independent variables u and v. Each "bond" in the model represents a partial derivative involving the two variables (the atoms joined by that bond). Finally, note that the formula displayed before this paragraph expresses $\partial w/\partial u$ as the sum of the products of the partial derivatives taken along all descending paths from w to u. Similarly, the sum of the products of the partial derivatives along all descending paths from w to v yields the correct formula

$$\frac{\partial w}{\partial v} = \frac{\partial w}{\partial x} \cdot \frac{\partial x}{\partial v} + \frac{\partial w}{\partial y} \cdot \frac{\partial y}{\partial v} + \frac{\partial w}{\partial z} \cdot \frac{\partial z}{\partial v}.$$

FIGURE 13.7.3 Diagram for $w = w(x, y, z)$, where $x = x(u, v)$, $y = y(u, v)$, and $z = z(u, v)$.

Theorem 2 describes the most general such situation.

THEOREM 2 The General Chain Rule
Suppose that w is a function of the variables $x_1, x_2, \ldots, x_m$ and that each of these is a function of the variables $t_1, t_2, \ldots, t_n$. If all these functions have continuous first-order partial derivatives, then

$$\frac{\partial w}{\partial t_i} = \frac{\partial w}{\partial x_1} \cdot \frac{\partial x_1}{\partial t_i} + \frac{\partial w}{\partial x_2} \cdot \frac{\partial x_2}{\partial t_i} + \cdots + \frac{\partial w}{\partial x_m} \cdot \frac{\partial x_m}{\partial t_i} \qquad (6)$$

for each i, $1 \leq i \leq n$.

Thus there is a formula in Eq. (6) for *each* of the independent variables $t_1, t_2, \ldots, t_n$, and the right-hand side of each such formula contains one typical chain rule term for each of the intermediate variables $x_1, x_2, \ldots, x_m$.

EXAMPLE 4 Suppose that

$$z = f(u, v), \qquad u = 2x + y, \qquad v = 3x - 2y.$$

Given the values $\partial z/\partial u = 3$ and $\partial z/\partial v = -2$ at the point $(u, v) = (3, 1)$, find the values $\partial z/\partial x$ and $\partial z/\partial y$ at the corresponding point $(x, y) = (1, 1)$.

Solution The relationships among the variables are shown in Fig. 13.7.4. The chain rule gives

$$\frac{\partial z}{\partial x} = \frac{\partial z}{\partial u} \cdot \frac{\partial u}{\partial x} + \frac{\partial z}{\partial v} \cdot \frac{\partial v}{\partial x} = 3 \cdot 2 + (-2) \cdot 3 = 0$$

FIGURE 13.7.4 Diagram for $z = z(u, v)$, where $u = u(x, y)$ and $v = v(x, y)$ (Example 4).

and

$$\frac{\partial z}{\partial y} = \frac{\partial z}{\partial u} \cdot \frac{\partial u}{\partial y} + \frac{\partial z}{\partial v} \cdot \frac{\partial v}{\partial y} = 3 \cdot 1 + (-2) \cdot (-2) = 7$$

at the indicated point $(x, y) = (1, 1)$. ◆

EXAMPLE 5 Let $w = f(x, y)$ where x and y are given in polar coordinates by the equations $x = r \cos \theta$ and $y = r \sin \theta$. Calculate

$$\frac{\partial w}{\partial r}, \quad \frac{\partial w}{\partial \theta}, \quad \text{and} \quad \frac{\partial^2 w}{\partial r^2}$$

in terms of r, θ, and the partial derivatives of w with respect to x and y (Fig. 13.7.5).

Solution Here x and y are intermediate variables; the independent variables are r and θ. First note that

$$\frac{\partial x}{\partial r} = \cos \theta, \quad \frac{\partial y}{\partial r} = \sin \theta, \quad \frac{\partial x}{\partial \theta} = -r \sin \theta, \quad \text{and} \quad \frac{\partial y}{\partial \theta} = r \cos \theta.$$

FIGURE 13.7.5 Diagram for $w = w(x, y)$, where $x = x(r, \theta)$ and $y = y(r, \theta)$ (Example 5).

Then

$$\frac{\partial w}{\partial r} = \frac{\partial w}{\partial x} \cdot \frac{\partial x}{\partial r} + \frac{\partial w}{\partial y} \cdot \frac{\partial y}{\partial r} = \frac{\partial w}{\partial x} \cos \theta + \frac{\partial w}{\partial y} \sin \theta \qquad (7a)$$

and
$$\frac{\partial w}{\partial \theta} = \frac{\partial w}{\partial x} \cdot \frac{\partial x}{\partial \theta} + \frac{\partial w}{\partial y} \cdot \frac{\partial y}{\partial \theta} = -r\frac{\partial w}{\partial x}\sin\theta + r\frac{\partial w}{\partial y}\cos\theta. \quad \text{(7b)}$$

Next,
$$\frac{\partial^2 w}{\partial r^2} = \frac{\partial}{\partial r}\left(\frac{\partial w}{\partial r}\right) = \frac{\partial}{\partial r}\left(\frac{\partial w}{\partial x}\cos\theta + \frac{\partial w}{\partial y}\sin\theta\right)$$
$$= \frac{\partial w_x}{\partial r}\cos\theta + \frac{\partial w_y}{\partial r}\sin\theta,$$

where $w_x = \partial w/\partial x$ and $w_y = \partial w/\partial y$. We apply Eq. (7a) to calculate $\partial w_x/\partial r$ and $\partial w_y/\partial r$, and we obtain

$$\frac{\partial^2 w}{\partial r^2} = \left(\frac{\partial w_x}{\partial x}\cdot\frac{\partial x}{\partial r} + \frac{\partial w_x}{\partial y}\cdot\frac{\partial y}{\partial r}\right)\cos\theta + \left(\frac{\partial w_y}{\partial x}\cdot\frac{\partial x}{\partial r} + \frac{\partial w_y}{\partial y}\cdot\frac{\partial y}{\partial r}\right)\sin\theta$$
$$= \left(\frac{\partial^2 w}{\partial x^2}\cos\theta + \frac{\partial^2 w}{\partial y\partial x}\sin\theta\right)\cos\theta + \left(\frac{\partial^2 w}{\partial x\partial y}\cos\theta + \frac{\partial^2 w}{\partial y^2}\sin\theta\right)\sin\theta.$$

Finally, because $w_{yx} = w_{xy}$, we get

$$\frac{\partial^2 w}{\partial r^2} = \frac{\partial^2 w}{\partial x^2}\cos^2\theta + 2\frac{\partial^2 w}{\partial x\partial y}\cos\theta\sin\theta + \frac{\partial^2 w}{\partial y^2}\sin^2\theta. \quad \text{(8)}$$

◆

EXAMPLE 6 Suppose that $w = f(u, v, x, y)$, where u and v are functions of x and y. Here x and y play dual roles as intermediate and independent variables. The chain rule yields

$$\frac{\partial w}{\partial x} = \frac{\partial f}{\partial u}\cdot\frac{\partial u}{\partial x} + \frac{\partial f}{\partial v}\cdot\frac{\partial v}{\partial x} + \frac{\partial f}{\partial x}\cdot\frac{\partial x}{\partial x} + \frac{\partial f}{\partial y}\cdot\frac{\partial y}{\partial x}$$
$$= \frac{\partial f}{\partial u}\cdot\frac{\partial u}{\partial x} + \frac{\partial f}{\partial v}\cdot\frac{\partial v}{\partial x} + \frac{\partial f}{\partial x},$$

because $\partial x/\partial x = 1$ and $\partial y/\partial x = 0$. Similarly,

$$\frac{\partial w}{\partial y} = \frac{\partial f}{\partial u}\cdot\frac{\partial u}{\partial y} + \frac{\partial f}{\partial v}\cdot\frac{\partial v}{\partial y} + \frac{\partial f}{\partial y}.$$

These results are consistent with the paths from w to x and from w to y in the molecular model shown in Fig. 13.7.6.

◆

FIGURE 13.7.6 Diagram for $w = f(u, v, x, y)$, where $u = u(x, y)$ and $v = v(x, y)$ (Example 6).

EXAMPLE 7 Consider a parametric curve $x = x(t)$, $y = y(t)$, $z = z(t)$ that lies on the surface $z = f(x, y)$ in space. Recall that if

$$\mathbf{T} = \left\langle \frac{dx}{dt}, \frac{dy}{dt}, \frac{dz}{dt} \right\rangle \quad \text{and} \quad \mathbf{N} = \left\langle \frac{\partial z}{\partial x}, \frac{\partial z}{\partial y}, -1 \right\rangle,$$

then $\mathbf{T}$ is tangent to the curve and $\mathbf{N}$ is normal to the surface. Show that $\mathbf{T}$ and $\mathbf{N}$ are everywhere perpendicular.

Solution The chain rule in Eq. (3) tells us that

$$\frac{dz}{dt} = \frac{\partial z}{\partial x}\cdot\frac{dx}{dt} + \frac{\partial z}{\partial y}\cdot\frac{dy}{dt}.$$

But this equation is equivalent to the vector equation

$$\left\langle \frac{\partial z}{\partial x}, \frac{\partial z}{\partial y}, -1 \right\rangle \cdot \left\langle \frac{dx}{dt}, \frac{dy}{dt}, \frac{dz}{dt} \right\rangle = 0.$$

Thus $\mathbf{N} \cdot \mathbf{T} = 0$, so $\mathbf{N}$ and $\mathbf{T}$ are perpendicular.

◆

Implicit Partial Differentiation

Sometimes we need to investigate a function $z = g(x, y)$ that is not defined explicitly by a formula giving z in terms of x and y, but instead is defined implicitly by an equation of the form $F(x, y, z) = 0$. The following implicit function theorem, proved in advanced calculus, guarantees the existence and differentiability of such implicitly defined functions under certain natural hypotheses.

THEOREM 3   Implicit Function Theorem

Suppose that the function $F(x_1, x_2, \ldots, x_n, z)$ is continuously differentiable near the point $(\mathbf{a}, b) = (a_1, a_2, \ldots, n, b)$ at which $F(\mathbf{a}, b) = 0$ and $D_z F(\mathbf{a}, b) \neq 0$. Then there exists a continuously differentiable function $z = g(x_1, x_2, \ldots, x_n)$ such that $g(\mathbf{a}) = b$ and $F(\mathbf{x}, g(\mathbf{x})) = 0$ for $\mathbf{x}$ near $\mathbf{a}$.

Moreover, the function $g(\mathbf{x})$ is uniquely defined for $\mathbf{x}$ near $\mathbf{a}$. In brief, Theorem 2 implies that the equation $F(x_1, x_2, \ldots, x_n, z) = 0$ implicitly defines one and only one continuously differentiable function $z = g(x_1, x_2, \ldots, x_n)$ near any point where $\partial F/\partial z \neq 0$. Knowing that the function g exists and is differentiable, we can calculate its partial derivatives by implicit differentiation of the given equation $F(x_1, x_2, \ldots, x_n, z) = 0$. Differentiating this equation with respect to x_i yields

$$\frac{\partial F}{\partial x_1} \cdot \frac{\partial x_1}{\partial x_i} + \cdots + \frac{\partial F}{\partial x_i} \cdot \frac{\partial x_i}{\partial x_i} + \cdots + \frac{\partial F}{\partial x_n} \cdot \frac{\partial x_n}{\partial x_i} + \frac{\partial F}{\partial z} \cdot \frac{\partial z}{\partial x_i} = 0. \tag{9}$$

But $\partial x_j/\partial x_i = 0$ unless $j = i$, and $\partial x_i/\partial x_i = 1$, so Eq. (9) reduces to the equation

$$\frac{\partial F}{\partial x_i} + \frac{\partial F}{\partial z} \cdot \frac{\partial z}{\partial x_i} = 0,$$

which (assuming that $\partial F/\partial z \neq 0$) we can solve to obtain the formula

$$\frac{\partial z}{\partial x_i} = -\frac{\partial F/\partial x_i}{\partial F/\partial z} = -\frac{F_{x_i}}{F_z} \tag{10}$$

for the ith partial derivative of $z = g(x_1, x_2, \ldots, x_n)$. In a specific example, it usually is just as simple to differentiate the given equation $F(x_1, x_2, \ldots, x_n, z) = 0$ as in (9), rather than applying the formula in (10).

EXAMPLE 8   Figure 13.7.7 shows the graph of the equation

$$F(x, y) = x^3 + y^3 - 3xy = 0 \tag{11}$$

(the folium of Descartes that we discussed in Example 3 of Section 4.1). With $n = 1$, x in place of x_1, and y in place of z, the implicit function theorem implies that this equation implicitly defines y as a function of x except possibly where

$$\frac{\partial F}{\partial y} = 3y^2 - 3x = 0.$$

By substituting $y^2 = x$ in Eq. (11), you can show that the only such points on the curve are the origin $(0, 0)$, where two branches of the curve intersect, and the point $(\sqrt[3]{4}, \sqrt[3]{2})$, where the figure shows a vertical tangent line. At any other point on the curve we can differentiate with respect to x in Eq. (11) to obtain

$$\frac{\partial F}{\partial x} \cdot \frac{dx}{dx} + \frac{\partial F}{\partial y} \cdot \frac{dy}{dx} = (3x^2 - 3y) \cdot 1 + (3y^2 - 3x) \cdot \frac{dy}{dx} = 0.$$

We can then solve for the slope

$$\frac{dy}{dx} = -\frac{x^2 - y}{y^2 - x}$$

of the line tangent to the curve at any point where there is not a vertical tangent line. ◆

FIGURE 13.7.7 Graph of the equation $F(x, y) = x^3 + y^3 - 3xy = 0$ (Example 8).

FIGURE 13.7.8 Graph of the equation $F(x, y, z) = x^4 + y^4 + z^4 + 4x^2y^2z^2 - 34 = 0$ (Example 9).

EXAMPLE 9 Figure 13.7.8 shows the graph of the equation

$$F(x, y, z) = x^4 + y^4 + z^4 + 4x^2y^2z^2 - 34 = 0. \tag{12}$$

With $n = 2$ and x and y in place of x_1 and x_2, the implicit function theorem implies that this equation implicitly defines z as a function of x and y except possibly where

$$\frac{\partial F}{\partial z} = 4z^3 + 8x^2y^2z = 4z(z^2 + 2x^2y^2) = 0.$$

The partial derivative is nonzero wherever $z \neq 0$, so it follows that z is defined as a function of x and y except at the points of the curve $x^4 + y^4 = 34$ in which the surface intersects the xy-plane (where $z = 0$). At any other point of the surface we can differentiate with respect to x and y in (12) to obtain

$$\frac{\partial F}{\partial x} \cdot \frac{\partial x}{\partial x} + \frac{\partial F}{\partial y} \cdot \frac{\partial y}{\partial x} + \frac{\partial F}{\partial z} \cdot \frac{\partial z}{\partial x} = (4x^3 + 8xy^2z^2) \cdot 1 + (4z^3 + 8x^2y^2z) \cdot \frac{\partial z}{\partial x} = 0$$

and

$$\frac{\partial F}{\partial x} \cdot \frac{\partial x}{\partial y} + \frac{\partial F}{\partial y} \cdot \frac{\partial y}{\partial y} + \frac{\partial F}{\partial z} \cdot \frac{\partial z}{\partial y} = (4y^3 + 8x^2yz^2) \cdot 1 + (4z^3 + 8x^2y^2z) \cdot \frac{\partial z}{\partial y} = 0.$$

We can then solve for

$$\frac{\partial z}{\partial x} = -\frac{x^3 + 2xy^2z^2}{z^3 + 2x^2y^2z} \quad \text{and} \quad \frac{\partial z}{\partial y} = -\frac{y^3 + 2x^2yz^2}{z^3 + 2x^2y^2z}.$$

For instance, at the point $(2, 1, 1)$ of the surface we find that $\partial z/\partial x = -\frac{4}{3}$ and $\partial z/\partial y = -1$. Hence the plane tangent to the surface at this point has equation

$$z - 1 = -\tfrac{4}{3}(x - 2) + (-1)(y - 1); \quad \text{that is,} \quad 4x + 3y + 3z = 14. \quad \blacklozenge$$

Matrix Form of the Chain Rule

The case $m = n = 2$ of the chain rule corresponds to the case of two intermediate variables (x and y, say) that are functions of two independent variables (u and v, say),

$$x = f(u, v), \qquad y = g(u, v). \tag{13}$$

These functions describe a **transformation** $T : \mathbf{R}^2_{uv} \to \mathbf{R}^2_{xy}$ from the coordinate plane $\mathbf{R}^2_{uv}$ of (u, v)-pairs to the coordinate plane $\mathbf{R}^2_{xy}$ of (x, y)-pairs. The **image** of the point (u, v) of $\mathbf{R}^2_{uv}$ is the point $T(u, v) = (f(u, v), g(u, v)) = (x, y)$ of $\mathbf{R}^2_{xy}$. The **derivative matrix** of the transformation T at the point (u, v) is then the 2×2 array

$$T'(u, v) = \begin{bmatrix} \dfrac{\partial x}{\partial u} & \dfrac{\partial x}{\partial v} \\ \dfrac{\partial y}{\partial u} & \dfrac{\partial y}{\partial v} \end{bmatrix} \tag{14}$$

of partial derivatives of the component functions in (13) of the transformation T (all evaluated at the point (u, v)).

EXAMPLE 10 The polar coordinate transformation $T : \mathbf{R}^2_{r\theta} \to \mathbf{R}^2_{xy}$ is defined by the familiar equations

$$x = r\cos\theta, \qquad y = r\sin\theta. \tag{15}$$

Its derivative matrix is given by

$$T'(r, \theta) = \begin{bmatrix} \dfrac{\partial x}{\partial r} & \dfrac{\partial x}{\partial \theta} \\ \dfrac{\partial y}{\partial r} & \dfrac{\partial y}{\partial \theta} \end{bmatrix} = \begin{bmatrix} \cos\theta & -r\sin\theta \\ \sin\theta & r\cos\theta \end{bmatrix}. \tag{16}$$

Now suppose that the dependent variable w is a function $F(x, y)$ of the intermediate variables x and y, and thereby is given by the composite function

$$G(u, v) = F(T(u, v)) = F(x(u, v), y(u, v)) \tag{17}$$

of the independent variables u and v (Fig. 13.7.9). The derivative matrices

$$F'(x, y) = \begin{bmatrix} \dfrac{\partial w}{\partial x} & \dfrac{\partial w}{\partial y} \end{bmatrix} \quad \text{and} \quad G'(u, v) = \begin{bmatrix} \dfrac{\partial w}{\partial u} & \dfrac{\partial w}{\partial v} \end{bmatrix} \tag{18}$$

of F and G are defined in analogy with (14)—there being a single row in each matrix, corresponding to the single dependent variable w. Those who are familiar with matrix multiplication will recognize that the two chain rule formulas

$$\frac{\partial w}{\partial u} = \frac{\partial w}{\partial x}\frac{\partial x}{\partial u} + \frac{\partial w}{\partial y}\frac{\partial y}{\partial u}, \quad \frac{\partial w}{\partial v} = \frac{\partial w}{\partial x}\frac{\partial x}{\partial v} + \frac{\partial w}{\partial y}\frac{\partial y}{\partial v}$$

are the "components" of the single matrix equation

$$G'(u, v) = F'(x, y) T'(u, v); \tag{19a}$$

that is,

$$\begin{bmatrix} \dfrac{\partial w}{\partial u} & \dfrac{\partial w}{\partial v} \end{bmatrix} = \begin{bmatrix} \dfrac{\partial w}{\partial x} & \dfrac{\partial w}{\partial y} \end{bmatrix} \begin{bmatrix} \dfrac{\partial x}{\partial u} & \dfrac{\partial x}{\partial v} \\ \dfrac{\partial y}{\partial u} & \dfrac{\partial y}{\partial v} \end{bmatrix}. \tag{19b}$$

Thus the chain rule for the situation indicated in Fig. 13.7.9 implies that *the derivative matrix of the composite function $G = F \circ T$ is the matrix product $G' = F'T'$.* ◆

FIGURE 13.7.9 Diagram for $w = F(x, y)$ where $(x, y) = (x(u, v), y(u, v)) = T(u, v)$

EXAMPLE 11 With the polar-coordinate derivative matrix $T'(r, \theta)$ in (16), the matrix multiplication in Eq. (19b) yields

$$\begin{bmatrix} \dfrac{\partial w}{\partial r} & \dfrac{\partial w}{\partial \theta} \end{bmatrix} = \begin{bmatrix} \dfrac{\partial w}{\partial x} & \dfrac{\partial w}{\partial y} \end{bmatrix} \begin{bmatrix} \cos\theta & -r\sin\theta \\ \sin\theta & r\cos\theta \end{bmatrix}$$

$$= \begin{bmatrix} \dfrac{\partial w}{\partial x}\cos\theta + \dfrac{\partial w}{\partial y}\sin\theta & -r\dfrac{\partial w}{\partial x}\sin\theta + r\dfrac{\partial w}{\partial y}\cos\theta \end{bmatrix}.$$

The components of this matrix equation are the scalar chain rule formulas

$$\frac{\partial w}{\partial r} = \frac{\partial w}{\partial x}\cos\theta + \frac{\partial w}{\partial y}\sin\theta, \quad \frac{\partial w}{\partial \theta} = -r\frac{\partial w}{\partial x}\sin\theta + r\frac{\partial w}{\partial y}\cos\theta$$

that we saw previously in Example 5. ◆

We have discussed here the 2×2 case of a general $m \times n$ matrix formulation of the multivariable chain rule. The 3×3 case and its application to spherical coordinates are discussed in Problems 58 through 61.

PROOF OF THE CHAIN RULE Given that $w = f(x, y)$ satisfies the hypotheses of Theorem 1, we choose a point t_0 at which we wish to compute dw/dt and write

$$a = g(t_0), \qquad b = h(t_0).$$

Let

$$\Delta x = g(t_0 + \Delta t) - g(t_0), \qquad \Delta y = h(t_0 + \Delta t) - h(t_0).$$

Then

$$g(t_0 + \Delta t) = a + \Delta x \quad \text{and} \quad h(t_0 + \Delta t) = b + \Delta y.$$

If

$$\Delta w = f(g(t_0 + \Delta t), h(t_0 + \Delta t)) - f(g(t_0), h(t_0))$$
$$= f(a + \Delta x, b + \Delta y) - f(a, b),$$

then what we need to compute is
$$\frac{dw}{dt} = \lim_{\Delta t \to 0} \frac{\Delta w}{\Delta t}.$$

The linear approximation theorem of Section 13.6 gives
$$\Delta w = f_x(a,b)\,\Delta x + f_y(a,b)\,\Delta y + \epsilon_1\,\Delta x + \epsilon_2\,\Delta y,$$

where ϵ_1 and ϵ_2 approach zero as $\Delta x \to 0$ and $\Delta y \to 0$. We note that both Δx and Δy approach zero as $\Delta t \to 0$, because both the derivatives
$$\frac{dx}{dt} = \lim_{\Delta t \to 0} \frac{\Delta x}{\Delta t} \quad \text{and} \quad \frac{dy}{dt} = \lim_{\Delta t \to 0} \frac{\Delta y}{\Delta t}$$

exist. Therefore,
$$\frac{dw}{dt} = \lim_{\Delta t \to 0} \frac{\Delta w}{\Delta t} = \lim_{\Delta t \to 0} \left[f_x(a,b)\frac{\Delta x}{\Delta t} + f_y(a,b)\frac{\Delta y}{\Delta t} + \epsilon_1 \frac{\Delta x}{\Delta t} + \epsilon_2 \frac{\Delta y}{\Delta t} \right]$$
$$= f_x(a,b)\frac{dx}{dt} + f_y(a,b)\frac{dy}{dt} + 0 \cdot \frac{dx}{dt} + 0 \cdot \frac{dy}{dt}.$$

Hence
$$\frac{dw}{dt} = \frac{\partial w}{\partial x} \cdot \frac{dx}{dt} + \frac{\partial w}{\partial y} \cdot \frac{dy}{dt}.$$

Thus we have established Eq. (3), writing $\partial w/\partial x$ and $\partial w/\partial y$ for the partial derivatives $f_x(a,b)$ and $f_y(a,b)$ in the final step. ◄

13.7 TRUE/FALSE STUDY GUIDE

13.7 CONCEPTS: QUESTIONS AND DISCUSSION

1. Give your own example of a composite function situation illustrating the general chain rule (Theorem 2), but with different numbers of independent, intermediate, and dependent variables than in any of the examples in this section.

2. Let C be a set in the xy-plane R^2. We might call C a **smooth curve** provided that every point of C has a neighborhood within which C agrees with the graph of a continuously differentiable function—either $y = f(x)$ or $x = g(y)$. Under what conditions on the function $F(x,y)$ does the implicit function theorem imply that the graph of the equation $F(x,y) = 0$ is a smooth curve? Explain.

3. Let S be a set in xyz-space R^3. We might call S a **smooth surface** provided that every point of S has a neighborhood within which S agrees with the graph of a continuously differentiable function—either $z = f(x,y)$ or $x = g(y,z)$ or $y = h(x,z)$. Under what conditions on the function $F(x,y,z)$ does the implicit function theorem imply that the graph of the equation $F(x,y,z) = 0$ is a smooth surface? Explain.

13.7 PROBLEMS

In Problems 1 through 4, find dw/dt both by using the chain rule and by expressing w explicitly as a function of t before differentiating.

1. $w = \exp(-x^2 - y^2);\quad x = t,\ y = \sqrt{t}$
2. $w = \dfrac{1}{u^2 + v^2};\quad u = \cos 2t,\ v = \sin 2t$
3. $w = \sin xyz;\quad x = t,\ y = t^2,\ z = t^3$
4. $w = \ln(u + v + z);\quad u = \cos^2 t,\ v = \sin^2 t,\ z = t^2$

In Problems 5 through 8, find $\partial w/\partial s$ and $\partial w/\partial t$.

5. $w = \ln(x^2 + y^2 + z^2);\quad x = s - t,\ y = s + t,\ z = 2\sqrt{st}$
6. $w = pq \sin r;\quad p = 2s + t,\ q = s - t,\ r = st$
7. $w = \sqrt{u^2 + v^2 + z^2};\quad u = 3e^t \sin s,\ v = 3e^t \cos s,\ z = 4e^t$
8. $w = yz + zx + xy;\quad x = s^2 - t^2,\ y = s^2 + t^2,\ z = s^2 t^2$

In Problems 9 through 12, find $\partial r/\partial x$, $\partial r/\partial y$, and $\partial r/\partial z$.

9. $r = e^{u+v+w};\quad u = yz,\ v = xz,\ w = xy$

10. $r = uvw - u^2 - v^2 - w^2$; $u = y+z$, $v = x+z$, $w = x+y$
11. $r = \sin(p/q)$; $p = \sqrt{xy^2z^3}$, $q = \sqrt{x+2y+3z}$
12. $r = \dfrac{p}{q} + \dfrac{q}{s} + \dfrac{s}{p}$; $p = e^{yz}$, $q = e^{xz}$, $s = e^{xy}$

In Problems 13 through 18, write chain rule formulas giving the partial derivative of the dependent variable p with respect to each independent variable.

13. $p = f(x, y)$; $x = x(u, v, w)$, $y = y(u, v, w)$
14. $p = f(x, y, z)$; $x = x(u, v)$, $y = y(u, v)$, $z = z(u, v)$
15. $p = f(u, v, w)$; $u = u(x, y, z)$, $v = v(x, y, z)$, $w = w(x, y, z)$
16. $p = f(v, w)$; $v = v(x, y, z, t)$, $w = w(x, y, z, t)$
17. $p = f(w)$; $w = w(x, y, z, u, v)$
18. $p = f(x, y, u, v)$; $x = x(s, t)$, $y = y(s, t)$, $u = u(s, t)$, $v = v(s, t)$

In Problems 19 through 24, find $\partial z/\partial x$ and $\partial z/\partial y$ as functions of x, y, and z, assuming that $z = f(x, y)$ satisfies the given equation.

19. $x^{2/3} + y^{2/3} + z^{2/3} = 1$
20. $x^3 + y^3 + z^3 = xyz$
21. $xe^{xy} + ye^{zx} + ze^{xy} = 3$
22. $x^5 + xy^2 + yz = 5$
23. $\dfrac{x^2}{a^2} + \dfrac{y^2}{b^2} + \dfrac{z^2}{c^2} = 1$
24. $xyz = \sin(x + y + z)$

In Problems 25 through 28, use the method of Example 6 to find $\partial w/\partial x$ and $\partial w/\partial y$ as functions of x and y.

25. $w = u^2 + v^2 + x^2 + y^2$; $u = x - y$, $v = x + y$
26. $w = \sqrt{uvxy}$; $u = \sqrt{x-y}$, $v = \sqrt{x+y}$
27. $w = xy\ln(u + v)$; $u = (x^2 + y^2)^{1/3}$, $v = (x^3 + y^3)^{1/2}$
28. $w = uv - xy$; $u = \dfrac{x}{x^2 + y^2}$, $v = \dfrac{y}{x^2 + y^2}$

In Problems 29 through 32, write an equation for the plane tangent at the point P to the surface with the given equation.

29. $x^2 + y^2 + z^2 = 9$; $P(1, 2, 2)$
30. $x^2 + 2y^2 + 2z^2 = 14$; $P(2, 1, -2)$
31. $x^3 + y^3 + z^3 = 5xyz$; $P(2, 1, 1)$
32. $z^3 + (x + y)z^2 + x^2 + y^2 = 13$; $P(2, 2, 1)$

33. The sun is melting a rectangular block of ice. When the block's height is 1 ft and the edge of its square base is 2 ft, its height is decreasing at 2 in./h and its base edge is decreasing at 3 in./h. What is the block's rate of change of volume V at that instant?

34. A rectangular box has a square base. Find the rate at which its volume and surface area are changing if its base edge is increasing at 2 cm/min and its height is decreasing at 3 cm/min at the instant when each dimension is 1 meter.

35. Falling sand forms a conical sandpile. When the sandpile has a height of 5 ft and its base radius is 2 ft, its height is increasing at 0.4 ft/min and its base radius is increasing at 0.7 ft/min. At what rate is the volume of the sandpile increasing at that moment?

36. A rectangular block has dimensions $x = 3$ m, $y = 2$ m, and $z = 1$ m. If x and y are increasing at 1 cm/min and 2 cm/min, respectively, while z is decreasing at 2 cm/min, are the block's volume and total surface area increasing or decreasing? At what rates?

37. The volume V (in cubic centimeters) and pressure p (in atmospheres) of n moles of an ideal gas satisfy the equation $pV = nRT$, where T is its temperature (in degrees Kelvin) and $R = 82.06$. Suppose that a sample of the gas has a volume of 10 L when the pressure is 2 atm and the temperature is 300°K. If the pressure is increasing at 1 atm/min and the temperature is increasing at 10°K/min, is the volume of the gas sample increasing or decreasing? At what rate?

38. The aggregate resistance R of three variable resistances R_1, R_2, and R_3 connected in parallel satisfies the *harmonic equation*

$$\dfrac{1}{R} = \dfrac{1}{R_1} + \dfrac{1}{R_2} + \dfrac{1}{R_3}.$$

Suppose that R_1 and R_2 are 100 Ω and are increasing at 1 Ω/s, while R_3 is 200 Ω and is decreasing at 2 Ω/s. Is R increasing or decreasing at that instant? At what rate?

39. Suppose that $x = h(y, z)$ satisfies the equation $F(x, y, z) = 0$ and that $F_x \neq 0$. Show that

$$\dfrac{\partial x}{\partial y} = -\dfrac{\partial F/\partial y}{\partial F/\partial x}.$$

40. Suppose that $w = f(x, y)$, $x = r\cos\theta$, and $y = r\sin\theta$. Show that

$$\left(\dfrac{\partial w}{\partial x}\right)^2 + \left(\dfrac{\partial w}{\partial y}\right)^2 = \left(\dfrac{\partial w}{\partial r}\right)^2 + \dfrac{1}{r^2}\left(\dfrac{\partial w}{\partial \theta}\right)^2.$$

41. Suppose that $w = f(u)$ and that $u = x + y$. Show that $\partial w/\partial x = \partial w/\partial y$.

42. Suppose that $w = f(u)$ and that $u = x - y$. Show that $\partial w/\partial x = -\partial w/\partial y$ and that

$$\dfrac{\partial^2 w}{\partial x^2} = \dfrac{\partial^2 w}{\partial y^2} = -\dfrac{\partial^2 w}{\partial x \partial y}.$$

43. Suppose that $w = f(x, y)$ where $x = u + v$ and $y = u - v$. Show that

$$\dfrac{\partial^2 w}{\partial x^2} - \dfrac{\partial^2 w}{\partial y^2} = \dfrac{\partial^2 w}{\partial u \partial v}.$$

44. Assume that $w = f(x, y)$ where $x = 2u + v$ and $y = u - v$. Show that

$$5\dfrac{\partial^2 w}{\partial x^2} + 2\dfrac{\partial^2 w}{\partial x \partial y} + 2\dfrac{\partial^2 w}{\partial y^2} = \dfrac{\partial^2 w}{\partial u^2} + \dfrac{\partial^2 w}{\partial v^2}.$$

45. Suppose that $w = f(x, y)$, $x = r\cos\theta$, and $y = r\sin\theta$. Show that

$$\dfrac{\partial^2 w}{\partial x^2} + \dfrac{\partial^2 w}{\partial y^2} = \dfrac{\partial^2 w}{\partial r^2} + \dfrac{1}{r}\dfrac{\partial w}{\partial r} + \dfrac{1}{r^2}\dfrac{\partial^2 w}{\partial \theta^2}.$$

[*Suggestion:* First find $\partial^2 w/\partial \theta^2$ by the method of Example 7. Then combine the result with Eqs. (7) and (8).]

46. Suppose that
$$w = \frac{1}{r} f\left(t - \frac{r}{a}\right)$$
and that $r = \sqrt{x^2 + y^2 + z^2}$. Show that
$$\frac{\partial^2 w}{\partial x^2} + \frac{\partial^2 w}{\partial y^2} + \frac{\partial^2 w}{\partial z^2} = \frac{1}{a^2} \frac{\partial^2 w}{\partial t^2}.$$

47. Suppose that $w = f(r)$ and that $r = \sqrt{x^2 + y^2 + z^2}$. Show that
$$\frac{\partial^2 w}{\partial x^2} + \frac{\partial^2 w}{\partial y^2} + \frac{\partial^2 w}{\partial z^2} = \frac{d^2 w}{dr^2} + \frac{2}{r} \frac{dw}{dr}.$$

48. Suppose that $w = f(u) + g(v)$, that $u = x - at$, and that $v = x + at$. Show that
$$\frac{\partial^2 w}{\partial t^2} = a^2 \frac{\partial^2 w}{\partial x^2}.$$

49. Assume that $w = f(u, v)$ where $u = x + y$ and $v = x - y$. Show that
$$\frac{\partial w}{\partial x} \frac{\partial w}{\partial y} = \left(\frac{\partial w}{\partial u}\right)^2 - \left(\frac{\partial w}{\partial v}\right)^2.$$

50. Given: $w = f(x, y)$, $x = e^u \cos v$, and $y = e^u \sin v$. Show that
$$\left(\frac{\partial w}{\partial x}\right)^2 + \left(\frac{\partial w}{\partial y}\right)^2 = e^{-2u}\left[\left(\frac{\partial w}{\partial u}\right)^2 + \left(\frac{\partial w}{\partial v}\right)^2\right].$$

51. Assume that $w = f(x, y)$ and that there is a constant α such that
$$x = u \cos \alpha - v \sin \alpha \quad \text{and} \quad y = u \sin \alpha + v \cos \alpha.$$
Show that
$$\left(\frac{\partial w}{\partial u}\right)^2 + \left(\frac{\partial w}{\partial v}\right)^2 = \left(\frac{\partial w}{\partial x}\right)^2 + \left(\frac{\partial w}{\partial y}\right)^2.$$

52. Suppose that $w = f(u)$, where
$$u = \frac{x^2 - y^2}{x^2 + y^2}.$$
Show that $xw_x + yw_y = 0$.

Suppose that the equation $F(x, y, z) = 0$ defines implicitly the three functions $z = f(x, y)$, $y = g(x, z)$, and $x = h(y, z)$. To keep track of the various partial derivatives, we use the notation

$$\left(\frac{\partial z}{\partial x}\right)_y = \frac{\partial f}{\partial x}, \quad \left(\frac{\partial z}{\partial y}\right)_x = \frac{\partial f}{\partial y}, \quad (20a)$$

$$\left(\frac{\partial y}{\partial x}\right)_z = \frac{\partial g}{\partial x}, \quad \left(\frac{\partial y}{\partial z}\right)_x = \frac{\partial g}{\partial z}, \quad (20b)$$

$$\left(\frac{\partial x}{\partial y}\right)_z = \frac{\partial h}{\partial y}, \quad \left(\frac{\partial x}{\partial z}\right)_y = \frac{\partial h}{\partial z}, \quad (20c)$$

In short, the general symbol $(\partial w/\partial u)_v$ denotes the derivative of w with respect to u, where w is regarded as a function of the independent variables u and v.

53. Using the notation in the equations in (20), show that
$$\left(\frac{\partial x}{\partial y}\right)_z \left(\frac{\partial y}{\partial z}\right)_x \left(\frac{\partial z}{\partial x}\right)_y = -1.$$
[*Suggestion:* Find the three partial derivatives on the right-hand side in terms of F_x, F_y, and F_z.]

54. Verify the result of Problem 53 for the equation
$$F(x, y, z) = x^2 + y^2 + z^2 - 1 = 0.$$

55. Verify the result of Problem 53 (with p, V, and T in place of x, y, and z) for the equation
$$F(p, V, T) = pV - nRT = 0$$
(n and R are constants), which expresses the ideal gas law.

56. Consider a given quantity of liquid whose pressure p, volume V, and temperature T satisfy a given "state equation" of the form $F(p, V, T) = 0$. The **thermal expansivity** α and **isothermal compressivity** β of the liquid are defined by
$$\alpha = \frac{1}{V}\frac{\partial V}{\partial T} \quad \text{and} \quad \beta = -\frac{1}{V}\frac{\partial V}{\partial p}.$$
Apply Theorem 3 first to calculate $\partial V/\partial p$ and $\partial V/\partial T$, and then to calculate $\partial p/\partial V$ and $\partial p/\partial T$. Deduce from the results that $\partial p/\partial T = \alpha/\beta$.

57. The thermal expansivity and isothermal compressivity of liquid mercury are $\alpha = 1.8 \times 10^{-4}$ and $\beta = 3.9 \times 10^{-6}$, respectively, in L-atm-°C units. Suppose that a thermometer bulb is exactly filled with mercury at 50°C. If the bulb can withstand an internal pressure of no more than 200 atm, can it be heated to 55°C without breaking? *Suggestion:* Apply the result of Problem 56 to calculate the increase in pressure with each increase of one degree in temperature.

58. Suppose that the transformation $T: \mathbf{R}^3_{uvw} \to \mathbf{R}^3_{xyz}$ is defined by the functions $x = x(u, v, w)$, $y = y(u, v, w)$, $z = z(u, v, w)$. Then its derivative matrix is defined by
$$T(u, v, w) = \begin{bmatrix} x_u & x_v & x_w \\ y_u & y_v & y_w \\ z_u & z_v & z_w \end{bmatrix}.$$
Calculate the derivative matrix of the linear transformation defined by $x = a_1 u + b_1 v + c_1 w$, $y = a_2 u + b_2 v + c_2 w$, $z = a_3 u + b_3 v + c_3 w$.

59. Calculate the derivative matrix of the spherical coordinate transformation T defined by $x = \rho \sin \phi \cos \theta$, $y = \rho \sin \phi \sin \theta$, $z = \rho \cos \phi$.

60. Suppose that $q = F(x, y, z)$ with 1×3 derivative matrix $F' = [F_x \ F_y \ F_z]$ and that $(x, y, z) = T(u, v, w)$ as in Problem 58. If $G = F \circ T$, deduce from the chain rule in Theorem 2 that $G' = F'T'$ (matrix product).

61. If $w = F(x, y, z)$, apply the results of Problems 59 and 60 to calculate by matrix multiplication the partial derivatives of w with respect to the spherical coordinates ρ, ϕ, and θ.

13.8 DIRECTIONAL DERIVATIVES AND THE GRADIENT VECTOR

Figure 13.8.1 shows temperatures (in degrees Fahrenheit) recorded at U.S. locations at 2:12 P.M. E.D.T. on Thursday, April 12, 2001. This plot of the U.S. temperature function $T = f(x, y)$ is contoured "by color"—that is, locations with the same temperature are shown in the same color. If we depart from an airport and fly due east (in the positive x-direction), then the rate of change of temperature (in degrees per mile) that we initially observe is given by the partial derivative $\partial T/\partial x = f_x$. If we fly due north, then $\partial T/\partial y = f_y$ gives the initial rate of change of temperature with respect to distance. But we need not fly either due east or due north. The *directional derivative* introduced in this section enables us to calculate the rate of change of a function in any specified direction.

FIGURE 13.8.1 Current temperatures (°F) recorded at 2:12 P.M. on April 12, 2001.

Directional Derivatives

Recall that the first-order partial derivatives of the function $z = f(x, y)$ are defined to be

$$f_x(x, y) = \lim_{h \to 0} \frac{f(x+h, y) - f(x, y)}{h} \quad \text{and} \quad f_y(x, y) = \lim_{h \to 0} \frac{f(x, y+h) - f(x, y)}{h}$$

wherever these limits exist. If we write $\mathbf{x} = \langle x, y \rangle$, then these partial derivatives may be described a bit more concisely in the form

$$f_x(\mathbf{x}) = \lim_{h \to 0} \frac{f(\mathbf{x} + h\mathbf{i}) - f(\mathbf{x})}{h}, \quad f_y(\mathbf{x}) = \lim_{h \to 0} \frac{f(\mathbf{x} + h\mathbf{j}) - f(\mathbf{x})}{h} \quad (1)$$

where $\mathbf{i} = \langle 1, 0 \rangle$ and $\mathbf{j} = \langle 0, 1 \rangle$ as usual. Thus f_x and f_y represent rates of change of z with respect to distance in the directions of the unit vectors $\mathbf{i}$ and $\mathbf{j}$. We get the definition of the *directional derivative* upon replacing $\mathbf{i}$ or $\mathbf{j}$ in (1) with an arbitrary specified unit vector $\mathbf{u}$.

DEFINITION Directional Derivative
The **directional derivative** of the function f at the point $\mathbf{x}$ in the direction of the unit vector $\mathbf{u}$ is

$$D_{\mathbf{u}} f(\mathbf{x}) = \lim_{h \to 0} \frac{f(\mathbf{x} + h\mathbf{u}) - f(\mathbf{x})}{h} \quad (2)$$

provided that this limit exists.

The function f in Eq. (2) can be a function of two or three or more variables. Comparing Eqs. (1) and (2), we see that the partial derivatives of a function of two variables x and y can be written as

$$f_x(x, y) = D_{\mathbf{i}} f(x, y) \quad \text{and} \quad f_y(x, y) = D_{\mathbf{j}} f(x, y).$$

Thus f_x and f_y are, indeed, the directional derivatives of f in the directions of the unit vectors **i** and **j**. Similarly, if f is a function of the three variables x, y, and z, then its partial derivatives

$$f_x = D_{\mathbf{i}} f, \quad f_y = D_{\mathbf{j}} f, \quad \text{and} \quad f_z = D_{\mathbf{k}} f$$

are the directional derivatives of f in the directions of the three standard unit vectors $\mathbf{i} = \langle 1, 0, 0 \rangle$, $\mathbf{j} = \langle 0, 1, 0 \rangle$, and $\mathbf{k} = \langle 0, 0, 1 \rangle$ in space.

The limit in Eq. (2) would still make sense if **u** were not a unit vector. But the *meaning* of directional derivatives is easiest to understand when **u** *is* a unit vector, and this is why we define $D_{\mathbf{u}} f(\mathbf{x})$ only when $|\mathbf{u}| = 1$. In Fig. 13.8.2 the unit vector **u** points in the direction from the fixed point P (with position vector **x**) to the point Q (with position vector $\mathbf{x} + h\mathbf{u}$). Then

$$\Delta w = f(Q) - f(P) = f(\mathbf{x} + h\mathbf{u}) - f(\mathbf{x})$$

is the increment in the function value $w = f(x, y, z)$ from the point P to the point Q. If we write $\Delta s = |\overrightarrow{PQ}| = h$ for the distance from P to Q, then the quotient

$$\frac{\Delta w}{\Delta s} = \frac{f(Q) - f(P)}{|\overrightarrow{PQ}|} = \frac{f(\mathbf{x} + h\mathbf{u}) - f(\mathbf{x})}{h}$$

is the *average rate of change* of w with respect to distance from P to Q. It is therefore natural to regard the limit

$$\frac{dw}{ds} = \lim_{\Delta s \to 0} \frac{\Delta w}{\Delta s} = \lim_{h \to 0} \frac{f(\mathbf{x} + h\mathbf{u}) - f(\mathbf{x})}{h} = D_{\mathbf{u}} f(\mathbf{x}) \quad (3)$$

as the **instantaneous rate of change** of w at P with respect to distance in the direction from P to Q. Some science and engineering texts may use the notation

$$\left. \frac{df}{ds} \right|_P = D_{\mathbf{u}} f(P),$$

or simply dw/ds as in Eq. (3), for the instantaneous rate of change of the function $w = f(x, y, z)$ at the point P, with respect to distance s in the direction of the unit vector **u**.

Calculation of Directional Derivatives

Equation (2) *defines* the directional derivative, but how do we actually *calculate* directional derivatives? To answer this question, we recall (from Eq. (18) in Section 13.6) that if the function $f(x_1, x_2, \ldots, x_n)$ is differentiable at $\mathbf{x} = \langle x_1, x_2, \ldots, x_n \rangle$, then its partial derivatives exist there; moreover,

$$\lim_{\mathbf{h} \to 0} \frac{f(\mathbf{x} + \mathbf{h}) - f(\mathbf{x}) - \nabla f(\mathbf{x}) \cdot \mathbf{h}}{|\mathbf{h}|} = 0 \quad (4)$$

where $\nabla f(\mathbf{x}) = \langle D_1 f(\mathbf{x}), D_2 f(\mathbf{x}), \ldots, D_n f(\mathbf{x}) \rangle$ is the gradient vector of f at **x**. If we substitute $\mathbf{h} = h\mathbf{u}$ where **u** is a unit vector and $h > 0$ (so that $|\mathbf{h}| = h$), then Eq. (4) implies that

$$\lim_{h \to 0} \frac{f(\mathbf{x} + \mathbf{h}) - f(\mathbf{x}) - \nabla f(\mathbf{x}) \cdot h\mathbf{u}}{h}$$

$$= \lim_{h \to 0} \left(\frac{f(\mathbf{x} + h\mathbf{u}) - f(\mathbf{x})}{h} - \nabla f(\mathbf{x}) \cdot \mathbf{u} \right) = D_{\mathbf{u}} f(\mathbf{x}) - \nabla f(\mathbf{x}) \cdot \mathbf{u} = 0.$$

In the last step we have used the definition in (2) of the directional derivative $D_{\mathbf{u}} f(\mathbf{x})$ and the fact that **x** and **u** play the role of constants as $h \to 0$. This proves the following theorem.

FIGURE 13.8.2 The first step in computing the rate of change of $f(x, y, z)$ in the direction of the unit vector **u**.

THEOREM 1 Calculation of Directional Derivatives

If the real-valued function f is differentiable at $\mathbf{x}$ and $\mathbf{u}$ is a unit vector, then the directional derivative $D_\mathbf{u} f(\mathbf{x})$ exists and is given by

$$D_\mathbf{u} f(\mathbf{x}) = \nabla f(\mathbf{x}) \cdot \mathbf{u}. \tag{5}$$

For instance, if $z = f(x, y)$ is a function of two variables, so that

$$\nabla f(x, y) = \langle f_x(x, y), f_y(x, y) \rangle \quad \text{and} \quad \mathbf{u} = \langle a, b \rangle,$$

then Eq. (5) gives

$$D_{\langle a,b \rangle} f(x, y) = \langle f_x(x, y), f_y(x, y) \rangle \cdot \langle a, b \rangle = a f_x(x, y) + b f_y(x, y). \tag{6}$$

If the unit vector $\mathbf{u}$ makes the counterclockwise angle θ with the positive x-axis (as in Fig. 13.8.3), then $\mathbf{u} = \langle \cos\theta, \sin\theta \rangle$, so Eq. (6) takes the form

$$D_\mathbf{u} f(x, y) = f_x(x, y) \cos\theta + f_y(x, y) \sin\theta = \frac{\partial w}{\partial x} \cos\theta + \frac{\partial w}{\partial y} \sin\theta. \tag{7}$$

FIGURE 13.8.3 The unit vector $\mathbf{u}$ of Eq. (7).

If $w = f(x, y, z)$ is a function of three variables and $\mathbf{u} = \langle a, b, c \rangle$ (still a unit vector), then Eq. (5) similarly yields

$$D_{\langle a,b,c \rangle} f(x, y, z) = a f_x(x, y, z) + b f_y(x, y, z) + c f_z(x, y, z). \tag{8}$$

EXAMPLE 1 Suppose that the temperature (in degrees Celsius) at the point (x, y) near an airport is given by

$$f(x, y) = \frac{1}{180}[7400 - 4x - 9y - (0.03)xy]$$

(with distances x and y measured in kilometers). Suppose that your aircraft takes off from this airport at the location $P(200, 200)$ and heads northeast in the direction specified by the vector $\mathbf{v} = \langle 3, 4 \rangle$. What initial rate of change of temperature will you observe?

Solution Because $\mathbf{v}$ is not a unit vector, we must first replace it with the unit vector $\mathbf{u}$ having the same direction:

$$\mathbf{u} = \frac{\mathbf{v}}{|\mathbf{v}|} = \frac{\langle 3, 4 \rangle}{\sqrt{3^2 + 4^2}} = \left\langle \frac{3}{5}, \frac{4}{5} \right\rangle.$$

Now we may use the formula in (6), which yields

$$D_\mathbf{u} f(x, y) = \left(\frac{3}{5}\right) \cdot \left(\frac{1}{180}[-4 - (0.03)y]\right) + \left(\frac{4}{5}\right) \cdot \left(\frac{1}{180}[-9 - (0.03)x]\right).$$

When we substitute $x = y = 200$ we find that

$$D_\mathbf{u} f(P) = \left(\frac{3}{5}\right) \cdot \left(-\frac{10}{180}\right) + \left(\frac{4}{5}\right) \cdot \left(-\frac{15}{180}\right) = -\frac{18}{180} = -0.1.$$

This instantaneous rate of change -0.1°C/km means that you will observe initially a decrease of 0.1°C in temperature per kilometer traveled. ◆

The Gradient Vector

In Section 13.6 we introduced the gradient vector informally as a notational device for simplifying the expression of certain multivariable formulas. Most of the remainder of this section is devoted to exploration of the meaning and geometric interpretation of gradient vectors, largely in two and three dimensions. We begin with a formal definition.

DEFINITION   Gradient Vector
The **gradient** of the differentiable real-valued function $f : \mathbf{R}^n \to \mathbf{R}$ is the vector-valued function $\nabla f : \mathbf{R}^n \to \mathbf{R}^n$ defined by

$$\nabla f(\mathbf{x}) = \langle D_1 f(\mathbf{x}), D_2 f(\mathbf{x}), \ldots, D_n f(\mathbf{x}) \rangle. \tag{9}$$

In particular, the gradient vectors of functions of two and three variables are given (respectively) by

$$\nabla f(P) = \frac{\partial f}{\partial x}\mathbf{i} + \frac{\partial f}{\partial y}\mathbf{j} \quad \text{and} \quad \nabla f(P) = \frac{\partial f}{\partial x}\mathbf{i} + \frac{\partial f}{\partial y}\mathbf{j} + \frac{\partial f}{\partial z}\mathbf{k}; \tag{10}$$

the partial derivatives in Eq. (10) are to be evaluated at the point P.

EXAMPLE 2 If $f(x, y, z) = yz + \sin xz + e^{xy}$, then the second formula in (10) gives

$$\nabla f(x, y, z) = (z \cos xz + ye^{xy})\mathbf{i} + (z + xe^{xy})\mathbf{j} + (y + x \cos xz)\mathbf{k}.$$

The value of this gradient vector at the point $(0, 7, 3)$ is

$$\nabla f(0, 7, 3) = (3 \cdot 1 + 7 \cdot 1)\mathbf{i} + (3 + 0 \cdot 1)\mathbf{j} + (7 + 0 \cdot 1)\mathbf{k} = 10\mathbf{i} + 3\mathbf{j} + 7\mathbf{k}. \blacklozenge$$

Theorem 1 says that if the function f is differentiable at $\mathbf{x}$ and $\mathbf{u}$ is a unit vector, then the directional derivative of f at $\mathbf{x}$ in the direction $\mathbf{u}$ is given by

$$D_\mathbf{u} f(\mathbf{x}) = \nabla f(\mathbf{x}) \cdot \mathbf{u}. \tag{11}$$

The chain rule has a similar gradient vector form. For instance, suppose that the differentiable vector-valued function

$$\mathbf{r}(t) = x(t)\mathbf{i} + y(t)\mathbf{j} + z(y)\mathbf{k}$$

is the position vector of a curve in $\mathbf{R}^3$ and that $f(x, y, z)$ is a differentiable function. Then the composition

$$f(\mathbf{r}(t)) = f(x(t), y(t), z(t))$$

is a differentiable function of t, and its (ordinary) chain-rule derivative with respect to t is

$$D_t[f(\mathbf{r}(t))] = D_t[f(x(t), y(t), z(t))] = \frac{\partial f}{\partial x} \cdot \frac{dx}{dt} + \frac{\partial f}{\partial y} \cdot \frac{dy}{dt} + \frac{\partial f}{\partial z} \cdot \frac{dz}{dt}.$$

We recognize here the dot product

$$D_t[f(\mathbf{r}(t))] = \nabla f(\mathbf{r}(t)) \cdot \mathbf{r}'(t), \tag{12}$$

where

$$\mathbf{r}'(t) = \frac{d\mathbf{r}}{dt} = \frac{dx}{dt}\mathbf{i} + \frac{dy}{dt}\mathbf{j} + \frac{dz}{dt}\mathbf{k}$$

is the velocity vector of the parametric curve $\mathbf{r}(t)$.

If $\mathbf{r}(t)$ is a *smooth* parametric curve with nonzero velocity vector $\mathbf{v}(t) = \mathbf{r}'(t)$, then $\mathbf{v} = v\mathbf{u}$ where $v = |\mathbf{v}|$ is the speed of motion along the curve and $\mathbf{u} = \mathbf{v}/v$ is the unit vector tangent to the curve (Section 12.6). Then Eq. (12) implies that

$$D_t[f(\mathbf{r}(t))] = \nabla f(\mathbf{r}(t)) \cdot \mathbf{r}'(t) = \nabla f(\mathbf{r}(t)) \cdot v\mathbf{u} = v \nabla f(\mathbf{r}(t)) \cdot \mathbf{u},$$

and hence in turn that

$$D_t[f(\mathbf{r}(t))] = v D_\mathbf{u} f(\mathbf{r}(t)). \tag{13}$$

With $w = f(\mathbf{r}(t))$, we may write $D_\mathbf{u} f(\mathbf{r}(t)) = dw/ds$ for the derivative of w with respect to (unit) distance along the parametrized curve, and $v = ds/dt$ for the speed. Then Eq. (13) takes the natural chain rule form

$$\frac{dw}{dt} = \frac{dw}{ds} \cdot \frac{ds}{dt}. \tag{14}$$

EXAMPLE 3 In Example 1 we found that the temperature function

$$w = f(x, y) = \frac{1}{180}[7400 - 4x - 9y - (0.03)xy]$$

(with temperature in degrees Celsius and distance in kilometers) has directional derivative

$$\frac{dw}{ds} = D_{\mathbf{u}} f(P) = -0.1 \frac{°C}{km}$$

at the point $P(200, 200)$ in the direction of the unit vector $\mathbf{u} = \langle \frac{3}{5}, \frac{4}{5} \rangle$. If a plane departs from an airport at P and flies in the direction $\mathbf{u}$ with speed $v = ds/dt = 5$ km/min, then Eq. (14) gives

$$\frac{dw}{dt} = \frac{dw}{ds} \cdot \frac{ds}{dt} = \left(-0.1 \frac{°C}{km}\right)\left(5 \frac{km}{min}\right) = -0.5 \frac{°C}{min}.$$

Thus an initial rate of decrease of a half-degree of temperature per minute is observed. ◆

EXAMPLE 4 Now suppose that the temperature function of Example 3 is replaced with

$$w = f(x, y, z) = \frac{1}{180}[7400 - 4x - 9y - (0.03)xy] - 2z.$$

The additional term $-2z$ corresponds to a decrease of 2°C in temperature per kilometer of altitude z. Suppose that a hawk hovering at the point $P(200, 200, 5)$ above the airport suddenly dives at a speed of 3 km/min in the direction specified by the vector $\langle 3, 4, -12 \rangle$. What instantaneous rate of change of temperature does the bird experience?

Solution The unit vector in the direction of the given vector $\langle 3, 4, -12 \rangle$ is

$$\mathbf{u} = \frac{3\mathbf{i} + 4\mathbf{j} - 12\mathbf{k}}{\sqrt{3^2 + 4^2 + (-12)^2}} = \frac{3}{13}\mathbf{i} + \frac{4}{13}\mathbf{j} - \frac{12}{13}\mathbf{k}.$$

The temperature gradient vector

$$\nabla f(x, y, z) = -\frac{1}{180}[4 + (0.03)y]\mathbf{i} - \frac{1}{180}[9 + (0.03)x]\mathbf{j} - 2\mathbf{k}$$

has the value

$$\nabla f(P) = -\frac{10}{180}\mathbf{i} - \frac{15}{180}\mathbf{j} - 2\mathbf{k}$$

at the initial position $P(200, 200, 5)$ of the hawk. Therefore the hawk's initial rate of change of temperature with respect to distance is

$$\frac{dw}{ds} = D_{\mathbf{u}} f(P) = \nabla f(P) \cdot \mathbf{u}$$

$$= \left(-\frac{10}{180}\right)\left(\frac{3}{13}\right) + \left(-\frac{15}{180}\right)\left(\frac{4}{13}\right) + (-2)\left(-\frac{12}{13}\right) = \frac{47}{26} \approx 1.808 \frac{°C}{km}.$$

Its speed is $ds/dt = 3$ km/min, so the time rate of change of temperature experienced by the hawk is

$$\frac{dw}{dt} = \frac{dw}{ds} \cdot \frac{ds}{dt} = \left(1.808 \frac{°C}{km}\right)\left(3 \frac{km}{min}\right) = 5.424 \frac{°C}{min}.$$

Thus the hawk initially gets warmer by almost 5.5 degrees per minute as it dives toward the ground. ◆

Interpretation of the Gradient Vector

The gradient vector ∇f has an important interpretation that involves the maximum possible value of the directional derivative of the differentiable function f at a given point P. If ϕ is the angle between $\nabla f(P)$ and the unit vector $\mathbf{u}$ (Fig. 13.8.4), then Eq. (11) gives

$$D_{\mathbf{u}} f(P) = \nabla f(P) \cdot \mathbf{u} = |\nabla f(P)|\,|\mathbf{u}|\cos\phi = |\nabla f(P)|\cos\phi$$

FIGURE 13.8.4 The angle ϕ between ∇f and the unit vector $\mathbf{u}$.

because $|\mathbf{u}| = 1$. The maximum possible value of $\cos\phi$ is 1, and this occurs when $\phi = 0$. This is so when $\mathbf{u}$ is the particular unit vector $\mathbf{m} = \nabla f(P)/|\nabla f(P)|$ that points in the direction of the gradient vector $\nabla f(P)$ itself. In this case the previous formula yields

$$D_{\mathbf{m}} f(P) = |\nabla f(P)|, \tag{15}$$

so the value of the directional derivative in this direction is equal to the length of the gradient vector. This argument establishes the following result.

THEOREM 2 Significance of the Gradient Vector
The maximum value of the directional derivative $D_{\mathbf{u}} f(P)$ is obtained when $\mathbf{u}$ is the unit vector in the direction of the gradient vector $\nabla f(P)$; that is, when $\mathbf{u} = \nabla f(P)/|\nabla f(P)|$. The value of the maximum directional derivative is $|\nabla f(P)|$, the length of the gradient vector.

Thus *the gradient vector ∇f points in the direction in which the function f increases the most rapidly, and its length is the rate of increase of f (with respect to distance) in that direction.* For instance, if the function f gives the temperature in space, then the gradient vector $\nabla f(P)$ points in the direction in which a hawk at P should initially fly to get warmer the fastest.

EXAMPLE 5 Recall the temperature function

$$w = f(x, y, z) = \frac{1}{180}[7400 - 4x - 9y - (0.03)xy] - 2z$$

of Example 4 (with distance in kilometers and temperature in degrees Celsius). In what direction should a hawk, starting at the point $P(200, 200, 5)$ at an altitude of 5 km, dive in order to get warmer the fastest? How rapidly will its temperature increase as it dives at a speed of 3 km/min? What will be its compass heading and angle of descent as it dives in this particular direction?

Solution In Example 4 we calculated the value

$$\nabla f(P) = -\frac{10}{180}\mathbf{i} - \frac{15}{180}\mathbf{j} - 2\mathbf{k}$$

of the gradient vector of f at the point $P(200, 200, 5)$. By Theorem 2, the maximum value

$$\frac{dw}{ds} = D_{\mathbf{m}} f(P) = |\nabla f(P)| = \sqrt{\left(-\frac{10}{180}\right)^2 + \left(-\frac{15}{180}\right)^2 + (-2)^2} \approx 2.0025$$

(°C/km) of the directional derivative of f at P is attained with the unit vector

$$\mathbf{m} = \frac{\nabla f(P)}{|\nabla f(P)|} \approx \frac{1}{2.0025}\left(-\frac{10}{180}\mathbf{i} - \frac{15}{180}\mathbf{j} - 2\mathbf{k}\right) = \frac{-10\mathbf{i} - 15\mathbf{j} - 360\mathbf{k}}{360.45}.$$

The speed of the hawk is $ds/dt = 3$ km/min, so the time rate of change of temperature experienced by the hawk is

$$\frac{dw}{dt} = \frac{dw}{ds} \cdot \frac{ds}{dt} \approx \left(2.0025\,\frac{°\text{C}}{\text{km}}\right)\left(3\,\frac{\text{km}}{\text{min}}\right) = 6.0075\,\frac{°\text{C}}{\text{min}}.$$

Thus the hawk initially gets warmer by slightly more than 6 °C/min as it dives toward the ground.

Figure 13.8.5 shows the third-quadrant vector $-10\mathbf{i} - 15\mathbf{j}$ that represents the hawk's (horizontal) compass heading of $\pi + \tan^{-1}(\frac{15}{10}) \approx 236.31°$ (about 56.31° south of west). The hawk is descending 360 meters vertically for every $\sqrt{10^2 + 15^2} \approx 18.028$ meters it flies horizontally. Hence its angle of descent (measured from the horizontal) is about $\tan^{-1}(360/18.028) \approx 87.13°$. ◆

FIGURE 13.8.5 The diving hawk's compass heading.

The Gradient Vector as a Normal Vector

Consider the graph of the equation

$$F(x, y, z) = 0, \qquad (16)$$

where the function F is continuously differentiable. The *implicit function theorem* stated in Section 13.7 (Theorem 3 there) implies that, near any point P where the partial derivative $\partial F/\partial z$ is nonzero, Eq. (16) defines z implicitly as a continuously differentiable function f of x and y. Thus the graph $F(x, y, z) = 0$ coincides—near P—with the surface $z = f(x, y)$. Similarly, the graph of Eq. (16) coincides with the surface of the form $x = g(y, z)$ near any point where $\partial F/\partial x$ is nonzero, and with a surface $y = h(x, z)$ near any point where $\partial F/\partial y$ is nonzero. In short, the graph of $F(x, y, z) = 0$ looks like a surface near any point P at which $\nabla F(P) \neq \mathbf{0}$ (so that at least one of the partial derivatives of F is nonzero). The next theorem implies that the gradient vector $\nabla F(P)$ is then normal to the surface $F(x, y, z) = 0$ at the point P.

THEOREM 3 Gradient Vector as Normal Vector
Suppose that $F(x, y, z)$ is continuously differentiable and let $P_0(x_0, y_0, z_0)$ be a point of the graph of the equation $F(x, y, z) = 0$ at which $\nabla F(P_0) \neq \mathbf{0}$. If $\mathbf{r}(t)$ is a differentiable curve on this surface with $\mathbf{r}(t_0) = \langle x_0, y_0, z_0 \rangle$ and $\mathbf{r}'(t_0) \neq \mathbf{0}$, then

$$\nabla F(P_0) \cdot \mathbf{r}'(t_0) = 0. \qquad (17)$$

Thus $\nabla F(P_0)$ is perpendicular to the tangent vector $\mathbf{r}'(t_0)$, as indicated in Fig. 13.8.6.

FIGURE 13.8.6 The gradient vector ∇F is normal to every curve in the surface $F(x, y, z) = 0$.

PROOF The statement that $\mathbf{r}(t)$ lies on the surface $F(x, y, z) = 0$ implies that $F(\mathbf{r}(t)) = 0$ for all t. Hence

$$0 = D_t F(\mathbf{r}(t_0)) = \nabla F(\mathbf{r}(t_0)) \cdot \mathbf{r}'(t_0) = \nabla F(P_0) \cdot \mathbf{r}'(t_0)$$

by the chain rule in the form in Eq. (12). Therefore the nonzero vectors $\nabla F(P_0)$ and $\mathbf{r}'(t_0)$ are perpendicular. ◂

Because the gradient vector $\nabla F(P_0)$ is perpendicular at P_0 to every curve on the surface through P_0, it is a **normal vector n** to the surface $F(x, y, z) = 0$ at the point P_0:

$$\mathbf{n} = \frac{\partial F}{\partial x}\mathbf{i} + \frac{\partial F}{\partial y}\mathbf{j} + \frac{\partial F}{\partial z}\mathbf{k}. \qquad (18)$$

If we write the explicit surface equation $z = f(x, y)$ in the form $F(x, y, z) = f(x, y) - z = 0$, then

$$\frac{\partial F}{\partial x}\mathbf{i} + \frac{\partial F}{\partial y}\mathbf{j} + \frac{\partial F}{\partial z}\mathbf{k} = \frac{\partial f}{\partial x}\mathbf{i} + \frac{\partial f}{\partial y}\mathbf{j} - \mathbf{k}.$$

Thus Eq. (18) agrees with the definition of a normal vector that we gave in Section 13.4 (Eq. (13) there).

If the tangent vector $\mathbf{T}$ to a curve is normal to the vector $\mathbf{n}$ at the point P, then $\mathbf{T}$ lies in the plane through P that is normal to $\mathbf{n}$. If the function F is continuously differentiable, we therefore *define* the **tangent plane** to the surface $F(x, y, z) = 0$ at a point $P(a, b, c)$ at which $\nabla F(P) \neq \mathbf{0}$ to be the plane through P that has the normal vector **n** given in Eq. (18). An equation of this tangent plane is then

$$F_x(a,b,c)(x-a) + F_y(a,b,c)(y-b) + F_z(a,b,c)(z-c) = 0. \quad (19)$$

EXAMPLE 6 Write an equation of the plane tangent to the ellipsoid $2x^2 + 4y^2 + z^2 = 45$ at the point $(2, -3, -1)$.

Solution If we write

$$F(x, y, z) = 2x^2 + 4y^2 + z^2 - 45,$$

then $F(x, y, z) = 0$ is an equation of the ellipsoid. Thus, by Theorem 3, a vector normal to the ellipsoidal surface at (x, y, z) is $\nabla F(x, y, z) = \langle 4x, 8y, 2z \rangle$, so

$$\nabla F(2, -3, -1) = 8\mathbf{i} - 24\mathbf{j} - 2\mathbf{k}$$

is normal to the ellipsoid at $(2, -3, -1)$. Equation (19) then gives the answer in the form

$$8(x-2) - 24(y+3) - 2(z+1) = 0;$$

that is, $4x - 12y - z = 45$. ◆

If F and G are continuously differentiable functions of three variables, then the intersection of the surfaces

$$F(x, y, z) = 0 \quad \text{and} \quad G(x, y, z) = 0 \quad (20)$$

will generally be some sort of curve C in space. More precisely, if P is a point of C where the two gradient vectors $\nabla F(P)$ and $\nabla G(P)$ are *not* collinear, then a general multivariable version of the implicit function theorem implies that near P the equations in (20) can be "solved for two of the variables in terms of the third." This means that the two equations implicitly define either x and y as functions of z, or y and z as functions of x, or x and z as functions of y. In any event, C is a smooth curve that passes through P. Because this curve lies on both surfaces, its tangent vector at P is perpendicular to both their normal vectors $\nabla F(P)$ and $\nabla G(P)$. It follows that the vector

$$\mathbf{T} = \nabla F(P) \times \nabla G(P) \quad (21)$$

is tangent at P to the curve C of intersection of the two surfaces $F(x, y, z) = 0$ and $G(x, y, z) = 0$. (See Fig. 13.8.7.)

EXAMPLE 7 The point $P(1, -1, 2)$ lies on both the paraboloid

$$F(x, y, z) = x^2 + y^2 - z = 0$$

and the ellipsoid

$$G(x, y, z) = 2x^2 + 3y^2 + z^2 - 9 = 0.$$

Write an equation of the plane through P that is normal to the curve of intersection of these two surfaces (Fig. 13.8.8).

Solution First we compute

$$\nabla F = \langle 2x, 2y, -1 \rangle \quad \text{and} \quad \nabla G = \langle 4x, 6y, 2z \rangle.$$

At $P(1, -1, 2)$ these two vectors are

$$\nabla F(1, -1, 2) = \langle 2, -2, -1 \rangle \quad \text{and} \quad \nabla G(1, -1, 2) = \langle 4, -6, 4 \rangle.$$

FIGURE 13.8.9 Gradient vectors and level curves for the function $F(x, y) = x^2 - 7xy + 2y^2$.

Hence a vector tangent at P to the curve of intersection of the paraboloid and the ellipsoid is

$$\mathbf{T} = \nabla F \times \nabla G = \begin{vmatrix} \mathbf{i} & \mathbf{j} & \mathbf{k} \\ 2 & -2 & -1 \\ 4 & -6 & 4 \end{vmatrix} = \langle -14, -12, -4 \rangle.$$

A slightly simpler vector parallel to $\mathbf{T}$ is $\mathbf{n} = \langle 7, 6, 2 \rangle$, and $\mathbf{n}$ is also normal to the desired plane through $(1, -1, 2)$. Therefore an equation of the plane is

$$7(x-1) + 6(y+1) + 2(z-2) = 0;$$

that is, $7x + 6y + 2z = 5$. ◆

A result analogous to Theorem 3 holds in two dimensions (and in higher dimensions). If the function F of two variables is continuously differentiable, then the graph of the equation $F(x, y) = 0$ looks like a smooth curve C near each point P at which $\nabla F(P) \neq \mathbf{0}$, and then the gradient vector $\nabla F(P)$ is normal to C at P. Consequently, if we use a computer algebra system to plot both a number of level curves and a "field" of different gradient vectors of the function $F(x, y)$, then (as illustrated in Fig. 13.8.9) the gradient vector at each point is normal to the level curve through that point.

EXAMPLE 8 Write an equation of the line tangent at the point $(1, 2)$ to the folium of Descartes with equation $F(x, y) = 2x^3 + 2y^3 - 9xy = 0$. (See Fig. 13.8.10.)

Solution The gradient of F is

$$\nabla F(x, y) = (6x^2 - 9y)\mathbf{i} + (6y^2 - 9x)\mathbf{j}.$$

So a vector normal to the folium at $(1, 2)$ is $\nabla F(1, 2) = -12\mathbf{i} + 15\mathbf{j}$. Hence the tangent line has equation $-12(x-1) + 15(y-2) = 0$. Simplified, this is $4x - 5y + 6 = 0$. ◆

FIGURE 13.8.10 The folium and its tangent (Example 8).

13.8 TRUE/FALSE STUDY GUIDE

13.8 CONCEPTS: QUESTIONS AND DISCUSSION

1. The partial derivatives $f_x(a, b)$ and $f_y(a, b)$ give the slopes (vertical rise per horizontal run) of the lines tangent to the x-curve $z = f(x, b)$ and the y-curve $z = f(a, y)$ through the point $(a, b, f(a, b))$ on the surface $z = f(x, y)$. What is an analogous interpretation of the directional derivative $D_\mathbf{u} f(a, b)$?

2. Suppose that you have a map showing level curves for the function $z = f(x, y)$ describing a mountain you're climbing. How can you use the level curves to sketch a path of "steepest ascent" from your present location on the mountain side to the peak of the mountain? This will be a path that at each point climbs as steeply as possible. Would your compass heading on such a path of steepest ascent always be directly toward the mountain peak?

13.8 PROBLEMS

In Problems 1 through 10, find the gradient vector ∇f at the indicated point P.

1. $f(x, y) = 3x - 7y;$ $P(17, 39)$
2. $f(x, y) = 3x^2 - 5y^2;$ $P(2, -3)$
3. $f(x, y) = \exp(-x^2 - y^2);$ $P(0, 0)$
4. $f(x, y) = \sin \frac{1}{4}\pi xy;$ $P(3, -1)$
5. $f(x, y, z) = y^2 - z^2;$ $P(17, 3, 2)$
6. $f(x, y, z) = \sqrt{x^2 + y^2 + z^2};$ $P(12, 3, 4)$
7. $f(x, y, z) = e^x \sin y + e^y \sin z + e^z \sin x;$ $P(0, 0, 0)$
8. $f(x, y, z) = x^2 - 3yz + z^3;$ $P(2, 1, 0)$
9. $f(x, y, z) = 2\sqrt{xyz};$ $P(3, -4, -3)$
10. $f(x, y, z) = (2x - 3y + 5z)^5;$ $P(-5, 1, 3)$

In Problems 11 through 20, find the directional derivative of f at P in the direction of $\mathbf{v}$; that is, find
$$D_{\mathbf{u}} f(P), \quad \text{where} \quad \mathbf{u} = \frac{\mathbf{v}}{|\mathbf{v}|}.$$

11. $f(x, y) = x^2 + 2xy + 3y^2$; $P(2, 1)$, $\mathbf{v} = \langle 1, 1 \rangle$
12. $f(x, y) = e^x \sin y$; $P(0, \pi/4)$, $\mathbf{v} = \langle 1, -1 \rangle$
13. $f(x, y) = x^3 - x^2 y + xy^2 + y^3$; $P(1, -1)$, $\mathbf{v} = 2\mathbf{i} + 3\mathbf{j}$
14. $f(x, y) = \tan^{-1}\left(\frac{y}{x}\right)$; $P(-3, 3)$, $\mathbf{v} = 3\mathbf{i} + 4\mathbf{j}$
15. $f(x, y) = \sin x \cos y$; $P(\pi/3, -2\pi/3)$, $\mathbf{v} = \langle 4, -3 \rangle$
16. $f(x, y, z) = xy + yz + zx$; $P(1, -1, 2)$, $\mathbf{v} = \langle 1, 1, 1 \rangle$
17. $f(x, y, z) = \sqrt{xyz}$; $P(2, -1, -2)$, $\mathbf{v} = \mathbf{i} + 2\mathbf{j} - 2\mathbf{k}$
18. $f(x, y, z) = \ln(1 + x^2 + y^2 - z^2)$; $P(1, -1, 1)$, $\mathbf{v} = 2\mathbf{i} - 2\mathbf{j} - 3\mathbf{k}$
19. $f(x, y, z) = e^{xyz}$; $P(4, 0, -3)$, $\mathbf{v} = \mathbf{j} - \mathbf{k}$
20. $f(x, y, z) = \sqrt{10 - x^2 - y^2 - z^2}$; $P(1, 1, -2)$, $\mathbf{v} = \langle 3, 4, -12 \rangle$

In Problems 21 through 28, find the maximum directional derivative of f at P and the direction in which it occurs.

21. $f(x, y) = 2x^2 + 3xy + 4y^2$; $P(1, 1)$
22. $f(x, y) = \arctan\left(\frac{y}{x}\right)$; $P(2, -3)$
23. $f(x, y) = \ln(x^2 + y^2)$; $P(3, 4)$
24. $f(x, y) = \sin(3x - 4y)$; $P(\pi/3, \pi/4)$
25. $f(x, y, z) = 3x^2 + y^2 + 4z^2$; $P(1, 5, -2)$
26. $f(x, y, z) = \exp(x - y - z)$; $P(5, 2, 3)$
27. $f(x, y, z) = \sqrt{xy^2 z^3}$; $P(2, 2, 2)$
28. $f(x, y, z) = \sqrt{2x + 4y + 6z}$; $P(7, 5, 5)$

In Problems 29 through 34, use the normal gradient vector to write an equation of the line (or plane) tangent to the given curve (or surface) at the given point P.

29. $\exp(25 - x^2 - y^2) = 1$; $P(3, 4)$
30. $2x^2 + 3y^2 = 35$; $P(2, 3)$
31. $x^4 + xy + y^2 = 19$; $P(2, -3)$
32. $3x^2 + 4y^2 + 5z^2 = 73$; $P(2, 2, 3)$
33. $x^{1/3} + y^{1/3} + z^{1/3} = 1$; $P(1, -1, 1)$
34. $xyz + x^2 - 2y^2 + z^3 = 14$; $P(5, -2, 3)$

The properties of gradient vectors listed in Problems 35 through 38 exhibit the close analogy between the gradient operator ∇ and the single-variable derivative operator D. Verify each, assuming that a and b are constants and that u and v are differentiable functions of x and y.

35. $\nabla(au + bv) = a\nabla u + b\nabla v$.
36. $\nabla(uv) = u\nabla v + v\nabla u$.
37. $\nabla\left(\frac{u}{v}\right) = \frac{v\nabla u - u\nabla v}{v^2}$ if $v \neq 0$.
38. If n is a positive integer, then $\nabla u^n = nu^{n-1}\nabla u$.
39. Show that the value of a differentiable function f decreases the most rapidly at P in the direction of the vector $-\nabla f(P)$, directly opposite to the gradient vector.

40. Suppose that f is a function of three independent variables x, y, and z. Show that $D_{\mathbf{i}} f = f_x$, $D_{\mathbf{j}} f = f_y$, and $D_{\mathbf{k}} f = f_z$.

41. Show that the equation of the line tangent to the conic section $Ax^2 + Bxy + Cy^2 = D$ at the point (x_0, y_0) is
$$(Ax_0)x + \tfrac{1}{2}B(y_0 x + x_0 y) + (Cy_0)y = D.$$

42. Show that the equation of the plane tangent to the quadric surface $Ax^2 + By^2 + Cz^2 = D$ at the point (x_0, y_0, z_0) is
$$(Ax_0)x + (By_0)y + (Cz_0)z = D.$$

43. Show that an equation of the plane tangent to the paraboloid $z = Ax^2 + By^2$ at the point (x_0, y_0, z_0) is $z + z_0 = 2Ax_0 x + 2By_0 y$.

44. Suppose that the temperature at the point (x, y, z) in space, with distance measured in kilometers, is given by
$$w = f(x, y, z) = 10 + xy + xz + yz$$
(in degrees Celsius). Find the rate of change (in degrees Celsius per kilometer) of temperature at the point $P(1, 2, 3)$ in the direction of the vector $\mathbf{v} = \mathbf{i} + 2\mathbf{j} - 2\mathbf{k}$.

45. Suppose that the function
$$w = f(x, y, z) = 10 + xy + xz + yz$$
of Problem 44 gives the temperature at the point (x, y, z) of space. (Units in this problem are in kilometers, degrees Celsius, and minutes.) What time rate of change (in degrees Celsius per minute) will a hawk observe as it flies through $P(1, 2, 3)$ at a speed of 2 km/min, heading directly toward the point $Q(3, 4, 4)$?

46. Suppose that the temperature w (in degrees Celsius) at the point (x, y) is given by
$$w = f(x, y) = 10 + (0.003)x^2 - (0.004)y^2.$$
In what direction $\mathbf{u}$ should a bumblebee at the point $(40, 30)$ initially fly in order to get warmer the most quickly? Find the directional derivative $D_{\mathbf{u}} f(40, 30)$ in this optimal direction $\mathbf{u}$.

47. Suppose that the temperature W (in degrees Celsius) at the point (x, y, z) in space is given by
$$W = 50 + xyz.$$
(a) Find the rate of change of temperature with respect to distance at the point $P(3, 4, 1)$ in the direction of the vector $\mathbf{v} = \langle 1, 2, 2 \rangle$. (The units of distance in space are feet.) (b) Find the maximal directional derivative $D_{\mathbf{u}} W$ at the point $P(3, 4, 1)$ and the direction $\mathbf{u}$ in which that maximum occurs.

48. Suppose that the temperature (in degrees Celsius) at the point (x, y, z) in space is given by the formula
$$W = 100 - x^2 - y^2 - z^2.$$
The units of distance in space are meters. (a) Find the rate of change of temperature at the point $P(3, -4, 5)$ in the direction of the vector $\mathbf{v} = 3\mathbf{i} - 4\mathbf{j} + 12\mathbf{k}$. (b) In what direction does W increase most rapidly at P? What is the value of the maximal directional derivative at P?

49. Suppose that the altitude z (in miles above sea level) of a certain hill is described by the equation $z = f(x, y)$, where
$$f(x, y) = \frac{1}{10}(x^2 - xy + 2y^2).$$

(a) Write an equation (in the form $z = ax + by + c$) of the plane tangent to the hillside at the point $P(2, 1, 0.4)$.
(b) Use $\nabla f(2, 1)$ to approximate the altitude of the hill above the point $(2.2, 0.9)$ in the xy-plane. Compare your result with the actual altitude at this point.

50. Find an equation for the plane tangent to the paraboloid $z = 2x^2 + 3y^2$ and, simultaneously, parallel to the plane $4x - 3y - z = 10$.

51. The cone with equation $z^2 = x^2 + y^2$ and the plane with equation $2x + 3y + 4z + 2 = 0$ intersect in an ellipse. Write an equation of the plane normal to this ellipse at the point $P(3, 4, -5)$ (Fig. 13.8.11).

52. It is apparent from geometry that the highest and lowest points of the ellipse of Problem 51 are those points where its tangent line is horizontal. Find those points.

53. Show that the sphere $x^2 + y^2 + z^2 = r^2$ and the cone $z^2 = a^2 x^2 + b^2 y^2$ are orthogonal (that is, have perpendicular tangent planes) at every point of their intersection (Fig. 13.8.12).

FIGURE 13.8.11 The cone and plane of Problems 51 and 52.

FIGURE 13.8.12 A cut-away view of the cone and sphere of Problem 53.

54. Suppose that $\mathcal{P}_1$ and $\mathcal{P}_2$ are planes tangent to the circular ellipsoid $x^2 + y^2 + 2z^2 = 2$ at the two points P_1 and P_2 having the same z-coordinate. Show that $\mathcal{P}_1$ and $\mathcal{P}_2$ intersect the z-axis at the same point.

55. A plane tangent to the surface $xyz = 1$ at a point in the first octant cuts off a pyramid from the first octant. Show that any two such pyramids have the same volume.

In Problems 56 through 61, the function $z = f(x, y)$ describes the shape of a hill; $f(P)$ is the altitude of the hill above the point $P(x, y)$ in the xy-plane. If you start at the point $(P, f(P))$ of this hill, then $D_{\mathbf{u}} f(P)$ is your rate of climb (rise per unit of horizontal distance) as you proceed in the horizontal direction $\mathbf{u} = a\mathbf{i} + b\mathbf{j}$. And the angle at which you climb while you walk in this direction is $\gamma = \tan^{-1}(D_{\mathbf{u}} f(P))$, as shown in Fig. 13.8.13.

56. You are standing at the point $(-100, -100, 430)$ on a hill that has the shape of the graph of
$$z = 500 - (0.003)x^2 - (0.004)y^2,$$
with x, y, and z given in feet. (a) What will be your rate of climb (*rise* over *run*) if you head northwest? At what angle from the horizontal will you be climbing? (b) Repeat part (a), except now you head northeast.

FIGURE 13.8.13 The cross section of the part of the graph above $\mathbf{u}$ (Problems 56 through 61).

57. You are standing at the point $(-100, -100, 430)$ on the hill of Problem 56. In what direction (that is, with what compass heading) should you proceed in order to climb the most steeply? At what angle from the horizontal will you initially be climbing?

58. Repeat Problem 56, but now you are standing at the point $P(100, 100, 500)$ on the hill described by
$$z = \frac{1000}{1 + (0.00003)x^2 + (0.00007)y^2}.$$

59. Repeat Problem 57, except begin at the point $P(100, 100, 500)$ of the hill of Problem 58.

60. You are standing at the point $(30, 20, 5)$ on a hill with the shape of the surface
$$z = 100 \exp\left(-\frac{x^2 + 3y^2}{701}\right).$$
(a) In what direction (with what compass heading) should you proceed in order to climb the most steeply? At what angle from the horizontal will you initially be climbing? (b) If, instead of climbing as in part (a), you head directly west (the negative x-direction), then at what angle will you be climbing initially?

61. (a) You are standing at the point where $x = y = 100$ (ft) on the side of a mountain whose height (in feet above sea level) is given by
$$z = \frac{1}{1000}(3x^2 - 5xy + y^2),$$
with the x-axis pointing east and the y-axis pointing north. If you head northeast, will you be ascending or descending? At what angle (in degrees) from the horizontal? (b) If you head 30° north of east, will you be ascending or descending? At what angle (in degrees) from the horizontal?

62. Suppose that the two surfaces $f(x, y, z) = 0$ and $g(x, y, z) = 0$ both pass through the point P where both gradient vectors $\nabla f(P)$ and $\nabla g(P)$ exist. (a) Show that the two surfaces are tangent at P if and only if $\nabla f(P) \times \nabla g(P) = \mathbf{0}$. (b) Show that the two surfaces are orthogonal at P if and only if $\nabla f(P) \cdot \nabla g(P) = 0$.

63. Suppose that the plane vectors $\mathbf{u}$ and $\mathbf{v}$ are not collinear and that the function $f(x, y)$ is differentiable at P. Show that the values of the directional derivatives $D_{\mathbf{u}} f(P)$ and $D_{\mathbf{v}} f(P)$ determine the value of the directional derivative of f at P in every other direction.

64. Show that the function $f(x, y) = (\sqrt[3]{x} + \sqrt[3]{y})^3$ is continuous at the origin and has directional derivatives in all directions there, but is not differentiable at the origin.

13.9 LAGRANGE MULTIPLIERS AND CONSTRAINED OPTIMIZATION

In Section 13.5 we discussed the problem of finding the maximum and minimum values attained by a function $f(x, y)$ at points of the plane region R, in the simple case in which R consists of the points on and within the simple closed curve C. We saw that any local maximum or minimum in the *interior* of R occurs at a point where $f_x(x, y) = 0 = f_y(x, y)$ or at a point where f is not differentiable (the latter usually signaled by the failure of f_x or f_y to exist). Here we discuss the very different matter of finding the maximum and minimum values attained by f at points of the *boundary* curve C.

If the curve C is the graph of the equation $g(x, y) = 0$, then our task is to maximize or minimize the function $f(x, y)$ subject to the **constraint,** or **side condition,**

$$g(x, y) = 0. \qquad (1)$$

We could in principle try to solve this constraint equation for $y = \phi(x)$ and then maximize or minimize the single-variable function $f(x, \phi(x))$ by the standard method of finding its critical points. But what if it is impractical or impossible to solve Eq. (1) explicitly for y in terms of x? An alternative approach that does not require that we first solve this equation is the **method of Lagrange multipliers.** It is named for its discoverer, the Italian-born French mathematician Joseph Louis Lagrange (1736–1813). The method is based on Theorem 1.

THEOREM 1 Lagrange Multiplier (with one constraint)
Let $f(x, y)$ and $g(x, y)$ be continuously differentiable functions. If the maximum (or minimum) value of $f(x, y)$ subject to the constraint

$$g(x, y) = 0 \qquad (1)$$

occurs at a point P where $\nabla g(P) \neq \mathbf{0}$, then

$$\nabla f(P) = \lambda \nabla g(P) \qquad (2)$$

for some constant λ.

PROOF Because $\nabla g(P) \neq \mathbf{0}$, the implicit function theorem implies that the graph C of the constraint equation $g(x, y) = 0$ agrees near $P(x_0, y_0)$ with the graph of a continuously differentiable single-variable function—either $y = \alpha(x)$ or $x = \beta(y)$. Either case provides a smooth parametric curve $\mathbf{r}(t)$ whose image agrees near P with C. For instance, in the case $y = \alpha(x)$ we define $\mathbf{r}(t) = \langle t, \alpha(t) \rangle$. If $\mathbf{r}(t_0) = \langle x_0, y_0 \rangle$, then $\mathbf{r}'(t_0) = \langle 1, \alpha'(t_0) \rangle \neq \mathbf{0}$ as indicated in Fig. 13.9.1. If $f(x, y)$ attains its maximum (or minimum) value on C at $P(x_0, y_0)$, then the composite function $F(t) = f(\mathbf{r}(t))$ attains its maximum (or minimum) value at $t = t_0$, so that $F'(t_0) = 0$. Therefore

$$F'(t_0) = \nabla f(\mathbf{r}(t_0)) \cdot \mathbf{r}'(t_0) = \nabla f(P) \cdot \mathbf{r}'(t_0) = 0 \qquad (3)$$

by the gradient vector form of the chain rule of Eq. (12) in Section 13.8.

Because $\mathbf{r}(t)$ lies on the curve $g(x, y) = 0$, the composite function $G(t) = g(\mathbf{r}(t))$ is constant-valued—$G(t) \equiv 0$—so $G'(t) \equiv 0$. Therefore

$$G'(t_0) = \nabla g(\mathbf{r}(t_0)) \cdot \mathbf{r}'(t_0) = \nabla g(P) \cdot \mathbf{r}'(t_0) = 0. \qquad (4)$$

Equations (3) and (4), when taken together, imply that the two-dimensional plane vectors $\nabla f(P)$ and $\nabla g(P)$ are both perpendicular to the nonzero vector $\mathbf{r}'(t_0)$, and are therefore collinear. Because $\nabla g(P) \neq \mathbf{0}$, it now follows that $\nabla f(P)$ must be a scalar multiple of $\nabla g(P)$, just as claimed in Eq. (2). ◄

FIGURE 13.9.1 The conclusion of Theorem 1 illustrated.

The Method

Let's see what steps we should follow to solve a problem by using Theorem 1—the method of Lagrange multipliers. First we need to identify a quantity $z = f(x, y)$ to be maximized or minimized, subject to the constraint $g(x, y) = 0$. Then Eq. (1) and the two scalar components of Eq. (2) yield three equations:

$$g(x, y) = 0, \tag{1}$$

$$f_x(x, y) = \lambda g_x(x, y), \quad \text{and} \tag{2a}$$

$$f_y(x, y) = \lambda g_y(x, y). \tag{2b}$$

Thus we have three equations that we can attempt to solve for the three unknowns x, y, and λ. The points (x, y) that we find (assuming that our efforts are successful) are the only possible locations for the extrema of f subject to the constraint $g(x, y) = 0$. The associated values of λ, called **Lagrange multipliers,** may be revealed as well but often are not of much interest. Finally, we calculate the value $f(x, y)$ at each of the solution points (x, y) in order to identify its maximum and minimum values.

We must bear in mind the additional possibility that the maximum or minimum (or both) of f may occur at a point where $g_x(x, y) = 0 = g_y(x, y)$. The Lagrange multiplier method may fail to locate these exceptional points, but they can usually be recognized as points where the graph of $g(x, y) = 0$ fails to be a smooth curve.

EXAMPLE 1 Find the points of the rectangular hyperbola $xy = 1$ that are closest to the origin $(0, 0)$.

Solution We need to minimize the distance $d = \sqrt{x^2 + y^2}$ from the origin of a point $P(x, y)$ on the curve $xy = 1$. But the algebra is simpler if instead we minimize the square

$$f(x, y) = x^2 + y^2$$

of this distance subject to the constraint

$$g(x, y) = xy - 1 = 0$$

that the point P lies on the hyperbola. Because

$$\frac{\partial f}{\partial x} = 2x, \quad \frac{\partial f}{\partial y} = 2y, \quad \text{and} \quad \frac{\partial g}{\partial x} = y, \quad \frac{\partial g}{\partial y} = x,$$

the Lagrange multiplier equations in (2a) and (2b) take the form

$$2x = \lambda y, \quad 2y = \lambda x.$$

If we multiply the first of these equations by x and the second by y, we can conclude that

$$2x^2 = \lambda xy = 2y^2$$

at $P(x, y)$. But the fact that $xy = 1 > 0$ implies that x and y have the same sign. Hence the fact that $x^2 = y^2$ implies that $x = y$. Substituting in $xy = 1$ then gives $x^2 = 1$, so it follows finally that either $x = y = 1$ or $x = y = -1$. The two resulting possibilities $(1, 1)$ and $(-1, -1)$ are indicated in Fig. 13.9.2. ◆

FIGURE 13.9.2 The level curve $f(x, y) = M$ and the constraint curve $g(x, y) = 0$ are tangent at a point P where the maximum or minimum value M is attained.

REMARK Example 1 illustrates an interesting geometric interpretation of Theorem 1. We see in Fig. 13.9.2 the constraint curve $g(x, y) = 0$ together with typical level curves of the function $f(x, y)$. Because the gradient vectors ∇f and ∇g are normal to the level curves of the functions f and g, respectively, it follows that the curves $f(x, y) = M$ and $g(x, y) = 0$ are tangent to one another at the point P where the two gradient vectors are collinear and f attains its maximum (or minimum) value M. In effect, the Lagrange multiplier criterion serves to select, from among the level curves of f, the one that is tangent to the constraint curve at P. Thus we see in Fig. 13.9.2 that the circle $x^2 + y^2 = 2$ and the hyperbola $xy = 1$ are, indeed, tangent at the two points $(1, 1)$ and $(-1, -1)$ where the squared distance $f(x, y) = x^2 + y^2$ is minimal subject to the constraint $g(x, y) = xy - 1$.

FIGURE 13.9.3 Cutting a rectangular beam from an elliptical log (Example 2).

EXAMPLE 2 In the sawmill problem of Example 5 in Section 3.6, we maximized the cross-sectional area of a rectangular beam cut from a circular log. Now we consider the elliptical log of Fig. 13.9.3, with semiaxes of lengths $a = 2$ ft and $b = 1$ ft. What is the maximal cross-sectional area of a rectangular beam cut as indicated from this elliptical log?

Solution The log is bounded by the ellipse $(x/2)^2 + y^2 = 1$; that is, $x^2 + 4y^2 = 4$. So with the coordinate system indicated in Fig. 13.9.3, we want to maximize the cross-sectional area

$$A = f(x, y) = 4xy \tag{5}$$

of the beam subject to the constraint

$$g(x, y) = x^2 + 4y^2 - 4 = 0. \tag{6}$$

Because

$$\frac{\partial f}{\partial x} = 4y, \quad \frac{\partial f}{\partial y} = 4x \quad \text{and} \quad \frac{\partial g}{\partial x} = 2x, \quad \frac{\partial g}{\partial y} = 8y,$$

Eqs. (2a) and (2b) give

$$4y = 2\lambda x, \quad 4x = 8\lambda y.$$

It is clear that neither $x = 0$ nor $y = 0$ gives the maximum area, so we can solve these two multiplier equations for

$$\frac{2y}{x} = \lambda = \frac{x}{2y}.$$

Thus $x^2 = 4y^2$ at the desired maximum. Because $x^2 + 4y^2 = 4$, it follows that $x^2 = 4y^2 = 2$. Because we seek (as in Fig. 13.9.3) a first-quadrant solution point (x, y), we conclude that $x = \sqrt{2}$, $y = 1/\sqrt{2}$ gives the maximum possible cross-sectional area $A_{\max} = 4(\sqrt{2})(1/\sqrt{2}) = 4$ ft² of a rectangular beam cut from the elliptical log. Note that this maximum area of 4 ft² is about 64% of the total cross-sectional area $A = \pi a b = 2\pi$ ft² of the original log. ◆

REMARK If we consider all four quadrants, then the condition $x^2 = 4y^2 = 2$ yields the *four* points $(\sqrt{2}, 1/\sqrt{2})$, $(-\sqrt{2}, 1/\sqrt{2})$, $(-\sqrt{2}, -1/\sqrt{2})$, and $(\sqrt{2}, -1/\sqrt{2})$. The function $f(x, y) = 4xy$ in Eq. (5) attains its maximum value $+4$ on the ellipse $x^2 + 4y^2 = 4$ at the first and third of these points and its minimum value -4 at the second and fourth points. The Lagrange multiplier method thus locates all of the global extrema of $f(x, y)$ on the ellipse.

In the applied maximum-minimum problems of Section 3.6, we typically began with a *formula* such as Eq. (5) of this section, expressing the quantity to be maximized in terms of *two* variables x and y, for example. We then used some available *relation* such as Eq. (6) between the variables x and y to eliminate one of them, such as y. Thus we finally obtained a single-variable *function* by substituting for y in terms of x in the original formula. As in Example 2, the Lagrange multiplier method frees us from the necessity of formulating the problem in terms of a single-variable function, and frequently leads to a solution process that is algebraically simpler and easier.

Lagrange Multipliers in Three Dimensions

Now suppose that $f(x, y, z)$ and $g(x, y, z)$ are continuously differentiable functions and that we want to find the points on the *surface*

$$g(x, y, z) = 0 \tag{7}$$

at which the function $f(x, y, z)$ attains its maximum and minimum values. Theorem 1 holds precisely as we have stated it, except with three independent variables rather than two. We leave the details to Problem 45, but an argument similar to the proof

Lagrange Multipliers and Constrained Optimization **SECTION 13.9** 921

of Theorem 1 shows that—at a maximum or minimum point P of $f(x, y, z)$ on the surface $g(x, y, z) = 0$—the two gradient vectors $\nabla f(P)$ and $\nabla g(P)$ are both perpendicular to every smooth curve on the surface through P. Hence they are both normal to the surface at P, and are therefore collinear. (See Fig. 13.9.4.) Because $\nabla g(P) \neq \mathbf{0}$, it follows that

$$\nabla f(P) = \lambda \nabla g(P) \tag{8}$$

for some scalar λ. This vector equation corresponds to three scalar equations. To find the possible locations of the extrema of f subject to the constraint g, we can attempt to solve simultaneously the four equations

FIGURE 13.9.4 The natural generalization of Theorem 1 holds for functions of three variables.

$$g(x, y, z) = 0, \tag{7}$$
$$f_x(x, y, z) = \lambda g_x(x, y, z), \tag{8a}$$
$$f_y(x, y, z) = \lambda g_y(x, y, z), \tag{8b}$$
$$f_z(x, y, z) = \lambda g_z(x, y, z) \tag{8c}$$

for the four unknowns x, y, z, and λ. If successful, we then evaluate $f(x, y, z)$ at each of the solution points (x, y, z) to see at which it attains its maximum and minimum values. In analogy to the two-dimensional case, we also check points at which the surface $g(x, y, z) = 0$ fails to be smooth. Thus the Lagrange multiplier method with one constraint is essentially the same in dimension three as in dimension two.

EXAMPLE 3 Find the maximum volume of a rectangular box inscribed in the ellipsoid $x^2/a^2 + y^2/b^2 + z^2/c^2 = 1$ with its faces parallel to the coordinate planes (Fig. 13.9.5).

Solution Let $P(x, y, z)$ be the vertex of the box that lies in the first octant (where x, y, and z are all positive). We want to maximize the volume $V(x, y, z) = 8xyz$ subject to the constraint

$$g(x, y, z) = \frac{x^2}{a^2} + \frac{y^2}{b^2} + \frac{z^2}{c^2} - 1 = 0.$$

FIGURE 13.9.5 A rectangular $2x \times 2y \times 2z$ box inscribed in an ellipsoid with semiaxes a, b, and c. The whole box is determined by its first-octant vertex $P(x, y, z)$.

Equations (8a), (8b), and (8c) give

$$8yz = \frac{2\lambda x}{a^2}, \quad 8xz = \frac{2\lambda y}{b^2}, \quad 8xy = \frac{2\lambda z}{c^2}.$$

Part of the art of mathematics lies in pausing for a moment to find an elegant way to solve a problem rather than rushing in headlong with brute force methods. Here, if we multiply the first equation by x, the second by y, and the third by z, we find that

$$2\lambda \frac{x^2}{a^2} = 2\lambda \frac{y^2}{b^2} = 2\lambda \frac{z^2}{c^2} = 8xyz.$$

Now $\lambda \neq 0$ because (at maximum volume) x, y, and z are nonzero. We conclude that

$$\frac{x^2}{a^2} = \frac{y^2}{b^2} = \frac{z^2}{c^2}.$$

The sum of the last three expressions is 1, because that is precisely the constraint condition in this problem. Thus each of these three expressions is equal to $\frac{1}{3}$. All three of x, y, and z are positive, and therefore

$$x = \frac{a}{\sqrt{3}}, \quad y = \frac{b}{\sqrt{3}}, \quad \text{and} \quad z = \frac{c}{\sqrt{3}}.$$

Therefore, the box of maximum volume has volume

$$V = V_{\max} = \frac{8}{3\sqrt{3}} abc.$$

Note that this answer is dimensionally correct—the product of the three *lengths* a, b, and c yields a *volume*. But because the volume of the ellipsoid is $V = \frac{4}{3}\pi abc$, and $[8/(3\sqrt{3})]/(4\pi/3) = 2/(\pi\sqrt{3}) \approx 0.37$, it follows that the maximal box occupies only about 37% of the volume of the circumscribed ellipsoid. Considering the 64% result in Example 2, would you consider this result plausible, or surprising? ◆

Problems that have Two Constraints

Suppose that we want to find the maximum and minimum values of the function $f(x, y, z)$ at points of the curve of intersection of the two surfaces

$$g(x, y, z) = 0 \quad \text{and} \quad h(x, y, z) = 0. \tag{9}$$

This is a maximum-minimum problem with *two* constraints. The Lagrange multiplier method for such situations is based on Theorem 2.

THEOREM 2 Lagrange Multipliers (with two constraints)

Suppose that $f(x, y, z)$, $g(x, y, z)$, and $h(x, y, z)$ are continuously differentiable functions. If the maximum (or minimum) value of $f(x, y, z)$ subject to the two constraints

$$g(x, y, z) = 0 \quad \text{and} \quad h(x, y, z) = 0 \tag{9}$$

occurs at a point P where the vectors $\nabla g(P)$ and $\nabla h(P)$ are nonzero and nonparallel, then

$$\nabla f(P) = \lambda_1 \nabla g(P) + \lambda_2 \nabla h(P) \tag{10}$$

for some two constants λ_1 and λ_2.

OUTLINE OF PROOF By an appropriate version of the implicit function theorem, the curve C of intersection of the two surfaces (Fig. 13.9.6) may be represented near P by a parametric curve $\mathbf{r}(t)$ with nonzero tangent vector $\mathbf{r}'(t)$. Let t_0 be the value of t such that $\mathbf{r}(t_0) = \overrightarrow{OP}$. We compute the derivatives at t_0 of the composite functions $f(\mathbf{r}(t))$, $g(\mathbf{r}(t))$, and $h(\mathbf{r}(t))$. We find—exactly as in the proof of Theorem 1—that

$$\nabla f(P) \cdot \mathbf{r}'(t_0) = 0, \quad \nabla g(P) \cdot \mathbf{r}'(t_0) = 0, \quad \text{and} \quad \nabla h(P) \cdot \mathbf{r}'(t_0) = 0.$$

These three equations imply that all three gradient vectors are perpendicular to the curve C at P and thus that they all lie in a single plane, the plane normal to the curve C at the point P.

Now $\nabla g(P)$ and $\nabla h(P)$ are nonzero and nonparallel, so $\nabla f(P)$ is the sum of its projections onto $\nabla g(P)$ and $\nabla h(P)$. (See Problem 65 of Section 12.2.) As illustrated in Fig. 13.9.7, this fact implies Eq. (10). ◂

FIGURE 13.9.6 The relation between the gradient vectors in the proof of Theorem 2.

In examples we prefer to avoid subscripts by writing λ and μ for the Lagrange multipliers λ_1 and λ_2 in the statement of Theorem 2. The equations in (9) and the three scalar components of the vector equation in (10) then give rise to the five simultaneous equations

$$g(x, y, z) = 0, \tag{9a}$$

$$h(x, y, z) = 0, \tag{9b}$$

$$f_x(x, y, z) = \lambda g_x(x, y, z) + \mu h_x(x, y, z), \tag{10a}$$

$$f_y(x, y, z) = \lambda g_y(x, y, z) + \mu h_y(x, y, z), \tag{10b}$$

$$f_z(x, y, z) = \lambda g_z(x, y, z) + \mu h_z(x, y, z) \tag{10c}$$

FIGURE 13.9.7 Geometry of the equation $\nabla f(P) = \lambda_1 \nabla g(P) + \lambda_2 \nabla h(P)$.

in the five unknowns x, y, z, λ, and μ.

FIGURE 13.9.8 The plane and paraboloid intersecting in the ellipse of Example 4.

EXAMPLE 4 The plane $x + y + z = 12$ intersects the paraboloid $z = x^2 + y^2$ in an ellipse (Fig. 13.9.8). Find the highest and lowest points on this ellipse.

Solution The height of the point (x, y, z) is z, so we want to find the maximum and minimum values of

$$f(x, y, z) = z \tag{11}$$

subject to the two conditions

$$g(x, y, z) = x + y + z - 12 = 0 \tag{12}$$

and

$$h(x, y, z) = x^2 + y^2 - z = 0. \tag{13}$$

The conditions in (10a) through (10c) yield

$$0 = \lambda + 2\mu x, \tag{14a}$$

$$0 = \lambda + 2\mu y, \tag{14b}$$

and

$$1 = \lambda - \mu. \tag{14c}$$

If μ were zero, then Eq. (14a) would imply that $\lambda = 0$, which contradicts Eq. (14c). Hence $\mu \neq 0$, and therefore the equations

$$2\mu x = -\lambda = 2\mu y$$

imply that $x = y$. Substituting $x = y$ into Eq. (13) gives $z = 2x^2$, and then Eq. (12) yields

$$2x^2 + 2x - 12 = 0;$$

$$2(x + 3)(x - 2) = 0.$$

Thus we obtain the two solutions $x = -3$ and $x = 2$. Because $y = x$ and $z = 2x^2$, the corresponding points of the ellipse are $P_1(2, 2, 8)$ and $P_2(-3, -3, 18)$. It's clear which is the lowest and which is the highest. ◆

More Variables, More Constraints

Many practical constrained optimization problems have more than three variables and/or more than two constraints. For instance, Problem 48 is a concrete plane geometry problem with four independent variables.

There is a general form of the Lagrange multiplier condition that applies to any such problem, whatever the numbers of variables and constraints. We need only adjoin an additional term to the right-hand side in Eq. (10) for each additional constraint. The resulting condition for maximizing or minimizing the value $f(x_1, x_2, \ldots, x_n)$ of a function of n variables subject to the k constraints

$$\begin{aligned} g_1(x_1, x_2, \ldots, x_n) &= 0, \\ g_2(x_1, x_2, \ldots, x_n) &= 0, \\ &\vdots \\ g_k(x_1, x_2, \ldots, x_n) &= 0 \end{aligned} \tag{15}$$

is

$$\nabla f(P) = \lambda_1 \nabla g_1(P) + \lambda_2 \nabla g_2(P) + \cdots + \lambda_k \nabla g_k(P), \tag{16}$$

where we write $P = (x_1, x_2, \ldots, x_n)$. This condition holds under the assumptions that the functions $f, g_1, g_2, \ldots,$ and g_k are continuously differentiable near the optimal point P, and that—in the language of linear algebra—the gradient vectors

$\nabla g_1(P), \nabla g_2(P), \ldots, \nabla g_k(P)$ are linearly independent in $\mathbf{R}^n$. The latter hypothesis means that no one of these k vectors can be expressed as a linear combination of the other $k-1$. The corresponding theorem is stated and proved in Chapter II of Edwards: *Advanced Calculus of Several Variables* (New York: Dover Publications, 1994).

Each of the gradient vectors in Eq. (16) has n components. When the resulting n "scalar component equations" are combined (Problem 61) with the k scalar equations in (15), we obtain the $k+n$ scalar equations

$$g_1(x_1, x_2, \ldots, x_n) = 0, \ldots, g_k(x_1, x_2, \ldots, x_n) = 0,$$
$$D_1 f(x_1, x_2, \ldots, x_n) = \lambda_1 D_1 g_1(x_1, x_2, \ldots, x_n) + \cdots + \lambda_k D_1 g_k(x_1, x_2, \ldots, x_n),$$
$$D_2 f(x_1, x_2, \ldots, x_n) = \lambda_1 D_2 g_1(x_1, x_2, \ldots, x_n) + \cdots + \lambda_k D_2 g_k(x_1, x_2, \ldots, x_n), \quad (17)$$
$$\vdots$$
$$D_n f(x_1, x_2, \ldots, x_n) = \lambda_1 D_n g_1(x_1, x_2, \ldots, x_n) + \cdots + \lambda_k D_n g_k(x_1, x_2, \ldots, x_n)$$

to solve for the $k+n$ unknowns $\lambda_1, \lambda_2, \ldots, \lambda_k, x_1, x_2, \ldots, x_n$.

For instance, suppose that we ask for the minimal distance between points $P(x, y, z)$ and $Q(u, v, w)$ on two different space curves, each of which is presented as the intersection of two surfaces. We have the six coordinates $x, y, z, u, v,$ and w of the two points and the four constraint equations of the four given surfaces. Then the system in (17) becomes a system of ten equations in the ten unknowns $x, y, z, u, v, w, \lambda_1, \lambda_2, \lambda_3,$ and λ_4. See Problem 65, where the two curves are skew lines in space. This is a comparatively simple case, but you surely will want to use a computer algebra system to solve the problem. (See the CD-ROM project material for this section.)

13.9 TRUE/FALSE STUDY GUIDE

13.9 CONCEPTS: QUESTIONS AND DISCUSSION

Give examples of continuously differentiable functions $f, g : \mathbf{R}^2 \to \mathbf{R}$ *satisfying the conditions in Questions 1 through 3.*

1. $f(x, y)$ attains a minimum value but no maximum value subject to the constraint $g(x, y) = 0$.
2. $f(x, y)$ attains neither a maximum value nor a minimum value subject to the constraint $g(x, y) = 0$.
3. $f(x, y)$ attains its maximum value subject to the constraint $g(x, y) = 0$ at a point P where $\nabla f(P) \neq \lambda \nabla g(P)$ for any λ. (In view of Theorem 1, how is this possible?)

13.9 PROBLEMS

In Problems 1 through 18, find the maximum and minimum values—if any—of the given function f subject to the given constraint or constraints.

1. $f(x, y) = 2x + y;\quad x^2 + y^2 = 1$
2. $f(x, y) = x + y;\quad x^2 + 4y^2 = 1$
3. $f(x, y) = x^2 - y^2;\quad x^2 + y^2 = 4$
4. $f(x, y) = x^2 + y^2;\quad 2x + 3y = 6$
5. $f(x, y) = xy;\quad 4x^2 + 9y^2 = 36$
6. $f(x, y) = 4x^2 + 9y^2;\quad x^2 + y^2 = 1$
7. $f(x, y, z) = x^2 + y^2 + z^2;\quad 3x + 2y + z = 6$
8. $f(x, y, z) = 3x + 2y + z;\quad x^2 + y^2 + z^2 = 1$
9. $f(x, y, z) = x + y + z;\quad x^2 + 4y^2 + 9z^2 = 36$
10. $f(x, y, z) = xyz;\quad x^2 + y^2 + z^2 = 1$
11. $f(x, y, z) = xy + 2z;\quad x^2 + y^2 + z^2 = 36$
12. $f(x, y, z) = x - y + z;\quad z = x^2 - 6xy + y^2$
13. $f(x, y, z) = x^2 y^2 z^2;\quad x^2 + 4y^2 + 9z^2 = 27$
14. $f(x, y, z) = x^2 + y^2 + z^2;\quad x^4 + y^4 + z^4 = 3$
15. $f(x, y, z) = x^2 + y^2 + z^2;\quad x + y + z = 1$ and $x + 2y + 3z = 6$
16. $f(x, y, z) = z;\quad x^2 + y^2 = 1$ and $2x + 2y + z = 5$

17. $f(x, y, z) = z;$ $x + y + z = 1$ and $x^2 + y^2 = 1$

18. $f(x, y, z) = x;$ $x + y + z = 12$ and $4y^2 + 9z^2 = 36$

19. Find the point on the line $3x + 4y = 100$ that is closest to the origin. Use Lagrange multipliers to minimize the *square* of the distance.

20. A rectangular open-topped box is to have volume 700 in.^{3} The material for its bottom costs 7¢/in.^{2} and the material for its four vertical sides costs 5¢/in.^{2} Use the method of Lagrange multipliers to find what dimensions will minimize the cost of the material used in constructing this box.

In Problems 21 through 34, use the method of Lagrange multipliers to solve the indicated problem from Section 13.5.

21. Problem 29
22. Problem 30
23. Problem 31
24. Problem 32
25. Problem 33
26. Problem 34
27. Problem 35
28. Problem 36
29. Problem 37
30. Problem 38
31. Problem 39
32. Problem 40
33. Problem 41
34. Problem 42

35. Find the point or points of the surface $z = xy + 5$ closest to the origin. [*Suggestion:* Minimize the *square* of the distance.]

36. A triangle with sides x, y, and z has fixed perimeter $2s = x + y + z$. Its area A is given by *Heron's formula:*

$$A = \sqrt{s(s-a)(s-b)(s-c)}.$$

Use the method of Lagrange multipliers to show that, among all triangles with the given perimeter, the one of largest area is equilateral. [*Suggestion:* Consider maximizing A^2 rather than A.]

37. Use the method of Lagrange multipliers to show that, of all triangles inscribed in the unit circle, the one of greatest area is equilateral. [*Suggestion:* Use Fig. 13.9.9 and the fact that the area of a triangle with sides a and b and included angle θ is given by the formula $A = \frac{1}{2}ab \sin\theta$.]

FIGURE 13.9.9 A triangle inscribed in a circle (Problem 37).

38. Find the points on the rotated ellipse $x^2 + xy + y^2 = 3$ that are closest to and farthest from the origin. [*Suggestion:* Write the Lagrange multiplier equations in the form

$$ax + by = 0,$$
$$cx + dy = 0.$$

These equations have a nontrivial solution *only if* $ad - bc = 0$. Use this fact to solve first for λ.]

39. Use the method of Problem 38 to find the points of the rotated hyperbola $x^2 + 12xy + 6y^2 = 130$ that are closest to the origin.

40. Find the points of the ellipse $4x^2 + 9y^2 = 36$ that are closest to the point $(1, 1)$ as well as the point or points farthest from it.

41. Find the highest and lowest points on the ellipse formed by the intersection of the cylinder $x^2 + y^2 = 1$ and the plane $2x + y - z = 4$.

42. Apply the method of Example 4 to find the highest and lowest points on the ellipse formed by the intersection of the cone $z^2 = x^2 + y^2$ and the plane $x + 2y + 3z = 3$.

43. Find the points on the ellipse of Problem 42 that are nearest the origin and those that are farthest from it.

44. The ice tray shown in Fig. 13.9.10 is to be made from material that costs 1¢/in.^{2} Minimize the cost function $f(x, y, z) = xy + 3xz + 7yz$ subject to the constraints that each of the 12 compartments is to have a square horizontal cross section and that the total volume (ignoring the partitions) is to be 12 in.^{3}

FIGURE 13.9.10 The ice tray of Problem 44.

45. Prove Theorem 1 for functions of three variables by showing that both of the vectors $\nabla f(P)$ and $\nabla g(P)$ are perpendicular at P to every curve on the surface $g(x, y, z) = 0$.

46. Find the lengths of the semiaxes of the ellipse of Example 4.

47. Figure 13.9.11 shows a right triangle with sides x, y, and z and fixed perimeter P. Maximize its area $A = \frac{1}{2}xy$ subject to the constraints $x + y + z = P$ and $x^2 + y^2 = z^2$. In particular, show that the optimal such triangle is isosceles (by showing that $x = y$).

FIGURE 13.9.11 A right triangle with fixed perimeter P (Problem 47).

FIGURE 13.9.12 A general triangle with fixed perimeter P (Problem 48).

48. Figure 13.9.12 shows a general triangle with sides x, y, and z and fixed perimeter P. Maximize its area

$$A = f(x, y, z, \alpha) = \tfrac{1}{2}xy \sin\alpha$$

subject to the constraints $x + y + z = P$ and

$$z^2 = x^2 + y^2 - 2xy \cos\alpha$$

(the law of cosines). In particular, show that the optimal such triangle is equilateral (by showing that $x = y = z$).

49. Figure 13.9.13 shows a hexagon with vertices $(0, \pm 1)$ and $(\pm x, \pm y)$ inscribed in the unit circle $x^2 + y^2 = 1$. Show that its area is maximal when it is a *regular* hexagon with equal sides and angles.

FIGURE 13.9.13 The inscribed hexagon of Problem 49.

50. When the hexagon of Fig. 13.9.13 is rotated around the y-axis, it generates a solid of revolution consisting of a cylinder and two cones (Fig. 13.9.14). What radius and cylinder height maximize the volume of this solid?

FIGURE 13.9.14 The solid of Problem 50.

In Problems 51 through 58, consider the square of the distance to be maximized or minimized. Use the numerical solution command in a computer algebra system as needed to solve the appropriate Lagrange multiplier equations.

51. Find the points of the parabola $y = (x-1)^2$ that are closest to the origin.

52. Find the points of the ellipse $4x^2 + 9y^2 = 36$ that are closest to and farthest from the point $(3, 2)$.

53. Find the first-quadrant point of the curve $xy = 24$ that is closest to the point $(1, 4)$.

54. Find the point of the surface $xyz = 1$ that is closest to the point $(1, 2, 3)$.

55. Find the points on the sphere with center $(1, 2, 3)$ and radius 6 that are closest to and farthest from the origin.

56. Find the points of the ellipsoid $4x^2 + 9y^2 + z^2 = 36$ that are closest to and farthest from the origin.

57. Find the points of the ellipse $4x^2 + 9y^2 = 36$ that are closest to and farthest from the straight line $x + y = 10$.

58. Find the points on the ellipsoid $4x^2 + 9y^2 + z^2 = 36$ that are closest to and farthest from the plane $2x + 3y + z = 10$.

59. Find the maximum possible volume of a rectangular box that has its base in the xy-plane and its upper vertices on the elliptic paraboloid $z = 9 - x^2 - 2y^2$.

60. The plane $4x + 9y + z = 0$ intersects the elliptic paraboloid $z = 2x^2 + 3y^2$ in an ellipse. Find the highest and lowest points on this ellipse.

61. Explain carefully how the equations in (17) result from those in (15) and (16). If you wish, consider only a nontrivial special case, such as the case $n = 4$ and $k = 3$.

62. (a) Suppose that $x_1, x_2, \ldots,$ and x_n are positive. Show that the minimum value of $f(\mathbf{x}) = x_1 + x_2 + \cdots + x_n$ subject to the constraint $x_1 x_2 \cdots x_n = 1$ is n. (b) Given n positive numbers $a_1, a_2, \ldots, a_n$, let

$$x_i = \frac{a_i}{(a_1 a_2 \cdots a_n)^{1/n}}$$

for $1 \leq i \leq n$ and apply the result in part (a) to deduce the **arithmetic-geometric mean inequality**

$$\sqrt[n]{a_1 a_2 \cdots a_n} \leq \frac{a_1 + a_2 + \cdots + a_n}{n}.$$

63. Figure 13.9.15 shows a moat of width $a = 10$ ft, filled with alligators, and bounded on each side by a wall of height $b = 6$ ft. Soldiers plan to bridge this moat by scaling a ladder placed across the nearer wall as indicated, anchored at the ground with a handy boulder, and with the upper end directly above the far wall on the opposite side of the moat. They naturally wonder what is the minimal length L of a ladder that will suffice for this purpose. This is a particular case of the problem of minimizing the length of a line segment in the uv-plane that joins the points $P(x, 0)$ and $Q(0, y)$ on the two coordinate axes and passes through the given first-quadrant point (a, b). Show that $L_{\min} = (a^{2/3} + b^{2/3})^{3/2}$ by minimizing the squared length $f(x, y) = x^2 + y^2$ subject to the constraint that $u = a$ and $v = b$ satisfy the uv-equation $u/x + v/y = 1$ of the line through P and Q.

FIGURE 13.9.15 The alligator-filled moat of Problem 63.

64. A three-dimensional analog of the two-dimensional problem in Problem 63 asks for the minimal area A of the triangle in uvw-space with vertices $P(x, 0, 0)$, $Q(0, y, 0)$, and $R(0, 0, z)$ on the three coordinate axes and passing through the given first-octant point (a, b, c). (a) First deduce from Miscellaneous Problem 51 of Chapter 12 that $A^2 = \frac{1}{4}(x^2 y^2 + x^2 z^2 + y^2 z^2)$. (b) If $a = b = c = 1$ then, by symmetry, $x = y = z$. Show in this case that $x = y = z = 3$, and thus that $A = \frac{9}{2}\sqrt{3}$. (c) Set up the Lagrange multiplier equations for minimizing the squared area A^2 subject to the constraint that the given coordinates (a, b, c) satisfy the uvw-equation $u/x + v/y + w/z = 1$ of the plane through the points P, Q, and R. In general, these equations have no known closed-form solution. Nevertheless, you can use a computer algebra system (as in the CD-ROM project material for this section) to approximate numerically the minimum value of A with given numerical values of a, b, and c. Show first that with $a = b = c = 1$ you get an accurate approximation to the exact value in part (b). Then repeat the process with your own selection of values of a, b, and c. [*Note:* This three-dimensional problem was motivated by the investigation of the n-dimensional version in David Spring's article "Solution of a Calculus Problem on Minimal Volume" in *The American Mathematical Monthly* (March 2001, pp. 217–221), where a Lagrange system of $n+1$ equations is reduced to a single nonlinear equation in a single unknown.]

65. Suppose that L_1 is the line of intersection of the planes $2x + y + 2z = 15$ and $x + 2y + 3z = 30$, and that L_2 is the line of intersection of the planes $x - y - 2z = 15$ and $3x - 2y - 3z = 20$. Find the closest points P_1 and P_2 on these two skew lines. Use a computer to solve the corresponding Lagrange multiplier system of 10 linear equations in 10 unknowns.

13.9 Project: Numerical Solution of Lagrange Multiplier Systems

The Lagrange multiplier problems in Examples 1 through 4 of this section are somewhat atypical in that the equations in these examples can be solved exactly and without great effort. Frequently a Lagrange multiplier problem leads to a system of equations that can be solved only numerically and approximately. The CD-ROM material for this section supplies typical computer algebra system commands for the numerical solution of such systems, plus a two-ladder moat problem that leads to a system of 12 nonlinear equations in seven coordinate variables and five Lagrange multipliers.

13.10 CRITICAL POINTS OF FUNCTIONS OF TWO VARIABLES

We saw in Section 13.5 that in order for the differentiable function $f(x, y)$ to have either a local minimum or a local maximum at an interior critical point $P(a, b)$ of its domain, it is a *necessary* condition that P be a *critical point* of f—that is, that

$$f_x(a, b) = 0 = f_y(a, b).$$

Here we give conditions *sufficient* to ensure that f has a local extremum at a critical point. The criterion stated in Theorem 1 involves the second-order partial derivatives of f at (a, b) and plays the role of the single-variable second derivative test (Section 4.6) for functions of two variables. To simplify the statement of this result, we use the following abbreviations:

$$A = f_{xx}(a, b), \qquad B = f_{xy}(a, b), \qquad C = f_{yy}(a, b), \qquad (1)$$

and

$$\Delta = AC - B^2 = f_{xx}(a, b) f_{yy}(a, b) - [f_{xy}(a, b)]^2. \qquad (2)$$

We outline a proof of Theorem 1 at the end of this section.

THEOREM 1 Two-Variable Second Derivative Test

Suppose that the function $f(x, y)$ has continuous second-order partial derivatives in a neighborhood of the critical point (a, b) at which its first-order partial derivatives all vanish. Let A, B, C, and Δ be defined as in Eqs. (1) and (2). Then:

- $f(a, b)$ is a local minimum value of f if $A > 0$ and $\Delta > 0$;
- $f(a, b)$ is a local maximum value of f if $A < 0$ and $\Delta > 0$;
- $f(a, b)$ is neither a local minimum nor a local maximum if $\Delta < 0$.

Thus f has *either* a local maximum *or* a local minimum at the critical point (a, b) provided that the **discriminant** $\Delta = AC - B^2$ is *positive*. In this case, $A = f_{xx}(a, b)$ plays the role of the second derivative of a single-variable function: There is a local minimum at (a, b) if $A > 0$ and a local maximum if $A < 0$.

928 CHAPTER 13 Partial Differentiation

FIGURE 13.10.1 The origin is a saddle point of the surface with equation $z = x^2 - y^2$.

If $\Delta < 0$, then f has *neither* a local maximum *nor* a local minimum at (a, b). In this case we call (a, b) a **saddle point** of f, thinking of the appearance of the hyperbolic paraboloid $f(x, y) = x^2 - y^2$ (Fig. 13.10.1), a typical example of this case.

Theorem 1 does not answer the question of what happens when $\Delta = 0$. In this case, the two-variable second derivative test fails—it gives no information. Moreover, at such a point (a, b), *anything* can happen, ranging from the local (indeed global) minimum of $f(x, y) = x^4 + y^4$ at $(0, 0)$ to the "monkey saddle" of Example 2.

In the case of a function $f(x, y)$ with several critical points, we must compute the quantities A, B, C, and Δ separately at each critical point in order to apply the test.

EXAMPLE 1 Locate and classify the critical points of

$$f(x, y) = 3x - x^3 - 3xy^2.$$

Solution This function is a polynomial, so all its partial derivatives exist and are continuous everywhere. When we equate its first partial derivatives to zero (to locate the critical points of f), we get

$$f_x(x, y) = 3 - 3x^2 - 3y^2 = 0 \quad \text{and} \quad f_y(x, y) = -6xy = 0.$$

The second of these equations implies that x or y must be zero; then the first implies that the other must be ± 1. Thus there are four critical points: $(1, 0)$, $(-1, 0)$, $(0, 1)$, and $(0, -1)$.

Critical Point	A	B	C	Δ	Type of Extremum
$(1, 0)$	-6	0	-6	36	Local maximum
$(-1, 0)$	6	0	6	36	Local minimum
$(0, 1)$	0	-6	0	-36	Saddle point
$(0, -1)$	0	6	0	-36	Saddle point

FIGURE 13.10.2 Critical-point analysis for the function of Example 1.

The second-order partial derivatives of f are

$$A = f_{xx}(x, y) = -6x, \quad B = f_{xy}(x, y) = -6y, \quad C = f_{yy}(x, y) = -6x.$$

Hence $\Delta = 36(x^2 - y^2)$ at each of the critical points. The table in Fig. 13.10.2 summarizes the situation at each of the four critical points, which are labeled in the contour plot in Fig. 13.10.3. Near the points $(\pm 1, 0)$ we see the nested "ellipse-like" contours that signal local extrema (Fig. 13.10.4), and near the points $(0, \pm 1)$ we see "hyperbola-like" contours that signal saddle points (Fig. 13.10.5). Figure 13.10.6 shows the critical points on the graph of $z = f(x, y)$. ◆

FIGURE 13.10.3 Level curves for the function of Example 1.

FIGURE 13.10.4 Level curves near the critical point $(1, 0)$.

FIGURE 13.10.5 Level curves near the critical point $(0, 1)$.

Local maximum
(1, 0, 2)

Saddle point
(0, 1, 0)

Local minimum
(−1, 0, −2)

FIGURE 13.10.6 Graph of the function of Example 1.

EXAMPLE 2 Find and classify the critical points of the function

$$f(x, y) = 6xy^2 - 2x^3 - 3y^4.$$

Solution When we equate the first-order partial derivatives to zero, we get the equations

$$f_x(x, y) = 6y^2 - 6x^2 = 0 \quad \text{and} \quad f_y(x, y) = 12xy - 12y^3 = 0.$$

It follows that

$$x^2 = y^2 \quad \text{and} \quad y(x - y^2) = 0.$$

The first of these equations gives $x = \pm y$. If $x = y$, the second equation implies that $y = 0$ or $y = 1$. If $x = -y$, the second equation implies that $y = 0$ or $y = -1$. Hence there are three critical points: $(0, 0)$, $(1, 1)$, and $(1, -1)$.

The second-order partial derivatives of f are

$$A = f_{xx}(x, y) = -12x, \quad B = f_{xy}(x, y) = 12y, \quad C = f_{yy}(x, y) = 12x - 36y^2.$$

These expressions give the data shown in the table in Fig. 13.10.7. The critical point test fails at $(0, 0)$, so we must find another way to test this point.

Critical Point	A	B	C	Δ	Type of Extremum
$(0, 0)$	0	0	0	0	Test fails
$(1, 1)$	−12	12	−24	144	Local maximum
$(1, −1)$	−12	−12	−24	144	Local maximum

FIGURE 13.10.7 Critical-point analysis for the function of Example 2.

We observe that $f(x, 0) = -2x^3$ and that $f(0, y) = -3y^4$. Hence, as we move away from the origin in the

Positive x-direction: f decreases;
Negative x-direction: f increases;
Positive y-direction: f decreases;
Negative y-direction: f decreases.

FIGURE 13.10.8 The monkey saddle of Example 2.

FIGURE 13.10.9 The monkey in its saddle (Example 2).

Consequently, f has neither a local maximum nor a local minimum at the origin. The graph of f is shown in Fig. 13.10.8. If a monkey were to sit with its rump at the origin and face the negative x-direction, then the directions in which $f(x, y)$ decreases would provide places for both its tail and its two legs to hang. That's why this particular surface is called a *monkey saddle* (Fig. 13.10.9). ◆

EXAMPLE 3 Find and classify the critical points of the function

$$f(x, y) = \tfrac{1}{3}x^4 + \tfrac{1}{2}y^4 - 4xy^2 + 2x^2 + 2y^2 + 3.$$

Solution When we equate to zero the first-order partial derivatives of f, we obtain the equations

$$f_x(x, y) = \tfrac{4}{3}x^3 - 4y^2 + 4x = 0, \tag{3}$$

$$f_y(x, y) = 2y^3 - 8xy + 4y = 0, \tag{4}$$

which are not as easy to solve as the corresponding equations in Examples 1 and 2. But if we write Eq. (4) in the form

$$2y(y^2 - 4x + 2) = 0,$$

we see that either $y = 0$ or

$$y^2 = 4x - 2. \tag{5}$$

If $y = 0$, then Eq. (3) reduces to the equation

$$\tfrac{4}{3}x^3 + 4x = \tfrac{4}{3}x(x^2 + 3) = 0,$$

whose only solution is $x = 0$. Thus one critical point of f is $(0, 0)$.

If $y \neq 0$, we substitute $y^2 = 4x - 2$ into Eq. (3) to obtain

$$\tfrac{4}{3}x^3 - 4(4x - 2) + 4x = 0;$$

that is,

$$\tfrac{4}{3}x^3 - 12x + 8 = 0.$$

Thus we need to solve the cubic equation

$$\phi(x) = x^3 - 9x + 6 = 0. \tag{6}$$

The graph of $\phi(x)$ in Fig. 13.10.10 shows that this equation has three real solutions with approximate values $x \approx -3$, $x \approx 1$, and $x \approx 3$. Using either graphical techniques or Newton's method (Section 3.8), you can obtain the values

$$x \approx -3.2899, \quad x \approx 0.7057, \quad x \approx 2.5842, \tag{7}$$

accurate to four decimal places. The corresponding values of y are given from Eq. (10) by

$$y = \pm\sqrt{4x - 2}, \tag{8}$$

FIGURE 13.10.10 The graph of $\phi(x) = x^3 - 9x + 6$ (Example 3).

but the first value of x in (7) yields *no* real value at all for y. Thus the two positive values of x in (7) add *four* critical points of $f(x, y)$ to the one critical point $(0, 0)$ already found.

These five critical points are listed in the table in Fig. 13.10.11, together with the corresponding values of

$$A = f_{xx}(x, y) = 4x^2 + 4, \qquad B = f_{xy}(x, y) = -8y,$$
$$C = f_{yy}(x, y) = 6y^2 - 8x + 4, \quad \Delta = AC - B^2$$

Critical Points of Functions of Two Variables SECTION 13.10   931

Critical Point	1	2	3	4	5
x	0.0000	0.7057	0.7057	2.5842	2.5842
y	0.0000	0.9071	−0.9071	2.8874	−2.8874
z	3.0000	3.7402	3.7402	−3.5293	−3.5293
A	4.00	5.99	5.99	30.71	30.71
B	0.00	−7.26	7.26	−23.10	23.10
C	4.00	3.29	3.29	33.35	33.35
Δ	16.00	−32.94	−32.94	490.62	490.62
Type	Local minimum	Saddle point	Saddle point	Local minimum	Local minimum

FIGURE 13.10.11 Classification of the critical points in Example 3.

(rounded to two decimal places) at each of these critical points. We see that $\Delta > 0$ and $A > 0$ at $(0, 0)$ and at $(2.5482, \pm 2.8874)$, so these points are local minimum points. But $\Delta < 0$ at $(0.7057, \pm 0.9071)$, so these two are saddle points. The level curve diagram in Fig. 13.10.12 shows how these five critical points fit together.

FIGURE 13.10.12 Level curves for the function of Example 3.

Finally, we observe that the behavior of $f(x, y)$ is approximately that of $\frac{1}{3}x^4 + \frac{1}{2}y^4$ when $|x|$ or $|y|$ is large, so the surface $z = f(x, y)$ must open upward and, therefore, have a global low point (but no global high point). Examining the values

$$f(0, 0) = 3 \quad \text{and} \quad f(2.5842, \pm 2.8874) \approx -3.5293,$$

we see that the global minimum value of $f(x, y)$ is approximately -3.5293. ◆

Proof of Theorem 1

It happens that the behavior of the function $f(x, y)$ near its critical point (a, b) is determined by the behavior near the origin $(0, 0)$ of the **quadratic form**

$$q(h, k) = Ah^2 + 2Bhk + Ck^2 \tag{9}$$

in h and k (A, B, and C are computed as in Eq. (1)). If $A \neq 0$, then you can verify readily that

$$q(h, k) = \frac{1}{A}[(Ah + Bk)^2 + \Delta k^2], \tag{10}$$

either by expanding the right-hand side in (10) or by completing the square in Eq. (9). The three parts of the following proposition correspond to the three cases in the conclusion of Theorem 1.

PROPOSITION Behavior of Quadratic Forms

1. If $\Delta > 0$ and $A > 0$, then $q(h, k) > 0$ unless h and k are both zero.
2. If $\Delta > 0$ and $A < 0$, then $q(h, k) < 0$ unless h and k are both zero.
3. If $\Delta < 0$, then every neighborhood of $(0, 0)$ contains points at which $q(h, k) > 0$ and points at which $q(h, k) < 0$.

The three parts of this proposition can be visualized by thinking of the graph of q as an upward-opening elliptic paraboloid in part 1, as a downward-opening paraboloid in part 2, and as a hyperbolic paraboloid with a saddle point in part 3.

PROOF Parts 1 and 2 of the proposition follow immediately by consideration of signs in Eq. (10), because the quantity within the brackets is positive if $\Delta > 0$ and h and k are not both zero, in which case the sign of $q(x, y)$ is the same as the sign of A.

Part 3 leads to several cases depending on the possible values of A, B, and C. If $A = C = 0$ and $\Delta = -B^2 < 0$, then $q(h, k) = 2Bhk$, so the conclusion in part 3 follows at once.

If $B = 0$ and $\Delta = AC < 0$, then A and C have different signs and $Q(h, k) = Ah^2 + Ck^2$, so again the conclusion in part 3 follows at once.

If $B \neq 0$ and $A \neq 0$, then the values $q(h, 0) = Ah^2$ and $q(h, -Ah/B) = \Delta k^2/A$ have different signs if $\Delta < 0$, so again the conclusion of part 3 follows. The analysis of the remaining case, in which $B \neq 0$ and $C \neq 0$, is similar. ◀

Now let us consider the critical point (a, b) of the function $f(x, y)$ of Theorem 1. Draw a circular disk centered at (a, b) as in Fig. 13.10.13. Because the second-order partial derivatives of f are continuous, we can make the radius of this disk so small that the quantity $f_{xx}(x, y) f_{yy}(x, y) - [f_{xy}(x, y)]^2$ has the same sign as the constant $\Delta = f_{xx}(a, b) f_{yy}(a, b) - [f_{xy}(a, b)]^2$ at every point (x, y) of the disk.

Now consider the single-variable function g defined by

$$g(t) = f(a + th, b + tk)$$

for $0 \leq t \leq 1$. Application of Taylor's formula (Section 11.4) to $g(t)$ gives

$$g(1) = g(0) + g'(0) + \tfrac{1}{2} g''(\bar{t}) \tag{11}$$

for some number $\bar{t}$ between 0 and 1. But the chain rule gives first

$$g'(t) = \frac{\partial f}{\partial x} \frac{dx}{dt} + \frac{\partial f}{\partial y} \frac{dy}{dt} = h f_x + k f_y,$$

FIGURE 13.10.13 The circular disk centered at the point (a, b).

and then
$$g''(t) = \frac{\partial}{\partial x}(hf_x + kf_y)\frac{dx}{dt} + \frac{\partial}{\partial y}(hf_x + kf_y)\frac{dy}{dt}$$
$$= h^2 f_{xx} + 2hk f_{xy} + k^2 f_{yy},$$

where the indicated partial derivatives of f are to be evaluated at the point $(x, y) = (a + th, b + tk)$. Consequently $g'(0) = 0$ because $f_x(a, b) = 0 = f_y(a, b)$, and

$$g''(\bar{t}) = \overline{A} h^2 + 2\overline{B} hk + \overline{C} k^2 \qquad (12)$$

where the coefficients $\overline{A}$, $\overline{B}$, and $\overline{C}$ in this quadratic form denote the values of the second derivatives f_{xx}, f_{xy}, and f_{yy} (respectively) at the point $(\bar{x}, \bar{y}) = (a + \bar{t}h, b + \bar{t}k)$.

Because $g(0) = f(a, b)$ and $g(1) = f(a + h, b + k)$, Eqs. (11) and (12) imply that

$$f(a + h, b + k) = f(a, b) + \tfrac{1}{2}(\overline{A} h^2 + 2\overline{B} hk + \overline{C} k^2). \qquad (13)$$

Now $\overline{\Delta} = \overline{A}\,\overline{C} - \overline{B}^2$ has the same sign as $\Delta = AC - B^2$. And if $A \neq 0$, then we may assume that the circular disk in Fig. 13.10.13 is so small that $\overline{A}$ has the same sign as A. Then the quadratic form

$$\bar{q}(h, k) = \overline{A} h^2 + 2\overline{B} hk + \overline{C} k^2$$

that appears in Eq. (13) exhibits the same behavior as the quadratic form $q(h, k)$ of Eq. (9). Theorem 1 now follows from the proposition on the behavior of quadratic forms. For instance, if Δ and A are both positive, then the values $q(h, k)$ and hence $\bar{q}(h, k)$ are positive unless h and k are both zero. Therefore Eq. (13) gives

$$f(a + h, b + k) = f(a, b) + \tfrac{1}{2}\bar{q}(h, k) > f(a, b)$$

at each point $(a + h, b + k)$—other than (a, b) itself—of the circular disk of Fig. 13.10.13. Thus $f(a, b)$ is a local minimum value in this first case of Theorem 1. The other two cases follow from similar arguments.

13.10 TRUE/FALSE STUDY GUIDE

13.10 CONCEPTS: QUESTIONS AND DISCUSSION

Give simple examples of your own, different from any that appear in this section, that illustrate the following situations.

1. The three cases in Theorem 1.
2. The fact that either a maximum or a minimum, or neither, can occur at a critical point at which $\Delta = AC - B^2 = 0$.

13.10 PROBLEMS

Find and classify the critical points of the functions in Problems 1 through 22. If a computer algebra system is available, check your results by means of contour plots like those in Figs. 13.10.14–13.10.17.

1. $f(x, y) = 2x^2 + y^2 + 4x - 4y + 5$
2. $f(x, y) = 10 + 12x - 12y - 3x^2 - 2y^2$
3. $f(x, y) = 2x^2 - 3y^2 + 2x - 3y + 7$
4. $f(x, y) = xy + 3x - 2y + 4$
5. $f(x, y) = 2x^2 + 2xy + y^2 + 4x - 2y + 1$
6. $f(x, y) = x^2 + 4xy + 2y^2 + 4x - 8y + 3$
7. $f(x, y) = x^3 + y^3 + 3xy + 3$ (Fig. 13.10.14)
8. $f(x, y) = x^2 - 2xy + y^3 - y$
9. $f(x, y) = 6x - x^3 - y^3$
10. $f(x, y) = 3xy - x^3 - y^3$

FIGURE 13.10.14 Contour plot for Problem 7.

11. $f(x, y) = x^4 + y^4 - 4xy$
12. $f(x, y) = x^3 + 6xy + 3y^2$
13. $f(x, y) = x^3 + 6xy + 3y^2 - 9x$ (Fig. 13.10.15)

FIGURE 13.10.15 Contour plot for Problem 13.

14. $f(x, y) = x^3 + 6xy + 3y^2 + 6x$
15. $f(x, y) = 3x^2 + 6xy + 2y^3 + 12x - 24y$
16. $f(x, y) = 3x^2 + 12xy + 2y^3 - 6x + 6y$
17. $f(x, y) = 4xy - 2x^4 - y^2$ (Fig. 13.10.16)

FIGURE 13.10.16 Contour plot for Problem 17.

18. $f(x, y) = 8xy - 2x^2 - y^4$
19. $f(x, y) = 2x^3 - 3x^2 + y^2 - 12x + 10$
20. $f(x, y) = 2x^3 + y^3 - 3x^2 - 12x - 3y$ (Fig. 13.10.17)
21. $f(x, y) = xy \exp(-x^2 - y^2)$
22. $f(x, y) = (x^2 + y^2) \exp(x^2 - y^2)$

FIGURE 13.10.17 Contour plot for Problem 20.

In Problems 23 through 25, first show that $\Delta = f_{xx} f_{yy} - (f_{xy})^2$ is zero at the origin. Then classify this critical point by visualizing the surface $z = f(x, y)$.

23. $f(x, y) = x^4 + y^4$
24. $f(x, y) = x^3 + y^3$
25. $f(x, y) = \exp(-x^4 - y^4)$

26. Let $f(s, t)$ denote the *square* of the distance between a typical point of the line $x = t$, $y = t + 1$, $z = 2t$ and a typical point of the line $x = 2s$, $y = s - 1$, $z = s + 1$. Show that the single critical point of f is a local minimum. Hence find the closest points on these two skew lines.

27. Let $f(x, y)$ denote the square of the distance from $(0, 0, 2)$ to a typical point of the surface $z = xy$. Find and classify the critical points of f.

28. Show that the surface
$$z = (x^2 + 2y^2) \exp(1 - x^2 - y^2)$$
looks like two mountain peaks joined by two ridges with a pit between them.

29. A wire 120 cm long is cut into three pieces of lengths x, y, and $120 - x - y$, and each piece is bent into the shape of a square. Let $f(x, y)$ denote the sum of the areas of these squares. Show that the single critical point of f is a local minimum. But surely it is possible to *maximize* the sum of the areas. Explain.

30. Show that the graph of the function
$$f(x, y) = xy \exp\left(\tfrac{1}{8}[x^2 + 4y^2]\right)$$
has a saddle point but no local extrema.

31. Find and classify the critical points of the function
$$f(x, y) = \sin \frac{\pi x}{2} \sin \frac{\pi y}{2}.$$

32. Let $f(x, y) = x^3 - 3xy^2$. (a) Show that its only critical point is $(0, 0)$ and that $\Delta = 0$ there. (b) By examining the behavior of $x^3 - 3xy^2$ on straight lines through the origin, show that the surface $z = x^3 - 3xy^2$ qualifies as a monkey saddle (Fig. 13.10.18).

FIGURE 13.10.18 The monkey saddle of Problem 32.

33. Repeat Problem 32 with $f(x, y) = 4xy(x^2 - y^2)$. Show that near the critical point $(0, 0)$ the surface $z = f(x, y)$

qualifies as a "dog saddle" for a dog with a very short tail (Fig. 13.10.19).

FIGURE 13.10.19 The dog saddle of Problem 33.

34. Let
$$f(x, y) = \frac{xy(x^2 - y^2)}{x^2 + y^2}.$$

Classify the behavior of f near the critical point $(0, 0)$.

In Problems 35 through 39, use a computer algebra program (as illustrated in the project material for this section) to approximate numerically and classify the critical point of the given function.

35. $f(x, y) = 2x^4 - 12x^2 + y^2 + 8x$
36. $f(x, y) = x^4 + 4x^2 - y^2 - 16x$
37. $f(x, y) = x^4 + 12xy + 6y^2 + 4x + 10$
38. $f(x, y) = x^4 + 8xy - 4y^2 - 16x + 10$
39. $f(x, y) = x^4 + 2y^4 - 12xy^2 - 20y^2$

13.10 Project: Critical Point Investigations

In the CD-ROM material for this project, the function

$$f(x, y) = 10 \exp\left(-x^2 - \tfrac{1}{2}xy - \tfrac{1}{2}y^2\right) \sin x \sin y \tag{1}$$

is used to illustrate computer algebra system techniques for the location and classification of critical points for functions of two variables, as follows:

- First, a surface graph shows the "big picture" that we want to investigate in detail. In Fig. 13.10.20 we see two peaks and two pits, as well as an apparent saddle point.
- Next, a contour graph as in Fig. 13.10.21 reveals the approximate location of each of these critical points.
- Then we set up the equations $f_x(x, y) = 0$ and $f_y(x, y) = 0$; we use a computer algebra `solve` command to approximate the critical points accurately—with the known approximate location of each critical point providing an initial guess for its calculation.
- Finally, we compute that information about the second-order partial derivatives needed to apply Theorem 1 to classify each critical point. And a contour plot in a small neighborhood of a critical point (as in Figs. 13.10.3 through 13.10.5) can provide satisfying visual corroboration of our results.

You can follow this agenda to investigate a function such as

$$f(x, y) = (ax^2 + 2bxy + cy^2) \exp(-x^2 - y^2) \tag{2}$$

FIGURE 13.10.20 Graph of the function in Eq. (1).

FIGURE 13.10.21 Contour plot for the function in Eq. (1).

FIGURE 13.10.22 Graph of the function in Eq. (3), with $p = 5$ and the minus sign.

where a, b, and c are selected integers, or the more exotic function

$$f(x, y) = 10\left(x^3 + y^5 \pm \frac{x}{p}\right)\exp(-x^2 - y^2) + \frac{1}{3}\exp(-(x-1)^2 - y^2) \quad (3)$$

where p is a small positive integer. With the plus sign in Eq. (3) you are likely to see a half-dozen critical points, but with the minus sign you can expect to see more (as in Fig. 13.10.22, in which $p = 5$ and there appears to be some "action" near the origin, in addition to the pairs of pits, peaks, and passes that are most evident).

CHAPTER 13 REVIEW: DEFINITIONS, CONCEPTS, RESULTS

Use the following list as a guide to concepts that you may need to review.

1. Graphs and level curves of functions of two variables.
2. Limits and continuity of functions of two or three variables.
3. Partial derivatives—definition and computation.
4. Geometric interpretation of partial derivatives and the plane tangent to the surface $z = f(x, y)$.
5. Absolute and local maxima and minima.
6. Necessary conditions for a local extremum.
7. Increments and differentials of functions of two or three variables.
8. The linear approximation theorem.
9. The chain rule for functions of several variables.
10. Directional derivatives—definition and computation.
11. The gradient vector and the chain rule.
12. Significance of the length and direction of the gradient vector.
13. The gradient vector as a normal vector; tangent plane to a surface $F(x, y, z) = 0$.
14. Constrained maximum-minimum problems and the Lagrange multiplier method.
15. Sufficient conditions for a local extremum of a function of two variables.

CHAPTER 13 MISCELLANEOUS PROBLEMS

1. Use polar coordinates to show that
$$\lim_{(x,y) \to (0,0)} \frac{x^2 y^2}{x^2 + y^2} = 0.$$

2. Use spherical coordinates to show that
$$\lim_{(x,y,z) \to (0,0,0)} \frac{x^3 + y^3 - z^3}{x^2 + y^2 + z^2} = 0.$$

3. Suppose that
$$g(x, y) = \frac{xy}{x^2 + y^2}$$

if $(x, y) \neq (0, 0)$; we *define* $g(0, 0)$ to be zero. Show that g is not continuous at $(0, 0)$.

4. Compute $g_x(0, 0)$ and $g_y(0, 0)$ for the function g of Problem 3.

5. Find a function $f(x, y)$ such that
$$f_x(x, y) = 2xy^3 + e^x \sin y$$
and
$$f_y(x, y) = 3x^2 y^2 + e^x \cos y + 1.$$

6. Prove that there is *no* function f with continuous second-order partial derivatives such that $f_x(x, y) = 6xy^2$ and $f_y(x, y) = 8x^2 y$.

7. Find the point or points on the paraboloid $z = x^2 + y^2$ at which the normal line passes through the point $(0, 0, 1)$.
8. Write an equation of the plane tangent to the surface
$$\sin xy + \sin yz + \sin xz = 1$$
at the point $(1, \pi/2, 0)$.
9. Prove that every line normal to the cone with equation $z = \sqrt{x^2 + y^2}$ intersects the z-axis.
10. Show that the function
$$u(x, t) = \frac{1}{\sqrt{4\pi kt}} \exp\left(-\frac{x^2}{4kt}\right)$$
satisfies the one-dimensional heat equation
$$\frac{\partial u}{\partial t} = k \frac{\partial^2 u}{\partial x^2}.$$
11. Show that the function
$$u(x, y, t) = \frac{1}{4\pi kt} \exp\left(-\frac{x^2 + y^2}{4kt}\right)$$
satisfies the two-dimensional heat equation
$$\frac{\partial u}{\partial t} = k\left(\frac{\partial^2 u}{\partial x^2} + \frac{\partial^2 u}{\partial y^2}\right).$$
12. Suppose that $f(x, y, z) = \sqrt[3]{xyz}$. (a) Show that the partial derivatives f_x, f_y, and f_z all exist at the origin. (b) Show that the directional derivative $D_{\mathbf{u}} f(0, 0, 0)$ exists if and only if the unit vector $\mathbf{u}$ is a linear combination of some two of the standard unit vectors $\mathbf{i}$, $\mathbf{j}$, and $\mathbf{k}$.
13. Define the partial derivatives $\mathbf{r}_x$ and $\mathbf{r}_y$ of the vector-valued function $\mathbf{r}(x, y) = \mathbf{i}x + \mathbf{j}y + \mathbf{k}f(x, y)$ by componentwise partial differentiation. Then show that the vector $\mathbf{r}_x \times \mathbf{r}_y$ is normal to the surface $z = f(x, y)$.
14. An open-topped rectangular box is to have total surface area 300 cm². Find the dimensions that maximize its volume.
15. You must build a rectangular shipping crate with volume 60 ft³. Its sides cost \$1/ft², its top costs \$2/ft², and its bottom costs \$3/ft². What dimensions would minimize the total cost of the box?
16. A pyramid is bounded by the three coordinate planes and by the plane tangent to the surface $xyz = 1$ at a point in the first octant. Find the volume of this pyramid (it is independent of the point of tangency).
17. Two resistors have resistances R_1 and R_2, respectively. When they are connected in parallel, the total resistance R of the resulting circuit satisfies the equation
$$\frac{1}{R} = \frac{1}{R_1} + \frac{1}{R_2}.$$
Suppose that R_1 and R_2 are measured to be 300 and 600 Ω (ohms) respectively, with a maximum error of 1% in each measurement. Use differentials to estimate the maximum error (in ohms) in the calculated value of R.
18. Consider a gas that satisfies van der Waals' equation. (See Problem 67 of Section 13.4.) Use differentials to approximate the change in its volume if p is increased from 1 atm to 1.1 atm and T is decreased from 313 K to 303 K.

19. Each of the semiaxes a, b, and c of an ellipsoid with volume $V = \frac{4}{3}\pi abc$ is measured with a maximum percentage error of 1%. Use differentials to estimate the maximum percentage error in the calculated value of V.
20. Two spheres have radii a and b, and the distance between their centers is $c < a + b$. Thus the spheres meet in a common circle. Let P be a point on this circle, and let $\mathcal{P}_1$ and $\mathcal{P}_2$ be the planes tangent at P to the two spheres. Find the angle between $\mathcal{P}_1$ and $\mathcal{P}_2$ in terms of a, b, and c. [*Suggestion:* Recall that the angle between two planes is, by definition, the angle between their normal vectors.]
21. Find every point on the surface of the ellipsoid $x^2 + 4y^2 + 9z^2 = 16$ at which the normal line at the point passes through the center $(0, 0, 0)$ of the ellipsoid.
22. Suppose that
$$F(x) = \int_{g(x)}^{h(x)} f(t)\,dt.$$
Show that
$$F'(x) = f(h(x))h'(x) - f(g(x))g'(x).$$
[*Suggestion:* Write $w = \int_u^v f(t)\,dt$ where $u = g(x)$ and $v = h(x)$.]
23. Suppose that $\mathbf{a}$, $\mathbf{b}$, and $\mathbf{c}$ are mutually perpendicular unit vectors in space and that f is a function of the three independent variables x, y, and z. Show that
$$\nabla f = \mathbf{a}(D_{\mathbf{a}} f) + \mathbf{b}(D_{\mathbf{b}} f) + \mathbf{c}(D_{\mathbf{c}} f).$$
24. Let $\mathbf{R} = \langle \cos\theta, \sin\theta, 0\rangle$ and $\Theta = \langle -\sin\theta, \cos\theta, 0\rangle$ be the polar-coordinates unit vectors. Given $f(x, y, z) = w(r, \theta, z)$, show that
$$D_{\mathbf{R}} f = \frac{\partial w}{\partial r} \quad \text{and} \quad D_\Theta f = \frac{1}{r}\frac{\partial w}{\partial \theta}.$$
Then conclude from Problem 23 that the gradient vector is given in cylindrical coordinates by
$$\nabla f = \frac{\partial w}{\partial r}\mathbf{R} + \frac{1}{r}\frac{\partial w}{\partial \theta}\Theta + \frac{\partial w}{\partial z}\mathbf{k}.$$
25. Suppose that you are standing at the point with coordinates $(-100, -100, 430)$ on a hill that has the shape of the graph of
$$z = 500 - (0.003)x^2 - (0.004)y^2$$
(in units of meters). In what (horizontal) direction should you move in order to maintain a constant altitude—that is, to neither climb nor descend the hill?
26. Suppose that the blood concentration in the ocean at the point (x, y) is given by
$$f(x, y) = A\exp(-k[x^2 + 2y^2]),$$
where A and k are positive constants. A shark always swims in the direction of ∇f. Show that its path is a parabola $y = cx^2$. [*Suggestion:* Show that the condition that $\langle dx/dt, dy/dt\rangle$ is a multiple of ∇f implies that
$$\frac{1}{x}\frac{dx}{dt} = \frac{1}{2y}\frac{dy}{dt}.$$
Then antidifferentiate this equation.]
27. Consider a plane tangent to the surface with equation $x^{2/3} + y^{2/3} + z^{2/3} = 1$. Find the sum of the squares of the x-, y-, and z-intercepts of this plane.

28. Find the points on the ellipse $x^2/a^2 + y^2/b^2 = 1$ (with $a \neq b$) where the normal line passes through the origin.

29. Let
$$f(x, y) = \frac{x^2 y^2}{x^2 + y^2}$$
if $(x, y) \neq (0, 0)$ and define $f(0, 0)$ to be 0. First show that f is differentiable at the origin. Then classify the origin as a critical point of f.

30. Find the point of the surface $z = xy + 1$ that is closest to the origin.

31. Use the method of Problem 38 in Section 13.9 to find the semiaxes of the rotated ellipse
$$73x^2 + 72xy + 52y^2 = 100.$$

32. Use the Lagrange multiplier method to show that the longest chord of the sphere $x^2 + y^2 + z^2 = 1$ has length 2. [*Suggestion:* There is no loss of generality in assuming that $(1, 0, 0)$ is one endpoint of the chord.]

33. Use the method of Lagrange multipliers, the law of cosines, and Fig. 13.9.9 to find the triangle of minimum perimeter inscribed in the unit circle.

34. When a current I enters two resistors, with resistances R_1 and R_2, that are connected in parallel, it splits into two currents I_1 and I_2 (with $I = I_1 + I_2$) in such a way to minimize the total power loss $R_1 I_1^2 + R_2 I_2^2$. Express I_1 and I_2 in terms of R_1, R_2, and I. Then derive the formula in Problem 17.

35. Use the method of Lagrange multipliers to find the points of the ellipse $x^2 + 2y^2 = 1$ that are closest to and farthest from the line $x + y = 2$. [*Suggestion:* Let $f(x, y, u, v)$ denote the square of the distance between the point (x, y) of the ellipse and the point (u, v) of the line.]

36. (a) Show that the maximum of
$$f(x, y, z) = x + y + z$$
at points of the sphere $x^2 + y^2 + z^2 = a^2$ is $a\sqrt{3}$. (b) Conclude from the result in part (a) that
$$(x + y + z)^2 \leq 3(x^2 + y^2 + z^2)$$
for any three numbers x, y, and z.

37. Generalize the method of Problem 36 to show that, for any n arbitrary real numbers $x_1, x_2, \ldots,$ and x_n,
$$\frac{x_1 + x_2 + \cdots + x_n}{n} \leq \sqrt{\frac{x_1^2 + x_2^2 + \cdots + x_n^2}{n}}.$$
Thus the *arithmetic mean* of the real numbers $x_1, x_2, \ldots, x_n$ is no greater than their *root-square mean*.

38. Find the maximum and minimum values of $f(x, y) = xy - x - y$ at points on and within the plane triangle with vertices $(0, 0)$, $(0, 1)$, and $(3, 0)$.

39. Find the maximum and minimum values of $f(x, y, z) = x^2 - yz$ at points of the sphere $x^2 + y^2 + z^2 = 1$.

40. Find the maximum and minimum values of $f(x, y) = x^2 y^2$ at points of the ellipse $x^2 + 4y^2 = 24$.

Locate and classify the critical points (local maxima, local minima, saddle points, and other points at which the tangent plane is horizontal) of the functions in Problems 41 through 50.

41. $f(x, y) = x^3 y - 3xy + y^2$
42. $f(x, y) = x^2 + xy + y^2 - 6x + 2$
43. $f(x, y) = x^3 - 6xy + y^3$
44. $f(x, y) = x^2 y + xy^2 + x + y$
45. $f(x, y) = x^3 y^2 (1 - x - y)$
46. $f(x, y) = x^4 - 2x^2 + y^2 + 4y + 3$
47. $f(x, y) = e^{xy} - 2xy$
48. $f(x, y) = x^3 - y^3 + x^2 + y^2$
49. $f(x, y) = (x - y)(xy - 1)$
50. $f(x, y) = (2x^2 + y^2) \exp(-x^2 - y^2)$

51. Given the data points (x_i, y_i) for $i = 1, 2, \ldots, n$, the **least-squares straight line** $y = mx + b$ is the line that best fits these data in the following sense. Let $d_i = y_i - (mx_i + b)$ be the *deviation* of the predicted value $mx_i + b$ from the true value y_i. Let
$$f(m, b) = d_1^2 + d_2^2 + \cdots + d_n^2 = \sum_{i=1}^{n} [y_i - (mx_i + b)]^2$$
be the sum of the squares of the deviations. The least-squares straight line is the one that minimizes this sum (Fig. 13.MP.1). Show how to choose m and b by minimizing f. [*Note:* The only variables in this computation are m and b.]

FIGURE 13.MP.1 Fitting the best straight line to the data points (x_i, y_i), $1 \leq i \leq n$ (Problem 51).

52. Let $f : \mathbf{R}^{2n} \to \mathbf{R}$ be defined for $(\mathbf{x}, \mathbf{y})$ in $\mathbf{R}^{2n}$ by
$$f(\mathbf{x}, \mathbf{y}) = \mathbf{x}^T \mathbf{y} = \sum_{i=1}^{n} x_i y_i.$$
Use Lagrange multipliers to show that the maximum value of $f(\mathbf{x}, \mathbf{y})$ subject to the constraints $|\mathbf{x}| = 1$ and $|\mathbf{y}| = 1$ is 1. Given any two vectors $\mathbf{a}$ and $\mathbf{b}$ in $\mathbf{R}^2$, write $\mathbf{x} = \mathbf{a}/|\mathbf{a}|$ and $\mathbf{y} = \mathbf{b}/|\mathbf{b}|$ to conclude that
$$\mathbf{a}^T \mathbf{b} \leq |\mathbf{a}| |\mathbf{b}|$$
(the **Cauchy-Schwarz inequality**).

MULTIPLE INTEGRALS

14

Henri Lebesgue (1875–1941)

Geometric problems of *measure*—dealing with concepts of length, area, and volume—can be traced back 40 centuries to the rise of civilizations in the fertile river valleys of Africa and Asia, when such issues as areas of fields and volumes of granaries became important. These problems led ultimately to the *integral,* which is used to calculate (among other things) areas and volumes of curvilinear figures. But only in the early twentieth century were certain long-standing difficulties with measure and integration finally resolved, largely as a consequence of the work of the French mathematician Henri Lebesgue.

In his 1902 thesis presented at the Sorbonne in Paris, Lebesgue introduced a new definition of the integral, generalizing Riemann's definition. In essence, to define the integral of the function f from $x = a$ to $x = b$, Lebesgue replaced Riemann's subdivision of the interval $[a, b]$ into nonoverlapping subintervals with a partition of $[a, b]$ into disjoint measurable sets $\{E_i\}$. The Riemann sum $\sum f(x_i^\star) \Delta x$ was thereby replaced with a sum of the form $\sum f(x_i^\star) m_i$, where m_i is the measure of the ith set E_i and $x_i^\star$ is a number in E_i. To see the advantage of the "Lebesgue integral," consider the fact that there exist differentiable functions whose derivatives are not integrable in the sense of Riemann. For such a function, the fundamental theorem of calculus in the form

$$\int_a^b f'(x)\, dx = f(b) - f(a)$$

fails to hold. But with his new definition of the integral, Lebesgue showed that a derivative function f' is integrable and that the fundamental theorem holds. Similarly, the equality of double and iterated integrals (Section 14.1) holds only under rather drastic restrictions if the Riemann definition of multiple integrals is used, but the Lebesgue integral resolves the difficulty.

For such reasons, the Lebesgue theory of measure and integration predominates in modern mathematical research, both pure and applied. For instance, the Lebesgue integral is basic to such diverse realms as applied probability and mathematical biology, the quantum theory of atoms and nuclei, and the information theory and electric signals processing of modern computer technology.

The Section 14.5 Project illustrates the application of multiple integrals to such concrete problems as the optimal design of race-car wheels.

We could use multiple integrals to determine the best design for the wheels of these soapbox derby cars.

14.1 DOUBLE INTEGRALS

This chapter is devoted to integrals of functions of two or three variables. Such integrals are called **multiple integrals.** The applications of multiple integrals include computation of area, volume, mass, and surface area in a wider variety of situations than can be handled with the single integral of Chapters 5 and 6.

The simplest sort of multiple integral is the *double integral*

$$\iint_R f(x, y)\, dA$$

of a continuous function $f(x, y)$ over the *rectangle*

$$R = [a, b] \times [c, d] = \{(x, y) \mid a \leq x \leq b, c \leq y \leq d\}$$

in the xy-plane. (We will see that dA represents here a differential element of area A.) Just as the definition of the single integral is motivated by the problem of computing areas, the definition of the double integral is motivated by the problem of computing the volume V of the solid of Fig. 14.1.1—a solid bounded above by the graph $z = f(x, y)$ of the nonnegative function f over the rectangle R in the xy-plane.

To define the *value*

$$V = \iint_R f(x, y)\, dA$$

FIGURE 14.1.1 We will use a double integral to compute the volume V.

of such a double integral, we begin with an approximation to V. To obtain this approximation, the first step is to construct a **partition** $\mathcal{P}$ of R into subrectangles $R_1, R_2, \ldots, R_k$ determined by the points

$$a = x_0 < x_1 < x_2 < \cdots < x_m = b$$

of $[a, b]$ and

$$c = y_0 < y_1 < y_2 < \cdots < y_n = d$$

of $[c, d]$. Such a partition of R into $k = mn$ rectangles is shown in Fig. 14.1.2. The order in which these rectangles are labeled makes no difference.

Next we choose an arbitrary point $(x_i^\star, y_i^\star)$ of the ith rectangle R_i for each i (where $1 \leq i \leq k$). The collection of points $S = \{(x_i^\star, y_i^\star) \mid 1 \leq i \leq k\}$ is called a **selection** for the partition $\mathcal{P} = \{R_i \mid 1 \leq i \leq k\}$. As a measure of the size of the rectangles of the partition $\mathcal{P}$, we define its **norm** $|\mathcal{P}|$ to be the maximum of the lengths of the diagonals of the rectangles $\{R_i\}$.

FIGURE 14.1.2 A partition $\mathcal{P}$ of the rectangle R.

Now consider a rectangular column that rises straight up from the xy-plane. Its base is the rectangle R_i and its height is the value $f(x_i^\star, y_i^\star)$ of f at the selected point $(x_i^\star, y_i^\star)$ of R_i. One such column is shown in Fig. 14.1.3. If ΔA_i denotes the area of R_i, then the volume of the ith column is $f(x_i^\star, y_i^\star)\, \Delta A_i$. The sum of the volumes of all such columns (Fig. 14.1.4) is the **Riemann sum**

$$\sum_{i=1}^{k} f(x_i^\star, y_i^\star)\, \Delta A_i, \tag{1}$$

an approximation to the volume V of the solid region that lies above the rectangle R and under the graph $z = f(x, y)$.

We would expect to determine the exact volume V by taking the limit of the Riemann sum in Eq. (1) as the norm $|\mathcal{P}|$ of the partition $\mathcal{P}$ approaches zero. We therefore define the **(double) integral** of the function f over the rectangle R to be

$$\iint_R f(x, y)\, dA = \lim_{|\mathcal{P}| \to 0} \sum_{i=1}^{k} f(x_i^\star, y_i^\star)\, \Delta A_i, \tag{2}$$

provided that this limit exists. (We will make the concept of the existence of such a

FIGURE 14.1.3 Approximating the volume under the surface by summing volumes of columns with rectangular bases.

FIGURE 14.1.4 Columns corresponding to a partition of the rectangle R.

limit more precise in Section 14.2.) It is proved in advanced calculus that the limit in Eq. (2) *does* exist if f is continuous on R. To motivate the introduction of the Riemann sum in Eq. (1), we assumed that f was nonnegative on R, but Eq. (2) serves to define the double integral over a rectangle whether or not f is nonnegative.

EXAMPLE 1 Approximate the value of the integral

$$\iint_R (4x^3 + 6xy^2)\,dA$$

over the rectangle $R = [1, 3] \times [-2, 1]$, by calculating the Riemann sum in (1) for the partition illustrated in Fig. 14.1.5, with the ith point $(x_i^\star, y_i^\star)$ selected as the center of the ith rectangle R_i (for each i, $1 \leq i \leq 6$).

Solution Each of the six partition rectangles shown in Fig. 14.1.5 is a unit square with area $\Delta A_i = 1$. With $f(x, y) = 4x^3 + 6xy^2$, the desired Riemann sum is therefore

$$\sum_{i=1}^{6} f(x_i^\star, y_i^\star)\,\Delta A_i = f(x_1^\star, y_1^\star)\,\Delta A_1 + f(x_2^\star, y_2^\star)\,\Delta A_2 + f(x_3^\star, y_3^\star)\,\Delta A_3$$
$$+ f(x_4^\star, y_4^\star)\,\Delta A_4 + f(x_5^\star, y_5^\star)\,\Delta A_5 + f(x_6^\star, y_6^\star)\,\Delta A_6$$
$$= f\left(\tfrac{3}{2}, -\tfrac{3}{2}\right)(1) + f\left(\tfrac{5}{2}, -\tfrac{3}{2}\right)(1) + f\left(\tfrac{3}{2}, -\tfrac{1}{2}\right)(1)$$
$$+ f\left(\tfrac{5}{2}, -\tfrac{1}{2}\right)(1) + f\left(\tfrac{3}{2}, \tfrac{1}{2}\right)(1) + f\left(\tfrac{5}{2}, \tfrac{1}{2}\right)(1)$$
$$= \tfrac{135}{4} \cdot 1 + \tfrac{385}{4} \cdot 1 + \tfrac{63}{4} \cdot 1 + \tfrac{265}{4} \cdot 1 + \tfrac{63}{4} \cdot 1 + \tfrac{265}{4} \cdot 1 = 294.$$

FIGURE 14.1.5 The partition in Example 1.

Thus we find that

$$\iint_R (4x^3 + 6xy^2)\,dA \approx 294,$$

but our calculation provides no information about the accuracy of this approximation. ◆

REMARK 1 The single-variable approximation methods of Section 5.9 all have analogs for double integrals. In Example 1 we calculated the **midpoint approximation** to the given double integral

$$\iint_R f(x, y)\,dA$$

Number of Subrectangles	Midpoint Approximation
6	294.00
24	307.50
96	310.88
384	311.72
1536	311.93
6144	311.98

FIGURE 14.1.6 Midpoint approximations to the integral in Example 1.

using a partition of the rectangle R into six subrectangles. The Riemann sum we calculated is the sum of the volumes of six rectangular columns or blocks. Each of these columns has a base consisting of one of the subrectangles in Fig. 14.1.5 and has height equal to the value $f(x_i^*, y_i^*)$ of the function at the *midpoint* of that subrectangle.

REMARK 2 If we subdivide each rectangle in Fig. 14.1.5 into four equal smaller rectangles, we get a partition of R into 24 subrectangles, and the corresponding Riemann sum is the sum of the volume of 24 rectangular columns with bases these 24 subrectangles. Suppose that we continue in this way, quadrupling the number of subrectangles (and of rectangular columns) at each step, and use a computer to calculate each time the Riemann sum defined by selecting the center of each subrectangle to calculate the height of the corresponding rectangular column. Then we get the midpoint approximations listed in Fig. 14.1.6 to the actual volume V that lies over the rectangle R and under the surface $z = f(x, y)$. (See Fig. 14.1.7.) Figure 14.1.8 shows the "rectangular block approximations" to V that correspond to partitions of R into 24, 96, and 384 subrectangles. In Example 2 we will see (much more easily) that the exact value of V is given by

$$V = \iint_R (4x^3 + 6xy^2)\, dA = 312.$$

Iterated Integrals

The direct evaluation of the limit in Eq. (2) is generally even less practical than the direct evaluation of the limit we used in Section 5.4 to define the single-variable integral. In practice, we shall calculate double integrals over rectangles by means of the **iterated integrals** that appear in Theorem 1.

FIGURE 14.1.7 The surface $z = 4x^3 + 6xy^2$ over the rectangle R.

THEOREM 1 Double Integrals as Iterated Single Integrals

Suppose that $f(x, y)$ is continuous on the rectangle $R = [a, b] \times [c, d]$. Then

$$\iint_R f(x, y)\, dA = \int_a^b \left(\int_c^d f(x, y)\, dy \right) dx = \int_c^d \left(\int_a^b f(x, y)\, dx \right) dy. \quad (3)$$

Theorem 1 tells us how to compute a double integral by means of two successive (or *iterated*) single-variable integrations, each of which we can compute by using the fundamental theorem of calculus (if the function f is sufficiently well-behaved on R).

(a) 24 blocks, $V \approx 307.50$

(b) 96 blocks, $V \approx 310.88$

(c) 384 blocks, $V \approx 311.72$

FIGURE 14.1.8 Midpoint sum approximations to the volume V under the surface $z = 4x^3 + 6xy^2$ with 24, 96, and 384 subrectangles.

Let us explain what we mean by the parentheses in the iterated integral

$$\int_a^b \int_c^d f(x, y)\, dy\, dx = \int_a^b \left(\int_c^d f(x, y)\, dy \right) dx. \qquad (4)$$

First we hold x constant and integrate with respect to y, from $y = c$ to $y = d$. The result of this first integration is the **partial integral of f with respect to y**, denoted by

$$\int_c^d f(x, y)\, dy,$$

and it is a function of x alone. Then we integrate this latter function with respect to x, from $x = a$ to $x = b$.

Similarly, we calculate the iterated integral

$$\int_c^d \int_a^b f(x, y)\, dx\, dy = \int_c^d \left(\int_a^b f(x, y)\, dx \right) dy \qquad (5)$$

by first integrating from a to b with respect to x (while holding y fixed) and then integrating the result from c to d with respect to y. The order of integration (either first with respect to x and then with respect to y, or the reverse) is determined by the order in which the differentials dx and dy appear in the iterated integrals in Eqs. (4) and (5). We almost always work "from the inside out." Theorem 1 guarantees that the value obtained is independent of the order of integration provided that f is continuous on R.

FIGURE 14.1.9 The inner limits of the first iterated integral (Example 2).

EXAMPLE 2 Compute the iterated integrals in Eqs. (4) and (5) for the function $f(x, y) = 4x^3 + 6xy^2$ on the rectangle $R = [1, 3] \times [-2, 1]$.

Solution The rectangle R is shown in Fig. 14.1.9, where the vertical segment (on which x is constant) corresponds to the inner integral in Eq. (4). Its endpoints lie at heights $y = -2$ and $y = 1$, which are, therefore, the limits on the inner integral. So Eq. (4) yields

$$\int_1^3 \left(\int_{-2}^1 (4x^3 + 6xy^2)\, dy \right) dx = \int_1^3 \left[4x^3 y + 2xy^3 \right]_{y=-2}^1 dx$$

$$= \int_1^3 [(4x^3 + 2x) - (-8x^3 - 16x)]\, dx$$

$$= \int_1^3 (12x^3 + 18x)\, dx$$

$$= \left[3x^4 + 9x^2 \right]_1^3 = 312.$$

The horizontal segment (on which y is constant) in Fig. 14.1.10 corresponds to the inner integral in Eq. (5). Its endpoints lie at $x = 1$ and $x = 3$ (the limits of integration for x), so Eq. (5) gives

$$\int_{-2}^1 \left(\int_1^3 (4x^3 + 6xy^2)\, dx \right) dy = \int_{-2}^1 \left[x^4 + 3x^2 y^2 \right]_{x=1}^3 dy$$

$$= \int_{-2}^1 [(81 + 27y^2) - (1 + 3y^2)]\, dy$$

$$= \int_{-2}^1 (80 + 24y^2)\, dy$$

$$= \left[80y + 8y^3 \right]_{-2}^1 = 312. \qquad \blacklozenge$$

FIGURE 14.1.10 The inner limits of the second iterated integral (Example 2).

When we note that iterated double integrals are almost always evaluated from the inside out, it becomes clear that the parentheses appearing on the right-hand sides in Eqs. (4) and (5) are unnecessary. They are, therefore, generally omitted, as in Examples 3 and 4. When $dy\,dx$ appears in the integrand, we integrate first with respect to y, whereas the appearance of $dx\,dy$ tells us to integrate first with respect to x.

EXAMPLE 3 See Fig. 14.1.11.

$$\int_0^\pi \int_0^{\pi/2} \cos x \cos y \, dy \, dx = \int_0^\pi \Big[\cos x \sin y\Big]_{y=0}^{\pi/2} dx$$
$$= \int_0^\pi \cos x \, dx = \Big[\sin x\Big]_0^\pi = 0.$$

FIGURE 14.1.11 Example 3.

EXAMPLE 4 See Fig. 14.1.12.

$$\int_0^1 \int_0^{\pi/2} (e^y + \sin x) \, dx \, dy = \int_0^1 \Big[xe^y - \cos x\Big]_{x=0}^{\pi/2} dy$$
$$= \int_0^1 \Big(\frac{1}{2}\pi e^y + 1\Big) dy$$
$$= \Big[\frac{1}{2}\pi e^y + y\Big]_0^1 = \frac{1}{2}\pi(e-1) + 1.$$

FIGURE 14.1.12 Example 4.

Iterated Integrals and Cross Sections

An outline of the proof of Theorem 1 illuminates the relationship between iterated integrals and the method of cross sections (for computing volumes) discussed in Section 6.2. First we partition $[a, b]$ into n equal subintervals, each of length $\Delta x = (b-a)/n$, and we also partition $[c, d]$ into n equal subintervals, each of length $\Delta y = (d-c)/n$. This gives n^2 rectangles, each of which has area $\Delta A = \Delta x\,\Delta y$. Choose a point $x_i^\star$ in $[x_{i-1}, x_i]$ for each i, $1 \leq i \leq n$. Then the average value theorem for single integrals (Section 5.6) gives a point $y_{ij}^\star$ in $[y_{j-1}, y_j]$ such that

$$\int_{y_{j-1}}^{y_j} f(x_i^\star, y)\, dy = f(x_i^\star, y_{ij}^\star)\, \Delta y.$$

This gives us the selected point $(x_i^\star, y_{ij}^\star)$ in the rectangle $[x_{i-1}, x_i] \times [y_{j-1}, y_j]$. Then

$$\iint_R f(x, y)\, dA \approx \sum_{i,j=1}^n f(x_i^\star, y_{ij}^\star)\, \Delta A = \sum_{i=1}^n \sum_{j=1}^n f(x_i^\star, y_{ij}^\star)\, \Delta y\, \Delta x$$
$$= \sum_{i=1}^n \left(\sum_{j=1}^n \int_{y_{j-1}}^{y_j} f(x_i^\star, y)\, dy\right) \Delta x$$
$$= \sum_{i=1}^n \left(\int_c^d f(x_i^\star, y)\, dy\right) \Delta x$$
$$= \sum_{i=1}^n A(x_i^\star)\, \Delta x,$$

where

$$A(x) = \int_c^d f(x, y)\, dy.$$

Moreover, the last sum is a Riemann sum for the integral

$$\int_a^b A(x)\, dx,$$

so the result of our computation is

$$\iint_R f(x,y)\,dA \approx \sum_{i=1}^{n} A(x_i^\star)\,\Delta x$$

$$\approx \int_a^b A(x)\,dx = \int_a^b \left(\int_c^d f(x,y)\,dy \right) dx.$$

We can convert this outline into a complete proof of Theorem 1 by showing that the preceding approximations become equalities when we take limits as $n \to +\infty$.

In case the function f is nonnegative on R, the function $A(x)$ introduced here gives the area of the vertical cross section of R perpendicular to the x-axis (Fig. 14.1.13). Thus the iterated integral in Eq. (4) expresses the volume V as the integral from $x = a$ to $x = b$ of the cross-sectional area function $A(x)$. Similarly, the iterated integral in Eq. (5) expresses V as the integral from $y = c$ to $y = d$ of the function

$$A(y) = \int_a^b f(x,y)\,dx,$$

which gives the area of a vertical cross section in a plane perpendicular to the y-axis. [Although it seems appropriate to use the notation $A(y)$ here, note that $A(x)$ and $A(y)$ are by no means the same function!]

FIGURE 14.1.13 The area of the cross section at x is
$A(x) = \int_c^d f(x,y)\,dy.$

14.1 TRUE/FALSE STUDY GUIDE

14.1 CONCEPTS: QUESTIONS AND DISCUSSION

1. Describe as completely as possible the analogy between
   - a single-variable integral $\int_I f(x)\,dx$ over an interval $I = [a, b]$
   and
   - a double integral $\iint_R f(x, y)\,dA$ over a rectangle $R = [a, b] \times [c, d]$.

   Discuss both the similarities and the differences.

2. Write the "double" Riemann sum

$$\sum_{i=1}^{m} \sum_{j=1}^{n} \cdots$$

   corresponding to subdivision of $[a, b]$ and $[c, d]$ into m subintervals each of length Δx and into n subintervals each of length Δy (respectively), together with selections $\{x_i^\star\}_{i=1}^{m}$ and $\{y_j^\star\}_{j=1}^{n}$ of points in these subintervals. What choices of these selections might correspond to left-hand, right-hand, and midpoint sums for single-variable integrals?

3. Can you describe a way of generalizing the idea of trapezoidal approximations for single-variable integrals to double-sum approximations for double integrals? Think of using trapezoidal approximations for the cross-sectional area integrals discussed at the end of this section.

14.1 PROBLEMS

1. Approximate the integral

$$\iint_R (4x^3 + 6xy^2)\,dA$$

of Example 1 using the partition shown in Fig. 14.1.5, but selecting each $(x_i^\star, y_i^\star)$ as (a) the lower left corner of the rectangle R_i; (b) the upper right corner of the rectangle R_i.

2. Approximate the integral

$$\iint_R (4x^3 + 6xy^2)\,dA$$

as in Problem 1, but selecting each $(x_i^\star, y_i^\star)$ as (a) the upper left corner of the rectangle R_i; (b) the lower right corner of the rectangle R_i.

In Problems 3 through 8, calculate the Riemann sum for

$$\iint_R f(x, y)\, dA$$

using the given partition and selection of points (x_i^*, y_i^*) for the rectangle R.

3. $f(x, y) = x + y$; $R = [0, 2] \times [0, 2]$; the partition $\mathcal{P}$ consists of four unit squares; each (x_i^*, y_i^*) is the center point of the ith rectangle R_i.

4. $f(x, y) = xy$; $R = [0, 2] \times [0, 2]$; the partition $\mathcal{P}$ consists of four unit squares; each (x_i^*, y_i^*) is the center point of the ith rectangle R_i.

5. $f(x, y) = x^2 - 2y$; $R = [2, 6] \times [-1, 1]$; the partition $\mathcal{P}$ consists of four equal rectangles of width $\Delta x = 2$ and height $\Delta y = 1$; each (x_i^*, y_i^*) is the lower left corner of the ith rectangle R_i.

6. $f(x, y) = x^2 + y^2$; $R = [0, 2] \times [0, 3]$; the partition $\mathcal{P}$ consists of six unit squares; each (x_i^*, y_i^*) is the upper right corner of the ith rectangle R_i.

7. $f(x, y) = \sin x \sin y$; $R = [0, \pi] \times [0, \pi]$; the partition $\mathcal{P}$ consists of four equal squares; each (x_i^*, y_i^*) is the center point of the ith rectangle R_i.

8. $f(x, y) = \sin 4xy$; $R = [0, 1] \times [0, \pi]$; the partition $\mathcal{P}$ consists of six equal rectangles of width $\Delta x = \frac{1}{2}$ and height $\Delta y = \frac{1}{3}\pi$; each (x_i^*, y_i^*) is the center point of the ith rectangle R_i.

In Problems 9 and 10, let L, M, and U denote the Riemann sums calculated for the given function f and the indicated partition $\mathcal{P}$ by selecting the lower left corners, midpoints, and upper right corners (respectively) of the rectangles in $\mathcal{P}$. Without actually calculating any of these Riemann sums, arrange them in increasing order of size.

9. $f(x, y) = x^2 y^2$; $R = [1, 3] \times [2, 5]$; the partition $\mathcal{P}$ consists of six unit squares.

10. $f(x, y) = \sqrt{100 - x^2 - y^2}$; $R = [1, 4] \times [2, 5]$; the partition $\mathcal{P}$ consists of nine unit squares.

Evaluate the iterated integrals in Problems 11 through 30.

11. $\displaystyle\int_0^2 \int_0^4 (3x + 4y)\, dx\, dy$

12. $\displaystyle\int_0^3 \int_0^2 x^2 y\, dx\, dy$

13. $\displaystyle\int_{-1}^2 \int_1^3 (2x - 7y)\, dy\, dx$

14. $\displaystyle\int_{-2}^1 \int_2^4 x^2 y^3\, dy\, dx$

15. $\displaystyle\int_0^3 \int_0^3 (xy + 7x + y)\, dx\, dy$

16. $\displaystyle\int_0^2 \int_2^4 (x^2 y^2 - 17)\, dx\, dy$

17. $\displaystyle\int_{-1}^2 \int_{-1}^2 (2xy^2 - 3x^2 y)\, dy\, dx$

18. $\displaystyle\int_1^3 \int_{-3}^{-1} (x^3 y - xy^3)\, dy\, dx$

19. $\displaystyle\int_0^{\pi/2} \int_0^{\pi/2} (\sin x \cos y)\, dx\, dy$

20. $\displaystyle\int_0^{\pi/2} \int_0^{\pi/2} (\cos x \sin y)\, dy\, dx$

21. $\displaystyle\int_0^1 \int_0^1 xe^y\, dy\, dx$

22. $\displaystyle\int_0^1 \int_{-2}^2 x^2 e^y\, dx\, dy$

23. $\displaystyle\int_0^1 \int_0^\pi e^x \sin y\, dy\, dx$

24. $\displaystyle\int_0^1 \int_0^1 e^{x+y}\, dx\, dy$

25. $\displaystyle\int_0^\pi \int_0^\pi (xy + \sin x)\, dx\, dy$

26. $\displaystyle\int_0^{\pi/2} \int_0^{\pi/2} (y - 1) \cos x\, dx\, dy$

27. $\displaystyle\int_0^{\pi/2} \int_1^e \frac{\sin y}{x}\, dx\, dy$

28. $\displaystyle\int_1^e \int_1^e \frac{1}{xy}\, dy\, dx$

29. $\displaystyle\int_0^1 \int_0^1 \left(\frac{1}{x+1} + \frac{1}{y+1}\right) dx\, dy$

30. $\displaystyle\int_1^2 \int_1^3 \left(\frac{x}{y} + \frac{y}{x}\right) dy\, dx$

In Problems 31 through 34, verify that the values of

$$\iint_R f(x, y)\, dA$$

given by the iterated integrals in Eqs. (4) and (5) are indeed equal.

31. $f(x, y) = 2xy - 3y^2$; $R = [-1, 1] \times [-2, 2]$

32. $f(x, y) = \sin x \cos y$; $R = [0, \pi] \times [-\pi/2, \pi/2]$

33. $f(x, y) = \sqrt{x + y}$; $R = [0, 1] \times [1, 2]$

34. $f(x, y) = e^{x+y}$; $R = [0, \ln 2] \times [0, \ln 3]$

35. Prove that

$$\lim_{n \to \infty} \int_0^1 \int_0^1 x^n y^n\, dx\, dy = 0.$$

36. Suppose that $f(x, y) = k$ is a constant-valued function and $R = [a, b] \times [c, d]$. Use Riemann sums to prove that

$$\iint_R k\, dA = k(b - a)(d - c).$$

37. Use Riemann sums to show, without calculating the value of the integral, that

$$0 \leqq \int_0^\pi \int_0^\pi \sin\sqrt{xy}\, dx\, dy \leqq \pi^2.$$

Problems 38 through 40 list properties of double integrals that are analogous to familiar properties of single integrals. In each case state the corresponding relation between Riemann sums associated with a given partition and selection for the rectangle R.

38. $\iint_R cf(x, y)\, dA = c \iint_R f(x, y)\, dA$ (c is a constant).

39. $\iint_R [f(x, y) + g(x, y)]\, dA$

$$= \iint_R f(x, y)\, dA + \iint_R g(x, y)\, dA.$$

40. If $f(x, y) \leqq g(x, y)$ at each point of R, then

$$\iint_R f(x, y)\, dA \leqq \iint_R g(x, y)\, dA.$$

14.1 Project: Midpoint Sums Approximating Double Integrals

Suppose that we divide the intervals $[a, b]$ and $[c, d]$ into m subintervals of length Δx and into n subintervals of length Δy (respectively). If u_i and v_j denote the midpoints of the ith subinterval of $[a, b]$ and the jth subinterval of $[c, d]$ (respectively), then (u_i, v_j) is the midpoint of the ijth subrectangle $[x_{i-1}, x_i] \times [y_{j-1}, y_j]$. We thereby obtain the midpoint sum approximation

$$S_{mn} = \sum_{i=1}^m \sum_{j=1}^n f(u_i, v_j)\, \Delta x\, \Delta y \approx \iint_R f(x, y)\, dA$$

to the double integral of the function f over the rectangle $R = [a, b] \times [c, d]$. Figure 14.1.14 illustrates the case in which $m = 3$ and $n = 2$. In the CD-ROM material for this project we illustrate the use of computer algebra systems to calculate midpoint sum approximations rapidly and efficiently.

FIGURE 14.1.14 The points used in the midpoint approximation.

14.2 DOUBLE INTEGRALS OVER MORE GENERAL REGIONS

Now we want to define and compute double integrals over regions more general than rectangles. Let the function f be defined on the plane region R, and suppose that R is **bounded**—that is, that R lies within some rectangle S. To define the (double) integral of f over R, we begin with a partition $\mathcal{Q}$ of the rectangle S into subrectangles. Some of the rectangles of $\mathcal{Q}$ will lie wholly within R, some will be outside R, and some will lie partly within and partly outside R. We consider the collection $\mathcal{P} = \{R_1, R_2, \ldots, R_k\}$ of all those rectangles in $\mathcal{Q}$ that lie *completely within* the region R. This collection $\mathcal{P}$ is called the **inner partition** of the region R determined by the partition $\mathcal{Q}$ of the rectangle S (Fig. 14.2.1). By the **norm** $|\mathcal{P}|$ of the inner partition $\mathcal{P}$ we mean the norm of the partition $\mathcal{Q}$ that determines $\mathcal{P}$. Note that $|\mathcal{P}|$ depends not only on $\mathcal{P}$ but on $\mathcal{Q}$ as well.

Using the inner partition $\mathcal{P}$ of the region R, we can proceed in much the same way as in Section 14.1. By choosing an arbitrary point $(x_i^\star, y_i^\star)$ in the ith rectangle R_i of $\mathcal{P}$ for $i = 1, 2, 3, \ldots, k$, we obtain a **selection** for the inner partition $\mathcal{P}$. Let us denote by ΔA_i the area of R_i. Then this selection gives the **Riemann sum**

$$\sum_{i=1}^k f(x_i^\star, y_i^\star)\, \Delta A_i$$

associated with the inner partition $\mathcal{P}$. In case f is nonnegative on R, this Riemann sum approximates the volume of the three-dimensional region that lies under the surface $z = f(x, y)$ and above the region R in the xy-plane. We therefore define the double integral of f over the region R by taking the limit of this Riemann sum as

FIGURE 14.2.1 The rectangular partition of S produces an associated inner partition (shown shaded) of the region R.

the norm $|\mathcal{P}|$ approaches zero. Thus

$$\iint_R f(x, y)\, dA = \lim_{|\mathcal{P}| \to 0} \sum_{i=1}^{k} f(x_i^\star, y_i^\star)\, \Delta A_i, \tag{1}$$

provided that this limit exists in the sense of the following definition.

DEFINITION The Double Integral
The **double integral** of the bounded function f over the plane region R is the number

$$I = \iint_R f(x, y)\, dA$$

provided that, for every $\epsilon > 0$, there exists a number $\delta > 0$ such that

$$\left| \sum_{i=1}^{k} f(x_i^\star, y_i^\star)\, \Delta A_i - I \right| < \epsilon$$

for every inner partition $\mathcal{P} = \{R_1, R_2, \ldots, R_k\}$ of R that has norm $|\mathcal{P}| < \delta$ and every selection of points $(x_i^\star, y_i^\star)$ in R_i ($i = 1, 2, \ldots, k$).

Thus the meaning of the limit in Eq. (1) is that the Riemann sum can be made arbitrarily close to the number

$$I = \iint_R f(x, y)\, dA$$

merely by choosing the norm of the inner partition $\mathcal{P}$ sufficiently small. In this case we say that the function f is **integrable** on the region R.

Note If R is a rectangle and we choose $S = R$ (so that an inner partition of R is simply a partition of R), then the preceding definition reduces to our earlier definition of a double integral over a rectangle. In advanced calculus the double integral of the function f over the bounded plane region R is shown to exist provided that f is continuous on R and the *boundary* of R is reasonably well-behaved. In particular, it suffices for the boundary of R to consist of a finite number of piecewise smooth simple closed curves (that is, each boundary curve consists of a finite number of smooth arcs).

EXAMPLE 1 Approximate the value of the integral

$$\iint_R (x + y)\, dA$$

where R is the region in the first quadrant bounded by the unit circle and the coordinate axes. Do so by calculating the sum in Eq. (1) for the inner partition and midpoint selection indicated in Fig. 14.2.2(a).

(a) 8 interior squares with $\Delta x = \Delta y = \frac{1}{4}$ (b) 41 interior squares with $\Delta x = \Delta y = \frac{1}{8}$ (c) 183 interior squares with $\Delta x = \Delta y = \frac{1}{16}$

FIGURE 14.2.2 Inner partitions of the quarter-circle R with $\Delta x = \Delta y = \frac{1}{4}$, $\Delta x = \Delta y = \frac{1}{8}$, and $\Delta x = \Delta y = \frac{1}{16}$.

Double Integrals over More General Regions SECTION 14.2   949

Solution The figure shows a partition of the unit square into 16 smaller squares each with side length $\Delta x = \Delta y = \frac{1}{4}$. The inner partition we use consists of the 8 small squares that are contained wholly within the quarter-circular region R. The midpoints of these squares are the 8 points $(\frac{1}{8}, \frac{1}{8})$, $(\frac{3}{8}, \frac{1}{8})$, $(\frac{5}{8}, \frac{1}{8})$, $(\frac{1}{8}, \frac{3}{8})$, $(\frac{3}{8}, \frac{3}{8})$, $(\frac{5}{8}, \frac{3}{8})$, $(\frac{1}{8}, \frac{5}{8})$, and $(\frac{3}{8}, \frac{5}{8})$. The corresponding Riemann sum is

$$S = \left[f\left(\tfrac{1}{8}, \tfrac{1}{8}\right) + f\left(\tfrac{3}{8}, \tfrac{1}{8}\right) + f\left(\tfrac{5}{8}, \tfrac{1}{8}\right) + f\left(\tfrac{1}{8}, \tfrac{3}{8}\right) \right.$$
$$\left. + f\left(\tfrac{3}{8}, \tfrac{3}{8}\right) + f\left(\tfrac{5}{8}, \tfrac{3}{8}\right) + f\left(\tfrac{1}{8}, \tfrac{5}{8}\right) + f\left(\tfrac{3}{8}, \tfrac{5}{8}\right) \right] \Delta x \, \Delta y$$
$$= \left[\left(\tfrac{1}{8} + \tfrac{1}{8}\right) + \left(\tfrac{3}{8} + \tfrac{1}{8}\right) + \left(\tfrac{5}{8} + \tfrac{1}{8}\right) + \left(\tfrac{1}{8} + \tfrac{3}{8}\right) \right.$$
$$\left. + \left(\tfrac{3}{8} + \tfrac{3}{8}\right) + \left(\tfrac{5}{8} + \tfrac{3}{8}\right) + \left(\tfrac{1}{8} + \tfrac{5}{8}\right) + \left(\tfrac{3}{8} + \tfrac{5}{8}\right) \right] \cdot \tfrac{1}{4} \cdot \tfrac{1}{4},$$

and thus

$$S = \frac{11}{32} = 0.34375 \approx 0.344.$$ ◆

n	N	S
4	8	0.344
8	41	0.494
16	183	0.580
32	770	0.625
64	3149	0.646
128	12,730	0.656
256	51,209	0.662
512	205,356	0.664
1024	822,500	0.665

FIGURE 14.2.3 The number n of subintervals in each direction, the number N of small squares in the inner partition, and the corresponding approximate Riemann sum S.

REMARK In Fig. 14.2.2(a) we began by dividing the unit intervals on the x- and y-axes into $n = 4$ subintervals each. Figures 14.2.2(b) and 14.2.2(c) show the inner partitions that result when we begin with $n = 8$ and $n = 16$ subintervals (respectively) in each direction. Suppose that we continue in this way, doubling the number n of subintervals in each direction at each step, and use a computer to calculate each time the midpoint Riemann sum corresponding to the resulting inner partition of the quarter-circular region R. Figure 14.2.3 shows the resulting approximations to the integral

$$\iint_R (x + y) \, dA;$$

we also show the total number N of interior squares used at each step. In Problem 51 we ask you to show (using a comparatively simple computation with iterated integrals) that the exact value of this integral is $\frac{2}{3}$. (Thus the approximation in Example 1 is not every impressive.)

FIGURE 14.2.4 A vertically simple region R.

Evaluation of Double Integrals

The explicit evaluation of Riemann sums as in Example 1 is cumbersome and inefficient. But for certain common types of regions, we can evaluate double integrals by using iterated integrals in much the same way as we do when the region is a rectangle. The plane region R is called **vertically simple** if it can be described by means of the inequalities

$$a \leqq x \leqq b, \qquad y_1(x) \leqq y \leqq y_2(x), \qquad (2)$$

where $y_1(x)$ and $y_2(x)$ are continuous functions of x on $[a, b]$. Such a region appears in Fig. 14.2.4. The region R is called **horizontally simple** if it can be described by the inequalities

$$c \leqq y \leqq d, \qquad x_1(y) \leqq x \leqq x_2(y), \qquad (3)$$

where $x_1(y)$ and $x_2(y)$ are continuous functions of y on $[c, d]$. The region in Fig. 14.2.5 is horizontally simple.

Theorem 1 tells us how to compute by iterated integration a double integral over a region R that is either vertically simple or horizontally simple.

FIGURE 14.2.5 A horizontally simple region R.

THEOREM 1 **Evaluation of Double Integrals**

Suppose that $f(x, y)$ is continuous on the region R. If R is the vertically simple region given in (2), then

$$\iint_R f(x, y)\, dA = \int_a^b \int_{y_1(x)}^{y_2(x)} f(x, y)\, dy\, dx. \qquad (4)$$

If R is the horizontally simple region given in (3), then

$$\iint_R f(x, y)\, dA = \int_c^d \int_{x_1(y)}^{x_2(y)} f(x, y)\, dx\, dy. \qquad (5)$$

Theorem 1 here includes Theorem 1 of Section 14.1 as a special case (when R is a rectangle), and it can be proved by a generalization of the argument we outlined there.

FIGURE 14.2.6 The vertically simple region of Example 2.

EXAMPLE 2 Compute in two different ways the integral

$$\iint_R xy^2\, dA,$$

where R is the first-quadrant region bounded by the two curves $y = \sqrt{x}$ and $y = x^3$.

Solution *Always sketch the region R of integration before attempting to evaluate a double integral.* As indicated in Figs. 14.2.6 and 14.2.7, the given region R is both vertically and horizontally simple. The vertical segment in Fig. 14.2.6 with endpoints on the curves $y = x^3$ and $y = \sqrt{x}$ corresponds to integrating first with respect to y:

$$\iint_R xy^2\, dA = \int_0^1 \int_{x^3}^{\sqrt{x}} xy^2\, dy\, dx = \int_0^1 \left[\frac{1}{3}xy^3\right]_{y=x^3}^{\sqrt{x}} dx$$

$$= \int_0^1 \left(\frac{1}{3}x^{5/2} - \frac{1}{3}x^{10}\right) dx = \frac{2}{21} - \frac{1}{33} = \frac{5}{77}.$$

We obtain $x = y^2$ and $x = y^{1/3}$ when we solve the equations $y = \sqrt{x}$ and $y = x^3$ for x in terms of y. The horizontal segment in Fig. 14.2.7 corresponds to integrating first with respect to x:

FIGURE 14.2.7 The horizontally simple region of Example 2.

$$\iint_R xy^2\, dA = \int_0^1 \int_{y^2}^{y^{1/3}} xy^2\, dx\, dy = \int_0^1 \left[\frac{1}{2}x^2 y^2\right]_{x=y^2}^{y^{1/3}} dy$$

$$= \int_0^1 \left(\frac{1}{2}y^{8/3} - \frac{1}{2}y^6\right) dy = \frac{3}{22} - \frac{1}{14} = \frac{5}{77}. \qquad \blacklozenge$$

EXAMPLE 3 Evaluate

$$\iint_R (6x + 2y^2)\, dA,$$

where R is the region bounded by the parabola $x = y^2$ and the straight line $x + y = 2$.

Solution The region R appears in Fig. 14.2.8. It is both horizontally and vertically simple. If we wished to integrate first with respect to y and then with respect to x, we would need to evaluate two integrals:

FIGURE 14.2.8 The vertically simple region of Example 3.

$$\iint_R f(x, y)\, dA = \int_0^1 \int_{-\sqrt{x}}^{\sqrt{x}} (6x + 2y^2)\, dy\, dx + \int_1^4 \int_{-\sqrt{x}}^{2-x} (6x + 2y^2)\, dy\, dx.$$

Double Integrals over More General Regions SECTION 14.2   951

The reason is that the formula of the function $y = y_2(x)$ describing the "top boundary curve" of R changes at the point $(1, 1)$, from $y = \sqrt{x}$ on the left to $y = 2 - x$ on the right. But as we see in Fig. 14.2.9, every *horizontal* segment in R extends from $x = y^2$ on the left to $x = 2 - y$ on the right. Therefore, integrating first with respect to x requires us to evaluate only *one* iterated integral:

$$\iint_R f(x,y)\,dA = \int_{-2}^{1} \int_{y^2}^{2-y} (6x + 2y^2)\,dx\,dy$$

$$= \int_{-2}^{1} \left[3x^2 + 2xy^2\right]_{x=y^2}^{2-y} dy$$

$$= \int_{-2}^{1} [3(2-y)^2 + 2(2-y)y^2 - 3(y^2)^2 - 2y^4]\,dy$$

$$= \int_{-2}^{1} (12 - 12y + 7y^2 - 2y^3 - 5y^4)\,dy$$

$$= \left[12y - 6y^2 + \frac{7}{3}y^3 - \frac{1}{2}y^4 - y^5\right]_{-2}^{1} = \frac{99}{2}.$$

FIGURE 14.2.9 The horizontally simple region of Example 3.

Example 3 shows that even when the region R is both vertically and horizontally simple, it may be easier to integrate in one order rather than the other because of the shape of R. We naturally prefer the easier route. The choice of the preferable order of integration may be influenced also by the nature of the function $f(x, y)$. It may be difficult—or even impossible—to compute a given iterated integral but easy to do so *after we reverse the order of integration.* Example 4 shows that the key to reversing the order of integration is this:

Find and sketch the region R over which
the integration is to be performed.

EXAMPLE 4 Evaluate

$$\int_0^2 \int_{y/2}^1 y e^{x^3}\,dx\,dy.$$

Solution We cannot integrate first with respect to x, as indicated, because $\exp(x^3)$ is known to have no elementary antiderivative. So we try to evaluate the integral by first reversing the order of integration. To do so, we sketch the region of integration specified by the limits in the given iterated integral.

The region R is determined by the inequalities

$$\tfrac{1}{2}y \leq x \leq 1 \quad \text{and} \quad 0 \leq y \leq 2.$$

Thus all points (x, y) of R lie between the horizontal lines $y = 0$ and $y = 2$ and between the two lines $x = y/2$ and $x = 1$. We draw the four lines $y = 0$, $y = 2$, $x = y/2$, and $x = 1$ and find that the region of integration is the shaded triangle that appears in Fig. 14.2.10.

Integrating first with respect to y, from $y_1(x) \equiv 0$ to $y_2(x) = 2x$, we obtain

$$\int_0^2 \int_{y/2}^1 y e^{x^3}\,dx\,dy = \int_0^1 \int_0^{2x} y e^{x^3}\,dy\,dx = \int_0^1 \left[\frac{1}{2}y^2\right]_{y=0}^{2x} e^{x^3}\,dx$$

$$= \int_0^1 2x^2 e^{x^3}\,dx = \left[\frac{2}{3}e^{x^3}\right]_{x=0}^{1} = \frac{2}{3}(e - 1).$$

FIGURE 14.2.10 The region of Example 4.

Properties of Double Integrals

We conclude this section by listing some formal properties of double integrals. Let c be a constant and f and g be continuous functions on a region R on which $f(x, y)$ attains a minimum value m and a maximum value M. Let $a(R)$ denote the area of the region R. If all the indicated integrals exist, then:

$$\iint_R cf(x, y)\, dA = c \iint_R f(x, y)\, dA, \tag{6}$$

$$\iint_R [f(x, y) + g(x, y)]\, dA = \iint_R f(x, y)\, dA + \iint_R g(x, y)\, dA, \tag{7}$$

$$m \cdot a(R) \leq \iint_R f(x, y)\, dA \leq M \cdot a(R), \tag{8}$$

$$\iint_R f(x, y)\, dA = \iint_{R_1} f(x, y)\, dA + \iint_{R_2} f(x, y)\, dA. \tag{9}$$

FIGURE 14.2.11 The regions of Eq. (9).

In Eq. (9), R_1 and R_2 are simply two nonoverlapping regions (with disjoint interiors) with union R (Fig. 14.2.11). We indicate in Problems 45 through 48 proofs of the properties in (6) through (9) for the special case in which R is a rectangle.

The property in Eq. (9) enables us to evaluate double integrals over a region R that is neither vertically nor horizontally simple. All that is necessary is to divide R into a finite number of simple regions $R_1, R_2, \ldots, R_n$. Then we integrate over each (converting each double integral into an iterated integral, as in the examples of this section) and add the results.

EXAMPLE 5 Let f be a function that is integrable on the region R of Fig. 14.2.12. Note that R is not simple, but is the union of the vertically simple region R_1 and the horizontally simple region R_2. Using the boundary curves labeled in the figure and the appropriate order of integration for each region, we see that

$$\iint_R f(x, y)\, dA = \iint_{R_1} f(x, y)\, dA + \iint_{R_2} f(x, y)\, dA$$

$$= \int_{-2}^{2} \int_{1}^{2+x^2/4} f(x, y)\, dy\, dx + \int_{-1}^{1} \int_{-1-y^2}^{1+y^2} f(x, y)\, dx\, dy. \quad \blacklozenge$$

FIGURE 14.2.12 The nonsimple region R is the union of the nonoverlapping simple regions R_1 and R_2.

14.2 TRUE/FALSE STUDY GUIDE

14.2 CONCEPTS: QUESTIONS AND DISCUSSION

1. Sketch a plane region that is (a) both horizontally simple and vertically simple; (b) horizontally simple but not vertically simple; (c) vertically simple but not horizontally simple; (d) neither horizontally nor vertically simple.

2. Sketch several different regions that are neither horizontally nor vertically simple but can be subdivided into different numbers of nonoverlapping regions, each of which is either horizontally simple or vertically simple. What about an annular region bounded by two concentric circles?

3. Construct several examples of double integrals that are readily evaluated by integrating in one order but not in the reverse order.

14.2 PROBLEMS

Evaluate the iterated integrals in Problems 1 through 14.

1. $\int_0^1 \int_0^x (1+x)\, dy\, dx$

2. $\int_0^2 \int_0^{2x} (1+y)\, dy\, dx$

3. $\int_0^1 \int_y^1 (x+y)\, dx\, dy$ (Fig. 14.2.13)

4. $\int_0^2 \int_{y/2}^1 (x+y)\, dx\, dy$ (Fig. 14.2.14)

FIGURE 14.2.13 Problem 3.

FIGURE 14.2.14 Problem 4.

5. $\int_0^1 \int_0^{x^2} xy\, dy\, dx$

6. $\int_0^1 \int_y^{\sqrt{y}} (x+y)\, dx\, dy$

7. $\int_0^1 \int_x^{\sqrt{x}} (2x-y)\, dy\, dx$ (Fig. 14.2.15)

8. $\int_0^2 \int_{-\sqrt{2y}}^{\sqrt{2y}} (3x+2y)\, dx\, dy$ (Fig. 14.2.16)

FIGURE 14.2.15 Problem 7.

FIGURE 14.2.16 Problem 8.

9. $\int_0^1 \int_{x^4}^x (y-x)\, dy\, dx$

10. $\int_{-1}^2 \int_{-y}^{y+2} (x+2y^2)\, dx\, dy$ (Fig. 14.2.17)

11. $\int_0^1 \int_0^{x^3} e^{y/x}\, dy\, dx$

12. $\int_0^\pi \int_0^{\sin x} y\, dy\, dx$ (Fig. 14.2.18)

13. $\int_0^3 \int_0^y \sqrt{y^2+16}\, dx\, dy$

14. $\int_1^{e^2} \int_0^{1/y} e^{xy}\, dx\, dy$

FIGURE 14.2.17 Problem 10.

FIGURE 14.2.18 Problem 12.

In Problems 15 through 24, evaluate the integral of the given function $f(x, y)$ over the plane region R that is described.

15. $f(x,y) = xy$; R is bounded by the parabola $y = x^2$ and the line $y = 4$.

16. $f(x,y) = x^2$; R is bounded by the parabola $y = 2 - x^2$ and the line $y = -4$.

17. $f(x,y) = x$; R is bounded by the parabolas $y = x^2$ and $y = 8 - x^2$.

18. $f(x,y) = y$; R is bounded by the parabolas $x = 1 - y^2$ and $x = y^2 - 1$.

19. $f(x,y) = x$; R is bounded by the x-axis and the curve $y = \sin x$, $0 \leq x \leq \pi$.

20. $f(x,y) = \sin x$; R is bounded by the x-axis and the curve $y = \cos x$, $-\pi/2 \leq x \leq \pi/2$.

21. $f(x,y) = 1/y$; R is the triangle bounded by the lines $y = 1$, $x = e$, and $y = x$.

22. $f(x,y) = xy$; R is the first-quadrant quarter circle bounded by $x^2 + y^2 = 1$ and the coordinate axes.

23. $f(x,y) = 1 - x$; R is the triangle with vertices $(0, 0)$, $(1, 1)$, and $(-2, 1)$.

24. $f(x,y) = 9 - y$; R is the triangle with vertices $(0, 0)$, $(0, 9)$, and $(3, 6)$.

In Problems 25 through 34, first sketch the region of integration, reverse the order of integration as in Examples 3 and 4, and finally evaluate the resulting integral.

25. $\int_{-2}^2 \int_{x^2}^4 x^2 y\, dy\, dx$

26. $\int_0^1 \int_{x^4}^x (x-1)\, dy\, dx$

27. $\int_{-1}^3 \int_{x^2}^{2x+3} x\, dy\, dx$

28. $\int_{-2}^2 \int_{y^2-4}^{4-y^2} y\, dx\, dy$

29. $\int_0^2 \int_{2x}^{4x-x^2} 1\, dy\, dx$

30. $\int_0^1 \int_y^1 e^{-x^2}\, dx\, dy$

31. $\int_0^\pi \int_x^\pi \frac{\sin y}{y}\, dy\, dx$

32. $\int_0^{\sqrt{\pi}} \int_y^{\sqrt{\pi}} \sin x^2\, dx\, dy$

33. $\int_0^1 \int_y^1 \frac{1}{1+x^4}\, dx\, dy$

34. $\int_0^1 \int_{\tan^{-1} y}^{\pi/4} \sec x\, dx\, dy$

In Problems 35 through 40, find the approximate value of

$$\iint_R x\, dA,$$

where R is the region bounded by the two given curves. Before integrating, use a calculator or computer to approximate (graphically or otherwise) the coordinates of the points of intersection of the given curves.

35. $y = x^3 + 1, \quad y = 3x^2$
36. $y = x^4, \quad y = x + 4$
37. $y = x^2 - 1, \quad y = \dfrac{1}{1+x^2}$
38. $y = x^4 - 16, \quad y = 2x - x^2$
39. $y = x^2, \quad y = \cos x$
40. $y = x^2 - 2x, \quad y = \sin x$

In Problems 41 through 44, the region R is the square with vertices $(\pm 1, 0)$ and $(0, \pm 1)$. Use the symmetry of this region around the coordinate axes to reduce the labor of evaluating the given integrals.

41. $\iint_R x\, dA$
42. $\iint_R x^2\, dA$
43. $\iint_R xy\, dA$
44. $\iint_R (x^2 + y^2)\, dA$

45. Use Riemann sums to prove Eq. (6) for the case in which R is a rectangle with sides parallel to the coordinate axes.

46. Use iterated integrals and familiar properties of single integrals to prove Eq. (7) for the case in which R is a rectangle with sides parallel to the coordinate axes.

47. Use Riemann sums to prove the inequalities in (8) for the case in which R is a rectangle with sides parallel to the coordinate axes.

48. Use iterated integrals and familiar properties of single integrals to prove Eq. (9) if R_1 and R_2 are rectangles with sides parallel to the coordinate axes and the right-hand edge of R_1 is the left-hand edge of R_2.

49. Use Riemann sums to prove that

$$\iint_R f(x, y)\, dA \leq \iint_R g(x, y)\, dA$$

if $f(x, y) \leq g(x, y)$ at each point of the region R, a rectangle with sides parallel to the coordinate axes.

50. Suppose that the continuous function f is integrable on the plane region R and that f attains a minimum value m and a maximum value M on R. Assume that R is *connected* in the following sense: For any two points (x_0, y_0) and (x_1, y_1) of R, there is a continuous parametric curve $\mathbf{r}(t)$ in R for which $\mathbf{r}(0) = \langle x_0, y_0 \rangle$ and $\mathbf{r}(1) = \langle x_1, y_1 \rangle$. Let $a(R)$ denote the area of R. Then deduce from (8) the *average value property* of double integrals:

$$\iint_R f(x, y)\, dA = f(\overline{x}, \overline{y}) \cdot a(R)$$

for some point $(\overline{x}, \overline{y})$ of R. [*Suggestion:* If $m = f(x_0, y_0)$ and $M = f(x_1, y_1)$, then you may apply the intermediate value property of the continuous function $f(\mathbf{r}(t))$.]

51. Show by iterated integration that the exact value of the integral in Example 1 is $\tfrac{2}{3}$.

In Problems 52 and 53, first approximate (as in Example 1) the integral

$$\iint_R f(x, y)\, dA$$

of the given function over the region R bounded by the unit circle and the coordinate axes in the first quadrant, except—unlike Example 1—use an inner partition resulting from the use of $n = 5$ subintervals in each direction. Then use iterated integrals to calculate the exact value of the double integral.

52. $f(x, y) = xy$
53. $f(x, y) = xy \exp(y^2)$

14.3 AREA AND VOLUME BY DOUBLE INTEGRATION

Our definition of the double integral $\iint_R f(x, y)\, dA$ was *motivated* in Section 14.2 by the problem of computing the volume of the solid

$$T = \{(x, y, z) \mid (x, y) \in R \text{ and } 0 \leq z \leq f(x, y)\}$$

that lies below the surface $z = f(x, y)$ and above the region R in the xy-plane. Such a solid appears in Fig. 14.3.1. Despite this geometric motivation, the actual definition of the double integral as a limit of Riemann sums does not depend on the concept of volume. We may, therefore, turn matters around and use the double integral to *define* volume.

DEFINITION Volume below $z = f(x, y)$

Suppose that the function f is continuous and nonnegative on the bounded plane region R. Then the **volume** V of the solid that lies below the surface $z = f(x, y)$ and above the region R is defined to be

$$V = \iint_R f(x, y)\, dA, \tag{1}$$

provided that this integral exists.

FIGURE 14.3.1 A solid region T with vertical sides and base R in the xy-plane.

FIGURE 14.3.2 The inner integral in Eq. (1) as the area of a region in the yz-plane.

FIGURE 14.3.3 The cross-sectional area is
$$A = \int_{y_1(x)}^{y_2(x)} f(x, y)\, dy.$$

It is of interest to note the connection between this definition and the cross-sectional approach to volume that we discussed in Section 6.2. If, for example, the region R is vertically simple, then the volume integral in Eq. (1) takes the form

$$V = \iint_R z\, dA = \int_a^b \int_{y_1(x)}^{y_2(x)} f(x, y)\, dy\, dx$$

in terms of iterated integrals. The inner integral

$$A(x) = \int_{y_1(x)}^{y_2(x)} f(x, y)\, dy$$

is equal to the area of the region in the yz-plane that lies below the curve

$$z = f(x, y) \quad (x \text{ fixed})$$

and above the interval $y_1(x) \leq y \leq y_2(x)$ (Fig. 14.3.2). But this is the projection of the cross section shown in Fig. 14.3.3. Hence the value of the inner integral is simply the area of the cross section of the solid region T in a plane perpendicular to the x-axis. Thus

$$V = \int_a^b A(x)\, dx,$$

and so in this case Eq. (1) reduces to "volume is the integral of cross-sectional area."

Volume by Iterated Integrals

A three-dimensional region T is typically described in terms of the surfaces that bound it. The first step in applying Eq. (1) to compute the volume V of such a region is to determine the region R in the xy-plane over which T lies. The second step is to determine the appropriate order of integration. This may be done in the following way:

If each vertical line in the xy-plane meets R in a *single* line segment, then R is vertically simple, and you may integrate first with respect to y. The limits on y will be the y-coordinates $y_1(x)$ and $y_2(x)$ of the endpoints of this line segment. (See Fig. 14.3.4.) The limits on x will be the endpoints a and b of the interval on the x-axis onto which R projects. Theorem 2 of Section 14.2 then gives

$$V = \iint_R f(x, y)\, dA = \int_a^b \int_{y_1(x)}^{y_2(x)} f(x, y)\, dy\, dx. \tag{2}$$

FIGURE 14.3.4 A vertically simple region.

Alternatively,

If each horizontal line in the xy-plane meets R in a *single* line segment, then R is horizontally simple, and you may integrate first with respect to x. In this case

$$V = \iint_R f(x, y)\, dA = \int_c^d \int_{x_1(y)}^{x_2(y)} f(x, y)\, dx\, dy. \tag{3}$$

As indicated in Fig. 14.3.5, $x_1(y)$ and $x_2(y)$ are the x-coordinates of the endpoints of this horizontal line segment, and c and d are the endpoints of the corresponding interval on the y-axis.

FIGURE 14.3.5 A horizontally simple region.

EXAMPLE 1 The rectangle R in the xy-plane consists of those points (x, y) for which $0 \leq x \leq 2$ and $0 \leq y \leq 1$. Find the volume V of the solid that lies below the surface $z = 1 + xy$ and above R (Fig. 14.3.6).

Solution Here $f(x, y) = 1 + xy$, so Eq. (1) yields

$$V = \iint_R z\, dA = \int_0^2 \int_0^1 (1 + xy)\, dy\, dx$$

$$= \int_0^2 \left[y + \frac{1}{2}xy^2 \right]_{y=0}^1 dx = \int_0^2 \left(1 + \frac{1}{2}x \right) dx = \left[x + \frac{1}{4}x^2 \right]_0^2 = 3. \quad \blacklozenge$$

FIGURE 14.3.6 The solid of Example 1.

The special case $f(x, y) \equiv 1$ in Eq. (1) gives the area

$$A = a(R) = \iint_R 1\, dA = \iint_R dA \tag{4}$$

of the plane region R. In this case the solid region T resembles a desert mesa (Fig. 14.3.7)—a solid cylinder with base R of area A and height 1. The volume of any such cylinder—not necessarily circular—is the product of its height and the area of its base. In this case, the iterated integrals in Eqs. (2) and (3) reduce to

$$A = \int_a^b \int_{y_{\text{bot}}}^{y_{\text{top}}} 1\, dy\, dx \quad \text{and} \quad A = \int_c^d \int_{x_{\text{left}}}^{x_{\text{right}}} 1\, dx\, dy,$$

FIGURE 14.3.7 The mesa.

respectively.

Area and Volume by Double Integration SECTION 14.3 957

EXAMPLE 2 Compute by double integration the area A of the region R in the xy-plane that is bounded by the parabola $y = x^2 - 2x$ and the line $y = x$.

Solution As indicated in Fig. 14.3.8, the line $y_{\text{top}} = x$ and the parabola $y_{\text{bot}} = x^2 - 2x$ intersect at the points $(0, 0)$ and $(3, 3)$. (These coordinates are easy to find by solving the equation $y_{\text{top}} = y_{\text{bot}}$.) Therefore,

$$A = \int_a^b \int_{y_{\text{bot}}}^{y_{\text{top}}} 1 \, dy \, dx = \int_0^3 \int_{x^2-2x}^x 1 \, dy \, dx$$

$$= \int_0^3 \Big[y\Big]_{y=x^2-2x}^x dx = \int_0^3 (3x - x^2) \, dx = \left[\frac{3}{2}x^2 - \frac{1}{3}x^3\right]_0^3 = \frac{9}{2}. \quad \blacklozenge$$

FIGURE 14.3.8 The region R of Example 2.

EXAMPLE 3 Find the volume of the wedge-shaped solid T that lies above the xy-plane, below the plane $z = x$, and within the cylinder $x^2 + y^2 = 4$. This wedge is shown in Fig. 14.3.9.

FIGURE 14.3.9 The wedge of Example 3.

FIGURE 14.3.10 Half of the base R of the wedge (Example 3).

Solution The base region R is a semicircle of radius 2, but by symmetry we may integrate over the first-quadrant quarter circle S alone and then double the result. A sketch of the quarter circle (Fig. 14.3.10) helps establish the limits of integration. We could integrate in either order, but integrating with respect to x first gives a slightly simpler computation of the volume V:

$$V = \iint_S z \, dA = 2\int_0^2 \int_0^{\sqrt{4-y^2}} x \, dx \, dy = 2\int_0^2 \left[\frac{1}{2}x^2\right]_{x=0}^{\sqrt{4-y^2}} dy$$

$$= \int_0^2 (4 - y^2) \, dy = \left[4y - \frac{1}{3}y^3\right]_0^2 = \frac{16}{3}.$$

As an exercise, you should integrate in the other order and verify that the result is the same. $\quad \blacklozenge$

Volume Between Two Surfaces

Suppose now that the solid region T lies above the plane region R, as before, but *between* the surfaces $z = z_1(x, y)$ and $z = z_2(x, y)$, where $z_1(x, y) \leqq z_2(x, y)$ for all (x, y) in R (Fig. 14.3.11). Then we get the volume V of T by subtracting the volume below $z = z_1(x, y)$ from the volume below $z = z_2(x, y)$, so

$$V = \iint_R [z_2(x, y) - z_1(x, y)] \, dA. \qquad (5)$$

FIGURE 14.3.11 The solid T has vertical sides and is bounded above and below by surfaces.

More briefly,

$$V = \iint_R (z_{\text{top}} - z_{\text{bot}}) \, dA$$

where $z_{\text{top}} = z_2(x, y)$ describes the top surface and $z_{\text{bot}} = z_1(x, y)$ the bottom surface of T. This is a natural generalization of the formula for the area of the plane region between the curves $y = z_1(x)$ and $y = z_2(x)$ over the interval $[a, b]$. Moreover, like that formula, Eq. (5) is valid even if $z_1(x, y)$, or both $z_1(x, y)$ and $z_2(x, y)$, are negative over part or all of the region R.

EXAMPLE 4 Find the volume V of the solid T bounded by the planes $z = 6$ and $z = 2y$ and by the parabolic cylinders $y = x^2$ and $y = 2 - x^2$. This solid is sketched in Fig. 14.3.12.

Solution Because the given parabolic cylinders are perpendicular to the xy-plane, the solid T has vertical sides. Thus we may think of T as lying between the planes $z_{\text{top}} = 6$ and $z_{\text{bot}} = 2y$ and above the xy-plane region R that is bounded by the parabolas $y = x^2$ and $y = 2 - x^2$. As indicated in Fig. 14.3.13, these parabolas intersect at the points $(-1, 1)$ and $(1, 1)$.

Integrating first with respect to y (for otherwise we would need two integrals), we get

$$V = \iint_R (z_{\text{top}} - z_{\text{bot}}) \, dA = \int_{-1}^{1} \int_{x^2}^{2-x^2} (6 - 2y) \, dy \, dx$$

$$= 2 \int_0^1 \left[6y - y^2 \right]_{y=x^2}^{2-x^2} dx \quad \text{(by symmetry)}$$

$$= 2 \int_0^1 \left([6 \cdot (2 - x^2) - (2 - x^2)^2] - [6x^2 - x^4] \right) dx$$

$$= 2 \int_0^1 (8 - 8x^2) \, dx = 16 \left[x - \frac{1}{3}x^3 \right]_0^1 = \frac{32}{3}. \quad \blacklozenge$$

FIGURE 14.3.12 The solid T of Example 4.

FIGURE 14.3.13 The region R of Example 4.

14.3 TRUE/FALSE STUDY GUIDE

14.3 CONCEPTS: QUESTIONS AND DISCUSSION

These questions involve "trick integrals." In each case the region R of integration is the unit disk $x^2 + y^2 \leq 1$ in the xy-plane, and the evaluation of the double integral by means of iterated single integrals might be tedious. But you should be able to evaluate the integral mentally *either by visualizing the volume represented by the integral or by exploiting symmetry (or both). Do so.*

1. $\iint_R \sqrt{1 - x^2 - y^2} \, dA$

2. $\iint_R (10 - x + y) \, dA$

3. $\iint_R \left(1 - \sqrt{x^2 + y^2} \right) dA$

4. $\iint_R \sqrt{x^2 + y^2} \, dA$

5. $\iint_R (5 - x^2 \sin x + y^3 \cos y) \, dA$

14.3 PROBLEMS

In Problems 1 through 10, use double integration to find the area of the region in the xy-plane bounded by the given curves.

1. $y = x$, $y^2 = x$
2. $y = x$, $y = x^4$
3. $y = x^2$, $y = 2x + 3$ (Fig. 14.3.14)
4. $y = 2x + 3$, $y = 6x - x^2$ (Fig. 14.3.15)

FIGURE 14.3.14 Problem 3.

FIGURE 14.3.15 Problem 4.

5. $y = x^2$, $x + y = 2$, $y = 0$
6. $y = (x-1)^2$, $y = (x+1)^2$, $y = 0$
7. $y = x^2 + 1$, $y = 2x^2 - 3$ (Fig. 14.3.16)
8. $y = x^2 + 1$, $y = 9 - x^2$ (Fig. 14.3.17)

FIGURE 14.3.16 Problem 7.

FIGURE 14.3.17 Problem 8.

9. $y = x$, $y = 2x$, $xy = 2$
10. $y = x^2$, $y = \dfrac{2}{1 + x^2}$

In Problems 11 through 26, find the volume of the solid that lies below the surface $z = f(x, y)$ and above the region in the xy-plane bounded by the given curves.

11. $z = 1 + x + y$; $x = 0$, $x = 1$, $y = 0$, $y = 1$
12. $z = 2x + 3y$; $x = 0$, $x = 3$, $y = 0$, $y = 2$
13. $z = y + e^x$; $x = 0$, $x = 1$, $y = 0$, $y = 2$
14. $z = 3 + \cos x + \cos y$; $x = 0$, $x = \pi$, $y = 0$, $y = \pi$ (Fig. 14.3.18)
15. $z = x + y$; $x = 0$, $y = 0$, $x + y = 1$
16. $z = 3x + 2y$; $x = 0$, $y = 0$, $x + 2y = 4$
17. $z = 1 + x + y$; $x = 1$, $y = 0$, $y = x^2$
18. $z = 2x + y$; $x = 0$, $y = 1$, $x = \sqrt{y}$
19. $z = x^2$; $y = x^2$, $y = 1$
20. $z = y^2$; $x = y^2$, $x = 4$

FIGURE 14.3.18 The surface of Problem 14.

21. $z = x^2 + y^2$; $x = 0$, $x = 1$, $y = 0$, $y = 2$
22. $z = 1 + x^2 + y^2$; $y = x$, $y = 2 - x^2$
23. $z = 9 - x - y$; $y = 0$, $x = 3$, $y = \frac{2}{3}x$
24. $z = 10 + y - x^2$; $y = x^2$, $x = y^2$
25. $z = 4x^2 + y^2$; $x = 0$, $y = 0$, $2x + y = 2$
26. $z = 2x + 3y$; $y = x^2$, $y = x^3$

In Problems 27 through 30, find the volume of the given solid.

27. The solid is bounded by the planes $x = 0$, $y = 0$, $z = 0$, and $3x + 2y + z = 6$.

28. The solid is bounded by the planes $y = 0$, $z = 0$, $y = 2x$, and $4x + 2y + z = 8$.

29. The solid lies under the hyperboloid $z = xy$ and above the triangle in the xy-plane with vertices $(1, 2)$, $(1, 4)$, and $(5, 2)$.

30. The solid lies under the paraboloid $z = 25 - x^2 - y^2$ and above the triangle in the xy-plane with vertices $(-3, -4)$, $(-3, 4)$, and $(5, 0)$.

In Problems 31 through 34, first set up an iterated integral that gives the volume of the given solid. Then use a computer algebra system (if available) to evaluate this integral.

31. The solid lies inside the cylinder $x^2 + y^2 = 1$, above the xy-plane, and below the plane $z = x + 1$ (Fig. 14.3.19).

FIGURE 14.3.19 The solid of Problem 31.

32. The solid lies above the xy-plane and below the paraboloid $z = 9 - x^2 - y^2$.

33. The solid lies inside both the cylinder $x^2 + y^2 = 1$ and the sphere $x^2 + y^2 + z^2 = 4$.

34. The solid lies inside the sphere $x^2 + y^2 + z^2 = 2$ and above the paraboloid $z = x^2 + y^2$.

35. Use double integration to find the volume of the tetrahedron in the first octant that is bounded by the coordinate planes and the plane with equation
$$\frac{x}{a} + \frac{y}{b} + \frac{z}{c} = 1$$
(Fig. 14.3.20). The numbers $a, b,$ and c are positive constants.

FIGURE 14.3.20 The tetrahedron of Problem 35.

FIGURE 14.3.21 The solid of Problem 37.

36. Suppose that $h > a > 0$. Show that the volume of the solid bounded by the cylinder $x^2 + y^2 = a^2$, the plane $z = 0$, and the plane $z = x + h$ is $V = \pi a^2 h$.

37. Find the volume of the first octant part of the solid bounded by the cylinders $x^2 + y^2 = 1$ and $y^2 + z^2 = 1$ (Fig. 14.3.21). [*Suggestion:* One order of integration is considerably easier than the other.]

38. Find by double integration the volume of the solid bounded by the surfaces $y = \sin x$, $y = -\sin x$, $z = \sin x$, and $z = -\sin x$ for $0 \leq x \leq \pi$.

In Problems 39 through 45, you may consult Chapter 7 or the integral table inside the back cover of this book to find antiderivatives of such expressions as $(a^2 - x^2)^{3/2}$.

39. Find the volume of a sphere of radius a by double integration.

40. Use double integration to find the formula $V = V(a, b, c)$ for the volume of an ellipsoid with semiaxes of lengths $a, b,$ and c.

41. Find the volume of the solid bounded below by the xy-plane and above by the paraboloid $z = 25 - x^2 - y^2$ by evaluating a double integral (Fig. 14.3.22).

42. Find the volume of the solid bounded by the two paraboloids $z = x^2 + 2y^2$ and $z = 12 - 2x^2 - y^2$ (Fig. 14.3.23).

FIGURE 14.3.22 The solid paraboloid of Problem 41.

FIGURE 14.3.23 The solid of Problem 42.

43. Find the volume removed when a vertical square hole of edge length R is cut directly through the center of a long horizontal solid cylinder of radius R.

44. Find the volume of the solid bounded by the two surfaces $z = x^2 + 3y^2$ and $z = 4 - y^2$ (Fig. 14.3.24).

FIGURE 14.3.24 The solid of Problem 44.

45. Find the volume V of the solid T bounded by the parabolic cylinders $z = x^2$, $z = 2x^2$, $y = x^2$, and $y = 8 - x^2$.

In Problems 46 and 47, use a computer algebra system to find (either approximately or exactly) the volume of the solid that lies under the surface $z = f(x, y)$ and above the region in the xy-plane that is bounded by $y = \cos x$ and $y = -\cos x$ for $-\pi/2 \leq x \leq \pi/2$.

46. $f(x, y) = 4 - x^2 - y^2$ **47.** $f(x, y) = \cos y$

48. Repeat Problem 47, but with $f(x, y) = |\sin x| \cos x$. Also try to exploit symmetry to evaluate the volume integral manually.

In Problems 49 through 51, the equations of a plane and a paraboloid are given. Use a computer algebra system to evaluate the double integral that gives the volume of the solid bounded by the two surfaces.

49. $z = 2x + 3$ and $z = x^2 + y^2$

50. $z = 4x + 4y$ and $z = x^2 + y^2 - 1$

51. $16x + 18y + z = 0$ and $z = 11 - 4x^2 - 9y^2$

52. Suppose that a square hole with sides of length 2 is cut symmetrically through the center of a sphere of radius 2. Use a computer algebra system to compute the volume thereby removed. Show that your result is (exactly or approximately) equal to the exact value
$$V = \frac{4}{3}\left(19\pi + 2\sqrt{2} - 54 \tan^{-1} \sqrt{2}\right).$$

53. Suppose that a square hole with sides of length 2 is cut off-center through a sphere of radius 4. Let S be the square cross section of the hole in an equatorial plane of the sphere. The midpoint C of S is at distance 2 from the center of the sphere, and the radius of the sphere that passes through C is perpendicular to two sides of S. Use a computer algebra system to show that about 10% of the whole volume of the sphere is removed when the hole is cut.

14.4 DOUBLE INTEGRALS IN POLAR COORDINATES

A double integral may be easier to evaluate after it has been transformed from rectangular xy-coordinates into polar $r\theta$-coordinates. This is likely to be the case when the region R of integration is a *polar rectangle*. A **polar rectangle** is a region described in polar coordinates by the inequalities

$$a \leqq r \leqq b, \qquad \alpha \leqq \theta \leqq \beta. \tag{1}$$

This polar rectangle is shown in Fig. 14.4.1. If $a = 0$, it is a sector of a circular disk of radius b. If $0 < a < b$, $\alpha = 0$, and $\beta = 2\pi$, it is an annular ring of inner radius a and outer radius b. Because the area of a circular sector with radius r and central angle θ is $\frac{1}{2}r^2\theta$, the area of the polar rectangle in (1) is

$$\begin{aligned} A &= \tfrac{1}{2}b^2(\beta - \alpha) - \tfrac{1}{2}a^2(\beta - \alpha) \\ &= \tfrac{1}{2}(a+b)(a-b)(\beta - \alpha) = \bar{r}\,\Delta r\,\Delta\theta, \end{aligned} \tag{2}$$

where $\Delta r = b - a$, $\Delta\theta = \beta - \alpha$, and $\bar{r} = \tfrac{1}{2}(a+b)$ is the *average radius* of the polar rectangle.

Suppose that we want to compute the value of the double integral

$$\iint_R f(x, y)\,dA,$$

where R is the polar rectangle in (1). Thus we want the volume of the solid with base R that lies below the surface $z = f(x, y)$ (Fig. 14.4.2). We defined in Section 14.1 the double integral as a limit of Riemann sums associated with partitions consisting of ordinary rectangles. We can define the double integral in terms of *polar partitions* as well, made up of polar rectangles. We begin with a partition

$$a = r_0 < r_1 < r_2 < \cdots < r_m = b$$

of $[a, b]$ into m subintervals all having the same length $\Delta r = (b-a)/m$ and a partition

$$\alpha = \theta_0 < \theta_1 < \theta_2 < \cdots < \theta_n = \beta$$

of $[\alpha, \beta]$ into n subintervals all having the same length $\Delta\theta = (\beta - \alpha)/n$. This gives the **polar partition** $\mathcal{P}$ of R into the $k = mn$ polar rectangles $R_1, R_2, \ldots, R_k$ indicated in Fig. 14.4.3. The **norm** $|\mathcal{P}|$ of this polar partition is the maximum of the lengths of the diagonals of its polar subrectangles.

Let the center point of R_i have polar coordinates $(r_i^\star, \theta_i^\star)$, where $r_i^\star$ is the average radius of R_i. Then the rectangular coordinates of this point are $x_i^\star = r_i^\star \cos\theta_i^\star$ and

FIGURE 14.4.1 A polar rectangle.

FIGURE 14.4.2 A solid region whose base is the polar rectangle R.

FIGURE 14.4.3 A polar partition of the polar rectangle R.

962 CHAPTER 14 Multiple Integrals

$y_i^\star = r_i^\star \sin\theta_i^\star$. Therefore the Riemann sum for the function $f(x, y)$ associated with the polar partition $\mathcal{P}$ is

$$\sum_{i=1}^{k} f(x_i^\star, y_i^\star)\,\Delta A_i,$$

where $\Delta A_i = r_i^\star \Delta r\,\Delta\theta$ is the area of the polar rectangle R_i [in part a consequence of Eq. (2)]. When we express this Riemann sum in polar coordinates, we obtain

$$\sum_{i=1}^{k} f(x_i^\star, y_i^\star)\,\Delta A_i = \sum_{i=1}^{k} f(r_i^\star \cos\theta_i^\star, r_i^\star \sin\theta_i^\star)\, r_i^\star\,\Delta r\,\Delta\theta$$

$$= \sum_{i=1}^{k} g(r_i^\star, \theta_i^\star)\,\Delta r\,\Delta\theta,$$

where $g(r, \theta) = r \cdot f(r\cos\theta, r\sin\theta)$. This last sum is simply a Riemann sum for the double integral

$$\int_\alpha^\beta \int_a^b g(r, \theta)\,dr\,d\theta = \int_\alpha^\beta \int_a^b f(r\cos\theta, r\sin\theta)\,r\,dr\,d\theta,$$

so it finally follows that

$$\iint_R f(x, y)\,dA = \lim_{|\mathcal{P}|\to 0}\sum_{i=1}^{k} f(x_i^\star, y_i^\star)\,\Delta A_i$$

$$= \lim_{\Delta r,\Delta\theta\to 0}\sum_{i=1}^{k} g(r_i^\star, \theta_i^\star)\,\Delta r\,\Delta\theta = \int_\alpha^\beta \int_a^b g(r, \theta)\,dr\,d\theta.$$

That is,

$$\iint_R f(x, y)\,dA = \int_\alpha^\beta \int_a^b f(r\cos\theta, r\sin\theta)\,r\,dr\,d\theta. \quad (3)$$

Thus we formally transform into polar coordinates a double integral over a polar rectangle of the form in (1) by substituting

$$x = r\cos\theta, \quad y = r\sin\theta, \quad dA = r\,dr\,d\theta \quad (4)$$

and inserting the appropriate limits of integration on r and θ. In particular, *note the "extra" r on the right-hand side* of Eq. (3). You may remember it by visualizing the "infinitesimal polar rectangle" of Fig. 14.4.4, with "area" $dA = r\,dr\,d\theta$.

FIGURE 14.4.4 The dimensions of the small polar rectangle suggest that its area is $dA = r\,dr\,d\theta$.

FIGURE 14.4.5 The paraboloid of Example 1.

EXAMPLE 1 Find the volume V of the solid shown in Fig. 14.4.5. This is the figure bounded below by the xy-plane and above by the paraboloid $z = 25 - x^2 - y^2$.

Solution The paraboloid intersects the xy-plane in the circle $x^2 + y^2 = 25$. We can compute the volume of the solid by integrating over the quarter of that circle that lies in the first quadrant (Fig. 14.4.6) and then multiplying the result by 4. Thus

$$V = 4\int_0^5 \int_0^{\sqrt{25-x^2}} (25 - x^2 - y^2)\,dy\,dx.$$

There is no difficulty in performing the integration with respect to y, but then we are confronted with the integrals

$$\int \sqrt{25-x^2}\,dx, \quad \int x^2\sqrt{25-x^2}\,dx, \quad \text{and} \quad \int (25-x^2)^{3/2}\,dx.$$

Let us instead transform the original integral into polar coordinates. Because $25 - x^2 - y^2 = 25 - r^2$ and because the quarter of the circular disk in the first quadrant

FIGURE 14.4.6 One-fourth of the domain of the integral of Example 1.

is described by

$$0 \leq r \leq 5, \quad 0 \leq \theta \leq \pi/2,$$

Eq. (3) yields the volume

$$V = 4 \int_0^{\pi/2} \int_0^5 (25 - r^2) \, r \, dr \, d\theta$$

$$= 4 \int_0^{\pi/2} \left[\frac{25}{2} r^2 - \frac{1}{4} r^4 \right]_{r=0}^5 d\theta = 4 \cdot \frac{625}{4} \cdot \frac{\pi}{2} = \frac{625\pi}{2}.$$ ◆

More General Polar-Coordinate Regions

If R is a more general region, then we can transform into polar coordinates the double integral

$$\iint_R f(x, y) \, dA$$

by expressing it as a limit of Riemann sums associated with "polar inner partitions" of the sort indicated in Fig. 14.4.7. Instead of giving the detailed derivation—a generalization of the preceding derivation of Eq. (3)—we shall simply give the results in one special case of practical importance.

Figure 14.4.8 shows a *radially simple* region R consisting of those points with polar coordinates that satisfy the inequalities

$$\alpha \leq \theta \leq \beta, \quad r_1(\theta) \leq r \leq r_2(\theta).$$

In this case, the formula

$$\iint_R f(x, y) \, dA = \int_\alpha^\beta \int_{r_1(\theta)}^{r_2(\theta)} f(r \cos \theta, r \sin \theta) \, r \, dr \, d\theta \quad (5)$$

FIGURE 14.4.7 A polar inner partition of the region R.

FIGURE 14.4.8 A radially simple region R.

gives the evaluation in polar coordinates of a double integral over R (under the usual assumption that the indicated integrals exist). Note that we integrate first with respect to r, with the limits $r_1(\theta)$ and $r_2(\theta)$ being the r-coordinates of a typical radial segment in R (Fig. 14.4.8).

Figure 14.4.9 shows how we can set up the iterated integral on the right-hand side of Eq. (5) in a formal way. First, a typical area element $dA = r \, dr \, d\theta$ is swept radially from $r = r_1(\theta)$ to $r = r_2(\theta)$. Second, the resulting strip is rotated from $\theta = \alpha$ to $\theta = \beta$ to sweep out the region R. Equation (5) yields the volume formula

$$V = \int_\alpha^\beta \int_{r_{\text{inner}}}^{r_{\text{outer}}} zr \, dr \, d\theta \quad (6)$$

for the volume V of the solid that lies above the region R of Fig. 14.4.8 and below the surface $z = f(x, y) = f(r \cos \theta, r \sin \theta)$.

Observe that Eqs. (3) and (5) for the evaluation of a double integral in polar coordinates take the form

$$\iint_R f(x, y) \, dA = \iint_S f(r \cos \theta, r \sin \theta) \, r \, dr \, d\theta. \quad (7)$$

The symbol S on the right-hand side represents the appropriate limits on r and θ such that the region R is swept out in the manner indicated in Fig. 14.4.9.

With $f(x, y) \equiv 1$, Eq. (7) reduces to the formula

$$A = a(R) = \iint_S r \, dr \, d\theta \quad (8)$$

FIGURE 14.4.9 Integrating first with respect to r and then with respect to θ.

964 CHAPTER 14 Multiple Integrals

for computing the area $a(R)$ of R by double integration in polar coordinates. Note again that the symbol S refers not to a new region in the xy-plane, but to a new description—in terms of polar coordinates—of the original region R.

EXAMPLE 2 Figure 14.4.10 shows the region R bounded on the inside by the circle $r = 1$ and on the outside by the limaçon $r = 2 + \cos\theta$. By following a typical radial line outward from the origin, we see that $r_{\text{inner}} = 1$ and $r_{\text{outer}} = 2 + \cos\theta$. Hence the area of R is

$$A = \int_\alpha^\beta \int_{r_{\text{inner}}}^{r_{\text{outer}}} r \, dr \, d\theta$$

$$= 2 \int_0^\pi \int_1^{2+\cos\theta} r \, dr \, d\theta \quad \text{(symmetry)}$$

$$= 2 \int_0^\pi \frac{1}{2}[(2+\cos\theta)^2 - 1^2] \, d\theta$$

$$= \int_0^\pi (3 + 4\cos\theta + \cos^2\theta) \, d\theta$$

$$= \int_0^\pi \left(3 + 4\cos\theta + \frac{1}{2} + \frac{1}{2}\cos 2\theta\right) d\theta$$

$$= \int_0^\pi \left(3 + \frac{1}{2}\right) d\theta = \frac{7}{2}\pi.$$

FIGURE 14.4.10 The region R of Example 2.

The cosine terms in the next-to-last integral contribute nothing, because upon integration they yield sine terms that are zero at both limits of integration. ◆

EXAMPLE 3 Find the volume of the solid region that is interior to both the sphere $x^2 + y^2 + z^2 = 4$ of radius 2 and the cylinder $(x-1)^2 + y^2 = 1$. This is the volume of material removed when an off-center hole of radius 1 is bored just tangent to a diameter all the way through a sphere of radius 2 (Fig. 14.4.11).

FIGURE 14.4.11 The sphere with off-center hole (Example 3).

Solution We need to integrate the function $f(x, y) = \sqrt{4 - x^2 - y^2}$ over the disk R that is bounded by the circle with center $(1, 0)$ and radius 1 (Fig. 14.4.12). The desired volume V is twice that of the part above the xy-plane, so

$$V = 2 \iint_R \sqrt{4 - x^2 - y^2} \, dA.$$

But this integral would be awkward to evaluate in rectangular coordinates, so we change to polar coordinates.

The circle of radius 1 in Fig. 14.4.12 is familiar from Section 10.2; its polar equation is $r = 2\cos\theta$. Therefore the region R is described by the inequalities

$$0 \leq r \leq 2\cos\theta, \quad -\pi/2 \leq \theta \leq \pi/2.$$

We shall integrate only over the upper half of R, taking advantage of the symmetry of the sphere-with-hole. This involves doubling, for a second time, the integral we write. So—using Eq. (5)—we find that

FIGURE 14.4.12 The small circle is the domain R of the integral of Example 3.

$$V = 4 \int_0^{\pi/2} \int_0^{2\cos\theta} \sqrt{4 - r^2} \, r \, dr \, d\theta$$

$$= 4 \int_0^{\pi/2} \left[-\frac{1}{3}(4 - r^2)^{3/2}\right]_{r=0}^{2\cos\theta} d\theta = \frac{32}{3} \int_0^{\pi/2} (1 - \sin^3\theta) \, d\theta.$$

Now we see from Formula (113) inside the back cover that

$$\int_0^{\pi/2} \sin^3\theta \, d\theta = \frac{2}{3},$$

and therefore

$$V = \frac{32}{3} \cdot \left(\frac{\pi}{2} - \frac{2}{3}\right) = \frac{16}{3}\pi - \frac{64}{9} \approx 9.64405.$$ ◆

In Example 4 we use a polar-coordinates version of the familiar volume formula

$$V = \iint_R (z_{\text{top}} - z_{\text{bot}})\,dA.$$

EXAMPLE 4 Find the volume of the solid that is bounded above by the paraboloid $z = 8 - r^2$ and below by the paraboloid $z = r^2$ (Fig. 14.4.13).

Solution The curve of intersection of the two paraboloids is found by simultaneous solution of the equations of the two surfaces. We eliminate z to obtain

$$r^2 = 8 - r^2; \quad \text{that is,} \quad r^2 = 4.$$

Hence the solid lies above the plane circular disk D with polar description $0 \leq r \leq 2$, and so the volume of the solid is

$$V = \iint_D (z_{\text{top}} - z_{\text{bot}})\,dA = \int_0^{2\pi} \int_0^2 [(8 - r^2) - r^2]\,r\,dr\,d\theta$$

$$= \int_0^{2\pi} \int_0^2 (8r - 2r^3)\,dr\,d\theta = 2\pi \left[4r^2 - \frac{1}{2}r^4\right]_0^2 = 16\pi.$$ ◆

FIGURE 14.4.13 The solid of Example 4.

EXAMPLE 5 Here we apply a standard polar-coordinates technique to show that

$$\int_0^\infty e^{-x^2}\,dx = \frac{\sqrt{\pi}}{2}. \tag{9}$$

REMARK This important improper integral converges because

$$\int_1^b e^{-x^2}\,dx \leq \int_1^b e^{-x}\,dx \leq \int_1^\infty e^{-x}\,dx = \frac{1}{e}.$$

(The first inequality is valid because $e^{-x^2} \leq e^{-x}$ for $x \geq 1$.) It follows that

$$\int_1^b e^{-x^2}\,dx$$

is a bounded and increasing function of b.

Solution Let V_b denote the volume of the region that lies below the surface $z = e^{-x^2-y^2}$ and above the square with vertices $(\pm b, \pm b)$ in the xy-plane (Fig. 14.4.14). Then

$$V_b = \int_{-b}^b \int_{-b}^b e^{-x^2-y^2}\,dx\,dy = \int_{-b}^b e^{-y^2}\left(\int_{-b}^b e^{-x^2}\,dx\right)dy$$

$$= \left(\int_{-b}^b e^{-x^2}\,dx\right)\left(\int_{-b}^b e^{-y^2}\,dy\right) = \left(\int_{-b}^b e^{-x^2}\,dx\right)^2 = 4\left(\int_0^b e^{-x^2}\,dx\right)^2.$$

It follows that the volume below $z = e^{-x^2-y^2}$ and above the entire xy-plane is

$$V = \lim_{b \to \infty} V_b = \lim_{b \to \infty} 4\left(\int_0^b e^{-x^2}\,dx\right)^2 = 4\left(\int_0^\infty e^{-x^2}\,dx\right)^2 = 4I^2,$$

where I denotes the value of the improper integral in (9).

FIGURE 14.4.14 The surface $z = e^{-x^2-y^2}$ (Example 5).

966 CHAPTER 14 Multiple Integrals

FIGURE 14.4.15 The surface $z = e^{-r^2}$ (Example 5).

Now we compute V by another method—by using polar coordinates. We take the limit, as $b \to +\infty$, of the volume below $z = e^{-x^2-y^2} = e^{-r^2}$ and above the circular disk with center $(0,0)$ and radius b (Fig. 14.4.15). This disk is described by $0 \leq r \leq b, 0 \leq \theta \leq 2\pi$, so we obtain

$$V = \lim_{b \to \infty} \int_0^{2\pi} \int_0^b re^{-r^2}\, dr\, d\theta = \lim_{b \to \infty} \int_0^{2\pi} \left[-\frac{1}{2}e^{-r^2}\right]_{r=0}^b d\theta$$

$$= \lim_{b \to \infty} \int_0^{2\pi} \frac{1}{2}\left[1 - e^{-b^2}\right] d\theta = \lim_{b \to \infty} \pi\left(1 - e^{-b^2}\right) = \pi.$$

We equate these two values of V, and it follows that $4I^2 = \pi$. Therefore, $I = \frac{1}{2}\sqrt{\pi}$, as desired. ◆

14.4 TRUE/FALSE STUDY GUIDE

14.4 CONCEPTS: QUESTIONS AND DISCUSSION

1. Describe a plane region R such that evaluation of $\iint_R f\, dA$ by iterated integration without subdividing the region R would require the use of rectangular coordinates, and another region such that this would require the use of polar coordinates.

2. Can you describe an integral $\iint_R f\, dA$ such that R is the unit square $0 \leq x \leq 1, 0 \leq y \leq 1$, but the integral is more easily evaluated in polar coordinates than in rectangular coordinates?

3. Can you describe an integral $\iint_R f\, dA$ such that R is the unit disk $0 \leq r \leq 1$ but the integral is more easily evaluated in rectangular coordinates than in polar coordinates?

14.4 PROBLEMS

In Problems 1 through 7, find the indicated area by double integration in polar coordinates.

1. The area bounded by the circle $r = 1$

2. The area bounded by the circle $r = 3\sin\theta$

3. The area bounded by the cardioid $r = 1 + \cos\theta$ (Fig. 14.4.16)

4. The area bounded by one loop of $r = 2\cos 2\theta$ (Fig. 14.4.17)

5. The area inside both the circles $r = 1$ and $r = 2\sin\theta$

6. The area inside $r = 2\cos\theta$ and outside the circle $r = 2$

FIGURE 14.4.16 The cardioid of Problem 3.

FIGURE 14.4.17 The rose of Problem 4.

7. The area inside the smaller loop of $r = 1 - 2\sin\theta$ (Fig. 14.4.18)

FIGURE 14.4.18 The limaçon of Problem 7.

In Problems 8 through 12, use double integration in polar coordinates to find the volume of the solid that lies below the given surface and above the plane region R bounded by the given curve.

8. $z = x^2 + y^2$; $r = 3$

9. $z = \sqrt{x^2 + y^2}$; $r = 2$

10. $z = x^2 + y^2$; $r = 2\cos\theta$

11. $z = 10 + 2x + 3y$; $r = \sin\theta$

12. $z = a^2 - x^2 - y^2$; $r = a$

In Problems 13 through 18, evaluate the given integral by first converting to polar coordinates.

13. $\int_0^1 \int_0^{\sqrt{1-y^2}} \dfrac{1}{1+x^2+y^2}\, dx\, dy$ (Fig. 14.4.19)

14. $\int_0^1 \int_0^{\sqrt{1-x^2}} \dfrac{1}{\sqrt{4-x^2-y^2}}\, dy\, dx$ (Fig. 14.4.19)

15. $\int_0^2 \int_0^{\sqrt{4-x^2}} (x^2+y^2)^{3/2}\, dy\, dx$

16. $\int_0^1 \int_x^1 x^2\, dy\, dx$

17. $\int_0^1 \int_0^{\sqrt{1-y^2}} \sin(x^2+y^2)\, dx\, dy$

18. $\int_1^2 \int_0^{\sqrt{2x-x^2}} \dfrac{1}{\sqrt{x^2+y^2}}\, dy\, dx$ (Fig. 14.4.20)

FIGURE 14.4.19 The quarter-circle of Problems 13 and 14.

FIGURE 14.4.20 The quarter-circle of Problem 18.

In Problems 19 through 22, find the volume of the solid that is bounded above and below by the given surfaces $z = z_1(x, y)$ and $z = z_2(x, y)$ and lies above the plane region R bounded by the given curve $r = g(\theta)$.

19. $z = 1$, $z = 3 + x + y$; $r = 1$

20. $z = 2 + x$, $z = 4 + 2x$; $r = 2$

21. $z = 0$, $z = 3 + x + y$; $r = 2\sin\theta$

22. $z = 0$, $z = 1 + x$; $r = 1 + \cos\theta$

Solve Problems 23 through 32 by double integration in polar coordinates.

23. Find the volume of a sphere of radius a by double integration.

24. Find the volume of the solid bounded by the paraboloids $z = 12 - 2x^2 - y^2$ and $z = x^2 + 2y^2$.

25. Suppose that $h > a > 0$. Show that the volume of the solid bounded by the cylinder $x^2 + y^2 = a^2$, the plane $z = 0$, and the plane $z = x + h$ is $V = \pi a^2 h$.

26. Find the volume of the wedge-shaped solid described in Example 3 of Section 14.3 (Fig. 14.4.21).

27. Find the volume bounded by the paraboloids $z = x^2 + y^2$ and $z = 4 - 3x^2 - 3y^2$.

28. Find the volume bounded by the paraboloids $z = x^2 + y^2$ and $z = 2x^2 + 2y^2 - 1$.

FIGURE 14.4.21 The wedge of Problem 26.

FIGURE 14.4.22 The fat ice-cream cone of Problem 29.

29. Find the volume of the "ice-cream cone" bounded by the sphere $x^2 + y^2 + z^2 = a^2$ and the cone $z = \sqrt{x^2+y^2}$. When $a = 1$ this solid is the one shown in Fig. 14.4.22.

30. Find the volume bounded by the paraboloid $z = r^2$, the cylinder $r = 2a\sin\theta$, and the plane $z = 0$.

31. Find the volume that lies below the paraboloid $z = r^2$ and above one loop of the lemniscate with equation $r^2 = 2\sin\theta$.

32. Find the volume that lies inside both the cylinder $x^2 + y^2 = 4$ and the ellipsoid $2x^2 + 2y^2 + z^2 = 18$.

33. If $0 < h < a$, then the plane $z = a - h$ cuts off a spherical segment of height h and radius b from the sphere $x^2 + y^2 + z^2 = a^2$ (Fig. 14.4.23). (a) Show that $b^2 = 2ah - h^2$. (b) Show that the volume of the spherical segment is $V = \frac{1}{6}\pi h(3b^2 + h^2)$.

34. Show by the method of Example 5 that

$$\int_0^\infty \int_0^\infty \dfrac{1}{(1+x^2+y^2)^2}\, dx\, dy = \dfrac{\pi}{4}.$$

35. Find the volume of the solid torus obtained by revolving the disk $r \le a$ around the line $x = b > a$ (Fig. 14.4.24). [*Suggestion:* If the area element $dA = r\, dr\, d\theta$ is revolved around the line, the volume generated is $dV = 2\pi(b-x)\, dA$. Express everything in polar coordinates.]

FIGURE 14.4.23 The spherical segment of Problem 33.

FIGURE 14.4.24 The torus of Problem 35 (the case $a = 1$, $b = 2$ is shown).

In Problems 36 through 40, use double integrals in polar coordinates to find the volumes of the indicated solids.

36. The solid lies above the plane $z = -3$ and below the paraboloid $z = 15 - 2x^2 - 2y^2$.

37. The solid is bounded above by the plane $z = y + 4$ and below by the paraboloid $z = x^2 + y^2 + y$.

38. The solid lies inside the cylinder $x^2 + y^2 = 4$, above the xy-plane, and below the plane $z = x + y + 3$.

39. The solid is bounded by the elliptical paraboloids $z = x^2 + 2y^2$ and $z = 12 - 2x^2 - y^2$.

40. The solid lies inside the ellipsoid $4x^2 + 4y^2 + z^2 = 80$ and above the paraboloid $z = 2x^2 + 2y^2$.

41. Find the volume removed when a circular hole of radius $a < b$ is bored symmetrically through the center of a sphere of radius b. [*Check:* It's about 35% of the volume of the sphere when $a = 1$ and $b = 2$.]

42. Suppose that a circular hole with radius 1 is cut off-center through a sphere of radius 4. The axis of the hole is at distance 2 from the center of the sphere. Use a computer algebra system to show that the volume of material removed is about 8% of the volume of the sphere.

43. Suppose that a hexagonal hole is cut symmetrically through the center of a sphere of radius 2. The cross section of the hole is a unit regular hexagon—a six-sided equiangular polygon with each side and "radius" of length 1. Use a computer algebra system to show that the volume of material removed is about 29% of the volume of the sphere. [To give your computer algebra system a more vigorous workout, you could try a pentagonal (five-sided) or heptagonal (seven-sided) hole, each with "radius" 1. With a unit 17-sided polygon, the volume of the material removed is over 34% of that of the sphere, close to the 35% figure cited in Problem 41.]

14.5 APPLICATIONS OF DOUBLE INTEGRALS

In Section 6.6 we discussed the *mass m* and *centroid* $(\overline{x}, \overline{y})$ of a plane region that corresponds to a thin plate or *lamina* of uniform (constant) density. This special case is amenable to calculation using single-variable integrals. Nevertheless, the double integral provides the proper setting for the general case of a lamina with variable density that occupies a bounded region R in the xy-plane. We suppose that the density of the lamina (in units of mass per unit area) at the point (x, y) is given by the continuous function $\delta(x, y)$.

Let $\mathcal{P} = \{R_1, R_2, \ldots, R_n\}$ be an inner partition of R, and choose a point $(x_i^\star, y_i^\star)$ in each subrectangle R_i (Fig. 14.5.1). Then the mass of the part of the lamina occupying R_i is approximately $\delta(x_i^\star, y_i^\star)\,\Delta A_i$, where ΔA_i denotes the area $a(R_i)$ of R_i. Hence the mass of the entire lamina is given approximately by

$$m \approx \sum_{i=1}^{n} \delta(x_i^\star, y_i^\star)\,\Delta A_i.$$

FIGURE 14.5.1 The area element $\Delta A_i = a(R_i)$.

As the norm $|\mathcal{P}|$ of the inner partition $\mathcal{P}$ approaches zero, this Riemann sum approaches the corresponding double integral over R. We therefore *define* the **mass** m of the lamina by means of the formula

$$m = \iint_R \delta(x, y)\,dA. \tag{1}$$

In brief,

$$m = \iint_R \delta\,dA = \iint_R dm$$

in terms of the density δ and the mass element

$$dm = \delta\,dA.$$

The coordinates $(\overline{x}, \overline{y})$ of the **centroid,** or *center of mass,* of the lamina are defined to be

$$\overline{x} = \frac{1}{m}\iint_R x\delta(x, y)\,dA, \tag{2}$$

$$\overline{y} = \frac{1}{m}\iint_R y\delta(x, y)\,dA. \tag{3}$$

Applications of Double Integrals   SECTION 14.5   969

You may prefer to remember these formulas in the form

$$\bar{x} = \frac{1}{m} \iint_R x\, dm, \qquad \bar{y} = \frac{1}{m} \iint_R y\, dm.$$

Thus $\bar{x}$ and $\bar{y}$ are the *average values* of x and y with respect to mass in the region R. The centroid $(\bar{x}, \bar{y})$ is the point of the lamina where it would balance horizontally if placed on the point of an ice pick (Fig. 14.5.2).

FIGURE 14.5.2 A lamina balanced on its centroid.

If the density function δ has the *constant* value $k > 0$, then the coordinates of $\bar{x}$ and $\bar{y}$ are independent of the specific value of k. (Why?) In such a case we will generally take $\delta \equiv 1$ in our computations. Moreover, in this case m will have the same numerical value as the area A of R, and $(\bar{x}, \bar{y})$ is then called the **centroid of the plane region** R.

Generally, we must calculate all three integrals in Eqs. (1) through (3) in order to find the centroid of a lamina. But sometimes we can take advantage of the following *symmetry principle:* If the plane region R (considered to be a lamina of constant density) is symmetric with respect to the line L—that is, if R is carried onto itself when the plane is rotated through an angle of 180° around the line L—then the centroid of R lies on L (Fig. 14.5.3). For example, the centroid of a rectangle (Fig. 14.5.4) is the point where the perpendicular bisectors of its sides meet, because these bisectors are also lines of symmetry.

In the case of a nonconstant density function δ, we require (for symmetry) that δ—as well as the region itself—be symmetric about the geometric line L of symmetry. That is, we require that $\delta(P) = \delta(Q)$ if (as in Fig. 14.5.3) the points P and Q are symmetrically located with respect to L. Then the centroid of the lamina R will lie on the line L of symmetry.

FIGURE 14.5.3 A line of symmetry.

FIGURE 14.5.4 The centroid of a rectangle.

EXAMPLE 1 Consider the semicircular disk of radius a shown in Fig. 14.5.5. If it has constant density $\delta \equiv 1$, then its mass is $m = \frac{1}{2}\pi a^2$ (numerically equal to its area), and by symmetry its centroid $C(\bar{x}, \bar{y})$ lies on the y-axis. Hence $\bar{x} = 0$, and we need only compute

$$\bar{y} = \frac{1}{m} \iint_R y\, dm$$

$$= \frac{2}{\pi a^2} \int_0^\pi \int_0^a (r \sin \theta)\, r\, dr\, d\theta \qquad \text{(polar coordinates)}$$

$$= \frac{2}{\pi a^2} \Big[-\cos \theta\Big]_0^\pi \left[\frac{1}{3}r^3\right]_0^a = \frac{2}{\pi a^2} \cdot 2 \cdot \frac{a^3}{3} = \frac{4a}{3\pi}.$$

FIGURE 14.5.5 The centroid of a semicircular disk (Example 1).

Thus the centroid of the semicircular lamina is located at the point $(0, 4a/3\pi)$. Note that the computed value for $\bar{y}$ has the dimensions of length (because a is a length), as it should. Any answer that has other dimensions would be suspect. ◆

EXAMPLE 2 A lamina occupies the region bounded by the line $y = x + 2$ and the parabola $y = x^2$ (Fig. 14.5.6). The density of the lamina at the point $P(x, y)$ is proportional to the square of the distance of P from the y-axis—thus $\delta(x, y) = kx^2$ (where k is a positive constant). Find the mass and centroid of the lamina.

Solution The line and the parabola intersect in the two points $(-1, 1)$ and $(2, 4)$, so Eq. (1) gives mass

$$m = \int_{-1}^{2} \int_{x^2}^{x+2} kx^2 \, dy \, dx = k \int_{-1}^{2} \left[x^2 y\right]_{y=x^2}^{x+2} dx$$

$$= k \int_{-1}^{2} (x^3 + 2x^2 - x^4) \, dx = \frac{63}{20} k.$$

FIGURE 14.5.6 The lamina of Example 2.

Then Eqs. (2) and (3) give

$$\bar{x} = \frac{20}{63k} \int_{-1}^{2} \int_{x^2}^{x+2} kx^3 \, dy \, dx = \frac{20}{63} \int_{-1}^{2} \left[x^3 y\right]_{y=x^2}^{x+2} dx$$

$$= \frac{20}{63} \int_{-1}^{2} (x^4 + 2x^3 - x^5) \, dx = \frac{20}{63} \cdot \frac{18}{5} = \frac{8}{7};$$

$$\bar{y} = \frac{20}{63k} \int_{-1}^{2} \int_{x^2}^{x+2} kx^2 y \, dy \, dx = \frac{20}{63} \int_{-1}^{2} \left[\frac{1}{2} x^2 y^2\right]_{y=x^2}^{x+2}$$

$$= \frac{10}{63} \int_{-1}^{2} (x^4 + 4x^3 + 4x^2 - x^6) \, dx = \frac{10}{63} \cdot \frac{531}{35} = \frac{118}{49}.$$

Thus the lamina of this example has mass $63k/20$, and its centroid is located at the point $(\frac{8}{7}, \frac{118}{49})$. ◆

EXAMPLE 3 A lamina is shaped like the first-quadrant quarter-circle of radius a shown in Fig. 14.5.7. Its density is proportional to distance from the origin—that is, its density at (x, y) is $\delta(x, y) = k\sqrt{x^2 + y^2} = kr$ (where k is a positive constant). Find its mass and centroid.

Solution First we change to polar coordinates, because both the shape of the boundary of the lamina and the formula for its density suggest that this will make the computations much simpler. Equation (1) then yields the mass to be

$$m = \iint_R \delta \, dA = \int_0^{\pi/2} \int_0^a kr^2 \, dr \, d\theta$$

$$= k \int_0^{\pi/2} \left[\frac{1}{3} r^3\right]_{r=0}^{a} = k \int_0^{\pi/2} \frac{1}{3} a^3 \, d\theta = \frac{k\pi a^3}{6}.$$

FIGURE 14.5.7 Finding mass and centroid (Example 3).

By symmetry of the lamina and its density function, the centroid lies on the line $y = x$. So Eq. (3) gives

$$\bar{x} = \bar{y} = \frac{1}{m} \iint_R y \delta \, dA = \frac{6}{k \pi a^3} \int_0^{\pi/2} \int_0^a kr^3 \sin \theta \, dr \, d\theta$$

$$= \frac{6}{\pi a^3} \int_0^{\pi/2} \left[\frac{1}{4} r^4 \sin \theta\right]_{r=0}^{a} d\theta = \frac{6}{\pi a^3} \cdot \frac{a^4}{4} \int_0^{\pi/2} \sin \theta \, d\theta = \frac{3a}{2\pi}.$$

Thus the given lamina has mass $\frac{1}{6} k\pi a^3$; its centroid is located at the point $(3a/2\pi, 3a/2\pi)$. ◆

Applications of Double Integrals   SECTION 14.5   971

FIGURE 14.5.8 A solid of volume $V = A \cdot d$ is generated by the area A as its centroid travels the distance $d = 2\pi r$ around a circle of radius r.

Volume and the First Theorem of Pappus

Now we can give a more general proof of the first theorem of Pappus, which was discussed from a single-variable viewpoint in Section 6.6.

FIRST THEOREM OF PAPPUS   Volume of Revolution

Suppose that a plane region R is revolved around an axis in its plane (Fig. 14.5.8), generating a solid of revolution with volume V. Assume that the axis does not intersect the interior of R. Then the volume

$$V = A \cdot d$$

of the solid is the product of the area A of R and the distance d traveled by the centroid of R.

FIGURE 14.5.9 A region R between the graphs of two functions.

FIGURE 14.5.10 A solid of revolution consisting of cylindrical shells.

PROOF   In Section 6.6 we treated the special case of a vertically simple region of the form illustrated in Fig. 14.5.9 and the corresponding volume of revolution illustrated in Fig. 14.5.10. More generally, let $\mathcal{P} = \{R_1, R_2, \ldots, R_n\}$ be an inner partition of R, let $(x_i^\star, y_i^\star)$ be the center of the rectangle R_i, and let ΔA_i denote the area of R_i. Then, by the formula for the volume of a cylindrical shell (Eq. (1) in Section 6.3), the volume obtained by revolving the rectangle R_i in a circle of radius $x_i^\star$ around the y-axis (for instance) is $\Delta V_i = 2\pi x_i^\star \Delta A_i$. Hence the volume of the entire solid of revolution is given approximately by

$$V \approx \sum_{i=1}^{n} \Delta V_i = \sum_{i=1}^{n} 2\pi x_i^\star \Delta A_i.$$

We see here a Riemann sum approximating the integral

$$V = \iint_R 2\pi x \, dA = 2\pi A \cdot \frac{1}{A} \iint_R x \, dA = 2\pi A \cdot \overline{x}$$

(using Eq. (2) with $\delta = 1$). But $d = 2\pi \overline{x}$ is the distance traveled by the centroid, so we conclude that $V = A \cdot d$, as desired.   ◂

FIGURE 14.5.11 A sphere of radius a generated by revolving a semicircular region of area $A = \frac{1}{2}\pi a^2$ around its diameter on the x-axis (Example 4). The centroid of the semicircle travels along a circle of circumference $d = 2\pi \overline{y}$.

EXAMPLE 4   Find the volume V of the sphere of radius a generated by revolving around the x-axis the semicircular region D of Example 1. See Fig. 14.5.11.

Solution   The area of D is $A = \frac{1}{2}\pi a^2$, and we found in Example 1 that $\overline{y} = 4a/3\pi$. Hence Pappus's theorem gives

$$V = 2\pi \overline{y} A = 2\pi \cdot \frac{4a}{3\pi} \cdot \frac{\pi a^2}{2} = \frac{4}{3}\pi a^3.$$ ◆

972 CHAPTER 14 Multiple Integrals

FIGURE 14.5.12 Rotating the circular disk around the y-axis to generated a torus (Example 5).

EXAMPLE 5 Consider the circular disk of Fig. 14.5.12, with radius a and center at the point $(b, 0)$ with $0 < a < b$. Find the volume V of the solid torus generated by revolving this disk around the y-axis. Such a torus is shown in Fig. 14.4.24.

Solution The centroid of the circle is at its center $(b, 0)$, so $\overline{x} = b$. Hence the centroid is revolved through the distance $d = 2\pi b$. Consequently,

$$V = d \cdot A = 2\pi b \cdot \pi a^2 = 2\pi^2 a^2 b.$$

Note that this result is dimensionally correct. ◆

Surface Area and the Second Theorem of Pappus

Centroids of plane *curves* are defined in analogy with centroids of plane regions, so we shall present this topic in less detail. It will suffice for us to treat only the case of constant density $\delta \equiv 1$ (such as a thin wire with unit mass per unit length). Then the centroid $(\overline{x}, \overline{y})$ of the plane curve C is defined by the formulas

$$\overline{x} = \frac{1}{s} \int_C x \, ds, \qquad \overline{y} = \frac{1}{s} \int_C y \, ds \qquad (4)$$

where s is the arc length of C.

The meaning of the integrals in Eq. (4) is that of the notation of Section 6.4. That is, ds is a symbol to be replaced (before the integral is evaluated) with either

$$ds = \sqrt{1 + \left(\frac{dy}{dx}\right)^2} \, dx \quad \text{or} \quad ds = \sqrt{1 + \left(\frac{dx}{dy}\right)^2} \, dy,$$

depending on whether C is a smooth arc of the form $y = f(x)$ or one of the form $x = g(y)$. Alternatively, we may have

$$ds = \sqrt{(dx)^2 + (dy)^2} = \sqrt{\left(\frac{dx}{dt}\right)^2 + \left(\frac{dy}{dt}\right)^2} \, dt$$

if C is presented in parametric form, as in Section 10.5.

EXAMPLE 6 Let J denote the upper half of the *circle* (not the disk) of radius a and center $(0, 0)$, represented parametrically by

$$x = a\cos t, \quad y = a\sin t, \qquad 0 \leq t \leq \pi.$$

The arc J is shown in Fig. 14.5.13. Find its centroid.

Solution Note first that $\overline{x} = 0$ by symmetry. The arc length of J is $s = \pi a$; the arc-length element is

$$ds = \sqrt{(-a\sin t)^2 + (a\cos t)^2} \, dt = a \, dt.$$

Hence the second formula in (4) yields

$$\overline{y} = \frac{1}{\pi a} \int_0^\pi (a\sin t) a \, dt = \frac{a}{\pi} \Big[-\cos t \Big]_0^\pi = \frac{2a}{\pi}.$$

FIGURE 14.5.13 The semicircular arc of Example 6.

Thus the centroid of the semicircular arc is located at the point $(0, 2a/\pi)$ on the y-axis. Note that the answer is both plausible and dimensionally correct. ◆

The first theorem of Pappus has an analogue for surface area of revolution.

SECOND THEOREM OF PAPPUS Surface Area of Revolution

Let the plane curve C be revolved around an axis in its plane that does not intersect the curve. Then the area

$$A = s \cdot d$$

of the surface of revolution generated is equal to the product of the length s of C and the distance d traveled by the centroid of C.

PROOF Let C be a smooth arc parametrized by $x = f(t), y = g(t), a \leqq t \leqq b$. If C is revolved around the y-axis (for instance), then by Eqs. (4) and (8) in Section 10.5 the resulting surface area of revolution is given by

$$A = \int_{t=a}^{b} 2\pi x \, ds = 2\pi s \cdot \frac{1}{s} \int_{t=a}^{b} x \, ds$$

$$= 2\pi s \cdot \overline{x} \quad \left(\text{where} \quad ds = \sqrt{[f'(t)]^2 + [g'(t)]^2} \, dt\right)$$

(using Eq. (4)). But $d = 2\pi \overline{x}$ is the distance traveled by the centroid, so we see that $A = s \cdot d$, and this concludes the proof. ◂

EXAMPLE 7 Find the surface area A of the sphere of radius a generated by revolving around the x-axis the semicircular arc of Example 6.

Solution Because we found that $\overline{y} = 2a/\pi$ and we know that $s = \pi a$, the second theorem of Pappus gives

$$A = 2\pi \overline{y} s = 2\pi \cdot \frac{2a}{\pi} \cdot \pi a = 4\pi a^2.$$

◆

EXAMPLE 8 Find the surface area A of the torus of Example 5.

Solution Now we think of revolving around the y-axis the circle (*not* the disk) of radius a centered at the point $(b, 0)$. Of course, the centroid of the circle is located at its center $(b, 0)$; this follows from the symmetry principle or can be verified by using computations such as those in Example 6. Hence the distance traveled by the centroid is $d = 2\pi b$. Because the circumference of the circle is $s = 2\pi a$, the second theorem of Pappus gives

$$A = 2\pi b \cdot 2\pi a = 4\pi^2 ab.$$

◆

Moments of Inertia

Let R be a plane lamina and L a straight line that may or may not lie in the xy-plane. Then the **moment of inertia** I of R around the axis L is defined to be

$$I = \iint_R p^2 \, dm, \tag{5}$$

where $p = p(x, y)$ denotes the perpendicular distance to L from the point (x, y) of R.

The most important case is that in which the axis of revolution is the z-axis, so $p = r = \sqrt{x^2 + y^2}$ (Fig. 14.5.14). In this case we call $I = I_0$ the **polar moment of inertia** of the lamina R. Thus the polar moment of inertia of R is defined to be

$$I_0 = \iint_R r^2 \delta(x, y) \, dA = \iint_R r^2 \, dm = \iint_R (x^2 + y^2) \, dm. \tag{6}$$

FIGURE 14.5.14 A lamina in the xy-plane in space.

It follows that

$$I_0 = I_x + I_y,$$

where

$$I_x = \iint_R y^2 \, dm = \iint_R y^2 \delta \, dA \tag{7}$$

and

$$I_y = \iint_R x^2 \, dm = \iint_R x^2 \delta \, dA. \tag{8}$$

Here I_x is the moment of inertia of the lamina around the x-axis and I_y is its moment of inertia around the y-axis.

An important application of moments of inertia involves *kinetic energy of rotation*. Consider a circular disk that is revolving around its center (the origin) with angular speed ω radians per second. A mass element dm at distance r from the origin is moving with (linear) velocity $v = r\omega$ (Fig. 14.5.15). Thus the kinetic energy of the mass element is

$$\tfrac{1}{2}(dm)v^2 = \tfrac{1}{2}\omega^2 r^2 \, dm.$$

FIGURE 14.5.15 The rotating disk.

Summing by integration over the whole disk, we find that its kinetic energy due to rotation at angular speed ω is

$$\text{KE}_{\text{rot}} = \iint_R \tfrac{1}{2}\omega^2 r^2 \, dm = \tfrac{1}{2}\omega^2 \iint_R r^2 \, dm;$$

that is,

$$\text{KE}_{\text{rot}} = \tfrac{1}{2} I_0 \omega^2. \tag{9}$$

Because linear kinetic energy has the formula $\text{KE} = \tfrac{1}{2}mv^2$, Eq. (9) suggests (correctly) that moment of inertia is the rotational analogue of mass.

EXAMPLE 9 Compute I_x for a lamina of constant density $\delta \equiv 1$ that occupies the region bounded by the curves $x = \pm y^4$, $-1 \leq y \leq 1$ (Fig. 14.5.16).

Solution Equation (7) gives

$$I_x = \int_{-1}^{1} \int_{-y^4}^{y^4} y^2 \, dx \, dy = \int_{-1}^{1} \left[xy^2 \right]_{x=-y^4}^{y^4} dy = \int_{-1}^{1} 2y^6 \, dy = \frac{4}{7}. \quad \blacklozenge$$

FIGURE 14.5.16 The lamina of Example 9.

The region of Example 9 resembles the cross section of an I beam. It is known that the stiffness, or resistance to bending, of a horizontal beam is proportional to the moment of inertia of its cross section with respect to a horizontal axis through the centroid of the cross section of the beam. Let us compare our I beam with a rectangular beam of equal height 2 and equal area

$$A = \int_{-1}^{1} \int_{-y^4}^{y^4} 1 \, dx \, dy = \frac{4}{5}.$$

The cross section of such a rectangular beam is shown in Fig. 14.5.17. Its width is $\frac{2}{5}$ and the moment of inertia of its cross section is

$$I_x = \int_{-1}^{1} \int_{-1/5}^{1/5} y^2 \, dx \, dy = \frac{4}{15}.$$

FIGURE 14.5.17 A rectangular beam for comparison with the I beam of Example 9.

Because the ratio of $\frac{4}{7}$ to $\frac{4}{15}$ is $\frac{15}{7}$, we see that the I beam is more than twice as strong as a rectangular beam of the same cross-sectional area. This strength is why I beams are commonly used in construction.

EXAMPLE 10 Find the polar moment of inertia of a circular lamina R of radius a and constant density δ centered at the origin.

Solution In Cartesian coordinates, the lamina R occupies the plane region $x^2 + y^2 \leq a^2$; in polar coordinates, this region has the much simpler description $0 \leq r \leq a$, $0 \leq \theta \leq 2\pi$. Equation (6) then gives

$$I_0 = \iint_R r^2 \delta \, dA = \int_0^{2\pi} \int_0^a \delta r^3 \, dr \, d\theta = \frac{\delta \pi a^4}{2} = \frac{1}{2} m a^2,$$

where $m = \delta \pi a^2$ is the mass of the circular lamina. ◆

Finally, the **radius of gyration** $\hat{r}$ of a lamina of mass m around an axis is defined to be

$$\hat{r} = \sqrt{\frac{I}{m}}, \qquad (10)$$

where I is the moment of inertia of the lamina around that axis. For example, the radii of gyration $\hat{x}$ and $\hat{y}$ around the y-axis and x-axis, respectively, are given by

$$\hat{x} = \sqrt{\frac{I_y}{m}} \quad \text{and} \quad \hat{y} = \sqrt{\frac{I_x}{m}}. \qquad (11)$$

Now suppose that this lamina lies in the right half-plane $x > 0$ and is symmetric around the x-axis. If it represents the face of a tennis racquet whose handle (considered of negligible weight) extends along the x-axis from the origin to the face, then the point $(\hat{x}, 0)$ is a plausible candidate for the racquet's "sweet spot" that delivers the maximum impact and control. (See Problem 56.)

The definition in Eq. (10) is motivated by considering a plane lamina R rotating with angular speed ω around the z-axis (Fig. 14.5.18). Then Eq. (10) yields

$$I_0 = m \hat{r}^2,$$

so it follows from Eq. (9) that the kinetic energy of the lamina is

$$KE = \tfrac{1}{2} m (\hat{r} \omega)^2.$$

Thus the kinetic energy of the rotating lamina equals that of a single particle of mass m revolving at the distance $\hat{r}$ from the axis of revolution.

FIGURE 14.5.18 A plane lamina rotating around the z-axis.

14.5 TRUE/FALSE STUDY GUIDE

14.5 CONCEPTS: QUESTIONS AND DISCUSSION

1. Suppose that a plane lamina has a line of symmetry. Must the centroid of the lamina lie on this line?
2. Must the centroid of a plane curve lie on the curve? Must the centroid of a plane region lie within the region? If not, provide counterexamples.

14.5 PROBLEMS

In Problems 1 through 10, find the centroid of the plane region bounded by the given curves. Assume that the density is $\delta \equiv 1$ for each region.

1. $x = 0$, $x = 4$, $y = 0$, $y = 6$
2. $x = 1$, $x = 3$, $y = 2$, $y = 4$
3. $x = -1$, $x = 3$, $y = -2$, $y = 4$
4. $x = 0$, $y = 0$, $x + y = 3$
5. $x = 0$, $y = 0$, $x + 2y = 4$
6. $y = 0$, $y = x$, $x + y = 2$
7. $y = 0$, $y = x^2$, $x = 2$
8. $y = x^2$, $y = 9$
9. $y = 0$, $y = x^2 - 4$
10. $x = -2$, $x = 2$, $y = 0$, $y = x^2 + 1$

In Problems 11 through 30, find the mass and centroid of the plane lamina with the indicated shape and density.

11. The triangular region bounded by $x = 0$, $y = 0$, and $x + y = 1$, with $\delta(x, y) = xy$

12. The triangular region of Problem 11, with $\delta(x, y) = x^2$
13. The region bounded by $y = 0$ and $y = 4 - x^2$, with $\delta(x, y) = y$
14. The region bounded by $x = 0$ and $x = 9 - y^2$, with $\delta(x, y) = x^2$
15. The region bounded by the parabolas $y = x^2$ and $x = y^2$, with $\delta(x, y) = xy$
16. The region of Problem 15, with $\delta(x, y) = x^2 + y^2$
17. The region bounded by the parabolas $y = x^2$ and $y = 2 - x^2$, with $\delta(x, y) = y$
18. The region bounded by $x = 0$, $x = e$, $y = 0$, and $y = \ln x$ for $1 \leq x \leq e$, with $\delta(x, y) \equiv 1$
19. The region bounded by $y = 0$ and $y = \sin x$ for $0 \leq x \leq \pi$, with $\delta(x, y) \equiv 1$
20. The region bounded by $y = 0$, $x = -1$, $x = 1$, and $y = \exp(-x^2)$, with $\delta(x, y) = |xy|$
21. The square with vertices $(0, 0)$, $(0, a)$, (a, a), and $(a, 0)$, with $\delta(x, y) = x + y$
22. The triangular region bounded by the coordinate axes and the line $x + y = a$ $(a > 0)$, with $\delta(x, y) = x^2 + y^2$
23. The region bounded by $y = x^2$ and $y = 4$; $\delta(x, y) = y$
24. The region bounded by $y = x^2$ and $y = 2x + 3$; $\delta(x, y) = x^2$
25. The region of Problem 19; $\delta(x, y) = x$
26. The semicircular region $x^2 + y^2 \leq a^2$, $y \geq 0$; $\delta(x, y) = y$
27. The region of Problem 26; $\delta(x, y) = r$ (the radial polar coordinate)
28. The region bounded by the cardioid with polar equation $r = 1 + \cos\theta$; $\delta(r, \theta) = r$ (Fig. 14.5.19)
29. The region inside the circle $r = 2\sin\theta$ and outside the circle $r = 1$; $\delta(x, y) = y$
30. The region inside the limaçon $r = 1 + 2\cos\theta$ and outside the circle $r = 2$; $\delta(r, \theta) = r$ (Fig. 14.5.20)

FIGURE 14.5.19 The cardioid of Problem 28.

FIGURE 14.5.20 The limaçon of Problem 30.

In Problems 31 through 35, find the polar moment of inertia I_0 of the indicated lamina.

31. The region bounded by the circle $r = a$; $\delta(x, y) = r^n$, where n is a fixed positive integer
32. The lamina of Problem 26
33. The disk bounded by $r = 2\cos\theta$; $\delta(x, y) = k$ (a positive constant)
34. The lamina of Problem 29
35. The region bounded by the right-hand loop of the lemniscate $r^2 = \cos 2\theta$; $\delta(x, y) = r^2$ (Fig. 14.5.21)

FIGURE 14.5.21 The leminscate of Problem 35.

In Problems 36 through 40, find the radii of gyration $\hat{x}$ and $\hat{y}$ of the indicated lamina around the coordinate axes.

36. The lamina of Problem 21
37. The lamina of Problem 23
38. The lamina of Problem 24
39. The lamina of Problem 27
40. The lamina of Problem 33
41. Find the centroid of the first quadrant of the circular disk $x^2 + y^2 \leq r^2$ by direct computation, as in Example 1.
42. Apply the first theorem of Pappus to find the centroid of the first quadrant of the circular disk $x^2 + y^2 \leq r^2$. Use the facts that $\bar{x} = \bar{y}$ (by symmetry) and that revolution of this quarter-disk around either coordinate axis gives a solid hemisphere with volume $V = \frac{2}{3}\pi r^3$.
43. Find the centroid of the arc that consists of the first-quadrant portion of the circle $x^2 + y^2 = r^2$ by direct computation, as in Example 6.
44. Apply the second theorem of Pappus to find the centroid of the quarter-circular arc of Problem 43. Note that $\bar{x} = \bar{y}$ (by symmetry) and that rotation of this arc around either coordinate axis gives a hemisphere with surface area $A = 2\pi r^2$.
45. Show by direct computation that the centroid of the triangle with vertices $(0, 0)$, $(r, 0)$, and $(0, h)$ is the point $(r/3, h/3)$. Verify that this point lies on the line from the vertex $(0, 0)$ to the midpoint of the opposite side of the triangle and two-thirds of the way from the vertex to the midpoint.
46. Apply the first theorem of Pappus and the result of Problem 45 to verify the formula $V = \frac{1}{3}\pi r^2 h$ for the volume of the cone obtained by revolving the triangle around the y-axis.
47. Apply the second theorem of Pappus to show that the lateral surface area of the cone of Problem 46 is $A = \pi r L$, where $L = \sqrt{r^2 + h^2}$ is the slant height of the cone.
48. (a) Find the centroid of the trapezoid shown in Fig. 14.5.22. (b) Apply the first theorem of Pappus and the result of part (a) to show that the volume of the conical frustum generated by revolving the trapezoid around the y-axis is

$$V = \frac{\pi h}{3}\left(r_1^2 + r_1 r_2 + r_2^2\right).$$

FIGURE 14.5.22 The trapezoid of Problem 48.

49. Apply the second theorem of Pappus to show that the lateral surface area of the conical frustum of Problem 48 is $a = \pi(r_1 + r_2)L$, where

$$L = \sqrt{(r_1 - r_2)^2 + h^2}$$

is its slant height.

50. (a) Apply the second theorem of Pappus to verify that the curved surface area of a right circular cylinder of height h and base radius r is $A = 2\pi rh$. (b) Explain how this follows also from the result of Problem 49.

51. (a) Find the centroid of the plane region shown in Fig. 14.5.23, which consists of a semicircular region of radius a sitting atop a rectangular region of width $2a$ and height b whose base is on the x-axis. (b) Then apply the first theorem of Pappus to find the volume generated by rotating this region around the x-axis.

FIGURE 14.5.23 The plane region of Problem 51(a).

52. (a) Consider the plane region of Fig. 14.5.24, bounded by $x^2 = 2py$, $x = 0$, and $y = h = r^2/2p$ ($p > 0$). Show that its area is $A = \frac{2}{3}rh$ and that the x-coordinate of its centroid is $\bar{x} = \frac{3}{8}r$. (b) Use Pappus's theorem and the result of part (a) to show that the volume of a paraboloid of revolution with radius r and height h is $V = \frac{1}{2}\pi r^2 h$.

FIGURE 14.5.24 The region of Problem 52.

53. A uniform rectangular plate with base length a, height b, and mass m is centered at the origin. Show that its polar moment of inertia is $I_0 = \frac{1}{12}m(a^2 + b^2)$.

54. The centroid of a uniform plane region is at $(0, 0)$, and the region has total mass m. Show that its moment of inertia about an axis perpendicular to the xy-plane at the point (x_0, y_0) is

$$I = I_0 + m(x_0^2 + y_0^2).$$

55. Suppose that a plane lamina consists of two nonoverlapping laminae. Show that its polar moment of inertia is the sum of theirs. Use this fact together with the results of Problems 53 and 54 to find the polar moment of inertia of the T-shaped lamina of constant density $\delta = k > 0$ shown in Fig. 14.5.25.

FIGURE 14.5.25 One lamina made of two simpler ones (Problem 55).

56. A racquet consists of a uniform lamina that occupies the region inside the right-hand loop of $r^2 = \cos 2\theta$ on the end of a handle (assumed to be of negligible mass) corresponding to the interval $-1 \leq x \leq 0$ (Fig. 14.5.26). Find the radius of gyration of the racquet around the line $x = -1$. Where is its sweet spot?

FIGURE 14.5.26 The racquet of Problem 56.

In Problems 57 through 60, find the mass m and centroid $(\bar{x}, \bar{y})$ of the indicated plane lamina R. You may use either a computer algebra system or the sine-cosine integrals of Formula (113) inside the back cover.

57. R is bounded by the circle with polar equation $r = 2\sin\theta$ and has density function $\delta(x, y) = y$

58. R is bounded by the circle with polar equation $r = 2\sin\theta$ and has density function $\delta(x, y) = y\sqrt{x^2 + y^2}$

59. R is the semicircular disk bounded by the x-axis and the upper half of the circle with polar equation $r = 2\cos\theta$ and has density function $\delta(x, y) = x$

60. R is the semicircular disk bounded by the x-axis and the upper half of the circle with polar equation $r = 2\cos\theta$ and has density function $\delta(x, y) = x^2 y^2$

14.5 Project: Optimal Design of Downhill Race-Car Wheels

To see moments of inertia in action, suppose that your club is designing an unpowered race car for the annual downhill derby. You have a choice of solid wheels, bicycle wheels with thin spokes, or even solid spherical wheels (like giant ball bearings). Which wheels will make the race car go the fastest?

FIGURE 14.5.27 A circular object rolling down an incline.

Imagine an experiment in which you roll various types of wheels down an incline to see which reaches the bottom the fastest (Fig. 14.5.27). Suppose that a wheel of radius a and mass M starts from rest at the top with potential energy $\text{PE} = Mgh$ and reaches the bottom with angular speed ω and (linear) velocity $v = a\omega$. Then (by conservation of energy) the wheel's initial potential energy has been transformed into a sum $\text{KE}_{\text{tr}} + \text{KE}_{\text{rot}}$ of translation kinetic energy $\text{KE}_{\text{tr}} = \frac{1}{2}Mv^2$ and rotational kinetic energy

$$\text{KE}_{\text{rot}} = \frac{1}{2}I_0\omega^2 = \frac{I_0 v^2}{2a^2}, \tag{1}$$

a consequence of Eq. (9) of this section. Thus

$$Mgh = \frac{1}{2}Mv^2 + \frac{I_0 v^2}{2a^2}. \tag{2}$$

Problems 1 through 8 explore the implications of this formula.

1. Suppose that the wheel's (polar) moment of inertia is given by

$$I_0 = kMa^2 \tag{3}$$

   for some constant k. (For instance, Example 10 gives $k = \frac{1}{2}$ for a wheel in the shape of a uniform solid disk.) Then deduce from Eq. (2) that

$$v = \sqrt{\frac{2gh}{1+k}}. \tag{4}$$

   Thus the smaller k is (and hence the smaller the wheel's moment of inertia), the faster the wheel will roll down the incline.

In Problems 2 through 8, take $g = 32$ ft/s^2 and assume that the vertical height of the incline is $h = 100$ ft.

2. Why does it follow from Eq. (4) that, whatever the wheel's design, the maximum velocity a circular wheel can attain on this incline is 80 ft/s (just under 55 mi/h)?

3. If the wheel is a uniform solid disk (like a medieval wooden wagon wheel) with $I_0 = \frac{1}{2}Ma^2$, what is its speed v at the bottom of the incline?

4. Answer Problem 3 if the wheel is shaped like a narrow bicycle tire, with its entire mass, in effect, concentrated at the distance a from its center. In this case, $I_0 = Ma^2$. (Why?)

5. Answer Problem 3 if the wheel is shaped like an annular ring (or washer) with outer radius a and inner radius b.

Example 3 and Problems 41 and 42 in Section 14.7 provide the moments of inertia needed in Problems 6 through 8. In each of these problems, find the velocity of the wheel when it reaches the bottom of the incline.

6. The wheel is a uniform solid sphere of radius a.
7. The wheel is a very thin, spherical shell whose entire mass is, in effect, concentrated at the distance a from its center.
8. The wheel is a spherical shell with outer radius a and inner radius $b = \frac{1}{2}a$.

Finally, what is your conclusion? What is the shape of the wheels that will yield the fastest downhill race car?

14.6 TRIPLE INTEGRALS

The definition of the triple integral is the three-dimensional version of the definition of the double integral of Section 14.2. Let $f(x, y, z)$ be continuous on the bounded space region T and suppose that T lies inside the rectangular block R determined by the inequalities

$$a \leq x \leq b, \quad c \leq y \leq d, \quad \text{and} \quad p \leq z \leq q.$$

We divide $[a, b]$ into subintervals of equal length Δx, $[c, d]$ into subintervals of equal length Δy, and $[p, q]$ into subintervals of equal length Δz. This generates a partition of R into smaller rectangular blocks (as in Fig. 14.6.1), each of volume $\Delta V = \Delta x \, \Delta y \, \Delta z$. Let $\mathcal{P} = \{T_1, T_2, \ldots, T_n\}$ be the collection of these smaller blocks that lie wholly within T. Then $\mathcal{P}$ is called an **inner partition** of the region T. The **norm** $|\mathcal{P}|$ of $\mathcal{P}$ is the length of a longest diagonal of any of the blocks T_i. If $(x_i^\star, y_i^\star, z_i^\star)$ is an arbitrarily selected point of T_i (for each $i = 1, 2, \ldots, n$), then the **Riemann sum**

$$\sum_{i=1}^{n} f(x_i^\star, y_i^\star, z_i^\star) \, \Delta V$$

is an approximation to the triple integral of f over the region T.

For example, if T is a solid body with density function f, then such a Riemann sum approximates its total mass. We define the **triple integral of f over T** by means of the equation

$$\iiint_T f(x, y, z) \, dV = \lim_{|\mathcal{P}| \to 0} \sum_{i=1}^{n} f(x_i^\star, y_i^\star, z_i^\star) \, \Delta V. \tag{1}$$

FIGURE 14.6.1 One small block in an inner partition of the bounded space region T.

It is proved in advanced calculus that this limit of Riemann sums exists as the norm $|\mathcal{P}|$ approaches zero provided that f is continuous on T and that the boundary of the region T is reasonably well-behaved. (For instance, it suffices for the boundary of T to consist of a finite number of smooth surfaces.)

Just as with double integrals, we ordinarily compute triple integrals by means of iterated integrals. If the region of integration is a rectangular block, as in Example 1, then we can integrate in any order we wish.

FIGURE 14.6.2 The rectangular block T of Example 1, for which $-1 \leq x \leq 1$, $2 \leq y \leq 3$, and $0 \leq z \leq 1$.

EXAMPLE 1 If $f(x, y, z) = xy + yz$ and T consists of those points (x, y, z) in space that satisfy the inequalities

$$-1 \leq x \leq 1, \quad 2 \leq y \leq 3, \quad \text{and} \quad 0 \leq z \leq 1$$

(Fig. 14.6.2), then

$$\iiint_T f(x, y, z)\, dV = \int_{-1}^{1} \int_{2}^{3} \int_{0}^{1} (xy + yz)\, dz\, dy\, dx$$

$$= \int_{-1}^{1} \int_{2}^{3} \left[xyz + \frac{1}{2} yz^2 \right]_{z=0}^{1} dy\, dx$$

$$= \int_{-1}^{1} \int_{2}^{3} \left(xy + \frac{1}{2} y \right) dy\, dx$$

$$= \int_{-1}^{1} \left[\frac{1}{2} xy^2 + \frac{1}{4} y^2 \right]_{y=2}^{3} dx$$

$$= \int_{-1}^{1} \left(\frac{5}{2} x + \frac{5}{4} \right) dx = \left[\frac{5}{4} x^2 + \frac{5}{4} x \right]_{-1}^{1} = \frac{5}{2}. \quad \blacklozenge$$

The applications of double integrals that we saw in earlier sections generalize immediately to triple integrals. If T is a solid body with the density function $\delta(x, y, z)$, then its **mass** m is given by

$$m = \iiint_T \delta\, dV. \tag{2}$$

The case $\delta \equiv 1$ gives the **volume**

$$V = \iiint_T dV \tag{3}$$

of T. The coordinates of its **centroid** are

$$\bar{x} = \frac{1}{m} \iiint_T x\delta\, dV, \tag{4a}$$

$$\bar{y} = \frac{1}{m} \iiint_T y\delta\, dV, \quad \text{and} \tag{4b}$$

$$\bar{z} = \frac{1}{m} \iiint_T z\delta\, dV. \tag{4c}$$

The **moments of inertia** of T around the three coordinate axes are

$$I_x = \iiint_T (y^2 + z^2)\delta\, dV, \tag{5a}$$

$$I_y = \iiint_T (x^2 + z^2)\delta\, dV, \quad \text{and} \tag{5b}$$

$$I_z = \iiint_T (x^2 + y^2)\delta\, dV. \tag{5c}$$

Iterated Triple Integrals

As indicated previously, we almost always evaluate triple integrals by iterated single integration. Suppose that the region T with piecewise smooth boundary is z-**simple:** Each line parallel to the z-axis intersects T (if at all) in a single line segment. In effect, this means that T can be described by the inequalities

$$z_1(x, y) \leq z \leq z_2(x, y), \quad (x, y) \text{ in } R,$$

Triple Integrals SECTION 14.6   981

where R is the vertical projection of T into the xy-plane. Then

$$\iiint_T f(x, y, z)\,dV = \iint_R \left(\int_{z_1(x,y)}^{z_2(x,y)} f(x, y, z)\,dz \right) dA. \tag{6}$$

In Eq. (6), we take $dA = dx\,dy$ or $dA = dy\,dx$, depending on the preferred order of integration over the set R. The limits $z_1(x, y)$ and $z_2(x, y)$ are the z-coordinates of the endpoints of the line segment in which the vertical line at (x, y) meets T (Fig. 14.6.3).

If the region R has the description

$$y_1(x) \leq y \leq y_2(x), \quad a \leq x \leq b,$$

then (integrating last with respect to x),

$$\iiint_T f(x, y, z)\,dV = \int_a^b \int_{y_1(x)}^{y_2(x)} \int_{z_1(x,y)}^{z_2(x,y)} f(x, y, z)\,dz\,dy\,dx.$$

FIGURE 14.6.3 Obtaining the limits of integration for z.

Thus the triple integral reduces in this case to three iterated single integrals. These can (in principle) be evaluated by using the fundamental theorem of calculus.

EXAMPLE 2 Find the mass m of the pyramid T of Fig. 14.6.4 if its density function is given by $\delta(x, y, z) = z$.

Solution The region T is bounded below by the xy-plane $z = 0$ and above by the plane $z = 6 - 3x - 2y$. Its base is the plane region R bounded by the x- and y-axes and the line $y = \frac{1}{2}(6 - 3x)$. Hence Eqs. (2) and (6) yield

$$m = \int_0^2 \int_0^{(6-3x)/2} \int_0^{6-3x-2y} z\,dz\,dy\,dx = \int_0^2 \int_0^{(6-3x)/2} \left[\frac{1}{2} z^2 \right]_{z=0}^{6-3x-2y} dy\,dx$$

$$= \frac{1}{2} \int_0^2 \int_0^{(6-3x)/2} (6 - 3x - 2y)^2\,dy\,dx = \frac{1}{2} \int_0^2 \left[-\frac{1}{6}(6 - 3x - 2y)^3 \right]_{y=0}^{(6-3x)/2} dx$$

$$= \frac{1}{12} \int_0^2 (6 - 3x)^3\,dx = \frac{1}{12} \left[-\frac{1}{12}(6 - 3x)^4 \right]_{x=0}^2 = \frac{6^4}{12^2} = 9.$$

FIGURE 14.6.4 The pyramid T of Example 2; its base is the triangle R in the xy-plane.

We leave as an exercise (Problem 45) to show that the coordinates of the centroid $(\bar{x}, \bar{y}, \bar{z})$ of the pyramid are given by

$$\bar{x} = \frac{1}{9} \int_0^2 \int_0^{(6-3x)/2} \int_0^{6-3x-2y} xz\,dz\,dy\,dx = \frac{2}{5},$$

$$\bar{y} = \frac{1}{9} \int_0^2 \int_0^{(6-3x)/2} \int_0^{6-3x-2y} yz\,dz\,dy\,dx = \frac{3}{5},$$

$$\bar{z} = \frac{1}{9} \int_0^2 \int_0^{(6-3x)/2} \int_0^{6-3x-2y} z^2\,dz\,dy\,dx = \frac{12}{5}. \quad \blacklozenge$$

FIGURE 14.6.5 To find the boundary of R, solve the equation $z_1(x, y) = z_2(x, y)$.

If the solid T is bounded by the *two* surfaces $z = z_1(x, y)$ and $z = z_2(x, y)$ (as in Fig. 14.6.5), then we can find the "base region" R in Eq. (6) as follows. Note that the equation $z_1(x, y) = z_2(x, y)$ determines a vertical cylinder (not necessarily circular) that passes through the curve of intersection of the two surfaces. (Why?) This cylinder intersects the xy-plane in the boundary curve C of the plane region R. In essence, we obtain the equation of the curve C by equating the height functions of the surfaces that form the top and bottom of the space region T.

FIGURE 14.6.6 The solid T of Example 3.

FIGURE 14.6.7 The circular disk R of Example 3.

EXAMPLE 3 Figure 14.6.6 shows the solid T bounded above by the plane $z = y + 2$ and below by the paraboloid $z = x^2 + y^2$. The equation

$$x^2 + y^2 = y + 2; \quad \text{that is,} \quad x^2 + \left(y - \tfrac{1}{2}\right)^2 = \tfrac{9}{4}$$

describes the boundary circle of the disk R of radius $\tfrac{3}{2}$ and with center $(0, \tfrac{1}{2})$ in the xy-plane (Fig. 14.6.7). Because this disk is not centered at the origin, the volume integral

$$V = \iint_R \left(\int_{z=x^2+y^2}^{y+2} dz \right) dA$$

is awkward to evaluate directly. In Example 5 we calculate V by integrating in a different order. ◆

We may integrate first with respect to either x or y if the space region T is either x-**simple** or y-**simple**. Such situations, as well as a z-simple solid, appear in Fig. 14.6.8. For example, suppose that T is y-simple, so that it has a description of the form

$$y_1(x, z) \leq y \leq y_2(x, z), \quad (x, z) \text{ in } R,$$

where R is the projection of T into the xz-plane. Then

$$\iiint_T f(x, y, z) \, dV = \iint_R \left(\int_{y_1(x,z)}^{y_2(x,z)} f(x, y, z) \, dy \right) dA, \tag{7}$$

where $dA = dx \, dz$ or $dA = dz \, dx$ and the limits $y_1(x, z)$ and $y_2(x, z)$ are the y-coordinates of the endpoints of the line segment in which a typical line parallel to the y-axis intersects T. If T is x-simple, we have

$$\iiint_T f(x, y, z) \, dA = \iint_R \left(\int_{x_1(y,z)}^{x_2(y,z)} f(x, y, z) \, dx \right) dA, \tag{8}$$

where $dA = dy \, dz$ or $dA = dz \, dy$ and R is the projection of T into the yz-plane.

EXAMPLE 4 Compute by triple integration the volume of the region T that is bounded by the parabolic cylinder $x = y^2$ and the planes $z = 0$ and $x + z = 1$. Also find the centroid of T given that it has constant density $\delta \equiv 1$.

COMMENT The three segments in Fig. 14.6.9 parallel to the coordinate axes indicate that the region T is simultaneously x-simple, y-simple, and z-simple. We may therefore integrate in any order we choose, so there are six ways to evaluate the integral. Here are three computations of the volume V of T.

FIGURE 14.6.8 Solids that are (a) z-simple, (b) y-simple, and (c) x-simple.

Triple Integrals SECTION 14.6   983

FIGURE 14.6.9 The region T of Example 4 is x-simple, y-simple, and z-simple.

FIGURE 14.6.10 The vertical projection of the solid region T into the xy-plane (Example 4, Solution 1).

Solution 1 The projection of T into the xy-plane is the region shown in Fig. 14.6.10, bounded by $x = y^2$ and $x = 1$. So Eq. (6) gives

$$V = \int_{-1}^{1} \int_{y^2}^{1} \int_{0}^{1-x} dz\, dx\, dy = 2\int_{0}^{1} \int_{y^2}^{1} (1-x)\, dx\, dy$$

$$= 2\int_{0}^{1} \left[x - \frac{1}{2}x^2 \right]_{x=y^2}^{1} dy = 2\int_{0}^{1} \left(\frac{1}{2} - y^2 + \frac{1}{2}y^4 \right) dy = \frac{8}{15}.$$

FIGURE 14.6.11 The vertical projection of the solid region T into the xz-plane (Example 4, Solution 2).

Solution 2 The projection of T into the xz-plane is the triangle bounded by the coordinate axes and the line $x + z = 1$ (Fig. 14.6.11), so Eq. (7) gives

$$V = \int_{0}^{1} \int_{0}^{1-x} \int_{-\sqrt{x}}^{\sqrt{x}} dy\, dz\, dx = 2\int_{0}^{1} \int_{0}^{1-x} \sqrt{x}\, dz\, dx$$

$$= 2\int_{0}^{1} (x^{1/2} - x^{3/2})\, dx = \frac{8}{15}.$$

Solution 3 The projection of T into the yz-plane is the triangle bounded by the y-axis and the parabola $z = 1 - y^2$ (Fig. 14.6.12), so Eq. (8) yields

$$V = \int_{-1}^{1} \int_{0}^{1-y^2} \int_{y^2}^{1-z} dx\, dz\, dy,$$

and evaluation of this integral again gives $V = \frac{8}{15}$.

FIGURE 14.6.12 The vertical projection of the solid region T into the yz-plane (Example 4, Solution 3).

Now for the centroid of T. Because the region T is symmetric with respect to the xz-plane, its centroid lies in this plane, and so $\bar{y} = 0$. We compute $\bar{x}$ and $\bar{z}$ by integrating first with respect to y:

$$\bar{x} = \frac{1}{V} \iiint_T x\, dV = \frac{15}{8} \int_{0}^{1} \int_{0}^{1-x} \int_{-\sqrt{x}}^{\sqrt{x}} x\, dy\, dz\, dx$$

$$= \frac{15}{4} \int_{0}^{1} \int_{0}^{1-x} x^{3/2}\, dz\, dx = \frac{15}{4} \int_{0}^{1} (x^{3/2} - x^{5/2})\, dx = \frac{3}{7};$$

similarly,

$$\bar{z} = \frac{1}{V}\iiint_T z\,dV = \frac{15}{8}\int_0^1 \int_0^{1-x} \int_{-\sqrt{x}}^{\sqrt{x}} z\,dy\,dz\,dx = \frac{2}{7}.$$

Thus the centroid of T is located at the point $(\frac{3}{7}, 0, \frac{2}{7})$. ◆

EXAMPLE 5 Find the volume of the *oblique segment of a paraboloid* bounded by the paraboloid $z = x^2 + y^2$ and the plane $z = y + 2$ (Fig. 14.6.13).

Solution The given region T is z-simple, but its projection into the xy-plane is bounded by the graph of the equation $x^2 + y^2 = y + 2$, which is a translated circle. It would be possible to integrate first with respect to z, but perhaps another choice will yield a simpler integral.

FIGURE 14.6.13 An oblique segment of a paraboloid (Example 5).

FIGURE 14.6.14 Projection of the segment of the paraboloid into the yz-plane (Example 5).

The region T is also x-simple, so we may integrate first with respect to x. The projection of T into the yz-plane is bounded by the line $z = y + 2$ and the parabola $z = y^2$, which intersect at the points $(-1, 1)$ and $(2, 4)$ (Fig. 14.6.14). The endpoints of a line segment in T parallel to the x-axis have x-coordinates $x = \pm\sqrt{z - y^2}$. Because T is symmetric with respect to the yz-plane, we can integrate from $x = 0$ to $x = \sqrt{z - y^2}$ and double the result. Hence T has volume

$$V = 2\int_{-1}^{2}\int_{y^2}^{y+2}\int_0^{\sqrt{z-y^2}} dx\,dz\,dy = 2\int_{-1}^{2}\int_{y^2}^{y+2} \sqrt{z - y^2}\,dz\,dy$$

$$= 2\int_{-1}^{2}\left[\frac{2}{3}(z - y^2)^{3/2}\right]_{z=y^2}^{y+2} dy = \frac{4}{3}\int_{-1}^{2}(2 + y - y^2)^{3/2}\,dy$$

$$= \frac{4}{3}\int_{-3/2}^{3/2}\left(\frac{9}{4} - u^2\right)^{3/2} du \quad \left(\text{completing the square;} \ u = y - \frac{1}{2}\right)$$

$$= \frac{27}{4}\int_{-\pi/2}^{\pi/2} \cos^4\theta\,d\theta \quad \left(u = \frac{3}{2}\sin\theta\right)$$

$$= \frac{27}{4} \cdot 2 \cdot \frac{1}{2} \cdot \frac{3}{4} \cdot \frac{\pi}{2} = \frac{81\pi}{32}.$$

In the final evaluation, we used symmetry—integrating from $\theta = 0$ to $\theta = \pi/2$ and doubling—and then Formula (113) (inside the back cover). ◆

14.6 TRUE/FALSE STUDY GUIDE

14.6 CONCEPTS: QUESTIONS AND DISCUSSION

1. Describe a region T in space such that you can calculate its volume by iterated integration in at least three different orders—integrating with respect to x first in one order, with respect to y first in another order, and finally with respect to z first. Then find its volume in each of these three ways.

2. (a) Give an example of a space region whose volume is most easily calculated by integrating first with respect to x. (b) Repeat, but with respect to y first. (c) Repeat, but with respect to z first.

14.6 PROBLEMS

In Problems 1 through 10, compute the value of the triple integral
$$\iiint_T f(x, y, z)\, dV.$$

1. $f(x, y, z) = x + y + z$; T is the rectangular box $0 \leq x \leq 2$, $0 \leq y \leq 3$, $0 \leq z \leq 1$.

2. $f(x, y, z) = xy \sin z$; T is the cube $0 \leq x \leq \pi$, $0 \leq y \leq \pi$, $0 \leq z \leq \pi$.

3. $f(x, y, z) = xyz$; T is the rectangular block $-1 \leq x \leq 3$, $0 \leq y \leq 2$, $-2 \leq z \leq 6$.

4. $f(x, y, z) = x + y + z$; T is the rectangular block of Problem 3.

5. $f(x, y, z) = x^2$; T is the tetrahedron bounded by the coordinate planes and the first octant part of the plane with equation $x + y + z = 1$.

6. $f(x, y, z) = 2x + 3y$; T is a first-octant tetrahedron as in Problem 5, except that the plane has equation $2x + 3y + z = 6$.

7. $f(x, y, z) = xyz$; T lies below the surface $z = 1 - x^2$ and above the rectangle $-1 \leq x \leq 0$, $0 \leq y \leq 2$ in the xy-plane.

8. $f(x, y, z) = 2y + z$; T lies below the surface with equation $z = 4 - y^2$ and above the rectangle $-1 \leq x \leq 1$, $-2 \leq y \leq 2$ in the xy-plane.

9. $f(x, y, z) = x + y$; T is the region between the surfaces $z = 2 - x^2$ and $z = x^2$ for $0 \leq y \leq 3$ (Fig. 14.6.15).

10. $f(x, y, z) = z$; T is the region between the surfaces $z = y^2$ and $z = 8 - y^2$ for $-1 \leq x \leq 1$.

In Problems 11 through 20, sketch the solid bounded by the graphs of the given equations. Then find its volume by triple integration.

11. $2x + 3y + z = 6$, $x = 0$, $y = 0$, $z = 0$
12. $z = y$, $y = x^2$, $y = 4$, $z = 0$ (Fig. 14.6.16)

FIGURE 14.6.16 The surfaces of Problem 12.

13. $y + z = 4$, $y = 4 - x^2$, $y = 0$, $z = 0$
14. $z = x^2 + y^2$, $z = 0$, $x = 0$, $y = 0$, $x + y = 1$
15. $z = 10 - x^2 - y^2$, $y = x^2$, $x = y^2$, $z = 0$
16. $x = z^2$, $x = 8 - z^2$, $y = -1$, $y = -3$
17. $z = x^2$, $y + z = 4$, $y = 0$, $z = 0$
18. $z = 1 - y^2$, $z = y^2 - 1$, $x + z = 1$, $x = 0$ (Fig. 14.6.17)
19. $y = z^2$, $z = y^2$, $x + y + z = 2$, $x = 0$
20. $y = 4 - x^2 - z^2$, $x = 0$, $y = 0$, $z = 0$, $x + z = 2$

FIGURE 14.6.15 The solid of Problem 9.

FIGURE 14.6.17 The surfaces of Problem 18.

In Problems 21 through 32, assume that the indicated solid has constant density $\delta \equiv 1$.

21. Find the centroid of the solid of Problem 12.

22. Find the centroid of the hemisphere
$$x^2 + y^2 + z^2 \leq R^2, \quad z \geq 0.$$

23. Find the centroid of the solid of Problem 17.

24. Find the centroid of the solid bounded by $z = 1 - x^2$, $z = 0$, $y = -1$, and $y = 1$.

25. Find the centroid of the solid bounded by $z = \cos x$, $x = -\pi/2$, $x = \pi/2$, $y = 0$, $z = 0$, and $y + z = 1$.

26. Find the moment of inertia around the z-axis of the solid of Problem 12.

27. Find the moment of inertia around the y-axis of the solid of Problem 24.

28. Find the moment of inertia around the z-axis of the solid cylinder $x^2 + y^2 \leq R^2$, $0 \leq z \leq H$.

29. Find the moment of inertia around the z-axis of the solid bounded by $x + y + z = 1$, $x = 0$, $y = 0$, and $z = 0$.

30. Find the moment of inertia around the z-axis of the cube with vertices $(\pm\frac{1}{2}, 3, \pm\frac{1}{2})$ and $(\pm\frac{1}{2}, 4, \pm\frac{1}{2})$.

31. Consider the solid paraboloid bounded by $z = x^2 + y^2$ and the plane $z = h > 0$. Show that its centroid lies on its axis of symmetry, two-thirds of the way from its "vertex" $(0, 0, 0)$ to its base.

32. Show that the centroid of a right circular cone lies on the axis of the cone and three-fourths of the way from the vertex to the base.

In Problems 33 through 40, the indicated solid has uniform density $\delta \equiv 1$ unless otherwise indicated.

33. For a cube with edge length a, find the moment of inertia around one of its edges.

34. The density at $P(x, y, z)$ of the first-octant cube with edge length a, faces parallel to the coordinate planes, and opposite vertices $(0, 0, 0)$ and (a, a, a) is proportional to the square of the distance from P to the origin. Find the coordinates of the centroid of this cube.

35. Find the moment of inertia around the z-axis of the cube of Problem 34.

36. The cube bounded by the coordinate planes and the planes $x = 1$, $y = 1$, and $z = 1$ has density $\delta = kz$ at the point $P(x, y, z)$ (k is a positive constant). Find its centroid.

37. Find the moment of inertia around the z-axis of the cube of Problem 36.

38. Find the moment of inertia around a diameter of a solid sphere of radius a.

39. Find the centroid of the first-octant region that is interior to the two cylinders $x^2 + z^2 = 1$ and $y^2 + z^2 = 1$ (Figs. 14.6.18 and 14.6.19).

40. Find the moment of inertia around the z-axis of the solid of Problem 39.

FIGURE 14.6.18 The intersecting cylinders of Problem 39.

FIGURE 14.6.19 The solid of intersection in Problem 39.

41. Find the volume bounded by the elliptic paraboloids $z = 2x^2 + y^2$ and $z = 12 - x^2 - 2y^2$. Note that this solid projects onto a circular disk in the xy-plane.

42. Find the volume bounded by the elliptic paraboloid $y = x^2 + 4z^2$ and the plane $y = 2x + 3$.

43. Find the volume of the elliptical cone bounded by $z = \sqrt{x^2 + 4y^2}$ and the plane $z = 1$. [*Suggestion:* Integrate first with respect to x.]

44. Find the volume of the region bounded by the paraboloid $x = y^2 + 2z^2$ and the parabolic cylinder $x = 2 - y^2$ (Fig. 14.6.20).

FIGURE 14.6.20 The surfaces of Problem 44.

45. Find the centroid of the pyramid in Example 2 with density $\delta(x, y, z) = z$.

46. Find the centroid of the parabolic segment (with density $\delta \equiv 1$) in Example 5.

*For Problems 47 through 52, the **average value** $\overline{f}$ of the function $f(x, y, z)$ at points of the space region T is defined to be*

$$\overline{f} = \frac{1}{V} \iiint_T f(x, y, z)\, dV$$

where V is the volume of T. For instance, if T is a solid with density $\delta \equiv 1$, then the coordinates $\overline{x}$, $\overline{y}$, and $\overline{z}$ of its centroid are the average values of the "coordinate functions" x, y, and z at points of T.

47. Find the average value of the density function $\delta(x, y, z) = z$ at points of the pyramid T of Example 2.

48. Suppose that T is the unit cube in the first octant with diagonally opposite vertices $(0, 0, 0)$ and $(1, 1, 1)$. Find the average of the "squared distance" $f(x, y, z) = x^2 + y^2 + z^2$ of points of T from the origin.

49. Let T be the cube of Problem 48. Find the average squared distance of points of T from its centroid.

50. Let T be the cube of Problem 48, but with density function $\delta(x, y, z) = x + y + z$ that varies linearly from 0 at the origin to 3 at the opposite vertex of T. Find the average value $\bar{\delta}$ of the density of T. Can you guess the value of $\bar{\delta}$ before evaluating the triple integral?

51. Find the average squared distance from the origin of points of the pyramid of Example 2.

52. Suppose that T is the pyramid of Example 2, but with density function $\delta \equiv 1$. Find the average squared distance of points of T from its centroid.

53. Use a computer algebra system to find the average distance of points of the cube T of Problem 48 from the origin. [Answer:
$$\frac{1}{24}\left[6\sqrt{3} - \pi + 8\ln\left(\sqrt{3} + \frac{1}{2}\sqrt{2}\right)\right.$$
$$\left. - 8\ln 2 + 16\ln\left(1 + \sqrt{3}\right)\right] \approx 0.960591956455.]$$

14.6 Project: Archimedes' Floating Paraboloid

Archimedes was interested in floating bodies and studied the possible position (see Fig. 14.6.21) of a floating right circular paraboloid of uniform density. For a paraboloid that floats in an "inclined position," he discovered how to determine its angle of inclination in terms of the volume and centroid of the "oblique segment" of the paraboloid that lies beneath the water line. The principles he introduced for this investigation (over 22 centuries ago) are still important in modern naval architecture.

FIGURE 14.6.21 How a uniform solid paraboloid might float.

For your own personal paraboloid to investigate, let T be the three-dimensional solid region bounded below by the paraboloid $z = x^2 + y^2$ and above by the plane $z = (b - a)y + ab$, where a and b are the smallest and largest nonzero digits (respectively) of your student I.D. number. (If $a = 1$ and $b = 2$ then T is the solid of Example 5.) In the following problems you can evaluate the triple integrals either by hand—consulting an integral table if you wish—or by using a computer algebra system.

1. Find the volume V of the solid oblique paraboloid T. Sketch a picture of T similar to Fig. 14.6.13. Can you see that T is symmetric with respect to the yz-plane? Describe the region R in the yz-plane that is the vertical projection of T. This plane region will determine the z-limits and the y-limits of your triple integral (as in Example 5).

2. Find the coordinates $(\bar{x}, \bar{y}, \bar{z})$ of the centroid C of T (assume that T has density $\delta \equiv 1$).

3. Find the coordinates of the point P at which a plane parallel to the original top plane $z = (b - a)y + ab$ is tangent to the paraboloid. Also find the coordinates of the point Q in which a vertical line through P intersects the top plane. According to Archimedes, the centroid C of Problem 2 should lie on the line PQ two-thirds of the way from P to Q. Is this so, according to your computations? (Compare with Problem 31 of this section.)

14.7 INTEGRATION IN CYLINDRICAL AND SPHERICAL COORDINATES

Suppose that $f(x, y, z)$ is a continuous function defined on the z-simple region T, which—because it is z-simple—can be described by

$$z_1(x, y) \leqq z \leqq z_2(x, y) \quad \text{for } (x, y) \text{ in } R$$

(where R is the projection of T into the xy-plane, as usual). We saw in Section 14.6 that

$$\iiint_T f(x, y, z)\, dV = \iint_R \left(\int_{z_1(x,y)}^{z_2(x,y)} f(x, y, z)\, dz \right) dA. \tag{1}$$

If we can describe the region R more naturally in polar coordinates than in rectangular coordinates, then it is likely that the integration over the plane region R will be simpler if it is carried out in polar coordinates.

We first express the inner partial integral of Eq. (1) in terms of r and θ by writing

$$\int_{z_1(x,y)}^{z_2(x,y)} f(x, y, z)\, dz = \int_{Z_1(r,\theta)}^{Z_2(r,\theta)} F(r, \theta, z)\, dz, \tag{2}$$

where

$$F(r, \theta, z) = f(r \cos\theta, r \sin\theta, z) \tag{3a}$$

and

$$Z_i(r, \theta) = z_i(r \cos\theta, r \sin\theta) \tag{3b}$$

for $i = 1, 2$. Substituting Eq. (2) into Eq. (1) with $dA = r\, dr\, d\theta$ (**important**) gives

$$\iiint_T f(x, y, z)\, dV = \iint_S \left(\int_{Z_1(r,\theta)}^{Z_2(r,\theta)} F(r, \theta, z)\, dz \right) r\, dr\, d\theta, \tag{4}$$

where F, Z_1, and Z_2 are the functions given in (3) and S represents the appropriate limits on r and θ needed to describe the plane region R in polar coordinates (as discussed in Section 14.4). The limits on z are simply the z-coordinates (in terms of r and θ) of a typical line segment joining the lower and upper boundary surfaces of T, as indicated in Fig. 14.7.1.

Thus the general formula for **triple integration in cylindrical coordinates** is

$$\iiint_T f(x, y, z)\, dV = \iiint_U f(r \cos\theta, r \sin\theta, z)\, r\, dz\, dr\, d\theta, \tag{5}$$

where U is not a region in xyz-space, but—as in Section 14.4—a representation of limits on z, r, and θ appropriate to describe the space region T in cylindrical coordinates. Before we integrate, we must replace the variables x and y with $r \cos\theta$ and $r \sin\theta$, respectively, but z is left unchanged. The cylindrical-coordinates volume element

$$dV = r\, dz\, dr\, d\theta$$

may be regarded informally as the product of dz and the polar-coordinates area element $dA = r\, dr\, d\theta$. It is a consequence of the formula $\Delta V = \bar{r}\, \Delta z\, \Delta r\, \Delta \theta$ for the volume of the *cylindrical block* shown in Fig. 14.7.2.

Integration in cylindrical coordinates is particularly useful for computations associated with solids of revolution. So that the limits of integration will be the simplest, the solid should usually be placed so that the axis of revolution is the z-axis.

FIGURE 14.7.1 The limits on z in a triple integral in cylindrical coordinates are determined by the lower and upper surfaces.

FIGURE 14.7.2 The volume of the cylindrical block is $\Delta V = \bar{r}\, \Delta z\, \Delta r\, \Delta \theta$.

EXAMPLE 1 Find the centroid of the first-octant portion T of the solid ball bounded by the sphere $r^2 + z^2 = a^2$. The solid T appears in Fig. 14.7.3.

Solution The volume of the first octant of the solid ball is $V = \frac{1}{8} \cdot \frac{4}{3}\pi a^3 = \frac{1}{6}\pi a^3$. Because $\bar{x} = \bar{y} = \bar{z}$ by symmetry, we need calculate only

$$\bar{z} = \frac{1}{V}\iiint_T z\, dV = \frac{6}{\pi a^3}\int_0^{\pi/2}\int_0^a\int_0^{\sqrt{a^2-r^2}} zr\, dz\, dr\, d\theta$$

$$= \frac{6}{\pi a^3}\int_0^{\pi/2}\int_0^a \frac{1}{2}r(a^2-r^2)\, dr\, d\theta$$

$$= \frac{3}{\pi a^3}\int_0^{\pi/2}\left[\frac{1}{2}a^2r^2 - \frac{1}{4}r^4\right]_{r=0}^a d\theta = \frac{3}{\pi a^3} \cdot \frac{\pi}{2} \cdot \frac{a^4}{4} = \frac{3a}{8}.$$

Thus the centroid is located at the point $(\frac{3}{8}a, \frac{3}{8}a, \frac{3}{8}a)$. Observe that the answer is both plausible and dimensionally correct. ◆

FIGURE 14.7.3 The first octant of the sphere (Example 1).

EXAMPLE 2 Find the volume and centroid of the solid T that is bounded by the paraboloid $z = b(x^2 + y^2)$ ($b > 0$) and the plane $z = h$ ($h > 0$).

Solution Figure 14.7.4 makes it clear that we get the radius of the circular top of T by equating $z = b(x^2+y^2) = br^2$ and $z = h$. This gives $a = \sqrt{h/b}$ for the radius of the circle over which the solid lies. Hence Eq. (4), with $f(x,y,z) \equiv 1$, gives the volume:

$$V = \iiint_T dV = \int_0^{2\pi}\int_0^a\int_{br^2}^h r\, dz\, dr\, d\theta = \int_0^{2\pi}\int_0^a (hr - br^3)\, dr\, d\theta$$

$$= 2\pi\left(\frac{1}{2}ha^2 - \frac{1}{4}ba^4\right) = \frac{\pi h^2}{2b} = \frac{1}{2}\pi a^2 h$$

(because $a^2 = h/b$).

By symmetry, the centroid of T lies on the z-axis, so all that remains is to compute $\bar{z}$:

FIGURE 14.7.4 The paraboloid of Example 2.

$$\bar{z} = \frac{1}{V}\iiint_T z\, dV = \frac{2}{\pi a^2 h}\int_0^{2\pi}\int_0^a\int_{br^2}^h rz\, dz\, dr\, d\theta$$

$$= \frac{2}{\pi a^2 h}\int_0^{2\pi}\int_0^a \left(\frac{1}{2}h^2 r - \frac{1}{2}b^2 r^5\right) dr\, d\theta$$

$$= \frac{4}{a^2 h}\left(\frac{1}{4}h^2 a^2 - \frac{1}{12}b^2 a^6\right) = \frac{2}{3}h,$$

again using the fact that $a^2 = h/b$. Therefore the centroid of T is located at the point $(0, 0, \frac{2}{3}h)$. Again, this answer is both plausible and dimensionally correct. ◆

FIGURE 14.7.5 Volume and centroid of a right circular paraboloid in terms of the circumscribed cylinder.

We can summarize the results of Example 2 as follows: The volume of a right circular paraboloid is *half* that of the circumscribed cylinder (Fig. 14.7.5), and its centroid lies on its axis of symmetry *two-thirds* of the way from the "vertex" at $(0, 0, 0)$ to its circular "base" at the top.

Spherical Coordinate Integrals

When the boundary surfaces of the region T of integration are spheres, cones, or other surfaces with simple descriptions in spherical coordinates, it is generally advantageous to transform a triple integral over T into spherical coordinates. Recall from Section 12.8 that the relationship between spherical coordinates (ρ, ϕ, θ) (shown in

Fig. 14.7.6) and rectangular coordinates (x, y, z) is given by

$$x = \rho \sin\phi \cos\theta, \qquad y = \rho \sin\phi \sin\theta, \qquad z = \rho \cos\phi. \tag{6}$$

Suppose, for example, that T is the **spherical block** determined by the simple inequalities

$$\rho_1 \leq \rho \leq \rho_2 = \rho_1 + \Delta\rho,$$
$$\phi_1 \leq \phi \leq \phi_2 = \phi_1 + \Delta\phi, \tag{7}$$
$$\theta_1 \leq \theta \leq \theta_2 = \theta_1 + \Delta\theta.$$

FIGURE 14.7.6 The spherical coordinates (ρ, ϕ, θ) of the point P.

As indicated by the dimensions labeled in Fig. 14.7.7, this spherical block is (if $\Delta\rho$, $\Delta\phi$, and $\Delta\theta$ are small) *approximately* a rectangular block with dimensions $\Delta\rho$, $\rho_1 \Delta\phi$, and $\rho_1 \sin\phi_2 \Delta\theta$. Thus its volume is approximately $\rho_1^2 \sin\phi_2 \Delta\rho \Delta\phi \Delta\theta$. It can be shown (see Problem 19 of Section 14.8) that the *exact* volume of the spherical block described in (7) is

$$\Delta V = \hat{\rho}^2 \sin\hat{\phi} \, \Delta\rho \, \Delta\phi \, \Delta\theta \tag{8}$$

for certain numbers $\hat{\rho}$ and $\hat{\phi}$ such that $\rho_1 < \hat{\rho} < \rho_2$ and $\phi_1 < \hat{\phi} < \phi_2$.

Now suppose that we partition each of the intervals $[\rho_1, \rho_2]$, $[\phi_1, \phi_2]$, and $[\theta_1, \theta_2]$ into n subintervals of lengths

$$\Delta\rho = \frac{\rho_2 - \rho_1}{n}, \quad \Delta\phi = \frac{\phi_2 - \phi_1}{n}, \quad \text{and} \quad \Delta\theta = \frac{\theta_2 - \theta_1}{n},$$

respectively. This produces a **spherical partition** $\mathcal{P}$ of the spherical block T into $k = n^3$ smaller spherical blocks $T_1, T_2, \ldots, T_k$; see Fig. 14.7.8. By Eq. (8), there exists a point $(\hat{\rho}_i, \hat{\phi}_i, \hat{\theta}_i)$ of the spherical block T_i such that its volume is $\Delta V_i = \hat{\rho}_i^2 \sin\hat{\phi}_i \Delta\rho \Delta\phi \Delta\theta$. The **norm** $|\mathcal{P}|$ of $\mathcal{P}$ is the length of the longest diagonal of any of the small spherical blocks $T_1, T_2, \ldots, T_k$.

If $(x_i^\star, y_i^\star, z_i^\star)$ are the rectangular coordinates of the point with spherical coordinates $(\hat{\rho}_i, \hat{\phi}_i, \hat{\theta}_i)$, then the definition of the triple integral as a limit of Riemann sums as the norm $|\mathcal{P}|$ approaches zero gives

$$\iiint_T f(x, y, z)\, dV = \lim_{|\mathcal{P}| \to 0} \sum_{i=1}^{k} f(x_i^\star, y_i^\star, z_i^\star) \Delta V_i$$

$$= \lim_{|\mathcal{P}| \to 0} \sum_{i=1}^{k} F(\hat{\rho}_i, \hat{\phi}_i, \hat{\theta}_i) \hat{\rho}_i^2 \sin\hat{\phi}_i \, \Delta\rho \, \Delta\phi \, \Delta\theta, \tag{9}$$

FIGURE 14.7.7 The volume of the spherical block is approximately $\rho_1^2 \sin\phi_2 \Delta\rho \Delta\phi \Delta\theta$.

FIGURE 14.7.8 The spherical block T divided into k smaller spherical blocks.

where

$$F(\rho, \phi, \theta) = f(\rho \sin\phi \cos\theta, \rho \sin\phi \sin\theta, \rho \cos\phi) \qquad (10)$$

is the result of substituting Eq. (6) into $f(x, y, z)$. But the right-hand sum in Eq. (9) is simply a Riemann sum for the triple integral

$$\int_{\theta_1}^{\theta_2} \int_{\phi_1}^{\phi_2} \int_{\rho_1}^{\rho_2} F(\rho, \phi, \theta)\, \rho^2 \sin\phi \, d\rho \, d\phi \, d\theta.$$

It therefore follows that

$$\iiint_T f(x, y, z)\, dV = \int_{\theta_1}^{\theta_2} \int_{\phi_1}^{\phi_2} \int_{\rho_1}^{\rho_2} F(\rho, \phi, \theta)\, \rho^2 \sin\phi \, d\rho \, d\phi \, d\theta. \qquad (11)$$

Thus we transform the integral

$$\iiint_T f(x, y, z)\, dV$$

into spherical coordinates by replacing the rectangular-coordinate variables x, y, and z with their expressions in Eq. (6) in terms of the spherical-coordinate variables ρ, ϕ, and θ. In addition, we write

$$dV = \rho^2 \sin\phi \, d\rho \, d\phi \, d\theta$$

for the volume element in spherical coordinates.

More generally, we can transform the triple integral

$$\iiint_T f(x, y, z)\, dV$$

into spherical coordinates whenever the region T is **centrally simple**—that is, whenever it has a spherical-coordinates description of the form

$$\rho_1(\phi, \theta) \leqq \phi \leqq \rho_2(\phi, \theta), \qquad \phi_1 \leqq \phi \leqq \phi_2, \qquad \theta_1 \leqq \theta \leqq \theta_2. \qquad (12)$$

If so, then

$$\iiint_T f(x, y, z)\, dV = \int_{\theta_1}^{\theta_2} \int_{\phi_1}^{\phi_2} \int_{\rho_1(\phi,\theta)}^{\rho_2(\phi,\theta)} F(\rho, \phi, \theta)\, \rho^2 \sin\phi \, d\rho \, d\phi \, d\theta. \qquad (13)$$

The limits on ρ in Eq. (13) are simply the ρ-coordinates (in terms of ϕ and θ) of the endpoints of a typical radial segment that joins the "inner" and "outer" parts of the boundary of T (Fig. 14.7.9). Thus the general formula for **triple integration in spherical coordinates** is

$$\iiint_T f(x, y, z)\, dV = \iiint_U f(\rho \sin\phi \cos\theta, \rho \sin\phi \sin\theta, \rho \cos\phi)\, \rho^2 \sin\phi \, d\rho \, d\phi \, d\theta,$$

(14)

FIGURE 14.7.9 A centrally simple region.

where, as before, U does not denote a region in xyz-space but rather indicates limits on ρ, ϕ, and θ appropriate to describe the region T in spherical coordinates.

EXAMPLE 3 A solid ball T with constant density δ is bounded by the spherical surface with equation $\rho = a$. Use spherical coordinates to compute its volume V and its moment of inertia I_z around the z-axis.

Solution The points of the ball T are described by the inequalities

$$0 \leqq \rho \leqq a, \qquad 0 \leqq \phi \leqq \pi, \qquad 0 \leqq \theta \leqq 2\pi.$$

We take $f = F \equiv 1$ in Eq. (11) and thereby obtain

$$V = \iiint_T dV = \int_0^{2\pi} \int_0^{\pi} \int_0^a \rho^2 \sin\phi \, d\rho \, d\phi \, d\theta$$

$$= \frac{1}{3}a^3 \int_0^{2\pi} \int_0^{\pi} \sin\phi \, d\phi \, d\theta$$

$$= \frac{1}{3}a^3 \int_0^{2\pi} \left[-\cos\phi\right]_{\phi=0}^{\pi} d\theta = \frac{2}{3}a^3 \int_0^{2\pi} d\theta = \frac{4}{3}\pi a^3.$$

The distance from the typical point (ρ, ϕ, θ) of the sphere to the z-axis is $r = \rho \sin\phi$, so the moment of inertia of the sphere around that axis is

$$I_z = \iiint_T r^2 \delta \, dV = \int_0^{2\pi} \int_0^{\pi} \int_0^a \delta \rho^4 \sin^3\phi \, d\rho \, d\phi \, d\theta$$

$$= \frac{1}{5}\delta a^5 \int_0^{2\pi} \int_0^{\pi} \sin^3\phi \, d\phi \, d\theta$$

$$= \frac{2}{5}\pi \delta a^5 \int_0^{\pi} \sin^3\phi \, d\phi = \frac{2}{5}\pi \delta a^5 \cdot 2 \cdot \frac{2}{3} = \frac{2}{5}ma^2,$$

where $m = \frac{4}{3}\pi a^3 \delta$ is the mass of the ball. (In evaluating the final integral, we used symmetry and Formula (113) inside the back cover.) The answer is dimensionally correct because it is the product of mass and the square of a distance. The answer is plausible because it implies that, for purposes of rotational inertia, the sphere acts as if its mass were concentrated about 63% of the way from the axis to the equator. ◆

EXAMPLE 4 Find the volume and centroid of the uniform "ice-cream cone" C that is bounded by the cone $\phi = \pi/6$ and the sphere $\rho = 2a\cos\phi$ of radius a. The sphere and the part of the cone within it are shown in Fig. 14.7.10.

Solution The ice-cream cone is described by the inequalities

$$0 \leqq \theta \leqq 2\pi, \qquad 0 \leqq \phi \leqq \frac{\pi}{6}, \qquad 0 \leqq \rho \leqq 2a\cos\phi.$$

Using Eq. (13) to compute its volume, we get

$$V = \int_0^{2\pi} \int_0^{\pi/6} \int_0^{2a\cos\phi} \rho^2 \sin\phi \, d\rho \, d\phi \, d\theta$$

$$= \frac{8}{3}a^3 \int_0^{2\pi} \int_0^{\pi/6} \cos^3\phi \sin\phi \, d\phi \, d\theta$$

$$= \frac{16}{3}\pi a^3 \left[-\frac{1}{4}\cos^4\phi\right]_0^{\pi/6} = \frac{7}{12}\pi a^3.$$

FIGURE 14.7.10 The ice-cream cone of Example 4 is the part of the cone that lies within the sphere.

Now for the centroid. It is clear by symmetry that $\bar{x} = \bar{y} = 0$. We may also assume that C has density $\delta \equiv 1$, so that the mass of C is numerically the same as its volume. Because $z = \rho \cos\phi$, the z-coordinate of the centroid of C is

$$\bar{z} = \frac{1}{V} \iiint_C z \, dV = \frac{12}{7\pi a^3} \int_0^{2\pi} \int_0^{\pi/6} \int_0^{2a\cos\phi} \rho^3 \cos\phi \sin\phi \, d\rho \, d\phi \, d\theta$$

$$= \frac{48a}{7\pi} \int_0^{2\pi} \int_0^{\pi/6} \cos^5\phi \sin\phi \, d\phi \, d\theta = \frac{96a}{7} \left[-\frac{1}{6}\cos^6\phi\right]_0^{\pi/6} = \frac{37a}{28}.$$

Hence the centroid of the ice-cream cone is located at the point $(0, 0, \frac{37}{28}a)$. ◆

14.7 TRUE/FALSE STUDY GUIDE

14.7 CONCEPTS: QUESTIONS AND DISCUSSION

1. Give examples of triple integrals that are most easily evaluated using (a) cylindrical rather than rectangular or spherical coordinates; (b) spherical rather than rectangular or cylindrical coordinates.
2. Describe a triple integral that you can most easily evaluate by using cylindrical coordinates and integrating first with respect to θ. Then evaluate it.
3. Describe a triple integral that you can most easily evaluate by using spherical coordinates and integrating first with respect to ϕ. Then evaluate it.

14.7 PROBLEMS

Solve Problems 1 through 20 by triple integration in cylindrical coordinates. Assume throughout that each solid has unit density unless another density function is specified.

1. Find the volume of the solid bounded above by the plane $z = 4$ and below by the paraboloid $z = r^2$.
2. Find the centroid of the solid of Problem 1.
3. Derive the formula for the volume of a sphere of radius a.
4. Find the moment of inertia around the z-axis of the solid sphere of Problem 3 given that the z-axis passes through its center.
5. Find the volume of the region that lies inside both the sphere $x^2 + y^2 + z^2 = 4$ and the cylinder $x^2 + y^2 = 1$.
6. Find the centroid of the half of the region of Problem 5 that lies on or above the xy-plane.
7. Find the mass of the cylinder $0 \leq r \leq a, 0 \leq z \leq h$ if its density at (x, y, z) is z.
8. Find the centroid of the cylinder of Problem 7.
9. Find the moment of inertia around the z-axis of the cylinder of Problem 7.
10. Find the volume of the region that lies inside both the sphere $x^2 + y^2 + z^2 = 4$ and the cylinder $x^2 + y^2 - 2x = 0$ (Fig. 14.7.11).

FIGURE 14.7.11 The sphere and cylinder of Problem 10.

11. Find the volume and centroid of the region bounded by the plane $z = 0$ and the paraboloid $z = 9 - x^2 - y^2$.
12. Find the volume and centroid of the region bounded by the paraboloids $z = x^2 + y^2$ and $z = 12 - 2x^2 - 2x^2$.
13. Find the volume of the region bounded by the paraboloids $z = 2x^2 + y^2$ and $z = 12 - x^2 - 2y^2$.
14. Find the volume of the region bounded below by the paraboloid $z = x^2 + y^2$ and above by the plane $z = 2x$ (Fig. 14.7.12).

FIGURE 14.7.12 The plane and paraboloid of Problem 14.

15. Find the volume of the region bounded above by the spherical surface $x^2 + y^2 + z^2 = 2$ and below by the paraboloid $z = x^2 + y^2$ (Fig. 14.7.13).

FIGURE 14.7.13 The sphere and paraboloid of Problem 15.

16. A homogeneous solid cylinder has mass m and radius a. Show that its moment of inertia around its axis of symmetry is $\frac{1}{2}ma^2$.
17. Find the moment of inertia I of a homogeneous solid right circular cylinder around a diameter of its base. Express I in terms of the radius a, the height h, and the (constant) density δ of the cylinder.
18. Find the centroid of a homogeneous solid right circular cylinder of radius a and height h.

19. Find the volume of the region bounded by the plane $z = 1$ and the cone $z = r$.

20. Show that the centroid of a homogeneous solid right circular cone lies on its axis three-quarters of the way from its vertex to its base.

Solve Problems 21 through 30 by triple integration in spherical coordinates.

21. Find the centroid of a homogeneous solid hemisphere of radius a.

22. Find the mass and centroid of the solid hemisphere $x^2 + y^2 + z^2 \leq a^2$, $z \geq 0$ if its density δ is proportional to distance z from its base—so $\delta = kz$ (where k is a positive constant).

23. Solve Problem 19 by triple integration in spherical coordinates.

24. Solve Problem 20 by triple integration in spherical coordinates.

25. Find the volume and centroid of the uniform solid that lies inside the sphere $\rho = a$ and above the cone $r = z$.

26. Find the moment of inertia I_z of the solid of Problem 25.

27. Find the moment of inertia around a tangent line of a solid homogeneous sphere of radius a and total mass m.

28. A spherical shell of mass m is bounded by the spheres $\rho = a$ and $\rho = 2a$, and its density function is $\delta = \rho^2$. Find its moment of inertia around a diameter.

29. Describe the surface $\rho = 2a \sin\phi$ and compute the volume of the region it bounds.

30. Describe the surface $\rho = 1 + \cos\phi$ and compute the volume of the region it bounds. Figure 14.7.14 may be useful.

FIGURE 14.7.14 The surface of Problem 30.

31. Find the moment of inertia around the x-axis of the region that lies inside both the cylinder $r = a$ and the sphere $\rho = 2a$.

32. Find the moment of inertia around the z-axis of the ice-cream cone of Example 4.

33. Find the mass and centroid of the ice-cream cone of Example 4 if its density at (x, y, z) is $\delta(x, y, z) = z$.

34. Find the moment of inertia of the ice-cream cone of Problem 33 around the z-axis.

35. Suppose that a gaseous spherical star of radius a has density function $\delta = k(1 - \rho^2/a^2)$, so its density varies from $\delta = k$ at its center to $\delta = 0$ at its boundary $\rho = a$. Show that its mass is $\frac{2}{5}$ that of a similar star with uniform density k.

36. Find the moment of inertia around a diameter of the gaseous spherical star of Problem 35.

37. (a) Use spherical coordinates to evaluate the integral

$$\iiint_B \exp(-\rho^3)\, dV$$

where B is the solid ball of radius a centered at the origin. (b) Let $a \to \infty$ in the result of part (a) to show that

$$\int_{-\infty}^{\infty} \int_{-\infty}^{\infty} \int_{-\infty}^{\infty} \exp(-(x^2 + y^2 + z^2)^{3/2})\, dx\, dy\, dz = \tfrac{4}{3}\pi.$$

38. Use the method of Problem 37 to show that

$$\int_{-\infty}^{\infty} \int_{-\infty}^{\infty} \int_{-\infty}^{\infty} (x^2 + y^2 + z^2)^{1/2}$$
$$\times \exp(-x^2 - y^2 - z^2)\, dx\, dy\, dz = 2\pi.$$

39. Find the average distance of points of a solid ball of radius a from the center of the ball. (The definition of the average value of a function precedes Problem 47 in Section 14.6.)

40. Find the average distance of the points of a solid ball of radius a from a fixed boundary point of the ball.

Problems 41 and 42 provide results that are needed in the Section 14.5 project.

41. A spherical shell of radius a and negligible thickness has area density δ, so its mass is $m = 4\pi\delta a^2$. Show that its moment of inertia about an axis of symmetry is $I_0 = \tfrac{2}{3}ma^2$.

42. A spherical shell has inner radius a, outer radius b, and uniform density δ. Show that its moment of inertia about an axis of symmetry is $I_0 = \tfrac{2}{5}mc^2$, where m is the mass of the shell and

$$c^2 = \frac{b^5 - a^5}{b^3 - a^3}.$$

43. A hole of radius $a < b$ is bored symmetrically through the center of a solid sphere of radius b and uniform density δ, leaving a "ring" of mass m. Show that the moment of inertia of this ring about its axis of symmetry is $I_0 = \tfrac{1}{5}m(3a^2 + 2b^2)$.

44. The three cylinders $x^2 + y^2 = 1$, $x^2 + z^2 = 1$, and $y^2 + z^2 = 1$ intersect as illustrated in Fig. 14.7.15(a); Fig. 14.7.15(b) shows a view directly from above, looking downward along the z-axis. Find the volume of the region that lies within all three cylinders.

FIGURE 14.7.15(a) The three intersecting cylinders of Problem 44.

FIGURE 14.7.15(b) The view looking down from a point high on the z-axis.

FIGURE 14.7.17 The system of Problem 47.

$$dV = \rho^2 \sin\phi \, d\rho \, d\phi \, d\theta$$

45. Figure 14.7.16 shows the bumpy sphere with spherical-coordinates equation $\rho = 6 + 3\cos 3\theta \sin 5\phi$. Use a computer algebra system to find the volume of the region enclosed by this bumpy sphere.

Then $2w \, dw = 2\rho c \sin\phi \, d\phi$ and $w \cos\alpha + \rho \cos\phi = c$. (Why?)]

48. Consider now the spherical shell $a \leq r \leq b$ with uniform density δ. Show that this shell exerts *no* net force on a point mass m located at the point $(0, 0, c)$ *inside* it—that is, with $|c| < a$. The computation will be the same as in Problem 47 except for the limits of integration on ρ and w.

49. If the earth were perfectly spherical with radius $R = 6370$ km, *uniform* density δ, and mass $M = \frac{4}{3}\pi\delta R^3$, then (according to Example 3) its moment of inertia about its polar axis would be $I = \frac{2}{5}MR^2$. In actuality, however, measurements from satellites indicate that

$$I = kMR^2 \qquad (15)$$

FIGURE 14.7.16 The bumpy sphere of Problem 45.

where $k \approx 0.371 < \frac{2}{5}$. The reason is that, instead of having a uniform interior, a more realistic model of the earth has a dense core covered with a lighter mantle a few thousand kilometers thick (Fig. 14.7.18). The density of the core is $\delta_1 \approx 11 \times 10^3$ kg/m^3 and that of the mantle is $\delta_2 \approx 5 \times 10^3$ kg/m^3. (a) With this core-mantle model, calculate the mass M of the earth and its polar moment of inertia I (using Problem 42) in terms of the unknown radius x of the spherical core. (b) Substitute your calculated values of M and I in Eq. (15) and use a computer algebra system to solve the resulting equation for x.

46. The bumpy sphere of Fig. 14.7.16 looks somewhat symmetrical. Is its centroid actually at the origin?

A crucial discovery of Newton (proved in his Principia Mathematica*) was the fact that the gravitational attraction of a uniform solid sphere (such as an idealized planet) is the same as though all of the mass of the planet were concentrated at its center. Problems 47 and 48 deal with this and a related fact.*

47. Consider a homogeneous spherical ball of radius a centered at the origin, with density δ and mass $M = \frac{4}{3}\pi a^3 \delta$. Show that the gravitational force **F** exerted by this ball on a point mass m located at the point $(0, 0, c)$, where $c > a$ (Fig. 14.7.17), is the same as though all the mass of the ball were concentrated at its center $(0, 0, 0)$. That is, show that $|\mathbf{F}| = GMm/c^2$. [*Suggestion:* By symmetry you may assume that the force is vertical, so that $\mathbf{F} = F_z\mathbf{k}$. Set up the integral

$$F_z = -\int_0^{2\pi}\int_0^a\int_0^\pi \frac{Gm\delta\cos\alpha}{w^2} \rho^2 \sin\phi \, d\phi \, d\rho \, d\theta.$$

Change the first variable of integration from ϕ to w by using the law of cosines:

$$w^2 = \rho^2 + c^2 - 2\rho c \cos\phi.$$

FIGURE 14.7.18 The core and mantle of the earth.

14.8 SURFACE AREA

Until now our concept of a surface has been the graph $z = f(x, y)$ of a function of two variables. Occasionally we have seen such a surface defined implicitly by an equation of the form $F(x, y, z) = 0$. Now we want to introduce the more precise concept of a *parametric surface*—the two-dimensional analogue of a parametric curve.

FIGURE 14.8.1 The uv-region R on which the transformation $\mathbf{r}$ is defined.

FIGURE 14.8.2 The parametric surface S in xyz-space.

A **parametric surface** S is the *image* of a function or transformation $\mathbf{r}$ that is defined on a region R in the uv-plane (Fig. 14.8.1) and has values in xyz-space (Fig. 14.8.2). The **image** under $\mathbf{r}$ of each point (u, v) in R is the point in xyz-space with position vector

$$\mathbf{r}(u, v) = \langle x(u, v), y(u, v), z(u, v) \rangle. \quad (1)$$

The parametric surface S is called **smooth** provided that the component functions of $\mathbf{r}$ have continuous partial derivatives with respect to u and v and, moreover, the vectors

$$\mathbf{r}_u = \frac{\partial \mathbf{r}}{\partial u} = \langle x_u, y_u, z_u \rangle = \frac{\partial x}{\partial u}\mathbf{i} + \frac{\partial y}{\partial u}\mathbf{j} + \frac{\partial z}{\partial u}\mathbf{k} \quad (2)$$

and

$$\mathbf{r}_v = \frac{\partial \mathbf{r}}{\partial v} = \langle x_v, y_v, z_v \rangle = \frac{\partial x}{\partial v}\mathbf{i} + \frac{\partial y}{\partial v}\mathbf{j} + \frac{\partial z}{\partial v}\mathbf{k} \quad (3)$$

are nonzero and nonparallel at each interior point of R. (Compare this with the definition of *smooth* parametric curve $\mathbf{r}(t)$ in Section 10.4.) We call the variables u and v the *parameters* for the surface S, in analogy with the single parameter t for a parametric curve.

FIGURE 14.8.3 A rectangle in the $r\theta$-plane; the domain of the function $z = g(r, \theta)$ of Example 1.

EXAMPLE 1 (a) We may regard the graph $z = f(x, y)$ of a function as a parametric surface with parameters x and y. In this case the transformation $\mathbf{r}$ from the xy-plane to xyz-space has the component functions

$$x = x, \qquad y = y, \qquad z = f(x, y). \quad (4)$$

(b) Similarly, we may regard a surface given in cylindrical coordinates by the graph of $z = g(r, \theta)$ as a parametric surface with parameters r and θ. The transformation $\mathbf{r}$ from the $r\theta$-plane (Fig. 14.8.3) to xyz-space (Fig. 14.8.4) is then given by

$$x = r\cos\theta, \qquad y = r\sin\theta, \qquad z = g(r, \theta). \quad (5)$$

(c) We may regard a surface given in spherical coordinates by $\rho = h(\phi, \theta)$ as a parametric surface with parameters ϕ and θ, and the corresponding transformation from the $\phi\theta$-plane to xyz-space is then given by

$$x = h(\phi, \theta)\sin\phi\cos\theta, \qquad y = h(\phi, \theta)\sin\phi\sin\theta, \qquad z = h(\phi, \theta)\cos\phi. \quad (6)$$

FIGURE 14.8.4 A cylindrical-coordinates surface in xyz-space (Example 1).

The concept of a parametric surface lets us treat all these special cases, and many others, with the same techniques. ◆

Surface Area of Parametric Surfaces

Now we want to define the *surface area* of the general smooth parametric surface given in Eq. (1). We begin with an inner partition of the region R—the domain of $\mathbf{r}$ in the uv-plane—into rectangles $R_1, R_2, \ldots, R_n$, each with dimensions Δu and Δv. Let (u_i, v_i) be the lower left-hand corner of R_i (as in Fig. 14.8.5). The image S_i of R_i under $\mathbf{r}$ will not generally be a rectangle in xyz-space; it will look more like a *curvilinear figure* on the image surface S, with $\mathbf{r}(u_i, v_i)$ as one "vertex" (Fig. 14.8.6). Let ΔS_i denote the area of this curvilinear figure S_i.

The parametric curves $\mathbf{r}(u, v_i)$ and $\mathbf{r}(u_i, v)$—with parameters u and v, respectively—lie on the surface S and meet at the point $\mathbf{r}(u_i, v_i)$. At this point of intersection, these two curves have the tangent vectors $\mathbf{r}_u(u_i, v_i)$ and $\mathbf{r}_v(u_i, v_i)$ shown in Fig. 14.8.7. Hence their vector product

$$\mathbf{N}(u_i, v_i) = \mathbf{r}_u(u_i, v_i) \times \mathbf{r}_v(u_i, v_i) \tag{7}$$

is a vector normal to S at the point $\mathbf{r}(u_i, v_i)$.

Now suppose that both Δu and Δv are small. Then the area ΔS_i of the curvilinear figure S_i should be approximately equal to the area ΔP_i of the parallelogram with adjacent sides $\mathbf{r}_u(u_i, v_i) \Delta u$ and $\mathbf{r}_v(u_i, v_i) \Delta v$ (Fig. 14.8.8). But the area of this parallelogram is

$$\Delta P_i = |\mathbf{r}_u(u_i, v_i) \Delta u \times \mathbf{r}_v(u_i, v_i) \Delta v| = |\mathbf{N}(u_i, v_i)| \, \Delta u \, \Delta v.$$

This means that the area $a(S)$ of the surface S should be given approximately by

$$a(S) = \sum_{i=1}^{n} \Delta S_i \approx \sum_{i=1}^{n} \Delta P_i,$$

so

$$a(S) \approx \sum_{i=1}^{n} |\mathbf{N}(u_i, v_i)| \, \Delta u \, \Delta v.$$

But this last sum is a Riemann sum for the double integral

$$\iint_R |\mathbf{N}(u, v)| \, du \, dv.$$

FIGURE 14.8.5 The rectangle R_i in the uv-plane.

FIGURE 14.8.6 The image of R_i is a curvilinear figure.

FIGURE 14.8.7 The vector $\mathbf{N}$ normal to the surface at $\mathbf{r}(u_i, v_i)$.

FIGURE 14.8.8 The area of the parallelogram P_i is an approximation to the area of the curvilinear figure S_i.

We are therefore motivated to *define* the **surface area** A of the smooth parametric surface S by

$$A = a(S) = \iint_R |\mathbf{N}(u,v)|\, du\, dv = \iint_R \left| \frac{\partial \mathbf{r}}{\partial u} \times \frac{\partial \mathbf{r}}{\partial v} \right| du\, dv. \qquad (8)$$

Surface Area in Rectangular Coordinates

In the case of the surface $z = f(x, y)$ for (x, y) in the region R in the xy-plane, the component functions of $\mathbf{r}$ are given by the equations in (4) with parameters x and y (in place of u and v). Then

$$\mathbf{N} = \frac{\partial \mathbf{r}}{\partial x} \times \frac{\partial \mathbf{r}}{\partial y} = \begin{vmatrix} \mathbf{i} & \mathbf{j} & \mathbf{k} \\ 1 & 0 & \dfrac{\partial f}{\partial x} \\ 0 & 1 & \dfrac{\partial f}{\partial y} \end{vmatrix} = -\frac{\partial f}{\partial x}\mathbf{i} - \frac{\partial f}{\partial y}\mathbf{j} + \mathbf{k},$$

so Eq. (8) takes the special form

$$A = a(S) = \iint_R \sqrt{1 + \left(\frac{\partial f}{\partial x}\right)^2 + \left(\frac{\partial f}{\partial y}\right)^2}\, dx\, dy = \iint_R \sqrt{1 + z_x^2 + z_y^2}\, dx\, dy. \qquad (9)$$

EXAMPLE 2 Find the area of the ellipse cut from the plane $z = 2x + 2y + 1$ by the cylinder $x^2 + y^2 = 1$ (Fig. 14.8.9).

Solution Here, R is the unit circle in the xy-plane with area

$$\iint_R 1\, dx\, dy = \pi,$$

so Eq. (9) gives the area of the ellipse to be

$$A = \iint_R \sqrt{1 + z_x^2 + z_y^2}\, dx\, dy$$

$$= \iint_R \sqrt{1 + 2^2 + 2^2}\, dx\, dy = \iint_R 3\, dx\, dy = 3\pi. \qquad \blacklozenge$$

FIGURE 14.8.9 The cylinder and plane of Example 2.

REMARK Computer-generated figures such as Fig. 14.8.9 could not be constructed easily without using parametric surfaces. For example, the vertical cylinder in Fig. 14.8.9 was generated by instructing the computer to plot the parametric surface defined on the $r\theta$-rectangle $-5 \leqq z \leqq 5, 0 \leqq \theta \leqq 2\pi$ by

$$\mathbf{r}(z, \theta) = \langle \cos\theta, \sin\theta, z \rangle.$$

Is it clear that the image of this transformation is the cylinder $x^2 + y^2 = 1, -5 \leqq z \leqq 5$?

Surface Area in Cylindrical Coordinates

Now consider a cylindrical-coordinates surface $z = g(r, \theta)$ parametrized by the equations in (5) for (r, θ) in a region R of the $r\theta$-plane. Then the normal vector is

$$\mathbf{N} = \frac{\partial \mathbf{r}}{\partial r} \times \frac{\partial \mathbf{r}}{\partial \theta} = \begin{vmatrix} \mathbf{i} & \mathbf{j} & \mathbf{k} \\ \cos\theta & \sin\theta & \dfrac{\partial z}{\partial r} \\ -r\sin\theta & r\cos\theta & \dfrac{\partial z}{\partial \theta} \end{vmatrix}$$

$$= \mathbf{i}\left(\frac{\partial z}{\partial \theta}\sin\theta - r\frac{\partial z}{\partial r}\cos\theta\right) - \mathbf{j}\left(\frac{\partial z}{\partial \theta}\cos\theta + r\frac{\partial z}{\partial r}\sin\theta\right) + r\mathbf{k}.$$

FIGURE 14.8.10 The part of the paraboloid $z = r^2$ inside the cylinder $r = 1$ (Example 3) is the same as the part beneath the plane $z = 1$. (Why?).

After some simplifications, we find that

$$|\mathbf{N}| = \sqrt{r^2 + r^2 \left(\frac{\partial z}{\partial r}\right)^2 + \left(\frac{\partial z}{\partial \theta}\right)^2}.$$

Then Eq. (8) yields the formula

$$A = \iint_R \sqrt{r^2 + (rz_r)^2 + (z_\theta)^2}\, dr\, d\theta \qquad (10)$$

for surface area in cylindrical coordinates.

EXAMPLE 3 Find the surface area cut from the paraboloid $z = r^2$ by the cylinder $r = 1$ (Fig. 14.8.10).

Solution Equation (10) gives area

$$A = \int_0^{2\pi} \int_0^1 \sqrt{r^2 + r^2 \cdot (2r)^2}\, dr\, d\theta = 2\pi \int_0^1 r\sqrt{1 + 4r^2}\, dr$$

$$= 2\pi \left[\frac{2}{3} \cdot \frac{1}{8}(1 + 4r^2)^{3/2}\right]_0^1 = \frac{\pi}{6}(5\sqrt{5} - 1) \approx 5.3304. \qquad \blacklozenge$$

In Example 3, you would get the same result if you first wrote $z = x^2 + y^2$, used Eq. (9), which gives

$$A = \iint_R \sqrt{1 + 4x^2 + 4y^2}\, dx\, dy,$$

and then changed to polar coordinates. In Example 4 it would be less convenient to begin with rectangular coordinates.

FIGURE 14.8.11 The spiral ramp of Example 4.

EXAMPLE 4 Find the area of the *spiral ramp* $z = \theta$, $0 \leq r \leq 1$, $0 \leq \theta \leq \pi$. This is the upper surface of the solid shown in Fig. 14.8.11.

Solution Equation (10) gives area

$$A = \int_0^\pi \int_0^1 \sqrt{r^2 + 1}\, dr\, d\theta = \frac{\pi}{2}\left[\sqrt{2} + \ln(1 + \sqrt{2})\right] \approx 3.6059.$$

We avoided a trigonometric substitution by using the table of integrals inside the back cover. $\blacklozenge$

FIGURE 14.8.12 The torus of Example 5.

EXAMPLE 5 Find the surface area of the torus generated by revolving the circle

$$(x - b)^2 + z^2 = a^2 \quad (0 < a < b)$$

in the xz-plane around the z-axis (Fig. 14.8.12).

Solution With the ordinary polar coordinate θ and the angle ψ of Fig. 14.8.13, the torus is described for $0 \leq \theta \leq 2\pi$ and $0 \leq \psi \leq 2\pi$ by the parametric equations

$$x = r\cos\theta = (b + a\cos\psi)\cos\theta,$$
$$y = r\sin\theta = (b + a\cos\psi)\sin\theta,$$
$$z = a\sin\psi.$$

When we compute $\mathbf{N} = \mathbf{r}_\theta \times \mathbf{r}_\psi$ and simplify, we find that

$$|\mathbf{N}| = a(b + a\cos\psi).$$

FIGURE 14.8.13 The circle that generates the torus of Example 5.

Hence the general surface-area formula, Eq. (8), gives area

$$A = \int_0^{2\pi} \int_0^{2\pi} a(b + a\cos\psi)\,d\theta\,d\psi = 2\pi a \Big[b\psi + a\sin\psi \Big]_0^{2\pi} = 4\pi^2 ab.$$

We obtained the same result in Section 14.5 with the aid of Pappus's first theorem.

14.8 TRUE/FALSE STUDY GUIDE

14.8 CONCEPTS: QUESTIONS AND DISCUSSION

1. Compare the calculations of the surface area of a sphere using (a) rectangular coordinates; (b) cylindrical coordinates; (c) spherical coordinates. (See Problem 18 of this section.)
2. We know that the volume of a solid ball of radius r is $V(r) = \frac{4}{3}\pi r^3$ and that the area of its spherical surface is $S(r) = 4\pi r^2$. Is it a coincidence that $V'(r) = S(r)$? Think about a thin spherical shell as "volume as product of thickness and area."

14.8 PROBLEMS

1. Find the area of the portion of the plane $z = x + 3y$ that lies inside the elliptical cylinder with equation
$$\frac{x^2}{4} + \frac{y^2}{9} = 1.$$

2. Find the area of the region in the plane $z = 1 + 2x + 2y$ that lies directly above the region in the xy-plane bounded by the parabolas $y = x^2$ and $x = y^2$.

3. Find the area of the part of the paraboloid $z = 9 - x^2 - y^2$ that lies above the plane $z = 5$.

4. Find the area of the part of the surface $2z = x^2$ that lies directly above the triangle in the xy-plane with vertices at $(0, 0)$, $(1, 0)$, and $(1, 1)$.

5. Find the area of the surface that is the graph of $z = x + y^2$ for $0 \leq x \leq 1$, $0 \leq y \leq 2$.

6. Find the area of that part of the surface of Problem 5 that lies above the triangle in the xy-plane with vertices at $(0, 0)$, $(0, 1)$, and $(1, 1)$.

7. Find by integration the area of the part of the plane $2x + 3y + z = 6$ that lies in the first octant.

8. Find the area of the ellipse that is cut from the plane $2x + 3y + z = 6$ by the cylinder $x^2 + y^2 = 2$.

9. Find the area that is cut from the saddle-shaped surface $z = xy$ by the cylinder $x^2 + y^2 = 1$.

10. Find the area that is cut from the surface $z = x^2 - y^2$ by the cylinder $x^2 + y^2 = 4$.

11. Find the surface area of the part of the paraboloid $z = 16 - x^2 - y^2$ that lies above the xy-plane.

12. Show by integration that the surface area of the conical surface $z = br$ between the planes $z = 0$ and $z = h = ab$ is given by $A = \pi aL$, where L is the slant height $\sqrt{a^2 + h^2}$ and a is the radius of the base of the cone.

13. Let the part of the cylinder $x^2 + y^2 = a^2$ between the planes $z = 0$ and $z = h$ be parametrized by $x = a\cos\theta$, $y = a\sin\theta$, $z = z$. Apply Eq. (8) to show that the area of this zone is $A = 2\pi ah$.

14. Consider the meridional zone of height $h = c - b$ that lies on the sphere $r^2 + z^2 = a^2$ between the planes $z = b$ and $z = c$, where $0 \leq b < c \leq a$. Apply Eq. (10) to show that the area of this zone is $A = 2\pi ah$.

15. Find the area of the part of the cylinder $x^2 + z^2 = a^2$ that lies within the cylinder $r^2 = x^2 + y^2 = a^2$.

16. Find the area of the part of the sphere $r^2 + z^2 = a^2$ that lies within the cylinder $r = a\sin\theta$.

17. (a) Apply Eq. (8) to show that the surface area of the surface $y = f(x, z)$, for (x, z) in the region R of the xz-plane, is given by
$$A = \iint_R \sqrt{1 + \left(\frac{\partial f}{\partial x}\right)^2 + \left(\frac{\partial f}{\partial z}\right)^2}\,dx\,dz.$$

(b) State and derive a similar formula for the area of the surface $x = f(y, z)$ for (y, z) in the region R of the yz-plane.

18. Suppose that R is a region in the $\phi\theta$-plane. Consider the part of the sphere $\rho = a$ that corresponds to (ϕ, θ) in R, parametrized by the equations in (6) with $h(\phi, \theta) = a$. Apply Eq. (8) to show that the surface area of this part of the sphere is
$$A = \iint_R a^2 \sin\phi\,d\phi\,d\theta.$$

19. (a) Consider the "spherical rectangle" defined by
$$\rho = a, \quad \phi_1 \leq \phi \leq \phi_2 = \phi_1 + \Delta\phi, \quad \theta_1 \leq \theta \leq \theta_2 = \theta_1 + \Delta\theta.$$

Apply the formula of Problem 18 and the average value property (see Problem 50 in Section 14.2) to show that the area of this spherical rectangle is $A = a^2 \sin\hat{\phi}\,\Delta\phi\,\Delta\theta$ for some $\hat{\phi}$ in (ϕ_1, ϕ_2). (b) Conclude from the result in part (a) that the volume of the spherical block defined by
$$\rho_1 \leq \rho \leq \rho_2 = \rho_1 + \Delta\rho, \quad \phi_1 \leq \phi \leq \phi_2, \quad \theta_1 \leq \theta \leq \theta_2$$

is
$$\Delta V = \tfrac{1}{3}(\rho_2^3 - \rho_1^3)\sin\hat{\phi}\,\Delta\phi\,\Delta\theta.$$

Finally, derive Eq. (8) of Section 14.7 by applying the mean value theorem to the function $f(\rho) = \rho^3$ on the interval $[\rho_1, \rho_2]$.

20. Describe the surface $\rho = 2a\sin\phi$. Why is it called a *pinched torus*? It is parametrized as in Eq. (6) with $h(\phi, \theta) = 2a\sin\phi$. Show that its surface area is $A = 4\pi^2 a^2$. Figure 14.8.14 may be helpful.

FIGURE 14.8.14 Cutaway view of the pinched torus of Problem 20.

21. The surface of revolution obtained when we revolve the curve $x = f(z), a \leq z \leq b$, around the z-axis is parametrized in terms of θ ($0 \leq \theta \leq 2\pi$) and z ($a \leq z \leq b$) by $x = f(z)\cos\theta$, $y = f(z)\sin\theta$, $z = z$. From Eq. (8) derive the surface-area formula
$$A = \int_0^{2\pi}\int_a^b f(z)\sqrt{1+[f'(z)]^2}\,dz\,d\theta.$$
This formula agrees with the area of a surface of revolution as defined in Section 6.4.

22. Apply the formula of Problem 18 in both parts of this problem. (a) Verify the formula $A = 4\pi a^2$ for the surface area of a sphere of radius a. (b) Find the area of that part of a sphere of radius a and center $(0,0,0)$ that lies inside the cone $\phi = \pi/6$.

23. Apply the result of Problem 21 to verify the formula $A = 2\pi rh$ for the lateral surface area of a right circular cylinder of radius r and height h.

24. Apply Eq. (9) to verify the formula $A = 2\pi rh$ for the lateral surface area of the cylinder $x^2 + z^2 = r^2, 0 \leq y \leq h$ of radius r and height h.

In Problems 25 through 28, use a computer algebra system first to plot and then to approximate (with four-place accuracy) the area of the part of the given surface S that lies above the square in the xy-plane defined by (a) $-1 \leq x \leq 1, -1 \leq y \leq 1$; (b) $|x| + |y| \leq 1$.

25. S is the paraboloid $z = x^2 + y^2$.
26. S is the cone $z = \sqrt{x^2 + y^2}$.
27. S is the hyperboloid $z = 1 + xy$.
28. S is the sphere $x^2 + y^2 + z^2 = 4$.

In Problems 29 through 32, a parametrization of a quadric surface is given. Use identities such as $\cos^2 t + \sin^2 t = 1$ *and* $\cosh^2 t - \sinh^2 t = 1$ *to identify these surfaces by means of the quadric surface equations listed in Section 12.7. For visual corroboration you can use the parametric plot command in a computer algebra system to plot each surface (with selected numerical values of the coefficients a, b, and c).*

29. $x = au\cos v, \ y = bu\sin v, \ z = cu^2; \ 0 \leq u \leq 1, \ 0 \leq v \leq 2\pi$
30. $x = a\sin u\cos v, \ y = b\sin u\sin v, \ z = c\cos u; \ 0 \leq u \leq \pi, \ 0 \leq v \leq 2\pi$
31. $x = a\sinh u\cos v, \ y = b\sinh u\sin v, \ z = c\cosh u; \ 0 \leq u \leq 1, \ 0 \leq v \leq 2\pi$
32. $x = a\cosh u\cos v, \ y = b\cosh u\sin v, \ z = c\sinh u; \ -1 \leq u \leq 1, \ 0 \leq v \leq 2\pi$

33. An ellipsoid with semiaxes a, b, and c is defined by the parametrization
$$x = a\sin\phi\cos\theta, \quad y = b\sin\phi\sin\theta, \quad z = c\cos\phi$$
($0 \leq \phi \leq \pi, 0 \leq \theta \leq 2\pi$) in terms of the angular spherical coordinates ϕ and θ. Use a computer algebra system to approximate (to four-place accuracy) the area of the ellipsoid with $a = 4, b = 3$, and $c = 2$.

34. (a) Generalize Example 5 to derive the parametric equations
$$x = (b + a\cos\psi)\cos\theta, \ y = (b + a\cos\psi)\sin\theta, \ z = c\sin\psi$$
($0 \leq \psi \leq 2\pi, 0 \leq \theta \leq 2\pi$) of the "elliptical torus" obtained by revolving around the z-axis the ellipse $(x-b)^2/a^2 + z^2/c^2 = 1$ (where $0 < a < b$) in the xz-plane. (b) Use a computer algebra system to approximate (to four-place accuracy) the area of the elliptical torus obtained as in part (a) with $a = 2$, $b = 3$, and $c = 1$. (c) Also approximate the perimeter of the ellipse of part (a). Are your results consistent with Pappus's theorem for the area of a surface of revolution?

14.9 CHANGE OF VARIABLES IN MULTIPLE INTEGRALS

We have seen in preceding sections that we can evaluate certain multiple integrals by transforming them from rectangular coordinates into polar or spherical coordinates. The technique of changing coordinate systems to evaluate a multiple integral is the multivariable analogue of substitution in a single integral. Recall from Section 5.7 that if $x = g(u)$, then
$$\int_a^b f(x)\,dx = \int_c^d f(g(u))\,g'(u)\,du, \qquad (1)$$

where $a = g(c)$ and $b = g(d)$. The method of substitution involves a "change of variables" that is tailored to the evaluation of a given integral.

Suppose that we want to evaluate the double integral

$$\iint_R F(x, y) \, dx \, dy.$$

A *change of variables* for this integral is determined by a continuously differentiable **transformation** T from the uv-plane to the xy-plane—that is, a function T that associates with the point (u, v) a point $(x, y) = T(u, v)$ given by equations of the form

$$x = f(u, v), \qquad y = g(u, v). \tag{2}$$

The point (x, y) is called the **image** of the point (u, v) under the transformation T. If no two different points in the uv-plane have the same image point in the xy-plane, then the transformation T is said to be **one-to-one.** In this case it may be possible to solve the equations in (2) for u and v in terms of x and y and thus obtain the equations

$$u = h(x, y), \qquad v = k(x, y). \tag{3}$$

of the **inverse transformation** T^{-1} from the xy-plane to the uv-plane.

Often it is convenient to visualize the transformation T geometrically in terms of its u-*curves* and v-*curves*. The u-**curves** of T are the images in the xy-plane of the *horizontal* lines in the uv-plane—on each such curve the value of u varies but v is constant. The v-**curves** of T are the images of the *vertical* lines in the uv-plane—on each of these, the value of v varies but u is constant. Note that the image under T of a rectangle bounded by horizontal and vertical lines in the uv-plane is a *curvilinear figure* bounded by u-curves and v-curves in the xy-plane (Fig. 14.9.1). If we know the equations in (3) of the inverse transformation, then we can find the u-curves and the v-curves quite simply by writing the equations

$$k(x, y) = C_1 \qquad (u\text{-curve on which } v = C_1 \text{ is constant})$$

and

$$h(x, y) = C_2 \qquad (v\text{-curve on which } u = C_2 \text{ is constant}).$$

FIGURE 14.9.1 The transformation T turns the rectangle S into the curvilinear figure R.

EXAMPLE 1 Determine the u-curves and the v-curves of the transformation T whose inverse T^{-1} is specified by the equations $u = xy$, $v = x^2 - y^2$.

Solution The u-curves are the hyperbolas

$$x^2 - y^2 = v = C_1 \quad \text{(constant)},$$

and the v-curves are the rectangular hyperbolas

$$xy = u = C_2 \quad \text{(constant)}.$$

These two familiar families of hyperbolas are shown in Fig. 14.9.2. ◆

FIGURE 14.9.2 The u-curves and v-curves of Example 1.

Change of Variables in Double Integrals

Now we shall describe the change of variables in a double integral that corresponds to the transformation T specified by the equations in (2). Let the region R in the xy-plane be the image under T of the region S in the uv-plane. Let $F(x, y)$ be continuous on R and let $\{S_1, S_2, \ldots, S_n\}$ be an inner partition of S into rectangles each with dimensions Δu by Δv. Each rectangle S_i is transformed by T into a curvilinear figure R_i in the xy-plane (Fig. 14.9.3). The images $\{R_1, R_2, \ldots, R_n\}$ under T of the rectangles S_i then constitute an inner partition of the region R (though into curvilinear figures rather than rectangles).

Let $(u_i^\star, v_i^\star)$ be the lower left-hand corner point of S_i, and write

$$(x_i^\star, y_i^\star) = (f(u_i^\star, v_i^\star), g(u_i^\star, v_i^\star))$$

for its image under T. The u-curve through $(x_i^\star, y_i^\star)$ has velocity vector

$$\mathbf{t}_u = \mathbf{i} f_u(u_i^\star, v_i^\star) + \mathbf{j} g_u(u_i^\star, v_i^\star) = \frac{\partial x}{\partial u}\mathbf{i} + \frac{\partial y}{\partial u}\mathbf{j},$$

and the v-curve through $(x_i^\star, y_i^\star)$ has velocity vector

$$\mathbf{t}_v = \mathbf{i} f_v(u_i^\star, v_i^\star) + \mathbf{j} g_v(u_i^\star, v_i^\star) = \frac{\partial x}{\partial v}\mathbf{i} + \frac{\partial y}{\partial v}\mathbf{j}.$$

Thus we can approximate the curvilinear figure R_i by a parallelogram P_i with edges that are "copies" of the vectors $\mathbf{t}_u \Delta u$ and $\mathbf{t}_v \Delta v$. These edges and the approximating parallelogram appear in Fig. 14.9.3.

Our strategy is to approximate the area ΔA_i of the curvilinear figure R_i with the area $a(P_i)$ of the parallelogram P_i. To calculate this approximating area, we recall from Section 12.3 that the area of a parallelogram spanned by two vectors $\mathbf{a}$ and $\mathbf{b}$ is the length $|\mathbf{a} \times \mathbf{b}|$ of their cross product. Therefore

$$\Delta A_i \approx a(P_i) = |(\mathbf{t}_u \Delta u) \times (\mathbf{t}_v \Delta v)| = |\mathbf{t}_u \times \mathbf{t}_v| \Delta u \Delta v. \qquad (4)$$

But

$$\mathbf{t}_u \times \mathbf{t}_v = \begin{vmatrix} \mathbf{i} & \mathbf{j} & \mathbf{k} \\ \frac{\partial x}{\partial u} & \frac{\partial y}{\partial u} & 0 \\ \frac{\partial x}{\partial v} & \frac{\partial y}{\partial v} & 0 \end{vmatrix} = \begin{vmatrix} \frac{\partial x}{\partial u} & \frac{\partial x}{\partial v} \\ \frac{\partial y}{\partial u} & \frac{\partial y}{\partial v} \end{vmatrix} \mathbf{k}. \qquad (5)$$

FIGURE 14.9.3 The effect of the transformation T. We estimate the area of $R_i = T(S_i)$ by computing the area of the parallelogram P_i.

The 2×2 determinant on the right in Eq. (5) is called the *Jacobian* of the transformation $T : \mathbf{R}^2_{uv} \to \mathbf{R}^2_{xy}$, after the German mathematician Carl Jacobi (1804–1851), who first investigated general changes of variables in double integrals.

DEFINITION The Jacobian

The **Jacobian** of the continuously differentiable transformation $T : \mathbf{R}^2_{uv} \to \mathbf{R}^2_{xy}$ is the (real-valued) function $J_T : \mathbf{R}^2_{uv} \to \mathbf{R}$ defined by

$$J_T(u, v) = \begin{vmatrix} x_u(u, v) & x_v(u, v) \\ y_u(u, v) & y_v(u, v) \end{vmatrix}. \qquad (6)$$

Another common and particularly suggestive notation for the Jacobian is

$$J_T = \frac{\partial(x, y)}{\partial(u, v)},$$

where the 2×2 pattern reminds us that both the dependent variables x and y are differentiated with respect to both the independent variables u and v.

Recall that we began with an inner partition $\{S_1, S_2, \ldots, S_n\}$ of the region S in the uv-plane, with the images of these rectangles forming a curvilinear partition $\{R_1, R_2, \ldots, R_n\}$ of the region $R = T(S)$ in the xy-plane. Now Eqs. (4) and (5) imply that the area ΔA_i of R_i is given approximately by

$$\Delta A_i \approx |J_T(u_i^\star, v_i^\star)| \Delta u \Delta v$$

in terms of the *absolute value* of the Jacobian determinant and the area $a(S_i) = \Delta u \Delta v$. Therefore, when we set up Riemann sums for approximating double integrals, we find that

$$\iint_R F(x, y)\, dx\, dy \approx \sum_{i=1}^{n} F(x_i^\star, y_i^\star)\, \Delta A_i$$

$$\approx \sum_{i=1}^{m} F(f(u_i^\star, v_i^\star), g(u_i^\star, v_i^\star)) |J_T(u_i^\star, v_i^\star)|\, \Delta u\, \Delta v$$

$$\approx \iint_S F(f(u, v), g(u, v)) |J_T(u, v)|\, du\, dv.$$

This discussion is, in fact, an outline of a proof of the following general **change-of-variables theorem**. To ensure the existence of the indicated double integrals, we assume that the boundaries of both regions R and S consist of a finite number of piecewise smooth curves. (See Fig. 14.9.4.)

FIGURE 14.9.4 The domains of $F(x, y)$ and $F(T(u, v)) = F(f(x, y), g(x, y))$.

THEOREM 1 Change of Variables

Suppose that the continuously differentiable transformation $T : \mathbf{R}^2_{uv} \to \mathbf{R}^2_{xy}$ takes the bounded region S in the uv-plane onto the bounded region R in the xy-plane, and is one-to-one from the interior of S to the interior of R. If $F(x, y)$ is continuous on R, then

$$\iint_R F(x, y)\, dx\, dy = \iint_S F(T(u, v)) |J_T(u, v)|\, du\, dv. \tag{7}$$

If we write $G(u, v) = F(T(u, v))$ for the result of substituting $x(u, v)$ and $y(u, v)$ for x and y in the original integrand $F(x, y)$, then the change-of-variables formula in (7) takes the form

$$\iint_R F(x, y)\, dx\, dy = \iint_S G(u, v) \left| \frac{\partial(x, y)}{\partial(u, v)} \right| du\, dv. \tag{8}$$

Thus we formally transform the integral $\iint_R F(x, y)\, dA$ by replacing the original variables x and y with $x(u, v)$ and $y(u, v)$, respectively, and writing

$$dA = \left| \frac{\partial(x, y)}{\partial(u, v)} \right| du\, dv$$

for the area element in terms of u and v.

Note the analogy between Eq. (8) and the single-variable formula in Eq. (1). In fact, if $g'(x) \neq 0$ on $[c, d]$ and we denote by α the smaller, and by β the larger, of the two limits c and d in Eq. (1), then Eq. (1) takes the form

$$\int_a^b f(x)\, dx = \int_\alpha^\beta f(g(u)) |g'(u)|\, du. \tag{1a}$$

Thus the Jacobian in Eq. (8) plays the role of the derivative $g'(u)$ in Eq. (1).

EXAMPLE 2 Suppose that the transformation T from the $r\theta$-plane to the xy-plane is determined by the polar equations

$$x = f(r, \theta) = r \cos\theta, \qquad y = g(r, \theta) = r \sin\theta.$$

The Jacobian of T is

$$\frac{\partial(x, y)}{\partial(r, \theta)} = \begin{vmatrix} \cos\theta & -r\sin\theta \\ \sin\theta & r\cos\theta \end{vmatrix} = r > 0,$$

so Eq. (8) reduces to the familiar formula

$$\iint_R F(x, y)\, dx\, dy = \iint_S F(r\cos\theta, r\sin\theta)\, r\, dr\, d\theta.$$

Given a particular double integral $\iint_R f(x, y)\, dx\, dy$, how do we find a *productive* change of variables? One standard approach is to choose a transformation T such that the boundary of R consists of u-curves and v-curves. In case it is more convenient to express u and v in terms of x and y, we can first compute $\partial(u, v)/\partial(x, y)$ explicitly and then find the needed Jacobian $\partial(x, y)/\partial(u, v)$ from the formula

$$\frac{\partial(x, y)}{\partial(u, v)} \cdot \frac{\partial(u, v)}{\partial(x, y)} = 1. \tag{9}$$

Equation (9) is a consequence of the chain rule. (See Problem 18.)

EXAMPLE 3 Suppose that R is the plane region of unit density that is bounded by the hyperbolas

$$xy = 1, \quad xy = 3 \quad \text{and} \quad x^2 - y^2 = 1, \quad x^2 - y^2 = 4.$$

Find the polar moment of inertia

$$I_0 = \iint_R (x^2 + y^2)\, dx\, dy$$

of this region.

Solution The hyperbolas bounding R are u-curves and v-curves if $u = xy$ and $v = x^2 - y^2$, as in Example 1. We can most easily write the integrand $x^2 + y^2$ in terms of u and v by first noting that

$$4u^2 + v^2 = 4x^2y^2 + (x^2 - y^2)^2 = (x^2 + y^2)^2,$$

so $x^2 + y^2 = \sqrt{4u^2 + v^2}$. Now

$$\frac{\partial(u, v)}{\partial(x, y)} = \begin{vmatrix} y & x \\ 2x & -2y \end{vmatrix} = -2(x^2 + y^2).$$

Hence Eq. (9) gives

$$\frac{\partial(x, y)}{\partial(u, v)} = -\frac{1}{2(x^2 + y^2)} = -\frac{1}{2\sqrt{4u^2 + v^2}}.$$

We are now ready to apply the change-of-variables theorem, with the regions S and R as shown in Fig. 14.9.5. With $F(x, y) = x^2 + y^2$, Eq. (8) gives

$$I_0 = \iint_R (x^2 + y^2)\, dx\, dy = \int_1^4 \int_1^3 \sqrt{4u^2 + v^2}\, \frac{1}{2\sqrt{4u^2 + v^2}}\, du\, dv$$

$$= \int_1^4 \int_1^3 \frac{1}{2}\, du\, dv = 3.$$

FIGURE 14.9.5 The transformation T and the new region S constructed in Example 3.

Example 4 is motivated by an important application. Consider an engine with an operating cycle that consists of alternate expansion and compression of gas in a piston. During one cycle the point (p, V), which gives the pressure and volume of this gas, traces a closed curve in the pV-plane. The work done by the engine—ignoring friction and related losses—is then equal (in appropriate units) to the area *enclosed by this curve,* called the *indicator diagram* of the engine. The indicator diagram for an ideal *Carnot engine* consists of two *isotherms* $xy = a, xy = b$ and two *adiabatics* $xy^\gamma = c, xy^\gamma = d$, where γ is the heat capacity ratio of the working gas in the piston. A typical value is $\gamma = 1.4$.

EXAMPLE 4 Find the area of the region R bounded by the curves $xy = 1$, $xy = 3$ and $xy^{1.4} = 1$, $xy^{1.4} = 2$ (Fig. 14.9.6).

Solution To force the given curves to be u-curves and v-curves, we define our change-of-variables transformation by $u = xy$ and $v = xy^{1.4}$. Then

$$\frac{\partial(u, v)}{\partial(x, y)} = \begin{vmatrix} y & x \\ y^{1.4} & (1.4)xy^{0.4} \end{vmatrix} = (0.4)xy^{1.4} = (0.4)v.$$

So

$$\frac{\partial(x, y)}{\partial(u, v)} = \frac{1}{\partial(u, v)/\partial(x, y)} = \frac{2.5}{v}.$$

FIGURE 14.9.6 Finding the area of the region R (Example 4).

Consequently, the change-of-variables theorem gives the formula

$$A = \iint_R 1 \, dx \, dy = \int_1^2 \int_1^3 \frac{2.5}{v} \, du \, dv = 5 \ln 2. \qquad \blacklozenge$$

Change of Variables in Triple Integrals

The change-of-variables formula for triple integrals is similar to Eq. (8). Suppose that S and $R = T(S)$ are regions that correspond under the continuously differentiable transformation $T : \mathbf{R}^3_{uvw} \to \mathbf{R}^3_{xyz}$. Then the Jacobian of T is the determinant

$$J_T(u, v, w) = \frac{\partial(x, y, z)}{\partial(u, v, w)} = \begin{vmatrix} \frac{\partial x}{\partial u} & \frac{\partial x}{\partial v} & \frac{\partial x}{\partial w} \\ \frac{\partial y}{\partial u} & \frac{\partial y}{\partial v} & \frac{\partial y}{\partial w} \\ \frac{\partial z}{\partial u} & \frac{\partial z}{\partial v} & \frac{\partial z}{\partial w} \end{vmatrix}. \qquad (10)$$

Then (under assumptions equivalent to those stated in Theorem 1) the change-of-variables formula for triple integrals is

$$\iiint_R F(x, y, z) \, dx \, dy \, dz = \iiint_S F(T(u, v, w)) \, |J_T(u, v, w)| \, du \, dv \, dw, \qquad (11)$$

in direct analogy to Eq. (7) for double integrals. That is,

$$\iiint_R F(x, y, z) \, dx \, dy \, dz = \iiint_S G(u, v, w) \left| \frac{\partial(x, y, z)}{\partial(u, v, w)} \right| du \, dv \, dw, \qquad (12)$$

where $G(u, v, w) = F(T(u, v, w)) = F(x(u, v, w), y(u, v, w), z(u, v, w))$ is the function obtained from $F(x, y, z)$ upon expressing the original variables x, y, and z in terms of the new variables u, v, and w.

EXAMPLE 5 If T is the spherical-coordinates transformation given by

$$x = \rho \sin \phi \cos \theta, \qquad y = \rho \sin \phi \sin \theta, \qquad z = \rho \cos \phi,$$

then the Jacobian of T is

$$\frac{\partial(x, y, z)}{\partial(\rho, \phi, \theta)} = \begin{vmatrix} \sin \phi \cos \theta & \rho \cos \phi \cos \theta & -\rho \sin \phi \sin \theta \\ \sin \phi \sin \theta & \rho \cos \phi \sin \theta & \rho \sin \phi \cos \theta \\ \cos \phi & -\rho \sin \phi & 0 \end{vmatrix} = \rho^2 \sin \phi.$$

Thus Eq. (11) reduces to the familiar formula

$$\iiint_R F(x, y, z) \, dx \, dy \, dz = \iiint_S G(\rho, \phi, \theta) \, \rho^2 \sin \phi \, d\rho \, d\phi \, d\theta.$$

The sign is correct because $\rho^2 \sin \phi \geq 0$ for ϕ in $[0, \pi]$. $\qquad \blacklozenge$

EXAMPLE 6 Find the volume of the solid torus R obtained by revolving around the z-axis the circular disk

$$(x-b)^2 + z^2 \leq a^2, \quad 0 < a < b \tag{13}$$

in the xz-plane.

Solution This is the torus of Example 5 of Section 14.8. Let us write u for the ordinary polar coordinate angle θ, v for the angle ψ of Fig. 14.8.13, and w for the distance from the center of the circular disk described by the inequality in (13). We then define the transformation T by means of the equations

$$x = (b + w\cos v)\cos u, \quad y = (b + w\cos v)\sin u, \quad z = w\sin v.$$

Then the solid torus R is the image under T of the region in uvw-space described by the inequalities

$$0 \leq u \leq 2\pi, \quad 0 \leq v \leq 2\pi, \quad 0 \leq w \leq a.$$

By a routine computation, we find that the Jacobian of T is

$$\frac{\partial(x,y,z)}{\partial(u,v,w)} = w(b + w\cos v).$$

Hence Eq. (11) with $F(x, y, z) \equiv 1$ yields volume

$$V = \iiint_T 1\,dx\,dy\,dz = \int_0^{2\pi}\int_0^{2\pi}\int_0^a (bw + w^2\cos v)\,dw\,du\,dv$$

$$= 2\pi \int_0^{2\pi}\left(\frac{1}{2}a^2 b + \frac{1}{3}a^3\cos v\right)dv = 2\pi^2 a^2 b,$$

which agrees with the value $V = 2\pi b \cdot \pi a^2$ given by Pappus's first theorem (Section 14.5). ◆

14.9 TRUE/FALSE STUDY GUIDE

14.9 CONCEPTS: QUESTIONS AND DISCUSSION

1. Explain why the change-of-variables formula involves the *absolute value* of the Jacobian, rather than the Jacobian itself.
2. Suppose that R is a given parallelogram in the xy-plane. Explain how to transform an integral $\iint_R F(x, y)\,dA$ into an integral over a rectangle in the uv-plane.
3. Suppose that your pocket computer contains a routine for the numerical evaluation of double integrals, but requires that the domain of integration be a rectangle. Given an integral $\iint_R F(x, y)\,dA$ where R is a region of the form $a \leq x \leq b$, $f(x) \leq y \leq g(x)$, describe a transformation that converts this integral into one that your pocket computer can evaluate.
4. Describe a strategy for evaluating an integral over the region R in the xy-plane that is bounded by a given rotated ellipse $ax^2 + bxy + cy^2 = 1$.

14.9 PROBLEMS

In Problems 1 through 6, solve for x and y in terms of u and v. Then compute the Jacobian $\partial(x,y)/\partial(u,v)$.

1. $u = x + y, \quad v = x - y$
2. $u = x - 2y, \quad v = 3x + y$
3. $u = xy, \quad v = y/x$
4. $u = 2(x^2 + y^2), \quad v = 2(x^2 - y^2)$
5. $u = x + 2y^2, \quad v = x - 2y^2$
6. $u = \dfrac{2x}{x^2 + y^2}, \quad v = -\dfrac{2y}{x^2 + y^2}$
7. Let R be the parallelogram bounded by the lines $x + y = 1$, $x + y = 2$ and $2x - 3y = 2$, $2x - 3y = 5$. Substitute $u = x+y$, $v = 2x - 3y$ to find its area

$$A = \iint_R 1\,dx\,dy.$$

8. Substitute $u = xy$, $v = y/x$ to find the area of the first-quadrant region bounded by the lines $y = x$, $y = 2x$ and the hyperbolas $xy = 1$, $xy = 2$ (Fig. 14.9.7).

FIGURE 14.9.7 The region of Problem 8.

9. Substitute $u = xy$, $v = xy^3$ to find the area of the first-quadrant region bounded by the curves $xy = 2$, $xy = 4$ and $xy^3 = 3$, $xy^3 = 6$ (Fig. 14.9.8).

FIGURE 14.9.8 The region of Problem 9.

10. Find the area of the first-quadrant region bounded by the curves $y = x^2$, $y = 2x^2$ and $x = y^2$, $x = 4y^2$ (Fig. 14.9.9). [*Suggestion:* Let $y = ux^2$ and $x = vy^2$.]

FIGURE 14.9.9 The region of Problem 10.

11. Use the method of Problem 10 to find the area of the first-quadrant region bounded by the curves $y = x^3$, $y = 2x^3$ and $x = y^3$, $x = 4y^3$.

12. Let R be the first-quadrant region bounded by the circles $x^2 + y^2 = 2x$, $x^2 + y^2 = 6x$ and the circles $x^2 + y^2 = 2y$, $x^2 + y^2 = 8y$. Use the transformation
$$u = \frac{2x}{x^2 + y^2}, \quad v = \frac{2y}{x^2 + y^2}$$
to evaluate the integral
$$\iint_R \frac{1}{(x^2 + y^2)^2}\, dx\, dy.$$

13. Use elliptical coordinates $x = 3r\cos\theta$, $y = 2r\sin\theta$ to find the volume of the region bounded by the xy-plane, the paraboloid $z = x^2 + y^2$, and the elliptic cylinder
$$\frac{x^2}{9} + \frac{y^2}{4} = 1.$$

14. Let R be the solid ellipsoid with outer boundary surface
$$\frac{x^2}{a^2} + \frac{y^2}{b^2} + \frac{z^2}{c^2} = 1.$$
Use the transformation $x = au$, $y = bv$, $z = cw$ to show that the volume of this ellipsoid is
$$V = \iiint_R 1\, dx\, dy\, dz = \frac{4}{3}\pi abc.$$

15. Find the volume of the region in the first octant that is bounded by the hyperbolic cylinders $xy = 1$, $xy = 4$; $xz = 1$, $xz = 9$; and $yz = 4$, $yz = 9$. [*Suggestion:* Let $u = xy$, $v = xz$, $w = yz$, and note that $uvw = x^2 y^2 z^2$.]

16. Use the transformation
$$x = \frac{r}{t}\cos\theta, \quad y = \frac{r}{t}\sin\theta, \quad z = r^2$$
to find the volume of the region R that lies between the paraboloids $z = x^2 + y^2$, $z = 4(x^2 + y^2)$ and the planes $z = 1$, $z = 4$.

17. Let R be the rotated elliptical region bounded by the graph of $x^2 + xy + y^2 = 3$. Let $x = u + v$ and $y = u - v$. Show that
$$\iint_R \exp(-x^2 - xy - y^2)\, dx\, dy$$
$$= 2 \iint_S \exp(-3u^2 - v^2)\, du\, dv.$$
Then substitute $u = r\cos\theta$, $v = \sqrt{3}\,(r\sin\theta)$ to evaluate the latter integral.

18. From the chain rule and from the following property of determinants, derive the relation in Eq. (9) between the Jacobians of a transformation and its inverse.
$$\begin{vmatrix} a_1 & b_1 \\ c_1 & d_1 \end{vmatrix} \cdot \begin{vmatrix} a_2 & b_2 \\ c_2 & d_2 \end{vmatrix} = \begin{vmatrix} a_1 a_2 + b_1 c_2 & a_1 b_2 + b_1 d_2 \\ a_2 c_1 + c_2 d_1 & b_2 c_1 + d_1 d_2 \end{vmatrix}.$$

19. Change to spherical coordinates to show that, for $k > 0$,
$$\int_{-\infty}^{+\infty}\int_{-\infty}^{+\infty}\int_{-\infty}^{+\infty} \sqrt{x^2 + y^2 + z^2}$$
$$\times \exp(-k(x^2 + y^2 + z^2))\, dx\, dy\, dz = \frac{2\pi}{k^2}.$$

20. Let R be the solid ellipsoid with constant density δ and boundary surface
$$\frac{x^2}{a^2} + \frac{y^2}{b^2} + \frac{z^2}{c^2} = 1.$$
Use ellipsoidal coordinates $x = a\rho\sin\phi\cos\theta$, $y = b\rho\sin\phi\sin\theta$, $z = c\rho\cos\phi$ to show that the mass of R is $M = \frac{4}{3}\pi\delta abc$.

21. Show that the moment of inertia of the ellipsoid of Problem 20 with respect to the z-axis is $I_z = \frac{1}{5}M(a^2 + b^2)$.

In Problems 22 through 26, use a computer algebra system (if necessary) to find the indicated centroids and moments of inertia.

22. The centroid of the plane region of Problem 8 (Fig. 14.9.7)
23. The centroid of the plane region of Problem 9 (Fig. 14.9.8)
24. The centroid of the plane region of Problem 10 (Fig. 14.9.9)
25. The moment of inertia around each coordinate axis of the solid ellipsoid of Problem 20
26. The centroid of the solid of Problem 16 and its moments of inertia around the coordinate axes
27. Write the triple integral that gives the average distance of points of the solid ellipsoid of Problem 20 from the origin. Then approximate that integral in the case $a = 4$, $b = 3$, and $c = 2$.

Problems 28 and 29 outline the use of double integrals to evaluate the famous infinite series

$$\zeta(2) = \sum_{n=1}^{\infty} \frac{1}{n^2} = 1 + \frac{1}{2^2} + \frac{1}{3^2} + \cdots$$

mentioned earlier in the Section 11.5 project. These problems are based on a calculation presented by Dirk Huylebrouck in his article "Similarity in Irrationality Proofs for π, $\ln 2$, $\zeta(2)$, and $\zeta(3)$," The American Mathematical Monthly (March 2001), 222–231.

28. Substitute the geometric series for $(1 - xy)^{-1}$ to show that

$$\int_0^1 \int_0^1 \frac{1}{1 - xy}\, dx\, dy = \zeta(2),$$

assuming the validity of termwise integration of the resulting series in powers of xy.

29. (a) First find a common denominator in the integrand, then make the substitution $u = x^2$, $v = y^2$ to show that

$$\int_0^1 \int_0^1 \left(\frac{1}{1 - xy} - \frac{1}{1 + xy} \right) dx\, dy = \frac{1}{2}\zeta(2).$$

(b) Add the equation in part (a) and the identity

$$\int_0^1 \int_0^1 \left(\frac{1}{1 - xy} + \frac{1}{1 + xy} \right) dx\, dy = 2 \int_0^1 \int_0^1 \frac{1}{1 - x^2 y^2}\, dx\, dy$$

to show that

$$\zeta(2) = \frac{4}{3} \int_0^1 \int_0^1 \frac{1}{1 - x^2 y^2}\, dx\, dy.$$

(c) Finally, use the transformation $T : \boldsymbol{R}_{uv}^2 \to \boldsymbol{R}_{xy}^2$ defined by $x = (\sin u)/(\cos v)$, $y = (\sin v)/(\cos u)$ to evaluate the final integral in part (b) and thereby obtain Euler's result that $\zeta(2) = \pi^2/6$. As indicated in Fig. 14.9.10, the transformation T carries the interior of the triangle $0 \leq u \leq (\pi/2) - v$, $0 \leq v \leq \pi/2$ in the uv-plane one-to-one to the interior of the unit square in the xy-plane.

FIGURE 14.9.10(a) Horizontal u-lines in the domain of the transformation T.

FIGURE 14.9.10(b) Their image u-curves in the range of the transformation T.

CHAPTER 14 REVIEW: DEFINITIONS, CONCEPTS, RESULTS

Use the following list as a guide to concepts that you may need to review.

1. Definition of the double integral as a limit of Riemann sums
2. Evaluation of double integrals by iterated single integration
3. Use of the double integral to find the volume between two surfaces above a given plane region
4. Transformation of the double integral $\iint_R f(x, y)\, dA$ into polar coordinates
5. Application of double integrals to find mass, centroids, and moments of inertia of plane laminae
6. The two theorems of Pappus
7. Definition of the triple integral as a limit of Riemann sums
8. Evaluation of triple integrals by iterated single integration
9. Applications of triple integrals to find volume, mass, centroids, and moments of inertia
10. Transformation of the triple integral $\iiint_T f(x, y, z)\, dV$ into cylindrical and spherical coordinates
11. The surface area of a parametric surface
12. The area of a surface $z = f(x, y)$ for (x, y) in the plane region R
13. The Jacobian of a transformation of coordinates
14. The transformation of a double or triple integral corresponding to a given change of variables

CHAPTER 14 MISCELLANEOUS PROBLEMS

In Problems 1 through 5, evaluate the given integral by first reversing the order of integration.

1. $\int_0^1 \int_{y^{1/3}}^1 \frac{1}{\sqrt{1+x^2}}\, dx\, dy$

2. $\int_0^1 \int_y^1 \frac{\sin x}{x}\, dx\, dy$

3. $\int_0^1 \int_x^1 \exp(-y^2)\, dy\, dx$

4. $\int_0^8 \int_{x^{2/3}}^4 x \cos y^4\, dy\, dx$

5. $\int_0^4 \int_{\sqrt{y}}^2 \frac{y \exp(x^2)}{x^3}\, dx\, dy$

6. The double integral
$$\int_0^\infty \int_x^\infty \frac{e^{-y}}{y}\, dy\, dx$$
is an improper integral over the unbounded region in the first quadrant between the lines $y = x$ and $x = 0$. Assuming that it is valid (it is) to reverse the order of integration, evaluate this integral by integrating first with respect to x.

7. Find the volume of the solid T that lies below the paraboloid $z = x^2 + y^2$ and above the triangle R in the xy-plane that has vertices at $(0, 0, 0)$, $(1, 1, 0)$, and $(2, 0, 0)$.

8. Find by integration in cylindrical coordinates the volume bounded by the paraboloids $z = 2x^2 + 2y^2$ and $z = 48 - x^2 - y^2$.

9. Use integration in spherical coordinates to find the volume and centroid of the solid region that is inside the sphere $\rho = 3$, below the cone $\phi = \pi/3$, and above the xy-plane $\phi = \pi/2$.

10. Find the volume of the solid bounded by the elliptic paraboloids $z = x^2 + 3y^2$ and $z = 8 - x^2 - 5y^2$.

11. Find the volume bounded by the paraboloid $y = x^2 + 3z^2$ and the parabolic cylinder $y = 4 - z^2$.

12. Find the volume of the region bounded by the parabolic cylinders $z = x^2$, $z = 2 - x^2$ and the planes $y = 0$, $y + z = 4$.

13. Find the volume of the region bounded by the elliptical cylinder $y^2 + 4z^2 = 4$ and the planes $x = 0$, $x = y + 2$.

14. Show that the volume of the solid bounded by the elliptical cylinder
$$\frac{x^2}{a^2} + \frac{y^2}{b^2} = 1$$
and the planes $z = 0$, $z = h + x$ (where $h > a > 0$) is $V = \pi a b h$.

15. Let R be the first-quadrant region bounded by the curve $x^4 + x^2 y^2 = y^2$ and the line $y = x$. Use polar coordinates to evaluate
$$\iint_R \frac{1}{(1+x^2+y^2)^2}\, dA.$$

In Problems 16 through 20, find the mass and centroid of a plane lamina with the given shape and density δ.

16. The region bounded by $y = x^2$ and $x = y^2$; $\delta(x, y) = x^2 + y^2$

17. The region bounded by $x = 2y^2$ and $y^2 = x - 4$; $\delta(x, y) = y^2$

18. The region between $y = \ln x$ and the x-axis over the interval $1 \leq x \leq 2$; $\delta(x, y) = 1/x$

19. The circle bounded by $r = 2\cos\theta$; $\delta(r, \theta) = k$ (a constant)

20. The region of Problem 19; $\delta(r, \theta) = r$

21. Use the first theorem of Pappus to find the y-coordinate of the centroid of the upper half of the ellipse
$$\frac{x^2}{a^2} + \frac{y^2}{b^2} = 1.$$
Employ the facts that the area of this semiellipse is $A = \pi a b/2$ and the volume of the ellipsoid it generates when rotated around the x-axis is $V = \frac{4}{3}\pi a b^2$.

22. (a) Use the first theorem of Pappus to find the centroid of the first-quadrant portion of the annular ring with boundary circles $x^2 + y^2 = a^2$ and $x^2 + y^2 = b^2$ (where $0 < a < b$). (b) Show that the limiting position of this centroid as $b \to a$ is the centroid of a quarter-circular arc, as we found in Problem 44 of Section 14.5.

23. Find the centroid of the region in the xy-plane bounded by the x-axis and the parabola $y = 4 - x^2$.

24. Find the volume of the solid that lies below the parabolic cylinder $z = x^2$ and above the triangle in the xy-plane bounded by the coordinate axes and the line $x + y = 1$.

25. Use cylindrical coordinates to find the volume of the ice-cream cone bounded above by the sphere $x^2 + y^2 + z^2 = 5$ and below by the cone $z = 2\sqrt{x^2 + y^2}$.

26. Find the volume and centroid of the ice-cream cone bounded above by the sphere $\rho = a$ and below by the cone $\phi = \pi/3$.

27. A homogeneous solid circular cone has mass M and base radius a. Find its moment of inertia around its axis of symmetry.

28. Find the mass of the first octant of the ball $\rho \leq a$ if its density at (x, y, z) is $\delta(x, y, z) = xyz$.

29. Find the moment of inertia around the x-axis of the homogeneous solid ellipsoid with unit density and boundary surface
$$\frac{x^2}{a^2} + \frac{y^2}{b^2} + \frac{z^2}{c^2} = 1.$$

30. Find the volume of the region in the first octant that is bounded by the sphere $\rho = a$, the cylinder $r = a$, the plane $z = a$, the xz-plane, and the yz-plane.

31. Find the moment of inertia around the z-axis of the homogeneous region of unit density that lies inside both the sphere $\rho = 2$ and the cylinder $r = 2\cos\theta$.

In Problems 32 through 34, a volume is generated by revolving a plane region R around an axis. To find the volume, set up a double integral over R by revolving an area element dA around the indicated axis to generate a volume element dV.

32. Find the volume of the solid obtained by revolving around the y-axis the region inside the circle $r = 2a\cos\theta$.

33. Find the volume of the solid obtained by revolving around the x-axis the region enclosed by the cardioid $r = 1 + \cos\theta$.

34. Find the volume of the solid torus obtained by revolving the disk $0 \leq r \leq a$ around the line $x = -b$, $|b| \geq a$.

35. Assume that the torus of Problem 34 has uniform density δ. Find its moment of inertia around its natural axis of symmetry.

Problems 36 through 42 deal with average distance. *The **average distance** $\bar{d}$ of the point (x_0, y_0) from the points of the plane region R with area A is defined to be*

$$\bar{d} = \frac{1}{A} \iint_R \sqrt{(x - x_0)^2 + (y - y_0)^2} \, dA.$$

The average distance of a point (x_0, y_0, z_0) from the points of a space region is defined analogously.

36. Show that the average distance of the points of a disk of radius a from its center is $2a/3$.

37. Show that the average distance of the points of a disk of radius a from a fixed point on its boundary is $32a/9\pi$.

38. A circle of radius 1 is interior to and tangent to a circle of radius 2. Find the average distance of the point of tangency from the points that lie between the two circles.

39. Show that the average distance of the points of a spherical ball of radius a from its center is $3a/4$.

40. Show that the average distance of the points of a spherical ball of radius a from a fixed point on its surface is $6a/5$.

41. A sphere of radius 1 is interior to and tangent to a sphere of radius 2. Find the average distance of the point of tangency from the set of all points between the two spheres.

42. A right circular cone has radius R and height H. Find the average distance of points of the cone from its vertex.

43. Find the surface area of the part of the paraboloid $z = 10 - r^2$ that lies between the two planes $z = 1$ and $z = 6$.

44. Find the surface area of the part of the surface $z = y^2 - x^2$ that is inside the cylinder $x^2 + y^2 = 4$.

45. Let A be the surface area of the zone on the sphere $\rho = a$ between the planes $z = z_1$ and $z = z_2$ (where $-a \leq z_1 < z_2 \leq a$). Use the formula of Problem 18 in Section 14.8 to show that $A = 2\pi a h$, where $h = z_2 - z_1$.

46. Find the surface area of the part of the sphere $\rho = 2$ that is inside the cylinder $x^2 + y^2 = 2x$.

47. A square hole with side length 2 is cut through a cone of height 2 and base radius 2; the centerline of the hole is the axis of symmetry of the cone. Find the area of the surface removed from the cone.

48. Numerically approximate the surface area of the part of the parabolic cylinder $2z = x^2$ that lies inside the cylinder $x^2 + y^2 = 1$.

49. A "fence" of variable height $h(t)$ stands above the plane curve $(x(t), y(t))$. Thus the fence has the parametrization $x = x(t)$, $y = y(t)$, $z = z$ for $a \leq t \leq b$, $0 \leq z \leq h(t)$. Apply Eq. (8) of Section 14.8 to show that the area of the fence is

$$A = \int_a^b \int_0^{h(t)} \left[\left(\frac{dx}{dt}\right)^2 + \left(\frac{dy}{dt}\right)^2\right]^{1/2} dz\, dt.$$

50. Apply the formula of Problem 49 to compute the area of the part of the cylinder $r = a \sin\theta$ that lies inside the sphere $r^2 + z^2 = a^2$.

51. Find the polar moment of inertia of the first-quadrant region of constant density δ that is bounded by the hyperbolas $xy = 1$, $xy = 3$ and $x^2 - y^2 = 1$, $x^2 - y^2 = 4$.

52. Substitute $u = x - y$ and $v = x + y$ to evaluate

$$\iint_R \exp\left(\frac{x-y}{x+y}\right) dx\, dy,$$

where R is bounded by the coordinate axes and the line $x + y = 1$.

53. Use ellipsoidal coordinates $x = a\rho \sin\phi \cos\theta$, $y = b\rho \sin\phi \sin\theta$, $z = c\rho \cos\phi$ to find the mass of the solid ellipsoid

$$\frac{x^2}{a^2} + \frac{y^2}{b^2} + \frac{z^2}{c^2} \leq 1$$

if its density at the point (x, y, z) is given by

$$\delta(x, y, z) = 1 - \frac{x^2}{a^2} - \frac{y^2}{b^2} - \frac{z^2}{c^2}.$$

54. Let R be the first-quadrant region bounded by the lemniscates $r^2 = 3\cos 2\theta$, $r^2 = 4\cos 2\theta$ and $r^2 = 3\sin 2\theta$, $r^2 = 4\sin 2\theta$ (Fig. 14.MP.1). Show that its area is

$$A = \frac{2\sqrt{17} - 5\sqrt{2}}{4}.$$

[*Suggestion:* Define the transformation T from the uv-plane to the $r\theta$-plane by $r^2 = u^{1/2} \cos 2\theta$, $r^2 = v^{1/2} \sin 2\theta$. Show first that

$$r^2 = \frac{uv}{u+v}, \qquad \theta = \frac{1}{2} \arctan \frac{u^{1/2}}{v^{1/2}}.$$

Then show that

$$\frac{\partial(r, \theta)}{\partial(u, v)} = -\frac{1}{16r(u+v)^{3/2}}.]$$

FIGURE 14.MP.1 The region R of Problem 54.

55. A 2-by-2 square hole is cut symmetrically through a sphere of radius $\sqrt{3}$. (See Fig. 14.MP.2.) (a) Show that the total surface area of the two pieces cut from the sphere is

$$A = \int_0^1 8\sqrt{3} \arcsin\left(\frac{1}{\sqrt{3-x^2}}\right) dx.$$

FIGURE 14.MP.2 Cutting a square hole through the sphere of Problem 55.

Then use Simpson's rule to approximate this integral. (b) (Difficult!) Show that the exact value of the integral in part (a) is $A = 4\pi(\sqrt{3} - 1)$. [*Suggestion:* First integrate by parts, then substitute $x = \sqrt{2}\sin\theta$.]

56. Show that the volume enclosed by the surface

$$x^{2/3} + y^{2/3} + z^{2/3} = a^{2/3}$$

is $V = \frac{4}{35}\pi a^3$. [*Suggestion:* Substitute $y = b\sin^3\theta$.]

57. Show that the volume enclosed by the surface

$$x^{1/3} + y^{1/3} + z^{1/3} = a^{1/3}$$

is $V = \frac{1}{210}a^3$. [*Suggestion:* Substitute $y = b\sin^6\theta$.]

58. Find the average of the *square* of the distance of points of the solid ellipsoid $(x/a)^2 + (y/b)^2 + (z/c)^2 \leq 1$ from the origin.

59. A cube C of edge length 1 is rotated around a line passing through two opposite vertices, thereby sweeping out a solid S of revolution. Find the volume of S. (*Answer:* $\pi/\sqrt{3} \approx 1.8138$.)

VECTOR CALCULUS 15

C. F. Gauss (1777–1855)

It is customary to list Archimedes, Newton, and Carl Friedrich Gauss as history's three preeminent mathematicians. Gauss was a precocious infant in a poor and uneducated family. He learned to calculate before he could talk and taught himself to read before beginning school in his native Brunswick, Germany. At age 14 he was already familiar with elementary geometry, algebra, and analysis. By age 18, when he entered the University of Göttingen, he had discovered empirically the *prime number theorem,* which implies that the number of primes p between 1 and n is about $n/(\ln n)$. This theorem was not proved rigorously until a century later.

During his first year at university, Gauss discovered conditions for the ruler-and-compass construction of regular polygons and demonstrated the constructability of the regular 17-gon (the first advance in this area since the similar construction of the regular pentagon in Euclid's *Elements* 2000 years earlier). In 1801 Gauss published his great treatise *Disquisitiones arithmeticae,* which summarized number theory to that time and set the pattern for nineteenth-century research in that area. This book established Gauss as a mathematician of uncommon stature, but another event thrust him into the public eye. On January 1, 1801, the new asteroid Ceres was observed, but it disappeared behind the sun a month later. In the following weeks, astronomers searched the skies in vain for Ceres' reappearance. It was Gauss who developed the method of least-squares approximations to predict the asteroid's future orbit on the basis of a handful of observations. When Gauss's three-month long computation was finished, Ceres was soon spotted in the precise location he had predicted. All this made Gauss famous as a mathematician and astronomer at the age of 25.

In 1807 Gauss became director of the astronomical observatory in Göttingen, where he remained until his death. His published work thereafter dealt mainly with physical science, although his unpublished papers show that he continued to work on theoretical mathematics ranging from infinite series and special functions to non-Euclidean geometry. His work on the shape of the earth's surface established the new subject of differential geometry, and his studies of the earth's magnetic and gravitational fields involved results such as the divergence theorem (Section 15.6).

The concept of curved space-time in Albert Einstein's general relativity theory traces back to the discovery of non-Euclidean geometry and Gauss's early investigations of differential geometry. A current application of relativity theory is the study of black holes. Space is itself thought to be severely warped in the vicinity of a black hole, with its immense gravitational attraction, and the mathematics required to analyze such a situation begins with the vector calculus of Chapter 15.

Schematic of mass swirling into a supermassive black hole at the center of the Milky Way galaxy.

15.1 VECTOR FIELDS

This chapter is devoted to topics in the calculus of vector fields of importance in science and engineering. A **vector field** defined on a region T in space is a vector-valued function $\mathbf{F}$ that associates with each point (x, y, z) of T a vector

$$\mathbf{F}(x, y, z) = \mathbf{i}P(x, y, z) + \mathbf{j}Q(x, y, z) + \mathbf{k}R(x, y, z). \tag{1}$$

We may more briefly describe the vector field $\mathbf{F}$ in terms of its *component functions* P, Q, and R by writing

$$\mathbf{F} = P\mathbf{i} + Q\mathbf{j} + R\mathbf{k} \quad \text{or} \quad \mathbf{F} = \langle P, Q, R \rangle.$$

Note that the components P, Q, and R of a vector function are *scalar* (real-valued) functions.

A **vector field** in the plane is similar except that neither z-components nor z-coordinates are involved. Thus a vector field on the plane region R is a vector-valued function $\mathbf{F}$ that associates with each point (x, y) of R a vector

$$\mathbf{F}(x, y) = \mathbf{i}P(x, y) + \mathbf{j}Q(x, y) \tag{2}$$

or, briefly, $\mathbf{F} = P\mathbf{i} + Q\mathbf{j}$ or $\mathbf{F} = \langle P, Q \rangle$.

It is useful to be able to visualize a given vector field $\mathbf{F}$. One common way is to sketch a collection of typical vectors $\mathbf{F}(x, y)$, each represented by an arrow of length $|\mathbf{F}(x, y)|$ and located with (x, y) as its initial point. This procedure is illustrated in Example 1.

EXAMPLE 1 Describe the vector field $\mathbf{F}(x, y) = x\mathbf{i} + y\mathbf{j}$.

Solution For each point (x, y) in the coordinate plane, $\mathbf{F}(x, y)$ is simply its position vector. It points directly away from the origin and has length

$$|\mathbf{F}(x, y)| = |x\mathbf{i} + y\mathbf{j}| = \sqrt{x^2 + y^2} = r,$$

equal to the distance from the origin to (x, y). Figure 15.1.1 shows some typical vectors representing this vector field. ◆

FIGURE 15.1.1 The vector field $\mathbf{F}(x, y) = x\mathbf{i} + y\mathbf{j}$.

Among the most important vector fields in applications are velocity vector fields. Imagine the steady flow of a fluid, such as the water in a river or the solar wind. By a *steady flow* we mean that the velocity vector $\mathbf{v}(x, y, z)$ of the fluid flowing through each point (x, y, z) is independent of time (although not necessarily independent of x, y, and z), so the pattern of the flow remains constant. Then $\mathbf{v}(x, y, z)$ is the **velocity vector field** of the fluid flow.

EXAMPLE 2 Suppose that the horizontal xy-plane is covered with a thin sheet of water that is revolving (rather like a whirlpool) around the origin with constant angular speed ω radians per second in the counterclockwise direction. Describe the associated velocity vector field.

Solution In this case we have a two-dimensional vector field $\mathbf{v}(x, y)$. At each point (x, y) the water is moving with speed $v = r\omega$ and tangential to the circle of radius $r = \sqrt{x^2 + y^2}$. The vector field

$$\mathbf{v}(x, y) = \omega(-y\mathbf{i} + x\mathbf{j}) \tag{3}$$

has length $r\omega$ and points in a generally counterclockwise direction, and

$$\mathbf{v} \cdot \mathbf{r} = \omega(-y\mathbf{i} + x\mathbf{j}) \cdot (x\mathbf{i} + y\mathbf{j}) = 0,$$

FIGURE 15.1.2 The velocity vector field $\mathbf{v}(x, y) = \omega(-y\mathbf{i} + x\mathbf{j})$, drawn for $\omega = 1$ (Example 2).

so $\mathbf{v}$ is tangent to the circle just mentioned. The velocity field determined by Eq. (3) is illustrated in Fig. 15.1.2. ◆

FIGURE 15.1.3 The vector field $\mathbf{F} = x\mathbf{i} + y\mathbf{j}$.

FIGURE 15.1.4 The vector field $\mathbf{F} = -y\mathbf{i} + x\mathbf{j}$.

REMARK Most computer algebra systems have the facility to plot vector fields. For instance, either the *Maple* command `fieldplot( [x,y], x=-2..2, y=-2..2 )` or the *Mathematica* command `PlotVectorField[ {x,y}, {x,-2,2}, {y,-2,2} ]` generates a computer plot like Fig. 15.1.3 of the vector field $\mathbf{F} = x\mathbf{i} + y\mathbf{j}$ of Example 1. The computer has scaled the vectors to a fixed maximum length so that the length of each vector as plotted is proportional to its actual length. Figure 15.1.4 shows a similar computer plot of the vector field $\mathbf{F} = -y\mathbf{i} + x\mathbf{j}$ of Example 2.

Equally important in physical applications are *force fields*. Suppose that some circumstance (perhaps gravitational or electrical in character) causes a force $\mathbf{F}(x, y, z)$ to act on a particle when it is placed at the point (x, y, z). Then we have a force field $\mathbf{F}$. Example 3 deals with what is perhaps the most common force field perceived by human beings.

EXAMPLE 3 Suppose that a mass M is fixed at the origin in space. When a particle of unit mass is placed at the point (x, y, z) other than the origin, it is subjected to a force $\mathbf{F}(x, y, z)$ of gravitational attraction directed toward the mass M at the origin. By Newton's inverse-square law of gravitation, the magnitude of $\mathbf{F}$ is $F = GM/r^2$, where $r = \sqrt{x^2 + y^2 + z^2}$ is the length of the position vector $\mathbf{r} = x\mathbf{i} + y\mathbf{j} + z\mathbf{k}$. It follows immediately that

$$\mathbf{F}(x, y, z) = -\frac{k\mathbf{r}}{r^3}, \quad (4)$$

where $k = GM$, because this vector has both the correct magnitude and the correct direction (toward the origin, for $\mathbf{F}$ is a multiple of $-\mathbf{r}$). A force field of the form in Eq. (4) is called an *inverse-square* force field. Note that $\mathbf{F}(x, y, z)$ is not defined at the origin and that $|\mathbf{F}| \to +\infty$ as $r \to 0^+$. Figure 15.1.5 illustrates an inverse-square force field. ◆

FIGURE 15.1.5 An inverse-square force field (Example 3).

The Gradient Vector Field

In Section 13.8 we introduced the gradient vector of the differentiable real-valued function $f(x, y, z)$. It is the vector ∇f defined as follows:

$$\nabla f = \mathbf{i}\frac{\partial f}{\partial x} + \mathbf{j}\frac{\partial f}{\partial y} + \mathbf{k}\frac{\partial f}{\partial z}. \quad (5)$$

The partial derivatives on the right-hand side of Eq. (5) are evaluated at the point (x, y, z). Thus $\nabla f(x, y, z)$ is a vector field: It is the **gradient vector field** of the function f and is sometimes denoted by grad f. According to Theorem 1 of Section 13.8, the vector $\nabla f(x, y, z)$ points in the direction in which the maximal directional derivative of f at (x, y, z) is obtained. For example, if $f(x, y, z)$ is the temperature at the point (x, y, z) in space, then you should move in the direction $\nabla f(x, y, z)$ in order to warm up the most quickly.

In the case of a two-variable scalar function $f(x, y)$ we suppress the third component in Eq. (5), so $\nabla f = \langle f_x, f_y \rangle = f_x\mathbf{i} + f_y\mathbf{j}$ defines a plane vector field.

EXAMPLE 4 With $f(x, y) = x^2 - y^2$, the gradient vector field $\nabla f = 2x\mathbf{i} - 2y\mathbf{j}$ plotted in Fig. 15.1.6 should remind you of a contour plot near a saddle point. ◆

The notation in Eq. (5) suggests the formal expression

$$\nabla = \mathbf{i}\frac{\partial}{\partial x} + \mathbf{j}\frac{\partial}{\partial y} + \mathbf{k}\frac{\partial}{\partial z}. \tag{6}$$

FIGURE 15.1.6 The gradient vector field $\nabla f = 2x\mathbf{i} - 2y\mathbf{j}$ of Example 4.

It is fruitful to think of ∇ as a *vector differential operator*. That is, ∇ is the operation that, when applied to the scalar function f, yields its gradient vector field ∇f. This operation behaves in several familiar and important ways like the operation D_x of single-variable differentiation. For a familiar example of this phenomenon, recall that in Chapter 13 we found the critical points of a function f of several variables to be those points at which $\nabla f(x, y, z) = \mathbf{0}$ and those at which $\nabla f(x, y, z)$ does not exist. As a computationally useful instance, suppose that f and g are functions and that a and b are constants. It then follows readily from Eq. (5) and from the linearity of partial differentiation that

$$\nabla(af + bg) = a\,\nabla f + b\,\nabla g. \tag{7}$$

Thus the gradient operator is *linear*. It also satisfies the product rule, as demonstrated in Example 5.

EXAMPLE 5 Given the differentiable functions $f(x, y, z)$ and $g(x, y, z)$, show that

$$\nabla(fg) = f\,\nabla g + g\,\nabla f. \tag{8}$$

Solution We apply the definition in Eq. (5) and the product rule for partial differentiation. Thus

$$\nabla(fg) = \mathbf{i}\frac{\partial(fg)}{\partial x} + \mathbf{j}\frac{\partial(fg)}{\partial y} + \mathbf{k}\frac{\partial(fg)}{\partial z}$$
$$= \mathbf{i}(fg_x + gf_x) + \mathbf{j}(fg_y + gf_y) + \mathbf{k}(fg_z + gf_z)$$
$$= f \cdot (\mathbf{i}g_x + \mathbf{j}g_y + \mathbf{k}g_z) + g \cdot (\mathbf{i}f_x + \mathbf{j}f_y + \mathbf{k}f_z) = f\,\nabla g + g\,\nabla f,$$

as desired. ◆

The Divergence of a Vector Field

Suppose that we are given the vector-valued function

$$\mathbf{F}(x, y, z) = \mathbf{i}P(x, y, z) + \mathbf{j}Q(x, y, z) + \mathbf{k}R(x, y, z)$$

with differentiable component functions P, Q, and R. Then the **divergence** of $\mathbf{F}$ is the scalar function div $\mathbf{F}$ defined as follows:

$$\text{div}\,\mathbf{F} = \nabla \cdot \mathbf{F} = \frac{\partial P}{\partial x} + \frac{\partial Q}{\partial y} + \frac{\partial R}{\partial z}. \tag{9}$$

Here *div* is an abbreviation for "divergence," and the alternative notation $\nabla \cdot \mathbf{F}$ is consistent with the formal expression for ∇ in Eq. (6). That is,

$$\nabla \cdot \mathbf{F} = \left\langle \frac{\partial}{\partial x}, \frac{\partial}{\partial y}, \frac{\partial}{\partial z} \right\rangle \cdot \langle P, Q, R \rangle = \frac{\partial P}{\partial x} + \frac{\partial Q}{\partial y} + \frac{\partial R}{\partial z}.$$

We will see in Section 15.6 that if $\mathbf{v}$ is the velocity vector field of a steady fluid flow, then the value of div $\mathbf{v}$ at the point (x, y, z) is essentially the net rate per unit volume at which fluid mass is flowing away (or "diverging") from the point (x, y, z).

EXAMPLE 6 If the vector field **F** is given by

$$\mathbf{F}(x, y, z) = (xe^y)\mathbf{i} + (z \sin y)\mathbf{j} + (xy \ln z)\mathbf{k},$$

then $P(x, y, z) = xe^y$, $Q(x, y, z) = z \sin y$, and $R(x, y, z) = xy \ln z$. Hence Eq. (9) yields

$$\operatorname{div} \mathbf{F} = \frac{\partial}{\partial x}(xe^y) + \frac{\partial}{\partial y}(z \sin y) + \frac{\partial}{\partial z}(xy \ln z) = e^y + z \cos y + \frac{xy}{z}.$$

For instance, the value of div **F** at the point $(-3, 0, 2)$ is

$$\nabla \cdot \mathbf{F}(-3, 0, 2) = e^0 + 2 \cos 0 + 0 = 3. \qquad \blacklozenge$$

The analogues of Eqs. (7) and (8) for divergence are the formulas

$$\nabla \cdot (a\mathbf{F} + b\mathbf{G}) = a \nabla \cdot \mathbf{F} + b \nabla \cdot \mathbf{G} \tag{10}$$

and

$$\nabla \cdot (f\mathbf{G}) = (f)(\nabla \cdot \mathbf{G}) + (\nabla f) \cdot \mathbf{G}. \tag{11}$$

We ask you to verify these formulas in the problems. Note that Eq. (11)—in which f is a scalar function and **G** is a vector field—is consistent in that f and $\nabla \cdot \mathbf{G}$ are scalar functions, whereas ∇f and **G** are vector fields, so the sum on the right-hand side makes sense (and is a scalar function).

The Curl of a Vector Field

The **curl** of the differentiable vector field $\mathbf{F} = P\mathbf{i} + Q\mathbf{j} + R\mathbf{k}$ is the following vector field, abbreviated as curl **F**:

$$\operatorname{curl} \mathbf{F} = \nabla \times \mathbf{F} = \begin{vmatrix} \mathbf{i} & \mathbf{j} & \mathbf{k} \\ \dfrac{\partial}{\partial x} & \dfrac{\partial}{\partial y} & \dfrac{\partial}{\partial z} \\ P & Q & R \end{vmatrix}. \tag{12}$$

When we evaluate the formal determinant in Eq. (12), we obtain

$$\operatorname{curl} \mathbf{F} = \mathbf{i}\left(\frac{\partial R}{\partial y} - \frac{\partial Q}{\partial z}\right) + \mathbf{j}\left(\frac{\partial P}{\partial z} - \frac{\partial R}{\partial x}\right) + \mathbf{k}\left(\frac{\partial Q}{\partial x} - \frac{\partial P}{\partial y}\right). \tag{13}$$

Although you may wish to memorize this formula, we recommend—because you will generally find it simpler—that in practice you set up and evaluate directly the formal determinant in Eq. (12). Example 7 shows how easy this is.

EXAMPLE 7 For the vector field **F** of Example 6, Eq. (12) yields

$$\operatorname{curl} \mathbf{F} = \begin{vmatrix} \mathbf{i} & \mathbf{j} & \mathbf{k} \\ \dfrac{\partial}{\partial x} & \dfrac{\partial}{\partial y} & \dfrac{\partial}{\partial z} \\ xe^y & z \sin y & xy \ln z \end{vmatrix}$$

$$= \mathbf{i}(x \ln z - \sin y) + \mathbf{j}(-y \ln z) + \mathbf{k}(-xe^y).$$

In particular, the value of curl **F** at the point $(3, \pi/2, e)$ is

$$\nabla \times \mathbf{F}(3, \pi/2, e) = 2\mathbf{i} - \tfrac{1}{2}\pi\mathbf{j} - 3e^{\pi/2}\mathbf{k}. \qquad \blacklozenge$$

We will see in Section 15.7 that if **v** is the velocity vector of a fluid flow, then the value of the vector curl **v** at the point (x, y, z) (where that vector is nonzero) determines the axis through (x, y, z) about which the fluid is rotating (or whirling or "curling") as well as the angular velocity of the rotation.

The analogues of Eqs. (10) and (11) for curl are the formulas

$$\nabla \times (a\mathbf{F} + b\mathbf{G}) = a(\nabla \times \mathbf{F}) + b(\nabla \times \mathbf{G}) \tag{14}$$

and

$$\nabla \times (f\mathbf{G}) = (f)(\nabla \times \mathbf{G}) + (\nabla f) \times \mathbf{G} \tag{15}$$

that we ask you to verify in the problems.

EXAMPLE 8 If the function $f(x, y, z)$ has continuous second-order partial derivatives, show that

$$\text{curl}(\text{grad} f) = \mathbf{0}.$$

Solution Direct computation yields

$$\nabla \times \nabla f = \begin{vmatrix} \mathbf{i} & \mathbf{j} & \mathbf{k} \\ \dfrac{\partial}{\partial x} & \dfrac{\partial}{\partial y} & \dfrac{\partial}{\partial z} \\ \dfrac{\partial f}{\partial x} & \dfrac{\partial f}{\partial y} & \dfrac{\partial f}{\partial z} \end{vmatrix}$$

$$= \mathbf{i}\left(\dfrac{\partial^2 f}{\partial y \, \partial z} - \dfrac{\partial^2 f}{\partial z \, \partial y}\right) + \mathbf{j}\left(\dfrac{\partial^2 f}{\partial z \, \partial x} - \dfrac{\partial^2 f}{\partial x \, \partial z}\right) + \mathbf{k}\left(\dfrac{\partial^2 f}{\partial x \, \partial y} - \dfrac{\partial^2 f}{\partial y \, \partial x}\right).$$

Therefore,

$$\nabla \times \nabla f = \mathbf{0}$$

because of the equality of continuous mixed second-order partial derivatives. ◆

15.1 TRUE/FALSE STUDY GUIDE

15.1 CONCEPTS: QUESTIONS AND DISCUSSION

1. Discuss the analogy between the differential operators

$$D = \dfrac{d}{dx} \quad \text{and} \quad \nabla = \mathbf{i}\dfrac{\partial}{\partial x} + \mathbf{j}\dfrac{\partial}{\partial y}$$

for functions of one and two variables (respectively).

2. What are the similarities and differences between the divergence and the curl of a vector field?

15.1 PROBLEMS

In Problems 1 through 10, illustrate the given vector field $\mathbf{F}$ by sketching several typical vectors in the field.

1. $\mathbf{F}(x, y) = \mathbf{i} + \mathbf{j}$
2. $\mathbf{F}(x, y) = 3\mathbf{i} - 2\mathbf{j}$
3. $\mathbf{F}(x, y) = x\mathbf{i} - y\mathbf{j}$
4. $\mathbf{F}(x, y) = 2\mathbf{i} + x\mathbf{j}$
5. $\mathbf{F}(x, y) = (x^2 + y^2)^{1/2}(x\mathbf{i} + y\mathbf{j})$
6. $\mathbf{F}(x, y) = (x^2 + y^2)^{-1/2}(x\mathbf{i} + y\mathbf{j})$
7. $\mathbf{F}(x, y, z) = \mathbf{j} + \mathbf{k}$
8. $\mathbf{F}(x, y, z) = \mathbf{i} + \mathbf{j} - \mathbf{k}$
9. $\mathbf{F}(x, y, z) = -x\mathbf{i} - y\mathbf{j}$
10. $\mathbf{F}(x, y, z) = x\mathbf{i} + y\mathbf{j} + z\mathbf{k}$

Match the gradient vector fields of the functions in Problems 11 through 14 with the computer-generated plots in Figs. 15.1.7 through 15.1.10.

FIGURE 15.1.7

FIGURE 15.1.8

FIGURE 15.1.9

FIGURE 15.1.10

Apply the definitions of gradient, divergence, and curl to establish the identities in Problems 25 through 31, in which a and b denote constants, f and g denote differentiable scalar functions, and **F** and **G** denote differentiable vector fields.

25. $\nabla(af + bg) = a\nabla f + b\nabla g$
26. $\nabla \cdot (a\mathbf{F} + b\mathbf{G}) = a\nabla \cdot \mathbf{F} + b\nabla \cdot \mathbf{G}$
27. $\nabla \times (a\mathbf{F} + b\mathbf{G}) = a(\nabla \times \mathbf{F}) + b(\nabla \times \mathbf{G})$
28. $\nabla \cdot (f\mathbf{G}) = (f)(\nabla \cdot \mathbf{G}) + (\nabla f) \cdot \mathbf{G}$
29. $\nabla \times (f\mathbf{G}) = (f)(\nabla \times \mathbf{G}) + (\nabla f) \times \mathbf{G}$
30. $\nabla\left(\dfrac{f}{g}\right) = \dfrac{g\nabla f - f\nabla g}{g^2}$
31. $\nabla \cdot (\mathbf{F} \times \mathbf{G}) = \mathbf{G} \cdot (\nabla \times \mathbf{F}) - \mathbf{F} \cdot (\nabla \times \mathbf{G})$

11. $f(x, y) = xy$
12. $f(x, y) = 2x^2 + y^2$
13. $f(x, y) = \sin \frac{1}{2}(x^2 + y^2)$
14. $f(x, y) = \sin \frac{1}{2}(y^2 - x^2)$

Establish the identities in Problems 32 through 34 under the assumption that the scalar functions f and g and the vector field **F** are twice continuously differentiable.

32. $\operatorname{div}(\operatorname{curl} \mathbf{F}) = 0$
33. $\operatorname{div}(\nabla fg) = f \operatorname{div}(\nabla g) + g \operatorname{div}(\nabla f) + 2(\nabla f) \cdot (\nabla g)$
34. $\operatorname{div}(\nabla f \times \nabla g) = 0$

In Problems 15 through 24, calculate the divergence and curl of the given vector field **F**.

15. $\mathbf{F}(x, y, z) = x\mathbf{i} + y\mathbf{j} + z\mathbf{k}$
16. $\mathbf{F}(x, y, z) = 3x\mathbf{i} - 2y\mathbf{j} - 4z\mathbf{k}$
17. $\mathbf{F}(x, y, z) = yz\mathbf{i} + xz\mathbf{j} + xy\mathbf{k}$
18. $\mathbf{F}(x, y, z) = x^2\mathbf{i} + y^2\mathbf{j} + z^2\mathbf{k}$
19. $\mathbf{F}(x, y, z) = xy^2\mathbf{i} + yz^2\mathbf{j} + zx^2\mathbf{k}$
20. $\mathbf{F}(x, y, z) = (2x - y)\mathbf{i} + (3y - 2z)\mathbf{j} + (7z - 3x)\mathbf{k}$
21. $\mathbf{F}(x, y, z) = (y^2 + z^2)\mathbf{i} + (x^2 + z^2)\mathbf{j} + (x^2 + y^2)\mathbf{k}$
22. $\mathbf{F}(x, y, z) = (e^{xz} \sin y)\mathbf{j} + (e^{xy} \cos z)\mathbf{k}$
23. $\mathbf{F}(x, y, z) = (x + \sin yz)\mathbf{i} + (y + \sin xz)\mathbf{j} + (z + \sin xy)\mathbf{k}$
24. $\mathbf{F}(x, y, z) = (x^2 e^{-z})\mathbf{i} + (y^3 \ln x)\mathbf{j} + (z \cosh y)\mathbf{k}$

Verify the identities in Problems 35 through 44, in which **a** is a constant vector, $\mathbf{r} = x\mathbf{i} + y\mathbf{j} + z\mathbf{k}$, and $r = |\mathbf{r}|$. Problems 37 and 38 imply that both the divergence and the curl of an inverse-square vector field vanish identically.

35. $\nabla \cdot \mathbf{r} = 3$ and $\nabla \times \mathbf{r} = 0$
36. $\nabla \cdot (\mathbf{a} \times \mathbf{r}) = 0$ and $\nabla \times (\mathbf{a} \times \mathbf{r}) = 2\mathbf{a}$
37. $\nabla \cdot \dfrac{\mathbf{r}}{r^3} = 0$
38. $\nabla \times \dfrac{\mathbf{r}}{r^3} = 0$
39. $\nabla r = \dfrac{\mathbf{r}}{r}$
40. $\nabla\left(\dfrac{1}{r}\right) = -\dfrac{\mathbf{r}}{r^3}$
41. $\nabla \cdot (r\mathbf{r}) = 4r$
42. $\nabla \cdot (\nabla r) = \dfrac{2}{r}$
43. $\nabla(\ln r) = \dfrac{\mathbf{r}}{r^2}$
44. $\nabla(r^{10}) = 10r^8\mathbf{r}$

15.2 LINE INTEGRALS

The single integral $\int_a^b f(x)\,dx$ might be described as an integral along the x-axis. We now define integrals along curves in space (or in the plane). Such integrals are called *line integrals* (although the phrase "curve integrals" might be more appropriate).

To motivate the definition of the line integral of the function f along the smooth space curve C with parametrization

$$x = x(t), \quad y = y(t), \quad z = z(t) \tag{1}$$

for $a \leqq t \leqq b$, we imagine a thin wire shaped like C (Fig. 15.2.1). Suppose that $f(x, y, z)$ denotes the density of the wire at the point (x, y, z), measured in units of mass per unit length—for example, grams per centimeter. Then we expect to compute the total mass m of the curved wire as some kind of integral of the function f. To *approximate* m, we begin with a partition

$$a = t_0 < t_1 < t_2 < \cdots < t_{n-1} < t_n = b$$

of $[a, b]$ into n subintervals, all with the same length $\Delta t = (b-a)/n$. These subdivision points of $[a, b]$ produce, via our parametrization, a physical subdivision of the wire

FIGURE 15.2.1 A wire of variable density in the shape of the smooth curve C from A (where $t = a$) to B (where $t = b$).

FIGURE 15.2.2 The partition of the interval $[a, b]$ determines a related partition of the curve C into short arcs.

into short curve segments (Fig. 15.2.2). We let P_i denote the point $(x(t_i), y(t_i), z(t_i))$ for $i = 0, 1, 2, \ldots, n$. Then the points $P_0, P_1, \ldots, P_n$ are the subdivision points of C.

From our study of arc length in Sections 10.4 and 12.6, we know that the arc length Δs_i of the segment of C from P_{i-1} to P_i is

$$\Delta s_i = \int_{t_{i-1}}^{t_i} \sqrt{[x'(t)]^2 + [y'(t)]^2 + [z'(t)]^2}\, dt$$

$$= \sqrt{[x'(t_i^\star)]^2 + [y'(t_i^\star)]^2 + [z'(t_i^\star)]^2}\, \Delta t \qquad (2)$$

for some number $t_i^\star$ in the interval $[t_{i-1}, t_i]$. This is a consequence of the average value theorem for integrals of Section 5.5.

Denote $x(t_i^\star)$ by $x_i^\star$ and similarly define $y_i^\star$ and $z_i^\star$. If we multiply the density of the wire at the point $(x_i^\star, y_i^\star, z_i^\star)$ by the length Δs_i of the segment of C containing that point, we obtain an estimate of the mass of that segment of C. So, after we sum over all the segments, we have an estimate of the total mass m of the wire:

$$m \approx \sum_{i=1}^{n} f(x(t_i^\star), y(t_i^\star), z(t_i^\star))\, \Delta s_i.$$

The limit of this sum as $\Delta t \to 0$ should be the actual mass m. This is our motivation for the definition of the line integral of the function f along the curve C, denoted by

$$\int_C f(x, y, z)\, ds.$$

DEFINITION Line Integral of a Function along a Curve

Suppose that the function $f(x, y, z)$ is defined at each point of the smooth curve C parametrized as in (1). Then the **line integral of f along C** is defined by

$$\int_C f(x, y, z)\, ds = \lim_{\Delta t \to 0} \sum_{i=1}^{n} f(x(t_i^\star), y(t_i^\star), z(t_i^\star))\, \Delta s_i, \qquad (3)$$

provided that this limit exists.

REMARK It can be shown that the limit in (3) always exists if the function f is continuous at each point of C. Recall from Section 10.4 that the curve C is *smooth* provided that the component functions in its parametrization have continuous derivatives that are never simultaneously zero.

When we substitute Eq. (2) into Eq. (3), we recognize the result as the limit of a Riemann sum. Therefore

$$\int_C f(x, y, z)\, ds = \int_a^b f(x(t), y(t), z(t))\sqrt{[x'(t)]^2 + [y'(t)]^2 + [z'(t)]^2}\, dt. \quad (4)$$

Thus we may evaluate the line integral $\int_C f(x, y, z)\, ds$ by expressing everything in terms of the parameter t, including the symbolic arc-length element

$$ds = \sqrt{\left(\frac{dx}{dt}\right)^2 + \left(\frac{dy}{dt}\right)^2 + \left(\frac{dz}{dt}\right)^2}\, dt.$$

As a consequence, the right-hand side in Eq. (4) is evaluated as *an ordinary single integral with respect to the real variable t.*

Line Integral with Respect to Arc Length

Because of the appearance of the arc-length element ds in Eq. (4), the line integral $\int_C f(x, y, z)\, ds$ is sometimes called the **line integral of the function f with respect to arc length along the curve C.**

A curve C that lies in the xy-plane may be regarded as a space curve for which z [and $z'(t)$] are zero. In this case we simply suppress the variable z in Eq. (4) and write

$$\int_C f(x, y)\, ds = \int_a^b f(x(t), y(t))\sqrt{[x'(t)]^2 + [y'(t)]^2}\, dt. \quad (5)$$

FIGURE 15.2.3 The vertical strip with base ds and height $f(x, y)$ has area $dA = f(x, y)\, ds$, so the whole fence with base curve C has area $A = \int dA = \int_C f(x, y)\, ds$.

In the case that f is positive-valued, Fig. 15.2.3 illustrates an interpretation of the line integral in Eq. (5) as the area of a "fence" whose base is the curve C in the xy-plane, with the height of the fence above the point (x, y) given by $f(x, y)$.

EXAMPLE 1 Evaluate the line integral

$$\int_C xy\, ds,$$

where C is the first-quadrant quarter-circle of radius 1 parametrized by $x = \cos t$, $y = \sin t$, $0 \leq t \leq \pi/2$ (Fig. 15.2.4).

FIGURE 15.2.4 The quarter-circle of Example 1.

Solution Here
$$ds = \sqrt{(-\sin t)^2 + (\cos t)^2}\, dt = dt,$$
so Eq. (5) yields
$$\int_C xy\, ds = \int_{t=0}^{\pi/2} \cos t \sin t\, dt = \left[\frac{1}{2}\sin^2 t\right]_0^{\pi/2} = \frac{1}{2}.$$

Let us now return to the physical wire and denote its density function by $\delta(x, y, z)$. The mass of a small piece of length Δs is $\Delta m = \delta\, \Delta s$, so we write
$$dm = \delta(x, y, z)\, ds$$
for its (symbolic) element of mass. Then the **mass** m of the wire and its **centroid** $(\bar{x}, \bar{y}, \bar{z})$ are defined as follows:

$$m = \int_C dm = \int_C \delta\, ds, \qquad \bar{x} = \frac{1}{m}\int_C x\, dm,$$
$$\bar{y} = \frac{1}{m}\int_C y\, dm, \qquad \bar{z} = \frac{1}{m}\int_C z\, dm. \tag{6}$$

Note the analogy with Eqs. (2) and (4) of Section 14.6. The **moment of inertia** of the wire around a given axis is
$$I = \int_C p^2\, dm, \tag{7}$$
where $p = p(x, y, z)$ denotes the perpendicular distance from the point (x, y, z) of the wire to the axis in question.

EXAMPLE 2 Find the centroid of a wire that has density $\delta = kz$ and the shape of the helix C (Fig. 15.2.5) with parametrization
$$x = 3\cos t, \quad y = 3\sin t, \quad z = 4t, \quad 0 \leqq t \leqq \pi.$$

Solution The mass element of the wire is
$$dm = \delta\, ds = kz\, ds = 4kt\sqrt{(-3\sin t)^2 + (3\cos t)^2 + 4^2}\, dt = 20kt\, dt.$$
Hence the formulas in (6) yield
$$m = \int_C \delta\, ds = \int_0^\pi 20kt\, dt = 10k\pi^2;$$
$$\bar{x} = \frac{1}{m}\int_C \delta x\, ds = \frac{1}{10k\pi^2}\int_0^\pi 60kt\cos t\, dt$$
$$= \frac{6}{\pi^2}\Big[\cos t + t\sin t\Big]_0^\pi = -\frac{12}{\pi^2} \approx -1.22;$$
$$\bar{y} = \frac{1}{m}\int_C \delta y\, ds = \frac{1}{10k\pi^2}\int_0^\pi 60kt\sin t\, dt$$
$$= \frac{6}{\pi^2}\Big[\sin t - t\cos t\Big]_0^\pi = \frac{6}{\pi} \approx 1.91;$$
$$\bar{z} = \frac{1}{m}\int_C \delta z\, ds = \frac{1}{10k\pi^2}\int_0^\pi 80kt^2\, dt$$
$$= \frac{8}{\pi^2}\left[\frac{1}{3}t^3\right]_0^\pi = \frac{8\pi}{3} \approx 8.38.$$

So the centroid of the wire is located close to the point $(-1.22, 1.91, 8.38)$.

FIGURE 15.2.5 The helical wire of Example 2. Does the centroid $(-1.22, 1.91, 8.38)$ lie on the wire?

Line Integrals with Respect to Coordinate Variables

We obtain a different kind of line integral by replacing Δs_i in Eq. (3) with

$$\Delta x_i = x(t_i) - x(t_{i-1}) = x'(t_i^\star)\,\Delta t.$$

The **line integral of f along C with respect to** x is defined to be

$$\int_C f(x, y, z)\,dx = \lim_{\Delta t \to 0} \sum_{i=1}^{n} f(x(t_i^\star), y(t_i^\star), z(t_i^\star))\,\Delta x_i.$$

Thus

$$\int_C f(x, y, z)\,dx = \int_a^b f(x(t), y(t), z(t)) x'(t)\,dt. \tag{8a}$$

Similarly, the **line integrals of f along C with respect to** y and **with respect to** z are given by

$$\int_C f(x, y, z)\,dy = \int_a^b f(x(t), y(t), z(t)) y'(t)\,dt \tag{8b}$$

and

$$\int_C f(x, y, z)\,dz = \int_a^b f(x(t), y(t), z(t)) z'(t)\,dt. \tag{8c}$$

The three integrals in (8) typically occur together. If P, Q, and R are continuous functions of the variables x, y, and z, then we write (indeed, *define*)

$$\int_C P\,dx + Q\,dy + R\,dz = \int_C P\,dx + \int_C Q\,dy + \int_C R\,dz. \tag{9}$$

REMARK Although it would be natural enough to write $\int_C (P\,dx + Q\,dy + R\,dz)$ on the right-hand side in Eq. (9), the parentheses are customarily omitted. Indeed, in more advanced vector calculus the *differential form* $P\,dx + Q\,dy + R\,dz$ is regarded as a single object that "hangs together" all by itself. For instance, one may see the abbreviations $\omega = P\,dx + Q\,dy + R\,dz$ for the differential form and $\int_C \omega$ for the line integral.

The line integrals in Eqs. (8) and (9) are evaluated by expressing x, y, z, dx, dy, and dz in terms of t as determined by a suitable parametrization of the curve C. The result is an ordinary single-variable integral. For instance, if C is a parametric plane curve parametrized over the interval $[a, b]$ by $\mathbf{r}(t) = \langle x(t), y(t) \rangle$, then

$$\int_C P\,dx + Q\,dy = \int_a^b [P(x(t), y(t)) \cdot x'(t) + Q(x(t), y(t)) \cdot y'(t)]\,dt.$$

EXAMPLE 3 Evaluate the line integral

$$\int_C y\,dx + z\,dy + x\,dz,$$

where C is the parametric curve $x = t, y = t^2, z = t^3, 0 \leqq t \leqq 1$.

Solution Because $dx = dt$, $dy = 2t\, dt$, and $dz = 3t^2\, dt$, substitution in terms of t yields

$$\int_C y\, dx + z\, dy + x\, dz = \int_0^1 t^2\, dt + t^3(2t\, dt) + t(3t^2\, dt)$$

$$= \int_0^1 (t^2 + 3t^3 + 2t^4)\, dt = \left[\frac{1}{3}t^3 + \frac{3}{4}t^4 + \frac{2}{5}t^5\right]_0^1 = \frac{89}{60}. \; \blacklozenge$$

The given parametrization of a smooth curve C determines an **orientation** or "positive direction" along the curve. As the parameter t increases from $t = a$ to $t = b$, the point $(x(t), y(t))$ moves along the curve from its initial point A to its terminal point B. Now think of a curve $-C$ with the *opposite orientation*. This new curve consists of the same points as C, but the parametrization of $-C$ traces these points in the opposite direction, from initial point B to terminal point A (Fig. 15.2.6). Because the arc-length differential $ds = \sqrt{[x'(t)]^2 + [y'(t)]^2 + [z'(t)]^2}\, dt$ is always positive (the square root is positive), the value of the line integral with respect to arc length is not affected by the reversal of orientation. That is,

$$\int_{-C} f(x, y, z)\, ds = \int_C f(x, y, z)\, ds. \qquad (10)$$

FIGURE 15.2.6 $\int_{-C} f\, ds = \int_C f\, ds$ but $\int_{-C} P\, dx + Q\, dy = -\int_C P\, dx + Q\, dy.$

In contrast, the signs of the derivatives $x'(t)$, $y'(t)$, and $z'(t)$ in Eqs. (8a), (8b), and (8c) are changed when the direction of the parametrization is reversed, so it follows that

$$\int_{-C} P\, dx + Q\, dy + R\, dz = -\int_C P\, dx + Q\, dy + R\, dz. \qquad (11)$$

Thus changing the orientation of the curve changes the *sign* of a line integral with respect to coordinate variables, but does not affect the value of a line integral with respect to arc length. It is proved in advanced calculus that, for either type of line integral, two one-to-one parametrizations of the same smooth curve give the same value if they agree in orientation.

EXAMPLE 4 The parametrization $x = 1 + 8t$, $y = 2 + 6t$ ($0 \leq t \leq 1$) of the line segment C from $A(1, 2)$ to $B(9, 8)$ in Fig. 15.2.7 gives $dx = 8\, dt$, $dy = 6\, dt$, and $ds = 10\, dt$. Hence we easily verify that

$$\int_C xy\, ds = \int_0^1 (1 + 8t)(2 + 6t) \cdot 10\, dt = 290$$

and

$$\int_C y\, dx + x\, dy = \int_0^1 [(2 + 6t) \cdot 8 + (1 + 8t) \cdot 6]\, dt = 70.$$

FIGURE 15.2.7 The line segment of Example 4.

The parametrization $x = 9 - 4t$, $y = 8 - 3t$ ($0 \leq t \leq 2$) of the oppositely oriented segment $-C$ from $B(9, 8)$ to $A(1, 2)$ gives $dx = -4\, dt$, $dy = -3\, dt$, and $ds = 5\, dt$, and we easily verify that

$$\int_{-C} xy\, ds = \int_0^2 (9 - 4t)(8 - 3t) \cdot 5\, dt = 290,$$

whereas

$$\int_{-C} y\, dx + x\, dy = \int_0^2 [(8 - 3t) \cdot (-4) + (9 - 4t) \cdot (-3)]\, dt = -70. \; \blacklozenge$$

If the curve C consists of a finite number of smooth curves joined at consecutive corner points, then we say that C is **piecewise smooth.** In such a case the value of a line integral along C is defined to be the sum of its values along the smooth segments

FIGURE 15.2.8 The curve $C = C_1 + C_2$ from P to R.

of C. For instance, with the piecewise smooth curve $C = C_1 + C_2$ of Fig. 15.2.8, we have

$$\int_C f(x, y, z)\, ds = \int_{C_1+C_2} f(x, y, z)\, ds = \int_{C_1} f(x, y, z)\, ds + \int_{C_2} f(x, y, z)\, ds.$$

EXAMPLE 5 Evaluate the line integral

$$\int_C y\, dx + 2x\, dy$$

for each of these three curves C (Fig. 15.2.9):

- C_1 The straight line segment in the plane from $A(1, 1)$ to $B(2, 4)$;
- C_2 The plane path from $A(1, 1)$ to $B(2, 4)$ along the graph of the parabola $y = x^2$; and
- C_3 The straight line in the plane from $A(1, 1)$ to $Q(2, 1)$ followed by the straight line from $Q(2, 1)$ to $B(2, 4)$.

FIGURE 15.2.9 The three arcs of Example 5.

Solution The straight line segment C_1 from A to B can be parametrized by $x = 1 + t$, $y = 1 + 3t$, $0 \leq t \leq 1$. Hence

$$\int_{C_1} y\, dx + 2x\, dy = \int_0^1 (1 + 3t)\, dt + 2(1 + t)(3\, dt)$$

$$= \int_0^1 (7 + 9t)\, dt = \frac{23}{2}.$$

Next, the arc C_2 of the parabola $y = x^2$ from A to B is "self-parametrizing": It has the parametrization $x = x$, $y = x^2$, $1 \leq x \leq 2$. So

$$\int_{C_2} y\, dx + 2x\, dy = \int_1^2 (x^2)(dx) + 2(x)(2x\, dx) = \int_1^2 5x^2\, dx = \frac{35}{3}.$$

Finally, along the straight line segment from $(1, 1)$ to $(2, 1)$ we have $y \equiv 1$ and (because y is a constant) $dy = 0$. Along the vertical segment from $(2, 1)$ to $(2, 4)$ we have $x \equiv 2$ and $dx = 0$. Therefore

$$\int_{C_3} y\, dx + 2x\, dy = \int_{x=1}^2 [(1)(dx) + (2x)(0)] + \int_{y=1}^4 [(y)(0) + (4)(dy)]$$

$$= \int_{x=1}^2 1\, dx + \int_{y=1}^4 4\, dy = 13. \qquad \blacklozenge$$

Example 5 shows that we may well obtain different values for the line integral from A to B if we evaluate it along different curves from A to B. Thus this line integral is *path-dependent*. We shall give in Section 15.3 a sufficient condition for the line integral

$$\int_C P\, dx + Q\, dy + R\, dz$$

to have the same value for *all* smooth or piecewise smooth curves C from A to B, and thus for the integral to be *independent of path*.

Line Integrals and Vector Fields

Suppose now that $\mathbf{F} = P\mathbf{i} + Q\mathbf{j} + R\mathbf{k}$ is a force field defined on a region that contains the curve C from the point A to the point B. Suppose also that C has a parametrization

$$\mathbf{r}(t) = \mathbf{i}x(t) + \mathbf{j}y(t) + \mathbf{k}z(t), \quad t \text{ in } [a, b],$$

1026 CHAPTER 15 Vector Calculus

FIGURE 15.2.10 The component of **F** along C from P_{i-1} to P_i is $\mathbf{F} \cdot \mathbf{T}$.

with a *nonzero* velocity vector

$$\mathbf{v} = \mathbf{i}\frac{dx}{dt} + \mathbf{j}\frac{dy}{dt} + \mathbf{k}\frac{dz}{dt}.$$

The speed associated with this velocity vector is

$$v = |\mathbf{v}| = \sqrt{\left(\frac{dx}{dt}\right)^2 + \left(\frac{dy}{dt}\right)^2 + \left(\frac{dz}{dt}\right)^2}.$$

Recall from Section 12.6 that the *unit tangent vector* to the curve C is

$$\mathbf{T} = \frac{\mathbf{v}}{v} = \frac{1}{v}\left(\frac{dx}{dt}\mathbf{i} + \frac{dy}{dt}\mathbf{j} + \frac{dz}{dt}\mathbf{k}\right).$$

We want to approximate the work W done by the force field $\mathbf{F}$ in moving a particle along the curve C from A to B. Subdivide C as indicated in Fig. 15.2.10. Think of $\mathbf{F}$ moving the particle from P_{i-1} to P_i, two consecutive division points of C. The work ΔW_i done is approximately the product of the distance Δs_i from P_{i-1} to P_i (measured along C) and the tangential component $\mathbf{F} \cdot \mathbf{T}$ of the force $\mathbf{F}$ at a typical point $(x(t_i^\star), y(t_i^\star), z(t_i^\star))$ between P_{i-1} and P_i. Thus

$$\Delta W_i \approx \mathbf{F}(x(t_i^\star), y(t_i^\star), z(t_i^\star)) \cdot \mathbf{T}(t_i^\star)\,\Delta s_i,$$

so the total work W is given approximately by

$$W \approx \sum_{i=1}^{n} \mathbf{F}(x(t_i^\star), y(t_i^\star), z(t_i^\star)) \cdot \mathbf{T}(t_i^\star)\,\Delta s_i.$$

This approximation suggests that we *define* the **work** W as

$$W = \int_C \mathbf{F} \cdot \mathbf{T}\,ds. \tag{12}$$

Thus *work is the integral with respect to arc length of the tangential component of the force.* Intuitively, we may regard $dW = \mathbf{F} \cdot \mathbf{T}\,ds$ as the infinitesimal element of work done by the tangential component $\mathbf{F} \cdot \mathbf{T}$ of the force in moving the particle along the arc-length element ds. The line integral in Eq. (12) is then the "sum" of all these infinitesimal elements of work.

It is customary to write

$$\mathbf{r} = x\mathbf{i} + y\mathbf{j} + z\mathbf{k} \quad \text{and} \quad d\mathbf{r} = \mathbf{i}\,dx + \mathbf{j}\,dy + \mathbf{k}\,dz.$$

Then

$$\mathbf{T}\,ds = \frac{\mathbf{v}}{v} \cdot v\,dt = \mathbf{v}\,dt$$

$$= \left(\frac{dx}{dt}\mathbf{i} + \frac{dy}{dt}\mathbf{j} + \frac{dz}{dt}\mathbf{k}\right)dt = \mathbf{i}\,dx + \mathbf{j}\,dy + \mathbf{k}\,dz,$$

so

$$\mathbf{T}\,ds = d\mathbf{r}.$$

With this notation, Eq. (12) takes the form

$$W = \int_C \mathbf{F} \cdot d\mathbf{r} \tag{13}$$

that is common in engineering and physics texts.

To evaluate the line integral in Eq. (12) or (13), we express its integrand and limit of integration in terms of the parameter t, as usual. Thus

$$W = \int_C \mathbf{F} \cdot \mathbf{T}\,ds$$

$$= \int_a^b (P\mathbf{i} + Q\mathbf{j} + R\mathbf{k}) \cdot \frac{1}{v}\left(\frac{dx}{dt}\mathbf{i} + \frac{dy}{dt}\mathbf{j} + \frac{dz}{dt}\mathbf{k}\right)v\,dt$$

$$= \int_a^b \left(P\frac{dx}{dt} + Q\frac{dy}{dt} + R\frac{dz}{dt}\right)dt.$$

Therefore,

$$W = \int_C P\,dx + Q\,dy + R\,dz. \tag{14}$$

This computation reveals an important relation between the two types of line integrals we have defined here.

THEOREM 1 Equivalent Line Integrals

Suppose that the vector field $\mathbf{F} = P\mathbf{i} + Q\mathbf{j} + R\mathbf{k}$ has continuous component functions and that $\mathbf{T}$ is the unit tangent vector to the smooth curve C. Then

$$\int_C \mathbf{F} \cdot \mathbf{T}\,ds = \int_C P\,dx + Q\,dy + R\,dz. \tag{15}$$

REMARK If the orientation of the curve C is reversed, then the sign of the right-hand integral in Eq. (15) is changed according to Eq. (11), whereas the sign of the left-hand integral is changed because $\mathbf{T}$ is replaced with $-\mathbf{T}$.

EXAMPLE 6 The work done by the force field $\mathbf{F} = y\mathbf{i} + z\mathbf{j} + x\mathbf{k}$ in moving a particle from $(0, 0, 0)$ to $(1, 1, 1)$ along the twisted cubic $x = t$, $y = t^2$, $z = t^3$ is given by the line integral

$$W = \int_C \mathbf{F} \cdot d\mathbf{r} = \int_C \mathbf{F} \cdot \mathbf{T}\,ds = \int_C y\,dx + z\,dy + x\,dz,$$

and we computed the value of this integral in Example 3. Hence $W = \frac{89}{60}$. ◆

EXAMPLE 7 Find the work done by the inverse-square force field

$$\mathbf{F}(x, y, z) = \frac{k\mathbf{r}}{r^3} = \frac{k(x\mathbf{i} + y\mathbf{j} + z\mathbf{k})}{(x^2 + y^2 + z^2)^{3/2}}$$

in moving a particle along the straight line segment C from $(0, 4, 0)$ to $(0, 4, 3)$.

Solution Along C we have $x = 0$, $y = 4$, and z varying from 0 to 3. Thus we choose z as the parameter:

$$x \equiv 0, \quad y \equiv 4, \quad \text{and} \quad z = z, \quad 0 \leqq z \leqq 3.$$

Because $dx = 0 = dy$, Eq. (14) gives

$$W = \int_C \frac{k(x\,dx + y\,dy + z\,dz)}{(x^2 + y^2 + z^2)^{3/2}}$$

$$= \int_0^3 \frac{kz}{(16 + z^2)^{3/2}}\,dz = \left[\frac{-k}{\sqrt{16 + z^2}}\right]_0^3 = \frac{k}{20}. \quad\blacklozenge$$

15.2 TRUE/FALSE STUDY GUIDE

15.2 CONCEPTS: QUESTIONS AND DISCUSSION

1. Contrast the definitions of $\int_C f\,ds$ and $\int_C f\,dx$ where C is a smooth curve in space. Describe physical measurements appropriate to both types of line integrals. Explain why one depends on the orientation or direction of integration along the curve C and the other does not.

2. Explain the relation between the line integrals

$$\int_C \mathbf{F} \cdot \mathbf{T}\,ds \quad \text{and} \quad \int_C P\,dx + Q\,dy + R\,dz.$$

In what way does each depend on the orientation of the curve C?

15.2 PROBLEMS

In Problems 1 through 5, evaluate the line integrals

$$\int_C f(x, y)\,ds, \quad \int_C f(x, y)\,dx, \quad \text{and} \quad \int_C f(x, y)\,dy$$

along the indicated parametric curve.

1. $f(x, y) = x^2 + y^2$; $x = 4t - 1$, $y = 3t + 1$, $-1 \leqq t \leqq 1$
2. $f(x, y) = x$; $x = t$, $y = t^2$, $0 \leqq t \leqq 1$
3. $f(x, y) = x + y$; $x = e^t + 1$, $y = e^t - 1$, $0 \leqq t \leqq \ln 2$
4. $f(x, y) = 2x - y$; $x = \sin t$, $y = \cos t$, $0 \leqq t \leqq \pi/2$
5. $f(x, y) = xy$; $x = 3t$, $y = t^4$, $0 \leqq t \leqq 1$

In Problems 6 through 10, evaluate

$$\int_C P(x, y)\,dx + Q(x, y)\,dy.$$

6. $P(x, y) = xy$, $Q(x, y) = x + y$; C is the part of the graph of $y = x^2$ from $(-1, 1)$ to $(2, 4)$
7. $P(x, y) = y^2$, $Q(x, y) = x$; C is the part of the graph of $x = y^3$ from $(-1, -1)$ to $(1, 1)$
8. $P(x, y) = y\sqrt{x}$, $Q(x, y) = x\sqrt{x}$; C is the part of the graph of $y^2 = x^3$ from $(1, 1)$ to $(4, 8)$
9. $P(x, y) = x^2 y$, $Q(x, y) = xy^3$; C consists of the line segments from $(-1, 1)$ to $(2, 1)$ and from $(2, 1)$ to $(2, 5)$
10. $P(x, y) = x + 2y$, $Q(x, y) = 2x - y$; C consists of the line segments from $(3, 2)$ to $(3, -1)$ and from $(3, -1)$ to $(-2, -1)$

In Problems 11 through 15, evaluate the line integral

$$\int_C \mathbf{F} \cdot \mathbf{T}\,ds$$

along the indicated path C.

11. $\mathbf{F}(x, y, z) = z\mathbf{i} + x\mathbf{j} - y\mathbf{k}$; C is parametrized by $x = t$, $y = t^2$, $z = t^3$, $0 \leqq t \leqq 1$.
12. $\mathbf{F}(x, y, z) = yz\mathbf{i} + xz\mathbf{j} + xy\mathbf{k}$; C is the straight line segment from $(2, -1, 3)$ to $(4, 2, -1)$.
13. $\mathbf{F}(x, y, z) = y\mathbf{i} - x\mathbf{j} + z\mathbf{k}$; $x = \sin t$, $y = \cos t$, $z = 2t$, $0 \leqq y \leqq \pi$.
14. $\mathbf{F}(x, y, z) = (2x + 3y)\mathbf{i} + (3x + 2y)\mathbf{j} + 3z^2\mathbf{k}$; C is the path from $(0, 0, 0)$ to $(4, 2, 3)$ that consists of three line segments parallel to the x-axis, the y-axis, and the z-axis, in that order.
15. $\mathbf{F}(x, y, z) = yz^2\mathbf{i} + xz^2\mathbf{j} + 2xyz\mathbf{k}$; C is the path from $(-1, 2, -2)$ to $(1, 5, 2)$ that consists of three line segments parallel to the z-axis, the x-axis, and the y-axis, in that order.

In Problems 16 through 18, evaluate

$$\int_C f(x, y, z)\,ds$$

for the given function $f(x, y, z)$ and the given path C.

16. $f(x, y, z) = xyz$; C is the straight line segment from $(1, -1, 2)$ to $(3, 2, 5)$.
17. $f(x, y, z) = 2x + 9xy$; C is the curve $x = t$, $y = t^2$, $z = t^3$, $0 \leqq t \leqq 1$.

18. $f(x, y, z) = xy$; C is the elliptical helix $x = 4\cos t$, $y = 9\sin t$, $z = 7t$, $0 \leq t \leq 5\pi/2$.

19. Find the centroid of a uniform thin wire shaped like the semicircle $x^2 + y^2 = a^2$, $a > 0$, $y \geq 0$.

20. Find the moments of inertia around the x- and y-axes of the wire of Problem 19.

21. Find the mass and centroid of a wire that has constant density $\delta = k$ and is shaped like the helix $x = 3\cos t$, $y = 3\sin t$, $z = 4t$, $0 \leq t \leq 2\pi$.

22. Find the moment of inertia $I_z = \int_C (x^2 + y^2)\, dm$ around the z-axis of the helical wire of Problem 21.

23. A wire shaped like the first-quadrant portion of the circle $x^2 + y^2 = a^2$ has density $\delta = kxy$ at the point (x, y). Find its mass, centroid, and moment of inertia around each coordinate axis.

24. A wire is shaped like the arch $x = t - \sin t$, $y = 1 - \cos t$ ($0 \leq t \leq 2\pi$) of a cycloid C and has constant density $\delta(x, y) \equiv k$. Find its mass, centroid, and moment of inertia $I_x = \int_C y^2\, dm$ around the x-axis.

25. A wire is shaped like the astroid $x = \cos^3 t$, $y = \sin^3 t$ ($0 \leq t \leq 2\pi$) and has constant density $\delta(x, y) \equiv k$. Find its moment of inertia $I_0 = \int_C (x^2 + y^2)\, dm$ around the origin.

*The **average distance** $\overline{D}$ from the fixed point P to points of the parametrized curve C is defined by*

$$\overline{D} = \frac{1}{s} \int_C D(x, y)\, ds$$

where s is the length of C and $D(x, y)$ denotes the distance from P to the variable point (x, y) of C. In Problems 26 through 31, compute the average distance, exactly if possible, else by using a computer algebra system to find it (either symbolically or, if necessary, numerically).

26. Use the standard trigonometric parametrization of a circle C of radius a to verify that the average distance of points of C from its center is $\overline{D} = a$.

27. Find (exactly) the average distance from the point $(a, 0)$ to points of the circle of radius a centered at the origin. [*Suggestion:* Use the law of cosines to find $D(x, y)$.]

28. Find the average distance from the origin to points of the cycloidal arch of Problem 24.

29. Find the average distance from the origin to points of the astroid of Problem 25.

30. Find the average distance from the origin to points of the helix of Problem 21.

31. The spiral parametrized by $x = e^{-t}\cos t$, $y = e^{-t}\sin t$ starts at $(1, 0)$ when $t = 0$ and closes in on the origin as $t \to \infty$. Use improper integrals to calculate the average distance from the origin to points of this spiral.

32. Find the work done by the inverse-square force field of Example 7 in moving a particle from $(1, 0, 0)$ to $(0, 3, 4)$. Integrate first along the line segment from $(1, 0, 0)$ to $(5, 0, 0)$ and then along a path on the sphere with equation $x^2 + y^2 + z^2 = 25$. The second integral is automatically zero. (Why?)

33. Imagine an infinitely long and uniformly charged wire that coincides with the z-axis. The electric force that it exerts on a unit charge at the point $(x, y) \neq (0, 0)$ in the xy-plane is

$$\mathbf{F}(x, y) = \frac{k(x\mathbf{i} + y\mathbf{j})}{x^2 + y^2}.$$

Find the work done by $\mathbf{F}$ in moving a unit charge along the straight line segment from (a) $(1, 0)$ to $(1, 1)$; (b) $(1, 1)$ to $(0, 1)$.

34. Show that if $\mathbf{F}$ is a *constant* force field, then it does zero work on a particle that moves once uniformly counterclockwise around the unit circle in the xy-plane.

35. Show that if $\mathbf{F} = k\mathbf{r} = k(x\mathbf{i} + y\mathbf{j})$, then $\mathbf{F}$ does zero work on a particle that moves once uniformly counterclockwise around the unit circle in the xy-plane.

36. Find the work done by the force field $\mathbf{F} = -y\mathbf{i} + x\mathbf{j}$ in moving a particle counterclockwise once around the unit circle in the xy-plane.

37. Let C be a curve on the unit sphere $x^2 + y^2 + z^2 = 1$. Explain why the inverse-square force field of Example 7 does zero work in moving a particle along C.

In Problems 38 through 40, the given curve C joins the points P and Q in the xy-plane. The point P represents the top of a ten-story building, and Q is a point on the ground 100 ft from the base of the building. A 150-lb person slides down a frictionless slide shaped like the curve C from P to Q under the influence of the gravitational force $\mathbf{F} = -150\mathbf{j}$. In each problem show that $\mathbf{F}$ does the same amount of work on the person, $W = 15000$ ft·lb, as if he or she had dropped straight down to the ground.

38. C is the straight line segment $y = x$ from $P(100, 100)$ to $Q(0, 0)$.

39. C is the circular arc $x = 100\sin t$, $y = 100\cos t$ from $P(0, 100)$ to $Q(100, 0)$.

40. C is the parabolic arc $y = x^2/100$ from $P(100, 100)$ to $Q(0, 0)$.

41. Now suppose that the 100-ft ten-story building of Problems 38 through 40 is a circular tower with a radius of 25 ft, and the fire-escape slide is a spiral (helical) ramp that encircles the tower once every two floors. Use a line integral to compute the work done by the gravitational force field $\mathbf{F} = -200\mathbf{k}$ on a 200-lb person who slides down this (frictionless) ramp from the top of the building to the ground.

42. An electric current I in a long straight wire generates a magnetic field $\mathbf{B}$ in the space surrounding the wire. The vector $\mathbf{B}$ is tangent to any circle C that is centered on the wire and lies in a plane perpendicular to the wire. *Ampere's law* implies that

$$\int_C \mathbf{B} \cdot d\mathbf{r} = \mu I$$

where μ is a certain electromagnetic constant. Deduce from this fact that the magnitude $B = |\mathbf{B}|$ of the magnetic field is proportional to the current I and inversely proportional to the distance r from the wire.

15.3 THE FUNDAMENTAL THEOREM AND INDEPENDENCE OF PATH

The fundamental theorem of calculus says, in effect, that differentiation and integration are inverse processes for single-variable functions. Specifically, part 2 of the fundamental theorem in Section 5.6 implies that

$$\int_a^b G'(t)\,dt = G(b) - G(a) \tag{1}$$

if the derivative G' is continuous on $[a, b]$. Theorem 1 here can be interpreted as saying that "gradient vector differentiation" and "line integration" are, similarly, inverse processes for multivariable functions.

THEOREM 1 The Fundamental Theorem for Line Integrals
Let f be a function of two or three variables and let C be a smooth curve parametrized by the vector-valued function $\mathbf{r}(t)$ for $a \leq t \leq b$. If f is continuously differentiable at each point of C, then

$$\int_C \nabla f \cdot d\mathbf{r} = f(\mathbf{r}(b)) - f(\mathbf{r}(a)). \tag{2}$$

PROOF We consider the three-dimensional case $f(x, y, z)$ illustrated in Fig. 15.3.1. Then $\nabla f = \langle \partial f/\partial x, \partial f/\partial y, \partial f/\partial z \rangle$, so Theorem 1 in Section 15.2 yields

$$\int_C \nabla f \cdot d\mathbf{r} = \int_C \frac{\partial f}{\partial x}\,dx + \frac{\partial f}{\partial y}\,dy + \frac{\partial f}{\partial z}\,dz$$

$$= \int_a^b \left(\frac{\partial f}{\partial x}\frac{dx}{dt} + \frac{\partial f}{\partial y}\frac{dy}{dt} + \frac{\partial f}{\partial z}\frac{dz}{dt} \right) dt.$$

By the multivariable chain rule (Section 13.7), the integrand here is the derivative $G'(t)$ of the composite function $G(t) = f(\mathbf{r}(t)) = f(x(t), y(t), z(t))$. Therefore it follows that

$$\int_C \nabla f \cdot d\mathbf{r} = \int_a^b G'(t)\,dt = G(b) - G(a) \quad \text{(by Eq. (1))}$$

$$= f(\mathbf{r}(b)) - f(\mathbf{r}(a)),$$

and so we have established Eq. (2), as desired. ◄

FIGURE 15.3.1 The path C of Theorem 1.

REMARK If we write A and B for the endpoints $\mathbf{r}(a)$ and $\mathbf{r}(b)$ of C, then Eq. (2) takes the form

$$\int_C \nabla f \cdot d\mathbf{r} = f(B) - f(A), \tag{3}$$

which is quite similar to Eq. (1).

EXAMPLE 1 If

$$f(x, y, z) = -\frac{k}{r} = -\frac{k}{\sqrt{x^2 + y^2 + z^2}},$$

then a brief computation shows that $\nabla f = \mathbf{F}$ is the inverse-square force field

$$\mathbf{F}(x, y, z) = \frac{k(x\mathbf{i} + y\mathbf{j} + z\mathbf{k})}{(x^2 + y^2 + z^2)^{3/2}}$$

of Example 7 in Section 15.2, where we calculated directly the work $W = k/20$ done by the force field $\mathbf{F}$ in moving a particle along a straight line segment from the point $A(0, 4, 0)$ to the point $B(0, 4, 3)$. Indeed, using Theorem 1 we find that the work done by **F** in moving a particle along *any* smooth path from A to B (that does not pass through the origin) is given by

$$W = \int_C \mathbf{F} \cdot d\mathbf{r} = \int_C \nabla f \cdot d\mathbf{r}$$
$$= f(0, 4, 3) - f(0, 4, 0) \quad \text{(by Eq. (3))}$$
$$= \left(-\frac{k}{5}\right) - \left(-\frac{k}{4}\right) = \frac{k}{20}.$$

◆

Independence of Path

We next apply the fundamental theorem for line integrals to discuss the question whether the integral

$$\int_C \mathbf{F} \cdot \mathbf{T} \, ds = \int_C \mathbf{F} \cdot d\mathbf{r} = \int_C P \, dx + Q \, dt + R \, dz \qquad (4)$$

(where $\mathbf{F} = \langle P, Q, R \rangle$) has the *same value* for *any* two curves with the same initial and terminal points.

DEFINITION Independence of Path
The line integral in Eq. (4) is said to be **independent of path in the region** D provided that, given any two points A and B of D, the integral has the same value along every piecewise smooth curve, or **path,** in D from A to B. In this case we may write

$$\int_C \mathbf{F} \cdot \mathbf{T} \, ds = \int_A^B \mathbf{F} \cdot \mathbf{T} \, ds \qquad (5)$$

because the value of the integral depends only on the points A and B, not on the particular choice of the path C joining them.

For a tangible interpretation of independence of path, let us think of walking along the curve C from point A to point B in the plane where a wind with velocity vector $\mathbf{w}(x, y)$ is blowing. Suppose that when we are at (x, y), the wind exerts a force $\mathbf{F} = k\mathbf{w}(x, y)$ on us, k being a constant that depends on our size and shape (and perhaps other factors as well). Then, by Eq. (12) of Section 15.2, the amount of work the wind does on us as we walk along C is given by

$$W = \int_C \mathbf{F} \cdot \mathbf{T} \, ds = k \int_C \mathbf{w} \cdot \mathbf{T} \, ds. \qquad (6)$$

This is the wind's contribution to our trip from A to B. In this context, the question of independence of path is whether or not the wind's work W depends on *which* path we choose from point A to point B.

EXAMPLE 2 Suppose that a steady wind blows toward the northeast with velocity vector $\mathbf{w} = 10\mathbf{i} + 10\mathbf{j}$ in fps units; its speed is $|\mathbf{w}| = 10\sqrt{2} \approx 14$ ft/s—about 10 mi/h. Assume that $k = 0.5$, so the wind exerts 0.5 lb of force for each foot per second of its velocity. Then $\mathbf{F} = 5\mathbf{i} + 5\mathbf{j}$, so Eq. (6) yields

$$W = \int_C \langle 5, 5 \rangle \cdot \mathbf{T} \, ds = \int_C 5 \, dx + 5 \, dy \qquad (7)$$

for the work done on us by the wind as we walk along C.

For instance, if C is the straight path $x = 10t$, $y = 10t$ ($0 \leqq x \leqq 1$) from $(0, 0)$ to $(10, 10)$, then Eq. (7) gives

$$W = \int_0^1 5 \cdot 10 \, dt + 5 \cdot 10 \, dt = 100 \int_0^1 1 \, dt = 100$$

ft·lb of work. Or, if C is the parabolic path $y = \frac{1}{10}x^2$, $0 \leq x \leq 10$ from the same initial point $(0, 0)$ to the same terminal point $(10, 10)$, then Eq. (7) yields

$$W = \int_0^{10} 5 \, dx + 5 \cdot \frac{1}{5} x \, dx = \int_0^{10} (5 + x) \, dx$$

$$= \left[5x + \frac{1}{2}x^2 \right]_0^{10} = 100$$

ft·lb of work, the same as before. We shall see that it follows from Theorem 2 of this section that the line integral in Eq. (7) is independent of path, so the wind does 100 ft·lb of work along *any* path from $(0, 0)$ to $(10, 10)$. ◆

EXAMPLE 3 Suppose that $\mathbf{w} = -2y\mathbf{i} + 2x\mathbf{j}$. This wind is blowing counterclockwise around the origin, as in a hurricane with its eye at $(0, 0)$. With $k = 0.5$ as before, $\mathbf{F} = -y\mathbf{i} + x\mathbf{j}$, so the work integral is

$$W = \int_C \mathbf{F} \cdot \mathbf{T} \, ds = \int_C -y \, dx + x \, dy. \tag{8}$$

If we walk from $(10, 0)$ to $(-10, 0)$ along the straight path C_1 through the eye of the hurricane, then the wind is always perpendicular to our unit tangent vector $\mathbf{T}$ (Fig. 15.3.2). Hence $\mathbf{F} \cdot \mathbf{T} = 0$, and therefore

$$W = \int_{C_1} \mathbf{F} \cdot \mathbf{T} \, ds = \int_{C_1} -y \, dx + x \, dy = 0.$$

But if we walk along the semicircular path C_2 shown in Fig. 15.3.2, then $\mathbf{w}$ remains tangent to our path, so $\mathbf{F} \cdot \mathbf{T} = |\mathbf{F}| = 10$ at each point. In this case,

$$W = \int_{C_2} -y \, dx + x \, dy = \int_{C_2} \mathbf{F} \cdot \mathbf{T} \, ds = 10 \cdot 10\pi = 100\pi.$$

The fact that we get different values along different paths from $(10, 0)$ to $(-10, 0)$ shows that the line integral in Eq. (8) is *not* independent of path. ◆

FIGURE 15.3.2 Around and through the eye of the hurricane (Example 2).

Theorem 2 tells us when a given line integral is independent of path and when it is not.

THEOREM 2 Independence of Path
The line integral $\int_C \mathbf{F} \cdot \mathbf{T} \, ds$ of the continuous vector field $\mathbf{F}$ is independent of path in the plane or space region D if and only if $\mathbf{F} = \nabla f$ for some function f defined on D.

PROOF Suppose that $\mathbf{F} = \nabla f = \langle \partial f/\partial x, \partial f/\partial y, \partial f/\partial z \rangle$ and that C is a piecewise smooth curve from A to B in D parametrized as usual with parameter t in $[a, b]$. Then the fundamental theorem in the form in Eq. (3) gives

$$\int_C \mathbf{F} \cdot \mathbf{T} \, ds = \int_C \nabla f \cdot \mathbf{T} \, ds = \int_C \nabla f \cdot d\mathbf{r} = f(B) - f(A).$$

This result shows that the value of the line integral depends only on the points A and B and is therefore independent of the choice of the particular path C. This proves the *if* part of Theorem 2.

To prove the *only if* part of Theorem 2, we suppose that the line integral is independent of path in D. Choose a *fixed* point $A_0 = A_0(x_0, y_0, z_0)$ in D, and let

$B = B(x, y, z)$ be an arbitrary point in D. Given any path C from A_0 to B in D, we *define* the function f by means of the equation

$$f(x, y, z) = \int_C \mathbf{F} \cdot \mathbf{T}\, ds = \int_{(x_0, y_0, z_0)}^{(x, y, z)} \mathbf{F} \cdot \mathbf{T}\, ds. \qquad (9)$$

Because of the hypothesis of independence of path, the resulting value of $f(x, y, z)$ depends only on (x, y, z) and not on the particular path C used.

To verify that $\nabla f = \mathbf{F}$, suppose that $\mathbf{F} = P\mathbf{i} + Q\mathbf{j} + R\mathbf{k}$. To show that $\partial f/\partial x = P$, we write

$$f(x+h, y, z) - f(x, y, z) = \int_{(x_0, y_0, z_0)}^{(x+h, y, z)} \mathbf{F} \cdot \mathbf{T}\, ds - \int_{(x_0, y_0, z_0)}^{(x, y, z)} \mathbf{F} \cdot \mathbf{T}\, ds$$

$$= \int_{(x, y, z)}^{(x+h, y, z)} \mathbf{F} \cdot \mathbf{T}\, ds.$$

In the last integral, we may take the path of integration to be the parametrized line segment L from (x, y, z) to $(x+h, y, z)$ defined by $\phi(t) = (x+th, y, z)$. Then $\phi'(t) = (h, 0, 0) = h\mathbf{i}$, so the unit tangent vector is $\mathbf{T} = \mathbf{i}$. Also, $dy = dz = 0$, so $ds = dx = h\, dt$ along this path. Therefore

$$f(x+h, y, z) - f(x, y, z) = \int_L \mathbf{F} \cdot \mathbf{T}\, ds = \int_0^1 P(\phi(t))h\, dt$$

$$= hP(\phi(\bar{t})) = hP(x + \bar{t}h, y, z)$$

for some $\bar{t}$ between 0 and 1 (by the average value theorem for single-variable integrals in Section 5.6). It follows that

$$\frac{\partial f}{\partial x} = \lim_{h \to 0} \frac{f(x+h, y, z) - f(x, y, z)}{h} = \lim_{h \to 0} P(x + \bar{t}h, y, z) = P(x, y, z)$$

by the continuity of P. It follows similarly that $\partial f/\partial y = Q$ and $\partial f/\partial z = R$, so $\nabla f = \mathbf{F}$ as desired. ◄

For a first application of Theorem 2, consider the force field $\mathbf{F} = -y\mathbf{i} + x\mathbf{j}$ that corresponds to the counterclockwise wind discussed in Example 3. Because the line integral $\int_C \mathbf{F} \cdot \mathbf{T}\, ds$ is *not* independent of path in any plane region that either includes or encloses the origin, it follows that $\mathbf{F}$ is not the gradient of any scalar function f.

By contrast, the force field $\mathbf{F} = 5\mathbf{i} + 5\mathbf{j}$, which corresponds to a constant wind blowing northeast, is obviously the gradient of the function $f(x, y) = 5x + 5y$. Therefore Theorem 2 implies that the line integral $\int_C \mathbf{F} \cdot \mathbf{T}\, ds$ *is* independent of path in the entire plane $\mathbf{R}^2$.

Similarly, the inverse-square force field $\mathbf{F}(x, y, z) = k\mathbf{r}/r^3$ of Example 1 is the gradient of the function $f(x, y, z) = -k/r$ (where $r = \sqrt{x^2 + y^2 + z^2}$). Hence Theorem 2 implies that the line integral $\int_C \mathbf{F} \cdot \mathbf{T}\, ds$ is independent of path in $\mathbf{R}^3$ minus the origin.

Conservative Vector Fields

DEFINITION Conservative Fields and Potential Functions
The vector field $\mathbf{F}$ defined on a region D is **conservative** provided that there exists a scalar function f defined on D such that

$$\mathbf{F} = \nabla f \qquad (10)$$

at each point of D. In this case f is called a **potential function** for the vector field $\mathbf{F}$.

For instance, Example 1 implies that $f(x, y, z) = -k/r$ is a potential function for the inverse-square force field $\mathbf{F}(x, y, z) = k\mathbf{r}/r^3$ (where $r = \sqrt{x^2 + y^2 + z^2}$).

COMMENT In some physical applications the scalar function f is called a *potential function* for the vector field $\mathbf{F}$ provided that $\mathbf{F} = -\nabla f$.

If the line integral $\int_C \mathbf{F} \cdot \mathbf{T}\, ds$ is known to be independent of path, then Theorem 2 guarantees that the vector field $\mathbf{F}$ is conservative and that Eq. (9) yields a potential function f for $\mathbf{F}$. In this case—because the value of the integral does not depend on the specific curve C from A to B—we may well write Eq. (3) in the form

$$\int_A^B \mathbf{F} \cdot \mathbf{T}\, ds = \int_A^B \nabla f \cdot d\mathbf{r} = f(B) - f(A) \tag{11}$$

that is still more reminiscent of the ordinary fundamental theorem.

EXAMPLE 4 Find a potential function for the conservative vector field

$$\mathbf{F}(x, y) = (6xy - y^3)\mathbf{i} + (4y + 3x^2 - 3xy^2)\mathbf{j}. \tag{12}$$

Solution Because we are given the information that $\mathbf{F}$ is a conservative field, the line integral $\int \mathbf{F} \cdot \mathbf{T}\, ds$ is independent of path by Theorem 2. Therefore we may apply Eq. (9) to find a scalar potential function f. Let C be the straight-line path from $A(0, 0)$ to $B(x_1, y_1)$ parametrized by $x = x_1 t$, $y = y_1 t$, $0 \leq t \leq 1$. Then Eq. (9) yields

$$f(x_1, y_1) = \int_A^B \mathbf{F} \cdot \mathbf{T}\, ds$$

$$= \int_A^B (6xy - y^3)\, dx + (4y + 3x^2 - 3xy^2)\, dy$$

$$= \int_0^1 \left(6x_1 y_1 t^2 - y_1^3 t^3\right)(x_1\, dt) + \left(4y_1 t + 3x_1^2 t^2 - 3x_1 y_1^2 t^3\right)(y_1\, dt)$$

$$= \int_0^1 \left(4y_1^2 t + 9x_1^2 y_1 t^2 - 4x_1 y_1^3 t^3\right) dt$$

$$= \left[2y_1^2 t^2 + 3x_1^2 y_1 t^3 - x_1 y_1^3 t^4\right]_0^1 = 2y_1^2 + 3x_1^2 y_1 - x_1 y_1^3.$$

At this point we delete the subscripts, because (x_1, y_1) is an arbitrary point of the plane. Thus we obtain the potential function

$$f(x, y) = 2y^2 + 3x^2 y - xy^3$$

for the vector field $\mathbf{F}$ in Eq. (12). As a check, we can differentiate f to obtain

$$\frac{\partial f}{\partial x} = 6xy - y^3, \qquad \frac{\partial f}{\partial y} = 4y + 3x^2 - 3xy^2. \qquad \blacklozenge$$

But how did we know in advance that the vector field $\mathbf{F}$ in Example 4 was conservative? The answer is provided by Theorem 3; a proof of this theorem based on Green's theorem is outlined in the next section.

THEOREM 3 Conservative Fields and Potential Functions

Suppose that the vector field $\mathbf{F} = P\mathbf{i} + Q\mathbf{j}$ is continuously differentiable in an open rectangle R in the xy-plane. Then $\mathbf{F}$ is conservative in R—and hence has a potential function $f(x, y)$ defined on R—if and only if, at each point of R,

$$\frac{\partial P}{\partial y} = \frac{\partial Q}{\partial x}. \tag{13}$$

Observe that the vector field **F** in Eq. (12), where $P(x, y) = 6xy - y^3$ and $Q(x, y) = 4y + 3x^2 - 3xy^2$, satisfies the criterion in Eq. (13) because

$$\frac{\partial P}{\partial y} = 6x - 3y^2 = \frac{\partial Q}{\partial x}.$$

When this sufficient condition for the existence of a potential function is satisfied, the method illustrated in Example 5 is usually an easier way to find a potential function than the evaluation of the line integral in Eq. (9)—the method used in Example 4.

EXAMPLE 5 Given

$$P(x, y) = 6xy - y^3 \quad \text{and} \quad Q(x, y) = 4y + 3x^2 - 3xy^2,$$

note that P and Q satisfy the condition $\partial P/\partial y = \partial Q/\partial x$. Find a potential function $f(x, y)$ such that

$$\frac{\partial f}{\partial x} = 6xy - y^3 \quad \text{and} \quad \frac{\partial f}{\partial y} = 4y + 3x^2 - 3xy^2. \tag{14}$$

Solution Upon integrating the first of these equations with respect to x, we get

$$f(x, y) = 3x^2 y - xy^3 + \xi(y), \tag{15}$$

where $\xi(y)$ is an "arbitrary function" of y alone; it acts as a "constant of integration" with respect to x, because its derivative with respect to x is zero. We next determine $\xi(y)$ by imposing the second condition in (14):

$$\frac{\partial f}{\partial y} = 3x^2 - 3xy^2 + \xi'(y) = 4y + 3x^2 - 3xy^2.$$

It follows that $\xi'(y) = 4y$, so $\xi(y) = 2y^2 + C$. When we set $C = 0$ and substitute the result into Eq. (15), we get the same potential function

$$f(x, y) = 3x^2 y - xy^3 + 2y^2$$

that we found by entirely different methods in Example 4. ◆

Conservative Force Fields and Conservation of Energy

Given a conservative force field **F**, it is customary in physics to introduce a minus sign and write $\mathbf{F} = -\nabla V$. Then $V(x, y, z)$ is called the **potential energy** at the point (x, y, z). With $f = -V$ in Eq. (11), we have

$$W = \int_A^B \mathbf{F} \cdot \mathbf{T}\, ds = V(A) - V(B), \tag{16}$$

and this means that the work W done by **F** in moving a particle from A to B is equal to the *decrease* in potential energy.

Here is the reason why the expression *conservative field* is used. Suppose that a particle of mass m moves from A to B under the influence of the conservative force **F**, with position vector $\mathbf{r}(t)$, $a \leq t \leq b$. Then Newton's law $\mathbf{F}(\mathbf{r}(t)) = m\mathbf{r}''(t) = m\mathbf{v}'(t)$ with $d\mathbf{r} = \mathbf{r}'(t)\, dt = \mathbf{v}(t)\, dt$ gives

$$\int_A^B \mathbf{F} \cdot \mathbf{T}\, ds = \int_a^b m\mathbf{v}'(t) \cdot \mathbf{v}(t)\, dt$$

$$= \int_a^b m D_t \left[\frac{1}{2}\mathbf{v}(t) \cdot \mathbf{v}(t)\right] dt = \left[\frac{1}{2}m[v(t)]^2\right]_a^b.$$

Thus with the abbreviations v_A for $v(a)$ and v_B for $v(b)$, we see that

$$\int_A^B \mathbf{F} \cdot d\mathbf{r} = \frac{1}{2}m(v_B)^2 - \frac{1}{2}m(v_A)^2. \tag{17}$$

By equating the right-hand sides of Eqs. (16) and (17), we get the formula

$$\tfrac{1}{2}m(v_A)^2 + V(A) = \tfrac{1}{2}m(v_B)^2 + V(B). \tag{18}$$

This is the law of **conservation of mechanical energy** for a particle moving under the influence of a *conservative* force field: Its **total energy**—the sum of its kinetic energy $\tfrac{1}{2}mv^2$ and its potential energy V—remains *constant*.

EXAMPLE 6 If we take $k = GMm$ in the calculation in Example 1, we see that the inverse-square gravitational force

$$\mathbf{F}(x, y, z) = -\frac{GMm\,\mathbf{r}}{r^3}$$

(exerted on a mass particle m by a mass M fixed at the origin) is the *negative* of the gradient of the potential energy function

$$V(x, y, z) = -\frac{GMm}{r}.$$

Hence Eq. (18) implies that the total energy of the mass particle moving with velocity v at distance r from the origin is the constant

$$E = \frac{1}{2}mv^2 - \frac{GMm}{r}.$$

It follows (for instance) that if—for whatever reason—the particle approaches the origin ($r \to 0$), then its velocity must increase without bound ($v \to +\infty$). ◆

15.3 TRUE/FALSE STUDY GUIDE

15.3 CONCEPTS: QUESTIONS AND DISCUSSION

1. Give several examples of line integrals that are *not* independent of the path.
2. Give several examples of a vector field $\mathbf{F}$ and a closed path C such that

$$\int_C \mathbf{F} \cdot \mathbf{T}\, ds \neq 0.$$

3. Give several examples of vector fields that are not conservative.

15.3 PROBLEMS

Determine whether the vector fields in Problems 1 through 16 are conservative. Find potential functions for those that are conservative (either by inspection or by using the method of Example 5).

1. $\mathbf{F}(x, y) = (2x + 3y)\mathbf{i} + (3x + 2y)\mathbf{j}$
2. $\mathbf{F}(x, y) = (4x - y)\mathbf{i} + (6y - x)\mathbf{j}$
3. $\mathbf{F}(x, y) = (3x^2 + 2y^2)\mathbf{i} + (4xy + 6y^2)\mathbf{j}$
4. $\mathbf{F}(x, y) = (2xy^2 + 3x^2)\mathbf{i} + (2x^2y + 4y^3)\mathbf{j}$
5. $\mathbf{F}(x, y) = (2y + \sin 2x)\mathbf{i} + (3x + \cos 3y)\mathbf{j}$
6. $\mathbf{F}(x, y) = (4x^2y - 5y^4)\mathbf{i} + (x^3 - 20xy^3)\mathbf{j}$
7. $\mathbf{F}(x, y) = \left(x^3 + \dfrac{y}{x}\right)\mathbf{i} + (y^2 + \ln x)\mathbf{j}$
8. $\mathbf{F}(x, y) = (1 + ye^{xy})\mathbf{i} + (2y + xe^{xy})\mathbf{j}$
9. $\mathbf{F}(x, y) = (\cos x + \ln y)\mathbf{i} + \left(\dfrac{x}{y} + e^y\right)\mathbf{j}$
10. $\mathbf{F}(x, y) = (x + \arctan y)\mathbf{i} + \dfrac{x + y}{1 + y^2}\mathbf{j}$
11. $\mathbf{F}(x, y) = (x \cos y + \sin y)\mathbf{i} + (y \cos x + \sin x)\mathbf{j}$
12. $\mathbf{F}(x, y) = e^{x-y}[(xy + y)\mathbf{i} + (xy + x)\mathbf{j}]$
13. $\mathbf{F}(x, y) = (3x^2y^3 + y^4)\mathbf{i} + (3x^3y^2 + y^4 + 4xy^3)\mathbf{j}$
14. $\mathbf{F}(x, y) = (e^x \sin y + \tan y)\mathbf{i} + (e^x \cos y + x \sec^2 y)\mathbf{j}$
15. $\mathbf{F}(x, y) = \left(\dfrac{2x}{y} - \dfrac{3y^2}{x^4}\right)\mathbf{i} + \left(\dfrac{2y}{x^3} - \dfrac{x^2}{y^2} + \dfrac{1}{\sqrt{y}}\right)\mathbf{j}$
16. $\mathbf{F}(x, y) = \dfrac{2x^{5/2} - 3y^{5/3}}{2x^{5/2}y^{2/3}}\mathbf{i} + \dfrac{3y^{5/3} - 2x^{5/2}}{3x^{3/2}y^{5/3}}\mathbf{j}$

In Problems 17 through 20, apply the method of Example 4 to find a potential function for the indicated vector field.

17. The vector field of Problem 3
18. The vector field of Problem 4
19. The vector field of Problem 13
20. The vector field of Problem 8

In Problems 21 through 26, show that the given line integral is independent of path in the entire xy-plane, then calculate the value of the line integral.

21. $\int_{(0,0)}^{(1,2)} (y^2 + 2xy)\,dx + (x^2 + 2xy)\,dy$

22. $\int_{(0,0)}^{(1,1)} (2x - 3y)\,dx + (2y - 3x)\,dy$

23. $\int_{(0,0)}^{(1,-1)} 2xe^y\,dx + x^2 e^y\,dy$

24. $\int_{(0,0)}^{(2,\pi)} \cos y\,dx - x \sin y\,dy$

25. $\int_{(\pi/2,\pi/2)}^{(\pi,\pi)} (\sin y + y\cos x)\,dx + (\sin x + x\cos y)\,dy$

26. $\int_{(0,0)}^{(1,-1)} (e^y + ye^x)\,dx + (e^x + xe^y)\,dy$

Find a potential function for each of the conservative vector fields in Problems 27 through 29.

27. $\mathbf{F}(x, y, z) = yz\mathbf{i} + xz\mathbf{j} + xy\mathbf{k}$

28. $\mathbf{F}(x, y, z) = (2x - y - z)\mathbf{i} + (2y - x)\mathbf{j} + (2z - x)\mathbf{k}$

29. $\mathbf{F}(x, y, z) = (y \cos z - yze^x)\mathbf{i} + (x \cos z - ze^x)\mathbf{j} - (xy \sin z + ye^x)\mathbf{k}$

30. Let $\mathbf{F}(x, y) = (-y\mathbf{i} + x\mathbf{j})/(x^2 + y^2)$ for x and y not both zero. Calculate the values of
$$\int_C \mathbf{F} \cdot \mathbf{T}\,ds$$
along both the upper and the lower halves of the circle $x^2 + y^2 = 1$ from $(1, 0)$ to $(-1, 0)$. Is there a function $f = f(x, y)$ defined for x and y not both zero such that $\nabla f = \mathbf{F}$? Why?

31. Show that if the force field $\mathbf{F} = P\mathbf{i} + Q\mathbf{j}$ is conservative, then $\partial P/\partial y = \partial Q/\partial x$. Show that the force field of Problem 30 satisfies the condition $\partial P/\partial y = \partial Q/\partial x$ but nevertheless is *not* conservative.

32. Suppose that the force field $\mathbf{F} = P\mathbf{i} + Q\mathbf{j} + R\mathbf{k}$ is conservative. Show that
$$\frac{\partial P}{\partial y} = \frac{\partial Q}{\partial x}, \quad \frac{\partial P}{\partial z} = \frac{\partial R}{\partial x}, \quad \text{and} \quad \frac{\partial Q}{\partial z} = \frac{\partial R}{\partial y}.$$

33. Apply Theorem 2 and the result of Problem 32 to show that
$$\int_C 2xy\,dx + x^2\,dy + y^2\,dz$$
is not independent of path.

34. Let $\mathbf{F}(x, y, z) = yz\mathbf{i} + (xz + y)\mathbf{j} + (xy + 1)\mathbf{k}$. Define the function f by
$$f(x, y, z) = \int_C \mathbf{F} \cdot \mathbf{T}\,ds,$$
where C is the straight line segment from $(0, 0, 0)$ to (x, y, z). Determine f by evaluating this line integral, then show that $\nabla f = \mathbf{F}$.

35. Let $f(x, y) = \tan^{-1}(y/x)$, which if $x > 0$ equals the polar angle θ for the point (x, y). (a) Show that
$$\mathbf{F} = \nabla f = \frac{-y\mathbf{i} + x\mathbf{j}}{x^2 + y^2}.$$
(b) Suppose that $A(x_1, y_1) = (r_1, \theta_1)$ and $B(x_2, y_2) = (r_2, \theta_2)$ are two points in the right half-plane $x > 0$ and that C is a smooth curve from A to B. Explain why it follows from the fundamental theorem for line integrals that $\int_C \mathbf{F} \cdot \mathbf{T}\,ds = \theta_2 - \theta_1$. (c) Suppose that C_1 is the upper half of the unit circle from $(1, 0)$ to $(-1, 0)$ and that C_2 is the lower half, oriented also from $(1, 0)$ to $(-1, 0)$. Show that
$$\int_{C_1} \mathbf{F} \cdot \mathbf{T}\,ds = \pi \quad \text{whereas} \quad \int_{C_2} \mathbf{F} \cdot \mathbf{T}\,ds = -\pi.$$
Why does this not contradict the fundamental theorem?

36. Let $\mathbf{F} = k\mathbf{r}/r^3$ be the inverse-square force field of Example 7 in Section 15.2. Show that the work done by $\mathbf{F}$ in moving a particle from a point at distance r_1 from the origin to a point at distance r_2 from the origin is given by
$$W = k\left(\frac{1}{r_1} - \frac{1}{r_2}\right).$$

37. Suppose that an earth satellite with mass $m = 10000$ kg travels in an elliptical orbit whose apogee (farthest point) and perigee (closest point) are, respectively, 11000 km and 9000 km from the center of the earth. Calculate the work done against the earth's gravitational force field $\mathbf{F} = -GMm\mathbf{r}/r^3$ in lifting the satellite from perigee to apogee. Use the values $M = 5.97 \times 10^{24}$ kg for the mass of the earth and $G = 6.67 \times 10^{-11}$ N·m²/kg² for the universal gravitational constant.

38. Calculate the work that must be done against the sun's gravitational force field in transporting the satellite of Problem 37 from the earth to Mars. Use the values $M = 1.99 \times 10^{30}$ kg for the mass of the sun, $r_E = 1.50 \times 10^8$ km for the distance from the sun to earth, and $r_M = 2.29 \times 10^8$ km for the distance from the sun to Mars.

15.4 GREEN'S THEOREM

Green's theorem relates a line integral around a simple closed plane curve C to an ordinary double integral over the plane region R with boundary C. [The curve C parametrized by $\mathbf{r}:[a, b] \to R^2$ is called **closed** if $\mathbf{r}(a) = \mathbf{r}(b)$ and **simple** if it has no other "self-intersections."] Suppose that the curve C is piecewise smooth—it consists of a finite number of parametric arcs with continuous nonzero velocity vectors. Then C has a unit tangent vector $\mathbf{T}$ everywhere except possibly at a finite number of *corner points*. The **positive,** or **counterclockwise,** direction along C is the

1038 CHAPTER 15 Vector Calculus

direction determined by a parametrization $\mathbf{r}(t)$ of C such that the region R remains on the *left* as the point $\mathbf{r}(t)$ traces the boundary curve C. That is, the vector obtained from the unit tangent vector $\mathbf{T}$ by a counterclockwise rotation through 90° always points *into* the region R (Fig. 15.4.1). The boundary curve C is said to be **positively oriented** if it is equipped with such a parametrization. The symbol

$$\oint_C P\,dx + Q\,dy$$

then denotes a line integral around C in the positive direction—that is, using a parametrization consistent with the positive orientation of the curve.

FIGURE 15.4.1 Positive orientation of the curve C: The region R within C is to the *left* of the unit tangent vector $\mathbf{T}$.

The following result first appeared (in an equivalent form) in a booklet on the applications of mathematics to electricity and magnetism, published privately in 1828 by the self-taught English mathematical physicist George Green (1793–1841).

GREEN'S THEOREM

Let C be a positively oriented piecewise-smooth simple closed curve that bounds the region R in the plane. Suppose that the functions $P(x, y)$ and $Q(x, y)$ have continuous first-order partial derivatives on R. Then

$$\oint_C P\,dx + Q\,dy = \iint_R \left(\frac{\partial Q}{\partial x} - \frac{\partial P}{\partial y}\right) dA. \tag{1}$$

PROOF First we give a proof for the case in which the region R is both horizontally simple and vertically simple. Then we indicate how to extend the result to more general regions.

Recall from Section 14.2 that if R is vertically simple, then it has a description of the form $g_1(x) \leqq y \leqq g_2(y)$, $a \leqq x \leqq b$. The boundary curve C is then the union of the four arcs C_1, C_2, C_3, and C_4 of Fig. 15.4.2, positively oriented as indicated there. Hence

$$\oint_C P\,dx = \int_{C_1} P\,dx + \int_{C_2} P\,dx + \int_{C_3} P\,dx + \int_{C_4} P\,dx.$$

The integrals along both C_2 and C_4 are zero, because on those two curves $x(t)$ is constant, so that $dx = x'(t)\,dt = 0$. Thus we need compute only the integrals along C_1 and C_3.

FIGURE 15.4.2 The boundary curve C is the union of the four arcs C_1, C_2, C_3, and C_4.

The point $(x, g_1(x))$ traces C_1 as x increases from a to b, whereas the point $(x, g_2(x))$ traces C_3 as x *decreases* from b to a. Hence

$$\oint_C P\,dx = \int_a^b P(x, g_1(x))\,dx + \int_b^a P(x, g_2(x))\,dx$$

$$= -\int_a^b [P(x, g_2(x)) - P(x, g_1(x))]\,dx = -\int_a^b \int_{g_1(x)}^{g_2(x)} \frac{\partial P}{\partial y}\,dy\,dx$$

by the fundamental theorem of calculus. Thus

$$\oint_C P\,dx = -\iint_R \frac{\partial P}{\partial y}\,dA. \tag{2}$$

In Problem 36 we ask you to show in a similar way that

$$\oint_C Q\,dy = +\iint_R \frac{\partial Q}{\partial x}\,dA \tag{3}$$

if the region R is horizontally simple. We then obtain Eq. (1), the conclusion of Green's theorem, by adding Eqs. (2) and (3). ◀

Green's Theorem SECTION 15.4   1039

The complete proof of Green's theorem for more general regions is beyond the scope of an elementary text. But the typical region R that appears in practice can be divided into smaller regions $R_1, R_2, \ldots, R_k$ that are both vertically and horizontally simple. Green's theorem for the region R then follows from the fact that it holds for each of the regions $R_1, R_2, \ldots, R_k$. (See Problem 37.)

For example, we can divide the horseshoe-shaped region R of Fig. 15.4.3 into the two regions R_1 and R_2, both of which are horizontally simple and vertically simple. We also subdivide the boundary C of R accordingly and write $C_1 \cup D_1$ for the boundary of R_1 and $C_2 \cup D_2$ for the boundary of R_2 (Fig. 15.4.3). Applying Green's theorem separately to the regions R_1 and R_2, we get

$$\oint_{C_1 \cup D_1} P\,dx + Q\,dy = \iint_{R_1} \left(\frac{\partial Q}{\partial x} - \frac{\partial P}{\partial y}\right) dA$$

and

$$\oint_{C_2 \cup D_2} P\,dx + Q\,dy = \iint_{R_2} \left(\frac{\partial Q}{\partial x} - \frac{\partial P}{\partial y}\right) dA.$$

FIGURE 15.4.3 Decomposing the region R into two horizontally and vertically simple regions by using a crosscut.

When we add these two equations, the result is Eq. (1), Green's theorem for the region R, because the two line integrals along D_1 and D_2 cancel. This occurs because D_1 and D_2 represent the same curve with opposite orientations, so

$$\int_{D_2} P\,dx + Q\,dy = -\int_{D_1} P\,dx + Q\,dy$$

by Eq. (11) of Section 15.2. It therefore follows that

$$\int_{C_1 \cup D_1 \cup C_2 \cup D_2} P\,dx + Q\,dy = \oint_{C_1 \cup C_2} P\,dx + Q\,dy = \oint_C P\,dx + Q\,dy.$$

Similarly, we could establish Green's theorem for the region shown in Fig. 15.4.4 by dividing it into the four simple regions indicated there.

FIGURE 15.4.4 Many important regions can be decomposed into simple regions by using one or more crosscuts.

EXAMPLE 1 Use Green's theorem to evaluate the line integral

$$\oint_C \left(2y + \sqrt{9 + x^3}\right) dx + \left(5x + e^{\arctan y}\right) dy,$$

where C is the positively oriented circle $x^2 + y^2 = 4$.

Solution With $P(x, y) = 2y + \sqrt{9 + x^3}$ and $Q(x, y) = 5x + e^{\arctan y}$, we see that

$$\frac{\partial Q}{\partial x} - \frac{\partial P}{\partial y} = 5 - 2 = 3.$$

Because C bounds R, a circular disk with area 4π, Green's theorem therefore implies that the given line integral is equal to

$$\iint_R 3\,dA = 3 \cdot 4\pi = 12\pi. \blacklozenge$$

REMARK Suppose that the force field $\mathbf{F}$ is defined by

$$\mathbf{F}(x, y) = \left(2y + \sqrt{9 + x^3}\right)\mathbf{i} + \left(5x + e^{\arctan y}\right)\mathbf{j} = P(x, y)\mathbf{i} + Q(x, y)\mathbf{j},$$

using the notation in Example 1. Then (as in Section 15.2) the work W done by the force field $\mathbf{F}$ in moving a particle counterclockwise once around the circle C of radius 2 is given by

$$W = \oint_C \mathbf{F} \cdot \mathbf{T}\,ds = \oint_C P\,dx + Q\,dy = \iint_R \left(\frac{\partial Q}{\partial x} - \frac{\partial P}{\partial y}\right) dA = \iint_R 3\,dA = 12\pi$$

as in Example 1.

EXAMPLE 2 Evaluate the line integral

$$\oint_C 3xy\,dx + 2x^2\,dy,$$

where C is the positively oriented boundary of the region R shown in Fig. 15.4.5. It is bounded above by the line $y = x$ and below by the parabola $y = x^2 - 2x$.

Solution To evaluate the line integral directly, we would need to parametrize separately the line and the parabola. Instead, we apply Green's theorem with $P(x, y) = 3xy$ and $Q(x, y) = 2x^2$, so

$$\frac{\partial Q}{\partial x} - \frac{\partial P}{\partial y} = 4x - 3x = x.$$

FIGURE 15.4.5 The region of Example 2.

Then

$$\oint_C 3xy\,dx + 2x^2\,dy = \iint_R x\,dA$$

$$= \int_0^3 \int_{x^2-2x}^x x\,dy\,dx = \int_0^3 \left[xy\right]_{y=x^2-2x}^x dx$$

$$= \int_0^3 (3x^2 - x^3)\,dx = \left[x^3 - \frac{1}{4}x^4\right]_0^3 = \frac{27}{4}. \quad\blacklozenge$$

In Examples 1 and 2 we found the double integral easier to evaluate directly than the line integral. Sometimes the situation is the reverse. The following consequence of Green's theorem illustrates the technique of evaluating a double integral $\iint_R f(x, y)\,dA$ by converting it into a line integral

$$\oint_C P\,dx + Q\,dy.$$

To do this we must be able to find functions $P(x, y)$ and $Q(x, y)$ such that

$$\frac{\partial Q}{\partial x} - \frac{\partial P}{\partial y} = f(x, y).$$

As in the proof of the following result, this is sometimes easy.

COROLLARY TO GREEN'S THEOREM
The area A of the region R bounded by the positively oriented piecewise-smooth simple closed curve C is given by

$$A = \frac{1}{2}\oint_C -y\,dx + x\,dy = -\oint_C y\,dx = \oint_C x\,dy. \quad (4)$$

PROOF With $P(x, y) = -y$ and $Q(x, y) \equiv 0$, Green's theorem gives

$$-\oint_C y\,dx = \iint_R 1\,dA = A.$$

Similarly, with $P(x, y) \equiv 0$ and $Q(x, y) = x$, we obtain

$$\oint_C x\,dy = \iint_R 1\,dA = A.$$

The third result may be obtained by averaging the left- and right-hand sides in the last two equations. Alternatively, with $P(x, y) = -y/2$ and $Q(x, y) = x/2$, Green's theorem gives

$$\frac{1}{2}\oint_C -y\,dx + x\,dy = \iint_R \left(\frac{1}{2} + \frac{1}{2}\right)dA = A.$$

EXAMPLE 3 Apply the corollary to Green's theorem to find the area A of the region R bounded by the ellipse $x^2/a^2 + y^2/b^2 = 1$.

Solution With the parametrization $x = a\cos t$, $y = b\sin t$, $0 \leq t \leq 2\pi$, Eq. (4) gives

$$A = \oint_R x\,dy = \int_0^{2\pi}(a\cos t)(b\cos t\,dt)$$

$$= \frac{1}{2}ab\int_0^{2\pi}(1+\cos 2t)\,dt = \pi ab.$$

FIGURE 15.4.6 An annular region—the boundary consists of two simple closed curves, one within the other.

By using the technique of subdividing a region into simpler ones, we can extend Green's theorem to regions with boundaries that consist of two or more simple closed curves. For example, consider the annular region R of Fig. 15.4.6, with boundary C consisting of the two simple closed curves C_1 and C_2. The positive direction along C—the direction for which the region R always lies on the left—is counterclockwise on the outer curve C_1 but clockwise on the inner curve C_2.

We divide R into two regions R_1 and R_2 by using two crosscuts, as shown in Fig. 15.4.7. Applying Green's theorem to each of these subregions, and noting cancellation of line integrals in opposite directions along the crosscuts, we get

$$\iint_R\left(\frac{\partial Q}{\partial x} - \frac{\partial P}{\partial y}\right)dA = \iint_{R_1}\left(\frac{\partial Q}{\partial x} - \frac{\partial P}{\partial y}\right)dA + \iint_{R_2}\left(\frac{\partial Q}{\partial x} - \frac{\partial P}{\partial y}\right)dA$$

$$= \oint_{C_1}(P\,dx + Q\,dy) + \oint_{C_2}(P\,dx + Q\,dy)$$

$$= \oint_C P\,dx + Q\,dy.$$

FIGURE 15.4.7 Two crosscuts convert the annular region into the union of two ordinary regions R_1 and R_2, each bounded by a single closed curve.

Thus we obtain Green's theorem for the given region R. What makes this proof work is that the opposite line integrals along the two crosscuts cancel each other. You may, of course, use any finite number of crosscuts.

EXAMPLE 4 Suppose that C is a positively oriented piecewise-smooth simple closed curve that encloses the origin $(0, 0)$. Show that

$$\oint_C \frac{-y\,dx + x\,dy}{x^2 + y^2} = 2\pi,$$

and also show that this integral is zero if C does *not* enclose the origin.

Solution With $P(x, y) = -y/(x^2 + y^2)$ and $Q(x, y) = x/(x^2 + y^2)$, a brief computation gives $\partial Q/\partial x - \partial P/\partial y \equiv 0$ when x and y are not both zero. If the region R bounded by C does not contain the origin, then P and Q and their derivatives are continuous on R. Hence Green's theorem implies that the integral in question is zero.

FIGURE 15.4.8 Use the small circle C_a if C encloses the origin (Example 4).

If C does enclose the origin, then we enclose the origin in a small circle C_a of radius a so small that C_a lies wholly within C (Fig. 15.4.8). We parametrize this circle by $x = a\cos t$, $y = a\sin t$, $0 \leq t \leq 2\pi$. Then Green's theorem, applied to the region R between C and C_a, gives

$$\oint_C \frac{-y\,dx + x\,dy}{x^2 + y^2} - \oint_{C_a} \frac{-y\,dx + x\,dy}{x^2 + y^2} = \iint_R 0\,dA = 0.$$

IMPORTANT The reason for the minus sign on the left-hand side is the fact that the positive orientation of C_a with respect to the region R is clockwise (as indicated in Fig. 15.4.8), whereas the selected parametrization determines a counterclockwise orientation of C_a. Therefore,

$$\oint_C \frac{-y\,dx + x\,dy}{x^2 + y^2} = \oint_{C_a} \frac{-y\,dx + x\,dy}{x^2 + y^2}$$

$$= \int_0^{2\pi} \frac{(-a\sin t)(-a\sin t\,dt) + (a\cos t)(a\cos t\,dt)}{(a\cos t)^2 + (a\sin t)^2}$$

$$= \int_0^{2\pi} 1\,dt = 2\pi. \qquad \blacklozenge$$

REMARK The result of Example 4 can be interpreted in terms of the polar-coordinate angle $\theta = \arctan(y/x)$. Because

$$d\theta = \frac{-y\,dx + x\,dy}{x^2 + y^2},$$

the line integral of Example 4 measures the net change in θ as we go around the curve C once in a counterclockwise direction. This net change is 2π if C encloses the origin and is zero otherwise.

PROOF OF THEOREM 3 IN SECTION 15.3 We now sketch a proof that if the vector field $\mathbf{F} = P\mathbf{i} + Q\mathbf{j}$ is continuously differentiable in an open rectangle R in the xy-plane, then $\mathbf{F}$ is conservative in R if and only if $\partial P/\partial y = \partial Q/\partial x$ at each point of R.

First suppose that $\mathbf{F}$ is conservative in R. Then there exists a function $f(x, y)$ defined on R such that

$$\nabla f = \frac{\partial f}{\partial x}\mathbf{i} + \frac{\partial f}{\partial y}\mathbf{j} = P\mathbf{i} + Q\mathbf{j} = \mathbf{F}$$

at each point of R. Then $P = \partial f/\partial x$ and $Q = \partial f/\partial y$, so it follows that

$$\frac{\partial P}{\partial y} = \frac{\partial}{\partial y}\left(\frac{\partial f}{\partial x}\right) = \frac{\partial^2 f}{\partial y\,\partial x} = \frac{\partial^2 f}{\partial x\,\partial y} = \frac{\partial}{\partial x}\left(\frac{\partial f}{\partial y}\right) = \frac{\partial Q}{\partial x},$$

as desired. The equality in the middle—where the order of partial differentiation is reversed—follows from the equality of mixed second-order partial derivatives of a function whose second-order partial derivatives are continuous.

Next, for the converse, suppose that $\partial P/\partial y = \partial Q/\partial x$ at each point of R. If we can show that line integrals of $\mathbf{F}$ are independent of the path in R, then it will follow from Theorem 2 in Section 15.3 that $\mathbf{F}$ is conservative in R, as desired. So let C_1 and C_2 be two smooth paths in R with the same initial point A and the same terminal point B, and let $C = C_1 \cup (-C_2)$ be the closed path that first follows C_1 from A to B and then follows the reversed path $-C_2$ from B back to A. If C is a *simple* closed path (one with no crossing points) and D is the region bounded by C, then Green's theorem gives

$$\oint_C \mathbf{F} \cdot \mathbf{T}\,ds = \oint_C P\,dx + Q\,dy = \iint_D \left(\frac{\partial Q}{\partial x} - \frac{\partial P}{\partial y}\right)dA = 0$$

because of the hypothesis that $\partial P/\partial y = \partial Q/\partial x$. But then

$$\oint_C \mathbf{F} \cdot \mathbf{T}\,ds = \int_{C_1} \mathbf{F} \cdot \mathbf{T}\,ds + \int_{-C_2} \mathbf{F} \cdot \mathbf{T}\,ds = \int_{C_1} \mathbf{F} \cdot \mathbf{T}\,ds - \int_{C_2} \mathbf{F} \cdot \mathbf{T}\,ds = 0.$$

Thus we may conclude that

$$\int_{C_1} \mathbf{F} \cdot \mathbf{T}\,ds = \int_{C_2} \mathbf{F} \cdot \mathbf{T}\,ds$$

for two such smooth paths C_1 and C_2 that together form a simple closed path. The more general case in which C has finitely many self-intersections can be treated by decomposing C into finitely many simple closed paths. Then the line integral around each of these simple closed paths is zero, so it follows by addition that

$$\oint_C \mathbf{F} \cdot \mathbf{T}\,ds = 0,$$

as needed to conclude that line integrals of **F** are independent of the path, and hence that **F** is conservative. A complete proof would require discussion of the possibility that C has infinitely many self-intersections. ◂

The Divergence and Flux of a Vector Field

Now let us consider the steady flow of a thin layer of fluid in the plane (perhaps like a sheet of water spreading across a floor). Let $\mathbf{v}(x, y)$ be its velocity vector field and $\delta(x, y)$ be the density of the fluid at the point (x, y). The term *steady flow* means that **v** and δ depend only on x and y and *not* on time t. We want to compute the rate at which the fluid flows out of the region R bounded by a positively oriented simple closed curve C (Fig. 15.4.9). We seek the net rate of outflow—the actual outflow minus the inflow.

Let Δs_i be a short segment of the curve C, and let (x_i^*, y_i^*) be an endpoint of Δs_i. Then the area of the portion of the fluid that flows out of R across Δs_i per unit time is approximately the area of the parallelogram in Fig. 15.4.9. This is the parallelogram spanned by the segment Δs_i and the vector $\mathbf{v}_i = \mathbf{v}(x_i^*, y_i^*)$. Suppose that $\mathbf{n}_i$ is the unit normal vector to C at the point (x_i^*, y_i^*), the normal that points *out* of R. Then the area of this parallelogram is

$$(|\mathbf{v}_i|\cos\theta)\,\Delta s_i = \mathbf{v}_i \cdot \mathbf{n}_i\,\Delta s_i,$$

where θ is the angle between $\mathbf{n}_i$ and $\mathbf{v}_i$.

We multiply this area by the density $\delta_i = \delta(x_i^*, y_i^*)$ and then add these terms over those values of i that correspond to a subdivision of the entire curve C. This gives the (net) total mass of fluid leaving R per unit of time; it is approximately

$$\sum_{i=1}^n \delta_i \mathbf{v}_i \cdot \mathbf{n}_i\,\Delta s_i = \sum_{i=1}^n \mathbf{F}_i \cdot \mathbf{n}_i\,\Delta s_i,$$

where $\mathbf{F} = \delta\mathbf{v}$. The line integral around C that this sum approximates is called the **flux of the vector field F across the curve** C. Thus the flux Φ of **F** across C is given by

$$\Phi = \oint_C \mathbf{F} \cdot \mathbf{n}\,ds, \tag{5}$$

where **n** is the *outer* unit normal vector to C (Fig. 15.4.10).

In the present case of fluid flow with velocity vector **v**, the flux Φ of $\mathbf{F} = \delta\mathbf{v}$ is the rate at which the fluid is flowing out of R across the boundary curve C, in units of mass per unit of time. But the same terminology is used for an arbitrary vector field $\mathbf{F} = M\mathbf{i} + N\mathbf{j}$. For example, we may speak of the flux of an electric or gravitational field across a curve C.

From Fig. 15.4.11 we see that the outer unit normal vector **n** is equal to $\mathbf{T} \times \mathbf{k}$. The unit tangent vector **T** to the curve C is

$$\mathbf{T} = \frac{1}{v}\left(\mathbf{i}\frac{dx}{dt} + \mathbf{j}\frac{dy}{dt}\right) = \mathbf{i}\frac{dx}{ds} + \mathbf{j}\frac{dy}{ds}$$

because $v = ds/dt$. Hence

$$\mathbf{n} = \mathbf{T} \times \mathbf{k} = \left(\mathbf{i}\frac{dx}{ds} + \mathbf{j}\frac{dy}{ds}\right) \times \mathbf{k}.$$

FIGURE 15.4.9 The area of the parallelogram approximates the fluid flow across Δs_i in unit time.

FIGURE 15.4.10 The flux Φ of the vector field **F** across the curve C is the net outflow minus the net inflow.

FIGURE 15.4.11 Computing the outer unit normal vector **n** from the unit tangent vector **T**.

1044 CHAPTER 15 Vector Calculus

But $\mathbf{i} \times \mathbf{k} = -\mathbf{j}$ and $\mathbf{j} \times \mathbf{k} = \mathbf{i}$. Thus we find that

$$\mathbf{n} = \mathbf{i}\frac{dy}{ds} - \mathbf{j}\frac{dx}{ds}. \tag{6}$$

Substituting the expression in Eq. (6) into the flux integral of Eq. (5) gives

$$\oint_C \mathbf{F} \cdot \mathbf{n}\, ds = \oint_C (M\mathbf{i} + N\mathbf{j}) \cdot \left(\mathbf{i}\frac{dy}{ds} - \mathbf{j}\frac{dx}{ds}\right) ds = \oint_C -N\, dx + M\, dy.$$

Applying Green's theorem to the last line integral with $P = -N$ and $Q = M$, we get

$$\oint_C \mathbf{F} \cdot \mathbf{n}\, ds = \iint_R \left(\frac{\partial M}{\partial x} + \frac{\partial N}{\partial y}\right) dA \tag{7}$$

for the flux of $\mathbf{F} = M\mathbf{i} + N\mathbf{j}$ across C.

The scalar function $\partial M/\partial x + \partial N/\partial y$ that appears in Eq. (7) is the **divergence** of the two-dimensional vector field $\mathbf{F} = M\mathbf{i} + N\mathbf{j}$ as defined in Section 15.1 and denoted by

$$\operatorname{div} \mathbf{F} = \nabla \cdot \mathbf{F} = \frac{\partial M}{\partial x} + \frac{\partial N}{\partial y}. \tag{8}$$

When we substitute Eq. (8) into Eq. (7), we obtain a **vector form of Green's theorem:**

$$\oint_C \mathbf{F} \cdot \mathbf{n}\, ds = \iint_R \nabla \cdot \mathbf{F}\, dA, \tag{9}$$

FIGURE 15.4.12 The circular disk R of radius r centered at (x_0, y_0).

with the understanding that $\mathbf{n}$ is the *outer* unit normal to C. Thus the flux of a vector field across a positively oriented simple closed curve C is equal to the double integral of its divergence over the region R bounded by C.

If the disk R with area $a(R)$ is bounded by a positively oriented circle C with radius r and center (x_0, y_0) (Fig. 15.4.12), then the average value property of double integrals (see Problem 50 in Section 14.2) gives

$$\oint_{C_r} \mathbf{F} \cdot \mathbf{n}\, ds = \iint_R \nabla \cdot \mathbf{F}\, dA = [\nabla \cdot \mathbf{F}(\bar{x}, \bar{y})] \cdot a(R)$$

for some point $(\bar{x}, \bar{y})$ in R. We assume that $\mathbf{F}$ is continuously differentiable, so it follows that

$$\nabla \cdot \mathbf{F}(\bar{x}, \bar{y}) \to \nabla \cdot \mathbf{F}(x_0, y_0) \quad \text{as} \quad (\bar{x}, \bar{y}) \to (x_0, y_0).$$

If we first divide both sides by $a(R) = \pi r^2$ and then take the limit as $r \to 0$, we see that

$$\nabla \cdot \mathbf{F}(x_0, y_0) = \lim_{r \to 0} \frac{1}{\pi r^2} \oint_{C_r} \mathbf{F} \cdot \mathbf{n}\, ds \tag{10}$$

because $(\bar{x}, \bar{y}) \to (x_0, y_0)$ as $r \to 0$.

In the case of our original fluid flow, with $\mathbf{F} = \delta\mathbf{v}$, Eq. (10) implies that the value of $\nabla \cdot \mathbf{F}$ at (x_0, y_0) is a measure of the rate at which the fluid is "diverging away" from the point (x_0, y_0).

EXAMPLE 5 The vector field $\mathbf{F} = -y\mathbf{i} + x\mathbf{j}$ is the velocity field of a steady-state counterclockwise rotation around the origin. Show that the flux of $\mathbf{F}$ across any simple closed curve C is zero (Fig. 15.4.13).

Solution This follows immediately from Eq. (9) because

$$\nabla \cdot \mathbf{F} = \frac{\partial}{\partial x}(-y) + \frac{\partial}{\partial y}(x) = 0. \qquad \blacklozenge$$

FIGURE 15.4.13 The flux $\oint \mathbf{F} \cdot \mathbf{n}\, ds$ of the vector field $\mathbf{F} = -y\mathbf{i} + x\mathbf{j}$ across the curve C is zero.

15.4 TRUE/FALSE STUDY GUIDE

15.4 CONCEPTS: QUESTIONS AND DISCUSSION

1. Sketch several different examples of bounded plane regions with multiple boundary curves. In each case indicate how to introduce crosscuts to divide the given region R into a union of simpler regions $R_1, R_2, \ldots, R_k$, each of which is bounded by a single simple closed curve, so that

$$\iint_R f(x,y)\,dA = \sum_{i=1}^{k}\left(\iint_{R_i} f(x,y)\,dA\right).$$

2. Sketch several examples of smooth closed paths in the plane that have self-intersections. In each case indicate how to decompose the given self-intersecting path C into simple closed paths $C_1, C_2, \ldots, C_k$ so that

$$\int_C \mathbf{F}\cdot\mathbf{T}\,ds = \sum_{i=1}^{k}\left(\int_{C_i} \mathbf{F}\cdot\mathbf{T}\,ds\right).$$

15.4 PROBLEMS

In Problems 1 through 12, apply Green's theorem to evaluate the integral

$$\oint_C P\,dx + Q\,dy$$

around the specified positively oriented closed curve C.

1. $P(x,y) = x + y^2$, $Q(x,y) = y + x^2$; C is the square with vertices $(\pm 1, \pm 1)$.

2. $P(x,y) = x^2 + y^2$, $Q(x,y) = -2xy$; C is the boundary of the triangle bounded by the lines $x = 0$, $y = 0$, and $x + y = 1$.

3. $P(x,y) = y + e^x$, $Q(x,y) = 2x^2 + \cos y$; C is the boundary of the triangle with vertices $(0, 0)$, $(1, 1)$, and $(2, 0)$.

4. $P(x,y) = x^2 - y^2$, $Q(x,y) = xy$; C is the boundary of the region bounded by the line $y = x$ and the parabola $y = x^2$.

5. $P(x,y) = -y^2 + \exp(e^x)$, $Q(x,y) = \arctan y$; C is the boundary of the region between the parabolas $y = x^2$ and $x = y^2$.

6. $P(x,y) = y^2$, $Q(x,y) = 2x - 3y$; C is the circle $x^2 + y^2 = 9$.

7. $P(x,y) = x - y$, $Q(x,y) = y$; C is the boundary of the region between the x-axis and the graph of $y = \sin x$ for $0 \le x \le \pi$.

8. $P(x,y) = e^x \sin y$, $Q(x,y) = e^x \cos y$; C is the right-hand loop of the graph of the polar equation $r^2 = 4\cos\theta$.

9. $P(x,y) = y^2$, $Q(x,y) = xy$; C is the ellipse with equation $x^2/9 + y^2/4 = 1$.

10. $P(x,y) = y/(1+x^2)$, $Q(x,y) = \arctan x$; C is the oval with equation $x^4 + y^4 = 1$.

11. $P(x,y) = xy$, $Q(x,y) = x^2$; C is the first-quadrant loop of the graph of the polar equation $r = \sin 2\theta$.

12. $P(x,y) = x^2$, $Q(x,y) = -y^2$; C is the cardioid with polar equation $r = 1 + \cos\theta$.

In Problems 13 through 16, use the corollary to Green's theorem to find the area of the indicated region.

13. The circle bounded by $x = a\cos t$, $y = a\sin t$, $0 \le t \le 2\pi$

14. The region between the x-axis and one arch of the cycloid with parametric equations $x = a(t - \sin t)$, $y = a(1 - \cos t)$

15. The region bounded by the astroid with parametric equations $x = \cos^3 t$, $y = \sin^3 t$, $0 \le t \le 2\pi$

16. The region between the graphs of $y = x^2$ and $y = x^3$

In Problems 17 through 20, use Green's theorem to calculate the work

$$W = \oint_C \mathbf{F}\cdot\mathbf{T}\,ds$$

done by the given force field $\mathbf{F}$ in moving a particle counterclockwise once around the indicated curve C.

17. $\mathbf{F} = -2y\mathbf{i} + 3x\mathbf{j}$ and C is the ellipse $x^2/9 + y^2/4 = 1$.

18. $\mathbf{F} = (y^2 - x^2)\mathbf{i} + 2xy\mathbf{j}$ and C is the circle $x^2 + y^2 = 9$.

19. $\mathbf{F} = 5x^2y^3\mathbf{i} + 7x^3y^2\mathbf{j}$ and C is the triangle with vertices $(0, 0)$, $(3, 0)$, and $(0, 6)$.

20. $\mathbf{F} = xy^2\mathbf{i} + 3x^2y\mathbf{j}$ and C is the boundary of the semicircular disk bounded by the x-axis and the circular arc $y = \sqrt{4 - x^2} \ge 0$.

In Problems 21 through 24, use Green's theorem in the vector form in Eq. (9) to calculate the outward flux

$$\Phi = \oint_C \mathbf{F}\cdot\mathbf{n}\,ds$$

of the given vector field across the indicated positively oriented closed curve C.

21. $\mathbf{F} = 2x\mathbf{i} + 3y\mathbf{j}$ and C is the ellipse of Problem 17.

22. $\mathbf{F} = x^3\mathbf{i} + y^3\mathbf{j}$ and C is the circle of Problem 18.

23. $\mathbf{F} = (3x + \sqrt{1+y^2})\mathbf{i} + (2y - \sqrt[3]{1+x^4})\mathbf{j}$ and C is the triangle of Problem 19.

24. $\mathbf{F} = (3xy^2 + 4x)\mathbf{i} + (3x^2y - 4y)\mathbf{j}$ and C is the closed curve of Problem 20.

25. Suppose that f is a twice differentiable scalar function of x and y. Show that
$$\nabla^2 f = \operatorname{div}(\nabla f) = \frac{\partial^2 f}{\partial x^2} + \frac{\partial^2 f}{\partial y^2}.$$

26. Show that $f(x, y) = \ln(x^2 + y^2)$ satisfies **Laplace's equation** $\nabla^2 f = 0$ except at the point $(0, 0)$.

27. Suppose that f and g are twice-differentiable functions. Show that
$$\nabla^2(fg) = f\nabla^2 g + g\nabla^2 f + 2\nabla f \cdot \nabla g.$$

28. Suppose that the function $f(x, y)$ is twice continuously differentiable in the region R bounded by the positively oriented piecewise-smooth curve C. Prove that
$$\oint_C \frac{\partial f}{\partial x} dy - \frac{\partial f}{\partial y} dx = \iint_R \nabla^2 f \, dx \, dy.$$

29. Let R be the plane region with area A enclosed by the positively oriented piecewise-smooth simple closed curve C. Use Green's theorem to show that the coordinates of the centroid of R are
$$\overline{x} = \frac{1}{2A}\oint_C x^2 \, dy, \qquad \overline{y} = -\frac{1}{2A}\oint_C y^2 \, dx.$$

30. Use the result of Problem 29 to find the centroid of (a) a semicircular region of radius a; (b) a quarter-circular region of radius a.

31. Suppose that a lamina shaped like the region of Problem 29 has constant density δ. Show that its moments of inertia around the coordinate axes are
$$I_x = -\frac{\delta}{3}\oint_C y^3 \, dx, \qquad I_y = \frac{\delta}{3}\oint_C x^3 \, dy.$$

32. Use the result of Problem 31 to show that the polar moment of inertia $I_0 = I_x + I_y$ of a circular lamina of radius a, centered at the origin and of constant density δ, is $\frac{1}{2}Ma^2$, where M is the mass of the lamina.

33. The loop of the folium of Descartes (with equation $x^3 + y^3 = 3xy$) appears in Fig. 15.4.14. Apply the corollary to Green's theorem (Eq. (4)) to find the area of this loop. [*Suggestion:* Set $y = tx$ to discover a parametrization of the loop. To obtain the area of the loop, use values of t that lie in the interval $[0, 1]$. This gives the half of the loop that lies below the line $y = x$.]

34. Find the area bounded by one loop of the curve $x = \sin 2t$, $y = \sin t$.

35. Let f and g be functions with continuous second-order partial derivatives in the region R bounded by the positively oriented piecewise-smooth simple closed curve C. Apply Green's theorem in vector form to show that
$$\oint_C f \nabla g \cdot \mathbf{n} \, ds = \iint_R [f(\nabla \cdot \nabla g) + (\nabla f) \cdot (\nabla g)] \, dA.$$
It was this formula rather than Green's theorem itself that appeared in Green's book of 1828.

36. Complete the proof of the simple case of Green's theorem by showing directly that
$$\oint_C Q \, dy = \iint_R \frac{\partial Q}{\partial x} \, dA$$
if the region R is horizontally simple.

37. Suppose that the bounded plane region R is divided into the nonoverlapping subregions $R_1, R_2, \ldots, R_k$. If Green's theorem, Eq. (1), holds for each of these subregions, explain why it follows that Green's theorem holds for R. State carefully any assumptions that you need to make.

38. (a) If C is the line segment from (x_1, y_1) to (x_2, y_2), show by direct evaluation of the line integral that
$$\int_C x \, dy - y \, dx = x_1 y_2 - x_2 y_1.$$
(b) Let $(0, 0)$, (x_1, y_1), and (x_2, y_2) be the vertices of a triangle taken in counterclockwise order. Deduce from part (a) and Green's theorem that the area of this triangle is $A = \frac{1}{2}(x_1 y_2 - x_2 y_1)$.

39. Use the result of Problem 38 to find the area of (a) the equilateral triangle with vertices $(1, 0)$, $(\cos \frac{2}{3}\pi, \sin \frac{2}{3}\pi)$, and $(\cos \frac{4}{3}\pi, \sin \frac{4}{3}\pi)$; (b) the regular pentagon with vertices $(1, 0)$, $(\cos \frac{2}{5}\pi, \sin \frac{2}{5}\pi)$, $(\cos \frac{4}{5}\pi, \sin \frac{4}{5}\pi)$, $(\cos \frac{6}{5}\pi, \sin \frac{6}{5}\pi)$, and $(\cos \frac{8}{5}\pi, \sin \frac{8}{5}\pi)$.

40. Let T be a one-to-one transformation from the region S (with boundary curve J) in the uv-plane to the region R (with boundary curve C) in the xy-plane. Then the change-of-variables formula in Section 14.9 implies that the area A of the region R is given by
$$\iint_R dx \, dy = \iint_S \left|\frac{\partial(x, y)}{\partial(u, v)}\right| du \, dv. \qquad (11)$$

Establish this formula by carrying out the following steps. (a) Use Eq. (4) to convert the left-hand side in Eq. (11) to a line integral around C. (b) Use the coordinate functions $x(u, v)$ and $y(u, v)$ of the transformation T to convert the line integral in part (a) to a line integral around J. (c) Apply Green's theorem to the line integral in part (b).

FIGURE 15.4.14 The loop of Problem 33.

41. Figure 15.4.15 shows the first-quadrant loop of the generalized folium of Descartes defined implicitly by the equation

$$x^{2n+1} + y^{2n+1} = (2n+1)x^n y^n \quad (12)$$

FIGURE 15.4.15 The first-quadrant loop of the generalized folium.

(where n is a positive integer). Your task here is to calculate the area A_n of the region bounded by this loop. Begin by substituting $y = tx$ to discover the parametrization

$$x = \frac{(2n+1)t^n}{t^{2n+1}+1}, \quad y = \frac{(2n+1)t^{n+1}}{t^{2n+1}+1} \quad (0 \leq t < \infty) \quad (13)$$

of the loop. A computer algebra system may be useful in showing that with this parametrization the area formula in Eq. (4) of this section yields

$$A_n = (2n+1)^2 \int_0^\infty \left[\frac{(2n+1)t^{2n}}{(t^{2n+1}+1)^3} - \frac{nt^{2n}}{(t^{2n+1}+1)^2} \right] dt. \quad (14)$$

You can now calculate A_n for $n = 1, 2, 3, \ldots$; you should find that $A_n = n + \frac{1}{2}$. (Do you need a computer algebra system for this?) But the improper integral in Eq. (14) should give you pause. Check your result by calculating (and then doubling) the area of the lower half of the loop indicated in Fig. 15.4.15—this involves only the integral from $t = 0$ to $t = 1$. (Why?)

15.5 SURFACE INTEGRALS

A *surface integral* is to surfaces in space what a line (or "curve") integral is to curves in the plane. Consider a curved, thin metal sheet shaped like the surface S. Suppose that this sheet has variable density, given at the point (x, y, z) by the known continuous function $f(x, y, z)$ in units such as grams per square centimeter of surface. We want to define the surface integral

$$\iint_S f(x, y, z)\, dS$$

in such a way that—upon evaluation—it gives the total mass of the thin metal sheet. In case $f(x, y, z) \equiv 1$, the numerical value of the integral should also equal the surface area of S.

As in Section 14.8, we assume that S is a smooth parametric surface described by the function or transformation

$$\mathbf{r}(u, v) = \langle x(u, v), y(u, v), z(u, v) \rangle = x\mathbf{i} + y\mathbf{j} + z\mathbf{k}$$

for (u, v) in a region D in the uv-plane. We suppose throughout that the component functions of $\mathbf{r}$ have continuous partial derivatives and also that the vectors $\mathbf{r}_u = \partial \mathbf{r}/\partial u$ and $\mathbf{r}_v = \partial \mathbf{r}/\partial v$ are nonzero and nonparallel at each interior point of D.

Recall how we computed the surface area A of S in Section 14.8. We began with an inner partition of D consisting of n rectangles $R_1, R_2, \ldots, R_n$, each Δu by Δv in size. The images under $\mathbf{r}$ of the rectangles are curvilinear figures filling most or all of the surface S, and these pieces of S are themselves approximated by parallelograms P_i of the sort shown in Fig. 15.5.1. This gave us the approximation

$$A \approx \sum_{i=1}^n \Delta S_i = \sum_{i=1}^n |\mathbf{N}(u_i, v_i)| \,\Delta u\, \Delta v, \quad (1)$$

FIGURE 15.5.1 Approximating surface area with parallelograms.

where the vector

$$\mathbf{N} = \frac{\partial \mathbf{r}}{\partial u} \times \frac{\partial \mathbf{r}}{\partial v} = \begin{vmatrix} \mathbf{i} & \mathbf{j} & \mathbf{k} \\ \dfrac{\partial x}{\partial u} & \dfrac{\partial y}{\partial u} & \dfrac{\partial z}{\partial u} \\ \dfrac{\partial x}{\partial v} & \dfrac{\partial y}{\partial v} & \dfrac{\partial z}{\partial v} \end{vmatrix} \quad (2)$$

is normal to S at the point $\mathbf{r}(u, v)$ and $\Delta S_i = |\mathbf{N}(u_i, v_i)| \Delta u \Delta v$ is the area of the parallelogram P_i that is tangent to the surface S at the point $\mathbf{r}(u_i, v_i)$.

If the surface S also has a density function $f(x, y, z)$, then we can approximate the total mass m of the surface by first multiplying each parallelogram area ΔS_i in Eq. (1) by the density $f(\mathbf{r}(u_i, v_i))$ at $\mathbf{r}(u_i, v_i)$ and then summing these estimates over all such parallelograms. Thus we obtain the approximation

$$m \approx \sum_{i=1}^{n} f(\mathbf{r}(u_i, v_i)) \, \Delta S_i = \sum_{i=1}^{n} f(\mathbf{r}(u_i, v_i)) \, |\mathbf{N}(u_i, v_i)| \, \Delta u \, \Delta v. \qquad (3)$$

This approximation is a Riemann sum for the **surface integral of the function f over the surface S**, denoted by

$$\iint_S f(x, y, z) \, dS = \iint_D f(\mathbf{r}(u, v)) \, |\mathbf{N}(u, v)| \, du \, dv$$

$$= \iint_D f(\mathbf{r}(u, v)) \left| \frac{\partial \mathbf{r}}{\partial u} \times \frac{\partial \mathbf{r}}{\partial v} \right| du \, dv. \qquad (4)$$

To evaluate the surface integral $\iint_S f(x, y, z) \, dS$, we simply use the parametrization $\mathbf{r}$ to express the variables x, y, and z in terms of u and v and formally replace the **surface area element** dS with

$$dS = |\mathbf{N}(u, v)| \, du \, dv = \left| \frac{\partial \mathbf{r}}{\partial u} \times \frac{\partial \mathbf{r}}{\partial v} \right| du \, dv. \qquad (5)$$

Expanding the cross product determinant in Eq. (2) gives

$$\mathbf{N} = \frac{\partial \mathbf{r}}{\partial u} \times \frac{\partial \mathbf{r}}{\partial v} = \frac{\partial(y, z)}{\partial(u, v)} \mathbf{i} + \frac{\partial(z, x)}{\partial(u, v)} \mathbf{j} + \frac{\partial(x, y)}{\partial(u, v)} \mathbf{k} \qquad (6)$$

in the Jacobian notation of Section 14.9, so the surface integral in Eq. (4) takes the form

$$\iint_S f(x, y, z) \, dS$$

$$= \iint_D f(x(u, v), y(u, v), z(u, v)) \sqrt{\left[\frac{\partial(y, z)}{\partial(u, v)}\right]^2 + \left[\frac{\partial(z, x)}{\partial(u, v)}\right]^2 + \left[\frac{\partial(x, y)}{\partial(u, v)}\right]^2} \, du \, dv.$$

$$(7)$$

This formula converts the surface integral into an *ordinary double integral* over the region D in the uv-plane, and is analogous to the formula (Eq. (4) of Section 15.2)

$$\int_C f(x, y, z) \, ds = \int_a^b f(x(t), y(t), z(t)) \sqrt{\left(\frac{dx}{dt}\right)^2 + \left(\frac{dy}{dt}\right)^2 + \left(\frac{dz}{dt}\right)^2} \, dt$$

that converts a line integral into an ordinary single integral.

In the important special case of a surface S described as a graph $z = h(x, y)$ of a function h defined on a region D in the xy-plane, we may use x and y (rather than u and v) as the parameters. The surface area element then takes the form

$$dS = \sqrt{1 + \left(\frac{\partial h}{\partial x}\right)^2 + \left(\frac{\partial h}{\partial y}\right)^2} \, dx \, dy \qquad (8)$$

(as in Eq. (9) of Section 14.8). The surface integral of f over S is then given by

$$\iint_S f(x, y, z)\, dS = \iint_D f(x, y, h(x, y)) \sqrt{1 + \left(\frac{\partial h}{\partial x}\right)^2 + \left(\frac{\partial h}{\partial y}\right)^2}\, dx\, dy. \quad (9)$$

Centroids and moments of inertia for surfaces are computed in much the same way as for curves (see Section 15.2), using surface integrals in place of line integrals. For example, suppose that the surface S has density $\delta(x, y, z)$ at the point (x, y, z) and total mass m. Then the z-component $\bar{z}$ of its centroid and its moment of inertia I_z around the z-axis are given by

$$\bar{z} = \frac{1}{m} \iint_S z\, \delta(x, y, z)\, dS \quad \text{and} \quad I_z = \iint_S (x^2 + y^2)\, \delta(x, y, z)\, dS.$$

EXAMPLE 1 Find the centroid of the unit-density hemispherical surface

$$z = \sqrt{a^2 - x^2 - y^2}, \quad x^2 + y^2 \leq a^2.$$

Solution By symmetry, $\bar{x} = 0 = \bar{y}$. A simple computation gives $\partial z/\partial x = -x/z$ and $\partial z/\partial y = -y/z$, so Eq. (8) takes the form

$$dS = \sqrt{1 + \left(\frac{\partial z}{\partial x}\right)^2 + \left(\frac{\partial z}{\partial y}\right)^2}\, dx\, dy = \sqrt{1 + \left(\frac{x}{z}\right)^2 + \left(\frac{y}{z}\right)^2}\, dx\, dy$$

$$= \frac{1}{z}\sqrt{x^2 + y^2 + z^2}\, dx\, dy = \frac{a}{z}\, dx\, dy.$$

Hence

$$\bar{z} = \frac{1}{2\pi a^2} \iint_D z \cdot \frac{a}{z}\, dx\, dy = \frac{1}{2\pi a} \iint_D 1\, dx\, dy = \frac{a}{2}.$$

Note in the final step that D is a circular disk of radius a in the xy-plane. This simplifies the computation of the last integral. ◆

EXAMPLE 2 Find the moment of inertia around the z-axis of the spherical surface $x^2 + y^2 + z^2 = a^2$, assuming that it has constant density $\delta = k$.

Solution The spherical surface of radius a is most easily parametrized in spherical coordinates:

$$x = a \sin\phi \cos\theta, \quad y = a \sin\phi \sin\theta, \quad z = a \cos\phi$$

for $0 \leq \phi \leq \pi$ and $0 \leq \theta \leq 2\pi$. Hence the sphere S is defined parametrically by

$$\mathbf{r}(\phi, \theta) = \mathbf{i}\, a \sin\phi \cos\theta + \mathbf{j}\, a \sin\phi \sin\theta + \mathbf{k}\, a \cos\phi.$$

As in Problem 18 of Section 14.8, the surface area element is then

$$dS = \left|\frac{\partial \mathbf{r}}{\partial \phi} \times \frac{\partial \mathbf{r}}{\partial \theta}\right| = a^2 \sin\phi\, d\phi\, d\theta.$$

Because

$$x^2 + y^2 = a^2 \sin^2\phi \cos^2\phi + a^2 \sin^2\phi \sin^2\phi = a^2 \sin^2\phi,$$

it follows that

$$I_z = \iint_S (x^2 + y^2)\, \delta\, dS = \int_0^{2\pi} \int_0^{\pi} k(a^2 \sin^2\phi)\, a^2 \sin\phi\, d\phi\, d\theta$$

$$= 2\pi \cdot ka^4 \cdot 2 \int_0^{\pi/2} \sin^3\phi\, d\phi = 4\pi k a^4 \cdot \frac{2}{3} \quad \text{(by integral formula 113)}$$

$$= \frac{2}{3} \cdot 4\pi k a^2 \cdot a^2 = \frac{2}{3} m a^2,$$

using in the final step the fact that the mass of the spherical surface with density k is $m = 4\pi k a^2$. Is this result both plausible and dimensionally correct? ◆

Surface Integrals With Respect to Coordinate Elements

The surface integral $\iint_S f(x, y, z)\, dS$ is an integral **respect to surface area,** and thus is analogous to the line integral $\int_C f(x, y)\, ds$ with respect to arc length. A second type of surface integral of the form

$$\iint_S P\, dy\, dz + Q\, dz\, dx + R\, dx\, dy$$

is analogous to the line integral $\int_C P\, dx + Q\, dy$ with respect to coordinate variables.

The definition of the integral $\iint_S R\, dx\, dy$, for instance—with $R(x, y, z)$ a scalar function (instead of f) and $dx\, dy$ an area element in the xy-plane (instead of the area element dS on the surface S)—is motivated by replacing the area element $\Delta S_i = |\mathbf{N}(u_i, v_i)|\, \Delta u\, \Delta v$ in the Riemann sum in Eq. (3) with the area $\Delta S_i \cos \gamma$ of its projection into the xy-plane (Fig. 15.5.2). The result is the Riemann sum

$$\sum_{i=1}^n R(\mathbf{r}(u_i, v_i)) \cos \gamma\, |\mathbf{N}(u_i, v_i)|\, \Delta u\, \Delta v \approx \iint_D R(\mathbf{r}(u, v)) \cos \gamma\, |\mathbf{N}(u, v)|\, du\, dv. \quad (10)$$

FIGURE 15.5.2 Finding the area of the projected parallelogram.

To calculate the factor $\cos \gamma$ in Eq. (10), we consider the unit normal vector

$$\mathbf{n} = \frac{\mathbf{N}}{|\mathbf{N}|} = \mathbf{i} \cos \alpha + \mathbf{j} \cos \beta + \mathbf{k} \cos \gamma \quad (11)$$

with direction cosines $\cos \alpha$, $\cos \beta$, and $\cos \gamma$. Using Eq. (6) we find that

$$\cos \alpha = \mathbf{n} \cdot \mathbf{i} = \frac{\mathbf{N} \cdot \mathbf{i}}{|\mathbf{N}|} = \frac{1}{|\mathbf{N}|} \frac{\partial(y, z)}{\partial(u, v)} \quad \text{and, similarly,}$$

$$\cos \beta = \frac{1}{|\mathbf{N}|} \frac{\partial(z, x)}{\partial(u, v)}, \qquad \cos \gamma = \frac{1}{|\mathbf{N}|} \frac{\partial(x, y)}{\partial(u, v)}. \quad (12)$$

Substitution for $\cos \gamma$ in (10) now yields the *definition*

$$\iint_S R(x, y, z)\, dx\, dy = \iint_S R(x, y, z) \cos \gamma\, dS$$

$$= \iint_D R(\mathbf{r}(u, v)) \frac{\partial(x, y)}{\partial(u, v)}\, du\, dv. \quad (13)$$

Similarly, we *define*

$$\iint_S P(x, y, z)\, dy\, dz = \iint_S P(x, y, z) \cos \alpha\, dS$$

$$= \iint_D P(\mathbf{r}(u, v)) \frac{\partial(y, z)}{\partial(u, v)}\, du\, dv \quad (14)$$

and

$$\iint_S Q(x, y, z)\, dz\, dx = \iint_S Q(x, y, z) \cos \beta\, dS$$

$$= \iint_D Q(\mathbf{r}(u, v)) \frac{\partial(z, x)}{\partial(u, v)}\, du\, dv. \quad (15)$$

Note The symbols z and x appear in the reverse of alphabetical order in Eq. (15). It is important to write them in the correct order because

$$\frac{\partial(x, z)}{\partial(u, v)} = \begin{vmatrix} x_u & x_v \\ z_u & z_v \end{vmatrix} = -\begin{vmatrix} z_u & z_v \\ x_u & x_v \end{vmatrix} = -\frac{\partial(z, x)}{\partial(u, v)}.$$

This implies that

$$\iint_S f(x, y, z)\, dx\, dz = -\iint_S f(x, y, z)\, dz\, dx.$$

In an ordinary *double integral*, the order in which the differentials are written simply indicates the order of integration. But in a *surface integral*, it instead indicates the order of appearance of the corresponding variables in the Jacobians in Eqs. (13) through (15).

The three integrals in Eqs. (13) through (15) typically occur together, and the general **surface integral with respect to coordinate area elements** is the sum

$$\iint_S P\, dy\, dz + Q\, dz\, dx + R\, dx\, dy = \iint_S (P\cos\alpha + Q\cos\beta + R\cos\gamma)\, dS; \quad (16)$$

that is,

$$\iint_S P\, dy\, dz + Q\, dz\, dx + R\, dx\, dy = \iint_D \left(P\frac{\partial(y,z)}{\partial(u,v)} + Q\frac{\partial(z,x)}{\partial(u,v)} + R\frac{\partial(x,y)}{\partial(u,v)} \right) du\, dv. \quad (17)$$

Equation (17) gives the evaluation procedure for the surface integral in Eq. (16): Substitute for x, y, z, and their derivatives in terms of u and v, then integrate over the appropriate region D in the uv-plane.

The relation between surface integrals with respect to surface area and with respect to coordinate areas is somewhat analogous to the formula

$$\int_C \mathbf{F}\cdot\mathbf{T}\, ds = \int_C P\, dx + Q\, dy + R\, dz$$

relating line integrals with respect to arc length and with respect to coordinates. Given the vector field $\mathbf{F} = P\mathbf{i} + Q\mathbf{j} + R\mathbf{k}$, Eq. (11) implies that

$$\mathbf{F}\cdot\mathbf{n} = P\cos\alpha + Q\cos\beta + R\cos\gamma, \quad (18)$$

so the equations in (12) yield

$$\iint_S \mathbf{F}\cdot\mathbf{n}\, dS = \iint_S P\, dy\, dz + Q\, dz\, dx + R\, dx\, dy. \quad (19)$$

Only the *sign* of the right-hand surface integral in Eq. (19) depends on the parametrization of S. The unit normal vector on the left-hand side is the vector provided by the parametrization of S via the equations in (12). In the case of a surface given by $z = h(x, y)$, with x and y used as the parameters u and v, this will be the *upper* normal, as you will see in Example 3.

EXAMPLE 3 Suppose that S is the surface $z = h(x, y)$, (x, y) in D. Then show that

$$\iint_S P\, dy\, dz + Q\, dz\, dx + R\, dx\, dy = \iint_D \left(-P\frac{\partial z}{\partial x} - Q\frac{\partial z}{\partial y} + R \right) dx\, dy, \quad (20)$$

where P, Q, and R in the second integral are evaluated at $(x, y, h(x, y))$.

Solution This is simply a matter of computing the three Jacobians in Eq. (17) with the parameters x and y. We note first that $\partial x/\partial x = 1 = \partial y/\partial y$ and that $\partial x/\partial y = 0 = \partial y/\partial x$. Hence

$$\frac{\partial(y, z)}{\partial(x, y)} = \begin{vmatrix} y_x & y_y \\ z_x & z_y \end{vmatrix} = -\frac{\partial z}{\partial x}, \quad \frac{\partial(z, x)}{\partial(x, y)} = \begin{vmatrix} z_x & z_y \\ x_x & x_y \end{vmatrix} = -\frac{\partial z}{\partial y},$$

and

$$\frac{\partial(x, y)}{\partial(x, y)} = \begin{vmatrix} x_x & x_y \\ y_x & y_y \end{vmatrix} = 1.$$

Equation (20) is an immediate consequence. ◆

The Flux of a Vector Field

One of the most important applications of surface integrals involves the computation of the flux of a vector field. To define the flux of the vector field **F** across the surface S, we assume that S has a *unit* normal vector field **n** that varies *continuously* from point to point of S. This condition excludes from our consideration one-sided (*nonorientable*) surfaces, such as the Möbius strip of Fig. 15.5.3. If S is a two-sided (*orientable*) surface, then there are two possible choices for **n**. For example, if S is a closed surface (such as a torus or sphere) that separates space, then we may choose for **n** either the outer normal vector (at each point of S) or the inner normal vector (Fig. 15.5.4). The unit normal vector defined in Eq. (11) may be either the outer normal or the inner normal; which of the two it is depends on how S has been parametrized.

FIGURE 15.5.3 The Möbius strip is an example of a one-sided surface.

FIGURE 15.5.4 Inner and outer normal vectors to a two-sided closed surface.

To define the concept of flux, suppose that we are given the vector field **F**, the orientable surface S, and a continuous unit normal vector field **n** on S. Then, in analogy with Eq. (5) in Section 15.4, we define the **flux Φ across S in the direction of n** by

$$\Phi = \iint_S \mathbf{F} \cdot \mathbf{n} \, dS. \tag{21}$$

For example, if $\mathbf{F} = \delta\mathbf{v}$, where **v** is the velocity vector field corresponding to the steady flow in space of a fluid of density δ and **n** is the *outer* unit normal vector for a closed surface S that bounds the space region T, then the flux determined by Eq. (21) is the net rate of flow of the fluid *out of* T across its boundary surface S in units such as grams per second.

EXAMPLE 4 Calculate the flux $\iint_S \mathbf{F} \cdot \mathbf{n} \, dS$, where $\mathbf{F} = v_0 \mathbf{k}$ and S is the hemispherical surface of radius a with equation $z = \sqrt{a^2 - x^2 - y^2}$ and with outer unit normal vector **n**. (See Fig. 15.5.5.)

FIGURE 15.5.5 The hemisphere S of Example 4.

Solution If we think of $\mathbf{F} = v_0 \mathbf{k}$ as the velocity vector field of a fluid that is flowing upward with constant speed v_0, then we can interpret the flux in question as the rate of flow (in cubic centimeters per second, for example) of the fluid across S. To calculate this flux, we note that

$$\mathbf{n} = \frac{x\mathbf{i} + y\mathbf{j} + z\mathbf{k}}{\sqrt{x^2 + y^2 + z^2}} = \frac{1}{a}(x\mathbf{i} + y\mathbf{j} + z\mathbf{k}).$$

Hence

$$\mathbf{F} \cdot \mathbf{n} = v_0 \mathbf{k} \cdot \frac{1}{a}(x\mathbf{i} + y\mathbf{j} + z\mathbf{k}) = \frac{v_0}{a} z,$$

so

$$\iint_S \mathbf{F} \cdot \mathbf{n} \, dS = \iint_S \frac{v_0}{a} z \, dS.$$

If we introduce spherical coordinates $z = a \cos\phi$, $dS = a^2 \sin\phi \, d\phi \, d\theta$ on the hemispherical surface, we get

$$\iint_S \mathbf{F} \cdot \mathbf{n} \, dS = \frac{v_0}{a} \int_0^{2\pi} \int_0^{\pi/2} (a\cos\phi)(a^2 \sin\phi) \, d\phi \, d\theta$$

$$= 2\pi a^2 v_0 \int_0^{\pi/2} \cos\phi \sin\phi \, d\phi = 2\pi a^2 v_0 \left[\frac{1}{2} \sin^2 \phi \right]_0^{\pi/2};$$

thus

$$\iint_S \mathbf{F} \cdot \mathbf{n} \, dS = \pi a^2 v_0.$$

This last quantity is equal to the flux of $\mathbf{F} = v_0 \mathbf{k}$ across the disk $x^2 + y^2 \leq a^2$ of area πa^2. If we think of the hemispherical region T bounded by the hemisphere S and the circular disk D that forms its base, it should be no surprise that the rate of inflow of an incompressible fluid across the disk D is equal to its rate of outflow across the hemisphere S. ◆

EXAMPLE 5 Find the flux of the vector field $\mathbf{F} = x\mathbf{i} + y\mathbf{j} + 3\mathbf{k}$ out of the region T bounded by the paraboloid $z = x^2 + y^2$ and the plane $z = 4$ (Fig. 15.5.6).

Solution Let S_1 denote the circular top, which has outer unit normal vector $\mathbf{n}_1 = \mathbf{k}$. Let S_2 be the parabolic part of this surface, with outer unit normal vector $\mathbf{n}_2$. The flux across S_1 is

$$\iint_{S_1} \mathbf{F} \cdot \mathbf{n}_1 \, dS = \iint_{S_1} 3 \, dS = 12\pi$$

because S_1 is a circular disk of radius 2.

Next, the computation in Example 3 gives

$$\mathbf{N} = \left\langle -\frac{\partial z}{\partial x}, -\frac{\partial z}{\partial y}, 1 \right\rangle = \langle -2x, -2y, 1 \rangle$$

FIGURE 15.5.6 The surface of Example 5.

for a vector normal to the paraboloid $z = x^2 + y^2$. Then $\mathbf{n} = \mathbf{N}/|\mathbf{N}|$ is an upper—and thus an *inner*—unit normal vector to the surface S_2. The unit *outer* normal vector is, therefore, $\mathbf{n}_2 = -\mathbf{n} = -\mathbf{N}/|\mathbf{N}|$, opposite to the direction of $\mathbf{N} = \langle -2x, -2y, 1 \rangle$. With parameters (x, y) in the circular disk $x^2 + y^2 \leq 4$ in the xy-plane, the surface-area element is $dS = |\mathbf{N}| \, dx \, dy$. Therefore, the outward flux across S_2 is

$$\iint_{S_2} \mathbf{F} \cdot \mathbf{n}_2 \, dS = -\iint_{S_2} \mathbf{F} \cdot \mathbf{n} \, dS = -\iint_D \mathbf{F} \cdot \frac{\mathbf{N}}{|\mathbf{N}|} |\mathbf{N}| \, dx \, dy$$

$$= -\iint_D \mathbf{F} \cdot \mathbf{N} \, dx \, dy = -\iint_D \langle x, y, 3 \rangle \cdot \langle -2x, -2y, 1 \rangle \, dx \, dy$$

$$= -\iint_D (3 - 2x^2 - 2y^2) \, dx \, dy.$$

We change to polar coordinates in the disk D of radius 2—so that $3 - 2x^2 - 2y^2 = 3 - 2r^2$ and $dx\,dy = r\,dr\,d\theta$—and find that

$$\iint_{S_2} \mathbf{F} \cdot \mathbf{n}_2\, dS = \int_0^{2\pi} \int_0^2 (2r^2 - 3)\, r\, dr\, d\theta = 2\pi \left[\frac{1}{2} r^4 - \frac{3}{2} r^2 \right]_0^2 = 4\pi.$$

Hence the total flux of $\mathbf{F}$ out of T is $16\pi \approx 50.27$. ◆

Another physical application of flux is to the flow of heat, which is mathematically quite similar to the flow of a fluid. Suppose that a body has temperature $u = u(x, y, z)$ at the point (x, y, z). Experiments indicate that the flow of heat in the body is described by the *heat-flow vector*

$$\mathbf{q} = -K\, \nabla u. \tag{22}$$

The number K—normally, but not always, a constant—is the *heat conductivity* of the body. The vector $\mathbf{q}$ points in the direction of heat flow, and its length is the rate of flow of heat across a unit area normal to $\mathbf{q}$. This flow rate is measured in units such as calories per second per square centimeter. If S is a closed surface within the body bounding the solid region T and $\mathbf{n}$ denotes the outer unit normal vector for S, then

$$\iint_S \mathbf{q} \cdot \mathbf{n}\, dS = -\iint_S K\, \nabla u \cdot \mathbf{n}\, dS \tag{23}$$

is the net rate of heat flow (in calories per second, for example) out of the region T across its boundary surface S.

EXAMPLE 6 Suppose that a uniform solid ball B of radius R is centered at the origin (Fig. 15.5.7) and that the temperature u within it is given by

$$u(x, y, z) = c(R^2 - x^2 - y^2 - z^2).$$

Thus the temperature of B is maximal at its center and is zero on its boundary. Find the rate of flow of heat across a sphere S of radius $a < R$ centered at the origin.

Solution Writing $\mathbf{r} = x\mathbf{i} + y\mathbf{j} + z\mathbf{k}$ for the position vector of a point (x, y, z) of B, we find that the heat flow vector $\mathbf{q}$ in Eq. (22) is

$$\mathbf{q} = -K\, \nabla u = -K \cdot c(-2x\mathbf{i} - 2y\mathbf{j} - 2z\mathbf{k}) = 2Kc\mathbf{r}.$$

Obviously the outer unit normal vector $\mathbf{n}$ at a point (x, y, z) of the sphere S is $\mathbf{n} = \mathbf{r}/a$, so

$$\mathbf{q} \cdot \mathbf{n} = 2Kc\mathbf{r} \cdot \frac{\mathbf{r}}{a} = 2Kca$$

FIGURE 15.5.7 The solid ball B of Example 6.

because $\mathbf{r} \cdot \mathbf{r} = a^2$ at points of S. Therefore the heat flow across the sphere S (with area $A(S) = 4\pi a^2$) is

$$\iint_S \mathbf{q} \cdot \mathbf{n}\, dS = \iint_S 2Kca\, dS = 2Kca \cdot 4\pi a^2 = 8Kc\pi a^3.$$ ◆

Still other applications of flux involve force fields rather than flow fields. For example, suppose that $\mathbf{F}$ is the gravitational field of a collection of fixed masses in space, so $\mathbf{F}(\mathbf{r})$ is the net force exerted on a unit mass located at $\mathbf{r}$. Then **Gauss's law** for inverse-square gravitational fields says that the (outward) flux of $\mathbf{F}$ across the closed surface S is

$$\Phi = \iint_S \mathbf{F} \cdot \mathbf{n}\, dS = -4\pi GM \tag{24}$$

where M is the total mass enclosed by S and G is the universal gravitational constant.

Gauss's law also applies to inverse-square electric fields. The electric field at $\mathbf{r}$ of a charge q located at the origin is $\mathbf{E} = q\mathbf{r}/(4\pi\epsilon_0|\mathbf{r}|^3)$, where $\epsilon_0 \approx 8.85 \times 10^{-12}$ in mks units (charge in coulombs). Then **Gauss's law** for electric fields says that the (outward) flux of $\mathbf{E}$ across the closed surface S is

$$\Phi = \iint_S \mathbf{E} \cdot \mathbf{n}\, dS = \frac{Q}{\epsilon_0} \quad (25)$$

where Q is the net (positive minus negative) charge enclosed by S.

15.5 TRUE/FALSE STUDY GUIDE

15.5 CONCEPTS: QUESTIONS AND DISCUSSION

1. Explain why an integral of the form $\iint_S f\, dS$ is defined even if S is a surface such as the Möbius strip in Fig. 15.5.3—which has no continuous unit normal vector field defined on the entire surface. Can the Möbius strip be subdivided into parametrized surfaces that *do* have continuous unit normal vector fields?

2. Explain why the value of a surface integral with respect to surface area does not depend on the orientation—that is, the direction of the normal vector $\mathbf{N} = \mathbf{r}_u \times \mathbf{r}_v$ provided by the surface parametrization—whereas the value of a surface integral with respect to coordinate area elements *does* depend on the orientation of the surface.

15.5 PROBLEMS

In Problems 1 through 6, evaluate the surface integral $\iint_S f(x, y, z)\, dS$.

1. $f(x, y, z) = x + y$; S is the first-octant part of the plane $x + y + z = 1$.

2. $f(x, y, z) = xyz$; S is the triangle with vertices $(3, 0, 0)$, $(0, 2, 0)$, and $(0, 0, 6)$.

3. $f(x, y, z) = y + z + 3$; S is the part of the plane $z = 2x + 3y$ that lies inside the cylinder $x^2 + y^2 = 9$.

4. $f(x, y, z) = z^2$; S is the part of the cone $z = \sqrt{x^2 + y^2}$ that lies inside the cylinder $x^2 + y^2 = 4$.

5. $f(x, y, z) = xy + 1$; S is the part of the paraboloid $z = x^2 + y^2$ that lies inside the cylinder $x^2 + y^2 = 4$.

6. $f(x, y, z) = (x^2 + y^2)z$; S is the hemisphere $z = \sqrt{1 - x^2 - y^2}$.

In Problems 7 through 12, find the moment of inertia $\iint_S (x^2 + y^2)\, dS$ *of the given surface S with respect to the z-axis. Assume that S has constant density $\delta \equiv 1$.*

7. S is the part of the plane $z = x + y$ that lies inside the cylinder $x^2 + y^2 = 9$.

8. S is the part of the surface $z = xy$ that lies inside the cylinder $x^2 + y^2 = 25$.

9. S is the part of the cylinder $x^2 + z^2 = 1$ that lies between the planes $y = -1$ and $y = 1$. As parameters on the cylinder use y and the polar angular coordinate in the xz-plane.

10. S is the part of the cone $z = \sqrt{x^2 + y^2}$ that lies between the planes $z = 2$ and $z = 5$.

11. S is the part of the sphere $x^2 + y^2 + z^2 = 25$ that lies above the plane $z = 3$.

12. S is the part of the sphere $x^2 + y^2 + z^2 = 25$ that lies outside the cylinder $x^2 + y^2 = 9$.

In Problems 13 through 18, evaluate the surface integral $\iint_S \mathbf{F} \cdot \mathbf{n}\, dS$, *where $\mathbf{n}$ is the upward-pointing unit normal vector to the given surface S.*

13. $\mathbf{F} = x\mathbf{i} + y\mathbf{j}$; S is the hemisphere $z = \sqrt{9 - x^2 - y^2}$.

14. $\mathbf{F} = x\mathbf{i} + y\mathbf{j} + z\mathbf{k}$; S is the first-octant part of the plane $2x + 2y + z = 3$.

15. $\mathbf{F} = 2y\mathbf{j} + 3z\mathbf{k}$; S is the part of the plane $z = 3x + 2$ that lies within the cylinder $x^2 + y^2 = 4$.

16. $\mathbf{F} = z\mathbf{k}$; S is the upper half of the spherical surface $\rho = 2$. [*Suggestion:* Use spherical coordinates.]

17. $\mathbf{F} = y\mathbf{i} - x\mathbf{j}$; S is the part of the cone $z = r$ that lies within the cylinder $r = 3$.

18. $\mathbf{F} = 2x\mathbf{i} + 2y\mathbf{j} + 3\mathbf{k}$; S is the part of the paraboloid $z = 4 - x^2 - y^2$ that lies above the xy-plane.

In Problems 19 through 24, calculate the outward flux of the vector field $\mathbf{F}$ across the given closed surface S.

19. $\mathbf{F} = x\mathbf{i} + 2y\mathbf{j} + 3z\mathbf{k}$; S is the boundary of the first-octant unit cube with opposite vertices $(0, 0, 0)$ and $(1, 1, 1)$.

20. $\mathbf{F} = 2x\mathbf{i} - 3y\mathbf{j} + z\mathbf{k}$; S is the boundary of the solid hemisphere $0 \leq z \leq \sqrt{4 - x^2 - y^2}$.

21. $\mathbf{F} = x\mathbf{i} - y\mathbf{j}$; S is the boundary of the solid first-octant pyramid bounded by the coordinate planes and the plane $3x + 4y + z = 12$.

22. $\mathbf{F} = 2x\mathbf{i} + 2y\mathbf{j} + 3\mathbf{k}$; S is the boundary of the solid paraboloid bounded by the xy-plane and $z = 4 - x^2 - y^2$.

23. $\mathbf{F} = z^2\mathbf{k}$; S is the boundary of the solid bounded by the paraboloids $z = x^2 + y^2$ and $z = 18 - x^2 - y^2$.

24. $\mathbf{F} = x^2\mathbf{i} + 2y^2\mathbf{j} + 3z^2\mathbf{k}$; S is the boundary of the solid bounded by the cone $z = \sqrt{x^2 + y^2}$ and the plane $z = 3$.

25. The first-octant part of the spherical surface $\rho = a$ has unit density. Find its centroid.

26. The conical surface $z = r$, $r \leq a$, has constant density $\delta = k$. Find its centroid and its moment of inertia around the z-axis.

27. The paraboloid $z = r^2$, $r \leq a$, has constant density δ. Find its centroid and moment of inertia around the z-axis.

28. Find the centroid of the part of the spherical surface $\rho = a$ that lies within the cone $r = z$.

29. Find the centroid of the part of the spherical surface $x^2 + y^2 + z^2 = 4$ that lies both inside the cylinder $x^2 + y^2 = 2x$ and above the xy-plane.

30. Suppose that the toroidal surface of Example 5 of Section 14.8 has uniform density and total mass M. Show that its moment of inertia around the z-axis is $\frac{1}{2}M(3a^2 + 2b^2)$.

In Problems 31 and 32, use a table of integrals or a computer algebra system (if necessary) to find the moment of inertia around the z-axis of the given surface S. Assume that S has constant density $\delta \equiv 1$.

31. S is the part of the parabolic cylinder $z = 4 - y^2$ that lies inside the rectangular cylinder $-1 \leq x \leq 1$, $-2 \leq y \leq 2$.

32. S is the part of the paraboloid $z = 4 - x^2 - y^2$ that lies inside the square cylinder $-1 \leq x \leq 1$, $-1 \leq y \leq 1$.

33. Let S denote the surface $z = h(x, y)$ for (x, y) in the region D in the xy-plane, and let γ be the angle between $\mathbf{k}$ and the upper normal vector $\mathbf{N}$ to S. Prove that

$$\iint_S f(x, y, z)\, dS = \iint_S f(x, y, h(x, y)) \sec \gamma \, dx\, dy.$$

34. Find a formula for

$$\iint_S P\, dy\, dz + Q\, dz\, dx + R\, dx\, dy$$

analogous to Eq. (20), but for the case of a surface S described explicitly by $x = h(y, z)$.

35. A uniform solid ball has radius 5 and its temperature u is proportional to the square of the distance from its center, with $u = 100$ at the boundary of the ball. If the heat conductivity of the ball is $K = 2$, find the rate of flow of heat across a concentric sphere of radius 3.

36. A uniform solid cylinder has radius 5 and height 10, and its temperature u is proportional to the square of the distance from its vertical axis, with $u = 100$ at the outer curved boundary of the cylinder. If the heat conductivity of the cylinder is $K = 2$, find the rate of flow of heat across a concentric cylinder of radius 3 and height 10.

In Problems 37 through 39, set up integrals giving the area and moment of inertia around the z-axis of the given surface S (assuming that S has constant density $\delta \equiv 1$). Use a computer algebra system—as illustrated in the project material for this section—to evaluate these integrals, symbolically if possible, numerically if necessary (with the numerical values $a = 4$, $b = 3$, and $c = 2$ of the given parameters).

37. S is the elliptic paraboloid $z = (x/a)^2 + (y/b)^2$ with parametrization $x = au \cos v$, $y = bu \sin v$, $z = u^2$, $0 \leq u \leq c$, $0 \leq v \leq 2\pi$.

38. S is the ellipsoid $(x/a)^2 + (y/b)^2 + (z/c)^2 = 1$ with parametrization $x = a \sin u \cos v$, $y = b \sin u \sin v$, $z = c \cos u$, $0 \leq u \leq \pi$, $0 \leq v \leq 2\pi$.

39. S is the hyperboloid $(x/a)^2 + (y/b)^2 - z^2 = 1$ with parametrization $x = a \cosh u \cos v$, $y = b \cosh u \sin v$, $z = \sinh u$, $-c \leq u \leq c$, $0 \leq v \leq 2\pi$. See Fig. 15.5.8, where the u-curves are hyperbolas and the v-curves are ellipses.

FIGURE 15.5.8 The hyperboloid of Problem 39.

40. The Möbius strip in Fig. 15.5.9 was generated by plotting the points

$$x = \left(4 + t\cos\tfrac{1}{2}\theta\right)\cos\theta, \qquad y = \left(4 + t\cos\tfrac{1}{2}\theta\right)\sin\theta,$$

$$z = t\sin\tfrac{1}{2}\theta$$

for $-1 \leq t \leq 1$, $0 \leq \theta \leq 2\pi$. This Möbius strip has width 2 and a circular centerline of radius 4. Set up integrals giving its area and moment of inertia (assume constant density $\delta \equiv 1$) around the z-axis, and use a computer algebra system to evaluate them numerically.

FIGURE 15.5.9 The Möbius strip of Problem 40.

41. Consider a homogeneous thin spherical shell S of radius a centered at the origin, with density δ and total mass $M = 4\pi a^2 \delta$. A particle of mass m is located at the point $(0, 0, c)$ with $c > a$. Use the method and notation of Problem 41 of Section 14.7 to show that the gravitational force of attraction between the particle and the spherical shell is

$$F = \iint_S \frac{Gm\delta}{w^2}\, dS = \frac{GMm}{c^2}.$$

15.5 Project: Surface Integrals and Rocket Nose Cones

Figure 15.5.10 shows a (curved) nose cone S of height $h = 1$ attached to a cylindrical rocket of radius $r = 1$ that is moving downward with velocity v through air of density δ (or, equivalently, the rocket is stationary and the air is streaming upward). In the *Principia Mathematica* Newton showed that (under plausible assumptions) the force of air resistance the rocket experiences is given by $F = 2\pi R \, \delta v^2$, and thus is proportional both to the density of the air and to the square of its velocity. The *drag coefficient* R is given by the surface integral

$$R = \frac{1}{\pi} \iint_S \cos^3 \phi \, dS,$$

where ϕ is the angle between the unit normal $\mathbf{n}$ and the direction of motion.

The integrals involved in Problems 1 through 5 of this project reduce to single-variable integrals that you should be able to evaluate by hand. The CD-ROM project material illustrates the use of a computer algebra system for the evaluation both of "nose cone integrals" and of more general surface integrals.

1. If the surface S of the nose cone is obtained by revolving the curve $y = y(x)$, with $y(0) = 0$ and $y(1) = 1$, around the y-axis, use the fact that $\cos\phi = dx/ds$ to show that

$$R = \int_0^1 \frac{2x}{1 + [y'(x)]^2} \, dx.$$

Use this integral to calculate the numerical value of R in the particular cases that follow.

2. $y = x$, so that S is an actual cone with 90° vertex angle.
3. $y = 1 - \sqrt{1 - x^2}$, so S is a hemisphere.
4. $y = x^2$, so S is a paraboloid.
5. For the flat-tipped conical frustum nose cone illustrated in Fig. 15.5.11 (still with $r = h = 1$), show that

$$R = \cos^2\alpha - 2\cos\alpha\sin\alpha + 2\sin^2\alpha$$

where α is the indicated angle. Then show that this drag coefficient is minimal when $\tan 2\alpha = 2$.

If you compare your numerical results, you should find that

- the cone and hemisphere offer the same resistance;
- the paraboloid offers less resistance than either; and
- the optimal flat-tipped conical frustum offers still less!

In an extraordinary *tour de force,* Newton determined the nose cone with minimum possible air resistance, allowing both a circular flat tip and a curved surface of resolution connecting the tip to the cylindrical body of the rocket—see C. Henry Edwards, "Newton's Nose-Cone Problem," *The Mathematica Journal* **7** (Winter 1997), pp. 75–82.

FIGURE 15.5.10 The nose cone S of height h and radius r.

FIGURE 15.5.11 The flat-tipped nose cone.

15.6 THE DIVERGENCE THEOREM

The *divergence theorem* is to surface integrals what Green's theorem is to line integrals. It lets us convert a surface integral over a closed surface into a triple integral over the enclosed region, or vice versa. The divergence theorem is known also as *Gauss's theorem,* and in some eastern European countries it is called *Ostrogradski's theorem.* The German "prince of mathematics" Carl Friedrich Gauss (1777–1855) used it to study inverse-square force fields; the Russian Michel Ostrogradski (1801–1861) used it to study heat flow. Both did their work in the 1830s.

The surface S is called **piecewise smooth** if it consists of a finite number of smooth parametric surfaces. It is called **closed** if it is the boundary of a bounded region in space. For example, the boundary of a cube is a closed piecewise smooth surface, as are the boundary of a pyramid and the boundary of a solid cylinder.

THE DIVERGENCE THEOREM

Suppose that S is a closed piecewise smooth surface that bounds the space region T and let the *outer* unit normal vector field $\mathbf{n}$ be continuous on each smooth piece of S. If the vector field $\mathbf{F}$ is continuously differentiable on T, then

$$\iint_S \mathbf{F} \cdot \mathbf{n}\, dS = \iiint_T \nabla \cdot \mathbf{F}\, dV. \tag{1}$$

Equation (1) is a three-dimensional analogue of the vector form of Green's theorem that we saw in Eq. (9) of Section 15.4:

$$\oint_C \mathbf{F} \cdot \mathbf{n}\, ds = \iint_R \nabla \cdot \mathbf{F}\, dA,$$

where $\mathbf{F}$ is a vector field in the plane, C is a piecewise smooth curve that bounds the plane region R, and $\mathbf{n}$ is the outer unit normal vector to C. The left-hand side of Eq. (1) is the flux of $\mathbf{F}$ across S in the direction of the outer unit normal vector $\mathbf{n}$.

Recall from Section 15.1 that the *divergence* $\nabla \cdot \mathbf{F}$ of the vector field $\mathbf{F} = P\mathbf{i} + Q\mathbf{j} + R\mathbf{k}$ is given in the three-dimensional case by

$$\operatorname{div} \mathbf{F} = \nabla \cdot \mathbf{F} = \frac{\partial P}{\partial x} + \frac{\partial Q}{\partial y} + \frac{\partial R}{\partial z}. \tag{2}$$

If $\mathbf{n}$ is given in terms of its direction cosines, as $\mathbf{n} = \langle \cos\alpha, \cos\beta, \cos\gamma \rangle$, then (by Eq. (18) in Section 15.5) we can write the divergence theorem in scalar form:

$$\iint_S (P\cos\alpha + Q\cos\beta + R\cos\gamma)\, dS = \iiint_T \left(\frac{\partial P}{\partial x} + \frac{\partial Q}{\partial y} + \frac{\partial R}{\partial z} \right) dV. \tag{3}$$

It is best to parametrize S so that the normal vector given by the parametrization is the outer normal. Then we can write Eq. (3) entirely in Cartesian form:

$$\iint_S P\, dy\, dz + Q\, dz\, dx + R\, dx\, dy = \iiint_T \left(\frac{\partial P}{\partial x} + \frac{\partial Q}{\partial y} + \frac{\partial R}{\partial z} \right) dV. \tag{4}$$

PARTIAL PROOF OF THE DIVERGENCE THEOREM We shall prove the divergence theorem only for the case in which the region T is simultaneously x-simple, y-simple, and z-simple. This guarantees that every straight line parallel to a coordinate axis intersects T, if at all, in a single point or a single line segment. It suffices for us to derive separately the equations

$$\iint_S P\, dy\, dz = \iiint_T \frac{\partial P}{\partial x}\, dV,$$

$$\iint_S Q\, dz\, dx = \iiint_T \frac{\partial Q}{\partial y}\, dV, \quad \text{and} \tag{5}$$

$$\iint_S R\, dx\, dy = \iiint_T \frac{\partial R}{\partial z}\, dV.$$

Then the sum of the equations in (5) is Eq. (4).

FIGURE 15.6.1 A z-simple space region bounded by the surfaces S_1, S_2, and S_3.

Because T is z-simple, it has the description

$$z_1(x, y) \leq z \leq z_2(x, y)$$

for (x, y) in D, the projection of T into the xy-plane. As in Fig. 15.6.1, we denote the lower surface $z = z_1(x, y)$ of T by S_1, the upper surface $z = z_2(x, y)$ by S_2, and the lateral surface between S_1 and S_2 by S_3. In the case of some simple surfaces, such as a spherical surface, there may be no surface S_3 to consider. But even if there is,

$$\iint_{S_3} R \, dx \, dy = \iint_{S_3} R \cos \gamma \, dS = 0, \tag{6}$$

because $\gamma = 90°$ at each point of the vertical cylinder S_3.

On the upper surface S_2, the unit upper normal vector corresponding to the parametrization $z = z_2(x, y)$ is the given outer unit normal vector $\mathbf{n}$, so Eq. (20) of Section 15.5 yields

$$\iint_{S_2} R \, dx \, dy = \iint_D R(x, y, z_2(x, y)) \, dx \, dy. \tag{7}$$

But on the lower surface S_1, the unit upper normal vector corresponding to the parametrization $z = z_1(x, y)$ is the inner normal vector $-\mathbf{n}$, so we must reverse the sign. Thus

$$\iint_{S_1} R \, dx \, dy = -\iint_D R(x, y, z_1(x, y)) \, dx \, dy. \tag{8}$$

We add Eqs. (6), (7), and (8). The result is that

$$\iint_S R \, dx \, dy = \iint_D [R(x, y, z_2(x, y)) - R(x, y, z_1(x, y))] \, dx \, dy$$

$$= \iint_D \left(\int_{z_1(x,y)}^{z_2(x,y)} \frac{\partial R}{\partial z} \, dz \right) dx \, dy.$$

Therefore

$$\iint_S R \, dx \, dy = \iiint_T \frac{\partial R}{\partial z} \, dV.$$

This is the third equation in (5), and we can derive the other two in the same way. ◄

FIGURE 15.6.2 The region of Example 1.

EXAMPLE 1 Let S be the surface (with outer unit normal vector $\mathbf{n}$) of the region T bounded by the planes $z = 0$, $y = 0$, $y = 2$, and the parabolic cylinder $z = 1 - x^2$ (Fig. 15.6.2). Apply the divergence theorem to compute

$$\iint_S \mathbf{F} \cdot \mathbf{n}\, dS$$

given $\mathbf{F} = (x + \cos y)\mathbf{i} + (y + \sin z)\mathbf{j} + (z + e^x)\mathbf{k}$.

Solution To evaluate the surface integral directly would be a lengthy project. But div $\mathbf{F} = 1 + 1 + 1 = 3$, so we can apply the divergence theorem easily:

$$\iint_S \mathbf{F} \cdot \mathbf{n}\, dS = \iiint_T \text{div } \mathbf{F}\, dV = \iiint_T 3\, dV.$$

We examine Fig. 15.6.2 to find the limits for the volume integral and thus obtain

$$\iint_S \mathbf{F} \cdot \mathbf{n}\, dS = \int_{-1}^{1} \int_0^2 \int_0^{1-x^2} 3\, dz\, dy\, dx = 12 \int_0^1 (1 - x^2)\, dx = 8. \quad \blacklozenge$$

EXAMPLE 2 Let S be the surface of the solid cylinder T bounded by the planes $z = 0$ and $z = 3$ and the cylinder $x^2 + y^2 = 4$. Calculate the outward flux

$$\iint_S \mathbf{F} \cdot \mathbf{n}\, dS$$

given $\mathbf{F} = (x^2 + y^2 + z^2)(x\mathbf{i} + y\mathbf{j} + z\mathbf{k})$.

Solution If we denote by P, Q, and R the component functions of the vector field $\mathbf{F}$, we find that

$$\frac{\partial P}{\partial x} = 2x \cdot x + (x^2 + y^2 + z^2) \cdot 1 = 3x^2 + y^2 + z^2.$$

Similarly,

$$\frac{\partial Q}{\partial y} = 3y^2 + z^2 + x^2 \quad \text{and} \quad \frac{\partial R}{\partial z} = 3z^2 + x^2 + y^2,$$

so

$$\text{div } \mathbf{F} = 5(x^2 + y^2 + z^2).$$

Therefore the divergence theorem yields

$$\iint_S \mathbf{F} \cdot \mathbf{n}\, dS = \iiint_T 5(x^2 + y^2 + z^2)\, dV.$$

Using cylindrical coordinates to evaluate the triple integral, we get

$$\iint_S \mathbf{F} \cdot \mathbf{n}\, dS = \int_0^{2\pi} \int_0^2 \int_0^3 5(r^2 + z^2) r\, dz\, dr\, d\theta$$

$$= 10\pi \int_0^2 \left[r^3 z + \frac{1}{3} r z^3 \right]_{z=0}^{3} dr$$

$$= 10\pi \int_0^2 (3r^3 + 9r)\, dr = 10\pi \left[\frac{3}{4} r^4 + \frac{9}{2} r^2 \right]_0^2 = 300\pi. \quad \blacklozenge$$

EXAMPLE 3 Suppose that the space region T is bounded by the smooth closed surface S with a parametrization that gives the outer unit normal vector to S. Show that the volume V of T is given by

$$V = \frac{1}{3} \iint_S x\,dy\,dz + y\,dz\,dx + z\,dx\,dy. \tag{9}$$

Solution Equation (9) follows immediately from Eq. (4) if we take $P(x, y, z) = x$, $Q(x, y, z) = y$, and $R(x, y, z) = z$. For example, if S is the spherical surface $x^2 + y^2 + z^2 = a^2$ with volume V, surface area A, and outer unit normal vector

$$\mathbf{n} = \langle \cos\alpha, \cos\beta, \cos\gamma \rangle = \left\langle \frac{x}{a}, \frac{y}{b}, \frac{z}{c} \right\rangle,$$

then Eq. (9) yields

$$V = \frac{1}{3} \iint_S x\,dy\,dz + y\,dz\,dx + z\,dx\,dy$$

$$= \frac{1}{3} \iint_S (x\cos\alpha + y\cos\beta + z\cos\gamma)\,dS$$

$$= \frac{1}{3} \iint_S \frac{x^2 + y^2 + z^2}{a}\,dS = \frac{1}{3}a \iint_S 1\,dS = \frac{1}{3}aA.$$

You should confirm that this result is consistent with the familiar formulas $V = \frac{4}{3}\pi a^3$ and $A = 4\pi a^2$. ◆

EXAMPLE 4 Show that the divergence of the vector field $\mathbf{F}$ at the point P is given by

$$\nabla \cdot \mathbf{F}(P) = \lim_{r \to 0} \frac{1}{v(B_r)} \iint_{S_r} \mathbf{F} \cdot \mathbf{n}\,dS, \tag{10}$$

where S_r is the sphere of radius r centered at P and $v(B_r) = \frac{4}{3}\pi r^3$ is the volume of the ball B_r that the sphere bounds.

Solution The divergence theorem gives

$$\iint_{S_r} \mathbf{F} \cdot \mathbf{n}\,dS = \iiint_{B_r} \nabla \cdot \mathbf{F}\,dV.$$

Then we apply the average value property of triple integrals, a result analogous to the double integral result of Problem 50 in Section 14.2. This yields

$$\iiint_{B_r} \nabla \cdot \mathbf{F}\,dV = [\nabla \cdot \mathbf{F}(\overline{P})] \cdot v(B_r)$$

for some point $\overline{P}$ of B_r. We assume that $\mathbf{F}$ is continuously differentiable, so it follows that

$$\nabla \cdot \mathbf{F}(\overline{P}) \to \nabla \cdot \mathbf{F}(P) \quad \text{as} \quad \overline{P} \to P.$$

Equation (10) follows after we divide both sides by $v(B_r)$ and then take the limit as $r \to 0$. ◆

For instance, suppose that $\mathbf{F} = \delta \mathbf{v}$ is the vector field of a fluid flow. We can interpret Eq. (10) as saying that $\nabla \cdot \mathbf{F}(P)$ is the net rate per unit volume that fluid mass is flowing away (or "diverging") from the point P. For this reason the point P is called a **source** if $\nabla \cdot \mathbf{F}(P) > 0$ but a **sink** if $\nabla \cdot \mathbf{F}(P) < 0$.

Heat in a conducting body can be treated mathematically as though it were a fluid flowing through the body. Miscellaneous Problems 25 through 27 at the end of this chapter ask you to apply the divergence theorem to show that if $u = u(x, y, z, t)$ is the temperature at the point (x, y, z) at the time t in a body through which heat is flowing, then the function u must satisfy the equation

$$\frac{\partial^2 u}{\partial x^2} + \frac{\partial^2 u}{\partial y^2} + \frac{\partial^2 u}{\partial z^2} = \frac{1}{k} \cdot \frac{\partial u}{\partial t}, \tag{11}$$

where k is a constant (the *thermal diffusivity* of the body). This is a *partial differential equation* called the **heat equation.** If both the initial temperature $u(x, y, z, 0)$ and the temperature on the boundary of the body are given, then its interior temperatures at future times are determined by the heat equation. A large part of advanced applied mathematics consists of techniques for solving such partial differential equations.

More General Regions and Gauss's Law

We can establish the divergence theorem for more general regions by the device of subdividing T into simpler regions, regions for which the preceding proof holds. For example, suppose that T is the shell between the concentric spherical surfaces S_a and S_b of radii a and b, with $0 < a < b$. The coordinate planes separate T into eight regions $T_1, T_2, \ldots, T_8$, each shaped as in Fig. 15.6.3. Let Σ_i denote the boundary of T_i and let $\mathbf{n}_i$ be the outer unit normal vector to Σ_i. We apply the divergence theorem to each of these eight regions and obtain

$$\iiint_T \nabla \cdot \mathbf{F} \, dV = \sum_{i=1}^{8} \iiint_{T_i} \nabla \cdot \mathbf{F} \, dV$$

$$= \sum_{i=1}^{8} \iint_{\Sigma_i} \mathbf{F} \cdot \mathbf{n}_i \, dS \quad \text{(divergence theorem)}$$

$$= \iint_{S_a} \mathbf{F} \cdot \mathbf{n}_a \, dS + \iint_{S_b} \mathbf{F} \cdot \mathbf{n}_b \, dS.$$

FIGURE 15.6.3 One octant of the shell between S_a and S_b.

Here we write $\mathbf{n}_a$ for the inner normal vector on S_a and $\mathbf{n}_b$ for the outer normal vector on S_b. The last equality holds because the surface integrals over the internal boundary surfaces (the surfaces in the coordinate planes) cancel in pairs—the normals are oppositely oriented there. As the boundary S of T is the union of the spherical surfaces S_a and S_b, it now follows that

$$\iiint_T \nabla \cdot \mathbf{F} \, dV = \iint_S \mathbf{F} \cdot \mathbf{n} \, dS.$$

This is the divergence theorem for the spherical shell T.

In a similar manner, the divergence theorem can be established for a region T that is bounded by two smooth closed surfaces S_1 and S_2 with S_1 interior to S_2, as in Fig. 15.6.4, where $\mathbf{n}_1$ and $\mathbf{n}_2$ denote the outward-pointing unit normal vectors to the two surfaces. Then the boundary S of T is the union of S_1 and S_2, and the outer unit normal vector field $\mathbf{n}$ on S consists of $-\mathbf{n}_1$ on the inner surface S_1 and $\mathbf{n}_2$ on the outer surface S_2 (both pointing out of T). Hence the divergence theorem takes the form

$$\iiint_T \nabla \cdot \mathbf{F} \, dV = \iint_S \mathbf{F} \cdot \mathbf{n} \, dS = \iint_{S_2} \mathbf{F} \cdot \mathbf{n}_2 \, dS - \iint_{S_1} \mathbf{F} \cdot \mathbf{n}_1 \, dS. \tag{12}$$

FIGURE 15.6.4 Nested closed surfaces S_1 and S_2.

For example, suppose that $\mathbf{F} = -GM\mathbf{r}/|\mathbf{r}|^3$ is the inverse-square gravitational force field of a mass M located at the origin. According to Problem 22, $\nabla \cdot \mathbf{F} = 0$ except at the origin. If S is a smooth surface enclosing M and S_a is a small sphere of radius a within S enclosing M, it then follows from Eq. (12) that (with $\mathbf{n}$ denoting the outer unit normal on each surface)

$$\iint_S \mathbf{F} \cdot \mathbf{n}\, dS = \iint_{S_a} \mathbf{F} \cdot \mathbf{n}\, dS$$

$$= \iint_{S_a} -\frac{GM\mathbf{r}}{|\mathbf{r}|^3} \cdot \frac{\mathbf{r}}{|\mathbf{r}|}\, dS = -\frac{GM}{a^2} \iint_{S_a} 1\, dS = -4\pi GM. \quad (13)$$

Thus we have established Gauss's law (Eq. (24) in Section 15.5) for the special case of a single point mass. The more general case of a collection of point masses within S can be established by enclosing each in its own small sphere. If we replace the constant GM in Eq. (13) with $Q/4\pi\epsilon_0$, we obtain similarly Gauss's law

$$\iint_S \mathbf{E} \cdot \mathbf{n}\, dS = \frac{Q}{\epsilon_0} \quad (14)$$

for the inverse-square electric field $\mathbf{E} = Q\mathbf{r}/(4\pi\epsilon_0|\mathbf{r}|^3)$ of a charge Q lying within S.

Another impressive consequence of the divergence theorem is Archimedes' law of buoyancy; see Problem 21 here and Problem 22 of Section 15.7.

15.6 TRUE/FALSE STUDY GUIDE

15.6 CONCEPTS: QUESTIONS AND DISCUSSION

1. The third equation in (5) is established in the "proof of the divergence theorem" included in this section. What changes in the derivation would be required to establish the first and second equations in (5)?

2. Let S_1 and S_2 be piecewise smooth surfaces in space with S_1 lying interior to S_2. Under what conditions on the vector field $\mathbf{F}$ can we conclude that

$$\iint_{S_1} \mathbf{F} \cdot \mathbf{n}\, dS = \iint_{S_2} \mathbf{F} \cdot \mathbf{n}\, dS?$$

If $\mathbf{F} = -k\mathbf{r}/|\mathbf{r}|^3$ is an inverse-square force field directed toward the origin, under what conditions on S_1 and S_2 can we conclude that the two flux integrals are equal?

15.6 PROBLEMS

In Problems 1 through 5, verify the divergence theorem by direct computation of both the surface integral and the triple integral of Eq. (1).

1. $\mathbf{F} = x\mathbf{i} + y\mathbf{j} + z\mathbf{k}$; S is the spherical surface with equation $x^2 + y^2 + z^2 = 1$.

2. $\mathbf{F} = |\mathbf{r}|\mathbf{r}$, where $\mathbf{r} = x\mathbf{i} + y\mathbf{j} + z\mathbf{k}$; S is the spherical surface with equation $x^2 + y^2 + z^2 = 9$.

3. $\mathbf{F} = x\mathbf{i} + y\mathbf{j} + z\mathbf{k}$; S is the surface of the cube bounded by the three coordinates planes and the three planes $x = 2$, $y = 2$, and $z = 2$.

4. $\mathbf{F} = xy\mathbf{i} + yz\mathbf{j} + xz\mathbf{k}$; S is the surface of Problem 3.

5. $\mathbf{F} = (x+y)\mathbf{i} + (y+z)\mathbf{j} + (z+x)\mathbf{k}$; S is the surface of the tetrahedron bounded by the three coordinates planes and the plane $x + y + z = 1$.

In Problems 6 through 14, use the divergence theorem to evaluate $\iint_S \mathbf{F} \cdot \mathbf{n}\, dS$, where $\mathbf{n}$ is the outer unit normal vector to the surface S.

6. $\mathbf{F} = x^2\mathbf{i} + y^2\mathbf{j} + z^2\mathbf{k}$; S is the surface of Problem 3.

7. $\mathbf{F} = x^3\mathbf{i} + y^3\mathbf{j} + z^3\mathbf{k}$; S is the surface of the cylinder bounded by $x^2 + y^2 = 9$, $z = -1$, and $z = 4$.

8. $\mathbf{F} = (x^2+y^2)(x\mathbf{i}+y\mathbf{j})$; S is the surface of the region bounded by the plane $z = 0$ and the paraboloid $z = 25 - x^2 - y^2$.

9. $\mathbf{F} = (x^2 + e^{-yz})\mathbf{i} + (y + \sin xz)\mathbf{j} + (\cos xy)\mathbf{k}$; S is the surface of Problem 5.

10. $\mathbf{F} = (xy^2 + e^{-y}\sin z)\mathbf{i} + (x^2 y + e^{-x}\cos z)\mathbf{j} + (\tan^{-1} xy)\mathbf{k}$; S is the surface of the region bounded by the paraboloid $z = x^2 + y^2$ and the plane $z = 9$.

11. $\mathbf{F} = (x^2 + y^2 + z^2)(x\mathbf{i} + y\mathbf{j} + z\mathbf{k})$; S is the surface of Problem 8.

12. $\mathbf{F} = \mathbf{r}/|\mathbf{r}|$, where $\mathbf{r} = x\mathbf{i} + y\mathbf{j} + z\mathbf{k}$; S is the sphere $\rho = 2$ of radius 2 centered at the origin.

13. $\mathbf{F} = x\mathbf{i} + y\mathbf{j} + 3\mathbf{k}$; S is the boundary of the region bounded by the paraboloid $z = x^2 + y^2$ and the plane $z = 4$.

14. $\mathbf{F} = (x^3 + e^z)\mathbf{i} + x^2 y\mathbf{j} + (\sin xy)\mathbf{k}$; S is the boundary of the region bounded by the parabolic cylinder $z = 4 - x^2$ and the planes $y = 0$, $z = 0$, and $y + z = 5$.

15. The **Laplacian** of the twice-differentiable scalar function f is defined to be $\nabla^2 f = \operatorname{div}(\operatorname{grad} f) = \nabla \cdot \nabla f$. Show that
$$\nabla^2 f = \frac{\partial^2 f}{\partial x^2} + \frac{\partial^2 f}{\partial y^2} + \frac{\partial^2 f}{\partial z^2}.$$

16. Let $\partial f / \partial n = \nabla f \cdot \mathbf{n}$ denote the directional derivative of the scalar function f in the direction of the outer unit normal vector $\mathbf{n}$ to the surface S that bounds the region T. Show that
$$\iint_S \frac{\partial f}{\partial n} \, dS = \iiint_T \nabla^2 f \, dV.$$

Use the notation of Problems 15 and 16 in Problems 17 through 19.

17. Suppose that $\nabla^2 f \equiv 0$ in the region T with boundary surface S. Show that
$$\iint_S f \frac{\partial f}{\partial n} \, dV = \iiint_T |\nabla f|^2 \, dV.$$

18. Apply the divergence theorem to $\mathbf{F} = f \nabla g$ to establish **Green's first identity**,
$$\iint_S f \frac{\partial g}{\partial n} \, dS = \iiint_T (f \nabla^2 g + \nabla f \cdot \nabla g) \, dV.$$

19. Interchange f and g in Green's first identity (Problem 18) to establish **Green's second identity**,
$$\iint_S \left(f \frac{\partial g}{\partial n} - g \frac{\partial f}{\partial n} \right) dS = \iiint_T (f \nabla^2 g - g \nabla^2 f) \, dV.$$

20. Suppose that f is a differentiable scalar function defined on the region T of space and that S is the boundary of T. Prove that
$$\iint_S f\mathbf{n} \, dS = \iiint_T \nabla f \, dV.$$

[*Suggestion:* Apply the divergence theorem to $\mathbf{F} = f\mathbf{a}$, where $\mathbf{a}$ is an arbitrary constant vector. *Note:* Integrals of vector-valued functions are defined by componentwise integration.]

21. **Archimedes' Law of Buoyancy** Let S be the surface of a body T submerged in a fluid of constant density δ. Set up coordinates so that positive values of z are measured *downward* from the surface. Then the pressure at depth z is $p = \delta g z$. The buoyant force exerted on the body by the fluid is
$$\mathbf{B} = -\iint_S p\mathbf{n} \, dS.$$
(Why?) Apply the result of Problem 20 to show that $\mathbf{B} = -W\mathbf{k}$, where W is the weight of the fluid displaced by the body. Because z is measured downward, the vector $\mathbf{B}$ is directed upward.

22. Let $\mathbf{r} = \langle x, y, z \rangle$, let $\mathbf{r}_0 = \langle x_0, y_0, z_0 \rangle$ be a fixed point, and suppose that
$$\mathbf{F}(x, y, z) = \frac{\mathbf{r} - \mathbf{r}_0}{|\mathbf{r} - \mathbf{r}_0|^3}.$$
Show that $\operatorname{div} \mathbf{F} = 0$ except at the point $\mathbf{r}_0$.

23. Apply the divergence theorem to compute the outward flux
$$\iint_S \mathbf{F} \cdot \mathbf{n} \, dS,$$
where $\mathbf{F} = |\mathbf{r}|\mathbf{r}$, $\mathbf{r} = x\mathbf{i} + y\mathbf{j} + z\mathbf{k}$, and S is the surface of Problem 8. [*Suggestion:* Integrate in cylindrical coordinates, first with respect to r and then with respect to z. For the latter integration, make a trigonometric substitution and then consult Eq. (9) of Section 8.3 for the antiderivative of $\sec^5 \theta$.]

24. Assume that Gauss's law in (13) holds for a uniform solid ball of mass M centered at the origin. Also assume by symmetry that the force $\mathbf{F}$ exerted by this mass on an exterior particle of unit mass is directed toward the origin. Apply Gauss's law with S being a sphere of radius r to show that $|\mathbf{F}| = GM/r^2$ at each point of S. Thus it follows that the solid ball acts (gravitationally) like a single point-mass M concentrated at its center.

25. Let $\mathbf{F}$ be the gravitational force field due to a uniform distribution of mass in the shell bounded by the concentric spherical surfaces $\rho = a$ and $\rho = b > a$. Apply Gauss's law in (13), with S being the sphere $\rho = r < a$, to show that $\mathbf{F}$ is zero at all points interior to this spherical shell.

26. Consider a solid spherical ball of radius a and constant density δ. Apply Gauss's law to show that the gravitational force on a particle of unit mass located at a distance $r < a$ from the center of the ball is given by $F = GM_r/r^2$, where $M_r = \frac{4}{3}\pi \delta r^3$ is the mass enclosed by a sphere of radius r. Thus the mass at a greater distance from the center of the ball exerts no net gravitational force on the particle.

27. Consider an infinitely long vertical straight wire with a uniform positive charge of q coulombs per meter. Assume by symmetry that the electric field vector $\mathbf{E}$ is at each point of space a horizontal radial vector directed away from the wire. Apply Gauss's law in (14), with S being a cylinder with the wire as its axis, to show that $|\mathbf{E}| = q/(2\pi \epsilon_0 r)$. Thus the electric field intensity is inversely proportional to distance r from the wire.

15.7 STOKES' THEOREM

In Section 15.4 we gave Green's theorem,

$$\oint_C P\,dx + Q\,dy = \iint_R \left(\frac{\partial Q}{\partial x} - \frac{\partial P}{\partial y}\right) dA, \tag{1}$$

in a vector form that is equivalent to a two-dimensional version of the divergence theorem. Another vector form of Green's theorem involves the curl of a vector field. Recall from Section 15.1 that if $\mathbf{F} = P\mathbf{i} + Q\mathbf{j} + R\mathbf{k}$ is a vector field, then curl $\mathbf{F}$ is the vector field given by

$$\operatorname{curl}\mathbf{F} = \nabla \times \mathbf{F} = \begin{vmatrix} \mathbf{i} & \mathbf{j} & \mathbf{k} \\ \dfrac{\partial}{\partial x} & \dfrac{\partial}{\partial y} & \dfrac{\partial}{\partial z} \\ P & Q & R \end{vmatrix}$$

$$= \left(\frac{\partial R}{\partial y} - \frac{\partial Q}{\partial z}\right)\mathbf{i} + \left(\frac{\partial P}{\partial z} - \frac{\partial R}{\partial x}\right)\mathbf{j} + \left(\frac{\partial Q}{\partial x} - \frac{\partial P}{\partial y}\right)\mathbf{k}. \tag{2}$$

The $\mathbf{k}$-component of $\nabla \times \mathbf{F}$ is the integrand of the double integral in Eq. (1). We know from Section 15.2 that we can write the line integral in Eq. (1) as

$$\oint_C \mathbf{F} \cdot \mathbf{T}\,ds,$$

where $\mathbf{T}$ is the positive-directed unit tangent vector to C. Consequently, we can rewrite Green's theorem in the form

$$\oint_C \mathbf{F} \cdot \mathbf{T}\,ds = \iint_R (\operatorname{curl}\mathbf{F}) \cdot \mathbf{k}\,dA. \tag{3}$$

Stokes' theorem is the generalization of Eq. (3) that we get by replacing the plane region R with a floppy two-dimensional version: an oriented bounded surface S in three-dimensional space with boundary C that consists of one or more simple closed curves in space.

An **oriented surface** is a piecewise smooth surface S together with a chosen *unit* normal vector field $\mathbf{n}$ that is continuous (that is, continuously turning) on each smooth piece of S. The positive orientation of the boundary C of an oriented surface S corresponds to the unit tangent vector $\mathbf{T}$ such that $\mathbf{n} \times \mathbf{T}$ always points *into* S (Fig. 15.7.1). Check that for a plane region with unit normal vector $\mathbf{k}$, the positive orientation of its outer boundary is counterclockwise.

FIGURE 15.7.1 Vectors, surface, and boundary curve mentioned in the statement of Stokes' theorem.

STOKES' THEOREM

Let S be an oriented, bounded, and piecewise smooth surface in space with positively oriented boundary C and unit normal vector field $\mathbf{n}$. Suppose that $\mathbf{T}$ is a positively oriented unit vector field tangent to C. If the vector field $\mathbf{F}$ is continuously differentiable in a space region containing S, then

$$\oint_C \mathbf{F} \cdot \mathbf{T}\,ds = \iint_S (\operatorname{curl}\mathbf{F}) \cdot \mathbf{n}\,dS. \tag{4}$$

Thus Stokes' theorem means that *the line integral around the boundary curve of the tangential component of* $\mathbf{F}$ *equals the surface integral of the normal component of* curl $\mathbf{F}$. Compare Eqs. (3) and (4).

This result first appeared publicly as a problem posed by George Stokes (1819–1903) on a prize examination for Cambridge University students in 1854. It had been stated in an 1850 letter to Stokes from the physicist William Thomson (Lord Kelvin, 1824–1907).

In terms of the components of $\mathbf{F} = P\mathbf{i} + Q\mathbf{j} + R\mathbf{k}$ and those of curl $\mathbf{F}$, we can recast Stokes' theorem—with the aid of Eq. (19) of Section 15.5—in its scalar form

$$\oint_C P\,dx + Q\,dy + R\,dz$$
$$= \iint_S \left(\frac{\partial R}{\partial y} - \frac{\partial Q}{\partial z}\right) dy\,dz + \left(\frac{\partial P}{\partial z} - \frac{\partial R}{\partial x}\right) dz\,dx + \left(\frac{\partial Q}{\partial x} - \frac{\partial P}{\partial y}\right) dx\,dy. \quad (5)$$

Here, as usual, the parametrization of S must correspond to the given unit normal vector $\mathbf{n}$.

To prove Stokes' theorem, we need only establish the equation

$$\oint_C P\,dx = \iint_S \left(\frac{\partial P}{\partial z}\,dz\,dx - \frac{\partial P}{\partial y}\,dx\,dy\right) \quad (6)$$

and the corresponding two equations that are the Q and R "components" of Eq. (5). Equation (5) itself then follows by adding the three results.

PARTIAL PROOF Suppose first that S is the graph of a function $z = f(x, y)$, (x, y) in D, where S has an upper unit normal vector and D is a region in the xy-plane bounded by the simple closed curve J (Fig. 15.7.2). Then

$$\oint_C P\,dx = \oint_J P(x, y, f(x, y))\,dx$$

$$= \oint_J p(x, y)\,dx \quad [\text{where } p(x, y) \equiv P(x, y, f(x, y))]$$

$$= -\iint_D \frac{\partial p}{\partial y}\,dx\,dy \quad \text{(by Green's theorem)}.$$

We now use the chain rule to compute $\partial p/\partial y$ and find that

$$\oint_C P\,dx = -\iint_D \left(\frac{\partial P}{\partial y} + \frac{\partial P}{\partial z}\frac{\partial z}{\partial y}\right) dx\,dy. \quad (7)$$

Next, we use Eq. (20) of Section 15.5:

$$\iint_S P\,dy\,dz + Q\,dz\,dx + R\,dx\,dy = \iint_D \left(-P\frac{\partial z}{\partial x} - Q\frac{\partial z}{\partial y} + R\right) dx\,dy.$$

In this equation we replace P with 0, Q with $\partial P/\partial z$, and R with $-\partial P/\partial y$. This gives

$$\iint_S \left(\frac{\partial P}{\partial z}\,dz\,dx - \frac{\partial P}{\partial y}\,dx\,dy\right) = \iint_D \left(-\frac{\partial P}{\partial z}\frac{\partial z}{\partial y} - \frac{\partial P}{\partial y}\right) dx\,dy. \quad (8)$$

Finally, we compare Eqs. (7) and (8) and see that we have established Eq. (6). If we can write the surface S in the forms $y = g(x, z)$ and $x = h(y, z)$, then we can derive the Q and R "components" of Eq. (5) in much the same way. This proves Stokes' theorem for the special case of a surface S that can be represented as a graph in all three coordinate directions. Stokes' theorem may then be extended to a more general oriented surface by the now-familiar method of subdividing it into simpler surfaces, to each of which the preceding proof is applicable. ◂

FIGURE 15.7.2 The surface S.

EXAMPLE 1 Apply Stokes' theorem to evaluate

$$\oint_C \mathbf{F} \cdot \mathbf{T}\,ds,$$

where C is the ellipse in which the plane $z = y + 3$ intersects the cylinder $x^2 + y^2 = 1$. Orient the ellipse counterclockwise as viewed from above and take $\mathbf{F}(x, y, z) = 3z\mathbf{i} + 5x\mathbf{j} - 2y\mathbf{k}$.

Solution The plane, cylinder, and ellipse appear in Fig. 15.7.3. The given orientation of C corresponds to the upward unit normal vector $\mathbf{n} = (-\mathbf{j} + \mathbf{k})/\sqrt{2}$ to the elliptical region S in the plane $z = y + 3$ bounded by C. Now

$$\operatorname{curl} \mathbf{F} = \begin{vmatrix} \mathbf{i} & \mathbf{j} & \mathbf{k} \\ \dfrac{\partial}{\partial x} & \dfrac{\partial}{\partial y} & \dfrac{\partial}{\partial z} \\ 3z & 5x & -2y \end{vmatrix} = -2\mathbf{i} + 3\mathbf{j} + 5\mathbf{k},$$

so

$$(\operatorname{curl} \mathbf{F}) \cdot \mathbf{n} = (-2\mathbf{i} + 3\mathbf{j} + 5\mathbf{k}) \cdot \frac{1}{\sqrt{2}}(-\mathbf{j} + \mathbf{k}) = \frac{-3+5}{\sqrt{2}} = \sqrt{2}.$$

Hence by Stokes' theorem,

$$\oint_C \mathbf{F} \cdot \mathbf{T}\, ds = \iint_S (\operatorname{curl} \mathbf{F}) \cdot \mathbf{n}\, dS = \iint_S \sqrt{2}\, dS = \sqrt{2} \cdot \operatorname{area}(S) = 2\pi,$$

because we can see from Fig. 15.7.3 that S is an ellipse with semiaxes 1 and $\sqrt{2}$. Thus its area is $\pi\sqrt{2}$. ◆

FIGURE 15.7.3 The ellipse of Example 1.

EXAMPLE 2 Apply Stokes' theorem to evaluate

$$\iint_S (\nabla \times \mathbf{F}) \cdot \mathbf{n}\, dS,$$

where $\mathbf{F} = 3z\mathbf{i} + 5x\mathbf{j} - 2y\mathbf{k}$ and S is the part of the parabolic surface $z = x^2 + y^2$ that lies below the plane $z = 4$ and whose orientation is given by the upper unit normal vector (Fig. 15.7.4).

Solution We parametrize the boundary circle C of S by $x = 2\cos t$, $y = 2\sin t$, $z = 4$ for $0 \leq t \leq 2\pi$. Then $dx = -2\sin t\, dt$, $dy = 2\cos t\, dt$, and $dz = 0$. So Stokes' theorem yields

$$\iint_S (\nabla \times \mathbf{F}) \cdot \mathbf{n}\, dS = \oint_C \mathbf{F} \cdot \mathbf{T}\, ds = \oint_C 3z\, dx + 5x\, dy - 2y\, dz$$

$$= \int_0^{2\pi} 3 \cdot 4 \cdot (-2\sin t\, dt) + 5 \cdot (2\cos t)(2\cos t\, dt) + 2 \cdot (2\sin t) \cdot 0$$

$$= \int_0^{2\pi} (-24\sin t + 20\cos^2 t)\, dt = \int_0^{2\pi} (-24\sin t + 10 + 10\cos 2t)\, dt$$

$$= \left[24\cos t + 10t + 5\sin 2t \right]_0^{2\pi} = 20\pi. \quad \blacklozenge$$

FIGURE 15.7.4 The parabolic surface of Example 2.

Just as the divergence theorem yields a physical interpretation of div $\mathbf{F}$ [Eq. (10) of Section 15.6], Stokes' theorem yields a physical interpretation of curl $\mathbf{F}$. Let S_r be a circular disk of radius r and area $a(S_r) = \pi r^2$, centered at the point P in space and perpendicular to the (fixed) unit vector $\mathbf{n}$. Let C_r be the positively oriented boundary circle of S_r (Fig. 15.7.5). Then Stokes' theorem and the average value property of double integrals together give

$$\oint_{C_r} \mathbf{F} \cdot \mathbf{T}\, ds = \iint_{S_r} (\nabla \times \mathbf{F}) \cdot \mathbf{n}\, dS = a(S_r)[\nabla \times \mathbf{F}(\overline{P})] \cdot \mathbf{n}$$

FIGURE 15.7.5 A physical interpretation of the curl of a vector field.

for some point $\overline{P}$ of S_r. We assume that $\mathbf{F}$ is continuously differentiable at P, so it follows that

$$\nabla \times \mathbf{F}(\overline{P}) \to \nabla \times \mathbf{F}(P) \quad \text{as} \quad \overline{P} \to P.$$

If we first divide both sides by $a(S_r)$ and then take the limit as $r \to 0$, we get

$$[\nabla \times \mathbf{F}(P)] \cdot \mathbf{n} = \lim_{r \to 0} \frac{1}{\pi r^2} \oint_{C_r} \mathbf{F} \cdot \mathbf{T}\, ds. \tag{9}$$

Equation (9) has a natural physical meaning. Suppose that $\mathbf{F} = \delta \mathbf{v}$, where $\mathbf{v}$ is the velocity vector field of the steady-state flow of a fluid with constant density δ. Then the value of the integral

$$\Gamma(C) = \oint_C \mathbf{F} \cdot \mathbf{T}\, ds \tag{10}$$

measures the rate of flow of fluid mass *around* the curve C and is therefore called the **circulation** of $\mathbf{F}$ around C. We see from Eq. (9) that

$$[\nabla \times \mathbf{F}(P)] \cdot \mathbf{n} \approx \frac{\Gamma(C_r)}{\pi r^2}$$

if C_r is a circle of very small radius r centered at P and perpendicular to $\mathbf{n}$. If it should happen that $\nabla \times \mathbf{F}(P) \neq \mathbf{0}$, it follows that $\Gamma(C_r)$ is greatest (for r fixed and small) when the unit vector $\mathbf{n}$ points in the direction of $\nabla \times \mathbf{F}(P)$. Hence the line through P determined by $\nabla \times \mathbf{F}(P)$ is the axis about which the fluid near P is revolving the most rapidly. A tiny paddle wheel placed in the fluid at P (see Fig. 15.7.6) would rotate the fastest if its axis lay along this line. It follows from Miscellaneous Problem 32 at the end of this chapter that $|\text{curl } \mathbf{F}| = 2\delta\omega$ in the case of a fluid revolving steadily around a fixed axis with constant angular speed ω (in radians per second). Thus $\nabla \times \mathbf{F}(P)$ indicates both the direction *and* rate of rotation of the fluid near P. Because of this interpretation, some older books use the notation "rot $\mathbf{F}$" for the curl, an abbreviation that has disappeared from general use.

FIGURE 15.7.6 The paddle-wheel interpretation of curl $\mathbf{F}$.

If $\nabla \times \mathbf{F} = \mathbf{0}$ everywhere, then the fluid flow and the vector field $\mathbf{F}$ are said to be **irrotational.** An infinitesimal straw placed in an irrotational fluid flow would be translated parallel to itself without rotating. A vector field $\mathbf{F}$ defined on a simply connected region D is irrotational if and only if it is conservative, which in turn is true if and only if the line integral

$$\int_C \mathbf{F} \cdot \mathbf{T}\, ds$$

is independent of the path in D. (The region D is said to be **simply connected** if every simple closed curve in D can be continuously shrunk to a point while staying inside D. The interior of a torus is an example of a space region that is *not* simply connected. It is true, though not obvious, that any piecewise smooth simple closed curve in a simply connected region D is the boundary of a piecewise smooth oriented surface in D.)

THEOREM 1 Conservative and Irrotational Fields
Let $\mathbf{F}$ be a vector field with continuous first-order partial derivatives in a simply connected region D in space. Then the vector field $\mathbf{F}$ is irrotational if and only if it is conservative; that is, $\nabla \times \mathbf{F} \equiv \mathbf{0}$ in D if and only if $\mathbf{F} = \nabla \phi$ for some scalar function ϕ defined on D.

OUTLINE OF PARTIAL PROOF A complete proof of the *if* part of Theorem 1 is easy; by Example 8 of Section 15.1, $\nabla \times (\nabla \phi) = \mathbf{0}$ for any twice-differentiable scalar function ϕ.

FIGURE 15.7.7 Two paths from P_0 to P in the simply connected space region D.

Here is a description of how we might show the *only if* part of the proof of Theorem 1. Assume that **F** is irrotational. Let $P_0(x_0, y_0, z_0)$ be a fixed point of D. Given an arbitrary point $P(x, y, z)$ of D, we would like to define

$$\phi(x, y, z) = \int_{C_1} \mathbf{F} \cdot \mathbf{T}\, ds, \tag{11}$$

where C_1 is a path in D from P_0 to P. But we must show that any *other* path C_2 from P_0 to P would give the *same* value for $\phi(x, y, z)$.

We assume, as suggested by Fig. 15.7.7, that C_1 and C_2 intersect only at their endpoints. Let $C = C_1 \cup (-C_2)$ be the closed path that first follows C_1 from P_0 to P and then follows the reversed path $-C_2$ from P back to P_0. Then it can be shown that the oriented closed curve C bounds an oriented surface S contained in D, and Stokes' theorem then gives

$$\int_{C_1} \mathbf{F} \cdot \mathbf{T}\, ds - \int_{C_2} \mathbf{F} \cdot \mathbf{T}\, ds = \oint_C \mathbf{F} \cdot \mathbf{T}\, ds = \iint_S (\nabla \times \mathbf{F}) \cdot \mathbf{n}\, dS = 0$$

because of the hypothesis that $\nabla \times \mathbf{F} \equiv \mathbf{0}$. This shows that the line integral $\int_C \mathbf{F} \cdot \mathbf{T}\, ds$ is *independent of path*, just as desired. In Problem 21 we ask you to complete this proof by showing that the function ϕ of Eq. (11) is the one whose existence is claimed in Theorem 1. That is, $\mathbf{F} = \nabla \phi$. ◄

EXAMPLE 3 Show that the vector field $\mathbf{F} = 3x^2\mathbf{i} + 5z^2\mathbf{j} + 10yz\mathbf{k}$ is irrotational. Then find a potential function $\phi(x, y, z)$ such that $\nabla \phi = \mathbf{F}$.

Solution To show that **F** is irrotational, we calculate

$$\nabla \times \mathbf{F} = \begin{vmatrix} \mathbf{i} & \mathbf{j} & \mathbf{k} \\ \dfrac{\partial}{\partial x} & \dfrac{\partial}{\partial y} & \dfrac{\partial}{\partial z} \\ 3x^2 & 5z^2 & 10yz \end{vmatrix} = (10z - 10z)\mathbf{i} = \mathbf{0}.$$

Hence Theorem 1 implies that **F** has a potential function ϕ. We can apply Eq. (11) to find ϕ explicitly. If C_1 is the straight line segment from $(0, 0, 0)$ to (u, v, w) that is parametrized by $x = ut$, $y = vt$, $z = wt$ for $0 \leq t \leq 1$, then Eq. (11) yields

$$\phi(u, v, w) = \int_{C_1} \mathbf{F} \cdot \mathbf{T}\, ds = \int_{(0,0,0)}^{(u,v,w)} 3x^2\, dx + 5z^2\, dy + 10yz\, dz$$

$$= \int_{t=0}^{1} (3u^2 t^2)(u\, dt) + (5w^2 t^2)(v\, dt) + (10vtwt)(w\, dt)$$

$$= \int_{t=0}^{1} (3u^3 t^2 + 15vw^2 t^2)\, dt = \left[u^3 t^3 + 5vwt^3 \right]_{t=0}^{1},$$

and thus

$$\phi(u, v, w) = u^3 + 5vw^2.$$

But because (u, v, w) is an arbitrary point of space, we have found that $\phi(x, y, z) = x^3 + 5yz^2$ is a scalar potential for **F**. As a check, we note that $\phi_x = 3x^2$, $\phi_y = 5z^2$, and $\phi_z = 10yz$, so $\nabla \phi = \mathbf{F}$, as desired. ◆

Application Suppose that **v** is the velocity field of a steady fluid flow that is both irrotational and incompressible—the density δ of the fluid is constant. Suppose that S is any closed surface that bounds a region T. Then, because of conservation of mass, the flux of **v** across S must be zero; the mass of fluid within S remains constant.

Hence the divergence theorem gives

$$\iiint_T \text{div}\,\mathbf{v}\,dV = \iint_S \mathbf{v}\cdot\mathbf{n}\,dS = 0.$$

Because this holds for *any* region T, it follows from the usual average value property argument that div $\mathbf{v} = 0$ everywhere. The scalar function ϕ provided by Theorem 1, for which $\mathbf{v} = \nabla\phi$, is called the **velocity potential** of the fluid flow. We substitute $\mathbf{v} = \nabla\phi$ into the equation div $\mathbf{v} = 0$ and thereby obtain

$$\text{div}(\nabla\phi) = \frac{\partial^2\phi}{\partial x^2} + \frac{\partial^2\phi}{\partial y^2} + \frac{\partial^2\phi}{\partial z^2} = 0. \tag{12}$$

Thus the velocity potential ϕ of an irrotational and incompressible fluid flow satisfies *Laplace's equation*.

Laplace's equation appears in numerous other applications. For example, consider a heated body whose temperature function $u = u(x, y, z)$ is independent of time t. Then $\partial u/\partial t \equiv 0$ in the heat equation, Eq. (11) of Section 15.6, shows that the "steady-state temperature" function $u(x, y, z)$ satisfies Laplace's equation

$$\frac{\partial^2 u}{\partial x^2} + \frac{\partial^2 u}{\partial y^2} + \frac{\partial^2 u}{\partial z^2} = 0. \tag{13}$$

These brief remarks should indicate how the mathematics of this chapter forms the starting point for investigations in a number of areas, including acoustics, aerodynamics, electromagnetism, meteorology, and oceanography. Indeed, the entire subject of vector calculus stems historically from its mathematical applications rather than from abstract mathematical considerations. The modern form of the subject is due primarily to J. Willard Gibbs (1839–1903), the first great American physicist, and the English electrical engineer Oliver Heaviside (1850–1925).

15.7 TRUE/FALSE STUDY GUIDE

15.7 CONCEPTS: QUESTIONS AND DISCUSSION

1. The P "component" of Eq. (5) was established in the partial proof of Stokes' theorem included in this section. What changes in the derivation would be required to establish the Q and R "components" of Eq. (5)?
2. Suppose that C_1 and C_2 are piecewise smooth closed curves in space, each being the boundary of a parametrized piecewise smooth disk. (Do C_1 and C_2 then necessarily form the boundary of some curvilinear annular ring?) Under what conditions on the vector field $\mathbf{F}$ can we conclude that

$$\oint_{C_1} \mathbf{F}\cdot\mathbf{T}\,ds = \oint_{C_2} \mathbf{F}\cdot\mathbf{T}\,ds?$$

15.7 PROBLEMS

In Problems 1 through 5, use Stokes' theorem for the evaluation of

$$\iint_S (\text{curl}\,\mathbf{F})\cdot\mathbf{n}\,dS.$$

1. $\mathbf{F} = 3y\mathbf{i} - 2x\mathbf{j} + xyz\mathbf{k}$; S is the hemispherical surface $z = \sqrt{4 - x^2 - y^2}$ with upper unit normal vector.
2. $\mathbf{F} = 2y\mathbf{i} + 3x\mathbf{j} + e^z\mathbf{k}$; S is the part of the paraboloid $z = x^2 + y^2$ below the plane $z = 4$ and with upper unit normal vector.
3. $\mathbf{F} = \langle xy, -2, \arctan x^2\rangle$; S is the part of the paraboloid $z = 9 - x^2 - y^2$ above the xy-plane and with upper unit normal vector.
4. $\mathbf{F} = yz\mathbf{i} + xz\mathbf{j} + xy\mathbf{k}$; S is the part of the cylinder $x^2 + y^2 = 1$ between the two planes $z = 1$ and $z = 3$ and with outer unit normal vector.
5. $\mathbf{F} = \langle yz, -xz, z^3\rangle$; S is the part of the cone $z = \sqrt{x^2 + y^2}$ between the two planes $z = 1$ and $z = 3$ and with upper unit normal vector.

In Problems 6 through 10, use Stokes' theorem to evaluate

$$\oint_C \mathbf{F} \cdot \mathbf{T}\, ds.$$

6. $\mathbf{F} = 3y\mathbf{i} - 2x\mathbf{j} + 3y\mathbf{k}$; C is the circle $x^2 + y^2 = 9$, $z = 4$, oriented counterclockwise as viewed from above.

7. $\mathbf{F} = 2z\mathbf{i} + x\mathbf{j} + 3y\mathbf{k}$; C is the ellipse in which the plane $z = x$ meets the cylinder $x^2 + y^2 = 4$, oriented counterclockwise as viewed from above.

8. $\mathbf{F} = y\mathbf{i} + z\mathbf{j} + x\mathbf{k}$; C is the boundary of the triangle with vertices $(0,0,0)$, $(2,0,0)$, and $(0,2,2)$, oriented counterclockwise as viewed from above.

9. $\mathbf{F} = \langle y-x, x-z, x-y \rangle$; C is the boundary of the part of the plane $x + 2y + z = 2$ that lies in the first octant, oriented counterclockwise as viewed from above.

10. $\mathbf{F} = y^2\mathbf{i} + z^2\mathbf{j} + x^2\mathbf{k}$; C is the intersection of the plane $z = y$ and the cylinder $x^2 + y^2 = 2y$, oriented counterclockwise as viewed from above.

In Problems 11 through 14, first show that the given vector field $\mathbf{F}$ is irrotational; then apply the method of Example 3 to find a potential function $\phi = \phi(x, y, z)$ for $\mathbf{F}$.

11. $\mathbf{F} = (3y - 2z)\mathbf{i} + (3x + z)\mathbf{j} + (y - 2x)\mathbf{k}$

12. $\mathbf{F} = (3y^3 - 10xz^2)\mathbf{i} + 9xy^2\mathbf{j} - 10x^2z\mathbf{k}$

13. $\mathbf{F} = (3e^z - 5y \sin x)\mathbf{i} + (5 \cos x)\mathbf{j} + (17 + 3xe^z)\mathbf{k}$

14. $\mathbf{F} = r^3\mathbf{r}$, where $\mathbf{r} = x\mathbf{i} + y\mathbf{j} + z\mathbf{k}$ and $r = |\mathbf{r}|$

15. Suppose that $\mathbf{r} = x\mathbf{i} + y\mathbf{j} + z\mathbf{k}$ and that $\mathbf{a}$ is a constant vector. Show that
    (a) $\nabla \cdot (\mathbf{a} \times \mathbf{r}) = 0$;
    (b) $\nabla \times (\mathbf{a} \times \mathbf{r}) = 2\mathbf{a}$;
    (c) $\nabla \cdot [(\mathbf{r} \cdot \mathbf{r})\mathbf{a}] = 2\mathbf{r} \cdot \mathbf{a}$;
    (d) $\nabla \times [(\mathbf{r} \cdot \mathbf{r})\mathbf{a}] = 2(\mathbf{r} \times \mathbf{a})$.

16. Prove that

$$\iint_S (\operatorname{curl} \mathbf{F}) \cdot \mathbf{n}\, dS$$

has the same value for all oriented surfaces S that have the same oriented boundary curve C.

17. Suppose that S is a closed surface. Prove in two different ways that

$$\iint_S (\operatorname{curl} \mathbf{F}) \cdot \mathbf{n}\, dS = 0:$$

(a) by using the divergence theorem, with T the region bounded outside by S, and (b) by using Stokes' theorem, with the aid of a simple closed curve C on S.

Line integrals, surface integrals, and triple integrals of vector-valued functions are defined by componentwise integration. Such integrals appear in Problems 18 through 20.

18. Suppose that C and S are as described in the statement of Stokes' theorem and that ϕ is a scalar function. Prove that

$$\oint_C \phi \mathbf{T}\, ds = \iint_S \mathbf{n} \times \nabla \phi\, dS.$$

[*Suggestion:* Apply Stokes' theorem with $\mathbf{F} = \phi\mathbf{a}$, where $\mathbf{a}$ is an arbitrary constant vector.]

19. Suppose that $\mathbf{a}$ and $\mathbf{r}$ are as in Problem 15. Prove that

$$\oint_C (\mathbf{a} \times \mathbf{r}) \cdot \mathbf{T}\, ds = 2\mathbf{a} \cdot \iint_S \mathbf{n}\, dS.$$

20. Suppose that S is a closed surface that bounds the region T. Prove that

$$\iint_S \mathbf{n} \times \mathbf{F}\, dS = \iiint_T \nabla \times \mathbf{F}\, dV.$$

[*Suggestion:* Apply the divergence theorem to $\mathbf{F} \times \mathbf{a}$, where $\mathbf{a}$ is an arbitrary constant vector.]

REMARK The formulas in Problem 20, the divergence theorem, and Problem 20 of Section 15.6 all fit the pattern

$$\iint_S \mathbf{n} \odot (\ )\, dS = \iiint_T \nabla \odot (\ )\, dV,$$

where $\odot$ denotes either ordinary multiplication, the dot product, or the vector product, and either a scalar function or a vector-valued function is placed within the parentheses, as appropriate.

21. Suppose that the line integral $\int_C \mathbf{F} \cdot \mathbf{T}\, ds$ is independent of path. If

$$\phi(x, y, z) = \int_{P_0}^{P_1} \mathbf{F} \cdot \mathbf{T}\, ds$$

as in Eq. (11), show that $\nabla \phi = \mathbf{F}$. [*Suggestion:* If L is the line segment from (x, y, z) to $(x + \Delta x, y, z)$, then

$$\phi(x + \Delta x, y, z) - \phi(x, y, z) = \int_L \mathbf{F} \cdot \mathbf{T}\, ds = \int_x^{x+\Delta x} P\, dx.]$$

22. Let T be the submerged body of Problem 21 in Section 15.6, with centroid

$$\mathbf{r}_0 = \frac{1}{V} \iiint_T \mathbf{r}\, dV.$$

The torque about $\mathbf{r}_0$ of Archimedes' buoyant force $\mathbf{B} = -W\mathbf{k}$ is given by

$$\mathbf{L} = \iint_S (\mathbf{r} - \mathbf{r}_0) \times (-\delta g z \mathbf{n})\, dS.$$

(Why?) Apply the result of Problem 20 of this section to prove that $\mathbf{L} = \mathbf{0}$. It follows that $\mathbf{B}$ acts along the vertical line through the centroid $\mathbf{r}_0$ of the submerged body. (Why?)

CHAPTER 15 REVIEW: DEFINITIONS, CONCEPTS, RESULTS

Use the following list as a guide to concepts that you may need to review.

1. Definition and evaluation of the line integral
$$\int_C f(x, y, z)\, ds$$

2. Definition and evaluation of the line integral
$$\int_C P\, dx + Q\, dy + R\, dz$$

3. Relationship between the two types of line integrals; the line integral of the tangential component of a vector field
4. Line integrals and independence of path
5. Green's theorem
6. Flux and the vector form of Green's theorem
7. The divergence of a vector field
8. Definition and evaluation of the surface integral
$$\iint_S f(x, y, z)\, dS$$

9. Definition and evaluation of the surface integral
$$\iint_S P\, dy\, dz + Q\, dz\, dx + R\, dx\, dy$$

10. Relationship between the two types of surface integrals; the flux of a vector field across a surface
11. The divergence theorem in vector and in scalar notation
12. The curl of a vector field
13. Stokes' theorem in vector and in scalar notation
14. The circulation of a vector field around a simple closed curve
15. Physical interpretation of the divergence and the curl of a vector field

CHAPTER 15 MISCELLANEOUS PROBLEMS

1. Evaluate the line integral
$$\int_C (x^2 + y^2)\, ds,$$
where C is the straight line segment from $(0, 0)$ to $(3, 4)$.

2. Evaluate the line integral
$$\int_C y^2\, dx + x^2\, dy,$$
where C is the part of the graph of $y = x^2$ from $(-1, 1)$ to $(1, 1)$.

3. Evaluate the line integral
$$\int_C \mathbf{F} \cdot \mathbf{T}\, ds,$$
where $\mathbf{F} = x\mathbf{i} + y\mathbf{j} + z\mathbf{k}$ and C is the curve $x = e^{2t}$, $y = e^t$, $z = e^{-t}$, $0 \leq t \leq \ln 2$.

4. Evaluate the line integral
$$\int_C xyz\, ds,$$
where C is the path from $(1, 1, 2)$ to $(2, 3, 6)$ consisting of three straight line segments, the first parallel to the x-axis, the second parallel to the y-axis, and the third parallel to the z-axis.

5. Evaluate the line integral
$$\int_C \sqrt{z}\, dx + \sqrt{x}\, dy + y^2\, dz,$$
where C is the curve $x = t$, $y = t^{3/2}$, $z = t^2$, $0 \leq t \leq 4$.

6. Apply Theorem 2 of Section 15.3 to show that the line integral
$$\int_C y^2\, dx + 2xy\, dy + z\, dz$$
from the fixed point A to the fixed point B is independent of the path C from A to B.

7. Apply Theorem 2 of Section 15.3 to show that the line integral
$$\int_C x^2 y\, dx + xy^2\, dy$$
is not independent of the path C from $(0, 0)$ to $(1, 1)$.

8. A wire shaped like the circle $x^2 + y^2 = a^2$, $z = 0$ has constant density and total mass M. Find its moment of inertia around (a) the z-axis; (b) the x-axis.

9. A wire shaped like the parabola $y = \frac{1}{2}x^2$, $0 \leq x \leq 2$, has density function $\delta = x$. Find its mass and its moment of inertia around the y-axis.

10. Find the work done by the force field $\mathbf{F} = z\mathbf{i} - x\mathbf{j} + y\mathbf{k}$ in moving a particle from $(1, 1, 1)$ to $(2, 4, 8)$ along the curve $y = x^2$, $z = x^3$.

11. Apply Green's theorem to evaluate the line integral
$$\oint_C x^2 y\, dx + xy^2\, dy,$$
where C is the boundary of the region between the two curves $y = x^2$ and $y = 8 - x^2$.

12. Evaluate the line integral
$$\oint_C x^2\, dy,$$

where C is the cardioid with polar equation $r = 1+\cos\theta$, by first applying Green's theorem and then changing to polar coordinates.

13. Let C_1 be the circle $x^2 + y^2 = 1$ and C_2 the circle $(x-1)^2 + y^2 = 9$. Show that if $\mathbf{F} = x^2 y\mathbf{i} - xy^2\mathbf{j}$, then

$$\oint_{C_1} \mathbf{F}\cdot\mathbf{n}\, ds = \oint_{C_2} \mathbf{F}\cdot\mathbf{n}\, ds$$

where $\mathbf{n}$ is an outer unit normal in the plane.

14. (a) Let C be the straight line segment from (x_1, y_1) to (x_2, y_2). Show that

$$\int_C -y\, dx + x\, dy = x_1 y_2 - x_2 y_1.$$

(b) Suppose that the vertices of a polygon are (x_1, y_1), $(x_2, y_2), \ldots, (x_n, y_n)$, named in counterclockwise order around the polygon. Apply the result in part (a) to show that the area of the polygon is

$$A = \frac{1}{2}\sum_{i=1}^{n}(x_i y_{i+1} - x_{i+1} y_i),$$

where $x_{n+1} = x_1$ and $y_{n+1} = y_1$.

15. Suppose that the line integral $\int_C P\, dx + Q\, dy$ is independent of the path in the plane region D. Prove that

$$\oint_C P\, dx + Q\, dy = 0$$

for every piecewise smooth simple closed curve C in D.

16. Use Green's theorem to prove that

$$\oint_C P\, dx + Q\, dy = 0$$

for every piecewise smooth simple closed curve C in the plane region D if and only if $\partial P/\partial y = \partial Q/\partial x$ at each point of D.

17. Evaluate the surface integral

$$\iint_S (x^2 + y^2 + 2z)\, dS,$$

where S is the part of the paraboloid $z = 2 - x^2 - y^2$ that lies above the xy-plane.

18. Suppose that $\mathbf{F} = (x^2 + y^2 + z^2)(x\mathbf{i} + y\mathbf{j} + z\mathbf{k})$ and that S is the spherical surface $x^2 + y^2 + z^2 = a^2$. Evaluate

$$\iint_S \mathbf{F}\cdot\mathbf{n}\, dS$$

without actually performing an antidifferentiation.

19. Let T be the solid bounded by the paraboloids

$$z = x^2 + 2y^2 \quad \text{and} \quad z = 12 - 2x^2 - y^2,$$

and suppose that $\mathbf{F} = x\mathbf{i} + y\mathbf{j} + z\mathbf{k}$. Find by evaluation of surface integrals the outward flux of $\mathbf{F}$ across the boundary of T.

20. Give a reasonable definition—in terms of a surface integral—of the average distance of the point P from points of the surface S. Then show that the average distance of a fixed point of a spherical surface of radius a from all points of the surface is $\frac{4}{3}a$.

21. Suppose that the surface S is the graph of the equation $x = g(y, z)$ for (y, z) in the region D of the yz-plane. Prove that

$$\iint_S P\, dy\, dz + Q\, dz\, dx + R\, dx\, dy$$

$$= \iint_D \left(P - Q\frac{\partial x}{\partial y} - R\frac{\partial x}{\partial z}\right) dy\, dz.$$

22. Suppose that the surface S is the graph of the equation $y = g(x, z)$ for (x, z) in the region D of the xz-plane. Prove that

$$\iint_S f(x, y, z)\, dS = \iint_D f(x, g(x, z), z) \sec\beta\, dx\, dz,$$

where $\sec\beta = \sqrt{1 + (\partial y/\partial x)^2 + (\partial y/\partial z)^2}$.

23. Let T be a region in space with volume V, boundary surface S, and centroid $(\bar{x}, \bar{y}, \bar{z})$. Use the divergence theorem to show that

$$\bar{z} = \frac{1}{2V}\iint_S z^2\, dx\, dy.$$

24. Apply the result of Problem 23 to find the centroid of the solid hemisphere

$$x^2 + y^2 + z^2 \leq a^2, \quad z \geq 0.$$

Problems 25 through 27 outline the derivation of the heat equation for a body with temperature $u = u(x, y, z, t)$ at the point (x, y, z) at time t. Denote by K its heat conductivity and by c its heat capacity, both assumed constant, and let $k = K/c$. Let B be a small solid ball within the body, and let S denote the boundary sphere of B.

25. Deduce from the divergence theorem and Eq. (23) of Section 15.5 that the rate of heat flow across S into B is

$$R = \iiint_B K\nabla^2 u\, dV.$$

26. The meaning of heat capacity is that, if Δu is small, then $(c\,\Delta u)\,\Delta V$ calories of heat are required to raise the temperature of the volume ΔV by Δu degrees. It follows that the rate at which the volume ΔV is absorbing heat is $c(\partial u/\partial t)\,\Delta V$. (Why?) Conclude that the rate of heat flow into B is

$$R = \iiint_B c\,\frac{\partial u}{\partial t}\, dV.$$

27. Equate the results of Problem 25 and 26, apply the average value property of triple integrals, and then take the limit as the radius of the ball B approaches zero. You should thereby obtain the heat equation

$$\frac{\partial u}{\partial t} = k\nabla^2 u.$$

28. For a *steady-state* temperature function (one that is independent of time t), the heat equation reduces to Laplace's equation,

$$\nabla^2 u = \frac{\partial^2 u}{\partial x^2} + \frac{\partial^2 u}{\partial y^2} + \frac{\partial^2 u}{\partial z^2} = 0.$$

(a) Suppose that u_1 and u_2 are two solutions of Laplace's equation in the region T and that u_1 and u_2 agree on its boundary surface S. Apply Problem 17 of Section 15.6 to the function $f = u_1 - u_2$ to conclude that $\nabla f = \mathbf{0}$ at each point of T. (b) From the facts that $\nabla f = \mathbf{0}$ in T and $f \equiv 0$ on S, conclude that $f \equiv 0$, so $u_1 \equiv u_2$. Thus the steady-state temperatures within a region are *determined* by the boundary-value temperatures.

29. Suppose that $\mathbf{r} = x\mathbf{i} + y\mathbf{j} + z\mathbf{k}$ and that $\phi(r)$ is a scalar function of $r = |\mathbf{r}|$. Compute
 (a) $\nabla \phi(r)$;
 (b) $\operatorname{div}[\phi(r)\mathbf{r}]$;
 (c) $\operatorname{curl}[\phi(r)\mathbf{r}]$.

30. Let S be the upper half of the torus obtained by revolving around the z-axis the circle $(y-a)^2 + z^2 = b^2$ ($a > b > 0$) in the yz-plane, with upper unit normal vector. Describe how to subdivide S to establish Stokes' theorem for it. How are the two boundary circles oriented?

31. Explain why the method of subdivision is not sufficient to establish Stokes' theorem for the Möbius strip of Fig. 15.5.3.

32. (a) Suppose that a fluid or a rigid body is rotating with angular speed ω radians per second around the line through the origin determined by the unit vector $\mathbf{u}$. Show that the velocity of the point with position vector $\mathbf{r}$ is $\mathbf{v} = \boldsymbol{\omega} \times \mathbf{r}$, where $\boldsymbol{\omega} = \omega \mathbf{u}$ is the angular velocity vector. Note that $|\mathbf{v}| = \omega |\mathbf{r}| \sin \theta$, where θ is the angle between $\mathbf{r}$ and $\boldsymbol{\omega}$. (b) Use the fact that $\mathbf{v} = \boldsymbol{\omega} \times \mathbf{r}$, established in part(a), to show that $\operatorname{curl} \mathbf{v} = 2\boldsymbol{\omega}$.

33. Consider an incompressible fluid flowing in space (no sources or sinks) with variable density $\delta(x, y, z, t)$ and velocity field $\mathbf{v}(x, y, z, t)$. Let B be a small ball with radius r and spherical surface S centered at the point (x_0, y_0, z_0). Then the amount of fluid within S at time t is

$$Q(t) = \iiint_B \delta \, dV,$$

and differentiation under the integral sign yields

$$Q'(t) = \iiint_B \frac{\partial \delta}{\partial t} \, dV.$$

(a) Consider fluid flow across S to get

$$Q'(t) = -\iint_S \delta \mathbf{v} \cdot \mathbf{n} \, dS,$$

where $\mathbf{n}$ is the outer unit normal vector to S. Now apply the divergence theorem to convert this into a volume integral. (b) Equate your two volume integrals for $Q'(t)$, apply the mean value theorem for integrals, and finally take limits as $r \to 0$ to obtain the **continuity equation**

$$\frac{\partial \delta}{\partial t} + \nabla \cdot (\delta \mathbf{v}) = 0.$$

APPENDICES

APPENDIX A: REAL NUMBERS AND INEQUALITIES

The **real numbers** are already familiar to you. They are just those numbers ordinarily used in most measurements. The mass, velocity, temperature, and charge of a body are measured with real numbers. Real numbers can be represented by **terminating** or **nonterminating** decimal expansions; in fact, every real number has a nonterminating decimal expansion because a terminating expansion can be padded with infinitely many zeros:

$$\frac{3}{8} = 0.375 = 0.375000000\ldots.$$

Any **repeating** decimal, such as

$$\frac{7}{22} = 0.31818181818\ldots,$$

represents a **rational** number, one that is the ratio of two integers. Conversely, every rational number is represented by a repeating decimal like the two displayed above. But the decimal expansion of an **irrational** number (a real number that is not rational), such as

$$\sqrt{2} = 1.414213562\ldots \quad \text{or} \quad \pi = 3.14159265358979\ldots,$$

is both nonterminating and nonrepeating.

The geometric interpretation of real numbers as points on the **real line** (or *real number line*) ***R*** should also be familiar to you. Each real number is represented by precisely one point of ***R***, and each point of ***R*** represents precisely one real number. By convention, the positive numbers lie to the right of zero and the negative numbers to the left, as in Fig. A.1.

FIGURE A.1 The real line ***R***.

The following properties of inequalities of real numbers are fundamental and often used:

If $a < b$ and $b < c$, then $a < c$.

If $a < b$, then $a + c < b + c$.

If $a < b$ and $c > 0$, then $ac < bc$.   **(1)**

If $a < b$ and $c < 0$, then $ac > bc$.

The last two statements mean that an inequality is preserved when its members are multiplied by a *positive* number but is *reversed* when they are multiplied by a *negative* number.

ABSOLUTE VALUE

The (nonnegative) distance along the real line between zero and the real number a is the **absolute value** of a, written $|a|$. Equivalently,

$$|a| = \begin{cases} a & \text{if } a \geq 0; \\ -a & \text{if } a < 0. \end{cases} \quad (2)$$

The notation $a \geq 0$ means that a is *either* greater than zero *or* equal to zero. Equation (2) implies that $|a| \geq 0$ for every real number a and that $|a| = 0$ if and only if $a = 0$.

EXAMPLE 1 As Fig. A.2 shows,

$$|4| = 4 \quad \text{and} \quad |-3| = 3.$$

Moreover, $|0| = 0$ and $|\sqrt{2} - 2| = 2 - \sqrt{2}$, the latter being true because $2 > \sqrt{2}$. Thus $\sqrt{2} - 2 < 0$, and hence

$$\left|\sqrt{2} - 2\right| = -(\sqrt{2} - 2) = 2 - \sqrt{2}. \quad \blacklozenge$$

FIGURE A.2 The absolute value of a real number is simply its distance from zero (Example 1).

The following properties of absolute values are frequently used:

$$\begin{aligned} |a| &= |-a| = \sqrt{a^2} \geq 0, \\ |ab| &= |a|\,|b|, \\ -|a| &\leq a \leq |a|, \\ \text{and} \quad |a| &< b \quad \text{if and only if} \quad -b < a < b. \end{aligned} \quad (3)$$

The **distance** between the real numbers a and b is defined to be $|a - b|$ (or $|b - a|$; there's no difference). This distance is simply the length of the line segment of the real line $\mathbf{R}$ with endpoints a and b (Fig. A.3).

The properties of inequalities and of absolute values in Eqs. (1) through (3) imply the following important theorem.

FIGURE A.3 The distance between a and b.

THEOREM 1 Triangle Inequality
For all real numbers a and b,

$$|a + b| \leq |a| + |b|. \quad (4)$$

PROOF There are several cases to consider, depending upon whether the two numbers a and b are positive or negative and which has the larger absolute value. If both are positive, then so is $a + b$; in this case,

$$|a + b| = a + b = |a| + |b|. \quad (5)$$

If $a > 0$ but $b < 0$ and $|b| < |a|$, then

$$0 < a + b < a,$$

so

$$|a + b| = a + b < a = |a| < |a| + |b|, \quad (6)$$

FIGURE A.4 The triangle inequality with $a > 0$, $b < 0$, and $|b| < |a|$.

as illustrated in Fig. A.4. The other cases are similar. In particular, we see that the triangle inequality is actually an equality [as in Eq. (5)] unless a and b have different signs, in which case it is a strict inequality [as in Eq. (6)]. ◂

INTERVALS

Suppose that S is a set (collection) of real numbers. It is common to describe S by the notation

$$S = \{x : \text{condition}\},$$

where the "condition" is true for those numbers x in S and false for those numbers x not in S. The most important sets of real numbers in calculus are *intervals*. If $a < b$, then the **open interval** (a, b) is defined to be the set

$$(a, b) = \{x : a < x < b\}$$

of real numbers, and the **closed interval** $[a, b]$ is

$$[a, b] = \{x : a \leqq x \leqq b\}.$$

Thus a closed interval contains its endpoints, whereas an open interval does not. We also use the **half-open intervals**

$$[a, b) = \{x : a \leqq x < b\} \quad \text{and} \quad (a, b] = \{x : a < x \leqq b\}.$$

Thus the open interval $(1, 3)$ is the set of those real numbers x such that $1 < x < 3$, the closed interval $[-1, 2]$ is the set of those real numbers x such that $-1 \leq x \leq 2$, and the half-open interval $(-1, 2]$ is the set of those real numbers x such that $-1 < x \leq 2$. In Fig. A.5 we show examples of such intervals as well as some **unbounded** intervals, which have forms such as

$$[a, +\infty) = \{x : x \geqq a\},$$
$$(-\infty, a] = \{x : x \leqq a\},$$
$$(a, +\infty) = \{x : x > a\},$$
$$\text{and} \quad (-\infty, a) = \{x : x < a\}.$$

FIGURE A.5 Some examples of intervals of real numbers.

The symbols $+\infty$ and $-\infty$, denoting "plus infinity" and "minus infinity," are merely notational conveniences and do *not* represent real numbers—the real line $\boldsymbol{R}$ does *not* have "endpoints at infinity." The use of these symbols is motivated by the brief and natural descriptions $[\pi, +\infty)$ and $(-\infty, 2)$ for the sets

$$\{x : x \geqq \pi\} \quad \text{and} \quad \{x : x < 2\}$$

of all real numbers x such that $x \geq \pi$ and $x < 2$, respectively.

INEQUALITIES

The set of solutions of an inequality involving a variable x is often an interval or a union of intervals, as in the next examples. The **solution set** of such an inequality is simply the set of all those real numbers x that satisfy the inequality.

EXAMPLE 2 Solve the inequality $2x - 1 < 4x + 5$.

Solution Using the properties of inequalities listed in (1), we proceed much as if we were solving an equation for x: We isolate x on one side of the inequality. Here we begin with

$$2x - 1 < 4x + 5$$

and it follows that

$$-1 < 2x + 5;$$
$$-6 < 2x;$$
$$-3 < x.$$

Hence the solution set is the unbounded interval $(-3, +\infty)$. ◆

EXAMPLE 3 Solve the inequality $-13 < 1 - 4x \leq 7$.

Solution We simplify the given inequality as follows:
$$-13 < 1 - 4x \leq 7;$$
$$-7 \leq 4x - 1 < 13;$$
$$-6 \leq 4x < 14;$$
$$-\tfrac{3}{2} \leq x < \tfrac{7}{2}.$$

Thus the solution set of the given inequality is the half-open interval $[-\tfrac{3}{2}, \tfrac{7}{2})$. ◆

EXAMPLE 4 Solve the inequality $|3 - 5x| < 2$.

Solution From the fourth property of absolute values in (3), we see that the given inequality is equivalent to
$$-2 < 3 - 5x < 2.$$
We now simplify as in the previous two examples:
$$-5 < -5x < -1;$$
$$\tfrac{1}{5} < x < 1.$$

Thus the solution set is the open interval $(\tfrac{1}{5}, 1)$. ◆

EXAMPLE 5 Solve the inequality
$$\frac{5}{|2x - 3|} < 1.$$

Solution It is usually best to begin by eliminating a denominator containing the unknown. Here we multiply each term by the *positive* quantity $|2x - 3|$ to obtain the equivalent inequality
$$|2x - 3| > 5.$$
It follows from the last property in (3) that this is so if and only if either
$$2x - 3 < -5 \quad \text{or} \quad 2x - 3 > 5.$$

The solutions of these *two* inequalities are the open intervals $(-\infty, -1)$ and $(4, +\infty)$, respectively. Hence the solution set of the original inequality consists of all those numbers x that lie in *either* of these two open intervals. ◆

The **union** of the two sets S and T is the set $S \cup T$ given by
$$S \cup T = \{x : \text{either } x \in S \text{ or } x \in T \text{ or both}\}.$$

Thus the solution set in Example 5 can be written in the form $(-\infty, -1) \cup (4, +\infty)$.

EXAMPLE 6 In accord with Boyle's law, the pressure p (in pounds per square inch) and volume V (in cubic inches) of a certain gas satisfy the condition $pV = 100$. Suppose that $50 \leq V \leq 150$. What is the range of possible values of the pressure p?

Solution If we substitute $V = 100/p$ in the given inequality $50 \leq V \leq 150$, we get
$$50 \leq \frac{100}{p} \leq 150.$$
It follows that *both*
$$50 \leq \frac{100}{p} \quad \text{and} \quad \frac{100}{p} \leq 150;$$
that is, that both
$$p \leq 2 \quad \text{and} \quad p \geq \tfrac{2}{3}.$$

Thus the pressure p must lie in the closed interval $[\tfrac{2}{3}, 2]$. ◆

The **intersection** of the two sets S and T is the set $S \cap T$ defined as follows:

$$S \cap T = \{x : \text{both } x \in S \text{ and } x \in T\}.$$

Thus the solution set in Example 6 is the set $(-\infty, 2] \cap [\frac{2}{3}, +\infty) = [\frac{2}{3}, 2]$.

APPENDIX A PROBLEMS

Simplify the expressions in Problems 1 through 12 by writing each without using absolute value symbols.

1. $|3 - 17|$
2. $|-3| + |17|$
3. $\left|-0.25 - \frac{1}{4}\right|$
4. $|5| - |-7|$
5. $|(-5)(4 - 9)|$
6. $\dfrac{|-6|}{|4| + |-2|}$
7. $|(-3)^3|$
8. $|3 - \sqrt{3}|$
9. $\left|\pi - \frac{22}{7}\right|$
10. $-|7 - 4|$
11. $|x - 3|$, given $x < 3$
12. $|x - 5| + |x - 10|$, given $|x - 7| < 1$

Solve the inequalities in Problems 13 through 31. Write each solution set in interval notation.

13. $2x - 7 < -3$
14. $1 - 4x > 2$
15. $3x - 4 \geq 17$
16. $2x + 5 \leq 9$
17. $2 - 3x < 7$
18. $6 - 5x > -9$
19. $-3 < 2x + 5 < 7$
20. $4 \leq 3x - 5 \leq 10$
21. $-6 \leq 5 - 2x < 2$
22. $3 < 1 - 5x < 7$
23. $|3 - 2x| < 5$
24. $|5x + 3| \leq 4$
25. $|1 - 3x| > 2$
26. $1 < |7x - 1| < 3$
27. $2 \leq |4 - 5x| \leq 4$
28. $\dfrac{1}{2x + 1} > 3$
29. $\dfrac{2}{7 - 3x} \leq -5$
30. $\dfrac{2}{|3x - 4|} < 1$
31. $\dfrac{1}{|1 - 5x|} \geq -\dfrac{1}{3}$

32. Solve the inequality $x^2 - x - 6 > 0$. [*Suggestion:* Conclude from the factorization $x^2 - x - 6 = (x - 3)(x + 2)$ that the quantities $x - 3$ and $x + 2$ are either both positive or both negative. Consider the two cases separately to deduce that the solution set is $(-\infty, -2) \cup (3, \infty)$.]

Use the method of Problem 32 to solve the inequalities in Problems 33 through 36.

33. $x^2 - 2x - 8 > 0$
34. $x^2 - 3x + 2 < 0$
35. $4x^2 - 8x + 3 \geq 0$
36. $2x \geq 15 - x^2$

37. In accord with Boyle's law, the pressure p (in pounds per square inch) and volume V (in cubic inches) of a certain gas satisfy the condition $pV = 800$. What is the range of possible values of the pressure, given $100 \leq V \leq 200$?

38. The relationship between the Fahrenheit temperature F and the Celsius temperature C is given by $F = 32 + \frac{9}{5}C$. If the temperature on a certain day ranged from a low of $70°F$ to a high of $90°F$, what was the range of the temperature in degrees Celsius?

39. An electrical circuit contains a battery supplying E volts in series with a resistance of R ohms, as shown in Fig. A.6. Then the current of I amperes that flows in the circuit satisfies Ohm's law, $E = IR$. If $E = 100$ and $25 < R < 50$, what is the range of possible values of I?

FIGURE A.6 A simple electric circuit.

40. The period T (in seconds) of a simple pendulum of length L (in feet) is given by $T = 2\pi\sqrt{L/32}$. If $3 < L < 4$, when is the range of possible values of T?

41. Use the properties of inequalities in (1) to show that the sum of two positive numbers is positive.

42. Use the properties of inequalities in (1) to show that the product of two positive numbers is positive.

43. Prove that the product of two negative numbers is positive and that the product of a positive number and a negative number is negative.

44. Suppose that $a < b$ and that a and b are either both positive or both negative. Prove that $1/a > 1/b$.

45. Apply the triangle inequality twice to show that

$$|a + b + c| \leq |a| + |b| + |c|$$

for arbitrary real numbers a, b, and c.

46. Write $a = (a - b) + b$ to deduce from the triangle inequality that

$$|a| - |b| \leq |a - b|$$

for arbitrary real numbers a and b.

47. Deduce from the definition in (2) that $|a| < b$ if and only if $-b < a < b$.

APPENDIX B: THE COORDINATE PLANE AND STRAIGHT LINES

Imagine the flat, featureless, two-dimensional plane of Euclid's geometry. Install a copy of the real number line **R**, with the line horizontal and the positive numbers to the right. Add another copy of **R** perpendicular to the first, with the two lines crossing where the number zero is located on each. The vertical line should have the positive numbers above the horizontal line, as in Fig. B.1; the negative numbers thus will be below it. The horizontal line is called the *x*-**axis** and the vertical line is called the *y*-**axis.**

With these added features, we call the plane the **coordinate plane,** because it's now possible to locate any point there by a pair of numbers, called the *coordinates of the point.* Here's how: If P is a point in the plane, draw perpendiculars from P to the coordinate axes, as shown in Fig. B.2. One perpendicular meets the *x*-axis at the *x*-**coordinate** (or **abscissa**) of P, labeled x_1 in Fig. B.2. The other meets the *y*-axis in the *y*-**coordinate** (or **ordinate**) y_1 of P. The pair of numbers (x_1, y_1), in that order, is called the **coordinate pair** for P, or simply the **coordinates** of P. To be concise, we speak of "the point $P(x_1, y_1)$."

FIGURE B.1 The coordinate plane.

FIGURE B.2 The point P has rectangular coordinates (x_1, y_1).

This coordinate system is called the **rectangular coordinate system,** or the **Cartesian coordinate system** (because its use was popularized, beginning in the 1630s, by the French mathematician and philosopher René Descartes [1596–1650]). The plane, thus coordinatized, is denoted by R^2 because two copies of **R** are used; it is known also as the **Cartesian plane.**

Rectangular coordinates are easy to use, because $P(x_1, y_1)$ and $Q(x_2, y_2)$ denote the same point if and only if $x_1 = x_2$ and $y_1 = y_2$. Thus when you know that P and Q are two different points, you may conclude that P and Q have different abscissas, different ordinates, or both.

The point of symmetry $(0, 0)$ where the coordinate axes meet is called the **origin.** All points on the *x*-axis have coordinates of the form $(x, 0)$. Although the *real number x* is not the same as the geometric point $(x, 0)$, there are situations in which it is useful to think of the two as the same. Similar remarks apply to points $(0, y)$ on the *y*-axis.

The concept of distance in the coordinate plane is based on the **Pythagorean theorem:** If ABC is a right triangle with its right angle at the point C, with hypotenuse of length c and the other two sides of lengths a and b (as in Fig. B.3), then

$$c^2 = a^2 + b^2. \tag{1}$$

The converse of the Pythagorean theorem is also true: If the three sides of a given triangle satisfy the Pythagorean relation in Eq. (1), then the angle opposite side c must be a right angle.

FIGURE B.3 The Pythagorean theorem.

The *distance* $d(P_1, P_2)$ between the points P_1 and P_2 is, by definition, the length of the straight-line segment joining P_1 and P_2. The following formula gives $d(P_1, P_2)$ in terms of the coordinates of the two points.

Distance Formula

The **distance** between the two points $P_1(x_1, y_1)$ and $P_2(x_2, y_2)$ is

$$d(P_1, P_2) = \sqrt{(x_2 - x_1)^2 + (y_2 - y_1)^2}. \tag{2}$$

PROOF If $x_1 \neq x_2$ and $y_1 \neq y_2$, then Eq. (2) follows from the Pythagorean theorem. Use the right triangle with vertices P_1, P_2, and $P_3(x_2, y_1)$ shown in Fig. B.4.

If $x_1 = x_2$, then P_1 and P_2 lie in a vertical line. In this case

$$d(P_1, P_2) = |y_1 - y_2| = \sqrt{(y_1 - y_2)^2}.$$

This agrees with Eq. (2) because $x_1 = x_2$. The remaining case ($y_1 = y_2$) is similar. ◄

APPENDIX B   A-7

FIGURE B.4 Use this triangle to deduce the distance formula.

FIGURE B.5 Is this a right triangle (Example 1)?

EXAMPLE 1 Show that the triangle PQR with vertices $P(1,0)$, $Q(5,4)$, and $R(-2,3)$ is a right triangle (Fig. B.5).

Solution The distance formula gives

$$a^2 = [d(P, Q)]^2 = (5-1)^2 + (4-0)^2 = 32,$$
$$b^2 = [d(P, R)]^2 = (-2-1)^2 + (3-0)^2 = 18, \text{ and}$$
$$c^2 = [d(Q, R)]^2 = (-2-5)^2 + (3-4)^2 = 50.$$

Because $a^2 + b^2 = c^2$, the *converse* of the Pythagorean theorem implies that RPQ is a right angle. (The right angle is at P because P is the vertex opposite the longest side, QR.) ◆

Another application of the distance formula is an expression for the coordinates of the midpoint M of the line segment $P_1 P_2$ with endpoints P_1 and P_2 (Fig. B.6). Recall from geometry that M is the one (and only) point of the line segment $P_1 P_2$ that is equally distant from P_1 and P_2. The following formula tells us that the coordinates of M are the *averages* of the corresponding coordinates of P_1 and P_2.

FIGURE B.6 The midpoint M.

Midpoint Formula

The **midpoint** of the line segment with endpoints $P_1(x_1, y_1)$ and $P_2(x_2, y_2)$ is the point $M(\bar{x}, \bar{y})$ with coordinates

$$\bar{x} = \tfrac{1}{2}(x_1 + x_2) \quad \text{and} \quad \bar{y} = \tfrac{1}{2}(y_1 + y_2). \tag{3}$$

PROOF If you substitute the coordinates of P_1, M, and P_2 in the distance formula, you find that $d(P_1, M) = d(P_2, M)$. All that remains is to show that M lies on the line segment $P_1 P_2$. We ask you to do this, and thus complete the proof, in Problem 31. ◄

STRAIGHT LINES AND SLOPE

We want to define the *slope* of a straight line, a measure of its rate of rise or fall from left to right. Given a nonvertical straight line L in the coordinate plane, choose two points $P_1(x_1, y_1)$ and $P_2(x_2, y_2)$ on L. Consider the **increments** Δx and Δy (read "delta x" and "delta y") in the x- and y-coordinates from P_1 to P_2. These are defined as follows:

$$\Delta x = x_2 - x_1 \quad \text{and} \quad \Delta y = y_2 - y_1. \tag{4}$$

Engineers (and others) call Δx the **run** from P_1 to P_2 and Δy the **rise** from P_1 to P_2, as in Fig. B.7. The **slope** m of the nonvertical line L is then defined to be the ratio of the rise to the run:

FIGURE B.7 The slope of a straight line.

$$m = \frac{\Delta y}{\Delta x} = \frac{y_2 - y_1}{x_2 - x_1}. \tag{5}$$

FIGURE B.8 The result of the slope computation does not depend on which two points of L are used.

This is also the definition of a line's slope in civil engineering (and elsewhere). In a surveying text you are likely to find the memory aid

$$\text{"slope} = \frac{\text{rise}}{\text{run}}\text{."}$$

Recall that corresponding sides of similar (that is, equal-angled) triangles have equal ratios. Hence, if $P_3(x_3, y_3)$ and $P_4(x_4, y_4)$ are two other points of L, then the similarity of the triangles in Fig. B.8 implies that

$$\frac{y_4 - y_3}{x_4 - x_3} = \frac{y_2 - y_1}{x_2 - x_1}.$$

Therefore, the slope m as defined in Eq. (5) does *not* depend on the particular choice of P_1 and P_2.

If the line L is horizontal, then $\Delta y = 0$. In this case Eq. (5) gives $m = 0$. If L is vertical, then $\Delta x = 0$, so the slope of L is *not defined*. Thus we have the following statements:

- Horizontal lines have slope zero.
- Vertical lines have no defined slope.

EXAMPLE 2

(a) The slope of the line through the points $(3, -2)$ and $(-1, 4)$ is

$$m = \frac{4 - (-2)}{(-1) - 3} = \frac{6}{-4} = -\frac{3}{2}.$$

(b) The points $(3, -2)$ and $(7, -2)$ have the same y-coordinate. Therefore, the line through them is horizontal and thus has slope zero.

(c) The points $(3, -2)$ and $(3, 4)$ have the same x-coordinate. Thus the line through them is vertical, and so its slope is undefined. ◆

EQUATIONS OF STRAIGHT LINES

Our immediate goal is to be able to write equations of given straight lines. That is, if L is a straight line in the coordinate plane, we wish to construct a mathematical sentence—an equation—about points (x, y) in the plane. We want this equation to be *true* when (x, y) is a point on L and *false* when (x, y) is not a point on L. Clearly this equation will involve x and y and some numerical constants determined by L itself. For us to write this equation, the concept of the slope of L is essential.

Suppose, then, that $P(x_0, y_0)$ is a fixed point on the nonvertical line L of slope m. Let $P(x, y)$ be any *other* point on L. We apply Eq. (5) with P and P_0 in place of P_1 and P_2 to find that

$$m = \frac{y - y_0}{x - x_0};$$

that is,
$$y - y_0 = m(x - x_0). \quad (6)$$

Because the point (x_0, y_0) satisfies Eq. (6), as does every other point of L, and because no other points of the plane can do so, Eq. (6) is indeed an equation for the given line L. In summary, we have the following result.

> ### The Point-Slope Equation
> The point $P(x, y)$ lies on the line with slope m through the fixed point (x_0, y_0) if and only if its coordinates satisfy the equation
> $$y - y_0 = m(x - x_0). \quad (6)$$

Equation (6) is called the **point-slope** equation of L, partly because the coordinates of the point (x_0, y_0) and the slope m of L may be read directly from this equation.

EXAMPLE 3 Write an equation for the straight line L through the points $P_1(1, -1)$ and $P_2(3, 5)$.

Solution The slope m of L may be obtained from the two given points:
$$m = \frac{5 - (-1)}{3 - 1} = 3.$$

Either P_1 or P_2 will do for the fixed point. We use $P_1(1, -1)$. Then, with the aid of Eq. (6), the point-slope equation of L is
$$y + 1 = 3(x - 1).$$

If simplification is appropriate, we may write $3x - y = 4$ or $y = 3x - 4$. ◆

Equation (6) can be written in the form
$$y = mx + b \quad (7)$$

where $b = y_0 - mx_0$ is a constant. Because $y = b$ when $x = 0$, the y-**intercept** of L is the point $(0, b)$ shown in Fig. B.9. Equations (6) and (7) are different forms of the equation of a straight line.

FIGURE B.9 The straight line with equation $y = mx + b$ has a slope m and y-intercept b.

> ### The Slope-Intercept Equation
> The point $P(x, y)$ lies on the line with slope m and y-intercept b if and only if the coordinates of P satisfy the equation
> $$y = mx + b. \quad (7)$$

Perhaps you noticed that both Eq. (6) and Eq. (7) can be written in the form of the general linear equation
$$Ax + By = C, \quad (8)$$

where A, B, and C are constants. Conversely, if $B \neq 0$, then Eq. (8) can be written in the form of Eq. (7) if we divide each term by B. Therefore Eq. (8) represents a straight line with its slope being the coefficient of x *after* solution of the equation for y. If $B = 0$, then Eq. (8) reduces to the equation of a vertical line: $x = K$ (where K is a constant). If $A = 0$ and $B \neq 0$, then Eq. (8) reduces to the equation of a horizontal line: $y = H$ (where H is a constant). Thus we see that Eq. (8) is always an equation of a straight line unless $A = B = 0$. Conversely, every straight line in the coordinate plane—even a vertical one—has an equation of the form in (8).

PARALLEL LINES AND PERPENDICULAR LINES

If the line L is not horizontal, then it must cross the x-axis. Then its **angle of inclination** is the angle ϕ measured counterclockwise from the positive x-axis to L. It follows that $0° < \phi < 180°$ if ϕ is measured in degrees. Figure B.10 makes it clear that this angle ϕ and the slope m of a nonvertical line are related by the equation

$$m = \frac{\Delta y}{\Delta x} = \tan \phi. \tag{9}$$

This is true because if ϕ is an acute angle in a right triangle, then $\tan \phi$ is the ratio of the leg opposite ϕ to the leg adjacent to ϕ.

Your intuition correctly assures you that two lines are parallel if and only if they have the same angle of inclination. So it follows from Eq. (9) that two parallel nonvertical lines have the same slope and that two lines with the same slope must be parallel. This completes the proof of Theorem 1.

FIGURE B.10 How is the angle of inclination ϕ related to the slope m?

THEOREM 1 Slopes of Parallel Lines
Two nonvertical lines are parallel if and only if they have the same slope.

Theorem 1 can also be proved without the use of the tangent function. The two lines shown in Fig. B.11 are parallel if and only if the two right triangles are similar, which is equivalent to the slopes of the lines being equal.

EXAMPLE 4 Write an equation of the line L that passes through the point $P(3, -2)$ and is parallel to the line L' with the equation $x + 2y = 6$.

Solution When we solve the equation of L' for y, we get $y = -\frac{1}{2}x + 3$. So L' has slope $m = -\frac{1}{2}$. Because L has the same slope, its point-slope equation is then

$$y + 2 = -\frac{1}{2}(x - 3);$$

if you prefer, $x + 2y = -1$. ◆

FIGURE B.11 Two parallel lines.

THEOREM 2 Slopes of Perpendicular Lines
Two lines L_1 and L_2 with slopes m_1 and m_2, respectively, are perpendicular if and only if

$$m_1 m_2 = -1. \tag{10}$$

That is, the slope of each is the *negative reciprocal* of the slope of the other.

PROOF If the two lines L_1 and L_2 are perpendicular and the slope of each exists, then neither is horizontal or vertical. Thus the situation resembles the one shown in Fig. B.12, in which the two lines meet at the point (x_0, y_0). It is easy to see that the two right triangles of the figure are similar, so equality of ratios of corresponding sides yields

$$m_2 = \frac{y_2 - y_0}{x_2 - x_0} = \frac{x_0 - x_1}{y_1 - y_0} = -\frac{x_1 - x_0}{y_1 - y_0} = -\frac{1}{m_1}.$$

Thus Eq. (10) holds if the two lines are perpendicular. This argument can be reversed to prove the converse—that the lines are perpendicular if $m_1 m_2 = -1$. ◂

FIGURE B.12 Illustration of the proof of Theorem 2.

EXAMPLE 5 Write an equation of the line L through the point $P(3, -2)$ that is perpendicular to the line L' with equation $x + 2y = 6$.

FIGURE B.13 Positive and negative slope; effect on ϕ.

Solution As we saw in Example 4, the slope of L' is $m' = -\frac{1}{2}$. By Theorem 2, the slope of L is $m = -1/m' = 2$. Thus L has the point-slope equation

$$y + 2 = 2(x - 3);$$

equivalently, $2x - y = 8$. ◆

You will find it helpful to remember that the *sign* of the slope m of the line L indicates whether L runs upward or downward as your eyes move from left to right. If $m > 0$, then the angle of inclination ϕ of L must be an acute angle, because $m = \tan \phi$. In this case, L "runs upward" to the right. If $m < 0$, then ϕ is obtuse, so L "runs downward." Figure B.13 shows the geometry behind these observations.

GRAPHICAL INVESTIGATION

Many mathematical problems require the simultaneous solution of a pair of linear equations of the form

$$a_1 x + b_1 y = c_1,$$
$$a_2 x + b_2 y = c_2. \tag{11}$$

The graph of these two equations consists of a pair of straight lines in the xy-plane. If these two lines are not parallel, then they must intersect at a single point whose coordinates (x_0, y_0) constitute the solution of (11). That is, $x = x_0$ and $y = y_0$ are the (only) values of x and y for which both equations in (11) are true.

In elementary algebra you studied various elimination and substitution methods for solving linear systems such as the one in (11). Example 6 illustrates an alternative *graphical method* that is sometimes useful when a graphing utility—a graphics calculator or a computer with a graphing program—is available.

FIGURE B.14 A calculator prepared to graph the lines in Eq. (12) (Example 6).

EXAMPLE 6 We want to investigate the simultaneous solution of the linear equations

$$10x - 8y = 17,$$
$$15x + 18y = 67. \tag{12}$$

With many graphics calculators, it is necessary first to solve each equation for y:

$$y = (17 - 10x)/(-8),$$
$$y = (67 - 15x)/18. \tag{13}$$

Figure B.14 shows a calculator prepared to graph the two lines represented by the equations in (12), and Fig. B.15 shows the result in the *viewing window* $-5 \leq x \leq 5$, $-5 \leq y \leq 5$.

FIGURE B.15 $-5 \leq x \leq 5$, $-5 \leq y \leq 5$ (Example 6).

Before proceeding, note that in Fig. B.15 the two lines *appear* to be perpendicular. But their slopes, $(-10)/(-8) = \frac{5}{4}$ and $(-15)/18 = -\frac{5}{6}$, are *not* negative

FIGURE B.16 $2 \leq x \leq 3$, $1 \leq y \leq 2$ (Example 6).

FIGURE B.17 $2.75 \leq x \leq 2.85$, $1.35 \leq y \leq 1.45$ (Example 6).

FIGURE B.18 $2.80 \leq x \leq 2.81$, $1.38 \leq y \leq 1.39$ (Example 6).

reciprocals of one another. It follows from Theorem 2 that the two linear are *not* perpendicular.

Figures B.16, B.17, and B.18 show successive magnifications produced by "zooming in" on the point of intersection of the two lines. The dashed-line box in each figure is the viewing window for the next figure. Looking at Fig. B.18, we see that the intersection point is given by the approximations

$$x \approx 2.807, \qquad y \approx 1.383, \tag{14}$$

rounded to three decimal places.

The result in (14) can be checked by equating the right-hand sides in (13) and solving for x. This gives $x = 421/150 \approx 2.8067$. Substituting the exact value of x into either equation in (13) then yields $y = 83/60 \approx 1.3833$.

The graphical method illustrated by Example 6 typically produces approximate solutions that are sufficiently accurate for practical purposes. But the method is especially useful for *nonlinear* equations, for which exact algebraic techniques of solution may not be available. ◆

APPENDIX B PROBLEMS

Three points A, B, and C lie on a single straight line if and only if the slope of AB is equal to the slope of BC. In Problems 1 through 4, plot the three given points and then determine whether or not they lie on a single line.

1. $A(-1, -2)$, $B(2, 1)$, $C(4, 3)$
2. $A(-2, 5)$, $B(2, 3)$, $C(8, 0)$
3. $A(-1, 6)$, $B(1, 2)$, $C(4, -2)$
4. $A(-3, 2)$, $B(1, 6)$, $C(8, 14)$

In Problems 5 and 6, use the concept of slope to show that the four points given are the vertices of a parallelogram.

5. $A(-1, 3)$, $B(5, 0)$, $C(7, 4)$, $D(1, 7)$
6. $A(7, -1)$, $B(-2, 2)$, $C(1, 4)$, $D(10, 1)$

In Problems 7 and 8, show that the three given points are the vertices of a right triangle.

7. $A(-2, -1)$, $B(2, 7)$, $C(4, -4)$
8. $A(6, -1)$, $B(2, 3)$, $C(-3, -2)$

In Problems 9 through 13, find the slope m and y-intercept b of the line with the given equation. Then sketch the line.

9. $2x = 3y$
10. $x + y = 1$
11. $2x - y + 3 = 0$
12. $3x + 4y = 6$
13. $2x = 3 - 5y$

In Problems 14 through 23, write an equation of the straight line L described.

14. L is vertical and has x-intercept 7.
15. L is horizontal and passes through $(3, -5)$.
16. L has x-intercept 2 and y-intercept -3.
17. L passes through $(2, -3)$ and $(5, 3)$.
18. L passes through $(-1, -4)$ and has slope $\frac{1}{2}$.
19. L passes through $(4, 2)$ and has angle of inclination $135°$.
20. L has slope 6 and y-intercept 7.
21. L passes through $(1, 5)$ and is parallel to the line with equation $2x + y = 10$.
22. L passes through $(-2, 4)$ and is perpendicular to the line with equation $x + 2y = 17$.
23. L is the perpendicular bisector of the line segment that has endpoints $(-1, 2)$ and $(3, 10)$.
24. Find the perpendicular distance from the point $(2, 1)$ to the line with equation $y = x + 1$.
25. Find the perpendicular distance between the parallel lines $y = 5x + 1$ and $y = 5x + 9$.
26. The points $A(-1, 6)$, $B(0, 0)$, and $C(3, 1)$ are three consecutive vertices of a parallelogram. What are the coordinates

of the fourth vertex? (What happens if the word *consecutive* is omitted?)

27. Prove that the diagonals of the parallelogram of Problem 26 bisect each other.

28. Show that the points $A(-1, 2)$, $B(3, -1)$, $C(6, 3)$, and $D(2, 6)$ are the vertices of a *rhombus*—a parallelogram with all four sides having the same length. Then prove that the diagonals of this rhombus are perpendicular to each other.

29. The points $A(2, 1)$, $B(3, 5)$, and $C(7, 3)$ are the vertices of a triangle. Prove that the line joining the midpoints of AB and BC is parallel to AC.

30. A **median** of a triangle is a line joining a vertex to the midpoint of the opposite side. Prove that the medians of the triangle of Problem 29 intersect in a single point.

31. Complete the proof of the midpoint formula in Eq. (3). It is necessary to show that the point M lies on the segment $P_1 P_2$. One way to do this is to show that the slope of MP_1 is equal to the slope of MP_2.

32. Let $P(x_0, y_0)$ be a point of the circle with center $C(0, 0)$ and radius r. Recall that the line tangent to the circle at the point P is perpendicular to the radius CP. Prove that the equation of this tangent line is $x_0 x + y_0 y = r^2$.

33. The Fahrenheit temperature F and the absolute temperature K satisfy a linear equation. Moreover, $K = 273.16$ when $F = 32$, and $K = 373.16$ when $F = 212$. Express K in terms of F. What is the value of F when $K = 0$?

34. The length L (in centimeters) of a copper rod is a linear function of its Celsius temperature C. If $L = 124.942$ when $C = 20$ and $L = 125.134$ when $C = 110$, express L in terms of C.

35. The owner of a grocery store finds that she can sell 980 gal of milk each week at \$1.69/gal and 1220 gal of milk each week at \$1.49/gal. Assume a linear relationship between price and sales. How many gallons would she then expect to sell each week at \$1.56/gal?

36. Figure B.19 shows the graphs of the equations

$$17x - 10y = 57,$$
$$25x - 15y = 17.$$

FIGURE B.19 The lines of Problem 36.

Are these two lines parallel? If not, find their point of intersection. If you have a graphing utility, find the solution by graphical approximation as well as by exact algebraic methods.

In Problems 37 through 46, use a graphics calculator or computer to approximate graphically (with three digits to the right of the decimal correct or correctly rounded) the solution of the given linear equation. Then check your approximate solution by solving the system by an exact algebraic method.

37. $2x + 3y = 5$
    $2x + 5y = 12$

38. $6x + 4y = 5$
    $8x - 6y = 13$

39. $3x + 3y = 17$
    $3x + 5y = 16$

40. $2x + 3y = 17$
    $2x + 5y = 20$

41. $4x + 3y = 17$
    $5x + 5y = 21$

42. $4x + 3y = 15$
    $5x + 5y = 29$

43. $5x + 6y = 16$
    $7x + 10y = 29$

44. $5x + 11y = 21$
    $4x + 10y = 19$

45. $6x + 6y = 31$
    $9x + 11y = 37$

46. $7x + 6y = 31$
    $11x + 11y = 47$

47. Justify the phrase "no other point of the plane can do so" that follows the first appearance of Eq. (6).

48. The discussion of the linear equation $Ax + By = C$ in Eq. (8) does not include a description of the graph of this equation if $A = B = 0$. What is the graph in this case?

APPENDIX C: REVIEW OF TRIGONOMETRY

In elementary trigonometry, the six basic trigonometric functions of an acute angle θ in a right triangle are defined as ratios between pairs of sides of the triangle. As in Fig. C.1, where "adj" stands for "adjacent," "opp" for "opposite," and "hyp" for "hypotenuse,"

$$\cos \theta = \frac{\text{adj}}{\text{hyp}}, \quad \sin \theta = \frac{\text{opp}}{\text{hyp}}, \quad \tan \theta = \frac{\text{opp}}{\text{adj}}, \quad (1)$$

$$\sec \theta = \frac{\text{hyp}}{\text{adj}}, \quad \csc \theta = \frac{\text{hyp}}{\text{opp}}, \quad \cot \theta = \frac{\text{adj}}{\text{opp}}.$$

FIGURE C.1 The sides and angle θ of a right triangle.

We generalize these definitions to *directed* angles of arbitrary size in the following way. Suppose that the initial side of the angle θ is the positive x-axis, so its vertex is at the origin. The angle is **directed** if a direction of rotation from its initial side to its terminal side is specified. We call θ a **positive angle** if this rotation is counterclockwise and a **negative angle** if it is clockwise.

Let $P(x, y)$ be the point at which the terminal side of θ intersects the *unit* circle $x^2 + y^2 = 1$. Then we define

$$\cos\theta = x, \qquad \sin\theta = y, \qquad \tan\theta = \frac{y}{x},$$
$$\sec\theta = \frac{1}{x}, \qquad \csc\theta = \frac{1}{y}, \qquad \cot\theta = \frac{x}{y}. \tag{2}$$

We assume that $x \neq 0$ in the case of $\tan\theta$ and $\sec\theta$ and that $y \neq 0$ in the case of $\cot\theta$ and $\csc\theta$. If the angle θ is positive and acute, then it is clear from Fig. C.2 that the definitions in (2) agree with the right triangle definitions in (1) in terms of the coordinates of P. A glance at the figure also shows which of the functions are positive for angles in each of the four quadrants. Figure C.3 summarizes this information.

Here we discuss primarily the two most basic trigonometric functions, the sine and the cosine. From (2) we see immediately that the other four trigonometric functions are defined in terms of $\sin\theta$ and $\cos\theta$ by

$$\tan\theta = \frac{\sin\theta}{\cos\theta}, \qquad \sec\theta = \frac{1}{\cos\theta},$$
$$\cot\theta = \frac{\cos\theta}{\sin\theta}, \qquad \csc\theta = \frac{1}{\sin\theta}. \tag{3}$$

Next, we compare the angles θ and $-\theta$ in Fig. C.4. We see that

$$\cos(-\theta) = \cos\theta \quad \text{and} \quad \sin(-\theta) = -\sin\theta. \tag{4}$$

Because $x = \cos\theta$ and $y = \sin\theta$ in (2), the equation $x^2 + y^2 = 1$ of the unit circle translates immediately into the **fundamental identity of trigonometry,**

$$\cos^2\theta + \sin^2\theta = 1. \tag{5}$$

Dividing each term of this fundamental identity by $\cos^2\theta$ gives the identity

$$1 + \tan^2\theta = \sec^2\theta. \tag{5'}$$

Similarly, dividing each term in Eq. (5) by $\sin^2\theta$ yields the identity

$$1 + \cot^2\theta = \csc^2\theta. \tag{5''}$$

(See Problem 9 of this appendix.)

In Problems 41 and 42 we outline derivations of the **addition formulas**

$$\sin(\alpha + \beta) = \sin\alpha \cos\beta + \cos\alpha \sin\beta, \tag{6}$$
$$\cos(\alpha + \beta) = \cos\alpha \cos\beta - \sin\alpha \sin\beta. \tag{7}$$

With $\alpha = \theta = \beta$ in Eqs. (6) and (7), we get the **double-angle formulas**

$$\sin 2\theta = 2\sin\theta \cos\theta, \tag{8}$$
$$\cos 2\theta = \cos^2\theta - \sin^2\theta \tag{9}$$
$$= 2\cos^2\theta - 1 \tag{9a}$$
$$= 1 - 2\sin^2\theta, \tag{9b}$$

where Eqs. (9a) and (9b) are obtained from Eq. (9) by use of the fundamental identity in Eq. (5).

If we solve Eq. (9a) for $\cos^2\theta$ and Eq. (9b) for $\sin^2\theta$, we get the **half-angle formulas**

$$\cos^2\theta = \tfrac{1}{2}(1 + \cos 2\theta), \tag{10}$$
$$\sin^2\theta = \tfrac{1}{2}(1 - \cos 2\theta). \tag{11}$$

Equations (10) and (11) are especially important in integral calculus.

FIGURE C.2 Using the unit circle to define the trigonometric functions.

FIGURE C.3 The signs of the trigonometric functions.

FIGURE C.4 The effect of replacing θ with $-\theta$ in the sine and cosine functions.

RADIAN MEASURE

FIGURE C.5 The radian measure of an angle.

Radians	Degrees
0	0
$\pi/6$	30
$\pi/4$	45
$\pi/3$	60
$\pi/2$	90
$2\pi/3$	120
$3\pi/4$	135
$5\pi/6$	150
π	180
$3\pi/2$	270
2π	360
4π	720

FIGURE C.6 Some radian-degree conversions.

FIGURE C.7 The area of a sector and arc length of a circular arc.

In elementary mathematics, angles frequently are measured in *degrees*, with 360° in one complete revolution. In calculus it is more convenient—and often essential—to measure angles in *radians*. The **radian measure** of an angle is the length of the arc it subtends in (that is, the arc it cuts out of) the unit circle when the vertex of the angle is at the center of the circle (Fig. C.5).

Recall that the area A and circumference C of a circle of radius r are given by the formulas

$$A = \pi r^2 \quad \text{and} \quad C = 2\pi r,$$

where the irrational number π is approximately 3.14159. Because the circumference of the unit circle is 2π and its central angle is 360°, it follows that

$$2\pi \text{ rad} = 360°; \qquad 180° = \pi \text{ rad} \approx 3.14159 \text{ rad}. \tag{12}$$

Using Eq. (12) we can easily convert back and forth between radians and degrees:

$$1 \text{ rad} = \frac{180°}{\pi} \approx 57° \, 17' \, 44.8'', \tag{12a}$$

$$1° = \frac{\pi}{180} \text{ rad} \approx 0.01745 \text{ rad}. \tag{12b}$$

Figure C.6 shows radian-degree conversions for some common angles.

Now consider an angle of θ radians at the center of a circle of radius r (Fig. C.7). Denote by s the length of the arc subtended by θ; denote by A the area of the sector of the circle bounded by this angle. Then the proportions

$$\frac{s}{2\pi r} = \frac{A}{\pi r^2} = \frac{\theta}{2\pi}$$

give the formulas

$$s = r\theta \qquad (\theta \text{ in radians}) \tag{13}$$

and

$$A = \tfrac{1}{2} r^2 \theta \qquad (\theta \text{ in radians}). \tag{14}$$

The definitions in (2) refer to trigonometric functions of *angles* rather than trigonometric functions of *numbers*. Suppose that t is a real number. Then the number $\sin t$ is, *by definition*, the sine of an angle of t radians—recall that a positive angle is directed counterclockwise from the positive x-axis, whereas a negative angle is directed clockwise. Briefly, $\sin t$ is the sine of an angle of t *radians*. The other trigonometric functions of the number t have similar definitions. Hence, when we write $\sin t$, $\cos t$, and so on, with t a real number, it is *always* in reference to an angle to t *radians*.

When we need to refer to the sine of an angle of t *degrees*, we will henceforth write $\sin t°$. The point is that $\sin t$ and $\sin t°$ are quite different functions of the variable t. For example, you would get

$$\sin 1° \approx 0.0175 \quad \text{and} \quad \sin 30° = 0.5$$

on a calculator set in degree mode. But in radian mode, a calculator would give

$$\sin 1 \approx 0.8415 \quad \text{and} \quad \sin 30 \approx -0.9880.$$

The relationship between the functions $\sin t$ and $\sin t°$ is

$$\sin t° = \sin\left(\frac{\pi t}{180}\right). \tag{15}$$

The distinction extends even to programming languages. In FORTRAN, the function `SIN` is the radian sine function, and you must write $\sin t°$ in the form `SIND(T)`. In BASIC you must write `SIN(Pi*T/180)` to get the correct value of the sine of an angle of t degrees.

FIGURE C.8 Periodicity of the sine and cosine functions.

An angle of 2π rad corresponds to one revolution around the unit circle. This implies that the sine and cosine functions have **period** 2π, meaning that

$$\sin(t + 2\pi) = \sin t,$$
$$\cos(t + 2\pi) = \cos t. \tag{16}$$

It follows from the equations in (16) that

$$\sin(t + 2n\pi) = \sin t \quad \text{and} \quad \cos(t + 2n\pi) = \cos t \tag{17}$$

for every integer n. This periodicity of the sine and cosine functions is evident in their graphs (Fig. C.8). From the equations in (3), the other four trigonometric functions also must be periodic, as their graphs in Figs. C.9 and C.10 show.

FIGURE C.9 The graphs of (a) the tangent function and (b) the cotangent function.

FIGURE C.10 The graphs of (a) the secant function and (b) the cosecant function.

We see from the equations in (2) that

$$\sin 0 = 0, \quad \sin \frac{\pi}{2} = 1, \quad \sin \pi = 0,$$
$$\cos 0 = 1, \quad \cos \frac{\pi}{2} = 0, \quad \cos \pi = -1. \tag{18}$$

The trigonometric functions of $\pi/6$, $\pi/4$, and $\pi/3$ (the radian equivalents of $30°$, $45°$, and $60°$, respectively) are easy to read from the well-known triangles of Fig. C.11. For instance,

$$\sin \frac{\pi}{6} = \cos \frac{\pi}{3} = \frac{1}{2} = \frac{\sqrt{1}}{2},$$

$$\sin \frac{\pi}{4} = \cos \frac{\pi}{4} = \frac{1}{\sqrt{2}} = \frac{\sqrt{2}}{2}, \quad \text{and} \tag{19}$$

$$\sin \frac{\pi}{3} = \cos \frac{\pi}{6} = \frac{\sqrt{3}}{2}.$$

FIGURE C.11 Familiar right triangles.

To find the values of trigonometric functions of angles larger than $\pi/2$, we can use their periodicity and the identities

$$\sin(\pi \pm \theta) = \mp \sin\theta,$$
$$\cos(\pi \pm \theta) = -\cos\theta \quad \text{and} \qquad (20)$$
$$\tan(\pi \pm \theta) = \pm\tan\theta$$

(Problems 38, 39, and 40) as well as similar identities for the cosecant, secant, and cotangent functions.

EXAMPLE 1

$$\sin\frac{5\pi}{4} = \sin\left(\pi + \frac{\pi}{4}\right) = -\sin\frac{\pi}{4} = -\frac{\sqrt{2}}{2};$$

$$\cos\frac{2\pi}{3} = \cos\left(\pi - \frac{\pi}{3}\right) = -\cos\frac{\pi}{3} = -\frac{1}{2};$$

$$\tan\frac{2\pi}{4} = \tan\left(\pi - \frac{\pi}{4}\right) = -\tan\frac{\pi}{4} = -1;$$

$$\sin\frac{7\pi}{6} = \sin\left(\pi + \frac{\pi}{6}\right) - \sin\frac{\pi}{6} = -\frac{1}{2};$$

$$\cos\frac{5\pi}{3} = \cos\left(2\pi - \frac{\pi}{3}\right) = \cos\left(-\frac{\pi}{3}\right) = \cos\frac{\pi}{3} = \frac{1}{2};$$

$$\sin\frac{17\pi}{6} = \sin\left(2\pi + \frac{5\pi}{6}\right) = \sin\frac{5\pi}{6}$$
$$= \sin\left(\pi - \frac{\pi}{6}\right) = \sin\frac{\pi}{6} = \frac{1}{2}.$$

♦

EXAMPLE 2 Find the solutions (if any) of the equation

$$\sin^2 x - 3\cos^2 x + 2 = 0$$

that lie in the interval $[0, \pi]$.

Solution Using the fundamental identity in Eq. (5), we substitute $\cos^2 x = 1 - \sin^2 x$ into the given equation to obtain

$$\sin^2 x - 3(1 - \sin^2 x) + 2 = 0;$$
$$4\sin^2 x - 1 = 0;$$
$$\sin x = \pm\tfrac{1}{2}.$$

Because $\sin x \geq 0$ for x in $[0, \pi]$, $\sin x = -\tfrac{1}{2}$ is impossible. But $\sin x = \tfrac{1}{2}$ for $x = \pi/6$ and for $x = \pi - \pi/6 = 5\pi/6$. These are the solutions of the given equation that lie in $[0, \pi]$.

♦

APPENDIX C PROBLEMS

Express in radian measure the angles in Problems 1 through 5.

1. 40°
2. −270°
3. 315°
4. 210°
5. −150°

In Problems 6 through 10, express in degrees the angles given in radian measure.

6. $\dfrac{\pi}{10}$
7. $\dfrac{2\pi}{5}$
8. 3π
9. $\dfrac{15\pi}{4}$
10. $\dfrac{23\pi}{60}$

In Problems 11 through 14, evaluate the six trigonometric functions of x at the given values.

11. $x = -\dfrac{\pi}{3}$
12. $x = \dfrac{3\pi}{4}$

13. $x = \dfrac{7\pi}{6}$ **14.** $x = \dfrac{5\pi}{3}$

Find all solutions x of each equation in Problems 15 through 23.

15. $\sin x = 0$ **16.** $\sin x = 1$
17. $\sin x = -1$ **18.** $\cos x = 0$
19. $\cos x = 1$ **20.** $\cos x = -1$
21. $\tan x = 0$ **22.** $\tan x = 1$
23. $\tan x = -1$

24. Suppose that $\tan x = \tfrac{3}{4}$ and that $\sin x < 0$. Find the values of the other five trigonometric functions of x.

25. Suppose that $\csc x = -\tfrac{5}{3}$ and that $\cos x > 0$. Find the values of the other five trigonometric functions of x.

Deduce the identities in Problems 26 and 27 from the fundamental identity

$$\cos^2 \theta + \sin^2 \theta = 1$$

and from the definitions of the other four trigonometric functions.

26. $1 + \tan^2 \theta = \sec^2 \theta$ **27.** $1 + \cot^2 \theta = \csc^2 \theta$

28. Deduce from the addition formulas for the sine and cosine the addition formula for the tangent:

$$\tan(x + y) = \frac{\tan x + \tan y}{1 - \tan x \tan y}.$$

In Problems 29 through 36, use the method of Example 1 to find the indicated values.

29. $\sin \dfrac{5\pi}{6}$ **30.** $\cos \dfrac{7\pi}{6}$
31. $\sin \dfrac{11\pi}{6}$ **32.** $\cos \dfrac{19\pi}{6}$
33. $\sin \dfrac{2\pi}{3}$ **34.** $\cos \dfrac{4\pi}{3}$
35. $\sin \dfrac{5\pi}{3}$ **36.** $\cos \dfrac{10\pi}{3}$

37. Apply the addition formula for the sine, cosine, and tangent functions (the latter from Problem 28) to show that if $0 < \theta < \pi/2$, then

(a) $\cos\left(\dfrac{\pi}{2} - \theta\right) = \sin \theta$;

(b) $\sin\left(\dfrac{\pi}{2} - \theta\right) = \cos \theta$;

(c) $\cot\left(\dfrac{\pi}{2} - \theta\right) = \tan \theta$.

The prefix *co-* is an abbreviation for the adjective *complementary*, which describes two angles whose sum is $\pi/2$. For example, $\pi/6$ and $\pi/3$ are complementary angles, so (a) implies that $\cos \pi/6 = \sin \pi/3$.

Suppose that $0 < \theta < \pi/2$. Derive the identities in Problems 38 through 40.

38. $\sin(\pi \pm \theta) = \mp \sin \theta$
39. $\cos(\pi \pm \theta) = -\cos \theta$
40. $\tan(\pi \pm \theta) = \pm \tan \theta$

41. The points $A(\cos \theta, -\sin \theta)$, $B(1, 0)$, $C(\cos \phi, \sin \phi)$, and $D(\cos(\theta + \phi), \sin(\theta + \phi))$ are shown in Fig. C.12; all are points on the unit circle. Deduce from the fact that the line segments AC and BD have the same length (because they are subtended by the same central angle $\theta + \phi$) that

$$\cos(\theta + \phi) = \cos \theta \cos \phi - \sin \theta \sin \phi.$$

FIGURE C.12 Deriving the cosine addition formula (Problem 41).

42. (a) Use the triangles shown in Fig. C.13 to deduce that

$$\sin\left(\theta + \frac{\pi}{2}\right) = \cos \theta \quad \text{and} \quad \cos\left(\theta + \frac{\pi}{2}\right) = -\sin \theta.$$

(b) Use the results of Problem 41 and part (a) to derive the addition formula for the sine function.

FIGURE C.13 Deriving the identities of Problem 42.

In Problems 43 through 48, find all solutions of the given equation that lie in the interval $[0, \pi]$.

43. $3 \sin^2 x - \cos^2 x = 2$ **44.** $\sin^2 x = \cos^2 x$
45. $2 \cos^2 x + 3 \sin^2 x = 3$ **46.** $2 \sin^2 x + \cos x = 2$
47. $8 \sin^2 x \cos^2 x = 1$ **48.** $\cos 2\theta - 3 \cos \theta = -2$

APPENDIX D: PROOFS OF THE LIMIT LAWS

Recall the definition of the limit:

$$\lim_{x \to a} F(x) = L$$

provided that, given $\epsilon > 0$, there exists a number $\delta > 0$ such that

$$0 < |x - a| < \delta \quad \text{implies that} \quad |F(x) - L| < \epsilon. \tag{1}$$

Note that the number ϵ comes *first*. Then a value of $\delta > 0$ must be found so that the implication in (1) holds. To prove that $F(x) \to L$ as $x \to a$, you must, in effect, be able to stop the next person you see and ask him or her to pick a positive number ϵ at random. Then you must *always* be ready to respond with a positive number δ. This number δ must have the property that the implication in (1) holds for your number δ and the given number ϵ. The **only** restriction on x is that

$$0 < |x - a| < \delta,$$

as given in (1).

To do all this, you will ordinarily need to give an explicit method—a recipe or formula—for producing a value of δ that works for each value of ϵ. As Examples 1 through 3 show, the method will depend on the particular function F under study as well as the values of a and L.

EXAMPLE 1 Prove that $\lim_{x \to 3} (2x - 1) = 5$.

Solution Given $\epsilon > 0$, we must find $\delta > 0$ such that

$$|(2x - 1) - 5| < \epsilon \quad \text{if} \quad 0 < |x - 3| < \delta.$$

Now

$$|(2x - 1) - 5| = |2x - 6| = 2|x - 3|,$$

so

$$0 < |x - 3| < \frac{\epsilon}{2} \quad \text{implies that} \quad |(2x - 1) - 5| < 2 \cdot \frac{\epsilon}{2} = \epsilon.$$

Hence, given $\epsilon > 0$, it suffices to choose $\delta = \epsilon/2$. This illustrates the observation that the required number δ is generally a function of the given number ϵ. ◆

EXAMPLE 2 Prove that $\lim_{x \to 2} (3x^2 + 5) = 17$.

Solution Given $\epsilon > 0$, we must find $\delta > 0$ such that

$$0 < |x - 2| < \delta \quad \text{implies that} \quad |(3x^2 + 5) - 17| < \epsilon.$$

Now

$$|(3x^2 + 5) - 17| = |3x^2 - 12| = 3 \cdot |x + 2| \cdot |x - 2|.$$

Our problem, therefore, is to show that $|x + 2| \cdot |x - 2|$ can be made as small as we please by choosing $x - 2$ sufficiently small. The idea is that $|x + 2|$ cannot be too large if $|x - 2|$ is fairly small. For example, if $|x - 2| < 1$, then

$$|x + 2| = |(x - 2) + 4| \leq |x - 2| + 4 < 5.$$

Therefore,

$$0 < |x - 2| < 1 \quad \text{implies that} \quad |(3x^2 + 5) - 17| < 15 \cdot |x - 2|.$$

Consequently, let us choose δ to be the minimum of the two numbers 1 and $\epsilon/15$. Then

$$0 < |x - 2| < \delta \quad \text{implies that} \quad |(3x^2 + 5) - 17| < 15 \cdot \frac{\epsilon}{15} = \epsilon,$$

as desired. ◆

EXAMPLE 3 Prove that

$$\lim_{x \to a} \frac{1}{x} = \frac{1}{a} \quad \text{if} \quad a \neq 0.$$

Solution For simplicity, we will consider only the case in which $a > 0$ (the case $a < 0$ is similar).

Suppose that $\epsilon > 0$ is given. We must find a number δ such that

$$0 < |x - a| < \delta \quad \text{implies that} \quad \left|\frac{1}{x} - \frac{1}{a}\right| < \epsilon.$$

Now

$$\left|\frac{1}{x} - \frac{1}{a}\right| = \left|\frac{a - x}{ax}\right| = \frac{|x - a|}{a|x|}.$$

The idea is that $1/|x|$ cannot be too large if $|x - a|$ is fairly small. For example, if $|x - a| < a/2$, then $a/2 < x < 3a/2$. Therefore,

$$|x| > \frac{a}{2}, \quad \text{so} \quad \frac{1}{|x|} < \frac{2}{a}.$$

In this case it would follow that

$$\left|\frac{1}{x} - \frac{1}{a}\right| < \frac{2}{a^2} \cdot |x - a|$$

if $|x - a| < a/2$. Thus, if we choose δ to be the minimum of the two numbers $a/2$ and $a^2\epsilon/2$, then

$$0 < |x - a| < \delta \quad \text{implies that} \quad \left|\frac{1}{x} - \frac{1}{a}\right| < \frac{2}{a^2} \cdot \frac{a^2\epsilon}{2} = \epsilon.$$

Therefore

$$\lim_{x \to a} \frac{1}{x} = \frac{1}{a} \quad \text{if} \quad a \neq 0,$$

as desired. ◆

We are now ready to give proofs of the limit laws stated in Section 2.2.

Constant Law

If $f(x) \equiv C$, a constant, then

$$\lim_{x \to a} f(x) = \lim_{x \to a} C = C.$$

PROOF Because $|C - C| = 0$, we merely choose $\delta = 1$, regardless of the previously given value of $\epsilon > 0$. Then, if $0 < |x - a| < \delta$, it is automatic that $|C - C| < \epsilon$. ◂

Addition Law

If $\lim_{x \to a} F(x) = L$ and $\lim_{x \to a} G(x) = M$, then

$$\lim_{x \to a} [F(x) + G(x)] = L + M.$$

PROOF Let $\epsilon > 0$ be given. Because L is the limit of $F(x)$ as $x \to a$, there exists a number $\delta_1 > 0$ such that

$$0 < |x - a| < \delta_1 \quad \text{implies that} \quad |F(x) - L| < \frac{\epsilon}{2}.$$

Because M is the limit of $G(x)$ as $x \to a$, there exists a number $\delta_2 > 0$ such that

$$0 < |x - a| < \delta_2 \quad \text{implies that} \quad |G(x) - M| < \frac{\epsilon}{2}.$$

Let $\delta = \min\{\delta_1, \delta_2\}$. Then $0 < |x - a| < \delta$ implies that

$$|(F(x) + G(x)) - (L + M)| \leq |F(x) - L| + |G(x) - M| < \frac{\epsilon}{2} + \frac{\epsilon}{2} = \epsilon.$$

Therefore

$$\lim_{x \to a} [F(x) + G(x)] = L + M,$$

as desired. ◂

Product Law

If $\lim_{x \to a} F(x) = L$ and $\lim_{x \to a} G(x) = M$, then

$$\lim_{x \to a} [F(x) \cdot G(x)] = L \cdot M.$$

PROOF Given $\epsilon > 0$, we must find a number $\delta > 0$ such that

$$0 < |x - a| < \delta \quad \text{implies that} \quad |F(x) \cdot G(x) - L \cdot M| < \epsilon.$$

But first, the triangle inequality gives the result

$$|F(x) \cdot G(x) - L \cdot M| = |F(x) \cdot G(x) - L \cdot G(x) + L \cdot G(x) - L \cdot M|$$
$$\leq |G(x)| \cdot |F(x) - L| + |L| \cdot |G(x) - M|. \quad (2)$$

Because $\lim_{x \to a} F(x) = L$, there exists $\delta_1 > 0$ such that

$$0 < |x - a| < \delta_1 \quad \text{implies that} \quad |F(x) - L| < \frac{\epsilon}{2(|M| + 1)}. \quad (3)$$

And because $\lim_{x \to a} G(x) = M$, there exists $\delta_2 > 0$ such that

$$0 < |x - a| < \delta_2 \quad \text{implies that} \quad |G(x) - M| < \frac{\epsilon}{2(|L| + 1)}. \quad (4)$$

Moreover, there is a *third* number $\delta_3 > 0$ such that

$$0 < |x - a| < \delta_3 \quad \text{implies that} \quad |G(x) - M| < 1,$$

which in turn implies that

$$|G(x)| < |M| + 1. \quad (5)$$

We now choose $\delta = \min\{\delta_1, \delta_2, \delta_3\}$. Then we substitute (3), (4), and (5) into (2) and, finally, see that $0 < |x - a| < \delta$ implies that

$$|F(x) \cdot G(x) - L \cdot M| < (|M| + 1) \cdot \frac{\epsilon}{2(|M| + 1)} + |L| \cdot \frac{\epsilon}{2(|L| + 1)}$$
$$< \frac{\epsilon}{2} + \frac{\epsilon}{2} = \epsilon,$$

as desired. The use of $|M| + 1$ and $|L| + 1$ in the denominators avoids the technical difficulty that arises should either L or M be zero. ◂

Substitution Law

If $\lim_{x \to a} g(x) = L$ and $\lim_{x \to L} f(x) = f(L)$, then
$$\lim_{x \to a} f(g(x)) = f(L).$$

PROOF Let $\epsilon > 0$ be given. We must find a number $\delta > 0$ such that
$$0 < |x - a| < \delta \quad \text{implies that} \quad |f(g(x)) - f(L)| < \epsilon.$$
Because $f(y) \to f(L)$ as $y \to L$, there exists $\delta_1 > 0$ such that
$$0 < |y - L| < \delta_1 \quad \text{implies that} \quad |f(y) - f(L)| < \epsilon. \qquad (6)$$
Also, because $g(x) \to L$ as $x \to a$, we can find $\delta > 0$ such that
$$0 < |x - a| < \delta \quad \text{implies that} \quad |g(x) - L| < \delta_1;$$
that is, such that
$$|y - L| < \delta_1,$$
where $y = g(x)$. From (6) we see that $0 < |x - a| < \delta$ implies that
$$|f(g(x)) - f(L)| = |f(y) - f(L)| < \epsilon,$$
as desired. ◂

Reciprocal Law

If $\lim_{x \to a} g(x) = L$ and $L \neq 0$, then
$$\lim_{x \to a} \frac{1}{g(x)} = \frac{1}{L}.$$

PROOF Let $f(x) = 1/x$. Then, as we saw in Example 3,
$$\lim_{x \to a} f(x) = \lim_{x \to a} \frac{1}{x} = \frac{1}{L} = f(L).$$
Hence the substitution law gives the result
$$\lim_{x \to a} \frac{1}{g(x)} = \lim_{x \to a} f(g(x)) = f(L) = \frac{1}{L},$$
as desired. ◂

Quotient Law

If $\lim_{x \to a} F(x) = L$ and $\lim_{x \to a} G(x) = M \neq 0$, then
$$\lim_{x \to a} \frac{F(x)}{G(x)} = \frac{L}{M}.$$

PROOF It follows immediately from the product and reciprocal laws that
$$\lim_{x \to a} \frac{F(x)}{G(x)} = \lim_{x \to a} F(x) \cdot \frac{1}{G(x)} = \left(\lim_{x \to a} F(x)\right)\left(\lim_{x \to a} \frac{1}{G(x)}\right) = L \cdot \frac{1}{M} = \frac{L}{M},$$
as desired. ◂

Squeeze Law

Suppose that $f(x) \leq g(x) \leq h(x)$ in some deleted neighborhood of a and that
$$\lim_{x \to a} f(x) = L = \lim_{x \to a} h(x).$$
Then
$$\lim_{x \to a} g(x) = L.$$

PROOF Given $\epsilon > 0$, we choose $\delta_1 > 0$ and $\delta_2 > 0$ such that

$$0 < |x - a| < \delta_1 \quad \text{implies that} \quad |f(x) - L| < \epsilon$$

and

$$0 < |x - a| < \delta_2 \quad \text{implies that} \quad |h(x) - L| < \epsilon.$$

Let $\delta = \min\{\delta_1, \delta_2\}$. Then $\delta > 0$. Moreover, if $0 < |x - a| < \delta$, then both $f(x)$ and $h(x)$ are points of the open interval $(L - \epsilon, L + \epsilon)$. So

$$L - \epsilon < f(x) \leq g(x) \leq h(x) < L + \epsilon.$$

Thus

$$0 < |x - a| < \delta \quad \text{implies that} \quad |g(x) - L| < \epsilon,$$

as desired. ◂

APPENDIX D PROBLEMS

In Problems 1 through 10, apply the definition of the limit to establish the given equality.

1. $\lim_{x \to a} x = a$
2. $\lim_{x \to 2} 3x = 6$
3. $\lim_{x \to 2} (x + 3) = 5$
4. $\lim_{x \to -3} (2x + 1) = -5$
5. $\lim_{x \to 1} x^2 = 1$
6. $\lim_{x \to a} x^2 = a^2$
7. $\lim_{x \to -1} (2x^2 - 1) = 1$
8. $\lim_{x \to a} \dfrac{1}{x^2} = \dfrac{1}{a^2}$
9. $\lim_{x \to a} \dfrac{1}{x^2 + 1} = \dfrac{1}{a^2 + 1}$
10. $\lim_{x \to a} \dfrac{1}{\sqrt{x}} = \dfrac{1}{\sqrt{a}}$ if $a > 0$

11. Suppose that
$$\lim_{x \to a} f(x) = L \quad \text{and} \quad \lim_{x \to a} f(x) = M.$$
Apply the definition of the limit to prove that $L = M$. Thus the limit of the function f at $x = a$ is unique if it exists.

12. Suppose that C is a constant and that $f(x) \to L$ as $x \to a$. Apply the definition of the limit to prove that
$$\lim_{x \to a} C \cdot f(x) = C \cdot L.$$

13. Suppose that $L \neq 0$ and that $f(x) \to L$ as $x \to a$. Use the method of Example 3 and the definition of the limit to show directly that
$$\lim_{x \to a} \dfrac{1}{f(x)} = \dfrac{1}{L}.$$

14. Use the algebraic identity
$$x^n - a^n = (x - a)(x^{n-1} + x^{n-2}a + x^{n-3}a^2 + \cdots + xa^{n-2} + a^{n-1})$$
to show directly from the definition of the limit that $\lim_{x \to a} x^n = a^n$ if n is a positive integer.

15. Apply the identity
$$\left|\sqrt{x} - \sqrt{a}\right| = \dfrac{|x - a|}{\sqrt{x} + \sqrt{a}}$$
to show directly from the definition of the limit that $\lim_{x \to a} \sqrt{x} = \sqrt{a}$ if $a > 0$.

16. Suppose that $f(x) \to f(a) > 0$ as $x \to a$. Prove that there exists a neighborhood of a on which $f(x) > 0$; that is, prove that there exists $\delta > 0$ such that
$$|x - a| < \delta \quad \text{implies that} \quad f(x) > 0.$$

APPENDIX E: THE COMPLETENESS OF THE REAL NUMBER SYSTEM

Here we present a self-contained treatment of those consequences of the completeness of the real number system that are relevant to this text. Our principal objective is to prove the intermediate value theorem and the maximum value theorem. We begin with the least upper bound property of the real numbers, which we take to be an axiom.

DEFINITION Upper Bound and Lower Bound

The set S of real numbers is said to be **bounded above** if there is a number b such that $x \leq b$ for every number x in S, and the number b is then called an **upper bound** for S. Similarly, if there is a number a such that $x \geq a$ for every number x in S, then S is said to be **bounded below**, and a is called a **lower bound** for S.

DEFINITION Least Upper Bound and Greatest Lower Bound
The number λ is said to be a **least upper bound** for the set S of real numbers provided that

1. λ is an upper bound for S, and
2. If b is an upper bound for S, then $\lambda \leqq b$.

Similarly, the number γ is said to be a **greatest lower bound** for S if γ is a lower bound for S and $\gamma \geqq a$ for every lower bound a of S.

EXERCISE Prove that if the set S has a least upper bound λ, then it is unique. That is, prove that if λ and μ are least upper bounds for S, then $\lambda = \mu$.

It is easy to show that the greatest lower bound γ of a set S, if any, is also unique. At this point you should construct examples to illustrate that a set with a least upper bound λ may or may not contain λ and that a similar statement is true of the set's greatest lower bound.

We now state the *completeness axiom* of the real number system.

Least Upper Bound Axiom
If the nonempty set S of real numbers has an upper bound, then it has a least upper bound.

By working with the set T consisting of the numbers $-x$, where x is in S, it is not difficult to show the following consequence of the least upper bound axiom: If the nonempty set S of real numbers is bounded below, then S has a greatest lower bound. Because of this symmetry, we need only one axiom, not two; results for least upper bounds also hold for greatest lower bounds, provided that some attention is paid to the directions of the inequalities.

The restriction that S be nonempty is annoying but necessary. If S is the "empty" set of real numbers, then 15 is an upper bound for S, but S has no least upper bound because $14, 13, 12, \ldots, 0, -1, -2, \ldots$ are also upper bounds for S.

DEFINITION Increasing, Decreasing, and Monotonic Sequences
The infinite sequence $x_1, x_2, x_3, \ldots, x_k, \ldots$ is said to be **nondecreasing** if $x_n \leqq x_{n+1}$ for every $n \geqq 1$. This sequence is said to be **nonincreasing** if $x_n \geqq x_{n+1}$ for every $n \geqq 1$. If the sequence $\{x_n\}$ is either nonincreasing or nondecreasing, then it is said to be **monotonic.**

Theorem 1 gives the **bounded monotonic sequence property** of the set of real numbers. (Recall that a set S of real numbers is said to be **bounded** if it is contained in an interval of the form $[a, b]$.)

THEOREM 1 Bounded Monotonic Sequences
Every bounded monotonic sequence of real numbers converges.

PROOF Suppose that the sequence
$$S = \{x_n\} = \{x_1, x_2, x_3, \ldots, x_k, \ldots\}$$
is bounded and nondecreasing. By the least upper bound axiom, S has a least upper bound λ. We claim that λ is the limit of the sequence $\{x_n\}$. Consider an open interval centered at λ—that is, an interval of the form $I = (\lambda - \epsilon, \lambda + \epsilon)$, where $\epsilon > 0$. Some terms of the sequence must lie within I, else $\lambda - \epsilon$ would be an upper bound for

S that is less than its least upper bound λ. But if x_N is in I, then—because we are dealing with a nondecreasing sequence—$x_N \leq x_k \leq \lambda$ for all $k \geq N$. That is, x_k is in I for all $k \geq N$. Because ϵ is an arbitrary positive number, λ is—almost by definition—the limit of the sequence $\{x_n\}$. Thus we have shown that a bounded nonincreasing sequence converges. A similar proof can be constructed for nonincreasing sequences by working with the greatest lower bound. ◄

Therefore, the least upper bound axiom implies the bounded monotonic sequence property of the real numbers. With just a little effort, you can prove that the two are logically equivalent. That is, if you take the bounded monotonic sequence property as an axiom, then the least upper bound property follows as a theorem. The *nested interval property* of Theorem 2 is also equivalent to the least upper bound property, but we shall prove only that it follows from the least upper bound property, because we have chosen the latter as the fundamental completeness axiom for the real number system.

THEOREM 2 Nested Interval Property of the Real Numbers

Suppose that $I_1, I_2, I_3, \ldots, I_n, \ldots$ is a sequence of closed intervals (so I_n is of the form $[a_n, b_n]$ for each positive integer n) such that

1. I_n contains I_{n+1} for each $n \geq 1$, and
2. $\lim_{n \to \infty} (b_n - a_n) = 0$.

Then there exists exactly one real number c such that c belongs to I_n for all n. Thus

$$\{c\} = I_1 \cap I_2 \cap I_3 \cap \cdots.$$

PROOF It is clear from hypothesis (2) of Theorem 2 that there is at most one such number c. The sequence $\{a_n\}$ of the left-hand endpoints of the intervals is a bounded (by b_1) nondecreasing sequence and thus has a limit a by the bounded monotonic sequence property. Similarly, the sequence $\{b_n\}$ has a limit b. Because $a_n \leq b_n$ for all n, it follows easily that $a \leq b$. It is clear that $a_n \leq a \leq b \leq b_n$ for all $n \geq 1$, so a and b belong to every interval I_n. But then hypothesis (2) of Theorem 2 implies that $a = b$, and clearly this common value—call it c—is the number satisfying the conclusion of Theorem 2. ◄

We can now use these results to prove several important theorems used in the text.

THEOREM 3 Intermediate Value Property of Continuous Functions

If the function f is continuous on the interval $[a, b]$ and $f(a) < K < f(b)$, then $K = f(c)$ for some number c in (a, b).

PROOF Let $I_1 = [a, b]$. Suppose that I_n has been defined for $n \geq 1$. We describe (inductively) how to define I_{n+1}, and this shows in particular how to define I_2, I_3, and so forth. Let a_n be the left-hand endpoint of I_n, b_n be its right-hand endpoint, and m_n be its midpoint. There are now three cases to consider: $f(m_n) > K$, $f(m_n) < K$, and $f(m_n) = K$.

If $f(m_n) > K$, then $f(a_n) < K < f(m_n)$; in this case, let $a_{n+1} = a_n$, $b_{n+1} = m_n$, and $I_{n+1} = [a_{n+1}, b_{n+1}]$.

If $f(m_n) < K$, then let $a_{n+1} = m_n$, $b_{n+1} = b_n$, and $I_{n+1} = [a_{n+1}, b_{n+1}]$.

If $f(m_n) = K$, then we simply let $c = m_n$ and the proof is complete. Otherwise, at each stage we bisect I_n and let I_{n+1} be the half of I_n on which f takes on values both above and below K.

It is easy to show that the sequence $\{I_n\}$ of intervals satisfies the hypotheses of Theorem 2. Let c be the (unique) real number common to all the intervals I_n. We will show that $f(c) = K$, and this will conclude the proof.

The sequence $\{b_n\}$ has limit c, so by the continuity of f, the sequence $\{f(b_n)\}$ has limit $f(c)$. But $f(b_n) > K$ for all n, so the limit of $\{f(b_n)\}$ can be no less than K; that is, $f(c) \geq K$. By considering the sequence $\{a_n\}$, it follows that $f(c) \leq K$ as well. Therefore, $f(c) = K$. ◄

LEMMA 1
If f is continuous on the closed interval $[a, b]$, then f is bounded there.

PROOF Suppose by way of contradiction that f is not bounded on $I_1 = [a, b]$. Bisect I_1 and let I_2 be either half of I_1 on which f is unbounded. (If f is unbounded on both halves, let $I_2 = I_1$.) In general, let I_{n+1} be a half of I_n on which f is unbounded.

Again it is easy to show that the sequence $\{I_n\}$ of closed intervals satisfies the hypotheses of Theorem 2. Let c be the number common to them all. Because f is continuous, there exists a number $\epsilon > 0$ such that f is bounded on the interval $(c - \epsilon, c + \epsilon)$. But for sufficiently large values of n, I_n is a subset of $(c - \epsilon, c + \epsilon)$. This contradiction shows that f must be bounded on $[a, b]$. ◄

THEOREM 4   Maximum Value Property of Continuous Functions
If the function f is continuous on the closed and bounded interval $[a, b]$, then there exists a number c in $[a, b]$ such that $f(x) \leq f(c)$ for all x in $[a, b]$.

PROOF Consider the set $S = \{f(x) \mid a \leq x \leq b\}$. By Lemma 1, this set is bounded, and it is certainly nonempty. Let λ be the least upper bound of S. Our goal is to show that λ is a value $f(x)$ of f.

With $I_1 = [a, b]$, bisect I_1 as before. Note that λ is the least upper bound of the values of f on at least one of the two halves of I_1; let I_2 be that half. Having defined I_n, let I_{n+1} be the half of I_n on which λ is the least upper bound of the values of f. Let c be the number common to all these intervals. It then follows from the continuity of f, much as in the proof of Theorem 3, that $f(c) = \lambda$. And it is clear that $f(x) \leq \lambda$ for all x in $[a, b]$. ◄

The technique we are using in these proof is called the *method of bisection*. We now use it once again to establish the *Bolzano–Weierstrass property* of the real number system.

DEFINITION   Limit Point
Let S be a set of real numbers. The number p is said to be a **limit point** of S if every open interval containing p also contains points of S other than p.

BOLZANO–WEIERSTRASS THEOREM
Every bounded infinite set of real numbers has a limit point.

PROOF Let I_0 be a closed interval containing the bounded infinite set S of real numbers. Bisect I_0. Let I_1 be one of the resulting closed half-intervals of I_0 that contains infinitely many points of S. If I_n has been chosen, let I_{n+1} be one of the closed half-intervals of I_n containing infinitely many points of S. An application of Theorem 2 yields a number p common to all the intervals I_n. If J is an open interval containing p, then J contains I_n for some sufficiently large value of n and thus contains infinitely many points of S. Therefore p is a limit point of S. ◂

Our final goal is in sight: We can now prove that a sequence of real numbers converges if and only if it is a *Cauchy sequence*.

DEFINITION Cauchy Sequence
The sequence $\{a_n\}_1^\infty$ is said to be a **Cauchy sequence** if, for every $\epsilon > 0$, there exists an integer N such that
$$|a_m - a_n| < \epsilon$$
for all $m, n \geqq N$.

LEMMA 2 Convergent Subsequences
Every bounded sequence of real numbers has a convergent subsequence.

PROOF If $\{a_n\}$ has only a finite number of values, then the conclusion of Lemma 2 follows easily. We therefore focus our attention on the case in which $\{a_n\}$ is an infinite set. It is easy to show that this set is also bounded, and thus we may apply the Bolzano–Weierstrass theorem to obtain a limit point p of $\{a_n\}$.

For each integer $k \geq 1$, let $a_{n(k)}$ be a term of the sequence $\{a_n\}$ such that

1. $n(k+1) > n(k)$ for all $k \geq 1$, and
2. $|a_{n(k)} - p| < \dfrac{1}{k}$.

It is then easy to show that $\{a_{n(k)}\}$ is a convergent (to p) subsequence of $\{a_n\}$. ◂

THEOREM 6 Convergence of Cauchy Sequences
A sequence of real numbers converges if and only if it is a Cauchy sequence.

PROOF It follows immediately from the triangle inequality that every convergent sequence is a Cauchy sequence. Thus suppose that the sequence $\{a_n\}$ is a Cauchy sequence.

Choose N such that
$$|a_m - a_n| < 1$$
if $m, n \geqq N$. It follows that if $n \geqq N$, then a_n lies in the closed interval $[a_N - 1, a_N + 1]$. This implies that the sequence $\{a_n\}$ is bounded, and thus by Lemma 2 it has a convergent subsequence $\{a_{n(k)}\}$. Let p be the limit of this subsequence.

We claim that $\{a_n\}$ itself converges to p. Given $\epsilon > 0$, choose M such that
$$|a_m - a_n| < \frac{\epsilon}{2}$$
if $m, n \geqq M$. Next choose K such that $n(K) \geqq M$ and
$$|a_{n(K)} - p| < \frac{\epsilon}{2}.$$
Then if $n \geqq M$,
$$|a_n - p| \leqq |a_n - a_{n(K)}| + |a_{n(K)} - p| < \epsilon.$$

Therefore, $\{a_n\}$ converges to p by definition. ◂

APPENDIX F: EXISTENCE OF THE INTEGRAL

When the basic computational algorithms of the calculus were discovered by Newton and Leibniz in the latter half of the seventeenth century, the logical rigor that had been a feature of the Greek method of exhaustion was largely abandoned. When computing the area A under the curve $y = f(x)$, for example, Newton took it as intuitively obvious that the area function existed, and he proceeded to compute it as the antiderivative of the height function $f(x)$. Leibniz regarded A as an infinite sum of infinitesimal area elements, each of the form $dA = f(x)\,dx$, but in practice computed the area

$$A = \int_a^b f(x)\,dx$$

by antidifferentiation just as Newton did—that is, by computing

$$A = \left[D^{-1} f(x)\right]_a^b.$$

The question of the *existence* of the area function—one of the conditions that a function f must satisfy in order for its integral to exist—did not at first seem to be of much importance. Eighteenth-century mathematicians were mainly occupied (and satisfied) with the impressive applications of calculus to the solution of real-world problems and did not concentrate on the logical foundations of the subject.

The first attempt at a precise definition of the integral and a proof of its existence for continuous functions was that of the French mathematician Augustin Louis Cauchy (1789–1857). Curiously enough, Cauchy was trained as an engineer, and much of his research in mathematics was in fields that we today regard as applications-oriented: hydrodynamics, waves in elastic media, vibrations of elastic membranes, polarization of light, and the like. But he was a prolific researcher, and his writings cover the entire spectrum of mathematics, with occasional essays into almost unrelated fields.

Around 1824, Cauchy defined the integral of a continuous function in a way that is familiar to us, as a limit of left-endpoint approximations:

$$\int_a^b f(x)\,dx = \lim_{\Delta x \to 0} \sum_{i=1}^n f(x_{i-1})\,\Delta x.$$

This is a much more complicated sort of limit than the ones we discussed in Chapter 2. Cauchy was not entirely clear about the nature of the limit process involved in this equation, nor was he clear about the precise role that the hypothesis of the continuity of f played in proving that the limit exists.

A complete definition of the integral, as we gave in Section 5.4, was finally produced in the 1850s by the German mathematician Georg Bernhard Riemann. Riemann was a student of Gauss; he met Gauss upon his arrival at Göttingen, Germany, for the purpose of studying theology, when he was about 20 years old and Gauss was about 70. Riemann soon decided to study mathematics and became known as one of the truly great mathematicians of the nineteenth century. Like Cauchy, he was particularly interested in applications of mathematics to the real world; his research emphasized electricity, heat, light, acoustics, fluid dynamics, and—as you might infer from the fact that Wilhelm Weber was a major influence on Riemann's education—magnetism. Riemann also made significant contributions to mathematics itself, particularly in the field of complex analysis. A major conjecture of his, involving the zeta function

$$\zeta(s) = \sum_{n=1}^{\infty} \frac{1}{n^s}, \tag{1}$$

remains unsolved to this day. This conjecture has important consequences in the theory of the distribution of prime numbers because

$$\zeta(k) = \prod \left(1 - \frac{1}{p^k}\right)^{-1},$$

where the product $\prod$ is taken over all primes p. [The zeta function is defined in Eq. (1) for complex numbers s to the right of the vertical line at $x = 1$ and is extended to other complex numbers by the requirement that it be differentiable.] Riemann died of tuberculosis shortly before his fortieth birthday.

Here we give a proof of the existence of the integral of a continuous function. We will follow Riemann's approach. Specifically, suppose that the function f is continuous on the closed and bounded interval $[a, b]$. We will prove that the definite integral

$$\int_a^b f(x)\,dx$$

exists. That is, we will demonstrate the existence of a number I that satisfies the following condition: For every $\epsilon > 0$ there exists $\delta > 0$ such that, for *every* Riemann sum R associated with *any* partition P with $|P| < \delta$,

$$|I - R| < \epsilon.$$

(Recall that the norm $|P|$ of the partition P is the length of the longest subinterval in the partition.) In other words, every Riemann sum associated with every sufficiently "fine" partition is close to the number I. If this happens, then the definite integral

$$\int_a^b f(x)\,dx$$

is said to **exist,** and I is its **value.**

Now we begin the proof. Suppose throughout that f is a function continuous on the closed interval $[a, b]$. Given $\epsilon > 0$, we need to show the existence of a number $\delta > 0$ such that

$$\left| I - \sum_{i=1}^{n} f(x_i^\star)\,\Delta x_i \right| < \epsilon \tag{2}$$

for every Riemann sum associated with any partition P of $[a, b]$ with $|P| < \delta$.

Given a partition P of $[a, b]$ into n subintervals that are *not necessarily of equal length*, let p_i be a point in the subinterval $[x_{i-1}, x_i]$ at which f attains its minimum value $f(p_i)$. Similarly, let $f(q_i)$ be its maximum value there. These numbers exist for $i = 1, 2, 3, \ldots, n$ because of the maximum value property of continuous functions (Theorem 4 of Appendix E).

In what follows we will denote the resulting lower and upper Riemann sums associated with P by

$$L(P) = \sum_{i=1}^{n} f(p_i)\,\Delta x_i \tag{3a}$$

and

$$U(P) = \sum_{i=1}^{n} f(q_i)\,\Delta x_i, \tag{3b}$$

respectively. Then Lemma 1 is obvious.

LEMMA 1
For any partition P of $[a, b]$, $L(P) \leq U(P)$.

Now we need a definition. The partition P' is called a **refinement** of the partition P if each subinterval of P' is contained in some subinterval of P. That is, P' is obtained from P by adding more points of subdivision to P.

LEMMA 2
Suppose that P' is a refinement of P. Then
$$L(P) \leq L(P') \leq U(P') \leq U(P). \tag{4}$$

PROOF The inequality $L(P') \leq U(P')$ is a consequence of Lemma 1. We will show that $L(P) \leq L(P')$; the proof that $U(P') \leq U(P)$ is similar.

The refinement P' is obtained from P by adding one or more points of subdivision to P. So all we need show is that the Riemann sum $L(P)$ cannot be decreased by adding a single point of subdivision. Thus we will suppose that the partition P' is obtained from P by dividing the kth subinterval $[x_{k-1}, x_k]$ of P into two subintervals $[x_{k-1}, z]$ and $[z, x_k]$ by means of the new subdivision point z.

The only resulting effect on the corresponding Riemann sum is to replace the term
$$f(p_k) \cdot (x_k - x_{k-1})$$
in $L(P)$ with the two-term sum
$$f(u) \cdot (z - x_{k-1}) + f(v) \cdot (x_k - z),$$
where $f(u)$ is the minimum of f on $[x_{k-1}, z]$ and $f(v)$ is the minimum of f on $[z, x_k]$. But
$$f(p_k) \leq f(u) \quad \text{and} \quad f(p_k) \leq f(v).$$
Hence
$$f(u) \cdot (z - x_{k-1}) + f(v) \cdot (x_k - z) \geq f(p_k) \cdot (z - x_{k-1}) + f(p_k) \cdot (x_k - z)$$
$$= f(p_k) \cdot (z - x_{k-1} + x_k - z)$$
$$= f(p_k) \cdot (x_k - x_{k-1}).$$

So the replacement of $f(p_k) \cdot (x_k - x_{k-1})$ cannot decrease the sum $L(P)$ in question, and therefore $L(P) \leq L(P')$. Because this is all we needed to show, we have completed the proof of Lemma 2. ◀

To prove that all the Riemann sums for sufficiently fine partitions are close to some number I, we must first give a construction of I. This is accomplished through Lemma 3.

LEMMA 3
Let P_n denote the regular partition of $[a, b]$ into 2^n subintervals of equal length. Then the (sequential) limit
$$I = \lim_{n \to \infty} L(P_n) \tag{5}$$
exists.

PROOF We begin with the observation that each partition P_{n+1} is a refinement of P_n, so (by Lemma 2)
$$L(P_1) \leq L(P_2) \leq \cdots \leq L(P_n) \leq \cdots.$$

Therefore $\{L(P_n)\}$ is a nondecreasing sequence of real numbers. Moreover,
$$L(P_n) = \sum_{i=1}^{2^n} f(p_i) \Delta x_i \leq M \sum_{i-1}^{2^n} \Delta x_i = M(b - a),$$
where M is the maximum value of f on $[a, b]$.

Theorem 1 of Appendix E guarantees that a bounded monotonic sequence of real numbers must converge. Thus the number

$$I = \lim_{n \to \infty} L(P_n)$$

exists. This establishes Eq. (5), and the proof of Lemma 3 is complete. ◄

It is proved in advanced calculus that if f is continuous on $[a, b]$, then—for every number $\epsilon > 0$—there exists a number $\delta > 0$ such that

$$|f(u) - f(v)| < \epsilon$$

for every two points u and v of $[a, b]$ such that

$$|u - v| < \delta.$$

This property of a function is called **uniform continuity** of f on the interval $[a, b]$. Thus the theorem from advanced calculus that we need to use states that every continuous function on a closed and bounded interval is uniformly continuous there.

Note The fact that f is continuous on $[a, b]$ means that for each number u in the interval and each $\epsilon > 0$, there exists $\delta > 0$ such that if v is a number in the interval with $|u - v| < \delta$, then $|f(u) - f(v)| < \epsilon$. But *uniform* continuity is a more stringent condition. It means that given $\epsilon > 0$, you can find not only a value δ_1 that "works" for u_1, a value δ_2 that works for u_2, and so on, but more: You can find a universal value of $\delta > 0$ that works for *all* values of u in the interval. This should not be obvious when you notice the possibility that $\delta_1 = 1, \delta_2 = \frac{1}{2}, \delta_3 = \frac{1}{3}$, and so on. In any case, it is clear that uniform continuity of f on an interval implies its continuity there.

Remember that throughout we have a continuous function f defined on the closed interval $[a, b]$.

LEMMA 4
Suppose that $\epsilon > 0$ is given. Then there exists a number $\delta > 0$ such that if P is a partition of $[a, b]$ with $|P| < \delta$ and P' is a refinement of P, then

$$|R(P) - R(P')| < \frac{\epsilon}{3} \tag{6}$$

for any two Riemann sums $R(P)$ associated with P and $R(P')$ associated with P'.

PROOF Because f must be uniformly continuous on $[a, b]$, there exists a number $\delta > 0$ such that if

$$|u - v| < \delta, \quad \text{then} \quad |f(u) - f(v)| < \frac{\epsilon}{3(b - a)}.$$

Suppose now that P is a partition of $[a, b]$ with $|P| < \delta$. Then

$$|U(P) - L(P)| = \sum_{i=1}^{n} |f(q_i) - f(p_i)| \Delta x_i < \frac{\epsilon}{3(b - a)} \sum_{i=1}^{n} \Delta x_i = \frac{\epsilon}{3}.$$

This is valid because $|p_i - q_i| < \delta$, for both p_i and q_i belong to the same subinterval $[x_{i-1}, x_i]$ of P, and $|P| < \delta$.

Now, as shown in Fig. F.1, we know that $L(P)$ and $U(P)$ differ by less than $\epsilon/3$. We know also that

$$L(P) \leqq R(P) \leqq U(P)$$

for every Riemann sum $R(P)$ associated with P. But

$$L(P) \leqq L(P') \leqq U(P') \leqq U(P)$$

FIGURE F.1 Part of the proof of Lemma 4.

by Lemma 2, because P' is a refinement of P; moreover,
$$L(P') \leq R(P') \leq U(P')$$
for every Riemann sum $R(P')$ associated with P'.

As Fig. F.1 shows, both the numbers $R(P)$ and $R(P')$ lie in the interval $[L(P), U(P)]$ of length less than $\epsilon/3$, so Eq. (6) follows. This concludes the proof of Lemma 4. ◂

THEOREM 1 Existence of the Integral
If f is continuous on the closed and bounded interval $[a, b]$, then the integral
$$\int_a^b f(x)\,dx$$
exists.

PROOF Suppose that $\epsilon > 0$ is given. We must show the existence of a number $\delta > 0$ such that, for every partition P of $[a, b]$ with $|P| < \delta$, we have
$$|I - R(P)| < \epsilon,$$
where I is the number given in Lemma 3 and $R(P)$ is an arbitrary Riemann sum for f associated with P.

We choose the number δ provided by Lemma 4 such that
$$|R(P) - R(P')| < \frac{\epsilon}{3}$$
if $|P| < \delta$ and P' is a refinement of P.

By Lemma 3, we can choose an integer N so large that
$$|P_N| < \delta \quad \text{and} \quad |L(P_N) - I| < \frac{\epsilon}{3}. \tag{7}$$

Given an arbitrary partition P such that $|P| < \delta$, let P' be a common refinement of both P and P_N. You can obtain such a partition P', for example, by using all the points of subdivision of both P and P_N to form the subintervals of $[a, b]$ that constitute P'.

Because P' is a refinement of both P and P_N and both the latter partitions have mesh less than δ, Lemma 4 implies that
$$|R(P) - R(P')| < \frac{\epsilon}{3} \quad \text{and} \quad |L(P_N) - R(P')| < \frac{\epsilon}{3}. \tag{8}$$

Here $R(P)$ and $R(P')$ are (arbitrary) Riemann sums associated with P and P', respectively.

Given an arbitrary Riemann sum $R(P)$ associated with the partition P with mesh less than δ, we see that
$$|I - R(P)| = |I - L(P_N) + L(P_N) - R(P') + R(P') - R(P)|$$
$$\leq |I - L(P_N)| + |L(P_N) - R(P')| + |R(P') - R(P)|.$$

In the last sum, both of the last two terms are less than $\epsilon/3$ by virtue of the inequalities in (8). We also know, by (7), that the first term is less than $\epsilon/3$. Consequently,
$$|I - R(P)| < \epsilon.$$

This establishes Theorem 1. ◂

We close with an example that shows that some hypothesis of continuity is required for integrability.

EXAMPLE 1 Suppose that f is defined for $0 \leq x \leq 1$ as follows:
$$f(x) = \begin{cases} 1 & \text{if } x \text{ is irrational;} \\ 0 & \text{if } x \text{ is rational.} \end{cases}$$

Then f is not continuous anywhere. (Why?) Given a partition P of $[0, 1]$, let p_i be a rational point and q_i an irrational point of the ith subinterval of P for each i, $1 \leq i \leq n$. As before, f attains its minimum value 0 at each p_i and its maximum value 1 at each q_i. Also

$$L(P) = \sum_{i=1}^{n} f(p_i) \Delta x_i = 0, \quad \text{whereas} \quad U(P) = \sum_{i=1}^{n} f(q_i) \Delta x_i = 1.$$

Thus if we choose $\epsilon = \frac{1}{2}$, then there is *no* number I that can lie within ϵ of both $L(P)$ and $U(P)$, no matter how small the mesh of P. It follows that f is *not* integrable on $[0, 1]$. ◆

REMARK This is not the end of the story of the integral. Integrals of highly discontinuous functions are important in many applications of physics, and near the beginning of the twentieth century a number of mathematicians, most notably Henri Lebesgue (1875–1941), developed more powerful integrals. The Lebesgue integral, in particular, always exists when the Riemann integral does, and gives the same value; but the Lebesgue integral is sufficiently powerful to integrate even functions that are continuous nowhere. It reports that

$$\int_0^1 f(x) \, dx = 1$$

for the function f of Example 1. Other mathematicians have developed integrals with domains far more general than sets of real numbers or subsets of the plane or space.

APPENDIX G: APPROXIMATIONS AND RIEMANN SUMS

Several times in Chapter 6 our attempt to compute some quantity Q led to the following situation. Beginning with a regular partition of an appropriate interval $[a, b]$ into n subintervals, each of length Δx, we found an approximation A_n to Q of the form

$$A_n = \sum_{i=1}^{n} g(u_i) h(v_i) \, \Delta x, \tag{1}$$

where u_i and v_i are two (generally different) points of the ith subinterval $[x_{i-1}, x_i]$. For example, in our discussion of surface area of revolution that precedes Eq. (8) of Section 6.4, we found the approximation

$$\sum_{i=1}^{n} 2\pi f(u_i) \sqrt{1 + [f'(v_i)]^2} \, \Delta x \tag{2}$$

to the area of the surface generated by revolving the curve $y = f(x)$, $a \leq x \leq b$, around the x-axis. (In Section 6.4 we wrote $x_i^{\star\star}$ for u_i and $x_i^{\star}$ for v_i.) Note that the expression in (2) is the same as the right-hand side in Eq. (1); take $g(x) = 2\pi f(x)$ and $h(x) = \sqrt{1 + [f'(x)]^2}$.

In such a situation we observe that if u_i and v_i were the *same* point $x_i^{\star}$ of $[x_{i-1}, x_i]$ for each i ($i = 1, 2, 3, \ldots, n$), then the approximation in Eq. (1) would be a Riemann sum for the function $g(x)h(x)$ on $[a, b]$. This leads us to suspect that

$$\lim_{\Delta x \to 0} \sum_{i=1}^{n} g(u_i) h(v_i) \, \Delta x = \int_a^b g(x) h(x) \, dx. \tag{3}$$

In Section 6.4, we assumed the validity of Eq. (3) and concluded from the approximation in (2) that the surface area of revolution ought to be defined to be

$$A = \lim_{\Delta x \to 0} \sum_{i=1}^{n} 2\pi f(u_i) \sqrt{1 + [f'(v_i)]^2} \, \Delta x = \int_a^b 2\pi f(x) \sqrt{1 + [f'(x)]^2} \, dx.$$

Theorem 1 guarantees that Eq. (3) holds under mild restrictions on the functions g and h.

THEOREM 1 A Generalization of Riemann Sums

Suppose that h and g' are continuous on $[a, b]$. Then

$$\lim_{\Delta x \to 0} \sum_{i=1}^{n} g(u_i) h(v_i) \, \Delta x = \int_a^b g(x) h(x) \, dx, \qquad (3)$$

where u_i and v_i are arbitrary points of the ith subinterval of a regular partition of $[a, b]$ into n subintervals, each of length Δx.

PROOF   Let M_1 and M_2 denote the maximum values on $[a, b]$ of $|g'(x)|$ and $|h(x)|$, respectively. Note that

$$\sum_{i=1}^{n} g(u_i) h(v_i) \, \Delta x = R_n + S_n, \quad \text{where} \quad R_n = \sum_{i=1}^{n} g(v_i) h(v_i) \, \Delta x$$

is a Riemann sum approaching $\int_a^b g(x) h(x) \, dx$ as $\Delta x \to 0$, and

$$S_n = \sum_{i=1}^{n} [g(u_i) - g(v_i)] h(v_i) \, \Delta x.$$

To prove Eq. (3) it is sufficient to show that $S_n \to 0$ as $\Delta x \to 0$. The mean value theorem gives

$$|g(u_i) - g(v_i)| = |g'(\bar{x}_i)| \cdot |u_i - v_i| \qquad [\bar{x}_i \text{ in } (u_i, v_i)]$$
$$\leqq M_1 \Delta x,$$

because both u_i and v_i are points of the interval $[x_{i-1}, x_i]$ of length Δx. Then

$$|S_n| \leqq \sum_{i=1}^{n} |g(u_i) - g(v_i)| \cdot |h(v_i)| \, \Delta x \leqq \sum_{i=1}^{n} (M_1 \Delta x) \cdot (M_2 \Delta x)$$

$$= (M_1 M_2 \Delta x) \sum_{i=1}^{n} \Delta x = M_1 M_2 (b - a) \Delta x,$$

from which it follows that $S_n \to 0$ as $\Delta x \to 0$, as desired.   ◂

As an application of Theorem 1, let us give a rigorous derivation of Eq. (2) of Section 6.3,

$$V = \int_a^b 2\pi x f(x) \, dx, \qquad (4)$$

for the volume of the solid generated by revolving around the y-axis the region between the graph of $y = f(x)$ and the x-axis for $a \leqq x \leqq b$. Beginning with the usual regular partition of $[a, b]$, let $f(x_i^{\flat})$ and $f(x_i^{\sharp})$ denote the minimum and maximum values of f on the ith subinterval $[x_{i-1}, x_i]$. Denote by $x_i^{\star}$ the midpoint of this subinterval. From Fig. G.1, we see that the part of the solid generated by revolving the region below $y = f(x)$, $x_{i-1} \leqq x \leqq x_i$, contains a cylindrical shell with average radius $x_i^{\star}$, thickness Δx, and height $f(x_i^{\flat})$ and is contained in another cylindrical shell with the same average radius and thickness but with height $f(x_i^{\sharp})$. Hence the volume ΔV_i of this part of the solid satisfies the inequalities

$$2\pi x_i^{\star} f(x_i^{\flat}) \, \Delta x \leqq \Delta V_i \leqq 2\pi x_i^{\star} f(x_i^{\sharp}) \, \Delta x.$$

We add these inequalities for $i = 1, 2, 3, \ldots, n$ and find that

$$\sum_{i=1}^{n} 2\pi x_i^{\star} f(x_i^{\flat}) \, \Delta x \leqq V \leqq \sum_{i=1}^{n} 2\pi x_i^{\star} f(x_i^{\sharp}) \, \Delta x.$$

FIGURE G.1 A careful estimate of the volume of a solid of revolution around the y-axis.

Because Theorem 1 implies that both of the last two sums approach $\int_a^b 2\pi f(x)\,dx$, the squeeze law of limits now implies Eq. (4).

We will occasionally need a generalization of Theorem 1 that involves the notion of a continuous function $F(x, y)$ of two variables. We say that F is *continuous* at the point (x_0, y_0) provided that the value $F(x, y)$ can be made arbitrarily close to $F(x_0, y_0)$ merely by choosing the point (x, y) sufficiently close to (x_0, y_0). We discuss continuity of functions of two variables in Chapter 13. Here it will suffice to accept the following facts: If $g(x)$ and $h(y)$ are continuous functions of the single variables x and y, respectively, then simple combinations such as

$$g(x) \pm h(y), \quad g(x)h(y), \quad \text{and} \quad \sqrt{[g(x)]^2 + [h(y)]^2}$$

are continuous functions of the two variables x and y.

Now consider a regular partition of $[a, b]$ into n subintervals, each of length Δx, and let u_i and v_i denote arbitrary points of the ith subinterval $[x_{i-1}, x_i]$. Theorem 2—we omit the proof—tells us how to find the limit as $\Delta x \to 0$ of a sum such as

$$\sum_{i=1}^{n} F(u_i, v_i)\,\Delta x.$$

THEOREM 2 A Further Generalization
Let $F(x, y)$ be continuous for x and y both in the interval $[a, b]$. Then, in the notation of the preceding paragraph,

$$\lim_{\Delta x \to 0} \sum_{i=1}^{n} F(u_i, v_i)\,\Delta x = \int_a^b F(x, x)\,dx. \tag{5}$$

Theorem 1 is the special case $F(x, y) = g(x)h(y)$ of Theorem 2. Moreover, the integrand $F(x, x)$ on the right in Eq. (5) is merely an ordinary function of the single variable x. As a formal matter, the integral corresponding to the sum in Eq. (5) is obtained by replacing the summation symbol with an integral sign, changing both u_i and v_i to x, replacing Δx with dx, and inserting the correct limits of integration. For example, if the interval $[a, b]$ is $[0, 4]$, then

$$\lim_{\Delta x \to 0} \sum_{i=1}^{n} \sqrt{9u_i^2 + v_i^4}\,\Delta x = \int_0^4 \sqrt{9x^2 + x^4}\,dx$$

$$= \int_0^4 x(9 + x^2)^{1/2}\,dx = \left[\frac{1}{3}(9 + x^2)^{3/2}\right]_0^4$$

$$= \frac{1}{3}\left[(25)^{3/2} - (9)^{3/2}\right] = \frac{98}{3}.$$

APPENDIX G PROBLEMS

In Problems 1 through 7, u_i and v_i are arbitrary points of the ith subinterval of a regular partition of $[a, b]$ into n subintervals, each of length Δx. Express the given limit as an integral from a to b, then compute the value of this integral.

1. $\lim\limits_{\Delta x \to 0} \sum\limits_{i=1}^{n} u_i v_i \, \Delta x; \quad a = 0, \ b = 1$

2. $\lim\limits_{\Delta x \to 0} \sum\limits_{j=1}^{n} (3u_j + 5v_j) \, \Delta x; \quad a = -1, \ b = 3$

3. $\lim\limits_{\Delta x \to 0} \sum\limits_{i=1}^{n} u_i \sqrt{4 - v_i^2} \, \Delta x; \quad a = 0, \ b = 2$

4. $\lim\limits_{\Delta x \to 0} \sum\limits_{i=1}^{n} \dfrac{u_i}{\sqrt{16 + v_i^2}} \, \Delta x; \quad a = 0, \ b = 3$

5. $\lim\limits_{\Delta x \to 0} \sum\limits_{i=1}^{n} \sin u_i \cos v_i \, \Delta x; \quad a = 0, \ b = \pi/2$

6. $\lim\limits_{\Delta x \to 0} \sum\limits_{i=1}^{n} \sqrt{\sin^2 u_i + \cos^2 v_i} \, \Delta x; \quad a = 0, \ b = \pi$

7. $\lim\limits_{\Delta x \to 0} \sum\limits_{k=1}^{n} \sqrt{u_k^4 + v_k^7} \, \Delta x; \quad a = 0, \ b = 2$

8. Explain how Theorem 1 applies to show that Eq. (8) of Section 6.4 follows from the discussion that precedes it in that section.

9. Use Theorem 1 to derive Eq. (10) of Section 6.4.

APPENDIX H: L'HÔPITAL'S RULE AND CAUCHY'S MEAN VALUE THEOREM

Here we give a proof of l'Hôpital's rule,

$$\lim_{x \to a} \frac{f(x)}{g(x)} = \lim_{x \to a} \frac{f'(x)}{g'(x)}, \qquad (1)$$

under the hypotheses of Theorem 1 in Section 7.2. The proof is based on a generalization of the mean value theorem due to the French mathematician Augustin Louis Cauchy. Cauchy used this generalization in the early nineteenth century to give rigorous proofs of several calculus results not previously established firmly.

CAUCHY'S MEAN VALUE THEOREM

Suppose that the functions f and g are continuous on the closed and bounded interval $[a, b]$ and differentiable on (a, b). Then there exists a number c in (a, b) such that

$$[f(b) - f(a)] g'(c) = [g(b) - g(a)] f'(c). \qquad (2)$$

REMARK 1 To see that this theorem is indeed a generalization of the (ordinary) mean value theorem, we take $g(x) = x$. Then $g'(x) \equiv 1$, and the conclusion in Eq. (2) reduces to the fact that

$$f(b) - f(a) = (b - a) f'(c)$$

for some number c in (a, b).

REMARK 2 Equation (2) has a geometric interpretation like that of the ordinary mean value theorem. Let us think of the equations $x = g(t)$, $y = f(t)$ as describing the motion of a point $P(x, y)$ moving along a curve C in the xy-plane as t increases from a to b (Fig. H.1). That is, $P(x, y) = P(g(t), f(t))$ is the location of the point P at time t. Under the assumption that $g(b) \neq g(a)$, the slope of the line L connecting the endpoints of the curve C is

$$m = \frac{f(b) - f(a)}{g(b) - g(a)}. \qquad (3)$$

But if $g'(c) \neq 0$, then the chain rule gives

$$\frac{dy}{dx} = \frac{dy/dt}{dx/dt} = \frac{f'(c)}{g'(c)} \qquad (4)$$

FIGURE H.1 The idea of Cauchy's mean value theorem.

for the slope of the line tangent to the curve C at the point $(g(c), f(c))$. But if $g(b) \neq g(a)$ and $g'(c) \neq 0$, then Eq. (2) may be written in the form

$$\frac{f(b) - f(a)}{g(b) - g(a)} = \frac{f'(c)}{g'(c)}, \tag{5}$$

so the two slopes in Eqs. (3) and (4) are equal. Thus Cauchy's mean value theorem implies that (under our assumptions) there is a point on the curve C where the tangent line is *parallel* to the line joining the endpoints of C. This is exactly what the (ordinary) mean value theorem says for an explicitly defined curve $y = f(x)$. This geometric interpretation motivates the following proof of Cauchy's mean value theorem.

PROOF The line L through the endpoints in Fig. H.1 has point-slope equation

$$y - f(a) = \frac{f(b) - f(a)}{g(b) - g(a)} [x - g(a)],$$

which can be rewritten in the form $Ax + By + C = 0$ with

$$A = g(b) - f(a), \quad B = -[g(b) - g(a)], \quad \text{and}$$
$$C = f(a)[g(b) - g(a)] - g(a)[f(b) - f(a)]. \tag{6}$$

According to Miscellaneous Problem 93 of Chapter 3, the (perpendicular) distance from the point (x_0, y_0) to the line L is

$$d = \frac{|Ax_0 + By_0 + C|}{\sqrt{A^2 + B^2}}.$$

Figure H.1 suggests that the point $(g(c), f(c))$ will maximize this distance d for points on the curve C.

We are motivated, therefore, to define the auxiliary function

$$\phi(t) = Ag(t) + Bf(t) + C, \tag{7}$$

with the constants A, B, and C as defined in (6). Thus $\phi(t)$ is essentially a constant multiple of the distance from $(g(t), f(t))$ to the line L in Fig. H.1.

Now $\phi(a) = 0 = \phi(b)$ (why?), so Rolle's theorem (Section 4.3) implies the existence of a number c in (a, b) such that

$$\phi'(c) = Ag'(c) + Bf'(c) = 0. \tag{8}$$

We substitute the values of A and B from Eq. (6) into (8) and obtain the equation

$$[f(b) - f(a)]g'(c) - [g(b) - g(a)]f'(c) = 0.$$

This is the same as Eq. (2) in the conclusion of Cauchy's mean value theorem, and the proof is complete. ◄

Note Although the assumptions that $g(b) \neq g(a)$ and $g'(c) \neq 0$ were needed for our geometric interpretation of the theorem, they were not used in its proof—only in the motivation for the method of proof.

PROOF OF L'HÔPITAL'S RULE Suppose that $f(x)/g(x)$ has the indeterminate form 0/0 at $x = a$. We may invoke continuity of f and g to allow the assumption that $f(a) = 0 = f(b)$. That is, we simply define $f(a)$ and $g(a)$ to be zero in case their values at $x = a$ are not originally given.

Now we restrict our attention to values of $x \neq a$ in a fixed neighborhood of a on which both f and g are differentiable. Choose one such value of x and hold it temporarily constant. Then apply Cauchy's mean value theorem on the interval $[a, x]$. (If $x < a$, use the interval $[x, a]$.) We find that there is a number z between a and x that behaves as c does in Eq. (2). Hence, by virtue of Eq. (2), we obtain the equation

$$\frac{f(x)}{g(x)} = \frac{f(x) - f(a)}{g(x) - g(a)} = \frac{f'(z)}{g'(z)}.$$

Now z depends on x, but z is trapped between x and a, so z is forced to approach a as $x \to a$. We conclude that

$$\lim_{x \to a} \frac{f(x)}{g(x)} = \lim_{z \to a} \frac{f'(z)}{g'(z)} = \lim_{x \to a} \frac{f'(x)}{g'(x)},$$

under the assumption that the right-hand limit exists. Thus we have verified l'Hôpital's rule in the form of Eq. (1). ◄

APPENDIX I: PROOF OF TAYLOR'S FORMULA

Several different proofs of Taylor's formula (Theorem 2 of Section 11.4) are known, but none of them seems very well motivated—each requires some "trick" to begin the proof. The trick we employ here (suggested by C. R. MacCluer) is to begin by introducing an auxiliary function $F(x)$, defined as follows:

$$F(x) = f(b) - f(x) - f'(x)(b - x) - \frac{f''(x)}{2!}(b - x)^2$$

$$- \cdots - \frac{f^{(n)}(x)}{n!}(b - x)^n - K(b - x)^{n+1}, \quad \textbf{(1)}$$

where the *constant* K is chosen so that $F(a) = 0$. To see that there *is* such a value of k, we could substitute $x = a$ on the right and $F(x) = F(a) = 0$ on the left in Eq. (1) and then solve routinely for K, but we have no need to do this explicitly.

Equation (1) makes it quite obvious that $F(b) = 0$ as well. Therefore, Rolle's theorem (Section 4.3) implies that

$$F'(z) = 0 \quad \textbf{(2)}$$

for some point z of the open interval (a, b) (under the assumption that $a < b$). To see what Eq. (2) means, we differentiate both sides of Eq. (1) and find that

$$F'(x) = -f'(x) + [f'(x) - f''(x)(b - x)]$$

$$+ \left[f''(x)(b - x) - \frac{1}{2!} f^{(3)}(x)(b - x)^2 \right]$$

$$+ \left[\frac{1}{2!} f^{(3)}(x)(b - x)^2 - \frac{1}{3!} f^{(4)}(x)(b - x)^3 \right]$$

$$+ \cdots + \left[\frac{1}{(n-1)!} f^{(n)}(x)(b - x)^{n-1} - \frac{1}{n!} f^{(n+1)}(x)(b - x)^n \right]$$

$$+ (n + 1)K(b - x)^n.$$

Upon careful inspection of this result, we see that all terms except the final two cancel in pairs. Thus the sum "telescopes" to give

$$F'(x) = (n+1)K(b-x)^n - \frac{f^{(n+1)}(x)}{n!}(b-x)^n. \tag{3}$$

Hence Eq. (2) means that

$$(n+1)K(b-z)^n - \frac{f^{(n+1)}(z)}{n!}(b-z)^n = 0.$$

Consequently we can cancel $(b-z)^n$ and solve for

$$K = \frac{f^{(n+1)}(z)}{(n+1)!}. \tag{4}$$

Finally, we return to Eq. (1) and substitute $x = a$, $f(x) = 0$, and the value of K given in Eq. (4). The result is the equation

$$0 = f(b) - f(a) - f'(a)(b-a) - \frac{f''(a)}{2!}(b-a)^2$$
$$- \cdots - \frac{f^{(n)}(a)}{n!}(b-a)^n - \frac{f^{(n+1)}(z)}{(n+1)!}(b-a)^{n+1},$$

which is equivalent to the desired Taylor's formula, Eq. (11) of Section 10.4. ◀

APPENDIX J: CONIC SECTIONS AS SECTIONS OF A CONE

FIGURE J.1 Finding an equation for a conic section.

The parabola, hyperbola, and ellipse that we studied in Chapter 10 were originally introduced by the ancient Greek mathematicians as plane sections (traces) of a right circular cone. Here we show that the intersection of a plane and a cone is, indeed, one of the three conic sections as defined in Chapter 10.

Figure J.1 shows the cone with equation $z = \sqrt{x^2 + y^2}$ and its intersection with a plane $\mathcal{P}$ that passes through the point $(0, 0, 1)$ and the line $x = c > 0$ in the xy-plane. An equation of $\mathcal{P}$ is

$$z = 1 - \frac{x}{c}. \tag{1}$$

The angle between $\mathcal{P}$ and the xy-plane is $\phi = \tan^{-1}(1/c)$. We want to show that the conic section obtained by intersecting the cone and the plane is

A parabola if $\phi = 45°$ $(c = 1)$,

An ellipse if $\phi < 45°$ $(c > 1)$,

A hyperbola if $\phi > 45°$ $(c < 1)$.

We begin by introducing uv-coordinates in the plane $\mathcal{P}$ as follows. The u-coordinate of the point (x, y, z) of $\mathcal{P}$ is $u = y$. The v-coordinate of the same point is its perpendicular distance from the line $x = c$. This explains the u- and v-axes indicated in Fig. J.1. Figure J.2 shows the cross section in the plane $y = 0$ exhibiting the relation between v, x, and z. We see that

$$z = v \sin \phi = \frac{v}{\sqrt{1+c^2}}. \tag{2}$$

Equations (1) and (2) give

$$x = c(1-z) = c\left(1 - \frac{v}{\sqrt{1+c^2}}\right). \tag{3}$$

FIGURE J.2 Computing coordinates in the uv-plane.

We had $z^2 = x^2 + y^2$ for the equation of the cone. We make the following substitutions in this equation: Replace y with u, and replace z and x with the expressions on the right-hand sides of Eqs. (2) and (3), respectively. These replacements yield

$$\frac{v^2}{1+c^2} = c^2\left(1 - \frac{v}{\sqrt{1+c^2}}\right)^2 + u^2.$$

After we simplify, this last equation takes the form

$$u^2 + \frac{c^2-1}{c^2+1}v^2 - \frac{2c^2}{\sqrt{1+c^2}}v + c^2 = 0. \tag{4}$$

This is the equation of the curve in the uv-plane. We examine the three cases for the angle ϕ.

Suppose first that $\phi = 45°$. Then $c = 1$, so Eq. (4) contains a term that includes u^2, another term that includes v, and a constant term. So the curve is a parabola; see Eq. (6) of Section 9.6.

Suppose next that $\phi < 45°$. Then $c > 1$, and both the coefficients of u^2 and v^2 in Eq.(4) are positive. Thus the curve is an ellipse; see Eq. (17) of Section 9.6.

Finally, if $\phi > 45°$, then $c < 1$, and the coefficients of u^2 and v^2 in Eq. (4) have opposite signs. So the curve is a hyperbola; see Eq. (26) of Section 9.6.

APPENDIX K: PROOF OF THE LINEAR APPROXIMATION THEOREM

Under the hypothesis of continuous differentiability of the linear approximation theorem stated in Section 13.6, we want to prove that the increment

$$\Delta f = f(\mathbf{a} + \mathbf{h}) - f(\mathbf{a})$$

is given by

$$\Delta f = \nabla f(\mathbf{a}) \cdot \mathbf{h} + \boldsymbol{\epsilon}(\mathbf{h}) \cdot \mathbf{h} \tag{1}$$

where $\boldsymbol{\epsilon}(\mathbf{h}) = \langle \epsilon_1(\mathbf{h}), \epsilon_2(\mathbf{h}), \ldots, \epsilon_n(\mathbf{h}) \rangle$ is a vector such that each element $\epsilon_i(\mathbf{h})$ approaches zero as $\mathbf{h} \to \mathbf{0}$. [Note the symbol Δ for "increment" and the inverted ∇ for "gradient" on the right-hand side in Eq. (1).]

To analyze the increment Δf, we split the jump from $\mathbf{a}$ to $\mathbf{a} + \mathbf{h}$ into n separate steps, in each of which only a single coordinate is changed. Let $\mathbf{e}_i$ denote the unit n-vector with 1 in the ith position, and write

$$\mathbf{a}_0 = \mathbf{a} \quad \text{and} \quad \mathbf{a}_i = \mathbf{a}_{i-1} + h_i \mathbf{e}_i \tag{2}$$

for $i = 1, 2, \ldots, n$, so that $\mathbf{a}_n = \mathbf{a} + \mathbf{h}$. Then

$$\Delta f = f(\mathbf{a}_n) - f(\mathbf{a}_0)$$
$$= [f(\mathbf{a}_n) - f(\mathbf{a}_{n-1})] + [f(\mathbf{a}_{n-1}) - f(\mathbf{a}_{n-2})] + \cdots$$
$$+ [f(\mathbf{a}_2) - f(\mathbf{a}_1)] + [f(\mathbf{a}_1) - f(\mathbf{a}_0)];$$

that is,

$$\Delta f = \sum_{i=1}^{n} [f(\mathbf{a}_i) - f(\mathbf{a}_{i-1})]. \tag{3}$$

The ith term in this sum is given by

$$f(\mathbf{a}_i) - f(\mathbf{a}_{i-1}) = f(a_1 + h_1, \ldots, a_{i-1} + h_{i-1}, a_i + h_i, a_{i+1}, \ldots, a_n)$$
$$- f(a_1 + h_1, \ldots, a_{i-1} + h_{i-1}, a_i, a_{i+1}, \ldots, a_n)$$
$$= g_i(1) - g_i(0),$$

where the differentiable function g_i is defined by

$$g_i(t) = f(a_1 + h_1, \ldots, a_{i-1} + h_{i-1}, a_i + th_i, a_{i+1}, \ldots, a_n).$$

The mean value theorem then yields

$$f(\mathbf{a}_i) - f(\mathbf{a}_{i-1}) = g_i(1) - g_i(0) = g_i'(\overline{t}_i)(1-0)$$
$$= D_i f(a_1 + h_1, \ldots, a_{i-1} + h_{i-1}, a_i + \overline{t}_i h_i, a_{i+1}, \ldots, a_n) \cdot h_i$$
$$= D_i f(\mathbf{a}_{i-1} + \overline{t}_i h_i \mathbf{e}_i) \cdot h_i$$

for some $\overline{t}_i$ between 0 and 1. Substitution in (2) then gives

$$\Delta f = \sum_{i=1}^{n} D_i f(\mathbf{a}_{i-1} + \overline{t}_i h_i \mathbf{e}_i) \cdot h_i$$
$$= \sum_{i=1}^{n} [D_i f(\mathbf{a}) + D_i f(\mathbf{a}_{i-1} + \overline{t}_i h_i \mathbf{e}_i) - D_i f(\mathbf{a})] \cdot h_i.$$

Thus

$$\Delta f = \sum_{i=1}^{n} [D_i f(\mathbf{a}) + \epsilon_i(\mathbf{h})] \cdot h_i$$
$$= \nabla f(\mathbf{a}) \cdot \mathbf{h} + \langle \epsilon_i(\mathbf{h}), \epsilon_i(\mathbf{h}), \ldots, \epsilon_i(\mathbf{h}) \rangle \cdot \mathbf{h}$$

where

$$\epsilon_i(\mathbf{h}) = D_i f(\mathbf{a}_{i-1} + \overline{t}_i h_i \mathbf{e}_i) - D_i f(\mathbf{a}) \to 0$$

(by continuity of $D_i f$ at $\mathbf{a}$) as $\mathbf{h} \to \mathbf{0}$ (and hence $\mathbf{a}_{i-1} \to \mathbf{a}$ by (2)). We have therefore established (1) and hence completed the proof. ◄

APPENDIX L: UNITS OF MEASUREMENT AND CONVERSION FACTORS

MKS SCIENTIFIC UNITS

- *Length* in meters (m); *mass* in kilograms (kg), *time* in seconds (s)
- *Force* in newtons (N); a force of 1 N imparts an acceleration of 1 m/s^2 to a mass of 1 kg.
- *Work* in joules (J); 1 J is the work done by a force of 1 N acting through a distance of 1 m.
- *Power* in watts (W); 1 W is 1 J/s.

BRITISH ENGINEERING UNITS (FPS)

- *Length* in feet (ft), *force* in pounds (lb), *time* in seconds (s)
- *Mass* in slugs; 1 lb of force imparts an acceleration of 1 ft/s^2 to a mass of 1 slug. A mass of m slugs at the surface of the earth has a *weight* of $w = mg$ pounds (lb), where $g \approx 32.17$ ft/s^2.
- *Work* in ft · lb, *power* in ft · lb/s.

CONVERSION FACTORS

$$1 \text{ in.} = 2.54 \text{ cm} = 0.0254 \text{ m}, \quad 1 \text{ m} \approx 3.2808 \text{ ft}$$
$$1 \text{ mi} = 5280 \text{ ft}; \quad 60 \text{ mi/h} = 88 \text{ ft/s}$$
$$1 \text{ lb} \approx 4.4482 \text{ N}; \quad 1 \text{ slug} \approx 14.594 \text{ kg}$$
$$1 \text{ hp} = 550 \text{ ft} \cdot \text{lb/s} \approx 745.7 \text{ W}$$

- *Gravitational acceleration:* $g \approx 32.17$ ft/s^2 ≈ 9.807 m/s^2
- *Atmospheric pressure:* 1 atm is the pressure exerted by a column of mercury 76 cm high; 1 atm ≈ 14.70 lb/in.^{2} $\approx 1.013 \times 10^5$ N/m^2
- *Heat energy:* 1 Btu ≈ 778 ft $\cdot$ lb ≈ 252 cal, 1 cal ≈ 4.184 J

APPENDIX M: FORMULAS FROM ALGEBRA, GEOMETRY, AND TRIGONOMETRY

LAWS OF EXPONENTS

$$a^m a^n = a^{m+n}, \quad (a^m)^n = a^{mn}, \quad (ab)^n = a^n b^n, \quad a^{m/n} = \sqrt[n]{a^m};$$

in particular,

$$a^{1/2} = \sqrt{a}.$$

If $a \neq 0$, then

$$a^{m-n} = \frac{a^m}{a^n}, \quad a^{-n} = \frac{1}{a^n}, \quad \text{and} \quad a^0 = 1.$$

QUADRATIC FORMULA

The quadratic equation

$$ax^2 + bx + c = 0 \quad (a \neq 0)$$

has solutions

$$x = \frac{-b \pm \sqrt{b^2 - 4ac}}{2a}.$$

FACTORING

$$a^2 - b^2 = (a-b)(a+b)$$
$$a^3 - b^3 = (a-b)(a^2 + ab + b^2)$$
$$a^4 - b^4 = (a-b)(a^3 + a^2 b + ab^2 + b^3)$$
$$= (a-b)(a+b)(a^2 + b^2)$$
$$a^5 - b^5 = (a-b)(a^4 + a^3 b + a^2 b^2 + ab^3 + b^4)$$

(The pattern continues.)

$$a^3 + b^3 = (a+b)(a^2 - ab + b^2)$$
$$a^5 + b^5 = (a+b)(a^4 - a^3 b + a^2 b^2 - ab^3 + b^4)$$
$$a^7 + b^7 = (a+b)(a^6 - a^5 b + a^4 b^2 - a^3 b^3 + a^2 b^4 - ab^5 + b^6)$$

(The pattern continues for odd exponents.)

BINOMIAL FORMULA

$$(a+b)^n = a^n + na^{n-1}b + \frac{n(n-1)}{1 \cdot 2} a^{n-2} b^2$$
$$+ \frac{n(n-1)(n-2)}{1 \cdot 2 \cdot 3} a^{n-3} b^3 + \cdots + nab^{n-1} + b^n$$

if n is a positive integer.

AREA AND VOLUME

In Fig. M.1, the symbols have the following meanings.

A: area b: length of base r: radius
B: area of base C: circumference V: volume
h: height ℓ: length w: width

Rectangle: $A = bh$

Parallelogram: $A = bh$

Triangle: $A = \frac{1}{2}bh$

Trapezoid: $A = \frac{1}{2}(b_1 + b_2)h$

Circle: $C = 2\pi r$ and $A = \pi r^2$

Rectangular parallelepiped:
$V = \ell w h$

Pyramid:
$V = \frac{1}{3}Bh$

Right circular cone:
$V = \frac{1}{3}\pi r^2 h = \frac{1}{3}Bh$

Right circular cylinder:
$V = \pi r^2 h = Bh$

Sphere:
$V = \frac{4}{3}\pi r^3$ and $A = 4\pi r^2$

FIGURE M.1 The basic geometric shapes.

PYTHAGOREAN THEOREM

In a right triangle with legs a and b and hypotenuse c,

$$a^2 + b^2 = c^2.$$

FORMULAS FROM TRIGONOMETRY

$$\sin(-\theta) = -\sin\theta$$

$$\cos(-\theta) = \cos\theta$$

$$\sin^2\theta + \cos^2\theta = 1$$

$$\sin 2\theta = 2\sin\theta\cos\theta$$

$$\cos 2\theta = \cos^2\theta - \sin^2\theta$$

$$\sin(\alpha + \beta) = \sin\alpha\cos\beta + \cos\alpha\sin\beta$$

$$\cos(\alpha + \beta) = \cos\alpha\cos\beta - \sin\alpha\sin\beta$$

$$\tan(\alpha + \beta) = \frac{\tan\alpha + \tan\beta}{1 - \tan\alpha\tan\beta}$$

$$\sin^2\frac{\theta}{2} = \frac{1 - \cos\theta}{2}$$

$$\cos^2\frac{\theta}{2} = \frac{1 + \cos\theta}{2}$$

For an arbitrary triangle (Fig. M.2):

Law of cosines: $\quad c^2 = a^2 + b^2 - 2ab\cos C.$

Law of sines: $\quad \dfrac{\sin A}{a} = \dfrac{\sin B}{b} = \dfrac{\sin C}{c}.$

FIGURE M.2 An arbitrary triangle.

APPENDIX N: THE GREEK ALPHABET

A	α	alpha	I	ι	iota	P	ρ	rho
B	β	beta	K	κ	kappa	Σ	σ	sigma
Γ	γ	gamma	Λ	λ	lambda	T	τ	tau
Δ	δ	delta	M	μ	mu	Υ	υ	upsilon
E	ϵ	epsilon	N	ν	nu	Φ	ϕ	phi
Z	ζ	zeta	Ξ	ξ	xi	X	χ	chi
H	η	eta	O	o	omicron	Ψ	ψ	psi
Θ	θ	theta	Π	π	pi	Ω	ω	omega

REFERENCES FOR FURTHER STUDY

References 2, 3, 7, and 10 may be consulted for historical topics pertinent to calculus. Reference 14 provides a more theoretical treatment of single-variable calculus topics than ours. References 4, 5, 8, and 15 include advanced topics in multivariable calculus. Reference 11 is a standard work on infinite series. References 1, 9, and 13 are differential equations textbooks. Reference 6 discusses topics in calculus together with computing and programming in BASIC. Those who would like to pursue the topic of fractals should look at reference 12.

1. Boyce, William E. and Richard C. DiPrima, *Elementary Differential Equations* (5th ed.). New York: John Wiley, 1991.
2. Boyer, Carl B., *A History of Mathematics* (2nd ed.). New York: John Wiley, 1991.
3. Boyer, Carl B., *The History of the Calculus and Its Conceptual Development.* New York: Dover Publications, 1959.
4. Buck, R. Creighton, *Advanced Calculus* (3rd ed.). New York: McGraw-Hill, 1977.
5. Courant, Richard and Fritz John, *Introduction to Calculus and Analysis.* Vols. I and II. New York: Springer-Verlag, 1982.
6. Edwards, C. H., Jr., *Calculus and the Personal Computer.* Englewood Cliffs, NJ: Prentice-Hall, 1986.
7. Edwards, C. H., Jr., *The Historical Development of the Calculus.* New York: Springer-Verlag, 1979.
8. Edwards, C. H., Jr., *Advanced Calculus of Several Variables.* New York: Academic Press, 1973.
9. Edwards, C. H., Jr. and David E. Penney, *Differential Equations with Boundary Value Problems: Computing and Modeling* (2nd ed.). Upper Saddle River, NJ: Prentice Hall, 2000.
10. Kline, Morris, *Mathematical Thought from Ancient to Modern Times.* Vols. I, II, and III. New York: Oxford University Press, 1972.
11. Knopp, Konrad, *Theory and Application of Infinite Series* (2nd ed.). New York: Hafner Press, 1990.
12. Peitgen, H.-O. and P. H. Richter, *The Beauty of Fractals.* New York: Springer-Verlag, 1986.
13. Simmons, George E., *Differential Equations with Applications and Historical Notes.* New York: McGraw-Hill, 1972.
14. Spivak, Michael E., *Calculus* (2nd ed.). Berkeley: Publish or Perish, 1980.
15. Taylor, Angus E. and W. Robert Mann, *Advanced Calculus* (3rd ed.). New York: John Wiley, 1983.

TEACHING OUTLINES CONTENTS

1 Functions, Graphs, and Models   T-3
2 Prelude to Calculus   T-4
3 The Derivative   T-5
4 Additional Applications of the Derivative   T-7
5 The Integral   T-9
6 Applications of the Integral   T-10
7 Calculus of Transcendental Functions   T-12
8 Techniques of Integration   T-13
9 Differential Equations   T-14
10 Polar Coordinates and Parametric Curves   T-15
11 Infinite Series   T-17
12 Vectors, Curves, and Surfaces in Space   T-19
13 Partial Differentiation   T-21
14 Multiple Integrals   T-23
15 Vector Calculus   T-25

TEACHING OUTLINES

Here are teaching outlines for each section of the text (other than those having no problems at the end, such as the introductory sections). If you've taught calculus several times, you might find them useful as a source of recommended problems. If you want more guidance, we've also included:

- A list of topics to cover.
- Notes on items to emphasize, possible pitfalls, and the like.
- A list of goals—skills and understanding we hope the students will acquire.

Your authors have taught calculus for a total of about 85 years. Our best advice: Have the students work lots of problems, especially those with no hints or answers, and never assign a problem you haven't worked yourself.

More about problems: Answers to many (but not all) odd-numbered problems appear in the back of the book. Complete solutions to all odd-numbered problems are available in the *Student Solutions Manual* (your bookstore may stock it; it's up to you, your calculus coordinator, or your department chairman to ask that they do *or* to insist that they do not). Solutions to *all* problems are available in the *Instructor's Manual,* which is not supposed to be available to students. Both manuals are also available online (available only to qualified instructors and faculty members).

Finally, remember that the textbook is *not* the course. Bring to the course your own experiences and those of your colleagues, current events, historical connections, and whatever else brings life and enthusiasm into the classroom. We have provided some enhancements through the True/False Study Guides that follow each section, the Concepts Questions that follow each section, and—following the Problems of many sections—the Projects, most of which require a graphing calculator and some of which require a microcomputer with symbolic algebra software.

CHAPTER 1 FUNCTIONS, GRAPHS, AND MODELS

1.1 Functions and Mathematical Modeling

Topics to Cover Function, domain, and range. Independent and dependent variable. Greatest integer function. If the domain is not specified, it's the largest set of real numbers for which the rule of the function makes sense. Intervals and interval notation.

Notes The key idea is that of *function*. Provide as many varied examples as time permits.

Goals The students should be able to distinguish between "formula" and "function" and should be able to construct their own examples of functions (complete with appropriate domains). As a first step toward mathematical modeling, the students should be able to construct functions to fit specific situations, such as those in Problems 36 through 47.

Problems 1, 2, 7, 8, 13, 14, 15, 16, 17, 18, 23, 24, 37, 38, 41, 42, 45, 46, 47, 48, 57, and 58.

1.2 Graphs of Equations and Functions

Topics to Cover The slope of a nonvertical line in the plane, the equation of such a line (and its point-slope form and slope-intercept form), and its angle of inclination. Horizontal and vertical lines. Parallel and perpendicular lines. Graph of an equation; example: circles. Translates of graphs; example: circles. Translation principle. Finding the center and radius of a general circle; completing the square. Graph of a function. Vertical line test. Graph of the greatest integer function. Parabolas. Finding the vertex of a parabola by completing the square. Application to finding maxima and minima of quadratic functions. Hints about the upcoming *tangent line*.

Notes The key idea is that of the *graph of a function.* Provide varied examples.

Goals The students should be able to sketch graphs of simple functions by hand. If graphing calculators are available, they should be able to use their calculators to construct graphs with given viewing windows and "zoom" to discover important local features (extrema, discontinuities, zeros). If their calculators show unexpected or incorrect results (at discontinuities, for example), take advantage of it.

Problems 1, 2, 3, 4, 5, 6, 9, 10, 11, 12, 15, 16, 17, 18, 21, 22, 23, 24, 29, 30, 33, 34, 43, 44, 49, 50, 51, 52, 65, 66, 73, and 74.

1.3 Polynomials and Algebraic Functions

Topics to Cover Power functions and their behavior as $x \to \pm\infty$. Negative and fractional powers. Combinations of functions: scalar multiple, sum, difference, product, and quotient. Domains of such combinations. Polynomials; the degree of a polynomial; zeros of a polynomial and the fundamental theorem of algebra (no proof, of course!). Rational functions; vertical asymptotes and discontinuities (very informally). Algebraic functions.

Notes The domains can be tricky. Provide plenty of examples.

Goals The students should be able to distinguish the varieties of functions discussed here.

Problems 1, 2, 5, 6, 7 through 20, 21, 28, 33, and 34.

1.4 Transcendental Functions

Topics to Cover Trigonometric functions (radians, periodicity, discontinuities of tangent and secant). Composition of functions; domain of a composition. Analysis of compositions, as in Example 5. Exponential functions; base; increasing and decreasing behavior. Logarithmic functions; logarithms and bases; common and natural logarithms (very informally). Comparative rates of increase of logarithmic functions, power functions, and exponential functions. Transcendental functions; transcendental equations; graphical (approximate) solution of transcendental equations. Optional: The subsection on "Can You Believe ...".

Notes This section is an introduction to the wide variety of functions.

Goals The students should learn that trigonometric functions exhibit periodic behavior, exponential functions exhibit rapidly increasing or rapidly decreasing behavior, and that both are unlike polynomials and rational functions.

Problems 1 through 10, 11, 12, 13, 14, 19, 20, 21, 22, 23, 24, 29, and 30; if graphing calculators are available, also 31, 32, 43, and 44.

1.5 Preview: What *Is* Calculus?

Topics to Cover Assign this section for reading. Key ideas: The tangent line problem; the area problem. Their connection through the fundamental theorem of calculus.

Chapter 1 Review

Problems 1, 6, 11, 14, 17, 18, 19, 24, 25 through 34, 35, 36, 43, 44, 45, and 46; if a graphing calculator is available, also 55, 56, 59, 60, 63, 64, and 65 through 70.

CHAPTER 2   PRELUDE TO CALCULUS

2.1 Tangent Lines and Slope Predictors

Topics to Cover The key idea is to develop the concept of the *line tangent to a curve at a point*. Our approach is to define instead the *slope* of such a line as the limiting value of slopes of appropriate secant lines; then we define the line *tangent* to the curve at the point P as the straight line through P with that limiting slope. To get to this concept, we need the simple concept of the increment Δx in a given value of x. The formula we obtain for the slope of the tangent line we call the *slope predictor* for the curve at the point of tangency. We proceed from the specific to the general: First we obtain the general slope predictor for the parabola with equation $y = x^2$, then the slope predictor in Eq. (7) for the slope of the line tangent to the graph of $y = f(x)$ at the point $(a, f(a))$. The [only] theorem of the section gives the general formula the slope predictor for $f(x) = px^2 + qx + r$, and this formula is used to a moderate extent in solving some of the problems at the end of the section. After a brief word about normal lines, the students should be ready to begin solving problems.

Notes This section is a foundation for the concept of the derivative, first introduced formally in Chapter 3, so it is important that the students understand the key ideas and become proficient at setting up the Newton quotient for finding the slope predictor ("derivative") and at the algebra of finding its limit as $\Delta x \to 0$.

Goals The students should understand how to find (in theory) the slope of a line tangent to an arbitrary curve at a given point on the curve and (in practice) how to find the slope of a line tangent to $f(x) = px^2 + qx + r$ at an arbitrary point of its graph.

Problems 1 through 12, 15 through 20, 25, 26, 28, 29, 30, 31, 33, 34, 35. If you are using graphing calculators, any of problems 36 through 48.

2.2 The Limit Concept

Topics to Cover The need for finding limits in order to find slopes; the necessity of having a precise definition of the limit; the idea of the limit. Your examples should include repeated instances of the situation in which

$$\lim_{x \to a} f(x) \neq f(a),$$

not only because the limit exists and is not equal to $f(a)$, but also because the limit does not exist or because $f(a)$ is undefined. If you are using graphing calculators, they can be of a great deal of help in illuminating the *symbolic* definition of the limit with *graphic* and *numerical* illustrations of limits. Cover the limit laws, emphasize their natural aspects, and use them to find a few limits (as in Examples 6 and 7). Don't omit the substitution law. The section continues with a gradual introduction to the derivative by means of a discussion of *slope-predictor functions*. It concludes with the use of conjugate expressions to help find limits (Example 13).

Notes Question 2 at the end of the section will be useful for testing your students' understanding of the substitution law of limits.

Goals Experience with using the limit laws, especially in finding slope-predictor functions; an awareness that care is required with the quotient law.

Problems 1 through 10, 19 through 26, 29 through 36, 37 through 40. The remaining problems require the use of a calculator; considering assigning any of 53 through 61, 63, and 64.

2.3 More About Limits

Topics to Cover The limits of $\sin x$ and $\cos x$ as $x \to 0$. The fundamental trigonometric limit:

$$\lim_{x \to 0} \frac{\sin x}{x} = 1. \quad (1)$$

Using the limit in (1) to find other trigonometric limits. The "squeeze law" of limits. One-sided limits. Theorem 2, relating one-sided and two-sided limits. One-sided limit laws. Existence of tangent lines—what if the limit of the Newton quotient is infinite? Infinite limits. Proof of Eq. (1). Formal definition of the limit.

Notes You will need to steer a thoughtful course between the Scylla of the precise epsilon-delta definition of the limit and the Charybdis of total informality. What is the composition of your classes? What are their majors? Will they be expected to write formal proofs in upcoming weeks (or semesters)?

Goals The students should acquire as thorough an understanding of the limit concept as time permits.

Problems 1 through 4; Problems 5 through 8 are more challenging. Problems 25 through 42, 59 through 52, 59, 61, 62, 67, and—if you have covered the formal definitions of the limit—Problems 75, 76, 78, and 79.

2.4 The Concept of Continuity

Topics to Cover "To find the limit of $f(x)$ as x approaches a, why can't I just substitute and get $f(a)$?" Answer: "This will give the correct answer if f is continuous at a." This is a major motive for the definition of continuity at a point, the first topic to cover. Also to cover: discontinuities (infinite, finite, and removable), continuity of combinations of continuous functions, that every polynomial is continuous, and that every rational function is continuous where defined (where its denominator is nonzero). Continuity of the trigonometric functions, Theorem 2 on the continuity of compositions, left and right continuity (so we can say that f is continuous on the closed interval $[a, b]$ even if f is undefined outside that interval), and continuity *on* the set S. The intermediate value property of continuous functions and its application to existence of solutions of certain equations.

Notes Continuity makes finding limits easy; in Chapter 3 we'll develop an easy sufficient condition for continuity (to wit, differentiability; see Theorem 2 in Section 3.4). Continuity on a closed interval has important consequences: the intermediate value theorem and the maximum value theorem (Theorem 1 in Section 3.5). These are key steps in the proof of the fundamental theorem of calculus and the proof of the existence of the definite integral, and have earlier applications throughout Chapters 3 and 4.

Goals Understanding what it means for a function to be continuous at a point or on an interval and the consequences of continuity. Recognizing and classifying discontinuities. The behavior of the graph of a function at and near a point where it is continuous; its behavior near a discontinuity. The intermediate value property of continuous functions and some of its consequences.

Problems 1, 4, 6, 7, 9, 12, 13, 15 through 24, 39, 40, 45, 46, 49 through 52, 55, 56, 60, 68, 69; if a graphing calculator is available, some of 71 through 78.

Chapter 2 Review

Problems 1, 5, 8, 10, 18, 21, 31, 37, 41, 42, 48, 51, 55, 56, 59, 61, 65, 66 (challenging).

CHAPTER 3 THE DERIVATIVE

3.1 The Derivative and Rates of Change

Topics to Cover The section title almost says it all: The definition of the derivative; the terminology (derivative, differentiation, differentiable); the fact that the derivative predicts the slope of the tangent line (not the other way around). The algebraic mechanics of differentiation. The special formula for the derivative of $f(x) = ax^2 + bx + c$. The $\Delta y / \Delta x$ notation and how it leads to the alternative notation dy/dx for the derivative of $y = f(x)$. The derivative's connection with rates of change; average and instantaneous rate of change. Position function; average and instantaneous velocity; velocity as the derivative of position (with respect to time). Vertical motion, acceleration; the position function of a particle in vertical motion.

Notes Memorize the definition of the derivative. Be able to state it with different names for the independent and dependent variables. At this point we let $h \to 0$ or $\Delta x \to 0$; the alternative definition with $x \to a$ for $f'(a)$ appears also in Eq. (2), but the former is used heavily in the opening sections of Chapter 3.

Goals The students should be able to find $f'(x)$ given $f(x)$ for such simple functions as appear in the end-of-section problems. They should also be sensitive to the phenomenon of $f'(x)$ failing to exist at certain points.

Problems 1, 3, 5, 8, 10, 15, 16, 17, 20, 21, 24, 27, 28, 30 through 35, 37, 39, 44, 49, 50, 58.

3.2 Basic Differentiation Rules

Topics to Cover Operator notation $D_x f(x)$ for $f'(x)$. Basic differentiation rules: The derivative of a constant (constant function), of x^n (for n a positive integer), of a linear combination, of polynomials; the product and reciprocal rules. Power rule for negative integral exponent; the quotient rule.

Notes The derivative of the product of three or more functions is mentioned briefly.

Goals The students should be able to work most of the problems at the end of the section.

Problems 1, 3, 5, 9, 12, 16, 18, 23, 33, 39, 40, 41, 44, 47, 48, 51, 53, 55, 56, 57, 58, 60, 61 through 65 (as a group), 66.

3.3 The Chain Rule

Topics to Cover The chain rule, first in Leibniz notation, then in function notation. The proof of the chain rule for the derivative of $f(g(x))$ for the case in which $g'(x)$ is never zero. (The complete proof appears in Section 4.2.) Special cases, such as the generalized power rule. Rate-of-change applications.

Notes You may wish to introduce the derivatives of the sine and cosine functions (informally) to provide further illustrations. With some students, the decomposition of $f(g(x))$ into its "components" f and g, step-by-step calculation of $f'(x)$, $g'(x)$, and $f'(g(x))$, followed by substitution in the formula in Eq. (4), is the only practical first step in learning the chain rule.

Goals As usual, the students should be able to work most of the end-of-section problems.

Problems Assign as many as your student will tolerate; you might consider including some (or all) of Problems 1, 3, 5, 6, 9, 11, 13, 16, 21, 22, 23, 24, 28, 30, 31, 35, 37 through 44, 45 through 48, 50, 51, 55, 57, 61, 65 through 68.

3.4 Derivatives of Algebraic Functions

Topics to Cover Power rule for rational exponents, generalized power rule (Theorem 1), vertical tangent lines, differentiability implies continuity (Theorem 2).

Notes There will be some examples of functions not differentiable at certain points in their domains. A little care in explanations and illustrations is a good idea.

It's also time to begin emphasizing speed and accuracy, and point out that dependence on the definition of the derivative will, in the future, only rarely be necessary. Also provide examples to illustrate that continuity does not imply differentiability.

Goals The students are now at the point where they should be able to find derivatives of all kinds of combinations of all the functions they know about other than the transcendental functions.

Problems 1, 2, 5, 8, 11, 17, 21, 23, 29, 30, 37, 38, 45 through 49, 51, 54, 57 through 63, 65, 67, 68, 70.

3.5 Maxima and Minima of Functions on Closed Intervals

Topics to Cover The definition of maximum and minimum value (global, but the word isn't used yet); relation to high and low points on the graph. Existence of extrema of a continuous function on a closed and bounded interval (Theorem 1). If you have time, examples to show that all the hypotheses of Theorem 1 are necessary. Local extrema. At a local extremum of a differentiable function, the derivative is zero (Theorem 2). Include the proof if you have time; only one case need be covered. Global extrema and the "closed interval maximum-minimum method." Locations of global extrema (Theorem 3). Finding global extrema.

Notes In finding global extrema, proceed from the simplest examples (find the global maximum value of $f(x) = x^2$ on the interval $-1 \leq x \leq 2$) to the more challenging, but leave the word problems for Section 3.6.

Goals The students should be able to find the global extrema of simple algebraic functions on closed intervals and should know criteria that guarantee their existence and their necessary locations.

Problems 1, 3, 4, 6, 8, 9, 10, 11, 13, 15, 18, 20, 25, 26, 27, 33, 40, 47 through 52. Problems 53 through 60 require a graphing calculator or computer.

3.6 Applied Optimization Problems

Topics to Cover A procedure for solving an applied optimization problem: **1.** Identify the quantity to be maximized or minimized. **2.** Express the dependent variable as a function of some independent variable (frequently with the aid of a sketch or diagram). **3.** Apply calculus. **4.** Identify the extrema. **5.** Answer the question posed in the original problem.

Notes Examples might include the largest rectangular corral with a long existing wall forming one of its side or (more difficult) with a short existing wall forming all or part of one of its sides; the open-topped box maximum volume obtained by cutting equal squares from the four corners of a rectangle and folding up the sides (if you want the solution to contain only simple rational numbers, choose the dimensions of the rectangle to be $a = r^2 - s^2$ by $b = r^2 - 2rs$ where r and s are positive integers such that $r > 2s$). Other examples might include rectangular corrals with various numbers of internal divider fences all parallel to two of the sides, cheapest boxes whose bottom, sides, and top are made of material of different costs per unit area, and the like. While working some of these problems, illustrate the five-step process discussed here. In part **2**, draw and carefully label a large, clear figure when possible. Work Example 5 so you can assign Problem 43. The discussions of plausibility and dimensions that follow Example 5 are very useful, especially for engineering students.

Goals The technique of solving applied optimization problems (in contrast to the rote mechanics thereof).

Problems 1, 2, 3, 6, 8, 12, 14, 15 (calculator suggested), 20, 25, 30, 32, 42, 43 (difficult), 46, 52, 62 (discontinuous function to be minimized). Your student will find these problems the most difficult so far in the course. You should definitely spend more than a single class period on this section—perhaps three or four—and give several short homework assignments.

3.7 Derivatives of Trigonometric Functions

Topics to Cover The derivatives of the six trigonometric functions and the chain-rule versions of these formulas. Rate-of-change and maximum-minimum applications.

Notes Prove that $D_x[\sin x] = \cos x$. Perhaps obtain the derivative of the cosine function as follows:

$$D_x[\cos x] = D_x\left[\sin\left(x + \tfrac{1}{2}\pi\right)\right] = \cos\left(x + \tfrac{1}{2}\pi\right) = -\sin x.$$

Goals Of course the students need to memorize the derivatives of the six trigonometric functions. But at this point they need strong reinforcement of what they should have learned earlier. Thus they need drill in routine differentiation involving the chain rule, the product rule, the quotient rule, and the like; they also need practice in solving rate-of-change problems and applied optimization problems in which the trigonometric functions play a prominent role.

Problems 1 through 8, 12, 16, 22, 36, 38, 42, 48, 54, 56, 60, 66, 70, 72, 74, 77, 82. More challenging: 81, 87, 88. Very challenging: 85.

3.8 Successive Approximations and Newton's Method

Topics to Cover Newton's method.

Notes You may wish to include a few examples of how Newton's method might fail, how to detect this, and how to prevent or remedy it. For efficient calculator implementation of Newton's method, your students will need calculators with two or three memory locations and several levels of parentheses.

Better still, a calculator that can "recall" the previous display makes Newton's method easy. For example, with a TI-85, you can approximate the solution of $f(x) = 0$ with initial guess $x_0 = a$ as follows.

```
a STO x ENTER

x - f(x)/f'(x) STO x ENTER
    (x₁ is displayed)

ENTRY ENTER       ( x₂ is displayed)

ENTRY ENTER       (x₃ is displayed, etc.)
```

In *Mathematica*, you could enter the commands

```
f[x] :=        (The formula for f(x) goes here.)

g[x] := N[ x - f[x]/f'[x], 20 ]

x = a

g[x]           (x₁ is displayed)

g[x]           (x₂ is displayed, etc.)
```

Goals The students should learn how to use Newton's method to solve equations involving differentiable functions of a single variable and (important) appreciate the geometry of the method.

Problems 1, 2, 6, 12, 18, 22, 29, 34, 38, 40.

Chapter 3 Review

Problems 2, 4, 6, 8, 19, 29, 37, 45, 49, 55, 61, 66, 68, 73, 78, 82 (long), 85, 88, 90, 103, 105, 112, 114, 118, 120.

CHAPTER 4   ADDITIONAL APPLICATIONS OF THE DERIVATIVE

4.1 Implicit Differentiation and Related Rates

Topics to Cover Implicitly defined functions, implicit differentiation, and related rates.

Notes The folium of Descartes with equation $x^3 + y^3 = 3xy$ is a very good standard example and it recurs frequently in the text. Mention that if $f(x) \equiv g(x)$, then $f'(x) = g'(x)$ where the previous identity holds, but to differentiate both sides of an *equation* is possible but pointless (see Problem 71 of Section 3.4).

Goals Enhancement of the students' understanding of how and when to use the chain rule.

Problems 1, 2, 5, 6, 8, 12, 18, 20, 26, 30, 31, 32, 35, 37, 44, 51, 54, 60, 63, 66.

4.2 Increments, Differentials, and Linear Approximation

Topics to Cover Increment, differential, linear approximation formula (Eqs. (1), (2), and (3)). The error in the linear approximation (Eq. (13)). Calculus using differentials.

Notes The proof of the chain rule is optional, but short and complete.

Goals The students should appreciate the geometry of the linear approximation and the behavior of the error in the approximation $dy \approx \Delta y$ as $\Delta x \to 0$.

Problems 1, 4, 5, 10, 11, 14, 16, 17 through 24, 25, 26, 29, 32, 33, 37, 40, 41, 43, 47, 49. If a graphical calculator or computer is available, 53 through 58.

4.3 Increasing and Decreasing Functions and the Mean Value Theorem

Topics to Cover The definitions of what it means for the function f to be *increasing* on an interval and *decreasing* on an interval. Rolle's theorem, the mean value theorem, and its three corollaries (especially the third).

Notes All five proofs are easy and suitable for classroom presentation. To find the intervals where f is increasing and those where it is decreasing, find the points at which $f'(x)$ can change sign: the points where $f'(x) = 0$ and those where f or f' is discontinuous. These points typically separate the x-axis into intervals; on each such interval, $f'(x)$ cannot change sign. Thus the sign of $f'(x)$ in each such interval can be determined by testing it at any convenient point of that interval. Numerous examples with many figures will help your students. There are several homework problems in which the student is asked to show that a certain equation has exactly one solution. Let them know that one efficient way to do so is to show first that the equation has *at least* one solution (usually as a consequence of the intermediate value theorem), then to show that the equation has *at most* one solution (usually with the aid of the first derivative).

Goals This is the first section in a sequence devoted to the use of calculus to find qualitatively accurate sketches of graphs, sketches that give more information than the usual computer graph.

Problems 1 through 18, 21, 22, 24, 25, 29, 33, 34, 37, 42, 43, 47, 49, 54, 55, 58.

4.4 The First Derivative Test and Applications

Topics to Cover Definitions of global (absolute) maximum and minimum, local (relative) maximum and minimum, global (or local) maximum (or minimum) *value, extremum*. Interior points and the first derivative test for local extrema. How you can sometimes use the first derivative to establish that a critical point is a *global* maximum or minimum (Theorem 2). Open-interval maximum-minimum problems.

Notes A few blackboard sketches and a brief verbal explanation is enough for the proofs of Theorems 1 and 2.

Goals This section is the second in the curve-sketching sequence but also had important applications in the identification of extrema, a key topic of the course.

Problems 1 through 13, 16, 17, 18, 27, 30, 34, 41, 43, 45, 47 (more difficult), 49, 51, 53.

4.5 Simple Curve Sketching

Topics to Cover We continue the development of curve-sketching techniques by examining the behavior of the function f as $x \to +\infty$ and as $x \to -\infty$ and the mechanics of beginning the sketch itself—first by plotting critical points and intercepts, then by using the increasing/decreasing behavior of f (from Section 4.4) to join these points with (generally) smooth curves.

Notes The section concludes with a brief discussion of the use of curve sketching to aid in finding the solutions of equations (in a single variable).

Goals As usual, the students should be able to use these new techniques to solve most of the problems at the end of the section.

Problems 1 through 4, 5 through 14, 15, 18 through 23, 27, 30, 37, 38, 42, 43, 49, 52.

4.6 Higher Derivatives and Concavity

Topics to Cover The second (and higher-order) derivatives; graphs that are "bending upward" (concave upward) and "bending downward" (concave downward); the second derivative and concavity. The second derivative test for identifying certain extrema. Inflection points and how to find them. Using all this information to enhance one's sketch of the graph of a function.

Notes This is a good point at which to review earlier curve-sketching techniques and to integrate the new material of this section with earlier material.

Goals At this point the students should be able to obtain graphs of elementary functions that are qualitatively quite accurate.

Problems 1, 4, 17, 21, 23, 24, 28, 29, 31, 33, 35, 36, 43, 48, 51, 52, 63 through 66, 77, 80, 84, 86.

4.7 Curve Sketching and Asymptotes

Topics to Cover Curve-sketching techniques are extended to include vertical asymptotes, horizontal asymptotes, and—if you wish—slant ("inclined" or "oblique") asymptotes. An eight-step curve-sketching strategy is given in concise form immediately before Example 8.

Notes This is the concluding section of the five on curve-sketching techniques. Additional fine points you may want to mention: the use of symmetry, the behavior of $f'(x)$ near a discontinuity of f, and the behavior of $f'(x)$ as $x \to \pm\infty$. Your students can also compare their results with those produced by a computer in problems such as 29 through 54.

Goals Students should now be able to show all the important features of the graph of a given elementary function. Ample opportunities exist among the problems at the end of the section.

Problems 1 through 6, 11, 12, 15, 16, 17, 21, 25, 28, 29, 34, 35, 36, 38, 41, 42, 47, 52, 69. If a graphing calculator or computer is available, also any (or even all) of Problems 55 through 68.

Chapter 4 Review
Problems 1, 2, 3, 8, 10, 13, 18, 19, 20, 23, 26, 27, 28, 31, 32, 33, 34, 36, 37, 40, 41, 42, 44, 45, 46, 50, 51, 55, 62, 63, 64, 68, 69, 71, 72, 78, 82, 83, 84, 85, 86, 90, 91, 94, 96, 100, 103 (more difficult), 104 (more difficult and tricky; there's an endpoint extremum).

CHAPTER 5   THE INTEGRAL

5.2 Antiderivatives and Initial Value Problems

Topics to Cover Real-world problems, mathematical modeling, and differential equations. Examples: Newton's law of cooling, Torricelli's law of draining. The definition of *antiderivative;* the most general antiderivative. Linearity of antidifferentiation. The integral sign, antiderivatives of specific simple functions. Simple differential equations and initial value problems. Motion of a particle moving in a straight line with prescribed acceleration and initial conditions; vertical motion under the influence of gravity.

Notes To verify that F is an antiderivative of f (on the interval I), simply verify that $F'(x) = f(x)$ (on I). Your students can also compare their "by-hand" answers with those obtained through a computer algebra program; sometimes the disparities are not easy to reconcile.

Goals Finding antiderivatives; correct use of notation; solution of simple initial value problems, including those involving vertical motion of a particle under constant gravitational acceleration.

Problems 1 through 6, 13 through 22, 27, 28, 31, 35 through 38, 45, 46, 47, 48, 57 through 62, 69, 72, 74, 77, 78, 79.

5.3 Elementary Area Computations

Topics to Cover The area of a bounded plane region as the limit of the areas of polygonal approximations to the region. The area between the graph of the nonnegative function f and the x-axis over the interval $a \leq x \leq b$ as the limit of the sums of areas of rectangles. Summation notation and simple summation formulas. Writing area approximations in summation notation. The exact computation of the area under the graph of $y = x^2$ over the interval $[0, 3]$ (Example 7).

Notes Don't hurry; this is new material but forms a vital foundation for much of the rest of the course. Note also that we *define* area as the limit of area approximations but that, nevertheless, the values we thereby obtain for areas are exact. There's an analogy with the earlier definition of the slope of the straight line tangent to the graph of a given function at a given point on its graph.

Goals The students should be able to write simple area approximations in summation notation.

Problems 1, 3, 5, 6, 7, 11, 13, 14, 15, 19, 24, 27, 29, 31, 39, 41, 47.

5.4 Riemann Sums and the Integral

Topics to Cover Partition, selection, Riemann sum, left-endpoint sum, right-endpoint sum, midpoint sum. Norm of a partition. The definite integral; notation—lower and upper limit, integrand. The definition of the definite integral as the limit of Riemann sums. Integrability. Theorem: If f is continuous on $[a, b]$ then f is integrable there. Perhaps evaluation "by hand" of

$$\int_a^b x^2\,dx,$$

similar to computations in Section 5.3. Simplification of the notation by use of regular partitions.

Notes For some students, this will be difficult; they need to memorize the definitions of the new terms as these ideas are key to setting up definite integrals for volume, work, and so forth in Chapter 6. The proof of Theorem 1 is in the Appendices but is not appropriate for most freshman calculus classes.

Goals Understanding the definition of the definite integral as the limit of Riemann sums.

Problems 1 through 6, 11 through 15, 21 through 25, 31 through 35, 44, 45, 51, perhaps 52 and 53; if a computer algebra system is available, 56 and 57.

5.5 Evaluation of Integrals

Topics to Cover Evaluation of the definite integral by means of the antiderivative. Integral of a constant, constant multiple property, sum property, interval union property, comparison property.

Notes Remind your students that we define the area between the graph of the nonnegative continuous function f and the x-axis over the interval $[a, b]$ to be

$$A = \int_a^b f(x)\,dx.$$

Goals Evaluation of definite integral by the evaluation theorem; understanding through use of the properties of the definite integral listed here.

Problems 1, 2, 3, 4, 9, 10, 12, 13, 19, 21, 25, 26, 29, 30, 37, 41, 44, 47, 50, 53, 55, 56, 63, 64.

5.6 The Fundamental Theorem of Calculus

Topics to Cover The average value of a function on an interval and the average value theorem. The fundamental theorem of calculus, its proof, and computational applications (including the solution of initial value problems).

Notes The proofs are educational and not difficult; this important section deserves more than one class period.

Goals Appreciation of the somewhat delicate relationship between the definite integral and the derivative.

Problems 1, 3, 4, 5, 10, 11, 12, 13, 14, 17, 19, 20, 23, 27, 28, 29, 32, 33, 36, 38, 41, 43 through 48, 50, 57, 63, 64, 65, 66.

5.7 Integration by Substitution

Topics to Cover Substitutions of the form $u = g(x)$ where x is the independent variable in the integrand. Care with differentials ($du = g'(x)\,dx$, and so forth). Substitution in the definite integral.

Notes Illustrate that effective substitutions are *sometimes* of the form $u = g(x)$ when the integrand has the form $f(g(x))$—but not always (try $f(x) = x\sqrt{x-1}$).

Goals The students should become proficient in integration by substitution but should not come to rely on it as a general panacea for finding all troublesome antiderivatives.

Problems 1 through 10, 11, 14, 19, 21, 22, 25 through 29, 31, 35, 40, 43, 45, 53, 54, 55, 56, 63, 64, 65, 67 through 70, 73.

5.8 Areas of Plane Regions

Topics to Cover The area bounded above by the graph of $y = f(x)$ and below by the graph of $y = g(x)$; the area bounded on the left by the graph of $x = h(y)$ and on the right by the graph of $x = k(y)$. Subdividing a region to find its area by adding the areas of regions each of which may be described in one of these ways.

Notes This easy section will give your student time to relax, but some will not know how to find the points of intersection of the graphs of $y = f(x)$ and $y = g(x)$. Note the *definitions* of area in the statements containing Eqs. (2) and (3).

Goals Finding areas of plane regions.

Problems 1 through 14, 16, 17, 19, 20, 23, 26, 31, 34, 37, 40, 46, 48, 50, 51, 54, 60.

5.9 Numerical Integration

Topics to Cover Left- and right-endpoint approximations, the trapezoidal and midpoint approximations, and (most important) Simpson's approximation, perhaps presented as a weighted average of the trapezoidal and midpoint approximations.

Notes Note that Simpson's approximation is not a Riemann sum. Emphasize that it generally does not give the *exact* value of the definite integral. Include the error estimate to underscore this point.

Goals Finding approximations to the definite integral when the fundamental theorem is unwieldy or inapplicable.

Problems 3, 4, 15, 16, 17, 25, 26 (if a calculator is available), 28, perhaps 32 and 33.

Chapter 5 Review

Problems 1, 2, 6, 7, 11, 15, 18, 21, 24, 27, 30, 31, 32, 34, 37, 40, 43, 50, 55, 58, 61, 65, 68, 71, 73, 76.

CHAPTER 6   APPLICATIONS OF THE INTEGRAL

6.1 Riemann Sum Approximations

Topics to Cover Review of the definitions of Riemann sum, the definite integral, and area (obtained as a limit of Riemann sums). Finding other quantities by integrals; for example, mass, total quantity, distance, volume (of water flowing into a tank at the rate $r = r(t)$), work done by a variable force. Use of units in setting up Riemann sums, as in Examples 1 and 2. Net distance and total distance. Fluid flow in circular pipes; Poiseuille's law of laminar flow and applications to cardiac output.

Notes This section reinforces the foundation idea of approximating quantities by setting up Riemann sums; although the material is a little complicated, it deserves careful classroom presentation.

Goals The students should be able to set up Riemann sums, find their limits, and evaluate the resulting definite integrals. They should also be able to do so in connection with finding physical quantities such as mass, net distance, total distance, and related quantities.

Problems 1 through 8, 11, 12, 15, 16, 19 through 26, 35 through 37 (as a group), 38 through 42, perhaps 46, and if you have covered Poiseuille's law thoroughly, 49 through 52.

6.2 Volumes by the Method of Cross Sections

Topics to Cover Cylinders (in general); base, height, volume. Volume as the integral of a cross-sectional area function. Cavalieri's principle. What happens if the cross sections are perpendicular to the y-axis. Volume of a solid of revolution around the x-axis; around the y-axis. Volume generated by revolving the region between two curves around an axis. Volumes of solids that aren't solids of revolution; for example, the wedge of Example 7.

Notes Students with high-school calculus will remember the formulas for volume of revolution around the coordinate axes but will probably have difficulties with finding volumes of more general solids. Some of the problems at the end of the section are concerned with such volumes. General advice to students: *Draw and label a slab!* Note also how Cavalieri's principle greatly reduces the dependence on the cumbersome Riemann sum notation.

Goals The students should be able to find the volume of a solid when a cross-sectional area function is given; they should also be able to find a suitable cross-sectional area function in the simpler cases.

Problems 1, 2, 7, 8, 10, 16, 18, 19, 23, 24, 25, 30, 39, 40, 41, 42, 46, 47 (more difficult), 49 (more difficult), 54, 56, 57 (more difficult).

6.3 Volumes by the Method of Cylindrical Shells

Topics to Cover Using the method of nested concentric cylindrical shells for finding the volume of a solid of revolution, including the volume generated by rotating the region between two curves around a horizontal or vertical line in a plane containing that region (almost always the xy-plane). Note that sometimes the method of cross sections is troublesome or even impossible; for example, see Problem 13. But the method of cylindrical shells is limited to volumes of solid of revolution.

Notes Don't let your students confuse the volume *of* the cylindrical shell with the volume *enclosed by* that shell (and its imaginary lids). If necessary, remove both lids from a cylindrical soup can and bring it to class. A Progresso® 538-gram soup can without lids has radius 42 mm, height 108 mm, and thickness 0.5 mm, for a total volume (of *metal* of approximately $2\pi \cdot 4.2 \cdot 10.8 \cdot 0.05 \approx$ 14 cm^3. But the volume it *encloses* is approximately $\pi \cdot (4.2)^2 \cdot 10.8 \approx 598$ cm^3. Also tell your student to draw a label a typical shell, then to express everything in terms of x or everything in terms of y. If the axis of revolution is parallel to the y-axis, then the independent variable must be x; if the axis is parallel to the x-axis, then the independent variable must be y.

Goals Simply finding volumes by the method of cylindrical shells.

Problems 1, 2, 6, 7, 11, 13, 14, 15, 18, 20, 25, 26, 35, 37, 38, 39, 42, 43, 47.

6.4 Arc Length and Surface Area of Revolution

Topics to Cover Smooth arc; smooth surface; the length of a smooth arc; the area of the surface generated by rotating a smooth arc around a horizontal or vertical line.

Notes Derivation of the arc-length formula is a good idea because it provides another review of the mean value theorem. Work Example 3 for your students; call their attention to the slightly tricky algebraic step in the second display there. Also mention the useful chart in Fig. 6.4.15.

Goals The students should be able to find arc length and surface area of revolution, as in the problems.

Problems 1 through 16, 21, 22, 27, 28, 29, 30, 33, 34, 36 (challenging), 38, 40, 41, 42.

6.5 Force and Work

Topics to Cover Work done by a constant force. Work done by a variable force as a definite integral. Elastic springs, work done against the force of gravity, work to fill or empty a tank. Force exerted by a liquid.

Notes Work is a good vehicle for a review of setting up Riemann sums.

Goals As usual, the students should be able to work most of the problems at the end of the section.

Problems 3, 4, 7, 8, 10, 11, 12, 13, 16 (long), 20, 22 and 23 (together), 25, 26, 30, 31, 33, 36.

6.6 Centroids of Plane Regions and Curves

Topics to Cover Law of the lever, center of mass (of a finite system of mass particles in the plane), moment (of a finite system of mass particles about the x- or y-axis). Center of mass of such a system. Generalization to bounded plane laminas of variable density by the method of setting up Riemann sums and finding their limits. Symmetry principle and additivity of moments. Integral formulas for centroids. First theorem of Pappus. Moments and centroids of curves (in the plane). Second theorem of Pappus.

Notes The theorems of Pappus can be used to find centroids if volumes (or surface areas) are known in advance.

Goals Finding centroids, of course; but just as important, yet another application of Riemann sums.

Problems 1, 4, 7, 8, 12, 13, 15, 16, 17, 21, 22, 29 (long), 31 (more difficult).

Chapter 6 Review
Problems 2, 4, 5, 6, 9, 10, 13, 18, 21, 23, 24, 25, 26, 32, 33, 34, 41, 47.

CHAPTER 7 CALCULUS OF TRANSCENDENTAL FUNCTIONS

7.1 Exponential and Logarithmic Functions

Topics to Cover Exponential functions, laws of exponents, exponential growth, the base a exponential function. Derivatives of exponential functions (somewhat intuitive). The number e, the natural exponential function, its graph, and the derivative of $f(x) = e^x$. Inverse functions, logarithm functions, laws of logarithms. The derivative of f^{-1}. The natural logarithm function, its graph, and its derivative. The derivative of $g(x) = \log_a x$. Chain rule versions of the differentiation formulas. Logarithmic differentiation.

Notes No great emphasis need be put on exponential or logarithm bases other than e (for the moment). Remind fearful students that "a logarithm is merely an exponent."

Goals The students need to become comfortable with the natural logarithm and exponential functions, their derivatives and graphs, their inverse function relationship, and routine differentiation using these functions. Additional practice with optimization problems requiring these new functions is also advisable.

Problems 1 through 6, 9, 10, 11, 18, 20, 22, 24, 28, 30, 32, 34, 36, 38, 40, 44, 46, 48, 50, 55, 56, 60, 65 and 66 (together), 72.

7.2 Indeterminate Forms and l'Hôpital's Rule

Topics to Cover Use of l'Hôpital's rule in the case of the indeterminate forms $0/0$ and ∞/∞, both as $x \to a$ and as $x \to \pm\infty$. Order of magnitude of e^x and $\ln x$ (rates of increase relative to polynomials as $x \to +\infty$, etc.). Applications to curve sketching.

Notes Caution your students not to use l'Hôpital's rule when it is not applicable (Example 3; see also Problem 23). The proof of the weak form given at the end of the section is useful in that it invokes the mean value theorem; it's time for a review.

Goals Correct use of l'Hôpital's rule when it's necessary and how to recognize when it's not applicable.

Problems 1 through 9, 11, 12, 13, 15, 25, 26, 31, 32, 35, 38, 43, 44, 55, 58, 59, 69, 71, 63 and 73 (together).

7.3 More Indeterminate Forms

Topics to Cover The indeterminate forms $0 \cdot \infty$, $\infty - \infty$, 0^0, ∞^0, and 1^∞. The number e as a limit.

Notes Note that 0^∞ is not indeterminate.

Goals The students should be able to find some rather difficult limits. Note that the form $\infty - \infty$ is one of the most difficult to work with.

Problems 1, 4, 7, 14, 15, 16, 17, 18, 19, 20, 23, 24, 29, 32, 35, 44.

7.4 The Natural Logarithm as an Integral

Topics to Cover Definition of $\ln x$ and its consequences: the graph of the natural logarithm function and the laws of logarithms. The definition of the number e. Logarithms and experimental data (optional). The definition of the natural exponential function as the inverse of the natural logarithm function. The graph of $y = e^x$. The theorem that $e^x = \exp x$ (Eq. (16)). Laws of exponents. General exponential functions. Derivatives and integrals involving these "new" functions. Logarithms to bases other than e.

Notes Note that the restriction that r be rational in defining and differentiating $f(x) = x^r$ is now removed—this occurs in the discussion between Eqs. (30) and (31). The formula in (35) is worth memorization.

Goals To put the natural logarithm and natural exponential functions on a logically sound basis and to review the mechanics of derivatives and integrals involving these functions.

Problems 1 through 35, 40, 41.

7.5 Inverse Trigonometric Functions

Topics to Cover One-to-one functions; review of inverse functions. The inverse tangent function (and the inverse cotangent function). The inverse sine function (and the inverse cosine function). The inverse secant function (and the inverse cosecant function). Antiderivatives such as those in Examples 4 through 7.

Notes The inverse cosine, cotangent, and cosecant functions are not needed for antidifferentiation, so there is no reason to emphasize them.

Goals Widening the range of functions that the student can antidifferentiate by elementary methods.

Problems 1, 3 through 12, 27, 31 through 44, 52, 58, 59, 63, 66, 67.

7.6 Hyperbolic Functions

Topics to Cover The hyperbolic and inverse hyperbolic functions; derivatives and integrals involving these functions.

Notes In many syllabi this will be an optional section. But some computer algebra systems give certain common antiderivatives in terms of inverse hyperbolic functions rather than in terms of natural logarithms, so students using such programs, and many engineering students, should have some exposure to the hyperbolic functions.

Goals Besides the obvious advantages in review of inverse functions, differentiation formulas, and the like, the section demonstrates the power of calculus in handling "new" functions.

Problems 1, 2, 4, 6, 8, 9, 10, 11, 12, 14, 15, 17, 18, 19, 20, 25, 26, 28, 29, 31, 33, 36, 39, 41, 42, 43, 44, 45, 46, 48, 53, 54, 55 (more difficult), 56, 57, 62.

Chapter 7 Review

Problems 1, 2, 3, 4, 5, 6, 8, 10, 11, 12, 14, 16, 19, 20, 22, 24, 25, 26, 31, 34, 37 (very difficult), 39, 42, 48, 49, 151, 53 (challenging), 55 through 59, 69 through 74 (if you have covered the hyperbolic functions), 75 through 80, 88 through 90 (if you have covered the hyperbolic functions), 95, 96, 101 (challenging). Also: Find $f'(x)$ if $f(x) = x^{1/\ln x}$. Work it before you assign it!

CHAPTER 8 TECHNIQUES OF INTEGRATION

8.2 Integral Tables and Simple Substitutions

Topics to Cover Use of simple (mostly algebraic) substitutions to transform a given integral into one that appears in a table of integrals.

Notes As usual, don't forget to substitute for dx. The key to some successful substitutions in

$$\int f(g(x))\,dx$$

is to find the "inner function" $g(x)$ and then to let $u = g(x)$. This will almost always simplify the problem if the integrand is actually of the form $\phi(g(x)) \cdot g'(x)$.

Goals Actually, to make the students *less* dependent on integral tables!

Problems 1 through 6, 9, 10, 12, 13, 14, 15, 19, 22, 27, 31 through 41, 52, 53, 55, 56, 57.

8.3 Integration by Parts

Topics to Cover The integration by parts formula in Eqs. (2) and (3). How to choose dv. Applying the technique twice successively, as in Examples 4 and 5. Reduction formulas (the one in Example 6 is particularly useful).

Notes Experience is more useful than advice when it comes to a useful choice for dv.

Goals The students should be able to work most of the end-of-section problems.

Problems 1 through 9, 14, 17, 18 (by parts), 20, 33, 38, 41, 49, 51, 55, 57, 58, 61 (long), 63, 68 (long).

8.4 Trigonometric Integrals

Topics to Cover The half-angle identities and their use in integrating even integral powers of sines, cosines, and their products. Integrating $\tan^2 x$ and $\cot^2 x$. The integrals of products of powers of sines and cosines. Integrating products of powers of secants and tangents. The difficult case—integrating $\sec^m x \tan^n x$ with m an odd positive integer and n an even nonnegative integer: Convert all tangent into secants, expand, and apply the reduction formula of Section 8.3.

Notes It may be time for a summary of the trigonometric formulas that are really necessary for this section.

Goals The students need to be able to work trigonometric integrals because they commonly occur when certain substitutions are used, as well in the method of partial fractions.

Problems 1 through 5, 7, 10, 11, 12, 17, 23, 24, 41, 44, 46, 49, 51, 56, 57, 59, 67, and (if a computer algebra system is available) 68.

8.5 Rational Functions and Partial Fractions

Topics to Cover An overview of the method—not a calculus technique, but an algebraic technique used to transform the integrand (a rational function) into something more tractable. Irreducible polynomials and proper rational fractions. Partial fractions associated with nonrepeated linear factors of the denominator; repeated linear factors; nonrepeated quadratic factors; repeated quadratic factors.

Notes This section may require two class meetings for thorough coverage. Computer algebra systems can be used to obtain partial fraction decompositions; the *Mathematica* command is `Apart[ p[x]/q[x] ]` (one of the few *Mathematica* commands with only a single argument). If your students are to find partial fraction decompositions by hand, some will need to be shown how to solve simultaneous linear equations efficiently and accurately. (We recommend the diagonalization process, which they may find useful in other courses in mathematics, statistics, or computer science.) Because integration by trigonometric substitution has yet to be covered, certain "natural" partial fractions problems may be too difficult at this point. Hence work any problem before assigning it for homework or using it as a test question.

Goals When and how to use the method of partial fractions.

Problems 1 through 18, 28, 31, 35, 38, 42, 46, 50, 59.

8.6 Trigonometric Substitutions

Topics to Cover The three basic substitutions, shown in the table in the first paragraph of the section.

Notes Care must be taken in simplifying the expression $\sqrt{x^2}$, especially in definite integrals. Some integrals may be computed either by trigonometric substitution or by the method of partial fractions; for example,

$$\int \frac{1}{x(x^2+1)}\,dx.$$

In such cases trigonometric substitution is usually simpler.

Goals When and how to use trigonometric substitution.

Problems 1 through 10, 14, 16, 25, 30, 31, 36, 38, 41, 44, 45, 49, 51.

8.7 Integrals Involving Quadratic Polynomials

Topics to Cover The technique of *completing the square*. (You could derive the quadratic formula as an application.) Completing the square in a quadratic expression to convert an integrand into a form suitable for a trigonometric substitution.

Notes This section completes the material on integration by partial fractions, as the latter sometimes leads to irreducible quadratic factors in inconvenient form (in the denominator or raised to large integral powers). Because

$$\int \frac{1}{x^2+x+1}\,dx$$

occurs frequently, it might be a good example for a [slightly lengthy] classroom demonstration; no trigonometric substitution is required in this example.

Goals Using completion of the square to help integrate expressions containing quadratic polynomials.

Problems 1 through 7, 9, 10, 11, 12, 22, 24, 25, 29, 30, 32, 34, 37 through 39 (as a group), 48, 49, 50, 55.

8.8 Improper Integrals

Topics to Cover The two principal kinds of improper integrals: Infinite integrand, unbounded interval of integration. How to evaluate each as a limit. The possibility that such an integral diverges (either to infinity or "by oscillation"). Statistics and probability integrals and applications.

Notes Include a discussion of what to do when the interval of integration has an interior point at which the integrand becomes unbounded. Explain what to do if the limits of integration are $-\infty$ and $+\infty$. Explain how to determine if an improper integral diverges. Mention that these are *not* Riemann integrals; we are *extending* the definition of the definite integral to cover cases important in physics, engineering, statistics, and applied mathematics.

Goals The correct evaluation of convergent improper integrals.

Problems 1 through 4, 8 through 12, 17, 18, 19, 21, 24, 25, 26, 28, 30, 31, 36, 38, 40, 44, 47 and 48 (together), 49 through 51 (together), 52, 55, 66 (computer required), and (if you have covered the material on probability and statistics) 71, 75, 77.

Chapter 8 Review

Problems Ideally, all 144 problems. More realistically: 1, 3, 5, 7, 14, 16, 20, 23, 32 (long), 35, 37, 38, 47, 51, 60, 61, 72, 81, 88, 91 (long), 94, 97, 110 and 111 (together), 117 (some will find it quite difficult), 119 (long), 127, 130, 133, 135, 139.

CHAPTER 9   DIFFERENTIAL EQUATIONS

9.1 Simple Equations and Models

Topics to Cover Differential equations, solutions, initial conditions, initial value problems. General and particular solutions. Very easy equations (one variable missing). The natural growth equation, population growth, radioactive decay (and radiocarbon dating), continuously compounded interest, Torricelli's law of draining.

Notes Even for students who studied calculus in high school, this material should be new; they may be shocked. Section 9.1 does, however, provide a relatively easy transition to differential equations, as it is a gentle and slow introduction, with plenty of real-world applications, building on what the students already know, and with almost no new notation.

Goals The student should be able to solve simple separable differential equations and initial value problems. It is much more difficult for them to formulate the differential equation associated with a real-world physical situation or even an abstract model thereof.

Problems 1 through 6, 9, 11 through 26, 30, 31, 32, 37, 38, 39, 41, 47 (difficult).

9.2 Slope Fields and Euler's Method

Topics to Cover Solution curves and slope fields. Euler's method for numerical approximation of the solution of a differential equation. Existence and uniqueness of solutions of certain initial value problems.

Notes Take a very geometric approach. The *Instructor's Manual* contains *Mathematica* routines for construction of slope fields.

Goals An appreciation of how much trouble it is to obtain accurate numerical approximations to solutions of initial value problems. Perhaps this will stimulate the students to take a deep interest in analytically obtained solutions.

Problems 1 through 8, 11 through 14, 21, 23 (if a computer algebra system is available), 30.

9.3 Separable Equations and Applications

Topics to Cover Separable differential equations and how to solve them. Newton's law of cooling and applications. Linear differential equations: Population growth with immigration, savings with continuous deposits.

Notes The applications are realistic and the techniques here are used by real people to solve real problems.

Goals Extending the student's ability to formulate and solve differential equations associated with simple physical and mathematical models.

Problems 1 through 8, 11 through 16, 21, 22, 23, 29, 31, 32, 34, 37, 41, 42, 43.

9.4 Linear Equations and Applications

Topics to Cover The definition of linear differential equation; standard form; integrating factor and solution by integration. Existence and uniqueness of linear initial value problems (Theorem 1). Mixture problems and motion with resistance.

Notes The technique for finding an integrating factor is not easily forgotten; the formula is very easy to forget.

Goals Solution of linear initial value problems and applications.

Problems 1, 2, 5, 6, 9, 10, 13, 14, 21, 23, 24, 26, 27, 32 through 36 (as a group), 39, 43.

9.5 Population Models

Topics to Cover The general population equation (Eq. (1)); bounded populations and the logistic equation; limited populations and carrying capacity; other applications of the logistic equation; predator-prey populations.

Notes Partial fraction decompositions will be required at times.

Goals For the students to develop an appreciation for the effectiveness and wide applicability of mathematical models.

Problems 1 through 6, 9, 10, 12, 13, 15, 17, 24 through 26 (as a group), 28 (long).

9.6 Linear Second-Order Equations

Topics to Cover Basic definitions; homogeneous equations. Linear combinations of solutions. Linearly independent solutions. General solutions. Equations with constant coefficients; the method of the characteristic equation (distinct real roots, repeated real roots, complex conjugate roots).

Notes This long section likely needs to be split over two class periods.

Goals The mechanics of solving linear second-order homogeneous equations with constant coefficients; an appreciation for the power of linearity.

Problems 1 through 8, 15 through 22, 27 through 31.

9.7 Mechanical Vibrations

Topics to Cover Mass-and-spring models; equilibrium position, spring constant, damping coefficient. Free undamped motion and natural frequency. Simple harmonic motion; period and frequency. Free damped motion: overdamped case, critically damped case, underdamped case. Forced oscillations and resonance; transient and steady-state solutions.

Notes This is a difficult section and will require more than one class meeting.

Goals The students should gain an appreciate of the power of differential equations in modeling simple mechanical systems and be able to solve simple systems on their own.

Problems 1 through 8, 11, 12, 15, 17, 19, 20, 31 through 36 (yes, a bit ambitious), 37.

Chapter 9 Review

Problems 1 through 5, 15, 20, 25, 27, 30, 32, 35, 38, 39, 40, 45, 50 and 51 (together), 55, 57.

CHAPTER 10 POLAR COORDINATES AND PARAMETRIC CURVES

10.1 Analytic Geometry and the Conic Sections

Topics to Cover The general Cartesian equation of a straight line; the circle. Symmetry properties that can be deduced from the Cartesian equation of a graph. The translation property. The conic sections: Let e be a fixed positive number and let L be the vertical line with equation $x = -p$. Determine the locus of a point $P(x, y)$ if its distance from the fixed point $F(p, 0)$ is e times its distance from L (Example 3).

Case 1: $e = 1$. Then we obtain $y^2 = 4px$, a parabola. Next, if $e \neq 1$, we obtain

$$\frac{(x-h)^2}{a^2} + \frac{y^2}{b^2} = 1$$

where

$$h = p\frac{1+e^2}{1-e^2} \quad \text{and} \quad b^2 = a^2(1-e^2).$$

Case 2: $e < 1$. Then the locus is an ellipse.
Case 3: $e > 1$. In this case the locus is a hyperbola.
Notes This section is a prerequisite for Section 10.6.
Goals The students should learn to derive and recognize (Cartesian) equations of straight lines, circles, and conic sections.
Problems 1 through 12, 17, 18, 21 through 30, 33, 35.

10.2 Polar Coordinates

Topics to Cover The pole, polar axis, radial coordinate, and angular coordinate. Polar coordinates. Graphs of polar-coordinate equations. Conversions from polar coordinates to rectangular coordinates and vice versa.

Notes Call your students' attention to the fact that every point in the plane has many different representations in polar coordinates. Demonstrate a variety of ways of plotting graphs of polar-coordinate equations (they will find this particularly difficult).

Goals The students should become as comfortable as possible with polar coordinates in the time allotted.

Problems 1 through 22, 24 through 28, 29 through 32 (as a group), 33 through 36 (as a group), 37 through 43, 47, 48, 53, 54, 57, 58, 61.

10.3 Area Computations in Polar Coordinates

Topics to Cover Riemann sums to approximate the area bounded by the graph of the polar equation $r = f(\theta)$ and the rays $\theta = \alpha$ and $\theta = \beta$. Area in polar coordinates as a definite integral. The area between two polar-coordinate curves.

Notes Possible examples: The area within the circle $r = \cos\theta$, the area within the cardioid $r = 1 + \cos\theta$, and the area within the limaçon $r = 1 + 2\cos\theta$.

Goals Finding the area enclosed by one or two graphs of equations in polar coordinates.

Problems 1 through 4, 7, 8, 10, 11, 12, 16, 17, 18, 20, 23, 25, 26, 29, 31, 32, 36, 38, 40.

10.4 Parametric Curves

Topics to Cover Definition of parametric curve and its graph, coordinate functions, elimination of the parameter, different parametrizations of the same curve. The cycloid (a slow and careful derivation of its parametric equations), definition of *smooth* parametric curve, lines tangent to smooth parametric curves, computing dy/dx and d^2y/dx^2 for such curves, polar graphs of parametric curves, dy/dx in terms of r and θ.

Notes Show your students how to sketch the graph of a parametric curve, both by eliminating the parameter and also when such elimination is impossible. Also show how to parametrize a given curve; examples might include the circle $x^2 + y^2 = a^2$ (parametrized by $x = a\cos t$, $y = a\sin t$, for instance) and the ellipse $(x/a)^2 + (y/b)^2 = 1$ (parametrized by $x = a\cos t$, $y = b\sin t$, for instance). Another example: The parabola $y = x^2$ is "self-parametrizing" with parametric equations $x = t$, $y = t^2$. Parametrize the first-quadrant loop of the folium of Descartes with Cartesian equation $x^2 + y^2 = 3xy$ as follows: Let L be a straight line through the origin with slope $t \geq 0$. This line meets the folium at the point (x, tx). When these coordinates are substituted into the equation of the folium, you can then solve for x, then for y, in terms of t, thereby parametrizing the loop. (This is Problem 30.) Computer note: If a plane curve has the parametrization $x = f(t)$, $y = g(t)$, then the *Mathematica* command

`ParametricPlot[{f[t], g[t]},{t, a, b}];`

plots this curve for $a \leqq t \leqq b$.

Goals Familiarity with parametrically defined curves; parametrizing a given plane curve. Finding the slope of the straight line tangent to a given parametric curve in terms of the parameter.

Problems 1 through 9, 14, 16, 17, 19, 22, 23, 25, 27, 31, 34 (long and difficult), 41, 42, 45 (computer recommended).

10.5 Integral Computations with Parametric Curves

Topics to Cover Area, volume, arc length, and surface area of revolution using parametric curves; parametric polar coordinates

Notes A good example is the semicircular arc $x = a\cos t$, $y = a\sin t$, $0 \leqq t \leqq \pi$. You can find the area bounded by this arc and the x-axis, the volume swept out when that area is rotated around the x-axis or around the y-axis, the length of the semicircle, and the surface area swept out when that arc is rotated around the x-axis. The "first" arch of the cycloid provides a more complex example; yet all the integrals remain elementary (see Example 2). Worth memorizing: The arc-length differential in polar coordinates (Eq. (10)).

Goals Facility with integral computations involving parametric equations as well as equations given in polar coordinates.

Problems 1, 2, 3, 5, 7 through 10, 12, 13, 16, 19, 21, 23 and 24 (if not worked in class), 26, 28 (a little long), 29 through 37. Problem 42 is quite challenging. If a computer algebra system is available, also problems 43, 47, 48, 53, and 55.

10.6 Conic Sections and Applications

Topics to Cover **1.** The focus-directrix definition of parabola; the resulting Cartesian equation if the directrix is vertical or horizontal. Completing the square to identify the vertex of a such parabola given its Cartesian equation, as in Example 2. Application: the reflection property of the parabola. **2.** The focus-directrix definition of ellipse; the resulting Cartesian equation if the directrix is vertical or horizontal. Vertices, major and minor axes. Determining if a Cartesian equation is that of an ellipse, as in Example 5. Applications: the reflection property of the ellipse; orbits of comets. **3.** The focus-directrix definition of hyperbola; the resulting Cartesian equation if the directrix is horizontal or vertical. Completing the square to identify a hyperbola given its Cartesian equation; vertices, transverse axis, conjugate axis, center, and asymptotes. Applications: the reflection property of the hyperbola; determination of the location of ships at sea. **4.** Conic sections in polar coordinates.

Notes The concluding subsection on conics in polar coordinates is the unifying concept in Section 10.6 and will be useful solving problems involving conic sections. It is difficult to say how much time should be allotted to Section 10.6; it would surely require several class meeting to cover all this material thoroughly.

Goals The analogies and dissimilarities among the conic sections, some of which are summarized in the table in the Chapter 10 Review section.

Problems Parabola problems: 1 through 4, 7 through 10, 11, 12, 17, 18. Ellipse problems: 19 through 24, 35 through 38. Hyperbola problems: 39 through 42, 45 through 48, 49 through 52. General problems: 53 through 62, 66, 68, 69, 75, 76, 78, 80, 83, 84, 90, 95 (difficult?).

Chapter 10 Review

Problems 1 through 8, 19 through 22, 28, 29, 31 through 36, 42, 43, 46, 47, 50, 51, 56, 60, 66, 71, 72, 75, 78, 80, 81, 82, 83 (difficult).

CHAPTER 11 INFINITE SERIES

11.2 Infinite Sequences

Topics to Cover The definition of an [infinite] sequence of real numbers. Subscript notation. The nth term of a sequence. Examples, including the Fibonacci sequence. Definition of the limit of a sequence. Using the limit laws (Chapter 2) to find limits of sequences. Using limits of functions, including l'Hôpital's rule, to find limits of sequences. Increasing, decreasing, and monotonic sequences. The bounded monotone sequence property.

Notes Consider a formal proof that

$$\lim_{n\to\infty} \frac{1}{n} = 0$$

directly from the definition of limit. Find limits using the limit laws; give some examples of sequences without limits (and explain why). It is easy to show that the recursively defined sequence

$$a_1 = \sqrt{2}, \quad a_{n+1} = \sqrt{2 + a_n} \quad \text{for } n \geq 1$$

(Problem 58, similar to Example 13) is bounded and increasing—therefore convergent—and then use limit laws to find its limit. The bounded monotonic sequence property is used frequently in many convergence tests for series; emphasize its importance. If appropriate, discuss its connection with the least upper bound property of the real number system.

Goals The definition of a sequence of real numbers and the definition of the limit of a sequence. The bounded monotone sequence property. Methods for finding limits of sequences.

Problems 1 through 22, 27, 28, 29, 30, 33, 35, 36, 43, 49, 51, 53, 56, 59, 64.

11.3 Infinite Series and Convergence

Topics to Cover Infinite series, summation notation, nth partial sum, the sequence of partial sums, the definition of the sum of an infinite series. Examples, including examples of series that do not converge (and why). Geometric series; the sum of a convergent geometric series. Termwise addition of series and multiplication of a series by a constant. The nth-term test for divergence. Divergence of the harmonic series (*per se* and as a counterexample to a "natural" conjecture). Series whose terms are eventually the same.

Notes Present as many examples as possible. Include "telescoping" series. Be sure that the students understand the difference between the sequence of *terms* of a series and its sequence of *partial sums*. Most important: the definition of the sum of a series and what it means for a series to converge. The proof in the text that the harmonic series diverges (Theorem 4) anticipates the integral test; you may want to present the following familiar alternative. Suppose that m is a positive integer and let $k = 2^m$. Then the kth partial sum of the harmonic series is

$$S_k = 1 + \frac{1}{2} + \left(\frac{1}{3} + \frac{1}{4}\right) + \left(\frac{1}{5} + \frac{1}{6} + \frac{1}{7} + \frac{1}{8}\right) + \cdots$$

$$+ \left(\frac{1}{2^{m-1}+1} + \frac{1}{2^{m-1}+2} + \cdots + \frac{1}{2^m}\right) \geq 1$$

$$+ \left(\frac{1}{2} + \frac{1}{2} + \cdots + \frac{1}{2}\right)$$

where the last pair of parentheses encloses m summands. Thus $S_k > (m+2)/2$, and it follows that $S_k > \frac{1}{2}\log_2 k$.

Because the sequence $\{S_n\}$ is increasing, $S_n \to +\infty$ as $n \to +\infty$. Therefore the harmonic series diverges.

Goals What it means for the number S to be the sum of a series, that a series may diverge even though the sequence of its terms approaches zero, the sum of a geometric series, and the technique of finding the sum of a series by first finding a formula for the nth partial sum (and then evaluating a limit).

Problems 1 through 10, 12 through 17, 20, 212, 22, 27, 28, 31, 35, 36, 37, 39, 40, 45, 46, 47, 48, 50, 52, 53, 55, 68 through 70.

11.4 Taylor Series and Taylor Polynomials

Topics to Cover Power series, Taylor polynomials. The nth-degree remainder $R_n(x)$ for $f(x)$ at $x = a$. Taylor's theorem, Taylor series, Maclaurin series. The Maclaurin series for e^x, $\sin x$, and $\cos x$.

Notes Emphasize the idea of approximating functions with polynomials. Important: The fact that the function f gives rises to a Taylor series centered at $x = c$ on some interval I centered at c does not imply that the series converges to $f(x)$ for any x in I (other than $x = c$). To show that the Taylor series converges to $f(x)$, you need to show that $R_n(x) \to 0$; it is not even enough to know that the series converges at x. You could also point out that the mean value theorem is a special case of Taylor's theorem.

Goals Derivation of Taylor polynomials and Taylor series; the remainder term; Taylor series of the most important transcendental functions.

Problems 1 through 8, 11 through 16, 20, 22 through 25, 27 through 34, 40 (long), 42, 44. If a computer algebra system is available, 45 through 48 and 58 and 59 (together).

11.5 The Integral Test

Topics to Cover We return to series of constant terms. The integral test (for positive-term series), p-series and their convergence or divergence, and the integral test remainder estimate.

Notes Emphasize that the integral test is *only* a test for convergence; the value of the integral is not closely related to the sum of the series. (Of course the integral test remainder estimate may be used to obtain close under- and overestimates of the sum of a convergent positive-term series.)

Goals When and how to use the integral test, familiarity with p-series, and approximations to sums of convergent positive-term series using ideas inherent in the integral test.

Problems 1 through 10, 12, 13, 15, 16, 23, 28, 31 through 33, 35, 36, 42, 45, 49, 50 (more difficult), and the last question in the Section 11.5 project.

11.6 Comparison Tests for Positive-Term Series

Topics to Cover The comparison test and the limit comparison test.

Notes These are tests that apply only to positive-term series. Give plenty of examples and explain how to choose a series appropriate for comparison (or limit comparison) with a given series. Provide an example in which the comparison test is unwieldy but the limit comparison test works smoothly. Give a proof of the comparison test if you have time; it's both short and educational. Note that l'Hôpital's rule will be needed in some of the problems.

Goals Correctly and effectively using these two new tests to check convergence and divergence of given series.

Problems 1 through 12, 23, 25, 28, 31, 33, 35 (more difficult), 36, 46, 48, 49, 50, 51. If a computer algebra program is available, 37 and 41.

11.7 Alternating Series and Absolute Convergence

Topics to Cover Alternating series and the alternating series test. The alternating series error estimate. Absolute convergence. Absolute convergence implies convergence (and its short proof). Conditional convergence. The ratio and root tests.

Notes This long section may require more than one class period. Note that the text first has a proof that an absolutely convergent series also converges, *without* using the phrase "absolutely convergent." Absolute convergence is defined next. Note that the ratio and root tests actually test for absolute convergence. Let your students discover that if $\sum |a_n|$ converges to S, then the number S does not give much information about the value of $\sum a_n$.

Goals If you plan to continue with power series, then the ratio and root tests are very important. If your emphasis is on convergence of numerical series, then the concept of absolute convergence is very important.

Problems 1 through 10, 15, 16, 17, 18, 21 through 28, 39, 40, 57, 59, 61 (more difficult), 65 (after reading through 62 through 64); if a computer algebra system is available, 45, 48, 50, and 51.

11.8 Power Series

Topics to Cover Review of what's already been covered in the area of power series. Convergence of power series; radius of convergence and interval of convergence. Power series in powers of $x - c$. Theorem 2: If f is infinitely differentiable in the interval I centered at $x = a$ and, for all x in I, $R_n(x) \to 0$ as $n \to +\infty$, then the Taylor series in powers of $x - a$ for the function f converges to $f(x)$ for each x in I. The binomial series (essential for showing that $\zeta(2) = \pi^2/6$ (Problem 68)). Term-by-term differentiation and integration of power series.

Notes This long section surely requires more than a single class period for thorough and careful coverage. The complete derivation of the binomial series is also quite lengthy.

Goals For the students to gain facility in working with power series.

Problems 1 through 7, 10, 12, 17, 18, 20, 26, 27, 29, 30 (more difficult), 31, 34, 37, 41, 44, 48, 49 through 52 (as a group), 53 through 55 and 59 (if you intend to cover Section 11.10), 65 (difficult).

11.9 Power Series Computations

Topics to Cover Using power series to approximate functions and definite integrals, especially when the numerical version of the power series is an alternating series (this makes the error estimates extremely simple, through crude). Adding and multiplying power series. Use of power series to evaluate indeterminate forms.

Notes This is advanced material. The numerical computations require patience, care, ingenuity, and attention to detail. Remember that for honesty, low estimates must be rounded *down* and high estimates must be rounded *up*. ("I do not mind lying, but I hate inaccuracy."—Samuel Butler, *Note-Books*)

Goals Increased facility in the manipulation of power series and increased applicability of the methods.

Problems 1, 4, 6, 11, 14, 17, 18, 22, 24, 27, 33 and 37 (together), 42, 48, 51. If a computer algebra system is available, 55, 61, and 62.

11.10 Series Solution of Differential Equations

Topics to Cover Overview of the power series method for solving differential equations. The identity principle and shift of index of summation. Power series definitions of functions.

Notes This is advanced material and Chapter 9 is a prerequisite. Note that some differential equations do not have power series solutions.

Goals Use of power series to solve differential equations, particularly those with coefficients slightly more complicated than constants.

Problems 1, 4, 5, 8, 12, 14, 15, 20, 23, 24 (difficult).

Chapter 11 Review

Problems 1, 3, 10, 12, 14, 16, 18, 23, 29, 30, 31, 33, 36, 37, 40, 41, 43 through 50, 53, 55, 63 through 66.

CHAPTER 12 VECTORS, CURVES, AND SURFACES IN SPACE

12.1 Vectors in the Plane

Topics to Cover Definition of vectors in the plane (two components), position vector of a point, length of a vector, the zero vector. Obtaining the components of the vector from P to Q from the coordinates of the points P and Q. Equality of vectors, addition of vectors, multiplication of a vector by a scalar, the difference of two vectors. Vectors with the same direction, vectors with opposite directions. Algebra of vector addition and scalar multiplication. The unit vectors **i** and **j**. Finding the unit vector **u** with the same direction as the given vector **a**.

Notes The idea of a vector will, to many students, be new and they will not be able to assimilate it rapidly.

Goals Vectors in the plane, vector notation, and algebraic properties of vectors.

Problems 1 through 14, 17 19, 21 through 33, 35, 36, 37, 38, 40, 41, 42, 44, 46, 47, 50, 52, 53, 54, 55.

12.2 Three-Dimensional Vectors

Topics to Cover Rectangular coordinates in space, the right-handed coordinate system, distance formula, equation of a circle with given center and radius. Vectors in space; length, equality, addition, multiplication by scalars. Unit vectors; the basic unit vectors **i**, **j**, and **k**. The parallelogram law for addition. Algebraic laws of vector addition and scalar multiplication. The dot product. Theorem 1: If θ is the angle between the vectors **a** and **b**, then $\mathbf{a} \cdot \mathbf{b} = |\mathbf{a}||\mathbf{b}| \cos \theta$. Test for perpendicular vectors. Direction angles, direction cosines, the component of **a** along **b**. Work: $W = \mathbf{F} \cdot \mathbf{D}$ if **F** is a constant force and moves a particle from P to Q where $\mathbf{D} = \overrightarrow{PQ}$.

Notes Include some two-dimensional examples; the idea is to unify the treatment of two- and three-dimensional vectors. Point out that the algebraic properties of three-dimensional vectors (addition and scalar multiplication) are exactly the same as in the two-dimensional case (Section 12.1). Use the law of cosines to *prove* Theorem 1.

Goals Familiarity with vectors in the plane and in space as well as with both their geometric and their algebraic properties.

Problems 1 through 4, 1 through 10, 13 through 16, 19 through 39, 41, 44, 47, 51, 54, 56, 58, 59, 60, 61, 62, 67, 69 and 70 (together).

12.3 The Cross Product of Vectors

Topics to Cover The cross (vector) product; that $\mathbf{a} \times \mathbf{b}$ is perpendicular both to **a** and to **b**. Determinants of order 2 and 3. The determinant form of the cross product. Anticommutativity of the cross product. Geometric significance of the length of **a** × **b** (see the discussion that includes Eq. (9)). Test for parallel vectors (corollary to Theorem 2). Algebraic properties of the cross product. The scalar triple product and its geometric significance.

Notes Important new idea: It's now easy to find a vector perpendicular to two given vectors in space. Suggestion: Prove Theorem 2 and some parts of Theorem 3. Show how the scalar triple product can be used to find the volume of a parallelepiped.

Goals The algebra and geometry of the cross product.

Problems 1 through 8, 11, 12, 13, 15, 17, 18, 19, 23, 25, 27, 35.

12.4 Lines and Planes in Space

Topics to Cover The vector equation of a line in space; its parametric and symmetric equations. The vector and scalar equations of a plane in space. Parallel planes; the angle between two planes (by definition, the angle between their normal vectors).

Notes Rather than asking students to memorize a half-dozen formulas for distance (point to plane, line to line, etc., etc.), show them the general procedure for finding the distance between one such object in space and another: First find a nonzero vector **n** normal to both objects, usually by computing a cross product. Then find a vector **c** that *connects* the two objects. The distance d between the objects is then the length of the projection of **c** in the direction of **n**; that is,

$$d = \frac{\mathbf{n} \cdot \mathbf{c}}{|\mathbf{n}|}.$$

One difficult case is that of finding the distance between two skew lines. In this case, begin by showing that any two skew lines lie in parallel planes (Problem 57). The most difficult case is that of finding the distance between a point and a line; see Problem 29 of Section 12.3 for a simple alternative approach to this problem.

Goals Using the concepts of Sections 12.1 through 12.4 to solve problems in three-dimensional analytic geometry; writing equations of lines and planes in space.

Problems 1, 2, 3, 5, 6, 9, 10, 12, 14, 18, 20, 21, 22, 24, 26, 28, 30, 32, 34, 36, 38, 40, 44, 48, 50, 52, 66. Also work Problems 55, 56, 59, and 60 *without* using the formulas in Problems 54 and 58.

12.5 Curves and Motion in Space

Topics to Cover The position vector of a moving point in space. Velocity, acceleration, speed, and scalar acceleration. Differentiation and integration of vector functions.

Notes If $\mathbf{r}(t) = \langle \cos t, \sin t \rangle$, then $v'(t) \neq a(t)$ (the time derivative of the *speed* need not equal the *scalar acceleration*). Prove a few of the differentiation formulas and remark on how natural they are. Present an example of finding the position of a particle whose acceleration, initial velocity, and initial position are known.

Goals Derivatives and integrals of vector functions and applications.

Problems 1 through 4, 6, 8, 12, 14, 16, 18, 20, 24, 25, 26, 30, 34, 40, 43 through 45, 50 and 51 (together), 52, 55, 56, 60, 62, 64.

12.6 Curvature and Acceleration

Topics to Cover Arc length, the arc-length parametrization of a space curve. The unit tangent vector for a *plane* curve. The curvature of a *plane* curve. Formulas for the curvature of a *plane* curve in terms of its parametrization $\langle x(t), y(t) \rangle$. The principal unit normal vector for a *plane* curve, the osculating circle, the radius of curvature, and the center of curvature. The unit tangent vector for a *space* curve. The curvature of a *space* curve. The principal unit normal vector; normal and tangential components of acceleration.

Notes This section demands extra preparation by the instructor. Don't forget to show that the curvature of a circle is a constant, the reciprocal of its radius.

Goals Analysis of plane and space curves using the concept of curvature; resolution of the acceleration vector into its normal and tangential components. The concluding subsections, beginning with the subsection on Newton, Kepler, and the Solar System, are optional, but it would be a shame to omit this material.

Problems 1, 2, 5, 6, 7, 8, 9, 10, 13 through 20, 22, 23, 25, 26, 27, 29, 31, 33 through 36, 38 through 41, 42 through 46, 48, 50, 51, 53, 54, 55, 56. If you covered the material on Newton, Kepler, and orbits of planets and satellites, also Problems 57 through 63.

12.7 Cylinders and Quadric Surfaces

Topics to Cover The graph of $f(x, y, z) = 0$. Planes, cylinders, and surfaces of revolution. The general quadratic surface with equation $Ax^2 + By^2 + Cz^2 + Dx + Ey + Fz + G = 0$. Classification of such surfaces: ellipsoid, elliptic paraboloid, hyperbolic paraboloid, elliptic cone, hyperboloid of one sheet, hyperboloid of two sheets, and degenerate cases. Appendix J covers conic sections as sections of a cone if you care to use it at this point.

Notes This material will be helpful to the students in Chapters 13 and 14 because it will help their ability to visualize surfaces, extrema, saddle points, and the like.

Goals Identification of quadratic surfaces; visualization of graphs of surfaces in space.

Problems 1 through 14, 17, 20, 24 through 30, 32, 33, 35, 36, 40, 42 through 47, 50, 51, 53, 55 through 60, 65 through 68.

12.8 Cylindrical and Spherical Coordinates

Topics to Cover Cylindrical and spherical coordinates. Graphs of cylindrical-coordinate and spherical-coordinate equations. Conversions between these and rectangular coordinates. Latitude and longitude.

Notes You can defer this section; insert it immediately before Section 14.7 (Integration in Cylindrical and Spherical Coordinates).

Goals Describing surfaces in cylindrical and spherical coordinates (preparation for triple integrals in cylindrical and spherical coordinates).

Problems 1 through 22, 24, 26, 28, 30, 34, 36, 38, 40, 44, 46, 48, 50, 54, 55, 60, 61. Also 56 through 59 and 62 if you covered latitude and longitude.

Chapter 12 Review
Problems 1 through 10, 12, 13, 16, 17, 18, 19, 20, 23, 24, 30, 31, 33, 34, 35, 36, 37, 38, perhaps 39 through 41, 42, 43, 45, 49, 50, 51.

CHAPTER 13 PARTIAL DIFFERENTIATION

13.2 Functions of Several Variables

Topics to Cover Functions of two and three variables; domain, independent and dependent variables, and graph. Level curves (in the domain of $f(x, y)$). Contour curves (on the graph of $z = f(x, y)$). Level surfaces (in the domain of $f(x, y, z)$). Isotherms and isobars.

Notes In addition to level curves and surfaces, the intersections of the graph of $z = f(x, y)$ with vertical planes parallel to the xz-plane or the yz-plane yield other curves that will help the student visualize the graph of $z = f(x, y)$.

Goals Understanding functions of several variables; visualizing the graph of a function of two variables.

Problems 1 through 8, 10, 12, 16, 18, 21, 22, 24, 26, 32, 34, 36, 43, 44, 47 through 52, 53 through 58.

13.3 Limits and Continuity

Topics to Cover Limits and continuity of a function of two variables. The general rule that sums, products, quotients, and compositions of continuous functions are continuous where defined. In particular, every polynomial (in any number of variables) is continuous everywhere and every rational function is continuous where its denominator is nonzero. Showing that a limit does not exist at (a, b) by showing that $f(x, y)$ approaches different limits as (x, y) approaches (a, b) along different straight lines (or, in tricky cases, along two different curves).

Notes Present Examples 8 and 9.

Goals Finding limits of functions of two and three variables; techniques for showing that certain limits do not exist.

Problems 2, 4, 10, 16, 17, 18, 21 through 46, 51 through 56.

13.4 Partial Derivatives

Topics to Cover Partial derivatives of $f(x, y)$. Computing partial derivatives by applying rules of single-variable calculus. The geometric interpretation of partial derivatives (as rate of change in a certain direction). The plane tangent to the graph of $z = f(x, y)$ at the point $P(a, b, f(a, b))$. How to write the equation of such a plane by finding a vector normal to it (and the graph) at the point P. Higher-order partial derivatives and equality of mixed partial derivatives.

Notes The concept of x-curves and y-curves provides a useful bridge from partial derivatives in the abstract to their geometric interpretation and the construction of tangent planes. But the first step is to show the students that the mechanics of partial differentiation are simple, as it relies so heavily on single-variable techniques. Provide motivation by providing analogies with goals of single-variable calculus (rates of change, optimization problems, approximation problems). Indicate that perfectly analogous techniques are used for functions of two or more variables.

Goals Computing partial derivatives, their geometric interpretation, and finding planes tangent to surfaces in space.

Problems 1, 2, 5, 6, 9 through 12, 20, 22, 28, 32, 36, 38, 40, 42, 44, 45 through 50 (more difficult than you might expect!), 55, 57, 59, 60, 64, 65, 73.

13.5 Multivariable Optimization Problems

Topics to Cover Definition and existence of global extrema. Local extrema; Theorem: If $f(x, y)$ attains a local extremum at $P(a, b)$ and both partial derivatives of f exist at P, then both are zero there. Note that these are not sufficient conditions; $z = x^2 - y^2$ has a saddle point at the origin. Critical points, boundary points of the domain of f, and their relation to extrema. Highest and lowest points on the graph of a function of two variables; applied optimization problems.

Notes Anything can happen at a point where both partial derivatives are zero; provide algebraic and geometric examples. Finding extrema. Example: $f(x, y) = xy - x - x + 4$ on the square with vertices at $(0,0)$, $(1,0)$, $(1,1)$, and $(0,1)$. Also Example 8. Also: What is the maximum possible volume of a rectangular box with no top and total surface area 300 m^2?

Goals Necessary and sufficient conditions for extrema, locating and identifying extrema, applied maximum-minimum problems.

Problems 1 through 4, 6, 8, 10, 14, 18, 22, 23, 24, 26, 28, 29, 30, 34, 36, 38, 40, 44, 45, 46, 53, 56, 60 through 63.

13.6 Increments and Linear Approximation

Topics to Cover Increments and differentials, linear approximation for a function of two variables (Eq. (8)). Repeat for functions of three variables. Differential of a function of n variables, linear approximation theorem. What it means for f to be continuously differentiable at a point. The error in the linear approximation. What it means for f to be differentiable at the point **a**. The relation between being continuously differentiable, differentiable, existence of all partial derivatives, and continuity.

Notes This is somewhat more difficult material.

Goals Understanding differentiability of a function of several variables and its consequences.

Problems 1 through 9, 10, 14, 17 through 22, 25, 27, 31, 33, 36, 38, 39, 43, 44, 45.

13.7 The Multivariable Chain Rule

Topics to Cover Functions from $\mathbf{R}^n$ to $\mathbf{R}^m$. Component functions, independent and dependent variables. Differentiability, continuous differentiability, and consequences. Independent, intermediate, and dependent variables and the multivariable chain rule in scalar notation. Special cases, implicit partial differentiation, and the implicit function theorem.

Notes This is somewhat more advanced material.

Goals A working knowledge of the chain rule.

Problems 1 through 4, 8, 9, 10, 13, 15, 17, 20, 22, 25, 29, 30, 35, 37, 38, 41, 42, 43, 45, 47, 50, 52, 56, 57, 58 and 59 (together).

13.8 Directional Derivatives and the Gradient Vector

Topics to Cover Directional derivative in the direction of the unit vector **u**. Calculation of directional derivatives (Theorem 2; Eq. (11)). The gradient vector. Geometric interpretation of the gradient vector (Theorem 2 and the paragraph that follows it). The gradient vector as a normal vector (Theorem 3). Using the gradient vector to find an equation of a plane tangent to a surface. Lower-dimensional analogy (Example 8).

Notes Mention the analogy between ∇ and D_x (from single-variable calculus). Also mention that this material generalizes to functions of three and more variables.

Goals Applications and geometry of the gradient vector.

Problems 1, 2, 5, 6, 7, 8, 11, 12, 17, 18, 21, 24, 25, 26, 30, 32, 35, 36, 42, 44, 47, 48, 49, 52, 53, 55, 64.

13.9 Lagrange Multipliers and Constrained Optimization

Topics to Cover The method of Lagrange multipliers, especially how it can be used to find the extrema of a differentiable function on the boundary of a set (only *ad hoc* methods were used in Section 13.5). The geometric interpretation of the method. Lagrange multipliers in three dimensions and with two (or even more) constraints. Solving applied optimization problems by the method of Lagrange multipliers.

Notes Encourage your students to think of most applied optimization problems as involving a quantity to be maximized (or minimized) subject to a *constraint* $C(x, y) = 0$ or $C(x, y, z) = 0$. When there is more than one constraint, the algebra can be challenging. It sometimes helps successively eliminate the Lagrange multipliers from the equations to be solved. The *Instructor's Manual* demonstrates other algebraic techniques that are sometimes effective.

Goals Using the Lagrange multiplier method to solve optimization problems, especially those resistant to the methods of Section 13.5.

Problems 1, 2, 6, 7, 8, 11, 12, 15, 16, 18, 20, 24, 26, 32, 38, 42, 43, 44, 51, 52, 57, 58, 60, and (if a computer algebra system is available) 65.

13.10 Critical Points of Functions of Two Variables

Topics to Cover The "second derivative test" for a function of two variables.

Notes You will need a list of examples for classroom presentation prepared in advance even though the topic is relatively simple.

Goals Classification of extrema of multivariable functions.

Problems 1, 2, 4, 5, 6, 7, 8, 10, 11, 12, 14, 18, 21, 23 through 25, 30, 34.

Chapter 13 Review

Problems 1 through 10, 15, 18, 21, 26, 27, 28, 32, 36 and 37 (together), 39, 41, 42, 43, 45 (lengthy), 46, 48, 51, perhaps 52.

CHAPTER 14 MULTIPLE INTEGRALS

14.1 Double Integrals

Topics to Cover Double integrals over rectangles in the plane with sides parallel to the coordinate axes. That is, let $[a, b]$ and $[c, d]$ be intervals on the x- and y-axes, respectively, and let $R = [a, b] \times [c, d]$. Partition these intervals to generate a partition $\mathcal{P}$ of R into rectangles; the *norm* of $\mathcal{P}$ is the maximum of the lengths of the diagonals of these rectangles. (That way, as the norm approaches zero, the bases and heights of all the rectangles approach zero in a "uniform" fashion.) Then a selection $(x_i^\star, y_i^\star)$ for $\mathcal{P}$ determines a Riemann sum

$$\sum_{i=1}^n f(x_i^\star, y_i^\star)\, \Delta A_i$$

for the function f defined on R, where ΔA_i is the area of the ith rectangle in the partition. If f is continuous on R, then—as the norm of $\mathcal{P}$ approaches zero—the limit of such sums exists and is denoted by

$$I = \iint_R f(x, y)\, dA.$$

Moreover, continuity of f on R makes it possible to evaluate this *double integral* by converting it into an iterated integral:

$$I = \int_c^d \left(\int_a^b f(x, y)\, dx \right) dy = \int_a^b \left(\int_c^d f(x, y)\, dy \right) dx.$$

Notes Iterated integrals are almost always evaluated from the "inside out," and thus the large parentheses in the last equation are unnecessary and almost always omitted. If $f(x, y) \geq 0$ on R, then the double integral may be interpreted as the volume of the region between the graph of f and the xy-plane over the rectangle R. If $f(x, y) \equiv 1$ on R, then the numerical value of the integral is also equal to the area of R. Even if not,

$$A(x) = \int_c^d f(x, y)\, dy$$

gives the cross-sectional area of the solid bounded above by the graph of $f(x, y)$ over R in a plane perpendicular to the x-axis at x. This justifies the present definition of volume, as this shows that (as in Section 6.2) volume is the integral of cross-sectional area. For various computer algebra commands for evaluating multiple integrals, see the *Instructor's Manual*.

Goals The definition of the double integral as the limit of Riemann sums, that this limit exists if f is continuous on the rectangle R, and that the double integral may in this case be evaluated by converting it into either of two iterated integrals—for which single-variable techniques suffice.

Problems 1, 2, 3, 4, 7, 9, 11 through 16, 19, 21, 23, 24, 27, 29, 31, 32, 35, 37, 40.

14.2 Double Integrals over More General Regions

Topics to Cover An inner partition of the bounded plane region R. Writing Riemann sums for a function f defined on R. If the limit of such sums exists as the norm of such inner partitions approaches zero, then it is denoted by

$$\iint_R f(x, y)\, dA.$$

(It does exist if f is continuous on R and the boundary of R is reasonably well-behaved ("piecewise smooth").) How to evaluate such integrals if R is either vertically simple or horizontally simple. Reversal of the order of integration in a given iterated integral. Useful general properties of double integrals in Eqs. (6) through (9).

Notes The limits of integration in an iterated integral over the plane region R are determined by the equations of the curves that bound R; they do *not* depend on the integrand $f(x, y)$. Advice: To set up an iterated integral, it is almost essential to *sketch the region R* and label its boundary curves with their equations. Assign several problems of the sort in which the order of integration is reversed; this compels the students to draw the region R and to label its boundary curves.

Goals The evaluation of double integrals over bounded plane regions; correct reversal of the order of integration in iterated integrals.

Problems 1 through 6, 11 through 22, 25 through 34, 41 through 44, 48 through 51.

14.3 Area and Volume by Double Integration

Topics to Cover The volume between the graph of $z = f(x, y) \geq 0$ and the xy-plane over the bounded plane region R. Using $f(x, y) \equiv 1$ to find the area of R. The volume between two surfaces.

Notes At appropriate points, you can show the students that the iterated integrals for volume reduce to integrals of cross-sectional area functions, thus making an important connection with Section 6.2.

Goals Setting up area and volume integrals in rectangular coordinates.

Problems 1 through 6, 10 through 15, 18, 22, 26 through 30, 31 through 34 if a computer algebra system is available, 37, 39, 41, 42, 43; if a computer algebra system is available, 52 and 53. Also the five problems in the Concepts: Questions and Discussion section.

14.4 Double Integrals in Polar Coordinates

Topics to Cover The polar rectangle R described in polar coordinates by $a \leqq r \leqq b$, $\alpha \leqq \theta \leqq \beta$. To evaluate the double integral

$$\iint_R f(x, y)\, dA$$

where R is such a polar rectangle, we evaluate the iterated integral

$$\int_\alpha^\beta \int_a^b f(r\cos\theta,\ r\sin\theta)\, r\, dr\, d\theta.$$

Note the presence of the factor r in the area differential $dA = r\, dr\, d\theta$. The methods of Section 14.2 may be used for plane regions that are radially simple. Examples 2 through 4 help make this clear.

Notes Double integrals in polar coordinates are almost always set up over regions that are radially simple, so polar iterated integrals will almost always be computed with respect to r first, θ last. The angular bounding rays $\theta = \alpha$ and $\theta = \beta$ are frequently missing, as in the integrals to find the areas enclosed by the circle $r = \sin\theta$ and the cardioid $r = 1 + \cos\theta$. This is not a problem. Finally, the main reason for choosing polar coordinates over rectangular coordinates is simplification of the description of the boundary of the domain R, resulting in simplification of the limits of integration. Not so common but almost as important is the simplification of the integrand, as in Problems 8, 9, 11, 12, 13, 14, 15, 17, and 18. The result in Example 5 is important in its own right, although the technique for evaluating the single integral is unusual.

Goals Use of polar coordinates to evaluate double integrals.

Problems 1 through 24, 26, 27, 29, 30, 34, 37, 39, 41. If a computer algebra system is available, 42 and 43.

14.5 Applications of Double Integrals

Topics to Cover Mass and centroid from the viewpoint of the double integral. Centroid, symmetry principle, first and second theorems of Pappus, moments of inertia, radius of gyration.

Notes The radius of gyration is optional, although Problem 56 needs this concept. We mention this because the integral required in Problem 56 is one of the most difficult in the book, can be done by hand with a little ingenuity, and resists most computer algebra systems. Applications to three-dimensional solids are postponed until the next section. Finally, to save work, advise the students to use symmetry whenever possible; moments are still additive (as in Section 6.6).

Goals Using double integrals in rectangular and polar coordinates to compute masses, centroids, and moments of inertia.

Problems 4, 6, 7, 9, 11, 12, 15, 16, 18, 19, 26, 27, 28, 35, 36, 39, 42, 43, 44, 53, 56 if you dare.

14.6 Triple Integrals

Topics to Cover A partition $\mathcal{P}$ of the bounded space region T, a selection S for T, the norm of $\mathcal{P}$, and the corresponding Riemann sum for the function f defined on T. The triple integral of f over T as the limit of such Riemann sums. (If f is continuous of T and the boundary of T consists of a finite number of piecewise smooth surfaces, then the definite integral exists.) Applications to volume, mass, centroid, and moments of inertia. Conversions of triple integrals into iterated integrals proceed as in the two-dimensional case.

Notes Keep the integrands simple to avoid formidable computational difficulties. The formulas for triple integrals are perfectly analogous to those for double integrals in Section 14.5, so should be easy to learn.

Goals Setting up and evaluating triple integrals in rectangular coordinates; applications.

Problems 1, 2, 5, 7, 9, 11 through 16, 21, 22, 24, 27, 28, 31, 32, 38, 41, 44, 48, 49, 52, and 53 if a computer algebra system is available.

14.7 Integration in Cylindrical and Spherical Coordinates

Topics to Cover Review of cylindrical and spherical coordinates (Section 12.8). Setting up triple integrals in cylindrical and spherical coordinates. The "translations"

$$dV = r\, dz\, dr\, d\theta \quad \text{and} \quad dV = \rho^2 \sin\phi\, d\rho\, d\phi\, d\theta.$$

Applications to volume, mass, centroids, and moments of inertia.

Notes You can cover this material very informally, or if you prefer you can use the machinery of cylindrical and spherical partitions, selections, norms, and Riemann sums to derive the results rigorously. The main thing is for the student to learn to convert awkward rectangular triple integrals into easier cylindrical or spherical triple integrals. You may wish to present the solution of Problem 47 in class because of its unique historical importance (it requires more than minimal advance preparation).

Goals Setting up and evaluating triple integrals in cylindrical and spherical coordinates.

Problems 1, 2, 3, 4, 5, 10, 12, 15, 16, 18, 20, 21, 27, 29, 30, 35, 37, 38, 39, 40, 44, 48, 49 (long).

14.8 Surface Area

Topics to Cover Parametric surfaces, the surface area of a smooth parametric surface; surface area in rectangular and cylindrical coordinates.

Notes The most difficult aspect of finding the area of a surface is finding a suitable parametrization. Give the students easy illustrations, such as the curved cylindrical surface $0 \leqq z \leqq H$, $r = R$, $0 \leqq \theta \leqq 2\pi$.

Goals Parametrizing surfaces in space and finding the areas of such surfaces.
Problems 1 through 5, 8, 9, 13 through 16, 20.

14.9 Change of Variables in Multiple Integrals

Topics to Cover Transformations from the uv-plane to the xy-plane. Inverse transformations, u-curves and v-curves. The Jacobian of a transformation. The change of variables theorem. How to change variables in double and triple integrals.

Notes Examples 2 and 5 are useful because they relate this new material to material with which the students are already familiar.

Goals Using change-of-variables techniques to evaluate multiple integrals.

Problems 1 through 14, 17, 19, 20, 21, 28 and 29 (together; more difficult).

Chapter 14 Review

Problems 1 through 4, 6, 8, 15, 18, 21, 25, 26, 27, 29, 33, 36 through 44, 47, 52 through 58, 59 (difficult).

CHAPTER 15 VECTOR CALCULUS

15.1 Vector Fields

Topics to Cover Vector fields in the plane and in space. Velocity vector fields and force fields. The gradient vector field. The divergence and curl of a vector field. The analogies between the single-variable derivative operator D_x and the gradient vector operator ∇.

Notes Physical interpretations of the divergence and curl come later. Algebraic properties are developed in Problems 25 through 44.

Goals The mechanics of computing gradient, divergence, and curl.

Problems 1, 3, 4, 6, 9, 10, 11 through 14, 18, 20, 21, 22, 23, 25 through 34, 37, 38, 39, 40, 44.

15.2 Line Integrals

Topics to Cover The line integral with respect to arc length. The mass, centroid, and moment of inertia of a wire (a piecewise smooth arc in space with density function $\delta(x, y, z)$). Line integrals with respect to the coordinate variables. The effect of reversal of orientation of the path. Piecewise smooth curves. Work as the line integral, with respect to arc length, of the tangential component of force. Theorem 1 on equivalent line integrals.

Notes The principal motivations are mass and work. The key to evaluating any line integral is to parametrize the path, then to express everything in terms of the parameter. This converts the integral into an ordinary integral of a function of a single real variable—the parameter.

Goals Evaluation of line integrals, especially those associated with work.

Problems 1, 2, 4, 5, 6, 7, 9, 10, 11, 12, 14, 16, 18, 19, 20, 24, 25, 26 through 30, 32, 34, 35, 36, 37, 40.

15.3 The Fundamental Theorem and Independent of Path

Topics to Cover Independence of path. Theorem: The line integral

$$\int_C \mathbf{F} \cdot \mathbf{T}\, ds$$

is independent of path in the simply connected plane region D if and only if $\mathbf{F} = \nabla f$ for some function f defined on D. Definition of conservative field and potential function. Theorem: $\mathbf{F} = \langle P, Q \rangle$ is conservative on the open rectangle R if and only if $P_y = Q_x$ on R. Potential energy and conservative force fields; the law of conservation of mechanical energy.

Notes The proofs of Theorems 1 and 2 give insight into how to solve many of the problems at the end of this section.

Goals Understanding the equivalences among these new concepts. Using scalar potentials to make the evaluation of line integrals simple when conservative fields are involved.

Problems 1 through 6, 13, 14, 17, 18, 21, 23, 24, 27, 28, 30, 31, 32, 33, 34, 36 and 37 (together).

15.4 Green's Theorem

Topics to Cover Green's theorem and its corollary (on finding the area of a plane region; all three formulas are useful). The divergence and flux of a vector field. The vector form of Green's theorem.

Notes We use the notation

$$\oint_C P\, dx + Q\, dy$$

to denote a line integral around the *closed* path C in the positive (counterclockwise) direction. Because the sign of the integral is reversed if the path is swept out in the negative direction, we use

$$-\oint_C P\,dx + Q\,dy$$

to denote a line integral around C in the negative (clockwise) direction.

Goals Use of Green's theorem to evaluate double integrals (by conversion to a contour integral) and to evaluate contour integrals (by conversion to a double integral); use of its corollary to evaluate areas of plane regions.

Problems 1 through 22, 25, 26, 27, 29 through 36, 38, 39, and 41 (a computer algebra system is helpful but not required).

15.5 Surface Integrals

Topics to Cover Surface integrals and the flux of a vector field across a surface.

Notes To evaluate a surface integral, convert it into an ordinary double integral, as in Eq. (7).

Goals Evaluation of surface integrals.

Problems 1 through 6, 8, 10, 13, 14, 16, 18, 19, 20, 25, 29, 30, 40 (if a computer algebra system is available), 41 (more difficult).

15.6 The Divergence Theorem

Topics to Cover Piecewise smooth closed surfaces and the divergence theorem. Physical interpretation of divergence.

Notes The partial proof of the divergence theorem in the text is suitable for classroom presentation.

Goals Use of the divergence theorem and some of its applications.

Problems 1, 2, 3, 4, 6, 7, 8, 10, 11, 13, 18, 21, 24; perhaps 26 and 27.

15.7 Stokes' Theorem

Topics to Cover Stokes' theorem, conservative and irrotational fields, and Green's theorem as a special case of Stokes' theorem. Physical interpretation of curl.

Notes The partial proof of the important Theorem 1 on conservative and irrotational fields is suitable for classroom presentation.

Goals Using Stokes' theorem to evaluate certain contour integrals and certain surface integrals.

Problems 1, 2, 4, 6, 7, 8, 10, 11, 12, 14, 15, 22.

Chapter 15 Review

Problems 1, 4, 6, 7, 8, 10, 11, 12, 17, 18, 19, 20, 23, 24, 29. All mathematics, physics, and engineering majors should work Problems 25 through 28 and 32. Everyone should work Problem 14!

INDEX

Entries in bold type indicate the page (or pages) where a term is formally defined.

A

Abel, Neils Henrik (1802–1829), 176
Abscissa, **A-6**
Absolute convergence, 731, **732**, 733
  implies convergence, 731
  and rearrangements, 733
Absolute maxima and minima, 145, **222**
  existence, 145
Absolute temperature, A-13
  (Problem 33)
Absolute value, **A-2**
Absolute value function, 15, 137
Acceleration, **110**, 279
  constant, 279
  gravitational, 110, 282
Acceleration vector, **807**
  normal, tangential components, **822**
  radial, transverse components, **825**
Acta Eruditorum (of Leibniz), 193
Addition formulas:
  arctangent, 476 (Problem 64)
  sine and cosine, 166, 758, A-14, A-18 (Problems 41–42)
  tangent, 714 (Problem 52), A-18 (Problem 28)
Additivity of moments, 417
Adiabat, 1005
Adiabatic expansion of gas, 465 (Problem 34)
Adriatic Sea, 595
Advanced Calculus (Taylor and Mann, 1983), 443
Advanced Calculus of Several Variables (Edwards, 1994), 924
A-frame house, 887 (Problem 55)
Age of universe example, 551–552
Airy functions, 764–766
Alanine, 778
Algebraic function, **30**
Aliasing, 41
Alligator population, 588, 593, 596 (Problems 12, 20, 25, 26)
Alternating series, **728**
  remainder estimate, 730
  text, 729
Alternative notation for derivatives, 115
Almagest (of Ptolemy), 771
Ampere's law, 1029 (Problem 42)
"An algorithm for the calculation of π," 712–713
Analytic Engine, 53
Angular momentum, **814** (Problem 42)

Angle:
  of inclination (of line), **12**, **A-10**
  between planes, **799**
Angular coordinate, **629**
Animal house, 161
Animal pen problem, 6, 18, 60, 93, 142
Annular ring, **381**
Anthill, 425 (Problem 34)
Antiderivative, **273**
  most general, 274
Antidifferentiation, **273**
  linearity, 276
Apéry, Roger, 722
Appalachian Trail, 396
Applied maximum-minimum problems, 152–153, 884–885
Approach curve, 823
Arc:
  length, **397**, 655, **817**, 846 (Problems 28–29)
  length in parametric form, 654
  smooth, **396**
Arc-length function, **817**
Arc-length parametrization, **818**
Archimedes (287–212 B.C.), 2, 187, 188, 271, 295, 345, 383, 387, 399, 426, 642 (Problem 39), 711, 987, 1013
  derivation of sphere volume, 387 (Problem 58), 426 (Problem 50)
  floating paraboloid, 987
  law of buoyancy, 1063, 1064 (Problem 21), 1071 (Problem 22)
arccos, **471**
  derivative and domain, 471
arccosh, **480**
  derivative, 481
  domain, 480
arccot, **468**
  derivative and domain, 468
arccoth, **480**
  derivative, 481
  domain, 480
arccsc, **473**
  derivative and domain, 473
arccsch, **480**
  derivative, 481
  domain, 480
arcsec, 471, **472**
  alternative definition, 472, 476 (Problem 63)
  derivative and domain, 472
arcsech, **480**
  derivative, 481
  domain, 480

arcsin, 469, **470**
  derivative and domain, 470
  Taylor series, 747
arcsinh, **480**
  derivative, 481
  domain, 480
arctan, 467, **468**
  addition formula, 476 (Problem 64)
  derivative and domain, 468
  Taylor series, 712, 746
arctanh, **480**
  derivative, 481
  domain, 480
Area, 47, 286, 342, 367
  within astroid, 658 (Problem 29), 1045 (Problem 15)
  between two curves, 337, 340
  bounded by circular arc, 175
  bounded by cycloid, 655, 1045 (Problem 14)
  bounded by graph of function, 272
  bounded by parametric curve, 654
  within cardioid, 638, 966 (Problem 3), 976 (Problem 28)
  of circle, 271, 308, 341, 372, 654, 966 (Problem 1–2), 1045 (Problem 13), A-15
  of circular sector, 520 (Problem 43)
  of conical frustum, 400
  of ellipse, 345 (Problem 47), 519 (Problem 42), 658 (Problem 45), 1041
  within folium of Descartes, 680 (Problem 83), 1046 (Problem 33)
  formulas, A-43
  of general plane region, 336
  within generalized folium, 1047 (Problem 41)
  by Green's theorem, 1040, 1073 (Problem 14)
  within lemniscate, 976 (Problem 35)
  within limaçon, 966 (Problem 7), 976 (Problem 30)
  as limit, 293
  of parabolic segment, 345 (Problems 48–49)
  of parallelogram, 791
  of plot of land, 795 (Problems 23–26)
  in polar coordinates, 638–640
  of polygon, 1073 (Problem 14)
  of polygonal figure, 286
  of regular pentagon, 1046 (Problem 39)
  of spherical surface, 399
  of spherical zone, 405 (Problem 43), 425 (Problem 28)

I-1

Area (*Cont.*)
  of surface of revolution, **401**
  of triangle, 791, 796 (Problem 35), 845 (Problem 5), 1046 (Problems 38–39)
  within two circles, 966 (Problem 5)
  within two lemniscates, 1011 (Problem 54)
  of unbounded region, 345 (Problem 50)
  under graph, 286
  under graph of quadratic function, 345 (Problem 52)
Area sums, 292
Arithmetic mean and root-square mean, 938 (Problem 37)
Arithmetic-geometric mean inequality, **926** (Problem 62)
Astroid:
  arc length, 404 (Problem 41), 658 (Problem 30)
  area enclosed, 658 (Problem 29), 1045 (Problem 15)
  surface area of revolution, 405 (Problem 42), 658 (Problem 31)
Astronomical unit (AU), **667**
Asymptote, 30, 256
  horizontal, **258**
  inclined (slant, oblique), **261**, 270 (Problem 103)
  vertical, **257**
Athens (Georgia), 20, 23, 35, 320
Atlanta (Georgia), 20, 844 (Problem 56)
Atm (unit of pressure), A-42
Automobile skid mark example, 281
Average distance, **1011**, 1029
  from origin to astroid, 1029 (Problem 29)
  from origin to cycloid, 1029 (Problem 28)
  from origin to helix, 1029 (Problem 30)
  from point to surface, 1073 (Problem 20)
  of points of ball from center, 994 (Problem 39), 1011 (Problem 39)
  of points of ball from fixed boundary point, 994 (Problem 40), 1011 (Problem 40)
  of points of circle from its center, 1029 (Problem 26)
  of points of circle from a fixed point, 1029 (Problem 27)
  of points of cone from vertex, 1011 (Problem 42)
  of points of cube from corner, 987 (Problem 53)
  of points of disk from center, 1011 (Problem 36)
  of points of disk from fixed boundary point, 1011 (Problem 37)
Average rate of change, **106**, **110**, **908**
Average value of function, **319**, **986**
Average value property of double integrals, 954 (Problem 50)
Average value theorem, 320, 944
Average velocity, **109**

B

Babbage, Charles (1791–1871), 53
Babylon, 176
Babylonian square root method, 176
Bach family, 545; *see also* **http://jan.ucc.nau.edu/~tas3/familyhis.html**
Bailey, D., 525 (Problem 50)
Barometric pressure, 619 (Problem 35)
Base:
  for exponential function, **37**, **430**, **461**
  for logarithmic function, **39**, **432**, **463**

Basic trigonometric limit, 75, 82
Basic unit vectors, **781**
Battle of Hastings, 667
Bead sliding down wire, 646
Beam, 896 (Problem 42)
Beckmann, Peter, 711
Bell-shaped curve, 533
Bending upward, downward, **243–244**
Bernoulli, Jacques (James, Jakob) (1654–1705), 545
Bernoulli, Jean (John, Johannes) (1667–1748), 489, 545, 646
Bessel function, 749 (Problems 57–60), 767 (Problem 24)
  of order 1 ($J_1(x)$), **749** (Problem 57)
  of order zero ($J_0(x)$), **743**
Beyer, William H., 490
Big Bang, 551
Big Frog, 358
Billiard table, 668
Binary event, **535**
Binomial series, 744, 749 (Problem 67)
Birdbath, 395 (Problem 47), 416 (Problem 40)
Black hole, 1013
Blood test, 486 (Problem 53)
Boas, R. P., Jr., 698
Bolzano-Weierstrass theorem, A-26
Borromean rings, 803
Borwein, Jonathan M., 713
Borwein, Peter B., 525 (Problem 50), 713
Bounce coefficient, 700 (Problems 64–65)
Bounded monotonic sequence property, 688, 689, 715, **A-24**
Bounded plane region, **947**
Bounded populations, 588
Bounded set of real numbers, A-23
Boyle's law, 49, A-4, A-5 (Problem 37)
Brachistochrone problem, 646
Brahe, Tycho (1546–1601), 771
Briggs, Henry (1561–1631), 427
Brunnian link, *see* Borromean rings
Btu (unit of heat energy), A-42
Bumpy sphere, 844 (Problem 64)
  centroid, 995 (Problem 46)
  volume, 995 (Problem 45)
Buoy, 616 (Problems 24–25)
Burrito, 162
Butterfly curve, 634
"Butterfly Curve, The," 634
Byron, Ada (1815–1852), 53
Byron, Lord (George Noel Gordon, 1788–1824), 53

C

c, 163
Cake, 574 (Problem 32)
cal (unit of heat energy), A-42
Calculus of variations, 849
Calgary (Alberta), 375
Carbon-14, 551
Card game, 701–702
Cardan, Girolamo (1501–1576), 176
  Cardan's formulas, 238
Cardiac output, 372, 373
Cardioid, **632**, 633, 636 (Problems 41–42), 637 (Problem 60), 638, 680 (Problem 65)
  arc length, 656
  surface area of revolution, 656
Caribou crossing, 23
Carnot engine, 1005
Cartesian coordinate system, **A-6**
Cascade of tanks, 586 (Problem 28)

Catenary, 485 (Problem 69), 545, 575 (Problem 43)
Cathode-ray tube, 808
Cauchy, Augustin Louis (1789–1857), A-28, A-36
Cauchy sequence, **A-27**
Cauchy's mean value theorem, A-36
Cauchy-Schwarz inequality, 787 (Problem 58), 938 (Problem 52)
Cavalieri, Bonaventura (1598–1647), 378
Cavalieri's principle, **378**
CEILING, 4
Celestial mechanics, 849
Celsius-Fahrenheit conversion, 49, 113, A-5 (Problem 38)
Center of curvature, **820**
Center of mass, 416, **417**
Central limit theorem, 535
Centrally simple region, **991**
Centroid, **151**, **417**, **418**, 969
  of bumpy sphere, 995 (Problem 46)
  of cone, 986 (Problem 32), 994 (Problem 20)
  of curve, **420**
  of cycloidal wire, 1029 (Problem 24)
  of cylinder, 993 (Problem 18)
  of hemisphere, 986 (Problem 22), 994 (Problem 21)
  of "ice-cream cone," 992, 1010 (Problem 26)
  of lamina, **968**
  of paraboloid, 986 (Problem 31)
  of plane curve, 972
  of semicircular disk, 969
  of solid, **980**
  of triangle, 422 (Problem 23)
  of wire, **1022**
Ceres (asteroid), 1013
Chain rule, 126
  formulas, 168
  in function notation, 128
  general (multivariable), 897, 899
  matrix form, 902–903
  multivariable, 897
  proof, 129 (with hole), 210 (complete)
  proof (multivariable), 903
Change of variables in triple integrals, 1006
Change-of-variables theorem, 1004
Chaos, 101
Characteristic (auxiliary) equation, **601**
Characteristic triangle, 193
Chaucer, Goeffrey (1340?–1400), 556
Chernobyl, 44
Chipmunks, 113
CHOP, 11
Chord (longest) of sphere, 938 (Problem 32)
Cider, 383
Circle:
  area, 297 (Problem 52), 308, 341, 372, 642 (Problem 37), 654, 657, A-15
  area within three, 642 (Problem 39)
  circumference, 297 (Problem 52), 403, 476 (Problem 67), A-15
  in parabola, 100
  parametric equations, 643
  polar equation, 630, 631, 632, 636 (Problems 37, 39–40)
Circle of curvature, **820**
Circular frequency, **611**
Circular lake, 270 (Problem 104)
Circulation, **1068**
City park problem, 165
Clarke, Arthur C., 286
Clement, Hal (Harry Clement Stubbs), 362

Clepsydra, 386 (Problem 52), 557 (Problem 47)
Closed curve, **1037**
    simple, **1037**
Closed interval, 4, **A-3**
Closed interval maximum-minimum method, 145
CN Tower (Toronto), 786
Coffee cup, 140–141
Coin toss game, 700 (Problems 68–69)
Collinear points, 845 (Problem 4)
Colorado, 853
Common logarithm, 39
Commuter train, 162
Completeness axiom, **A-24**
Complex number, 183
    conjugate, **183**
    real, imaginary parts, 183
Component of **a** along **b**, 785
Componentwise differentiation, 805
Composition (of functions), **36**, 91
    continuity, 91
    derivative, 126
Computer algebra systems, 492
Concavity, **246**
    test, 247
Cone:
    generator, 626
    inscribed in inverted cone, 191
    inscribed in sphere, 190
    lateral surface area, 422 (Problem 25)
    nappes, 626
    with square hole, 1011 (Problem 47)
    volume, 380, 422 (Problem 24)
Conic section, 623, **624**, 626–628; *see also* Ellipse, Hyperbola, Parabola
    eccentricity, 626, **627**
    focus, **627**
    in polar coordinates, 674
    review, 679
    as sections of cone, A-39
Conical tank (draining), 124
Conjugate, 72, 75
    of complex number, **183**
Connected plane region (arcwise), 954 (Problem 50)
Conservation of mechanical energy, 1036
Conservative and irrotational vector fields, 1068
Conservative vector field, **1033**
    origin for terminology, 1035
    and potential function (theorem), 1034; (proof), 1042–1043
Constant law (for limits), 67
Constraint, **918**
Continued fraction, 691, 768 (Problem 47), 769 (Problem 65)
Continuity:
    of compositions, 91
    implied by differentiability, 138
    of multivariable function, **862**
    one-sided, **93**
    at a point, **88**
    of polynomials, 94
    of trigonometric functions, 91
    of vector-valued function, **804**
Continuity equation, 1074 (Problem 33)
Continuous function:
    on closed interval, 93, **94**
    combinations, 90
    composition, 91, 92
    definition, **90**
    intermediate value property, 94
    and polynomial roots, 92
Continuously differentiable function, **893**

Contour curve, 853
Convergence of sequence, **178**, **684**
Coordinate axes in space, **778**
Coordinate function, **643**
Coordinate plane, **A-6**
Coordinate planes, **779**
Coordinates, **A-6**
Copernicus, Nicolas (1473–1543), 771
Coplanar points, 793
Core-mantle model of earth, 995 (Problem 49)
Corner points, 396
$\cosh x$, **477**, 545, 575 (Problem 43)
Cost:
    additional, **154**
    fixed, **154**
    total, **154**
$\coth x$, **477**
Critical point, 145, 233, **881**
    classification, 224–226
Cross product (of vectors), **788**
    algebraic properties, 792
    not associative, 794 (Problem 11)
    not commutative, 790, 792, 795 (Problem 27)
    geometric significance, 790
    length, 790
    and parallel vectors, 791
    perpendicularity, 788
Cross section, **376**
Cross-sectional area function, **377**
Crossbow, 282, 587 (Problem 41)
Crosscut, 1041
$\operatorname{csch} x$, **477**
Cube, rotated, sweeps out volume, 1012 (Problem 59)
Curl, **1017**
    identities (with divergence and gradient), 1019 (Problems 25–44)
Curvature, 818, **819**, **821**
    at inflection point, 847 (Problem 42)
    in polar coordinates, 847 (Problem 47)
    of space curves, 821–822
Curve sketching, 232–267
    and solution of equations, 237
    strategy, 260
Cusp, 138, 646
Cycloid, **645**, 651 (Problem 38), 1029 (Problem 24)
    arc length, 655
    area under arch, 655, 1045 (Problem 14)
    area of revolution, 658 (Problems 24, 38)
    as brachistochrone, 646
    geometric construction of tangent, 650 (Problem 33)
    parametric equations, 645
    surface area of revolution, 658 (Problem 38)
    volume of revolution, 659 (Problem 39), 680 (Problem 67)
Cylinder, 376, **831**
    base, **376**
    circular, **376**
    elliptic, **832**
    height, **376**
    inscribed in cone, 162
    parabolic, **832**
    ruling, **831**
    surface area, 423 (Problem 28)
    volume, 377
Cylindrical coordinates, **838**
Cylindrical shell, **388**
    average radius, thickness, **388**

D

Damped motion (of mass on spring), 610–612
    circular frequency, **611**
    pseudoperiod, **611**
    time-varying amplitude, **611**
Dase, Zacharias (1824–1861), 712
Dashpot, 607
    damping constant, **607**
Decreasing function, 111, **212**, 217, 233
Decreasing quantity, 107
Definite integral, 286, **302**
    evaluation, 309, 310
    existence, A-29 through A-33
    as a limit, 301
    by substitution, 331, 332
Degree (of polynomial), **27**
Degree measure, 165
del Ferro, Scipione (1465–1526), 176
Denali National Park (Alaska), 619 (Problem 35)
Dependent variable, **3**, **898**
Dependent-independent variable notation (for derivatives), 115
Derivative, **45**, 58, 70, **102**
    alternative notation, 115
    of composition (chain rule), 126
    of constant, 115–116
    directional, **907**
    generalized power rule, 129, 133, 135, 463
    higher, 242
    left- and right-hand, **114**
    of linear combination, 117
    nth, 242
    partial, 868
    of polynomial, 118
    of product, 120–121, 193
    of quadratic function, 104
    of quotient, 122
    second, 242
    of sine and cosine, 166
    third, **242**
    of trigonometric functions, 166–168
    of vector-valued function, **805**
    see also specific functions by name (sinh, arctan, etc.)
Derivative vector, **805**
Descartes, René (1596–1650), 1, 195, 623, 624, A-6
    folium, **195**, 200 (Problems 29, 32), 203, 650 (Problem 30), 680 (Problem 81), 901, 915
Determinant, **789**
Determinism, 621 (Problems 64–67)
Diagonals of rhombus, 846 (Problem 18)
Diana, 286
Dice game, 696, 700 (Problem 70), 701
Dictionary of Scientific Biography, 545
Difference:
    of functions, **25**
    of vectors, **774**
Difference Engine, 53
Difference quotient, 57
Differentiability implies continuity, 138
Differentiable function, **102**
    multivariable, **894**
Differential, **204**, **209**, **889**, **892**, **893**
Differential calculus, 272
Differential equation, **272**, **546**
    and determinism, 621 (Problems 64–67)
    equilibrium solution, 579
    existence, uniqueness of solution, 564
    general solution, 278, **546**
    implicit solution, **547**
    initial condition, 278, **546**

Differential equation (*Cont.*)
    initial value problem, **546**
    integrating factor, **575**
    linear, **571**
    linear first-order, **575**, 579
    logistic, 560
    with one variable missing, 547
    particular solution, 278, **546**
    second-order, **598**
    separable, **568**
    singular solution, 570
    solution, **546**
Differential Equations: Computing and Modeling (2000), 564
Differential form, 1023
Differential geometry, 1013
Differential notation, 104–105, 115
Differentiation, **102** (*see also* Derivative)
    implicit, **194**
    logarithmic, 438
    of power of function, 134
    of quadratic functions, 104
    of vector-valued functions, 806
    see also specific functions by name (sin, arctanh, etc.)
Differentiation and integration of power series, 745–747
Diffusion of heat, 187
Diffusion of information, 573
Dimensions, 157
Dinosaur, 620 (Problem 46)
Diophantus (*floruit* A.D. 250), 623
Directed line segment, 772
Direction angles, cosines, **784**
Directional derivative, **907**
    calculation, 909
Discontinuity, 15, 35, **88**
    finite jump, 89
    infinite, 15, 89
    removable, 89
Discothèques, 231 (Problem 48)
Discourse on the Method, 1
Discriminant, **927**
Disease spread, 573
Displacement, 370
Disquisitiones arithmeticae (Gauss, 1801), 1013
Distance, 368, **A-2**, **A-6**
    between lines, 795 (Problem 31), 927 (Problem 65), 934 (Problem 26)
    between parallel planes, 802 (Problem 58), 846 (Problem 15)
    net, 370
    origin to plane, 845–846 (Problem 13)
    point to line, 788 (Problem 66), 795 (Problem 29)
    point to plane, 795 (Problem 30), 802 (Problem 54), 846 (Problem 14)
    total, **370**
Distance formula, 13
    in space, **779**
Divergence, **1016**, 1044
    identities (with curl and gradient), 1019 (Problems 25–44)
Divergence theorem, 1013, 1057, 1058
    partial proof, 1058–1059
DNA Tower (Kings Park, Perth), 804
Dodecahedral die, 701
Dog saddle, 934 (Problem 33)
Dog sled, 787 (Problem 56)
Domain:
    of single-variable function, **2**, **4**
    of function of two or three variables, **850**

Doomsday, 592–593
Dot product (of vectors), **782**
    algebraic properties, 782
    geometric interpretation, 783
    see also Vector
Double helix, 804
Double Helix, The (James D. Watson, 1968), 804
Double integral, **940**, **948**
    average value property, 954 (Problem 50)
    evaluation, 950
    properties, 947 (Problems 38–40), 952
Double-angle formulas, A-14
Doubling time, 39
Downhill Derby, 48
Drug elimination, 552–553
    elimination constant, time, 553
Dummy variable, 302

E

e, 39, 74, 430, 431, 441, **457**, 489, 696, 709, 711, 731
    irrationality, 769 (Problem 63)
    as a limit, 452–453
    as the sum of a series, 489, 500 (Problem 61), 709, 724
Earth orbit, 830 (Problem 58)
Earth satellite, 1037 (Problems 37–38)
Eccentricity (of conic section), 626, **627**
Einstein, Albert (1879–1955), 1013
Elastic springs, 406–407
    natural length, **406**
    spring constant, **407**
Elementary function, **346**, 428
Elements (of Euclid), 271
Elements of Differential and Integral Calculus (1929), 677 (Problem 75)
Ellipse, 627, **664**
    alternative definition, 668
    applications to planetary orbits, 667–668
    arc length, 404 (Problem 36), 520 (Problem 46), 661
    area, 345 (Problem 47), 519 (Problem 42), 658 (Problem 25), 1041
    as conic section, 626
    diameter, **680** (Problem 71)
    directrix, **664**
    eccentricity, **664**
    focus, **664**
    highest, lowest points, 917 (Problem 52), 923, 925 (Problem 42), 926 (Problem 60)
    major, minor axis, **665**
    perimeter, 757 (Problems 61, 62), 1001 (Problem 34)
    points closest to origin, 925 (Problems 38, 43)
    reflection property, 668, 678 (Problem 81)
    semiaxes, **665**
    vertex, **665**
Ellipsoid, **833**
    of revolution, 833
    surface area, 454 (Problem 47), 486 (Problem 38), 520 (Problems 52–53), 658 (Problem 25)
    volume, 385 (Problem 36), 394 (Problem 37), 426 (Problem 47), 960 (Problem 40), 1008 (Problem 14)
Ellipsoidal coordinates, 1008 (Problem 20), 1011 (Problem 53)
Elliptic integral, 660
Elliptical cone, **834**

Elliptical paraboloid, **834**
Elliptical torus, 1001 (Problem 34)
Empire State Building, 285
Enigma, 74, 623
Epicycle, 771
Epicycloid, 652, 680 (Problems 64–65)
Epitrochoid, 652, 660 (Problem 54)
Equality of vectors, **773**
Equation:
    differential, **272**
    general linear, 12
    of tangent plane, 872
Equilibrium population, 590
Equilibrium position (of mass on spring), **607**
    static, **607**
Equivalent line integrals, 1027
erf, *see* Error function
Error:
    absolute, **206**
    in linear approximation, 207, **893**
    relative, **206**
Error estimates:
    Simpson's approximation, 356
    trapezoidal and midpoint approximations, 355
Error function, **534**, 585, 965 (Example 5)
Escape velocity, 532
Estes Park (Colorado), 98
Etruscans, 701
Euler, Leonhard (1707–1783), 457, 489, 531, 561, 681, 722, 849
Euler's constant (γ), **721** (Problem 50)
Euler's formula, 489, 604, 711, 713
Euler's method, **562**
    step size, **562**
Evaluation theorem (for integrals), 309, 310
Even function, **172**
"Exception that proves the rule," 390
Existence:
    of cube roots, 98 (Problem 66)
    of (definite) integral, 303, 526, A-29 through A-33
    of double integral, 948
    of solution of differential equation, 564
    of solution of equation, 95
    of $\sqrt{2}$, 95
    of tangent line, 79
Exotic graphs, 267
exp, *see* Natural exponential function
Exponential decay, 549
Exponential function, **37**, **428**
    base a, **430**, **461**
    derivative, 430–432
    general, 461–462
    natural, 431, **459**

F

Factor theorem, 238
Fahrenheit-Celsius conversion, 49, 113, A-5 (Problem 38)
Fairbanks (Alaska, "North to the Future"), 844 (Problems 57–59)
Falling rock example, 469
Farris, Frank A., 660 (Problem 55)
Fay, Temple H., 634
Federal Express letter, 23
Feedlot, 158
Fermat, Pierre de (1601–1665), 1, 195, 623, 624
Fermat's "last theorem," 623, 722
Fermat's principle of least time, 158
Ferrari, Ludovico (1522–1565), 176
Fibonacci, Leonardo (of Pisa; 1170?–*post* 1240), 683
    see also Sequence

Figure-eight curve, 633, 637 (Problem 52), 642 (Problem 34), 660 (Problems 50–52)
First derivative test:
    for global extrema, 228
    for local extrema, 224
Five billionth hexagesimal digit of π, 525 (Problem 50)
Five-leaved rose, 637 (Problem 51)
Flat spots on graph, 255 (Problem 92)
Fleas (proverbial), 184
Floating paraboloid, 987
Floor, **4**, 16
Fluid flow (in circular pipes), 371
Fluorocarbons, 620 (Problem 58)
Flux (of vector field), **1043**
    across surface, **1052**
Focus (of conic section), **627**
Folium of Descartes, **195**, 200 (Problems 29, 32), 203, 650 (Problem 30), 680 (Problem 81), 901, 915, 1046 (Problem 33)
    arc length, 658 (Problem 37)
    curvature, 829 (Problem 54)
    folium-like curve, 651 (Problem 41)
    generalized, 1047 (Problem 41)
Foot-pound, 786
Force, A-41
    exerted by liquid, 412–413
    (gravitational) exerted by rod, 538 (Problems 55–56)
    moment, **794**
    perpendicular to direction of motion, 829 (Problem 51)
Force field, 1015
    inverse-square, 1015
Force function, 406
Forced oscillations, 612–615
    resonance, **614**
    steady periodic solution, **615**
    transient solution, **614**
Four-leaved rose, 632, 637 (Problem 47), 659 (Problems 45–46)
Four-step process (for differentiation), 102
Fractal images, 101, 182–185
Free motion (of mass on spring), **608**
    damped, 610–612
    natural frequency, **608**
Freezer, 620 (Problem 57)
From the Earth to the Moon (1865), 532
Function, **2** (*see also* Power function, Rational function, etc.)
    absolute value, 15, 137
    average value, **319**
    behavior at infinity, 232–233
    continuous, **88**, 90
    continuously differentiable, **893**
    critical points, 233
    defined implicitly, 194
    dependent, independent variable, **851**
    differentiable (multivariable), **894**
    discontinuous, **88**
    domain, **850**
    elementary, **346**
    even, **172**
    greatest integer, **4**, 16, 78, 149
    increasing, decreasing, 111, **212**, 217, 233–234
    increasing without bound, 80, **256**
    integrable, **302**
    with interesting discontinuities, 22 (Problem 56)
    inverse, **433**
    inverse pairs, 433
    maximum, minimum value, **878**
    of n variables, **865**
    not integrable, 307 (Problems 54–55), A-33
    odd, **172**
    one-to-one, **467**
    position, **279**
    quadratic, 16
    root, 134
    smooth, **396**
    trigonometric, *see* Trigonometric functions
    of two, three variables, **850**
    vector-valued, **804**
    with zero derivative, 216
Function notation for derivatives, 115
Functions with equal derivatives, 217
Fundamental identity of trigonometry, **A-14**
Fundamental theorem of algebra, 27
Fundamental theorem of calculus, 47, 272, 318, 321, 328, 490, 939
    and initial value problems, 324
    for line integrals, 1030
    for vector-valued functions, 809

G

g, 282, A-42
Gabriel's horn, 537 (Problems 49–51)
Galilei, Galileo (1564–1642), 664
γ, *see* Euler's constant
Gamma function, **531**, 537 (Problems 47–48), 749 (Problem 64)
Gauss, Carl Friedrich (1777–1855), 295, 1013, 1057, A-28
Gauss's law, 1062–1063, 1064 (Problems 24–27)
    for electric fields, 1055
    for inverse-square gravitational fields, 1054
Gauss's theorem (divergence theorem), 1057
General chain rule, 899
General linear equation, 12
General population equation, **588**
General solution (of differential equation), 278
Generalized power rule, 129, 133, 135
Geometric series, **694**
    ratio, **694**
    sum, 694
Geosynchronous orbit, 828
Gibbs, Josiah Willard (1839–1903), 1070
Gizeh (Egypt), 48, 409
Glass pane, 700 (Problem 71)
Global extrema, **145**, **222**, **878**, **879**
    first derivative test, 228
    types, 881
Gotham City, 114
Gradient vector, **892**, **910**
    analogy with D_x, 916 (Problems 35–38), 1018
    in cylindrical coordinates, 937 (Problem 24)
    identities (with divergence and curl), 1019 (Problems 25–44)
    interpretation, significance, 912
    linearity, 1016
    as normal vector, 913
    and product rule, 1016
Gradient vector field, **1015**
    divergence, **1016**
Grain warehouse, 486 (Problem 51)
Grand Lake (Colorado), 98
Granville, William Anthony (1863–1943), 677 (Problem 75)

H

Graph:
    of equation, **13**, **830**
    of equation in cylindrical coordinates, **839**
    of equation in three variables, **780**
    of function, **14**, **852**
    of parametric curve, **643**
    of polar equation, **630**
    with no tangent (at the origin), 80
Gravitation, 101
    attraction by spherical ball or shell, 995 (Problems 47–48), 1056 (Problem 41), 1064 (Problem 24)
Gravitational acceleration, 110
Gravitational attraction, 538 (Problems 56–57)
Great pyramid, 409
Greatest integer function, **4**, 16, 78, 149
Greatest lower bound, **A-24**
Greek alphabet, A-44
Green, George (1793–1841), 1038
Green's first identity, **1064** (Problem 18)
Green's second identity, **1064** (Problem 19)
Green's theorem, 1038
    corollary (area), 1040, 1073 (Problem 14)
    vector form, 1044
Greenwich (England), 842
Gyration (radius of), **975**
Gzyx, 114, 186

H

Hailstone, 133, 586 (Problem 30)
Half-angle identities, 501, A-14
Half-open interval, **4**
Halley, Edmund (1656–1742), 667
Halley's comet, 667
Hanging cable, 484–485 (Problems 69–70), 545
Hardy, G. H. (1877–1947), 681
Harmonic equation, 905 (Problem 38)
Harmonic function, **877** (Problem 69), 878 (Problem 70)
Harmonic series, **697**, 717, 736 (Problem 61)
    divergence, 697
    slow divergence, 698
Hat surface, 856
Hawsehole, 202 (Problem 60)
Heart rate, 465 (Problem 33)
Heat capacity, 1073 (Problem 26)
Heat conductivity, 1054
Heat diffusion, 187
Heat equation, **1062**, 1074 (Problem 28)
    derivation, 1073 (Problems 25–27)
    one-dimensional, 876 (Problem 55), 877 (Problem 61), 937 (Problem 10)
    two-dimensional, 876 (Problem 56), 937 (Problem 11)
Heat flow, 1054
Heaviside, Oliver (1850–1925), 1070
Heliocentric system, 771
Helix, 804, 817
Heptagonal hole, 968 (Problem 43)
Heron's formula, 925 (Problem 36)
Hexagonal hole, 968 (Problem 43)
High air pollution forecast, 854
Historical Development of the Calculus, The (C. H. Edwards, Jr.), 296, 383
History of π, A (Peter Beckmann), 711
Hole (square) through cone, 1011 (Problem 47)
Hole through cylinder, 960 (Problem 43)
Hole through earth, 616–617 (Problem 26)

Hole through sphere, 385 (Problem 46),
  390, 394 (Problem 43),
  844 (Problem 55),
  960 (Problems 52–53), 964,
  968 (Problems 41–43),
  994 (Problem 43),
  1012 (Problem 55)
Hooke's law, 406, 607
  spring constant, **607**
Hopper, Grace Murray (1906–1992), 53
Hopper emptying, 201 (Problem 37)
Horizontally simple region, **949**
Horsepower, **408**, 786
Huylebrouck, Dirk, 1009
Hyakutake (comet), 678 (Problem 77)
Hyperbola, 24, 627, **629** (Problem 35)
  applications, 673–674
  branches, 626, 628, **669**
  as conic section, 626
  conjugate axis, **670**
  construction of points thereon,
    680 (Problem 76)
  difference definition, 678 (Problems
    87–88)
  directrix, **668**
  eccentricity, **668**
  focus, **668**
  reflection property, 673, 678 (Problem 87)
  transverse axis, **669**
  vertex, **669**
Hyperbolic functions, 477–485, 545
  definitions, 477
  derivatives and integrals, 478–480
  graphs, 478
  identities, 477
  inverses, 480–483
  see also sinh, cosh, arcsinh, arctanh, etc.
Hyperbolic paraboloid, **836**
Hyperbolic substitution, 518–519
Hyperboloid:
  of one sheet, **835**
  of two sheets, **835**
Hypertension, 376 (Problem 49)
Hypocycloid, **651** (Problems 34–36),
  680 (Problem 68)
  of four cusps, see Astroid
Hypotrochoid, 652

I

i, 238, 711
i, 775, 781
I beam, 974
Ice block melting, 201 (Problem 36)
Ice tray, 925 (Problem 44)
Icecap (polar), 810
Idea of the limit, 64
Ideal gas law, 850, 877 (Problem 63),
  905 (Problem 37)
Implicit differentiation, **194**
Implicit function theorem, 901
Implicit partial differentiation, 901
Implicitly defined function, 194
Improper integral, **526**
  convergent, divergent, **527**, **529**
Increasing function, 111, **212**, 217, 233
Increasing quantity, 107
Increment, 54, 104, **106**, **204**, **889**, **892**, **A-7**
Indefinite integral, **274**
Independence of path, **1031**, 1032
Independent variable, **3**, **898**
Indeterminate form:
  $\infty - \infty$, **450**
  ∞/∞, 443
  ∞^0, 451

1^∞, 451
$0/0$, **441**
$0 \cdot \infty$, **449**
0^∞ not indeterminate, 452, 453
0^0, 451, 455 (Problem 52)
Index of refraction, **163**
Index of summation, **290**
Indicator diagram, 1005
Inequalities, A-1
  solving, A-3
Inequality (arithmetic-geometric mean),
  926 (Problem 62)
Infinite discontinuity, 15
Infinite limit, 80
Infinite product, 500–501 (Problem 68),
  768 (Problems 49–50),
  769 (Problem 64)
Infinite radical, 688, 691
Infinite sequence, **682**
  bounded, **688**
  convergent, divergent, **684**
  Fibonacci, **683**, 689 (Problems 55–56),
    768 (Problem 48)
  increasing, decreasing, etc., **688**, **A-24**
  and l'Hôpital's rule, 687
  limit, **684**
  limit laws, 685
  limits of functions and sequences, 687
  monotonic, **688**, **A-24**
  nth term, **682**
  recursively defined, 683, 690 (Problems
    53–60), 691
  remarkable, 691 (Problem 64)
  squeeze law, 685
  substitution law, 685
Infinite series, **691**
  absolutely convergent, 731–733
  alternating, **728**
  alternating harmonic, 728,
    736 (Problem 61)
  binomial, 744, 749 (Problem 67)
  comparison test, 723
  conditionally convergent, **732**
  convergent, divergent, **692**
  divergent to infinity, **698**
  divergent by oscillation, 698
  domination, **723**
  eventually the same, 698
  geometric, **694**; see also Geometric series
  harmonic, **697**; see also Harmonic series
  integral test, 716
  limit comparison test, 725
  nth partial sum, **692**
  nth term, **691**
  nth-term test for divergence, 696
  positive-term, **715**
  p-series, **717**
  ratio test, 733
  rearrangement, 726
  root test, 734
  sequence of partial sums, **602**
  sum, **692**
  Taylor, see Taylor series
  telescoping, 694, 700 (Problems 50–60)
  term, **691**
  termwise addition and
    multiplication, 695
  see also Power series, etc.
Inflection point, **248**
  test, 248
Initial condition (for differential
  equation), 278
Initial value problem, **278**, 324
Inner partition, **947**
  norm, **947**
  selection, **947**

Instantaneous rate of change, 105, **106**, **111**,
  869, **908**
Instantaneous velocity, **109**
Integrable function, **302**, **948**
Integral, 47, 298
  comparison properties, 315,
    317 (Problems 60–61)
  of constant, 313
  constant multiple property, 313,
    317 (Problem 59)
  definite, 286, **302**
  double, **940**, **948**
  evaluation, 309, 310, 950
  existence, 303, A-29 through A-33
  improper, **526**
  indefinite, **274**
  interval union property, 314,
    317 (Problem 62)
  iterated, **942**
  as a limit, 301
  as the limit of a sequence, 303
  line, **1020**
  multiple, 940
  partial, **943**
  sum property, 313
  triple, **979**
Integral calculus, 272
Integral test, 716
Integral test remainder estimate, 718
Integrand, **302**
Integrating factor, **575**
Integration:
  by hyperbolic substitution, 518–519
  by parts, 494
  of products of secants and tangents,
    503–506
  of products of sines and cosines, 502–503
  by rationalizing substitution,
    542 (Problem 120)
  by special substitution, 542 (Eqs. (1)–(5))
  strategy, 539–540
  by substitution, **329**, 490
  triple, **979**
  triple, in cylindrical coordinates, 988
  triple, in spherical coordinates, 991
  of vector-valued functions, 809–811
Interest (compound), 454 (Problem 48), 552,
  556 (Problems 21, 26, 27), 683
  effective annual interest rate, 552
Interior point, **223**, **879**
Intermediate value property, theorem,
  94, A-25
Intermediate variable, **898**
Internet, 557 (Problem 38)
Intersection (of sets), **A-5**
Interstate Highway 80, 221 (Problem 47)
Interval, **4**, **A-3**
Introductio in Analysin Infinitorium, 489
Inverse function, **433**
  derivatives, 435
  examples of pairs, 433
Inverse hyperbolic functions, 480–483
  identities involving ln x, 482
  see also arcsinh, arctanh, etc.
Inverse sine, inverse tangent, etc., see arcsin,
  arctan, etc.
Inverse-square force field, 1015,
  1019 (Problems 37–38), 1030,
  1037 (Problem 36)
Inverse-square law of gravitational attraction,
  772, 825, 826, 1036
Inverse trigonometric functions:
  derivatives, 468–473
  domain and derivative table, 473
  integrals, 473–474
  see also arcsin, arctan, etc.

Involute of circle, **659** (Problems 40–42)
Irrational number, A-1
Irreducible quadratic polynomial, **509**
Irrotational field, **1068**
 and conservative field, 1068
Isobar, isotherm, **854**, 1005
Isoperimetric problem, 849
Isothermal compressivity,
 906 (Problems 56–57)

J

j, 775, 781
Jacobi, Carl (1804–1851), 1003
Jacobian **1003**
Jerk, 823
Joule (J, unit of work), 786, A-41
Juneau (Alaska, "North to the Future"), 317
Jupiter (planet), 667, 830 (Problem 62)

K

k, 781
Kahoutek (comet), 678 (Problem 77)
Kangaroos, 105
Keenory, Brendon, 786
Kepler, Johannes (1571–1630), 459, 624,
 771, 825
Kepler's equation, 187
Kepler's laws of planetary motion, 771, 825
 second, 677 (Problem 69), 678 (Problem 96), 826, 830 (Problem 56)
 third, 459
Key (to reversing order of integration), 951
Khufu, 48, 409
Kinetic energy of rotation, 974
Kiss, *see* Osculum
Kite frame, 164
Kosmo, 285
Kristiansand (Norway), 216

L

Labrador Sea, 673
Ladder problem, 187, 202 (Problems 51, 57),
 270 (Problem 106)
Lagrange, Joseph Louis (1736–1813),
 849, 918
 method of Lagrange multipliers, **918**
Lagrange multiplier, **919**
Lake (circular), 270 (Problem 104)
Lake Erie, 48, 581
Lake Huron, 581
Lake Ontario, 581, 585
Lamborghini, 556
Laplace equation:
 three-dimensional, 877 (Problem 60),
  1070, 1074 (Problem 28)
 two-dimensional, 877 (Problem 69),
  1046 (Problem 26)
Laplacian, **1064** (Problem 15)
Latitude and longitude, 842–843
Laurel leaf, 195
Law of conservation of angular
 momentum, 814
Law of conservation of mechanical
 energy, 1036
Law of cosines, 783, A-44
Law of laminar flow, 372
Law of the lever, **416**
Law of sines, A-44
Laws of exponents, 428, 461–462
Laws of logarithms, 434, 457, 464
Leading coefficient, 31

Least-squares approximations, 1013
Least-squares straight line, **938** (Problem 51)
Least upper bound, **690**, **A-24**
Least upper bound property, 689, A-24
Lebesgue, Henri (1875–1941), 939, A-33
Leçons sur le calcul des fonctions
 (Lagrange, 1806), 849
Left-endpoint approximation, **347**
Left-endpoint sum, 299
Left-hand derivative, 114
Left-hand limit, **78**
Leibniz, Gottfried Wilhelm (1646–1716), 2,
 47, 193, 209, 275, 286, 302, 308, 318,
 365, 545, 646, A-28
 method of characteristic triangle, 193
Leibniz's series, 712, 729 (Example 1),
 769 (Problem 62)
Lemniscate, 200 (Problem 35), 632, 636
 (Problem 45), 637 (Problem 46)
 surface area of revolution, 658 (Problem 32), 680 (Problem 66)
Length, A-41
 of cross product, 790
 of smooth arc, **397**, **817**
 of vector, **772**, **780**, **865**
Leningrad, *see* St. Petersburg
Level curve, **853**
Level surface, **854**
l'Hôpital, Guillaume-François-Antoine de
 (Marquis de Sante-Mesme, Comte
 d'Entremont) (1661–1704),
 442, 545
 l'Hôpital's own example, 448 (Problem 69)
l'Hôpital's rule, 442, 443, 545, A-36
 proof, 446, 447, A-38
 see also Indeterminate form
$li(x)$, 365
Lifetime (of light bulb), 268 (Problem 32)
Limaçon, 636 (Problems 38, 43–44), 639, 640,
 659 (Problems 47–48)
Limit, 56, 64, **83**, **A-19**
 basic trigonometric, 75
 of composition, 70
 of $f(x, y)$, **861**
 idea of, 64
 infinite, 80
 at infinity, **257**
 intuitive idea, 860
 laws (multivariable), 862–863
 lower (of integral), **302**
 one-sided, 67, 77
 uniqueness, A-23 (Problem 11)
 upper (of integral), **302**
 of vector-valued function, **804**
Limit laws, 67–68, 70, 76
 multivariable, 862–863
 one-sided, 79
 proofs, A-20 through A-23
Limit point, **A-26**
Limiting population, **590**
Limiting speed, 584
Limiting velocity, 560
Line:
 angle of inclination, **A-10**
 parametric equations, **796**
 point-slope equation, **A-9**
 slope-intercept equation, **A-9**
 symmetric equations, **797**
 tangent to curve, 45
 vector equation, **796**
Line integral, **1020**
 equivalent, 1027
 fundamental theorem of
  calculus, 1030
 path-dependent, path-independent,
  1025, **1031**, 1032

 with respect to arc length, **1021**
 with respect to coordinate variable, **1023**
Linear approximation, 204, 205, **890**
 error, **893**
Linear approximation theorem, 893
 proof, A-40
Linear combination, **117**
 derivative, 117
 of solutions of differential equation, 598
 of vectors, 775
Linear differential equation, **571**
 first-order, **575**, 579
 solution method, 577
Linear equation, 12, 624
Linearity property:
 of antidifferentiation, 276
 of limits, 117
Line-through-point method, 885
Linguistics, 553, 556 (Problems 30, 36, 37)
Lissajous curves, 644, 660 (Problem 53)
Littlewood, J. E. (1885–1977), 681
ln, *see* Natural logarithm
ln 2, 356, 360, 456, 714–715 (Problems 57, 59),
 727, 736 (Problem 61),
 769 (Problem 62), 1009
ln 3, 769 (Problem 66)
Local extremum, **144**, **222**, **879**
 finding, 880–881
 first derivative test, 224
Locus, **624**
Logarithm, **39**
 laws, 434
 natural, **436**, 455
Logarithm function, 39
 base a, **432**, **463**
 common, **432**
 derivative, 436
$\log_2 3$, 440 (Problem 72)
Logarithmic differentiation, 438
Logarithmic spiral, 642 (Problem 41), 649,
 651 (Problem 39)
Logarithms and experimental data, 458
Logistic equation, 560, 588–595, **589**
 competition situation, 592
 joint proportion situation, 592
 limited environment situation, 591
London, 842, 844 (Problem 62)
Longest chord of sphere,
 938 (Problem 32)
Longley, William Raymond
 (1880–1965), 677
Longs Peak (Colorado), 853
Lovely curve, 660 (Problem 55)
Lower bound, **A-23**
Lower limit (of integration), **302**
Loxodrome, **39**
Lunar orbit, 830 (Problem 59)

M

MacCluer, C. R., A-38
Machin, John (1680–1751), 712
Maclaurin, Colin (1698–1746), 710
Maclaurin series, **710**, **742**
Madras (India), 681
Magnitude, *see* Vector (length)
Mandelbrot, Benoit, 623
Mandelbrot set, 623
Mann, W. R., 443
Maserati, 586 (Problem 31)
Mass, 368, A-41
 of cycloidal wire, 1029 (Problem 24)
 of lamina, **968**
 of solid, **980**
 of wire, 1019, **1022**

Mass on spring, 607
    dashpot, 607
    external force, **607**
    free undamped motion, 608–610
    natural frequency, 608
Mathematical modeling, 5, 7
Maximum and minimum problems, 152–165, 884–885, etc.
    on open intervals, 226–228
    see also key words in statement of problem
Maximum and minimum value, **142**, **222**, **878**
    existence, 879, A-26
    global (absolute), **142**, **222**, **878**
    local (relative), **144**, **222**, **879**
Maximum and minimum value property, 143
Mean (arithmetic and root-square), 938 (Problem 37)
Mean value theorem, 213
    corollaries, 216–218
    geometric formulation, 213
    statement, proof, 215–216
Mécanique analytique (Lagrange, 1788), 849
Median (of triangle), **A-13** (Problem 30)
Mercury (planet), 678 (Problem 78), 827, 830 (Problem 57)
Meridian, **842**
Meridional zone, 1000 (Problem 14)
Mesa, 956
Mesklin, 362, 363
Methane, 788 (Problem 70)
Methanol, 596 (Problem 17)
Method, The (of Archimedes), 271
Method of bisection, A-26
Method of characteristic triangle, 193
Method of exhaustion, 383
Method of Lagrange multipliers, **918**
Method of substitution, 490
Metropolis, 114
Mexico, 44
Michaud's syndrome, 596 (Problem 16)
Micronote on a functional equation, 466
Midpoint, **780**, 845 (Problem 1), **A-7**
Midpoint approximation, **350**, **940**
Midpoint sum, 300
Miel, George, 713
Minivan, 203 (Problem 68)
Mirifici Logarithmorum Canonis Descriptio (John Napier, 1614), 427
Mission of Gravity, 362
Mixture problems, 580–582
Möbius strip, 1052, 1055, 1056 (Problem 40), 1074 (Problem 31)
Model rocket, 363 (Problem 38)
Moment, **416**
    additivity, 417
    of cycloidal wire, 1029 (Problem 24)
    of force, **794**
Moment of inertia, **973**
    of cone, 1010 (Problem 27)
    of cube, 986 (Problems 30, 33)
    of cylinder, 986 (Problem 28), 993 (Problem 16)
    polar, **973**
    of solid, **980**
    of solid sphere, 986 (Problem 38), 991, 993 (Problem 4)
    of wire, **1022**
Money market example, 38
Monkey, 415 (Problem 28)
Monkey saddle, 928, 930, 934 (Problem 32)
Moon orbit perimeter, 757 (Problem 62)
Mortgage, 574 (Problem 33), 620 Problem 55)
Most general antiderivative, 274

Motion of projectiles, 811–813
    central force field, 815 (Problem 62)
    constant speed, 814 (Problem 40), 815 (Problem 55)
    with Coriolis acceleration, 816 (Problem 66)
    uniform circular, 815 (Problem 61)
Motion with resistance, 583–584
Motion in a straight line, 279
    vertical, 282
Mt. McKinley (Denali National Park, Alaska), 619 (Problem 35)
Multiplicity (of factor of polynomial), **510**
Mysterium Cosmographicum (Kepler, 1596), 771

N

n-dimensional space, **865**
Napier, John (Baron of Merchiston, 1550–1617), 427
Nappe, 626
NASA 0012 airfoil, 31
National actuarial examination, 677 (Problem 76)
Natural exponential equation, **549**
Natural exponential function, **431**, **459**
    derivative, 431
    order of magnitude, 444–446
    and powers of e, 460
Natural frequency (of mass on spring), **608**
Natural growth equation, 548, **549**
Natural logarithm, 39, 74, **436**, **455**
    derivative, 436
    graph, 456
    order of magnitude, 444–446, 487 (Problem 101)
Natural population growth, 546
n-dimensional space, **865**
Nebraska, 221
Negative angle, **A-14**
Negative of vector, **774**
Neighborhood, **64**
Nested interval property, A-25
Nested radical, *see* Infinite radical
Net distance, **370**
N-event sample, **535**
New York, 842, 844 (Problem 62)
Newfoundland, 673
Newton, Sir Isaac (1642–1727), 2, 47, 101, 176, 193, 286, 308, 318, 365, 545, 624, 646, 667, 710, 744, 757 (Problem 51), 772, 825, 995, 1013, 1057, A-28
Newton (N, unit of force), A-41
Newton's first law of motion, 815 (Problem 60)
Newton's law of cooling, 272, 570, 574, 619 (Problem 32)
Newton's law of gravitation, 407, 825, 826
Newton's method, 101, 178
"Newton's Nose-Cone Problem" (Edwards, 1997), 1057
Newton's second law of motion, 583, 607, 808
    with calculators and computers, 181–182
    and computer graphics, 182–185
Newton's wine barrel, 386 (Problem 51)
Non-Euclidean geometry, 1013
Nonorientable surface, 1052
Nonterminating decimal expansion, A-1
Norm (of partition), **302**
Normal line, **59**
North pole, 353, 810, 844 (Problem 59)
Norway, 216
Nose cones, 1057
Nuclear waste disposal, 587 (Problem 40)

O

Oblique segment of paraboloid, 984
Observatory volume, 385 (Problem 39)
Octant (first), **779**
Odd function, **172**
Ohm's law, 49, A-5 (Problem 39)
Oil field problem, 10, 22, 190
Oil refinery, 127
Oil slick, 201 (Problem 39)
One-sided continuity, **93**
One-sided limit, 67, **77**
One-to-one function, **467**
One-to-one transformation, **1002**
    inverse, **1002**
Onion, 136
Open interval, **4**, **A-3**
Open interval maximum-minimum problems, 226–228
Open-topped box problem, 11, 153, 161, 190
Operator notation for derivatives, 115
Order of magnitude (of e^x and $\ln x$), 444–446, 487 (Problem 101)
Ordinate, **A-6**
Orientable surface, 1052
Orientation (of curve), **1024**
Oriented surface, **1065**
Origin, **A-6**
Osculating circle, **820**, 825
Osculating plane, **846** (Problem 24)
Osculum, 820
Oslo (Norway), 216
Ostrich, 201 (Problem 40)
Ostrogradski, Michel (1801–1861), 1057
Ozone problem, 44

P

Paint roller, 309
Paper folding problem, 174
Pappus:
    first theorem, 420, 971
    second theorem, 421, 973
Parabola, 16, 627, **661**, 677 (Problems 67, 75)
    arc length, 520 (Problem 44)
    area of segment, 345 (Problems 48–49)
    axis, **662**
    as conic section, 626
    directrix, **661**
    focus, **661**
    reflection property, **663**
    surface area of revolution, 520 (Problem 45)
    and tangent line, 58, 677 (Problem 67)
    vertex, 17, **662**
Parabolic approximation, 354
Paraboloid surface area, 402
Paraboloid volume, 385 (Problem 43), 423 (Problem 30)
    with hole, 394 (Problem 44)
Parallel lines, A-10
Parallel planes, **799**
Parallel resistors, 937 (Problem 17), 938 (Problem 34)
Parallelogram area, 791, 847 (Problem 36)
Parallelogram diagonals, 778 (Problem 53)
Parallelogram law (of vector addition), 773
Parameter, **643**
Parametric curve, **643**, **803**
    coordinate functions, **803**
    with different parametrizations, 643
    graph, **643**
    oriented, **1024**
    piecewise smooth, **1024**
    smooth, **646**
    tangent line, 646

Parametric equations, **643**, 803
Parametric polar coordinates, 656
Parametric surface, **996**
    image, **996**
    smooth, **996**
Partial derivative, **868**, 873–875
    geometric interpretation, 870
    notation, 868
    second and higher order, 874–875
Partial differential equation, 1062
"Partial sums of infinite series, and how they grow," 698
Particular solution (of differential equation), 278
Partition, **298**, **940**
    inner, **979**
    norm, **940**, **979**, **990**
    regular, **303**
    selection, **298**, **940**
    spherical, **990**
Path, **1031**
Pendulum, 49, 268 (Problem 31), 359, 644, 896 (Problems 39–40), A-5 (Problem 40)
Pennsylvania Turnpike, 216
Pentagon area, 1046 (Problem 39)
Pentagonal hole, 968 (Problem 43)
Periodicity (of trigonometric functions), 34, A-16
Perpendicular lines, A-10
Perpendicular vector test, 783
Perpendicularity of cross product, 788
Perpetual annuity, 532, 538 (Problem 54)
Perth (Australia), 804
Phenylethylamine, 574 (Problem 35)
π, 271, 295, 360, 361, 429, 489, 500–501 (Problem 68), 528, 542 (Problems 110–111), 681, 683, 696, 711, 712, 714 (Problem 54), 719, 720, 721, 749 (Problems 56, 63), 1009, A-1
    five billionth hexagesimal digit, 525 (Problem 50)
Piecewise smooth curve, **1024**
Piecewise smooth surface, **1058**
    closed, **1058**
Pinched torus, 1001 (Problem 20)
Plaine Discovery of the Whole Revelation of Saint John, The (John Napier, 1593), 427
Plane:
    normal vector, **798**
    scalar equation, **798**
    tangent to surface, **872**
    vector equation, **798**
Plane analytic geometry, 624
Planetarium, 271
Planetary motion, 458–459
Plausibility, 157
Plouffe, S., 525 (Problem 50)
Point of discontinuity, 16
Point-slope equation, **12**, **A-9**
Poiseuille, Jean-Louis-Marie (Jean Louis, 1799–1869), 372, 376
Poiseuille's law, 372
Polar coordinates, **629**
    angular coordinate, **629**
    polar axis, **629**
    pole, **629**
    radial coordinate, **629**
Polar curves as parametric curves, 648
Polar equation, 630
Polar icecap, 810
Polar partition, **961**
    norm, **961**
Polar rectangle, **961**
Polygon area, 1073 (Problem 14)

Polynomial, **27**, 90
    approximations, 703
    continuity, 94, 863
    degree n, **27**
    derivative, 118
    leading coefficient, 31
    see also Taylor polynomial
Pop-top can, 165, 231 (Problem 55)
Population growth, 549–550, 556 (Problems 22, 23, 33)
    annual growth rate, **549**
    birth rate, 587
    bounded, 588
    carrying capacity, 560, 589, **590**
    death rate, 587
    general equation, **588**
    with immigration, 571–572
    limiting population, 560, 589, **590**
    world, 549
Position function, **108**, **279**
Position vector, **772**, **780**, **804**
Positions of ships at sea, 673
Positive angle, **A-14**
Positive direction (on curve), **1037**
Post office problem, 9, 161, 887 (Problems 47–48)
Potassium nitrate, 596 (Problem 17)
Potential energy, **1035**
Potential function, **1033**, 1034
Pound (lb, unit of force), A-41
Power, **408**, 786, A-41
Power function, **24**, **27**, **458**
    general, **463**
Power line problem, 163, 165
Power rule, 116, 134
    for arbitrary (real) exponents, 463
    generalized, 129, 133, 135
    for negative integers, 121
    for positive integers, 11
Power series, **737**
    adding and multiplying, 752
    convergence, 738
    to define functions, 764–766
    differentiation, integration, 745–747
    identity principle, 759
    and indeterminate forms, 753
    interval of convergence, **738**, **741**
    in powers of $x - c$, **741**
    radius of convergence, **738**, **741**
    representation of $f(x)$, **741**
    solution of differential equations, 758–763
    for tan x, 767 (Problem 25)
Predator-prey populations, 594–595
Present value (of a future dollar), 532
Pressure, **412**
Prime number theorem, 1013
Prime numbers, 365, 683, A-29
Prince of mathematics, *see* Gauss
Principal unit normal vector, **820**, **821**
Principia Mathematica, 101, 772, 825, 995, 1057
Principle of least time, 158
Probability, 533
Product (of functions), **25**
Product law (for limits), 68
Product rule (for derivatives), 119–120, 193
    extended, 121
Profit, 368
Projectile, 62
    range, **664**, 677 (Problems 72–74), 896 (Problem 41)
    see also Trajectory
Proper rational function, **509**
p-series, **717**
Pseudoperiod, **611**

Ptolemy (Claudius Ptolemaeus, c. 100–c. 170), 771
Pudding (containing proof), 181
Pyramid:
    with inscribed sphere, 230 (Problem 47)
    volume, 378, 385 (Problem 44)
Pythagorean theorem, 847 (Problem 51), A-6, A-43
    converse, A-7

Q

Quadratic form, **931**, 932
Quadratic formula, 11, 176
Quadratic function, 16
Quadric surface, **833**
Quadrilateral, 778 (Problem 54)
Quartic polynomial, 29
Quotient (of functions), **25**
Quotient law (for limits), 68
Quotient rule (for derivatives), 119, 122

R

Racquet, 975, 977 (Problem 56)
Radial component of acceleration, **825**
Radial coordinate, **629**
Radially simple region, 963
Radian measure, 165, **A-15**
Radioactive decay, 550–552, 556 (Problems 31, 32, 35), 619 (Problem 31)
    decay constant, **550**
    half-life, **550**
Radiocarbon dating, 551–552, 556 (Problems 24, 25)
Radius of curvature, **820**
Radius of gyration, **975**
Raft (mnemonic), 840
Railroad track, 187, 829 (Problem 55), 847 (Problem 49)
Rain gutter, 888 (Problem 59)
Raindrop, 131
Ramanujan, Srinivasa (1887–1920), 681, 713
"Ramanujan and pi," 713
Random variable, **533**
    mean value, **533**
    normal, **533**
    standard deviation, **533**
Range:
    of function, **2**
    of projectile, **173**, 191, 677 (Problems 72–74), 896 (Problem 41)
Rate of change, 105, 130
    average, **106**, **110**
    instantaneous, 105, **106**, **110**
Rational function, **29**, 90
Rational number, 695, 700 (Problems 38–43), **A-1**
Rationalizing substitution, 542 (Problem 120)
Real line, Real number, A-1
Rearrangement of infinite series, 726, 737 (Problems 63–65)
Reciprocal rule, 121
Rectangle:
    inscribed in circle, 162, 174
    inscribed in ellipse, 162
    inscribed in semicircle, 171
    rotated around one side, 10
Rectangular beam, 160
Rectangular coordinate system, **A-6**
Rectangular coordinates in space, 778, **779**
    coordinate axes, **778**
    first octant, **779**
    right-handed, **778**

Rectangular hyperbola, 24
Rectilinear motion, 279
Recurrence relation, 760
Reduction formula, 499 (Problems 49–54)
    for $\cos^k \theta$, 524
    for $\sec^n x$, 497, 524
    for $\sin^m x \cos^n x$, 541 (Problem 107)
    for $\tan^n x$, 506
    for $x^k \exp(-x^2)$, 538 (Problem 61)
    for $x^m (\ln x)^n$, 500 (Problem 62), 541 (Problem 106)
Reflecting telescope, 673
Regular partition, **303**
Regular polygons, 1013
Related rates problems, 196
    steps in solution, 197
Remainder (in infinite series), **718**, **730**
    alternating series estimate, 730
    estimating, 726
    integral test estimate, 718
Repeated substitution, 186
Repeated tabulation, 7
Repeating decimal, 695, 700 (Problems 38–43), A-1
Resonance, **614**, 618 (Problem 37)
Reversing order of integration, 951–952
    key, 951
Review of conic sections, 679
Rhombus, **A-13** (Problem 28)
    diagonals, 846 (Problem 18)
Riemann, G. F. Bernhard (1826–1866), 299, 365, 939, A-28
Riemann hypothesis, 722
Riemann sum, 298, **299**, 366, **940**, **947**, **979**
    computations, 303
    generalized, A-34
Riemann surface, 365
Riemann zeta function, **722**, A-28
Right-endpoint approximation, **347**
Right-endpoint sum, 300
Right-hand derivative, 114
Right-hand limit, **77**
Rise, **A-7**
Rocket nose cone, 1057
Rocky Mountain National Park (Colorado), 853
Rod carried around corner, 228, 230 (Problem 45)
Rolle, Michel (1652–1719), 213
Rolle's theorem, 213
    proof, 214
Root of continuous function, 92
Root function, 134
Root law (for limits), 68
Root-square mean and arithmetic mean, 938 (Problem 37)
Rose (polar curve), 632
Rotating cube, 1012 (Problem 59, *not easy!*)
ROUND, **4**, 11
Ruler-and-compass constructions, 1013
Rumor, 596 (Problem 27)
Run, **A-7**
Ruritania, 596 (Problem 15)

S

Saddle point, **836**, **928**
St. John's (Newfoundland), 673
St. Petersburg (Russia), 844 (Problems 57–59)
Sales decline, 553, 556 (Problem 29)
San Francisco, 844 (Problem 56)
Sandwich theorem, 76

Satellite (communications), 828
Satellite launch, 408
Savings account, 572
Sawmill problem, 156, 163, 175, 920
Sawtooth function, **16**, 89
Scalar, **772**
Scalar acceleration, **807**
Scalar multiple:
    of function, **25**
    of vector, **774**
Scalar product, *see* Vector, Dot product
Scalar triple product, **792**, 795 (Problem 28)
    and volume of parallelepiped, 793
Scherk's minimal surface, 877 (Problem 68)
Secant line, 54, 104
sech x, 477
Second derivative, **242**
    significance of sign, 242–246
Second derivative test, 244
    for functions of two variables, 927
Second difference quotient, 448 (Problem 68)
Second-order differential equation, **598**
    with constant coefficients, 600
    general solution, **600**
    homogeneous, **598**
    linear, **598**
    solution, **598**
Selection (for partition), **298**
Semicubical parabola, 397
Separable (differential equation), **568**
Separation of variables, 545, 547–548
Sequence (convergence), **178**
    see also Infinite sequence
Series, *see* Infinite series
Service station, 414 (Problem 16)
Seventeen-sided hole, 968 (Problem 43)
sgn, 89
Shapiro, H. N., 466
Shark population, 595
Shark swimming, 937 (Problem 26)
Shift of index of summation, 760–761
Shockwave lithotripsy, 668
Side condition, *see* Constraint
Sign function, **86**
"Similarity in Irrationality Proofs for π, $\ln 2$, $\zeta(2)$, and $\zeta(3)$," 1009
Simple closed curve, **1037**
Simple harmonic motion, **609**
    frequency, **609**
    period, **609**
Simply connected region, **1068**
Simpson's approximation, **352**, 360
Sine curve arc length, 404 (Problem 36), 520 (Problem 46)
Singular solution (of differential equation), 570
sinh x, **477**
Sink, **1061**
Sioux City, 375
Skew lines, **797**, 845 (Problem 10), 927 (Problem 65), 934 (Problem 26)
Skid mark example, 281
Slide rule, 427
Slope, **12**, **A-7**
    of horizontal line, A-8
    of parallel lines, A-10
    of perpendicular lines, A-10
    of vertical line, A-8
    of tangent line, 57, 63, 102, 105
Slope field (direction field), **558**
Slope-intercept equation, **12**, **A-9**
Slope predictor, 45, 54, 56, 58, **59**, 70–72, 102, 105

Slug (unit of mass), A-41
Smith, Percey Franklyn (1867–1956), 677
Smoky alchemical experiments, 101
Smooth arc, function, **396**, **646**
Smooth curve, surface, **904**, **996**, 1020
Snell's law, **163**, 164
Snowball (melting), 114, 133
Snowplow, 575 (Problems 41–42)
Soft drink can, 165, 231 (Problem 55)
Solar panel, 850
Solid of revolution, **378**
"Solution of a Calculus Problem on Minimal Volume," 927 (Problem 64)
Solution curve (of differential equation), **548**, **558**
Solutions (of differential equation), 278
    independent, **599**
    linear combination, **598**
Source, **1061**
Spacecraft problem, 286
Special Functions (Andrews, Askey, and Roy, 1999), 724
Special substitution (for integration), 542–543 (Eqs. (1)–(5))
Spectrum, 101
Speed, **109**, **807**, 818
    of light, 163
    limiting, 584
Sphere, **780**
    bumpy, 844 (Problem 64)
    inscribed in circular cylinder, 271
    inscribed in cone, 174
    inscribed in pyramid, 230
    longest chord, 938 (Problem 32)
    surface area, 375 (Problem 46), 399, 422, 454 (Problem 47), 654, 973
    volume, 375 (Problem 46), 379, 387 (Problem 58), 420, 654, 960 (Problem 39), 967 (Problem 23), 971, 993 (Problem 3)
Sphere with hole, 385 (Problem 46), 390, 394 (Problem 43), 844 (Problem 55), 960 (Problems 52–53), 964, 968 (Problems 41–43), 994 (Problem 43)
Spherical block, **990**
Spherical coordinates, **840**
Spherical hailstone, 133
Spherical partition, **990**
    norm, **990**
Spherical raindrop, 131
Spherical segment, 187, 188, 394 (Problem 38)
Spherical snowball, 133
Spiral of Archimedes, 637 (Problem 50), 642 (Problem 39), 648, 651 (Problem 37)
    arc length, 658 (Problem 27)
    curvature, 847 (Problem 48)
Spiral ramp area, 999
Spring, David, 927 (Problem 64)
Spring constant, **407**
$\sqrt{2}$, 95, 176, 179, 691 (Problem 63), 696, A-1
$\sqrt{5}$, 769 (Problem 65)
Squeeze law, 76
Squirrels, 596 (Problem 18)
Standard Mathematical Tables and Formulas, 490
Steady periodic solution, **615**
Stirling's series, 769 (Problem 61)
Stokes, George (1819–1903), 1065
Stokes' theorem, 1065
    partial proof, 1066
Stonehenge example, 551
Stop sign, 112

INDEX   I-11

Strait of Messina, 405
Strategy for integration, 539–540
Strength of beam, 160
Strophoid, 680 (Problem 80)
Submarine example, 353, 810
Substitution law (for limits), 70
Substitution method for integration, 329
    in definite integrals, 331
    in trigonometric integrals, 330
Sum (of functions), **25**
Sum law (for limits), 67
summa, 275
Summation:
    index, **290**
    notation, 290
    rules, 290
    term, **290**
Sure-fire check, 275
Surface, **830**
    orientable, nonorientable, 1052
    oriented, **1065**
    piecewise smooth, **1058**
    of revolution, **832**
    trace, **831**
Surface area:
    of cone, 422 (Problem 25),
        976 (Problem 47)
    of conical frustum, 400,
        404 (Problem 39)
    in cylindrical coordinates, 998–999
    of ellipsoid, 454 (Problem 47),
        486 (Problem 38),
        520 (Problems 52–53),
        658 (Problem 25)
    of elliptical torus, 1001 (Problem 34)
    of meridional zone, 1000 (Problem 14)
    of paraboloid, 402, 520 (Problem 45)
    in parametric form, 654
    of pinched torus, 1001 (Problem 20)
    in rectangular coordinates, 998
    of right circular cylinder,
        423 (Problem 28)
    of rotated astroid, 658 (Problem 31)
    of rotated cardioid, 656
    of rotated cycloid, 658 (Problem 24)
    of rotated lemniscate,
        658 (Problem 32)
    of segment of conic section, 271
    of smooth parametric surface, **998**
    of sphere, 271, 375 (Problem 46), 399,
        404 (Problem 40), 422,
        425 (Problem 29),
        454 (Problem 47),
        654, 973
    of spherical zone, 405 (Problem 43),
        425 (Problem 28)
    of spiral ramp, 999
    of torus, 422, 520 (Problem 49),
        658 (Problem 28),
        973, 999
Surface integral, **1048**, **1051**
    surface area element, **1048**
Surface of revolution, **399**, **832**
    area, **401**
    area in parametric form, 654
Suspension bridge, 405 (Problems 45–46)
Sweet spot, 975, 977 (Problem 56)
Symmetric difference quotient,
    448 (Problem 67)
Symmetry principle, 417, 969
Symmetry properties, 625
    in polar coordinates, 632
Syracuse ("near the marsh";
    Trinacria, later Sicily), 271

T

Tablecloth problem, 51
Tangent line, 45, 54, 57, 102, 124 (Problems 54–60, 66–71), 192 (Problems 118, 120), 805
    existence, 79
    slope, 63, 105
    vertical, **137**
Tangent-line approximation, *see* Midpoint approximation
Tangent plane, **872**, **913**
    normal vector, 873
Tangent vector, **805**
tanh x, **477**
    Taylor series, 769 (Problem 58)
Tartaglia (Niccolò Fontana of Brescia,
    c. 1500–1557), 176
Taxicab problem, 23
Taylor, A. E., 443
Taylor, Brooke (1685–1731), 707
Taylor polynomial, **705**
    with remainder, **707**
Taylor series, **708**
    arcsin x, 747
    arcsinh x, 769 (Problem 59)
    arctan x, 712, 746
    cos x, 710, 737
    cosh x, 714 (Problems 43–44), 742
    e^x, 709, 737
    representation of $f(x)$, **741**
    sin x, 710, 737
    sinh x, 714 (Problems 43–44), 743
    tanh x, 769 (Problem 58)
Taylor's formula, **707**, A-38
Tennis racquet, 975, 977 (Problem 56)
Tent design, 164, 231 (Problem 49)
Term (in summation), **290**
Terminating decimal expansion, A-1
Tetrahedron, 788 (Problem 69),
    847 (Problem 51)
Théorie des fonctions analytiques (Lagrange, 1797), 849
Theory and Application of Infinite Series
    (K. Knopp, 1971), 752
Thermal diffusivity, 1062
Thermal expansivity, **906**, (Problems 56–57)
Thomson, William (Lord Kelvin,
    1824–1907), 1065
Three-leaved rose, 637 (Problems 48–49),
    659 (Problems 43–44)
Threshold population, **593**
Tides (oceanic), 172
Time lag of economic prosperity, 595
Time-varying amplitude, 611
Top volume, 500 (Problem 65)
Toronto (Canada), 786
Torque, **814** (Problem 42)
Torricelli's law of draining, 203 (Problem 66),
    272, 387, 546, 553–555,
    557 (Problems 39–47)
Torsion, **846** (Problems 30–32)
Torus, 844 (Problem 63)
    elliptical, 1001 (Problem 34)
    moment of inertia, 1011 (Problem 35)
    pinched, 1001 (Problem 20)
    surface area, 422, 520 (Problem 49),
        658 (Problem 28), 973, 999
    volume, 386 (Problem 49), 394 (Problem 39), 420, 972, 1007,
        1011 (Problem 34)
Total distance, **370**
Toughest integral in the book, 977
    (Problem 56)
Tour de force, 1057

Trajectory (of projectile), 62, 664, 811,
    814 (Problems 43–49),
    846 (Problem 20)
    range, **664**, 677 (Problems 72–74), **814**
Transcendental equation, 40
Transformation (of coordinate plane),
    902, **1002**
    derivative matrix, **902**
    image, **902**, **1002**
    inverse, **1002**
    one-to-one, **1002**
Transient solution, **614**
Translates of graphs, 13
Translation principle, 14, 18, 625
Transverse component of acceleration, **825**
Trapezoid:
    inscribed in circle, 162
    inscribed in semicircle, 174
    of maximal area, 190
Trapezoidal approximation, **348**
Trefoil knot, 803
Triangle:
    area, 791, 845 (Problem 5)
    inscribed in circle, 925 (Problem 37),
        938 (Problem 33)
Triangle inequality, 787 (Problem 59), A-2,
    A-5 (Problems 45–46)
Triangle law (of vector addition), 773
"Trick integrals," 958 (Problems 1–5)
Trigonometric formulas, A-43
Trigonometric functions, 34, 167, **A-13**
    (triangular), **A-14** (circular)
    derivatives, 166–168
Triple integral, **979**
    in cylindrical coordinates, 988
    in spherical coordinates, 991
Trochoid, **652**, 680 (Problem 63)
Tumor, 621 (Problems 62–63)
Tycho, *see* Brahe

U

u-curve, **1002**
Unbounded interval, **4**
Underwater cable, 163
Unicycle model of car, 617 (Problem 30)
Uniform continuity, **A-31**
Union (of sets), **A-4**
Unit binormal vector, **846** (Problem 30)
Unit tangent vector, **818**, **821**
Unit vector, **775**, **781**
U.S. population, 108, 571, 591,
    597 (Problem 29)
U.S. Senate, 668
Upper bound, **690**, **A-23**
Upper limit (of integral), **302**
Uranium isotopes, 551

V

Vacuum pump, 700 (Problem 67)
Value (of function), **2**
    maximum and minimum, **142**
van der Waals' equation, 255 (Problem 89),
    877 (Problem 67), 937 (Problem 18)
Variable, **3**
v-curve, **1002**
Vector, vector quantity, **772**
    acceleration, **807**
    angle between, **783**
    bisecting angle, 787 (Problem 64)
    component of **a** along **b**, **785**
    components, **772**
    cross product, *see* Cross product
    difference, **774**

Vector, vector quantity (*Cont.*)
    direction angles, **784**
    direction cosines, **784**
    dot product, **782**
    equality, **773**, **781**
    length, **772**, **780**
    negative of, **774**
    opposite direction, **774**
    parallel, **783**, **787**, 791
    parallelogram law of addition, 773, 781
    perpendicular, **783**
    position, **780**
    resolution into components, 776
    same direction, **774**
    scalar multiple, **774**, **781**
    scalar triple product, **792**
    in space, 780–785
    sum, **773**, **781**
    torque, **794**
    triangle law of addition, 773
    unit, **774**, **781**
    velocity, **807**
    zero, **773**
Vector algebra, 773–775, 777 (Problems 39–42), 781, 792
Vector differential operator, 1016
Vector field, **1014**
    component function, 1014
    conservative, **1033**
    curl, **1017**
    divergence, **1016**
    flux, **1043**, **1052**
    irrotational, **1068**
    and potential function, **1033**
Vector form of Green's theorem, 1044
Vector product, *see* Cross product
Vector triple product, **796** (Problem 32)
Vector-valued function, **804**
    continuity, **805**
    derivative, **805**
    limit, **804**
Velocity, 108–109, **279**
    average, 108, **109**
    escape, 532
    instantaneous, **109**
    limiting, 560
Velocity potential, **1070**
Velocity vector, 772, **807**
    apparent, 778
    true, 778
Velocity vector field, **1014**
Verhulst, Pierre-François (1804–1849), 48, 590
Verne, Jules (1828–1905), 532
Vertical line test, 15
Vertical motion, 109–110, 282
Vertical tangent line, **137**
Vertically simple region, **949**
Villabuena, 165
Voltaire, François-Marie Jean Arouet (1694–1778), 101
Volterra, Vito (1860–1940), 595
Volume, 368, **378**, **380**, 940, **954**, **980**
    between two surfaces, 957–958

of birdbath, 395 (Problem 47), 416 (Problem 40)
within bumpy sphere, 995 (Problem 45)
of cone, 271, 380, 422 (Problem 24), 976 (Problem 46)
of conical frustum, 424 (Problem 14)
of cylinder, 377
of ellipsoid, 271, 385 (Problem 36), 394 (Problem 37), 426 (Problem 47), 960 (Problem 40), 1008 (Problem 14)
of elliptical cone, 424 (Problem 15)
formulas, A-43
of "ice-cream cone," 967 (Problem 29), 992, 1010 (Problems 25–26)
of intersecting cylinders, 386 (Problem 47)
of intersecting spheres, 387 (Problems 56–57)
by iterated integration, 955–957
of oblique segment of paraboloid, 984
of observatory, 385 (Problem 39)
of paraboloid, 271, 385 (Problem 43), 423 (Problem 30)
of paraboloid with hole, 394 (Problem 44)
in parametric form, 654
of pyramid, 378, 385 (Problem 44), 793
of region within sphere and cylinder, 993 (Problem 10)
of segment of ellipsoid, 424 (Problem 16)
of segment of hyperboloid, 425 (Problem 17)
within rotated cycloid, 659 (Problem 39)
swept out by rotating cube, 1012 (Problem 59)
of solid of revolution, 378, **379**
of solid of revolution, parametric form, 654
of sphere, 271, 375, 379, 387 (Problem 58), 420, 426 (Problem 50), 654, 960 (Problem 39), 971, 993 (Problem 3)
of sphere with hole, 385 (Problem 46), 390, 394 (Problem 43)
of spherical segment, 386 (Problem 48), 394 (Problem 38), 967 (Problem 33)
of tetrahedron, 960 (Problem 35)
within three cylinders, 994 (Problem 44)
of top, 500 (Problem 65)
of torus, 386 (Problem 49), 394 (Problem 39), 420, 967 (Problem 35), 972, 1007, 1011 (Problem 34)
within two cylinders, 960 (Problem 37)
of unbounded region, 385 (Problem 38)
of wedge (of Archimedes), 193, 383, 957, 967 (Problem 26)

W

Wallis, John (1616–1703), 500–501 (Problem 68)

Washer, **381**
Washington Monument, 285
Water clock, *see* Clepsydra
Water trough problem, 158–159, 174
Water volume formula, 119, 124, 125, 161
Watson, James D., 804
Watt (W, unit of power), A-41
Wave equation (one-dimensional), 877 (Problems 57, 59)
Weber, Wilhelm (1804–1891), A-28
Wedge (of Archimedes), 383
Weierstrass, Karl (1815–1897), 83
Weight, **407**
Wesleyville (Newfoundland), 673
"Wheels on Wheels on Wheels—Surprising Symmetry," 660 (Problem 55)
Whispering Gallery, 48, 668
Wiggles, 255 (Problem 91)
Wiles, Andrew, 623
Wind from the Sun, The, 286
Wine barrel volume, 386 (Problem 51)
Wire wrapped around earth, 211 (Problem 48)
Work, 368, 405, **406**, 785, **1026**, A-41
    to compress gas, 415 (Problem 22)
    to empty tank, 410–411
    to fill tank, 408–410
    by steam engine, 415 (Problem 23)

X

x-axis, **A-6**
x-coordinate, **A-6**
x-curve, 870
x-simple region, **982**

Y

y-axis, **A-6**
y-coordinate, **A-6**
y-curve, 871
y-intercept, **12**, **A-9**
y-simple region, **982**

Z

Zembla, 574 (Problem 31)
Zeno of Elea (490?–430 B.C.), 682
Zero, 737 (Problem 65)
Zero of function, **27**
Zero vector, **773**
$\zeta(2)$, 719, 722, 747, 750 (Problem 68), 1009 (Problems 28–29)
$\zeta(3)$, 722, 1009
$\zeta(4)$, 722
$\zeta(6)$, 722
$\zeta(8)$, 722
$\zeta(n)$, 722
Zorg, 362
z-simple, **980**

TABLE OF INTEGRALS

ELEMENTARY FORMS

1. $\int u\, dv = uv - \int v\, du$

2. $\int u^n\, du = \dfrac{1}{n+1} u^{n+1} + C \quad \text{if } n \neq -1$

3. $\int \dfrac{du}{u} = \ln|u| + C$

4. $\int e^u\, du = e^u + C$

5. $\int a^u\, du = \dfrac{a^u}{\ln a} + C$

6. $\int \sin u\, du = -\cos u + C$

7. $\int \cos u\, du = \sin u + C$

8. $\int \sec^2 u\, du = \tan u + C$

9. $\int \csc^2 u\, du = -\cot u + C$

10. $\int \sec u \tan u\, du = \sec u + C$

11. $\int \csc u \cot u\, du = -\csc u + C$

12. $\int \tan u\, du = \ln|\sec u| + C$

13. $\int \cot u\, du = -\ln|\csc u| + C$

14. $\int \sec u\, du = \ln|\sec u + \tan u| + C$

15. $\int \csc u\, du = -\ln|\csc u + \cot u| + C$

16. $\int \dfrac{du}{\sqrt{a^2 - u^2}} = \sin^{-1} \dfrac{u}{a} + C$

17. $\int \dfrac{du}{a^2 + u^2} = \dfrac{1}{a} \tan^{-1} \dfrac{u}{a} + C$

18. $\int \dfrac{du}{a^2 - u^2} = \dfrac{1}{2a} \ln\left|\dfrac{u+a}{u-a}\right| + C$

19. $\int \dfrac{du}{u\sqrt{u^2 - a^2}} = \dfrac{1}{a} \sec^{-1} \left|\dfrac{u}{a}\right| + C$

TRIGONOMETRIC FORMS

20. $\int \sin^2 u\, du = \dfrac{1}{2} u - \dfrac{1}{4} \sin 2u + C$

21. $\int \cos^2 u\, du = \dfrac{1}{2} u + \dfrac{1}{4} \sin 2u + C$

22. $\int \tan^2 u\, du = \tan u - u + C$

23. $\int \cot^2 u\, du = -\cot u - u + C$

24. $\int \sin^3 u\, du = -\dfrac{1}{3}(2 + \sin^2 u)\cos u + C$

25. $\int \cos^3 u\, du = \dfrac{1}{3}(2 + \cos^2 u)\sin u + C$

26. $\int \tan^3 u\, du = \dfrac{1}{2} \tan^2 u + \ln|\cos u| + C$

27. $\int \cot^3 u\, du = -\dfrac{1}{2} \cot^2 u - \ln|\sin u| + C$

28. $\int \sec^3 u\, du = \dfrac{1}{2} \sec u \tan u + \dfrac{1}{2} \ln|\sec u + \tan u| + C$

29. $\int \csc^3 u\, du = -\dfrac{1}{2} \csc u \cot u + \dfrac{1}{2} \ln|\csc u - \cot u| + C$

30. $\int \sin au \sin bu\, du = \dfrac{\sin(a-b)u}{2(a-b)} - \dfrac{\sin(a+b)u}{2(a+b)} + C \quad \text{if } a^2 \neq b^2$

31. $\int \cos au \cos bu\, du = \dfrac{\sin(a-b)u}{2(a-b)} + \dfrac{\sin(a+b)u}{2(a+b)} + C \quad \text{if } a^2 \neq b^2$

32. $\int \sin au \cos bu\, du = -\dfrac{\cos(a-b)u}{2(a-b)} - \dfrac{\cos(a+b)u}{2(a+b)} + C \quad \text{if } a^2 \neq b^2$

33. $\int \sin^n u\, du = -\dfrac{1}{n} \sin^{n-1} u \cos u + \dfrac{n-1}{n} \int \sin^{n-2} u\, du$

34. $\int \cos^n u\, du = \dfrac{1}{n} \cos^{n-1} u \sin u + \dfrac{n-1}{n} \int \cos^{n-2} u\, du$

35. $\int \tan^n u\, du = \dfrac{1}{n-1} \tan^{n-1} u - \int \tan^{n-2} u\, du \quad \text{if } n \neq 1$

36. $\int \cot^n u\, du = -\dfrac{1}{n-1} \cot^{n-1} u - \int \cot^{n-2} u\, du \quad \text{if } n \neq 1$

37. $\int \sec^n u\, du = \dfrac{1}{n-1} \sec^{n-2} u \tan u + \dfrac{n-2}{n-1} \int \sec^{n-2} u\, du \quad \text{if } n \neq 1$

38. $\int \csc^n u\, du = -\dfrac{1}{n-1} \csc^{n-2} u \cot u + \dfrac{n-2}{n-1} \int \csc^{n-2} u\, du \quad \text{if } n \neq 1$

39a. $\int \sin^n u \cos^m u\, du = -\dfrac{\sin^{n-1} u \cos^{m+1} u}{n+m} + \dfrac{n-1}{n+m} \int \sin^{n-2} u \cos^m u\, du \quad \text{if } n \neq -m$

39b. $\int \sin^n u \cos^m u\, du = -\dfrac{\sin^{n+1} u \cos^{m-1} u}{n+m} + \dfrac{m-1}{n+m} \int \sin^n u \cos^{m-2} u\, du \quad \text{if } m \neq -n$

40. $\int u \sin u\, du = \sin u - u \cos u + C$

41. $\int u \cos u\, du = \cos u + u \sin u + C$

42. $\int u^n \sin u\, du = -u^n \cos u + n \int u^{n-1} \cos u\, du$

43. $\int u^n \cos u\, du = u^n \sin u - n \int u^{n-1} \sin u\, du$

TA-1

(Table of Integrals continues from previous page)

FORMS INVOLVING $\sqrt{u^2 \pm a^2}$

44. $\int \sqrt{u^2 \pm a^2}\, du = \dfrac{u}{2}\sqrt{u^2 \pm a^2} \pm \dfrac{a^2}{2}\ln\left|u + \sqrt{u^2 \pm a^2}\right| + C$

45. $\int \dfrac{du}{\sqrt{u^2 \pm a^2}} = \ln\left|u + \sqrt{u^2 \pm a^2}\right| + C$

46. $\int \dfrac{\sqrt{u^2 + a^2}}{u}\, du = \sqrt{u^2 + a^2} - a\ln\left(\dfrac{a + \sqrt{u^2 + a^2}}{u}\right) + C$

47. $\int \dfrac{\sqrt{u^2 - a^2}}{u}\, du = \sqrt{u^2 - a^2} - a\sec^{-1}\dfrac{u}{a} + C$

48. $\int u^2\sqrt{u^2 \pm a^2}\, du = \dfrac{u}{8}(2u^2 \pm a^2)\sqrt{u^2 \pm a^2} - \dfrac{a^4}{8}\ln\left|u + \sqrt{u^2 \pm a^2}\right| + C$

49. $\int \dfrac{u^2\, du}{\sqrt{u^2 \pm a^2}} = \dfrac{u}{2}\sqrt{u^2 \pm a^2} \mp \dfrac{a^2}{2}\ln\left|u + \sqrt{u^2 \pm a^2}\right| + C$

50. $\int \dfrac{du}{u^2\sqrt{u^2 \pm a^2}} = \mp \dfrac{\sqrt{u^2 \pm a^2}}{a^2 u} + C$

51. $\int \dfrac{\sqrt{u^2 \pm a^2}}{u^2}\, du = -\dfrac{\sqrt{u^2 \pm a^2}}{u} + \ln\left|u + \sqrt{u^2 \pm a^2}\right| + C$

52. $\int \dfrac{du}{(u^2 \pm a^2)^{3/2}} = \pm \dfrac{u}{a^2\sqrt{u^2 \pm a^2}} + C$

53. $\int (u^2 \pm a^2)^{3/2}\, du = \dfrac{u}{8}(2u^2 \pm 5a^2)\sqrt{u^2 \pm a^2} + \dfrac{3a^4}{8}\ln\left|u + \sqrt{u^2 \pm a^2}\right| + C$

FORMS INVOLVING $\sqrt{a^2 - u^2}$

54. $\int \sqrt{a^2 - u^2}\, du = \dfrac{u}{2}\sqrt{a^2 - u^2} + \dfrac{a^2}{2}\sin^{-1}\dfrac{u}{a} + C$

55. $\int \dfrac{\sqrt{a^2 - u^2}}{u}\, du = \sqrt{a^2 - u^2} - a\ln\left|\dfrac{a + \sqrt{a^2 - u^2}}{u}\right| + C$

56. $\int \dfrac{u^2\, du}{\sqrt{a^2 - u^2}} = -\dfrac{u}{2}\sqrt{a^2 - u^2} + \dfrac{a^2}{2}\sin^{-1}\dfrac{u}{a} + C$

57. $\int u^2\sqrt{a^2 - u^2}\, du = \dfrac{u}{8}(2u^2 - a^2)\sqrt{a^2 - u^2} + \dfrac{a^4}{8}\sin^{-1}\dfrac{u}{a} + C$

58. $\int \dfrac{du}{u^2\sqrt{a^2 - u^2}} = -\dfrac{\sqrt{a^2 - u^2}}{a^2 u} + C$

59. $\int \dfrac{\sqrt{a^2 - u^2}}{u^2}\, du = -\dfrac{\sqrt{a^2 - u^2}}{u} - \sin^{-1}\dfrac{u}{a} + C$

60. $\int \dfrac{du}{u\sqrt{a^2 - u^2}} = -\dfrac{1}{a}\ln\left|\dfrac{a + \sqrt{a^2 - u^2}}{u}\right| + C$

61. $\int \dfrac{du}{(a^2 - u^2)^{3/2}} = \dfrac{u}{a^2\sqrt{a^2 - u^2}} + C$

62. $\int (a^2 - u^2)^{3/2}\, du = \dfrac{u}{8}(5a^2 - 2u^2)\sqrt{a^2 - u^2} + \dfrac{3a^4}{8}\sin^{-1}\dfrac{u}{a} + C$

EXPONENTIAL AND LOGARITHMIC FORMS

63. $\int ue^u\, du = (u - 1)e^u + C$

64. $\int u^n e^u\, du = u^n e^u - n\int u^{n-1} e^u\, du$

65. $\int \ln u\, du = u\ln u - u + C$

66. $\int u^n \ln u\, du = \dfrac{u^{n+1}}{n+1}\ln u - \dfrac{u^{n+1}}{(n+1)^2} + C$

67. $\int e^{au}\sin bu\, du = \dfrac{e^{au}}{a^2 + b^2}(a\sin bu - b\cos bu) + C$

68. $\int e^{au}\cos bu\, du = \dfrac{e^{au}}{a^2 + b^2}(a\cos bu + b\sin bu) + C$

INVERSE TRIGONOMETRIC FORMS

69. $\int \sin^{-1} u\, du = u\sin^{-1} u + \sqrt{1 - u^2} + C$

70. $\int \tan^{-1} u\, du = u\tan^{-1} u - \dfrac{1}{2}\ln(1 + u^2) + C$

71. $\int \sec^{-1} u\, du = u\sec^{-1} u - \ln\left|u + \sqrt{u^2 - 1}\right| + C$

72. $\int u\sin^{-1} u\, du = \dfrac{1}{4}(2u^2 - 1)\sin^{-1} u + \dfrac{u}{4}\sqrt{1 - u^2} + C$

73. $\int u\tan^{-1} u\, du = \dfrac{1}{2}(u^2 + 1)\tan^{-1} u - \dfrac{u}{2} + C$

74. $\int u\sec^{-1} u\, du = \dfrac{u^2}{2}\sec^{-1} u - \dfrac{1}{2}\sqrt{u^2 - 1} + C$

75. $\int u^n \sin^{-1} u\, du = \dfrac{u^{n+1}}{n+1}\sin^{-1} u - \dfrac{1}{n+1}\int \dfrac{u^{n+1}}{\sqrt{1 - u^2}}\, du$ if $n \neq -1$

76. $\int u^n \tan^{-1} u\, du = \dfrac{u^{n+1}}{n+1}\tan^{-1} u - \dfrac{1}{n+1}\int \dfrac{u^{n+1}}{1 + u^2}\, du$ if $n \neq -1$

77. $\int u^n \sec^{-1} u\, du = \dfrac{u^{n+1}}{n+1}\sec^{-1} u - \dfrac{1}{n+1}\int \dfrac{u^n}{\sqrt{u^2 - 1}}\, du$ if $n \neq -1$

(Table of Integrals continues from previous page)

HYPERBOLIC FORMS

78. $\int \sinh u \, du = \cosh u + C$

79. $\int \cosh u \, du = \sinh u + C$

80. $\int \tanh u \, du = \ln (\cosh u) + C$

81. $\int \coth u \, du = \ln |\sinh u| + C$

82. $\int \text{sech } u \, du = \tan^{-1} |\sinh u| + C$

83. $\int \text{csch } u \, du = \ln \left| \tanh \frac{u}{2} \right| + C$

84. $\int \sinh^2 u \, du = \frac{1}{4} \sinh 2u - \frac{u}{2} + C$

85. $\int \cosh^2 u \, du = \frac{1}{4} \sinh 2u + \frac{u}{2} + C$

86. $\int \tanh^2 u \, du = u - \tanh u + C$

87. $\int \coth^2 u \, du = u - \coth u + C$

88. $\int \text{sech}^2 u \, du = \tanh u + C$

89. $\int \text{csch}^2 u \, du = -\coth u + C$

90. $\int \text{sech } u \tanh u \, du = -\text{sech } u + C$

91. $\int \text{csch } u \coth u \, du = -\text{csch } u + C$

MISCELLANEOUS ALGEBRAIC FORMS

92. $\int u(au + b)^{-1} \, du = \frac{u}{a} - \frac{b}{a^2} \ln |au + b| + C$

93. $\int u(au + b)^{-2} \, du = \frac{1}{a^2} \left(\ln |au + b| + \frac{b}{au + b} \right) + C$

94. $\int u(au + b)^n \, du = \frac{(au + b)^{n+1}}{a^2} \left(\frac{au + b}{n + 2} - \frac{b}{n + 1} \right) + C$ if $n \neq -1, -2$

95. $\int \frac{du}{(a^2 \pm u^2)^n} = \frac{1}{2a^2(n - 1)} \left(\frac{u}{(a^2 \pm u^2)^{n-1}} + (2n - 3) \int \frac{du}{(a^2 \pm u^2)^{n-1}} \right)$ if $n \neq 1$

96. $\int u \sqrt{au + b} \, du = \frac{2}{15a^2} (3au - 2b)(au + b)^{3/2} + C$

97. $\int u^n \sqrt{au + b} \, du = \frac{2}{a(2n + 3)} \left(u^n (au + b)^{3/2} - nb \int u^{n-1} \sqrt{au + b} \, du \right)$

98. $\int \frac{u \, du}{\sqrt{au + b}} = \frac{2}{3a^2} (au - 2b) \sqrt{au + b} + C$

99. $\int \frac{u^n \, du}{\sqrt{au + b}} = \frac{2}{a(2n + 1)} \left(u^n \sqrt{au + b} - nb \int \frac{u^{n-1} \, du}{\sqrt{au + b}} \right)$

100a. $\int \frac{du}{u \sqrt{au + b}} = \frac{1}{\sqrt{b}} \ln \left| \frac{\sqrt{au + b} - \sqrt{b}}{\sqrt{au + b} + \sqrt{b}} \right| + C$ if $b > 0$

100b. $\int \frac{du}{u \sqrt{au + b}} = \frac{2}{\sqrt{-b}} \tan^{-1} \sqrt{\frac{au + b}{-b}} + C$ if $b < 0$

101. $\int \frac{du}{u^n \sqrt{au + b}} = -\frac{\sqrt{au + b}}{b(n - 1)u^{n-1}} - \frac{(2n - 3)a}{(2n - 2)b} \int \frac{du}{u^{n-1} \sqrt{au + b}}$ if $n \neq 1$

102. $\int \sqrt{2au - u^2} \, du = \frac{u - a}{2} \sqrt{2au - u^2} + \frac{a^2}{2} \sin^{-1} \frac{u - a}{a} + C$

103. $\int \frac{du}{\sqrt{2au - u^2}} = \sin^{-1} \frac{u - a}{a} + C$

104. $\int u^n \sqrt{2au - u^2} \, du = -\frac{u^{n-1}(2au - u^2)^{3/2}}{n + 2} + \frac{(2n + 1)a}{n + 2} \int u^{n-1} \sqrt{2au - u^2} \, du$

105. $\int \frac{u^n \, du}{\sqrt{2au - u^2}} = -\frac{u^{n-1}}{n} \sqrt{2au - u^2} + \frac{(2n - 1)a}{n} \int \frac{u^{n-1} \, du}{\sqrt{2au - u^2}}$

106. $\int \frac{\sqrt{2au - u^2}}{u} \, du = \sqrt{2au - u^2} + a \sin^{-1} \frac{u - a}{a} + C$

107. $\int \frac{\sqrt{2au - u^2}}{u^n} \, du = \frac{(2au - u^2)^{3/2}}{(3 - 2n)au^n} + \frac{n - 3}{(2n - 3)a} \int \frac{\sqrt{2au - u^2}}{u^{n-1}} \, du$

108. $\int \frac{du}{u^n \sqrt{2au - u^2}} = \frac{\sqrt{2au - u^2}}{a(1 - 2n)u^n} + \frac{n - 1}{(2n - 1)a} \int \frac{du}{u^{n-1} \sqrt{2au - u^2}}$

109. $\int \left(\sqrt{2au - u^2} \right)^n \, du = \frac{u - a}{n + 1} (2au - u^2)^{n/2} + \frac{na^2}{n + 1} \int \left(\sqrt{2au - u^2} \right)^{n-2} du$

110. $\int \frac{du}{\left(\sqrt{2au - u^2} \right)^n} = \frac{u - a}{(n - 2)a^2} \left(\sqrt{2au - u^2} \right)^{2-n} + \frac{n - 3}{(n - 2)a^2} \int \frac{du}{\left(\sqrt{2au - u^2} \right)^{n-2}}$

DEFINITE INTEGRALS

111. $\int_0^\infty u^n e^{-u} \, du = \Gamma(n + 1) = n!$ $(n \geq 0)$

112. $\int_0^\infty e^{-au^2} \, du = \frac{1}{2} \sqrt{\frac{\pi}{a}}$ $(a > 0)$

113. $\int_0^{\pi/2} \sin^n u \, du = \int_0^{\pi/2} \cos^n u \, du = \begin{cases} \dfrac{1 \cdot 3 \cdot 5 \cdot \cdots \cdot (n - 1)}{2 \cdot 4 \cdot 6 \cdot \cdots \cdot n} \dfrac{\pi}{2} & \text{if } n \text{ is an even integer and } n \geq 2 \\ \dfrac{2 \cdot 4 \cdot 6 \cdot \cdots \cdot (n - 1)}{3 \cdot 5 \cdot 7 \cdot \cdots \cdot n} & \text{if } n \text{ is an odd integer and } n \geq 3 \end{cases}$

LICENSE AGREEMENT

YOU SHOULD CAREFULLY READ THE FOLLOWING TERMS AND CONDITIONS BEFORE BREAKING THE SEAL ON THE PACKAGE. AMONG OTHER THINGS, THIS AGREEMENT LICENSES THE ENCLOSED SOFTWARE TO YOU AND CONTAINS WARRANTY AND LIABILITY DISCLAIMERS. BY BREAKING THE SEAL ON THE PACKAGE, YOU ARE ACCEPTING AND AGREEING TO THE TERMS AND CONDITIONS OF THIS AGREEMENT. IF YOU DO NOT AGREE TO THE TERMS OF THIS AGREEMENT, DO NOT BREAK THE SEAL. YOU SHOULD PROMPTLY RETURN THE PACKAGE UNOPENED.

LICENSE.

Subject to the provisions contained herein, Prentice-Hall, Inc. ("PH") hereby grants to you a non-exclusive, non-transferable license to use the object code version of the computer software product ("Software") contained in the package on a single computer of the type identified on the package.

SOFTWARE AND DOCUMENTATION.

PH shall furnish the Software to you on media in machine-readable object code form and may also provide the standard documentation ("Documentation") containing instructions for operation and use of the Software.

LICENSE TERM AND CHARGES.

The term of this license commences upon delivery of the Software to you and is perpetual unless earlier terminated upon default or as otherwise set forth herein.

TITLE.

Title, and ownership right, and intellectual property rights in and to the Software and Documentation shall remain in PH and/or in suppliers to PH of programs contained in the Software. The Software is provided for your own internal use under this license. This license does not include the right to sublicense and is personal to you and therefore may not be assigned (by operation of law or otherwise) or transferred without the prior written consent of PH. You acknowledge that the Software in source code form remains a confidential trade secret of PH and/or its suppliers and therefore you agree not to attempt to decipher or decompile, modify, disassemble, reverse engineer or prepare derivative works of the Software or develop source code for the Software or knowingly allow others to do so. Further, you may not copy the Documentation or other written materials accompanying the Software.

UPDATES.

This license does not grant you any right, license, or interest in and to any improvements, modifications, enhancements, or updates to the Software and Documentation. Updates, if available, may be obtained by you at PH's then current standard pricing, terms, and conditions.

LIMITED WARRANTY AND DISCLAIMER.

PH warrants that the media containing the Software, if provided by PH, is free from defects in material and workmanship under normal use for a period of sixty (60) days from the date you purchased a license to it.

THIS IS A LIMITED WARRANTY AND IT IS THE ONLY WARRANTY MADE BY PH. THE SOFTWARE IS PROVIDED 'AS IS' AND PH SPECIFICALLY DISCLAIMS ALL WARRANTIES OF ANY KIND, EITHER EXPRESS OR IMPLIED, INCLUDING, BUT NOT LIMITED TO, THE IMPLIED WARRANTY OF MERCHANTABILITY AND FITNESS FOR A PARTICULAR PURPOSE. FURTHER, COMPANY DOES NOT WARRANT, GUARANTY OR MAKE ANY REPRESENTATIONS REGARDING THE USE, OR THE RESULTS OF THE USE, OF THE SOFTWARE IN TERMS OF CORRECTNESS, ACCURACY, RELIABILITY, CURRENTNESS, OR OTHERWISE AND DOES NOT WARRANT THAT THE OPERATION OF ANY SOFTWARE WILL BE UNINTERRUPTED OR ERROR FREE. COMPANY EXPRESSLY DISCLAIMS ANY WARRANTIES NOT STATED HEREIN. NO ORAL OR WRITTEN INFORMATION OR ADVICE GIVEN BY PH, OR ANY PH DEALER, AGENT, EMPLOYEE OR OTHERS SHALL CREATE, MODIFY OR EXTEND A WARRANTY OR IN ANY WAY INCREASE THE SCOPE OF THE FOREGOING WARRANTY, AND NEITHER SUBLICENSEE OR PURCHASER MAY RELY ON ANY SUCH INFORMATION OR ADVICE. If the media is subjected to accident, abuse, or improper use; or if you violate the terms of this Agreement, then this warranty shall immediately be terminated. This warranty shall not apply if the Software is used on or in conjunction with hardware or programs other than the unmodified version of hardware and programs with which the Software was designed to be used as described in the Documentation.

LIMITATION OF LIABILITY.

Your sole and exclusive remedies for any damage or loss in any way connected with the Software are set forth below. UNDER NO CIRCUMSTANCES AND UNDER NO LEGAL THEORY, TORT, CONTRACT, OR OTHERWISE, SHALL PH BE LIABLE TO YOU OR ANY OTHER PERSON FOR ANY INDIRECT, SPECIAL, INCIDENTAL, OR CONSEQUENTIAL DAMAGES OF ANY CHARACTER INCLUDING, WITHOUT LIMITATION, DAMAGES FOR LOSS OF GOODWILL, LOSS OF PROFIT, WORK STOPPAGE, COMPUTER FAILURE OR MALFUNCTION, OR ANY AND ALL OTHER COMMERCIAL DAMAGES OR LOSSES, OR FOR ANY OTHER DAMAGES EVEN IF PH SHALL HAVE BEEN INFORMED OF THE POSSIBILITY OF SUCH DAMAGES, OR FOR ANY CLAIM BY ANY OTHER PARTY. PH'S THIRD PARTY PROGRAM SUPPLIERS MAKE NO WARRANTY, AND HAVE NO LIABILITY WHATSOEVER, TO YOU. PH's sole and exclusive obligation and liability and your exclusive remedy shall be: upon PH's election, (i) the replacement of your defective media; or (ii) the repair or correction of your defective media if PH is able, so that it will conform to the above warranty; or (iii) if PH is unable to replace or repair, you may terminate this license by returning the Software. Only if you inform PH of your problem during the applicable warranty period will PH be obligated to honor this warranty. You may contact PH to inform PH of the problem as follows:

SOME STATES OR JURISDICTIONS DO NOT ALLOW THE EXCLUSION OF IMPLIED WARRANTIES OR LIMITATION OR EXCLUSION OF CONSEQUENTIAL DAMAGES, SO THE ABOVE LIMITATIONS OR EXCLUSIONS MAY NOT APPLY TO YOU. THIS WARRANTY GIVES YOU SPECIFIC LEGAL RIGHTS AND YOU MAY ALSO HAVE OTHER RIGHTS WHICH VARY BY STATE OR JURISDICTION.

MISCELLANEOUS.

If any provision of this Agreement is held to be ineffective, unenforceable, or illegal under certain circumstances for any reason, such decision shall not affect the validity or enforceability (i) of such provision under other circumstances or (ii) of the remaining provisions hereof under all circumstances and such provision shall be reformed to and only to the extent necessary to make it effective, enforceable, and legal under such circumstances. All headings are solely for convenience and shall not be considered in interpreting this Agreement. This Agreement shall be governed by and construed under New York law as such law applies to agreements between New York residents entered into and to be performed entirely within New York, except as required by U.S. Government rules and regulations to be governed by Federal law.

YOU ACKNOWLEDGE THAT YOU HAVE READ THIS AGREEMENT, UNDERSTAND IT, AND AGREE TO BE BOUND BY ITS TERMS AND CONDITIONS. YOU FURTHER AGREE THAT IT IS THE COMPLETE AND EXCLUSIVE STATEMENT OF THE AGREEMENT BETWEEN US THAT SUPERSEDES ANY PROPOSAL OR PRIOR AGREEMENT, ORAL OR WRITTEN, AND ANY OTHER COMMUNICATIONS BETWEEN US RELATING TO THE SUBJECT MATTER OF THIS AGREEMENT.

U.S. GOVERNMENT RESTRICTED RIGHTS.

Use, duplication or disclosure by the Government is subject to restrictions set forth in subparagraphs (a) through (d) of the Commercial Computer-Restricted Rights clause at FAR 52.227-19 when applicable, or in subparagraph (c) (1) (ii) of the Rights in Technical Data and Computer Software clause at DFARS 252.227-7013, and in similar clauses in the NASA FAR Supplement.